120TH YEAR

WISDEN

CRICKETERS' ALMANACK

1983

EDITED BY JOHN WOODCOCK

PUBLISHED FOR THE PROPRIETORS JOHN WISDEN AND CO LTD, A SUBSIDIARY COMPANY OF GRAYS OF CAMBRIDGE (INTERNATIONAL) LTD, BY QUEEN ANNE PRESS, MACDONALD AND CO (PUBLISHERS) LTD,
MAXWELL HOUSE, 74 WORSHIP STREET, LONDON EC2A 2EN
LIMP EDITION £8.95 CASED EDITION £9.95

PREFACE

Much was made of the fact that in the 1982 *Wisden*, the year following an English victory over Australia, there was no Englishman among the Five Cricketers of the Year. This was not because none merited it, but that those who did, such as Botham and Brearley, had already been one.

It was in 1889 that the then editor, C. F. Pardon, first picked out Six Great Bowlers, honouring them with "medallion portraits". Since then they have, at different times, become Nine Great Batsmen (1890), Five Great Wicket-keepers (1891), The Five Great All-Round Cricketers of the Year (1894), Five Great Players of the Season (1899), Mr R. E. Foster and Four Young Cricketers (1901), Lord Hawke and Four Cricketers of the Year (1909) and Five Members of the MCC Team in Australia (1912). In 1913, the almanack's golden jubilee, John Wisden appeared in solitary splendour, as, subsequently, did P. F. Warner in 1921 and J. B. Hobbs in 1926.

Since 1926 the feature has not varied. Except when it was suspended during the Second War it has always been The Five Cricketers of the Year. Never in any of its guises has the same player been chosen twice, unless it is considered that Sir Pelham Warner and Sir Jack Hobbs were. This year there *is* an Englishman in the list – Trevor Jesty, the Hampshire all-rounder, who finished a fine season in a blaze of glory.

For company he has the outstanding bowler of the season and his colleague in the Hampshire side, Malcolm Marshall; India's irrepressible all-rounder, Kapil Dev; Pakistan's captain and another wonderfully whole-hearted cricketer, Imran Khan; and Alvin Kallicharran, who, in spite of being disowned by West Indies for having played in South Africa, produced one sparkling innings after another.

Kallicharran was not the only cricketer to be excommunicated. The time has come when first-class cricketers go to South Africa at their peril, if they do so as members of a team, though not without the promise of rich financial reward. Graham Johnson of Kent, who has been going to South Africa, on and off, since 1973, and has participated in the development and expansion of cricket there for all races, takes a dispassionate look at an acute human problem.

There is an appreciation of Michael Brearley by John Arlott, two of the outstandingly able people in the cricket world. Norman Harris salutes his fellow New Zealander, Glenn Turner, for having joined the select band who have scored a century of centuries. As the debate develops about the future of the first-class game in England, Philip Carling writes with a close working knowledge of county cricket and its fight for survival. With Ian Botham and Kapil Dev constantly threatening the records of fast scoring in Test cricket, Gerald Brodribb recalls what has been achieved by other great hitters of the ball. And Dick Williamson, who has had a seat in the press box at Headingley for the last 50 years, reveals some fascinating statistics about Yorkshire exiles.

It is an increasing worry to know how best to make room for everything one would like to carry. But that has always been so. As long ago as 1895, Sydney Pardon wrote in his Preface that "the question of space becomes more and more pressing". By its very nature the record section is bound to expand. So, indeed, are the births and deaths. Close students will note a number of changes in this 120th edition, all of inclusion or adjustment rather than omission.

I am indebted to a host of helpers. Between them, like the game itself, they "girdle the earth". There are correspondents in each cricketing country and in every English county without whose help and vigilance one's task would hardly be possible. Graeme Wright, my assistant editor, and Christine Forrest have again been towers of strength. To the secretariat at Lord's, the masters-in-charge of schools cricket, the photographers and the county secretaries, to John Arlott for his book reviews, R. L. Arrowsmith for writing so many of the obituaries, Robert Brooke for taking such care of Births and Deaths, and to Terry Cooper of the Press Association for helping with so many bits and pieces I offer special thanks. Since the 1982 edition went to the printers Michael Fordham has died. He was all an editor could ask for as a statistician, being conscientious, patient, willing and loyal. Barry McCaully, his successor, inspires a similar confidence.

JOHN WOODCOCK

Longparish,
Hampshire.

LIST OF CONTRIBUTORS

The Editor acknowledges with gratitude the assistance afforded in the preparation of the Almanack by the following:

H. E. Abel (Surrey)
Jack Arlidge (Sussex)
John Arlott
Robert L. Arrowsmith
Chris Aspin
Philip August
Jack Bannister
Geoff Beane (Warwickshire)
Brian Bearshaw (Lancashire)
Scyld Berry
J. Watson Blair (Scotland)
Henry Blofeld
Dick Brittenden
Gerald Brodribb
Robert Brooke
Sue Bullen
C. R. Buttery (New Zealand)
John Callaghan (Yorkshire)
Michael Carey
P. G. Carling
Terry Cooper (Middlesex)
Geoffrey Copinger
Tony Cozier (West Indies)
Patrick Eagar
Paton Fenton (Oxford University)
John Fogg
Bill Frindall
Nigel Fuller (Essex)
Ghulam Mustafa Khan (Pakistan)
Stephen Green
David Hallett (Cambridge University)
Laurance Hancock
Norman Harris
Brian Hayward (Hampshire)
Eric Hill (Somerset)
Arthur Holden (Zimbabwe)
Dr Grenville Holland
Ken Ingman (ESCA)
V. H. Isaacs (Limited-overs records)
Robert Jobson
Graham Johnson
Martin Johnson (Leicestershire)
Ken Kelly
Brian Langley
Stephanie Lawrence
John Lawson (Nottinghamshire)
Alan Lee
Edward Liddle
Barry McCaully
Peter Mackinnon (Australia)
Michael Melford
Chris Moore (Worcestershire)
Dudley Moore (Kent)
Gerald Mortimer (Derbyshire)
Brian Osborne
Michael Owen-Smith
Gerald Pawle
A. L. A. Pichanick
Netta Rheinberg
Dicky Rutnagur
Geoffrey Saulez
Peter Sichel (South Africa)
Derek Scott (Ireland)
Bill Smith
Peter Smith
Philip Snow
F. S. Speakman (Northamptonshire)
P. N. Sundaresan (India)
John Thicknesse
J. B. G. Thomas (Glamorgan)
P. T. Thomson
Gerry Vaidyasekera (Sri Lanka)
Geoffrey J. Wheeler (Gloucestershire)
A. H. Wiggett
Dick Williamson
A. S. R. Winlaw

★ ★ ★ ★ ★

Limp edition ISBN 0356 09382 4

Cased edition ISBN 0356 09381 6

CONTENTS

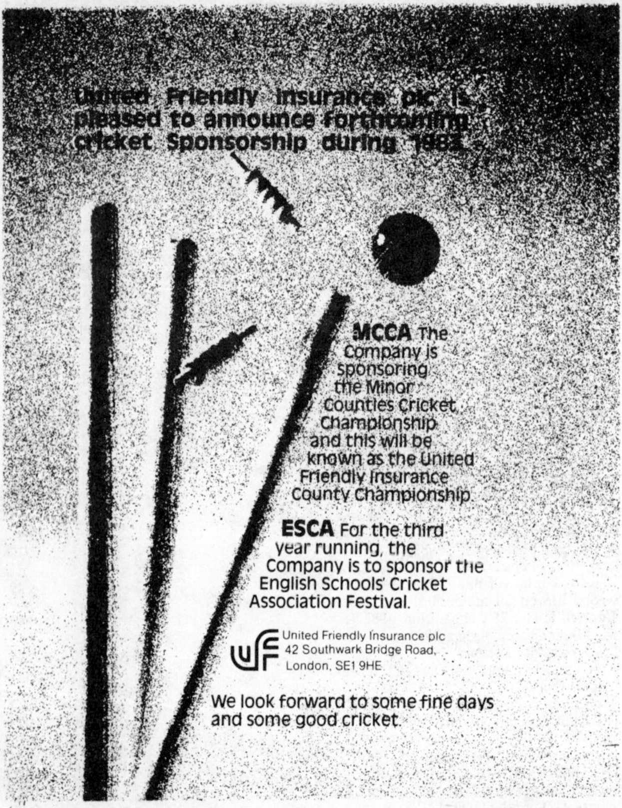
United Friendly Insurance plc is pleased to announce forthcoming cricket Sponsorship during
MCCA The Company is sponsoring the Minor Counties Cricket Championship and this will be known as the United Friendly Insurance County Championship.
ESCA For the third year running, the Company is to sponsor the English Schools' Cricket Association Festival.
United Friendly Insurance plc
42 Southwark Bridge Road,
London, SE1 9HE
We look forward to some fine days and some good cricket.

INDEX

Note: For reasons of space, certain entries which appear in alphabetical order in sections of the Almanack are not included in this index. These include names that appear in Test Cricketers, Births and Deaths of Cricketers, Individual batting and bowling performances in the 1982 first-class season, and Oxford and Cambridge Blues.

c. = catches; d. = dismissals; r. = runs; w. = wickets.

**Signifies not out or an unbroken partnership*

A

B

Grasshopper
Sports
CRICKET
EQUIPMENT
Designed by players
used by champions
for 100yrs.
Produced and sold by
FRANK BRYAN LTD
BROMYARD ROAD · WORCESTER

C

GM
GUNN & MOORE
fine bats, built by craftsmen
HAND MADE
GM
GUNN & MOORE
The Autograph
Write for further details and free colour leaflet.
GUNN & MOORE LTD., 119/121 Stanstead Road, Forest Hill, London, SE23 1HJ.

Special County
IMPERIAL
NULLI SECUNDUS
5½ OZS
MADE IN ENGLAND
CONFORMING TO
M.C.C
REGULATIONS

D

E

F

G

H

I

J

K

L

M

N

O

P

Q

R

S

T

U

V

W

EASTERN MAGIC

[*Ken Kelly*

Abdul Qadir of Pakistan, whose flighted leg-breaks and googlies revived a dying art in England in 1982.

O TEMPORA! O MORES!

[*West Australian Newspapers Ltd*

[*Patrick Eagar*

Above: Umpire Crafter separates Dennis Lillee and Javed Miandad as they bring cricket into disrepute in a Test match at Perth. *Below:* Robin Jackman shows Wasim Bari the pavilion after bowling him in the third Test between England and Pakistan at Headingley. Although thoroughly offensive, such gestures invariably pass unpunished.

NEAR TO DEATH

[*Sporting Pictures (UK) Ltd*

This horrifying picture, more like someone facing a firing-squad than playing cricket for Yorkshire, illustrates the danger of short-pitched bowling and the reason why helmets have become standard wear. The batsman is David Bairstow, the bowler was Sylvester Clarke of Surrey.

OUT OF BOUNDS

[*Colorsport*

The Wanderers Stadium, Johannesburg, March 13, 1982. Geoff Boycott and Graham Gooch open against South Africa on the controversial tour which led to the suspension, for three years, of fifteen Englishmen from Test cricket.

ENGLAND'S TEAM v INDIA AT LORD'S

[*Patrick Eagar*

Back row: D. W. Randall, C. J. Tavaré, P. J. W. Allott, D. R. Pringle, P. H. Edmonds, G. Cook, A. J. Lamb. *Front row:* R. W. Taylor, D. I. Gower, R. G. D. Willis (*captain*), I. T. Botham, G. Miller.

RISING PASSIONS

[*Patrick Eagar*

Qadir bowls, Botham sweeps, up goes the appeal, the fielders close in on the umpire (David Constant): a typical scene from last summer's Test matches between England and Pakistan.

CAPTAINS FACE THE CAMERA

[*Ken Kelly*

A regular feature of modern Test matches is the television interview. Here Bob Willis and Imran Khan answer questions from Peter West of the BBC after England had won their series against Pakistan.

[*Patrick Eagar*

M. D. MARSHALL (West Indies and Hampshire)

[*Patrick Eagar*

T. E. JESTY (Hampshire)

[*Patrick Eagar*

KAPIL DEV (India and Northamptonshire)

[*Ken Kelly*

A. I. KALLICHARRAN (West Indies and Warwickshire)

[*Patrick Eagar*

IMRAN KHAN (Pakistan and Sussex)

FIVE CRICKETERS OF THE YEAR

IMRAN KHAN

In the early part of last season, before he had turned into the glamorous public figure he was soon to become, Imran Khan was playing as usual for Sussex in the County Championship. During their game at Edgbaston, Imran hooked a ball from one of Warwickshire's pace bowlers down to the fine-leg fielder, who caught it but then carried it over the boundary: not out. Nothing daunted, Imran tried another hook-shot at the very next ball, and gave a simple catch to square leg. On seeing this indiscretion, a Sussex colleague commented: "He would be a great player if only he used his head."

By the end of the season Imran *had* combined thoughtfulness with a natural ability which had always been outstanding. What brought about this transformation, as Imran readily admits, was his appointment to the captaincy of his native Pakistan. This sense of responsibility turned a fine cavalier into a great cricketer.

Whether the newly transformed Imran had become the equal of Ian Botham as an all-rounder made one of the liveliest debates of the summer. On the one hand, Imran did not have the batting record in Test cricket which Botham had; on the other, Imran as a pace bowler probably had the edge over Botham as he then was. Indeed some critics, Mike Brearley amongst them, rated Imran as the best of all contemporary bowlers even at the relatively advanced age of 29.

IMRAN KHAN NIAZI was born in Lahore on November 25, 1952. His father was a Pathan landowner in the region to the north of Baluchistan. His mother was one of three sisters of the Burki tribal family: one sister gave birth to Javed Burki, who became an Oxford Blue and captain of Pakistan; the other gave birth to Majid Khan, a Cambridge Blue and captain of Pakistan. Like his cousins, Imran was born to affluent circumstances in which he could devote as much time as he wished to the development of his cricket. The school which he attended, Aitchison College in Lahore, is considered the most prestigious in Pakistan, and there he was guided by one of the country's best coaches, Abdurrabb. During his schooldays he also slipped while climbing a tree, and broke his left arm when trying to cling on to a branch. The arm was set badly in hospital and has given Imran trouble ever since – not in his bowling, but he has to practise constantly at holding his bat, otherwise his grip stiffens up.

In 1971, at the age of eighteen, he was chosen to tour England and made his Test début there. In his one Test match, at Edgbaston, he had no success as an in-swing bowler, being far too immature at that age, as he himself knew; so much so that he returned to school after the tour, joining Worcester Royal Grammar, from where he gained admission to Keble College, Oxford. According to Imran, being university captain in 1974 was little use in giving him experience of later office, but he developed his batting at Oxford to the extent of two centuries in a match against Nottinghamshire. He also launched his reputation for being able to deliver a fearsome bouncer that would swing in at a right-handed batsman's head. Worcestershire, not surprisingly after the help they had given him, were dismayed when he decided to leave after only one full season with them.

Imran's sudden move, which brought him a three-month suspension in early 1977, took him to Brighton, where the swinging pace of life and of the Hove pitches was more to his taste. There he became a dashing No. 5 batsman, and experimented with his bowling action until he had mastered the out-swinger. He considers that his time spent with World Series Cricket was decisive in making him a complete bowler, for while Mike Procter advised him on his run-up, John Snow assisted him in turning his left shoulder more towards fine leg, to help achieve the out-swinger. Imran feels that he has been technically competent as a fast bowler only since 1979-80.

Unfortunately for Imran, Pakistan had no more than a handful of Test matches over the next two years in which he could display his full prowess. When he did have the chance to prove himself, in Australia in 1981-82, he was judged to be the player of the three-match series. During that series against Australia he overtook Fazal Mahmood's record of 139 wickets for Pakistan. Having missed their following two Tests against Sri Lanka, after joining the boycott by senior players, he took fourteen wickets against them in Lahore to register his best Test performance.

His feat, therefore, against England last season, of taking 21 wickets in three Tests, was nothing extraordinary by his recent standards, which have been of the highest. He began with six wickets in England's first innings at Edgbaston, bowled with magnificent stamina in their second innings at Lord's, and took another eight wickets at Headingley. His run-up made a most exhilarating spectacle as he charged in, leaning forward from the waist, and leapt at the crease; so did the end-product of some extremely fast, in-dipping yorkers and virtually unplayable out-swingers.

This much, however, was expected of Imran Khan. The surprise was his common-sensical approach to batting now that he had the captaincy. It had been given to him as a compromise candidate in the dispute between Javed Miandad and Pakistan's senior players, but he was more tactically astute than a mere novice. He could justify not taking a new ball on the last afternoon at Lord's – a tactic which he thinks is too often "a cliché" – by arguing that Mudassar did not know how to use one. As to the charge of over-using Abdul Qadir in the third Test, Imran felt it was sheer bad luck that Qadir had one of those "off" days to which every leg-spinner is subject. But Imran primarily places the blame for his 2–1 defeat – with much justification – on the ill-discipline of his batsmen.

Imran's own batting, meanwhile, was progressing so rapidly that his No. 7 position, and record of only one Test century, had become false labels by the time of Headingley. There he scored more runs in the match than anyone else, and he was dismissed only once, when hitting out with the last man in. The maturity with which he chose his strokes was astonishing to those who had known him only as a Sussex player.

Having won belated fame in his 30th year, Imran's private life became a regular subject of discussion in certain newspapers. As he was not married at the time, and handsome of face and build, the matter of his future wife was widely speculated upon. Imran himself, however, said that he did not intend marriage so long as he was playing full-time cricket, which could keep the females amongst his admirers in suspense for the next two or three years at least. – A.S.I.B.

TREVOR JESTY

When TREVOR EDWARD JESTY mauled the bowling of Bob Willis and his Warwickshire side on the penultimate day of the first-class season, it was a vivid, silent expression of his frustration at being overlooked yet again for international recognition when every formline suggested his moment had come at last. Just 48 hours earlier, the squad to tour Australia under Willis had been announced. There was no place for Jesty and now, at the age of 34 and with comfortably his best season drawing to a close, he wondered in vain just what he was expected to do before being selected for England.

That the England captain was present, indeed on the receiving end, as Jesty concluded his 1982 business with a 64-minute century almost murderous in its intent, was an appropriate irony. Little was said between the two over that weekend and, although both Willis and chairman of selectors Peter May were subsequently to say Jesty had been "unlucky", it was small consolation for one who was dolefully aware that he would never have a better chance of realising his ambition.

When considering Jesty's achievements in 1982, the most striking is undoubtedly his total of eight first-class centuries, the most made in a season for Hampshire since that prodigious batsman Phil Mead managed ten, from a larger programme of matches, 49 years earlier. Jesty was also, and this is a much more obscure statistic, the first English-registered player to top his county's batting averages since Peter Sainsbury in 1967; for fifteen years the presence of Barry Richards, Gordon Greenidge and, for one year, Chris Smith kept Hampshire's home-bred talent in the shadows. But in 1982, although Greenidge was far from idle, averaging 46 and consistently giving the Hampshire innings a conscientious start, he could not compare with Jesty.

The argument against Jesty as a Test candidate has generally been that he is inconsistent. Certainly, as indicated by the ten years it took him to register a maiden century, his potential long remained somewhat unfulfilled. But he will point out justifiably that until recent years he was always batted in the lower middle order for Hampshire and given little chance to build an innings.

Born on June 2, 1948, he was not short of opportunities in early life, despite attending Privet Secondary Modern School in his native Gosport, where cricket was not a major part of the sporting curriculum. His stroke of luck at this stage was the presence among his masters of one F. J. Davies, a keen follower of the game and Jesty's first significant influence. "Perhaps", he recalled now in his quiet, level manner, "he took an interest in me because I showed some aptitude for the game, but the standard of cricket was very poor. The only competitive games were a handful of inter-house and inter-school affairs." Nevertheless, he did enough to attract attention. He played for Hampshire Schools, then the English Schools colts side, and finally for the full English Schools XI, an honour which must have smoothed his path into a county career.

Much of his cricket had already been played among the Hampshire clubs. Trevor's brother Aubrey, ten years his senior, was a very capable cricketer who was offered a place on the county staff as a wicket-keeper but preferred to complete his apprenticeship in the Portsmouth dockyard. Aubrey's weekend cricket was played for the powerful Gosport Amateurs club, and his young brother, taken along as scorer, dreamed that one day he would play for the same team. But it was not to be. Trevor was ready and willing to play club cricket at the age of twelve, but the Amateurs considered he was not up to their level. Consequently he joined the neighbouring Gosport Cricket Club and played at a lower standard.

Jesty remembers the surprise with which he received the letter from Hampshire, inviting him to join them. "I had no doubts about accepting, but funnily enough I had never really considered a career in cricket up to that point", he said. Suitably grateful, however, he withdrew an application for a job with a yacht company near his home and made his Hampshire début in 1966, aged eighteen. By this stage the emphasis of his talents was unclear. At school, he had often begun a match as wicket-keeper, then removed his pads and bowled if things became sticky. Although he never kept wicket for Hampshire, he tended to do most other things and, remarkably, it was not until 1975 that he settled into what seems to be his optimum batting position at No. 4.

Trevor married in 1970 and, soon afterwards, it was his wife Jacqueline who helped him over one of the personal crises of his career. It would not be stretching a point to report that he seldom saw eye to eye with Richard Gilliat, Hampshire's captain of the time, and they clashed heatedly when Jesty was hardly bowled in Championship matches one year. He contemplated changing counties and was fleetingly prepared to give up the game altogether, but Jacqueline and the county's coach, Geoff Keith, talked him out of both options. The episode serves to illustrate how badly Jesty wants to be thought of as an all-rounder, rather than just as a batsman who can turn his arm over. In 1982 his seamers, bowled with a pleasantly high action from a gentle run-up, captured 35 wickets at only 21 apiece, good enough to make him the second Englishman in the national bowling averages.

To most, however, he has always been a batsman first. A strokemaker who, in appearance at the crease and in a certain fluency of stroke, has often been compared with Barry Richards, a colleague he much admired. He loves to get on the front foot and drive and, if he has a noticeable weakness, opponents claim it is when he is forced on to the back foot against the fastest of bowling.

The season of 1982 began like so many others for Jesty. Vice-captain now, a responsibility easing the disillusionment which has sometimes affected his outlook, he had more early success with the ball than the bat. But at the end of May he made 164 not out against the Indian tourists and then, a month later, he dented the pride and reputation of Pakistan's leg-spinner, Abdul Qadir, taking 26 off a single over from him on the way to

133. That, Jesty said, was the most satisfying innings he played. And it was only the beginning.

Towards the end of July, Hampshire were short of runs and Jesty sat meditatively in his hotel room on one of those long, away-trip evenings. What he decided upon amounted to a bold change of style. Someone in the side had to drop anchor and play long, restrained innings, he reasoned, so why should he not do it himself. "From the next innings I played, I put all idea of quick runs out of my mind early on. I was content to stay and accumulate, and if it took me twice as long as my usual time for a hundred, that didn't matter." The success of the scheme was astonishing. In the final ten first-class matches of Hampshire's season, Jesty scored six centuries and a total of 1,079 runs. During one four-day period in which nobody seemed able to bowl to him, he made three hundreds, one in the John Player League. That same week a long-standing bogey was broken, Jacqueline being present to see all the runs. "She had never seen me score a hundred before and I had begun to believe she brought me bad luck", Trevor admitted.

The season ended with that 134 against Warwickshire and a win to confirm third place in the Championship for Hampshire; as well, ironically, as with the biggest disappointment of his career. – A.L.

ALVIN KALLICHARRAN

In a tortured 1982 season, when they usually had to sit and suffer, Warwickshire's followers could at least take comfort from the disciplined brilliance of ALVIN ISAAC KALLICHARRAN. The little West Indian left-hander was the only batsman on the county circuit to score 2,000 first-class runs, hitting three double-centuries and five other hundreds in the Schweppes Championship. He also played one great innings in limited-overs cricket, his 141 not out against Somerset at Taunton securing a shock NatWest Trophy quarter-final success. One shot in this innings will be particularly treasured by those who saw it. When the 6ft 8in Joel Garner came round the wicket to bounce one at him, perfectly positioned, 5ft 5in Kallicharran hooked his towering adversary high over square leg for 6 with stunning power.

Captain Bob Willis provided an apt testimony when he said: "Alvin's Taunton knock contained a myriad of high-class shots." His stock-in-trade pulls and hooks were supplemented by a series of silken drives on the rise through the off. Somerset came apart at the seams.

Not that a bonanza summer was unexpected. A sequence of events paved the way for Kallicharran's prolific output. Following two lean series, against England and Pakistan, he was dropped by West Indies, having scored 4,399 runs for them in 66 Tests at an average of 44. Then Transvaal stepped in with a lucrative winter contract. The first West Indian to compete in South Africa's Currie Cup, he averaged nearly 60 to finish third in the national list and inspire Transvaal to win the Benson and Hedges Floodlit Cup.

Banned by West Indies for having been to South Africa, Kallicharran returned to Birmingham with fire in his belly, a profusion of runs bursting to get out of him. And there was the added incentive of his 1983 county benefit being just a year away. Behind the sunny smile lies a steely, resolute character. His first century came at Dartford, followed by a career-best 235 at Worcester, his maiden double-hundred in first-class cricket.

Then, the day after Warwickshire had been swept aside for 43 by Sussex, he lifted them out of the dumps with 210 at Leicester. Gloucestershire were next on the list, being taken for 173 at Nuneaton. A week later came the Southport saga, Kallicharran scoring an undefeated 230 in an English record fourth-wicket stand of 470 with Geoff Humpage.

Edgbaston had yet to sample a Kallicharran special, but any voodoo was dispelled with 195 against Surrey, followed by 109 not out in the return against Worcestershire. Finally came the climax at Southampton. Kallicharran, the country's leading run-maker, versus Malcolm Marshall, the leading wicket-taker – a contest to savour. Kallicharran countered Marshall's extreme pace with unrivalled expertise, his second-innings 131 raising him past 2,000 runs for the first time in his career. Eight centuries in a summer equalled the Warwickshire record held jointly by R. E. S. Wyatt (1937) and Rohan Kanhai (1972).

Like Kanhai, Kallicharran is a product of Port Mourant in Berbice, Guyana, the same club which produced Basil Butcher, Joe Solomon, John Trim, Ivan Madray and the Christiani brothers, Cyril and Robert, all of whom played for West Indies. His father Isaac, a rice and coconut farmer, captained Port Mourant.

He was born on March 21, 1949, at Paidama, a rural settlement. He had four brothers and six sisters. When, as a youngster, he would sneak off the farm to practise cricket, his punishment was "No food". Times were hard; he knew the score. Like so many of his countrymen he learnt his cricket in back streets and backyards, batting with any stick or branch he could find. The ball would be hewn from the bark of a tree, hence his corrugated right shin from getting into line at an early age. His impeccable technique was largely self-taught.

Uncle Ramjee, a Port Mourant shopkeeper, was the key benefactor during his youth, giving him the dollar a week which he needed to pay his club fees, and "Kalli" soon made his mark at Port Mourant School. Size proved no handicap. In 1966 he was selected for a West Indian Schools tournament. A couple of 90s against the Windward/Leeward Islands and Trinidad earned him trials for Guyana. At sixteen and a half he became the youngest player ever to represent Guyana in the Shell Shield. Another influential benefactor in his rise to fame was a Guyanan rum-manufacturer, Robert White, who bought Kallicharran his kit and provided him with work.

A postal strike frustrated Glamorgan's bid to sign the promising young left-hander, and instead Alan Smith, after a flying visit to the Caribbean, brought him to Warwickshire in 1971. That winter he marked his Test début with an unbeaten 100 against New Zealand in the fourth Test at Georgetown, followed by 101 at Port-of-Spain. Two innings, two hundreds. He averaged 36.75 in his first full series, at home against

Australia, and on his début tour to England, in 1973, he averaged 46.78 overall; 42.40 in the three Tests. In the return series with England, he played a thrilling innings on the first day of the first Test, at Port-of-Spain, walking off towards the pavilion apparently undefeated on 142. Spotting that Kallicharran had not gone through the formality of grounding his bat at the non-striker's end, Tony Greig threw down the stumps. He had to be given out by umpire Douglas Sang Hue, but in the interests of peace and harmony it was agreed overnight that the decision be revoked.

Kallicharran's 1976 tour of England was ruined by a shoulder dislocation that necessitated an operation. It prevented him from throwing a cricket ball for a whole year but his recovery was total, restoring one of the best throwing arms in the game. By autumn 1980, however, following a lean series against England in England, his Test appearances were numbered.

He had been, briefly, at the centre of the storm which broke around Mr Packer in the English summer of 1977. Having signed for World Series Cricket, he discovered that he was in breach of another contract with a Queensland radio station. His subsequent, much-publicised withdrawal led to his being appointed captain of West Indies midway through the 1977-78 series against Australia in West Indies. With Clive Lloyd, from whom he took over, and the other Packer West Indians unavailable, Kallicharran had mixed fortunes as a Test captain, though his influence and experience were of inestimable value to West Indies during a difficult and unsettled period in their cricket history. If, for political reasons, his Test career proves now to be over, there are, on the evidence of his 1982 form, both for Warwickshire and Transvaal, still many runs to come, at county and provincial level, from one of cricket's most nimble talents. – R.H.J.

KAPIL DEV

India's tour of England made a quiet start to the summer. But the Test series was lent excitement by the rivalry between Ian Botham and an Indian who, by his exuberant performances, challenged the title unofficially held by Botham of being the finest contemporary all-rounder. During the series against England, Kapil Dev again proved himself a fine fast-medium bowler, but it was his batting which secured for him the "player of the series" award. His scores were 41, 89, 65 and 97; and every time he went in, after the first of those innings, he seemed to be on course for the fastest Test century ever made in terms of deliveries received.

Only in recent decades have Test centuries been regularly recorded in terms of deliveries as well as minutes, and it was considered that the one by Roy Fredericks off 71 balls at Perth in 1975-76 was the fastest until research discovered that Jack Gregory's at Johannesburg in 1921-22 came from four balls fewer. Kapil Dev, in his second innings of the Lord's Test, hit 89 off 55 balls. Although he fell short of the record then, it would be surprising if he does not break it on some occasion in his career, so quick is his eye, so clean his hitting, so laughing and cavalier his manner.

This amateurish, or at least old-fashioned, approach is readily comprehensible if seen against his background. KAPIL DEV NIKHANJ was born in Chandigarh, a model Welwyn Garden-type city in the northern foothills of India, which serves as the capital of Punjab and of Haryana, being on the border of the two states. Kapil Dev, a Punjabi, plays for Haryana. His official date of birth is given as January 6, 1959, although in that part of India the year of birth is not always registered at the time and can be altered to suit convenience. As it stands, however, Kapil Dev goes into history as the youngest man to have made 1,000 Test runs and taken 100 Test wickets.

His parents came from what is now Pakistan. They emigrated at Partition from near Rawalpindi – if they had not, Kapil Dev might have been opening the bowling for Pakistan with Imran Khan. After a while of wandering, Kapil Dev's father settled in Chandigarh to become a building and timber contractor in the new city. The family business remains prosperous: in other words Kapil Dev does not play cricket for a living but for pleasure.

Batting, however, had been no pleasure for Kapil Dev in his Test matches away from home before he arrived in England last summer. Until then his average in Tests abroad was under 13, and runs had deserted him to such an extent on India's tour of Australia and New Zealand – he made 82 runs in eleven innings, being over-careful he thinks – that some Indian critics were questioning his classification as an all-rounder. From the start, in the first Test at Lord's, he refuted them.

By his own admission, India's position in their first innings at Lord's was the most awkward he faced: hounded by Bob Willis and Botham, India were 45 for five wickets. Kapil Dev had to be circumspect, but clearly the chafing shackles were going to be thrown off at the next opportunity. That came on the fourth evening, after Dilip Vengsarkar had worn down England's bowling but India were still in arrears in the follow-on. Kapil Dev then hit 89 out of the 117 runs which India added in fifteen overs. Test cricket can have seldom seen such exuberance. His runs might have come off even fewer than 55 balls if Dilip Doshi had not been the last man in and Kapil Dev forced to neglect some runs in order to keep the strike. When he finished off his evening's work by taking England's first three wickets in four overs, he had enjoyed as glorious a session of play as any immortal of the game.

In the second Test at Old Trafford, Kapil Dev reached his 50 off 33 balls, well on course again for breaking the record. India, once again, were under pressure to avert the follow-on: but after Kapil had emerged at 173 for six wickets, the remaining 53 runs required were scored in even time. Towards the end of his innings of 65 he slowed down, which does not suit him or his special talent. For Kapil Dev as a batsman has the almost unique ability to launch himself straight into fourth gear, with over-drive his variation.

His cleanness of hitting and precision of timing were repeated at The Oval. Again India faced the follow-on: when Kapil Dev entered their last five wickets still had to make 147. He promptly hit, between interruptions, 97 off 92 balls in 102 minutes. When Botham offered the bait of a slower ball, the uncomplicated Kapil put it straight into the distant Vauxhall stand. During what was otherwise a promising first term of captaincy by Willis, Kapil Dev's partnership of 130 in 27 overs with Syed Kirmani threw England into some disorder.

Before returning to Northamptonshire after the series, Kapil Dev enjoyed a mid-season working holiday in the United States, which may again exemplify his attitude to the game. When back with his county the carefree hitting continued with two whirlwind hundreds in the Championship, one on an under-prepared pitch at Eastbourne. His 50 would arrive in even time, his century – if it came – in about two hours. Dennis Brookes said he had seen no-one at Northampton with such a gift for hitting and timing since Colin Milburn.

Less to Northamptonshire's delight, the amateur attitude – playing for the pleasure of it – has manifested itself in Kapil Dev's bowling as well. Understandably, as India's one quick bowler, he has been worked to the full during an intensive Test programme. It was the opportunity to take the new ball in 25 Test matches in the space of only one year and 110 days which helped him to his world record of performing the Test double in the shortest-ever time. (Botham reached his 1,000 Test runs and 100 wickets in longer time but four fewer Tests.) The last thing he needs in India's off-season is the grind of daily bowling.

As he remains the only strike bowler on India's horizon, Kapil Dev may soon decide to devote his energies to India's cause to the exclusion of the county game. But even if he is lost to the English scene, he will not be forgotten after his all-round displays of rubbery exuberance, which were enough to evoke the memory of Learie Constantine. – A.S.I.B.

MALCOLM MARSHALL

Cricketers seldom agree on the relative merits of fast bowlers. Debates about the fastest, bounciest or most difficult to play will invariably rage unresolved through a tour or a season. But not in 1982. Then, almost without exception, the batsmen on the county circuit nominated MALCOLM DENZIL MARSHALL, born in St Michael, Barbados, on April 18, 1958, as the quickest they encountered.

This accolade was remarkable enough for its unanimity, but there was more. Fast bowlers as a race are often treated with suspicion, if not outright resentment, by the men they attack day by day. But Marshall somehow earned an element of admiration, for his ability, his workrate – if one can apply such a clichéd soccer word to him – and his cheerful Barbadian humour.

He has shown much resourcefulness since the May day in 1979 on which he made his Hampshire début, and his sense of humour has been needed. Not long off the plane from the sand, surf and sun of his homeland, Marshall found himself running in to bowl against Glamorgan while the English climate played one of its more eccentric tricks – snow fell on the Southampton ground. Undeterred, though maybe mystified, he took nine wickets in the match, figures which he never quite lived up to during the rest of that summer. He finished with 47 wickets and less than 200 runs, missed virtually all the following season owing to the West Indians' tour, and then, in 1981, made his first significant impact on county cricket, taking 68 wickets despite missing one-third of Hampshire's matches.

The improvement accelerated dramatically in 1982. Suddenly, this man with the wispy beard, searching eyes and infectious grin was no longer just one in the pack of West Indian bowlers in the English game; he was looking like the best. He had learnt how to bowl in English conditions and he could do it for as long as he was allowed. His total of 134 wickets was 44 more than his closest challenger, Nick Cook, who also happened to be the only other leading bowler to get through more than 800 overs in the season. Marshall's total output of 822 was startling for a strike bowler; the traditional county workhorses were well behind.

This, according to those close to him, is Marshall's greatest asset, and his willingness to bowl is matched by a stamina seldom seen in the game. It was one of captain Nick Pocock's most teasing problems – just how many overs to give Marshall in the hope that he might make another break. Trevor Jesty, who led Hampshire while Pocock was absent injured, confirms: "I set out to give him spells of five or six overs, but he always wants to go on bowling, and sometimes it can be very difficult to get the ball off him."

Marshall had a great deal to live up to when he arrived with Hampshire. For the previous five years, Roberts had been taking the new ball, and with his loss of enthusiasm and subsequent departure, the county's followers quite naturally feared the worst. Who could possibly fill such boots? But Marshall came well qualified. He had just passed his 21st birthday and already he had represented West Indies, in India and Sri Lanka. What is more, he had an inbuilt affection for his new employers. As a boy in Barbados, playing cricket on the beaches and dreaming of one day bowling fast in England, his adopted counties had been Middlesex and Hampshire.

Incentive was another motivator. West Indies' quartet of pace bowlers was well established and Marshall was just one of a cluster trying hard to break in. He had time on his side, maybe, but there was a degree of impatience in him. He wanted to play Test cricket and he saw the county game as a showcase. It is said he put on a yard of pace to impress Clive Lloyd whenever the West Indies captain happened to be at the receiving end. His persistence paid off, at least to the extent that he became the regular fifth seamer in the squad.

Marshall has many of the traits of the typical West Indian. His walk is jaunty, his speech liltingly rushed, his ego large. He wears his name on a gold pendant hung round his neck, dresses sharply and remains, at 24, an eligible bachelor, delighting in soul music, reggae and a good party. But if the popular conception of the Barbadian remains dominated by *mañana,* then Marshall is a misfit. Tomorrow, for him, will never be good enough. He wants to be the best today and is prepared to work to achieve his aims.

He is a great believer in training, particularly the specific muscle exercises for quick bowlers, and he completes his own routine of them religiously before play each day. He sees bowling as a business, but like most high-fliers in that branch of industry, remains convinced he is very nearly as good a batsman. He made runs, too, in 1982, and for all his devastation with the ball, one wonders if he derived more private pleasure from making his maiden first-class century against Lancashire – yes, Clive Lloyd's county again.

Marshall, a dressing-room joker with a love of laughter, combined to remarkable effect last season with a tall, rather serious newcomer named Kevin Emery who, to his great credit, was not often overshadowed by his more illustrious new-ball partner. Emery finished with 83 wickets, a handsome collection in his début season, though how many he would have taken with an inferior bowler at the other end is a moot point.

Twelve times during the season, Marshall took five wickets in an innings – a figure not equalled for Hampshire since the days of Derek Shackleton. On four occasions he finished with ten wickets in a match, and Hampshire's diligent statistician Vic Isaacs provided a deeper insight into his success with the revelation that a huge proportion of his wickets were "bowler's victims" – 27 bowled, 37 lbw and a further 25 caught by wicket-keeper Parks. His eight for 71 against Worcestershire was a career best, but the performances which may live longer in the memory came at The Oval and Bournemouth. Against Surrey, he took seven for 38, dismissing the home side for 100 and securing an extraordinary 3-run win; and on an unpleasant pitch at Dean Park his five wickets hurried out Somerset for 74 when they needed only 85 to win.

Marshall is below six feet, small for a fast bowler, and at twelve stone he is no heavyweight either. But on that sprinting, low-slung approach, his balance invariably seems perfect, the delivery merely a flowing continuation. The results have impressed England's best players for several years, never more so than now. Dennis Amiss sums up: "He is as quick as Imran Khan at his best and that means he is the fastest around. He has learnt to keep the ball up and bowl to get people out rather than to stop them scoring. And he has the ability to move the ball late and sharply, either in the air or off the pitch."

His tally of wickets in 1982 was the highest by any individual since the Championship was reduced in matches. That, and many more statistics, add to the testimonials that Malcolm Marshall received in 1982 for a phenomenal season. – A.L.

NOTES BY THE EDITOR

In 1982, as in 1981, politics cast a shadow across the cricket fields of the world. For this and other reasons it was a disturbing year. Towards the end of 1981 two of the game's outstanding cricketers, Dennis Lillee of Australia and Javed Miandad, who was captaining Pakistan, had been involved in an ugly scuffle in a Test match in Perth; early in 1982 fourteen English cricketers were banned for three years from playing Test cricket for touring South Africa together. To umpire in a Test match, not least in England, was to run the risk of becoming profoundly disaffected. The English season closed with most of the seventeen first-class counties in financial difficulties, and no sooner had England's series against Australia, in the winter of 1982-83, begun than shameful scenes, again in Perth, caused concern.

Although the Australian Cricket Board, under urging from Lord's, had given proper priority to the Test matches, over the one-day triangular tournament which is now a regular feature of the Australian season, they had sanctioned from their marketing agents a distasteful film aimed at promoting England's tour. This caricatured, in a gratuitously offensive and quite erroneous way, the English view of Australia's chances. In the event it was a number of Englishmen, bearing Union Jacks and under the influence of drink, who invaded the field during the first Test match in Perth and grappled with the Australian fielders.

In England last summer, during the matches against Pakistan, there were times when Trent Bridge and Edgbaston sounded like football grounds. The same has begun to happen on Sundays at John Player League matches and at Lord's in the one-day finals. For some years now, on high days and holidays, the Hill at Sydney and the southern stand at Melbourne have been places where no-one wanting an agreeable day at the cricket would choose to go. The unruliness which has removed so much of the pleasure from watching football is even less compatible with cricket.

If, in Perth, young expatriate Englishmen started the trouble, as they clearly did, the players themselves, particularly Lillee, have much to answer for, owing to their inflammatory gestures on the field of play. In Mr Packer's World Series Cricket these were necessary because of the absence of any authentic atmosphere. Test cricket is competitive enough without them. When, in Perth, a blow was aimed at Alderman, the Australian bowler, by one of England's so-called supporters, and some of the Australian side retaliated by setting on him, it was another sad manifestation of the violence that is the bane of modern sport.

That said, the year under review was not without its redeeming aspects. Public interest in the game remains undiminished. If this is not reflected in attendance figures, except in India, it is undoubtedly true. As a pointer, *Wisden* 1982 appeared in the best-selling lists (the "top ten") for fourteen successive weeks. No fewer than 20,538,533 telephone calls, a staggering total, were made to the British Telecom Recorded Cricket Service by people wanting to know the latest cricket scores. After losing what must have been a gruesomely boring series in India, England, back home, avenged this defeat and then beat Pakistan. There was some magnificent cricket from, in turn, the game's three best all-rounders – Ian Botham of England, Kapil Dev of India and Imran Khan of Pakistan. Great, too, was one's delight at seeing Abdul Qadir, a genuine leg-break and googly bowler, being given the chance to practise, successfully, a dying art.

A New England Captain

Expressing a modern misconception, Bob Willis, the England captain, wrote: "As for the way everyone's been going into raptures over leg-spin bowling, it doesn't win Test matches." Within a few weeks of his having said this, Qadir had tied Australia's batsmen into all manner of knots, and been, without the slightest doubt, the cause of an Australian defeat. To imply that leg-spin is archaic is to disparage one of the great traditions of the game.

Except for this, and his intransigence in allowing The Oval Test match against India to peter out, Willis made a capital start to his late and unexpected accession to the England captaincy. Pakistan provided strong opposition. They, too, were under a new captain. Blending the many talents and emotions of a Pakistan team has proved, for the years of their existence, to be one of the most difficult jobs in cricket. Himself an indomitable player, Imran led them, with more than a hint of autocracy, to their first Test victory at Lord's. Only the mercurial ways of his batsmen, and England's determination, personified in Willis's own unstinting efforts, prevented Pakistan from winning the series as well.

Umpires in Need of Support

Imran, so handsomely athletic, has many followers. Even they, though, must have thought it a pity that he was so specifically critical of the umpiring in the Test matches between England and Pakistan. The frustration of having lost to England, whom he considered to be a weaker side than his own, led him into this; but if the public debate which he provoked persuades the game's governing bodies to be more forthright in their support of umpires, good will come of it.

Not that there can be any certainty that it will. The International Cricket Conference have an undistinguished record when it comes to taking a strong line. Once again they allowed their annual meeting to pass in 1982 without insisting that in every country a minimum number of overs should be bowled, weather permitting, in a day's play in a Test match. After a series in India, in which England, to their undying shame, took as long to bowl their overs as India, and although, by the time of the ICC meeting at Lord's, the same two sides were finding a mandatory 96 overs in a day's play comfortably manageable, reasons were still found for evading the issue. For the way in which they put off until tomorrow what they should do today, and allow themselves to become so politically compromised, the ICC are in danger of forfeiting all credibility as a ruling authority.

That umpires find themselves at the centre of some controversy or other more often than they used to is not, I am sure, because they are any less efficient. Their job is simply more exacting than it was. Partly because of all the money that is at stake, partly for reasons of nationalism, partly because there are fewer easy Test victories than there were, partly because the ball moves about more than it did, partly because of the frenzied way in which players appeal, and by no means least because of television, the man in the white coat is now under constant pressure. Trial by television is not something to which only football referees are subjected.

Just how contagious animosity on the cricket field is, was to be seen at Hove in the last of the four-day "Tests" between the best young players of England and West Indies. Having given both sides a dressing-down for their behaviour, the umpires, both of them on the first-class list, said that they had no wish to stand in such a game again.

Appealing Gets Out of Control

In England last summer the Pakistanis got themselves a bad name as headstrong appealers. England's batsmen, unable to tell Qadir's googly from his leg-break, were regularly hit on the pads. From as far afield as wide mid-on or deep third man would come a piercing cry for leg-before. The fielders close to the bat would turn on the umpire as though to dare him to deny them their appeal. Anyone watching on television would be enlightened by that merciless invention, the slow-motion replay, not once but many times over. By nightfall, millions of viewers, many of them not remotely interested in cricket, would be taking sides in a way that never used to happen.

Much needs to be done to take the heat out of this aspect of the game. As could be seen from the pictures of the incident which finally caused Imran to give vent to his feelings – the dismissal of Sikander Bakht in Pakistan's second innings at Headingley – the England players could be just as indiscriminate in their appealing as the Pakistanis. In the weeks that followed, some suggested that only the bowler and wicket-keeper should have the right to appeal, some that there should be no appealing at all, some that instant replays should be more discreetly used, others that the umpires themselves should have access to a television monitor, or that there should be an independent panel who did, and who could be called upon for its opinion. On a different tack, Mr A. G. Pawson, at 94 one of the oldest surviving first-class cricketers, was at a loss to know why, in the case of a leg-before decision, the bowler's umpire seems never to refer to his colleague at square-leg to determine, perhaps more precisely, the height of the bounce of the ball.

What tended to be forgotten, but never must be, was that, right or wrong, the umpire's decision is final and has always to be accepted as such. That is as paramount now as it was 100 years ago. Nor should the principle that batsmen be given the benefit of an umpire's doubt be undermined. In the course of an English season, in first-class cricket let alone at lower levels, one does see batsmen given out when it is hard to believe that in the umpire's mind there cannot have been some element of uncertainty. This, I believe, is more common than it was. I am thinking, as an example, of catches at the wicket down the leg side, when at the bowler's end there is no visible deflection and therethe sound that is heard could equally well be buckle as bat.

Pakistan a Stronger Side than India

The days are gone when Pakistan were easily beaten. So long as Qadir retains his form, the chances of their losing in Pakistan will be slender. If and when it looks like happening I am not sure the crowds there will allow it, they are so quick to riot. Despite the heroics of Kapil Dev in England last summer, India were a good deal more vulnerable than Pakistan. To be chosen to play for England against India, ahead of one's nearest rivals, was the surest way of winning a place in the side for Australia. Allan Lamb's fortunes say it all: having averaged 50 against India, he made 6, 5, 33, 0, 0 and 4 against Pakistan.

When it came to picking the party to tour Australia, the selectors seemed altogether uncertain as to what to make of the evidence before them. In the end they left the many supporters of Trevor Jesty and Mike Gatting as irate as Frank Woolley's were when Maurice Leyland was preferred to him in 1928-29 ("the worst crime since the Crucifixion" wrote G. J. V. Weigall) or Fred Trueman's in 1954-55 when he, too, was left behind.

The Question of Eligibility

The choice of Lamb, a first-generation South African of English parentage, focused attention on the matter of eligibility for England and whether or not the rules need revising. At present a cricketer is qualified if:

(a) He was born in the British Isles.
(b) His father or mother was born in the British Isles and he himself has lived there for four consecutive years without in that time having played in a Test match for the country of his birth.
(c) He has lived in the British Isles for ten consecutive years and has not in that time played in a Test match for the country of his birth.
(d) He has lived in the British Isles since the day before his fourteenth birthday and has not played in a Test match for the country of his birth.

Among others, this brings into the net Brian Davison, the prolific Zimbabwean who has played since 1970 for Leicestershire. Were Davison English, as distinct from being qualified to play for England, he would surely be in the England side. It might be simpler and more satisfactory if the rules were rewritten so that to play for England it became necessary to take up British citizenship, in the same way that Kepler Wessels, another South African, has become a naturalised Australian.

The South African Dilemma

It was ironic, some thought absurd, that Lamb should be acceptable for England but not the fifteen Englishmen, captained by Graham Gooch, who toured South Africa, Lamb's home country, in the spring of 1982 and were disqualified from Test cricket for three years for having done so. Having had their submission for re-entry into the Test fold persistently rejected, despite meeting in every detail the original conditions for this to happen, South Africa have run out of patience and decided that only with the aid of a cheque book can they give the game there the stimulus of international competition which it needs. They are, accordingly, offering cricketers the chance to become mercenaries. By the end of 1982 a team of Sri Lankans (the equivalent, perhaps, of Sri Lanka's second eleven) had been slipped into South Africa, there, at the expense of their cricket careers at home, to earn more money in a few weeks than they could normally do in a lifetime.

There are, inevitably, unattractive aspects to this. For one thing, any such operation is likely to be conspiratorially planned, if only to keep the protestors at bay. Although the Englishmen who went to South Africa (twelve of them had won Test caps, all except Amiss within the previous eighteen months) were not in breach of the Gleneagles Agreement as it is interpreted by the British Government (they would have been, of course, had they been an "official" team), they must have known that there would be repercussions. Five of the party had only recently returned from the England tour of India, which Mrs Gandhi had threatened to prohibit because of the connections of two of them (Boycott and Cook) with cricket in South Africa. It was hardly surprising, when Gooch, Boycott, Emburey, Lever and Underwood turned up in Johannesburg in March, that the Indians felt let down. In the autumn of 1981 the Test and County Cricket Board had warned, by letter, all county cricketers that if they went as members of a team to South Africa (the distinction between going collectively and to coach was clearly drawn) they might have to pay for it.

The Prime Minister's View

In the event, the reaction to their unheralded arrival in South Africa was little short of hysterical. Although they had widespread public support, the English players became, overnight, pawns in a fiercely political game. Predictably, the cricket boards of both India and Pakistan, guided by their governments, threatened to call off their forthcoming visits to England should they be expected to play against the English "rebels". One English county, Northamptonshire, so feared the financial consequences of such a cancellation that they called for a life ban, no less, on the offending players. The Prime Minister, on the other hand, refused to condemn them. Speaking in Parliament, Mrs Thatcher said "we do not have the power to prevent any sportsmen or women from visiting South Africa or anywhere else. If we did we would no longer be a free country." Trapped in the maelstrom, the TCCB, by imposing a three-year ban – "to preserve international multi-racial cricket" – bowed to political pressures to the consternation not only of the players concerned but also of the average cricket follower.

In politics, which this was, even a week is a long time. Three years is an eternity, as it is in a cricketer's career. In time the players appealed for some remission of their sentence. But again politics took over. When the

West Indians were asked how they would view it if the players' suspensions were to be reduced from three years to two, they withheld their approval. This although, less than a month before, the ICC had agreed "unanimously" that on no account should one country be allowed to influence the team selection of another.

If that was not hypocritical, what is? I am sure that at all times the TCCB proceeded, as they thought, in good faith. They did all they could, once they had got wind of the tour, to dissuade the players from embarking on it. For all that, to act as they ultimately did, without doing anything for the cause of cricket in South Africa, smacked more of expediency than strength. A one-year suspension, with a future tightening of players' contracts, would have been ample. And knowing the West Indians as I do, and the importance they attach to playing cricket against England, quite apart from the joy they get from beating them, I believe that, come 1984, their politicians, like everyone else, would have accepted some reduction of the ban.

Structure of the English Game

If it was not the South African issue that was exercising the TCCB, it was the structure and viability of first-class cricket in England. For one reason and another, primarily the decline in revenue between Australia's tour of England in 1981 and the visits of India and Pakistan in 1982, several counties are having difficulty balancing their books. Although, as the result of a decision taken in 1981, each county will play 24 Championship matches in 1983, there is still a move for these to be replaced by sixteen four-day games, played in mid-week with the weekends being set aside for the one-day competitions.

This, it is said, would reduce a county's running costs, free their Test players for a higher proportion of Championship matches, and provide a better preparation for Test cricket. Against that, it would reduce the amount of cricket available to county members, who form the backbone of every county club; and if Parkinson's Law were to apply ("Work expands to meet the time available for its completion . . ."), as it well might, the cricket would be unlikely to gain in attraction. Unless a financial necessity, it would seem to be advocating change for change's sake. It is not irrelevant that in Australia, where Sheffield Shield matches are played over four days, there are many who feel they would be better played over three.

Changes at Lord's

Meanwhile there has been something of a struggle for power at Lord's, the significance of which may become more apparent with time. It came to a head in the autumn of 1982, when Mr G. O. Allen, for the last half-century the game's most influential and dedicated administrator, resigned as one of MCC's representatives on the Cricket Council, the governing body of English cricket. He did so in protest at the way, through a realignment of voting rights, the TCCB had been assured of what he feels amounts to control of the Council. A few weeks earlier, Mr Allen had celebrated his 80th birthday at a candlelit dinner, given in his honour, in the Long Room at Lord's. The only other dinner of its kind, at any rate in living memory, was to Sir Pelham Warner in 1953.

Commenting on his resignation, Mr Allen said that he believed the Cricket Council, being the governing body of the game in England, should be fully representative of all levels of cricket. While accepting that the TCCB now provides most of the money for official coaching schemes, as well as for the more recreational branches of English cricket, Mr Allen expressed strong opposition to a national game being virtually controlled by a body that is mainly concerned with its professional side. An analogy might be if the Football Association were to come under the ordinance of the Football League.

Founded in 1968, the Cricket Council previously comprised, in equal measure, representatives of the TCCB, the National Cricket Association (embracing clubs and schools) and MCC, each with five votes. The Minor Counties Cricket Association had one vote, Scotland and Ireland a seat on the Council but no vote. MCC owed the strength of its representation to having been, for the best part of 200 years, the Council's predecessor as the ruling body of English cricket, as well as being the lawmakers of the game and a club with a unique standing in the cricket world. Mr Allen is afraid that the Council's new constitution, which follows the recommendation of a Working Party and gives the TCCB eight votes, the NCA five and MCC only three (the Minor Counties have lost theirs), will make it no more than a rubber stamp for the TCCB.

How will the TCCB exercise its potential control? That is crucial. Since its inception, also in 1968 (before that it had acted, as the Advisory County Cricket Committee, in a recommendatory capacity to MCC), it has become a major commercial concern, vigorously administered. In recent years the corridors of power at Lord's have not always echoed with compatibility. It is, in many ways, a good thing that the tennis and squash courts there are to be redeveloped to house the TCCB and the NCA. The TCCB, especially, has outgrown the Pavilion in which, with the NCA, it has been the guest of MCC. If, besides running its own show, namely English Test and county cricket, the TCCB is now to have, should it wish, the final word in matters affecting the 25,000 clubs and 150,000 players who form the heart and soul of cricket in these islands, Mr Allen may have been right to sound a warning. He and MCC stand for cricket with a capital "C"; the TCCB, as it has to be, is more commercialistic.

In Australia, where the marketing people have been given a large say in who does what, and where and how, the character of the game has been quite drastically changed. With sponsorship taking an ever firmer hold, it is not impossible to imagine something similar happening in England. I hardly think it will – but it could. Beware the small, executive sub-committee of businessmen, to whom the charm of cricket is little more than a technicality: that was the burden of Mr Allen's message.

Brearley's Influence

After being pursued almost to the finishing line by Leicestershire, Middlesex won the 1982 Schweppes County Championship. That they did so in the year of Michael Brearley's retirement was entirely fitting. Few cricketers, if any, can have achieved so much by reading the game so astutely as Brearley, and by finding out how to get the best out of each player. With a combination of intelligence, coercion, wisdom and care he has had a profound influence on the modern game. Although a good enough batsman to have scored 45 first-class hundreds, it was less as a player than as a presence that he made his considerable impact. At the age of 50, another prominent student of the psychology of cricket, Ray Illingworth, returned to captain the Yorkshire side, driven to doing so by feeling the need to get out into the middle to coax and coach his players. The relatively new role of cricket manager, which Illingworth holds in Yorkshire, is thought by some counties to be an extravagance and by others to be of the first importance.

Brearley considers that his most tangible contribution to the game was to pave the way for the introduction of the helmet. That he should think so is not only interesting but typically pragmatic. Whether or not the helmet has made cricket a better game is open to question. That it has made the batsman's existence a safer one is not. What I am afraid has happened is that the amount of wanton short-pitched bowling has increased, not despite the helmet but because of it. The sight of a tailender heavily protected does nothing to deter the bowler from unleashing bouncers at him, as he never would have done a few years ago. Willis found this in one of last summer's Test matches. While batting against Imran at Edgbaston, he was obliged to take such frequent evasive action that he ricked his neck badly enough to miss the next Test, at Lord's. Sir Garfield Sobers, when in England in September to play in a match for "old soldiers" at The Oval, observed that had Ken Barrington been able to shelter behind a helmet, no-one would ever have got him out.

Midland Hospitality

For a second time the ICC Trophy, confined to associate members of the Conference (the winners qualify for the World Cup of the following year), was played in the Midlands. Although dogged by bad weather it was a splendidly cosmopolitan tournament, which attracted sixteen entries and much generous hospitality. Since winning it in 1979, Sri Lanka have become a full-fledged Test-playing country and given the full England side a nasty fright in Colombo. It may not be very long before Zimbabwe, Sri Lanka's successors as winners of the Trophy, are themselves promoted to Test status. They have a good side and in Andrew Pycroft an outstanding batsman.

Dominance of Overseas Players

In English county cricket overseas players were again pre-eminent, occupying seven of the first ten places in the batting averages and nine of the first eleven in the bowling figures. With Jesty and Gatting both being left behind, and several of the other most successful Englishmen under suspension, the England team that went to Australia consisted mostly of players who had been buried well down the averages. Under their new chairman, P. B. H. May, the selectors had a difficult job. Most vitally, perhaps, they had been deprived by the TCCB ban of all their best opening batsmen.

Spinners' Revival

Despite pitches being covered for a second year running, spin bowlers, especially of the left-arm orthodox variety, were more prominent than for some time, an indication, perhaps, that the TCCB's call for matches to be begun on drier, firmer pitches, which would eventually take turn, did not go unanswered. Middlesex and Leicestershire, the two leading sides in the Championship, both owed much to their spin bowlers – or, to put it another way, to being able to field a balanced attack.

Lessons from the Averages

Not since 1934 had as many as fourteen batsmen averaged over 50 in an English season, and seldom before have bowlers had to pay such a high price for their wickets. There used to be three times as many bowlers with an average of under 20. The fact that there are now no drying wickets, because of full covering, may partly account for this, as well as the almost total absence of wrist-spinners to make short work of numbers nine, ten and eleven. There are also fewer "rabbits" about, to whom batting is an insoluble mystery.

Financial Worries

As the season of 1982 ended, a patchy one so far as the weather was concerned, the financial problems of many counties were reflected in the number of players who were not re-engaged. In hard times, the much higher wages which first-class cricketers have come to expect must inevitably mean smaller staffs. The withdrawal, in November, of the Schweppes sponsorship of the County Championship brought further anxiety to those whose job it is to keep the game solvent. Schweppes came into cricket in 1977. They are to leave it at the end of the 1983 season, to concentrate on "other marketing objectives". By then they will have put something like £1 million into the game, a splendid contribution. With the Prudential Assurance Company also withdrawing their invaluable support of the one-day internationals after this year's World Cup, the TCCB became urgently occupied with the search for successors. In that it attracts less television coverage than one-day cricket, the Championship, although the foremost competition and the one which the players value most highly, is not necessarily the most attractive target for potential sponsors.

Random Thoughts

To finish with, a few random thoughts. In a book of facts and figures, none is more remarkable than that which appears in the account of the

Test match between India and England in Madras: while India were scoring 455 runs between losing their second wicket on a Wednesday afternoon and their third on a Friday morning, it was estimated that 75,000 Indians first saw the light of day – many of them, no doubt, with a natural eye for games. As, in England, umpires referred to their light meters, rather than to their own judgement, there were times when I found myself wondering whether they, the meters, might not be a mixed blessing. Lloyd Budd, now retired after fourteen years on the first-class umpires' list, will be missed not only for his admirably steady standards but for the way he considered the long-suffering spectators by keeping the action going. And when, say from third man, a fielder, under no particular pressure, returns the ball to the top of the stumps, was he always applauded by the rest of his side? Actors are not, by their fellow-actors, when they get their lines right. But customs are constantly changing. The game is never quite the same from one season to the next. As has been said before now, it never has been what it was. To those who love it, though, it remains, despite the politicians, an incomparable pastime.

BREARLEY TAKES HIS LEAVE

[Ken Kelly

On a misty September morning at Worcester, Mike Brearley, having led Middlesex to victory in the match which ensured them of the Schweppes Championship, takes his leave of first-class cricket to the applause of the Worcestershire fieldsmen.

J. M. BREARLEY – SUCCESS THROUGH PERCEPTIVENESS

By JOHN ARLOTT

Comfortably before lunch on Tuesday, September 14, 1982, at Worcester, J. M. – Mike – Brearley made the final run in Middlesex's ten-wicket win over Worcestershire. He had been applauded on to the field at the start of the match; and he was applauded off it, into the retirement he had planned and announced. He walked into the pavilion for the fourth, and last, time as captain of the county champions.

There is little doubt that he was one of the best – certainly the most sustainedly successful – captain international cricket has known. A shrewd and experienced North country professional and Test selector summed it up in the words: "This man is as good a captain on the field as Illingworth; off it, he must be far and away the best we have had." He added: "If only he could get some more runs there could never be any question about him." Runs, though, are not a yardstick of captaincy, only a reinforcement of selection.

Mike Brearley's record as a Test captain is excelled only by Sir Donald Bradman who, it will be conceded, had – by comparison with his opponents – stronger sides under his command. In short, Brearley captained England in 31 Test matches, of which they won eighteen and lost four; while, of nine series, seven were won, one drawn and one lost. In his eleven years as captain of Middlesex they won the County Championship three times and shared it once, against five and one shared in their previous 89 years in the competition. They were twice winners and once losing finalists in the Gillette Cup; once Benson and Hedges Cup finalists; once runners-up and twice third in the John Player League.

His achievement that will live in the imagination of all those who lived through it – or who read of it in the future – is the taking over of the 1981 England team, one down to Australia, which had all the look of a beaten side, and transforming it, almost incredibly, into the winner of the rubber by three to one. Much credit, of course, must go to Ian Botham for his amazing all-round cricket. Yet Botham had been in the losing team Brearley took over. After that Brearley stepped down from the England captaincy, as he did from that of his county a year later, on a note of triumph.

The simple explanation for his success was expressed by the Australian fast bowler, Rodney Hogg, not generally known for his perspicacity, when he said "I reckon Brearley has got a degree in people". The salient points of his make-up are intellectual quality, clarity of mind and common sense – which are by no means the same thing, nor always found in the same person – and human perception. He would not claim the finest brain cricket has known. Indeed, he has argued that Edward Craig, his contemporary at Cambridge, was superior both mentally and as a batsman. It is, though, as certain as may be that his was the most effective intellect ever closely applied to the game. His clarity of mind enabled him to pierce the woolly romanticism and anachronistic feudalism which for so long obscured the truth of cricket. His common sense was reflected in his recognition of the need for Kerry Packer to be accepted into the body of cricket; and that, if players were not better treated financially, the available talent would ebb even further away.

His understanding – both intuitive and tutored – of human beings proved a major asset in his captaincy. He was able to reach, sympathise with and – in the current term – motivate cricketers as few, if any, others have done. If that capacity proved helpful, it also led to some of his major griefs, for his depth of understanding made his failures in human relationships the more agonising.

His career is absorbing to follow, if only for its many-sidedness. Invariably cricketers who achieve so much have been single-minded about the game. Mike Brearley has never seen it as an exclusive interest so much as the finest of games, set in a world of more important matters. That has enabled him to detach himself mentally from a match in which he was deeply involved and to assess it objectively.

Yet he could not be so detached about his own performance. Throughout his career as captain of England he was deeply – often inhibitingly – concerned about his batting form in Test matches. Clear-mindedly recognising his own potential, he was idealist enough to appreciate how far he often fell short of it. Had he played under a captain as sympathetic as himself, the problem might have been solved. In the event, although he often batted freely and fluently in county cricket, when he played for England anxiety drove him constantly into over-care. This frequently cost him his wicket. In short he was, like all good batsmen, basically an instinctive player: not even he could quite impose thought on the high-speed reactions of batting against pace. Thus his best Test innings were defensive: salvage operations conducted with an eye to survival. History, surely, will say that his captaincy and fine slip-catching compensated for the deficiency.

He was born in Harrow on April 28, 1942. His father, Horace Brearley, who came from Yorkshire, was a good enough batsman to play as an amateur for that county once and, after he moved south, twice for Middlesex. He employed encouragement to help his son towards a success in cricket which was soon evident. At fourteen he won a place in the first XI of City of London School, and held it for five years.

He began his 21-year career in first-class cricket for Cambridge University against Surrey, at Fenner's, on April 29, 1961, as wicket-keeper and No. 8 batsman. His 76 was the highest score of the match for Cambridge. Within three weeks he had gained the respect of some stern critics with 73 and 89, by far the highest Cambridge scores, against Benaud's Australians. By the time of the University match he had made his first and second centuries and been top scorer in ten Cambridge innings. Against Oxford his 27, which held the unsteady Cambridge innings together, was bettered only by Jefferson's lusty 54 at No. 9. With

1,158 runs at 44.53 he was second to Craig (1,342 at 47.92) in the University averages. Selection for the Gentlemen against the Players at Lord's put an unusual seal of achievement on his first season; but brought him only two – relatively unsuccessful – matches for Middlesex.

Next year he was less successful for Cambridge until his century against Oxford; and he scored 143 for once out for Middlesex. He was praised for his captaincy of the University at Lord's in 1963, when he made 790 runs at 30.38. Then, in 1964, came his best season. The first man since F. S. Jackson in 1892 and 1893 to captain Cambridge in consecutive seasons, he made his second century against Oxford and finished top of the University averages, 25 ahead of the next man, with 1,313 at 57.08. And he set a new Cambridge record individual aggregate of 4,068. He was chosen to captain the President of MCC's XI against the Australians and, with a top score of 67 out of 179 for seven, saved the match. Over the entire season only Tom Graveney and Eric Russell made more than his 2,179 runs. The Cricket Writers' Club elected him Young Cricketer of 1964 and he was, almost inevitably, chosen for the winter's tour of South Africa.

That would have been a considerable series of performances for an undergraduate in the days when they could devote their time to cricket without fear of the examiners. Brearley, however, not only kept wicket through two of those four seasons but, changing academic horses in mid-stream, he achieved a first in Classics and a two-one in Moral Sciences. In addition he was joint-top in the Civil Service examination.

In South Africa the competition of more experienced players kept him out of the Test team, but he contrived to see those facets of that country and its people which are not usually shown to visiting cricketers. Back in England, he played regularly for Middlesex and, like many before him, found a first full county season as an opening batsman a trying experience. He was, though, not afraid to graft, and in that summer he probably learnt more about going in first against the new ball than in any other phase of his career.

It is possible that, in 1966, Mike Brearley might have advanced from a highly talented and promising batsman to a great one. That was the next logical step in his progress. But he became, once again, preoccupied with studies, and took a post-graduate course in philosophy at Cambridge. He found time to play a few matches for Cambridgeshire, where he was intrigued by keeping wicket to Johnny Wardle's left-arm mixture of finger spin, the Chinaman, and its complementary googly. He turned out twice, too, for the University, for whom he scored a century against a powerful Yorkshire bowling side. Although that was not the hardening process old pros would have prescribed for an aspiring 24-year-old batsman, the selectors were happy to send him as captain of the MCC Under-25 team to Pakistan. There his batting was remarkable. His 312 not out against Northern Zone was one of the rare instances of a triple-century being made in a day; and he scored 223 against Pakistan in the second representative match. He averaged 132 for the tour; more than twice as many as any other member of a side which included Dennis Amiss, Keith Fletcher and Alan Ormrod.

Whatever conclusion may be drawn about his absence from the first-class scene in 1966, it must be virtually certain that the development of his batting lost crucial momentum when research at Cambridge and teaching in the Universities of California and Newcastle kept him out of first-class cricket in 1967, and restricted him to the latter part of the 1968, 1969 and 1970 seasons. That may appear contradictory when the best part of his career lay ahead. He had yet to become the outstanding captain of his, or perhaps any other age, but he was never again such an outstanding batsman among his contemporaries as he had been when he returned from Pakistan.

In 1971 he gave up university teaching in order to take up the Middlesex captaincy. Outside cricket in the following years he developed his long-standing interest in psychotherapy. He set about not merely captaining but rebuilding a Middlesex side which had not had major success since the Championship title of 1949. In 1975, though eleventh in the table, Middlesex performed the then unique feat of reaching both finals – of the Gillette and Benson and Hedges – only to lose both. Brearley's own performance and confidence steadily improved, his average rising through 33, 30, 34 and 44, until, in 1975, he was top of the county's batting figures, in aggregate and average, and sixth in the national averages.

In 1976, in a characteristically perceptive move, he recruited Alan Jones, the former Sussex and Somerset bowler, who provided the extra edge of penetration to give Middlesex their first county title for 29 years. In the same season Brearley was chosen for England – as a batsman, it should be noted. Opening the innings in the first two Tests against West Indies he scored 0, 17, 40 and 13. He was picked for the tour to India, Sri Lanka and the Centenary Test of 1977 in Australia, as vice-captain to Tony Greig. First in aggregate and second in average for the entire Indian tour, he made only 215 at 26.87 in the Tests. Still, he made top score in both the third and fifth Test matches and, most valuably, steadied the English second innings in the anniversary game at Melbourne.

Then came the Packer defections, which Brearley probably understood as clearly as and with less bias than anyone else in cricket, though he refused to take part in the operation. Because of his share in it, Greig was dropped from the captaincy, playing under Brearley, who inherited it, in the 1977 home series against Australia, who employed all their Packer men. Brearley played two useful innings; but that mattered little beside the fact that Australia were beaten by three-nothing.

In addition, Middlesex finished equal first in the Championship with Kent and won the Gillette Cup. Brearley, despite his absences at Tests, was top of their averages with a figure of 68.33. After captaining England in the first two – drawn – Tests in Pakistan, Brearley had his arm broken by a ball from Sikander Bakht, who was not more than fast-medium, and returned home without going on to New Zealand.

The injury seemed subsequently to unsettle him and he had an abject batting year. But again results gave his reply: Middlesex finished third in the Championship; England beat Pakistan two-nothing, New Zealand three-nothing, and Australia, on their own pitches but without their Packer players, five-one. In 1979, India were beaten three-one but, although Brearley's batting revived, Middlesex, an unhappy fourteenth, experienced their worst season under his captaincy.

In 1979-80 Australia, at full Packer-reinforced strength, were waiting to take revenge for, above all, the humiliation of a year before. They did so most effectively from a playing point of view. Despite Botham's spirited resistance, the bowling of Dennis Lillee and Geoff Dymock, and the batting of Greg and Ian Chappell and Allan Border, were too much for England. Australia won all three matches of the series. Brearley batted resolutely enough to average 34.20; better than his figures against some substantially less hostile attacks. This was his one real defeat.

Unfortunately Lillee chose to bait Brearley in an offensive and childish manner; while a section of the crowd at Melbourne treated him in a fashion which the Australian manager, in an official statement, said made him "ashamed to be an Australian". This was England's first experience of the new, Packer-inspired commercialisation of Australian cricket. Brearley was pressured to accept playing conditions already rejected by the TCCB, and the Australian authorities behaved less than honestly in portraying him, through the media, as a "whingeing Pom". Brearley never behaved better nor with more dignity.

The Golden Jubilee Test at Bombay, played on the way home from Australia and lifted to considerable heights by Botham's splendid all-round cricket, did something to wash away the unpleasant taste. More happily, Brearley led Middlesex to yet another Championship and the Gillette Cup; and then decided to allow himself another couple of seasons before he retired. Nevertheless, he decided that his studies in psychoanalysis would prevent him from touring in the following winter. The selectors needed to "blood" his successor; and Botham inherited, with unhappy results for his own playing performances over more than a year. Subsequently, in 1981, after an English defeat at Trent Bridge and an unhappy draw at Lord's, Botham resigned his office and the selectors recalled Brearley. He can hardly have contemplated the task with pleasure, but under his calm, tactically skilful, and friendly leadership, and through the amazing all-round performances of the revived Botham, England won the third, fourth and fifth Tests; at Headingley, Edgbaston and Old Trafford respectively.

So to 1982; another Championship and retirement. He has gone with regret but not bitterness. He realises that he will miss the companionship, the humour and the excitement of the first-class game but he is clear on what he wants to do. He hopes still to play some cricket, preferably of a competitive kind, and he will, surely, contribute much on the cricket committee of the TCCB. For the two years until he completes his studies and qualifies as a psychoanalyst, he will practise as a psychotherapist. He has already worked in a clinic for disturbed adolescents and is convinced of his destiny in this field.

It would be foolish to pretend that Mike Brearley is the usual type of county cricketer. He is a serious man; an idealist in matters of morals, but also a realist. Happy to accept, and content that he had earned, a benefit of £31,000 in 1978, he had always believed that cricketers in general were underpaid in view of the risks their career implies. He has campaigned along those lines; not merely for himself. He was an early, active, and wise member of the Cricketers' Association which is, in effect, the players' trade union.

Much of his influence over his players stemmed from his friendly approach. Physically lean and wiry, even at 40, his hair greying, there is an engagingly boyish quality about his easy smile and a frankness about his expression confirmed by honesty. He remains a most interesting character who has displayed so many facets that one waits, intrigued, for the next.

J. M. Brearley's first-class career consisted of 454 matches to the end of the 1982 season. In 767 innings, 102 of them not out, he scored 25,168 runs, average 37.84, with 45 hundreds. His highest score was 312 not out, made in one day, for MCC Under-25 v North Zone at Peshawar, 1966-67. He took 418 catches, made 12 stumpings and captured 3 wickets for 192 runs, average 64.00.

TURNER MARCHES ON

By NORMAN HARRIS

In retrospect, it almost seems that Glenn Turner was destined to score his 100th hundred on May 29. One would hardly say he had tried *not* to reach the milestone on some other day on some other ground. But, after a run of low scores, a gloriously fine Saturday at Worcester suddenly seemed the obvious setting.

It was also clear that Turner would not want to "just score 100" in adding his name to the eighteen players who had previously registered the feat. He would surely want to do so in particularly glittering fashion. Securing 100 before lunch was the most obvious way. Almost inevitably, he achieved it.

The occasion seemed even more appropriate, with Billy Ibadulla on hand to come out to the middle with a celebratory gin and tonic. It was Ibadulla, once a coach in Dunedin, New Zealand, who had encouraged Turner to go to England and arrange a trial with Warwickshire. It was Warwickshire who had not been able to offer him a contract, and against whom Turner has always scored particularly heavily. And it was Warwickshire's bowlers who were now suffering again. With Turner 128 at lunch, the afternoon offered a further challenge; as the runs mounted up it became clear that he was after his 300. He reached it at 5.36 and at the declaration, six minutes later, was 311 not out.

The performance brought to mind other famous scorers of many runs, notably Bradman. Certainly the great Australian run-maker scored centuries far more often than Turner or anyone else, especially in Test matches. But it is difficult to think of any batsman, Bradman included, who could respond to particular challenges with more certainty and flair. There was another celebrated example of this in 1973 when Turner, touring England with the New Zealanders, achieved the rare feat (only six others have done it) of scoring 1,000 runs before the end of May. He needed 93 in his last possible innings, at Northampton; the wet wicket was, by his own judgement, "dangerous", and the opposition bowlers included Bishen Bedi. There was also the factor that cricket is reckoned the last game on earth where such targets can be pursued with confidence. Yet when the Worcestershire captain, Norman Gifford, was told the previous evening that Turner needed 93 runs he said, simply, "If that's what he needs he'll get them". So he did, even though the first day's play was quite short and he had to resume the next morning needing another 23 runs.

There have also been six occasions when Turner has scored two hundreds in a match, most notably when New Zealand gained their first victory against Australia at Christchurch in 1974. The fall of wickets around him has seemed to provide extra stimulus, for he has twice carried his bat in Test matches and when he did it in a 1981 county match against Glamorgan, his unbeaten 141 out of 169 constituted a record 83.4 per cent of the total.

His initial season in first-class cricket, as a schoolboy in New Zealand, might not have promised such an abundance of runs. But it did indicate

[*Ken Kelly*

The milestone achieved, Glenn Turner puts down his bat, temporarily, to celebrate his 100th hundred with a gin and tonic, brought out, appropriately, by Billy Ibadulla who, while coaching in New Zealand, recognised Turner's potential and arranged trials for him in England.

the character and the technique: once he scored just 3 runs in an entire morning session, and he recalls wryly that his defensive technique was so sound that he "didn't even get any runs from snicks". Further evidence of character was to be found in his giving up his job as an insurance clerk and working in a bakery for ten months in order to save the money for his trip to England – a very big gamble in itself.

Several seasons were to pass before, quite suddenly, he shed his reputation for slow scoring. Having established himself with Worcestershire, he decided to try to gain – and give – some pleasure with his batting. He drove the ball with great power for one who, even in his mid-twenties, looked unusually slender and boyish. There was also an aesthetic quality in his stroke-play which made it quite distinctive. In silhouette there would have been no mistaking the front foot *en point*, the full follow-through of the bat without the wrists "breaking" and an overall impression of the bat being long and pointed like a sword.

Two points of technique contributed to this. Firstly, the hands were kept high up the bat handle, very much in the approved manner for those who wish to drive well. Secondly, the top hand was kept around the back of the handle, in a grip which has been termed "the jug handle". To many observers, this should have militated against making the drive with a full follow-through. But Turner seemed to gain satisfaction from proving otherwise, a point he emphasised in calling his autobiography *My Way*.

Criticism was a most effective motivation, as were the sort of uncomplimentary comments which sometimes get passed on the field of play. In Turner's case this was the more so because of a distaste for coarse or unprofessional behaviour. His most striking (perhaps only) display of aggression in a Test match was the result of being "talked at" by the Australians, his answer being to hit off-spinner Ashley Mallett through and over the off-side for 8 fours in three overs.

An independent streak, and his belief in his monetary worth as a leading professional, caused him to fall out with the New Zealand cricket authorities and, sadly, to withdraw for some years from Test cricket. In 1978 he opted to continue playing for Worcestershire and help organise his benefit rather than tour with the visiting New Zealanders. Even to some of his colleagues and friends that decision seemed almost perverse, since his appearances in Test matches that summer would have been welcomed by cricket lovers in Worcestershire and might well have been to the advantage of his benefit. As much in his mind as his dispute with the New Zealand authorities was probably his belief that he should be seen to be working hard in support of his benefit committee.

Since then, while at the height of his powers, he has covered Test series in New Zealand as a television commentator instead of playing in them. This has deprived him of the opportunity of playing against the best Test teams, with the fastest bowlers of his time, a fact which has had to be entered as a caveat by critics ranking him among the "greats". Nor, when scoring all the runs he did against West Indies in 1971-72 and against Australia in New Zealand in 1973-74, did he, other than very rarely, dominate the bowling.

Perhaps circumstances will still allow him to prove this point. If not, how will history assess him? A remarkable record-breaker? That seems a little unfair, as it ignores his match-winning efforts at all levels of cricket and, most particularly, it fails to recognise the aesthetic element in his batting. Yet, however unsatisfactory, that at the moment is as it may be.

At the end of the English season of 1982, Turner himself viewed his innings at Worcester on May 29 as the most satisfying of all his achievements. In fact, though it hardly seemed so at the time, he is aware now that the day could have been even more momentous. He could have passed the highest score ever made in a day (345 by C. G. Macartney for the Australians against Nottinghamshire in 1921) had Worcestershire not declared when he was on 311, with 48 minutes of the day remaining.

G. M. TURNER – FIRST-CLASS CAREER

Season		*M*	*I*	*NO*	*R*	*HS*	*Avge*	*50*	*100*
1964-65	(NZ)	6	10	1	126	28	14.00	0	0
1965-66	(NZ)	6	11	4	330	95	47.14	3	0
1966-67	(NZ)	6	11	1	224	64	22.40	1	0
1967		2	3	1	23	14	11.50	0	0
1968		25	44	3	1,182	106*	28.82	9	1
1968-69	(NZ)	10	16	1	708	167	47.20	3	2
1969†		23	41	7	1,146	124	33.70	7	1
1969-70	(I/P)	7	13	1	458	110	38.16	4	1
	(A)	3	6	0	205	99	34.16	2	0
	(NZ)	5	9	1	160	57	20.00	1	0
1970		25	46	7	2,379	154*	61.00	9	10
1970-71	(NZ)	8	16	1	517	76	34.46	4	0
	(A)	1	1	0	8	8	8.00	0	0
1971		19	31	4	1,126	179	41.70	6	2
1971-72	(NZ)	5	10	3	424	101*	60.57	2	1
	(WI/Ber.)	12	17	2	1,284	259	85.60	3	4
1972		21	38	4	1,764	170	51.88	6	7
1972-73	(Rh)	2	3	0	143	91	47.66	1	0
	(NZ)	8	14	1	644	132	49.53	1	2
	(A)	1 (did not bat)							
1973†		26	44	8	2,416	153*	67.11	12	9
1973-74	(A)	6	10	1	265	106*	29.44	0	1
	(NZ)	4	7	1	449	110*	74.83	2	2
1974		20	31	9	1,332	202*	60.54	5	3
1974-75	(Rh)	1	2	0	36	27	18.00	0	0
	(NZ)	8	15	1	838	186*	59.85	2	4
1975		17	29	5	1,362	214*	56.75	8	3
1975-76	(Rh)	2	4	1	162	74	54.00	1	0
	(NZ)	11	20	4	1,244	177*	77.75	5	5
	(SA)	3	6	0	157	66	26.16	1	0
1976		20	37	2	1,752	169	50.05	10	4
1976-77	(P/I)	7	13	0	423	113	32.53	2	1
	(NZ)	9	16	2	750	177*	53.57	5	1
1977		22	38	5	1,380	153	41.81	6	3
1978		22	38	7	1,711	202*	55.19	4	6
1979		18	31	2	1,669	150*	57.55	5	8
1979-80	(NZ)	7	13	0	327	136	25.15	1	1
1980		21	35	4	1,817	228*	58.61	7	7
1981		24	42	4	2,101	168	55.28	6	9
1982		9	16	3	1,171	311*	90.07	3	5
		452	787	101	34,213	311*	49.87	147	103

† *Includes New Zealand tour to England as well as matches for Worcestershire.*

Notes: Turner's 311* for Worcestershire v Warwickshire at Worcester in 1982 was the highest innings played in England since J. D. Robertson's 331* for Middlesex v Worcestershire at Worcester in 1949. (R. B. Simpson, for Australia v England at Manchester in 1964, was dismissed at 311.)

Turner's 72 hundreds for Worcestershire are a record for the county. The previous best was 70, by D. Kenyon. His ten hundreds for Worcestershire in 1970 established a new record for the county in a season, surpassing the nine by C. F. Walters in 1933.

When he scored 109 for Worcestershire v Lancashire at Southport in 1979, Turner became the first batsman to score 100 against all seventeen first-class counties. (I. V. A. Richards equalled this feat in 1981.)

Of Turner's 103 hundreds, six were scored before lunch: v Nottinghamshire at Worcester, 1973; v Surrey at Worcester, 1978; v Warwickshire at Birmingham, 1980; v Northamptonshire at Stourbridge (1st innings), 1981; v Warwickshire at Worcester, 1982; v Lancashire at Worcester, 1982.

Turner is unique in that he has the highest individual innings for a county in all the major English competitions: 311* in the County Championship, 117* in the Gillette Cup, 105 in the NatWest Bank Trophy, 143* in the Benson and Hedges Cup and 147 in the John Player League. In the John Player League, his aggregate of 6,144 runs at the end of the 1982 season was the highest for the competition, no other batsman having scored 6,000 runs.

G. M. TURNER'S 100 HUNDREDS

106*	Worcestershire v Middlesex at Worcester, 1968
167	Otago v Wellington at Dunedin, 1968-69
123	South Island v West Indians at Dunedin, 1968-69
124	New Zealanders v Middlesex at Lord's, 1969
110	New Zealand v Pakistan at Dacca, 1969-70
122	Worcestershire v Essex at Worcester, 1970
137	Worcestershire v Hampshire at Southampton, 1970
154*	Worcestershire v Gloucestershire at Bristol, 1970
112	Worcestershire v Leicestershire at Worcester, 1970
106	Worcestershire v Warwickshire at Birmingham,1970
118*	Worcestershire v Somerset at Worcester, 1970
110*	Worcestershire v Northamptonshire at Wellingborough, 1970
142*	Worcestershire v Derbyshire at Chesterfield, 1970
140	Worcestershire v Yorkshire at Worcester, 1970
133*	Worcestershire v Warwickshire at Worcester, 1970
179	Worcestershire v Pakistanis at Worcester, 1971
101	Worcestershire v Essex at Worcester, 1971
101*	Otago v Wellington at Wellington, 1971-72
202	New Zealanders v President of WIBC's XI at Montego Bay, 1971-72
223*	New Zealand v West Indies at Kingston, 1971-72
259	New Zealanders v Guyana at Georgetown, 1971-72
259	New Zealand v West Indies at Georgetown, 1971-72
111	Worcestershire v Cambridge University at Cambridge, 1972
156	Worcestershire v Warwickshire at Worcester, 1972
122 128*	Worcestershire v Warwickshire at Birmingham, 1972
170	Worcestershire v Gloucestershire at Bristol, 1972
154	Worcestershire v Essex at Leyton, 1972
107	Worcestershire v Nottinghamshire at Nottingham, 1972
132	Otago v Auckland at Auckland, 1972-73
131	Otago v Wellington at Dunedin, 1972-73
151*	New Zealanders v D. H. Robins' XI at Eastbourne, 1973
143	New Zealanders v Worcestershire at Worcester, 1973
153*	New Zealanders v MCC at Lord's, 1973
111	New Zealanders v Northamptonshire at Northampton, 1973
121*	New Zealanders v Surrey at The Oval, 1973
109*	Worcestershire v Glamorgan at Cardiff, 1973
110	Worcestershire v Leicestershire at Leicester, 1973

106*	Worcestershire v Essex at Chelmsford, 1973
140	Worcestershire v Nottinghamshire at Worcester, 1973
106*	New Zealanders v Tasmania at Launceston, 1973-74
101 110*	New Zealand v Australia at Christchurch, 1973-74
138*	Worcestershire v Kent at Worcester, 1974
202*	Worcestershire v Cambridge University at Cambridge, 1974
181	Worcestershire v Gloucestershire at Cheltenham, 1974
135 108	Otago v Northern Districts at Gisborne, 1974-75
105 186*	Otago v Central Districts at Dunedin, 1974-75
100*	Worcestershire v Nottinghamshire at Worcester, 1975
214*	Worcestershire v Oxford University at Worcester, 1975
154*	Worcestershire v Glamorgan at Swansea, 1975
177*	Otago v Wellington at Wellington, 1975-76
104	Otago v Auckland at Dunedin, 1975-76
115	Otago v Northern Districts at Dunedin, 1975-76
121*	Otago v Indians at Dunedin, 1975-76
117	New Zealand v India at Christchurch, 1975-76
169	Worcestershire v Nottinghamshire at Nottingham, 1976
135*	Worcestershire v Somerset at Bath, 1976
150	Worcestershire v Sussex at Hove, 1976
120	Worcestershire v Northamptonshire at Northampton, 1976
113	New Zealand v India at Kanpur, 1976-77
177*	Northern Districts v Central Districts at Napier, 1976-77
153	Worcestershire v Hampshire at Worcester, 1977
141*	Worcestershire v Glamorgan at Swansea, 1977
131	Worcestershire v Somerset at Worcester, 1977
127	Worcestershire v Northamptonshire at Northampton, 1978
155*	Worcestershire v Hampshire at Portsmouth, 1978
150	Worcestershire v Surrey at Worcester, 1978
101	Worcestershire v Essex at Chelmsford, 1978
202*	Worcestershire v Warwickshire at Birmingham, 1978
115	Worcestershire v Gloucestershire at Worcester, 1978
148*	Worcestershire v Yorkshire at Worcester, 1979
109	Worcestershire v Lancashire at Southport, 1979
118	Worcestershire v Sussex at Worcester, 1979
131	Worcestershire v Surrey at Guildford, 1979
120	Worcestershire v Leicestershire at Leicester, 1979
150*	Worcestershire v Nottinghamshire at Worcester, 1979
108	Worcestershire v Warwickshire at Worcester, 1979
135	Worcestershire v Glamorgan at Worcester, 1979
136	Otago v Auckland at Alexandra, 1979-80
228*	Worcestershire v Gloucestershire at Worcester, 1980
100	Worcestershire v Middlesex at Worcester, 1980
115	Worcestershire v Yorkshire at Bradford, 1980
101	Worcestershire v Warwickshire at Birmingham, 1980
182*	Worcestershire v Derbyshire at Worcester, 1980
168	Worcestershire v Essex at Colchester, 1980
103*	Worcestershire v Kent at Worcester, 1980
104*	Worcestershire v Sussex at Worcester, 1981
101	Worcestershire v Essex at Worcester, 1981
168	Worcestershire v Yorkshire at Worcester, 1981
161 101	Worcestershire v Northamptonshire at Stourbridge, 1981
111	Worcestershire v Gloucestershire at Worcester, 1981
130	Worcestershire v Glamorgan at Swansea, 1981
147* 139	Worcestershire v Warwickshire at Worcester, 1981
239*	Worcestershire v Oxford University at Oxford, 1982
311*	Worcestershire v Warwickshire at Worcester, 1982

Of Turner's 100 hundreds, 75 were scored in England, 18 in New Zealand, 4 in the West Indies and 1 each in Australia, India and Pakistan.

MAKERS OF 100 HUNDREDS

	Innings needed	*Début*	*Year achieved*	*Age*	*Career 100s*
D. G. Bradman (*NSW/SA*)..........	295	1927-28	1947-48	39	117
D. C. S. Compton (*Middx*)..........	552	1936	1952	34	123
L. Hutton (*Yorks.*)....................	619	1934	1951	35	129
G. Boycott (*Yorks.*)...................	645	1962	1977	37	128
W. R. Hammond (*Glos.*)...........	679	1920	1935	32	167
H. Sutcliffe (*Yorks.*)..................	700	1919	1932	37	149
E. H. Hendren (*Middx*)..............	740	1907	1928-29	39	170
G. M. Turner (*Otago/ND/Worcs.*)	779	1964-65	1982	35	103
J. B. Hobbs (*Surrey*)..................	821	1905	1923	40	197
A. Sandham (*Surrey*).................	871	1911	1935	44	107
C. P. Mead (*Hants*)....................	892	1905	1927	40	153
L. E. G. Ames (*Kent*)................	915	1926	1950	44	102
G. E. Tyldesley (*Lancs.*)............	919	1909	1934	45	102
T. W. Graveney (*Glos/Worcs.*).....	940	1948	1964	37	122
J. H. Edrich (*Surrey*).................	945	1956	1977	40	103
F. E. Woolley (*Kent*)..................	1,031	1906	1929	42	145
M. C. Cowdrey (*Kent*)...............	1,035	1950	1973	40	107
T. W. Hayward (*Surrey*)............	1,076	1893	1913	42	104
W. G. Grace (*Glos.*)..................	1,113	1865	1895	46	126

THE CONTINUING STRUGGLE FOR SURVIVAL

By PHILIP CARLING

(Formerly Chief Executive of Nottinghamshire, now Secretary-Designate of Glamorgan)

For most of its history, county cricket has lurched from one financial crisis to another. Only during the two immediate post-war periods did large crowds invade county grounds to provide relative security for clubs and players alike. Yet in spite of seemingly regular predictions that the end for cricket, or rather professional cricket, was nigh, the game has survived for the most part in a form which would have been immediately recognisable to its practitioners in late Victorian England. This thought is at the same time both reassuring and worrying. It is reassuring because the warmth of feeling for the game throughout English society has seen it safely through these crises; it is worrying lest today's administrators rely too heavily on this history of survival.

Cricket has traditionally provided for its professionals no more than a reasonable way of life and the hope, not always realised, of a rewarding benefit which would provide secondary employment when limbs or faculties forced a reluctant retirement. It became abruptly apparent, however, during the 1960s, that the game could not for very much longer support such an existence, even for a quite small number of players. As a result, a period of commercialism began with the advent of the knockout cup, sponsored on its inception by Gillette Industries Limited. Along with the growing awareness of the need to attract spectators back to cricket came the realisation that cricket could not survive without commercial support. It would be industry which would replace the wealthy benefactors of inter-war years. But there would be an important difference. Sponsorship is a reward-seeking, commercial activity and not an exercise in altruism. Cricket would have to adjust to its new partner and to a new image.

The limited-overs knockout competition was to bring its own problems. Above all, attitudes changed, and success on the field, previously the plaything of a small group of the more heavily populated counties, became paramount. Whereas overseas players helped to redress the county population imbalance, they increased the pressure to win. Financial rewards for international cricketers needed to be improved and the best English cricketers did not expect to lag behind the cricketing mercenaries.

The profound shock waves which swept through the cricket establishment worldwide at the formation of World Series Cricket in 1977 are proof that the commercial opportunities which offered themselves, once the Gillette sponsorship was adopted, were declined. Cricket was admittedly saved for the seventies, but other sports were left to capitalise on the interest newly shown by business and commercial organisations. Open tennis saw players' earnings multiply many times over, and golf's great achievement in Britain was to increase substantially the prize-money for the winner of its Open Championship while subjugating the size of the winner's purse to the prestige and traditional value of winning itself – proof that heavy commercialisation need not necessarily detract from tradition and the purity of a game.

Much of it had happened before. The parallels between William Clarke's operation in the mid-nineteenth century and World Series Cricket are obvious. Clarke, in earning for himself considerable sums of money, clashed frequently with the established county game, with Lord's, and eventually with a rival organisation set up by James Dean and John Wisden, two of his own players who believed his profit margins were excessive. The immediate rewards offered by World Series Cricket in 1977 were too good for a large number of international cricketers to refuse, but such an experiment, parasitic as it was and superimposed on the established game, could not survive as a long-term threat. The commercial success of the Melbourne Centenary Test match in March, 1977, underlined both cricket's commercial potential at the highest level and the relatively poor rewards accepted until then by its top players. Thus World Series Cricket provided a logical if unwelcome jolt for the professional game. It provoked a new approach and a greater acceptance of the need for further commercialism. It posed many new problems, but solving them also helped to overcome previously unresolved difficulties. As a result, a hesitant acceptance of the need to improve cricketers' salaries, particularly at the highest level, has been at the heart of the flurry of commercial activity undertaken both by individual counties and centrally by the Test and County Cricket Board since 1977. Professional cricket could survive only if it could provide a rewarding career for its players.

Necessity has indeed proved the mother of invention. The marketing department of the Test and County Cricket Board, now a full-time operation, oversees an income to English cricket approaching £3 million. Ironically, as it became apparent that the prices charged for national sponsorships were commercially unrealistic and could be increased, Gillette were the first major casualty. To a large extent, they were the victims of their own success. Gillette's name had become synonymous with cricket's knockout cup during a sponsorship lasting eighteen years. The popularity of the competition had increased the value of a sponsorship which started at £6,500 to a startling £250,000, a sum which rather more than compensates for inflation. Gillette declined the increased cost and the National Westminster Bank were pleased to become involved in cricket. Gillette departed from the scene content that their long involvement with the game had been beneficial both to their own company objectives and to cricket.

Of course the John Player League (1969) and the Benson and Hedges Cup (1972) had been in existence well before 1977. The former had been a competition designed for purely commercial reasons and sold simultaneously to the sponsor and to television. Both have proved successful, and the price to their sponsors has been dramatically increased in 1982 and 1983 respectively. In a further heightening of commercialism, the County Championship became the Schweppes Championship in 1977. The major innovation, however, was the sponsorship of Test matches in England by the Cornhill Insurance Group.

This was a sponsorship hurriedly undertaken in the confusion which followed the formation of World Series Cricket, and represented something of a gamble for the Cornhill company. It has proved so successful that the Test and County Cricket Board has been able more than to double its asking price for a continuation of the agreement in 1983 – a price which Cornhill are prepared to pay. The Cornhill sponsorship of Test cricket in England is acknowledged as one of the outstanding successes in the general field of sports sponsorship. Public awareness of the Cornhill name increased from 2 per cent to 17 per cent as a direct result of their sponsorship and put the company into the top five in insurance for instant recognition.

This new, more business-like approach to the finances of the game, adopted in recent years at national level, has been mirrored, again of necessity, at county level, with considerable local success. The counties have been forced to use their facilities and their grounds to the full. Investment has been made in executive boxes, entertaining suites and, in some counties, in the building of squash courts. Local firms have responded to this encouragement, and the partnerships at county level between business and cricket have increased considerably the game's income. In recent years perimeter advertising and lotteries have also bolstered the game. Both have produced huge sums of money. Cricket has achieved more television time than any other sport, and the advertising industry has been quick to take advantage of the sites on cricket grounds. Counties have managed to swell their coffers in a way previously undreamt of.

The fruits of this dramatic growth of commercialism reached their peak in 1981. An entertaining and heavily attended Ashes series coincided with this peak, and nearly all the first-class counties reported profits for the year. Surpluses in excess of six figures were returned in some cases. To underline this achievement it has to be remembered that global expenditure on cricket and cricketers had almost trebled in a little over three years. But the financial situation changed considerably in 1982, and although there is a strong temptation to place the blame for this on a poorly-attended Test series with India, that would be hiding the whole truth. The fear must be that if income has been maximised both nationally and in the counties, and yet, as in 1982, large losses still result, then cricket has still not got the equation right. Although there are still pockets of income to be tapped, we are left with the harrowing thought that another financial crisis is imminent. There are signs that income from perimeter advertising and from lotteries is decreasing, and the recession has led to a rationalisation of business involvement at county level.

A number of solutions have been advanced: more cricket, less cricket, a four-day County Championship with one-day cricket at weekends. Cricketing arguments augment and sometimes override financial considerations. The only certain conclusion is that administrators cannot rely on the game's history of survival. There remains a general short-sightedness in the county game. It was always stressed by the TCCB that receipts from an Australian series would produce considerably more income for each county than the Test matches of 1982, against India and Pakistan. With West Indies coming second in the league table of attendances, it seems financially advisable to make sure that they and Australia do not come to England in successive years.

Yet the sharp fluctuation in financial fortunes between 1981 and 1982 does suggest poor county budgeting, which, in most cases, is an annual exercise. It means, effectively, that a county will spend virtually all its income in any one year to try to achieve success on the field. Pressure from the Cricketers' Association for a minimum earnings level for all cricketers and the move to longer contracts for players have played havoc with one-year budgets. A more sophisticated financial approach is required. The high number of redundant players at the end of 1982 is testimony to this.

Cricket, then, must be flexible, adaptable and financially more far-seeing. A central decision-making body would, I think, be a great boost for the game. The somewhat unwieldy democracy of the TCCB committee system is hard-pressed to react quickly enough to the ever-changing demands of the 1980s. At the end of the 1981 season there was a general feeling that two additional County Championship games would be beneficial. In the light of the financial euphoria at the time, the Championship programme was increased to 24 matches for each county in 1983. It is generally agreed that for financial reasons this decision would not have been taken at the end of the 1982 season. Yet a change for 1984 would have to be made almost before the start of the 1983 season, and there is understandable reluctance to reject an experiment before it has begun.

The committee system, able to call upon a wealth of expertise throughout the country, could, I believe, be made more efficient at national level by an executive body which has both foresight and teeth. Without this, cricket will continue to lurch from one financial crisis to another when there is no need. Until still more financial sophistication is applied, neither four-day Championship cricket nor more limited-overs matches will provide long-term security. By creating a real executive, the decision-making process could be quickened throughout the entire administration of the professional game.

SOUTH AFRICA: PROGRESS TOWARDS NON-RACIAL CRICKET

By GRAHAM JOHNSON, the Kent cricketer

My initial contact with South African cricket came in 1973, as a member of a strong Derrick Robins XI. The situation was illuminating: it was the first non-racial cricket tour of South Africa, and sharing a room with John Shepherd, a West Indian, gave me an insight into many questions.

In 1978 I was asked by Barclays National Bank of South Africa to spend an English winter in Johannesburg, developing and expanding their already considerable cricket coaching programme and playing in the top Johannesburg league for a non-racial club. With this becoming an annual visit I have gained an intimate knowledge by personal contact of the aspirations and problems of cricket in Johannesburg, and, by contact with the other provinces and the personalities involved, of the situation in other areas.

Two points are central to the Barclays' philosophy in cricket development. It is insisted that the scheme benefits cricketers of *all* races (although in prevailing circumstances the major portion of the budget is directed towards non-white cricketers) and the involvement is viewed as a long-term commitment to the establishment of cricket in areas where it has not previously thrived. Taking the population groups within South Africa, cricket in general is well established in the Asian, Coloured and white areas, but is a relatively new sport in most African areas.

Thus for people to expect that with the coming of non-racial cricket within South Africa some eight years ago, representative sides would immediately become markedly more non-white was unfounded. Few non-white cricketers were of a calibre to compete for places on merit with white players who had had world exposure for the development of their talents. It made one realise what an enigma Basil D'Oliveira was, and that his amazing example should not be held as a yardstick for the average product of non-white cricket. A goal to be achieved yes, but not the "norm".

Having established the framework in which equal development and opportunity can take place, there is bound to be a lead-in period before the talent develops sufficiently for the non-white players whom the public expect to see representing South Africa, and playing at provincial level, to do so in any numbers. Initially the non-white representation has to come from the Coloured and Asian groups. Almost certainly it will be some time before an African cricketer wears a Springbok cap. Nevertheless, given time, I can see no reason why the development of African cricket should not be along the lines of South African football, which has become an African-dominated sport. It is important that the public overseas accepts this perspective and appreciates that a lot of good is being done within South African cricket and South African sport in general, even if the whole South African XI does not come from Soweto.

Within the Barclays scheme in Johannesburg, evidence of this development has been seen since 1978 with non-white cricketers gaining selection for the Transvaal Schools under fourteen, under fifteen, open-age group and the senior Transvaal B team on merit. This trend is happening throughout the country, and in the different population groups the progression is bound to continue. There has been an honest and sincere effort by the South African cricket authorities to overcome deep-seated internal problems and prejudices. They have challenged the laws of the land so that their belief in non-racial sport may be realised. It cannot be said of cricket that it is a cosmetic selection of a few talented non-white players for representative sides. It is a major commitment, and one can understand the disappointment of South African cricket representatives, who have made considerable steps forward in their sport, when international bodies seem so reluctant to acknowledge these improvements.

Within South African cricket there is a split allegiance between the South African Cricket Union, the almost universally-recognised governing body, and the more politically motivated South African Cricket Board with its predominantly Asian and Coloured membership. This causes continual internal problems, especially for the non-white cricketer. To say that either camp truly has the support of the non-white cricketer is to over-simplify a complicated issue. There is an ebb and flow between the two sides; and that such a difference of opinion exists in a country of so many population groups, with further divisions within each group, is hardly surprising. Despite their different ways of going about them, their aims are basically the same. When different personalities run the SACB set-up, the current differences may be looked back on in years to come as a passing phase. What would be hypocritical is if either side were to adopt an unyielding stance and so create what in effect would be a reverse apartheid system within the game.

Tours such as that by the English SAB XI, provided they are handled correctly, can do a great deal to further changes within South Africa. There is a valid view expressed – about the future of South Africa – that socio-economic trends and principles decree that attitudes and therefore, eventually, laws will *have* to change, and that commercial companies and their attitudes will have a big part to play in forming the country's future. Why, in that case, can the same attitudes and ideas not be applied to cricket and other sports, which, to those playing them, are "businesses"? The idea of a cricket world split in two, comprising those with and without contacts with South Africa, is disastrous. World cricket can't afford it and South Africa would rather avoid it. But unless constructive contact is made and South Africa's advances are recognised, without threatening a rupture in the world game, there is a real danger that entrepreneurs within South Africa will successfully develop their activities.

I was once asked what I was "trying to do" in Johannesburg. I replied that, whether through the coaching programme or by playing club cricket, I hoped to help create a system in which everybody had an equal opportunity to play the game; and in which people could meet on equal terms afterwards, learning, through contact, more about each other. Without such contact messages are misunderstood and false images built up, either within the country itself or externally. The philosophy can be applied, I believe, at international level and can help to ensure the natural development of the game.

THE FASTEST HUNDREDS IN TEST CRICKET

By GERALD BRODRIBB

In theory, Test matches should provide cricket at its best – with great batsmen matched against great bowlers. Inevitably, though, fear of losing, defensive tactics and time-wasting have at times blunted the spirit of adventure. Since Test cricket began a hundred years ago there have been over 900 matches, producing nearly 1,500 centuries. In only twelve of these has a batsman reached his hundred at the rate of a run-a-minute. It is these memorable innings that are recalled here.

Time as a basis for calculation is not completely satisfactory, but as the truer basis of "balls received" is a recent development, it is the only way of reckoning innings of earlier days. When watching cricket today, the spectator witnesses at least 25 per cent fewer balls in a day compared with first-class cricket of some decades ago, owing to the much slower over-rate. The player is thereby robbed of action, and the spectator of entertainment. Here, in chronological order, are the Test hundreds in which runs were made at the sort of rate Ian Botham scored them against Australia in 1981 or Kapil Dev, against Engand last summer, while making 89 in 55 balls at Lord's and 97 in 93 balls at The Oval.

G. J. Bonnor, 128 for Australia against England at Sydney, 1884-85. After England had scored 269, Australia, on a difficult wicket, were 119 for six when Bonnor, 6ft 6in tall, came in. Soon, at 134, the seventh wicket fell. Bonnor, now joined by Jones, had started shakily and at the tea interval he had scored 15 runs in 30 minutes. But afterwards the giant slogger chanced his arm. He reached 50 in 65 minutes and, thanks to a slip chance when 99, 100 in 100 minutes. When, finally, he was caught he had made 128 out of 169 in 115 minutes, the last 113 of them coming in only 85 minutes. He hit four 5s (the old Australian equivalent of a 6), and fourteen 4s. Australia gained a lead of 40, and won the match by eight wickets.

J. T. Brown, 140 for England against Australia at Melbourne, 1894-95. With the series level at two matches apiece, much interest had been aroused. In a high-scoring fifth and final Test, England were left 297 runs to win. On the last morning, with the weather threatening to spoil the finish, they were 28 for two when Brown came in to join Ward. Encouraged by the strains of "Rule, Britannia", played on a tin whistle, Brown immediately attacked. He reached 35 in sixteen minutes and 50 in 28 minutes, which still remains the fastest fifty in Test cricket. He arrived at 102 out of 144 in 91 minutes, and continued to hit out until, with England in sight of victory, he was caught for 140 scored in 145 minutes. His innings was chanceless, and many of his runs came from powerful cuts.

J. Darling, 160 for Australia against England at Sydney, 1897-98. In the last match of the series England had scored 335 and 178 to Australia's 239. The home team, therefore, needed 275 to win. In Australia's first innings Richardson's fast bowling had gained him eight wickets. This prompted the left-handed Darling (already with two centuries in the series to his credit) to decide that the best hope of victory was to make an all-out attack on Richardson. Going in first, he reached 50 out of 57 in 40 minutes, and 100 in 91 minutes. By then he had hit twenty 4s, driving with immense power. After surviving two skimming chances he was eventually caught off Richardson for 160 out of 252 made in 165 minutes. Victory soon followed. In all Darling hit as many as 30 4s and no great fast bowler can ever have been more deliberately or courageously attacked as Richardson was. In 21.4 overs he took two for 110.

G. L. Jessop, 104 for England against Australia at The Oval, 1902. England, 2–0 down in the series, needed 263 runs to win the fifth Test, and Jessop came in at the fall of the fifth wicket at 48. To quote H. S. Altham: "He *found* the ball at once." Jessop reached 50 out of 70 in 43 minutes. He increased his attack, his hundred coming up in 75 minutes. After one more boundary he was caught at square leg, having made 104 out of 139 in 77 minutes and having hit a 5 and seventeen 4s, some of which would today have counted as 6. With unusual foresight one newspaper kept a ball-by-ball record, so we know that his fifty came in 23 scoring strokes off 38 balls, and his hundred off 40 strokes from 76 balls. Jessop said that he was much satisfied at having shown restraint in not hitting across the line. Some restraint! After Jessop was seventh out England still wanted 76 to win, but they gained a famous one-wicket victory.

J. H. Sinclair, 104 for South Africa against Australia at Cape Town, 1902-03. South Africa, in their first innings, had collapsed for 85 in reply to Australia's 252, but in their second innings, Sinclair, coming in at 81 for two, attacked at once. With huge hits he reached 100 in 80 minutes, only to be stumped for 104 off almost the last ball of the day. His last 64 runs came in 33 minutes, including a spell that produced 34 runs off eight consecutive balls: 446 off Howell and 24464 off Hopkins. Standing 6ft 4in tall, he hit six 6s (all out of the ground), as well as eight 4s, and it is thought that at least four of these 4s would today have counted as 6s.

V. T. Trumper, 185 not out for Australia against England at Sydney, 1903-04. In a historic match Australia began their second innings 292 behind an England score of 577 (R. E. Foster 287), and at 191 for three they were in a doubtful position. Trumper, who had opened in the first innings, came in fifth and at tea had scored 7 in twenty minutes. After tea, in spite of disturbance over a controversial run-out, Trumper played superbly. He reached 50 in 60 minutes, and 100 in 94 minutes, and at the close he was 119 not out, his last 60 runs having come in 40 minutes. The score was 367 for five and Australia were back in the game. Next day 20,000 spectators turned up to see Trumper take his score to 185 before he ran out of partners. He had made his runs out of 294 and given no chance in an innings lasting 230 minutes. The wicket had now deteriorated, and when England, needing 194 to win, lost their fourth wicket at 82, it seemed that Trumper's innings had brought victory in sight. But this was not to be.

P. W. Sherwell, 115 for South Africa against England at Lord's, 1907. After England had scored 428 off 127 overs from an over-rate of almost 23 overs an hour, South Africa were all out for 140. In the follow-on, Sherwell, South Africa's wicket-keeper and captain, went in first and scored 115 out of 153 in 105 minutes, reaching his hundred in 95 minutes. He gave no chance, and thanks to him, with the last day being rained off, South Africa saved the match.

J. M. Gregory, 119 for Australia against South Africa at Johannesburg, 1921-22. The Australians, who had toured England so successfully in 1921, paid a short visit to South Africa on their way home. On the opening day of the second of the three Test matches, Gregory, going in fourth, put on 209 for the third wicket with Collins (203) in only 97 minutes. This is still the fastest double-century stand in Test cricket. Of these 209 runs, Gregory, a tall left-hander with a free style, made 119 before being stumped. He reached 100 in 70 minutes, which remains the fastest Test century, both in time and on the basis of balls received. It has recently been calculated that Gregory received only 67 balls. He hit two 6s and seventeen 4s, but was lucky to survive three chances after passing 68. He also took seven wickets with his aggressive bowling.

D. G. Bradman, 334 for Australia against England at Leeds, 1930. On the opening day Australia scored 458 for three, Bradman's share being 309. He reached 50 in even time, 102 out of 127 in 95 minutes, and at lunch he was 105 out of 134. He added 115 between lunch and tea, and another 89 after tea. This was the fastest double-century and triple-century in Anglo-Australian Tests and for sustained fast scoring has few equals.

S. J. McCabe, 189 not out for Australia against South Africa at Johannesburg, 1935-36. In a remarkable match Australia needed 399 runs to win after South Africa had fought back with a score of 491 (Nourse 231). They reached 85 for one before bad light ended the third day's play. Of these McCabe had scored 59, reaching 50 in 40 minutes with ten 4s. Next morning, on a turning, dusty pitch, he continued to hit while Fingleton kept his end up. When Fingleton was out for 40, the two had put on 177 runs of which McCabe had made 148. He reached 100 in 91 minutes, 150 in 145 minutes, and at lunch he was 159. By mid-afternoon, with Australia 274 for two and victory in sight, lightning and thunder clouds encircled the ground. It was so dark that the South African captain appealed against the light on the grounds that the fielders could no longer see the ball leave McCabe's bat. This unique appeal was upheld, and within minutes the field was under water. McCabe's innings (29 4s) seemed to Fingleton "like a crazy dream".

R. Benaud, 121 for Australia against West Indies at Kingston, Jamaica, 1954-55. After West Indies had scored 357, Australia replied with 758 for eight declared. Five batsmen made centuries, the most dramatic of them being Benaud's. Coming in eighth, with the score 597 for six, he reached 50 in 38 minutes and 100 in 78 minutes, and when finally caught he had made 121 out of 161 in 96 minutes. He hit two 6s and eighteen 4s, five of them off consecutive balls from Dewdney. His hitting, for all its power, was admirably controlled.

B. R. Taylor, 124 for New Zealand against West Indies at Auckland, 1968-69. In what was the first century made by a New Zealander against West Indies, Taylor, primarily an opening bowler but also a powerful left-handed hitter, went in No. 8 at 152 for six. He reached 50 in 30 minutes and 100 in 86 minutes. When out he had made 124 in 110 minutes, including five 6s and fourteen 4s. A notable match ensued. This was Taylor's second century in first-class cricket, both of them in Test matches.

Another remarkable Test innings, worthy of mention, was R. C. Fredericks's 169 for West Indies against Australia at Perth in 1975-76. In reply to Australia's 329 on a fast pitch, opener Fredericks hooked his second ball from Lillee for 6, almost on to the sightscreen. Within 45 minutes, he reached 50 off 33 balls. His opening partner, Julien, was out for 25 in the tenth over with the score at 91. At lunch, when only fourteen overs had been bowled in the 90-minute session, the score was 130 for one. Fredericks's hundred came up in 116 minutes off only 71 balls, and he continued to savage the bowling until he was third out at 258 for a score of 169. West Indies went on to score 585, made at a rate of six runs an over off Lillee, Thomson, Gilmour, Walker and Mallett. This is the second-fastest Test hundred based on balls received. The comparatively slow *time* shows how much a leisurely over-rate can distort the balance between balls received and time taken.

Two other memorable spells of fast scoring were by McCabe, in his 232 against England at Trent Bridge in 1938, when he scored his last 72 runs out of 77 in 28 minutes, and by Botham in his 118 against Australia at Old Trafford in 1981 when he scored his last 90 runs off 49 balls in 53 minutes.

Now that more sophisticated methods of scoring provide a balls received basis, a new approach to records is possible. On the evidence available it seems that the fewest balls received for reaching a Test hundred are:

67 by Gregory in his 119 against South Africa, 1921-22
71 by Fredericks in his 169 against Australia, 1975-76
76 by Jessop in his 104 against Australia, 1902
85 by C. H. Lloyd in his 163 against India at Bangalore, 1974-75
86 by Botham in his 118 against Australia, 1981
87 by Botham in his 149 not out against Australia at Leeds, 1981.

Almost all these innings were ones that mattered vitally to the fortunes of the batting side, either in fighting back from probable defeat or producing a dramatic victory. The batsmen concerned would no doubt have echoed, as a man, Jessop's modest remark after his own finest hour: "Things just went my way."

THE YORKSHIRE CONNECTION

By C. R. WILLIAMSON

(As a journalist, the writer has espoused the cause of Yorkshire cricket for more than 50 years.)

Yorkshire's failure to win any of the four major competitions since their Gillette Cup victory in 1969 has led to more and more pressure being applied on the county's authorities to abandon the age-old and rigid policy of employing only players born within its borders. The irony of it is that Yorkshire, wanted by many of their members to import "outsiders", continue to supply players to other counties in much the same profusion as they have done since the beginning of cricket time. Such has been the succession of these exiles that Yorkshire have long been viewed as the universal providers of players for literally all their competitors.

The subject induced in me an urge to dig into the past, with the idea of presenting a complete picture of the position since the 1914-18 war. What emerges is that there has been such a persistent and widespread exodus, mostly of players not considered competent enough to command a regular place in the Yorkshire team, that Yorkshire-born cricketers who have turned out, during that period, with other counties far exceed the century! I do not guarantee to have included all of them, though the following must be just about a complete list. The notation (1) indicates those who played before the 1939-45 war and (2) those who have played since.

Derbyshire: George R. Langdale (1), Arnold Hamer (2), Charlie Lee (2), William Oates (2), Alan Revill (2), David Smith (2), Brian Bolus (2), Phil Sharpe (2), John Walters (2), Steve Oldham (2), Barry Wood (2), John Hampshire (2). (In 1972 Fred Trueman played in a number of one-day, but not first-class, matches.)

Essex: H. P. Crabtree (1), F. W. Appleyard (2), Bill Greensmith (2), Dick Horsfall (2), Paul Gibb (2), Gordon Barker (2), Ian King (2), Jim Laker (2), Rodney Cass (2), Roger Wrightson (2), Neil Smith (2).

Glamorgan: Eddie Bates (1), Thompson Bell (1), Arnold Dyson (1), Dick Horsfall (2).

Gloucestershire: Frank McHugh (2), Peter Rochford (2), Julian Shackleton (2), Richard Doughty (2).

Hampshire: Walter Livsey (1), Gilbert Dawson (2), Derek Shackleton (2), Clifford Walker (2).

Kent: James Allan (2), Geoffrey Smith (2), Peter Shenton (2), David Baker (2).

Lancashire: Harry Makepeace (1), Phil King (2), Peter Greenwood (2), J. M. Cownley (2), Gordon Hodgson (2), Peter Lever (2), Barry Wood (2), Graham Atkinson (2), Kevin Hayes (2).

Leicestershire: Frank Prentice (1), Jack Firth (2), Gerald Smithson (2), Jack van Geloven (2), Peter Broughton (2), Willie Watson (2), Harold Bird (2), Bernard Cromack (2), Jackie Birkenshaw (2), Ray Illingworth (2), Peter Stringer (2), Chris Balderstone (2), Peter Booth (2), Tim Boon (2).

Middlesex: Don Bennett (2).

Northamptonshire: E. J. H. Dixon (1), Dennis Brookes (1), Norman Grimshaw (1), Ken Fiddling (2), Fred Jakeman (2), Jack Webster (2), Desmond Barrick (2), Douglas Greasley (2), Peter Pickering (2), Peter Shenton (2), Arthur Wells (2), Ronald Jakeman (2), Bob Platt (2), John Swinburne (2), Geoff Cook (2), Norman Maltby (2), Neil Mallender (2).

Nottinghamshire: Freddie Stocks (2), Ken Smales (2), Jack Kelly (2), David Baker (2), Barry Whittingham (2), Keith Gillhouley (2), David Pullan (2), William Rhodes (2), Brian Bolus (2), Mike Smedley (2), Barry Stead (2), Mike Bore (2).

Somerset: Ernest Robson (1), Johnny Lawrence (2), George R. Langdale (2), Miles Coope (2), Ellis Robinson (2), J. D. Stenton (2), David Kitson (2), Gerald Tordoff (2), Colin Atkinson (2), Graham Atkinson (2), Lewis Pickles (2), Michael Walker (2), Tony Clarkson (2), Brian Close (2).

Surrey: Fred Berry (1), Jim Laker (2).

Sussex: Terry Gunn (2), Peter Ledden (2), Chris Fletcher (2).

Warwickshire: Norman Kilner (1), Albert Hayhurst (1), J. Buckingham (1), Norman Horner (2), Eddie Leadbeater (2), Ian King (2), Mike Hellawell (2), Edwin Legard (2), Jack Waring (2), James Allan (2), Chris Clifford (2), John Claughton (2), Chris Lethbridge (2), Simon Sutcliffe (2), Peter Hartley (2).

Worcestershire: Dick Burrows (1), A. W. Robinson (1), George Brook (1), Syd Buller (1), Victor Fox (1), Vernon Grimshaw (1), Phil King (1), George Dews (2), Joe Lister (2), John Ashman (2), John Whitehead (2), Roy Booth (2), J. C. Scholey (2), Duncan Fearnley (2), Rodney Cass (2), Nigel Boyns (2), Jackie Birkenshaw (2), Richard Illingworth (2).

It will be seen that Ian King (Essex and Warwickshire), Phil King (Worcestershire and Lancashire), Langdale (Derbyshire and Somerset), Shenton (Kent and Northamptonshire), Horsfall (Essex and Glamorgan), Baker (Kent and Nottinghamshire), Laker (Surrey and Essex), Bolus (Nottinghamshire and Derbyshire), Wood (Lancashire and Derbyshire) and Birkenshaw (Leicestershire and Worcestershire) have turned out for two counties other than Yorkshire. Derbyshire, Essex, Leicestershire, Northamptonshire, Nottinghamshire, Somerset, Warwickshire and Worcestershire have all built up such a formidable colony of Yorkshire "emigrants" as to assume, in each case, the equivalent of at least a complete eleven. According to my researches, the county which has gone longest without aid from the broad acres is Glamorgan, their last Yorkshireman having been Dick Horsfall in 1956.

In a match at Trent Bridge in July, 1964, Yorkshiremen in action numbered sixteen – the Yorkshire eleven plus Bolus, Smedley, Rhodes, Gillhouley and Baker of Nottinghamshire, whose staff at the time included two other Yorkshiremen, Stead and Whittingham.

Bringing the whole of the past within the scope of this survey, Yorkshiremen who have appeared in Test cricket after having left home for service elsewhere also form more than a complete "team". All these sixteen have turned out for England when with other counties: Albert Ward, Willis Cuttell, Harry Makepeace, Peter Lever and Barry Wood (all Lancashire), Walter Lees and Jim Laker (both Surrey), Willie Watson, Ray Illingworth, Jackie Birkenshaw and Chris Balderstone (all

Leicestershire), Dennis Brookes and Geoff Cook (both Northamptonshire), Derek Shackleton (Hampshire), Brian Bolus (Nottinghamshire), and Brian Close (Somerset). And, lest we forget – Yorkshiremen Frank Mitchell (South Africa) and Hanson Carter (Australia) played *against* England in Tests in the days of long ago.

Imagine it – more than 100 Yorkshiremen with other counties within a 60-year spell. And nothing could be more certain than that there will be many to be added to that company as the seasons come and go.

If and when Yorkshire do open their doors to "foreigners", we are bound to be reminded of the very few who, born outside their boundaries, have appeared in their team. The last to do so, in 1951, was Geoffrey Keighley, who, born in the South of France, was a special case, his forebears for many generations having hailed from Yorkshire's West Riding. Between the wars the club compromised their principles in the case of three amateurs – W. E. Blackburn, W. E. Harbord and R. T. Stanyforth. They were under the impression, though, until the mid-fifties, that Blackburn, who had been an Army officer in the 1914-18 war, was a native of Sawley, which is in Yorkshire, when in fact he was born at Clitheroe in Lancashire. Lord Hawke, as is well known, was born in Lincolnshire of Yorkshire parents. A matter of less general knowledge is that E. J. Radcliffe, who succeeded Lord Hawke in the team captaincy, first saw daylight at Tiverton in Devon.

Nothing, perhaps, could emphasise Yorkshire's opposition to "outsiders" more strikingly than the fact that there has not been a single professional throughout this century who was permitted to find and retain a place in their ranks. Cecil Parkin came nearest to it, being introduced for the match against Gloucestershire at Headingley in July, 1906, but he was promptly "shown the door" when it transpired that he had been born on the "wrong" side of the Tees in Durham.

TEST CRICKETERS

FULL LIST FROM 1877 TO SEPTEMBER 1, 1982

These lists have been compiled on a home and abroad basis, appearances abroad being printed in *italics*.

Abbreviations. E: England. A: Australia. SA: South Africa. WI: West Indies. NZ: New Zealand. In: India. P: Pakistan. SL: Sri Lanka.

All appearances are placed in this order of seniority. Hence, any England cricketer playing against Australia in England has that achievement recorded first and the remainder of his appearances at home (if any) set down before passing to matches abroad. Although the distinction between amateur and professional was abolished in 1963, initials of English professionals before that date are still given in brackets. The figures immediately following each name represent the total number of appearances in *all* Tests.

Where the season embraces two different years, the first year is given; i.e. 1876 indicates 1876-77.

When South Africa left the British Commonwealth in 1961 they ceased membership of the Imperial Cricket Conference, which in 1965 was renamed the International Cricket Conference. The rules of membership were changed then so that, although Pakistan have left the Commonwealth, they remain members of ICC.

ENGLAND

Number of Test cricketers: 499

Abel (R.) 13: v A 1888 (3) 1896 (3) 1902 (2); *v A 1891 (3); v SA 1888 (2)*

Absolom, C.A. 1: *v A 1878*

Allen (D. A.) 39: v A 1961 (4) 1964 (1); v SA 1960 (2); v WI 1963 (2) 1966 (1); v P 1962 (4); *v A 1962 (1) 1965 (4); v SA 1964 (4); v WI 1959 (5); v NZ 1965 (3); v In 1961 (5); v P 1961 (3)*

Allen, G. O. 25: v A 1930 (1) 1934 (2); v WI 1933 (1); v NZ 1931 (3); v In 1936 (3); *v A 1932 (5) 1936 (5); v WI 1947 (3); v NZ 1932 (2)*

Allom, M. J. C. 5: *v SA 1930 (1); v NZ 1929 (4)*

Allott, P. J. W. 5: v A 1981 (1); v In 1982 (2); *v In 1981 (1); v SL 1981 (1)*

Ames (L. E. G.) 47: v A 1934 (5) 1938 (2); v SA 1929 (1) 1935 (4); v WI 1933 (3); v NZ 1931 (3) 1937 (3); v In 1932 (1); *v A 1932 (5) 1936 (5); v SA 1938 (5); v WI 1929 (4) 1934 (4); v NZ 1932 (2)*

Amiss, D. L. 50: v A 1968 (1) 1975 (2) 1977 (2); v WI 1966 (1) 1973 (3) 1976 (1); v NZ 1973 (3); v In 1967 (2) 1971 (1) 1974 (3); v P 1967 (1) 1971 (3) 1974 (3); *v A 1974 (5) 1976 (1); v WI 1973 (5) v NZ 1974 (2); v In 1972 (3) 1976 (5); v P 1972 (3)*

Andrew (K. V.) 2: v WI 1963 (1); *v A 1954 (1)*

Appleyard (R.) 9: v A 1956 (1); v SA 1955 (1); v P 1954 (1); *v A 1954 (4); v NZ 1954 (2)*

Archer, A. G. 1: *v SA 1898*

Armitage (T.) 2: *v A 1876 (2)*

Arnold (E. G.) 10: v A 1905 (4); v SA 1907 (2); *v A 1903 (4)*

Arnold, G. G. 34: v A 1972 (3) 1975 (1); v WI 1973 (3); v NZ 1969 (1) 1973 (3); v In 1974 (2); v P 1967 (2) 1974 (3); *v A 1974 (4); v WI 1973 (3); v NZ 1974 (2); v In 1972 (4); v P 1972 (3)*

Arnold (J.) 1: v NZ 1931

Astill (W. E.) 9: *v SA 1927 (5); v WI 1929 (4)*

Athey, C. W. J. 3: v A 1980 (1); *v WI 1980 (2)*

Attewell (W.) 10: v A 1890 (1); *v A 1884 (5) 1887 (1) 1891 (3)*

Bailey, T. E. 61: v A 1953 (5) 1956 (4); v SA 1951 (2) 1955 (5); v WI 1950 (2) 1957 (4); v NZ 1949 (4) 1958 (4); v P 1954 (3); *v A 1950 (4) 1954 (5) 1958 (5); v SA 1956 (5); v WI 1953 (5); v NZ 1950 (2) 1954 (2)*
Bairstow, D. L. 4: v A 1980 (1); v WI 1980 (1); v In 1979 (1); *v WI 1980 (1)*
Bakewell (A. H.) 6: v SA 1935 (2); v WI 1933 (1); v NZ 1931 (2); *v In 1933 (1)*
Balderstone J. C. 2: v WI 1976 (2)
Barber, R. W. 28: v A 1964 (1) 1968 (1); v SA 1960 (1) 1965 (3); v WI 1966 (2); v NZ 1965 (3); *v A 1965 (5); v SA 1964 (4); v In 1961 (5); v P 1961 (3)*
Barber (W.) 2: v SA 1935 (2)
Barlow, G. D. 3: v A 1977 (1); *v In 1976 (2)*
Barlow (R. G.) 17: v A 1882 (1) 1884 (3) 1886 (3); *v A 1881 (4) 1882 (4) 1886 (2)*
Barnes (S. F.) 27: v A 1902 (1) 1909 (3) 1912 (3); v SA 1912 (3); *v A 1901 (3) 1907 (5) 1911 (5); v SA 1913 (4)*
Barnes (W.) 21: v A 1880 (1) 1882 (1) 1884 (2) 1886 (2) 1888 (3) 1890 (2); *v A 1882 (4) 1884 (5) 1886 (1)*
Barnett (C. J.) 20: v A 1938 (3) 1948 (1); v SA 1947 (3); v WI 1933 (1); v NZ 1937 (3); v In 1936 (1); *v A 1936 (5); v In 1933 (3)*
Barratt (F.) 5: v SA 1929 (1); *v NZ 1929 (4)*
Barrington (K. F.) 82: v A 1961 (5) 1964 (5) 1968 (3); v SA 1955 (2) 1960 (4) 1965 (3); v WI 1963 (5) 1966 (2); v NZ 1965 (2); v In 1959 (5) 1967 (3); v P 1962 (4) 1967 (3); *v A 1962 (5) 1965 (5); v SA 1964 (5); v WI 1959 (5) 1967 (5); v NZ 1962 (3); v In 1961 (5) 1963 (1); v P 1961 (2)*
Barton (V. A.) 1: *v SA 1891*
Bates (W.) 15: *v A 1881 (4) 1882 (4) 1884 (5) 1886 (2)*
Bean (G.) 3: *v A 1891 (3)*
Bedser (A. V.) 51: v A 1948 (5) 1953 (5); v SA 1947 (2) 1951 (5) 1955 (1); v WI 1950 (3); v NZ 1949 (2); v In 1946 (3) 1952 (4); v P 1954 (2); *v A 1946 (5) 1950 (5) 1954 (1); v SA 1948 (5); v NZ 1946 (1) 1950 (2)*
Berry (R.) 2: v WI 1950 (2)
Binks, J. G. 2: *v In 1963 (2)*
Bird M. C. 10: *v SA 1909 (5) 1913 (5)*
Birkenshaw J. 5: *v WI 1973 (2); v In 1972 (2); v P 1972 (1)*
Bligh, Hon. I. F. W. 4: *v A 1882 (4)*
Blythe (C.) 19: v A 1905 (1) 1909 (2); v SA 1907 (3); *v A 1901 (5) 1907 (1); v SA 1905 (5) 1909 (2)*
Board (J. H.) 6: *v SA 1898 (2) 1905 (4)*
Bolus, J. B. 7: v WI 1963 (2); *v In 1963 (5)*
Booth (M. W.) 2: *v SA 1913 (2)*
Bosanquet, B. J. T. 7: v A 1905 (3); *v A 1903 (4)*
Botham, I. T. 54: v A 1977 (2) 1980 (1) 1981 (6); v WI 1980 (5); v NZ 1978 (3); v In 1979 (4) 1982 (3); v P 1978 (3) 1982 (3); *v A 1978 (6) 1979 (3); v WI 1980 (4); v NZ 1977 (3); v In 1979 (1) 1981 (6); v SL 1981 (1)*
Bowden, M. P. 2: *v SA 1888 (2)*
Bowes (W. E.) 15: v A 1934 (3) 1938 (2); v SA 1935 (4); v WI 1939 (2); v In 1932 (1) 1946 (1); *v A 1932 (1); v NZ 1932 (1)*
Bowley (E. H.) 5: v SA 1929 (2); *v NZ 1929 (3)*
Boycott, G. 108: v A 1964 (4) 1968 (3) 1972 (2) 1977 (3) 1980 (1) 1981 (6); v SA 1965 (2); v WI 1966 (4) 1969 (3) 1973 (3) 1980 (5); v NZ 1965 (2) 1969 (3) 1973 (3) 1978 (2); v In 1967 (2) 1971 (1) 1974 (1) 1979 (4); v P 1967 (1) 1971 (2); *v A 1965 (5) 1970 (5) 1978 (6) 1979 (3); v SA 1964 (5); v WI 1967 (5) 1973 (5) 1980 (4); v NZ 1965 (2) 1977 (3); v In 1979 (1) 1981 (4); v P 1977 (3)*
Bradley, W. M. 2: v A 1899 (2)
Braund (L. C.) 23: v A 1902 (5); v SA 1907 (3); *v A 1901 (5) 1903 (5) 1907 (5)*
Brearley, J. M. 39: v A 1977 (5) 1981 (4); v WI 1976 (2); v NZ 1978 (3); v In 1979 (4); v P 1978 (3); *v A 1976 (1) 1978 (6) 1979 (3); v In 1976 (5) 1979 (1); v P 1977 (2)*
Brearley, W. 4: v A 1905 (2) 1909 (1); v SA 1912 (1)
Brennan, D. V. 2: v SA 1951 (2)
Briggs (John) 33: v A 1886 (3) 1888 (3) 1893 (2) 1896 (1) 1899 (1); *v A 1884 (5) 1886 (2) 1887 (1) 1891 (3) 1894 (5) 1897 (5); v SA 1888 (2)*
Brockwell (W.) 7: v A 1893 (1) 1899 (1); *v A 1894 (5)*
Bromley-Davenport, H. R. 4: *v SA 1895 (3) 1898 (1)*

Brookes (D.) 1: *v WI 1947*
Brown (A.) 2: *v In 1961 (1); v P 1961 (1)*
Brown, D. J. 26: v A 1968 (4); v SA 1965 (2); v WI 1966 (1) 1969 (3); v NZ 1969 (1); v In 1967 (2): *v A 1965 (4); v WI 1967 (4); v NZ 1965 (2); v P 1968 (3)*
Brown, F. R. 22: v A 1953 (1); v SA 1951 (5); v WI 1950 (1); v NZ 1931 (2) 1937 (1) 1949 (2); v In 1932 (1); *v A 1950 (5); v NZ 1932 (2) 1950 (2)*
Brown (G.) 7: v A 1921 (3); *v SA 1922 (4)*
Brown (J. T.) 8: v A 1896 (2) 1899 (1); *v A 1894 (5)*
Buckenham (C. P.) 4: *v SA 1909 (4)*
Butcher, A. R. 1: v In 1979
Butcher, R. O. 3: *v WI 1980 (3)*
Butler (H. J.) 2: v SA 1947 (1); *v WI 1947 (1)*
Butt (H. R.) 3: *v SA 1895 (3)*

Calthorpe, Hon. F. S. G. 4: *v WI 1929 (4)*
Carr, A. W. 11: v A 1926 (4); v SA 1929 (2); *v SA 1922 (5)*
Carr, D. B. 2: *v In 1951 (2)*
Carr, D. W. 1: v A 1909
Cartwright, T. W. 5: v A 1964 (2); v SA 1965 (1); v NZ 1965 (1); *v SA 1964 (1)*
Chapman, A. P. F. 26: v A 1926 (4) 1930 (4); v SA 1924 (2); v WI 1928 (3); *v A 1924 (4) 1928 (4); v SA 1930 (5)*
Charlwood (H. R. J.) 2: *v A 1876 (2)*
Chatterton (W.) 1: *v SA 1891*
Christopherson, S. 1: v A 1884
Clark (E. W.) 8: v A 1934 (2); v SA 1929 (1); v WI 1933 (2); *v In 1933 (3)*
Clay, J. C. 1: v SA 1935
Close (D. B.) 22: v A 1961 (1); v SA 1955 (1); v WI 1957 (2) 1963 (5) 1966 (1) 1976 (3); v NZ 1949 (1); v In 1959 (1) 1967 (3); v P 1967 (3); *v A 1950 (1)*
Coldwell (L. J.) 7: v A 1964 (2); v P 1962 (2); *v A 1962 (2); v NZ 1962 (1)*
Compton (D. C. S.) 78: v A 1938 (4) 1948 (5) 1953 (5) 1956 (1); v SA 1947 (5) 1951 (4) 1955 (5); v WI 1939 (3) 1950 (1); v NZ 1937 (1) 1949 (4); v In 1946 (3) 1952 (2); v P 1954 (4); *v A 1946 (5) 1950 (4) 1954 (4); v SA 1948 (5) 1956 (5); v WI 1953 (5); v NZ 1946 (1) 1950 (2)*
Cook (C.) 1: v SA 1947
Cook, G. 4: v In 1982 (3); *v SL 1981 (1)*
Cope, G. A. 3: *v P 1977 (3)*
Copson (W. H.) 3: v SA 1947 (1); v WI 1939 (2)
Cornford (W. L.) 4: *v NZ 1929 (4)*
Cottam, R. M. H. 4: *v In 1972 (2); v P 1968 (2)*
Coventry, Hon. C. J. 2: *v SA 1888 (2)*
Cowdrey, M. C. 114: v A 1956 (5) 1961 (4) 1964 (3) 1968 (4); v SA 1955 (1) 1960 (5) 1965 (3); v WI 1957 (5) 1963 (2) 1966 (4); v NZ 1958 (4) 1965 (3); v In 1959 (5); v P 1962 (4) 1967 (2) 1971 (1); *v A 1954 (5) 1958 (5) 1962 (5) 1965 (4) 1970 (3) 1974 (5); v SA 1956 (5); v WI 1959 (5) 1967 (5); v NZ 1954 (2) 1958 (2) 1962 (3) 1965 (3) 1970 (1); v In 1963 (3); v P 1968 (3)*
Coxon (A.) 1: v A 1948
Cranston, J. 1: v A 1890
Cranston, K. 8: v A 1948 (1); v SA 1947 (3); *v WI 1947 (4)*
Crapp (J. F.) 7: v A 1948 (3); *v SA 1948 (4)*
Crawford J. N. 12: v SA 1907 (2); *v A 1907 (5); v SA 1905 (5)*
Cuttell (W. R.) 2: *v SA 1898 (2)*

Dawson, E. W. 5: *v SA 1927 (1); v NZ 1929 (4)*
Dean (H.) 3: v A 1912 (2); v SA 1912 (1)
Denness, M. H. 28: v A 1975 (1); v NZ 1969 (1); v In 1974 (3); v P 1974 (3); *v A 1974 (5); v WI 1973 (5); v NZ 1974 (2); v In 1972 (5); v P 1972 (3)*
Denton (D.) 11: v A 1905 (1); *v SA 1905 (5) 1909 (5)*
Dewes, J. G. 5: v A 1948 (1); v WI 1950 (2); *v A 1950 (2)*

Dexter, E. R. 62: v A 1961 (5) 1964 (5) 1968 (2); v SA 1960 (5); v WI 1963 (5); v NZ 1958 (1) 1965 (2); v In 1959 (2); v P 1962 (5); *v A 1958 (2) 1962 (5); v SA 1964 (5); v WI 1959 (5); v NZ 1958 (2) 1962 (3); v In 1961 (5); v P 1961 (3)*
Dilley, G. R. 16: v A 1981 (3); v WI 1980 (3); *v A 1979 (2); v WI 1980 (4); v In 1981 (4)*
Dipper (A. E.) 1: v A 1921
Doggart, G. H. G. 2: v WI 1950 (2)
D'Oliveira, B. L. 44: v A 1968 (2) 1972 (5); v WI 1966 (4) 1969 (3); v NZ 1969 (3); v In 1967 (2) 1971 (3); v P 1967 (3) 1971 (3); *v A 1970 (6); v WI 1967 (5); v NZ 1970 (2); v P 1968 (3)*
Dollery (H. E.) 4: v A 1948 (2); v SA 1947 (1); v WI 1950 (1)
Dolphin (A.) 1: *v A 1920*
Douglas, J. W. H. T. 23: v A 1912 (1) 1921 (5); v SA 1924 (1); *v A 1911 (5) 1920 (5) 1924 (1); v SA 1913 (5)*
Downton, P. R. 4: v A 1981 (1); *v WI 1980 (3)*
Druce, N. F. 5: *v A 1897 (5)*
Ducat (A.) 1: v A 1921
Duckworth (G.) 24: v A 1930 (5); v SA 1924 (1) 1929 (4) 1935 (1); v WI 1928 (1); v In 1936 (3); *v A 1928 (5); v SA 1930 (3); v NZ 1932 (1)*
Duleepsinhji, K. S. 12: v A 1930 (4); v SA 1929 (1); v NZ 1931 (3); *v NZ 1929 (4)*
Durston (F. J.) 1: v A 1921

Edmonds, P. H. 21: v A 1975 (2); v NZ 1978 (3); v In 1979 (4) 1982 (3); v P 1978 (3); *v A 1978 (1); v NZ 1977 (3); v P 1977 (2)*
Edrich, J. H. 77: v A 1964 (3) 1968 (5) 1972 (5) 1975 (4); v SA 1965 (1); v WI 1963 (3) 1966 (1) 1969 (3) 1976 (2); v NZ 1965 (1) 1969 (3); v In 1967 (2) 1971 (3) 1974 (3); v P 1971 (3) 1974 (3); *v A 1965 (5) 1970 (6) 1974 (4); v WI 1967 (5); v NZ 1965 (3) 1970 (2) 1974 (2); v In 1963 (2); v P 1968 (3)*
Edrich, W. J. 39: v A 1938 (4) 1948 (5) 1953 (3); v SA 1947 (4); v WI 1950 (2); v NZ 1949 (4); v In 1946 (1); v P 1954 (1); *v A 1946 (5) 1954 (4); v SA 1938 (5); v NZ 1946 (1)*
Elliott (H.) 4: v WI 1928 (1); *v SA 1927 (1); v In 1933 (2)*
Emburey, J. E. 22: v A 1980 (1) 1981 (4); v WI 1980 (3); v NZ 1978 (1); *v A 1978 (4); v WI 1980 (4); v In 1979 (1) 1981 (3); v SL 1981 (1)*
Emmett (G. M.) 1: v A 1948
Emmett (T.) 7: *v A 1876 (2) 1878 (1) 1881 (4)*
Evans, A. J. 1: v A 1921
Evans (T. G.) 91: v A 1948 (5) 1953 (5) 1956 (5); v SA 1947 (5) 1951 (3) 1955 (3); v WI 1950 (3) 1957 (5); v NZ 1949 (4) 1958 (5); v In 1946 (1) 1952 (4) 1959 (2); v P 1954 (4); *v A 1946 (4) 1950 (5) 1954 (4) 1958 (3); v SA 1948 (3) 1956 (5); v WI 1947 (4) 1953 (4); v NZ 1946 (1) 1950 (2) 1954 (2)*

Fagg (A. E.) 5: v WI 1939 (1); v In 1936 (2); *v A 1936 (2)*
Fane, F. L. 14: *v A 1907 (4); v SA 1905 (5) 1909 (5)*
Farnes, K. 15: v A 1934 (2) 1938 (4); *v A 1936 (2); v SA 1938 (5); v WI 1934 (2)*
Farrimond (W.) 4: v SA 1935 (1); *v SA 1930 (2); v WI 1934 (1)*
Fender, P. G. H. 13: v A 1921 (2); v SA 1924 (2) 1929 (1); *v A 1920 (3); v SA 1922 (5)*
Ferris, J. J. 1: *v SA 1891*
Fielder (A.) 6: *v A 1903 (2) 1907 (4)*
Fishlock (L. B.) 4: v In 1936 (2) 1946 (1); *v A 1946 (1)*
Flavell (J. A.) 4: v A 1961 (2) 1964 (2)
Fletcher, K. W. R. 59: v A 1968 (1) 1972 (1) 1975 (2); v WI 1973 (3); v NZ 1969 (2) 1973 (3); v In 1971 (2) 1974 (3); v P 1974 (3); *v A 1970 (5) 1974 (5) 1976 (1); v WI 1973 (4); v NZ 1970 (1) 1974 (2); v In 1972 (5) 1976 (3) 1981 (6); v P 1968 (3) 1972 (3); v SL 1981 (1)*
Flowers (W.) 8: v A 1893 (1); *v A 1884 (5) 1886 (2)*
Ford, F. G. J. 5: *v A 1894 (5)*
Foster, F. R. 11: v A 1912 (3); v SA 1912 (3); *v A 1911 (5)*
Foster, R. E. 8: v SA 1907 (3); *v A 1903 (5)*
Fothergill (A. J.) 2: *v SA 1888 (2)*
Fowler, G. 1: v P 1982
Freeman (A. P.) 12: v SA 1929 (3); v WI 1928 (3); *v A 1924 (2); v SA 1927 (4)*
Fry, C. B. 26: v A 1899 (5) 1902 (3) 1905 (4) 1909 (3) 1912 (3); v SA 1907 (3) 1912 (3); *v SA 1895 (2)*

Gatting, M. W. 22: v A 1980 (1) 1981 (6); v WI 1980 (4); v P 1982 (3); *v WI 1980 (1); v NZ 1977 (1); v In 1981 (5); v P 1977 (1)*
Gay, L. H. 1: *v A 1894*
Geary (G.) 14: v A 1926 (2) 1930 (1) 1934 (2); v SA 1924 (1) 1929 (3); *v A 1928 (4); v SA 1927 (2)*
Gibb, P. A. 8: v In 1946 (2); *v A 1946 (1); v SA 1938 (5)*
Gifford, N. 15: v A 1964 (2) 1972 (3); v NZ 1973 (2); v In 1971 (2); v P 1971 (2); *v In 1972 (2); v P 1972 (2)*
Gilligan, A. E. R. 11: v SA 1924 (4); *v A 1924 (5); v SA 1922 (2)*
Gilligan, A. H. H. 4: *v NZ 1929 (4)*
Gimblett (H.) 3: v WI 1939 (1); v In 1936 (2)
Gladwin (C.) 8: v SA 1947 (2); v NZ 1949 (1); *v SA 1948 (5)*
Goddard (T. W.) 8: v A 1930 (1); v WI 1939 (2); v NZ 1937 (2); *v SA 1938 (3)*
Gooch, G. A. 42: v A 1975 (2) 1980 (1) 1981 (5); v WI 1980 (5); v NZ 1978 (3); v In 1979 (4); v P 1978 (2); *v A 1978 (6) 1979 (2); v WI 1980 (4); v In 1979 (1) 1981 (6); v SL 1981 (1)*
Gover (A. R.) 4: v NZ 1937 (2); v In 1936 (1) 1946 (1)
Gower, D. I. 44: v A 1980 (1) 1981 (5); v WI 1980 (1); v NZ 1978 (3); v In 1979 (4) 1982 (3); v P 1978 (3) 1982 (3); *v A 1978 (6) 1979 (3); v WI 1980 (4); v In 1979 (1) 1981 (6); v SL 1981 (1)*
Grace, E. M. 1: v A 1880
Grace, G. F. 1: v A 1880
Grace, W. G. 22: v A 1880 (1) 1882 (1) 1884 (3) 1886 (3) 1888 (3) 1890 (2) 1893 (2) 1896 (3) 1899 (1); *v A 1891 (3)*
Graveney (T. W.) 79: v A 1953 (5) 1956 (2) 1968 (5); v SA 1951 (1) 1955 (5); v WI 1957 (4) 1966 (4) 1969 (1); v NZ 1958 (4); v In 1952 (4) 1967 (3); v P 1954 (3) 1962 (4) 1967 (3); *v A 1954 (2) 1958 (5) 1962 (3); v WI 1953 (5) 1967 (5); v NZ 1954 (2) 1958 (2); v In 1951 (4); v P 1968 (3)*
Greenhough (T.) 4: v SA 1960 (1); v In 1959 (3)
Greenwood (A.) 2: *v A 1876 (2)*
Greig, A. W. 58: v A 1972 (5) 1975 (4) 1977 (5); v WI 1973 (3) 1976 (5); v NZ 1973 (3); v In 1974 (3); v P 1974 (3); *v A 1974 (6) 1976 (1); v WI 1973 (5); v NZ 1974 (2); v In 1972 (5) 1976 (5); v P 1972 (3)*
Greig, I. A. 2: v P 1982 (2)
Grieve, B. A. F. 2: *v SA 1888 (2)*
Griffith, S. C. 3: *v SA 1948 (2); v WI 1947 (1)*
Gunn (G.) 15: v A 1909 (1); *v A 1907 (5) 1911 (5); v WI 1929 (4)*
Gunn (J.) 6: v A 1905 (1); *v A 1901 (5)*
Gunn (W.) 11: v A 1888 (2) 1890 (2) 1893 (3) 1896 (1) 1899 (1); *v A 1886 (2)*

Haig, N. E. 5: v A 1921 (1); *v WI 1929 (4)*
Haigh (S.) 11: v A 1905 (2) 1909 (1) 1912 (1); *v SA 1898 (2) 1905 (5)*
Hallows (C.) 2: v A 1921 (1); v WI 1928 (1)
Hammond, W. R. 85: v A 1930 (5) 1934 (5) 1938 (4); v SA 1929 (4) 1935 (5); v WI 1928 (3) 1933 (3) 1939 (3); v NZ 1931 (3) 1937 (3); v In 1932 (1) 1936 (2) 1946 (3); *v A 1928 (5) 1932 (5) 1936 (5) 1946 (4); v SA 1927 (5) 1930 (5) 1938 (5); v WI 1934 (4); v NZ 1932 (2) 1946 (1)*
Hampshire, J. H. 8: v A 1972 (1) 1975 (1); v WI 1969 (2); *v A 1970 (2); v NZ 1970 (2)*
Hardinge (H. T. W.) 1: v A 1921
Hardstaff (J.) 5: *v A 1907 (5)*
Hardstaff (J. jun.) 23: v A 1938 (2) 1948 (1); v SA 1935 (1); v WI 1939 (3); v NZ 1937 (3); v In 1936 (2) 1946 (2); *v A 1936 (5) 1946 (1); v WI 1947 (3)*
Harris, Lord 4: v A 1880 (1) 1884 (2); *v A 1878 (1)*
Hartley, J. C. 2: *v SA 1905 (2)*
Hawke, Lord 5: *v SA 1895 (3) 1898 (2)*
Hayes (E. G.) 5: v A 1909 (1); v SA 1912 (1); *v SA 1905 (3)*
Hayes, F. C. 9: v WI 1973 (3) 1976 (2); *v WI 1973 (4)*
Hayward (T. W.) 35: v A 1896 (2) 1899 (5) 1902 (1) 1905 (5) 1909 (1); v SA 1907 (3); *v A 1897 (5) 1901 (5) 1903 (5); v SA 1895 (3)*
Hearne (A.) 1: *v SA 1891*
Hearne (F.) 2: *v SA 1888 (2)*

Hearne (G. G.) 1: *v SA 1891*
Hearne (J. T.) 12: v A 1896 (3) 1899 (3); *v A 1897 (5); v SA 1891 (1)*
Hearne (J. W.) 24: v A 1912 (3) 1921 (1) 1926 (1); v SA 1912 (2) 1924 (3); *v A 1911 (5) 1920 (2) 1924 (4); v SA 1913 (3)*
Hemmings, E. E. 2: v P 1982 (2)
Hendren (E. H.) 51: v A 1921 (2) 1926 (5) 1930 (2) 1934 (4); v SA 1924 (5) 1929 (4); v WI 1928 (1); *v A 1920 (5) 1924 (5) 1928 (5); v SA 1930 (5); v WI 1929 (4) 1934 (4)*
Hendrick, M. 30: v A 1977 (3) 1980 (1) 1981 (2); v WI 1976 (2) 1980 (2); v NZ 1978 (2); v In 1974 (3) 1979 (4); v P 1974 (2); *v A 1974 (2) 1978 (5); v NZ 1974 (1) 1977 (1)*
Heseltine, C. 2: v SA 1895 (2)
Higgs, K. 15: v A 1968 (1); v WI 1966 (5); v SA 1965 (1); v In 1967 (1); v P 1967 (3); *v A 1965 (1); v NZ 1965 (3)*
Hill (A.) 2: *v A 1876 (2)*
Hill, A. J. L. 3: *v SA 1895 (3)*
Hilton (M. J.) 4: v SA 1951 (1); v WI 1950 (1); *v In 1951 (2)*
Hirst (G. H.) 24: v A 1899 (1) 1902 (4) 1905 (3) 1909 (4); v SA 1907 (3); *v A 1897 (4) 1903 (5)*
Hitch (J. W.) 7: v A 1912 (1) 1921 (1); v SA 1912 (1); *v A 1911 (3) 1920 (1)*
Hobbs (J. B.) 61: v A 1909 (3) 1912 (3) 1921 (1) 1926 (5) 1930 (5); v SA 1912 (3) 1924 (4) 1929 (1); v WI 1928 (2); *v A 1907 (4) 1911 (5) 1920 (5) 1924 (5) 1928 (5); v SA 1909 (5) 1913 (5)*
Hobbs, R. N. S. 7: v In 1967 (3); v P 1967 (1) 1971 (1); *v WI 1967 (1); v P 1968 (1)*
Hollies (W. E.) 13: v A 1948 (1); v SA 1947 (3); v WI 1950 (2); v NZ 1949 (4); *v WI 1934 (3)*
Holmes, E. R. T. 5: v SA 1935 (1); *v WI 1934 (4)*
Holmes (P.) 7: v A 1921 (1); v In 1932 (1); *v SA 1927 (5)*
Hone, L. 1: *v A 1878*
Hopwood (J. L.) 2: v A 1934 (2)
Hornby, A. N. 3: v A 1882 (1) 1884 (1); *v A 1878 (1)*
Horton (M. J.) 2: v In 1959 (2)
Howard, N. D. 4: *v In 1951 (4)*
Howell (H.) 5: v A 1921 (1); v SA 1924 (1); *v A 1920 (3)*
Howorth (R.) 5: v SA 1947 (1); *v WI 1947 (4)*
Humphries (J.) 3: *v A 1907 (3)*
Hunter (J.) 5: *v A 1884 (5)*
Hutchings, K. L. 7: v A 1909 (2); *v A 1907 (5)*
Hutton (L.) 79: v A 1938 (3) 1948 (4) 1953 (5); v SA 1947 (5) 1951 (5); v WI 1939 (3) 1950 (3); v NZ 1937 (3) 1949 (4); v In 1946 (3) 1952 (4); v P 1954 (2); *v A 1946 (5) 1950 (5) 1954 (5); v SA 1938 (4) 1948 (5); v WI 1947 (2) 1953 (5); v NZ 1950 (2) 1954 (2)*
Hutton, R. A. 5: v In 1971 (3); v P 1971 (2)

Iddon (J.) 5: v SA 1935 (1); *v WI 1934 (4)*
Ikin (J. T.) 18: v SA 1951 (3) 1955 (1); v In 1946 (2) 1952 (2); *v A 1946 (5); v NZ 1946 (1); v WI 1947 (4)*
Illingworth (R.) 61: v A 1961 (2) 1968 (3) 1972 (5); v SA 1960 (4); v WI 1966 (2) 1969 (3) 1973 (3); v NZ 1958 (1) 1965 (1) 1969 (3) 1973 (3); v In 1959 (2) 1967 (3) 1971 (3); v P 1962 (1) 1967 (1) 1971 (3); *v A 1962 (2) 1970 (6); v WI 1959 (5); v NZ 1962 (3) 1970 (2)*
Insole, D. J. 9: v A 1956 (1); v SA 1955 (1); v WI 1950 (1) 1957 (1); *v SA 1956 (5)*

Jackman, R. D. 4: v P 1982 (2); *v WI 1980 (2)*
Jackson, F. S. 20: v A 1893 (2) 1896 (3) 1899 (5) 1902 (5) 1905 (5)
Jackson (H. L.) 2: v A 1961 (1); v NZ 1949 (1)
Jameson, J. A. 4: v In 1971 (2); *v WI 1973 (2)*
Jardine, D. R. 22: v WI 1928 (2) 1933 (2); v NZ 1931 (3); v In 1932 (1); *v A 1928 (5) 1932 (5); v NZ 1932 (1); v In 1933 (3)*
Jenkins (R. O.) 9: v WI 1950 (2); v In 1952 (2); *v SA 1948 (5)*
Jessop, G. L. 18: v A 1899 (1) 1902 (4) 1905 (1) 1909 (2); v SA 1907 (3) 1912 (2); *v A 1901 (5)*
Jones, A. O. 12: v A 1899 (1) 1905 (2) 1909 (2); *v A 1901 (5) 1907 (2)*
Jones, I. J. 15: v WI 1966 (2); *v A 1965 (4); v WI 1967 (5); v NZ 1965 (3); v In 1963 (1)*
Jupp (H.) 2: *v A 1876 (2)*
Jupp, V. W. C. 8: v A 1921 (2); v WI 1928 (2); *v SA 1922 (4)*

Keeton (W. W.) 2: v A 1934 (1); v WI 1939 (1)
Kennedy (A. S.) 5: *v SA 1922 (5)*
Kenyon (D.) 8: v A 1953 (2); v SA 1955 (3); *v In 1951 (3)*
Killick, E. T. 2: v SA 1929 (2)
Kilner (R.) 9: v A 1926 (4); v SA 1924 (2); *v A 1924 (3)*
King (J. H.) 1: v A 1909
Kinneir (S. P.) 1: *v A 1911*
Knight (A. E.) 3: *v A 1903 (3)*
Knight (B. R.) 29: v A 1968 (2); v WI 1966 (1) 1969 (3); v NZ 1969 (2); v P 1962 (2); *v A 1962 (1) 1965 (2); v NZ 1962 (3) 1965 (2); v In 1961 (4) 1963 (5); v P 1961 (2)*
Knight, D. J. 2: v A 1921 (2)
Knott, A. P. E. 95: v A 1968 (5) 1972 (5) 1975 (4) 1977 (5) 1981 (2); v WI 1969 (3) 1973 (3) 1976 (5) 1980 (4); v NZ 1969 (3) 1973 (3); v In 1971 (3) 1974 (3); v P 1967 (2) 1971 (3) 1974 (3); *v A 1970 (6) 1974 (6) 1976 (1); v WI 1967 (2) 1973 (5); v NZ 1970 (1) 1974 (2); v In 1972 (5) 1976 (5); v P 1968 (3) 1972 (3)*
Knox, N. A. 2: v SA 1907 (2)

Laker (J. C.) 46: v A 1948 (3) 1953 (3) 1956 (5); v SA 1951 (2) 1955 (1); v WI 1950 (1) 1957 (4); v NZ 1949 (1) 1958 (4); v In 1952 (4); v P 1954 (1); *v A 1958 (4); v SA 1956 (5); v WI 1947 (4) 1953 (4)*
Lamb, A. J. 6: v In 1982 (3); v P 1982 (3)
Langridge (James) 8: v SA 1935 (1); v WI 1933 (2); v In 1936 (1) 1946 (1); *v In 1933 (3)*
Larkins, W. 6: v A 1981 (1); v WI 1980 (3); *v A 1979 (1); v In 1979 (1)*
Larter (J. D. F.) 10: v SA 1965 (2); v NZ 1965 (1); v P 1962 (1); *v NZ 1962 (3); v In 1963 (3)*
Larwood (H.) 21: v A 1926 (2) 1930 (3); v SA 1929 (3); v WI 1928 (2); v NZ 1931 (1); *v A 1928 (5) 1932 (5)*
Leadbeater (E.) 2: *v In 1951 (2)*
Lee (H. W.) 1: *v SA 1930*
Lees (W. S.) 5: *v SA 1905 (5)*
Legge G. B. 5: *v SA 1927 (1); v NZ 1929 (4)*
Leslie, C. F. H. 4: *v A 1882 (4)*
Lever, J. K. 20: v A 1977 (3); v WI 1980 (1); v In 1979 (1); *v A 1976 (1) 1978 (1) 1979 (1); v NZ 1977 (1); v In 1976 (5) 1979 (1) 1981 (2); v P 1977 (3)*
Lever, P. 17: v A 1972 (1) 1975 (1); v In 1971 (1); v P 1971 (3); *v A 1970 (5) 1974 (2); v NZ 1970 (2) 1974 (2)*
Leveson Gower, H. D. G. 3: *v SA 1909 (3)*
Levett, W. H. V. 1: *v In 1933*
Lewis, A. R. 9: v NZ 1973 (1); *v In 1972 (5); v P 1972 (3)*
Leyland (M.) 41: v A 1930 (3) 1934 (5) 1938 (1); v SA 1929 (5) 1935 (4); v WI 1928 (1) 1933 (1); v In 1936 (2); *v A 1928 (1) 1932 (5) 1936 (5); v SA 1930 (5); v WI 1934 (3)*
Lilley (A. A.) 35: v A 1896 (3) 1899 (4) 1902 (5) 1905 (5) 1909 (5); v SA 1907 (3); *v A 1901 (5) 1903 (5)*
Lillywhite (James jun.) 2: *v A 1876 (2)*
Lloyd, D. 9: v In 1974 (2); v P 1974 (3); *v A 1974 (4)*
Loader (P. J.) 13: v SA 1955 (1); v WI 1957 (2); v NZ 1958 (3); v P 1954 (1); *v A 1958 (2); v SA 1956 (4)*
Lock (G. A. R.) 49: v A 1953 (2) 1956 (4) 1961 (3); v SA 1955 (3); v WI 1957 (3) 1963 (3); v NZ 1958 (5); v In 1952 (2); v P 1962 (3); *v A 1958 (4); v SA 1956 (1); v WI 1953 (5) 1967 (2); v NZ 1958 (2); v In 1961 (5); v P 1961 (2)*
Lockwood (W. H.) 12: v A 1893 (2) 1899 (1) 1902 (4); *v A 1894 (5)*
Lohmann (G. A.) 18: v A 1886 (3) 1888 (3) 1890 (2) 1896 (1); *v A 1886 (2) 1887 (1) 1891 (3); v SA 1895 (3)*
Lowson (F. A.) 7: v SA 1951 (2) 1955 (1); *v In 1951 (4)*
Lucas, A. P. 5: v A 1880 (1) 1882 (1) 1884 (2); *v A 1878 (1)*
Luckhurst, B. W. 21: v A 1972 (4); v WI 1973 (2); v In 1971 (3); v P 1971 (3); *v A 1970 (5); 1974 (2); v NZ 1970 (2)*
Lyttelton, Hon. A. 4: v A 1880 (1) 1882 (1) 1884 (2)

Macaulay (G. G.) 8: v A 1926 (1); v SA 1924 (1); v WI 1933 (2); *v SA 1922 (4)*
MacBryan, J. C. W. 1: v SA 1924
McConnon (J. E.) 2: v P 1954 (2)

McGahey, C. P. 2: *v A 1901 (2)*
MacGregor, G. 8: v A 1890 (2) 1893 (3); *v A 1891 (3)*
McIntyre (A. J. W.) 3: v SA 1955 (1); v WI 1950 (1); *v A 1950 (1)*
MacKinnon, F. A. 1: *v A 1878*
MacLaren, A. C. 35: v A 1896 (2) 1899 (4) 1902 (5) 1905 (4) 1909 (5); *v A 1894 (5) 1897 (5) 1901 (5)*
McMaster, J. E. P. 1: *v SA 1888*
Makepeace (H.) 4: *v A 1920 (4)*
Mann, F. G. 7: v NZ 1949 (2); *v SA 1948 (5)*
Mann, F. T. 5: *v SA 1922 (5)*
Marks, V. J. 1: v P 1982
Marriott, C. S. 1: v WI 1933
Martin (F.) 2: v A 1890 (1); *v SA 1891 (1)*
Martin, J. W. 1: v SA 1947
Mason, J. R. 5: *v A 1897 (5)*
Matthews (A. D. G.) 1: v NZ 1937
May, P. B. H. 66: v A 1953 (2) 1956 (5) 1961 (4); v SA 1951 (2) 1955 (5); v WI 1957 (5); v NZ 1958 (5); v In 1952 (4) 1959 (3); v P 1954 (4); *v A 1954 (5) 1958 (5); v SA 1956 (5); v WI 1953 (5) 1959 (3); v NZ 1954 (2) 1958 (2)*
Mead (C. P.) 17: v A 1921 (2); *v A 1911 (4) 1928 (1); v SA 1913 (5) 1922 (5)*
Mead (W.) 1: v A 1899
Midwinter (W. E.) 4: *v A 1881 (4)*
Milburn, C. 9: v A 1968 (2); v WI 1966 (4); v In 1967 (1); v P 1967 (1); *v P 1968 (1)*
Miller, A. M. 1: *v SA 1895*
Miller, G. 27: v A 1977 (2); v WI 1976 (1); v NZ 1978 (2); v In 1979 (3) 1982 (1); v P 1978 (3) 1982 (1); *v A 1978 (6) 1979 (1); v WI 1980 (1); v NZ 1977 (3); v P 1977 (3)*
Milligan, F. W. 2: *v SA 1898 (2)*
Millman (G.) 6: v P 1962 (2); *v In 1961 (2); v P 1961 (2)*
Milton (C. A.) 6: v NZ 1958 (2); v In 1959 (2); *v A 1958 (2)*
Mitchell (A.) 6: v SA 1935 (2); v In 1936 (1); *v In 1933 (3)*
Mitchell, F. 2: *v SA 1898 (2)*
Mitchell (T. B.) 5: v A 1934 (2); v SA 1935 (1); *v A 1932 (1); v NZ 1932 (1)*
Mitchell-Innes, N. S. 1: v SA 1935
Mold (A. W.) 3: v A 1893 (3)
Moon, L. J. 4: *v SA 1905 (4)*
Morley (F.) 4: v A 1880 (1); *v A 1882 (3)*
Mortimore (J. B.) 9: v A 1964 (1); v In 1959 (2); *v A 1958 (1); v NZ 1958 (2); v In 1963 (3)*
Moss (A. E.) 9: v A 1956 (1); v SA 1960 (2); v In 1959 (3); *v WI 1953 (1) 1959 (2)*
Murdoch, W. L. 1: *v SA 1891*
Murray, J. T. 21: v A 1961 (5); v WI 1966 (1); v In 1967 (3); v P 1962 (3) 1967 (1); *v A 1962 (1); v SA 1964 (1); v NZ 1962 (1) 1965 (1); v In 1961 (3); v P 1961 (1)*

Newham (W.) 1: *v A 1887*
Nichols (M. S.) 14: v A 1930 (1); v SA 1935 (4); v WI 1933 (1) 1939 (1); *v NZ 1929 (4); v In 1933 (3)*

Oakman (A. S. M.) 2: v A 1956 (2)
O'Brien, T. C. 5: v A 1884 (1) 1888 (1); *v SA 1895 (3)*
O'Connor (J.) 4: v SA 1929 (1); *v WI 1929 (3)*
Old, C. M. 46: v A 1975 (3) 1977 (2) 1980 (1) 1981 (2); v WI 1973 (1) 1976 (2) 1980 (1); v NZ 1973 (2) 1978 (1); v In 1974 (3); v P 1974 (3) 1978 (3); *v A 1974 (2) 1976 (1) 1978 (1); v WI 1973 (4) 1980 (1); v NZ 1974 (1) 1977 (2); v In 1972 (4) 1976 (4); v P 1972 (1) 1977 (1)*
Oldfield (N.) 1: v WI 1939

Padgett (D. E. V.) 2: v SA 1960 (2)
Paine (G. A. E.) 4: *v WI 1934 (4)*
Palairet, L. C. H. 2: v A 1902 (2)
Palmer, C. H. 1: *v WI 1953*
Palmer, K. E. 1: *v SA 1964*

Parfitt (P. H.) 37: v A 1964 (4) 1972 (3); v SA 1965 (2); v WI 1969 (1); v NZ 1965 (2); v P 1962 (5); *v A 1962 (2); v SA 1964 (5); v NZ 1962 (3) 1965 (3); v In 1961 (2) 1963 (3); v P 1961 (2)*
Parker (C. W. L.) 1: v A 1921
Parker, P. W. G. 1: v A 1981
Parkhouse (W. G. A.) 7: v WI 1950 (2); v In 1959 (2); *v A 1950 (2); v NZ 1950 (1)*
Parkin (C. H.) 10: v A 1921 (4); v SA 1924 (1); *v A 1920 (5)*
Parks (J. H.) 1: v NZ 1937
Parks (J. M.) 46: v A 1964 (5); v SA 1960 (5) 1965 (3); v WI 1963 (4) 1966 (4); v NZ 1965 (3); v P 1954 (1); *v A 1965 (5); v SA 1964 (5); v WI 1959 (1) 1967 (3); v NZ 1965 (2); v In 1963 (5)*
Pataudi, Nawab of, 3: v A 1934 (1); *v A 1932 (2)*
Paynter (E.) 20: v A 1938 (4); v WI 1939 (2); v NZ 1931 (1) 1937 (2); v In 1932 (1); *v A 1932 (3); v SA 1938 (5); v NZ 1932 (2)*
Peate (E.) 9: v A 1882 (1) 1884 (3) 1886 (1); *v A 1881 (4)*
Peebles, I. A. R. 13: v A 1930 (2); v NZ 1931 (3); *v SA 1927 (4) 1930 (4)*
Peel (R.) 20: v A 1888 (3) 1890 (1) 1893 (1) 1896 (1); *v A 1884 (5) 1887 (1) 1891 (3) 1894 (5)*
Penn, F. 1: v A 1880
Perks (R. T. D.) 2: v WI 1939 (1); *v SA 1938 (1)*
Philipson, H. 5: *v A 1891 (1) 1894 (4)*
Pilling (R.) 8: v A 1884 (1) 1886 (1) 1888 (1); *v A 1881 (4) 1887 (1)*
Place (W.) 3: *v WI 1947 (3)*
Pocock, P. I. 17: v A 1968 (1); v WI 1976 (2); *v WI 1967 (2) 1973 (4); v In 1972 (4); v P 1968 (1) 1972 (3)*
Pollard (R.) 4: v A 1948 (2); v In 1946 (1); *v NZ 1946 (1)*
Poole (C. J.) 3: *v In 1951 (3)*
Pope (G. H.) 1: v SA 1947
Pougher (A. D.) 1: *v SA 1891*
Price, J. S. E. 15: v A 1964 (2) 1972 (1); v In 1971 (3); v P 1971 (1); *v SA 1964 (4); v In 1963 (4)*
Price (W. F. F.) 1: v A 1938
Prideaux, R. M. 3: v A 1968 (1); *v P 1968 (2)*
Pringle, D. R. 4: v In 1982 (3); v P 1982 (1)
Pullar (G.) 28: v A 1961 (5); v SA 1960 (3); v In 1959 (3); v P 1962 (2); *v A 1962 (4); v WI 1959 (5); v In 1961 (3); v P 1961 (3)*

Quaife (Wm) 7: v A 1899 (2); *v A 1901 (5)*

Radley, C. T. 8: v NZ 1978 (3); v P 1978 (3); *v NZ 1977 (2)*
Randall, D. W. 33: v A 1977 (5); v In 1979 (3) 1982 (3); v P 1982 (3); *v A 1976 (1) 1978 (6) 1979 (2); v NZ 1977 (3); v In 1976 (4); v P 1977 (3)*
Ranjitsinhji, K. S. 15: v A 1896 (2) 1899 (5) 1902 (3); *v A 1897 (5)*
Read, H. D. 1: v SA 1935
Read (J. M.) 17: v A 1882 (1) 1890 (2) 1893 (1); *v A 1884 (5) 1886 (2) 1887 (1) 1891 (3); v SA 1888 (2)*
Read, W. W. 18: v A 1884 (2) 1886 (3) 1888 (3) 1890 (2) 1893 (2); *v A 1882 (4) 1887 (1); v SA 1891 (1)*
Relf (A. E.) 13: v A 1909 (1); *v A 1903 (2); v SA 1905 (5) 1913 (5)*
Rhodes (H. J.) 2: v In 1959 (2)
Rhodes (W.) 58: v A 1899 (3) 1902 (5) 1905 (4) 1909 (4) 1912 (3) 1921 (1) 1926 (1); v SA 1912 (3); *v A 1903 (5) 1907 (5) 1911 (5) 1920 (5); v SA 1909 (5) 1913 (5); v WI 1929 (4)*
Richardson (D. W.) 1: v WI 1957
Richardson (P. E.) 34: v A 1956 (5); v WI 1957 (5) 1963 (1); v NZ 1958 (4); *v A 1958 (4); v SA 1956 (5); v NZ 1958 (2); v In 1961 (5); v P 1961 (3)*
Richardson (T.) 14: v A 1893 (1) 1896 (3); *v A 1894 (5) 1897 (5)*
Richmond (T. L.) 1: v A 1921
Ridgway (F.) 5: *v In 1951 (5)*
Robertson (J. D.) 11: v SA 1947 (1); v NZ 1949 (1); *v WI 1947 (4); v In 1951 (5)*
Robins, R. W. V. 19: v A 1930 (2); v SA 1929 (1) 1935 (3); v WI 1933 (2); v NZ 1931 (1) 1937 (3); v In 1932 (1) 1936 (2); *v A 1936 (4)*
Roope, G. R. J. 21: v A 1975 (1) 1977 (2); v WI 1973 (1); v NZ 1973 (3) 1978 (1); v P 1978 (3); *v NZ 1977 (3); v In 1972 (2); v P 1972 (2) 1977 (3)*

Root (C. F.) 3: v A 1926 (3)
Rose, B. C. 9: v WI 1980 (3); *v WI 1980 (1); v NZ 1977 (2); v P 1977 (3)*
Royle, V. P. F. A. 1: *v A 1878*
Rumsey, F. E. 5: v A 1964 (1); v SA 1965 (1); v NZ 1965 (3)
Russell (A. C.) 10: v A 1921 (2); *v A 1920 (4); v SA 1922 (4)*
Russell, W. E. 10: v SA 1965 (1); v WI 1966 (2); v P 1967 (1); *v A 1965 (1); v NZ 1965 (3); v In 1961 (1); v P 1961 (1)*

Sandham (A.) 14: v A 1921 (1); v SA 1924 (2); *v A 1924 (2); v SA 1922 (5); v WI 1929 (4)*
Schultz, S. S. 1: *v A 1878*
Scotton (W. H.) 15: v A 1884 (1) 1886 (3); *v A 1881 (4) 1884 (5) 1886 (2)*
Selby (J.) 6: *v A 1876 (2) 1881 (4)*
Selvey, M. W. W. 3: v WI 1976 (2); *v In 1976 (1)*
Shackleton (D.) 7: v SA 1951 (1); v WI 1950 (1) 1963 (4); *v In 1951 (1)*
Sharp (J.) 3: v A 1909 (3)
Sharpe (J. W.) 3: v A 1890 (1); *v A 1891 (2)*
Sharpe, P. J. 12: v A 1964 (2); v WI 1963 (3) 1969 (3); v NZ 1969 (3); *v In 1963 (1)*
Shaw (A.) 7: v A 1880 (1); *v A 1876 (2) 1881 (4)*
Sheppard, Rev. D. S. 22: v A 1956 (2); v WI 1950 (1) 1957 (2); v In 1952 (2); v P 1954 (2) 1962 (2); *v A 1950 (2) 1962 (5); v NZ 1950 (1) 1963 (3)*
Sherwin (M.) 3: v A 1888 (1); *v A 1886 (2)*
Shrewsbury (A.) 23: v A 1884 (2) 1886 (3) 1890 (2) 1893 (3); *v A 1881 (4) 1884 (5) 1886 (2) 1887 (1)*
Shuter, J. 1: v A 1888
Shuttleworth, K. 5: v P 1971 (1); *v A 1970 (2); v NZ 1970 (2)*
Simpson, R. T. 27: v A 1953 (3); v SA 1951 (3); v WI 1950 (3); v NZ 1949 (2); v In 1952 (2); v P 1954 (3); *v A 1950 (5) 1954 (1); v SA 1948 (1); v NZ 1950 (2) 1954 (2)*
Simpson-Hayward, G. H. 5: *v SA 1909 (5)*
Sims (J. M.) 4: v SA 1935 (1); v In 1936 (1); *v A 1936 (2)*
Sinfield (R. A.) 1: v A 1938
Smailes (T. F.) 1: v In 1946
Smith, A. C. 6: *v A 1962 (4); v NZ 1962 (2)*
Smith, C. A. 1: *v SA 1888*
Smith (C. I. J.) 5: v NZ 1937 (1); *v WI 1934 (4)*
Smith (D.) 2: v SA 1935 (2)
Smith (D. R.) 5: *v In 1961 (5)*
Smith (D. V.) 3: v WI 1957 (3)
Smith (E. J.) 11: v A 1912 (3); v SA 1912 (3); *v A 1911 (4); v SA 1913 (1)*
Smith (H.) 1: v WI 1928
Smith, M. J. K. 50: v A 1961 (1) 1972 (3); v SA 1960 (4) 1965 (3); v WI 1966 (1); v NZ 1958 (3) 1965 (3); v In 1959 (2); *v A 1965 (5); v SA 1964 (5); v WI 1959 (5); v NZ 1965 (3); v In 1961 (4) 1963 (5); v P 1961 (3)*
Smith (T. P. B.) 4: v In 1946 (1); *v A 1946 (2); v NZ 1946 (1)*
Smithson (G. A.) 2: *v WI 1947 (2)*
Snow, J. A. 49: v A 1968 (5) 1972 (5) 1975 (4); v SA 1965 (1); v WI 1966 (3) 1969 (3) 1973 (1) 1976 (3); v NZ 1965 (1) 1969 (2) 1973 (3); v In 1967 (3) 1971 (2); v P 1967 (1); *v A 1970 (6); v WI 1967 (4); v P 1968 (2)*
Southerton (J.) 2: *v A 1876 (2)*
Spooner, R. H. 10: v A 1905 (2) 1909 (2) 1912 (3); v SA 1912 (3)
Spooner (R. T.) 7: v SA 1955 (1); *v In 1951 (5); v WI 1953 (1)*
Stanyforth, R. T. 4: *v SA 1927 (4)*
Staples (S. J.) 3: *v SA 1927 (3)*
Statham (J. B.) 70: v A 1953 (1) 1956 (3) 1961 (4); v SA 1951 (2) 1955 (4) 1960 (5) 1965 (1); v WI 1957 (3) 1963 (2); v NZ 1958 (2); v In 1959 (3); v P 1954 (4) 1962 (3); *v A 1954 (5) 1958 (4) 1962 (5); v SA 1956 (4); v WI 1953 (4) 1959 (3); v NZ 1950 (1) 1954 (2); v In 1951 (5)*
Steel, A. G. 13: v A 1880 (1) 1882 (1) 1884 (3) 1886 (3) 1888 (1); *v A 1882 (4)*
Steele, D. S. 8: v A 1975 (3); v WI 1976 (5)
Stevens, G. T. S. 10: v A 1926 (2); *v SA 1922 (1) 1927 (5); v WI 1929 (2)*
Stevenson, G. B. 2: *v WI 1980 (1); v In 1979 (1)*

Stewart (M. J.) 8: v WI 1963 (4); v P 1962 (2); *v In 1963 (2)*
Stoddart, A. E. 16: v A 1893 (3) 1896 (2); *v A 1887 (1) 1891 (3) 1894 (5) 1897 (2)*
Storer (W.) 6: v A 1899 (1); *v A 1897 (5)*
Street (G. B.) 1: *v SA 1922*
Strudwick (H.) 28: v A 1921 (2) 1926 (5); v SA 1924 (1); *v A 1911 (1) 1920 (4) 1924 (5); v SA 1909 (5) 1913 (5)*
Studd, C. T. 5: v A 1882 (1); *v A 1882 (4)*
Studd, G. B. 4: *v A 1882 (4)*
Subba Row, R. 13: v A 1961 (5); v SA 1960 (4); v NZ 1958 (1); v In 1959 (1); *v WI 1959 (2)*
Sugg (F. H.) 2: v A 1888 (2)
Sutcliffe (H.) 54: v A 1926 (5) 1930 (4) 1934 (4); v SA 1924 (5) 1929 (5) 1935 (2); v WI 1928 (3) 1933 (2); v NZ 1931 (2); v In 1932 (1); *v A 1924 (5) 1928 (4) 1932 (5); v SA 1927 (5); v NZ 1932 (2)*
Swetman (R.) 11: v In 1959 (3); *v A 1958 (2); v WI 1959 (4); v NZ 1958 (2)*

Tate (F. W.) 1: v A 1902
Tate (M. W.) 39: v A 1926 (5) 1930 (5); v SA 1924 (5) 1929 (3) 1935 (1); v WI 1928 (3); v NZ 1931 (1); *v A 1924 (5) 1928 (5); v SA 1930 (5); v NZ 1932 (1)*
Tattersall (R.) 16: v A 1953 (1); v SA 1951 (5); v P 1954 (1); *v A 1950 (2); v NZ 1950 (2); v In 1951 (5)*
Tavaré, C. J. 17: v A 1981 (2); v WI 1980 (2); v In 1982 (3); v P 1982 (3); *v In 1981 (6); v SL 1981 (1)*
Taylor (K.) 3: v A 1964 (1); v In 1959 (2)
Taylor, R. W. 42: v A 1981 (3); v NZ 1978 (3); v In 1979 (3) 1982 (3); v P 1978 (3) 1982 (3); *v A 1978 (6) 1979 (3); v NZ 1970 (1) 1977 (3); v In 1979 (1) 1981 (6); v P 1977 (3); v SL 1981 (1)*
Tennyson, Hon. L. H. 9: v A 1921 (4); *v SA 1913 (5)*
Thompson (G. J.) 6: v A 1909 (1); *v SA 1909 (5)*
Thomson, N. I. 5: *v SA 1964 (5)*
Titmus (F. J.) 53: v A 1964 (5); v SA 1955 (2) 1965 (3); v WI 1963 (4) 1966 (3); v NZ 1965 (3); v P 1962 (2) 1967 (2); *v A 1962 (5) 1965 (5) 1974 (4); v SA 1964 (5); v WI 1967 (2); v NZ 1962 (3); v In 1963 (5)*
Tolchard, R. W. 4: *v In 1976 (4)*
Townsend, C. L. 2: v A 1899 (2)
Townsend, D. C. H. 3: *v WI 1934 (3)*
Townsend (L. F.) 4: *v WI 1929 (1); v In 1933 (3)*
Tremlett (M. F.) 3: *v WI 1947 (3)*
Trott (A. E.) 2: *v SA 1898 (2)*
Trueman (F. S.) 67: v A 1953 (1) 1956 (2) 1961 (4) 1964 (4); v SA 1955 (1) 1960 (5); v WI 1957 (5) 1963 (5); v NZ 1958 (5) 1965 (2); v In 1952 (4) 1959 (5); v P 1962 (4); *v A 1958 (3) 1962 (5); v WI 1953 (3) 1959 (5); v NZ 1958 (2) 1962 (2)*
Tufnell, N. C. 1: *v SA 1909*
Turnbull, M. J. 9: v WI 1933 (2); v In 1936 (1); *v SA 1930 (5); v NZ 1929 (1)*
Tyldesley (E.) 14: v A 1921 (3) 1926 (1); v SA 1924 (1); v WI 1928 (3); *v A 1928 (1): v SA 1927 (5)*
Tyldesley (J. T.) 31: v A 1899 (2) 1902 (5) 1905 (5) 1909 (4); v SA 1907 (3); *v A 1901 (5) 1903 (5); v SA 1898 (2)*
Tyldesley (R. K.) 7: v A 1930 (2); v SA 1924 (4); *v A 1924 (1)*
Tylecote, E. F. S. 6: v A 1886 (2); *v A 1882 (4)*
Tyler (E. J.) 1: *v SA 1895*
Tyson (F. H.) 17: v A 1956 (1); v SA 1955 (2); v P 1954 (1); *v A 1954 (5) 1958 (2); v SA 1956 (2); v NZ 1954 (2) 1958 (2)*

Ulyett (G.) 25: v A 1882 (1) 1884 (3) 1886 (3) 1888 (2) 1890 (1); *v A 1876 (2) 1878 (1) 1881 (4) 1884 (5) 1887 (1); v SA 1888 (2)*
Underwood, D. L. 86: v A 1968 (4) 1972 (2) 1975 (4) 1977 (5); v WI 1966 (2) 1969 (2) 1973 (3) 1976 (5) 1980 (1); v NZ 1969 (3) 1973 (1); v In 1971 (1) 1974 (3); v P 1967 (2) 1971 (1) 1974 (3); *v A 1970 (5) 1974 (5) 1976 (1) 1979 (3); v WI 1973 (4); v NZ 1970 (2) 1974 (2); v In 1972 (4) 1976 (5) 1979 (1) 1981 (6); v P 1968 (3) 1972 (2); v SL 1981 (1)*

Valentine, B. H. 7: *v SA 1938 (5); v In 1933 (2)*
Verity (H.) 40: v A 1934 (5) 1938 (4); v SA 1935 (4); v WI 1933 (2) 1939 (1); v NZ 1931 (2) 1937 (1); v In 1936 (3); *v A 1932 (4) 1936 (5); v SA 1938 (5); v NZ 1932 (1); v In 1933 (3)*
Vernon, G. F. 1: *v A 1882*
Vine (J.) 2: *v A 1911 (2)*
Voce (W.) 27: v NZ 1931 (1) 1937 (1); v In 1932 (1) 1936 (1) 1946 (1); *v A 1932 (4) 1936 (5) 1946 (2); v SA 1930 (5); v WI 1929 (4); v NZ 1932 (2)*

Waddington (A.) 2: *v A 1920 (2)*
Wainwright (E.) 5: v A 1893 (1); *v A 1897 (4)*
Walker (P. M.) 3: v SA 1960 (3)
Walters, C. F. 11: v A 1934 (5); v WI 1933 (3); *v In 1933 (3)*
Ward (A.) 7: v A 1893 (2); *v A 1894 (5)*
Ward, A. 5: v WI 1976 (1); v NZ 1969 (3); v P 1971 (1)
Wardle (J. H.) 28: v A 1953 (3) 1956 (1); v SA 1951 (2) 1955 (3); v WI 1950 (1) 1957 (1); v P 1954 (4); *v A 1954 (4); v SA 1956 (4); v WI 1947 (1) 1953 (2); v NZ 1954 (2)*
Warner, P. F. 15: v A 1909 (1) 1912 (1); v SA 1912 (1); *v A 1903 (5); v SA 1898 (2) 1905 (5)*
Warr, J. J. 2: *v A 1950 (2)*
Warren (A. R.) 1: v A 1905
Washbrook (C.) 37: v A 1948 (4) 1956 (3); v SA 1947 (5); v WI 1950 (2); v NZ 1937 (1) 1949 (2); v In 1946 (3); *v A 1946 (5) 1950 (5); v SA 1948 (5); v NZ 1946 (1) 1950 (1)*
Watkins (A. J.) 15: v A 1948 (1); v NZ 1949 (1); v In 1952 (3); *v SA 1948 (5); v In 1951 (5)*
Watson (W.) 23: v A 1953 (3) 1956 (2); v SA 1951 (5) 1955 (1); v NZ 1958 (2); v In 1952 (1); *v A 1958 (2); v WI 1953 (5); v NZ 1958 (2)*
Webbe, A. J. 1: *v A 1878*
Wellard (A. W.) 2: v A 1938 (1); v NZ 1937 (1)
Wharton (A.) 1: v NZ 1949
White, J. C. 15: v A 1921 (1) 1930 (1); v SA 1929 (3); v WI 1928 (1); *v A 1928 (5); v SA 1930 (4)*
White (D. W.) 2: v *P 1961 (2)*
Whysall (W. W.) 4: v A 1930 (1); *v A 1924 (3)*
Wilkinson (L. L.) 3: *v SA 1938 (3)*
Willey, P. 20: v A 1980 (1) 1981 (4); v WI 1976 (2) 1980 (5); v In 1979 (1); *v A 1979 (3); v WI 1980 (4)*
Willis, R. G. D. 74: v A 1977 (5) 1981 (6); v WI 1973 (1) 1976 (2) 1980 (4); v NZ 1978 (3); v In 1974 (1) 1979 (3) 1982 (3); v P 1974 (1) 1978 (3) 1982 (2); *v A 1970 (4) 1974 (5) 1976 (1) 1978 (6) 1979 (3); v WI 1973 (3); v NZ 1970 (1) 1977 (3); v In 1976 (5) 1981 (5); v P 1977 (3); v SL 1981 (1)*
Wilson, C. E. M. 2: *v SA 1898 (2)*
Wilson, D. 6: *v NZ 1970 (1); v In 1963 (5)*
Wilson, E. R. 1: *v A 1920*
Wood (A.) 4: v A 1938 (1); v WI 1939 (3)
Wood, B. 12: v A 1972 (1) 1975 (3); v WI 1976 (1); v P 1978 (1); *v NZ 1974 (2); v In 1972 (3); v P 1972 (1)*
Wood, G. E. C. 3: v SA 1924 (3)
Wood (H.) 4: v A 1888 (1); *v SA 1888 (2) 1891 (1)*
Wood (R.) 1: *v A 1886*
Woods S. M. J. 3: *v SA 1895 (3)*
Woolley (F. E.) 64: v A 1909 (1) 1912 (3) 1921 (5) 1926 (5) 1930 (2) 1934 (1); v SA 1912 (3) 1924 (5) 1929 (3); v NZ 1931 (1); v In 1932 (1); *v A 1911 (5) 1920 (5) 1924 (5); v SA 1909 (5) 1913 (5) 1922 (5); v NZ 1929 (4)*
Woolmer, R. A. 19: v A 1975 (2) 1977 (5) 1981 (2); v WI 1976 (5) 1980 (2); *v A 1976 (1); v In 1976 (2)*
Worthington (T. S.) 9: v In 1936 (2); *v A 1936 (3); v NZ 1929 (4)*
Wright, C. W. 3: *v SA 1895 (3)*
Wright (D. V. P.) 34: v A 1938 (3) 1948 (1); v SA 1947 (4); v WI 1939 (3) 1950 (1); v NZ 1949 (1); v In 1946 (2); *v A 1946 (5) 1950 (5); v SA 1938 (3) 1948 (3); v NZ 1946 (1) 1950 (2)*

Wyatt, R. E. S. 40: v A 1930 (1) 1934 (4); v SA 1929 (2) 1935 (5); v WI 1933 (2); v In 1936 (1); *v A 1932 (5) 1936 (2); v SA 1927 (5) 1930 (5); v WI 1929 (2) 1934 (4); v NZ 1932 (2)*
Wynyard, E. G. 3: v A 1896 (1); *v SA 1905 (2)*

Yardley, N. W. D. 20: v A 1948 (5); v SA 1947 (5); v WI 1950 (3); *v A 1946 (5); v SA 1938 (1); v NZ 1946 (1)*
Young (H. I.) 2: v A 1899 (2)
Young (J. A.) 8: v A 1948 (3); v SA 1947 (1); v NZ 1949 (2); *v SA 1948 (2)*
Young, R. A. 2: *v A 1907 (2)*

AUSTRALIA

Number of Test cricketers: 314

A'Beckett, E. L. 4: v E 1928 (2); v SA 1931 (1); *v E 1930 (1)*
Alderman, T. M. 14: v WI 1981 (2); v P 1981 (3); *v E 1981 (6); v NZ 1981 (3)*
Alexander, G. 2: v E 1884 (1); *v E 1880 (1)*
Alexander, H. H. 1: v E 1932
Allan, F. E. 1: v E 1878
Allan, P. J. 1: v E 1965
Allen, R. C. 1: v E 1886
Andrews, T. J. E. 16: v E 1924 (3); *v E 1921 (5) 1926 (5); v SA 1921 (3)*
Archer, K. A. 5: v E 1950 (3); v WI 1951 (2)
Archer, R. G. 19: v E 1954 (4); v SA 1952 (1); *v E 1953 (3) 1956 (5); v WI 1954 (5); v P 1956 (1)*
Armstrong, W. W. 50: v E 1901 (4) 1903 (3) 1907 (5) 1911 (5) 1920 (5); v SA 1910 (5); *v E 1902 (5) 1905 (5) 1909 (5) 1921 (5); v SA 1902 (3)*

Badcock, C. L. 7: v E 1936 (3); *v E 1938 (4)*
Bannerman, A. C. 28: v E 1878 (1) 1881 (3) 1882 (4) 1884 (4) 1886 (1) 1887 (1) 1891 (3); *v E 1880 (1) 1882 (1) 1884 (3) 1888 (3) 1893 (3)*
Bannerman, C. 3: v E 1876 (2) 1878 (1)
Bardsley, W. 41: v E 1911 (4) 1920 (5) 1924 (3); v SA 1910 (5); *v E 1909 (5) 1912 (3) 1921 (5) 1926 (5); v SA 1912 (3) 1921 (3)*
Barnes, S. G. 13: v E 1946 (4); v In 1947 (3); *v E 1938 (1) 1948 (4); v NZ 1945 (1)*
Barnett, B. A. 4: *v E 1938 (4)*
Barrett, J. E. 2: *v E 1890 (2)*
Beard, G. R. 3: *v P 1979 (3)*
Benaud, J. 3: v P 1972 (2); *v WI 1972 (1)*
Benaud, R. 63: v E 1954 (5) 1958 (5) 1962 (5); v SA 1952 (4) 1963 (4); v WI 1951 (1) 1960 (5); *v E 1953 (3) 1956 (5) 1961 (4); v SA 1957 (5); v WI 1954 (5); v In 1956 (3) 1959 (5); v P 1956 (1) 1959 (3)*
Blackham, J. McC. 35: v E 1876 (2) 1878 (1) 1881 (4) 1882 (4) 1884 (2) 1886 (1) 1887 (1) 1891 (3) 1894 (1); *v E 1880 (1) 1882 (1) 1884 (3) 1886 (3) 1888 (3) 1890 (2) 1893 (3)*
Blackie, D. D. 3: v E 1928 (3)
Bonnor, G. J. 17: v E 1882 (4) 1884 (3); *v E 1880 (1) 1882 (1) 1884 (3) 1886 (2) 1888 (3)*
Booth, B. C. 29: v E 1962 (5) 1965 (3); v SA 1963 (4); v P 1964 (1); *v E 1961 (2) 1964 (5); v WI 1964 (5); v In 1964 (3); v P 1964 (1)*
Border, A. R. 42: v E 1978 (3) 1979 (3); v WI 1979 (3) 1981 (3); v In 1980 (3); v NZ 1980 (3); v P 1978 (2) 1981 (3); *v E 1980 (1) 1981 (6); v NZ 1981 (3); v In 1979 (6); v P 1979 (3)*
Boyle, H. F. 12: v E 1878 (1) 1881 (4) 1882 (1) 1884 (1); *v E 1880 (1) 1882 (1) 1884 (3)*
Bradman, D. G. 52: v E 1928 (4) 1932 (4) 1936 (5) 1946 (5); v SA 1931 (5); v WI 1930 (5); v In 1947 (5); *v E 1930 (5) 1934 (5) 1938 (4) 1948 (5)*
Bright, R. J. 14: v E 1979 (1); v WI 1979 (1); *v E 1977 (3) 1980 (1) 1981 (5); v P 1979 (3)*
Bromley, E. H. 2: v E 1932 (1); *v E 1934 (1)*
Brown, W. A. 22: v E 1936 (2); v In 1947 (3); *v E 1934 (5) 1938 (4) 1948 (2); v SA 1935 (5); v NZ 1945 (1)*

Bruce, W. 14: v E 1884 (2) 1891 (3) 1894 (4); *v E 1886 (2) 1893 (3)*
Burge, P. J. 42: v E 1954 (1) 1958 (1) 1962 (3) 1965 (4); v SA 1963 (5); v WI 1960 (2); *v E 1956 (3) 1961 (5) 1964 (5); v SA 1957 (1); v WI 1954 (1); v In 1956 (3) 1959 (2) 1964 (3); v P 1959 (2) 1964 (1)*
Burke, J. W. 24: v E 1950 (2) 1954 (2) 1958 (5); v WI 1951 (1); *v E 1956 (5); v SA 1957 (5); v In 1956 (3); v P 1956 (1)*
Burn, K. E. 2: *v E 1890 (2)*
Burton, F. J. 2: v E 1886 (1) 1887 (1)

Callaway, S. T. 3: v E 1891 (2) 1894 (1)
Callen, I. W. 1: v In 1977
Carkeek, W. 6: *v E 1912 (3); v SA 1912 (3)*
Carlson, P. H. 2: v E 1978 (2)
Carter, H. 28: v E 1907 (5) 1911 (5) 1920 (2); v SA 1910 (5); *v E 1909 (5) 1921 (4); v SA 1921 (2)*
Chappell, G. S. 76: v E 1970 (5) 1974 (6) 1976 (1) 1979 (3); v WI 1975 (6) 1979 (3) 1981 (3); v NZ 1973 (3) 1980 (3); v In 1980 (3); v P 1972 (3) 1976 (3) 1981 (3); *v E 1972 (5) 1975 (4) 1977 (5) 1980 (1); v WI 1972 (5); v NZ 1973 (3) 1976 (2) 1981 (3); v P 1979 (3)*
Chappell, I. M. 75: v E 1965 (2) 1970 (6) 1974 (6) 1979 (2); v WI 1968 (5) 1975 (6) 1979 (1); v NZ 1973 (3); v In 1967 (4); v P 1964 (1) 1972 (3); *v E 1968 (5) 1972 (5) 1975 (4); v SA 1966 (5) 1969 (4); v WI 1972 (5); v NZ 1973 (3); v In 1969 (5)*
Chappell, T. M. 3: *v E 1981 (3)*
Charlton, P. C. 2: *v E 1890 (2)*
Chipperfield, A. G. 14: v E 1936 (3); *v E 1934 (5) 1938 (1); v SA 1935 (5)*
Clark, W. M. 10: v In 1977 (5); v P 1978 (1); *v WI 1977 (4)*
Colley, D. J. 3: *v E 1972 (3)*
Collins, H. L. 19: v E 1920 (5) 1924 (5); *v E 1921 (3) 1926 (3); v SA 1921 (3)*
Coningham, A. 1: v E 1894
Connolly, A. N. 29; v E 1965 (1) 1970 (1); v SA 1963 (3); v WI 1968 (5); v In 1967 (3); *v E 1968 (5); v SA 1969 (4); v In 1964 (2); 1969 (5)*
Cooper, B. B. 1: v E 1876
Cooper, W. H. 2: v E 1881 (1) 1884 (1)
Corling, G. E. 5: *v E 1964 (5)*
Cosier, G. J. 18: v E 1976 (1) 1978 (2); v WI 1975 (3); v In 1977 (4); v P 1976 (3); *v WI 1977 (3); v NZ 1976 (2)*
Cottam, W. J. 1: v E 1886
Cotter, A. 21: v E 1903 (2) 1907 (2) 1911 (4); v SA 1910 (5); *v E 1905 (3) 1909 (5)*
Coultard, G. 1: v E 1881
Cowper, R. M. 27: v E 1965 (4); v In 1967 (4); v P 1964 (1); *v E 1964 (1) 1968 (4); v SA 1966 (5); v WI 1964 (5); v In 1964 (2); v P 1964 (1)*
Craig, I. D. 11: v SA 1952 (1); *v E 1956 (2); v SA 1957 (5); v In 1956 (2); v P 1956 (1)*
Crawford, W. P. A. 4: *v E 1956 (1); v In 1956 (3)*

Darling, J. 34: v E 1894 (5) 1897 (5) 1901 (3); *v E 1896 (3) 1899 (5) 1902 (5) 1905 (5); v SA 1902 (3)*
Darling, L. S. 12: v E 1932 (2) 1936 (1); *v E 1934 (4): v SA 1935 (5)*
Darling, W. M. 14: v E 1978 (4); v In 1977 (1); v P 1978 (1); *v WI 1977 (3); v In 1979 (5)*
Davidson, A. K. 44; v E 1954 (3) 1958 (5) 1962 (5); v WI 1960 (4); *v E 1953 (5) 1956 (2) 1961 (5); v SA 1957 (5); v In 1956 (1) 1959 (5); v P 1956 (1) 1959 (3)*
Davis, I. C. 15: v E 1976 (1); v NZ 1973 (3); v P 1976 (3); *v E 1977 (3); v NZ 1973 (3) 1976 (2)*
De Courcy, J. H. 3: *v E 1953 (3)*
Dell, A. R. 2: v E 1970 (1); v NZ 1973 (1)
Donnan, H. 5: v E 1891 (2); *v E 1896 (3)*
Dooland, B. 3: v E 1946 (2); v In 1947 (1)
Duff, R. A. 22: v E 1901 (4) 1903 (5); *v E 1902 (5) 1905 (5); v SA 1902 (3)*
Duncan, J. R. F. 1: v E 1970
Dymock, G. 21: v E 1974 (1) 1978 (3) 1979 (3); v WI 1979 (2); v NZ 1973 (1); v P 1978 (1); *v NZ 1973 (2); v In 1979 (5); v P 1979 (3)*
Dyson, J. 19: v WI 1981 (2); v NZ 1980 (3); v In 1977 (3) 1980 (3); *v E 1981 (5); v NZ 1981 (3)*

Eady, C. J. 2: v E 1901 (1); *v E 1896 (1)*
Eastwood, K. H. 1: v E 1970
Ebeling, H. I. 1: *v E 1934*
Edwards, J. D. 3: *v E 1888 (3)*
Edwards, R. 20: v E 1974 (5); v P 1972 (2); *v E 1972 (4) 1975 (4); v WI 1972 (5)*
Edwards, W. J. 3: v E 1974 (3)
Emery, S. H. 4: *v E 1912 (2); v SA 1912 (2)*
Evans, E. 6: v E 1881 (2) 1882 (1) 1884 (1); *v E 1886 (2)*

Fairfax, A. G. 10: v E 1928 (1); v WI 1930 (5); *v E 1930 (4)*
Favell, L. E. 19: v E 1954 (4) 1958 (2); v WI 1960 (4); *v WI 1954 (2); v In 1959 (4); v P 1959 (3)*
Ferris, J. J. 8: v E 1886 (2) 1887 (1); *v E 1888 (3) 1890 (2)*
Fingleton, J. H. 18: v E 1932 (3) 1936 (5); v SA 1931 (1); *v E 1938 (4); v SA 1935 (5)*
Fleetwood-Smith, L. O'B. 10: v E 1936 (3); *v E 1938 (4); v SA 1935 (3)*
Francis, B. C. 3: *v E 1972 (3)*
Freeman, E. W. 11: v WI 1968 (4); v In 1967 (2); *v E 1968 (2); v SA 1969 (2); v In 1969 (1)*
Freer, F. W. 1: v E 1946

Gannon, J. B. 3: v In 1977 (3)
Garrett, T. W. 19: v E 1876 (2) 1878 (1) 1881 (3) 1882 (3) 1884 (3) 1886 (2) 1887 (1); *v E 1882 (1) 1886 (3)*
Gaunt, R. A. 3: v SA 1963 (1); *v E 1961 (1); v SA 1957 (1)*
Gehrs, D. R. A. 6: v E 1903 (1); v SA 1910 (4); *v E 1905 (1)*
Giffen, G. 31: v E 1881 (3) 1882 (4) 1884 (3) 1891 (3) 1894 (5); *v E 1882 (1) 1884 (3) 1886 (3) 1893 (3) 1896 (3)*
Giffen, W. F. 3: v E 1886 (1) 1891 (2)
Gilmour, G. J. 15: v E 1976 (1); v WI 1975 (5); v NZ 1973 (2); v P 1976 (3); *v E 1975 (1); v NZ 1973 (1) 1976 (2)*
Gleeson, J. W. 29: v E 1970 (5); v WI 1968 (5); v In 1967 (4); *v E 1968 (5) 1972 (3); v SA 1969 (4); v In 1969 (3)*
Graham, H. 6: v E 1894 (2); *v E 1893 (3) 1896 (1)*
Gregory, D. W. 3: v E 1876 (2) 1878 (1)
Gregory, E. J. 1: v E 1876
Gregory, J. M. 24: v E 1920 (5) 1924 (5) 1928 (1); *v E 1921 (5) 1926 (5); v SA 1921 (3)*
Gregory, R. G. 2: v E 1936 (2)
Gregory, S. E. 58: v E 1891 (1) 1894 (5) 1897 (5) 1901 (5) 1903 (4) 1907 (2) 1911 (1); *v E 1890 (2) 1893 (3) 1896 (3) 1899 (5) 1902 (5) 1905 (3) 1909 (5) 1912 (3); v SA 1902 (3) 1912 (3)*
Grimmett, C. V. 37: v E 1924 (1) 1928 (5) 1932 (3); v SA 1931 (5); v WI 1930 (5); *v E 1926 (3) 1930 (5) 1934 (5); v SA 1935 (5)*
Groube, T. U. 1: *v E 1880*
Grout, A. T. W. 51: v E 1958 (5) 1962 (2) 1965 (5); v SA 1963 (5); v WI 1960 (5); *v E 1961 (5) 1964 (5); v SA 1957 (5); v WI 1964 (5); v In 1959 (4) 1964 (1); v P 1959 (3) 1964 (1)*
Guest, C. E. J. 1: v E 1962

Hamence, R. A. 3: v E 1946 (1); v In 1947 (2)
Hammond, J. R. 5: *v WI 1972 (5)*
Harry, J. 1: v E 1894
Hartigan, R. J. 2: v E 1907 (2)
Hartkopf, A. E. V. 1: v E 1924
Harvey, M. R. 1: v E 1946
Harvey, R. N. 79: v E 1950 (5) 1954 (5) 1958 (5) 1962 (5); v SA 1952 (5); v WI 1951 (5) 1960 (4); v In 1947 (2); *v E 1948 (2) 1953 (5) 1956 (5) 1961 (5); v SA 1949 (5) 1957 (4); v WI 1954 (5); v In 1956 (3) 1959 (5); v P 1956 (1) 1959 (3)*
Hassett, A. L. 43: v E 1946 (5) 1950 (5); v SA 1952 (5); v WI 1951 (4); v In 1947 (4); *v E 1938 (4) 1948 (5) 1953 (5); v SA 1949 (5); v NZ 1945 (1)*
Hawke, N. J. N. 27: v E 1962 (1) 1965 (4); v SA 1963 (4); v In 1967 (1); v P 1964 (1); *v E 1964 (5) 1968 (2); v SA 1966 (2); v WI 1964 (5); v In 1964 (1); v P 1964 (1)*
Hazlitt, G. R. 9: v E 1907 (2) 1911 (1); *v E 1912 (3); v SA 1912 (3)*
Hendry, H. S. T. L. 11: v E 1924 (1) 1928 (4); *v E 1921 (4); v SA 1921 (2)*

Hibbert, P. A. 1: v In 1977
Higgs, J. D. 22: v E 1978 (5) 1979 (1); v WI 1979 (1); v NZ 1980 (3); v In 1980 (2); *v WI 1977 (4); v In 1979 (6)*
Hilditch, A. M. J. 9: v E 1978 (1); v P 1978 (2); *v In 1979 (6)*
Hill, C. 49: v E 1897 (5) 1901 (5) 1903 (5) 1907 (5) 1911 (5); v SA 1910 (5); *v E 1896 (3) 1899 (3) 1902 (5) 1905 (5); v SA 1902 (3)*
Hill, J. C. 3: *v E 1953 (2); v WI 1954 (1)*
Hoare, D. E. 1: v WI 1960
Hodges, J. H. 2: v E 1876 (2)
Hogg, R. M. 22: v E 1978 (6); v WI 1979 (2); v NZ 1980 (2); v In 1980 (2); v P 1978 (2); *v E 1981 (2); v In 1979 (6)*
Hole, G. B. 18: v E 1950 (1) 1954 (3); v SA 1952 (4); v WI 1951 (5); *v E 1953 (5)*
Hookes, D. W. 8: v E 1976 (1); v WI 1979 (1); *v E 1977 (5); v P 1979 (1)*
Hopkins, A. J. Y. 20: v E 1901 (2) 1903 (5); *v E 1902 (5) 1905 (3) 1909 (2); v SA 1902 (3)*
Horan, T. P. 15: v E 1876 (1) 1878 (1) 1881 (4) 1882 (4) 1884 (4); *v E 1882 (1)*
Hordern, H. V. 7: v E 1911 (5): v SA 1910 (2)
Hornibrook, P. M. 6: v E 1928 (1); *v E 1930 (5)*
Howell, W. P. 18: v E 1897 (3) 1901 (4) 1903 (3); *v E 1899 (5) 1902 (1); v SA 1902 (2)*
Hughes, K. J. 48: v E 1978 (6) 1979 (3); v WI 1979 (3) 1981 (3); v NZ 1980 (3); v In 1977 (2) 1980 (3); v P 1978 (2) 1981 (3); *v E 1977 (1) 1980 (1) 1981 (6); v NZ 1981 (3); v In 1979 (6); v P 1979 (3)*
Hunt, W. A. 1: v SA 1931
Hurst, A. G. 12: v E 1978 (6); v NZ 1973 (1); v In 1977 (1); v P 1978 (2); *v In 1979 (2)*
Hurwood, A. 2: v WI 1930 (2)

Inverarity, R. J. 6: v WI 1968 (1); *v E 1968 (2) 1972 (3)*
Iredale, F. A. 14: v E 1894 (5) 1897 (4); *v E 1896 (2) 1899 (3)*
Ironmonger, H. 14: v E 1928 (2) 1932 (4); v SA 1931 (4); v WI 1930 (4)
Iverson, J. B. 5: v E 1950 (5)

Jackson, A. 8: v E 1928 (2); v WI 1930 (4); *v E 1930 (2)*
Jarman, B. N. 19: v E 1962 (3); v WI 1968 (4); v In 1967 (4); v P 1964 (1); *v E 1968 (4); v In 1959 (1); 1964 (2)*
Jarvis, A. H. 11: v E 1884 (3) 1894 (4); *v E 1886 (2) 1888 (2)*
Jenner, T. J. 9: v E 1970 (2) 1974 (2); v WI 1975 (1); *v WI 1972 (4)*
Jennings, C. B. 6: *v E 1912 (3); v SA 1912 (3)*
Johnson I. W. 45: v E 1946 (4) 1950 (5) 1954 (4); v SA 1952 (1); v WI 1951 (4); v In 1947 (4); *v E 1948 (4) 1956 (5); v SA 1949 (5); v WI 1954 (5); v NZ 1945 (1); v In 1956 (2); v P 1956 (1)*
Johnson, L. J. 1: v In 1947
Johnston W. A. 40: v E 1950 (5) 1954 (4); v SA 1952 (5); v WI 1951 (5); v In 1947 (4); *v E 1948 (5) 1953 (3); v SA 1949 (5); v WI 1954 (4)*
Jones, E. 19: v E 1894 (1) 1897 (5) 1901 (2); *v E 1896 (3) 1899 (5) 1902 (2); v SA 1902 (1)*
Jones, S. P. 12: v E 1881 (2) 1884 (4) 1886 (1) 1887 (1); *v E 1882 (1) 1886 (3)*
Joslin, L. R. 1: v In 1967

Kelleway, C. 26: v E 1911 (4) 1920 (5) 1924 (5) 1928 (1); v SA 1910 (5); *v E 1912 (3); v SA 1912 (3)*
Kelly, J. J. 36: v E 1897 (5) 1901 (5) 1903 (5); *v E 1896 (3) 1899 (5) 1902 (5) 1905 (5); v SA 1902 (3)*
Kelly, T. J. D. 2: v E 1876 (1) 1878 (1)
Kendall, T. 2: v E 1876 (2)
Kent, M. F. 3: *v E 1981 (3)*
Kippax, A. F. 22: v E 1924 (1) 1928 (5) 1932 (1); v SA 1931 (4); v WI 1930 (5); *v E 1930 (5) 1934 (1)*
Kline L. F. 13: v E 1958 (2); v WI 1960 (2); *v SA 1957 (5); v In 1959 (3); v P 1959 (1)*

Laird, B. M. 18: v E 1979 (2); v WI 1979 (3) 1981 (3); v P 1981 (3); *v E 1980 (1) 1981 (3); v P 1979 (3)*
Langley, G. R. A. 26: v E 1954 (2); v SA 1952 (5); v WI 1951 (5); *v E 1953 (4) 1956 (3); v WI 1954 (4); v In 1956 (2); v P 1956 (1)*

Laughlin, T. J. 3: v E 1978 (1); *v WI 1977 (2)*
Laver, F. 15: v E 1901 (1) 1903 (1); *v E 1899 (4) 1905 (5) 1909 (4)*
Lawry, W. M. 67: v E 1962 (5) 1965 (5) 1970 (5); v SA 1963 (5); v WI 1968 (5); v In 1967 (4); v P 1964 (1); *v E 1961 (5) 1964 (5) 1968 (4); v SA 1966 (5) 1969 (4); v WI 1964 (5); v In 1964 (3) 1969 (5); v P 1964 (1)*
Lawson, G. F. 5: v WI 1981 (1); v NZ 1980 (1); *v E 1981 (3)*
Lee, P. K. 2: v E 1932 (1); v SA 1931 (1)
Lillee, D. K. 63: v E 1970 (2) 1974 (6) 1976 (1) 1979 (3); v WI 1975 (5) 1979 (3) 1981 (3); v NZ 1980 (3); v In 1980 (3); v P 1972 (3) 1976 (3) 1981 (3); *v E 1972 (5) 1975 (4) 1980 (1) 1981 (6); v WI 1972 (1); v NZ 1976 (2) 1981 (3); v P 1979 (3)*
Lindwall, R. R. 61: v E 1946 (4) 1950 (5) 1954 (4) 1958 (2); v SA 1952 (4); v WI 1951 (5); v In 1947 (5); *v E 1948 (5) 1953 (5) 1956 (4); v SA 1949 (4); v WI 1954 (5); v NZ 1945 (1); v In 1956 (3) 1959 (2); v P 1956 (1) 1959 (2)*
Love, H. S. B. 1: v E 1932
Loxton, S. J. E. 12: v E 1950 (3); v In 1947 (1); *v E 1948 (3); v SA 1949 (5)*
Lyons, J. J. 14: v E 1886 (1) 1891 (3) 1894 (3) 1897 (1); *v E 1888 (1) 1890 (2) 1893 (3)*

McAlister, P. A. 8: v E 1903 (2) 1907 (4); *v E 1909 (2)*
Macartney, C. G. 35: v E 1907 (5) 1911 (1) 1920 (2); v SA 1910 (4); *v E 1909 (5) 1912 (3) 1921 (5) 1926 (5); v SA 1912 (3) 1921 (2)*
McCabe, S. J. 39: v E 1932 (5) 1936 (5); v SA 1931 (5); v WI 1930 (5); *v E 1930 (5) 1934 (5) 1938 (4); v SA 1935 (5)*
McCool, C. L. 14: v E 1946 (5); v In 1947 (3); *v SA 1949 (5) v NZ 1945 (1)*
McCormick, E. L. 12: v E 1936 (4); *v E 1938 (3); v SA 1935 (5)*
McCosker, R. B. 25: v E 1974 (3) 1976 (1) 1979 (2); v WI 1975 (4) 1979 (1); v P 1976 (3); *v E 1975 (4) 1977 (5); v NZ 1976 (2)*
McDonald, C. C. 47: v E 1954 (2) 1958 (5); v SA 1952 (5); v WI 1951 (1) 1960 (5); *v E 1956 (5) 1961 (3); v SA 1957 (5); v WI 1954 (5); v In 1956 (2) 1959 (5); v P 1956 (1) 1959 (3)*
McDonald, E. A. 11: v E 1920 (3); *v E 1921 (5); v SA 1921 (3)*
McDonnell, P. S. 19: v E 1881 (4) 1882 (3) 1884 (2) 1886 (2) 1887 (1); *v E 1880 (1) 1884 (3) 1888 (3)*
McIlwraith, J. 1: *v E 1886*
Mackay K. D. 37: v E 1958 (5) 1962 (3); v WI 1960 (5); *v E 1956 (3) 1961 (5); v SA 1957 (5); v In 1956 (3) 1959 (5); v P 1959 (3)*
McKenzie, G. D. 60: v E 1962 (5) 1965 (4) 1970 (3); v SA 1963 (5); v WI 1968 (5); v In 1967 (2); v P 1964 (1); *v E 1961 (3) 1964 (5) 1968 (5); v SA 1966 (5) 1969 (3); v WI 1964 (5); v In 1964 (3) 1969 (5); v P 1964 (1)*
McKibbin, T. R. 5: v E 1894 (1) 1897 (2); *v E 1896 (2)*
McLaren, J. W. 1: v E 1911
Maclean, J. A. 4: v E 1978 (4)
McLeod, C. E. 17: v E 1894 (1) 1897 (5) 1901 (2) 1903 (3); *v E 1899 (1) 1905 (5)*
McLeod, R. W. 6: v E 1891 (3); *v E 1893 (3)*
McShane, P. G. 3: v E 1884 (1) 1886 (1) 1887 (1)
Maddocks, L. V. 7: v E 1954 (3); *v E 1956 (2); v WI 1954 (1); v In 1956 (1)*
Mailey, A. A. 21: v E 1920 (5) 1924 (5); *v E 1921 (3) 1926 (5); v SA 1921 (3)*
Mallett, A. A. 38: v E 1970 (2) 1974 (5) 1979 (1); v WI 1968 (1) 1975 (6) 1979 (1); v NZ 1973 (3); v P 1972 (2); *v E 1968 (1) 1972 (2) 1975 (4) 1980 (1); v SA 1969 (1); v NZ 1973 (3); v In 1969 (5)*
Malone, M. F. 1: *v E 1977*
Mann, A. L. 4: v In 1977 (4)
Marr, A. P. 1: v E 1884
Marsh, R. W. 83: v E 1970 (6) 1974 (6) 1976 (1) 1979 (3); v WI 1975 (6) 1979 (3) 1981 (3); v NZ 1973 (3) 1980 (3); v In 1980 (3); v P 1972 (3) 1976 (3) 1981 (3); *v E 1972 (5) 1975 (4) 1977 (5) 1980 (1) 1981 (6); v WI 1972 (5); v NZ 1973 (3) 1976 (2) 1981 (3); v P 1979 (3)*
Martin, J. W. 8: v SA 1963 (1); v WI 1960 (3); *v SA 1966 (1); v In 1964 (2); v P 1964 (1)*
Massie, H. H. 9: v E 1881 (4) 1882 (3) 1884 (1); *v E 1882 (1)*
Massie, R. A. L. 6: v P 1972 (2); *v E 1972 (4)*
Matthews, T. J. 8: v E 1911 (2); *v E 1912 (3); v SA 1912 (3)*
Mayne, E. R. 4: *v E 1912 (1); v SA 1912 (1) 1921 (2)*
Mayne, L. C. 6: *v SA 1969 (2); v WI 1964 (3); v In 1969 (1)*

Meckiff, I. 18: v E 1958 (4); v SA 1963 (1); v WI 1960 (2); *v SA 1957 (4); v In 1959 (5); v P 1959 (2)*
Meuleman, K. D. 1: *v NZ 1945*
Midwinter, W. E. 8: v E 1876 (2) 1882 (1) 1886 (2); *v E 1884 (3)*
Miller, K. R. 55: v E 1946 (5) 1950 (5) 1954 (4); v SA 1952 (4); v WI 1951 (5); v In 1947 (5); *v E 1948 (5) 1953 (5) 1956 (5); v SA 1949 (5); v WI 1954 (5); v NZ 1945 (1); v P 1956 (1)*
Minnett, R. B. 9: v E 1911 (5); *v E 1912 (1); v SA 1912 (3)*
Misson, F. M. 5: v WI 1960 (3); *v E 1961 (2)*
Moroney, J. R. 7: v E 1950 (1); v WI 1951 (1); *v SA 1949 (5)*
Morris, A. R. 46: v E 1946 (5) 1950 (5) 1954 (4); v SA 1952 (5); v WI 1951 (4); v In 1947 (4); *v E 1948 (5) 1953 (5); v SA 1949 (5); v WI 1954 (4)*
Morris, S. 1: v E 1884
Moses, H. 6: v E 1886 (2) 1887 (1) 1891 (2) 1894 (1)
Moss, J. K. 1: v P 1978
Moule, W. H. 1: *v E 1880*
Murdoch, W. L. 18: v E 1876 (1) 1878 (1) 1881 (4) 1882 (4) 1884 (1); *v E 1880 (1) 1882 (1) 1884 (3) 1890 (2)*
Musgrove, H. 1: v E 1884

Nagel, L. E. 1: v E 1932
Nash, L. J. 2: v E 1936 (1); v SA 1931 (1)
Nitschke, H. C. 2: v SA 1931 (2)
Noble, M. A. 42: v E 1897 (4) 1901 (5) 1903 (5) 1907 (5); *v E 1899 (5) 1902 (5) 1905 (5) 1909 (5); v SA 1902 (3)*
Noblet, G. 3: v SA 1952 (1); v WI 1951 (1); *v SA 1949 (1)*
Nothling, O. E. 1: v E 1928

O'Brien, L. P. J. 5: v E 1932 (2) 1936 (1); *v SA 1935 (2)*
O'Connor, J. D. A. 4: v E 1907 (3); *v E 1909 (1)*
Ogilvie, A. D. 5: v In 1977 (3); *v WI 1977 (2)*
O'Keeffe, K. J. 24: v E 1970 (2) 1976 (1); v NZ 1973 (3); v P 1972 (2) 1976 (3); *v E 1977 (3); v WI 1972 (5); v NZ 1973 (3) 1976 (2)*
Oldfield, W. A. 54: v E 1920 (3) 1924 (5) 1928 (5) 1932 (4) 1936 (5); v SA 1931 (5); v WI 1930 (5); *v E 1921 (1) 1926 (5) 1930 (5) 1934 (5); v SA 1921 (1) 1935 (5)*
O'Neill, N. C. 42: v E 1958 (5) 1962 (5); v SA 1963 (4); v WI 1960 (5); *v E 1961 (5) 1964 (4); v WI 1964 (4); v In 1959 (5) 1964 (2); v P 1959 (3)*
O'Reilly, W. J. 27: v E 1932 (5) 1936 (5); v SA 1931 (2); *v E 1934 (5) 1938 (4); v SA 1935 (5); v NZ 1945 (1)*
Oxenham, R. K. 7: v E 1928 (3); v SA 1931 (1); v WI 1930 (3)

Palmer, G. E. 17: v E 1881 (4) 1882 (4) 1884 (2); *v E 1880 (1) 1884 (3) 1886 (3)*
Park, R. L. 1: v E 1920
Pascoe, L. S. 14: v E 1979 (2); v WI 1979 (1) 1981 (1); v NZ 1980 (3); v In 1980 (3); *v E 1977 (3) 1980 (1)*
Pellew, C. E. 10: v E 1920 (4); *v E 1921 (5); v SA 1921 (1)*
Philpott, P. I. 8: v E 1965 (3); *v WI 1964 (5)*
Ponsford, W. H. 29: v E 1924 (5) 1928 (2) 1932 (3); v SA 1931 (4); v WI 1930 (5); *v E 1926 (2) 1930 (4) 1934 (4)*
Pope, R. J. 1: v E 1884

Ransford, V. S. 20: v E 1907 (5) 1911 (5); v SA 1910 (5); *v E 1909 (5)*
Redpath, I. R. 66: v E 1965 (1) 1970 (6) 1974 (6); v SA 1963 (1); v WI 1968 (5) 1975 (6); v In 1967 (3); v P 1972 (3); *v E 1964 (5) 1968 (5); v SA 1966 (5) 1969 (4); v WI 1972 (5); v NZ 1973 (3); v In 1964 (2) 1969 (5); v P 1964 (1)*
Reedman, J. C. 1: v E 1894
Renneberg, D. A. 8: v In 1967 (3); *v SA 1966 (5)*
Richardson, A. J. 9: v E 1924 (4); *v E 1926 (5)*
Richardson, V. Y. 19: v E 1924 (3) 1928 (2) 1932 (5); *v E 1930 (4); v SA 1935 (5)*
Rigg, K. E. 8: v E 1936 (3); v SA 1931 (4); v WI 1930 (1)
Ring, D. T. 13: v SA 1952 (5); v WI 1951 (5); v In 1947 (1); *v E 1948 (1) 1953 (1)*

Rixon, S. J. 10: v In 1977 (5); *v WI 1977 (5)*
Robertson, W. R. 1: v E 1884
Robinson, R. D. 3: *v E 1977 (3)*
Robinson, R. H. 1: v E 1936
Rorke, G. F. 4: v E 1958 (2); *v In 1959 (2)*
Rutherford, J. W. 1: *v In 1956*
Ryder, J. 20: v E 1920 (5) 1924 (3) 1928 (5); *v E 1926 (4); v SA 1921 (3)*

Saggers, R. A. 6: *v E 1948 (1); v SA 1949 (5)*
Saunders, J. V. 14: v E 1901 (1) 1903 (2) 1907 (5); *v E 1902 (4); v SA 1902 (2)*
Scott, H. J. H. 8: v E 1884 (2); *v E 1884 (3) 1886 (3)*
Sellers, R. H. D. 1: *v In 1964*
Serjeant, C. S. 12: v In 1977 (4); *v E 1977 (3); v WI 1977 (5)*
Sheahan, A. P. 31: v E 1970 (2); v WI 1968 (5); v NZ 1973 (2); v In 1967 (4); v P 1972 (2); *v E 1968 (5) 1972 (2); v SA 1969 (4); v In 1969 (5)*
Shepherd, B. K. 9: v E 1962 (2); v SA 1963 (4); v P 1964 (1); *v WI 1964 (2)*
Sievers, M. W. 3: v E 1936 (3)
Simpson, R. B. 62: v E 1958 (1) 1962 (5) 1965 (3); v SA 1963 (5); v WI 1960 (5); v In 1967 (3) 1977 (5); v P 1964 (1); *v E 1961 (5) 1964 (5); v SA 1957 (5) 1966 (5); v WI 1964 (5) 1977 (5); v In 1964 (3); v P 1964 (1)*
Sincock, D. J. 3: v E 1965 (1); v P 1964 (1); *v WI 1964 (1)*
Slater, K. N. 1: v E 1958
Sleep, P. R. 3: v P 1978 (1); *v In 1979 (2)*
Slight, J. 1: *v E 1880*
Smith, D. B. M. 2: *v E 1912 (2)*
Spofforth, F. R. 18: v E 1876 (1) 1878 (1) 1881 (1) 1882 (4) 1884 (3) 1886 (1); *v E 1882 (1) 1884 (3) 1886 (3)*
Stackpole, K. R. 43: v E 1965 (2) 1970 (6); v WI 1968 (5); v NZ 1973 (3); v P 1972 (1); *v E 1972 (5); v SA 1966 (5) 1969 (4); v WI 1972 (4); v NZ 1973 (3); v In 1969 (5)*
Stevens, G. B. 4: *v In 1959 (2); v P 1959 (2)*

Taber, H. B. 16: v WI 1968 (1); *v E 1968 (1); v SA 1966 (5); 1969 (4); v In 1969 (5)*
Tallon, D. 21: v E 1946 (5) 1950 (5); v In 1947 (5); *v E 1948 (4) 1953 (1); v NZ 1945 (1)*
Taylor, J. M. 20: v E 1920 (5) 1924 (5); *v E 1921 (5) 1926 (3); v SA 1921 (2)*
Thomas, G. 8: v E 1965 (3); *v WI 1964 (5)*
Thompson, N. 2: v E 1876 (2)
Thoms, G. R. 1: v WI 1951
Thomson, A. L. 4: v E 1970 (4)
Thomson, J. R. 42: v E 1974 (5) 1979 (1); v WI 1975 (6) 1979 (1) 1981 (2); v In 1977 (5); v P 1972 (1) 1976 (1) 1981 (3); *v E 1975 (4) 1977 (5); v WI 1977 (5); v NZ 1981 (3)*
Thurlow, H. M. 1: v SA 1931
Toohey, P. M. 15: v E 1978 (5) 1979 (1); v WI 1979 (1); v In 1977 (5); *v WI 1977 (3)*
Toshack, E. R. H. 12: v E 1946 (5); v In 1947 (2); *v E 1948 (4); v NZ 1945 (1)*
Travers, J. P. F. 1: v E 1901
Tribe, G. E. 3: v E 1946 (3)
Trott, A. E. 3: v E 1894 (3)
Trott, G. H. S. 24: v E 1891 (3) 1894 (5) 1897 (5); *v E 1888 (3) 1890 (2) 1893 (3) 1896 (3)*
Trumble, H. 32: v E 1894 (1) 1897 (5) 1901 (5) 1903 (4); *v E 1890 (2) 1893 (3) 1896 (3) 1899 (5) 1902 (3); v SA 1902 (1)*
Trumble, J. W. 7: v E 1884 (4); *v E 1886 (3)*
Trumper, V. T. 48: v E 1901 (5) 1903 (5) 1907 (5) 1911 (5); v SA 1910 (5); *v E 1899 (5) 1902 (5) 1905 (5) 1909 (5); v SA 1902 (3)*
Turner, A. 14: v WI 1975 (6); v P 1976 (3); *v E 1975 (3); v NZ 1976 (2)*
Turner, C. T. B. 17: v E 1886 (2) 1887 (1) 1891 (3) 1894 (3); *v E 1888 (3) 1890 (2) 1893 (3)*

Veivers, T. R. 21: v E 1965 (4); v SA 1963 (3); v P 1964 (1); *v E 1964 (5); v SA 1966 (4); v In 1964 (3); v P 1964 (1)*

Waite, M. G. 2: *v E 1938 (2)*
Walker, M. H. N. 34: v E 1974 (6); 1976 (1); v WI 1975 (3); v NZ 1973 (1); v P 1972 (2) 1976 (2); *v E 1975 (4); 1977 (5); v WI 1972 (5); v NZ 1973 (3) 1976 (2)*

Wall, T. W. 18: v E 1928 (1) 1932 (4); v SA 1931 (3); v WI 1930 (1); *v E 1930 (5) 1934 (4)*
Walters, F. H. 1: v E 1884
Walters, K. D. 74: v E 1965 (5) 1970 (6) 1974 (6) 1976 (1); v WI 1968 (4); v NZ 1973 (3) 1980 (3); v In 1967 (2) 1980 (3); v P 1972 (1) 1976 (3); *v E 1968 (5) 1972 (4) 1975 (4) 1977 (5); v SA 1969 (4); v WI 1972 (5); v NZ 1973 (3) 1976 (2); v In 1969 (5)*
Ward, F. A. 4: v E 1936 (3); *v E 1938 (1)*
Watkins, J. R. 1: v P 1972
Watson, G. D. 5: *v E 1972 (2); v SA 1966 (3)*
Watson, W. 4: v E 1954 (1); *v WI 1954 (3)*
Wellham, D. M. 4: v WI 1981 (1); v P 1981 (2); *v E 1981 (1)*
Whatmore, D. F. 7: v P 1978 (2); *v In 1979 (5)*
Whitney, M. R. 2: *v E 1981 (2)*
Whitty, W. J. 14: v E 1911 (2); v SA 1910 (5); *v E 1909 (1) 1912 (3); v SA 1912 (3)*
Wiener, J. M. 6: v E 1979 (2); v WI 1979 (2); *v P 1979 (2)*
Wilson, J. W. 1: *v In 1956*
Wood, G. M. 37: v E 1978 (6); v WI 1981 (3); v NZ 1980 (3); v In 1977 (1) 1980 (3); v P 1978 (1) 1981 (3); *v E 1980 (1) 1981 (6); v WI 1977 (5); v NZ 1981 (3); v In 1979 (2)*
Woodcock, A. J. 1: v NZ 1973
Woodfull, W. M. 35: v E 1928 (5) 1932 (5); v SA 1931 (5); v WI 1930 (5); *v E 1926 (5) 1930 (5) 1934 (5)*
Woods, S. M. J. 3: *v E 1888 (3)*
Worrall, J. 11: v E 1884 (1) 1887 (1) 1894 (1) 1897 (1); *v E 1888 (3) 1899 (4)*
Wright, K. J. 10: v E 1978 (2); v P 1978 (2); *v In 1979 (6)*

Yallop, G. N. 32: v E 1978 (6); v WI 1975 (3); v In 1977 (1); v P 1978 (1) 1981 (1); *v E 1980 (1) 1981 (6); v WI 1977 (4); v In 1979 (6); v P 1979 (3)*
Yardley, B. 25: v E 1978 (4); v WI 1981 (3); v In 1977 (1) 1980 (2); v P 1978 (1) 1981 (3); *v WI 1977 (5); v NZ 1981 (3); v In 1979 (3)*

SOUTH AFRICA

Number of Test cricketers: 235

Adcock, N. A. T. 26: v E 1956 (5); v A 1957 (5); v NZ 1953 (5) 1961 (2); *v E 1955 (4) 1960 (5)*
Anderson, J. H. 1: v A 1902
Ashley, W. H. 1: v E 1888

Bacher, A. 12: v A 1966 (5) 1969 (4); *v E 1965 (3)*
Balaskas, X. C. 9: v E 1930 (2) 1938 (1); v A 1935 (3); *v E 1935 (1); v NZ 1931 (2)*
Barlow, E. J. 30: v E 1964 (5); v A 1966 (5) 1969 (4); v NZ 1961 (5); *v E 1965 (3); v A 1963 (5); v NZ 1963 (3)*
Baumgartner, H. V. 1: v E 1913
Beaumont, R. 5: v E 1913 (2); *v E 1912 (1); v A 1912 (2)*
Begbie, D. W. 5: v E 1948 (3); v A 1949 (2)
Bell, A. J. 16: v E 1930 (3); *v E 1929 (3) 1935 (3); v A 1931 (5); v NZ 1931 (2)*
Bisset, M. 3: v E 1898 (2) 1909 (1)
Bissett, G. F. 4: v E 1927 (4)
Blanckenberg, J. M. 18: v E 1913 (5) 1922 (5); v A 1921 (3); *v E 1924 (5)*
Bland, K. C. 21: v E 1964 (5); v A 1966 (1); v NZ 1961 (5); *v E 1965 (3); v A 1963 (4); v NZ 1963 (3)*
Bock, E. G. 1: v A 1935
Bond, G. E. 1: v E 1938
Botten, J. T. 3: *v E 1965 (3)*
Brann, W. H. 3: v E 1922 (3)
Briscoe, A. W. 2: v E 1938 (1); v A 1935 (1)
Bromfield, H. D. 9: v E 1964 (3); v NZ 1961 (5); *v E 1965 (1)*
Brown, L. S. 2: *v A 1931 (1); v NZ 1931 (1)*
Burger, C. G. de V. 2: v A 1957 (2)

Burke, S. F. 2: v E 1964 (1); v NZ 1961 (1)
Buys, I. D. 1: v E 1922

Cameron, H. B. 26: v E 1927 (5) 1930 (5); *v E 1929 (4) 1935 (5); v A 1931 (5); v NZ 1931 (2)*
Campbell, T. 5: v E 1909 (4); *v E 1912 (1)*
Carlstein, P. R. 8: v A 1957 (1); *v E 1960 (5); v A 1963 (2)*
Carter, C. P. 10: v E 1913 (2); v A 1921 (3); *v E 1912 (2) 1924 (3)*
Catterall, R. H. 24: v E 1922 (5) 1927 (5) 1930 (4); *v E 1924 (5) 1929 (5)*
Chapman, H. W. 2: v E 1913 (1); v A 1921 (1)
Cheetham, J. E. 24: v E 1948 (1); v A 1949 (3); v NZ 1953 (5); *v E 1951 (5) 1955 (3); v A 1952 (5); v NZ 1952 (2)*
Chevalier, G. A. 1: v A 1969
Christy, J. A. J. 10: v E 1930 (1); *v E 1929 (2); v A 1931 (5); v NZ 1931 (2)*
Chubb, G. W. A. 5: *v E 1951 (5)*
Cochran, J. A. K. 1: v E 1930
Coen, S. K. 2: v E 1927 (2)
Commaille, J. M. M. 12: v E 1909 (5) 1927 (2); *v E 1924 (5)*
Conyngham, D. P. 1: v E 1922
Cook, F. J. 1: v E 1895
Cooper, A. H. C. 1: v E 1913
Cox, J. L. 3: v E 1913 (3)
Cripps, G. 1: v E 1891
Crisp, R. J. 9: v A 1935 (4); *v E 1935 (5)*
Curnow, S. H. 7: v E 1930 (3); *v A 1931 (4)*

Dalton, E. L. 15: v E 1930 (1) 1938 (4); v A 1935 (1); *v E 1929 (1) 1935 (4); v A 1931 (2); v NZ 1931 (2)*
Davies, E. Q. 5: v E 1938 (3); v A 1935 (2)
Dawson, O. C. 9: v E 1948 (4); *v E 1947 (5)*
Deane, H. G. 17: v E 1927 (5) 1930 (2); *v E 1924 (5) 1929 (5)*
Dixon, C. D. 1: v E 1913
Dower, R. R. 1: v E 1898
Draper, R. G. 2: v A 1949 (2)
Duckworth, C. A. R. 2: v E 1956 (2)
Dumbrill, R. 5: v A 1966 (2); *v E 1965 (3)*
Duminy, J. P. 3: v E 1927 (2); *v E 1929 (1)*
Dunell, O. R. 2: v E 1888 (2)
Du Preez, J. H. 2: v A 1966 (2)
Du Toit, J. F. 1: v E 1891
Dyer, D. V. 3: *v E 1947 (3)*

Elgie, M. K. 3: v NZ 1961 (3)
Endean, W. R. 28: v E 1956 (5); v A 1957 (5); v NZ 1953 (5); *v E 1951 (1) 1955 (5); v A 1952 (5); v NZ 1952 (2)*

Farrer, W. S. 6: v NZ 1961 (3); *v NZ 1963 (3)*
Faulkner, G. A. 25: v E 1905 (5) 1909 (5); *v E 1907 (3) 1912 (3) 1924 (1); v A 1910 (5) 1912 (3)*
Fellows-Smith, J. P. 4: *v E 1960 (4)*
Fichardt, C. G. 2: v E 1891 (1) 1895 (1)
Finlason, C. E. 1: v E 1888
Floquet, C. E. 1: v E 1909
Francis, H. H. 2: v E 1898 (2)
Francois, C. M. 5: v E 1922 (5)
Frank, C. N. 3: v A 1921 (3)
Frank, W. H. B. 1: v E 1895
Fuller, E. R. H. 7: v A 1957 (1); *v E 1955 (2); v A 1952 (2); v NZ 1952 (2)*
Fullerton, G. M. 7: v A 1949 (2); *v E 1947 (2) 1951 (3)*
Funston, K. J. 18: v E 1956 (3); v A 1957 (5); v NZ 1953 (3); *v A 1952 (5); v NZ 1952 (2)*

Gamsy, D. 2: v A 1969 (2)

Gleeson, R. A. 1: v E 1895
Glover, G. K. 1: v E 1895
Goddard, T. L. 41: v E 1956 (5) 1964 (5); v A 1957 (5) 1966 (5) 1969 (3); *v E 1955 (5) 1960 (5); v A 1963 (5); v NZ 1963 (3)*
Gordon, N. 5: v E 1938 (5)
Graham, R. 2: v E 1898 (2)
Grieveson, R. E. 2: v E 1938 (2)
Griffin, G. M. 2: *v E 1960 (2)*

Hall, A. E. 7: v E 1922 (4) 1927 (2) 1930 (1)
Hall, G. G. 1: v E 1964
Halliwell, E. A. 8: v E 1891 (1) 1895 (3) 1898 (1); v A 1902 (3)
Halse, C. G. 3: *v A 1963 (3)*
Hands, P. A. M. 7: v E 1913 (5); v A 1921 (1); *v E 1924 (1)*
Hands, R. H. M. 1: v E 1913
Hanley, M. A. 1: v E 1948
Harris, T. A. 3: v E 1948 (1); *v E 1947 (2)*
Hartigan, G. P. D. 5: v E 1913 (3); *v E 1912 (1); v A 1912 (1)*
Harvey, R. L. 2: v A 1935 (2)
Hathorn, C. M. H. 12: v E 1905 (5); v A 1902 (3); *v E 1907 (3); v A 1910 (1)*
Hearne, F. 4: v E 1891 (1) 1895 (3)
Hearne, G. A. L. 3: v E 1922 (2); *v E 1924 (1)*
Heine, P. S. 14: v E 1956 (5); v A 1957 (4); v NZ 1961 (1); *v E 1955 (4)*
Hime, C. F. W. 1: v E 1895
Hutchinson, P. 2: v E 1888 (2)

Ironside, D. E. J. 3: v NZ 1953 (3)
Irvine, B. L. 4: v A 1969 (4)

Johnson, C. L. 1: v E 1895
Jones, P. S. T. 1: v A 1902

Keith, H. J. 8: v E 1956 (3); *v E 1955 (4); v A 1952 (1)*
Kempis, G. A. 1: v E 1888
Kotze, J. J. 3: v A 1902 (2); *v E 1907 (1)*
Kuys, F. 1: v E 1898

Lance, H. R. 13: v A 1966 (5) 1969 (3); v NZ 1961 (2); *v E 1965 (3)*
Langton, A. B. C. 15: v E 1938 (5); v A 1935 (5); *v E 1935 (5)*
Lawrence, G. B. 5: v NZ 1961 (5)
Le Roux, F. le S. 1: v E 1913
Lewis, P. T. 1: v E 1913
Lindsay, D. T. 19: v E 1964 (3); v A 1966 (5) 1969 (2); *v E 1965 (3); v A 1963 (3); v NZ 1963 (3)*
Lindsay, J. D. 3: *v E 1947 (3)*
Lindsay, N. V. 1: v A 1921
Ling, W. V. S. 6: v E 1922 (3); v A 1921 (3)
Llewellyn, C. B. 15: v E 1895 (1) 1898 (1); v A 1902 (3); *v E 1912 (3); v A 1910 (5) 1912 (2)*
Lundie, E. B. 1: v E 1913

Macaulay, M. J. 1: v E 1964
McCarthy, C. N. 15: v E 1948 (5); v A 1949 (5); *v E 1951 (5)*
McGlew, D. J. 34: v E 1956 (1); v A 1957 (5); v NZ 1953 (5) 1961 (5); *v E 1951 (2) 1955 (5) 1960 (5); v A 1952 (4); v NZ 1952 (2)*
McKinnon, A. H. 8: v E 1964 (2); v A 1966 (2); v NZ 1961 (1); *v E 1960 (1) 1965 (2)*
McLean, R. A. 40: v E 1956 (5) 1964 (2); v A 1957 (4); v NZ 1953 (4) 1961 (5); *v E 1951 (3) 1955 (5) 1960 (5); v A 1952 (5); v NZ 1952 (2)*
McMillan, Q. 13: v E 1930 (5); *v E 1929 (2); v A 1931 (4); v NZ 1931 (2)*
Mann, N. B. F. 19: v E 1948 (5); v A 1949 (5); *v E 1947 (5) 1951 (4)*

Mansell, P. N. F. 13: *v E 1951 (2) 1955 (4); v A 1952 (5); v NZ 1952 (2)*
Markham, L. A. 1: v E 1948
Marx, W. F. E. 3: v A 1921 (3)
Meintjes, D. J. 2: v E 1922 (2)
Melle, M. G. 7: v A 1949 (2); *v E 1951 (1); v A 1952 (4)*
Melville, A. 11: v E 1938 (5) 1948 (1); *v E 1947 (5)*
Middleton, J. 6: v E 1895 (2) 1898 (2); v A 1902 (2)
Mills, C. 1: v E 1891
Milton, W. H. 3: v E 1888 (2) 1891 (1)
Mitchell, B. 42: v E 1930 (5) 1938 (5) 1948 (5); v A 1935 (5); *v E 1929 (5) 1935 (5) 1947 (5); v A 1931 (5); v NZ 1931 (2)*
Mitchell, F. 3: *v E 1912 (1); v A 1912 (2)*
Morkel, D. P. B. 16: v E 1927 (5); *v E 1929 (5); v A 1931 (5); v NZ 1931 (1)*
Murray, A. R. A. 10: v NZ 1953 (4); *v A 1952 (4); v NZ 1952 (2)*

Nel, J. D. 6: v A 1949 (5) 1957 (1)
Newberry, C. 4: v E 1913 (4)
Newson, E. S. 3: v E 1930 (1) 1938 (2)
Nicholson, F. 4: v A 1935 (4)
Nicolson, J. F. W. 3: v E 1927 (3)
Norton, N. O. 1: v E 1909
Nourse, A. D. 34: v E 1938 (5) 1948 (5); v A 1935 (5) 1949 (5); *v E 1935 (4) 1947 (5) 1951 (5)*
Nourse, A. W. 45: v E 1905 (5) 1909 (5) 1913 (5) 1922 (5); v A 1902 (3) 1921 (3); *v E 1907 (3) 1912 (3) 1924 (5); v A 1910 (5) 1912 (3)*
Nupen, E. P. 17: v E 1922 (4) 1927 (5) 1930 (3); v A 1921 (2) 1935 (1); *v E 1924 (2)*

Ochse, A. E. 2: v E 1888 (2)
Ochse, A. L. 3: v E 1927 (1); *v E 1929 (2)*
O'Linn, S. 7: v NZ 1961 (2); *v E 1960 (5)*
Owen-Smith, H. G. 5: *v E 1929 (5)*

Palm, A. W. 1: v E 1927
Parker, G. M. 2: *v E 1924 (2)*
Parkin, D. C. 1: v E 1891
Partridge, J. T. 11: v E 1964 (3); *v A 1963 (5); v NZ 1963 (3)*
Pearse, O. C. 3: *v A 1910 (3)*
Pegler, S. J. 16: v E 1909 (1); *v E 1912 (3) 1924 (5); v A 1910 (4) 1912 (3)*
Pithey, A. J. 17: v E 1956 (3) 1964 (5); *v E 1960 (2); v A 1963 (4); v NZ 1963 (3)*
Pithey, D. B. 8: v A 1966 (2); *v A 1963 (3); v NZ 1963 (3)*
Plimsoll, J. B. 1: *v E 1947*
Pollock, P. M. 28: v E 1964 (5); v A 1966 (5) 1969 (4); v NZ 1961 (3); *v E 1965 (3); v A 1963 (5); v NZ 1963 (3)*
Pollock, R. G. 23: v E 1964 (5); v A 1966 (5) 1969 (4); *v E 1965 (3); v A 1963 (5); v NZ 1963 (1)*
Poore, R. M. 3: v E 1895 (3)
Pothecary, J. E. 3: *v E 1960 (3)*
Powell, A. W. 1: v E 1898
Prince, C. F. H. 1: v E 1898
Procter, M. J. 7: v A 1966 (3) 1969 (4)
Promnitz, H. L. E. 2: v E 1927 (2)

Quinn, N. A. 12: v E 1930 (1); *v E 1929 (4); v A 1931 (5); v NZ 1931 (2)*

Reid, N. 1: v A 1921
Richards, A. R. 1: v E 1895
Richards, B. A. 4: v A 1969 (4)
Richards, W. H. 1: v E 1888
Robertson, J. B. 3: v A 1935 (3)
Rose-Innes, A. 2: v E 1888 (2)
Routledge, T. W. 4: v E 1891 (1) 1895 (3)

Rowan, A. M. B. 15: v E 1948 (5); *v E 1947 (5) 1951 (5)*
Rowan, E. A. B. 26: v E 1938 (4) 1948 (4); v A 1935 (3); 1949 (5); *v E 1935 (5) 1951 (5)*
Rowe, G. A. 5: v E 1895 (2) 1898 (2); v A 1902 (1)

Samuelson, S. V. 1: v E 1909
Schwarz, R. O. 20: v E 1905 (5) 1909 (4); *v E 1907 (3) 1912 (1); v A 1910 (5) 1912 (2)*
Seccull, A. W. 1: v E 1895
Seymour, M. A. 7: v E 1964 (2); v A 1969 (1); *v A 1963 (4)*
Shalders, W. A. 12: v E 1898 (1) 1905 (5); v A 1902 (3); *v E 1907 (3)*
Shepstone, G. H. 2: v E 1895 (1) 1898 (1)
Sherwell, P. W. 13: v E 1905 (5); *v E 1907 (3); v A 1910 (5)*
Siedle, I. J. 18: v E 1927 (1) 1930 (5); v A 1935 (5); *v E 1929 (3) 1935 (4)*
Sinclair, J. H. 25: v E 1895 (3) 1898 (2) 1905 (5) 1909 (4); v A 1902 (3); *v E 1907 (3); v A 1910 (5)*
Smith, C. J. E. 3: v A 1902 (3)
Smith, F. W. 3: v E 1888 (2) 1895 (1)
Smith, V. I. 9: v A 1949 (3) 1957 (1); *v E 1947 (4) 1955 (1)*
Snooke, S. D. 1: *v E 1907*
Snooke, S. J. 26: v E 1905 (5) 1909 (5) 1922 (3); *v E 1907 (3) 1912 (3); v A 1910 (5) 1912 (2)*
Solomon, W. R. 1: v E 1898
Stewart, R. B. 1: v E 1888
Stricker, L. A. 13: v E 1909 (4); *v E 1912 (2); v A 1910 (5) 1912 (2)*
Susskind, M. J. 5: *v E 1924 (5)*

Taberer, H. M. 1: v A 1902
Tancred, A. B. 2: v E 1888 (2)
Tancred, L. J. 14: v E 1905 (5) 1913 (1); v A 1902 (3); *v E 1907 (1) 1912 (2); v A 1912 (2)*
Tancred, V. M. 1: v E 1898
Tapscott, G. L. 1: v E 1913
Tapscott, L. E. 2: v E 1922 (2)
Tayfield, H. J. 37: v E 1956 (5); v A 1949 (5) 1957 (5); v NZ 1953 (5); *v E 1955 (5) 1960 (5); v A 1952 (5); v NZ 1952 (2)*
Taylor, A. I. 1: v E 1956
Taylor, D. 2: v E 1913 (2)
Taylor, H. W. 42: v E 1913 (5) 1922 (5) 1927 (5) 1930 (4); v A 1921 (3); *v E 1912 (3) 1924 (5) 1929 (3); v A 1912 (3) 1931 (5); v NZ 1931 (1)*
Theunissen, N. H. G. de J. 1: v E 1888
Thornton, P. G. 1: v A 1902
Tomlinson, D. S. 1: *v E 1935*
Traicos, A. J. 3: v A 1969 (3)
Trimborn, P. H. J. 4: v A 1966 (3) 1969 (1)
Tuckett, L. 9: v E 1948 (4); *v E 1947 (5)*
Tuckett, L. R. 1: v E 1913

Van der Bijl, P. G. V. 5: v E 1938 (5)
Van der Merwe, E. A. 2: v A 1935 (1); *v E 1929 (1)*
Van der Merwe, P. L. 15: v E 1964 (2); v A 1966 (5); *v E 1965 (3); v A 1963 (3); v NZ 1963 (2)*
Van Ryneveld, C. B. 19: v E 1956 (5); v A 1957 (4); v NZ 1953 (5); *v E 1951 (5)*
Varnals, G. D. 3: v E 1964 (3)
Viljoen, K. G. 27: v E 1930 (3) 1938 (4) 1948 (2); v A 1935 (4); *v E 1935 (4) 1947 (5); v A 1931 (4); v NZ 1931 (1)*
Vincent, C. L. 25: v E 1927 (5) 1930 (5); *v E 1929 (4) 1935 (4); v A 1931 (5); v NZ 1931 (2)*
Vintcent, C. H. 3: v E 1888 (2) 1891 (1)
Vogler, A. E. E. 15: v E 1905 (5) 1909 (5); *v E 1907 (3); v A 1910 (2)*

Wade, H. F. 10: v A 1935 (5); *v E 1935 (5)*
Wade, W. W. 11: v E 1938 (3) 1948 (5); v A 1949 (3)
Waite, J. H. B. 50: v E 1956 (5); 1964 (2); v A 1957 (5); v NZ 1953 (5) 1961 (5); *v E 1951 (4) 1955 (5) 1960 (5); v A 1952 (5) 1963 (4); v NZ 1952 (2) 1963 (3)*

Walter, K. A. 2: v NZ 1961 (2)
Ward, T. A. 23: v E 1913 (5) 1922 (5); v A 1921 (3); *v E 1912 (2) 1924 (5); v A 1912 (3)*
Watkins, J. C. 15: v E 1956 (2); v A 1949 (3); v NZ 1953 (3); *v A 1952 (5); v NZ 1952 (2)*
Wesley, C. 3: *v E 1960 (3)*
Westcott, R. J. 5: v A 1957 (2); v NZ 1953 (3)
White, G. C. 17: v E 1905 (5) 1909 (4); *v E 1907 (3) 1912 (2); v A 1912 (3)*
Willoughby, J. T. I. 2: v E 1895 (2)
Wimble, C. S. 1: v E 1891
Winslow, P. L. 5: v A 1949 (2); *v E 1955 (3)*
Wynne, O. E. 6: v E 1948 (3); v A 1949 (3)

Zulch, J. W. 16: v E 1909 (5) 1913 (3); v A 1921 (3); *v A 1910 (5)*

WEST INDIES

Number of Test cricketers: 176

Achong, E. 6: v E 1929 (1) 1934 (2); *v E 1933 (3)*
Alexander, F. C. M. 25: v E 1959 (5); v P 1957 (5); *v E 1957 (2); v A 1960 (5); v In 1958 (5); v P 1958 (3)*
Ali, Imtiaz 1: v In 1975
Ali, Inshan 12: v E 1973 (2); v A 1972 (3); v In 1970 (1); v P 1976 (1); v NZ 1971 (3); *v E 1973 (1); v A 1975 (1)*
Allan, D. W. 5: v A 1964 (1); v In 1961 (2); *v E 1966 (2)*
Asgarali, N. 2: *v E 1957 (2)*
Atkinson, D. St E. 22: v E 1953 (4); v A 1954 (4); v P 1957 (1); *v E 1957 (2); v A 1951 (2); v NZ 1951 (1) 1955 (4); v In 1948 (4)*
Atkinson, E. St E. 8: v P 1957 (3); *v In 1958 (3); v P 1958 (2)*
Austin, R. A. 2: v A 1977 (2)

Bacchus, S. F. A. 19: v A 1977 (2); *v E 1980 (5); v A 1981 (2); v In 1978 (6); v P 1980 (4)*
Baichan, L. 3: *v A 1975 (1); v P 1974 (2)*
Barrow, I. 11: v E 1929 (1) 1934 (1); *v E 1933 (3) 1939 (1); v A 1930 (5)*
Barrett, A. G. 6: v E 1973 (2); v In 1970 (2); *v In 1974 (2)*
Bartlett, E. L. 5: *v E 1928 (1); v A 1930 (4)*
Betancourt, N. 1: v E 1929
Binns, A. P. 5: v A 1954 (1); v In 1952 (1); *v NZ 1955 (3)*
Birkett, L. S. 4 *v A 1930 (4)*
Boyce, K. D. 21: v E 1973 (4); v A 1972 (4); v In 1970 (1); *v E 1973 (3); v A 1975 (4); v In 1974 (3); v P 1974 (2)*
Browne, C. R. 4: v E 1929 (2); *v E 1928 (2)*
Butcher, B. F. 44: v E 1959 (2) 1967 (5); v A 1964 (5); *v E 1963 (5) 1966 (5) 1969 (3); v A 1968 (5); v NZ 1968 (3); v In 1958 (5) 1966 (3); v P 1958 (3)*
Butler, L. 1: v A 1954
Bynoe, M. R. 4: *v In 1966 (3); v P 1958 (1)*

Camacho, G. S. 11: v E 1967 (5); v In 1970 (2); *v E 1969 (2); v A 1968 (2)*
Cameron, F. J. 5: *v In 1948 (5)*
Cameron, J. H. 2: *v E 1939 (2)*
Carew, G. M. 4: v E 1934 (1) 1947 (2); *v In 1948 (1)*
Carew, M. C. 19: v E 1967 (1); v NZ 1971 (3); v In 1970 (3); *v E 1963 (2) 1966 (1) 1969 (1); v A 1968 (5); v NZ 1968 (3)*
Challenor, G. 3: *v E 1928 (3)*
Chang, H. S. 1: *v In 1978*
Christiani, C. M. 4: v E 1934 (4)
Christiani, R. J. 22: v E 1947 (4) 1953 (1); v In 1952 (2); *v E 1950 (4); v A 1951 (5); v NZ 1951 (1); v In 1948 (5)*
Clarke, C. B. 3: *v E 1939 (3)*
Clarke, S. T. 11: v A 1977 (1); *v A 1981 (1); v In 1978 (5); v P 1980 (4)*

Constantine, L. N. 18: v E 1929 (3) 1934 (3); *v E 1928 (3) 1933 (1) 1939 (3); v A 1930 (5)*
Croft, C. E. H. 27: v E 1980 (4); v A 1977 (2); v P 1976 (5); *v E 1980 (3); v A 1979 (3) 1981 (3); v NZ 1979 (3); v P 1980 (4)*

Da Costa, O. C. 5: v E 1929 (1) 1934 (1); *v E 1933 (3)*
Daniel, W. W. 5: v In 1975 (1); *v E 1976 (4)*
Davis, B. A. 4: v A 1964 (4)
Davis, C. A. 15: v A 1972 (2); v NZ 1971 (5); v In 1970 (4); *v E 1969 (3); v A 1968 (1)*
De Caires, F. I. 3: v E 1929 (3)
Depeiza, C. C. 5: v A 1954 (3); *v NZ 1955 (2)*
Dewdney, T. 9: v A 1954 (2); v P 1957 (3); *v E 1957 (1); v NZ 1955 (3)*
Dowe, U. G. 4: v A 1972 (1); v NZ 1971 (1); v In 1970 (2)
Dujon, P. J. 3: *v A 1981 (3)*

Edwards, R. M. 5: *v A 1968 (2); v NZ 1968 (3)*

Ferguson, W. 8: v E 1947 (4) 1953 (1); *v In 1948 (3)*
Fernandes, M. P. 2: v E 1929 (1); *v E 1928 (1)*
Findlay, T. M. 10: v A 1972 (1); v NZ 1971 (5); v In 1970 (2); *v E 1969 (2)*
Foster, M. L. C. 14: v E 1973 (1); v A 1972 (4) 1977 (1); v NZ 1971 (3); v In 1970 (2); v P 1976 (1); *v E 1969 (1) 1973 (1)*
Francis, G. N. 10: v E 1929 (1); *v E 1928 (3) 1933 (1); v A 1930 (5)*
Frederick, M. C. 1: v E 1953
Fredericks, R. C. 59: v E 1973 (5); v A 1972 (5); v NZ 1971 (5); v In 1970 (4) 1975 (4); v P 1976 (5); *v E 1969 (3) 1973 (3) 1976 (5); v A 1968 (4) 1975 (6); v NZ 1968 (3); v In 1974 (5); v P 1974 (2)*
Fuller, R. L. 1: v E 1934
Furlonge, H. A. 3: v A 1954 (1); *v NZ 1955 (2)*

Ganteaume, A. G. 1: v E 1947
Garner, J. 28: v E 1980 (4); v A 1977 (2); v P 1976 (5); *v E 1980 (5); v A 1979 (3) 1981 (3); v NZ 1979 (3); v P 1980 (3)*
Gaskin, B. B. M. 2: v E 1947 (2)
Gibbs, G. L. R. 1: v A 1954
Gibbs, L. R. 79: v E 1967 (5) 1973 (5); v A 1964 (5) 1972 (5); v NZ 1971 (2); v In 1961 (5) 1970 (1); v P 1957 (4); *v E 1963 (5) 1966 (5) 1969 (3) 1973 (3); v A 1960 (3) 1968 (5) 1975 (6); v NZ 1968 (3); v In 1958 (1) 1966 (3) 1974 (5); v P 1958 (3) 1974 (2)*
Gilchrist, R. 13: v P 1957 (5); *v E 1957 (4); v In 1958 (4)*
Gladstone, G. 1: v E 1929
Goddard, J. D. C. 27: v E 1947 (4); *v E 1950 (4) 1957 (5); v A 1951 (4); v NZ 1951 (2) 1955 (3); v In 1948 (5)*
Gomes, H. A. 22: v E 1980 (4); v A 1977 (3); *v E 1976 (2); v A 1981 (3); v In 1978 (6); v P 1980 (4)*
Gomez, G. E. 29: v E 1947 (4) 1953 (4); v In 1952 (4); *v E 1939 (2) 1950 (4); v A 1951 (5); v NZ 1951 (1); v In 1948 (5)*
Grant, G. C. 12: v E 1934 (4); *v E 1933 (3); v A 1930 (5)*
Grant, R. S. 7: v E 1934 (4); *v E 1939 (3)*
Greenidge, A. E. 6: v A 1977 (2); *v In 1978 (4)*
Greenidge, C. G. 36: v E 1980 (4); v A 1977 (2); v P 1976 (5); *v E 1976 (5) 1980 (5); v A 1975 (2) 1979 (3) 1981 (2); v NZ 1979 (3); v In 1974 (5)*
Greenidge, G. A. 5: v A 1972 (3); v NZ 1971 (2)
Grell, M. G. 1: v E 1929
Griffith, C. C. 28: v E 1959 (1) 1967 (4); v A 1964 (5); *v E 1963 (5) 1966 (5); v A 1968 (3); v NZ 1968 (2); v In 1966 (3)*
Griffith, H. C. 13: v E 1929 (3); *v E 1928 (3) 1933 (2); v A 1930 (5)*
Guillen, S. C. 5: *v A 1951 (3); v NZ 1951 (2)*

Hall, W. W. 48: v E 1959 (5) 1967 (4); v A 1964 (5); v In 1961 (5); *v E 1963 (5) 1966 (5); v A 1960 (5) 1968 (2); v NZ 1968 (1); v In 1958 (5) 1966 (3); v P 1958 (3)*
Haynes, D. L. 24: v E 1980 (4); v A 1977 (2); *v E 1980 (5); v A 1979 (3) 1981 (3); v NZ 1979 (3); v P 1980 (4)*

Headley, G. A. 22: v E 1929 (4) 1934 (4) 1947 (1) 1953 (1); *v E 1933 (3) 1939 (3); v A 1930 (5); v In 1948 (1)*
Headley, R. G. A. 2: *v E 1973 (2)*
Hendriks, J. L. 20: v A 1964 (4); v In 1961 (1); *v E 1966 (3) 1969 (1); v A 1968 (5); v NZ 1968 (3); v In 1966 (3)*
Hoad, E. L. G. 4: v E 1929 (1); *v E 1928 (1) 1933 (2)*
Holder, V. A. 40: v E 1973 (1); v A 1972 (3) 1977 (3); v NZ 1971 (4); v In 1970 (3) 1975 (1); v P 1976 (1); *v E 1969 (3) 1973 (2) 1976 (4); v A 1975 (3); v In 1974 (4) 1978 (6); v P 1974 (2)*
Holding, M. A. 31: v E 1980 (4); v In 1975 (4); *v E 1976 (4) 1980 (5); v A 1975 (5) 1979 (3) 1981 (3); v NZ 1979 (3)*
Holford, D. A. J. 24: v E 1967 (4); v NZ 1971 (5); v In 1970 (1) 1975 (2); v P 1976 (1); *v E 1966 (5); v A 1968 (2); v NZ 1968 (3); v In 1966 (1)*
Holt, J. K. 17: v E 1953 (5); v A 1954 (5); *v In 1958 (5); v P 1958 (2)*
Howard, A. B. 1: v NZ 1971
Hunte, C. C. 44: v E 1959 (5); v A 1964 (5); v In 1961 (5); v P 1957 (5); *v E 1963 (5) 1966 (5); v A 1960 (5); v In 1958 (5) 1966 (3); v P 1958 (1)*
Hunte, E. A. C. 3: v E 1929 (3)
Hylton, L. G. 6: v E 1934 (4); *v E 1939 (2)*

Johnson, H. H. H. 3: v E 1947 (1); *v E 1950 (2)*
Johnson, T. F. 1: *v E 1939*
Jones, C. M. 4: v E 1929 (1) 1934 (3)
Jones, P. E. 9: v E 1947 (1); *v E 1950 (2); v A 1951 (1); v In 1948 (5)*
Julien, B. D. 24: v E 1973 (5); v In 1975 (4); v P 1976 (1); *v E 1973 (3) 1976 (2); v A 1975 (3); v In 1974 (4); v P 1974 (2)*
Jumadeen, R. R. 12: v A 1972 (1) 1977 (2); v NZ 1971 (1); v In 1975 (4); v P 1976 (1); *v E 1976 (1); v In 1978 (2)*

Kallicharran, A. I. 66: v E 1973 (5); v A 1972 (5) 1977 (5); v NZ 1971 (2); v In 1975 (4); v P 1976 (5); *v E 1973 (3) 1976 (3) 1980 (5); v A 1975 (6) 1979 (3); v NZ 1979 (3); v In 1974 (5) 1978 (6); v P 1974 (2) 1980 (4)*
Kanhai, R. B. 79: v E 1959 (5) 1967 (5) 1973 (5); v A 1964 (5) 1972 (5); v In 1961 (5) 1970 (5); v P 1957 (5); *v E 1957 (5) 1963 (5) 1966 (5) 1973 (3); v A 1960 (5) 1968 (5); v In 1958 (5) 1966 (3); v P 1958 (3)*
Kentish, E. S. M. 2: v E 1947 (1) 1953 (1)
King, C. L. 9: v P 1976 (1); *v E 1976 (3) 1980 (1); v A 1979 (1); v NZ 1979 (3)*
King, F. M. 14: v E 1953 (3); v A 1954 (4); v In 1952 (5); *v NZ 1955 (2)*
King, L. A. 2: v E 1967 (1); v In 1961 (1)

Lashley, P. D. 4: *v E 1966 (2); v A 1960 (2)*
Legall, R. 4: v In 1952 (4)
Lewis, D. M. 3: v In 1970 (3)
Lloyd, C. H. 85: v E 1967 (5) 1973 (5) 1980 (4); v A 1972 (3) 1977 (2); v NZ 1971 (2); v In 1970 (5) 1975 (4); v P 1976 (5); *v E 1969 (3) 1973 (3) 1976 (5) 1980 (4); v A 1968 (4) 1975 (6) 1979 (2) 1981 (3); v NZ 1968 (3) 1979 (3); v In 1966 (3) 1974 (5); v P 1974 (2) 1980 (4)*

McMorris, E. D. A. 13: v E 1959 (4); v In 1961 (4); v P 1957 (1); *v E 1963 (2) 1966 (2)*
McWatt, C. A. 6: v E 1953 (5); v A 1954 (1)
Madray, I. S. 2: v P 1957 (2)
Marshall, M. D. 12: v E 1980 (1); *v E 1980 (4); v In 1978 (3); v P 1980 (4)*
Marshall, N. E. 1: v A 1954
Marshall, R. E. 4: *v A 1951 (2); v NZ 1951 (2)*
Martin, F. R. 9: v E 1929 (1); *v E 1928 (3); v A 1930 (5)*
Martindale, E. A. 10: v E 1934 (4); *v E 1933 (3) 1939 (3)*
Mattis, E. H. 4: v E 1980 (4)
Mendonca, I. L. 2: v In 1961 (2)
Merry, C. A. 2: *v E 1933 (2)*
Miller, R. 1: v In 1952
Moodie, G. H. 1: v E 1934

Murray, D. A. 19: v E 1980 (4); v A 1977 (3); *v A 1981 (2); v In 1978 (6); v P 1980 (4)*
Murray, D. L. 62: v E 1967 (5) 1973 (5); v A 1972 (4) 1977 (2); v In 1975 (4); v P 1976 (5); *v E 1963 (5) 1973 (3) 1976 (5) 1980 (5); v A 1975 (6) 1979 (3); v NZ 1979 (3); v In 1974 (5); v P 1974 (2)*

Nanan, R. 1: *v P 1980*
Neblett, J. M. 1: v E 1934
Noreiga, J. M. 4: v In 1970 (4)
Nunes, R. K. 4: v E 1929 (1); *v E 1928 (3)*
Nurse, S. M. 29: v E 1959 (1) 1967 (5); v A 1964 (4); v In 1961 (1); *v E 1966 (5); v A 1960 (3) 1968 (5); v NZ 1968 (3); v In 1966 (2)*

Padmore, A. L. 2: v In 1975 (1); *v E 1976 (1)*
Pairaudeau, B. H. 13: v E 1953 (2); v In 1952 (5): *v E 1957 (2); v NZ 1955 (4)*
Parry, D. R. 12: v A 1977 (5); *v NZ 1979 (1); v In 1978 (6)*
Passailaigue, C. C. 1: v E 1929
Phillip, N. 9: v A 1977 (3); *v In 1978 (6)*
Pierre, L. R. 1: v E 1947

Rae, A. F. 15: v In 1952 (2); *v E 1950 (4); v A 1951 (3); v NZ 1951 (1); v In 1948 (5)*
Ramadhin, S. 43: v E 1953 (5) 1959 (4); v A 1954 (4); v In 1952 (4); *v E 1950 (4) 1957 (5); v A 1951 (5) 1960 (2); v NZ 1951 (2) 1955 (4); v In 1958 (2); v P 1958 (2)*
Richards, I. V. A. 47: v E 1980 (4); v A 1977 (2); v In 1975 (4); v P 1976 (5); *v E 1976 (4) 1980 (5); v A 1975 (6) 1979 (3) 1981 (3); v In 1974 (5); v P 1974 (2) 1980 (4)*
Rickards, K. R. 2: v E 1947 (1); *v A 1951 (1)*
Roach, C. A. 16: v E 1929 (4) 1934 (1); *v E 1928 (3) 1933 (3); v A 1930 (5)*
Roberts, A. M. E. 40: v E 1973 (1) 1980 (3); v A 1977 (2); v In 1975 (2); v P 1976 (5); *v E 1976 (5) 1980 (3); v A 1975 (5) 1979 (3) 1981 (2); v NZ 1979 (2); v In 1974 (5); v P 1974 (2)*
Roberts, A. T. 1: *v NZ 1955*
Rodriguez, W. V. 5: v E 1967 (1); v A 1964 (1); v In 1961 (2); *v E 1963 (1)*
Rowe, L. G. 30: v E 1973 (5); v A 1972 (3); v NZ 1971 (4); v In 1975 (4); *v E 1976 (2); v A 1975 (6) 1979 (3); v NZ 1979 (3)*

St Hill, E. L. 2: v E 1929 (2)
St Hill, W. H. 3: v E 1929 (1); *v E 1928 (2)*
Scarlett, R. G. 3: v E 1959 (3)
Scott, A. P. H. 1: v In 1952
Scott, O. C. 8: v E 1929 (1); *v E 1928 (2); v A 1930 (5)*
Sealey, B. J. 1: *v E 1933*
Sealy, J. E. D. 11: v E 1929 (2) 1934 (4); *v E 1939 (3); v A 1930 (2)*
Shepherd, J. N. 5: v In 1970 (2); *v E 1969 (3)*
Shillingford, G. C. 7: v NZ 1971 (2); v In 1970 (3); *v E 1969 (2)*
Shillingford, I. T. 4: v A 1977 (1); v P 1976 (3)
Shivnarine, S. 8: v A 1977 (3); *v In 1978 (5)*
Singh, C. K. 2: v E 1959 (2)
Small, J. A. 3: v E 1929 (1); *v E 1928 (2)*
Smith, C. W. 5: v In 1961 (1); *v A 1960 (4)*
Smith, O. G. 26: v A 1954 (4); v P 1957 (5); *v E 1957 (5); v NZ 1955 (4); v In 1958 (5); v P 1958 (3)*
Sobers, G. S. 93: v E 1953 (1) 1959 (5) 1967 (5) 1973 (4); v A 1954 (4) 1964 (5); v NZ 1971 (5); v In 1961 (5); 1970 (5); v P 1957 (5); *v E 1957 (5) 1963 (5) 1966 (5) 1969 (3) 1973 (3); v A 1960 (5) 1968 (5); v NZ 1955 (4) 1968 (3); v In 1958 (5) 1966 (3); v P 1958 (3)*
Solomon, J. S. 27: v E 1959 (2); v A 1964 (4); v In 1961 (4); *v E 1963 (5); v A 1960 (5); v In 1958 (4); v P 1958 (3)*
Stayers, S. C. 4: v In 1961 (4)
Stollmeyer, J. B. 32: v E 1947 (2) 1953 (5); v A 1954 (2); v In 1952 (5); *v E 1939 (3) 1950 (4); v A 1951 (5); v NZ 1951 (2); v In 1948 (4)*
Stollmeyer, V. H. 1: *v E 1939*

Taylor, J. 3: v P 1957 (1); *v In 1958 (1); v P 1958 (1)*

Trim, J. 4: v E 1947 (1); *v A 1951 (1); v In 1948 (2)*

Valentine, A. L. 36: v E 1953 (3); v A 1954 (3); v In 1952 (5) 1961 (2); v P 1957 (1); *v E 1950 (4) 1957 (2); v A 1951 (5) 1960 (5); v NZ 1951 (2) 1955 (4)*
Valentine, V. A. 2: *v E 1933 (2)*

Walcott, C. L. 44: v E 1947 (4) 1953 (5) 1959 (2); v A 1954 (5); v In 1952 (5); v P 1957 (4); *v E 1950 (4) 1957 (5); v A 1951 (3); v NZ 1951 (2); v In 1948 (5)*
Walcott, L. A. 1: v E 1929
Watson, C. 7: v E 1959 (5); v In 1961 (1); *v A 1960 (1)*
Weekes, E. D. 48: v E 1947 (4) 1953 (4); v A 1954 (5) v In 1952 (5); v P 1957 (5); *v E 1950 (4) 1957 (5); v A 1951 (5); v NZ 1951 (2) 1955 (4); v In 1948 (5)*
Weekes, K. H. 2: *v E 1939 (2)*
White, W. A. 2: v A 1964 (2)
Wight, C. V. 2: v E 1929 (1); *v E 1928 (1)*
Wight, G. L. 1: v In 1952
Wiles, C. A. 1: *v E 1933*
Willett, E. T. 5: v A 1972 (3); *v In 1974 (2)*
Williams, A. B. 7: v A 1977 (3); *v In 1978 (4)*
Williams, E. A. V. 4: v E 1947 (3); *v E 1939 (1)*
Wishart, K. L. 1: v E 1934
Worrell, F. M. M. 51: v E 1947 (3) 1953 (4) 1959 (4); v A 1954 (4); v In 1952 (5) 1961 (5); *v E 1950 (4) 1957 (5) 1963 (5); v A 1951 (5) 1960 (5); v NZ 1951 (2)*

NEW ZEALAND

Number of Test cricketers: 150

Alabaster, J. C. 21: v E 1962 (2); v WI 1955 (1); v In 1967 (4); *v E 1958 (2); v SA 1961 (5); v WI 1971 (2); v In 1955 (4); v P 1955 (1)*
Allcott, C. F. W. 6: v E 1929 (2); v SA 1931 (1); *v E 1931 (3)*
Anderson, R. W. 9: v E 1977 (3); *v E 1978 (3); v P 1976 (3)*
Anderson, W. M. 1: v A 1945
Andrews, B. 2: *v A 1973 (2)*

Badcock, F. T. 7: v E 1929 (3) 1932 (2); v SA 1931 (2)
Barber, R. T. 1: v WI 1955
Bartlett, G. A. 10: v E 1965 (2); v In 1967 (2); v P 1964 (1); *v SA 1961 (5)*
Barton, P. T. 7: v E 1962 (3); *v SA 1961 (4)*
Beard, D. D. 4: v WI 1951 (2) 1955 (2)
Beck, J. E. F. 8: v WI 1955 (4); *v SA 1953 (4)*
Bell, W. 2: *v SA 1953 (2)*
Bilby, G. P. 2: v E 1965 (2)
Blair, R. W. 19: v E 1954 (1) 1958 (2) 1962 (2); v SA 1952 (2) 1963 (3); v WI 1955 (2) *v E 1958 (3); v SA 1953 (4)*
Blunt, R. C. 9: v E 1929 (4); v SA 1931 (2); *v E 1931 (3)*
Bolton, B. A. 2: v E 1958 (2)
Boock, S. L. 12: v E 1977 (3); v WI 1979 (3); v P 1978 (3); *v E 1978 (3)*
Bracewell, B. P. 5: v P 1978 (1); *v E 1978 (3); v A 1980 (1)*
Bracewell, J. G. 4: v In 1980 (1); *v A 1980 (3)*
Bradburn, W. P. 2: v SA 1963 (2)
Burgess, M. G. 50: v E 1970 (1) 1977 (3); v A 1973 (1) 1976 (2); v WI 1968 (2); v In 1967 (4) 1975 (3); v P 1972 (3) 1978 (3); *v E 1969 (2) 1973 (3) 1978 (3); v A 1980 (3); v WI 1971 (5); v In 1969 (3) 1976 (3); v P 1969 (3) 1976 (3)*
Burke, C. 1: v A 1945
Burtt, T. B. 10: v E 1946 (1) 1950 (2); v SA 1952 (1); v WI 1951 (2); *v E 1949 (4)*
Butterfield, L. A. 1: v A 1945

Cairns, B. L. 26: v E 1974 (1) 1977 (1); v A 1976 (1) 1981 (3); v WI 1979 (3); v In 1975 (1) 1980 (3); v P 1978 (3); *v E 1978 (2); v A 1973 (1) 1980 (3); v In 1976 (2); v P 1976 (2)*

Cameron, F. J. 19: v E 1962 (3); v SA 1963 (3); v P 1964 (3); *v E 1965 (2); v SA 1961 (5); v In 1964 (1); v P 1964 (2)*
Cave, H. B. 19: v E 1954 (2); v WI 1955 (3); *v E 1949 (4) 1958 (2); v In 1955 (5); v P 1955 (3)*
Chapple, M. E. 14: v E 1954 (1) 1965 (1); v SA 1952 (1) 1963 (3); v WI 1955 (1); *v SA 1953 (5) 1961 (2)*
Chatfield, E. J. 5: v E 1974 (1) 1977 (1); v A 1976 (2) 1981 (1)
Cleverley, D. C. 2: v SA 1931 (1); v A 1945 (1)
Collinge, R. O. 35: v E 1970 (2) 1974 (2) 1977 (3); v A 1973 (3); v In 1967 (2) 1975 (3); v P 1964 (3) 1972 (2);*v E 1965 (3) 1969 (1) 1973 (3) 1978 (1); v In 1964 (2) 1976 (1); v P 1964 (2) 1976 (2)*
Colquhoun, I. A. 2: v E 1954 (2)
Coney, J. V. 18: v A 1973 (2) 1981 (3); v WI 1979 (3); v In 1980 (3); v P 1978 (3); *v A 1973 (2); 1980 (2)*
Congdon, B. E. 61: v E 1965 (3) 1970 (2) 1974 (2) 1977 (3); v A 1973 (3) 1976 (2); v WI 1968 (3); v In 1967 (4) 1975 (3); v P 1964 (3) 1972 (3); *v E 1965 (3) 1969 (3) 1973 (3) 1978 (3); v A 1973 (3); v WI 1971 (5); v In 1964 (3) 1969 (3); v P 1964 (1) 1969 (3)*
Cowie, J. 9: v E 1946 (1); v A 1945 (1); *v E 1937 (3) 1949 (4)*
Cresswell G. F. 3: v E 1950 (2); *v E 1949 (1)*
Cromb, I. B. 5: v SA 1931 (2); *v E 1931 (3)*
Crowe, M. D. 3: v A 1981 (3)
Cunis R. S. 20: v E 1965 (3) 1970 (2); v SA 1963 (1); v WI 1968 (3); *v E 1969 (1); v WI 1971 (5); v In 1969 (3); v P 1969 (2)*

D'Arcy, J. W. 5: *v E 1958 (5)*
Dempster, C. S. 10: v E 1929 (4) 1932 (2); v SA 1931 (2); *v E 1931 (2)*
Dempster, E. W. 5: v SA 1952 (1); *v SA 1953 (4)*
Dick, A. E. 17: v E 1962 (3); v SA 1963 (2); v P 1964 (2); *v E 1965 (2); v SA 1961 (5); v P 1964 (3)*
Dickinson, G. R. 3: v E 1929 (2); v SA 1931 (1)
Donnelly, M. P. 7: *v E 1937 (3) 1949 (4)*
Dowling, G. T. 39: v E 1962 (3) 1970 (2); v In 1967 (4); v SA 1963 (1); v WI 1968 (3); v P 1964 (2); *v E 1965 (3) 1969 (3); v SA 1961 (4); v WI 1971 (2); v In 1964 (4) 1969 (3); v P 1964 (2) 1969 (3)*
Dunning, J. A. 4: v E 1932 (1); *v E 1937 (3)*

Edgar, B. A. 18: v A 1981 (3); v WI 1979 (3); v In 1980 (3); v P 1978 (3); *v E 1978 (3); v A 1980 (3)*
Edwards, G. N. 8: v E 1977 (1); v A 1976 (2); v In 1980 (3); *v E 1978 (2)*
Emery, R. W. G. 2: v WI 1951 (2)

Fisher, F. E. 1: v SA 1952
Foley, H. 1: v E 1929
Freeman, D. L. 2: v E 1932 (2)

Gallichan, N. 1: *v E 1937*
Gedye, S. G. 4: v SA 1963 (3); v P 1964 (1)
Guillen, S. C. 3: v WI 1955 (3)
Guy, J. W. 12: v E 1958 (2); v WI 1955 (2); *v SA 1961 (2); v In 1955 (5); v P 1955 (1)*

Hadlee, D. R. 26: v E 1974 (2) 1977 (1); v A 1973 (3) 1976 (1); v In 1975 (3); v P 1972 (2); *v E 1969 (2) 1973 (3); v A 1973 (3); v In 1969 (3); v P 1969 (3)*
Hadlee, R. J. 38: v E 1977 (3); v A 1973 (2) 1976 (2) 1981 (3); v WI 1979 (3); v In 1975 (2) 1980 (3); v P 1972 (1) 1978 (3); *v E 1973 (1) 1978 (3); v A 1973 (3) 1980 (3); v In 1976 (3); v P 1976 (3)*
Hadlee, W. A. 11: v E 1946 (1) 1950 (2); v A 1945 (1); *v E 1937 (3) 1949 (4)*
Harford, N. S. 8: *v E 1958 (4); v In 1955 (2); v P 1955 (2)*
Harford, R. I. 3: v In 1967 (3)
Harris, P. G. Z. 9: v P 1964 (1); *v SA 1961 (5); v In 1955 (1); v P 1955 (2)*
Harris, R. M. 2: v E 1958 (2)
Hastings, B. F. 31: v E 1974 (2); v A 1973 (3); v WI 1968 (3); v In 1975 (1); v P 1972 (3); *v E 1969 (3) 1973 (3); v A 1973 (3); v WI 1971 (5); v In 1969 (2); v P 1969 (3)*

Hayes, J. A. 15: v E 1950 (2) 1954 (1); v WI 1951 (2); *v E 1958 (4); v In 1955 (5); v P 1955 (1)*
Henderson, M. 1: v E 1929
Hough, K. W. 2: v E 1958 (2)
Howarth, G. P. 28: v E 1974 (2) 1977 (3); v A 1976 (2) 1981 (3); v WI 1979 (3); v In 1980 (3); v P 1978 (3); *v E 1978 (3); v A 1980 (2); v In 1976 (2); v P 1976 (2)*
Howarth, H. J. 30: v E 1970 (2) 1974 (2); v A 1973 (3) 1976 (2); v In 1975 (2); v P 1972 (3); *v E 1969 (3) 1973 (2); v WI 1971 (5); v In 1969 (3); v P 1969 (3)*

James, K. C. 11: v E 1929 (4) 1932 (2); v SA 1931 (2); *v E 1931 (3)*
Jarvis, T. W. 13: v E 1965 (1); v P 1972 (3); *v WI 1971 (4); v In 1964 (2); v P 1964 (3)*

Kerr, J. L. 7: v E 1932 (2); v SA 1931 (1); *v E 1931 (2) 1937 (2)*

Lees, W. K. 17: v E 1977 (2); v A 1976 (1); v WI 1979 (3); v P 1978 (3); *v A 1980 (2); v In 1976 (3); v P 1976 (3)*
Leggat, I. B. 1: *v SA 1953*
Leggat, J. G. 9: v E 1954 (1); v SA 1952 (1); v WI 1951 (1) 1955 (1); *v In 1955 (3); v P 1955 (2)*
Lissette, A. F. 2: v WI 1955 (2)
Lowry, T. C. 7: v E 1929 (4); *v E 1931 (3)*

MacGibbon, A. R. 26: v E 1950 (2) 1954 (2); v SA 1952 (1); v WI 1955 (3); *v E 1958 (5); v SA 1953 (5); v In 1955 (5); v P 1955 (3)*
McEwan, P. E. 3: v WI 1979 (1); *v A 1980 (2)*
McGirr, H. M. 2: v E 1929 (2)
McGregor, S. N. 25: v E 1954 (2) 1958 (2); v SA 1963 (3); v WI 1955 (4); v P 1964 (2); *v SA 1961 (5); v In 1955 (4); v P 1955 (3)*
McLeod E. G. 1: v E 1929
McMahon T. G. 5: v WI 1955 (1); *v In 1955 (3); v P 1955 (1)*
McRae, D. A. N. 1: v A 1945
Matheson, A. M. 2: v E 1929 (1); *v E 1931 (1)*
Meale, T. 2: *v E 1958 (2)*
Merritt, W. E. 6: v E 1929 (4); *v E 1931 (2)*
Meuli, E. M. 1: v SA 1952
Milburn, B. D. 3: v WI 1968 (3)
Miller, L. S. M. 13: v SA 1952 (2); v WI 1955 (3); *v E 1958 (4); v SA 1953 (4)*
Mills, J. E. 7: v E 1929 (3) 1932 (1); *v E 1931 (3)*
Moir, A. M. 17: v E 1950 (2) 1954 (2) 1958 (2); v SA 1952 (1); v WI 1951 (2) 1955 (1); *v E 1958 (2); v In 1955 (2); v P 1955 (3)*
Moloney D. A. R. 3: *v E 1937 (3)*
Mooney, F. L. H. 14: v E 1950 (2); v SA 1952 (2); v WI 1951 (2); *v E 1949 (3); v SA 1953 (5)*
Morgan, R. W. 20: v E 1965 (2) 1970 (2); v WI 1968 (1); v P 1964 (2); *v E 1965 (3); v WI 1971 (3); v In 1964 (4); v P 1964 (3)*
Morrison, B. D. 1: v E 1962
Morrison, J. F. M. 17: v E 1974 (2); v A 1973 (3) 1981 (3); v In 1975 (3); *v A 1973 (3); v In 1976 (1); v P 1976 (2)*
Motz, R. C. 32: v E 1962 (2) 1965 (3); v SA 1963 (2); v WI 1968 (3): v In 1967 (4); v P 1964 (3); *v E 1965 (3) 1969 (3); v SA 1961 (5); v In 1964 (3); v P 1964 (1)*
Murray, B. A. G. 13: v E 1970 (1); v In 1967 (4); *v E 1969 (2); v In 1969 (3); v P 1969 (3)*

Newman J. 3: v E 1932 (2); v SA 1931 (1)

O'Sullivan, D. R. 11: v In 1975 (1); v P 1972 (1); *v A 1973 (3); v In 1976 (3); v P 1976 (3)*
Overton, G. W. F. 3: *v SA 1953 (3)*

Page, M. L. 14: v E 1929 (4) 1932 (2); v SA 1931 (2); *v E 1931 (3) 1937 (3)*
Parker, J. M. 36: v E 1974 (2) 1977 (3); v A 1973 (3) 1976 (2); v WI 1979 (3); v In 1975 (3); v P 1972 (1) 1978 (2); *v E 1973 (3) 1978 (2); v A 1973 (3) 1980 (3); v In 1976 (3); v P 1976 (3)*

Parker, N. M. 3: *v In 1976 (2); v P 1976 (1)*
Petherick, P. J. 6: v A 1976 (1); *v In 1976 (3); v P 1976 (2)*
Petrie, E. C. 14: v E 1958 (2) 1965 (3); *v E 1958 (5); v In 1955 (2); v P 1955 (2)*
Playle, W. R. 8: v E 1962 (3); *v E 1958 (5)*
Pollard, V. 32: v E 1965 (3) 1970 (1); v WI 1968 (3); v In 1967 (4); v P 1972 (1); *v E 1965 (3) 1969 (3) 1973 (3); v In 1964 (4) 1969 (1); v P 1964 (3) 1969 (3)*
Poore, M. B. 14: v E 1954 (1); v SA 1952 (1); *v SA 1953 (5); v In 1955 (4); v P 1955 (3)*
Puna, N. 3: v E 1965 (3)

Rabone, G. O. 12: v E 1954 (2); v SA 1952 (1); v WI 1951 (2); *v E 1949 (4); v SA 1953 (3)*
Redmond, R. E. 1: v P 1972
Reid, J. F. 4: v In 1980 (3); v P 1978 (1)
Reid, J. R. 58: v E 1950 (2) 1954 (2) 1958 (2) 1962 (3); v SA 1952 (2) 1963 (3); v WI 1951 (2) 1955 (4); v P 1964 (3); *v E 1949 (2) 1958 (5) 1965 (3); v SA 1953 (5) 1961 (5); v In 1955 (5) 1964 (4); v P 1955 (3) 1964 (3)*
Roberts, A. D. G. 7: v In 1975 (2); *v In 1976 (3); v P 1976 (2)*
Roberts, A. W. 5: v E 1929 (1); v SA 1931 (2); *v E 1937 (2)*
Rowe, C. G. 1: v A 1945

Scott, R. H. 1: v E 1946
Scott, V. J. 10: v E 1946 (1) 1950 (2); v A 1945 (1); v WI 1951 (2); *v E 1949 (4)*
Shrimpton, M. J. F. 10: v E 1962 (2) 1965 (3) 1970 (2); v SA 1963 (1); *v A 1973 (2)*
Sinclair, B. W. 21: v E 1962 (3) 1965 (3); v SA 1963 (3); v In 1967 (2); v P 1964 (2); *v E 1965 (3); v In 1964 (2); v P 1964 (3)*
Sinclair, I. M. 2: v WI 1955 (2)
Smith, F. B. 4: v E 1946 (1); v WI 1951 (1); *v E 1949 (2)*
Smith, H. D. 1: v E 1932
Smith, I. D. S. 7: v A 1981 (3); v In 1980 (3); *v A 1980 (1)*
Snedden, C. A. 1: v E 1946
Snedden, M. C. 6: v A 1981 (3); v In 1980 (3)
Sparling, J. T. 11: v E 1958 (2) 1962 (1); v SA 1963 (2); *v E 1958 (3); v SA 1961 (3)*
Sutcliffe, B. 42: v E 1946 (1) 1950 (2) 1954 (2) 1958 (2); v SA 1952 (2); v WI 1951 (2) 1955 (2); *v E 1949 (4) 1958 (4) 1965 (1); v SA 1953 (5); v In 1955 (5) 1964 (4); v P 1955 (3) 1964 (3)*

Taylor, B. R. 30: v E 1965 (1); v WI 1968 (3); v In 1967 (3); v P 1972 (3); *v E 1965 (2) 1969 (2) 1973 (3); v WI 1971 (4); v In 1964 (3) 1969 (2); v P 1964 (3) 1969 (1)*
Taylor, D. D. 3: v E 1946 (1); v WI 1955 (2)
Thomson, K. 2: v In 1967 (2)
Tindill, E. W. T. 5: v E 1946 (1); v A 1945 (1); *v E 1937 (3)*
Troup, G. B. 12: v A 1981 (2); v WI 1979 (3); v In 1980 (2); v P 1978 (2); *v A 1980 (2); v In 1976 (1)*
Truscott, P. B. 1: v P 1964
Turner, G. M. 39: v E 1970 (2) 1974 (2); v A 1973 (3) 1976 (2); v WI 1968 (3); v In 1975 (3); v P 1972 (3); *v E 1969 (2) 1973 (3); v A 1973 (2); v WI 1971 (5); v In 1969 (3) 1976 (3); v P 1969 (1) 1976 (2)*

Vivian, G. E. 5: *v WI 1971 (4); v In 1964 (1)*
Vivian, H. G. 7: v E 1932 (1); v SA 1931 (1); *v E 1931 (2) 1937 (3)*

Wadsworth, K. J. 33: v E 1970 (2) 1974 (2); v A 1973 (3); v In 1975 (3); v P 1972 (3); *v E 1969 (3) 1973 (3); v A 1973 (3); v WI 1971 (5); v In 1969 (3); v P 1969 (3)*
Wallace, W. M. 13: v E 1946 (1) 1950 (2); v A 1945 (1); v SA 1952 (2); *v E 1937 (3) 1949 (4)*
Ward, J. T. 8: v SA 1963 (1); v In 1967 (1); v P 1964 (1); *v E 1965 (1); v In 1964 (4)*
Watt, L. 1: v E 1954
Webb, M. G. 3: v E 1970 (1); v A 1973 (1); *v WI 1971 (1)*
Webb, P. N. 2: v WI 1979 (2)
Weir, G. L. 11: v E 1929 (3) 1932 (2); v SA 1931 (2); *v E 1931 (3) 1937 (1)*
Whitelaw, P. E. 2: v E 1932 (2)
Wright, J. G. 20: v E 1977 (3); v A 1981 (3); v WI 1979 (3); v In 1980 (3); v P 1978 (3); *v E 1978 (2); v A 1980 (3)*

Yuile, B. W. 17: v E 1962 (2); v WI 1968 (3); v In 1967 (1); v P 1964 (3); *v E 1965 (1); v In 1964 (3) 1969 (1); v P 1964 (1) 1969 (2)*

INDIA

Number of Test cricketers: 158

Adhikari, H. R. 21: v E 1951 (3); v A 1956 (2); v WI 1948 (5) 1958 (1); v P 1952 (2); *v E 1952 (3); v A 1947 (5)*
Ali, S. Abid, 29: v E 1972 (4); v A 1969 (1); v WI 1974 (2); v NZ 1969 (3); *v E 1971 (3) 1974 (3); v A 1967 (4); v WI 1970 (5); v NZ 1967 (4)*
Ali, S. Nazir, 2: v E 1933 (1); *v E 1932 (1)*
Ali, S. Wazir, 7: v E 1933 (3); *v E 1932 (1) 1936 (3)*
Amarnath, L. 24: v E 1933 (3) 1951 (3); v WI 1948 (5); v P 1952 (5); *v E 1946 (3); v A 1947 (5)*
Amarnath, M. 26: v E 1976 (2); v A 1969 (1) 1979 (1); v WI 1978 (2); v NZ 1976 (3); *v E 1979 (2); v A 1977 (5); v WI 1975 (4); v NZ 1975 (3); v P 1978 (3)*
Amarnath, S. 8: v E 1976 (2): *v WI 1975 (2); v NZ 1975 (1); v P 1978 (3)*
Amar Singh 7: v E 1933 (3); *v E 1932 (1) 1936 (3)*
Amir Elahi 1: *v A 1947*
Apte, A. L. 1: *v E 1959*
Apte, M. L. 7: v P 1952 (2); *v WI 1952 (5)*

Baig, A. A. 10: v A 1959 (3); v WI 1966 (2); v P 1960 (3); *v E 1959 (2)*
Banerjee, S. A. 1: v WI 1948
Banerjee, S. N. 1: v WI 1948
Bedi, B. S. 67: v E 1972 (5) 1976 (5); v A 1969 (5); v WI 1966 (2) 1974 (4) 1978 (3); v NZ 1969 (3) 1976 (3); *v E 1967 (3) 1971 (3) 1974 (3) 1979 (3); v A 1967 (2) 1977 (5); v WI 1970 (5) 1975 (4); v NZ 1967 (4) 1975 (2); v P 1978 (3)*
Bhandari, P. 3: v A 1956 (1); v NZ 1955 (1); *v P 1954 (1)*
Binny, R. M. H. 9: v E 1979 (1); v P 1979 (6); *v A 1980 (1); v NZ 1980 (1)*
Borde, C. G. 55: v E 1961 (5) 1963 (5); v A 1959 (5) 1964 (3) 1969 (1); v WI 1958 (4) 1966 (3); v NZ 1964 (4); v P 1960 (5); *v E 1959 (4) 1967 (3); v A 1967 (4); v WI 1961 (5); v NZ 1967 (4)*

Chandrasekhar, B. S. 58: v E 1963 (4) 1972 (5) 1976 (5); v A 1964 (2); v WI 1966 (3) 1974 (4) 1978 (4); v NZ 1964 (2) 1976 (3); *v E 1967 (3) 1971 (3) 1974 (2) 1979 (1); v A 1967 (2) 1977 (5); v WI 1975 (4); v NZ 1975 (3); v P 1978 (3)*
Chauhan, C. P. S. 40: v E 1972 (2); v A 1969 (1) 1979 (6); v WI 1978 (6); v NZ 1969 (2); v P 1979 (6); *v E 1979 (4); v A 1977 (4) 1980 (3); v NZ 1980 (3); v P 1978 (3)*
Chowdhury, N. R. 2: v E 1951 (1); v WI 1948 (1)
Colah, S. H. M. 2: v E 1933 (1); *v E 1932 (1)*
Contractor, N. J. 31: v E 1961 (5); v A 1956 (1) 1959 (5); v WI 1958 (5); v NZ 1955 (4); v P 1960 (5); *v E 1959 (4); v WI 1961 (2)*

Dani, H. T. 1: v P 1952
Desai, R. B. 28: v E 1961 (4) 1963 (2); v A 1959 (3); v WI 1958 (1); v NZ 1964 (3); v P 1960 (5); *v E 1959 (5); v A 1967 (1); v WI 1961 (3); v NZ 1967 (1)*
Dilawar Hussain 3: v E 1933 (2); *v E 1936 (1)*
Divecha, R. V. 5: v E 1951 (2); v P 1952 (1); *v E 1952 (2)*
Doshi, D. R. 27: v E 1979 (1) 1981 (6); v A 1979 (6); v P 1979 (6); *v E 1982 (3); v A 1980 (3); v NZ 1980 (2)*
Durani, S. A. 29: v E 1961 (5) 1963 (5) 1972 (3); v A 1959 (1) 1964 (3); v WI 1966 (1); v NZ 1964 (3); *v WI 1961 (5) 1970 (3)*

Engineer, F. M. 46: v E 1961 (4) 1972 (5); v A 1969 (5); v WI 1966 (1) 1974 (5); v NZ 1964 (4) 1969 (2); *v E 1967 (3) 1971 (3) 1974 (3); v A 1967 (4); v WI 1961 (3); v NZ 1967 (4)*

Gadkari, C. V. 6: *v WI 1952 (3); v P 1954 (3)*

Gaekwad, A. D. 21: v E 1976 (4); v WI 1974 (3) 1978 (5); v NZ 1976 (3); *v E 1979 (2); v A 1977 (1); v WI 1975 (3)*
Gaekwad, D. K. 11: v WI 1958 (1); v P 1952 (2) 1960 (1); *v E 1952 (1) 1959 (4); v WI 1952 (2)*
Gaekwad, H. G. 1: v P 1952
Gandotra, A. 2: v A 1969 (1); v NZ 1969 (1)
Gavaskar, S. M. 78: v E 1972 (5) 1976 (5) 1979 (1) 1981 (6); v A 1979 (6); v WI 1974 (2) 1978 (6); v NZ 1976 (3); v P 1979 (6); *v E 1971 (3) 1974 (3) 1979 (4) 1982 (3); v A 1977 (5) 1980 (3); v WI 1970 (4) 1975 (4); v NZ 1975 (3) 1980 (3); v P 1978 (3)*
Ghavri, K. D. 39: v E 1976 (3) 1979 (1); v A 1979 (6); v WI 1974 (3) 1978 (6); v NZ 1976 (2); v P 1979 (6); *v E 1979 (4); v A 1977 (3) 1980 (3); v NZ 1980 (1); v P 1978 (1)*
Ghorpade, J. M. 8: v A 1956 (1); v WI 1958 (1); v NZ 1955 (1); *v E 1959 (3); v WI 1952 (2)*
Ghulam Ahmed 22: v E 1951 (2); v A 1956 (2); v WI 1948 (3) 1958 (2); v NZ 1955 (1); v P 1952 (4); *v E 1952 (4); v P 1954 (4)*
Gopalan, M. J. 1: v E 1933
Gopinath, C. D. 8: v E 1951 (3); v A 1959 (1); v P 1952 (1); *v E 1952 (1); v P 1954 (2)*
Guard, G. M. 2: v A 1959 (1); v WI 1958 (1)
Guha, S. 4: v A 1969 (3); *v E 1967 (1)*
Gul Mahomed 8: v P 1952 (2); *v E 1946 (1); v A 1947 (5)*
Gupte, B. P. 3: v E 1963 (1); v NZ 1964 (1); v P 1960 (1)
Gupte, S. P. 36: v E 1951 (1) 1961 (2); v A 1956 (3); v WI 1958 (5); v NZ 1955 (5); v P 1952 (2) 1960 (3); *v E 1959 (5); v WI 1952 (5); v P 1954 (5)*

Hafeez, A. 3: *v E 1946 (3)*
Hanumant Singh 14: v E 1963 (2); v A 1964 (3); v WI 1966 (2); v NZ 1964 (4) 1969 (1); *v E 1967 (2)*
Hardikar, M. S. 2: v WI 1958 (2)
Hazare, V. S. 30: v E 1951 (5); v WI 1948 (5); v P 1952 (3); *v E 1946 (3) 1952 (4); v A 1947 (5); v WI 1952 (5)*
Hindlekar, D. D. 4: *v E 1936 (1) 1946 (3)*

Ibrahim, K. C. 4: v WI 1948 (4)
Indrajitsinhji, K. S. 4: v A 1964 (3); v NZ 1969 (1)
Irani, J. K. 2: *v A 1947 (2)*

Jai, L. P. 1: v E 1933
Jaisimha, M. L. 39: v E 1961 (5) 1963 (5); v A 1959 (1) 1964 (3); v WI 1966 (2); v NZ 1964 (4) 1969 (1); v P 1960 (4); *v E 1959 (1); v A 1967 (2); v WI 1961 (4) 1970 (3); v NZ 1967 (4)*
Jamshedji, R. J. 1: v E 1933
Jayantilal, K. 1: *v WI 1970*
Jilani, M. Baqa 1: *v E 1936*
Joshi, P. G. 12: v E 1951 (2); v A 1959 (1); v WI 1958 (1); v P 1952 (1) 1960 (1); *v E 1959 (3); v WI 1952 (3)*

Kanitkar, H. S. 2: v WI 1974 (2)
Kapil Dev 41: v E 1979 (1) 1981 (6); v A 1979 (6); v WI 1978 (6); v P 1979 (6); *v E 1979 (4) 1982 (3); v A 1980 (3); v NZ 1980 (3); v P 1978 (3)*
Kardar, A. H. (*see* Hafeez)
Kenny, R. B. 5: v A 1959 (4); v WI 1958 (1)
Khan, M. Jahangir, 4: *v E 1932 (1) 1936 (3)*
Kirmani, S. M. H. 57: v E 1976 (5) 1979 (1) 1981 (6); v A 1979 (6); v WI 1978 (6); v NZ 1976 (3); v P 1979 (6); *v E 1982 (3); v A 1977 (5) 1980 (3); v WI 1975 (4); v NZ 1975 (3) 1980 (3); v P 1978 (3)*
Kirti Azad 4: v E 1981 (3); *v NZ 1980 (1)*
Kischenchand, G. 5: v P 1952 (1); *v A 1947 (4)*
Kripal Singh, A. G. 14: v E 1961 (3) 1963 (2); v A 1956 (2) 1964 (1); v WI 1958 (1); v NZ 1955 (4); *v E 1959 (1)*
Krishnamurthy, P. 5: *v WI 1970 (5)*
Kulkarni, U. N. 4: *v A 1967 (3); v NZ 1967 (1)*
Kumar, V. V. 2: v E 1961 (1); v P 1960 (1)

Kunderan, B. K. 18: v E 1961 (1) 1963 (5); v A 1959 (3); v WI 1966 (2); v NZ 1964 (1); v P 1960 (2); *v E 1967 (2); v WI 1961 (2)*

Lall Singh 1: *v E 1932*

Madan Lal 25: v E 1976 (2) 1981 (6); v WI 1974 (2); v NZ 1976 (1); *v E 1974 (2) 1982 (3); v A 1977 (2); v WI 1975 (4); v NZ 1975 (3)*
Maka, E. S. 2: v P 1952 (1); *v WI 1952 (1)*
Malhotra, A. 3: v E 1981 (2); *v E 1982 (1)*
Manjrekar, V. L. 55: v E 1951 (2) 1961 (5) 1963 (4); v A 1956 (3) 1964 (3); v WI 1958 (4); v NZ 1955 (5) 1964 (1); v P 1952 (3) 1960 (5); *v E 1952 (4) 1959 (2); v WI 1952 (4) 1961 (5); v P 1954 (5)*
Mankad, A. V. 21: v E 1976 (1); v A 1969 (5); v WI 1974 (1) 1976 (1); v NZ 1969 (2); *v E 1971 (3) 1974 (1); v A 1977 (3); v WI 1970 (3)*
Mankad, V. 44: v E 1951 (5); v A 1956 (3); v WI 1948 (5) 1958 (2); v NZ 1955 (4); v P 1952 (4); *v E 1946 (3) 1952 (3); v A 1947 (5); v WI 1952 (5); v P 1954 (5)*
Mansur Ali Khan (*see* Pataudi)
Mantri, M. K. 4: v E 1951 (1); *v E 1952 (2); v P 1954 (1)*
Meherhomji, K. R. 1: *v E 1936*
Mehra, V. L. 8: v E 1961 (1) 1963 (2); v NZ 1955 (2); *v WI 1961 (3)*
Merchant, V. M. 10: v E 1933 (3) 1951 (1); *v E 1936 (3) 1946 (3)*
Milkha Singh, A. G. 4: v E 1961 (1); v A 1959 (1); v P 1960 (2)
Modi, R. S. 10: v E 1951 (1); v WI 1948 (5); v P 1952 (1); *v E 1946 (3)*
Muddiah, V. M. 2: v A 1959 (1); v P 1960 (1)
Mushtaq Ali 11: v E 1933 (2); 1951 (1); v WI 1948 (3); *v E 1936 (3) 1946 (2)*

Nadkarni, R. G. 41: v E 1961 (1) 1963 (5); v A 1959 (5) 1964 (3); v WI 1958 (1) 1966 (1); v NZ 1955 (1) 1964 (4); v P 1960 (4); *v E 1959 (4); v A 1967 (3); v WI 1961 (5); v NZ 1967 (4)*
Naik, S. S. 3: v WI 1974 (2); *v E 1974 (1)*
Naoomal Jeoomal 3: v E 1933 (2); *v E 1932 (1)*
Narasimha Rao, M. V. 4: v A 1979 (2); v WI 1978 (2)
Navle, J. G. 2: v E 1933 (1); *v E 1932 (1)*
Nayak, S. V. 2: *v E 1982 (2)*
Nayudu, C. K. 7: v E 1933 (3); *v E 1932 (1) 1936 (3)*
Nayudu, C. S. 11: v E 1933 (2) 1951 (1); *v E 1936 (2) 1946 (2); v A 1947 (4)*
Nissar, Mahomed 6: v E 1933 (2); *v E 1932 (1) 1936 (3)*
Nyalchand, K. 1: v P 1952

Pai, A. M. 1: v NZ 1969
Palia, P. E. 2: *v E 1932 (1) 1936 (1)*
Parkar, G. A. 1: *v E 1982*
Parkar, R. D. 2: v E 1972 (2)
Parsana, D. D. 2: v WI 1978 (2)
Patankar, C. T. 1: v NZ 1955
Pataudi sen., Nawab of, 3: *v E 1946 (3)*
Pataudi jun., Nawab of (now Mansur Ali Khan) 46: v E 1961 (3) 1963 (5) 1972 (3); v A 1964 (3) 1969 (5); v WI 1966 (3) 1974 (4); v NZ 1964 (4) 1969 (3); *v E 1967 (3); v A 1967 (3); v WI 1961 (3); v NZ 1967 (4)*
Patel, B. P. 21: v E 1976 (5); v WI 1974 (3); v NZ 1976 (3); *v E 1974 (2); v A 1977 (2); v WI 1975 (3); v NZ 1975 (3)*
Patel, J. M. 7: v A 1956 (2) 1959 (3); v NZ 1955 (1); *v P 1954 (1)*
Patil, S. M. 15: v E 1979 (1) 1981 (4); v P 1979 (2); *v E 1982 (2); v A 1980 (3); v NZ 1980 (3)*
Patil, S. R. 1: v NZ 1955
Patiala, Yuvraj of, 1: v E 1933
Phadkar, D. G. 31: v E 1951 (4); v A 1956 (1); v WI 1948 (4) 1958 (1); v NZ 1955 (4); v P 1952 (2); *v E 1952 (4); v A 1947 (4); v WI 1952 (4); v P 1954 (3)*
Prasanna, E. A. S. 49: v E 1961 (1) 1972 (3) 1976 (4); v A 1969 (5); v WI 1966 (1) 1974 (5); v NZ 1969 (3); *v E 1967 (3) 1974 (2); v A 1967 (4) 1977 (4); v WI 1961 (1) 1970 (3) 1975 (1); v NZ 1967 (4) 1975 (3); v P 1978 (2)*
Punjabi, P. H. 5: *v P 1954 (5)*

Rai Singh, K. 1: *v A 1947*
Rajinder Pal 1: v E 1963
Rajindernath, V. 1: v P 1952
Ramaswami, C. 2: *v E 1936 (2)*
Ramchand, G. S. 33: v A 1956 (3) 1959 (5); v WI 1958 (3); v NZ 1955 (5); v P 1952 (3); *v E 1952 (4); v WI 1952 (5); v P 1954 (5)*
Ramji, L. 1: v E 1933
Rangachari, C. R. 4: v WI 1948 (2); *v A 1947 (2)*
Rangnekar, K. M. 3: *v A 1947 (3)*
Ranjane, V. B. 7: v E 1961 (3) 1963 (1); v A 1964 (1); v WI 1958 (1); *v WI 1961 (1)*
Reddy, B. 4: *v E 1979 (4)*
Rege, M. R. 1: v WI 1948
Roy, A. 4: v A 1969 (2); v NZ 1969 (2)
Roy, Pankaj 43: v E 1951 (5); v A 1956 (3) 1959 (5); v WI 1958 (5); v NZ 1955 (3); v P 1952 (3) 1960 (1); *v E 1952 (4) 1959 (5); v WI 1952 (4); v P 1954 (5)*
Roy, Pranab 2: v E 1981 (2)

Sardesai, D. N. 30: v E 1961 (1) 1963 (5) 1972 (1); v A 1964 (3) 1969 (1); v WI 1966 (2); v NZ 1964 (3); *v E 1967 (1) 1971 (3); v A 1967 (2); v WI 1961 (3) 1970 (5)*
Sarwate, C. T. 9: v E 1951 (1); v WI 1948 (2); *v E 1946 (1); v A 1947 (5)*
Saxena, R. C. 1: *v E 1967*
Sen, P. 14: v E 1951 (2); v WI 1948 (5); v P 1952 (2); *v E 1952 (2); v A 1947 (3)*
Sengupta, A. K. 1: v WI 1958
Sharma, P. 5: v E 1976 (2); v WI 1974 (2); *v WI 1975 (1)*
Shastri, R. J. 11: v E 1981 (6); *v E 1982 (3); v NZ 1980 (2)*
Shinde, S. G. 7: v E 1951 (3); v WI 1948 (1); *v E 1946 (1) 1952 (2)*
Shodhan, D. H. 3: v P 1952 (1); *v WI 1952 (2)*
Sohoni, S. W. 4: v E 1951 (1); *v E 1946 (2); v A 1947 (1)*
Solkar, E. D. 27: v E 1972 (5) 1976 (1); v A 1969 (4); v WI 1974 (4); v NZ 1969 (1); *v E 1971 (3) 1974 (3); v WI 1970 (5) 1975 (1)*
Sood, M. M. 1: v A 1959
Srikkanth, K. 4: v E 1981 (4)
Srinivasan, T. E. 1: *v NZ 1980*
Subramanya, V. 9: v WI 1966 (2); v NZ 1964 (1); *v E 1967 (2); v A 1967 (2); v NZ 1967 (2)*
Sunderram, G. 2: v NZ 1955 (2)
Surendranath, R. 11: v A 1959 (2); v WI 1958 (2); v P 1960 (2); *v E 1959 (5)*
Surti, R. F. 26: v E 1963 (1); v A 1964 (2) 1969 (1); v WI 1966 (2); v NZ 1964 (1) 1969 (2); v P 1960 (2); *v E 1967 (2); v A 1967 (4); v WI 1961 (5); v NZ 1967 (4)*
Swamy, V. N. 1: v NZ 1955

Tamhane, N. S. 21: v A 1956 (3) 1959 (1); v WI 1958 (4); v NZ 1955 (4); v P 1960 (2); *v E 1959 (2); v P 1954 (5)*
Tarapore, K. K. 1: v WI 1948

Umrigar, P. R. 59: v E 1951 (5) 1961 (4); v A 1956 (3) 1959 (3); v WI 1948 (1) 1958 (5); v NZ 1955 (5); v P 1952 (5) 1960 (5); *v E 1952 (4) 1959 (4); v WI 1952 (5) 1961 (5); v P 1954 (5)*

Vengsarkar, D. B. 51: v E 1976 (1) 1979 (1) 1981 (6); v A 1979 (6); v WI 1978 (6); v P 1979 (5); *v E 1979 (4) 1982 (3); v A 1977 (5) 1980 (3); v WI 1975 (2); v NZ 1975 (3) 1980 (3); v P 1978 (3)*
Venkataraghavan, S. 50: v E 1972 (2) 1976 (1); v A 1969 (5) 1979 (3); v WI 1966 (2) 1974 (2) 1978 (6); v NZ 1964 (4) 1969 (2) 1976 (3); *v E 1967 (1) 1971 (3) 1974 (2) 1979 (4); v A 1977 (1); v WI 1970 (5) 1975 (3); v NZ 1975 (1)*
Viswanath, G. R. 84: v E 1972 (5) 1976 (5) 1979 (1) 1981 (6); v A 1969 (4) 1979 (6); v WI 1974 (5) 1978 (6); v NZ 1976 (3); v P 1979 (6); *v E 1971 (3) 1974 (3) 1979 (4) 1982 (3); v A 1977 (5) 1980 (3); v WI 1970 (3) 1975 (4); v NZ 1975 (3) 1980 (3); v P 1978 (3)*

Vizianagram, Maharaj Sir Vijaya 3: *v E 1936 (3)*

Wadekar, A. L. 37: v E 1972 (5); v A 1969 (5); v WI 1966 (2); v NZ 1969 (3); *v E 1967 (3) 1971 (3) 1974 (3); v A 1967 (4); v WI 1970 (5); v NZ 1967 (4)*

Yadav, N. S. 15: v E 1979 (1) 1981 (1); v A 1979 (5); v P 1979 (5); *v A 1980 (2); v NZ 1980 (1)*
Yajurvindra Singh 4: v E 1976 (2); v A 1979 (1); *v E 1979 (1)*
Yashpal Sharma 25: v E 1979 (1) 1981 (2); v A 1979 (6); v P 1979 (6); *v E 1979 (3) 1982 (3); v A 1980 (3); v NZ 1980 (1)*
Yograj Singh 1: *v NZ 1980*

Note: Hafeez, on going later to Oxford University, took his correct name, Kardar.

PAKISTAN

Number of Test cricketers: 93

Abdul Kadir 4: v A 1964 (1); *v A 1964 (1); v NZ 1964 (2)*
Abdul Qadir 11: v E 1977 (3); v WI 1980 (2); *v E 1982 (3); v In 1979 (3)*
Afaq Hussain 2: v E 1961 (1); *v A 1964 (1)*
Aftab Baloch 2: v WI 1974 (1); v NZ 1969 (1)
Aftab Gul 6: v E 1968 (2); v NZ 1969 (1); *v E 1971 (3)*
Agha Saadat Ali 1: v NZ 1955
Agha Zahid 1: v WI 1974
Alim-ud-Din 25: v E 1961 (2); v A 1956 (1) 1959 (1); v WI 1958 (1); v NZ 1955 (3); v In 1954 (5); *v E 1954 (3) 1962 (3); v WI 1957 (5); v In 1960 (1)*
Amir Elahi 5: *v In 1952 (5)*
Anwar Hussain 4: *v In 1952 (4)*
Anwar Khan 1: *v NZ 1978*
Arif Butt 3: *v A 1964 (1); v NZ 1964 (2)*
Ashraf Ali 2: v SL 1981 (2)
Asif Iqbal 58: v E 1968 (3) 1972 (3); v A 1964 (1); v WI 1974 (2); v NZ 1964 (3) 1969 (3) 1976 (3); v In 1978 (3); *v E 1967 (3) 1971 (3) 1974 (3); v A 1964 (1) 1972 (3) 1976 (3) 1978 (2); v WI 1976 (5); v NZ 1964 (3) 1972 (3) 1978 (2); v In 1979 (6)*
Asif Masood 16: v E 1968 (2) 1972 (1); v WI 1974 (2); v NZ 1969 (1); *v E 1971 (3) 1974 (3); v A 1972 (3) 1976 (1)*
Azhar Khan 1: v A 1979
Azmat Rana 1: v A 1979

Burki, J. 25: v E 1961 (3); v A 1964 (1); v NZ 1964 (3) 1969 (1); *v E 1962 (5) 1967 (3); v A 1964 (1); v NZ 1964 (3); v In 1960 (5)*

D'Souza, A. 6: v E 1961 (2); v WI 1958 (1); *v E 1962 (3)*

Ehtesham-ud-Din 5: v A 1979 (1); *v E 1982 (1); v In 1979 (3)*

Farooq Hamid 1: *v A 1964*
Farrukh Zaman 1: v NZ 1976
Fazal Mahmood 34: v E 1961 (1); v A 1956 (1) 1959 (2); v WI 1958 (3); v NZ 1955 (2); v In 1954 (4); *v E 1954 (4) 1962 (2); v WI 1957 (5); v In 1952 (5) 1960 (5)*

Ghazali, M. E. Z. 2: *v E 1954 (2)*
Ghulam Abbas 1: *v E 1967*
Gul Mahomed 1: v A 1956

Hanif Mohammad 55: v E 1961 (3) 1968 (3); v A 1956 (1) 1959 (3) 1964 (1); v WI 1958 (1); v NZ 1955 (3) 1964 (3) 1969 (1); v In 1954 (5); *v E 1954 (4) 1962 (5) 1967 (3); v A 1964 (1); v WI 1957 (5); v NZ 1964 (3); v In 1952 (5) 1960 (5)*

Haroon Rashid 18: v E 1977 (3); v A 1979 (2); v SL 1981 (2); *v E 1978 (3) 1982 (1); v A 1976 (1) 1978 (1); v WI 1976 (5); v NZ 1978 (1)*
Haseeb Ahsan 12: v E 1961 (2); v A 1959 (1); v WI 1958 (1); *v WI 1957 (3); v In 1960 (5)*

Ibadulla, K. 4: v A 1964 (1); *v E 1967 (2); v NZ 1964 (1)*
Ijaz Butt 8: v A 1959 (2); v WI 1958 (3); *v E 1962 (3)*
Ijaz Faqih 2: v WI 1980 (1); *v A 1981 (1)*
Imran Khan 42: v A 1979 (2); v WI 1980 (4); v NZ 1976 (3); v In 1978 (3); v SL 1981 (1); *v E 1971 (1) 1974 (3) 1982 (3); v A 1976 (3) 1978 (2) 1981 (3); v WI 1976 (5); v NZ 1978 (2); v In 1979 (5)*
Imtiaz Ahmed 41: v E 1961 (3); v A 1956 (1) 1959 (3); v WI 1958 (3); v NZ 1955 (3); v In 1954 (5); *v E 1954 (4) 1962 (4); v WI 1957 (5); v In 1952 (5) 1960 (5)*
Intikhab Alam 47: v E 1961 (2) 1968 (3) 1972 (3); v A 1959 (1) 1964 (1); v WI 1974 (2); v NZ 1964 (3) 1969 (3) 1976 (3); *v E 1962 (3) 1967 (3) 1971 (3) 1974 (3); v A 1964 (1) 1972 (3); v WI 1976 (1); v NZ 1964 (3) 1972 (3); v In 1960 (3)*
Iqbal Qasim 32: v E 1977 (3); v A 1979 (3); v WI 1980 (4); v In 1978 (3); v SL 1981 (3); *v E 1978 (3); v A 1976 (3) 1981 (2); v WI 1976 (2); v In 1979 (6)*
Israr Ali 4: v A 1959 (2); *v In 1952 (2)*

Javed Akhtar 1: *v E 1962*
Javed Miandad 43: v E 1977 (3); v A 1979 (3); v WI 1980 (4); v NZ 1976 (3); v In 1978 (3); v SL 1981 (3); *v E 1978 (3) 1982 (3); v A 1976 (3) 1978 (2) 1981 (3); v WI 1976 (1); v NZ 1978 (3); v In 1979 (6)*

Kardar, A. H. 23: v A 1956 (1); v NZ 1955 (3); v In 1954 (5); *v E 1954 (4); v WI 1957 (5); v In 1952 (5)*
Khalid Hassan 1: *v E 1954*
Khalid Wazir 2: *v E 1954 (2)*
Khan Mohammad 13: v A 1956 (1); v NZ 1955 (3); v In 1954 (4); *v E 1954 (2); v WI 1957 (2); v In 1952 (1)*

Liaqat Ali 5: v E 1977 (2); v WI 1974 (1); *v E 1978 (2)*

Mahmood Hussain 27: v E 1961 (1); v WI 1958 (3); v NZ 1955 (1); v In 1954 (5); *v E 1954 (2) 1962 (3); v WI 1957 (3); v In 1952 (4) 1960 (5)*
Majid J. Khan 62: v E 1968 (3) 1972 (3); v A 1964 (1) 1979 (3); v WI 1974 (2) 1980 (4); v NZ 1964 (3) 1976 (3); v In 1978 (3); v SL 1981 (1); *v E 1967 (3) 1971 (2) 1974 (3) 1982 (1); v A 1972 (3) 1976 (3) 1978 (2) 1981 (3); v WI 1976 (5); v NZ 1972 (3) 1978 (2); v In 1979 (6)*
Mansoor Akhtar 7: v WI 1980 (2); v SL 1981 (1); *v E 1982 (3); v A 1981 (1)*
Maqsood Ahmed 16: v NZ 1955 (2); v In 1954 (5); *v E 1954 (4); v In 1952 (5)*
Mathias, Wallis 21: v E 1961 (1); v A 1956 (1) 1959 (2); v WI 1958 (3); v NZ 1955 (1); *v E 1962 (3); v WI 1957 (5); v In 1960 (5)*
Miran Bux 2: v In 1954 (2)
Mohammad Aslam 1: *v E 1954*
Mohammad Farooq 7: v NZ 1964 (3); *v E 1962 (2); v In 1960 (2)*
Mohammad Ilyas 10: v E 1968 (2); v NZ 1964 (3); *v E 1967 (1); v A 1964 (1); v NZ 1964 (3)*
Mohammad Munaf 4: v E 1961 (2); v A 1959 (2)
Mohammad Nazir 8: v E 1972 (1); v WI 1980 (4); v NZ 1969 (3)
Mohsin Khan 13: v E 1977 (1); v SL 1981 (2); *v E 1978 (3) 1982 (3); v A 1978 (1) 1981 (2); v NZ 1978 (1)*
Mudassar Nazar 26: v E 1977 (3); v A 1979 (3); v In 1978 (2); v SL 1981 (1); *v E 1978 (3) 1982 (3); v A 1976 (1) 1978 (1) 1981 (3); v NZ 1978 (1); v In 1979 (5)*
Mufasir-ul-Haq 1: *v NZ 1964*
Munir Malik 3: v A 1959 (1); *v E 1962 (2)*
Mushtaq Mohammad 57: v E 1961 (3) 1968 (3) 1972 (3); v WI 1958 (1) 1974 (2); v NZ 1969 (2) 1976 (3); v In 1978 (3); *v E 1962 (5) 1967 (3) 1971 (3) 1974 (3); v A 1972 (3) 1976 (3) 1978 (2); v WI 1976 (5); v NZ 1972 (2) 1978 (3); v In 1960 (5)*

Nasim-ul-Ghani 29: v E 1961 (2); v A 1959 (2) 1964 (1); v WI 1958 (3); *v E 1962 (5) 1967 (2); v A 1964 (1) 1972 (1); v WI 1957 (5); v NZ 1964 (3); v In 1960 (4)*
Naushad Ali 6: v NZ 1964 (3); *v NZ 1964 (3)*

Nazar Mohammad 5: *v In 1952 (5)*
Nazir Junior (*see* Mohammad Nazir)
Niaz Ahmed 2: v E 1968 (1); *v E 1967 (1)*

Pervez Sajjad 19: v E 1968 (1) 1972 (2); v A 1964 (1); v NZ 1964 (3) 1969 (3); *v E 1971 (3); v NZ 1964 (3) 1972 (3)*

Rashid Khan 2: v SL 1981 (2)
Rehman, S. F. 1: *v WI 1957*
Rizwan-uz-Zaman 3: v SL 1981 (2); *v A 1981 (1)*

Sadiq Mohammad 41: v E 1972 (3) 1977 (2); v WI 1974 (1) 1980 (3); v NZ 1969 (3) 1976 (3); v In 1978 (1); *v E 1971 (3) 1974 (3) 1978 (3); v A 1972 (3) 1976 (2); v WI 1976 (5); v NZ 1972 (3); v In 1979 (3)*
Saeed Ahmed 41: v E 1961 (3) 1968 (3); v A 1959 (3) 1964 (1); v WI 1958 (3); v NZ 1964 (3); *v E 1962 (5) 1967 (3) 1971 (1); v A 1964 (1) 1972 (2); v WI 1957 (5); v NZ 1964 (3); v In 1960 (5)*
Salah-ud-Din 5: v E 1968 (1); v NZ 1964 (3) 1969 (1)
Saleem Altaf 21: v E 1972 (3); v NZ 1969 (2); v In 1978 (1); *v E 1967 (2) 1971 (2); v A 1972 (3) 1976 (2); v WI 1976 (3); v NZ 1972 (3)*
Salim Malik 2: v SL 1981 (2)
Salim Yousuf 1: v SL 1981
Sarfraz Nawaz 43: v E 1968 (1) 1972 (2) 1977 (2); v A 1979 (3); v WI 1974 (2) 1980 (2); v NZ 1976 (3); v In 1978 (3); *v E 1974 (3) 1978 (2) 1982 (1); v A 1972 (2) 1976 (2) 1978 (2) 1981 (3); v WI 1976 (4); v NZ 1972 (3) 1978 (3)*
Shafiq Ahmad 6: v E 1977 (3); v WI 1980 (2); *v E 1974 (1)*
Shafqat Rana 5: v E 1968 (2); v A 1964 (1); v NZ 1969 (2)
Shahid Israr 1: v NZ 1976
Shahid Mahmood 1: *v E 1962*
Sharpe, D. 3: v A 1959 (3)
Shuja-ud-Din 19: v E 1961 (2); v A 1959 (3); v WI 1958 (3); v NZ 1955 (3); v In 1954 (5); *v E 1954 (3)*
Sikander Bakht 25: v E 1977 (2); v WI 1980 (1); v NZ 1976 (1); v In 1978 (2); *v E 1978 (3) 1982 (2); v A 1978 (2) 1981 (3); v WI 1976 (1); v NZ 1978 (3); v In 1979 (5)*

Tahir Naqqash 5: v SL 1981 (3); *v E 1982 (2)*
Talat Ali 10: v E 1972 (3); *v E 1978 (2); v A 1972 (1); v NZ 1972 (1) 1978 (3)*
Taslim Arif 6: v A 1979 (3); v WI 1980 (2); *v In 1979 (1)*
Tauseef Ahmed 6: v A 1979 (3); v SL 1981 (3)

Waqar Hassan 21: v A 1956 (1) 1959 (1); v WI 1958 (1); v NZ 1955 (3); v In 1954 (5); *v E 1954 (4); v WI 1957 (1); v In 1952 (5)*
Wasim Bari 64: v E 1968 (3) 1972 (3) 1977 (3); v WI 1974 (2) 1980 (2); v NZ 1969 (3) 1976 (2); v In 1978 (3); *v E 1967 (3) 1971 (3) 1974 (3) 1978 (3) 1982 (3); v A 1972 (3) 1976 (3) 1978 (2) 1981 (3); v WI 1976 (5); v NZ 1972 (3) 1978 (3); v In 1979 (6)*
Wasim Raja 44: v E 1972 (1) 1977 (3); v A 1979 (3); v WI 1974 (2) 1980 (4); v NZ 1976 (1); v SL 1981 (3); *v E 1974 (2) 1978 (3) 1982 (1); v A 1978 (1) 1981 (3); v WI 1976 (5); v NZ 1972 (3) 1978 (3); v In 1979 (6)*
Wazir Mohammad 20: v A 1956 (1) 1959 (1); v WI 1958 (3); v NZ 1955 (2); v In 1954 (5); *v E 1954 (2); v WI 1957 (5); v In 1952 (1)*

Younis Ahmed 2: v NZ 1969 (2)

Zaheer Abbas 49: v E 1972 (2); v A 1979 (2); v WI 1974 (2) 1980 (3); v NZ 1969 (1) 1976 (3); v In 1978 (3); v SL 1981 (1); *v E 1971 (3) 1974 (3) 1982 (3); v A 1972 (3) 1976 (3) 1978 (2) 1982 (2); v WI 1976 (3); v NZ 1972 (3) 1978 (2); v In 1979 (5)*
Zulfiqar Ahmed 9: v A 1956 (1); v NZ 1955 (3); *v E 1954 (2); v In 1952 (3)*

SRI LANKA

Number of Test cricketers: 15

de Mel, A. L. F. 4: v E 1981 (1); *v P 1981 (3)*
de Silva, D. S. 4: v E 1981 (1); *v P 1981 (3)*
de Silva, G. R. A. 3: v E 1981 (1); *v P 1981 (2)*
Dias, R. L. 4: v E 1981 (1); *v P 1981 (3)*

Goonatillake, H. M. 4: v E 1981 (1); *v P 1981 (3)*

Jayasekera, R. S. A. 1: *v P 1981 (1)*

Kaluperuma, L. W. 2: v E 1981 (1); *v P 1981 (1)*

Madugalle, R. S. 4: v E 1981 (1); *v P 1981 (3)*
Mendis, R. L. S. 4: v E 1981 (1); *v P 1981 (3)*

Ranasinghe, A. N. 1: *v P 1981 (1)*
Ranatunga, A. 3: v E 1981 (1); *v P 1981 (2)*
Ratnayeke, J. R. 2: *v P 1981 (2)*

Warnapura, B. 3: v E 1981 (1); *v P 1981 (2)*
Wettimuny, S. 4: v E 1981 (1); *v P 1981 (3)*
Wijesuriya, R. G. C. E. 1: *v P 1981 (1)*

TWO COUNTRIES

Twelve cricketers have appeared for two countries in Test matches, namely:

Amir Elahi, *India and Pakistan.*
J. J. Ferris, *Australia and England.*
S. C. Guillen, *West Indies and NZ.*
Gul Mahomed, *India and Pakistan.*
F. Hearne, *England and South Africa.*
A. H. Kardar, *India and Pakistan.*
W. E. Midwinter, *England and Australia.*
F. Mitchell, *England and South Africa.*
W. L. Murdoch, *Australia and England.*
Nawab of Pataudi, sen., *England and India.*
A. E. Trott, *Australia and England.*
S. M. J. Woods, *Australia and England.*

MOST TEST APPEARANCES FOR EACH COUNTRY

England: M. C. Cowdrey 114.
Australia: R. N. Harvey 79.
South Africa: J. H. B. Waite 50.
West Indies: G. S. Sobers 93.
New Zealand: B. E. Congdon 61.
India: G. R. Viswanath 84.
Pakistan: Wasim Bari 64.

MOST TEST APPEARANCES AS CAPTAIN FOR EACH COUNTRY

England: P. B. H. May 41.
Australia: R. B. Simpson 39.
South Africa: H. W. Taylor 18.
West Indies: C. H. Lloyd 49.
New Zealand: J. R. Reid 34.
India: Nawab of Pataudi, jun., 40.
Pakistan: A. H. Kardar 23.

ENGLAND v REST OF THE WORLD

The following were awarded England caps for playing against the Rest of the World in England in 1970, although the five matches played are now generally considered not to have rated as full Tests: D. L. Amiss (1). G. Boycott (2), D. J. Brown (2), M. C. Cowdrey (4), M. H. Denness (1), B. L. D'Oliveira (4), J. H. Edrich (2), K. W. R. Fletcher (4), A. W. Greig (3), R. Illingworth (5), A. Jones (1), A. P. E. Knott (5), P. Lever (1), B. W. Luckhurst (5), C. M. Old (2), P. J. Sharpe (1), K. Shuttleworth (1), J. A. Snow (5), D. L. Underwood (3), A. Ward (1), D. Wilson (2).

CRICKET RECORDS

Amended by BARRY McCAULLY to end of 1982 season in England

Unless stated to be of a minor character, all records apply only to first-class cricket including some performances in the distant past which have always been recognised as of exceptional merit.

*Denotes not out or an unbroken partnership.

(A), (SA), (WI), (NZ), (I), (P) or (SL) indicates either the nationality of the player, or the country in which the record was made.

INDEX

BATTING

BOWLING AND FIELDING

ALL-ROUND CRICKET

THE SIDES

TEST MATCH RECORDS

MISCELLANEOUS

BATTING RECORDS

INDIVIDUAL SCORES OF 300 OR MORE

499	Hanif Mohammad	Karachi v Bahawalpur at Karachi	1958-59
452*	D. G. Bradman	NSW v Queensland at Sydney	1929-30
443*	B. B. Nimbalkar	Maharashtra v Kathiawar at Poona	1948-49
437	W. H. Ponsford	Victoria v Queensland at Melbourne	1927-28

429	W. H. Ponsford	Victoria v Tasmania at Melbourne	1922-23
428	Aftab Baloch	Sind v Baluchistan at Karachi	1973-74
424	A. C. MacLaren	Lancashire v Somerset at Taunton	1895
385	B. Sutcliffe	Otago v Canterbury at Christchurch	1952-53
383	C. W. Gregory	NSW v Queensland at Brisbane	1906-07
369	D. G. Bradman	South Australia v Tasmania at Adelaide	1935-36
365*	C. Hill	South Australia v NSW at Adelaide	1900-01
365*	G. S. Sobers	West Indies v Pakistan at Kingston	1957-58
364	L. Hutton	England v Australia at The Oval	1938
359*	V. M. Merchant	Bombay v Maharashtra at Bombay	1943-44
359	R. B. Simpson	NSW v Queensland at Brisbane	1963-64
357*	R. Abel	Surrey v Somerset at The Oval	1899
357	D. G. Bradman	South Australia v Victoria at Melbourne	1935-36
356	B. A. Richards	South Australia v W. Australia at Perth	1970-71
355	B. Sutcliffe	Otago v Auckland at Dunedin	1949-50
352	W. H. Ponsford	Victoria v NSW at Melbourne	1926-27
350	Rashid Israr	Habib Bank v National Bank at Lahore	1976-77
345	C. G. Macartney	Australians v Nottinghamshire at Nottingham	1921
344*	G. A. Headley	Jamaica v Lord Tennyson's XI at Kingston	1931-32
344	W. G. Grace	MCC v Kent at Canterbury	1876
343*	P. A. Perrin	Essex v Derbyshire at Chesterfield	1904
341	G. H. Hirst	Yorkshire v Leicestershire at Leicester	1905
340*	D. G. Bradman	NSW v Victoria at Sydney	1928-29
340	S. M. Gavaskar	Bombay v Bengal at Bombay	1981-82
338*	R. C. Blunt	Otago v Canterbury at Christchurch	1931-32
338	W. W. Read	Surrey v Oxford University at The Oval	1888
337*	Pervez Akhtar	Railways v Dera Ismail Khan at Lahore	1964-65
337†	Hanif Mohammad	Pakistan v West Indies at Bridgetown	1957-58
336*	W. R. Hammond	England v New Zealand at Auckland	1932-33
336	W. H. Ponsford	Victoria v South Australia at Melbourne	1927-28
334	D. G. Bradman	Australia v England at Leeds	1930
333	K. S. Duleepsinhji	Sussex v Northamptonshire at Hove	1930
332	W. H. Ashdown	Kent v Essex at Brentwood	1934
331*	J. D. Robertson	Middlesex v Worcestershire at Worcester	1949
325*	H. S. T. L. Hendry	Victoria v New Zealanders at Melbourne	1925-26
325	C. L. Badcock	South Australia v Victoria at Adelaide	1935-36
325	A. Sandham	England v West Indies at Kingston	1929-30
324	J. B. Stollmeyer	Trinidad v British Guiana at Port-of-Spain	1946-47
324	Waheed Mirza	Karachi Whites v Quetta at Karachi	1976-77
323	A. L. Wadekar	Bombay v Mysore at Bombay	1966-67
322	E. Paynter	Lancashire v Sussex at Hove	1937
321	W. L. Murdoch	NSW v Victoria at Sydney	1881-82
319	Gul Mahomed	Baroda v Holkar at Baroda	1946-47
318*	W. G. Grace	Gloucestershire v Yorkshire at Cheltenham	1876
317	W. R. Hammond	Gloucestershire v Nottinghamshire at Gloucester	1936
316*	V. S. Hazare	Maharashtra v Baroda at Poona	1939-40
316*	J. B. Hobbs	Surrey v Middlesex at Lord's	1926
316	R. H. Moore	Hampshire v Warwickshire at Bournemouth	1937
315*	T. W. Hayward	Surrey v Lancashire at The Oval	1898
315*	P. Holmes	Yorkshire v Middlesex at Lord's	1925
315*	A. F. Kippax	NSW v Queensland at Sydney	1927-28
314*	C. L. Walcott	Barbados v Trinidad at Port-of-Spain	1945-46
313	H. Sutcliffe	Yorkshire v Essex at Leyton	1932
312*	W. W. Keeton	Nottinghamshire v Middlesex at The Oval	1939
312*	J. M. Brearley	MCC Under 25 v North Zone at Peshawar	1966-67
311*	G. M. Turner	Worcestershire v Warwickshire at Worcester	1981-82
311	J. T. Brown	Yorkshire v Sussex at Sheffield	1897
311	R. B. Simpson	Australia v England at Manchester	1964
311	Javed Miandad	Karachi Whites v National Bank at Karachi	1974-75
310*	J. H. Edrich	England v New Zealand at Leeds	1965
310	H. Gimblett	Somerset v Sussex at Eastbourne	1948

309	V. S. Hazare	The Rest v Hindus at Bombay	1943-44
308*	F. M. M. Worrell	Barbados v Trinidad at Bridgetown	1943-44
307	M. C. Cowdrey	MCC v South Australia at Adelaide	1962-63
307	R. M. Cowper	Australia v England at Melbourne	1965-66
306*	A. Ducat	Surrey v Oxford University at The Oval	1919
306*	E. A. B. Rowan	Transvaal v Natal at Johannesburg	1939-40
305*	F. E. Woolley	MCC v Tasmania at Hobart	1911-12
305*	F. R. Foster	Warwickshire v Worcestershire at Dudley	1914
305*	W. H. Ashdown	Kent v Derbyshire at Dover	1935
304*	P. H. Tarilton	Barbados v Trinidad at Bridgetown	1919-20
304*	A. W. Nourse	Natal v Transvaal at Johannesburg	1919-20
304*	E. D. Weekes	West Indians v Cambridge University at Cambridge	1950
304	R. M. Poore	Hampshire v Somerset at Taunton	1899
304	D. G. Bradman	Australia v England at Leeds	1934
303*	W. W. Armstrong	Australians v Somerset at Bath	1905
303*	Mushtaq Mohammad	Karachi Blues v Karachi University at Karachi	1967-68
302*	P. Holmes	Yorkshire v Hampshire at Portsmouth	1920
302*	W. R. Hammond	Gloucestershire v Glamorgan at Bristol	1934
302	W. R. Hammond	Gloucestershire v Glamorgan at Newport	1939
302	L. G. Rowe	West Indies v England at Bridgetown	1973-74
301*	E. H. Hendren	Middlesex v Worcestershire at Dudley	1933
301	W. G. Grace	Gloucestershire v Sussex at Bristol	1896
300*	V. T. Trumper	Australians v Sussex at Hove	1899
300*	F. B. Watson	Lancashire v Surrey at Manchester	1928
300*	Imtiaz Ahmed	PM's XI v Commonwealth XI at Bombay	1950-51
300	J. T. Brown	Yorkshire v Derbyshire at Chesterfield	1898
300	D. C. S. Compton	MCC v N. E. Transvaal at Benoni	1948-49
300	R. Subba Row	Northamptonshire v Surrey at The Oval	1958

† *Hanif Mohammad batted for 16 hours 10 minutes – the longest innings in first-class cricket.*

HIGHEST INDIVIDUAL SCORES FOR TEAMS

For English Teams in Australia

307	M. C. Cowdrey	MCC v South Australia at Adelaide	1962-63
287	R. E. Foster	England v Australia at Sydney	1903-04

Against Australians in England

364	L. Hutton	England v Australia at The Oval	1938
219	A. Sandham	Surrey at The Oval (record for any county)	1934

For Australian Teams in England

345	C. G. Macartney	v Nottinghamshire at Nottingham	1921
334	D. G. Bradman	Australia v England at Leeds	1930

Against English Teams in Australia

307	R. M. Cowper	Australia v England at Melbourne	1965-66
280	A. J. Richardson	South Australia v MCC at Adelaide	1922-23

For Each First-Class County

Derbyshire	274	G. Davidson v Lancashire at Manchester	1896
Essex	343*	P. A. Perrin v Derbyshire at Chesterfield	1904
Glamorgan	287*	D. E. Davies v Gloucestershire at Newport	1939
Gloucestershire	318*	W. G. Grace v Yorkshire at Cheltenham	1876
Hampshire	316	R. H. Moore v Warwickshire at Bournemouth	1937
Kent	332	W. H. Ashdown v Essex at Brentwood	1934
Lancashire	424	A. C. MacLaren v Somerset at Taunton	1895
Leicestershire	252*	S. Coe v Northamptonshire at Leicester	1914
Middlesex	331*	J. D. Robertson v Worcestershire at Worcester	1949

Northamptonshire..	300	R. Subba Row v Surrey at The Oval	1958
Nottinghamshire..	312*	W. W. Keeton v Middlesex at The Oval†	1939
Somerset	310	H. Gimblett v Sussex at Eastbourne	1948
Surrey	357*	R. Abel v Somerset at The Oval	1899
Sussex	333	K. S. Duleepsinhji v Northamptonshire at Hove	1930
Warwickshire	305*	F. R. Foster v Worcestershire at Dudley	1914
Worcestershire	311*	G. M. Turner v Warwickshire at Worcester	1982
Yorkshire	341	G. H. Hirst v Leicestershire at Leicester	1905

† *On this date Eton played Harrow at Lord's*

HIGHEST IN A MINOR COUNTY MATCH

323*	F. E. Lacey	Hampshire v Norfolk at Southampton	1887

HIGHEST IN MINOR COUNTIES CHAMPIONSHIP

282	E. Garnett	Berkshire v Wiltshire at Reading	1908
254	H. E. Morgan	Glamorgan v Monmouthshire at Cardiff	1901
253*	G. J. Whittaker	Surrey II v Gloucestershire II at The Oval	1950
253	A. Booth	Lancashire II v Lincolnshire at Grimsby	1950
252	J. A. Deed	Kent II v Surrey II at The Oval (on début)	1924

HIGHEST FOR ENGLISH PUBLIC SCHOOL

278	J. L. Guise	Winchester v Eton at Eton	1921

HIGHEST IN OTHER MATCHES

628*	A. E. J. Collins, Clark's House v North Town at Clifton College. (A Junior House match. His innings of 6 hours 50 minutes was spread over four afternoons.)	1899
566	C. J. Eady, Break-o'-Day v Wellington at Hobart	1901-02
515	D. R. Havewalla, B.B. and C.I. Rly v St Xavier's at Bombay	1933-34
506*	J. C. Sharp, Melbourne GS v Geelong College at Melbourne	1914-15
502*	Chaman Lal, Mehandra Coll., Patiala v Government Coll., Rupar at Patiala	1956-57
485	A. E. Stoddart, Hampstead v Stoics at Hampstead	1886
475*	Mohammad Iqbal, Muslim Model HS v Islamia HS, Sialkot at Lahore	1958-59
466*	G. T. S. Stevens, Beta v Lambda (University College School House match) at Neasden	1919
459	J. A. Prout, Wesley College v Geelong College at Geelong	1908-09

HUNDRED ON DEBUT IN ENGLAND

(The following list does not include instances of players who have previously appeared in first-class cricket outside England.)

146*	D. G. Aslett	Kent v Hampshire at Bournemouth	1981
107*	G. Barker	Essex v Canadians at Clacton	†1954
116*	B. L. Bisgood	Somerset v Worcestershire at Worcester	1907
107*	H. O. Bloomfield	Surrey v Northamptonshire at Northampton	1921
124	G. J. Bryan	Kent v Nottinghamshire at Nottingham	†1920
100	J. F. Byrne	Warwickshire v Leicestershire at Birmingham	1897
118	A. P. F. Chapman	Cambridge University v Essex at Cambridge	1920
113	G. J. Chidgey	Free Foresters v Cambridge University at Cambridge	1962
100*	E. A. Clark	Middlesex v Cambridge University at Cambridge	1959
112	J. A. Claughton	Oxford University v Gloucestershire at Oxford	†1976

101*	S. H. Day	Kent v Gloucestershire at Cheltenham	†1897
	At the time, Day was a schoolboy at Malvern, aged 18		
108	E. W. Dillon	London County v Worcestershire at Crystal Palace.	1900
215*	G. H. G. Doggart	Cambridge University v Lancashire at Cambridge..	1948
137	C. H. M. Ebden	Cambridge U. v Leveson Gower's XI at Cambridge.	1902
108	A. Fairbairn	Middlesex v Somerset at Taunton	†‡1947
123	H. Gimblett	Somerset v Essex at Frome	1935
101	P. M. Hall	Oxford University v Free Foresters at Oxford	1919
101	R. P. Hammond-Chambers-Borgnis	Combined Services v New Zealanders at Portsmouth	1937
156	M. N. Harbottle	Army v Oxford University at Camberley	1938
110*	A. J. Harvey-Walker	Derbyshire v Oxford University at Burton-on-Trent	†1971
124	P. Hearn	Kent v Warwickshire at Gillingham	1947
101	K. A. Higgs	Sussex v Worcestershire at Hove	1920
103*	A. L. Hilder	Kent v Essex at Gravesend	†1924
139*	J. E. Hill	Warwickshire v Nottinghamshire at Nottingham	1894
158*	J. H. Human	Cambridge U. v Leveson Gower's XI at Eastbourne.	1932
146*	J. S. Johnson	Minor Counties v Indians at Wellington	1979
111*	C. F. H. Leslie	Oxford University v MCC and Ground at Oxford...	1881
100*	A. W. Lilley	Essex v Nottinghamshire at Nottingham	†1978
154	A. Lockett	Minor Counties v West Indians at Exeter	†1928
108	A. C. MacLaren	Lancashire v Sussex at Hove	1890
124	N. Miller	Surrey v Sussex at Hove	1899
116	M. D. Moxon	Yorkshire v Essex at Leeds	†1981
106*	W. Murray Wood	Oxford University v Gloucestershire at Oxford	1936
104	M. Nichol	Worcestershire v West Indians at Worcester	1928
101	A. H. C. Parnaby	Minor Counties v Oxford University at Oxford	1939
101	C. A. L. Payne	MCC and Ground v Derbyshire at Lord's	1905
138*	F. B. Pinch	Glamorgan v Worcestershire at Swansea	1921
124	H. C. Pretty	Surrey v Nottinghamshire at The Oval	1899
149	H. R. J. Rhys	Free Foresters v Cambridge University at Cambridge.	1929
195*	J. Ricketts	Lancashire v Surrey at The Oval	1867
137	J. G. C. Scott	Sussex v Oxford University at Eastbourne	1907
108	D. R. Shepherd	Gloucestershire v Oxford University at Oxford	1965
135	J. K. E. Slack	Cambridge University v Middlesex at Cambridge...	1954
114	F. W. Stocks	Nottinghamshire v Kent at Nottingham	1946
110	N. R. Taylor	Kent v Sri Lankans at Canterbury	1979
110	Hon. L. H. Tennyson	MCC and Ground v Oxford University at Lord's	†1913
125	G. S. Tuck	Royal Navy v New Zealanders at Portsmouth	1927
106	J. B. Turner	Minor Counties v Pakistanis at Jesmond	1974
100*	C. T. Tyson	Yorkshire v Hampshire at Southampton	1921
151	H. Venn	Warwickshire v Worcestershire at Birmingham	1919
102	I. D. Walker	Middlesex v Surrey Club at The Oval	1862
131*	R. Whitehead	Lancashire v Nottinghamshire at Manchester	1908
173	J. Whitehouse	Warwickshire v Oxford University at Oxford	1971
117*	E. R. Wilson	A. J. Webbe's XI v Cambridge University at Cambridge	1899
124	L. Winslow	Sussex v Gloucestershire at Hove	1875

† *In second innings.*

‡ *A. Fairbairn (Middlesex) in 1947 scored hundreds in the second innings of his first two matches in first-class cricket: 108 Middlesex v Somerset at Taunton, 110* Middlesex v Nottinghamshire at Nottingham.*

★ ★ ★ ★ ★

Notes: T. Marsden made 227 on début, playing for Sheffield and Leicester v Nottingham at Sheffield in 1826.

A number of players abroad have also made a hundred on a first appearance.

The highest innings on début was hit by W. F. E. Marx when he made 240 for Transvaal against Griqualand West at Johannesburg in 1920-21.

There are three instances of a cricketer making two separate hundreds on début: A. R. Morris, New South Wales, 148 and 111 against Queensland in 1940-41, N. J. Contractor, Gujarat, 152 and 102* against Baroda in 1952-53, and Aamer Malik, Lahore "A", 132* and 110* against Railways in 1979-80.

J. S. Solomon, British Guiana, scored a hundred in each of his first three innings in first-class cricket: 114* v Jamaica; 108 v Barbados in 1956-57; 121 v Pakistanis in 1957-58.

R. Watson-Smith, Border, scored 310 runs before he was dismissed in first-class cricket, including not-out centuries in his first two innings: 183* v Orange Free State and 125* v Griqualand West in 1969-70.

G. R. Viswanath and D. M. Wellham alone have scored 100 on both their début in first-class cricket and in Test cricket. Viswanath scored 230 for Mysore v Andhra in 1967-68 and 137 for India v Australia in 1969-70. Wellham scored 100 for New South Wales v Victoria in 1980-81 and 103 for Australia v England in 1981.

MOST INDIVIDUAL HUNDREDS

(35 or More)

	Hundreds Total	Hundreds Abroad	100th 100		Hundreds Total	Hundreds Abroad	100th 100
J. B. Hobbs	197	22	1923	T. W. Graveney	122	31	1964
E. H. Hendren	170	19	1928	D. G. Bradman	117	41†	1947
W. R. Hammond	167	33	1935	M. C. Cowdrey	107	27	1973
C. P. Mead	153	8	1927	A. Sandham	107	20	1935
H. Sutcliffe	149	14	1932	T. W. Hayward	104	4	1913
F. E. Woolley	145	10	1929	J. H. Edrich	103	13	1977
G. Boycott	132	27	1977	G. M. Turner	103	25	1982
L. Hutton	129	24	1951	L. E. G. Ames	102	13	1950
W. G. Grace	126	1	1895	E. Tyldesley	102	8	1934
D. C. S. Compton	123	31	1952				

† *Scored outside Australia.*

J. W. Hearne	96	C. H. Lloyd	70	A. I. Kallicharran	57
Zaheer Abbas	95	Majid J. Khan	70	L. B. Fishlock	56
C. B. Fry	94	D. Denton	69	C. A. Milton	56
W. J. Edrich	86	M. J. K. Smith	69	C. Hallows	55
G. S. Sobers	86	G. S. Chappell	68	Hanif Mohammad	55
J. T. Tyldesley	86	R. E. Marshall	68	A. Jones	55
P. B. H. May	85	R. N. Harvey	67	W. Watson	55
R. E. S. Wyatt	85	P. Holmes	67	D. J. Insole	54
J. Hardstaff, jun	83	J. D. Robertson	67	W. W. Keeton	54
R. B. Kanhai	83	P. A. Perrin	66	R. G. Pollock	54
D. L. Amiss	82	S. M. Gavaskar	65	W. Bardsley	53
M. Leyland	80	R. T. Simpson	64	A. E. Dipper	53
B. A. Richards	79	I. V. A. Richards	63	G. L. Jessop	53
K. F. Barrington	76	G. Gunn	62	James Seymour	53
J. G. Langridge	76	G. H. Hirst	60	E. H. Bowley	52
C. Washbrook	76	R. B. Simpson	60	D. B. Close	52
H. T. W. Hardinge	75	P. F. Warner	60	A. Ducat	52
R. Abel	74	I. M. Chappell	59	E. R. Dexter	51
D. Kenyon	74	A. L. Hassett	59	J. M. Parks	51
Mushtaq Mohammad	72	V. S. Hazare	59	W. W. Whysall	51
J. O'Connor	72	A. Shrewsbury	59	G. Cox, jun	50
Wm. Quaife	72	A. E. Fagg	58	H. E. Dollery	50
K. S. Ranjitsinhji	72	P. H. Parfitt	58	K. S. Duleepsinhji	50
D. Brookes	71	W. Rhodes	58	H. Gimblett	50
A. C. Russell	71	K. W. R. Fletcher	57	W. M. Lawry	50

F. B. Watson	50	B. Sutcliffe	44	P. J. Burge	38
C. G. Macartney	49	B. L. D'Oliveira	43	J. F. Crapp	38
M. J. Stewart	49	A. F. Kippax	43	R. C. Fredericks	38
K. G. Suttle	49	H. Makepeace	43	V. L. Manjrekar	38
P. R. Umrigar	49	V. M. Merchant	43	A. W. Nourse	38
W. M. Woodfull	49	E. J. Barlow	42	N. Oldfield	38
C. J. Barnett	48	J. H. Hampshire	42	Rev. J. H. Parsons	38
C. G. Greenidge	48	James Langridge	42	C. T. Radley	38
W. Gunn	48	H. W. Parks	42	W. W. Read	38
E. G. Hayes	48	T. F. Shepherd	42	J. Sharp	38
B. W. Luckhurst	48	V. T. Trumper	42	L. J. Todd	38
Javed Miandad	47	J. Gunn	41	J. Arnold	37
A. C. MacLaren	47	M. J. Harris	41	G. Brown	37
W. H. Ponsford	47	K. S. McEwan	41	G. M. Emmett	37
M. J. Procter	47	K. R. Miller	41	P. N. Kirsten	37
J. Iddon	46	A. D. Nourse	41	H. W. Lee	37
A. R. Morris	46	J. H. Parks	41	D. Lloyd	37
W. W. Armstrong	45	R. M. Prideaux	41	M. A. Noble	37
Asif Iqbal	45	G. Pullar	41	E. Oldroyd	37
L. G. Berry	45	W. E. Russell	41	H. S. Squires	37
J. M. Brearley	45	M. J. Smith	40	R. T. Virgin	37
A. W. Carr	45	G. R. Viswanath	40	C. J. B. Wood	37
B. F. Davison	45	C. L. Walcott	40	N. F. Armstrong	36
C. Hill	45	D. M. Young	40	W. Place	36
N. C. O'Neill	45	W. H. Ashdown	39	Shafiq Ahmed	36
E. Paynter	45	J. B. Bolus	39	A. L. Wadekar	36
Rev. D. S. Sheppard	45	W. A. Brown	39	E. D. Weekes	36
K. D. Walters	45	R. J. Gregory	39	Younis Ahmed	36
H. H. I. Gibbons	44	W. R. D. Payton	39	C. S. Dempster	35
A. Mitchell	44	J. R. Reid	39	D. R. Jardine	35
P. E. Richardson	44	F. M. M. Worrell	39	B. H. Valentine	35
Sadiq Mohammad	44	F. L. Bowley	38		

TWO SEPARATE HUNDREDS IN A MATCH

Seven times: W. R. Hammond, Zaheer Abbas.

Six times: J. B. Hobbs, G. M. Turner.

Five times: C. B. Fry.

Four times: D. G. Bradman, G. S. Chappell, J. H. Edrich, L. B. Fishlock, T. W. Graveney, H. T. W. Hardinge, E. H. Hendren, G. L. Jessop, P. A. Perrin, B. Sutcliffe, H. Sutcliffe.

Three times: L. E. G. Ames, I. M. Chappell, D. C. S. Compton, M. C. Cowdrey, D. Denton, K. S. Duleepsinhji, R. E. Foster, R. C. Fredericks, S. M. Gavaskar, W. G. Grace, G. Gunn, M. R. Hallam, Hanif Mohammad, M. J. Harris, T. W. Hayward, V. S. Hazare, L. Hutton, A. Jones, P. B. H. May, C. P. Mead, A. C. Russell, J. T. Tyldesley.

Twice: D. L. Amiss, B. J. T. Bosanquet, G. Boycott, C. C. R. Dacre, G. M. Emmett, A. E. Fagg, L. E. Favell, H. Gimblett, C. G. Greenidge, C. Hallows, R. A. Hamence, A. L. Hassett, G. A. Headley, D. W. Hookes, Javed Miandad, J. H. King, A. F. Kippax, J. G. Langridge, H. W. Lee, E. Lester, C. B. Llewellyn, C. G. Macartney, R. B. McCosker, C. A. Milton, A. R. Morris, P. H. Parfitt, Nawab of Pataudi jun., E. Paynter, C. Pinch, R. G. Pollock, R. M. Prideaux, W. Rhodes, B. A. Richards, Pankaj Roy, Sadiq Mohammad, James Seymour, R. B. Simpson, G. S. Sobers, E. Tyldesley, C. L. Walcott, W. W. Whysall.

Notes: W. Lambert scored 107 and 157 for Sussex v Epsom at Lord's in 1817 and it was not until W. G. Grace made 130 and 102* for South of the Thames v North of the Thames at Canterbury in 1868 that the feat was repeated.

T. W. Hayward (Surrey) set up a unique record in 1906 when in one week – six days – he hit four successive hundreds, 144 and 100 v Nottinghamshire at Nottingham and 143 and 125 v Leicestershire at Leicester.

D. W. Hookes (South Australia) scored four successive hundreds in eleven days at Adelaide in 1976-77: 185 and 105 v Queensland (tied match) and 135 and 156 v New South Wales.

A. E. Fagg alone has scored two double-hundreds in the same match: 244 and 202* for Kent v Essex at Colchester, 1938.

L. G. Rowe is alone in scoring hundreds in each innings on his first appearance in Test cricket: 214 and 100* for West Indies v New Zealand at Kingston in 1971-72.

Zaheer Abbas (Gloucestershire) set a unique record in 1976 by twice scoring a double hundred and a hundred in the same match without being dismissed: 216* and 156* v Surrey at The Oval and 230* and 104* v Kent at Canterbury. In 1977 he achieved this feat for a third time, scoring 205* and 108* v Sussex at Cheltenham, and in 1981 for a fourth time, scoring 215* and 150* v Somerset at Bath.

M. R. Hallam (Leicestershire), opening the batting each time, achieved the following treble: 210* and 157 v Glamorgan at Leicester, 1959; 203* and 143* v Sussex at Worthing, 1961; 107* and 149* v Worcestershire at Leicester, 1965. In the last two matches he was on the field the whole time, as was C. J. B. Wood when he scored 107* and 117* for Leicestershire against Yorkshire at Bradford, 1911.

W. L. Foster, 140 and 172*, and R. E. Foster, 134 and 101*, for Worcestershire v Hampshire at Worcester in July 1899, were the first brothers each to score two separate hundreds in the same first-class match.

The brothers I. M. Chappell, 145 and 121, and G. S. Chappell, 247* and 133, for Australia v New Zealand at Wellington in 1973-74, became the first players on the same side each to score a hundred in each innings of a Test match.

G. Gunn, 183, and G. V. Gunn, 100*, for Nottinghamshire v Warwickshire at Birmingham in 1931, provide the only instance of father and son each hitting a century in the same innings of a first-class match.

BATSMEN WHO HAVE SCORED 25,000 RUNS

	Career	*R*	*I*	*NO*	*HI*	*100s*	*Avge*
J. B. Hobbs	1905-34	61,237	1,315	106	316*	197	50.65
F. E. Woolley	1906-38	58,969	1,532	85	305*	145	40.75
E. H. Hendren	1907-38	57,611	1,300	166	301*	170	50.80
C. P. Mead	1905-36	55,061	1,340	185	280*	153	47.67
†W. G. Grace	1865-1908	54,896	1,493	105	344	126	39.55
W. R. Hammond	1920-51	50,551	1,005	104	336*	167	56.10
H. Sutcliffe	1919-45	50,138	1,088	123	313	149	51.95
T. W. Graveney	1948-72	47,793	1,223	159	258	122	44.91
T. W. Hayward	1893-1914	43,551	1,138	96	315*	104	41.79
M. C. Cowdrey	1950-76	42,719	1,130	134	307	107	42.89
G. Boycott	1962-82	42,269	885	134	261*	132	56.28
A. Sandham	1911-38	41,284	1,000	79	325	107	44.82
L. Hutton	1934-60	40,140	814	91	364	129	55.51
M. J. K. Smith	1951-75	39,832	1,091	139	204	69	41.84
W. Rhodes	1898-1930	39,802	1,528	237	267*	58	30.83
J. H. Edrich	1956-78	39,790	979	104	310*	103	45.47
R. E. S. Wyatt	1923-57	39,404	1,141	157	232	85	40.04
D. C. S. Compton	1936-64	38,942	839	88	300	123	51.85
E. Tyldesley	1909-36	38,874	961	106	256*	102	45.46
J. T. Tyldesley	1895-1923	37,897	994	62	295*	86	40.60
J. W. Hearne	1909-36	37,252	1,025	116	285*	96	40.98
L. E. G. Ames	1926-51	37,248	951	95	295	102	43.51
D. Kenyon	1946-67	37,002	1,159	59	259	74	33.63
W. J. Edrich	1934-58	36,965	964	92	267*	86	42.39
J. M. Parks	1949-76	36,673	1,227	172	205*	51	34.76
D. Denton	1894-1920	36,479	1,163	70	221	69	33.37
G. H. Hirst	1891-1929	36,323	1,215	151	341	60	34.13
Wm. Quaife	1894-1928	36,012	1,203	186	255*	72	35.38
R. E. Marshall	1945-72	35,725	1,053	59	228*	68	35.94

	Career	*R*	*I*	*NO*	*HI*	*100s*	*Avge*
G. Gunn	1902-32	35,208	1,061	82	220	62	35.96
D. L. Amiss	1960-82	35,158	911	98	262*	82	43.24
A. Jones	1957-82	34,990	1,131	70	204*	55	32.97
D. B. Close	1949-82	34,859	1,218	170	198	52	33.26
J. G. Langridge	1928-55	34,380	984	66	250*	76	37.45
G. M. Turner	1964-82	34,213	787	101	311*	103	49.87
C. Washbrook	1933-64	34,101	906	107	251*	76	42.67
M. Leyland	1920-48	33,659	932	101	263	80	40.50
H. T. W. Hardinge	1902-33	33,519	1,021	103	263*	75	36.51
R. Abel	1881-1904	33,124	1,007	73	357*	74	35.46
K. W. R. Fletcher	1962-82	32,880	989	143	228*	57	38.86
C. A. Milton	1948-74	32,150	1,078	125	170	56	33.73
J. D. Robertson	1937-59	31,914	897	46	331*	67	37.50
J. Hardstaff, jun.	1930-55	31,847	812	94	266	83	44.35
James Langridge	1924-53	31,716	1,058	157	167	42	35.20
K. F. Barrington	1953-68	31,714	831	136	256	76	45.63
Mushtaq Mohammad	1957-82	30,974	838	103	303*	72	42.14
C. B. Fry	1892-1921	30,886	658	43	258*	94	50.22
D. Brookes	1934-59	30,874	925	70	257	71	36.10
P. Holmes	1913-35	30,574	810	84	315*	67	42.11
R. T. Simpson	1944-63	30,546	852	55	259	64	38.32
L. G. Berry	1924-51	30,225	1,056	57	232	45	30.25
K. G. Suttle	1949-71	30,225	1,064	92	204*	49	31.09
Zaheer Abbas	1965-82	30,069	648	79	274*	95	52.84
P. A. Perrin	1896-1928	29,709	918	91	343*	66	35.92
P. F. Warner	1894-1929	29,028	875	75	244	60	36.28
J. O'Connor	1921-39	28,875	906	80	248	72	34.95
T. E. Bailey	1945-67	28,642	1,072	215	205	28	33.42
R. B. Kanhai	1955-77	28,639	663	82	256	83	49.29
E. H. Bowley	1912-34	28,378	859	47	283	52	34.94
G. S. Sobers	1953-74	28,315	609	93	365*	86	54.87
A. E. Dipper	1908-32	28,075	865	69	252*	53	35.27
D. G. Bradman	1927-49	28,067	338	43	452*	117	95.14
B. A. Richards	1964-82	27,768	559	57	356	79	55.31
P. B. H. May	1948-63	27,592	618	77	285*	85	51.00
A. C. Russell	1908-30	27,545	719	59	273	71	41.73
C. H. Lloyd	1963-82	27,334	643	85	242*	70	48.98
E. G. Hayes	1896-1926	27,318	896	48	276	48	32.21
A. E. Fagg	1932-57	27,291	803	46	269*	58	36.05
James Seymour	1900-26	27,238	911	62	218*	53	32.08
Majid J. Khan	1961-82	26,699	684	58	241	70	42.65
P. H. Parfitt	1956-74	26,924	845	104	200*	58	36.33
G. L. Jessop	1894-1914	26,698	855	37	286	53	32.63
J. H. Hampshire	1961-82	26,666	870	106	183*	42	34.90
D. E. Davies	1924-54	26,566	1,033	79	287*	32	27.84
M. J. Stewart	1954-72	26,492	898	93	227*	49	32.90
A. Shrewsbury	1875-1902	26,439	811	90	267	59	36.66
P. E. Richardson	1949-65	26,055	794	41	185	44	34.60
M. H. Denness	1959-80	25,886	838	65	195	33	33.48
H. Makepeace	1906-30	25,799	778	66	203	43	36.23
W. Gunn	1880-1904	25,791	850	72	273	48	33.15
W. Watson	1939-64	25,670	753	109	257	55	39.86
G. Brown	1908-33	25,649	1,012	52	232*	37	26.71
G. M. Emmett	1936-59	25,602	865	50	188	37	31.41
J. B. Bolus	1956-75	25,598	833	81	202*	39	34.03
W. E. Russell	1956-72	25,525	796	64	193	41	34.87
C. J. Barnett	1927-54	25,389	821	45	259	48	32.71
L. B. Fishlock	1931-52	25,376	699	54	253	56	39.34
D. J. Insole	1947-63	25,237	743	72	219*	54	37.61
J. Vine	1896-1922	25,171	920	79	202	34	29.92

	Career	R	I	NO	HI	100s	Avge
J. M. Brearley..........	1961-82	25,168	767	102	312*	45	37.84
R. M. Prideaux........	1958-75	25,136	808	75	202*	41	34.29
J. H. King...............	1895-1926	25,122	988	69	227*	34	27.34

†*In recent years some statisticians have removed from W. G. Grace's record a number of matches which they consider not to have been first-class. The above figures are those which became universally accepted upon appearance in W. G. Grace's obituary in the* Wisden *of 1916. Some works of reference give his career record as being 54,211–1,478–104–344–124–39.45. These figures also appeared in the 1981 edition of* Wisden.

Note: K. S. Ranjitsinhji (1893-1920) had career figures of 24,692–500–62–285*–72–56.37.

1,000 RUNS IN A SEASON

(Includes Overseas Tours and Seasons)

28 times: W. G. Grace 2,000 (6); F. E. Woolley 3,000 (1), 2,000 (12).

27 times: M. C. Cowdrey 2,000 (2); C. P. Mead 3,000 (2), 2,000 (9).

26 times: J. B. Hobbs 3,000 (1), 2,000 (16).

25 times: E. H. Hendren 3,000 (3), 2,000 (12).

24 times: Wm. Quaife 2,000 (1); H. Sutcliffe 3,000 (3), 2,000 (12).

23 times: G. Boycott 2,000 (3).

22 times: T. W. Graveney 2,000 (7); W. R. Hammond 3,000 (3), 2,000 (9), A. Jones.

21 times: D. Denton 2,000 (5); J. H. Edrich 2,000 (6); W. Rhodes 2,000 (2).

20 times: D. B. Close; G. Gunn; T. W. Hayward 3,000 (2), 2,000 (8); James Langridge 2,000 (1); J. M. Parks 2,000 (3); A. Sandham 2,000 (8); M. J. K. Smith 3,000 (1), 2,000 (5); C. Washbrook 2,000 (2).

19 times: D. L. Amiss 2,000 (2); J. W. Hearne 2,000 (4); G. H. Hirst 2,000 (3); D. Kenyon 2,000 (7); E. Tyldesley 3,000 (1), 2,000 (5); J. T. Tyldesley 3,000 (1), 2,000 (4).

18 times: L. G. Berry 2,000 (1); K. W. R. Fletcher; H. T. W. Hardinge 2,000 (5); R. E. Marshall 2,000 (6); P. A. Perrin; G. M. Turner 2,000 (3); R. E. S. Wyatt 2,000 (5).

17 times: L. E. G. Ames 3,000 (1), 2,000 (5); T. E. Bailey 2,000 (1); D. Brookes 2,000 (6); D. C. S. Compton 3,000 (1), 2,000 (5); L. Hutton 3,000 (1), 2,000 (8); J. G. Langridge 2,000 (11); M. Leyland 2,000 (3); K. G. Suttle 2,000 (1).

16 times: D. G. Bradman 2,000 (4); D. E. Davies 2,000 (1); E. G. Hayes 2,000 (2); C. A. Milton 2,000 (1); J. O'Connor 2,000 (4); James Seymour 2,000 (1); Zaheer Abbas 2,000 (2).

15 times: G. Barker; K. F. Barrington 2,000 (3); E. H. Bowley 2,000 (4); M. H. Denness; A. E. Dipper 2,000 (5); H. E. Dollery 2,000 (2); W. J. Edrich 3,000 (1), 2,000 (8); J. H. Hampshire; P. Holmes 2,000 (7); Mushtaq Mohammad; R. B. Nicholls 2,000 (1); P. H. Parfitt 2,000 (3); W. G. A. Parkhouse 2,000 (1); B. A. Richards 2,000 (1); J. D. Robertson 2,000 (9); G. S. Sobers; M. J. Stewart 2,000 (1).

Notes: F. E. Woolley reached 1,000 runs in 28 consecutive seasons (1907-1938). C. P. Mead did so 27 seasons in succession (1906-1936).

Outside England, 1,000 runs in a season has been reached most times by D. G. Bradman (in 12 seasons in Australia).

Three batsmen have scored 1,000 runs in a season in each of four different countries: G. S. Sobers in West Indies, England, India and Australia; M. C. Cowdrey and G. Boycott in England, South Africa, West Indies and Australia.

FOUR HUNDREDS OR MORE IN SUCCESSION

Six in succession: C. B. Fry 1901; D. G. Bradman 1938-39; M. J. Procter 1970-71.
Five in succession: E. D. Weekes 1955-56.

Four in succession: D. G. Bradman 1931-32, 1948-49; D. C. S. Compton 1946-47; N. J. Contractor 1957-58; K. S. Duleepsinhji 1931; C. B. Fry 1911; W. R. Hammond 1936-37, 1945-46; H. T. W. Hardinge 1913; T. W. Hayward 1906; J. B. Hobbs 1920, 1925; D. W. Hookes 1976-77; P. N. Kirsten 1976-77; J. G. Langridge 1949; C. G. Macartney 1921; K. S. McEwan 1977; P. B. H. May 1956-57; V. M. Merchant 1941-42; A. Mitchell 1933; Nawab of Pataudi sen. 1931; L. G. Rowe 1971-72; P. Roy 1962-63; Sadiq Mohammad 1976; Saeed Ahmed 1961-62; H. Sutcliffe 1931, 1939; E. Tyldesley 1926; W. W. Whysall 1930; F. E. Woolley 1929; Zaheer Abbas 1970-71.

MOST HUNDREDS IN A SEASON

Eighteen: D. C. S. Compton in 1947. These included six hundreds against the South Africans in which matches his average was 84.78. His aggregate for the season was 3,816, also a record.

Sixteen: J. B. Hobbs in 1925, when aged 42, played 16 three-figure innings in first-class matches. It was during this season that he exceeded the number of hundreds obtained in first-class cricket by W. G. Grace.

Fifteen: W. R. Hammond in 1938.

Fourteen: H. Sutcliffe in 1932.

Thirteen: G. Boycott in 1971, D. G. Bradman in 1938, C. B. Fry in 1901, W. R. Hammond in 1933 and 1937, T. W. Hayward in 1906, E. H. Hendren in 1923, 1927 and 1928, C. P. Mead in 1928, and H. Sutcliffe in 1928 and 1931.

FAST FIFTIES

Minutes			
8†	C. C. Inman (57)	Leicestershire v Nottinghamshire at Nottingham	1965
11	C. I. J. Smith (66)	Middlesex v Gloucestershire at Bristol	1938
14	S. J. Pegler (50)	South Africans v Tasmania at Launceston	1910-11
14	F. T. Mann (53)	Middlesex v Nottinghamshire at Lord's	1921
14	H. B. Cameron (56)	Transvaal v Orange Free State at Johannesburg	1934-35
14	C. I. J. Smith (52)	Middlesex v Kent at Maidstone	1935

† *Full tosses were bowled to expedite a declaration.*

FAST HUNDREDS

Minutes			
35	P. G. H. Fender (113*)	Surrey v Northamptonshire at Northampton	1920
37	C. M. Old (107)	Yorkshire v Warwickshire at Birmingham	1977
40	G. L. Jessop (101)	Gloucestershire v Yorkshire at Harrogate	1897
42	G. L. Jessop (191)	Gentlemen of South v Players of South at Hastings	1907
43	A. H. Hornby (106)	Lancashire v Somerset at Manchester	1905
44	R. N. S. Hobbs (100)	Essex v Australians at Chelmsford	1975

Note: The fastest known hundred in terms of balls received is off 45 balls by R. N. S. Hobbs (above) and by B. L. Cairns for Otago v Wellington at Lower Hutt, 1979-80, his time being 52 minutes. P. G. H. Fender is calculated to have made his hundred off not fewer than 40 balls and not more than 46.

FAST DOUBLE-HUNDREDS

Minutes			
120	G. L. Jessop (286)	Gloucestershire v Sussex at Hove	1903
120	C. H. Lloyd (201*)	West Indians v Glamorgan at Swansea	1976
130	G. L. Jessop (234)	Gloucestershire v Somerset at Bristol	1905
131	V. T. Trumper (293)	Australians v Canterbury at Christchurch	1913-14

FAST TRIPLE-HUNDREDS

Minutes			
181	D. C. S. Compton (300)	MCC v N. E. Transvaal at Benoni	1948-49
205	F. E. Woolley (305*)	MCC v Tasmania at Hobart	1911-12
205	C. G. Macartney (345)	Australians v Nottinghamshire at Nottingham	1921
213	D. G. Bradman (369)	South Australia v Tasmania at Adelaide	1935-36

FAST SCORING

P. G. H. Fender, for Surrey v Northamptonshire at Northampton in 1920, scored 113* out of 171 in forty-two minutes. He reached 50 in nineteen minutes and 100 in thirty-five minutes. Fender and H. A. Peach added 171 (unfinished) in forty-two minutes for the sixth wicket.

C. I. J. Smith, in June 1938, made 69 in twenty minutes for Middlesex against Sussex at Lord's, and ten days later against Gloucestershire at Bristol he scored 66 in eighteen minutes – the first 50 coming in eleven minutes.

E. B. Alletson, for Nottinghamshire v Sussex at Hove in 1911, scored 189 out of 227 runs obtained while at the wicket in ninety minutes. He went from 50 to 189 in thirty minutes.

For Auckland v Otago at Dunedin in 1936-37, P. E. Whitelaw and W. N. Carson added 445 runs for the third wicket in 268 minutes – a world record.

Worcestershire, set to make 131 in forty minutes against Nottinghamshire at Worcester in 1951, hit off the runs in thirty-five minutes for the loss of D. Kenyon's wicket. The other batsmen were G. Dews and R. O. Jenkins.

Kent scored 219 in seventy-one minutes when beating Gloucestershire at Dover, 1937. They averaged 9 runs an over.

H. Sutcliffe (194) and M. Leyland (45) hit 102 off six consecutive overs for Yorkshire v Essex at Scarborough, 1932.

J. B. Hobbs (47) and J. N. Crawford (48) made 96 without loss in thirty-two minutes at The Oval, 1919, after Kent left Surrey to get 95 in forty-two minutes.

RECORD HIT

The Rev. W. Fellows, while at practice on the Christ Church ground at Oxford in 1856, drove a ball bowled by Charles Rogers 175 yards from hit to pitch.

MOST PERSONAL SIXES IN AN INNINGS

15	J. R. Reid (296)	Wellington v N. Districts at Wellington	1962-63
13	Majid J. Khan (147*)	Pakistanis v Glamorgan at Swansea	1967
13	C. G. Greenidge (273*)	D. H. Robins' XI v Pakistanis at Eastbourne	1974
13	C. G. Greenidge (259)	Hampshire v Sussex at Southampton	1975

12	Gulfraz Khan (207)	Railways v Universities at Lahore	1976-77
11	C. K. Nayudu (153)	Hindus v MCC at Bombay	1926-27
11	C. J. Barnett (194)	Gloucestershire v Somerset at Bath	1934
11	R. Benaud (135)	Australians v T. N. Pearce's XI at Scarborough	1953

Note: W. J. Stewart (Warwickshire) hit seventeen 6s in the match v Lancashire, at Blackpool, 1959; ten in his first innings of 155 and seven in his second innings of 125.

MOST PERSONAL BOUNDARIES IN AN INNINGS

68	P. A. Perrin (343*)	Essex v Derbyshire at Chesterfield	1904
65	A. C. MacLaren (424)	Lancashire v Somerset at Taunton	1895
64	Hanif Mohammad (499)	Karachi v Bahawalpur at Karachi	1958-59
57	J. H. Edrich (310*)	England v New Zealand at Leeds	1965
55	C. W. Gregory (383)	NSW v Queensland at Brisbane	1906-07
54	G. H. Hirst (341)	Yorkshire v Leicestershire at Leicester	1905
53	A. W. Nourse (304*)	Natal v Transvaal at Johannesburg	1919-20
51	W. G. Grace (344)	MCC v Kent at Canterbury	1876
51	C. G. Macartney (345)	Australians v Nottinghamshire at Nottingham	1921
50	D. G. Bradman (369)	South Australia v Tasmania at Adelaide	1935-36
50	A. Ducat (306*)	Surrey v Oxford University at The Oval	1919
50	B. B. Nimbalkar (443*)	Maharashtra v Kathiawar at Poona	1948-49
50	J. R. Reid (296)	Wellington v N. Districts at Wellington	1962-63

Note: Boundaries include sixes.

MOST RUNS SCORED OFF ONE OVER

(All instances refer to six-ball overs)

36	G. S. Sobers	off M. A. Nash, Nottinghamshire v Glamorgan at Swansea (six 6s)	1968
34	F. C. Hayes	off M. A. Nash, Lancashire v Glamorgan at Swansea (646666)	1977
34	E. B. Alletson	off E. H. Killick, Nottinghamshire v Sussex at Hove (46604446; including two no-balls)	1911
32	C. C. Inman	off N. W. Hill, Leicestershire v Nottinghamshire at Nottingham (466664; full tosses were provided for him to hit)	1965
32	C. C. Smart	off G. Hill, Glamorgan v Hampshire at Cardiff (664664)	1935
32	I. R. Redpath	off N. Rosendorff, Australians v Orange Free State at Bloemfontein (666644)	1969-70
32	P. W. G. Parker	off A. I. Kallicharran, Sussex v Warwickshire at Birmingham (466664)	1982
31	A. W. Wellard	off F. E. Woolley, Somerset v Kent at Wells (666661)	1938
31	M. H. Bowditch (1) and M. J. Procter (30)	off A. A. Mallett, Western Province v Australians at Cape Town (Procter hit five 6s)	1969-70
30	D. G. Bradman	off A. P. Freeman, Australians v England XI at Folkestone (466464)	1934
30	H. B. Cameron	off H. Verity, South Africans v Yorkshire at Sheffield (444666)	1935
30	D. T. Lindsay	off W. T. Greensmith, South African Fezela XI v Essex at Chelmsford (066666 to win the match)	1961
30	Majid J. Khan	off R. C. Davis, Pakistanis v Glamorgan at Swansea (606666)	1967
30	A. W. Wellard	off T. R. Armstrong, Somerset v Derbyshire at Wells (066666)	1936

30	D. Wilson	off R. N. S. Hobbs, Yorkshire v MCC at Scarborough (466266)	1966
30	P. L. Winslow	off J. T. Ikin, South Africans v Lancashire at Manchester (446646)	1955
30	Zaheer Abbas	off D. Breakwell, Gloucestershire v Somerset at Taunton (466626)	1979

Note: The greatest number of runs scored off an eight-ball over is 34 (40446664) by R. M. Edwards off M. C. Carew, Governor-General's XI v West Indians at Auckland, 1968-69.

300 RUNS IN ONE DAY

345	C. G. Macartney	Australians v Nottinghamshire at Nottingham	1921
334	W. H. Ponsford	Victoria v New South Wales at Melbourne	1926-27
333	K. S. Duleepsinhji	Sussex v Northamptonshire at Hove	1930
331*	J. D. Robertson	Middlesex v Worcestershire at Worcester	1949
325*	B. A. Richards	S. Australia v W. Australia at Perth	1970-71
322†	E. Paynter	Lancashire v Sussex at Hove	1937
318	C. W. Gregory	New South Wales v Queensland at Brisbane	1906-07
316†	R. H. Moore	Hampshire v Warwickshire at Bournemouth	1937
315*	R. C. Blunt	Otago v Canterbury at Christchurch	1931-32
312*	J. M. Brearley	MCC Under 25 v North Zone at Peshawar	1966-67
311*	G. M. Turner	Worcestershire v Warwickshire at Worcester	1981-82
309*	D. G. Bradman	Australia v England at Leeds	1930
307*	W. H. Ashdown	Kent v Essex at Brentwood	1934
306*	A. Ducat	Surrey v Oxford University at The Oval	1919
305*	F. R. Foster	Warwickshire v Worcestershire at Dudley	1914

† *E. Paynter's 322 and R. H. Moore's 316 were scored on the same day: July 28, 1937.*

HIGHEST PARTNERSHIPS

577	V. S. Hazare (288) and Gul Mahomed (319), fourth wicket, Baroda v Holkar at Baroda	1946-47
574*	F. M. M. Worrell (255*) and C. L. Walcott (314*), fourth wicket, Barbados v Trinidad at Port-of-Spain	1945-46
561	Waheed Mirza (324) and Mansoor Akhtar (224*), first wicket, Karachi Whites v Quetta at Karachi	1976-77
555	P. Holmes (224*) and H. Sutcliffe (313), first wicket, Yorkshire v Essex at Leyton	1932
554	J. T. Brown (300) and J. Tunnicliffe (243), first wicket, Yorkshire v Derbyshire at Chesterfield	1898
502*	F. M. M. Worrell (308*) and J. D. C. Goddard (218*), fourth wicket, Barbados v Trinidad at Bridgetown	1943-44
490	E. H. Bowley (283) and J. G. Langridge (195), first wicket, Sussex v Middlesex at Hove	1933
487*	G. A. Headley (344*) and C. C. Passailaigue (261*), sixth wicket, Jamaica v Lord Tennyson's XI at Kingston	1931-32
470	A. I. Kallicharran (230*) and G. W. Humpage (254), fourth wicket, Warwickshire v Lancashire at Southport	1982
465*	J. A. Jameson (240*) and R. B. Kanhai (213*), second wicket, Warwickshire v Gloucestershire at Birmingham	1974
456	W. H. Ponsford (248) and E. R. Mayne (209), first wicket, Victoria v Queensland at Melbourne	1923-24
456	Khalid Irtiza (290) and Aslam Ali (236), third wicket, United Bank v Multan at Karachi	1975-76
455	B. B. Nimbalkar (443*) and K. V. Bhandarkar (205), second wicket, Maharashtra v Kathiawar at Poona	1948-49
451	D. G. Bradman (244) and W. H. Ponsford (266), second wicket, Australia v England, Fifth Test, at The Oval	1934
451*	S. Desai (218*) and R. M. H. Binny (211*), first wicket, Karnataka v Kerala at Chikmagalur	1977-78

PARTNERSHIPS FOR FIRST WICKET

561	Waheed Mirza and Mansoor Akhtar, Karachi Whites v Quetta at Karachi.	1976-77
555	P. Holmes and H. Sutcliffe, Yorkshire v Essex at Leyton	1932
554	J. T. Brown and J. Tunnicliffe, Yorkshire v Derbyshire at Chesterfield	1898
490	E. H. Bowley and J. G. Langridge, Sussex v Middlesex at Hove	1933
456	E. R. Mayne and W. H. Ponsford, Victoria v Queensland at Melbourne	1923-24
451*	S. Desai and R. M. H. Binney, Karnataka v Kerala at Chikmagalur	1977-78
428	J. B Hobbs and A. Sandham, Surrey v Oxford University at The Oval	1926
424	J. F. W. Nicholson and I. J. Siedle, Natal v Orange Free State at Bloemfontein	1926-27
418	Kamal Najamuddin and Khalid Alvi, Karachi v Railways at Karachi	1980-81
413	V. Mankad and P. Roy, India v New Zealand at Madras (world Test record)	1955-56
405	C. P. S. Chauhan and M. S. Gupte, Maharashtra v Vidarbha at Poona	1972-73
395	D. M. Young and R. B. Nicholls, Gloucestershire v Oxford University at Oxford	1962
391	A. O. Jones and A. Shrewsbury, Nottinghamshire v Gloucestershire at Bristol.	1899
390	G. L. Wight and G. L. R. Gibbs, B. Guiana v Barbados at Georgetown	1951-52
390	B. Dudleston and J. F. Steele, Leicestershire v Derbyshire at Leicester	1979
389	Majid J. Khan and Shafiq Ahmed, Punjab A v Sind A at Karachi	1974-75
387	G. M. Turner and T. W. Jarvis, New Zealand v West Indies at Georgetown.	1971-72
382	R. B. Simpson and W. M. Lawry, Australia v West Indies at Bridgetown	1964-65
380	H. Whitehead and C. J. B. Wood, Leicestershire v Worcestershire at Worcester	1906
379	R. Abel and W. Brockwell, Surrey v Hampshire at The Oval	1897
378	J. T. Brown and J. Tunnicliffe, Yorkshire v Sussex at Sheffield	1897
377*	N. F. Horner and Khalid Ibadulla, Warwickshire v Surrey at The Oval	1960
375	W. H. Ponsford and W. M. Woodfull, Victoria v New South Wales at Melbourne	1926-27
373	B. Sutcliffe and L. Watt, Otago v Auckland at Auckland	1950-51
368	A. C. MacLaren and R. H. Spooner, Lancashire v Gloucestershire at Liverpool	1903
368	E. H. Bowley and J. H. Parks, Sussex v Gloucestershire at Hove	1929
367*	G. D. Barlow and W. N. Slack, Middlesex v Kent at Lord's	1981
364	R. Abel and D. L. A. Jephson, Surrey v Derbyshire at The Oval	1900
361	N. Oldfield and V. Broderick, Northamptonshire v Scotland at Peterborough.	1953
359	L. Hutton and C. Washbrook, England v South Africa at Johannesburg	1948-49
355	A. F. Rae and J. B. Stollmeyer, West Indians v Sussex at Hove	1950
352	T. W. Hayward and J. B. Hobbs, Surrey v Warwickshire at The Oval	1909
350*	C. Washbrook and W. Place, Lancashire v Sussex at Manchester	1947

FIRST-WICKET HUNDREDS IN BOTH INNINGS

B. Sutcliffe and D. D. Taylor, for Auckland v Canterbury in 1948-49, scored for the first wicket 220 in the first innings and 286 in the second innings. This is the only instance of two double-century opening stands in the same match.

T. W. Hayward and J. B. Hobbs in 1907 accomplished a performance without parallel by scoring over 100 together for Surrey's first wicket four times in one week: 106 and 125 v Cambridge University at The Oval, and 147 and 105 v Middlesex at Lord's.

L. Hutton and C. Washbrook, in three consecutive Test match innings which they opened together for England v Australia in 1946-47, made 138 in the second innings at Melbourne, and 137 and 100 at Adelaide. They also opened with 168 and 129 at Leeds in 1948.

J. B. Hobbs and H. Sutcliffe, in three consecutive Test match innings which they opened together for England v Australia in 1924-25, made 157 and 110 at Sydney and 283 at Melbourne. On 26 occasions – 15 times in Test matches – Hobbs and Sutcliffe took part in a three-figure first-wicket partnership. Seven of these stands exceeded 200.

G. Boycott and J. H. Edrich, in three consecutive Test match innings which they opened together for England v Australia in 1970-71, made 161* in the second innings at Melbourne, and 107 and 103 at Adelaide.

In 1971 R. G. A. Headley and P. J. Stimpson of Worcestershire shared in first-wicket hundred partnerships on each of the first four occasions they opened the innings together: 125 and 147 v Northamptonshire at Worcester, 102 and 128* v Warwickshire at Birmingham.

J. B. Hobbs during his career, which extended from 1905 to 1934, helped to make 100 or more for the first wicket in first-class cricket 166 times – 15 of them in 1926, when in consecutive innings he helped to make 428, 182, 106 and 123 before a wicket fell. As many as 117 of the 166 stands were made for Surrey. In all first-class matches Hobbs and A. Sandham shared 66 first-wicket partnerships of 100 or more runs.

P. Holmes and H. Sutcliffe made 100 or more runs for the first wicket of Yorkshire on 69 occasions; J. B. Hobbs and A. Sandham for Surrey on 63 occasions; W. W. Keeton and C. B. Harris of Nottinghamshire on 46; T. W. Hayward and J. B. Hobbs of Surrey on 40; G. Gunn and W. W. Whysall of Nottinghamshire on 40; J. D. Robertson and S. M. Brown of Middlesex on 34; C. B. Fry and J. Vine of Sussex on 33; R. E. Marshall and J. R. Gray of Hampshire on 33; D. E. Davies and A. H. Dyson of Glamorgan on 32; and G. Boycott and R. G. Lumb of Yorkshire on 26.

J. Douglas and A. E. Stoddart in 1896 scored over 150 runs for the Middlesex first wicket three times within a fortnight. In 1901, J. Iremonger and A. O. Jones obtained over 100 for the Nottinghamshire first wicket four times within eight days, scoring 134 and 144* v Surrey at The Oval, 238 v Essex at Leyton, and 119 v Derbyshire at Welbeck.

J. W. Lee and F. S. Lee, brothers, for Somerset in 1934, scored over 100 runs thrice in succession in the County Championship.

W. G. Grace and A. E. Stoddart, in three consecutive innings against the Australians in 1893, made over 100 runs for each opening partnership.

C. Hallows and F. B. Watson, in consecutive innings for Lancashire in 1928, opened with 200, 202, 107, 118; reached three figures twelve times, 200 four times.

H. Sutcliffe, in the period 1919-1939 inclusive, shared in 145 first-wicket partnerships of 100 runs or more.

There were four first-wicket hundred partnerships in the match between Somerset and Cambridge University at Taunton in 1960. G. Atkinson and R. T. Virgin scored 172 and 112 for Somerset and R. M. Prideaux and A. R. Lewis 198 and 137 for Cambridge University.

PARTNERSHIP RECORDS FOR ALL COUNTRIES

Best First-Wicket Stands

Pakistan	561	Waheed Mirza (324) and Mansoor Akhtar (224*), Karachi Whites v Quetta at Karachi	1976-77
English	555	P. Holmes (224*) and H. Sutcliffe (313), Yorkshire v Essex at Leyton	1932
Australian	456	W. H. Ponsford (248) and E. R. Mayne (209), Victoria v Queensland at Melbourne	1923-24
Indian	451*	S. Desai (218*) and R. M. H. Binny (211*), Karnataka v Kerala at Chikmagalur	1977-78
South African	424	J. F. W. Nicolson (252*) and I. J. Siedle (174), Natal v Orange Free State at Bloemfontein	1926-27
West Indian	390	G. L. Wight (262*) and G. L. R. Gibbs (216), British Guiana v Barbados at Georgetown	1951-52
New Zealand	387	G. M. Turner (259) and T. W. Jarvis (182), New Zealand v West Indies at Georgetown	1971-72

Best Second-Wicket Stands

English	465*	J. A. Jameson (240*) and R. B. Kanhai (213*), Warwickshire v Gloucestershire at Birmingham	1974
Indian	455	B. B. Nimbalkar (443*) and K. V. Bhandarkar (205), Maharashtra v Kathiawar at Poona	1948-49

Australian	451	W. H. Ponsford (266) and D. G. Bradman (244), Australia v England at The Oval	1934
West Indian	446	C. C. Hunte (260) and G. S. Sobers (365*), West Indies v Pakistan at Kingston	1957-58
Pakistan	426	Arshad Pervez (220) and Mohsin Khan (220), Habib Bank v Income Tax Dept at Lahore	1977-78
South African	305	S. K. Coen (165) and J. M. M Commaille (186), Orange Free State v Natal at Bloemfontein	1926-27
New Zealand	301	C. S. Dempster (180) and C. F. W. Allcott (131), New Zealanders v Warwickshire at Birmingham	1927

Best Third-Wicket Stands

Pakistan	456	Khalid Irtiza (290) and Aslam Ali (236), United Bank v Multan at Karachi	1975-76
New Zealand	445	P. E. Whitelaw (195) and W. N. Carson (290), Auckland v Otago at Dunedin	1936-37
West Indian	434	J. B. Stollmeyer (324) and G. E. Gomez (190), Trinidad v British Guiana at Port-of-Spain	1946-47
English	424*	W. J. Edrich (168*) and D. C. S. Compton (252*), Middlesex v Somerset at Lord's	1948
Indian	410†	L. Amarnath (262) and R. S. Modi (156), India in England v The Rest at Calcutta	1946-47
Australian	390*	J. M. Wiener (221*) and J. K. Moss (200*), Victoria v Western Australia at Melbourne	1981-82
South African	341	E. J. Barlow (201) and R. G. Pollock (175), South Africa v Australia at Adelaide	1963-64

† *415 runs were added for this wicket for India v England at Madras in 1981-82 in two separate partnerships. See Highest Test Wicket Partnerships for details.*

Best Fourth-Wicket Stands

Indian	577	V. S. Hazare (288) and Gul Mahomed (319), Baroda v Holkar at Baroda	1946-47
West Indian	574*	C. L. Walcott (314*) and F. M. M. Worrell (255*), Barbados v Trinidad at Port-of-Spain	1945-46
English	470	A. I. Kallicharran (230*) and G. W. Humpage (254), Warwickshire v Lancashire at Southport	1982
Australian	424	I. S. Lee (258) and S. O. Quin (210), Victoria v Tasmania at Melbourne	1933-34
Pakistan	350	Mushtaq Mohammad (201) and Asif Iqbal (175), Pakistan v New Zealand at Dunedin	1972-73
South African	342	E. A. B. Rowan (196) and P. J. M. Gibb (203), Transvaal v N. E. Transvaal at Johannesburg	1952-53
New Zealand	324	J. R. Reid (188*) and W. M. Wallace (197), New Zealanders v Cambridge University at Cambridge	1949

Best Fifth-Wicket Stands

Australian	405	S. G. Barnes (234) and D. G. Bradman (234), Australia v England at Sydney	1946-47
English	393	E. G. Arnold (200*) and W. B. Burns (196), Worcestershire v Warwickshire at Birmingham	1909
Indian	360	Uday Merchant (217) and M. N. Raiji (170), Bombay v Hyderabad at Bombay	1947-48
Pakistan	355	Altaf Shah (276) and Tariq Bashir (196), House Building Finance Corporation v Multan at Multan	1976-77
South African	338	R. G. Pollock (194) and A. L. Wilmot (152), Eastern Province v Natal at Port Elizabeth	1975-76

West Indian	335	B. F. Butcher (151) and C. H. Lloyd (201*), West Indians v Glamorgan at Swansea	1969
New Zealand	266	B. Sutcliffe (355) and W. S. Haig (67), Otago v Auckland at Dunedin	1949-50

Best Sixth-Wicket Stands

West Indian	487*	G. A. Headley (344*) and C. C. Passailaigue (261*), Jamaica v Lord Tennyson's XI at Kingston	1931-32
Australian	428	M. A. Noble (284) and W. W. Armstrong (172*), Australians v Sussex at Hove	1902
English	411	R. M. Poore (304) and E. G. Wynyard (225), Hampshire v Somerset at Taunton	1899
Indian	371	V. M. Merchant (359*) and R. S. Modi (168), Bombay v Maharashtra at Bombay	1943-44
Pakistan	353	Salah-ud-Din (256) and Zaheer Abbas (197), Karachi v East Pakistan at Karachi	1968-69
South African	244*	J. M. M. Commaille (132*) and A. W. Palm (106*), Western Province v Griqualand West at Johannesburg	1923-24
New Zealand	220	G. M. Turner (223*) and K. J. Wadsworth (78), New Zealand v West Indies at Kingston	1971-72

Best Seventh-Wicket Stands

West Indian	347	D. St E. Atkinson (219) and C. C. Depeiza (122), West Indies v Australia at Bridgetown	1954-55
English	344	K. S. Ranjitsinhji (230) and W. Newham (153), Sussex v Essex at Leyton	1902
Australian	335	C. W. Andrews (253) and E. C. Bensted (155), Queensland v New South Wales at Sydney	1934-35
Pakistan	308	Waqar Hassan (189) and Imtiaz Ahmed (209), Pakistan v New Zealand at Lahore	1955-56
South African	299	B. Mitchell (159) and A. Melville (153), Transvaal v Griqualand West at Kimberley	1946-47
Indian	274	K. C. Ibrahim (250) and K. M. Rangnekar (138), Bijapur XI v Bengal XI at Bombay	1942-43
New Zealand	265	J. L. Powell (164) and N. Dorreen (105*), Canterbury v Otago at Christchurch	1929-30

Best Eighth-Wicket Stands

Australian	433	A. Sims (184*) and V. T. Trumper (293), An Australian XI v Canterbury at Christchurch	1913-14
English	292	R. Peel (210*) and Lord Hawke (166), Yorkshire v Warwickshire at Birmingham	1896
West Indian	255	E. A. V. Williams (131*) and E. A. Martindale (134), Barbados v Trinidad at Bridgetown	1935-36
Pakistan	240	Gulfraz Khan (207) and Raja Sarfraz (102), Railways v Universities at Lahore	1976-77
Indian	236	C. T. Sarwate (235) and R. P. Singh (88), Holkar v Delhi and District at Delhi	1949-50
South African	222	D. P. B. Morkel (114) and S. S. L. Steyn (261*), Western Province v Border at Cape Town	1929-30
New Zealand	190*	J. E. Mills (104*) and C. F. W. Allcott (102*), New Zealanders v Civil Service at Chiswick	1927

Best Ninth-Wicket Stands

English	283	A. Warren (123) and J. Chapman (165), Derbyshire v Warwickshire at Blackwell	1910
Indian	245	V. S. Hazare (316*) and N. D. Nagarwalla (98), Maharashtra v Baroda at Poona	1939-40
New Zealand	239	H. B. Cave (118) and I. B. Leggat (142*), Central Districts v Otago at Dunedin	1952-53
Australian	232	C. Hill (365*) and E. Walkley (53), South Australia v New South Wales at Adelaide	1900-01
South African	221	N. V. Lindsay (160*) and G. R. McCubbin (97), Transvaal v Rhodesia at Bulawayo	1922-23
Pakistan	190	Asif Iqbal (146) and Intikhab Alam (51), Pakistan v England at The Oval	1967
West Indian	155*†	A. Persaud (85) and K. C. Glasgow (102), Demerara v Berbice at Rose Hall	1976-77

† 201 runs were added for this wicket in two separate partnerships; K. C. Glasgow retired hurt and was replaced by C. E. H. Croft when 155 had been added.

Best Tenth-Wicket Stands

Australian	307	A. F. Kippax (260*), and J. E. H. Hooker (62), New South Wales v Victoria at Melbourne	1928-29
Indian	249	C. T. Sarwate (124*) and S. N. Banerjee (121), Indians v Surrey at The Oval	1946
English	235	F. E. Woolley (185) and A. Fielder (112*), Kent v Worcestershire at Stourbridge	1909
Pakistan	196*	Nadeem Yousuf (202*) and Maqsood Kundi (109*) Muslim Commercial Bank v National Bank at Lahore	1981-82
New Zealand	184	R. C. Blunt (338*) and W. Hawkesworth (21), Otago v Canterbury at Christchurch	1931-32
South African	174	H. R. Lance (168) and D. Mackay-Coghill (57*), Transvaal v Natal at Johannesburg	1965-66
West Indian	138	E. L. G. Hoad (149*) and H. C. Griffith (84), West Indians v Sussex at Hove	1933

Note: All the English record wicket partnerships were made in the County Championship.

HIGHEST AGGREGATES IN A SEASON: OVER 3,000

	Season	*I*	*NO*	*R*	*HI*	*100s*	*Avge*
D. C. S. Compton	1947	50	8	3,816	246	18	90.85
W. J. Edrich	1947	52	8	3,539	267*	12	80.43
T. W. Hayward	1906	61	8	3,518	219	13	66.37
L. Hutton	1949	56	6	3,429	269*	12	68.58
F. E. Woolley	1928	59	4	3,352	198	12	60.94
H. Sutcliffe	1932	52	7	3,336	313	14	74.13
W. R. Hammond	1933	54	5	3,323	264	13	67.81
E. H. Hendren	1928	54	7	3,311	209*	13	70.44
R. Abel	1901	68	8	3,309	247	7	55.15
W. R. Hammond	1937	55	5	3,252	217	13	65.04
M. J. K. Smith	1959	67	11	3,245	200*	8	57.94
E. H. Hendren	1933	65	9	3,186	301*	11	56.89
C. P. Mead	1921	52	6	3,179	280*	10	69.10
T. W. Hayward	1904	63	5	3,170	203	11	54.65
K. S. Ranjitsinhji	1899	58	8	3,159	197	8	63.18
C. B. Fry	1901	43	3	3,147	244	13	78.67
K. S. Ranjitsinhji	1900	40	5	3,065	275	11	87.57

	Season	I	NO	R	HI	100s	Avge
L. E. G. Ames	1933	57	5	3,058	295	9	58.80
J. T. Tyldesley	1901	60	5	3,041	221	9	55.29
C. P. Mead	1928	50	10	3,027	180	13	75.67
J. B. Hobbs	1925	48	5	3,024	266*	16	70.32
E. Tyldesley	1928	48	10	3,024	242	10	79.57
W. E. Alley	1961	64	11	3,019	221*	11	56.96
W. R. Hammond	1938	42	2	3,011	271	15	75.27
E. H. Hendren	1923	51	12	3,010	200*	13	77.17
H. Sutcliffe	1931	42	11	3,006	230	13	96.96
J. H. Parks	1937	63	4	3,003	168	11	50.89
H. Sutcliffe	1928	44	5	3,002	228	13	76.97

Note: W. G. Grace scored 2,739 runs in 1871 – the first batsman to reach 2,000 runs in a season. He made ten hundreds and twice exceeded 200, with an average of 78.25 in all first-class matches. At the time, the over consisted of four balls.

HIGHEST AGGREGATES IN A SEASON: OVER 2,000

Since Reduction of Championship Matches in 1969

	Season	I	NO	R	HI	100s	Avge
Zaheer Abbas	1976	39	5	2,554	230*	11	75.11
G. Boycott	1971	30	5	2,503	233	13	100.12
G. M. Turner	1973	44	8	2,416	153*	9	67.11
G. M. Turner	1970	46	7	2,379	154*	10	61.00
Zaheer Abbas	1981	36	10	2,306	215*	10	88.69
J. H. Edrich	1969	39	7	2,238	181	8	69.93
M. J. Harris	1971	45	1	2,238	177	9	50.86
R. T. Virgin	1970	47	0	2,223	178	7	47.29
I. V. A. Richards	1977	35	2	2,161	241*	7	65.48
J. B. Bolus	1970	53	9	2,143	147*	2	48.70
A. I. Kallicharran	1982	37	5	2,120	235	8	66.25
D. L. Amiss	1976	38	6	2,110	203	8	65.92
G. M. Turner	1981	42	4	2,101	168	9	55.28
Javed Miandad	1981	37	7	2,083	200*	8	69.43
Majid J. Khan	1972	38	4	2,074	204	8	61.00
G. Boycott	1970	42	5	2,051	260*	4	55.43
A. J. Lamb	1981	43	9	2,049	162	5	60.26
J. H. Edrich	1971	44	1	2,031	195*	6	47.23
D. L. Amiss	1978	41	3	2,030	162	7	53.42

Note: The feat was not achieved in 1974, 1975, 1979 or 1980.

HIGHEST BATTING AVERAGES IN AN ENGLISH SEASON

(Qualification: 12 innings)

	Season	I	NO	R	HI	100s	Avge
D. G. Bradman	1938	26	5	2,429	278	13	115.66
G. Boycott	1979	20	5	1,538	175*	6	102.53
W. A. Johnston	1953	17	16	102	28*	0	102.00
G. Boycott	1971	30	5	2,503	233	13	100.12
D. G. Bradman	1930	36	6	2,960	334	10	98.66
H. Sutcliffe	1931	42	11	3,006	230	13	96.96
R. M. Poore	1899	21	4	1,551	304	7	91.23
D. R. Jardine	1927	14	3	1,002	147	5	91.09
D. C. S. Compton	1947	50	8	3,816	246	18	90.85
G. M. Turner	1982	16	3	1,171	311*	5	90.07

	Season	*I*	*NO*	*R*	*HI*	*100s*	*Avge*
D. G. Bradman........	1948	31	4	2,428	187	11	89.92
Zaheer Abbas..........	1981	36	10	2,306	215*	10	88.69
K. S. Ranjitsinhji......	1900	40	5	3,065	275	11	87.57
D. R. Jardine...........	1928	17	4	1,133	193	3	87.15
W. R. Hammond......	1946	26	5	1,783	214	7	84.90
D. G. Bradman........	1934	27	3	2,020	304	7	84.16
R. B. Kanhai............	1975	22	9	1,073	178*	3	82.53
J. B. Hobbs.............	1928	38	7	2,542	200*	12	82.00
C. B. Fry.................	1903	40	7	2,683	234	9	81.30
W. J. Edrich............	1947	52	8	3,539	267*	12	80.43
E. D. Weekes..........	1950	33	4	2,310	304*	7	79.65
E. Tyldesley............	1928	48	10	3,024	242	10	79.57
Nawab of Pataudi sen.	1934	15	3	945	214*	3	78.75
A. Shrewsbury..........	1887	23	2	1,653	267	8	78.71
C. B. Fry.................	1901	43	3	3,147	244	13	78.67
W. G. Grace............	1871	39	4	2,739	268	10	78.25
J. B. Hobbs.............	1926	41	3	2,949	316*	10	77.60
W. H. Ponsford........	1934	27	4	1,784	281*	5	77.56
E. H. Hendren.........	1923	51	12	3,010	200*	13	77.17
H. Sutcliffe..............	1928	44	5	3,002	228	13	76.97
W. R. Hammond......	1934	35	4	2,366	302*	8	76.32
G. S. Sobers............	1970	32	9	1,742	183	7	75.73
C. P. Mead..............	1928	50	10	3,027	180	13	75.67
C. Hallows...............	1927	44	13	2,343	233*	7	75.58
W. R. Hammond......	1938	42	2	3,011	271	15	75.27
Zaheer Abbas..........	1976	39	5	2,554	230*	11	75.11

HIGHEST AGGREGATES OUTSIDE ENGLAND

	Season	*I*	*NO*	*R*	*HI*	*100s*	*Avge*
In Australia							
D. G. Bradman........	1928-29	24	6	1,690	340*	7	93.88
In South Africa							
J. R. Reid...............	1961-62	30	2	1,915	203	7	68.39
In West Indies							
E. H. Hendren.........	1929-30	18	5	1,765	254*	6	135.76
In New Zealand							
G. M. Turner...........	1975-76	20	4	1,244	177*	5	77.75
In India							
C. G. Borde............	1964-65	28	3	1,604	168	6	64.16
In Pakistan							
Zaheer Abbas..........	1973-74	24	5	1,597	174	5	84.05

Note: In more than one country, the following aggregates of over 2,000 runs have been recorded.

S. M. Gavaskar (I/P).	1978-79	30	6	2,121	205	10	88.37
J. R. Reid (SA/A/NZ)	1961-62	36	2	2,083	203	7	61.26
R. B. Simpson (I/P/A/WI)............	1964-65	34	4	2,063	201	8	68.76

1,000 RUNS IN MAY

Three batsmen have scored 1,000 runs in May, and four others – D. G. Bradman twice – have made 1,000 runs before June. Their innings-by-innings records are as follows:

	Runs	*Avge*
W. G. Grace, May 9 to May 30, 1895 (22 days): 13, 103, 18, 25, 288, 52, 257, 73*, 18, 169..................................	1,016	112.88

"W.G." was within two months of completing his 47th year.

	Runs	*Avge*
W. R. Hammond, May 7 to May 31, 1927 (25 days):		
27, 135, 108, 128, 17, 11, 99, 187, 4, 30, 83, 7, 192, 14	1,042	74.42
Hammond scored his 1,000th run on May 28, thus equalling "W.G.'s" record of 22 days.		
C. Hallows, May 5 to May 31, 1928 (27 days):		
100, 101, 51*, 123, 101*, 22, 74, 104, 58, 34*, 232	1,000	125.00
T. W. Hayward, April 16 to May 31, 1900:		
120*, 55, 108, 131*, 55, 193, 120, 5, 6, 3, 40, 146, 92	1,074	97.63
D. G. Bradman, April 30 to May 31, 1930:		
236, 185*, 78, 9, 48*, 66, 4, 44, 252*, 32, 47*	1,001	143.00
On April 30 Bradman scored 75 not out.		
D. G. Bradman, April 30 to May 31, 1938:		
258, 58, 137, 278, 2, 143, 145*, 5, 30*	1,056	150.85
Bradman scored 258 on April 30, and his 1,000th run on May 27.		
W. J. Edrich, April 30 to May 31, 1938:		
104, 37, 115, 63, 20*, 182, 71, 31, 53*, 45, 15, 245, 0, 9, 20*	1,010	84.16
Edrich scored 21 not out on April 30. All his runs were scored at Lord's.		
G. M. Turner, April 24 to May 31, 1973:		
41, 151*, 143, 85, 7, 8, 17*, 81, 13, 53, 44, 153*, 3, 2, 66*, 30, 10*, 111	1,018	78.30

1,000 RUNS IN TWO SEPARATE MONTHS

Only four batsmen, C. B. Fry, K. S. Ranjitsinhji, H. Sutcliffe and L. Hutton, have scored over 1,000 runs in each of two months in the same season. L. Hutton, by scoring 1,294 in June 1949, made more runs in a single month than anyone else. He also made 1,050 in August 1949.

OUT HANDLED THE BALL

J. Grundy	MCC v Kent at Lord's	1857
G. Bennett	Kent v Sussex at Hove	1872
W. H. Scotton	Smokers v Non-Smokers at East Melbourne	1886-87
C. W. Wright	Nottinghamshire v Gloucestershire at Bristol	1893
E. Jones	South Australia v Victoria at Melbourne	1894-95
A. W. Nourse	South Africans v Sussex at Hove	1907
E. T. Benson	MCC v Auckland at Auckland	1929-30
A. W. Gilbertson	Otago v Auckland at Auckland	1952-53
W. R. Endean	South Africa v England at Cape Town	1956-57
P. J. Burge	Queensland v New South Wales at Sydney	1958-59
Dildar Awan	Services v Lahore at Lahore	1959-60
Mahmood-ul-Hasan	Karachi University v Railways-Quetta at Karachi	1960-61
Ali Raza	Karachi Greens v Hyderabad at Karachi	1961-62
Mohammad Yusuf	Rawalpindi v Peshawar at Peshawar	1962-63
A. Rees	Glamorgan v Middlesex at Lord's	1965
Pervez Akhtar	Multan v Karachi Greens at Sahiwal	1971-72
Javed Mirza	Railways v Punjab at Lahore	1972-73
R. G. Pollock	Eastern Province v Western Province at Cape Town	1973-74
C. I. Dey	Northern Transvaal v Orange Free State at Bloemfontein	1973-74
Nasir Valika	Karachi Whites v National Bank at Karachi	1974-75
Haji Yousuf	National Bank v Railways at Lahore	1974-75
Masood-ul-Hasan	PIA v National Bank 'B' at Lyallpur	1975-76
D. K. Pearse	Natal v Western Province at Cape Town	1978-79
A. M. J. Hilditch	Australia v Pakistan at Perth	1978-79
Musleh-ud-Din	Railways v Lahore at Lahore	1979-80

OUT OBSTRUCTING THE FIELD

C. A. Absolom	Cambridge University v Surrey at The Oval	1868
T. Straw	Worcestershire v Warwickshire at Worcester	1899
T. Straw	Worcestershire v Warwickshire at Birmingham	1901
J. P. Whiteside	Leicestershire v Lancashire at Leicester	1901
L. Hutton	England v South Africa at The Oval	1951
J. A. Hayes	Canterbury v Central Districts at Christchurch	1954-55
D. D. Deshpande	Madhya Pradesh v Uttar Pradesh at Benares	1956-57
M. Mehra	Railways v Delhi at Delhi	1959-60
K. Ibadulla	Warwickshire v Hampshire at Coventry	1963
Kaiser	Dera Ismail Khan v Pakistan W.R. at Lahore	1964-65
Qasim Feroze	Bahawalpur v Universities at Lahore	1974-75
T. Quirk	Northern Transvaal v Border at East London	1978-79

Note: This method of dismissal has occurred twice in the *John Player League:*

R. W. Tolchard	Leicestershire v Middlesex at Lord's	1972
D. J. S. Taylor	Somerset v Warwickshire at Birmingham	1980

OUT HIT THE BALL TWICE

H. E. Bull	MCC v Oxford University at Lord's	1864
H. R. J. Charlwood	Sussex v Surrey at Hove	1872
R. G. Barlow	North v South at Lord's	1878
P. S. Wimble	Transvaal v Griqualand West at Kimberley	1892-93
G. B. Nicholls	Somerset v Gloucestershire at Bristol	1896
A. A. Lilley	Warwickshire v Yorkshire at Birmingham	1897
J. H. King	Leicestershire v Surrey at The Oval	1906
A. P. Binns	Jamaica v British Guiana at Georgetown	1956-57
K. Bavanna	Andhra v Mysore at Guntur	1963-64
Zaheer Abbas	PIA 'A' v Karachi Blues at Karachi	1969-70

BOWLING AND FIELDING RECORDS

FOUR WICKETS WITH CONSECUTIVE BALLS

J. Wells	Kent v Sussex at Brighton	1862
G. Ulyett	Lord Harris's XI v New South Wales at Sydney	1878-79
G. Nash	Lancashire v Somerset at Manchester	1882
J. B. Hide	Sussex v MCC and Ground at Lord's	1890
F. J. Shacklock	Nottinghamshire v Somerset at Nottingham	1893
A. D. Downes	Otago v Auckland at Dunedin	1893-94
F. Martin	MCC and Ground v Derbyshire at Lord's	1895
A. W. Mold	Lancashire v Nottinghamshire at Nottingham	1895
W. Brearley†	Lancashire v Somerset at Manchester	1905
S. Haigh	MCC v Army XI at Pretoria	1905-06
A. E. Trott‡	Middlesex v Somerset at Lord's	1907
F. A. Tarrant	Middlesex v Gloucestershire at Bristol	1907
A. Drake	Yorkshire v Derbyshire at Chesterfield	1914
S. G. Smith	Northamptonshire v Warwickshire at Birmingham	1914
H. A. Peach	Surrey v Sussex at The Oval	1924
A. F. Borland	Natal v Griqualand West at Kimberley	1926-27
J. E. H. Hooker†	New South Wales v Victoria at Sydney	1928-29

R. K. Tyldesley†	Lancashire v Derbyshire at Derby	1929
R. J. Crisp	Western Province v Griqualand West at Johannesburg	1931-32
R. J. Crisp	Western Province v Natal at Durban	1933-34
A. R. Gover	Surrey v Worcestershire at Worcester	1935
W. H. Copson	Derbyshire v Warwickshire at Derby	1937
W. A. Henderson	N.E. Transvaal v Orange Free State at Bloemfontein	1937-38
F. Ridgway	Kent v Derbyshire at Folkestone	1951
A. K. Walker §	Nottinghamshire v Leicestershire at Leicester	1956
S. N. Mohol	Board of Control President's XI v Minister for Small Savings' XI at Poona	1965-66
P. I. Pocock	Surrey v Sussex at Eastbourne	1972

† *Not all in the same innings.*

‡ *Trott achieved another hat-trick in the same innings of this, his benefit match.*

§ *Walker dismissed Firth with the last ball of the first innings and Lester, Tompkin and Smithson with the first three balls of the second innings, a feat without parallel.*

Notes: In their match with England at The Oval in 1863, Surrey lost four wickets in the course of a four-ball over from G. Bennett.

Sussex lost five wickets in the course of the final (six-ball) over of their match with Surrey at Eastbourne in 1972. P. I. Pocock, who had taken three wickets in his previous over, captured four more, taking in all seven wickets with eleven balls, a feat unique in first-class matches. (The eighth wicket fell to a run-out.)

P. G. H. Fender (Surrey) took six Middlesex wickets with eleven balls (including five with seven) at Lord's in 1927.

HAT-TRICKS

Double Hat-Trick

Besides Trott's performance, which is given in the preceding section, the following instances are recorded of players having performed the hat-trick twice in the same match, Rao doing so in the same innings.

A. Shaw	Nottinghamshire v Gloucestershire at Nottingham	1884
T. J. Matthews	Australia v South Africa at Manchester	1912
C. W. L. Parker	Gloucestershire v Middlesex at Bristol	1924
R. O. Jenkins	Worcestershire v Surrey at Worcester	1949
J. S. Rao	Services v Northern Punjab at Amritsar	1963-64
Amin Lakhani	Combined XI v Indians at Multan	1978-79

Five Wickets with Six Consecutive Balls

W. H. Copson	Derbyshire v Warwickshire at Derby	1937
W. A. Henderson	N.E. Transvaal v Orange Free State at Bloemfontein	1937-38
P. I. Pocock	Surrey v Sussex at Eastbourne	1972

Most Hat-Tricks

Seven times: D. V. P. Wright.
Six times: T. W. Goddard, C. W. L. Parker.
Five times: S. Haigh, V. W. C. Jupp, A. E. G. Rhodes, F. A. Tarrant.
Four times: R. G. Barlow, J. T. Hearne, J. C. Laker, G. A. R. Lock, G. G. Macaulay, T. J. Matthews, M. J. Procter, T. Richardson, F. R. Spofforth, F. S. Trueman.
Three times: W. M. Bradley, H. J. Butler, W. H. Copson, R. J. Crisp, J. W. H. T. Douglas, J. A. Flavell, A. P. Freeman, G. Giffen, K. Higgs, A. Hill, W. A. Humphries, R. D. Jackman, R. O. Jenkins, A. S. Kennedy, W. H. Lockwood, E. A. McDonald, T. L. Pritchard, J. S. Rao, A. Shaw, J. B. Statham, M. W. Tate, H. Trumble, D. Wilson, G. A. Wilson.

Unusual Hat-Tricks

All "Stumped":	by W. H. Brain off C. L. Townsend, Gloucestershire v Somerset at Cheltenham	1893
All "Caught":	by G. J. Thompson off S. G. Smith, Northamptonshire v Warwickshire at Birmingham	1914
	by Cyril White off R. Beesly, Border v Griqualand West at Queenstown	1946-47
	by G. O. Dawkes (wicket-keeper) off H. L. Jackson, Derbyshire v Worcestershire at Kidderminster	1958
All "LBW":	H. Fisher, Yorkshire v Somerset at Sheffield	1932
	J. A. Flavell, Worcestershire v Lancashire at Manchester	1963
	M. J. Procter, Gloucestershire v Essex at Westcliff	1972
	B. J. Ikin, Griqualand West v OFS at Kimberley	1973-74
	M. J. Procter, Gloucestershire v Yorkshire at Cheltenham	1979

TEN WICKETS IN ONE INNINGS

	O	*M*	*R*		
E. Hinkly (Kent)				v England at Lord's	1848
J. Wisden (North)				v South at Lord's	1850
V. E. Walker (England)	43	17	74	v Surrey at The Oval	1859
E. M. Grace (MCC)	32.2	7	69	v Gents of Kent at Canterbury	1862
V. E. Walker (Middlesex)	44.2		104	v Lancashire at Manchester	1865
G. Wootton (All England)	31.3	9	54	v Yorkshire at Sheffield	1865
W. Hickton (Lancashire)	36.2	19	46	v Hampshire at Manchester	1870
S. E. Butler (Oxford)	24.1	11	38	v Cambridge at Lord's	1871
James Lillywhite (South)	60.2	22	129	v North at Canterbury	1872
W. G. Grace (MCC)	46.1	15	92	v Kent at Canterbury	1873
A. Shaw (MCC)	36.2	8	73	v North at Lord's	1874
E. Barratt (Players)	29	11	43	v Australians at The Oval	1878
G. Giffen (Australian XI)	26	10	66	v The Rest at Sydney	1883-84
W. G. Grace (MCC)	36.2	17	49	v Oxford University at Oxford	1886
G. Burton (Middlesex)	52.3	25	59	v Surrey at The Oval	1888
†A. E. Moss (Canterbury)	21.3	10	28	v Wellington at Christchurch	1889-90
S. M. J. Woods (Cambridge U.)	31	6	69	v Thornton's XI at Cambridge	1890
T. Richardson (Surrey)	15.3	3	45	v Essex at The Oval	1894
H. Pickett (Essex)	27	11	32	v Leicestershire at Leyton	1895
E. J. Tyler (Somerset)	34.3	15	49	v Surrey at Taunton	1895
W. P. Howell (Australians)	23.2	14	28	v Surrey at The Oval	1899
C. H. G. Bland (Sussex)	25.2	0	48	v Kent at Tonbridge	1899
J. Briggs (Lancashire)	28.5	7	55	v Worcestershire at Manchester	1900
A. E. Trott (Middlesex)	14.2	5	42	v Somerset at Taunton	1900
F. Hinds (A. B. St Hill's XI)	19.1	6	36	v Trinidad at Port-of-Spain	1900-01
A. Fielder (Players)	24.5	1	90	v Gentlemen at Lord's	1906
E. G. Dennett (Gloucestershire)	19.4	7	40	v Essex at Bristol	1906
A. E. E. Vogler (E. Province)	12	2	26	v Griqualand West at Johannesburg	1906-07
C. Blythe (Kent)	16	7	30	v Northamptonshire at Northampton	1907
A. Drake (Yorkshire)	8.5	0	35	v Somerset at Weston-super-Mare	1914
F. A. Tarrant (Maharaja of Cooch Behar's XI)	35.4	4	90	v Lord Willingdon's XI at Poona	1918-19
W. Bestwick (Derbyshire)	19	2	40	v Glamorgan at Cardiff	1921
A. A. Mailey (Australians)	28.4	5	66	v Gloucestershire at Cheltenham	1921
C. W. L. Parker (Glos.)	40.3	13	79	v Somerset at Bristol	1921
T. Rushby (Surrey)	17.5	4	43	v Somerset at Taunton	1921
J. C. White (Somerset)	42.2	11	76	v Worcestershire at Worcester	1921

	O	M	R		
G. C. Collins (Kent)............	19.3	4	65	v Nottinghamshire at Dover....	1922
H. Howell (Warwickshire).....	25.1	5	51	v Yorkshire at Birmingham.....	1923
A. S. Kennedy (Players).......	22.4	10	37	v Gentlemen at The Oval.......	1927
G. O. Allen (Middlesex).......	25.3	10	40	v Lancashire at Lord's............	1929
A. P. Freeman (Kent)..........	42	9	131	v Lancashire at Maidstone......	1929
G. Geary (Leicestershire)......	16.2	8	18	v Glamorgan at Pontypridd.....	1929
C. V. Grimmett (Australians)	22.3	8	37	v Yorkshire at Sheffield..........	1930
A. P. Freeman (Kent)..........	30.4	8	53	v Essex at Southend..............	1930
H. Verity (Yorkshire)..........	18.4	6	36	v Warwickshire at Leeds.........	1931
A. P. Freeman (Kent)..........	36.1	9	79	v Lancashire at Manchester.....	1931
V. W. C. Jupp (Northants)....	39	6	127	v Kent at Tunbridge Wells......	1932
H. Verity (Yorkshire)..........	19.4	16	10	v Nottinghamshire at Leeds.....	1932
T. W. Wall (South Australia).	12.4	2	36	v New South Wales at Sydney.	1932-33
T. B. Mitchell (Derbyshire)...	19.1	4	64	v Leicestershire at Leicester....	1935
J. Mercer (Glamorgan).........	26	10	51	v Worcestershire at Worcester.	1936
T. W. Goddard (Glos.).........	28.4	4	113	v Worcestershire at Cheltenham	1937
T. F. Smailes (Yorkshire)......	17.1	5	47	v Derbyshire at Sheffield........	1939
E. A. Watts (Surrey)............	24.1	8	67	v Warwickshire at Birmingham	1939
W. E. Hollies (Warwickshire)	20.4	4	49	v Nottinghamshire at Birmingham..............................	1946
J. M. Sims (East)................	18.4	2	90	v West at Kingston................	1948
T. E. Bailey (Essex).............	39.4	9	90	v Lancashire at Clacton..........	1949
J. K. R. Graveney (Glos.).....	18.4	2	66	v Derbyshire at Chesterfield....	1949
R. Berry (Lancashire)..........	36.2	9	102	v Worcestershire at Blackpool.	1953
S. P. Gupte (Bombay)..........	24.2	7	78	v Combined XI at Bombay.....	1954-55
J. C. Laker (Surrey)............	46	18	88	v Australians at The Oval.......	1956
J. C. Laker (England)..........	51.2	23	53	v Australia at Manchester.......	1956
G. A. R. Lock (Surrey)........	29.1	18	54	v Kent at Blackheath............	1956
K. Smales (Nottinghamshire).	41.3	20	66	v Gloucestershire at Stroud.....	1956
P. Chatterjee (Bengal)..........	19	11	20	v Assam at Jorhat................	1956-57
J. D. Bannister (Warwickshire)	23.3	11	41	v Comb. Services at Birmingham	1959
A. J. G. Pearson (Cambridge University)......................	30.3	8	78	v Leicestershire at Loughborough........................	1961
N. I. Thomson (Sussex)........	34.2	19	49	v Warwickshire at Worthing....	1964
P. J. Allan (Queensland)......	15.6	3	61	v Victoria at Melbourne........	1965-66
I. J. Brayshaw (W. Australia)	17.6	4	44	v Victoria at Perth...............	1967-68
Shahid Mahmood (Karachi Whites)...........................	25	5	58	v Khairpur at Karachi............	1969-70

† *On début in first-class cricket.*

MOST WICKETS IN A MATCH

19-90	J. C. Laker	England v Australia at Manchester......................	1956
17-48	C. Blythe	Kent v Northamptonshire at Northampton...........	1907
17-50	C. T. B. Turner	Australians v England XI at Hastings..................	1888
17-54	W. P. Howell	Australians v Western Province at Cape Town......	1902-03
17-56	C. W. L. Parker	Gloucestershire v Essex at Gloucester.................	1925
17-67	A. P. Freeman	Kent v Sussex at Hove..	1922
17-89	W. G. Grace	Gloucestershire v Nottinghamshire at Cheltenham..	1877
17-89	F. C. L. Matthews	Nottinghamshire v Northants at Nottingham.........	1923
17-91	H. Dean	Lancashire v Yorkshire at Liverpool..................	1913
17-91	H. Verity	Yorkshire v Essex at Leyton.............................	1933
17-92	A. P. Freeman	Kent v Warwickshire at Folkestone.....................	1932
17-103	W. Mycroft	Derbyshire v Hampshire at Southampton.............	1876
17-106	G. R. Cox	Sussex v Warwickshire at Horsham.....................	1926
17-106	T. W. Goddard	Gloucestershire v Kent at Bristol........................	1939
17-119	W. Mead	Essex v Hampshire at Southampton.....................	1895
17-137	W. Brearley	Lancashire v Somerset at Manchester..................	1905

17-159	S. F. Barnes	England v South Africa at Johannesburg	1913-14
17-201	G. Giffen	South Australia v Victoria at Adelaide	1885-86
17-212	J. C. Clay	Glamorgan v Worcestershire at Swansea	1937

Notes: H. A. Arkwright took eighteen wickets for 96 runs in a 12-a-side match for Gentlemen of MCC v Gentlemen of Kent at Canterbury in 1861.

W. Mead took seventeen wickets for 205 runs for Essex v Australians at Leyton in 1893, the year before Essex were raised to first-class status.

F. P. Fenner took seventeen wickets for Cambridge Town Club v University of Cambridge at Cambridge in 1844.

OUTSTANDING ANALYSES

(Also see Ten Wickets in One Innings)

	O	*M*	*R*	*W*		
H. Verity (Yorkshire)	19.4	16	10	10	v Nottinghamshire at Leeds	1932
G. Elliott (Victoria)	19	17	2	9	v Tasmania at Launceston	1857-58
Ahad Khan (Railways)	6.3	4	7	9	v Dera Ismail Khan at Lahore	1964-65
J. C. Laker (England)	14	12	2	8	v The Rest at Bradford	1950
D. Shackleton (Hampshire)	11.1	7	4	8	v Somerset at Weston-super-Mare	1955
E. Peate (Yorkshire)	16	11	5	8	v Surrey at Holbeck	1883
F. R. Spofforth (Australians)	8.3	6	3	7	v England XI at Birmingham	1884
W. A. Henderson (N.E. Transvaal)	9.3	7	4	7	v Orange Free State at Bloemfontein	1937-38
Rajinder Goel (Haryana)	7	4	4	7	v Jammu and Kashmir at Chandigarh	1977-78
V. I. Smith (South Africans)	4.5	3	1	6	v Derbyshire at Derby	1947
S. Cosstick (Victoria)	21.1	20	1	6	v Tasmania at Melbourne	1868-69
Israr Ali (Bahawalpur)	11	10	1	6	v Dacca U. at Bahawalpur	1957-58
A. D. Pougher (MCC)	3	3	0	5	v Australians at Lord's	1896
G. R. Cox (Sussex)	6	6	0	5	v Somerset at Weston-super-Mare	1921
R. K. Tyldesley (Lancashire)	5	5	0	5	v Leicestershire at Manchester	1924
P. T. Mills (Gloucestershire)	6.4	6	0	5	v Somerset at Bristol	1928

SIXTEEN OR MORE WICKETS IN A DAY

17-48	C. Blythe	Kent v Northamptonshire at Northampton	1907
17-91	H. Verity	Yorkshire v Essex at Leyton	1933
17-106	T. W. Goddard	Gloucestershire v Kent at Bristol	1939
16-38	T. Emmett	Yorkshire v Cambridgeshire at Hunslet	1869
16-52	J. Southerton	South v North at Lord's	1875
16-69	T. G. Wass	Nottinghamshire v Lancashire at Liverpool	1906
16-38	A. E. E. Vogler	E. Province v Griqualand West at Johannesburg	1906-07
16-103	T. G. Wass	Nottinghamshire v Essex at Nottingham	1908
16-83	J. C. White	Somerset v Worcestershire at Bath	1919

200 OR MORE WICKETS IN A SEASON

	Season	*O*	*M*	*R*	*W*	*Avge*
A. P. Freeman........	1928	1,976.1	423	5,489	304	18.05
A. P. Freeman........	1933	2,039	651	4,549	298	15.26
T. Richardson.........	1895‡	1,690.1	463	4,170	290	14.37
C. T. B. Turner**.....	1888†	2,427.2	1,127	3,307	283	11.68
A. P. Freeman........	1931	1,618	360	4,307	276	15.60
A. P. Freeman........	1930	1,914.3	472	4,632	275	16.84
T. Richardson.........	1897‡	1,603.4	495	3,945	273	14.45
A. P. Freeman........	1929	1,670.5	381	4,879	267	18.27
W. Rhodes.............	1900	1,553	455	3,606	261	13.81
J. T. Hearne...........	1896‡	2,003.1	818	3,670	257	14.28
A. P. Freeman........	1932	1,565.5	404	4,149	253	16.39
W. Rhodes.............	1901	1,565	505	3,797	251	15.12
T. W. Goddard.......	1937	1,478.1	359	4,158	248	16.76
W. C. Smith...........	1910	1,423.3	420	3,225	247	13.05
T. Richardson.........	1896‡	1,656.2	526	4,015	246	16.32
A. E. Trott............	1899‡	1,772.4	587	4,086	239	17.09
T. W. Goddard.......	1947	1,451.2	344	4,119	238	17.30
M. W. Tate............	1925	1,694.3	472	3,415	228	14.97
J. T. Hearne...........	1898‡	1,802.2	781	3,120	222	14.05
C. W. L. Parker......	1925	1,512.3	478	3,311	222	14.91
G. A. Lohmann......	1890‡	1,759.1	737	2,998	220	13.62
M. W. Tate............	1923	1,608.5	331	3,061	219	13.97
C. F. Root.............	1925	1,493.2	416	3,770	219	17.21
C. W. L. Parker......	1931	1,320.4	386	3,125	219	14.26
H. Verity...............	1936	1,289.3	463	2,847	216	13.18
G. A. R. Lock........	1955	1,408.4	497	3,109	216	14.39
C. Blythe...............	1909	1,273.5	343	3,128	215	14.54
E. Peate.................	1882†	1,853.1	868	2,466	214	11.52
A. W. Mold............	1895‡	1,629	598	3,400	213	15.96
W. Rhodes.............	1902	1,306.3	405	2,801	213	13.15
C. W. L. Parker......	1926	1,739.5	556	3,920	213	18.40
J. T. Hearne...........	1893‡	1,741.4	667	3,492	212	16.47
A. P. Freeman........	1935	1,503.2	320	4,562	212	21.51
G. A. R. Lock........	1957	1,194.1	449	2,550	212	12.02
A. E. Trott............	1900	1,547.1	363	4,923	211	23.33
G. G. Macaulay......	1925	1,338.2	307	3,268	211	15.48
H. Verity...............	1935	1,279.2	453	3,032	211	14.36
J. Southerton..........	1870†	1,876.5	709	3,074	210	14.63
G. A. Lohmann......	1888†	1,649.1	783	2,280	209	10.90
C. H. Parkin..........	1923	1,356.2	356	3,543	209	16.94
G. H. Hirst............	1906	1,306.1	271	3,434	208	16.50
F. R. Spofforth.......	1884†	1,577	653	2,774	207	13.25
A. W. Mold............	1894‡	1,288.3	456	2,548	207	12.30
C. W. L Parker.......	1922	1,294.5	445	2,712	206	13.16
A. S. Kennedy........	1922	1,346.4	366	3,444	205	16.80
M. W. Tate............	1924	1,469.5	465	2,818	205	13.74
E. A. McDonald.....	1925	1,249.4	282	3,828	205	18.67
A. P. Freeman........	1934	1,744.4	440	4,753	205	23.18
C. W. L. Parker......	1924	1,303.5	411	2,913	204	14.27
G. A. Lohmann......	1889‡	1,614.1	646	2,714	202	13.43
H. Verity...............	1937	1,386.2	487	3,168	202	15.68
A. Shaw.................	1878†	2,630	1,586	2,203	201	10.96
E. G. Dennett........	1907	1,216.2	305	3,227	201	16.05
A. R. Gover..........	1937	1,219.4	191	3,816	201	18.98
C. H. Parkin..........	1924	1,162.5	357	2,735	200	13.67
T. W. Goddard.......	1935	1,553	384	4,073	200	20.36
A. R. Gover..........	1936	1,159.2	185	3,547	200	17.73

	Season	*O*	*M*	*R*	*W*	*Avge*
T. W. Goddard.......	1939§	819	139	2,973	200	14.86
R. Appleyard.........	1951	1,313.2	391	2,829	200	14.14

† *Indicates 4-ball overs;* ‡ *5-ball overs. All others were 6-ball overs except* § *8-ball overs.*
** *Exclusive of matches not reckoned as first-class.*

Notes: In four consecutive seasons (1928-31), A. P. Freeman took 1,122 wickets, and in eight consecutive seasons (1928-35), 2,090 wickets. In each of these eight seasons he took over 200 wickets.

T. Richardson took 1,005 wickets in four consecutive seasons (1894-97).

In 1896, J. T. Hearne took his 100th wicket as early as June 12. In 1931, C. W. L. Parker did the same and A. P. Freeman obtained his 100th wicket a day later.

C. T. B. Turner is the only bowler to take over 100 wickets in first-class matches in a season in Australia – 106 wickets in twelve matches, 1887-88.

100 OR MORE WICKETS IN A SEASON

Since Reduction of Championship Matches in 1969

	Season	*O*	*M*	*R*	*W*	*Avge*
M. D. Marshall.......	1982	822	225	2,108	134	15.73
L. R. Gibbs...........	1971	1,024.1	295	2,475	131	18.89
R. D. Jackman........	1980	746.2	220	1,864	121	15.40
A. M. E. Roberts....	1974	727.4	198	1,621	119	13.62
B. S. Bedi.............	1974	1,085.3	307	2,760	112	24.64
P. G. Lee..............	1975	799.5	199	2,067	112	18.45
D. L. Underwood....	1978	815.1	359	1,594	110	14.49
R. M. H. Cottam.....	1969	989.1	252	2,294	109	21.04
M. J. Procter..........	1977	777.3	226	1,967	109	18.04
T. W. Cartwright.....	1969	880.5	373	1,748	108	16.18
M. J. Procter..........	1969	639.3	160	1,623	108	15.02
P. J. Sainsbury........	1971	845.5	332	1,874	107	17.51
D. J. Shepherd........	1970	1,123.3	420	2,031	106	19.16
J. K. Lever............	1978	681.1	160	1,610	106	15.18
J. K. Lever............	1979	700	166	1,834	106	17.30
D. L. Underwood....	1979	799.2	335	1,575	106	14.85
N. Gifford.............	1970	965.5	331	2,092	105	19.92
F. J. Titmus...........	1970	1,106.3	320	2,804	105	26.70
B. S. Bedi.............	1973	864.2	307	1,884	105	17.94
R. J. Hadlee..........	1981	708.4	231	1,564	105	14.89
T. W. Cartwright.....	1971	976.4	407	1,852	104	17.80
Intikhab Alam........	1971	1,097.4	244	2,950	104	28.36
F. J. Titmus...........	1971	1,065.1	341	2,355	104	22.64
D. Wilson.............	1969	964.1	384	1,772	102	17.37
R. N. S. Hobbs.......	1970	736	178	2,183	102	21.40
D. L. Underwood....	1971	945.5	368	1,986	102	19.47
D. L. Underwood....	1969	808.3	355	1,561	101	15.45
P. G. Lee..............	1973	740.3	181	1,901	101	18.82
Sarfraz Nawaz........	1975	728.4	175	2,051	101	20.30
M. W. W. Selvey.....	1978	743.5	199	1,929	101	19.09
D. R. Doshi...........	1980	961.2	268	2,700	101	26.73
I. T. Botham..........	1978	605.2	143	1,640	100	16.40

Note: The feat was not achieved in 1972 or 1976.

1,500 WICKETS OR MORE IN A CAREER

	Career	*W*	*R*	*Avge*
W. Rhodes	1898-1930	4,187	69,993	16.71
A. P. Freeman	1914-36	3,776	69,577	18.42
C. W. L. Parker	1903-35	3,278	63,821	19.46
J. T. Hearne	1888-1923	3,061	54,342	17.75
T. W. Goddard	1922-52	2,979	59,116	19.84
†W. G. Grace	1865-1908	2,876	51,545	17.92
A. S. Kennedy	1907-36	2,874	61,044	21.24
D. Shackleton	1948-69	2,857	53,303	18.65
G. A. R. Lock	1946-71	2,844	54,710	19.23
F. J. Titmus	1949-82	2,830	63,313	22.37
M. W. Tate	1912-37	2,784	50,567	18.16
G. H. Hirst	1891-1929	2,739	51,300	18.72
C. Blythe	1899-1914	2,506	42,136	16.81
W. E. Astill	1906-39	2,431	57,781	23.76
J. C. White	1909-37	2,356	43,759	18.57
W. E. Hollies	1932-57	2,323	48,656	20.94
F. S. Trueman	1949-69	2,304	42,154	18.29
J. B. Statham	1950-68	2,260	36,995	16.36
R. T. D. Perks	1930-55	2,233	53,770	24.07
J. Briggs	1879-1900	2,221	35,390	15.93
D. J. Shepherd	1950-72	2,218	47,298	21.32
E. G. Dennett	1903-26	2,147	42,568	19.82
D. L. Underwood	1963-82	2,118	41,970	19.81
T. Richardson	1892-1905	2,105	38,794	18.42
T. E. Bailey	1945-67	2,082	48,170	23.13
F. E. Woolley	1906-38	2,068	41,066	19.85
G. Geary	1912-38	2,063	41,339	20.03
D. V. P. Wright	1932-57	2,056	49,305	23.98
R. Illingworth	1951-82	2,040	41,072	20.13
J. Newman	1906-30	2,032	51,211	25.20
A. Shaw	1864-97	2,021	24,496	12.12
S. Haigh	1895-1913	2,012	32,091	15.94
H. Verity	1930-39	1,956	29,146	14.90
J. C. Laker	1946-65	1,944	35,789	18.40
W. Attewell	1881-1900	1,932	29,745	15.39
A. V. Bedser	1939-60	1,924	39,281	20.41
W. Mead	1892-1913	1,916	36,388	18.99
A. E. Relf	1900-21	1,897	39,724	20.94
P. G. H. Fender	1910-36	1,894	47,457	25.05
J. W. H. T. Douglas	1901-30	1,893	44,159	23.32
J. H. Wardle	1946-58	1,846	35,027	18.97
G. R. Cox	1895-1928	1,843	42,138	22.86
M. S. Nichols	1924-39	1,841	39,845	21.64
J. W. Hearne	1909-36	1,839	44,927	24.43
G. G. Macaulay	1920-35	1,837	32,440	17.65
J. B. Mortimore	1950-75	1,807	41,904	23.18
G. A. Lohmann	1884-98	1,805	25,110	13.91
C. Cook	1946-64	1,782	36,578	20.52
R. Peel	1882-99	1,754	28,446	16.21
H. L. Jackson	1947-63	1,733	30,101	17.36
N. Gifford	1960-82	1,720	39,244	22.81
T. P. B. Smith	1929-52	1,697	45,193	26.63
J. Southerton	1854-79	1,680	24,257	14.43
A. E. Trott	1892-1911	1,674	35,316	21.09
A. W. Mold	1889-1901	1,673	26,012	15.54
T. G. Wass	1896-1920	1,666	34,091	20.46
V. W. C. Jupp	1909-38	1,658	38,166	23.01
C. Gladwin	1939-58	1,653	30,265	18.30

	Career	*W*	*R*	*Avge*
W. E. Bowes............	1928-47	1,639	27,470	16.76
A. W. Wellard..........	1927-50	1,614	39,292	24.34
N. I. Thomson..........	1952-72	1,597	32,866	20.57
J. Mercer................	1919-47	1,593	37,302	23.41
G. J. Thompson.........	1897-1922	1,591	30,060	18.89
T. Emmett...............	1866-88	1,582	21,147	13.36
J. M. Sims................	1929-53	1,582	39,401	24.90
Intikhab Alam...........	1957-82	1,571	43,472	27.67
W. Voce..................	1927-52	1,558	35,961	23.08
A. R. Gover..............	1928-48	1,555	36,753	23.63
B. S. Bedi................	1961-81	1,547	33,478	21.64
T. W. Cartwright........	1952-77	1,536	29,357	19.11
K. Higgs..................	1958-82	1,531	36,196	23.64
James Langridge.........	1924-53	1,530	34,524	22.56
J. A. Flavell..............	1949-67	1,529	32,847	21.48
C. F. Root................	1910-33	1,512	31,933	21.11
R. K. Tyldesley..........	1919-35	1,509	25,980	17.21

†*In recent years some statisticians have removed from W. G. Grace's record a number of matches which they consider not to have been first-class. The above figures are those which became universally accepted upon appearance in W. G. Grace's obituary in the* Wisden *of 1916. Some works of reference give his career record as being 2,809–50,999–18.15. These figures also appeared in the 1981 edition of* Wisden.

100 WICKETS IN A SEASON EIGHT TIMES OR MORE

23 times: W. Rhodes 200 wkts (3).

20 times: D. Shackleton.

17 times: A. P. Freeman 300 wkts (1), 200 wkts (7).

16 times: T. W. Goddard 200 wkts (4), C. W. L. Parker 200 wkts (5), R. T. D. Perks, F. J. Titmus.

15 times: J. T. Hearne 200 wkts (3), G. H. Hirst 200 wkts (1), A. S. Kennedy 200 wkts (1).

14 times: C. Blythe 200 wkts (1), W. E. Hollies, G. A. R. Lock 200 wkts (2), M. W. Tate 200 wkts (3), J. C White.

13 times: J. B. Statham.

12 times: J. Briggs, E. G. Dennett 200 wkts (1), C. Gladwin, D. J. Shepherd, N. I. Thomson, F. S. Trueman.

11 times: A. V. Bedser, G. Geary, S. Haigh, J. C. Laker, M. S. Nichols, A. E. Relf.

10 times: W. Attewell, W. G. Grace, R. Illingworth, H. L. Jackson, V. W. C. Jupp, G. G. Macaulay 200 wkts (1), W. Mead, T. B. Mitchell, T. Richardson 200 wkts (3), R. K. Tyldesley, J. H. Wardle, T. G. Wass, D. V. P. Wright.

9 times: W. E. Astill, T. E. Bailey, W. E. Bowes, C. Cook, R. Howorth, J. Mercer, A. W. Mold 200 wkts (2), J. Newman, C. F. Root 200 wkts (1), A. Shaw 200 wkts (1), J. Southerton 200 wkts (1), D. L. Underwood, H. Verity 200 wkts (3).

8 times: T. W. Cartwright, H. Dean, J. A. Flavell, A. R. Gover 200 wkts (2), H. Larwood, G. A. Lohmann 200 wkts (3), R. Peel, J. M. Sims, F. A. Tarrant, R. Tattersall, G. J. Thompson, G. E. Tribe, A. W. Wellard, F. E. Woolley, J. A. Young.

100 WICKETS IN A SEASON OVERSEAS

W		*Season*	*R*	*Avge*
116	M. W. Tate........................	1926-27 (I)	1,599	13.78
106	C. T. B. Turner..................	1887-88 (A)	1,441	13.59
106	R. Benaud.........................	1957-58 (SA)	2,056	19.39
104	S. F. Barnes.......................	1913-14 (SA)	1,117	10.74

ALL-ROUND CRICKET

20,000 RUNS AND 2,000 WICKETS IN A CAREER

	Career	*R*	*Avge*	*W*	*Avge*	*'Doubles'*
W. E. Astill.....	1906-39	22,726	22.54	2,431	23.76	9
T. E. Bailey......	1945-67	28,642	33.42	2,082	23.13	8
W. G. Grace.....	1865-1908	54,896	39.55	2,876	17.99	8
G. H. Hirst......	1891-1929	36,323	34.13	2,739	18.72	14
R. Illingworth...	1951-82	24,063	28.37	2,040	20.13	6
W. Rhodes.......	1898-1930	39,802	30.83	4,187	16.71	16
M. W. Tate......	1912-37	21,717	25.01	2,784	18.16	8
F. J. Titmus......	1949-82	21,588	23.11	2,830	22.37	8
F. E. Woolley...	1906-38	58,969	40.75	2,068	19.85	8

THE DOUBLE

2,000 RUNS AND 200 WICKETS IN A SEASON

1906 G. H. Hirst 2,385 runs and 208 wickets

3,000 RUNS AND 100 WICKETS IN A SEASON

1937 J. H. Parks 3,003 runs and 101 wickets

2,000 RUNS AND 100 WICKETS IN A SEASON

	Season	*R*	*W*
W. G. Grace..........	1873	2,139	106
W. G. Grace..........	1876	2,622	129
C. L. Townsend......	1899	2,440	101
G. L. Jessop..........	1900	2,210	104
G. H. Hirst...........	1904	2,501	132
G. H. Hirst...........	1905	2,266	110
W. Rhodes............	1909	2,094	141
W. Rhodes............	1911	2,261	117
F. A. Tarrant.........	1911	2,030	111
J. W. Hearne.........	1913	2,036	124
J. W. Hearne.........	1914	2,116	123
F. E. Woolley.........	1914	2,272	125
J. W. Hearne.........	1920	2,148	142
V. W. C. Jupp........	1921	2,169	121
F. E. Woolley.........	1921	2,101	167
F. E. Woolley.........	1922	2,022	163
F. E. Woolley.........	1923	2,091	101
L. F. Townsend.......	1933	2,268	100
D. E. Davies..........	1937	2,012	103
James Langridge......	1937	2,082	101
T. E Bailey............	1959	2,011	100

1,000 RUNS AND 200 WICKETS IN A SEASON

	Season	*R*	*W*
A. E. Trott...........	1899	1,175	239
A. E. Trott...........	1900	1,337	211
A. S. Kennedy........	1922	1,129	205
M. W. Tate...........	1923	1,168	219
M. W. Tate...........	1924	1,419	205
M. W. Tate...........	1925	1,290	228

The double feat of scoring 1,000 runs and taking 100 wickets in one season of first-class cricket has been accomplished as follows, the last instance being by F. J. Titmus in 1967:

Sixteen times: W. Rhodes. **Fourteen times:** G. H. Hirst.
Ten times: V. W. C. Jupp. **Nine times:** W. E. Astill.
Eight times: T. E. Bailey, W. G. Grace, M. S. Nichols, A. E. Relf, F. A. Tarrant, M. W. Tate, F. J. Titmus, F. E. Woolley.
Seven times: G. E. Tribe.
Six times: P. G. H. Fender, R. Illingworth, James Langridge.
Five times: J. W. H. T. Douglas, J. W. Hearne, A. S. Kennedy, J. Newman.
Four times: E. G. Arnold, J. Gunn, R. Kilner, B. R. Knight.
Three times: W. W. Armstrong (Australians), L. C. Braund, G. Giffen (Australians), N. E. Haig, R. Howorth, C. B. Llewellyn, J. B. Mortimore, Ray Smith, S. G. Smith, L. F. Townsend, A. W. Wellard.

Note: A complete list of those performing the feat once or twice will be found on p.202 of the 1982 *Wisden*.

WICKET-KEEPER'S DOUBLE

	Season	*R*	*D*
L. E. G. Ames	1928	1,919	121
L. E. G. Ames	1929	1,795	127
L. E. G. Ames	1932	2,482	100
J. T. Murray	1957	1,025	104

1,000 RUNS AND 50 WICKETS IN A SEASON

Since Reduction of Championship Matches in 1969

Season		*R*	*Avge*	*W*	*Avge*
1969	A. W. Greig	1,130	27.56	69	23.60
	Mushtaq Mohammad	1,831	59.06	78	24.38
	G. S. Sobers	1,023	42.62	54	24.42
1970	A. W. Greig	1,008	24.00	59	27.69
	Mushtaq Mohammad	1,482	36.14	58	28.50
	G. S. Sobers	1,742	75.73	64	24.06
	P. M. Walker	1,049	24.39	60	26.65
1971	M. A. Buss	1,337	31.83	62	26.59
	A. W. Greig	1,242	27.00	77	29.07
	R. A. Hutton	1,009	31.53	80	20.35
	Mushtaq Mohammad	1,660	33.87	52	27.25
	M. J. Procter	1,786	45.79	65	18.95
	G. S. Sobers	1,485	46.40	53	30.96
1972	K. D. Boyce	1,023	30.08	82	20.20
	Mushtaq Mohammad	1,949	59.06	57	19.82
	M. J. Procter	1,219	40.63	58	16.55
1974	Imran Khan	1,016	36.28	60	30.13
1975	A. W. Greig	1,699	47.19	56	33.41
	C. E. B. Rice	1,155	33.00	53	25.98
1976	I. T. Botham	1,022	34.06	66	28.48
	Imran Khan	1,092	40.44	65	23.41
	M. J. Procter	1,209	34.54	68	28.05
1977	C. E. B. Rice	1,300	35.13	50	22.26
1978	M. J. Procter	1,655	50.15	69	23.89
1979	J. R. T. Barclay	1,093	32.14	52	24.03
	M. J. Procter	1,241	38.78	81	18.91
	C. E. B. Rice	1,297	41.83	58	19.63
	P. Willey	1,109	41.07	52	32.63

Season		R	Avge	W	Avge
1980	M. J. Procter	1,081	34.87	51	18.25
1981	C. E. B. Rice	1,462	56.23	65	19.20
1982	I. T. Botham	1,241	44.32	66	22.98
	R. C. Ontong	1,204	31.68	64	32.17
	D. N. Patel	1,104	26.92	50	30.62
	P. Willey	1,783	50.94	51	26.88

HUNDRED AND HAT-TRICK

W. G. Grace, MCC v Kent at Canterbury; 123, five for 82, and six for 47 including hat-trick (12-a-side) ... 1874

G. Giffen, Australians v Lancashire at Manchester; 13, 113, and six for 55 including hat-trick ... 1884

W. E. Roller, Surrey v Sussex at The Oval; 204, four for 28 including hat-trick, and two for 16. (Unique instance of 200 and hat-trick.) ... 1885

W. B. Burns, Worcestershire v Gloucestershire at Worcester; 102*, three for 56, including hat-trick, and two for 21 ... 1913

V. W. C. Jupp, Sussex v Essex at Colchester; 102, six for 61, including hat-trick, and six for 78 ... 1921

R. E. S. Wyatt, MCC v Ceylon at Colombo; 124 and five for 39 including hat-trick. 1926-27

L. N. Constantine, West Indians v Northamptonshire at Northampton; seven for 45, including hat-trick, 107 (five 6s), and six for 67 ... 1928

D. E Davies, Glamorgan v Leicestershire at Leicester; 139, four for 27, and three for 31 including hat-trick ... 1937

V. M. Merchant, Dr C. R. Pereira's XI v Sir Homi Mehta's XI at Bombay; 1, 142, three for 31 including hat-trick, and no wicket for 17 ... 1946-47

M. J. Procter, Gloucestershire v Essex at Westcliff-on-Sea; 51, 102, three for 43, and five for 30 including hat-trick (all lbw) ... 1972

M. J. Procter, Gloucestershire v Leicestershire at Bristol; 122, no wkt for 32, and seven for 26 including hat-trick ... 1979

HUNDRED AND TEN WICKETS IN ONE INNINGS

V. E. Walker, England v Surrey at The Oval; ten for 74, four for 17, 20* and 108. 1859

E. M. Grace, MCC v Gentlemen of Kent at Canterbury; five for 77, ten for 69, and 192* ... 1862

W. G. Grace, MCC v Oxford University at Oxford; two for 60, ten for 49, and 104. 1886

F. A. Tarrant, Maharaja of Cooch Behar's XI v Lord Willingdon's XI at Poona; ten for 90, one for 22, 182* and 8* ... 1918-19

HUNDRED IN EACH INNINGS AND FIVE WICKETS TWICE

G. H. Hirst, Yorkshire v Somerset at Bath; six for 70, five for 45, 111 and 117*. 1906

WICKET-KEEPING RECORDS

MOST DISMISSALS IN A CAREER

	Ct	St	Total
J. T. Murray (1952-75)	1,270	257	1,527
R. W. Taylor (1960-82)	1,359	167	1,526
H. Strudwick (1902-27)	1,215	253	1,468

	Ct	*St*	*Total*
F. H. Huish (1895-1914)	952	376	1,328
D. Hunter (1889-1909)	955	372	1,327
B. Taylor (1949-73)	1,082	212	1,294
H. R. Butt (1890-1912)	971	291	1,262
A. P. E. Knott (1965-82)	1,090	123	1,213
J. H. Board (1891-1915)	852	354	1,206
H. Elliott (1920-47)	904	302	1,206
J. M. Parks (1949-76)	1,089	93	1,182
R. Booth (1951-70)	946	176	1,122
L. E. G. Ames (1926-51)	698	415	1,113
G. Duckworth (1923-47)	751	339	1,090
H. W. Stephenson (1948-64)	752	332	1,084
J. G. Binks (1955-75)	895	176	1,071
T. G. Evans (1939-69)	811	249	1,060
A. Long (1960-80)	922	124	1,046
G. O. Dawkes (1937-61)	896	146	1,042
W. L. Cornford (1921-47)	656	344	1,000

100 OR MORE DISMISSALS IN A SEASON

127 (79ct, 48st)	L. E. G. Ames, Kent	1929
121 (69ct, 52st)	L. E. G. Ames, Kent	1928
110 (62ct, 48st)	H. Yarnold, Worcestershire	1949
107 (77ct, 30st)	G. Duckworth, Lancashire	1928
107 (96ct, 11st)	J. G. Binks, Yorkshire	1960
104 (82ct, 22st)	J. T. Murray, Middlesex	1957
102 (70ct, 32st)	F. H. Huish, Kent	1913
102 (95ct, 7st)	J. T. Murray, Middlesex	1960
101 (85ct, 16st)	R. Booth, Worcestershire	1960
100 (62ct, 38st)	F. H. Huish, Kent	1911
100 (36ct, 64st)	L. E. G. Ames, Kent	1932
100 (91ct, 9st)	R. Booth, Worcestershire	1964

TEN OR MORE DISMISSALS IN A MATCH

12 (8ct, 4st)	E. Pooley	Surrey v Sussex at The Oval	1868
12 (9ct, 3st)	D. Tallon	Queensland v New South Wales at Sydney	1938-39
12 (9ct, 3st)	H. B. Taber	New South Wales v South Australia at Adelaide	1968-69
11 (all ct)	A. Long	Surrey v Sussex at Hove	1964
11 (all ct)	R. W. Marsh	Western Australia v Victoria at Perth	1975-76
11 (all ct)	D. L. Bairstow	Yorkshire v Derbyshire at Scarborough	1982
10 (5ct, 5st)	H. Phillips	Sussex v Surrey at The Oval	1872
10 (2ct, 8st)	E. Pooley	Surrey v Kent at The Oval	1878
10 (9ct, 1st)	T. W. Oates	Nottinghamshire v Middlesex at Nottingham	1906
10 (1ct, 9st)	F. H. Huish	Kent v Surrey at The Oval	1911
10 (9ct, 1st)	J. C. Hubble	Kent v Gloucestershire at Cheltenham	1923
10 (8ct, 2st)	H. Elliott	Derbyshire v Lancashire at Manchester	1935
10 (7ct, 3st)	P. Corrall	Leicestershire v Sussex at Hove	1936
10 (9ct, 1st)	R. A. Saggers	New South Wales v Combined XI at Brisbane	1940-41
10 (all ct)	A. E. Wilson	Gloucestershire v Hampshire at Portsmouth	1953
10 (7ct, 3st)	B. N. Jarman	South Australia v New South Wales at Adelaide	1961-62
10 (all ct)	L. A. Johnson	Northamptonshire v Sussex at Worthing	1963
10 (all ct)	R. W. Taylor	Derbyshire v Hampshire at Chesterfield	1963
10 (8ct, 2st)	L. A. Johnson	Northamptonshire v Warwickshire at Birmingham	1965
10 (9ct, 1st)	R. C. Jordon	Victoria v South Australia at Melbourne	1970-71

10 (all ct)	R. W. Marsh†	Western Australia v South Australia at Perth	1976-77
10 (6ct, 4st)	Taslim Arif	National Bank v Punjab at Lahore	1978-79
10 (9ct, 1st)	Arif-ud-Din	United Bank v Karachi 'B' at Karachi	1978-79
10 (all ct)	R. W. Taylor	England v India at Bombay	1979-80
10 (all ct)	R. J. Parks	Hampshire v Derbyshire at Portsmouth	1981

† *Marsh also scored a hundred (104), a unique "double".*

SEVEN OR MORE DISMISSALS IN AN INNINGS

8 (all ct)	A. T. W. Grout	Queensland v Western Australia at Brisbane	1959-60
7 (4ct, 3st)	E. J. Smith	Warwickshire v Derbyshire at Birmingham	1926
7 (6ct, 1st)	W. Farrimond	Lancashire v Kent at Manchester	1930
7 (all ct)	W. F. F. Price	Middlesex v Yorkshire at Lord's	1937
7 (3ct, 4st)	D. Tallon	Queensland v Victoria at Brisbane	1938-39
7 (all ct)	R. A. Saggers	New South Wales v Combined XI at Brisbane	1940-41
7 (1ct, 6st)	H. Yarnold	Worcestershire v Scotland at Dundee	1951
7 (4ct, 3st)	J. W. Brown	Scotland v Ireland at Dublin	1957
7 (6ct, 1st)	N. Kirsten	Border v Rhodesia at East London	1959-60
7 (all ct)	M. S. Smith	Natal v Border at East London	1959-60
7 (all ct)	K. V. Andrew	Northamptonshire v Lancashire at Manchester	1962
7 (all ct)	A. Long	Surrey v Sussex at Hove	1964
7 (all ct)	R. M. Schofield	Central Districts v Wellington at Wellington	1964-65
7 (all ct)	R. W. Taylor	Derbyshire v Glamorgan at Derby	1966
7 (6ct, 1st)	H. B. Taber	New South Wales v South Australia at Adelaide	1968-69
7 (6ct, 1st)	E. W. Jones	Glamorgan v Cambridge University at Cambridge	1970
7 (6ct, 1st)	S. Benjamin	Central Zone v North Zone at Bombay	1973-74
7 (all ct)	R. W. Taylor	Derbyshire v Yorkshire at Chesterfield	1975
7 (6ct, 1st)	Shahid Israr	Karachi Whites v Quetta at Karachi	1976-77
7 (all ct)	J. A. Maclean	Queensland v Victoria at Melbourne	1977-78
7 (5ct, 2st)	Taslim Arif	National Bank v Punjab at Lahore	1978-79
7 (all ct)	Wasim Bari	Pakistan v New Zealand at Auckland	1978-79
7 (all ct)	R. W. Taylor	England v India at Bombay	1979-80
7 (all ct)	D. L. Bairstow	Yorkshire v Derbyshire at Scarborough	1982

WICKET-KEEPERS' HAT-TRICKS

W. H. Brain, Gloucestershire v Somerset at Cheltenham, 1893 – three stumpings off successive balls from C. L. Townsend.

G. O. Dawkes, Derbyshire v Worcestershire at Kidderminster, 1958 – three catches off successive balls from H. L. Jackson.

MOST CATCHES – EXCLUDING WICKET-KEEPERS

In a Career

1,018	F. E. Woolley (1906-38)	811	D. B. Close (1949-82)
877	W. G. Grace (1865-1908)	786	J. G. Langridge (1928-55)
830	G. A. R. Lock (1946-71)	755	E. H. Hendren (1907-38)
819	W. R. Hammond (1920-51)	755	C. A. Milton (1948-74)

In a Season

78	W. R. Hammond	1928	65	W. R. Hammond	1925
77	M. J. Stewart	1957	65	P. M. Walker	1959
73	P. M. Walker	1961	65	D. W. Richardson	1961
71	P. J. Sharpe	1962	64	J. Tunnicliffe	1904
70	J. Tunnicliffe	1901	64	K. F. Barrington	1957
69	J. G. Langridge	1955	64	G. A. R. Lock	1957
69	P. M. Walker	1960	63	K. J. Grieves	1950
65	J. Tunnicliffe	1895	63	C. A. Milton	1956

In a Match

10	W. R. Hammond	Gloucestershire v Surrey at Cheltenham	1928
8	W. B. Burns	Worcestershire v Yorkshire at Bradford	1907
8	A. H. Bakewell	Northamptonshire v Essex at Leyton	1928
8	W. R. Hammond	Gloucestershire v Worcestershire at Cheltenham	1932
8	K. J. Grieves	Lancashire v Sussex at Manchester	1951
8	C. A. Milton	Gloucestershire v Sussex at Hove	1952
8	G. A. R. Lock	Surrey v Warwickshire at The Oval	1957
8	J. M. Prodger	Kent v Gloucestershire at Cheltenham	1961
8	P. M. Walker	Glamorgan v Derbyshire at Swansea	1970
8	Javed Miandad	Habib Bank v Universities at Lahore	1977-78

In an Innings

7	M. J. Stewart	Surrey v Northamptonshire at Northampton	1957
7	A. S. Brown	Gloucestershire v Nottinghamshire at Nottingham	1966

THE SIDES

HIGHEST TOTALS

1,107	Victoria v New South Wales at Melbourne	1926-27
1,059	Victoria v Tasmania at Melbourne	1922-23
951-7 dec.	Sind v Baluchistan at Karachi	1973-74
918	New South Wales v South Australia at Sydney	1900-01
912-8 dec.	Holkar v Mysore at Indore	1945-46
910-6 dec.	Railways v Dera Ismail Khan at Lahore	1964-65
903-7 dec.	England v Australia at The Oval	1938
887	Yorkshire v Warwickshire at Birmingham	1896
849	England v West Indies at Kingston	1929-30
843	Australians v Oxford and Cambridge Universities Past and Present at Portsmouth	1893

HIGHEST FOR EACH FIRST-CLASS COUNTY

Derbyshire	645	v Hampshire at Derby	1898
Essex	692	v Somerset at Taunton	1895
Glamorgan	587-8	v Derbyshire at Cardiff	1951
Gloucestershire	653-6	v Glamorgan at Bristol	1928
Hampshire	672-7	v Somerset at Taunton	1899
Kent	803-4	v Essex at Brentwood	1934
Lancashire	801	v Somerset at Taunton	1895

Leicestershire	701-4	v Worcestershire at Worcester	1906
Middlesex	642-3	v Hampshire at Southampton	1923
Northamptonshire	557-6	v Sussex at Hove	1914
Nottinghamshire	739-7	v Leicestershire at Nottingham	1903
Somerset	675-9	v Hampshire at Bath	1924
Surrey	811	v Somerset at The Oval	1899
Sussex	705-8	v Surrey at Hastings	1902
Warwickshire	657-6	v Hampshire at Birmingham	1899
Worcestershire	633	v Warwickshire at Worcester	1906
Yorkshire	887	v Warwickshire at Birmingham	1896

LOWEST TOTALS

12	Oxford University v MCC and Ground at Oxford	†1877
12	Northamptonshire v Gloucestershire at Gloucester	1907
13	Auckland v Canterbury at Auckland	1877-78
13	Nottinghamshire v Yorkshire at Nottingham	1901
15	MCC v Surrey at Lord's	1839
15	Victoria v MCC at Melbourne	†1903-04
15	Northamptonshire v Yorkshire at Northampton	†1908
15	Hampshire v Warwickshire at Birmingham	1922
	(Following on, Hampshire scored 521 and won by 155 runs.)	
16	MCC and Ground v Surrey at Lord's	1872
16	Derbyshire v Nottinghamshire at Nottingham	1879
16	Surrey v Nottinghamshire at The Oval	1880
16	Warwickshire v Kent at Tonbridge	1913
16	Trinidad v Barbados at Bridgetown	1941-42
16	Border v Natal at East London (first innings)	1959-60
17	Gentlemen of Kent v Gentlemen of England at Lord's	1850
17	Gloucestershire v Australians at Cheltenham	1896
18	The 'B's v England at Lord's	1831
18	Kent v Sussex at Gravesend	†1867
18	Tasmania v Victoria at Melbourne	1868-69
18	Australians v MCC and Ground at Lord's	†1896
18	Border v Natal at East London (second innings)	1959-60
19	Sussex v Surrey at Godalming	1830
19	Sussex v Nottinghamshire at Hove	†1873
19	MCC and Ground v Australians at Lord's	1878
19	Wellington v Nelson at Nelson	1885-86

† *Signifies that one man was absent.*

Note: At Lord's in 1810, The 'B's, with one man absent, were dismissed by England for 6.

LOWEST TOTAL IN A MATCH

34	(16 and 18) Border v Natal at East London	1959-60
42	(27 and 15) Northamptonshire v Yorkshire at Northampton	1908

Note: Northamptonshire batted one man short in each innings.

LOWEST FOR EACH FIRST-CLASS COUNTY

Derbyshire	16	v Nottinghamshire at Nottingham	1879
Essex	30	v Yorkshire at Leyton	1901
Glamorgan	22	v Lancashire at Liverpool	1924
Gloucestershire	17	v Australians at Cheltenham	1896
Hampshire	15	v Warwickshire at Birmingham	1922

Kent	18	v Sussex at Gravesend	1867
Lancashire	25	v Derbyshire at Manchester	1871
Leicestershire	25	v Kent at Leicester	1912
Middlesex	20	v MCC at Lord's	1864
Northamptonshire	12	v Gloucestershire at Gloucester	1907
Nottinghamshire	13	v Yorkshire at Nottingham	1901
Somerset	25	v Gloucestershire at Bristol	1947
Surrey	16	v Nottinghamshire at The Oval	1880
Sussex	19	v Nottinghamshire at Hove	1873
Warwickshire	16	v Kent at Tonbridge	1913
Worcestershire	24	v Yorkshire at Huddersfield	1903
Yorkshire	23	v Hampshire at Middlesbrough	1965

HIGHEST MATCH AGGREGATES

2,376 for 38 wickets	Maharashtra v Bombay at Poona	1948-49
2,078 for 40 wickets	Bombay v Holkar at Bombay	1944-45
1,981 for 35 wickets	England v South Africa at Durban	1938-39
1,929 for 39 wickets	New South Wales v South Australia at Sydney	1925-26
1,911 for 34 wickets	New South Wales v Victoria at Sydney	1908-09
1,905 for 40 wickets	Otago v Wellington at Dunedin	1923-24

In England

1,723 for 31 wickets	England v Australia at Leeds	1948
1,601 for 29 wickets	England v Australia at Lord's	1930
1,507 for 28 wickets	England v West Indies at The Oval	1976
1,502 for 28 wickets	MCC v New Zealanders at Lord's	1927
1,499 for 31 wickets	T. N. Pearce's XI v Australians at Scarborough	1961
1,496 for 24 wickets	England v Australia at Nottingham	1938
1,494 for 37 wickets	England v Australia at The Oval	1934

LOWEST MATCH AGGREGATE

105 for 31 wickets	MCC v Australians at Lord's	1878

Note: The lowest aggregate since 1900 is 158 for 22 wickets, Surrey v Worcestershire at The Oval, 1954.

HIGHEST FOURTH INNINGS TOTALS

(Unless otherwise stated, the side making the runs won the match.)

654-5 England v South Africa at Durban 1938-39
(After being set 696 to win. The match was left drawn on the tenth day.)

604 Maharashtra v Bombay at Poona 1948-49
(After being set 959 to win.)

576-8 Trinidad v Barbados at Port-of-Spain 1945-46
(After being set 672 to win. Match drawn on fifth day.)

572 New South Wales v South Australia at Sydney 1907-08
(After being set 593 to win.)

529-9 Combined XI v South Africans at Perth 1963-64
(After being set 579 to win. Match drawn on fourth day.)

518	Victoria v Queensland at Brisbane (After being set 753 to win.)	1926-27
507-7	Cambridge University v MCC and Ground at Lord's	1896
502-6	Middlesex v Nottinghamshire at Nottingham (Game won by an unfinished stand of 271; a county record.)	1925
502-8	Players v Gentlemen at Lord's	1900
500-7	South African Universities v Western Province at Stellenbosch	1978-79

LARGEST VICTORIES

Largest Innings Victories

Inns and 851 runs:	Railways (910-6 dec.) v Dera Ismail Khan (Lahore)	1964-65
Inns and 666 runs:	Victoria (1,059) v Tasmania (Melbourne)	1922-23
Inns and 656 runs:	Victoria (1,107) v New South Wales (Melbourne)	1926-27
Inns and 605 runs:	New South Wales (918) v South Australia (Sydney)	1900-01
Inns and 579 runs:	England (903-7 dec.) v Australia (The Oval)	1938
Inns and 575 runs:	Sind (951-7 dec.) v Baluchistan (Karachi)	1973-74
Inns and 527 runs:	New South Wales (713) v South Australia (Adelaide)	1908-09
Inns and 517 runs:	Australians (675) v Nottinghamshire (Nottingham)	1921

Largest Victories by Runs Margin

685 runs:	New South Wales (235 and 761-8 dec.) v Queensland (Sydney)	1929-30
675 runs:	England (521 and 342-8 dec.) v Australia (Brisbane)	1928-29
638 runs:	New South Wales (304 and 770) v South Australia (Adelaide)	1920-21
625 runs:	Sargodha (376 and 416) v Lahore Municipal Corporation (Faisalabad)	1978-79
609 runs:	Muslim Commercial Bank (575 and 282-0 dec.) v WAPDA (Lahore).	1977-78
571 runs:	Victoria (304 and 649) v South Australia (Adelaide)	1926-27
562 runs:	Australia (701 and 327) v England (The Oval)	1934

Victory Without Losing a Wicket

Lancashire (166-0 dec. and 66-0) beat Leicestershire by ten wickets (Manchester)	1956
Karachi 'A' (277-0 dec.) beat Sind 'A' by an innings and 77 runs (Karachi)	1957-58
Railways (236-0 dec. and 16-0) beat Jammu and Kashmir by ten wickets (Srinagar)	1960-61
Karnataka (451-0 dec.) beat Kerala by an innings and 186 runs (Chikmagalur)	1977-78

TIED MATCHES IN FIRST-CLASS CRICKET

There have been 27 tied matches since the First World War.

Somerset v Sussex at Taunton (The last Sussex batsman not allowed to bat under Law 45 [subsequently Law 17 and now Law 31])	1919
Orange Free State v Eastern Province at Bloemfontein (Eastern Province had two wickets to fall.)	1925-26
Essex v Somerset at Chelmsford (Although Essex had one man to go in, MCC ruled that the game should rank as a tie. The ninth wicket fell half a minute before time.)	1926
Gloucestershire v Australians at Bristol	1930
Victoria v MCC at Melbourne (Victoria's third wicket fell to the last ball of the match when one run was needed to win.)	1932-33
Worcestershire v Somerset at Kidderminster	1939

Southern Punjab v Baroda at Patiala	1945-46
Essex v Northamptonshire at Ilford	1947
Hampshire v Lancashire at Bournemouth	1947
D. G. Bradman's XI v A. L. Hassett's XI at Melbourne	1948-49
Hampshire v Kent at Southampton	1950
Sussex v Warwickshire at Hove	1952
Essex v Lancashire at Brentwood	1952
Northamptonshire v Middlesex at Peterborough	1953
Yorkshire v Leicestershire at Huddersfield	1954
Sussex v Hampshire at Eastbourne	1955
Victoria v New South Wales at Melbourne	1956-57
T. N. Pearce's XI v New Zealanders at Scarborough	1958
Essex v Gloucestershire at Leyton	1959
Australia v West Indies (First Test) at Brisbane	1960-61
Bahawalpur v Lahore 'B' at Bahawalpur	1961-62
Hampshire v Middlesex at Portsmouth	1967
England XI v England Under 25 XI at Scarborough	1968
Yorkshire v Middlesex at Bradford	1973
Sussex v Essex at Hove	1974
South Australia v Queensland at Adelaide	1976-77
Central Districts v England XI at New Plymouth	1977-78
Peshawar v Allied Bank at Peshawar	1979-80

Note: Since 1948 a tie has been recognised only when the scores are level with all the wickets down in the fourth innings. This ruling applies to all grades of cricket, and in the case of a one-day match to the second innings, provided that the match has not been brought to a further conclusion.

MATCHES BEGUN AND FINISHED IN ONE DAY

Since 1900. A fuller list may be found in the Wisden *of 1981 and preceding editions.*

Yorkshire v Worcestershire at Bradford, May 7	1900
MCC and Ground v London County at Lord's, May 20	1903
Transvaal v Orange Free State at Johannesburg, December 30	1906
Middlesex v Gentlemen of Philadelphia at Lord's, July 20	1908
Gloucestershire v Middlesex at Bristol, August 26	1909
Eastern Province v Orange Free State at Port Elizabeth, December 26	1912
Kent v Sussex at Tonbridge, June 21	1919
Lancashire v Somerset at Manchester, May 21	1925
Madras v Mysore at Madras, November 4	1934
Ireland v New Zealanders at Dublin, September 11	1937
Derbyshire v Somerset at Chesterfield, June 11	1947
Lancashire v Sussex at Manchester, July 12	1950
Surrey v Warwickshire at The Oval, May 16	1953
Somerset v Lancashire at Bath, June 6 (H. T. F. Buse's benefit)	1953
Kent v Worcestershire at Tunbridge Wells, June 15	1960

A WISDEN RECORD

At a sale of sporting memorabilia at the Phillips auction rooms, London, in November 1982, a record price of £800 was paid for an 1869 edition, in original paper covers, of *Wisden Cricketers' Almanack*. A bound run of *Wisdens* from 1880 for 1937 went for the sale's top price of £3,000.

TEST MATCH RECORDS

SCORERS OF 2,000 RUNS IN TESTS

FOR ENGLAND

	T	*I*	*NO*	*R*	*HI*	*100s*	*Avge*
G. Boycott................	108	193	23	8,114	246*	22	47.72
M. C. Cowdrey...........	114	188	15	7,624	182	22	44.06
W. R. Hammond.........	85	140	16	7,249	336*	22	58.45
L. Hutton..................	79	138	15	6,971	364	19	56.67
K. F. Barrington..........	82	131	15	6,806	256	20	58.67
D. C. S. Compton........	78	131	15	5,807	278	17	50.06
J. B. Hobbs................	61	102	7	5,410	211	15	56.94
J. H. Edrich................	77	127	9	5,138	310*	12	43.54
T. W. Graveney...........	79	123	13	4,882	258	11	44.38
H. Sutcliffe.................	54	84	9	4,555	194	16	60.73
P. B. H. May..............	66	106	9	4,537	285*	13	46.77
E. R. Dexter...............	62	102	8	4,502	205	9	47.89
A. P. E. Knott............	95	149	15	4,389	135	5	32.75
D. L. Amiss................	50	88	10	3,612	262*	11	46.30
A. W. Greig................	58	93	4	3,599	148	8	40.43
E. H. Hendren............	51	83	9	3,525	205*	7	47.63
F. E. Woolley..............	64	98	7	3,283	154	5	36.07
K. W. R. Fletcher........	59	96	14	3,272	216	7	39.90
I. T. Botham...............	54	82	3	2,996	208	11	37.92
D. I. Gower................	44	75	7	2,897	200*	4	42.60
M. Leyland.................	41	65	5	2,764	187	9	46.06
C. Washbrook.............	37	66	6	2,569	195	6	42.81
G. A. Gooch..............	42	75	4	2,540	153	4	35.77
B. L. D'Oliveira..........	44	70	8	2,484	158	5	40.06
W. J. Edrich...............	39	63	2	2,440	219	6	40.00
T. G. Evans................	91	133	14	2,439	104	2	20.49
L. E. G. Ames............	47	72	12	2,434	149	8	40.56
W. Rhodes.................	58	98	21	2,325	179	2	30.19
T. E. Bailey................	61	91	14	2,290	134*	1	29.74
M. J. K. Smith...........	50	78	6	2,278	121	3	31.63
P. E. Richardson.........	34	56	1	2,061	126	5	37.47

FOR AUSTRALIA

	T	*I*	*NO*	*R*	*HI*	*100s*	*Avge*
D. G. Bradman...........	52	80	10	6,996	334	29	99.94
G. S. Chappell............	76	134	16	6,291	247*	20	53.31
R. N. Harvey.............	79	137	10	6,149	205	21	48.41
K. D. Walters..............	74	125	14	5,357	250	15	48.26
I. M. Chappell............	75	136	10	5,345	196	14	42.42
W. M. Lawry..............	67	123	12	5,234	210	13	47.15
R. B. Simpson............	62	111	7	4,869	311	10	46.81
I. R. Redpath.............	66	120	11	4,737	171	8	43.45
A. R. Morris...............	46	79	3	3,533	206	12	46.48
C. Hill........................	49	89	2	3,412	191	7	39.21
R. W. Marsh..............	83	131	11	3,362	132	3	28.01
V. T. Trumper............	48	89	8	3,163	214*	8	39.04
K. J. Hughes..............	48	86	5	3,121	213	7	38.53

	T	*I*	*NO*	*R*	*HI*	*100s*	*Avge*
C. C. McDonald..........	47	83	4	3,107	170	5	39.32
A. L. Hassett..............	43	69	3	3,073	198*	10	46.56
A. R. Border.............	42	75	12	3,057	162	9	48.52
K. R. Miller................	55	87	7	2,958	147	7	36.97
W. W. Armstrong........	50	84	10	2,863	159*	6	38.68
K. R. Stackpole...........	43	80	5	2,807	207	7	37.42
N. C. O'Neill..............	42	69	8	2,779	181	6	45.55
S. J. McCabe...............	39	62	5	2,748	232	6	48.21
W. Bardsley................	41	66	5	2,469	193*	6	40.47
G. M. Wood...............	37	72	5	2,318	126	7	34.59
W. M. Woodfull..........	35	54	4	2,300	161	7	46.00
P. J. Burge.................	42	68	8	2,290	181	4	38.16
S. E. Gregory..............	58	100	7	2,282	201	4	24.53
R. Benaud..................	63	97	7	2,201	122	3	24.45
C. G. Macartney..........	35	55	4	2,131	170	7	41.78
W. H. Ponsford...........	29	48	4	2,122	266	7	48.22
G. N. Yallop...............	32	61	3	2,101	172	6	36.22
R. M. Cowper.............	27	46	2	2,061	307	5	46.84

FOR SOUTH AFRICA

	T	*I*	*NO*	*R*	*HI*	*100s*	*Avge*
B. Mitchell.................	42	80	9	3,471	189*	8	48.88
A. D. Nourse.............	34	62	7	2,960	231	9	53.81
H. W. Taylor..............	42	76	4	2,936	176	7	40.77
E. J. Barlow...............	30	57	2	2,516	201	6	45.74
T. L. Goddard............	41	78	5	2,516	112	1	34.46
D. J. McGlew.............	34	64	6	2,440	255*	7	42.06
J. H. B. Waite............	50	86	7	2,405	134	4	30.44
R. G. Pollock..............	23	41	4	2,256	274	7	60.97
A. W. Nourse.............	45	83	8	2,234	111	1	29.78
R. A. McLean............	40	73	3	2,120	142	5	30.28

FOR WEST INDIES

	T	*I*	*NO*	*R*	*HI*	*100s*	*Avge*
G. S. Sobers...............	93	160	21	8,032	365*	26	57.78
R. B. Kanhai..............	79	137	6	6,227	256	15	47.53
C. H. Lloyd...............	85	143	10	5,831	242*	14	43.84
E. D. Weekes.............	48	81	5	4,455	207	15	58.61
A. I. Kallicharran.........	66	109	10	4,399	187	12	44.43
R. C. Fredericks..........	59	109	7	4,334	169	8	42.49
I. V. A. Richards.........	47	74	4	4,129	291	13	58.98
F. M. M. Worrell.........	51	87	9	3,860	261	9	49.48
C. L. Walcott..............	44	74	7	3,798	220	15	56.68
C. C. Hunte................	44	78	6	3,245	260	8	45.06
B. F. Butcher..............	44	78	6	3,104	209*	7	43.11
C. G. Greenidge..........	36	63	3	2,569	134	5	42.81
S. M. Nurse................	29	54	1	2,523	258	6	47.60
G. A. Headley............	22	40	4	2,190	270*	10	60.83
J. B. Stollmeyer...........	32	56	5	2,159	160	4	42.33
L. G. Rowe................	30	49	2	2,047	302	7	43.55

FOR NEW ZEALAND

	T	*I*	*NO*	*R*	*HI*	*100s*	*Avge*
B. E. Congdon	61	114	7	3,448	176	7	32.22
J. R. Reid	58	108	5	3,431	142	6	33.31
G. M. Turner	39	70	6	2,920	259	7	45.62
B. Sutcliffe	42	76	8	2,727	230*	5	40.10
M. G. Burgess	50	92	6	2,684	119*	5	31.20
G. T. Dowling	39	77	3	2,306	239	3	31.16

FOR INDIA

	T	*I*	*NO*	*R*	*HI*	*100s*	*Avge*
S. M. Gavaskar	78	137	9	6,792	221	24	53.06
G. R. Viswanath	84	145	10	5,935	222	14	43.96
P. R. Umrigar	59	94	8	3,631	223	12	42.22
V. L. Manjrekar	55	92	10	3,209	189*	7	39.13
C. G. Borde	55	97	11	3,062	177*	5	35.60
D. B. Vengsarkar	51	83	8	2,869	157*	6	38.25
Nawab of Pataudi jun.	46	83	3	2,792	203*	6	34.90
F. M. Engineer	46	87	3	2,611	121	2	31.08
Pankaj Roy	43	79	4	2,441	173	5	32.54
V. S. Hazare	30	52	6	2,192	164*	7	47.65
A. L. Wadekar	37	71	3	2,113	143	1	31.07
V. Mankad	44	72	5	2,109	231	5	31.47
C. P. S. Chauhan	40	68	2	2,084	97	0	31.57
M. L. Jaisimha	39	71	4	2,056	129	3	30.68
D. N. Sardesai	30	55	4	2,001	212	5	39.23

FOR PAKISTAN

	T	*I*	*NO*	*R*	*HI*	*100s*	*Avge*
Majid J. Khan	62	105	5	3,931	167	8	39.31
Hanif Mohammad	55	97	8	3,915	337	12	43.98
Mushtaq Mohammad	57	100	7	3,643	201	10	39.17
Asif Iqbal	58	99	7	3,575	175	11	38.85
Javed Miandad	43	74	13	3,222	206	7	52.81
Zaheer Abbas	49	85	6	3,154	274	7	39.92
Saeed Ahmed	41	78	4	2,991	172	5	40.41
Sadiq Mohammad	41	74	2	2,579	166	5	35.81
Wasim Raja	44	73	12	2,311	117*	2	37.88
Imtiaz Ahmed	41	72	1	2,079	209	3	29.28

TEST BATTING AVERAGE OVER 50

(Qualification: 20 innings)

Avge		*T*	*I*	*NO*	*R*	*HI*	*100s*
99.94	D. G. Bradman (*A*)......	52	80	10	6,996	334	29
60.97	R. G. Pollock (*SA*).......	23	41	4	2,256	274	7
60.83	G. A. Headley (*WI*).....	22	40	4	2,190	270*	10
60.73	H. Sutcliffe (*E*)...........	54	84	9	4,555	194	16
59.23	E. Paynter (*E*)............	20	31	5	1,540	243	4
58.98	I. V. A. Richards (*WI*)..	47	74	4	4,129	291	13
58.67	K. F. Barrington (*E*).....	82	131	5	6,806	256	20
58.61	E. D. Weekes (*WI*)......	48	81	5	4,455	207	15
58.45	W. R. Hammond (*E*)....	85	140	16	7,249	336*	22
57.78	G. S. Sobers (*WI*)........	93	160	21	8,032	365*	26
56.94	J. B. Hobbs (*E*)..........	61	102	7	5,410	211	15
56.68	C. L. Walcott (*WI*).......	44	74	7	3,798	220	15
56.67	L. Hutton (*E*).............	79	138	15	6,971	364	19
55.00	E. Tyldesley (*E*)..........	14	20	2	990	122	3
54.20	C. A. Davis (*WI*).........	15	29	5	1,301	183	4
53.81	A. D. Nourse (*SA*).......	34	62	7	2,960	231	9
53.31	G. S. Chappell (*A*).......	76	134	16	6,291	247*	20
53.06	S. M. Gavaskar (*I*).......	78	137	9	6,792	221	24
52.81	Javed Miandad (*P*).......	43	74	13	3,222	206	7
51.62	J. Ryder (*A*)..............	20	32	5	1,394	201*	3
50.06	D. C. S. Compton (*E*)..	78	131	15	5,807	278	17

HUNDRED ON TEST DEBUT

C. Bannerman (165*).......	Australia v England at Melbourne.......................	1876-77
W. G. Grace (152)..........	England v Australia at The Oval........................	1880
H. Graham (107)............	Australia v England at Lord's............................	1893
K. S. Ranjitsinhji (154*)...	England v Australia at Manchester......................	1896
P. F. Warner (132*).........	England v South Africa at Johannesburg.............	1898-99
R. A. Duff (104)............	Australia v England at Melbourne.......................	1901-02
R. E. Foster (287)...........	England v Australia at Sydney...........................	1903-04
G. Gunn (119)................	England v Australia at Sydney...........................	1907-08
R. J. Hartigan (116)........	Australia v England at Adelaide.........................	1907-08
H. L. Collins (104)..........	Australia v England at Sydney...........................	1920-21
W. H. Ponsford (110)......	Australia v England at Sydney...........................	1924-25
A. Jackson (164).............	Australia v England at Adelaide.........................	1928-29
G. A. Headley (176)........	West Indies v England at Bridgetown..................	1929-30
J. E. Mills (117).............	New Zealand v England at Wellington................	1929-30
Nawab of Pataudi (102)....	England v Australia at Sydney...........................	1932-33
B. H. Valentine (136)......	England v India at Bombay...............................	1933-34
L. Amarnath (118)..........	India v England at Bombay...............................	1933-34
P. A. Gibb (106)............	England v South Africa at Johannesburg.............	1938-39
S. C. Griffith (140)..........	England v West Indies at Port-of-Spain...............	1947-48
A. G. Ganteaume (112)...	West Indies v England at Port-of-Spain...............	1947-48
J. W. Burke (101*)..........	Australia v England at Adelaide.........................	1950-51
P. B. H. May (138).........	England v South Africa at Leeds........................	1951
D. H. Shodhan (110).......	India v Pakistan at Calcutta..............................	1952-53
B. H. Pairaudeau (115)....	West Indies v India at Port-of-Spain...................	1952-53
O. G. Smith (104)...........	West Indies v Australia at Kingston....................	1954-55
A. G. Kripal Singh (100*).	India v New Zealand at Hyderabad.....................	1955-56
C. C. Hunte (142)...........	West Indies v Pakistan at Bridgetown.................	1957-58
C. A. Milton (104*).........	England v New Zealand at Leeds.......................	1958

A. A. Baig (112)	India v England at Manchester	1959
Hanumant Singh (105)	India v England at Delhi	1963-64
Khalid Ibadulla (166)	Pakistan v Australia at Karachi	1964-65
B. R. Taylor (105)	New Zealand v India at Calcutta	1964-65
K. D. Walters (155)	Australia v England at Brisbane	1965-66
J. H. Hampshire (107)	England v West Indies at Lord's	1969
G. R. Viswanath (137)	India v Australia at Kanpur	1969-70
G. S. Chappell (108)	Australia v England at Perth	1970-71
†L. G. Rowe (214, 100*)	West Indies v New Zealand at Kingston	1971-72
A. I. Kallicharran (100*)	West Indies v New Zealand at Georgetown	1971-72
R. E. Redmond (107)	New Zealand v Pakistan at Auckland	1972-73
F. C. Hayes (106*)	England v West Indies at The Oval	1973
C. G. Greenidge (107)	West Indies v India at Bangalore	1974-75
L. Baichan (105*)	West Indies v Pakistan at Lahore	1974-75
G. J. Cosier (109)	Australia v West Indies at Melbourne	1975-76
S. Amarnath (124)	India v New Zealand at Auckland	1975-76
Javed Miandad (163)	Pakistan v New Zealand at Lahore	1976-77
A. B. Williams (100)	West Indies v Australia at Georgetown	1977-78
D. M. Wellham (103)	Australia v England at The Oval	1981
Salim Malik (100*)	Pakistan v Sri Lanka at Karachi	1981-82

† *L. G. Rowe is the only batsman to score a hundred in each innings on début.*

300 RUNS IN FIRST TEST MATCH

314	L. G. Rowe (214, 100*)	West Indies v New Zealand at Kingston	1971-72
306	R. E. Foster (287, 19)	England v Australia at Sydney	1903-04

HUNDRED AND TEN WICKETS IN A TEST MATCH

I. T. Botham	114 and thirteen for 106	England v India at Bombay	1979-80

HUNDRED AND FIVE WICKETS IN ONE TEST INNINGS

J. H. Sinclair	106 and six for 26	South Africa v England at Cape Town	1898-99
G. A. Faulkner	123 and five for 120	South Africa v England at Johannesburg	1909-10
C. Kelleway	114 and five for 33	Australia v South Africa at Manchester	1912
J. M. Gregory	100 and seven for 69	Australia v England at Melbourne	1920-21
V. Mankad	184 and five for 196	India v England at Lord's	1952
D. St E. Atkinson	219 and five for 56	West Indies v Australia at Bridgetown	1954-55
K. R. Miller	109 and six for 107	Australia v West Indies at Kingston	1954-55
R. Benaud	100 and five for 84	Australia v South Africa at Johannesburg	1957-58
O. G. Smith	100 and five for 90	West Indies v India at Delhi	1958-59
P. R. Umrigar	172* and five for 107	India v West Indies at Port-of-Spain	1961-62
G. S. Sobers	104 and five for 63	West Indies v India at Kingston	1961-62
†B. R. Taylor	105 and five for 86	New Zealand v India at Calcutta	1964-65
G. S. Sobers	174 and five for 41	West Indies v England at Leeds	1966
Mushtaq Mohammad	201 and five for 49	Pakistan v New Zealand at Dunedin	1972-73
A. W. Greig	148 and six for 164	England v West Indies at Bridgetown	1973-74
Mushtaq Mohammad	121 and five for 28	Pakistan v West Indies at Port-of-Spain	1976-77
I. T. Botham	103 and five for 73	England v New Zealand at Christchurch	1977-78
I. T. Botham	108 and eight for 34	England v Pakistan at Lord's	1978
I. T. Botham	114 and six for 58 (1st innings), seven for 48 (2nd innings)	England v India at Bombay	1979-80
I. T. Botham	149* and six for 95	England v Australia at Leeds	1981

† *Taylor's feat was on Test début.*

TWO SEPARATE HUNDREDS IN A TEST MATCH

Three times: S. M. Gavaskar v West Indies (1970-71), v Pakistan (1978-79), v West Indies (1978-79).

Twice in one series: C. L. Walcott v Australia (1954-55).

Twice: H. Sutcliffe v Australia (1924-25), v South Africa (1929); G. A. Headley v England (1929-30 and 1939); G. S. Chappell v New Zealand (1973-74), v West Indies (1975-76).

Once: W. Bardsley v England (1909); A. C. Russell v South Africa (1922-23); W. R. Hammond v Australia (1928-29); E. Paynter v South Africa (1938-39); D. C. S. Compton v Australia (1946-47); A. R. Morris v England (1946-47); A. Melville v England (1947); B. Mitchell v England (1947); D. G. Bradman v India (1947-48); V. S. Hazare v Australia (1947-48); E. D. Weekes v India (1948-49); J. Moroney v South Africa (1949-50); G. S. Sobers v Pakistan (1957-58); R. B. Kanhai v Australia (1960-61); Hanif Mohammad v England (1961-62); R. B. Simpson v Pakistan (1964-65); K. D. Walters v West Indies (1968-69); †L. G. Rowe v New Zealand (1971-72); I. M. Chappell v New Zealand (1973-74); G. M. Turner v Australia (1973-74); C. G. Greenidge v England (1976); G. P. Howarth v England (1977-78); ‡A. R. Border v Pakistan (1979-80).

† *L. G. Rowe's two hundreds were on his Test début.*

‡ *A. R. Border scored 150* ad 153 to become the first batsman to score 150 in each innings of a Test match.*

HUNDRED AND DOUBLE-HUNDRED IN SAME TEST

K. D. Walters (Australia)	242 and 103 v West Indies (Sydney)	1968-69
S. M. Gavaskar (India)	124 and 220 v West Indies (Port-of-Spain)	1970-71
†L. G. Rowe (West Indies)	214 and 100* v New Zealand (Kingston)	1971-72
G. S. Chappell (Australia)	247* and 133 v New Zealand (Wellington)	1973-74

† *On Test début*

MOST RUNS IN A TEST SERIES

	T	*I*	*NO*	*R*	*HI*	*100s*	*Avge*		
D. G. Bradman	5	7	0	974	334	4	139.14	A v E	1930
W. R. Hammond	5	9	1	905	251	4	113.12	E v A	1928-29
R. N. Harvey	5	9	0	834	205	4	92.66	A v SA	1952-53
I. V. A. Richards	4	7	0	829	291	3	118.42	WI v E	1976
C. L. Walcott	5	10	0	827	155	5	82.70	WI v A	1954-55
G. S. Sobers	5	8	2	824	365*	3	137.33	WI v P	1957-58
D. G. Bradman	5	9	0	810	270	3	90.00	A v E	1936-37
D. G. Bradman	5	5	1	806	299*	4	201.50	A v SA	1931-32
E. D. Weekes	5	7	0	779	194	4	111.28	WI v I	1948-49
†S. M. Gavaskar	4	8	3	774	220	4	154.80	I v WI	1970-71
D. G. Bradman	5	8	0	758	304	2	94.75	A v E	1934
D. C. S. Compton	5	8	0	753	208	4	94.12	E v SA	1947

† *Gavaskar's aggregate was achieved in his first Test series.*

CARRYING BAT THROUGH TEST INNINGS

(Figures in brackets show side's total)

A. B. Tancred	26*	(47)	South Africa v England (Cape Town)	1888-89
J. E. Barrett	67*	(176)	Australia v England (Lord's)	1890
R. Abel	132*	(307)	England v Australia (Sydney)	1891-92
P. F. Warner	132*	(237)	England v South Africa (Johannesburg)	1898-99
W. W. Armstrong	159*	(309)	Australia v South Africa (Johannesburg)	1902-03
J. W. Zulch	43*	(103)	South Africa v England (Cape Town)	1909-10

W. Bardsley	193*	(383)	Australia v England (Lord's)	1926
W. M. Woodfull	30*	(66)‡	Australia v England (Brisbane)	1928-29
W. M. Woodfull	73*	(193)†	Australia v England (Adelaide)	1932-33
W. A. Brown	206*	(422)	Australia v England (Lord's)	1938
L. Hutton	202*	(344)	England v West Indies (The Oval)	1950
L. Hutton	156*	(272)	England v Australia (Adelaide)	1950-51
Nazar Mohammad	124*	(331)	Pakistan v India (Lucknow)	1952-53
F. M. M. Worrell	191*	(372)	West Indies v England (Nottingham)	1957
T. L. Goddard	56*	(99)	South Africa v Australia (Cape Town)	1957-58
D. J. McGlew	127*	(292)	South Africa v New Zealand (Durban)	1961-62
C. C. Hunte	60*	(131)	West Indies v Australia (Port-of-Spain)	1964-65
G. M. Turner	43*	(131)	New Zealand v England (Lord's)	1969
W. M. Lawry	49*	(107)	Australia v India (Delhi)	1969-70
W. M. Lawry	60*	(116)†	Australia v England (Sydney)	1970-71
G. M. Turner	223*	(386)	New Zealand v West Indies (Kingston)	1971-72
I. R. Redpath	159*	(346)	Australia v New Zealand (Auckland)	1973-74
G. Boycott	99*	(215)	England v Australia (Perth)	1979-80

† *One man absent.* ‡ *Two men absent.*

Notes: G. M. Turner (223*) holds the record for the highest score by a player carrying his bat through a Test innings. He is also the youngest player to do so, being 22 years 63 days old when he first achieved the feat (1969).

D. L. Amiss (262*) batted throughout England's second innings of 432 for nine v West Indies at Kingston, 1973-74, the tenth wicket adding 40, unbroken, in fifty-three minutes.

D. L. Haynes (55 and 105) opened the batting and was last man out in each innings for West Indies v New Zealand at Dunedin, 1979-80.

FASTEST TEST FIFTIES

Minutes			
28	J. T. Brown	England v Australia at Melbourne	1894-95
29	S. A. Durani	India v England at Kanpur	1963-64
30	E. A. V. Williams	West Indies v England at Bridgetown	1947-48
30	B. R. Taylor	New Zealand v West Indies at Auckland	1968-69
33	C. A. Roach	West Indies v England at The Oval	1933
34	C. R. Browne	West Indies v England at Georgetown	1929-30

FASTEST TEST HUNDREDS

Minutes			
70	J. M. Gregory	Australia v South Africa at Johannesburg	1921-22
75	G. L. Jessop	England v Australia at The Oval	1902
78	R. Benaud	Australia v West Indies at Kingston	1954-55
80	J. H. Sinclair	South Africa v Australia at Cape Town	1902-03
86	B. R. Taylor	New Zealand v West Indies at Auckland	1968-69

Note: The fastest known hundred in a Test match in terms of balls received is off 67 balls by J. M. Gregory for Australia v South Africa at Johannesburg, 1921-22. R. C. Fredericks, for West Indies v Australia at Perth, 1975-76, reached his hundred off 71 balls. I. T. Botham, for England v Australia in 1981, reached three figures off 87 balls in the third Test match and off 86 balls in the fifth.

FASTEST TEST DOUBLE-HUNDREDS

Minutes			
214	D. G. Bradman	Australia v England at Leeds	1930
223	S. J. McCabe	Australia v England at Nottingham	1938
226	V. T. Trumper	Australia v South Africa at Adelaide	1910-11
234	D. G. Bradman	Australia v England at Lord's	1930
240	W. R. Hammond	England v New Zealand at Auckland	1932-33
241	S. E. Gregory	Australia v England at Sydney	1894-95
245	D. C. S. Compton	England v Pakistan at Nottingham	1954

FASTEST TEST TRIPLE-HUNDREDS

Minutes			
287	W. R. Hammond	England v New Zealand at Auckland	1932-33
336	D. G. Bradman	Australia v England at Leeds	1930

MOST RUNS IN A DAY BY A BATSMAN

309	D. G. Bradman	Australia v England at Leeds	1930
295	W. R. Hammond	England v New Zealand at Auckland	1932-33
273	D. C. S. Compton	England v Pakistan at Nottingham	1954
271	D. G. Bradman	Australia v England at Leeds	1934

MOST RUNS IN A DAY (BOTH SIDES)

588	England (398 for six), India (190 for no wkt) at Manchester	1936
522	England (503 for two), South Africa (19 for no wkt) at Lord's	1924
508	England (221 for two), South Africa (287 for six) at The Oval	1935

MOST RUNS IN A DAY (ONE SIDE)

503	England (503 for two) v South Africa at Lord's	1924
494	Australia (494 for six) v South Africa at Sydney	1910-11
475	Australia (475 for two) v England at The Oval	1934
471	England (471 for eight) v India at The Oval	1936
458	Australia (458 for three) v England at Leeds	1930
455	Australia (455 for one) v England at Leeds	1934

SLOWEST INDIVIDUAL TEST BATTING

2* in 80 minutes	C. E. H. Croft, West Indies v Australia at Brisbane	1979-80
3* in 100 minutes	J. T. Murray, England v Australia at Sydney	1962-63
5 in 102 minutes	M. A. K. Pataudi, India v England at Bombay	1972-73
8 in 120 minutes	T. E. Bailey, England v South Africa at Leeds	1955
9 in 120 minutes	W. Newham, England v Australia at Sydney	1887-88
9 in 125 minutes	T. W. Jarvis, New Zealand v India at Madras	1964-65
10* in 133 minutes	T. G. Evans, England v Australia at Adelaide	1946-47
18 in 194 minutes	W. R. Playle, New Zealand v England at Leeds	1958
20 in 195 minutes	Hanif Mohammad, Pakistan v England at Lord's	1954
21 in 210 minutes	P. G. Z. Harris, New Zealand v Pakistan at Karachi	1955-56
28* in 250 minutes	J. W. Burke, Australia v England at Brisbane	1958-59
31 in 264 minutes	K. D. Mackay, Australia v England at Lord's	1956
35 in 332 minutes	C. J. Tavaré, England v India at Madras	1981-82
40 in 289 minutes	H. L. Collins, Australia v England at Manchester	1921
45 in 318 minutes	Shuja-ud-Din, Pakistan v Australia at Lahore	1959-60
55 in 336 minutes	B. A. Edgar, New Zealand v Australia at Wellington	1981-82
57 in 346 minutes	G. S. Camacho, West Indies v England at Bridgetown	1967-68
58 in 367 minutes	Ijaz Butt, Pakistan v Australia at Karachi	1959-60
68 in 458 minutes	T. E. Bailey, England v Australia at Brisbane	1958-59
99 in 505 minutes	M. L. Jaisimha, India v Pakistan at Kanpur	1960-61
105 in 575 minutes	D. J. McGlew, South Africa v Australia at Durban	1957-58
114 in 591 minutes	Mudassar Nazar, Pakistan v England at Lahore	1977-78
197* in 682 minutes	F. M. M. Worrell, West Indies v England at Bridgetown	1959-60
259 in 705 minutes	G. M. Turner, New Zealand v West Indies at Georgetown	1971-72
337 in 970 minutes	Hanif Mohammad, Pakistan v West Indies at Bridgetown	1957-58

Note: C. J. Tavaré scored 147 in 710 minutes in two innings (69 in 287 minutes and 78 in 423 minutes) for England v Australia at Manchester, 1981.

SLOWEST TEST HUNDREDS

557 minutes	Mudassar Nazar, Pakistan v England at Lahore	1977-78
545 minutes	D. J. McGlew, South Africa v Australia at Durban	1957-58
488 minutes	P. E. Richardson, England v South Africa at Johannesburg	1956-57

Note: The slowest for any Test in England is 458 minutes by K. W. R. Fletcher, England v Pakistan, The Oval, 1974.

LOWEST TEST SCORES IN FULL DAY'S PLAY

95 At Karachi, October 11, 1956. Australia 80 all out; Pakistan 15 for two (first day, 5½ hours).

104 At Karachi, December 8, 1959. Pakistan 0 for no wicket to 104 for five v Australia (fourth day, 5½ hours).

106 At Brisbane, December 9, 1958. England 92 for two to 198 all out v Australia (fourth day, 5 hours). *England were dismissed five minutes before the close of play, leaving no time for Australia to start their second innings.*

112 At Karachi, October 15, 1956. Australia 138 for six to 187 all out; Pakistan 63 for one (fourth day, 5½ hours).

117 At Madras, October 19, 1956. India 117 for five v Australia (first day, 5½ hours).

122 At Port Elizabeth, March 4, 1957. England's last wicket fell after the first twenty minutes without addition. South Africa then made 122 for seven in five and a half hours (third day, 6 hours).

122 At Brisbane, December 8, 1958. Australia 156 for six to 186 all out; England 92 for two (third day, 5 hours).

122 At Melbourne, January 3, 1959. Australia 282 for seven to 308 all out and 9 for one; England 87 all out (fourth day, 5 hours). *There were two intervals between innings, amounting to twenty minutes.*

122 At Melbourne, December 30, 1978. Australia 243 for four to 258 all out; England 107 for eight (second day, 6 hours).

123 At Hyderabad, January 4, 1978. England 123 for two to 191 all out; Pakistan 55 for one (third day, 5½ hours).

124 At Dacca, November 17, 1959. Pakistan 74 for four to 134 all out; Australia 64 for one (fourth day, 5½ hours).

124 At Kanpur, December 23, 1959. India 226 for six to 291 all out; Australia 59 for two (fourth day, 5½ hours).

128 At Bridgetown, February 9, 1954. England 53 for two to 181 for nine v West Indies (third day, 5 hours).

In England

151 At Lord's, August 26, 1978. England 175 for two to 289 all out; New Zealand 37 for seven (third day, 6 hours).

159 At Leeds, July 10, 1971. Pakistan 208 for four to 350 all out; England 17 for one (third day, 6 hours).

HIGHEST MATCH AGGREGATES

Runs	*Wkts*			*Days played*
1,981	35	South Africa v England at Durban	1938-39	10†
1,815	34	West Indies v England at Kingston	1929-30	9‡
1,764	39	Australia v West Indies at Adelaide	1968-69	5
1,753	40	Australia v England at Adelaide	1920-21	6

Runs	*Wkts*			*Days played*
1,723	31	England v Australia at Leeds	1948	5
1,661	36	West Indies v Australia at Bridgetown	1954-55	6
1,646	40	Australia v South Africa at Adelaide	1910-11	6
1,644	38	Australia v West Indies at Sydney	1968-69	6
1,640	24	West Indies v Australia at Bridgetown	1964-65	6
1,640	33	Australia v Pakistan at Melbourne	1972-73	5
1,619	40	Australia v England at Melbourne	1924-25	7
1,611	40	Australia v England at Sydney	1924-25	7
1,601	29	England v Australia at Lord's	1930	4

† *No play on one day.* ‡ *No play on two days.*

LOWEST MATCH AGGREGATES

(For a completed match)

Runs	*Wkts*			*Days played*
234	29	Australia v South Africa at Melbourne	1931-32	3†
291	40	England v Australia at Lord's	1888	2
295	28	New Zealand v Australia at Wellington	1945-46	2
309	29	West Indies v England at Bridgetown	1934-35	3
323	30	England v Australia at Manchester	1888	2
363	40	England v Australia at The Oval	1882	2
374	40	Australia v England at Sydney	1887-88	5‡
378	30	England v South Africa at The Oval	1912	2
382	30	South Africa v England at Cape Town	1888-89	2
389	38	England v Australia at The Oval	1890	2
390	30	England v New Zealand at Lord's	1958	3
392	40	England v Australia at The Oval	1896	3

† *No play on one day.* ‡ *No play on two days.*

HIGHEST FOURTH INNINGS TOTALS

To win

406-4	India v West Indies at Port-of-Spain	1975-76
404-3	Australia v England at Leeds	1948

To draw

654-5	England (needing 696 to win) v South Africa at Durban	1938-39
429-8	India (needing 438 to win) v England at The Oval	1979

To lose

445	India (lost by 47 runs) v Australia at Adelaide	1977-78
440	New Zealand (lost by 38 runs) v England at Nottingham	1973

HIGHEST TEST WICKET PARTNERSHIPS

413 for 1st	V. Mankad (231) and P. Roy (173) for India v New Zealand at Madras	1955-56
451 for 2nd	W. H. Ponsford (266) and D. G. Bradman (244) for Australia v England at The Oval	1934
370 for 3rd†	W. J. Edrich (189) and D. C. S. Compton (208) for England v South Africa at Lord's	1947
411 for 4th	P. B. H. May (285*) and M. C. Cowdrey (154) for England v West Indies at Birmingham	1957
405 for 5th	S. G. Barnes (234) and D. G. Bradman (234) for Australia v England at Sydney	1946-47
346 for 6th	J. H. W. Fingleton (136) and D. G. Bradman (270) for Australia v England at Melbourne	1936-37
347 for 7th	D. St E. Atkinson (219) and C. C. Depeiza (122) for West Indies v Australia at Bridgetown	1954-55
246 for 8th	L. E. G. Ames (137) and G. O. Allen (122) for England v New Zealand at Lord's	1931
190 for 9th	Asif Iqbal (146) and Intikhab Alam (51) for Pakistan v England at The Oval	1967
151 for 10th	B. F. Hastings (110) and R. O. Collinge (68*) for New Zealand v Pakistan at Auckland	1972-73

† 415 runs were added between the fall of the 2nd and 3rd wickets for India v England at Madras in 1981-82. D. B. Vengsarkar retired hurt after he and G. R. Viswanath had added 99 runs and Viswanath and Yashpal Sharma added another 316.

BOWLERS WITH 75 WICKETS IN TESTS

FOR ENGLAND

	T	*Balls*	*R*	*W*	*Avge*	*5 W/i*	*10 W/m*
F. S. Trueman	67	15,178	6,625	307	21.57	17	3
D. L. Underwood	85	21,527	7,579	289	26.22	16	6
R. G. D. Willis	74	14,302	6,712	267	25.13	14	—
J. B. Statham	70	16,032	6,261	252	24.84	9	1
I. T. Botham	54	12,767	5,807	249	23.32	20	4
A. V. Bedser	51	15,941	5,876	236	24.89	15	5
J. A. Snow	49	12,021	5,387	202	26.66	8	1
J. C. Laker	46	12,009	4,099	193	21.23	9	3
S. F. Barnes	27	7,873	3,106	189	16.43	24	7
G. A. R. Lock	49	13,063	4,452	174	25.58	9	3
M. W. Tate	39	12,571	4,055	155	26.16	7	1
F. J. Titmus	53	15,124	4,931	153	32.22	7	—
H. Verity	40	11,143	3,510	144	24.37	5	2
C. M. Old	46	8,858	4,020	143	28.11	4	—
A. W. Greig	58	9,802	4,541	141	32.20	6	2
T. E. Bailey	61	9,712	3,856	132	29.21	5	1
W. Rhodes	58	8,220	3,425	127	26.96	6	1
D. A. Allen	39	11,297	3,778	122	30.96	4	—
R. Illingworth	61	11,934	3,807	122	31.20	3	—
J. Briggs	33	5,332	2,094	118	17.74	9	4
G. G. Arnold	34	7,650	3,254	115	28.29	6	—
G. A. Lohmann	18	3,821	1,205	112	10.75	9	5
D. V. P. Wright	34	8,141	4,224	108	39.11	6	1
R. Peel	20	5,216	1,715	102	16.81	6	2
J. H. Wardle	28	6,597	2,080	102	20.39	5	1

	T	*Balls*	*R*	*W*	*Avge*	*5 W/i*	*10 W/m*
C. Blythe	19	4,438	1,863	100	18.63	9	4
W. Voce	27	6,360	2,733	98	27.88	3	2
T. Richardson	14	4,485	2,220	88	25.22	11	4
M. Hendrick	30	6,208	2,248	87	25.83	—	—
W. R. Hammond	85	7,967	3,140	83	37.83	2	—
F. E. Woolley	64	6,495	2,815	83	33.91	4	1
G. O. Allen	25	4,392	2,379	81	29.37	5	1
D. J. Brown	26	5,098	2,237	79	28.31	2	—
H. Larwood	21	4,969	2,212	78	28.35	4	1
F. H. Tyson	17	3,452	1,411	76	18.56	4	1

FOR AUSTRALIA

	T	*Balls*	*R*	*W*	*Avge*	*5 W/i*	*10 W/m*
D. K. Lillee	63	16,478	7,568	328	23.07	22	7
R. Benaud	63	19,093	6,704	248	27.03	16	1
G. D. McKenzie	60	17,681	7,328	246	29.78	16	3
R. R. Lindwall	61	13,666	5,257	228	23.05	12	—
C. V. Grimmett	37	14,573	5,231	216	24.21	21	7
A. K. Davidson	44	11,665	3,828	186	20.58	14	2
J. R. Thomson	42	8,959	4,620	172	26.86	6	—
K. R. Miller	55	10,474	3,905	170	22.97	7	1
W. A. Johnston	40	11,048	3,825	160	23.90	7	—
W. J. O'Reilly	27	10,024	3,254	144	22.59	11	3
H. Trumble	32	8,099	3,072	141	21.78	9	3
M. H. N. Walker	34	10,094	3,792	138	27.47	6	—
A. A. Mallett	38	9,990	3,940	132	29.84	6	1
M. A. Noble	42	7,109	3,027	121	25.01	9	2
I. W. Johnson	45	8,773	3,182	109	29.19	3	—
G. Giffen	31	6,325	2,791	103	27.09	7	1
A. N. Connolly	29	7,818	2,981	102	29.22	4	—
C. T. B. Turner	17	5,195	1,670	101	16.53	11	2
A. A. Mailey	21	6,117	3,358	99	33.91	6	2
B. Yardley	25	6,531	2,818	95	29.66	4	1
F. R. Spofforth	18	4,185	1,731	94	18.41	7	4
J. W. Gleeson	29	8,857	3,367	93	36.20	3	—
N. J. N. Hawke	27	6,974	2,677	91	29.41	6	1
A. Cotter	21	4,633	2,549	89	28.64	7	—
W. W. Armstrong	50	8,052	2,923	87	33.59	3	—
J. M. Gregory	24	5,581	2,648	85	31.15	4	—
R. M. Hogg	22	4,652	1,937	82	23.62	5	2
J. V. Saunders	14	3,565	1,797	79	22.74	6	—
G. Dymock	21	5,545	2,116	78	27.12	5	1
G. E. Palmer	17	4,519	1,678	78	21.51	6	2

FOR SOUTH AFRICA

	T	*Balls*	*R*	*W*	*Avge*	*5 W/i*	*10 W/m*
H. J. Tayfield	37	13,568	4,405	170	25.91	14	2
T. L. Goddard	41	11,735	3,226	123	26.22	5	—
P. M. Pollock	28	6,522	2,806	116	24.18	9	1
N. A. T. Adcock	26	6,423	2,195	104	21.10	5	—
C. L. Vincent	25	5,863	2,631	84	31.32	3	—
G. A. Faulkner	25	4,227	2,180	82	26.58	4	—

FOR WEST INDIES

	T	*Balls*	*R*	*W*	*Avge*	*5 W/i*	*10 W/m*
L. R. Gibbs............	79	27,115	8,989	309	29.09	18	2
G. S. Sobers............	93	21,599	7,999	235	34.03	6	—
W. W. Hall.............	48	10,415	5,066	192	26.38	9	1
A. M. E. Roberts......	40	9,674	4,481	173	25.90	10	2
S. Ramadhin...........	43	13,939	4,577	158	28.96	10	1
M. A. Holding.........	31	7,162	3,194	139	22.97	10	2
A. L. Valentine........	36	12,961	4,215	139	30.32	8	2
C. E. H. Croft..........	27	6,165	2,913	125	23.30	3	—
J. Garner................	28	6,648	2,560	124	20.64	2	—
V. A. Holder...........	40	9,095	3,627	109	33.27	3	—
C. C. Griffith..........	28	5,631	2,683	94	28.54	5	—

FOR NEW ZEALAND

	T	*Balls*	*R*	*W*	*Avge*	*5 W/i*	*10 W/m*
R. J. Hadlee...........	38	9,498	4,464	169	26.41	13	3
R. O. Collinge..........	35	7,689	3,393	116	29.25	3	—
B. R. Taylor............	30	6,334	2,953	111	26.60	4	—
R. C. Motz.............	32	7,034	3,148	100	31.48	5	—
H. J. Howarth..........	30	8,833	3,178	86	36.95	2	—
J. R. Reid..............	58	7,719	2,837	85	33.37	1	—

FOR INDIA

	T	*Balls*	*R*	*W*	*Avge*	*5 W/i*	*10 W/m*
B. S. Bedi...............	67	21,364	7,637	266	28.71	14	1
B. S. Chandrasekhar..	58	15,963	7,199	242	29.74	16	2
E. A. S. Prasanna.....	49	14,353	5,742	189	30.38	10	2
V. Mankad.............	44	14,686	5,235	162	32.31	8	2
Kapil Dev...............	41	9,133	4,620	157	29.42	11	1
S. P. Gupte.............	36	11,284	4,402	149	29.54	12	1
S. Venkataraghavan...	50	13,442	4,944	145	34.09	3	1
K. D. Ghavri...........	39	7,042	3,656	109	33.54	4	—
D. R. Doshi............	27	7,979	2,730	97	28.14	4	—
R. G. Nadkarni........	41	9,175	2,559	88	29.07	4	1
S. A. Durani...........	29	6,446	2,657	75	35.42	3	1

FOR PAKISTAN

	T	*Balls*	*R*	*W*	*Avge*	*5 W/i*	*10 W/m*
Imran Khan............	40	10,592	4,587	179	25.62	12	2
Fazal Mahmood........	34	9,870	3,437	139	24.72	13	4
Intikhab Alam..........	47	10,475	4,492	125	35.93	5	2
Sarfraz Nawaz..........	43	10,581	4,387	136	32.25	4	1
Iqbal Qasim............	29	7,362	2,744	89	30.83	3	2
Mushtaq Mohammad.	57	5,260	2,310	79	29.24	3	—

Note: Only G. S. Sobers (West Indies), R. Benaud (Australia) and I. T. Botham (England) have scored 2,000 runs and taken 200 wickets.

MOST WICKETS IN A TEST MATCH

19-90	J. C. Laker	England v Australia at Manchester	1956
17-159	S. F. Barnes	England v South Africa at Johannesburg	1913-14
16-137†	R. A. L. Massie	Australia v England at Lord's	1972
15-28	J. Briggs	England v South Africa at Cape Town	1888-89
15-45	G. A. Lohmann	England v South Africa at Port Elizabeth	1895-96
15-99	C. Blythe	England v South Africa at Leeds	1907
15-104	H. Verity	England v Australia at Lord's	1934
15-124	W. Rhodes	England v Australia at Melbourne	1903-04
14-90	F. R. Spofforth	Australia v England at The Oval	1882
14-99	A. V. Bedser	England v Australia at Nottingham	1953
14-102	W. Bates	England v Australia at Melbourne	1882-83
14-116	Imran Khan	Pakistan v Sri Lanka at Lahore	1981-82
14-124	J. M. Patel	India v Australia at Kanpur	1959-60
14-144	S. F. Barnes	England v South Africa at Durban	1913-14
14-149	M. A. Holding	West Indies v England at The Oval	1976
14-199	C. V. Grimmett	Australia v South Africa at Adelaide	1931-32

† *On Test début.*

Notes: The best for South Africa is 13-165 by H. J. Tayfield against Australia at Melbourne, 1952-53.

The best for New Zealand is 11-58 by R. J. Hadlee against India at Wellington, 1975-76.

MOST WICKETS IN A TEST INNINGS

10-53	J. C. Laker	England v Australia at Manchester	1956
9-28	G. A. Lohmann	England v South Africa at Johannesburg	1895-96
9-37	J. C. Laker	England v Australia at Manchester	1956
9-69	J. M. Patel	India v Australia at Kanpur	1959-60
9-86	Sarfraz Nawaz	Pakistan v Australia at Melbourne	1978-79
9-95	J. M. Noreiga	West Indies v India at Port-of-Spain	1970-71
9-102	S. P. Gupte	India v West Indies at Kanpur	1958-59
9-103	S. F. Barnes	England v South Africa at Johannesburg	1913-14
9-113	H. J. Tayfield	South Africa v England at Johannesburg	1956-57
9-121	A. A. Mailey	Australia v England at Melbourne	1920-21
8-7	G. A. Lohmann	England v South Africa at Port Elizabeth	1895-96
8-11	J. Briggs	England v South Africa at Cape Town	1888-89
8-29	S. F. Barnes	England v South Africa at The Oval	1912
8-29	C. E. H. Croft	West Indies v Pakistan at Port-of-Spain	1976-77
8-31	F. Laver	Australia v England at Manchester	1909
8-31	F. S. Trueman	England v India at Manchester	1952
8-34	I. T. Botham	England v Pakistan at Lord's	1978
8-35	G. A. Lohmann	England v Australia at Sydney	1886-87
8-38	L. R. Gibbs	West Indies v India at Bridgetown	1961-62
8-43†	A. E. Trott	Australia v England at Adelaide	1894-95
8-43	H. Verity	England v Australia at Lord's	1934
8-43	R. G. D. Willis	England v Australia at Leeds	1981
8-51	D. L. Underwood	England v Pakistan at Lord's	1974
8-52	V. Mankad	India v Pakistan at Delhi	1952-53
8-53	G. B. Lawrence	South Africa v New Zealand at Johannesburg	1961-62
8-53†	R. A. L. Massie	Australia v England at Lord's	1972
8-55	V. Mankad	India v England at Madras	1951-52
8-56	S. F. Barnes	England v South Africa at Johannesburg	1913-14
8-58	G. A. Lohmann	England v Australia at Sydney	1891-92
8-58	Imran Khan	Pakistan v Sri Lanka at Lahore	1981-82
8-59	C. Blythe	England v South Africa at Leeds	1907
8-59	A. A. Mallett	Australia v Pakistan at Adelaide	1972-73
8-65	H. Trumble	Australia v England at The Oval	1902

8-68	W. Rhodes	England v Australia at Melbourne	1903-04
8-69	H. J. Tayfield	South Africa v England at Durban	1956-57
8-69	Sikander Bakht	Pakistan v India at Delhi	1979-80
8-70	S. J. Snooke	South Africa v England at Johannesburg	1905-06
8-71	G. D. McKenzie	Australia v West Indies at Melbourne	1968-69
8-72	S. Venkataraghavan	India v New Zealand at Delhi	1964-65
8-76	E. A. S. Prasanna	India v New Zealand at Auckland	1975-76
8-79	B. S. Chandrasekhar	India v England at Delhi	1972-73
8-81	L. C. Braund	England v Australia at Melbourne	1903-04
8-84†	R. A. L. Massie	Australia v England at Lord's	1972
8-86	A. W. Greig	England v West Indies at Port-of-Spain	1973-74
8-92	M. A. Holding	West Indies v England at The Oval	1976
8-94	T. Richardson	England v Australia at Sydney	1897-98
8-104†	A. L. Valentine	West Indies v England at Manchester	1950
8-107	B. J. T. Bosanquet	England v Australia at Nottingham	1905
8-126	J. C. White	England v Australia at Adelaide	1928-29
8-143	M. H. N. Walker	Australia v England at Melbourne	1974-75

† *On Test début.*

Note: The best for New Zealand is 7-23 by R. J. Hadlee against India at Wellington, 1975-76.

MOST WICKETS IN A TEST SERIES

	T	*R*	*W*	*Avge*		
S. F. Barnes	4	536	49	10.93	England v South Africa	1913-14
J. C. Laker	5	442	46	9.60	England v Australia	1956
C. V. Grimmett	5	642	44	14.59	Australia v South Africa	1935-36
T. M. Alderman	6	893	42	21.26	Australia v England	1981
R. M. Hogg	6	527	41	12.85	Australia v England	1978-79
A. V. Bedser	5	682	39	17.48	England v Australia	1953
D. K. Lillee	6	870	39	22.30	Australia v England	1981
M. W. Tate	5	881	38	23.18	England v Australia	1924-25
W. J. Whitty	5	632	37	17.08	Australia v South Africa	1910-11
H. J. Tayfield	5	636	37	17.18	South Africa v England	1956-57
A. E. E. Vogler	5	783	36	21.75	South Africa v England	1909-10
A. A. Mailey	5	946	36	26.27	Australia v England	1920-21
G. A. Lohmann	3	203	35	5.80	England v South Africa	1895-96
B. S. Chandrasekhar	5	662	35	18.91	India v England	1972-73

TEST HAT-TRICKS

F. R. Spofforth	Australia v England at Melbourne	1878-79
W. Bates	England v Australia at Melbourne	1882-83
J. Briggs	England v Australia at Sydney	1891-92
G. A. Lohmann	England v South Africa at Port Elizabeth	1895-96
J. T. Hearne	England v Australia at Leeds	1899
H. Trumble	Australia v England at Melbourne	1901-02
H. Trumble	Australia v England at Melbourne	1903-04
T. J. Matthews† T. J. Matthews	Australia v South Africa at Manchester	1912
M. J. C. Allom‡	England v New Zealand at Christchurch	1929-30
T. W. Goddard	England v South Africa at Johannesburg	1938-39
P. J. Loader	England v West Indies at Leeds	1957
L. F. Kline	Australia v South Africa at Cape Town	1957-58
W. W. Hall	West Indies v Pakistan at Lahore	1958-59
G. M. Griffin	South Africa v England at Lord's	1960
L. R. Gibbs	West Indies v Australia at Adelaide	1960-61
P. J. Petherick‡	New Zealand v Pakistan at Lahore	1976-77

† *T. J. Matthews did the hat-trick in each innings of the same match.*

‡ *On Test début.*

MOST BALLS BOWLED IN A TEST MATCH

S. Ramadhin (West Indies) sent down 774 balls in 129 overs against England at Birmingham, 1957. It was the most delivered by any bowler in a Test, beating H. Verity's 766 for England against South Africa at Durban, 1938-39. In this match Ramadhin also bowled the most balls (588) in any single first-class innings, including Tests.

It should be noted that six balls were bowled to the over in the Australia v England Test series of 1928-29 and 1932-33, when the eight-ball over was otherwise in force in Australia.

WICKET-KEEPING RECORDS

Most Dismissals in a Test Career

	T	*Ct*	*St*	*Total*
R. W. Marsh (Australia)	83	291	11	302
A. P. E. Knott (England)	95	250	19	269
T. G. Evans (England)	91	173	46	219
D. L. Murray (West Indies)	62	181	8	189
A. T. W. Grout (Australia)	51	163	24	187
Wasim Bari (Pakistan)	64	153	20	173
J. H. B. Waite (South Africa)	50	124	17	141
S. M. H. Kirmani (India)	57	106	30	136
W. A. Oldfield (Australia)	54	78	52	130
J. M. Parks (England)†	46	103	11	114

† J. M. Parks's figures include two catches taken in three Tests in which he did not keep wicket.

Note: K. J. Wadsworth (92ct, 4st) made most dismissals for New Zealand.

Most Dismissals in a Test Series

26 (26ct)	R. W. Marsh	Australia v West Indies (6 Tests)	1975-76
26 (23ct, 3st)	J. H. B. Waite	South Africa v New Zealand	1961-62
24 (21ct, 3st)	A. P. E. Knott	England v Australia (6 Tests)	1970-71
24 (24ct)	D. T. Lindsay	South Africa v Australia	1966-67
24 (22ct, 2st)	D. L. Murray	West Indies v England	1963
23 (22ct, 1st)	F. C. M. Alexander	West Indies v England	1959-60
23 (21ct, 2st)	A. E. Dick	New Zealand v South Africa	1961-62
23 (20ct, 3st)	A. T. W. Grout	Australia v West Indies	1960-61
23 (22ct, 1st)	A. P. E. Knott	England v Australia (6 Tests)	1974-75
23 (21ct, 2st)	R. W. Marsh	Australia v England	1972
23 (23ct)	R. W. Marsh	Australia v England (6 Tests)	1981
23 (16ct, 7st)	J. H. B. Waite	South Africa v New Zealand	1953-54
22 (22ct)	S. J. Rixon	Australia v India	1977-78
21 (20ct, 1st)	A. T. W. Grout	Australia v England	1961
21 (16ct, 5st)	G. R. A. Langley	Australia v West Indies	1951-52
21 (13ct, 8st)	R. A. Saggers	Australia v South Africa	1949-50
21 (15ct, 6st)	H. Strudwick	England v South Africa	1913-14
20 (18ct, 2st)	T. G. Evans	England v South Africa	1956-57
20 (17ct, 3st)	A. T. W. Grout	Australia v England	1958-59
20 (16ct, 4st)	G. R. A. Langley	Australia v West Indies	1954-55
20 (19ct, 1st)	H. B. Taber	Australia v South Africa	1966-67
20 (16ct, 4st)	D. Tallon	Australia v England	1946-47
20 (18ct, 2st)	R. W. Taylor	England v Australia (6 Tests)	1978-79

Most Dismissals in One Test

10 (all ct)	R. W. Taylor	England v India at Bombay	1979-80
9 (8ct, 1st)	G. R. A. Langley	Australia v England at Lord's	1956
9 (all ct)	D. A. Murray	West Indies v Australia at Melbourne	1981-82
8 (6ct, 2st)	L. E. G. Ames	England v West Indies at The Oval	1933
8 (6ct, 2st)	A. T. W. Grout	Australia v Pakistan at Lahore	1959-60
8 (all ct)	A. T. W. Grout	Australia v England at Lord's	1961
8 (all ct)	J. J. Kelly	Australia v England at Sydney	1901-02
8 (all ct)	G. R. A. Langley	Australia v West Indies at Kingston	1954-55
8 (all ct)	J. M. Parks	England v New Zealand at Christchurch	1965-66
8 (all ct)	D. T. Lindsay	South Africa v Australia at Johannesburg	1966-67
8 (7ct, 1st)	H. B. Taber	Australia v South Africa at Johannesburg	1966-67
8 (all ct)	Wasim Bari	Pakistan v England at Leeds	1971
8 (all ct)	R. W. Marsh	Australia v West Indies at Melbourne	1975-76
8 (all ct)	R. W. Marsh	Australia v New Zealand at Christchurch	1976-77

Most Dismissals in a Test Innings

7 (all ct)	Wasim Bari	Pakistan v New Zealand at Auckland	1978-79
7 (all ct)	R. W. Taylor	England v India at Bombay	1979-80
6 (all ct)	A. T. W. Grout	Australia v South Africa at Johannesburg	1957-58
6 (all ct)	D. T. Lindsay	South Africa v Australia at Johannesburg	1966-67
6 (all ct)	J. T. Murray	England v India at Lord's	1967
6 (5ct, 1st)	S. M. H. Kirmani	India v New Zealand at Christchurch	1975-76

MOST CATCHES – EXCLUDING WICKET-KEEPERS

In a Test Career

M. C. Cowdrey (England)	120 in 114 matches
R. B. Simpson (Australia)	110 in 62 matches
W. R. Hammond (England)	110 in 85 matches
G. S. Sobers (West Indies)	109 in 93 matches
I. M. Chappell (Australia)	105 in 75 matches

In a Test Series

15	J. M. Gregory	Australia v England	1920-21
14	G. S. Chappell	Australia v England (6 Tests)	1974-75
13	R. B. Simpson	Australia v South Africa	1957-58
13	R. B. Simpson	Australia v West Indies	1960-61

In One Test

7	G. S. Chappell	Australia v England at Perth	1974-75
7	Yajurvindra Singh	India v England at Bangalore	1976-77
6	A. Shrewsbury	England v Australia at Sydney	1887-88
6	A. E. E. Vogler	South Africa v England at Durban	1909-10

6	F. E. Woolley	England v Australia at Sydney	1911-12
6	J. M. Gregory	Australia v England at Sydney	1920-21
6	B. Mitchell	South Africa v Australia at Melbourne	1931-32
6	V. Y. Richardson	Australia v South Africa at Durban	1935-36
6	R. N. Harvey	Australia v England at Sydney	1962-63
6	M. C. Cowdrey	England v West Indies at Lord's	1963
6	E. D. Solkar	India v West Indies at Port-of-Spain	1970-71
6	G. S. Sobers	West Indies v England at Lord's	1973
6	I. M. Chappell	Australia v New Zealand at Adelaide	1973-74
6	A. W. Greig	England v Pakistan at Leeds	1974
6	D. F. Whatmore	Australia v India at Kanpur	1979-80

In a Test Innings

5	V. Y. Richardson	Australia v South Africa at Durban	1935-36
5	Yajurvindra Singh	India v England at Bangalore	1976-77

SAME CAPTAIN WINNING TOSS IN ALL FIVE TESTS

Hon. F. S. Jackson, for England v Australia	1905
M. A. Noble, for Australia v England	1909
H. G. Deane, for South Africa v England	1927-28
J. D. C. Goddard, for West Indies v India	1948-49
A. L. Hassett, for Australia v England	1953
M. C. Cowdrey, for England v South Africa	1960
Nawab of Pataudi jun., for India v England	1963-64
G. S. Sobers, for West Indies v England	1966
G. S. Sobers, for West Indies v New Zealand	1971-72

Notes: P. B. H. May (3) and M. C. Cowdrey (2) won the toss in all five Tests for England in West Indies, 1959-60.

I. M. Chappell won the toss in five of the six Tests against England in Australia, 1974-75.

G. S. Chappell won the toss in five of the six Tests against West Indies in Australia, 1975-76.

G. N. Yallop won the toss in five of the six Tests against England in Australia, 1978-79.

K. W. R. Fletcher won the toss in five of the six Tests against India in India, 1981-82.

HUNDREDS BY RIVAL CAPTAINS IN THE SAME TEST

J. W. H. T. Douglas (119) and H. W. Taylor (109), South Africa v England at Durban	1913-14
W. M. Woodfull (155) and A. P. F. Chapman (121), England v Australia at Lord's	1930
W. R. Hammond (240) and D. G. Bradman (102*), England v Australia at Lord's	1938
W. R. Hammond (140) and A. Melville (103), South Africa v England at Durban	1938-39
L. Hutton (145) and A. L. Hassett (104), England v Australia at Lord's	1953
P. B. H. May (117) and D. J. McGlew (104*), England v South Africa at Manchester	1955
J. R. Reid (142) and D. J. McGlew (120), South Africa v New Zealand at Johannesburg	1961-62
R. B. Simpson (311) and E. R. Dexter (174), England v Australia at Manchester	1964
G. S. Sobers (113*) and M. C. Cowdrey (101), West Indies v England at Kingston	1967-68
W. M. Lawry (151) and G. S. Sobers (113), Australia v West Indies at Sydney	1968-69
G. S. Sobers (142) and B. E. Congdon (126), West Indies v New Zealand at Bridgetown	1971-72

R. B. Kanhai (105) and I. M. Chappell (106*), West Indies v Australia at Bridgetown....... 1972-73
B. E. Congdon (132) and I. M. Chappell (145 and 121), New Zealand v Australia at Wellington....... 1973-74
S. M. Gavaskar (205) and A. I. Kallicharran (187), India v West Indies at Bombay 1978-79
Javed Miandad (106*) and G. S. Chappell (235), Pakistan v Australia at Faisalabad 1979-80

YOUNGEST TEST PLAYERS

Years	*Days*			
15	124	Mushtaq Mohammad.	Pakistan v West Indies at Lahore	1958-59
16	191	Aftab Baloch	Pakistan v New Zealand at Dacca	1969-70
16	248	Nasim-ul-Ghani	Pakistan v West Indies at Bridgetown	1957-58
16	352	Khalid Hassan	Pakistan v England at Nottingham	1954
17	122	J. E. D. Sealy	West Indies v England at Bridgetown	1929-30
17	239	I. D. Craig	Australia v South Africa at Melbourne	1952-53
17	245	G. S. Sobers	West Indies v England at Kingston	1953-54
17	265	V. L. Mehra	India v New Zealand at Bombay	1955-56
17	300	Hanif Mohammad	Pakistan v India at Delhi	1952-53
17	341	Intikhab Alam	Pakistan v Australia at Karachi	1959-60
18	13	A. G. Milkha Singh	India v Australia at Madras	1959-60
18	26	Majid J. Khan	Pakistan v Australia at Karachi	1964-65
18	31	M. R. Bynoe	West Indies v Pakistan at Lahore	1958-59
18	41	Salah-ud-Din	Pakistan v New Zealand at Rawalpindi	1964-65
18	44	Khalid Wazir	Pakistan v England at Lord's	1954
18	105	J. B. Stollmeyer	West Indies v England at Lord's	1939
18	149	D. B. Close	England v New Zealand at Manchester	1949
18	173	A. T. Roberts	West Indies v New Zealand at Auckland	1955-56
18	186	Haseeb Ahsan	Pakistan v West Indies at Bridgetown	1957-58
18	190	Imran Khan	Pakistan v England at Birmingham	1971
18	197	D. L. Freeman	New Zealand v England at Christchurch	1932-33
18	232	T. W. Garrett	Australia v England at Melbourne	1876-77
18	242	A. P. H. Scott	West Indies v India at Kingston	1952-53
18	249	B. S. Chandrasekhar	India v England at Bombay	1963-64
18	260	Mohammad Ilyas	Pakistan v Australia at Melbourne	1964-65
18	267	H. G. Vivian	New Zealand v England at The Oval	1931
18	270	R. J. Shastri	India v New Zealand at Wellington	1980-81
18	295	R. O. Collinge	New Zealand v Pakistan at Wellington	1964-65
18	312	S. Venkataraghavan	India v New Zealand at Madras	1964-65
18	316	B. P. Bracewell	New Zealand v England at The Oval	1978

OLDEST PLAYERS ON TEST DEBUT

Years	*Days*			
49	119	J. Southerton	England v Australia at Melbourne	1876-77
47	284	Miran Bux	Pakistan v India at Lahore	1954-55
46	253	D. D. Blackie	Australia v England at Sydney	1928-29
46	237	H. Ironmonger	Australia v England at Brisbane	1928-29
42	242	N. Betancourt	West Indies v England at Port-of-Spain	1929-30
41	337	E. R. Wilson	England v Australia at Sydney	1920-21
41	27	R. J. D. Jamshedji	India v England at Bombay	1933-34
40	345	C. A. Wiles	West Indies v England at Manchester	1933
40	216	S. P. Kinneir	England v Australia at Sydney	1911-12
40	110	H. W. Lee	England v South Africa at Johannesburg	1930-31
40	56	G. W. A. Chubb	South Africa v England at Nottingham	1951
40	37	C. Ramaswami	India v England at Manchester	1936

OLDEST TEST PLAYERS

(Age on final day of their last Test match)

Years	*Days*			
52	165	W. Rhodes	England v West Indies at Kingston	1929-30
50	327	H. Ironmonger	Australia v England at Sydney	1932-33
50	320	W. G. Grace	England v Australia at Nottingham	1899
50	303	G. Gunn	England v West Indies at Kingston	1929-30
49	139	J. Southerton	England v Australia at Melbourne	1876-77
47	302	Miran Bux	Pakistan v India at Peshawar	1954-55
47	249	J. B. Hobbs	England v Australia at The Oval	1930
47	87	F. E. Woolley	England v Australia at The Oval	1934
46	309	D. D. Blackie	Australia v England at Adelaide	1928-29
46	206	A. W. Nourse	South Africa v England at The Oval	1924
46	202	H. Strudwick	England v Australia at The Oval	1926
46	41	E. H. Hendren	England v West Indies at Kingston	1934-35
45	245	G. O. Allen	England v West Indies at Kingston	1947-48
45	215	P. Holmes	England v India at Lord's	1932
45	140	D. B. Close	England v West Indies at Manchester	1976
44	341	E. G. Wynyard	England v South Africa at Johannesburg	1905-06
44	317	J. M. M. Commaille	South Africa v England at Cape Town	1927-28
44	238	R. Abel	England v Australia at Manchester	1902
44	236	G. A. Headley	West Indies v England at Kingston	1953-54
44	105	Amir Elahi	Pakistan v India at Calcutta	1952-53

MOST CONSECUTIVE TEST APPEARANCES

85	G. S. Sobers, West Indies	Port-of-Spain 1954-55 to Port-of-Spain 1971-72
80	G. R. Viswanath, India	Georgetown 1970-71 to The Oval 1982
71	I. M. Chappell, Australia	Adelaide 1965-66 to Melbourne 1975-76
65	A. P. E. Knott, England	Auckland 1970-71 to The Oval 1977
62	S. M. Gavaskar, India	Bombay 1974-75 to The Oval 1982
61	R. B. Kanhai, West Indies	Birmingham 1957 to Sydney 1968-69
58†	A. W. Greig, England	Manchester 1972 to The Oval 1977
58†	J. R. Reid, New Zealand	Manchester 1949 to Leeds 1965
52	I. T. Botham, England	Wellington 1977-78 to The Oval 1982
52	R. W. Marsh, Australia	Brisbane 1970-71 to The Oval 1977
52	P. B. H. May, England	The Oval 1953 to Leeds 1959
52	F. E. Woolley, England	The Oval 1909 to The Oval 1926
51	G. S. Chappell, Australia	Perth 1970-71 to The Oval 1977

† *Indicates complete Test career.*

SUMMARY OF ALL TEST MATCHES

To end of 1982 season in England

ENGLAND

Against	*W*	*L*	*D*	*T*	*Total*
Australia	82	93	71	0	246
South Africa	46	18	38	0	102
West Indies	21	25	34	0	80
New Zealand	27	1	25	0	53
India	28	8	31	0	67
Pakistan	13	2	21	0	36
Sri Lanka	1	0	0	0	1
Totals	218	147	220	0	585

AUSTRALIA

Against	*W*	*L*	*D*	*T*	*Total*
England	93	82	71	0	246
South Africa	29	11	13	0	53
West Indies	26	13	12	1	52
New Zealand	8	2	5	0	15
India	20	8	11	0	39
Pakistan	9	5	6	0	20
Totals	185	121	118	1	425

SOUTH AFRICA

Against	*W*	*L*	*D*	*T*	*Total*
England	18	46	38	0	102
Australia	11	29	13	0	53
New Zealand	9	2	6	0	17
Totals	38	77	57	0	172

WEST INDIES

Against	*W*	*L*	*D*	*T*	*Total*
England	25	21	34	0	80
Australia	13	26	12	1	52
New Zealand	5	3	9	0	17
India	17	5	21	0	43
Pakistan	7	4	8	0	19
Totals	67	59	84	1	211

NEW ZEALAND

Against	*W*	*L*	*D*	*T*	*Total*
England	1	27	25	0	53
Australia	2	8	5	0	15
South Africa	2	9	6	0	17
West Indies	3	5	9	0	17
India	4	10	11	0	25
Pakistan	1	8	12	0	21
Totals	13	67	68	0	148

INDIA

Against	*W*	*L*	*D*	*T*	*Total*
England	8	28	31	0	67
Australia	8	20	11	0	39
West Indies	5	17	21	0	43
New Zealand	10	4	11	0	25
Pakistan	4	3	17	0	24
Totals	35	72	91	0	198

PAKISTAN

Against	*W*	*L*	*D*	*T*	*Total*
England	2	13	21	0	36
Australia	5	8	7	0	20
West Indies	4	7	8	0	19
New Zealand	8	1	12	0	21
India	3	4	17	0	24
Sri Lanka	2	0	1	0	3
Totals	24	33	66	0	123

SRI LANKA

Against	*W*	*L*	*D*	*T*	*Total*
England	0	1	0	0	1
Pakistan	0	2	1	0	3
Totals	0	3	1	0	4

ENGLAND v AUSTRALIA

	Captains					
Season	*England*	*Australia*	*T*	*E*	*A*	*D*
1876-77	James Lillywhite	D. W. Gregory	2	1	1	0
1878-79	Lord Harris	D. W. Gregory	1	0	1	0
1880	Lord Harris	W. L. Murdoch	1	1	0	0
1881-82	A. Shaw	W. L. Murdoch	4	0	2	2
1882	A. N. Hornby	W. L. Murdoch	1	0	1	0

THE ASHES

	Captains						
Season	*England*	*Australia*	*T*	*E*	*A*	*D*	*Held by*
1882-83	Hon. Ivo Bligh	W. L. Murdoch	4*	2	2	0	E
1884	Lord Harris[1]	W. L. Murdoch	3	1	0	2	E
1884-85	A. Shrewsbury	T. Horan[2]	5	3	2	0	E
1886	A. G. Steel	H. J. H. Scott	3	3	0	0	E
1886-87	A. Shrewsbury	P. S. McDonnell	2	2	0	0	E
1887-88	W. W. Read	P. S. McDonnell	1	1	0	0	E
1888	W. G. Grace[3]	P. S. McDonnell	3	2	1	0	E
1890†	W. G. Grace	W. L. Murdoch	2	2	0	0	E
1891-92	W. G. Grace	J. McC. Blackham	3	1	2	0	A
1893	W. G. Grace[4]	J. McC. Blackham	3	1	0	2	E
1894-95	A. E. Stoddart	G. Giffen[5]	5	3	2	0	E
1896	W. G. Grace	G. H. S. Trott	3	2	1	0	E
1897-98	A. E. Stoddart[6]	G. H. S. Trott	5	1	4	0	A
1899	A. C. MacLaren[7]	J. Darling	5	0	1	4	A
1901-02	A. C. MacLaren	J. Darling[8]	5	1	4	0	A
1902	A. C. MacLaren	J. Darling	5	1	2	2	A
1903-04	P. F. Warner	M. A. Noble	5	3	2	0	E
1905	Hon. F. S. Jackson	J. Darling	5	2	0	3	E
1907-08	A. O. Jones[9]	M. A. Noble	5	1	4	0	A

	Captains						
Season	*England*	*Australia*	*T*	*E*	*A*	*D*	*Held by*
1909	A. C. MacLaren	M. A. Noble	5	1	2	2	A
1911-12	J. W. H. T. Douglas	C. Hill	5	4	1	0	E
1912	C. B. Fry	S. E. Gregory	3	1	0	2	E
1920-21	J. W. H. T. Douglas	W. W. Armstrong	5	0	5	0	A
1921	Hon. L. H. Tennyson[10]	W. W. Armstrong	5	0	3	2	A
1924-25	A. E. R. Gilligan	H. L. Collins	5	1	4	0	A
1926	A. W. Carr[11]	H. L. Collins[12]	5	1	0	4	E
1928-29	A. P. F. Chapman[13]	J. Ryder	5	4	1	0	E
1930	A. P. F. Chapman[14]	W. M. Woodfull	5	1	2	2	A
1932-33	D. R. Jardine	W. M. Woodfull	5	4	1	0	E
1934	R. E. S. Wyatt[15]	W. M. Woodfull	5	1	2	2	A
1936-37	G. O. Allen	D. G. Bradman	5	2	3	0	A
1938†	W. R. Hammond	D. G. Bradman	4	1	1	2	A
1946-47	W. R. Hammond[16]	D. G. Bradman	5	0	3	2	A
1948	N. W. D. Yardley	D. G. Bradman	5	0	4	1	A
1950-51	F. R. Brown	A. L. Hassett	5	1	4	0	A
1953	L. Hutton	A. L. Hassett	5	1	0	4	E
1954-55	L. Hutton	I. W. Johnson[17]	5	3	1	1	E
1956	P. B. H. May	I. W. Johnson	5	2	1	2	E
1958-59	P. B. H. May	R. Benaud	5	0	4	1	A
1961	P. B. H. May[18]	R. Benaud[19]	5	1	2	2	A
1962-63	E. R. Dexter	R. Benaud	5	1	1	3	A
1964	E. R. Dexter	R. B. Simpson	5	0	1	4	A
1965-66	M. J. K. Smith	R. B. Simpson[20]	5	1	1	3	A
1968	M. C. Cowdrey[21]	W. M. Lawry[22]	5	1	1	3	A
1970-71†	R. Illingworth	W. M. Lawry[23]	6	2	0	4	E
1972	R. Illingworth	I. M. Chappell	5	2	2	1	E
1974-75	M. H. Denness[24]	I. M. Chappell	6	1	4	1	A
1975	A. W. Greig[25]	I. M. Chappell	4	0	1	3	A
1976-77‡	A. W. Greig	G. S. Chappell	1	0	1	0	—
1977	J. M. Brearley	G. S. Chappell	5	3	0	2	E
1978-79	J. M. Brearley	G. N. Yallop	6	5	1	0	E
1979-80‡	J. M. Brearley	G. S. Chappell	3	0	3	0	—
1980‡	I. T. Botham	G. S. Chappell	1	0	0	1	—
1981	J. M. Brearley[26]	K. J. Hughes	6	3	1	2	E
	In Australia		129	48	64	17	
	In England		117	34	29	54	
	Totals		246	82	93	71	

* *The Ashes were awarded in 1882-83 after a series of three matches which England won 2-1. A fourth unofficial match was played, each innings being played on a different pitch, and this was won by Australia.*

† *The matches at Manchester in 1890 and 1938 and at Melbourne (Third Test) in 1970-71 were abandoned without a ball being bowled and are excluded.*

‡ *The Ashes were not at stake in these series.*

Notes: The following deputised for the official touring captain or were appointed by the home authority for only a minor proportion of the series:

[1] A. N. Hornby (First). [2] W. L. Murdoch (First), H. H. Massie (Third), J. McC. Blackham (Fourth). [3] A. G. Steel (First). [4] A. E. Stoddart (First). [5] J. McC. Blackham (First). [6] A. C. MacLaren (First, Second and Fifth). [7] W. G. Grace (First). [8] H. Trumble (Fourth and Fifth). [9] F. L. Fane (First, Second and Third). [10] J. W. H. T. Douglas (First and Second). [11] A. P. F. Chapman (Fifth). [12] W. Bardsley (Third and Fourth). [13] J. C. White (Fifth). [14] R. E. S. Wyatt (Fifth). [15] C. F. Walters (First). [16] N. W. D. Yardley (Fifth). [17] A. R. Morris (Second). [18] M. C. Cowdrey (First and Second). [19] R. N. Harvey (Second). [20] B. C. Booth (First and Third). [21] T. W. Graveney (Fourth). [22] B. N. Jarman (Fourth). [23] I. M. Chappell (Seventh). [24] J. H. Edrich (Fourth). [25] M. H. Denness (First). [26] I. T. Botham (First and Second).

HIGHEST INNINGS TOTALS

By England

903-7 dec.	The Oval	1938
658-8 dec.	Nottingham	1938
636 ..	Sydney	1928-29
627-9 dec.	Manchester	1934
611 ..	Manchester	1964

By Australia

729-6 dec.	Lord's	1930
701 ..	The Oval	1934
695 ..	The Oval	1930
659-8 dec.	Sydney	1946-47
656-8 dec.	Manchester	1964
645 ..	Brisbane	1946-47
604 ..	Melbourne	1936-37
601-8 dec.	Brisbane	1954-55
600 ..	Melbourne	1924-25

LOWEST INNINGS TOTALS

By England

45 ..	Sydney	1886-87
52 ..	The Oval	1948
53 ..	Lord's	1888

By Australia

36 ..	Birmingham	1902
42 ..	Sydney	1887-88
44 ..	The Oval	1896

INDIVIDUAL HUNDREDS IN THE MATCHES 1876-77–1981

For England (169)

132*	R. Abel, Sydney	1891-92
120	L. E. G. Ames, Lord's	1934
185	R. W. Barber, Sydney	1965-66
134	W. Barnes, Adelaide	1884-85
129	C. J. Barnett, Adelaide	1936-37
126	C. J. Barnett, Nottingham	1938
132*	K. F. Barrington, Adelaide	1962-63
101	K. F. Barrington, Sydney	1962-63
256	K. F. Barrington, Manchester	1964
102	K. F. Barrington, Adelaide	1965-66
115	K. F. Barrington, Melbourne	1965-66
119*	I. T. Botham, Melbourne	1979-80
149*	I. T. Botham, Leeds	1981
118	I. T. Botham, Manchester	1981
113	G. Boycott, The Oval	1964
142*	G. Boycott, Sydney	1970-71
119*	G. Boycott, Adelaide	1970-71
107	G. Boycott, Nottingham	1977
191	G. Boycott, Leeds	1977
128*	G. Boycott, Lord's	1980
137	G. Boycott, The Oval	1981
103*	L. C. Braund, Adelaide	1901-02
102	L. C. Braund, Sydney	1903-04
121	J. Briggs, Melbourne	1884-85
140	J. T. Brown, Melbourne	1894-95
121	A. P. F. Chapman, Lord's	1930
102†	D. C. S. Compton, Nottingham	1938
147 / 103*	D. C. S. Compton, Adelaide	1946-47
184	D. C. S. Compton, Nottingham	1948
145*	D. C. S. Compton, Manchester	1948
102	M. C. Cowdrey, Melbourne	1954-55
100*	M. C. Cowdrey, Sydney	1958-59
113	M. C. Cowdrey, Melbourne	1962-63
104	M. C. Cowdrey, Melbourne	1965-66
104	M. C. Cowdrey, Birmingham	1968
188	M. H. Denness, Melbourne	1974-75
180	E. R. Dexter, Birmingham	1961
174	E. R. Dexter, Manchester	1964
158	B. L. D'Oliveira, The Oval	1968
117	B. L. D'Oliveira, Melbourne	1970-71
173†	K. S. Duleepsinhji, Lord's	1930
120†	J. H. Edrich, Lord's	1964
109	J. H. Edrich, Melbourne	1965-66
103	J. H. Edrich, Sydney	1965-66
164	J. H. Edrich, The Oval	1968
115*	J. H. Edrich, Perth	1970-71
130	J. H. Edrich, Adelaide	1970-71
175	J. H. Edrich, Lord's	1975
119	W. J. Edrich, Sydney	1946-47
111	W. J. Edrich, Leeds	1948
146	K. W. R. Fletcher, Melbourne	1974-75
287†	R. E. Foster, Sydney	1903-04

144	C. B. Fry, The Oval........	1905
102	D. I. Gower, Perth.........	1978-79
152†	W. G. Grace, The Oval....	1880
170	W. G. Grace, The Oval....	1886
111	T. W. Graveney, Sydney..	1954-55
110	A. W. Greig, Brisbane.....	1974-75
119†	G. Gunn, Sydney............	1907-08
122*	G. Gunn, Sydney............	1907-08
102*	W. Gunn, Manchester......	1893
251	W. R. Hammond, Sydney.	1928-29
200	W. R. Hammond, Melbourne.......................	1928-29
119* 177	W. R. Hammond, Adelaide	1928-29
113	W. R. Hammond, Leeds..	1930
112	W. R. Hammond, Sydney.	1932-33
101	W. R. Hammond, Sydney.	1932-33
231*	W. R. Hammond, Sydney.	1936-37
240	W. R. Hammond, Lord's..	1938
169*	J. Hardstaff jun., The Oval..	1938
130	T. W. Hayward, Manchester.......................	1899
137	T. W. Hayward, The Oval	1899
114	J. W. Hearne, Melbourne.	1911-12
127*	E. H. Hendren, Lord's.....	1926
169	E. H. Hendren, Brisbane..	1928-29
132	E. H. Hendren, Manchester	1934
126*	J. B. Hobbs, Melbourne...	1911-12
187	J. B. Hobbs, Adelaide.....	1911-12
178	J. B. Hobbs, Melbourne...	1911-12
107	J. B. Hobbs, Lord's.........	1912
122	J. B. Hobbs, Melbourne...	1920-21
123	J. B. Hobbs, Adelaide.....	1920-21
115	J. B. Hobbs, Sydney........	1924-25
154	J. B. Hobbs, Melbourne...	1924-25
119	J. B. Hobbs, Adelaide.....	1924-25
119	J. B. Hobbs, Lord's.........	1926
100	J. B. Hobbs, The Oval.....	1926
142	J. B. Hobbs, Melbourne...	1928-29
126	K. L. Hutchings, Melbourne.......................	1907-08
100†	L. Hutton, Nottingham....	1938
364	L. Hutton, The Oval.......	1938
122*	L. Hutton, Sydney...........	1946-47
156*	L. Hutton, Adelaide........	1950-51
145	L. Hutton, Lord's...........	1953
103	Hon. F. S. Jackson, The Oval.........................	1893
118	Hon. F. S. Jackson, The Oval.........................	1899
128	Hon. F. S. Jackson, Manchester......................	1902
144*	Hon. F. S. Jackson, Leeds	1905
113	Hon. F. S. Jackson, Manchester......................	1905
104	G. L. Jessop, The Oval....	1902
106*	A. P. E. Knott, Adelaide.	1974-75
135	A. P. E. Knott, Nottingham	1977
137†	M. Leyland, Melbourne....	1928-29
109	M. Leyland, Lord's.........	1934
153	M. Leyland, Manchester...	1934
110	M. Leyland, The Oval......	1934
126	M. Leyland, Brisbane......	1936-37
111*	M. Leyland, Melbourne....	1936-37
187	M. Leyland, The Oval......	1938
131	B. W. Luckhurst, Perth....	1970-71
109	B. W. Luckhurst, Melbourne.......................	1970-71
120	A. C. MacLaren, Melbourne.......................	1894-95
109	A. C. MacLaren, Sydney..	1897-98
124	A. C. MacLaren, Adelaide.........................	1897-98
116	A. C. MacLaren, Sydney..	1901-02
140	A. C. MacLaren, Nottingham.....................	1905
117	H. Makepeace, Melbourne	1920-21
104	P. B. H. May, Sydney......	1954-55
101	P. B. H. May, Leeds.......	1956
113	P. B. H. May, Melbourne.	1958-59
182*	C. P. Mead, The Oval......	1921
102†	Nawab of Pataudi, Sydney	1932-33
216*	E. Paynter, Nottingham....	1938
174†	D. W. Randall, Melbourne	1976-77
150	D. W. Randall, Sydney....	1978-79
154*†	K. S. Ranjitsinhji, Manchester.......................	1896
175	K. S. Ranjitsinhji, Sydney.	1897-98
117	W. W. Read, The Oval....	1884
179	W. Rhodes, Melbourne....	1911-12
104	P. E. Richardson, Manchester.......................	1956
135*	A. C. Russell, Adelaide...	1920-21
101	A. C. Russell, Manchester	1921
102*	A. C. Russell, The Oval...	1921
105	J. Sharp, The Oval..........	1909
113	Rev. D. S. Sheppard, Manchester.................	1956
113	Rev. D. S. Sheppard, Melbourne.................	1962-63
105*	A. Shrewsbury, Melbourne.......................	1884-85
164	A. Shrewsbury, Lord's.....	1886
106	A. Shrewsbury, Lord's.....	1893
156*	R. T. Simpson, Melbourne	1950-51
135*	A. G. Steel, Sydney.........	1882-83
148	A. G. Steel, Lord's.........	1884
134	A. E. Stoddart, Adelaide..	1891-92
173	A. E. Stoddart, Melbourne	1894-95
112†	R. Subba Row, Birmingham..........................	1961
137	R. Subba Row, The Oval.	1961
115†	H. Sutcliffe, Sydney.........	1924-25
176 127	H. Sutcliffe, Melbourne....	1924-25
143	H. Sutcliffe, Melbourne....	1924-25
161	H. Sutcliffe, The Oval.....	1926
135	H. Sutcliffe, Melbourne....	1928-29
161	H. Sutcliffe, The Oval.....	1930
194	H. Sutcliffe, Sydney.........	1932-33
138	J. T. Tyldesley, Birmingham..........................	1902

100	J. T. Tyldesley, Leeds	1905
112*	J. T. Tyldesley, The Oval.	1905
149	G. Ulyett, Melbourne	1881-82
117	A. Ward, Sydney	1894-95
112	C. Washbrook, Melbourne	1946-47
143	C. Washbrook, Leeds	1948
109†	W. Watson, Lord's	1953
133*	F. E. Woolley, Sydney	1911-12
123	F. E. Woolley, Sydney	1924-25
149	R. A. Woolmer, The Oval	1975
120	R. A. Woolmer, Lord's	1977
137	R. A. Woolmer, Manchester	1977

† *Signifies hundred on first appearance in England–Australia Tests.*

Note: In consecutive innings in 1928-29, W. R. Hammond scored 251 at Sydney, 200 and 32 at Melbourne, and 119* and 177 at Adelaide.

For Australia (189)

133*	W. W. Armstrong, Melbourne	1907-08
158	W. W. Armstrong, Sydney	1920-21
121	W. W. Armstrong, Adelaide	1920-21
123*	W. W. Armstrong, Melbourne	1920-21
118	C. L. Badcock, Melbourne	1936-37
165*†	C. Bannerman, Melbourne	1876-77
136 } 130 }	W. Bardsley, The Oval	1909
193*	W. Bardsley, Lord's	1926
234	S. G. Barnes, Sydney	1946-47
141	S. G. Barnes, Lord's	1948
128	G. J. Bonnor, Sydney	1884-85
112	B. C. Booth, Brisbane	1962-63
103	B. C. Booth, Melbourne	1962-63
115	A. R. Border, Perth	1979-80
123*	A. R. Border, Manchester	1981
106*	A. R. Border, The Oval	1981
112	D. G. Bradman, Melbourne	1928-29
123	D. G. Bradman, Melbourne	1928-29
131	D. G. Bradman, Nottingham	1930
254	D. G. Bradman, Lord's	1930
334	D. G. Bradman, Leeds	1930
232	D. G. Bradman, The Oval	1930
103*	D. G. Bradman, Melbourne	1932-33
304	D. G. Bradman, Leeds	1934
244	D. G. Bradman, The Oval	1934
270	D. G. Bradman, Melbourne	1936-37
212	D. G. Bradman, Adelaide	1936-37
169	D. G. Bradman, Melbourne	1936-37
144*	D. G. Bradman, Nottingham	1938
102*	D. G. Bradman, Lord's	1938
103	D. G. Bradman, Leeds	1938
187	D. G. Bradman, Brisbane.	1946-47
234	D. G. Bradman, Sydney	1946-47
138	D. G. Bradman, Nottingham	1948
173*	D. G. Bradman, Leeds	1948
105	W. A. Brown, Lord's	1934
133	W. A. Brown, Nottingham	1938
206*	W. A. Brown, Lord's	1938
181	P. J. Burge, The Oval	1961
103	P. J Burge, Sydney	1962-63
160	P. J. Burge, Leeds	1964
120	P. J. Burge, Melbourne	1965-66
101*†	J. W. Burke, Adelaide	1950-51
108†	G. S. Chappell, Perth	1970-71
131	G. S. Chappell, Lord's	1972
113	G. S. Chappell, The Oval.	1972
144	G. S. Chappell, Sydney	1974-75
102	G. S. Chappell, Melbourne	1974-75
112	G. S. Chappell, Manchester	1977
114	G. S. Chappell, Melbourne	1979-80
111	I. M. Chappell, Melbourne	1970-71
104	I. M. Chappell, Adelaide	1970-71
118	I. M. Chappell, The Oval.	1972
192	I. M. Chappell, The Oval.	1975
104†	H. L. Collins, Sydney	1920-21
162	H. L. Collins, Adelaide	1920-21
114	H. L. Collins, Sydney	1924-25
307	R. M. Cowper, Melbourne	1965-66
101	J. Darling, Sydney	1897-98
178	J. Darling, Adelaide	1897-98
160	J. Darling, Sydney	1897-98
104†	R. A. Duff, Melbourne	1901-02
146	R. A. Duff, The Oval	1905
102	J. Dyson, Leeds	1981
170*	R. Edwards, Nottingham	1972
115	R. Edwards, Perth	1974-75
100	J. H. Fingleton, Brisbane	1936-37
136	J. H. Fingleton, Melbourne	1936-37
161	G. Giffen, Sydney	1894-95
107†	H. Graham, Lord's	1893
105	H. Graham, Sydney	1894-95
100	J. M. Gregory, Melbourne	1920-21
201	S. E. Gregory, Sydney	1894-95
103	S. E. Gregory, Lord's	1896
117	S. E. Gregory, The Oval	1899
112	S. E. Gregory, Adelaide	1903-04
116†	R. J. Hartigan, Adelaide	1907-08
112†	R. N. Harvey, Leeds	1948

122	R. N. Harvey, Manchester	1953
162	R. N. Harvey, Brisbane....	1954-55
167	R. N. Harvey, Melbourne.	1958-59
114	R. N. Harvey, Birmingham	1961
154	R. N. Harvey, Adelaide...	1962-63
128	A. L. Hassett, Brisbane....	1946-47
137	A. L. Hassett, Nottingham	1948
115	A. L. Hassett, Nottingham	1953
104	A. L. Hassett, Lord's.......	1953
112	H. S. T. L. Hendry, Sydney	1928-29
188	C. Hill, Melbourne..........	1897-98
135	C. Hill, Lord's................	1899
119	C. Hill, Sheffield............	1902
160	C. Hill, Adelaide............	1907-08
124	T. P. Horan, Melbourne...	1881-82
129	K. J. Hughes, Brisbane....	1978-79
117	K. J. Hughes, Lord's.......	1980
140	F. A. Iredale, Adelaide....	1894-95
108	F. A. Iredale, Manchester.	1896
164†	A. Jackson, Adelaide.......	1928-29
147	C. Kelleway, Adelaide.....	1920-21
100	A. F. Kippax, Melbourne.	1928-29
130	W. M. Lawry, Lord's.......	1961
102	W. M. Lawry, Manchester	1961
106	W. M. Lawry, Manchester	1964
166	W. M. Lawry, Brisbane....	1965-66
119	W. M. Lawry, Adelaide...	1965-66
108	W. M. Lawry, Melbourne.	1965-66
135	W. M. Lawry, The Oval...	1968
100	R. R. Lindwall, Melbourne	1946-47
134	J. J. Lyons, Sydney.........	1891-92
170	C. G. Macartney, Sydney.	1920-21
115	C. G. Macartney, Leeds...	1921
133*	C. G. Macartney, Lord's..	1926
151	C. G. Macartney, Leeds...	1926
109	C. G. Macartney, Manchester.......................	1926
187*	S. J. McCabe, Sydney......	1932-33
137	S. J. McCabe, Manchester	1934
112	S. J. McCabe, Melbourne.	1936-37
232	S. J. McCabe, Nottingham	1938
104*	C. L. McCool, Melbourne	1946-47
127	R. B. McCosker, The Oval	1975
107	R. B. McCosker, Nottingham..........................	1977
170	C. C. McDonald, Adelaide.........................	1958-59
133	C. C. McDonald, Melbourne.......................	1958-59
147	P. S. McDonnell, Sydney..	1881-82
103	P. S. McDonnell, The Oval	1884
124	P. S. McDonnell, Adelaide.........................	1884-85
112	C. E. McLeod, Melbourne	1897-98
110*	R. W. Marsh, Melbourne.	1976-77
141*	K. R. Miller, Adelaide.....	1946-47
145*	K. R. Miller, Sydney.......	1950-51
109	K. R. Miller, Lord's........	1953
155	A. R. Morris, Melbourne.	1946-47
122 } 124* }	A. R. Morris, Adelaide....	1946-47
105	A. R. Morris, Lord's.......	1948
182	A. R. Morris, Leeds........	1948
196	A. R. Morris, The Oval...	1948
206	A. R. Morris, Adelaide....	1950-51
153	A. R. Morris, Brisbane....	1954-55
153*	W. L. Murdoch, The Oval	1880
211	W. L. Murdoch, The Oval	1884
133	M. A. Noble, Sydney.......	1903-04
117	N. C. O'Neill, The Oval...	1961
100	N. C. O'Neill, Adelaide...	1962-63
116	C. E. Pellew, Melbourne..	1920-21
104	C. E. Pellew, Adelaide.....	1920-21
110†	W. H. Ponsford, Sydney...	1924-25
128	W. H. Ponsford, Melbourne.......................	1924-25
110	W. H. Ponsford, The Oval.	1930
181	W. H. Ponsford, Leeds....	1934
266	W. H. Ponsford, The Oval.	1934
143*	V. S. Ransford, Lord's.....	1909
171	I. R. Redpath, Perth........	1970-71
105	I. R. Redpath, Sydney.....	1974-75
100	A. J. Richardson, Leeds...	1926
138	V. Y. Richardson, Melbourne.......................	1924-25
201*	J. Ryder, Adelaide..........	1924-25
112	J. Ryder, Melbourne........	1928-29
102	H. J. H. Scott, The Oval..	1884
311	R. B. Simpson, Manchester	1964
225	R. B. Simpson, Adelaide..	1965-66
207	K. R. Stackpole, Brisbane	1970-71
136	K. R. Stackpole, Adelaide	1970-71
114	K. R. Stackpole, Nottingham..........................	1972
108	J. M. Taylor, Sydney.......	1924-25
143	G. H. S. Trott, Lord's.....	1896
135*	V. T. Trumper, Lord's.....	1899
104	V. T. Trumper, Manchester	1902
185*	V. T. Trumper, Sydney....	1903-04
113	V. T. Trumper, Adelaide..	1903-04
166	V. T. Trumper, Sydney....	1907-08
113	V. T. Trumper, Sydney....	1911-12
155†	K. D. Walters, Brisbane...	1965-66
115	K. D. Walters, Melbourne	1965-66
112	K. D. Walters, Brisbane...	1970-71
103	K. D. Walters, Perth.......	1974-75
103†	D. M. Wellham, The Oval	1981
100	G. M. Wood, Melbourne..	1978-79
112	G. M. Wood, Lord's........	1980
141	W. M. Woodfull, Leeds....	1926
117	W. M. Woodfull, Manchester.......................	1926
111	W. M. Woodfull, Sydney..	1928-29
107	W. M. Woodfull, Melbourne......................	1928-29
102	W. M. Woodfull, Melbourne......................	1928-29
155	W. M. Woodfull, Lord's...	1930
102†	G. N. Yallop, Brisbane....	1978-79
121	G. N. Yallop, Sydney......	1978-79
114	G. N. Yallop, Manchester.	1981

† *Signifies hundred on first appearance in England–Australia Tests.*

Notes: D. G. Bradman's scores in 1930 were 8 and 131 at Nottingham, 254 and 1 at Lord's, 334 at Leeds, 14 at Manchester, and 232 at The Oval.

D. G. Bradman scored a hundred in eight successive Tests against England in which he batted – three in 1936-37, three in 1938 and two in 1946-47. He was injured and unable to bat at The Oval in 1938.

W. H. Ponsford and K. D. Walters each hit hundreds in their first two Tests.

C. Bannerman and H. Graham each scored their maiden hundred in first-class cricket in their first Test.

No right-handed batsman has obtained two hundreds for Australia in a Test match against England, and no left-handed batsman for England against Australia.

H. Sutcliffe, in his first two games for England, scored 59 and 115 at Sydney and 176 and 127 at Melbourne in 1924-25. In the latter match, which lasted into the seventh day, he was on the field throughout except for 86 minutes, namely 27 hours and 52 minutes.

C. Hill made 98 and 97 at Adelaide in 1901-02, and F. E. Woolley 95 and 93 at Lord's in 1921.

H. Sutcliffe in 1924-25, C. G. Macartney in 1926 and A. R. Morris in 1946-47 made three hundreds in consecutive innings.

J. B. Hobbs and H. Sutcliffe shared eleven first-wicket three-figure partnerships.

L. Hutton and C. Washbrook twice made three-figure stands in each innings, at Adelaide in 1946-47 and at Leeds in 1948.

H. Sutcliffe, during his highest score of 194, v Australia in 1932-33, took part in three stands each exceeding 100, viz. 112 with R. E. S. Wyatt for the first wicket, 188 with W. R. Hammond for the second wicket, and 123 with the Nawab of Pataudi for the third wicket. In 1903-04 R. E. Foster, in his historic innings of 287, added 192 for the fifth wicket with L. C. Braund, 115 for the ninth with A. E. Relf, and 130 for the tenth with W. Rhodes.

When L. Hutton scored 364 at The Oval in 1938 he added 382 for the second wicket with M. Leyland, 135 for the third wicket with W. R. Hammond and 215 for the sixth wicket with J. Hardstaff jun.

D. C. S. Compton and A. R. Morris at Adelaide in 1946-47 provide the only instance of a player on each side hitting two separate hundreds in a Test match.

G. S. and I. M. Chappell at The Oval in 1972 provide the first instance in Test matches of brothers each scoring hundreds in the same innings.

G. Boycott (191 at Leeds, 1977) is the only batsman to score his hundredth first-class century in a Test match.

RECORD PARTNERSHIPS FOR EACH WICKET

For England

323 for 1st	J. B. Hobbs and W. Rhodes at Melbourne	1911-12
382 for 2nd†	L. Hutton and M. Leyland at The Oval	1938
262 for 3rd	W. R. Hammond and D. R. Jardine at Adelaide	1928-29
222 for 4th	W. R. Hammond and E. Paynter at Lord's	1938
206 for 5th	E. Paynter and D. C. S. Compton at Nottingham	1938
215 for 6th	L. Hutton and J. Hardstaff jun. at The Oval	1938
	G. Boycott and A. P. E. Knott at Nottingham	1977
143 for 7th	F. E. Woolley and J. Vine at Sydney	1911-12
124 for 8th	E. H. Hendren and H. Larwood at Brisbane	1928-29
151 for 9th	W. H. Scotton and W. W. Read at The Oval	1884
130 for 10th†	R. E. Foster and W. Rhodes at Sydney	1903-04

For Australia

244 for 1st	R. B. Simpson and W. M. Lawry at Adelaide	1965-66
451 for 2nd†	W. H. Ponsford and D. G. Bradman at The Oval	1934
276 for 3rd	D. G. Bradman and A. L. Hassett at Brisbane	1946-47
388 for 4th†	W. H. Ponsford and D. G. Bradman at Leeds	1934
405 for 5th†	S. G. Barnes and D. G. Bradman at Sydney	1946-47
346 for 6th†	J. H. Fingleton and D. G. Bradman at Melbourne	1936-37
165 for 7th	C. Hill and H. Trumble at Melbourne	1897-98

243 for 8th†	R. J. Hartigan and C. Hill at Adelaide	1907-08
154 for 9th†	S. E. Gregory and J. McC. Blackham at Sydney	1894-95
127 for 10th†	J. M. Taylor and A. A. Mailey at Sydney	1924-25

† *Denotes record partnership against all countries.*

MOST RUNS IN A SERIES

England in England	562 (average 62.44)	D. C. S. Compton	1948
England in Australia	905 (average 113.12)	W. R. Hammond	1928-29
Australia in England	974 (average 139.14)	D. G. Bradman	1930
Australia in Australia	810 (average 90.00)	D. G. Bradman	1936-37

TEN WICKETS OR MORE IN A MATCH

For England (36)

13-163 (6-42, 7-121)	S. F. Barnes, Melbourne	1901-02
14-102 (7-28, 7-74)	W. Bates, Melbourne	1882-83
10-105 (5-46, 5-59)	A. V. Bedser, Melbourne	1950-51
14-99 (7-55, 7-44)	A. V. Bedser, Nottingham	1953
11-102 (6-44, 5-58)	C. Blythe, Birmingham	1909
11-176 (6-78, 5-98)	I. T. Botham, Perth	1979-80
10-253 (6-125, 4-128)	I. T. Botham, The Oval	1981
11-74 (5-29, 6-45)	J. Briggs, Lord's	1886
12-136 (6-49, 6-87)	J. Briggs, Adelaide	1891-92
10-148 (5-34, 5-114)	J. Briggs, The Oval	1893
10-179 (5-102, 5-77)†	K. Farnes, Nottingham	1934
10-60 (6-41, 4-19)	J. T. Hearne, The Oval	1896
11-113 (5-58, 6-55)	J. C. Laker, Leeds	1956
19-90 (9-37, 10-53)	J. C. Laker, Manchester	1956
10-124 (5-96, 5-28)	H. Larwood, Sydney	1932-33
11-76 (6-48, 5-28)	W. H. Lockwood, Manchester	1902
12-104 (7-36, 5-68)	G. A. Lohmann, The Oval	1886
10-87 (8-35, 2-52)	G. A. Lohmann, Sydney	1886-87
10-142 (8-58, 2-84)	G. A. Lohmann, Sydney	1891-92
12-102 (6-50, 6-52)†	F. Martin, The Oval	1890
10-58 (5-18, 5-40)	R. Peel, Sydney	1887-88
11-68 (7-31, 4-37)	R. Peel, Manchester	1888
15-124 (7-56, 8-68)	W. Rhodes, Melbourne	1903-04
10-156 (5-49, 5-107)†	T. Richardson, Manchester	1893
11-173 (6-39, 5-134)	T. Richardson, Lord's	1896
13-244 (7-168, 6-76)	T. Richardson, Manchester	1896
10-204 (8-94, 2-110)	T. Richardson, Sydney	1897-98
11-228 (6-130, 5-98)†	M. W. Tate, Sydney	1924-25
11-88 (5-58, 6-30)	F. S. Trueman, Leeds	1961
10-130 (4-45, 6-85)	F. H. Tyson, Sydney	1954-55
10-82 (4-37, 6-45)	D. L. Underwood, Leeds	1972
11-215 (7-113, 4-102)	D. L. Underwood, Adelaide	1974-75
15-104 (7-61, 8-43)	H. Verity, Lord's	1934
10-57 (6-41, 4-16)	W. Voce, Brisbane	1936-37
13-256 (5-130, 8-126)	J. C. White, Adelaide	1928-29
10-49 (5-29, 5-20)	F. E. Woolley, The Oval	1912

For Australia (34)

10-239 (4-129, 6-110)	L. O'B. Fleetwood-Smith, Adelaide	1936-37
10-160 (4-88, 6-72)	G. Giffen, Sydney	1891-92
11-82 (5-45, 6-37)†	C. V. Grimmett, Sydney	1924-25
10-201 (5-107, 5-94)	C. V. Grimmett, Nottingham	1930
10-122 (5-65, 5-57)	R. M. Hogg, Perth	1978-79
10-66 (5-30, 5-36)	R. M. Hogg, Melbourne	1978-79
12-175 (5-85, 7-90)†	H. V. Hordern, Sydney	1911-12
10-161 (5-95, 5-66)	H. V. Hordern, Sydney	1911-12
10-164 (7-88, 3-76)	E. Jones, Lord's	1899
10-181 (5-58, 5-123)	D. K. Lillee, The Oval	1972
11-165 (6-26, 5-139)	D. K. Lillee, Melbourne	1976-77
11-138 (6-60, 5-78)	D. K. Lillee, Melbourne	1979-80
11-159 (7-89, 4-70)	D. K. Lillee, The Oval	1981
11-85 (7-58, 4-27)	C. G. Macartney, Leeds	1909
10-302 (5-160, 5-142)	A. A. Mailey, Adelaide	1920-21
13-236 (4-115, 9-121)	A. A. Mailey, Melbourne	1920-21
16-137 (8-84, 8-53)†	R. A. L. Massie, Lord's	1972
10-152 (5-72, 5-80)	K. R. Miller, Lord's	1956
13-77 (7-17, 6-60)	M. A. Noble, Melbourne	1901-02
11-103 (5-51, 6-52)	M. A. Noble, Sheffield	1902
10-129 (5-63, 5-66)	W. J. O'Reilly, Melbourne	1932-33
11-129 (4-75, 7-54)	W. J. O'Reilly, Nottingham	1934
10-122 (5-66, 5-56)	W. J. O'Reilly, Leeds	1938
11-165 (7-68, 4-97)	G. E. Palmer, Sydney	1881-82
10-126 (7-65, 3-61)	G. E. Palmer, Melbourne	1882-83
13-110 (6-48, 7-62)	F. R. Spofforth, Melbourne	1878-79
14-90 (7-46, 7-44)	F. R. Spofforth, The Oval	1882
11-117 (4-73, 7-44)	F. R. Spofforth, Sydney	1882-83
10-144 (4-54, 6-90)	F. R. Spofforth, Sydney	1884-85
12-89 (6-59, 6-30)	H. Trumble, The Oval	1896
10-128 (4-75, 6-53)	H. Trumble, Manchester	1902
12-173 (8-65, 4-108)	H. Trumble, The Oval	1902
12-87 (5-44, 7-43)	C. T. B. Turner, Sydney	1887-88
10-63 (5-27, 5-36)	C. T. B. Turner, Lord's	1888

† *Signifies ten wickets or more on first appearance in England-Australia Tests.*

Note: J. Briggs, J. C. Laker, T. Richardson in 1896, R. M. Hogg, A. A. Mailey, H. Trumble and C. T. B. Turner took ten wickets or more in successive Tests. J. Briggs was omitted, however, from the England team for the first Test match in 1893.

MOST WICKETS IN A SERIES

England in England	46 (average 9.60)	J. C. Laker	1956
England in Australia	38 (average 23.18)	M. W. Tate	1924-25
Australia in England	42 (average 21.26)	T. M. Alderman (6 Tests)	1981
Australia in Australia	41 (average 12.85)	R. M. Hogg (6 Tests)	1978-79

WICKET-KEEPING – MOST DISMISSALS

	M	*Ct*	*St*	*Total*
†R. W. Marsh (Australia)	37	113	7	120
A. P. E. Knott (England)	34	97	8	105
†W. A. Oldfield (Australia)	38	59	31	90
A. A. Lilley (England)	32	65	19	84
A. T. W. Grout (Australia)	22	69	7	76
T. G. Evans (England)	31	63	12	75

† *The number of catches by R. W. Marsh (113) and stumpings by W. A. Oldfield (31) are respective records in England–Australia Tests.*

SCORERS OF OVER 2,000 RUNS

	T	*I*	*NO*	*R*	*HI*	*Avge*
D. G. Bradman	37	63	7	5,028	334	89.78
J. B. Hobbs	41	71	4	3,636	187	54.26
G. Boycott	38	71	9	2,945	191	47.50
W. R. Hammond	31	58	3	2,852	251	51.85
H. Sutcliffe	27	46	5	2,741	194	66.85
C. Hill	41	76	1	2,660	188	35.46
J. H. Edrich	32	57	3	2,644	175	48.96
M. C. Cowdrey	43	75	4	2,433	113	34.26
L. Hutton	27	49	6	2,428	364	56.46
R. N. Harvey	37	68	5	2,416	167	38.34
V. T. Trumper	40	74	5	2,263	185*	32.79
W. M. Lawry	29	51	5	2,233	166	48.54
G. S. Chappell	30	55	6	2,230	144	45.51
S. E Gregory	52	92	7	2,193	201	25.80
W. W. Armstrong	42	71	9	2,172	158	35.03
I. M. Chappell	30	56	4	2,138	192	41.11
K. F. Barrington	23	39	6	2,111	256	63.96
A. R. Morris	24	43	2	2,080	206	50.73

BOWLERS WITH 100 WICKETS

	T	*Balls*	*R*	*W*	*5 W/i*	*Avge*
D. K. Lillee	28	8,090	3,322	163	11	20.38
H. Trumble	31	7,895	2,945	141	9	20.88
M. A. Noble	39	6,845	2,860	115	9	24.86
R. R. Lindwall	29	6,728	2,559	114	6	22.44
R. G. D. Willis	30	6,295	2,860	110	6	26.00
W. Rhodes	41	5,791	2,616	109	6	24.00
S. F. Barnes	20	5,749	2,288	106	12	21.58
C. V. Grimmett	22	9,224	3,439	106	11	32.44
D. L. Underwood	29	8,000	2,770	105	4	26.38
A. V. Bedser	21	7,065	2,859	104	7	27.49
G. Giffen	31	6,325	2,791	103	7	27.09
W. J. O'Reilly	19	7,864	2,587	102	8	25.36
R. Peel	20	5,216	1,715	102	6	16.81
C. T. B. Turner	17	5,195	1,670	101	11	16.53

ENGLAND v SOUTH AFRICA

	Captains					
Season	*England*	*South Africa*	*T*	*E*	*SA*	*D*
1888-89	C. A. Smith[1]	O. R. Dunell[2]	2	2	0	0
1891-92	W. W. Read	W. H. Milton	1	1	0	0
1895-96	Lord Hawke[3]	E. A. Halliwell[4]	3	3	0	0
1898-99	Lord Hawke	M. Bisset	2	2	0	0
1905-06	P. F. Warner	P. W. Sherwell	5	1	4	0
1907	R. E. Foster	P. W. Sherwell	3	1	0	2
1909-10	H. D. G. Leveson Gower[5]	S. J. Snooke	5	2	3	0
1912	C. B. Fry	F. Mitchell[6]	3	3	0	0
1913-14	J. W. H. T. Douglas	H. W. Taylor	5	4	0	1

	Captains					
Season	*England*	*South Africa*	*T*	*E*	*SA*	*D*
1922-23	F. T. Mann	H. W. Taylor	5	2	1	2
1924	A. E. R. Gilligan[7]	H. W. Taylor	5	3	0	2
1927-28	R. T. Stanyforth[8]	H. G. Deane	5	2	2	1
1929	J. C. White[9]	H. G. Deane	5	2	0	3
1930-31	A. P. F. Chapman	H. G. Deane[10]	5	0	1	4
1935	R. E. S. Wyatt	H. F. Wade	5	0	1	4
1938-39	W. R. Hammond	A. Melville	5	1	0	4
1947	N. W. D. Yardley	A. Melville	5	3	0	2
1948-49	F. G. Mann	A. D. Nourse	5	2	0	3
1951	F. R. Brown	A. D. Nourse	5	3	1	1
1955	P. B. H. May	J. E. Cheetham[11]	5	3	2	0
1956-57	P. B. H. May	C. B. van Ryneveld[12]	5	2	2	1
1960	M. C. Cowdrey	D. J. McGlew	5	3	0	2
1964-65	M. J. K. Smith	T. L. Goddard	5	1	0	4
1965	M. J. K. Smith	P. L. van der Merwe	3	0	1	2
	In South Africa		58	25	13	20
	In England		44	21	5	18
	Totals		102	46	18	38

Notes: The following deputised for the official touring captain or were appointed by the home authority for only a minor proportion of the series:

[1] M. P Bowden (Second). [2] W. H. Milton (Second). [3] Sir T. C. O'Brien (First). [4] A. R. Richards (Third). [5] F. L. Fane (Fourth and Fifth). [6] L. J. Tancred (Second and Third). [7] J. W. H. T. Douglas (Fourth). [8] G. T. S. Stevens (Fifth). [9] A. W. Carr (Fourth and Fifth). [10] E. P. Nupen (First), H. B. Cameron (Fourth and Fifth). [11] D. J. McGlew (Third and Fourth). [12] D. J. McGlew (Second).

HIGHEST INNINGS TOTALS

By England

654-5	Durban	1938-39
608 ..	Johannesburg	1948-49
559-9 dec.	Cape Town	1938-39
554-8 dec.	Lord's	1947
551 ..	Nottingham	1947
534-6 dec.	The Oval	1935
531-2 dec.	Lord's	1924
531 ..	Johannesburg	1964-65

By South Africa

538 ..	Leeds	1951
533 ..	Nottingham	1947
530 ..	Durban	1938-39
521-8 dec.	Manchester	1955
513-8 dec.	Cape Town	1930-31
502 ..	Port Elizabeth	1964-65
501-7 dec.	Cape Town	1964-65
500 ..	Leeds	1955

LOWEST INNINGS TOTALS

By England

76 ..	Leeds	1907
92 ..	Cape Town	1898-99
110 ..	Port Elizabeth	1956-57

By South Africa

30 ..	Port Elizabeth	1895-96
30 ..	Birmingham	1924
35 ..	Cape Town	1898-99

INDIVIDUAL HUNDREDS IN THE MATCHES 1888-89–1965

For England (87)

120	R. Abel, Cape Town	1888-89
148*	L. E. G. Ames, The Oval	1935
115	L. E. G. Ames, Cape Town	1938-39
148*	K. F. Barrington, Durban.	1964-65
121	K. F. Barrington, Johannesburg	1964-65
117	G. Boycott, Port Elizabeth	1964-65
104†	L. C. Braund, Lord's	1907
208	D. C. S. Compton, Lord's	1947
163†	D. C. S. Compton, Nottingham	1947
115	D. C. S. Compton, Manchester	1947
113	D. C. S. Compton, The Oval	1947
114	D. C. S. Compton, Johannesburg	1948-49
112	D. C. S. Compton, Nottingham	1951
158	D. C. S. Compton, Manchester	1955
101	M. C. Cowdrey, Cape Town	1956-57
155	M. C. Cowdrey, The Oval	1960
105	M. C. Cowdrey, Nottingham	1965
104	D. Denton, Johannesburg.	1909-10
172	E. R. Dexter, Johannesburg	1964-65
119†	J. W. H. T. Douglas, Durban	1913-14
219	W. J. Edrich, Durban	1938-39
191	W. J. Edrich, Manchester.	1947
189	W. J. Edrich, Lord's	1947
143	F. L. Fane, Johannesburg.	1905-06
129	C. B. Fry, The Oval	1907
106†	P. A. Gibb, Johannesburg	1938-39
120	P. A. Gibb, Durban	1938-39
138*	W. R. Hammond, Birmingham	1929
101*	W. R. Hammond, The Oval	1929
136*	W. R. Hammond, Durban	1930-31
181	W. R. Hammond, Cape Town	1938-39
120	W. R. Hammond, Durban	1938-39
140	W. R. Hammond, Durban	1938-39
122	T. W. Hayward, Johannesburg	1895-96
132	E. H. Hendren, Leeds	1924
142	E. H. Hendren, The Oval	1924
124	A. J. L. Hill, Cape Town.	1895-96
187	J. B. Hobbs, Cape Town..	1909-10
211	J. B. Hobbs, Lord's	1924
100	L. Hutton, Leeds	1947
158	L. Hutton, Johannesburg..	1948-49
123	L. Hutton, Johannesburg..	1948-49
100	L. Hutton, Leeds	1951
110*	D. J. Insole, Durban	1956-57
102	M. Leyland, Lord's	1929
161	M. Leyland, The Oval	1935
136*	F. G. Mann, Port Elizabeth	1948-49
138†	P. B. H. May, Leeds	1951
112	P. B. H. May, Lord's	1955
117	P. B. H. May, Manchester	1955
102	C. P. Mead, Johannesburg	1913-14
117	C. P. Mead, Port Elizabeth	1913-14
181	C. P. Mead, Durban	1922-23
122*	P. H. Parfitt, Johannesburg	1964-65
108*	J. M. Parks, Durban	1964-65
117†, 100	E. Paynter, Johannesburg.	1938-39
243	E. Paynter, Durban	1938-39
175	G. Pullar, The Oval	1960
152	W. Rhodes, Johannesburg	1913-14
117†	P. E. Richardson, Johannesburg	1956-57
108	R. W. V. Robins, Manchester	1935
140, 111	A. C. Russell, Durban	1922-23
137	R. T. Simpson, Nottingham	1951
121	M. J. K. Smith, Cape Town	1964-65
119†	R. H. Spooner, Lord's	1912
122	H. Sutcliffe, Lord's	1924
102	H. Sutcliffe, Johannesburg	1927-28
114	H. Sutcliffe, Birmingham..	1929
100	H. Sutcliffe, Lord's	1929
104, 109*	H. Sutcliffe, The Oval	1929
100*	M. W. Tate, Lord's	1929
122†	E. Tyldesley, Johannesburg	1927-28
100	E. Tyldesley, Durban	1927-28
112	J. T. Tyldesley, Cape Town	1898-99
112	B. H. Valentine, Cape Town	1938-39
132*†	P. F. Warner, Johannesburg	1898-99
195	C. Washbrook, Johannesburg	1948-49
111	A. J. Watkins, Johannesburg	1948-49
134*	H. Wood, Cape Town	1891-92
115*	F. E. Woolley, Johannesburg	1922-23
134*	F. E. Woolley, Lord's	1924
154	F. E. Woolley, Manchester	1929
113	R. E. S. Wyatt, Manchester	1929
149	R. E. S. Wyatt, Nottingham	1935

For South Africa (58)

138	E. J. Barlow, Cape Town.	1964-65
144*	K. C. Bland, Johannesburg	1964-65
127	K. C. Bland, The Oval	1965
120	R. H. Catterall, Birmingham	1924

120	R. H. Catterall, Lord's	1924
119	R. H. Catterall, Durban	1927-28
117	E. L. Dalton, The Oval	1935
102	E. L. Dalton, Johannesburg	1938-39
116*	W. R. Endean, Leeds	1955
123	G. A. Faulkner, Johannesburg	1909-10
112	T. L. Goddard, Johannesburg	1964-65
102	C. M. H. Hathorn, Johannesburg	1905-06
104*	D. J. McGlew, Manchester	1955
133	D. J. McGlew, Leeds	1955
142	R. A. McLean, Lord's	1955
100	R. A. McLean, Durban	1956-57
109	R. A. McLean, Manchester	1960
103	A. Melville, Durban	1938-39
189 } 104* }	A. Melville, Nottingham	1947
117	A. Melville, Lord's	1947
123	B. Mitchell, Cape Town	1930-31
164*	B. Mitchell, Lord's	1935
128	B. Mitchell, The Oval	1935
109	B. Mitchell, Durban	1938-39
120 } 189* }	B. Mitchell, The Oval	1947
120	B. Mitchell, Cape Town	1948-49
120	A. D. Nourse, Cape Town	1938-39
103	A. D. Nourse, Durban	1938-39
149	A. D. Nourse, Nottingham	1947
115	A. D. Nourse, Manchester	1947
129*	A. D. Nourse, Johannesburg	1948-49
112	A. D. Nourse, Cape Town	1948-49
208	A. D. Nourse, Nottingham	1951
129	H. G. Owen-Smith, Leeds	1929
154	A. J. Pithey, Cape Town	1964-65
137	R. G. Pollock, Port Elizabeth	1964-65
125	R. G. Pollock, Nottingham	1965
156*	E. A. B. Rowan, Johannesburg	1948-49
236	E. A. B. Rowan, Leeds	1951
115	P. W. Sherwell, Lord's	1907
141	I. J. Siedle, Cape Town	1930-31
106	J. H. Sinclair, Cape Town	1898-99
109	H. W. Taylor, Durban	1913-14
176	H. W. Taylor, Johannesburg	1922-23
101	H. W. Taylor, Johannesburg	1922-23
102	H. W. Taylor, Durban	1922-23
101	H. W. Taylor, Johannesburg	1927-28
121	H. W. Taylor, The Oval	1929
117	H. W. Taylor, Cape Town	1930-31
125	P. G. V. van der Bijl, Durban	1938-39
124	K. G. Viljoen, Manchester	1935
125	W. W. Wade, Port Elizabeth	1948-49
113	J. H. B. Waite, Manchester	1955
147	G. C. White, Johannesburg	1905-06
118	G. C. White, Durban	1909-10
108	P. L. Winslow, Manchester	1955

† *Signifies hundred on first appearance in England–South Africa Tests.*

Notes: P. F. Warner carried his bat through the second innings.

The highest score by a South African batsman on début is 93* by A. W. Nourse at Johannesburg in 1905-06.

P. N. F. Mansell made 90 at Leeds in 1951, the best on début in England.

RECORD PARTNERSHIP FOR EACH WICKET

For England

359 for 1st†	L. Hutton and C. Washbrook at Johannesburg	1948-49
280 for 2nd	P. A. Gibb and W. J. Edrich at Durban	1938-39
370 for 3rd†	W. J. Edrich and D. C. S. Compton at Lord's	1947
197 for 4th	W. R. Hammond and L. E. G. Ames at Cape Town	1938-39
237 for 5th	D. C. S. Compton and N. W. D. Yardley at Nottingham	1947
206* for 6th	K. F. Barrington and J. M. Parks at Durban	1964-65
115 for 7th	M. C. Bird and J. W. H. T. Douglas at Durban	1913-14
154 for 8th	C. W. Wright and H. R. Bromley-Davenport at Johannesburg	1895-96
71 for 9th	H. Wood and J. T. Hearne at Cape Town	1891-92
92 for 10th	A. C. Russell and A. E. R. Gilligan at Durban	1922-23

For South Africa

260 for 1st†	I. J. Siedle and B. Mitchell at Cape Town	1930-31
198 for 2nd†	E. A. B. Rowan and C. B. van Ryneveld at Leeds	1951
319 for 3rd	A. Melville and A. D. Nourse at Nottingham	1947

214 for 4th†	H. W. Taylor and H. G. Deane at The Oval	1929
157 for 5th†	A. J. Pithey and J. H. B. Waite at Johannesburg	1964-65
171 for 6th	J. H. B. Waite and P. L. Winslow at Manchester	1955
123 for 7th	H. G. Deane and E. P. Nupen at Durban	1927-28
109* for 8th	B. Mitchell and L. Tuckett at The Oval	1947
137 for 9th†	E. L. Dalton and A. B. C. Langton at The Oval	1935
103 for 10th†	H. G. Owen-Smith and A. J. Bell at Leeds	1929

† *Denotes record partnership against all countries.*

MOST RUNS IN A SERIES

England in England	753 (average 94.12)	D. C. S. Compton	1947
England in South Africa	653 (average 81.62)	E. Paynter	1938-39
South Africa in England	621 (average 69.00)	A. D. Nourse	1947
South Africa in South Africa	582 (average 64.66)	H. W. Taylor	1922-23

TEN WICKETS OR MORE IN A MATCH

For England (23)

11-110 (5-25, 6-85)†	S. F. Barnes, Lord's	1912
10-115 (6-52, 4-63)	S. F. Barnes, Leeds	1912
13-57 (5-28, 8-29)	S. F. Barnes, The Oval	1912
10-105 (5-57, 5-48)	S. F. Barnes, Durban	1913-14
17-159 (8-56, 9-103)	S. F. Barnes, Johannesburg	1913-14
14-144 (7-56, 7-88)	S. F. Barnes, Durban	1913-14
12-112 (7-58, 5-54)	A. V. Bedser, Manchester	1951
11-118 (6-68, 5-50)	C. Blythe, Cape Town	1905-06
15-99 (8-59, 7-40)	C. Blythe, Leeds	1907
10-104 (7-46, 3-58)	C. Blythe, Cape Town	1909-10
15-28 (7-17, 8-11)	J. Briggs, Cape Town	1888-89
13-91 (6-54, 7-37)†	J. J. Ferris, Cape Town	1891-92
10-207 (7-115, 3-92)	A. P. Freeman, Leeds	1929
12-171 (7-71, 5-100)	A. P. Freeman, Manchester	1929
12-130 (7-70, 5-60)	G. Geary, Johannesburg	1927-28
11-90 (6-7, 5-83)	A. E. R. Gilligan, Birmingham	1924
10-119 (4-64, 6-55)	J. C. Laker, The Oval	1951
15-45 (7-38, 8-7)†	G. A. Lohmann, Port Elizabeth	1895-96
12-71 (9-28, 3-43)	G. A. Lohmann, Johannesburg	1895-96
11-97 (6-63, 5-34)	J. B. Statham, Lord's	1960
12-101 (7-52, 5-49)	R. Tattersall, Lord's	1951
12-89 (5-53, 7-36)	J. H. Wardle, Cape Town	1956-57
10-175 (5-95, 5-80)	D. V. P. Wright, Lord's	1947

For South Africa (6)

11-112 (4-49, 7-63)†	A. E. Hall, Cape Town	1922-23
11-150 (5-63, 6-87)	E. P. Nupen, Johannesburg	1930-31
10-87 (5-53, 5-34)	P. M. Pollock, Nottingham	1965
12-127 (4-57, 8-70)	S. J. Snooke, Johannesburg	1905-06
13-192 (4-79, 9-113)	H. J. Tayfield, Johannesburg	1956-57
12-181 (5-87, 7-94)	A. E. E. Vogler, Johannesburg	1909-10

† *Signifies ten wickets or more on first appearance in England–South Africa Tests.*

Note: S. F. Barnes took ten wickets or more in his first five Tests v South Africa and in six of his seven Tests v South Africa. A. P. Freeman and G. A. Lohmann took ten wickets or more in successive matches.

MOST WICKETS IN A SERIES

England in England	34 (average 8.29)	S. F. Barnes	1912
England in South Africa	49 (average 10.93)	S. F. Barnes	1913-14
South Africa in England	26 (average 21.84)	H. J. Tayfield	1955
South Africa in England	26 (average 22.57)	N. A. T. Adcock	1960
South Africa in South Africa	37 (average 17.18)	H. J. Tayfield	1956-57

ENGLAND v WEST INDIES

	Captains					
Season	*England*	*West Indies*	*T*	*E*	*WI*	*D*
1928	A. P. F. Chapman	R. K. Nunes	3	3	0	0
1929-30	Hon. F. S. G. Calthorpe	E. L. G. Hoad[1]	4	1	1	2
1933	D. R. Jardine[2]	G. C. Grant	3	2	0	1
1934-35	R. E. S. Wyatt	G. C. Grant	4	1	2	1
1939	W. R. Hammond	R. S. Grant	3	1	0	2
1947-48	G. O. Allen[3]	J. D. C. Goddard[4]	4	0	2	2
1950	N. W. D. Yardley[5]	J. D. C. Goddard	4	1	3	0
1953-54	L. Hutton	J. B. Stollmeyer	5	2	2	1
1957	P. B. H. May	J. D. C. Goddard	5	3	0	2
1959-60	P. B. H. May[6]	F. C. M. Alexander	5	1	0	4

THE WISDEN TROPHY

	Captains						
Season	*England*	*West Indies*	*T*	*E*	*WI*	*D*	*Held by*
1963	E. R. Dexter	F. M. Worrell	5	1	3	1	WI
1966	M. C. Cowdrey[7]	G. S. Sobers	5	1	3	1	WI
1967-68	M. C. Cowdrey	G. S. Sobers	5	1	0	4	E
1969	R. Illingworth	G. S. Sobers	3	2	0	1	E
1973	R. Illingworth	R. B. Kanhai	3	0	2	1	WI
1973-74	M. H. Denness	R. B. Kanhai	5	1	1	3	WI
1976	A. W. Greig	C. H. Lloyd	5	0	3	2	WI
1980	I. T. Botham	C. H. Lloyd[8]	5	0	1	4	WI
1980-81†	I. T. Botham	C. H. Lloyd	4	0	2	2	WI
	In England		44	14	15	15	
	In West Indies		36	7	10	19	
	Totals		80	21	25	34	

† *The Test match at Georgetown, scheduled as the second of the series, was cancelled owing to political pressure.*

Notes: The following deputised for the official touring captain or were appointed by the home authority for only a minor proportion of the series:

[1] N. Betancourt (Second), M. P. Fernandes (Third), R. K. Nunes (Fourth). [2] R. E. S. Wyatt (Third). [3] K. Cranston (First). [4] G. A. Headley (First), G. E. Gomez (Second). [5] F. R. Brown (Fourth). [6] M. C. Cowdrey (Fourth and Fifth). [7] M. J. K. Smith (First), D. B. Close (Fifth). [8] I. V. A. Richards (Fifth).

HIGHEST INNINGS TOTALS

By England			By West Indies		
849 ..	Kingston	1929-30	687-8 dec.	The Oval	1976
619-6 dec.	Nottingham	1957	681-8 dec.	Port-of-Spain	1953-54
583-4 dec.	Birmingham	1957	652-8 dec.	Lord's	1973
568 ..	Port-of-Spain	1967-68	596-8 dec.	Bridgetown	1973-74
537 ..	Port-of-Spain	1953-54	583-9 dec.	Kingston	1973-74
527 ..	The Oval	1966	563-8 dec.	Bridgetown	1959-60
			558 ..	Nottingham	1950

LOWEST INNINGS TOTALS

By England			By West Indies		
71 ..	Manchester	1976	86 ..	The Oval (2nd Inns).	1957
103 ..	Kingston	1934-35	89 ..	The Oval (1st Inns)..	1957
103 ..	The Oval	1950	91 ..	Birmingham	1963
107 ..	Port-of-Spain	1934-35	97 ..	Lord's	1933

Note: West Indies' lowest total in West Indies is 103 at Kingston, 1934-35.

INDIVIDUAL HUNDREDS IN THE MATCHES 1928–1980-81

For England (77)

105	L. E. G. Ames, Port-of-Spain	1929-30
149	L. E. G. Ames, Kingston	1929-30
126	L. E. G. Ames, Kingston	1934-35
174	D. L. Amiss, Port-of-Spain	1973-74
262*	D. L. Amiss, Kingston	1973-74
118	D. L. Amiss, Georgetown	1973-74
203	D. L. Amiss, The Oval	1976
107†	A. H. Bakewell, The Oval	1933
128†	K. F. Barrington, Bridgetown	1959-60
121	K. F. Barrington, Port-of-Spain	1959-60
143	K. F. Barrington, Port-of-Spain	1967-68
116	G. Boycott, Georgetown	1967-68
128	G. Boycott, Manchester	1969
106	G. Boycott, Lord's	1969
112	G. Boycott, Port-of-Spain.	1973-74
104*	G. Boycott, St John's	1980-81
120†	D. C. S. Compton, Lord's	1939
133	D. C. S. Compton, Port-of-Spain	1953-54
154†	M. C. Cowdrey, Birmingham	1957
152	M. C. Cowdrey, Lord's	1957
114	M. C. Cowdrey, Kingston.	1959-60
119	M. C. Cowdrey, Port-of-Spain	1959-60
101	M. C. Cowdrey, Kingston.	1967-68
148	M. C. Cowdrey, Port-of-Spain	1967-68
136*†	E. R. Dexter, Bridgetown	1959-60
110	E. R. Dexter, Georgetown	1959-60
146	J. H. Edrich, Bridgetown	1967-68
104	T. G. Evans, Manchester	1950
129*	K. W. R. Fletcher, Bridgetown	1973-74
123	G. A. Gooch, Lord's	1980
116	G. A. Gooch, Bridgetown	1980-81
153	G. A. Gooch, Kingston	1980-81
154*	D. I. Gower, Kingston	1980-81
258	T. W. Graveney, Nottingham	1957
164	T. W. Graveney, The Oval	1957
109	T. W. Graveney, Nottingham	1966
165	T. W. Graveney, The Oval	1966
118	T. W. Graveney, Port-of-Spain	1967-68
148	A. W. Greig, Bridgetown.	1973-74
121	A. W. Greig, Georgetown	1973-74
116	A. W. Greig, Leeds	1976
140†	S. C. Griffith, Port-of-Spain	1947-48
138	W. R. Hammond, The Oval	1939
107†	J. H. Hampshire, Lord's	1969
106*†	F. C. Hayes, The Oval	1973
205*	E. H. Hendren, Port-of-Spain	1929-30
123	E. H. Hendren, Georgetown	1929-30

159 J. B. Hobbs, The Oval..... 1928
196† L. Hutton, Lord's........... 1939
165* L. Hutton, The Oval....... 1939
202* L. Hutton, The Oval....... 1950
169 L. Hutton, Georgetown.... 1953-54
205 L. Hutton, Kingston........ 1953-54
113 R. Illingworth, Lord's...... 1969
127 D. R. Jardine, Manchester 1933
116 A. P. E. Knott, Leeds...... 1976
135 P. B. H. May, Port-of-Spain 1953-54
285* P. B. H. May, Birmingham 1957
104 P. B. H. May, Nottingham 1957
126* C. Milburn, Lord's.......... 1966
112† J. T. Murray, The Oval.... 1966
101*† J. M. Parks, Port-of-Spain 1959-60
107 W. Place, Kingston......... 1947-48
126 P. E. Richardson, Nottingham........................... 1957
107 P. E. Richardson, The Oval 1957
133 J. D. Robertson, Port-of-Spain......................... 1947-48
152† A. Sandham, Bridgetown.. 1929-30
325 A. Sandham, Kingston..... 1929-30
108 M. J. K. Smith, Port-of-Spain......................... 1959-60
106† D. S. Steele, Nottingham.. 1976
100† R. Subba Row, Georgetown......................... 1959-60
122† E. Tyldesley, Lord's........ 1928
114† C. Washbrook, Lord's...... 1950
102 C. Washbrook, Nottingham.......................... 1950
116† W. Watson, Kingston...... 1953-54
100* P. Willey, The Oval........ 1980
102* P. Willey, St John's......... 1980-81

For West Indies (80)

105 I. Barrow, Manchester..... 1933
133 B. F. Butcher, Lord's...... 1963
209* B. F. Butcher, Nottingham 1966
107 G. M. Carew, Port-of-Spain 1947-48
103 C. A. Davis, Lord's......... 1969
150 R. C. Fredericks, Birmingham........................... 1973
138 R. C. Fredericks, Lord's.. 1976
109 R. C. Fredericks, Leeds... 1976
112† A. G. Ganteaume, Port-of-Spain......................... 1947-48
134 }
101 } C. G. Greenidge, Manchester....................... 1976
115 C. G. Greenidge, Leeds... 1976
184 D. L. Haynes, Lord's...... 1980
176† G. A. Headley, Bridgetown 1929-30
114 }
112 } G. A. Headley, Georgetown 1929-30
223 G. A. Headley, Kingston.. 1929-30
169* G. A. Headley, Manchester 1933
270* G. A. Headley, Kingston.. 1934-35
106 }
107 } G. A. Headley, Lord's..... 1939
105* D. A. J. Holford, Lord's.. 1966
166 J. K. Holt, Bridgetown.... 1953-54
182 C. C. Hunte, Manchester.. 1963
108* C. C. Hunte, The Oval.... 1963
135 C. C. Hunte, Manchester.. 1966
121 B. D. Julien, Lord's........ 1973
158 A. I. Kallicharran, Port-of-Spain......................... 1973-74
119 A. I. Kallicharran, Bridgetown......................... 1973-74
110 R. B. Kanhai, Port-of-Spain 1959-60
104 R. B. Kanhai, The Oval... 1966
153 R. B. Kanhai, Port-of-Spain 1967-68
150 R. B. Kanhai, Georgetown 1967-68
157 R. B. Kanhai, Lord's....... 1973
118† C. H. Lloyd, Port-of-Spain 1967-68
113* C. H. Lloyd, Bridgetown.. 1967-68
132 C. H. Lloyd, The Oval.... 1973
101 C. H. Lloyd, Manchester.. 1980
100 C. H. Lloyd, Bridgetown.. 1980-81
137 S. M. Nurse, Leeds......... 1966
136 S. M. Nurse, Port-of-Spain 1967-68
106 A. F. Rae, Lord's........... 1950
109 A. F. Rae, The Oval....... 1950
232† I. V. A. Richards, Nottingham........................... 1976
135 I. V. A. Richards, Manchester....................... 1976
291 I. V. A. Richards, The Oval 1976
145 I. V. A. Richards, Lord's. 1980
182* I. V. A. Richards, Bridgetown......................... 1980-81
114 I. V. A. Richards, St John's 1980-81
122 C. A. Roach, Bridgetown. 1929-30
209 C. A. Roach, Georgetown 1929-30
120 L. G. Rowe, Kingston..... 1973-74
302 L. G. Rowe, Bridgetown.. 1973-74
123 L. G. Rowe, Port-of-Spain 1973-74
161† O. G. Smith, Birmingham 1957
168 O. G. Smith, Nottingham. 1957
226 G. S. Sobers, Bridgetown. 1959-60
147 G. S. Sobers, Kingston..... 1959-60
145 G. S. Sobers, Georgetown 1959-60
102 G. S. Sobers, Leeds......... 1963
161 G. S. Sobers, Manchester. 1966
163* G. S. Sobers, Lord's........ 1966
174 G. S. Sobers, Leeds......... 1966
113* G. S. Sobers, Kingston..... 1967-68
152 G. S. Sobers, Georgetown 1967-68
150* G. S. Sobers, Lord's........ 1973
168* C. L. Walcott, Lord's...... 1950
220 C. L. Walcott, Bridgetown 1953-54
124 C. L. Walcott, Port-of-Spain......................... 1953-54
116 C. L. Walcott, Kingston... 1953-54

141	E. D. Weekes, Kingston...	1947-48
129	E. D. Weekes, Nottingham	1950
206	E. D. Weekes, Port-of-Spain...	1953-54
137	K. H. Weekes, The Oval..	1939
131*	F. M. M. Worrell, Georgetown...	1947-48
261	F. M. M. Worrell, Nottingham...	1950
138	F. M. M. Worrell, The Oval	1950
167	F. M. M. Worrell, Port-of-Spain...	1953-54
191*	F. M. M. Worrell, Nottingham...	1957
197*	F. M. M. Worrell, Bridgetown...	1959-60

† *Signifies hundred on first appearance in England–West Indies Tests. S. C. Griffith provides the only instance for England of a player hitting his maiden century in first-class cricket in his first Test.*

RECORD PARTNERSHIPS FOR EACH WICKET

For England

212 for 1st	C. Washbrook and R. T. Simpson at Nottingham...	1950
266 for 2nd	P. E. Richardson and T. W. Graveney at Nottingham...	1957
264 for 3rd	L. Hutton and W. R. Hammond at The Oval...	1939
411 for 4th†	P. B. H. May and M. C. Cowdrey at Birmingham...	1957
130* for 5th	C. Milburn and T. W. Graveney at Lord's...	1966
163 for 6th	A. W. Greig and A. P. E. Knott at Bridgetown...	1973-74
197 for 7th†	M. J. K. Smith and J. M. Parks at Port-of-Spain...	1959-60
217 for 8th	T. W. Graveney and J. T. Murray at The Oval...	1966
109 for 9th	G. A. R. Lock and P. I. Pocock at Georgetown...	1967-68
128 for 10th	K. Higgs and J. A. Snow at The Oval...	1966

For West Indies

206 for 1st	R. C. Fredericks and L. G. Rowe at Kingston...	1973-74
249 for 2nd	L. G. Rowe and A. I. Kallicharran at Bridgetown...	1973-74
338 for 3rd†	E. D. Weekes and F. M. M. Worrell at Port-of-Spain...	1953-54
399 for 4th†	G. S. Sobers and F. M. M. Worrell at Bridgetown...	1959-60
265 for 5th†	S. M. Nurse and G. S. Sobers at Leeds...	1966
274* for 6th†	G. S. Sobers and D. A. J. Holford at Lord's...	1966
155* for 7th‡	G. S. Sobers and B. D. Julien at Lord's...	1973
99 for 8th	C. A. McWatt and J. K. Holt at Georgetown...	1953-54
63* for 9th	G. S. Sobers and W. W. Hall at Port-of-Spain...	1967-68
67* for 10th	M. A. Holding and C. E. H. Croft at St John's...	1980-81

† *Denotes record partnership against all countries.*
‡ *231 runs were added for this wicket in two separate partnerships: G. S. Sobers retired ill and was replaced by K. D. Boyce when 155 had been added.*

TEN WICKETS OR MORE IN A MATCH

For England (10)

11-98 (7-44, 4-54)	T. E. Bailey, Lord's...	1957
10-93 (5-54, 5-39)	A. P. Freeman, Manchester...	1928
13-156 (8-86, 5-70)	A. W. Greig, Port-of-Spain...	1973-74
11-48 (5-28, 6-20)	G. A. R. Lock, The Oval...	1957
11-96 (5-37, 6-59)†	C. S. Marriott, The Oval...	1933
10-142 (4-82, 6-60)	J. A. Snow, Georgetown...	1967-68
10-195 (5-105, 5-90)†	G. T. S. Stevens, Bridgetown...	1929-30
11-152 (6-100, 5-52)	F. S. Trueman, Lord's...	1963
12-119 (5-75, 7-44)	F. S. Trueman, Birmingham...	1963
11-149 (4-79, 7-70)	W. Voce, Port-of-Spain...	1929-30

For West Indies (10)

11-147 (5-70, 6-77)†	K. D. Boyce, The Oval	1973
11-229 (5-137, 6-92)	W. Ferguson, Port-of-Spain	1947-48
11-157 (5-59, 6-98)†	L. R. Gibbs, Manchester	1963
10-106 (5-37, 5-69)	L. R. Gibbs, Manchester	1966
14-149 (8-92, 6-57)	M. A. Holding, The Oval	1976
10-96 (5-41, 5-55)†	H. H. H. Johnson, Kingston	1947-48
11-152 (5-66, 6-86)	S. Ramadhin, Lord's	1950
10-123 (5-60, 5-63)	A. M. E. Roberts, Lord's	1976
11-204 (8-104, 3-100)†	A. L. Valentine, Manchester	1950
10-160 (4-121, 6-39)	A. L. Valentine, The Oval	1950

† *Signifies ten wickets or more on first appearance in England–West Indies Tests.*

Note: F. S. Trueman took ten wickets or more in successive matches.

ENGLAND v NEW ZEALAND

	Captains					
Season	*England*	*New Zealand*	*T*	*E*	*NZ*	*D*
1929-30	A. H. H. Gilligan	T. C. Lowry	4	1	0	3
1931	D. R. Jardine	T. C. Lowry	3	1	0	2
1932-33	D. R. Jardine[1]	M. L. Page	2	0	0	2
1937	R. W. V. Robins	M. L. Page	3	1	0	2
1946-47	W. R. Hammond	W. A. Hadlee	1	0	0	1
1949	F. G. Mann[2]	W. A. Hadlee	4	0	0	4
1950-51	F. R. Brown	W. A. Hadlee	2	1	0	1
1954-55	L. Hutton	G. O. Rabone	2	2	0	0
1958	P. B. H. May	J. R. Reid	5	4	0	1
1958-59	P. B. H. May	J. R. Reid	2	1	0	1
1962-63	E. R. Dexter	J. R. Reid	3	3	0	0
1965	M. J. K. Smith	J. R. Reid	3	3	0	0
1965-66	M. J. K. Smith	B. W. Sinclair[3]	3	0	0	3
1969	R. Illingworth	G. T. Dowling	3	2	0	1
1970-71	R. Illingworth	G. T. Dowling	2	1	0	1
1973	R. Illingworth	B. E Congdon	3	2	0	1
1974-75	M. H. Denness	B. E. Congdon	2	1	0	1
1977-78	G. Boycott	M. G. Burgess	3	1	1	1
1978	J. M. Brearley	M. G. Burgess	3	3	0	0
	In New Zealand		26	11	1	14
	In England		27	16	0	11
	Totals		53	27	1	25

Notes: The following deputised for the official touring captain or were appointed by the home authority for only a minor proportion of the series:

[1]R. E. S. Wyatt (Second). [2]F. R. Brown (Third and Fourth). [3]M. E. Chapple (First).

HIGHEST INNINGS TOTALS

By England

593-6 dec.	Auckland	1974-75
562-7 dec.	Auckland	1962-63
560-8 dec.	Christchurch	1932-33
550 ..	Christchurch	1950-51
548-7 dec.	Auckland	1932-33
546-4 dec.	Leeds	1965

By New Zealand

551-9 dec.	Lord's	1973
484 ..	Lord's	1949
469-9 dec.	Lord's	1931
440 ..	Wellington	1929-30
440 ..	Nottingham	1973

LOWEST INNINGS TOTALS

By England			By New Zealand		
64	Wellington	1977-78	26	Auckland	1954-55
181	Christchurch	1929-30	47	Lord's	1958
187	Manchester	1937	65	Christchurch	1970-71
190	Lord's	1969	67	Leeds	1958
			67	Lord's	1978

INDIVIDUAL HUNDREDS IN THE MATCHES 1929-30–1978

For England (55)

122†	G. O. Allen, Lord's	1931
137†	L. E. G. Ames, Lord's	1931
103	L. E. G. Ames, Christchurch	1932-33
138*†	D. L. Amiss, Nottingham	1973
164*	D. L. Amiss, Christchurch	1974-75
134*	T. E. Bailey, Christchurch	1950-51
126†	K. F. Barrington, Auckland	1962-63
163	K. F. Barrington, Leeds	1965
137	K. F. Barrington, Birmingham	1965
103	I. T. Botham, Christchurch	1977-78
109	E. H. Bowley, Auckland	1929-30
115	G. Boycott, Leeds	1973
131	G. Boycott, Nottingham	1978
114	D. C. S. Compton, Leeds	1949
116	D. C. S. Compton, Lord's	1949
128*	M. C. Cowdrey, Wellington	1962-63
119	M. C. Cowdrey, Lord's	1965
181	M. H. Denness, Auckland	1974-75
141	E. R. Dexter, Christchurch	1958-59
100	B. L. D'Oliveira, Christchurch	1970-71
117	K. S. Duleepsinhji, Auckland	1929-30
109	K. S. Duleepsinhji, The Oval	1931
310*†	J. H. Edrich, Leeds	1965
155	J. H. Edrich, Lord's	1969
115	J. H. Edrich, Nottingham	1969
100	W. J. Edrich, The Oval	1949
178	K. W. R. Fletcher, Lord's	1973
216	K. W. R. Fletcher, Auckland	1974-75
111†	D. I. Gower, The Oval	1978
139†	A. W. Greig, Nottingham	1973
100*	W. R. Hammond, The Oval	1931
227	W. R. Hammond, Christchurch	1932-33
336*	W. R. Hammond, Auckland	1932-33
140	W. R. Hammond, Lord's	1937
114†	J. Hardstaff jun., Lord's	1937
103	J. Hardstaff jun., The Oval	1937
100	L. Hutton, Manchester	1937
101	L. Hutton, Leeds	1949
206	L. Hutton, The Oval	1949
125†	B. R. Knight, Auckland	1962-63
101	A. P. E. Knott, Auckland	1970-71
196	G. B. Legge, Auckland	1929-30
113*	P. B. H. May, Leeds	1958
101	P. B. H. May, Manchester	1958
124*	P. B. H. May, Auckland	1958-59
104*†	C. A. Milton, Leeds	1958
131*†	P. H. Parfitt, Auckland	1962-63
158	C. T. Radley, Auckland	1977-78
100†	P. E. Richardson, Birmingham	1958
121†	J. D. Robertson, Lord's	1949
111	P. J. Sharpe, Nottingham	1969
103†	R. T. Simpson, Manchester	1949
117†	H. Sutcliffe, The Oval	1931
109*	H. Sutcliffe, Manchester	1931
103*	C. Washbrook, Leeds	1949

For New Zealand (21)

104	M. G. Burgess, Auckland	1970-71
105	M. G. Burgess, Lord's	1973
104	B. E. Congdon, Christchurch	1965-66
176	B. E. Congdon, Nottingham	1973
175	B. E. Congdon, Lord's	1973
136	C. S. Dempster, Wellington	1929-30
120	C. S. Dempster, Lord's	1931
206	M. P. Donnelly, Lord's	1949
116	W. A. Hadlee, Christchurch	1946-47
122 / 102	G. P. Howarth, Auckland	1977-78
123	G. P. Howarth, Lord's	1978
117†	J. E. Mills, Wellington	1929-30
104	M. L. Page, Lord's	1931
121	J. M. Parker, Auckland	1974-75
116	V. Pollard, Nottingham	1973
105*	V. Pollard, Lord's	1973
100	J. R. Reid, Christchurch	1962-63
114	B. W. Sinclair, Auckland	1965-66
101	B. Sutcliffe, Manchester	1949
116	B. Sutcliffe, Christchurch	1950-51

† *Signifies hundred on first appearance in England–New Zealand Tests.*

RECORD PARTNERSHIPS FOR EACH WICKET

For England

147 for 1st	L. Hutton and R. T. Simpson at The Oval	1949
369 for 2nd	J. H. Edrich and K. F. Barrington at Leeds	1965
245 for 3rd	W. R. Hammond and J. Hardstaff jun. at Lord's	1937
266 for 4th	M. H. Denness and K. W. R. Fletcher at Auckland	1974-75
242 for 5th	W. R. Hammond and L. E. G. Ames at Christchurch	1932-33
240 for 6th†	P. H. Parfitt and B. R. Knight at Auckland	1962-63
149 for 7th	A. P. E. Knott and P. Lever at Auckland	1970-71
246 for 8th†	L. E. G. Ames and G. O. Allen at Lord's	1931
163* for 9th†	M. C. Cowdrey and A. C. Smith at Wellington	1962-63
59 for 10th	A. P. E. Knott and N. Gifford at Nottingham	1973

For New Zealand

276 for 1st	C. S. Dempster and J. E. Mills at Wellington	1929-30
131 for 2nd	B. Sutcliffe and J. R. Reid at Christchurch	1950-51
190 for 3rd	B. E. Congdon and B. F. Hastings at Lord's	1973
142 for 4th	M. L. Page and R. C. Blunt at Lord's	1931
177 for 5th	B. E. Congdon and V. Pollard at Nottingham	1973
117 for 6th	M. G. Burgess and V. Pollard at Lord's	1973
104 for 7th	B. Sutcliffe and V. Pollard at Birmingham	1965
104 for 8th	A. W. Roberts and D. A. R. Moloney at Lord's	1937
64 for 9th	J. Cowie and T. B. Burtt at Christchurch	1946-47
57 for 10th	F. L. H. Mooney and J. Cowie at Leeds	1949

† *Denotes record partnership against all countries.*

TEN WICKETS OR MORE IN A MATCH

For England (7)

11-140 (6-101, 5-39)	I. T. Botham, Lord's	1978
10-149 (5-98, 5-51)	A. W. Greig, Auckland	1974-75
11-65 (4-14, 7-51)	G. A. R. Lock, Leeds	1958
11-84 (5-31, 6-53)	G. A. R. Lock, Christchurch	1958-59
11-70 (4-38, 7-32)†	D. L. Underwood, Lord's	1969
12-101 (6-41, 6-60)	D. L. Underwood, The Oval	1969
12-97 (6-12, 6-85)	D. L. Underwood, Christchurch	1970-71

For New Zealand (2)

10-140 (4-73, 6-67)	J. Cowie, Manchester	1937
10-100 (4-74, 6-26)	R. J. Hadlee, Wellington	1977-78

† *Signifies ten wickets or more on first appearance in England–New Zealand Tests.*

Note: D. L. Underwood took twelve wickets in successive matches against New Zealand in 1969 and 1970-71.

HAT-TRICK AND FOUR WICKETS IN FIVE BALLS

M. J. C. Allom, in his first Test match, v New Zealand at Christchurch in 1929-30, dismissed C. S. Dempster, T. C. Lowry, K. C. James, and F. T. Badcock to take four wickets in five balls (w-www).

ENGLAND v INDIA

Season	Captains: England	India	T	E	I	D
1932	D. R. Jardine	C. K. Nayudu	1	1	0	0
1933-34	D. R. Jardine	C. K. Nayudu	3	2	0	1
1936	G. O. Allen	Maharaj of Vizianagram	3	2	0	1
1946	W. R. Hammond	Nawab of Pataudi sen.	3	1	0	2
1951-52	N. D Howard[1]	V. S. Hazare	5	1	1	3
1952	L. Hutton	V. S. Hazare	4	3	0	1
1959	P. B. H. May[2]	D. K. Gaekwad[3]	5	5	0	0
1961-62	E. R. Dexter	N. J. Contractor	5	0	2	3
1963-64	M. J. K. Smith	Nawab of Pataudi jun.	5	0	0	5
1967	D. B. Close	Nawab of Pataudi jun.	3	3	0	0
1971	R. Illingworth	A. L. Wadekar	3	0	1	2
1972-73	A. R. Lewis	A. L. Wadekar	5	1	2	2
1974	M. H. Denness	A. L. Wadekar	3	3	0	0
1976-77	A. W. Greig	B. S. Bedi	5	3	1	1
1979	J. M. Brearley	S. Venkataraghavan	4	1	0	3
1979-80	J. M. Brearley	G. R. Viswanath	1	1	0	0
1981-82	K. W. R. Fletcher	S. M. Gavaskar	6	0	1	5
1982	R. G. D. Willis	S. M. Gavaskar	3	1	0	2
	In England		32	20	1	11
	In India		35	8	7	20
	Totals		67	28	8	31

Notes: The 1932 Indian touring team was captained by the Maharaj of Porbandar but he did not play in the Test match.

The following deputised for the official touring captain or were appointed by the home authority for only a minor proportion of the series:

[1]D. B. Carr (Fifth). [2]M. C. Cowdrey (Fourth and Fifth). [3]P. Roy (Second).

HIGHEST INNINGS TOTALS

By England

633-5 dec.	Birmingham	1979
629 ..	Lord's	1974
594 ..	The Oval	1982
571-8 dec.	Manchester	1936
559-8 dec.	Kanpur	1963-64
550-4 dec.	Leeds	1967
537 ..	Lord's	1952
500-8 dec.	Bombay	1961-62

By India

510 ..	Leeds	1967
487 ..	Delhi	1981-82
485-9 dec.	Bombay	1951-52
481-4 dec.	Madras	1981-82
467-8 dec.	Kanpur	1961-62
466 ..	Delhi	1961-62
463-4	Delhi	1963-64

LOWEST INNINGS TOTALS

By England

101 ..	The Oval	1971
102 ..	Bombay (2nd Inns)	1981-82
134 ..	Lord's	1936
159 ..	Madras	1972-73
163 ..	Calcutta	1972-73
166 ..	Bombay (1st Inns)	1981-82

By India

42 ..	Lord's	1974
58 ..	Manchester (1st Inns)	1952
82 ..	Manchester(2ndInns)	1952
83 ..	Madras	1976-77
92 ..	Birmingham	1967
93 ..	Lord's	1936
96 ..	Lord's	1979
98 ..	The Oval	1952

INDIVIDUAL HUNDREDS IN THE MATCHES 1932–1982

For England (55)

188	D. L. Amiss, Lord's	1974
179	D. L. Amiss, Delhi	1976-77
151*	K. F. Barrington, Bombay	1961-62
172	K. F. Barrington, Kanpur	1961-62
113*	K. F. Barrington, Delhi	1961-62
137	I. T. Botham, Leeds	1979
114	I. T. Botham, Bombay	1979-80
142	I. T. Botham, Kanpur	1981-82
128	I. T. Botham, Manchester	1982
208	I. T. Botham, The Oval	1982
246*†	G. Boycott, Leeds	1967
155	G. Boycott, Birmingham	1979
125	G. Boycott, The Oval	1979
105	G. Boycott, Delhi	1981-82
160	M. C. Cowdrey, Leeds	1959
107	M. C. Cowdrey, Calcutta	1963-64
151	M. C. Cowdrey, Delhi	1963-64
118	M. H. Denness, Lord's	1974
100	M. H. Denness, Birmingham	1974
126*	E. R. Dexter, Kanpur	1961-62
109†	B. L. D'Oliveira, Leeds	1967
100*	J. H. Edrich, Manchester	1974
104	T. G. Evans, Lord's	1952
113	K. W. R. Fletcher, Bombay	1972-73
123*	K. W. R. Fletcher, Manchester	1974
129	G. A. Gooch, Madras	1981-82
200*†	D. I. Gower, Birmingham	1979
175†	T. W. Graveney, Bombay	1951-52
151	T. W. Graveney, Lord's	1967
148	A. W. Greig, Bombay	1972-73
106	A. W. Greig, Lord's	1974
103	A. W. Greig, Calcutta	1976-77
167	W. R. Hammond, Manchester	1936
217	W. R. Hammond, The Oval	1936
205*	J. Hardstaff jun., Lord's	1946
150	L. Hutton, Lord's	1952
104	L. Hutton, Manchester	1952
107	R. Illingworth, Manchester	1971
127	B. R. Knight, Kanpur	1963-64
107	A. J. Lamb, The Oval	1982
125	A. R. Lewis, Kanpur	1972-73
214*	D. Lloyd, Birmingham	1974
101	B. W. Luckhurst, Manchester	1971
106	P. B. H. May, Nottingham	1959
121	P. H. Parfitt, Kanpur	1963-64
131	G. Pullar, Manchester	1959
119	G. Pullar, Kanpur	1961-62
126	D. W. Randall, Lord's	1982
119	D. S. Sheppard, The Oval	1952
100†	M. J. K. Smith, Manchester	1959
149	C. J. Tavaré, Delhi	1981-82
136†	B. H. Valentine, Bombay	1933-34
102	C. F. Walters, Madras	1933-34
137*†	A. J. Watkins, Delhi	1951-52
128	T. S. Worthington, The Oval	1936

For India (41)

118†	L. Amarnath, Bombay	1933-34
112†	A. A. Baig, Manchester	1959
121	F. M. Engineer, Bombay	1972-73
101	S. M. Gavaskar, Manchester	1974
108	S. M. Gavaskar, Bombay	1976-77
221	S. M. Gavaskar, The Oval	1979
172	S. M. Gavaskar, Bangalore	1981-82
105†	Hanumant Singh, Delhi	1963-64
164*	V. S. Hazare, Delhi	1951-52
155	V. S. Hazare, Bombay	1951-52
127	M. L. Jaisimha, Delhi	1961-62
129	M. L. Jaisimha, Calcutta	1963-64
116	Kapil Dev, Kanpur	1981-82
192	B. K. Kunderan, Madras	1963-64
100	B. K. Kunderan, Delhi	1963-64
133	V. L. Manjrekar, Leeds	1952
189*	V. L. Manjrekar, Delhi	1961-62
108	V. L. Manjrekar, Madras	1963-64
184	V. Mankad, Lord's	1952
114	V. M. Merchant, Manchester	1936
128	V. M. Merchant, The Oval	1946
154	V. M. Merchant, Delhi	1951-52
112	Mushtaq Ali, Manchester	1936
122*	R. G. Nadkarni, Kanpur	1963-64
103	Nawab of Pataudi jun., Madras	1961-62
203*	Nawab of Pataudi jun., Delhi	1963-64
148	Nawab of Pataudi jun., Leeds	1967
129*	S. M. Patil, Manchester	1982
115	D. G. Phadkar, Calcutta	1951-52
140	P. Roy, Bombay	1951-52
111	P. Roy, Madras	1951-52
130*	P. R. Umrigar, Madras	1951-52
118	P. R. Umrigar, Manchester	1959
147*	P. R. Umrigar, Kanpur	1961-62
103	D. B. Vengsarkar, Lord's	1979
157	D. B. Vengsarkar, Lord's	1982
113	G. R. Viswanath, Bombay	1972-73
113	G. R. Viswanath, Lord's	1979
107	G. R. Viswanath, Delhi	1981-82
222	G. R. Viswanath, Madras	1981-82
140	Yashpal Sharma, Madras	1981-82

† *Signifies hundred on first appearance in England–India Tests.*

RECORD PARTNERSHIPS FOR EACH WICKET

For England

159 for 1st	P. E. Richardson and G. Pullar at Bombay	1961-62
221 for 2nd	D. L. Amiss and J. H. Edrich at Lord's	1974
169 for 3rd	R. Subba Row and M. J. K. Smith at The Oval	1959
266 for 4th	W. R. Hammond and T. S. Worthington at The Oval	1936
254 for 5th†	K. W. R. Fletcher and A. W. Greig at Bombay	1972-73
171 for 6th	I. T. Botham and R. W. Taylor at Bombay	1979-80
125 for 7th	D. W. Randall and P. H. Edmonds at Lord's	1982
168 for 8th	R. Illingworth and P. Lever at Manchester	1971
83 for 9th	K. W. R. Fletcher and N. Gifford at Madras	1972-73
70 for 10th	P. J. W. Allott and R. G. D. Willis at Lord's	1982

For India

213 for 1st	S. M. Gavaskar and C. P. S. Chauhan at The Oval	1979
192 for 2nd	F. M. Engineer and A. L. Wadekar at Bombay	1972-73
316 for 3rd†‡	G. R. Viswanath and Yashpal Sharma at Madras	1981-82
222 for 4th†	V. S. Hazare and V. L. Manjrekar at Leeds	1952
190* for 5th	Nawab of Pataudi jun. and C. G. Borde at Delhi	1963-64
130 for 6th	S. M. H. Kirmani and Kapil Dev at The Oval	1982
169 for 7th	Kapil Dev and Yashpal Sharma at Kanpur	1981-82
128 for 8th	R. J. Shastri and S. M. H. Kirmani at Delhi	1981-82
104 for 9th	R. J. Shastri and Madan Lal at Delhi	1981-82
51 for 10th	R. G. Nadkarni and B. S. Chandrasekhar at Calcutta	1963-64

† *Denotes record partnership against all countries.*

‡ *415 runs were added between the fall of the 2nd and 3rd wickets: D. B. Vengsarkar retired hurt when he and Viswanath had added 99 runs.*

TEN WICKETS OR MORE IN A MATCH

For England (6)

10-78 (5-35, 5-43)†	G. O. Allen, Lord's	1936
11-145 (7-49, 4-96)†	A. V. Bedser, Lord's	1946
11-93 (4-41, 7-52)	A. V. Bedser, Manchester	1946
13-106 (6-58, 7-48)	I. T. Botham, Bombay	1979-80
10-70 (7-46, 3-24)†	J. K. Lever, Delhi	1976-77
11-153 (7-49, 4-104)	H. Verity, Madras	1933-34

For India (2)

10-177 (6-105, 4-72)	S. A. Durani, Madras	1961-62
12-108 (8-55, 4-53)	V. Mankad, Madras	1951-52

† *Signifies ten wickets or more on first appearance in England–India Tests.*

Note: A. V. Bedser took eleven wickets in a match in the first two Tests of his career.

ENGLAND v PAKISTAN

Season	Captains: England	Captains: Pakistan	T	E	P	D
1954	L. Hutton[1]	A. H. Kardar	4	1	1	2
1961-62	E. R. Dexter	Imtiaz Ahmed	3	1	0	2
1962	E. R Dexter[2]	Javed Burki	5	4	0	1
1967	D. B. Close	Hanif Mohammad	3	2	0	1
1968-69	M. C. Cowdrey	Saeed Ahmed	3	0	0	3
1971	R. Illingworth	Intikhab Alam	3	1	0	2
1972-73	A. R. Lewis	Majid J. Khan	3	0	0	3
1974	M. H. Denness	Intikhab Alam	3	0	0	3
1977-78	J. M. Brearley[3]	Wasim Bari	3	0	0	3
1978	J. M. Brearley	Wasim Bari	3	2	0	1
1982	R. G. D. Willis[4]	Imran Khan	3	2	1	0
	In England		24	12	2	10
	In Pakistan		12	1	0	11
	Totals		36	13	2	21

Notes: [1]D. S. Sheppard captained in Second and Third Tests. [2]M. C. Cowdrey captained in Third Test. [3]G. Boycott captained in Third Test. [4]D. I. Gower captained in Second Test.

HIGHEST INNINGS TOTALS

By England

558-6 dec.	Nottingham	1954
545 ..	The Oval	1974
544-5 dec.	Birmingham	1962
507 ..	Karachi	1961-62
502-7	Karachi	1968-69

By Pakistan

608-7 dec.	Birmingham	1971
600-7 dec.	The Oval	1974
569-9 dec.	Hyderabad	1972-73

LOWEST INNINGS TOTALS

By England

130 ..	The Oval (1st Inns)	1954
143 ..	The Oval (2nd Inns)	1954

By Pakistan

87 ..	Lord's	1954
90 ..	Manchester	1954

Note: The lowest totals made in Pakistan are: England 191 at Hyderabad, 1977-78; Pakistan 199 at Karachi, 1972-73.

INDIVIDUAL HUNDREDS IN THE MATCHES 1954–1982

For England (34)

112	D. L. Amiss, Lahore	1972-73
158	D. L. Amiss, Hyderabad	1972-73
183	D. L. Amiss, The Oval	1974
139†	K. F. Barrington, Lahore	1961-62
148	K. F. Barrington, Lord's	1967
109*	K. F. Barrington, Nottingham	1967
142	K. F. Barrington, The Oval	1967
100†	I. T. Botham, Birmingham	1978
108	I. T. Botham, Lord's	1978
121*	G. Boycott, Lord's	1971
112	G. Boycott, Leeds	1971
100*	G. Boycott, Hyderabad	1977-78
278	D. C. S. Compton, Nottingham	1954
159†	M. C. Cowdrey, Birmingham	1962
182	M. C. Cowdrey, The Oval	1962

100	M. C. Cowdrey, Lahore	1968-69
205	E. R. Dexter, Karachi	1961-62
172	E. R. Dexter, The Oval	1962
114*	B. L. D'Oliveira, Dacca	1968-69
122	K. W. R. Fletcher, The Oval	1974
153	T. W. Graveney, Lord's	1962
114	T. W. Graveney, Nottingham	1962
105	T. W. Graveney, Karachi	1968-69
116	A. P. E. Knott, Birmingham	1971
108*†	B. W. Luckhurst, Birmingham	1971
139	C. Milburn, Karachi	1968-69
111	P. H. Parfitt, Karachi	1961-62
101*	P. H. Parfitt, Birmingham	1962
119	P. H. Parfitt, Leeds	1962
101*	P. H. Parfitt, Nottingham	1962
165	G. Pullar, Dacca	1961-62
106†	C. T. Radley, Birmingham	1978
105	D. W. Randall, Birmingham	1982
101	R. T. Simpson, Nottingham	1954

For Pakistan (22)

109	Alim-ud-Din, Karachi	1961-62
146	Asif Iqbal, The Oval	1967
104*	Asif Iqbal, Birmingham	1971
102	Asif Iqbal, Lahore	1972-73
138†	Javed Burki, Lahore	1961-62
140	Javed Burki, Dacca	1961-62
101	Javed Burki, Lord's	1962
111 } 104 }	Hanif Mohammad, Dacca	1961-62
187*	Hanif Mohammad, Lord's	1967
122†	Haroon Rashid, Lahore	1977-78
108	Haroon Rashid, Hyderabad	1977-78
138	Intikhab Alam, Hyderabad	1972-73
200	Mohsin Khan, Lord's	1982
114†	Mudassar Nazar, Lahore	1977-78
100*	Mushtaq Mohammad, Nottingham	1962
100	Mushtaq Mohammad, Birmingham	1971
157	Mushtaq Mohammad, Hyderabad	1972-73
101	Nasim-ul-Ghani, Lord's	1962
119	Sadiq Mohammad, Lahore	1972-73
274†	Zaheer Abbas, Birmingham	1971
240	Zaheer Abbas, The Oval	1974

† *Signifies hundred on first appearance in England–Pakistan Tests.*

Note: Three batsmen – Majid J. Khan, Mushtaq Mohammad and D. L. Amiss – were dismissed for 99 at Karachi, 1972-73: the only instance in Test matches.

RECORD PARTNERSHIPS FOR EACH WICKET

For England

198 for 1st	G. Pullar and R. W. Barber at Dacca	1961-62
248 for 2nd	M. C. Cowdrey and E. R. Dexter at The Oval	1962
201 for 3rd	K. F. Barrington and T. W. Graveney at Lord's	1967
188 for 4th	E. R. Dexter and P. H. Parfitt at Karachi	1961-62
192 for 5th	D. C. S. Compton and T. E. Bailey at Nottingham	1954
153* for 6th	P. H. Parfitt and D. A. Allen at Birmingham	1962
159 for 7th	A. P. E. Knott and P. Lever at Birmingham	1971
99 for 8th	P. H. Parfitt and D. A. Allen at Leeds	1962
76 for 9th	T. W. Graveney and F. S. Trueman at Lord's	1962
79 for 10th	R. W. Taylor and R. G. D. Willis at Birmingham	1982

For Pakistan

122 for 1st	Hanif Mohammad and Alim-ud-Din at Dacca	1961-62
291 for 2nd†	Zaheer Abbas and Mushtaq Mohammad at Birmingham	1971
180 for 3rd	Mudassar Nazar and Haroon Rashid at Lahore	1977-78
153 for 4th	Javed Burki and Mushtaq Mohammad at Lahore	1961-62
	Mohsin Khan and Zaheer Abbas at Lord's	1982
197 for 5th	Javed Burki and Nasim-ul-Ghani at Lord's	1962
145 for 6th	Mushtaq Mohammad and Intikhab Alam at Hyderabad	1972-73
51 for 7th	Saeed Ahmed and Nasim-ul-Ghani at Nottingham	1962
130 for 8th†	Hanif Mohammad and Asif Iqbal at Lord's	1967
190 for 9th†	Asif Iqbal and Intikhab Alam at The Oval	1967
62 for 10th	Sarfraz Nawaz and Asif Masood at Leeds	1974

† *Denotes record partnership against all countries.*

TEN WICKETS OR MORE IN A MATCH

For England (1)

13-71 (5-20, 8-51) D. L. Underwood, Lord's.. 1974

For Pakistan (1)

12-99 (6-53, 6-46) Fazal Mahmood, The Oval.. 1954

FOUR WICKETS IN FIVE BALLS

C. M. Old, v Pakistan at Birmingham in 1978, dismissed Wasim Raja, Wasim Bari, Iqbal Qasim and Sikander Bakht to take four wickets in five balls (ww-ww).

ENGLAND v SRI LANKA

	Captains					
Season	*England*	*Sri Lanka*	*T*	*E*	*SL*	*D*
1981-82	K. W. R. Fletcher	B. Warnapura	1	1	0	0

The only match played, at Colombo, produced no individual centuries or century partnerships. The best performances were as follows:

Highest score for England: 89 by D. I. Gower.
Sri Lanka: 77 by R. L. Dias.

Best bowling in an innings for England: 6-33 by J. E. Emburey.
Sri Lanka: 4-70 by A. L. F. de Mel.

Best match bowling for England: 8-95 by D. L. Underwood.
Sri Lanka: 5-103 by A. L. F. de Mel.

Best wicket partnership for England: 83 for the 3rd by C. J. Tavaré and D. I. Gower.
Sri Lanka: 99 for the 5th by R. S. Madugalle and A. Ranatunga.

AUSTRALIA v SOUTH AFRICA

	Captains					
Season	*Australia*	*South Africa*	*T*	*A*	*SA*	*D*
1902-03*S*	J. Darling	H. M. Taberer[1]	3	2	0	1
1910-11*A*	C. Hill	P. W. Sherwell	5	4	1	0
1912*E*	S. E. Gregory	F. Mitchell[2]	3	2	0	1
1921-22*S*	H. L. Collins	H. W. Taylor	3	1	0	2
1931-32*A*	W. M. Woodfull	H. B. Cameron	5	5	0	0
1935-36*S*	V. Y. Richardson	H. F. Wade	5	4	0	1
1949-50*S*	A. L. Hassett	A. D. Nourse	5	4	0	1
1952-53*A*	A. L. Hassett	J. E. Cheetham	5	2	2	1
1957-58*S*	I. D. Craig	C. B. van Ryneveld[3]	5	3	0	2
1963-64*A*	R. B. Simpson[4]	T. L. Goddard	5	1	1	3
1966-67*S*	R. B. Simpson	P. L. van der Merwe	5	1	3	1
1969-70*S*	W. M. Lawry	A. Bacher	4	0	4	0
	In South Africa......................		30	15	7	8
	In Australia..........................		20	12	4	4
	In England...........................		3	2	0	1
	Totals..................................		53	29	11	13

S Played in South Africa. A Played in Australia. E Played in England.

Notes: The following deputised for the official touring captain or were appointed by the home authority for only a minor proportion of the series:
[1]J. H. Anderson (Second), E. A. Halliwell (Third). [2]L. J. Tancred (Third). [3]D. J. McGlew (First). [4]R. Benaud (First).

HIGHEST INNINGS TOTALS

By Australia

578 ..	Melbourne	1910-11
554 ..	Melbourne	1931-32
549-7 dec.	Port Elizabeth	1949-50

By South Africa

622-9 dec.	Durban	1969-70
620 ..	Johannesburg	1966-67
595 ..	Adelaide	1963-64

LOWEST INNINGS TOTALS

By Australia

75 ..	Durban	1949-50
143 ..	Johannesburg	1966-67
147 ..	Durban	1966-67
153 ..	Melbourne	1931-32

By South Africa

36 } 45 } ..	†Melbourne	1931-32
80 ..	Melbourne	1910-11
85 ..	Johannesburg	1902-03
85 ..	Cape Town	1902-03

† *The aggregate of 81 (12 extras) for two innings is the smallest in Test cricket.*

INDIVIDUAL HUNDREDS IN THE MATCHES 1902-03–1969-70

For Australia (55)

159*	W. W. Armstrong, Johannesburg	1902-03
132	W. W. Armstrong, Melbourne	1910-11
132†	W. Bardsley, Sydney	1910-11
121	W. Bardsley, Manchester	1912
164	W. Bardsley, Lord's	1912
122	R. Benaud, Johannesburg	1957-58
100	R. Benaud, Johannesburg	1957-58
169†	B. C. Booth, Brisbane	1963-64
102*	B. C. Booth, Sydney	1963-64
226†	D. G. Bradman, Brisbane	1931-32
112	D. G. Bradman, Sydney	1931-32
167	D. G. Bradman, Melbourne	1931-32
299*	D. G. Bradman, Adelaide	1931-32
121	W. A. Brown, Cape Town	1935-36
189	J. W. Burke, Cape Town	1957-58
109†	A. G. Chipperfield, Durban	1935-36
203	H. L. Collins, Johannesburg	1921-22
112	J. H. Fingleton, Cape Town	1935-36
108	J. H. Fingleton, Johannesburg	1935-36
118	J. H. Fingleton, Durban	1935-36
119	J. M. Gregory, Johannesburg	1921-22
178	R. N. Harvey, Cape Town	1949-50
151*	R. N. Harvey, Durban	1949-50
116	R. N. Harvey, Port Elizabeth	1949-50
100	R. N. Harvey, Johannesburg	1949-50
109	R. N. Harvey, Brisbane	1952-53
190	R. N. Harvey, Sydney	1952-53
116	R. N. Harvey, Adelaide	1952-53
205	R. N. Harvey, Melbourne	1952-53
112†	A. L. Hassett, Johannesburg	1949-50
167	A. L. Hassett, Port Elizabeth	1949-50
163	A. L. Hassett, Adelaide	1952-53
142†	C. Hill, Johannesburg	1902-03
191	C. Hill, Sydney	1910-11
100	C. Hill, Melbourne	1910-11
114	C. Kelleway, Manchester	1912
102	C. Kelleway, Lord's	1912
157	W. M. Lawry, Melbourne	1963-64
101†	S. J. E. Loxton, Johannesburg	1949-50
137	C. G. Macartney, Sydney	1910-11
116	C. G. Macartney, Durban	1921-22
149	S. J. McCabe, Durban	1935-36
189*	S. J. McCabe, Johannesburg	1935-36

154	C. C. McDonald, Adelaide	1952-53
118 } 101* }	J. Moroney, Johannesburg	1949-50
111	A. R. Morris, Johannesburg	1949-50
157	A. R. Morris, Port Elizabeth	1949-50
127†	K. E. Rigg, Sydney	1931-32
142	J. Ryder, Cape Town	1921-22
153	R. B. Simpson, Cape Town	1966-67
134	K. R. Stackpole, Cape Town	1966-67
159	V. T. Trumper, Melbourne	1910-11
214*	V. T. Trumper, Adelaide	1910-11
161	W. M. Woodfull, Melbourne	1931-32

For South Africa (36)

114†	E. J. Barlow, Brisbane	1963-64
109	E. J. Barlow, Melbourne	1963-64
201	E. J. Barlow, Adelaide	1963-64
127	E. J. Barlow, Cape Town	1969-70
110	E. J. Barlow, Johannesburg	1969-70
126	K. C. Bland, Sydney	1963-64
162*	W. R. Endean, Melbourne	1952-53
204	G. A. Faulkner, Melbourne	1910-11
115	G. A. Faulkner, Adelaide	1910-11
122*	G. A. Faulkner, Manchester	1912
152	C. N. Frank, Johannesburg	1921-22
102	B. L. Irvine, Port Elizabeth	1969-70
182	D. T. Lindsay, Johannesburg	1966-67
137	D. T. Lindsay, Durban	1966-67
131	D. T. Lindsay, Johannesburg	1966-67
108	D. J. McGlew, Johannesburg	1957-58
105	D. J. McGlew, Durban	1957-58
231	A. D. Nourse, Johannesburg	1935-36
114	A. D. Nourse, Cape Town	1949-50
111	A. W. Nourse, Johannesburg	1921-22
122	R. G. Pollock, Sydney	1963-64
175	R. G. Pollock, Adelaide	1963-64
209	R. G. Pollock, Cape Town	1966-67
105	R. G. Pollock, Port Elizabeth	1966-67
274	R. G. Pollock, Durban	1969-70
140	B. A. Richards, Durban	1969-70
126	B. A. Richards, Port Elizabeth	1969-70
143	E. A. B. Rowan, Durban	1949-50
101	J. H. Sinclair, Johannesburg	1902-03
104	J. H. Sinclair, Cape Town	1902-03
103	S. J. Snooke, Adelaide	1910-11
111	K. G. Viljoen, Melbourne	1931-32
115	J. H. B. Waite, Johannesburg	1957-58
134	J. H. B. Waite, Durban	1957-58
105	J. W. Zulch, Adelaide	1910-11
150	J. W. Zulch, Sydney	1910-11

† *Signifies hundred on first appearance in Australia–South Africa Tests.*

RECORD PARTNERSHIPS FOR EACH WICKET

For Australia

233 for 1st	J. H. Fingleton and W. A. Brown at Cape Town	1935-36
275 for 2nd	C. C. McDonald and A. L. Hassett at Adelaide	1952-53
242 for 3rd	C. Kelleway and W. Bardsley at Lord's	1912
168 for 4th	R. N. Harvey and K. R. Miller at Sydney	1952-53
143 for 5th	W. W. Armstrong and V. T. Trumper at Melbourne	1910-11
107 for 6th	C. Kelleway and V. S. Ransford at Melbourne	1910-11
160 for 7th	R. Benaud and G. D. McKenzie at Sydney	1963-64
83 for 8th	A. G. Chipperfield and C. V. Grimmett at Durban	1935-36
78 for 9th	D. G. Bradman and W. J. O'Reilly at Adelaide	1931-32
	K. D. Mackay and I. Meckiff at Johannesburg	1957-58
82 for 10th	V. S. Ransford and W. J. Whitty at Melbourne	1910-11

For South Africa

176 for 1st	D. J. McGlew and T. L. Goddard at Johannesburg	1957-58
173 for 2nd	L. J. Tancred and C. B. Llewellyn at Johannesburg	1902-03
341 for 3rd†	E. J. Barlow and R. G. Pollock at Adelaide	1963-64

206 for 4th	C. N. Frank and A. W. Nourse at Johannesburg	1921-22
129 for 5th	J. H. B. Waite and W. R. Endean at Johannesburg	1957-58
200 for 6th†	R. G. Pollock and H. R. Lance at Durban	1969-70
221 for 7th	D. T. Lindsay and P. L. van der Merwe at Johannesburg	1966-67
124 for 8th†	A. W. Nourse and E. A. Halliwell at Johannesburg	1902-03
85 for 9th	R. G. Pollock and P. M. Pollock at Cape Town	1966-67
53 for 10th	L. A. Stricker and S. J. Pegler at Adelaide	1910-11

† *Denotes record partnership against all countries.*

TEN WICKETS OR MORE IN A MATCH

For Australia (5)

14-199 (7-116, 7-83)	C. V. Grimmett, Adelaide	1931-32
10-88 (5-32, 5-56)	C. V. Grimmett, Cape Town	1935-36
10-110 (3-70, 7-40)	C. V. Grimmett, Johannesburg	1935-36
13-173 (7-100, 6-73)	C. V. Grimmett, Durban	1935-36
11-24 (5-6, 6-18)	H. Ironmonger, Melbourne	1931-32

For South Africa (2)

10-116 (5-43, 5-73)	C. B. Llewellyn, Johannesburg	1902-03
13-165 (6-84, 7-81)	H. J. Tayfield, Melbourne	1952-53

Note: C. V. Grimmett took ten wickets or more in three consecutive matches in 1935-36.

AUSTRALIA v WEST INDIES

	Captains						
Season	*Australia*	*West Indies*	*T*	*A*	*WI*	*T*	*D*
1930-31*A*	W. M. Woodfull	G. C. Grant	5	4	1	0	0
1951-52*A*	A. L. Hassett[1]	J. D. C. Goddard[2]	5	4	1	0	0
1954-55*W*	I. W. Johnson	D. S. Atkinson[3]	5	3	0	0	2
1960-61*A*	R. Benaud	F. M. M. Worrell	5†	2	1	1	1

THE FRANK WORRELL TROPHY

	Captains							
Season	*Australia*	*West Indies*	*T*	*A*	*WI*	*T*	*D*	*Held by*
1964-65*W*	R. B. Simpson	G. S. Sobers	5	1	2	0	2	WI
1968-69*A*	W. M. Lawry	G. S. Sobers	5	3	1	0	1	A
1972-73*W*	I. M. Chappell	R. B. Kanhai	5	2	0	0	3	A
1975-76*A*	G. S. Chappell	C. H. Lloyd	6	5	1	0	0	A
1977-78*W*	R. B. Simpson	A. I. Kallicharran[4]	5	1	3	0	1	WI
1979-80*A*	G. S. Chappell	C. H. Lloyd[5]	3	0	2	0	1	WI
1981-82*A*	G. S. Chappell	C. H. Lloyd	3	1	1	0	1	WI
	In Australia		32	19	8	1	4	
	In West Indies		20	7	5	0	8	
	Totals		52	26	13	1	12	

† *The First Test at Brisbane resulted in a tie. This is the only instance of a Test match resulting in a tie.*

A Played in Australia. W Played in West Indies.

Notes: The following deputised for the official touring captain or were appointed by the home authority for only a minor proportion of the series:

[1] A. R. Morris (Third). [2] J. B. Stollmeyer (Fifth). [3] J. B. Stollmeyer (Second and Third). [4] C. H. Lloyd (First and Second). [5] D. L. Murray (First).

HIGHEST INNINGS TOTALS

By Australia			By West Indies		
758-8 dec.	Kingston	1954-55	616 ..	Adelaide	1968-69
668 ..	Bridgetown	1954-55	585 ..	Perth	1975-76
650-6 dec.	Bridgetown	1964-65	573 ..	Bridgetown	1964-65
619 ..	Sydney	1968-69	510	Bridgetown	1954-55
600-9 dec.	Port-of-Spain	1954-55			

LOWEST INNINGS TOTALS

By Australia			By West Indies		
82 ..	Adelaide	1951-52	78 ..	Sydney	1951-52
90 ..	Port-of-Spain	1977-78	90 ..	Sydney	1930-31
94 ..	Port-of-Spain	1977-78	99 ..	Melbourne	1930-31

Note: West Indies' lowest total in West Indies is 109 at Georgetown, 1972-73.

INDIVIDUAL HUNDREDS IN THE MATCHES 1930-31–1981-82

For Australia (60)

128	R. G. Archer, Kingston	1954-55
121	R. Benaud, Kingston	1954-55
117	B. C. Booth, Port-of-Spain	1964-65
126	A. R. Border, Adelaide	1981-82
223	D. G. Bradman, Brisbane	1930-31
152	D. G. Bradman, Melbourne	1930-31
106	G. S. Chappell, Bridgetown	1972-73
123 / 109*	‡G. S. Chappell, Brisbane	1975-76
182*	G. S. Chappell, Sydney	1975-76
124	G. S. Chappell, Brisbane	1979-80
117†	I. M. Chappell, Brisbane	1968-69
165	I. M. Chappell, Melbourne	1968-69
106*	I. M. Chappell, Bridgetown	1972-73
109	I. M. Chappell, Georgetown	1972-73
156	I. M. Chappell, Perth	1975-76
109†	G. J. Cosier, Melbourne	1975-76
143	R. M. Cowper, Port-of-Spain	1964-65
102	R. M. Cowper, Bridgetown	1964-65
127*†	J. Dyson, Sydney	1981-82
133	R. N. Harvey, Kingston	1954-55
133	R. N. Harvey, Port-of-Spain	1954-55
204	R. N. Harvey, Kingston	1954-55
132	A. L. Hassett, Sydney	1951-52
102	A. L. Hassett, Melbourne	1951-52
130*†	K. J. Hughes, Brisbane	1979-80
100*	K. J. Hughes, Melbourne	1981-82
146†	A. F. Kippax, Adelaide	1930-31
210	W. M. Lawry, Bridgetown	1964-65
105	W. M. Lawry, Brisbane	1968-69
205	W. M. Lawry, Melbourne	1968-69
151	W. M. Lawry, Sydney	1968-69
118	R. R. Lindwall, Bridgetown	1954-55
109*	R. B. McCosker, Melbourne	1975-76
110	C. C. McDonald, Port-of-Spain	1954-55
127	C. C. McDonald, Kingston	1954-55
129	K. R. Miller, Sydney	1951-52
147	K. R. Miller, Kingston	1954-55
137	K. R. Miller, Bridgetown	1954-55
109	K. R. Miller, Kingston	1954-55
111	A. R. Morris, Port-of-Spain	1954-55
181†	N. C. O'Neill, Brisbane	1960-61
183	W. H. Ponsford, Sydney	1930-31
109	W. H. Ponsford, Brisbane	1930-31
132	I. R. Redpath, Sydney	1968-69
102	I. R. Redpath, Melbourne	1975-76
103	I. R. Redpath, Adelaide	1975-76
101	I. R. Redpath, Melbourne	1975-76
124	C. S. Serjeant, Georgetown	1977-78
201	R. B. Simpson, Bridgetown	1964-65
142	K. R. Stackpole, Kingston	1972-73
122	P. M. Toohey, Kingston	1977-78
136	A. Turner, Adelaide	1975-76
118	K. D. Walters, Sydney	1968-69
110	K. D. Walters, Adelaide	1968-69
242 / 103	K. D. Walters, Sydney	1968-69
102*	K. D. Walters, Bridgetown	1972-73
112	K. D. Walters, Port-of-Spain	1972-73
126	G. M. Wood, Georgetown	1977-78

‡ *G. S. Chappell is the only player to score hundreds in both innings of his first Test as captain.*

For West Indies (49)

108	F. C. M. Alexander, Sydney	1960-61
219	D. S. Atkinson, Bridgetown	1954-55
117	B. F. Butcher, Port-of-Spain	1964-65
101	B. F. Butcher, Sydney	1968-69
118	B. F. Butcher, Adelaide	1968-69
122	C. C. Depeiza, Bridgetown	1954-55
125†	M. L. C. Foster, Kingston	1972-73
169	R. C. Fredericks, Perth	1975-76
101†	H. A. Gomes, Georgetown	1977-78
115	H. A. Gomes, Kingston	1977-78
126	H. A. Gomes, Sydney	1981-82
124*	H. A. Gomes, Adelaide	1981-82
102*	G. A. Headley, Brisbane	1930-31
105	G. A. Headley, Sydney	1930-31
110	C. C. Hunte, Melbourne	1960-61
101	A. I. Kallicharran, Brisbane	1975-76
127	A. I. Kallicharran, Port-of-Spain	1977-78
126	A. I. Kallicharran, Kingston	1977-78
106	A. I. Kallicharran, Adelaide	1979-80
117, 115	R. B. Kanhai, Adelaide	1960-61
129	R. B. Kanhai, Bridgetown	1964-65
121	R. B. Kanhai, Port-of-Spain	1964-65
105	R. B. Kanhai, Bridgetown	1972-73
129†	C. H. Lloyd, Brisbane	1968-69
178	C. H. Lloyd, Georgetown	1972-73
149	C. H. Lloyd, Perth	1975-76
102	C. H. Lloyd, Melbourne	1975-76
121	C. H. Lloyd, Adelaide	1979-80
123*	F. R. Martin, Sydney	1930-31
201	S. M. Nurse, Bridgetown	1964-65
137	S. M. Nurse, Sydney	1968-69
101	I. V. A. Richards, Adelaide	1975-76
140	I. V. A. Richards, Brisbane	1979-80
107	L. G. Rowe, Brisbane	1975-76
104†	O. G. Smith, Kingston	1954-55
132	G. S. Sobers, Brisbane	1960-61
168	G. S. Sobers, Sydney	1960-61
110	G. S. Sobers, Adelaide	1968-69
113	G. S. Sobers, Sydney	1968-69
104	J. B. Stollmeyer, Sydney	1951-52
108	C. L. Walcott, Kingston	1954-55
126, 110	C. L. Walcott, Port-of-Spain	1954-55
155, 110	C. L. Walcott, Kingston	1954-55
139	E. D. Weekes, Port-of-Spain	1954-55
100†	A. B. Williams, Georgetown	1977-78
108	F. M. M. Worrell, Melbourne	1951-52

† *Signifies hundred on first appearance in Australia–West Indies Tests.*

Note: F. C. M. Alexander hit the only hundred of his career in a Test match.

RECORD PARTNERSHIPS FOR EACH WICKET

For Australia

382 for 1st†	W. M. Lawry and R. B. Simpson at Bridgetown	1964-54
298 for 2nd	W. M. Lawry and I. M. Chappell at Melbourne	1968-69
295 for 3rd†	C. C. McDonald and R. N. Harvey at Kingston	1954-55
336 for 4th	W. M. Lawry and K. D. Walters at Sydney	1968-69
220 for 5th	K. R. Miller and R. G. Archer at Kingston	1954-55
206 for 6th	K. R. Miller and R. G. Archer at Bridgetown	1954-55
134 for 7th	A. K. Davidson and R. Benaud at Brisbane	1960-61
137 for 8th	R. Benaud and I. W. Johnson at Kingston	1954-55
97 for 9th	K. D. Mackay and J. W. Martin at Melbourne	1960-61
73 for 10th	J. W. Gleeson and A. N. Connolly at Sydney	1968-69

For West Indies

145 for 1st	C. C. Hunte and B. A. Davis at Bridgetown	1964-65
165 for 2nd	M. C. Carew and R. B. Kanhai at Brisbane	1968-69
242 for 3rd	C. L. Walcott and E. D. Weekes at Port-of-Spain	1954-55
198 for 4th	L. G. Rowe and A. I. Kallicharran at Brisbane	1975-76
210 for 5th	R. B. Kanhai and M. L. C. Foster at Kingston	1972-73
165 for 6th	R. B. Kanhai and D. L. Murray at Bridgetown	1972-73
347 for 7th†‡	D. St E. Atkinson and C. C. Depeiza at Bridgetown	1954-55
82 for 8th	H. A. Gomes and A. M. E. Roberts at Adelaide	1981-82
122 for 9th†	D. A. J. Holford and J. L. Hendriks at Adelaide	1968-69
56 for 10th	J. Garner and C. E. H. Croft at Brisbane	1979-80

† *Denotes record partnership against all countries.*

‡ *The 347 partnership for the 7th wicket is the highest for this wicket in first-class cricket.*

TEN WICKETS OR MORE IN A MATCH

For Australia (7)

11-222 (5-135, 6-87)†	A. K. Davidson, Brisbane	1960-61
11-183 (7-87, 4-96)†	C. V. Grimmett, Adelaide	1930-31
10-115 (6-72, 4-43)	N. J. N. Hawke, Georgetown	1964-65
11-79 (7-23, 4-56)	H. Ironmonger, Melbourne	1930-31
10-127 (7-83, 3-44)	D. K. Lillee, Melbourne	1981-82
10-159 (8-71, 2-88)	G. D. McKenzie, Melbourne	1968-69
10-185 (3-87, 7-98)	B. Yardley, Sydney	1981-82

For West Indies (2)

10-113 (7-55, 3-58)	G. E. Gomez, Sydney	1951-52
11-107 (5-45, 6-62)	M. A. Holding, Melbourne	1981-82

† *Signifies ten wickets or more on first appearance in Australia–West Indies Tests.*

AUSTRALIA v NEW ZEALAND

	Captains					
Season	*Australia*	*New Zealand*	*T*	*A*	*NZ*	*D*
1945-46*N*	W. A. Brown	W. A. Hadlee	1	1	0	0
1973-74*A*	I. M. Chappell	B. E. Congdon	3	2	0	1
1973-74*N*	I. M. Chappell	B. E. Congdon	3	1	1	1
1976-77*N*	G. S. Chappell	G. M. Turner	2	1	0	1
1980-81*A*	G. S. Chappell	G. P. Howarth[1]	3	2	0	1
1981-82*N*	G. S. Chappell	G. P. Howarth	3	1	1	1
	In Australia		6	4	0	2
	In New Zealand		9	4	2	3
	Totals		15	8	2	5

A Played in Australia. N Played in New Zealand.

Note: The following deputised for the official touring captain: [1]M. G. Burgess (Second).

HIGHEST INNINGS TOTALS

By Australia			**By New Zealand**		
552 ..	Christchurch	1976-77	484 ..	Wellington	1973-74
511-6 dec.	Wellington	1973-74	387 ..	Auckland	1981-82

Note: The highest totals made in Australia are: Australia 477 at Adelaide, 1973-74; New Zealand 312 at Sydney, 1973-74.

LOWEST INNINGS TOTALS

By Australia			**By New Zealand**		
162 ..	Sydney	1973-74	42 } ..	Wellington	1945-46
188 ..	Melbourne	1980-81	54 }		

Note: Australia's lowest total in New Zealand is 210 at Auckland, 1981-82. New Zealand's lowest total in Australia is 200 at Melbourne, 1973-74.

INDIVIDUAL HUNDREDS IN THE MATCHES 1945-46–1981-82

For Australia (14)

247* / 133	G. S. Chappell, Wellington	1973-74
176	G. S. Chappell, Christchurch	1981-82
145 / 121	I. M. Chappell, Wellington	1973-74
101	G. J. Gilmour, Christchurch	1976-77
132	R. W. Marsh, Adelaide	1973-74
159*	I. R. Redpath, Auckland	1973-74
122†	K. R. Stackpole, Melbourne	1973-74
104*	K. D. Walters, Auckland	1973-74
250	K. D. Walters, Christchurch	1976-77
107	K. D. Walters, Melbourne	1980-81
111†	G. M. Wood, Brisbane	1980-81
100	G. M. Wood, Auckland	1981-82

For New Zealand (9)

132	B. E. Congdon, Wellington	1973-74
107*	B. E. Congdon, Christchurch	1976-77
161	B. A. Edgar, Auckland	1981-82
101	B. F. Hastings, Wellington	1973-74
117	J. F. M. Morrison, Sydney	1973-74
108	J. M. Parker, Sydney	1973-74
101 / 110*	G. M. Turner, Christchurch	1973-74
141	J. G. Wright, Christchurch	1981-82

† *Signifies hundred on first appearance in Australia–New Zealand Tests.*

Notes: G. S. and I. M. Chappell at Wellington in 1973-74 provide the only instance in Test matches of brothers both scoring a hundred in each innings and in the same Test.

G. S. Chappell's match aggregate of 380 (247* and 133) for Australia at Wellington in 1973-74 is the record in Test matches.

RECORD PARTNERSHIPS FOR EACH WICKET

For Australia

106 for 1st	G. M. Wood and B. M. Laird at Auckland	1981-82
141 for 2nd	I. R. Redpath and I. M. Chappell at Wellington	1973-74
264 for 3rd	I. M. Chappell and G. S. Chappell at Wellington	1973-74
106 for 4th	I. R. Redpath and I. C. Davis at Christchurch	1973-74
93 for 5th	G. S. Chappell and K. D. Walters at Christchurch	1976-77
92 for 6th	G. S Chappell and R. W Marsh at Christchurch	1981-82
217 for 7th†	K. D. Walters and G. J. Gilmour at Christchurch	1976-77
93 for 8th	G. J. Gilmour and K. J. O'Keeffe at Auckland	1976-77
57 for 9th	R. W. Marsh and L. S. Pascoe at Perth	1980-81
60 for 10th	K. D. Walters and J. D. Higgs at Melbourne	1980-81

For New Zealand

107 for 1st	G. M. Turner and J. M. Parker at Auckland	1973-74
108 for 2nd	G. M. Turner and J. F. M. Morrison at Wellington	1973-74
125 for 3rd	G. P. Howarth and J. M. Parker at Melbourne	1980-81
229 for 4th†	B. E. Congdon and B. F. Hastings at Wellington	1973-74
88 for 5th	J. V. Coney and M. G. Burgess at Perth	1980-81
105 for 6th	M. G. Burgess and R. J. Hadlee at Auckland	1976-77
66 for 7th	K. J. Wadsworth and D. R. Hadlee at Adelaide	1973-74
53 for 8th	B. A. Edgar and R. J. Hadlee at Brisbane	1980-81
73 for 9th	H. J. Howarth and D. R. Hadlee at Christchurch	1976-77
47 for 10th	H. J. Howarth and M. G. Webb at Wellington	1973-74

† *Denotes record partnership against all countries.*

TEN WICKETS OR MORE IN A MATCH

For Australia (1)

11-123 (5-51, 6-72) D. K. Lillee, Auckland.. 1976-77

Note: The best match figures by a New Zealand bowler are 9-166 (5-82, 4-84), R. O. Collinge at Auckland, 1973-74, and 9-146 (3-89, 6-57), R. J. Hadlee at Melbourne, 1980-81.

AUSTRALIA v INDIA

Season	*Captains* *Australia*	*India*	*T*	*A*	*I*	*D*
1947-48*A*	D. G. Bradman	L. Amarnath	5	4	0	1
1956-57*I*	I. W. Johnson[1]	P. R. Umrigar	3	2	0	1
1959-60*I*	R. Benaud	G. S. Ramchand	5	2	1	2
1964-65*I*	R. B. Simpson	Nawab of Pataudi jun.	3	1	1	1
1967-68*A*	R. B. Simpson[2]	Nawab of Pataudi jun.[3]	4	4	0	0
1969-70*I*	W. M. Lawry	Nawab of Pataudi jun.	5	3	1	1
1977-78*A*	R. B. Simpson	B. S. Bedi	5	3	2	0
1979-80*I*	K. J. Hughes	S. M. Gavaskar	6	0	2	4
1980-81*A*	G. S. Chappell	S. M. Gavaskar	3	1	1	1
	In Australia.......................		17	12	3	2
	In India............................		22	8	5	9
	Totals..............................		39	20	8	11

A Played in Australia. I Played in India.

Notes: The following deputised for the official touring captain or were appointed by the home authority for only a minor proportion of the series:
[1]R. R. Lindwall (Second). [2]W. M. Lawry (Third and Fourth). [3]C. G. Borde (First).

HIGHEST INNINGS TOTALS

By Australia			**By India**		
674 ..	Adelaide...............	1947-48	510-7 dec.	Delhi....................	1979-80
575-8 dec.	Melbourne.............	1947-48	458-8 dec.	Bombay................	1979-80
529 ..	Melbourne.............	1967-68	457-5 dec.	Bangalore..............	1979-80
528 ..	Adelaide...............	1980-81	445 ..	Adelaide...............	1977-78
523-7 dec.	Bombay.................	1956-57	419 ..	Adelaide...............	1980-81
505 ..	Adelaide...............	1977-78	402 ..	Perth....................	1977-78

LOWEST INNINGS TOTALS

By Australia			**By India**		
83 ..	Melbourne.............	1980-81	58 ..	Brisbane (1st Inns)...	1947-48
105 ..	Kanpur..................	1959-60	67 ..	Melbourne.............	1947-48
107 ..	Sydney..................	1947-48	98 ..	Brisbane (2nd Inns)..	1947-48
107 ..	Delhi....................	1969-70			

Note: India's lowest total in India is 135 at Delhi, 1959-60.

INDIVIDUAL HUNDREDS IN THE MATCHES 1947-48–1980-81

For Australia (36)

112	S. G. Barnes, Adelaide....	1947-48
162†	A. R. Border, Madras......	1979-80
124	A. R. Border, Melbourne.	1980-81
185†	D. G. Bradman, Brisbane.	1947-48
132 / 127*	D. G. Bradman, Melbourne	1947-48
201	D. G. Bradman, Adelaide	1947-48
161	J. W. Burke, Bombay......	1956-57
204†	G. S. Chappell, Sydney....	1980-81
151	I. M. Chappell, Melbourne	1967-68
138	I. M. Chappell, Delhi......	1969-70
108	R. M. Cowper, Adelaide..	1967-68
165	R. M. Cowper, Sydney.....	1967-68
101	L. E. Favell, Madras........	1959-60
153	R. N. Harvey, Melbourne.	1947-48
140	R. N. Harvey, Bombay....	1956-57
114	R. N. Harvey, Delhi........	1959-60
102	R. N. Harvey, Bombay....	1959-60
198*	A. L. Hassett, Adelaide...	1947-48
100	K. J. Hughes, Madras......	1979-80
213	K. J. Hughes, Adelaide....	1980-81
100	W. M. Lawry, Melbourne.	1967-68
105	A. L. Mann, Perth..........	1977-78
100*	A. R. Morris, Melbourne.	1947-48
163	N. C. O'Neill, Bombay....	1959-60
113	N. C. O'Neill, Calcutta....	1959-60
114	A. P. Sheahan, Kanpur....	1969-70
103	R. B. Simpson, Adelaide..	1967-68
109	R. B. Simpson, Melbourne	1967-68
176	R. B. Simpson, Perth......	1977-78
100	R. B. Simpson, Adelaide..	1977-78
103†	K. R. Stackpole, Bombay.	1969-70
102	K. D. Walters, Madras.....	1969-70
125	G. M. Wood, Adelaide....	1980-81
121†	G. N. Yallop, Adelaide....	1977-78
167	G. N. Yallop, Calcutta.....	1979-80

For India (23)

100	M. Amarnath, Perth........	1977-78
108	N. J. Contractor, Bombay.	1959-60
113†	S. M. Gavaskar, Brisbane.	1977-78
127	S. M. Gavaskar, Perth.....	1977-78
118	S. M. Gavaskar, Melbourne	1977-78
115	S. M. Gavaskar, Delhi.....	1979-80
123	S. M. Gavaskar, Bombay..	1979-80
116 / 145	V. S. Hazare, Adelaide....	1947-48
101	M. L. Jaisimha, Brisbane..	1967-68
101*	S. M. H. Kirmani, Bombay	1979-80
116	V. Mankad, Melbourne....	1947-48
111	V. Mankad, Melbourne....	1947-48
128*†	Nawab of Pataudi, Madras	1964-65
174	S. M. Patil, Adelaide.......	1980-81
123	D. G. Phadkar, Adelaide..	1947-48
109	G. S. Ramchand, Bombay	1956-57
112	D. B. Vengsarkar, Bangalore..........................	1979-80
137†	G. R. Viswanath, Kanpur.	1969-70
161*	G. R. Viswanath, Bangalore..........................	1979-80
131	G. R. Viswanath, Delhi....	1979-80
114	G. R. Viswanath, Melbourne........................	1980-81
100*	Yashpal Sharma, Delhi....	1979-80

† *Signifies hundred on first appearance in Australia–India Tests.*

RECORD PARTNERSHIPS FOR EACH WICKET

For Australia

191 for 1st	R. B. Simpson and W. M. Lawry at Melbourne........................	1967-68
236 for 2nd	S. G. Barnes and D. G. Bradman at Adelaide..........................	1947-48
222 for 3rd	A. R. Border and K. J. Hughes at Madras.............................	1979-80
159 for 4th	R. N. Harvey and S. J. E. Loxton at Melbourne......................	1947-48
223* for 5th	A. R. Morris and D. G. Bradman at Melbourne......................	1947-48
151 for 6th	T. R. Veivers and B. N. Jarman at Bombay............................	1964-65
64 for 7th	T. R. Veivers and J. W. Martin at Madras..............................	1964-65
73 for 8th	T. R. Veivers and G. D. McKenzie at Madras.........................	1964-65
87 for 9th	I. W. Johnson and W. P. A. Crawford at Madras.....................	1956-57
52 for 10th	K. J. Wright and J. D. Higgs at Delhi..................................	1979-80

For India

192 for 1st	S. M. Gavaskar and C. P. S. Chauhan at Bombay	1979-80
193 for 2nd	S. M. Gavaskar and M. Amarnath at Perth	1977-78
159 for 3rd	S. M. Gavaskar and G. R. Viswanath at Delhi	1979-80
159 for 4th	D. B. Vengsarkar and G. R. Viswanath at Bangalore	1979-80
109 for 5th	A. A. Baig and R. B. Kenny at Bombay	1959-60
188 for 6th	V. S. Hazare and D. G. Phadkar at Adelaide	1947-48
132 for 7th	V. S. Hazare and H. R. Adhikari at Adelaide	1947-48
127 for 8th	S. M. H. Kirmani and K. D. Ghavri at Bombay	1979-80
57 for 9th	S. M. H. Kirmani and K. D. Ghavri at Sydney	1980-81
39 for 10th	C. G. Borde and B. S. Chandrasekhar at Calcutta	1964-65

TEN WICKETS OR MORE IN A MATCH

For Australia (7)

11-105 (6-52, 5-53)	R. Benaud, Calcutta	1956-57
12-124 (5-31, 7-93)	A. K. Davidson, Kanpur	1959-60
11-166 (5-99, 7-67)	G. Dymock, Kanpur	1979-80
10-91 (6-58, 4-33)†	G. D. McKenzie, Madras	1964-65
10-151 (7-66, 3-85)	G. D. McKenzie, Melbourne	1967-68
10-144 (5-91, 5-53)	A. A. Mallett, Madras	1969-70
11-31 (5-2, 6-29)†	E. R. H. Toshack, Brisbane	1947-48

For India (6)

10-194 (5-89, 5-105)	B. S. Bedi, Perth	1977-78
12-104 (6-52, 6-52)	B. S Chandrasekhar, Melbourne	1977-78
10-130 (7-49, 3-81)	Ghulam Ahmed, Calcutta	1956-57
11-122 (5-31, 6-91)	R. G. Nadkarni, Madras	1964-65
14-124 (9-69, 5-55)	J. M. Patel, Kanpur	1959-60
10-174 (4-100, 6-74)	E. A. S. Prasanna, Madras	1969-70

† *Signifies ten wickets or more on first appearance in Australia–India Tests.*

AUSTRALIA v PAKISTAN

	Captains					
Season	*Australia*	*Pakistan*	*T*	*A*	*P*	*D*
1956-57*P*	I. W. Johnson	A. H. Kardar	1	0	1	0
1959-60*P*	R. Benaud	Fazal Mahmood[1]	3	2	0	1
1964-65*P*	R. B. Simpson	Hanif Mohammad	1	0	0	1
1964-65*A*	R. B. Simpson	Hanif Mohammad	1	0	0	1
1972-73*A*	I. M. Chappell	Intikhab Alam	3	3	0	0
1976-77*A*	G. S. Chappell	Mushtaq Mohammad	3	1	1	1
1978-79*A*	G. N. Yallop[2]	Mushtaq Mohammad	2	1	1	0
1979-80*P*	G. S. Chappell	Javed Miandad	3	0	1	2
1981-82*A*	G. S. Chappell	Javed Miandad	3	2	1	0
	In Pakistan		8	2	2	4
	In Australia		12	7	3	2
	Totals		20	9	5	6

A Played in Australia. P Played in Pakistan.

Notes: [1]Imtiaz Ahmed captained in Second Test. [2]K. J. Hughes captained in Second Test.

HIGHEST INNINGS TOTALS

By Australia			By Pakistan		
617 ..	Faisalabad	1979-80	574-8 dec.	Melbourne	1972-73
585 ..	Adelaide	1972-73	500-8 dec.	Melbourne	1981-82

Note: Pakistan's highest total in Pakistan is 420-9 dec. at Lahore, 1979-80.

LOWEST INNINGS TOTALS

By Australia			By Pakistan		
80 ..	Karachi	1956-57	62 ..	Perth	1981-82

Note: Australia's lowest total in Australia is 125 at Melbourne, 1981-82. Pakistan's lowest total in Pakistan is 134 at Dacca, 1959-60.

INDIVIDUAL HUNDREDS IN THE MATCHES 1956-57–1981-82

For Australia (22)

142	J. Benaud, Melbourne	1972-73
105†	A. R. Border, Melbourne	1978-79
150* / 153	A. R. Border, Lahore	1979-80
116*	G. S. Chappell, Melbourne	1972-73
121	G. S. Chappell, Melbourne	1976-77
235	G. S. Chappell, Faisalabad	1979-80
201	G. S. Chappell, Brisbane	1981-82
196	I. M. Chappell, Adelaide	1972-73
168	G. J. Cosier, Melbourne	1976-77
105†	I. C. Davis, Adelaide	1976-77
106	K. J. Hughes, Perth	1981-82
105	R. B. McCosker, Melbourne	1976-77
118†	R. W. Marsh, Adelaide	1972-73
134	N. C. O'Neill, Lahore	1959-60
135	I. R. Redpath, Melbourne	1972-73
127	A. P. Sheahan, Melbourne	1972-73
153† / 115	R. B. Simpson, Karachi	1964-65
107	K. D. Walters, Adelaide	1976-77
100	G. M. Wood, Melbourne	1981-82
172	G. N. Yallop, Faisalabad	1979-80

For Pakistan (17)

152*	Asif Iqbal, Adelaide	1976-77
120	Asif Iqbal, Sydney	1976-77
134*	Asif Iqbal, Perth	1978-79
101*	Hanif Mohammad, Karachi	1959-60
104	Hanif Mohammad, Melbourne	1964-65
129*	Javed Miandad, Perth	1978-79
106*	Javed Miandad, Faisalabad	1979-80
166†	Khalid Ibadulla, Karachi	1964-65
158	Majid J. Khan, Melbourne	1972-73
108	Majid J. Khan, Melbourne	1978-79
110*	Majid J. Khan, Lahore	1979-80
121	Mushtaq Mohammad, Sydney	1972-73
137	Sadiq Mohammad, Melbourne	1972-73
105	Sadiq Mohammad, Melbourne	1976-77
166	Saeed Ahmed, Lahore	1959-60
210*	Taslim Arif, Faisalabad	1979-80
101	Zaheer Abbas, Adelaide	1976-77

† *Signifies hundred on first appearance in Australia–Pakistan Tests.*

RECORD PARTNERSHIPS FOR EACH WICKET

For Australia

134 for 1st	I. C Davis and A. Turner at Melbourne	1976-77
233 for 2nd	A. P. Sheahan and J. Benaud at Melbourne	1972-73
179 for 3rd	K. J. Hughes and G. S. Chappell at Faisalabad	1979-80
217 for 4th	G.S. Chappell and G. N. Yallop at Faisalabad	1979-80
171 for 5th	G. S. Chappell and G. J. Cosier at Melbourne	1976-77
139 for 6th	R. M. Cowper and T. R. Veivers at Melbourne	1964-65
134 for 7th	A. R. Border and G. R. Beard at Lahore	1979-80
117 for 8th	G. J. Cosier and K. J. O'Keeffe at Melbourne	1976-77
83 for 9th	J. R. Watkins and R. A. L. Massie at Sydney	1972-73
52 for 10th	D. K. Lillee and M. H. N. Walker at Sydney	1976-77

For Pakistan

249 for 1st†	Khalid Ibadulla and Abdul Kadir at Karachi	1964-65
195 for 2nd	Sadiq Mohammad and Majid J. Khan at Melbourne	1972-73
223* for 3rd†	Taslim Arif and Javed Miandad at Faisalabad	1979-80
128 for 4th	Javed Miandad and Zaheer Abbas at Melbourne	1981-82
139 for 5th	Mushtaq Mohammad and Asif Iqbal at Sydney	1972-73
115 for 6th	Asif Iqbal and Javed Miandad at Sydney	1976-77
104 for 7th	Intikhab Alam and Wasim Bari at Adelaide	1972-73
111 for 8th	Majid J. Khan and Imran Khan at Lahore	1979-80
56 for 9th	Intikhab Alam and Afaq Hussain at Melbourne	1964-65
87 for 10th	Asif Iqbal and Iqbal Qasim at Adelaide	1976-77

† *Denotes record partnership against all countries.*

TEN WICKETS OR MORE IN A MATCH

For Australia (2)

10-111 (7-87, 3-24)†	R. J. Bright, Karachi	1979-80
10-135 (6-82, 4-53)	D. K. Lillee, Melbourne	1976-77

For Pakistan (4)

13-114 (6-34, 7-80)†	Fazal Mahmood, Karachi	1956-57
12-165 (6-102, 6-63)	Imran Khan, Sydney	1976-77
11-118 (4-69, 7-49)	Iqbal Qasim, Karachi	1979-80
11-125 (2-39, 9-86)	Sarfraz Nawaz, Melbourne	1978-79

† *Signifies ten wickets or more on first appearance in Australia–Pakistan Tests.*

SOUTH AFRICA v NEW ZEALAND

	Captains					
Season	*South Africa*	*New Zealand*	*T*	*SA*	*NZ*	*D*
1931-32*N*	H. B. Cameron	M. L. Page	2	2	0	0
1952-53*N*	J. E Cheetham	W. M. Wallace	2	1	0	1
1953-54*S*	J. E Cheetham	G. O. Rabone[1]	5	4	0	1
1961-62*S*	D. J. McGlew	J. R. Reid	5	2	2	1
1963-64*N*	T. L. Goddard	J. R. Reid	3	0	0	3
	In New Zealand		7	3	0	4
	In South Africa		10	6	2	2
	Totals		17	9	2	6

N Played in New Zealand. S Played in South Africa.

Note: [1]B. Sutcliffe captained in Fourth and Fifth Tests.

HIGHEST INNINGS TOTALS

For South Africa in South Africa: 464 at Johannesburg, 1961-62.
in New Zealand: 524-8 at Wellington, 1952-53.

For New Zealand in South Africa: 505 at Cape Town, 1953-54.
in New Zealand: 364 at Wellington, 1931-32.

LOWEST INNINGS TOTALS

For South Africa in South Africa: 148 at Johannesburg, 1953-54.
in New Zealand: 223 at Dunedin, 1963-64.

For New Zealand in South Africa: 79 at Johannesburg, 1953-54.
in New Zealand: 138 at Dunedin, 1963-64.

INDIVIDUAL HUNDREDS IN THE MATCHES 1931-32–1963-64

For South Africa (11)

122*	X. C. Balaskas, Wellington	1931-32
103†	J. A. J. Christy, Christchurch	1931-32
116	W. R. Endean, Auckland	1952-53
255*†	D. J. McGlew, Wellington	1952-53
127*	D. J. McGlew, Durban	1961-62
120	D. J. McGlew, Johannesburg	1961-62
101	R. A. McLean, Durban	1953-54
113	R. A. McLean, Cape Town	1961-62
113†	B. Mitchell, Christchurch	1931-32
109†	A. R. A. Murray, Wellington	1952-53
101	J. H. B. Waite, Johannesburg	1961-62

For New Zealand (7)

109	P. T. Barton, Port Elizabeth	1961-62
101	P. G. Z. Harris, Cape Town	1961-62
107	G. O. Rabone, Durban	1953-54
135	J. R. Reid, Cape Town	1953-54
142	J. R. Reid, Johannesburg	1961-62
138	B. W. Sinclair, Auckland	1963-64
100†	H. G. Vivian, Wellington	1931-32

† *Signifies hundred on first appearance in South Africa–New Zealand Tests.*

RECORD PARTNERSHIPS FOR EACH WICKET

For South Africa

196 for 1st	J. A. J. Christy and B. Mitchell at Christchurch	1931-32
76 for 2nd	J. A. J. Christy and H. B. Cameron at Wellington	1931-32
112 for 3rd	D. J. McGlew and R. A. McLean at Johannesburg	1961-62
135 for 4th	K. J. Funston and R. A. McLean at Durban	1953-54
130 for 5th	W. R. Endean and J. E. Cheetham at Auckland	1952-53
83 for 6th	K. C. Bland and D. T. Lindsay at Auckland	1963-64
246 for 7th†	D. J. McGlew and A. R. A. Murray at Wellington	1952-53
95 for 8th	J. E. Cheetham and H. J. Tayfield at Cape Town	1953-54
60 for 9th	P. M. Pollock and N. A. T. Adcock at Port Elizabeth	1961-62
47 for 10th	D. J. McGlew and H. D. Bromfield at Port Elizabeth	1961-62

For New Zealand

126 for 1st	G. O. Rabone and M. E. Chapple at Cape Town	1953-54
51 for 2nd	W. P. Bradburn and B. W. Sinclair at Dunedin	1963-64
94 for 3rd	M. B. Poore and B. Sutcliffe at Cape Town	1953-54
171 for 4th	B. W. Sinclair and S. N. McGregor at Auckland	1963-64
174 for 5th	J. R. Reid and J. E. F. Beck at Cape Town	1953-54
100 for 6th	H. G. Vivian and F. T. Badcock at Wellington	1931-32
84 for 7th	J. R. Reid and G. A. Bartlett at Johannesburg	1961-62
73 for 8th	P. G. Z. Harris and G. A. Bartlett at Durban	1961-62
69 for 9th	C. F. W. Allcott and I. B. Cromb at Wellington	1931-32
49* for 10th	A. E. Dick and F. J. Cameron at Cape Town	1961-62

† *Denotes record partnership against all countries.*

TEN WICKETS OR MORE IN A MATCH

For South Africa (1)

11-196 (6-128, 5-68)† S. F. Burke, Cape Town 1961-62

† *Signifies ten wickets or more on first appearance in South Africa–New Zealand Tests.*

Note: The best match figures by a New Zealand bowler are 8-180 (4-61, 4-119), J. C. Alabaster at Cape Town, 1961-62.

WEST INDIES v NEW ZEALAND

Season	*Captains* *West Indies*	*New Zealand*	*T*	*WI*	*NZ*	*D*
1951-52*N*	J. D. C. Goddard	B. Sutcliffe	2	1	0	1
1955-56*N*	D. St E. Atkinson	J. R. Reid[1]	4	3	1	0
1968-69*N*	G. S. Sobers	G. T. Dowling	3	1	1	1
1971-72*W*	G. S. Sobers	G. T. Dowling[2]	5	0	0	5
1979-80*N*	C. H. Lloyd	G. P. Howarth	3	0	1	2
	In New Zealand		12	5	3	4
	In West Indies		5	0	0	5
	Totals		17	5	3	9

N Played in New Zealand. *W Played in West Indies.*

Notes: The following deputised for the official touring captain or were appointed by the home authority for only a minor proportion of the series:

[1] H. B. Cave (First). [2] B. E. Congdon (Third, Fourth and Fifth).

HIGHEST INNINGS TOTALS

By West Indies

564-8	Bridgetown	1971-72
546-6 dec.	Auckland	1951-52
508-4 dec.	Kingston	1971-72

By New Zealand

543-3 dec.	Georgetown	1971-72
460	Christchurch	1979-80
422	Bridgetown	1971-72

LOWEST INNINGS TOTALS

For West Indies in West Indies: 133 at Bridgetown, 1971-72.
in New Zealand: 77 at Auckland, 1955-56.
For New Zealand in West Indies: 162 at Port-of-Spain, 1971-72.
in New Zealand: 74 at Dunedin, 1955-56.

INDIVIDUAL HUNDREDS IN THE MATCHES 1951-52–1979-80

By West Indies (20)

109†	M. C. Carew, Auckland	1968-69	258	S. M. Nurse, Christchurch	1968-69
183	C. A. Davis, Bridgetown	1971-72	214† / 100*	L. G. Rowe, Kingston	1971-72
163	R. C. Fredericks, Kingston	1971-72	100	L. G. Rowe, Christchurch	1979-80
105†	D. L. Haynes, Dunedin	1979-80	142	G. S. Sobers, Bridgetown	1971-72
122	D. L. Haynes, Christchurch	1979-80	152	J. B. Stollmeyer, Auckland	1951-52
100*†	A. I. Kallicharran, Georgetown	1971-72	115	C. L. Walcott, Auckland	1951-52
101	A. I. Kallicharran, Port-of-Spain	1971-72	123	E. D. Weekes, Dunedin	1955-56
100*	C. L. King, Christchurch	1979-80	103	E. D. Weekes, Christchurch	1955-56
168†	S. M. Nurse, Auckland	1968-69	156	E. D. Weekes, Wellington	1955-56
			100	F. M. M. Worrell, Auckland	1951-52

By New Zealand (12)

101	M. G. Burgess, Kingston	1971-72	105	B. F. Hastings, Bridgetown	1971-72
166*	B. E. Congdon, Port-of-Spain	1971-72	147	G. P. Howarth, Christchurch	1979-80
126	B. E. Congdon, Bridgetown	1971-72	182	T. W. Jarvis, Georgetown	1971-72
127	B. A. Edgar, Auckland	1979-80	124†	B. R. Taylor, Auckland	1968-69
103	R. J. Hadlee, Christchurch	1979-80	223*	G. M. Turner, Kingston	1971-72
117*	B. F. Hastings, Christchurch	1968-69	259	G. M. Turner, Georgetown	1971-72

† *Signifies hundred on first appearance in West Indies–New Zealand Tests.*

Notes: E. D. Weekes in 1955-56 made three hundreds in consecutive innings.

L. G. Rowe and A. I. Kallicharran each scored hundreds in their first two innings in Test cricket, Rowe being the only batsman to do so in his first match.

RECORD PARTNERSHIPS FOR EACH WICKET

For West Indies

225 for 1st	C. G. Greenidge and D. L. Haynes at Christchurch	1979-80
269 for 2nd	R. C. Fredericks and L. G. Rowe at Kingston	1971-72
174 for 3rd	S. M. Nurse and B. F. Butcher at Auckland	1968-69
162 for 4th	E. D. Weekes and O. G. Smith at Dunedin	1955-56
	C. G. Greenidge and A. I. Kallicharran at Christchurch	1979-80
189 for 5th	F. M. M. Worrell and C. L. Walcott at Auckland	1951-52
254 for 6th	C. A. Davis and G. S. Sobers at Bridgetown	1971-72
143 for 7th	D. St E. Atkinson and J. D. C. Goddard at Christchurch	1955-56
75 for 8th	J. D. C. Goddard and S. Ramadhin at Dunedin	1955-56
56 for 9th	D. A. J. Holford and V. A. Holder at Port-of-Spain	1971-72
31 for 10th	T. M. Findlay and G. C. Shillingford at Bridgetown	1971-72

For New Zealand

387 for 1st†	G. M. Turner and T. W. Jarvis at Georgetown	1971-72
139 for 2nd	G. M. Turner and B. E. Congdon at Port-of-Spain	1971-72
75 for 3rd	B. E. Congdon and B. F. Hastings at Christchurch	1968-69
175 for 4th	B. E. Congdon and B. F. Hastings at Bridgetown	1971-72
110 for 5th	B. F. Hastings and V. Pollard at Christchurch	1968-69
220 for 6th†	G. M. Turner and K. J. Wadsworth at Kingston	1971-72
98 for 7th	J. V. Coney and R. J. Hadlee at Christchurch	1979-80
136 for 8th†	B. E. Congdon and R. S. Cunis at Port-of-Spain	1971-72
62* for 9th	V. Pollard and R. S. Cunis at Auckland	1968-69
41 for 10th	B. E. Congdon and J. C. Alabaster at Port-of-Spain	1971-72

† *Denotes record partnership against all countries.*

TEN WICKETS OR MORE IN A MATCH

For New Zealand (2)

11-102 (5-34, 6-68)†	R. J. Hadlee, Dunedin	1979-80
10-166 (4-71, 6-95)	G. B. Troup, Auckland	1979-80

† *Signifies ten wickets or more on first appearance in West Indies–New Zealand Tests.*

Note: The best match figures by a West Indian bowler are 9-125 (5-86, 4-39), S. Ramadhin at Christchurch, 1951-52, and 9-81 (6-23, 3-58), S. Ramadhin at Dunedin, 1955-56.

WEST INDIES v INDIA

	Captains					
Season	*West Indies*	*India*	*T*	*WI*	*I*	*D*
1948-49*I*	J. D. C. Goddard	L. Amarnath	5	1	0	4
1952-53*W*	J. B. Stollmeyer	V. S. Hazare	5	1	0	4
1958-59*I*	F. C. M. Alexander	Ghulam Ahmed[1]	5	3	0	2
1961-62*W*	F. M. M. Worrell	N. J. Contractor[2]	5	5	0	0
1966-67*I*	G. S. Sobers	Nawab of Pataudi jun.	3	2	0	1
1970-71*W*	G. S. Sobers	A. L. Wadekar	5	0	1	4
1974-75*I*	C. H. Lloyd	Nawab of Pataudi jun.[3]	5	3	2	0
1975-76*W*	C. H. Lloyd	B. S. Bedi	4	2	1	1
1978-79*I*	A. I. Kallicharran	S. M. Gavaskar	6	0	1	5
	In India		24	9	3	12
	In West Indies		19	8	2	9
	Totals		43	17	5	21

I Played in India. W Played in West Indies.

Notes: The following deputised for the official touring captain or were appointed by the home authority for only a minor proportion of the series:

[1]P. R. Umrigar (First), V. Mankad (Fourth), H. R. Adhikari (Fifth). [2]Nawab of Pataudi jun. (Third, Fourth and Fifth). [3]S. Venkataraghavan (Second).

HIGHEST INNINGS TOTALS

By West Indies

644-8 dec.	Delhi	1958-59
631-8 dec.	Kingston	1961-62
631 ..	Delhi	1948-49
629-6 dec.	Bombay	1948-49
614-5 dec.	Calcutta	1958-59
604-6 dec.	Bombay	1974-75

By India

644-7 dec.	Kanpur	1978-79
566-8 dec.	Delhi	1978-79
454 ..	Delhi	1948-49
444 ..	Kingston	1952-53
427 ..	Port-of-Spain	1970-71
424 ..	Bombay	1978-79

LOWEST INNINGS TOTALS

By West Indies

151 ..	Madras	1978-79
154 ..	Madras (2nd Inns)	1974-75
172 ..	Delhi	1978-79
192 ..	Madras (1st Inns)	1974-75

By India

97† ..	Kingston	1975-76
98 ..	Port-of-Spain	1961-62
118 ..	Bangalore	1974-75
124 ..	Calcutta	1958-59

† *Five men absent hurt.*

Note: West Indies' lowest score in West Indies is 214 at Port-of-Spain, 1970-71.

INDIVIDUAL HUNDREDS IN THE MATCHES 1948-49–1978-79

For West Indies (55)

250	S. F. A. Bacchus, Kanpur	1978-79
103	B. F. Butcher, Calcutta	1958-59
142	B. F. Butcher, Madras	1958-59
107†	R. J. Christiani, Delhi	1948-49
125*	C. A. Davis, Georgetown	1970-71
105	C. A. Davis, Port-of-Spain	1970-71
100	R. C. Fredericks, Calcutta	1974-75
104	R. C. Fredericks, Bombay	1974-75
101†	G. E. Gomez, Delhi	1948-49
107†	C. G. Greenidge, Bangalore	1974-75
123	J. K. Holt, Delhi	1958-59
101	C. C. Hunte, Bombay	1966-67
124†	A. I. Kallicharran, Bangalore	1974-75
103*	A. I. Kallicharran, Port-of-Spain	1975-76
187	A. I. Kallicharran, Bombay	1978-79
256	R. B. Kanhai, Calcutta	1958-59
138	R. B. Kanhai, Kingston	1961-62
139	R. B. Kanhai, Port-of-Spain	1961-62
158*	R. B. Kanhai, Kingston	1970-71
163	C. H. Lloyd, Bangalore	1974-75
242*	C. H. Lloyd, Bombay	1974-75
102	C. H. Lloyd, Bridgetown	1975-76
125†	E. D. A. McMorris, Kingston	1961-62
115†	B. H. Pairaudeau, Port-of-Spain	1952-53
104	A. F. Rae, Bombay	1948-49
109	A. F. Rae, Madras	1948-49
192*	I. V. A. Richards, Delhi	1974-75
142	I. V. A. Richards, Bridgetown	1975-76
130	I. V. A. Richards, Port-of-Spain	1975-76
177	I. V. A. Richards, Port-of-Spain	1975-76
100	O. G. Smith, Delhi	1958-59
142*†	G. S. Sobers, Bombay	1958-59
198	G. S. Sobers, Kanpur	1958-59
106*	G. S. Sobers, Calcutta	1958-59
153	G. S. Sobers, Kingston	1961-62
104	G. S. Sobers, Kingston	1961-62
108*	G. S. Sobers, Georgetown	1970-71
178*	G. S. Sobers, Bridgetown	1970-71
132	G. S. Sobers, Port-of-Spain	1970-71
100*	J. S. Solomon, Delhi	1958-59
160	J. B. Stollmeyer, Madras	1948-49
104*	J. B. Stollmeyer, Port-of-Spain	1952-53
152†	C. L. Walcott, Delhi	1948-49
108	C. L. Walcott, Calcutta	1948-49
125	C. L. Walcott, Georgetown	1952-53
118	C. L. Walcott, Kingston	1952-53
128†	E. D. Weekes, Delhi	1948-49
194	E. D. Weekes, Bombay	1948-49
162 } 101 }	E. D. Weekes, Calcutta	1948-49
207	E. D. Weekes, Port-of-Spain	1952-53
161	E. D. Weekes, Port-of-Spain	1952-53
109	E. D. Weekes, Kingston	1952-53
111	A. B. Williams, Calcutta	1978-79
237	F. M. M. Worrell, Kingston	1952-53

For India (40)

114*†	H. R. Adhikari, Delhi	1948-49	122	V. S. Hazare, Bombay	1948-49
101*	M. Amarnath, Kanpur	1978-79	126*	Kapil Dev, Delhi	1978-79
163*	M. L. Apte, Port-of-Spain	1952-53	118	V. L. Manjrekar, Kingston	1952-53
109	C. G. Borde, Delhi	1958-59	112	R. S. Modi, Bombay	1948-49
121	C. G. Borde, Bombay	1966-67	106†	Mushtaq Ali, Calcutta	1948-49
125	C. G. Borde, Madras	1966-67	115*	B. P. Patel, Port-of-Spain	1975-76
104	S. A. Durani, Port-of-Spain	1961-62	150	P. Roy, Kingston	1952-53
109	F. M. Engineer, Madras	1966-67	212	D. N. Sardesai, Kingston	1970-71
102	A. D. Gaekwad, Kanpur	1978-79	112	D. N. Sardesai, Port-of-Spain	1970-71
116	S. M. Gavaskar, Georgetown	1970-71	150	D. N. Sardesai, Bridgetown	1970-71
117*	S. M. Gavaskar, Bridgetown	1970-71	102	E. D. Solkar, Bombay	1974-75
124 / 220	S. M. Gavaskar, Port-of-Spain	1970-71	130	P. R. Umrigar, Port-of-Spain	1952-53
156	S. M. Gavaskar, Port-of-Spain	1975-76	117	P. R. Umrigar, Kingston	1952-53
102	S. M. Gavaskar, Port-of-Spain	1975-76	172*	P. R. Umrigar, Port-of-Spain	1961-62
205	S. M. Gavaskar, Bombay	1978-79	157*	D. B. Vengsarkar, Calcutta	1978-79
107 / 182*	S. M. Gavaskar, Calcutta	1978-79	109	D. B Vengsarkar, Delhi	1978-79
120	S. M. Gavaskar, Delhi	1978-79	139	G. R. Viswanath, Calcutta	1974-75
134*	V. S. Hazare, Bombay	1948-49	112	G. R. Viswanath, Port-of-Spain	1975-76
			124	G. R. Viswanath, Madras	1978-79
			179	G. R. Viswanath, Kanpur	1978-79

† *Signifies hundred on first appearance in West Indies–India Tests.*

RECORD PARTNERSHIPS FOR EACH WICKET

For West Indies

239 for 1st†	J. B. Stollmeyer and A. F. Rae at Madras	1948-49
255 for 2nd	E. D. A. McMorris and R. B. Kanhai at Kingston	1961-62
220 for 3rd	I. V. A. Richards and A. I. Kallicharran at Bridgetown	1975-76
267 for 4th	C. L. Walcott and G. E. Gomez at Delhi	1948-49
219 for 5th	E. D. Weekes and B. H. Pairaudeau at Port-of-Spain	1952-53
250 for 6th	C. H. Lloyd and D. L. Murray at Bombay	1974-75
127 for 7th	G. S. Sobers and I. L. Mendonca at Kingston	1961-62
124 for 8th†	I. V. A. Richards and K. D. Boyce at Delhi	1974-75
106 for 9th	R. J. Christiani and D. St E. Atkinson at Delhi	1948-49
98* for 10th†	F. M. M. Worrell and W. W. Hall at Port-of-Spain	1961-62

For India

153 for 1st	S. M. Gavaskar and C. P. S. Chauhan at Bombay	1978-79
344* for 2nd†	S. M. Gavaskar and D. B Vengsarkar at Calcutta	1978-79
159 for 3rd	M. Amarnath and G. R. Viswanath at Port-of-Spain	1975-76
172 for 4th	G. R. Viswanath and A. D. Gaekwad at Kanpur	1978-79
204 for 5th†	S. M. Gavaskar and B. P. Patel at Port-of-Spain	1975-76
137 for 6th	D. N. Sardesai and E. D. Solkar at Kingston	1970-71
186 for 7th†	D. N. Sardesai and E. D. Solkar at Bridgetown	1970-71
94 for 8th	R. G. Nadkarni and F. M. Engineer at Kingston	1961-62
122 for 9th	D. N. Sardesai and E. A. S. Prasanna at Kingston	1970-71
62 for 10th	D. N. Sardesai and B. S. Bedi at Bridgetown	1970-71

† *Denotes record partnership against all countries.*

TEN WICKETS OR MORE IN A MATCH

For West Indies (2)

11-126 (6-50, 5-76)	W. W. Hall, Kanpur	1958-59
12-121 (7-64, 5-57)	A. M. E. Roberts, Madras	1974-75

For India (2)

11-235 (7-157, 4-78)†	B. S Chandrasekhar, Bombay	1966-67
10-223 (9-102, 1-121)	S. P. Gupte, Kanpur	1958-59

† *Signifies ten wickets or more on first appearance in West Indies–India Tests.*

WEST INDIES v PAKISTAN

Season	*Captains* *West Indies*	*Pakistan*	*T*	*WI*	*P*	*D*
1957-58*W*	F. C. M. Alexander	A. H. Kardar	5	3	1	1
1958-59*P*	F. C. M. Alexander	Fazal Mahmood	3	1	2	0
1974-75*P*	C. H. Lloyd	Intikhab Alam	2	0	0	2
1976-77*W*	C. H. Lloyd	Mushtaq Mohammad	5	2	1	2
1980-81*P*	C. H. Lloyd	Javed Miandad	4	1	0	3
	In West Indies		10	5	2	3
	In Pakistan		9	2	2	5
	Totals		19	7	4	8

P Played in Pakistan. W Played in West Indies.

HIGHEST INNINGS TOTALS

For West Indies in West Indies: 790-3 dec. at Kingston, 1957-58
in Pakistan: 493 at Karachi, 1974-75.

For Pakistan in West Indies: 657-8 dec. at Bridgetown, 1957-58.
in Pakistan: 406-8 dec. at Karachi, 1974-75.

LOWEST INNINGS TOTALS

For West Indies in West Indies: 154 at Port-of-Spain, 1976-77
in Pakistan: 76 at Dacca, 1958-59.

For Pakistan in West Indies: 106 at Bridgetown, 1957-58
in Pakistan: 104 at Lahore, 1958-59.

INDIVIDUAL HUNDREDS IN THE MATCHES 1957-58–1980-81

For West Indies (17)

105*†	L. Baichan, Lahore	1974-75
120	R. C. Fredericks, Port-of-Spain	1976-77
100	C. G. Greenidge, Kingston	1976-77
142†	C. C. Hunte, Bridgetown	1957-58
260	C. C. Hunte, Kingston	1957-58
114	C. C. Hunte, Georgetown	1957-58
101	B. D. Julien, Karachi	1974-75
115	A. I. Kallicharran, Karachi	1974-75
217	R. B. Kanhai, Lahore	1958-59
157	C. H. Lloyd, Bridgetown	1976-77
120*	I. V. A. Richards, Multan	1980-81
120	I. T. Shillingford, Georgetown	1976-77
365*	G. S. Sobers, Kingston	1957-58
125 109*	G. S. Sobers, Georgetown	1957-58
145	C. L. Walcott, Georgetown	1957-58
197†	E. D. Weekes, Bridgetown	1957-58

Pakistan (14)

135	Asif Iqbal, Kingston	1976-77
337†	Hanif Mohammad, Bridgetown	1957-58
103	Hanif Mohammad, Karachi	1958-59
122	Imtiaz Ahmed, Kingston	1957-58
123	Imran Khan, Lahore	1980-81
100	Majid J. Khan, Karachi	1974-75
167	Majid J. Khan, Georgetown	1976-77
123	Mushtaq Mohammad, Lahore	1974-75
121	Mushtaq Mohammad, Port-of-Spain	1976-77
150	Saeed Ahmed, Georgetown	1957-58
107*	Wasim Raja, Karachi	1974-75
117*	Wasim Raja, Bridgetown	1976-77
106	Wazir Mohammad, Kingston	1957-58
189	Wazir Mohammad, Port-of-Spain	1957-58

† *Signifies hundred on first appearance in West Indies–Pakistan Tests.*

RECORD PARTNERSHIPS FOR EACH WICKET

For West Indies

182 for 1st	R. C. Fredericks and C. G. Greenidge at Kingston	1976-77
446 for 2nd†	C. C. Hunte and G. S. Sobers at Kingston	1957-58
162 for 3rd	R. B. Kanhai and G. S. Sobers at Lahore	1958-59
188* for 4th	G. S. Sobers and C. L. Walcott at Kingston	1957-58
185 for 5th	E. D. Weekes and O. G. Smith at Bridgetown	1957-58
151 for 6th	C. H. Lloyd and D. L. Murray at Bridgetown	1976-77
70 for 7th	C. H. Lloyd and J. Garner at Bridgetown	1976-77
50 for 8th	B. D. Julien and V. A. Holder at Karachi	1974-75
46 for 9th	J. Garner and C. E. H. Croft at Port-of-Spain	1976-77
44 for 10th	R. Nanan and S. T. Clarke at Faisalabad	1980-81

For Pakistan

159 for 1st‡	Majid J. Khan and Zaheer Abbas at Georgetown	1976-77
178 for 2nd	Hanif Mohammad and Saeed Ahmed at Karachi	1958-59
169 for 3rd	Saeed Ahmed and Wazir Mohammad at Port-of-Spain	1957-58
154 for 4th	Wazir Mohammad and Hanif Mohammad at Port-of-Spain	1957-58
87 for 5th	Mushtaq Mohammad and Asif Iqbal at Kingston	1976-77
166 for 6th	Wazir Mohammad and A. H. Kardar at Kingston	1957-58
128 for 7th	Wasim Raja and Wasim Bari at Karachi	1974-75
73 for 8th	Imran Khan and Sarfraz Nawaz at Port-of-Spain	1976-77
73 for 9th	Wasim Raja and Sarfraz Nawaz at Bridgetown	1976-77
133 for 10th†	Wasim Raja and Wasim Bari at Bridgetown	1976-77

† *Denotes record partnership against all countries.*

‡ *219 runs were added for this wicket in two separate partnerships: Sadiq Mohammad retired hurt and was replaced by Zaheer Abbas when 60 had been added. The highest partnership by two opening batsmen is 152 by Hanif Mohammad and Imtiaz Ahmed at Bridgetown, 1957-58.*

TEN WICKETS OR MORE IN A MATCH

For Pakistan (1)

12-100 (6-34, 6-66) Fazal Mahmood, Dacca... 1958-59

Note: The best match figures by a West Indian bowler are 9-187 (5-66, 4-121), A. M. E. Roberts at Lahore, 1974-75, and 9-95 (8-29, 1-66), C. E. H. Croft at Port-of-Spain, 1976-77.

NEW ZEALAND v INDIA

Season	*Captains* *New Zealand*	*India*	*T*	*NZ*	*I*	*D*
1955-56*I*	H. B. Cave	P. R. Umrigar[1]	5	0	2	3
1964-65*I*	J. R. Reid	Nawab of Pataudi jun.	4	0	1	3
1967-68*N*	G. T. Dowling[2]	Nawab of Pataudi jun.	4	1	3	0
1969-70*I*	G. T. Dowling	Nawab of Pataudi jun.	3	1	1	1
1975-76*N*	G. M. Turner	B. S. Bedi[3]	3	1	1	1
1976-77*I*	G. M. Turner	B. S. Bedi	3	0	2	1
1980-81*N*	G. P. Howarth	S. M. Gavaskar	3	1	0	2
	In India................................		15	1	6	8
	In New Zealand.....................		10	3	4	3
	Totals..................................		25	4	10	11

I Played in India. N Played in New Zealand.

Notes: [1] Ghulam Ahmed captained in First Test. [2] B. W. Sinclair captained in First Test. [3] S. M. Gavaskar captained in First Test.

HIGHEST INNINGS TOTALS

For New Zealand in New Zealand: 502 at Christchurch, 1967-68.
in India: 462-9 dec. at Calcutta, 1964-65.
450-2 dec. at Delhi, 1955-56.
For India in New Zealand: 414 at Auckland, 1975-76.
in India: 537-3 dec. at Madras, 1955-56.

LOWEST INNINGS TOTALS

For New Zealand in New Zealand: 100 at Wellington, 1980-81.
in India: 127 at Bombay, 1969-70.
For India in New Zealand: 81 at Wellington, 1975-76.
in India: 88 at Bombay, 1964-65.

INDIVIDUAL HUNDREDS IN THE MATCHES 1955-56–1980-81

For New Zealand (16)

120 G. T. Dowling, Bombay... 1964-65
143 G. T. Dowling, Dunedin.. 1967-68
239 G. T. Dowling, Christchurch....................... 1967-68
102† J. W. Guy, Hyderabad..... 1955-56
137* G. P. Howarth, Wellington 1980-81
104 J. M. Parker, Bombay...... 1976-77
123* J. F. Reid, Christchurch... 1980-81

120	J. R. Reid, Calcutta	1955-56	105†	B. R. Taylor, Calcutta	1964-65
119*	J. R. Reid, Delhi	1955-56	117	G. M. Turner, Christchurch	1975-76
137*†	B. Sutcliffe, Hyderabad	1955-56	113	G. M. Turner, Kanpur	1976-77
230*	B. Sutcliffe, Delhi	1955-56	110	J. G. Wright, Auckland	1980-81
151*	B. Sutcliffe, Calcutta	1964-65			

For India (20)

124†	S. Amarnath, Auckland	1975-76	153	Nawab of Pataudi jun., Calcutta	1964-65
109	C. G. Borde, Bombay	1964-65	113	Nawab of Pataudi jun., Delhi	1964-65
116†	S. M. Gavaskar, Auckland	1975-76	106*	G. S. Ramchand, Calcutta	1955-56
119	S. M. Gavaskar, Bombay	1976-77	173	P. Roy, Madras	1955-56
100*†	A. G. Kripal Singh, Hyderabad	1955-56	100	P. Roy, Calcutta	1955-56
177	V. L. Manjrekar, Delhi	1955-56	200*	D. N. Sardesai, Bombay	1964-65
118†	V. L. Manjrekar, Hyderabad	1955-56	106	D. N. Sardesai, Delhi	1964-65
102*	V. L. Manjrekar, Madras	1964-65	223†	P. R. Umrigar, Hyderabad	1955-56
231	V. Mankad, Madras	1955-56	103*	G. R. Viswanath, Kanpur	1976-77
223	V. Mankad, Bombay	1955-56	143	A. L. Wadekar, Wellington	1967-68

† *Signifies hundred on first appearance in New Zealand–India Tests. B. R. Taylor provides the only instance for New Zealand of a player scoring his maiden hundred in first-class cricket in his first Test.*

RECORD PARTNERSHIPS FOR EACH WICKET

For New Zealand

126 for 1st	B. A. G. Murray and G. T. Dowling at Christchurch	1967-68
155 for 2nd	G. T. Dowling and B. E. Congdon at Dunedin	1967-68
222* for 3rd†	B. Sutcliffe and J. R. Reid at Delhi	1955-56
103 for 4th	G. T. Dowling and M. G. Burgess at Christchurch	1967-68
119 for 5th	G. T. Dowling and K. Thomson at Christchurch	1967-68
87 for 6th	J. W. Guy and A. R. MacGibbon at Hyderabad	1955-56
163 for 7th	B. Sutcliffe and B. R. Taylor at Calcutta	1964-65
81 for 8th	V. Pollard and G. E. Vivian at Calcutta	1964-65
69 for 9th	M. G. Burgess and J. C. Alabaster at Dunedin	1967-68
61 for 10th	J. T. Ward and R. O. Collinge at Madras	1964-65

For India

413 for 1st†	V. Mankad and P. Roy at Madras	1955-56
204 for 2nd	S. M. Gavaskar and S. Amarnath at Auckland	1975-76
238 for 3rd	P. R. Umrigar and V. L. Manjrekar at Hyderabad	1955-56
171 for 4th	P. R. Umrigar and A. G. Kripal Singh at Hyderabad	1955-56
127 for 5th	V. L. Manjrekar and G. S. Ramchand at Delhi	1955-56
193* for 6th†	D. N. Sardesai and Hanumant Singh at Bombay	1964-65
116 for 7th	B. P. Patel and S. M. H. Kirmani at Wellington	1975-76
143 for 8th†	R. G. Nadkarni and F. M. Engineer at Madras	1964-65
105 for 9th	S. M. H. Kirmani and B. S. Bedi at Bombay	1976-77
	S. M. H. Kirmani and N. S. Yadav at Auckland	1980-81
57 for 10th	R. B. Desai and B. S. Bedi at Dunedin	1967-68

† *Denotes record partnership against all countries.*

TEN WICKETS OR MORE IN A MATCH

For New Zealand (1)

11-58 (4-35, 7-23)	R. J. Hadlee, Wellington	1975-76

For India (2)

11-140 (3-64, 8-76)	E. A. S. Prasanna, Auckland	1975-76
12-152 (8-72, 4-80)	S. Venkataraghavan, Delhi	1964-65

NEW ZEALAND v PAKISTAN

Season	*Captains* *New Zealand*	*Pakistan*	*T*	*NZ*	*P*	*D*
1955-56*P*	H. B. Cave	A. H. Kardar	3	0	2	1
1964-65*N*	J. R. Reid	Hanif Mohammad	3	0	0	3
1964-65*P*	J. R. Reid	Hanif Mohammad	3	0	2	1
1969-70*P*	G. T. Dowling	Intikhab Alam	3	1	0	2
1972-73*N*	B. E. Congdon	Intikhab Alam	3	0	1	2
1976-77*P*	G. M. Turner[1]	Mushtaq Mohammad	3	0	2	1
1978-79*N*	M. G. Burgess	Mushtaq Mohammad	3	0	1	2
	In Pakistan		12	1	6	5
	In New Zealand		9	0	2	7
	Totals		21	1	8	12

N Played in New Zealand. P Played in Pakistan.

Note: [1] J. M. Parker captained in Third Test.

HIGHEST INNINGS TOTALS

For New Zealand in New Zealand { 402 at Auckland, 1972-73. / 402 at Napier, 1978-79.
in Pakistan: 482-6 dec. at Lahore, 1964-65.

For Pakistan in New Zealand: 507-6 dec. at Dunedin, 1972-73.
in Pakistan: 565-9 dec. at Karachi, 1976-77.
561 at Lahore, 1955-56.

LOWEST INNINGS TOTALS

For New Zealand in New Zealand: 156 at Dunedin, 1972-73.
in Pakistan: 70 at Dacca, 1955-56.

For Pakistan in New Zealand: 187 at Wellington, 1964-65.
in Pakistan: 114 at Lahore, 1969-70.

INDIVIDUAL HUNDREDS IN THE MATCHES 1955-56–1978-79

For New Zealand (11)

119*	M. G. Burgess, Dacca	1969-70
111	M. G. Burgess, Lahore	1976-77
129†	B. A. Edgar, Christchurch	1978-79
110	B. F. Hastings, Auckland	1972-73
114	G. P. Howarth, Napier	1978-79
152	W. K. Lees, Karachi	1976-77

111	S. N. McGregor, Lahore	1955-56	130	B. W. Sinclair, Lahore	1964-65
107†	R. E. Redmond, Auckland	1972-73	110†	G. M. Turner, Dacca	1969-70
128	J. R. Reid, Karachi	1964-65			

For Pakistan (22)

175	Asif Iqbal, Dunedin	1972-73	126	Mohammad Ilyas, Karachi	1964-65
166	Asif Iqbal, Lahore	1976-77	201	Mushtaq Mohammad, Dunedin	1972-73
104	Asif Iqbal, Napier	1978-79	101	Mushtaq Mohammad, Hyderabad	1976-77
103	Hanif Mohammad, Dacca	1955-56	107	Mushtaq Mohammad, Karachi	1976-77
100*	Hanif Mohammad, Christchurch	1964-65	166	Sadiq Mohammad, Wellington	1972-73
203*	Hanif Mohammad, Lahore	1964-65	103*	Sadiq Mohammad, Hyderabad	1976-77
209	Imtiaz Ahmed, Lahore	1955-56	172	Saeed Ahmed, Karachi	1964-65
163†	Javed Miandad, Lahore	1976-77	189	Waqar Hassan, Lahore	1955-56
206	Javed Miandad, Karachi	1976-77	135	Zaheer Abbas, Auckland	1978-79
160*	Javed Miandad, Christchurch	1978-79			
110	Majid J. Khan, Auckland	1972-73			
112	Majid J. Khan, Karachi	1976-77			
119*	Majid J. Khan, Napier	1978-79			

† *Signifies hundred on first appearance in New Zealand–Pakistan Tests.*

Note: Mushtaq and Sadiq Mohammad, at Hyderabad in 1976-77, provide the fourth instance in Test matches, after the Chappells (thrice), of brothers each scoring hundreds in the same innings.

RECORD PARTNERSHIPS FOR EACH WICKET

For New Zealand

159 for 1st	R. E. Redmond and G. M. Turner at Auckland	1972-73
195 for 2nd†	J. G. Wright and G. P. Howarth at Napier	1978-79
178 for 3rd	B. W. Sinclair and J. R. Reid at Lahore	1964-65
128 for 4th	B. F. Hastings and M. G. Burgess at Wellington	1972-73
183 for 5th†	M. G. Burgess and R. W. Anderson at Lahore	1976-77
91 for 6th	M. G. Burgess and W. K. Lees at Karachi	1976-77
186 for 7th†	W. K. Lees and R. J. Hadlee at Karachi	1976-77
100 for 8th	B. W. Yuile and D. R. Hadlee at Karachi	1969-70
96 for 9th†	M. G. Burgess and R. S. Cunis at Dacca	1969-70
151 for 10th†	B. F. Hastings and R. O. Collinge at Auckland	1972-73

For Pakistan

147 for 1st‡	Sadiq Mohammad and Majid J. Khan at Karachi	1976-77
114 for 2nd	Mohammad Ilyas and Saeed Ahmed at Rawalpindi	1964-65
171 for 3rd	Sadiq Mohammad and Majid J. Khan at Wellington	1972-73
350 for 4th†	Mushtaq Mohammad and Asif Iqbal at Dunedin	1972-73
281 for 5th†	Javed Miandad and Asif Iqbal at Lahore	1976-77
217 for 6th†	Hanif Mohammad and Majid J. Khan at Lahore	1964-65
308 for 7th†	Waqar Hassan and Imtiaz Ahmed at Lahore	1955-56
72 for 8th	Asif Iqbal and Imran Khan at Lahore	1976-77
52 for 9th	Intikhab Alam and Arif Butt at Auckland	1964-65
65 for 10th	Salah-ud-Din and Mohammad Farooq at Rawalpindi	1964-65

† *Denotes record partnership against all countries.*

‡ *In the preceding Test of this series, at Hyderabad, 164 runs were added for this wicket by Sadiq Mohammad, Majid J. Khan and Zaheer Abbas. Sadiq Mohammad retired hurt after 136 had been scored.*

TEN WICKETS OR MORE IN A MATCH

For Pakistan (3)

10-182 (5-91, 5-91)	Intikhab Alam, Dacca	1969-70
11-130 (7-52, 4-78)	Intikhab Alam, Dunedin	1972-73
11-79 (5-37, 6-42)†	Zulfiqar Ahmed, Karachi	1955-56

† *Signifies ten wickets or more on first appearance in New Zealand–Pakistan Tests.*

Note: The best match figures by a New Zealand bowler are 9-70 (4-36, 5-34), F. J. Cameron at Auckland, 1964-65.

INDIA v PAKISTAN

	Captains					
Season	*India*	*Pakistan*	*T*	*I*	*P*	*D*
1952-53*I*	L. Amarnath	A. H. Kardar	5	2	1	2
1954-55*P*	V. Mankad	A. H. Kardar	5	0	0	5
1960-61*I*	N . J. Contractor	Fazal Mahmood	5	0	0	5
1978-79*P*	B. S. Bedi	Mushtaq Mohammad	3	0	2	1
1979-80*I*	S. M. Gavaskar[1]	Asif Iqbal	6	2	0	4
	In India		16	4	1	11
	In Pakistan		8	0	2	6
	Totals		24	4	3	17

I Played in India. P Played in Pakistan.

Note: [1]G. R. Viswanath captained in Sixth Test.

HIGHEST INNINGS TOTALS

For India in India: 539-9 dec. at Madras, 1960-61.
in Pakistan: 465 at Lahore, 1978-79.

For Pakistan in India: 448-8 dec. at Madras, 1960-61.
in Pakistan: 539-6 dec. at Lahore, 1978-79.
503-8 dec. at Faisalabad, 1978-79.

LOWEST INNINGS TOTALS

For India in India: 106 at Lucknow, 1952-53.
in Pakistan: 145 at Karachi, 1954-55.

For Pakistan in India: 150 at Delhi, 1952-53.
in Pakistan: 158 at Dacca, 1954-55.

INDIVIDUAL HUNDREDS IN THE MATCHES 1952-53–1979-80

For India (13)

177*	C. G. Borde, Madras	1960-61
111, 137	S. M. Gavaskar, Karachi	1978-79
166	S. M. Gavaskar, Madras	1979-80
146*	V. S. Hazare, Bombay	1952-53
110†	D. H. Shodhan, Calcutta	1952-53
102	P. R. Umrigar, Bombay	1952-53
108	P. R. Umrigar, Peshawar	1954-55

115	P. R. Umrigar, Kanpur....	1960-61	146*	D. B. Vengsarkar, Delhi..	1979-80
117	P. R. Umrigar, Madras....	1960-61	145†	G. R. Viswanath, Faisalabad........................	1978-79
112	P. R. Umrigar, Delhi.......	1960-61			

For Pakistan (14)

103*	Alim-ud-Din, Karachi......	1954-55	101	Mushtaq Mohammad, Delhi.........................	1960-61
104†	Asif Iqbal, Faisalabad......	1978-79	124*	Nazar Mohammad, Lucknow.........................	1952-53
142	Hanif Mohammad, Bahawalpur.......................	1954-55	121†	Saeed Ahmed, Bombay....	1960-61
160	Hanif Mohammad, Bombay	1960-61	103	Saeed Ahmed, Madras.....	1960-61
135	Imtiaz Ahmed, Madras.....	1960-61	176†	Zaheer Abbas, Faisalabad	1978-79
154*†	Javed Miandad, Faisalabad	1978-79	235*	Zaheer Abbas, Lahore.....	1978-79
100	Javed Miandad, Karachi...	1978-79			
126	Mudassar Nazar, Bangalore	1979-80			

† *Signifies hundred on first appearance in India–Pakistan Tests.*

RECORD PARTNERSHIPS FOR EACH WICKET

For India

192 for 1st	S. M. Gavaskar and C. P. S. Chauhan at Lahore......................	1978-79
117 for 2nd	S. M. Gavaskar and M. Amarnath at Karachi.........................	1978-79
130* for 3rd	P. Roy and V. L. Manjrekar at Dacca..................................	1954-55
183 for 4th	V. S. Hazare and P. R. Umrigar at Bombay...........................	1952-53
177 for 5th	P. R. Umrigar and C. G. Borde at Madras.............................	1960-61
82 for 6th	C. G. Borde and R. G. Nadkarni at Bombay...........................	1960-61
95 for 7th	S. M. H. Kirmani and Kapil Dev at Bombay...........................	1979-80
84 for 8th	K. D. Ghavri and Kapil Dev at Karachi................................	1978-79
149 for 9th†	P. G. Joshi and R. B. Desai at Bombay................................	1960-61
109 for 10th†	H. R. Adhikari and Ghulam Ahmed at Delhi..........................	1952-53

For Pakistan

162 for 1st	Hanif Mohammad and Imtiaz Ahmed at Madras.......................	1960-61
246 for 2nd	Hanif Mohammad and Saeed Ahmed at Bombay.......................	1960-61
166 for 3rd	Zaheer Abbas and Asif Iqbal at Faisalabad............................	1978-79
255 for 4th	Zaheer Abbas and Javed Miandad at Faisalabad......................	1978-79
155 for 5th	Alim-ud-Din and A. H. Kardar at Karachi.............................	1954-55
154 for 6th	Javed Miandad and Mushtaq Mohammad at Karachi.................	1978-79
88 for 7th	Mushtaq Mohammad and Intikhab Alam at Calcutta................	1960-61
82 for 8th	Wasim Raja and Iqbal Qasim at Kanpur................................	1979-80
60 for 9th	Wasim Bari and Iqbal Qasim at Bangalore............................	1979-80
104 for 10th	Zulfiqar Ahmed and Amir Elahi at Madras............................	1952-53

† *Denotes record partnership against all countries.*

TEN WICKETS OR MORE IN A MATCH

For India (2)

11-146 (4-90, 7-56)	Kapil Dev, Madras..	1979-80
13-131 (8-52, 5-79)†	V. Mankad, Delhi..	1952-53

For Pakistan (3)

12-94 (5-52, 7-42)	Fazal Mahmood, Lucknow..	1952-53
10-175 (4-135, 6-40)	Iqbal Qasim, Bombay..	1979-80
11-190 (8-69, 3-121)	Sikander Bakht, Delhi...	1979-80

† *Signifies ten wickets or more on first appearance in India–Pakistan Tests.*

PAKISTAN v SRI LANKA

	Captains					
Season	*Pakistan*	*Sri Lanka*	*T*	*P*	*SL*	*D*
1981-82*P*	Javed Miandad	B. Warnapura[1]	3	2	0	1

P Played in Pakistan.

Note: [1]L. R. D. Mendis deputised for the official touring captain in the Second Test.

HIGHEST INNINGS TOTALS

For Pakistan: 500-7 dec. at Lahore, 1981-82.
For Sri Lanka: 454 at Faisalabad, 1981-82.

LOWEST INNINGS TOTALS

For Pakistan: 270 at Faisalabad, 1981-82.
For Sri Lanka: 149 at Karachi, 1981-82.

INDIVIDUAL HUNDREDS IN THE MATCHES 1981-82

For Pakistan (4)

153† Haroon Rashid, Karachi... 1981-82
129 Mohsin Khan, Lahore...... 1981-82
100*† Salim Malik, Karachi....... 1981-82
134† Zaheer Abbas, Lahore..... 1981-82

For Sri Lanka (2)

109 R. L. Dias, Lahore......... 1981-82
157 S. Wettimuny, Faisalabad. 1981-82

† *Signifies hundred on first appearance in Pakistan–Sri Lanka Tests.*

RECORD PARTNERSHIPS FOR EACH WICKET

For Pakistan

79 for 1st	Mudassar Nazar and Mohsin Khan at Lahore	1981-82
151 for 2nd	Mohsin Khan and Majid J. Khan at Lahore	1981-82
92 for 3rd	Mohsin Khan and Javed Miandad at Faisalabad	1981-82
161 for 4th	Salim Malik and Javed Miandad at Karachi	1981-82
41 for 5th	Wasim Raja and Haroon Rashid at Karachi	1981-82
100 for 6th	Zaheer Abbas and Imran Khan at Lahore	1981-82
104 for 7th	Haroon Rashid and Tahir Naqqash at Karachi	1981-82
29 for 8th	Ashraf Ali and Iqbal Qasim at Faisalabad	1981-82
127 for 9th	Tahir Naqqash and Rashid Khan at Karachi	1981-82
48 for 10th	Rashid Khan and Tauseef Ahmed at Faisalabad	1981-82

For Sri Lanka

77 for 1st	S. Wettimuny and H. M. Goonatillake at Faisalabad	1981-82
217 for 2nd	S. Wettimuny and R. L. Dias at Faisalabad	1981-82
62 for 3rd	S. Wettimuny and R. L. Dias at Lahore	1981-82
47 for 4th	R. L. Dias and J. R. Ratnayeke at Karachi	1981-82
58 for 5th	R. L. Dias and L. R. D. Mendis at Lahore	1981-82
30 for 6th	A. Ranatunga and D. S. de Silva at Karachi	1981-82
	R. L. Dias and D. S. de Silva at Lahore	1981-82

43 for 7th	L. R. D. Mendis and D. S. de Silva at Karachi	1981-82
61 for 8th	R. S. Madugalle and D. S. de Silva at Faisalabad	1981-82
40* for 9th	A. L. F. de Mel and L. W. Kaluperuma at Faisalabad	1981-82
22 for 10th	H. M. Goonatillake and G. R. A. de Silva at Karachi	1981-82

TEN WICKETS OR MORE IN A MATCH

For Pakistan (1)

14-116 (8-58, 6-58)	Imran Khan, Lahore	1981-82

Note: The best match figures by a Sri Lankan bowler are 9-162 (4-103, 5-59) by D. S. de Silva at Faisalabad, 1981-82.

MISCELLANEOUS

RELATIONS IN TEST CRICKET

FATHERS AND SONS

England

J. Hardstaff (5 Tests, 1907-08) and J. Hardstaff jun. (23 Tests, 1935–1948).
Sir L. Hutton (79 Tests, 1937–1954-55) and R. A. Hutton (5 Tests, 1971).
F. T. Mann (5 Tests, 1922-23) and F. G. Mann (7 Tests, 1948-49–1949).
J. H. Parks (1 Test, 1937) and J. M. Parks (46 Tests, 1954–1967-68).
F. W. Tate (1 Test, 1902) and M. W. Tate (39 Tests, 1924–1935).
C. L. Townsend (2 Tests, 1899) and D. C. H. Townsend (3 Tests, 1934-35).

Australia

E. J. Gregory (1 Test, 1876-77) and S. E. Gregory (58 Tests, 1890–1912).

South Africa

F. Hearne (4 Tests, 1891-92–1895-96) and G. A. L. Hearne (3 Tests, 1922-23–1924).
F. Hearne also played 2 Tests for England in 1888-89.
J. D. Lindsay (3 Tests, 1947) and D. T. Lindsay (19 Tests, 1963-64–1969-70).
A. W. Nourse (45 Tests, 1902-03–1924) and A. D. Nourse (34 Tests, 1935–1951).
L. R. Tuckett (1 Test, 1913-14) and L. Tuckett (9 Tests, 1947–1948-49).

West Indies

G. A. Headley (22 Tests, 1929-30–1953-54) and R. G. A. Headley (2 Tests, 1973).
O. C. Scott (8 Tests, 1928–1930-31) and A. P. H. Scott (1 Test, 1952-53).

New Zealand

W. M. Anderson (1 Test, 1945-46) and R. W. Anderson (9 Tests, 1976-77–1978).
W. A. Hadlee (11 Tests, 1937–1950-51) and D. R. Hadlee (26 Tests, 1969–1977-78); R. J. Hadlee (38 Tests, 1972-73–1981-82).
H. G. Vivian (7 Tests, 1931–1937) and G. E. Vivian (5 Tests, 1964-65–1971-72).

India

L. Amarnath (24 Tests, 1933-34–1952-53) and M. Amarnath (26 Tests, 1969-70–1979-80); S. Amarnath (8 Tests, 1975-76–1978-79).
D. K. Gaekwad (11 Tests, 1952–1960-61) and A. D. Gaekwad (21 Tests, 1974-75–1979).
Nawab of Pataudi (Iftikhar Ali Khan) (3 Tests, 1946) and Nawab of Pataudi (Mansur Ali Khan) (46 Tests, 1961-62–1974-75).
Nawab of Pataudi sen. also played 3 Tests for England, 1932-33–1934.
V. Mankad (44 Tests, 1946–1958-59) and A. V. Mankad (22 Tests, 1969-70–1977-78).
Pankaj Roy (43 Tests, 1951-52–1960-61) and Pranab Roy (2 Tests, 1981-82).

India and Pakistan
M. Jahangir Khan (4 Tests, 1932–1936) and Majid J. Khan (62 Tests, 1964-65–1982).
S. Wazir Ali (7 Tests, 1932–1936) and Khalid Wazir (2 Tests, 1954).

Pakistan
Nazar Mohammad (5 Tests, 1952-53) and Mudassar Nazar (26 Tests, 1976-77–1982).

GRANDFATHERS AND GRANDSONS

Australia
V. Y. Richardson (19 Tests, 1924-25–1935-36) and G. S. Chappell (76 Tests, 1970-71–1981-82); I. M. Chappell (75 Tests, 1964-65–1979-80); T. M. Chappell (3 Tests, 1981).

GREAT-GRANDFATHER AND GREAT-GRANDSON

Australia
W. H. Cooper (2 Tests, 1881-82 and 1884-85) and A. P. Sheahan (31 Tests, 1967-68–1973-74).

BROTHERS IN SAME TEST TEAM

England
E. M., G. F. and W. G. Grace: 1 Test, 1880.
C. T. and G. B. Studd: 4 Tests, 1882-83.
A. and G. G. Hearne: 1 Test, 1891-92.
F. Hearne, their brother, played in this match for South Africa.
D. W. and P. E. Richardson: 1 Test, 1957.

Australia
E. J. and D. W. Gregory: 1 Test, 1876-77.
C. and A. C. Bannerman: 1 Test, 1878-79.
G. and W. F. Giffen: 2 Tests, 1891-92.
G. H. S. and A. E. Trott: 3 Tests, 1894-95.
I. M. and G. S. Chappell: 43 Tests, 1970-71–1979-80.

South Africa
S. J. and S. D. Snooke: 1 Test, 1907.
R. H. M. and P. A. M. Hands: 1 Test, 1913-14.
E. A. B. and A. M. B. Rowan: 9 Tests, 1948-49–1951.
P. M. and R. G. Pollock: 23 Tests, 1963-64–1969-70.
A. J. and D. B. Pithey: 5 Tests, 1963-64.

West Indies
G. C. and R. S. Grant: 4 Tests, 1934-35.
J. B. and V. H. Stollmeyer: 1 Test, 1939.
D. St E. and E. St E. Atkinson: 1 Test, 1957-58.

New Zealand
D. R. and R. J. Hadlee: 10 Tests, 1973–1977-78.
H. J. and G. P. Howarth: 4 Tests, 1974-75–1976-77.
J. M. and N. M. Parker: 3 Tests, 1976-77.
B. P. and J. G. Bracewell: 1 Test, 1980-81.

India
S. Wazir Ali and S. Nazir Ali: 2 Tests, 1932–1933-34.
L. Ramji and Amar Singh: 1 Test, 1933-34.
C. K. and C. S. Nayudu: 4 Tests, 1933-34–1936.
A. G. Kripal Singh and A. G. Milkha Singh: 1 Test, 1961-62.
S. and M. Amarnath: 8 Tests, 1975-76–1978-79.

Pakistan
Wazir and Hanif Mohammad: 18 Tests, 1952-53–1959-60.
Wazir and Mushtaq Mohammad: 1 Test, 1958-59.
Hanif and Mushtaq Mohammad: 19 Tests, 1960-61–1969-70.
Hanif, Mushtaq and Sadiq Mohammad: 1 Test, 1969-70.
Mushtaq and Sadiq Mohammad: 26 Tests, 1969-70–1978–79.

TEST MATCH GROUNDS

In Chronological Sequence

	City and Ground	*Date of First Test*	*Match*
1.	Melbourne, Melbourne Cricket Ground	March 15, 1877	Australia v England
2.	London, Kennington Oval	September 6, 1880	England v Australia
3.	Sydney, Sydney Cricket Ground (No. 1)	February 17, 1882	Australia v England
4.	Manchester, Old Trafford	July 11, 1884	England v Australia

This match was due to have started on July 10, but rain prevented any play.

5.	London, Lord's	July 21, 1884	England v Australia
6.	Adelaide, Adelaide Oval	December 12, 1884	Australia v England
7.	Port Elizabeth, St George's Park	March 12, 1889	South Africa v England
8.	Cape Town, Newlands	March 25, 1889	South Africa v England
9.	Johannesburg, Old Wanderers*	March 2, 1896	South Africa v England
10.	Nottingham, Trent Bridge	June 1, 1899	England v Australia
11.	Leeds, Headingley	June 29, 1899	England v Australia
12.	Birmingham, Edgbaston	May 29, 1902	England v Australia
13.	Sheffield, Bramall Lane*	July 3, 1902	England v Australia
14.	Durban, Lord's*	January 1, 1910	South Africa v England
15.	Durban, Kingsmead	January 18,1923	South Africa v England
16.	Brisbane, Exhibition Ground*	November 30, 1928	Australia v England
17.	Christchurch, Lancaster Park	January 10, 1930	New Zealand v England
18.	Bridgetown, Kensington Oval	January 11, 1930	West Indies v England
19.	Wellington, Basin Reserve	January 24, 1930	New Zealand v England
20.	Port-of-Spain, Queen's Park Oval	February 1, 1930	West Indies v England
21.	Auckland, Eden Park	February 17, 1930	New Zealand v England

This match was due to have started on February 14, but rain prevented any play on the first two days. February 16 was a Sunday.

22.	Georgetown, Bourda	February 21, 1930	West Indies v England
23.	Kingston, Sabina Park	April 3, 1930	West Indies v England
24.	Brisbane, Woolloongabba	November 27, 1931	Australia v South Africa
25.	Bombay, Gymkhana Ground*	December 15, 1933	India v England
26.	Calcutta, Eden Gardens	January 5, 1934	India v England
27.	Madras, Chepauk	February 10, 1934	India v England
28.	Delhi, Feroz Shah Kotla	November 10, 1948	India v West Indies
29.	Bombay, Brabourne Stadium*	December 9, 1948	India v West Indies
30.	Johannesburg, Ellis Park*	December 27, 1948	South Africa v England
31.	Kanpur, Green Park (Modi Stadium)	January 12, 1952	India v England
32.	Lucknow, University Ground*	October 25, 1952	India v Pakistan
33.	Dacca, Dacca Stadium*	January 1, 1955	Pakistan v India
34.	Bahawalpur, Dring Stadium	January 15, 1955	Pakistan v India
35.	Lahore, Lawrence Gardens (Bagh-i-Jinnah)*	January 29, 1955	Pakistan v India
36.	Peshawar, Gymkhana Ground	February 13, 1955	Pakistan v India
37.	Karachi, National Stadium	February 26, 1955	Pakistan v India
38.	Dunedin, Carisbrook	March 11, 1955	New Zealand v England
39.	Hyderabad, Fateh Maidan (Lal Bahadur Stadium)	November 19, 1955	India v New Zealand

	City and Ground	Date of First Test	Match
40.	Madras Corporation Stadium*	January 6, 1956	India v New Zealand
41.	Johannesburg, New Wanderers	December 24, 1956	South Africa v England
42.	Lahore, Gaddafi Stadium	November 21, 1959	Pakistan v Australia
43.	Rawalpindi, Rawalpindi Club Ground	March 27, 1965	Pakistan v New Zealand
44.	Nagpur, Vidarbha Cricket Association Ground	October 3, 1969	India v New Zealand
45.	Perth, Western Australian Cricket Association Ground	December 11, 1970	Australia v England
46.	Hyderabad, Niaz Stadium	March 16, 1973	Pakistan v England
47.	Bangalore, Karnataka Cricket Association Ground	November 22, 1974	India v West Indies
48.	Bombay, Wankhede Stadium	January 23, 1975	India v West Indies
49.	Faisalabad, Iqbal Park	October 16, 1978	Pakistan v India
50.	Napier, McLean Park	February 16, 1979	New Zealand v Pakistan
51.	Multan, Ibn-e-Qasim Bagh Stadium	December 30, 1980	Pakistan v West Indies
52.	St John's (Antigua), Recreation Ground	March 27, 1981	West Indies v England
53.	Colombo, Saravanamuttu Oval	February 17, 1982	Sri Lanka v England

* *Denotes no longer used for Test matches. In some instances the ground is no longer in existence.*

ENGLAND v REST OF THE WORLD

In 1970, owing to the cancellation of the South African tour to England, a series of matches was arranged, with the trappings of a full Test series, between England and the Rest of the World. It was played for the Guinness Trophy.

Captains: England	Captains: Rest	M	E	R
R. Illingworth	G. S. Sobers	5	1	4

HIGHEST TOTALS FOR AN INNINGS

By England	By Rest of the World
409 at Birmingham	563-9 at Birmingham

LOWEST TOTALS FOR AN INNINGS

By England	By Rest of the World
127 at Lord's	276 at Nottingham

INDIVIDUAL HUNDREDS IN THE MATCHES

For England (3)

157 G. Boycott, The Oval
110 B. L. D'Oliveira, Birmingham
113* B. W. Luckhurst, Nottingham

For Rest of the World (8)

119 E. J. Barlow, Lord's	101 C. H. Lloyd, Birmingham
142 E. J. Barlow, Nottingham	114 R. G. Pollock, The Oval
100 R. B. Kanhai, The Oval	183 G. S. Sobers, Lord's
114* C. H. Lloyd, Nottingham	114 G. S. Sobers, Leeds

TEN WICKETS OR MORE IN A MATCH

For Rest of the World (1)

12-142 (7-64, 5-78) E. J. Barlow, Leeds.

Note: The best match figures by an England bowler were 7-106 (4-43, 3-63), B. L. D'Oliveira, Nottingham; 7-130 (4-59, 3-71), A. W. Greig, Nottingham; and 7-117 (7-83, 0-34), P. Lever, The Oval.

HAT-TRICK AND FOUR WICKETS IN FIVE BALLS

E. J. Barlow (Rest of the World), Leeds.

APPEARANCES FOR REST OF THE WORLD

E. J. Barlow (5), F. M. Engineer (2), L. R. Gibbs (4), Intikhab Alam (5), R. B. Kanhai (5), C. H. Lloyd (5), G. D. McKenzie (3), D. L. Murray (3), Mushtaq Mohammad (2), P. M. Pollock (1), R. G. Pollock (5), M. J. Procter (5), B. A. Richards (5), G. S. Sobers (5).

Note: A list of those players who appeared for England in these matches may be found on page 152.

GENTLEMEN v PLAYERS

The highest individual scores were:

266*	J. B. Hobbs	Scarborough.	1925	215	W. G. Grace	The Oval.....	1870
247	R. Abel	The Oval.....	1901	203	T. W. Hayward	The Oval.....	1904
241	L. Hutton	Scarborough.	1953	201	L. E. G. Ames	Folkestone...	1933
232*	C. B. Fry	Lord's.........	1903	195	R. Abel	The Oval.....	1899
223	C. P. Mead	Scarborough.	1911	194*	E. H. Hendren	The Oval.....	1932
217	W. G. Grace	Hove..........	1871				

Notes: W. G. Grace made no fewer than fifteen hundreds for Gentlemen v Players. On his 58th birthday – at The Oval in July 1906 – he scored 74.

J. B. Hobbs in all matches under this title scored sixteen hundreds, and had an aggregate of 4,052 runs with an average of 54.75.

The match, first played in 1806, has not been contested since 1962, owing to the abolition of the amateur status in first-class cricket.

There were 137 matches played at Lord's from 1806; Players won 68, Gentlemen won 41, and 28 were drawn. Individual hundreds and results since 1919 appeared in *Wisden* 1963, page 358.

LARGE ATTENDANCES

Test Series

943,000	Australia v England (5 Tests)	1936-37
In England		
549,650	England v Australia (5 Tests)	1953

Test Match

†350,534	Australia v England, Melbourne (Third Test)	1936-37
325,000+	India v England, Calcutta (Second Test)	1972-73
In England		
158,000+	England v Australia, Leeds (Fourth Test)	1948
137,915	England v Australia, Lord's (Second Test)	1953

Test Match Day

90,800	Australia v West Indies, Melbourne (Fifth Test, 2nd day)	1960-61

Other First-Class Matches in England

80,000+	Surrey v Yorkshire, The Oval (3 days)	1906
78,792	Yorkshire v Lancashire, Leeds (3 days)	1904
76,617	Lancashire v Yorkshire, Manchester (3 days)	1926

† *Although no official figures are available, the attendance at the Fourth Test between India and England at Calcutta, 1981-82, was thought to have exceeded this figure.*

LORD'S CRICKET GROUND

Lord's and the MCC were founded in 1787. The Club has enjoyed an uninterrupted career since that date, but there have been three grounds known as Lord's. The first (1787-1810) was situated where Dorset Square now is; the second (1809-13), at North Bank, had to be abandoned owing to the cutting of the Regent's Canal; and the third, opened in 1814, is the present one at St John's Wood. It was not until 1866 that the freehold of Lord's was secured by the MCC. The present pavilion was erected in 1890 at a cost of £21,000.

HIGHEST INDIVIDUAL SCORES MADE AT LORD'S

316*	J. B. Hobbs	Surrey v Middlesex	1926
315*	P. Holmes	Yorkshire v Middlesex	1925
281*	W. H. Ponsford	Australians v MCC	1934
278	W. Ward	MCC v Norfolk (with E. H. Budd, T. Vigne and F. Ladbroke)	1820
278	D. G. Bradman	Australians v MCC	1938
277*	E. H. Hendren	Middlesex v Kent	1922

HIGHEST TOTALS OBTAINED AT LORD'S

First-Class Matches

729-6	Australia v England	1930
665	West Indians v Middlesex	1939
652-8	West Indies v England	1973
629	England v India	1974
612-8	Middlesex v Nottinghamshire	1921

610-5	Australians v Gentlemen	1948
609-8	Cambridge University v MCC and Ground	1913
608-7	Middlesex v Hampshire	1919
607	MCC and Ground v Cambridge University	1902

Minor Match

735-9	MCC and Ground v Wiltshire	1888

BIGGEST HIT AT LORD'S

The only known instance of a batsman hitting a ball over the present pavilion at Lord's occurred when A. E. Trott, appearing for MCC against Australians on July 31, August 1, 2, 1899, drove M. A. Noble so far and high that the ball struck a chimney pot and fell behind the building.

THROWING THE CRICKET BALL

140 yards 2 feet, Robert Percival, on the Durham Sands, Co. Durham Racecourse	1884
140 yards 9 inches, Ross Mackenzie, at Toronto	1872

Notes: W. F. Forbes, on March 16, 1876, threw 132 yards at the Eton College Sports. He was then 18 years of age.

William Yardley, while a boy at Rugby, threw 100 yards with his right hand and 78 yards with his left .

Charles Arnold, of Cambridge, once threw 112 yards with the wind and 108 against. W. H. Game, at The Oval in 1875, threw the ball 111 yards and then back the same distance. W. G. Grace threw 109 yards one way and back 105, and George Millyard 108 with the wind and 103 against. At The Oval in 1868, W. G. Grace made three successive throws of 116, 117 and 118 yards, and then threw back over 100 yards. D. G. Foster (Warwickshire) threw 133 yards, and in 1930 he made a Danish record with 120.1 metres – about 130 yards.

DATES OF FORMATION OF COUNTY CLUBS NOW FIRST-CLASS

County	First known county organisation	Present Club Original date	Present Club Reorganisation, if substantial
Derbyshire	November 4, 1870	November 4, 1870	—
Essex	By May, 1790	January 14, 1876	—
Glamorgan	1863	July 6, 1888	—
Gloucestershire	November 3, 1863	1871	—
Hampshire	April 3, 1849	August 12, 1863	July, 1879
Kent	August 6, 1842	March 1, 1859	December 6, 1870
Lancashire	January 12, 1864	January 12, 1864	—
Leicestershire	By August, 1820	March 25, 1879	—
Middlesex	December 15, 1863	February 2, 1864	—
Northamptonshire	1820	1820	July 31, 1878
Nottinghamshire	March/April, 1841	March/April, 1841	December 11, 1866
Somerset	October 15, 1864	August 18, 1875	—
Surrey	August 22, 1845	August 22, 1845	—
Sussex	June 16, 1836	March 1, 1839	August, 1857
Warwickshire	May, 1826	1882	—
Worcestershire	1844	March 5, 1865	—
Yorkshire	March 7, 1861	January 8, 1863	December 10, 1891

DATES OF FORMATION OF CLUBS IN THE CURRENT MINOR COUNTIES CHAMPIONSHIP

County	*First known county organisation*	*Present Club*
Bedfordshire	May, 1847	November 3, 1899
Berkshire	By May, 1841	March 17, 1895
Buckinghamshire	November, 1864	January 15, 1891
Cambridgeshire	March 13, 1844	June 6, 1891
Cheshire	1819	September 29, 1908
Cornwall	1813	November 12, 1894
Cumberland	January 2, 1884	April 10, 1948
Devon	1824	November 26, 1899
Dorset	1862 *or* 1871	February 5, 1896
Durham	January 24, 1874	May 10, 1882
Hertfordshire	1838	March 8, 1876
Lincolnshire	1853	September 28, 1906
Norfolk	January 11, 1827	October 14, 1876
Northumberland	1834	December, 1895
Oxfordshire	1787	December 14, 1921
Shropshire	1819 *or* 1829	June 28, 1956
Staffordshire	November 24, 1871	November 24, 1871
Suffolk	July 27, 1864	August, 1932
Wiltshire	February 24, 1881	January, 1893

CONSTITUTION OF COUNTY CHAMPIONSHIP

There are references in the sporting press to a champion county as early as 1825, but the list is not continuous and in some years only two counties contested the title. The earliest reference in any cricket publication is from 1864, and at this time there were eight leading counties who have come to be regarded as first-class from that date – Cambridgeshire, Hampshire, Kent, Middlesex, Nottinghamshire, Surrey, Sussex and Yorkshire. The newly formed Lancashire club began playing inter-county matches in 1865, Gloucestershire in 1870 and Derbyshire in 1871, and they are therefore regarded as first-class from these respective dates. Cambridgeshire dropped out after 1871, Hampshire, who had not played inter-county matches in certain seasons, after 1885, and Derbyshire after 1887. Somerset, who had played matches against the first-class counties since 1879, were regarded as first-class from 1882 to 1885, and were admitted formally to the Championship in 1891. In 1894, Derbyshire, Essex, Leicestershire and Warwickshire were granted first-class status, but did not compete in the Championship until 1895 when Hampshire returned. Worcestershire, Northamptonshire and Glamorgan were admitted to the Championship in 1899, 1905 and 1921 respectively and are regarded as first-class from these dates. An invitation in 1921 to Buckinghamshire to enter the Championship was declined, owing to the lack of necessary playing facilities, and an application by Devon in 1948 was unsuccessful.

MOST COUNTY CHAMPIONSHIP APPEARANCES

763	W. Rhodes	Yorkshire	1898-1930
707	F. E. Woolley	Kent	1906-38
665	C. P. Mead	Hampshire	1906-36

MOST CONSECUTIVE COUNTY CHAMPIONSHIP APPEARANCES

423	K. G. Suttle	Sussex	1954-69
412	J. G. Binks	Yorkshire	1955-69
399	J. Vine	Sussex	1899-1914
344	E. H. Killick	Sussex	1898-1912
326	C. N. Woolley	Northamptonshire	1913-31
305	A. H. Dyson	Glamorgan	1930-47
301	B. Taylor	Essex	1961-72

Notes: J. Vine made 417 consecutive appearances for Sussex in *all* first-class matches between July 1900 and September 1914.

J. G. Binks did not miss a Championship match for Yorkshire between making his début in June 1955 and retiring at the end of the 1969 season.

CHAMPION COUNTY SINCE 1864

Note: The earliest county champions were decided usually by the fewest matches lost, but in 1888 an unofficial points system was introduced. In 1890, the Championship was constituted officially. Since 1977, it has been sponsored by Schweppes.

1864	Surrey
1865	Nottinghamshire
1866	Middlesex
1867	Yorkshire
1868	Nottinghamshire
1869	Nottinghamshire Yorkshire
1870	Yorkshire
1871	Nottinghamshire
1872	Nottinghamshire
1873	Gloucestershire Nottinghamshire
1874	Gloucestershire
1875	Nottinghamshire
1876	Gloucestershire
1877	Gloucestershire
1878	Undecided
1879	Nottinghamshire Lancashire
1880	Nottinghamshire
1881	Lancashire
1882	Nottinghamshire Lancashire
1883	Nottinghamshire
1884	Nottinghamshire
1885	Nottinghamshire
1886	Nottinghamshire
1887	Surrey
1888	Surrey
1889	Surrey Lancashire Nottinghamshire
1890	Surrey
1891	Surrey
1892	Surrey
1893	Yorkshire
1894	Surrey
1895	Surrey
1896	Yorkshire
1897	Lancashire
1898	Yorkshire
1899	Surrey
1900	Yorkshire
1901	Yorkshire
1902	Yorkshire
1903	Middlesex
1904	Lancashire
1905	Yorkshire
1906	Kent
1907	Nottinghamshire
1908	Yorkshire
1909	Kent
1910	Kent
1911	Warwickshire
1912	Yorkshire
1913	Kent
1914	Surrey
1919	Yorkshire
1920	Middlesex
1921	Middlesex
1922	Yorkshire
1923	Yorkshire
1924	Yorkshire
1925	Yorkshire
1926	Lancashire
1927	Lancashire
1928	Lancashire
1929	Nottinghamshire
1930	Lancashire
1931	Yorkshire
1932	Yorkshire
1933	Yorkshire
1934	Lancashire
1935	Yorkshire
1936	Derbyshire
1937	Yorkshire
1938	Yorkshire
1939	Yorkshire
1946	Yorkshire
1947	Middlesex
1948	Glamorgan
1949	Middlesex Yorkshire
1950	Lancashire Surrey
1951	Warwickshire
1952	Surrey
1953	Surrey
1954	Surrey
1955	Surrey
1956	Surrey
1957	Surrey
1958	Surrey
1959	Yorkshire
1960	Yorkshire
1961	Hampshire
1962	Yorkshire
1963	Yorkshire
1964	Worcestershire
1965	Worcestershire
1966	Yorkshire
1967	Yorkshire
1968	Yorkshire
1969	Glamorgan
1970	Kent
1971	Surrey
1972	Warwickshire
1973	Hampshire
1974	Worcestershire
1975	Leicestershire
1976	Middlesex
1977	Middlesex Kent
1978	Kent
1979	Essex
1980	Middlesex
1981	Nottinghamshire
1982	Middlesex

Notes: The title has been won outright as follows: Yorkshire 31 times, Surrey 18, Nottinghamshire 13, Lancashire 8, Middlesex 8, Kent 6, Gloucestershire 3, Warwickshire 3, Worcestershire 3, Glamorgan 2, Hampshire 2, Derbyshire 1, Essex 1, Leicestershire 1.

Eight times the title has been shared as follows: Nottinghamshire 5, Lancashire 4, Middlesex 2, Surrey 2, Yorkshire 2, Gloucestershire 1, Kent 1.

The earliest date the Championship has been won in any season since it was expanded in 1895 was August 12, 1910, by Kent.

THE MINOR COUNTIES CHAMPIONS

1895	Norfolk, Durham, Worcestershire
1896	Worcestershire
1897	Worcestershire
1898	Worcestershire
1899	Northamptonshire, Buckinghamshire
1900	Glamorgan, Durham, Northamptonshire
1901	Durham
1902	Wiltshire
1903	Northamptonshire
1904	Northamptonshire
1905	Norfolk
1906	Staffordshire
1907	Lancashire II
1908	Staffordshire
1909	Wiltshire
1910	Norfolk
1911	Staffordshire
1912	In abeyance
1913	Norfolk
1920	Staffordshire
1921	Staffordshire
1922	Buckinghamshire
1923	Buckinghamshire
1924	Berkshire
1925	Buckinghamshire
1926	Durham
1927	Staffordshire
1928	Berkshire
1929	Oxfordshire
1930	Durham
1931	Leicestershire II
1932	Buckinghamshire
1933	Undecided
1934	Lancashire II
1935	Middlesex II
1936	Hertfordshire
1937	Lancashire II
1938	Buckinghamshire
1939	Surrey II
1946	Suffolk
1947	Yorkshire II
1948	Lancashire II
1949	Lancashire II
1950	Surrey II
1951	Kent II
1952	Buckinghamshire
1953	Berkshire
1954	Surrey II
1955	Surrey II
1956	Kent II
1957	Yorkshire II
1958	Yorkshire II
1959	Warwickshire II
1960	Lancashire II
1961	Somerset II
1962	Warwickshire II
1963	Cambridgeshire
1964	Lancashire II
1965	Somerset II
1966	Lincolnshire
1967	Cheshire
1968	Yorkshire II
1969	Buckinghamshire
1970	Bedfordshire
1971	Yorkshire II
1972	Bedfordshire
1973	Shropshire
1974	Oxfordshire
1975	Hertfordshire
1976	Durham
1977	Suffolk
1978	Devon
1979	Suffolk
1980	Durham
1981	Durham
1982	Oxfordshire

SECOND ELEVEN CHAMPIONS

1959	Gloucestershire
1960	Northamptonshire
1961	Kent
1962	Worcestershire
1963	Worcestershire
1964	Lancashire
1965	Glamorgan
1966	Surrey
1967	Hampshire
1968	Surrey
1969	Kent
1970	Kent
1971	Hampshire
1972	Nottinghamshire
1973	Essex
1974	Middlesex
1975	Surrey
1976	Kent
1977	Yorkshire
1978	Sussex
1979	Warwickshire
1980	Glamorgan
1981	Hampshire
1982	Worcestershire

HONOURS' LIST

In 1982, the following were decorated for services to cricket.

New Year's Honours: R. W. Abbott (Australia) MBE; G. F. Goddard (to cricket in Scotland) MBE; R. W. Marsh (Australia) MBE; R. G. D. Willis (England) MBE.

Queen's Birthday Honours: A. V. Bedser (England) CBE; A. Jones (to cricket in Wales) MBE.

FEATURES OF 1982

Double-Hundreds

311*	G. M. Turner	Worcestershire v Warwickshire at Worcester (County record).
254	G. W. Humpage	Warwickshire v Lancashire at Southport.
239*	G. M. Turner	Worcestershire v Oxford University at Oxford.
235	A. I. Kallicharran	Warwickshire v Worcestershire at Worcester.
230*	A. I. Kallicharran	Warwickshire v Lancashire at Southport.
212*	A. W. Stovold	Gloucestershire v Northamptonshire at Northampton.
211*	Mudassar Nazar	Pakistanis v Sussex at Hove.
210	A. I. Kallicharran	Warwickshire v Leicestershire at Leicester.
209*	S. P. Henderson	Cambridge University v Middlesex at Cambridge.
208	I. T. Botham	England v India at The Oval.
206*	M. C. J. Nicholas	Hampshire v Oxford University at Oxford.
203*	W. N. Slack	Middlesex v Oxford University at Oxford.
203*	Mohsin Khan	Pakistanis v Leicestershire at Leicester.
203	R. A. Woolmer	Kent v Sussex at Tunbridge Wells.
200*	J. A. Ormrod	Worcestershire v Gloucestershire at Worcester.
200	Mohsin Khan	Pakistan v England at Lord's.

Hundred in Each Innings of a Match

123	119	R. J. Boyd-Moss	Cambridge University v Warwickshire at Cambridge.
126	128*	G. Fowler	Lancashire v Warwickshire at Southport.
164*	123*	P. N. Kirsten	Derbyshire v Surrey at Derby.
132*	102*	J. W. Lloyds	Somerset v Northamptonshire at Northampton.
162*	107	Zaheer Abbas	Gloucestershire v Lancashire at Gloucester.

Fastest Hundred

52 minutes: I. T. Botham for Somerset v Warwickshire at Taunton.

Hundred Before Lunch

B. F. Davison, Leicestershire v Middlesex at Uxbridge (1st day).
G. M. Turner, Worcestershire v Warwickshire at Worcester (1st day).
G. M. Turner, Worcestershire v Lancashire at Worcester (3rd day).
Zaheer Abbas, Pakistanis v Derbyshire at Chesterfield (3rd day).

First to 1,000 Runs

M. W. Gatting (Middlesex) on June 26.

First to 2,000 Runs

A. I. Kallicharran (Warwickshire) on September 14.

1,000 Runs and 50 Wickets

I. T. Botham (Somerset)........... 1,241 runs and 66 wickets.
R. C. Ontong (Glamorgan)........ 1,205 runs and 64 wickets.
D. N. Patel (Worcestershire)...... 1,104 runs and 50 wickets.
P. Willey (Northamptonshire)..... 1,783 runs and 51 wickets.

100 Wickets and 500 Runs

M. D. Marshall (Hampshire)...... 134 wickets and 633 runs.

Carrying Bat Through Completed Innings

J. C. Balderstone (114* out of 246), Leicestershire v Essex at Colchester.
C. G. Greenidge (157* out of 270), Hampshire v Glamorgan at Cardiff.
W. Larkins (118* out of 223), Northamptonshire v Yorkshire at Northampton.
J. G. Wright (141* out of 259), Derbyshire v Nottinghamshire at Chesterfield.

Partnerships of 250 and Over

470 (4th wicket) A. I. Kallicharran (230*) and G. W. Humpage (254), Warwickshire v Lancashire at Southport – English record.
319 (1st wicket) Mudassar Nazar (211*) and Mohsin Khan (151), Pakistanis v Sussex at Hove.
316* (2nd wicket) A. R. Butcher (187*) and D. M. Smith (105*), Surrey v Warwickshire at Birmingham.
291 (1st wicket) G. M. Turner (311*) and J. A. Ormrod (79), Worcestershire v Warwickshire at Worcester.
278 (1st wicket) G. Cook (112*) and W. Larkins (186), Northamptonshire v Yorkshire at Middlesbrough.
256* (6th wicket) C. J. Tavaré (168*) and A. P. E. Knott (115*), Kent v Essex at Chelmsford.
251* (3rd wicket) C. G. Greenidge (183*) and T. E. Jesty (135*), Hampshire v Glamorgan at Portsmouth.

Highest Innings Totals

616 for six declared: Kent v Oxford University at Oxford.
594: England v India at The Oval.
536 for seven declared: Surrey v Worcestershire at Worcester.
523 for four declared: Warwickshire v Lancashire at Southport.
502: Essex v Warwickshire at Colchester.
501 for one declared: Worcestershire v Warwickshire at Worcester.

Lowest Innings Totals

43†: Warwickshire v Sussex at Birmingham.
56: Hampshire v Nottinghamshire at Nottingham.
57: Kent v Nottinghamshire at Nottingham.
57: Somerset v Middlesex at Weston-super-Mare.

†*Nine wickets fell.*

Eight Wickets or More in an Innings

Nine for 61	W. W. Daniel	Middlesex v Glamorgan at Swansea.
Eight for 56	A. M. E. Roberts	Leicestershire v Glamorgan at Leicester.
Eight for 68	K. I. Hodgson	Cambridge University v Glamorgan at Cambridge.
Eight for 70	G. Miller	Derbyshire v Leicestershire at Coalville.
Eight for 71	M. D. Marshall	Hampshire v Worcestershire at Southampton.
Eight for 80	P. H. Edmonds	Middlesex v Sussex at Lord's.

Thirteen or More Wickets in a Match

Fourteen for 94 (6–38 & 8–56)	A. M. E. Roberts	Leicestershire v Glamorgan at Leicester.
Thirteen for 122 (7–44 & 6–78)	Abdul Qadir	Pakistanis v Sussex at Hove.

First to 100 Wickets

M. D. Marshall (Hampshire) on August 25.

Eight or More Dismissals in a Match by a Wicket-keeper

Eleven	D. L. Bairstow (11ct)	Yorkshire v Derbyshire at Scarborough.
Eight	D. E. East (8ct)	Essex v Derbyshire at Southend.
	E. W. Jones (8ct)	Glamorgan v Essex at Cardiff.
	A. P. E. Knott (7ct, 1st)	Kent v Leicestershire at Canterbury.

Career Aggregate Milestones

35,000 runs:	D. L. Amiss.
30,000 runs:	Zaheer Abbas.
25,000 runs:	J. M. Brearley.
20,000 runs:	S. M. Gavaskar, I. V. A. Richards.
15,000 runs:	C. E. B. Rice.
10,000 runs:	P. W. Denning, B. R. Hardie, W. Larkins, A. W. Stovold, C. J. Tavaré.
100 hundreds:	G. M. Turner.
50 hundreds:	A. I. Kallicharran.
1,000 wickets:	J. N. Shepherd.
500 wickets:	P. Carrick, W. W. Daniel, D. A. Graveney, T. E. Jesty, N. Phillip, C. E. Waller.

County Caps Awarded in 1982

Derbyshire	K. J. Barnett, J. H. Hampshire.
Essex	D. E. East, D. R. Pringle.
Glamorgan	D. A. Francis, B. J. Lloyd.
Hampshire	M. C. J. Nicholas, R. J. Parks.
Kent	N. R. Taylor.
Lancashire	J. Abrahams, C. E. H. Croft.
Leicestershire	N. G. B. Cook.
Nottinghamshire	M. Hendrick.
Somerset	J. W. Lloyds.
Surrey	M. A. Lynch, D. J. Thomas.
Sussex	A. C. S. Pigott, C. M. Wells.
Warwickshire	G. C. Small.
Yorkshire	S. N. Hartley, K. Sharp.

No caps were awarded by Gloucestershire, Middlesex, Northamptonshire, and Worcestershire.

FIELDING IN 1982

76	R. J. Parks (70ct, 6st)
74	D. E. East (65ct, 9st)
64	B. N. French (61ct, 3st)
61	D. L. Bairstow (57ct, 4st)
61	P. R. Downton (51ct, 10st)
55	C. J. Richards (52ct, 3st)
55	G. Sharp (48ct, 7st)
53	A. P. E. Knott (46ct, 7st)
52	R. W. Taylor (48ct, 4st)
51	R. W. Tolchard (44ct, 7st)
50	G. W. Humpage (49ct, 1st)
49	I. J. Gould (44ct, 5st)
46	D. J. Humphries (41ct, 5st)
45	A. J. Brassington (37ct, 8st)
44	D. J. S. Taylor (40ct, 4st)
41	E. W. Jones (37ct, 4st)
30	J. W. Lloyds
28	M. W. Gatting
27	J. F. Steele
26	G. Cook
26	C. S. Cowdrey
26	J. M. Rice
25	C. Maynard (20ct, 5st)
25	J. R. T. Barclay
25	G. A. Gooch
25	C. E. B. Rice
24	J. Abrahams
24	Javed Miandad
24	D. G. Moir
24	C. P. Phillipson
24	A. W. Stovold
23	C. F. E. Goldie (19ct, 4st)
23	C. G. Greenidge
22	C. W. J. Athey
21	T. Davies (20ct, 1st)
21	R. O. Butcher
21	R. E. East
21	P. W. G. Parker
21	W. N. Slack
21	B. Wood
20	N. G. B. Cook
20	G. W. Johnson
20	D. N. Patel
20	N. E. J. Pocock
20	C. T. Radley

R. W. Tolchard's total includes ten catches taken as a fielder.

FIRST-CLASS AVERAGES, 1982

BATTING

(Qualification: 8 innings, average 10.00)

**Signifies not out.*   *† Denotes a left-handed batsman.*

	I	NO	R	HI	Avge	100s
G. M. Turner (*Worcestershire*)	16	3	1,171	311*	90.07	5
Zaheer Abbas (*Gloucestershire and Pakistanis*)	25	4	1,475	162*	70.23	5
†A. I. Kallicharran (*Warwickshire*)	37	5	2,120	235	66.25	8
P. N. Kirsten (*Derbyshire*)	37	7	1,941	164*	64.70	8
G. Boycott (*Yorkshire*)	37	6	1,913	159	61.70	6
M. W. Gatting (*Middlesex*)	34	6	1,651	192	58.96	6
T. E. Jesty (*Hampshire*)	36	8	1,645	164*	58.75	8
†J. G. Wright (*Derbyshire*)	39	6	1,830	190	55.45	7
B. F. Davison (*Leicestershire*)	37	4	1,800	172	54.54	7
†Younis Ahmed (*Worcestershire*)	29	6	1,247	122	54.21	4
J. Simmons (*Lancashire*)	21	12	487	79*	54.11	0
P. Willey (*Northamptonshire*)	41	6	1,783	145	50.94	5
†D. M. Smith (*Surrey*)	25	4	1,065	160	50.71	3
Javed Miandad (*Glamorgan and Pakistanis*)	29	8	1,051	105*	50.04	1
D. P. Hughes (*Lancashire*)	36	9	1,303	126*	48.25	3
C. J. Tavaré (*Kent*)	36	4	1,522	168*	47.56	3
D. W. Randall (*Nottinghamshire*)	33	4	1,369	130*	47.20	4
J. M. Brearley (*Middlesex*)	32	9	1,083	165	47.08	3
S. J. O'Shaughnessy (*Lancashire*)	19	7	560	62	46.66	0
A. J. Lamb (*Northamptonshire*)	30	2	1,302	140	46.50	5
†D. I. Gower (*Leicestershire*)	35	2	1,530	176*	46.36	2
C. G. Greenidge (*Hampshire*)	41	8	1,526	183*	46.24	3
I. V. A. Richards (*Somerset*)	31	2	1,324	181*	45.65	4
W. Larkins (*Northamptonshire*)	44	3	1,863	186	45.43	5
†B. C. Rose (*Somerset*)	32	8	1,090	173*	45.41	2
Imran Khan (*Sussex and Pakistanis*)	20	7	588	85	45.23	0
R. J. Boyd-Moss (*Cambridge University and Northamptonshire*)	41	5	1,602	137	44.50	5
R. S. Cowan (*Oxford University and Sussex*)	16	4	533	143*	44.41	2
I. T. Botham (*Somerset*)	29	1	1,241	208	44.32	3
G. A. Gooch (*Essex*)	38	1	1,632	149	44.10	3
†W. N. Slack (*Middlesex*)	40	6	1,499	203*	44.08	2
†M. R. Benson (*Kent*)	30	5	1,100	137	44.00	3
C. W. J. Athey (*Yorkshire*)	38	7	1,339	134	43.19	4
Kapil Dev (*Northamptonshire and Indians*)	20	2	770	103	42.77	2
P. Bainbridge (*Gloucestershire*)	33	8	1,069	103	42.76	2
R. A. Woolmer (*Kent*)	22	3	809	203	42.57	2
R. O. Butcher (*Middlesex*)	28	3	1,058	197	42.32	3
B. R. Hardie (*Essex*)	39	5	1,432	161	42.11	1
†G. Fowler (*Lancashire*)	35	2	1,387	150	42.03	5
†C. H. Lloyd (*Lancashire*)	29	2	1,135	100	42.03	1
J. H. Hampshire (*Derbyshire*)	36	6	1,256	101*	41.86	1
K. S. McEwan (*Essex*)	37	3	1,421	150*	41.79	3
†S. P. Henderson (*Cambridge U.*)	16	3	531	209*	40.84	1
L. Potter (*Kent*)	21	2	775	118	40.78	2

	I	NO	R	HI	Avge	100s
G. Miller (*Derbyshire*)	26	7	772	98	40.63	0
K. R. Pont (*Essex*)	24	7	687	89	40.41	0
†D. Lloyd (*Lancashire*)	36	2	1,371	114	40.32	5
G. P. Howarth (*Surrey*)	32	3	1,158	156*	39.93	4
†A. R. Butcher (*Surrey*)	43	5	1,514	187*	39.84	4
M. C. J. Nicholas (*Hampshire*)	42	9	1,312	206*	39.75	3
D. W. Varey (*Cambridge University*)	17	3	548	156*	39.14	1
K. W. R. Fletcher (*Essex*)	36	4	1,249	124	39.03	3
J. C. Balderstone (*Leicestershire*)	41	3	1,482	148	39.00	4
A. P. Wells (*Sussex*)	9	3	233	70	38.83	0
D. A. Francis (*Glamorgan*)	33	5	1,076	142*	38.42	2
G. W. Humpage (*Warwickshire*)	41	4	1,407	254	38.02	4
D. L. Amiss (*Warwickshire*)	38	1	1,404	156	37.94	1
K. P. Tomlins (*Middlesex*)	17	1	607	146	37.93	2
A. M. Ferreira (*Warwickshire*)	10	2	303	112*	37.87	1
†J. Abrahams (*Lancashire*)	32	5	1,013	124	37.51	1
Asif Iqbal (*Kent*)	17	2	558	115*	37.20	1
D. S. Steele (*Northamptonshire*)	36	13	853	74*	37.08	0
†T. A. Lloyd (*Warwickshire*)	45	5	1,432	122	35.80	2
†Sadiq Mohammad (*Gloucestershire*)	29	1	998	91	35.64	0
†A. Jones (*Glamorgan*)	47	5	1,491	146*	35.50	4
E. A. Baptiste (*Kent*)	12	3	319	69*	35.44	0
A. P. E. Knott (*Kent*)	32	5	942	115*	34.88	1
J. D. Birch (*Nottinghamshire*)	35	6	1,011	125	34.86	2
N. E. Briers (*Leicestershire*)	38	4	1,175	106	34.55	1
N. R. Taylor (*Kent*)	43	4	1,340	143*	34.35	3
R. G. P. Ellis (*Oxford University and Middlesex*)	25	1	823	105*	34.29	1
J. E. Emburey (*Middlesex*)	27	5	752	100*	34.18	1
J. G. Varey (*Oxford University*)	12	5	239	68	34.14	0
B. Dudleston (*Gloucestershire*)	12	1	373	111	33.90	1
D. R. Pringle (*Cambridge University and Essex*)	26	4	741	127	33.68	1
J. D. Love (*Yorkshire*)	29	6	773	123	33.60	2
C. E. B. Rice (*Nottinghamshire*)	36	3	1,095	144	33.18	1
A. W. Stovold (*Gloucestershire*)	42	1	1,350	212*	32.92	2
C. M. Wells (*Sussex*)	41	3	1,248	126	32.84	3
†G. S. Clinton (*Surrey*)	23	4	622	172*	32.73	2
C. J. C. Rowe (*Glamorgan*)	39	6	1,071	105	32.45	1
B. Hassan (*Nottinghamshire*)	34	4	970	89*	32.33	0
K. J. Barnett (*Derbyshire*)	25	5	642	120	32.10	2
M. A. Lynch (*Surrey*)	38	2	1,155	141*	32.08	3
G. S. le Roux (*Sussex*)	28	5	737	83	32.04	0
D. G. Aslett (*Kent*)	28	3	794	82	31.76	0
R. M. Carter (*Northamptonshire*)	19	6	411	79	31.61	0
G. Cook (*Northamptonshire*)	43	2	1,285	125	31.34	3
K. S. Mackintosh (*Surrey*)	10	7	94	31	31.33	0
K. A. Hayes (*Oxford University and Lancashire*)	22	3	594	152	31.26	1
G. R. J. Roope (*Surrey*)	25	7	560	108	31.11	1
R. G. Williams (*Northamptonshire*)	39	4	1,087	141	31.05	2
A. M. Green (*Sussex*)	26	1	776	99	31.04	0
†R. J. Hadlee (*Nottinghamshire*)	28	2	807	131	31.03	2
G. D. Mendis (*Sussex*)	42	2	1,240	114	31.00	2
†R. D. V. Knight (*Surrey*)	40	4	1,114	111	30.94	2
C. T. Radley (*Middlesex*)	28	3	773	141*	30.92	2
R. C. Ontong (*Glamorgan*)	43	4	1,205	152*	30.89	3
R. D. Jackman (*Surrey*)	22	8	430	68	30.71	0
I. S. Anderson (*Derbyshire*)	26	4	671	103*	30.50	1
I. P. Butcher (*Leicestershire*)	9	3	182	71*	30.33	0

	I	*NO*	*R*	*HI*	*Avge*	*100s*
S. N. Hartley (*Yorkshire*)	30	9	635	114	30.23	1
A. J. Hignell (*Gloucestershire*)	28	6	664	72	30.18	0
†K. Sharp (*Yorkshire*)	18	2	478	115	29.87	1
R. Marsden (*Oxford University*)	10	1	264	60	29.33	0
†N. A. Felton (*Somerset*)	12	0	346	71	28.83	0
D. L. Bairstow (*Yorkshire*)	30	9	603	77	28.71	0
S. Turner (*Essex*)	28	4	679	83	28.29	0
J. R. T. Barclay (*Sussex*)	33	6	761	95	28.18	0
†B. C. Broad (*Gloucestershire*)	41	0	1,153	97	28.12	0
R. T. Robinson (*Nottinghamshire*)	38	3	984	109	28.11	1
R. W. Tolchard (*Leicestershire*)	38	8	843	93*	28.10	0
P. H. Edmonds (*Middlesex*)	22	4	505	92	28.05	0
G. J. Toogood (*Oxford University*)	18	4	392	83	28.00	0
P. A. Neale (*Worcestershire*)	44	8	1,006	79*	27.94	0
P. W. Romaines (*Gloucestershire*)	24	2	609	186	27.68	1
T. S. Curtis (*Worcestershire*)	17	4	359	59*	27.61	0
T. M. Lamb (*Northamptonshire*)	13	8	137	39*	27.40	0
G. Monkhouse (*Surrey*)	10	5	137	63*	27.40	0
†J. W. Lloyds (*Somerset*)	39	3	981	132*	27.25	2
J. A. Ormrod (*Worcestershire*)	38	2	981	200*	27.25	1
J. A. Hopkins (*Glamorgan*)	41	5	978	124	27.16	1
N. Phillip (*Essex*)	32	3	783	79	27.00	0
R. G. D. Willis (*Warwickshire*)	22	9	351	72	27.00	0
D. N. Patel (*Worcestershire*)	42	1	1,104	133	26.92	1
Asif Din (*Warwickshire*)	34	2	855	102	26.71	1
†D. J. Humphries (*Worcestershire*)	37	5	852	98	26.62	0
R. G. Lumb (*Yorkshire*)	33	1	844	81	26.37	0
P. W. G. Parker (*Sussex*)	43	9	896	106	26.35	1
P. A. Slocombe (*Somerset*)	23	1	579	78	26.31	0
P. M. Roebuck (*Somerset*)	40	3	958	90	25.89	0
†P. W. Denning (*Somerset*)	22	1	541	91*	25.76	0
B. N. French (*Nottinghamshire*)	34	6	721	79	25.75	0
D. A. Graveney (*Gloucestershire*)	30	11	489	55*	25.73	0
C. S. Cowdrey (*Kent*)	35	4	794	72*	25.61	0
D. J. Capel (*Northamptonshire*)	22	4	460	60*	25.55	0
P. A. Smith (*Warwickshire*)	16	1	383	68	25.53	0
E. E. Hemmings (*Nottinghamshire*)	25	8	432	127*	25.41	1
B. Wood (*Derbyshire*)	38	4	851	124*	25.02	1
†A. L. Jones (*Glamorgan*)	38	2	900	88	25.00	0
C. J. Richards (*Surrey*)	38	9	716	117*	24.68	1
K. D. Smith (*Warwickshire*)	34	6	691	67	24.67	0
P. A. Todd (*Nottinghamshire*)	21	2	461	117*	24.26	2
†D. J. Thomas (*Surrey*)	20	3	409	64	24.05	0
†I. J. Gould (*Sussex*)	32	3	695	94	23.96	0
N. F. M. Popplewell (*Somerset*)	24	5	451	55	23.73	0
G. B. Stevenson (*Yorkshire*)	19	4	356	115*	23.73	1
†K. I. Hodgson (*Cambridge University*)	10	1	213	50	23.66	0
J. N. Shepherd (*Gloucestershire*)	34	9	590	67*	23.60	0
T. Davies (*Glamorgan*)	16	4	283	66*	23.58	0
P. Carrick (*Yorkshire*)	21	3	423	93	23.50	0
A. J. Wright (*Gloucestershire*)	19	2	399	65	23.47	0
M. J. Weston (*Worcestershire*)	31	1	704	93	23.46	0
G. C. Holmes (*Glamorgan*)	10	1	210	68	23.33	0
A. Sidebottom (*Yorkshire*)	18	8	233	44*	23.30	0
C. Lethbridge (*Warwickshire*)	21	5	369	87*	23.06	0
†D. R. Turner (*Hampshire*)	21	1	459	96	22.95	0
J. P. C. Mills (*Cambridge University*)	17	0	389	98	22.88	0
A. Needham (*Surrey*)	20	6	319	134*	22.78	1
M. D. Marshall (*Hampshire*)	31	3	633	116*	22.60	1
†R. M. Ellison (*Kent*)	11	3	179	46*	22.37	0

	I	NO	R	HI	Avge	100s
R. S. Luddington (*Oxford University*)..	14	1	290	65	22.30	0
†G. D. Barlow (*Middlesex*).................	12	3	199	37*	22.11	0
P. J. W. Allott (*Lancashire*)..............	15	5	220	41*	22.00	0
†A. Kennedy (*Lancashire*)..................	12	1	242	43	22.00	0
N. E. J. Pocock (*Hampshire*).............	30	2	616	164	22.00	1
S. A. B. Daniels (*Glamorgan*)...........	15	6	197	73	21.88	0
D. E. East (*Essex*).........................	32	8	525	78	21.87	0
H. L. Alleyne (*Worcestershire*)...........	9	3	130	32	21.66	0
N. G. Cowley (*Hampshire*)................	28	1	584	104	21.62	1
G. W. Johnson (*Kent*)......................	34	7	582	86	21.55	0
J. W. Southern (*Hampshire*)..............	21	7	300	50*	21.42	0
V. J. Marks (*Somerset*).....................	33	5	599	71*	21.39	0
A. W. Lilley (*Essex*)........................	14	1	276	67	21.23	0
†R. E. Hayward (*Hampshire*)..............	9	1	169	59	21.12	0
R. A. Cobb (*Leicestershire*)...............	37	1	760	64	21.11	0
G. Sharp (*Northamptonshire*).............	26	7	401	58*	21.10	0
P. R. Downton (*Middlesex*)...............	25	2	483	65	21.00	0
I. Cockbain (*Lancashire*)..................	25	1	492	98	20.50	0
†S. J. G. Doggart (*Cambridge U.*)........	13	1	242	64	20.16	0
A. Hill (*Derbyshire*).........................	14	3	219	54	19.90	0
A. M. E. Roberts (*Leicestershire*).......	20	3	338	47	19.88	0
M. A. Garnham (*Leicestershire*).........	17	2	298	57	19.86	0
J. F. Steele (*Leicestershire*)...............	31	6	496	63	19.84	0
S. Oldham (*Derbyshire*)...................	18	10	156	35*	19.50	0
J. M. Rice (*Hampshire*).....................	44	4	777	69	19.42	0
†N. Gifford (*Worcestershire*)...............	15	7	155	31*	19.37	0
A. E. Warner (*Worcestershire*)...........	17	2	287	67	19.13	0
H. R. Moseley (*Somerset*).................	19	13	113	24*	18.83	0
I. A. Greig (*Sussex*).........................	28	1	507	109	18.77	1
N. F. Williams (*Middlesex*)...............	11	5	112	27*	18.66	0
J. D. Inchmore (*Worcestershire*).........	19	3	294	68	18.37	0
†B. W. Reidy (*Lancashire*).................	13	2	199	37	18.09	0
†C. H. Dredge (*Somerset*)..................	26	8	317	54*	17.61	0
M. A. Fell (*Nottinghamshire*).............	18	0	315	108	17.50	1
†M. W. Stovold (*Gloucestershire*).........	9	0	155	52	17.22	0
E. J. O. Hemsley (*Worcestershire*)......	24	1	393	49	17.08	0
N. G. B. Cooke (*Leicestershire*).........	25	8	284	37	16.70	0
R. E. East (*Essex*)...........................	23	2	344	58	16.38	0
J. Garner (*Somerset*)........................	11	5	98	40*	16.33	0
S. T. Clarke (*Surrey*)........................	25	0	408	52	16.32	0
T. J. Boon (*Leicestershire*)................	14	1	210	90	16.15	0
C. J. Tunnicliffe (*Derbyshire*)............	19	2	273	40	16.05	0
K. Saxelby (*Nottinghamshire*)............	15	5	160	59*	16.00	0
R. K. Illingworth (*Worcestershire*).......	16	4	191	47*	15.91	0
D. J. S. Taylor (*Somerset*)................	26	5	334	67	15.90	0
P. R. Oliver (*Warwickshire*)..............	9	0	143	46	15.88	0
N. J. B. Illingworth (*Nottinghamshire*).	14	4	158	49	15.80	0
†G. J. Parsons (*Leicestershire*)............	32	7	392	51	15.68	0
I. Folley (*Lancashire*).......................	15	4	165	36	15.00	0
†A. J. Webster (*Worcestershire*)...........	10	5	75	25	15.00	0
E. W. Jones (*Glamorgan*)..................	21	3	268	65	14.88	0
M. K. Bore (*Nottinghamshire*)...........	8	5	44	23*	14.66	0
W. W. Daniel (*Middlesex*)................	15	9	88	21	14.66	0
C. P. Phillipson (*Sussex*)..................	22	3	274	64	14.42	0
Sarfraz Nawaz (*Northamptonshire and Pakistanis*)......................................	9	1	115	26	14.37	0
R. J. Parks (*Hampshire*)....................	30	5	350	44	14.00	0
†C. M. Old (*Yorkshire*)......................	18	3	207	32	13.80	0
†C. Penn (*Kent*)...............................	8	4	54	30	13.50	0
N. A. Mallender (*Northamptonshire*)...	17	8	121	42	13.44	0

	I	*NO*	*R*	*HI*	*Avge*	*100s*
R. P. Moulding (*Oxford University*)....	20	2	242	67	13.44	0
C. Maynard (*Warwickshire and Lancashire*).................................	20	3	227	40	13.35	0
B. J. Lloyd (*Glamorgan*)....................	32	8	318	48	13.25	0
J. G. Thomas (*Glamorgan*)................	13	0	172	84	13.23	0
G. C. Small (*Warwickshire*)...............	29	5	309	57*	12.87	0
C. F. E. Goldie (*Cambridge U.*).........	9	0	115	31	12.77	0
C. E. H. Croft (*Lancashire*)..............	12	3	109	20	12.11	0
C. E. Waller (*Sussex*).......................	27	12	181	50	12.06	0
R. W. Taylor (*Derbyshire*)	29	5	286	54	11.91	0
†K. E. Cooper (*Nottinghamshire*).........	26	5	247	38*	11.76	0
D. L. Underwood (*Kent*)..................	22	11	129	30	11.72	0
F. D. Stephenson (*Gloucestershire*).....	10	1	105	63	11.66	0
S. R. Barwick (*Glamorgan*)...............	17	6	126	24	11.45	0
†M. A. Nash (*Glamorgan*)..................	20	1	216	37	11.36	0
P. G. Newman (*Derbyshire*)	22	4	204	39*	11.33	0
J. P. Agnew (*Leicestershire*)...............	12	1	122	56	11.09	0
T. M. Tremlett (*Hampshire*)..............	22	3	209	48	11.00	0
M. S. Scott (*Worcestershire*)..............	11	0	118	37	10.72	0
A. J. Pollock (*Cambridge University*)...	8	2	63	19	10.50	0
A. C. S. Pigott (*Sussex*)....................	23	7	167	40	10.43	0

BOWLING

(Qualification: 10 wickets in 10 innings)

† *Denotes left-arm bowler.*

	O	*M*	*R*	*W*	*Avge*	*BB*
R. J. Hadlee (*Nottinghamshire*)..........	403.5	122	889	61	14.57	7-25
M. D. Marshall (*Hampshire*).............	822	225	2,108	134	15.73	8-71
M. W. Gatting (*Middlesex*)...............	135	40	343	21	16.33	5-34
Imran Khan (*Sussex and Pakistanis*)....	484.4	134	1,079	64	16.85	7-52
W. W. Daniel (*Middlesex*)................	469.4	107	1,245	71	17.53	9-61
J. Garner (*Somerset*)........................	259.1	76	583	33	17.66	6-23
M. Hendrick (*Nottinghamshire*)..........	244.2	86	473	26	18.19	5-21
G. S. le Roux (*Sussex*)......................	467	116	1,210	65	18.61	5-15
A. M. E. Roberts (*Leicestershire*).......	428.2	114	1,081	55	19.65	8-56
F. D. Stephenson (*Gloucestershire*).....	197.2	40	632	32	19.75	5-64
S. T. Clarke (*Surrey*)........................	659.3	162	1,696	85	19.95	6-63
†J. F. Steele (*Leicestershire*)...............	470.2	134	1,075	52	20.67	5-4
T. E. Jesty (*Hampshire*)....................	288.1	89	750	35	21.42	6-71
K. Saxelby (*Nottinghamshire*)............	292.4	68	799	37	21.59	4-18
†M. K. Bore (*Nottinghamshire*)...........	279.1	104	609	28	21.75	6-134
N. G. Cowans (*Middlesex*)................	222.3	50	721	33	21.84	5-28
L. B. Taylor (*Leicestershire*).............	582.1	153	1,465	67	21.86	5-24
†P. H. Edmonds (*Middlesex*)..............	789	242	1,768	80	22.10	8-80
†D. L. Underwood(*Kent*)...................	690.4	223	1,751	78	22.44	7-79
N. Phillip (*Essex*).............................	584.1	107	1,842	82	22.46	6-50
W. N. Slack (*Middlesex*)...................	81	18	225	10	22.50	3-17
S. J. Malone (*Hampshire*)	150.5	35	505	22	22.95	7-55
I. T. Botham (*Somerset*)...................	491.4	113	1,517	66	22.98	5-46
J. E. Emburey (*Middlesex*)................	764.5	198	1,787	77	23.20	5-50
†N. G. B. Cook (*Leicestershire*)..........	847.1	260	2,093	90	23.25	7-63
J. G. Thomas (*Glamorgan*)...............	140	25	514	22	23.36	5-61

	O	*M*	*R*	*W*	*Avge*	*BB*
†J. K. Lever (*Essex*)	543.5	112	1,683	72	23.37	6-48
D. R. Pringle (*Cambridge University and Essex*)	433.1	122	1,087	46	23.63	6-33
K. St J. D. Emery (*Hampshire*)	659	152	1,969	83	23.72	6-51
†J. W. Southern (*Hampshire*)	439.5	118	1,314	55	23.89	5-51
T. M. Tremlett (*Hampshire*)	353.3	114	766	32	23.93	5-59
R. D. Jackman (*Surrey*)	674.1	196	1,751	73	23.98	6-28
J. D. Inchmore (*Worcestershire*)	326.2	68	841	35	24.02	7-53
G. A. Gooch (*Essex*)	230	72	541	22	24.59	7-14
A. Sidebottom (*Yorkshire*)	495.2	95	1,538	62	24.80	6-31
E. E. Hemmings (*Nottinghamshire*)	666.1	199	1,611	64	25.17	6-76
K. E. Cooper (*Nottinghamshire*)	685	191	1,719	68	25.27	6-46
I. A. Greig (*Sussex*)	581.1	131	1,723	68	25.33	5-46
†D. P. Hughes (*Lancashire*)	292.3	79	789	31	25.45	4-22
Sarfraz Nawaz (*Northamptonshire and Pakistanis*)	327.4	72	920	36	25.55	6-92
B. J. Griffiths (*Northamptonshire*)	411.1	91	1,200	46	26.08	5-71
C. M. Old (*Yorkshire*)	458.2	125	1,229	47	26.14	6-76
J. Simmons (*Lancashire*)	538.4	152	1,284	49	26.20	5-57
S. J. O'Shaughnessy (*Lancashire*)	209.2	34	710	27	26.29	4-66
†D. S. Steele (*Northamptonshire*)	755	245	1,846	70	26.37	6-59
S. P. Hughes (*Middlesex*)	218.5	30	723	27	26.77	4-28
P. Willey (*Northamptonshire*)	670.1	223	1,371	51	26.88	6-17
R. M. Ellison (*Kent*)	153.5	35	433	16	27.06	3-12
†P. J. Hacker (*Derbyshire*)	174.1	25	677	25	27.08	5-51
K. I. Hodgson (*Cambridge University*)	198.1	42	625	23	27.17	8-68
†D. G. Moir (*Derbyshire*)	811.5	231	2,076	76	27.31	6-63
†R. E. East (*Essex*)	490.5	141	1,231	45	27.35	6-80
A. C. S. Pigott (*Sussex*)	477	92	1,684	61	27.60	7-74
†I. Folley (*Lancashire*)	309	76	758	27	28.07	4-40
H. R. Moseley (*Somerset*)	320	68	985	35	28.14	5-40
†D. A. Graveney (*Gloucestershire*)	498.4	145	1,242	44	28.22	7-37
R. G. D. Willis (*Warwickshire*)	446	89	1,444	51	28.31	6-45
V. J. Marks (*Somerset*)	700.4	199	1,951	68	28.69	7-51
G. R. Dilley (*Kent*)	563.2	124	1,839	64	28.73	6-71
P. M. Such (*Nottinghamshire*)	232.1	51	737	25	29.48	5-112
†C. E. Waller (*Sussex*)	605	171	1,627	55	29.58	7-67
D. L. Acfield (*Essex*)	565.2	129	1,332	45	29.60	4-35
M. W. W. Selvey (*Middlesex*)	254.5	74	597	20	29.85	3-47
K. S. Mackintosh (*Surrey*)	304.2	59	1,023	34	30.08	6-61
P. I. Pocock (*Surrey*)	233	64	632	21	30.09	5-73
G. Miller (*Derbyshire*)	455.3	135	1,058	35	30.22	8-70
A. M. Ferreira (*Warwickshire*)	243.3	49	789	26	30.34	5-109
C. E. H. Croft (*Lancashire*)	304	60	1,003	33	30.39	7-88
G. C. Small (*Warwickshire*)	589.1	106	1,925	63	30.55	7-68
D. N. Patel (*Worcestershire*)	572.2	146	1,531	50	30.62	7-46
S. R. Barwick (*Glamorgan*)	323.2	79	981	32	30.65	5-44
W. W. Davis (*Glamorgan*)	390.5	70	1,296	42	30.85	7-101
J. W. Lloyds (*Somerset*)	469.3	102	1,463	46	31.80	7-88
D. Surridge (*Gloucestershire*)	561	159	1,507	47	32.06	5-78
J. N. Shepherd (*Gloucestershire*)	743.1	175	2,026	63	32.15	6-75
S. Oldham (*Derbyshire*)	507.5	98	1,544	48	32.16	7-78
R. C. Ontong (*Glamorgan*)	639.1	130	2,059	64	32.17	6-50
P. J. W. Allott (*Lancashire*)	453	128	1,172	36	32.55	5-58
G. B. Stevenson (*Yorkshire*)	443.4	95	1,474	45	32.75	5-72
†C. J. Tunnicliffe (*Derbyshire*)	383.1	92	1,213	37	32.78	5-73
G. Monkhouse (*Surrey*)	131.3	27	395	12	32.91	3-40
†M. A. Nash (*Glamorgan*)	418.2	103	1,276	38	33.57	5-35
C. Lethbridge (*Warwickshire*)	304.3	68	977	29	33.68	5-68
R. G. Williams (*Northamptonshire*)	274	75	747	22	33.95	4-25

	O	M	R	W	Avge	BB
G. W. Johnson (*Kent*)	330.4	84	892	26	34.30	5-36
A. J. Pollock (*Cambridge University*)	115.5	18	483	14	34.50	5-108
C. H. Dredge (*Somerset*)	446.5	109	1,214	35	34.68	3-33
S. P. Perryman (*Worcestershire*)	430.1	111	1,216	35	34.74	6-49
†N. Gifford (*Worcestershire*)	500	157	1,080	31	34.83	6-48
L. L. McFarlane (*Lancashire*)	223.5	43	946	27	35.03	6-59
R. J. Doughty (*Gloucestershire*)	149.1	19	533	15	35.53	6-43
N. F. Williams (*Middlesex*)	236.4	33	819	23	35.60	4-38
†P. Carrick (*Yorkshire*)	568.5	144	1,425	40	35.62	6-90
†D. J. Thomas (*Surrey*)	426.4	109	1,284	36	35.66	4-39
S. Turner (*Essex*)	453	117	1,080	30	36.00	4-53
A. P. Pridgeon (*Worcestershire*)	463	103	1,184	32	37.00	4-39
N. A. Mallender (*Northamptonshire*)	562.2	131	1,860	50	37.20	7-41
A. E. Warner (*Worcestershire*)	202.1	34	707	19	37.21	4-73
N. G. Cowley (*Hampshire*)	310.1	86	895	24	37.29	6-48
H. L. Alleyne (*Worcestershire*)	207.3	44	599	16	37.43	4-92
C. S. Cowdrey (*Kent*)	166.3	39	533	14	38.07	3-45
†D. Lloyd (*Lancashire*)	297.2	68	801	21	38.14	4-36
K. B. S. Jarvis (*Kent*)	636	145	2,078	54	38.48	5-94
G. J. Parsons (*Leicestershire*)	518.1	89	1,931	50	38.62	5-25
B. J. Lloyd (*Glamorgan*)	687.2	138	2,201	55	40.01	5-58
†M. R. Davis (*Somerset*)	145	19	481	12	40.08	3-36
N. J. B. Illingworth (*Nottinghamshire*)	164.1	29	565	14	40.35	5-89
A. I. Kallicharran (*Warwickshire*)	154.2	21	578	14	41.28	3-32
P. G. Newman (*Derbyshire*)	458.3	73	1,661	40	41.52	4-59
S. A. B. Daniels (*Glamorgan*)	223.2	37	836	20	41.80	3-49
Kapil Dev (*Northamptonshire and Indians*)	395.2	77	1,214	29	41.86	5-39
I. V. A. Richards (*Somerset*)	265.3	75	671	16	41.93	3-6
T. M. Lamb (*Northamptonshire*)	308.5	77	850	20	42.50	5-37
J. P. Agnew (*Leicestershire*)	203.5	27	816	19	42.94	4-55
†J. H. Childs (*Gloucestershire*)	656.3	201	1,681	38	44.23	5-112
†R. K. Illingworth (*Worcestershire*)	260.4	59	811	18	45.05	4-85
†B. W. Reidy (*Lancashire*)	137	32	457	10	45.70	3-33
C. J. C. Rowe (*Glamorgan*)	265.2	57	898	19	47.26	3-67
J. Cumbes (*Warwickshire*)	349.1	71	993	21	47.28	4-47
A. J. Webster (*Worcestershire*)	202.1	36	716	15	47.73	5-87
P. Bainbridge (*Gloucestershire*)	301	77	915	19	48.15	6-59
S. P. Sutcliffe (*Warwickshire*)	554.4	114	1,799	37	48.62	5-151
R. D. V. Knight (*Surrey*)	266.2	61	762	15	50.80	3-34
A. Needham (*Surrey*)	357	72	1,167	22	53.04	5-91
P. A. Smith (*Warwickshire*)	136	21	536	10	53.60	2-12
E. A. Baptiste (*Kent*)	186.4	45	671	12	55.91	3-41
Asif Din (*Warwickshire*)	284.1	60	1,128	20	56.40	5-100
J. Abrahams (*Lancashire*)	316.1	61	921	16	57.56	2-19
†R. W. M. Palmer (*Cambridge U.*)	219.4	34	849	14	60.64	4-96
S. P. Ridge (*Oxford University*)	240.1	32	829	13	63.76	4-128
J. R. T. Barclay (*Sussex*)	230.2	58	702	11	63.81	3-44
B. Wood (*Derbyshire*)	231.2	54	690	10	69.00	2-0

The following bowlers took ten wickets but bowled in fewer than ten innings:

K. R. Pont (*Essex*)	62	11	158	10	15.80	5-17
†S. J. Dennis (*Yorkshire*)	95	16	365	12	30.41	5-42
N. A. Foster (*Essex*)	125	29	425	12	35.41	3-32
I. J. Curtis (*Oxford University*)	214.4	45	659	15	43.93	5-140
†T. J. Taylor (*Oxford University and Lancashire*)	165	25	541	10	54.10	5-118

INDIVIDUAL SCORES OF 100 AND OVER

There were 281 three-figure innings in first-class cricket in 1982, seventeen more than in 1981. The list includes 209 hit in the County Championship and 53 in other first-class games, but not the seven hit by the Indian touring team nor the twelve by the Pakistani touring team, which can be found in their respective sections.

**Signifies not out.*

T. E. Jesty (8)
164* Hants v Indians, Southampton
135* Hants v Glam., Portsmouth
134 Hants v Warw., Southampton
133 Hants v Pakistanis, Bournemouth
123 Hants v Worcs., Southampton
121 Hants v Glos., Bournemouth
109 Hants v Yorks., Bournemouth
106 Hants v Essex, Chelmsford

A. I. Kallicharran (8)
235 Warw. v Worcs., Worcester
230* Warw. v Lancs., Southport
210 Warw. v Leics., Leicester
195 Warw. v Surrey, Birmingham
173 Warw. v Glos., Nuneaton
131 Warw. v Hants., Southampton
109* Warw. v Worcs., Birmingham
105 Warw. v Kent, Dartford

P. N. Kirsten (8)
164* } 123 } Derby. v Surrey, Derby
143 Derby. v Glos., Gloucester
140* Derby. v Yorks., Scarborough
121* Derby. v Leics., Derby
113 Derby. v Essex, Southend
105* Derby. v Sussex, Chesterfield
102 Derby. v Leics., Coalville

B. F. Davison (7)
172 Leics. v Hants, Southampton
139* Leics. v Worcs., Worcester
119 Leics. v Glam., Leicester
111 Leics. v Surrey, Leicester
110* Leics. v Essex, Colchester
100* Leics. v Kent, Canterbury
100 Leics. v Middx, Uxbridge

J. G. Wright (7)
190 Derby. v Yorks., Derby
185* Derby. v Northants, Derby
157 Derby. v Northants, Northampton
141* Derby. v Notts., Chesterfield
107 Derby. v Hants, Derby
106 Derby. v Essex, Chesterfield
103* Derby. v Middx, Lord's

G. Boycott (6)
159 Yorks. v Worcs., Sheffield
152* Yorks. v Warw., Leeds
138 Yorks. v Northants, Northampton
134 Yorks. v Glam., Leeds
129 Yorks. v Somerset, Weston-super-Mare
122* Yorks. v Sussex, Scarborough

M. W. Gatting (6)
192 Middx v Surrey, The Oval
164* Middx v Cambridge U., Cambridge
141 Middx v Yorks., Lord's
140 Middx v Derby., Lord's
133* Middx v Lancs., Lord's
114 Middx v Kent, Tunbridge Wells

R. J. Boyd-Moss (5)
137 Northants v Derby., Northampton
123 } 119 } Cambridge U. v Warw., Cambridge
114* Northants v Glos., Northampton
100 Cambridge U. v Oxford U., Lord's

G. Fowler (5)
150 Lancs. v Warw., Birmingham
126 } 128* } Lancs. v Warw., Southport
122 Lancs. v Essex, Liverpool
100 Lancs. v Glos., Gloucester

A. J. Lamb (5)
140 Northants v Hants, Northampton
140 Northants v Oxford U., Oxford
107* England v India, The Oval
106 Northants v Essex, Chelmsford
102 Northants v Leics., Leicester

W. Larkins (5)
186 Northants v Yorks., Middlesbrough
137 Northants v Somerset, Northampton
118* Northants v Yorks., Northampton
110* Northants v Worcs., Northampton
105 Northants v Derby., Northampton

D. Lloyd (5)
114 Lancs. v Derby., Manchester
112* Lancs. v Northants, Manchester
112 Lancs. v Hants, Southampton
108 Lancs. v Glos., Gloucester
103 Lancs. v Kent, Manchester

G. M. Turner (5)
311* Worcs. v Warw., Worcester
239* Worcs. v Oxford U., Oxford
118 Worcs. v Kent, Hereford
115 Worcs. v Lancs., Worcester
112 Worcs. v Yorks., Sheffield

P. Willey (5)
145 Northants v Derby., Derby
140 Northants v Essex, Northampton
117 Northants v Glam., Swansea
102 Northants v Lancs., Manchester
100* Northants v Oxford U., Oxford

C. W. J. Athey (4)
140* Yorks. v Surrey, The Oval
134 Yorks. v Derby., Derby
100 Yorks. v Glam., Leeds
100 Yorks. v Kent, Leeds

J. C. Balderstone (4)
148 Leics. v Middx, Uxbridge
118 Leics. v Glam., Leicester
114* Leics. v Essex, Colchester
103* Leics. v Glos., Leicester

A. R. Butcher (4)
187* Surrey v Warw., Birmingham
162 Surrey v Worcs., Worcester
151 Surrey v Leics., Leicester
131 Surrey v Oxford U., Oxford

G. P. Howarth (4)
156* Surrey v Glam., Guildford
126* Surrey v Yorks., The Oval
121 Surrey v Derby., Derby
112 Surrey v Middx, Lord's

G. W. Humpage (4)
254 Warw. v Lancs., Southport
146 Warw. v Northants, Birmingham
121* Warw. v Oxford U., Oxford
113 Warw. v Somerset, Taunton

A. Jones (4)
146* Glam. v Worcs., Worcester
136* Glam. v Kent, Canterbury
103 Glam. v Notts., Swansea
103 Glam. v Cambridge U., Cambridge

D. W. Randall (4)
130* MCC v Indians, Lord's
126 England v India, Lord's
122 Notts. v Worcs., Worcester
105 England v Pakistan, Birmingham

I. V. A. Richards (4)
181* Somerset v Pakistanis, Taunton
178 Somerset v Lancs., Taunton
146 Somerset v Kent, Taunton
135 Somerset v Warw., Birmingham

Younis Ahmed (4)
122 Worcs. v Leics., Worcester
114* Worcs. v Glos., Worcester
114 Worcs. v Notts., Worcester
110 Worcs. v Warw., Birmingham

M. R. Benson (3)
137 Kent v Sussex, Hove
120 Kent v Oxford U., Oxford
107 Kent v Worcs., Hereford

I. T. Botham (3)
208 England v India, The Oval
131* Somerset v Warw., Taunton
128 England v India, Manchester

J. M. Brearley (3)
165 Middx v Northants, Lord's
135 Middx v Notts., Nottingham
100* Middx v Sussex, Hove

R. O. Butcher (3)
197 Middx v Yorks., Lord's
173 Middx v Glos., Cheltenham
122 Middx v Glam., Swansea

G. Cook (3)
125 Northants v Leics., Leicester
112* Northants v Yorks., Middlesbrough
101 Northants v Glos., Bristol

K. W. R. Fletcher (3)
124 Essex v Northants, Northampton
122 Essex v Surrey, Chelmsford
120 Essex v Middx, Lord's

G. A. Gooch (3)
149 Essex v Kent, Canterbury
140 Essex v Surrey, The Oval
127 Essex v Kent, Chelmsford

C. G. Greenidge (3)
183* Hants v Glam., Portsmouth
157* Hants v Glam., Cardiff
156 Hants v Indians, Southampton

D. P. Hughes (3)
126* Lancs. v Yorks., Leeds
111 Lancs. v Derby., Derby
106 Lancs. v Cambridge U., Cambridge

M. A. Lynch (3)
141* Surrey v Glam., Guildford
118 Surrey v Notts., The Oval
102 Surrey v Sussex, The Oval

K. S. McEwan (3)
150* Essex v Derby., Chesterfield
128 Essex v Warw., Colchester
116 Essex v Derby., Southend

M. C. J. Nicholas (3)
206* Hants v Oxford U., Oxford
127* Hants v Sussex, Basingstoke
107* Hants v Pakistanis, Bournemouth

R. C. Ontong (3)
152* Glam. v Glos., Swansea
110 Glam. v Surrey, Guildford
106* Glam. v Cambridge U., Cambridge

D. M. Smith (3)
160 Surrey v Worcs., Worcester
105* Surrey v Warw., Birmingham
100* Surrey v Yorks., The Oval

C. J. Tavaré (3)
168* Kent v Essex, Chelmsford
125 Kent v Oxford U., Oxford
122* Kent v Somerset, Taunton

N. R. Taylor (3)
143* Kent v Warw., Dartford
127 Kent v Oxford U., Oxford
100 Kent v Middx, Tunbridge Wells

C. M. Wells (3)
126 Sussex v Kent, Hove
123* Sussex v Notts., Hove
100* Sussex v Glos., Bristol

Zaheer Abbas (3)
162* } Glos. v Lancs., Gloucester
107 }
144 Glos. v Oxford U., Oxford

P. Bainbridge (2)
103 Glos. v Yorks., Bradford
101* Glos. v Glam., Swansea

K. J. Barnett (2)
120 Derby. v Warw., Birmingham
100* Derby. v Glam., Derby

J. D. Birch (2)
125 Notts. v Leics., Nottingham
102* Notts. v Lancs., Nottingham

G. S. Clinton (2)
172* Surrey v Oxford U., Oxford
102 Surrey v Leics., Leicester

R. S. Cowan (2)
143* Oxford U. v Northants, Oxford
108 Oxford U. v Kent, Oxford

D. A. Francis (2)
142* Glam. v Kent, Canterbury
127 Glam. v Somerset, Taunton

D. I. Gower (2)
176* Leics. v Pakistanis, Leicester
111 Leics. v Somerset, Taunton

R. J. Hadlee (2)
131 Notts. v Surrey, The Oval
100* Notts. v Worcs., Worcester

Kapil Dev (2)
103 Northants v Sussex, Eastbourne
100* Northants v Derby., Northampton

R. D. V. Knight (2)
111 Surrey v Pakistanis, The Oval
104* Surrey v Oxford U., Oxford

T. A. Lloyd (2)
122 Warw. v Glam., Cardiff
120 Warw. v Worcs., Birmingham

J. W. Lloyds (2)
132*}
102*} Somerset v Northants, Northampton

J. D. Love (2)
123 Yorks. v Surrey, The Oval
110 Yorks. v Derby., Derby

G. D. Mendis (2)
114 Sussex v Pakistanis, Hove
104 Sussex v Lancs., Manchester

L. Potter (2)
118 Kent v Indians, Canterbury
108 Kent v Middx, Lord's

C. T. Radley (2)
141* Middx v Kent, Tunbridge Wells
106 Middx v Warw., Coventry

B. C. Rose (2)
173* Somerset v Glos., Bristol
102* Somerset v Warw., Birmingham

W. N. Slack (2)
203* Middx v Oxford U., Oxford
114 Middx v Cambridge U., Cambridge

A. W. Stovold (2)
212* Glos. v Northants, Northampton
100 Glos. v Warw., Nuneaton

P. A. Todd (2)
117* Notts. v Yorks., Worksop
104* Notts. v Cambridge U., Cambridge

K. P. Tomlins (2)
146 Middx v Oxford U., Oxford
138 Middx v Notts., Lord's

R. G. Williams (2)
141 Northants v Cambridge U., Cambridge
106* Northants v Oxford U., Oxford

R. A. Woolmer (2)
203 Kent v Sussex, Tunbridge Wells
126 Kent v Oxford U., Oxford

The following each played one three-figure innings:

J. Abrahams, 124, Lancs. v Surrey, Manchester; D. L. Amiss, 156, Warw. v Somerset, Birmingham; I. S. Anderson, 103*, Derby. v Hants, Derby; Asif Din, 102, Warw. v Middx, Coventry; Asif Iqbal, 115*, Kent v Warw., Dartford.
N. E. Briers, 106, Leics. v Yorks., Hinckley.
N. G. Cowley, 104, Hants v Leics., Southampton; M. D. Crowe, 104, D. B. Close's XI v Pakistanis, Scarborough.
B. Dudleston, 111, Glos. v Hants, Bournemouth.
R. G. P. Ellis, 105*, Oxford U. v Surrey, Oxford; J. E. Emburey, 100*, Middx v Northants, Lord's.
M. A. Fell, 108, Notts. v Essex, Nottingham; A. M. Ferreira, 112*, Warw. v Indians, Birmingham.
I. A. Greig, 109, Sussex v Warw., Birmingham.
S. J. Halliday, 113*, Oxford U. v Kent, Oxford; J. H. Hampshire, 101*, Derby. v Lancs., Derby; B. R. Hardie, 161, Essex v Indians, Chelmsford; S. N. Hartley, 114, Yorks. v Glos., Bradford; K. A. Hayes, 152, Oxford U. v Warw., Oxford; E. E. Hemmings, 127*, Notts. v Yorks., Worksop; S. P. Henderson, 209*, Cambridge U. v Middx, Cambridge; J. A. Hopkins, 124, Glam. v Surrey, Guildford.
A. P. E. Knott, 115*, Kent v Essex, Chelmsford.
C. H. Lloyd, 100, Lancs. v Yorks., Manchester.
M. D. Marshall, 116*, Hants v Lancs., Southampton.
A. Needham, 134*, Surrey v Lancs., Manchester.
J. A. Ormrod, 200*, Worcs. v Glos., Worcester.
P. W. G. Parker, 106, Sussex v Leics., Hove; D. N. Patel, 133, Worcs. v Surrey, Worcester; N. E. J. Pocock, 164, Hants v Lancs., Southampton; D. R. Pringle, 127, Cambridge U. v Glam., Cambridge.

C. E. B. Rice, 144, Notts. v Derby., Nottingham; C. J. Richards, 117*, Surrey v Notts., The Oval; R. T. Robinson, 109, Notts. v Sussex, Hove; P. W. Romaines, 186, Glos. v Warw., Nuneaton; G. R. J. Roope, 108, Surrey v Northants, Northampton; C. J. C. Rowe, 105, Glam. v Somerset, Taunton.

K. Sharp, 115, Yorks. v Indians, Bradford; G. B. Stevenson, 115*, Yorks. v Warw., Birmingham.

D. W. Varey, 156*, Cambridge U. v Northants, Cambridge.

B. Wood, 124*, Derby. v Notts., Nottingham.

TEN WICKETS IN A MATCH

There were 23 instances of bowlers taking ten or more wickets in a match in first-class cricket in 1982, six fewer than in 1981. The list includes nineteen in the County Championship, one by the Pakistani touring side and three in other first-class matches.

M. D. Marshall (4)
11-107 Hants v Sussex, Eastbourne
11-128 Hants v Worcs., Southampton
10-76 Hants v Surrey, The Oval
10-109 Hants v Kent, Maidstone

P. H. Edmonds (2)
12-120 Middx v Sussex, Lord's
10-107 Middx v Hants, Uxbridge

The following each took ten wickets in a match on one occasion:

Abdul Qadir, 13-122, Pakistanis v Sussex, Hove.

S. T. Clarke, 10-109, Surrey v Northants, Northampton; N. G. B. Cook, 12-130, Leics. v Essex, Colchester.

W. W. Daniel, 11-97, Middx v Glam., Swansea; G. R. Dilley, 10-116, Kent v Leics., Canterbury.

K. St J. D. Emery, 10-101, Hants v Glam., Portsmouth.

J. Garner, 11-80, Somerset v Hants, Bournemouth.

K. I. Hodgson, 10-139, Cambridge U. v Glam., Cambridge.

J. K. Lever, 10-136, Essex v Derby., Southend.

N. A. Mallender, 10-96, Northants v Derby., Northampton; S. J. Malone, 12-110, Hants v Oxford U., Oxford; G. Miller, 12-138, Derby. v Leics., Coalville.

R. C. Ontong, 10-126, Glam. v Glos., Bristol.

N. Phillip, 11-91, Essex v Cambridge U., Cambridge.

A. M. E. Roberts, 14-94, Leics. v Glam., Leicester.

D. S. Steele, 10-149, Northants v Essex, Chelmsford.

D. L. Underwood, 10-124, Kent v Hants, Bournemouth.

SIX WICKETS IN AN INNINGS

There were 92 instances of bowlers taking six or more wickets in an innings in first-class cricket in 1982, two more than in 1981. The list includes 80 in the County Championship, six by the Pakistani touring side, one by the Indian touring side and five in other first-class matches.

M. D. Marshall (7)
8-71 Hants v Worcs., Southampton
7-38 Hants v Surrey, The Oval
7-48 Hants v Sussex, Eastbourne
6-41 Hants v Yorks., Bournemouth
6-55 Hants v Kent, Maidstone
6-60 Hants v Derby., Derby
6-103 Hants v Essex, Chelmsford

N. G. B. Cook (6)
7-63 Leics. v Somerset, Taunton
7-81 Leics. v Sussex, Hove
6-17 Leics. v Essex, Colchester
6-32 Leics. v Middx, Uxbridge
6-51 Leics. v Essex, Leicester
6-113 Leics. v Essex, Colchester

V. J. Marks (4)
7-51 Somerset v Notts., Nottingham
7-59 Somerset v Essex, Chelmsford
7-121 Somerset v Warw., Birmingham
6-128 Somerset v Lancs., Taunton

Abdul Qadir (3)
7-44 Pakistanis v Sussex, Hove
6-71 Pakistanis v Leics., Leicester
6-78 Pakistanis v Sussex, Hove

W. W. Daniel (3)
9-61 Middx v Glam., Swansea
6-37 Middx v Surrey, The Oval
6-60 Middx v Yorks., Sheffield

G. R. Dilley (3)
6-71 Kent v Leics., Canterbury
6-87 Kent v Worcs., Hereford
6-96 Kent v Surrey, The Oval

P. H. Edmonds (3)
8-80 Middx v Sussex, Lord's
6-31 Middx v Notts., Lord's
6-48 Middx v Hants, Uxbridge

J. W. Lloyds (3)
7-88 Somerset v Essex, Chelmsford
6-62 Somerset v Worcs., Worcester
6-114 Somerset v Glam., Swansea

A. M. E. Roberts (3)
8-56 Leics. v Glam., Leicester
6-38 Leics. v Glam., Leicester
6-61 Leics. v Warw., Leicester

S. T. Clarke (2)
6-63 Surrey v Notts., The Oval
6-70 Surrey v Sussex, Hove

R. E. East (2)
6-80 Essex v Somerset, Chelmsford
6-105 Essex v Northants, Chelmsford

K. St J. D. Emery (2)
6-51 Hants v Glam., Portsmouth
6-67 Hants v Essex, Chelmsford

J. Garner (2)
6-23 Somerset v Hants, Bournemouth
6-42 Somerset v Worcs., Taunton

R. J. Hadlee (2)
7-25 Notts. v Hants, Nottingham
6-65 Notts. v Lancs., Manchester

N. Phillip (2)
6-50 Essex v Cambridge U., Cambridge
6-60 Essex v Surrey, Chelmsford

A. C. S. Pigott (2)
7-74 Sussex v Northants, Eastbourne
6-81 Sussex v Notts., Hove

S. Oldham (2)
7-78 Derby. v Warw., Birmingham
6-63 Derby. v Somerset, Derby

R. G. D. Willis (2)
6-45 Warw. v Derby., Birmingham
6-101 England v India, Lord's

The following each took six wickets in an innings on one occasion:

P. Bainbridge, 6-59, Glos. v Glam., Swansea; M. K. Bore, 6-134, Notts. v Middx, Nottingham.

P. Carrick, 6-90, Yorks. v Worcs., Sheffield; K. E. Cooper, 6-46, Notts. v Lancs., Manchester; N. G. Cowley, 6-48, Hants v Leics., Southampton; C. E. H. Croft, 7-88; Lancs. v Derby., Manchester.

W. W. Davis, 7-101, Glam. v Notts., Swansea; D. R. Doshi, 6-102, India v England, Manchester; R. J. Doughty, 6-43, Glos. v Glam., Bristol.

N. Gifford, 6-48, Worcs. v Notts., Nottingham; G. A. Gooch, 7-14, Essex v Worcs., Ilford; D. A. Graveney, 7-37, Glos. v Worcs., Bristol.

E. E. Hemmings, 6-76, Notts., v Glam., Swansea; K. I. Hodgson, 8-68, Cambridge U. v Glam., Cambridge.

Imran Khan, 7-52, Pakistan v England, Birmingham; J. D. Inchmore, 7-53, Worcs. v Glos., Bristol.

R. D. Jackman, 6-28, Surrey v Sussex, The Oval; T. E. Jesty, 6-71, Hants v Leics., Southampton.

J. K. Lever, 6-48, Essex v Derby., Southend.

L. L. McFarlane, 6-59, Lancs. v Warw., Southport; K. S. Mackintosh, 6-61, Surrey v Middx, Lord's; N. A. Mallender, 7-41, Northants v Derby., Northampton; S. J. Malone, 7-55, Hants v Oxford U., Oxford; G. Miller, 8-70, Derby. v Leics., Coalville; D. G. Moir, 6-63, Derby. v Yorks., Scarborough; Mudassar Nazar, 6-32, Pakistan v England, Lord's.

C. M. Old, 6-76, Yorks. v Warw., Birmingham; R. C. Ontong, 6-50, Glam. v Glos., Bristol.

D. N. Patel, 7-46, Worcs. v Lancs., Worcester; S. P. Perryman, 6-49, Worcs. v Lancs., Blackpool; D. R. Pringle, 6-33, Cambridge U. v Lancs., Cambridge.

Sarfraz Nawaz, 6-92, Pakistanis v Surrey, The Oval; J. N. Shepherd, 6-75, Glos. v Sussex, Hastings; A. Sidebottom, 6-31, Yorks. v Derby., Scarborough; G. C. Small, 6-78, Warw. v Yorks., Birmingham; D. S. Steele, 6-59, Northants v Hants, Northampton.

D. L. Underwood, 7-79, Kent v Hants, Bournemouth.

C. E. Waller, 7-67, Sussex v Surrey, Hove; P. Willey, 6-17, Northants v Sussex, Eastbourne.

STATUS OF MATCHES IN THE UK

(*a*) **Automatic First-Class Matches**

The following matches of three or more days duration should automatically be considered first-class:

(i) County Championship matches.

(ii) Official representative tourist matches from ICC full member countries, unless specifically excluded.

(iii) MCC v any first-class county.

(iv) Oxford v Cambridge and either University against first-class counties.

(v) Scotland v Ireland.

(*b*) **Excluded from First-Class Status**

The following matches of three or more days duration should not normally be accorded first-class status:

(i) County "friendly" matches.

(ii) Matches played by Scotland or Ireland, other than their annual match against each other.

(iii) Unofficial tourist matches, unless circumstances are exceptional.

(iv) MCC v Oxford/Cambridge.

(v) Matches involving privately raised teams, unless included officially in a touring team's itinerary.

(*c*) **Consideration of Doubtful Status**

Matches played by unofficial touring teams of exceptional ability can be considered in advance and decisions taken accordingly.

Certain other matches comprising 22 recognised first-class cricketers might also be considered in advance.

THE INDIANS IN ENGLAND, 1982

It hardly seemed satisfactory that a tour by England to India should be followed almost immediately by one by India to England. But that is as it was, and it gave England the chance to avenge their defeat, suffered on the sub-continent, a few months earlier. Of the three Test matches, England won the first and drew the last two. Although poorly attended, the series contained some good and interesting cricket, to which Sunil Gavaskar's Indian side, the tenth to visit England in an official capacity, made a generous contribution.

Of the sixteen players, three, Ghulam Parkar, Suru Nayak and Randhir Singh, arrived uncapped. Ashok Malhotra and Pranab Roy had each played in only two Test matches. The others were widely experienced. Besides Gavaskar himself, the world's most prolific opening batsman, they included a glorious all-round cricketer in Kapil Dev, whose jousts with Botham were among the features of the summer, two seasoned batsmen of high quality in Dilip Vengsarkar and Gundappa Viswanath (Gavaskar's brother-in-law), a top-class wicket-keeper in Syed Kirmani, and a successfully teasing orthodox left-arm spinner in Dilip Doshi.

That they managed to win only one of their twelve first-class matches was because of their bowling, which was very short of depth. Madan Lal, at medium pace, occasionally moved the ball about effectively, and Ravi Shastri, only nineteen, showed promise as a tall spinner (orthodox left-arm). At Lord's in the first Test and at Old Trafford in the second they had England at 166 for six and 161 for five respectively, without being able to press home their advantage.

By his own exceptional standards, Gavaskar had a lean tour. This was partly due to his wanting, in the matches outside the Tests, to make sure that he did not deprive his supporting batsmen of the chance of a good innings. He was also unable to bat in the third Test at The Oval, after being hit on the shin by a drive from Botham while fielding at silly-point. Despite this India, needing a massive 395 to avoid following on, added a total of 410 to the 379 for eight they had made, also when under pressure, at Old Trafford. Of the 24 Test hundreds Gavaskar had made when the series ended, only four had been against England.

Vengsarkar scored a brilliant 157 in the first Test and made more runs on the tour than anyone else, though still fewer than three of the Pakistanis who followed the Indians to England. At his best, as he was at Lord's, Vengsarkar has few superiors. The failure of two of the specialist openers, Roy and Parkar, to adapt easily to English conditions led to Shastri being sent in first in the last two Tests. By making 66 in India's first innings at The Oval, he responded well to the challenge.

One of the outstanding innings of the whole of the 1982 season was Sandeep Patil's 129 not out in the second Test. An unexpected selection for the match, because of poor form, he rivalled Botham with the power and range of his strokeplay. Malhotra, like Roy a diminutive, quick-footed newcomer, showed what he was capable of in a dazzling innings of 154 not out against Kent at Canterbury.

There was much less bowling potential. Shivlal Yadav, the only off-spinner, despite having had success against Australia, paid dearly for his few wickets. The tireless Kapil Dev was too often the only real hope of an early break.

THE INDIANS IN ENGLAND, 1982

[*Patrick Eagar*

Back row: P. Roy, Yashpal Sharma, A. Malhotra, G. A. Parkar. *Middle row:* N. S. Yadav, Randhir Singh, R. J. Shastri, Kapil Dev, S. M. Patil, S. V. Nayak, D. R. Doshi, G. Saulez (*scorer*). *Front row:* Raj Singh (*manager*), D. B. Vengsarkar, G. R. Viswanath, S. M. Gavaskar (*captain*), Madan Lal, S. M. H. Kirmani, C. Nagaraj (*assistant manager*).

After taking eight wickets in the first Test he picked up only two more in the series, a likely sign of his being overworked.

The side was admirably managed by Raj Singh, a former player for India's Central Zone with a strong sense of history and tradition. They could field very well, with Parkar a sparkling cover-point, and they were never to be taken for granted. Their one victory came in a chase against the clock against Hampshire at Southampton. Their only defeat, other than in the two one-day internationals and their warm-up match at Arundel, was in the first Test. – J. W.

INDIAN TOUR RESULTS

Test matches—Played 3: Lost 1, Drawn 2.

First-class matches—Played 12: Won 1, Lost 1, Drawn 10.

Win—Hampshire.

Loss—England.

Draws—England (2), Essex, Gloucestershire, Kent, Northamptonshire, Nottinghamshire, MCC, Warwickshire, Yorkshire.

Non first-class matches—Played 5: Won 1, Lost 3, Drawn 2. *Win*—Ireland. *Losses*—Lavinia, Duchess of Norfolk's XI, England (2). *Draws*—Oxford & Cambridge Univs, Ireland.

TEST MATCH AVERAGES

ENGLAND – BATTING

	T	*I*	*NO*	*R*	*HI*	*Avge*
I. T. Botham............	3	3	0	403	208	134.33
D. W. Randall.........	3	3	0	221	126	73.66
A. J. Lamb.............	3	5	1	207	107	51.75
C. J. Tavaré.............	3	5	1	178	75*	44.50
P. J. W. Allott.........	2	2	1	44	41*	44.00
D. I. Gower.............	3	5	1	152	47	38.00
P. H. Edmonds........	3	3	0	90	64	30.00
G. Cook..................	3	5	0	138	66	27.60
R. G. D. Willis........	3	3	1	35	28	17.50
D. R. Pringle...........	3	3	0	39	23	13.00
R. W. Taylor............	3	4	1	36	31	12.00

Played in one Test: G. Miller 98.

* *Signifies not out.*

BOWLING

	O	*M*	*R*	*W*	*Avge*
R. G. D. Willis........	88	11	330	15	22.00
D. R. Pringle...........	82	22	219	7	31.28
I. T. Botham............	93.3	16	320	9	35.55
P. H. Edmonds........	102.2	35	261	6	43.50
P. J. W. Allott.........	49	9	147	2	73.50

Also bowled: G. Cook 1–0–4–0; G. Miller 16–4–51–1.

INDIA – BATTING

	T	*I*	*NO*	*R*	*HI*	*Avge*
S. M. Patil	2	2	1	191	129*	191.00
Kapil Dev	3	4	0	292	97	73.00
G. R. Viswanath	3	5	1	189	75*	47.25
D. B. Vengsarkar	3	5	0	193	157	38.60
S. M. H. Kirmani	3	4	1	110	58	36.66
S. M. Gavaskar	3	3	0	74	48	24.66
Yashpal Sharma	3	5	1	98	38	24.50
R. J. Shastri	3	5	0	93	66	18.60
Madan Lal	3	4	0	52	26	13.00
S. V. Nayak	2	3	1	19	11	9.50
D. R. Doshi	3	3	2	9	5*	9.00

Played in one Test: A. Malhotra 5, 0; G. A. Parkar 6, 1.

* *Signifies not out.*

BOWLING

	O	*M*	*R*	*W*	*Avge*
D. R. Doshi	157.1	38	455	13	35.00
Kapil Dev	133	21	439	10	43.90
Madan Lal	102.1	30	291	6	48.50
R. J. Shastri	116.3	29	275	4	68.75

Also bowled: S. V. Nayak 38.3–6–132–1; S. M. Patil 14–1–48–1; Yashpal Sharma 3–2–1–0.

INDIAN AVERAGES – FIRST-CLASS MATCHES

BATTING

	M	*I*	*NO*	*R*	*HI*	*Avge*
G. R. Viswanath	9	12	3	561	106*	62.33
Madan Lal	9	15	10	309	58*	61.80
D. B. Vengsarkar	9	13	2	610	157	55.45
S. M. Gavaskar	8	10	0	438	172	43.80
Yashpal Sharma	9	15	5	418	77*	41.80
Kapil Dev	8	11	0	438	97	39.81
S. V. Nayak	10	13	6	253	67*	36.14
G. A. Parkar	7	14	2	433	146	36.08
A. Malhotra	8	15	1	462	154*	33.00
S. M. H. Kirmani	9	12	3	265	65	29.44
R. J. Shastri	9	15	2	359	74	27.61
S. M. Patil	9	16	1	390	129*	26.00
P. Roy	7	12	0	174	51	14.50
D. R. Doshi	9	4	2	11	5*	5.50
N. S. Yadav	7	2	1	1	1*	1.00
Randhir Singh	5	3	0	0	0	0.00

* *Signifies not out.*

BOWLING

	O	*M*	*R*	*W*	*Avge*
Madan Lal	246.1	49	763	22	34.68
S. M. Patil	60	9	155	4	38.75
D. R. Doshi	345.3	78	1,003	25	40.12
Kapil Dev	255.4	45	810	20	40.50
R. J. Shastri	269.5	69	634	15	42.26
S. V. Nayak	205.3	39	645	14	46.07
Randhir Singh	131	24	418	7	59.71
N. S. Yadav	195	33	604	7	86.28

Also bowled: S. M. Gavaskar 5–0–23–0; A. Malhotra 9–1–37–1; P. Roy 1–0–14–0; D. B. Vengsarkar 0.2–0–2–0; Yashpal Sharma 10–2–32–0.

FIELDING

S. M. H. Kirmani 15 (11ct, 4st), D. B. Vengsarkar 9, G. A. Parkar 8 (7ct, 1st), G. R. Viswanath 8, R. J. Shastri 6, Yashpal Sharma 6, Kapil Dev 5, A. Malhotra 5, S. M. Gavaskar 3, S. V. Nayak 3, Madan Lal 1, S. M. Patil 1, P. Roy 1.

HUNDREDS FOR INDIANS

The following eight three-figure innings were played for the Indians, seven in first-class matches and one in a non first-class match.

S. M. Gavaskar (2)
172 v Warwickshire at Birmingham
†120 v Oxford & Cambridge Univs at Cambridge

G. R. Viswanath (2)
106* v Northamptonshire at Northampton
100 v Hampshire at Southampton

A. Malhotra (1)
154* v Kent at Canterbury

G. A. Parkar (1)
146 v Yorkshire at Bradford

S. M. Patil (1)
129* v England at Manchester (Second Test)

D. B. Vengsarkar (1)
157 v England at Lord's (First Test)

**Signifies not out.* †*Not first-class.*

HUNDREDS AGAINST INDIANS

The following twelve three-figure innings were played against the Indians, eleven in first-class matches and one in a non first-class match.

I. T. Botham (2)
208 for England at The Oval (Third Test)
128 for England at Manchester (Second Test)

D. W. Randall (2)
130* for MCC at Lord's
126 for England at Lord's (First Test)

A. M. Ferreira (1)
112* for Warwickshire at Birmingham

C. G. Greenidge (1)
156 for Hampshire at Southampton

B. R. Hardie (1)
161 for Essex at Chelmsford

T. E. Jesty (1)
164* for Hampshire at Southampton

A. J. Lamb (1)
107 for England at The Oval (Third Test)

L. Potter (1)
118 for Kent at Canterbury

Sadiq Mohammad (1)
†107* for Lavinia, Duchess of Norfolk's XI at Arundel

K. Sharp (1)
115 for Yorkshire at Bradford

**Signifies not out.*   †*Not first-class.*

Note: Those matches which follow and which were not first-class are signified by the use of a dagger.

†LAVINIA, DUCHESS OF NORFOLK'S XI v INDIANS

At Arundel, May 5. Lavinia, Duchess of Norfolk's XI won by ten wickets. Indians 201 for five (45 overs) (Yashpal Sharma 66 not out, A. Malhotra 54, G. A. Parkar 35); Lavinia, Duchess of Norfolk's XI 202 for no wkt (44.5 overs) (Sadiq Mohammad 107 not out, A. W. Stovold 90 not out).

WARWICKSHIRE v INDIANS

At Birmingham, May 9, 10, 11. Drawn. A glut of runs on the last day, 474, closed a match in which an outright result was never likely. The tourists, dismissed for 243 before tea on the first day, hit back by capturing three wickets for 68 by the close. Lloyd went on to score 87, but the batting honours went to Asif Din, whose 91 was the highest score of his career. Ferreira, 44 not out at the start of the final day, went on to his first century for the county, hitting a 6 and fifteen 4s as he took Warwickshire to their highest total against a touring team. Willis also made his highest-ever score, after which the small crowd were treated to a fluent 172 (four 6s, twenty 4s) by the Indian captain while his side enjoyed some batting practice.

Indians

*S. M. Gavaskar c Maynard b Hogg	32	– c Lloyd b Small	172
P. Roy c Maynard b Willis	9	– b Small	8
D. B. Vengsarkar b Lloyd	72	– (5) not out	57
G. R. Viswanath c Asif Din b Ferreira	67		
A. Malhotra lbw b Willis	1	– (3) c and b Cumbes	79
S. M. Patil lbw b Ferreira	0	– (4) lbw b Cumbes	4
Kapil Dev lbw b Ferreira	0	– (6) c Smith b Small	6
S. V. Nayak b Lloyd	28	– (7) not out	3
†S. M. H. Kirmani b Small	15		
N. S. Yadav not out	1		
D. R. Doshi c Smith b Small	2		
B 4, l-b 8, w 1, n-b 3	16	B 8, l-b 11, n-b 3	22
1/33 2/57 3/174 4/175 5/177 6/177 7/220 8/225 9/241	243	1/23 2/191 3/195 4/331 5/341 (5 wkts)	351

Bowling: *First Innings*—Willis 14–6–17–2; Small 12.3–1–47–2; Ferreira 21–2–67–3; Hogg 12–2–30–1; Cumbes 6–0–31–0; Asif Din 2–0–6–0; Lloyd 7–0–29–2. *Second Innings*—Willis 8–0–33–0; Small 10–2–45–3; Ferreira 3–0–19–0; Hogg 9–2–28–0; Cumbes 27–3–97–2; Asif Din 12–1–64–0; Lloyd 5–0–43–0.

Warwickshire

A. I. Kallicharran b Nayak	2
T. A. Lloyd st Kirmani b Yadav	87
K. D. Smith b Patil	13
P. R. Oliver lbw b Nayak	2
Asif Din lbw b Kapil Dev	91
†C. Maynard c Patil b Kapil Dev	40
A. M. Ferreira not out	112
*R. G. D. Willis c Kapil Dev b Malhotra	72
B 19, n-b 9	28
1/3 2/31 3/34 4/178 5/241 6/272 7/447 (7 wkts dec.)	447

G. C. Small, J. Cumbes and W. Hogg did not bat.

Bowling: Kapil Dev 26–4–86–2; Nayak 28–7–87–2; Patil 18–3–27–1; Yadav 33–10–68–1; Doshi 34–7–87–0; Roy 1–0–14–0; Malhotra 9–1–37–1; Gavaskar 2–0–13–0.

Umpires: B. J. Meyer and D. G. L. Evans.

NOTTINGHAMSHIRE v INDIANS

At Nottingham, May 12, 13, 14. Drawn. Acting-captain Birch manufactured some late excitement, when a draw seemed inevitable, by setting the tourists to score 134 to win in nineteen overs. Had Kapil Dev stayed longer – he was caught at long-off by Hemmings for 40 – the Indians would probably have met their target, but in the end they finished on the defensive. Nottinghamshire, without five regulars, had been bowled out for 141 on the opening day, Kapil Dev taking five for 39, but they were able to restrict the Indian lead to 118 through Saxelby's career-best four for 47 and four for 52 by Bore. Roy took four hours over his half-century. Nottinghamshire batted much better in their second innings, and half-centuries by Randall and Robinson paved the way for Birch's initiative.

Nottinghamshire

R. T. Robinson c Kirmani b Kapil Dev	14	– b Madan Lal	52
B. Hassan c Yashpal b Kapil Dev	7	– c Vengsarkar b Randhir	44
D. W. Randall b Patil	29	– c Kirmani b Shastri	51
*J. D. Birch run out	6	– c Vengsarkar b Shastri	27
M. J. Harris c Kirmani b Kapil Dev	41	– not out	43
†C. W. Scott c Madan Lal b Kapil Dev	14	– not out	17
N. J. B. Illingworth c Shastri b Kapil Dev	0		
E. E. Hemmings b Madan Lal	6		
K. Saxelby not out	2		
K. E. Cooper c Parkar b Patil	19		
M. K. Bore b Randhir	0		
L-b 1, n-b 2	3	L-b 8, n-b 9	17
1/11 2/24 3/39 4/77 5/102 6/102 7/118 8/120 9/139	141	1/70 2/135 3/170 4/196 (4 wkts dec.)	251

Bowling: *First Innings*—Kapil Dev 16–4–39–5; Madan Lal 14–4–40–1; Randhir 10–1–31–1; Patil 10–1–26–2; Shastri 1–0–2–0. *Second Innings*—Kapil Dev 21.4–8–60–0; Randhir 21–3–54–1; Madan Lal 18–3–42–1; Shastri 31–11–69–2; Patil 1–0–2–0; Yashpal 2–0–7–0.

Indians

P. Roy c Hassan b Hemmings	51		
G. A. Parkar c Hemmings b Saxelby	30	– c Bore b Cooper	13
Yashpal Sharma c Randall b Saxelby	3	– c Scott b Cooper	9
S. M. Patil c Randall b Bore	34	– b Saxelby	0
D. B. Vengsarkar c Robinson b Bore	28	– (6) not out	18
*S. M. Gavaskar c Hassan b Bore	23	– (1) run out	10
Kapil Dev c Illingworth b Hemmings	4	– (5) c Hemmings b Cooper	40
R. J. Shastri c Scott b Saxelby	24		
†S. M. H. Kirmani c Birch b Bore	32	– (7) c Harris b Hemmings	4
Madan Lal not out	13	– (8) not out	2
Randhir Singh lbw b Saxelby	0		
B 4, l-b 6, w 7	17	L-b 1	1
1/41 2/53 3/106 4/144 5/172 6/185 7/185 8/241 9/249	259	1/22 2/24 3/32 4/36 5/89 6/95 (6 wkts)	97

Bowling: *First Innings*—Cooper 25–10–57–0; Saxelby 22.2–8–47–4; Illingworth 12–2–42–0; Bore 35–19–52–4; Hemmings 24–9–44–2. *Second Innings*—Cooper 7–1–38–3; Saxelby 2–0–24–1; Hemmings 7–0–31–1; Bore 2.3–1–3–0.

Umpires: H. D. Bird and A. G. T. Whitehead.

YORKSHIRE v INDIANS

At Bradford, May 15, 17, 18. Drawn. Gavaskar hammered Yorkshire's weakened attack on an easy-paced pitch, hitting four 6s and nine 4s in a stay of 95 minutes. Even after his dismissal runs continued to come easily, although Taylor, on his first-class début, had the satisfaction of capturing two wickets. Although the tourists' spin bowling was good enough to pose problems even in unfavourable conditions, Sharp, opening in the place of Boycott, made a splendid century in reply, reaching 50 out of 87 and going to three figures with his seventeenth boundary. Hartley's declaration, 116 in arrears, invited reciprocation, but an eventual target of 288 in three hours asked a lot of Yorkshire, and they had not shown much interest when the weather brought an early finish.

Indians

*S. M. Gavaskar c and b Dennis	79		
†G. A. Parkar c Athey b Whiteley	146	– (1) lbw b Dennis	28
A. Malhotra run out	22	– c Carrick b Whiteley	8
G. R. Viswanath c Bairstow b Taylor	45		
Yashpal Sharma not out	48	– (4) c Taylor b Whiteley	26
R. J. Shastri c Bairstow b Taylor	21	– (2) run out	29
Kapil Dev (did not bat)		– (5) b Carrick	30
Madan Lal (did not bat)		– (6) not out	28
S. V. Nayak (did not bat)		– (7) not out	14
B 2, l-b 8, w 1, n-b 4	15	L-b 2, w 5, n-b 1	8
1/128 2/201 3/279 4/317 5/376 (5 wkts dec.)	376	1/58 2/72 3/76 4/128 5/128 (5 wkts dec.)	171

N. S. Yadav and D. R. Doshi did not bat.

Bowling: *First Innings*—Stevenson 15–4–44–0; Dennis 16–1–71–1; Taylor 14.4–1–76–2; Hartley 2–0–15–0; Whiteley 19–0–93–1; Carrick 22–6–62–0. *Second Innings*—Taylor 7–1–31–0; Dennis 13–5–32–1; Stevenson 6–4–7–0; Whiteley 13–1–59–2; Carrick 14–3–34–1.

Yorkshire

R. G. Lumb c Kapil Dev b Doshi	52	– not out	15
K. Sharp c Kapil Dev b Doshi	115	– not out	20
C. W. J. Athey not out	61		
J. D. Love retired hurt	3		
*S. N. Hartley b Yadav	16		
†D. L. Bairstow not out	4		
B 4, l-b 1, n-b 4	9		
1/127 2/203 3/247 (3 wkts dec.)	260	(no wkt)	35

G. B. Stevenson, P. Carrick, N. S. Taylor, S. J. Dennis and J. P. Whiteley did not bat.

Bowling: *First Innings*—Kapil Dev 8–2–26–0; Madan Lal 11–1–48–0; Nayak 8–2–22–0; Yadav 17–4–48–1; Doshi 26.1–4–85–2; Shastri 14–8–22–0. *Second Innings*—Kapil Dev 6–1–9–0; Madan Lal 6–1–17–0; Shastri 2–0–5–0; Nayak 1–0–4–0.

Umpires: D. J. Constant and N. T. Plews.

MCC v INDIANS

At Lord's, May 19, 20, 21. Drawn. An MCC side chosen by the England selectors had the better of the match. Against some modest Indian bowling Randall made a successful return to representative cricket after a lapse of two years, adding 166 in 155 minutes on the first day with Tavaré and 116 with Gower. Amid frequent interruptions on the second day the Indians reached 178 for eight, Vengsarkar saving them from a much lower score. Further good batting from Tavaré preceded an MCC declaration on the last day which asked the Indians to score 266 to win in 195 minutes, something they never seriously attempted. MCC were captained by Gower, a possible portent of things to come, and on the last day it was announced that Fletcher, who had led England in India, would be replaced by Willis for the Test series against India.

MCC

G. Cook lbw b Madan Lal	14	– c Vengsarkar b Madan Lal 18
C. J. Tavaré c Viswanath b Madan Lal	99	– not out 75
D. W. Randall not out	130	– run out 4
M. W. Gatting lbw b Madan Lal	3	– not out 27
*D. I. Gower c and b Nayak	55	
G. Miller not out	8	
L-b 9, w 1	10	B 1, l-b 1 2
1/28 2/194 3/204 4/302	(4 wkts dec.) 319	1/41 2/50 (2 wkts dec.) 126

D. R. Pringle, V. J. Marks, †C. J. Richards, G. R. Dilley and P. J. W. Allott did not bat.

Bowling: *First Innings*—Randhir 22–4–72–0; Madan Lal 19–2–63–3; Nayak 16–0–80–1; Yadav 24–3–94–0. *Second Innings*—Randhir 9–3–16–0; Madan Lal 12–0–41–1; Nayak 9–1–32–0; Yadav 7–0–35–0.

Indians

P. Roy c Cook b Dilley	9	– b Pringle 7
G. A. Parkar c Richards b Dilley	0	– c Gower b Cook 92
D. B. Vengsarkar c Miller b Dilley	96	
*G. R. Viswanath lbw b Pringle	32	
A. Malhotra c Richards b Pringle	5	– (3) c Miller b Marks 18
S. M. Patil c Allott b Pringle	7	– (4) b Miller 3
†S. M. H. Kirmani run out	4	– (6) not out 4
Madan Lal not out	19	– (5) not out 11
S. V. Nayak lbw b Dilley	0	
N. S. Yadav b Dilley	0	
Randhir Singh lbw b Allott	0	
L-b 4, n-b 4	8	B 5, l-b 3 8
1/5 2/32 3/98 4/116 5/139 6/152 7/171 8/171 9/179	180	1/17 2/79 3/112 4/135 (4 wkts) 143

Bowling: *First Innings*—Dilley 19–4–69–5; Allott 22.4–7–50–1; Pringle 17–3–53–3; Miller 1–1–0–0. *Second Innings*—Dilley 6–2–11–0; Allott 10–7–12–0; Pringle 5–4–5–1; Marks 16–4–43–1; Miller 15–3–42–1; Cook 2–0–18–1; Randall 1–0–4–0.

Umpires: D. O. Oslear and A. G. T. Whitehead.

KENT v INDIANS

At Canterbury, May 22, 23, 24. Drawn. Kent's young openers, Taylor and Potter, shared in an opening stand of 101 off 35 overs, Potter falling 4 short of his century after batting for almost four hours and hitting twelve 4s. After a disastrous start, a tremendous unbroken fourth-wicket stand of 198 in 188 minutes between Malhotra and Yashpal Sharma rescued the Indians and enabled them to declare 20 runs behind. Yashpal hit nine 4s while Malhotra, who batted for 249 minutes, hit 23 boundaries. When Kent batted again, Potter compensated for his first innings' disappointment with a stroke-laden 100 out of 123 in 140 minutes with one 6 and fourteen 4s. But for a stoppage for bad light he might have had a hundred before lunch. Tavaré's declaration set the Indians 269 to win in two hours and the game understandably fizzled out into a tame draw.

Kent

L. Potter c Malhotra b Kapil Dev	96	– c Kapil Dev b Shastri 118
N. R. Taylor c Malhotra b Shastri	62	– c Nayak b Doshi 18
*C. J. Tavaré b Doshi	39	
M. R. Benson c Kirmani b Nayak	9	– (3) not out 41
A. G. E. Ealham c Shastri b Doshi	16	– (6) not out 31
C. S. Cowdrey c Roy b Nayak	7	– (5) c Kapil Dev b Shastri 19
G. W. Johnson not out	18	– (4) lbw b Doshi 12
G. R. Dilley c Shastri b Randhir	33	
E. A. Baptiste not out	14	
L-b 1, n-b 7	8	B 1, l-b 4, n-b 4 9
1/101 2/191 3/207 4/220 5/237 6/237 7/283 (7 wkts dec.)	302	1/124 2/147 3/166 4/193 (4 wkts dec.) 248

†S. N. V. Waterton and L. J. Wood did not bat.

Bowling: *First Innings*—Kapil Dev 19–2–66–1; Nayak 13–3–40–2; Randhir 19–2–82–1; Yashpal 3–0–13–0; Shastri 11–2–40–1; Doshi 22.1–8–53–2. *Second Innings*—Randhir 10–1–48–0; Nayak 7–2–8–0; Doshi 32–3–110–2; Kapil Dev 4–0–9–0; Shastri 26–1–64–2.

Indians

*S. M. Gavaskar c Waterton b Baptiste	19	
P. Roy b Baptiste	3	– (1) c Tavaré b Cowdrey 20
A. Malhotra not out	154	
S. M. Patil b Baptiste	18	– b Potter 0
Yashpal Sharma not out	77	
R. J. Shastri (did not bat)		– (2) run out 4
S. V. Nayak (did not bat)		– (3) not out 37
†S. M. H. Kirmani (did not bat)		– (5) not out 5
B 2, l-b 3, w 1, n-b 5	11	L-b 1, n-b 1 2
1/27 2/28 3/84 (3 wkts dec.)	282	1/15 2/40 3/43 (3 wkts) 68

Kapil Dev, Randhir Singh and D. R. Doshi did not bat.

Bowling: *First Innings*—Dilley 17–7–35–0; Baptiste 22–5–78–3; Cowdrey 20–4–60–0; Johnson 20–7–40–0; Wood 12–1–58–0. *Second Innings*—Dilley 5–1–5–0; Baptiste 6–2–14–0; Cowdrey 9–2–20–1; Johnson 2–0–7–0; Potter 5–1–20–1.

Umpires: H. D. Bird and D. G. L. Evans.

†IRELAND v INDIANS

At Belfast, May 26. Drawn, after rain prevented further play. Indians 179 for two (43.5 overs) (P. Roy 84, S. M. Patil 45, G. A. Parkar 35); Ireland did not bat.

†IRELAND v INDIANS

At Belfast, May 27. Indians won by five wickets. Ireland 134 for nine (50 overs) (E. A. McDermott 50; D. R. Doshi four for 11); Indians 137 for five (41.3 overs) (R. J. Shastri 43, Madan Lal 37).

HAMPSHIRE v INDIANS

At Southampton, May 29, 30, 31. Indians won by three wickets. They gained plenty of batting practice, as well as their first win of the tour, but Hampshire did declare twice and they lost a total of only eight wickets. After early setbacks Hampshire's fortunes were lifted by an enterprising third-wicket stand of 117 between Nicholas and Jesty, the latter going on to his hundred in four hours and eventually to a career-best, undefeated 164 (21 4s) in five hours. The Indians lost Parkar before the close, but next day Viswanath made his first century of the tour and shared in half-century stands with Kirmani and Madan Lal before he was fifth out. Gavaskar's declaration 7 runs later enabled Hampshire to set up a good finish, Greenidge taking the principal role in a second-wicket partnership of 181 in 40 overs with Nicholas. He reached his century, made out of 162, in 176 minutes and then celebrated by hitting five 6s. The declaration left the tourists to score 296 in 227 minutes and, boosted by stands such as the 64 in nine overs for the fourth wicket between Vengsarkar and Kapil Dev, they got home with 23 balls to spare.

Hampshire

C. G. Greenidge lbw b Kapil Dev	4	– b Doshi	156
J. M. Rice lbw b Madan Lal	28	– c Kirmani b Kapil Dev	16
M. C. J. Nicholas c Vengsarkar b Doshi	72	– not out	54
T. E. Jesty not out	164	– not out	1
*N. E. J. Pocock b Madan Lal	29		
N. G. Cowley c Gavaskar b Doshi	13		
T. M. Tremlett c Kirmani b Doshi	1		
†R. J. Parks not out	16		
L-b 3, w 1, n-b 5	9	B 1, l-b 5, n-b 3	9
1/4 2/44 3/161 4/214 5/265 6/281 (6 wkts dec.)	336	1/53 2/234 (2 wkts dec.)	236

J. W. Southern, K. St J. D. Emery and S. J. Malone did not bat.

Bowling: *First Innings*—Kapil Dev 10–2–34–1; Madan Lal 17–2–73–2; Nayak 13–2–38–0; Yadav 30–2–96–0; Doshi 28–8–86–3. *Second Innings*—Kapil Dev 12–1–42–1; Madan Lal 7–1–11–0; Nayak 11–2–45–0; Yadav 12–3–55–0; Patil 5–1–25–0; Doshi 14–3–39–1; Gavaskar 3–0–10–0.

Indians

G. A. Parkar c Parks b Malone	19	– (2) c Parks b Emery	32
†S. M. H. Kirmani b Southern	65	– (7) c Southern b Malone	26
Kapil Dev lbw b Tremlett	26	– (5) c Tremlett b Southern	40
G. R. Viswanath b Cowley	100	– (8) not out	21
S. M. Patil b Southern	23	– (4) c and b Tremlett	7
Madan Lal not out	32	– (9) not out	4
S. V. Nayak b Southern	2	– (6) c Tremlett b Southern	33
*S. M. Gavaskar (did not bat)		– (1) c Nicholas b Tremlett	29
D. B. Vengsarkar (did not bat)		– (3) c and b Cowley	86
B 2, l-b 2, n-b 6	10	B 5, l-b 8, w 3, n-b 4	20
1/43 2/93 3/155 4/201 5/270 6/277 (6 wkts dec.)	277	1/72 2/107 3/120 4/184 5/230 6/262 7/287 (7 wkts)	298

N. S. Yadav and D. R. Doshi did not bat.

Bowling: *First Innings*—Emery 14–1–62–0; Malone 11–1–42–1; Tremlett 9–4–17–1; Cowley 26–7–63–1; Southern 23.4–3–83–3. *Second Innings*—Malone 19.2–2–74–1; Emery 14–1–56–1; Tremlett 5–1–30–2; Southern 11–0–64–2; Cowley 11–0–54–1.

Umpires: B. J. Meyer and P. B. Wight.

†ENGLAND v INDIA

First Prudential Trophy Match

At Leeds, June 2. England won by nine wickets. Following a violent hailstorm the previous afternoon, lasting for only twenty minutes but leaving cars parked round the ground with water up to their hubcaps, the first of the two Prudential Trophy matches had a controversial beginning. Having pleaded in vain that the pitch was unfit for play at the time appointed for the start – the covers had leaked during the storm – India's captain lost the toss and led his side to a heavy defeat. With the ball moving about, as much because of the heavy atmosphere as any dampness in the pitch, India reached 193, after being 68 for five, thanks to a punishing innings of 60 in 37 balls by Kapil Dev. England were steered home by Wood, ably supported by Tavaré and the South African, Lamb, making his first appearance for a representative English side. The match ended with lightning flashing across the sky.

Wood was Man of the Match. The attendance was 10,000, the takings £47,000.

India

*S. M. Gavaskar c Botham b Allott	38
G. A. Parkar c Tavaré b Willis	10
D. B. Vengsarkar c Taylor b Botham	5
G. R. Viswanath b Botham	9
S. M. Patil c Taylor b Botham	0
Yashpal Sharma c Taylor b Allott	20
R. J. Shastri run out	18
Kapil Dev run out	60
†S. M. H. Kirmani c Taylor b Botham	11
S. V. Nayak c Tavaré b Willis	3
Madan Lal not out	1
B 4, l-b 9, w 1, n-b 4	18
1/30 2/54 3/58 4/59 5/68 6/113 7/114 8/154 9/192 (55 overs)	193

Bowling: Willis 11–0–32–2; Dilley 5–1–20–0; Allott 11–4–21–2; Botham 11–0–56–4; Wood 7–2–17–0; Miller 10–0–29–0.

England

B. Wood not out	78
C. J. Tavaré lbw b Madan Lal	66
A. J. Lamb not out	35
B 1, l-b 7, w 3, n-b 4	15
1/135 (1 wkt, 50.1 overs)	194

D. I. Gower, I. T. Botham, D. W. Randall, G. Miller, G. R. Dilley, †R. W. Taylor, P. J. W. Allott and *R. G. D. Willis did not bat.

Bowling: Kapil Dev 9–2–21–0; Madan Lal 9–3–21–1; Nayak 9–0–37–0; Patil 7–0–29–0; Shastri 11–0–37–0; Yashpal 5.1–0–34–0.

Umpires: D. J. Constant and D. O. Oslear.

†ENGLAND v INDIA

Second Prudential Trophy Match

At The Oval, June 4. England won by 114 runs to win the Prudential Trophy. They were handed the initiative when India put them in on a lovely morning and a good pitch. Their 276 for nine was based on a sparkling third-wicket partnership of 159 in 27 overs, a Prudential Trophy record, between Lamb and Gower, and only the slowness of the outfield prevented England from passing 300. Bowling as effectively as they had batted, England took India's first five wickets for only 42 runs, but in poor light after tea, with storm-clouds threatening, Kapil Dev, Madan Lal and Shastri saved India from a heavier defeat.

Lamb was Man of the Match. The attendance was 10,208, the takings £62,063.50.

England

B. Wood b Patil	15	G. R. Dilley c Yashpal b Madan Lal	1
C. J. Tavaré b Patil	27	†R. W. Taylor not out	3
A. J. Lamb c and b Madan Lal	99	P. J. W. Allott run out	5
D. I. Gower c Vengsarkar b Yashpal	76	B 3, l-b 10, w 6, n-b 3	22
I. T. Botham run out	4		
D. W. Randall run out	24	1/43 2/53 3/212 (9 wkts, 55 overs)	276
G. Miller run out	0	4/218 5/260 6/260 7/267 8/268 9/276	

*R. G. D. Willis did not bat.

Bowling: Kapil Dev 11–1–39–0; Madan Lal 11–0–50–2; Nayak 11–1–48–0; Patil 11–0–37–2; Shastri 8–0–53–0; Yashpal 3–0–27–1.

India

*S. M. Gavaskar c Willis b Miller	15	†S. M. H. Kirmani c Botham b Miller	8
G. A. Parkar c Botham b Willis	2	Madan Lal not out	53
D. B. Vengsarkar c Taylor b Dilley	15	R. J. Shastri not out	9
Yashpal Sharma lbw b Allott	2	B 1, l-b 3, w 2	6
A. Malhotra b Botham	4		
S. M. Patil b Miller	1	1/5 2/28 3/36 (8 wkts, 55 overs)	162
Kapil Dev c Gower b Wood	47	4/42 5/42 6/43 7/66 8/131	

S. V. Nayak did not bat.

Bowling: Willis 7–2–10–1; Dilley 7–1–19–1; Botham 9–2–22–1; Allott 8–3–24–1; Miller 11–3–27–3; Wood 11–0–51–1; Tavaré 2–0–3–0.

Umpires: D. G. L. Evans and B. J. Meyer.

NORTHAMPTONSHIRE v INDIA

At Northampton, June 5, 6, 7. Drawn. Play ended early on the first afternoon and only the last two hours were possible on the second day, but Viswanath lifted the gloom with a splendid century full of stylish strokeplay. He scored 86 out of the Indians' 180 for five before the first storm, and next day he quickly reached his century before declaring, having hit seventeen 4s and batted three hours. That Northamptonshire gained a lead of 1 was due to a career-best 79 by their 22-year-old opener, Carter, who was deputising as opener for the "unacceptable" Larkins. He showed immense determination in a four-hour stay that included only four boundaries. For India the final day belonged to Nayak, who took five for 54 in conditions that did not give much help and then, when the Indians decided to bat out the game, enthusiastically attacked Northamptonshire's varied bowling for an unbeaten 67.

Indians

P. Roy lbw b Sarfraz	6	– lbw b Williams	17
†G. A. Parkar lbw b Sarfraz	1	– lbw b Griffiths	5
D. B. Vengsarkar c Capel b Griffiths	19		
*G. R. Viswanath not out	106		
A. Malhotra b Griffiths	15	– (3) c and b Mallender	10
Yashpal Sharma c Sharp b Capel	10	– (4) lbw b Williams	56
R. J. Shastri not out	25	– (6) not out	15
S. V. Nayak (did not bat)		– (5) not out	67
L-b 6, w 4, n-b 11	21	B 8, l-b 13, w 1, n-b 5	27
1/6 2/18 3/64 (5 wkts dec.)	203	1/17 2/30 3/56 (4 wkts)	197
4/91 5/127		4/166	

N. S. Yadav, D. R. Doshi and Randhir Singh did not bat.

Bowling: *First Innings*—Sarfraz 10–3–21–2; Griffiths 14–2–36–2; Mallender 11–1–44–0; Carter 6–2–18–0; Steele 7–2–26–0; Capel 7–0–37–1. *Second Innings*—Mallender 9–6–10–1; Griffiths 8–2–15–1; Williams 18–5–50–2; Wild 6–2–26–0; Steele 12–2–42–0; A. J. Lamb 2-1-1–0; Sharp 3–0–19–0; Cook 1–0–7–0.

Northamptonshire

*G. Cook c Viswanath b Nayak	3
R. M. Carter c Viswanath b Shastri	79
R. G. Williams c Parkar b Doshi	14
A. J. Lamb c Vengsarkar b Randhir	25
D. J. Capel c Parkar b Nayak	4
D. J. Wild c Shastri b Nayak	16
D. S. Steele b Yadav	10
†G. Sharp c Vengsarkar b Nayak	22
Sarfraz Nawaz c Parkar b Shastri	26
N. A. Mallender c Vengsarkar b Nayak	0
B. J. Griffiths not out	0
L-b 3, w 2	5
1/15 2/50 3/84 4/89 5/121 6/133 7/172 8/177 9/194	204

Bowling: Randhir 13–1–36–1; Nayak 22–7–54–5; Doshi 17–3–47–1; Yadav 15–3–37–1; Shastri 8.5–2–25–2.

Umpires: K. E. Palmer and C. T. Spencer.

ENGLAND v INDIA

First Cornhill Test

At Lord's, June 10, 11, 12, 14, 15. England won by seven wickets. Despite a first-innings collapse by India, the almost inevitable rain on a Lord's Saturday and a comfortable England win, this was a Test match worth remembering. Botham and Kapil Dev both held the stage in their spectacular styles, and the fourth day was highly entertaining.

Randall and Edmonds returned to England duty after more than two years absence, while Lamb and Pringle earned first caps and Miller was twelfth man.

Kapil Dev briskly accounted for England's early batsmen, reaching 150 Test wickets when Viswanath held a stinging catch off Tavaré. Botham, promoted to No. 5, and Gower improved England's position with a rich display of strokes, Botham especially hitting the ball with great ferocity. They both departed to excellent diving catches and Randall had the responsibility of organising the repair of another unpromising situation. Though never fluent for sustained periods, he achieved this successfully in an alliance with Edmonds, who batted as well as he ever has in a Test match, making his highest score at this level. Randall, 84 overnight, when England were 278 for six, took his time in arriving at a personally important century. He batted 354 minutes, hitting eleven 4s and one 6. Contributions by Taylor, Allott and Willis, whose last-wicket partnership of 70 set a record for England against India, were prosaic preludes to India's downfall, which began just before tea on the second day when Botham beat Parkar.

The ball started to bounce awkwardly and to move off a reasonably helpful pitch, and England's pace attack was too straight for all but Gavaskar. He and Kapil Dev improved 45 for five to 92 before the close. Gavaskar had given the impression that he could stay for ever, but he was dismissed twice in the two and a half hours of play that proved possible on the Saturday and India were left with little apparent hope. First Botham bowled him through a drive with a splendid ball, and then, after India had followed on, Willis unshipped him with one of a series of menacing lifters that was jabbed to backward short leg.

India began the Monday at 67 for two in their second innings, and although Shastri performed the night-watchman's job well, India slipped to 110 for four before Yashpal

Sharma joined Vengsarkar in offering prolonged resistance. Vengsarkar made 86 between lunch and tea and played some glorious strokes; powerful, yet with the wristiness and ease of the best Indian players. He batted 331 minutes, with 21 4s, and he and Yashpal saw off eight overs of the new ball. Then Willis, bowling near his fastest, took four wickets in four overs, including three in a span of nine balls.

This brought in Kapil Dev, who took the match into a fifth day with a spectacularly violent piece of batting, which he followed, when India were all out, with an inspired new-ball burst. Hitting thirteen 4s and three 6s, with his bat making the sound of gunfire, he was soon on course for the fastest Test century of all time. When he was caught at short mid-wicket, he had received only 55 balls. When England batted again, he whipped out Cook, Tavaré and a highly superfluous night-watchman – Taylor – in eight balls, and England were, embarrassingly, 23 for three at the end of a day that contained 331 runs. Lamb's flurry of boundaries efficiently ended the game on the last morning.

The inauguration of the 96-overs-per-day minimum was generally agreed to be a success, with the sides working through their overs in a few minutes over the scheduled six hours. The match was watched by 50,217 people, who paid £211,408. – T.C.

England

G. Cook lbw b Kapil Dev	4	– lbw b Kapil Dev	10
C. J. Tavaré c Viswanath b Kapil Dev	4	– b Kapil Dev	3
A. J. Lamb lbw b Kapil Dev	9	– (4) not out	37
D. I. Gower c Viswanath b Kapil Dev	37	– (5) not out	14
I. T. Botham c Malhotra b Madan Lal	67		
D. W. Randall c Parkar b Kapil Dev	126		
D. R. Pringle c Gavaskar b Doshi	7		
P. H. Edmonds c Kirmani b Madan Lal	64		
†R. W. Taylor c Viswanath b Doshi	31	– (3) c Malhotra b Kapil Dev	1
P. J. W. Allott not out	41		
*R. G. D. Willis b Madan Lal	28		
B 1, l-b 5, n-b 9	15	L-b 2	2
1/5 2/18 3/37 4/96 5/149 6/166 7/291 8/363 9/363	433	1/11 2/13 3/18 (3 wkts)	67

Bowling: *First Innings*—Kapil Dev 43–8–125–5; Madan Lal 28.1–6–99–3; Shastri 34–10–73–0; Doshi 40–7–120–2; Yashpal 3–2–1–0. *Second Innings*—Kapil Dev 10–1–43–3; Madan Lal 2–1–2–0; Doshi 5–3–11–0; Shastri 2–0–9–0.

India

*S. M. Gavaskar b Botham	48	– c Cook b Willis	24
G. A. Parkar lbw b Botham	6	– b Willis	1
D. B. Vengsarkar lbw b Willis	2	– c Allott b Willis	157
G. R. Viswanath b Botham	1	– (5) c Taylor b Pringle	3
Yashpal Sharma lbw b Pringle	4	– (6) b Willis	37
A. Malhotra lbw b Pringle	5	– (7) c Taylor b Willis	0
Kapil Dev c Cook b Willis	41	– (8) c Cook b Botham	89
R. J. Shastri c Cook b Willis	4	– (4) b Allott	23
†S. M. H. Kirmani not out	6	– c Gower b Willis	3
Madan Lal c Tavaré b Botham	6	– lbw b Pringle	15
D. R. Doshi c Taylor b Botham	0	– not out	4
L-b 1, n-b 4	5	L-b 2, n-b 11	13
1/17 2/21 3/22 4/31 5/45 6/112 7/116 8/116 9/128	128	1/6 2/47 3/107 4/110 5/252 6/252 7/254 8/275 9/341	369

Bowling: *First Innings*—Botham 19.4–3–46–5; Willis 16–2–41–3; Pringle 9–4–16–2; Edmonds 2–1–5–0; Allott 4–1–15–0. *Second Innings*—Botham 31.5–7–103–1; Willis 28–3–101–6; Pringle 19–4–58–2; Allott 17–3–51–1; Edmonds 15–6–39–0; Cook 1–0–4–0.

Umpires: D. G. L. Evans and B. J. Meyer.

†OXFORD & CAMBRIDGE UNIVS v INDIANS

At Cambridge, June 17, 18. Drawn. On a perfect pitch, two days were never enough to provide a positive result, and the Indians devoted themselves to practice; spin bowler Shastri proved a successful opening bat, falling 7 short of a century, while Gavaskar stroked a serene 120. Earlier, Ellis had provided the backbone of the Universities' innings, his 90 coming in 150 minutes, and he gave their second innings stability until a quick partnership of 77 between Pringle and Hayes took them towards the declaration. However, the touring side declined to accept the invitation to score 169 in 70 minutes.

Oxford & Cambridge Univs

D. W. Varey b Randhir	18	– b Randhir	0
R. G. P. Ellis c and b Yadav	90	– b Yadav	45
R. J. Boyd-Moss c sub b Yadav	63	– c Yashpal b Nayak	22
S. P. Henderson b Doshi	38	– c Nayak b Shastri	31
*D. R. Pringle c and b Yadav	22	– (6) st Yashpal b Doshi	51
K. A. Hayes b Yadav	18	– (5) c Nayak b Doshi	62
S. J. G. Doggart c Yashpal b Yadav	25	– b Doshi	14
J. G. Varey not out	3	– not out	2
K. I. Hodgson not out	2		
B 1, l-b 5, n-b 3	9	B 5, w 1, n-b 1	7
1/18 2/174 3/187 4/221 5/251 6/261 7/284 (7 wkts dec.)	288	1/1 2/41 3/88 4/108 5/185 6/217 7/234 (7 wkts dec.)	234

†C. F. E. Goldie and R. W. M. Palmer did not bat.

Bowling: *First Innings*—Randhir 8–1–32–1; Kapil Dev 5–0–16–0; Nayak 8–1–22–0; Doshi 23–6–70–1; Shastri 11–0–32–0; Yadav 28–1–107–5. *Second Innings*—Randhir 7–2–39–1; Nayak 6–0–22–1; Yadav 16–0–66–1; Shastri 12–1–44–1; Doshi 13.4–4–43–3; Kapil Dev 2–0–13–0.

Indians

P. Roy b Pringle	20	– lbw b Pringle	3
R. J. Shastri b Doggart	93	– not out	24
S. M. Gavaskar st Goldie b Boyd-Moss	120		
†Yashpal Sharma c Hayes b Doggart	55	– (3) not out	24
Kapil Dev b Boyd-Moss	0		
S. V. Nayak not out	23		
*G. R. Viswanath b Boyd-Moss	29		
L-b 11, n-b 3	14		
1/50 2/160 3/301 4/301 5/301 6/354 (6 wkts dec.)	354	1/3 (1 wkt)	51

S. M. Patil, N. S. Yadav, Randhir Singh and D. R. Doshi did not bat.

Bowling: *First Innings*—Palmer 11–2–59–0; Pringle 9–3–25–1; J. G. Varey 10–2–34–0; Hodgson 18–5–60–0; Doggart 23–5–82–2; Boyd-Moss 11.1–1–58–3; Ellis 2–0–22–0. *Second Innings*—Palmer 5–1–16–0; Pringle 4–0–16–1; Boyd-Moss 2–0–17–0; Doggart 2–0–2–0.

Umpires: D. O. Oslear and R. Julian.

GLOUCESTERSHIRE v INDIANS

At Bristol, June 19, 20, 21. Drawn. Madan Lal had Gloucestershire on the run when rain ended play five minutes after tea on the third day, with the touring side holding an obvious chance of victory. The pitch, its preparation having been hampered by the unsettled weather, was reported as unsatisfactory by the umpires because of cracks in it and the very low bounce, but the teams managed none the less to provide some entertaining cricket and the Indians were always intent on forcing a result. Madan Lal's all-round form was outstanding. In partnership with Yashpal Sharma, he rescued the Indians' first innings from 138 for five, and followed this by making an early breach in the Gloucestershire innings before Broad and Bainbridge repaired the damage in a lively partnership of 97. The Indians took up the challenge provided by Graveney's declaration, even though the start of the third day was delayed for 70 minutes by rain, and then the light was so poor that Childs and Graveney had to bowl, with a damp ball, to keep the players on the field. Madan Lal completed his second unbeaten half-century, and when Gloucestershire set out to score 246 in 170 minutes he swung the ball appreciably in the heavy atmosphere, ensuring that survival could be the county batsmen's sole aim.

Indians

P. Roy c and b Graveney	32		
R. J. Shastri b Lawrence	51	– b Surridge	20
A. Malhotra lbw b Surridge	21	– c Brassington b Graveney	37
*G. R. Viswanath lbw b Bainbridge	1		
S. M. Patil st Brassington b Childs	20	– (4) st Brassington b Graveney	34
†Yashpal Sharma not out	50	– not out	40
Madan Lal not out	51	– (5) not out	58
S. V. Nayak (did not bat)		– (1) b Lawrence	6
B 8, l-b 6, w 2, n-b 3	19	B 4, w 1	5
1/79 2/98 3/99 4/138 5/138 (5 wkts dec.)	245	1/24 2/36 3/97 4/104 (4 wkts dec.)	200

S. M. H. Kirmani, D. R. Doshi and N. S. Yadav did not bat.

Bowling: *First Innings*—Lawrence 16–2–50–1; Surridge 27–10–57–1; Bainbridge 20–5–47–1; Childs 27.1–8–57–1; Graveney 16–8–15–1. *Second Innings*—Lawrence 7–1–24–1; Surridge 8–1–36–1; Bainbridge 5–0–24–0; Childs 21–5–43–0; Graveney 21–7–42–2; Cunningham 4–0–13–0; M. W. Stovold 1–0–13–0.

Gloucestershire

A. W. Stovold lbw b Madan Lal	12	– (2) c Yashpal b Madan Lal	0
B. C. Broad lbw b Shastri	73	– (1) c Yashpal b Madan Lal	0
Sadiq Mohammad b Doshi	9	– (5) not out	15
†A. J. Brassington c Kirmani b Nayak	0		
M. W. Stovold lbw b Madan Lal	3	– (3) b Madan Lal	9
P. Bainbridge b Shastri	61	– not out	7
E. J. Cunningham not out	11	– (4) lbw b Madan Lal	8
*D. A. Graveney not out	12		
B 9, l-b 10	19		
1/16 2/34 3/37 4/56 5/153 6/174 (6 wkts dec.)	200	1/0 2/5 3/17 4/26 (4 wkts)	39

J. H. Childs, D. V. Lawrence and D. Surridge did not bat.

Bowling: *First Innings*—Madan Lal 12–3–35–2; Nayak 10–1–33–1; Yadav 16–1–49–0; Doshi 16–4–41–1; Shastri 10.3–4–23–2. *Second Innings*—Madan Lal 7–0–28–4; Nayak 6–3–11–0; Shastri 1–1–0–0.

Umpires: J. Birkenshaw and W. E. Alley.

ENGLAND v INDIA

Second Cornhill Test

At Manchester, June 24, 25, 26, 27, 28. Drawn. There was not one day in this match that was free of bad weather. No play was possible after lunch on the second day and none at all on the last. The previous Test, at Lord's, had produced enough cricket of quality to raise interest in this match, yet the total attendance for the four days on which play was possible was 21,611 – with takings amounting to only £71,986.

Despite an encouraging weather forecast, the crowd on the Sunday, the fourth day, was the thinnest. The abstainers missed a batting feast, the like of which is rare in modern Test cricket. No fewer than 334 runs were scored from 93 overs, with Viswanath, Kirmani, Patil and Kapil Dev excelling themselves in mending severe damage inflicted the previous evening by Willis and Pringle.

The pitch was bare enough at the Stretford end for England to play two spinners, Miller being included in preference to the uncapped Jarvis, of Kent, who was standing by to replace an injured Allott. India, having found four bowlers inadequate in the first Test, found room for the medium-paced Nayak, omitting Parkar and promoting Shastri to open the innings with Gavaskar. Their other change was Patil for Malhotra, although Patil's record against the counties was no recommendation for his inclusion.

England won the toss for the seventh time in as many Tests against India and batted. Although the air was heavy with moisture, there were the doubts about the durability of the pitch to be considered. In the event, the ball moved about and Kapil Dev and Madan Lal posed a threat which Cook and Tavaré, with some luck, survived, staying together nearly until tea and putting on 106. Yet this healthy start, painstakingly achieved (Cook took 173 balls to make 66) was frittered away. At Tavaré's exit, England were 161 for four. Randall was out at the same score, to a ball from Doshi that turned and bounced. Doshi bowled superbly on the first day for his three economical wickets.

England's fortunes were revived as quickly and dramatically as they had been dissipated, Botham making 50 off 46 balls, with a 6 and ten 4s. On the second day, about half an hour after the start, Botham, having added only 7 to his overnight 60, took a painful blow on the toe of his left foot from a full toss by Nayak. Treatment brought no relief and Botham summoned a runner, but any discomfort Botham must have felt was minimal compared to the agony he inflicted on India's bowlers. For the next frenzied hour, he drove, cut and pulled with brutal power, and when he reached his tenth Test century – his fourth against India – he had scored 32 runs since his injury off only twenty balls, seven of which were boundary hits.

After the battering they had taken from Botham, who, when he played on to Shastri via his back leg, had made 128 (169 balls, two 6s, nineteen 4s) and added 169 with Miller, India could not have been distressed when rain, starting at lunchtime, ended the second day. Further delays next morning and afternoon meant that England batted almost until five o'clock on the third day. Miller, ninth out after a stay of 324 minutes, missed his maiden first-class hundred by only 2 runs.

India had seventeen overs to face before the close that evening, and were immediately in trouble against Willis. At 5, Shastri, the makeshift opener, was caught close in, fending off a short ball, and in Willis's next over Gavaskar fell to a brilliant catch at second slip by Tavaré. Before the end of the day, Vengsarkar, forcing Pringle off the back foot, was caught at fourth slip and India were 25 for 3. The first stage of their recovery was brought about by the overnight partnership between Viswanath and night-watchman Kirmani, who, batting bravely and responsibly, lifted the score to 112 before Viswanath top-edged a square-cut to Taylor.

Once this partnership was split, two more wickets fell before, at 173, Patil, then 25, was joined by Kapil Dev. India still needed 52 runs to save the follow-on. The partners conferred and, seemingly, decided on clearly defined roles, Kapil's part being to play in the only manner he knows. Patil relinquished the authority with which he had started and the follow-on mark was quickly left behind. Willis came in for heavy punishment as Kapil Dev hit 65 (one 6, nine 4s) off 55 balls in a partnership of 96 with Patil.

After Kapil's exit Patil, who had just reached 50, staged a spectacular assault, of which Willis was again the chief victim. In his first over with the second new ball, which included a no-ball, Willis was hit for six 4s, a new Test record. The fifth of them took Patil to his century, his last 50 runs having come in even time off 51 balls. – D.J.R.

England

G. Cook b Doshi	66
C. J. Tavaré b Doshi	57
A. J. Lamb c Viswanath b Madan Lal	9
D. I. Gower c Shastri b Madan Lal	9
I. T. Botham b Shastri	128
D. W. Randall c Kirmani b Doshi	0
G. Miller c Vengsarkar b Doshi	98
D. R. Pringle st Kirmani b Doshi	23
P. H. Edmonds c Kirmani b Madan Lal	12
†R. W. Taylor not out	1
*R. G. D. Willis c Gavaskar b Doshi	6
B 2, l-b 5, n-b 9	16
1/106 2/117 3/141 4/161 5/161 6/330 7/382 8/413 9/419	425

Bowling: Kapil Dev 36–5–109–0; Madan Lal 35–9–104–3; Nayak 12–1–50–0; Doshi 47.1–17–102–6; Shastri 23–8–44–1.

India

*S. M. Gavaskar c Tavaré b Willis	2
R. J. Shastri c Cook b Willis	0
D. B. Vengsarkar c Randall b Pringle	12
G. R. Viswanath c Taylor b Botham	54
†S. M. H. Kirmani b Edmonds	58
Yashpal Sharma b Edmonds	10
S. M. Patil not out	129
Kapil Dev c Taylor b Miller	65
Madan Lal b Edmonds	26
S. V. Nayak not out	2
B 6, l-b 2, w 3, n-b 10	21
1/5 2/8 3/25 4/112 5/136 6/173 7/269 8/366	(8 wkts) 379

D. R. Doshi did not bat.

Bowling: Willis 17–2–94–2; Pringle 15–4–33–1; Edmonds 37–12–94–3; Botham 19–4–86–1; Miller 16–4–51–1.

Umpires: H. D. Bird and B. J. Meyer.

ESSEX v INDIANS

At Chelmsford, July 3, 4, 5. Drawn. The tourists' failure to field anything like their strongest side was in keeping with a disappointing contest. Hardie, though experiencing some alarms against the spinners, batted with commendable concentration throughout his six-hour effort, hitting eleven 4s before being needlessly run out. Phillip's robust effort – 50 of his runs came in boundaries – served to enliven proceedings. Malhotra performed well for the tourists, but it needed an eighth-wicket stand between Parkar and Nayak to avert the follow-on. Pont and McEwan were the chief contributors when Essex went in a second time, but the game ended in a tame draw after India had been set 254 in 170 minutes.

Essex

B. R. Hardie run out	161	– c Vengsarkar b Nayak	20
A. W. Lilley lbw b Nayak	0	– lbw b Randhir	0
K. R. Pont c Parkar b Yadav	21	– not out	58
D. R. Pringle c Malhotra b Yadav	0	– c Parkar b Shastri	10
K. S. McEwan c Yashpal b Yadav	12	– st Parkar b Yadav	52
*K. W. R. Fletcher c sub b Shastri	17		
N. Phillip b Randhir	79		
S. Turner b Randhir	7		
†D. E. East lbw b Madan Lal	2	– (6) not out	32
R. E. East b Madan Lal	10		
D. L. Acfield not out	2		
B 5, l-b 16, w 2, n-b 2	25	L-b 2, n-b 1	3
1/8 2/90 3/92 4/114 5/152 6/294 7/308 8/321 9/325	336	1/0 2/36 3/57 4/134	(4 wkts dec.) 175

Bowling: *First Innings*—Randhir 18–6–50–2; Nayak 12–1–40–1; Madan Lal 16–1–64–2; Patil 7–1–14–0; Shastri 33–8–55–1; Yadav 24–4–77–3; Yashpal 2–0–11–0. *Second Innings*—Randhir 9–3–29–1; Nayak 11–2–19–1; Madan Lal 5–1–10–0; Shastri 15–3–54–1; Yadav 17–3–45–1; Patil 5–2–13–0; Vengsarkar 0.2–0–2–0.

Indians

P. Roy c D. E. East b Pringle	1	– c Lilley b Phillip	11
R. J. Shastri lbw b Phillip	3	– st D. E. East b R. E. East	74
A. Malhotra c D. E. East b Pringle	85	– c D. E. East b R. E. East	2
S. M. Patil c R. E. East b Pringle	10	– c McEwan b R. E. East	39
Yashpal Sharma lbw b Pringle	1		
D. B. Vengsarkar lbw b Phillip	41		
*Madan Lal b Pringle	4	– (5) not out	35
†G. A. Parkar not out	60	– (7) not out	0
S. V. Nayak not out	44		
Randhir Singh (did not bat)		– (6) b R. E. East	0
L-b 4, n-b 5	9	B 5, l-b 2, n-b 3	10
1/5 2/12 3/29 4/35 5/129 6/133 7/175	(7 wkts dec.) 258	1/27 2/42 3/100 4/166 5/166	(5 wkts) 171

N. S. Yadav did not bat.

Bowling: *First Innings*—Phillip 14–2–41–2; Pringle 19–5–59–5; Turner 7–0–35–0; R. E. East 19–5–30–0; Acfield 17–2–46–0; Pont 9–1–38–0. *Second Innings*—Phillip 5–1–12–1; Pringle 5–2–13–0; Turner 8–2–16–0; R. E. East 15–4–49–4; Acfield 6–1–23–0; Fletcher 4–0–22–0; McEwan 2–0–26–0.

Umpires: J. van Geloven and P. B. Wight.

ENGLAND v INDIA

Third Cornhill Test

At The Oval, July 8, 9, 10, 12, 13. Drawn. Though left drawn after a highly unprepossessing last day, a result which gave England a 1–0 win in the series, the third and final Test had, like its predecessors, its share of excitement and drama. Notable was the batting of Botham, Lamb and Kapil Dev, and a cruel injury to Gavaskar, who took no further part in the match after a stroke by Botham broke a bone in his left shin on the first day.

Despite their captain's absence, and in the face of a huge total, India batted boldly and with a good deal of character, avoiding the follow-on, albeit with seven wickets down. The match then died a lingering death on the fifth day with England delaying their declaration until India were right out of contention and not asking batsmen who were under pressure for their places to sacrifice their wickets.

While India were unchanged, England brought back Allott and omitted Miller, opting for four seam bowlers rather than the variety of an extra spinner. In the event, a mild pitch offered negligible help to anyone although, having been under water less than a week earlier, it had its hazards on the first morning when Cook and Tavaré figured in their second successive century opening stand. This was a good example of sensible batting providing a platform for pyrotechnics later. As the pitch became more straightforward under hot sunshine, Botham and Lamb provided entertainment of the highest quality in a partnership which had added 144 in 28 overs by the end of the day. Crucially, it also brought about Gavaskar's injury when Botham, forcing Shastri off the back foot, struck him a fearsome blow as he fielded close in at silly-point.

Lamb was run out after completing his maiden Test century, but Botham went on, with increasing power and majesty, to his highest score at this level and to one of the fastest double-centuries in Test history. When he reached 200 off 220 balls in 268 minutes, it was the third fastest by an Englishman, after Hammond (240 minutes) and Compton (245 minutes). In terms of balls received, it may have been the fastest ever. The Indians found it virtually impossible to bowl to him as he drove with rare ferocity, one straight 6 off Doshi leaving its mark for posterity in the shape of a hole in the pavilion roof. When he was caught, off his controversial reverse sweep, he had hit four 6s and nineteen 4s.

Inevitably there was a sense of anti-climax after his departure, and poor light prevented a logical England declaration before the close of the second day, with Randall falling 5 short of his second century of the series. India then counter-attacked spiritedly, Shastri, Viswanath and Patil making half-centuries of varying nature and, after 42 overs had been lost to bad light on the fourth morning, Kapil Dev crashing 97 from 93 balls. Kirmani batted sensibly in support of Kapil Dev, and the pair added a record 130 for India's sixth wicket, beating the 105 made by Hazare and Phadkar at Leeds in 1952. Though lacking Botham's discipline, Kapil Dev's was a hugely entertaining innings, played in adversity, and included two 6s and fourteen 4s; by the time he was caught from a stroke aimed at taking him to three figures, India had virtually avoided the follow-on.

When they were all out, 184 behind, Kapil still had enough energy left to produce a testing, high-class piece of new-ball bowling which bothered England, even though the pitch was at its mildest. He removed the unlucky Cook and the last day was highly academic, not dissimilar to many seen in India during the previous winter, but accepted rather more decorously there than by a small but noisy Oval crowd.

The total attendance was 26,348, the receipts £121,678. – M. J. C.

England

G. Cook c Shastri b Patil	50	– c Yashpal b Kapil Dev	8
C. J. Tavaré b Kapil Dev	39	– not out	75
A. J. Lamb run out	107	– b Doshi	45
D. I. Gower c Kirmani b Shastri	47	– c and b Nayak	45
I. T. Botham c Viswanath b Doshi	208		
D. W. Randall st Kirmani b Shastri	95		
D. R. Pringle st Kirmani b Doshi	9		
P. H. Edmonds c sub (G. A. Parkar) b Doshi	14		
†R. W. Taylor lbw b Shastri	3		
P. J. W. Allott c Yashpal b Doshi	3		
*R. G. D. Willis not out	1		
B 3, l-b 5, n-b 10	18	B 6, l-b 8, n-b 4	18
1/96 2/96 3/185 4/361 5/512 6/534 7/562 8/569 9/582	594	1/12 2/94 3/191 (3 wkts dec.)	191

Bowling: *First Innings*—Kapil Dev 25–4–109–1; Madan Lal 26–8–69–0; Nayak 21–5–66–0; Patil 14–1–48–1; Doshi 46–6–175–4; Shastri 41.3–8–109–3. *Second Innings*—Kapil Dev 19–3–53–1; Madan Lal 11–6–17–0; Doshi 19–5–47–1; Shastri 16–3–40–0; Nayak 5.3–0–16–1.

India

R. J. Shastri c Botham b Willis	66	– c Taylor b Willis	0
D. B. Vengsarkar c Edmonds b Botham	6	– (3) c Taylor b Pringle	16
G. R. Viswanath lbw b Willis	56	– (4) not out	75
Yashpal Sharma c Gower b Willis	38	– (5) not out	9
S. M. Patil c sub (N. R. Taylor) b Botham	62		
†S. M. H. Kirmani b Allott	43		
Kapil Dev c Allott b Edmonds	97		
Madan Lal c Taylor b Edmonds	5		
S. V. Nayak b Edmonds	11	– (2) c Taylor b Pringle	6
D. R. Doshi not out	5		
*S. M. Gavaskar absent hurt			
B 3, l-b 5, n-b 13	21	L-b 3, n-b 2	5
1/21 2/134 3/135 4/232 5/248 6/378 7/394 8/396 9/410	410	1/0 2/18 3/43 (3 wkts)	111

Bowling: *First Innings*—Willis 23–4–78–3; Botham 19–2–73–2; Allott 24–4–69–1; Pringle 28–5–80–0; Edmonds 35.2–11–89–3. *Second Innings*—Willis 4–0–16–1; Pringle 11–5–32–2; Edmonds 13–5–34–0; Allott 4–1–12–0: Botham 4–0–12–0.

Umpires: H. D. Bird and A. G. T. Whitehead.

THE PAKISTANIS IN ENGLAND, 1982

The Pakistanis, paying their seventh visit to England, were a strong and experienced side, led for the first time by Imran Khan. England, who did well to beat them, were helped by an unsteadiness of temperament which tended at vital moments to be Pakistan's undoing. In terms of pure cricketing ability, Pakistan, man for man, were at least as good a side.

The tour began with their making a succession of large scores against understrength county opposition. Imran felt that this resulted in their going into the first Test match critically short of hard cricket, a not uncommon grievance among touring captains. His other complaint, which had become an obsession by the end of the third and last Test match, concerned the umpiring. In various unguarded statements, both Imran and the team's manager, Intikhab Alam, one of his country's most popular cricketers, blamed the umpires for Pakistan's defeat.

With two of the three Test matches being played on pitches which allowed much movement off the seam, the bat was regularly beaten. This led to a lot of frenzied appealing by the players of both sides. The failure of England's batsmen to distinguish Abdul Qadir's googly from his leg-break meant that he, too, was forever rapping the pads and letting forth an impassioned appeal. The Pakistanis felt they had "the worst of the deal" in the first and third Tests. Imran's opposite number, Bob Willis, refused, wisely, to be drawn on the subject, as did Gower when, at Lord's, he led England in Willis's absence. The concensus here was that if either side benefited more than the other from close decisions it was Pakistan.

From the start of the first of the two one-day internationals, at Trent Bridge, it was clear that Pakistan could expect a lot of rowdily vocal, expatriate support. This added to the somewhat disputatious nature of an exciting Test series. The days have long gone when Pakistan came meekly to the slaughter. Imran is one of the world's outstanding all-rounders. He led a fine, if volatile, batting side, and in Qadir he had the best leg-spinner in the game. The rest of the bowling was not quite good enough. Unluckily, too, by the time of the last Test match Sarfraz Nawaz and Tahir Naqqash were both injured. Although slightly past his best, Sarfraz had played a useful part in Pakistan's victory at Lord's, while Tahir had bowled effectively in the first Test at Edgbaston. Ehtesham-ud-Din, who was summoned from the Bolton and District Association to make up the side at Headingley, was, hardly surprisingly, hopelessly unprepared.

Although Zaheer Abbas, Mudassar Nazar and Javed Miandad all scored almost at will outside the Test matches, only Mohsin played a big Test innings. His 200 at Lord's was a brilliant piece of cricket, raising him to the top rank of Pakistani batsmen after being unable, for several years, to get beyond the fringes of the Test side. He is a fine stylist, upstanding and correct. For such a prolific scorer in English county cricket, Zaheer's Test failures were a big disappointment. The extravagantly talented Javed, who was run out in two of his first three Test innings, has yet to make more than 54 in a Test in England.

Majid Khan, another with his best days behind him, found runs hard to get. Wasim Raja, an accomplished all-rounder, rather lacked opportunity, especially in the early days when runs were flowing freely. Mudassar, on the other hand, son of Nazar Mohammad, also a Test cricketer, proved himself a

THE PAKISTANIS IN ENGLAND, 1982

[*Ken Kelly*

Back row: Iqbal Qasim, Mudassar Nazar, Salim Yousuf, Sikander Bakht, Mohsin Khan, Tahir Naqqash, Mansoor Akhtar, Salim Malik, Haroon Rashid, Abdul Qadir. *Front row:* Wasim Raja, Wasim Bari, Majid Khan, Intikhab Alam (*manager*), Imran Khan (*captain*), Zaheer Abbas, Sarfraz Nawaz, Javed Miandad.

most spirited all-rounder, his bowling spells in the second and third Tests, at a friendly medium-pace, taking everyone by surprise.

Jalal-ud-Din, not a member of the original party but sent for when injuries began to diminish it, was himself injured by the time of the third Test. Iqbal Qasim was kept out of the Test side by Qadir, who, for the first month of the tour, carried all before him. If less deadly in the Tests, Qadir's mysteries still unsettled England's batsmen. His wickets in the Lord's victory were an invaluable contribution.

Imran, though, was the commanding figure of the tour. If he had a failing, other than picking out the umpires for criticism, it was in trying to do too much of the Test bowling himself. Being so much the most dangerous of the faster bowlers, the temptation was obvious. He led from the front, never sparing himself in any of his bowling spells, batting with more application than those higher in the order, and handling his side with authority. It is much to be hoped that the hint which he dropped after the last Test match, that he might not still be playing in 1986, when Pakistan tour England next, does not materialise. – J. W.

PAKISTANI TOUR RESULTS

Test matches – Played 3: Won 1, Lost 2.

First-class matches – Played 15: Won 5, Lost 4, Drawn 6.

Wins – England, Derbyshire, Glamorgan, Sussex, Worcestershire.

Losses – England (2), Hampshire, D. B. Close's XI.

Draws – England B, Lancashire, Leicestershire, Middlesex, Somerset, Surrey.

Non first-class matches – Played 4: Won 1, Lost 2, Drawn 1. *Win* – Minor Counties. *Losses* – England (2). *Draw* – Scotland.

Note: In addition to the matches listed above, the touring team played two non first-class games of 40 overs each side which were not included in the original itinerary. The first, at Swansea on July 4, the Sunday of the first-class game v Glamorgan, was rained off after 23 overs when the Pakistanis were 74 for four. The second, at the Scarborough Festival, was on September 3, the third day scheduled for the first-class match v D. B. Close's XI, and the Pakistanis won by 83 runs.

TEST MATCH AVERAGES

ENGLAND – BATTING

	T	*I*	*NO*	*R*	*HI*	*Avge*
C. J. Tavaré	3	6	0	216	82	36.00
D. I. Gower	3	6	0	197	74	32.83
D. W. Randall	3	6	0	168	105	28.00
I. T. Botham	3	6	0	163	69	27.16
R. W. Taylor	3	6	2	108	54	27.00
M. W. Gatting	3	6	1	111	32*	22.20
E. E. Hemmings	2	4	0	41	19	10.25
R. D. Jackman	2	3	0	28	17	9.33
A. J. Lamb	3	6	0	48	33	8.00
I. A. Greig	2	4	0	26	14	6.50

Played in two Tests: R. G. D. Willis 0*, 28*, 1*. Played in one Test: G. Fowler, 9, 86; V. J. Marks 7, 12*; G. Miller 47, 5; D. R. Pringle 5, 14.

* *Signifies not out.*

BOWLING

	O	M	R	W	Avge
R. G. D. Willis	74	14	222	10	22.20
I. T. Botham	150.5	33	478	18	26.55
I. A. Greig	31.2	6	114	4	28.50
R. D. Jackman	105	30	247	8	30.87
E. E. Hemmings	56.1	12	149	3	49.66

Also bowled: M. W. Gatting 10–3–21–0; V. J. Marks 7–1–31–1; G. Miller 9.4–2–27–2; D. R. Pringle 26–9–62–0.

PAKISTAN – BATTING

	T	I	NO	R	HI	Avge
Mohsin Khan	3	6	1	310	200	62.00
Imran Khan	3	5	1	212	67*	53.00
Javed Miandad	3	6	1	178	54	35.60
Mansoor Akhtar	3	5	0	154	58	30.80
Wasim Bari	3	5	2	82	24*	27.33
Zaheer Abbas	3	5	0	131	75	26.20
Tahir Naqqash	2	3	0	53	39	17.66
Mudassar Nazar	3	5	0	85	65	17.00
Abdul Qadir	3	5	1	56	18*	14.00
Sikander Bakht	2	4	1	16	7	5.33

Played in one Test: Ehtesham-ud-Din 0, 0*; Haroon Rashid 1; Majid J. Khan 21, 10; Wasim Raja 26, 16. Sarfraz Nawaz did not bat.

**Signifies not out.*

BOWLING

	O	M	R	W	Avge
Mudassar Nazar	54	18	104	10	10.40
Tahir Naqqash	52	20	117	7	16.71
Imran Khan	178.1	48	390	21	18.57
Sarfraz Nawaz	37	9	78	3	26.00
Abdul Qadir	160.5	48	406	10	40.60
Sikander Bakht	75	19	179	3	59.66

Also bowled: Ehtesham-ud-Din 14–4–46–1; Wasim Raja 2.3–2–0–1.

PAKISTANI TOUR AVERAGES – FIRST-CLASS MATCHES

BATTING

	M	I	NO	R	HI	Avge
Mudassar Nazar	11	16	6	825	211*	82.50
Zaheer Abbas	9	12	3	664	148*	73.77
Mohsin Khan	13	20	3	1,248	203*	73.41
Imran Khan	9	8	4	291	67*	72.75
Javed Miandad	10	13	6	450	105*	64.28
Mansoor Akhtar	11	17	2	595	153	39.66
Haroon Rashid	10	13	3	331	90	33.10
Wasim Bari	11	7	2	162	45	32.40
Majid J. Khan	11	17	3	403	88	28.78

	M	*I*	*NO*	*R*	*HI*	*Avge*
Wasim Raja............	12	12	2	247	50*	24.70
Tahir Naqqash..........	6	4	0	65	39	16.25
Abdul Qadir............	12	9	3	93	21*	15.50
Salim Yousuf...........	4	4	1	38	15*	12.66
Salim Malik............	5	7	1	68	25*	11.33
Sikander Bakht.........	12	7	2	29	9	5.80
Iqbal Qasim............	7	4	1	9	5	3.00

Also batted: Ehtesham-ud-Din (2 matches) 0, 0*; Intikhab Alam (1 match) 0, 4; Jalal-ud-Din (3 matches) 10, 0; Sarfraz Nawaz (6 matches) 7.

**Signifies not out.*

BOWLING

	O	*M*	*R*	*W*	*Avge*
Mudassar Nazar........	139	35	368	21	17.52
Imran Khan.............	290.3	76	621	35	17.74
Abdul Qadir............	452.4	123	1,187	57	20.82
Sarfraz Nawaz..........	127	24	351	16	21.93
Sikander Bakht.........	326	86	959	27	35.51
Tahir Naqqash..........	160	44	537	15	35.80
Wasim Raja.............	117.4	30	346	9	38.44
Iqbal Qasim............	161.1	36	434	12	36.16

Also bowled: Ehtesham-ud-Din 28–9–81–1; Intikhab Alam 6–0–17–1; Jalal-ud-Din 56–19–123–4; Javed Miandad 3–0–16–0; Majid J. Khan 22–9–57–2; Mansoor Akhtar 16.3–6–43–1; Mohsin Khan 5–0–32–1; Salim Malik 1–0–5–0; Zaheer Abbas 0.1–0–0–0.

FIELDING

Wasim Bari 29 (22ct, 7st), Javed Miandad 14, Haroon Rashid 8, Majid J. Khan 8, Salim Yousuf 7 (5ct, 2st), Mansoor Akhtar 5, Mohsin Khan 5, Wasim Raja 5, Mudassar Nazar 4, Salim Malik 4, Abdul Qadir 3, Sikander Bakht 3, Tahir Naqqash 3, Iqbal Qasim 2, Zaheer Abbas 2, Sarfraz Nawaz 1.

HUNDREDS FOR PAKISTANIS

The following thirteen three-figure innings were played for the Pakistanis, twelve in first-class matches and one in a non first-class match.

Mohsin Khan (4)
- 203* v Leicestershire at Leicester
- 200 v England at Lord's (Second Test)
- 165* v Worcestershire at Worcester
- 151 v Sussex at Hove

Mudassar Nazar (4)
- 211* v Sussex at Hove
- 163* v Glamorgan at Swansea
- 103* v England B at Leicester
- 100* v Derbyshire at Chesterfield

Zaheer Abbas (2)
- 148* v Derbyshire at Chesterfield
- 147 v Worcestershire at Worcester

Javed Miandad (1)
105* v Somerset at Taunton

Mansoor Akhtar (1)
153 v Somerset at Taunton

Wasim Raja (1)
†174 v Scotland at Glasgow

**Signifies not out.* *†Not first-class.*

HUNDREDS AGAINST PAKISTANIS

The following nine three-figure innings were played against the Pakistanis, eight in first-class matches and one in a non first-class match.

M. D. Crowe (1)
104 for D. B. Close's XI at Scarborough

D. I. Gower (1)
176* for Leicestershire at Leicester

T. E. Jesty (1)
133 for Hampshire at Bournemouth

R. D. V. Knight (1)
111 for Surrey at The Oval

A. J. Lamb (1)
†118 for England at Nottingham (First Prudential Trophy Match)

G. D. Mendis (1)
114 for Sussex at Hove

M. C. J. Nicholas (1)
107* for Hampshire at Bournemouth

D. W. Randall (1)
105 for England at Birmingham (First Test)

I. V. A. Richards (1)
181* for Somerset at Taunton

**Signifies not out.* *†Not first-class.*

Note: Those matches which follow and which were not first-class are signified by the use of a dagger.

MIDDLESEX v PAKISTANIS

At Lord's, June 23, 24, 25. Drawn. In a rain-ruined match, Middlesex relaxed rather too much from their pursuit of trophies on several fronts. Play was possible for only half the first and second days and not at all on the third, but even in that time Middlesex were thoroughly outplayed. Only Slack, showing immense calm, countered the assorted seam bowlers in the first innings, although Gatting struck four boundaries in his brief stay. In Pakistan's innings Majid hooked his second ball for 6, but it was not long before Imran, seeking a positive result, declared well in arrears. Immediately he showed Middlesex that their first-innings toils were tame as, full of accuracy and hostility, he sent the first four batsmen back to the pavilion.

Middlesex

W. N. Slack b Mudassar	64	– c Miandad b Imran	9
G. D. Barlow c Miandad b Sarfraz	8	– b Imran	0
C. T. Radley c Miandad b Sarfraz	2	– c Bari b Imran	2
K. P. Tomlins b Sikander	3		
R. O. Butcher st Bari b Qasim	7	– not out	9
R. J. Maru c Zaheer b Sikander	13	– not out	2
*M. W. Gatting lbw b Mudassar	18	– (4) c Bari b Imran	4
†P. R. Downton b Mudassar	7		
K. D. James b Raja	1		
N. F. Williams not out	6		
L-b 9, n-b 6	15	W 2, n-b 2	4
1/138 2/45 3/56 4/68 5/96 6/124 7/131 8/138 9/144 (9 wkts dec.)	144	1/1 2/13 3/18 4/23 (4 wkts)	30

W. G. Merry did not bat.

Bowling: *First Innings*—Imran 13–5–15–0; Sarfraz 17–4–41–2; Sikander 17–4–48–2; Qasim 4–1–4–1; Mudassar 6–1–21–3; Raja 1.1–1–0–1. *Second Innings*—Imran 7–1–10–4; Sikander 5–0–14–0; Qasim 3–3–0–0; Raja 2–1–2–0.

Pakistanis

Mudassar Nazar not out	12
Mohsin Khan b James	1
Majid J. Khan not out	12
L-b 1, n-b 5	6
1/4 (1 wkt dec.)	31

Javed Miandad, Zaheer Abbas, Wasim Raja, *Imran Khan, Sarfraz Nawaz, †Wasim Bari, Iqbal Qasim and Sikander Bakht did not bat.

Bowling: Williams 6–1–12–0; James 6–1–13–1.

Umpires: D. Archer and K. E. Palmer.

SUSSEX v PAKISTANIS

At Hove, June 26, 27, 28. Pakistanis won by an innings and 13 runs. An opening partnership of 319 on the first day between Mudassar Nazar and Mohsin Khan, playing disciplined cricket with very few errors, sentenced a below-strength Sussex to hard grafting in an attempt to prevent an overwhelming victory for the tourists. Mohsin hit eighteen 4s in his five-hour stay, while Mudassar's unbeaten 211 contained 22 4s. Yet when the home side batted, following Zaheer's declaration after Saturday's run-spree, wickets tumbled regularly to the leg-spin of Abdul Qadir, who bewitched seven batsmen in the first innings, and another six when Sussex followed on, all of them during a mesmerising spell of 49 balls at a cost of only 17 runs. With Wasim Raja also bowling leg-spinners at the other end, spectators had the unusual treat of viewing what the Pakistan team manager Intikhab Alam, himself an exponent, had described as "a dying art". Mendis and Colin Wells delayed the inevitable defeat with a fighting second-wicket stand of 171, Mendis hitting one 6 and eleven 4s in his first century of the season.

Pakistanis

Mudassar Nazar not out	211
Mohsin Khan run out	151
Majid J. Khan c and b Phillipson	0
Javed Miandad not out	52
B 8, l-b 4, w 1, n-b 23	36
1/319 2/324 (2 wkts dec.)	450

Haroon Rashid, Wasim Raja, *Zaheer Abbas, †Wasim Bari, Tahir Naqqash, Abdul Qadir and Sikander Bakht did not bat.

Bowling: Pigott 23–4–87–0; Jones 3–0–11–0; C. M. Wells 13.1–3–20–0; Waller 34–6–100–0; Green 24–2–92–0; A. P. Wells 12–1–42–0; Phillipson 14–0–57–1; Gould 3.5–0–5–0.

Sussex

G. D. Mendis c sub b Qadir	48	– lbw b Qadir	114
J. R. P. Heath lbw b Sikander	10	– c and b Sikander	12
C. M. Wells st Bari b Qadir	28	– c Mudassar b Qadir	59
A. M. Green b Qadir	30	– c Miandad b Qadir	3
†I. J. Gould st Bari b Qadir	32	– (6) c Tahir b Qadir	11
C. P. Phillipson c Majid b Raja	17	– (5) b Tahir	3
A. P. Wells c Miandad b Qadir	17	– st Bari b Qadir	4
A. C. S. Pigott st Bari b Qadir	0	– not out	2
C. E Waller not out	6	– c Majid b Qadir	3
A. N. Jones b Qadir	0	– absent hurt	
*P. W. G. Parker absent hurt		– absent hurt	
B 1, l-b 7, w 1, n-b 12	21	L-b 7, n-b 10	17
1/26 2/88 3/103 4/156 5/185 6/187 7/194 8/205 9/209	209	1/23 2/194 3/196 4/201 5/215 6/221 7/222 8/228	228

Bowling: *First Innings*—Sikander 12–3–62–1; Tahir 11–0–49–0; Qadir 23.1–6–44–7; Mudassar 3–0–7–0; Raja 14–7–26–1. *Second Innings*—Sikander 11–2–47–1; Tahir 18–7–33–1; Qadir 30.3–7–78–6; Raja 8–2–32–0; Majid 3–1–5–0; Miandad 3–0–16–0.

Umpires: R. S. Herman and D. O. Oslear.

HAMPSHIRE v PAKISTANIS

At Bournemouth, June 30, July 1, 2. Hampshire won by six wickets, so gaining their first victory over a touring team since beating the Indians in 1932. Batting first on a slow pitch of variable bounce, the Pakistanis scored at over a run a minute, the substance of their innings coming from Mansoor Akhtar and Haroon Rashid, who put on 77 in nineteen overs for the third wicket, and Wasim Raja and Wasim Bari, whose sixth-wicket partnership realised 69 in sixteen overs. Sarfraz removed Rice and Nicholas in the fifth over of the Hampshire innings and Qadir dismissed Robin Smith, the 18-year-old South African who was making his first-class début in England, before the close, but rain prevented any play on the second day. Pocock closed Hampshire's innings before the start of the third day, and Majid responded by declaring after just 80 minutes, leaving Hampshire 213 minutes plus twenty overs in which to score 317. Two wickets fell for 3 runs, but then Nicholas and Jesty put on 175 in 119 minutes to put Hampshire right on course. Jesty punished Qadir for 26 in one over (a 6 and five 4s) before he was third out at 178, having made his runs off 133 balls in 119 minutes and having hit three 6s and twenty 4s. Nicholas saw Hampshire home with nine balls remaining, his unbeaten century, including one 5 and thirteen 4s, taking 279 minutes.

Pakistanis

Mohsin Khan c Parks b Malone	17	– lbw b Malone	0
Mansoor Akhtar b Rice	87	– not out	40
*Majid J. Khan b Jesty	8	– c Jesty b Nicholas	45
Haroon Rashid c Nicholas b Southern	32	– not out	7
Salim Malik c Jesty b Southern	12		
Wasim Raja c Smith b Southern	40		
†Wasim Bari c Smith b Southern	45		
Sarfraz Nawaz c Emery b Cowley	7		
Tahir Naqqash c Southern b Cowley	12		
Abdul Qadir not out	21		
Iqbal Qasim not out	3		
B 3, l-b 9, n-b 4	16	B 2, l-b 3, w 1, n-b 3	9
1/45 2/78 3/155 4/156 5/180 6/249 7/258 8/262 9/287	(9 wkts dec.) 300	1/0 2/92	(2 wkts dec.) 101

Bowling: *First Innings*—Emery 7–1–24–0; Malone 8–1–50–1; Jesty 9–3–20–1; Rice 19–5–76–1; Southern 26–7–88–4; Cowley 13.3–3–26–2. *Second Innings*—Malone 7–2–35–1; Emery 4–0–19–0; Rice 6–1–25–0; Nicholas 3–0–13–1.

Hampshire

J. M. Rice lbw b Sarfraz	5	– c Raja b Sarfraz	0
M. C. J. Nicholas c Bari b Sarfraz	2	– not out	107
R. A. Smith b Qadir	8	– c Haroon b Tahir	1
T. E. Jesty not out	45	– b Tahir	133
R. E. Hayward b Qadir	7	– c Bari b Sarfraz	31
*N. E. J. Pocock not out	10	– not out	29
B 1, l-b 1, n-b 6	8	B 4, l-b 2, n-b 12	18
1/8 2/9 3/39 4/54	(4 wkts dec.) 85	1/0 2/3 3/178 4/261	(4 wkts) 319

N. G. Cowley, †R. J. Parks, J. W. Southern, K. St J. D. Emery and S. J. Malone did not bat.

Bowling: *First Innings*—Sarfraz 7–2–20–2; Tahir 8–1–40–0; Qadir 6–2–17–2. *Second Innings*—Sarfraz 16–2–56–2; Tahir 12–3–49–2; Qadir 24–4–114–0; Qasim 18.3–4–57–0; Raja 5–0–25–0.

Umpires: R. S. Herman and A. G. T. Whitehead.

GLAMORGAN v PAKISTANIS

At Swansea, July 3, 5. Pakistanis won by an innings and 73 runs. Glamorgan continued their dismal season by being completely outplayed by the Pakistani tourists, and suffered considerably from lack of interest at the turnstiles. As they had at Hove a week earlier, the Pakistanis spent Saturday amassing a formidable total under the direction of Mudassar Nazar, who this time remained unbeaten for a splendid 163. Majid displayed for his former county the touch he regained at Bournemouth during the week, and there was a half-century from Wasim Raja before Imran's declaration left time for a wicket apiece for himself and Sikander before the close. On Monday, only Ontong and Rowe offered any resistance as Qadir's leg-spin produced five wickets in the first innings and four in the second for a mere 51 runs. It was a poor effort by the Welshmen, who normally put up a confident show against touring teams.

Pakistanis

Mudassar Nazar not out	163	Wasim Raja not out	50
Mansoor Akhtar c Davies b Barwick	26	L-b 2, w 3, n-b 4	9
Majid J. Khan c Davies b Barwick	88		—
Haroon Rashid b Ontong	20	1/42 2/214	(4 wkts dec.) 356
Salim Malik c Davies b Ontong	0	3/247 4/247	

*Imran Khan, †Wasim Bari, Abdul Qadir, Iqbal Qasim and Sikander Bakht did not bat.

Bowling: Nash 12–4–43–0; Davis 20–1–74–0; Barwick 17–2–69–2; Ontong 16–1–81–2; Lloyd 19.4–1–80–0.

Glamorgan

A. Jones b Sikander	17	– b Imran	0
J. A. Hopkins c Majid b Imran	4	– run out	24
D. A. Francis lbw b Sikander	12	– c Bari b Sikander	0
†T. Davies c Bari b Imran	6	– (7) not out	14
R. C. Ontong c Majid b Mudassar	33	– (4) b Mudassar	41
C. J. C. Rowe b Qadir	48	– (5) c Haroon b Sikander	8
A. L. Jones not out	12	– (6) c Bari b Mudassar	0
M. A. Nash st Bari b Qadir	4	– b Qadir	5
*B. J. Lloyd c and b Qadir	9	– c Haroon b Qadir	18
S. R. Barwick b Qadir	0	– lbw b Qadir	2
W. W. Davis lbw b Qadir	0	– c sub b Qadir	6
B 4, l-b 5, n-b 1	10	B 4, l-b 5, n-b 1	10
	—		—
1/21 2/21 3/35 4/51 5/121 6/129 7/135 8/150 9/154	155	1/0 2/1 3/63 4/83 5/83 6/84 7/90 8/118 9/122	128

Bowling: *First Innings*—Imran 14–7–10–2; Sikander 17–8–38–2; Qadir 10.1–2–31–5; Mudassar 12–3–41–1; Qasim 9–2–25–0. *Second Innings*—Imran 12–3–29–1; Sikander 14–4–41–2; Qadir 7–2–20–4; Mudassar 10–1–28–2.

Umpires: W. E. Alley and W. L. Budd.

SOMERSET v PAKISTANIS

At Taunton, July 7, 8, 9. Drawn. On an easy pitch Mansoor, with two 6s and 23 4s in a sparkling 66 overs, led the establishing opening partnership of 226 in 53 overs with Mohsin before the spinners and Dredge quietened the batting down. Sarfraz, who later developed 'flu, Qadir and Sikander steadily reduced Somerset to 147 for seven before Richards, in a splendid 72-over effort, found a useful partner in Dredge. Dropped at 2 and 16, Dredge helped Richards to a new Somerset eighth-wicket record of 153 in 32 overs, the West Indian ending with 25 4s. After overnight and morning rain, Miandad moved smoothly to 100 in 60 overs on the final day, hitting three 6s and seven 4s, but the third declaration of the match offered an unrealistic target of 263 in 140 minutes. A hostile Imran and Sikander threatened severely in the opening stages but, with Richards unlikely to bat because of a slight injury, Slocombe, through 29 difficult overs, and Popplewell, dropped when 13, ensured against defeat. Consequently the final half-hour was not used.

Pakistanis

Mohsin Khan c Lloyds b Marks	85		
Mansoor Akhtar c Davis b Dredge	153		
Majid J. Khan c Lloyds b Dredge	16	– c Rose b Lloyds	47
Javed Miandad c Dredge b Lloyds	29	– (1) not out	105
Zaheer Abbas st Gard b Lloyds	36	– (2) c Davis b Moseley	41
Wasim Raja not out	14	– (4) c and b Marks	3
*Imran Khan (did not bat)		(5) not out	12
B 7, l-b 2, n-b 2	11	B 4, l-b 3, n-b 3	10
1/226 2/253 3/264 4/315 5/344 (5 wkts dec.)	344	1/83 2/182 3/185 (3 wkts dec.)	218

Sarfraz Nawaz, †Wasim Bari, Sikander Bakht and Abdul Qadir did not bat.

Bowling: *First Innings*—Moseley 8–0–33–0; Davis 7–0–46–0; Dredge 15–3–48–2; Richards 9–2–36–0; Marks 36–10–96–1; Popplewell 2–0–15–0; Lloyds 16.4–4–59–2. *Second Innings*—Moseley 9–0–31–1; Davis 13–2–41–0; Marks 12.2–3–45–1; Dredge 6–1–12–0; Popplewell 10–1–47–0; Richards 5–1–12–0; Lloyds 4–0–20–1.

Somerset

P. M. Roebuck b Qadir	15	– c Bari b Sikander	1
J. W. Lloyds c Miandad b Sarfraz	16	– c Mansoor b Imran	0
I. V. A. Richards not out	181		
N. F. M. Popplewell c Majid b Qadir	0	– not out	29
P. A. Slocombe c Mohsin b Sikander	19	– (3) c Bari b Raja	17
*B. C. Rose c Miandad b Sikander	11		
V. J. Marks b Sikander	0	– (5) not out	2
†T. Gard lbw b Imran	0		
C. H. Dredge not out	34		
B 9, l-b 10, w 4, n-b 1	24	B 1, l-b 3, n-b 1	5
1/27 2/58 3/58 4/117 5/140 6/146 7/147 (7 wkts dec.)	300	1/0 2/6 3/51 (3 wkts)	54

M. R. Davis and H. R. Moseley did not bat.

Bowling: *First Innings*—Imran 23.5–2–80–1; Sikander 20–1–85–3; Sarfraz 5–0–15–1; Qadir 27–3–80–2; Raja 3–0–16–0. *Second Innings*—Imran 7–3–6–1; Sikander 9–6–11–1; Qadir 7–2–19–0; Majid 5–3–8–0; Mansoor 1.3–0–4–0; Raja 1–0–1–1.

Umpires: D. J. Constant and D. G. L. Evans.

WORCESTERSHIRE v PAKISTANIS

At Worcester, July 10, 11, 12. Pakistanis won by an innings and 93 runs. A Worcestershire side minus seven capped players lacked the batsmen with experience to counter the spin combination of Iqbal Qasim and Abdul Qadir. Nor could their second-string attack, with opening bowler Newport making his first appearance, restrain the Pakistani strokemakers, whose innings began with 100 in 80 minutes. Neale twice played solidly, his second half-century threatening to thwart the tourists for a time on the third day, when almost three hours were lost to rain and bad light. Humphries, seeing others perish on the back foot, struck out with success, but the highlight for the disappointingly few supporters came in the last hour and a quarter on Sunday. Weston, with sixteen boundaries, plundered 86 out of a total of 94 for the first wicket. Earlier in the day Mohsin, 91 not out overnight, had taken his score to 165 before retiring with a jarred wrist and Zaheer had placed the ball effortlessly to all parts of the ground as the tourists amassed their highest total to date.

Worcestershire

M. J. Weston c Mudassar b Tahir	20	– c Yousuf b Qasim	93
M. S. Scott c Miandad b Tahir	0	– lbw b Qadir	6
*P. A. Neale lbw b Tahir	68	– lbw b Qasim	59
E. J. O. Hemsley b Qadir	8	– c Miandad b Qasim	8
D. N. Patel c Yousuf b Mudassar	0	– b Qadir	1
D. B. D'Oliveira lbw b Qadir	8	– c sub b Qadir	1
†D. J. Humphries c Mansoor b Qasim	46	– b Imram	1
P. J. Newport lbw b Qadir	8	– lbw b Qadir	7
R. K. Illingworth b Qadir	0	– c sub b Qasim	0
A. E. Warner b Qasim	15	– c Tahir b Qasim	4
S. P. Perryman not out	0	– not out	2
B 5, l-b 3, w 1, n-b 6	15	L-b 2, w 1, n-b 1	4
1/4 2/39 3/65 4/72 5/97 6/145 7/169 8/169 9/180	188	1/94 2/102 3/122 4/123 5/143 6/163 7/180 8/180 9/180	186

Bowling: *First Innings*—Imran 9–0–35–0; Tahir 15–4–60–3; Mudassar 9–4–21–1; Qadir 14–5–30–4; Qasim 12–4–27–2. *Second Innings*—Imran 9–2–17–1; Tahir 5–0–38–0; Qasim 29.4–8–52–5; Qadir 26–8–75–4.

Pakistanis

Mudassar Nazar c and b Illingworth	75
Mohsin Khan retired hurt	165
Mansoor Akhtar lbw b Patel	2
Zaheer Abbas c Illingworth b Perryman	147
Javed Miandad not out	35
Majid J. Khan c Humphries b Weston	8
*Imran Khan not out	21
L-b 8, n-b 6	14
1/164 2/175 3/408 4/424 (4 wkts dec.)	467

†Salim Yousuf, Iqbal Qasim, Abdul Qadir and Tahir Naqqash did not bat.

Bowling: Warner 12–1–64–0; Newport 11–0–64–0; Weston 18.4–0–61–1; Perryman 26–4–91–1; Illingworth 30–3–126–1; Patel 19–3–47–1.

Umpires: K. E. Palmer and N. T. Plews.

†SCOTLAND v PAKISTANIS

At Glasgow, July 14, 15. Drawn. Pakistanis 351 for four dec. (Wasim Raja 174, Javed Miandad 54 not out, Mudassar Nazar 47, Zaheer Abbas 41 not out); Scotland 111 for five (W. A. Donald 53 not out; Imran Khan five for 24).

ENGLAND v PAKISTAN

First Prudential Trophy Match

At Nottingham, July 17. England won by seven wickets. During an opening partnership of 102 in 26 overs between Mudassar and Mohsin, Pakistan, who had won the toss, seemed to have laid the foundation of a larger total than the 250 for six with which they finished. Some good slow bowling by Hemmings, playing in his first match at this level, and Miller, brilliantly supported in the field, slowed Pakistan down. In reply England, gradually gaining momentum, were comfortably within reach of their target once Lamb had survived a hard chance to deep mid-on off Iqbal Qasim when he was 12. Lamb's 118, made in 34 overs, contained fourteen 4s and won him the Man of the Match award. The behaviour of a large crowd, watching in glorious weather, left much to be desired, the ground being frequently invaded by over-enthusiastic spectators.

The attendance was 10,231.

Pakistan

Mudassar Nazar run out	51	*Imran Khan not out	16
Mohsin Khan b Botham	47	Sarfraz Nawaz not out	2
Zaheer Abbas lbw b Pringle	53	B 4, l-b 4, w 6, n-b 2	16
Javed Miandad c Willis b Pringle	28		
Majid J. Khan c Willis b Botham	23	1/102 2/103 3/175 (6 wkts, 55 overs)	250
Wasim Raja c Hemmings b Botham	14	4/208 5/222 6/238	

†Wasim Bari, Iqbal Qasim and Sikander Bakht did not bat.

Bowling: Willis 11–1–46–0; Botham 11–0–57–3; Pringle 11–1–50–2; Miller 11–1–36–0; Hemmings 11–1–45–0.

England

D. I. Gower c Bari b Sikander	17	I. T. Botham not out	10
C. J. Tavaré b Imran	48	L-b 11, w 5, n-b 6	22
A. J. Lamb c Bari b Imran	118		
M. W. Gatting not out	37	1/25 2/132 3/234 (3 wkts, 47.1 overs)	252

D. W. Randall, G. Miller, D. R. Pringle, E. E. Hemmings, †R. W. Taylor and *R. G. D. Willis did not bat.

Bowling: Imran 11–2–35–2; Sarfraz 11–3–43–0; Sikander 7–0–34–1; Qasim 7–0–49–0; Mudassar 5.1–0–26–0; Majid 4–0–25–0; Raja 2–0–18–0.

Umpires: D. G. L. Evans and A. G. T. Whitehead.

ENGLAND v PAKISTAN

Second Prudential Trophy Match

At Manchester, July 19. England won by 73 runs. England's second victory, which assured them of the Prudential Trophy, was no less convincing than their first. Batting first this time, after Pakistan had put them in, they reached 295 for eight, the second largest total recorded in these matches. Gatting and Botham set it up with a violent partnership of 84 in eleven overs, Botham's 49, scored off only 29 balls, containing four 6s, all off the slow left-arm spin of Iqbal Qasim. Needing to score at 5.38 runs an over to win, Pakistan found the risks that this involved too great, only Wasim Raja and Imran Khan, in a stand of 60, causing England any concern. Gatting was Man of the Match. For England the Man of the Series was Lamb, for Pakistan, Mudassar.

The attendance was 21,770.

England

D. I. Gower c Bari b Mudassar	33	D. R. Pringle not out	34
C. J. Tavaré run out	16	E. E. Hemmings c Qasim b Tahir	1
A. J. Lamb c Bari b Qasim	27	†R. W. Taylor not out	1
M. W. Gatting run out	76	L-b 16, w 10	26
I. T. Botham c Raja b Imran	49		
D. W. Randall run out	6	1/32 2/54 3/101 (8 wkts, 55 overs)	295
G. Miller b Imran	26	4/185 5/217 6/226 7/280 8/284	

*R. G. D. Willis did not bat.

Bowling: Imran 11–1–48–2; Tahir 10–0–37–1; Sikander 11–0–42–0; Mudassar 11–0–50–1; Qasim 8–0–76–1; Majid 4–1–16–0.

Pakistan

Mudassar Nazar run out	31
Mohsin Khan b Pringle	17
Zaheer Abbas c Randall b Pringle	13
Mansoor Akhtar run out	28
Majid J. Khan b Miller	5
Wasim Raja c Botham b Willis	60
*Imran Khan c Gower b Miller	31
Tahir Naqqash run out	1
†Wasim Bari b Hemmings	4
Iqbal Qasim lbw b Botham	13
Sikander Bakht not out	2
L-b 14, w 2, n-b 1	17
1/52 2/55 3/82 4/97 5/123 6/183 7/200 8/201 9/213 (49.4 overs)	222

Bowling: Willis 8–0–36–1; Botham 8.4–0–40–1; Miller 11–1–56–2; Pringle 11–0–43–2; Hemmings 11–3–30–1.

Umpires: D. J. Constant and H. D. Bird

LEICESTERSHIRE v PAKISTANIS

At Leicester, July 21, 22, 23. Drawn. The Pakistani attack laboured on the first day when Gower struck 29 boundaries in his unbeaten 176, after being dropped by Wasim Raja when 4. It was his highest innings for the county, and with Butcher, who made a career-best 71 not out, he shared an unbroken fourth-wicket partnership of 198. Earlier Cobb, too, had taken advantage of the fast outfield to hit six 4s as well as one 6. The next day, however, the touring side put the Leicestershire innings in truer perspective with an invigorating opening partnership of 111 in 68 minutes, Mohsin going on to reach 203 not out with one 6 and 25 4s. After Majid's declaration, 3 runs behind, Gower, with the first Test only a week away, was given little opportunity to evaluate Qadir, who bowled only six overs in the first innings and now dismissed him in his second over. Thereafter survival became the theme as Qadir collected another five wickets, and Leicestershire had much to be thankful for in the intelligent methods employed by Boon in a career-best innings and Tolchard's assured footwork and strokeplay against even the best spin bowling. When bad light ended play early, Haroon had struck a confident 44 in an hour, but Leicestershire's declaration had not precipitated any hopes of a win to either side.

Leicestershire

J. C. Balderstone b Sikander	4	– lbw b Sikander	4
R. A. Cobb b Tahir	42	– c Raja b Tahir	13
T. J. Boon c Majid b Sikander	44	– st Yousuf b Qasim	90
D. I. Gower not out	176	– b Qadir	16
I. P. Butcher not out	71	– c Tahir b Qadir	1
*†R. W. Tolchard (did not bat)		– c Qasim b Qadir	61
D. A. Wenlock (did not bat)		– c sub b Qadir	2
G. J. Parsons (did not bat)		– st Yousuf b Qadir	4
N. G. B. Cook (did not bat)		– c Yousuf b Qadir	5
A. M. E. Roberts (did not bat)		– not out	22
J. P. Agnew (did not bat)		– not out	0
B 6, l-b 3, n-b 8	17	B 9, l-b 3, n-b 11	23
1/6 2/70 3/156 (3 wkts dec.)	354	1/8 2/29 3/55 4/72 5/205 6/208 7/209 8/213 9/240 (9 wkts dec.)	241

Bowling: *First Innings*—Sikander 23–7–54–2; Tahir 23–2–107–1; Mansoor 8–4–23–0; Qadir 6–2–15–0; Qasim 13–0–54–0; Raja 20–4–59–0; Majid 3–1–20–0; Malik 1–0–5–0. *Second Innings*—Sikander 16–5–35–1; Tahir 16–7–44–1; Qadir 39–14–71–6; Qasim 20–4–68–1.

Pakistanis

Mohsin Khan not out	203		
Mansoor Akhtar c Tolchard b Wenlock	65	– c Tolchard b Roberts	5
*Majid J. Khan b Cook	42	– (4) not out	6
Haroon Rashid c Balderstone b Cook	8	– (1) not out	44
Salim Malik not out	25		
†Salim Yousuf (did not bat)		– (3) lbw b Parsons	6
B 4, l-b 3, n-b 1	8		
1/111 2/231 3/269 (3 wkts dec.)	351	1/18 2/24 (2 wkts)	61

Wasim Raja, Abdul Qadir, Tahir Naqqash, Iqbal Qasim and Sikander Bakht did not bat.

Bowling: *First Innings*—Agnew 16.3–0–101–0; Parsons 15–1–87–0; Roberts 13–3–41–0; Wenlock 12–2–41–1; Cook 18–2–63–2; Balderstone 4–1–10–0. *Second Innings*—Roberts 5–2–13–1; Parsons 6–2–18–1; Agnew 3.2–0–25–0; Wenlock 2–0–5–0.

Umpires: D. J. Constant and B. J. Meyer.

DERBYSHIRE v PAKISTANIS

At Chesterfield, July 24, 25, 26. Pakistanis won by 140 runs. The tourists resolved some of their doubts in the final match before the first Test, Sarfraz taking part only on the first day and Imran not bowling until the second innings. Jefferies, a South African left-arm opening bowler from Western Province, took three wickets in an erratic Pakistani first innings which was punctuated by rash as well as handsome strokes. The second of Taylor's five catches was the 1,500th dismissal of his first-class career. Miller batted soundly before Derbyshire declared but all else was overshadowed by Zaheer's innings on the final day. He scored a century before lunch in only 105 minutes and stepped up the rate to reach 148 (two 6s, twenty 4s) in 130. Imran declared when Mudassar, inevitably playing second fiddle, reached 100, setting Derbyshire to score 303 in 225 minutes, but with Wright and Kirsten rested, the target was beyond them.

Pakistanis

Mudassar Nazar c Miller b Jefferies	22	– not outout	100
Mohsin Khan c Taylor b Oldham	22	– c Hampshire b Jefferies	42
Mansoor Akhtar c Taylor b Jefferies	1	– c Miller b Jefferies	0
Zaheer Abbas c Taylor b Jefferies	51	– not outout	148
Wasim Raja c Taylor b Newman	14		
Haroon Rashid c Taylor b Oldham	43		
*Imran Khan not out	46		
†Wasim Bari b Moir	35		
Abdul Qadir c Moir b Miller	0		
Sikander Bakht b Miller	4		
L-b 1, w 2, n-b 19	22	B 1, l-b 3, n-b 5	9
1/49 2/49 3/72 4/96 5/165 6/168 7/241 8/248 9/260 (9 wkts dec.)	260	1/78 2/78 (2 wkts dec.)	299

Sarfraz Nawaz did not bat.

Bowling: *First Innings*—Oldham 16–0–41–2; Newman 14–1–67–1; Wood 3–0–14–0; Jefferies 16–2–57–3; Miller 14.5–3–49–2; Moir 5–1–10–1; *Second Innings*—Newman 16–1–61–0; Jefferies 12–1–52–2; Wood 3–1–17–0; Miller 16.4–2–57–0; Moir 17–4–76–0; Anderson 4–0–19–0; Barnett 1–0–8–0.

Derbyshire

*B. Wood b Qadir	39	– (2) b Imran	13
I. S. Anderson c Zaheer b Mudassar	18	– (1) lbw b Imran	2
K. J. Barnett c Bari b Sikander	37	– lbw b Imran	27
J. H. Hampshire lbw b Qadir	37	– b Sikander	40
G. Miller not out	72	– c Bari b Imran	40
J. E. Morris c Haroon b Mudassar	6	– c Bari b Sikander	12
†R. W. Taylor b Mansoor	21	– b Sikander	0
S. T. Jefferies not out	14	– c Bari b Sikander	0
P. G. Newman (did not bat)		– lbw b Raja	7
D. G. Moir (did not bat)		– c Mudassar b Raja	0
S. Oldham (did not bat)		– not out	8
L-b 7, n-b 6	13	B 4, l-b 4, n-b 5	13
1/42 2/88 3/113 4/145 5/171 6/236	(6 wkts dec.) 257	1/13 2/23 3/86 4/91 5/125 6/133 7/137 8/147 9/153	162

Bowling: *First Innings*—Sarfraz 10–3–16–0; Sikander 25–5–75–1; Qadir 26–9–50–2; Mudassar 17–5–43–2; Raja 19–5–44–0; Mansoor 7–2–16–1; Zaheer 0.1–0–0–0. *Second Innings*—Imran 14.3–3–27–4; Sikander 16–3–68–4; Mudassar 6–0–22–0; Qadir 8–5–7–0; Raja 14–5–25–2.

Umpires: P. J. Eele and D. R. Shepherd.

ENGLAND v PAKISTAN

First Cornhill Test

At Birmingham, July 29, 30, 31, August 1. England won by 113 runs, a comfortable-looking margin which belies the finely balanced fulcrum on which the game was poised before Pakistan began their second innings. Then, with the visitors needing 313 for victory, Botham and Willis took the first six wickets for 77, and although Imran and Tahir offered some late-order resistance, the game ended a day early in front of a 9,000 Sunday crowd with England preserving an impressive ground record of twelve wins, seven draws and only one defeat since Test cricket was first staged at Edgbaston in 1902.

After overnight injury scares which brought Cook and Small away from their county games and increased the England party to fourteen, these two players were not needed. Back trouble kept Pringle out of the side, Hemmings and Greig gained their first caps, and Gatting was recalled after a summer of prolific scoring. Sarfraz was unfit for Pakistan, Tahir Naqqash deputising. Majid Khan was omitted from their original twelve.

The pitch looked a good, even one for batting, an impression which turned out to be misleading. After Willis had won his fourth successive toss as captain, England batted under blue skies and hot sunshine, their innings opened by a makeshift partnership of Tavaré and Randall. The latter raced away with 16 from the first nine balls of the match. He was then bowled, offering no stroke to Imran, who later in the day was to show what a dramatic effect a world-class fast bowler can have, even when batsmen appear to be set.

Just before tea England were 164 for two, but the Pakistan captain had Gower caught behind the wicket for 74, easily the most fluent innings of the day, and then bowled Botham with a fast break-back. Tavaré, though still there, made no more effort to wrest the initiative from the bowlers than in his previous innings as a Test opener. Imran made short work of the tail to finish with seven for 52, but Pakistan's leg-spinner, Abdul Qadir, had a day to satisfy the connoisseur. Only Gower played him with any degree of comfort. Despite an unsuitably low and slow pitch, he spun his web around everyone else, notably Greig.

Replying to a moderate-looking 272, Pakistan lost Mudassar before the close, in Botham's opening over, to a high-looking leg-before decision. But many of their wickets which fell at encouragingly regular intervals for the England bowlers on the second day owed too little to ill fortune and too much to a self-destructive approach. Mohsin and Imran were both out hooking recklessly, and Javed tried to hit Hemmings out of the ground in the latter's first over in Test cricket. Greig bowled tidily, helped by the sort of apparent fortune which tended to be associated with his elder brother, and so, instead of gaining a substantial lead, Pakistan subsided to 251 all out after a performance that was profligate even by their standards.

England's second innings was in keeping with the untidy quality of much of the cricket played in the match, though this added paradoxically to the crowd's enjoyment, for the final outcome was becoming increasingly unpredictable. Prior to lunch on the third day England, at one stage, were 137 for two, with Randall on his way to an invaluable, improvised hundred that owed little to orthodoxy and hardly encouraged the belief that he can be turned into a Test opener. Tahir dismissed Gower, Gatting, Botham (first ball) and Miller in quick succession, and when Imran ended Randall's priceless innings for 105, England were only 209 ahead with two wickets remaining. But wicket-keeper Taylor, helped first by Hemmings and then by Willis, squeezed 103 runs from an attack which rather lost its tactical way. The result was that Pakistan started their second innings needing over 300 to win, a target seldom achieved in Test cricket.

The measure of this became apparent in Botham's opening over, bowled in the sort of heavy atmosphere a top-class swing bowler dreams about. In six balls he removed Mudassar, who had entered the match with a tour average of 291.5 and who departed from it with one of 145.75, and Mansoor. Thereafter Pakistan's approach was no less undisciplined than in their first innings. Within an hour and a half they were 77 for six after 22 overs. Willis bowled a very fast spell, reminiscent of his match-winning one against Australia at Leeds in 1981, and with Botham bowling 21 overs unchanged and showing splendid stamina, the game was won and lost.

The total attendance was 41,000 and the takings were £139,323. – J.D.B.

England

D. W. Randall b Imran	17	– b Imran	105
C. J. Tavaré c Miandad b Qadir	54	– c Mohsin b Imran	17
A. J. Lamb c Bari b Sikander	6	– lbw b Tahir	5
D. I. Gower c Bari b Imran	74	– c Mudassar b Tahir	13
I. T. Botham b Imran	2	– (6) lbw b Tahir	0
M. W. Gatting b Tahir	17	– (5) c Bari b Tahir	5
G. Miller b Imran	47	– b Tahir	5
I. A. Greig c sub (Haroon Rashid) b Imran	14	– b Qadir	7
E. E. Hemmings lbw b Imran	2	– c Mansoor b Qadir	19
†R. W. Taylor lbw b Imran	1	– c Qadir b Raja	54
*R. G. D. Willis not out	0	– not out	28
B 4, l-b 10, w 6, n-b 18	38	B 10, l-b 11, w 7, n-b 5	33
1/29 2/37 3/164 4/172 5/179 6/228 7/263 8/265 9/271	272	1/62 2/98 3/127 4/137 5/137 6/146 7/170 8/188 9/212	291

Bowling: *First Innings*—Imran 25.3–11–52–7; Tahir 15–4–46–1; Sikander 18–5–58–1; Mudassar 5–2–8–0; Qadir 29–7–70–1. *Second Innings*—Imran 32–5–84–2; Sikander 13–5–34–0; Qadir 40–10–100–2; Tahir 18–7–40–5; Raja 2.3–2–0–1.

Pakistan

Mudassar Nazar lbw b Botham	0	– lbw b Botham	0
Mohsin Khan c Willis b Botham	26	– lbw b Botham	35
Tahir Naqqash c Taylor b Greig	12	– (9) c and b Hemmings	39
Mansoor Akhtar c Miller b Hemmings	58	– (3) c Taylor b Botham	0
Javed Miandad c Willis b Hemmings	30	– (4) run out	10
Zaheer Abbas lbw b Greig	40	– (5) c Taylor b Willis	4
Wasim Raja c Tavaré b Willis	26	– (6) c Gower b Willis	16
*Imran Khan c Taylor b Willis	22	– (7) b Miller	65
†Wasim Bari not out	16	– (8) c Taylor b Botham	12
Abdul Qadir lbw b Greig	7	– c Randall b Miller	9
Sikander Bakht c Hemmings b Greig	1	– not out	1
B 5, l-b 2, w 1, n-b 5	13	L-b 3, n-b 5	8
1/0 2/29 3/53 4/110 5/164 6/198 7/217 8/227 9/248	251	1/0 2/0 3/38 4/54 5/66 6/77 7/98 8/151 9/178	199

Bowling: *First Innings*—Botham 24–1–86–2; Greig 14.2–3–53–4; Willis 15–3–42–2; Hemmings 24–5–56–2; Miller 2–1–1–0. *Second Innings*—Botham 21–7–70–4; Willis 14–2–49–2; Greig 4–1–19–0; Hemmings 10–4–27–1; Miller 7.4–1–26–2.

Umpires: D. G. L. Evans and K. E. Palmer.

†MINOR COUNTIES v PAKISTANIS

At Slough, August 5, 6. Pakistanis won by seven wickets. Bailey's early declaration on the shortened first day backfired when, to the delight of a large crowd, Mansoor's flowing strokeplay took the Pakistanis to a lead of 26 in only 110 minutes. For a second time McEvoy anchored the Minor Counties innings, with only O'Brien and Smith resisting for long as Qasim and Wasim Raja swept through the batting. The tourists found no difficulty in scoring 154 in 230 minutes, and with Mansoor hitting one 6 and ten 4s in his second half-century, the match finished with two hours to spare.

Minor Counties

M. S. A. McEvoy c Miandad b Majid	39	– c Jalal b Qasim	61
S. G. Plumb b Mudassar	13	– run out	3
D. G. Ottley lbw b Tahir	20	– b Jalal	6
*D. Bailey b Mudassar	21	– lbw b Qasim	9
N. A. Riddell not out	2	– c Mansoor b Raja	0
W. M. Osman c Majid b Raja	8	– c Majid b Raja	12
N. T. O'Brien (did not bat)		– lbw b Qasim	39
†A. Griffiths (did not bat)		– b Miandad	4
J. A. Smith (did not bat)		– b Qasim	26
D. G. Nicholls (did not bat)		– b Raja	2
A. W. Allin (did not bat)		– not out	0
B 1, l-b 5, w 2, n-b 3	11	B 4, l-b 10, n-b 3	17
1/24 2/76 3/104 4/106 5/114	(5 wkts dec.) 114	1/20 2/60 3/83 4/86 5/88 6/110 7/115 8/154 9/171	179

Bowling: *First Innings*—Tahir 8–0–25–1; Jalal 8–3–24–0; Mudassar 6–2–18–2; Raja 2.3–1–6–1; Qasim 11–4–26–0; Majid 3–1–4–1. *Second Innings*—Tahir 12–3–28–0; Jalal 10–1–18–1; Mudassar 3–0–13–0; Raja 20.3–6–36–3; Qasim 19–7–36–4; Miandad 6–3–17–1; Malik 5–0–14–0.

Pakistanis

Mudassar Nazar st Griffiths b Allin	28	– c and b Nicholls	23
Mansoor Akhtar not out	83	– st Griffiths b Bailey	51
Majid J. Khan not out	27	– c Plumb b Bailey	29
Salim Malik (did not bat)		– not out	29
Javed Miandad (did not bat)		– not out	18
B 1, w 1	2	B 4	4
1/59	(1 wkt dec.) 140	1/53 2/95 3/112	(3 wkts) 154

*Zaheer Abbas, †Salim Yousuf, Iqbal Qasim, Jalal-ud-Din, Tahir Naqqash and Wasim Raja did not bat.

Bowling: *First Innings*—Smith 13–1–53–0; Nicholls 6–3–19–0; Allin 11–3–40–1; O'Brien 5–0–26–0. *Second Innings*—Smith 7–2–26–0; Nicholls 6–0–36–1; Allin 9–0–51–0; Bailey 7–1–31–2; Plumb 2–0–6–0.

Umpires: T. G. Wilson and D. B. Harrison.

SURREY v PAKISTANIS

At The Oval, August 7, 8, 9. Drawn. Mohsin Khan and Zaheer Abbas sparkled on a first day reduced by 100 minutes through bad light, and with Surrey labouring for 60 overs over 154 in reply, most of the interest centred on the last six hours. Then, Haroon Rashid took over the role of entertainer with his highest score on two tours of England; and with Zaheer playing his second major innings, Pakistan were able to leave Surrey to score 304 in 226 minutes to win. They began as if a draw was inevitable, but Knight galvanised them into action with a 6, a 5 and fifteen 4s in 111 in 168 minutes. First with Smith and then Roope, he guided Surrey closer to their target. They wanted 136 from the last twenty overs, 64 from ten, and then 37 from five. In the end they fell short by 13 runs. At the same time, Pakistan, needing just one more wicket, were as near to victory. Sarfraz Nawaz had proved that the finger injury which kept him out of the first Test had mended by bowling three increasingly impressive spells. He took two wickets in the first, one in the second, and three for 24 in six overs in the third. Among his victims was Knight, one of four batsmen to edge sharply moving deliveries into his stumps.

Pakistanis

Mudassar Nazar c Lynch b Thomas	43	– (6) not out	2
Mohsin Khan c Smith b Thomas	79		
Majid J. Khan c Richards b Thomas	13	– (1) lbw b Thomas	36
Haroon Rashid run out	1	– (2) c Knight b Monkhouse	90
Javed Miandad not out	24	– (3) lbw b Monkhouse	17
*Zaheer Abbas not out	60	– (4) not out	50
Wasim Raja (did not bat)		– (5) c Richards b Monkhouse	5
B 2, l-b 8, n-b 9	19	B 2, l-b 6, w 4, n-b 6	18
1/99 2/116 3/130 4/154 (4 wkts dec.)	239	1/105 2/140 3/156 4/193 (4 wkts dec.)	218

Sarfraz Nawaz, †Wasim Bari, Jalal-ud-Din and Sikander Bakht did not bat.

Bowling: *First Innings*—Thomas 23–6–72–3; Mackintosh 18–1–65–0; Monkhouse 24–9–58–0; Needham 9–4–17–0; Knight 5–1–8–0. *Second Innings*—Thomas 15–3–58–1; Mackintosh 14–4–40–0; Monkhouse 12–4–40–3; Needham 10.3–2–53–0; Knight 2–0–9–0.

Surrey

A. R. Butcher c Raja b Sikander	1	– b Sarfraz	17
D. B. Pauline c Raja b Mudassar	9	– run out	9
D. M. Smith c Sikander b Jalal	30	– b Sarfraz	35
M. A. Lynch run out	0	– lbw b Sarfraz	14
*R. D. V. Knight b Raja	26	– b Sarfraz	111
G. R. J. Roope not out	34	– b Sarfraz	46
†C. J. Richards c Sikander b Raja	27	– (8) c Raja b Mudassar	15
D. J. Thomas c Bari b Sikander	0	– (7) run out	6
A. Needham lbw b Raja	5	– not out	4
G. Monkhouse not out	11	– c Miandad b Sarfraz	4
K. S. Mackintosh (did not bat)		– not out	1
L-b 3, w 1, n-b 7	11	B 4, l-b 11, w 1, n-b 13	29
1/3 2/37 3/42 4/49 5/103 6/131 7/134 8/139 (8 wkts dec.)	154	1/25 2/39 3/56 4/140 5/250 6/257 7/280 8/282 9/289 (9 wkts)	291

Bowling: *First Innings*—Sarfraz 15–4–33–0; Sikander 14–5–34–2; Jalal 8–2–16–1; Mudassar 11–2–26–1; Raja 12–3–34–3. *Second Innings*—Sarfraz 20–0–92–6; Sikander 15–2–63–0; Jalal 4–1–7–0; Mudassar 11–1–55–1; Raja 7–0–45–0.

Umpires: C. Cook and R. Palmer.

ENGLAND v PAKISTAN

Second Cornhill Test

At Lord's, August 12, 13, 14, 15, 16. Pakistan won by ten wickets, a margin which reflected their superiority but failed to record the tension of the closing stages as the Pakistanis sought only their second-ever victory over England. The first had been in 1954, at The Oval, in the fourth Test of Pakistan's first Test series in England.

It in no way detracts from Pakistan's win to say that England were handicapped by the limitations of their attack once Willis pronounced himself unfit, ironically as a result of a neck injury incurred avoiding Imran's bouncers at Birmingham. Into his place came Jackman, for his first Test in England, while Gower, with little experience at the job, assumed the captaincy. Pringle was recalled for Miller, who was unwell, and Marks was twelfth man. Pakistan brought in Haroon Rashid for Wasim Raja and Sarfraz for Sikander. England, for the first time in the summer, lost the toss and Imran elected to bat.

Both the quality of England's bowling and the nature of the pitch were shown in true perspective when Mohsin drove back Botham's first ball for 4. Before lunch, taken with Pakistan 107 for one, the batsmen had disdained wearing helmets, and these did not reappear until the 89th over, when Pringle took the new ball and with his third delivery had Zaheer, then 28, dropped by Tavaré at second slip. Had England held their catches, the day might have ended differently than with Pakistan 295 for three. Mohsin, whose delightful batting was resplendent with cover drives and forceful strokes off his legs, was let off twice: once when 72, at first slip by Pringle, and again shortly after reaching his second Test hundred (153 balls, fourteen 4s) when he gave Jackman the hardest of caught-and-bowled chances.

On Friday a brief stoppage for showers in the morning, a four-hour delay after lunch, and Gower's strengthening of his on-side field meant that it took Mohsin, 159 overnight, until six o'clock to become only the second post-war batsman to score 200 in a Lord's Test. M. P. Donnelly, 206 in 1949, was the other, though he did not have to wait for four hours on 199. Mohsin's 200 came off 383 balls, took 491 minutes, and included 23 4s. Three balls later he flicked Jackman uppishly behind square leg to Tavaré.

Imran's overnight declaration brought early reward when Tavaré played on, but Randall and Lamb negotiated the most fiery of spells from Imran to bring up 50 after ten overs. Eight overs later, Randall played down the wrong line to Sarfraz, and soon after lunch Lamb, early on the drive, was taken by forward short-leg, diving forward. Pakistan's attacking bowling and fielding, allied to a slow over-rate, restrained both Gower and Botham. The England captain, unusually inhibited, had managed only one 4 by tea, by which time he had lost Botham, sweeping Qadir to square leg.

In the evening session, England's later batsmen were severely embarrassed by Qadir's mixture of leg-spin, googlies and top-spin. Only Gatting looked confident, and he had guided England to within 3 runs of the follow-on figure when, with Jackman just in, he accepted the umpires' offer of bad light. Perhaps he should have batted on, for next morning, after pushing Imran's third ball for a single, he saw Jackman adjudged lbw to the last.

So Sunday's play, the first such at Lord's, began with high drama before many of the 11,200 spectators had gathered. (It was to end in cheap farce after most of them had gone home.) The drama was heightened by an amazing spell of bowling by Mudassar who, coming on for the tenth over, accounted for Randall, Lamb and Gower in six balls for no runs. Lamb apart, his victims fell as much to their own imperfections as to his medium-pace seam and swing.

Tavaré and Botham, however, dug in, Tavaré remaining on 0 for 67 minutes. Rain and bad light prevented any play in the afternoon, and in the evening they resisted further the speed of Imran and the guile of Qadir. When Mudassar was brought back for the first time since his morning spell of 5–2–11–3, the umpires conferred and went off for bad light. It was then seven o'clock. They reappeared 37 minutes later, allowed Mudassar one maiden over in the pleasant sunshine, looked at their light meters, and brought the day to a somewhat banal close.

Monday began darker and cloudier than the previous evening, precipitating an early stoppage and increasing the possibility of England being saved by the weather. Soon after midday Mudassar made the vital breakthrough, getting one to lift and having Botham well caught at backward point and persuading Gatting to flash fatally at a long-hop. After lunch, taken when England were 140 for five, Pringle again fell close in to Qadir and Greig, playing back, gave Mudassar his sixth wicket. Tavaré, however, went on, venturing a selection of fine strokes, and just after three o'clock he saw England past an innings defeat. His 50, off 236 balls, had absorbed 352 minutes and was second only to T. E. Bailey's at Brisbane in 1957-58 as the slowest on record. When, finally, he succumbed outside off stump to Imran's persistent hostility, he had batted for 6 hours, 47 minutes and hit six 4s.

With Tahir and Sarfraz unfit, Imran's bowling resources were limited, yet it was not until the 117th over, as Taylor and Jackman were edging England towards safety, that he took the new ball. This gave Qadir that extra bounce to remove Jackman.

Pakistan's target was 76 from eighteen overs, and from the start Gower's Sunday field was never going to match the confident strokeplay and brilliant running of Mohsin and Miandad. The first two overs realised 13 runs; in the eighth they were halfway there; by the twelfth, with dark clouds threatening, only 10 more were needed. And when, in the fourteenth, Miandad cut Hemmings for 4, the Pakistani faithful raced on to the field to acclaim their heroes and the victory which sent the two teams level to Leeds for the deciding match of the series.

The attendance for the five days was 74,889, with takings of £329,254. – G.A.W.

Pakistan

Mohsin Khan c Tavaré b Jackman	200	– not out	39
Mudassar Nazar c Taylor b Jackman	20		
Mansoor Akhtar c Lamb b Botham	57		
Javed Miandad run out	6	– (2) not out	26
Zaheer Abbas b Jackman	75		
Haroon Rashid lbw b Botham	1		
*Imran Khan c Taylor b Botham	12		
Tahir Naqqash c Gatting b Jackman	2		
†Wasim Bari not out	24		
Abdul Qadir not out	18		
B 3, l-b 8, n-b 2	13	B 1, l-b 10, w 1	12
1/53 2/197 3/208 4/361 5/364 6/380 7/382 8/401	(8 wkts dec.) 428		(no wkt) 77

Sarfraz Nawaz did not bat.

Bowling: *First Innings*—Botham 44–8–148–3; Jackman 36–5–110–4; Pringle 26–9–62–0; Greig 13–2–42–0; Hemmings 20–3–53–0. *Second Innings*—Botham 7–0–30–0; Jackman 4–0–22–0; Hemmings 2.1–0–13–0.

England

D. W. Randall b Sarfraz	29	– b Mudassar	9
C. J. Tavaré b Sarfraz	8	– c Miandad b Imran	82
A. J. Lamb c Haroon b Tahir	33	– lbw b Mudassar	0
*D. I. Gower c Mansoor b Imran	29	– c Bari b Mudassar	0
I. T. Botham c Mohsin b Qadir	31	– c Sarfraz b Mudassar	69
M. W. Gatting not out	32	– c Bari b Mudassar	7
D. R. Pringle c Haroon b Qadir	5	– c Miandad b Qadir	14
I. A. Greig lbw b Qadir	3	– lbw b Mudassar	2
E. E. Hemmings b Sarfraz	6	– c Bari b Imran	14
†R. W. Taylor lbw b Qadir	5	– not out	24
R. D. Jackman lbw b Imran	0	– c Haroon b Qadir	17
B 11, l-b 12, w 13, n-b 10	46	B 10, l-b 19, w 5, n-b 4	38
1/16 2/69 3/89 4/157 5/173 6/187 7/197 8/217 9/226	227	1/9 2/9 3/9 4/121 5/132 6/171 7/180 8/224 9/235	276

Bowling: *First Innings*—Imran 23–4–55–2; Sarfraz 23–4–56–3; Tahir 12–4–25–1; Qadir 24–9–39–4; Mudassar 4–1–6–0. *Second Innings*—Imran 42–13–84–2; Sarfraz 14–5–22–0; Qadir 37.5–15–94–2; Mudassar 19–7–32–6; Tahir 7–5–6–0.

Umpires: H. D. Bird and D. J. Constant.

ENGLAND B v PAKISTANIS

At Leicester, August 18, 19, 20. Drawn. A disappointing match, watched by few people and badly affected by rain, ended in the draw that had seemed inevitable after the first day. On an easy-paced pitch, Hampshire's Emery bowled well in Pakistan's first innings, albeit assisted by some careless shots. England captain Marks declared 1 run behind, and Mudassar's accomplished century persuaded Majid to set a target of 193 in two hours. Aggressive batting by Kent's Taylor suggested that England were interested, but when he and Parker departed in quick succession, the chase was abandoned. Rain, in any case, brought about a premature close.

Pakistanis

Mohsin Khan c Cook b Emery	24	– c Neale b Dilley	12
Mudassar Nazar b Jarvis	9	– not out	103
*Majid J. Khan c Gould b Jarvis	3	– c Roebuck b Cook	9
Salim Malik lbw b Emery	6	– c Parker b Cook	0
Wasim Raja lbw b Emery	30	– c Neale b Cook	38
Haroon Rashid c Gould b Emery	13	– not out	12
Javed Miandad not out	10		
Iqbal Qasim c Gould b Dilley	1		
†Salim Yousuf not out	15		
B 2, l-b 1, n-b 18	21	B 4, l-b 2, w 2, n-b 9	17
1/17 2/30 3/42 4/68 5/89 6/106 7/109 (7 wkts dec.)	132	1/53 2/87 3/89 4/165 (4 wkts dec.)	191

Sikander Bakht and Jalul-ud-Din did not bat.

Bowling: *First Innings*—Dilley 17–5–41–1; Jarvis 10–3–24–2; Emery 16–3–46–4. *Second Innings*—Dilley 8–3–27–1; Jarvis 12–4–28–0; Emery 6–0–31–0; Cook 20–5–66–3; Marks 8–0–22–0.

England B

G. Fowler c Malik b Qasim	25	– b Qasim	21
N. R. Taylor b Sikander	18	– c Qasim b Jalal	32
P. M. Roebuck c Yousuf b Jalal	31	– not out	13
P. W. G. Parker not out	29	– c Malik b Qasim	4
P. A. Neale not out	14	not out	0
B 1, l-b 6, n-b 7	14	L-b 3, n-b 1	4
1/38 2/66 3/100 (3 wkts dec.)	131	1/35 2/62 3/74 (3 wkts)	74

*V. J. Marks, †I. J. Gould, G. R. Dilley, N. G. B. Cook, K. St J. D. Emery and K. B. S. Jarvis did not bat.

Bowling: *First Innings*—Sikander 13–3–27–1; Jalal 21–9–43–1; Qasim 18–3–47–1. *Second Innings*—Sikander 6–1–27–0; Jalal 8–1–29–1; Qasim 5–0–14–2.

Umpires: C. Cook and R. Julian.

LANCASHIRE v PAKISTANIS

At Manchester, August 21, 22, 23. Drawn. The first two days of the match were lost to rain and play started on the third only after lunch. Main interest centred around Imran Khan, who had to go to hospital for a check-up, and Ehtesham-ud-Din, who played in four Tests in the 1970s and had been called out of league cricket to assist the injury-hit tourists. Imran bowled only three overs at half pace before going to hospital for an examination which ended with Intikhab, the team's manager, saying that the injury was not believed to be serious. Ehtesham was called out of the Bolton Association where he had been playing for Daisy Hill.

Lancashire

G. Fowler c Haroon b Majid	27	D. P. Hughes not out	1
D. Lloyd st Bari b Majid	55	B 2, l-b 4, n-b 8	14
A. Kennedy not out	17		
†C. Maynard c Mansoor b Qadir	6	1/92 2/92 3/111 (3 wkts dec.)	120

*C. H. Lloyd, J. Abrahams, J. Simmons, P. J. W. Allott, L. L. McFarlane and P. G. Lee did not bat.

Bowling: Imran 3–2–2–0; Ehtesham 14–5–35–0; Sikander 10–5–21–0; Qadir 10–1–24–1; Majid 11–4–24–2.

Pakistanis

Mudassar Nazar lbw b Allott	0
Mansoor Akhtar not out	53
Majid J. Khan not out	39
L-b 1	1
1/0 (1 wkt)	93

Javed Miandad, Haroon Rashid, Wasim Raja, *Imran Khan, †Wasim Bari, Abdul Qadir, Sikander Bakht and Ehtesham-ud-Din did not bat.

Bowling: Allott 6–3–9–1; McFarlane 5–0–22–0; Hughes 7–2–32–0; Lee 5–1–17–0; Abrahams 3–0–10–0; D. Lloyd 1–0–2–0.

Umpires: K. Ibadulla and A. Jepson.

ENGLAND v PAKISTAN

Third Cornhill Test

At Leeds, August 26, 27, 28, 30, 31. England won by three wickets. With Willis, having recovered from his neck injury, back in command England gained the victory they needed to take their second series of the summer. It was accompanied, all the same, by another undistinguished batting stumble which came close to allowing Pakistan to create a piece of cricketing history with their first success in a series against England. Requiring 219 to win, which should have been a formality once they had moved to 168 for the loss of only Tavaré, England suddenly turned their innings into a desperate scramble on the fourth evening when five wickets went down for the addition of 21 runs before Botham gratefully accepted a bad light offer to calm English nerves. Botham also went on the final morning before the last 29 runs were secured.

England's eventual victory to take the series 2-1 was accompanied, as at Edgbaston, by claims from Pakistan's captain, Imran Khan, that umpiring errors, one of which, he said, allowed Gower to survive a catch behind in the early stages of his first-innings 74, cost his side the match and the series. If errors were made, the main reason why Pakistan failed to take an exciting and fascinating series was their own reckless batting, particularly in their second innings when conditions were at their least difficult on a wicket which encouraged seam bowling throughout the five days.

It was easy to understand Imran's disappointment after his own heroic efforts with both bat and ball which were to earn him the "Man of the Match" award for the second time in the series as well as the "Man of the Series" award. Apart from his readiness to criticise the umpires and his failure to curb the excessive appealing from his team, he had a magnificent series, his first as his country's captain.

Pakistan's aspirations at Headingley were handicapped before the start when injury ruled out three of their quicker bowlers, forcing them to enrol the portly Ehtesham-ud-Din from the Bolton Association side, Daisy Hill, as Imran's new-ball partner. Pakistan made two other changes following their Lord's victory, Sikander and Majid both being in the side. England abandoned the policy adopted in the first two Tests of being without a recognised opening batsman by awarding a first cap to the Lancashire left-hander, Graeme Fowler. Marks replaced Hemmings and made his Test début.

Imran having won the toss and chosen to bat, Pakistan's first innings contained only one partnership of note; that of 100 between Mudassar and Miandad for the third wicket after Mohsin and Mansoor had gone to the new ball. With only four specialist bowlers at his command, and the pitch of little help to spin, Willis used himself and Botham in short bursts while Jackman courageously kept the other end going for 4 hours 35 minutes, broken only by lunch and tea. Once Botham had removed Mudassar to make Pakistan 119 for three, England made good progress, Jackman being rewarded with three wickets from his 37-over spell. Among them was that of Majid, who became the leading Test run-maker in Pakistan's history during his innings of 21, overtaking Hanif's total of 3,915. Pakistan needed the steadying influence of an unbeaten 67 by Imran to climb to 275, fewer than Imran wanted but still beyond the capabilities of England once he had exchanged his bat for the ball and taken five for 49 in 25 overs.

England's first innings, like Pakistan's, contained only one productive partnership in which Botham gave a glimpse of what he had achieved on the same ground the year before against Australia. In a stay of just an hour he made 57 out of a stand of 69 with Gower, destroying the leg-spin bowling of Qadir before falling to a fine running catch by Haroon, fielding as substitute for Ehtesham, who had pulled a muscle. Imran removed Tavaré, Gatting and Lamb in nine deliveries, and England's plight would have been worse if Qadir's appeal for a catch behind off Gower, when the batsman was 7, had been rewarded. Gower survived, however, to lend support to Botham and to bat altogether for 234 minutes.

Pakistan's first-innings lead of 19 was soon forgotten when they batted again. By the end of Willis's opening over Mohsin and Mudassar were both out, Mohsin caught behind driving loosely against the first ball and Mudassar edging the fifth and his own first, a rising delivery, to third slip. For a while Miandad entertained and threatened in his second half-century of the match, but attempting a full-blooded drive he was caught behind. It was the very stroke he had urged his partner Mansoor to ignore during their third-wicket stand of 78. Miandad was the first of five victims for Botham, Imran the last, out after having seen Sikander given caught at short leg when, as was clearly evident from television pictures, his bat missed the ball. With help from Qadir and Sikander, Imran again played with a discipline lacking from his senior batsmen.

Fowler and Tavaré, left to negotiate the first nine overs of England's second innings on the third evening, took the score into three figures when, after the weekend, the match was resumed. While Tavaré played his familiar deadpan role, Fowler, driving superbly, reached his first Test half-century just before the third of the day's brief stoppages for rain. He lost Tavaré soon afterwards, but Gatting took over and victory looked safe that day when they reached 168. By then the light had deteriorated, but the batsmen twice spurned the chance of going off, Fowler having settled into his role and Gatting mindful of an indifferent forecast for the final day. Although the decision was undoubtedly right at the time it was to have a disastrous effect later. With Ehtesham unable to bowl, Imran turned to Mudassar to fill in, and as in the second Test at Lord's the opening batsman rewarded him.

Mudassar's medium pace accounted for Fowler, caught behind after a 262-minute stay which included eleven boundaries. Lamb and Gower soon followed, giving Mudassar a three for 11 spell in sixteen balls, and when Gatting and Randall both fell leg-before to Imran, England had slipped to 189 for six, victory still 30 runs away. However, the overnight break gave England the chance to escape from the panic of the previous evening and only 50 deliveries were needed on the last morning to secure the additional 29 runs required, despite the loss of Botham to the eleventh ball. Marks and Taylor saw England home, although not without alarms. The 42 extras in England's second innings undermined Pakistan's stirring effort.

Receipts were £189,800 and the total attendance 50,300 – P.S.

Pakistan

Mohsin Khan c Taylor b Botham	10	– c Taylor b Willis	0
Mudassar Nazar b Botham	65	– c Botham b Willis	0
Mansoor Akhtar c Gatting b Willis	0	– c Randall b Botham	39
Javed Miandad c Fowler b Willis	54	– c Taylor b Botham	52
Zaheer Abbas c Taylor b Jackman	8	– lbw b Botham	4
Majid J. Khan lbw b Jackman	21	– c Gower b Botham	10
*Imran Khan not out	67	– c Randall b Botham	46
†Wasim Bari b Jackman	23	– c Taylor b Willis	7
Abdul Qadir c Willis b Botham	5	– b Jackman	17
Sikander Bakht c Tavaré b Willis	7	– c Gatting b Marks	7
Ehtesham-ud-Din b Botham	0	– not out	0
B 1, l-b 7, w 4, n-b 3	15	L-b 6, w 4, n-b 7	17
1/16 2/19 3/119 4/128 5/160 6/168 7/207 8/224 9/274	275	1/0 2/3 3/81 4/85 5/108 6/115 7/128 8/169 9/199	199

Bowling: *First Innings*—Willis 26–6–76–3; Botham 24.5–9–70–4; Jackman 37–14–74–3; Marks 5–0–23–0; Gatting 8–2–17–0. *Second Innings*—Willis 19–3–55–3; Botham 30–8–74–5; Jackman 28–11–41–1; Gatting 2–1–4–0; Marks 2–1–8–1.

England

C. J. Tavaré c sub (Haroon Rashid) b Imran	22	– c Majid b Imran	33
G. Fowler b Ehtesham	9	– c Bari b Mudassar	86
M. W. Gatting lbw b Imran	25	– lbw b Imran	25
A. J. Lamb c Mohsin b Imran	0	– lbw b Mudassar	4
D. I. Gower c sub (Haroon) b Sikander	74	– c Bari b Mudassar	7
I. T. Botham c sub (Haroon) b Sikander	57	– c Majid b Mudassar	4
D. W. Randall run out	8	– lbw b Imran	0
V. J. Marks b Qadir	7	– not out	12
†R. W. Taylor c Miandad b Imran	18	– not out	6
R. D. Jackman c Mohsin b Imran	11		
*R. G. D. Willis not out	1		
B 4, l-b 10, w 2, n-b 8	24	B 19, l-b 16, w 1, n-b 6	42
1/15 2/67 3/69 4/77 5/146 6/159 7/170 8/209 9/255	256	1/103 2/168 3/172 4/187 5/189 6/189 7/199	(7 wkts) 219

Bowling: *First Innings*—Imran 25.2–7–49–5; Ehtesham 14–4–46–1; Sikander 24–5–47–2; Qadir 22–5–87–1; Mudassar 4–1–3–0. *Second Innings*—Sikander 20–4–40–0; Imran 30.2–8–66–3; Qadir 8–2–16–0; Mudassar 22–7–55–4.

Umpires: D. J. Constant and B. J. Meyer.

D. B. CLOSE'S XI v PAKISTANIS

At Scarborough, September 1, 2. D. B. Close's XI won by an innings and 46 runs. Brian Close, extending his first-class career at the age of 51, inflicted on the Pakistanis the heaviest defeat of their tour. Yet Mohsin, with ten sparkling boundaries in his fifty, and then Haroon looked to be building a useful score following Stephenson's early inroads. After lunch, though, Stephenson destroyed the middle order with three wickets in five balls. By the close, Close's XI were 165 for three, just 12 behind, with Crowe, a young New Zealand Test batsman from the Yorkshire League, 56 not out. Next day he went on to a near-faultless hundred, Stephenson struck an uncomplicated 63, and the tourists needed 180 to avoid an innings defeat. Instead they succumbed to the left-arm spin of Gifford and finally to the leg-spin of the former Pakistan captain, Mushtaq, who took the last two wickets with successive balls. Mohsin, hitting two 6s and eleven 4s in his 85, threatened to take the match into its third day, but Gatting's fine catch at extra cover ensured that the Festival organisers would have to arrange a 40-overs match between the two sides on the Friday.

Pakistanis

Mohsin Khan b Gatting	52	– c Gatting b Mushtaq		85
Mansoor Akhtar c Bairstow b Stephenson	2	– c and b Stephenson		7
Salim Malik b Stephenson	19	– lbw b Allott		6
Wasim Raja c Bairstow b Gatting	0	– c Close b Stephenson		11
Haroon Rashid c Lloyd b Stephenson	50	– c Bairstow b Gifford		10
†Salim Yousuf c Haynes b Stephenson	6	– c Crowe b Gifford		11
*Intikhab Alam lbw b Stephenson	0	– c Crowe b Gifford		4
Iqbal Qasim c Haynes b Gifford	5	– (9) c Lloyd b Mushtaq		0
Sikander Bakht c Bairstow b Allott	9	– (10) not out		0
Jalal-ud-Din b Allott	10	– (11) b Mushtaq		0
Abdul Qadir not out	16	– (8) st Bairstow b Gifford		0
L-b 7, w 1	8			
1/12 2/57 3/66 4/95 5/134 6/134 7/135 8/143 9/151	177	1/8 2/29 3/59 4/76 5/110 6/116 7/116 8/125 9/134		134

Bowling: *First Innings*—Allott 13.2–5–28–2; Stephenson 15–3–64–5; King 4–1–11–0; Gatting 8–3–26–2; Mushtaq 1–0–14–0; Gifford 7–1–26–1. *Second Innings*—Stephenson 7–0–26–2; Allott 8–2–37–1; Gatting 6–2–13–0; Gifford 11–2–24–4; Mushtaq 10.4–2–34–3.

D. B. Close's XI

D. L. Haynes lbw b Sikander	4
M. D. Crowe lbw b Intikhab	104
D. Lloyd c Yousuf b Mohsin	35
C. L. King c and b Qadir	22
M. W. Gatting b Jalal	48
Mushtaq Mohammad lbw b Qadir	23
*D. B. Close not out	26
†D. L. Bairstow c Malik b Qadir	0
F. D. Stephenson c Malik b Qadir	63
P. J. W. Allott not out	11
B 6, l-b 11, n-b 4	21
1/8 2/61 3/94 4/195 5/245 6/264 7/264 8/341 (8 wkts dec.)	357

N. Gifford did not bat.

Bowling: Sikander 8–3–30–1; Jalal 15–6–28–1; Qadir 28–3–106–4; Mohsin 5–0–32–1; Qasim 29–7–86–0; Raja 9–1–37–0; Intikhab 6–0–17–1.

Umpires: J van Geloven and B. Leadbeater.

PAKISTAN v AUSTRALIA, 1982–83

Following their tour of England in 1982, Pakistan returned home to play a three-Test series against Australia, captained by K. J. Hughes in the absence of G. S. Chappell. Pakistan, led by Imran Khan, won all three Test matches by decisive margins, the leg-spin and googly bowling of Abdul Qadir accounting for 22 wickets in the series.

First Test: at Karachi, September 22, 23, 24, 26, 27. Pakistan won by nine wickets. Australia 284 (J. Dyson 87, A. R. Border 55 not out, K. J. Hughes 54, B. M. Laird 32; Tahir Naqqash four for 61) and 179 (R. J. Bright 32 not out, R. W. Marsh 32; Abdul Qadir five for 76); Pakistan 419 for nine dec. (Zaheer Abbas 91, Haroon Rashid 82, Mohsin Khan 58, Mudassar Nazar 52 not out, Mansoor Akhtar 32, Javed Miandad 32; R. J. Bright three for 96) and 47 for one.

Second Test: at Faisalabad, September 30, October 1, 2, 4, 5. Pakistan won by an innings and 3 runs. Pakistan 501 for six dec. (Zaheer Abbas 126, Mansoor Akhtar 111, Mudassar Nazar 79, Mohsin Khan 76, Haroon Rashid 51; G. F. Lawson four for 96); Australia 168 (G. M. Wood 49, G. M. Ritchie 34; Abdul Qadir four for 76) and 330 (G. M. Ritchie 106 not out, B. M. Laird 60, J. Dyson 43, A. R. Border 31; Abdul Qadir seven for 142).

Third Test: at Lahore, October 14, 15, 16, 18, 19. Pakistan won by nine wickets. Australia 316 (G. M. Wood 85, G. F. Lawson 57 not out, B. Yardley 40; Imran Khan four for 45, Jalal-ud-Din three for 77) and 214 (J. Dyson 51, K. J. Hughes 39, G. M. Wood 30; Imran Khan four for 35); Pakistan 467 for seven dec. (Javed Miandad 138, Mohsin Khan 135, Zaheer Abbas 52, Extras 45, Imran Khan 39 not out) and 64 for one (Mudassar Nazar 39 not out).

Full details of the Australian tour of Pakistan will appear in the 1984 edition of Wisden.

THE ICC TROPHY, 1982

By PHILIP SNOW

In 1979, the only previous time the Associate Members (the non-Test-playing countries) of the International Cricket Conference had been in competition, May, the month chosen, had been the wettest in Midlands' history since 1722, seriously affecting results. The winners – Sri Lanka, subsequently promoted to Full Membership, and Canada – then joined the Test countries in the Prudential World Cup. The second competition, held in 1982 and arranged for June to reduce chances of rain, was dominated by the worst second half of a June in the Midlands this century. Three out of nine rounds of inter-country contests were abandoned virtually without a ball bowled. For some countries this meant sharing points with almost certainly weaker opponents from whom they might otherwise have gained maximum points.

All teams stayed in a single Solihull hotel – a kaleidoscopic scene of bright and sombre blazers and ties and of every spectrum of complexion. Hospitality on Midlands Club Cricket Conference grounds was often first-class. The organisation of the ICC Trophy Midlands Committee under the chairmanship of R. J. Evans, involving 225 inter-country and club matches, 450 umpires and 151 grounds for the concentrated period of five weeks, was little short of remarkable.

Compared with 1979, Denmark, a semi-finalist, did not compete. Nor did Argentina. New were Gibraltar, Hong Kong, Kenya (separated from East Africa), West Africa and Zimbabwe who, in their first year of Associate Membership, included five who had played first-class cricket in South Africa (one, John Traicos, in Test matches) before Rhodesia became independent. Zimbabwe met some counties in three-day matches before the competition started, as had Sri Lanka in 1979. No country ever dismissed Zimbabwe (except Fiji in a friendly match). The batting of David Houghton, John Heron, Andrew Pycroft and Kevin Curran (also an all-rounder) looked professional and, like their varied but accurate bowling, was well adapted to the limited-overs game. It was no surprise that they should win. The other finalists, Bermuda, had gained from their 1979 experience when they did less well than expected. This time Gladstone Brown, Winston Reid and Colin Blades showed reliable batting force, compiling the next highest scoring-rate after Zimbabwe. A quirk of weather favoured their getting in an extra result, albeit in a twenty-over match.

Travelling from ranges (including return) of 24,000 miles (Fiji 4,000 miles further than the next most distant, Papua New Guinea) to 300 miles in the case of the nearest, Holland, the Associate Members were unhappy in being allotted only a single place to compete for in the 1983 World Cup finals, as compared with two in 1979.

Papua New Guinea, totally indigenous, made the most of their opportunities, accomplishing a high scoring-rate, not least through Vavine Pala, an uninhibited left-handed hitter. They achieved the surprise of the competition by narrowly defeating Canada. Canada's scoring-rate was marginally higher (third after Zimbabwe and Bermuda) but although less strong than in 1979 they were deprived by the weather of possible wins against

ZIMBABWE, WINNERS OF THE ICC TROPHY, 1982

[*Ken Kelly*

Back row: L. Watson (*assistant manager*), D. L. Houghton, A. T. Hodgson, I. P. Butchart, G. Scott, E. J. Hough, P. W. E. Rawson, Mohammad Dudhia, K. M. Curran, G. C. Wallace. *Front row:* A. J. Pycroft, J. G. Heron, D. A. G. Fletcher (*captain*), D. Ellman-Brown (*manager*), A. J. Traicos, R. D. Brown, V. R. Hogg.

weaker countries. Their leading performers were predominantly West Indian and Pakistani. Bangladesh, with a lower scoring-rate than Holland and Fiji and winning by 1 run against Malaysia, were perhaps flattered in reaching the semi-final. They lost the third place play-off to Papua New Guinea.

Highest-scoring batsmen in the competition were the Dutch left-handers, Rob Elferink and Rob Lifmann. Holland were specially helped by rain in the result with Fiji, who were deprived by rain of possible wins in at least two matches. Fiji's virtually indigenous players were of a uniform standard of competence. Singapore (mostly Indian or Chinese) and East Africa (almost wholly Indian) were rather in Fiji's position as regards absence of pre-eminent players and effect of weather on results: Kenya (Indian in composition) and Hong Kong also kept fairly level on these counts in their first appearances. Pakistanis and West Indians mostly formed the United States team, which was a little stronger than in 1979. Gibraltar gained valuable experience in this their first competition but needed to score more quickly. Israel, preoccupied with Middle East conflict and internal dissent, defaulted in the last match (against Canada). The indigenous West Africans suffered the most abandonments (five); Malaysia (Indian and Chinese) were enthusiastic but unsuccessful. Each team was supposed to play seven matches; but nowhere is the calamitous effect of the weather better demonstrated than in the following tables.

Group One

	Won	*Lost*	*No Result*	*Pts*	*Scoring-rate*
Zimbabwe	5	0	2	24	5.5
Papua New Guinea	4	2	1	18	3.8
Canada	3	1	3	18	4.0
Kenya	3	2	2	16	3.4
Hong Kong	2	3	2	12	3.0
United States	1	2	4	12	3.6
Gibraltar	0	3	4	8	2.4
Israel	0	5	2	4	2.6

Group Two

	Won	*Lost*	*No Result*	*Pts*	*Scoring-rate*
Bermuda	6	0	1	26	5.2
Bangladesh	4	1	2	20	3.2
Holland	3	1	3	18	3.6
Singapore	1	2	4	12	3.0
Fiji	1	3	3	10	3.6
East Africa	1	3	3	10	2.82
West Africa	0	2	5	10	2.83
Malaysia	0	4	3	6	3.0

JUNE 16

Group 1

Zimbabwe 332 for four (D. L. Houghton 135, K. M. Curran 126 not out); USA 141 (37.5 overs) (P. W. Rawson four for 34). *Zimbabwe won by 191 runs.*

Gibraltar 80 (34.3 overs); Kenya 81 for one (14.2 overs) (A. Rehman 53 not out). *Kenya won by nine wickets.*

Hong Kong 100 (48.1 overs); Papua New Guinea 101 for six (25.3 overs). *Papua New Guinea won by four wickets.*

Group 2

Bermuda 348 for nine (W. Reid 128, G. Brown 100, C. Blades 42; Z. Mat three for 54, K. Kamalanathan three for 74); Malaysia 64 (29.1 overs) B. Banerji 34, E. G. James five for 2). *Bermuda won by 284 runs.*

Bangladesh 246 (59.4 overs) (G. Ashraf 77); West Africa 170 for nine. *Bangladesh won by 76 runs.*

Holland 150 for nine; East Africa 127 (51.5 overs). *Holland won by 23 runs.*

JUNE 18

Group 1

Gibraltar 42 for four (18 overs) v USA. *No result.*

Zimbabwe 192 for four (25 overs) (D. L. Houghton 73, J. G. Heron 50); Kenya 71 for four (25 overs). *Zimbabwe won by 121 runs.*

Hong Kong 207 for seven (45 overs) (A. A. Lorimer 53); Israel 84 (38.2 overs). *Hong Kong won by 123 runs.*

Group 2

Fiji 31 for two (14 overs) v Malaysia. *No result.*

West Africa v Holland. *No result: abandoned without a ball being bowled.*

East Africa v Singapore. *No result: abandoned without a ball being bowled.*

JUNE 21

Group 1

USA v Kenya. *No result: abandoned without a ball being bowled.*

Zimbabwe v Gibraltar. *No result: abandoned without a ball being bowled.*

Israel 167 for nine (S. B. Perlman 75 not out); Papua New Guinea 171 for one (N. R. Agonia 86 not out, T. Vai 75 not out). *Papua New Guinea won by nine wickets.*

Hong Kong v Canada. *No result: abandoned without a ball being bowled.*

Group 2

Bangladesh 143 (W. A. Bourne four for 33); East Africa 117. *Bangladesh won by 26 runs.*

Holland v Singapore. *No result: abandoned without a ball being bowled.*

Bermuda 153 for five (20 overs) (C. Blades 45 not out, N. A. Gibbons 39); Fiji 102 for six (20 overs) (T. Korocowiri 30 not out). *Bermuda won by 51 runs.*

JUNE 23

Group 1

USA v Papua New Guinea. *No result: abandoned without a ball being bowled.*

Gibraltar v Canada. *No result: abandoned without a ball being bowled.*

Israel 74 for six (24 overs) v Kenya. *No result.*

Group 2

Fiji v West Africa. *No result: abandoned without a ball being bowled.*

Malaysia v East Africa. *No result: abandoned without a ball being bowled.*

Bangladesh v Singapore. *No result: abandoned without a ball being bowled.*

JUNE 25

Group 1

USA v Hong Kong. *No result: abandoned without a ball being bowled.*

Canada 9 for no wkt (9 overs) v Zimbabwe. *No result.*

Israel 42 for two (10 overs) v Gibraltar. *No result.*

Group 2

Fiji v Bangladesh. *No result: abandoned without a ball being bowled.*

Bermuda v Holland. *No result: abandoned without a ball being bowled.*

West Africa v Singapore. *No result: abandoned without a ball being bowled.*

JUNE 28

Group 1

Israel 65 (31.2 overs) (A. J. Traicos four for 21); Zimbabwe 66 for one (7 overs). *Zimbabwe won by nine wickets.*

Gibraltar 129 for eight (40 overs); Hong Kong 130 for two (29.2 overs) (D. Reeve 56 not out, D. G. Greenwood 56 not out). *Hong Kong won by eight wickets.*

Papua New Guinea 231 for seven (56 overs) (V. Pala 101 not out); Canada 211 (54.4 overs) (T. Javed 50; K. Vuivagi four for 26). *Papua New Guinea won by 20 runs.*

Group 2

Holland 251 for six (60 overs) (R. Elferink 154 not out, R. Lifmann 43); Fiji 79 for two. *Holland won on faster scoring-rate.*

East Africa 53 for two (25.1 overs) v West Africa. *No result.*

Singapore 115 (45.1 overs) (W. H. Trott four for 27, E. A. James three for 19); Bermuda 116 for four (23.3 overs) (N. A. Gibbons 48). *Bermuda won by six wickets.*

Bangladesh 122 for seven (25 overs); Malaysia 121 for six (25 overs). *Bangladesh won by 1 run.*

JUNE 30

Group 1

Canada 233 (T. Javed 68); USA 95 (R. J. Stevens four for 26). *Canada won by 138 runs.*

Papua New Guinea 94; Zimbabwe 96 for one. *Zimbabwe won by nine wickets.*

Hong Kong 105 for nine; Kenya 108 for seven. *Kenya won by three wickets.*

Group 2

East Africa 220 for seven (K. W. Arnold 54, D. C. Patel 52, B. K. Bouri 49); Fiji 132 (C. A. C. Browne 36, R. G. Jepsen 30; B. K. Desai four for 21). *East Africa won by 88 runs.*

Bangladesh 67 (31 overs) (L. Thomas four for 13, W. H. Trott three for 12, A. King three for 23); Bermuda 70 for three (16 overs). *Bermuda won by seven wickets.*

Malaysia 128; Singapore 129 for four (F. J. R. Martens 67). *Singapore won by six wickets.*

JULY 2

Group 1

Israel 157 (52 overs); USA 158 for two (32.3 overs) (N. Lashkari 76 not out, K. Khan 65 not out). *USA won by eight wickets.*

Gibraltar 55 (36 overs) (V. Pala four for 30); Papua New Guinea 58 for one. *Papua New Guinea won by nine wickets.*

Canada 242 for eight (I. F. Kirmani 107); Kenya 197 (53.5 overs) (G. Musa 53, C. Neblett four for 26). *Canada won by 45 runs.*

Group 2

West Africa 219 for nine (58 overs) (S. Elliott 75, J. Onyechi 53) v Malaysia. *No result.*

Bermuda 240 (55.4 overs) (L. Thomas 68, E. G. James 51; B. K. Desai three for 31, W. A. Bourne three for 55); East Africa 175 for eight (56 overs) (D. C. Patel 64). *Bermuda won by 65 runs.*

Holland 163 for eight; Bangladesh 167 for four (35.4 overs). *Bangladesh won by six wickets.*

JULY 5

Group 1

Hong Kong 192 for four (A. A. Lorimer 72 not out); Zimbabwe 196 for three (A. J. Pycroft 83 not out, J. G. Heron 51). *Zimbabwe won by seven wickets.*

Kenya 200 for eight (H. S. Mehta 52); Papua New Guinea 173 (W. Maha 52). *Kenya won by 27 runs.*

Israeli XI 246 (R. J. Cottle 90); Canada 247 (C. Neblett 79). *Canada won by default – Israel out of competition.*

Group 2

West Africa 249 (58.4 overs) (S. Elliott 67, J. Onyechi 53, D. Otegbeye 47, E. Henshaw 42; E. A. James four for 41); Bermuda 252 for three (48.5 overs) (C. Blades 82 not out, G. Brown 78 not out, S. Lightbourne 44). *Bermuda won by seven wickets.*

Holland 301 for three (R. Lifmann 155 not out, R. Schoonheim 117); Malaysia 176. *Holland won by 125 runs.*

Fiji 219 for eight (I. G. Vuli 31 not out, R. G. Jepsen 30, S. Sekinini 30; M. Rajalingham five for 39); Singapore 205 (F. J. R. Martens 35, A. Dass 35; I. G. Vuli three for 30). *Fiji won by 14 runs.*

SEMI-FINALS

BANGLADESH v ZIMBABWE

At West Bromwich, Dartmouth, July 7. Zimbabwe won by eight wickets.

Bangladesh

Omar Khalid b Hough	20	*Shafiqul Haque b Curran	1
Nazeem Shiraji c Houghton b Hough	0	Samiur Rahman c Houghton b Curran	5
Gazi Ashraf lbw b Hogg	10	Dipu Rai Chowdhury not out	15
Raquibul Hassan c Houghton b Curran	35	Anwarul Ameen Azhar lbw b Rawson	2
Rafiqul Alam run out	4	B 2, l-b 10, w 1	13
Jahangir Shah Badsha b Curran	19	1/2 2/21 3/44 4/45 5/97 (55.2 overs)	124
Sadrul Anam run out	0	6/97 7/100 8/102 9/113	

Bowling: Hogg 8–1–13–1; Hough 12–2–28–2; Rawson 9.2–5–11–1; Fletcher 4–0–17–0; Curran 12–1–31–4; Traicos 10–3–11–0.

Zimbabwe

†D. L. Houghton lbw b Chowdhury	1		
J. G. Heron not out	63	L-b 6, w 1, n-b 1	8
K. M. Curran b Rahman	44		
A. J. Pycroft not out	10	1/4 2/107 (2 wkts, 29.3 overs)	126

*D. A. G. Fletcher, C. A. T. Hodgson, R. D. Brown, P. W. E. Rawson, A. J. Traicos, E. J. Hough and V. R. Hogg did not bat.

Bowling: Chowdhury 4–0–16–1; Rahman 5.3–0–30–1; Badsha 6–0–26–0; Khalid 3–0–16–0; Azhar 11–0–30–0.

Umpires: T. J. Cox and F. J. Law.

BERMUDA v PAPUA NEW GUINEA

At Mitchell and Butler's, July 7. Bermuda won by six wickets.

Papua New Guinea

K. Vuivagi c Douglas b Trott	2	G. Ravu b Bailey	8
V. Patu b King	0	K. Ila run out	2
T. Vai c Reid b James	23	K. Kalo not out	0
T. Ao c Douglas b King	0		
W. Maha c Bailey b Trott	2	L-b 4, w 5, n-b 3	12
*A. Leka c Douglas b James	18		
V. Pala c Tucker b Bailey	72	1/9 2/9 3/14 4/19 5/48 (39 overs)	153
R. Ila c Reid b Gibbons	14	6/48 7/129 8/142 9/147	

Bowling: Trott 12–4–30–2; King 8–2–23–2; James 8–0–34–2; Gibbons 7–1–36–1; Lightbourne 2–0–17–0; Bailey 2–1–1–2.

Bermuda

G. A. Brown b Kalo	0	J. Tucker not out	28
W. A. Reid b Ao	24		
S. Lightbourne c R. Ila b K. Ila	26	B 1, l-b 4, w 2, n-b 1	8
N. A. Gibbons b K. Ila	0		
*C. Blades not out	69	1/0 2/51 3/52 4/55 (4 wkts, 42.4 overs)	155

J. L. O. Bailey, †A. C. Douglas, E. G. James, A. King and W. H. Trott did not bat.

Bowling: Kalo 10–3–35–1; Ravu 6–0–34–0; Ao 12–2–32–1; K. Ila 9–2–22–2; Pala 4–1–18–0; Leka 1–0–6–0.

Umpires: J. B. Morris and P. D. Ogden.

THIRD PLACE MATCH

At Bournville, July 9. Bangladesh 224 (Yousuf Rahman 115, Nazeem Shiraji 52; L. Aukopi five for 14); Papua New Guinea 225 for seven (W. Maha 60). *Papua New Guinea won by three wickets.*

FINAL

BERMUDA v ZIMBABWE

At Leicester County Ground, July 10. Zimbabwe won by five wickets.

Man of the Match: A. J. Pycroft.

Bermuda

G. A. Brown c Traicos b Rawson	48
W. A. Reid b Hogg	13
S. Lightbourne b Fletcher	32
N. A. Gibbons b Fletcher	1
*C. Blades c Curran b Rawson	45
E. G. James run out	8
J. Tucker lbw b Hogg	18
†A. C. Douglas not out	36
J. L. O. Bailey c Hough b Fletcher	4
A. King not out	5
B 1, l-b 15, w 1, n-b 4	21
1/27 2/74 3/78 4/135 5/151 6/161 7/197 8/210 (8 wkts, 60 overs)	231

W. H. Trott did not bat.

Bowling: Hogg 10–0–35–2; Hough 8–3–28–0; Rawson 12–1–48–2; Traicos 12–3–25–0; Fletcher 9–1–34–3; Curran 9–1–40–0.

Zimbabwe

†D. L. Houghton lbw b Trott	8
J. G. Heron c and b Gibbons	9
K. M. Curran lbw b Blades	30
A. J. Pycroft c Lightbourne b Gibbons	82
*D. A. G. Fletcher c Douglas b Blades	13
C. A. T. Hodgson not out	57
R. D. Brown not out	12
B 1, l-b 8, w 10, n-b 2	21
1/22 2/30 3/78 4/110 5/177 (5 wkts, 54.3 overs)	232

P. W. E. Rawson, A. J. Traicos, E. J. Hough and V. R. Hogg did not bat.

Bowling: Trott 11.3–1–27–1; King 3–0–10–0; James 11–1–41–0; Gibbons 12–0–64–2; Blades 12–2–39–2; Bailey 5–0–30–0.

Umpires: J. A. Walker and R. Burrows.

THE CRICKET COUNCIL

The Cricket Council, which was set up in 1968 and reconstituted in 1974, acts as the governing body for cricket in the United Kingdom. It is composed of the following, the officers listed being those for 1981–82.

President: G. H. G. Doggart.
Chairman: C. H. Palmer.
Chairman of Public Relations and Promotion Sub-Committee: F. M. Turner.
5 Representatives of Test and County Cricket Board: F. G. Mann, J. K. R. Graveney, D. J. Insole, C. S. Rhoades, A. G. Waterman.
5 Representatives of National Cricket Association: J. D. Robson, F. R. Brown, F. H. Elliott, J. Lane, J. G. Overy.
5 Representatives of Marylebone Cricket Club: D. G. Clark (vice-chairman), G. O. Allen, J. G. W. Davies, C. G. A. Paris, W. H. Webster.
1 Representative of Minor Counties Cricket Association: R. A. C. Forrester.
1 Representative (non-voting) of Irish Cricket Union: D. Scott.
1 Representative (non-voting) of Scottish Cricket Union: R. W. Barclay.

Secretary – D. B. Carr; *Deputy Secretary* – J. A. Bailey; *Secretary, PR and Promotion* – P. M. Lush.

THE TEST AND COUNTY CRICKET BOARD

The TCCB was set up in 1968 to be responsible for Test matches, official tours, and First-Class and Minor Counties competitions. It is composed of representatives from – 17 First-Class Counties; Marylebone Cricket Club; Minor Counties Cricket Association.

Oxford University Cricket Club and Cambridge University Cricket Club attend as observers.

Officers 1981-82

Chairman: F. G. Mann.
Chairmen of Committees: F. G. Mann (Adjudication, Executive); F. R. Brown (County Pitches); D. J. Insole (Cricket, Overseas Tours); O. S. Wheatley (Discipline); A. G. Waterman (Finance and General Purposes); B. Coleman (PR and Marketing); D. R. W. Silk (Registration); P. B. H. May (Selection); D. B. Carr (Umpires); M. D. Vockins (Under 25 and Second XI Competitions).

Secretary – D. B. Carr; *Assistant Secretary (Admin.)* – B. Langley; *Assistant Secretary (Cricket)* – M. E. Gear; *PR and Marketing Manager* – P. M. Lush; *Promotions Officer* – R. J. Roe.

THE NATIONAL CRICKET ASSOCIATION

With the setting up of the Cricket Council in 1968 it was necessary to form a separate organisation to represent the interests of all cricket below the first-class game, and it is the National Cricket Association that carries out this function. It comprises – Representatives from 50 County Cricket Associations and Representatives from 16 national cricketing organisations.

Officers 1981-82

President: F. R. Brown.
Chairman: J. D. Robson.
Secretary: B. J. Aspital.
Director of Coaching: K. V. Andrew.
Hon. Treasurer: D. A. Jackson.
Assistant Secretary: P. G. M. August.

THE MARYLEBONE CRICKET CLUB, 1982

At the 195th Annual Meeting of MCC, held at Lord's on May 5, 1982, Mr G. O. Allen was reappointed a Trustee of the club. As the result of a postal ballot the practice of the Committee's indicating its recommendations in regard to certain candidates nominated for election to the Committee is to be continued, the voting being 3,251 in favour of this and 1,441 against. A postal ballot conducted to establish members' views on Sunday cricket being played at Lord's resulted in a quite substantial majority (3,799 to 1,990) in favour of it. The surplus of income over expenditure was £3,400 before taxation, a large reduction on 1980-81, owing partly to an increase in match expenses of £29,656, including the costs of two overseas tours. The membership of the club numbered 18,179 on December 31, 1981, when the number of candidates on the waiting list was 7,571. In 1981, 234 members had died, 86 had resigned and 135 had allowed their memberships to lapse.

Among notable personalities connected with the game whose deaths were reported were Captain the Lord Cornwallis, for nearly 50 years either a member of the Committee, a Trustee or a Life Vice-President of MCC, K. F. Barrington, an England batsman of great distinction and determination who died while on tour, as assistant-manager, with the England team in West Indies, J. H. Fingleton, famous as an Australian Test cricketer as well as his country's outstanding writer on the game, T. W. Wall, also an Australian Test player, A. D. Nourse, one of South Africa's greatest cricketers, G. Ashton, the oldest of a celebrated trio of cricketing brothers and a former member of the MCC committee, G. Geary, a fine England bowler, L. G. Crawley, famed as a striker of both a cricket and a golf ball, A. B. Sellers, one of Yorkshire's most successful captains, B. O. Allen, captain of Gloucestershire before and after the Second World War, and E. H. King and O. J. Wait, both former members of the MCC Committee. The club also mourned the loss of Admiral of the Fleet Lord Fraser of North Cape, the last surviving war leader to have been given Honorary Life Membership in 1946.

Sir Anthony Tuke was nominated by G. H. G. Doggart to succeed him as President of MCC on October 1, 1982. Aged 61, Sir Anthony was chairman of Barclays Bank from 1973 until 1981, the post he now holds with the Rio Tinto-Zinc Corporation. He was chairman of the British Olympic Appeal Committee in 1980 and has been for some time a member of the Finance sub-committee of the club.

The Annual General Meeting was followed immediately by a Special General Meeting, at which the Committee's proposal to reintroduce associate membership (the Committee had asked to be empowered to elect up to 2,000 of these) was rejected. Further business which it had been the intention to deal with at this Special General Meeting, concerning subscriptions and the development of new offices at Lord's, was deferred until an additional Special General Meeting, called for August 3, 1982.

Meanwhile, at the request of the requisite minimum of 50, the actual number being 58, a Special General Meeting was also held on July 6, 1982, to vote on three resolutions calling for a reduction in the size of the Committee, and if this were approved to amend the administration of the club by further changes of rule. Considering that the first resolution was, in effect, one of No Confidence, the Committee put the matter to a postal ballot, at the same time reminding members of the way the club operates. The total votes cast, postal and at the meeting, were 1,625 for the No Confidence resolution, and 3,694 against it. The other resolutions, being dependent on this first one, were not therefore discussed.

At the Special General Meeting on August 3, 1982, also preceded by a postal ballot, an increase in subscriptions with effect from January 1, 1983, was approved by 3,694 to 1,173. The Committee's proposal to develop the Tennis and Squash building to house the offices of the Test and County Cricket Board and the National Cricket Association, to renovate the Tennis and Squash courts, and also to rebuild the Middlesex CCC office alongside, was approved by 3,764 votes to 645.

MCC v NOTTINGHAMSHIRE

At Lord's, May 1, 3, 4. Drawn. Bad weather marred the start of the season at headquarters. After a delayed start on the first day MCC, having won the toss, reached 269 for eight, Gower, not long back from India, showing fine form and Marks playing freely. On the second day, half of which was lost to rain, Nottinghamshire, batting cautiously, reached 131 for three. Two declarations on the last day, culminating in Nottinghamshire being left to score 264 to win in 155 minutes plus twenty overs, came to nothing when heavy rain, at and after tea, brought the match to an end. Todd had the unenviable distinction of making a "king pair", Newman dismissing him with the first ball in each of Nottinghamshire's innings.

MCC

A. R. Butcher c Robinson b Illingworth	19 – (2) c Birch b Randall	43
G. Cook c Rice b Hadlee	39 – (1) c French b Hadlee	9
D. I. Gower c Hemmings b Cooper	47 – c French b Randall	62
P. W. G. Parker lbw b Hemmings	13 – (5) not out	5
*K. W. R. Fletcher c Birch b Cooper	11	
I. A. Greig c and b Cooper	4	
V. J. Marks not out	71	
P. H. Edmonds b Hemmings	9	
†C. J. Richards b Hemmings	13 – (4) c Todd b Randall	3
P. J. W. Allott not out	30	
L-b 9, n-b 4	13 B 1, l-b 1, w 1	3
1/41 2/78 3/106 4/137 5/140 6/159 7/184 8/210	(8 wkts dec.) 269 1/13 2/110 3/114 4/125	(4 wkts dec.) 125

P. G. Newman did not bat.

Bowling: *First Innings*—Hadlee 23–7–49–1; Hendrick 20–6–50–0; Cooper 22–8–60–3; Illingworth 12–0–51–1; Hemmings 15–4–46–3. *Second Innings*—Hadlee 7–5–4–1; Hendrick 7–2–22–0; Illingworth 5–1–26–0; Cooper 9–2–24–0; Hemmings 4–1–12–0; Robinson 4–0–19–0; Randall 3.5–1–15–3.

Nottinghamshire

P. A. Todd b Newman	0 – c Gower b Newman	0
R. T. Robinson b Greig	11 – not out	28
D. W. Randall not out	52 – b Marks	32
*C. E. B. Rice c Butcher b Edmonds	46	
J. D. Birch not out	15	
L-b 2, n-b 5	7 N-b 1	1
1/0 2/19 3/96	(3 wkts dec.) 131 1/0 2/61	(2 wkts) 61

N. J. B. Illingworth, E. E. Hemmings, K. E. Cooper, †B. N. French, R. J. Hadlee and M. Hendrick did not bat.

Bowling: *First Innings*—Newman 12–5–31–1; Allott 16–3–50–0; Greig 11–2–29–1; Edmonds 4–1–14–1. *Second Innings*—Newman 6–3–8–1; Allott 4–1–17–0; Greig 3–1–2–0; Marks 8.2–1–15–1; Edmonds 7–0–18–0.

Umpires: B. Leadbeater and R. Palmer.

At Lord's, May 19, 20, 21. MCC drew with INDIANS (see Indian tour section).

At Lord's, May 25. Drawn. MCC 242 for three dec. (N. E. Briers 113 not out); MCC Young Cricketers 199 for eight (R. N. Berry 96).

At Oxford, June 5, 7, 8. MCC beat OXFORD UNIVERSITY by eight wickets (see Oxford University section).

At Roehampton, June 23, 24, 25. MCC v CAMBRIDGE UNIVERSITY. Abandoned.

At Lord's, July 8, 9. Drawn. MCC 223 for no wkt dec. (S. G. Plumb 111 not out, R. A. B. Ezekowitz 107 not out) and 201 for five dec.; Scotland 167 for five dec. (R. S. Weir 61, W. A. Donald 53) and 206 for seven (R. S. Weir 102 not out).

At Eglinton, Co. Derry, July 27, 28, 29. MCC drew with IRELAND (see Other Matches, 1982).

MCC HONORARY LIFE MEMBERS, 1982

England: Sir Cyril Hawker, J. D. B. Robertson, W. H. Webster.

Honorary Cricket Members: J. M. Brearley, R. T. Simpson.

MCC ENGLAND HONORARY CRICKET MEMBERS

C. J. Barnett
W. E. Bowes
H. Larwood
W. Voce
L. E. G. Ames, CBE
Sir Leonard Hutton
D. C. S. Compton, CBE
D. V. P. Wright
J. T. Ikin
T. G. Evans, CBE
C. Washbrook
A. V. Bedser, CBE
W. J. Edrich, DFC
J. C. Laker
P. B. H. May, CBE
W. Watson
P. E. Richardson
T. E. Bailey
M. J. K. Smith, OBE
J. Hardstaff
J. B. Statham, CBE
F. S. Trueman
T. W. Graveney, OBE
G. A. R. Lock
C. Milburn
D. A. Allen
R. W. Barber
E. R. Dexter
P. H. Parfitt
F. H. Tyson
M. C. Cowdrey, CBE
J. T. Murray, MBE
J. M. Parks
D. B. Close
B. L. D'Oliveira, OBE
R. Illingworth, CBE
G. Pullar
F. J. Titmus, MBE
J. H. Wardle
D. J. Brown
M. H. Denness
R. T. Simpson
J. M. Brearley, OBE

OTHER MATCHES AT LORD'S, 1982

June 10, 11, 12, 14, 15. First Cornhill Test. ENGLAND beat INDIA by seven wickets (See Indian tour section).

OXFORD UNIVERSITY v CAMBRIDGE UNIVERSITY

June 26, 28, 29. Cambridge University won by seven wickets. For the first time in its 138 years' history the University match was won on a declaration. After Ellis had set Cambridge to score 272 in 210 minutes, a dashing 100 by Boyd-Moss helped them home with five overs to spare. This departure from the uncompromising combat of former years was dictated partly by the modern approach to the match and partly by the loss through rain of seven hours' play on the first two days when Ellis and others batted with spirit for Oxford. Though the Cambridge captain, D. R. Pringle, had preferred to play for England in the second Test, Cambridge had promised to be the stronger of two sides of modest bowling. In the last innings, Boyd-Moss and Henderson made 144 together in 22 overs against Oxford bowlers who could not contain them enough to force them into taking excessive and perhaps costly risks. John Varey, bowling for Oxford, gave the 1982 match another place in history by taking the wicket of his twin brother, David.

Oxford University

*R. G. P. Ellis (*Haileybury and St Edmund Hall*) c Goldie b Hodgson	86	– c Henderson b Pollock	14
R. Marsden (*Merchant Taylors' and Christ Church*) lbw b Palmer	13	– b Boyd-Moss	39
K. A. Hayes (*QEGS, Blackburn and Merton*) retired hurt	13		
R. S. Cowan (*Lewes Priory CS and Magdalen*) c Goldie b Hodgson	33	– (3) c Mills b Pollock	4
G. J. Toogood (*N. Bromsgrove HS and Lincoln*) c Henderson b Hodgson	31	– (4) c Barrington b Boyd-Moss	38
†R. S. Luddington (*KCS, Wimbledon and St Edmund Hall*) b Boyd-Moss	6	– (7) c Henderson b Boyd-Moss	7
R. P. Moulding (*Haberdashers' Aske's and Christ Church*) not out	20	– (5) c Mills b Boyd-Moss	8
J. G. Varey (*Birkenhead and St Edmund Hall*) not out	32	– (6) not out	12
S. P. Ridge (*Dr Challenors, Amersham and Worcester*) (did not bat)		– (8) not out	2
L-b 10, w 1, n-b 4	15	B 6, l-b 4, n-b 2	12
1/58 2/125 3/188 4/189 5/199 (5 wkts dec.)	249	1/17 2/25 3/64 4/104 5/113 6/127 (6 wkts dec.)	136

I. J. Curtis (*Whitgift and Lincoln*) and T. J. Taylor (*Stockport GS and Magdalen*) did not bat.

Bowling: *First Innings*—Palmer 17–2–52–1; Pollock 3–1–19–0; Hodgson 26–4–89–3; Ellison 6–1–23–0; Boyd-Moss 11–1–51–1. *Second Innings*—Palmer 10–0–35–0; Pollock 7–1–16–2; Hodgson 3–0–20–0; Boyd-Moss 9–0–42–4; Varey 1–0–4–0; Ellison 2–0–7–0.

Cambridge University

*J. P. C. Mills (*Oundle and Corpus Christi*) c sub b Ellis	9	– lbw b Ridge	11
D. W. Varey (*Birkenhead and Pembroke*) c Cowan b Varey	22	– retired hurt	16
R. J. Boyd-Moss (*Bedford and Magdalene*) not out	41	– c sub b Curtis	100
S. P. Henderson (*Downside and Magdalene*) not out	39	– c Ridge b Taylor	50
W. E. J. Barrington (*Lancing and St Catharine's*) (did not bat)		– not out	48
K. I. Hodgson (*Oundle and Downing*) (did not bat)		– not out	36
L-b 1, w 1, n-b 1	3	B 1, l-b 9, n-b 1	11
1/19 2/50 (2 wkt dec.)	114	1/26 2/178 3/190 (3 wkts)	272

S. J. G. Doggart (*Winchester and Magdalene*), †C. F. E. Goldie (*St Paul's and Pembroke*), A. J. Pollock (*Shrewsbury and Trinity*), C. C. Ellison (*Tonbridge and Homerton*) and R. W. M. Palmer (*Bedford and St Catharine's*) did not bat.

Bowling: *First Innings*—Cowan 7–0–49–0; Ridge 6–0–14–0; Ellis 4–0–18–1; Taylor 5–0–17–0; Varey 2–0–13–1. *Second Innings*—Cowan 6–0–42–0; Ridge 8–1–33–1; Curtis 22–2–119–1; Varey 3–0–19–0; Taylor 16–4–46–1; Ellis 1–0–2–0.

Umpires: J. Birkenshaw and W. L. Budd.

OXFORD v CAMBRIDGE, RESULTS AND HUNDREDS

The University match dates back to 1827. Altogether there have been 138 official matches, Cambridge winning 53 and Oxford 45, with 40 drawn. Results since 1950:

1950	Drawn
1951	Oxford won by 21 runs
1952	Drawn
1953	Cambridge won by two wickets
1954	Drawn
1955	Drawn
1956	Drawn
1957	Cambridge won by an innings and 186 runs
1958	Cambridge won by 99 runs
1959	Oxford won by 85 runs
1960	Drawn
1961	Drawn
1962	Drawn
1963	Drawn
1964	Drawn
1965	Drawn
1966	Oxford won by an innings and 9 runs
1967	Drawn
1968	Drawn
1969	Drawn
1970	Drawn
1971	Drawn
1972	Cambridge won by an innings and 25 runs
1973	Drawn
1974	Drawn
1975	Drawn
1976	Oxford won by ten wickets
1977	Drawn
1978	Drawn
1979	Cambridge won by an innings and 52 runs
1980	Drawn
1981	Drawn
1982	Cambridge won by seven wickets

Seventy-three three-figure innings have been played in the University matches. For those scored before 1919 see 1940 *Wisden*. Those subsequent to 1919 include the six highest, as shown here:

238*	Nawab of Pataudi	1931	Oxford
211	G. Goonesena	1957	Cam.
201*	M. J. K. Smith	1954	Oxford
201	A. Ratcliffe	1931	Cam.
200	Majid J. Khan	1970	Cam.
193	D. C. H. Townsend	1934	Oxford

170	M. Howell	1919 Oxford	116*	D. R. W. Silk	1953 Cam.
167	B. W. Hone	1932 Oxford	116	M. C. Cowdrey	1953 Oxford
158	P. M. Roebuck	1975 Cam.	115	A. W. Allen	1934 Cam.
157	D. R. Wilcox	1932 Cam.	114*	D. R. Owen-Thomas	1972 Cam.
155	F. S. Goldstein	1968 Oxford	114	J. F. Pretlove	1955 Cam.
149	J. T. Morgan	1929 Cam.	113*	J. M. Brearley	1962 Cam.
146	R. O'Brien	1956 Cam.	113	E. R. T. Holmes	1927 Oxford
146	D. R. Owen-Thomas	1971 Cam.	112*	E. D. Fursdon	1975 Oxford
145*	H. E. Webb	1948 Oxford	111*	G. W. Cook	1957 Cam.
145	D. P. Toft	1967 Oxford	109	C. H. Taylor	1923 Oxford
142	M. P. Donnelly	1946 Oxford	108	F. G. H. Chalk	1934 Oxford
136	E. T. Killick	1930 Cam.	106	Nawab of Pataudi	1929 Oxford
135	H. A. Pawson	1947 Oxford	105	E. J. Craig	1961 Cam.
131	Nawab of Pataudi	1960 Oxford	104	H. J. Enthoven	1924 Cam.
129	H. J. Enthoven	1925 Cam.	104	M. J. K. Smith	1955 Oxford
127	D. S. Sheppard	1952 Cam.	103*	A. R. Lewis	1962 Cam.
124	A. K. Judd	1927 Cam.	103*	D. R. Pringle	1979 Cam.
124	A. Ratcliffe	1932 Cam.	102*	A. P. F. Chapman	1922 Cam.
122	P. A. Gibb	1938 Cam.	101*	R. W. V. Robins	1928 Cam.
121	J. N. Grover	1937 Oxford	101	N. W. D. Yardley	1937 Cam.
119	J. M. Brearley	1964 Cam.	100*	M. Manasseh	1964 Oxford
118	H. Ashton	1921 Cam.	100	P. J. Dickinson	1939 Cam.
118	D. R. W. Silk	1954 Cam.	100	N. J. Cosh	1967 Cam.
117	M. J. K. Smith	1956 Oxford	100	R. J. Boyd-Moss	1982 Cam.

* *Signifies not out.*

Highest Totals

503	Oxford	1900	432-9	Cambridge	1936
457	Oxford	1947	431	Cambridge	1932
453-8	Oxford	1931	425	Cambridge	1938

Lowest Totals

32	Oxford	1878	42	Oxford	1890
39	Cambridge	1858	47	Cambridge	1838

Notes: A. P. F. Chapman and M. P. Donnelly enjoy the following distinction: Chapman scored a century at Lord's in the University match (102*, 1922); for Gentlemen v Players (160, 1922), (108, 1926); and for England v Australia (121, 1930). M. P. Donnelly scored a century at Lord's in the University match (142, 1946); for Gentlemen v Players (162*, 1947); and for New Zealand v England (206, 1949).

A. Ratcliffe's 201 for Cambridge remained a record for the match for only one day, being beaten by the Nawab of Pataudi's 238* for Oxford next day.

M. J. K. Smith (Oxford) is the only player who has scored three hundreds; 201* in 1954, 104 in 1955, and 117 in 1956. His aggregate, 477, surpassed the previous best, 457, by the Nawab of Pataudi, 1929–31.

The following players have scored two hundreds: W. Yardley (Cambridge) 100 in 1870 and 130 in 1872; H. J. Enthoven (Cambridge) 104 in 1924 and 129 in 1925; Nawab of Pataudi (Oxford) 106 in 1929 and 238* in 1931; A. Ratcliffe (Cambridge) 201 in 1931 and 124 in 1932; D. R. W. Silk (Cambridge) 116* in 1953 and 118 in 1954; J. M. Brearley (Cambridge) 113* in 1962 and 119 in 1964; D. R. Owen-Thomas (Cambridge) 146 in 1971 and 114* in 1972.

F. C. Cobden, in the Oxford v Cambridge match in 1870, performed the hat-trick by taking the last three wickets and won an extraordinary game for Cambridge by two runs. The feat is without parallel in first-class cricket. Cobden obtained the last three Oxford wickets in each innings – a curious coincidence. Other hat-tricks, all for Cambridge, have been credited to A. G. Steel (1879), P. H. Morton (1880), J. F. Ireland (1911), and R. G. H. Lowe (1926).

S. E. Butler, in the 1871 match, took all the wickets in the Cambridge first innings. The feat is unique in University matches. He bowled 24.1 overs. In the follow-on he took five wickets for 57, making fifteen for 95 runs in the match.

P. R. Le Couteur scored 160 and took eleven Cambridge wickets for 66 runs in 1910 – the best all-round performance in the history of the match.

D. W. Jarrett (Oxford 1975, Cambridge 1976) and S. M. Wookey (Cambridge 1975-76, Oxford 1978) are alone in gaining cricket Blues for both Universities.

ETON v HARROW

July 3. Drawn. The oldest fixture at Lord's was played there for the first time as a one-day match. Eton, in scoring 216 for three declared and then taking the first five Harrow wickets for 45 runs, held the upper hand for most of the day. But in the final hour Field and fifteen-year-old Nirmalalingham, from Sri Lanka, stoutly defended to save the match with an undefeated partnership of 63. After Eton had been put in to bat, Fleming and Gibbs took full advantage of the easy-paced pitch in an opening partnership of 72. Brooks and Berry then added 114 for the third wicket before Eton's declaration, awaited, left Harrow 217 to win in 150 minutes.

Eton

M. V. Fleming b Raper	52
D. N. Gibbs b Beard	28
N. H. Brooks not out	71
J. P. Berry b Raper	45
B 2, l-b 8, w 2, n-b 8	20
1/72 2/102 3/216 (3 wkts dec.)	216

J. W. M. Barlow, W. A. B. Russell, G. F. Baring, *C. A. Watt, †P. A. D. Inkin, C. E. Pettifer and E. Brassey did not bat.

Bowling: Murray 19–4–60–0; Rogerson 5–1–18–0; Raper 15.4–2–50–2; Beard 28–6–60–1; Hay 2–0–8–0.

Harrow

*†J. F. Turner c Watt b Brassey	5
J. W. S. Raper c Inkin b Pettifer	20
J. M. H. Ford c Barlow b Fleming	7
W. A. Menpes-Smith c Brassey b Watt	8
N. F. M. Hay run out	3
J. D. R. Field not out	19
D. R. Nirmalalingham not out	37
B 7, l-b 2	9
1/16 2/30 3/38 4/41 5/45 (5 wkts)	108

R. C. A. Kinnison, J. R. Rogerson, D. St J. B. Beard and P. R. G. Murray did not bat.

Bowling: Brassey 10–4–18–1; Pettifer 13–5–23–1; Fleming 8–7–1–1; Watt 9–2–42–1; Barlow 7–3–15–0.

Umpires: R. O. Hounsell and A. E. D. Smith.

ETON v HARROW, RESULTS AND HUNDREDS

Of the 147 matches played Eton have won 49, Harrow 44 and 54 have been drawn. This is the generally published record, but Harrow men object strongly to the first game in 1805 being treated as a regular contest between the two schools, contending that it is no more correct to count that one than the fixture of 1857 which has been rejected.

The matches played during the war years 1915-18 and 1940-45 are not reckoned as belonging to the regular series.

Results since 1950:

1950	Drawn
1951	Drawn
1952	Harrow won by seven wickets
1953	Eton won by ten wickets
1954	Harrow won by nine wickets
1955	Eton won by 38 runs
1956	Drawn
1957	Drawn
1958	Drawn
1959	Drawn
1960	Harrow won by 124 runs
1961	Harrow won by an innings and 12 runs
1962	Drawn
1963	Drawn
1964	Eton won by eight wickets
1965	Harrow won by 48 runs
1966	Drawn
1967	Drawn
1968	Harrow won by seven wickets
1969	Drawn
1970	Eton won by 97 runs
1971	Drawn
1972	Drawn
1973	Drawn
1974	Harrow won by eight wickets
1975	Harrow won by an innings and 151 runs
1976	Drawn
1977	Eton won by six wickets
1978	Drawn
1979	Drawn
1980	Drawn
1981	Drawn
1982	Drawn

Forty-five three-figure innings have been played in matches between these two schools. Those since 1918:

161*	M. K. Fosh	1975 Harrow
159	E. W. Dawson	1923 Eton
158	I. S. Akers-Douglas	1928 Eton
153	N. S. Hotchkin	1931 Eton
151	R. M. Tindall	1976 Harrow
135	J. C. Atkinson-Clark	1930 Eton
115	E. Crutchley	1939 Harrow
112	A. W. Allen	1931 Eton
112*	T. M. H. James	1978 Harrow
111	R. A. A. Holt	1937 Harrow
109	K. F. H. Hale	1929 Eton
109	N. S Hotchkin	1932 Eton
107	W. N. Coles	1946 Eton
106	D. M. Smith	1966 Eton
104	R. Pulbrook	1932 Harrow
103	L. G. Crawley	1921 Harrow
103	T. Hare	1947 Eton
102*	P. H. Stewart-Brown	1923 Harrow
102	R. V. C. Robins	1953 Eton
100	R. H. Cobbold	1923 Eton
100*	P. V. F. Cazalet	1926 Eton
100	A. N. A. Boyd	1934 Eton
100*	P. M. Studd	1935 Harrow
100	S. D. D. Sainsbury	1947 Eton
100	M. J. J. Faber	1968 Eton

* *Signifies not out.*

In 1904, D. C. Boles of Eton, making 183, set up a new record for the match, beating the 152 obtained for Eton in 1841 by Emilius Bayley, afterwards the Rev. Sir John Robert Laurie Emilius Bayley Laurie. M. C. Bird, Harrow, in 1907, scored 100 not out and 131, the only batsman who has made two 100s in the match. N. S. Hotchkin, Eton, played the following innings: 1931, 153; 1932, 109 and 96; 1933, 88 and 12.

July 24. Benson and Hedges Cup final. SOMERSET beat NOTTINGHAMSHIRE by nine wickets (See Benson and Hedges Cup section).

MCC SCHOOLS v NATIONAL ASSOCIATION OF YOUNG CRICKETERS

July 28, 29. MCC Schools won by five wickets. Having chosen to bat, Bailey declared NAYC's first innings before tea on the first day. MCC Schools then went to 115 for four, the full day's play producing 382 runs, eleven wickets and 123 overs. Morris, hurt while fielding, did not participate on the second day, when Cowdrey deputised as captain. After the third declaration of the match, NAYC set MCC Schools 270 to win – a tall order without Morris. However, the diminutive Matthews hit a splendid hundred, Cowdrey 54, and the target was reached with five overs to spare. Cotterell and Golding both bowled left-arm spin well for their respective sides.

National Association of Young Cricketers

*S. J. Bailey (*Staffordshire*) c Gill b Rose	10	– b Talbot	50
A. Middleton (*Hampshire*) b Ellcock	33	– c and b Golding	27
R. Pepper (*Kent*) b Ellcock	33	– c Ellcock b Golding	2
P. A. Redfarn (*Cambridgeshire*) c Gill b Rose	50	– c Fairbrother b Talbot	5
P. Caley (*Suffolk*) c Morris b Golding	64	– b Golding	16
C. K. Bullen (*Surrey*) c Matthews b Golding	5	– b Golding	21
T. A. Cotterell (*Surrey*) b Golding	23	– lbw b Golding	17
C. Shaw (*Yorkshire*) not out	44	– not out	12
K. Moye (*Essex*) not out	0		
†J. M. Robinson (*Warwickshire*) (did not bat)		– c Gill b Talbot	9
L-b 3, w 1, n-b 1	5	B 1, l-b 3, w 2, n-b 5	11
1/27 2/67 3/93 4/170 5/200 6/200 7/239 (7 wkts dec.)	267	1/65 2/83 3/87 4/94 5/108 6/144 7/153 8/170 (8 wkts dec.)	170

A. M. Babington (*Surrey*) did not bat.

Bowling: *First Innings*—Ellcock 19–8–70–2; Pick 9–3–22–0; Rose 19–6–72–2; Talbot 11–3–35–0; Golding 16–5–63–3. *Second Innings*—Ellcock 8–1–39–0; Pick 5–1–20–0; Rose 4–0–13–0; Talbot 9.5–1–49–3; Golding 13–4–38–5.

MCC Schools

M. Gouldstone (*Braintree College*) c Caley b Cotterell	15	– c Bullen b Cotterell	35
W. J. P. Matthews (*Bablake*) b Moye	4	– c Shaw b Cotterell	100
N. H. Fairbrother (*Lymm*) c Babington b Cotterell	60	– c Cotterell b Bullen	0
G. R. Cowdrey (*Tonbridge*) c and b Cotterell	27	– c and b Bullen	54
*H. Morris (*Blundell's*) b Bullen	2		
G. D. Rose (*Northumberland Pk, Tottenham*) not out	43	– b Cotterell	32
R. C. Talbot (*Richard Huish College*) b Cotterell	11		
A. K. Golding (*Colchester RGS*) not out	3	– not out	15
†P. Gill (*Grange School, Oldham*) (did not bat)		– not out	19
B 1, l-b 1, w 1	3	B 3, l-b 7, w 6	16
1/15 2/28 3/82 4/99 5/123 6/155 (6 wkts dec.)	168	1/65 2/66 3/158 4/233 5/237 (5 wkts)	271

R. A. Pick (*High Pavement College, Nottingham*) and R. M. Ellcock (*Malvern*) did not bat.

Bowling: *First Innings*—Moye 6–3–10–1; Babington 5–1–10–0; Cotterell 26.3–6–67–4; Bullen 27–5–78–1; Caley 1–1–0–0. *Second Innings*—Moye 3–0–17–0; Babington 9–0–51–0; Cotterell 17–3–92–3; Bullen 14–2–50–2; Shaw 8.5–1–45–0.

Umpires: A. E. Bishop and T. A. Brown.

After this match, the following were selected to play for NCA Young Cricketers against Combined Services: S. J. Bailey (*captain*), W. J. P. Matthews, N. H. Fairbrother, G. R. Cowdrey, P. A. Redfarn, G. D. Rose, C. K. Bullen, T. A. Cotterell, A. K. Golding, P. Gill and R. A. Pick.

July 30. NCA Young Cricketers won on faster scoring-rate. NCA Young Cricketers 283 for five (55 overs) (S. J. Bailey 131, N. H. Fairbrother 68, W. J. P. Matthews 50); Combined Services 119 for four (33 overs) (R. C. Moylan-Jones 57).

August 12, 13, 14, 15, 16. Second Cornhill Test. ENGLAND lost to PAKISTAN by ten wickets (See Pakistan tour section).

JOHN HAIG TROPHY FINAL

August 28. Scarborough won by 4 runs, taking the club title for the fifth time, in the last season of John Haig's sponsorship. Scarborough, electing to bat, lost four wickets to run-outs, only Pincher standing his ground. Finchley, after a fine start from Selwood and Milton, also suffered four run-outs, and steady bowling by Pincher, backed by splendid fielding, left them 5 runs short of victory.

Scarborough

A. J. Moor run out	30
C. H. Stephenson run out	12
A. Dalby c Johns b Selwood	2
W. L. Pincher not out	61
*B. Rennard run out	0
D. Byas run out	23
J. Precious c Milton b Alldis	8
†M. Brown b Alldis	2
C. C. Clifford not out	2
L-b 7, n-b 3	10
1/43 2/48 3/48 4/48 5/81 6/108 7/114 (7 wkts, 45 overs)	150

N. J. West and P. Ellis did not bat.

Bowling: Herbert 9–0–19–0; Edrupt 9–4–12–0; Selwood 9–3–20–1; Milton 9–3–22–0; Alldis 8–0–53–2; Bharadia 1–0–14–0.

Finchley

T. Selwood lbw b Pincher	49
*M. E. Milton c Moor b Clifford	39
P. Halstead run out	10
D. Foskett lbw b Pincher	0
†R. Johns run out	5
J. S. Alldis run out	7
W. Puri run out	8
W. Jordan not out	3
K. Bharadia b Dalby	0
R. M. Edrupt not out	1
B 2, l-b 16, w 2, n-b 4	24
1/72 2/95 3/96 4/114 5/114 6/134 7/136 8/143 (8 wkts, 45 overs)	146

S. Herbert did not bat.

Bowling: Ellis 9–1–35–0; West 9–5–13–0; Moor 5–1–14–0; Clifford 9–0–36–1; Pincher 9–0–16–2; Dalby 4–1–8–1.

Umpires: W. Harvey and P. S. G. Stevens.

NATIONAL CLUB CRICKET CHAMPIONSHIP WINNERS 1969-1982

D. H. Robins Cup

1969 HAMPSTEAD beat Finchley by seven wickets.
1970 CHELTENHAM beat Stockport by three wickets.
1971 BLACKHEATH beat Ealing by eight wickets.
1972 SCARBOROUGH beat Brentham by six wickets.
1973 WOLVERHAMPTON beat The Mote by five wickets.
1974 SUNBURY beat Tunbridge Wells by seven wickets.
1975 YORK beat Blackpool by six wickets.

John Haig Trophy

1976 SCARBOROUGH beat Dulwich by five wickets.
1977 SOUTHGATE beat Bowdon by six wickets.
1978 CHELTENHAM beat Bishop's Stortford by 15 runs.
1979 SCARBOROUGH beat Reading by two wickets.
1980 MOSELEY beat Gosport Borough by nine wickets.
1981 SCARBOROUGH beat Blackheath by 57 runs.
1982 SCARBOROUGH beat Finchley by 4 runs.

From 1983 the championship will be sponsored by William Younger.

SAMUEL WHITBREAD NATIONAL VILLAGE CHAMPIONSHIP FINAL

August 29. St Fagans (South Wales) won by six wickets, in their second successive victory, a feat previously accomplished only by Troon of Cornwall. Collingham (Nottinghamshire), after being put in, could muster only 148 from their 40 overs, Driscoll, the wicket-keeper, taking out his bat for 63. England, formerly of St Fagans, hit a brisk 42. The hard-hitting Stevens, held back until the 36th over, won the match for St Fagans by hitting the last 16 runs required in five balls.

Collingham

*J. Kirkham c Stevens b Howe	25	G. Croft b Needham	0
†G. Driscoll not out	63	L. Norris lbw b Needham	1
N. Weeks c Madley b Painter	3	N. Crookes run out	0
R. England c Madley b Robertson	42	B 2, l-b 8, w 2	12
M. Bossart b Robertson	0		
M. Smalley b Needham	2	1/41 2/54 3/128 (9 wkts, 40 overs)	148
J. Beckitt run out	0	4/128 5/133 6/134 7/139 8/147 9/148	

P. Wright did not bat.

Bowling: Howe 9–1–30–1; Jones 4–0–24–0; Painter 9–0–42–1; Robertson 9–2–19–2; Needham 9–1–21–3.

St Fagans

G. Lewis lbw b Crookes	15	R. Stevens not out	16
D. Mason c Weeks b Norris	43	L-b 6, w 2, n-b 1	9
*P. J. Needham b Wright	21		
D. Painter not out	39	1/27 2/54 (4 wkts, 37.4 overs)	149
D. Williams b Smalley	6	3/125 4/133	

D. Mason, B. Brooks, †P. Madley, S. Robertson and S. Howe did not bat.

Bowling: Crookes 9–0–36–1; Wright 9–1–20–1; Norris 5.4–0–30–1; Weeks 4–0–14–0; Croft 2–0–9–0; Smalley 3–0–14–1; England 5–0–17–0.

Umpires: P. C. Young and R. W. D. Giles.

VILLAGE CRICKET CHAMPIONSHIP WINNERS 1972-1982

Sponsored by John Haig Ltd

1972 TROON (Cornwall) beat Astwood Bank (Worcestershire) by seven wickets.
1973 TROON (Cornwall) beat Gowerton (Glamorgan) by 12 runs.
1974 BOMARSUND (Northumberland) beat Collingham (Nottinghamshire) by three wickets. (*Played at Edgbaston after being rained off at Lord's*)
1975 GOWERTON (Glamorgan) beat Isleham (Cambridgeshire) by six wickets.
1976 TROON (Cornwall) beat Sessay (Yorkshire) by 18 runs.
1977 COOKLEY (Worcestershire) beat Lindal Moor (Cumbria) by 28 runs.

Sponsored by *The Cricketer*

1978 LINTON PARK (Kent) beat Toft (Cheshire) by four wickets.

Sponsored by Samuel Whitbread and Co. Ltd

1979 EAST BIERLEY (Yorkshire) beat Ynysygerwyn (Glamorgan) by 92 runs.
1980 MARCHWIEL (Clwyd) beat Longparish (Hampshire) by 79 runs.
1981 ST FAGANS (Glamorgan) beat Broad Oak (Yorkshire) by 22 runs.
1982 ST FAGANS (Glamorgan) beat Collingham (Nottinghamshire) by six wickets.

September 4. NatWest Bank Trophy final. SURREY beat WARWICKSHIRE by nine wickets (See NatWest Bank Trophy section).

SCHWEPPES COUNTY CHAMPIONSHIP, 1982

The Championship in 1982 epitomised Mike Brearley's tenure of the Middlesex captaincy. Unarguably the strongest three-day side, Middlesex led throughout, resisting the challenges of various pretenders who threatened and then faded. They were worthy champions and the winners of £13,000.

Leicestershire improved from a mid-table placing in 1981 to take the £6,500 runners-up prize. Only a bad spell in June precluded an even stronger challenge from them. Third-placed Hampshire recovered from a dismal start, maintaining their advance of the previous season without ever quite challenging for top spot. They won £3,250. The fourth prize of £1,650 went to the 1981 champions, Nottinghamshire, whose early challenge died with a poor July. Fifth-placed Surrey's expected late surge never materialised, while for the third successive season Somerset (sixth) owed their final respectability to a late run after earlier disappointments.

Sussex mounted such a strong mid-season challenge that on July 10 they were only one bonus point behind Middlesex. They then lost their way, their batting especially wanting for consistency as they sank to mid-table. Northamptonshire also achieved a mid-way position, a satisfactory outcome after a disastrous start had seen them without a victory until mid-July; their late improvement owed much to their positive batting. Of the other mid-table sides, Yorkshire's hopes of a high placing when they rallied under Ray Illingworth's captaincy did not materialise, their improvement in July being countered by a late decline. Derbyshire also faded steadily after reaching third place in mid-season. Kent, undergoing a transitionary period, did well early

SCHWEPPES CHAMPIONSHIP TABLE

					Bonus points		
*Win = 16 points**	*Played*	*Won*	*Lost*	*Drawn*	*Batting*	*Bowling*	*Points*
1 –Middlesex (4)	22	12	2	8	59	74	325
2 –Leicestershire (8)	22	10	4	8	57	69	286
3 –Hampshire (7)	22	8	6	8	48	74	250
4 –Nottinghamshire (1)	21	7	7	7	44	65	221
5 –Surrey (6)	22	6	6	10	56	62	214
6 –Somerset (3)	22	6	6	10	51	66	213
7 –Essex (5)	22	5	5	12	57	75	212
8 –Sussex (2)	22	6	7	9	43	68	207
9 –Northamptonshire (15)	22	5	3	14	61	54	195
10 –Yorkshire (10)	21	5	1	15	48	51	179
11 –Derbyshire (12)	22	4	3	15	45	64	173
12 –Lancashire (16)	22	4	3	15	48	55	167
13 –Kent (9)	22	3	4	15	55	63	166
14 –Worcestershire (11)	22	3	5	14	43	54	141
15 –Gloucestershire (13)	22	2	9	11	46	55	133
16 –Glamorgan (14)	22	1	8	13	43	60	119
17 –Warwickshire (17)	22	0	8	14	58	53	111

1981 positions in brackets.

**Worcestershire total includes 12 points for a win in a match reduced to one innings.*

The following match was abandoned and is not included in the above table: June 26, 28, 29 – Yorkshire v Nottinghamshire at Harrogate.

on, and although, subsequently, their young players found the going more difficult, they stayed comfortably clear of the bottom places.

For the whole of the last month the last four positions were occupied by Worcestershire, Gloucestershire, Glamorgan and Warwickshire. None of them ever looked likely to move forward. For the bottom pair, the season was one of almost unrelieved woe, though Glamorgan did manage a late victory which enabled them to push Warwickshire into bottom place for the second successive season.

REGULATIONS FOR SCHWEPPES CHAMPIONSHIP

(As applied in 1982)

1. Prize-money

First (Middlesex)	£13,000
Second (Leicestershire)	£6,500
Third (Hampshire)	£3,250
Fourth (Nottinghamshire)	£1,650
Winner of each match	£150
Each bonus point	£5

2. Scoring of Points

(*a*) For a win. 16 points, plus any points scored in the first innings.

(*b*) In a tie, each side to score eight points, plus any points scored in the first innings.

(*c*) If the scores are equal in a drawn match, the side batting in the fourth innings to score eight points, plus any points scored in the first innings.

(*d*) **First Innings Points** (awarded only for performances **in the first 100 overs** of each first innings and retained whatever the result of the match).

(i) A maximum of four batting points to be available as under:
150 to 199 runs – 1 point; 200 to 249 runs – 2 points; 250 to 299 runs – 3 points; 300 runs or over – 4 points.

(ii) A maximum of four bowling points to be available as under:
3 to 4 wickets taken – 1 point; 5 to 6 wickets taken – 2 points; 7 to 8 wickets taken – 3 points; 9 to 10 wickets taken – 4 points.

(*e*) If play starts when less than eight hours playing time remains and a one innings match is played, no first innings points shall be scored. The side winning on the one innings to score 12 points.

(*f*) The side which has the highest aggregate of points gained at the end of the season shall be the Champion County. Should any sides in the Schweppes Championship table be equal on points the side with most wins will have priority.

3. Hours of Play

1st and 2nd days	11.00 a.m. to 6.30 p.m.
3rd day	11.00 a.m. to 6.00 p.m.

Play may cease on the last day up to 30 minutes earlier than the scheduled time for cessation of play by mutual agreement of the captains.

Intervals

Lunch: 1.15 p.m. to 1.55 p.m. (1st and 2nd days)
1.00 p.m. to 1.40 p.m. (3rd day)

Tea: 4.10 p.m. to 4.30 p.m. (1st and 2nd days)
3.40 p.m. to 4.00 p.m. (3rd day)

4. Declarations

Law 14 will apply, but, in addition, a captain may also forfeit his first innings, subject to the provisions set out in Law 14.2. If, owing to weather conditions, the match has not started when less than eight hours playing time remains, the first innings of each side shall automatically be forfeited and a one-innings match played.

5. Over-rate Fines

In 1982, the minimum over-rate to be achieved by counties, before a financial penalty was imposed, was 19.00 overs per hour. In assessing any fines, of which counties paid half and players half, the season was divided into two parts (11 matches) and fines graded on the following basis per half season:
Under 19.00 overs per hour – £1,000
Under 18.50 overs per hour – £1,500
Under 18.00 overs per hour – £2,000
Under 17.50 overs per hour – £2,500

(Additional £500 penalty for each 0.5 o.p.h. below these rates.)

When calculating the over-rate, an allowance of two minutes was made for each wicket taken. In the event of a player from either side being seriously injured and having to leave the field, any such time, additional to the two minutes, was also a deductable allowance. The contribution to be made by each player to any fine was to be decided by the county concerned.

OVER-RATE AND RUN-RATE IN SCHWEPPES CHAMPIONSHIP, 1982

	Over-rate per hour			*Run-rate per*
	1st half	*2nd half*	*Total*	*100 balls*
Derbyshire (11)	†*18.67*	19.49	19.11 (12)	49.10 (16)
Essex (7)	19.18	19.31	19.25 (6)	55.99 (2)
Glamorgan (16)	19.33	19.09	19.21 (7=)	45.10 (17)
Gloucestershire (15)	19.10	19.18	19.14 (10)	49.40 (15)
Hampshire (3)	19.08	†*18.86*	18.73 (14)	50.31 (11)
Kent (13)	**18.06*	**18.02*	18.04 (17)	50.90 (8)
Lancashire (12)	19.34	20.54	20.02 (1=)	50.83 (9)
Leicestershire (2)	19.49	20.54	20.02 (1=)	49.53 (14)
Middlesex (1)	19.42	19.18	19.30 (3)	53.37 (5)
Northamptonshire (9)	†*18.95*	19.41	19.21 (7=)	53.73 (4)
Nottinghamshire (4)	19.06	19.46	19.29 (4=)	51.50 (7)
Somerset (6)	19.05	19.32	19.17 (9)	50.71 (10)
Surrey (5)	**18.31*	†*18.69*	18.52 (16)	58.58 (1)
Sussex (8)	†*18.51*	†*18.78*	18.65 (15)	49.83 (13)
Warwickshire (17)	19.42	19.17	19.29 (4=)	52.63 (6)
Worcestershire (14)	19.07	19.18	19.13 (11)	53.85 (3)
Yorkshire (10)	†*18.75*	19.10	18.94 (13)	50.03 (12)
1982 average rate			19.06	51.38
1981 average rate			18.62	50.86
1980 average rate			18.95	50.47
1979 average rate			19.36	48.37
1978 average rate			19.45	47.53

**£1,500 fine.* *†£1,000 fine.*

1982 Championship positions are shown in parentheses after name of county.

SCHWEPPES CHAMPIONSHIP STATISTICS FOR 1982

County	For Runs	For Wickets	For Average	Against Runs	Against Wickets	Against Average
Derbyshire	9,148	274	33.38	9,644	284	33.95
Essex	9,075	275	33.00	8,810	323	27.27
Glamorgan	8,961	315	28.44	10,009	272	36.79
Gloucestershire	9,131	321	28.44	8,914	249	35.79
Hampshire	8,026	305	26.31	8,194	353	23.21
Kent	8,973	296	30.31	8,946	273	32.76
Lancashire	8,940	256	34.92	8,517	266	32.01
Leicestershire	9,063	310	29.23	8,866	336	26.38
Middlesex	8,490	238	35.67	8,276	354	23.37
Northamptonshire	10,094	276	36.57	9,227	276	33.43
Nottinghamshire	8,134	294	27.66	7,798	314	24.83
Somerset	8,593	308	27.89	8,097	274	29.55
Surrey	9,333	290	32.18	9,392	300	31.30
Sussex	8,250	299	27.59	8,089	310	26.09
Warwickshire	9,559	307	31.13	9,861	222	44.41
Worcestershire	8,726	313	27.87	9,577	260	36.83
Yorkshire	8,353	241	34.65	8,632	252	34.25
	150,849	4,918	30.67	150,849	4,918	30.67

COUNTY CHAMPIONSHIP – MATCH RESULTS 1864-1982

County	Years of Play	Played	Won	Lost	Tied	Drawn
Derbyshire	1871-87; 1895-1982	1,926	476	723	—	727
Essex	1895-1982	1,890	512	567	5	806
Glamorgan	1921-1982	1,424	322	502	—	600
Gloucestershire	1870-1982	2,167	653	810	1	703
Hampshire	1864-85; 1895-1982	1,999	520	710	4	765
Kent	1864-1982	2,286	853	706	2	725
Lancashire	1865-1982	2,365	910	473	3	979
Leicestershire	1895-1982	1,856	393	725	1	737
Middlesex	1864-1982	2,068	783	532	5	748
Northamptonshire	1905-1982	1,623	384	595	2	642
Nottinghamshire	1864-1982	2,197	670	584	—	943
Somerset	1882-85; 1891–1982	1,897	458	804	3	632
Surrey	1864-1982	2,443	994	534	4	911
Sussex	1864-1982	2,339	671	814	4	850
Warwickshire	1895-1982	1,870	493	554	1	822
Worcestershire	1899-1982	1,811	440	665	1	705
Yorkshire	1864-1982	2,468	1,162	396	2	908
Cambridgeshire	1864-69; 1871	19	8	8	—	3
		34,648	10,702	10,702	38	13,206

DERBYSHIRE

President: The Duke of Devonshire
Chairman: D. C. Robinson
Chairman, Cricket Committee: C. S. Elliott
Secretary/Chief Executive: R. Pearman
County Ground, Nottingham Road, Derby
DE2 6DA (Telephone: 0332-683211)
Captain: B. Wood
Coach: P. E. Russell

The spectacular batting of Peter Kirsten and John Wright dominated a season which began with considerable optimism and ended both disappointingly and unhappily. During May, the new pavilion at Derby was opened by the Duke of Devonshire, there was a comfortable Championship victory over Somerset, and Derbyshire were going well in the one-day competitions. By September, there was considerable unrest within the club. Barry Wood's somewhat inflexible style of man-management caused increasing disquiet and he was openly critical of the committee who, while confirming him as captain, offered him a playing contract for only one year.

Wood found that full-time captaincy was a different matter from taking over for half a season, as had happened in 1981 when he led Derbyshire to victory in the NatWest Bank Trophy. He was often in conflict with his players and performances inevitably suffered. Derbyshire's best hopes of success had seemed to lie in the one-day competitions, and in the first half of the season they did achieve some notable victories in the Benson and Hedges Cup and the John Player League. But defeat came in the quarter-finals of the Benson and Hedges, they made a swift exit from the NatWest Bank Trophy, and after July 18, when they beat Middlesex in a Sunday match at Lord's, Derbyshire did not register a victory in any competition. Wood, an increasingly isolated figure but still a formidable competitor, had failed to make the best use of his resources and there was some surprise at the committee's unanimity in reappointing him as captain.

The summer will be remembered more happily for the marvellous displays of Wright and Kirsten, who engaged in friendly rivalry to overtake the county record of six centuries in a season, set by Leslie Townsend in 1933 and equalled by Kirsten in 1980. Kirsten finished with eight Championship hundreds and Wright with seven; but it was no mere accumulation of runs, for three of the county's four Schweppes Championship victories – against Leicestershire at Derby and Coalville and Northamptonshire at Derby – came from their ability to make big scores in pursuit of a target. Derbyshire's 350 for three which beat Northamptonshire was the highest fourth innings score in their history. Supporters were disappointed when Kirsten was given permission to take 1983 off to explore business opportunities in South Africa, strenuous attempts being made to persuade him to change his mind.

There were other positive advances. Geoff Miller, who decided to stay with Derbyshire after having obtained his release in 1981, regained his England place, and the batting was strengthened by the development of Kim Barnett and Iain Anderson. Both scored maiden hundreds. Barnett was awarded his county cap, but it was sad to see his leg-spin so neglected. John Hampshire was also capped and, while not making quite the impact expected of him, proved a wise partner for the overseas batsmen and a comfortingly solid figure at No. 4.

David Steele's return to Northamptonshire gave Dallas Moir, the 6ft 8in left-arm spinner born in Malta of Scottish parents, an opportunity which he seized eagerly. Moir's height gave him the ability to achieve steep bounce on responsive pitches and, although he encountered few of those, his craft developed visibly as he learnt and gained in confidence. He was the county's leading wicket-taker in his first full season. Miller, who achieved the best figures of his career with eight for 70 against Leicestershire at Coalville, might with advantage have bowled more overs in partnership with his fellow-spinner. Strange, too, was the treatment of Peter Hacker, who, after being registered from Nottinghamshire, took 23 wickets in the first six Championship games. He was then injured and, after being unable to regain a place, released at the end of the season.

Especially in view of Paul Newman's disappointing form, more use might have been made of Hacker who, although erratic, achieved a better striking-rate than anybody. Although the medium-paced bowlers, Colin Tunnicliffe and Steve Oldham, had their days, greater penetration was required. Bob Taylor kept wicket as immaculately as ever and, when he was playing for England, Bernard Maher again proved an able and promising deputy. Taylor ended the season one short of John Murray's world record of 1,527 dismissals and it is remarkable to consider that three Derbyshire wicket-keepers span 62 years, Harry Elliott, George Dawkes and now Taylor. What the county need to rediscover is their traditional bowling strength if they are to become regular challengers for honours. – J.G.M.

DERBYSHIRE 1982

[*Bill Smith*

Back row: S. Oldham, J. H. Hampshire, P. G. Newman, D. G. Moir, K. J. Barnett, I. S. Anderson, P. J. Hacker. *Front row:* R. W. Taylor, P. N. Kirsten, B. Wood (*captain*), J. G. Wright, C. J. Tunnicliffe.

DERBYSHIRE RESULTS

All first-class matches – Played 23: Won 4, Lost 4, Drawn 15.

County Championship matches – Played 22: Won 4, Lost 3, Drawn 15.

Bonus points – Batting 45, Bowling 64.

Competition placings – Schweppes County Championship, 11th; NatWest Bank Trophy, 2nd round; Benson and Hedges Cup, q-f; John Player League, 12th eq.

COUNTY CHAMPIONSHIP AVERAGES

BATTING

	Birthplace	*M*	*I*	*NO*	*R*	*HI*	*Avge*
P. N. Kirsten c	*Pietermaritzburg, SA*	21	37	7	1,941	164*	64.70
J. G. Wright c	*Darfield, NZ*	21	39	6	1,830	190	55.45
J. H. Hampshire c	*Thurnscoe*	21	34	6	1,179	101*	42.10
G. Miller c	*Chesterfield*	12	20	5	502	61	33.46
I. S. Anderson	*Derby*	16	24	4	651	103*	32.55
K. J. Barnett c	*Stoke-on-Trent*	17	23	5	578	120	32.11
B. Wood c	*Ossett*	20	36	4	799	124*	24.96
A. Hill c	*Buxworth*	7	14	3	219	54	19.90
S. Oldham c	*Sheffield*	20	17	9	148	35*	18.50
C. J. Tunnicliffe c	*Derby*	16	19	2	273	40	16.05
P. G. Newman	*Leicester*	17	21	4	197	39*	11.58
P. J. Hacker	*Nottingham*	8	4	2	22	10*	11.00
B. J. M. Maher	*Hillingdon*	10	11	5	49	15*	8.16
R. W. Taylor c	*Stoke-on-Trent*	12	17	2	121	45	8.06
D. G. Moir	*Mtarfa, Malta*	22	21	1	136	25	6.80

Also batted: R. J. Finney (*Darley Dale*) (1 match) 39; A. Watts (*Chapeltown*) (1 match) 0.

**Signifies not out.* c *Denotes county cap.*

BOWLING

	O	*M*	*R*	*W*	*Avge*	*BB*
D. G. Moir	789.5	226	1,990	75	26.53	6-63
P. J. Hacker	174.1	25	677	25	27.08	5-51
G. Miller	382.2	120	832	29	28.68	8-70
S. Oldham	491.5	98	1,503	46	32.67	7-78
C. J. Tunnicliffe	383.1	92	1,213	37	32.78	5-73
P. G. Newman	410.3	63	1,494	37	40.37	4-59
B. Wood	225.2	53	659	10	65.90	2-0

Also bowled: I. S. Anderson 58.4–22–157–5; K. J. Barnett 42.3–8–139–0; R. J. Finney 14–5–40–1; J. H. Hampshire 4–1–26–0; A. Hill 1–0–4–0; P. N. Kirsten 121–28–348–9; A. Watts 9–1–31–0; J. G. Wright 3–0–29–0.

HUNDREDS

The following twenty three-figure innings were played for Derbyshire in County Championship matches – P. N. Kirsten (8) 143 v Gloucestershire (Gloucester), 121* v Leicestershire (Derby), 102 v Leicestershire (Coalville), 113 v Essex (Southend), 164* and 123* v Surrey (Derby), 105* v Sussex (Chesterfield), 140* v Yorkshire (Scarborough); J. G. Wright (7) 141* v Nottinghamshire (Chesterfield), 103* v Middlesex (Lord's), 106 v Essex (Chesterfield), 190 v Yorkshire (Derby), 185* v Northamptonshire (Derby), 157 v Northamptonshire (Northampton), 107 v Hampshire (Derby); K. J. Barnett (2) 120 v Warwickshire (Birmingham), 100* v Glamorgan (Derby); I. S. Anderson (1) 103* v Hampshire (Derby); J. H. Hampshire (1) 101* v Lancashire (Derby); B. Wood (1) 124* v Nottinghamshire (Nottingham).

At Worcester, May 5, 6, 7. DERBYSHIRE drew with WORCESTERSHIRE.

DERBYSHIRE v SOMERSET

At Derby, May 12, 13, 14. Derbyshire won by nine wickets. Derbyshire 23 pts, Somerset 5 pts. Oldham produced the best figures of his career (six for 63) in Somerset's first innings, and his return would have been more impressive but for an innings of carefree brilliance by Botham, who scored 63 (58 of them in boundaries) in 51 minutes. For Derbyshire, Miller batted almost as well and Wood, supported by Finney on his first-class début, gave them a lead of 72 which was exploited by spinners Miller and Moir. Wright and Kirsten made short work of the victory target. The match inaugurated the new Derby pavilion, and was played on the first pitch produced by groundsman Barry Marsh, who succeeded Walter Goodyear.

Somerset

*B. C. Rose c and b Oldham	2	– lbw b Hacker	27
J. W. Lloyds b Oldham	3	– c Kirsten b Hacker	8
P. A. Slocombe c Wright b Hacker	0	– b Miller	41
P. M. Roebuck c Hampshire b Miller	37	– c Miller b Moir	17
P. W. Denning c Wood b Finney	24	– c Miller b Kirsten	13
I. T. Botham c Miller b Oldham	63	– b Miller	26
V. J. Marks c Miller b Oldham	28	– (8) b Moir	6
†D. J. S. Taylor c Wood b Oldham	10	– (9) c Hampshire b Oldham	13
C. H. Dredge c Kirsten b Miller	35	– (7) c Miller b Moir	4
R. J. McCool c Miller b Oldham	7	– c Finney b Oldham	12
H. R. Moseley not out	4	– not out	3
B 1, l-b 4, w 1	6	B 1, l-b 2, n-b 4	7
1/2 2/5 3/23 4/62 5/76 6/143 7/165 8/173 9/205	219	1/30 2/37 3/64 4/97 5/135 6/143 7/147 8/160 9/164	177

Bonus points – Somerset 2, Derbyshire 4.

Bowling: *First Innings*—Oldham 19–3–63–6; Hacker 16–3–57–1; Finney 13–5–37–1; Miller 17–5–38–2; Moir 3–0–18–0. *Second Innings*—Oldham 12.4–2–34–2; Finney 1–0–3–0; Hacker 7–2–23–2; Miller 19–8–32–2; Moir 25–6–60–3; Kirsten 6–1–18–1.

Derbyshire

A. Hill lbw b Moseley	22	– c Botham b Marks 13
J. G. Wright c Marks b Moseley	16	– not out 59
P. N. Kirsten c Lloyds b Marks	11	– not out 31
J. H. Hampshire c and b Moseley	45	
G. Miller c Lloyds b Marks	61	
*B. Wood lbw b Dredge	62	
R. J. Finney c and b Marks	39	
†R. W. Taylor c Taylor b Dredge	10	
D. G. Moir c McCool b Botham	5	
S. Oldham not out	9	
P. J.Hacker c Slocombe b Moseley	2	
B 1, l-b 4, n-b 4	9	L-b 2, n-b 3 5
1/40 2/43 3/61 4/142 5/179 6/251 7/272 8/273 9/288	291	1/40 (1 wkt) 108

Bonus points – Derbyshire 3, Somerset 3 (Score at 100 overs: 288-8).

Bowling: *First Innings*—Botham 17–3–55–1; Moseley 15.3–2–40–4; Marks 41–14–103–3; Dredge 19–8–39–2; McCool 9–0–45–0. *Second Innings*—Botham 6–1–15–0; Moseley 1–0–7–0; Marks 13–1–44–1; Lloyds 5–0–19–0; McCool 8–2–18–0.

Umpires: K. Ibadulla and B. J. Meyer.

At Manchester, May 19, 20, 21. DERBYSHIRE drew with LANCASHIRE.

DERBYSHIRE v NOTTINGHAMSHIRE

At Chesterfield, May 29, 31, June 1. Drawn. Derbyshire 6 pts, Nottinghamshire 7 pts. Nottinghamshire were on top throughout without being able to force victory on a good pitch. Rice and Birch added 144 in 32 overs and, after Moir had taken three wickets in three overs, the innings was sustained by Saxelby, who scored his maiden 50, and Hemmings. Hadlee's aggressive bowling had Derbyshire in trouble, but his fellow-New Zealander, Wright, carried his bat. His 141, which included eighteen 4s, was an example of concentration and technique. Randall and French enabled Nottinghamshire to set a target of 272 in 114 minutes plus twenty overs but Derbyshire never approached this after losing three wickets quickly. Miller and Taylor batted defiantly and Wood, despite a wrist strain, saw out the final overs.

Nottinghamshire

R. T. Robinson lbw b Hacker	12	– c Wright b Newman 6
M. A. Fell c Hill b Wood	11	– c Wright b Newman 4
D. W. Randall c Miller b Newman	18	– c Moir b Hacker 67
*C. E. B. Rice b Oldham	87	– b Oldham 30
J. D. Birch c Taylor b Moir	60	– b Newman 6
R. J. Hadlee c Taylor b Moir	0	– c Taylor b Oldham 3
†B. N. French c Hampshire b Moir	3	– c Hill b Hacker 55
E. E. Hemmings c Oldham b Moir	43	– not out 18
K. Saxelby not out	59	– not out 4
K. E. Cooper c Newman b Miller	4	
M. Hendrick not out	4	
B 2, l-b 9, w 1, n-b 7	19	L-b 8, w 2, n-b 7 17
1/23 2/39 3/43 4/187 5/191 6/198 7/202 8/304 9/310 (9 wkts dec.)	320	1/6 2/13 3/77 4/94 5/100 6/139 7/197 (7 wkts dec.) 210

Bonus points – Nottinghamshire 4, Derbyshire 4.

Bowling: *First Innings*—Oldham 20–6–45–1; Newman 13–5–50–1; Hacker 14–1–68–1; Wood 14–5–45–1; Miller 16–5–31–1; Moir 23–4–62–4. *Second Innings*—Oldham 24–9–45–2; Newman 18–0–78–3; Moir 14–4–30–0; Miller 4–1–9–0; Hacker 10–0–31–2.

Derbyshire

*B. Wood c French b Hendrick	19	– (8) not out	2
J. G. Wright not out	141	– (1) b Hendrick	5
P. N Kirsten lbw b Hadlee	0	– lbw b Hadlee	20
J. H. Hampshire c Randall b Hendrick	12	– b Hemmings	0
G. Miller c Hendrick b Hadlee	44	– c and b Hemmings	53
A. Hill b Hadlee	0	– (2) c Fell b Hemmings	5
†R. W. Taylor b Hemmings	1	– (6) c Hadlee b Hemmings	25
P. G. Newman c Fell b Hemmings	5	– (7) not out	2
D. G. Moir c Robinson b Hemmings	25		
S. Oldham c Cooper b Hadlee	3		
P. J. Hacker c and b Hadlee	0		
B 1, l-b 4, w 1, n-b 3	9	B 8, l-b 1, n-b 2	11
1/27 2/31 3/59 4/134 5/134 6/139 7/145 8/242 9/259	259	1/6 2/16 3/18 4/43 5/97 6/116	(6 wkts) 123

Bonus points – Derbyshire 2, Nottinghamshire 3 (Score at 100 overs: 249-8).

Bowling: *First Innings*—Hadlee 26.5–8–64–5; Hendrick 21–8–35–2; Hemmings 35–10–66–3; Cooper 12–0–45–0; Saxelby 6–0–36–0; Fell 1–0–4–0. *Second Innings*—Hadlee 11–4–18–1; Hendrick 10–5–12–1; Hemmings 29–5–48–4; Cooper 2–1–1–0; Fell 9–3–33–0.

Umpires: D. G. L. Evans and A. G. T. Whitehead.

At Lord's, June 2, 3, 4. DERBYSHIRE drew with MIDDLESEX.

At Gloucester, June 5, 7, 8. DERBYSHIRE drew with GLOUCESTERSHIRE.

DERBYSHIRE v ESSEX

At Chesterfield, June 9, 10, 11. Drawn. Derbyshire 4 pts, Essex 8 pts. Rain on the first morning cost 140 minutes and Derbyshire, put in, laboured in conditions which assisted the seam bowlers. When Hampshire, who had held the innings together, was run out off the last ball of the 100 overs, Wood declared. Essex were more enterprising, McEwan scoring his first century of the season. He batted for five hours, four minutes, hitting eighteen 4s, and caused the temporary withdrawal of umpire Bird on the second afternoon, struck on the right calf by a sweep. When Derbyshire were left to save the game, Wright hit his fourth hundred in twelve days (three in the Championship and one in the John Player League) before Hampshire steered them to safety.

Derbyshire

*B. Wood c D. E. East b Lever	0		
J. G. Wright c Phillip b Foster	34	– (1) c Fletcher b Gooch	106
P. N. Kirsten b Foster	22	– lbw b Foster	4
J. H. Hampshire run out	64	– not out	81
A. Hill lbw b Turner	28	– (2) c D. E. East b Lever	24
D. G. Moir lbw b Turner	0		
K. J. Barnett c D. E. East b Foster	9	– (5) c D. E. East b Gooch	0
†B. J. M. Maher b Lever	0	– (6) not out	11
P. G. Newman lbw b Lever	18		
S. Oldham not out	0		
B 4, l-b 9, w 2, n-b 9	24	L-b 4, n-b 11	15
1/0 2/57 3/76 4/136 5/136 6/153 7/158 8/194 9/199	(9 wkts dec.) 199	1/57 2/68 3/185 4/192	(4 wkts) 241

P. J. Hacker did not bat.

Bonus points – Derbyshire 1, Essex 4.

Bowling: *First Innings*—Lever 30–9–67–3; Phillip 12–2–26–0; Foster 24–9–32–3; Turner 23–7–37–2; Gooch 7–4–11–0; Acfield 4–3–2–0. *Second Innings*—Lever 14–2–45–1; Phillip 7–0–29–0; Foster 8–0–45–1; Gooch 20–6–55–2; Acfield 17–4–28–0; Turner 5–2–14–0; Lilley 3–0–10–0.

Essex

G. A. Gooch c Wright b Newman	7	†D. E. East b Newman	17
B. R. Hardie b Hacker	36	N. A. Foster not out	36
*K. W. R. Fletcher c Wood b Hacker	16		
K. S. McEwan not out	150	B 1, l-b 9, w 2, n-b 7	19
A. W. Lilley c Maher b Moir	26		—
N. Phillip b Moir	23	1/13 2/59 3/68 4/113 (7 wkts dec.)	386
S. Turner b Moir	56	5/173 6/261 7/304	

J. K. Lever and D. L. Acfield did not bat.

Bonus points – Essex 4, Derbyshire 3.

Bowling: Oldham 10–1–34–0; Newman 30–2–116–2; Hacker 15–2–74–2; Moir 23–4–93–3; Wood 18–5–50–0; Kirsten 1–1–0–0.

Umpires H. D. Bird and K. E. Palmer.

At Canterbury, June 19, 21, 22. DERBYSHIRE drew with KENT.

DERBYSHIRE v LEICESTERSHIRE

At Derby, June 26, 28, 29. Derbyshire won by eight wickets. Derbyshire 20 pts. A week of rain had left the pitch damp, and after a delayed start this was exploited by Moir, who took five wickets for the first time, and Tunnicliffe. Although there was less than an hour of play on the second day, two declarations set up a finish. Derbyshire put on 39 in seventeen minutes before closing their first innings, and then Wood encouraged Leicestershire by using spinners and occasional bowlers. Indeed, in three of the four innings, left-arm spinners (Cook twice and Moir) opened the bowling. Tolchard set Derbyshire 229 and Leicestershire bowled 32 overs in the 94 minutes before the final hour. Kirsten, who hit two 6s and ten 4s in 140 minutes, made the target appear easy, and with Hampshire joining him in an unbroken stand of 179, Derbyshire won with 22 balls to spare.

Leicestershire

J. C. Balderstone c Oldham b Tunnicliffe	8	– c Hampshire b Moir	9
R. A. Cobb c Maher b Moir	6	– c Wood b Tunnicliffe	8
N. E. Briers c Wood b Moir	1	– c Moir b Anderson	36
B. F. Davison c Kirsten b Moir	61	– b Moir	45
*R. W. Tolchard b Tunnicliffe	22	– c Wright b Anderson	53
J. F. Steele c Wright b Tunnicliffe	3	– not out	12
†M. A. Garnham c and b Moir	0		
G. J. Parsons c Kirsten b Anderson	9		
N. G. B. Cook not out	7	– (7) not out	2
J. P. Agnew lbw b Moir	0		
L. B. Taylor b Tunnicliffe	0		
B 2, l-b 1, n-b 6	9	B 4, l-b 3, w 1, n-b 2	10
	—		—
1/15 2/16 3/25 4/71	126	1/9 2/47 3/72 (5 wkts dec.)	175
5/82 6/93 7/115 8/121 9/125		4/157 5/164	

Bonus points – Derbyshire 4.

Bowling: *First Innings*—Oldham 4–1–9–0; Tunnicliffe 21.5–7–53–4; Moir 25–8–40–5; Anderson 7–0–15–1. *Second Innings*—Tunnicliffe 4–0–18–1; Moir 15–6–15–2; Barnett 11–2–34–0; Anderson 5.4–0–43–2; Hampshire 4–1–26–0; Wright 3–0–29–0.

Derbyshire

*B. Wood not out	39	– b Cook	12
D. G. Moir b Cook	7		
J. G. Wright not out	18	– (2) c Garnham b Steele	25
P. N. Kirsten (did not bat)		– (3) not out	121
J. H. Hampshire (did not bat)		– (4) not out	62
B 3, l-b 3, n-b 3	9	L-b 8, n-b 1	9
1/34 (1 wkt dec.)	73	1/34 2/50 (2 wkts)	229

K. J. Barnett, I. S. Anderson, †B. J. M. Maher, C. J. Tunnicliffe, P. G. Newman and S. Oldham did not bat.

Bowling: *First Innings*—Taylor 11–5–21–0; Cook 8.3–5–7–1; Parsons 4–0–7–0; Steele 3–1–4–0; Agnew 2–0–25–0. *Second Innings*—Taylor 3–0–25–0; Cook 21–2–78–1; Steele 13–0–46–1; Balderstone 3–0–19–0; Parsons 6–0–33–0; Agnew 2.2–0–19–0.

Umpires: P. J. Eele and N. T. Plews.

DERBYSHIRE v YORKSHIRE

At Derby, July 3, 5, 6. Drawn. Derbyshire 6 pts, Yorkshire 3 pts. Love, with his first century of the season, and Lumb pulled Yorkshire's first innings round after Moir had taken three wickets cheaply. The partnership of 242 between Wright and Anderson was the highest for any Derbyshire wicket against Yorkshire, and Wright, on his 28th birthday, flawlessly reached a new career best with 190, including three 6s and twenty 4s. Kirsten, captain in place of Wood, committed Derbyshire to bowling out Yorkshire again by batting into the third day, and they appeared to have a chance of their first Championship victory over Yorkshire for 25 years when Oldham dismissed Boycott and Love with successive balls. However, Athey, who reached 50 out of 60 and 100 out of 124, dominated the rest of the day in passing his previous best score.

Yorkshire

G. Boycott st Taylor b Moir	20	– c Wright b Oldham	7
R. G. Lumb c and b Moir	74	– lbw b Newman	0
C. W. J. Athey c Taylor b Moir	0	– c Wright b Miller	134
S. N. Hartley c Kirsten b Moir	2	– (5) not out	52
J. D. Love c Hampshire b Tunnicliffe	110	– (4) c Taylor b Oldham	0
†D. L. Bairstow b Newman	21	– not out	1
G. B. Stevenson b Newman	37		
P. Carrick not out	3		
C. M. Old b Newman	15		
L-b 2, w 1, n-b 6	9	B 2, l-b 1, n-b 3	6
1/40 2/40 3/52 4/173 5/228 6/259 7/275 8/291 (8 wkts dec.)	291	1/1 2/41 3/41 4/174 (4 wkts)	200

*R. Illingworth and P. W. Jarvis did not bat.

Bonus points – Yorkshire 3, Derbyshire 2 (Score at 100 overs: 258-5).

Bowling: *First Innings*—Newman 13.2–4–39–3; Tunnicliffe 18–8–52–1; Oldham 21–6–54–0; Moir 38–14–83–4; Miller 14–2–54–0. *Second Innings*—Newman 12–4–37–1; Tunnicliffe 2–0–4–0; Moir 30–9–76–0; Miller 21–11–45–1; Oldham 12–5–21–2; Kirsten 8–3–9–0; Barnett 2–0–2–0.

Derbyshire

J. G. Wright c Old b Jarvis	190	D. G. Moir b Old	1
I. S. Anderson c Bairstow b Boycott	82	S. Oldham not out	1
*P. N. Kirsten lbw b Old	45	J. H. Hampshire absent hurt	
K. J. Barnett c and b Stevenson	74	B 2, l-b 7, w 1, n-b 1	11
G. Miller lbw b Stevenson	0		
†R. W. Taylor b Jarvis	7	1/242 2/308 3/335	473
C. J. Tunnicliffe c Athey b Stevenson	32	4/336 5/350 6/405	
P. G. Newman lbw b Stevenson	30	7/454 8/465 9/473	

Bonus points – Derbyshire 4 (Score at 100 overs: 308-1).

Bowling: Old 31–7–70–2; Jarvis 25–4–100–2; Carrick 24–5–64–0; Illingworth 22–6–68–0; Stevenson 24–3–114–4; Athey 5–0–27–0; Boycott 7–1–19–1.

Umpires: D. Archer and B. J. Meyer.

DERBYSHIRE v NORTHAMPTONSHIRE

At Derby, July 7, 8, 9. Derbyshire won by seven wickets. Derbyshire 21 pts, Northamptonshire 8 pts. Willey began explosively after Northamptonshire had been put in, reaching 50 in only 36 minutes and going on to his first Championship hundred since 1979. Boyd-Moss also batted well, whereas Derbyshire were in trouble on the second day, especially against Mallender. Despite a lead of 167 on a pitch showing signs of wear, Sharp did not enforce the follow-on and, after Moir had taken five for 53, he set Derbyshire to score 347 in 305 minutes. Wright was again outstanding, hitting 33 4s in his unbeaten 185 and becoming the second batsman (after Gatting) to reach 1,000 runs for the season. His stand of 125 with Kirsten gave Derbyshire the initiative and they won with seventeen balls to spare for the loss of only three wickets. It was the highest fourth-innings total in their history, passing the 344 against Hampshire at Southampton in 1911.

Northamptonshire

R. M. Carter c and b Tunnicliffe	35	– c Hampshire b Moir	7
W. Larkins lbw b Newman	5	– c Barnett b Moir	36
P. Willey c Barnett b Tunnicliffe	145	– b Moir	27
R. G. Williams c Anderson b Moir	19	– c Anderson b Kirsten	6
D. J. Capel c Moir b Kirsten	17	– not out	35
R. J. Boyd-Moss b Moir	88	– c Kirsten b Moir	3
D. S. Steele lbw b Tunnicliffe	23	– c Wood b Moir	16
*†G. Sharp c Newman b Tunnicliffe	9	– not out	44
N. A. Mallender not out	2		
T. M. Lamb not out	5		
B 1, l-b 5, n-b 16	22	L-b 1, w 1, n-b 3	5
1/12 2/135 3/171 4/211 5/249 6/324 7/354 8/362	(8 wkts dec.) 370	1/27 2/57 3/70 4/92 5/96 6/124	(6 wkts dec.) 179

B. J. Griffiths did not bat.

Bonus points – Northamptonshire 4, Derbyshire 3.

Bowling: *First Innings*—Tunnicliffe 22-5-72-4; Newman 20–2–79–1; Oldham 13–0–60–0; Wood 13–2–46–0; Moir 26–5–72–2; Kirsten 6–0–19–1. *Second Innings*—Tunnicliffe 3–0–6–0; Newman 4–1–16–0; Oldham 4–0–11–0; Moir 24–8–53–5; Kirsten 14–0–43–1; Barnett 6–0–27–0; Wood 1–0–18–0.

Derbyshire

*B. Wood b Capel	33	– c Larkins b Steele	28
D. G. Moir c Carter b Mallender	10		
J. G. Wright lbw b Steele	38	– (2) not out	185
P. N. Kirsten c Lamb b Griffiths	10	– (3) b Steele	68
J. H. Hampshire c Williams b Griffiths	0	– (4) lbw b Griffiths	17
K. J. Barnett c Steele b Mallender	22	– (5) not out	42
I. S. Anderson c Sharp b Mallender	27		
C. J. Tunnicliffe c Griffiths b Mallender	38		
P. G. Newman lbw b Williams	1		
†B. J. M. Maher not out	1		
S. Oldham b Mallender	6		
B 3, l-b 3, w 2, n-b 9	17	B 1, w 2, n-b 7	10
1/19 2/59 3/76 4/80 5/111 6/126 7/190 8/196 9/196	203	1/52 2/177 3/236	(3 wkts) 350

Bonus points – Derbyshire 2, Northamptonshire 4.

Bowling: *First Innings*—Griffiths 15–3–33–2; Mallender 16–5–30–5; Steele 22–9–44–1; Lamb 12–1–34–0; Capel 3–0–19–1; Willey 8–2–26–0; Williams 6–6–0–1; *Second Innings*—Griffiths 13–1–61–1; Mallender 5–0–43–0; Williams 6–6–0–1. *Second Innings*—Griffiths 13–1–61–1; Mallender 5–0–43–0; Willey 29–6–77–0; Steele 27–8–79–2; Williams 10–3–27–0; Lamb 9.1–0–53–0.

Umpires: D. Archer and B. J. Meyer.

At Coalville, July 10, 12, 13. DERBYSHIRE beat LEICESTERSHIRE by five wickets.

At Southend, July 17, 19, 20. DERBYSHIRE lost to ESSEX by 85 runs.

At Chesterfield, July 24, 25, 26. DERBYSHIRE lost to PAKISTANIS by 140 runs (See Pakistani tour section).

DERBYSHIRE v SURREY

At Derby, July 31, August 2, 3. Drawn. Derbyshire 5 pts, Surrey 5 pts. Surrey prospered after being put in, passing 400 on the first day. Howarth reached a sound century in 233 minutes, hitting seventeen 4s, while Lynch's entertaining 94 included two 6s and eleven 4s. Kirsten then became the first Derbyshire player since 1965 to score two centuries in a match and, in the process, hit his fourth hundred in five Championship innings. He also equalled the county record, which he already shared with L. F. Townsend, of six in a season. Rain halted play before tea on the second day and Derbyshire declared after avoiding the follow-on. Kirsten's unbeaten 164 in the first innings occupied 279 minutes (one 6 and 22 4s); his 123 not out in the second took 173 minutes (one 6, twelve 4s). Surrey survived several missed chances before setting Derbyshire 294 at 96 an hour, and despite Kirsten's stand of 196 with Hampshire, they finished 54 short.

Surrey

A. R. Butcher c Maher b Oldham	9 – c Maher b Hacker	28
G. S. Clinton c Oldham b Newman	4 – run out	3
G. P. Howarth c Wood b Moir	121 – c Wood b Moir	1
*R. D. V. Knight b Moir	49 – c and b Moir	0
M. A. Lynch c Wood b Moir	94 – b Moir	72
†C. J. Richards c Barnett b Oldham	47 – not out	16
D. J. Thomas c Hacker b Newman	21 – c Maher b Hacker	2
A. Needham c Anderson b Oldham	14 – b Moir	4
S. T. Clarke c Kirsten b Oldham	24 – b Oldham	13
R. D. Jackman not out	1 – not out	0
K. S. Mackintosh not out	2	
B 2, l-b 6, w 2, n-b 5	15 L-b 3, w 1, n-b 1	5
1/6 2/21 3/134 4/279 5/306 6/336 7/372 8/379 9/398	(9 wkts dec.) 401 1/10 2/17 3/17 4/108 5/108 6/110 7/119 8/138	(8 wkts dec.) 144

Bonus points – Surrey 4, Derbyshire 2 (Score at 100 overs: 339-6).

Bowling: *First Innings*—Oldham 22–4–88–4; Newman 16–2–64–2; Hacker 10–1–54–0; Wood 22–4–48–0; Kirsten 13–2–44–0; Moir 30–2–85–3; Barnett 1–0–3–0. *Second Innings*—Oldham 3–0–13–1; Newman 7–1–43–0; Hacker 7–1–40–2; Moir 13.4–3–43–4.

Derbyshire

*B. Wood c Howarth b Jackman	0 – c Butcher b Jackman	13
J. G. Wright lbw b Jackman	8 – c Thomas b Jackman	9
P. N. Kirsten not out	164 – not out	123
J. H. Hampshire c and b Needham	40 – c Butcher b Mackintosh	85
K. J. Barnett c Knight b Jackman	21 – not out	8
I. S. Anderson not out	11	
B 4, l-b 2, w 2	8 L-b 2	2
1/1 2/22 3/141 4/217	(4 wkts dec.) 252 1/18 2/31 3/227	(3 wkts) 240

†B. J. M. Maher, P. G. Newman, D. G. Moir, S. Oldham and P. J. Hacker did not bat.

Bonus points – Derbyshire 3, Surrey 1.

Bowling: *First Innings*—Clarke 15–4–39–0; Jackman 22–2–77–3; Thomas 12–3–26–0; Knight 4–1–19–0; Mackintosh 8–1–29–0; Needham 18–2–54–1. *Second Innings*—Clarke 8–1–22–0; Jackman 16–1–65–2; Thomas 8–0–48–0; Needham 9–1–35–0; Butcher 5–1–33–0; Lynch 3–1–9–0; Mackintosh 6.3–0–26–1.

Umpires: J. Birkenshaw and J. van Geloven.

At Birmingham, August 7, 9, 10. DERBYSHIRE drew with WARWICKSHIRE.

DERBYSHIRE v LANCASHIRE

At Derby, August 11, 12, 13. Drawn. Derbyshire 4 pts, Lancashire 6 pts. Having won the toss, Lancashire set off eagerly before Tunnicliffe dismissed both openers, and from then on the batting became increasingly pedestrian. Hughes reached his century in 231 minutes with eight 4s, but Lancashire fell well short of a fourth batting point. Hampshire scored his first century for Derbyshire, in 197 minutes with a 6 and eight 4s, and also passed 1,000 runs for the fifteenth time in his career before Wood declared. Rain cut 100 minutes from the final day, and the game drifted away tediously. Moir, in his first full season, took his 50th wicket when he dismissed O'Shaughnessy.

Lancashire

D. Lloyd b Tunnicliffe	12	– lbw b Moir	2
G. Fowler b Tunnicliffe	29	– c Wright b Anderson	57
I. Cockbain c Maher b Tunnicliffe	39	– (4) c Anderson b Moir	33
*C. H. Lloyd b Kirsten	34		
D. P. Hughes c Anderson b Moir	111	– (7) not out	21
J. Abrahams not out	90	– (8) not out	19
S. J. O'Shaughnessy not out	5	– (6) c and b Moir	8
I. Folley (did not bat)		(3) b Oldham	0
†C. Maynard (did not bat)		(5) c Anderson b Moir	37
B 2, l-b 2, n-b 8	12	B 1, l-b 2, n-b 1	4
1/34 2/44 3/100 4/153 5/302 (5 wkts dec.)	332	1/5 2/16 3/85 4/99 5/117 6/144 (6 wkts dec.)	181

J. Simmons and P. J. W. Allott did not bat.

Bonus points – Lancashire 3, Derbyshire 1 (Score at 100 overs: 274-4).

Bowling: *First Innings*—Tunnicliffe 25–11–65–3; Newman 19–4–52–0; Oldham 27–3–64–0; Kirsten 7–1–23–1; Moir 23–5–65–1; Wood 18–2–51–0. *Second Innings*—Newman 9–5–26–0; Moir 39–21–48–4; Oldham 6–0–23–1; Kirsten 3–0–22–0; Anderson 29–19–43–1; Tunnicliffe 3–1–7–0; Barnett 10–6–8–0.

Derbyshire

*B. Wood c Maynard b D. Lloyd	67
J. G. Wright c Simmons b Allott	1
P. N. Kirsten b D. Lloyd	63
J. H. Hampshire not out	101
K. J. Barnett run out	2
I. S. Anderson b Abrahams	24
C. J. Tunnicliffe lbw b Allott	8
P. G. Newman c C. H. Lloyd b Allott	13
†B. J. M. Maher not out	15
B 2, l-b 9	11
1/11 2/110 3/141 4/150 5/196 6/210 7/262 (7 wkts dec.)	305

D. G. Moir and S. Oldham did not bat.

Bonus points – Derbyshire 3, Lancashire 3 (Score at 100 overs: 264-7).

Bowling: Allott 34–11–74–3; Folley 6–1–20–0; O'Shaughnessy 6–1–26–0; Simmons 20–3–47–0; Hughes 12–2–36–0; D. Lloyd 23.1–5–68–2; Abrahams 6–0–23–1.

Umpires: C. T. Spencer and C. Cook.

At Northampton, August 14, 16, 17. DERBYSHIRE lost to NORTHAMPTONSHIRE by 236 runs.

DERBYSHIRE v SUSSEX

At Chesterfield, August 21, 23, 24. Drawn. Derbyshire 5 pts, Sussex 4 pts. With bad light curtailing the first two days and the third washed out, the match never took any shape, though it was given distinction by Kirsten, who set a Derbyshire record with his seventh century of the season. This passed L. F. Townsend's six in 1933, a total which Kirsten equalled in 1980. The South African reached three figures in 183 minutes, having hit fourteen 4s in another fine display. Barclay and Phillipson were absent with influenza on the second day and, after a brisk start, Sussex were contained, Parker occupying 60 overs in compiling an unbeaten 58.

Derbyshire

*B. Wood lbw b le Roux	16	– not out	0
J. G. Wright c Greig b Waller	79	– not out	0
P. N. Kirsten not out	105		
G. Miller c Phillipson b Pigott	52		
K. J. Barnett c Gould b le Roux	18		
I. S. Anderson b Waller	6		
†R. W. Taylor not out	10		
L-b 4, w 2, n-b 8	14		
1/73 2/124 3/209 4/241 5/287	(5 wkts dec.) 300		(no wkt) 0

P. J. Hacker, C. J. Tunnicliffe, D. G. Moir and S. Oldham did not bat.

Bonus points – Derbyshire 4, Sussex 2.

Bowling: *First Innings*—le Roux 25–7–63–2; Pigott 24–5–78–1; Greig 27.5–11–90–0; Waller 22–6–55–2. *Second Innings*—le Roux 2–2–0–0; Pigott 1–1–0–0.

Sussex

G. D. Mendis c and b Tunnicliffe	36
A. M. Green c Tunnicliffe b Oldham	21
C. M. Wells c Taylor b Tunnicliffe	9
P. W. G. Parker not out	58
G. S. le Roux c and b Moir	24
†I. J. Gould not out	38
L-b 5, n-b 11	16
1/53 2/72 3/79 4/142	(4 wkts dec.) 202

*J. R. T. Barclay, I. A. Greig, C. P. Phillipson, C. E. Waller and A. C. S. Pigott did not bat.

Bonus points – Sussex 2, Derbyshire 1.

Bowling: Oldham 13–3–36–1; Hacker 12–2–52–0; Tunnicliffe 16–7–27–2; Moir 28–13–42–1; Wood 2–2–0–0; Miller 13–4–29–0.

Umpires: W. L. Budd and R. Palmer.

At Nottingham, August 28, 30, 31. DERBYSHIRE drew with NOTTINGHAMSHIRE.

DERBYSHIRE v HAMPSHIRE

At Derby, September 1, 2, 3. Drawn. Derbyshire 6 pts, Hampshire 6 pts. Overseas players dominated the first day. Wright equalled Kirsten's county record, set nine days earlier, reaching his seventh century of the season in 191 minutes with sixteen 4s. He and Tunnicliffe were the only ones to look remotely comfortable against the excellent Marshall after Derbyshire had been put in. Marshall's eleventh five-wickets haul of the season took his total to 121, and he captured his 250th wicket for Hampshire. Struggling at 102 for seven, Hampshire recovered through Tremlett, Southern and Emery, the last-named doubling his aggregate for the season. Against some accommodating bowling, Anderson completed his maiden century (187 minutes, eleven 4s) before Hampshire were set 281 in 112 minutes plus the final hour. Despite a sparkling innings from Turner, the target was too steep.

Derbyshire

*B. Wood b Marshall	5	– b Southern	18
J. G. Wright lbw b Marshall	107	– b Tremlett	65
I. S. Anderson lbw b Jesty	10	– (4) not out	103
J. H. Hampshire c Jesty b Marshall	6	– (5) c Tremlett b Southern	61
G. Miller not out	22	– (6) not out	34
K. J. Barnett b Marshall	8		
†R. W. Taylor b Marshall	0	– (3) c Pocock b Southern	0
C. J. Tunnicliffe b Marshall	28		
P. G. Newman c Parks b Tremlett	5		
D. G. Moir b Emery	9		
A. Watts b Tremlett	0		
L-b 6, w 3	9	L-b 9, n-b 6	15
1/17 2/62 3/94 4/156 5/156 6/167 7/190 8/204 9/204	209	1/32 2/32 3/113 4/219 (4 wkts dec.)	296

Bonus points – Derbyshire 2, Hampshire 4.

Bowling: *First Innings*—Marshall 26–9–60–6; Emery 21–7–50–1; Jesty 14–4–40–1; Tremlett 20.5–3–50–2; Southern 1–1–0–0. *Second Innings*—Marshall 10–2–21–0; Emery 11–2–63–0; Southern 32–3–119–3; Tremlett 8–1–23–1; Pocock 12.5–1–55–0.

Hampshire

C. G. Greenidge c Taylor b Tunnicliffe	28	– c and b Tunnicliffe	18
J. M. Rice lbw b Newman	0	– c Wood b Miller	45
M. C. J. Nicholas c Anderson b Miller	44	– st Taylor b Moir	9
T. E. Jesty c Hampshire b Tunnicliffe	5	– c Watts b Newman	38
D. R. Turner run out	0	– not out	61
*N. E. J. Pocock c Wood b Moir	8	– c Anderson b Miller	3
M. D. Marshall c Taylor b Moir	6	– not out	0
T. M. Tremlett run out	48		
†R. J. Parks c and b Wood	12		
J. W. Southern not out	50		
K. St J. D. Emery not out	18		
L-b 6	6	L-b 2, n-b 3	5
1/6 2/42 3/52 4/52 5/66 6/72 7/104 8/146 9/162 (9 wkts dec.)	225	1/39 2/74 3/77 4/166 5/179 (5 wkts)	179

Bonus points – Hampshire 2, Derbyshire 4.

Bowling: *First Innings*—Tunnicliffe 23–5–49–2; Newman 16–2–43–1; Miller 15–6–36–1; Moir 30–8–74–2; Wood 5–2–9–1; Watts 5–1–8–0. *Second Innings*—Tunnicliffe 10–3–25–1; Newman 5–0–31–1; Watts 4–0–23–0; Moir 13–4–42–1; Miller 9–0–38–2; Barnett 2–0–15–0.

Umpires: A. Jepson and M. J. Kitchen.

At Scarborough, September 8, 9, 10. DERBYSHIRE lost to YORKSHIRE by six wickets.

DERBYSHIRE v GLAMORGAN

At Derby, September 11, 13, 14. Drawn. Derbyshire 7 pts, Glamorgan 5 pts. Aided by fine catches from Kirsten and Miller, Derbyshire cut through Glamorgan's first innings, but their own batting proved equally frail until Barnett was under way. His second Championship century, made in 219 minutes with eleven 4s, put Derbyshire 47 ahead and brought him a county cap. Thomas deservedly took five wickets for the first time. Glamorgan's second innings dragged on into the 153rd over before Lloyd set Derbyshire 281 to win in 90 minutes plus twenty overs. Brilliant batting by Wright and Kirsten, plus a forthright half-century by Hampshire, almost took them to victory but they finished 13 short with two wickets standing. Taylor, without a second-innings victim, was left one short of John Murray's world record of 1,527 dismissals.

Glamorgan

A. Jones c Miller b Tunnicliffe	14	– b Moir	54
A. L. Jones c Kirsten b Tunnicliffe	8	– c and b Miller	55
D. A. Francis c Tunnicliffe b Miller	19	– c Barnett b Miller	53
R. C. Ontong run out	20	– b Moir	25
C. J. C. Rowe b Newman	33	– (6) c and b Moir	42
J. A. Hopkins c Taylor b Tunnicliffe	24	– (5) c Kirsten b Moir	6
H. Morris c Taylor b Newman	63	– not out	42
J. G. Thomas c Taylor b Newman	15	– b Moir	0
†E. W. Jones b Tunnicliffe	0	– lbw b Newman	13
*B. J. Lloyd b Moir	13	– c Wood b Newman	1
S. R. Barwick not out	14	– not out	23
B 1, l-b 2, n-b 8	11	B 2, l-b 4, w 4, n-b 3	13
1/19 2/22 3/57 4/75 5/101 6/152 7/168 8/169 9/207	234	1/101 2/117 3/166 4/182 5/213 6/263 7/263 8/285 9/287 (9 wkts dec.)	327

Bonus points – Glamorgan 2, Derbyshire 4.

Bowling: *First Innings*—Tunnicliffe 17–10–44–4; Newman 12.5–1–60–3; Moir 19–3–56–1; Miller 25–8–35–1; Wood 10–4–28–0. *Second Innings*—Newman 14–2–40–2; Wood 4–1–8–0; Miller 60–22–118–2; Kirsten 19–12–31–0; Moir 52–13–112–5; Anderson 2–2–0–0; Barnett 1.3–0–5–0.

Derbyshire

I. S. Anderson lbw b Thomas	3	– (2) b Ontong	38
J. G. Wright c Lloyd b Thomas	17	– (1) lbw b Ontong	44
P. N. Kirsten c E. W. Jones b Thomas	1	– st E. W. Jones b Rowe	92
J. H. Hampshire b Thomas	40	– (5) not out	57
G. Miller lbw b Barwick	23	– (8) c Lloyd b Thomas	5
K. J. Barnett not out	100	– c and b Ontong	11
*B. Wood c E. W. Jones b Ontong	19	– c Hopkins b Rowe	0
†R. W. Taylor c A. Jones b Rowe	9		
C. J. Tunnicliffe lbw b Thomas	10	– (4) c Thomas b Lloyd	3
P. G. Newman not out	39	– (9) b Thomas	2
D. G. Moir (did not bat)		– not out	0
B 4, l-b 6, w 2, n-b 8	20	L-b 7, w 1, n-b 8	16
1/8 2/27 3/32 4/73 5/105 6/160 7/177 8/202 (8 wkts dec.)	281	1/54 2/154 3/157 4/220 5/247 6/255 7/265 8/268 (8 wkts)	268

Bonus points – Derbyshire 3, Glamorgan 3 (Score at 100 overs: 277-8).

Bowling: *First Innings*—Thomas 23–6–61–5; Barwick 23–7–54–1; Ontong 15.4–3–46–1; Rowe 32–6–83–1; Lloyd 7–1–17–0. *Second Innings*—Thomas 6–0–30–2; Barwick 4–0–15–0; Lloyd 8–0–37–1; Ontong 21–1–101–3; Rowe 13–1–69–2.

Umpires: B. Leadbeater and J. van Geloven.

ESSEX

President: T. N. Pearce, OBE, TD
Chairman: A. G. Waterman
Chairman, Cricket Committee: D. J. Insole, CBE
Secretary/General Manager: P. J. Edwards
County Ground, New Writtle Street,
Chelmsford CM2 0PG
(Telephone: 0245-354533)
Captain: K. W. R. Fletcher

Essex can look back on 1982 only with disappointment. Taking into account the quality of the players at their disposal, to finish among the also-rans must be tantamount to failure. During a disastrous May they virtually surrendered their John Player League title by losing their first four matches, were eliminated from the Benson and Hedges Cup, and lost their opening two Championship games. Although they came back well enough during the next few weeks to inspire hopes of ending with honours, these were not fulfilled. In the final reckoning, Essex had to settle for seventh place in the Championship and fifth in the John Player League and to reflect upon a heavy defeat in the NatWest Bank Trophy at Headingley, where Fletcher's misfortune in losing the toss on a morning greatly in favour of the Yorkshire bowlers condemned his side to defeat.

The early summer setbacks were due to all-round inconsistency. Of the batsmen, only Keith Fletcher managed to strike any sort of form in the first few weeks, a fact which said much for his character. Within three weeks of the start of the season he lost the England captaincy, which he had held in India during the winter. The news came as a great disappointment to him. But his answer was to put together a string of fine scores during the first half of the season. Graham Gooch, on the other hand, struggled uncharacteristically most of this time. Whether the three-year Test ban imposed on him for having played in South Africa earlier in the year was the major reason is open to debate. The fact remains that when mid-July arrived he was still short of 500 first-class runs and out of sorts, despite establishing a new limited-overs record with an astonishing innings of 198 not out against Sussex in the Benson and Hedges Cup. Later he was to rediscover his confidence and form to such a degree that he finished as the county's leading run-maker with over 1,600 runs, the final ten Championship matches bringing him three centuries in addition to eight other scores of over fifty.

Brian Hardie, the 1983 beneficiary, could lay claim to being his side's most consistent gatherer of runs. His only century was against the Indian tourists but he came near to reaching 1,500 runs, as did Ken McEwan. Like Gooch and Fletcher, McEwan collected three Championship hundreds, but his most effective contributions were reserved for John Player League matches. In that competition he amassed 676 runs, more than 250 more than his closest Essex rival, and broke his own county record with an undefeated 156 against Warwickshire at Colchester.

Norbert Phillip, a shy man off the field, proved a tough and formidable foe on it as he enjoyed his best season with bat and ball since joining the club in 1978. Sharing the new ball with Lever, he took 82 first-class wickets, while an aggregate of just under 800 runs confirmed him as a splendid all-rounder. Together with Stuart Turner and Keith Pont, Phillip ensured that the middle-order produced its fair share of runs with a mixture of resolution and enterprise.

Lever, as has come to be expected of him over the years, obtained his quota of wickets, but Ray East and David Acfield, the two spinners, were subjected to a great deal of frustration. Like other members of their art, they suffered largely from the fact that they seldom, if ever, encountered pitches best suited to their talents.

One of the biggest plus factors was the continued improvement of David East. In his first full season, he confirmed his rich potential with superb displays behind the stumps and fully earned his county cap, awarded near the end of the season.

There were, of course, disappointments too. Alan Lilley, a young stroke-player of whom much was and still is expected, seldom looked like building on his promise of the previous year, while Derek Pringle, despite his elevation to Test status, proved something of an enigma. His selection for England stemmed from his deeds with Cambridge University: in the more demanding world of the county circuit he has yet to strike the form to be expected of a Test player. Although yet to make the sort of impact that demands a county cap, he was awarded one upon his selection for the tour of Australia.

Neil Foster, a young fast bowler who enjoyed much success at schoolboy level, will be hoping for a change of fortune in 1983. He forced his way into the side at the beginning of the season, only for a back injury, for which he underwent an operation, to keep him on the sidelines for the greater part of the summer.

At the end of the season, Gary Sainsbury and Neil Smith were not re-engaged. Wicket-keeper Smith, who joined the staff in 1973, was a regular until losing his place to East, while left-arm paceman Sainsbury, despite several fine performances at second-team level, found few first-team opportunities because of the form and fitness of Lever. – N.F.

ESSEX 1982

[*Bill Smith*

Back row: K. S. McEwan, N. Smith, A. W. Lilley, G. A. Gooch, K. R. Pont, B. R. Hardie, D. E. East. *Front row:* S. Turner, R. E. East, K. W. R. Fletcher (*captain*), J. K. Lever, D. L. Acfield.

ESSEX RESULTS

All first-class matches – Played 24: Won 6, Lost 5, Drawn 13.

County Championship matches – Played 22: Won 5, Lost 5, Drawn 12.

Bonus points – Batting 57, Bowling 75.

Competition placings – Schweppes County Championship, 7th; NatWest Bank Trophy, q-f; Benson and Hedges Cup – 3rd in Group C; John Player League, 5th eq.

COUNTY CHAMPIONSHIP AVERAGES

BATTING

	Birthplace	*M*	*I*	*NO*	*R*	*HI*	*Avge*
G. A. Gooch[c]	*Leytonstone*	22	37	1	1,597	149	44.36
K. S. McEwan[c]	*Bedford, SA*	22	34	3	1,306	150*	42.12
K. W. R. Fletcher[c] ...	*Worcester*	22	34	4	1,221	124	40.70
B. R. Hardie[c]	*Stenhousemuir*	22	36	5	1,207	94	38.93
K. R. Pont[c]	*Wanstead*	14	21	6	576	89	38.40
S. Turner[c]	*Chester*	21	26	4	661	83	30.04
N. Phillip[c]	*Bioche, Dominica*	22	30	3	684	73	25.33
A. W. Lilley	*Ilford*	8	11	1	236	67	23.60
D. R. Pringle[c]	*Nairobi, Kenya*	6	9	1	152	54	19.00
D. E. East[c]	*Clapton*	22	29	7	413	61	18.77
R. E. East[c]	*Manningtree*	19	21	2	276	44	14.52
J. K. Lever[c]	*Stepney*	18	19	3	89	22*	5.56
D. L. Acfield[c]	*Chelmsford*	19	16	12	20	4*	5.00

Also batted: N. A. Foster (*Colchester*) (4 matches) 0, 7, 36*; R. J. Leiper (*Woodford Green*) (1 match) 3, 0.

**Signifies not out.* [c] *Denotes county cap.*

BOWLING

	O	*M*	*R*	*W*	*Avge*	*BB*
K. R. Pont	53	10	120	10	12.00	5-17
D. R. Pringle	161.5	40	388	17	22.82	4-53
G. A. Gooch	225	72	510	22	23.18	7-14
J. K. Lever	543.5	112	1,683	72	23.37	6-48
N. Phillip	537.2	98	1,698	68	24.97	6-60
R. E. East	446.5	128	1,130	41	27.56	6-80
D. L. Acfield	525.2	119	1,247	45	27.71	4-35
S. Turner	418	109	984	26	37.84	4-53

Also bowled: K. W. R. Fletcher 16.1–0–134–2; N. A. Foster 82–18–286–8; B. R. Hardie 7–1–20–0; A. W. Lilley 3–0–10–0; K. S. McEwan 11–0–94–1.

HUNDREDS

The following nine three-figure innings were played for Essex in County Championship matches – K. W. R. Fletcher (3) 120 v Middlesex (Lord's), 122 v Surrey (Chelmsford), 124 v Northamptonshire (Northampton); G. A. Gooch (3) 149 v Kent (Canterbury), 140 v Surrey (The Oval), 127 v Kent (Chelmsford); K. S. McEwan (3) 150* v Derbyshire (Chesterfield), 116 v Derbyshire (Southend), 128 v Warwickshire (Colchester).

At Lord's, May 5, 6, 7. ESSEX lost to MIDDLESEX by two wickets.

At Hove, May 12, 13, 14. ESSEX lost to SUSSEX by ten wickets.

At Cambridge, May 19, 20, 21. ESSEX beat CAMBRIDGE UNIVERSITY by an innings and 42 runs.

ESSEX v SURREY

At Chelmsford, May 29, 31, June 1. Essex won by 209 runs. Essex 22 pts, Surrey 4pts. After winning the toss, Essex lost half their wickets for a mere 80 and needed the determination of Turner, on a pitch which helped both spin and seam on the first day, to achieve respectability. For the most part watchful defence dominated proceedings, but even so he managed three 6s in his innings spanning 61 overs. Pocock relished the conditions, but the Surrey batsmen hardly complemented his efforts. The opening day closed with them 49 for six, and only Clarke's spirited hitting on the second morning spared them from following on. A masterful innings by Fletcher, containing thirteen boundaries in four hours, and aggressive knocks by Gooch and Lilley enabled Essex to set a target of 385. Surrey never looked like offering a serious challenge, although Lynch and Clarke put together an exciting eighth-wicket partnership of 61 in only five overs. Surrey's cause was hardly helped by the back injury which prevented Pocock from bowling in Essex's second innings.

Essex

B. R. Hardie lbw b Jackman	21	– (2) b Jackman	3
G. A. Gooch c Richards b Knight	19	– (1) c Roope b Clarke	71
*K. W. R. Fletcher b Clarke	8	– b Jackman	122
K. S. McEwan c Roope b Pocock	14	– lbw b Clarke	3
A. W. Lilley lbw b Pocock	13	– st Richards b Butcher	67
N. Phillip c Knight b Pocock	27	– not out	11
S. Turner c Lynch b Pocock	74		
†D. E. East b Pocock	11		
R. E. East lbw b Clarke	18		
J. K. Lever b Clarke	1		
D. L. Acfield not out	1		
B 7, l-b 13, n-b 1	21	B 1, l-b 8, w 1, n-b 1	11
1/42 2/42 3/57 4/71 5/80 6/129 7/146 8/190 9/196	228	1/16 2/127 3/142 4/258 5/288 (5 wkts dec.)	288

Bonus points – Essex 2, Surrey 4.

Bowling: *First Innings*—Clarke 21–4–50–3; Jackman 25–14–29–1; Knight 7–2–30–1; Pocock 35.1–12–73–5; Needham 6–0–21–0; Butcher 1–0–4–0. *Second Innings*—Clarke 15–3–49–2; Jackman 16.3–3–57–2; Knight 14–0–59–0; Needham 15–3–49–0; Butcher 16–2–63–1.

Surrey

A. R. Butcher c D. E. East b Phillip	4	– lbw b Lever	8
G. S. Clinton run out	1	– c Lilley b Lever	3
*R. D. V. Knight b Phillip	14	– b Phillip	21
D. M. Smith b Lever	3	– (5) c D. E. East b Lever	9
M. A. Lynch lbw b Phillip	4	– (6) lbw b Acfield	69
G. R. J. Roope c D. E. East b Lever	11	– (7) c R. E. East b Lever	7
†C. J. Richards run out	8	– (4) c D. E. East b Turner	4
A. Needham lbw b Phillip	14	– c D. E. East b Lever	1
S. T. Clarke b Phillip	40	– c Gooch b Phillip	31
R. D. Jackman not out	23	– not out	12
P. I. Pocock lbw b Phillip	1	– absent injured	
L-b 6, w 2, n-b 1	9	L-b 1, w 1, n-b 8	10
1/5 2/5 3/21 4/24 5/39 6/41 7/54 8/94 9/122	132	1/7 2/18 3/23 4/41 5/67 6/77 7/94 8/155 9/175	175

Bonus points – Essex 4.

Bowling: *First Innings*—Lever 16–4–63–2; Phillip 15.1–1–60–6. *Second Innings*—Lever 17–4–61–5; Phillip 15–1–80–2; Turner 2–0–4–1; R. E. East 2–0–12–0; Acfield 2–0–8–1.

Umpires: K. E. Palmer and R. S. Herman.

ESSEX v SOMERSET

At Chelmsford, June 5, 7, 8. Essex won by 173 runs. Essex 22 pts, Somerset 4 pts. Following a splendid second-wicket partnership of 134 between Hardie and Fletcher, Essex collapsed dramatically on a pitch showing distinct signs of wear on the opening day. Off-spinner Marks was chiefly responsible, achieving a career best as Essex lost their last eight wickets for 44. Somerset, in turn, were routed by Lever, Acfield and Phillip, leaving Essex with a lead of 127 which, thanks to Fletcher's fifth Championship score of 50 or more in seven innings, they increased substantially to set their opponents a massive target of 377 on the final day – this despite a personal-best performance by off-spinner Lloyds. Phillip destroyed Somerset's innings by capturing three wickets in his first three overs, including that of Richards, first ball. Rose offered sound resistance and received good support from Denning and Botham. But in the end East spun Essex to an easy victory with several hours to spare.

Essex

G. A. Gooch c Taylor b Botham	5	– b Marks	34
B. R. Hardie c Taylor b Marks	76	– c Popplewell b Lloyds	47
*K. W. R. Fletcher b Marks	72	– c Taylor b Lloyds	61
K. S. McEwan c Denning b Marks	26	– c sub b Lloyds	13
A. W. Lilley c Bryant b Popplewell	7	– c and b Lloyds	5
N. Phillip c sub b Marks	9	– b Lloyds	0
S. Turner c Lloyds b Popplewell	8	– c Rose b Lloyds	21
†D. E. East lbw b Marks	8	– (9) not out	14
R. E. East not out	3	– (8) c Ollis b Lloyds	44
J. K. Lever c Lloyds b Marks	0	– b Botham	4
D. L. Acfield c Richards b Marks	4		
B 7, l-b 1, w 1, n-b 11	20	B 3, l-b 3	6
1/8 2/142 3/194 4/203 5/207 6/223 7/227 8/234 9/234	238	1/74 2/95 3/115 4/125 5/127 6/165 7/218 8/243 9/249 (9 wkts dec.)	249

Bonus points – Essex 2, Somerset 4.

Bowling: *First Innings*—Botham 6–3–12–1; Bryant 10–1–62–0; Dredge 13–3–33–0; Marks 24.5–8–59–7; Lloyds 6–3–20–0; Richards 3–1–9–0; Popplewell 13–6–23–2. *Second Innings*—Botham 16.2–1–54–1; Dredge 5–1–16–0; Marks 22–6–56–1; Popplewell 6–0–29–0; Lloyds 28–4–88–7.

Somerset

J. W. Lloyds c Turner b Phillip	27	– lbw b Phillip	5
R. L. Ollis lbw b Phillip	1	– lbw b Phillip	1
I. V. A. Richards c Lilley b Lever	3	– c D. E. East b Phillip	0
*B. C. Rose c D. E. East b Lever	2	– not out	83
P. W. Denning c D. E. East b Acfield	21	– b R. E. East	33
I. T. Botham c R. E. East b Lever	0	– c Turner b Acfield	46
N. F. M. Popplewell b Acfield	13	– c D. E. East b R. E. East	12
V. J. Marks b Lever	1	– c Fletcher b R. E. East	1
†D. J. S. Taylor lbw b Acfield	11	– c Gooch b R. E. East	4
C. H. Dredge not out	12	– c D. E. East b R. E. East	11
M. Bryant c Fletcher b R. E. East	6	– st D. E. East b R. E. East	0
B 3, l-b 1, w 4, n-b 6	14	L-b 6, n-b 1	7
1/3 2/6 3/12 4/55 5/56 6/74 7/75 8/85 9/100	111	1/4 2/4 3/15 4/85 5/142 6/165 7/171 8/177 9/203	203

Bonus points – Essex 4.

Bowling: *First Innings*—Lever 19–5–28–4; Phillip 13–2–31–2; Turner 3–2–4–0; Acfield 13–2–22–3; R. E. East 4.5–0–12–1. *Second Innings*—Lever 8–2–13–0; Phillip 6–0–34–3; Acfield 30–10–58–1; R. E. East 27–6–80–6; Fletcher 1–0–7–0; Turner 2–0–4–0.

Umpires: D. J. Constant and C. Cook.

At Chesterfield, June 9, 10, 11. ESSEX drew with DERBYSHIRE.

At Liverpool, June 12, 14, 15. ESSEX drew with LANCASHIRE.

ESSEX v WORCESTERSHIRE

At Ilford, June 19, 21, 22. Drawn. Essex 7 pts, Worcestershire 3 pts. The final day's play was washed out, thus depriving Essex of almost certain victory. Alleyne, displaying plenty of hostility, had posed the chief problems when Essex were put in by Neale, but Hardie, Fletcher and Phillip batted with commendable determination. Worcestershire, in reply, had no answer to Phillip and the swing of Gooch. Pressed into action as a front-line bowler because Lever and Foster were injured, Gooch emerged with the amazing career-best figures of seven for 14 from eleven overs. Following on 188 behind, the visitors quickly lost another wicket, but then were rescued by the rain.

Essex

G. A. Gooch c Hemsley b Inchmore	10
B. R. Hardie b Alleyne	55
A. W. Lilley hit wkt b Alleyne	9
K. S. McEwan b Alleyne	20
*K. W. R. Fletcher c Humphries b Alleyne	45
K. R. Pont c Ormrod b Gifford	2
N. Phillip c Humphries b Pridgeon	61
S. Turner not out	24
†D. E. East not out	10
L-b 12, n-b 4	16
1/32 2/47 3/101 4/102 5/119 6/194 7/234 (7 wkts dec.)	252

R. E. East and D. L. Acfield did not bat.

Bonus points – Essex 3, Worcestershire 3.

Bowling: Alleyne 30.3–5–92–4; Pridgeon 20–6–40–1; Inchmore 26–9–44–1; Gifford 15–6–34–1; Weston 7–1–26–0.

Worcestershire

M. J. Weston c Hardie b Gooch	15	– lbw b Phillip	3
J. A. Ormrod lbw b Phillip	9	– not out	6
D. N. Patel c D. E. East b Gooch	0		
*P. A. Neale c R. E. East b Gooch	0		
E. J. O. Hemsley lbw b Phillip	0		
D. B. D'Oliveira lbw b Gooch	10		
†D. J. Humphries lbw b Phillip	11		
J. D. Inchmore b Gooch	9		
H. L. Alleyne b Gooch	0		
N. Gifford not out	4	(3) not out	8
A. P. Pridgeon c D. E. East b Gooch	1		
L-b 2, n-b 3	5		
1/25 2/25 3/25 4/25 5/25 6/44 7/50 8/50 9/60	64	1/8	(1 wkt) 17

Bonus points – Essex 4.

Bowling: *First Innings*—Phillip 15–4–29–3; Turner 4–0–16–0; Gooch 11–5–14–7. *Second Innings*—Phillip 5–2–6–1; Gooch 5–0–11–0.

Umpires: D. G. L. Evans and C. T. Spencer.

ESSEX v YORKSHIRE

At Ilford, June 23, 24, 25. Drawn. Essex 3 pts, Yorkshire 1 pt. This match marked the return of Illingworth who, at the age of 50, came out of retirement in an attempt to revive Yorkshire's flagging fortunes. However, in a rain-ruined encounter, he did not perform with either bat or ball. As in the previous match, Gooch again proved a lively proposition in overcast conditions and the visitors were made to struggle for runs. Lumb, for example, needed as many overs for his 52, and the innings was in the 78th over before Yorkshire gained their only bonus point. In contrast, Essex hurried to 84 in seventeen overs by the close of the second day, but only eleven balls were bowled on the final day before rain washed out further play. A feature of the Yorkshire innings was the tidy wicket-keeping of David East, who picked up five catches before the visitors declared.

Yorkshire

G. Boycott c D. E. East b Gooch	9
R. G. Lumb c D. E. East b Gooch	52
C. W. J. Athey c R. E. East b Gooch	18
J. D. Love b Gooch	2
S. N. Hartley c Gooch b Phillip	7
†D. L. Bairstow c D. E. East b Phillip	16
P. Carrick c D. E. East b Turner	11
A. Sidebottom not out	26
C. M. Old c D. E. East b Phillip	2
G. B. Stevenson not out	1
L-b 2, w 2, n-b 4	8
1/23 2/66 3/70 4/87 5/96 6/111 7/132 8/147	(8 wkts dec.) 152

*R. Illingworth did not bat.

Bonus points – Yorkshire 1, Essex 3.

Bowling: Phillip 23.4–5–47–3; Turner 23–9–37–1; Gooch 29–10–60–4; R. E. East 2–2–0–0.

Essex

G. A. Gooch b Old	28
B. R. Hardie not out	44
A. W. Lilley not out	11
B 1, l-b 4, n-b 2	7
1/50	(1 wkt) 90

*K. W. R. Fletcher, K. S. McEwan, K. R. Pont, N. Phillip, S. Turner, †D. E. East, R. E. East and D. L. Acfield did not bat.

Bowling: Old 9.5–0–48–1; Stevenson 6–1–29–0; Athey 3–0–6–0.

Umpires: D. G. L. Evans and C. T. Spencer.

At CHELMSFORD, July 3, 4, 5. ESSEX drew with INDIANS (See Indian tour section).

At NOTTINGHAM, July 7, 8, 9. ESSEX beat NOTTINGHAMSHIRE by ten wickets.

At NORTHAMPTON, July 10, 12, 13. ESSEX drew with NORTHAMPTONSHIRE.

ESSEX v DERBYSHIRE

At Southend, July 17, 19, 20. Essex won by 85 runs. Essex 23 pts, Derbyshire 4 pts. A pitch full of bounce encouraged bowlers and strokemakers alike and so provided much entertaining cricket. After Gooch had gone to the first ball, McEwan cut and drove with great assurance, hitting twenty boundaries during his three-and-a-half hour stay. Pont helped him add 137 before the innings folded late in the afternoon against Wood, Newman and Oldham. Lever's hostility proved too much for the visitors as, 38 for three over the weekend, they finished 132 adrift on first innings. Hardie and McEwan, again, scored freely, allowing Fletcher to set Derbyshire the massive target of 394 at a run a minute. They started disastrously, but the elegant Kirsten and Hampshire set the innings alight with a stand of 158 in 140 minutes, Kirsten's fourth Championship hundred of the summer including fifteen 4s. He struck three more before, like Hampshire, he was magnificently caught behind by David East, one of the game's outstanding performers. Hampshire hit eleven 4s and a 6 in his 95, but Lever, Turner and Ray East eventually saw Essex home.

Essex

G. A. Gooch c Maher b Oldham	0	– c Wright b Oldham	31
B. R. Hardie c Hampshire b Newman	27	– c Moir b Newman	77
*K. W. R. Fletcher c Maher b Oldham	10	– c Moir b Newman	35
K. S. McEwan c Moir b Tunnicliffe	116	– lbw b Moir	63
K. R. Pont c Anderson b Newman	38	– not out	35
N. Phillip c and b Wood	17		
S. Turner lbw b Newman	8		
†D. E. East lbw b Wood	0		
R. E. East c Wood b Oldham	16		
J. K. Lever not out	2		
D. L. Acfield b Newman	1		
B 1, l-b 6, n-b 20	27	B 1, l-b 7, n-b 12	20
1/0 2/24 3/57 4/194 5/221 6/225 7/225 8/252 9/257	262	1/86 2/155 3/158 4/261 (4 wkts dec.)	261

Bonus points – Essex 3, Derbyshire 4.

Bowling: *First Innings*—Oldham 20–8–50–3; Tunnicliffe 20.4–2–76–1; Newman 19.1–3–59–4; Wood 16–3–45–2; Moir 2–1–5–0. *Second Innings*—Oldham 18–2–66–1; Newman 15–2–75–2; Tunnicliffe 8–2–39–0; Moir 11.2–4–42–1; Wood 6–1–19–0.

Derbyshire

*B. Wood c Acfield b Phillip	20	– c D. E. East b Lever 16
J. G. Wright c D. E. East b Phillip	13	– c Hardie b Lever 2
D. G. Moir lbw b Lever	1	– (10) b R. E. East 0
P. N. Kirsten c McEwan b Lever	23	– (3) c D. E. East b Lever 113
J. H. Hampshire lbw b Lever	3	– c D. E. East b Turner 95
K. J. Barnett c D. E. East b Phillip	6	– c Pont b Turner 19
I. S. Anderson c D. E. East b Lever	3	– c D. E. East b R. E. East 11
C. J. Tunnicliffe c Pont b Lever	37	– c R. E. East b Turner 16
P. G. Newman not out	11	– c Fletcher b Turner 17
†B. J. M. Maher lbw b Lever	0	– (4) c D. E. East b Lever 1
S. Oldham c Pont b Turner	3	– not out 8
L-b 1, w 1, n-b 8	10	L-b 6, n-b 4 10
1/35 2/36 3/38 4/45 5/55 6/64 7/87 8/127 9/127	130	1/3 2/32 3/47 4/205 5/249 6/258 7/281 8/287 9/287 308

Bonus points – Essex 4.

Bowling: *First Innings*—Lever 18–5–48–6; Phillip 16–2–65–3; Turner 1.3–0–7–1. *Second Innings*—Lever 23–7–88–4; Phillip 16–2–53–0; Turner 21–1–74–4; Acfield 10–1–36–0; R. E. East 21–4–47–2.

Umpires: D. O. Oslear and Khizar Hayat.

ESSEX v MIDDLESEX

At Southend, July 21, 22, 23. Drawn. Essex 7 pts, Middlesex 6 pts. An absorbing contest was ruined by several stoppages for bad light on the final day when, with Middlesex chasing 285 in 185 minutes, both teams were entertaining thoughts of victory. Gooch, struggling for his true form, showed great determination in his two half-centuries, and Hardie batted pugnaciously in both innings. Pringle's second-innings fifty represented his best for Essex to date. The match, in which Brearley inserted his rivals, was noted for two incidents. During the Essex first innings, Turner was twice caught by Edmonds but was allowed to bat on because umpire Oslear ruled "no-ball", bowlers Cowans and Hughes having exceeded the one-bouncer-per-over rule. Then, in the Middlesex first innings, Downton, batting with Tomlins as his runner, was given run out while standing at the bowler's end. When Downton played the ball into the covers, both he and Tomlins raced through for a single, so contravening the law, which states that a batsman who has a runner may not himself run.

Essex

G. A. Gooch b Edmonds	60	– c Brearley b Edmonds 87
B. R. Hardie lbw b Selvey	43	– c Butcher b Cowans 43
D. R. Pringle c Downton b Cowans	5	– (4) not out 51
K. S. McEwan b Edmonds	20	– (5) c Butcher b Edmonds 7
*K. W. R. Fletcher c Edmonds b Emburey	43	– (6) run out 13
K. R. Pont c Brearley b Hughes	2	– (7) c sub b Edmonds 0
N. Phillip b Cowans	26	– (8) b Cowans 14
S. Turner c Downton b Hughes	21	– (9) not out 1
†D. E. East b Hughes	6	– (3) lbw b Selvey 23
R. E. East st Downton b Emburey	7	
J. K. Lever not out	5	
B 1, l-b 1, w 2, n-b 8	12	B 10, l-b 10, n-b 4 24
1/71 2/79 3/124 4/139 5/142 6/192 7/231 8/233 9/244	250	1/67 2/156 3/189 4/199 5/223 6/223 7/256 (7 wkts dec.) 263

Bonus points – Essex 3, Middlesex 4.

Bowling: *First Innings*—Cowans 12–3–41–2; Selvey 16–4–41–1; Hughes 18–0–77–3; Edmonds 21–8–37–2; Slack 2–0–6–0; Gatting 3–0–6–0; Emburey 10–1–30–2. *Second Innings*—Selvey 10–2–30–1; Cowans 12.2–2–56–2; Edmonds 27–7–80–3; Emburey 11–0–38–0; Hughes 13–5–35–0.

Middlesex

W. N. Slack b Pringle	50	– (2) c Gooch b Lever	16
*J. M. Brearley c D. E. East b Pringle	28	– (1) not out	22
K. P. Tomlins lbw b Lever	14	– not out	3
M. W. Gatting c R. E. East b Lever	5		
R. O. Butcher run out	4		
†P. R. Downton run out	46		
J. E. Emburey st D. E. East b R. E. East	27		
P. H. Edmonds c D. E. East b Lever	2		
M. W. W. Selvey not out	36		
N. G. Cowans c D. E. East b R. E. East	10		
S. P. Hughes c Fletcher b Phillip	0		
L-b 5, w 1, n-b 1	7	L-b 3, w 1, n-b 2	6
1/37 2/72 3/78 4/86 5/128 6/172 7/177 8/200 9/224	229	1/36	(1 wkt) 47

Bonus points – Middlesex 2, Essex 4.

Bowling: *First Innings*—Lever 26–9–67–3; Phillip 15–2–43–1; Pringle 25–5–61–2; Turner 14–3–27–0; R. E. East 11–2–24–2. *Second Innings*—Lever 8–4–9–1; R. E. East 5–1–15–0; Phillip 3–1–13–0; Hardie 2–0–2–0; Fletcher 1–0–2–0; Gooch 1–1–0–0.

Umpires: D. O. Oslear and Khizar Hayat.

At Leicester, July 24, 26, 27. ESSEX lost to LEICESTERSHIRE by 25 runs.

At Cardiff, July 31, August 2, 3. ESSEX beat GLAMORGAN by seven wickets.

At Canterbury, August 7, 9, 10. ESSEX drew with KENT.

ESSEX v HAMPSHIRE

At Chelmsford, August 11, 12, 13. Drawn. Essex 5 pts, Hampshire 8 pts. The weather robbed Hampshire of victory after they had dictated play throughout. After more than four hours had been lost on the final day, they came to a point where they needed 86 to win from eight overs, but despite the efforts of Greenidge, Jesty and Rice they fell short by 11 runs. Fletcher's decision to bat soon proved misguided as the combination of poor strokes and Emery's fast-medium pace reduced them to 63 for six in the thirteenth over, and only the staunch efforts of Turner staved off total embarrassment. When Hampshire batted, Jesty showed his class with his fourth century of the summer, hitting fourteen 4s and a 6 during his 185-minute stay. Phillip, first with Turner and then with David East, ensured that an innings defeat was avoided, despite Marshall's attempts to bring the match to a rapid conclusion.

Essex

G. A. Gooch c Greenidge b Emery	12	– c Parks b Marshall	1
B. R. Hardie c Parks b Emery	12	– lbw b Tremlett	34
*K. W. R. Fletcher c Greenidge b Emery	0	– b Tremlett	19
K. S. McEwan c Greenidge b Emery	3	– b Emery	23
K. R. Pont c Pocock b Marshall	12	– c Parks b Marshall	5
N. Phillip c Parks b Emery	6	– c and b Tremlett	73
S. Turner c Greenidge b Marshall	58	– c Greenidge b Marshall	21
†D. E. East c Tremlett b Southern	27	– lbw b Marshall	41
R. E. East c Tremlett b Marshall	12	– c Pocock b Marshall	0
J. K. Lever b Emery	8	– c Jesty b Marshall	6
D. L. Acfield not out	0	– not out	0
L-b 8, w 2, n-b 15	25	B 7, l-b 16, w 5, n-b 10	38
1/18 2/19 3/26 4/46 5/61 6/63 7/128 8/151 9/174	175	1/3 2/59 3/98 4/103 5/120 6/170 7/255 8/255 9/255	261

Bonus points – Essex 1, Hampshire 4.

Bowling: *First Innings*—Marshall 14–4–54–3; Emery 13.1–1–67–6; Southern 7–2–22–1; Tremlett 7–3–7–0. *Second Innings*—Marshall 28–5–103–6; Emery 21–3–48–1; Tremlett 28–12–35–3; Southern 8–2–37–0.

Hampshire

C. G. Greenidge lbw b Lever	33	– b Phillip	25
J. M. Rice c and b R. E. East	69	– (4) not out	17
M. C. J. Nicholas run out	39	– c R. E. East b Phillip	0
T. E. Jesty c Hardie b Turner	106	– (2) not out	27
*N. E. J. Pocock b Turner	24		
N. G. Cowley lbw b Phillip	7		
M. D. Marshall c Lever b Phillip	5		
T. M. Tremlett c Hardie b Acfield	8		
†R. J. Parks c D. E. East b Acfield	1		
J. W. Southern not out	31		
K. St J. D. Emery lbw b Phillip	5		
B 8, l-b 4, n-b 11	23	L-b 6	6
1/60 2/146 3/154 4/223 5/239 6/249 7/300 8/310 9/314	351	1/38 2/38	(2 wkts) 75

Bonus points – Hampshire 4, Essex 4 (Score at 100 overs: 336-9).

Bowling: *First Innings*—Lever 25–5–109–1; Phillip 19.3–1–66–3; Turner 23–3–74–2; Gooch 8–1–17–0; Acfield 24–6–50–2; R. E. East 6–2–12–1. *Second Innings*—Phillip 4–0–42–2; Lever 4–0–27–0.

Umpires: D. O. Oslear and M. J. Kitchen.

At Cheltenham, August 14, 16, 17. ESSEX drew with GLOUCESTERSHIRE.

ESSEX v WARWICKSHIRE

At Colchester, August 21, 23, 24. Drawn. Essex 8 pts, Warwickshire 4 pts. Essex's prospects were washed out by rain after they had forced their opponents to follow on 253 runs behind. Only 80 minutes of play were possible on the final day before the elements had the final say. The Essex run-feast on the opening day was led by McEwan, whose 128 in 140 minutes included four 6s and fourteen 4s, and he was going for a fourth 6 in one over off Sutcliffe when he was caught on the long-on boundary. The Smith brothers, David and Paul, provided the backbone of the visitors' reply, with the latter making his Championship best. Acfield and East struck quickly for Essex to have Warwickshire 16 for two at the end of the second day, still 237 in arrears, but overnight thoughts of victory were soon dampened on Tuesday.

Essex

G. A. Gooch c K. D. Smith b Sutcliffe. 72	†D. E. East c K. D. Smith b Sutcliffe.. 1
B. R. Hardie b Kallicharran.............. 86	R. E. East c Ferreira b Small............ 20
*K. W. R. Fletcher c Humpage b Sutcliffe. 15	J. K. Lever c Willis b Kallicharran...... 8
K. S. McEwan c Small b Sutcliffe.......128	D. L. Acfield not out........................ 0
D. R. Pringle c Asif Din b Sutcliffe.... 54	L-b 7, n-b 4........................... 11
N. Phillip b Kallicharran................... 24	1/130 2/164 3/211 4/363 5/367 6/423 502
S. Turner c Lethbridge b Willis.......... 83	7/428 8/467 9/498

Bonus Points – Essex 4, Warwickshire 2 (Score at 100 overs: 385-5).

Bowling: Willis 12–0–58–1; Small 12–0–70–1; Ferreira 7–0–42–0; Sutcliffe 43–8–151–5; Kallicharran 46.3–9–134–3; Asif Din 6–1–29–0; Lethbridge 1–0–7–0.

Warwickshire

K. D. Smith b R. E. East	50	– c Gooch b Acfield	2
T. A. Lloyd c Gooch b Lever	17	– not out	42
A. I. Kallicharran c D. E. East b Phillip	26	– c Acfield b R. E. East	3
†G. W. Humpage c Hardie b Phillip	1	– c R. E. East b Lever	11
Asif Din c Gooch b Phillip	1	– c Lever b Pringle	32
A. M. Ferreira lbw b Pringle	21	– not out	16
P. A. Smith lbw b Acfield	68		
C. Lethbridge c D. E. East b Phillip	34		
G. C. Small b R. E. East	8		
*R. G. D. Willis c Gooch b Acfield	2		
S. P. Sutcliffe not out	1		
B 1, l-b 11, w 3, n-b 5	20	L-b 3, n-b 4	7
1/31 2/64 3/70 4/76 5/127 6/129 7/197 8/231 9/238	249	1/12 2/15 3/48 4/91 (4 wkts)	113

Bonus points – Warwickshire 2, Essex 4.

Bowling: *First Innings*—Lever 11–1–30–1; Phillip 16–4–80–4; R. E. East 31–10–45–2; Pringle 11–3–36–1; Acfield 14.1–3–38–2. *Second Innings*—Lever 14.3–2–49–1; Phillip 9–0–39–0; Acfield 6–4–4–1; R. E. East 2–2–0–1; Pringle 3–0–14–1.

Umpires: P. J. Eele and K. E. Palmer.

ESSEX v LEICESTERSHIRE

At Colchester, August 25, 26, 27. Leicestershire won by six wickets. Leicestershire 21 pts, Essex 2 pts. Leicestershire, set 203 in 55 minutes plus twenty overs, achieved a splendid victory, reaching their objective with sixteen balls to spare. Davison, promoted to open the innings, struck a brilliant century off only 80 balls, 30 runs coming from 6s. With Roberts he enjoyed a third-wicket stand of 75 in only 29 minutes, the West Indian collecting four 6s *en route*. On the opening day Cook had routed Essex, and with six wickets in the second innings he returned match figures of twelve for 130. However, Essex did do themselves justice in their second innings, Gooch thumping 88 in 82 minutes, 58 of them in boundaries, and Pont batting with great assurance before being last out chasing quick runs. Leicestershire's first innings was built around the solid defence of Balderstone, who carried his bat during an effort lasting almost six and a half hours.

Essex

G. A. Gooch lbw b Taylor	5	– b Cook	88
B. R. Hardie c Tolchard b Parsons	47	– c Cobb b Steele	19
*K. W. R. Fletcher c Butcher b Taylor	3	– b Cook	25
K. S. McEwan st Tolchard b Cook	19	– c Steele b Cook	7
K. R. Pont c Balderstone b Cook	9	– c Butcher b Steele	89
N. Phillip not out	27	– c sub b Cook	16
S. Turner b Cook	9	– c Balderstone b Cook	19
†D. E. East c Butcher b Roberts	7	– lbw b Cook	4
R. E. East lbw b Cook	0	– c Cook b Parsons	13
J. K. Lever c Balderstone b Cook	4	– st Tolchard b Steele	9
D. L. Acfield b Cook	0	– not out	0
L-b 4, w 1, n-b 5	10	B 4, l-b 11, w 1, n-b 3	19
1/6 2/24 3/62 4/87 5/92 6/113 7/135 8/136 9/140	140	1/115 2/121 3/130 4/188 5/208 6/249 7/260 8/288 9/303	308

Bonus points – Leicestershire 4.

Bowling: *First Innings*—Taylor 19–3–62–2; Roberts 17–5–38–1; Parsons 11–1–13–1; Cook 12.5–6–17–6. *Second Innings*—Taylor 3–0–13–0; Roberts 15–3–36–0; Cook 36–8–113–6; Parsons 7–0–47–1; Steele 27.2–7–80–3.

Leicestershire

J. C. Balderstone not out	114	– c Gooch b Lever	12
R. A. Cobb lbw b Phillip	0		
N. E. Briers b Acfield	36	– st D. E. East b Acfield	7
B. F. Davison c McEwan b Acfield	0	– (2) not out	110
I. P. Butcher run out	0		
*†R. W. Tolchard c D. E. East b Turner	30	– (5) lbw b Acfield	0
A. M. E. Roberts b Turner	43	– (4) c McEwan b Lever	42
G. J. Parsons b Lever	2		
J. F. Steele b Acfield	7	– (6) not out	24
N. G. B. Cook c Fletcher b R. E. East	0		
L. B. Taylor c Fletcher b R. E. East	0		
B 1, l-b 11, w 1, n-b 1	14	L-b 8	8
1/4 2/81 3/81 4/81 5/142 6/210 7/217 8/245 9/246	246	1/35 2/75 3/150 4/156	(4 wkts) 203

Bonus points – Leicestershire 1, Essex 2 (Score at 100 overs: 193-5).

Bowling: *First Innings*—Lever 15–1–45–1; Phillip 14–5–22–1; R. E. East 38.1–17–66–2; Acfield 41–8–77–3; Turner 15–4–22–2. *Second Innings*—Lever 12–0–54–2; Phillip 2–0–11–0; R. E. East 8–0–80–0; Acfield 8.2–0–50–2.

Umpires: K. E. Palmer and P. J. Eele.

At The Oval, August 28, 30, 31. ESSEX drew with SURREY.

ESSEX v KENT

At Chelmsford, September 1, 2, 3. Drawn. Essex 8 pts, Kent 2 pts. An unbroken sixth-wicket partnership between Tavaré and Knott, who came together shortly before lunch, easily earned Kent a draw. Tavaré batted some five hours for his career-best score, reaching his 100 in 215 minutes, while Knott's century came in 192 minutes. Both hit thirteen 4s in reaching three figures. In contrast, Kent had been easily dismissed in the first innings, only Taylor offering any resistance. Essex flourished through Gooch, whose 127 in just under three and a quarter hours included twenty boundaries. Pont also batted well as he and Turner saw the home side to maximum bonus points.

Kent

N. R. Taylor c D. E. East b Lever	65	– c Hardie b Lever 2
M. R. Benson lbw b Lever	8	– c D. E. East b Lever 13
*C. J. Tavaré lbw b Lever	0	– (4) not outout 168
D. G. Aslett c Gooch b Pringle	19	– (5) c Fletcher b Pringle 5
C. S. Cowdrey lbw b Turner	4	– (6) c Pont b Gooch 10
†A. P. E. Knott b Gooch	9	– (7) not out 115
R. M. Ellison lbw b Lever	1	
G. W. Johnson not out	11	
G. R. Dilley lbw b Phillip	3	
D. L. Underwood c Pont b Phillip	1	– (3) c Fletcher b Pringle 30
K. B. S. Jarvis lbw b Phillip	0	
B 2, l-b 4, w 1, n-b 1	8	L-b 4, w 2, n-b 4 10
1/31 2/35 3/68 4/84 5/103 6/104 7/119 8/127 9/129	129	1/9 2/20 3/78 4/84 5/97 (5 wkts dec.) 353

Bonus points – Essex 4.

Bowling: *First Innings*—Lever 25–8–57–4; Phillip 7.4–3–13–3; Acfield 1–0–5–0; Pringle 14–3–25–1; Turner 8–3–17–1; Gooch 5–3–4–1. *Second Innings*—Lever 18–0–59–2; Phillip 12–0–31–0; Acfield 22–3–70–0; Turner 15–4–61–0; Pringle 15–5–32–2; Gooch 15.5–4–58–1; Pont 11–3–32–0.

Essex

G. A. Gooch b Underwood	127	– c Johnson b Dilley 0
B. R. Hardie lbw b Underwood	28	– not out 2
K. S. McEwan c Johnson b Jarvis	26	
*K. W. R. Fletcher c Tavaré b Jarvis	11	
D. R. Pringle c Tavaré b Jarvis	2	
K. R. Pont not out	58	
N. Phillip c Taylor b Underwood	3	
S. Turner not out	30	
†D. E. East (did not bat)		– (3) not out 15
L-b 14, w 1	15	W 1 1
1/85 2/148 3/170 4/174 5/213 6/219	(6 wkts dec.) 300	1/0 (1 wkt) 18

J. K. Lever and D. L. Acfield did not bat.

Bonus points – Essex 4, Kent 2.

Bowling: *First Innings*—Dilley 16.5–0–88–0; Jarvis 18–1–71–3; Ellison 9–1–40–0; Underwood 29–7–51–3; Cowdrey 12–2–31–0; Aslett 1–0–4–0. *Second Innings*—Dilley 2–2–0–1; Aslett 4–1–8–0; Taylor 3–1–9–0.

Umpires: W. E. Alley and J. Birkenshaw.

ESSEX v NORTHAMPTONSHIRE

At Chelmsford, September 11, 13, 14. Northamptonshire won by 159 runs. Northamptonshire 23 pts, Essex 7 pts. On a wearing pitch, Essex were spun to defeat after being set a target of 328 in 240 minutes, though only nine minutes remained when the visitors, already in the twentieth over, gained their deserved success. Steele was the chief destroyer, finishing with ten or more wickets in a match for only the third time in his long career. Lamb batted brilliantly in Northamptonshire's first innings, taking only 145 minutes to amass his runs and hitting two 6s and eighteen 4s before a superb mid-wicket boundary catch by Pont ended his assault. Gooch, with eleven boundaries, caught the eye in Essex's reply before Steele began to make an impact. Consistent batting down the order enabled Northamptonshire to declare a second time, whereupon Essex lost Gooch quickly to Mallender, who was later ordered out of the attack by umpire Meyer for persistently running on to the pitch during his follow-through.

Northamptonshire

*G. Cook c and b Phillip	5	– c Hardie b R. E. East	29
W. Larkins lbw b Lever	25	– c Pont b R. E. East	44
P. Willey c D. E. East b Phillip	43	– c Gooch b R. E. East	30
A. J. Lamb c Pont b Acfield	106	– st D. E. East b Acfield	35
R. G. Williams run out	21	– c Gooch b R. E. East	26
R. J. Boyd-Moss c Pont b Acfield	5	– b R. E. East	24
D. J. Capel c Acfield b R. E. East	45	– st D. E. East b R. E. East	6
D. S. Steele c Acfield b Pringle	42	– not out	16
†G. Sharp c Lever b R. E. East	15	– not out	23
T. M. Lamb not out	30		
N. A. Mallender not out	20		
L-b 8, w 1, n-b 10	19	B 12, l-b 1, w 1, n-b 4	18
1/5 2/48 3/130 4/193 5/207 6/214 7/291 8/314 9/329 (9 wkts dec.)	376	1/57 2/84 3/141 4/159 5/201 6/205 7/216 (7 wkts dec.)	251

Bonus points – Northamptonshire 4, Essex 3 (Score at 100 overs: 329-8).

Bowling: *First Innings*—Lever 16–1–80–1; Phillip 22–5–50–2; Pringle 22–6–58–1; Acfield 28–4–99–2; R. E. East 22–4–70–2. *Second Innings*—Lever 4–0–28–0; Phillip 5–0–22–0; R. E. East 35–9–105–6; Acfield 33–9–78–1.

Essex

G. A. Gooch c Sharp b Steele	61	– lbw b Mallender	7
B. R. Hardie b Mallender	12	– c Cook b Steele	30
*K. W. R. Fletcher c and b Steele	10	– b Steele	23
K. S. McEwan c Larkins b Steele	38	– b Williams	21
D. R. Pringle b Steele	11	– lbw b Steele	7
K. R. Pont b Willey	49	– c Larkins b Williams	11
N. Phillip b Steele	32	– c Capel b Steele	20
†D. E. East not out	35	– (9) c Cook b Steele	1
R. E. East not out	14	– (8) c Larkins b Willey	28
J. K. Lever (did not bat)		– c Larkins b Willey	0
D. L. Acfield (did not bat)		– not out	0
B 11, l-b 10, n-b 17	38	L-b 10, n-b 10	20
1/35 2/91 3/110 4/127 5/190 6/240 7/252 (7 wkts dec.)	300	1/17 2/69 3/74 4/102 5/104 6/134 7/140 8/144 9/159	168

Bonus points – Essex 4, Northamptonshire 3.

Bowling: *First Innings*—Mallender 11–1–30–1; T. M. Lamb 11–4–21–0; Steele 37.2–12–105–5; Capel 8–0–39–0; Willey 25–6–55–1; Williams 5–1–12–0; *Second Innings*—Mallender 7.4–0–31–1; T. M. Lamb 5–0–11–0; Steele 26–11–44–5; Willey 17.2–5–32–2; Williams 19–8–30–2.

Umpires: B. J. Meyer and N. T. Plews.

THE ART OF CRICKET

"The Art of Cricket", an exhibition of works of art connected with the game, is being shown in 1983 at the University of Nottingham Art Gallery (June), The Fine Art Society, Bond Street, London (July and August) and York City Art Gallery (September).

GLAMORGAN

President: His Honour Judge Rowe Harding
Chairman: O. S. Wheatley
Chairman, Cricket Committee: G. Craven
Secretary: P. B. Clift.
Secretary Designate: P. G. Carling
6 High Street, Cardiff CF1 2PW
(Telephone: 0222-29956)
Captain: 1982 – Javed Miandad and B. J. Lloyd;
1983 – M. W. W. Selvey
Chief Coach: T. W. Cartwright

Glamorgan in 1982 did not improve on their disappointing 1981 record, dropping two places in the Schweppes Championship and holding tenth place in the John Player League only through a rally in the second half of the season. In the Benson and Hedges Cup, they won only one of their four matches and were dismissed by Warwickshire in the second round of the NatWest Bank Trophy. The one Championship victory was achieved in the penultimate match at Bristol.

Javed Miandad could play only during the first half of the season before moving off to join the Pakistani touring team. He was missed as a brilliant, fast-scoring, match-winning batsman, though, strange to relate, the batting improved slightly during the season while the bowling fell away. Indeed, the attack became one of the easiest to score off in the Championship. Not only was the cost of wicket-taking far too high to clinch matches that could have been won, but the bowling lacked the hostility to finish off later batsmen and remains the county's major problem.

Glamorgan did find one new young batsman and, possibly, one young bowler. Hugh Morris, an eighteen-year-old Blundell's schoolboy, came into the side in August and played a few innings of high promise; Gregory Thomas, towards the end of the summer, showed promise with his medium-paced bowling. Another player, Arthur Francis, flourished as a batsman, nine seasons after his début in the first team, with 1,076 first-class runs and two good centuries. Three others passed 1,000 runs – Alan Jones, Rodney Ontong and Charles Rowe – while two more, John Hopkins and Alan Lewis Jones, went near.

For Alan Jones, the senior professional, it was a fine performance, in his 43rd year, to reach a four-figure aggregate, which he accomplished for the 22nd consecutive season. He also achieved his 50th century for the county and was awarded the MBE for his services to cricket in Wales. Modest, popular and sporting, he has always applied himself well in good times and bad.

Rowe, signed from Kent, did encouragingly well, but Hopkins did not regain the consistency that originally marked him as a player of considerable promise. Ontong was the leading all-rounder with 1,205 runs and 64 wickets in first-class matches, but the county's bowling was unhelpfully similar in style. Ontong and the new captain, Barry Lloyd, bore the brunt of the attack. Malcolm Nash's 38 wickets cost him 33 runs apiece while Steve Barwick was rarely completely fit. Nash, too, was frequently injured. It was unfortunate that Ezra Moseley, one of Glamorgan's imports from West Indies in recent years, did not deliver a single ball during the season as the result of a back injury. He had had a splendid first season in 1981. Winston Davis, a little-known West Indian from St Vincent, was sent for to deputise for Moseley and collected 42 wickets for 30 runs apiece. Owing to a lack of control in his run-up he conceded many no-balls, however.

The wicket-keeping duties were shared by Eifion Jones, at the age of 40, and 21-year-old Terry Davies, a player of much promise. But the team's catching was inconsistent, many chances going to ground.

Phil Clift, a worthy and loyal Glamorgan servant, had a testimonial season. In his 46 years of service with the county, as player, assistant-coach, coach, assistant-secretary and secretary, he worked hard and with a quiet enthusiasm. During the close season Philip Carling, formerly at Trent Bridge, was appointed as his successor. – J.B.G.T.

GLAMORGAN 1982

[*Bill Smith*

Back row: G. C. Holmes, A. L. Jones, R. C. Ontong, S. R. Barwick, C. J. C. Rowe, J. A. Hopkins. *Front row:* A. Jones, A. E. Cordle, Javed Miandad (*captain*), B. J. Lloyd, M. A. Nash, T. Davies.

GLAMORGAN RESULTS

All first-class matches – Played 25: Won 1, Lost 9, Drawn 15.

County Championship matches – Played 22: Won 1, Lost 8, Drawn 13.

Bonus points – Batting 43, Bowling 60.

Competition placings – Schweppes County Championship, 16th; NatWest Bank Trophy, 2nd round; Benson and Hedges Cup, 4th in Group D; John Player League, 10th eq.

COUNTY CHAMPIONSHIP AVERAGES

BATTING

	Birthplace	*M*	*I*	*NO*	*R*	*HI*	*Avge*
H. Morris	*Cardiff*	4	6	3	213	63	71.00
Javed Miandad c	*Karachi, Pakistan*	8	16	2	601	96*	42.92
D. A. Francis c	*Clydach*	18	31	5	1,064	142*	40.92
A. Jones c	*Velindre*	22	42	5	1,242	146*	33.56
C. J. C. Rowe	*Hong Kong*	22	34	5	888	105	30.62
R. C. Ontong c	*Johannesburg, SA*	22	39	3	1,019	152*	28.30
J. A. Hopkins c	*Maesteg*	21	38	5	923	124	27.96
A. L. Jones	*Alltwen*	19	33	1	839	88	26.21
T. Davies	*St Albans*	8	13	3	211	66*	21.10
G. C. Holmes	*Newcastle-on-Tyne*	5	8	1	139	46*	19.85
S. A. B. Daniels	*Darlington*	9	13	5	151	73	18.87
E. W. Jones c	*Velindre*	14	20	3	268	65	15.76
B. J. Lloyd c	*Neath*	22	28	8	278	48	13.90
J. G. Thomas	*Garnswllt*	9	13	0	172	84	13.23
M. A. Nash c	*Abergavenny*	13	16	1	197	37	13.13
S. R. Barwick	*Neath*	12	13	5	95	23*	11.87
W. W. Davis	*St Vincent, WI*	12	11	6	52	20*	10.40

Also batted: M. J. Llewellyn c (*Clydach*) (1 match) 25, 0; M. N. Davies (*Maesteg*) (1 match) did not bat.

* *Signifies not out.* c *Denotes county cap.*

BOWLING

	O	*M*	*R*	*W*	*Avge*	*BB*
J. G. Thomas	140	25	514	22	23.36	5-61
W. W. Davis	370.5	69	1,222	42	29.09	7-101
S. R. Barwick	266.2	59	836	28	29.85	5-44
R. C. Ontong	615.1	128	1,922	62	31.00	6-50
M. A. Nash	336.2	77	1,048	31	33.80	5-35
B. J. Lloyd	564.5	96	1,898	45	42.17	5-155
S. A. B. Daniels	187.4	33	737	15	49.13	3-65
C. J. C. Rowe	189.2	35	732	12	61.00	3-95

Also bowled: G. C. Holmes 10–3–31–0; Javed Miandad 101.4–31–293–7; A. Jones 1–1–0–0.

HUNDREDS

The following nine three-figure innings were played for Glamorgan in County Championship matches – A. Jones (3) 146* v Worcestershire (Worcester), 136* v Kent (Canterbury), 103 v Nottinghamshire (Swansea); D. A. Francis (2) 127 v Somerset (Taunton), 142* v Kent (Canterbury); R. C. Ontong (2) 152* v Gloucestershire (Swansea), 110 v Surrey (Guildford); J. A. Hopkins (1) 124 v Surrey (Guildford); C. J. C. Rowe (1) 105 v Somerset (Taunton).

At Cambridge, April 21, 22, 23. GLAMORGAN drew with CAMBRIDGE UNIVERSITY.

At Birmingham, May 5, 6, 7. GLAMORGAN drew with WARWICKSHIRE.

At Leeds, May 12, 13, 14. GLAMORGAN drew with YORKSHIRE.

GLAMORGAN v LEICESTERSHIRE

At Cardiff, May 19, 20, 21. Leicestershire won by an innings and 9 runs. Leicestershire 23 pts, Glamorgan 3 pts. Glamorgan suffered a heavy defeat in their first home match of the Championship, mainly because they eased their grip on Leicestershire's first innings and allowed them to recover from 97 for four at lunch and 115 for five in the 54th over. Garnham led the fight-back, riding his luck, while Tolchard dug in at the other end until the arrival of Parsons, whereupon he too attacked the flagging bowlers until a shortage of partners denied him a well-merited hundred. When Glamorgan batted, Roberts exploded, taking five for 27 and forcing them to follow on 193 runs behind. Holmes batted bravely for his 46 not out, but the second innings was no sounder and the third day commenced with Glamorgan still 115 behind with only five second-innings wickets standing. Miandad and Francis delayed the inevitable but Leicestershire were not required to bat again.

Leicestershire

J. C. Balderstone b Nash	8
R. A. Cobb c Miandad b Ontong	7
N. E. Briers c and b Miandad	40
B. F. Davison c Lloyd b Nash	23
I. P. Butcher b Lloyd	23
*R. W. Tolchard not out	93
†M. A. Garnham c Miandad b Barwick	53
A. M. E. Roberts c E. W. Jones b Miandad	11
G. J. Parsons c Barwick b Nash	43
N. G. B. Cook lbw b Lloyd	10
L. B. Taylor c Ontong b Lloyd	0
B 6, l-b 7, n-b 3	16
1/14 2/34 3/63 4/97 5/115 6/191 7/202 8/287 9/327	327

Bonus points – Leicestershire 3, Glamorgan 3 (Score at 100 overs: 275-7).

Bowling: Nash 27–5–72–3; Ontong 26–9–79–1; Barwick 13–2–53–1; Lloyd 21.4–4–55–3; Miandad 15–3–30–2; Rowe 7–4–22–0.

Glamorgan

A. Jones c Butcher b Roberts	5	– lbw b Parsons	15
J. A. Hopkins lbw b Roberts	1	– c Davison b Parsons	0
R. C. Ontong c Parsons b Taylor	25	– b Parsons	27
*Javed Miandad c Garnham b Parsons	7	– lbw b Taylor	51
C. J. C. Rowe b Roberts	2	– (6) st Garnham b Cook	3
D. A. Francis c Tolchard b Taylor	0	– (8) not out	23
G. C. Holmes not out	46	– (5) b Taylor	5
M. A. Nash c Davison b Cook	13	– (10) c Cobb b Taylor	37
†E. W. Jones b Roberts	3	– b Taylor	2
B. J. Lloyd lbw b Roberts	1	– (7) lbw b Roberts	6
S. R. Barwick c Tolchard b Cook	15	– b Roberts	2
B 3, l-b 4, w 1, n-b 8	16	B 3, l-b 2, n-b 8	13
1/1 2/11 3/24 4/29 5/31 6/69 7/85 8/97 9/105	134	1/0 2/39 3/43 4/55 5/81 6/105 7/122 8/136 9/178	184

Bonus points – Leicestershire 4.

Bowling: *First Innings*—Roberts 18–8–27–5; Taylor 17–4–30–2; Parsons 11–1–40–1; Cook 15.2–8–21–2. *Second Innings*—Roberts 18.4–6–33–2; Parsons 18–5–68–3; Taylor 21–8–31–4; Cook 16–6–39–1.

Umpires: W. L. Budd and K. E. Palmer.

GLAMORGAN v GLOUCESTERSHIRE

At Swansea, May 29, 31, June 1. Drawn. Glamorgan 5 pts, Gloucestershire 8 pts. A record last-wicket stand by uncapped players, Terry Davies and Daniels, saved Glamorgan's first innings. They put on 143 to pass the previous best of 140, which was set at Swansea the previous July. However, Gloucestershire, with an unbeaten century by Bainbridge, passed Glamorgan's total and declared at 325 for six on the second afternoon. Glamorgan, 129 for one overnight, batted into the next afternoon as Ontong hit a career-best 152 not out which included three 6s and twenty 4s and occupied four hours. Javed's declaration set Gloucestershire 305 at 100 an hour, but even with Nash absent from Glamorgan's attack after pulling a hamstring, they never managed to keep up with the clock.

Glamorgan

A. Jones c Brassington b Surridge	7	– b Surridge	94
J. A. Hopkins c Graveney b Shepherd	4	– c Brassington b Surridge	4
R. C. Ontong c Stovold b Shepherd	4	– not out	152
*Javed Miandad b Bainbridge	29	– c Brassington b Bainbridge	27
C. J. C. Rowe c Brassington b Bainbridge	55	– c Brassington b Bainbridge	21
A. L. Jones b Bainbridge	4		
G. C. Holmes lbw b Bainbridge	37		
M. A. Nash c Brassington b Shepherd	10		
B. J. Lloyd c Childs b Bainbridge	9		
†T. Davies not out	66		
S. A. B. Daniels b Bainbridge	73	– (6) not out	1
L-b 5, w 3, n-b 2	10	B 1, l-b 17, w 2, n-b 2	22
1/9 2/14 3/27 4/82 5/92 6/117 7/134 8/165 9/165	308	1/29 2/171 3/254 4/304 (4 wkts dec.)	321

Bonus points – Glamorgan 3, Gloucestershire 4 (Score at 100 overs: 264-9).

Bowling: *First Innings*—Shepherd 33–5–116–3; Surridge 29–9–79–1; Bainbridge 28.2–8–59–6; Childs 9–3–19–0; Sadiq 7–0–25–0. *Second Innings*—Shepherd 14–2–48–0; Surridge 26–4–57–2; Bainbridge 22–5–74–2; Childs 13–1–62–0; Graveney 11–1–46–0; Broad 4–0–12–0.

Gloucestershire

A. W. Stovold b Nash	28	– (2) c and b Ontong	4
Sadiq Mohammad b Nash	33	– (3) c Daniels b Rowe	15
B. C. Broad c and b Nash	16	– (1) c Hopkins b Lloyd	25
Zaheer Abbas c Miandad b Lloyd	39	– c Lloyd b Rowe	60
P. Bainbridge not out	101	– b Lloyd	1
A. J. Hignell c and b Ontong	31	– not out	50
J. N. Shepherd b Daniels	1	– not out	9
*D. A. Graveney not out	55		
B 8, l-b 4, n-b 9	21	W 3, n-b 5	8
1/45 2/66 3/86 4/140 5/198 6/215 (6 wkts dec.)	325	1/20 2/39 3/79 4/88 5/134 (5 wkts)	172

†A. J. Brassington, J. H. Childs and D. Surridge did not bat.

Bonus points – Gloucestershire 4, Glamorgan 2.

Bowling: *First Innings*—Nash 20–6–39–3; Daniels 14–3–54–1; Ontong 21–4–72–1; Lloyd 19–2–83–1; Miandad 9–1–36–0; Holmes 5–1–17–0; Rowe 1–0–3–0. *Second Innings*—Nash 2–1–4–0; Ontong 6–3–7–1; Daniels 3–0–26–0; Lloyd 21–6–63–2; Rowe 16–0–60–2; Miandad 3–1–4–0.

Umpires: A. Jepson and N. T. Plews.

GLAMORGAN v SOMERSET

At Swansea, June 2, 3, 4. Drawn. Glamorgan 4 pts, Somerset 8 pts. Dropped catches cost Glamorgan dearly on the first day when Rose denied himself a century by declaring as soon as Somerset obtained maximum batting points. Glamorgan, having withstood Moseley and Dredge in the evening, replied next day with 226, of which Hopkins collected a patient 75. Lloyds' off-spinners reaped most reward for Somerset, but it was the seam of Barwick that had the visitors struggling at 83 for five by the close. Roebuck and Rose again steadied Somerset, whose declaration demanded too much of Glamorgan (271 in 185 minutes) but almost produced a victory for themselves. At the close, Glamorgan were 84 runs short with three wickets standing, including that of Rowe whose unbeaten 58 included twelve boundaries.

Somerset

J. W. Lloyds c Miandad b Barwick	44	– lbw b Barwick	25
P. M. Roebuck c Davies b Daniels	90	– retired ill	53
I. V. A. Richards run out	11	– lbw b Daniels	9
*B. C. Rose not out	97	– (8) not out	63
P. W. Denning run out	21	– c Ontong b Barwick	2
N. F. M. Popplewell c Rowe b Lloyd	10	– (4) c Davies b Barwick	5
P. A. Slocombe c A. L. Jones b Rowe	0	– (6) c Miandad b Barwick	0
†D. J. S. Taylor not out	14	– (7) lbw b Barwick	4
C. H. Dredge (did not bat)		– c Davies b Miandad	0
M . R. Davis (did not bat)		– c Hopkins b Daniels	9
H. R. Moseley (did not bat)		– not out	9
L-b 5, n-b 8	13	B 1, l-b 5, n–b 11	17
1/103 2/119 3/192 4/242 5/265 6/266 (6 wkts dec.)	300	1/48 2/63 3/72 4/74 5/74 6/83 7/162 8/184 (8 wkts dec.)	196

Bonus points – Somerset 4, Glamorgan 2.

Bowling: *First Innings*—Ontong 17–3–47–0; Daniels 18–1–81–1; Barwick 21–2–69–1; Lloyd 23–4–54–1; Rowe 11.3–3–36–1. *Second Innings*—Ontong 8–1–23–0; Barwick 21–7–44–5; Daniels 16.4–5–54–2; Lloyd 25–7–32–0; Miandad 14–7–26–1.

Glamorgan

A. Jones c Taylor b Lloyds	43 – c Lloyds b Dredge	16
J. A. Hopkins c Denning b Davis	75 – b Lloyds	31
R. C. Ontong b Davis	4 – (4) c Taylor b Lloyds	25
*Javed Miandad c Popplewell b Lloyds	32 – (3) c Slocombe b Dredge	27
C. J. C. Rowe c Moseley b Lloyds	2 – not out	58
A. L. Jones c and b Lloyds	36 – c sub b Richards	12
G. C. Holmes b Lloyds	4 – c Lloyds b Richards	6
†T. Davies c Taylor b Davis	0 – c Lloyds b Richards	2
S. A. B. Daniels c Popplewell b Lloyds	11	
B. J. Lloyd c sub b Dredge	6 – (9) not out	0
S. R. Barwick not out	0	
B 1, l-b 6, w 1, n-b 5	13	B 4, l-b 4, n-b 2 10
1/80 2/85 3/122 4/128 5/178 6/182 7/184 8/212 9/219	226	1/22 2/72 3/92 4/112 5/127 6/137 7/161 (7 wkts) 187

Bonus points – Glamorgan 2, Somerset 4.

Bowling: *First Innings*—Moseley 9.4–2–26–0; Dredge 17.2–9–23–1; Lloyds 30–9–114–6; Davis 13–2–36–3; Richards 4–1–14–0. *Second Innings*—Dredge 12–0–38–2; Davis 5–0–26–0; Lloyds 27–6–107–2; Richards 13–9–6–3.

Umpires: A. Jepson and N. T. Plews.

At Manchester, June 5, 7, 8. GLAMORGAN lost to LANCASHIRE by 206 runs.

GLAMORGAN v MIDDLESEX

At Swansea, June 9, 10, 11. Middlesex won by ten wickets. Middlesex 24 pts, Glamorgan 5 pts. Glamorgan continued their season dismally by being outplayed by the Championship leaders, who dismissed them for 191 on the first day and, with Butcher in devastating form, raced away to a comfortable lead at 257 for four by the close. Gatting enjoyed a splendid day as captain, capturing five Glamorgan wickets for 34 and scoring 73 of his 81 runs. Middlesex went on to 352 (from 84.2 overs) on the second day and then had Glamorgan struggling at 63 for three. On the third day Daniel continued his run of superb form, finishing with nine for 61, the best figures of his career, as he dismissed Glamorgan for 202.

Glamorgan

A. Jones lbw b Daniel	7 – c Slack b Daniel	17
J. A. Hopkins c Butcher b Gatting	39 – c Slack b Daniel	0
R. C. Ontong c Butcher b Kemp	0 – run out	17
A. L. Jones lbw b Williams	8 – (6) c Downton b Daniel	43
C. J. C. Rowe c Downton b Emburey	12 – c Emburey b Daniel	23
*Javed Miandad c Radley b Gatting	66 – (4) c Kemp b Daniel	52
D. A. Francis c Emburey b Gatting	5 – c Gatting b Daniel	1
†T. Davies c Emburey b Gatting	32 – lbw b Daniel	34
M. A. Nash c Butcher b Daniel	4 – c Radley b Daniel	0
B. J. Lloyd b Gatting	0 – not out	1
S. R. Barwick not out	2 – c Slack b Daniel	4
L-b 4, w 2, n-b 10	16	L-b 3, n-b 7 10
1/16 2/18 3/36 4/65 5/95 6/113 7/173 8/189 9/189	191	1/9 2/25 3/53 4/93 5/117 6/127 7/196 8/196 9/197 202

Bonus points – Glamorgan 1, Middlesex 4.

Bowling: *First Innings*—Daniel 15.2–6–36–2; Williams 12–2–35–1; Kemp 8–1–21–1; Gatting 12–2–34–5; Emburey 8–0–36–1; Maru 3–1–13–0. *Second Innings*—Daniel 21.4–6–61–9; Williams 15–2–73–0; Kemp 8–2–28–0; Gatting 11–7–17–0; Emburey 1–0–10–0; Maru 6–3–3–0.

Middlesex

W. N. Slack c Davies b Barwick	37	– not out	11
G. D. Barlow c Miandad b Nash	4	– not out	31
C. T. Radley lbw b Nash	18		
*M. W. Gatting c Hopkins b Lloyd	81		
R. O. Butcher c Barwick b Ontong	122		
J. E. Emburey run out	0		
†P.R. Downton b Nash	41		
N. J. Kemp lbw b Barwick	14		
N. F. Williams b Barwick	0		
R. J. Maru lbw b Nash	18		
W. W. Daniel not out	11		
L-b 2, w 2, n-b 2	6	L-b 2, n-b 1	3
1/12 2/60 3/60 4/255 5/262 6/267 7/289 8/289 9/318	352	(no wkt)	45

Bonus points – Middlesex 4, Glamorgan 4.

Bowling: *First Innings*—Nash 26.2–4–95–4; Ontong 20–2–94–1; Barwick 17–6–42–3; Lloyd 16–0–73–1; Miandad 5–0–42–0. *Second Innings*—Nash 3–1–11–0; Barwick 3–1–7–0; Miandad 2–0–12–0; Lloyd 2.2–1–12–0; A. Jones 1–1–0–0.

Umpires: B. Leadbeater and D. R. Shepherd.

GLAMORGAN v WARWICKSHIRE

At Cardiff, June 12, 14, 15. Drawn. Glamorgan 5 pts, Warwickshire 8 pts. Warwickshire, after being put in to bat on a leisurely pitch, batted throughout Saturday for their 391 for seven, with Lloyd (122) and Humpage (90 not out) enjoying an attack which never really threatened. Lloyd, who the previous week had been hit on the jaw while batting, struck fifteen boundaries in his century. On Monday, Hopkins was forced to retire for a while after being hit in the face trying to hook Paul Smith, but it was the medium pace of Lethbridge that did the damage as Glamorgan struggled to avoid the follow-on. Warwickshire, batting a second time, reached 89 for four and were all out on the third day for 169, leaving Glamorgan 311 to win in 280 minutes. Given their current form this was well beyond them, and they were in difficulties when bad light and rain prompted an early finish. Only Ontong, following a good bowling performance, and Rowe revealed enthusiasm with the bat.

Warwickshire

*D. L. Amiss lbw b Nash	32	– c Rowe b Daniels	38
T. A. Lloyd c Daniels b Lloyd	122	– c A. L. Jones b Ontong	42
A. I. Kallicharran c Nash b Lloyd	38	– (6) lbw b Barwick	9
†G. W. Humpage not out	90	– (3) b Daniels	1
K. D. Smith c Lloyd b Ontong	0	– (4) c Davies b Ontong	4
Asif Din lbw b Nash	13	– (5) c A. L. Jones b Ontong	55
P. A. Smith st Davies b Lloyd	35	– c Rowe b Barwick	0
C. Lethbridge c Nash b Barwick	15	– c Daniels b Barwick	3
G. C. Small not out	14	– c A. L. Jones b Barwick	7
D. M. Smith (did not bat)		– c Davies b Ontong	0
J. Cumbes (did not bat)		– not out	0
B 12, l-b 12, n-b 8	32	B 2, l-b 2, w 1, n-b 5	10
1/64 2/181 3/214 4/216 5/248 6/319 7/366	(7 wkts dec.) 391	1/79 2/83 3/88 4/89 5/145 6/145 7/160 8/161 9/168	169

Bonus points – Warwickshire 4, Glamorgan 2 (Score at 100 overs: 333-6).

Bowling: *First Innings*—Nash 24–6–62–2; Barwick 15–4–56–1; Ontong 20–2–67–1; Daniels 14–1–65–0; Lloyd 36.1–7–92–3; Rowe 1–1–0–0; Miandad 3–0–17–0. *Second Innings*—Nash 7–1–29–0; Ontong 20–4–61–4; Lloyd 1–0–2–0; Daniels 9–1–57–2; Barwick 4–1–10–4.

Glamorgan

A. Jones c Humpage b Small	0	– run out	14
J. A. Hopkins lbw b Lethbridge	10	– lbw b Lethbridge	6
R. C. Ontong c P. A. Smith b Small	7	– lbw b Small	56
*Javed Miandad b Asif Din	68	– b Lethbridge	27
C. J. C. Rowe b Lethbridge	20	– not out	43
A. L. Jones c Cumbes b Asif Din	72	– c Humpage b Small	0
†T. Davies run out	8	– c Humpage b Small	7
S. A. B. Daniels not out	10	– not out	3
M. A. Nash b Lethbridge	19		
B. J. Lloyd lbw b Lethbridge	0		
S. R. Barwick b Lethbridge	14		
L-b 20, w 1, n-b 1	22	L-b 8, w 1, n-b 1	10
1/3 2/16 3/58 4/161 5/180 6/194 7/202 8/230 9/230	250	1/21 2/29 3/74 4/126 5/140 6/162	(6 wkts) 166

Bonus points – Glamorgan 3, Warwickshire 4.

Bowling: *First Innings*—Small 18–8–30–2; P. A. Smith 12–3–35–0; Cumbes 10–0–37–0; Lethbridge 24.5–5–68–5; D. M. Smith 2–0–12–0; Asif Din 20–7–46–2. *Second Innings*—Small 14–4–29–3; Cumbes 17–2–34–0; Lethbridge 17–3–54–2; Asif Din 6–2–37–0; D. M. Smith 2–0–2–0.

Umpires: B. Leadbeater and D. R. Shepherd.

GLAMORGAN v OXFORD UNIVERSITY

At Swansea, June 19, 21, 22. Drawn. Despite achieving a good position on the third day, Glamorgan were unable to force a victory. Their attack was never able to break through some defiant batting by the University. On the first day Oxford recovered from 80 for five to 250 all out through Armstrong, Edbrooke and Luddington. In turn Glamorgan fell from 50 without loss to 86 for four by the close. That they recovered on the second day was due to Alan Jones, who narrowly missed a deserved century, and Davies and Rowe, who both hit half-centuries. Oxford, in their second innings on a curtailed third day, were in danger of defeat at 81 for six before Luddington played out time.

Oxford University

*R. G. P. Ellis c T. Davies b Nash	15	– c T. Davies b Barwick	7
R. Marsden lbw b Barwick	12	– retired hurt	21
K. A. Hayes c Hopkins b Nash	0	– b Daniels	10
P. A. N. Armstrong c Holmes b Rowe	34	– b Lloyd	0
R. P. Moulding b Nash	0	– c A. L. Jones b Nash	10
R. M. Edbrooke not out	84	– c T. Davies b Rowe	16
†R. S. Luddington b Rowe	65	– not out	62
S. P. Ridge c M. N. Davies b Rowe	4	– b Rowe	0
T. J. Taylor c Rowe b Lloyd	20	– not out	17
I. J. Curtis c sub b Lloyd	0		
J. J. Cassidy b Lloyd	0		
B 4, l-b 7, n-b 5	16	L-b 5, w 4, n-b 2	11
1/28 2/28 3/28 4/28 5/80 6/175 7/189 8/236 9/240	250	1/8 2/38 3/51 4/59 5/81 6/81	(6 wkts) 154

Bowling: *First Innings*—Nash 20–8–40–3; Daniels 7–0–22–0; Barwick 8–4–19–1; Rowe 29–7–67–3; Lloyd 25.3–6–57–3; Holmes 8–1–29–0. *Second Innings*—Nash 18–5–57–1; Daniels 7–3–9–1; Lloyd 26–15–30–1; Barwick 10–5–18–1; Rowe 15–7–29–2.

Glamorgan

A. Jones c Ridge b Curtis	98	*B. J. Lloyd lbw b Curtis	4
J. A. Hopkins c and b Curtis	27	S. A. B. Daniels b Taylor	16
G. C. Holmes b Taylor	3	S. R. Barwick st Luddington b Curtis	24
A. L. Jones b Curtis	5	B 2, l-b 13, w 1, n-b 2	18
M. N. Davies c Hayes b Taylor	0		
†T. Davies c Hayes b Taylor	52		317
C. J. C. Rowe not out	60	1/51 2/64 3/69 4/82 5/193 6/197	
M. A. Nash c Moulding b Taylor	10	7/218 8/233 9/270	

Bowling: Ridge 12–4–28–0; Cassidy 4–2–12–0; Curtis 53–18–140–5; Taylor 47–11–118–5; Hayes 1–0–1–0.

Umpires: R. Palmer and M. J. Kitchen.

GLAMORGAN v WORCESTERSHIRE

At Cardiff, June 23, 24, 25. Drawn. Glamorgan 4 pts, Worcestershire 2 pts. Rain and bad light ruined this match, allowing only nine overs on the first day in the last 25 minutes, when Worcestershire made 10 without loss. On the second day they were all out for 217 as Lloyd and Daniels each captured three wickets and Glamorgan's fielders snapped up the chances that came their way. Worcestershire had again omitted Turner in preference to Alleyne, but the West Indian fast bowler, though causing both openers painful blows, failed to shift either Alan Jones or Hopkins as Glamorgan built a steady reply. Jones had already passed the half-century mark when stumps were drawn, and rain decided the result by preventing any play at all on the third day.

Worcestershire

M. J. Weston c A. L. Jones b Daniels	9	J. D. Inchmore c Rowe b Lloyd	38
J. A. Ormrod c T. Davies b Nash	11	H. L. Alleyne lbw b Daniels	0
Younis Ahmed c A. L. Jones b Daniels	33	A. P. Pridgeon b Lloyd	21
D. N. Patel c Francis b Nash	8	B 1, l-b 8, n-b 2	11
*P. A. Neale c Nash b Ontong	14		
E. J. O. Hemsley c A. Jones b Lloyd	13	1/26 2/34 3/49	217
†D. J. Humphries c Nash b Ontong	28	4/75 5/92 6/108	
R. K. Illingworth not out	31	7/129 8/174 9/174	

Bonus points – Worcestershire 2, Glamorgan 4.

Bowling: Nash 22–9–52–2; Ontong 25–8–45–2; Lloyd 17.1–2–44–3; Daniels 19–2–65–3.

Glamorgan

A. Jones c and b Patel	53
J. A. Hopkins not out	24
†T. Davies not out	4
L-b 4, n-b 1	5
1/76	(1 wkt) 86

D. A. Francis, R. C. Ontong, C. J. C. Rowe, A. L. Jones, M. N. Davies, *B. J. Lloyd, M. A. Nash and S. A. B. Daniels did not bat.

Bowling: Alleyne 11–7–14–0; Pridgeon 9–1–30–0; Inchmore 7–1–24–0; Weston 2–0–6–0; Patel 2–0–7–1.

Umpires: M. J. Kitchen and R. Palmer.

At Swansea, July 3, 5. GLAMORGAN lost to PAKISTANIS by an innings and 73 runs (See Pakistani tour section).

GLAMORGAN v HAMPSHIRE

At Cardiff, July 10, 12, 13. Hampshire won by 116 runs. Hampshire 19 pts, Glamorgan 4 pts. Batting on winning the toss, Hampshire fell to 37 for four before the brilliant Greenidge, who remained the scourge of the Glamorgan bowlers, carried his bat through 281 minutes for 157, which featured two 6s and 21 4s. In 29 overs Glamorgan mustered 54 for the loss of two wickets before the end of the first day, and when Monday's play was washed out they declared at this total. Hampshire followed with a declaration which set Glamorgan 287 to win at a run a minute, but this was far too big a task for them and they lost with an hour remaining. Including the Sunday League match, Greenidge took 287 runs off the Glamorgan attack without once being dismissed.

Hampshire

C. G. Greenidge not out	157	– not out	38
J. M. Rice lbw b Nash	0	– not out	27
M. C. J. Nicholas c Barwick b Nash	7		
T. E. Jesty lbw b Davis	9		
R. E. Hayward c Davies b Davis	2		
*N. E. J. Pocock b Barwick	20		
N. G. Cowley c Francis b Nash	31		
M. D. Marshall b Nash	10		
†R. J. Parks b Lloyd	4		
J. W. Southern c Nash b Davis	12		
K. St J. D. Emery c Nash b Davis	0		
B 1, l-b 3, w 3, n-b 11	18	L-b 4, w 1	5
1/2 2/16 3/31 4/37 5/84 6/171 7/195 8/231 9/270	270	(no wkt dec.)	70

Bonus Points – Hampshire 3, Glamorgan 4.

Bowling: *First Innings*—Nash 20–5–63–4; Davis 22–5–72–4; Barwick 12–2–48–1; Ontong 12–2–30–0; Lloyd 16–7–39–1. *Second Innings*—Nash 5–1–22–0; Davis 8–2–27–0; Ontong 4–0–16–0.

Glamorgan

A. Jones not out	22	– c Hayward b Emery	34
J. A. Hopkins c Cowley b Emery	0	– c Jesty b Emery	2
D. A. Francis b Marshall	25	– lbw b Emery	16
†T. Davies not out	2	– (7) lbw b Marshall	15
R. C. Ontong (did not bat)		– (4) c Parks b Marshall	10
C. J. C. Rowe (did not bat)		– (5) b Emery	27
A. L. Jones (did not bat)		– (6) c Rice b Southern	3
M. A. Nash (did not bat)		– b Southern	9
*B. J. Lloyd (did not bat)		– not out	15
S. R. Barwick (did not bat)		– st Parks b Southern	9
W. W. Davis (did not bat)		– st Parks b Southern	12
L-b 2, n-b 3	5	B 1, l-b 11, w 2, n-b 4	18
1/0 2/45 (2 wkts dec.)	54	1/4 2/32 3/52 4/94 5/103 6/113 7/133 8/133 9/150	170

Bowling: *First Innings*—Marshall 8–4–8–1; Emery 7–1–16–1; Jesty 7–0–12–0; Cowley 7–4–13–0. *Second Innings*—Marshall 19–6–46–2; Emery 15–4–19–4; Jesty 12–4–35–0; Southern 16.1–2–50–4; Cowley 2–1–2–0.

Umpires: D. J. Constant and P. J. Eele.

At Taunton, July 17, 19, 20. GLAMORGAN drew with SOMERSET.

At Portsmouth, July 21, 22, 23. GLAMORGAN lost to HAMPSHIRE by an innings and 78 runs.

At Worcester, July 28, 29, 30. GLAMORGAN drew with WORCESTERSHIRE.

GLAMORGAN v ESSEX

At Cardiff, July 31, August 2, 3. Essex won by seven wickets. Essex 20 pts, Glamorgan 6 pts. In dire straits after collapsing to 78 for five, Glamorgan recovered to 226 for eight off 113 overs by the close of the first day, thanks to a patient 67 not out by Rowe. Next morning they went on to 256 and then reduced Essex to 154 for nine before Fletcher declared. Batting a second time, Glamorgan reached 99 for three and ended the second day with a lead of 201, poised for their first Championship victory of 1982. But in keeping with the season's uncertainty, they failed miserably on the third day. Bundled out for the addition of just 37 runs as Pont returned career-best figures, they were unable to contain the Essex all-rounder and his captain, who struck one 6 and seven 4s while guiding his side to a convincing win with 2.4 overs to spare. For Eifion Jones, Glamorgan's 40-year-old wicket-keeper, there was the consolation of equalling the county record of eight catches in a match.

Glamorgan

A. Jones c Gooch b Turner	23	– (9) c R. E. East b Gooch	7
A. L. Jones c D. E. East b Phillip	1	– (1) lbw b Turner	46
D. A. Francis c Gooch b Phillip	35	– c R. E. East b Pont	11
R. C. Ontong lbw b Phillip	6	– c sub b Acfield	1
J. A. Hopkins c Pont b Gooch	0	– (2) lbw b Turner	32
C. J. C. Rowe c D. E. East b Gooch	77	– (5) c D. E. East b Pont	11
†E. W. Jones b Phillip	27	– (6) c D. E. East b Pont	0
J. G. Thomas b Phillip	1	– (7) c Fletcher b Pont	10
*B. J. Lloyd lbw b Lever	35	– (8) b Phillip	4
S. A. B. Daniels not out	23	– b Pont	2
W. W. Davis b Gooch	0	– not out	0
L-b 11, w 2, n-b 15	28	L-b 6, w 2, n-b 6	14
1/7 2/45 3/74 4/78 5/78 6/154 7/161 8/202 9/256	256	1/67 2/93 3/94 4/101 5/109 6/112 7/124 8/126 9/129	138

Bonus points – Glamorgan 2, Essex 3 (Score at 100 overs: 201-7).

Bowling: *First Innings*—Lever 26.5–6–70–1; Phillip 30–12–40–5; Gooch 24.2–7–37–3; Turner 24.1–10–24–1; Acfield 12–1–34–0; R. E. East 11–5–23–0. *Second Innings*—Phillip 16–3–24–1; Gooch 11.5–4–33–1; Turner 18–3–36–2; Acfield 9–5–14–1; Pont 13–3–17–5.

Essex

G. A. Gooch c Lloyd b Ontong	2	– c E. W. Jones b Thomas	24
†D. E. East c E. W. Jones b Davis	5	– b Daniels	38
*K. W. R. Fletcher c E. W. Jones b Thomas	7	– not out	83
K. S. McEwan b Daniels	36	– c E. W. Jones b Thomas	28
K. R. Pont c E. W. Jones b Thomas	5	– not out	47
N. Phillip c E. W. Jones b Davis	33		
S. Turner c E. W. Jones b Thomas	1		
R. E. East c E. W. Jones b Ontong	18		
B. R. Hardie not out	19		
J. K. Lever c Francis b Lloyd	4		
D. L. Acfield not out	4		
L-b 5, w 3, n-b 12	20	B 3, l-b 5, w 2, n-b 11	21
1/7 2/11 3/45 4/67 5/67 6/72 7/120 8/132 9/148 (9 wkts dec.)	154	1/49 2/90 3/156 (3 wkts)	241

Bonus points – Essex 1, Glamorgan 4.

Bowling: *First Innings*—Davis 17–1–52–2; Ontong 14–5–28–2; Thomas 8–3–24–3; Daniels 9–1–23–1; Lloyd 4–1–7–1. *Second Innings*—Ontong 10.2–3–37–0; Davis 21–4–63–0; Daniels 17–4–47–1; Thomas 9–1–32–2; Lloyd 14–4–41–0.

Umpires: D. R. Shepherd and A. G. T. Whitehead.

GLAMORGAN v NORTHAMPTONSHIRE

At Swansea, August 7, 9, 10. Drawn. Glamorgan 3 pts, Northamptonshire 3 pts. On the third day Northamptonshire made a brave effort to achieve victory, though on such a good wicket it had needed three declarations to achieve the chance of a decisive result. On the first day Glamorgan had declared at 296 for five after 112 overs, to which Northamptonshire had replied with 23 for one by the close. Rain interfered on the second day when Larkins and Willey took the visitors to 157 for two, at which Cook declared before the start of the third day. Glamorgan's second declaration, set up by A. L. Jones and Francis, gave Northamptonshire three hours in which to get 318, and they set about their task with panache. Larkins and Willey put on 170 in 116 minutes, Willey going on to his fifth century of the season in 146 minutes before he was fifth out at 247, and only when the seventh wicket fell at 272 was the chase abandoned.

Glamorgan

A. Jones lbw b T. M. Lamb	87	– c Steele b Mallender	3
A. L. Jones lbw b Kapil Dev	10	– lbw b T. M. Lamb	88
D. A. Francis c Cook b T. M. Lamb	49	– not out	68
R. C. Ontong b Willey	33	– not out	14
J. A. Hopkins not out	72		
C. J. C. Rowe st Sharp b Steele	13		
H. Morris not out	21		
L-b 5, w 1, n-b 5	11	L-b 3, w 1, n-b 1	5
1/37 2/140 3/155 4/212 5/242 (5 wkts dec.)	296	1/11 2/138 (2 wkts dec.)	178

*B. J. Lloyd, †E. W. Jones, W. W. Davis and S. R. Barwick did not bat.

Bonus points – Glamorgan 3, Northamptonshire 2 (Score at 100 overs: 255-5).

Bowling: *First Innings*—Kapil Dev 18–3–59–1; Mallender 18–3–55–0; T. M. Lamb 23–9–41–2; Larkins 2–0–15–0; Willey 33–10–70–1; Steele 17–4–41–1; Williams 1–0–4–0. *Second Innings*—Kapil Dev 9–1–34–0; Mallender 9–2–22–1; T. M. Lamb 12–4–42–1; Willey 9–4–21–0; Steele 6–1–14–0; Williams 10–1–40–0.

Northamptonshire

*G. Cook lbw b Ontong	3	– c Rowe b Davis	0
W. Larkins not out	82	– c E. W. Jones b Davis	78
T. M. Lamb b Davis	5	– (9) not out	1
P. Willey not out	49	– (3) c A. L. Jones b Lloyd	117
A. J. Lamb (did not bat)		– (4) c Rowe b Barwick	2
Kapil Dev (did not bat)		– (5) c Ontong b Barwick	5
R. G. Williams (did not bat)		– (6) c Hopkins b Lloyd	39
R. J. Boyd-Moss (did not bat)		– (7) run out	8
D. S. Steele (did not bat)		– (8) not out	12
B 4, l-b 3, n-b 11	18	L-b 10, n-b 12	22
1/10 2/42 (2 wkts dec.)	157	1/0 2/170 3/179 4/196 5/247 6/260 7/272 (7 wkts)	284

†G. Sharp and N. A. Mallender did not bat.

Bonus points – Northamptonshire 1.

Bowling: *First Innings*—Davis 8–1–43–1; Ontong 12–4–32–1; Barwick 7–0–29–0; Lloyd 8–0–27–0; Rowe 2–0–8–0. *Second Innings*—Davis 19–0–99–2; Ontong 7–1–34–0; Barwick 16–1–78–2; Lloyd 5–0–35–2; Rowe 6–2–16–0.

Umpires: K. E. Palmer and P. B. Wight.

At Canterbury, August 11, 12, 13. GLAMORGAN drew with KENT.

At Guildford, August 14, 16, 17. GLAMORGAN lost to SURREY by two wickets.

GLAMORGAN v NOTTINGHAMSHIRE

At Swansea, August 21, 23, 24. Drawn. Glamorgan 6 pts, Nottinghamshire 6 pts. Batting on the first day, the visitors began brightly with a century opening stand from Hassan and Robinson, but needed Hadlee's belligerent 91 to obtain maximum points as Glamorgan's new signing, Winston Davis, enjoyed his best performance with seven for 101. In reply, Glamorgan had made 69 for one by the close, and on the second day Alan Jones battled bravely for his 55th century. Nottinghamshire, batting a second time, lost three wickets while increasing their lead to 182, which they built further on the third morning before rain brought the match to a premature end.

Nottinghamshire

B. Hassan hit wkt b Davis	73	– b Ontong	26
R. T. Robinson b Ontong	59	– run out	26
D. W. Randall b Davis	18	– c E. W. Jones b Ontong	2
*C. E. B. Rice b Davis	28	– c and b Davis	54
J. D. Birch b Davis	0	– lbw b Ontong	28
R. J. Hadlee c E. W. Jones b Lloyd	91	– not out	30
†B. N. French c Rowe b Davis	11	– not out	2
E. E. Hemmings lbw b Davis	1		
K. Saxelby c Lloyd b Davis	0		
K. E. Cooper not out	18		
P. M. Such lbw b Lloyd	0		
B 5, l-b 7, n-b 7	19	B 1, l-b 9, w 1, n-b 23	34
1/119 2/158 3/175 4/175 5/212 6/244 7/261 8/264 9/318	318	1/51 2/54 3/69 4/151 5/176 (5 wkts)	202

Bonus points – Nottinghamshire 4, Glamorgan 4.

Bowling: *First Innings*—Nash 20–2–71–0; Davis 26–6–101–7; Thomas 6–0–41–0; Lloyd 10.5–0–40–2; Ontong 16–4–43–1; Rowe 1–0–3–0. *Second Innings*—Davis 13–2–51–1; Nash 6–1–16–0; Ontong 18.4–1–79–3; Thomas 6–2–22–0.

Glamorgan

A. Jones c Rice b Hemmings	103	*B. J. Lloyd b Hemmings	6
A. L. Jones lbw b Saxelby	0	M. A. Nash c Randall b Hemmings	6
D. A. Francis b Cooper	56	W. W. Davis not out	1
R. C. Ontong c Rice b Cooper	3		
J. A. Hopkins c Such b Hemmings	14	B 5, l-b 3, n-b 8	16
C. J. C. Rowe c French b Saxelby	32		—
J. G. Thomas c French b Hemmings	3	1/1 2/169 3/169 4/176 5/200 6/203	249
†E. W. Jones c Such b Hemmings	9	7/230 8/235 9/247	

Bonus points – Glamorgan 2, Nottinghamshire 2 (Score at 100 overs: 209-6).

Bowling: Saxelby 26–6–61–2; Cooper 32–10–63–2; Hemmings 47.2–19–76–6; Such 10–3–33–0.

Umpires: C. T. Spencer and D. O. Oslear

GLAMORGAN v SUSSEX

At Cardiff, August 25, 26, 27. Drawn. Glamorgan 3 pts, Sussex 4 pts. Put in to bat, Glamorgan recovered from a poor start through A. L. Jones and eighteen-year-old Hugh Morris, captain of the England Schools XI, whose 55 revealed his potential. Rain, which affected the first day, also disturbed the second and prompted Sussex to declare at 49 for two before the start of the third in the hope of obtaining a win. Glamorgan's own declaration at 70 for two left their visitors to get 301 in 195 minutes, but they ended 53 short with three wickets remaining. Parker and le Roux made a bold effort with 93 in 35 minutes for the fifth wicket.

Glamorgan

A. Jones c Phillipson b Greig	9	– not out	34
A. L. Jones c Barclay b le Roux	71	– lbw b le Roux	10
J. A. Hopkins lbw b le Roux	7	– c Waller b Pigott	8
R. C. Ontong c Greig b Pigott	31	– not out	10
C. J. C. Rowe lbw b Wells	9		
H. Morris c Barclay b Greig	55		
†T. Davies c Barclay b Greig	8		
J. G. Thomas c Wells b Pigott	6		
*B. J. Lloyd lbw b Greig	48		
S. R. Barwick c Pigott b Greig	7		
W. W. Davis not out	7		
B 4, l-b 8, w 6, n-b 3	21	L-b 5, w 3	8
	—		—
1/18 2/41 3/118 4/135 5/135 6/166 7/179 8/250 9/260	279	1/26 2/54 (2 wkts dec.)	70

Bonus points – Glamorgan 3, Sussex 4.

Bowling: *First Innings*—le Roux 30–7–68–2; Pigott 16–3–66–2; Greig 36–6–103–5; Wells 7–3–9–1; Waller 1–0–4–0; Barclay 4–1–8–0. *Second Innings*—le Roux 4–1–18–1; Pigott 5.4–1–15–1; Greig 7–1–29–0.

Sussex

G. D. Mendis lbw b Davis	2	– b Barwick	6
A. M. Green not out	27	– lbw b Ontong	59
C. M. Wells c Hopkins b Davis	0	– c Davies b Barwick	31
P. W. G. Parker not out	8	– c Lloyd b Ontong	68
I. A. Greig (did not bat)		– b Ontong	2
G. S. le Roux (did not bat)		– b Ontong	50
C. P. Phillipson (did not bat)		– b Davis	8
*J. R. T. Barclay (did not bat)		– not out	1
C. E. Waller (did not bat)		– not out	5
B 1, l-b 1, w 1, n-b 9	12	B 3, l-b 3, n-b 12	18
1/2 2/4 (2 wkts dec.)	49	1/23 2/84 3/115 4/123 5/216 6/239 7/241 (7 wkts)	248

†D. J. Smith and A. C. S. Pigott did not bat.

Bowling: *First Innings*—Davis 8–3–16–2; Thomas 6–2–10–0; Barwick 7–3–11–0; Lloyd 1–1–0–0. *Second Innings*—Barwick 11–4–35–2; Davis 12–2–25–1; Lloyd 21–4–97–0; Rowe 6–2–16–0; Ontong 16.4–2–57–4.

Umpires: D. O. Oslear and P. B. Wight.

At Leicester, September 1, 2, 3. GLAMORGAN lost to LEICESTERSHIRE by an innings and 58 runs.

At Bristol, September 8, 9, 10. GLAMORGAN beat GLOUCESTERSHIRE by four wickets.

At Derby, September 11, 13, 14. GLAMORGAN drew with DERBYSHIRE.

PLAYERS' SALARIES

The Test and County Cricket Board and the Cricketers' Association agreed, in September 1982, a pay rise of just under seven per cent for capped county players, to apply in 1983. This raised their minimum salary to £6,250. There were also increases of between £125 and £225 for uncapped members of county staffs aged between 17 and 21, their salaries now ranging from £2,150 to £3,650.

Mr J. D. Bannister, secretary of the Association, said that in reaching agreement, account had been taken of the poor financial returns for the 1982 season, due partly to a reduction, from 1981, in Test match takings. The collapse of a Sports Space Advertising Company had also hit several of the first-class counties – Lancashire, Surrey, Warwickshire and Nottinghamshire to the tune of £40,000 or more.

GLOUCESTERSHIRE

Patron: The Duke of Beaufort, KG
President: T. L. Robinson
Chairman: D. N. Perry
Chairman, Cricket Committee: D. G. Stone
Secretary/Cricket Manager: 1982 – A. S. Brown. Phoenix County Ground, Nevil Road, Bristol BS7 9EJ. (Telephone: 0272-45216)
Captain: D. A. Graveney
Coach: G. G. Wiltshire

There were few bright spots for Gloucestershire in a 1982 season which was just as difficult as most of their supporters must have feared. The team dropped from twelfth to fifteenth in the Championship, failed to survive the qualifying rounds of the Benson and Hedges Cup, and went out of the NatWest Bank Trophy at the quarter-final stage.

The batting held up fairly well, even after Zaheer Abbas had left to join the Pakistani touring side, but an attack based on medium-pace and left-arm spin lacked the cutting edge of speed. On only two occasions did Gloucestershire manage to dismiss the opposition twice, losing to Worcestershire by 11 runs the first time and beating Yorkshire by five wickets at Bradford the other. The only other first-class victory was in a single-innings match against Hampshire.

An attempt to remedy the situation was made by the signing of a West Indian fast bowler, Franklyn Stephenson, who in seven mid-week Championship games took 25 wickets and looked a splendid prospect. Under registration regulations it was not possible to play both him and Sadiq, so when Stephenson was in the side the batting had to be weakened. Stephenson bowled the side into a winning position against Middlesex, only for the advantage to be squandered, as it was in later games against Hampshire and Glamorgan. Apart from Stephenson, only David Graveney managed to take his wickets at less than 30 runs apiece. John Childs, the other left-arm spinner, of whom great things had been hoped, lost form to such an extent that his number of Championship wickets was almost halved.

Gloucestershire had many reasons to be thankful for the efforts of John Shepherd, their winter signing from Kent. He showed that even at the age of 38 there was plenty of good cricket left in him. He bowled with great heart and intelligence, often having to toil through long spells because of the lack of back-up bowling. David Surridge, his new-ball partner for most of the season, had a useful first campaign after his entry into county cricket had been delayed by two years because of back trouble.

Andy Stovold and Chris Broad were a more than adequate opening pair, although the left-handed Broad too often got out when a big score was in prospect. Paul Romaines, at his second attempt to establish himself in the first-class game, played one fine, match-saving innings of 186 against Warwickshire, but otherwise found it difficult to dictate to bowlers. Phil Bainbridge again looked one of the best young batsmen in the country, but his season was curtailed when he had a finger broken on a bad pitch at Leicester, causing him to miss the next five matches. In Bainbridge's absence, and with Alastair Hignell right out of form, the assistant-coach, Barry Dudleston, was brought in to fill the breach and showed he had lost little of his ability. Although he lost his coaching post in an end-of-season economy drive, he was offered a match contract.

Tony Wright, a young batsman from Hertfordshire, was given a chance in the last ten matches and made some useful scores, while another player of obvious potential is the England Young Cricketers' wicket-keeper, Jack Russell, who played in the NatWest Bank Trophy game against Middlesex which was lost by 3 runs. This was just about Gloucestershire's best team performance of the season, apart, perhaps, from the second-round victory by nine wickets over Nottinghamshire at Trent Bridge. – G.J.W.

GLOUCESTERSHIRE 1982

[*Bill Smith*

Back row: P. Bainbridge, P. W. Romaines, A. J. Wright, B. C. Broad, F. D. Stephenson, D. Surridge, J. N. Shepherd, R. C. Russell, B. Avery (*scorer*).
Front row: B. Dudleston, D. A. Graveney (*captain*), A. S. Brown (*secretary/manager*), J. H. Childs, A. W. Stovold.

GLOUCESTERSHIRE RESULTS

All first-class matches – Played 24: Won 3, Lost 9, Drawn 12.

County Championship matches – Played 22: Won 2, Lost 9, Drawn 11.

Bonus points – Batting 46, Bowling 55.

Competition placings – Schweppes County Championship, 15th; NatWest Bank Trophy, q-f; Benson and Hedges Cup, 3rd in Group D; John Player League, 14th.

COUNTY CHAMPIONSHIP AVERAGES

BATTING

	Birthplace	*M*	*I*	*NO*	*R*	*HI*	*Avge*
Zaheer Abbas c	*Sialkot, Pakistan*	6	12	1	667	162*	60.63
P. Bainbridge c	*Stoke-on-Trent*	17	31	7	1,001	103	41.70
Sadiq Mohammad c	*Junagadh, India*	14	27	0	974	91	36.07
A. W. Stovold c	*Bristol*	22	40	1	1,338	212*	34.30
B. Dudleston	*Bebington*	6	12	1	373	111	33.90
A. J. Hignell c	*Cambridge*	15	28	6	664	72	30.18
P. W. Romaines	*Bishop Auckland*	13	22	1	561	186	26.71
B. C. Broad c	*Bristol*	20	38	0	985	97	25.92
D. A. Graveney c	*Bristol*	21	28	9	457	55*	24.05
A. J. Wright	*Stevenage*	10	19	2	399	65	23.47
J. N. Shepherd	*St Andrew, Barbados*	21	33	8	533	67*	21.32
R. C. Russell	*Stroud*	4	6	1	81	41	16.20
M. W. Stovold	*Bristol*	3	6	0	96	52	16.00
R. J. Doughty	*Bridlington*	5	5	1	58	29	14.50
A. J. Brassington c	*Bagnall*	18	19	5	141	35	10.07
J. H. Childs c	*Plymouth*	19	21	5	132	34*	8.25
D. Surridge	*Bishop's Stortford*	16	17	7	61	12	6.10
F. D. Stephenson	*St James, Barbados*	7	9	1	42	15	5.25
E. J. Cunningham	*Oxford*	3	4	1	7	5	2.33

Also batted: D. P. Simpkins (*Chippenham*) (1 match) 0, 1*; C. R. Trembath (*London*) (1 match) 8*.

**Signifies not out.* c *Denotes county cap.*

BOWLING

	O	*M*	*R*	*W*	*Avge*	*BB*
F. D. Stephenson	175.2	37	542	25	21.68	5-69
D. A. Graveney	430.4	118	1,134	39	29.07	7-37
D. Surridge	491.2	134	1,319	41	32.17	5-78
J. N. Shepherd	709.1	162	1,962	60	32.70	6-75
R. J. Doughty	149.1	19	533	15	35.53	6-43
J. H. Childs	551.2	158	1,514	33	45.87	5-112
P. Bainbridge	276	72	844	18	46.88	6-59

Also bowled: B. C. Broad 34–7–87–2; B. Dudleston 37–10–108–3; Sadiq Mohammad 101.4–20–305–7; D. P. Simpkins 2–0–15–0; C. R. Trembath 23.2–2–98–0; Zaheer Abbas 2–0–15–0.

HUNDREDS

The following eight three-figure innings were played for Gloucestershire in County Championship matches – P. Bainbridge (2) 101* v Glamorgan (Swansea), 103 v Yorkshire (Bradford); A. W. Stovold (2) 100 v Warwickshire (Nuneaton), 212* v Northamptonshire (Northampton); Zaheer Abbas (2) 162* and 107 v Lancashire (Gloucester); B. Dudleston (1) 111 v Hampshire (Bournemouth); P. W. Romaines (1) 186 v Warwickshire (Nuneaton).

At Oxford, May 5, 6, 7. GLOUCESTERSHIRE beat OXFORD UNIVERSITY by ten wickets.

GLOUCESTERSHIRE v WORCESTERSHIRE

At Bristol, May 12, 13, 14. Worcestershire won by 11 runs. Worcestershire 22 pts, Gloucestershire 5 pts. Only three batsmen passed 50 on an untypically sporting Bristol pitch, which nevertheless produced an enthralling encounter. Worcestershire needed a captain's innings from Neale for their two batting points as Surridge emphasised his complete recovery from pre-season surgery, and later in the day and next morning Inchmore exploited the inconsistent bounce at one end to give Worcestershire a lead of 64. With Childs suffering from flu, Graveney shouldered the responsibility of the bowling with no mean skill and Worcestershire would have foundered but for Younis' fluent 84. Requiring 249 for victory, at tea on the third day it seemed as if Gloucestershire would win easily. They were then 171 for three with Zaheer in complete control, having put on 65 in seventeen overs with Bainbridge. However, both departed immediately afterwards, the bowlers quickly regained control, and although Childs was summoned from his sick-bed, Worcestershire won in the penultimate over.

Worcestershire

G. M. Turner b Surridge	4	– lbw b Surridge	0
J. A. Ormrod c and b Surridge	27	– (7) b Graveney	10
D. N. Patel run out	30	– (2) b Graveney	47
Younis Ahmed b Bainbridge	3	– c and b Graveney	84
*P. A. Neale b Surridge	61	– (3) c and b Shepherd	4
E. J. O. Hemsley lbw b Shepherd	22	– (5) c Stovold b Graveney	0
†D. J. Humphries c Bainbridge b Surridge	33	– (6) c Sadiq b Graveney	0
J. D. Inchmore c Shepherd b Surridge	9	– (9) c Stovold b Graveney	9
N. Gifford lbw b Graveney	11	– (8) not out	10
A. P. Pridgeon c Stovold b Graveney	2	– c Stovold b Graveney	6
S. P. Perryman not out	0	– c Brassington b Shepherd	0
B 5, l-b 14, w 1	20	B 4, l-b 10	14
1/4 2/52 3/55 4/85 5/124 6/173 7/185 8/208 9/219	222	1/2 2/29 3/100 4/100 5/100 6/154 7/157 8/169 9/179	184

Bonus points – Worcestershire 2, Gloucestershire 4.

Bowling: *First Innings*—Surridge 28–4–78–5; Shepherd 19–3–55–1; Bainbridge 10–4–23–1; Childs 20–7–40–0; Graveney 8.2–4–6–2. *Second Innings*—Surridge 15–6–33–1; Shepherd 31.3–8–77–2; Bainbridge 7–2–23–0; Graveney 25–12–37–7.

Gloucestershire

A. W. Stovold c Neale b Inchmore	27 – b Inchmore	1
B. C. Broad lbw b Pridgeon	16 – c Neale b Patel	40
Sadiq Mohammad c Gifford b Perryman	36 – c Gifford b Perryman	18
Zaheer Abbas c Hemsley b Inchmore	0 – lbw b Pridgeon	91
P. Bainbridge b Inchmore	2 – b Patel	14
†A. J. Brassington b Inchmore	2 – (9) c Patel b Pridgeon	5
A. J. Hignell lbw b Perryman	13 – (6) c Gifford b Patel	23
J. N. Shepherd c Turner b Inchmore	33 – (7) lbw b Patel	16
*D. A. Graveney c Turner b Inchmore	8 – (8) b Pridgeon	13
J. H. Childs b Inchmore	0 – c Gifford b Pridgeon	1
D. Surridge not out	0 – not out	2
B 6, l-b 13, w 1, n-b 1	21 B 4, l-b 5, n-b 4	13
1/41 2/57 3/57 4/69 5/77 6/107 7/128 8/152 9/157	158 1/3 2/29 3/106 4/171 5/171 6/202 7/215 8/229 9/233	237

Bonus points – Gloucestershire 1, Worcestershire 4.

Bowling: *First Innings*—Pridgeon 23–6–46–1; Inchmore 24–7–53–7; Perryman 8–2–27–2; Gifford 3–1–11–0. *Second Innings*—Pridgeon 22.2–6–56–4; Inchmore 17–2–51–1; Perryman 12–3–36–1; Gifford 27–6–62–0; Patel 21–12–19–4.

Umpires: M. J. Kitchen and W. E. Alley.

At Hastings, May 19, 20, 21. GLOUCESTERSHIRE lost to SUSSEX by seven wickets.

At Swansea, May 29, 31, June 1. GLOUCESTERSHIRE drew with GLAMORGAN.

GLOUCESTERSHIRE v LANCASHIRE

At Gloucester, June 2, 3, 4. Drawn. Gloucestershire 4 pts, Lancashire 7 pts. Zaheer's achievement of equalling Walter Hammond's world record by completing separate hundreds in a match for the seventh time was the main feature of this tame draw. Zaheer, still suffering from the after-effects of a virus infection, found little support, other than from Sadiq, in a first innings which was abruptly ended by Croft, who was far too quick for the tailenders. Against an attack with little to offer but accuracy, Fowler and David Lloyd were so restrained in making their centuries that Lancashire only just managed three batting points before Hughes provided some much-needed acceleration. Although Gloucestershire lost two wickets clearing the deficit, their Pakistani batsmen ended any thoughts of defeat, putting on 162 in two hours. And an hour's interruption for bad light on the third afternoon removed all hopes of a declaration. Zaheer gave his wicket away after hitting a celebratory six to mark his 93rd century.

Gloucestershire

A. W. Stovold c and b Folley	12 – c D. Lloyd b McFarlane	30
B. C. Broad b McFarlane	0 – lbw b Croft	29
Sadiq Mohammad c Kennedy b Abrahams	43 – c Croft b Abrahams	91
Zaheer Abbas not out	162 – c and b Abrahams	107
P. Bainbridge b D. Lloyd	15 – b Kennedy	39
A. J. Hignell c Fowler b Abrahams	12 – not out	38
J. N. Shepherd b Croft	10 – not out	8
*D. A. Graveney b Croft	0	
†A. J. Brassington c Abrahams b Croft	1	
J. H. Childs c Scott b Croft	0	
D. Surridge b McFarlane	3	
B 1, l-b 5, n-b 3	9 B 3, l-b 1, w 2, n-b 2	8
1/4 2/14 3/121 4/168 5/217 6/248 7/248 8/258 9/258	267 1/45 2/64 3/226 4/277 5/329	(5 wkts) 350

Bonus points – Gloucestershire 3, Lancashire 4.

Bowling: *First Innings*—Folley 6–0–26–1; McFarlane 12.5–1–62–2; Croft 10–0–39–4; Reidy 6–2–19–0; Abrahams 20–1–52–2; D. Lloyd 16–2–60–1. *Second Innings*—Croft 11–1–37–1; McFarlane 8–2–31–1; D. Lloyd 13–3–46–0; Folley 9–0–25–0; Reidy 7–0–41–0; Abrahams 31–6–77–2; Hughes 16–3–57–0; Kennedy 7–2–17–1; Fowler 5–2–11–0.

Lancashire

A. Kennedy c Brassington b Shepherd	0
G. Fowler c and b Graveney	100
D. Lloyd b Bainbridge	108
*C. H. Lloyd c Stovold b Surridge	44
D. P. Hughes not out	66
J. Abrahams b Bainbridge	33
B. W. Reidy not out	1
B 5, l-b 14, w 1, n-b 3	23
1/2 2/184 3/248 4/281 5/369 (5 wkts dec.)	375

I. Folley, †C. J. Scott, C. E. H. Croft and L. L. McFarlane did not bat.

Bonus points – Lancashire 3, Gloucestershire 1 (Score at 100 overs: 255-3).

Bowling: Shepherd 32–11–82–1; Surridge 30–10–81–1; Bainbridge 28–8–84–2; Childs 15–2–54–0; Graveney 14–1–51–1.

Umpires: R. Palmer and D. Archer.

GLOUCESTERSHIRE v DERBYSHIRE

At Gloucester, June 5, 7, 8. Drawn. Gloucestershire 5 pts, Derbyshire 6 pts. Derbyshire's ninth-wicket pair played safely through the last ten overs of a match which came to life after heavy rain had forced its way through the covers. Prior to that, a placid pitch had produced consistent scoring from the time that Wood put Gloucestershire in. Romaines deputised ably for the injured Broad. Kirsten's nimble stroke-making saw Derbyshire to maximum batting points for the first time in the season, Hampshire proving a sound partner in a third-wicket partnership of 123 in two hours; and although Wood declared 53 runs behind, by the close of the second day he must have scented victory when Gloucestershire, disrupted by injury and illness, had lost five for 117. Then came the rain, which delayed the resumption on the third day until two o'clock. Moir worked his way through the rest of the Gloucestershire batting, but Derbyshire were left only 140 minutes in which to score 248 f r victory. On a drying pitch they lost wickets steadily to Childs and Graveney before Hill and Taylor settled for the draw.

Gloucestershire

A. W. Stovold c Wood b Oldham	60	– c Miller b Oldham	0
P. W. Romaines c Barnett b Moir	20	– c Hill b Kirsten	25
Sadiq Mohammad c Hill b Miller	85	– (6) st Taylor b Moir	33
Zaheer Abbas b Kirsten	30	– b Miller	4
P. Bainbridge c Hill b Kirsten	34	– (8) not out	23
A. J. Hignell not out	52	– (3) b Miller	23
J. N. Shepherd not out	57	– (5) c and b Kirsten	28
*D. A. Graveney (did not bat)		– (7) c and b Moir	28
†A. J. Brassington (did not bat)		– c Wood b Kirsten	14
J. H. Childs (did not bat)		– c Barnett b Moir	0
D. Surridge (did not bat)		– c Hampshire b Moir	6
B 4, l-b 6, w 1, n-b 5	16	L-b 3, n-b 7	10
1/63 2/110 3/196 4/216 5/262 (5 wkts dec.)	354	1/0 2/45 3/49 4/87 5/92 6/143 7/150 8/177 9/180	194

Bonus points – Gloucestershire 4, Derbyshire 2 (Score at 100 overs: 332-5).

Bowling: *First Innings*—Oldham 10–2–28–1; Tunnicliffe 11–2–40–0; Miller 34–14–76–1; Moir 27–7–94–1; Wood 4–1–22–0; Kirsten 14–1–51–2; Barnett 5–0–27–0. *Second Innings*—Oldham 7–0–28–1; Tunnicliffe 8–2–29–0; Miller 19–7–46–2; Moir 23.2–11–46–4; Kirsten 10–3–25–3; Barnett 3–0–10–0.

Derbyshire

*B. Wood b Shepherd	10	(2) run out	4
J. G. Wright c Shepherd b Graveney	36	(1) c Hignell b Childs	40
P. N. Kirsten lbw b Childs	143	c Zaheer b Graveney	11
J. H. Hampshire c Romaines b Childs	52	c Bainbridge b Childs	40
G. Miller not out	38	b Childs	0
A. Hill not out	7	(9) not out	1
C. J. Tunnicliffe (did not bat)	–	(6) b Graveney	40
D. G. Moir (did not bat)	–	(7) st Brassington b Graveney	4
K. J. Barnett (did not bat)	–	(8) c and b Graveney	6
*R. W. Taylor (did not bat)	–	not out	4
B 5, l-b 5, n-b 5	15	L-b 6, n-b 1	7
1/11 2/80 3/203 4/282 (4 wkts dec.)	301	1/33 2/55 3/59 4/60 5/119 6/137 7/151 8/153 (8 wkts)	157

S. Oldham did not bat.

Bonus points – Derbyshire 4, Gloucestershire 1.

Bowling: *First Innings*—Shepherd 11–4–34–1; Surridge 20–8–41–0; Childs 30–7–94–2; Sadiq 2–1–4–0; Graveney 32.1–4–99–1; Bainbridge 3–0–14–0. *Second Innings*—Surridge 2–0–22–0; Shepherd 6–1–15–0; Childs 19.5–6–64–3; Graveney 15–4–49–4.

Umpires: R. Palmer and D. Archer.

At Worcester, June 9, 10, 11. GLOUCESTERSHIRE drew with WORCESTERSHIRE.

At The Oval, June 12, 14, 15. GLOUCESTERSHIRE lost to SURREY by five wickets.

At Bristol, June 19, 20, 21. GLOUCESTERSHIRE drew with INDIANS (See Indian tour section).

At Bath, June 23, 24, 25. GLOUCESTERSHIRE drew with SOMERSET.

GLOUCESTERSHIRE v HAMPSHIRE

At Bristol, June 26, 28, 29. Gloucestershire won by four wickets. Gloucestershire 16 pts. Gloucestershire's first Championship win of the season was gained in unusual circumstances. With no play possible until after four o'clock on the second day, the captains decided to forfeit first innings and play for 16 points. Had the match started twenty minutes later, they would have had to play a single-innings game for 12 points as per regulations. It then looked as if the game might end in record time. Hampshire, having decided to bat on a damp pitch, found themselves 21 for five in no time at all as Stephenson marked his home début with some lively bowling. Surridge supported him with unstinting accuracy. However, Marshall and Parks ensured the match would run into the final day, though the start of this was delayed by rain and play eventually continued into the evening session. Gloucestershire, needing only 100, were given a lively start by Stovold, but after that the batsmen became over-cautious, and so played into the hands of the bowlers. Cowley's off-breaks were treated with enormous respect, and it needed some sensible aggression from Shepherd to settle the issue.

Hampshire

J. M. Rice (did not bat)	– b Surridge	1
V. P. Terry (did not bat)	– lbw b Surridge	9
M. C. J. Nicholas (did not bat)	– b Stephenson	2
T. E Jesty (did not bat)	– c Brassington b Surridge	6
D. R. Turner (did not bat)	– c Brassington b Shepherd	15
*N. E. J. Pocock (did not bat)	– b Stephenson	0
N. G. Cowley (did not bat)	– lbw b Surridge	7
M. D. Marshall (did not bat)	– c Bainbridge b Stephenson	21
†R. J. Parks (did not bat)	– c Hignell b Stephenson	25
J. W. Southern (did not bat)	– b Shepherd	9
K. St J. D. Emery (did not bat)	– not out	1
	B 1, l-b 1, n-b 1	3
	1/3 2/13 3/13 4/20 5/21 6/34 7/46 8/79 9/93	99

Bowling: Stephenson 23–6–48–4; Surridge 19–8–26–4; Shepherd 10.5–5–18–2; Graveney 1–0–4–0.

Hampshire forfeited their first innings.

Gloucestershire

A. W. Stovold (did not bat)	– b Jesty	29
P. W. Romaines (did not bat)	– b Cowley	25
P. Bainbridge (did not bat)	– c Terry b Emery	11
A. J. Hignell (did not bat)	– b Emery	3
E. J. Cunningham (did not bat)	– c Terry b Cowley	5
J. N. Shepherd (did not bat)	– not out	16
F. D. Stephenson (did not bat)	– lbw b Marshall	4
*D. A. Graveney (did not bat)	– not out	2
	L-b 1, w 1, n-b 4	6
	1/38 2/65 3/73 4/78 5/90 6/95	(6 wkts) 101

†A. J. Brassington, J. H. Childs and D. Surridge did not bat.

Bowling: Marshall 10–2–39–1; Emery 12–3–37–2; Jesty 4–2–10–1; Cowley 9.4–7–9–2.

Gloucestershire forfeited their first innings.

Umpires: D. J. Constant and R. Julian.

GLOUCESTERSHIRE v SUSSEX

At Bristol, July 7, 8. Sussex won by an innings and 88 runs. Sussex 23 pts, Gloucestershire 2 pts. Gloucestershire, submitting tamely to persistent pace bowling, lost eighteen wickets on the second and final day of the match. The home batsmen lacked the application shown by Colin Wells, who battled through 84 overs for his unbeaten 100 which put Sussex in a position to dictate the course of the game. Sussex had found it slow going against Childs and Graveney, but the value of Wells's innings was immediately put into perspective when le Roux took two cheap wickets before the close of the first day. Next morning, despite the low bounce and the heat, the South African, ably assisted by Greig and Arnold (on his first outing of the season), had Gloucestershire all out before lunch. When they went in again 238 behind, Stovold was dismissed for a "pair" by le Roux before he retired to rest a groin strain. The steadfast Broad kept one end secure for two hours, but he was poorly supported and Sussex's overwhelming success was rarely in doubt.

Sussex

G. D. Mendis st Brassington b Childs	67	A. C. S. Pigott lbw b Stephenson	18
A. M. Green b Stephenson	29	C. E. Waller c Stovold b Surridge	12
C. M. Wells not out	100	G. G. Arnold not out	0
P. W. G. Parker b Graveney	5	L-b 9	9
*J. R. T. Barclay lbw b Graveney	11		—
†I. J. Gould c Romaines b Graveney	24	1/77 2/113 3/128 (9 wkts dec.)	308
G. S. le Roux lbw b Bainbridge	8	4/162 5/200 6/222	
I. A. Greig b Stephenson	25	7/251 8/291 9/306	

Bonus points – Sussex 3, Gloucestershire 2 (Score at 100 overs: 251-6).

Bowling: Stephenson 17.1–3–45–3; Surridge 15–2–58–1; Bainbridge 14–3–49–1; Childs 34–14–68–1; Graveney 32–12–79–3.

Gloucestershire

A. W. Stovold c and b le Roux	0	– lbw b le Roux	0
B. C. Broad lbw b le Roux	18	– c Barclay b Greig	44
†A. J. Brassington c Waller b le Roux	1	– (9) c Gould b Greig	14
P. W. Romaines lbw b Waller	17	– (3) lbw b Arnold	9
P. Bainbridge c Parker b Greig	4	– (4) c Barclay b Arnold	8
A. J. Hignell c Gould b Arnold	4	– (5) st Gould b Waller	6
E. J. Cunningham c Greig b Arnold	0	– (6) b Barclay	1
F. D. Stephenson lbw b Greig	0	– (7) c Green b Greig	14
*D. A. Graveney b le Roux	16	– (8) b Pigott	20
J. H. Childs b le Roux	0	– not out	11
D. Surridge not out	5	– c Barclay b Greig	9
B 1, l-b 1, w 1, n-b 2	5	L-b 13, n-b 1	14
	—		—
1/0 2/15 3/22 4/26 5/36 6/36 7/37 8/60 9/65	70	1/0 2/15 3/43 4/67 5/80 6/80 7/101 8/121 9/135	150

Bonus points – Sussex 4.

Bowling: *First Innings*—le Roux 11.3–4–15–5; Pigott 2–0–10–0; Arnold 13–8–9–2; Greig 10–2–28–2; Waller 4–3–3–1. *Second Innings*—le Roux 1.5–1–1–1; Arnold 11–5–12–2; Greig 22–5–66–4; Pigott 10–2–29–1; Waller 15–11–20–1; Barclay 3–1–8–1.

Umpires: J. Birkenshaw and K. E. Palmer.

At Bradford, July 10, 12, 13. GLOUCESTERSHIRE beat YORKSHIRE by five wickets.

GLOUCESTERSHIRE v NORTHAMPTONSHIRE

At Bristol, July 17, 19, 20. Northamptonshire won by nine wickets. Northamptonshire 23 pts, Gloucestershire 4 pts. Northamptonshire's first Championship victory of the season was earned by the spin of Willey and Steele, who shared sixteen wickets, and Steele also played a valuable innings when Northants might have lost their grip. The brisk manner in which Stovold and Broad began gave promise of a big Gloucestershire total, but once Steele and Willey were in harness the pattern changed completely, only Sadiq showing the skill necessary to combat the turning ball. Cook, with his third Championship century of the summer, and Larkins were full of positive strokeplay, but on Monday afternoon Sadiq's leg-spinners so bemused the middle-order batsmen that Northamptonshire were in danger of losing their advantage. However, Steele, a formidable No. 8, put the innings back on course. Gloucestershire never looked likely to save the game. Steele, although frequently no-balled for over-stepping, finished with match figures of nine for 148 while Willey was a valuable ally against batsmen too easily pinned to the crease.

Gloucestershire

A. W. Stovold c Sharp b Steele	63	– run out	41
B. C. Broad c Sharp b Willey	28	– c Steele b Griffiths	9
P. W. Romaines c Steele b Willey	2	– b Steele	7
Sadiq Mohammad b Williams	53	– b Steele	50
A. J. Hignell c Larkins b Steele	0	– c Cook b Steele	3
P. Bainbridge c Carter b Steele	25	– c Cook b Steele	12
J. N. Shepherd c Sharp b Willey	13	– c Carter b Willey	17
*D. A. Graveney not out	28	– c Capel b Steele	6
†A. J. Brassington b Willey	1	– lbw b Willey	10
J. H. Childs c Sharp b Williams	0	– not out	18
D. Surridge b Steele	12	– c Cook b Willey	0
L-b 1, w 1, n-b 17	19	B 5, l-b 4, n-b 11	20
1/98 2/100 3/111 4/117 5/166 6/202 7/202 8/208 9/209	244	1/27 2/61 3/66 4/77 5/117 6/149 7/154 8/173 9/173	193

Bonus points – Gloucestershire 2, Northamptonshire 4.

Bowling: *First Innings*—Griffiths 5–1–27–0; Lamb 5–0–21–0; Carter 2–0–17–0; Willey 36–13–74–4; Steele 28–9–77–4; Williams 7–3–9–2. *Second Innings*—Griffiths 8–1–28–1; Lamb 2–1–2–0; Willey 38.3–12–59–3; Steele 44–17–71–5; Williams 6–3–13–0.

Northamptonshire

*G. Cook c and b Graveney	101	– not out	18
W. Larkins b Surridge	92	– c Hignell b Surridge	0
P. Willey c Romaines b Sadiq	33	– not out	21
R. J. Boyd-Moss c and b Graveney	27		
R. G. Williams st Brassington b Graveney	4		
D. J. Capel b Sadiq	1		
R. M. Carter c Bainbridge b Sadiq	7		
D. S. Steele not out	74		
†G. Sharp b Surridge	37		
T. M. Lamb b Surridge	0		
B. J. Griffiths st Brassington b Sadiq	16		
B 1, l-b 4, w 1, n-b 3	9	L-b 1	1
1/175 2/207 3/257 4/261 5/261 6/266 7/287 8/363 9/363	401	1/1	(1 wkt) 40

Bonus points – Northamptonshire 3, Gloucestershire 2 (Score at 100 overs: 263-5).

Bowling: *First Innings*—Surridge 27–7–82–3; Shepherd 28–3–79–0; Childs 27–5–90–0; Graveney 44–14–99–3; Sadiq 18.4–6–42–4. *Second Innings*—Surridge 3–0–9–1; Shepherd 2–0–10–0; Childs 7–3–13–0; Graveney 6–4–7–0.

Umpires: W. L. Budd and C. Cook.

At Nuneaton, July 21, 22, 23. GLOUCESTERSHIRE drew with WARWICKSHIRE.

At Northampton, July 28, 29, 30. GLOUCESTERSHIRE drew with NORTHAMPTON-SHIRE.

At Leicester, July 31, August 2. GLOUCESTERSHIRE lost to LEICESTERSHIRE by an innings and 45 runs.

GLOUCESTERSHIRE v NOTTINGHAMSHIRE

At Cheltenham, August 7, 9, 10. Nottinghamshire won by 106 runs. Nottinghamshire 21 pts, Gloucestershire 4 pts. After losing five of their six previous Championship games, Nottinghamshire returned to form as their off-spinners Hemmings and Such bemused initially and later winkled out the Gloucestershire batsmen. Hemmings enjoyed a match return of nine for 104, while young Such had match figures of seven for 143. Gloucestershire had no off-spinner and were handicapped further by Graveney's inability to bowl because of a back injury. Yet they needed only three bowlers to dismiss their opponents on the first day when, without Hadlee's 64, Nottinghamshire would have been sorely embarrassed. However, when the day ended with Gloucestershire at 94 for seven after 44 overs it was the home side who were up against it. Hemmings saw to it that there was no recovery on the Monday, and when Nottinghamshire batted a second time only Childs posed much of a threat. Gloucestershire were left with more than a day to get 371, and when it was reported that Hemmings might not be able to bowl, because of a badly bruised toe, they appeared to have an outside chance. But wearing one boot larger than the other to protect the injury, Hemmings proved his fitness for the second Test against Pakistan, and he would have returned even better figures but for a lively ninth-wicket stand of 62 between Graveney and Childs, the latter making a career-best 34 not out.

Nottinghamshire

R. T. Robinson b Surridge	43	– (2) b Childs	14
B. Hassan c Brassington b Shepherd	3	– (1) c sub b Surridge	85
D. W. Randall c Sadiq b Surridge	10	– c Stovold b Childs	27
*C. E. B. Rice c Stovold b Childs	34	– c Stovold b Childs	58
J. D. Birch c Graveney b Childs	13	– not out	43
R. J. Hadlee c Brassington b Childs	64	– c Stovold b Childs	3
†B. N. French c Brassington b Shepherd	8	– c Wright b Childs	2
E. E. Hemmings c Stovold b Shepherd	5	– not out	32
K. Saxelby c Romaines b Shepherd	9		
K. E. Cooper c Broad b Childs	1		
P. M. Such not out	0		
L-b 4, w 2, n-b 1	7	B 2, l-b 15, w 1, n-b 2	20
1/7 2/20 3/94 4/94 5/127 6/155 7/181 8/187 9/193	197	1/38 2/83 3/178 4/203 5/217 6/227 (6 wkts dec.)	284

Bonus points – Nottinghamshire 1, Gloucestershire 4.

Bowling: *First Innings*—Surridge 22–8–51–2; Shepherd 25.5–5–86–4; Childs 24–12–53–4. *Second Innings*—Surridge 20–8–37–1; Shepherd 25.5–6–66–0; Childs 38–11–112–5; Sadiq 6–1–22–0; Dudleston 7–0–27–0.

Gloucestershire

B. C. Broad c Hassan b Cooper	11	– (2) c Rice b Hemmings	19
A. W. Stovold c Robinson b Saxelby	16	– (1) c Hassan b Such	58
P. W. Romaines c Hassan b Hemmings	10	– c Hadlee b Hemmings	0
B. Dudleston b Cooper	8	– c Rice b Such	43
Sadiq Mohammad c and b Hemmings	19	– c and b Such	31
A. J. Wright b Such	20	– c Robinson b Such	12
J. N. Shepherd c French b Such	5	– c Hassan b Such	4
†A. J. Brassington c Hassan b Hemmings	2	– b Hemmings	7
J. H. Childs c Hadlee b Hemmings	0	– (10) not out	34
*D. A. Graveney not out	16	– (9) c Hadlee b Saxelby	42
D. Surridge c Such b Hemmings	0	– lbw b Hemmings	0
L-b 4	4	B 4, l-b 10	14
1/18 2/32 3/40 4/46 5/83 6/91 7/92 8/94 9/111	111	1/48 2/48 3/117 4/132 5/156 6/160 7/169 8/201 9/263	264

Bonus points – Nottinghamshire 4.

Bowling: *First Innings*—Saxelby 4–1–11–1; Cooper 12–4–34–2; Hemmings 21.3–8–31–5; Such 13–5–31–2. *Second Innings*—Cooper 10–2–44–0; Such 30–6–112–5; Hemmings 32.5–14–73–4; Saxelby 9–2–21–1.

Umpires: A. Jepson and B. Leadbeater.

GLOUCESTERSHIRE v MIDDLESEX

At Cheltenham, August 11, 12, 13. Drawn. Gloucestershire 6 pts, Middlesex 7 pts. At the end of the first day it seemed as if Gloucestershire might repeat their famous 1980 victory over the champions-elect. Middlesex were then 30 for five, reeling from a fine spell of new-ball bowling by Stephenson, after Gloucestershire's fragile lower order had collapsed to Cowans, who took five wickets for the second successive day. A splendid innings by Broad must have made acting-captain Emburey regret his decision to insert Gloucestershire, and they had reached 227 before the fifth wicket fell and Cowans ran through the tail. On the second morning, Middlesex lost only one further wicket before saving the follow-on and by then Butcher, missed at second slip when 19, was established. Continuing to ride his luck – he was dropped three times in all – he hit a glorious 173 to put Middlesex back in control, his last 71 runs coming in only 47 minutes as he hammered two 6s and nine 4s in that time. The tenth wicket realised 92 before Butcher was last out, providing Shepherd with his 1,000th first-class wicket. Middlesex seemed to be on their way to victory when they took three quick second-innings wickets, but no play was possible until early afternoon on the last day, and further interruptions for rain helped Gloucestershire hold out.

Gloucestershire

A. W. Stovold c Downton b Daniel	27	– c Downton b Cowans	2
B. C. Broad c Butcher b Slack	75	– c Tomlins b Hughes	16
P. W. Romaines c Downton b Hughes	30	– c Downton b Hughes	25
B. Dudleston c Tomlins b Emburey	10	– c Butcher b Hughes	0
A. J. Wright c Tomlins b Cowans	35	– b Edmonds	19
*J. N. Shepherd lbw b Cowans	43	– c Tomlins b Edmonds	24
†R. C. Russell c Downton b Slack	0	– not out	25
F. D. Stephenson lbw b Cowans	0	– c Downton b Daniel	15
D. P. Simpkins lbw b Cowans	0	– not out	1
J. H. Childs not out	10		
D. Surridge b Cowans	2		
B 3, l-b 6, n-b 6	15	B 8, l-b 1, n-b 5	14
1/66 2/129 3/151 4/160 5/227 6/232 7/233 8/233 9/238	247	1/9 2/28 3/28 4/67 5/81 6/109 7/132	(7 wkts) 141

Bonus points – Gloucestershire 2, Middlesex 4.

Bowling: *First Innings*—Cowans 15–6–34–5; Hughes 10–1–36–1; Daniel 10–1–34–1; Edmonds 30–10–62–0; Emburey 14–3–50–1; Slack 6–1–16–2. *Second Innings*—Cowans 4–2–10–1; Daniel 11–3–30–1; Hughes 13–3–35–3; Slack 4–1–5–0; Emburey 11–1–24–0; Edmonds 17–9–23–2.

Middlesex

C. R. Cook b Stephenson	2
W. N. Slack c Russell b Stephenson	7
K. P. Tomlins lbw b Shepherd	8
C. T. Radley lbw b Stephenson	6
R. O. Butcher c Dudleston b Shepherd	173
P. H. Edmonds run out	0
†P. R. Downton c Romaines b Stephenson	6
*J. E. Emburey c Shepherd b Stephenson	35
N. G. Cowans b Shepherd	14
W. W. Daniel lbw b Shepherd	10
S. P. Hughes not out	5
L-b 5, n-b 6	11
1/9 2/14 3/25 4/25 5/26 6/55 7/129 8/162 9/185	277

Bonus points – Middlesex 3, Gloucestershire 4.

Bowling: Stephenson 26–9–69–5; Surridge 25–8–78–0; Shepherd 24.3–8–79–4; Childs 8–0–25–0; Simpkins 2–0–15–0.

Umpires: A. Jepson and B. Leadbeater.

GLOUCESTERSHIRE v ESSEX

At Cheltenham, August 14, 16, 17. Drawn. Gloucestershire 7 pts, Essex 6 pts. McEwan played Essex back into this match after they were in some danger at 59 for four, battling hard early on and then, once Pont had dropped anchor at the other end, going through his full range of strokes. His last 50 runs came in just over an hour. Pont's stubborn half-century and some forthright batting by Turner and Ray East enabled Essex to declare only 19 behind. In their second innings Gloucestershire were dogged but uninspiring. Fletcher gave his spinners plenty of work in the hope of a declaration, but when it came Essex required 256 in 130 minutes. Undeterred, however, they went off at such a rate that when Gooch was out in the seventh over he had scored 44 out of 62 from only 23 balls. After thirteen overs they were 107, but by then five wickets had fallen. McEwan was splendidly caught at mid-wicket, Turner was stumped far from home, and as rain set in Essex gave up the chase.

Gloucestershire

A. W. Stovold c Turner b Acfield	83	– c D. E. East b Lever	13
B. C. Broad c Gooch b Lever	13	– c McEwan b R. E. East	66
P. W. Romaines c Gooch b Lever	6	– c and b Acfield	59
B. Dudleston lbw b Lever	0	– b Acfield	47
Sadiq Mohammad c Gooch b Turner	75	– c D. E. East b Acfield	7
A. J. Wright c and b Turner	43	– c Fletcher b R. E. East	12
J. N. Shepherd not out	67	– c Gooch b R. E. East	14
*D. A. Graveney c Gooch b R. E. East	5	– not out	4
R. J. Doughty c Hardie b R. E. East	6		
†A. J. Brassington c Gooch b Lever	11		
J. H. Childs b Lever	0		
B 3, l-b 6, w 1, n-b 3	13	B 3, l-b 10, n-b 1	14
1/27 2/63 3/67 4/130 5/217 6/228 7/257 8/275 9/322	322	1/27 2/113 3/169 4/193 5/214 6/222 7/236 (7 wkts dec.)	236

Bonus points – Gloucestershire 4, Essex 3 (Score at 100 overs: 308-8).

Bowling: *First Innings*—Lever 22–4–78–5; Phillip 12–1–50–0; Turner 13–3–40–2; R. E. East 24–8–65–2; Acfield 29–5–62–1; Gooch 5–2–14–0. *Second Innings*—Lever 7–2–26–1; Phillip 10–2–28–0; Acfield 35–5–79–3; R. E. East 31.5–3–89–3.

Essex

G. A. Gooch b Doughty	5	– b Shepherd	44
B. R. Hardie c Brassington b Shepherd	10	– not out	30
†D. E. East lbw b Doughty	6	– (6) c Brassington b Graveney	0
*K. W. R. Fletcher lbw b Broad	11	– (7) not out	0
K. S. McEwan c Sadiq b Childs	91	– (3) c Dudleston b Shepherd	13
K. R. Pont b Childs	50		
N. Phillip c Stovold b Childs	6	– (4) c Brassington b Shepherd	7
S. Turner not out	64	– (5) st Brassington b Graveney	11
R. E. East c Shepherd b Graveney	34		
J. K. Lever b Shepherd	5		
D. L. Acfield not out	3		
B 4, l-b 7, w 1, n-b 6	18	L-b 2	2
1/10 2/20 3/29 4/55 5/158 6/172 7/219 8/272 9/287 (9 wkts dec.)	303	1/62 2/78 3/90 4/107 5/107 (5 wkts)	107

Bonus points – Essex 3, Gloucestershire 3 (Score at 100 overs: 256-7).

Bowling: *First Innings*—Shepherd 25.2–9–48–2; Doughty 22–4–70–2; Childs 28–6–88–3; Broad 15–5–23–1; Graveney 21–5–56–1. *Second Innings*—Shepherd 8–1–44–3; Doughty 3–0–33–0; Childs 2–0–23–0; Graveney 3–1–5–2.

Umpires: W. L. Budd and K. Ibadulla.

At Folkestone, August 21, 23, 24. GLOUCESTERSHIRE drew with KENT.

At Bournemouth, August 25, 26, 27. GLOUCESTERSHIRE lost to HAMPSHIRE by eight wickets.

GLOUCESTERSHIRE v SOMERSET

At Bristol, August 28, 30, 31. Drawn. Gloucestershire 3 pts, Somerset 7 pts. Once Somerset had obtained a first-innings lead of 198, largely through the efforts of Rose, Gloucestershire had no option but to play for a draw, and this they comfortably achieved on a pitch which grew slower and easier as the match progressed. Rose hit a 6 and 24 4s in his chanceless, unbeaten 173, which occupied 236 minutes, and his fifth-wicket partnership of 222 with Slocombe was only 13 short of the county record. The poor light at the end of the second day influenced his decision to go for a big advantage rather than declare, but with Botham and Marks away on Test duty he lacked the resources to bowl Gloucestershire out a second time, and this time the home batsmen were in no mood to surrender.

Gloucestershire

A. W. Stovold b Garner	27	– b Richards	37
B. C. Broad c Gard b Moseley	6	– lbw b Richards	65
Sadiq Mohammad c Gard b Dredge	57	– c Popplewell b Roebuck	66
A. J. Hignell lbw b Dredge	72	– c Gard b Lloyds	41
A. J. Wright b Garner	2	– c Felton b Slocombe	65
P. Bainbridge b Lloyds	39	– c Richards b Lloyds	17
J. N. Shepherd run out	8	– not out	24
*D. A. Graveney lbw b Moseley	8		
†A. J. Brassington c Gard b Moseley	10		
J. H. Childs b Moseley	1		
D. Surridge not out	0		
B 1, l-b 6, n-b 3	10	B 7, l-b 4, w 1, n-b 1	13
1/8 2/46 3/167 4/168 5/176 6/187 7/227 8/237 9/239	240	1/72 2/133 3/208 4/218 5/264 6/328 (6 wkts)	328

Bonus points – Gloucestershire 2, Somerset 4.

Bowling: *First Innings*—Garner 22–4–53–2; Moseley 15.2–2–50–4; Dredge 21–8–49–2; Richards 9–4–13–0; Lloyds 23–6–57–1; Popplewell 2–0–8–0. *Second Innings*—Garner 19–6–35–0; Moseley 2–1–5–0; Dredge 11–0–36–0; Lloyds 34–4–118–2; Richards 32–6–79–2; Roebuck 12–1–40–1; Slocombe 1.2–0–2–1.

Somerset

P. M. Roebuck c Brassington b Graveney.	63
J. W. Lloyds c and b Bainbridge	38
I. V. A. Richards c and b Childs	58
N. A. Felton c Sadiq b Graveney	0
P. A. Slocombe b Graveney	78
*B. C. Rose not out	173
N. F. M. Popplewell not out	18
L-b 4, w 2, n-b 4	10
1/71 2/158 3/160 4/168 5/390 (5 wkts dec.)	438

J. Garner, †T. Gard, C. H. Dredge and H. R. Moseley did not bat.

Bonus points – Somerset 3, Gloucestershire 1 (Score at 100 overs: 267-4).

Bowling: Shepherd 30–6–80–0; Surridge 30–6–109–0; Graveney 38–8–116–3; Bainbridge 15–0–53–1; Childs 24–5–70–1.

Umpires: H. D. Bird and D. O. Oslear.

GLOUCESTERSHIRE v GLAMORGAN

At Bristol, September 8, 9, 10. Glamorgan won by four wickets. Glamorgan 21 pts, Gloucestershire 7 pts. Having been outplayed for much of the first two days Glamorgan rallied with great determination to win their first Championship match of the season with five balls to spare. They had almost all the last day to score 315 on a pitch playing easily, but even allowing for the shortcomings of the Gloucestershire attack, it was a commendable effort. Yet at 93 for six in their first innings Glamorgan were in danger of following on until they were rescued by a dour partnership of 70 between Eifion Jones and young Hugh Morris. Doughty's six for 43 was his best for Gloucestershire, who then batted carelessly when a little more application would have set Glamorgan a stiffer target. Ontong celebrated his 27th birthday with six for 50. Glamorgan batted consistently throughout their second innings, and though a late stutter against the admirable Shepherd left them needing 38 from the last nine overs, Eifion Jones settled the match by hitting Doughty for 6.

Gloucestershire

A. W. Stovold c E. W. Jones b Ontong	33	– c Ontong b Barwick	11
B. C. Broad lbw b Ontong	37	– c Morris b Ontong	5
Sadiq Mohammad c and b Ontong	2	– b Ontong	11
A. J. Hignell b Lloyd	2	– c E. W. Jones b Thomas	43
P. Bainbridge c E. W. Jones b Ontong	84	– c sub b Ontong	24
A. J. Wright lbw b Davis	29	– lbw b Ontong	23
J. N. Shepherd c E. W. Jones b Davis	4	– c sub b Ontong	9
*D. A. Graveney c E. W. Jones b Davis	25	– not out	23
†R. C. Russell lbw b Davis	0	– lbw b Ontong	2
R. J. Doughty c Davis b Lloyd	29	– b Thomas	14
J. H. Childs not out	10	– b Davis	18
B 17, l-b 3, w 1, n-b 12	33	B 5, l-b 2, w 1, n-b 12	20
1/75 2/83 3/86 4/92 5/151 6/159 7/221 8/221 9/263	288	1/18 2/19 3/61 4/93 5/114 6/134 7/139 8/142 9/179	203

Bonus points – Gloucestershire 3, Glamorgan 4.

Bowling: *First Innings*—Davis 23–3–69–4; Barwick 6–2–24–0; Ontong 22–5–76–4; Lloyd 26.4–8–72–2; Thomas 3–0–14–0. *Second Innings*—Barwick 15–2–50–1; Ontong 26–8–50–6; Thomas 18–3–62–2; Lloyd 7–1–19–0; Davis 0.5–0–2–1.

Glamorgan

A. Jones c Sadiq b Shepherd	4	– c Sadiq b Graveney	68
A. L. Jones c Hignell b Doughty	2	– c Stovold b Childs	44
D. A. Francis lbw b Shepherd	26	– b Shepherd	63
R. C. Ontong c Russell b Doughty	38	– (5) b Shepherd	3
J. G. Thomas c Childs b Doughty	0	– (7) c Stovold b Shepherd	12
C. J. C. Rowe b Shepherd	4	– (4) c Wright b Sadiq	70
H. Morris b Doughty	11	– (6) not out	21
†E. W. Jones c Bainbridge b Childs	65	– not out	29
*B. J. Lloyd lbw b Doughty	0		
S. R. Barwick c Broad b Doughty	2		
W. W. Davis not out	0		
B 10, l-b 6, w 9	25	B 2, l-b 5, w 1, n-b 1	9
1/6 2/6 3/71 4/72 5/76 6/93 7/163 8/165 9/177	177	1/80 2/136 3/234 4/250 5/257 6/277	(6 wkts) 319

Bonus points – Glamorgan 1, Gloucestershire 4.

Bowling: *First Innings*—Shepherd 30–10–58–3; Doughty 20.2–5–43–6; Bainbridge 19–12–28–0; Childs 13–4–23–1. *Second Innings*—Shepherd 27–8–78–3; Doughty 14.1–2–50–0; Bainbridge 6–1–14–0; Childs 25–6–75–1; Graveney 21–7–47–1; Sadiq 24–7–46–1.

Umpires: C. T. Spencer and P. B. Wight.

I ZINGARI RESULTS, 1982

Matches – 31: Won 11, Lost 8, Drawn 9, Abandoned 3.

May 8	Honourable Artillery Company	Lost by 69 runs
May 9	Staff College, Camberley	Won by six wkts
May 15	Royal Engineers	Lost by five wkts
May 16	Royal Artillery	Won by 95 runs
May 22	Eton Ramblers	Lost by two wkts
May 23	Royal Military Academy, Sandhurst	Abandoned
May 29	Eton College 1st XI	Lost by seven wkts
May 29	Eton College 2nd XI (XXII)	Drawn
June 5	Hurlingham CC	Won by three wkts
June 5	Charterhouse School	Lost by seven wkts
June 6	Lord Porchester's XI	Drawn
June 12	Royal Regiment of Fusiliers	Drawn
June 15	Winchester College	Won by seven wkts
June 19	Guards Brigade CC	Drawn
June 20	Lavinia, Duchess of Norfolk's XI	Lost by 36 runs
June 26	Harrow School	Abandoned
June 26	Hon. H. M. Herbert's XI	Abandoned
July 3	Green Jackets Club	Drawn
July 4	London New Zealand CC	Won by four wkts
July 11	Captain R. H. Hawkins's XI	Lost by 60 runs
July 17	Bradfield Waifs	Drawn
July 17, 18	N. S. Agar's XI	Won by six wkts
July 25	Royal Armoured Corps	Drawn
July 31, August 1	South Wales Hunts XI	Won by ten wkts
August 7	Band of Brothers	Won by 51 runs
August 8	R. Leigh Pemberton's XI	Won by 30 runs
August 21	J. H. Pawle's XI	Lost by six wkts
August 22	Harrow Wanderers	Drawn
August 28	Hampshire Hogs	Drawn
September 5	Rickling Green CC	Won by one wkt
September 11	J. H. Weatherby's XI	Won by six wkts

HAMPSHIRE

President: R. Aird, MC, TD
Chairman: G. Ford, MC
Chairman, Cricket Committee: C. J. Knott
Secretary: A. K. James
Northlands Road, Southampton SO9 2TY
(Telephone: 0703-24155)
Captain: N. E. J. Pocock
Coach: P. J. Sainsbury

Hampshire's commitment to positive cricket saw them finish third in the Schweppes Championship and thus enjoy their best season since 1975. The improvement of 1981 had been meaningful and was further continued with a brand of exciting cricket which produced a series of thrilling finishes and a climb of four places up the table. Without doubt players and supporters would have settled for third place at the start of the season and the team's performance certainly pleased Nick Pocock, an enterprising captain. Yet he was left with a lingering disappointment that Hampshire had not won the Championship.

Pocock cited three games in August – against Sussex, Essex and Worcestershire – which he believed Hampshire could have won. He reasoned that had they done so, the extra points would not only have put more pressure on Middlesex, the eventual champions, but given his own side added impetus. Nevertheless, Pocock had every right to be pleased with what was achieved, both in terms of the quality of Hampshire's cricket and in entertaining the public.

There was no indication at the start of the season that Hampshire would be successful. Pocock missed almost the whole of the first month because of injury, and by the beginning of June Hampshire were propping up the table. However, victories over Surrey at The Oval and Lancashire at Southampton emphasised the strength of their recovery. They beat the Pakistanis at Bournemouth, to record their first success over a touring team for 50 years, and then put themselves in contention for honours by winning four of their next five Championship matches.

Hampshire's good performances in the Championship owed much to the individual achievements of Malcolm Marshall and Trevor Jesty. Marshall, a genuinely fast bowler with a fine, rhythmic action, was the only bowler in the country to take 100 wickets, and his total of 134 wickets broke the record for a 22-match Championship season. In addition, he took five or more wickets in an innings twelve times, the best by a Hampshire bowler since 1963 when Derek Shackleton did so on thirteen occasions. His century against Lancashire furnished evidence of his emergence as an all-rounder.

Marshall's hostile and penetrating bowling was undoubtedly the biggest single factor in Hampshire's high finish, but this in no way detracts from the splendid batting of Jesty, who must be considered unlucky not to have been called up for Test duty. He scored centuries against Pakistan and India, and his total of eight hundreds was the most in a season by a Hampshire batsman since Phil Mead collected ten in 1933. He was the third-highest placed Englishman in the first-class batting averages and he achieved an almost similar ranking in the bowling.

Hampshire's bowling also received a welcome boost from the introduction of Kevin Emery, who took 83 wickets in first-class cricket and represented England B against the touring Pakistanis. To be in partnership with Marshall was an obvious benefit, but his was a splendid achievement. Spin bowling was again not Hampshire's strongest point, although John Southern trebled his haul of wickets from the previous year. Nigel Cowley, an all-rounder, began the season with a century and a career-best bowling return of six for 48, but this form was not maintained. Tim Tremlett often bowled well in a supporting role.

In addition to Jesty, Gordon Greenidge and Mark Nicholas scored over 1,000 runs. Greenidge played a match-winning innings against Surrey at The Oval, but, judged by his own high standards, was not at his consistent best. Nicholas confirmed his promise, being awarded his county cap, as was Bobby Parks, who finished the season with 76 victims, two more than any other wicket-keeper in the country.

Hampshire made no impact in the limited-overs knockout competitions. They lost all four of their Benson and Hedges Cup group matches, while in the NatWest Bank Trophy they began with a victory over Derbyshire before losing in the quarter-finals to Surrey, the eventual winners. They finished sixth in the John Player League.

HAMPSHIRE 1982

[*Bill Smith*

Back row: V. H. Isaacs (*scorer*), M. C. J. Nicholas, K. St J. D. Emery, J. W. Southern, T. M. Tremlett, R. E. Hayward, R. J. Parks. *Front row:* N. G. Cowley, C. G. Greenidge, N. E. J. Pocock (*captain*), T. E. Jesty, J. M. Rice, M. D. Marshall.

HAMPSHIRE RESULTS

All first-class matches – Played 25: Won 10, Lost 7, Drawn 8.

County Championship matches – Played 22: Won 8, Lost 6, Drawn 8.

Bonus points – Batting 48, Bowling 74.

Competition placings – Schweppes County Championship, 3rd; NatWest Bank Trophy, q-f; Benson and Hedges Cup, 5th in Group C; John Player League, 5th eq.

COUNTY CHAMPIONSHIP AVERAGES

BATTING

	Birthplace	*M*	*I*	*NO*	*R*	*HI*	*Avge*
T. E. Jesty[c]	*Gosport*	20	32	5	1,302	135*	48.22
C. G. Greenidge[c]	*St Peter, Barbados*	20	39	8	1,366	183*	44.06
M. C. J. Nicholas[c]	*London*	21	37	6	871	127*	28.09
M. D. Marshall[c]	*St Michael, Barbados*	22	31	3	633	116*	22.60
D. R. Turner[c]	*Chippenham*	14	20	1	425	96	22.36
N. G. Cowley[c]	*Shaftesbury*	20	27	1	571	104	21.96
J. W. Southern[c]	*King's Cross*	16	21	7	300	50*	21.42
N. E. J. Pocock[c]	*Maracaibo, Venezuela*	20	27	0	548	164	20.29
J. M. Rice[c]	*Chandler's Ford*	21	40	4	728	69	20.22
R. E. Hayward	*Hillingdon*	4	6	0	102	59	17.00
R. J. Parks[c]	*Cuckfield*	22	29	4	334	44	13.36
V. P. Terry	*Osnabruck, WG*	3	5	2	35	16*	11.66
T. M. Tremlett	*Wellington, Som.*	14	20	3	190	48	11.17
S. J. Malone	*Chelmsford*	3	5	2	13	4	4.33
K. St J. D. Emery	*Swindon*	21	26	15	37	18*	3.36

Also batted: M. J. Bailey (*Cheltenham*) (1 match) 3.

**Signifies not out.* [c] *Denotes county cap.*

BOWLING

	O	*M*	*R*	*W*	*Avge*	*BB*
M. D. Marshall	822	225	2,108	134	15.73	8-71
T. E. Jesty	279.1	86	730	34	21.47	6-71
K. St J. D. Emery	598	146	1,731	78	22.19	6-51
J. W. Southern	350.1	96	1,024	44	23.27	5-51
T. M. Tremlett	299.3	89	665	24	27.70	5-59
N. G. Cowley	244.4	69	734	20	36.70	6-48

Also bowled: M. J. Bailey 18–4–76–2; S. J. Malone 58–12–194–6; N. E. J. Pocock 12.5–1–55–0; J. M. Rice 36.3–4–139–2; D. R. Turner 1–0–1–0.

HUNDREDS

The following twelve three-figure innings were played for Hampshire in County Championship matches – T. E. Jesty (6) 135* v Glamorgan (Portsmouth), 106 v Essex (Chelmsford), 123 v Worcestershire (Southampton), 121 v Gloucestershire (Bournemouth), 109 v Yorkshire (Bournemouth), 134 v Warwickshire (Southampton); C. G. Greenidge (2) 157* v Glamorgan (Cardiff), 183* v Glamorgan (Portsmouth); N. G. Cowley (1) 104 v Leicestershire (Southampton); M. D. Marshall (1) 116* v Lancashire (Southampton); M. C. J. Nicholas (1) 127* v Sussex (Basingstoke); N. E. J. Pocock (1) 164 v Lancashire (Southampton).

HAMPSHIRE v LEICESTERSHIRE

At Southampton, May 5, 6, 7. Drawn. Hampshire 8 pts, Leicestershire 7 pts. Leicestershire lost Balderstone and Gower cheaply, but Davison was in splendid form. He failed by just 1 run to score a hundred before lunch and went on to score 172 (one 6 and 27 4s) before he was last out. Tolchard, with 24, was the next highest scorer. Emery bowled well on his début, but Hampshire's most successful bowler was Jesty, who took six wickets in an innings for the sixth time in his career. A wet outfield delayed the start of the second day, when Leicestershire grabbed the initiative by removing seven men for 165. However, Hampshire were rallied by Cowley, dropped at 59, and Parks, who produced an eighth-wicket partnership of 121 in 26 overs. Cowley took 143 minutes over his second century in six seasons, hitting two 6s, a 5 and fourteen 4s. On the third day, Hampshire opened the door to possible victory by taking four quick wickets after lunch when Leicestershire, at 178 for seven, led by only 152 with 158 minutes left. Cowley, the off-spinner, returned career-best figures of six for 48, but Hampshire found the task of scoring 195 in 95 minutes too tough a task.

Leicestershire

J. C. Balderstone c Hayward b Marshall	6	– c Marshall b Cowley	40
J. F. Steele c Parks b Jesty	19	– lbw b Jesty	22
D. I. Gower c Parks b Emery	5	– lbw b Jesty	15
B. F. Davison c Terry b Emery	172	– b Cowley	29
N. E. Briers c Parks b Marshall	7	– c Parks b Southern	18
*R. W. Tolchard lbw b Jesty	24	– b Cowley	6
†M. A. Garnham lbw b Jesty	5	– not out	38
A. M. E. Roberts b Jesty	0	– c Rice b Cowley	18
N. G. B. Cook c Greenidge b Jesty	4	– b Cowley	4
J. P. Agnew b Jesty	18	– c Rice b Cowley	4
L. B. Taylor not out	0	– run out	2
B 4, l-b 9, w 1, n-b 7	21	B 8, l-b 10	18
1/13 2/24 3/84 4/127 5/210 6/222 7/230 8/237 9/279	281	1/60 2/82 3/92 4/142 5/144 6/156 7/178 8/201 9/211	214

Bonus points – Leicestershire 3, Hampshire 4.

Bowling: *First Innings*—Marshall 20–6–56–2; Emery 25.3–4–84–2; Jesty 27–6–71–6; Rice 10–0–49–0. *Second Innings*—Marshall 21.4–6–44–0; Emery 11–6–16–0; Rice 7–3–18–0; Jesty 12–4–31–2; Cowley 24–10–48–6; Southern 15–8–39–1.

Hampshire

C. G. Greenidge c Briers b Cook	26	– not out	40
J. M. Rice c Garnham b Taylor	5	– lbw b Taylor	18
V. P. Terry lbw b Taylor	5	– not out	16
*T. E. Jesty c Davison b Agnew	31		
D. R. Turner c Davison b Roberts	22		
R. E. Hayward c Tolchard b Agnew	9		
N. G. Cowley b Briers	104		
M. D. Marshall b Taylor	15		
†R. J. Parks c Balderstone b Agnew	44		
J. W. Southern not out	6		
K. St J. D. Emery not out	0		
B 17, l-b 8, n-b 9	34	L-b 3, n-b 4	7
1/12 2/40 3/92 4/93 5/120 6/131 7/165 8/286 9/298	(9 wkts dec.) 301	1/48	(1 wkt) 81

Bonus points – Hampshire 4, Leicestershire 4.

Bowling: *First Innings*—Roberts 22–7–52–1; Taylor 20–7–63–3; Agnew 17.3–2–73–3; Cook 17–3–42–1; Steele 6–0–26–0; Briers 3–0–11–1. *Second Innings*—Roberts 8–3–23–0; Taylor 8–0–33–1; Agnew 2–0–14–0; Cook 1–0–4–0.

Umpires: W. E. Alley and K. E. Palmer.

At Oxford, May 12, 13, 14. HAMPSHIRE beat OXFORD UNIVERSITY by an innings and 62 runs.

At Trent Bridge, May 19, 20, 21. HAMPSHIRE lost to NOTTINGHAMSHIRE by 272 runs.

At Southampton, May 29, 30, 31. HAMPSHIRE lost to INDIANS by three wickets (See Indian tour section).

HAMPSHIRE v KENT

At Bournemouth, June 2, 3, 4. Kent won by six wickets. Kent 23 pts, Hampshire 5 pts. Hampshire fell away badly after Greenidge and Rice, who was easily top scorer, had given them a useful start. However, Kent also ran into trouble, losing Woolmer, Taylor and Potter for 30 runs before Aslett and Cowdrey, captaining the side, shored up the innings with a fourth-wicket partnership of 136. An excellent half-century by Knott then saw Kent establish a lead of 116 on first innings. Thanks to an unbeaten 52 by Jesty, Hampshire ended the second day at 148 for four, but next morning he fell first ball to Underwood, who made all the Hampshire batsmen struggle and finished with seven for 79. Kent knocked off the runs for the loss of four wickets, but with the pitch taking spin they could have struggled if faced with a bigger target.

Hampshire

C. G. Greenidge c Potter b Jarvis	22	– lbw b Jarvis	33
J. M. Rice b Penn	60	– lbw b Jarvis	0
M. C. J. Nicholas c Baptiste b Jarvis	5	– c Cowdrey b Underwood	20
T. E. Jesty c Woolmer b Underwood	2	– b Underwood	52
*N. E. J. Pocock b Jarvis	7	– c Woolmer b Underwood	6
N. G. Cowley st Knott b Underwood	26	– c Hinks b Underwood	20
M. D. Marshall b Baptiste	14	– c Taylor b Baptiste	32
T. M. Tremlett b Underwood	0	– c Knott b Underwood	2
†R. J. Parks lbw b Baptiste	6	– not out	14
J. W. Southern lbw b Baptiste	0	– c Aslett b Underwood	8
K. St J. D. Emery not out	0	– c Aslett b Underwood	0
B 1, l-b 6, n-b 9	16	B 1, l-b 14, w 1, n-b 18	34
1/56 2/86 3/101 4/101 5/121 6/143 7/148 8/154 8/155	158	1/1 2/62 3/88 4/98 5/146 6/167 7/194 8/196 9/220	221

Bonus points – Hampshire 1, Kent 4.

Bowling: *First Innings*—Jarvis 16–6–46–3; Baptiste 11.3–1–41–3; Underwood 23–11–45–3; Penn 5–1–10–1. *Second Innings*—Jarvis 20–7–53–2; Baptiste 14–7–27–1; Penn 9–3–21–0; Underwood 32.2–6–79–7; Aslett 2–0–7–0.

Kent

R. A. Woolmer lbw b Marshall	10	– c and b Southern	32
N. R. Taylor b Emery	16	– c Parks b Marshall	3
L. Potter b Marshall	0	– lbw b Cowley	54
D. G. Aslett b Cowley	80	– not out	11
*C. S. Cowdrey c Parks b Emery	49	– c Rice b Southern	4
S. G. Hinks c Tremlett b Marshall	1	– not out	2
†A. P. E. Knott c Emery b Marshall	65		
E. A. Baptiste lbw b Marshall	7		
C. Penn lbw b Southern	2		
D. L. Underwood c Cowley b Southern	9		
K. B. S. Jarvis not out	3		
B 16, l-b 9, w 1, n-b 6	32		
1/22 2/26 3/30 4/166 5/179 6/186 7/199 8/222 9/254	274	1/7 2/89 3/89 4/95	(4 wkts) 106

Bonus points – Kent 3, Hampshire 4.

Bowling: *First Innings*—Marshall 31.2–10–84–5; Emery 13–3–45–2; Jesty 10–4–12–0; Tremlett 8–3–11–0; Southern 28–9–77–2; Cowley 4–0–13–1. *Second Innings*—Marshall 4–1–9–1; Emery 3–0–9–0; Southern 14–4–42–2; Cowley 14–2–46–1.

Umpires: M. J. Kitchen and J. van Geloven.

At The Oval, June 5, 7, 8. HAMPSHIRE beat SURREY by 3 runs.

HAMPSHIRE v LANCASHIRE

At Southampton, June 9, 10, 11. Hampshire won by ten wickets. Hampshire 24 pts, Lancashire 5 pts. Marshall, capturing four wickets as Lancashire slumped to 77 for five, made an early impression on a match in which he was to make significant contributions. Only through the experience of Hughes and Simmons, who made his first fifty of the season, did Lancashire rally to relative respectability. Hampshire, too, made a bad start, losing Greenidge, Rice and Jesty for 21, but Pocock, the captain, swung the game their way in a fifth-wicket partnership of 171 with the reliable Cowley. Pocock saw Hampshire reach 312 before he was sixth out for a career-best 164, made in 280 minutes and containing 24 4s, whereupon the innings was dominated by Marshall, whose first century for Hampshire featured four 6s and thirteen 4s. Lancashire, facing a deficit of 248, soon lost their openers, but David Lloyd led a determined fight-back, batting 284 minutes for his hundred, and sharing century stands with Clive Lloyd and Hughes. However, his departure triggered a collapse and Hampshire were left to score 112 for victory in eighteen overs – a target they achieved with eight balls to spare.

Lancashire

I. Cockbain c Parks b Tremlett	31	– c Parks b Emery	15
G. Fowler c Pocock b Marshall	2	– c Tremlett b Marshall	6
D. Lloyd c Rice b Marshall	0	– b Jesty	112
*C. H. Lloyd c Southern b Marshall	11	– (5) lbw b Marshall	60
D. P. Hughes c Rice b Jesty	40	– (6) b Cowley	65
J. Abrahams b Marshall	0	– (4) b Marshall	17
B. W. Reidy c Parks b Emery	15	– not out	33
†C. Maynard b Jesty	20	– c Parks b Emery	1
J. Simmons c Rice b Marshall	50	– b Emery	27
C. E. H. Croft c Parks b Emery	18	– run out	1
L. L. McFarlane not out	4	– lbw b Jesty	0
L-b 5, n-b 14	19	B 7, l-b 8, w 2, n-b 5	22
1/23 2/23 3/40 4/70 5/77 6/103 7/128 8/145 9/190	210	1/24 2/28 3/67 4/185 5/292 6/296 7/301 8/347 9/358	359

Bonus points – Lancashire 2, Hampshire 4.

Bowling: *First Innings*—Marshall 18.1–7–48–5; Emery 20–5–55–2; Tremlett 15–8–22–1; Jesty 18–5–56–2; Southern 2–0–10–0. *Second Innings*—Marshall 32–9–108–3; Emery 26–7–71–3; Cowley 26–11–54–1; Jesty 16.3–5–42–2; Southern 17–4–62–0.

Hampshire

C. G. Greenidge b McFarlane	9	– not out	62
J. M. Rice c Abrahams b Croft	4	– not out	50
M. C. J. Nicholas lbw b Simmons	31		
T. E Jesty c Hughes b Croft	2		
*N. E. J. Pocock c Reidy b HughesHughes	164		
N. G. Cowley c C. H. Lloyd b Hughes	71		
M. D. Marshall not outout	116		
T. M. Tremlett c Abrahams b Hughes	2		
†R. J. Parks run out	28		
J. W. Southern not out	16		
B 3, l-b 6, w 1, n-b 5	15	L-b 2, w 1	3
1/11 2/17 3/21 4/90 5/261 6/312 7/334 8/438	(8 wkts dec.) 458		(no wkt) 115

K. St J. D. Emery did not bat.

Bonus points – Hampshire 4, Lancashire 3 (Score at 100 overs: 338-7).

Bowling: *First Innings*—Croft 27–3–102–2; McFarlane 23–3–102–1; Reidy 18–6–58–0; Simmons 22–6–53–1; D. Lloyd 8–1–36–0; Abrahams 7–0–29–0; Hughes 14–0–63–3. *Second Innings*—Croft 8.4–0–62–0; McFarlane 5–0–36–0; Simmons 3–0–14–0.

Umpires: C. Cook and A. G. T. Whitehead.

At Bath, June 19, 21, 22. HAMPSHIRE drew with SOMERSET.

HAMPSHIRE v SUSSEX

At Basingstoke, June 23, 24, 25. Drawn. Hampshire 4 pts. After rain prevented any play on the first day, both sides showed enterprise on the second. Having been put in, Hampshire lost Terry at 1, but Rice and Nicholas prospered in a second-wicket stand which harvested 196 in 66 overs. Nicholas was unbeaten on 127, a Championship best which contained a 6 and 21 4s, when Hampshire declared. Marshall removed Heath and Parker in three deliveries as Sussex lost wickets cheaply, but they played their part towards making a game of it by declaring 96 behind, before taking Hampshire's first second-innings wicket at 4. However, further rain thwarted the efforts of both sides, washing out the third day completely.

Hampshire

J. M. Rice c and b Waller	60	– c Gould b le Roux	2
V. P. Terry c Gould b le Roux	0	– not out	5
M. C. J. Nicholas not outout	127	– not out	0
T. E. Jesty not out	5		
B 4, l-b 5, n-b 1	10	L-b 1	1
1/1 2/197 (2 wkts dec.)	202	1/4 (1 wkt)	8

D. R. Turner, *N. E. J. Pocock, N. G. Cowley, M. D. Marshall, T. M. Tremlett, †R. J. Parks and K. St J. D. Emery did not bat.

Bonus points – Hampshire 2.

Bowling: *First Innings*—le Roux 6–3–11–1; Pigott 7–2–30–0; Greig 10–3–26–0; Waller 23–5–60–1; Barclay 18.2–6–50–0; Wells 5–0–15–0. *Second Innings*—le Roux 4–1–5–1; Pigott 3–2–2–0.

Sussex

G. D. Mendis b Emery	5	I. A. Greig not out	18
J. R. P. Heath lbw b Marshall	19	C. P. Phillipson not out	4
C. M Wells lbw b Marshall	20	B 6, l-b 6, n-b 1	13
P. W. G. Parker c Nicholas b Marshall	0		
†I. J. Gould b Jesty	27	1/13 2/29 3/29 (6 wkts dec.)	106
G. S. le Roux c Parks b Marshall	0	4/67 5/68 6/101	

*J. R. T. Barclay, A. C. S. Pigott and C. E. Waller did not bat.

Bonus points – Hampshire 2.

Bowling: Marshall 16–3–42–4; Emery 8–3–29–1; Jesty 7.5–1–22–1.

Umpires: D. J. Constant and J. Birkenshaw.

At Bristol, June 26, 28, 29. HAMPSHIRE lost to GLOUCESTERSHIRE by four wickets.

At Bournemouth, June 30, July 1, 2. HAMPSHIRE beat PAKISTANIS by six wickets (See Pakistani tour section).

At Maidstone, July 3, 5, 6. HAMPSHIRE beat KENT by 45 runs.

At Cardiff, July 10, 12, 13. HAMPSHIRE beat GLAMORGAN by 116 runs.

HAMPSHIRE v SURREY

At Portsmouth, July 17, 19, 20. Surrey won by two wickets. Surrey 23 pts, Hampshire 5 pts. Hampshire, having been put in on a green wicket, were indebted to the pugnacious Turner, who, playing in the absence of the injured Jesty, shared useful partnerships with Nicholas, Hayward and Pocock before he was sixth out, having batted for 265 minutes and narrowly missed a century. Surrey's consistent reply gave them a lead of 92 before Knight's declaration, and Hampshire had reduced this to 67, with all their wickets intact, by the close. However, they lost Greenidge and Rice to lifting deliveries from Clarke early on Tuesday, and but for an enterprising partnership of 133 in 44 overs from Nicholas and Turner, Surrey's task might have been negligible. They captured five wickets for 9 runs in eight overs to get back in the game, but still needed to get 130 in 50 minutes plus twenty overs for victory. Thanks principally to Thomas and Lynch, they did so with three balls and two wickets to spare.

Hampshire

C. G. Greenidge lbw b Jackman	6	– c Smith b Clarke	8
J. M. Rice lbw b Thomas	11	– c Thomas b Clarke	20
M. C. J. Nicholas lbw b Thomas	21	– lbw b Jackman	81
D. R. Turner c Howarth b Roope	96	– c Richards b Knight	46
R. E. Hayward c Roope b Needham	16	– b Knight	7
*N. E. J. Pocock b Roope	19	– c Richards b Jackman	0
N. G. Cowley lbw b Clarke	22	– lbw b Jackman	0
M. D. Marshall b Thomas	7	– (9) b Jackman	20
†R. J. Parks c Clarke b Jackman	15	– (10) not out	10
T. M. Tremlett not out	9	– (8) lbw b Clarke	11
K. St J. D. Emery not out	1	– c Smith b Clarke	0
B 10, l-b 14, w 4	28	B 6, l-b 10, n-b 2	18
1/25 2/25 3/72 4/125 5/181 6/205 7/222 8/237 9/241 (9 wkts dec.)	251	1/26 2/39 3/172 4/176 5/177 6/179 7/181 8/208 9/213	221

Bonus points – Hampshire 2, Surrey 3 (Score at 100 overs: 241-8).

Bowling: *First Innings*—Clarke 21–5–49–1; Jackman 28–8–66–2; Thomas 22–9–28–3; Knight 12–4–23–0; Needham 9–1–27–1; Roope 13–4–30–2. *Second Innings*—Clarke 23.4–6–53–4; Jackman 23–6–58–4; Knight 19–5–39–2; Roope 6–3–16–0; Butcher 2–0–15–0; Needham 3–0–22–0.

Surrey

A. R. Butcher c Parks b Emery	32	– c Parks b Marshall	9
G. P. Howarth c Greenidge b Rice	46	– b Emery	8
D. M. Smith lbw b Marshall	50	– b Marshall	9
*R. D. V. Knight c Pocock b Tremlett	25	– (5) c Turner b Emery	14
M. A. Lynch c Nicholas b Cowley	35	– (4) lbw b Emery	25
G. R. J. Roope c Rice b Cowley	21	– (7) c Parks b Marshall	5
†C. J. Richards c Turner b Tremlett	28	– (8) c Parks b Marshall	7
D. J. Thomas not out	50	– (6) not out	30
A. Needham not out	25	– (10) not out	1
S. T. Clarke (did not bat)		– (9) b Emery	9
B 3, l-b 13, w 1, n-b 14	31	B 6, l-b 8	14
1/46 2/140 3/154 4/201 5/229 6/237 7/289 (7 wkts dec.)	343	1/18 2/20 3/32 4/64 5/75 6/84 7/102 8/119 (8 wkts)	131

R. D. Jackman did not bat.

Bonus points – Surrey 4, Hampshire 3 (Score at 100 overs: 301-7).

Bowling: *First Innings*—Marshall 23.2–9–66–1; Emery 17–3–60–1; Tremlett 28–8–63–2; Rice 18–1–64–1; Cowley 18–5–59–2. *Second Innings*—Marshall 16.3–1–64–4; Emery 12–0–38–4; Tremlett 4–0–15–0.

Umpires: K. Ibadulla and R. Palmer.

HAMPSHIRE v GLAMORGAN

At Portsmouth, July 21, 22, 23. Hampshire won by an innings and 78 runs. Hampshire 24 pts, Glamorgan 1 pt. On a pitch of uneven bounce, Glamorgan, having chosen to bat, slumped from 76 for one to 103 for seven in seven overs and were dismissed for 164 as Emery returned a career-best six for 51. Yet when Hampshire went in, they took just 28 overs to overhaul Glamorgan, and Greenidge was unbeaten at the close on 108 – his fourth successive century against Glamorgan – in a score of 220 for two. Moreover, Hampshire were to lose no further wickets as they raced to 435 for two in 96 overs before declaring. Greenidge, who completed 1,000 runs for the season, and Jesty shared an unbroken partnership of 251 – a Hampshire record for any wicket against Glamorgan – with Greenidge batting for 320 minutes in all and hitting two 6s and 28 4s. Jesty's unbeaten 135, his first Championship century for two years, took 204 minutes and included a 6 and 22 4s. Glamorgan, needing 271 to avoid an innings defeat, were soon in trouble and were 134 for seven by the close. However, there was resistance from Francis and Lloyd on the final morning, when Hampshire spent 95 minutes taking the three remaining wickets. Emery had match figures of ten for 101.

Glamorgan

A. Jones c Parks b Emery	26	– (6) lbw b Tremlett	6
A. L. Jones c Parks b Emery	53	– c Parks b Emery	11
D. A. Francis c Parks b Marshall	3	– not out	77
R. C. Ontong run out	1	– c Rice b Marshall	0
J. A. Hopkins lbw b Emery	0	– (1) lbw b Tremlett	19
C. J. C. Rowe c Parks b Emery	1	– (5) c Parks b Tremlett	5
†E. W. Jones c Pocock b Emery	0	– c Pocock b Tremlett	7
S. A. B. Daniels b Emery	22	– c Greenidge b Emery	4
*B. J. Lloyd not out	30	– c Jesty b Emery	36
M. A. Nash b Tremlett	15	– c Rice b Emery	0
W. W. Davis lbw b Rice	0	– lbw b Tremlett	10
B 3, l-b 2, w 1, n-b 7	13	B 4, l-b 4, n-b 10	18
1/48 2/76 3/77 4/78 5/80 6/80 7/103 8/123 9/163	164	1/21 2/37 3/38 4/44 5/50 6/64 7/92 8/170 9/174	193

Bonus points – Glamorgan 1, Hampshire 4.

Bowling: *First Innings*—Marshall 19–2–41–1; Emery 22–6–51–6; Jesty 6–1–25–0; Tremlett 9–3–26–1; Rice 1.3–0–8–1. *Second Innings*—Emery 23–10–50–4; Marshall 24–7–43–1; Tremlett 32.3–15–59–5; Cowley 6–1–19–0; Jesty 1–0–4–0.

Hampshire

C. G. Greenidge not out	183
J. M. Rice c Francis b Davis	57
M. C. J. Nicholas c E. W. Jones b Davis	4
T. E. Jesty not out	135
B 19, l-b 11, w 4, n-b 22	56
1/176 2/184 (2 wkts dec.)	435

D. R. Turner, *N. E. J. Pocock, N. G. Cowley, M. D. Marshall, †R. J. Parks, T. M. Tremlett and K. St J. D. Emery did not bat.

Bonus points – Hampshire 4.

Bowling: Nash 14–3–56–0; Davis 23–3–93–2; Ontong 19–3–71–0; Daniels 11–3–58–0; Lloyd 21–3–79–0; Rowe 8–2–22–0.

Umpires: K. Ibadulla and R. Palmer.

HAMPSHIRE v SOMERSET

At Bournemouth, July 31, August 2. Hampshire won by 10 runs. Hampshire 20 pts, Somerset 5 pts. Hampshire gained a remarkable win in two days after seemingly facing certain defeat when Somerset needed only 83 for victory. The 'Big Birds' ruled the first day: Somerset's Joel Garner and the Red Arrows. A nearby display by the RAF team appeared to upset Hampshire's concentration, but Garner disturbed them even more, at one stage taking six wickets for 9 runs in 8.1 overs. Not that Somerset found batting much easier. By the close they led by only 18 with three wickets in hand. The second day saw 23 wickets fall. Initially, Garner cracked an unbeaten 40 to boost Somerset's advantage to 75, and he soon made inroads when Hampshire batted a second time. On a deteriorating pitch, he collected another five wickets while Jesty hit a defiant fifty, finishing with match figures of eleven for 80 as Hampshire were skittled for 157. Somerset's task of scoring 83 seemed a mere formality, but at 38 for two Jesty came on to take four for 8 and, with Marshall bowling throughout, Hampshire took the final wicket off the last ball of the extra ten overs.

Hampshire

C. G. Greenidge c Roebuck b Dredge	24	– c Taylor b Garner	20
J. M. Rice c Taylor b Davis	18	– c Marks b Garner	2
M. C. J. Nicholas c Roebuck b Davis	0	– c Davis b Dredge	2
T. E. Jesty c Felton b Moseley	23	– lbw b Garner	50
D. R. Turner b Garner	15	– c Dredge b Garner	0
*N. E. J. Pocock c Lloyds b Garner	15	– lbw b Davis	20
N. G. Cowley c Lloyds b Garner	16	– c Rose b Marks	26
M. D. Marshall c Dredge b Garner	0	– b Dredge	25
T. M. Tremlett c Marks b Garner	2	– not out	3
†R. J. Parks c Taylor b Garner	0	– b Dredge	5
K. St J. D. Emery not out	0	– c Taylor b Garner	0
L-b 3, n-b 3	6	L-b 2, n-b 2	4
1/47 2/47 3/51 4/72 5/94 6/110 7/110 8/112 9/112	119	1/22 2/23 3/49 4/50 5/85 6/103 7/149 8/149 9/156	157

Bonus points – Somerset 4.

Bowling: *First Innings*—Garner 16.1–7–23–6; Moseley 8–0–18–1; Dredge 16–4–39–1; Davis 10–2–33–2. *Second Innings*—Garner 18.2–5–57–5; Dredge 18–5–40–3; Moseley 7–1–22–0; Davis 5–0–19–1; Marks 6–1–15–1.

Somerset

P. M. Roebuck c Nicholas b Marshall	8	– b Marshall	4
J. W. Lloyds lbw b Emery	12	– c Greenidge b Emery	9
N. A. Felton c Parks b Marshall	20	– c Parks b Jesty	19
*B. C. Rose c Pocock b Emery	21	– c Rice b Marshall	6
P. W. Denning c Turner b Jesty	25	– lbw b Marshall	9
V. J. Marks c Rice b Jesty	20	– b Jesty	0
†D. J. S. Taylor c Parks b Jesty	1	– c Tremlett b Marshall	4
C. H. Dredge c Nicholas b Jesty	8	– c Parks b Marshall	6
M. R. Davis c Greenidge b Marshall	4	– c Greenidge b Jesty	0
J. Garner not out	40	– c Parks b Jesty	2
H. R. Moseley c Parks b Emery	9	– not out	7
B 10, l-b 4, w 2, n-b 10	26	B 2, l-b 4	6
1/15 2/49 3/63 4/96 5/121 6/126 7/127 8/137 9/166	194	1/9 2/13 3/38 4/38 5/39 6/44 7/55 8/58 9/60	72

Bonus points – Somerset 1, Hampshire 4.

Bowling: *First Innings*—Marshall 19–5–47–3; Emery 21–5–53–3; Tremlett 11–3–37–0; Jesty 7–2–31–4. *Second Innings*—Marshall 16–3–37–5; Emery 5–0–21–1; Jesty 10–4–8–4.

Umpires: N. T. Plews and C. T. Spencer.

At Eastbourne, August 7, 9, 10. HAMPSHIRE drew with SUSSEX.

At Chelmsford, August 11, 12, 13. HAMPSHIRE drew with ESSEX.

HAMPSHIRE v WORCESTERSHIRE

At Southampton, August 14, 16, 17. Worcestershire won by one wicket. Worcestershire 21 pts, Hampshire 7 pts. A game of changing fortunes was not settled until the fifth ball of the final over, which Perryman hit for a winning 6. On the first day, Hampshire, put in on a damp pitch, lost five wickets for 18 in ten overs, Webster claiming three in seven balls without cost. However, Jesty led a splendid recovery, scoring his fifth century of the season and so completing 1,000 runs. He batted with skill for 281 minutes, hitting a 6 and twelve 4s, before he was last out. Worcestershire were then shattered by the superb fast bowling of Marshall, who produced career-best figures of eight for 71, and Hampshire were soon extending a first-innings lead of 92. They added 117 in 90 minutes on the third morning before the declaration set Worcestershire a target of 284 in 255 minutes. Thanks to Weston, Ormrod, Patel and Younis, they looked to be cruising to a comfortable victory, and when nine overs remained they needed only 33 with eight wickets in hand. But then seven wickets tumbled, four of them to Southern, and when he began the final over they still needed 7 to win with three wickets in hand. Pridgeon took 2 off the first ball, but was bowled by the next; the third produced a leg-bye; the fourth saw the dismissal of Patel, who had earlier featured in a third-wicket partnership of 145 in 92 minutes; the fifth brought Perryman his moment of glory.

Hampshire

C. G. Greenidge lbw b Pridgeon	3	– c Perryman b Webster	38
J. M. Rice b Pridgeon	1	– lbw b Perryman	39
M. C. J. Nicholas c Humphries b Webster	9	– (4) not out	59
T. E. Jesty b Webster	123	– (5) not out	30
*N. E. J. Pocock c Ormrod b Webster	1		
N. G. Cowley c Humphries b Webster	0		
M. D. Marshall c Patel b Pridgeon	44		
T. M. Tremlett lbw b Webster	6	– (3) c Ormrod b Webster	2
†R. J. Parks c Weston b Gifford	36		
J. W. Southern b Pridgeon	17		
S. J. Malone not out	3		
L-b 14, w 1, n-b 1	16	L-b 18, w 2, n-b 3	23
1/1 2/14 3/16 4/18 5/18 6/101 7/140 8/202 9/239	259	1/67 2/79 3/125 (3 wkts dec.)	191

Bonus points – Hampshire 3, Worcestershire 4.

Bowling: *First Innings*—Pridgeon 29–5–75–4; Webster 23.1–2–87–5; Perryman 11–1–45–0; Gifford 22–9–36–1. *Second Innings*—Pridgeon 16–2–60–0; Perryman 14–5–43–1; Webster 18–6–39–2; Gifford 7–1–26–0.

Worcestershire

M. J. Weston c Parks b Marshall	0 – lbw b Tremlett	49
J. A. Ormrod lbw b Marshall	9 – lbw b Marshall	45
D. N. Patel c Parks b Marshall	30 – c Parks b Southern	89
Younis Ahmed c Tremlett b Marshall	34 – c Pocock b Marshall	59
*P. A. Neale lbw b Jesty	0 – c Tremlett b Southern	2
T. S. Curtis c Nicholas b Marshall	29 – c Greenidge b Southern	3
†D. J. Humphries c Parks b Marshall	0 – b Marshall	5
A. P. Pridgeon b Marshall	5 – (9) b Southern	3
N. Gifford not out	31 – (8) run out	2
A. J. Webster b Malone	0 – not out	0
S. P. Perryman c Greenidge b Marshall	14 – not out	6
L-b 7, w 7, n-b 1	15 B 7, l-b 6, w 9, n-b 1	23
1/4 2/31 3/78 4/83 5/83 6/86 7/107 8/120 9/131	167 1/104 2/106 3/251 4/260 (9 wkts) 5/266 6/271 7/276 8/279 9/280	286

Bonus points – Worcestershire 1, Hampshire 4.

Bowling: *First Innings*—Marshall 22.5–7–71–8; Malone 8–1–36–1; Jesty 10–5–22–1; Tremlett 8–2–23–0. *Second Innings*—Marshall 24–8–57–3; Malone 9–2–25–0; Jesty 5–0–18–0; Tremlett 17–1–65–1; Cowley 6–0–50–0; Southern 8.5–1–48–4.

Umpires: P. J. Eele and A. Jepson.

At Northampton, August 21, 23, 24. HAMPSHIRE drew with NORTHAMPTONSHIRE.

HAMPSHIRE v GLOUCESTERSHIRE

At Bournemouth, August 25, 26, 27. Hampshire won by eight wickets. Hampshire 23 pts, Gloucestershire 7 pts. Gloucestershire's first innings owed much to Dudleston, their assistant-coach and Second XI captain, who shared a fourth-wicket stand of 146 in 32 overs with Hignell. He batted for 258 minutes, hitting two 6s and twelve 4s, before becoming Marshall's 100th wicket of the season. From 244 for three, Gloucestershire slumped to 272 all out, but they soon had Hampshire in trouble at 63 for five. However, Jesty's sixth century of the season, in four hours, rallied the home side. Well supported by Tremlett and Marshall, Jesty's innings was a masterpiece of concentration and technical excellence. He reached his 100 with a 6, the only one in an innings which included nineteen 4s. On a difficult wicket, Gloucestershire encountered immediate problems when they batted again, Marshall taking five wickets for the ninth time in the season, and Hampshire were left to make just 63.

Gloucestershire

A. W. Stovold c Parks b Emery	50 – c Parks b Emery	11
B. C. Broad lbw b Emery	5 – c Pocock b Jesty	25
B. Dudleston lbw b Marshall	111 – b Marshall	9
M. W. Stovold c Parks b Jesty	5 – c Parks b Emery	0
A. J. Hignell c Greenidge b Southern	63 – lbw b Marshall	6
A. J. Wright lbw b Cowley	13 – (7) c Pocock b Marshall	2
J. N. Shepherd b Marshall	4 – (8) c Nicholas b Southern	0
F. D. Stephenson lbw b Marshall	0 – (10) c Parks b Marshall	6
*D. A. Graveney c Greenidge b Southern	1 – not out	8
†A. J. Brassington not out	2 – (6) b Marshall	0
J. H. Childs b Southern	1 – c Marshall b Southern	8
L-b 4, w 3, n-b 10	17 L-b 5, w 4	9
1/17 2/91 3/98 4/244 5/261 6/268 7/268 8/269 9/269	272 1/23 2/39 3/40 4/53 5/53 6/54 7/55 8/59 9/69	84

Bonus points – Gloucestershire 3, Hampshire 4.

Bowling: *First Innings*—Marshall 16–1–48–3; Emery 15–3–75–2; Tremlett 10–5–19–0; Jesty 17–4–41–1; Cowley 11–0–54–1; Southern 11.3–5–18–3. *Second Innings*—Marshall 13–5–33–5; Emery 10–2–25–2; Jesty 5–4–4–1; Southern 7.4–2–13–2.

Hampshire

C. G. Greenidge lbw b Shepherd	28	– not out	37
J. M. Rice b Stephenson	0	– b Stephenson	5
M. C. J. Nicholas b Stephenson	7	– c Childs b Graveney	12
T. E. Jesty c A. W. Stovold b Childs	121	– not out	9
*N. E. J. Pocock lbw b Shepherd	8		
N. G. Cowley c Hignell b Childs	1		
T. M. Tremlett c A. W. Stovold b Graveney	31		
M. D. Marshall b Graveney	54		
†R. J. Parks c Dudleston b Childs	17		
J. W. Southern b Stephenson	11		
K. St J. D. Emery not out	2		
B 5, l-b 7, n-b 2	14	L-b 1	1
1/5 2/31 3/37 4/48 5/63 6/155 7/236 8/280 9/280	294	1/21 2/41	(2 wkts) 64

Bonus points – Hampshire 3, Gloucestershire 4 (Score at 100 overs: 280-9).

Bowling: *First Innings*—Stephenson 25.2–5–67–3; Shepherd 30–9–64–2; Childs 22–4–79–3; Graveney 21–13–29–2; Broad 3–0–16–0; Dudleston 5–1–25–0. *Second Innings*—Stephenson 7–1–25–1; Shepherd 7–3–15–0; Graveney 6–3–6–1; Childs 5.3–1–17–0.

Umpires: W. E. Alley and W. L. Budd.

HAMPSHIRE v YORKSHIRE

At Bournemouth, August 28, 30, 31. Drawn. Hampshire 6 pts, Yorkshire 5 pts. Jesty, with his seventh century of the season, again provided the backbone of the Hampshire innings on a wicket which took spin on the first afternoon. After taking 70 minutes to reach double figures, Turner gave useful assistance, helping Jesty in a fourth-wicket stand of 101. Jesty batted for three and a half hours and hit eighteen 4s. Yorkshire lost two wickets for 17, but Boycott and Hartley patiently launched a recovery before the last eight wickets fell for 51 as Marshall finished with six for 41. Half-centuries by Nicholas and Jesty enabled Hampshire to declare and set Yorkshire a target of 227 in two and threequarter hours on a wearing pitch. It seldom looked on against tight bowling and fielding, but thanks to some brave batting they were just 10 runs short at the close, while Hampshire needed two more wickets.

Hampshire

C. G. Greenidge lbw b Stevenson	8	– lbw b Old	12
J. M. Rice lbw b Illingworth	26	– c Boycott b Old	16
M. C. J. Nicholas b Old	26	– c Lumb b Stevenson	51
T. E. Jesty run out	109	– b Stevenson	58
D. R. Turner b Old	42	– c Bairstow b Stevenson	3
*N. E. J. Pocock c Athey b Carrick	2	– c Hartley b Carrick	0
M. D. Marshall st Bairstow b Carrick	0	– c Sidebottom b Carrick	1
†R. J. Parks b Sidebottom	3	– not out	8
J. W. Southern b Sidebottom	24	– c Old b Carrick	3
M. J. Bailey b Sidebottom	3		
K. St J. D. Emery not out	0		
L-b 6, n-b 6	12	B 2, l-b 6, w 1, n-b 6	15
1/13 2/51 3/99 4/200 5/205 6/209 7/218 8/229 9/252	255	1/15 2/36 3/146 4/150 5/151 6/155 7/155 8/167	(8 wkts dec.) 167

Bonus points – Hampshire 3, Yorkshire 4 (Score at 100 overs: 252-9).

Bowling: *First Innings*—Old 20–5–47–2; Stevenson 11–2–34–1; Sidebottom 16.1–4–36–3; Carrick 36–1–69–2; Illingworth 20–9–57–1. *Second Innings*—Old 11–3–21–2; Stevenson 12–3–35–3; Carrick 25.1–5–58–3; Sidebottom 6–1–15–0; Illingworth 13–5–23–0.

Yorkshire

G. Boycott c Southern b Bailey	72	– lbw b Marshall	24
R. G. Lumb lbw b Emery	0	– b Emery	13
C. W. J. Athey lbw b Marshall	3	– st Parks b Southern	7
S. N. Hartley c Rice b Marshall	51	– (5) not out	45
K. Sharp c Rice b Bailey	4	– (6) c Rice b Southern	39
†D. L. Bairstow lbw b Marshall	0	– (8) c Pocock b Southern	44
P. Carrick b Marshall	25	– (9) st Parks b Southern	5
A. Sidebottom lbw b Marshall	4	– (10) not out	1
C. M. Old b Marshall	10	– (4) c Pocock b Marshall	32
G. B. Stevenson c Rice b Southern	4	– (7) c Jesty b Southern	0
*R. Illingworth not out	2		
B 3, l-b 15, w 2, n-b 1	21	B 5, l-b 1, w 1	7
1/5 2/17 3/145 4/149 5/150 6/150 7/173 8/189 9/190	196	1/23 2/36 3/64 4/85 5/140 6/140 7/204 8/213	(8 wkts) 217

Bonus points – Yorkshire 1, Hampshire 3 (Score at 100 overs: 180-7).

Bowling: *First Innings*—Marshall 32–13–41–6; Emery 25–8–39–1; Southern 32.5–12–60–1; Jesty 6–3–8–0; Bailey 9–3–27–2. *Second Innings*—Marshall 17–1–44–2; Emery 6–1–11–1; Southern 21–2–106–5; Bailey 9–1–49–0.

Umpires: W. E. Alley and J. Birkenshaw.

At Derby, September 1, 2, 3. HAMPSHIRE drew with DERBYSHIRE.

At Uxbridge, September 8, 9, 10. HAMPSHIRE lost to MIDDLESEX by 106 runs.

HAMPSHIRE v WARWICKSHIRE

At Southampton, September 11, 13, 14. Hampshire won by 37 runs. Hampshire 24 pts, Warwickshire 5 pts. Following the early loss of Tremlett, Greenidge and Nicholas added 130 in 29 overs and Greenidge, the dominant partner, seemed set for a century when he gave a return catch to Ferreira. Nicholas had made 67 when, with the total 202, he suffered a depressed fracture of the left cheekbone after being hit by a lifting delivery from Small. Warwickshire were dismissed for 191, with Marshall taking five for 74 and breaking Lance Gibbs's record of 131 wickets for a 22-match Championship. Hampshire added to their lead as Jesty set a post-war Hampshire record by hitting his eighth century of the season, contributing 95 to the 111 runs he and Tremlett put on for the third wicket and reaching his century in 64 minutes. In all he batted for 82 minutes (101 balls) for his 134, which included two 6s and 22 4s. Hampshire's declaration set Warwickshire a target of 377 in 330 minutes, and they were facing defeat at 157 for five. But then Kallicharran and Ferreira put on 115 in fifteen overs for the sixth wicket, Kallicharran becoming the only player to score 2,000 runs in the season. He batted for 221 minutes, hitting a 6 and fourteen 4s, giving rise to Warwickshire's hopes with every stroke until he was seventh out at 311 just before the start of the final twenty overs.

Hampshire

C. G. Greenidge c and b Ferreira	85 – c Smith b Willis	31
T. M. Tremlett c Lloyd b Small	1 – b Asif Din	30
M. C. J. Nicholas retired hurt	67	
T. E. Jesty b Small	35 – c Amiss b Willis	134
D. R. Turner c Lethbridge b Willis	8 – (3) c Lloyd b Sutcliffe	13
*N. E. J. Pocock c Small b Lethbridge	25	
N. G. Cowley b Asif Din	33 – (6) not out	6
M. D. Marshall c Smith b Asif Din	14 – (5) not out	28
†R. J. Parks lbw b Asif Din	3	
J. W. Southern b Sutcliffe	17	
K. St J. D. Emery not out	1	
L-b 4, n-b 13	17	B 8, l-b 4, w 5, n-b 2 19
1/2 2/132 3/193 4/226 5/243 6/268 7/279 8/304 9/306	306	1/45 2/68 3/179 4/226 (4 wkts dec.) 261

Bonus points – Hampshire 4, Warwickshire 4.

Bowling: *First Innings*—Willis 13–4–37–1; Small 10–5–14–2; Ferreira 17–6–62–1; Lethbridge 9–0–46–1; Sutcliffe 32–11–72–1; Asif Din 17.1–5–58–3. *Second Innings*—Small 14–1–61–0; Willis 13–1–46–2; Sutcliffe 20–5–65–1; Ferreira 8–2–32–0; Asif Din 5–0–38–1.

Warwickshire

T. A. Lloyd b Marshall	8 – b Jesty	27
K. D. Smith c Pocock b Marshall	6 – c Greenidge b Tremlett	28
A. I. Kallicharran run out	27 – c Pocock b Emery	131
D. L. Amiss lbw b Marshall	31 – c Jesty b Tremlett	0
†G. W. Humpage c Greenidge b Emery	1 – c Parks b Tremlett	6
Asif Din b Marshall	31 – c Parks b Cowley	20
A. M. Ferreira c Greenidge b Tremlett	23 – b Marshall	38
C. Lethbridge b Marshall	43 – c Parks b Emery	33
G. C. Small st Parks b Southern	3 – c Parks b Southern	10
*R. G. D. Willis not out	8 – b Emery	1
S. P. Sutcliffe c sub b Southern	1 – not out	2
L-b 6, n-b 3	9	B 22, l-b 7, w 12, n-b 2 43
1/14 2/16 3/71 4/77 5/77 6/130 7/143 8/170 9/190	191	1/48 2/86 3/86 4/96 5/157 6/270 7/311 8/326 9/329 339

Bonus points – Warwickshire 1, Hampshire 4.

Bowling: *First Innings*—Marshall 26–8–74–5; Emery 17–5–51–1; Southern 4.5–0–22–2; Tremlett 15–7–24–1; Jesty 6–2–11–0. *Second Innings*—Marshall 17–2–53–1; Emery 15–3–64–3; Tremlett 19–2–64–3; Jesty 4–0–18–1; Cowley 20–6–54–1; Southern 11.2–0–43–1.

Umpires: D. J. Constant and D. O. Oslear.

THE WRIGLEY TROPHY INDOOR SIX-A-SIDE FINALS

1976 Durham City beat Enville by 47 runs.
1977 Scarborough beat Headington United by 87 runs.
1978 Percy Main beat Dunstable Town by 43 runs.
1979 Ickenham beat Leamington by 44 runs.
1980 Percy Main beat Narborough and Littlethorpe by five wickets.
1981 Wanstead beat Newport by 92 runs.
1982 Percy Main (104) beat Wanstead (76) by 28 runs.

KENT

Patron: HRH The Duke of Kent
President: 1982 – Major O'B. ffrench Blake;
1983 – F. O. A. G. Bennett
Chairman: H. J. Pocock
Chairman, Cricket Committee: A. H. Phebey
Secretary: M. D. Fenner
St Lawrence Ground, Old Dover Road,
Canterbury, CT1 3NZ
(Telephone: 0227-56886)
Cricket Manager: B. W. Luckhurst
Captain: 1982 – Asif Iqbal; 1983 – C. J. Tavaré
Director of Youth Coaching: J. C. T. Page

Kent's transitional period continued, amid valid pleas for patience as everyone inside and outside the club began to appreciate that good players do not necessarily become so overnight. Nor are results forthcoming quickly in such times. The glory-winning side of the 1970s was not built in a day.

The 1982 season had started promisingly. Kent qualified for the Benson and Hedges Cup quarter-finals, there to be knocked out, and soon revealed themselves as contenders for the John Player League title – a reputation they maintained throughout the summer. On the other hand, their fall at the first hurdle in the NatWest Bank Trophy could not have been more painful, and, having registered their second Championship victory at Tunbridge Wells at the beginning of June, they had to wait until the last match of the season for their third.

Accepting the period of transition, unpalatable though that may be for fans reared on success, there were definite consolations. These were to be found mainly in the batting department, where established players like Bob Woolmer and Chris Tavaré were in fine form until the former was laid low by a fractured cheek-bone at the beginning of July. He was missed, not only for his batting but also for his bowling which had been useful in the first half of the summer.

The left-handed Mark Benson, the young batting success of the previous summer, established himself in his second season, despite an interruption caused by a broken finger. On his return to the side he enjoyed a run of eleven successive first-class innings in which he nine times passed 50 and twice went on to score a century. Neil Taylor, who had waited for a regular place since scoring a century on his début against Sri Lanka in 1979, took his opportunity by scoring 643 runs in his opening twelve first-class innings, including three centuries, and collected the Gold Award in three of his first four Benson and Hedges Cup games. He reached 1,000 runs in his first full season.

Laurie Potter, reared in Australia but qualified for Kent and England by birth, was taking his opportunities in fine style until the captaincy of

Young England against Young West Indies restricted his appearances in the closing stages of the season. A right-handed batsman with obvious talent, he also bowls left-arm medium pace; it was surprising he was not called upon more often in the latter capacity. Derek Aslett, another century-maker on his début, in 1981, had to combat the problems of being in and out of the side, but he did so remarkably well. He was given the chance to bowl his leg-spin, recalling past exponents of that art in Kent, and once enjoyed a spell of eighteen overs.

Christopher Cowdrey, in his first full season in the side, rather lacked consistency, a fault which could never be attributed to his fielding and catching, always of the highest standard and often phenomenal. Graham Johnson benefited briefly when promoted in the batting order, while Alan Knott, who kept wicket consistently well, had a productive season with the bat despite going in lower than he probably should. He still scored over 900 runs and Kent often relied on him and other lower-order players to get them out of trouble, particularly when Tavaré was missing.

Young bowlers are badly needed. Kevin Jarvis could not repeat his success of the previous summer and there was no doubt in the first half of the season that Kent missed John Shepherd, now with Gloucestershire. Apart from Woolmer, they did not then have a recognised third seam bowler available. This meant that Chris Penn, an eighteen-year-old, was pressed into service earlier than he might have expected, but he showed such promise that he won recognition for Young England.

Richard Ellison, now finished with his studies, had looked distinctly promising in the last half of 1981. He again had only the second half of 1982 in which to show that he is an all-rounder of promise – and did. The season could have been a lot worse had Derek Underwood not bowled so consistently well. In the end, though, the main bowling consolation was provided by Graham Dilley, who had dedicated himself, backed by manager Brian Luckhurst, to do things his way throughout the summer. His gradual recovery of confidence culminated in a good end to the season.

For the last six weeks of the summer Kent agreed with the suggestion of the captain, Asif Iqbal, that he should stand down to give younger players a chance. One to benefit was the Antiguan all-rounder, Eldine Baptiste, who showed all-round promise. Asif's gesture enabled the county to evaluate the captaincy capabilities of Cowdrey and Tavaré. Apart from Asif, it was also the final season on the staff for another former captain, Alan Ealham, who took a well-deserved benefit after long and distinguished service, including three seasons in charge of the side.

Reflecting on the pleasure and entertainment that Asif had provided for Kent, it was a pity that he should have had to curtail his final summer. He did not play for Kent again after four days of cricket against Middlesex at Lord's, so bowing out in the manner in which he would have wished, leading Kent to a 1-run John Player League victory. He leaves Kent with two spells of captaining them as the highlights of his English career. – D.M.

KENT 1982

[*Bill Smith*

Back row: S. G. Hinks, C. Penn, G. R. Dilley, D. G. Aslett, G. D. Spelman. *Middle row:* C. Lewis (*scorer*), B. W. Luckhurst (*manager*), E. A. Baptiste, S. Marsh, S. N. V. Waterton, L. Potter, N. R. Taylor, M. R. Benson, J. C. T. Page (*director of youth coaching*), D. O'Donnell (*physiotherapist*). *Front row:* C. J. Tavaré, A. G. E. Ealham, K. B. S. Jarvis, A. P. E. Knott, Asif Iqbal (*captain*), D. L. Underwood, C. S. Cowdrey, G. W. Johnson, R. A. Woolmer.

KENT RESULTS

All first-class matches – Played 24: Won 3, Lost 4, Drawn 17.

County Championship matches – Played 22: Won 3, Lost 4, Drawn 15.

Bonus points – Batting 55, Bowling 63.

Competition placings – Schweppes County Championship, 13th; NatWest Bank Trophy, 2nd round; Benson and Hedges Cup, q-f; John Player League, 4th.

COUNTY CHAMPIONSHIP AVERAGES

BATTING

	Birthplace	*M*	*I*	*NO*	*R*	*HI*	*Avge*
C. J. Tavaré c	*Orpington*	11	21	2	790	168*	41.57
M. R. Benson c	*Shoreham*	14	27	4	930	137	40.43
R. A. Woolmer c	*Kanpur, India*	12	21	3	683	203	37.94
Asif Iqbal c	*Hyderabad, India*	11	17	2	558	115*	37.20
A. P. E. Knott c	*Belvedere*	21	32	5	942	115*	34.88
E. A. Baptiste	*Antigua*	8	11	2	305	69*	33.88
L. Potter	*Bexleyheath*	11	19	2	561	108	33.00
N. R. Taylor c	*Orpington*	21	38	4	1,083	143*	31.85
D. G. Aslett	*Dover*	15	27	2	743	82	29.72
C. S. Cowdrey c	*Farnborough*	20	32	4	726	72*	25.92
R. M. Ellison	*Ashford*	7	11	3	179	46*	22.37
G. W. Johnson c	*Beckenham*	20	31	6	541	86	21.64
C. Penn	*Dover*	7	8	4	54	30	13.50
D. L. Underwood c	*Bromley*	22	22	11	129	30	11.72
S. G. Hinks	*Northfleet*	2	4	1	35	18	11.66
G. R. Dilley c	*Dartford*	19	26	7	166	32	8.73
K. B. S. Jarvis c	*Dartford*	20	15	4	21	6	1.90

Also batted: S. Marsh (*Westminster*) (1 match) 10*.

**Signifies not out.* c *Denotes county cap.*

BOWLING

	O	*M*	*R*	*W*	*Avge*	*BB*
D. L. Underwood	690.4	223	1,751	78	22.44	7-79
R. M. Ellison	153.5	35	433	16	27.06	3-12
G. R. Dilley	466.2	96	1,595	54	29.53	6-71
G. W. Johnson	286.4	69	796	25	31.84	5-36
C. S. Cowdrey	130.3	32	432	13	33.23	3-45
K. B. S. Jarvis	585	128	1,961	49	40.02	5-94

Also bowled: D. G. Aslett 70.1–8–289–6; E. A. Baptiste 158.4–38–579–9; M. R. Benson 4–0–28–0; S. G. Hinks 1.4–1–5–0; C. Penn 93.4–17–327–7; L. Potter 8–3–13–1; N. R. Taylor 17–5–83–4; R. A. Woolmer 49–14–127–4.

HUNDREDS

The following ten three-figure innings were played for Kent in County Championship matches – M. R. Benson (2) 107 v Worcestershire (Hereford), 137 v Sussex (Hove); C. J. Tavaré (2) 122* v Somerset (Taunton), 168* v Essex (Chelmsford); N. R. Taylor (2) 143* v Warwickshire (Dartford), 100 v Middlesex (Tunbridge Wells); Asif Iqbal (1) 115* v Warwickshire (Dartford); A. P. E. Knott (1) 115* v Essex (Chelmsford); L. Potter (1) 108 v Middlesex (Lord's); R. A. Woolmer (1) 203 v Sussex (Tunbridge Wells).

At Oxford, May 1, 3, 4. KENT drew with OXFORD UNIVERSITY.

At The Oval, May 5, 6, 7. KENT lost to SURREY by 18 runs.

KENT v WARWICKSHIRE

At Dartford, May 12, 13, 14. Drawn. Kent 7 pts, Warwickshire 6 pts. Kent, put in to bat, were indebted to an unbeaten innings by Taylor on the ground where he plays his club cricket. He reached his century in 225 minutes, hitting ten 4s, and had most support from Asif and Cowdrey, the former cracking 52 out of 79 in 76 minutes with seven 4s. Warwickshire, beginning badly, recovered on the second day as Lloyd batted soundly. Underwood, however, always posed a considerable threat, and Warwickshire declared 45 behind. Woolmer reached 51 out of 82 in 75 minutes, with nine 4s; Tavaré passed his half-century mark in 97 minutes with seven 4s; and on the final day Asif completed a brilliant century in 112 minutes with nineteen 4s before setting Warwickshire a target of 343 in 225 minutes, plus the final twenty overs. Thanks to Amiss and Kallicharran, who put on 144 in 38 overs, they had a great chance of victory. Kallicharran reached his century in 172 minutes with fourteen 4s and two 6s, and Humpage and Oliver continued the attack before Underwood checked Warwickshire's advance. The final over saw their last-wicket pair holding out for a draw with the target just 16 runs away.

Kent

R. A. Woolmer lbw b Small	4	– c Humpage b Cumbes	55
N. R. Taylor not out	143	– lbw b Willis	2
C. J. Tavaré c Oliver b Smith	26	– b Asif Din	66
M. R. Benson lbw b Hogg	0	– c and b Asif Din	0
*Asif Iqbal c Asif Din b Small	55	– not out	115
C. S. Cowdrey c and b Hogg	42	– (7) not out	17
G. W. Johnson c Humpage b Smith	0		
G. R. Dilley b Asif Din	3	– (6) c Amiss b Cumbes	32
†S. Marsh not out	10		
L-b 10, w 1, n-b 6	17	B 4, l-b 4, w 1, n-b 1	10
1/11 2/57 3/58 4/151 5/250 6/257 7/274 (7 wkts dec.)	300	1/7 2/96 3/101 4/166 5/236 (5 wkts dec.)	297

D. L. Underwood and K. B. S. Jarvis did not bat.

Bonus points – Kent 4, Warwickshire 3.

Bowling: *First Innings*—Willis 14–7–38–0; Small 14–2–48–2; Hogg 20–5–54–2; Smith 15–2–47–2; Cumbes 13.1–2–54–0; Asif Din 10–2–42–1. *Second Innings*—Willis 5–3–11–1; Small 11–2–38–0; Asif Din 20–2–88–2; Smith 9–2–36–0; Hogg 4–1–21–0; Cumbes 21–4–81–2; Lloyd 5–1–12–0.

Warwickshire

D. L. Amiss c Marsh b Jarvis	12	– c Marsh b Woolmer	54
T. A. Lloyd c Cowdrey b Underwood	87	– lbw b Dilley	9
A. I. Kallicharran c Woolmer b Underwood	10	– run out	105
†G. W. Humpage c Cowdrey b Dilley	22	– c Tavaré b Underwood	64
P. R. Oliver c Asif Iqbal b Cowdrey	26	– lbw b Underwood	46
Asif Din b Underwood	27	– b Jarvis	5
P. A. Smith b Underwood	13	– c Johnson b Underwood	10
*R. G. D. Willis b Underwood	4	– b Jarvis	1
G. C. Small not out	30	– c Woolmer b Underwood	4
J. Cumbes not out	4	– not out	0
W. Hogg (did not bat)		– not out	0
B 2, l-b 9, n-b 9	20	B 8, l-b 16, w 1, n-b 4	29
1/14 2/49 3/95 4/168 5/175 6/208 7/212 8/233 (8 wkts dec.)	255	1/16 2/160 3/197 4/286 5/306 6/314 7/318 8/327 9/327 (9 wkts)	327

Bonus points – Warwickshire 3, Kent 3.

Bowling: *First Innings*—Jarvis 16–4–50–1; Dilley 15–6–27–1; Cowdrey 9–3–31–1; Underwood 36–14–63–5; Johnson 23.5–7–64–0. *Second Innings*—Jarvis 20–4–80–2; Dilley 17–4–81–1; Cowdrey 1–0–5–0; Underwood 35–9–104–4; Woolmer 11–3–28–1.

Umpires: C. T. Spencer and P. B. Wight.

At Canterbury, May 22, 23, 24. KENT drew with INDIANS (See Indian tour section).

At Taunton, May 29, 31, June 1. KENT drew with SOMERSET.

At Bournemouth, June 2, 3, 4. KENT beat HAMPSHIRE by six wickets.

KENT v MIDDLESEX

At Tunbridge Wells, June 5, 7, 8. Middlesex won by an innings and 72 runs. Middlesex 24 pts, Kent 4 pts. A century by Taylor in 3 hours, 40 minutes, with two 6s and eight 4s, was the feature of the Kent innings. Aslett, who reached 50 in 115 minutes, helped in a stand of 116 off 42 overs, but generally the Middlesex spinners, Edmonds and Emburey, bowling all but 29 overs of the innings, were in command. Gatting hit a brilliant stroke-laden century in the Middlesex reply, reaching 100 out of 167 in 138 minutes with four 6s and nine 4s and featuring in a stand of 184 off 41 overs with Radley. In contrast to Gatting's, Radley's was an accumulator's hundred, lasting six hours and including one 6 and six 4s. Facing substantial arrears, Kent's batsmen offered little resistance to the pace of Daniel, supported by the spin of Edmonds, and were dismissed in 114 minutes.

Kent

R. A. Woolmer st Downton b Edmonds	25 – c Downton b Williams	2
N. R. Taylor c Kemp b Emburey	100 – lbw b Daniel	1
C. J. Tavaré c Brearley b Edmonds	1 – b Daniel	2
D. G. Aslett c Slack b Emburey	53 – c Gatting b Daniel	13
*Asif Iqbal c Edmonds b Daniel	13 – c Kemp b Daniel	21
C. S. Cowdrey b Edmonds	30 – c Downton b Daniel	14
†A. P. E. Knott st Downton b Edmonds	24 – c Gatting b Edmonds	1
C. Penn c Gatting b Emburey	7 – not out	11
G. R. Dilley not out	3 – c Daniel b Emburey	5
D. L. Underwood c Slack b Emburey	8 – c Gatting b Edmonds	7
K. B. S. Jarvis c Kemp b Emburey	0 – c Daniel b Edmonds	4
B 4, l-b 3, w 1, n-b 4	12 L-b 1, w 1, n-b 7	9
1/61 2/63 3/179 4/190 5/199 6/236 7/265 8/265 9/276	276 1/2 2/7 3/7 4/33 5/46 6/47 7/72 8/78 9/86	90

Bonus points – Kent 3, Middlesex 4.

Bowling: *First Innings*—Daniel 14–5–26–1; Williams 10–1–64–0; Edmonds 42–12–91–4; Kemp 5–0–15–0; Emburey 28.5–8–68–5. *Second Innings*—Daniel 14–5–37–5; Williams 4–0–14–1; Edmonds 6.5–3–18–3; Emburey 6–2–12–1.

Middlesex

*J. M. Brearley c Cowdrey b Dilley	33
W. N. Slack c Dilley b Underwood	51
†P. R. Downton run out	7
C. T. Radley not out	141
M. W. Gatting run out	114
R. O. Butcher b Dilley	35
J. E. Emburey c Knott b Jarvis	3
P. H. Edmonds lbw b Jarvis	2
N. J. Kemp lbw b Dilley	1
N. F. Williams b Jarvis	24
W. W. Daniel not out	5
L-b 11, w 1, n-b 10	22
1/56 2/80 3/105 4/289 5/334 6/343 7/351 8/360 9/420 (9 wkts dec.)	438

Bonus points – Middlesex 4, Kent 1 (Score at 100 overs: 320-4).

Bowling: Jarvis 40–13–113–3; Dilley 37–4–148–3; Underwood 24–7–75–1; Cowdrey 4–1–16–0; Penn 15–4–38–0; Woolmer 7–0–23–0; Aslett 1–0–3–0.

Umpires: B. J. Meyer and J. van Geloven.

KENT v SUSSEX

At Tunbridge Wells, June 9, 10, 11. Kent won by ten wickets. Kent 24 pts, Sussex 3 pts. le Roux, with a 6 and six 4s in his 75-minute half-century, saved Sussex from an even more modest total before Woolmer played the innings of the week on his "home" ground. His double-century was the first by a Kent player against Sussex in a first-class game, occupied five hours, 42 minutes, and included three 6s and 23 4s. Asif, who struck seven 4s in racing to 50 in 65 minutes, shared in a stand of 164 off 30 overs. Kent's sizeable lead did not deter the Sussex openers, Mendis and Gould, who hit 120 off 40 overs, but then the batting faltered and only a late stand of 72 between le Roux and Barclay made it necessary for Kent to bat again.

Sussex

G. D. Mendis c Jarvis b Penn	29 – c Woolmer b Underwood	52
I. J. Gould c Johnson b Potter	6 – c Potter b Penn	65
C. M. Wells c Knott b Woolmer	41 – b Penn	8
P. W. G. Parker c Cowdrey b Penn	26 – c Knott b Jarvis	1
Imran Khan c Woolmer b Jarvis	7 – c Woolmer b Jarvis	39
I. A. Greig c Cowdrey b Jarvis	5 – c Knott b Underwood	1
G. S. le Roux c sub b Underwood	78 – b Cowdrey	42
*J. R. T. Barclay b Jarvis	1 – c Jarvis b Johnson	23
†D. J. Smith b Underwood	1 – run out	0
A. C. S. Pigott c and b Underwood	1 – lbw b Cowdrey	3
C. E. Waller not out	1 – not out	1
L-b 6, n-b 2	8 L-b 2, w 1, n-b 13	16
1/12 2/76 3/84 4/92 5/98 6/150 7/155 8/181 9/197	204 1/120 2/129 3/130 4/155 5/173 6/175 7/247 8/247 9/249	251

Bonus points – Sussex 2, Kent 4.

Bowling: *First Innings*—Jarvis 22–7–49–3; Potter 4–1–9–1; Cowdrey 6–1–19–0; Woolmer 9–3–22–1; Underwood 13.1–4–34–3; Penn 15–2–63–2. *Second Innings*—Jarvis 21–4–67–2; Penn 13–3–61–2; Potter 4–2–4–0; Underwood 31–9–70–2; Johnson 11–4–16–1; Aslett 1–0–5–0; Cowdrey 4.3–2–12–2.

Kent

R. A. Woolmer c Imran b Greig	203 – not out	22
L. Potter c Mendis b Barclay	43 – not out	12
D. G. Aslett c Smith b Greig	19	
*Asif Iqbal c Waller b Pigott	73	
C. S. Cowdrey c Parker b Waller	27	
†A. P. E. Knott c Parker b Greig	30	
G. W. Johnson c le Roux b Wells	8	
C. Penn b Pigott	0	
D. L. Underwood not out	6	
B 8, l-b 5, w 1, n-b 1	15 L-b 1	1
1/125 2/166 3/330 4/364 5/395 6/413 7/418 8/424	(8 wkts dec.) 424	(no wkt) 35

N. R. Taylor and K. B. S. Jarvis did not bat.

Bonus points – Kent 4, Sussex 1 (Score at 100 overs: 373-4).

Bowling: *First Innings*—Imran 15–6–24–0; le Roux 14–2–30–0; Greig 29–3–132–3; Pigott 16–2–67–2; Waller 17–2–66–1; Barclay 22–4–72–1; Wells 4–0–18–1. *Second Innings*—Gould 5.4–2–18–0; Parker 5–0–16–0.

Umpires: D. J. Constant and J. van Geloven.

At Nottingham, June 12, 14, 15. KENT lost to NOTTINGHAMSHIRE by ten wickets.

KENT v DERBYSHIRE

At Canterbury, June 19, 21, 22. Drawn. Kent 4 pts, Derbyshire 4 pts. Rain ruined this match, with two and a half hours lost on the first day when Kent were put in. Tavaré returned to form with a half-century in 110 minutes (eight 4s) and Asif reached 50 in 103 minutes. Rain interfered again on the second day when, following a Kent declaration, Derbyshire declared 99 behind. Kent's second innings, begun in the evening, was never resumed as the weather prevented any play at all on the final day.

Kent

R. A. Woolmer c Moir b Tunnicliffe	12 – not out	16
N. R. Taylor b Miller	40 – not out	4
C. J. Tavaré c Taylor b Tunnicliffe	54	
*Asif Iqbal c Taylor b Oldham	65	
C. S. Cowdrey c Miller b Tunnicliffe	7	
G. W. Johnson c Miller b Oldham	20	
†A. P. E. Knott c Newman b Tunnicliffe	22	
G. R. Dilley c Moir b Tunnicliffe	3	
C. Penn not out	4	
D. L. Underwood not out	6	
L-b 6, w 1, n-b 10	17	L-b 4, n-b 4 8
1/37 2/74 3/142 4/171 5/191 6/218 7/238 8/238	(8 wkts dec.) 250	(no wkt) 28

K. B. S. Jarvis did not bat.

Bonus points – Kent 3, Derbyshire 3.

Bowling: *First Innings*—Oldham 23.4–9–52–2; Newman 17–1–62–0; Tunnicliffe 24–3–73–5; Wood 12–3–36–0; Miller 3–0–10–1; Moir 1–1–0–0. *Second Innings*—Oldham 3–0–8–0; Newman 3–0–12–0; Moir 1–1–0–0.

Derbyshire

*B. Wood b Jarvis	45	G. Miller not out	25
J. G. Wright c Cowdrey b Dilley	22	L-b 5, n-b 1	6
P. N. Kirsten c Knott b Jarvis	16		
J. H. Hampshire not out	37	1/63 2/81 3/98	(3 wkts dec.) 151

D. G. Moir, K. J. Barnett, †R. W. Taylor, C. J. Tunnicliffe, S. Oldham and P. G. Newman did not bat.

Bonus points – Derbyshire 1, Kent 1.

Bowling: Jarvis 14–6–33–2; Dilley 11–4–28–1; Cowdrey 8–1–37–0; Penn 11.4–1–42–0; Woolmer 2–1–2–0; Underwood 2–0–3–0.

Umpires: W. L. Budd and R. S. Herman.

At Leicester, June 23, 24, 25. KENT drew with LEICESTERSHIRE.

KENT v HAMPSHIRE

At Maidstone, July 3, 5, 6. Hampshire won by 45 runs. Hampshire 21 pts, Kent 5 pts. Pace and seam bowlers generally dominated on a wicket of uneven bounce. In Hampshire's first innings Knott took six catches and for the sixth time in his career equalled the county's wicket-keeping record for the number of dismissals in an innings. A crucial blow for Kent was the injury to Woolmer, who took no further part in the match after sustaining a fractured cheek-bone when he was struck in the face by a ball from Marshall on the first evening. Kent's last five wickets fell for 12 runs in ten overs, all to Marshall. Pocock, who reached 50 in 81 minutes with two 6s and seven 4s, and Hayward, whose 50 took 176 minutes with eight 4s, put on 98 in 91 minutes, and Kent needed 282 to win in 270 minutes. Spearheaded by Asif, who reached 52 out of 76 in 58 minutes, they made a brave effort. Knott and Cowdrey continued the victory bid, adding 66 in 56 minutes, but Marshall dismissed them both and Hampshire got home with 5.2 overs to spare.

Hampshire

C. G. Greenidge c Knott b Cowdrey	46	– c Asif b Dilley	32
J. M. Rice c Knott b Jarvis	11	– c Cowdrey b Jarvis	9
M. C. J. Nicholas c Knott b Jarvis	1	– lbw b Dilley	49
T. E. Jesty c Asif b Cowdrey	24	– c Asif b Cowdrey	1
R. E. Hayward c Knott b Dilley	9	– b Dilley	59
*N. E. J. Pocock c and b Dilley	0	– c Cowdrey b Jarvis	62
N. G. Cowley b Cowdrey	35	– c Jarvis b Underwood	9
M. D. Marshall c Knott b Jarvis	10	– c Knott b Underwood	22
†R. J. Parks c Knott b Dilley	25	– c Jarvis b Underwood	12
J. W. Southern lbw b Woolmer	10	– b Underwood	1
K. St J. D. Emery not out	0	– not out	0
B 1, l-b 5, n-b 2	8	L-b 17, n-b 10	27
1/29 2/32 3/77 4/89 5/90 6/101 7/135 8/144 9/179	179	1/27 2/57 3/62 4/126 5/224 6/237 7/270 8/270 9/272	283

Bonus points – Hampshire 1, Kent 4.

Bowling: *First Innings*—Jarvis 19–7–46–3; Dilley 16.3–3–70–3; Cowdrey 20–6–45–3; Underwood 2–0–10–0; Woolmer 1–1–0–1. *Second Innings*—Jarvis 27–7–77–2; Dilley 25–6–56–3; Underwood 15.1–5–34–4; Cowdrey 16–5–61–1; Johnson 13–5–28–0.

Kent

R. A. Woolmer retired hurt	3	– absent injured	
N. R. Taylor c Rice b Marshall	40	– c Nicholas b Emery	13
C. J. Tavaré c Parks b Marshall	68	– c Pocock b Marshall	39
M. R. Benson b Jesty	1	– (1) lbw b Jesty	1
*Asif Iqbal c Parks b Emery	10	– (4) c Rice b Cowley	75
C. S Cowdrey c Hayward b Jesty	14	– c Parks b Marshall	31
†A. P. E. Knott c Parks b Marshall	18	– lbw b Marshall	36
G. W. Johnson c Parks b Marshall	0	– (5) lbw b Marshall	13
G. R. Dilley c Parks b Marshall	5	– (8) c Marshall b Cowley	5
D. L. Underwood not out	2	– (9) not out	11
K. B. S. Jarvis b Marshall	0	– (10) b Emery	0
B 1, l-b 8, n-b 11	20	L-b 6, w 1, n-b 5	12
1/61 2/62 3/92 4/123 5/169 6/169 7/173 8/181 9/181	181	1/10 2/20 3/133 4/150 5/153 6/219 7/222 8/230 9/236	236

Bonus points – Kent 1, Hampshire 4.

Bowling: *First Innings*—Marshall 27.5–9–55–6; Emery 23–5–49–1; Jesty 24–11–57–2. *Second Innings*—Marshall 21–5–54–4; Emery 18.4–4–77–2; Jesty 11–1–32–1; Cowley 22–7–60–2; Southern 3–2–1–0.

Umpires: A. Jepson and D. R. Shepherd.

KENT v SURREY

At Maidstone, July 7, 8, 9. Drawn. Kent 5 pts, Surrey 8 pts. Surrey, put in, replied by registering four batting points, thanks to the left-handed Thomas scoring a career best. He batted 126 minutes for his 64, hitting a 6 and eleven 4s, after his side had been struggling at 250 for eight in the 76th over. Kent lost half their side for 105 in 50 overs, but Knott hit 50 out of 65 in 55 minutes with eight 4s. Clinton, playing against his old county, increased Surrey's lead on the second evening and next morning Knight was able to set Kent 321 to win in 260 minutes – a little more than 4 an over. Again Kent began badly, losing half their side for 92 before Knott helped Potter add 67 in 54 minutes. Potter, batting for three hours and hitting sixteen 4s, stayed to the premature end, caused by bad light, and Kent had staved off defeat.

Surrey

G. S. Clinton lbw b Ellison	33	– c Knott b Jarvis	61
D. B. Pauline c Taylor b Underwood	26	– c Cowdrey b Underwood	22
D. M. Smith c Johnson b Jarvis	36	– c Knott b Johnson	17
*R. D. V. Knight c Potter b Underwood	57	– (5) c Johnson b Underwood	8
M. A. Lynch c Johnson b Underwood	40	– (4) c Asif b Underwood	22
G. R. J. Roope c Taylor b Johnson	9	– not out	41
†C. J. Richards c Asif b Johnson	13	– c Knott b Ellison	20
D. J. Thomas c Knott b Ellison	64		
S. T. Clarke b Johnson	16		
R. D. Jackman c Dilley b Ellison	17		
R. G. L. Cheatle not out	1		
L-b 6, w 1, n-b 7	14	L-b 6	6
1/62 2/62 3/131 4/186 5/211 6/211 7/230 8/250 9/308	326	1/50 2/103 3/113 4/134 5/141 6/197 (6 wkts dec.)	197

Bonus points – Surrey 4, Kent 3 (Score at 100 overs: 307-8).

Bowling: *First Innings*—Jarvis 20–3–62–1; Dilley 13–3–64–0; Ellison 16–1–41–3; Underwood 26–10–72–3; Johnson 26–11–72–3; Cowdrey 1–0–1–0. *Second Innings*—Jarvis 10–1–39–1; Ellison 14.2–1–52–1; Underwood 23–8–69–3; Johnson 15–6–31–1.

Kent

N. R. Taylor c Clarke b Cheatle	37	– b Jackman	0
L. Potter lbw b Jackman	5	– not out	90
M. R. Benson c Richards b Thomas	29	– c Lynch b Clarke	2
*Asif Iqbal c Clarke b Thomas	23	– c and b Jackman	15
G. W. Johnson b Clarke	0	– c Knight b Cheatle	21
C. S. Cowdrey lbw b Jackman	5	– c Richards b Knight	13
†A. P. E. Knott c Richards b Clarke	53	– c Roope b Jackman	38
R. M. Ellison st Richards b Lynch	29	– not out	2
G. R. Dilley b Thomas	1		
D. L. Underwood not out	2		
K. B. S. Jarvis c Thomas b Clarke	1		
B 4, l-b 12, w 1, n-b 1	18	L-b 4, w 1	5
1/17 2/71 3/96 4/101 5/105 6/138 7/181 8/196 9/196	203	1/0 2/7 3/26 4/77 5/92 6/159 (6 wkts)	186

Bonus points – Kent 2, Surrey 4.

Bowling: *First Innings*—Clarke 23.4–9–44–3; Thomas 19–7–33–3; Cheatle 15–3–50–1; Jackman 13–6–32–2; Knight 6–0–19–0; Pauline 1–0–3–0; Lynch 1–0–4–1. *Second Innings*—Clarke 14–2–32–1; Jackman 13–2–45–3; Thomas 8–2–31–0; Cheatle 10–1–37–1; Knight 5–0–34–1; Lynch 1–0–2–0.

Umpires: A. Jepson and D. R. Shepherd.

At Hereford, July 21, 22, 23. KENT drew with WORCESTERSHIRE.

At Hove, July 28, 29, 30. KENT drew with SUSSEX.

At Lord's, July 31, August 2, 3. KENT drew with MIDDLESEX.

KENT v ESSEX

At Canterbury, August 7, 9, 10. Drawn. Kent 6 pts, Essex 6 pts. Gooch, reaching 50 in two hours with six 4s, and McEwan added 75 off nineteen overs for the third wicket to give Essex a great start, but once Cowdrey had dismissed them both, Essex collapsed. Kent made a poor start and, against the pace of Pringle and the off-spin of Acfield, were dismissed 39 runs behind, having managed a run-rate of just over 2 an over throughout their innings. Batting again, Gooch blasted the Kent attack, his 103 out of 143 coming in 95 minutes with two 6s and fifteen 4s. Fletcher was able to set Kent 301 to win in four and a quarter hours, and for a time Benson and Aslett threatened to put them on target. However, Kent faltered, and although Essex endeavoured to keep them in the hunt the challenge petered out. Cowdrey, who hit 50 in 67 minutes with two 6s and five 4s, ensured that Kent saved the game.

Essex

G. A. Gooch c Baptiste b Cowdrey	71	– c Benson b Johnson	149
B. R. Hardie c Knott b Dilley	25	– c Johnson b Cowdrey	26
*K. W. R. Fletcher b Underwood	19	– st Knott b Underwood	43
K. S. McEwan c Baptiste b Cowdrey	47	– c Tavaré b Johnson	4
D. R. Pringle b Baptiste	21		
K. R. Pont c Johnson b Baptiste	0	– not out	1
N. Phillip b Jarvis	5	– (5) not out	25
S. Turner c Knott b Jarvis	4		
†D. E. East run out	20		
R. E. East c Knott b Baptiste	22		
D. L. Acfield not out	2		
L-b 3, w 1, n-b 8	12	B 3, l-b 5, w 1, n-b 4	13
1/30 2/93 3/168 4/168 5/171 6/194 7/194 8/199 9/228	248	1/99 2/217 3/223 4/244 (4 wkts dec.)	261

Bonus points – Essex 2, Kent 4.

Bowling: *First Innings*—Dilley 7–1–39–1; Jarvis 22–4–73–2; Baptiste 20.1–5–57–3; Underwood 20–8–48–1; Cowdrey 9–5–19–2. *Second Innings*—Jarvis 10–1–59–0; Baptiste 9–2–46–0; Cowdrey 9–0–49–1; Underwood 16–0–60–1; Johnson 11–0–34–2.

Kent

M. R. Benson lbw b Acfield	48	– b Acfield	51
N. R. Taylor c D. E. East b Pringle	12	– lbw b Pringle	8
C. J. Tavaré b Pringle	24	– b Acfield	22
D. G. Aslett lbw b Acfield	31	– st D. E. East b Acfield	56
G. W. Johnson lbw b Phillip	10	– lbw b Pringle	41
*C. S. Cowdrey c Gooch b Pringle	13	– not out	72
†A. P. E. Knott c and b Acfield	40	– run out	1
E. A. Baptiste b Acfield	11	– lbw b Pringle	14
G. R. Dilley c D. E. East b Pringle	0	– b R. E. East	5
D. L. Underwood not out	7	– not out	0
K. B. S. Jarvis b Phillip	1		
B 4, l-b 4, w 2, n-b 2	12	B 5, l-b 5, w 1, n-b 3	14
1/16 2/83 3/90 4/101 5/121 6/178 7/197 8/200 9/206	209	1/25 2/78 3/99 4/181 5/203 6/204 7/231 8/265 (8 wkts)	284

Bonus points – Kent 2, Essex 4 (Score at 100 overs: 209-9).

Bowling: *First Innings*—Phillip 20.4–4–55–2; Pringle 27–9–53–4; Turner 22–9–23–0; Gooch 8–4–6–0; Acfield 16–4–37–4; R. E. East 8–3–23–0. *Second Innings*—Phillip 9–0–43–0; Pringle 20.5–4–45–3; Acfield 25–3–84–3; Turner 11–1–32–0; R. E. East 13–0–48–1; Fletcher 1–0–18–0.

Umpires: D. J. Constant and P. J. Eele.

KENT v GLAMORGAN

At Canterbury, August 11, 12, 13. Drawn. Kent 6 pts, Glamorgan 6 pts. A career-best innings by Francis, who batted for 356 minutes, hitting twelve 4s, was the feature of the Glamorgan innings, though Eifion Jones subsequently gave them a good boost with 50 in 68 minutes, including seven 4s. Kent lost half their side for 144 in 46 overs after Benson had scored 50 in 96 minutes (six 4s), but Baptiste, reaching his maiden first-class fifty in 100 minutes, with six 4s and Ellison added 86 off 21 overs to allow Cowdrey to declare only 68 behind. Glamorgan began their second innings with a century stand, and Alan Jones compiled his 50th century for the county in 200 minutes, hitting a 6 and fifteen 4s. Kent, needing 304 to win in four hours, began badly, but Potter's 50 out of 89 (one 6 and six 4s) in 92 minutes and Benson's 50 in 94 minutes (six 4s) saw the game poised for an interesting finish when the rain proved the unwelcome but decisive factor.

Glamorgan

A. Jones c Benson b Cowdrey	37	– not out	136
A. L. Jones c Knott b Jarvis	10	– c Taylor b Jarvis	53
D. A. Francis not out	142	– c Cowdrey b Underwood	3
R. C. Ontong c Knott b Jarvis	0	– c Ellison b Aslett	21
J. A. Hopkins b Johnson	48	– not out	7
C. J. C. Rowe run out	8		
J. G. Thomas c Benson b Underwood	9		
†E. W. Jones b Ellison	58		
*B. J. Lloyd not out	24		
B 1, l-b 14, w 3, n-b 14	32	B 1, l-b 10, n-b 4	15
1/22 2/65 3/67 4/177 5/197 6/219 7/326 (7 wkts dec.)	368	1/128 2/132 3/201 (3 wkts dec.)	235

M. A. Nash and W. W. Davis did not bat.

Bonus points – Glamorgan 3, Kent 2 (Score at 100 overs: 288-6).

Bowling: *First Innings*—Jarvis 25–3–95–2; Ellison 23–6–63–1; Baptiste 16–5–58–0; Cowdrey 4–1–7–1; Underwood 20–6–34–1; Johnson 18–2–61–1; Aslett 5–0–18–0. *Second Innings*—Jarvis 17–6–32–1; Baptiste 6–1–26–0; Ellison 6–1–21–0; Johnson 20–5–46–0; Aslett 6–1–33–1; Underwood 9–3–34–1; Benson 4–0–28–0.

Kent

L. Potter lbw b Nash	0	– c E. W. Jones b Ontong	52
N. R. Taylor c and b Nash	36	– c E. W. Jones b Nash	1
D. G. Aslett lbw b Davis	6	– lbw b Davis	17
M. R. Benson c E. W. Jones b Davis	51	– not out	56
G. W. Johnson run out	32	– c Rowe b Ontong	4
*C. S. Cowdrey c and b Davis	6	– (7) not out	12
†A. P. E. Knott c Nash b Davis	15		
E. A. Baptiste not out	69	– (6) c A. L. Jones b Ontong	10
R. M. Ellison c Francis b Lloyd	35		
D. L. Underwood not out	10		
B 4, l-b 17, w 2, n-b 17	40	B 4, l-b 2, w 1, n-b 5	12
1/0 2/22 3/64 4/136 5/144 6/148 7/182 8/268 (8 wkts dec.)	300	1/10 2/43 3/101 4/123 5/136 (5 wkts)	164

K. B. S. Jarvis did not bat.

Bonus points – Kent 4, Glamorgan 3.

Bowling: *First Innings*—Nash 17–7–35–2; Davis 23–5–83–4; Thomas 11–4–44–0; Ontong 16–4–63–0; Lloyd 12–3–35–1. *Second Innings*—Nash 12–2–47–1; Davis 12–5–20–1; Lloyd 10–1–38–0; Ontong 11–1–42–3; Thomas 1–0–5–0.

Umpires: B. J. Meyer and P. J. Eele.

At Leeds, August 14, 16, 17. KENT drew with YORKSHIRE.

KENT v GLOUCESTERSHIRE

At Folkestone, August 21, 23, 24. Drawn. Kent 7 pts, Gloucestershire 6 pts. Woolmer, returning to the first-class scene after six weeks' absence with a fractured cheek-bone, settled quickly into his stride, reaching his half-century out of 85 in 128 minutes. Benson continued in his fine form with eight 4s in his 50, and he and Cowdrey added 97 off 30 overs for the fifth wicket. Then Cowdrey, whose 50 occupied two hours, ten minutes, and Knott put on 72 at almost 5 an over before the declaration. Gloucestershire made a sound start, Broad batting three and a half hours and hitting ten 4s and Sadiq slightly longer with eight 4s. Following Graveney's declaration on achieving maximum batting points, Kent were moving smoothly into a position from which to set a target when rain intervened. Benson again reached 50 (in 99 minutes with six 4s), the ninth time in eleven successive innings he had passed the half-century mark.

Kent

R. A. Woolmer b Childs	67		
N. R. Taylor c Brassington b Doughty	8	– (1) c Brassington b Shepherd	13
C. J. Tavaré b Doughty	42	– c Brassington b Shepherd	0
M. R. Benson c Stovold b Doughty	81	– (2) not out	59
G. W. Johnson b Shepherd	16	– (4) not out	59
*C. S. Cowdrey c Stovold b Graveney	54		
†A. P. E. Knott not out	44		
B 1, l-b 7, w 2, n-b 2	12	B 1, w 1, n-b 1	3
1/22 2/113 3/130 4/155 5/252 6/324 (6 wkts dec.)	324	1/41 2/49 (2 wkts)	134

E. A. Baptiste, G. R. Dilley, D. L. Underwood and K. B. S. Jarvis did not bat.

Bonus points – Kent 4, Gloucestershire 2.

Bowling: *First Innings*—Shepherd 25–8–51–1; Doughty 21–1–80–3; Trembath 17–2–62–0; Childs 19–1–73–1; Graveney 17.1–3–46–1. *Second Innings*—Shepherd 19–3–58–2; Doughty 12–1–37–0; Trembath 6.2–0–36–0.

Gloucestershire

A. W. Stovold c Knott b Dilley	37
B. C. Broad c Benson b Woolmer	97
P. W. Romaines retired hurt	0
Sadiq Mohammad c and b Underwood	90
A. J. Wright c Dilley b Johnson	14
J. N. Shepherd c Tavaré b Baptiste	7
*D. A. Graveney b Dilley	22
R. J. Doughty c Johnson b Dilley	7
C. R. Trembath not out	8
†A. J. Brassington not out	0
B 4, l-b 6, n-b 11	21
1/88 2/184 3/214 4/233 5/281 6/289 7/299 (7 wkts dec.)	303

J. H. Childs did not bat.

Bonus points – Gloucestershire 4, Kent 3.

Bowling: Dilley 22–4–72–3; Jarvis 16–4–55–0; Baptiste 20–4–56–1; Underwood 14–3–41–1; Woolmer 8–3–15–1; Johnson 11–2–43–1.

Umpires: R. Julian and N. T. Plews.

KENT v NORTHAMPTONSHIRE

At Folkestone, August 25, 26, 27. Drawn. Kent 8 pts, Northamptonshire 4 pts. Kent, despite a splendid innings of more than two and threequarter hours by Aslett, were struggling at 169 for five after 65 overs, but Knott and Baptiste hit them out of trouble, putting on 75 in seventeen overs and Knott hitting six 4s in his 92-minute 50. Northamptonshire looked set for a substantial reply when Larkins raced to 50 in 88 minutes, but they lost their last nine wickets for 75 runs in 30 overs. Kent, too, found batting difficult, but Taylor held firm for more than two and a half hours and eventually Northamptonshire were left with 4 hours 25 minutes to make 321 to win. They were given a good start by Cook and Larkins, who reached his second 50 of the match in 84 minutes, and Boyd-Moss kept up the effort with seven 4s in a 78-minute half-century. At 246 for eight in the twelfth of the last twenty overs Northamptonshire still looked in danger of defeat, but Sharp averted that threat with a half-century in even time.

Kent

N. R. Taylor c Sharp b Steele	28	– c Sharp b Griffiths	56
L. Potter c Kapil Dev b Mallender	8	– c Sharp b Mallender	8
D. G. Aslett b Williams	82	– c Willey b Griffiths	18
M. R. Benson c Steele b Griffiths	25	– b Mallender	7
*G. W. Johnson c and b Steele	6	– lbw b Kapil Dev	7
†A. P. E. Knott not out	69	– c Kapil Dev b Griffiths	21
E. A. Baptiste b Griffiths	42	– c Cook b Griffiths	43
R. M. Ellison lbw b Mallender	15	– not out	25
G. R. Dilley not out	2	– c and b Griffiths	1
D. L. Underwood (did not bat)		– not out	10
B 3, l-b 10, n-b 10	23	L-b 4, n-b 12	16
1/21 2/83 3/155 4/165 5/169 6/244 7/286 (7 wkts dec.)	300	1/13 2/44 3/59 4/77 5/118 6/125 7/190 8/198 (8 wkts dec.)	212

K. B. S. Jarvis did not bat.

Bonus points – Kent 4, Northamptonshire 3.

Bowling: *First Innings*—Kapil Dev 20–6–57–0; Mallender 18–4–45–2; Griffiths 20–6–61–2; Steele 14–4–41–2; Willey 10–3–24–0; Williams 17–4–49–1. *Second Innings*—Kapil Dev 18–2–59–1; Mallender 20–5–47–2; Griffiths 23–5–71–5; Steele 5–0–19–0.

Northamptonshire

*G. Cook c Benson b Dilley	21	– lbw b Dilley	37
W. Larkins c Knott b Jarvis	68	– b Dilley	71
P. Willey c Baptiste b Jarvis	28	– c Knott b Dilley	0
R. J. Boyd-Moss c Johnson b Underwood	0	– c Benson b Ellison	54
R. G. Williams c Knott b Jarvis	34	– c Johnson b Ellison	17
Kapil Dev b Jarvis	4	– c Baptiste b Ellison	0
D. S. Steele b Ellison	14	– lbw b Jarvis	15
R. J. Bailey c Knott b Ellison	4	– c Dilley b Underwood	3
†G. Sharp c Johnson b Ellison	3	– not out	58
N. A. Mallender not out	1	– not out	5
B. J. Griffiths b Jarvis	6		
L-b 3, n-b 6	9	L-b 3, n-b 10	13
1/41 2/117 3/120 4/120 5/133 6/174 7/179 8/181 9/185	192	1/81 2/83 3/167 4/171 5/175 6/200 7/208 8/246 (8 wkts)	273

Bonus points – Northamptonshire 1, Kent 4.

Bowling: *First Innings*—Dilley 16–2–52–1; Jarvis 23–4–94–5; Underwood 7–4–10–1; Ellison 13–6–12–3; Baptiste 2–0–15–0. *Second Innings*—Dilley 23–4–88–3; Jarvis 15–2–71–1; Ellison 21.5–8–51–3; Underwood 10–2–28–1; Baptiste 4–1–22–0.

Umpires: R. Julian and N. T. Plews.

At Manchester, August 28, 30, 31. KENT drew with LANCASHIRE.

At Chelmsford, September 1, 2, 3. KENT drew with ESSEX.

KENT v LEICESTERSHIRE

At Canterbury, September 11, 13, 14. Kent won by 39 runs. Kent 23 pts, Leicestershire 6 pts. Taylor, batting 156 minutes and hitting twelve 4s, was the mainstay of the Kent innings, which never mastered an attack spearheaded by Taylor's pace and Cook's slow left-arm spin. Leicestershire began disastrously as Dilley snapped up three wickets for 32 in his first 9.5 overs, and only a bold innings from Roberts, who hit a 6 and seven 4s in his 47-minute stay, kept their arrears to 50. Kent also struggled, despite Tavaré's 50 in 97 minutes with nine 4s, but on the final day Knott, with 50 in 77 minutes (eight 4s), and Ellison revived them before Parsons, with a spell of three for 2 in twelve balls, wrapped up the innings. Needing 292 to win in 230 minutes, Leicestershire started badly and had only Gower and Davison to resist the pace of Dilley, who had a good match, and the spin of Underwood. Davison had the satisfaction of hitting his seventh century of the season – made in 174 minutes with two 6s and nine 4s – to equal the Leicestershire record held by Willie Watson and Les Berry, but it was Kent who, with 4.5 overs to spare, had the satisfaction of ending the season on a winning note.

Kent

M. R. Benson lbw b Parsons	16	– c Tolchard b Roberts	4
N. R. Taylor c Tolchard b Taylor	82	– c Roberts b Cook	41
*C. J. Tavaré b Cook	34	– c Taylor b Cook	52
D. G. Aslett c Steele b Cook	27	– lbw b Roberts	24
C. S. Cowdrey lbw b Taylor	2	– c Briers b Steele	5
†A. P. E. Knott b Roberts	34	– c Davison b Steele	57
R. M. Ellison c and b Cook	14	– not out	46
G. W. Johnson c and b Steele	12	– c Tolchard b Parsons	0
G. R. Dilley c Steele b Taylor	5	– lbw b Parsons	0
D. L. Underwood not out	10	– c Tolchard b Parsons	2
K. B. S. Jarvis b Steele	0	– c Tolchard b Parsons	6
L-b 12, w 2	14	L-b 3, n-b 1	4
1/46 2/123 3/152 4/166 5/166 6/219 7/223 8/238 9/242	250	1/4 2/97 3/107 4/128 5/134 6/221 7/222 8/226 9/230	241

Bonus points – Kent 3, Leicestershire 4.

Bowling: *First Innings*—Taylor 24–5–83–3; Roberts 20–7–41–1; Parsons 13–4–39–1; Steele 9.1–5–16–2; Cook 26–11–57–3; Balderstone 1–1–0–0. *Second Innings*—Roberts 21–8–63–2; Parsons 17.3–4–55–4; Taylor 12–2–17–0; Cook 26–7–56–2; Steele 18–5–46–2.

Leicestershire

J. C. Balderstone c Knott b Dilley	4	– lbw b Dilley	0
R. A. Cobb c Ellison b Dilley	5	– c Cowdrey b Underwood	14
D. I. Gower c Knott b Ellison	26	– c Knott b Dilley	80
B. F. Davison c and b Dilley	19	– not out	100
N. G. B. Cook c Knott b Ellison	37	– (10) b Underwood	0
N. E. Briers b Jarvis	10	– (5) c Tavaré b Ellison	7
*†R. W. Tolchard not out	31	– (6) c Knott b Underwood	12
G. J. Parsons c Knott b Dilley	2	– (9) c Tavaré b Dilley	12
J. F. Steele c Tavaré b Dilley	8	– (8) b Underwood	0
A. M. E. Roberts c Knott b Dilley	47	– (7) st Knott b Underwood	13
L. B. Taylor c Jarvis b Ellison	0	– c Tavaré b Dilley	7
L-b 4, w 2, n-b 5	11	L-b 6, w 1	7
1/4 2/21 3/38 4/58 5/81 6/123 7/128 8/142 9/197	200	1/0 2/63 3/129 4/152 5/179 6/195 7/205 8/230 9/231	252

Bonus points – Leicestershire 2, Kent 4.

Bowling: *First Innings*—Dilley 27–7–71–6; Jarvis 20–6–40–1; Underwood 14–6–19–0; Ellison 14.4–2–40–3; Cowdrey 2–0–19–0. *Second Innings*—Dilley 12.1–2–45–4; Jarvis 11–0–38–0; Underwood 23–6–80–5; Ellison 11–0–60–1; Johnson 4–0–22–0.

Umpires: R. S. Herman and K. E. Palmer.

WHITBREAD SCHOLARSHIPS

The Whitbread Brewery Scholarships, first awarded in 1976, were instituted to help young cricketers further their experience by playing for a season in Australia. Scholarships have been awarded to the following:

1976-77: C. W. J. Athey (Yorkshire), I. T. Botham (Somerset), M. W. Gatting (Middlesex), G. B. Stevenson (Yorkshire).
1977-78: C. S. Cowdrey (Kent), J. E. Emburey (Middlesex), J. A. Hopkins (Glamorgan), J. D. Love (Yorkshire).
1978-79: J. P. Agnew (Leicestershire), M. W. Gatting (Middlesex), W. Larkins (Northamptonshire), C. J. Tavaré (Kent).
1979-80: K. J. Barnett (Derbyshire), D. N. Patel (Worcestershire), A. C. S. Pigott (Sussex), R. G. Williams (Northamptonshire).
1980-81: N. G. B. Cook (Leicestershire), W. Hogg (Lancashire), D. M. Smith (Surrey).
1981-82: M. R. Benson (Kent), N. A. Foster (Essex), P. G. Newman (Derbyshire).
1982-83: D. J. Capel (Northamptonshire), R. K. Illingworth (Worcestershire), C. Penn (Kent), D. J. Thomas (Surrey).

ESSO SCHOLARSHIPS

The four young Australian cricketers who received Esso Scholarships to play in England in 1982 were: M. C. Dolman (South Australia, to Warwickshire), K. MacLeay (Western Australia, to Sussex), G. M. Ritchie (Queensland, to Middlesex), S. B. Smith (New South Wales, to Essex).

LANCASHIRE

Patron: HM The Queen
President: 1982 – J. L. Hopwood;
1983 – Edwin Kay
Chairman: C. S. Rhoades
Secretary: C. D. Hassell
County Cricket Ground, Old Trafford,
Manchester M16 0PX
(Telephone: 061-872 5533)
Cricket Manager: J. D. Bond
Captain: C. H. Lloyd
Coach: J. S. Savage

On the surface Lancashire had another disappointing year. They did manage to move up four places in the Championship but were still in the bottom half of the table for the seventh successive year, matching their poor performances in the 1960s. They moved up one position to eleventh in the John Player League and for only the second time in thirteen years were knocked out in their opening round of the NatWest Bank Trophy. They had their best run in the Benson and Hedges Cup since 1974, but defeat at Trent Bridge, just when supporters were thinking of a visit to Lord's, will long be remembered. Yet there were signs of moving forward with more young players making an impression and raising hopes for the future. There were no signs, either, of decline in the old faithfuls, David Lloyd, David Hughes and Jack Simmons.

David Lloyd, in his eighteenth season, had his best year since 1972, scoring five centuries, topping 1,300 runs and averaging more than 40. He returned to his more familiar role as opening batsman in July, sharing the position with a fellow-Accringtonian, Graeme Fowler, who distinguished himself by winning an England cap and being chosen to tour Australia in only his second full season in first-class cricket. Fowler, after averaging 40 in 1981, surpassed this by averaging almost 43 and scoring five centuries in the middle two months of the season, three of them against Warwickshire. Frank Hayes was unfortunately out of action nearly all season with injury, but there was some consolation for him in the award of a benefit in 1983. Hughes, however, took the chance provided by Hayes's absence to concentrate, as in 1981, on his batting and scored 1,300 runs at an average of 46.

Perhaps the success story of the season centred around John Abrahams, who was capped the month before his 30th birthday. He was in his tenth season in the first-class game and responded by reaching 1,000 runs for the first time, during his last innings of the season at Taunton. Abrahams has kept going through the years with loyal, uncomplaining service and proved a credit to the game. He matured noticeably almost from the day he received his cap.

Clive Lloyd was the fifth player to reach 1,000 runs, getting there for the seventh time for Lancashire during their last home game. He scored only one century but still kept his average above 40. Simmons, with the help of a high percentage of not outs, averaged 54 an innings and was also the leading wicket-taker, good going for a player in his 42nd year.

The bowling, however, was again not penetrative enough. Colin Croft, the West Indian fast bowler who played with moderate success in 1977 and 1978, promised much on his return and then spent almost the whole of the second half of the season out of the game with injury. Paul Allott, after a wonderful season in 1981, found life harder in 1982. He, too, was upset by injury, missing several games and reaching the last four matches of the season with only fourteen wickets for 558 runs for Lancashire. He played twice for England but missed the tour of Australia.

There was plenty of youthful promise, particularly from Ian Folley and Steve O'Shaughnessy. Folley maintained his place in the team after taking six wickets in the opening match and showed immense potential with his left-arm medium-paced bowling. O'Shaughnessy, who had his 21st birthday near the end of the season, got into the team for only the second half of the summer but swiftly established himself as a middle-order batsman and medium-paced bowler. His batting was particularly impressive with seven half-centuries in eleven matches to finish with more than 500 runs and an average of over 46.

Near the end of the season Lancashire released four senior players including Peter Lee, who took 100 wickets in a season twice, in 1973 and 1975. He took 496 wickets for Lancashire, the last being that of Geoff Boycott in the Roses match at Old Trafford in August. Opening-batsman Andrew Kennedy, a former winner of the Cricket Writers' award as Young Cricketer of the Year (1975), who at one time looked destined to be a future captain of Lancashire, all-rounder Bernard Reidy and wicket-keeper Chris Scott were also not re-engaged.

Two of Lancashire's four Championship wins were tributes to their ability to fight back from daunting positions. They beat Warwickshire by ten wickets after conceding 523 for four declared on the opening day at Southport and beat Somerset by 14 runs at Taunton after entering the final day of the season 56 runs behind with the first four batsmen out. A fine finale to any season. – B.B.

LANCASHIRE 1982

[*Bill Smith*

Back row: J. Abrahams, I. Folley, G. Fowler, C. E. H. Croft, I. Cockbain, C. Maynard, L. L. McFarlane. *Front row:* J. Simmons, D. P. Hughes, C. H. Lloyd (*captain*), D. Lloyd, B. W. Reidy.

LANCASHIRE RESULTS

All first-class matches – Played 24: Won 4, Lost 4, Drawn 16.

County Championship matches – Played 22: Won 4, Lost 3, Drawn 15.

Bonus points – Batting 48, Bowling 55.

Competition placings – Schweppes County Championship, 12th; NatWest Bank Trophy, 2nd round; Benson and Hedges Cup, s-f; John Player League, 10th eq.

COUNTY CHAMPIONSHIP AVERAGES

BATTING

	Birthplace	*M*	*I*	*NO*	*R*	*HI*	*Avge*
J. Simmons c	*Clayton-le-Moors*	17	21	12	487	79*	54.11
D. P. Hughes c	*Newton-le-Willows*	21	33	8	1,196	126*	47.84
S. J. O'Shaughnessy	*Bury*	11	19	7	560	62	46.66
G. Fowler c	*Accrington*	18	30	2	1,219	150	43.53
C. H. Lloyd c	*Georgetown, BG*	20	29	2	1,135	100	42.03
D. Lloyd c	*Accrington*	20	32	2	1,223	114	40.76
J. Abrahams c	*Cape Town, SA*	21	30	5	995	124	39.80
A. Kennedy c	*Blackburn*	7	9	0	189	43	21.00
I. Cockbain	*Bootle*	14	25	1	492	98	20.50
B. W. Reidy c	*Bramley Meade*	8	11	2	151	33*	16.77
I. Folley	*Burnley*	16	13	4	133	36	14.77
P. J. W. Allott c	*Altrincham*	11	9	2	101	30	14.42
C. E. H. Croft c	*Demerara, Guyana*	12	12	3	109	20	12.11
C. Maynard	*Haslemere*	15	18	3	181	37	12.06
C. J. Scott	*Swinton*	6	6	1	29	15	5.80
L. L. McFarlane	*Portland, Jamaica*	11	8	3	16	8	3.20

Also batted: F. C. Hayes c (*Preston*) (2 matches) 43, 21*; K. A. Hayes (*Thurnscoe*) (3 matches) 90, 4*, 9; P. G. Lee c (*Arthingworth*) (2 matches) 0; G. J. Speak (*Chorley*) (2 matches) 1, 7; R. G. Watson (*Rawtenstall*) (1 match) 11, 4; N. H. Fairbrother (*Warrington*); T. J. Taylor (*Romiley*), M. A. Wallwork (*Salford*) and M. Watkinson (*Westhoughton*) (1 match each) did not bat.

**Signifies not out.* c *Denotes county cap.*

BOWLING

	O	*M*	*R*	*W*	*Avge*	*BB*
J. Simmons	538.4	152	1,284	49	26.20	5-57
S. J. O'Shaughnessy	209.2	34	710	27	26.29	4-66
D. P. Hughes	264.1	73	688	26	26.46	4-22
P. J. W. Allott	290	79	734	27	27.18	5-58
C. E. H. Croft	304	60	1,003	33	30.39	7-88
L. L. McFarlane	198.5	38	855	27	31.66	6-59
I. Folley	280	67	694	21	33.04	3-20
D. Lloyd	288.2	67	784	21	37.33	4-36
B. W. Reidy	133	30	450	10	45.00	3-33
J. Abrahams	293.3	58	838	16	52.37	2-19

Also bowled: I. Cockbain 2–2–0–0; G. Fowler 7–3–13–0; A. Kennedy 9–2–28–1; P. G. Lee 27–2–84–2; G. J. Speak 43–4–144–1; T. J. Taylor 16–1–72–1; M. Watkinson 13–4–45–1.

HUNDREDS

The following fourteen three-figure innings were played for Lancashire in County Championship matches – G. Fowler (5) 100 v Gloucestershire (Gloucester), 122 v Essex (Liverpool), 150 v Warwickshire (Birmingham), 126 and 128* v Warwickshire (Southport); D. Lloyd (5) 114 v Derbyshire (Manchester), 108 v Gloucestershire (Gloucester), 112 v Hampshire (Southampton), 112* v Northamptonshire (Manchester), 103 v Kent (Manchester); D. P. Hughes (2) 126* v Yorkshire (Leeds), 111 v Derbyshire (Derby); J. Abrahams (1) 124 v Surrey (Manchester); C. H. Lloyd (1) 100 v Yorkshire (Manchester).

LANCASHIRE v NOTTINGHAMSHIRE

At Manchester, May 5, 6. Nottinghamshire won by an innings and 37 runs. Nottinghamshire 23 pts, Lancashire 4 pts. Nottinghamshire began the defence of their Championship title in convincing style, winning in two days on an unreliable pitch. Cooper dominated the opening day with afternoon figures of six for 14, and on the second day, with Randall, Birch and Hadlee scoring half-centuries, Nottinghamshire took a first-innings lead of 166. Batting a second time, Lancashire lost their opening batsmen before a run had been scored and they were unable to recover in the face of hostile bowling by Hadlee. McFarlane, formerly of Bedfordshire and Northamptonshire, made his début for Lancashire, and Croft was back in the team after a three-year absence.

Lancashire

A. Kennedy b Hadlee	21	– c French b Hadlee	0
I. Cockbain c French b Hendrick	11	– c Randall b Hendrick	0
D. Lloyd lbw b Hadlee	5	– lbw b Cooper	14
*C. H. Lloyd c French b Cooper	21	– c Hemmings b Hadlee	13
J. Abrahams c Hendrick b Cooper	40	– lbw b Hadlee	14
D. P. Hughes c French b Cooper	0	– c French b Cooper	3
J. Simmons lbw b Cooper	1	– lbw b Hadlee	41
†C. J. Scott c Randall b Cooper	0	– c French b Cooper	15
P. J. W. Allott c Hadlee b Cooper	9	– not out	8
C. E. H. Croft not out	2	– c French b Hadlee	16
L. L. McFarlane c Randall b Hadlee	1	– lbw b Hadlee	0
B 1, l-b 4, n-b 4	9	L-b 5	5
1/29 2/37 3/44 4/70 5/70 6/86 7/88 8/113 9/118	120	1/0 2/0 3/31 4/31 5/49 6/53 7/97 8/105 9/129	129

Bonus points – Nottinghamshire 4.

Bowling: *First Innings*—Hadlee 17.1–6–27–3; Hendrick 16–9–18–1; Cooper 31–13–46–6; Hemmings 6–2–20–0. *Second Innings*—Hadlee 17.5–3–65–6; Hendrick 10–3–26–1; Cooper 17–9–33–3.

Nottinghamshire

P. A. Todd c McFarlane b Allott	4
R. T. Robinson c Scott b Croft	12
D. W. Randall b Croft	61
*C. E. B. Rice b Allott	39
J. D. Birch b McFarlane	71
R. J. Hadlee b Simmons	59
†B. N. French c Croft b McFarlane	10
N. J. B. Illingworth not out	11
E. E. Hemmings c Croft b McFarlane	2
K. E. Cooper b McFarlane	0
M. Hendrick b Simmons	0
B 4, l-b 6, w 7	17
1/7 2/21 3/104 4/164 5/245 6/265 7/273 8/279 9/285	286

Bonus points – Nottinghamshire 3, Lancashire 4.

Bowling: Croft 23–3–96–2; Allott 21–3–76–2; McFarlane 15–3–64–4; Simmons 13.4–3–33–2.

Umpires: D. J. Constant and J. van Geloven.

At Cambridge, May 12, 13, 14. LANCASHIRE lost to CAMBRIDGE UNIVERSITY by seven wickets.

At Manchester, May 15. Lancashire beat Surrey by nine wickets. Surrey 246 for eight (55 overs) (R. D. V. Knight 88, A. R. Butcher 50; I. Folley four for 58); Lancashire 248 for one (53 overs) (A. Kennedy 131 not out, I. Cockbain 80 not out).

LANCASHIRE v DERBYSHIRE

At Manchester, May 19, 20, 21. Drawn. Lancashire 7 pts, Derbyshire 6 pts. A fourth-wicket partnership of 92 between Hill and Hampshire helped Derbyshire recover from 50 for three, but they provided the only real resistance to Croft, whose hostile bowling earned him seven wickets. Folley, making his Championship début for Lancashire, started encouragingly by taking the other three. Lancashire took a lead of 71 after a third-wicket partnership of 106 between their two Lloyds. Clive was out for 73 in the over before lunch, but David took control of the innings with a resolute 114 in five hours, ten minutes. However, any faint hopes Lancashire had of winning were denied them by Kirsten.

Derbyshire

*B. Wood c Simmons b Croft	17	– lbw b Reidy	36
J. G. Wright c Scott b Folley	24	– c Speak b Reidy	39
P. N. Kirsten lbw b Folley	0	– b Simmons	81
J. H. Hampshire c C. H. Lloyd b Folley	54	– lbw b D. Lloyd	30
A. Hill c Scott b Croft	54	– (7) not out	13
I. S. Anderson lbw b Croft	8	– (5) not out	33
†R. W. Taylor c Scott b Croft	3	– (6) c Reidy b Simmons	0
C. J. Tunnicliffe b Croft	0		
D. G. Moir lbw b Croft	3		
S. Oldham b Croft	23		
P. J. Hacker not out	10		
L-b 14, w 1, n-b 5	20	B 1, l-b 3, w 1, n-b 5	10
1/36 2/36 3/50 4/142 5/165 6/175 7/175 8/180 9/185	216	1/81 2/81 3/186 4/202 5/216	(5 wkts) 242

Bonus points – Derbyshire 2, Lancashire 4.

Bowling: *First Innings*—Croft 33–7–88–7; Folley 20–3–37–3; Reidy 15–1–42–0; Speak 10–1–25–0; D. Lloyd 1–0–4–0. *Second Innings*—Croft 20–2–81–0; Folley 10–3–20–0; Speak 5–0–24–0; D. Lloyd 19–4–49–1; Simmons 16–4–42–2; Reidy 5–1–16–2.

Lancashire

A. Kennedy lbw b Oldham	3
G. Fowler c Taylor b Oldham	12
D. Lloyd c Tunnicliffe b Hacker	114
*C. H. Lloyd c and b Anderson	73
I. Cockbain lbw b Oldham	7
B. W. Reidy c Taylor b Hacker	19
I. Folley c Taylor b Hacker	36
†C. J. Scott b Hacker	1
C. E. H. Croft c Anderson b Tunnicliffe	3
G. J. Speak lbw b Hacker	1
J. Simmons not out	3
B 7, l-b 3, n-b 5	15
1/8 2/17 3/123 4/137 5/176 6/259 7/265 8/274 9/284	287

Bonus points – Lancashire 3, Derbyshire 4.

Bowling: Oldham 17–4–57–3; Tunnicliffe 23–3–68–1; Hacker 18.1–1–51–5; Wood 18–6–47–0; Anderson 10–1–29–1; Moir 6–1–15–0; Kirsten 2–1–5–0.

Umpires: C. T. Spencer and P. B. Wight.

At Leeds, May 29, 30, 31. LANCASHIRE drew with YORKSHIRE.

At Gloucester, June 2, 3, 4. LANCASHIRE drew with GLOUCESTERSHIRE.

LANCASHIRE v GLAMORGAN

At Manchester, June 5, 7, 8. Lancashire won by 206 runs. Lancashire 22 pts, Glamorgan 4 pts. Hughes, run out attempting a sharp single to bring him his third century of the season, led Lancashire's recovery on the first day after four wickets had fallen for 43 runs, all to Ontong. Glamorgan collapsed on the second morning and went into the final day needing 338 for victory, a target well beyond their capabilities. Four bowlers shared the wickets in Lancashire's first win of the season, including Croft and Abrahams who were capped during the match. Abrahams, 29, had made his début in 1973, was in his 126th first-class match, and was the country's most senior uncapped player.

Lancashire

I. Cockbain lbw b Ontong	9	– lbw b Barwick	36
G. Fowler c Davies b Ontong	18	– b Lloyd	52
D. Lloyd lbw b Ontong	8	– c Miandad b Ontong	30
*C. H. Lloyd c Davies b Ontong	0	– not out	53
D. P. Hughes run out	99	– lbw b Lloyd	17
J. Abrahams c Hopkins b Miandad	39	– b Daniels	1
B. W. Reidy c Davies b Daniels	9		
I. Folley c Davies b Barwick	18		
P. J. W. Allott c Miandad b Lloyd	17		
C. E. H. Croft c Davies b Lloyd	17	– (7) c A. Jones b Lloyd	2
†C. J. Scott not out	0		
B 2, l-b 4	6	B 12, l-b 7, n-b 2	21
1/27 2/30 3/32 4/43 5/130 6/145 7/206 8/206 9/239	240	1/81 2/99 3/147 4/194 5/203 6/212 (6 wkts dec.)	212

Bonus points – Lancashire 2, Glamorgan 4.

Bowling: *First Innings*—Daniels 15–3–58–1; Barwick 24–6–53–1; Ontong 24–9–53–4; Lloyd 7.2–3–22–2; Miandad 17–5–48–1. *Second Innings*—Ontong 18–5–52–1; Barwick 9–2–22–1; Daniels 11–2–29–1; Lloyd 22.4–3–83–3; Miandad 3–2–5–0.

Glamorgan

A. Jones c Fowler b Allott	2	– lbw b Reidy	17
J. A. Hopkins c Allott b Folley	36	– c Fowler b Croft	23
R. C. Ontong c Cockbain b Allott	11	– lbw b Reidy	4
B. J. Lloyd b Croft	0	– (10) not out	1
*Javed Miandad c C. H. Lloyd b Croft	4	– (4) lbw b Reidy	16
C. J. C. Rowe c D. Lloyd b Croft	0	– (5) b Croft	1
A. L. Jones c Hughes b Folley	12	– (6) c Reidy b Abrahams	49
D. A. Francis run out	16	– (7) b D. Lloyd	5
†T. Davies run out	25	– (8) b D. Lloyd	8
S. A. B. Daniels c Scott b Reidy	0	– (9) b D. Lloyd	0
S. R. Barwick not out	3	– lbw b Abrahams	0
B 1, l-b 3, n-b 2	6	L-b 3, n-b 4	7
1/9 2/32 3/34 4/49 5/49 6/63 7/72 8/103 9/103	115	1/23 2/31 3/49 4/58 5/70 6/80 7/130 8/130 9/130	131

Bonus points – Lancashire 4.

Bowling: *First Innings*—Croft 20–7–42–3; Allott 15–5–27–2; Folley 15–4–30–2; Reidy 8–4–10–1. *Second Innings*—Allott 16–8–15–0; Croft 17–5–24–2; Reidy 17–5–33–3; Abrahams 9.3–2–22–2; D. Lloyd 17–10–23–3; Folley 6–1–7–0.

Umpires: J. Birkenshaw and R. S. Herman.

At Southampton, June 9, 10, 11. LANCASHIRE lost to HAMPSHIRE by ten wickets.

LANCASHIRE v ESSEX

At Liverpool, June 12, 14, 15. Drawn. Lancashire 3 pts, Essex 8 pts. Lancashire were unable to get on top of a varied Essex attack in their first innings, despite passing 100 with only two wickets down. Fletcher closed Essex's first innings as soon as he had maximum batting points, although centuries were there for the taking both for himself and McEwan. Lancashire batted much better second time round on the perfect Aigburth pitch, but with Essex waiting for the declaration, rain ended the game soon after two o'clock. Fowler hit six 6s in his second century of the season, Hughes's unbeaten 85 occupied only just over 40 minutes, and Lancashire's last 122 runs came in half an hour.

Lancashire

G. Fowler c D. E. East b Acfield	37	– c Hardie b Fletcher	122
I. Cockbain c Turner b Phillip	2	– lbw b Phillip	3
*D. Lloyd lbw b Phillip	29	– c Acfield b Phillip	20
F. C. Hayes b Foster	43		
D. P. Hughes c R. E. East b Turner	6	– not out	85
J. Abrahams b R. E. East	53	– (4) c Hardie b Fletcher	90
B. W. Reidy c Turner b Acfield	8	– (6) c Acfield b McEwan	29
†C. Maynard c Hardie b Foster	1	– (7) not out	2
J. Simmons b R. E. East	34		
C. E. H. Croft c R. E. East b Phillip	12		
L. L. McFarlane not out	0		
L-b 3, n-b 9	12	B 5, l-b 3, w 1, n-b 7	16
1/8 2/51 3/114 4/120 5/133 6/147 7/155 8/216 9/237	237	1/3 2/45 3/228 4/279 5/352 (5 wkts)	367

Bonus points – Lancashire 2, Essex 4.

Bowling: *First Innings*—Phillip 22.4–6–63–3; Foster 14–2–57–2; Turner 22–9–36–1; R. E. East 13–5–31–2; Acfield 13–4–38–2. *Second Innings*—Phillip 21–8–43–2; Turner 20–7–50–0; R. E. East 16–5–39–0; Acfield 14–3–31–0; Fletcher 13–0–103–2; McEwan 6–0–64–1; Gooch 18–10–21–0.

Essex

G. A. Gooch lbw b Reidy	66
B. R. Hardie c Cockbain b Croft	18
A. W. Lilley c and b Simmons	39
K. S. McEwan not out	92
*K. W. R. Fletcher not out	73
B 1, w 1, n-b 10	12
1/29 2/133 3/133 (3 wkts dec.)	300

N. Phillip, S. Turner, †D. E. East, N. A. Foster, R. E. East and D. L. Acfield did not bat.

Bonus points – Essex 4, Lancashire 1.

Bowling: Croft 23–7–64–1; McFarlane 14–3–62–0; Simmons 29–8–81–1; Reidy 18–5–48–1; D. Lloyd 7.2–0–28–0; Abrahams 3–0–5–0.

Umpires: A. Jepson and N. T. Plews.

At Lord's, June 19, 21, 22. LANCASHIRE drew with MIDDLESEX.

At The Oval, June 23, 24, 25. LANCASHIRE drew with SURREY.

At Worcester, June 26, 28, 29. LANCASHIRE lost to WORCESTERSHIRE by 89 runs.

At Birmingham, July 7, 8, 9. LANCASHIRE drew with WARWICKSHIRE.

LANCASHIRE v SURREY

At Manchester, July 10, 12, 13. Lancashire won by four wickets. Lancashire 22 pts, Surrey 5 pts. A magnificent maiden century from Needham, who went in to bat at 74 for seven, and a last-wicket partnership of 172 with Jackman, revived Surrey's first innings. The tenth-wicket stand was only 1 run short of the Surrey record, set in 1921 by Sandham and Ducat against Essex at Leyton. Abrahams averted any danger of the follow-on with his highest Championship innings. Surrey found Simmons difficult to overcome in their second innings, but with Jackman getting his second half-century of the match, they were able to set Lancashire a target of 252 in 164 minutes. This they achieved in a thrilling finish with two balls remaining, Clive Lloyd and Abrahams having played the major parts.

Surrey

D. B. Pauline lbw b Simmons	2	– c D. Lloyd b Folley	1
G. S. Clinton c Hayes b O'Shaughnessy	12		
G. P. Howarth c Maynard b Folley	29	– (4) c Hughes b Simmons	17
*R. D. V. Knight c C. H. Lloyd b O'Shaughnessy	6	– (9) not out	17
M. A. Lynch lbw b O'Shaughnessy	0	– c Hughes b Simmons	9
G. R. J. Roope c Fowler b Simmons	8	– not out	49
†C. J. Richards c and b Abrahams	63	– c C. H. Lloyd b Simmons	6
D. J. Thomas lbw b Speak	0		
A. Needham not out	134	– (2) c Abrahams b Simmons	1
S. T. Clarke c Maynard b Abrahams	0	– (8) c Speak b Simmons	6
R. D. Jackman b Hughes	60	– (3) st Maynard b D. Lloyd	68
L-b 6, w 1, n-b 3	10	L-b 2	2
1/6 2/17 3/39 4/47 5/53 6/62 7/74 8/152 9/152	324	1/1 2/7 3/50 4/63 5/127 6/138 7/144 (7 wkts dec.)	176

Bonus points – Surrey 1, Lancashire 4 (Score at 100 overs: 197-9).

Bowling: *First Innings*—Folley 16–4–28–1; Speak 24–3–78–1; Simmons 33–14–54–2; O'Shaughnessy 29–6–89–3; Hughes 17.1–7–37–1; D. Lloyd 3–0–9–0; Abrahams 14–6–19–2. *Second Innings*—Speak 4–0–17–0; Simmons 25–7–57–5; Folley 11–2–29–1; O'Shaughnessy 5–2–6–0; D. Lloyd 15–4–52–1; Abrahams 4–0–13–0.

Lancashire

D. Lloyd c Roope b Jackman	6	lbw b Thomas	36
G. Fowler c Howarth b Jackman	11	c Roope b Needham	21
†C. Maynard c Richards b Clarke	8	b Needham	1
*C. H. Lloyd lbw b Knight	34	b Lynch	76
D. P. Hughes b Needham	20	run out	21
J. Abrahams c Howarth b Needham	124	run out	58
S. J. O'Shaughnessy b Needham	11	(8) not out	0
J. Simmons b Needham	2	(7) not out	31
I. Folley c Roope b Needham	14		
G. J. Speak b Clarke	7		
K. A. Hayes not out	4		
L-b 7, n-b 1	8	B 2, l-b 2, n-b 4	8
1/11 2/28 3/28 4/70 5/92 6/136 7/159 8/190 9/208	249	1/43 2/58 3/62 4/144 5/162 6/250 (6 wkts)	252

Bonus points – Lancashire 2, Surrey 4.

Bowling: *First Innings*—Clarke 23–8–45–2; Jackman 15–5–42–2; Thomas 10–1–26–0; Needham 30.3–7–91–5; Knight 8–2–23–1; Lynch 8–2–14–0. *Second Innings*—Clarke 10.4–2–42–0; Jackman 4–0–7–0; Needham 15–1–113–2; Thomas 10–2–30–1; Lynch 9–1–52–1.

Umpires: W. L. Budd and B. J. Meyer.

LANCASHIRE v NORTHAMPTONSHIRE

At Manchester, July 21, 22, 23. Drawn. Lancashire 6 pts, Northamptonshire 6 pts. More than 1,100 runs were scored on a dry pitch taking spin. David Lloyd, missed twice in the slips off Mallender, and Fowler gave Lancashire a century start, but ground was lost to the spinners before Abrahams, Simmons and O'Shaughnessy reasserted control. Willey's century, which took 165 minutes and included eighteen boundaries, enabled him to reach 1,000 runs for the season for the first time since 1976 and Northamptonshire declared 67 runs behind. David Lloyd then hit his fourth century of the season, O'Shaughnessy his second fifty of the game, and Northamptonshire were set 283 to win in 185 minutes. They scored the first 100 in an hour, but when Hughes took four wickets they settled for a draw. Lancashire fielded with only ten men for the first 50 minutes as Clive Lloyd, their captain, was away from the ground on personal business and so could not be replaced by a substitute fielder.

Lancashire

D. Lloyd c and b Willey	61	not out	112
G. Fowler c Sharp b Steele	66	b Willey	35
K. A. Hayes lbw b Willey	9		
D. P. Hughes c Boyd-Moss b Steele	14	b Steele	4
*C. H. Lloyd hit wkt b Steele	28		
J. Abrahams c Mallender b Williams	49		
S. J. O'Shaughnessy c Cook b T. M. Lamb	56	(3) b T. M. Lamb	50
J. Simmons not out	79	(5) not out	5
†C. Maynard c Cook b Steele	10		
B 6, l-b 9, n-b 10	25	L-b 7, n-b 2	9
1/106 2/133 3/161 4/180 5/203 6/277 7/356 8/397 (8 wkts dec.)	397	1/77 2/201 3/206 (3 wkts dec.)	215

I. Folley and L. L. McFarlane did not bat.

Bonus points – Lancashire 4, Northamptonshire 2 (Score at 100 overs: 301-6).

Bowling: *First Innings*—Griffiths 11.1–2–42–0; Mallender 22–6–93–0; T. M. Lamb 20.5–6–56–1; Willey 30–9–52–2; Steele 28.5–7–82–4; Williams 13–3–47–1. *Second Innings*—Mallender 6–1–21–0; T. M. Lamb 9–0–38–1; Willey 19–4–34–1; Steele 18–2–54–1; Williams 18–4–59–0.

Northamptonshire

*G. Cook c C. H. Lloyd b D. Lloyd	61	– c and b Abrahams	66
W. Larkins c Maynard b Folley	4	– b Hughes	44
P. Willey c C. H. Lloyd b Hughes	102	– c and b Hughes	34
A. J. Lamb st Maynard b Hughes	30	– c Abrahams b Hughes	25
R. G. Williams c and b Abrahams	27	– c Hughes b Simmons	4
R. J. Boyd-Moss not out	62	– c C. H. Lloyd b Hughes	3
D. S. Steele not out	32	– not out	32
†G. Sharp (did not bat)		– not out	1
B 8, l-b 1, n-b 3	12	B 6, l-b 8	14
1/4 2/131 3/195 4/204 5/260 (5 wkts dec.)	330	1/116 2/118 3/180 4/183 5/187 6/187 (6 wkts)	223

N. A. Mallender, T. M. Lamb and B. J. Griffiths did not bat.

Bonus points – Northamptonshire 4, Lancashire 2 (Score at 100 overs: 302-5).

Bowling: *First Innings*—McFarlane 14–6–55–0; Folley 7–2–21–1; O'Shaughnessy 2–0–9–0; Simmons 24–0–53–0; D. Lloyd 16–3–42–1; Abrahams 22–2–75–1; Hughes 23–10–63–2. *Second Innings*—McFarlane 9–1–49–0; Folley 3–0–24–0; Simmons 13–1–46–1; Hughes 22–7–50–4; Abrahams 13–1–40–1; D. Lloyd 3–3–0–0.

Umpires: D. G. L. Evans and B. Leadbeater.

LANCASHIRE v WARWICKSHIRE

At Southport, July 28, 29, 30. Lancashire won by ten wickets. Lancashire 21 pts, Warwickshire 6 pts. In one of the most remarkable matches in the history of the County Championship, Lancashire won with the utmost ease after Warwickshire had scored 523 for four declared on the opening day. Kallicharran, with his third double-century of the season, and Humpage, with a career-best 254, shared in a stand of 470 in 293 minutes, the biggest for the fourth wicket in English cricket, beating the 448 by Abel and Hayward for Surrey against Yorkshire at The Oval in 1899. It was the highest partnership for any Warwickshire wicket, beating Jameson's and Kanhai's 465 against Gloucestershire at Edgbaston in 1974, was the ninth highest stand ever, and the fourth best in the Championship. Humpage's thirteen 6s were the most by an Englishman in one innings. On the second day of this eventful match, Warwickshire manager David Brown became the first substitute to take a wicket in county cricket when he stood in for Small, who was standing by for England in the morning and back in the match in the afternoon. Lancashire declared 109 behind after a century in 109 minutes from Fowler, and on the third day McFarlane had a career-best bowling performance to set up an astonishing victory for Lancashire, for whom Fowler hit a second century. Having hurt himself fielding on the opening day, Fowler batted with a runner on the second and third days.

Warwickshire

*D. L. Amiss c Abrahams b McFarlane	6	– c Scott b McFarlane	24
R. I. H. B. Dyer c Simmons b McFarlane	0	– c Abrahams b McFarlane	0
T. A. Lloyd c Scott b Folley	23	– b McFarlane	0
A. I. Kallicharran not out	230	– (5) c D. Lloyd b O'Shaughnessy	0
†G. W. Humpage b D. Lloyd	254	– (6) c Abrahams b O'Shaughnessy	21
Asif Din (did not bat)		– (4) c Hughes b O'Shaughnessy	21
S. H. Wootton (did not bat)		– b McFarlane	0
C. Lethbridge (did not bat)		– c Hughes b Folley	18
G. C. Small (did not bat)		– lbw b McFarlane	0
P. J. Hartley (did not bat)		– c Scott b McFarlane	16
S. P. Sutcliffe (did not bat)		– not out	7
B 1, l-b 6, w 1, n-b 2	10	B 1, l-b 2, w 1	4
1/5 2/6 3/53 4/523 (4 wkts dec.)	523	1/1 2/1 3/47 4/47 5/47 6/47 7/76 8/81 9/99	111

Bonus points – Warwickshire 4, Lancashire 1 (Score at 100 overs: 441-3).

Bowling: *First Innings*—McFarlane 11–2–90–2; Folley 15–3–64–1; O'Shaughnessy 15–2–62–0; Simmons 20–2–97–0; Hughes 20–2–79–0; Abrahams 15–3–76–0; D. Lloyd 10.1–1–45–1. *Second Innings*—McFarlane 20–3–59–6; Folley 11–5–19–1; O'Shaughnessy 7.1–0–29–3; Simmons 1–1–0–0.

Lancashire

G. Fowler b Asif Din	126	– not out	128
D. Lloyd c Humpage b Small	10	– not out	88
†C. J. Scott lbw b Brown (sub)	9		
I. Cockbain c Amiss b Kallicharran	98		
*C. H. Lloyd c Humpage b Kallicharran	45		
D. P. Hughes c Small b Kallicharran	14		
J. Abrahams not out	51		
S. J. O'Shaughnessy not out	26		
L-b 13, w 3, n-b 19	35	L-b 2, n-b 8	10
1/34 2/109 3/194 4/305 5/327 6/333 (6 wkts dec.)	414	(no wkt)	226

J. Simmons, I. Folley and L. L. McFarlane did not bat.

Bonus points – Lancashire 4, Warwickshire 2 (Score at 100 overs: 357-6).

Bowling: *First Innings*—Small 15–4–38–1; Hartley 14–0–66–0; Sutcliffe 38–9–103–0; Lethbridge 14–5–58–0; D. J. Brown (sub) 13–3–47–1; Asif Din 6–1–35–1; Kallicharran 13–3–32–3. *Second Innings*—Small 11–2–30–0; Hartley 9–1–38–0; Sutcliffe 19–5–60–0; Lethbridge 9–2–27–0; Asif Din 5–0–25–0; Kallicharran 6–0–35–0; Lloyd 1–0–1–0.

Umpires: H. D. Bird and J. van Geloven.

At Nottingham, July 31, August 2, 3. LANCASHIRE drew with NOTTINGHAMSHIRE.

LANCASHIRE v YORKSHIRE

At Manchester, August 7, 9, 10. Drawn. Lancashire 4 pts, Yorkshire 2 pts. Some seven hours of play were lost to rain on the first two days, which ended with Lancashire having closed their first innings after Clive Lloyd's only century of the season. It was, however, his sixth Roses century, a record for Lancashire. Yorkshire forfeited their first innings on the final day, Lancashire declared in the ninth over of their second innings, but the target of 341 was too demanding.

Lancashire

D. Lloyd lbw b Sidebottom	31	
G. Fowler lbw b Ramage	4	– (1) not out 17
I. Cockbain b Ramage	0	– (2) not out 13
*C. H. Lloyd c Carrick b Taylor	100	
D. P. Hughes b Sidebottom	6	
J. Abrahams c Bairstow b Hartley	41	
S. J. O'Shaughnessy not out	41	
J. Simmons not out	61	
B 8, l-b 5, n-b 13	26	
1/29 2/31 3/53 4/79 5/201 6/207	(6 wkts dec.) 310	(no wkt dec.) 30

†C. Maynard, P. J. W. Allott and P. G. Lee did not bat.

Bonus points – Lancashire 4, Yorkshire 2.

Bowling: *First Innings*—Ramage 23–7–69–2; Taylor 24.3–7–72–1; Sidebottom 19–4–60–2; Hartley 13–3–37–1; Illingworth 5–1–10–0; Carrick 10–3–36–0. *Second Innings*—Athey 4.1–0–16–0; Hartley 4–1–14–0.

Yorkshire

G. Boycott (did not bat)	– lbw b Lee	62
R. G. Lumb (did not bat)	– c D. Lloyd b Allott	15
C. W. J. Athey (did not bat)	– c Maynard b Simmons	2
J. D. Love (did not bat)	– not out	38
S. N. Hartley (did not bat)	– not out	15
	B 6, w 1, n-b 3	10
	1/19 2/44 3/110	(3 wkts) 142

†D. L. Bairstow, P. Carrick, A. Sidebottom, A. Ramage, N. S. Taylor and *R. Illingworth did not bat.

Bowling: Allott 15–6–19–1; Lee 10–0–19–1; Simmons 14–4–33–1; O'Shaughnessy 8–1–32–0; Hughes 7–3–7–0; D. Lloyd 14–8–11–0; Abrahams 12–6–9–0; Fowler 2–1–2–0; Cockbain 2–2–0–0.

Yorkshire forfeited their first innings.

Umpires: B. J. Meyer and D. R. Shepherd.

At Derby, August 11, 12, 13. LANCASHIRE drew with DERBYSHIRE.

At Leicester, August 14, 16, 17. LANCASHIRE drew with LEICESTERSHIRE.

At Manchester, August 21, 22, 23. LANCASHIRE drew with PAKISTANIS (See Pakistani tour section).

LANCASHIRE v WORCESTERSHIRE

At Blackpool, August 25, 26, 27. Drawn. Lancashire 7 pts, Worcestershire 4 pts. Allott, who had taken only fourteen wickets in nine matches for Lancashire, had his best performance of the season after the start of the game had been delayed until 1.45 p.m. Worcestershire, who won the toss, lost their last five wickets for 14 runs, three of them to O'Shaughnessy who proved Lancashire's best batsmen on the second day when less than three hours of play were possible. A bright innings by Hughes the following morning gave Lancashire a lead of 132, and with Worcestershire collapsing against the spin of Hughes and Simmons, the prospect of an innings win opened up. However, Humphries scored an undefeated half-century to deny Lancashire.

Worcestershire

J. A. Ormrod c Maynard b Allott	3	– c Simmons b Allott	9
M. J. Weston c Simmons b McFarlane	8	– c Simmons b Hughes	24
D. N. Patel c C. H. Lloyd b McFarlane	0	– c C. H. Lloyd b Simmons	12
Younis Ahmed lbw b Allott	30	– c O'Shaughnessy b Hughes	4
*P. A. Neale b D. Lloyd	26	– lbw b Simmons	5
T. S. Curtis b O'Shaughnessy	35	– b Hughes	2
†D. J. Humphries b Allott	16	– not out	55
R. K. Illingworth b O'Shaughnessy	0	– lbw b Simmons	0
A. E. Warner b O'Shaughnessy	9	– c D. Lloyd b Abrahams	23
A. J. Webster b Allott	4	– not out	0
S. P. Perryman not out	0		
B 9, l-b 4, n-b 1	14	B 9, l-b 2, w 1, n-b 2	14
1/11 2/11 3/19 4/60 5/87 6/131 7/131 8/135 9/145	145	1/26 2/47 3/54 4/59 5/59 6/61 7/66 8/142 (8 wkts)	148

Bonus points – Lancashire 4.

Bowling: *First Innings*—Allott 14.1–4–32–4; McFarlane 4–0–26–2; Folley 5–2–6–0; Simmons 18–7–31–0; D. Lloyd 13–6–17–1; O'Shaughnessy 6–1–19–3. *Second Innings*—Allott 10–4–16–1; McFarlane 3–0–11–0; O'Shaughnessy 10–4–24–0; Hughes 17–8–23–3; Simmons 25–16–31–3; D. Lloyd 8–1–24–0; Abrahams 4–3–5–1.

Lancashire

D. Lloyd lbw b Webster	0
I. Cockbain c Curtis b Illingworth	29
S. J. O'Shaughnessy c Younis b Perryman	58
*C. H. Lloyd b Perryman	35
D. P. Hughes c Humphries b Perryman	93
J. Abrahams c Curtis b Perryman	0
J. Simmons c Humphries b Perryman	10
†C. Maynard b Perryman	2
P. J. W. Allott c Humphries b Webster	14
I. Folley not out	10
L. L. McFarlane b Warner	3
B 3, l-b 7, n-b 13	23
1/0 2/58 3/127 4/178 5/178 6/212 7/215 8/251 9/271	277

Bonus points – Lancashire 3, Worcestershire 4.

Bowling: Webster 29–4–113–2; Warner 6.1–4–6–1; Patel 15–3–33–0; Illingworth 15–4–53–1; Perryman 26–6–49–6.

Umpires: B. Leadbeater and C. T. Spencer.

LANCASHIRE v KENT

At Manchester, August 28, 30, 31. Drawn. Lancashire 4 pts, Kent 1 pt. Allott's best bowling performance of a disappointing summer for him gave Lancashire the chance to take a commanding position by the end of the first day, only 54 behind with eight wickets standing. But with the second day lost to rain, Lancashire declared on the last morning at their Saturday score. A fine innings by Aslett, plus an explosive half-century from Baptiste, allowed Kent to set Lancashire a target of 273 for victory in 175 minutes. An opening stand of 83 was followed by one of 82 between the two Lloyds, with David hitting his fifth century of the season in 128 minutes. Then Jarvis dismissed them both in one over, and although Hughes kept Lancashire in the hunt, they were unable to make it.

Kent

R. A. Woolmer lbw b O'Shaughnessy	14	– c Abrahams b Watkinson	29
N. R. Taylor lbw b O'Shaughnessy	0	– lbw b Allott	9
D. G. Aslett lbw b Allott	37	– b D. Lloyd	60
M. R. Benson c Maynard b Abrahams	48	– c Hughes b O'Shaughnessy	8
*G. W. Johnson lbw b Allott	10	– b Taylor	25
E. A. Baptiste lbw b Allott	20	– not out	51
†A. P. E. Knott c Allott b Abrahams	1	– not out	22
R. M. Ellison lbw b Allott	0		
G. R. Dilley not out	17		
D. L. Underwood b Allott	0		
K. B. S. Jarvis lbw b O'Shaughnessy	5		
L-b 3, n-b 4	7	L-b 8, n-b 6	14
1/0 2/28 3/92 4/111 5/136 6/137 7/137 8/138 9/138	159	1/28 2/52 3/62 4/128 5/160 (5 wkts dec.)	218

Bonus points – Kent 1, Lancashire 4.

Bowling: *First Innings*—Allott 25–8–58–5; O'Shaughnessy 14.3–4–24–3; Watkinson 5–3–21–0; Taylor 3–0–15–0; Abrahams 15–6–30–2; D. Lloyd 1–0–4–0. *Second Innings*—Allott 7–0–22–1; O'Shaughnessy 11–3–37–1; Watkinson 8–1–24–1; Abrahams 11–4–42–0; Taylor 13–1–57–1; D. Lloyd 3–0–22–1.

Lancashire

D. Lloyd b Jarvis	29	– c Johnson b Jarvis	103
I. Cockbain c Johnson b Ellison	43	– c and b Baptiste	21
S. J. O'Shaughnessy not out	25	– (8) not out	9
†C. Maynard not out	1	– (7) b Underwood	5
*C. H. Lloyd (did not bat)		– (3) lbw b Jarvis	31
D. P. Hughes (did not bat)		– (4) not out	63
J. Abrahams (did not bat)		– (5) c Johnson b Dilley	0
P. J. W. Allott (did not bat)		– (6) run out	5
L-b 2, n-b 5	7	B 2, l-b 2, n-b 6	10
1/42 2/96 (2 wkts dec.)	105	1/83 2/165 3/166 4/169 5/185 6/204 (6 wkts)	247

N. H. Fairbrother, M. Watkinson and T. J. Taylor did not bat.

Bowling: *First Innings*—Dilley 7–2–20–0; Jarvis 7–1–43–1; Ellison 7–2–14–1; Baptiste 4–1–19–0; Underwood 4–4–0–0; Johnson 1–0–2–0. *Second Innings*—Dilley 13–2–45–1; Jarvis 8–1–28–2; Ellison 4–1–14–0; Underwood 17.3–1–96–1; Baptiste 6–0–38–1; Aslett 3–0–16–0.

Umpires: R. S. Herman and B. Leadbeater.

LANCASHIRE v SUSSEX

At Manchester, September 8, 9, 10. Drawn. Lancashire 4 pts, Sussex 5 pts. Sussex were unable to take full advantage of an opening stand of 187 in 64 overs between Mendis and

Green, the scoring tempo declining so much that Sussex were only 255 for two after 100 overs. Fowler followed his fine innings for England by batting more than four hours before Lancashire declared 14 behind. All but one of Sussex's second-innings wickets fell to spin and Lancashire were left with 132 minutes in which to score 238. They sacrificed wickets in their attempt, but with seven of the last twenty overs remaining and only two wickets standing the game was ended by bad light.

Sussex

G. D. Mendis lbw b Simmons	104	– b Hughes	6
A. M. Green c Hughes b Simmons	82	– b Simmons	18
*J. R. T. Barclay c Hughes b Simmons	39	– (4) lbw b D. Lloyd	53
P. W. G. Parker c Fowler b Hughes	22	– (5) st Maynard b Simmons	0
C. M. Wells lbw b Allott	24	– (6) b Hughes	33
A. P. Wells not out	15	– (7) b Abrahams	39
†I. J. Gould run out	15	– (8) c Folley b Simmons	18
G. S. le Roux (did not bat)		– (3) c C. H. Lloyd b Hughes	0
I. A. Greig (did not bat)		– c Hughes b Simmons	31
C. E. Waller (did not bat)		– not out	9
A. C. S. Pigott (did not bat)		– st Maynard b Folley	4
B 3, l-b 6, n-b 5	14	B 4, l-b 6, n-b 2	12
1/187 2/195 3/257 4/260 5/296 6/315	(6 wkts dec.) 315	1/17 2/17 3/46 4/48 5/95 6/152 7/154 8/202 9/212	223

Bonus points – Sussex 3 (Score at 100 overs: 255-2).

Bowling: *First Innings*—Allott 21.5–3–72–1; Folley 20–5–38–0; O'Shaughnessy 16–0–60–0; Simmons 36–11–68–3; Hughes 14–2–30–1; Abrahams 7–0–19–0; D. Lloyd 4–0–14–0. *Second Innings*—Allott 7–3–14–0; Folley 11.5–2–19–1; Simmons 26–10–60–4; Hughes 12–3–24–3; O'Shaughnessy 3–0–13–0; D. Lloyd 11–3–23–1; Abrahams 18–3–58–1.

Lancashire

D. Lloyd lbw b le Roux	7	– c Mendis b Greig	11
G. Fowler c Greig b Barclay	91	– c Parker b Greig	11
I. Cockbain c Parker b Greig	11	– run out	2
J. Abrahams st Gould b Barclay	27	– c Greig b Barclay	32
*C. H. Lloyd c Gould b le Roux	50	– c Greig b Barclay	60
D. P. Hughes c Greig b Green	44	– c and b Barclay	7
S. J. O'Shaughnessy not out	54	– c C. M. Wells b Waller	10
J. Simmons not out	8	– (10) not out	5
†C. Maynard (did not bat)		– (8) not out	5
I. Folley (did not bat)		– (9) b Green	5
B 5, l-b 4	9	L-b 4	4
1/16 2/50 3/111 4/188 5/188 6/281	(6 wkts dec.) 301	1/18 2/22 3/50 4/83 5/115 6/134 7/142 8/147	(8 wkts) 152

P. J. W. Allott did not bat.

Bonus points – Lancashire 4, Sussex 2.

Bowling: *First Innings*—le Roux 15–3–38–2; Pigott 24–5–68–0; Greig 9–2–20–1; Barclay 25–6–70–2; Waller 25–5–72–0; Green 2–0–24–1. *Second Innings*—Pigott 4–1–12–0; Greig 5–0–19–2; Waller 13–2–49–1; Green 4–0–24–1; Barclay 10–3–44–3.

Umpires: J. Birkenshaw and D. O. Oslear.

At Taunton, September 11, 13, 14. LANCASHIRE beat SOMERSET by 14 runs.

LEICESTERSHIRE

President: W. Bentley, MBE
Chairman: C. H. Palmer
Chairman, Cricket Committee: J. J. Palmer
Secretary/Cricket Manager: F. M. Turner
County Cricket Ground, Grace Road,
Leicester LE2 8AD
(Telephone: 0533-831880/832128)
Captain: R. W. Tolchard
Coach: K. Higgs

Despite the absence of any tangible evidence, in the way of trophies, Leicestershire enjoyed their most satisfactory season since 1975, when they won both the Championship and the Benson and Hedges Cup under Ray Illingworth's leadership. Their run of eight victories in twelve matches at one stage pulled them to within two points of the eventual county champions, Middlesex, with two matches left; but they then produced perhaps their worst performance of the season at Trent Bridge, and conceded the title.

Leicestershire's charge began, after a good May but a thoroughly unhappy June, with a six-wicket victory over Middlesex, the runaway leaders, at Uxbridge in the first week of July. That win owed much to some fine spin bowling by Nick Cook, who went into the game with only twenty Championship wickets under his belt yet was to take his tally for the county to 87 by the end of the season, persuading many that the England selectors would have been well advised to take him to Australia.

There were hints, too, that Brian Davison, Rhodesian-born but recently qualified as "English" by registration, might make the tour. He proved a sparkling exception to the general rule that players do not prosper in their benefit seasons, totalling 1,800 runs, only 18 short of his best-ever aggregate in 1976. Davison also went into the Leicestershire record books when scoring an unbeaten century in his final innings at Canterbury (he also recorded a hundred in his first innings of the summer at Southampton), thus taking his season's tally of centuries to seven and equalling the previous county record set jointly by Les Berry and Willie Watson. Davison's aggressive batting played a major part in Leicestershire's success.

Davison had sound support from three other batsmen who passed 1,000 runs for Leicestershire in the season, including David Gower, who achieved it in his last innings. Gower scored his runs in only 21 visits to the crease, his county appearances being restricted by the heavy demands of Test cricket. He served Leicestershire splendidly, a remarkable feature of his season being the number of runs he scored in the John Player League. In just nine innings he passed 50 six times, scoring 669 runs, including three centuries, and finishing with an average only narrowly short of three figures. Nigel Briers confirmed the promise he had shown the previous season, scoring only one century but consistently making runs at No. 5 or, when Gower was absent, at No. 3.

Chris Balderstone had his best-ever season with the bat, scoring nearly 1,500 runs. His was largely an anchor role at the head of the innings, but when the situation demanded it he played as attractively as anyone. Still "youthful" at 41, Balderstone also took many breathtaking close-to-the-wicket catches when Leicestershire were sweeping all before them in July and August. His opening partner, Russell Cobb, made a good impression in the first half of the season, without making any substantial scores, but struggled to maintain form in the latter stages.

With one or two faster pitches being prepared at Grace Road than for a long time, Les Taylor, Andy Roberts and Gordon Parsons all took 50 wickets or more, and Jonathan Agnew impressed with his pace and new-found control until injury ruled him out midway through Leicestershire's strong surge. Taylor confirmed the good impressions he had made in South Africa during the winter, both with Natal and the SA Breweries English XI. His connection with the latter probably cost him a Test place.

Roberts, who had bowled well in 1981 without much luck, was at times back to the fearsome pace he generated in the mid-seventies. Leicestershire signed him to play full-time in 1983, after two years of being committed at the weekends to Lancashire League cricket. Parsons, without the pace of Roberts or Taylor, but with an ability to swing the ball both ways, despite having often to bowl from the less favourable end, progressed in leaps and bounds once he had learnt to channel his aggression. His batting also improved, to the extent that he became regarded almost as an all-rounder; his powerful hitting saw him elevated in the order when the occasion arose. These twin qualities made him an important member of the one-day squad.

Leicestershire were well served for bowling, lacking only a regular off-spinner by way of balance. Paddy Clift, who bowls off-spin when required, suffered Achilles' tendon damage for the second successive season and played in only four Championship games. To offset this, John Steele took 50 wickets in the Championship with his left-arm spin to go with Cook's total.

Leicestershire's Championship success came in a season when they were expected to mount more serious challenges in the limited-overs competitions. They won five of their last six games to finish third in the John Player League, thanks largely to Gower's brilliant batting, but they batted badly when chasing a modest Nottinghamshire total in a Benson and Hedges quarter-final. Their NatWest ambitions were halted in the second round by Botham and Garner at Taunton. – M.J.

LEICESTERSHIRE 1982

[*Bill Smith*

Back row: L. W. Barratt (*scorer*), R. A. Cobb, N. E. Briers, J. P. Agnew, L. B. Taylor, G. J. Parsons, N. G. B. Cook, D. A. Wenlock, D. Jones (*physiotherapist*). *Front row:* J. F. Steele, D. I. Gower, R. W. Tolchard (*captain*), J. C. Balderstone, B. F. Davison.

LEICESTERSHIRE RESULTS

All first-class matches – Played 25: Won 10, Lost 4, Drawn 11.

County Championship matches – Played 22: Won 10, Lost 4, Drawn 8.

Bonus points – Batting 57, Bowling 69.

Competition placings – Schweppes County Championship, r/u; NatWest Bank Trophy, 2nd round; Benson and Hedges Cup, q-f; John Player League, 3rd.

COUNTY CHAMPIONSHIP AVERAGES

BATTING

	Birthplace	*M*	*I*	*NO*	*R*	*HI*	*Avge*
B. F. Davison c	*Bulawayo, Rhodesia*	21	35	4	1,789	172	57.70
D. I. Gower c	*Tunbridge Wells*	9	16	0	716	111	44.75
J. C. Balderstone c	*Huddersfield*	22	39	3	1,474	148	40.94
N. E. Briers c	*Leicester*	22	37	4	1,081	106	32.75
R. W. Tolchard c	*Torquay*	22	37	8	782	93*	26.96
M. A. Garnham	*Johannesburg, SA*	9	14	2	280	57	23.33
P. B. Clift c	*Salisbury, Rhodesia*	4	4	1	63	24	21.00
R. A. Cobb	*Leicester*	19	31	1	600	63	20.00
A. M. E. Roberts	*Urlings Village, Antigua*	12	19	2	316	47	18.58
I. P. Butcher	*Farnborough*	4	5	1	71	31	17.75
J. F. Steele c	*Stafford*	19	29	5	423	58	17.62
N. G. B. Cook c	*Leicester*	21	23	7	263	37	16.43
G. J. Parsons	*Slough*	21	29	6	359	51	15.60
J. P. Agnew	*Macclesfield*	8	11	0	122	56	11.09
L. B. Taylor c	*Earl Shilton*	20	23	8	119	25	7.93
T. J. Boon	*Doncaster*	6	8	0	58	21	7.25

Also batted: G. Forster (*Seaham*) (1 match) 2; D. A. Wenlock (*Leicester*) (1 match) 4; K. Higgs c (*Sandyford*) (1 match) did not bat.

**Signifies not out.* c *Denotes county cap.*

BOWLING

	O	*M*	*R*	*W*	*Avge*	*BB*
A. M. E. Roberts	410.2	109	1,027	54	19.01	8-56
J. F. Steele	448.2	130	1,026	50	20.52	5-4
L. B. Taylor	564.1	148	1,411	66	21.37	5-24
N. G. B. Cook	767.2	243	1,832	80	22.90	7-63
J. P. Agnew	157	24	609	18	33.83	4-55
G. J. Parsons	456.1	81	1,649	44	37.47	5-25

Also bowled: J. C. Balderstone 75–22–177–7; N. E. Briers 19–2–75–2; P. B. Clift 77–21–194–3; R. A. Cobb 4–2–5–0; D. I. Gower 5–2–10–0; G. Forster 17–3–48–0; K. Higgs 19–5–64–1; D. A. Wenlock 2–0–8–0.

HUNDREDS

The following thirteen three-figure innings were played for Leicestershire in County Championship matches – B. F. Davison (7) 172 v Hampshire (Southampton), 111 v Surrey (Leicester), 100 v Middlesex (Uxbridge), 139* v Worcestershire (Worcester), 110* v Essex (Colchester), 119 v Glamorgan (Leicester), 100* v Kent (Canterbury); J. C. Balderstone (4) 148 v Middlesex (Uxbridge), 103* v Gloucestershire (Leicester), 114* v Essex (Colchester), 118 v Glamorgan (Leicester); N. E. Briers (1) 106 v Yorkshire (Hinckley); D. I. Gower (1) 111 v Somerset (Taunton).

At Southampton, May 5, 6, 7. LEICESTERSHIRE drew with HAMPSHIRE.

LEICESTERSHIRE v SURREY

At Leicester, May 12, 13, 14. Leicestershire won by five wickets. Leicestershire 24 pts, Surrey 7 pts. Leicestershire, putting Surrey in on a green but true pitch, were thwarted by a 205-minute century from opener Clinton and a fluent 89 from Smith. Richards and Smith shared a sixth-wicket partnership of 103 in 73 minutes. Leicestershire's reply was built on a second-wicket stand of 165 between Balderstone and Gower which ended when Gower was run out for 99. Balderstone, who batted for four and threequarter hours, also missed his century. Butcher then confirmed the easy nature of the pitch with an unbeaten 151, including eighteen 4s, before Surrey's declaration left Leicestershire to make 288 in 175 minutes. Gower launched the chase with ten 4s, in a run-a-minute 61, and Davison hammered 111 (two 6s, fifteen 4s) in only two hours. When the final twenty overs were signalled, Leicestershire still required 127 runs, but Garnham kept the momentum going and Roberts accomplished a memorable victory – with 25 balls to spare – with two straight 6s off Pocock into the pavilion.

Surrey

A. R. Butcher c Gower b Taylor	15	– (2) not out	151
G. S. Clinton c Roberts b Parsons	102	– (1) c Tolchard b Agnew	5
*R. D. V. Knight c Briers b Parsons	17	– b Parsons	12
G. R. J. Roope c Tolchard b Taylor	14	– (5) c Steele b Roberts	4
M. A. Lynch c Briers b Agnew	6	– (6) lbw b Steele	47
D. M. Smith c Steele b Roberts	89	– (7) not out	25
†C. J. Richards lbw b Parsons	61		
S. T. Clarke b Roberts	26		
R. D. Jackman c Balderstone b Agnew	15		
P. I. Pocock b Roberts	0	– (4) lbw b Agnew	7
P. H. L. Wilson not out	0		
L-b 6, w 1, n-b 6	13	B 1, l-b 5, n-b 3	9
1/38 2/89 3/112 4/126 5/200 6/303 7/333 8/358 9/358	358	1/14 2/50 3/68 4/84 5/178	(5 wkts dec.) 260

Bonus points – Surrey 4, Leicestershire 4.

Bowling: *First Innings*—Roberts 21–2–69–3; Taylor 18–4–48–2; Parsons 22–2–123–3; Agnew 14.1–2–71–2; Steele 13–4–29–0; Briers 2–1–5–0. *Second Innings*—Roberts 14–3–36–1; Agnew 18–3–72–2; Parsons 15–2–55–1; Steele 23–1–78–1; Balderstone 4–1–10–0.

Leicestershire

J. C. Balderstone b Wilson	94 – b Clarke	17
J. F. Steele c Richards b Clarke	3	
D. I. Gower run out	99 – c Butcher b Pocock	61
B. F. Davison c Smith b Pocock	31 – c Clarke b Pocock	111
N. E. Briers c Smith b Wilson	13 – (2) c Smith b Clarke	8
*R. W. Tolchard c Lynch b Pocock	0 – not out	15
†M. A. Garnham c Smith b Pocock	24 – (5) c Smith b Jackman	55
A. M. E. Roberts lbw b Clarke	20 – (7) not out	15
G. J. Parsons c Clinton b Clarke	22	
J. P. Agnew c Lynch b Clarke	4	
L. B. Taylor not out	6	
B 4, l-b 9, n-b 2	15	B 4, l-b 5, n-b 1 10
1/5 2/170 3/228 4/239 5/240 6/259 7/293 8/301 9/316	331	1/22 2/28 3/142 4/220 5/273 (5 wkts) 292

Bonus points – Leicestershire 4, Surrey 3 (Score at 100 overs: 303-8).

Bowling: *First Innings*—Clarke 29–4–101–4; Jackman 18–5–43–0; Knight 10–2–45–0; Wilson 22–5–57–2; Pocock 29–9–70–3. *Second Innings*—Clarke 13–1–70–2; Jackman 6–3–19–1; Knight 5–0–42–0; Wilson 22–5–46–0; Pocock 18.5–2–105–2.

Umpires: B. Leadbeater and J. van Geloven.

At Cardiff, May 19, 20, 21. LEICESTERSHIRE beat GLAMORGAN by an innings and 9 runs.

LEICESTERSHIRE v NORTHAMPTONSHIRE

At Leicester, May 29, 31, June 1. Drawn. Leicestershire 5 pts, Northamptonshire 7 pts. Cook, with fifteen 4s, and Lamb (two 6s, eleven 4s) both scored first-day centuries, figuring in a third-wicket partnership of 197 on an easy-paced pitch. Leicestershire found batting a little more difficult, Balderstone battling for four hours for his 98, and Briers taking 75 minutes to reach double figures. Only Gower played with real assurance. Willey's hard-hit 88 enabled Cook to set Leicestershire a target of 269 in three hours, and half-centuries from Gower and Davison gave them hope. But Davison's dismissal sparked the fall of three wickets for only 9 runs, and Leicestershire, needing 146 from the final twenty overs, settled for the draw.

Northamptonshire

*G. Cook c Briers b Steele	125 – c Garnham b Taylor	3
W. Larkins c Gower b Clift	24 – c and b Cook	28
P. Willey c Garnham b Taylor	14 – (4) not out	88
A. J. Lamb c Briers b Cook	102 – (5) c Briers b Cook	13
D. J. Capel c Parsons b Cook	15 – (6) b Balderstone	0
D. S. Steele not out	49 – (7) c Cook b Balderstone	0
R. M. Carter not out	18 – (8) b Balderstone	18
N. A. Mallender (did not bat)	– (3) c Tolchard b Balderstone	42
†G. Sharp (did not bat)	– c Taylor b Cook	11
Sarfraz Nawaz (did not bat)	– not out	14
B 2, l-b 2, w 1, n-b 2	7	B 1, l-b 8, w 5, n-b 2 16
1/43 2/68 3/265 4/275 5/313	(5 wkts dec.) 354	1/13 2/65 3/123 4/142 5/148 6/148 7/194 8/214 (8 wkts dec.) 233

B. J. Griffiths did not bat.

Bonus points – Northamptonshire 4, Leicestershire 1 (Score at 100 overs: 304-4).

Bowling: *First Innings*—Taylor 19–2–52–1; Parsons 16–3–65–0; Clift 22–4–69–1; Cook 36–11–88–2; Briers 1–0–4–0; Steele 17–4–50–1; Balderstone 9–1–19–0. *Second Innings*—Taylor 15–4–46–1; Parsons 2–1–4–0; Cook 32–7–116–3; Balderstone 19–6–51–4.

Leicestershire

J. C. Balderstone c Cook b Steele	98	– run out	5
J. F. Steele c Steele b Griffiths	5	– (8) not out	12
D. I. Gower c Carter b Mallender	54	– c Griffiths b Willey	52
B. F. Davison c Sarfraz b Steele	14	– c Sarfraz b Mallender	52
N. E. Briers c Larkins b Sarfraz	71	– (2) c and b Griffiths	5
*R. W. Tolchard b Griffiths	16	– c Sarfraz b Steele	17
†M. A. Garnham c Mallender b Steele	1	– (5) c Steele b Willey	0
P. B. Clift c Lamb b Steele	17	– (7) c Carter b Willey	18
G. J. Parsons run out	4	– not out	4
N. G. B. Cook not out	19		
L. B. Taylor not out	2		
L-b 7, n-b 11	18	B 5, w 1, n-b 3	9
1/33 2/121 3/136 4/202 (9 wkts dec.)	319	1/9 2/17 3/112 (7 wkts)	174
5/232 6/241 7/271 8/291 9/300		4/112 5/121 6/138 7/169	

Bonus points – Leicestershire 4, Northamptonshire 3 (Score at 100 overs: 300-8).

Bowling: *First Innings*—Sarfraz 14–3–38–1; Griffiths 21–7–55–2; Steele 33–8–96–4; Mallender 13–3–40–1; Willey 22–0–69–0; Capel 1–0–3–0. *Second Innings*—Sarfraz 3–0–12–0; Griffiths 6–1–17–1; Steele 24–7–81–1; Willey 21–10–49–3; Mallender 1–0–4–1; Cook 1–0–2–0.

Umpires: H. D. Bird and D. R. Shepherd.

LEICESTERSHIRE v YORKSHIRE

At Hinckley, June 2, 3, 4. Drawn. Leicestershire 7 pts, Yorkshire 4 pts. Leicestershire's first-innings crawl on a friendly wicket had much to do with the absence of Gower, on England duty, and Davison, who withdrew at the last minute with an elbow injury. Briers, having made 58 in 44 overs on the first day, cut loose on the second morning to reach his century and take his side to maximum batting points. Taylor, operating on his old club ground, took five wickets as Yorkshire tumbled to 124 for six, and the visitors were indebted to Lumb's 70 for avoiding the follow-on. They declared 100 behind and Leicestershire, trying to make up for four hours lost to the weather, flung the bat before setting Yorkshire 242 in 160 minutes. Boycott batted with urgency; but on a wicket starting to take spin, Yorkshire gave up the chase when Athey was fifth out and 72 were still needed off ten overs.

Leicestershire

J. C. Balderstone lbw b Sidebottom	67	– c Whiteley b Jarvis	6
J. F. Steele c Love b Carrick	40	– b Old	0
R. A. Cobb c Athey b Whiteley	41	– (6) c Whiteley b Carrick	20
N. E. Briers st Bairstow b Carrick	106	– (3) c Bairstow b Sidebottom	19
*R. W. Tolchard lbw b Sidebottom	45	– (4) c Athey b Old	30
A. M. E. Roberts c Sharp b Carrick	0	– (8) not out	22
†M. A Garnham lbw b Old	6	– (5) b Sidebottom	15
G. J. Parsons not out	1	– (7) c Lumb b Carrick	9
L. B. Taylor (did not bat)		– c Whiteley b Sidebottom	5
I. P. Butcher (did not bat)		– not out	5
L-b 15, n-b 8	23	L-b 5, n-b 5	10
1/103 2/122 3/200 4/298 (7 wkts dec.)	329	1/1 2/11 3/49 (8 wkts dec.)	141
5/301 6/321 7/329		4/62 5/89 6/106 7/109 8/131	

N. G. B. Cook did not bat.

Bonus points – Leicestershire 4, Yorkshire 2 (Score at 100 overs: 305-5).

Bowling: *First Innings*—Old 21–7–42–1; Jarvis 10–0–45–0; Sidebottom 25–4–72–2; Carrick 41–13–106–3; Whiteley 10–0–41–1. *Second Innings*—Old 13–3–43–2; Jarvis 7–1–23–1; Sidebottom 10.1–1–45–3; Carrick 5–0–20–2.

Yorkshire

G. Boycott b Roberts	17	– b Steele	56
R. G. Lumb c Cobb b Steele	70	– b Cook	21
C. W. J. Athey lbw b Taylor	3	– (5) st Garnham b Cook	50
J. D. Love c Garnham b Taylor	3	– (6) c Cobb b Cook	27
K. Sharp c Steele b Taylor	32	– (4) b Cook	21
†D. L. Bairstow lbw b Taylor	7	– (7) not out	8
P. Carrick b Taylor	11	– (8) not out	2
A. Sidebottom not out	44		
*C. M. Old c Garnham b Roberts	22	– (3) b Steele	4
J. P. Whiteley not out	5		
L-b 7, w 1, n-b 7	15	B 1, w 2	3
1/34 2/37 3/41 4/94 5/104 6/124 7/169 8/217	(8 wkts dec.) 229	1/44 2/56 3/78 4/130 5/170 6/190	(6 wkts) 192

P. W. Jarvis did not bat.

Bonus points – Yorkshire 2, Leicestershire 3.

Bowling: *First Innings*—Roberts 24–6–70–2; Taylor 22–7–52–5; Parsons 15.5–1–74–0; Cook 7–1–15–0; Steele 5–2–3–1. *Second Innings*—Roberts 12–2–27–0; Taylor 3–0–13–0; Parsons 2–1–2–0; Cook 18–3–74–4; Steele 15–1–73–2; Balderstone 2–2–0–0.

Umpires: H. D. Bird and D. R. Shepherd.

LEICESTERSHIRE v ZIMBABWEANS

At Leicester, June 5, 7, 9. Drawn. Zimbabwe's refreshingly cavalier approach, although not reflected later in a laggardly declaration, got them out of trouble from 19 for three on the opening morning. Agnew was extremely hostile, but Brown rode his luck, Butchart hit out powerfully, and both reached half-centuries. Young Cobb reaffirmed his promise with a stylish 64 for Leicestershire, captained for only his second time by Gower, who declared with a lead of 35. Heron and Pycroft tucked into some wayward second-innings bowling – Leicestershire's attack was blunted somewhat when Agnew pulled a rib muscle – and Fletcher set a target of 252 in little over two hours. Leicestershire made no attempt, but they were momentarily in trouble by losing four wickets in a careless twenty minutes either side of five o'clock.

Zimbabweans

J. G. Heron hit wkt b Agnew	1	– b Forster	83
†D. L. Houghton c Davison b Parsons	0	– c Cobb b Clift	12
R. D. Brown run out	51	– c Garnham b Parsons	16
A. J. Pycroft c Cook b Parsons	6	– b Steele	50
*D. A. G. Fletcher run out	19	– c Forster b Cook	22
C. A. T. Hodgson st Garnham b Cook	47	– b Steele	33
G. C. Wallace c Garnham b Parsons	34	– b Cook	43
I. P. Butchart c Parsons b Clift	54	– c Davison b Clift	14
P. W. E. Rawson lbw b Clift	13	– not out	2
A. J. Traicos not out	12	– c and b Cook	0
E. J. Hough not out	0		
B 1, l-b 5, w 2, n-b 4	12	L-b 9, n-b 2	11
1/3 2/6 3/19 4/83 5/95 6/156 7/180 8/230 9/241	(9 wkts dec.) 249	1/38 2/84 3/142 4/178 5/197 6/234 7/266 8/286 9/286	(9 wkts dec.) 286

Bowling: *First Innings*—Agnew 19–2–54–1; Parsons 16–3–64–3; Clift 18–3–51–2; Cook 10–2–47–1; Forster 4–1–21–0. *Second Innings*—Agnew 8–1–27–0; Parsons 12–0–48–1; Clift 18–3–49–2; Cook 24.5–5–73–3; Forster 9–2–29–1; Steele 22–4–49–2.

Leicestershire

J. F. Steele c Wallace b Traicos	63	(7) not out	10
R. A. Cobb lbw b Traicos	64	b Traicos	26
T. J. Boon lbw b Butchart	1	(1) c Houghton b Hough	8
†M. A. Garnham c Houghton b Rawson	8	(3) lbw b Traicos	10
*D. I. Gower st Houghton b Traicos	32	(4) c and b Traicos	0
B. F. Davison b Hough	6	(5) lbw b Butchart	5
P. B. Clift c Houghton b Butchart	45	(6) not out	15
G. Forster not out	22		
G. J. Parsons not out	9		
B 4, l-b 11, w 1, n-b 18	34	B 1, l-b 3	4
1/112 2/120 3/134 4/186 5/192 6/213 7/261 (7 wkts dec.)	284	1/20 2/46 3/46 4/51 5/55 (5 wkts)	78

N. G. B. Cook and J. P. Agnew did not bat.

Bowling: *First Innings*—Hough 21–8–49–1; Fletcher 13–3–39–0; Rawson 22–5–69–1; Traicos 30–9–71–3; Butchart 7–3–22–2. *Second Innings*—Hough 6–0–24–1; Fletcher 8–1–15–0; Rawson 8–3–11–0; Traicos 12–8–5–3; Butchart 4–0–11–1; Wallace 3–1–8–0.

Umpires: J. H. Harris and M. J. Kitchen,

LEICESTERSHIRE v WARWICKSHIRE

At Leicester, June 9, 10, 11. Drawn. Leicestershire 5 pts, Warwickshire 7 pts. Despite a dreadful first day, when Kallicharran plundered their erratic attack for 210, including 30 boundaries, Leicestershire looked set for victory by the second evening. Briers' sparkling unbeaten 58 saw Leicestershire to maximum batting points, and Tolchard's declaration, 79 behind, paid off as Warwickshire crashed to 58 for six against Roberts. But a run-a-minute partnership of 89 for the eighth wicket between Paul Smith and Lethbridge held up Leicestershire until after lunch on the final day. Faced with an unexpectedly difficult target of 257 in three and a half hours, they batted poorly, with the notable exception of Garnham. Tolchard, hardly encouraged by his own slow scoring, called off the chase early, while Warwickshire never threatened to win themselves despite taking seven wickets.

Warwickshire

*D. L. Amiss c Steele b Roberts	49	c Briers b Roberts	0
T. A. Lloyd retired hurt	3	b Higgs	32
A. I. Kallicharran b BalderstoneBalderstone	210	lbw b Parsons	7
†G. W. Humpage c Garnham b Parsons	25	b Roberts	11
K. D. Smith c Tolchard b Balderstone	19	b Roberts	0
Asif Din b Roberts	16	c Garnham b Parsons	1
P. A. Smith c Steele b Parsons	30	(8) b Roberts	59
C. Lethbridge not out	17	(9) c Cobb b Roberts	47
G. C. Small (did not bat)	–	(10) c Davison b Parsons	13
S. P. Sutcliffe (did not bat)	–	(11) not out	0
J. Cumbes (did not bat)	–	(7) b Roberts	1
B 5, l-b 6, w 1	12	L-b 4, w 1, n-b 1	6
1/157 2/231 3/296 4/322 5/343 6/381 (6 wkts dec.)	381	1/0 2/9 3/40 4/40 5/53 6/54 7/61 8/150 9/177	177

Bonus points – Warwickshire 4, Leicestershire 1 (Score at 100 overs: 323-4).

Bowling: *First Innings*—Roberts 25–4–79–2; Parsons 28.3–2–130–2; Higgs 13–4–46–0; Cook 19–6–43–0; Steele 17–5–37–0; Balderstone 10–0–34–2. *Second Innings*—Roberts 25.2–5–61–6; Parsons 20–4–71–3; Higgs 6–1–18–1; Cook 8–6–5–0; Balderstone 5–1–16–0.

Leicestershire

J. C. Balderstone c Humpage b Lethbridge	51	– c Lethbridge b Small	7
J. F. Steele c P. A. Smith b Sutcliffe	58	– (9) not out	4
R. A. Cobb c Humpage b Small	33	– (2) lbw b Sutcliffe	33
B. F. Davison lbw b Lethbridge	42	– c P. A. Smith b Small	12
N. E. Briers not out	58	– (3) c Humpage b Small	9
*R. W. Tolchard c Humpage b Lethbridge	5	– (5) not out	50
†M. A. Garnham c Cumbes b Sutcliffe	21	– (6) st Humpage b Sutcliffe	57
A. M. E. Roberts c K. D. Smith b Sutcliffe	16	– (7) c Sutcliffe b Lethbridge	3
G. J. Parsons not out	0	– (8) b Sutcliffe	10
B 1, l-b 6, w 9, n-b 2	18	B 1, l-b 9, n-b 1	11
1/99 2/131 3/178 4/214 5/228 6/269 7/297 (7 wkts dec.)	302	1/17 2/39 3/57 4/89 5/161 6/166 7/180 (7 wkts)	196

N. G. B. Cook and K. Higgs did not bat.

Bonus points – Leicestershire 4, Warwickshire 3.

Bowling: *First Innings*—Small 19–3–53–1; Cumbes 14–2–37–0; P. A. Smith 10–0–34–0; Lethbridge 27–4–87–3; Asif Din 2–1–5–0; Sutcliffe 28–9–68–3. *Second Innings*—Small 14–2–41–3; P. A. Smith 2–1–6–0; Cumbes 3–1–4–0; Lethbridge 20–4–53–1; Sutcliffe 21–3–73–3; Asif Din 3–3–0–0; Amiss 1–0–8–0.

Umpires: D. O. Oslear and M. J. Kitchen.

At Cambridge, June 19, 20, 21. LEICESTERSHIRE drew with CAMBRIDGE UNIVERSITY.

LEICESTERSHIRE v KENT

At Leicester, June 23, 24, 25. Drawn. Rain having washed out the first two days, a one-innings match was started, promptly, on the final day. Leicestershire put Kent in on a spongy wicket, and Roberts and Taylor were soon taking pieces out of the damp surface. Woolmer, though, found a splendid touch after a slow start and, driving fluently, had made 42 of a half-century opening partnership with Taylor when he was bowled by Balderstone. Soon afterwards the rain, never far away, halted play after 85 minutes, and at 1.35 pm, with the ground awash, the match was abandoned.

Kent

R. A. Woolmer b Balderstone	42
N. R. Taylor not out	9
D. G. Aslett not out	4
1/50 (1 wkt)	55

L. Potter, C. Penn, *Asif Iqbal, C. S. Cowdrey, +A. P. E. Knott, G. W. Johnson, G. R. Dilley and D. L. Underwood did not bat.

Bowling: Roberts 8–7–1–0; Taylor 3–2–4–0; Cook 12–6–16–0; Parsons 4–1–25–0; Balderstone 4–1–9–1.

Leicestershire

J. C. Balderstone, R. A. Cobb, N. E. Briers, B. F. Davison, *R. W. Tolchard, T. J. Boon, †M. A. Garnham, G. J. Parsons, A. M. E. Roberts, L. B. Taylor and N. G. B. Cook.

Umpires: R. S. Herman and A. G. T. Whitehead.

At Derby, June 26, 28, 29. LEICESTERSHIRE lost to DERBYSHIRE by eight wickets.

At Uxbridge, July 7, 8, 9. LEICESTERSHIRE beat MIDDLESEX by six wickets.

LEICESTERSHIRE v DERBYSHIRE

At Coalville, July 10, 12, 13. Derbyshire won by five wickets. Derbyshire 22 pts, Leicestershire 6 pts. Despite Miller's career-best eight for 70, with all his victims either bowled or caught close to the wicket, splendid half-centuries by Davison and Balderstone suggested that Tolchard had won a good toss on a pitch taking spin almost from the start. This theory was reinforced when Steele undermined the Derbyshire reply with a spell of five for 10 in 61 balls, the visitors' narrow lead being heavily dependent on the century second-wicket stand between Anderson and Kirsten, and an unbeaten fifty from Miller. When Davison and Balderstone again scored half-centuries, Derbyshire's target of 207 at a run a minute looked well out of reach. But Kirsten, surviving four dropped catches, rose above the conditions and took heavy toll of some poor Leicestershire bowling. When he was out Derbyshire were almost home, and they finally won with fifteen balls to spare.

Leicestershire

J. C. Balderstone b Miller	57	– run out	75
R. A. Cobb c and b Oldham	3	– c Anderson b Miller	22
N. E. Briers b Moir	33	– lbw b Miller	0
B. F. Davison b Miller	72	– b Miller	60
J. F. Steele b Miller	8	– (6) run out	0
*†R. W. Tolchard c Anderson b Miller	9	– (5) run out	27
T. J. Boon c Anderson b Miller	1	– c Wright b Miller	1
G. J. Parsons c Wood b Miller	3	– c Wright b Oldham	0
N. G. B. Cook not out	21	– run out	22
J. P. Agnew c Moir b Miller	14	– c Hampshire b Moir	0
L. B. Taylor b Miller	2	– not out	0
B 5, l-b 4, w 1, n-b 1	11	B 5, l-b 5, n-b 5	15
1/13 2/92 3/116 4/153 5/169 6/173 7/195 8/196 9/230	234	1/44 2/52 3/167 4/171 5/171 6/174 7/176 8/217 9/218	222

Bonus points – Leicestershire 2, Derbyshire 4.

Bowling: *First Innings*—Oldham 7–0–25–1; Tunnicliffe 6–1–28–0; Moir 35–13–83–1; Miller 44.2–11–70–8; Kirsten 6–1–17–0. *Second Innings*—Tunnicliffe 12.5–0–26–0; Oldham 13–1–27–1; Moir 27–5–65–1; Miller 33–7–68–4; Kirsten 7–1–21–0.

Derbyshire

*B. Wood lbw b Taylor	4	– c Balderstone b Taylor 10
I. S. Anderson c Tolchard b Taylor	79	– (7) not out 11
P. N. Kirsten c Davison b Taylor	84	– b Agnew 102
J. H. Hampshire b Steele	6	– c Briers b Steele 2
G. Miller not out	50	– lbw b Taylor 7
K. J. Barnett c Davison b Steele	0	– not out 17
J. G. Wright c Briers b Steele	2	– (2) c Balderstone b Steele 60
C. J. Tunnicliffe c Davison b Steele	0	
D. G. Moir b Steele	1	
†B. J. M. Maher lbw b Taylor	11	
S. Oldham b Cook	10	
B 1, l-b 1, n-b 1	3	N-b 1 1
1/6 2/164 3/175 4/181 5/181 6/195 7/195 8/202 9/219	250	1/18 2/120 3/124 4/146 5/199 (5 wkts) 210

Bonus points – Derbyshire 2, Leicestershire 4 (Score at 100 overs: 225-9).

Bowling: *First Innings*—Taylor 28–8–58–4; Parsons 13–5–21–0; Cook 24.2–7–60–1; Agnew 10–3–40–0; Steele 31–8–60–5; Balderstone 2–0–8–0. *Second Innings*—Taylor 16–1–65–2; Parsons 5–1–21–0; Cook 13–0–55–0; Steele 18.4–2–54–2; Agnew 5–0–14–1.

Umpires: B. Leadbeater and P. B. Wight.

At Hove, July 17, 19, 20. LEICESTERSHIRE beat SUSSEX by 13 runs.

At Leicester, July 21, 22, 23. LEICESTERSHIRE drew with PAKISTANIS (See Pakistani tour section).

LEICESTERSHIRE v ESSEX

At Leicester, July 24, 26, 27. Leicestershire won by 25 runs. Leicestershire 23 pts, Essex 5 pts. Batsmen always struggled on a wicket that often saw the ball shoot through at ankle height. Essex collapsed in their first innings against the left-arm spin of Cook, but Leicestershire, 70 ahead on first innings, declined just as dramatically in their second innings. Essex's target of 183 to win was far from easy, but when Gooch's watchful 85 (two 6s, nine 4s in 103 minutes) took them to within 45 with seven wickets in hand, they seemed certain winners. However, Parsons struck back to destroy them with a career-best five for 25, supplementing his invaluable 41 not out in Leicestershire's first innings. Gooch was the first of Parsons's victims, caught down the leg side by Tolchard, and soon afterwards Essex lost four wickets at 152. Leicestershire clinched their improbable win when East was run out, and so climbed to second in the Championship table.

Leicestershire

J. C. Balderstone lbw b Turner	10	– lbw b Lever	3
R. A. Cobb c Hardie b Lever	63	– lbw b Phillip	15
D. I. Gower lbw b Lever	37	– c D. E. East b Phillip	9
B. F. Davison c Lever b Acfield	59	– lbw b Pringle	45
N. E. Briers b Acfield	40	– lbw b Phillip	5
*†R. W. Tolchard b Acfield	6	– c Hardie b Pringle	10
G. J. Parsons not out	41	– (8) b Lever	0
J. F. Steele c McEwan b Acfield	6	– (7) b Phillip	9
N. G. B. Cook b R. E. East	12	– c D. E. East b Lever	0
J. P. Agnew b R. E. East	2	– b Phillip	7
L. B. Taylor b R. E. East	0	– not out	4
B 3, l-b 9, w 1	13	L-b 4, n-b 1	5
1/36 2/106 3/141 4/204 5/227 6/232 7/238 8/283 9/287	289	1/6 2/15 3/40 4/56 5/88 6/91 7/92 8/92 9/107	112

Bonus points – Leicestershire 3, Essex 3 (Score at 100 overs: 255-7).

Bowling: *First Innings*—Lever 16–2–40–2; Phillip 10–1–25–0; Pringle 16–2–55–0; Turner 16–4–40–1; Acfield 24–8–56–4; R. E. East 27–9–60–3. *Second Innings*—Lever 18–3–31–3; Phillip 18–7–42–5; Turner 9–3–25–0; Pringle 8–3–9–2.

Essex

G. A. Gooch st Tolchard b Cook	50	– c Tolchard b Parsons	85
B. R. Hardie lbw b Taylor	82	– b Taylor	5
D. R. Pringle c and b Cook	0	– lbw b Cook	1
K. S. McEwan c Agnew b Cook	32	– b Steele	20
*K. W. R. Fletcher c Tolchard b Taylor	2	– b Steele	25
N. Phillip b Cook	22	– b Parsons	0
S. Turner b Taylor	12	– lbw b Parsons	7
J. K. Lever lbw b Cook	0	– (10) c Tolchard b Parsons	0
†D. E. East lbw b Taylor	1	– (8) lbw b Parsons	0
R. E. East c Tolchard b Cook	5	– (9) run out	4
D. L. Acfield not out	0	– not out	0
B 5, l-b 7, n-b 1	13	B 1, l-b 9	10
1/95 2/107 3/171 4/173 5/182 6/204 7/206 8/214 9/214	219	1/17 2/28 3/94 4/138 5/138 6/152 7/152 8/152 9/152	157

Bonus points – Essex 2, Leicestershire 4.

Bowling: *First Innings*—Taylor 23–6–54–4; Agnew 14–3–59–0; Parsons 9–1–42–0; Cook 24.3–8–51–6. *Second Innings*—Taylor 17–7–42–1; Agnew 12–1–36–0; Cook 14–3–26–1; Parsons 13–5–25–5; Steele 21.2–13–18–2.

Umpires: R. Julian and B. Leadbeater.

LEICESTERSHIRE v GLOUCESTERSHIRE

At Leicester, July 31, August 2. Leicestershire won by an innings and 45 runs. Leicestershire 22 pts, Gloucestershire 1 pt. In contrast to their previous home match, which they won on a pitch with no bounce, Leicestershire won easily, inside two days, on a green wicket with a surfeit of lift for pace bowlers. Gloucestershire's Bainbridge had to retire with a broken finger after being hit by Agnew in the first innings. However, Graveney, the Gloucestershire captain, did not blame the conditions for his side's heavy defeat; rather their poor batting and the extra pace of the Leicestershire attack, particularly from Taylor and Agnew. Taylor's combined return was eight for 33 from 25 overs, and he had to leave the field, suffering from heat exhaustion, with four second-innings wickets still available. Wicket-keeper Tolchard took seven catches in the match, John Steele six, all at second slip. Balderstone's 333-minute 103 not out was the only major innings, but it attracted some criticism when Leicestershire failed to collect a third batting point in 100 overs, despite having only four wickets down.

Leicestershire

J. C. Balderstone not out	103	*†R. W. Tolchard not out	0
R. A. Cobb c Graveney b Broad	27		
N. E. Briers b Surridge	38	L-b 10, n-b 6	16
B. F. Davison c Dudleston b Childs	39		—
T. J. Boon c and b Bainbridge	21	1/60 2/148 3/197 4/242 (4 wkts dec.)	244

J. F. Steele, G. J. Parsons, N. G. B. Cook, J. P. Agnew and L. B. Taylor did not bat.

Bonus points – Leicestershire 2, Gloucestershire 1 (Score at 100 overs: 242-4).

Bowling: Surridge 22–5–55–1; Shepherd 21.4–6–43–0; Bainbridge 30–11–72–1; Broad 5–0–13–1; Childs 23–9–45–1.

Gloucestershire

A. W. Stovold c Tolchard b Agnew	1	– c Steele b Parsons	31
B. C. Broad c Tolchard b Taylor	7	– lbw b Agnew	11
P. W. Romaines c Steele b Agnew	1	– c Balderstone b Taylor	13
B. Dudleston c Tolchard b Agnew	22	– lbw b Cook	6
P. Bainbridge retired hurt	12	– absent hurt	
A. J. Wright c Steele b Taylor	0	– (5) c Steele b Taylor	0
J. N. Shepherd c Tolchard b Parsons	0	– (6) c Steele b Taylor	0
*D. A. Graveney lbw b Taylor	0	– (7) c Tolchard b Cook	6
†R. C. Russell c Tolchard b Taylor	13	– (8) c Tolchard b Steele	41
J. H. Childs c Steele b Taylor	4	– (9) b Parsons	8
D. Surridge not out	0	– (10) not out	8
L-b 6, n-b 4	10	L-b 2, w 1, n-b 2	5
	—		—
1/1 2/7 3/9 4/41 5/42 6/47 7/61 8/69 9/70	70	1/28 2/53 3/66 4/66 5/66 6/66 7/80 8/109 9/129	129

Bonus points – Leicestershire 4.

Bowling: *First Innings*—Taylor 13.2–4–24–5; Agnew 14–4–16–3; Parsons 9–3–20–1. *Second Innings*—Taylor 12–7–9–3; Agnew 12–1–42–1; Parsons 11–2–37–2; Cook 18–10–36–2; Steele 0.3–0–0–1.

Umpires: M. J. Kitchen and D. O. Oslear.

At Worcester, August 7, 9, 10. LEICESTERSHIRE drew with WORCESTERSHIRE.

LEICESTERSHIRE v NOTTINGHAMSHIRE

At Leicester, August 11, 12. Leicestershire won by ten wickets. Leicestershire 23 pts. Nottinghamshire 6 pts. High-class fast bowling on a lively green pitch by Roberts and Taylor, who took fifteen wickets between them, hurried Leicestershire to victory soon after tea on the second day and kept them in second place in the Championship. Nottinghamshire did not possess firepower of a similar calibre, as Hendrick was absent injured, Rice was playing purely as a batsman (he faced a total of six balls), and Hadlee's hamstring ailment caused him to bowl off a short run. Leicestershire, from 180 for eight, were indebted for their healthy lead of 51 to a last-wicket flourish of 49 from Cook and, compiling his highest-ever score, Taylor. Nottinghamshire then collapsed in only 95 minutes. Their top-scorer, Birch, was still in hospital, having an elbow struck by Roberts x-rayed, when the innings closed.

Nottinghamshire

P. A. Todd c Cook b Roberts	4	– (3) b Roberts	14
R. T. Robinson b Roberts	10	– (1) lbw b Taylor	0
B. Hassan c Tolchard b Taylor	26	– (2) lbw b Roberts	8
*C. E. B. Rice c Tolchard b Roberts	0	– lbw b Taylor	0
J. D. Birch b Roberts	13	– retired hurt	25
R. J. Hadlee c Cook b Taylor	20	– c Tolchard b Taylor	1
†B. N. French b Parsons	79	– b Roberts	5
I. L. Pont lbw b Cook	2	– (9) c and b Roberts	3
K. Saxelby c Roberts b Steele	40	– (8) c Cobb b Roberts	0
K. E. Cooper c and b Steele	3	– b Taylor	8
P. M. Such not out	0	– not out	1
L-b 10, w 1, n-b 8	19	L-b 1, w 1, n-b 3	5
1/4 2/16 3/16 4/37 5/76 6/116 7/123 8/211 9/216	216	1/4 2/19 3/20 4/33 5/34 6/47 7/56 8/67 9/70	70

Bonus points – Nottinghamshire 2, Leicestershire 4.

Bowling: *First Innings*—Roberts 16–4–53–4; Taylor 20–4–58–2; Parsons 13–2–48–1; Cook 16–9–25–1; Steele 8.5–2–13–2. *Second Innings*—Roberts 13–3–37–5; Taylor 12.4–1–28–4.

Leicestershire

J. C. Balderstone c French b Saxelby	21	– not out	15
R. A. Cobb c and b Cooper	27	– not out	5
N. E. Briers c Rice b Hadlee	11		
B. F. Davison b Hadlee	51		
T. J. Boon lbw b Hadlee	13		
*†R. W. Tolchard c Rice b Saxelby	6		
J. F. Steele c Todd b Such	15		
A. M. E. Roberts c Cooper b Such	25		
G. J. Parsons c Saxelby b Such	24		
N. G. B. Cook not out	33		
L. B. Taylor c Todd b Cooper	25		
B 5, l-b 4, n-b 7	16		
1/34 2/54 3/74 4/122 5/127 6/150 7/164 8/180 9/218	267	(no wkt)	20

Bonus points – Leicestershire 3, Nottinghamshire 4.

Bowling: *First Innings*—Saxelby 18–4–46–2; Cooper 33–14–66–2; Hadlee 18–7–44–3; Such 23–6–79–3; Pont 3–1–16–0. *Second Innings*—Pont 5.1–1–17–0; Such 5–2–3–0.

Umpires: D. R. Shepherd and P. B. Wight.

LEICESTERSHIRE v LANCASHIRE

At Leicester, August 14, 16, 17. Drawn. Leicestershire 5 pts, Lancashire 3 pts. The absence of Roberts, and the return to the Lancashire side of Croft after injury, persuaded Leicestershire, who gave a Championship début to off-spinner Forster, to prepare a dry, grassless wicket. Davison's aggressive batting, and a run-a-minute seventh-wicket partnership of 94 between Parsons and Steele made up for other batting deficiencies, although with Croft aggravating his back strain and bowling only seven overs in the match, their total was disappointing. On the slow-turning pitch, Cockbain (52 in 62 overs) and O'Shaughnessy (55 in 78 overs) played with exaggerated caution, and Lancashire still needed 13 from nineteen balls for a second batting point when rain curtailed the second day's play at tea. Clive Lloyd declared next morning, when the start was delayed by 90 minutes, and although Leicestershire swung the bat, Tolchard's declaration, setting 249 in 145 minutes, was considered unrealistic. Clive Lloyd, alternately becalmed then cutting loose, seemed unsure whether or not the chase was on, but once he went the accent remained solely on defence.

Leicestershire

J. C. Balderstone c and b D. Lloyd	52	– c and b Simmons	14
R. A. Cobb b Croft	0	– lbw b O'Shaughnessy	9
N. E. Briers c Abrahams b Simmons	45	– c and b Simmons	38
B. F. Davison c Allott b Simmons	60	– b O'Shaughnessy	31
T. J. Boon c sub b Hughes	2	– (7) c sub b Simmons	3
*†R. W. Tolchard c C. H. Lloyd b Hughes	13	– (5) b Simmons	9
G. J. Parsons b O'Shaughnessy	51	– (6) c Abrahams b Simmons	8
J. F. Steele run out	44	– b O'Shaughnessy	8
N. G. B. Cook c Allott b Simmons	13	– run out	7
L. B. Taylor not out	6	– not out	6
G. Forster c Abrahams b Simmons	2		
L-b 7, n-b 3	10	B 2, l-b 1, n-b 1	4
1/9 2/96 3/128 4/155 5/177 6/181 7/275 8/289 9/296	298	1/11 2/44 3/85 4/99 5/104 6/115 7/115 8/129 9/137 (9 wkts dec.)	137

Bonus points – Leicestershire 3, Lancashire 2 (Score at 100 overs: 261-6).

Bowling: *First Innings*—Allott 22–7–59–0; Croft 7–3–11–1; O'Shaughnessy 15–1–59–1; Abrahams 6–3–19–0; Simmons 33.1–13–59–4; D. Lloyd 8–1–18–1; Hughes 21–5–63–2. *Second Innings*—Allott 11–3–33–0; O'Shaughnessy 10.3–1–39–3; Simmons 14–1–57–5; Abrahams 1–0–4–0.

Lancashire

G. Fowler c Balderstone b Parsons	1	– lbw b Taylor	0
I. Cockbain lbw b Taylor	52	– st Tolchard b Cook	7
S. J. O'Shaughnessy c Forster b Steele	55	– st Tolchard b Cook	34
D. P. Hughes not out	36	– (5) c Cobb b Steele	13
*C. H. Lloyd c sub b Steele	2	– (4) c Briers b Cook	68
J. Abrahams c sub b Steele	2	– not out	17
J. Simmons not out	15	– not out	11
B 12, l-b 6, n-b 6	24	L-b 2, n-b 2	4
1/1 2/103 3/146 4/150 5/166 (5 wkts dec.)	187	1/0 2/20 3/73 4/126 5/130 (5 wkts)	154

D. Lloyd, †C. Maynard, P. J. W. Allott and C. E. H. Croft did not bat.

Bonus points – Lancashire 1, Leicestershire 2.

Bowling: *First Innings*—Taylor 19–8–16–1; Parsons 11–3–21–1; Cook 31.5–12–64–0; Steele 27–10–47–3; Forster 8–3–15–0. *Second Innings*—Taylor 6–1–17–1; Parsons 2–0–8–0; Cook 22.4–3–69–3; Forster 9–0–33–0; Steele 10–5–23–1.

Umpires: D. R. Shepherd and P. B. Wight.

At Taunton, August 21, 23, 24. LEICESTERSHIRE beat SOMERSET by 160 runs.

At Colchester, August 25, 26, 27. LEICESTERSHIRE beat ESSEX by six wickets.

At Northampton, August 28, 30, 31. LEICESTERSHIRE drew with NORTHAMPTONSHIRE.

LEICESTERSHIRE v GLAMORGAN

At Leicester, September 1, 2, 3. Leicestershire won by an innings and 58 runs. Leicestershire 24 pts, Glamorgan 4 pts. Glamorgan, put in on a green pitch, had no answer to Roberts, who recorded match figures of fourteen for 94, his highest-ever match aggregate, and whose eight for 56 in the second innings was his best return for Leicestershire. Six of his wickets, for 29 runs, came in a fiery eleven-over spell after lunch on the third day. Their only first-innings resistance was a stand of 85 between Francis and Ontong until Nash and Davis, hitting out vigorously, put on 53 for the final wicket. Balderstone's anchor innings of 118 was complemented by dazzling displays from Gower and Davison. Balderstone and Gower added 135 in 34 overs, Balderstone and Davison 207 in 43. Davison's century, his sixth of the season, came in exactly two hours and featured three 6s and twelve 4s.

Glamorgan

A. Jones c Balderstone b Roberts	11	– c Tolchard b Roberts	14
A. L. Jones c Tolchard b Roberts	3	– lbw b Roberts	4
D. A. Francis c Cook b Parsons	40	– (4) lbw b Roberts	28
R. C. Ontong b Cook	43	– (5) lbw b Parsons	0
J. A. Hopkins lbw b Roberts	8	– (6) c Tolchard b Roberts	19
C. J. C. Rowe c Tolchard b Parsons	16	– (7) lbw b Roberts	39
J. G. Thomas c Tolchard b Roberts	4	– (3) c Briers b Parsons	19
†E. W. Jones b Roberts	6	– b Roberts	0
*B. J. Lloyd b Roberts	12	– b Roberts	12
M. A. Nash c Parsons b Cook	33	– not out	2
W. W. Davis not out	20	– lbw b Roberts	1
B 1, l-b 7, w 2, n-b 2	12	B 1, l-b 5, w 1	7
1/5 2/15 3/100 4/105 5/121 6/125 7/132 8/144 9/155	208	1/7 2/31 3/39 4/39 5/83 6/92 7/92 8/134 9/143	145

Bonus points – Glamorgan 2, Leicestershire 4.

Bowling: *First Innings*—Roberts 27–9–38–6; Taylor 14–5–26–0; Parsons 25–4–87–2; Clift 9–3–8–0; Cook 14.1–5–37–2. *Second Innings*—Roberts 22.5–8–56–8; Taylor 17–8–32–0; Parsons 8–4–12–2; Cook 12–4–27–0; Clift 3–1–11–0.

Leicestershire

J. C. Balderstone b Lloyd	118	A. M. E. Roberts b Rowe	27
R. A. Cobb c E. W. Jones b Nash	3		
D. I. Gower lbw b Lloyd	77	B 11, l-b 10, n-b 24	45
B. F. Davison c Thomas b Lloyd	119		
N. E. Briers not out	21	1/11 2/146 3/353	(6 wkts dec.) 411
*†R. W. Tolchard run out	1	4/373 5/374 6/411	

P. B. Clift, G. J. Parsons, N. G. B. Cook and L. B. Taylor did not bat.

Bonus points – Leicestershire 4, Glamorgan 2.

Bowling: Nash 11–1–49–1; Davis 14–2–33–0; Ontong 14–0–64–0; Thomas 8–0–37–0; Lloyd 28–1–121–3; Rowe 11.5–2–62–1.

Umpires: H. D. Bird and R. S. Herman.

At Nottingham, September 8, 9, 10. LEICESTERSHIRE lost to NOTTINGHAMSHIRE by an innings and 105 runs.

At Canterbury, September 11, 13, 14. LEICESTERSHIRE lost to KENT by 39 runs.

MIDDLESEX

Patron: HRH The Duke of Edinburgh
President: W. H. Webster, CBE
Chairman: F. G. Mann, DSO, MC
Chairman, Cricket Committee: R. V. C. Robins
Secretary: A. J. Wright
Lord's Cricket Ground, St John's Wood, London NW8 8QN (Telephone: 01-289 1300)
Captain: 1982 – J. M. Brearley, OBE; 1983 – M. W. Gatting
Coach: D. Bennett

The Middlesex players were determined that their retirement gift to Mike Brearley should be a trophy – all four if possible. They embarked on their prize-gathering so skilfully, remaining unbeaten until the middle of June, by when they had played sixteen matches in three competitions, that the four-timer began to look something less than an impossibility.

But this inspired start could not be maintained. Lancashire, in the Benson and Hedges Cup quarter-final, and Surrey, in the NatWest Bank semi-final, both old and successful one-day opponents of Middlesex, ended hopes of a farewell Lord's final for Brearley. A run of three consecutive John Player League defeats also transformed a six-point lead into a six-point deficit, although four wins in the last five games kept Middlesex in second place, their highest in the League's fourteen seasons.

There remained the Championship. Middlesex were always winning this most cherished title, even though Leicestershire enlivened the later weeks by reducing the Middlesex lead from 47 points on August 17 to only two on September 5. The first of twelve Championship victories came in the opening match against Essex, by two wickets. The others were all by wider, often huge, margins. There was a remarkable mid-summer sequence – punctuated by a few draws and the defeat by Leicestershire – of six wins, five by an innings and the other by ten wickets.

With Leicestershire closing fast, Middlesex managed an important victory over Surrey. They then lost at Hove before moving to the verge of the title in the last home match by beating Hampshire at Uxbridge and clinching it at Worcester on September 11. The captain made the winning hit of that final game, ending another fruitful season with the bat. He and Wilf Slack, consistent and phlegmatic, provided a model opening pair.

So Brearley departed after a dozen seasons of captaincy, festooned with honours at Test and county level. The Middlesex successes were crammed into his final eight seasons, the necessary spade-work having been undertaken in the previous four years. In 1971 he inherited a side disunited and unsuccessful with, at times, an aversion to attacking cricket that was the despair of their dwindling supporters. Brearley restored purposeful cricket to Lord's, while winning four Championships (one shared) and two Gillette Cups. As the best county side of a generation they were a credit also to their coach, Don Bennett.

What made Middlesex's pre-season prospects even more promising than usual, besides the full-time availability of Brearley, was the Test ban on John Emburey. Had he played for England, Middlesex would have found no adequate replacement. Emburey and Phil Edmonds reforged their spin alliance in the second half of the season, when Edmonds confirmed his rehabilitation by taking wickets at a faster striking-rate and more economically than Emburey. They both acknowledged their debt to the other.

Another decision taken at higher than county level, the omission of Gatting from the Test series against India, also proved fundamental to Middlesex's cause. Early in the season Gatting was the most commanding English batsman: his strokes were, as always, powerful and well produced, and he discovered the confidence, bordering on arrogance, reminiscent of some of the best overseas players. For those who watched Gatting in 1976, when Middlesex were on their way to their first Championship of this era, and noted his promise, 1981 and 1982 were rewarding summers. It was a major surprise that he was not required for Australia, especially as he was the highest qualified Englishman in the national averages. Neatly enough, he occupied the same position in the bowling averages, one of the highlights of his year being a return of five wickets when captain at Swansea.

The only player to represent the champions in Australia was, in fact, Norman Cowans. Mike Selvey and Neil Williams had failed to take wickets, and Cowans, who had hinted at exceptional speed in a handful of games in 1981, was pressed into action on recovering from injury. Apart from one short, spectacular morning at Weston, he did not collect wickets in large quantities. He was sometimes wild, but was almost always extremely fast; faster, when his fine action was working smoothly, than Wayne Daniel. Cowans and Hughes are fortunate to be able to observe and partner Daniel, who remained a constant stand-by for Brearley when the game dragged, as well as his chief strike bowler. If a wicket were needed, Brearley was usually able to urge Daniel into another effort with the old ball.

Of the other regulars, Clive Radley overcame a lean spell with characteristic resolution and was a key man in limited-overs cricket. Roland Butcher frequently did the hard work of playing himself in without cashing in. He passed 49 only five times – not enough for one of the most breathtaking stroke-players in the game. But Middlesex could afford the odd batting lapses. Paul Downton and, especially, Emburey, who achieved a vastly elevated status as a batsman, were usually to be relied on for late-order runs. – T.C.

MIDDLESEX 1982

[*Bill Smith*

Back row: H. Sharpe (*scorer*), D. Bennett (*coach*), C. R. Cook, W. N. Slack, N. J. Kemp, W. G. Merry, A. G. Smith, N. G. Cowans, K. D. James, N. F. Williams, P. R. Downton, R. O. Butcher, J. Miller (*physiotherapist*). *Middle row:* W. W. Daniel, G. D. Barlow, M. W. W. Selvey, M. W. Gatting, J. M. Brearley (*captain*), P. H. Edmonds, C. T. Radley, J. E. Emburey. *Front row:* G. M. Ritchie, R. J. Maru, S. P. Hughes, C. P. Metson, K. D. Tomlins.

MIDDLESEX RESULTS

All first-class matches – Played 25: Won 14, Lost 2, Drawn 9.

County Championship matches – Played 22: Won 12, Lost 2, Drawn 8.

Bonus points – Batting 59, Bowling 74.

Competition placings – Schweppes County Championship, winners; NatWest Bank Trophy, s-f; Benson and Hedges Cup, q-f; John Player League, r/u.

COUNTY CHAMPIONSHIP AVERAGES

BATTING

	Birthplace	*M*	*I*	*NO*	*R*	*HI*	*Avge*
M. W. Gatting c	*Kingsbury*	16	21	2	1,273	192	67.00
J. M. Brearley c	*Harrow*	19	31	9	1,023	165	46.50
R. O. Butcher c	*St Philip, Barbados*	19	25	2	1,013	197	44.04
W. N. Slack c	*Troumaca, St Vincent*	22	36	5	1,109	85	35.77
J. E. Emburey c	*Peckham*	22	26	4	734	100*	33.36
K. P. Tomlins	*Kingston-upon-Thames*	11	15	1	458	138	32.71
C. T. Radley c	*Hertford*	19	25	3	697	141*	31.68
R. G. P. Ellis	*Paddington*	3	5	0	157	55	31.40
N. J. Kemp	*Bromley*	4	5	2	84	46*	28.00
P. H. Edmonds c	*Lusaka, N. Rhodesia*	16	17	3	368	92	26.28
G. D. Barlow c	*Folkestone*	4	7	2	121	37*	24.20
M. W. W. Selvey c	*Chiswick*	9	6	1	114	36*	22.80
P. R. Downton c	*Farnborough, Kent*	22	24	2	476	65	21.63
N. F. Williams	*Hope Well, St Vincent*	9	10	4	106	27*	17.66
W. W. Daniel c	*St Philip, Barbados*	19	15	9	88	21	14.66
N. G. Cowans	*Enfield St Mary, Jamaica*	11	10	1	63	16	7.00
S. P. Hughes c	*Kingston-upon-Thames*	10	8	4	27	18	6.75

Also batted: C. R. Cook (*Edgware*) (2 matches) 2, 36; R. J. Maru (*Nairobi, Kenya*) (2 matches) 18, 12; J. D. Monteith (*Lisburn*) (1 match) 36, 1; F. J. Titmus (*St Pancras*) (1 match) 1*; W. G. Merry (*Newbury*) (1 match) did not bat.

* *Signifies not out.* c *Denotes county cap.*

BOWLING

	O	*M*	*R*	*W*	*Avge*	*BB*
M. W. Gatting	111	32	283	19	14.89	5-34
W. W. Daniel	469.4	107	1,245	71	17.53	9-61
P. H. Edmonds	635.1	195	1,348	71	18.98	8-80
N. G. Cowans	222.3	50	721	33	21.84	5-28
J. E. Emburey	689.5	167	1,629	74	22.01	5-50
W. N. Slack	81	18	225	10	22.50	3-17
S. P. Hughes	218.5	30	723	27	26.77	4-28
M. W. W. Selvey	223.5	65	524	17	30.82	3-47
N. F. Williams	173.4	24	622	15	41.46	4-40

Also bowled: J. M. Brearley 1–0–3–0; R. O. Butcher 1–0–10–0; N. J. Kemp 37–6–110–2; R. J. Maru 17–7–40–0; W. G. Merry 15.2–3–42–1; J. D. Monteith 6–1–18–0; C. T. Radley 4–0–27–0; K. P. Tomlins 10.3–1–59–2; F. J. Titmus 25–4–92–3.

HUNDREDS

The following fifteen three-figure innings were played for Middlesex in County Championship matches – M. W. Gatting (5) 140 v Derbyshire (Lord's), 114 v Kent (Tunbridge Wells), 133* v Lancashire (Lord's), 192 v Surrey (The Oval), 141 v Yorkshire (Lord's); J. M. Brearley (3) 165 v Northamptonshire (Lord's), 135 v Nottinghamshire (Nottingham), 100* v Sussex (Hove); R. O. Butcher (3) 122 v Glamorgan (Swansea), 173 v Gloucestershire (Cheltenham), 197 v Yorkshire (Lord's); C. T. Radley (2) 141* v Kent (Tunbridge Wells), 106 v Warwickshire (Coventry); J. E. Emburey (1) 100* v Northamptonshire (Lord's); K. P. Tomlins (1) 138 v Nottinghamshire (Lord's).

At Cambridge, April 28, 29, 30. MIDDLESEX beat CAMBRIDGE UNIVERSITY by eight wickets.

MIDDLESEX v ESSEX

At Lord's, May 5, 6, 7. Middlesex won by two wickets. Middlesex 18 pts, Essex 4 pts. Gooch drove the second ball of the match to the cover boundary and generally gave the Lord's county season an invigorating start. Rain washed out the afternoon and the first two sessions on the second day, but by the time Fletcher declared a few minutes before the close he had shown his ability to progress under difficult conditions. He was 74 overnight and eventually batted only three hours, taking advantage of some stiff-shouldered bowling. Events moved swiftly before the start on the third day, with Brearley declaring and Fletcher forfeiting. Foster disturbed a promising start as Middlesex embarked on their pursuit of 348 in the day, but Gatting commanded the afternoon in an innings punctuated with violent strokes. When he left, Essex looked winners, but Emburey, arriving at 220 for five, found a series of able partners. Williams, coming in with fourteen overs left and 59 wanted, saw Emburey hit three 4s off the next five balls before himself contributing a hook for 6 against Phillip and the winning boundary off Lever – a cool performance on his competitive début.

Essex

G. A. Gooch c Downton b Daniel	58
B. R. Hardie b Daniel	50
*K. W. R. Fletcher c Daniel b Edmonds	120
K. S. McEwan b Emburey	14
A. W. Lilley lbw b Emburey	20
N. Phillip c Downton b Daniel	37
S. Turner c Daniel b Selvey	28
†D. E. East not out	10
R. E. East lbw b Selvey	1
L-b 10, w 1, n-b 6	17
1/96 2/139 3/178 4/200 5/310 6/322 7/348 8/355 (8 wkts dec.)	355

J. K. Lever and N. A. Foster did not bat.

Bonus points – Essex 4, Middlesex 2 (Score at 100 overs: 330-6).

Bowling: Daniel 31–3–102–3; Selvey 22.2–4–63–2; Williams 19–0–74–0; Emburey 16–3–41–2; Edmonds 19–1–58–1.

Essex forfeited their second innings.

Middlesex

*J. M. Brearley not out	4	– lbw b Lever	59
W. N. Slack not out	4	– c McEwan b Foster	19
G. D. Barlow (did not bat)		– lbw b Phillip	4
M. W. Gatting (did not bat)		– c Phillip b R. E. East	90
C. T. Radley (did not bat)		– b Foster	25
P. H. Edmonds (did not bat)		– c Gooch b R. E. East	19
J. E. Emburey (did not bat)		– not out	67
†P. R. Downton (did not bat)		– c Fletcher b R. E. East	2
M. W. W. Selvey (did not bat)		– c Lever b Phillip	17
N. F. Williams (did not bat)		– not out	27
		L-b 18, n-b 1	19
(no wkt dec.)	8	1/45 2/49 3/148 4/200 5/220 6/232 7/246 8/289 (8 wkts)	348

W. W. Daniel did not bat.

Bowling: *First Innings*—Lever 2–1–6–0; Phillip 1–0–2–0. *Second Innings*—Lever 22.2–3–57–1; Phillip 14–3–73–2; Foster 22–4–83–2; Turner 11–2–30–0; R. E. East 31–10–69–3; Gooch 4–0–17–0.

Umpires: B. Leadbeater and R. Palmer.

MIDDLESEX v NORTHAMPTONSHIRE

At Lord's, May 12, 13, 14. Middlesex won by nine wickets. Middlesex 24 pts, Northamptonshire 4 pts. Middlesex enjoyed virtually unbroken command and won comfortably shortly after tea. Cook, having put Middlesex in, was soon having second thoughts as Brearley indicated his supreme form by outscoring Slack on the slowish pitch. Griffiths worked tirelessly and testingly all day, and his afternoon wickets gave his side a glimpse of a breakthrough, but Emburey continued his fine early-season form, cracking the ball around with considerable strength. Brearley batted for five hours, but Emburey needed exactly half that time for his maiden century. Northamptonshire lost fourteen wickets on the second day, but all the batsmen, bar the unfortunate Cook, had something to show for their efforts between the regular tumble of wickets. Lamb, with aggression, and Steele, with customary prudence, achieved limited success, but Lamb had been disposed of a second time when Northamptonshire began the last day at 107 for four. Carter, emulating Steele's defiance, did not fall until after lunch, while Steele resisted for 220 minutes, both helped by a deterioration in Middlesex's catching standards.

Middlesex

*J. M. Brearley c Mallender b Griffiths	165	– not out	21
W. N. Slack lbw b Griffiths	44	– c Cook b Sarfraz	1
G. D. Barlow c Cook b Griffiths	2	– not out	37
M. W. Gatting c Steele b Griffiths	17		
C. T. Radley c Yardley b Griffiths	3		
J. E. Emburey not out	100		
P. H. Edmonds not out	25		
B 4, l-b 8, w 2, n-b 9	23	L-b 4, n-b 4	8
1/112 2/138 3/176 4/184 5/312 (5 wkts dec.)	379	1/9 (1 wkt)	67

†P. R. Downton, N. F. Williams, M. W. W. Selvey and W. W. Daniel did not bat.

Bonus points – Middlesex 4, Northamptonshire 2 (Score at 100 overs: 345-5).

Bowling: *First Innings*—Sarfraz 22–3–71–0; Griffiths 32–7–105–5; Carter 10–2–28–0; Mallender 19–5–70–0; Steele 16–2–48–0; Williams 8–2–34–0. *Second Innings*—Sarfraz 7–1–12–1; Griffiths 3–0–11–0; Williams 7.5–2–23–0; Mallender 4–0–13–0.

Northamptonshire

*G. Cook c and b Selvey	12	– c Brearley b Williams	9
W. Larkins b Daniel	8	– b Edmonds	38
R. G. Williams c Downton b Daniel	9	– b Edmonds	14
A. J. Lamb c Downton b Selvey	55	– lbw b Emburey	18
D. S. Steele b Williams	52	– c Williams b Daniel	66
T. J. Yardley b Emburey	39	– c Emburey b Daniel	18
R. M. Carter not out	28	– c Radley b Emburey	40
†G. Sharp c and b Emburey	4	– not out	5
Sarfraz Nawaz lbw b Emburey	4	– lbw b Daniel	4
N. A. Mallender b Edmonds	3	– b Williams	3
B. J. Griffiths c Radley b Edmonds	0	– b Williams	0
L-b 6	6	B 4, l-b 6	10
1/20 2/21 3/59 4/124 5/170 6/185 7/191 8/195 9/220	220	1/14 2/47 3/70 4/83 5/114 6/197 7/213 8/221 9/225	225

Bonus points – Northamptonshire 2, Middlesex 4.

Bowling: *First Innings*—Daniel 19–5–61–2; Selvey 18–5–56–2; Emburey 18–6–31–3; Williams 14–2–42–1; Edmonds 13.5–4–22–2; Slack 2–1–2–0. *Second Innings*—Daniel 21–5–39–3; Selvey 9–5–13–0; Emburey 26–6–50–2; Williams 16.4–4–38–3; Edmonds 40–14–75–2.

Umpires: J. Birkenshaw and A. Jepson.

At Oxford, May 19, 20, 21. MIDDLESEX beat OXFORD UNIVERSITY by an innings and 107 runs.

MIDDLESEX v SUSSEX

At Lord's, May 29, 31, June 1. Middlesex won by 68 runs. Middlesex 22 pts, Sussex 5 pts. Imran's inability to bowl in the first innings was well camouflaged by first Greig and then Pigott. Slack, the only man to top 50 in the match, underpinned a useful-looking Middlesex start, but Greig beat him and then Pigott took five quick wickets. The Sussex batsmen played some handsome strokes on the second morning, but nobody had the application needed against the spinners on a pitch giving marginal help. Middlesex's second-innings start was vital to the result, and it was ended by Imran and Barclay during a twenty-over spell which cost just 20 runs. On the last morning Kemp, making his Championship début for Middlesex, saw the score from 125 for seven to the declaration, which set 262 in four hours. Again all the Sussex batsmen thought they had found the answer to Edmonds, only to be disillusioned before doing too much damage. There were two good catches in the middle distance and Gatting took three at short leg as Edmonds achieved career-best figures and a win with an hour in hand.

Middlesex

*J. M. Brearley b Greig	7	– c Parker b Barclay	33
W. N. Slack lbw b Greig	85	– st Gould b Barclay	36
G. D. Barlow c le Roux b Greig	13	– (4) b Imran	30
M. W. Gatting b Waller	24	– (3) lbw b Waller	8
C. T. Radley c Waller b Pigott	32	– c and b Waller	2
J. E. Emburey b Pigott	13	– b Imran	9
P. H. Edmonds lbw b Pigott	11	– lbw b Imran	0
N. J. Kemp not out	22	– not out	46
†P. R. Downton c Parker b Pigott	2	– c Phillipson b Barclay	9
N. F. Williams c Gould b Pigott	0	– not out	10
W. W. Daniel b Greig	3		
B 1, l-b 15, n-b 2	18	B 4, l-b 10, w 2	16
1/24 2/58 3/111 4/175 5/185 6/202 7/203 8/205 9/205	230	1/67 2/78 3/89 4/99 5/124 6/124 7/125 8/155 (8 wkts dec.)	199

Bonus points – Middlesex 2, Sussex 4.

Bowling: *First Innings*—le Roux 14–4–22–0; Pigott 19–6–47–5; Greig 26.4–5–63–4; Barclay 10–3–39–0; Waller 14–3–41–1. *Second Innings*—Imran 25–13–28–3; le Roux 7–1–20–0; Pigott 3–0–9–0; Waller 33–7–78–2; Barclay 27–9–48–3.

Sussex

G. D. Mendis c Downton b Williams	2 – c Gatting b Edmonds	4
*J. R. T. Barclay lbw b Kemp	8 – (9) c Gatting b Edmonds	6
C. M. Wells c Kemp b Emburey	39 – c Gatting b Edmonds	16
P. W. G. Parker st Downton b Edmonds	12 – c Daniel b Edmonds	31
Imran Khan c Downton b Daniel	34 – c Barlow b Daniel	40
I. A. Greig c Gatting b Edmonds	7 – (7) c Emburey b Edmonds	9
†I. J. Gould c Barlow b Emburey	16 – (2) st Downton b Emburey	22
C. P. Phillipson c Radley b Edmonds	0 – b Edmonds	26
G. S. le Roux not out	17 – (6) c Emburey b Edmonds	35
A. C. S. Pigott st Downton b Emburey	13 – not out	1
C. E. Waller c Daniel b Edmonds	5 – b Edmonds	0
B 3, l-b 6, w 2, n-b 4	15 L-b 3	3
1/3 2/32 3/54 4/93 5/110 6/125 7/130 8/131 9/158	168 1/19 2/33 3/49 4/100 5/129 6/149 7/168 8/188 9/193	193

Bonus points – Sussex 1, Middlesex 4.

Bowling: *First Innings*—Daniel 12–5–27–1; Williams 10–2–35–1; Edmonds 20.4–3–40–4; Kemp 3–0–13–1; Emburey 15–3–38–3; *Second Innings*—Daniel 9–1–20–1; Williams 1–0–13–0; Emburey 25–5–77–1; Edmonds 28.5–5–80–8.

Umpires: W. E. Alley and P. J. Eele.

MIDDLESEX v DERBYSHIRE

At Lord's, June 2, 3, 4. Drawn. Middlesex 4 pts, Derbyshire 2 pts. The first day was halted before tea by a thunderstorm, before which Kirsten and Hampshire had displayed a few shots to make up for a torpid start. Emburey worked productively on the second morning, but the match was making no progress until Brearley galvanised it by declaring during tea. Derbyshire, 85 for one overnight, were allowed to build towards a declaration with attractive batting from Wright and Kirsten again. Middlesex were set 348 in 247 minutes, and the early departure of Brearley and Radley merely paved the way for another of Gatting's early-season specials. Slack batted with far greater urgency than in the first innings, and as Gatting blazed off his shots Emburey and then Edmonds gave him wonderful support. The strokeplay reached its zenith during the 25 overs of the 152-run Gatting-Edmonds stand. Middlesex wanted 123 from the last twenty overs and 69 from the final ten, but rain then cost them two crucial overs and Williams and Daniel were not able to make 16 from the last two overs.

Derbyshire

A. Hill b Emburey	14 – st Downton b Emburey	18
J. G. Wright c Slack b Williams	9 – not out	103
*P. N. Kirsten c Slack b Daniel	47 – not out	80
J. H. Hampshire b Emburey	40	
K. J. Barnett c Gatting b Emburey	24	
I. S. Anderson c Gatting b Emburey	9	
†B. J. M. Maher c Gatting b Edmonds	4	
P. G. Newman b Emburey	12	
D. G. Moir st Downton b Edmonds	25	
S. Oldham not out	22	
B 1, l-b 14, w 1, n-b 6	22 L-b 1, n-b 6	7
1/17 2/56 3/98 4/143 5/153 6/158 7/168 8/191 9/228	(9 wkts dec.) 228 1/45	(1 wkt dec.) 208

P. J. Hacker did not bat.

Bonus points – Derbyshire 2, Middlesex 4.

Bowling: *First Innings*—Daniel 20–4–31–1; Williams 19–4–38–1; Edmonds 21.3–6–60–2; Kemp 10–2–27–0; Emburey 28–9–50–5. *Second Innings*—Daniel 8–2–16–0; Williams 5–2–14–0; Emburey 28–3–65–1; Kemp 3–1–6–0; Edmonds 24–4–84–0; Gatting 2–1–4–0; Brearley 1–0–3–0; Radley 1–0–9–0.

Middlesex

*J. M. Brearley	not out	43	c Hacker b Newman	6
W. N. Slack	not out	42	c Anderson b Hacker	46
C. T. Radley	(did not bat)		c Maher b Newman	9
M. W. Gatting	(did not bat)		c Anderson b Oldham	140
R. O. Butcher	(did not bat)		c Maher b Hacker	4
J. E. Emburey	(did not bat)		run out	40
P. H. Edmonds	(did not bat)		b Hacker	67
N. J. Kemp	(did not bat)		c Newman b Oldham	1
†P. R. Downton	(did not bat)		c sub b Oldham	5
N. F. Williams	(did not bat)		not out	5
W. W. Daniel	(did not bat)		not out	3
	L-b 2, n-b 2	4	B 1, l-b 10, n-b 3	14
	(no wkt)	89	1/11 2/31 3/84 4/88 5/170 6/322 7/323 8/329 9/331 (9 wkts)	340

Bowling: *First Innings*—Newman 11–3–25–0; Oldham 10–2–18–0; Hacker 10–4–27–0; Moir 9–3–12–0; Anderson 1–0–3–0. *Second Innings*—Newman 13–1–72–2; Oldham 17–0–99–3; Hacker 19–3–86–3; Moir 13–1–45–0; Anderson 4–0–24–0.

Umpires: W. E. Alley and P. J. Eele.

At Tunbridge Wells, June 5, 7, 8. MIDDLESEX beat KENT by an innings and 72 runs.

At Swansea, June 9, 10, 11. MIDDLESEX beat GLAMORGAN by ten wickets.

At Sheffield, June 12, 14, 15. MIDDLESEX drew with YORKSHIRE.

MIDDLESEX v LANCASHIRE

At Lord's, June 19, 21, 22. Drawn. Middlesex 6 pts, Lancashire 4 pts. A match with no play on the third day would not normally be memorable, but Clive Lloyd, Gatting and Butcher touched their best in contrasting exhibitions of batsmanship. Hayes, too, might have contributed, but his return to his old form was abruptly ended when he slipped as he started for a run and broke a bone in his foot. Lancashire, put in, batted sedately throughout Saturday, and Lloyd's over-powering presence remained a threat over the weekend. However, he added only 1 run to his score. Croft swept through the early Middlesex batting before the balance of bat and ball underwent a transformation swift even by cricket's drastic fluctuations. Croft's lift allowed him to hit Butcher and Gatting on the hands, but they hit his bowling with increasing ferocity. Their cutting and hooking of the short stuff was both brave and spectacular, and even in bad light they refused to go off. Butcher hooked Allott for two 6s, Gatting hit one 6 and fourteen 4s in all, and their breath-taking performance had added 178 in 35 overs before Croft showed his resilience by taking two quick wickets.

Lancashire

A. Kennedy c Downton b Daniel	33	P. J. W. Allott b Daniel	2
G. Fowler c Downton b Edmonds	28	I. Folley not out	26
F. C. Hayes retired hurt	21	C. E. H. Croft b Merry	20
*C. H. Lloyd lbw b Selvey	93	B 6, l-b 11, w 1, n-b 5	23
D. P. Hughes c and b Selvey	12		—
J. Abrahams b Emburey	6	1/57 2/71 3/141	280
J. Simmons b Emburey	0	4/166 5/166 6/198	
†C. Maynard c Radley b Emburey	16	7/215 8/245 9/280	

Bonus points – Lancashire 2, Middlesex 3 (Score at 100 overs: 234-7).

Bowling: Daniel 23–7–48–2; Selvey 28–10–58–2; Merry 15.2–3–42–1; Gatting 4–2–8–0; Edmonds 27–5–71–1; Emburey 15–4–30–3.

Middlesex

*J. M. Brearley c sub b Croft	0	J. E. Emburey c Kennedy b Simmons	17
W. N. Slack c Allott b Croft	15	†P. R. Downton not out	0
C. T. Radley c Hughes b Allott	1	B 5, l-b 5, n-b 4	14
M. W. Gatting not out	133		—
R. O. Butcher c Lloyd b Croft	82	1/1 2/6 3/24	(6 wkts) 267
P. H. Edmonds c sub b Croft	5	4/202 5/229 6/266	

W. G. Merry, M. W. W. Selvey and W. W. Daniel did not bat.

Bonus points – Middlesex 3, Lancashire 2.

Bowling: Croft 26–3–100–4; Allott 13–1–67–1; Folley 5–0–18–0; Kennedy 2–0–11–0; Simmons 14–2–57–1.

Umpires: D. Archer and K. E. Palmer.

At Lord's, June 23, 24, 25. MIDDLESEX drew with PAKISTANIS (See Pakistani tour section).

At The Oval, June 26, 28, 29. MIDDLESEX drew with SURREY.

MIDDLESEX v LEICESTERSHIRE

At Uxbridge, July 7, 8, 9. Leicestershire won by six wickets. Leicestershire 24 pts, Middlesex 5 pts. Middlesex pleasure at putting Leicestershire in and taking two wickets in the first five overs was swiftly transformed. Davison's arrival signalled unbroken control for Leicestershire and Middlesex lost in the Championship for the first time in the season. Davison was at his devastating best, scoring a century before lunch despite coming in at No. 4. He hit two 6s in making 53 in his first 40 minutes and played handsome strokes more or less as he wanted until he was out in the last over before the interval. Balderstone and Tolchard added 148 in the afternoon, and Leicestershire ended a most satisfactory day with two wickets for Taylor. Cook achieved some turn on the second day, removing Gatting and Butcher in successive balls, but Tomlins sustained the innings for 150 minutes and continued as opener when Middlesex followed on. However, he, Brearley and Gatting had all gone by the start of the third day, which began with two early wickets from long-hops by Roberts. Downton and Emburey battled determinedly, but Leicestershire's chief worry was rain, which halted their innings twice before they won with nine overs remaining.

Leicestershire

J. C. Balderstone c Butcher b Slack	148	– c Butcher b Emburey	14
R. A. Cobb c Downton b Williams	0	– c Radley b Emburey	20
N. E. Briers c Butcher b Daniel	1		
B. F. Davison c and b Williams	100	– (3) not out	25
*R. W. Tolchard not out	80	– c Downton b Gatting	2
†M. A. Garnham b Slack	0	– not out	5
J. F. Steele b Slack	1		
G. J. Parsons c Butcher b Daniel	16		
A. M. E. Roberts b Hughes	4	– (4) b Emburey	6
N. G. B. Cook run out	5		
L. B. Taylor c Daniel b Emburey	17		
L-b 8, w 1, n-b 18	27	B 2, l-b 1	3
1/7 2/9 3/169 4/317 5/317 6/320 7/345 8/350 9/359	399	1/23 2/50 3/58 4/61 (4 wkts)	75

Bonus points – Leicestershire 4, Middlesex 4 (Score at 100 overs: 364-9).

Bowling: *First Innings*—Daniel 16–2–53–2; Williams 9–2–34–2; Gatting 16–0–53–0; Hughes 15–2–65–1; Emburey 35.3–6–119–1; Slack 7–1–17–3; Tomlins 7–1–31–0. *Second Innings*—Daniel 5–1–15–0; Hughes 2–0–14–0; Emburey 9.2–3–26–3; Gatting 5–0–17–1.

Middlesex

*J. M. Brearley c Garnham b Taylor	5	– (3) c Tolchard b Briers	1
W. N. Slack c Cook b Taylor	10	– (1) c Steele b Roberts	57
†P. R. Downton lbw b Cook	40	– (5) c and b Steele	65
C. T. Radley c Cobb b Taylor	6	– (7) lbw b Parsons	20
M. W. Gatting c Balderstone b Cook	21	– (4) lbw b Roberts	22
R. O. Butcher c Tolchard b Cook	0	– c Parsons b Roberts	13
K. P. Tomlins c and b Cook	51	– (2) c and b Steele	44
J. E. Emburey c Tolchard b Cook	10	– b Roberts	61
N. F. Williams lbw b Cook	4	– c Garnham b Taylor	18
S. P. Hughes run out	0	– (11) not out	0
W. W. Daniel not out	8	– (10) lbw b Taylor	0
L-b 2, w 2, n-b 1	5	B 4, l-b 5, w 3	12
1/13 2/21 3/33 4/68 5/68 6/91 7/117 8/134 9/143	160	1/88 2/89 3/125 4/140 5/156 6/229 7/231 8/305 9/313	313

Bonus points – Middlesex 1, Leicestershire 4.

Bowling: *First Innings*—Roberts 16–2–38–0; Taylor 18–3–42–3; Cook 25.4–13–32–6; Parsons 12–1–43–0; Steele 1–1–0–0. *Second Innings*—Roberts 22.3–7–53–4; Taylor 17–3–60–2; Cook 31–8–87–0; Parsons 10–2–29–1; Steele 22–5–42–2; Briers 4–0–24–1; Balderstone 3–0–6–0.

Umpires: C. T. Spencer and P. B. Wight.

At Nottingham, July 10, 12, 13. MIDDLESEX beat NOTTINGHAMSHIRE by an innings and 15 runs.

MIDDLESEX v NOTTINGHAMSHIRE

At Lord's, July 17, 19, 20. Middlesex won by an innings and 111 runs. Middlesex 23 pts, Nottinghamshire 2 pts. On a pitch that could not be trusted, and against a second-string Nottinghamshire attack which strove for accuracy, Middlesex batted ponderously on the first day. Tomlins showed industry and a fair range of strokes in his maiden first-class century. Middlesex added 50 on the second morning, and then the match quickened drastically. Nottinghamshire began their first innings at noon and the game ended at 12.50 on the third day. The Middlesex new-ball bowlers made an early strike, Hughes collected two important wickets, and the spinners always had too much in their armoury for the later batsmen. Nottinghamshire were 82 for three in their second innings at the end of the second day, and Edmonds took five for 11 on the last to wrap up Middlesex's second innings win over Nottinghamshire within a week.

Middlesex

*J. M. Brearley c Hassan b Cooper	7
W. N. Slack c French b Illingworth	13
K. P. Tomlins c Fell b Illingworth	138
R. O. Butcher c French b Pont	30
C. T. Radley c Illingworth b Fell	45
†P. R. Downton c Robinson b Illingworth	22
J. E. Emburey b Illingworth	30
P. H. Edmonds c French b Cooper	41
N. G. Cowans b Illingworth	2
W. W. Daniel c Robinson b Cooper	21
S. P. Hughes not out	0
B 1, l-b 4, n-b 9	14
1/11 2/26 3/73 4/190 5/237 6/271 7/312 8/317 9/362	363

Bonus points – Middlesex 3, Nottinghamshire 2 (Score at 100 overs: 272-6).

Bowling: Cooper 37.1–13–77–3; Pont 23–2–93–1; Illingworth 31–6–89–5; Such 23–3–70–0; Fell 8–1–20–1.

Nottinghamshire

R. T. Robinson c Downton b Cowans	0	– b Emburey	40
B. Hassan c Radley b Daniel	4	– b Cowans	0
M. A. Fell c Brearley b Emburey	11	– c Brearley b Edmonds	34
*C. E. B. Rice c Brearley b Hughes	12	– (5) c Radley b Emburey	19
J. D. Birch c Radley b Edmonds	32	– (6) c Butcher b Edmonds	0
P. Johnson c Downton b Hughes	4	– (7) c Downton b Edmonds	7
†B. N. French c Slack b Emburey	11	– (8) c Brearley b Edmonds	4
I. L. Pont c Tomlins b Emburey	16	– (9) c Radley b Edmonds	8
N. J. B. Illingworth not out	12	– (4) c Slack b Emburey	9
K. E. Cooper c Daniel b Edmonds	6	– not out	7
P. M. Such lbw b Emburey	0	– c Downton b Edmonds	0
B 2, l-b 2, w 1, n-b 1	6	B 3, l-b 1, n-b 6	10
1/5 2/5 3/28 4/28 5/34 6/69 7/90 8/100 9/114	114	1/4 2/80 3/80 4/102 5/103 6/114 7/120 8/129 9/132	138

Bonus points – Middlesex 4.

Bowling: *First Innings*—Daniel 10–2–22–1; Cowans 9–4–15–1; Emburey 20.4–9–30–4; Hughes 8–1–15–2; Edmonds 11–4–26–2. *Second Innings*—Daniel 3–0–6–0; Cowans 6–3–22–1; Emburey 31–16–49–3; Hughes 5–0–13–0; Edmonds 29.4–16–31–6; Slack 2–0–7–0.

Umpires: M. J. Kitchen and P. B. Wight.

At Southend, July 21, 22, 23. MIDDLESEX drew with ESSEX.

MIDDLESEX v KENT

At Lord's, July 31, August 2, 3. Drawn. Middlesex 5 pts, Kent 5 pts. Middlesex put Kent in but gained no profit from the move. Potter and Taylor did not score for five overs before gradually gaining command in the 105 minutes to lunch, which brought 86 runs. Taylor, hit on the cheek-bone, was forced to retire when 39, but Potter went on to a most responsible first Championship century. On Monday, Kent had Johnson, 55 overnight, and the restored

Taylor to push them from 259 for five to their declaration, following which Middlesex struggled as Johnson and Underwood exploited the slow turn. Brearley, who batted low down because of a neck injury, and Emburey improved matters and the third batting point was achieved on the last morning. Potter played another innings ideally suited to the context, Knott and Dilley provided acceleration, and Middlesex were set 254 in 162 minutes. Butcher hit six 4s and two 6s in his 36-minute stay, but this was just too brief an innings to give his side a chance. They needed 147 from the last twenty overs, and the chase was abandoned with 67 needed from seven overs.

Kent

N. R. Taylor b Cowans	58	– c Downton b Daniel	7
L. Potter lbw b Emburey	108	– c sub b Emburey	55
D. G. Aslett lbw b Selvey	12	– c Radley b Edmonds	9
*Asif Iqbal c Cowans b Daniel	5		
G. W. Johnson c Edmonds b Selvey	86	– (4) c sub b Edmonds	18
C. S. Cowdrey lbw b Edmonds	2	– (5) c Emburey b Edmonds	24
†A. P. E. Knott c Cowans b Emburey	9	– (6) c Slack b Tomlins	42
R. M. Ellison c Radley b Edmonds	10	– (7) run out	2
G. R. Dilley c Daniel b Selvey	1	– (8) b Tomlins	23
C. Penn not out	0	– (9) not out	0
B 1, l-b 10, w 2, n-b 8	21	B 4, l-b 4, w 2, n-b 1	11
1/125 2/142 3/207 4/212 5/229 6/260 7/310 8/312 9/312 (9 wkts dec.)	312	1/11 2/41 3/76 4/122 5/127 6/134 7/170 8/191 (8 wkts dec.)	191

D. L. Underwood did not bat.

Bonus points – Kent 3, Middlesex 2 (Score at 100 overs: 252-5).

Bowling: *First Innings*—Selvey 28.3–13–47–3; Daniel 17–5–34–1; Cowans 18–2–76–1; Edmonds 34–10–74–2; Emburey 22–5–51–2; Slack 4–1–9–0. *Second Innings*—Cowans 5–1–17–0; Daniel 5–1–6–1; Selvey 3–2–4–0; Emburey 15–4–52–1; Edmonds 13–3–43–3; Slack 1–0–2–0; Radley 3–0–18–0; Tomlins 3.3–0–28–2; Butcher 1–0–10–0.

Middlesex

W. N. Slack b Johnson	32	– c Ellison b Aslett	15
†P. R. Downton c Potter b Dilley	1	– (6) not out	7
K. P. Tomlins b Dilley	33	– (2) c Penn b Underwood	62
R. O. Butcher c Aslett b Underwood	20	– (3) c Knott b Dilley	49
C. T. Radley c Aslett b Johnson	40	– not out	40
J. E. Emburey not out	73	– (4) st Knott b Underwood	7
P. H. Edmonds c Penn b Taylor	5		
*J. M. Brearley not out	31		
L-b 6, n-b 9	15	L-b 4, n-b 3	7
1/13 2/72 3/73 4/110 5/154 6/179 (6 wkts dec.)	250	1/29 2/102 3/119 4/154 (4 wkts)	187

M. W. W. Selvey, N. G. Cowans and W. W. Daniel did not bat.

Bonus points – Middlesex 3, Kent 2.

Bowling: *First Innings*—Dilley 15.3–5–37–2; Ellison 12–5–21–0; Penn 6–1–16–0; Aslett 7–1–23–0; Johnson 28–7–76–2; Underwood 27–8–57–1; Taylor 1–0–5–1. *Second Innings*—Dilley 7–1–17–1; Ellison 2–1–4–0; Johnson 9–0–49–0; Underwood 13–1–74–2; Aslett 8–1–35–1; Penn 2–1–1–0.

Umpires: B. J. Meyer and R. Palmer.

At Weston-super-Mare, August 7, 9, 10. MIDDLESEX beat SOMERSET by an innings and 75 runs.

At Cheltenham, August 11, 12, 13. MIDDLESEX drew with GLOUCESTERSHIRE.

At Coventry, August 14, 16, 17. MIDDLESEX beat WARWICKSHIRE by an innings and 66 runs.

MIDDLESEX v YORKSHIRE

At Lord's, August 21, 23, 24. Drawn. Middlesex 8 pts, Yorkshire 2 pts. Yorkshire were never able to catch up after falling at the first when Daniel had Lumb lbw and then found an even better ball to end Boycott's run of high scores. The other batsmen played capably before 120 for four became 147 for nine against Edmonds and Hughes, but Bairstow gave a typical flourish to the end of the innings. Middlesex were not too promisingly placed themselves on the Saturday after Brearley, third ball, and Radley had gone. Slack, too, went early, but this merely served to bring together Gatting and Butcher, who treated the spectators to violent strokeplay of the highest class. Balls of quite respectable length and line were dismissed disdainfully as they added 237, Gatting playing the major role. In the twilight conditions of mid-afternoon, he refused an offer of bad light and cut and hooked the pace bowlers with increasing frequency and power. Butcher, whose 197 included six 6s and eighteen 4s, and Emburey hit the last 116 of their 156 stand off sixteen overs with the new ball as Butcher, with a declaration impending, sought his double-century. Yorkshire then survived a fiery burst from Cowans and were required to resist for 50 minutes on the last day before rain ended the game.

Yorkshire

G. Boycott lbw b Daniel	2	– not out	40
R. G. Lumb lbw b Daniel	0	– b Edmonds	34
C. W. J. Athey lbw b Hughes	20	– not out	1
S. N. Hartley b Emburey	54		
K. Sharp c Downton b Emburey	16		
†D. L. Bairstow not out	54		
P. Carrick b Hughes	2		
A. Sidebottom c Slack b Edmonds	1		
G. B. Stevenson c Brearley b Edmonds	4		
A. Ramage lbw b Hughes	0		
*R. Illingworth lbw b Emburey	15		
B 4, l-b 3, w 1, n-b 6	14		
1/0 2/5 3/37 4/79 5/120 6/132 7/133 8/146 9/147	182	1/73	(1 wkt) 75

Bonus points – Yorkshire 1, Middlesex 4.

Bowling: *First Innings*—Cowans 14–4–40–0; Daniel 11–3–33–2; Hughes 10–0–31–3; Slack 3–0–3–0; Emburey 13.1–4–28–3; Edmonds 20–10–33–2. *Second Innings*—Cowans 7–0–24–0; Daniel 10–2–27–0; Edmonds 9.1–4–13–1; Emburey 5–0–11–0; Hughes 1–1–0–0.

Middlesex

*J. M. Brearley b Ramage	4	J. E. Emburey not out	43
W. N. Slack c Lumb b Carrick	41	B 6, l-b 11, n-b 11	28
C. T. Radley lbw b Stevenson	7		
M. W. Gatting st Bairstow b Carrick	141	1/4 2/36 3/68 4/305 5/461	(5 wkts dec.) 461
R. O. Butcher run out	197		

†P. R. Downton, P. H. Edmonds, S. P. Hughes, N. G. Cowans and W. W. Daniel did not bat.

Bonus points – Middlesex 4, Yorkshire 1 (Score at 100 overs: 345-4).

Bowling: Ramage 23–2–106–1; Stevenson 26–4–120–1; Sidebottom 19.1–0–75–0; Carrick 37–9–80–2; Illingworth 4–0–17–0; Hartley 9–2–35–0.

Umpires: C. Cook and Khizar Hayat.

MIDDLESEX v SURREY

At Lord's, August 25, 26, 27. Middlesex won by 58 runs. Middlesex 18 pts, Surrey 5 pts. The match began and ended with little dramas involving Titmus. His arrival at Lord's was a chance matter and, as Brearley believed that the pitch would help spin, the 49-year-old player was recalled to action. Brearley's assessment was justified, though not at first. Middlesex intentions of compiling a large score at whatever pace – Slack batted five hours – were set back when Mackintosh took three wickets in four balls, the intervening delivery being a no-ball. Rain, missed chances, the slowness of the pitch and the well-organised batting of Butcher and Howarth enabled Surrey to reach the third morning unscathed at 180 for no wicket. They continued until lunch, whereupon Middlesex hurried to set a target, which, with tea abandoned, set Surrey a generous 161 in 135 minutes. Now the pitch and circumstances vindicated Brearley, and his final appearance at Lord's was marked by a triumph he did much to engineer. Edmonds took three of the first four wickets, and when he withdrew with an injured back Middlesex had Titmus to step in with three timely wickets. Clarke hit three 6s and one 4 in scoring all 35 of the runs made while he was there, but Titmus removed him with one of three catches in the deep by Cowans and Middlesex won with 7.3 overs in hand.

Middlesex

*J. M. Brearley c Lynch b Monkhouse	43	– c and b Needham	27
W. N. Slack b Needham	79	– not out	71
K. P. Tomlins c Smith b Knight	9	– c Thomas b Mackintosh	51
R. O. Butcher c Knight b Needham	36	– not out	0
C. T. Radley c Richards b Mackintosh	40		
J. E. Emburey b Mackintosh	13		
†P. R. Downton c Clarke b Mackintosh	24		
P. H. Edmonds hit wkt b Mackintosh	0		
N. G. Cowans b Mackintosh	0		
W. W. Daniel c Monkhouse b Mackintosh	3		
F. J. Titmus not out	1		
B 5, l-b 13, n-b 10	28	B 5, l-b 1, n-b 2	8
1/84 2/107 3/173 4/202 5/240 6/247 7/247 8/248 9/272	276	1/47 2/146 (2 wkts dec.)	157

Bonus points – Middlesex 2, Surrey 3 (Score at 100 overs: 248-8).

Bowling: *First Innings*—Clarke 17–6–35–0; Thomas 25–14–43–0; Monkhouse 11–2–28–1; Mackintosh 25–10–61–6; Needham 25–10–63–2; Knight 8–2–18–1. *Second Innings*—Clarke 2–0–13–0; Thomas 3–0–16–0; Needham 13–0–44–1; Mackintosh 6–0–27–1; Butcher 4–0–24–0; Lynch 6–0–25–0.

Surrey

A. R. Butcher c Downton b Edmonds	82	– c Brearley b Edmonds	1
G. P. Howarth c Emburey b Daniel	112	– c Cowans b Emburey	8
D. M. Smith lbw b Cowans	19	– lbw b Emburey	17
*R. D. V. Knight not out	16	– (5) c Butcher b Edmonds	7
M. A. Lynch b Emburey	22	– (4) c and b Edmonds	3
†C. J. Richards not out	0	– b Emburey	5
S. T. Clarke (did not bat)		– c Cowans b Titmus	35
D. J. Thomas (did not bat)		– c Slack b Titmus	7
A. Needham (did not bat)		– c Cowans b Emburey	11
G. Monkhouse (did not bat)		– lbw b Titmus	0
K. S. Mackintosh (did not bat)		– not out	0
B 7, l-b 13, w 1, n-b 1	22	B 6, l-b 2	8
1/188 2/233 3/235 4/272 (4 wkts dec.)	273	1/3 2/13 3/24 4/40 5/49 6/70 7/84 8/100 9/102	102

Bonus points – Surrey 2 (Score at 100 overs: 204-1).

Bowling: *First Innings*—Cowans 5–0–35–1; Daniel 9–0–24–1; Edmonds 43–16–67–1; Emburey 43–11–76–1; Titmus 15–3–49–0. *Second Innings*—Daniel 2–0–3–0; Edmonds 11–3–24–3; Emburey 13.3–2–24–4; Titmus 10–1–43–3.

Umpires: C. Cook and Khizar Hayat.

At Hove, August 28, 30, 31. MIDDLESEX lost to SUSSEX by three wickets.

MIDDLESEX v HAMPSHIRE

At Uxbridge, September 8, 9, 10. Middlesex won by 106 runs. Middlesex 22 pts, Hampshire 5 pts. On a pitch that accepted spin freely it was predictable that the higher class of the Middlesex slow bowlers would prove decisive. The win lifted Middlesex to the verge of the title and proved a most satisfying farewell for Brearley to the county's supporters. Not that his start was promising: his helmet jerked on to his wicket second ball as Hampshire's fast bowlers took an early grip. Slack batted judiciously, Butcher belligerently and Monteith surprised by organising the second batting point. Brearley had the spinners in early action. Emburey had Greenidge, sweeping, caught near the boundary and Jesty caught close in within three balls, and Hampshire ended the day 93 for five. Turner was out at the start of the second day, but the late batsmen fought defiantly to close the gap. Middlesex looked like being masters of their own destiny on the backs of typical half-centuries from Brearley and Gatting and some fine strokes from Ellis, but the last six wickets were somewhat carelessly tossed away. Daniel struck twice on the second evening and Edmonds had the important wickets of Greenidge and Turner in his first fourteen balls on the last day. When Daniel whipped out Jesty, the game – which finished on the stroke of lunch – was decided.

Middlesex

W. N. Slack c Turner b Marshall	68	– (2) c Rice b Marshall	26
*J. M. Brearley hit wkt b Emery	0	– (1) c Rice b Cowley	50
R. G. P. Ellis b Marshall	6	– c Cowley b Southern	45
M. W. Gatting c Jesty b Marshall	3	– st Parks b Southern	50
R. O. Butcher run out	42	– c Greenidge b Cowley	0
†P. R. Downton c Turner b Emery	14	– c Jesty b Southern	17
J. E. Emburey lbw b Marshall	15	– b Southern	3
P. H. Edmonds c Rice b Southern	5	– lbw b Marshall	4
N. G. Cowans c Nicholas b Southern	0	– (10) b Marshall	2
J. D. Monteith b Southern	36	– (9) b Southern	1
W. W. Daniel not out	4	– not out	2
B 1, l-b 7, n-b 6	14	B 6, l-b 8, w 1	15
1/4 2/18 3/22 4/89 5/135 6/153 7/160 8/180 9/181	207	1/40 2/122 3/158 4/158 5/196 6/201 7/208 8/210 9/213	215

Bonus points – Middlesex 2, Hampshire 4.

Bowling: *First Innings*—Marshall 20–3–67–4; Emery 17–6–51–2; Jesty 7–4–15–0; Cowley 16–6–26–0; Southern 11.4–3–34–3. *Second Innings*—Marshall 17–5–48–3; Emery 8–0–26–0; Cowley 19–2–75–2; Southern 27.2–12–51–5.

Hampshire

C. G. Greenidge c Daniel b Emburey	10	– c Emburey b Edmonds	14
J. M. Rice c Downton b Daniel	15	– c Gatting b Daniel	11
M. C. J. Nicholas c Brearley b Edmonds	8	– lbw b Daniel	0
T. E. Jesty c Slack b Emburey	4	– c Downton b Daniel	26
D. R. Turner b Emburey	30	– lbw b Edmonds	0
*N. E. J. Pocock c Brearley b Edmonds	18	– b Daniel	16
N. G. Cowley c Gatting b Edmonds	18	– run out	21
M. D. Marshall c Brearley b Edmonds	29	– c Brearley b Edmonds	9
†R. J. Parks c Downton b Edmonds	14	– st Downton b Emburey	13
J. W. Southern not out	18	– c Gatting b Edmonds	23
K. St J. D. Emery c Gatting b Edmonds	0	– not out	0
B 4, l-b 6, n-b 4	14	B 2, l-b 2, n-b 1	5
1/21 2/39 3/43 4/43 5/87 6/98 7/140 8/145 9/178	178	1/17 2/17 3/47 4/54 5/60 6/79 7/88 8/113 9/128	138

Bonus points – Hampshire 1, Middlesex 4.

Bowling: *First Innings*—Daniel 9–0–23–1; Cowans 3–0–14–0; Emburey 25–5–61–3; Edmonds 23.5–7–48–6; Monteith 6–1–18–0. *Second Innings*—Daniel 14–6–31–4; Cowans 8–2–24–0; Edmonds 22.3–4–59–4; Emburey 5–1–19–1.

Umpires: R. Julian and A. G. T. Whitehead.

At Worcester, September 11, 13, 14. MIDDLESEX beat WORCESTERSHIRE by ten wickets.

NORTHAMPTONSHIRE

President: D. Brookes
Chairman: D. C. Lucas
Chairman, Cricket Committee: A. P. Arnold
Secretary: K. C. Turner
County Ground, Wantage Road,
Northampton NN1 4TJ
(Telephone: 0604-32917)
Captain: G. Cook
Coach: B. L. Reynolds

After three Lord's finals in successive years, and four in six seasons, Northamptonshire failed in their strongest department recently, only beating Scotland in the Benson and Hedges Cup, and Ireland in the NatWest Bank Trophy. The one cup consolation was the Tilcon Trophy at Harrogate. These lapses notwithstanding, 1982 was an enjoyable season, with both team and individual progress. Northamptonshire rose from fifteenth to ninth in the Schweppes County Championship and from last to eighth in the John Player League.

The outstanding feature was their splendid batting record. They gathered more batting bonus points in the Championship than any other county. Starting with what many of their supporters thought was the best first five batsmen in any county side, this department was further strengthened by the return of David Steele, after a spell with Derbyshire, the splendid progress of the Cambridge Blue, Robin Boyd-Moss, and the discovery of David Capel, a nineteen-year-old local batsman. The county's 1981 England players, Peter Willey and Wayne Larkins, having been on the controversial South African tour, were banned from Test cricket. Leaving aside any debate on that subject, this was certainly a great boon to Northamptonshire, their batting providing the highlights of an excellent scoring season.

Larkins laid claim to being one of the country's foremost opening batsmen with some magnificent displays. Apart from a record 1,863 runs in the first-class game, he also scored 976 in one-day matches. Yet Willey matched him for masterly cricket, moving up to No. 3 and producing his finest form since 1976 when he was first selected for England. Lacking a county century since 1979, he this time hit five, all stamped with powerful strokeplay. He also took 51 first-class wickets at 26 each and supporters voted him their Player of the Year for his all-round excellence.

The third most prolific run-getter was Boyd-Moss, who won the Commercial Union award for the best young batsman in the country and showed remarkable progress with stylish and successful attacking performances. When Allan Lamb was away playing for England, Boyd-Moss got more chances of batting higher up the order. Three established batsmen, skipper Geoff Cook, Lamb and Richard Williams, all just topped the 1,000 mark for the county, though without consistently producing their best form. Lamb, who played only twelve first-class matches for the county because of Test calls, finished the season at his best and ended up top of the averages. Cook had a spell of splendid form in mid-season but struggled early on and again after being left out of the Pakistan series.

The Indian Test all-rounder, Kapil Dev, made a spectacular impact in his nine innings for the county. Supporters described him as a big-hitting successor to Colin Milburn. After Jim Yardley had dropped out to become second-team captain and assistant-coach, Capel had the chance to show his high potential. He played for Young England against Young West Indies three times as also did another of the county's up-and-coming players, Duncan Wild. Capel was rewarded for his promising play with a Whitbread Scholarship to Australia. For all this, and although Steele found himself batting at No. 7 or 8 after twenty years in the higher positions, Northamptonshire's first Championship win did not come until July 20.

Hit by injuries and lack of form, the bowlers could not initially turn to advantage several winning positions. A pre-season disc operation sidelined Tim Lamb until June; Sarfraz Nawaz joined the Pakistanis after eight matches; the discovery of 1981, Neil Mallender, had early run-up problems. As much as anyone it was Steele who changed the picture as pitches began to suit him more. His left-arm slow bowling, aided by the off-spin of Willey and Williams, brought him no fewer than 70 wickets, 58 of them in the last two months of the season. With Mallender also finding his form there were two more wins in August and another two in September to raise hopes for 1983. The great lack was a strike bowler after Sarfraz had gone. The hard-working Jim Griffiths was another hit by injuries, and Kapil Dev's bowling (nine wickets for 404 runs) failed to match his batting. – F.S.

NORTHAMPTONSHIRE 1982

[*Bill Smith*

Back row: R. G. Williams, R. J. Boyd-Moss, D. J. Capel, B. J. Griffiths, T. M. Lamb, Kapil Dev, N. A. Mallender. *Front row:* P. Willey, G. Sharp, G. Cook (*captain*), W. Larkins, A. J. Lamb.

NORTHAMPTONSHIRE RESULTS

All first-class matches – Played 25: Won 6, Lost 3, Drawn 16.

County Championship matches – Played 22: Won 5, Lost 3, Drawn 14.

Bonus points – Batting 61, Bowling 54.

Competition placings – Schweppes County Championship, 9th; NatWest Bank Trophy, 2nd round; Benson and Hedges Cup, 4th in Group B; John Player League, 8th.

COUNTY CHAMPIONSHIP AVERAGES

BATTING

	Birthplace	*M*	*I*	*NO*	*R*	*HI*	*Avge*
A. J. Lamb c	*Langebaanweg, SA*	10	17	1	882	140	55.12
Kapil Dev	*Chandigarh, India*	6	9	2	332	103	47.42
P. Willey c	*Sedgefield*	21	38	4	1,605	145	47.20
W. Larkins c	*Roxton*	22	40	3	1,728	186	46.70
R. J. Boyd-Moss	*Hatton, Ceylon*	14	24	4	885	137	44.25
D. S. Steele c	*Stoke-on-Trent*	22	33	12	775	74*	36.90
G. Cook c	*Wellingborough*	17	31	2	1,014	125	34.96
R. M. Carter	*King's Lynn*	9	16	5	289	40	26.27
D. J. Wild	*Northampton*	5	5	2	76	29	25.33
T. M. Lamb c	*Hartford*	12	12	7	126	39*	25.20
D. J. Capel	*Northampton*	12	19	3	402	60*	25.12
R. G. Williams c	*Bangor*	21	35	3	795	87*	24.84
G. Sharp c	*West Hartlepool*	22	24	7	360	58*	21.17
T. J. Yardley c	*Chaddesley Corbett*	3	5	0	89	39	17.80
N. A. Mallender	*Kirk Sandall*	21	16	8	121	42	15.12
Sarfraz Nawaz c	*Lahore, Pakistan*	6	6	1	65	25	13.00
B. J. Griffiths c	*Wellingborough*	7	10	3	39	16	5.57

Also batted: R. J. Bailey (*Stoke-on-Trent*) (2 matches) 10, 4, 3.

* *Signifies not out.* c *Denotes county cap.*

BOWLING

	O	*M*	*R*	*W*	*Avge*	*BB*
D. S. Steele	673.2	219	1,623	67	24.22	6-59
B. J. Griffiths	367.1	81	1,102	41	26.87	5-71
Sarfraz Nawaz	169.4	39	477	17	28.05	4-33
P. Willey	580.5	182	1,211	41	29.53	6-17
N. A. Mallender	491.2	105	1,670	47	35.53	7-41
R. G. Williams	208	54	596	16	37.25	3-23
T. M. Lamb	286.5	66	811	19	42.68	5-37

Also bowled: R. J. Boyd-Moss 2–0–26–0; D. J. Capel 79.5–5–373–3; R. M. Carter 32–5–127–2; G. Cook 2–0–7–0; Kapil Dev 139.4–32–404–9; W. Larkins 12–0–58–1; D. J. Wild 36.3–5–126–3.

HUNDREDS

The following nineteen three-figure innings were played for Northamptonshire in County Championship matches – W. Larkins (5) 118* v Yorkshire (Northampton), 137 v Somerset (Northampton), 186 v Yorkshire (Middlesbrough), 110* v Worcestershire (Northampton), 105 v Derbyshire (Northampton); P. Willey (4) 145 v Derbyshire (Derby), 140 v Essex (Northampton), 102 v Lancashire (Manchester), 117 v Glamorgan (Swansea); G. Cook (3) 125 v Leicestershire (Leicester), 112* v Yorkshire (Middlesbrough), 101 v Gloucestershire (Bristol); A. J. Lamb (3) 102 v Leicestershire (Leicester), 140 v Hampshire (Northampton), 106 v Essex (Chelmsford); R. J. Boyd-Moss (2) 114* v Gloucestershire (Northampton), 137 v Derbyshire (Northampton); Kapil Dev (2) 103 v Sussex (Eastbourne), 100* v Derbyshire (Northampton).

At Oxford, April 24, 26, 27. NORTHAMPTONSHIRE drew with OXFORD UNIVERSITY.

NORTHAMPTONSHIRE v YORKSHIRE

At Northampton, May 5, 6, 7. Drawn. Northamptonshire 5 pts, Yorkshire 8 pts. Boycott dominated the opening day with a typical century, reaching three figures just before tea and going on to 138 before being eighth out, just before the declaration. The home pace attack restricted Yorkshire to 166 for five before Bairstow slammed 77 out of 129 in 98 minutes, and finally Stevenson hit an unbeaten 34 in eighteen minutes. Despite injuring his back while fielding, Larkins showed splendid form in carrying his bat through a stuttering Northamptonshire innings to save the follow-on, but another of the South African tourists, Sidebottom, ensured that Northants finished up well in arrears. Big hitting by Carrick, Love and Bairstow hurried Yorkshire's second declaration, enabling Old to set a target of 335 in 255 minutes. Larkins accepted the challenge with a 59 that included ten 4s, but after his dismissal the game dwindled to a draw, despite a bright little innings from Allan Lamb.

Yorkshire

G. Boycott c Cook b Mallender	138	– c A. J. Lamb b Griffiths	3
R. G. Lumb c Sharp b Sarfraz	6		
C. W. J. Athey lbw b Larkins	18	– c Yardley b Mallender	12
J. D. Love lbw b Sarfraz	29	– (5) not out	64
K. Sharp lbw b Griffiths	27	– (2) lbw b Mallender	20
S. N. Hartley lbw b Griffiths	2	– lbw b Sarfraz	2
†D. L. Bairstow c Mallender b Griffiths	77	– not out	27
P. Carrick c Willey b Mallender	5	– (4) b Sarfraz	44
G. B. Stevenson not out	34		
*C. M. Old not out	9		
B 4, l-b 10, n-b 9	23	B 6, l-b 10, n-b 1	17
1/9 2/49 3/92 4/162 5/166 6/295 7/323 8/327 (8 wkts dec.)	368	1/7 2/33 3/46 4/102 5/106 (5 wkts dec.)	189

A. Sidebottom did not bat.

Bonus points – Yorkshire 4, Northamptonshire 3.

Bowling: *First Innings*—Sarfraz 27–5–76–2; Griffiths 21–5–59–3; Mallender 22–3–115–2; Larkins 9–0–38–1; Willey 13–1–32–0; Steele 5–0–25–0. *Second Innings*—Sarfraz 17–4–52–2; Griffiths 19–7–45–1; Mallender 11–0–56–2; Steele 2–0–19–0.

Northamptonshire

*G. Cook c Boycott b Stevenson	10	– c Bairstow b Old	17
W. Larkins not out	118	– lbw b Hartley	59
R. G. Williams c Bairstow b Sidebottom	35	– c Bairstow b Sidebottom	0
A. J. Lamb lbw b Sidebottom	1	– lbw b Stevenson	34
P. Willey c Lumb b Sidebottom	5	– not out	13
D. S. Steele b Stevenson	0	– not out	29
T. J. Yardley c Carrick b Sidebottom	17		
†G. Sharp c Lumb b Old	5		
Sarfraz Nawaz c Stevenson b Hartley	18		
N. A. Mallender b Stevenson	4		
B. J. Griffiths lbw b Sidebottom	0		
L-b 8, n-b 2	10	L-b 6, n-b 2	8
1/21 2/91 3/101 4/107 5/108 6/136 7/149 8/203 9/220	223	1/55 2/60 3/99 4/113	(4 wkts) 160

Bonus points – Northamptonshire 2, Yorkshire 4.

Bowling: *First Innings*—Old 23–8–56–1; Stevenson 26–6–74–3; Sidebottom 22–5–57–5; Hartley 10–4–17–1; Carrick 4–2–9–0. *Second Innings*—Old 14–5–29–1; Stevenson 14–2–50–1; Sidebottom 14–3–40–1; Hartley 10–5–28–1; Carrick 5–3–5–0.

Umpires: R. S. Herman and R. Julian.

At Lord's, May 12, 13, 14. NORTHAMPTONSHIRE lost to MIDDLESEX by nine wickets.

NORTHAMPTONSHIRE v SURREY

At Northampton, May 19, 20, 21. Surrey won by 95 runs. Surrey 23 pts, Northamptonshire 4 pts. Sarfraz and Griffiths had reduced Surrey to 55 for four on a lively wicket before Roope (one 6, fourteen 4s) and Smith (one 6, ten 4s) pursued a policy of aggression so effectively that they put on 152 in 99 minutes. Clarke and Jackman emphasised the difficult nature of the wicket with fiery bowling that brought them five wickets each and earned Surrey a lead of 139. Indeed, Northamptonshire were in danger of following on until Sarfraz and Carter put on 49 in 46 minutes. When Surrey batted a second time they struggled against Sarfraz, Griffiths and Carter, but Knight, with ten 4s in his 65, ensured that Northamptonshire had to face a final target of 311, reduced to 274 for the loss of Larkins by the close of play. Next day Northamptonshire lost Willey in the first over but were progressing promisingly when Clarke, Jackman and Pocock took control and the innings collapsed. Clarke finished with match figures of ten for 109.

Surrey

A. R. Butcher lbw b Mallender	19	– c Sharp b Sarfraz	4
G. S. Clinton c Lamb b Sarfraz	2	– b Carter	27
*R. D. V. Knight c Larkins b Griffiths	6	– c Steele b Griffiths	65
G. R. J. Roope run out	108	– c Sharp b Sarfraz	4
M. A. Lynch b Sarfraz	7	– lbw b Carter	0
D. M. Smith c Yardley b Mallender	74	– c Carter b Griffiths	19
†A. J. Stewart c Larkins b Sarfraz	9	– c Sharp b Sarfraz	16
S. T. Clarke c Larkins b Griffiths	10	– c Lamb b Griffiths	13
R. D. Jackman c Sarfraz b Mallender	19	– not out	6
P. I. Pocock c Willey b Griffiths	1	– c Carter b Mallender	0
P. H. L . Wilson not out	4	– lbw b Sarfraz	3
B 1, l-b 5, n-b 7	13	B 1, l-b 12, n-b 1	14
1/11 2/27 3/35 4/55 5/207 6/238 7/246 8/252 9/259	272	1/4 2/73 3/92 4/93 5/129 6/133 7/151 8/163 9/164	171

Bonus points – Surrey 3, Northamptonshire 4.

Bowling: *First Innings*—Sarfraz 18–4–72–3; Griffiths 24–5–57–3; Mallender 21.1–3–69–3; Carter 4–1–21–0; Willey 11–4–40–0. *Second Innings*—Sarfraz 14.4–3–33–4; Griffiths 14–0–58–3; Mallender 17–5–40–1; Carter 9–1–26–2.

Northamptonshire

P. Willey b Jackman	18	– lbw b Clarke	26
W. Larkins c Butcher b Clarke	15	– b Clarke	2
D. S. Steele c Stewart b Clarke	8	– c Stewart b Clarke	36
A. J. Lamb lbw b Clarke	17	– c Clarke b Jackman	63
R. G. Williams c Stewart b Clarke	0	– run out	35
T. J. Yardley c Stewart b Jackman	15	– c Knight b Jackman	0
R. M. Carter c Roope b Jackman	24	– not out	19
†*G. Sharp c Lynch b Jackman	0	– b Clarke	2
Sarfraz Nawaz lbw b Clarke	25	– b Pocock	0
N. A. Mallender not out	2	– c Smith b Pocock	0
B. J. Griffiths lbw b Jackman	0	– b Clarke	3
B 1, l-b 7, n-b 1	9	B 14, l-b 13, w 2	29
1/33 2/37 3/64 4/64 5/76 6/82 7/82 8/131 9/133	133	1/5 2/41 3/116 4/165 5/169 6/189 7/192 8/195 9/199	215

Bonus points – Surrey 4.

Bowling: *First Innings*—Clarke 19–4–58–5; Jackman 19.2–7–39–5; Wilson 9–5–20–0; Knight 3–1–7–0. *Second Innings*—Clarke 23.5–5–51–5; Jackman 23–10–53–2; Pocock 24–10–42–2; Wilson 7–1–23–0; Knight 6–2–17–0.

Umpires: W. E. Alley and K. Ibadulla.

At Leicester, May 29, 31, June 1. NORTHAMPTONSHIRE drew with LEICESTERSHIRE.

NORTHAMPTONSHIRE v NOTTINGHAMSHIRE

At Northampton, June 2, 3, 4. Drawn. Northamptonshire 7 pts, Nottinghamshire 3 pts. Nottinghamshire, facing a target of 246 in 165 minutes, looked promising while Todd, Hadlee and Rice were batting, but the spin of Willey and Steele caused a collapse and it required stout defence from the ninth-wicket pair, Hemmings and Bore, in the closing stages to stave off defeat. On the first day, interrupted by rain, Cook dominated the Northamptonshire batting with a masterly 81, while an unusually subdued Willey and an aggressive Williams both hit half-centuries before the declaration. Nottinghamshire began badly against Sarfraz and Griffiths; then Birch inspired a rally. However, Willey caused further setbacks, and despite a recovery by Cooper and Hemmings, Nottinghamshire were all out in the final over of the second day with a deficit of 58. Striving to set a target, Northamptonshire regularly lost wickets but Willey, Williams, Sharp and Carter produced sufficient runs to make the afternoon interesting.

Northamptonshire

*G. Cook c Cooper b Bore	81	– c Todd b Hadlee	2
W. Larkins c Todd b Hadlee	17	– lbw b Hadlee	10
P. Willey b Cooper	51	– c Todd b Hemmings	47
D. J. Capel lbw b Bore	14	– b Hemmings	19
R. G. Williams not out	52	– run out	42
D. S. Steele b Bore	12	– run out	9
R. M. Carter not out	14	– c and b Robinson	24
†G. Sharp (did not bat)		– c Hadlee b Birch	28
N. A. Mallender (did not bat)		– not out	1
B 1, l-b 11	12	B 1, l-b 3, n-b 1	5
1/25 2/137 3/162 4/166 5/220 (5 wkts dec.)	253	1/2 2/15 3/66 4/86 5/108 6/139 7/185 8/187 (8 wkts dec.)	187

Sarfraz Nawaz and B. J. Griffiths did not bat.

Bonus points – Northamptonshire 3, Nottinghamshire 2.

Bowling: *First Innings*—Hadlee 13–5–21–1; Hendrick 15–7–34–0; Cooper 20.1–3–73–1; Hemmings 20–9–55–0; Bore 30–10–58–3. *Second Innings*—Hadlee 8–2–21–2; Hendrick 7–2–17–0; Bore 12–3–34–0; Cooper 11–2–30–0; Hemmings 17–4–39–2; Robinson 3–0–22–1; Birch 2.3–0–19–1.

Nottinghamshire

P. A. Todd lbw b Sarfraz	3	– b Willey	35
R. T. Robinson c Capel b Griffiths	5	– lbw b Sarfraz	8
†B. N. French b Griffiths	4	– c Willey b Mallender	8
*C. E. B. Rice c Willey b Sarfraz	24	– (5) c Carter b Willey	30
J. D. Birch c Sharp b Willey	64	– (6) st Sharp b Steele	2
M. A. Fell c Carter b Willey	37	– (7) lbw b Williams	3
R. J. Hadlee c Cook b Willey	1	– (4) b Steele	17
E. E. Hemmings c Sharp b Griffiths	16	– (9) not out	2
K. E. Cooper c Larkins b Sarfraz	24	– (8) b Willey	12
M. K. Bore b Griffiths	7	– not out	4
M. Hendrick not out	1		
B 1, l-b 4, w 1, n-b 3	9	L-b 6, n-b 7	13
1/6 2/13 3/22 4/71 5/135 6/144 7/147 8/181 9/194	195	1/21 2/52 3/66 4/96 5/106 6/106 7/122 8/123 (8 wkts)	134

Bonus points – Nottinghamshire 1, Northamptonshire 4.

Bowling: *First Innings*—Sarfraz 24–7–54–3; Griffiths 18.3–4–53–4; Mallender 16–5–45–0; Willey 13–6–12–3; Capel 3–0–22–0. *Second Innings*—Sarfraz 7–3–9–1; Griffiths 5–1–13–0; Willey 20–12–33–3; Steele 11–7–28–2; Mallender 4–0–38–1; Williams 5–5–0–1.

Umpires: B. Leadbeater and K. E. Palmer.

At Northampton, June 5, 6, 7. NORTHAMPTONSHIRE drew with INDIANS (See Indian tour section).

At Cambridge, June 9, 10, 11. NORTHAMPTONSHIRE beat CAMBRIDGE UNIVERSITY by 133 runs.

NORTHAMPTONSHIRE v SOMERSET

At Northampton, June 12, 14, 15. Drawn. Northamptonshire 4 pts, Somerset 4 pts. On a batsman's wicket, runs were always abundant. Even so, Somerset found a final target of 357 in 200 minutes too formidable a task, especially when 34 minutes were lost through rain. However, opener Lloyds enjoyed a personal triumph, taking advantage of Somerset's decision not to chase victory by hitting his second unbeaten century in the game: in the first innings he struck a career-best 132 (one 6, twenty 4s) in 204 minutes; second time round he got 102 (one 6, seventeen 4s) in 124 minutes. Each time Roebuck was the capable junior partner in three-figure opening stands, and altogether Somerset scored 355 for one in the match. On the first day Northamptonshire, put in, had scored 137 for one off 44 overs (Larkins 80 not out) before rain called a halt, and on Monday they added another 165 in 110 minutes before declaring. Larkins (five 6s, fourteen 4s) was in superb form in a stay of 210 minutes, and the batting fairly sparkled as Willey (twelve 4s) helped him to add 117 in 76 minutes. Willey (one 6, nine 4s) again struck powerfully when Northamptonshire batted a second time, and a fine display of free hitting by Williams and Capel produced 129 in 86 minutes, the nineteen-year-old Capel displaying great potential in his first Championship half-century.

Northamptonshire

W. Larkins c Dredge b Russom	137	– c Richards b Bryant	8
R. M. Carter c Russom b Bryant	28	– lbw b Dredge	17
P. Willey c Lloyds b Russom	65	– c Richards b Russom	70
R. G. Williams lbw b Popplewell	26	– not out	87
D. J. Capel b Popplewell	13	– not out	60
D. S. Steele not out	9		
D. J. Wild not out	18		
L-b 4, n-b 2	6	B 1, l-b 9, w 5	15
1/99 2/216 3/235 4/266 5/275 (5 wkts dec.)	302	1/9 2/55 3/128 (3 wkts dec.)	257

*†G. Sharp, Sarfraz Nawaz, N. A. Mallender and B. J. Griffiths did not bat.

Bonus points – Northamptonshire 4, Somerset 2.

Bowling: *First Innings*—Dredge 16–3–53–0; Bryant 11–2–67–1; Russom 13–2–49–2; Popplewell 17–3–43–2; Marks 19.4–4–74–0; Richards 2–0–10–0. *Second Innings*—Dredge 12–4–32–1; Bryant 6–0–29–1; Popplewell 5–0–28–0; Marks 27–8–76–0; Russom 3–0–15–1; Richards 16–3–57–0; Rose 1–0–5–0.

Somerset

P. M. Roebuck c Willey b Steele	51	– not out	38
J. W. Lloyds not out	132	– not outout	102
I. V. A. Richards not out	6		
B 5, l-b 5, n-b 4	14	B 4, l-b 5, w 1, n-b 2	12
1/195 (1 wkt dec.)	203	(no wkt)	152

P. W. Denning, *B. C. Rose, N. F. M. Popplewell, V. J. Marks, †D. J. S. Taylor, C. H. Dredge, M. Bryant and N. Russom did not bat.

Bonus points – Somerset 2.

Bowling: *First Innings*—Sarfraz 12–4–38–0; Griffiths 10–1–33–0; Mallender 8–2–16–0; Capel 4–0–17–0; Wild 4–0–15–0; Steele 12.3–4–26–1; Willey 10–1–44–0. *Second Innings*—Sarfraz 4–2–10–0; Griffiths 3–2–7–0; Steele 12–2–41–0; Williams 4–0–19–0; Capel 7–1–23–0; Wild 6–0–16–0; Carter 4–1–19–0; Mallender 4–2–5–0.

Umpires: J. Birkenshaw and D. O. Oslear.

At Middlesbrough, June 19, 21, 22. NORTHAMPTONSHIRE drew with YORKSHIRE.

NORTHAMPTONSHIRE v WARWICKSHIRE

At Northampton, June 23, 24, 25. Drawn. When rain delayed the start until after lunch on the second day, acting-captains Sharp and Amiss bid for a result by sacrificing bonus points and both declaring after an hour's batting. The main features were a first Championship wicket by Warwickshire's pace bowler, Maguire, and a fierce, unbeaten 44 by Williams (two 6s, five 4s) in even time. Warwickshire then reached 96 for three by the end of the day through lively batting by Amiss and Kallicharran, but more rain on the final morning ended the game. In the 34 minutes of play possible, Kallicharran just had time to reach his half-century by hitting a 6 on to the press box roof.

Warwickshire

*D. L. Amiss c Mallender b Griffiths	10	– b Willey	41
T. A. Lloyd not out	28	– c Larkins b Griffiths	14
A. I. Kallicharran lbw b Capel	2	– not out	52
†G. W. Humpage (did not bat)		– run out	6
J. Cumbes (did not bat)		– lbw b Lamb	2
K. D. Smith (did not bat)		– not out	2
N-b 1	1	L-b 2, n-b 4	6
1/21 2/41	(2 wkts dec.) 41	1/30 2/68 3/94 4/115	(4 wkts) 123

Asif Din, R. I. H. B. Dyer, C. Lethbridge, G. C. Small and K. R. Maguire did not bat.

Bowling: *First Innings*—Griffiths 6–3–6–1; Mallender 6–1–28–0; Lamb 2–0–6–0; Capel 1.5–1–0–1. *Second Innings*—Griffiths 18–4–40–1; Mallender 3–0–13–0; Willey 23–9–34–1; Williams 7–0–19–0; Steele 4–0–10–0; Lamb 2.2–1–1–1.

Northamptonshire

W. Larkins c Humpage b Maguire	4
R. M. Carter not out	6
P. Willey lbw b Small	3
R. G. Williams not out	44
L-b 1, n-b 7	8
1/6 2/9	(2 wkts dec.) 65

D. J. Capel, D. S Steele, D. J. Wild, *†G. Sharp, T. M. Lamb, N. A. Mallender and B. J. Griffiths did not bat.

Bowling: Small 5–2–13–1; Maguire 4–0–32–1; Lethbridge 3–1–4–0; Cumbes 3–1–8–0.

Umpires: C. Cook and N. T. Plews.

At Derby, July 7, 8, 9. NORTHAMPTONSHIRE lost to DERBYSHIRE by seven wickets.

NORTHAMPTONSHIRE v ESSEX

At Northampton, July 10, 12, 13. Drawn. Northamptonshire 4 pts, Essex 8 pts. Willey defied a challenge for victory by Essex, who had declared with a first-innings lead of 197, hoping to bowl out Northamptonshire a second time. He batted superbly for four and a half hours for 140, hitting two 6s and nineteen 4s, helped first by Larkins and then by Williams in stands that made a draw inevitable. On the first day Turner took advantage of helpful conditions to claim four of the first seven Northamptonshire wickets at a cost of 26 runs before Boyd-Moss fought back with an excellent 61, Mallender joining him in a half-century eighth-wicket stand. The second day was devoted completely to a prolific run-getting display by Essex, capitalising on a fine start by Gooch. Fletcher hit a stylish century, Hardie narrowly missed one, and the hard-hitting McEwan and Pont both gathered half-centuries in the race to the declaration. But with batting conditions so good, and with Willey in peak form, the Essex bowlers found it was their turn to toil in vain.

Northamptonshire

R. M. Carter b Lever	3	– lbw b Lever	1
W. Larkins b Turner	26	– c R. E. East b Gooch	50
P. Willey c Phillip b Gooch	32	– c R. E. East b Pont	140
R. G. Williams st D. E. East b Acfield	50	– c and b Pont	37
D. J. Capel b Turner	22	– lbw b Pont	5
R. J. Boyd-Moss lbw b R. E. East	61	– not out	24
D. S. Steele b Turner	1	– not out	36
*†G. Sharp c D. E. East b Turner	4		
N. A. Mallender lbw b Phillip	16		
T. M. Lamb b Gooch	14		
B. J. Griffiths not out	10		
L-b 5, n-b 8	13	B 2, l-b 4, w 1, n-b 7	14
1/15 2/50 3/89 4/129 5/151 6/164 7/172 8/227 9/234	252	1/7 2/136 3/222 4/245 5/248 (5 wkts)	307

Bonus points – Northamptonshire 3, Essex 4.

Bowling: *First Innings*—Lever 14–2–36–1; Phillip 17–2–66–1; Turner 27–7–53–4; R. E. East 16–9–17–1; Acfield 11–1–31–1; Gooch 15–2–36–2. *Second Innings*—Lever 17–3–53–1; Phillip 9–1–43–0; Turner 5–1–15–0; Acfield 27–10–45–0; Gooch 13–4–36–1; R. E. East 9–4–5–0; Pont 18–3–48–3; Hardie 5–1–18–0; McEwan 5–0–30–0.

Essex

G. A. Gooch c Carter b Griffiths	48
B. R. Hardie c Steele b Griffiths	94
*K. W. R. Fletcher c Sharp b Griffiths	124
K. S. McEwan c Boyd-Moss b Steele	61
K. R. Pont not out	50
N. Phillip c Sharp b Lamb	23
S. Turner c Griffiths b Lamb	19
†D. E. East not out	5
B 1, l-b 15, n-b 9	25
1/89 2/224 3/337 4/349 5/395 6/437 (6 wkts dec.)	449

R. E. East, J. K. Lever and D. L. Acfield did not bat.

Bonus points – Essex 4, Northamptonshire 1 (Score at 100 overs: 346-3).

Bowling: Griffiths 28–7–80–3; Mallender 25–7–86–0; Lamb 35–3–126–2; Capel 10–0–58–0; Steele 20–7–53–1; Willey 2–1–5–0; Carter 3–0–16–0.

Umpires: D. R. Shepherd and J. van Geloven.

At Bristol, July 17, 19, 20. NORTHAMPTONSHIRE beat GLOUCESTERSHIRE by nine wickets.

At Manchester, July 21, 22, 23. NORTHAMPTONSHIRE drew with LANCASHIRE.

NORTHAMPTONSHIRE v GLOUCESTERSHIRE

At Northampton, July 28, 29, 30. Drawn. Northamptonshire 4 pts, Gloucestershire 7 pts. Set to score 285 in 172 minutes, Northamptonshire approached their task adventurously and settled for a draw only in the last two overs when eight wickets were down and they were 33 short. They were inspired initially by hard hitting from Willey with a 47-minute half-century, followed by a first Championship century (in 138 minutes) from Boyd-Moss, who hit two 6s and twelve 4s as he increased his first-ever 1,000 runs in a season, achieved during his first-innings fifty. The Cambridge Blue was helped later by Capel and Sharp, but then Stephenson and Childs applied the brake. The first day had featured a career-best 212 not out (two 6s, 24 4s) in 360 minutes by Andy Stovold, who shared three-figure partnerships with Broad and Dudleston. He reached his second hundred in 113 minutes. In his nineteenth over Mallender was banned for the rest of the innings, by umpire Khizar Hayat, for following through on to the wicket, and on the first afternoon Cook, the home captain, was called off the field to report for standby duty by England at Edgbaston. However, he returned next day to bat at No. 7, and later to declare 47 runs behind. Gloucestershire achieved their second declaration through a stirring third-wicket stand of 167 in 117 minutes by Dudleston and Bainbridge.

Gloucestershire

A. W. Stovold not out	212		
B. C. Broad c Sharp b Steele	61	– c and b Mallender	29
P. W. Romaines c Sharp b Mallender	11	– (1) b Willey	18
B. Dudleston b Williams	39	– (3) not out	78
P. Bainbridge c Cook b Williams	0	– (4) c Sharp b Wild	89
A. J. Wright not out	23	– (5) not out	14
B 2, l-b 9	11	B 8, l-b 1	9
1/139 2/157 3/264 4/272 (4 wkts dec.)	357	1/47 2/47 3/214 (3 wkts dec.)	237

J. N. Shepherd, *D. A. Graveney, †R. C. Russell, F. D. Stephenson and J. H. Childs did not bat.

Bonus points – Gloucestershire 4, Northamptonshire 1 (Score at 100 overs: 316-4).

Bowling: *First Innings*—Mallender 18.3–4–50–1; Lamb 23–5–76–0; Capel 8–0–51–0; Wild 11.3–2–45–0; Willey 18–4–53–0; Steele 21–9–39–1; Williams 9–1–32–2. *Second Innings*—Mallender 12–2–46–1; Lamb 11–1–34–0; Steele 11–1–53–0; Willey 19–8–33–1; Williams 5–0–22–0; Wild 9–0–35–1; Cook 1–0–5–0.

Northamptonshire

W. Larkins c Childs b Shepherd	44	– (2) c Russell b Stephenson	8
D. J. Wild c Shepherd b Stephenson	21	– (9) c and b Stephenson	1
P. Willey c and b Shepherd	10	– c Dudleston b Childs	59
R. J. Boyd-Moss c Wright b Graveney	53	– not out	114
R. G. Williams lbw b Stephenson	14	– c Shepherd b Childs	0
D. J. Capel b Dudleston	46	– b Childs	25
*G. Cook st Russell b Graveney	47	– (1) c Russell b Stephenson	12
D. S. Steele st Russell b Dudleston	0	– lbw b Stephenson	0
†G. Sharp c and b Dudleston	18	– (7) b Childs	19
T. M. Lamb not out	39	– not out	1
N. A. Mallender not out	4		
B 3, l-b 5, w 1, n-b 5	14	B 2, l-b 10, w 1	13
1/56 2/79 3/80 4/116 5/183 6/207 7/207 8/237 9/279 (9 wkts dec.)	310	1/22 2/25 3/112 4/120 5/199 6/242 7/243 8/247 (8 wkts)	252

Bonus points – Northamptonshire 3, Gloucestershire 3 (Score at 100 overs: 250-8).

Bowling: *First Innings*—Stephenson 24–6–64–2; Shepherd 25–7–73–2; Childs 30–14–52–0; Graveney 19–3–71–2; Dudleston 19–8–36–3. *Second Innings*—Stephenson 13.5–1–73–4; Shepherd 2–0–16–0; Childs 23–7–65–4; Graveney 10–1–65–0; Dudleston 6–1–20–0.

Umpires: D. J. Constant and Khizar Hayat.

NORTHAMPTONSHIRE v WORCESTERSHIRE

At Northampton, July 31, August 2, 3. Drawn. Northamptonshire 6 pts, Worcestershire 3 pts. Rain and bad light ended play 30 minutes early as Northamptonshire strove for five more wickets after Worcestershire had made little attempt to chase a target of 272 in 203 minutes. Ormrod and Neale took 25 overs to score 64 for the second wicket. Rain had shortened the first day, when Northamptonshire lost six wickets for 158 with Inchmore bowling effectively. However, the veteran Steele and youthful Wild took their partnership to 73 on the second morning and Cook was able to declare with a second bonus point. With Tim Lamb finding conditions to his liking and returning his season's best figures, Worcestershire were bundled out for 112 in 41.3 overs before tea. At one time they were 49 for seven, but Alleyne and Humphries rallied the innings with some aggressive batting. Northamptonshire's second innings was dominated by Larkins, who hit one 6 and thirteen 4s in a superb unbeaten 110 out of 183 on a wicket where no other batsman reached 50.

Northamptonshire

*G. Cook lbw b Pridgeon	8	– c Humphries b Pridgeon	5
W. Larkins c Patel b Alleyne	13	– not out	110
P. Willey c and b Inchmore	49	– c Humphries b Inchmore	23
R. J. Boyd-Moss b Inchmore	11	– b Alleyne	14
R. G. Williams c Humphries b Alleyne	7	– b Alleyne	0
D. J. Capel lbw b Inchmore	20	– c Humphries b Alleyne	0
D. S. Steele not out	47	– c Hemsley b Pridgeon	19
D. J. Wild c Weston b Gifford	29	– not out	7
†G. Sharp st Humphries b Gifford	2		
T. M. Lamb not out	1		
L-b 7, n-b 6	13	B 3, l-b 2	5
1/21 2/23 3/58 4/70 5/111 6/115 7/188 8/192 (8 wkts dec.)	200	1/9 2/50 3/76 4/76 5/100 6/146 (6 wkts dec.)	183

N. A. Mallender did not bat.

Bonus points – Northamptonshire 2, Worcestershire 3.

Bowling: *First Innings*—Alleyne 28–4–79–2; Pridgeon 26–8–47–1; Inchmore 22–7–40–3; Gifford 20–8–21–2; Patel 1–1–0–0. *Second Innings*—Alleyne 21–5–70–3; Pridgeon 14–2–42–2; Inchmore 3–0–6–1; Gifford 24–6–60–0.

Worcestershire

M. J. Weston lbw b Steele	10	– c Sharp b Mallender	2
J. A. Ormrod c Capel b Lamb	9	– c Sharp b Steele	25
*P. A. Neale c Sharp b Mallender	8	– b Willey	37
D. N. Patel c Steele b Wild	8	– (6) b Willey	0
T. S. Curtis b Lamb	8	– (4) not out	28
E. J. O. Hemsley lbw b Lamb	0	– (5) c Sharp b Willey	12
†D. J. Humphries run out	23	– not out	2
J. D. Inchmore lbw b Wild	1		
N. Gifford c Sharp b Lamb	8		
H. L. Alleyne c Cook b Lamb	32		
A. P. Pridgeon not out	1		
L-b 3, n-b 1	4	B 2, l-b 2, n-b 2	6
1/14 2/24 3/39 4/47 5/47 6/47 7/49 8/70 9/94	112	1/4 2/68 3/68 4/102 5/102 (5 wkts)	112

Bonus points – Northamptonshire 4.

Bowling: *First Innings*—Mallender 13–3–52–1; Lamb 20.3–8–37–5; Steele 2–1–4–1; Wild 6–3–15–2. *Second Innings*—Mallender 12–2–41–1; Lamb 8–3–17–0; Steele 18–9–24–1; Willey 15–10–9–3; Williams 4–0–15–0.

Umpires: D. J. Constant and Khizar Hayat.

At Swansea, August 7, 9, 10. NORTHAMPTONSHIRE drew with GLAMORGAN.

At Eastbourne, August 11, 12. NORTHAMPTONSHIRE beat SUSSEX by an innings and 58 runs.

NORTHAMPTONSHIRE v DERBYSHIRE

At Northampton, August 14, 16, 17. Northamptonshire won by 236 runs. Northamptonshire 22 pts, Derbyshire 4 pts. Pace bowler Mallender routed Derbyshire on the final afternoon with a career-best seven for 41, giving him match figures of ten for 96. After tea, when Derbyshire were 75 for four, having been set to score 354 in 252 minutes, he took five wickets for 6 runs in a seventeen-ball spell. Northamptonshire had begun the last day 171 in front with four top batsmen out, but Kapil Dev and Boyd-Moss tore into the Derbyshire attack with furious hitting, putting on 182 in 98 minutes to hasten the declaration. Kapil Dev, with one 6 and eleven 4s, completed his second century in successive games, while Boyd-Moss had one 6 and nine 4s in his 80 not out. In the first innings, Boyd-Moss had scored a career-best 137 (three 6s, eighteen 4s) and shared a fourth-wicket stand of 170 in 40 overs with Williams before Kapil Dev provided his own brand of fireworks with an unbeaten 65 that included four 6s and four 4s. His 50 came off 30 balls. Larkins, too, was among the runs, reaching his fifth century (fourteen 4s) of the season in 163 minutes, and later Wright featured strongly in Derbyshire's reply with 157 (23 4s) to follow his 186 against Northamptonshire at Derby in July.

Northamptonshire

*G. Cook c and b Moir	20	– c Maher b Newman	1
W. Larkins c Moir b Wood	105	– c Anderson b Tunnicliffe	29
P. Willey c Tunnicliffe b Moir	0	– c and b Tunnicliffe	7
R. J. Boyd-Moss c Oldham b Moir	137	– not out	80
R. G. Williams c Moir b Tunnicliffe	58	– c sub b Moir	4
Kapil Dev not out	65	– not out	100
D. S. Steele not out	3		
L-b 6, n-b 6	12	L-b 1, n-b 6	7
1/78 2/78 3/155 4/325 5/377 (5 wkts dec.)	400	1/1 2/35 3/39 4/46 (4 wkts dec.)	228

D. J. Wild, †G. Sharp, N. A. Mallender and B. J. Griffiths did not bat.

Bonus points – Northamptonshire 4, Derbyshire 1 (Score at 100 overs: 356-4).

Bowling: *First Innings*—Oldham 15–2–59–0; Tunnicliffe 19.2–2–95–1; Newman 13–2–50–0; Wood 23–3–78–1; Moir 34–9–106–3. *Second Innings*—Oldham 12–2–79–0; Newman 5–0–23–1; Tunnicliffe 12–1–53–2; Moir 16.3–3–66–1.

Derbyshire

*B. Wood c Boyd-Moss b Mallender	3	– c Kapil Dev b Mallender	42
J. G. Wright b Mallender	157	– c Sharp b Mallender	20
P. N. Kirsten st Sharp b Steele	48	– c Kapil Dev b Mallender	5
K. J. Barnett c Cook b Willey	46	– lbw b Williams	12
I. S. Anderson b Willey	0	– lbw b Griffiths	5
C. J. Tunnicliffe not out	13	– (7) c Boyd-Moss b Mallender	6
P. G. Newman c Steele b Mallender	0	– (8) b Kapil Dev	14
†B. J. M. Maher not out	4	– (10) c Steele b Mallender	0
J. H. Hampshire (did not bat)		– (6) not out	6
D. G. Moir (did not bat)		– (9) c Kapil Dev b Mallender	0
S. Oldham (did not bat)		– lbw b Mallender	0
B 1, l-b 2, n-b 1	4	L-b 6, n-b 1	7
1/3 2/101 3/240 4/240 5/266 6/266	(6 wkts dec.) 275	1/28 2/34 3/54 4/67 5/93 6/99 7/99 8/103 9/103	117

Bonus points – Derbyshire 3, Northamptonshire 2.

Bowling: *First Innings*—Kapil Dev 18–5–33–0; Mallender 16–2–55–3; Willey 8–1–21–2; Griffiths 12–0–53–0; Steele 31–14–55–1; Williams 15–3–54–0. *Second Innings*—Kapil Dev 14.2–5–32–1; Mallender 19–9–41–7; Willey 7–4–8–0; Steele 8–4–13–0; Griffiths 4–2–2–1; Williams 6–1–14–1.

Umpires: A. G. T. Whitehead and R. Julian.

NORTHAMPTONSHIRE v HAMPSHIRE

At Northampton, August 21, 23, 24. Drawn. Northamptonshire 7 pts, Hampshire 6 pts. Rain prevented any play on the third day when a good finish seemed likely. Hampshire were 109 behind on the first innings and had lost Greenidge without scoring when bad light ended play the previous night. In their first innings Hampshire had problems against the left-arm spin of Steele, who took six wickets in a long stint and was later to play his part with the bat as Northamptonshire moved positively towards a declaration. Willey and Allan Lamb made up for the early loss of openers Larkins and Cook, with Lamb, given a chance at 26, producing his best form. His brilliant strokeplay took him to 140 (two 6s, 21 4s), and there was a lively 36 (seven 4s) from Kapil Dev before Steele and Sharp helped to build a lead from which victory could be forced. But then the weather took a hand.

Hampshire

C. G. Greenidge b Steele	62	– c Williams b Kapil Dev	0
J. M. Rice c Cook b Steele	29	– not out	0
M. C. J. Nicholas b Steele	6	– not out	0
T. E. Jesty c Sharp b Steele	46		
D. R. Turner b Williams	30		
*N. E. J. Pocock b Mallender	53		
N. G. Cowley b Steele	11		
M. D. Marshall c Boyd-Moss b Willey	1		
†R. J. Parks lbw b Steele	1		
J. W. Southern not out	8		
K. St J. D. Emery lbw b Kapil Dev	1		
B 11, l-b 6, n-b 3	20		
1/65 2/98 3/103 4/169 5/193 6/233 7/234 8/235 9/267	268	1/0	(1 wkt) 0

Bonus points – Hampshire 3, Northamptonshire 3 (Score at 100 overs: 260-8).

Bowling: *First Innings*—Kapil Dev 11.4–3–34–1; Griffiths 5–1–28–0; Mallender 8–1–30–1; Steele 41–19–59–6; Willey 33–14–65–1; Williams 8–1–32–1. *Second Innings*—Kapil Dev 1–1–0–1; Griffiths 0.3–0–0–0.

Northamptonshire

*G. Cook lbw b Marshall	23
W. Larkins b Emery	0
P. Willey b Southern	51
A. J. Lamb c and b Emery	140
R. G. Williams b Southern	6
R. J. Boyd-Moss c Nicholas b Marshall	7
Kapil Dev c Jesty b Southern	36
D. S. Steele not out	44
†G. Sharp c Parks b Emery	32
N. A. Mallender not out	8
B 13, l-b 11, n-b 6	30
1/2 2/52 3/145 4/163 5/176 6/229 7/299 8/363 (8 wkts dec.)	377

B. J. Griffiths did not bat.

Bonus points – Northamptonshire 4, Hampshire 3 (Score at 100 overs: 350-7).

Bowling: Marshall 28–4–84–2; Emery 21–7–48–3; Cowley 24–4–96–0; Southern 41–10–118–3; Turner 1–0–1–0.

Umpires: J. Birkenshaw and P. B. Wight.

At Folkestone, August 25, 26, 27. NORTHAMPTONSHIRE drew with KENT.

NORTHAMPTONSHIRE v LEICESTERSHIRE

At Northampton, August 28, 30, 31. Drawn. Northamptonshire 4 pts, Leicestershire 7 pts. A typical back-to-the-wall innings by Steele halted Leicestershire's victory bid and hampered their Championship challenge. Set to score 224 in three hours, Northamptonshire had quickly lost three leading batsmen and were continuing to slump against Parsons, Cook and John Steele when David Steele batted stubbornly for 88 minutes, helped by an equally determined Sharp, who stayed to the end and ensured a draw. The first two days had seen the brothers Steele in control as spin bowlers, each taking five wickets. On the first day, when Leicestershire struggled to 263, David took five for 50, but on the Monday it was John's turn, his five for 45 helping Leicestershire gain a first-innings lead of 37. Nick Cook had effected a breakthrough after Geoff Cook had taken 151 minutes over his half-century and Larkins, Willey and Boyd-Moss had combined to boost Northamptonshire to a likely score of 176 for three. Then seven wickets fell for another 50 as two stoppages for rain contributed to break the batsmen's concentration.

Leicestershire

J. C. Balderstone c Boyd-Moss b Steele	28	– c Sharp b Kapil Dev	17
R. A. Cobb c Cook b Willey	49	– (5) run out	50
N. E. Briers c Sharp b Steele	35	– (2) c Boyd-Moss b Mallender	6
B. F. Davison b Steele	68	– c sub b Kapil Dev	20
I. P. Butcher c Willey b Steele	12	– (3) c Willey b Mallender	31
*†R. W. Tolchard c Sharp by Steele	13	– not out	24
G. J. Parsons b Kapil Dev	7	– b Lamb	0
J. F. Steele c and b Mallender	18		
N. G. B. Cook run out	3		
D. A. Wenlock c and b Kapil Dev	4		
P. B. Clift not out	4	– (8) c Boyd-Moss b Steele	24
L-b 7, n-b 15	22	B 4, l-b 5, n-b 5	14
1/60 2/114 3/157 4/189 5/221 6/222 7/252 8/252 9/255	263	1/12 2/26 3/59 4/102 5/145 6/145 7/186 (7 wkts dec.)	186

Bonus points – Leicestershire 3, Northamptonshire 2 (Score at 100 overs: 252-6).

Bowling: *First Innings*—Kapil Dev 10.4–5–17–2; Mallender 19–4–68–1; Griffiths 8–2–15–0; Steele 27.5–5–50–5; Willey 35–11–74–1; Williams 6.1–1–17–0. *Second Innings*—Kapil Dev 13–1–57–2; Mallender 9–1–41–2; Lamb 17–7–43–1; Steele 8.5–3–29–1; Willey 1–0–2–0.

Northamptonshire

*G. Cook c Steele b Cook	56	– b Cook	22
W. Larkins lbw b Clift	47	– c Balderstone b Parsons	0
P. Willey c Balderstone b Steele	40	– c Cook b Parsons	10
R. J. Boyd-Moss b Cook	31	– c Davison b Cook	11
R. G. Williams c and b Steele	1	– lbw b Steele	32
Kapil Dev b Steele	6	– b Steele	13
D. S. Steele c and b Cook	12	– c Steele b Cook	33
†G. Sharp c Balderstone b Steele	3	– not out	24
T. M. Lamb c Wenlock b Steele	11	– not out	0
N. A. Mallender run out	9		
B. J. Griffiths not out	0		
B 1, l-b 3, n-b 6	10	L-b 1, n-b 1	2
1/78 2/143 3/159 4/176 5/188 6/188 7/197 8/211 9/221	226	1/1 2/31 3/33 4/60 5/76 6/91 7/143 (7 wkts)	147

Bonus points – Northamptonshire 2, Leicestershire 4.

Bowling: *First Innings*—Parsons 14–6–24–0; Clift 16–1–62–1; Cook 34.3–13–77–3; Steele 25–11–45–5; Wenlock 2–0–8–0. *Second Innings*—Parsons 8–1–27–2; Clift 13–5–30–0; Cook 24–8–57–3; Steele 15–5–31–2; Balderstone 3–3–0–0.

Umpires: K. Ibadulla and R. Palmer.

At Birmingham, September 8, 9, 10. NORTHAMPTONSHIRE beat WARWICKSHIRE by five wickets.

At Chelmsford, September 11, 13, 14. NORTHAMPTONSHIRE beat ESSEX by 159 runs.

ADDRESSES OF REPRESENTATIVE BODIES

INTERNATIONAL CRICKET CONFERENCE: J. A. Bailey, Lord's Ground, London NW8 8QN.

ENGLAND: Cricket Council, D. B. Carr, Lord's Ground, London NW8 8QN.

AUSTRALIA: Australian Cricket Board, D. L. Richards, 70 Jolimont Street, Jolimont, Victoria 3002.

SOUTH AFRICA: South African Cricket Union, Charles Fortune, PO Box 55009, Northlands 2116, Transvaal.

WEST INDIES: West Indies Cricket Board of Control, G. S. Camacho, 27 Salisbury Avenue, Kingston 6, Jamaica.

INDIA: Board of Control for Cricket in India, A. W. Kanmadikar, E-4 Radio Colony, Indore (MP).

NEW ZEALAND: New Zealand Cricket Council, G. T. Dowling, PO Box 958, Christchurch.

PAKISTAN: Board of Control for Cricket in Pakistan, A. A. K. Abbasi, Gaddafi Stadium, Lahore.

SRI LANKA: Board of Control for Cricket in Sri Lanka, Nuski Mohamed, 35 Maitland Place, Colombo 7.

ARGENTINA: Argentine Cricket Association, R. H. Gooding, c/o The English Club, 25 de Mayo 586, 1002 Buenos Aires.

BANGLADESH: Bangladesh Cricket Control Board, K. Z. Islam, The Stadium, Dacca.

BERMUDA: Bermuda Cricket Board of Control, Wilton L. Smith, PO Box 992, Hamilton.

CANADA: Canadian Cricket Association, K. D. Wilson, 1306–1261 Nelson Street, Vancouver, British Columbia.

DENMARK: Danish Cricket Association, Peter S. Hargreaves, Lykkesborg Alle 7, 2860 Soborg.

EAST AFRICA: East African Cricket Conference, A. E. Dudhia, PO Box 1198, Lusaka, Zambia.

FIJI: Fiji Cricket Association, P. I. Knight, PO Box 300, Suva.

GIBRALTAR: Gibraltar Cricket Association, T. J. Finlayson (acting sec.), 21 Sandpits House, Withams Road.

HONG KONG: Hong Kong Cricket Association, S. K. Sipahimalani, Centre for Media Resources, University of Hong Kong, Knowles Bldg, Pokfulam Road.

ISRAEL: Israel Cricket Association, G. Kandeli, 35/7 Minz Street, Petach Tiqua.

KENYA: Kenya Cricket Association, K. G. Purohit, PO Box 46480, Nairobi.

MALAYSIA: Malaysian Cricket Association, Daljit Singh Gill, c/o High Court (Mahkamah Tinggi), Kuala Lumpur.

NETHERLANDS: Royal Netherlands Cricket Association, P. J. Trijzelaar, Willem de Zwijgerlaan 96A, The Hague.

PAPUA NEW GUINEA: Papua New Guinea Cricket Board of Control, N. R. Agonia, PO Box 812, Port Moresby.

SINGAPORE: Singapore Cricket Association, J. C. Cooke, c/o The Singapore Commission, 3rd Floor, Maya Puri Bldg, Jalah Sultan, Bandar Seri Begawan, Brunei.

USA: United States Cricket Association, Naseeruddin Khan, 2361 Hickory Road, Plymouth Meeting, Pennsylvania 19462.

WEST AFRICA: West Africa Cricket Conference, Lt-Col. W. A. Jibunch; c/o Cricket Secretariat, National Sports Commission, PO Box 145, Lagos, Nigeria.

ZIMBABWE: Zimbabwe Cricket Union, A. L. A. Pichanik, PO Box 452, Harare.

BRITISH UNIVERSITIES SPORTS FEDERATION: 28 Woburn Square, London WC1.

CLUB CRICKET CONFERENCE: D. J. Annetts, 353 West Barnes Lane, New Malden, Surrey, KT3 6JF.

ENGLAND SCHOOLS' CRICKET ASSOCIATION: C. J. Cooper, 68 Hatherley Road, Winchester, Hampshire SO22 6RR.

IRISH CRICKET UNION: D. Scott, 45 Foxrock Park, Foxrock, Co. Dublin.

MINOR COUNTIES CRICKET ASSOCIATION: Laurance Hancock, 4 Kingsland Avenue, Oakhill, Stoke-on-Trent, ST4 5LA.

NATIONAL CRICKET ASSOCIATION: B. J. Aspital, Lord's Ground, London, NW8 8QN.

SCARBOROUGH FESTIVAL: Secretary, North Marine Road, Scarborough, Yorkshire.

SCOTTISH CRICKET UNION: R. W. Barclay, Admin. Office, 8 Frederick Street, Edinburgh, EH2 2HB.

THE SPORTS COUNCIL: Emlyn B. Jones, 70 Brompton Road, London, SW3 1EX.

UMPIRES: ASSOCIATION OF CRICKET UMPIRES: L. J. Cheeseman, 16 Ruden Way, Epsom Downs, Surrey, KT17 3LN.

WOMEN'S CRICKET ASSOCIATION: 70 Brompton Road, London SW3 1HA.

The addresses of MCC, the First-Class Counties, and Minor Counties are given at the head of each separate section.

NOTTINGHAMSHIRE

President: Dr J. B. Cochrane, FRCOG
Chairman: J. R. Heatley
Chairman, Cricket Committee: J. R. Heatley
Secretary: B. Robson
County Cricket Ground, Trent Bridge,
Nottingham NG2 6AG
(Telephone: 0602-821525)
Cricket Manager: K. A. Taylor
Captain: C. E. B. Rice

In theory, the 1982 season at Trent Bridge promised to be every bit as profitable as the Championship year that had preceded it. In practice, the promise was not fully realised.

The addition of Derbyshire's Mike Hendrick should have given an attack, already boasting the pace of Richard Hadlee and Clive Rice and the off-spin of Eddie Hemmings, extra variety, quality and penetration. But unfortunately for Nottinghamshire followers, the anticipation generated by the thought of Hadlee, Rice and Hendrick all firing together was never fulfilled. Only once – in the final of the Benson and Hedges Cup – did they all bowl in the same fixture, though even then none was 100 per cent fit and there was nothing they could do to change the course of Somerset's victory surge.

Had all three been able to bowl in even 75 per cent of the fixtures, Nottinghamshire would have been confident of repeating their Championship effort of 1982, but there were occasions when not one of the trio was fit to bowl. Hadlee, again the spearhead, bowled only just over half his number of overs of the previous year; Hendrick missed the second half of the season, and Rice, plagued by a neck injury, managed only 79 overs all summer.

Mindful of that, Nottinghamshire took some satisfaction from finishing fourth in the Championship, following a late flourish in which they won their last two games – against Leicestershire, the runners-up, and Sussex. Yet the season started well enough for the defending champions, who won four and drew two of their first six fixtures. Then injuries and Test calls took their toll, and five successive defeats left them in no position to mount a significant challenge.

The final placing in the John Player League – they finished joint fifth to equal their previous best season in 1975 – left them to reflect on what might have been had they not been stripped of their top performers for so long.

The high spot of the season came in reaching a Lord's final for the first time. In the Benson and Hedges Cup, Nottinghamshire won all four qualifying games, had a thrilling 2-run victory over Leicestershire in the quarter-finals, and a brilliant batting display by Hadlee, in the semi-final against Lancashire, saw them through to the final. Once there, they were overwhelmed in a way which mirrored the nerves of experiencing a major occasion for the first time. Their batting on the day was so poor that it gave the bowlers nothing at which to aim.

Overall, it was again a season when the Nottinghamshire bowlers were asked to cement over the cracks in the batting. Although they finished fourth in the Championship, only three counties earned fewer batting bonus points, all of them just one point less. The attack, even allowing for the inactivity of Hadlee, Rice and Hendrick, performed creditably for the most part, with Kevin Cooper, who bowled as many overs as these three put together, having a productive summer with 68 wickets at 25.27 each from all first-class matches.

There were also encouraging signs for the future from Kevin Saxelby, despite injury problems of his own in mid-season. He emerged as a genuine shock bowler with a promising future. Perhaps the most enlightening breakthrough was made, however, by an eighteen-year-old off-spinner, Peter Such, who responded splendidly to the challenge thrust upon him only a few weeks after leaving school. Injury to Mike Bore and the Test call that went out to Hemmings left Nottinghamshire to plunge Such into the first-class fray with immediate results. His consistency of line and length belied his inexperience, and his haul of seven for 143 in the victory over Gloucestershire was not a solitary success.

The batting again lacked the depth and consistency required of a side with title ambitions. Only Rice and his steadily improving vice-captain, John Birch, reached 1,000 runs. Apart from them, the belligerent strokeplay of Hadlee, the reliability of Basharat Hassan and the promise of Tim Robinson, there were a lot of shortcomings.

In Mark Fell, who produced a maiden hundred against Essex in his first full season of first-class cricket, and Paul Johnson, who was called up for the Young England side against their West Indian counterparts, Nottinghamshire possess two batsmen of whom much is expected. Bruce French, freely recognised as one of the top wicket-keepers in the country, had a fine season, with 64 first-class victims and more than 700 runs. He must be on the fringe of international selection.

Sadly, economic measures dictated that two other hopefuls, Neil Weightman and Ian Pont, would not be retained. Two other familiar faces will also not be around the Trent Bridge scene any more. In another cost-cutting exercise Nottinghamshire have parted company with their assistant-manager, Bob White, who was running the Second Eleven, and opener Paul Todd, who indicated that he would like to leave after twelve years on the staff. – J.L.

NOTTINGHAMSHIRE 1982

[*Bill Smith*

Back row: M. K. Bore, R. T. Robinson, K. Saxelby, P. A. Todd, K. E. Cooper, B. N. French. *Front row:* E. E. Hemmings, B. Hassan, J. D. Birch, C. E. B. Rice (*captain*), D.W. Randall, M. Hendrick.

NOTTINGHAMSHIRE RESULTS

All first-class matches – Played 24: Won 8, Lost 7, Drawn 9. Abandoned 1.

County Championship matches – Played 21: Won 7, Lost 7, Drawn 7. Abandoned 1.

Bonus points – Batting 44, Bowling 65.

Competition placings – Schweppes County Championship, 4th; NatWest Bank Trophy, 2nd round; Benson and Hedges Cup, r/u; John Player League, 5th eq.

COUNTY CHAMPIONSHIP AVERAGES

BATTING

	Birthplace	*M*	*I*	*NO*	*R*	*HI*	*Avge*
D. W. Randall c	*Retford*	10	16	1	653	122	43.53
J. D. Birch c	*Nottingham*	19	31	5	940	125	36.15
E. E. Hemmings c	*Leamington Spa*	15	19	8	385	127*	35.00
B. Hassan c	*Nairobi, Kenya*	17	31	4	918	89*	34.00
C. E. B. Rice c	*Johannesburg, SA*	21	35	3	1,049	144	32.78
R. J. Hadlee c	*Christchurch, NZ*	17	28	2	807	131	31.03
R. T. Robinson	*Sutton-in-Ashfield*	19	34	2	879	109	27.46
B. N. French c	*Warsop*	21	33	6	681	79	25.22
M. K. Bore c	*Hull*	6	7	5	44	23*	22.00
P. A. Todd c	*Morton*	10	17	1	305	117*	19.06
M. A. Fell	*Newark*	10	18	0	315	108	17.50
K. Saxelby	*Worksop*	13	14	4	158	59*	15.80
P. Johnson	*Newark*	4	7	1	90	37*	15.00
N. J. B. Illingworth	*Chesterfield*	8	12	4	109	46*	13.62
K. E. Cooper c	*Hucknall*	20	24	4	190	33*	9.50
M. Hendrick c	*Darley Dale*	9	10	4	54	29	9.00
I. L. Pont	*Brentwood*	4	7	1	32	16	5.33
P. M. Such	*Helensburgh*	8	9	3	3	2	0.50

**Signifies not out.* c *Denotes county cap.*

BOWLING

	O	*M*	*R*	*W*	*Avge*	*BB*
R. J. Hadlee	373.5	110	836	59	14.16	7-25
M. Hendrick	217.2	78	401	26	15.42	5-21
M. K. Bore	203.2	73	466	21	22.19	6-134
K. Saxelby	268.2	60	728	32	22.75	4-18
K. E. Cooper	586	163	1,445	57	25.35	6-46
E. E. Hemmings	514.3	157	1,241	48	25.85	6-76
P. M. Such	232.1	51	737	25	29.48	5-112
N. J. B. Illingworth	100.1	19	325	10	32.50	5-89

Also bowled: J. D. Birch 2.3–0–19–1; M. A. Fell 45–7–146–1; I. L. Pont 78.5–13–302–3; C. E. B. Rice 78.5–25–206–6; R. T. Robinson 3–0–22–1.

HUNDREDS

The following ten three-figure innings were played for Nottinghamshire in County Championship matches – J. D. Birch (2) 102* v Lancashire (Nottingham), 125 v Leicestershire (Nottingham); R. J. Hadlee (2) 131 v Surrey (The Oval), 100* v Worcestershire (Worcester); M. A. Fell (1) 108 v Essex (Nottingham); E. E. Hemmings (1) 127* v Yorkshire (Worksop); D. W. Randall (1) 122 v Worcestershire (Worcester); C. E. B. Rice (1) 144 v Derbyshire (Nottingham); R. T. Robinson (1) 109 v Sussex (Hove); P. A. Todd (1) 117* v Yorkshire (Worksop).

At Cambridge, April 24, 26, 27. NOTTINGHAMSHIRE beat CAMBRIDGE UNIVERSITY by ten wickets.

At Lord's, May 1, 3, 4. NOTTINGHAMSHIRE drew with MCC.

At Manchester, May 5, 6. NOTTINGHAMSHIRE beat LANCASHIRE by an innings and 37 runs.

At Nottingham, May 12, 13, 14. NOTTINGHAMSHIRE drew with INDIANS (See Indian tour section).

NOTTINGHAMSHIRE v HAMPSHIRE

At Nottingham, May 19, 20, 21. Nottinghamshire won by 272 runs. Nottinghamshire 21 pts, Hampshire 4 pts. On a wicket of eccentric bounce, Nottinghamshire completed a comfortable victory before lunch on the final day. They struggled themselves after being put in to bat, and with Malone and Marshall exploiting the conditions it was left to French, Hadlee and Hendrick to give their score respectability. Hadlee then destroyed Hampshire with a return of seven for 25, and after French had top scored for the second time in the match with 65 not out, Nottinghamshire set the visitors a daunting 329 to win. It was never realistic and Hampshire had the dubious distinction of being bowled out for what was then the season's lowest total twice in the same match. After their first-innings 70, they slumped to 56 all out with Hendrick taking five for 21 and the improving Saxelby four for 18. Hadlee, for once, was not responsible for the annihilation.

Nottinghamshire

R. T. Robinson c Nicholas b Marshall	0	– b Emery	35
P. A. Todd c Parks b Marshall	0	– c Rice b Emery	0
B. Hassan c Turner b Malone	23	– retired hurt	28
*C. E. B. Rice c Parks b Malone	20	– c Parks b Tremlett	7
M. A. Fell lbw b Malone	1	– b Marshall	36
R. J. Hadlee c Rice b Malone	37	– c Parks b Emery	0
†B. N. French c Tremlett b Jesty	38	– not out	65
E. E. Hemmings c Jesty b Marshall	3	– not out	15
K. Saxelby run out	4		
M. Hendrick c and b Jesty	29		
M. K. Bore not out	5		
B 2, l-b 7, n-b 11	20	B 8, l-b 10, w 2, n-b 12	32
1/0 2/1 3/37 4/50 5/67 6/92 7/95 8/110 9/163	180	1/0 2/62 3/102 4/107 5/170 (5 wkts dec.)	218

Bonus points – Nottinghamshire 1, Hampshire 4.

Bowling: *First Innings*—Marshall 23–6–53–3; Emery 14–5–32–0; Malone 15–4–53–4; Jesty 6.5–1–22–2. *Second Innings*—Marshall 24–5–52–1; Emery 15–5–40–3; Malone 15–3–42–0; Tremlett 22–5–41–1; Jesty 5–2–11–0.

Hampshire

C. G. Greenidge retired hurt	3	– (5) c French b Hendrick	6
J. M. Rice c Hendrick b Hadlee	9	– (1) c French b Hendrick	4
T. M. Tremlett c French b Hendrick	5	– (2) c Hadlee b Hendrick	0
M. C. J. Nicholas c Rice b Hendrick	21	– (3) c French b Saxelby	7
*T. E. Jesty lbw b Hadlee	15	– (4) c Todd b Hadlee	5
D. R. Turner lbw b Hadlee	0	– c Todd b Saxelby	3
N. G. Cowley c French b Hadlee	0	– c French b Saxelby	8
M. D. Marshall lbw b Hadlee	9	– b Hendrick	17
†R. J. Parks c Hendrick b Hadlee	0	– c Fell b Hendrick	0
K. St J. D. Emery not out	0	– b Saxelby	1
S. J. Malone c Fell b Hadlee	2	– not out	2
B 4, l-b 2	6	B 1, n-b 2	3
1/17 2/27 3/44 4/44 5/44 6/68 7/68 8/68 9/70	70	1/0 2/8 3/13 4/23 5/27 6/31 7/45 8/46 9/49	56

Bonus points – Nottinghamshire 4.

Bowling: *First Innings*—Hadlee 18.2–6–25–7; Hendrick 16–7–21–2; Saxelby 7–1–18–0. *Second Innings*—Hadlee 10–4–14–1; Hendrick 13.5–6–21–5; Saxelby 9–4–18–4.

Umpires: R.Palmer and J. van Geloven.

At Chesterfield, May 29, 30, June 1. NOTTINGHAMSHIRE drew with DERBYSHIRE.

At Northampton, June 2, 3, 4. NOTTINGHAMSHIRE drew with NORTHAMPTONSHIRE.

NOTTINGHAMSHIRE v WORCESTERSHIRE

At Nottingham, June 5, 7, 8. Nottinghamshire won by nine wickets. Nottinghamshire 23 pts, Worcestershire 5 pts. Amid controversy over the uneven bounce of the pitch, Nottinghamshire again completed an emphatic victory before lunch on the final day. Worcestershire on the opening day were bowled out for 166, with paceman Warner retired hurt with a broken thumb, and only an unorthodox 54 by Turner and an unbeaten 35 by Inchmore, who was also struck on the hand, prevented a total collapse. With Younis using the new ball in place of Warner, Nottinghamshire built a useful first-innings lead before their seamers got to work again. Turner was forced to retire hurt after being hit by Hendrick, and although there was resistance from Younis, Hemsley and Humphries, Worcestershire were unable to leave Nottinghamshire a challenging target. They needed just 63 to win and Robinson and Randall, who had been largely responsible for giving Nottinghamshire a first-innings lead, saw them home after the loss of Todd.

Worcestershire

G. M. Turner b Hadlee	54	– retired hurt	9
J. A. Ormrod c French b Hendrick	1	– c Todd b Saxelby	1
D. N. Patel hit wkt b Hadlee	5	– c French b Hadlee	6
Younis Ahmed c Hemmings b Hendrick	0	– c French b Hendrick	65
*P. A. Neale lbw b Saxelby	16	– c Hemmings b Saxelby	9
E. J. O. Hemsley b Saxelby	16	– c Hendrick b Cooper	47
†D. J. Humphries c French b Saxelby	6	– not out	32
J. D. Inchmore not out	35	– b Hadlee	12
A. E. Warner retired hurt	15	– absent hurt	
N. Gifford c Rice b Hadlee	11	– (9) b Hadlee	0
A. P. Pridgeon b Hendrick	1	– (10) c Todd b Hendrick	0
L-b 5, w 1	6	B 1, l-b 3, n-b 1	5
1/12 2/35 3/46 4/68 5/95 6/99 7/116 8/163 9/166	166	1/16 2/21 3/47 4/129 5/144 6/185 7/185 8/186	186

Bonus points – Worcestershire 1, Nottinghamshire 4.

Bowling: *First Innings*—Hadlee 15–4–59–3; Hendrick 12–0–56–3; Saxelby 10–1–33–3; Cooper 6–0–12–0. *Second Innings*—Hadlee 12–1–56–3; Hendrick 19–5–49–2; Saxelby 10–1–37–2; Hemmings 9–3–26–0; Cooper 4–1–13–1.

Nottinghamshire

P. A. Todd lbw b Pridgeon	0	– b Pridgeon	12
R. T. Robinson c Humphries b Pridgeon	65	– not out	28
D. W. Randall c Younis b Patel	76	– not out	16
*C. E. B. Rice st Humphries b Gifford	42		
J. D. Birch c Patel b Gifford	46		
†B. N. French b Gifford	9		
R. J. Hadlee c Patel b Gifford	19		
E. E. Hemmings c Neale b Patel	0		
K. Saxelby not out	1		
K. E. Cooper c Turner b Gifford	2		
M. Hendrick c Younis b Gifford	5		
B 7, l-b 14, n-b 4	25	W 4, n-b 3	7
1/0 2/128 3/194 4/208 5/237 6/282 7/282 8/282 9/284	290	1/32	(1 wkt) 63

Bonus points – Nottinghamshire 3, Worcestershire 4.

Bowling: *First Innings*—Pridgeon 29–8–73–2; Younis 5–1–14–0; Hemsley 5–0–19–0; Gifford 33.5–15–48–6; Patel 15–5–50–2; Inchmore 12–1–61–0. *Second Innings*—Pridgeon 9–2–23–1; Inchmore 4–1–17–0; Gifford 6–1–16–0.

Umpires: A. Jepson and D. R. Shepherd.

†At Nottingham, June 9. Nottinghamshire beat Zimbabweans by 76 runs. Nottinghamshire 218 for three (44 overs) (C. E. B. Rice 60, J. D. Birch 58 not out, R. T. Robinson 45, B. Hassan 35); Zimbabweans 142 (44 overs) (A. J. Pycroft 41; N. J. B. Illingworth three for 34).

NOTTINGHAMSHIRE v KENT

At Nottingham, June 12, 14, 15. Nottinghamshire won by ten wickets. Nottinghamshire 21 pts, Kent 5 pts. Nottinghamshire produced their third successive home victory following another remarkable performance by their seam attack. Kent, who surprisingly had volunteered to bat after winning the toss, collapsed to 60 for six before Knott, with a typically impish half-century, and Johnson restored some form of respectability. Hadlee, Hendrick and Cooper, who all took three wickets, caused continual problems. Nottinghamshire, aiming for quick runs to compensate for four hours lost to the weather, slid from 96 without loss to 183 all out against the spin of Underwood and Johnson, who took five wickets each to keep Nottinghamshire's lead to 26. However, in the final half-hour of the second day Hendrick reduced Kent to 3 for four, taking all four wickets in the space of nine balls. When play resumed on the final day Hadlee removed Aslett and Asif with successive deliveries, and although Cowdrey, Knott and Hinks all reached double figures, Kent's meagre total left Nottinghamshire to score just 32 for victory.

Kent

R. A. Woolmer lbw b Hadlee	3	– c Rice b Hendrick	1
L. Potter c French b Hadlee	0	– c Hadlee b Hendrick	0
D. G. Aslett c Birch b Hendrick	6	– (6) lbw b Hadlee	0
*Asif Iqbal c Birch b Saxelby	9	– (7) lbw b Hadlee	0
C. S. Cowdrey c French b Cooper	11	– (8) c Rice b Hemmings	21
S. G. Hinks lbw b Cooper	18	– (4) c Birch b Cooper	14
†A. P. E. Knott lbw b Hadlee	52	– (9) c French b Cooper	13
G. W. Johnson c Cooper b Hendrick	35	– (10) c French b Cooper	1
G. R. Dilley c and b Hendrick	11	– (5) b Hendrick	0
D. L. Underwood c Fell b Cooper	4	– (3) c Rice b Hendrick	2
K. B. S. Jarvis not out	0	– not out	0
B 5, l-b 2, w 1	8	L-b 5	5
1/0 2/7 3/23 4/25 5/51 6/60 7/132 8/144 9/153	157	1/1 2/2 3/3 4/3 5/8 6/8 7/29 8/55 9/55	57

Bonus points – Kent 1, Nottinghamshire 4.

Bowling: *First Innings*—Hadlee 23–9–47–3; Hendrick 20.3–7–27–3; Saxelby 17–5–40–1; Cooper 14–6–21–3; Hemmings 9–3–14–0. *Second Innings*—Hadlee 10–2–13–2; Hendrick 10–6–4–4; Hemmings 7–1–18–1; Cooper 5.1–1–17–3.

Nottinghamshire

B. Hassan c Aslett b Johnson	66	– (2) not out	15
R. T. Robinson st Knott b Underwood	41	– (1) not out	14
†B. N. French c Woolmer b Underwood	0		
*C. E. B. Rice c Potter b Underwood	39		
J. D. Birch c Woolmer b Johnson	2		
M. A. Fell c Knott b Underwood	11		
R. J. Hadlee c Cowdrey b Underwood	17		
E. E. Hemmings not out	5		
K. Saxelby c Jarvis b Johnson	0		
K. E. Cooper c Underwood b Johnson	0		
M. Hendrick c Woolmer b Johnson	0		
N-b 2	2	L-b 4, w 1, n-b 1	6
1/96 2/101 3/117 4/131 5/153 6/177 7/178 8/179 9/179	183	(no wkt)	35

Bonus points – Nottinghamshire 1, Kent 4.

Bowling: *First Innings*—Jarvis 8–4–18–0; Dilley 10–0–36–0; Underwood 25–9–70–5; Cowdrey 6–0–21–0; Johnson 14.2–3–36–5. *Second Innings*—Jarvis 2–0–11–0; Dilley 2–0–8–0; Hinks 1.4–1–5–0; Aslett 1–0–5–0.

Umpires: W. E. Alley and C. T. Spencer.

NOTTINGHAMSHIRE v WARWICKSHIRE

At Nottingham, June 19, 21, 22. Drawn. Nottinghamshire 1 pt. No play was possible on the second and third days, and very little on the first, when Warwickshire were put in to bat.

Warwickshire

D. L. Amiss c Randall b Hendrick	4	K. D. Smith not out	0
T. A. Lloyd c Hassan b Saxelby	12	B 3, l-b 3, n-b 1	7
A. I. Kallicharran not out	32		
†G. W. Humpage c Robinson b Hemmings	19	1/16 2/20 3/69	(3 wkts) 74

Asif Din, S. H. Wootton, C. Lethbridge, G. C. Small, *R. G. D. Willis and J. Cumbes did not bat.

Bonus points – Nottinghamshire 1.

Bowling: Hendrick 9–4–12–1; Saxelby 9–1–19–1; Hemmings 9–4–15–1; Cooper 7–1–20–0; Illingworth 1–0–1–0.

Nottinghamshire

R. T. Robinson, B. Hassan, D. W. Randall, *C. E. B. Rice, J. D. Birch, †B. N. French, E. E. Hemmings, N. J. B. Illingworth, K. Saxelby, K. E. Cooper and M. Hendrick.

Umpires: P. J. Eele and B. J. Meyer.

At Harrogate, June 26, 28, 29. YORKSHIRE v NOTTINGHAMSHIRE. Abandoned.

NOTTINGHAMSHIRE v ESSEX

At Nottingham, July 7, 8, 9. Essex won by ten wickets. Essex 23 pts, Nottinghamshire 4 pts. Nottinghamshire were beaten in the Championship for the first time in a year – and comprehensively beaten too. Essex, having decided to bat, were dithering on 103 for five before half-centuries by Phillip and David East turned their total into one of match-winning proportions. Lever made immediate inroads into the Nottinghamshire innings, and resistance from Fell and French was insufficient to prevent the follow-on. Nottinghamshire lost four wickets for 50 before Fell, in only his fifth first-class game, scored the first Championship century of the season for the county, and in doing so passed his career best twice in the same match. French, too, again showed application, but Essex retained their grip. Gooch and Hardie, who completed his fifty with the winning hit, had little trouble taking Essex to victory.

Essex

G. A. Gooch c French b Cooper	4	– not out	33
B. R. Hardie c and b Illingworth	13	– not out	50
*K. W. R. Fletcher c Fell b Rice	30		
K. S. McEwan b Hendrick	35		
K. R. Pont c French b Cooper	7		
N. Phillip lbw b Hemmings	59		
S. Turner c French b Cooper	31		
†D. E. East c French b Cooper	61		
R. E. East c French b Cooper	0		
J. K. Lever not out	22		
D. L. Acfield c French b Illingworth	3		
B 4, l-b 6, w 1, n-b 9	20	B 2, n-b 1	3
1/9 2/26 3/76 4/92 5/103 6/185 7/225 8/225 9/282	285		(no wkt) 86

Bonus points – Essex 3, Nottinghamshire 4.

Bowling: *First Innings*—Hendrick 19–3–44–1; Cooper 27–6–53–5; Illingworth 12.1–2–59–2; Rice 18–5–46–1; Hemmings 20–4–63–1. *Second Innings*—Cooper 9–1–35–0; Hemmings 11–3–34–0; Illingworth 3–0–14–0.

Nottinghamshire

B. Hassan run out	9	– c Gooch b Phillip	3
R. T. Robinson c Hardie b Lever	5	– c D. E. East b Lever	11
M. A. Fell c R. E. East b Lever	40	– c Gooch b Lever	108
J. D. Birch lbw b Lever	0	– (5) c D. E. East b Lever	17
*C. E. B. Rice c D. E. East b Lever	4	– (4) c Pont b Lever	0
N. J. B. Illingworth b Lever	2	– (8) not out	5
†B. N. French c D. E. East b Phillip	40	– (6) lbw b Acfield	68
E. E. Hemmings c D. E. East b Turner	8	– (7) lbw b Acfield	22
K. E. Cooper run out	9	– lbw b Acfield	1
M. Hendrick not out	1	– c McEwan b Acfield	0
P. A. Todd absent ill		– absent ill	
L-b 1, n-b 3	4	L-b 9, n-b 3	12
1/15 2/15 3/15 4/20 5/36 6/68 7/109 8/113 9/122	122	1/5 2/22 3/25 4/50 5/164 6/226 7/246 8/247 9/247	247

Bonus points – Essex 4.

Bowling: *First Innings*—Lever 16–2–63–5; Phillip 10–3–32–1; R. E. East 1–1–0–0; Gooch 1–0–2–0; Turner 8.2–3–21–1. *Second Innings*—Lever 13–3–55–4; Phillip 12–0–47–1; Turner 4–1–13–0; Gooch 7–2–31–0; R. E. East 21–7–54–0; Acfield 19.5–6–35–4.

Umpires: C. Cook and R. Palmer.

NOTTINGHAMSHIRE v MIDDLESEX

At Nottingham, July 10, 12, 13. Middlesex won by an innings and 15 runs. Middlesex 23 pts, Nottinghamshire 2 pts. Nottinghamshire were conclusively beaten at home for the second successive match as Middlesex stretched their lead at the top of the table. Middlesex, put in to bat, lost Slack and Tomlins cheaply before Brearley and Gatting came together in a stand of 164 that dictated the course of the game. Gatting batted three hours for his 96, while Brearley stayed more than twice as long for 135. He decided to bat on into the second day in the hope of forcing the follow-on, and his bowlers responded accordingly. Hassan top-scored in both innings, but Nottinghamshire perished and an innings victory was completed by Middlesex with more than a session of play to spare.

Middlesex

*J. M. Brearley b Bore	135
W. N. Slack b Cooper	2
K. P. Tomlins c French b Cooper	4
M. W. Gatting lbw b Bore	96
R. O. Butcher c French b Cooper	29
J. E. Emburey c Hassan b Cooper	18
C. T. Radley c Robinson b Bore	21
N. G. Cowans st French b Bore	10
†P. R. Downton lbw b Bore	28
M. W. W. Selvey c and b Bore	13
S. P. Hughes not out	2
B 1, l-b 13, w 5, n-b 6	25
1/4 2/15 3/179 4/252 5/289 6/309 7/329 8/346 9/376	383

Bonus points – Middlesex 3, Nottinghamshire 1 (Score at 100 overs: 279-4).

Bowling: Cooper 42–10–121–4; Hendrick 19–6–25–0; Illingworth 11–2–39–0; Rice 11–1–39–0; Bore 49.5–14–134–6.

Nottinghamshire

B. Hassan c Brearley b Emburey	48	– (2) c Slack b Gatting 70
R. T. Robinson b Cowans	37	– (1) c Butcher b Emburey 8
M. A. Fell c Slack b Selvey	4	– c Downton b Cowans 0
*C. E. B. Rice c Radley b Cowans	8	– c Radley b Cowans 17
J. D. Birch b Gatting	11	– c Gatting b Emburey 8
P. Johnson lbw b Hughes	4	– b Slack 23
†B. N. French lbw b Emburey	1	– lbw b Gatting 17
N. J. B. Illingworth c Downton b Emburey	7	– lbw b Gatting 0
K. E. Cooper b Emburey	12	– b Cowans 21
M. Hendrick c Slack b Hughes	14	– (11) not out 0
M. K. Bore not out	23	– (10) retired hurt 2
B 4, l-b 8, w 1, n-b 8	21	B 4, l-b 1, w 5, n-b 2 12
1/78 2/85 3/94 4/116 5/125 6/125 7/130 8/151 9/152	190	1/22 2/44 3/61 4/104 5/143 6/146 7/146 8/159 9/178 178

Bonus points – Nottinghamshire 1, Middlesex 4.

Bowling: *First Innings*—Selvey 22–8–38–1; Cowans 12–4–21–2; Hughes 21.2–2–50–2; Emburey 18–6–32–4; Slack 6–2–22–0; Gatting 3–0–6–1. *Second Innings*—Cowans 15–4–40–3; Selvey 6–0–24–0; Emburey 23–7–43–2; Hughes 12–2–38–0; Slack 4–2–6–1; Gatting 8–3–15–3.

Umpires: C. Cook and R. Palmer.

At Lord's, July 17, 19, 20. NOTTINGHAMSHIRE lost to MIDDLESEX by an innings and 111 runs.

NOTTINGHAMSHIRE v YORKSHIRE

At Worksop, July 21, 22, 23. Yorkshire won by two wickets. Yorkshire 22 pts, Nottinghamshire 6 pts. The defending champions lost their fourth successive Championship fixture after Yorkshire had taken on the challenge of scoring 305 for victory in 210 minutes plus twenty overs. Yet Nottinghamshire had dominated much of the earlier play once they had recovered from being 127 for seven on the first day. Hemmings, scoring a first-ever century in 174 minutes with one 6 and fourteen 4s, took them to 329 for nine, to which Yorkshire, owing much to Boycott's 91, replied with 206. Todd's first Championship century of the summer came in 171 minutes and opened the way for Rice's declaration. Boycott, Lumb, Athey and Love responded to the target, and although wickets fell at regular intervals from Yorkshire's being 192 for one, they scrambled to victory.

Nottinghamshire

P. A. Todd c Old b Stevenson	10	– not out 117
R. T. Robinson c Bairstow b Sidebottom	28	– c Bairstow b Sidebottom 34
D. W. Randall c Bairstow b Sidebottom	34	– lbw b Sidebottom 0
B. Hassan c sub b Illingworth	21	– not out 21
*C. E. B. Rice c Hartley b Sidebottom	20	
J. D. Birch c Bairstow b Sidebottom	0	
R. J. Hadlee lbw b Sidebottom	3	
†B. N. French c Lumb b Boycott	19	
E. E. Hemmings not out	127	
N. J. B. Illingworth c Sidebottom b Boycott	13	
K. E. Cooper not out	33	
B 1, l-b 13, n-b 7	21	B 1, l-b 2, n-b 6 9
1/19 2/68 3/81 4/117 5/118 6/124 7/127 8/192 9/239	(9 wkts dec.) 329	1/101 2/101 (2 wkts dec.) 181

Bonus points – Nottinghamshire 2, Yorkshire 4 (Score at 100 overs: 247-9).

Bowling: *First Innings*—Old 10–2–25–0; Stevenson 18–3–69–1; Sidebottom 26–3–85–5; Hartley 15–2–43–0; Illingworth 24–11–28–1; Carrick 13–5–20–0; Boycott 9–2–14–2; Athey 6–0–24–0. *Second Innings*—Hartley 8–3–23–0; Sidebottom 16–3–39–2; Carrick 22–7–70–0; Illingworth 14–4–39–0; Boycott 1–0–1–0.

Yorkshire

G. Boycott c Birch b Hadlee	91	– st French b Cooper	82
R. G. Lumb c Hassan b Hadlee	1	– b Cooper	43
C. W. J. Athey c Hassan b Hemmings	5	– c French b Hemmings	76
J. D. Love b Cooper	0	– (5) b Hemmings	39
S. N. Hartley c Rice b Hemmings	9	– (9) run out	2
†D. L. Bairstow c French b Illingworth	32	– c Robinson b Hemmings	5
P. Carrick lbw b Cooper	34	– c Rice b Hadlee	5
A. Sidebottom c Cooper b Rice	18	– (10) not out	6
C. M. Old c Hassan b Hadlee	0	– not out	19
G. B. Stevenson c Hemmings b Rice	3	– (4) b Rice	18
*R. Illingworth not out	1		
B 4, l-b 5, n-b 3	12	B 1, l-b 6, n-b 3	10
1/15 2/20 3/25 4/40 5/87 6/150 7/198 8/198 9/205	206	1/78 2/192 3/215 4/267 5/268 6/277 7/279 8/280	(8 wkts) 305

Bonus points – Yorkshire 2, Nottinghamshire 4.

Bowling: *First Innings*—Hadlee 16.5–5–33–3; Cooper 19–4–33–2; Hemmings 30–6–83–2; Illingworth 10–3–35–1; Rice 10–6–10–2. *Second Innings*—Hadlee 21.5–6–74–1; Cooper 23–5–57–2; Hemmings 23–6–90–3; Illingworth 4–1–15–0; Rice 12.5–2–59–1.

Umpires: J. Birkenshaw and P. J. Eele.

At The Oval, July 28, 29, 30. NOTTINGHAMSHIRE lost to SURREY by ten wickets.

NOTTINGHAMSHIRE v LANCASHIRE

At Nottingham, July 31, August 2, 3. Drawn. Nottinghamshire 5 pts, Lancashire 5 pts. Lancashire, set to get 261 for victory in 220 minutes, did not see their final target being realistically possible and the game ended in a draw. Having invited Nottinghamshire to bat at the outset, they made breakthroughs from the start, reducing the home side to 84 for five before Birch and Hadlee came to the rescue. An innings of 64 not out by Simmons that revealed all his character and courage took Lancashire to a 1-run lead and it was left for Nottinghamshire to make the pace afresh. Their second-innings 261 revolved around Birch's first Championship hundred at Trent Bridge, but it took him 264 minutes. Although the asking-rate seemed within the capabilities of Clive Lloyd, Lancashire decided on survival rather than victory.

Nottinghamshire

P. A. Todd c Simmons b McFarlane	4	– b McFarlane	4
B. Hassan c Scott b Folley	14	– c Abrahams b O'Shaughnessy	29
M. A. Fell b McFarlane	0	– (6) lbw b Simmons	0
*C. E. B. Rice c Abrahams b Folley	6	– c Simmons b O'Shaughnessy	33
J. D. Birch st Scott b Simmons	56	– not out	102
P. Johnson c Simmons b O'Shaughnessy	11	– (3) c Cockbain b Lee	4
R. J. Hadlee c Scott b McFarlane	60	– c Abrahams b Simmons	12
†B. N. French c Abrahams b McFarlane	8	– c Simmons b O'Shaughnessy	25
N. J. B. Illingworth c Abrahams b Folley	1	– c Abrahams b O'Shaughnessy	3
K. Saxelby b Simmons	1	– run out	25
K. E. Cooper not out	0	– lbw b Simmons	6
L-b 2, n-b 1	3	B 3, l-b 11, w 3, n-b 1	18
1/4 2/6 3/17 4/44 5/84 6/119 7/158 8/161 9/164	164	1/5 2/16 3/60 4/83 5/98 6/142 7/186 8/196 9/248	261

Bonus points – Nottinghamshire 1, Lancashire 4.

Bowling: *First Innings*—McFarlane 14–5–37–4; Folley 11–5–20–3; Lee 7–1–31–0; O'Shaughnessy 6–0–28–1; Simmons 18.3–9–27–2; Abrahams 6–0–18–0. *Second Innings*—McFarlane 1–0–6–1; Folley 17–4–28–0; Lee 10–1–34–1; O'Shaughnessy 19–3–66–4; Simmons 28.2–10–47–3; Hughes 16–4–39–0; Abrahams 3–0–14–0; D. Lloyd 9–3–9–0.

Lancashire

D. Lloyd c French b Hadlee	17	– c French b Saxelby	56
I. Cockbain c Hadlee b Rice	17	– lbw b Hadlee	2
S. J. O'Shaughnessy c French b Hadlee	0	– c French b Rice	1
*C. H. Lloyd c Illingworth b Cooper	3	– not out	45
D. P. Hughes c Rice b Cooper	17	– not out	22
J. Abrahams c French b Hadlee	14		
†C. J. Scott c French b Saxelby	4		
J. Simmons not out	64		
I. Folley c Rice b Cooper	5		
L. L. McFarlane b Illingworth	8		
P. G. Lee c Fell b Saxelby	0		
B 2, l-b 4, n-b 10	16	B 1, l-b 3, w 1, n-b 2	7
1/23 2/25 3/32 4/54 5/66 6/81 7/83 8/107 9/162	165	1/7 2/34 3/81	(3 wkts) 133

Bonus points – Lancashire 1, Nottinghamshire 4.

Bowling: *First Innings*—Hadlee 22–4–26–3; Saxelby 20.2–7–24–2; Cooper 17–4–45–3; Rice 17–7–37–1; Fell 4–0–15–0; Illingworth 3–1–2–1. *Second Innings*—Hadlee 12–4–11–1; Saxelby 10–3–38–1; Cooper 13–2–38–0; Rice 10–4–15–1; Fell 6–1–21–0; Illingworth 2–0–3–0.

Umpires: D. Archer and H. D. Bird.

At Cheltenham, August 7, 9, 10. NOTTINGHAMSHIRE beat GLOUCESTERSHIRE by 106 runs.

At Leicester, August 11, 12. NOTTINGHAMSHIRE lost to LEICESTERSHIRE by 10 wickets.

NOTTINGHAMSHIRE v SOMERSET

At Nottingham, August 14, 16, 17. Somerset won by 104 runs. Somerset 19 pts, Nottinghamshire 6 pts. Career-best figures by Marks helped Somerset to victory after Nottinghamshire had lost quick wickets in their bid to score 252 in 170 minutes. Robinson's 77 – his top score of the season – kept Nottinghamshire in with a chance, but after he had gone, the only resistance to Somerset came in a last-wicket partnership between French and teenager Such, who stayed together for eleven overs. Such's off-spin had again impressed as Nottinghamshire bowled out Somerset for 289 in the first innings, but rain prevented Nottinghamshire from building a lead and also robbed Hassan of the time in which to make his first century in five years. Quick scoring and two declarations set up the finish, with Somerset emerging successful in a match that saw both teams considerably below strength.

Somerset

J. W. Lloyds b Saxelby	50	– not out	86
P. M. Roebuck c Pont b Saxelby	1	– c Hadlee b Saxelby	19
I. V. A. Richards c Fell b Such	29	– b Such	3
N. A. Felton c Saxelby b Such	61		
P. A. Slocombe b Cooper	4	– (4) not out	50
*B. C. Rose c French b Saxelby	24		
N. F. M. Popplewell lbw b Such	6		
V. J. Marks c Rice b Cooper	64		
M. R. Davis c Cooper b Saxelby	5		
†T. Gard c and b Such	31		
H. R. Moseley not out	0		
B 4, l-b 7, w 3	14	L-b 2, n-b 2	4
1/2 2/74 3/101 4/115 5/162 6/179 7/202 8/215 9/285	289	1/42 2/46 (2 wkts dec.)	162

Bonus points – Somerset 3, Nottinghamshire 4 (Score at 100 overs: 289-9).

Bowling: *First Innings*—Saxelby 25–5–51–4; Cooper 28–4–53–2; Pont 19–3–69–0; Such 29–4–102–4. *Second Innings*—Saxelby 8–2–21–1; Cooper 2–0–14–0; Such 22.4–5–70–1; Fell 17–2–53–0.

Nottinghamshire

B. Hassan not out	89	– b Moseley	1
R. T. Robinson b Marks	14	– c Davis b Marks	77
P. A. Todd c Gard b Richards	48	– st Gard b Marks	14
*C. E. B. Rice not out	35	– c Felton b Marks	16
R. J. Hadlee (did not bat)		– c Moseley b Marks	16
M. A. Fell (did not bat)		– c Roebuck b Richards	7
†B. N. French (did not bat)		– not out	10
K. Saxelby (did not bat)		– b Marks	1
I. L. Pont (did not bat)		– c Lloyds b Marks	0
K. E. Cooper (did not bat)		– b Marks	0
P. M. Such (did not bat)		– c Gard b Moseley	2
B 3, l-b 8, n-b 3	14	B 2, n-b 1	3
1/28 2/135 (2 wkts dec.)	200	1/7 2/27 3/57 4/115 5/131 6/134 7/135 8/135 9/135	147

Bonus points – Nottinghamshire 2.

Bowling: *First Innings*—Moseley 7–1–26–0; Davis 18–1–54–0; Marks 18–6–53–1; Lloyds 15–4–28–0; Richards 11–3–25–1. *Second Innings*—Moseley 2.3–0–12–2; Davis 9–2–33–0; Marks 20–6–51–7; Lloyds 11–5–44–0; Richards 4–2–4–1.

Umpires: C. Cook and R. S. Herman.

At Swansea, August 21, 23, 24. NOTTINGHAMSHIRE drew with GLAMORGAN.

NOTTINGHAMSHIRE v DERBYSHIRE

At Nottingham, August 28, 30, 31. Drawn. Nottinghamshire 5 pts, Derbyshire 5 pts. Both captains, Rice and Wood, scored their first centuries of the season in a match which ended with Derbyshire resisting Nottinghamshire's late challenge for victory. Set to score 262 in 155 minutes, Derbyshire had lost five wickets for 11 runs against spinners Hemmings and Such before Barnett and Maher negotiated the final overs. Initially Wood paid heavily for the mistake of asking Nottinghamshire to bat, for Rice, reaching his century in 202 minutes, went on to make 144 of their total of 400 for five. However, Wood then led Derbyshire's reply with 124 not out in 272 minutes, but delays for rain did not help the sides set up a challenging finish.

Nottinghamshire

B. Hassan b Tunnicliffe	77	– c Maher b Newman	17
R. T. Robinson c Moir b Tunnicliffe	1	– c Miller b Moir	37
P. Johnson retired hurt	37		
*C. E. B. Rice run out	144	– not out	33
J. D. Birch c Maher b Moir	30	– (3) c Wood b Moir	6
R. J. Hadlee c Barnett b Moir	13	– (5) c Barnett b Moir	0
†B. N. French not out	67	– (6) not out	6
E. E. Hemmings not out	17		
B 2, l-b 7, n-b 5	14	L-b 7, w 1, n-b 5	13
1/8 2/157 3/216 4/234 5/353 (5 wkts dec.)	400	1/35 2/58 3/81 4/83 (4 wkts dec.)	112

K. Saxelby, K. E. Cooper and P. M. Such did not bat.

Bonus points – Nottinghamshire 4, Derbyshire 2 (Score at 100 overs: 376-5).

Bowling: *First Innings*—Oldham 20.3–3–70–0; Tunnicliffe 25–5–109–2; Miller 11–3–42–0; Newman 9–1–46–0; Wood 15–3–42–0; Moir 23–4–69–2; Barnett 1–0–8–0. *Second Innings*—Tunnicliffe 4–1–12–0; Newman 8–1–15–1; Moir 13–0–59–3; Miller 8–2–13–0.

Derbyshire

*B. Wood not out	124	– c Hadlee b Cooper	31
I. S. Anderson st French b Such	45	– c French b Hadlee	12
P. N. Kirsten c Hadlee b Saxelby	27	– b Such	29
J. H. Hampshire c Cooper b Hemmings	38	– (5) c Hassan b Hemmings	0
G. Miller c Robinson b Hemmings	1	– (6) c Rice b Such	3
C. J. Tunnicliffe not out	1	– (4) b Hemmings	5
K. J. Barnett (did not bat)		– not out	9
P. G. Newman (did not bat)		– c French b Such	0
†B. J. M. Maher (did not bat)		– not out	2
B 6, l-b 3, n-b 6	15	B 4, l-b 2, w 1, n-b 1	8
1/104 2/160 3/223 4/240 (4 wkts dec.)	251	1/36 2/59 3/78 4/79 5/88 6/88 7/89 (7 wkts)	99

D. G. Moir and S. Oldham did not bat.

Bonus points – Derbyshire 3, Nottinghamshire 1.

Bowling: *First Innings*—Saxelby 19–5–49–1; Cooper 14–4–37–0; Hemmings 29.5–5–79–2; Hadlee 15–7–32–0; Such 11–0–39–1. *Second Innings*—Hadlee 6–1–15–1; Saxelby 5–0–27–0; Cooper 8–3–14–1; Hemmings 21–12–17–2; Such 14–5–18–3.

Umpires: D. G. L. Evans and M. J. Kitchen.

At Worcester, September 1, 2, 3. NOTTINGHAMSHIRE drew with WORCESTERSHIRE.

NOTTINGHAMSHIRE v LEICESTERSHIRE

At Nottingham, September 8, 9, 10. Nottinghamshire won by an innings and 105 runs. Nottinghamshire 24 pts, Leicestershire 3 pts. This defeat virtually eliminated any hope Leicestershire had of winning the Championship. Nottinghamshire won the toss and built an impressive total of 400 on the opening day, Birch hitting nineteen boundaries in his stay of 190 minutes. Leicestershire hit immediate problems in their reply, the swing of Cooper creating the most havoc as they tumbled to 144 all out, which meant they had to score 256 to make Nottinghamshire bat again. Balderstone and Davison resisted for a time in a third-wicket stand of 45, but Hemmings and Bore, bowling spinners, took four wickets each as Leicestershire perished for a second time, Nottinghamshire completing victory in the afternoon session of the final day.

Nottinghamshire

B. Hassan c Davison b Roberts	14
R. T. Robinson lbw b Taylor	12
D. W. Randall c Tolchard b Taylor	65
*C. E. B. Rice b Cook	46
J. D. Birch b Taylor	125
R. J. Hadlee c Steele b Taylor	20
†B. N. French c Davison b Taylor	31
E. E. Hemmings lbw b Parsons	49
K. Saxelby lbw b Parsons	10
K. E. Cooper b Steele	6
M. K. Bore not out	3
B 4, l-b 4, n-b 11	19
1/27 2/45 3/131 4/161 5/193 6/287 7/355 8/371 9/388	400

Bonus points – Nottinghamshire 4, Leicestershire 3 (Score at 100 overs: 355-7).

Bowling: Roberts 24–0–96–1; Taylor 26–4–101–5; Cook 31–10–67–1; Parsons 18–0–87–2; Steele 17–2–28–1; Balderstone 1–0–2–0.

Leicestershire

J. C. Balderstone b Hemmings	42	– lbw b Hemmings	48
R. A. Cobb b Saxelby	0	– c Hassan b Hemmings	6
D. I. Gower c Hemmings b Cooper	6	– c Hemmings b Cooper	6
B. F. Davison c Hemmings b Cooper	1	– b Saxelby	26
N. E. Briers c Birch b Hemmings	36	– c French b Bore	12
*†R. W. Tolchard c French b Cooper	11	– c Rice b Bore	3
J. F. Steele c French b Saxelby	18	– lbw b Hemmings	0
A. M. E. Roberts c Hemmings b Cooper	0	– c sub b Hemmings	4
G. J. Parsons b Saxelby	10	– not out	14
N. G. B. Cook not out	4	– c Randall b Bore	22
L. B. Taylor c Randall b Hemmings	0	– c Rice b Bore	0
L-b 1, n-b 15	16	B 1, l-b 3, w 1, n-b 5	10
1/1 2/15 3/31 4/84 5/110 6/110 7/110 8/135 9/143	144	1/16 2/35 3/80 4/106 5/106 6/109 7/109 8/115 9/151	151

Bonus points – Nottinghamshire 4.

Bowling: *First Innings*—Saxelby 15–2–40–3; Cooper 20–6–40–4; Bore 6–3–5–0; Hemmings 20–4–43–3. *Second Innings*—Saxelby 11–5–20–1; Cooper 16–5–26–1; Hemmings 35–15–70–4; Bore 15.3–6–25–4.

Umpires: D. G. L. Evans and B. Leadbeater.

At Hove, September 11, 13, 14. NOTTINGHAMSHIRE beat SUSSEX by six wickets.

SOMERSET

President: C. R. M. Atkinson
Chairman: J. M. Jeffrey
Chairman, Cricket Committee: 1982 – R. C. Kerslake
Secretary: 1982 – D. G. Seward; 1983 – A. S. Brown
County Cricket Ground, St James's Street, Taunton TA1 1JT. (Telephone: 0823-72946)
Captain: B. C. Rose
Coach: P. J. Robinson

It is a measure of current Somerset expectations that a season containing the first-ever successful defence of the Benson and Hedges Cup and sixth position in the Schweppes Championship was regarded as something of a disappointment. Being made favourites for all four competitions hardly assisted a realistic appraisal; especially, as it happened, in view of many injuries. Most of the team were affected at some time, but, most critically, Joel Garner missed much of the year with knee and shoulder ailments. Vivian Richards, troubled by a nagging winter finger injury, testimonial year duties, and understandable cricket-weariness after nine crowded years, had some unusually thin periods, reaching his sustained best only at the end. He made more first-class runs than anyone else in the team, but his one-day batting was well below his best. Garner and Richards, at peak form, make the difference between a good side and a winning one.

Most of Somerset's luck came in the Benson and Hedges. Without Garner they were thrashed by Middlesex, and squeezed through by 12 and 13 runs against Glamorgan and Gloucestershire respectively. The full team were at their commanding best for the remaining three matches, both semi-final and final opponents being considerably weakened. The loss of four early John Player League matches could hardly be overcome. Two of the best performances came, after losing the toss, in the NatWest Bank Trophy, before progress in that competition was ended by the devastating brilliance of Kallicharran. Not until late July was the second Championship victory achieved. Then three late wins earned a good position before a shuddering shock in the final match brought a salutary, costly lesson.

Jeremy Lloyds made the biggest advance, earning his cap while nearing 1,000 runs (including two centuries in a match) and 50 wickets. Peter Roebuck, promoted to open the innings, acquitted himself usefully, although suffering a lot of failures, while Peter Denning, before missing the final month, did some fine things in the one-day matches. Once again, however, the openers rarely came off together, Richards usually facing a glossy ball on arrival. Batting down the order, Brian Rose scored 1,000 stabilising runs, while his fifth year of captaincy, perhaps his most difficult, was handled steadily with few dramatics but few important errors. Vic Marks, whose wider, representative recognition was much approved, bowled very well in the one-day games, took 68 first-class wickets, and produced a number of valuable bursts of batting aggression. Ian Botham's limited county appearances were marked, unforgettably, by some fantastic batting, which always threatened to, and often did, turn a match on its ear.

Colin Dredge and Hallam Moseley strove as manfully as ever and had their good days; but in the frequent absence of Garner they were less effective than previously. Phil Slocombe recovered from a dreadful start and regained his place with some sterling efforts. Derek Taylor set the seal on a splendid wicket-keeping/batting contribution with an excellent retirement year, leaving the way clear for Trevor Gard to establish himself in the side. Nigel Popplewell, although blossoming with some lively batting at important times, had a disappointing season and was unable to command a regular place.

Three newcomers registered claims for the future. Nigel Felton, a well-organised twenty-year-old left-hander, displays high potential; the left-arm seamer, Mark Davis, also twenty, should develop well when he can stay clear of minor injury; and sixteen-year-old Gary Palmer, son of the Test match umpire and former Somerset all-rounder, Ken Palmer, showed plenty of ability and competitiveness in his two outings.

Although there were any number of wet days, the weather was mostly kind for the "big" occasions. Even when title hopes had vanished, gates remained encouragingly high. After more complaints about the square at Weston-super-Mare, both that and the one at Bath were relaid in September, but Taunton provided an interesting variety of pitches, and the development of its catering, spectator and player facilities has been so well done that it is now among the best and most profitable of the provincial centres. Indeed, a successful floodlit match between Somerset and a West Indian team, the first on an English county ground, together with a World Cup qualifying game, could point the way to a continuing healthy future. – E.H.

SOMERSET 1982

[*Bill Smith*

Back row: V. J. Marks, P. W. Denning, P. M. Roebuck, J. Garner, C. H. Dredge, J. W. Lloyds, N. F. M. Popplewell. *Front row:* I. V. A. Richards, I. T. Botham, B. C. Rose (*captain*), D. J. S. Taylor, H. R. Moseley.

SOMERSET RESULTS

All first-class matches – Played 23: Won 6, Lost 6, Drawn 11.

County Championship matches – Played 22: Won 6, Lost 6, Drawn 10.

Bonus points – Batting 51, Bowling 66.

Competition placings – Schweppes County Championship, 6th; NatWest Bank Trophy, q-f; Benson and Hedges Cup, winners; John Player League, 9th.

COUNTY CHAMPIONSHIP AVERAGES

BATTING

	Birthplace	*M*	*I*	*NO*	*R*	*HI*	*Avge*
B. C. Rose c	*Dartford*	20	31	8	1,079	173*	46.91
I. V. A. Richards c	*St John's, Antigua*	19	30	1	1,143	178	39.41
I. T. Botham c	*Heswall*	11	20	1	675	131*	35.52
N. A. Felton	*Guildford*	8	12	0	346	71	28.83
J. W. Lloyds c	*Penang, Malaya*	22	37	3	965	132*	28.38
P. A. Slocombe c	*Weston-super-Mare*	12	21	1	543	78	27.15
P. M. Roebuck c	*Oxford*	21	36	2	898	90	26.41
P. W. Denning c	*Chewton Mendip*	14	22	1	541	91*	25.76
N. F. M. Popplewell	*Chislehurst*	15	22	4	422	55	23.44
V. J. Marks c	*Middle Chinnock*	18	28	2	507	67	19.50
H. R. Moseley c	*Christ Church, Barbados*	17	19	13	113	24*	18.83
J. Garner c	*Barbados*	10	11	5	98	40*	16.33
D. J. S. Taylor c	*Amersham*	17	26	5	334	67	15.90
C. H. Dredge c	*Frome*	19	25	7	283	54*	15.72
T. Gard	*South Petherton*	5	4	1	37	31	12.33
M. R. Davis	*Kilve*	8	12	2	65	21*	6.50

Also batted: M. Bryant (*Camborne*) (2 matches) 6, 0; R. J. McCool (*Taunton*) (1 match) 7,12; R. L. Ollis (*Clifton*) (1 match) 1, 1; G. V. Palmer (*Taunton*) (1 match) 6, 27; N. Russom (*Finchley*) (1 match) did not bat.

**Signifies not out.* c *Denotes county cap.*

BOWLING

	O	*M*	*R*	*W*	*Avge*	*BB*
J. Garner	259.1	76	583	33	17.66	6-23
I. T. Botham	247.2	64	719	39	18.43	5-48
V. J. Marks	613	180	1,699	63	26.96	7-51
H. R. Moseley	303	68	921	34	27.08	5-40
J. W. Lloyds	448.5	98	1,384	43	32.18	7-88
M. R. Davis	125	17	394	12	32.83	3-36
C. H. Dredge	425.5	105	1,154	33	34.96	3-33
I. V. A. Richards	251.3	72	623	16	38.93	3-6

Also bowled: M. Bryant 27–3–158–2; R. J. McCool 17–2–63–0; G. V. Palmer 17–3–57–0; N. F. M. Popplewell 82–16–258–6; P. M. Roebuck 39–5–109–1; B. C. Rose 1–0–5–0; N. Russom 16–2–64–3; P. A. Slocombe 3.2–0–10–1; D. J. S. Taylor 3–2–1–0.

HUNDREDS

The following eight three-figure innings were played for Somerset in County Championship matches – I. V. A. Richards (3) 146 v Kent (Taunton), 135 v Warwickshire (Birmingham), 178 v Lancashire (Taunton); J. W. Lloyds (2) 132* and 102* v Northamptonshire (Northampton); B. C. Rose (2) 102* v Warwickshire (Birmingham), 173* v Gloucestershire (Bristol); I. T. Botham (1) 131* v Warwickshire (Taunton).

SOMERSET v SUSSEX

At Taunton, May 5, 6, 7. Drawn. Somerset 6 pts, Sussex 5 pts. A dry, fast, unreliable pitch made batting difficult throughout and a painful business against bowlers of extreme pace. Somerset, put in, were saved by Botham, who hit two 6s and ten 4s in sixteen overs on the first day, when only two and a quarter hours' play was possible. Next morning Marks, through 30 overs, and Popplewell, in 44, courageously and luckily extended the effort. When Sussex batted Barclay, dropped twice, remained for all but eight of the overs bowled and received good support, first from Wells and Parker and then, after a collapse against Moseley and Dredge, from some aggressive hitting by le Roux. With a lead of only 20, and with Imran and le Roux very hostile and the pitch nasty, the sound opening stand between Rose and Lloyds was vital, for thereafter only Denning and Botham made any progress. Rose's declaration required 171 in 108 minutes, and though a fine third-wicket stand of 81 in nineteen overs between Mendis and Parker opened up Sussex hopes, they went with the dismissal of Parker with 60 needed in six overs.

Somerset

*B. C. Rose b le Roux	8	– c Gould b Greig	43
J. W. Lloyds c Gould b le Roux	11	– c Gould b Greig	22
P. A. Slocombe lbw b Greig	10	– c Phillipson b le Roux	8
P. M. Roebuck c Greig b le Roux	0	– c Waller b le Roux	1
P. W. Denning c Gould b Pigott	2	– c Greig b Pigott	20
I. T. Botham c Phillipson b Imran	66	– c Parker b Pigott	20
N. F. M. Popplewell not out	43	– c Greig b Imran	4
V. J. Marks b Pigott	51	– c Gould b Pigott	8
†D. J. S. Taylor c Phillipson b le Roux	12	– not out	7
C. H. Dredge c le Roux b Greig	5	– c Waller b le Roux	4
H. R. Moseley c Barclay b le Roux	0		
B 1, l-b 3	4	B 5, l-b 7, w 1	13
1/8 2/25 3/25 4/30 5/100 6/104 7/184 8/204 9/211	212	1/55 2/73 3/77 4/85 5/116 6/125 7/134 8/139 9/150 (9 wkts dec.)	150

Bonus points – Somerset 2, Sussex 4.

Bowling: *First Innings*—le Roux 19.1–5–47–5; Imran 21–7–48–1; Pigott 13–3–27–2; Greig 20–5–86–2. *Second Innings*—le Roux 15.5–2–45–3; Imran 13–3–42–1; Greig 12–4–24–2; Pigott 8–3–26–3; Barclay 1–1–0–0.

Sussex

G. D. Mendis lbw b Moseley	17	– not out	49
*J. R. T. Barclay b Moseley	47		
C. M. Wells run out	27	– lbw b Moseley	13
P. W. G. Parker lbw b Botham	30	– c Taylor b Botham	39
Imran Khan c Taylor b Dredge	7	– not out	13
I. A. Greig c Taylor b Moseley	5		
C. P. Phillipson lbw b Moseley	0		
†I. J. Gould lbw b Dredge	12	– (2) c Taylor b Botham	0
G. S. le Roux c Taylor b Botham	30		
A. C. S. Pigott c Taylor b Moseley	3		
C. E. Waller not out	4		
L-b 8, n-b 2	10	L-b 9, n-b 2	11
1/23 2/66 3/101 4/112 5/117 6/117 7/146 8/182 9/184	192	1/3 2/30 3/111 (3 wkts)	125

Bonus points – Sussex 1, Somerset 4.

Bowling: *First Innings*—Botham 14–6–33–2; Moseley 27–10–40–5; Dredge 23–6–80–2; Popplewell 7–1–22–0; Marks 1–0–7–0; Roebuck 1–1–0–0. *Second Innings*—Botham 15–2–47–2; Moseley 6–1–20–1; Dredge 8.2–0–47–0.

Umpires: D. R. Shepherd and C. Cook.

At Derby, May 12, 13, 14. SOMERSET lost to DERBYSHIRE by nine wickets.

At Worcester, May 19, 20, 21. SOMERSET beat WORCESTERSHIRE by five wickets.

SOMERSET v KENT

At Taunton, May 29, 31, June 1. Drawn. Somerset 7 pts, Kent 7 pts. In very hot weather the dry pitch gave some early unevenness which increased, but never unacceptably. Richards, with his first century of the summer, in 55 overs, and Rose established the Somerset total before Tavaré, with a well-planned 80-over response, led the reply. Kent conceded a lead of 60, but with Richards injured only Roebuck, patient over 59 overs, resisted Underwood for long. Botham, relishing the change bowler, Taylor, struck four 6s and four 4s in 41 balls. Kent were set 261 to win in 175 minutes. Woolmer, dropped before scoring, led a splendid start of 88 in 21 overs, but Marks slowed the scoring, taking wickets steadily until Kent, with fifteen overs and five wickets (one of them the injured Johnson) left, gave up the chase with 100 required. Eleven overs later so did Somerset, leaving Taylor undefeated after a skilful, resourceful innings of 49 overs.

Somerset

P. M. Roebuck b Dilley	9	– c Tavaré b Underwood	73
J. W. Lloyds c Woolmer b Underwood	41	– c sub b Underwood	25
I. V. A. Richards c Cowdrey b Johnson	146		
*B. C. Rose c Tavaré b Johnson	89	– c Knott b Penn	4
P. W. Denning st Knott b Underwood	21	– c and b Taylor	13
I. T. Botham c Asif b Underwood	20	– c Dilley b Taylor	47
N. F. M. Popplewell not out	18	– (3) b Penn	23
V. J. Marks c Penn b Underwood	9	– (7) c Penn b Underwood	5
†D. J. S. Taylor not out	6	– (8) not out	0
C. H. Dredge (did not bat)		– (9) not out	4
L-b 3	3	B 5, l-b 1	6
1/26 2/92 3/247 4/307 5/329 6/329 7/338 (7 wkts dec.)	362	1/48 2/106 3/110 4/138 5/142 6/184 7/196 (7 wkts dec.)	200

H. R. Moseley did not bat.

Bonus points – Somerset 4, Kent 3.

Bowling: *First Innings*—Jarvis 18–3–75–0; Dilley 17–5–59–1; Penn 13–0–64–0; Underwood 23–9–65–4; Woolmer 7–2–23–0; Johnson 19–6–48–2; Cowdrey 3–0–25–0. *Second Innings*—Jarvis 11–1–33–0; Dilley 13–1–45–0; Underwood 28–15–47–3; Taylor 12–4–58–2; Penn 4–1–11–2.

Kent

R. A. Woolmer c Marks b Dredge	31	– c Popplewell b Dredge	50
N. R. Taylor lbw b Dredge	7	– not out	81
C. J. Tavaré not out	122	– run out	9
*Asif Iqbal c and b Lloyds	47	– st Taylor b Marks	20
C. S. Cowdrey c Rose b Lloyds	34	– c Dredge b Marks	16
†A. P. E. Knott lbw b Dredge	5	– c Denning b Marks	5
G. R. Dilley c Rose b Marks	7	– not out	6
C. Penn c sub b Marks	30		
G. W. Johnson not out	1		
B 4, l-b 13, w 1	18	L-b 5	5
1/44 2/45 3/114 4/172 5/183 6/203 7/297 (7 wkts dec.)	302	1/88 2/102 3/128 4/156 5/161 (5 wkts)	192

D. L. Underwood and K. B. S. Jarvis did not bat.

Bonus points – Kent 4, Somerset 3.

Bowling: *First Innings*—Botham 14–6–27–0; Moseley 11–2–38–0; Marks 25.5–6–98–2; Dredge 18–4–52–3; Lloyds 29–9–69–2. *Second Innings*—Botham 4–0–42–0; Moseley 2–0–9–0; Marks 22–3–73–3; Lloyds 11–2–32–0; Dredge 10–0–31–1.

Umpires: J. Birkenshaw and R. Julian.

At Swansea, June 2, 3, 4. SOMERSET drew with GLAMORGAN.

At Chelmsford, June 5, 7, 8. SOMERSET lost to ESSEX by 173 runs.

At Northampton, June 12, 14, 15. SOMERSET drew with NORTHAMPTONSHIRE.

SOMERSET v HAMPSHIRE

At Bath, June 19, 21, 22. Drawn. Somerset 6 pts, Hampshire 7 pts. On a dry pitch which always helped seam movement, Hampshire enjoyed a useful start, suffered a collapse in mid-innings, and effected a recovery, notably through Cowley and Southern, who added 70 for the ninth wicket. For a period on Monday morning the pitch was distinctly fiery, and Somerset slipped to 110 for six as Emery achieved his best performance. But a remarkable counter-attack from Botham, hitting four 6s and eight 4s in 38 balls, changed things, and a diligent innings by Denning over 42 overs saw the deficit kept to 11. Greenidge took Hampshire further ahead but rain destroyed the final day.

Hampshire

C. G. Greenidge c Taylor b Dredge	35	– not out	48
J. M. Rice c Denning b Popplewell	29	– c Marks b Dredge	20
M. C. J. Nicholas lbw b Botham	37	– not out	10
T. E. Jesty c Taylor b Botham	16		
D. R. Turner c Taylor b Moseley	2		
*N. E. J. Pocock c Taylor b Botham	12		
N. G. Cowley c Taylor b Botham	50		
M. D. Marshall c Taylor b Richards	14		
†R. J. Parks c Moseley b Marks	14		
J. W. Southern not out	30		
K. St J. D. Emery lbw b Botham	0		
B 6, l-b 11, n-b 3	20	B 5, l-b 2	7
1/46 2/78 3/117 4/126 5/142 6/143 7/160 8/189 9/259	259	1/64	(1 wkt) 85

Bonus points – Hampshire 3, Somerset 4.

Bowling: *First Innings*—Botham 23.3–7–48–5; Moseley 16–4–41–1; Popplewell 13–3–45–1; Dredge 18–6–44–1; Richards 16–7–28–1; Marks 12–2–33–1. *Second Innings*—Botham 6–1–28–0; Moseley 9–1–33–0; Dredge 9–1–15–1; Richards 3–1–2–0.

Somerset

P. M. Roebuck lbw b Marshall	7
J. W. Lloyds lbw b Emery	16
C. H. Dredge c Pocock b Emery	17
I. V. A. Richards lbw b Marshall	25
*B. C. Rose c Rice b Jesty	7
P. W. Denning c Cowley b Emery	45
V. J. Marks c Rice b Emery	12
I. T. Botham c Southern b Jesty	66
†D. J. S. Taylor b Emery	6
N. F. M. Popplewell lbw b Marshall	19
H. R. Moseley not out	0
B 4, l-b 6, w 1, n-b 17	28
1/15 2/42 3/45 4/76 5/84 6/110 7/193 8/201 9/247	248

Bonus points – Somerset 2, Hampshire 4.

Bowling: Marshall 25.1–8–71–3; Emery 23–4–80–5; Cowley 1–0–5–0; Jesty 19–7–64–2.

Umpires: B. Leadbeater and K. Ibadulla.

SOMERSET v GLOUCESTERSHIRE

At Bath, June 23, 24, 25. Drawn. Somerset 3 pts, Gloucestershire 3 pts. The only play possible was on a full second day. Somerset, put in, faltered as the 23-year-old Stephenson took two wickets in his first four overs of county cricket and then recovered, principally through Denning in 44 overs and Rose in 36 overs. Despite a useful bowl by Richards, Stovold and Hignell laid the foundation of a suitable reply.

Somerset

P. M. Roebuck lbw b Shepherd	30
J. W. Lloyds c Brassington b Stephenson	2
I. V. A. Richards lbw b Stephenson	12
*B. C. Rose b Shepherd	45
P. W. Denning c and b Graveney	51
N. F. M. Popplewell c Brassington b Surridge	26
V. J. Marks b Surridge	2
†D. J. S. Taylor lbw b Surridge	8
J. Garner not out	9
C. H. Dredge not out	1
L-b 5, n-b 9	14
1/7 2/22 3/82 4/130 5/173 6/175 7/185 8/191	(8 wkts dec.) 200

H. R. Moseley did not bat.

Bonus points – Somerset 2, Gloucestershire 3.

Bowling: Stephenson 16–2–45–2; Surridge 20.1–5–36–3; Shepherd 16–0–59–2; Bainbridge 9–1–27–0; Graveney 10–4–19–1.

Gloucestershire

A. W. Stovold c Taylor b Richards	42	E. J. Cunningham not out	1
B. C. Broad lbw b Richards	23	B 1, l-b 1, n-b 2	4
P. Bainbridge lbw b Richards	1		
A. J. Hignell not out	33	1/40 2/52 3/97	(3 wkts) 104

P. W. Romaines, *D. A. Graveney, F. D. Stephenson, J. N. Shepherd, †A. J. Brassington and D. Surridge did not bat.

Bonus points – Somerset 1.

Bowling: Garner 8–0–30–0; Dredge 5–1–15–0; Richards 13–3–26–3; Moseley 7–2–20–0; Popplewell 2–0–9–0; Marks 2–2–0–0.

Umpires: B. Leadbeater and K. Ibadulla.

At Birmingham, June 26, 28, 29. SOMERSET drew with WARWICKSHIRE.

At Taunton, July 7, 8, 9. SOMERSET drew with PAKISTANIS (See Pakistani tour section).

At Hove, July 10, 12, 13. SOMERSET beat SUSSEX by 19 runs.

SOMERSET v GLAMORGAN

At Taunton, July 17, 19, 20. Drawn. Somerset 1 pt, Glamorgan 6 pts. On a dry, variable pitch showing occasional venom, Somerset collapsed as Nash, Davis and Ontong took advantage of conditions conducive to swing. A slow, patient innings, with two Somerset bowlers injured, brought Francis his highest score in 137 overs and 7 hours, 24 minutes, Rowe helping him to add 184 in 79 overs. Roebuck and Slocombe set about reducing arrears of 255 with a century opening stand but then Lloyd and Davis dashed Somerset to 180 for four, still 75 behind with five and a half hours of the match left. However, Denning, who retired hurt with a badly damaged arm when 85, then returned to lead a most courageous recovery through 53 overs. Marks attacked briskly; Lloyds, batting late because of a torn arm muscle, struck out splendidly; and an obdurate stay of 22 overs by Davis eventually put victory beyond Glamorgan, whose final requirement, not heeded, was 209 to win in 70 minutes.

Somerset

P. M. Roebuck c E. W. Jones b Nash	0	– st E. W. Jones b Lloyd	66
J. W. Lloyds c A. Jones b Davis	13	– (8) c E. W. Jones b Davis	89
*I. V. A. Richards lbw b Davis	11	– (4) b Davis	36
P. A. Slocombe b Nash	0	– (2) b Davis	63
N. F. M. Popplewell c A. L. Jones b Nash	25	– c and b Lloyd	22
P. W. Denning c E. W. Jones b Nash	13	– not out	91
V. J. Marks c Francis b Ontong	5	– lbw b Daniels	50
†D. J. S. Taylor c E. W. Jones b Ontong	1	– (9) b Lloyd	3
C. H. Dredge b Nash	4	– (3) c sub b Lloyd	0
M. R. Davis lbw b Ontong	0	– c Hopkins b Ontong	6
H. R. Moseley not out	0	– b Lloyd	13
L-b 3, w 2, n-b 1	6	B 9, l-b 12, w 1, n-b 2	24
1/8 2/22 3/23 4/31 5/58 6/67 7/73 8/73 9/77	78	1/137 2/137 3/169 4/180 5/218 6/289 7/399 8/443 9/457	463

Bonus points – Glamorgan 4.

Bowling: *First Innings*—Davis 12–4–27–2; Nash 17–3–35–5; Ontong 5.5–2–10–3. *Second Innings*—Nash 17–6–37–0; Davis 32–7–95–3; Lloyd 40–4–155–5; Ontong 17–6–40–1; Rowe 24–4–75–0; Daniels 6–1–37–1.

Glamorgan

A. Jones lbw b Davis	15	– not out	8
A. L. Jones lbw b Richards	28	– not out	13
D. A. Francis c and b Dredge	127		
R. C. Ontong b Dredge	15		
J. A. Hopkins c Taylor b Davis	0		
C. J. C. Rowe c Richards b Moseley	105		
†E. W. Jones c Slocombe b Moseley	12		
*B. J. Lloyd b Moseley	1		
S. A. B. Daniels not out	2		
M. A. Nash b Dredge	13		
W. W. Davis not out	1		
B 5, l-b 4, w 1, n-b 4	14	N-b 1	1
1/23 2/60 3/100 4/107 5/291 6/306 7/315 8/315 9/331	(9 wkts dec.) 333		(no wkt) 22

Bonus points – Glamorgan 2, Somerset 1 (Score at 100 overs: 221-4).

Bowling: *First Innings*—Davis 16–2–35–2; Moseley 22–5–75–3; Dredge 28–12–33–3; Marks 42–13–93–0; Richards 23–7–35–1; Lloyds 7–2–15–0; Roebuck 12–1–33–0. *Second Innings*—Dredge 2–1–7–0; Moseley 2–0–5–0; Taylor 3–2–1–0; Slocombe 2–0–8–0.

Umpires: J. Birkenshaw and R. Julian.

At The Oval, July 21, 22, 23. SOMERSET beat SURREY by two wickets.

At Bournemouth, July 31, August 2. SOMERSET lost to HAMPSHIRE by 10 runs.

SOMERSET v MIDDLESEX

At Weston-super-Mare, August 7, 9, 10. Middlesex won by an innings and 75 runs. Middlesex 24 pts, Somerset 5 pts. Dogged batting on an unreliable pitch by Roebuck, for 67 overs, Richards and Rose presaged a collapse, with eight wickets falling for 40 runs. Middlesex were themselves in trouble at 139 for five, but with Garner injured, gritty batting by Radley through 62 overs, and a brisk 34 overs from Downton, they established a vital lead. A vicious, lifting pitch, ably exploited by Cowans and Hughes, brought an astonishing collapse on the last morning, all ten wickets falling in the final 46 deliveries of the match.

Somerset

P. M. Roebuck c Butcher b Cowans	58	– c Downton b Cowans	10
J. W. Lloyds c Downton b Emburey	16	– c Downton b Hughes	10
I. V. A. Richards c Edmonds b Cowans	35	– c Downton b Hughes	0
*B. C. Rose b Hughes	53	– c sub b Cowans	9
P. W. Denning b Cowans	0	– c Emburey b Cowans	5
I. T. Botham c Gatting b Hughes	7	– b Cowans	0
V. J. Marks b Hughes	0	– c Tomlins b Hughes	5
†D. J. S. Taylor c Radley b Edmonds	2	– c Tomlins b Hughes	8
C. H. Dredge c Gatting b Edmonds	1	– run out	4
M. R. Davis not out	0	– (11) b Cowans	0
J. Garner c Butcher b Edmonds	1	– (10) not out	5
B 8, l-b 3, n-b 3	14	L-b 1	1
1/24 2/76 3/147 4/147 5/160 6/166 7/171 8/177 9/181	187	1/21 2/21 3/24 4/29 5/35 6/40 7/44 8/52 9/54	57

Bonus points – Somerset 1, Middlesex 4.

Bowling: *First Innings*—Cowans 15–4–41–3; Hughes 18–6–48–3; Emburey 14–2–33–1; Edmonds 32.2–11–43–3; Slack 4–2–8–0. *Second Innings*—Cowans 7.1–1–28–5; Hughes 7–1–28–4.

Middlesex

*J. M. Brearley c Dredge b Botham	7	P. H. Edmonds not out	28
W. N. Slack c Lloyds b Botham	62	N. G. Cowans c Taylor b Lloyds	8
K. P. Tomlins lbw b Dredge	6	S. P. Hughes st Taylor b Marks	2
M. W. Gatting c Garner b Davis	13		
C. T. Radley c Marks b Dredge	82	B 6, l-b 8, n-b 3	17
R. O. Butcher c and b Lloyds	0		
†P. R. Downton c Taylor b Marks	59	1/9 2/20 3/56 4/122 5/139 6/230	319
J. E. Emburey c Denning b Marks	35	7/254 8/301 9/312	

Bonus points – Middlesex 4, Somerset 4 (Score at 100 overs: 312-9).

Bowling: Garner 13–3–31–0; Botham 18–5–52–2; Dredge 13–5–24–2; Davis 7–1–25–1; Marks 27.3–5–99–3; Lloyds 21–4–67–2; Richards 3–1–4–0.

Umpires: W. L. Budd and J. van Geloven.

SOMERSET v YORKSHIRE

At Weston-super-Mare, August 11, 12, 13. Drawn. Somerset 5 pts, Yorkshire 5 pts. On an unreliable pitch, which fortunately lacked pace, Somerset recovered well from Old's opening burst of three for 18. Felton, in his second match, batted with much maturity and in company with Rose added a vital 119 in 36 overs before Slocombe and Popplewell steadily reinforced the restored position. The last three wickets occupied half an hour of the second day, Carrick emerging with the best figures, whereupon Boycott, hitting eighteen 4s in 94 overs, and Lumb, with a 6 and seven 4s, laid the foundations of a most determined reply. Boycott escaped a difficult chance when 54, but whether or not this might have influenced the outcome became academic when the final day was washed out by rain.

Somerset

P. M. Roebuck b Old	0	C. H. Dredge not out	19
J. W. Lloyds c Bairstow b Old	30	M. R. Davis b Sidebottom	5
I. V. A. Richards c Carrick b Old	36	H. R. Moseley c Love b Carrick	7
N. A. Felton c Bairstow b Sidebottom	71	B 7, l-b 7, w 1, n-b 10	25
*B. C. Rose c Bairstow b Hartley	45		
P. A. Slocombe c Athey b Carrick	59	1/0 2/67 3/68	388
N. F. M. Popplewell c Bairstow b Carrick	55	4/187 5/213 6/283	
†D. J. S. Taylor b Carrick	36	7/344 8/366 9/381	

Bonus points – Somerset 4, Yorkshire 2 (Score at 100 overs: 300-6).

Bowling: Ramage 21–2–101–0; Old 22–9–50–3; Sidebottom 26–4–104–2; Illingworth 28–11–54–0; Hartley 7–1–23–1; Carrick 24.4–13–31–4.

Yorkshire

G. Boycott b Lloyds	129	A. Ramage not out	4
R. G. Lumb c Lloyds b Davis	81	B 3, l-b 1, n-b 9	13
C. W. J. Athey b Lloyds	2		
J. D. Love b Lloyds	14	1/178 2/187	(4 wkts) 250
S. N. Hartley not out	7	3/218 4/246	

†D. L. Bairstow, P. Carrick, C. M. Old, A. Sidebottom and *R. Illingworth did not bat.

Bonus points – Yorkshire 3, Somerset 1.

Bowling: Moseley 18–7–41–0; Davis 18–4–42–1; Lloyds 32–6–84–3; Dredge 6–2–4–0; Richards 16–5–52–0; Roebuck 6–0–14–0.

Umpires: W. L. Budd and J. van Geloven.

At Nottingham, August 14, 16, 17. SOMERSET beat NOTTINGHAMSHIRE by 104 runs.

SOMERSET v LEICESTERSHIRE

At Taunton, August 21, 23, 24. Leicestershire won by 160 runs with 77 balls to spare. Leicestershire 24 pts, Somerset 4 pts. Against a weakened attack, on a slowish pitch accepting early spin, Cobb and Gower established a strong position which was well sustained by Briers and Tolchard. Gower hit one 6 and thirteen 4s in 71 overs. Somerset struggled throughout, though the stern rearguard efforts of Felton, for 57 overs, and Slocombe, plus 28 from the last-wicket pair, meant they narrowly avoided the follow-on. After a crisp start on the Monday evening, Balderstone (one 6 and ten 4s) and Briers (eleven 4s) added a hectic 92 in the first half-hour of the final day, allowing Tolchard to set a target of 338 in 320 minutes. With Cook returning career-best figures, only Felton (26 overs) and Slocombe (30 overs) stood in Leicestershire's way, though a brave ninth-wicket stand of 53 in 24 overs between sixteen-year-old Palmer, in his first game, and Davis, with a damaged foot, threatened to combine with the weather to thwart the visitors. However, after a 35-minute stoppage for rain, the conditions improved sufficiently for Leicestershire to complete an important victory.

Leicestershire

J. C. Balderstone c Slocombe b Davis	0	– c Lloyds b Marks	88
R. A. Cobb st Gard b Lloyds	63		
D. I. Gower c Lloyds b Marks	111		
B. F. Davison b Lloyds	14		
N. E. Briers not out	91	– (2) not out	93
*†R. W. Tolchard b Marks	50		
G. J. Parsons not out	21		
L-b 7, n-b 7	14	B 3, l-b 3, n-b 2	8
1/2 2/159 3/187 4/209 5/310 (5 wkts dec.)	364	1/189 (1 wkt dec.)	189

J. F. Steele, P. B. Clift, N. G. B. Cook and L. B. Taylor did not bat.

Bonus points – Leicestershire 4, Somerset 2 (Score at 100 overs: 311-5).

Bowling: *First Innings*—Moseley 18–3–79–0; Davis 14–3–56–1; Palmer 7–3–15–0; Richards 7–2–16–0; Marks 37–10–102–2; Lloyds 23–1–82–2. *Second Innings*—Moseley 10–2–38–0; Palmer 10–0–42–0; Richards 12–1–61–0; Marks 11.2–3–40–1.

Somerset

P. M. Roebuck c and b Clift	29	(2) c Tolchard b Cook	16
*B. C. Rose b Parsons	4	(5) b Cook	1
†T. Gard lbw b Taylor	3	(8) c Gower b Steele	3
I. V. A. Richards c Balderstone b Taylor	36	(3) b Cook	0
J. W. Lloyds c Balderstone b Cook	1	(1) c and b Steele	33
N. A. Felton b Parsons	59	(4) c Steele b Cook	32
P. A. Slocombe b Parsons	17	(6) lbw b Cook	25
V. J. Marks c Tolchard b Steele	18	(7) c Gower b Cook	9
G. V. Palmer c Cobb b Parsons	6	lbw b Cook	27
M. R. Davis c and b Cook	14	not out	21
H. R. Moseley not out	18	lbw b Taylor	1
B 8, l-b 2, n-b 1	11	B 5, l-b 2, n-b 2	9
1/13 2/16 3/60 4/61 5/76 6/140 7/169 8/177 9/188	216	1/33 2/42 3/54 4/55 5/100 6/116 7/123 8/123 9/176	177

Bonus points – Somerset 2, Leicestershire 4.

Bowling: *First Innings*—Taylor 21–6–36–2; Parsons 23–4–88–4; Cook 30.5–9–49–2; Clift 11–5–8–1; Steele 14–6–24–1. *Second Innings*—Taylor 12.1–4–30–1; Parsons 6–1–18–0; Cook 35–14–63–7; Steele 27–10–51–2; Clift 3–2–6–0.

Umpires: R. S. Herman and A. G. T. Whitehead.

At Bristol, August 28, 30, 31. SOMERSET drew with GLOUCESTERSHIRE.

SOMERSET v WARWICKSHIRE

At Taunton, September 1, 2, 3. Somerset won by five wickets. Somerset 20 pts, Warwickshire 6 pts. Rain and bad light took two hours from the first day as useful half-centuries by the openers and a busy 90 not out by Humpage followed three dropped chances. In perfect weather, Humpage went to his century, in 170 minutes, on the second day, and following the declaration Somerset slipped to 63 for four against the seam bowlers, helped by Lethbridge's two superb gully catches. Botham's lively 32-ball interlude against the spinners and steady efforts from Felton and Rose rescued matters, but after the declaration, 92 behind, Marks and Lloyds broke through remarkably to seize the initiative for Somerset. On the final morning, though, an unexpected ninth-wicket stand of 115 in 22 overs between Lethbridge – making his highest score with two 6s and eleven 4s in 42 overs – and Willis swung the game Warwickshire's way again. Needing 309 in 270 minutes, Somerset faltered to 57 for three before Richards, with two 6s and twelve 4s in 31 overs, and Slocombe, through 41 overs, set the scene for the astonishing finale. Botham arrived with 160 needed in 145 minutes, and in 65 minutes he scored 131 by way of ten 6s and twelve 4s, getting Somerset home with 80 minutes to spare. He scored 17 in 25 minutes before tea and the rest in 40 minutes afterwards, registering the fastest 100 of the season in 52 minutes from 56 balls.

Warwickshire

K. D. Smith c Gard b Marks	67 – c Slocombe b Marks	15
T. A. Lloyd b Marks	55 – b Botham	4
D. L. Amiss lbw b Botham	1 – b Marks	26
G. W. Humpage c Botham b Marks	113 – b Lloyds	1
Asif Din c and b Botham	24 – hit wkt b Marks	7
P. A. Smith c Lloyds b Marks	1 – c Marks b Lloyds	2
†G. A. Tedstone not out	9 – b Garner	7
C. Lethbridge not out	16 – not out	87
G. C. Small (did not bat)	– c Lloyds b Marks	1
*R. G. D. Willis (did not bat)	– b Dredge	48
S. P. Sutcliffe (did not bat)	– c Gard b Dredge	0
B 10, l-b 4	14 B 12, l-b 1, n-b 5	18
1/88 2/89 3/188 4/251 5/252 6/279 (6 wkts dec.)	300 1/13 2/28 3/61 4/61 5/70 6/70 7/96 8/97 9/212	216

Bonus points – Warwickshire 4, Somerset 2.

Bowling: *First Innings*—Garner 12–2–41–0; Botham 10–2–24–2; Dredge 14–1–59–0; Marks 40–13–94–4; Lloyds 10–2–27–0; Richards 8.3–0–41–0. *Second Innings*—Garner 17–5–25–1; Botham 14–3–41–1; Richards 6–0–18–0; Marks 19–9–47–4; Lloyds 12–3–50–2; Roebuck 2–1–5–0; Dredge 3.2–0–12–2.

Somerset

J. W. Lloyds b Lethbridge	22 – lbw b Willis	20
P. M. Roebuck b Willis	7 – c Lloyd b Small	0
I. V. A. Richards c Lethbridge b P. A. Smith	26 – b Humpage	85
N. A. Felton c Humpage b Sutcliffe	43 – b Sutcliffe	10
P. A. Slocombe c Lethbridge b P. A. Smith	0 – c Humpage b P. A. Smith	50
I. T. Botham st Tedstone b Sutcliffe	41 – not out	131
*B. C. Rose not out	40 – not out	0
V. J. Marks not out	21	
L-b 6, w 1, n-b 1	8 L-b 5, n-b 11	16
1/12 2/57 3/59 4/63 5/116 6/176 (6 wkts dec.)	208 1/10 2/34 3/57 4/149 5/307 (5 wkts)	312

J. Garner, †T. Gard and C. H. Dredge did not bat.

Bonus points – Somerset 2, Warwickshire 2.

Bowling: *First Innings*—Willis 5–2–13–1; Small 6–0–21–0; Lethbridge 5–1–12–1; P. A. Smith 5–1–12–2; Sutcliffe 18.3–1–70–2; Asif Din 5–0–23–0; Lloyd 13–1–49–0. *Second Innings*—Willis 8–0–35–1; Small 7–0–34–1; Sutcliffe 23–5–124–1; Lethbridge 1–0–14–0; Humpage 5–0–17–1; Asif Din 5–1–19–0; P. A. Smith 3–0–49–1; Amiss 0.1–0–4–0.

Umpires: D. O. Oslear and N. T. Plews.

SOMERSET v WORCESTERSHIRE

At Taunton, September 8, 9. Somerset won by an innings and 18 runs. Somerset 24 pts, Worcestershire 4 pts. Match figures of nine for 74 by Garner and eight for 79 by Botham in a match lasting only 137.4 overs told the tale of a green, lively pitch in cloudy conditions. Worcestershire were put in and Garner, running out Weston then completing Somerset's first hat-trick since 1958, accounted for four wickets with the first four balls of the fifth over of the match. Younis sustained a broken finger from the only ball he faced, which then hit his wicket, and he took no further part in the match. Curtis, with a courageous, skilled innings lasting 26 overs, gained some support from the tail in the first innings, and later

Neale, in twenty overs, plus a belligerent fourteen overs by Humphries (one 6 and ten 4s) gave substance to the second. After severe early difficulties, Somerset's decisive response was led by Richards – "caught" first ball off a Warner no-ball, he hit a 6 and twelve 4s – and underlined by Botham, who struck five 6s and twelve 4s while receiving only 51 deliveries.

Worcestershire

J. A. Ormrod b Garner	1	– b Garner	6
M. J. Weston run out	6	– lbw b Dredge	18
D. N. Patel c Garner b Botham	4	– b Garner	1
Younis Ahmed hit wkt b Garner	0	– absent injured	
*P. A. Neale c Lloyds b Garner	0	– (4) c Richards b Botham	23
T. S. Curtis c Roebuck b Botham	47	– (5) lbw b Garner	11
†D. J. Humphries c Botham b Garner	2	– (6) c Slocombe b Botham	60
R. K. Illingworth c Marks b Garner	17	– (7) lbw b Botham	17
A. E. Warner c Dredge b Garner	0	– (8) b Botham	16
H. L. Alleyne b Botham	32	– (9) not out	8
S. P. Perryman not out	10	– (10) b Botham	4
W 1	1	B 1, l-b 2, w 1, n-b 1	5
1/7 2/7 3/7 4/7 5/21 6/24 7/60 8/60 9/95	120	1/26 2/26 3/29 4/46 5/100 6/129 7/146 8/165 9/169	169

Bonus points – Somerset 4.

Bowling: *First Innings*—Garner 15–4–42–6; Botham 10.1–2–29–3; Dredge 9–0–48–0. *Second Innings*—Garner 18–9–32–3; Dredge 21–5–82–1; Botham 7.4–1–50–5.

Somerset

J. W. Lloyds c Humphries b Warner	13
P. M. Roebuck c Humphries b Warner	22
I. V. A. Richards c Humphries b Alleyne	77
N. A. Felton c Ormrod b Perryman	11
P. A. Slocombe c Humphries b Alleyne	33
I. T. Botham b Perryman	98
*B. C. Rose c Patel b Perryman	15
V. J. Marks b Perryman	5
†T. Gard not out	0
C. H. Dredge c Humphries b Perryman	2
L-b 20, w 1, n-b 10	31
1/28 2/79 3/136 4/146 5/269 6/297 7/304 8/305 9/307 (9 wkts dec.)	307

J. Garner did not bat.

Bonus points – Somerset 4, Worcestershire 4.

Bowling: Alleyne 21–2–69–2; Warner 13–3–85–2; Perryman 19.5–5–74–5; Patel 3–0–48–0.

Umpires: C. Cook and A. Jepson.

SOMERSET v LANCASHIRE

At Taunton, September 11, 13, 14. Lancashire won by 14 runs. Lancashire 21 pts, Somerset 8 pts. Put in, Lancashire were rescued from Botham's opening burst by Clive Lloyd and O'Shaughnessy, who batted 33 overs for his half-century. Somerset owed everything to Richards, whose masterly innings occupied 77 overs, contained two 6s and eighteen 4s and was well supported by Slocombe in a stand of 176. Lancashire's spinners swiftly despatched the tail, but then their batsmen slumped to 66 for four. O'Shaughnessy, with eleven 4s in his highest score, Abrahams, and Clive Lloyd, with two 6s and ten 4s, effected a recovery, but it was curious that Garner did not bowl on the last day, while Botham bowled only four overs. Somerset needed 134 in 200 minutes but collapsed initially against the seamers and, despite the efforts of Slocombe, Botham and Marks, slumped to 80 for eight against the spinners. Dredge and Taylor batted doggedly and only eight overs remained when David Lloyd took the final wicket to end a remarkable day which had begun with Lancashire 56 runs behind with only six wickets left.

Lancashire

D. Lloyd lbw b Botham	3	– st Taylor b Marks	2
G. Fowler run out	19	– b Marks	12
I. Cockbain c Richards b Botham	7	– c Slocombe b Garner	4
J. Abrahams c Richards b Botham	6	– (5) b Marks	26
*C. H. Lloyd lbw b Moseley	32	– (7) b Marks	79
D. P. Hughes c Lloyds b Botham	5	– (4) b Lloyds	33
S. J. O'Shaughnessy lbw b Garner	55	– (6) b Marks	62
R. G. Watson run out	11	– c Taylor b Marks	4
†C. Maynard c Taylor b Dredge	10	– c Slocombe b Botham	20
I. Folley c Felton b Dredge	5	– not out	2
P. J. W. Allott not out	4	– b Botham	12
L-b 3, w 1, n-b 4	8	B 5, l-b 11, w 2, n-b 1	19
1/11 2/29 3/39 4/40 5/49 6/94 7/138 8/146 9/160	165	1/14 2/21 3/39 4/66 5/129 6/180 7/198 8/261 9/261	275

Bonus points – Lancashire 1, Somerset 4.

Bowling: *First Innings*—Garner 20–4–62–1; Botham 14–3–44–4; Dredge 11.5–3–29–2; Moseley 7–2–22–1; Marks 1–1–0–0. *Second Innings*—Garner 14–8–13–1; Botham 6.5–2–20–2; Marks 44–14–128–6; Lloyds 13–6–36–1; Moseley 8–3–33–0; Dredge 10–2–26–0.

Somerset

P. M. Roebuck c Maynard b Folley	6	– c Maynard b Allott	0
J. W. Lloyds lbw b Allott	2	– c Maynard b Allott	2
I. V. A. Richards b Hughes	178	– (6) b D. Lloyd	5
N. A. Felton b O'Shaughnessy	17	– (3) lbw b O'Shaughnessy	3
P. A. Slocombe c Maynard b O'Shaughnessy	56	– (4) run out	20
*I. T. Botham st Maynard b Hughes	5	– (5) c Maynard b Hughes	30
V. J. Marks c Cockbain b O'Shaughnessy	13	– c Hughes b D. Lloyd	16
†D. J. S. Taylor c Maynard b O'Shaughnessy	8	– c Maynard b D. Lloyd	11
J. Garner c and b Hughes	6	– b D. Lloyd	0
C. H. Dredge c C. H. Lloyd b Hughes	1	– c Maynard b Allott	18
H. R. Moseley not out	2	– not out	5
B 5, l-b 1, n-b 7	13	L-b 7, n-b 2	9
1/3 2/42 3/90 4/266 5/272 6/277 7/295 8/302 9/303	307	1/2 2/3 3/15 4/43 5/54 6/78 7/80 8/80 9/103	119

Bonus points – Somerset 4, Lancashire 4.

Bowling: *First Innings*—Allott 14–5–30–1; Folley 17–4–50–1; O'Shaughnessy 21.1–3–72–4; Abrahams 19–2–61–0; D. Lloyd 15–0–59–0; Hughes 10–2–22–4. *Second Innings*—Allott 15–2–29–3; Folley 3–0–5–0; O'Shaughnessy 5–2–16–1; D. Lloyd 15.4–1–36–4; Hughes 11–4–18–1; Abrahams 2–0–6–0.

Umpires: J. Birkenshaw and C. T. Spencer.

POT-HOLES

Customs men confiscated a consignment of cricket bats which arrived at Heathrow Airport from India in August 1982 and were found to have been hollowed out and filled with cannabis. Charges were subsequently brought.

SURREY

Patron: HM The Queen
President: Brigadier G. A. Rimbault, CBE, DSO, MC, DL
Chairman: D. H. Newton
Chairman, Cricket Committee: J. C. Laker
Secretary: I. F. B. Scott-Browne
Kennington Oval, London SE11 5SS
(Telephone: 01-582 6660)
Cricket Manager: M. J. Stewart
Captain: R. D. V. Knight
Coach: D. Gibson

Surrey finished the 1982 season with something in their hands at last. After three abortive visits in three years to Lord's, for the 1979 and 1981 finals of the Benson and Hedges Cup and the 1980 Gillette Cup final, they walked away with the NatWest Bank Trophy. Moreover, they earned it in style, dismissing Warwickshire for 158 and scoring 159 for the loss of only one wicket.

Rounding off the season so successfully created justifiable optimism at a time of gradual change. Monte Lynch, David Smith and Jack Richards are firmly established; Dave Thomas, Andy Needham, Graham Monkhouse and Kevin Mackintosh are following along the right lines – and they are all in their early or middle twenties. Graham Roope, after the best part of twenty years of excellent service, had had to make way for the younger school and was looking for another county.

There was an annoying inconsistency in the Surrey batting at the start of the season, and with Intikhab's leg-spin gone for good and Pat Pocock, with his off-breaks, absent almost throughout because of a nasty back condition, the spin bowling needed to follow up an effective pace attack was inadequate. Opponents who should have been winkled out in their second innings, when pitches had begun to wear, were allowed to slip through the net. As a result, although Surrey occupied fourth place in the Championship table for much of the season, and at the end of July were briefly second, in the end they had to settle for fifth position.

Needham went some of the way to making up for Pocock's absence, but his tally of 22 wickets from thirteen three-day matches was disappointing. He had his big day on returning to the first team early in July, scoring his maiden century and taking a career-best five for 91 against Lancashire at Old Trafford. Unfortunately, in celebrating he rather overstepped the mark and was dropped from the next match by the manager, Micky Stewart.

Pocock was by no means the only player to fall foul of injury. Grahame Clinton suffered in almost every part of the body – thumb, back and shoulder in turn; Smith had a longish lay-off with a neck complaint and then fractured a thumb; and Alan Butcher had to overcome a wrist injury before ending the season full of runs – as he had in 1981.

Geoff Howarth, deputising as one of the opening batsmen for Clinton, helped give the innings many worthwhile beginnings. He and Butcher both hit four centuries in first-class matches. Butcher, Richards and also Thomas could consider themselves unlucky to miss selection in the England team for the Australian tour. Butcher had been no less uncertain than his colleagues at the start of the summer, when the pitches at The Oval provided inconsistent bounce; but in the end he hit most runs, 1,514, in all first-class games and played six innings over 50 in one-day matches, including 86 not out in the NatWest final.

Of the seventeen Championship centuries scored by Surrey players, only five were recorded at The Oval. Howarth and Lynch managed one apiece at Guildford and Butcher and Smith did likewise at Worcester, where a total of 536 for seven declared was the highest of the season in the competition.

Sylvester Clarke and Robin Jackman again proved as good an opening pair of bowlers as any in the country, taking 85 and 73 wickets respectively in three-day cricket and 25 and 22 in one-day games. Jackman, in his late thirties, was spared the Sunday frolics but did better than anybody in the knockout tournaments. His six for 22 against Hampshire in the NatWest was an outstanding performance. This was followed by selection for his first home Test appearance and subsequently a place in the side for Australia.

Clarke, as hostile as ever, steered clear of serious injury for the first time since joining Surrey, and along with Lynch and Roger Knight, who again captained the team with distinction, he played in every Championship match. After doubts had been expressed about Clarke's action, the Test and County Cricket Board filmed it while Surrey were playing at Derby at the beginning of August and deemed it fair.

Hugh Wilson, like Roope, was not retained. Surrey hoped that in releasing him at the early age of 24 he would have plenty of time to continue his career with another county and rediscover the form which made him an England prospect three years earlier. Roope's departure saddened many. Few over the last two decades had latched on to so many sparkling catches close to the wicket, and although he could not make the Test field regularly, the winning of 21 caps between 1972 and 1978 reflected his all-round ability. – H.E.A.

SURREY 1982

[*Bill Smith*

Back row: D. B. Pauline, I. R. Payne, K. S. Mackintosh, N. J. Falkner, G. S. Clinton, M. A. Lynch. *Middle row:* J. Hill (*scorer*), R. G. L. Cheatle, G. Monkhouse, D. M. Smith, P. H. L. Wilson, D. J. Thomas, A. Needham, A. J. Stewart, D. Gibson (*coach*). *Front row:* S. T. Clarke, G. R. J. Roope, P. I. Pocock, R. D. V. Knight (*captain*), M. J. Stewart (*manager*), A. R. Butcher, R. D. Jackman, G. P. Howarth, C. J. Richards.

SURREY RESULTS

All first-class matches – Played 24: Won 6, Lost 6, Drawn 12.

County Championship matches – Played 22: Won 6, Lost 6, Drawn 10.

Bonus points – Batting 56, Bowling 62.

Competition placings – Schweppes County Championship, 5th; NatWest Bank Trophy, winners; Benson and Hedges Cup, 4th in Group C; John Player League, 12th eq.

COUNTY CHAMPIONSHIP AVERAGES

BATTING

	Birthplace	*M*	*I*	*NO*	*R*	*HI*	*Avge*
D. M. Smith c	*Balham*	13	23	4	1,000	160	52.63
A. R. Butcher c	*Croydon*	20	37	5	1,293	187*	40.40
G. P. Howarth c	*Auckland, NZ*	18	31	3	1,125	156*	40.17
R. D. Jackman c	*Simla, India*	17	18	8	350	68	35.00
M. A. Lynch c	*Georgetown, BG*	22	36	2	1,141	141*	33.55
K. S. Mackintosh	*Surbiton*	10	9	6	93	31	31.00
G. Monkhouse	*Carlisle*	7	8	4	122	63*	30.50
G. R. J. Roope c	*Fareham*	13	23	6	480	108	28.23
D. J. Thomas c	*Solihull*	16	18	3	403	64	26.86
R. D. V. Knight c	*Streatham*	22	36	3	873	99	26.45
C. J. Richards c	*Penzance*	21	33	9	597	117*	24.87
G. S. Clinton c	*Sidcup*	13	22	3	450	102	23.68
A. Needham	*Calow*	11	16	3	282	134*	21.69
S. T. Clarke c	*Christ Church, Barbados*	22	25	0	408	52	16.32
D. B. Pauline	*Aberdeen*	2	4	0	51	26	12.75
P. H. L. Wilson	*Guildford*	3	4	2	20	13	10.00
P. I. Pocock c	*Bangor*	7	8	2	32	10*	5.33

Also batted: R. G. L. Cheatle (*London*) (4 matches) 27*, 1*; A. J. Stewart (*Merton*) (1 match) 9, 16.

* *Signifies not out.* c *Denotes county cap.*

BOWLING

	O	*M*	*R*	*W*	*Avge*	*BB*
S. T. Clarke	659.3	162	1,696	85	19.95	6-63
R. D. Jackman	541.2	159	1,429	61	23.42	6-28
K. S. Mackintosh	236.2	44	808	28	28.85	6-61
P. I. Pocock	233	64	632	21	30.09	5-73
D. J. Thomas	388.4	100	1,154	32	36.06	4-39
A. Needham	309.3	56	1,032	21	49.14	5-91
R. D. V. Knight	254.2	57	743	15	49.53	3-34

Also bowled: A. R. Butcher 83–12–367–4; R. G. L. Cheatle 49–9–183–3; M. A. Lynch 51.5–8–208–4; G. Monkhouse 95.3–14–297–9; D. B. Pauline 1–0–3–0; C. J. Richards 4–0–14–0; G. R. J. Roope 32–14–81–3; P. H. L. Wilson 73.4–18–209–4.

HUNDREDS

The following seventeen three-figure innings were played for Surrey in County Championship matches – G. P. Howarth (4) 121 v Derbyshire (Derby), 156* v Glamorgan (Guildford), 112 v Middlesex (Lord's), 126* v Yorkshire (The Oval); A. R. Butcher (3) 151* v Leicestershire (Leicester), 187* v Warwickshire (Birmingham), 162 v Worcestershire (Worcester); M. A. Lynch (3) 118 v Nottinghamshire (The Oval), 141* v Glamorgan (Guildford), 102 v Sussex (The Oval); D. M. Smith (3) 105* v Warwickshire (Birmingham), 160 v Worcestershire (Worcester), 100* v Yorkshire (The Oval); G. S. Clinton (1) 102 v Leicestershire (Leicester); A. Needham (1) 134* v Lancashire (Manchester); C. J. Richards (1) 117* v Nottinghamshire (The Oval); G. R. J. Roope (1) 108 v Northamptonshire (Northampton).

SURREY v KENT

At The Oval, May 5, 6, 7. Surrey won by 18 runs. Surrey 19 pts, Kent 4 pts. Both counties started the season in the right spirit with sporting declarations aimed at making up for a blank second day; and both had a chance of victory. With a target of 248 in 210 minutes, Kent were set on their way with an opening stand of 79 between Woolmer, who contributed 62, and Taylor and looked likely winners at 203 for five. But the innings was all over 26 runs later and Surrey were home with two overs and two balls to spare. The ever-menacing fast bowling of Clarke had done the trick, his pace and bounce bringing four for 6 in the spell. On the first day, Kent had put Surrey in on a greenish wicket, only to find Clarke in their way, this time as a batsman. He reached 50 off 29 balls and with Richards put on 74 in 38 minutes so that Surrey saw out a showery first day with a total higher than seemed likely. England-hopeful Dilley did his best to make an early impression with six for 96, though Clarke hit him for three 6s and took two more off Jarvis.

Surrey

A. R. Butcher c Johnson b Dilley	0	– not out	59
G. S. Clinton c Woolmer b Dilley	2	– not out	27
*R. D. V. Knight c Tavaré b Cowdrey	13		
G. P. Howarth b Jarvis	46		
M. A. Lynch c Knott b Cowdrey	0		
G. R. J. Roope c Knott b Dilley	7		
†C. J. Richards not out	52		
R. D. Jackman b Jarvis	2		
S. T. Clarke c Cowdrey b Dilley	52		
P. I. Pocock b Dilley	6		
P. H. L. Wilson b Dilley	13		
B 1, l-b 7, w 1, n-b 3	12	L-b 3, n-b 1	4
1/2 2/5 3/43 4/43 5/68 6/77 7/80 8/154 9/173	205	(no wkt dec.)	90

Bonus points – Surrey 2, Kent 4.

Bowling: *First Innings*—Jarvis 24–5–77–2; Dilley 22.2–1–96–6; Cowdrey 8–4–6–2; Woolmer 4–1–14–0. *Second Innings*—Jarvis 8–0–47–0; Dilley 9–1–35–0; Cowdrey 1–0–4–0.

Kent

R. A. Woolmer lbw b Jackman	0	– c Roope b Pocock	62
N. R. Taylor lbw b Jackman	2	– b Wilson	82
C. J. Tavaré c Butcher b Knight	28	– b Knight	10
M. R. Benson not out	15	– c Richards b Clarke	20
*Asif Iqbal not out	0	– b Clarke	12
C. S. Cowdrey (did not bat)		– b Clarke	10
†A. P. E. Knott (did not bat)		– run out	3
G. W. Johnson (did not bat)		– b Clarke	6
G. R. Dilley (did not bat)		– not out	13
D. L. Underwood (did not bat)		– c Richards b Clarke	0
K. B. S. Jarvis (did not bat)		– c Richards b Wilson	1
B 1, l-b 1, n-b 1	3	B 2, l-b 4, w 3, n-b 1	10
1/3 2/6 3/48 (3 wkts dec.)	48	1/79 2/110 3/175 4/189 5/203 6/207 7/213 8/228 9/228	229

Bonus points – Surrey 1.

Bowling: *First Innings*—Clarke 5–2–7–0; Jackman 7–3–24–2; Knight 3–1–14–1. *Second Innings*—Clarke 17–2–52–5; Jackman 12–3–55–0; Knight 7–1–31–1; Wilson 13.4–2–63–2; Pocock 3–0–18–1.

Umpires: H. D. Bird and N. T. Plews.

At Leicester, May 12, 13, 14. SURREY lost to LEICESTERSHIRE by five wickets.

†At Manchester, May 15 (not first-class). SURREY lost to LANCASHIRE by nine wickets.

At Northampton, May 19, 20, 21. SURREY beat NORTHAMPTONSHIRE by 95 runs.

At Chelmsford, May 29, 31, June 1. SURREY lost to ESSEX by 209 runs.

SURREY v HAMPSHIRE

At The Oval, June 5, 7, 8. Hampshire won by 3 runs. Hampshire 20 pts, Surrey 6 pts. Hampshire finished a match of much-changing fortunes with their first Championship victory of the summer, gained two hours into the third day. Not far from the pitch on which England and India had managed runs fairly comfortably the day before this game, batsmen on both sides found the job hazardous. Some 24 minutes were lost during the three days while injuries were treated on the field. First Clarke and Jackman had the batsmen ducking and weaving after Hampshire had been put in; then Marshall and Emery had their turn. Saturday ended with nineteen wickets down for 304 runs and Surrey 8 runs ahead with their last pair, Jackman and Monkhouse, together. However, they continued boisterously on the Monday, stretching the lead to 66 with a partnership of 76 before the ball took over once more. Surrey, in their second innings, lost five wickets for 13 runs – four to Marshall for 6 – chasing 105 to win, and although they recovered sufficiently to challenge, with their tenth-wicket stand again the best of the innings, Hampshire had the final say. Marshall's second-innings return of seven for 38 was a personal best, and in the circumstances, innings of 84 by Greenidge and 67 by Lynch were of outstanding quality.

Hampshire

C. G. Greenidge c Richards b Clarke	8	– c Howarth b Thomas	84
J. M. Rice c Roope b Clarke	23	– c Richards b Clarke	0
M. C. J. Nicholas c Clarke b Monkhouse	17	– b Thomas	14
T. E. Jesty c Lynch b Clarke	55	– lbw b Jackman	0
*N. E. J. Pocock c Lynch b Thomas	5	– (9) b Clarke	2
N. G. Cowley c Richards b Jackman	0	– b Jackman	1
M. D. Marshall c Richards b Jackman	25	– (5) c Clinton b Thomas	24
T. M. Tremlett c Richards b Clarke	0	– (7) run out	3
†R. J. Parks not out	7	– (8) c Howarth b Clarke	5
K. St J. D. Emery c Richards b Jackman	1	– not out	5
S. J. Malone b Jackman	2	– b Thomas	4
L-b 5	5	B 8, l-b 7, w 2, n-b 11	28
1/16 2/45 3/61 4/79 5/80 6/122 7/122 8/142 9/144	148	1/5 2/42 3/46 4/118 5/119 6/131 7/157 8/159 9/162	170

Bonus points – Surrey 4.

Bowling: *First Innings*—Clarke 16–3–44–4; Jackman 14.3–0–52–4; Monkhouse 5–0–23–1; Thomas 8–3–24–1. *Second Innings*—Clarke 20–7–33–3; Jackman 18–3–52–2; Thomas 17–5–39–4; Knight 6–1–18–0.

Surrey

A. R. Butcher c Parks b Emery	3	– c Tremlett b Marshall	5
G. S. Clinton lbw b Marshall	5	– c Parks b Marshall	4
*R. D. V. Knight c Cowley b Marshall	0	– lbw b Marshall	0
G. P. Howarth lbw b Marshall	19	– lbw b Marshall	0
M. A. Lynch c Greenidge b Malone	67	– c Parks b Emery	0
G. R. J. Roope lbw b Emery	1	– c Parks b Marshall	9
†C. J. Richards c Tremlett b Emery	1	– lbw b Emery	13
D. J. Thomas c Cowley b Tremlett	17	– c Pocock b Marshall	37
S. T. Clarke b Tremlett	6	– c Pocock b Marshall	7
G. Monkhouse b Tremlett	14	– (11) not out	8
R. D. Jackman not out	49	– (10) b Emery	6
B 4, l-b 11, w 1, n-b 16	32	B 2, l-b 6, n-b 4	12
1/7 2/7 3/22 4/78 5/81 6/93 7/127 8/127 9/138	214	1/8 2/10 3/10 4/11 5/13 6/37 7/37 8/55 9/68	101

Bonus points – Surrey 2, Hampshire 4.

Bowling: *First Innings*—Marshall 20–7–38–3; Emery 19–4–72–3; Malone 8–2–28–1; Jesty 1–0–8–0; Tremlett 10.1–1–36–3. *Second Innings*—Marshall 20.1–6–38–7; Emery 17–4–41–3; Malone 3–0–10–0.

Umpires: D. G. L. Evans and A. G. T. Whitehead.

At Oxford, June 9, 10, 11. SURREY drew with OXFORD UNIVERSITY.

SURREY v GLOUCESTERSHIRE

At The Oval, June 12, 14, 15. Surrey won by five wickets. Surrey 20 pts, Gloucestershire 4 pts. Both captains did their best to make up for the loss of all but 70 minutes of the first day, though the final gesture by Graveney seemed over-generous. Having seen Roope hit a sparkling 53 (one 6, eight 4s) in even time on the second day and watched his own Zaheer account for all 32 runs taken off the first three overs of the third afternoon, he still left Surrey 2 hours, 23 minutes plus twenty overs in which to score 253 to win. Moreover,

Graveney's bowling resources were not all that strong, as became obvious as Surrey paced their effort with some ease. Butcher and Clinton laid the foundation with a partnership of 82, and Butcher then helped Knight in a stand of 76 in fifteen overs. Hignell gave a reminder of his rugby prowess when he ran round the square-leg boundary and, with a full-length dive, took a catch to end Butcher's gallop.

Gloucestershire

A. W. Stovold b Jackman	12	– c Lynch b Jackman	24
B. C. Broad lbw b Clarke	40	– c Clarke b Jackman	23
Sadiq Mohammad c Richards b Clarke	10	– c Lynch b Monkhouse	5
Zaheer Abbas c Richards b Clarke	39	– c Clinton b Butcher	58
P. Bainbridge c Richards b Jackman	57	– not out	44
A. J. Hignell b Jackman	29	– not out	4
J. N. Shepherd c Howarth b Thomas	14		
*D. A. Graveney b Thomas	21		
R. J. Doughty not out	2		
B 6, l-b 3, w 2, n-b 4	15	L-b 3, n-b 2	5
1/15 2/40 3/104 4/111 5/195 6/198 7/234 8/239 (8 wkts dec.)	239	1/49 2/50 3/70 4/133 (4 wkts dec.)	163

†A. J. Brassington and D. Surridge did not bat.

Bonus points – Gloucestershire 2, Surrey 3.

Bowling: *First Innings*—Clarke 31–7–76–3; Jackman 33–15–58–3; Thomas 16.4–3–51–2; Knight 6–2–16–0; Monkhouse 3–1–5–0; Butcher 3–1–18–0. *Second Innings*—Clarke 14–3–33–0; Jackman 14–4–25–2; Thomas 8–3–14–0; Monkhouse 7–2–19–1; Lynch 5–0–36–0; Butcher 5–0–31–1.

Surrey

A. R. Butcher b Shepherd	33	– c Hignell b Bainbridge	79
G. S. Clinton c Brassington b Doughty	14	– c Brassington b Shepherd	39
*R. D. V. Knight c and b Doughty	19	– b Shepherd	54
G. P. Howarth c Stovold b Doughty	7	– lbw b Shepherd	12
M. A. Lynch c Brassington b Shepherd	5	– c Doughty b Shepherd	30
G. R. J. Roope not out	53	– not out	16
†C. J. Richards not out	11	– not out	4
L-b 5, n-b 3	8	B 1, l-b 14, w 4	19
1/49 2/49 3/70 4/79 5/102 (5 wkts dec.)	150	1/82 2/158 3/186 4/217 5/232 (5 wkts)	253

S. T. Clarke, D. J. Thomas, R. D. Jackman and G. Monkhouse did not bat.

Bonus points – Surrey 1, Gloucestershire 2.

Bowling: *First Innings*—Surridge 4–0–27–0; Shepherd 16–2–67–2; Doughty 12.4–3–48–3. *Second Innings*—Doughty 10–0–49–0; Shepherd 24–1–81–4; Surridge 5–0–24–0; Bainbridge 17.4–2–80–1.

Umpires: D. J. Constant and P. J. Eele.

At Hove, June 19, 21, 22. SURREY drew with SUSSEX.

SURREY v LANCASHIRE

At The Oval, June 23, 24, 25. Drawn. Surrey 2 pts, Lancashire 2 pts. In between the rain that washed out the first and last days, Surrey, put in, had the better of things, scoring 128 for five off 35 overs whereas Lancashire spent 30 overs struggling to 78 for five. Surrey's innings featured an unlucky dismissal for Butcher, whose helmet was knocked off on to his wicket, and bright batting by Lynch, who hit off-spinner Simmons for three 6s in four balls. Clive Lloyd took 40 minutes over 8 runs, which emphasised Lancashire's difficulties in facing Surrey's livelier attack.

Surrey

A. R. Butcher hit wkt b Croft......... 0	G. R. J. Roope not out........................ 20
G. S. Clinton c Reidy b Simmons.... 40	†C. J. Richards not out........................ 14
*R. D. V. Knight lbw b Croft......... 0	B 2, w 1, n-b 1........................... 4
G. P. Howarth c Reidy b Folley...... 14	
M. A. Lynch c Lloyd b Folley......... 36	1/2 2/2 3/45 4/91 5/95 (5 wkts dec.) 128

D. J. Thomas, S. T. Clarke, R. D. Jackman and R. G. L. Cheatle did not bat.

Bonus points – Lancashire 2.

Bowling: Croft 8–4–23–2; McFarlane 5–2–11–0; Folley 12–3–35–2; Reidy 3–0–19–0; Simmons 7–1–36–1.

Lancashire

A. Kennedy c Lynch b Thomas....... 31	B. W. Reidy b Clarke.......................... 5
G. Fowler c Richards b Jackman..... 2	J. Simmons not out.............................. 6
†C. Maynard c Butcher b Thomas.... 18	L-b 1.. 1
*C. H. Lloyd c Richards b Thomas.. 8	
D. P. Hughes not out..................... 7	1/14 2/33 3/58 4/62 5/67 (5 wkts) 78

J. Abrahams, I. Folley, C. E. H. Croft and L. L. McFarlane did not bat.

Bonus points – Surrey 2.

Bowling: Clarke 11–2–30–1; Jackman 10–6–9–1; Thomas 9–0–38–3.

Umpires: W. E. Alley and P. B. Wight.

SURREY v MIDDLESEX

At The Oval, June 26, 28, 29. Drawn. Surrey 3 pts, Middlesex 5 pts. Although Gatting surpassed his previous highest score and Williams and Daniel bowled with great fire, Middlesex, top of the table with five wins in eight games, found victory just beyond them as both sides tried to make up for the loss of much of the first day. After losing four wickets to Jackman in scoring 53, Middlesex reached a substantial first innings through a stand of 148 in 96 minutes between Gatting and Emburey. Gatting completed a chanceless century in three and a quarter hours and went on to 192 (three 6s and 25 4s) in just under five hours – in the process becoming the first of the season to 1,000 runs. Still, it needed three declarations to keep the game going, with Surrey's final target 250 at roughly five an over. They were never able to keep up with that, and after their heart had been broken by Daniel as the score went from 70 for two to 93 for eight with nineteen overs left, it needed courageous batting from Clinton, who had a damaged thumb, and Jackman to save the day. The two were still together when bad light and rain brought an end with two overs remaining. Daniel's six for 37 included a spell of three for 6 in thirteen balls.

Middlesex

*J. M. Brearley lbw b Jackman	6	– not out	40
W. N. Slack lbw b Jackman	14	– run out	2
C. T. Radley c Richards b Jackman	6	– b Thomas	0
M. W. Gatting c Thomas b Clarke	192	– c sub b Roope	16
R. O. Butcher lbw b Jackman	2	– not out	5
K. P. Tomlins c and b Cheatle	24		
J. E. Emburey c Clarke b Thomas	54		
†P. R. Downton c Richards b Knight	1		
M. W. W. Selvey run out	6		
N. F. Williams not out	14		
B 2, l-b 7, w 2	11		
1/6 2/19 3/44 4/53 5/139 6/287 7/288 8/296 9/330 (9 wkts dec.)	330	1/9 2/9 3/44 (3 wkts dec.)	63

W. W. Daniel did not bat.

Bonus points – Middlesex 4, Surrey 3 (Score at 100 overs: 327-8).

Bowling: *First Innings*—Clarke 24.4–7–69–1; Jackman 27–9–55–4; Thomas 17–2–82–1; Knight 21–2–52–1; Cheatle 12–3–61–1. *Second Innings*—Thomas 7–0–25–1; Roope 8–5–25–1; Lynch 2–0–13–0.

Surrey

A. R. Butcher c Gatting b Williams	23	– c Gatting b Williams	1
G. P. Howarth c Downton b Williams	18	– c Downton b Daniel	30
*R. D. V. Knight lbw b Williams	0	– c Tomlins b Daniel	13
M. A. Lynch c Butcher b Williams	30	– lbw b Gatting	15
G. R. J. Roope not out	30	– b Daniel	10
†C. J. Richards not out	34	– c Radley b Daniel	4
D. J. Thomas (did not bat)		– c Emburey b Daniel	0
G. S. Clinton (did not bat)		– not out	26
S. T. Clarke (did not bat)		– c and b Daniel	0
R. D. Jackman (did not bat)		– not out	12
L-b 1, w 2, n-b 6	9	B 9, l-b 6, w 1, n-b 10	26
1/40 2/41 3/65 4/80 (4 wkts dec.)	144	1/1 2/46 3/70 4/72 5/78 6/78 7/93 8/93 (8 wkts)	137

R. G. L. Cheatle did not bat.

Bonus points – Middlesex 1.

Bowling: *First Innings*—Daniel 9–1–53–0; Williams 9–0–40–4; Selvey 3–0–13–0; Emburey 6–0–19–0; Gatting 6–2–10–0. *Second Innings*—Selvey 7–1–27–0; Williams 7–2–19–1; Daniel 16–4–37–6; Gatting 9–3–18–1; Emburey 5–2–10-0.

Umpires: W. E. Alley and P. B. Wight.

At Maidstone, July 7, 8, 9. SURREY drew with KENT.

At Manchester, July 10, 12, 13. SURREY lost to LANCASHIRE by four wickets.

At Portsmouth, July 17, 19, 20. SURREY beat HAMPSHIRE by two wickets.

SURREY v SOMERSET

At The Oval, July 21, 22, 23. Somerset won by two wickets. Somerset 20 pts, Surrey 6 pts. Monkhouse, with his maiden half-century, and Mackintosh put on 88 in 99 minutes to rescue Surrey from 125 for eight to 213 for nine, an all-out total as Smith had suffered a fractured left thumb from a ball by Garner, who had already accounted for Butcher with his first ball of the match. However, when Somerset batted, only Richards, who reached 50 (nine 4s) in 54 minutes, played Clarke confidently and Surrey batted again 66 runs ahead. Again worried by Garner, this time in concert with Botham, they were able to set a victory target of 201, and at 153 for seven the task looked beyond Somerset. Then came a challenge from Marks and Dredge in a stand of 37, and the West Countrymen managed the victory they wanted to take to Lord's the following day for the final of the Benson and Hedges Cup. A pitch of uncertain bounce helped produce the low scores.

Surrey

A. R. Butcher c Taylor b Garner	0	– c Richards b Botham	2
G. P. Howarth b Dredge	34	– b Botham	7
D. M. Smith retired hurt	2	– absent injured	
*R. D. V. Knight c Popplewell b Moseley	5	– (3) c Garner b Botham	43
M. A. Lynch c Garner b Moseley	9	– (4) c Botham b Garner	10
G. R. J. Roope c sub b Marks	41	– (5) c Taylor b Garner	7
†C. J. Richards c and b Moseley	7	– (6) lbw b Garner	4
A. Needham lbw b Moseley	0	– (7) lbw b Botham	32
S. T. Clarke c sub b Moseley	11	– (9) c Taylor b Garner	6
G. Monkhouse not out	63	– (8) c Taylor b Garner	17
K. S. Mackintosh b Garner	31	– (10) not out	1
B 1, l-b 8, w 1	10	B 1, l-b 4	5
1/0 2/10 3/31 4/66 5/79 6/87 7/103 8/125 9/213	213	1/10 2/11 3/22 4/38 5/42 6/105 7/126 8/128 9/134	134

Bonus points – Surrey 2, Somerset 4.

Bowling: *First Innings*—Garner 25.2–6–61–2; Moseley 18–3–57–5; Dredge 21–5–37–1; Popplewell 3–1–3–0; Marks 8–1–24–1; Richards 1–0–4–0; Roebuck 6–1–17–0. *Second Innings*—Garner 20.2–9–28–5; Botham 17–7–34–4; Moseley 6–2–9–0; Marks 14–5–34–0; Lloyds 4–0–13–0; Dredge 5–1–11–0.

Somerset

J. W. Lloyds c Richards b Clarke	17	– c Roope b Clarke	0
P. M. Roebuck b Clarke	0	– c Richards b Knight	51
I. V. A. Richards c Howarth b Mackintosh	64	– c and b Clarke	9
*B. C. Rose b Monkhouse	20	– (8) c Richards b Knight	6
I. T. Botham b Monkhouse	3	– c Richards b Mackintosh	0
N. F. M. Popplewell c Monkhouse b Mackintosh	7	– (4) c Richards b Knight	48
V. J. Marks c Lynch b Clarke	9	– (6) c Butcher b Mackintosh	44
†D. J. S. Taylor b Clarke	10	– (7) c Roope b Mackintosh	0
C. H. Dredge b Clarke	5	– not out	34
J. Garner c Lynch b Knight	7	– not out	2
H. R. Moseley not out	0		
B 4, l-b 1	5	B 4, l-b 6	10
1/5 2/32 3/105 4/107 5/110 6/120 7/131 8/136 9/143	147	1/0 2/10 3/98 4/99 5/143 6/144 7/153 8/190	(8 wkts) 204

Bonus points – Surrey 4.

Bowling: *First Innings*—Clarke 17–2–42–5; Mackintosh 14–0–62–2; Monkhouse 7–0–23–2; Knight 4.2–1–15–1. *Second Innings*—Clarke 20.2–5–57–2; Mackintosh 23–5–58–3; Monkhouse 8–1–30–0; Needham 4–2–5–0; Knight 17–5–34–3; Roope 5–2–10–0.

Umpires: D. Archer and A. Jepson.

SURREY v NOTTINGHAMSHIRE

At The Oval, July 28, 29, 30. Surrey won by ten wickets. Surrey 24 pts, Nottinghamshire 5 pts. Surrey, having beaten Nottinghamshire in the John Player League the previous Sunday, inflicted a second defeat on the reigning champions. They began with a strange uncertainty after being put in but recovered to record their first total over 400 of the summer. Howarth and Knight put on 116 for the third wicket and Lynch and Richards 75 for the fourth. Lynch batted just over two hours, hitting two 6s and thirteen 4s, for Surrey's first three-figure innings at The Oval in 1982, and on the second day Richards completed his maiden hundred, batting 207 minutes and hitting one 6 and seventeen 4s. Nottinghamshire's innings was brought to life by an exciting century (seven 6s, twelve 4s) from Hadlee in 137 minutes. He simmered down Clarke, who had taken the first four wickets for 25 runs, but found little support and Nottinghamshire followed on 186 behind. Hadlee batted brightly again, and Rice sparkled with 62 in 117 minutes, but once more the support was minimal and Surrey needed to score only 2 runs in mid-afternoon on the third day for a victory which took them to second in the table.

Surrey

A. R. Butcher b Pont	24	– not out	4
G. S. Clinton lbw b Hadlee	6	– not out	0
G. P. Howarth b Pont	74		
*R. D. V. Knight b Such	54		
M. A. Lynch c Such b Illingworth	118		
†C. J. Richards not out	117		
G. Monkhouse b Hadlee	5		
A. Needham c Such b Cooper	5		
S. T. Clarke c Rice b Cooper	4		
R. D. Jackman c French b Cooper	4		
K. S. Mackintosh not out	17		
B 2, l-b 6, w 2, n-b 12	22		
1/17 2/43 3/159 4/234 5/330 6/338 7/361 8/365 9/377	(9 wkts dec.) 450		(no wkt) 4

Bonus points – Surrey 4, Nottinghamshire 2 (Score at 100 overs: 338-5).

Bowling: *First Innings*—Hadlee 35–8–79–2; Cooper 32–5–121–3; Illingworth 23–4–68–1; Pont 28.4–6–107–2; Such 17–5–53–1. *Second Innings*—Such 1–0–4–0.

Nottinghamshire

P. A. Todd b Clarke	9	– lbw b Jackman	27
B. Hassan b Clarke	1	– c Howarth b Monkhouse	26
M. A. Fell b Clarke	0	– b Jackman	8
*C. E. B. Rice c Richards b Mackintosh	31	– c Clarke b Mackintosh	62
J. D. Birch c Richards b Clarke	13	– lbw b Clarke	5
†B. N. French c Richards b Mackintosh	4	– c Richards b Mackintosh	6
R. J. Hadlee c Jackman b Needham	131	– c Mackintosh b Needham	37
I. L. Pont b Mackintosh	0	– not out	3
N. J. B. Illingworth not out	46	– b Clarke	0
K. E. Cooper c Howarth b Clarke	17	– c Jackman b Clarke	0
P. M. Such lbw b Clarke	0	– c Clinton b Needham	0
B 5, l-b 5, w 1, n-b 1	12	B 6, l-b 6, n-b 1	13
1/6 2/6 3/15 4/45 5/53 6/94 7/114 8/229 9/264	264	1/41 2/57 3/104 4/122 5/141 6/152 7/184 8/184 9/186	187

Bonus points – Nottinghamshire 3, Surrey 4.

Bowling: *First Innings*—Clarke 17.4–3–63–6; Jackman 18–5–52–0; Mackintosh 12–2–72–3; Monkhouse 7–0–19–0; Needham 11–2–46–1. *Second Innings*—Clarke 17–7–36–3; Jackman 11–1–58–2; Mackintosh 10–2–32–2; Monkhouse 6–2–11–1; Needham 15.4–6–37–2.

Umpires: W. L. Budd and R. S. Herman.

At Derby, July 31, August 2, 3. SURREY drew with DERBYSHIRE.

At The Oval, August 7, 8, 9. SURREY drew with PAKISTANIS (See Pakistani tour section).

At Birmingham, August 11, 12, 13. SURREY drew with WARWICKSHIRE.

SURREY v GLAMORGAN

At Guildford, August 14, 16, 17. Surrey won by two wickets. Surrey 22 pts, Glamorgan 6 pts. Batsmen enjoyed themselves on the small Guildford ground, 1,356 runs being hit during the match for the loss of 26 wickets on an easy-paced pitch. The final slaughter of the bowling came from Lynch, who plundered eight 6s and eight 4s in taking 141 runs off 112 balls – his highest score to date – as Surrey completed an exciting win. Only his captain and some of the locals were less than happy. Knight found the roof of his car dented by one of the 6s and several nearby houses lost some slates. Other three-figure innings on this batsman's paradise came from Hopkins (one 6, ten 4s) and Ontong (fifteen 4s) for Glamorgan and Howarth (one 6, 21 4s) for Surrey. And there was a landmark for Alan Jones, in his 25th season for Glamorgan. During one of the few short innings, of 11, he marked the completion of 1,000 runs against every first-class county. Surrey conceded first innings by 2 runs but emerged on top in the end as Butcher, with eight 4s in his 54 in 65 minutes, and then Lynch stormed towards the target of 319 in two and threequarter hours. Surrey required 68 off the last ten overs and then 26 off three, but Lynch eased matters with 16 off six balls from Barwick. The final over began with only 5 runs wanted and Monkhouse got those with a 4 and a single.

Glamorgan

A. Jones c Richards b Thomas	11	– b Clarke	3
A. L. Jones c Knight b Mackintosh	30	– c Mackintosh b Needham	36
D. A. Francis run out	52	– b Clarke	0
R. C. Ontong lbw b Mackintosh	88	– c Needham b Butcher	110
J. A. Hopkins c Richards b Mackintosh	19	– c Thomas b Needham	124
C. J. C. Rowe not out	51	– not out	19
J. G. Thomas b Clarke	84	– c Mackintosh b Needham	9
†E. W. Jones b Thomas	11	– not out	0
*B. J. Lloyd not out	3		
L-b 3, w 1, n-b 7	11	B 4, l-b 8, n-b 3	15
1/18 2/65 3/161 4/202 5/209 6/334 7/349 (7 wkts dec.)	360	1/10 2/10 3/58 4/259 5/298 6/311 (6 wkts dec.)	316

S. R. Barwick and W. W. Davis did not bat.

Bonus points – Glamorgan 4, Surrey 2 (Score at 100 overs: 333-5).

Bowling: *First Innings*—Clarke 23–5–47-1; Thomas 17–4–80–2; Monkhouse 17–2–48–0; Mackintosh 20–4–76–3; Knight 14–3–30–0; Needham 16–2–68–0. *Second Innings*—Clarke 16–4–30–2; Thomas 3–0–20–0; Mackintosh 5–0–14–0; Lynch 10–2–30–0; Needham 38.2–4–102–3; Butcher 29–5–105–1.

Surrey

A. R. Butcher c Ontong b Thomas	60	– c Hopkins b Rowe	54
G. P. Howarth not out	156	– c Thomas b Lloyd	26
D. M. Smith st E. W. Jones b Rowe	24	– (5) b Barwick	25
*R. D. V. Knight c Lloyd b Rowe	10	– (6) c Thomas b Ontong	4
M. A. Lynch c Barwick b Rowe	20	– (3) not out	141
†C. J. Richards lbw b Lloyd	0	– (8) c sub b Barwick	21
D. J. Thomas not out	58	– c Lloyd b Barwick	12
S. T. Clarke (did not bat)		– (4) b Lloyd	17
A. Needham (did not bat)		– c sub b Barwick	0
G. Monkhouse (did not bat)		– not out	11
L-b 13, w 2, n-b 15	30	B 1, l-b 4, n-b 6	11
1/84 2/138 3/172 4/210 5/213 (5 wkts dec.)	358	1/49 2/103 3/138 4/220 5/231 6/251 7/287 8/288 (8 wkts)	322

K. S. Mackintosh did not bat.

Bonus points – Surrey 4, Glamorgan 2.

Bowling: *First Innings*—Davis 16–4–59–0; Barwick 7–1–32–0; Thomas 5–0–30–1; Ontong 12–2–43–0; Rowe 18–4–95–3; Lloyd 21–4–69–1. *Second Innings*—Davis 5–0–24–0; Ontong 14–0–60–1; Rowe 12–0–83–1; Lloyd 13–0–81–2; Barwick 8.2–0–63–4.

Umpires: R. Palmer and B. J. Meyer.

At Worcester, August 21, 23, 24. SURREY drew with WORCESTERSHIRE.

At Lord's, August 25, 26, 27. SURREY lost to MIDDLESEX by 58 runs.

SURREY v ESSEX

At The Oval, August 28, 30, 31. Drawn. Surrey 7 pts, Essex 5 pts. The return of Pocock with his off-spin after a three-month lay-off because of back trouble gave the Surrey attack a more balanced look, but even so Essex, helped by a whirlwind 34 from Gooch to dampen Clarke's enthusiasm and a determined 75 in 175 minutes by Pont, compiled a useful 276 on the first day. Surrey looked to have things well in hand as Butcher and Howarth put on 171 for the first wicket in reply, but then Acfield dismissed Howarth, Butcher (thirteen 4s) and Knight for 2 runs in eighteen balls. With the difference a mere 28 and Essex unable to commence on the second evening because of the weather, the match fizzled out. Gooch recorded his second Championship century of the summer, hitting four 6s and ten 4s during a stay of just over four hours, but by the end wicket-keeper Richards was bowling in his pads, such was the state of the game.

Essex

G. A. Gooch c Pocock b Clarke	34	– c Howarth b Needham 140
B. R. Hardie c Butcher b Thomas	9	– c Richards b Mackintosh 8
R. J. Leiper c Howarth b Thomas	3	– c Butcher b Clarke 0
K. S. McEwan c and b Mackintosh	49	– c sub b Clarke 28
*K. W. R. Fletcher c Smith b Clarke	26	– not out 60
K. R. Pont c Richards b Mackintosh	75	– not out 31
N. Phillip c Lynch b Clarke	21	
S. Turner c Howarth b Knight	26	
†D. E. East c Butcher b Pocock	6	
J. K. Lever b Pocock	11	
D. L. Acfield not out	2	
B 4, l-b 5, w 4, n-b 1	14	B 8, l-b 4, n-b 2 14
1/43 2/47 3/57 4/124 5/134 6/156 7/214 8/233 9/272	276	1/20 2/25 3/103 4/207 (4 wkts dec.) 281

Bonus points – Essex 3, Surrey 4.

Bowling: *First Innings*—Clarke 20–2–75–3; Thomas 17–6–43–2; Mackintosh 20.4–1–68–2; Knight 14–6–22–1; Needham 2–0–11–0; Pocock 15–5–43–2. *Second Innings*—Clarke 18–4–41–2; Thomas 13–2–48–0; Mackintosh 7–2–22–1; Pocock 32–8–57–0; Knight 4–0–15–0; Needham 23–10–46–1; Butcher 7–2–24–0; Richards 4–0–14–0.

Surrey

A. R. Butcher c D. E. East b Acfield	90
G. P. Howarth b Acfield	76
D. M. Smith c Leiper b Pont	27
*R. D. V. Knight c D. E. East b Acfield	6
M. A. Lynch lbw b Pont	38
†C. J. Richards b Phillip	16
D. J. Thomas c Gooch b Acfield	7
A. Needham lbw b Phillip	15
S. T. Clarke c Leiper b Phillip	0
K. S. Mackintosh c McEwan b Lever	9
P. I. Pocock not out	7
B 2, l-b 7, n-b 4	13
1/171 2/172 3/178 4/241 5/250 6/265 7/280 8/280 9/290	304

Bonus points – Surrey 3, Essex 2 (Score at 100 overs: 267-6).

Bowling: Lever 18.3–5–50–1; Phillip 14–1–49–3; Turner 20–4–63–0; Acfield 37–7–76–4; Pont 11–1–23–2; Gooch 11–3–30–0.

Umpires: C. T. Spencer and Khizar Hayat.

SURREY v SUSSEX

At The Oval, September 1, 2, 3. Drawn. Surrey 6 pts, Sussex 5 pts. Lynch, with a century, and Jackman, with six for 13 in a 48-ball spell, enabled Surrey to hold the upper hand, but with the first day's cricket confined to half an hour by rain, and Sussex not starting their first innings until 4.10 on the second day, there was never much hope of a result. Sussex, finally left to get 274 in just over two and a half hours, disintegrated to 19 for four but, with Clarke absent all day because of a damaged knee, Barclay and le Roux were able to show that the wound was mostly self-inflicted. The splendid first-innings century from Lynch came after he had been dropped before scoring by Wells, who 132 minutes later caught him at deep mid-off. By then Lynch had 102 runs to his name, having hit three 6s and nine 4s.

Surrey

A. R. Butcher lbw b le Roux	8	– b Pigott	13
G. P. Howarth lbw b Pigott	28	– lbw b Greig	24
D. M. Smith c Greig b le Roux	53	– c A. P. Wells b Waller	44
*R. D. V. Knight b Pigott	6	– c and b Pigott	14
M. A. Lynch c C. M. Wells b Waller	102	– not out	23
†C. J. Richards c Green b le Roux	0	– not out	5
D. J. Thomas c Mendis b Pigott	28		
S. T. Clarke b Pigott	20		
R. D. Jackman c Greig b Pigott	1		
K. S. Mackintosh c Smith b Greig	22		
P. I. Pocock not out	10		
B 8, l-b 9, n-b 1	18	B 1, l-b 3	4
1/14 2/60 3/74 4/154 5/154 6/235 7/257 8/258 9/269	296	1/35 2/40 3/67 4/115 (4 wkts dec.)	127

Bonus points – Surrey 3, Sussex 4.

Bowling: *First Innings*—le Roux 18–2–75–3; Pigott 23–1–85–5; Greig 22.3–2–71–1; Waller 13–2–47–1. *Second Innings*—le Roux 4–0–18–0; Pigott 13–1–57–2; Greig 8–0–31–1; Waller 3–0–17–1.

Sussex

G. D. Mendis b Pocock	48	– lbw b Thomas	1
A. M. Green lbw b Jackman	56	– b Jackman	0
C. M. Wells b Pocock	6	– c Lynch b Pocock	14
P. W. G. Parker not out	19	– run out	0
A. P. Wells lbw b Jackman	1		
I. A. Greig b Jackman	0		
G. S. le Roux c Smith b Jackman	0	– (6) not out	30
*J. R. T. Barclay lbw b Jackman	3	– (5) not out	10
C. E. Waller b Jackman	0		
A. C. S. Pigott not out	0		
B 5, l-b 7, n-b 5	17	B 4, l-b 8, n-b 4	16
1/97 2/117 3/127 4/133 5/139 6/139 7/145 8/149 (8 wkts dec.)	150	1/1 2/4 3/5 4/19 (4 wkts)	71

†D. J. Smith did not bat.

Bonus points – Sussex 1, Surrey 3.

Bowling: *First Innings*—Clarke 7–3–17–0; Jackman 20–7–28–6; Mackintosh 5–2–9–0; Thomas 5–2–9–0; Knight 7–2–12–0; Pocock 20–2–58–2. *Second Innings*—Jackman 8–4–10–1; Thomas 11–6–14–1; Pocock 14–8–12–1; Mackintosh 3–1–14–0; Butcher 3–1–5–0.

Umpires: Khizar Hayat and C. T. Spencer.

SURREY v YORKSHIRE

At The Oval, September 11, 13, 14. Drawn. Surrey 4 pts, Yorkshire 3 pts. Surrey inserted Yorkshire in the belief that it was the more likely way to retain fourth place in the Championship and so earn £1,650, but the policy backfired when Yorkshire made a typically workmanlike 393 before declaring well into the second day. And although Knight did the only sensible thing, calling in his players 136 behind, Illingworth was again Yorkshire personified in setting a target of 346 in 220 minutes. Smith, with a fine 75 to add to his first-innings century, did his best to make the figure seem realistic, but well before the end Surrey were fighting to avoid defeat and Nottinghamshire relegated them to fifth place by winning at Hove. In Surrey's first innings, Smith (fourteen 4s) had been helped by Howarth (one 6, fifteen 4s) in a fine, unbroken stand of 232 in 148 minutes to cancel out a partnership of 192 between Athey and Love. Boycott's 27 and 37 left him 87 short of 2,000 runs for the season.

Yorkshire

G. Boycott c Richards b Thomas	27	– c Richards b Pocock	37
M. D. Moxon hit wkt b Jackman	40	– b Pocock	54
C. W. J. Athey not out	114	– c Lynch b Butcher	19
S. N. Hartley c Knight b Clarke	3	– b Lynch	28
K. Sharp lbw b Pocock	15	– b Lynch	52
J. D. Love c Richards b Thomas	123	– c Knight b Clarke	1
†D. L. Bairstow c Richards b Jackman	1	– c Richards b Clarke	1
A. Sidebottom c Smith b Mackintosh	12	– not out	7
G. B. Stevenson b Mackintosh	34		
S. J. Dennis not out	5		
B 2, l-b 10, w 1, n-b 6	19	B 4, l-b 3, n-b 3	10
1/70 2/70 3/84 4/116 5/308 6/313 7/336 8/382 (8 wkts dec.)	393	1/94 2/111 3/119 4/178 5/187 6/191 7/209 (7 wkts dec.)	209

*R. Illingworth did not bat.

Bonus points – Yorkshire 3, Surrey 1 (Score at 100 overs: 268-4).

Bowling: *First Innings*—Clarke 12–6–26–1; Jackman 32–9–92–2; Thomas 28–8–75–2; Mackintosh 22–5–76–2; Knight 10–5–21–0; Pocock 23–5–84–1. *Second Innings*—Thomas 12–2–27–0; Jackman 9–3–22–0; Pocock 20–3–70–2; Mackintosh 3–0–12–0; Lynch 6.5–2–23–2; Butcher 5–0–32–1; Clarke 6–2–13–2.

Surrey

A. R. Butcher c Boycott b Stevenson	14	– c Bairstow b Dennis	47
G. P. Howarth not out	126	– b Illingworth	43
D. M. Smith not out	100	– c Love b Dennis	75
M. A. Lynch (did not bat)		– run out	0
*R. D. V. Knight (did not bat)		– b Sidebottom	35
D. J. Thomas (did not bat)		– c Athey b Sidebottom	8
†C. J. Richards (did not bat)		– lbw b Sidebottom	3
S. T. Clarke (did not bat)		– b Sidebottom	3
R. D. Jackman (did not bat)		– not out	40
K. S. Mackintosh (did not bat)		– not out	11
L-b 7, w 1, n-b 9	17	B 2, l-b 7, w 7, n-b 13	29
1/25 (1 wkt dec.)	257	1/89 2/117 3/117 4/194 5/229 6/235 7/235 8/253 (8 wkts)	294

P. I. Pocock did not bat.

Bonus points – Surrey 3.

Bowling: *First Innings*—Dennis 15–1–73–0; Stevenson 9–0–32–1; Sidebottom 10–3–59–0; Illingworth 11–1–48–0; Hartley 6–0–28–0. *Second Innings*—Dennis 19–3–80–2; Stevenson 13–2–52–0; Sidebottom 18–2–66–4; Illingworth 16–0–67–1.

Umpires: K. Ibadulla and A. G. T. Whitehead.

SUSSEX

President: S. Cama
Chairman: Dr D. Rice
Chairman, Cricket & Ground Sub-committee: G. L. Everitt
Chief Executive: R. G. Stevens
County Ground, Eaton Road, Hove BN3 3AN
(Telephone: 0273-732161)
Captain: J. R. T. Barclay
Coach: S. J. Storey

At the start of the season there was justifiable confidence that Sussex were strong enough, with the right balance of youth and experience, to win one of the four competitions. As the County Championship had always eluded them, and following their spirited bid to foil Nottinghamshire the previous season, it was hoped that this would be the 1982 prize. After an encouraging start hopes soared, but later in the season inconsistency proved a fatal handicap, while Imran Khan's great all-round ability was badly missed when he took over the captaincy of Pakistan. Time after time the early batsmen failed, and only in the John Player League did Sussex produce really reliable form. In this competition they lost only one match, picking up 58 points, a record for the League, and finishing twelve points ahead of runners-up Middlesex.

In Imran's absence Garth le Roux, the giant South African, displayed impressive all-round form, his exploits with the bat being as vigorous as his fast bowling. In the John Player League, in particular, he became a firm favourite with Sussex supporters, who even formed an unofficial fan club, including a vociferous "male voice choir". With 83 against Surrey, le Roux went near to a first first-class century for Sussex. In addition to his batting, he took most wickets, 65; it was a splendid season for him.

Two of the younger players emerged with great credit from the campaign: Allan Green, a 22-year-old opening batsman from Pulborough, and Alan Wells, brother of Colin, a twenty-year-old all-rounder. Green proved a dependable partner for Gehan Mendis, looking to have a good temperament, possessing some handsome strokes, and having the ability to keep the score moving. At times he outpaced even the aggressive Mendis. Alan Wells played a number of hard-hitting knocks, and he, too, appeared to have the right temperament. Indeed the Wells brothers, from Newhaven, gave the club further encouragement to think that their youth policy is succeeding, and that the towns and villages of Sussex, where cricketing roots lie deep, can still produce their share of first-class players.

Once again John Barclay led the side as though thriving on the difficult and complex business of captaincy, setting a stirring example with his zest and enthusiasm. If there were occasional errors of judgement they were made in the worthwhile cause of enterprising cricket, and he received loyal support from his vice-captain, Paul Parker, another enthusiast of the game. Parker, however, did not strike the form which had earned him Test recognition in 1981, while Mendis, whose international aspirations had been equally high in April, was also disappointingly inconsistent. Ian Greig did catch the selectorial eye, making his Test début in July, but he, too, could not quite recapture his exciting form of the previous season. Tony Pigott, who had to shoulder quite a burden of pace bowling with Imran away and Geoff Arnold plagued with injury, stuck to his task manfully. To see his express-train approach and energetic delivery was to marvel at such a recovery from the serious back injury which had threatened to end his career. Ian Gould not only kept wicket efficiently; he also played many sparkling innings, especially as Mendis's opening partner in Sunday League matches.

Apart from the Eastbourne week and one or two Sunday games at Hove, support was again very disappointing, especially during a summer in which Sussex was one of the driest parts of the country. In the decisive Sunday League match against Middlesex the county ground was bursting at the seams, with around 7,000 spectators inside. Beer sales in the Sussex Cricketer bars during the luncheon interval totalled £1,000, and £2,500 by the end of a thirsty day. Except for the bad behaviour of one small section of the crowd this was reminiscent of the early 1960s when Sussex were such a successful one-day side.

A. Crole-Rees, formerly chairman of the club, became chairman of the Welfare Association, a post he had previously held. The Sussex Cricket Society produced an interesting 200th edition of its popular newsletter, and assisted in the establishment of a picnic area on the county ground. The season ended in such delightful weather that spectators and players seemed reluctant to disperse. – J.A.

SUSSEX 1982

[*Bill Smith*

Back row: L. V. Chandler (*scorer*), I. J. Gould, C. M. Wells, C. P. Phillipson, G. S. le Roux, A. P. Wells, I. A. Greig, S. J. Storey (*coach*). *Front row:* A. C. S. Pigott, Imran Khan, J. R. T. Barclay (*captain*), P. W. G. Parker, C. E. Waller, G. D. Mendis.

SUSSEX RESULTS

All first-class matches – Played 23: Won 6, Lost 8, Drawn 9.

County Championship matches – Played 22: Won 6, Lost 7, Drawn 9.

Bonus points – Batting 43, Bowling 68.

Competition placings – Schweppes County Championship, 8th; NatWest Bank Trophy, 1st round; Benson and Hedges Cup, s-f; John Player League, winners.

COUNTY CHAMPIONSHIP AVERAGES

BATTING

	Birthplace	*M*	*I*	*NO*	*R*	*HI*	*Avge*
A. P. Wells	*Newhaven*	4	7	3	212	70	53.00
Imran Khan c	*Lahore, Pakistan*	7	12	3	297	85	33.00
A. M. Green	*Pulborough*	13	24	1	743	99	32.30
C. M. Wells c	*Newhaven*	22	39	3	1,161	126	32.25
G. S. le Roux c	*Cape Town, SA*	20	28	5	737	83	32.04
G. D. Mendis c	*Colombo, Ceylon*	22	40	2	1,078	104	28.36
J. R. T. Barclay c	*Bonn, WG*	22	33	6	761	95	28.18
P. W. G. Parker c	*Bulawayo, Rhodesia*	22	39	7	845	106	26.40
I. J. Gould c	*Slough*	18	30	3	652	94	24.14
I. A. Greig c	*Queenstown, SA*	18	23	1	477	109	21.68
C. P. Phillipson c	*Brindaban, India*	15	20	3	254	64	14.94
C. E. Waller c	*Guildford*	22	25	11	172	50	12.28
A. C. S. Pigott c	*London*	22	21	6	165	40	11.00
G. G. Arnold c	*Earlsfield*	3	5	4	11	8*	11.00

Also batted: R. S. Cowan (*Hamlin, WG*) (1 match) 0, 18*; J. R. P. Heath (*Turner's Hill*) (2 matches) 17, 3, 19; A. N. Jones (*Woking*) (3 matches) 29, 5, 5; D. J. Smith (*Brighton*) (5 matches) 1, 0, 0; A. Willows (*Portslade*) (1 match) 0*, 4.

* *Signifies not out.* c *Denotes county cap.*

BOWLING

	O	*M*	*R*	*W*	*Avge*	*BB*
Imran Khan	194.1	58	458	29	15.79	4-26
G. S. le Roux	467	116	1,210	65	18.61	5-15
I. A. Greig	535.5	122	1,578	63	25.04	5-46
A. C. S. Pigott	454	88	1,597	61	26.18	7-74
C. E. Waller	571	165	1,527	55	27.76	7-67
J. R. T. Barclay	230.2	58	702	11	63.81	3-44

Also bowled: G. G. Arnold 59–23–89–6; R. S. Cowan 9–0–34–0; I. J. Gould 5.4–2–18–0; A. M. Green 36–4–182–6; A. N. Jones 26–5–89–4; P. W. G. Parker 5–0–16–0; C. M. Wells 56.3–9–175–5; A. Willows 17–4–39–0.

HUNDREDS

The following six three-figure innings were played for Sussex in County Championship matches – C. M. Wells (3) 100* v Gloucestershire (Bristol), 126 v Kent (Hove), 123* v Nottinghamshire (Hove); I. A. Greig (1) 109 v Warwickshire (Birmingham); G. D. Mendis (1) 104 v Lancashire (Manchester); P. W. G. Parker (1) 106 v Leicestershire (Hove).

At Taunton, May 5, 6, 7. SUSSEX drew with SOMERSET.

SUSSEX v ESSEX

At Hove, May 12, 13, 14. Sussex won by ten wickets. Sussex 24 pts, Essex 5 pts. When the teams met on a nearby strip in the John Player League a few days previously, Essex had been given first knock and bowled out for a modest total. Fletcher, winning the toss this time, repaid the courtesy but his gamble misfired. The three-day wicket was much more placid, and Sussex built up a massive 378, even though the innings began with Barclay receiving a painful blow to the face from a ball by Foster and being unable to take any further part. Lever persevered to take five wickets, but it was a different story when the Essex batsmen took strike against the Sussex pace battery. Only Gooch and Fletcher got among the runs, McEwan ran out of partners, and by early afternoon on the second day Essex were following on 208 in arrears. At tea they were 46 for three; next morning they had been bowled out again. Pigott's lively deliveries sent back the first four batsmen for 53, but David East battled away gamely for a career-best 36 not out. The Sussex catching was first class, especially Phillipson's at second slip. Sussex, needing only 37 to win, went to lunch with maximum points in the bag.

Sussex

G. D. Mendis c Hardie b Phillip	54	– not out	8
*J. R. T. Barclay retired hurt	1		
C. M. Wells c Hardie b Lever	12		
P. W. G. Parker lbw b Lever	0		
Imran Khan c Lilley b R. E. East	85		
I. A. Greig c Turner b Phillip	13		
C. P. Phillipson hit wkt b Lever	21		
†I. J. Gould b Phillip	74	– (2) not out	26
G. S. le Roux c D. E. East b Lever	69		
A. C. S. Pigott c D. E. East b Lever	23		
C. E. Waller not out	0		
B 1, l-b 19, w 1, n-b 5	26	B 2, l-b 3, n-b 1	6
1/42 2/42 3/110 4/136 5/173 6/242 7/308 8/372 9/378	378		(no wkt) 40

Bonus points – Sussex 4, Essex 4.

Bowling: *First Innings*—Lever 27.4–7–91–5; Foster 14–3–69–0; Phillip 18–2–81–3; Turner 22–2–72–0; R. E. East 10–0–39–1. *Second Innings*—Turner 6–2–13–0; Gooch 5–0–17–0; Fletcher 0.1–0–4–0.

Essex

G. A. Gooch c and b Pigott	56	– c Phillipson b Pigott	3
B. R. Hardie b Imran	1	– c Parker b Pigott	25
*K. W. R. Fletcher c Phillipson b Imran	64	– c Wells b Pigott	3
K. S. McEwan not out	28	– c le Roux b Pigott	31
A. W. Lilley c Gould b le Roux	0	– b le Roux	39
N. Phillip run out	1	– c Phillipson b le Roux	56
S. Turner c Mendis b Greig	3	– b Imran	22
†D. E. East lbw b Imran	5	– not out	36
R. E. East c sub b le Roux	7	– c Parker b Greig	10
J. K. Lever b le Roux	0	– lbw b Imran	0
N. A. Foster b Imran	0	– c Gould b Imran	7
B 1, l-b 3, w 1	5	B 4, l-b 6, n-b 2	12
1/7 2/104 3/131 4/132 5/133 6/139 7/146 8/163 9/163	170	1/21 2/30 3/44 4/84 5/136 6/185 7/189 8/220 9/220	244

Bonus points – Essex 1, Sussex 4.

Bowling: *First Innings*—Imran 20–6–40–4: le Roux 17–6–39–3; Greig 16–4–54–1; Pigott 10–3–32–1. *Second Innings*—Imran 20.5–2–75–3; le Roux 14–1–44–2; Pigott 13–2–53–4; Greig 12–2–42–1; Waller 7–0–18–0.

Umpires: W. L. Budd and D. R. Shepherd.

SUSSEX v GLOUCESTERSHIRE

At Hastings, May 19, 20, 21. Sussex won by seven wickets. Sussex 22 pts, Gloucestershire 4 pts. This was Sussex's fifth successive victory in all competitions, and they shaped like a strongly balanced side. Gloucestershire badly missed Zaheer Abbas, who was unwell, and might have been beaten in two days but for a fighting eighth-wicket stand of 64 between Graveney, the captain, and wicket-keeper Brassington on the second evening. Consequently Sussex had to bat till just after lunch on the final day for their victory. Imran batted and bowled to Test-match standards and Wells, with contributions of 88 and 35, played an important role. Shepherd, the former Kent and West Indies all-rounder, toiled magnificently to take six for 75 in the first innings, bowling unchanged on the slowish wicket until the final few overs.

Gloucestershire

A. W. Stovold c Parker b le Roux	9	– c Gould b Pigott	54
B. C. Broad c Gould b Imran	4	– c Waller b Imran	14
Sadiq Mohammad c Gould b Imran	3	– c Phillipson b Greig	12
P. Bainbridge c Phillipson b le Roux	5	– c Phillipson b Imran	5
M. W. Stovold c Barclay b Pigott	20	– c Gould b le Roux	8
A. J. Hignell c Waller b Greig	0	– c Greig b Pigott	13
J. N. Shepherd c Phillipson b Imran	30	– c Parker b Pigott	10
*D. A. Graveney lbw b Greig	5	– c le Roux b Waller	49
†A. J. Brassington not out	7	– b le Roux	35
J. H. Childs c Gould b Imran	0	– b Imran	8
D. Surridge c Gould b Greig	10	– not out	3
L-b 3, n-b 2	5	L-b 7, w 2, n-b 2	11
1/13 2/17 3/17 4/29 5/34 6/50 7/67 8/81 9/83	98	1/34 2/53 3/61 4/73 5/108 6/122 7/122 8/196 9/210	222

Bonus points – Sussex 4.

Bowling: *First Innings*—Imran 15–7–26–4; le Roux 8–3–23–2; Greig 17.1–7–25–3; Pigott 6–0–19–1. *Second Innings*—Imran 22–7–44–3; le Roux 16.2–2–69–2; Greig 16–4–36–1; Barclay 2–0–5–0; Pigott 17–6–50–3; Waller 7–4–7–1.

Sussex

G. D. Mendis c Sadiq b Shepherd	5	– b Childs	22
*J. R. T. Barclay c Bainbridge b Surridge	9	– c Brassington b Surridge	17
C. M. Wells c A. W. Stovold b Surridge	88	– c Brassington b Bainbridge	35
P. W. G. Parker lbw b Shepherd	33	– not out	25
Imran Khan c A. W. Stovold b Shepherd	31	– not out	1
G. S. le Roux c Hignell b Shepherd	7		
I. A. Greig c and b Surridge	8		
†I. J. Gould b Surridge	14		
C. P. Phillipson not out	8		
A. C. S. Pigott c Broad b Shepherd	1		
C. E. Waller c A. W. Stovold b Shepherd	3		
L-b 7, n-b 4	11	L-b 2, n-b 2	4
1/12 2/16 3/103 4/164 5/174 6/187 7/191 8/211 9/212	218	1/37 2/64 3/96	(3 wkts) 104

Bonus points — Sussex 2, Gloucestershire 4.

Bowling: *First Innings*—Surridge 30–6–74–4; Shepherd 33.1–5–75–6; Bainbridge 13–4–44–0; Childs 9–4–14–0. *Second Innings*—Surridge 13.1–5–29–1; Shepherd 12–2–30–0; Childs 9–2–19–1; Bainbridge 3–1–12–1.

Umpires: C. Cook and P. J. Eele.

At Lord's, May 29, 31, June 1. SUSSEX lost to MIDDLESEX by 68 runs.

At Birmingham, June 5, 7, 8. SUSSEX beat WARWICKSHIRE by 269 runs.

At Tunbridge Wells, June 9, 10, 11. SUSSEX lost to KENT by ten wickets.

SUSSEX v WORCESTERSHIRE

At Hove, June 12, 14. Sussex won by an innings and 37 runs. Sussex 23 pts, Worcestershire 3 pts. Without Turner, Younis Ahmed and Gifford, and on a fast and green wicket, the visitors were twice bowled out cheaply, the match being all over just before tea on the second day. Indeed, such was the speed of Worcestershire's demise in the first innings that Scott, called up as a late replacement for Younis, could not reach the ground in time to bat. Imran and le Roux kept up a torrid attack, breaking the back of the Worcestershire innings and each taking six wickets in the match. The Sussex fielding, a pleasing feature of the season to date, was again on form with some exciting catches being held, including several by the energetic Gould behind the stumps. Neale's 40, as he strove to bring respectability to the Worcestershire second innings, was a true captain's effort, and Alleyne displayed lively form with bat and ball, providing a rich West Indian flavour in his mixture of the orthodox and improvised.

Worcestershire

M. J. Weston c Pigott b le Roux	3	– b le Roux	10
J. A. Ormrod c Barclay b Imran	3	– c Phillipson b le Roux	14
D. N. Patel c Gould b Imran	4	– c Gould b le Roux	8
*P. A. Neale c Barclay b le Roux	8	– c le Roux b Wells	40
E. J. O. Hemsley c Gould b Greig	25	– b Greig	24
†D. J. Humphries c Phillipson b Greig	7	– (7) lbw b Wells	0
J. D. Inchmore c Waller b le Roux	1	– (8) c Gould b Greig	3
H. L. Alleyne b Imran	23	– (9) b Imran	20
A. P. Pridgeon c Gould b Greig	1	– (10) not out	14
S. P. Perryman not out	0	– (11) c Phillipson b Imran	0
M. S. Scott absent		– (6) b Imran	14
B 1, l-b 6, w 2, n-b 1	10	L-b 3, n-b 3	6
1/5 2/9 3/17 4/25 5/34 6/39 7/77 8/81 9/85	85	1/16 2/29 3/36 4/95 5/99 6/99 7/109 8/128 9/153	153

Bonus points – Sussex 4.

Bowling: *First Innings*—Imran 8.3–2–23–3; le Roux 9–4–23–3; Greig 6–0–29–3. *Second Innings*—le Roux 10–1–46–3; Greig 12–3–53–2; Imran 8.2–0–33–3; Wells 6–0–15–2.

Sussex

G. D. Mendis c and b Alleyne	29	*J. R. T. Barclay b Perryman	7
C. P. Phillipson lbw b Pridgeon	10	C. E. Waller not out	9
C. M. Wells b Inchmore	3		
P. W. G. Parker c Patel b Inchmore	74	L-b 17, n-b 21	38
†I. J. Gould run out	66		
Imran Khan c Humphries b Perryman	23	1/34 2/45 3/67 4/162 (8 wkts dec.)	275
I. A. Greig b Perryman	16	5/219 6/255 7/258 8/275	

G. S. le Roux and A. C. S. Pigott did not bat.

Bonus points – Sussex 3, Worcestershire 3.

Bowling: Alleyne 22–6–49–1; Pridgeon 19–3–58–1; Inchmore 18–1–70–2; Perryman 15–3–60–3.

Umpires: C. Cook and K. Ibadulla.

SUSSEX v SURREY

At Hove, June 19, 21, 22. Drawn. Sussex 7 pts, Surrey 5 pts. By the time Sussex had built up a lead of 155, with seven wickets in hand, at the close on the second evening, an interesting finish looked in prospect. Then came the rain to wash out the entire third day. However, there had been much to entertain the Hove faithful, especially a thrilling 83 by le Roux, sprinkled with fierce and disciplined shots, exciting fast bowling by Clarke (six for 70 in the first innings), and controlled left-arm spin bowling by Waller which earned him seven wickets against his former county.

Sussex

G. D. Mendis c Roope b Clarke	0	– b Clarke	17
J. R. P. Heath c Butcher b Clarke	17	– lbw b Jackman	3
C. M. Wells c Butcher b Jackman	45	– lbw b Clarke	0
P. W. G. Parker lbw b Clarke	3	– not out	10
†I. J. Gould b Thomas	16	– not out	55
*J. R. T. Barclay b Clarke	87		
I. A. Greig b Clarke	18		
G. S. le Roux c Lynch b Thomas	83		
C. P. Phillipson b Clarke	19		
A. C. S. Pigott not out	2		
C. E. Waller not out	4		
B 4, l-b 12, n-b 3	19		
1/0 2/42 3/53 4/85 5/89 6/122 7/252 8/296 9/309 (9 wkts dec.)	313	1/20 2/20 3/20 (3 wkts)	85

Bonus points – Sussex 3, Surrey 3 (Score at 100 overs: 262-7).

Bowling: *First Innings*—Clarke 31–7–70–6; Jackman 35–9–96–1; Knight 16–3–37–0; Thomas 22–5–56–2; Cheatle 12–2–35–0. *Second Innings*—Clarke 10–4–18–2; Jackman 8–1–43–1; Thomas 7–2–24–0.

Surrey

A. R. Butcher lbw b Greig	32	S. T. Clarke c Parker b Waller	22
G. S. Clinton lbw b Waller	34	R. D. Jackman c Barclay b Waller	15
*R. D. V. Knight c Parker b Waller	69	R. G. L. Cheatle not out	27
G. P. Howarth run out	0		
M. A. Lynch c Parker b Greig	25	B 2, l-b 1, n-b 3	6
G. R. J. Roope c Parker b Waller	5		
†C. J. Richards c le Roux b Waller	3	1/47 2/106 3/106 4/144 5/153	243
D. J. Thomas b Waller	5	6/163 7/177 8/188 9/202	

Bonus points – Surrey 2, Sussex 4.

Bowling: le Roux 11–4–25–0; Pigott 10–1–39–0; Greig 18–3–49–2; Barclay 21–5–57–0; Waller 26.3–4–67–7.

Umpires: D. J. Constant and P. B. Wight.

At Basingstoke, June 23, 24, 25. SUSSEX drew with HAMPSHIRE.

At Hove, June 26, 27, 28. SUSSEX lost to PAKISTANIS by an innings and 13 runs (See Pakistani tour section).

At Bristol, July 7, 8. SUSSEX beat GLOUCESTERSHIRE by an innings and 88 runs.

SUSSEX v SOMERSET

At Hove, July 10, 12, 13. Somerset won by 19 runs. Somerset 24 pts, Sussex 5 pts. A magnificent game, in which fortunes fluctuated throughout between two well-matched sides, ended with Sussex in full cry to meet a target of 254 in 200 minutes and last-man Arnold being run out with three overs remaining. Somerset's first-innings total of 356 for eight looked to be a match-winner when the first three Sussex wickets tumbled for 27 on Monday morning, but from 93 for five they battled to 295, and by the close Pigott had Somerset in difficulties at 52 for five. The last day's play was particularly exciting as Richards, in bed with influenza the previous day, slammed the ball to distant parts of the ground, one 6 disappearing over the Arthur Gilligan Stand to smash the windows of a flat behind. Gould, the Sussex wicket-keeper, was equally belligerent when Sussex were chasing runs, knocking up 94 in 90 minutes to take his side so near to what would have been a notable victory.

Somerset

J. W. Lloyds c Phillipson b Green	10	– (9) lbw b Greig	1
P. M. Roebuck c Gould b Waller	70	– c Phillipson b Pigott	2
I. V. A. Richards b Greig	33	– (8) st Gould b Waller	69
*B. C. Rose b Greig	12	– (3) c and b Pigott	5
P. W. Denning c Phillipson b Barclay	46	– c Greig b Pigott	3
N. F. M. Popplewell lbw b Greig	28	– (1) lbw b Arnold	1
V. J. Marks run out	67	– (5) hit wkt b Waller	24
†D. J. S. Taylor not out	36	– (6) c Barclay b Waller	52
J. Garner c Mendis b Waller	26	– not out	0
C. H. Dredge not out	12	– (7) c Gould b Green	22
H. R. Moseley (did not bat)		– c Greig b Waller	0
B 2, l-b 8, n-b 6	16	B 7, l-b 1, n-b 5	13
1/51 2/63 3/180 4/202 5/231 6/303 7/303 8/338 (8 wkts dec.)	356	1/3 2/3 3/11 4/12 5/47 6/83 7/183 8/186 9/192	192

Bonus points – Somerset 4, Sussex 2 (Score at 100 overs: 303-6).

Bowling: *First Innings*—Pigott 12–3–34–0; Arnold 8–3–26–0; Greig 27–4–102–3; Waller 35–7–94–2; Barclay 26–9–51–1; Green 7–1–33–1. *Second Innings*—Pigott 9–3–29–3; Arnold 7–2–10–1; Waller 16.5–2–67–4; Greig 17–3–36–1; Barclay 9–2–28–0; Green 3–1–9–1.

Sussex

G. D. Mendis c Lloyds b Marks	16	– c Taylor b Moseley	18
A. M. Green c Taylor b Moseley	9	– c Popplewell b Marks	21
C. M. Wells c Taylor b Marks	65	– b Marks	27
P. W. G. Parker c Dredge b Moseley	0	– c Rose b Marks	14
*J. R. T. Barclay c Rose b Lloyds	17	– (8) not out	16
†I. J. Gould b Lloyds	2	– run out	94
I. A. Greig c sub b Popplewell	68	– (5) c Moseley b Marks	19
C. P. Phillipson c Lloyds b Marks	64	– (7) lbw b Richards	6
A. C. S. Pigott c Denning b Marks	12	– c Taylor b Dredge	1
C. E. Waller lbw b Dredge	10	– b Moseley	2
G. G. Arnold not out	8	– run out	1
B 12, l-b 3, w 2, n-b 7	24	B 2, l-b 12, w 1	15
1/27 2/27 3/27 4/90 5/93 6/149 7/265 8/266 9/287	295	1/31 2/63 3/74 4/93 5/130 6/168 7/211 8/219 9/232	234

Bonus points – Sussex 3, Somerset 4 (Score at 100 overs: 293-9).

Bowling: *First Innings*—Garner 3–1–3–0; Moseley 13–5–24–2; Dredge 12–1–46–1; Marks 39.5–13–93–4; Lloyds 30–5–97–2; Popplewell 3–0–8–1. *Second Innings*—Moseley 11–2–48–2; Dredge 13–3–33–1; Marks 24–8–82–4; Lloyds 8–3–29–0; Richards 7–1–27–1.

Umpires: W. E. Alley and D. G. L. Evans.

SUSSEX v LEICESTERSHIRE

At Hove, July 17, 19, 20. Leicestershire won by 13 runs. Leicestershire 22 pts, Sussex 5 pts. An exciting finish had spectators applauding every run as the Sussex tailenders struck out boldly in an attempt to reach a target of 249. Waller, who shared a ninth-wicket stand of 60 off eight overs with Pigott, hit 50 off 28 balls with nine robust 4s, but Cook's left-arm spin, which brought him seven for 81 to equal his previous best – also against Sussex – had the final say. In the first innings, Leicestershire's other spinner, Steele, claimed five for only 4 runs as spin proved deadlier than pace on a wicket usually friendlier towards the speed merchants. Parker's 205-minute century in that innings was the outstanding batting performance before Waller's spirited last-ditch effort.

Leicestershire

J. C. Balderstone b Waller	16	– c Barclay b Greig	20
R. A. Cobb lbw b Greig	32	– c Gould b le Roux	21
N. E. Briers c Barclay b le Roux	69	– c Barclay b Waller	10
B. F. Davison c and b le Roux	14	– lbw b le Roux	11
T. J. Boon c Gould b Greig	1	– b Greig	16
*†R. W. Tolchard b Greig	4	– b Greig	57
J. F. Steele b Arnold	6	– not out	40
G. J. Parsons c Gould b Greig	1	– st Gould b Waller	2
N. G. B. Cook not out	29	– lbw b Greig	0
J. P. Agnew b le Roux	0	– c sub b Waller	17
L. B. Taylor c le Roux b Pigott	13	– run out	0
B 2, l-b 15, w 1, n-b 5	23	L-b 4, w 2, n-b 4	10
1/45 2/73 3/92 4/95 5/99 6/145 7/146 8/171 9/171	208	1/31 2/50 3/60 4/71 5/112 6/166 7/171 8/172 9/203	204

Bonus points – Leicestershire 2, Sussex 4.

Bowling: *First Innings*—le Roux 23–7–50–3; Arnold 16–4–19–1; Greig 24–7–58–4; Pigott 14.3–5–44–1; Waller 17–7–14–1. *Second Innings*—le Roux 18–6–35–2; Arnold 4–1–13–0; Greig 27–12–39–4; Pigott 13–3–31–0; Waller 30.5–13–55–3; Barclay 5–0–21–0.

Sussex

G. D. Mendis lbw b Agnew	4	– c Davison b Cook	72
A. M. Green lbw b Agnew	11	– run out	0
C. M. Wells lbw b Taylor	0	– c and b Cook	52
P. W. G. Parker c Cook b Agnew	106	– c Tolchard b Cook	11
C. E. Waller b Agnew	18	– (9) b Cook	50
*J. R. T. Barclay c Cook b Steele	14	– (8) st Tolchard b Steele	6
†I. J. Gould c and b Steele	0	– (6) c Boon b Cook	4
G. S. le Roux c Boon b Steele	0	– (5) c Parsons b Cook	17
I. A. Greig c Cobb b Steele	1	– (7) st Tolchard b Cook	4
A. C. S. Pigott c Davison b Steele	1	– lbw b Agnew	11
G. G. Arnold not out	0	– not out	2
L-b 6, n-b 3	9	L-b 6	6
1/2 2/24 3/67 4/75 5/158 6/158 7/158 8/162 9/164	164	1/0 2/100 3/120 4/157 5/162 6/166 7/167 8/173 9/233	235

Bonus points – Sussex 1, Leicestershire 4.

Bowling: *First Innings*—Taylor 16–4–44–1; Agnew 17–4–55–4; Parsons 9–2–30–0; Cook 7–1–22–0; Steele 7.3–4–4–5. *Second Innings*—Taylor 17–4–35–0; Agnew 9–1–24–1; Steele 11–0–66–1; Parsons 4–0–23–0; Cook 19.1–0–81–7.

Umpires: D. Archer and C. T. Spencer.

SUSSEX v KENT

At Hove, July 28, 29, 30. Drawn. Sussex 4 pts, Kent 8 pts. A splendid attacking century by Benson, after Kent had lost three batsmen at 48, highlighted a daunting score of 353 for eight for Sussex to approach. They collapsed to be skittled out for 152, only the 22-year-old opening batsman, Green, displaying any confidence or powers of concentration. Cowdrey held five spectacular close-to-the-wicket catches. Following on, Sussex fared far better, and were once again indebted to Green, who went desperately close to following his first half-century in first-class cricket with his maiden century – all in one day. His seventeen boundaries were crisply stroked, especially his drives through extra-cover. Wells (one 6, twenty 4s) and le Roux, 70 not out, hurried Sussex along to their declaration. Now, with Kent requiring 234 to win in 150 minutes, the game had become transformed. But with the prospect of a keen battle to savour, it started to rain for the first time in weeks.

Kent

L. Potter c Gould b le Roux	13
N. R. Taylor c Barclay b Jones	35
M. R. Benson c Gould b Jones	137
D. G. Aslett lbw b le Roux	0
G. W. Johnson c Gould b le Roux	40
*C. S. Cowdrey c Green b Jones	61
†A. P. E. Knott b Pigott	32
E. A. Baptiste c Waller b le Roux	20
G. R. Dilley not out	14
D. L. Underwood not out	0
N-b 1	1
1/48 2/48 3/48 4/125 5/287 6/287 7/319 8/341	(8 wkts dec.) 353

K. B. S. Jarvis did not bat.

Bonus points – Kent 4, Sussex 3.

Bowling: le Roux 22–7–49–4; Pigott 26–3–105–1; Jones 16–3–59–3; Waller 16–2–62–0; Barclay 7–1–58–0; Wells 9–1–19–0.

Sussex

G. D. Mendis c Cowdrey b Dilley	4	– c and b Aslett	72
A. M. Green c Cowdrey b Underwood	57	– c and b Aslett	95
C. P. Phillipson c Cowdrey b Dilley	3	– (8) b Aslett	11
C. M. Wells c Dilley b Jarvis	18	– (3) c Dilley b Taylor	126
P. W. G. Parker c Cowdrey b Dilley	7	– (4) c Knott b Aslett	6
*J. R. T. Barclay c Knott b Underwood	1	– (5) c Cowdrey b Dilley	24
†I. J. Gould c Aslett b Underwood	0	– (6) c Taylor b Underwood	12
G. S. le Roux c Knott b Dilley	1	– (7) not out	70
C. E. Waller c Cowdrey b Underwood	5		
A. C. S. Pigott not out	6		
A. N. Jones b Underwood	29		
L-b 3, n-b 18	21	B 3, l-b 3, w 1, n-b 11	18
1/20 2/58 3/95 4/97 5/103 6/103 7/104 8/105 9/110	152	1/160 2/192 3/202 4/238 5/251 6/423 7/434 (7 wkts dec.)	434

Bonus points – Sussex 1, Kent 4.

Bowling: *First Innings*—Dilley 15–7–43–4; Jarvis 8–1–29–1; Underwood 17.3–11–21–5; Baptiste 11–5–38–0. *Second Innings*—Dilley 23–7–67–1; Jarvis 18–5–54–0; Baptiste 12–1–62–0; Underwood 27–7–63–1; Aslett 29.1–4–119–4; Johnson 18–4–40–0; Taylor 1–0–11–1.

Umpires: W. E. Alley and C. T. Spencer.

At Scarborough, July 31, August 2, 3. SUSSEX lost to YORKSHIRE by six wickets.

SUSSEX v HAMPSHIRE

At Eastbourne, August 7, 9, 10. Drawn. Sussex 6 pts, Hampshire 4 pts. Despite the splendid bowling of Marshall, who captured seven wickets for 48, Sussex took a first-innings lead of 70 and, 63 for four when the first of the final twenty overs was bowled, they needed just 108 to win. Marshall, however, was again bowling in tireless fashion, Barclay and Greig were run out as they attempted to accelerate the scoring-rate, and finally it needed an innings of grit and determination from Phillipson, shielding his partners from Marshall, to stave off defeat.

Hampshire

C. G. Greenidge c Greig b le Roux	6	– b Waller	38
J. M. Rice c Gould b Pigott	0	– c Greig b le Roux	15
M. C. J. Nicholas c Barclay b Pigott	5	– c le Roux b Waller	73
D. R. Turner c Gould b Pigott	25	– c Barclay b Pigott	14
*N. E. J. Pocock c Green b Greig	50	– c Phillipson b le Roux	8
N. G. Cowley b Greig	20	– lbw b le Roux	28
M. D. Marshall b Greig	19	– (8) b le Roux	42
T. M. Tremlett not out	17	– (7) c Barclay b Pigott	10
†R. J. Parks c Gould b le Roux	9	– c Gould b Pigott	3
J. W. Southern c Phillipson b Greig	3	– lbw b le Roux	3
K. St J. D. Emery c le Roux b Greig	1	– not out	0
L-b 1, n-b 4	5	L-b 1, w 1, n-b 4	6
1/6 2/8 3/11 4/82 5/109 1/109 7/132 8/152 9/157	160	1/43 2/59 3/95 4/117 5/172 6/186 7/234 8/234 9/238	240

Bonus points – Hampshire 1, Sussex 4.

Bowling: *First Innings*—le Roux 20–6–49–2; Pigott 18–5–47–3; Greig 22.4–7–46–5; Waller 7–1–13–0. *Second Innings*—le Roux 28.2–5–60–5; Pigott 19–3–45–3; Greig 27–7–55–0; Waller 27–11–59–2; Barclay 5–2–15–0.

Sussex

G. D. Mendis c Greenidge b Marshall	31	– lbw b Marshall	1
A. M. Green c Greenidge b Southern	19	– b Marshall	6
C. M. Wells c Parks b Marshall	0	– c Nicholas b Emery	27
P. W. G. Parker c Greenidge b Marshall	6	– c Pocock b Marshall	25
*J. R. T. Barclay lbw b Marshall	61	– (8) run out	5
C. P. Phillipson lbw b Marshall	7	– (7) not out	23
†I. J. Gould lbw b Cowley	11	– (5) b Marshall	5
G. S. le Roux lbw b Marshall	16	– (6) c Rice b Southern	18
I. A. Greig c and b Marshall	62	– run out	0
C. E. Waller lbw b Emery	0	– not out	0
A. C. S. Pigott not out	0		
B 4, l-b 5, n-b 8	17	L-b 8, n-b 4	12
1/52 2/57 3/58 4/71 5/81 6/100 7/131 8/228 9/230	230	1/2 2/31 3/39 4/48 5/78 6/102 7/110 8/115 (8 wkts)	122

Bonus points – Sussex 2, Hampshire 3 (Score at 100 overs: 204-7).

Bowling: *First Innings*—Marshall 33–16–48–7; Emery 15.4–4–43–1; Tremlett 22–6–34–0; Southern 24–11–37–1; Cowley 15–3–51–1. *Second Innings*—Marshall 19–5–59–4; Emery 12–3–25–1; Southern 5–1–15–1; Tremlett 6–1–11–0.

Umpires: D. G. L. Evans and K. Ibadulla.

SUSSEX v NORTHAMPTONSHIRE

At Eastbourne, August 11, 12. Northamptonshire won by an innings and 58 runs. Northamptonshire 23 pts, Sussex 4 pts. On a dusty, wearing wicket which the umpires reported to the TCCB as being unsatisfactory for first-class cricket, Sussex were twice schemed out by Steele and Willey. Nevertheless, the Northamptonshire spin bowlers were helped by some hesitant and timid batting, this being by far the most disappointing Sussex display of the season to date. The visitors' total of 261 had included a masterly 81 by Larkins, who displayed a responsible approach as well as enterprise, and three towering 6s and eleven 4s in a most entertaining century by Kapil Dev, very much a young man in a hurry. Pigott toiled away in his whirlwind fashion for a reward of seven wickets, and then it was the turn of Steele and Willey to spin their side to victory in a day and a half.

Northamptonshire

*G. Cook c Barclay b Waller	6
W. Larkins b Waller	81
P. Willey c and b Pigott	23
R. J. Boyd-Moss c Barclay b Pigott	1
R. G. Williams c Parker b Jones	23
Kapil Dev lbw b Pigott	103
D. S. Steele lbw b Pigott	3
R. J. Bailey c Waller b Pigott	10
†G. Sharp c Barclay b Pigott	0
N. A. Mallender c Barclay b Pigott	1
B. J. Griffiths not out	4
B 2, l-b 1, n-b 3	6
1/36 2/110 3/116 4/116 5/199 6/210 7/222 8/232 9/256	261

Bonus points – Northamptonshire 3, Sussex 4.

Bowling: le Roux 11–2–33–0; Pigott 20.1–4–74–7; Wells 5–2–24–0; Waller 27–7–96–2; Barclay 11–3–25–0; Jones 2–0–3–1.

Sussex

G. D. Mendis b Willey	21	– c Kapil Dev b Willey	35
A. M. Green c Cook b Steele	19	– c Sharp b Steele	14
C. M. Wells b Willey	0	– c Bailey b Steele	5
P. W. G. Parker st Sharp b Willey	2	– c Sharp b Steele	5
*J. R. T. Barclay not out	14	– run out	1
†I. J. Gould c Steele b Willey	3	– run out	0
G. S. le Roux st Sharp b Steele	4	– b Willey	2
C. P. Phillipson c Williams b Steele	0	– c Kapil Dev b Steele	4
C. E. Waller b Steele	1	– lbw b Steele	5
A. C. S. Pigott b Willey	0	– not out	20
A. N. Jones c Sharp b Willey	5	– st Sharp b Willey	5
B 9, l-b 1, n-b 5	15	B 8, l-b 5, n-b 10	23
1/44 2/46 3/52 4/52 5/59 6/64 7/70 8/75 9/76	84	1/50 2/61 3/67 4/74 5/75 6/75 7/82 8/84 9/100	119

Bonus points – Northamptonshire 4.

Bowling: *First Innings*—Kapil Dev 5–0–15–0; Griffiths 2–0–4–0; Steele 15–4–27–4; Mallender 3–0–6–0; Willey 10.5–4–17–6. *Second Innings*—Kapil Dev 1–0–7–0; Griffiths 1–0–16–0; Willey 20.1–3–41–3; Steele 20–9–32–5.

Umpires: D. G. L. Evans and K. Ibadulla.

At Chesterfield, August 21, 23, 24. SUSSEX drew with DERBYSHIRE.

At Cardiff, August 25, 26, 27. SUSSEX drew with GLAMORGAN.

SUSSEX v MIDDLESEX

At Hove, August 28, 30, 31. Sussex won by three wickets. Sussex 21 pts, Middlesex 5 pts. An absorbing match, with fortunes fluctuating right to the end, contained a number of splendid individual performances. Following an unbeaten, even-time century in which he hit a 6 and seventeen 4s, Brearley set Sussex a victory target of 252 in three hours. They made a most purposeful start with Mendis and Green putting on 168 for the first wicket, Green narrowly missing a maiden century after displaying admirable coolness, but then wickets tumbled quickly and it needed the experience of Waller and the power and exuberance of Alan Wells to see Sussex through. Wells ended their exciting eighth-wicket partnership by lifting a ball from Emburey over the boundary for the winning runs. The victory was just reward for Barclay's enterprise in declaring 53 runs behind after Middlesex had solidly compiled 300 in their first innings.

Middlesex

W. N. Slack c le Roux b Greig	27	– c Green b Pigott	1
*J. M. Brearley b Greig	58	– not out	100
R. G. P. Ellis b Waller	50	– c Green b Waller	55
R. O. Butcher c and b Waller	32	– c Pigott b C. M. Wells	33
C. T. Radley c Barclay b le Roux	6	– not out	0
K. P. Tomlins c Smith b le Roux	5		
J. E. Emburey b Greig	44		
†P. R. Downton c le Roux b Pigott	47		
W. W. Daniel lbw b Greig	16		
N. G. Cowans not out	1		
B 3, l-b 6, w 1, n-b 8	18	B 3, l-b 4, n-b 2	9
1/45 2/140 3/149 4/174 5/192 6/192 7/275 8/303 9/304 (9 wkts dec.)	304	1/1 2/108 3/197 (3 wkts dec.)	198

S. P. Hughes did not bat.

Bonus points – Middlesex 3, Sussex 2 (Score at 100 overs: 269-6).

Bowling: *First Innings*—le Roux 20–5–64–2; Pigott 10–1–50–1; Greig 32–8–85–4; C. M. Wells 8–2–24–0; Barclay 7–1–17–0; Waller 29–20–46–2. *Second Innings*—le Roux 5–1–16–0; Pigott 7–0–41–1; Greig 7–1–43–0; Waller 11–0–68–1; C. M. Wells 2.3–0–13–1; Green 1–0–8–0.

Sussex

G. D. Mendis run out	15	– c Emburey b Daniel	66
A. M. Green c Downton b Daniel	6	– c Downton b Daniel	99
*J. R. T. Barclay c Downton b Daniel	64	– (7) c sub b Emburey	2
P. W. G. Parker c Butcher b Cowans	0	– run out	2
C. M. Wells b Emburey	29	– (3) c Cowans b Daniel	5
I. A. Greig lbw b Emburey	55	– c Cowans b Emburey	1
G. S. le Roux not out	46	– (5) b Emburey	7
A. P. Wells not out	12	– not out	45
C. E. Waller (did not bat)		– not out	15
B 6, l-b 3, n-b 15	24	L-b 3, n-b 9	12
1/11 2/26 3/26 4/73 5/161 6/233 (6 wkts dec.)	251	1/168 2/178 3/180 4/183 5/185 6/199 7/201 (7 wkts)	254

†D. J. Smith and A. C. S. Pigott did not bat.

Bonus points – Sussex 3, Middlesex 2.

Bowling: *First Innings*—Daniel 14.2–3–61–2; Cowans 19–3–45–1; Emburey 30–5–57–2; Hughes 15–2–35–0; Slack 10–2–29–0. *Second Innings*—Cowans 10–2–43–0; Daniel 10–1–38–3; Hughes 11–0–67–0; Emburey 19.5–1–79–3; Slack 4–0–15–0.

Umpires: N. T. Plews and A. G. T. Whitehead.

At The Oval, September 1, 2, 3. SUSSEX drew with SURREY.

At Manchester, September 8, 9, 10. SUSSEX drew with LANCASHIRE.

SUSSEX v NOTTINGHAMSHIRE

At Hove, September 11, 13, 14. Nottinghamshire won by six wickets. Nottinghamshire 22 pts, Sussex 5 pts. More than 1,000 runs were scored on a splendid batting wicket on which the visitors, chasing a victory target of 268, achieved it with two overs to spare. In the Sussex second innings, the highest of the match, the Wells brothers shared a stand of 98 through 30 overs, Colin's unbeaten 123 being generously sprinkled with hefty blows, mainly to or over mid-wicket. However, Robinson, following his century in the first innings, Randall, in a lively romp, and some robust blows by Rice took Nottinghamshire to a deserved win and fourth position in the Championship.

Sussex

G. D. Mendis c Randall b Saxelby	0	– c Robinson b Hadlee	51
A. M. Green c Rice b Saxelby	15	– c French b Hadlee	20
*J. R. T. Barclay c Rice b Hadlee	95	– run out	3
P. W. G. Parker lbw b Bore	8	– c French b Hadlee	23
C. M. Wells lbw b Bore	0	– (6) not out	123
A. P. Wells b Hadlee	70	– (7) c French b Cooper	30
R. S. Cowan b Hadlee	0	– (8) not out	18
†D. J. Smith lbw b Hadlee	0		
C. E. Waller c Rice b Hadlee	5		
A. C. S. Pigott c Hadlee b Cooper	40		
A. Willows not out	0	– (5) b Bore	4
B 6, l-b 7, w 1, n-b 10	24	B 1, l-b 6, n-b 5	12
1/1 2/19 3/35 4/35 5/163 6/173 7/173 8/179 9/257	257	1/68 2/77 3/82 4/107 5/123 6/221 (6 wkts dec.)	284

Bonus points – Sussex 2, Nottinghamshire 3 (Score at 100 overs: 249-8).

Bowling: *First Innings*—Saxelby 19–4–72–2; Cooper 22.3–10–45–1; Bore 29–17–33–2; Hemmings 19–3–62–0; Hadlee 16–6–21–5. *Second Innings*—Saxelby 11–1–46–0; Cooper 24–10–68–1; Hadlee 25–7–59–3; Bore 18–6–45–1; Hemmings 16–6–54–0.

Nottinghamshire

B. Hassan c Smith b Pigott	22	– b Waller	37
R. T. Robinson c Cowan b Pigott	109	– b Waller	79
D. W. Randall b Waller	16	– lbw b Waller	76
*C. E. B. Rice c and b Pigott	0	– not out	58
J. D. Birch b Waller	30	– (6) not out	11
R. J. Hadlee c Pigott b Green	32	– (5) c C. M. Wells b Waller	5
†B. N. French c and b Green	30		
E. E. Hemmings c Smith b Pigott	18		
K. Saxelby not out	4		
K. E. Cooper c Smith b Pigott	0		
M. K. Bore b Pigott	0		
L-b 2, w 1, n-b 10	13	L-b 1, n-b 2	3
1/46 2/82 3/85 4/128 5/172 6/235 7/267 8/270 9/274	274	1/84 2/159 3/232 4/244 (4 wkts)	269

Bonus points – Nottinghamshire 3, Sussex 3 (Score at 100 overs: 274-8).

Bowling: *First Innings*—Pigott 19.4–4–81–6; C. M. Wells 7–1–16–0; Waller 41–23–71–2; Willows 13–4–23–0; Cowan 7–0–22–0; Green 13–2–48–2. *Second Innings*—Pigott 14–2–103–0; Cowan 2–0–12–0; Waller 23–2–77–4; Willows 4–0–16–0; Green 6–0–36–0; C. M. Wells 3–0–22–0.

Umpires: P. J. Eele and M. J. Kitchen.

THE ASHES

The Ashes were originated in 1882 when, on August 29, Australia defeated the full strength of England on English soil for the first time. The Australians won by the narrow margin of 7 runs and the following day the *Sporting Times* printed a mock obituary notice, written by Shirley Brooks, son of an editor of *Punch*, which read:

> "In affectionate remembrance of English Cricket which died at The Oval, 29th August, 1882. Deeply lamented by a large circle of sorrowing friends and acquaintances, R.I.P. N.B. The body will be cremated and the Ashes taken to Australia."

The following winter the Hon. Ivo Bligh, afterwards Lord Darnley, set out to Australia to recover these mythical Ashes. Australia won the first match by nine wickets, but England won the next two, and the real ashes came into being when some Melbourne women burnt a bail used in the third game and presented the ashes in an urn to Ivo Bligh.

When Lord Darnley died in 1927, the urn, by a bequest in his will, was given to MCC, and it held a place of honour in the Long Room at Lord's until 1953 when, with other cricket treasures, it was moved to the newly built Imperial Cricket Memorial near the pavilion. There it stands permanently, together with the velvet bag in which the urn was originally given to Lord Darnley and the scorecard of the 1882 match.

★ ★ ★ ★

Note: At the time of the 1982 centenary of The Oval Test match, evidence was provided that the Ashes were the remains of a ball, that they were presented to the Hon. Ivo Bligh around Christmas 1882, and that they were handed over to the England captain by Sir William Clarke. This account does not tally with the version by Florence, Countess of Darnley (the Hon. Ivo Bligh's widow) and by members of her family. Possibly more than one presentation of some ashes took place on the 1882-83 tour in view of the great interest shown in Australia towards Ivo Bligh and his cricketing mission.

WARWICKSHIRE

President: Lord Aylesford
Chairman: C. C. Goodway
Chairman, Cricket Committee: R. E. Hitchcock
Secretary: A. C. Smith
County Ground, Edgbaston,
Birmingham B5 7QU
(Telephone: 021-440 4292)
Cricket Manager: D. J. Brown
Captain: R. G. D. Willis, MBE
Coach: A. S. M. Oakman

The season which marked 100 years of Warwickshire cricket came and went with sadly little to celebrate. Instead, there was much heart-searching about a woeful string of results which sent the club carrying two wooden spoons into 1983. For the first time they failed to win a single Championship match; they plunged from third place in 1981 to the foot of the John Player League, winning only three times, and they never emerged from the qualifying stages of the Benson and Hedges Cup. They let some daylight into an otherwise gloomy campaign by battling their way to the final of the NatWest Bank Trophy, although, once there, they were well beaten by Surrey.

Having finished at the bottom of the Championship in 1981, for the first time since 1919, the club embarked on the new campaign with much leeway to make up and a playing staff still lacking balance. There was some confidence that the batsmen would come up with the runs, but this was countered by fears that the bowling, which had been the prime cause of the trouble in 1981, would again not be up to the task. In the event, nagging inconsistencies marked the form of the specialist batsmen, while the loss of Dilip Doshi, the prolonged absence of Willie Hogg, and a sapping spate of injuries to other bowlers, were crushing blows. A salient factor, too, was the absence from so many fixtures of England's captain, Bob Willis, and his inability to produce match-winning bowling performances when he was able to turn out for the county. Willis's difficulty in making the switch from the international scene to the bread-and-butter game was no help to the team's morale.

The batting did turn up one shining exception to the rule in Alvin Kallicharran, whose scintillating displays did much to chase away the shadows. In the final Championship match at Southampton he became the only player in the country to top 2,000 runs. In all he hit three double-centuries and five singles in equalling the county's record for a season. His third double, an unbeaten 230, was compiled in a record English fourth-wicket stand of 470 with Geoff Humpage against Lancashire at

Southport. Humpage, who registered four centuries, on that occasion scored a career-best 254, which included thirteen 6s, equalling the highest number in a first-class match in England and the most by an English batsman.

By early June, Warwickshire were on the bottom of the table. Six drawn games followed, in the last of which the club, because of injuries, were obliged to call up their manager, David Brown. Yorkshire then beat them at Leeds, but after making the biggest total ever recorded at Nuneaton, they failed to press home their advantage against Gloucestershire. Despite the big Kallicharran-Humpage stand at Southport, they lost that match by ten wickets, and they were outplayed by Middlesex at Coventry. After drawn games against Essex and Worcestershire an unhappy season closed with defeats by Somerset, Northamptonshire and Hampshire.

Amiss, who led the side in Willis's absence, came up with 1,404 Championship runs, having benefited in the second half of the season by dropping down the order. Andy Lloyd, in all first-class matches, beat Amiss's aggregate by 28, but a lapse in mid-season cost him what seemed to be becoming a bright chance of selection for the tour of Australia. If Asif Din failed to maintain his 1981 promise with the bat, this was offset by his contribution as a spin-bowler in a trying season for the attack. He always stuck to his task well, sending down 252 overs in the Championship and remaining an enthusiastic member of the side. Chris Lethbridge, too, had more bowling to do and took 29 Championship wickets from the 302 overs he was given, compared with 105 in 1981.

Anton Ferreira had the misfortune to begin the season with Achilles' tendon trouble. This finally led to an operation before he returned to finish with 26 wickets at 30.34 and underline the considerable difference he might have made had he been available throughout. In the event a big burden was thrown on to Gladstone Small, who faced up to it so successfully that he was rewarded by being put on standby for England against Pakistan at Edgbaston. Even so, afflicted by tiredness and bronchitis, and after run-up trouble causing him to be frequently no-balled, he rather fell away towards the end of the season. Kallicharran, not envisaged as a regular bowler when the season began, did some useful work with his gentle off-spin. – G.B.

WARWICKSHIRE 1982

[*Ken Kelly*

Back row: Asif Din, C. Lethbridge, P. R. Oliver, A. M. Ferreira, G. C. Small, S. P. Sutcliffe, T. A. Lloyd, G. A. Tedstone. *Front row:* K. D. Smith, D. L. Amiss, R. G. D. Willis (*captain*), A. I. Kallicharran, G. W. Humpage.

WARWICKSHIRE RESULTS

All first-class matches – Played 25: Won 1, Lost 8, Drawn 16.

County Championship matches – Played 22, Won 0, Lost 8, Drawn 14.

Bonus points – Batting 58, Bowling 53.

Competition placings – Schweppes County Championship, 17th; NatWest Bank Trophy, r/u; Benson and Hedges Cup, 3rd in Group B; John Player League, 17th.

COUNTY CHAMPIONSHIP AVERAGES

BATTING

	Birthplace	*M*	*I*	*NO*	*R*	*HI*	*Avge*
A. I. Kallicharran[c]	Berbice, BG	21	36	5	2,118	235	68.32
D. L. Amiss[c]	Birmingham	21	38	1	1,404	156	37.94
G. W. Humpage[c]	Birmingham	22	38	3	1,264	254	36.11
P. J. Lewington	Finchampstead	4	5	4	35	15*	35.00
T. A. Lloyd[c]	Oswestry	22	40	4	1,156	122	32.11
C. Lethbridge	Castleford	15	20	5	369	87*	24.60
K. D. Smith[c]	Jesmond	17	30	5	604	67	24.16
A. M. Ferreira	Pretoria, SA	6	9	1	191	41	23.87
P. A. Smith	Jesmond	8	14	0	329	68	23.50
Asif Din	Kampala, Uganda	21	30	0	681	102	22.70
R. G. D. Willis[c]	Sunderland	12	15	5	215	63*	21.50
G. A. Tedstone	Southport	2	4	2	36	18*	18.00
P. R. Oliver	West Bromwich	5	7	0	115	46	16.42
R. I. H. B. Dyer	Hertford	5	5	1	58	31*	14.50
G. C. Small[c]	St George, Barbados	22	28	4	252	36	10.50
P. J. Hartley	Keighley	3	4	1	31	16	10.33
J. Cumbes	East Didsbury	11	14	7	33	7*	4.71
W. Hogg	Ulverston	3	4	2	9	8	4.50
S. P. Sutcliffe	Watford	13	16	6	35	20	3.50

Also batted: D. J. Brown[c] (*Walsall*) (3 matches †) 7*; K. R. Maguire (*Marston Green*) (3 matches) 2, 1, 0; D. M. Smith (*Coventry*) (1 match) 0; S. H. Wootton (*Perivale*) (3 matches) 3, 0.

† *Includes one match as temporary substitute for G. C. Small (Test match stand-by) when he bowled.*

* *Signifies not out.* [c] *Denotes county cap.*

BOWLING

	O	*M*	*R*	*W*	*Avge*	*BB*
A. M. Ferreira	175.2	41	568	19	29.89	5-109
G. C. Small	500.4	86	1,646	51	32.27	7-68
C. Lethbridge	301.3	67	961	29	33.13	5-68
R. G. D. Willis	262	58	842	24	35.08	6-45
A. I. Kallicharran	154.2	21	578	14	41.28	3-32
S. P. Sutcliffe	533.4	107	1,755	37	47.43	5-151
Asif Din	252.1	55	999	20	49.95	5-100
J. Cumbes	228.1	50	654	12	54.50	3-65

Also bowled: D. L. Amiss 2.1–0–18–0; D. J. Brown 51–8–204–4 (including 13–3–47–1 when substituting for G. C. Small); R. I. H. B. Dyer 1–0–2–0; P. J. Hartley 57–11–215–2; W. Hogg 58.3–9–198–4; G. W. Humpage 27–6–74–2; P. J. Lewington 89.1–19–294–3; T. A. Lloyd 80–23–266–3; K. R. Maguire 35–6–123–1; D. M. Smith 4–0–14–0; P. A. Smith 94–16–362–7.

HUNDREDS

The following fifteen three-figure innings were played for Warwickshire in County Championship matches – A. I. Kallicharran (8) 105 v Kent (Dartford), 235 v Worcestershire (Worcester), 210 v Leicestershire (Leicester), 173 v Gloucestershire (Nuneaton), 230* v Lancashire (Southport), 195 v Surrey (Birmingham), 109* v Worcestershire (Birmingham), 131 v Hampshire (Southampton); G. W. Humpage (3) 254 v Lancashire (Southport), 113 v Somerset (Taunton), 146 v Northamptonshire (Birmingham); T. A. Lloyd (2) 122 v Glamorgan (Cardiff), 120 v Worcestershire (Birmingham); D. L. Amiss (1) 156 v Somerset (Birmingham); Asif Din (1) 102 v Middlesex (Coventry).

At Cambridge, May 1, 3, 4. WARWICKSHIRE drew with CAMBRIDGE UNIVERSITY.

WARWICKSHIRE v GLAMORGAN

At Birmingham, May 5, 6, 7. Drawn. Warwickshire 6 pts, Glamorgan 7 pts. Warwickshire managed an honourable draw in a match in which two and threequarter hours were lost to rain. After Ontong's bold 73 had given Glamorgan a healthy total, Warwickshire began well, topping 200 for the loss of only two wickets thanks to a stand of 102 in 77 minutes between Lloyd and Humpage, Humpage hitting fifteen boundaries. But then the innings folded, leaving them 23 in arrears. Asif Din's leg-spin yielded a creditable and promising five for 100 as Glamorgan were dismissed for 190.

Glamorgan

A. Jones c Amiss b Small	45	– c Amiss b Asif Din	14
J. A. Hopkins c Lloyd b Cumbes	33	– run out	5
R. C. Ontong lbw b Ferreira	73	– c Hogg b Lloyd	3
*Javed Miandad c Asif Din b Willis	35	– (7) not out	96
C. J. C. Rowe b Ferreira	23	– (4) c Amiss b Asif Din	0
G. C. Holmes lbw b Ferreira	6	– (5) c Amiss b Asif Din	29
D. A. Francis c Ferreira b Hogg	14	– (6) b Asif Din	14
M. J. Llewellyn c Oliver b Small	25	– b Lloyd	0
†E. W. Jones lbw b Ferreira	22	– c Humpage b Asif Din	4
B. J. Lloyd not out	6	– lbw b Hogg	6
M. A. Nash b Cumbes	1	– b Small	4
B 4, l-b 9, w 1, n-b 6	20	B 11, l-b 2, n-b 2	15
1/72 2/83 3/177 4/201 5/215 6/230 7/247 8/273 9/297	303	1/22 2/30 3/30 4/32 5/71 6/120 7/125 8/164 9/180	190

Bonus points – Glamorgan 3, Warwickshire 3 (Score at 100 overs: 267-7).

Bowling: *First Innings*—Willis 24–3–58–1; Hogg 17–1–53–1; Small 22–6–64–2; Ferreira 29–10–48–4; Cumbes 19.1–3–60–2. *Second Innings*—Willis 5–2–8–0; Small 5–2–14–1; Hogg 4–0–15–1; Asif Din 30–9–100–5; Lloyd 26–15–38–2.

Warwickshire

D. L. Amiss c Miandad b Lloyd	39
T. A. Lloyd c Hopkins b Ontong	74
A. I. Kallicharran c Francis b Lloyd	18
†G. W. Humpage c Hopkins b Nash	78
P. R. Oliver b Ontong	4
Asif Din c Nash b Ontong	2
A. M. Ferreira c Ontong b Miandad	4
*R. G. D. Willis not out	27
G. C. Small lbw b Miandad	3
J. Cumbes c Hopkins b Lloyd	6
W. Hogg b Miandad	1
B 4, l-b 9, n-b 11	24
1/67 2/98 3/203 4/218 5/234 6/243 7/251 8/258 9/275	280

Bonus points – Warwickshire 3, Glamorgan 4.

Bowling: Nash 15–4–47–1; Ontong 28–5–85–3; Lloyd 16–2–56–3; Rowe 5–2–16–0; Miandad 26.4–10–52–3.

Umpires: D. G. L. Evans and B. J. Meyer.

At Birmingham, May 8, 9, 10. WARWICKSHIRE drew with INDIANS (See Indian tour section).

At Dartford, May 12, 13, 14. WARWICKSHIRE drew with KENT.

WARWICKSHIRE v YORKSHIRE

At Birmingham, May 19, 20, 21. Yorkshire won by nine wickets. Yorkshire 23 pts, Warwickshire 5 pts. An extraordinary last-wicket stand of 149 in 140 minutes between Boycott and Stevenson on the second day left Warwickshire in a precarious position after they had been dismissed for 158. Stevenson's unbeaten 115 made him only the eighth No. 11 to score a century in first-class cricket, and the stand was Yorkshire's best ever for the tenth wicket, the previous record having stood since 1898. Yorkshire gained a lead of 134, and although Amiss battled in his second innings to reach 75, Warwickshire were only 14 ahead with three wickets remaining at the start of the last day. Boycott saw Yorkshire home to their easy victory.

Warwickshire

D. L. Amiss c Bairstow b Stevenson	39	– c Boycott b Old	75
T. A. Lloyd b Stevenson	12	– b Old	5
A. I. Kallicharran b Sidebottom	11	– c Bairstow b Sidebottom	8
†G. W. Humpage b Boycott	4	– c Sidebottom b Old	18
P. R. Oliver c Hartley b Boycott	16	– b Stevenson	9
Asif Din c Athey b Old	13	– c Boycott b Old	5
P. A. Smith c Bairstow b Old	15	– c Boycott b Sidebottom	16
G. C. Small b Old	22	– (9) c Bairstow b Old	5
*R. G. D. Willis b Stevenson	12	– (10) not out	2
J. Cumbes c Lumb b Sidebottom	4	– (8) c Sharp b Old	0
W. Hogg not out	0	– c Bairstow b Sidebottom	8
B 2, l-b 3, w 1, n-b 4	10	L-b 5, w 2, n-b 8	15
1/21 2/43 3/58 4/87 5/92 6/114 7/121 8/148 9/158	158	1/7 2/21 3/50 4/77 5/94 6/148 7/148 8/152 9/156	166

Bonus points – Warwickshire 1, Yorkshire 4.

Bowling: *First Innings*—Old 20–7–52–3; Stevenson 18–5–41–3; Sidebottom 15.1–4–30–2; Boycott 6–1–15–2; Carrick 5–1–10–0. *Second Innings*—Old 27–8–76–6; Sidebottom 21.3–7–34–3; Stevenson 9–2–30–1; Carrick 2–1–1–0; Boycott 4–0–10–0.

Yorkshire

G. Boycott b Asif Din	79	– not out	21
R. G. Lumb lbw b Small	1	– lbw b Small	4
C. W. J. Athey lbw b Small	0	– not out	5
K. Sharp c Smith b Willis	0		
S. N. Hartley c Amiss b Willis	7		
†D. L. Bairstow c Humpage b Small	30		
P. Carrick lbw b Small	0		
J. P. Whiteley c Humpage b Small	1		
A. Sidebottom c Humpage b Small	13		
*C. M. Old b Small	27		
G. B. Stevenson not out	115		
B 5, l-b 4, w 7, n-b 3	19	L-b 2, n-b 1	3
1/2 2/2 3/9 4/35 5/89 6/89 7/91 8/108 9/143	292	1/26	(1 wkt) 33

Bonus points – Yorkshire 3, Warwickshire 4.

Bowling: *First Innings*—Willis 23–4–71–2; Small 29–7–68–7; Hogg 7–0–41–0; Cumbes 20–8–34–0; Asif Din 12–4–27–1; Smith 5–0–32–0. *Second Innings*—Willis 2–0–3–0; Small 7–0–13–1; Hogg 6.3–2–14–0.

Umpires: R. Julian and M. J. Kitchen.

At Worcester, May 29, 31, June 1. WARWICKSHIRE drew with WORCESTERSHIRE.

At Oxford, June 2, 3, 4. WARWICKSHIRE beat OXFORD UNIVERSITY by nine wickets.

WARWICKSHIRE v SUSSEX

At Birmingham, June 5, 7, 8. Sussex won by 269 runs. Sussex 24 pts, Warwickshire 6 pts. Warwickshire returned to the bottom of the Championship table with this embarrassingly heavy defeat after making a promising start by having Sussex 86 for seven. However, a timely century by Greig restored them to 302 by the end of the first day and next morning they added a further 41. Despite Kallicharran's 89, Warwickshire were dismissed for 205 in 61.3 overs, and this made unlikely their final task of 313 to win in five hours. Parker, in Sussex's second innings, had taken 32 runs off an over by Kallicharran as they powered their way to a declaration. Warwickshire collapsed against Imran, le Roux and Waller and were routed for 43, only Kallicharran reaching double figures.

Sussex

G. D. Mendis c Smith b Cumbes	26	– c Amiss b Sutcliffe	32
C. P. Phillipson c Humpage b Cumbes	1	– c Humpage b Willis	35
C. M. Wells c Amiss b Cumbes	12	– c Willis b Asif Din	0
P. W. G. Parker c Humpage b Willis	6	– not out	84
Imran Khan c Kallicharran b Small	5	– not out	12
†I. J. Gould c Kallicharran b Small	16		
G. S. le Roux c Humpage b Sutcliffe	53		
I. A. Greig b Kallicharran	109		
*J. R. T. Barclay c Willis b Small	77		
A. C. S. Pigott b Sutcliffe	5		
C. E. Waller not out	8		
B 4, l-b 11, w 2, n-b 8	25	B 2, l-b 4, w 1, n-b 4	11
1/15 2/34 3/47 4/53 5/83 6/87 7/199 8/283 9/292	343	1/67 2/67 3/108 (3 wkts dec.)	174

Bonus points – Sussex 4, Warwickshire 4 (Score at 100 overs: 302-9).

Bowling: *First Innings*—Willis 19–6–37–1; Small 21.1–4–68–3; Cumbes 25–9–65–3; Asif Din 5–1–19–0; Sutcliffe 22–1–78–2; Kallicharran 19–3–51–1. *Second Innings*—Willis 8–0–30–1; Small 10–0–34–0; Cumbes 10–2–27–0; Sutcliffe 8–2–31–1; Asif Din 2–1–4–1; Kallicharran 2–0–37–0.

Warwickshire

D. L. Amiss b le Roux	6	– c Waller b le Roux	2
T. A. Lloyd c Gould b le Roux	5	– c Gould b Imran	4
A. I. Kallicharran b Waller	89	– c Wells b Waller	12
†G. W. Humpage c and b Waller	22	– c Parker b le Roux	0
K. D. Smith lbw b Greig	2	– c Greig b le Roux	0
Asif Din c Gould b Imran	39	– b Imran	5
G. C. Small c Gould b Greig	3	– b Waller	5
*R. G. D. Willis c le Roux b Waller	28	– c Parker b Waller	9
S. P. Sutcliffe b Imran	2	– c Imran b Waller	0
J. Cumbes not out	0	– not out	4
P. R. Oliver absent hurt		– absent hurt	
L-b 7, n-b 2	9	B 1, l-b 1	2
1/12 2/25 3/105 4/110 5/149 6/156 7/193 8/202 9/205	205	1/7 2/11 3/11 4/15 5/21 6/27 7/31 8/34 9/43	43

Bonus points – Warwickshire 2, Sussex 4.

Bowling: *First Innings*—Imran 16.3–4–61–2; le Roux 6–2–21–2; Waller 25–6–55–3; Barclay 4–1–21–0; Greig 10–1–38–2. *Second Innings*—Imran 9–1–14–2; le Roux 9–3–16–3; Waller 6.2–3–11–4.

Umpires: H. D. Bird and P. B. Wight.

At Leicester, June 9, 10, 11. WARWICKSHIRE drew with LEICESTERSHIRE.

At Cardiff, June 12, 14, 15. WARWICKSHIRE drew with GLAMORGAN.

At Nottingham, June 19, 21, 22. WARWICKSHIRE drew with NOTTINGHAMSHIRE.

At Northampton, June 23, 24, 25. WARWICKSHIRE drew with NORTHAMPTONSHIRE.

WARWICKSHIRE v SOMERSET

At Birmingham, June 26, 28, 29. Drawn. Warwickshire 5 pts, Somerset 7 pts. A rain-marred first day, on which Somerset made 150 for two, eventually produced an unfortunate stalemate. Richards and Rose both went on to complete centuries as Somerset pursued bonus points, delaying their declaration until the captain was 102 not out. Warwickshire replied in kind, prolonging their innings in search of maximum batting points, which were achieved with three balls to spare. Amiss's first Championship century of the season – he was 68 not out in Warwickshire's overnight 119 for one – dominated an otherwise meaningless last day.

Somerset

J. W. Lloyds c Lloyd b Small	22		
P. M. Roebuck c Humpage b Small	0		
I. V. A. Richards c and b Cumbes	135		
*B. C. Rose not out	102		
N. F. M. Popplewell b Cumbes	5		
V. J. Marks not out	14		
C. H. Dredge (did not bat)	–	(1) not out	54
H. R. Moseley (did not bat)	–	(2) not out	24
B 12, l-b 9, w 2, n-b 4	27	B 4, l-b 1	5
1/1 2/44 3/250 4/284	(4 wkts dec.) 305		(no wkt) 83

P. W. Denning, †D. J. S. Taylor and J. Garner did not bat.

Bonus points – Somerset 4, Warwickshire 1.

Bowling: *First Innings*—Small 24–1–87–2; Maguire 11–1–33–0; Lethbridge 13–4–47–0; Cumbes 32.5–9–85–2; Asif Din 3–2–5–0; Kallicharran 13–4–19–0; Lloyd 1–0–2–0. *Second Innings*—Asif Din 7–1–35–0; Lloyd 6–2–37–0; Amiss 1–0–6–0.

Warwickshire

*D. L. Amiss b Lloyds	156
T. A. Lloyd c Richards b Marks	20
A. I. Kallicharran c Richards b Garner	33
†G. W. Humpage b Marks	8
K. D. Smith c Rose b Marks	34
Asif Din c Lloyds b Marks	8
R. I. H. B. Dyer not out	31
C. Lethbridge c Roebuck b Marks	8
G. C. Small c and b Marks	5
J. Cumbes b Marks	0
K. R. Maguire lbw b Lloyds	2
B 11, l-b 6, n-b 1	18
1/48 2/130 3/143 4/207 5/271 6/277 7/297 8/308 9/308	323

Bonus points – Warwickshire 4, Somerset 3 (Score at 100 overs: 301-7).

Bowling: Garner 18–3–47–1; Dredge 5–1–21–0; Marks 51–18–121–7; Richards 16–4–42–0; Popplewell 11–2–40–0; Lloyds 11.5–2–34–2.

Umpires: A. G. T. Whitehead and D. Archer.

WARWICKSHIRE v LANCASHIRE

At Birmingham, July 7, 8, 9. Drawn. Warwickshire 4 pts, Lancashire 5 pts. Seriously weakened by injuries to bowlers, Warwickshire recalled their manager, David Brown, to play in a high-scoring match which ran into a dead end. Amiss and Lloyd batted well for Warwickshire, who totalled 303, but Lancashire enjoyed themselves immensely on the second day, Fowler scoring a career-best 150 as they moved to a declaration at 498 for seven. Warwickshire had no alternative but to stave off defeat, and Amiss and Lloyd were again to the fore in an opening stand of 150, though Lancashire were hampered by a finger injury to off-spinner Simmons. Kallicharran took the opportunity to complete his 1,000 runs for the season.

Warwickshire

D. L. Amiss c C. H. Lloyd b D. Lloyd	84	– c C. H. Lloyd b Hughes	76
T. A. Lloyd c and b Simmons	35	– c C. H. Lloyd b Simmons	74
A. I. Kallicharran b D. Lloyd	74	– c Maynard b Hughes	37
†G. W. Humpage c Croft b D. Lloyd	7	– not out	39
K. D . Smith c Hughes b Simmons	19	– not out	4
Asif Din lbw b Simmons	26		
R. I. H. B. Dyer lbw b Simmons	10		
G. C. Small c Maynard b Folley	21		
P. J. Hartley c Maynard b Folley	4		
S. P. Sutcliffe lbw b Folley	0		
*D. J. Brown not out	7		
B 4, l-b 5, n-b 7	16	B 1, l-b 5, w 1, n-b 1	8
1/68 2/196 3/209 4/214 5/258 6/259 7/292 8/292 9/292	303	1/150 2/156 3/213 (3 wkts)	238

Bonus points – Warwickshire 3, Lancashire 1 (Score at 100 overs: 253-4).

Bowling: *First Innings*—Croft 16–6–40–0; Folley 17.1–7–23–3; McFarlane 14–3–56–0; Simmons 37–10–79–4; Abrahams 21–7–46–0; D. Lloyd 20–5–43–3. *Second Innings*—Croft 5–4–5–0; McFarlane 10–2–34–0; Folley 5–1–6–0; Abrahams 13–0–47–0; D. Lloyd 8–2–22–0; Hughes 31–11–65–2; Simmons 24–6–51–1.

Lancashire

D. Lloyd c Brown b Sutcliffe	83
G. Fowler c Amiss b Sutcliffe	150
†C. Maynard lbw b Sutcliffe	7
*C. H. Lloyd c Humpage b Brown	17
D. P. Hughes b Small	43
K. A. Hayes c Hartley b Kallicharran	90
J. Abrahams b Sutcliffe	51
J. Simmons not out	21
C. E. H. Croft not out	8
B 10, l-b 8, w 4, n-b 6	28
1/199 2/231 3/262 4/296 5/354 6/457 7/483 (7 wkts dec.)	498

I. Folley and L. L. McFarlane did not bat.

Bonus points – Lancashire 4, Warwickshire 1 (Score at 100 overs: 330-4).

Bowling: Small 22–4–69–1; Brown 17–1–66–1; Asif Din 12–0–63–0; Hartley 16–6–66–0; Sutcliffe 50–8–154–4; Kallicharran 11–0–52–1.

Umpires: W. L. Budd and M. J. Kitchen.

At Leeds, July 17, 19, 20. WARWICKSHIRE lost to YORKSHIRE by nine wickets.

WARWICKSHIRE v GLOUCESTERSHIRE

At Nuneaton, July 21, 22, 23. Drawn. Warwickshire 8 pts, Gloucestershire 4 pts. Having moved into a strong position by the end of the second day, Warwickshire were denied their first Championship win of the season by Stovold's century and a career-best 186 from Romaines (three 6s, 25 4s in four and threequarter hours). After dismissing Gloucestershire for 240, Warwickshire replied with the highest total ever put together in the 52 years of first-class cricket at the Nuneaton ground. Kallicharran hit his fourth century (one 6, 30 4s) of the summer, and Willis made his highest-ever Championship score, figuring in a last-wicket stand of 72 with Sutcliffe. Gloucestershire, faced with scoring 206 to avert an innings defeat, were never in danger as Bainbridge joined Romaines in another big stand after the dismissal of Stovold.

Gloucestershire

A. W. Stovold b Small	26	– c Humpage b Willis 100
B. C. Broad lbw b Small	13	– lbw b Lethbridge 25
P. W. Romaines c Asif Din b Willis	12	– c Asif Din b Kallicharran 186
M. W. Stovold c Humpage b Willis	52	– lbw b Sutcliffe 11
P. Bainbridge c Dyer b Lethbridge	5	– not out 75
A. J. Wright b Lethbridge	65	– c Asif Din b Lethbridge 8
*D. A. Graveney c Humpage b Willis	0	
J. N. Shepherd lbw b Lethbridge	31	
F. D. Stephenson c Humpage b Asif Din	3	– (7) not out 0
†A. J. Brassington not out	8	
D. Surridge lbw b Lethbridge	1	
B 9, l-b 10, w 4, n-b 1	24	B 6, l-b 7, w 10, n-b 6 29
1/43 2/48 3/65 4/70 5/181 6/181 7/201 8/207 9/231	240	1/58 2/190 3/244 4/412 5/428 (5 wkts dec.) 434

Bonus points – Gloucestershire 2, Warwickshire 4.

Bowling: *First Innings*—Willis 17–3–64–3; Small 19–5–43–2; Lethbridge 21.1–6–56–4; Sutcliffe 13–5–24–0; Asif Din 7–1–29–1. *Second Innings*—Small 16–2–41–0; Willis 19–5–60–1; Lethbridge 12–0–45–2; Sutcliffe 38–7–107–1; Kallicharran 9–1–48–1; Asif Din 15–4–52–0; Lloyd 11–2–50–0; Dyer 1–0–2–0.

Warwickshire

D. L. Amiss c Graveney b Shepherd	33
R. I. H. B. Dyer b Surridge	17
T. A. Lloyd b Shepherd	24
A. I. Kallicharran lbw b Bainbridge	173
G. C. Small c Brassington b Shepherd	22
†G. W. Humpage b Surridge	17
S. H. Wootton lbw b Surridge	3
Asif Din c Brassington b Stephenson	48
C. Lethbridge c Bainbridge b Surridge	2
*R. G. D. Willis not out	63
S. P. Sutcliffe b Bainbridge	20
B 6, l-b 10, w 2, n-b 6	24
1/56 2/66 3/97 4/162 5/205 6/218 7/352 8/356 9/374	446

Bonus points – Warwickshire 4, Gloucestershire 2 (Score at 100 overs: 342-6).

Bowling: Stephenson 23–4–106–1; Surridge 37–6–137–4; Shepherd 37–12–87–3; Bainbridge 19–4–63–2; Graveney 11–0–29–0.

Umpires: M. J. Kitchen and J. van Geloven.

At Southport, July 28, 29, 30. WARWICKSHIRE lost to LANCASHIRE by ten wickets.

WARWICKSHIRE v DERBYSHIRE

At Birmingham, August 7, 9, 10. Drawn. Warwickshire 7 pts, Derbyshire 4 pts. The loss of time through bad light at the end of the second day was crucial in denying Warwickshire their first Championship victory. On the opening morning, Willis's best bowling for the county for four seasons had Derbyshire out for a modest 128, and a fourth-wicket stand of 126 between Amiss and Humpage saw their side to what might have been a winning lead of 156. When bad light halted play Derbyshire, at 70 for two, were still 86 behind, and they were 118 for four when Anderson joined Barnett. However, Barnett chose this day to reach his maiden century, and when Derbyshire were all out, Warwickshire were left to score an impossible 203 in only 21 overs.

Derbyshire

*B. Wood b Willis	2	– c Humpage b Ferreira	37
J. G. Wright b Willis	39	– c Humpage b Lethbridge	11
P. N. Kirsten b Small	4	– b Small	19
J. H. Hampshire b Willis	1	– c Ferreira b Lewington	36
K. J. Barnett c Asif Din b Ferreira	4	– c Humpage b Ferreira	120
I. S. Anderson c Asif Din b Willis	2	– c Asif Din b Ferreira	89
†R. W. Taylor c Humpage b Willis	2	– b Small	0
C. J. Tunnicliffe c Humpage b Willis	16	– b Small	9
P. G. Newman lbw b Ferreira	0	– lbw b Kallicharran	8
D. G. Moir b Lewington	12	– c Humpage b Small	0
S. Oldham not out	35	– not out	15
L-b 4, n-b 7	11	B 9, n-b 5	14
1/21 2/42 3/51 4/52 5/56 6/60 7/63 8/70 9/79	128	1/49 2/57 3/84 4/118 5/306 6/311 7/325 8/335 9/339	358

Bonus points – Warwickshire 4.

Bowling: *First Innings*—Willis 22–8–45–6; Small 10–1–37–1; Ferreira 18–7–24–2; Lewington 6.5–3–4–1; Lethbridge 4–1–7–0. *Second Innings*—Willis 9–4–19–0; Small 24–3–89–4; Ferreira 21–6–47–3; Lethbridge 18–4–46–1; Lewington 27–8–75–1; Asif Din 17–3–68–0; Kallicharran 0.5–0–0–1.

Warwickshire

T. A. Lloyd c Taylor b Oldham	19	– (4) not out	12
K. D. Smith c Moir b Oldham	7		
A. I. Kallicharran b Oldham	14	– (2) not out	24
D. L. Amiss c Barnett b Oldham	60	– (3) c Anderson b Oldham	12
†G. W. Humpage c Moir b Oldham	60	– (1) c sub b Tunnicliffe	11
Asif Din c Wood b Oldham	16		
A. M. Ferreira c Barnett b Oldham	25		
C. Lethbridge lbw b Newman	4		
G. C. Small c Barnett b Newman	36		
P. J. Lewington not out	15		
*R. G. D. Willis b Newman	1		
B 4, l-b 3, w 20	27	N-b 1	1
1/26 2/27 3/43 4/169 5/178 6/204 7/209 8/232 9/283	284	1/16 2/30	(2 wkts) 60

Bonus points – Warwickshire 3, Derbyshire 4.

Bowling: *First Innings*—Oldham 30–9–78–7; Newman 25.2–4–90–3; Moir 7–1–13–0; Tunnicliffe 20–6–63–0; Wood 5–1–13–0. *Second Innings*—Oldham 3–0–27–1; Tunnicliffe 2–0–14–1; Kirsten 4–1–17–0; Moir 4–3–1–0.

Umpires: Khizar Hayat and R. S. Herman.

WARWICKSHIRE v SURREY

At Birmingham, August 11, 12, 13. Drawn. Warwickshire 4 pts, Surrey 5 pts. With three hours lost to rain, the captains contrived an exciting end to this high-scoring match, and Warwickshire, chasing an elusive victory, were almost there when Knight was ninth out at 228, Surrey having been set 273 in 135 minutes after three declarations. However, the last pair survived the final twenty balls safely. Warwickshire's big total was highlighted by another splendid innings from Kallicharran, who missed a fourth double-century of the season by only 5 runs after Lloyd had completed 1,000 for the season with his 89. Butcher held the stage when Surrey replied, hitting two 6s and 31 4s in his stand of 316 with Smith, who was also unbeaten with a century when Knight made his surprising declaration 129 runs in arrears.

Warwickshire

T. A. Lloyd c Richards b Clarke	89	– b Mackintosh	60
K. D. Smith c Howarth b Needham	21	– not out	49
A. I. Kallicharran c Richards b Monkhouse	195	– lbw b Monkhouse	14
D. L. Amiss c Needham b Thomas	49	– not out	10
†G. W. Humpage c Monkhouse b Knight	15		
Asif Din lbw b Thomas	12		
P. A. Smith c sub b Monkhouse	21		
G. C. Small c Howarth b Thomas	11		
P. J. Lewington not out	0		
B 6, l-b 15, w 5, n-b 8	34	L-b 2, w 1, n-b 7	10
1/89 2/141 3/258 4/291 5/356 6/428 7/443 8/447 (8 wkts dec.)	447	1/89 2/120 (2 wkts dec.)	143

S. P. Sutcliffe and *D. J. Brown did not bat.

Bonus points – Warwickshire 4, Surrey 1 (Score at 100 overs: 326-4).

Bowling: *First Innings*—Clarke 13–6–24–1; Thomas 32–6–123–3; Mackintosh 20–3–71–0; Monkhouse 14.3–2–62–2; Needham 28–4–82–1; Knight 18–4–51–1. *Second Innings*—Thomas 8–1–34–0; Mackintosh 16.1–4–46–1; Monkhouse 10–2–29–1; Needham 8–1–24–0.

Surrey

A. R. Butcher not out	187	– lbw b Brown	11
G. P. Howarth c Lloyd b Small	0	– lbw b Brown	3
D. M. Smith not out	105	– c Asif Din b Small	18
*R. D. V. Knight (did not bat)		– c P. A. Smith b Kallicharran	99
M. A. Lynch (did not bat)		– c Kallicharran b Sutcliffe	15
S. T. Clarke (did not bat)		– c P. A. Smith b Sutcliffe	37
†C. J. Richards (did not bat)		– c K. D. Smith b Sutcliffe	10
D. J. Thomas (did not bat)		– c Humpage b Sutcliffe	13
A. Needham (did not bat)		– c and b Kallicharran	13
G. Monkhouse (did not bat)		– not out	4
K. S. Mackintosh (did not bat)		– not out	0
B 1, l-b 9, w 2, n-b 14	26	L-b 8, n-b 3	11
1/2 (1 wkt dec.)	318	1/12 2/23 3/35 4/97 5/154 6/167 7/208 8/224 9/228 (9 wkts)	234

Bonus points – Surrey 4.

Bowling: *First Innings*—Small 10–2–67–1; Brown 14–4–54–0; P. A. Smith 8–1–44–0; Sutcliffe 17–3–58–0; Asif Din 1–0–12–0; Lewington 18–4–57–0. *Second Innings*—Small 9–0–32–1; Brown 7–0–37–2; Sutcliffe 12–0–72–4; Lewington 5–0–47–0; Kallicharran 6–0–35–2; Asif Din 1–1–0–0.

Umpires: R. S. Herman and Khizar Hayat.

WARWICKSHIRE v MIDDLESEX

At Coventry, August 14, 16, 17. Middlesex won by an innings and 66 runs. Middlesex 23 pts, Warwickshire 3 pts. A century by Radley and big contributions from Slack and Edmonds enabled Middlesex to declare at their first-day score, and after that Warwickshire were always struggling. They began their reply disastrously, losing their first four wickets for only 10, but were rescued by a stand of 142 by two of their younger players, Asif Din and Paul Smith. Asif Din battled bravely to his maiden century, but with Kallicharran unable to bat the innings folded with Warwickshire 186 in arrears. Although Amiss held out for 108 minutes when they followed on, the depth of the Middlesex bowling was a decisive factor, and the Championship leaders won with nearly four hours to spare.

Middlesex

C. R. Cook c Lloyd b Cumbes	36	P. H. Edmonds not out	62
W. N. Slack c Humpage b Cumbes	72	M. W. W. Selvey c P. A. Smith b Small	17
K. P. Tomlins lbw b Cumbes	6	W. W. Daniel not out	2
C. T. Radley b Small	106	L-b 10, w 4, n-b 21	35
R. O. Butcher c Small b Sutcliffe	11		
*J. E. Emburey c Cumbes b P. A. Smith	12	1/84 2/100 3/142 4/173 (8 wkts dec.)	360
†P. R. Downton lbw b P. A. Smith	1	5/225 6/227 7/331 8/357	

S. P. Hughes did not bat.

Bonus points – Middlesex 3, Warwickshire 2 (Score at 100 overs: 282-6).

Bowling: Small 19–0–64–2; Maguire 20–5–58–0; Cumbes 31–7–70–3; P. A. Smith 25–6–67–2; Sutcliffe 16–5–49–1; Kallicharran 3–0–17–0.

Warwickshire

T. A. Lloyd c and b Daniel	0	– c Radley b Edmonds	25
K. D. Smith lbw b Selvey	4	– b Emburey	16
*D. L. Amiss b Daniel	6	– lbw b Slack	41
†G. W. Humpage b Selvey	0	– c Slack b Edmonds	1
Asif Din c Butcher b Daniel	102	– c Butcher b Emburey	2
P. A. Smith c Radley b Edmonds	45	– lbw b Slack	14
G. C. Small not out	9	– b Edmonds	0
S. P. Sutcliffe lbw b Daniel	0	– c Cook b Daniel	1
J. Cumbes b Daniel	1	– not out	7
K. R. Maguire b Hughes	1	– c Radley b Daniel	0
A. I. Kallicharran absent hurt		– absent hurt	
B 3, l-b 2, n-b 1	6	B 2, l-b 6, n-b 5	13
1/0 2/10 3/10 4/10 5/152 6/166 7/166 8/168 9/174	174	1/41 2/64 3/72 4/83 5/103 6/110 7/110 8/120 9/120	120

Bonus points – Warwickshire 1, Middlesex 4.

Bowling: *First Innings*—Daniel 19–5–55–5; Selvey 8–3–17–2; Hughes 5.5–0–26–1; Emburey 12–2–26–0; Edmonds 20–6–30–1; Slack 4–0–14–0. *Second Innings*—Daniel 11.5–3–29–2; Hughes 6–1–17–0; Slack 4–2–8–2; Emburey 17–9–21–2; Edmonds 18–6–32–3.

Umpires: W. E. Alley and B. Leadbeater.

At Colchester, August 21, 23, 24. WARWICKSHIRE drew with ESSEX.

At Rathmines, Dublin, August 25, 26. Drawn. Warwickshire 345 for four dec. (K. D. Smith 161 not out, A. I. Kallicharran 96; G. W. Humpage 48) and 167 for eight dec. (A. I. Kallicharran 51 not out; P. M. O'Reilly four for 50); Ireland 269 for six dec. (J. A. Prior 119, J. D. Monteith 52; G. C. Small three for 48) and 127 for two (M. F. Cohen 59 not out, I. J. Anderson 38 not out).

WARWICKSHIRE v WORCESTERSHIRE

At Birmingham, August 28, 30, 31. Drawn. Warwickshire 6 pts, Worcestershire 5 pts. On a pitch which assisted spin, Patel dispelled any hopes Warwickshire may have held of gaining their first Championship win. He claimed five wickets for 76 when Warwickshire were faced with scoring 341 in 200 minutes, dealing crucial blows by removing the three potential match-winners, Amiss, Kallicharran and Humpage, and Warwickshire were hanging on with nine wickets lost at the close. Younis led the Worcestershire scoring with 110 on the opening day, but in-form Kallicharran replied with an unbeaten 109 as Warwickshire declared with only three wickets down. Kallicharran earned his runs the hard way, his innings being four times interrupted by the weather.

Worcestershire

J. A. Ormrod c Humpage b Sutcliffe	39	– c Humpage b Small	0
M. J. Weston b Ferreira	11	– c Humpage b Lloyd	63
D. N. Patel b Ferreira	16	– (4) c Lethbridge b Sutcliffe	23
Younis Ahmed b Lewington	110	– (5) not out	33
*P. A. Neale c Humpage b Ferreira	21	– (6) not out	60
T. S. Curtis c Lloyd b Ferreira	51		
†D. J. Humphries c Asif Din b Sutcliffe	3		
P. J. Newport lbw b Sutcliffe	6		
A. E. Warner b Small	67		
A. J. Webster not out	3	– (3) b Lethbridge	25
S. P. Perryman b Ferreira	3		
B 1, l-b 10, w 4, n-b 23	38	B 12, l-b 2, n-b 4	18
1/36 2/60 3/99 4/193 5/243 6/254 7/264 8/342 9/365	368	1/1 2/84 3/122 4/126 (4 wkts dec.)	222

Bonus points – Worcestershire 4, Warwickshire 3 (Score at 100 overs: 342-8).

Bowling: *First Innings*—Small 12–1–57–1; Ferreira 29.2–3–109–5; Lethbridge 12–7–24–0; Sutcliffe 34–10–97–3; Lewington 16–3–43–1. *Second Innings*—Small 7–0–23–1; Ferreira 9–3–29–0; Lethbridge 7–1–13–1; Lewington 9–1–25–0; Sutcliffe 5–1–22–1; Lloyd 10–1–55–1; Asif Din 9–1–37–0.

Warwickshire

T. A. Lloyd c Younis b Warner	6	– c Patel b Webster	120
K. D. Smith c Humphries b Webster	36	– c Curtis b Newport	42
A. I. Kallicharran not out	109	– b Patel	17
*D. L. Amiss b Newport	54	– c Newport b Patel	8
†G. W. Humpage not out	23	– lbw b Patel	34
Asif Din (did not bat)		– lbw b Warner	28
A. M. Ferreira (did not bat)		– lbw b Patel	1
C. Lethbridge (did not bat)		– c Humphries b Warner	4
G. C. Small (did not bat)		– b Patel	1
P. J. Lewington (did not bat)		– not out	4
S. P. Sutcliffe (did not bat)		– not out	0
B 2, l-b 8, n-b 12	22	L-b 11, w 1, n-b 3	15
1/8 2/110 3/203 (3 wkts dec.)	250	1/105 2/155 3/167 4/213 5/259 6/262 7/269 8/270 9/270 (9 wkts)	274

Bonus points – Warwickshire 3, Worcestershire 1.

Bowling: *First Innings*—Warner 7–0–42–1; Webster 16–4–53–1; Patel 4–2–8–0; Perryman 19–4–78–0; Newport 13–1–47–1. *Second Innings*—Warner 10–0–34–2; Webster 16–1–70–1; Perryman 10–1–57–0; Newport 3–0–22–1; Patel 20–6–76–5.

Umpires: D. R. Shepherd and J. van Geloven.

At Taunton, September 1, 2, 3. WARWICKSHIRE lost to SOMERSET by five wickets.

WARWICKSHIRE v NORTHAMPTONSHIRE

At Birmingham, September 8, 9, 10. Northamptonshire won by five wickets. Northamptonshire 22 pts, Warwickshire 8 pts. A furious onslaught by Allan Lamb sent Warwickshire tumbling to another home defeat as Northamptonshire met their target of 331 in 175 minutes. Lamb began his innings in the first of the last twenty overs, scored 75 in half an hour, and finished undefeated with 95. In one over from Kallicharran he hit three 6s and three 4s. The first day had been dominated by Humpage, whose 146 was his third Championship century of the season and contained two 6s and 24 4s, to which Lamb had replied by missing a century by only 3 runs.

Warwickshire

T. A. Lloyd c A. J. Lamb b Mallender	0	– b T. M. Lamb	34
K. D. Smith c Steele b T. M. Lamb	25	– c Sharp b Mallender	54
A. I. Kallicharran c Boyd-Moss b Mallender	68	– lbw b T. M. Lamb	3
D. L. Amiss c Steele b T. M. Lamb	42	– b Steele	32
G. W. Humpage lbw b Mallender	146	– b Mallender	42
Asif Din c Capel b Steele	37	– c Boyd-Moss b Williams	34
A. M. Ferreira c Sharp b Mallender	22	– c Capel b Williams	41
†G. A. Tedstone not out	18	– c Willey b Williams	2
C. Lethbridge b Mallender	0	– not out	7
G. C. Small c Larkins b T. M. Lamb	2	– not out	3
*R. G. D. Willis not out	2		
L-b 7, n-b 12	19	B 15, l-b 5, n-b 10	30
1/0 2/80 3/102 4/221 5/318 6/347 7/366 8/366 9/373 (9 wkts dec.)	381	1/73 2/82 3/115 4/167 5/195 6/235 7/262 8/269 (8 wkts dec.)	282

Bonus points – Warwickshire 4, Northamptonshire 2 (Score at 100 overs: 327-5).

Bowling: *First Innings*—Mallender 27–4–97–5; Capel 20–2–87–0; T. M. Lamb 33–7–91–3; Larkins 1–0–5–0; Steele 22–8–63–1; Willey 11–2–19–0. *Second Innings*—Mallender 19–9–42–2; Capel 11–2–43–0; T. M. Lamb 19–4–48–2; Willey 8–1–13–0; Steele 23–6–57–1; Boyd-Moss 2–0–26–0; Williams 10–2–23–3.

Northamptonshire

*G. Cook c Lethbridge b Small	15	– c Smith b Kallicharran	87
W. Larkins c Kallicharran b Willis	7	– b Small	5
P. Willey b Ferreira	20	– c and b Asif Din	96
A. J. Lamb c Smith b Ferreira	97	– not out	95
R. G. Williams b Ferreira	8	– c and b Small	14
R. J. Boyd-Moss c Humpage b Willis	63	– run out	4
D. J. Capel c Kallicharran b Ferreira	44	– not out	15
D. S. Steele c Tedstone b Humpage	31		
†G. Sharp not out	13		
T. M. Lamb b Asif Din	19		
B 1, l-b 3, n-b 12	16	B 2, l-b 10, n-b 5	17
1/22 2/24 3/58 4/71 5/217 6/223 7/298 8/300 9/333 (9 wkts dec.)	333	1/20 2/188 3/222 4/290 5/300 (5 wkts)	333

N. A. Mallender did not bat.

Bonus points – Northamptonshire 4, Warwickshire 4.

Bowling: *First Innings*—Willis 15–4–70–2; Small 11–2–41–1; Ferreira 29–4–126–4; Lethbridge 5–0–26–0; Kallicharran 2–0–13–0; Humpage 12–3–30–1; Asif Din 4–1–11–1. *Second Innings*—Willis 12–1–46–0; Small 10.3–1–52–2; Ferreira 8–0–49–0; Lethbridge 7–1–38–0; Kallicharran 9–0–68–1; Asif Din 7–0–63–1.

Umpires: W. E. Alley and N. T. Plews.

At Southampton, September 11, 13, 14. WARWICKSHIRE lost to HAMPSHIRE by 37 runs.

WORCESTERSHIRE

President: J. J. Roberts
Chairman: Dr J. A. Burnett
Chairman, Cricket Committee: M. Jones
Secretary: M. D. Vockins
County Ground, New Road, Worcester
WR2 4QQ (Telephone: 0905-422694)
Captain: P. A. Neale
Coach: B. L. D'Oliveira, OBE

Worcestershire's only tangible success in 1982 was provided by their crop of up-and-coming youngsters who brought the Second Eleven Championship to New Road for the first time for twenty years. Now, supporters and officials alike must be hoping history will repeat itself, for the last such triumph preceded the winning of two successive County Championships in 1964 and 1965.

On the overall evidence of an otherwise disappointing 1982, the return of such successful days is a long way away, though the emergence of Martin Weston and the Yorkshire-born Richard Illingworth, plus the potential already underlined by Tim Curtis, Alan Warner, Andy Webster and Damian D'Oliveira, are promising signs. Against such promise, though, must be weighed the loss of Glenn Turner, who has severed his seventeen-year association with the county. He has been Worcestershire's match-winner on so many occasions in recent years that it will be nigh impossible to replace him. Gone, too, are the guile and experience of Norman Gifford, and another long-serving stalwart, Ted Hemsley, has been released. It was a case, the committee decided, of out with the old and in with the new.

Worcestershire entered the 1982 season under their third captain in three years, although Phil Neale, having taken over from Turner, was excused some early engagements to try to help Lincoln City clinch promotion to the Second Division of the Football League. It was always going to be a difficult baptism for him as captain, not least because of the new laws governing overseas players, which prevented Turner and Hartley Alleyne from playing in the same side.

Turner opened up with his 99th century in the first match of the season, scoring an unbeaten 239 against Oxford University. On May 29, against Warwickshire, he completed his 100th hundred with one of the greatest innings of his career. It had to be seen to be believed: 128 out of 181 for none at lunch; 254 out of 389 for one at tea; 300 in 336 minutes, and 311 not out out of 501 for one declared. Two more centuries took him past Don Kenyon's record of 70 hundreds for Worcestershire, and another against Kent at Hereford, in what proved to be his final Championship match, left him with a first-class average of 90.07. An appendix operation at the end of July cut short a season in which he felt he was batting as well as at any time in his career.

But scoring runs without Turner was not Worcestershire's biggest problem. Younis Ahmed, after a month out through injury, came back with three typically fluent centuries; Dipak Patel, who played in every game, completed the modern "double" of 1,000 runs and 50 wickets, while Alan Ormrod and Neale, though both disappointed with their final aggregates, were only fractionally short of the four-figure mark. David Humphries, too, who never let the side down behind the stumps, proved his worth with the bat, reaching a new best aggregate of 852 runs.

Where Worcestershire were again found wanting was in their continued failure to bowl out the opposition. Patel was the only bowler to take 50 wickets, collecting a career-best seven for 46 against Lancashire. John Inchmore might have done so but for a back injury late in the season. But without a penetrating strike bowler, Worcestershire were never likely to make much impression in the Championship, their fourteenth place being fairly predictable.

There was more early cause for optimism in the limited-overs games, especially after they won five one-day warm-up matches and four of their first five games in the Benson and Hedges Cup and John Player League. Even then, it was not until August 22, when they beat Surrey on faster scoring-rate in the Sunday League, that they registered their first home victory in one-day cricket. In the NatWest Bank Trophy, fortunes hit rock bottom with an amazing defeat by Yorkshire, who, at the end of a rain-affected day, were 40 for four off sixteen overs in reply to Worcestershire's 286 for five. Next day, against all the odds, Yorkshire knocked off the 247 runs needed for a victory which finally destroyed Worcestershire's confidence and prompted a policy of giving youth its fling for most of the remainder of the season.

Given the chance, Curtis established a regular place in the middle order and generally acquitted himself well; Webster, with the ability to extract extra bounce, underlined his progress with five for 87 in a rare win over Hampshire; while Illingworth's performances, capped by his success for Young England against their West Indies counterparts, won him a Whitbread Scholarship to winter in Australia. Weston scored a spectacular Sunday League century against Somerset, having earlier produced one of the most remarkable innings of the season when he hit 86 out of an opening stand of 94 in eighteen overs with Mark Scott against the Pakistani tourists.

Behind the scenes, Basil D'Oliveira, the coach, has assembled several more young players with the ability to make the grade. Steve Watkins and David Banks are two young batsmen to watch out for, while seventeen-year-old Ricardo Ellcock, a Barbadian from Malvern College, provided sufficient pace and hostility on his début in the final game against Middlesex to look another genuine discovery. – C.O.M.

WORCESTERSHIRE 1982

[*Bill Smith*

Back row: D. N. Patel. Younis Ahmed. M. J. Weston. A. P. Pridgeon. S. P. Perryman. M. S. Scott. D. J. Humphries. *Front row:* G. M. Turner. N. Gifford. P. A. Neale (*captain*). J. A. Ormrod. E. J. O. Hemsley.

WORCESTERSHIRE RESULTS

All first-class matches – Played 25: Won 3, Lost 5, Drawn 17.

County Championship matches – Played 22: Won 3, Lost 5, Drawn 14.

Bonus points – Batting 43, Bowling 54.

Competition placings – Schweppes County Championship, 14th; NatWest Bank Trophy, 2nd round; Benson and Hedges Cup, 3rd in Group A; John Player League, 15th.

COUNTY CHAMPIONSHIP AVERAGES

BATTING

	Birthplace	*M*	*I*	*NO*	*R*	*HI*	*Avge*
G. M. Turner c	*Dunedin, NZ*	8	15	2	932	311*	71.69
Younis Ahmed c	*Jullundur, Pakistan*	16	26	4	1,039	122	47.22
D. N. Patel c	*Nairobi, Kenya*	22	38	1	1,085	133	29.32
D. J. Humphries c	*Alveley*	22	33	5	784	98	28.00
T. S. Curtis	*Chislehurst*	10	17	4	359	59*	27.61
P. A. Neale c	*Scunthorpe*	22	37	6	851	79*	27.45
J. A. Ormrod c	*Ramsbottom*	20	37	2	915	200*	26.14
A. E. Warner	*Birmingham*	10	15	2	268	67	20.61
M. J. Weston	*Worcester*	15	27	1	526	68	20.23
H. L. Alleyne c	*Bridgetown, Barbados*	7	8	2	121	32	20.16
N. Gifford c	*Ulverston*	12	15	7	155	31*	19.37
J. D. Inchmore c	*Ashington*	13	18	3	273	68	18.20
E. J. O. Hemsley c	*Stoke-on-Trent*	13	20	1	336	49	17.68
R. K. Illingworth	*Bradford*	9	12	2	171	47*	17.10
A. J. Webster	*Burton upon Trent*	8	10	5	75	25	15.00
M. S. Scott	*Muswell Hill*	4	7	0	100	37	14.28
A. P. Pridgeon c	*Wall Heath*	14	16	4	110	21	9.16
S. P. Perryman	*Birmingham*	12	16	8	56	14	7.00

Also batted: D. B. D'Oliveira (*Cape Town, SA*) (2 matches) 10, 4, 18*; R. M. Ellcock (1 match) 0, 13*; P. J. Newport (*High Wycombe*) (2 matches) 6, 11, 6*.

**Signifies not out. c Denotes county cap.*

BOWLING

	O	*M*	*R*	*W*	*Avge*	*BB*
J. D. Inchmore	289.4	57	778	32	24.31	7-53
D. N. Patel	490.2	124	1,328	46	28.86	7-46
S. P. Perryman	350.1	82	1,027	31	33.12	6-49
A. E. Warner	190.1	33	643	19	33.84	4-73
R. K. Illingworth	219.4	55	638	17	37.52	4-85
A. P. Pridgeon	424	92	1,109	29	38.24	4-39
H. L. Alleyne	193.3	42	558	14	39.85	4-92
N. Gifford	417	121	944	23	41.04	6-48
A. J. Webster	202.1	36	716	15	47.73	5-87

Also bowled: T. S. Curtis 2–0–7–0; R. M. Ellcock 26.1–2–90–3; E. J. O. Hemsley 20.4–1–80–1; P. A. Neale 4–0–16–0; J. A. Ormrod 1–0–5–0; P. J. Newport 36–1–174–6; M. J. Weston 57.3–8–215–5; Younis Ahmed 5–1–14–0.

HUNDREDS

The following ten three-figure innings were played for Worcestershire in County Championship matches – G. M. Turner (4) 311* v Warwickshire (Worcester), 115 v Lancashire (Worcester), 112 v Yorkshire (Sheffield), 118 v Kent (Hereford); Younis Ahmed (4) 114* v Gloucestershire (Worcester), 122 v Leicestershire (Worcester), 110 v Warwickshire (Birmingham), 114 v Nottinghamshire (Worcester); J. A. Ormrod (1) 200* v Gloucestershire (Worcester); D. N. Patel (1) 133 v Surrey (Worcester).

At Oxford, April 28, 29, 30. WORCESTERSHIRE drew with OXFORD UNIVERSITY.

WORCESTERSHIRE v DERBYSHIRE

At Worcester, May 5, 6, 7. Drawn. Worcestershire 5 pts, Derbyshire 5 pts. On an awkward pitch of uneven bounce and movement, Warner marked his first-class début with four wickets, while Hampshire, on his first appearance for the visitors, worked hard for his 34. Before the close Worcestershire lost their first three wickets for 12 runs, two falling to Derbyshire's other newcomer, Hacker, who next day finished with five. Worcestershire called in Bernard Flack, the TCCB Inspector of Pitches, for advice on the troublesome wicket, which favoured the seamers to such an extent that on the final day Derbyshire scored only 65 runs before lunch. Set a target of 252 in 164 minutes, Worcestershire abandoned any idea of chasing victory when they received only nine overs in 45 minutes.

Derbyshire

*B. Wood c Humphries b Warner	24	– c Turner b Perryman	24
J. G. Wright c Humphries b Warner	10	– c Hemsley b Perryman	60
P. N. Kirsten c Humphries b Pridgeon	22	– b Pridgeon	31
J. H. Hampshire b Perryman	34	– c Younis b Perryman	17
A. Hill c Hemsley b Warner	1	– b Perryman	19
G. Miller run out	21	– b Warner	39
†R. W. Taylor b Pridgeon	45	– b Warner	3
P. G. Newman c Younis b Perryman	0	– not out	18
D. G. Moir c Neale b Warner	10	– c Ormrod b Perryman	11
S. Oldham c Hemsley b Pridgeon	12	– not out	0
P. J. Hacker not out	10		
L-b 6, n-b 3	9	B 6, l-b 12, n-b 7	25
1/16 2/58 3/58 4/60 5/91 6/137 7/137 8/154 9/177	198	1/50 2/101 3/125 4/155 5/182 6/204 7/205 8/240 (8 wkts dec.)	247

Bonus points – Derbyshire 1, Worcestershire 4.

Bowling: *First Innings*—Warner 24–3–73–4; Pridgeon 26.2–6–66–3; Perryman 24–7–43–2; Gifford 4–3–7–0. *Second Innings*—Pridgeon 26–11–52–1; Warner 26–9–60–2; Perryman 36.2–9–97–5; Gifford 8–4–13–0.

Worcestershire

G. M. Turner c Hacker b Newman	4	– b Hacker	27
J. A. Ormrod b Hacker	39	– c Kirsten b Moir	47
*P. A. Neale c Hampshire b Hacker	5	– (7) not out	11
Younis Ahmed b Hacker	0	– not out	36
D. N. Patel b Wood	48	– (3) c and b Moir	46
E. J. O. Hemsley b Hacker	0	– c sub b Hacker	0
†D. J. Humphries lbw b Wood	52	– (5) c Kirsten b Wood	11
A. E. Warner c Taylor b Hacker	19		
N. Gifford c Taylor b Newman	11		
A. P. Pridgeon not out	4		
S. P. Perryman c Taylor b Newman	0		
B 2, l-b 4, n-b 6	12	L-b 4, w 1, n-b 9	14
1/4 2/12 3/12 4/93 5/94 6/150 7/173 8/184 9/194	194	1/42 2/124 3/131 4/143 5/143 (5 wkts)	192

Bonus points – Worcestershire 1, Derbyshire 4.

Bowling: *First Innings*—Newman 19.5–3–73–3; Hacker 23–3–61–5; Oldham 17–4–37–0; Wood 2–2–0–2; Miller 5–2–10–0; Moir 1–0–1–0. *Second Innings*—Hacker 13–2–53–2; Newman 12–2–45–0; Oldham 5–0–24–0; Wood 8–2–22–1; Moir 2–0–12–2; Miller 3–1–15–0; Kirsten 1–0–3–0; Hill 1–0–4–0.

Umpires: D. O. Oslear and C. T. Spencer.

At Bristol, May 12, 13, 14. WORCESTERSHIRE beat GLOUCESTERSHIRE by 11 runs.

WORCESTERSHIRE v SOMERSET

At Worcester, May 19, 20, 21. Somerset won by five wickets. Somerset 21 pts, Worcestershire 4 pts. Somerset, needing exactly 100, made hard work of securing their first Championship win of the season. Pridgeon bowled Worcestershire back into contention with four for 24 in 50 balls as Somerset slipped to 51 for five, but then Rose and Popplewell arrested the slide and saw the visitors to victory with 22 balls to spare. Worcestershire's Richard Illingworth marked his first-class début with three wickets, but the bowling honours went to Somerset off-spinner Lloyds with six wickets in Worcestershire's first innings.

Worcestershire

G. M. Turner c Taylor b Moseley	6	– lbw b Moseley	4
J. A. Ormrod b Lloyds	21	– c Slocombe b Botham	12
D. N. Patel c Roebuck b Botham	30	– lbw b Lloyds	26
Younis Ahmed b Lloyds	7	– c Taylor b Lloyds	39
*P. A. Neale c Rose b Botham	29	– c and b Lloyds	40
E. J. O. Hemsley b Davis	10	– st Taylor b Richards	15
†D. J. Humphries not out	69	– c Taylor b Botham	30
R. K. Illingworth b Lloyds	8	– c Rose b Richards	1
J. D. Inchmore lbw b Lloyds	0	– c Lloyds b Richards	3
A. P. Pridgeon b Lloyds	17	– c Popplewell b Moseley	19
S. P. Perryman c Roebuck b Lloyds	0	not out	0
L-b 1, n-b 1	2	B 2, l-b 5, n-b 2	9
1/9 2/57 3/57 4/94 5/94 6/127 7/146 8/150 9/199	199	1/9 2/35 3/67 4/101 5/144 6/144 7/148 8/152 9/194	198

Bonus points – Worcestershire 1, Somerset 4.

Bowling: *First Innings*—Botham 16–6–28–2; Moseley 13–2–56–1; Davis 10–0–35–1; Lloyds 30–7–62–6; Richards 6–3–16–0. *Second Innings*—Botham 11.5–3–36–2; Moseley 11–3–27–2; Lloyds 28–7–92–3; Richards 20–8–34–3.

Somerset

P. M. Roebuck c Humphries b Illingworth	50 – lbw b Pridgeon	10
P. A. Slocombe b Perryman	27 – lbw b Inchmore	2
I. V. A. Richards c Illingworth b Perryman	5 – b Pridgeon	1
*B. C. Rose c Turner b Illingworth	33 – not out	40
P. W. Denning b Patel	71 – c and b Pridgeon	12
I. T. Botham c Perryman b Illingworth	0 – c Neale b Pridgeon	6
N. F. M. Popplewell b Patel	11 – not out	23
J. W. Lloyds b Patel	6	
†D. J. S. Taylor c Humphries b Patel	67	
H. R. Moseley not out	11	
M. R. Davis b Inchmore	1	
B 6, l-b 9, n-b 1	16 L-b 5, n-b 2	7
1/66 2/74 3/115 4/126 5/126 6/137 7/157 8/268 9/295	298 1/6 2/7 3/18 4/40 5/51	(5 wkts) 101

Bonus points – Somerset 1, Worcestershire 3 (Score at 100 overs: 184-7).

Bowling: *First Innings*—Pridgeon 17–4–33–0; Inchmore 20.2–5–39–1; Perryman 29–7–67–2; Illingworth 27–8–61–3; Patel 43–12–82–4. *Second Innings*—Pridgeon 17–3–39–4; Inchmore 10–0–35–1; Patel 6.2–1–20–0.

Umpires: B. J. Meyer and D. R. Shepherd.

WORCESTERSHIRE v WARWICKSHIRE

At Worcester, May 29, 31, June 1. Drawn. Worcestershire 5 pts, Warwickshire 3 pts. Turner launched an amazing assault on the Warwickshire attack to complete his 100th century in first-class cricket, going on to compile a career-best 311 not out in Worcestershire's total of 501 for one declared on the opening day. His triple-hundred was a record for Worcestershire, beating Fred Bowley's 276 against Hampshire in 1914, and he became the first batsman to top 300 runs in a day in England since J. D. Robertson achieved the feat for Middlesex, against Worcestershire, in 1949. Turner reached his first 50 in 34 minutes, was 128 at lunch out of a total of 181, and in all he batted for 343 minutes, hitting two 6s and 39 4s. But Kallicharran, with a career-best 235, ensured that Warwickshire avoided the follow-on, although in their second innings, needing 289 to win in 197 minutes, they were always batting to save the game as the spinners achieved increasing turn from the wearing wicket.

Worcestershire

G. M. Turner not out	311 – c and b Small	32
J. A. Ormrod c Cumbes b Lethbridge	79 – c Humpage b Lethbridge	43
D. N. Patel not out	88 – b Lethbridge	22
Younis Ahmed (did not bat)	– c Willis b Sutcliffe	10
*P. A. Neale (did not bat)	– not out	17
†D. J. Humphries (did not bat)	– c and b Kallicharran	5
A. P. Pridgeon (did not bat)	– b Sutcliffe	12
N. Gifford (did not bat)	– not out	14
B 1, l-b 19, n-b 3	23 B 2, l-b 4, n-b 6	12
1/291	(1 wkt dec.) 501 1/50 2/103 3/106 4/124 5/129 6/152	(6 wkts dec.) 167

E. J. O. Hemsley, R. K. Illingworth and S. P. Perryman did not bat.

Bonus points – Worcestershire 4 (Score at 100 overs: 433-1).

Bowling: *First Innings*—Willis 12–0–76–0; Small 7–0–54–0; Cumbes 9–0–58–0; Lethbridge 20–1–94–1; Sutcliffe 40–5–127–0; Asif Din 10–1–29–0; Lloyd 7–1–22–0; Kallicharran 7–0–18–0. *Second Innings*—Willis 5–1–17–0; Small 8–3–33–1; Lethbridge 11–5–26–2; Sutcliffe 16–3–60–2; Kallicharran 7–1–19–1.

Warwickshire

D. L. Amiss run out	64	– c Humphries b Gifford	21
T. A. Lloyd c Ormrod b Pridgeon	0	– c Turner b Gifford	3
A. I. Kallicharran c Perryman b Patel	235	– b Patel	35
†G. W. Humpage e Patel b Illingworth	15	– c Patel b Illingworth	23
K. D. Smith c Pridgeon b Gifford	31	– not out	62
Asif Din c Humphries b Illingworth	12	– c Turner b Illingworth	39
C. Lethbridge c Neale b Illingworth	0	– not out	2
G. C. Small c Gifford b Patel	0		
*R. G. D. Willis c Humphries b Illingworth	7		
S. P. Sutcliffe not out	1		
J. Cumbes not out	4		
B 2, l-b 8, n-b 1	11	B 1, l-b 9, n-b 2	12
1/4 2/168 3/217 4/283 5/326 6/346 7/347 8/364 9/372	(9 wkts dec.) 380	1/34 2/35 3/81 4/101 5/188	(5 wkts) 197

Bonus points – Warwickshire 3, Worcestershire 1 (Score at 100 overs: 296-4).

Bowling: *First Innings*—Pridgeon 15–2–54–1; Perryman 10–0–20–0; Gifford 41–11–100–1; Patel 40–8–110–2; Illingworth 37–9–85–4. *Second Innings*—Pridgeon 7–2–15–0; Perryman 4–1–9–0; Gifford 20–1–59–2; Patel 13–3–60–1; Illingworth 19–7–42–2.

Umpires: W. L. Budd and C. Cook.

WORCESTERSHIRE v ZIMBABWEANS

At Worcester, June 2, 3, 4. Drawn. Thunder and lightning produced a dramatic but unsatisfactory ending to a match which deserved better treatment throughout from the elements. A rain-interrupted first day saw Worcestershire lose three wickets for 117, including that of D'Oliveira on his first-class début. Next morning, in humid conditions, Weston added 7 to his overnight score, and only Younis looked comfortable against the off-spin of Traicos, the former South African Test player, who bowled unchanged as Worcestershire lost six wickets for 99 before lunch. A heavy storm, which flooded the ground and dampened the wicket before it was covered, precipitated the Zimbabwean declaration overnight, and they looked to be reaping rewards for their policy as Worcestershire struggled to 98 for seven by lunch on the final morning. However, Younis, aided by Illingworth, held out as the wicket eased, and the declaration, setting 248 in two and a half hours, had virtually decided the outcome before the storm which sent the players running for shelter.

Worcestershire

M. J. Weston st Houghton b Traicos	63	– (6) c Brown b Rawson	2
M. S. Scott lbw b Dudhia	8	– (1) b Dudhia	4
D. B. D'Oliveira c Traicos b Curran	21	– (8) c Traicos b Rawson	3
E. J. O. Hemsley c Houghton b Traicos	17	– c and b Rawson	24
Younis Ahmed c Brown b Traicos	63	– (7) not out	75
*P. A. Neale b Rawson	1	– (2) c Traicos b Dudhia	12
†D. J. Humphries lbw b Traicos	0	– (5) c Pycroft b Rawson	21
D. N. Patel b Traicos	6	– (3) c Fletcher b Rawson	12
R. K. Illingworth not out	5	– not out	15
J. D. Inchmore lbw b Fletcher	21		
H. L. Alleyne not out	9		
L-b 8	8	B 2, l-b 10, n-b 1	13
1/14 2/66 3/99 4/144 5/147 6/148 7/182 8/185 9/206	(9 wkts dec.) 222	1/13 2/30 3/36 4/79 5/80 6/87 7/97	(7 wkts dec.) 181

Bowling: *First Innings*—Hogg 11–3–30–0; Dudhia 7–2–16–1; Fletcher 9–2–26–1; Curran 6–0–31–1; Traicos 27–7–56–5; Rawson 17–3–55–1. *Second Innings*—Hogg 12–1–43–0; Dudhia 7–3–13–2; Rawson 15–1–42–5; Curran 2–0–16–0; Traicos 17–4–54–0.

Zimbabweans

J. G. Heron b Inchmore	16	– (2) st Humphries b Patel	16
†D. L. Houghton hit wkt b Alleyne	0	– (1) not out	24
R. D. Brown lbw b Alleyne	3	– b Patel	6
A. J. Pycroft not out	62		
*D. A. G. Fletcher not out	56		
K. M. Curran (did not bat)		(4) not out	0
B 7, l-b 9, n-b 3	19	L-b 2, n-b 4	6
1/4 2/11 3/45 (3 wkts dec.)	156	1/24 2/52 (2 wkts)	52

G. M. Scott, P. W. E. Rawson, M. H. E. M. Dudhia, A. J. Traicos and V. R. Hogg did not bat.

Bowling: *First Innings*—Alleyne 9–1–26–2; Inchmore 8–0–22–1; Weston 9–3–10–0; Illingworth 10–0–47–0; Patel 9–2–32–0. *Second Innings*—Alleyne 5–1–15–0; Inchmore 7–3–8–0; Patel 7–0–23–2; Illingworth 1–1–0–0.

Umpires: W. L. Budd and J. H. Harris.

At Nottingham, June 5, 7, 8. WORCESTERSHIRE lost to NOTTINGHAMSHIRE by nine wickets.

WORCESTERSHIRE v GLOUCESTERSHIRE

At Worcester, June 9, 10, 11. Drawn. Worcestershire 5 pts, Gloucestershire 4 pts. With only six wickets falling for 806 runs on the first two days, a draw was always inevitable, though Gifford raised home hopes on the final afternoon with four wickets as Gloucestershire, set 318 in 212 minutes, played out time. Ormrod, having reached 200 not out in 5 hours, 42 minutes, with eighteen boundaries, was only 4 short of his career best when Worcestershire declared their first innings. Gloucestershire, thanks to Zaheer and Sadiq, declared only 49 behind, but by the end of the second day Worcestershire were back in the driving seat at 117 without loss, with Ormrod 65 and Weston having just completed his first Championship half-century. When Sadiq ended Ormrod's bid for his second century of the match, he had batted over nine hours for his 293 runs.

Worcestershire

M. J. Weston c Hignell b Graveney	14	– c Shepherd b Childs	51
J. A. Ormrod not out	200	– b Sadiq	93
D. N. Patel st Brassington b Sadiq	27	– c Brassington b Doughty	4
Younis Ahmed not out	114		
*P. A. Neale (did not bat)		– (4) not out	79
E. J. O. Hemsley (did not bat)		– (5) not out	34
B 4, l-b 10	14	L-b 4, n-b 3	7
1/47 2/123 (2 wkts dec.)	369	1/119 2/129 3/192 (3 wkts dec.)	268

†D. J. Humphries, J. D. Inchmore, N. Gifford, A. P. Pridgeon and H. L. Alleyne did not bat.

Bonus points – Worcestershire 4 (Score at 100 overs: 323-2).

Bowling: *First Innings*—Shepherd 18–3–53–0; Doughty 15–1–62–0; Graveney 31–6–80–1; Childs 21–3–55–0; Sadiq 24–3–90–1; Zaheer 2–0–15–0. *Second Innings*—Shepherd 6–1–25–0; Doughty 19–2–61–1; Sadiq 20–2–76–1; Graveney 12–4–33–0; Childs 21–7–42–1; Broad 5–2–13–0; Bainbridge 2–0–11–0.

Gloucestershire

A. W. Stovold c Humphries b Inchmore	17 – c and b Gifford	68
B. C. Broad c Ormrod b Patel	36 – lbw b Alleyne	14
Sadiq Mohammad b Gifford	72 – b Gifford	22
Zaheer Abbas lbw b Gifford	77 – c Hemsley b Gifford	0
P. Bainbridge not out	55 – c and b Patel	62
A. J. Hignell not out	44 – b Gifford	11
J. N. Shepherd (did not bat)	– not out	9
*D. A. Graveney (did not bat)	– not out	5
B 8, l-b 6, w 1, n-b 4	19 L-b 4, w 1, n-b 1	6
1/38 2/89 3/205 4/222 (4 wkts dec.)	320 1/25 2/68 3/68 4/155 5/171 6/183 (6 wkts)	197

R. J. Doughty, †A. J. Brassington and J. H. Childs did not bat.

Bonus points – Gloucestershire 4, Worcestershire 1.

Bowling: *First Innings*—Alleyne 20–2–74–0; Pridgeon 6–0–18–0; Gifford 35–8–97–2; Inchmore 6–1–9–1; Patel 24–6–76–1; Weston 4–0–24–0; Hemsley 1–0–3–0. *Second Innings*—Alleyne 13–5–29–1; Pridgeon 7–3–19–0; Inchmore 3–0–12–0; Gifford 24–8–73–4; Patel 15–2–58–1.

Umpires: P. B. Wight and R. S. Herman.

At Hove, June 12, 14. WORCESTERSHIRE lost to SUSSEX by an innings and 37 runs.

At Ilford, June 19, 21, 22. WORCESTERSHIRE drew with ESSEX.

At Cardiff, June 23, 24, 25. WORCESTERSHIRE drew with GLAMORGAN.

WORCESTERSHIRE v LANCASHIRE

At Worcester, June 26, 28, 29. Worcestershire won by 89 runs. Worcestershire 12 pts. Although the umpires deemed the pitch unfit for a prompt start on the final morning, after the first two days had been lost to rain, the captains agreed to proceed with a one-innings match. Turner equalled Don Kenyon's record of 70 centuries for Worcestershire, reaching his hundred in 81 minutes, with eighteen boundaries, off only 80 balls. It was the sixth time in his career he had completed a century before lunch. Patel, with a career-best seven for 46, and young Illingworth, both assisted by some splendid catching, bowled in unison to dismiss Lancashire for 175 after Kennedy and Fowler had given them a good start.

Worcestershire

G. M. Turner c Reidy b McFarlane	115
J. A. Ormrod c Lloyd b Simmons	23
*P. A. Neale b McFarlane	31
Younis Ahmed c Hughes b Simmons	32
D. N. Patel b McFarlane	34
M. J. Weston b McFarlane	6
†D. J. Humphries c Croft b Simmons	0
J. D. Inchmore not out	6
A. E. Warner not out	3
B 4, l-b 4, w 3, n-b 3	14
1/104 2/174 3/174 4/234 5/248 6/249 7/253 (7 wkts dec.)	264

R. K. Illingworth and A. J. Webster did not bat.

Bowling: Croft 7–1–35–0; Folley 5–0–34–0; Reidy 9–0–46–0; Simmons 24–3–71–3; McFarlane 16–2–64–4.

Lancashire

A. Kennedy c Younis b Patel	38	I. Folley b Patel	3
G. Fowler c Younis b Patel	28	C. E. H. Croft c Patel b Illingworth	2
†C. Maynard b Patel	17	L. L. McFarlane not out	0
*D. Lloyd c Weston b Patel	12		
D. P. Hughes c Neale b Patel	39	B 5, l-b 12, w 2, n-b 2	21
J. Abrahams c Webster b Illingworth	0		
J. Simmons c Younis b Illingworth	13	1/66 2/89 3/105 4/131 5/132 6/168	175
B. W. Reidy c Turner b Patel	2	7/168 8/170 9/173	

Bowling: Warner 6–1–16–0; Webster 7–1–24–0; Patel 20–9–46–7; Inchmore 5–0–17–0; Illingworth 13.3–2–51–3.

Umpires: D. G. L. Evans and K. E. Palmer.

†At Broughty Ferry, July 3, 4, 5 (not first-class). Drawn. Worcestershire 369 for eight dec. (G. M. Turner 125, D. N. Patel 84; G. F. Goddard four for 114) and 189 for eight dec. (Younis Ahmed 53; W. A. Morton four for 46); Scotland 316 for five dec. (W. A. Donald 92, R. S. Weir 58 not out, R. G. Swan 53) and 128 for three.

At Sheffield, July 7, 8, 9. WORCESTERSHIRE drew with YORKSHIRE.

At Worcester, July 10, 11, 12. WORCESTERSHIRE drew with PAKISTANIS (See Pakistani tour section).

WORCESTERSHIRE v KENT

At Hereford, July 21, 22, 23. Drawn. Worcestershire 6 pts, Kent 8 pts. Kent killed the game by batting to tea on the final day and setting a target of 288 in two hours. However, this did not stop Turner blazing his way to 66 out of 97 in 69 minutes, and for the second time in the match he reached his half-century off only 54 balls. In the final 45 minutes on the first day he had hit 60 out of an opening stand of 69 with Scott, topping 1,000 runs for the season in the process, but next day it took him another 106 minutes to complete his third century in successive Championship matches. Dilley took four wickets for 15 runs in four overs to arrest Worcestershire's advance, but Humphries put on 62 for the ninth wicket with Illingworth, and 37 with last-man Webster to enable Worcestershire to match Kent's first-innings total.

Kent

N. R. Taylor lbw b Warner	2	– (2) run out	38
L. Potter b Webster	39	– (1) c Inchmore b Illingworth	44
C. J. Tavaré c D'Oliveira b Inchmore	13	– c Neale b Patel	10
M. R. Benson c and b Patel	107	– c Humphries b Patel	80
D. G. Aslett b Patel	75	– lbw b Illingworth	11
*C. S. Cowdrey c Scott b Patel	38	– c D'Oliveira b Patel	27
†A. P. E. Knott c Patel b Inchmore	6	– not out	56
G. W. Johnson not out	12	– not out	12
G. R. Dilley not out	1		
B 1, l-b 13, w 1, n-b 13	28	B 2, l-b 3, n-b 4	9
1/7 2/49 3/71 4/228 5/294 6/294 7/314 (7 wkts dec.)	321	1/77 2/95 3/110 4/148 5/213 6/218 (6 wkts dec.)	287

D. L. Underwood and K. B. S. Jarvis did not bat.

Bonus points – Kent 4, Worcestershire 2 (Score at 100 overs: 300-6).

Bowling: *First Innings*—Warner 13–1–39–1; Inchmore 17.3–4–36–2; Webster 16–3–55–1; Patel 37–10–81–3; Illingworth 9–2–26–0; Hemsley 13–1–56–0. *Second Innings*—Warner 10–1–40–0; Inchmore 10–5–11–0; Patel 41–8–101–3; Illingworth 40–13–107–2; Webster 5–1–19–0.

Worcestershire

G. M. Turner c Cowdrey b Jarvis	118	– c Johnson b Jarvis	66
M. S. Scott b Johnson	4	– c Cowdrey b Dilley	0
*P. A. Neale b Underwood	7	– not out	32
D. N. Patel b Dilley	56		
E. J. O. Hemsley c Knott b Dilley	13		
D. B. D'Oliveira c Cowdrey b Dilley	4	– (4) not out	18
†D. J. Humphries not out	60		
J. D. Inchmore c Benson b Dilley	6		
A. E. Warner b Underwood	1		
R. K. Illingworth c Cowdrey b Dilley	27		
A. J. Webster c Knott b Dilley	12		
L-b 4, n-b 9	13	L-b 5, n-b 1	6
1/69 2/81 3/185 4/205 5/209 6/214 7/220 8/221 9/283	321	1/1 2/97 (2 wkts)	122

Bonus points – Worcestershire 4, Kent 4 (Score at 100 overs: 309-9).

Bowling: *First Innings*—Jarvis 18–0–91–1; Dilley 27–5–87–6; Underwood 35–14–75–2; Johnson 26–6–55–1. *Second Innings*—Dilley 5–1–22–1; Jarvis 10–1–54–1; Underwood 5–0–17–0; Cowdrey 3–1–10–0; Aslett 2–0–13–0.

Umpires: A. G. T. Whitehead and R. Julian.

WORCESTERSHIRE v GLAMORGAN

At Worcester, July 28, 29, 30. Drawn. Worcestershire 6 pts, Glamorgan 5 pts. Worcestershire needed a dogged 59 not out from Curtis, playing his first Championship match of the season, to get them off the hook when it was looking as if Glamorgan would win their first Championship match for almost a year. He batted 161 minutes to give Worcestershire a lead of 274, which was more than enough to save the game. On a slow, unresponsive wicket, Ontong, with four for 19 in twelve overs, and Thomas, who had a match return of seven for 102, had Worcestershire struggling on the final morning until the last two wickets put on 71.

Worcestershire

M. J. Weston c E. W. Jones b Davis	0	– lbw b Thomas	43
J. A. Ormrod c Hopkins b Thomas	24	– c Lloyd b Davis	3
*P. A. Neale b Thomas	46	– lbw b Thomas	33
D. N. Patel b Daniels	43	– lbw b Ontong	19
T. S. Curtis c Francis b Davis	7	– not out	59
E. J. O. Hemsley c Rowe b Thomas	39	– c E. W. Jones b Davis	16
†D. J. Humphries b Thomas	48	– c E. W. Jones b Ontong	1
R. K. Illingworth not out	47	– c E. W. Jones b Ontong	0
J. D. Inchmore c Lloyd b Davis	68	– b Ontong	11
N. Gifford not out	25	– c E. W. Jones b Thomas	9
A. P. Pridgeon (did not bat)		– not out	3
B 5, l-b 10, w 1, n-b 4	20	L-b 10, w 2, n-b 15	27
1/0 2/67 3/98 4/117 5/134 6/216 7/219 8/320 (8 wkts dec.)	367	1/17 2/78 3/95 4/112 5/136 6/138 7/139 8/153 9/193 (9 wkts dec.)	224

Bonus points – Worcestershire 4, Glamorgan 3.

Bowling: *First Innings*—Davis 31–5–101–3; Ontong 8–2–32–0; Thomas 16–2–52–4; Lloyd 28–5–85–0; Daniels 13–4–53–1; Rowe 4–1–24–0. *Second Innings*—Davis 25–5–67–2; Thomas 14–2–50–3; Daniels 12–2–30–0; Lloyd 9–4–20–0; Ontong 19–8–30–4.

Glamorgan

A. Jones not out	146	– c Humphries b Inchmore	2
A. L. Jones lbw b Pridgeon	1	– c and b Inchmore	23
D. A. Francis c Weston b Patel	5	– not out	58
S. A. B. Daniels b Inchmore	0		
R. C. Ontong c and b Patel	44	– (4) c Humphries b Inchmore	1
J. A. Hopkins c and b Gifford	45	– (5) not out	34
C. J. C. Rowe not out	45		
B 15, l-b 9, w 2, n-b 5	31	B 1, n-b 6	7
1/6 2/24 3/24 4/116 5/218 (5 wkts dec.)	317	1/19 2/35 3/45 (3 wkts)	125

†E. W. Jones, J. G. Thomas, *B. J. Lloyd and W. W. Davis did not bat.

Bonus points – Glamorgan 2, Worcestershire 2 (Score at 100 overs: 249-5).

Bowling: *First Innings*—Pridgeon 18–2–40–1; Inchmore 16–3–56–1; Patel 28–9–54–2; Gifford 29–8–57–1; Weston 10–3–21–0; Illingworth 17–3–58–0. *Second Innings*—Pridgeon 7–0–35–0; Inchmore 7–1–30–3; Gifford 3–1–3–0; Patel 8–0–29–0; Illingworth 6–1–16–0; Ormrod 1–0–5–0.

Umpires: A. G. T. Whitehead and D. R. Shepherd.

At Northampton, July 31, August 2, 3. WORCESTERSHIRE drew with NORTHAMPTONSHIRE.

WORCESTERSHIRE v LEICESTERSHIRE

At Worcester, August 7, 9, 10. Drawn. Worcestershire 8 pts, Leicestershire 5 pts. Tolchard's decision to bat until 22 minutes after tea on the final day prompted angry reactions from New Road spectators, who accorded Davison a hostile reception as he walked off with an unbeaten 139, made in 261 minutes with one 6 and sixteen 4s. Tolchard's defence was that three of his bowlers were not fully fit, but in setting Worcestershire 236 to win in 88 minutes he forced a farcical finish. Inchmore produced his best bowling return of the season at New Road in Leicestershire's first innings, and then Younis marked his return after a month out through injury with a typically stylish 122. Weston, with a Championship-best 68, helped Worcestershire build a lead of 56 and gain maximum bonus points for the first time.

Leicestershire

J. C. Balderstone b Gifford	35	– c Patel b Inchmore 4
R. A. Cobb c Humphries b Inchmore	7	– b Inchmore 11
D. I. Gower c Younis b Inchmore	4	– c and b PatelPatel 74
B. F. Davison lbw b Pridgeon	14	– not out 139
N. E. Briers c Pridgeon b Inchmore	33	– b Patel 13
*†R. W. Tolchard c Humphries b Alleyne	2	– (7) not out 6
J. F. Steele b Inchmore	33	
G. J. Parsons c Gifford b Inchmore	13	– (6) st Humphries b Patel 30
N. G. B. Cook c Inchmore b Gifford	9	
J. P. Agnew b Gifford	56	
L. B. Taylor not out	24	
B 1, l-b 5, n-b 11	17	B 2, l-b 9, n-b 3 14
1/16 2/20 3/51 4/71 5/76 6/105 7/128 8/152 9/172	247	1/9 2/28 3/174 4/210 5/270 (5 wkts dec.) 291

Bonus points – Leicestershire 2, Worcestershire 4.

Bowling: *First Innings*—Alleyne 24–5–76–1; Inchmore 24–4–59–5; Pridgeon 23–5–63–1; Gifford 25.1–12–28–3; Patel 3–1–4–0. *Second Innings*—Alleyne 3–1–6–0; Inchmore 8.5–0–26–2; Pridgeon 10–5–19–0; Weston 9.1–2–33–0; Gifford 31–5–89–0; Patel 30–4–88–3; Neale 4–0–16–0.

Worcestershire

J. A. Ormrod lbw b Agnew	10	– (2) c and b Steele 5
M. J. Weston c Tolchard b Taylor	68	– (1) not out 5
*P. A. Neale c Tolchard b Parsons	21	
Younis Ahmed b Cook	122	– (3) not out 12
D. N. Patel c Parsons b Steele	11	
T. S. Curtis c sub b Cook	39	
†D. J. Humphries st Tolchard b Cook	12	
J. D. Inchmore not out	3	
H. L. Alleyne not out	6	
B 1, l-b 5, n-b 5	11	B 1, w 2 3
1/40 2/75 3/116 4/159 5/257 6/285 7/296 (7 wkts dec.)	303	1/5 (1 wkt) 25

N. Gifford and A. P. Pridgeon did not bat.

Bonus points – Worcestershire 4, Leicestershire 3.

Bowling: *First Innings*—Taylor 21–7–41–1; Agnew 8–0–49–1; Parsons 20–2–87–1; Cook 27–10–56–3; Steele 15–5–28–1; Briers 9–1–31–0. *Second Innings*—Steele 10–6–4–1; Balderstone 9–6–3–0; Gower 5–2–10–0; Cobb 4–2–5–0.

Umpires: H. D. Bird and W. E. Alley.

At Southampton, August 14, 16, 17. WORCESTERSHIRE beat HAMPSHIRE by one wicket.

WORCESTERSHIRE v SURREY

At Worcester, August 21, 23, 24. Drawn. Worcestershire 4 pts, Surrey 5 pts. Rain washed out all but 25 minutes of the final day's play after the captains had reached an interesting compromise. Worcestershire declared 231 behind, still needing 82 to avoid the follow-on, which Surrey agreed not to enforce. Surrey, put in, had batted throughout the first day to reach 419 for two, with Butcher (twenty 4s), and Smith adding 225 for the second wicket in 193 minutes. Knight batted for 90 minutes more on the second morning and Surrey amassed the highest Championship score of the season, Smith making a career-best 160 in 323 minutes. Knight was 95 not out when he declared. Patel thwarted Surrey's hopes of getting Worcestershire in again by the end of the day with a defiant 133, his first Championship century of the season and including two 6s and sixteen 4s, with 22 coming off one over from Needham.

Surrey

A. R. Butcher b Patel	162	– not out	20
G. P. Howarth c Younis b Weston	25	– not out	15
D. M. Smith b Pridgeon	160		
*R. D. V. Knight not out	95		
M. A. Lynch b Webster	2		
†C. J. Richards lbw b Webster	0		
D. J. Thomas c Pridgeon b Perryman	44		
A. Needham b Weston	12		
B 6, l-b 19, w 9, n-b 2	36	L-b 1	1
1/74 2/299 3/431 4/440 5/440 6/519 7/536	(7 wkts dec.) 536		(no wkt) 36

S. T. Clarke, R. D. Jackman and K. S. Mackintosh did not bat.

Bonus points – Surrey 4 (Score at 100 overs: 322-2).

Bowling: *First Innings*—Pridgeon 25–0–92–1; Webster 29–6–99–2; Perryman 23–2–91–1; Weston 14.2–0–63–2; Gifford 23–1–82–0; Patel 30–4–73–1. *Second Innings*—Pridgeon 3.2–0–14–0; Webster 3–0–21–0.

Worcestershire

M. J. Weston c Richards b Jackman	21
J. A. Ormrod c Needham b Mackintosh	57
D. N. Patel c Richards b Thomas	133
Younis Ahmed lbw b Needham	34
*P. A. Neale not out	36
T. S. Curtis not out	10
B 6, l-b 1, n-b 7	14
1/49 2/122 3/197 4/291 (4 wkts dec.)	305

†D. J. Humphries, N. Gifford, A. P. Pridgeon A. J. Webster and S. P. Perryman did not bat.

Bonus points – Worcestershire 4, Surrey 1.

Bowling: Clarke 14–5–40–0; Jackman 22–5–66–1; Thomas 14–2–47–1; Needham 20–0–92–1; Mackintosh 10–2–33–1; Butcher 3–0–13–0.

Umpires: B. J. Meyer and M. J. Kitchen.

At Blackpool, August 25, 26, 27. WORCESTERSHIRE drew with LANCASHIRE.

At Birmingham, August 28, 30, 31. WORCESTERSHIRE drew with WARWICKSHIRE.

WORCESTERSHIRE v NOTTINGHAMSHIRE

At Worcester, September 1, 2, 3. Drawn. Worcestershire 5 pts, Nottinghamshire 8 pts. Worcestershire looked well on the way to achieving a target of 280 in 200 minutes while Younis was hitting his fourth hundred of the season, including three 6s and sixteen 4s. But after Hemmings had him caught in the deep, they lost momentum and duly settled for a draw. Randall, with his first Championship hundred of the season, and Hadlee put on 142 in Nottinghamshire's first innings before Randall provided Patel with his 50th wicket of the summer. Worcestershire were indebted to Humphries, who hit eighteen fours in his 98, for avoiding the follow-on and restricting Nottinghamshire to a lead of 49. Only Younis and Patel, who hit 48 in 29 minutes, including 40 off nineteen deliveries from Hemmings, had earlier batted with any authority.

Nottinghamshire

B. Hassan lbw b Warner	10	– c Perryman b Newport	52
R. T. Robinson run out	0	– lbw b Perryman	9
D. W. Randall c Webster b Patel	122	– b Newport	45
*C. E. B. Rice c Patel b Warner	5	– c sub b Newport	8
J. D. Birch c Curtis b Patel	67	– not out	54
R. J. Hadlee not out	100	– c Warner b Newport	16
†B. N. French b Warner	8	– not out	27
E. E. Hemmings not out	2		
B 5, l-b 4, n-b 3	12	B 2, l-b 9, w 1, n-b 7	19
1/0 2/12 3/18 4/150 5/292 6/313 (6 wkts dec.)	326	1/37 2/105 3/115 4/130 5/146 (5 wkts dec.)	230

K. E. Cooper, M. K. Bore and P. M. Such did not bat.

Bonus points – Nottinghamshire 4, Worcestershire 2.

Bowling: *First Innings*—Warner 28–5–92–3; Perryman 20–5–51–0; Webster 16–1–79–0; Patel 20–6–63–2; Newport 5–0–29–0. *Second Innings*—Warner 9–2–36–0; Perryman 30–7–81–1; Webster 6–1–18–0; Newport 15–0–76–4.

Worcestershire

J. A. Ormrod b Hemmings	15	– lbw b Cooper	3
M. J. Weston b Such	15	– c French b Cooper	2
D. N. Patel c Birch b Such	48	– (5) c and b Bore	39
Younis Ahmed c and b Hemmings	50	– c Rice b Hemmings	114
*P. A. Neale c Randall b Bore	1	– (3) c Hassan b Such	31
T. S. Curtis lbw b Such	0	– (8) not out	8
†D. J. Humphries c Birch b Such	98	– (6) c Hadlee b Bore	4
A. E. Warner c Hadlee b Hemmings	17	– (7) c Bore b Hemmings	9
P. J. Newport lbw b Bore	11	– not out	6
A. J. Webster lbw b Bore	1		
S. P. Perryman not out	10		
B 2, l-b 7, n-b 2	11	B 9, l-b 2	11
1/27 2/45 3/94 4/105 5/110 6/142 7/174 8/207 9/215	277	1/3 2/10 3/65 4/162 5/178 6/209 7/213 (7 wkts)	227

Bonus points – Worcestershire 3, Nottinghamshire 4.

Bowling: *First Innings*—Hadlee 4–1–12–0; Cooper 8–4–20–0; Hemmings 27–8–103–3; Such 23.3–4–94–4; Bore 19–6–37–3. *Second Innings*—Cooper 8–0–30–2; Hemmings 20–3–62–2; Bore 24–8–95–2; Such 10–3–29–1.

Umpires: C. Cook and R. Julian.

At Taunton, September 8, 9. WORCESTERSHIRE lost to SOMERSET by an innings and 18 runs.

WORCESTERSHIRE v MIDDLESEX

At Worcester, September 11, 13, 14. Middlesex won by ten wickets. Middlesex 24 pts, Worcestershire 5 pts. Brearley fittingly hit the winning runs in his final game for Middlesex, who coasted home by ten wickets with two sessions to spare. Humphries and Patel had provided the only resistance as Middlesex dismissed the home side for 168 in their first innings to clinch the four points they needed to be sure of the Championship title. Weston, with only three wickets for 300 runs all summer, then removed the first three Middlesex batsmen for 62, but Butcher and Edmonds led the recovery which produced a lead of 214. Weston and the Worcestershire tail delayed the inevitable until the final morning, when Middlesex were left needing 50 runs to win.

Worcestershire

M. S. Scott b Cowans	8	– (2) b Gatting	37
J. A. Ormrod c Gatting b Cowans	9	– (1) b Cowans	4
D. N. Patel c Brearley b Gatting	44	– c Downton b Cowans	16
*P. A. Neale c Downton b Slack	12	– lbw b Gatting	50
M. J. Weston lbw b Slack	6	– c Downton b Hughes	64
T. S. Curtis b Hughes	2	– lbw b Gatting	20
†D. J. Humphries b Emburey	56	– c Butcher b Gatting	0
R. K. Illingworth c Emburey b Cowans	4	– c Emburey b Hughes	19
A. E. Warner c Daniel b Emburey	14	– c Slack b Hughes	22
S. P. Perryman not out	5	– run out	4
R. M. Ellcock lbw b Emburey	0	– not out	13
B 3, w 1, n-b 4	8	B 1, l-b 11, n-b 2	14
1/17 2/26 3/51 4/64 5/67 6/112 7/134 8/150 9/168	168	1/20 2/41 3/109 4/116 5/140 6/140 7/182 8/220 9/235	263

Bonus points – Worcestershire 1, Middlesex 4.

Bowling: *First Innings*—Daniel 11–2–33–0; Cowans 13–2–50–3; Hughes 9–1–34–1; Slack 4–0–14–2; Gatting 2–1–9–1; Edmonds 3–2–2–0; Emburey 9–2–18–3. *Second Innings*—Cowans 13–4–45–2; Hughes 18.4–2–59–3; Daniel 5–2–13–0; Edmonds 6–2–22–0; Slack 7–2–29–0; Emburey 14–3–38–0; Gatting 12–4–43–4.

Middlesex

W. N. Slack b Weston	18	– not out	32
*J. M. Brearley c Curtis b Weston	31	– not out	14
R. G. P. Ellis c Warner b Weston	1		
M. W. Gatting c Illingworth b Perryman	61		
R. O. Butcher b Illingworth	94		
J. E. Emburey b Illingworth	2		
†P. R. Downton c Illingworth b Perryman	20		
P. H. Edmonds c Perryman b Ellcock	92		
S. P. Hughes lbw b Ellcock	18		
N. G. Cowans lbw b Ellcock	16		
W. W. Daniel not out	0		
B 9, l-b 14, w 1, n-b 5	29	L-b 3, n-b 1	4
1/50 2/54 3/62 4/191 5/202 6/228 7/271 8/327 9/372	382		(no wkt) 50

Bonus points – Middlesex 4, Worcestershire 4 (Score at 100 overs: 372-9).

Bowling: *First Innings*—Ellcock 20.1–1–80–3; Warner 6–0–22–0; Perryman 32–8–85–2; Weston 11–2–42–3; Illingworth 33–6–124–2. *Second Innings*—Ellcock 6–1–10–0; Perryman 7–4–14–0; Illingworth 3.1–0–15–0; Curtis 2–0–7–0.

Umpires: D. G. L. Evans and R. Palmer.

YORKSHIRE

Patron: HRH The Duchess of Kent
President: N. W. D. Yardley
Chairman: M. G. Crawford
Chairman, Cricket Committee: J. R. Burnet
Secretary: J. Lister
Headingley Cricket Ground, Leeds LS6 3BU
(Telephone: 0532-787394)
Cricket Manager: R. Illingworth, CBE
Captain: 1982 – C. M. Old and R. Illingworth; 1983 – R. Illingworth
Coach: D. E. V. Padgett

The erratic nature of Yorkshire cricket was reflected in the fortunes of their former England seam bowler, Chris Old, who began the summer as club captain only to find himself surplus to requirements in September. The decline in his fortunes resulted from an unhappy start to the programme, particularly in the one-day competitions, with only one victory in nine games – and that against the Minor Counties.

In one of the most controversial moves of even Yorkshire's trouble-strewn recent history, Old was replaced by the manager, Ray Illingworth, who resumed his playing career at Ilford fifteen days after his 50th birthday. Not even Illingworth's experience and tactical skill, however, could compensate for the lack of consistency and, in some cases, application as the side continued to perform some way below expectations.

The hard fact that the committee had to face was that in four years of change things had taken a distinct turn for the worse. When Geoff Boycott was removed from the captaincy in 1978, Yorkshire were fourth in the Championship and seventh in the Sunday League, figures which compare favourably with tenth and sixteenth respectively in 1982. Even so, it could be argued that Illingworth had held things together reasonably well in difficult circumstances and his reappointment was a formality. No generally acceptable alternative could be found, and as this is to be his last campaign the horizon remains clouded by doubt.

Although at the end of the season he was offered only a one-year contract (which he accepted) Boycott once again stood head and shoulders above any other batsman in terms of dedication and ability. He achieved the rare feat of being on the field throughout both matches against Warwickshire and also made the decisive contribution to four of the five first-class victories. Largely under his influence, Yorkshire proved difficult to beat in the Championship. Bill Athey also made over 1,000 runs with impressive fluency. But the county seldom looked like bowling out the opposition either cheaply or in quick time.

Old, reduced to his Sunday League run on a number of occasions by a persistent back strain, lacked a yard of pace. Arnold Sidebottom produced bursts of hostility but also had injury problems, while Alan Ramage, of whom so much was hoped, had his season ruined by a bad groin strain which limited his opportunity and wrecked his rhythm. In the circumstances, heavy responsibility fell on the shoulders of Graham Stevenson, who managed to take five wickets in an innings only once and also had difficulties with his back.

In 1983 prospects may be shaped by the form of Ramage and youngsters Paul Jarvis, Nick Taylor and Simon Dennis. There will also be interest in the work of Phil Carrick, who, responding to Illingworth's shrewd handling, gradually developed the attacking quality of his left-arm spin to the point at which, at the end of the 1982 season, he believed himself to be bowling better than at any stage of his career. As a bowler Illingworth was understandably a much less potent force than in the past, but he batted resolutely and accepted more than his share of bad luck as an off-spinner with professional calm.

Boycott and Stevenson had the satisfaction of becoming the first pair for 50 years to break the record for any Yorkshire wicket. They added 148 for the tenth at Edgbaston, removing Lord Hawke and David Hunter from the yearbook, with Stevenson's 115 representing the highest not out score made by a No. 11 batsman in first-class cricket.

The picture on the one-day front was one of much gloom, with the side slumping to their lowest Sunday League placing. After remarkable displays against Worcestershire and Essex had swept them into the semi-finals of the NatWest Bank Trophy, form and fortune deserted them there, too, against an injury-hit Warwickshire. The bowling lacked accuracy under pressure, with the part-time left-arm seam bowler Steve Stuchbury being as impressive as anyone. Jarvis also earned high marks, including the county's first Sunday League hat-trick, but Illingworth acknowledged that a better relationship between the bowling and field placings would have to be established if any progress is to be made.

Not the least of the worrying signs concerned a serious decline in membership, which helped to strain finances already being hit by below-average Sunday attendances. – J.C.

YORKSHIRE 1982

[*Bill Smith*

Back row: M. D. Moxon, S. N. Hartley, A. Sidebottom, J. D. Love, S. Stutchbury, P. W. Jarvis. *Front row:* C. W. J. Athey, G. Boycott, R. Illingworth (*captain*), D. L. Bairstow, P. Carrick.

YORKSHIRE RESULTS

All first-class matches – Played 22: Won 5, Lost 1, Drawn 16. Abandoned 1.

County Championship matches – Played 21: Won 5, Lost 1, Drawn 15. Abandoned 1.

Bonus points – Batting 48, Bowling 51.

Competition placings – Schweppes County Championship, 10th; NatWest Bank Trophy, s-f; Benson and Hedges Cup, 5th in Group A; John Player League, 16th.

COUNTY CHAMPIONSHIP AVERAGES

BATTING

	Birthplace	*M*	*I*	*NO*	*R*	*HI*	*Avge*
G. Boycott c	*Fitzwilliam*	21	37	6	1,913	159	61.70
M. D. Moxon	*Barnsley*	2	4	0	197	67	49.25
C. W. J. Athey c	*Middlesbrough*	21	37	6	1,278	134	41.22
J. D. Love c	*Leeds*	17	28	5	770	123	33.47
S. N. Hartley c	*Shipley*	19	29	9	619	114	30.95
D. L. Bairstow c	*Bradford*	21	28	8	599	77	29.95
R. G. Lumb c	*Doncaster*	19	31	0	777	81	25.06
G. B. Stevenson c	*Ackworth*	16	19	4	356	115*	23.73
P. Carrick c	*Leeds*	19	21	3	423	93	23.50
A. Sidebottom c	*Barnsley*	19	18	8	233	44*	23.30
K. Sharp c	*Leeds*	9	16	1	343	52	22.86
R. Illingworth c	*Pudsey*	13	6	2	86	33	21.50
C. M. Old c	*Middlesbrough*	16	18	3	207	32	13.80

Also batted: P. A. Booth (*Huddersfield*) (1 match) 0*; S. J. Dennis (*Scarborough*) (2 matches) 5*; P. W. Jarvis (*Redcar*) (6 matches) 0*, 7, 0; A. Ramage (*Guisborough*) (4 matches) 4*, 0; N. S. Taylor (*Holmfirth*) (3 matches) 0*; J. P. Whiteley (*Otley*) (3 matches) 1, 5*.

**Signifies not out.* c *Denotes county cap.*

BOWLING

	O	*M*	*R*	*W*	*Avge*	*BB*
A. Sidebottom	495.2	95	1,538	62	24.80	6-31
C. M. Old	458.2	125	1,229	47	26.14	6-76
S. J. Dennis	66	10	262	10	26.20	5-42
G. B. Stevenson	422.4	87	1,423	45	31.62	5-72
P. Carrick	532.5	135	1,329	39	34.07	6-90

Also bowled: C. W. J. Athey 27.1–1–98–0; P. A. Booth 10–3–22–0; G. Boycott 57.2–13–120–8; S. N. Hartley 116–27–373–6; R. Illingworth 223.4–66–587–9; P. W. Jarvis 132–25–434–8; J. D. Love 3–3–0–0; A. Ramage 90–14–381–5; N. S. Taylor 62.3–14–186–6; J. P. Whiteley 16–0–71–1.

HUNDREDS

The following fourteen three-figure innings were played for Yorkshire in County Championship matches – G. Boycott (6) 138 v Northamptonshire (Northampton), 134 v Glamorgan (Leeds), 159 v Worcestershire (Sheffield), 152* v Warwickshire (Leeds), 122* v Sussex (Scarborough), 129 v Somerset (Weston-super-Mare); C. W. J. Athey (4) 100 v Glamorgan (Leeds), 134 v Derbyshire (Derby), 100 v Kent (Leeds), 114* v Surrey (The Oval); J. D. Love (2) 110 v Derbyshire (Derby), 123 v Surrey (The Oval); S. N. Hartley (1) 114 v Gloucestershire (Bradford); G. B. Stevenson (1) 115* v Warwickshire (Birmingham).

At Northampton, May 5, 6, 7. YORKSHIRE drew with NORTHAMPTONSHIRE.

YORKSHIRE v GLAMORGAN

At Leeds, May 12, 13, 14. Drawn. Yorkshire 7 pts, Glamorgan 6 pts. Yorkshire were put in on an easy-paced pitch, with Glamorgan presumably hoping for a third-day declaration, but an attack lacking any excesses of pace and spin could not contain Boycott, while Athey and Love also scored readily. Hopkins, despite a painful elbow injury, held the Glamorgan innings together. With batsmen in total command, Yorkshire were in a difficult position with regard to their declaration on the last day, when Athey completed a splendid century, and they finally set Glamorgan a target of 307 in just over three hours. This was reasonable enough, as the side batting last had an obvious advantage, but it was beyond Glamorgan's capabilities.

Yorkshire

G. Boycott lbw b Rowe	134	– lbw b Ontong	15
R. G. Lumb c Francis b Nash	10	– c Hopkins b Ontong	67
C. W. J. Athey c Hopkins b Lloyd	77	– b Ontong	100
J. D. Love c Holmes b Lloyd	65	– (5) c Ontong b Nash	4
K. Sharp lbw b Ontong	5	– (6) not out	19
S. N. Hartley not out	40	– (7) not out	15
†D. L. Bairstow c E. W. Jones b Ontong	13		
G. B. Stevenson c Barwick b Nash	9	– (4) c Barwick b Ontong	14
*C. M. Old not out	0		
B 4, l-b 13, w 3, n-b 7	27	B 2, l-b 9, n-b 3	14
1/20 2/189 3/285 4/294 5/317 6/355 7/375 (7 wkts dec.)	380	1/34 2/174 3/202 4/205 5/210 (5 wkts dec.)	248

P. Carrick and A. Sidebottom did not bat.

Bonus points – Yorkshire 4, Glamorgan 2 (Score at 100 overs: 321-5).

Bowling: *First Innings*—Nash 27–7–95–2; Ontong 28–10–73–2; Barwick 15–5–25–0; Lloyd 24–3–86–2; Miandad 4–0–21–0; Holmes 5–2–14–0; Rowe 10–1–39–1. *Second Innings*—Nash 24–2–111–1; Ontong 23–4–80–4; Barwick 8–1–16–0; Lloyd 2–0–27–0.

Glamorgan

A. Jones b Stevenson	4	– lbw b Sidebottom	12
J. A. Hopkins c Old b Sidebottom	80	– not out	64
B. J. Lloyd b Sidebottom	2		
R. C. Ontong c Old b Sidebottom	75	– (3) lbw b Carrick	19
*Javed Miandad c Old b Carrick	50	– (4) not out	14
C. J. C. Rowe b Stevenson	18		
D. A. Francis run out	30		
G. C. Holmes c Bairstow b Sidebottom	6		
†E. W. Jones not out	0		
M. A. Nash c Bairstow b Stevenson	31		
B 5, l-b 5, w 1, n-b 15	26	L-b 1, n-b 2	3
1/5 2/18 3/112 4/141 5/196 6/265 7/273 8/288 9/322 (9 wkts dec.)	322	1/26 2/75 (2 wkts)	112

S. R. Barwick did not bat.

Bonus points – Glamorgan 4, Yorkshire 3 (Score at 100 overs: 314-8).

Bowling: *First Innings*—Old 19–4–40–0; Stevenson 25.1–6–68–3; Sidebottom 31–7–83–4; Hartley 3–0–27–0; Carrick 22–3–68–1; Athey 4–0–10–0. *Second Innings*—Old 5–1–13–0; Stevenson 8–3–15–0; Sidebottom 7–2–21–1; Carrick 17–3–36–1; Athey 1–0–7–0; Hartley 10–4–17–0; Love 3–3–0–0.

Umpires: D. J. Constant and N. T. Plews.

At Bradford, May 15, 17, 18. YORKSHIRE drew with INDIANS (See Indian tour section).

At Birmingham, May 19, 20, 21. YORKSHIRE beat WARWICKSHIRE by nine wickets.

YORKSHIRE v LANCASHIRE

At Leeds, May 29, 30, 31. Drawn. Yorkshire 6 pts, Lancashire 5 pts. A seaming pitch made life hard for the early Lancashire batsmen, although Yorkshire were handicapped by a back injury which limited Old to his Sunday League run-up. A century by Hughes rescued his side from a possible collapse, while Abrahams survived several alarms to assist impressively. Yorkshire similarly recovered from a hesitant start, thanks to Athey and the aggressive Bairstow. Adventurous Lancashire batting set up the prospect of a challenging conclusion, with Yorkshire's target 290 in three hours. Boycott and Lumb made 144 in two hours, but a hostile spell by Croft, who had a defensive field for much of the time, ensured a draw.

Lancashire

A. Kennedy c Bairstow b Sidebottom	20	– c sub b Carrick	43
G. Fowler c Carrick b Taylor	32	– c Love b Old	2
D. Lloyd b Old	21	– c Carrick b Sidebottom	81
*C. H. Lloyd lbw b Old	5	– c Bairstow b Taylor	15
D. P. Hughes not out	126	– c Jarvis b Taylor	44
J. Abrahams c Bairstow b Old	57	– not out	38
B. W. Reidy c Bairstow b Sidebottom	19	– c Sidebottom b Carrick	11
I. Folley b Old	4	– not out	5
P. J. W. Allott run out	30		
C. E. H. Croft not out	8		
L-b 15, w 6, n-b 8	29	L-b 3, w 4, n-b 9	16
1/38 2/76 3/84 4/87 5/221 6/254 7/272 8/336 (8 wkts dec.)	351	1/7 2/93 3/132 4/193 5/205 6/224 (6 wkts dec.)	255

†M. A. Wallwork did not bat.

Bonus points – Lancashire 3, Yorkshire 2 (Score at 100 overs: 272-6).

Bowling: *First Innings*—Old 35–13–91–4; Jarvis 21–3–68–0; Sidebottom 24–7–71–2; Taylor 12–2–45–1; Carrick 21–8–47–0. *Second Innings*—Old 6–2–33–1; Jarvis 8–1–33–0; Taylor 13–1–42–2; Sidebottom 12–3–43–1; Carrick 21–2–88–2.

Yorkshire

G. Boycott c Kennedy b Croft	13	– c Wallwork b Reidy	68
R. G. Lumb run out	29	– c Hughes b Reidy	72
C. W. J. Athey b Abrahams	90	– (4) not out	38
J. D. Love lbw b Allott	0	– (6) c Wallwork b Croft	4
K. Sharp c Abrahams b Allott	43	– c Wallwork b Croft	0
†D. L. Bairstow not out	70	– (3) b Croft	7
P. Carrick b Reidy	44		
A. Sidebottom not out	7	– (7) not out	1
B 7, l-b 6, w 2, n-b 6	21	L-b 6, n-b 1	7
1/43 2/73 3/74 4/188 5/188 6/280 (6 wkts dec.)	317	1/144 2/150 3/176 4/176 5/196 (5 wkts)	197

*C. M. Old, N. S. Taylor and P. W. Jarvis did not bat.

Bonus points – Yorkshire 4, Lancashire 2.

Bowling: *First Innings*—Croft 27–4–103–1; Allott 19–5–52–2; Folley 12–3–40–0; Reidy 13–5–40–1; Abrahams 11–3–29–1; D. Lloyd 6–0–20–0; Hughes 1–0–12–0. *Second Innings*—Folley 6–1–22–0; Croft 15.2–1–51–3; Reidy 14–1–78–2; Allott 10–1–39–0; D. Lloyd 1–1–0–0.

Umpires: D. J. Constant and D. O. Oslear.

At Hinckley, June 2, 3, 4. YORKSHIRE drew with LEICESTERSHIRE.

†At Sheffield, June 10 (not first-class). YORKSHIRE beat ZIMBABWEANS by three wickets. Zimbabweans 202 (56.3 overs) (D. A. G. Fletcher 53, K. M. Curran 33; P. W. Jarvis three for 47); Yorkshire 203 for seven (59.3 overs) (G. Boycott 98 not out; D. A. G. Fletcher three for 30).

YORKSHIRE v MIDDLESEX

At Sheffield, June 12, 14, 15. Drawn. Yorkshire 6 pts, Middlesex 5 pts. Daniel had Yorkshire in trouble after they had been put in on a pitch lacking in bounce and allowing some movement off the seam, but the last two wickets added 52. Middlesex, surviving a poor start, were accelerating under Gatting's influence when Stevenson brought about a collapse in which five wickets fell for 10 runs in 28 balls. Love, in brilliant form, led Yorkshire into a commanding position as the Middlesex bowling faltered under pressure, but rain ended the match more than two and a half hours early to thwart Yorkshire. There were thirteen lbw victims – a record for a Yorkshire match.

Yorkshire

G. Boycott lbw b Selvey	6	– lbw b Gatting	34
R. G. Lumb lbw b Daniel	3	– c Maru b Emburey	27
C. W. J. Athey lbw b Daniel	47	– c Brearley b Gatting	0
J. D. Love c Gatting b Selvey	0	– (5) not out	81
K. Sharp b Daniel	47	– (6) c Downton b Daniel	3
S. N. Hartley c Downton b Daniel	18	– (7) not out	60
†D. L. Bairstow c Downton b Daniel	18		
P. Carrick b Selvey	0	– (4) lbw b Daniel	6
A. Sidebottom c Downton b Gatting	13		
*C. M. Old c Brearley b Daniel	29		
G. B. Stevenson not out	8		
B 2, l-b 9, n-b 3	14	B 6, l-b 4, w 7, n-b 8	25
1/7 2/9 3/13 4/107 5/116 6/146 7/147 8/151 9/180	203	1/65 2/66 3/79 4/85 5/103 (5 wkts dec.)	236

Bonus points – Yorkshire 2, Middlesex 4.

Bowling: *First Innings*—Daniel 21.3–3–60–6; Selvey 31–7–66–3; Emburey 6–2–13–0; Williams 8–1–29–0; Gatting 8–3–21–1. *Second Innings*—Daniel 12–3–21–2; Williams 15–0–60–0; Selvey 12–1–27–0; Emburey 17–6–44–1; Gatting 10–4–22–2; Maru 8–3–24–0; Slack 3–1–13–0.

Middlesex

*J. M. Brearley lbw b Old	25	– not out	18
W. N. Slack lbw b Stevenson	3	– lbw b Old	0
C. T. Radley lbw b Stevenson	30	– b Stevenson	11
M. W. Gatting lbw b Stevenson	38	– not out	8
R. O. Butcher lbw b Old	0		
J. E. Emburey b Stevenson	3		
†P. R. Downton c Athey b Sidebottom	12		
N. F. Williams lbw b Old	4		
M. W. W. Selvey c Hartley b Boycott	25		
R. J. Maru lbw b Old	12		
W. W. Daniel not out	0		
L-b 4, n-b 2	6	L-b 2	2
1/4 2/37 3/98 4/99 5/99 6/103 7/108 8/134 9/158	158	1/5 2/22 (2 wkts)	39

Bonus points – Middlesex 1, Yorkshire 4.

Bowling: *First Innings*—Old 20–5–48–4; Stevenson 17–5–46–4; Sidebottom 16–3–57–1; Boycott 2.3–1–1–1. *Second Innings*—Old 6–2–11–1; Stevenson 6–0–19–1; Sidebottom 0.5–0–7–0.

Umpires: R. Julian and K. E. Palmer.

YORKSHIRE v NORTHAMPTONSHIRE

At Middlesbrough, June 19, 21, 22. Drawn. Yorkshire 1 pt, Northamptonshire 5 pts. Rain ruined a contest that Northamptonshire dominated from the start. Given first use of an easy-paced pitch, they thrashed some very poor bowling, Larkins and Cook setting up a series of records. Their opening partnership of 278 was the best for the county against Yorkshire, and Larkins's 186 became the highest in the same context. Griffiths extracted far more life from the pitch when Yorkshire batted, and only a determined third-wicket stand of 95 in 28 overs prevented total embarrassment. The last day was washed out, much to Yorkshire's relief.

Northamptonshire

*G. Cook not out	112
W. Larkins c Bairstow b Hartley	186
P. Willey c Bairstow b Old	16
A. J. Lamb c Bairstow b Sidebottom	49
L-b 9, w 1, n-b 9	19
1/278 2/302 3/382 (3 wkts dec.)	382

R. G. Williams, D. J. Capel, D. S. Steele, †G. Sharp, N. A. Mallender, T. M. Lamb and B. J. Griffiths did not bat.

Bonus points – Northamptonshire 4, Yorkshire 1.

Bowling: Old 25–5–101–1; Stevenson 21–2–104–0; Sidebottom 8.4–0–60–1; Hartley 8–0–41–1; Carrick 13–2–27–0; Whiteley 6–0–30–0.

Yorkshire

G. Boycott c Mallender b Capel	9
R. G. Lumb c Mallender b Griffiths	18
C. W. J. Athey lbw b Griffiths	54
J. D. Love st Sharp b Steele	41
S. N. Hartley not out	1
†D. L. Bairstow not out	5
L-b 1, n-b 13	14
1/30 2/38 3/133 4/136 (4 wkts)	142

P. Carrick, A. Sidebottom, *C. M. Old, G. B. Stevenson and J. P. Whiteley did not bat.

Bonus points – Northamptonshire 1.

Bowling: Griffiths 11–3–22–2; Mallender 9–1–46–0; Capel 3–0–11–1; T. M. Lamb 7–2–13–0; Willey 5–2–14–0; Steele 12–6–20–1; Williams 1–0–2–0.

Umpires: H. D. Bird and J. van Geloven.

At Ilford, June 23, 24, 25. YORKSHIRE drew with ESSEX.

YORKSHIRE v NOTTINGHAMSHIRE

At Harrogate, June 26, 28, 29. Abandoned.

At Derby, July 3, 5, 6. YORKSHIRE drew with DERBYSHIRE.

YORKSHIRE v WORCESTERSHIRE

At Sheffield, July 7, 8, 9. Drawn. Yorkshire 6 pts, Worcestershire 4 pts. On a pitch that allowed some turn, Carrick returned his best figures for four years, but Worcestershire were saved by the resourceful Turner, whose 71st century for the county put him at the head of that particular list. He batted for 200 minutes, hitting fourteen boundaries, and his brilliance was matched by only Boycott. The Yorkshire opener's 129th first-class century equalled Len Hutton's record and, well supported by Carrick, he gave his side a tremendous advantage. With Illingworth injured, Boycott led Yorkshire on the last day, when the absence of spin support for Carrick and several responsible innings enabled Worcestershire to escape with a draw.

Worcestershire

G. M. Turner c Boycott b Carrick	112	– c Old b Carrick	70
M. S. Scott b Carrick	13	– c Bairstow b Sidebottom	24
*P. A. Neale c Illingworth b Carrick	30	– lbw b Stevenson	6
Younis Ahmed lbw b Sidebottom	6	– (9) c Bairstow b Old	8
D. N. Patel c Bairstow b Sidebottom	7	– c Bairstow b Old	53
E. J. O. Hemsley c Stevenson b Carrick	1	– (4) c Old b Carrick	49
†D. J. Humphries b Stevenson	25	– (6) b Jarvis	30
J. D. Inchmore c Lumb b Carrick	1	– (7) b Jarvis	58
N. Gifford c Illingworth b Carrick	4	– (11) not out	7
A. E. Warner c Bairstow b Old	43	– (8) c Stevenson b Carrick	10
A. J. Webster not out	8	– (10) not out	22
B 5, l-b 9, n-b 3	17	B 1, l-b 17, n-b 7	25
1/61 2/123 3/140 4/161	267	1/105 2/105 3/128 (9 wkts dec.)	362
5/164 6/204 7/209 8/214 9/217		4/174 5/243 6/257 7/270 8/329 9/337	

Bonus points – Worcestershire 3, Yorkshire 4.

Bowling: *First Innings*—Old 7.3–0–27–1; Jarvis 4–0–24–0; Stevenson 16–4–51–1; Carrick 31–7–90–6; Sidebottom 18–1–58–2. *Second Innings*—Old 16–5–54–2; Stevenson 21–3–76–1; Jarvis 13–4–32–2; Carrick 46–19–107–3; Sidebottom 16–3–53–1; Illingworth 1–0–1–0; Hartley 2–0–6–0; Athey 4–1–8–0.

Yorkshire

G. Boycott c Humphries b Inchmore	159
R. G. Lumb c Patel b Webster	21
C. W. J. Athey b Patel	44
S. N. Hartley st Humphries b Patel	11
†D. L. Bairstow c Gifford b Warner	5
P. Carrick c Webster b Hemsley	93
A. Sidebottom c Hemsley b Patel	2
C. M. Old b Patel	1
G. B. Stevenson c Humphries b Warner	19
*R. Illingworth c Inchmore b Warner	30
P. W. Jarvis not out	0
B 7, l-b 15, w 1, n-b 16	39
1/56 2/175 3/201 4/210 5/307 6/314 7/316 8/361 9/421	424

Bonus points – Yorkshire 2, Worcestershire 1 (Score at 100 overs: 239-4).

Bowling: Warner 32–4–98–3; Inchmore 29–5–82–1; Webster 18–6–39–1; Gifford 16–6–22–0; Patel 51–12–142–4; Hemsley 1.4–0–2–1.

Umpires: R. S. Herman and K. Ibadulla.

YORKSHIRE v GLOUCESTERSHIRE

At Bradford, July 10, 12, 13. Gloucestershire won by five wickets. Gloucestershire 22 pts, Yorkshire 6 pts. A century by Hartley rescued Yorkshire on a pitch that gave some help to the bowlers, but a late rush for bonus points cost wickets. Gloucestershire, too, collapsed early on, but then Bainbridge and Romaines made 154 from 55 overs. Badly repaired footholds at the pavilion end handicapped the bowlers on the last day, when the admirably accurate Shepherd took five for 9 in 23 balls, Yorkshire lost six wickets for 17 runs, and Gloucestershire cruised to victory, Hignell speeding them on their way with some forceful strokeplay.

Yorkshire

*G. Boycott lbw b Shepherd	5	– c Stovold b Surridge	33
R. G. Lumb run out	2	– run out	14
C. W. J. Athey c Shepherd b Surridge	22	– b Childs	73
J. D. Love b Shepherd	6	– c Hignell b Surridge	3
S. N. Hartley run out	114	– c Shepherd b Surridge	0
†D. L. Bairstow b Surridge	55	– (10) not out	9
G. B. Stevenson c Broad b Graveney	18	– c Graveney b Shepherd	0
P. Carrick c and b Surridge	2	– (6) c Childs b Shepherd	41
C. M. Old c Sadiq b Graveney	10	– (8) c Brassington b Shepherd	0
A. Sidebottom not out	15	– (9) c and b Shepherd	8
P. W. Jarvis b Graveney	7	– c Brassington b Shepherd	0
L-b 10, w 6, n-b 7	23	L-b 4, w 1, n-b 1	6
1/8 2/8 3/20 4/70 5/217 6/242 7/246 8/246 9/263	279	1/27 2/79 3/87 4/87 5/170 6/170 7/170 8/170 9/187	187

Bonus points – Yorkshire 3, Gloucestershire 4 (Score at 100 overs: 277-9).

Bowling: *First Innings*—Shepherd 19–5–49–2; Surridge 27–8–67–3; Bainbridge 13–2–52–0; Childs 26–11–45–0; Graveney 15–4–33–3; Broad 2–0–10–0. *Second Innings*—Surridge 22–11–29–3; Shepherd 14.3–2–43–5; Bainbridge 17–4–62–0; Childs 6–3–25–1; Graveney 7–0–22–0.

Gloucestershire

B. C. Broad c Athey b Stevenson	0	– c Lumb b Old	20
A. W. Stovold c Athey b Stevenson	5	– c Athey b Carrick	37
P. W. Romaines c Athey b Jarvis	74	– c Athey b Jarvis	11
Sadiq Mohammad c Jarvis b Stevenson	8	– c Carrick b Stevenson	27
A. J. Hignell c Love b Old	0	– c sub b Jarvis	45
P. Bainbridge c Athey b Sidebottom	103	– not out	35
J. N. Shepherd c sub b Sidebottom	2	– not out	16
*D. A. Graveney not out	41		
†A. J. Brassington not out	11		
B 1, l-b 12, w 3, n-b 6	22	B 2, l-b 6, w 1, n-b 1	10
1/2 2/5 3/25 4/26 5/180 6/187 7/225 (7 wkts dec.)	266	1/42 2/72 3/72 4/139 5/172 (5 wkts)	201

J. H. Childs and D. Surridge did not bat.

Bonus points – Gloucestershire 2, Yorkshire 3 (Score at 100 overs: 233-7).

Bowling: *First Innings*—Old 25–9–66–1; Stevenson 24–5–57–3; Jarvis 19–4–49–1; Sidebottom 21–5–56–2; Carrick 11–4–10–0; Boycott 5–1–6–0. *Second Innings*—Old 12–0–35–1; Stevenson 10–0–57–1; Sidebottom 2–0–15–0; Carrick 15–2–60–1; Jarvis 9–3–24–2.

Umpires: D. O. Oslear and R. S. Herman.

YORKSHIRE v WARWICKSHIRE

At Leeds, July 17, 19, 20. Yorkshire won by nine wickets. Yorkshire 24 pts, Warwickshire 4 pts. There was sufficient movement off the seam on the first day to worry Yorkshire, who were grateful for Boycott's patience in a slow but vital innings. Warwickshire wasted their chances with inaccurate bowling, and Humpage took off the pads to become first change. Carrick played well as Yorkshire dominated, and after Illingworth had declared a remarkable spell by left-arm seamer Dennis, in his first Championship game of the season, brought about the follow-on. Amiss played with ringing authority throughout, but lacked support, although Kallicharran was very aggressive in the first innings after being dropped at slip early in his innings. As Yorkshire won with ease, Boycott achieved the rare distinction of being on the field throughout the whole match.

Yorkshire

G. Boycott not out	152	– not out	24
R. G. Lumb c Smith b Hartley	4	– lbw b Lethbridge	10
C. W. J. Athey c Amiss b Lethbridge	13	– not out	21
J. D. Love c Lloyd b Lethbridge	13		
S. N. Hartley c Humpage b Lethbridge	18		
†D. L. Bairstow c Humpage b Hartley	34		
P. Carrick c Oliver b Sutcliffe	75		
G. B. Stevenson c and b Sutcliffe	6		
C. M. Old b Lethbridge	20		
B 1, l-b 11, w 5, n-b 13	30	L-b 6, w 1, n-b 2	9
1/7 2/37 3/63 4/108 5/174 6/325 7/338 8/365 (8 wkts dec.)	365	1/21 (1 wkt)	64

S. J. Dennis and *R. Illingworth did not bat.

Bonus points – Yorkshire 4, Warwickshire 3 (Score at 100 overs: 344-7).

Bowling: *First Innings*—Small 20–4–68–0; Hartley 18–4–45–2; Humpage 10–3–27–0; Lethbridge 31.3–9–84–4; Sutcliffe 19–1–84–2; Lewington 5–0–27–0. *Second Innings*—Small 8–3–8–0; Lethbridge 9–3–25–1; Lewington 2.2–0–16–0; Sutcliffe 1–0–6–0.

Warwickshire

*D. L. Amiss c Athey b Dennis	73	– c Bairstow b Hartley	94
K. D. Smith b Dennis	3	– c Old b Dennis	2
T. A. Lloyd b Stevenson	3	– b Stevenson	7
A. I. Kallicharran b Dennis	59	– c Hartley b Stevenson	8
†G. W. Humpage b Dennis	0	– c Athey b Old	55
P. R. Oliver b Dennis	1	– (7) c Illingworth b Dennis	13
C. Lethbridge b Stevenson	3	– (8) lbw b Old	26
G. C. Small lbw b Old	7	– (9) c Stevenson b Dennis	7
P. J. Hartley lbw b Old	3	– (10) not out	8
P. J. Lewington not out	11	– (6) c Stevenson b Illingworth	5
S. P. Sutcliffe c Bairstow b Boycott	0	– lbw b Stevenson	0
B 4, l-b 12, n-b 10	26	B 2, l-b 1, w 2, n-b 6	11
1/26 2/32 3/141 4/145 5/158 6/159 7/164 8/173 9/186	189	1/24 2/60 3/78 4/158 5/168 6/190 7/192 8/220 9/235	236

Bonus points – Warwickshire 1, Yorkshire 4.

Bowling: *First Innings*—Old 16–6–32–2; Stevenson 18–8–46–2; Dennis 15–1–42–5; Hartley 5–1–18–0; Carrick 5–0–12–0; Illingworth 1–0–1–0; Boycott 2.5–1–12–1. *Second Innings*—Dennis 17–5–67–3; Stevenson 16.3–3–55–3; Old 18–3–56–2; Carrick 8–1–19–0; Hartley 3–0–11–1; Boycott 3–0–14–0; Illingworth 1–0–3–1.

Umpires: P. J. Eele and N. T. Plews.

At Worksop, July 21, 22, 23. YORKSHIRE beat NOTTINGHAMSHIRE by two wickets.

YORKSHIRE v SUSSEX

At Scarborough, July 31, August 2, 3. Yorkshire won by six wickets. Yorkshire 19 pts, Sussex 3 pts. Yorkshire completed a hat-trick of Championship victories for the first time since 1978, thanks largely to a generous declaration by Barclay. On a slow pitch advantageous to the batsmen, there was some elegant strokeplay from Wells, Boycott, Lumb and Parker in particular as both teams worked hard to make up for time lost to the weather on the first day. Barclay, hoping to press the Sussex challenge in the top-of-the-table struggle, set a last-day target of 251 in 195 minutes. Boycott responded with an innings of the highest quality, although he came close to being lbw first ball to le Roux. He hit thirteen 4s and one rare 6 as Yorkshire raced home with fourteen balls to spare, sharing partnerships of 93 in 75 minutes with Hartley and 87 in 65 minutes with Love.

Sussex

G. D. Mendis c Bairstow b Illingworth	44	– b Ramage	7
A. M. Green lbw b Sidebottom	26	– c Athey b Carrick	34
C. M. Wells not out	71	– c Hartley b Carrick	37
*J. R. T. Barclay c Bairstow b Ramage	8	– (8) not out	30
P. W. G. Parker c Jarvis b Sidebottom	7	– (4) not out	69
†I. J. Gould b Sidebottom	10	– c Jarvis b Carrick	1
G. S. le Roux not out	24	– (5) c Boycott b Carrick	6
C. P. Phillipson (did not bat)		– (7) c Athey b Illingworth	4
B 3, l-b 2, n-b 8	13	L-b 5, w 1, n-b 3	9
1/53 2/88 3/126 4/147 5/162 (5 wkts dec.)	203	1/14 2/64 3/105 4/113 5/115 6/122 (6 wkts dec.)	197

C. E. Waller, A. C. S. Pigott and A. N. Jones did not bat.

Bonus points – Sussex 2, Yorkshire 2.

Bowling: *First Innings*—Ramage 17–3–73–1; Jarvis 11–4–23–0; Sidebottom 19–1–55–3; Boycott 4–1–5–0; Illingworth 11–6–20–1; Hartley 2–1–4–0; Carrick 8–4–10–0. *Second Innings*—Ramage 6–0–32–1; Jarvis 5–1–13–0; Sidebottom 4–1–17–0; Illingworth 17.4–4–57–1; Carrick 22–5–69–4.

Yorkshire

G. Boycott lbw b Pigott	52	– not out	122
R. G. Lumb lbw b Waller	46		
C. W. J. Athey c Parker b Pigott	19	– (2) lbw b le Roux	5
J. D. Love not out	19	– c Phillipson b Waller	56
S. N. Hartley c and b Waller	4	– (3) c Phillipson b Waller	35
†D. L. Bairstow not out	4	– (5) b Waller	19
P. Carrick (did not bat)		– not out	10
L-b 3, w 1, n-b 2	6	B 1, l-b 3, n-b 1	5
1/96 2/102 3/141 4/146 (4 wkts dec.)	150	1/22 2/115 3/202 4/237 (4 wkts)	252

A. Sidebottom, A. Ramage, *R. Illingworth and P. W. Jarvis did not bat.

Bonus points – Yorkshire 1, Sussex 1.

Bowling: *First Innings*—le Roux 11–4–23–0; Pigott 14–1–59–2; Jones 8–2–27–0; Waller 15.5–6–35–2. *Second Innings*—le Roux 17–2–49–1; Pigott 10–1–33–0; Barclay 13–0–65–0; Waller 19.4–1–100–3.

Umpires: A. Jepson and R. Julian.

At Manchester, August 7, 9, 10. YORKSHIRE drew with LANCASHIRE.

At Weston-super-Mare, August 11, 12, 13. YORKSHIRE drew with SOMERSET.

YORKSHIRE v KENT

At Leeds, August 14, 16, 17. Drawn. Yorkshire 4 pts, Kent 4 pts. A determined innings by Athey, whose century occupied five and a half hours, gave Yorkshire a good start on a pitch allowing some assistance for the spinners. Cowdrey, Kent's young captain, may, in fact, have missed a trick by not using off-spinner Johnson until after tea. Rain complicated the issue, but two declarations set up a situation which left Kent requiring 250 to win in three and a quarter hours. Yorkshire enjoyed some early success and Carrick hurried them on their way towards a likely victory, but Cowdrey showed both resolution and a reliable technique in holding the fort. Four overs were lost to bad light in the closing stages as Jarvis frustrated Yorkshire's increasingly desperate attempts to collect a further 16 points.

Yorkshire

G. Boycott b Underwood	69	– not out	41
R. G. Lumb c Johnson b Jarvis	5	– c Aslett b Johnson	34
C. W. J. Athey c Baptiste b Johnson	100	– not out	28
J. D. Love c Johnson b Underwood	27		
S. N. Hartley lbw b Underwood	0		
†D. L. Bairstow c Knott b Johnson	12		
G. B. Stevenson c Aslett b Johnson	29		
P. Carrick c Aslett b Johnson	5		
A. Sidebottom c Knott b Underwood	16		
*R. Illingworth st Knott b Johnson	5		
N. S. Taylor not out	0		
B 1, l-b 12, w 1, n-b 22	36	L-b 2, n-b 4	6
1/20 2/130 3/187 4/187 5/232 6/271 7/278 8/288 9/304	304	1/49 (1 wkt dec.)	109

Bonus points – Yorkshire 3, Kent 3 (Score at 100 overs: 288-7).

Bowling: *First Innings*—Dilley 16–6–34–0; Jarvis 19–6–43–1; Underwood 35–14–62–4; Baptiste 21–5–63–0; Cowdrey 4–0–14–0; Johnson 12.3–1–52–5. *Second Innings*—Dilley 4–0–15–0; Jarvis 4–0–15–0; Underwood 9–2–41–0; Johnson 6–0–21–1; Baptiste 2–0–11–0.

Kent

L. Potter c Athey b Carrick	26	– lbw b Stevenson	4
N. R. Taylor c Bairstow b Taylor	0	– b Taylor	2
D. G. Aslett lbw b Illingworth	37	– lbw b Sidebottom	31
M. R. Benson not out	57	– c Boycott b Carrick	6
G. W. Johnson not out	24	– b Carrick	11
*C. S. Cowdrey (did not bat)		– not out	51
†A. P. E. Knott (did not bat)		– b Carrick	4
E. A. Baptiste (did not bat)		– c and b Carrick	18
G. R. Dilley (did not bat)		– lbw b Illingworth	0
D. L. Underwood (did not bat)		– lbw b Illingworth	2
K. B. S. Jarvis (did not bat)		– not out	0
L-b 8, n-b 12	20	B 4, l-b 3, w 2, n-b 4	13
1/0 2/52 3/114 (3 wkts dec.)	164	1/5 2/22 3/39 4/53 5/77 6/81 7/121 8/122 9/128 (9 wkts)	142

Bonus points – Kent 1, Yorkshire 1.

Bowling: *First Innings*—Stevenson 11–4–23–0; Taylor 7–2–9–1; Sidebottom 9–3–22–0; Carrick 15–2–51–1; Illingworth 12–3–39–1. *Second Innings*—Stevenson 6–1–12–1–; Taylor 6–2–18–1; Carrick 24–5–56–4; Sidebottom 9–3–11–1; Illingworth 14–5–32–2.

Umpires: J. van Geloven and N. T. Plews.

At Lord's, August 21, 23, 24. YORKSHIRE drew with MIDDLESEX.

At Bournemouth, August 28, 30, 31. YORKSHIRE drew with HAMPSHIRE.

YORKSHIRE v DERBYSHIRE

At Scarborough, September 8, 9, 10. Yorkshire won by six wickets. Yorkshire 22 pts, Derbyshire 4 pts. Derbyshire, sent in on a slow pitch, collapsed as nine wickets fell for 46 runs in 23 overs, with Bairstow establishing a Yorkshire record of seven catches in an innings. Sidebottom's six for 31 was the best return for the county in an innings throughout the season. Yorkshire themselves struggled against the spin of Moir, who took six wickets in an innings for the first time, but a 72-run ninth-wicket partnership between Illingworth and Sidebottom ensured an important lead. Bairstow went on to equal the world record for catches in a match – eleven – as Derbyshire battled grimly in their second innings. Kirsten's unbeaten 140 in 247 minutes, including three 6s and eighteen 4s, was his eighth century of the season and set a record for Derbyshire. Yorkshire experienced few problems in making the necessary runs, as Moxon, in his first Championship game of the season, revealed splendid form. Booth, a seventeen-year-old left-arm spinner from Huddersfield, made his first-class début for Yorkshire.

Derbyshire

I. S. Anderson c Bairstow b Sidebottom	29	–	b Sidebottom	11
J. G. Wright c Love b Boycott	27	–	c Boycott b Old	9
P. N. Kirsten c Bairstow b Stevenson	36	–	not out	140
J. H. Hampshire c Bairstow b Sidebottom	10	–	c Love b Stevenson	7
G. Miller c Athey b Sidebottom	12	–	c Athey b Stevenson	12
*B. Wood c Bairstow b Old	0	–	c Bairstow b Stevenson	17
†R. W. Taylor lbw b Old	1	–	c Bairstow b Sidebottom	1
C. J. Tunnicliffe c Bairstow b Sidebottom	6	–	b Stevenson	5
P. G. Newman c Bairstow b Sidebottom	1	–	c Bairstow b Stevenson	1
D. G. Moir c Bairstow b Sidebottom	0	–	c Bairstow b Sidebottom	12
S. Oldham not out	1	–	run out	0
B 4, l-b 2, n-b 8	14		L-b 3, w 2, n-b 17	22
1/46 2/91 3/108 4/118 5/125 6/125 7/134 8/135 9/136	137		1/21 2/34 3/60 4/80 5/138 6/143 7/150 8/157 9/222	237

Bonus points – Yorkshire 4.

Bowling: *First Innings*—Old 16–4–30–2; Stevenson 10–1–42–1; Boycott 8–3–20–1; Sidebottom 15.5–5–31–6; Booth 1–1–0–0. *Second Innings*—Old 10–2–33–1; Stevenson 27–9–72–5; Sidebottom 17.5–3–61–3; Illingworth 9–0–23–0; Booth 9–2–22–0; Hartley 1–0–1–0; Boycott 5–2–3–0.

Yorkshire

G. Boycott b Miller	57	–	lbw b Oldham	4
M. D. Moxon st Taylor b Moir	36	–	c Taylor b Tunnicliffe	67
C. W. J. Athey b Moir	0	–	c Wright b Tunnicliffe	58
S. N. Hartley c Wood b Moir	1	–	(5) not out	16
J. D. Love b Moir	0	–	(6) not out	1
†D. L. Bairstow c Anderson b Moir	24			
C. M. Old c Taylor b Moir	5	–	(4) c and b Oldham	2
A. Sidebottom c Miller b Wood	39			
G. B. Stevenson b Newman	3			
*R. Illingworth c Hampshire b Wood	33			
P. A. Booth not out	0			
B 1, l-b 10, n-b 8	19		B 1, l-b 5, n-b 4	10
1/67 2/69 3/79 4/79 5/115 6/122 7/133 8/142 9/214	217		1/14 2/122 3/126 4/137	(4 wkts) 158

Bonus points – Yorkshire 2, Derbyshire 4.

Bowling: *First Innings*—Oldham 16–4–31–0; Tunnicliffe 17–3–45–0; Newman 18–3–36–1; Wood 4.2–1–12–2; Moir 35–16–63–6; Miller 8–1–11–1. *Second Innings*—Newman 13–2–37–0; Oldham 17–3–40–2; Moir 5–2–24–0; Wood 5–0–20–0; Tunnicliffe 5.3–2–21–2; Miller 1–0–6–0.

Umpires: H. D. Bird and K. Ibadulla.

At The Oval, September 11, 13, 14. YORKSHIRE drew with SURREY.

FUTURE TOURS

1983	Indians to West Indies Australians to Sri Lanka World Cup in England New Zealanders to England Pakistanis to Sri Lanka West Indians to India
1983-84	Pakistanis and West Indians to Australia England to New Zealand and Pakistan
1984	Australians to West Indies West Indians to England Sri Lankans to England New Zealanders to Pakistan
1984-85	England to India and Sri Lanka West Indians and Sri Lankans to Australia Pakistanis to New Zealand
1985	New Zealanders to West Indies Sri Lankans to Pakistan Australians to England Indians to Pakistan
1985-86	Pakistanis to West Indies Indians and New Zealanders to Australia England to West Indies
1986	Australians to New Zealand Indians to Sri Lanka Indians to England New Zealanders to England Australians to India West Indians to Pakistan New Zealanders to India and Sri Lanka (Provisional)
1986-87	England and West Indians to Australia Pakistanis to Sri Lanka West Indians to New Zealand (Provisional)
1987	World Cup in England (June) or in Pakistan (September) Pakistanis to England Sri Lankans to England (if no World Cup in England) Sri Lankans to Pakistan West Indians to India
1987-88	England to Pakistan and New Zealand New Zealanders and Sri Lankans to Australia
1988	Australians to West Indies West Indians to England Sri Lankans to England Australians to Pakistan
1988-89	England to India and Sri Lanka West Indians and Pakistanis to Australia Pakistanis to New Zealand
1989	Indians to West Indies Australians to England
1989-90	England to West Indies

THE UNIVERSITIES IN 1982

OXFORD

President – LORD BLAKE
(The Queen's)

Hon. Treasurer – DR S. R. PORTER
(St Cross)

Captain – R. G. P. ELLIS
(Haileybury and St Edmund Hall)

Secretary – K. A. HAYES
(Queen Elizabeth GS, Blackburn and Merton)

Captain for 1983 – G. J. TOOGOOD
(North Bromsgrove HS and Lincoln)

Secretary – A. J. T. MILLER
(Haileybury and St Edmund Hall)

Two factors contributed to a good season in the Parks. It was one of the driest ever, with only three hours of play lost to rain, and with the square in correspondingly better condition the Parks became a batsman's paradise. The eight first-class matches played there produced a record number of centuries (21) and an abundance of humbling bowling figures, with the undergraduates as the chief sufferers. As the averages suggest, Oxford possessed a desperately weak attack, though this was partly compensated for by a much-improved performance by the batsmen.

Five centuries were scored for the university and in contrast to recent years there were no total collapses. Indeed, there were some remarkable recoveries, and in a number of matches the dark blues successfully avoided an innings defeat through diligent batting in the second innings. The relative strength and weakness of the side were exemplified in the match against Kent when Oxford recovered from 86 for six to reach 306 for eight declared through centuries by Simon Halliday and Ralph Cowan. Kent replied with a massive 616 for six with Woolmer, Taylor, Tavaré and Benson scoring centuries, so that from what looked a position of safety, Oxford found themselves needing over 300 to avoid an innings defeat. In the event rain came to their rescue. Oxford's other centuries came from Richard Ellis, Kevin Hayes and Cowan. Giles Toogood, John Varey, Bob Marsden and wicket-keeper Richard Luddington all performed soundly, but Halliday disappointed after his maiden hundred and was omitted from the team for Lord's.

Much hard bowling was done by Ridge and Cowan, at a fairly gentle medium pace; both were pretty heavily punished. Varey, an all-rounder who was

OXFORD UNIVERSITY 1982

[*Bill Smith*

Back row: P. A. N. Armstrong, J. G. Varey, I. J. Curtis, S. P. Ridge, R. Marsden, R. S. Luddington, G. J. Toogood. *Front row:* T. J. Taylor, R. S. Cowan, R. G. P. Ellis (*captain*), K. A. Hayes, R. P. Moulding.

occasionally thrust into the role of new-ball bowler, also paid heavily for his wickets. Despite this, Ellis set extravagantly attacking fields. The best bowling came from the two slow left-armers, Timothy Taylor and Ian Curtis. Unfortunately neither was able to play regularly owing to academic commitments, and when they did turn out their lack of match practice told.

It was hardly surprising that the visiting professionals reaped a big haul against such bowling. Worcestershire's Turner hit the highest score, 239 not out, while Nicholas of Hampshire and Slack of Middlesex also scored double-hundreds.

Oxford's contribution to the Benson and Hedges Cup competition was disappointing; but Ellis's declaration in the University Match, which Cambridge won, made for a good, positive finish. – P.F.

OXFORD UNIVERSITY RESULTS

First-class matches – Played 10: Lost 5, Drawn 5.

FIRST-CLASS AVERAGES – BATTING

	M	*I*	*NO*	*R*	*HI*	*Avge*
R. S. Cowan	7	14	3	515	143*	46.81
S. J. Halliday	4	7	1	213	113*	35.50
R. G. P. Ellis	10	20	1	666	105*	35.05
J. G. Varey	7	12	5	239	68	34.14
R. Marsden	5	10	1	264	60	29.33
K. A. Hayes	10	19	2	491	152	28.88
G. J. Toogood	9	18	4	392	83	28.00
J. R. Chessher	3	4	1	67	47	22.33
R. S. Luddington	10	14	1	290	65	22.30
R. P. Moulding	10	20	2	242	67	13.44
A. D. Gilfillan	3	4	1	40	31	13.33
S. P. Ridge	10	13	5	64	22	8.00
M. P. Lawrence	4	5	2	20	18	6.66
H. T. Rawlinson	4	6	0	30	21	5.00

Played in five matches: I. J. Curtis 0*, 20*, 0. Played in four matches: T. J. Taylor 0, 20, 17*. Played in one match: P. A. N. Armstrong 34, 0; J. J. Cassidy 0; P. J. Crowe 11, 0; R. M. Edbrooke 84*, 16; A. J. T. Miller 0, 20.

* *Signifies not out.*

BOWLING

	O	*M*	*R*	*W*	*Avge*	*BB*
I. J. Curtis	214.4	45	659	15	43.93	5-140
T. J. Taylor	149	24	469	9	52.11	5-118
S. P. Ridge	240.1	32	829	13	63.76	4-128
H. T. Rawlinson	96.1	9	435	5	87.00	2-102
R. S. Cowan	131	18	559	6	93.16	2-75

Also bowled: J. J. Cassidy 4–2–12–0; P. J. Crowe 36–4–121–1; R. G. P. Ellis 61–14–182–4; A. D. Gilfillan 51–5–218–2; K. A. Hayes 21–1–96–0; M. P. Lawrence 99–20–366–2; G. J. Toogood 3–0–22–0; J. G. Varey 132–15–550–3.

OXFORD UNIVERSITY v NORTHAMPTONSHIRE

At Oxford, April 24, 26, 27. Drawn. Northamptonshire's first innings was dominated by Lamb and Willey, who added 215 for the fourth wicket. Cook's declaration was made immediately Willey had completed his century and Oxford made a spirited reply on a good pitch. Their soccer Blue, Cowan, hit a career-best 143, and with Toogood and Chessher making promising débuts Oxford declared at 338 for five. They had the visitors 77 for four in the second innings but an unbeaten 106 by Williams enabled Cook to declare a second time and set Oxford 240 to win in 150 minutes. The challenge was not accepted.

Northamptonshire

*G. Cook c Ridge b Cowan	28	– c Luddington b Cowan	22
W. Larkins c Ellis b Curtis	42	– (6) b Curtis	25
R. G. Williams c Hayes b Curtis	31	– not out	106
A. J. Lamb c Cowan b Taylor	140		
P. Willey not out	100	– (8) not out	14
T. J. Yardley not out	20	– (5) b Curtis	2
D. S. Steele (did not bat)		– (2) b Ridge	3
†G. Sharp (did not bat)		– (4) c Toogood b Taylor	19
Sarfraz Nawaz (did not bat)		– (7) lbw b Taylor	17
B 2, l-b 1, w 1, n-b 1	5	B 2, l-b 1	3
1/43 2/96 3/107 4/322 (4 wkts dec.)	366	1/5 2/39 3/75 4/77 5/151 6/192 (6 wkts dec.)	211

N. A. Mallender and B. J. Griffiths did not bat.

Bowling: *First Innings*—Ridge 13–1–43–0; Cowan 19–1–91–1; Varey 7–2–24–0; Curtis 35–4–108–2; Taylor 23–3–95–1. *Second Innings*—Ridge 17–1–51–1; Curtis 19–3–54–2; Cowan 8–2–37–1; Taylor 23–5–66–2.

Oxford University

*R. G. P. Ellis lbw b Willey	34	– lbw b Willey	27
R. P. Moulding c Cook b Willey	1	– c Sharp b Sarfraz	0
K. A. Hayes c Sharp b Griffiths	27	– c Yardley b Steele	37
R. S. Cowan not out	143	– not out	12
G. J. Toogood c Sharp b Griffiths	54	– not out	1
J. R. Chessher run out	47		
J. G. Varey not out	4		
B 1, l-b 3, n-b 24	28	L-b 8, n-b 8	16
1/23 2/65 3/77 4/230 5/315 (5 wkts dec.)	338	1/9 2/56 3/91 (3 wkts)	93

†R. S. Luddington, T. J. Taylor, I. J. Curtis and S. P. Ridge did not bat.

Bowling: *First Innings*—Sarfraz 17–5–62–0; Griffiths 18–6–35–2; Steele 25–7–62–0; Willey 20–5–63–2; Larkins 5–2–8–0; Mallender 13–2–59–0; Williams 8–1–21–0. *Second Innings*—Sarfraz 4–1–9–1; Mallender 11–3–28–0; Steele 7–3–12–1; Griffiths 4–0–12–0; Willey 10–4–16–1.

Umpires: D. J. Constant and M. J. Kitchen.

†OXFORD UNIVERSITY v CAMBRIDGE UNIVERSITY

At Oxford, April 25. Oxford University won by 62 runs. Oxford University 265 for five (R. P. Moulding 80, R. G. P. Ellis 58); Cambridge University 205 (S. P. Henderson 85; I. J. Curtis four for 30).

OXFORD UNIVERSITY v WORCESTERSHIRE

At Oxford, April 28, 29, 30. Drawn. Turner hit a career-best 239 not out against a weak Oxford attack, putting on 169 with Ormrod for the first wicket and an unbroken 188 with Younis before Neale declared at 401 for two. He batted a little over five hours, hitting one 6 and 29 4s. The University were rescued by Cowan and Toogood, who had put on 153 against Northamptonshire in the opening game. This time they added 118 after the first four wickets had fallen for 65, but the remaining batsmen failed and the innings closed at 211. Oxford followed on needing 190 to avoid an innings defeat, but Ellis and Moulding virtually made a draw certain with an opening partnership of 162 – Oxford's biggest of the season.

Worcestershire

J. A. Ormrod c Toogood b Rawlinson	66
G. M. Turner not out	239
*P. A. Neale lbw b Cowan	1
Younis Ahmed not out	70
B 13, l-b 11, w 1	25
1/169 2/213 (2 wkts dec.)	401

D. N. Patel, E. J. O. Hemsley, †D. J. Humphries, J. D. Inchmore, N. Gifford, A. P. Pridgeon and S. P. Perryman did not bat.

Bowling: Ridge 10–0–51–0; Cowan 12–2–33–1; Taylor 35–1–127–0; Curtis 24.1–2–85–0; Rawlinson 10–0–57–1; Hayes 4–0–23–0.

Oxford University

*R. G. P. Ellis lbw b Perryman	25	– lbw b Patel	92
R. P. Moulding c Humphries b Perryman	2	– (3) b Gifford	67
K. A. Hayes c Turner b Pridgeon	0	– (4) not out	23
†R. S. Luddington lbw b Gifford	15		
R. S. Cowan c Humphries b Inchmore	76	– (2) c Ormrod b Gifford	3
G. J. Toogood b Inchmore	83	– (5) not out	5
J. R. Chessher c Humphries b Pridgeon	1		
H. T. Rawlinson c Humphries b Perryman	1		
S. P. Ridge b Pridgeon	0		
T. J. Taylor run out	0		
I. J. Curtis not out	0		
B 1, l-b 2, w 1, n-b 4	8	B 4, l-b 7, n-b 1	12
1/20 2/27 3/27 4/65 5/183 6/185 7/191 8/198 9/198	211	1/162 2/172 3/189 (3 wkts)	202

Bowling: *First Innings*—Pridgeon 25–6–51–3; Perryman 30–12–62–3; Inchmore 13.4–5–22–2; Gifford 18–6–31–1; Patel 10–1–37–0. *Second Innings*—Pridgeon 14–5–24–0; Perryman 24–13–36–0; Inchmore 8–3–11–0; Gifford 47–27–55–2; Patel 37–16–64–1; Neale 2–2–0–0.

Umpires: D. J. Constant and M. J. Kitchen.

OXFORD UNIVERSITY v KENT

At Oxford, May 1, 3, 4. Drawn. Heavy rain and bad light after tea on the third day saved Oxford from a heavy defeat. In a remarkable match in which six centuries were scored, Oxford, having declared at 306 for eight, found themselves requiring 310 to avoid an innings defeat after Kent had replied with a massive 616 for six. Oxford in their first innings slumped to 86 for six after winning the toss but staged a magnificent recovery through Cowan and Halliday, who added 129 for the seventh wicket. Cowan hit his second century of the season and Halliday, a rugger Blue, scored an unbeaten maiden century before the declaration.

Kent clinically cut the university's bowling to pieces, their first four batsmen all enjoying hundreds before falling in the 120s.

Oxford University

*R. G. P. Ellis c Marsh b Jarvis	3	– b Dilley	8
H. T. Rawlinson b Spelman	21	– b Dilley	0
K. A. Hayes c Marsh b Jarvis	5	– c Woolmer b Dilley	7
R. S. Cowan b Aslett	108	– c Marsh b Jarvis	0
G. J. Toogood c Marsh b Spelman	0	– not out	15
R. P. Moulding c Aslett b Woolmer	5	– lbw b Spelman	2
J. R. Chessher c and b Woolmer	1	– not out	18
S. J. Halliday not out	113		
†R. S. Luddington c Cowdrey b Johnson	12		
S. P. Ridge not out	6		
B 5, l-b 7, w 3, n-b 17	32	B 1, l-b 2, n-b 2	5
1/6 2/20 3/62 4/62 5/78 6/86 7/215 8/244 (8 wkts dec.)	306	1/8 2/16 3/17 4/17 5/34 (5 wkts)	55

A. D. Gilfillan did not bat.

Bowling: *First Innings*—Dilley 15–3–35–0; Jarvis 17–4–58–2; Cowdrey 7–1–21–0; Spelman 16–5–44–2; Woolmer 11–6–13–2; Johnson 20–6–49–1; Aslett 14–2–54–1. *Second Innings*—Dilley 10–3–21–3; Jarvis 12–6–7–1; Spelman 7–3–22–1; Johnson 2–2–0–0.

Kent

R. A. Woolmer run out	126
N. R. Taylor b Gilfillan	127
C. J. Tavaré c Moulding b Ridge	125
M. R. Benson c Toogood b Ridge	120
D. G. Aslett not out	51
*C. S. Cowdrey c Toogood b Gilfillan	42
G. W. Johnson b Ridge	11
B 2, l-b 6, w 5, n-b 1	14
1/227 2/278 3/507 4/509 5/582 6/616 (6 wkts dec.)	616

G. D. Spelman, G. R. Dilley, K. B. S. Jarvis and †S. Marsh did not bat.

Bowling: Ridge 43.1–3–161–3; Cowan 23–8–80–0; Rawlinson 22–3–95–0; Hayes 12–0–51–0; Gilfillan 39–2–177–2; Toogood 3–0–22–0; Ellis 6–0–16–0.

Umpires: K. Ibadulla and A. Jepson.

†At Cambridge, May 2. OXFORD UNIVERSITY lost to CAMBRIDGE UNIVERSITY by seven wickets.

OXFORD UNIVERSITY v GLOUCESTERSHIRE

At Oxford, May 5, 6, 7. Gloucestershire won by ten wickets. Ellis hit a punishing 65 after Oxford had been put in, and stubborn knocks by tailenders Luddington and Gilfillan helped the dark blues to a respectable 230, but Oxford soon ran into trouble when Gloucestershire batted. Leg-spinner Gilfillan had already broken a finger while batting, and when Cowan broke down with back trouble after four overs the university were reduced to three bowlers. Broad and Romaines softened up the weakened attack in the morning with a partnership of 101 and Zaheer cut loose later with 144 in a little over three hours. Having recovered arrears of 181 Oxford at 207 for five looked set to hold out for a draw. But when Surridge took the new ball, the last five wickets fell for 10 runs and Gloucestershire hit off the 37 runs required for victory without loss.

Oxford University

*R. G. P. Ellis b Shepherd	65	– c Trembath b Childs	36
G. J. Toogood c Brassington b Trembath	7	– c Graveney b Surridge	9
K. A. Hayes c Brassington b Trembath	0	– lbw b Graveney	52
R. S. Cowan c Brassington b Shepherd	37	– (5) not out	60
R. P. Moulding b Shepherd	8	– (6) c Childs b Graveney	5
S. J. Halliday b Childs	1	– (7) c Graveney b Surridge	27
J. G. Varey b Childs	6	– (8) lbw b Surridge	0
†R. S. Luddington b Trembath	38	– (4) lbw b Childs	13
P. J. Crowe b Trembath	11	– b Surridge	0
S. P. Ridge not out	13	– c Shepherd b Trembath	5
A. D. Gilfillan c Brassington b Trembath	31	– run out	0
L-b 4, n-b 9	13	W 3, n-b 7	10
1/37 2/37 3/86 4/101 5/107 6/135 7/145 8/175 9/190	230	1/38 2/49 3/119 4/119 5/136 6/207 7/207 8/207 9/216	217

Bowling: *First Innings*—Trembath 19.1–4–91–5; Surridge 18–7–52–0; Childs 26–18–14–2; Shepherd 25–7–60–3. *Second Innings*—Surridge 16.4–7–43–4; Trembath 7–1–30–1; Graveney 31–12–51–2; Childs 31–12–53–2; Shepherd 9–6–4–0; Broad 5–1–17–0; Romaines 5–2–9–0.

Gloucestershire

B. C. Broad lbw b Ridge	95		
P. W. Romaines c Luddington b Crowe	32	– (1) not out	16
Zaheer Abbas b Ridge	144		
M. W. Stovold c sub b Ridge	47		
S. J. Windaybank lbw b Ridge	8	– (2) not out	10
J. N. Shepherd not out	57		
*D. A. Graveney not out	20		
B 2, l-b 3, w 3	8	B 4, l-b 3, w 3, n-b 1	11
1/101 2/160 3/321 4/325 5/352	(5 wkts dec.) 411		(no wkt) 37

C. R. Trembath, †A. J. Brassington, J. H. Childs and D. Surridge did not bat.

Bowling: *First Innings*—Ridge 36–6–128–4; Crowe 31–4–105–1; Cowan 4–0–11–0; Gilfillan 3–2–1–0; Varey 25–2–116–0; Ellis 12–2–42–0. *Second Innings*—Ridge 6–3–5–0; Crowe 5–0–16–0; Hayes 1–1–0–0; Ellis 1–0–5–0.

Umpires: K. Ibadulla and A. Jepson.

OXFORD UNIVERSITY v HAMPSHIRE

At Oxford, May 12, 13, 14. Hampshire won by an innings and 62 runs. The university bowlers were thrashed by Nicholas and the batsmen later destroyed by the medium-fast bowling of Malone. Hampshire lost Tremlett and Terry for 51 after Turner had won the toss, but the game changed when Nicholas joined Smith. They added 138 before Smith was caught for 71, and as the bowlers wilted Nicholas plundered his way to a career-best 206 not out which included one 6 and 29 4s. Oxford lost half their batting for 75 but recovered to 169 thanks to the eighth-wicket pair, Varey and Ridge. Malone's seven for 55 gave him career-best figures, and in the follow-on he picked up another five wickets at similar cost to finish with match figures of twelve for 110.

Hampshire

C. L. Smith c Varey b Ridge	71
T. M. Tremlett c Luddington b Ridge	18
V. P. Terry lbw b Varey	6
M. C. J. Nicholas not out	206
*D. R. Turner c Moulding b Cowan	34
R. E. Hayward not out	29
B 2, l-b 2, w 2	6
1/42 2/51 3/189 4/266 (4 wkts dec.)	370

N. G. Cowley, †R. J. Parks, J. W. Southern, K. Stevenson and S. J. Malone did not bat.

Bowling: Ridge 17–6–37–2; Cowan 15–2–58–1; Varey 25–1–109–1; Gilfillan 9–1–40–0; Lawrence 29–5–120–0.

Oxford University

*R. G. P. Ellis c Smith b Malone	15	– c Southern b Malone	15
G. J. Toogood c Parks b Stevenson	3	– c Parks b Malone	16
K. A. Hayes c Parks b Malone	23	– (4) b Malone	13
R. S. Cowan b Malone	19	– (3) c Stevenson b Southern	10
R. P. Moulding c Nicholas b Tremlett	6	– c and b Malone	13
S. J. Halliday c Cowley b Tremlett	4	– (7) c Parks b Tremlett	15
J. G. Varey c Cowley b Malone	68	– (8) c Smith b Tremlett	5
†R. S. Luddington lbw b Malone	1	– (6) lbw b Tremlett	32
S. P. Ridge b Malone	22	– b Malone	4
A. D. Gilfillan not out	2	– c and b Southern	7
M. P. Lawrence b Malone	0	– not out	0
L-b 3, w 1, n-b 2	6	B 3, l-b 4, w 1, n-b 1	9
1/6 2/40 3/49 4/71 5/75 6/79 7/80 8/166 9/167	169	1/33 2/38 3/58 4/58 5/75 6/120 7/125 8/130 9/139	139

Bowling: *First Innings*—Stevenson 14–6–35–1; Malone 23.3–7–55–7; Tremlett 19–7–44–2; Cowley 9–3–11–0; Southern 11–4–18–0. *Second Innings*—Malone 24–10–55–5; Stevenson 8–4–21–0; Tremlett 21–13–10–3; Southern 18–8–37–2; Cowley 6–4–7–0.

Umpires: K. E. Palmer and R. Palmer.

OXFORD UNIVERSITY v MIDDLESEX

At Oxford, May 19, 20, 21. Middlesex won by an innings and 107 runs. Oxford suffered their heaviest defeat of the season after Ellis and Marsden had given them a sound start with 73 and Moulding had contributed an attractive 48. However, the remaining batsmen disappointed, and when Middlesex replied, Slack thrashed the undergraduates for an unbeaten 203 which included a 6 and 24 4s. He added 241 for the third wicket with Tomlins, who went on to score a career-best 146. Oxford's hopes of saving the match were wrecked by Williams, who dismissed the first four batsmen for 10 runs in a four-over spell. Miller and Varey held out for two hours, but Maru completed the mopping up, claiming four for 30 with his slow left-arm spin.

Oxford University

*R. G. P. Ellis b Maru	35 – c Cook b Williams	8
R. Marsden b Williams	46 – b Williams	4
K. A. Hayes b Merry	24 – lbw b Williams	0
G. J. Toogood c Butcher b Kemp	15 – lbw b Emburey	28
A. J. T. Miller c Downton b Kemp	0 – (6) c Merry b Maru	20
R. P. Moulding b Maru	48 – (5) c Barlow b Williams	0
J. G. Varey c Emburey b Maru	23 – c and b Maru	48
H. T. Rawlinson c and b Merry	4 – run out	0
†R. S. Luddington c Slack b Emburey	10 – c Barlow b Maru	2
S. P. Ridge b Emburey	0 – not out	4
M. P. Lawrence not out	2 – c Merry b Maru	18
B 4, l-b 5, w 2, n-b 10	21 L-b 2, n-b 9	11
1/73 2/94 3/123 4/124 5/131 6/176 7/201 8/220 9/226	228 1/7 2/7 3/15 4/15 5/54 6/84 7/87 8/111 9/121	143

Bowling: *First Innings*—Williams 21–4–58–1; Merry 26–7–54–2; Emburey 18–10–19–2; Kemp 20–6–53–2; Maru 16.2–9–18–3; Tomlins 1–0–5–0. *Second Innings*—Williams 15–2–38–4; Merry 13–6–16–0; Kemp 9–1–17–0; Emburey 20–10–22–1; Maru 21–10–30–4; Tomlins 2–0–9–0.

Middlesex

W. N. Slack not out	203	*J. E. Emburey not out	18
G. D. Barlow c and b Varey	28		
R. O. Butcher c Ellis b Rawlinson	29	B 11, l-b 5, n-b 1	17
K. P. Tomlins c Ellis b Rawlinson	146		
C. R. Cook b Lawrence	0	1/57 2/112 3/353 4/355 5/445 (5 wkts dec.)	478
N. J. Kemp c Luddington b Ridge	37		

†P. R. Downton, N. F. Williams, R. J. Maru and W. G. Merry did not bat.

Bowling: Ridge 24–1–100–1; Varey 19–1–88–1; Lawrence 39–6–142–1; Rawlinson 28.1–4–117–2; Ellis 4–0–14–0.

Umpires: J. H. Harris and R. S. Herman.

†OXFORD UNIVERSITY v FREE FORESTERS

At Oxford, May 29, 31, June 1 (not first-class). Free Foresters won by 104 runs. Free Foresters 323 for seven dec. (P. Davy 80, A. H. Barker 53 not out, R. Gracey 51) and 237 for seven dec. (J. O. D. Orders 89, D. A. Stewart 60); Oxford University 257 for eight dec. (K. A. Hayes 60) and 199 (R. S. Cowan 70; R. Gracey five for 38).

OXFORD UNIVERSITY v WARWICKSHIRE

At Oxford, June 2, 3, 4. Warwickshire won by nine wickets. Warwickshire's acting-captain Humpage was the architect of his side's win with a little more than two overs to spare. Humpage, who was bowled first ball in the first innings, seized on an over-generous declaration which left Warwickshire to score 229 in 150 minutes and set up the win with an unbeaten 121. He put on 129 in 78 minutes with Lloyd and was the dominant partner in an unbroken partnership of 101 with Asif Din. Initially Oxford had produced some of their most positive batting when they won the toss. Marsden and Hayes flayed the Warwickshire attack in a partnership of 154, Hayes going on to a career-best 152 – the highest score by an Oxford batsman since Imran Khan's 170 against Northamptonshire in 1974.

Oxford University

*R. G. P. Ellis b Small	35	– c Tedstone b Small	2
R. Marsden run out	60	– c Lloyd b Small	9
K. A. Hayes c Tedstone b Cumbes	152	– (4) c K. D. Smith b P. A. Smith	32
R. S. Cowan c Lloyd b Small	10	– (5) c Lloyd b Cumbes	0
G. J. Toogood not out	31	– (6) c Tedstone b Cumbes	26
R. P. Moulding not out	7	– (7) c Cumbes b Small	28
†R. S. Luddington (did not bat)		– (3) lbw b Cumbes	0
J. G. Varey (did not bat)		– not out	28
S. P. Ridge (did not bat)		– c K. D. Smith b Cumbes	0
I. J. Curtis (did not bat)		– not out	20
L-b 4, w 2, n-b 4	10	B 5, l-b 8, n-b 4	17
1/47 2/201 3/224 4/277 (4 wkts dec.)	305	1/2 2/5 3/23 4/24 5/57 6/88 7/110 8/116 (8 wkts dec.)	162

M. P. Lawrence did not bat.

Bowling: *First Innings*—Small 20–6–41–2; Lethbridge 3–1–16–0; P. A. Smith 10–1–43–0; Cumbes 24–6–60–1; Sutcliffe 17–4–40–0; D. M. Smith 12–2–45–0; Humpage 3–0–5–0; Asif Din 11–1–41–0; Lloyd 2–1–4–0. *Second Innings*—Small 18–8–40–3; Cumbes 28–7–47–4; P. A. Smith 8–0–36–1; Asif Din 7–3–18–0; Sutcliffe 4–3–4–0.

Warwickshire

T. A. Lloyd c Luddington b Lawrence	24	– b Curtis	63
*G. W. Humpage b Cowan	0	– not out	121
Asif Din c Ellis b Curtis	15	– not out	38
K. D. Smith b Curtis	64		
P. A. Smith c and b Cowan	20		
†G. A. Tedstone lbw b Curtis	9		
D. M. Smith c Ellis b Curtis	27		
C. Lethbridge run out	0		
G. C. Small not out	57		
S. P. Sutcliffe not out	17		
L-b 3, w 1, n-b 2	6	L-b 8	8
1/2 2/39 3/39 4/97 5/114 6/153 7/153 8/171 (8 wkts dec.)	239	1/129 (1 wkt)	230

J. Cumbes did not bat.

Bowling: *First Innings*—Ridge 8–1–17–0; Cowan 24–3–75–2; Curtis 42–15–57–4; Lawrence 10–4–32–1; Varey 16–2–52–0. *Second Innings*—Cowan 13–0–83–0; Varey 9–0–42–0; Curtis 19.3–1–96–1; Hayes 1–0–1–0.

Umpires: J. D. Morley and A. G. T. Whitehead.

†OXFORD UNIVERSITY v MCC

At Oxford, June 5, 7, 8 (not first-class). MCC won by eight wickets. Former England and Yorkshire slow left-arm bowler Don Wilson took seven Oxford second-innings wickets in a marathon spell of 40 overs as the university, having required 156 to avoid an innings defeat, were dismissed for 260. MCC hit off the 105 runs required for victory for the loss of two wickets.

Oxford University 186 (N. P. D. Ross five for 29) and 260 (R. S. Luddington 73; D. Wilson seven for 102); MCC 342 for seven dec. (E. A. Clark 71, R. G. Abeynaike 64, N. P. D. Ross 63, J. A. Claughton 51) and 105 for two (E. A. Clark 67 not out).

OXFORD UNIVERSITY v SURREY

At Oxford, June 9, 10, 11. Drawn. After Clinton had amassed an unbeaten career-best 172 in Surrey's first innings, Oxford made a positive reply with Hayes and Marsden putting on 104 for the second wicket. Once again, however, the later batsmen capitulated rather than capitalised and Surrey batted again with a lead of 69, which Alan Butcher and Knight extended rapidly with an opening partnership of 227. Butcher's 131 included seventeen boundaries and Knight's declaration, made soon after he had completed his century, asked the dark blues to score 331 in four hours. At 42 for four they faced defeat but were rescued by Ellis, who had demoted himself in the order, and Halliday. They added 101 for the fifth wicket and Ellis went on to a maiden century (sixteen 4s), having saved the match.

Surrey

A. R. Butcher c Marsden b Rawlinson	10	– c Rawlinson b Ellis	131
G. S. Clinton not out	172		
*R. D. V. Knight c Hayes b Ridge	0	– (2) not out	104
G. P. Howarth c and b Ellis	33		
†C. J. Richards c Ellis b Rawlinson	61		
R. D. Jackman lbw b Ellis	52		
A. Needham not out	9	– (3) not out	19
L-b 3, n-b 5	8	B 4, l-b 3	7
1/20 2/21 3/79 4/189 5/318 (5 wkts dec.)	345	1/227 (1 wkt dec.)	261

K. S. Mackintosh, M. S. Butcher, C. K. Bullen and P. H. L. Wilson did not bat.

Bowling: *First Innings*—Ridge 24–2–96–1; Varey 12–4–27–0; Rawlinson 22–1–102–2; Ellis 17–8–40–2; Lawrence 20–4–72–0. *Second Innings*—Ridge 16–3–65–0; Varey 14–3–60–0; Ellis 16–4–45–1; Rawlinson 14–1–64–0; Lawrence 1–1–0–0; Hayes 2–0–20–0.

Oxford University

*R. G. P. Ellis lbw b Jackman	39	– (4) not out	105
R. Marsden run out	49	– (1) c Jackman b Mackintosh	11
K. A. Hayes c Howarth b Wilson	65	– c Mackintosh b Needham	8
G. J. Toogood c Needham b Mackintosh	28	– (2) b Wilson	2
R. P. Moulding c M. S. Butcher b Mackintosh	12	– c Needham b Mackintosh	0
S. J. Halliday c Richards b Mackintosh	18	– c Knight b A. R. Butcher	35
J. G. Varey b Jackman	0	– not out	13
H. T. Rawlinson b Mackintosh	4		
†R. S. Luddington st Richards b Jackman	27		
S. P. Ridge not out	4		
M. P. Lawrence b Jackman	0		
B 3, l-b 12, n-b 15	30	B 3, l-b 8, n-b 2	13
1/55 2/159 3/169 4/208 5/219 6/220 7/226 8/250 9/276	276	1/13 2/13 3/42 4/42 5/143 (5 wkts)	187

Bowling: *First Innings*—Jackman 25.5–6–66–4; Wilson 18–4–41–1; Mackintosh 24–4–77–4; Clinton 1–0–11–0; Knight 5–3–2–0; Needham 11–6–25–0; A. R. Butcher 4–0–21–0; Howarth 2–1–3–0. *Second Innings*—Wilson 12–4–33–1; Mackintosh 12–6–33–2; Needham 17–4–40–1; Jackman 5–1–9–0; Bullen 9–0–29–0; A. R. Butcher 11–4–23–1; Richards 1–0–5–0; M. S. Butcher 1–0–2–0.

Umpires: W. L. Budd and K. Ibadulla.

†OXFORD UNIVERSITY v AUSTRALIAN UNIVERSITIES

At Oxford, June 12, 14, 15 (not first-class). Australian Universities won by six wickets. Oxford University 240 for seven dec. (R. G. P. Ellis 51) and 252 for five dec. (R. M.

Edbrooke 101, P. N. Huxford 55); Australian Universities 225 for nine dec. (S. Campbell 64 not out, J. Dixon 52; J. G. Varey six for 43) and 270 for four (J. Robson 92 not out, L. Robinson 82, J. Dixon 57).

At Swansea, June 19, 21, 22. OXFORD UNIVERSITY drew with GLAMORGAN.

At Lord's, June 26, 28, 29. OXFORD UNIVERSITY lost to CAMBRIDGE UNIVERSITY by seven wickets (See other matches at Lord's, 1982).

CAMBRIDGE

President – SIR JOHN BUTTERFIELD
(Downing)

Hon. Treasurer – PROFESSOR A. D. BUCKINGHAM
(Pembroke)

Captain – D. R. PRINGLE
(Felsted and Fitzwilliam)

Secretary – S. J. G. DOGGART
(Winchester and Magdalene)

Captain for 1983 – S. P. HENDERSON
(Downside and Magdalene)

Secretary – D. W. VAREY
(Birkenhead and Pembroke)

Not since the days of Majid Khan had Cambridge cricket been so dominated by the ability of one man as it was in 1982 when Derek Pringle, blossoming under the pressures of captaincy, grew from a promising colt to an England all-rounder. In fact, when beating Lancashire the university gained their first victory over a county side since Majid inspired three such victories in 1971.

Just to prove, though, that they were not a one-man team, Cambridge achieved the ultimate success by beating Oxford at Lord's without the help of Pringle, who, despite some pressure to the contrary, opted to play for England in the second Test against India, this coinciding with the University match. Robin Boyd-Moss, gaining the confidence of a maiden century against Warwickshire, immediately scored a second hundred in the same match. That done he made a match-winning century at Lord's before carrying his run-making into county cricket.

Stephen Henderson was another to make an impact with the bat, scoring his maiden century against Middlesex, a brilliant innings of 209 not out. The talented left-hander did not, however, always score the runs expected of him. Another century-maker in a largely dry Fenner's season was the opening batsman, David Varey, while more than once Peter Mills, his usual partner, went close to three figures. In Pringle's absence, the side was well led at Lord's by Mills, himself a son of the 1948 Cambridge captain.

Pringle started the season with a century when playing just as a batsman, being unable to bowl because of a persistent ankle injury suffered in pre-season training. While he concentrated on his batting he made runs freely, soon being up with the leaders in the first-class averages. Once he was able to bowl, his victims kept him for a while among the leading wicket-takers as well. The knowledge that Pringle was likely to make runs or take wickets, if not both, took the pressure off his colleagues and allowed them to gather confidence.

Bowling was more difficult, despite a remarkable start to the season when, on the first day, Keith Hodgson took the first eight wickets against Glamorgan. Hitting the seam with encouraging regularity he looked a threat for the season, but injury dulled his edge. Cambridge always found it difficult to bowl sides out without a major contribution from Pringle. The wicket-keeper, Chris Goldie, reached a modern record of dismissals in a season for Cambridge with 23 victims.

Away from Fenner's, university cricket was given a boost by the regular selection of Oxbridge graduates in England's two Test series. From Cambridge came Greig and Edmonds, besides Pringle; from Oxford came Marks and Tavaré. Two former captains, Imran Khan (Oxford) and Majid (Cambridge), also appeared in the summer's Test matches. – D.H.

CAMBRIDGE UNIVERSITY RESULTS

First-class matches – Played 9: Won 2, Lost 4, Drawn 3.

FIRST-CLASS AVERAGES – BATTING

	M	*I*	*NO*	*R*	*HI*	*Avge*
D. R. Pringle	6	10	3	521	127	74.42
R. J. Boyd-Moss	9	17	1	717	123	44.81
S. P. Henderson	9	16	3	531	209*	40.84
D. W. Varey	9	17	3	548	156*	39.14
W. E. J. Barrington	4	6	1	174	59	34.80
K. I. Hodgson	8	10	1	213	50	23.66
J. P. C. Mills	9	17	0	389	98	22.88
S. J. G. Doggart	9	13	1	242	64	20.16
C. C. Ellison	7	7	4	56	16	18.66
C. F. E. Goldie	9	9	0	115	31	12.77
A. J. Pollock	7	8	2	63	19	10.50
R. W. M. Palmer	9	8	5	20	12	6.66

Played in two matches: R. S. Dutton 0, 0*, 0. Played in one match: A. G. Davies 13, 4; P. D. Griffiths 1, 0.

* *Signifies not out.*

CAMBRIDGE UNIVERSITY 1982

[*Bill Smith*

Back row: B. Taylor (*coach*), S. P. Henderson, R. W. M. Palmer, W. E. J. Barrington, K. I. Hodgson, A. J. Pollock, R. J. Gowar, H. Shipp (*scorer*).
Front row: C. F. E. Goldie, S. J. G. Doggart, J. P. C. Mills (*captain*), R. J. Boyd-Moss, D. W. Varey.

BOWLING

	O	*M*	*R*	*W*	*Avge*	*BB*
D. R. Pringle	117.2	37	288	13	22.15	6-33
R. J. Boyd-Moss	64	15	233	9	25.88	4-42
K. I. Hodgson	198.1	42	625	23	27.17	8-68
A. J. Pollock	115.5	18	483	14	34.50	5-108
R. W. M. Palmer	219.4	34	849	14	60.64	4-96
C. C. Ellison	96.5	20	314	5	62.80	3-30
S. J. G. Doggart	182.4	29	623	7	89.00	2-30

Also bowled: R. S. Dutton 19–1–130–0; P. D. Griffiths 9–2–39–0; S. P. Henderson 6–3–8–0; D. W. Varey 1–0–4–0.

CAMBRIDGE UNIVERSITY v GLAMORGAN

At Cambridge, April 21, 22, 23. Drawn. There was an eventful start to the season with Hodgson taking the first eight wickets to fall on the opening day and Alan Jones scoring his 52nd century, hitting twelve 4s in his 205-minute innings. The county declared on the first evening and by stumps Cambridge had lost both openers. Their situation improved next day, however, when Pringle hit a century which included a 6 and eighteen 4s. On the final morning Ontong completed the fastest of the match's three hundreds with a 6 and seventeen 4s to enable the county to set a fourth-innings target of 326 in four and threequarter hours. This was always too steep for the undergraduates, who took the opportunity to obtain batting practice.

Glamorgan

A. Jones c Goldie b Hodgson	103	– c Goldie b Hodgson	31
A. L. Jones c Goldie b Hodgson	24	– c Goldie b Hodgson	20
R. C. Ontong b Hodgson	6	– not out	106
C. J. C. Rowe b Hodgson	23	– c Varey b Doggart	44
M. J. Llewellyn c Henderson b Hodgson	2	– not out	61
G. C. Holmes st Goldie b Doggart	68		
†E. W. Jones c Henderson b Hodgson	0		
*B. J. Lloyd c Goldie b Hodgson	9		
M. A. Nash b Hodgson	0		
S. A. B. Daniels not out	30		
S. R. Barwick not out	5		
B 3, l-b 7, w 1	11	L-b 2, w 2	4
1/62 2/92 3/126 4/128 5/196 6/196 7/212 8/212 9/269	(9 wkts dec.) 281	1/48 2/53 3/126	(3 wkts dec.) 266

Bowling: *First Innings*—Palmer 22–3–73–0; Dutton 6–0–29–0; Hodgson 32–12–68–8; Doggart 20–3–55–1; Ellison 8–1–28–0; Henderson 4–3–6–0; Boyd-Moss 8–3–11–0. *Second Innings*—Palmer 13–2–66–0; Dutton 4–1–22–0; Hodgson 22–5–71–2; Doggart 20–1–86–1; Boyd-Moss 7–3–17–0.

Cambridge University

J. P. C. Mills c E. W. Jones b Nash	0 – c Lloyd b Rowe	56
D. W. Varey c E. W. Jones b Daniels	0 – b Rowe	41
R. J. Boyd-Moss c A. L. Jones b Nash	15 – c A. L. Jones b Nash	18
†C. F. E. Goldie c E. W. Jones b Daniels	13	
*D. R. Pringle b Lloyd	127 – not out	73
S. J. G. Doggart b Daniels	8 – b Daniels	34
K. I. Hodgson c Llewellyn b Lloyd	34	
S. P. Henderson c Ontong b Lloyd	0 – (4) c A. L. Jones b Lloyd	23
C. C. Ellison st E. W. Jones b Lloyd	15	
R. S. Dutton lbw b Lloyd	0	
R. W. M. Palmer not out	0	
B 4, l-b 2, w 1, n-b 3	10 – B 1, l-b 5, w 5	11
1/0 2/2 3/27 4/31 5/50 6/155 7/160 8/209 9/215	222 – 1/78 2/115 3/125 4/153 5/256	(5 wkts) 256

Bowling: *First Innings*—Nash 18–5–50–2; Daniels 16–1–49–3; Lloyd 23.2–9–58–5; Barwick 12–3–22–0; Ontong 3–0–27–0; Rowe 5–2–6–0. *Second Innings*—Nash 14–4–38–1; Daniels 5.4–0–19–1; Barwick 10–6–17–0; Lloyd 28–11–78–1; Rowe 27–6–64–2; Ontong 5–1–29–0.

Umpires: J. Birkenshaw and D. G. L. Evans.

CAMBRIDGE UNIVERSITY v NOTTINGHAMSHIRE

At Cambridge, April 24, 26, 27. Nottinghamshire won by ten wickets. Boyd-Moss, Pringle (again) and Doggart scored freely against the county champions but in the end Hemmings's off-spin made too many demands on the technique of undergraduate batsmen. The county's innings was one of fits and starts, with a lack of practice being the main problem for the batsmen. When Cambridge batted a second time they displayed their usual frailties, owing everything to another innings of substance by Boyd-Moss, who batted for 207 minutes – all but seven minutes of the university's innings. The task facing Nottinghamshire was never difficult, and on a fast Fenner's wicket Todd hit his hundred in 75 minutes, his two 6s and sixteen 4s taking his boundary tally for the match to 29.

Cambridge University

J. P. C. Mills c Randall b Cooper	0 – c French b Cooper	1
D. W. Varey c Todd b Cooper	10 – lbw b Illingworth	22
R. J. Boyd-Moss c Hassan b Hemmings	52 – b Bore	82
*D. R. Pringle c Randall b Hemmings	81 – (5) b Illingworth	8
S. P. Henderson lbw b Hemmings	0 – (4) b Illingworth	13
S. J. G. Doggart c Todd b Hemmings	64 – c Birch b Hemmings	6
K. I. Hodgson c Hassan b Hemmings	13 – (8) c sub b Hemmings	11
†C. F. E. Goldie c French b Bore	28 – (7) c French b Cooper	1
C. C. Ellison not out	1 – lbw b Bore	3
R. S. Dutton not out	0 – lbw b Cooper	0
R. W. M. Palmer (did not bat)	– not out	0
B 7, l-b 2, n-b 1	10 – L-b 7	7
1/0 2/19 3/151 4/151 5/152 6/172 7/243 8/259	(8 wkts dec.) 259 – 1/2 2/46 3/66 4/82 5/99 6/104 7/121 8/153 9/154	154

Bowling: *First Innings*—Cooper 18–6–46–2; Bore 27–6–65–1; Illingworth 20–4–63–0; Hemmings 30.3–8–71–5; Weightman 1–0–4–0. *Second Innings*—Cooper 18–1–49–3; Illingworth 15–3–58–3; Bore 11.2–5–23–2; Hemmings 15–8–17–2.

Nottinghamshire

P. A. Todd c Goldie b Palmer	52	– (2) not out 104
†B. N. French c Palmer b Hodgson	40	
D. W. Randall lbw b Palmer	0	– (1) not out 29
B. Hassan lbw b Hodgson	1	
*J. D. Birch b Ellison	23	
N. I. Weightman lbw b Palmer	36	
N. J. B. Illingworth c Goldie b Hodgson	49	
E. E. Hemmings c Doggart b Palmer	0	
M. J. Harris not out	31	
K. E. Cooper not out	38	
B 7, l-b 2, w 1	10	L-b 1 1
1/74 2/74 3/83 4/114 5/118 6/172 7/178 8/232	(8 wkts dec.) 280	(no wkt) 134

M. K. Bore did not bat.

Bowling: *First Innings*—Dutton 4–0–44–0; Palmer 18–2–96–4; Hodgson 22–4–55–3; Ellison 8–2–20–1; Doggart 19–3–55–0. *Second Innings*—Dutton 5–0–35–0; Palmer 7–0–26–0; Doggart 6.4–1–38–0; Boyd-Moss 4–0–34–0.

Umpires: D. G. L. Evans and J. Birkenshaw.

†At Oxford, April 25. CAMBRIDGE UNIVERSITY lost to OXFORD UNIVERSITY by 62 runs.

CAMBRIDGE UNIVERSITY v MIDDLESEX

At Cambridge, April 28, 29, 30. Middlesex won by eight wickets. On the first day a double-hundred by graduate freshman Henderson helped the university recover from a precarious start. In sharing a stand of 220 runs for the fourth wicket with Mills, who was out 2 short of what would have been his first hundred for Cambridge, Henderson, an uncomplicated, hard-hitting left-hander, reached his 50 in 44 minutes and his maiden century in 84 minutes. His 200 took 239 minutes and included 33 4s. Brearley, on his 40th birthday, scored 60 against his old university while Slack made a most sedate century before the county declared 149 behind. Pringle's response after some rapid scoring set Middlesex 292 to win in three and a half hours, but his bowlers were incapable of restraining Gatting, who, having reached his hundred in 146 minutes, launched a furious assault. He hit 26 off one over from Doggart – 6, 4, 6, 2, 4, 4 – and, after hitting a 6 and twelve 4s in his century, he had three more 6s and six 4s in his unbeaten 164 as Middlesex romped home with eight overs in hand.

Cambridge University

J. P. C. Mills st Downton b Edmonds	98	– lbw b Selvey 10
D. W. Varey b Selvey	0	– not out 51
R. J. Boyd-Moss c Barlow b Williams	14	– (4) c Slack b Williams 0
*D. R. Pringle c Slack b Williams	0	– (3) not out 72
S. P. Henderson not out	209	
S. J. G. Doggart c Gatting b Selvey	16	
K. I. Hodgson c and b Edmonds	25	
B 9, l-b 7, w 1, n-b 1	18	B 3, l-b 4, n-b 2 9
1/1 2/41 3/50 4/270 5/317 6/380	(6 wkts dec.) 380	1/31 2/33 (2 wkts dec.) 142

A. J. Pollock, †C. F. E. Goldie, C. C. Ellison and R. W. M. Palmer did not bat.

Bowling: *First Innings*—Selvey 20–6–52–2; Merry 15–1–76–0; Williams 13–0–69–2; Edmonds 26.3–7–85–2; Emburey 26–8–80–0. *Second Innings*—Selvey 11–3–21–1; Williams 8–2–20–1; Merry 7–1–13–0; Edmonds 14–4–42–0; Emburey 11–3–37–0.

Middlesex

*J. M. Brearley lbw b Pringle	60		
W. N. Slack c Mills b Pollock	114		
G. D. Barlow not out	36	– lbw b Doggart	6
M. W. Gatting not out	3	– (2) not out	164
C. T. Radley (did not bat)		– (1) st Goldie b Doggart	72
P. H. Edmonds (did not bat)		– (4) not out	38
B 7, n-b 11	18	L-b 9, w 1, n-b 2	12
1/135 2/228 (2 wkts dec.)	231	1/145 2/169 (2 wkts)	292

J. E. Emburey, †P. R. Downton, M. W. W. Selvey, N. F. Williams and W. G. Merry did not bat.

Bowling: *First Innings*—Palmer 10.2–0–51–0; Pringle 16–3–41–1; Ellison 10–1–35–0; Hodgson 6–0–27–0; Pollock 9–0–41–1; Doggart 4–1–18–0. *Second Innings*—Palmer 7–0–37–0; Pringle 9.3–0–45–0; Hodgson 5–1–24–0; Pollock 9–1–55–0; Doggart 13–2–77–2; Ellison 9–1–42–0.

Umpires: A. G. T. Whitehead and J. Holder.

CAMBRIDGE UNIVERSITY v WARWICKSHIRE

At Cambridge, May 1, 3, 4. Drawn. Boyd-Moss, who had shown good early-season form, scored a deserved maiden hundred and celebrated by scoring a second in the same match. Lloyd led the county's reply and looked set to become another Fenner's century-maker before falling on 95. On the third morning Boyd-Moss completed his second century, in 160 minutes, sharing a 127-run stand for the second wicket with the promising Varey, but soon after Pringle's declaration rain ruined the likelihood of another interesting finish.

Cambridge University

J. P. C. Mills c Humpage b Hogg	4	– c K. D. Smith b Hogg	9
D. W. Varey lbw b Ferreira	24	– lbw b Ferreira	63
R. J. Boyd-Moss lbw b Smith	123	– c Humpage b Ferreira	119
S. P. Henderson c Humpage b Cumbes	2	– c and b Cumbes	15
*D. R. Pringle c Humpage b Small	37		
S. J. G. Doggart run out	7	– (5) not out	47
K. I. Hodgson c Ferreira b Hogg	20		
A. J. Pollock b Smith	13	– (6) not out	5
†C. F. E. Goldie c Kallicharran b Small	19		
C. C. Ellison c K. D. Smith b Ferreira	16		
R. W. M. Palmer not out	2		
L-b 4, n-b 3	7	B 2, l-b 3, w 1, n-b 1	7
1/4 2/48 3/62 4/127 5/157 6/200 7/227 8/240 9/272	274	1/14 2/141 3/186 4/232 (4 wkts dec.)	265

Bowling: *First Innings*—Hogg 16–5–45–2; Small 18–3–51–2; Ferreira 25.1–6–60–2; Cumbes 16–3–38–1; P. A. Smith 17–2–73–2. *Second Innings*—Hogg 10–0–38–1; Ferreira 19–0–75–2; Small 10–0–55–0; Cumbes 20–2–66–1; P. A. Smith 7–2–22–0; Lloyd 1–0–2–0.

Warwickshire

K. D. Smith c Pringle b Palmer	10	– (2) not out	0
T. A. Lloyd c Goldie b Palmer	95	– (1) not out	7
†G. W. Humpage b Pollock	22		
P. R. Oliver run out	26		
Asif Din not out	30		
P. A. Smith not out	34		
B 1, l-b 12, w 7, n-b 7	27		
1/25 2/78 3/146 4/184 (4 wkts dec.)	244	(no wkt)	7

*A. I. Kallicharran, A. M. Ferreira, G. C. Small, J. Cumbes and W. Hogg did not bat.

Bowling: *First Innings*—Palmer 18–8–57–2; Pringle 18–5–47–0; Pollock 14–3–30–1; Ellison 11–1–44–0; Doggart 16–4–39–0. *Second Innings*—Palmer 3–1–7–0; Pringle 2.4–2–0–0.

Umpires: A. G. T. Whitehead and J. Holder.

†CAMBRIDGE UNIVERSITY v OXFORD UNIVERSITY

At Cambridge, May 2. Cambridge University won by seven wickets. Oxford University 233 (R. T. Rawlinson 59; A. J. Pollock four for 39); Cambridge University 234 for three (R. J. Boyd-Moss 100, J. P. C. Mills 72 not out).

†CAMBRIDGE UNIVERSITY v SUFFOLK

At Cambridge, May 6, 7. Drawn. Suffolk 182 for eight dec. (S. M. Clements 50; R. J. Gowar four for 29) and 274 for six dec. (S. M. Clements 100, A. G. Warrington 51); Cambridge University 229 for six dec. (N. I. Holcombe 98; P. D. Barker four for 55) and 95 for seven.

†CAMBRIDGE UNIVERSITY v NORFOLK

At Cambridge, May 11. Drawn. Cambridge University 210 for nine (D. W. Varey 57, W. E. J. Barrington 53); Norfolk 169 for nine (P. J. Mir 66).

CAMBRIDGE UNIVERSITY v LANCASHIRE

At Cambridge, May 12, 13, 14. Cambridge University won by seven wickets. Cambridge University's first victory over a first-class county for eleven years was a great personal triumph for Pringle, who led his side by example to celebrate his selection for MCC against the Indians. At the outset there was little indication of what was to come as Hughes and Lloyd provided the core of a solid total and the university middle order collapsed against the medium pace of Folley. However, Hodgson and wicket-keeper Goldie set about a revival that took Cambridge to within 30 of their visitors, and when Lancashire batted again Pringle claimed a career-best six for 33. Cambridge's target was 159 on a wicket whose quality was being questioned, but there appeared to be nothing wrong with it as Pringle, batting with increasing power, and Henderson shared a century partnership to take the students to a long-awaited victory.

Lancashire

A. Kennedy c Henderson b Hodgson	19	– lbw b Pringle	17
J. Abrahams c Goldie b Pringle	4	– c Varey b Pringle	14
F. C. Hayes lbw b Pringle	0	– b Pringle	9
*D. Lloyd c Goldie b Ellison	54	– (6) c Goldie b Ellison	4
D. P. Hughes c Boyd-Moss b Pollock	106	– c Goldie b Pringle	0
B. W. Reidy b Pollock	37	– (4) c Varey b Pringle	11
I. Folley c Goldie b Palmer	17	– c Doggart b Pringle	15
†C. J. Scott c and b Doggart	1	– c Henderson b Ellison	9
P. J. W. Allott c Henderson b Doggart	23	– run out	11
L. L. McFarlane c Boyd-Moss b Pringle	11	– st Goldie b Ellison	12
G. J. Speak not out	4	– not out	15
L-b 8, n-b 20	28	B 1, l-b 4, w 1, n-b 5	11
1/21 2/23 3/65 4/159 5/220 6/247 7/256 8/279 9/285	304	1/29 2/39 3/51 4/51 5/58 6/60 7/82 8/94 9/105	128

Bowling: *First Innings*—Palmer 14–3–39–1; Pringle 18.1–7–54–3; Hodgson 18–5–72–1; Ellison 14–5–37–1; Doggart 10–3–30–2; Pollock 7–0–44–2. *Second Innings*—Palmer 8–2–32–0; Pringle 27–13–33–6; Ellison 17.5–7–30–3; Hodgson 14–5–22–0.

Cambridge University

D. W. Varey lbw b Allott	16	– c Hughes b Folley	28
J. P. C. Mills c Scott b Folley	73	– c Reidy b Folley	15
R. J. Boyd-Moss c Kennedy b Allott	39	– c Speak b Hughes	3
*D. R. Pringle c Kennedy b Folley	24	– not out	61
S. P. Henderson c Kennedy b Folley	8	– not out	46
S. J. G. Doggart c Kennedy b Folley	1		
K. I. Hodgson c Folley b Hughes	50		
A. J. Pollock c Abrahams b Hughes	19		
†C. F. E. Goldie c McFarlane b Hughes	31		
C. C. Ellison not out	0		
R. W. M. Palmer c McFarlane b Hughes	3		
L-b 5, n-b 5	10	L-b 4, n-b 2	6
1/20 2/86 3/131 4/151 5/161 6/162 7/226 8/271 9/271	274	1/39 2/44 3/56 (3 wkts)	159

Bowling: *First Innings*—Allott 21–6–62–2; McFarlane 15–3–59–0; Speak 6–1–14–0; Folley 19–4–40–4; Lloyd 8–1–15–0; Abrahams 13–3–46–0; Hughes 8.2–2–28–4. *Second Innings*—Allott 13–6–26–0; McFarlane 5–2–10–0; Reidy 4–2–7–0; Hughes 13–2–41–1; Folley 10–5–24–2; Speak 4–1–18–0; Abrahams 6.4–0–27–0.

Umpires: P. J. Eele and J. Morley.

†CAMBRIDGE UNIVERSITY v CLUB CRICKET CONFERENCE

At Cambridge, May 18. Club Cricket Conference won by nine wickets. Cambridge University 123 (G. Black five for 26); Club Cricket Conference 124 for one (M. E. Milton 72 not out).

CAMBRIDGE UNIVERSITY v ESSEX

At Cambridge, May 18, 20, 21. Essex won by an innings and 42 runs. For the first time in the season all the university batsmen failed, and without Pringle – away on MCC duty – there was no-one to rescue them. Phillip and Foster bundled them out in a little over two hours. Essex batted unspectacularly until the two Easts shared a jolly eighth-wicket stand of 139 in

111 minutes. In the second innings, Boyd-Moss, Henderson and débutant Barrington all made half-centuries, but Phillip proved too lively for the tail, wrapping up the match within an hour on the final day and finishing with match figures of eleven for 91.

Cambridge University

D. W. Varey lbw b Phillip	7	– lbw b Phillip	3
*J. P. C. Mills run out	24	– c Turner b Foster	19
R. J. Boyd-Moss c McEwan b Phillip	2	– st D. E. East b Turner	81
S. P. Henderson c D. E. East b Phillip	8	– b Turner	52
W. E. J. Barrington c R. E. East b Phillip	2	– c and b Phillip	59
S. J. G. Doggart c R. E. East b Phillip	10	– c R. E. East b Turner	10
A. G. Davies b Turner	13	– lbw b Phillip	4
A. J. Pollock b Foster	0	– c and b Phillip	5
†C. F. E. Goldie b Foster	4	– c D. E. East b Phillip	8
C. C. Ellison not out	11	– not out	10
R. W. M. Palmer c R. E. East b Foster	12	– lbw b Phillip	0
L-b 4, n-b 2	6	B 2, l-b 3, n-b 2	7
1/28 2/32 3/40 4/43 5/48 6/61 7/64 8/74 9/74	99	1/15 2/23 3/88 4/205 5/219 6/232 7/239 8/240 9/258	258

Bowling: *First Innings*—Foster 16–7–46–3; Phillip 12–2–41–5; Turner 5–2–6–1; R. E. East 2–2–0–0. *Second Innings*—Foster 27–4–93–1; Phillip 15.5–4–50–6; Acfield 17–7–16–0; Turner 15–4–39–3; R. E. East 8–2–22–0; Gooch 5–0–31–0.

Essex

*G. A. Gooch b Pollock	35
B. R. Hardie c Davies b Palmer	44
A. W. Lilley c Henderson b Doggart	40
K. S. McEwan c Davies b Pollock	51
K. R. Pont c Davies b Boyd-Moss	32
S. Turner b Boyd-Moss	11
N. Phillip c Ellison b Pollock	20
†D. E. East c Palmer b Pollock	78
R. E. East b Boyd-Moss	58
N. A. Foster b Pollock	15
D. L. Acfield not out	1
B 1, l-b 6, w 1, n-b 6	14
1/57 2/116 3/134 4/199 5/215 6/230 7/242 8/381 9/382	399

Bowling: Palmer 23–1–102–1; Pollock 30.5–7–108–5; Ellison 11–1–48–0; Henderson 2–0–2–0; Doggart 16–3–57–1; Boyd-Moss 24–8–68–3.

Umpires: H. D. Bird and J. Morley.

†CAMBRIDGE UNIVERSITY v CAMBRIDGESHIRE

At Cambridge, May 22. Drawn. Cambridge University 200 for six dec. (G. Nienon 51 not out); Cambridgeshire 174 for five.

†CAMBRIDGE UNIVERSITY v AUSTRALIAN UNIVERSITIES

At Cambridge, June 5, 7, 8 (not first-class). Drawn. Cambridge University 190 (W. E. J. Barrington 71; J. Maguire four for 57) and 293 for seven dec. (R. J. Boyd-Moss 100, D. R. Pringle 53; S. Campbell five for 107); Australian Universities 203 (R. W. M. Palmer four for 48) and 204 for five (D. Robertson 70, J. Robson 50).

CAMBRIDGE UNIVERSITY v NORTHAMPTONSHIRE

At Cambridge, June 9, 10, 11. Northamptonshire won by 133 runs. Without Pringle, away on England duty, the university attack was exposed by Willey and Williams – the latter reaching his hundred in 135 minutes. Willey needed only 40 minutes for his fifty but was dismissed by Boyd-Moss, a county colleague, in a bizarre over. The bowler was struck for two boundaries by Willey and then twice bowled 4 wides before having the batsman stumped off a ball way outside his off stump. In the Cambridge reply Varey hit a maiden hundred in 258 minutes and was close to carrying his bat when Mills declared with nine wickets down. Northamptonshire again batted freely before declaring, and spinners Steele, Williams and Willey worked their way through the Cambridge batting in three and a half hours.

Northamptonshire

M. J. Bamber c Varey b Hodgson	27	– (2) b Pollock	31
W. Larkins c Goldie b Hodgson	16	– (1) c Varey b Hodgson	52
P. Willey st Goldie b Boyd-Moss	64		
R. G. Williams c Boyd-Moss b Palmer	141		
D. J. Capel b Pollock	33	– not out	21
D. S. Steele not out	65		
R. M. Carter not out	5	– (4) c Goldie b Pollock	38
D. J. Wild (did not bat)		– (3) c Goldie b Palmer	21
T. M. Lamb (did not bat)		– (6) not out	11
B 1, l-b 4, w 8, n-b 8	21	L-b 3, w 1, n-b 1	5
1/44 2/69 3/138 4/229 5/339 (5 wkts dec.)	372	1/62 2/94 3/125 4/168 (4 wkts dec.)	179

*†G. Sharp and N. A. Mallender did not bat.

Bowling: *First Innings*—Palmer 19–5–63–1; Pollock 19–3–95–1; Hodgson 16–1–72–2; Doggart 24–1–73–0; Boyd-Moss 1–0–10–1; Griffiths 7–1–38–0. *Second Innings*—Palmer 13–3–48–1; Pollock 14–1–58–2; Hodgson 9–1–29–1; Doggart 14–3–38–0; Griffiths 2–1–1–0.

Cambridge University

*J. P. C. Mills b Mallender	9	– (2) c Sharp b Steele	31
D. W. Varey not out	156	– (1) c Sharp b Mallender	17
R. J. Boyd-Moss c Sharp b T. M. Lamb	0	– c Capel b Steele	16
S. P. Henderson b Wild	2	– c Steele b Williams	30
W. E. J. Barrington b Willey	45	– c Carter b Willey	20
S. J. G. Doggart b Willey	7	– c Sharp b Willey	5
K. I. Hodgson c Sharp b Capel	8	– b Willey	0
A. J. Pollock b Capel	4	– c Carter b Williams	17
†C. F. E. Goldie b Willey	10	– c Sharp b Williams	1
P. D. Griffiths b Willey	1	– c Sharp b Williams	0
R. W. M. Palmer not out	3	– not out	0
B 4, l-b 8, n-b 15	27	B 1, l-b 3, n-b 5	9
1/16 2/24 3/26 4/129 5/153 6/168 7/198 8/221 9/228 (9 wkts dec.)	272	1/18 2/68 3/75 4/109 5/111 6/138 7/146 8/146 9/146	146

Bowling: *First Innings*—Mallender 18–11–31–1; T. M. Lamb 16–9–29–1; Wild 10–3–30–1; Steele 20.4–9–41–0; Willey 32–15–45–4; Williams 21–5–55–0; Capel 8–3–14–2. *Second Innings*—Mallender 9–3–18–1; T. M. Lamb 6–2–10–0; Capel 4–0–8–0; Steele 10–3–40–2; Willey 27.2–17–36–3; Williams 19–10–25–4.

Umpires: P. J. Eele and N. T. Plews.

†CAMBRIDGE UNIVERSITY v COMBINED SERVICES

At Cambridge, June 12, 13, 14 (not first-class). Drawn. Combined Services 163 (R. Evans 64; R. W. M. Palmer seven for 45) and 280 for four dec. (R. de Caires 95, R. C. Moylan-Jones 93); Cambridge University 160 for three dec. (J. P. C. Mills 71 not out) and 206 for seven (R. J. Boyd-Moss 57; K. J. Winder five for 83).

CAMBRIDGE UNIVERSITY v LEICESTERSHIRE

At Cambridge, June 19, 21, 22. Drawn. Rain ruined all three days against opponents who, in the past, had traditionally opened the Fenner's season. The county initially experienced trouble against Pringle and Hodgson before Gower, captaining Leicestershire, and Briers put on 141 for the fifth wicket. Varey again made runs for Cambridge, who declared 26 behind. But only 40 minutes' play was possible on the final day.

Leicestershire

I. P. Butcher b Pringle	14	– not out	25
R. A. Cobb c Goldie b Hodgson	10	– lbw b Palmer	5
T. J. Boon c Henderson b Pringle	4	– not out	5
N. E. Briers b Hodgson	94		
†M. A. Garnham lbw b Pringle	0		
*D. I. Gower run out	77		
D. A. Wenlock c Varey b Hodgson	9		
G. J. Parsons c Henderson b Palmer	20		
G. Forster c Henderson b Palmer	4		
N. G. B. Cook not out	16		
B 1, l-b 5, n-b 2	8	L-b 2, w 1, n-b 2	5
1/28 2/28 3/33 4/33 5/174 6/213 7/220 8/229 9/256 (9 wkts dec.)	256	1/18 (1 wkt)	40

L. B. Taylor did not bat.

Bowling: *First Innings*—Palmer 11.2–0–49–2; Pringle 22–7–54–3; Hodgson 24–4–71–3; Pollock 3–1–17–0; Doggart 20–4–57–0. *Second Innings*—Palmer 6–2–16–1; Pringle 4–0–14–0; Hodgson 1.1–0–5–0.

Cambridge University

D. W. Varey c Boon b Briers	72
J. P. C. Mills lbw b Taylor	20
R. J. Boyd-Moss c Butcher b Briers	12
S. P. Henderson st Garnham b Wenlock	34
W. E. J. Barrington lbw b Parsons	0
*D. R. Pringle c and b Cook	38
S. J. G. Doggart lbw b Wenlock	27
K. I. Hodgson b Wenlock	16
A. J. Pollock not out	0
B 5, l-b 5, w 1	11
1/50 2/86 3/141 4/141 5/175 6/190 7/229 8/230 (8 wkts dec.)	230

†C. F. E. Goldie and R. W. M. Palmer did not bat.

Bowling: Taylor 18–5–54–1; Parsons 13–2–65–1; Wenlock 14.1–5–50–3; Briers 5–2–11–2; Forster 14–5–27–0; Cook 7–3–12–1.

Umpires: D. O. Oslear and R. Julian.

†CAMBRIDGE UNIVERSITY v QUIDNUNCS

At Cambridge, June 20. Quidnuncs won by 10 runs. Quidnuncs 208 for six dec. (N. H. C. Cooper 75; R. J. Boyd-Moss four for 72); Cambridge University 198 (M. E. Allbrook four for 70, R. J. A. Huxter four for 84).

†At Roehampton, June 23, 24, 25. CAMBRIDGE UNIVERSITY v MCC. Abandoned.

At Lord's, June 26, 28, 29. CAMBRIDGE UNIVERSITY beat OXFORD UNIVERSITY by seven wickets (See Other Matches at Lord's, 1982).

FESTIVAL FOR BLIND CRICKETERS

The first festival for blind cricketers was held at Durham University on the weekend of June 5–6, 1982. Four teams took part in the festival: Avon, Barclays Bank, Northern Alliance (an amalgam of teams from Leeds and Manchester) and Worcester College Old Boys.

Cricket for the blind and visually handicapped has been played for more than 30 years, but in the last decade it has so gained in prominence and popularity that there are now twelve teams playing on a fairly regular basis. Modifications to the rules of cricket as understood by sighted players are essential. The ball used is much larger and softer, being a Frido size 5 white football which is filled with ball-bearings so that it rattles and can be heard each time that it bounces or strikes the bat. The wicket is shortened to eighteen yards. The stumps are rather larger – 35 inches high and 10 inches wide – and are in the form of a stout wooden frame which can also act as a reference point of touch to the blind batsmen and bowlers alike. Furthermore, because the ball is essentially silent until it strikes the ground, the bowler must call to the batsman as he releases the ball and the ball must also bounce at least once before it reaches a visually handicapped batsman (a "partial") and twice before reaching a totally blind batsman (a "total"). A "total" fielder can also take a catch after the ball has bounced once, and an accepted tactic is for the "totals" to field close to the wicket where their chances of collecting a first-bounce catch are higher. Furthermore, a "total" is allowed two lbw decisions and two hit-wickets per innings and he cannot be stumped or run out (although his runner can). In competition all teams must field at least four "totals" in any eleven. Despite these amended rules and concessions, the essential spirit of the game has not been forfeited.

One innovation at the festival was the introduction of a new acoustic ball developed by the Department of Applied Physics in the university. A soft-plastic ball, rather smaller than the Frido size 5 presently used, was implanted with an electronic module. This module contained a rechargeable battery, two miniature loudspeakers and some integrated circuit electronics, which were encapsulated in silicone rubber and surrounded by a glassfibre sheath for electrical and mechanical protection. Continuous operation for at least ten hours was found to be possible before recharging. The output "beep" of the balls used had a pitch and frequency that were effectively constant, although they could be tuned to the players' preference.

Although not used in the competitive matches, this new ball was tested by the blind cricketers during the festival – with mixed response. The bowlers enjoyed using it, in part because they could get greater purchase on the rather smaller ball and hence send it down more quickly. This benefit could be removed simply by making the new generation of balls to size 5. The fielders found the new ball easier to track. However, the "total" batsmen, although they could hear the inward flight of the ball from the moment it left the bowler's hand, had no sense of bounce or of when the ball pitched. This problem could probably be remedied by introducing a gravity sensor into the circuit so that whenever the ball bounced the "beep" momentarily changed pitch. Experience with the blind players indicated that further research on the acoustic prototype was necessary.

Despite a humid and thundery weekend, all the matches were completed. The favourites, Worcester College Old Boys, played true to form and won all three of their matches. The BASRAB Durham Trophy was presented to Worcester's captain, David Sheridan, by Jim Oliver on behalf of Barclays Bank, who had sponsored the event.

Scores: Northern Alliance 62 for six; Worcester College OB 64 for three. Avon 107 for four (Carpenter 43, Fisher 44 not out); Northern Alliance 99 for eight (Bond 42). Barclays 100 for five; Avon 64 for nine. Barclays 79 for eight; Worcester College OB 80 for two (Baxter 38 not out). Worcester College OB 100 for seven; Avon 70. Barclays 128 for three (Loten 54 not out); Northern Alliance 44 (Jones four for 1).

OXFORD AND CAMBRIDGE BLUES

From 1919-1982

Blues prior to 1919 are omitted, except some of special interest for personal or family reasons.

OXFORD

Aamer Hameed (Central Model HS and Punjab U.) 1979
Abell, G. E. B. (Marlborough) 1924, 1926-27
Allan, J. M. (Edinburgh Academy) 1953-56
Allerton, J. W. O. (Stowe) 1969
Allison, D. F. (Greenmore Coll.) 1970
Altham, H. S. (Repton) 1911-12
Arenhold, J. A. (Diocesan Coll., SA) 1954

Baig, A. A. (Aliya and Osmania U., India) 1959-62
Baig, M. A. (Osmania U., India) 1962-64
Bailey, J. A. (Christ's Hospital) (Capt. in 1958) 1956-58
Ballance, T. G. L. (Uppingham) 1935, 1937
Barber, A. T. (Shrewsbury) (Capt. in 1929) 1927-29
Barker, A. H. (Charterhouse) 1964-65, 1967
Barlow, E. A. (Shrewsbury) 1932-34
Barnard, F. H. (Charterhouse) 1922, 1924
Barnes, R. G. (Harrow) 1906-07
Bartlett, J. H. (Chichester) 1946, 1951
Barton, M. R. (Winchester) 1936-37
Bell, G. F. (Repton) 1919
Belle, B. H. (Forest School) 1936
Benn, A. (Harrow) 1935
Benson, E. T. (Blundell's) 1928-29
Bettington, R. H. B. (The King's School, Parramatta) (Capt. in 1923) 1920-23
Bickmore, A. F. (Clifton) 1920-21
Bird, W. S. (Malvern) (Capt. in 1906) 1904-06
Birrell, H. B. (St Andrews, SA) 1953-54
Blagg, P. H. (Shrewsbury) 1939
Blaikie, K. G. (Maritzburg Coll., SA) 1924
Blake, P. D. S. (Eton) (Capt. in 1952) 1950-52
Bloy, N. C. F. (Dover) 1946-47
Bonham-Carter, M. (Winchester) 1902
Boobbyer, B. (Uppingham) 1949-52
Bosanquet, B. J. T. (Eton) 1898-1900
Botton, N. D. (King Edward's, Bath) 1974
Bowman, R. C. (Fettes) 1957
Bradshaw, W. H. (Malvern) 1930-31
Brett, P. J. (Winchester) 1929
Brettell, D. N. (Cheltenham) 1977
Brooke, R. H. J. (St Edward's, Oxford) 1932
Brooks, R. A. (Quintin and Bristol U.) 1967
Bruce, Hon. C. N. (later Lord Aberdare) (Winchester) 1907-08
Burchnall, R. L. (Winchester) 1970-71
Burki, J. (St Mary's, Rawalpindi and Punjab U.) 1958-60
Burton, M. St J. W. (Umtali HS. Rhodesia and Rhodes U.) (Capt. in 1970) 1969-71
Bury, T. E. O. (Charterhouse) 1980
Bush, J. E. (Magdalen Coll. Sch.) 1952
Butterworth, R. E. C. (Harrow) 1927

Campbell, A. N. (Berkhamsted) 1970
Campbell, I. P. (Canford) 1949-50
Campbell, I. P. F. (Repton) (Capt. in 1913) 1911-13
Cantlay, C. P. T. (Radley) 1975
Carr, D. B. (Repton) (Capt. in 1950) 1949-51
Carroll, P. R. (Newington Coll. and Sydney U.) 1971
Cazalet, P. V. F. (Eton) 1927
Chalk, F. G. H. (Uppingham) (Capt. in 1934) 1931-34
Chesterton, G. H. (Malvern) 1949
Claughton, J. A. (King Edward's, Birmingham) (Capt. in 1978) 1976-79
Clements, S. M. (Ipswich) (Capt. in 1979) 1976, 1979
Clube, S. V. M. (St John's, Leatherhead) 1956
Corlett, S. C. (Worksop) 1971-72
Corran, A. J. (Gresham's) 1958-60
Coutts, I. D. F. (Dulwich) 1952
Cowan, R. S. (Lewes Priory CS) 1980-82
Cowdrey, M. C. (Tonbridge) (Capt. in 1954) 1952-54
Coxon, A. J. (Harrow CS) 1952
Crawley, A. M. (Harrow) 1927-30
Crutchley, G. E. V. (Harrow) 1912
Curtis, I. J. (Whitgift) 1980, 1982
Cushing, V. G. B. (KCS Wimbledon) 1973
Cuthbertson, J. L. (Rugby) 1962-63

Darwall-Smith, R. F. H. (Charterhouse) 1935-38
Davidson, W. W. (Brighton) 1947-48
Davis, F. J. (Blundell's) 1963
Delisle, G. P. S. (Stonyhurst) 1955-56
de Saram, F. C. (Royal Coll., Colombo) 1934-35
Dillon, E. W. (Rugby) 1901-02
Divecha, R. V. (Podar HS and Bombay U.) 1950-51

Dixon, E. J. H. (St Edward's, Oxford) (Capt. in 1939) 1937-39
Donnelly, M. P. (New Plymouth BHS and Canterbury U., NZ) (Capt. in 1947) 1946-47
Dowding, A. L. (St Peter's, Adelaide) (Capt. in 1953) 1952-53
Drybrough, C. D. (Highgate) (Capt. in 1961-62) 1960-62
Duff, A. R. (Radley) 1960-61
Dyer, A. W. (Mill Hill) 1965-66
Dyson, E. M. (QEGS, Wakefield) 1958
Dyson, J. H. (Charterhouse) 1936

Eagar, E. D. R. (Cheltenham) 1939
Eagar, M. A. (Rugby) 1956-59
Easter, J. N. C. (St Edward's, Oxford) 1967-68
Eggar, J. D. (Winchester) 1938
Ellis, R. G. P. (Haileybury) (Capt. in 1982) 1981-82
Elviss, R. W. (Leeds GS) 1966-67
Evans, E. N. (Haileybury) 1932
Evans, G. (St Asaph) 1939
Ezekowitz, R. A. B. (Westville BHS, Durban and Cape Town U., SA) 1980-81

Faber, M. J. J. (Eton) 1972
Fane, F. L. (Charterhouse) 1897-98
Fasken, D. K. (Wellington) 1953-55
Fellows-Smith, J. P. (Durban HS, SA) 1953-55
Fillary, E. W. J. (St Lawrence) 1963-65
Findlay, W. (Eton) (Capt. in 1903) 1901-03
Fisher, P. B. (St Ignatius, Enfield) 1975-78
Ford, N. M. (Harrow) 1928-30
Foster, G. N. (Malvern) 1905-08
Foster, H. K. (Malvern) 1894-96
Foster, R. E. (Malvern) (Capt. in 1900) 1897-1900
Franklin, H. W. F. (Christ's Hospital) 1924
Fraser, J. N. (Church of England GS, Melbourne and Melbourne U.) 1912-13
Frazer, J. E. (Winchester) 1924
Fry, C. A. (Repton) 1959-61
Fry, C. B. (Repton) (Capt. in 1894) 1892-95
Fursdon, E. D. (Sherborne) 1974-75

Gamble, N. W. (Stockport GS) 1967
Garland-Wells, H. M. (St Paul's) 1928-30
Garofall, A. R. (Latymer Upper) 1967-68
Garthwaite, P. F. (Wellington) 1929
Gibbs, P. J. K. (Hanley GS) 1964-66
Gibson, I. (Manchester GS) 1955-58
Gilbert, H. A. (Charterhouse) 1907-09
Gilliat, I. A. W. (Charterhouse) 1925
Gilliat, R. M. C. (Charterhouse) (Capt. in 1966) 1964-67
Gilligan, F. W. (Dulwich) (Capt. in 1920) 1919-20
Glover, T. R. (Lancaster RGS) (Capt. in 1975) 1973-75
Goldstein, F. S. (Falcon Coll., Bulawayo) (Capt. in 1968-69) 1966-69
Green, D. M. (Manchester GS) 1959-61
Greenstock, J. W. (Malvern) 1925-27
Grover, J. N. (Winchester) (Capt. in 1938) 1936-38
Groves, M. G. M. (Diocesan Coll., SA) 1964-66
Guest, M. R. J. (Rugby) 1964-66
Guise, J. L. (Winchester) (Capt. in 1925) 1924-25
Gurr, D. R. (Aylesbury GS) 1976-77

Halliday, J. G. (City of Oxford HS) 1935
Halliday, S. J. (Downside) 1980
Hamblin, C. B. (King's, Canterbury) 1971-73
Hamilton, A. C. (Charterhouse) 1975
Harris, C. R. (Buckingham RLS) 1964
Harris, Hon. G. R. C. (Lord Harris) (Eton) 1871-72, 1874
Hart, T. M. (Strathallan) 1931-32
Hayes, K. A. (QEGS, Blackburn) 1981-82
Heal, M. G. (St Brendan's, Bristol) 1970, 1972
Heard, H. (QE Hosp. Sch.) 1969-70
Hedges, L. P. (Tonbridge) 1920-22
Henderson, D. (St Edward's, Oxford) 1950
Henley, D. F. (Harrow) 1947
Hewetson, E. P. (Shrewsbury) 1923-25
Hiller, R. B. (Bec) 1966
Hill-Wood, C. K. H. (Eton) 1928-30
Hill-Wood, D. J. (Eton) 1928
Hobbs, J. A. D. (Liverpool Coll.) 1957
Hofmeyr, M. B. (Pretoria, SA) (Capt. in 1951) 1949-51
Holdsworth, R. L. (Repton) 1919-22
Holmes, E. R. T. (Malvern) (Capt. in 1927) 1925-27
Hone, B. W. (Adelaide U.) (Capt. in 1933) 1931-33
Hopkins, H. O. (St Peter's, Adelaide) 1923
Howell, M. (Repton) (Capt. in 1919) 1914, 1919
Hurst, C. S. (Uppingham) (Capt. in 1909) 1907-09
Huxford, P. N. (Richard Hale) 1981

Imran Khan (Aitchison Coll., Lahore and Worcester RGS) (Capt. in 1974) 1973-75

Jackson, K. L. T. (Rugby) 1934
Jakobson, T. R. (Charterhouse) 1961
Jardine, D. R. (Winchester) 1920-21, 1923
Jardine, M. R. (Fettes) (Capt. in 1891) 1889-92
Jarrett, D. W. (Wellington) 1975
Jenkins, V. G. J. (Llandovery) 1933
Johns, R. L. (St Albans and Keele U.) 1970
Jones, A. K. C. (Solihull) (Capt. in 1973) 1971-73

Jones, P. C. H. (Milton HS. Rhodesia and Rhodes U.) (Capt. in 1972) 1971-72
Jose, A. D. (Adelaide U.) 1950-51
Jowett, D. C. P. R. (Sherborne) 1952-55
Jowett, R. L. (Bradford GS) 1957-59

Kamm, A. (Charterhouse) 1954
Kardar, A. H. (Islamia Coll. and Punjab U.) 1947-49
Kayum, D. A. (Selhurst GS and Chatham House GS) 1977-78
Keighley, W. G. (Eton) 1947-48
Kentish, E. S. M. (Cornwall Coll, Jamaica) 1956
Key, K. J. (Clifton) 1884-87
Khan, A. J. (Aitchison Coll., Lahore and Punjab U.) 1968-69
Kimpton, R. C. M. (Melbourne U.) 1935, 1937-38
Kingsley, P. G. T. (Winchester) (Capt. in 1930) 1928-30
Kinkead-Weekes, R. C. (Eton) 1972
Knight, D. J. (Malvern) 1914, 1919
Knight, J. M. (Oundle) 1979
Knight, N. S. (Uppingham) 1934
Knott, C. H. (Tonbridge) (Capt. in 1924) 1922-24
Knott, F. H. (Tonbridge) (Capt. in 1914) 1912-14
Knox, F. P. (Dulwich) (Capt. in 1901) 1899-1901

Lamb, Hon. T. M. (Shrewsbury) 1973-74
Lee, R. J. (Church of England GS and Sydney U.) 1972-74
Legard, A. R. (Winchester) 1932, 1935
Legge, G. B. (Malvern) (Capt. in 1926) 1925-26
L'Estrange, M. G. (St Aloysius Coll. and Sydney U.) 1977, 1979
Leveson Gower, H. D. G. (Winchester) (Capt. in 1896) 1893-96
Lewis, D. J. (Cape Town U.) 1951
Lindsay, W. O'B. (Harrow) 1931
Lloyd, M. F. D. (Magdalen Coll. Sch.) 1974
Lomas, J. M. (Charterhouse) 1938-39
Lowe, J. C. M. (Uppingham) 1907-09
Lowndes, W. G. L. F. (Eton) 1921
Luddington, R. S. (KCS, Wimbledon) 1982
Lyon, B. H. (Rugby) 1922-23
Lyon, G. W. F. (Brighton) 1925

McBride, W. N. (Westminster) 1926
McCanlis, M. A. (Cranleigh) (Capt. in 1928) 1926-28
Macindoe, D. H. (Eton) (Capt. in 1946) 1937-39, 1946
McIntosh, R. I. F. (Uppingham) 1927-28
M'Iver, C. D. (Forest School) 1903-04
McKinna, G. H. (Manchester GS) 1953
Majendie, N. L. (Winchester) 1962-63
Mallett, A. W. H. (Dulwich) 1947-48
Mallett, N. V. H. (St Andrew's Coll. and Cape Town U.) 1981
Manasseh, M. (Epsom) 1964
Marie, G. V. (Western Australia U. and Reading U.) (Capt. in 1979, but injury prevented him playing v Cambridge) 1978
Marks, V. J. (Blundell's) (Capt. in 1976-77) 1975-78
Marsden, R. (Merchant Taylors', Northwood) 1982
Marshall, J. C. (Rugby) 1953
Marsham, A. J. B. (Eton) 1939
Marsham, C. D. B. (Private) (Capt. in 1857-58) 1854-58
Marsham, C. H. B. (Eton) (Capt. in 1902) 1900-02
Marsham, C. J. B. (Private) 1851
Marsham, R. H. B. (Private) 1856
Marsland, G. P. (Rossall) 1954
Martin, J. D. (Magdalen Coll. Sch.) (Capt. in 1965) 1962-63, 1965
Matthews, M. H. (Westminster) 1936-37
Maudsley, R. H. (Malvern) 1946-47
May, B. (Prince Edward's, Salisbury and Cape Town U.) (Capt. in 1971) 1970-72
Mayhew, J. F. N. (Eton) 1930
Melville, A. (Michaelhouse, SA) (Capt. in 1931-32) 1930-33
Melville, C. D. M. (Michaelhouse, SA) 1957
Metcalfe, S. G. (Leeds GS) 1956
Millener, D. J. (Auckland GS and Auckland U.) 1969-70
Minns, R. E. F. (King's, Canterbury) 1962-63
Mitchell, W. M. (Dulwich) 1951-52
Mitchell-Innes, N. S. (Sedbergh) (Capt. in 1936) 1934-37
Monro, R. W. (Harrow) 1860
Moore, D. N. (Shrewsbury) (Capt. in 1931, when he did not play v Cambridge owing to illness) 1930
Morgan, A. H. (Hastings GS) 1969
Morrill, N. D. (Sandown GS and Millfield) 1979
Moulding, R. P. (Haberdashers' Aske's) (Capt. in 1981) 1978-82
Mountford, P. N. G. (Bromsgrove) 1963
Murray-Wood, W. (Mill Hill) 1936

Naumann, F. C. G. (Malvern) 1914, 1919
Neate, F. W. (St Paul's) 1961-62
Neser, V. H. (South African Coll., Cape Town) 1921
Newman, G. C. (Eton) 1926-27
Newton-Thompson, J. O. (Diocesan Coll., SA) 1946
Niven, R. A. (Berkhamsted) 1968-69, 1973
Nunn, J. A. (Sherborne) 1926-27

O'Brien, T. C. (St Charles' College, Notting-Hill) 1884-85

Oldfield, P. C. (Repton) 1932-33
Orders, J. O. D. (Winchester) 1978-81
Owen-Smith, H. G. (Diocesan College, SA) 1931-33

Palairet, L. C. H. (Repton) (Capt. in 1892-93) 1890-93
Palairet, R. C. N. (Repton) 1893-94
Pataudi, Nawab of (Chief's College, Lahore) 1929-31
Pataudi, Nawab of (Winchester) (Capt. in 1961, when he did not play v Cambridge owing to a car accident and 1963) 1960, 1963
Pathmanathan, G. (Royal Coll., Colombo and Sri Lanka U.) 1975-78
Patten, M. (Winchester) 1922-23
Paver, R. G. L. (Fort Victoria HS and Rhodes U.) 1973-74
Pawson, A. C. (Winchester) 1903
Pawson, A. G. (Winchester) (Capt. in 1910) 1908-11
Pawson, H. A. (Winchester) (Capt. in 1948) 1947-48
Pearce, J. P. (Ampleforth) 1979
Pearse, G. V. (Maritzburg Coll., SA) 1919
Peebles, I. A. R. (Glasgow Academy) 1930
Pershke, W. J. (Uppingham) 1938
Pether, S. (Magdalen Coll. Sch.) 1939
Phillips, J. B. M. (King's, Canterbury) 1955
Piachaud, J. D. (St Thomas's, Colombo) 1958-61
Pithey, D. B. (Plumtree HS and Cape Town U.) 1961-62
Porter, S. R. (Peers School) 1973
Potter, I. C. (King's, Canterbury) 1961-62
Potts, H. J. (Stand GS) 1950
Price, V. R. (Bishop's Stortford) (Capt. in 1921) 1919-22
Proud, R. B. (Winchester) 1939
Pycroft, J. (Bath) 1836

Raikes, D. C. G. (Shrewsbury) 1931
Raikes, G. B. (Shrewsbury) 1894-95
Raikes, T. B. (Winchester) 1922-24
Randolph, B. M. (Charterhouse) 1855-56
Raybould, J. G. (Leeds GS) 1959
Richardson, J. V. (Uppingham) 1925
Ridge, S. P. (Dr Challenors) 1982
Ridley, G. N. S. (Milton HS, Rhodesia) (Capt. in 1967) 1965-68
Ridley, R. M. (Clifton) 1968-70
Robertson-Glasgow, R. C. (Charterhouse) 1920-23
Robinson, G. A. (Preston Cath. Coll.) 1971
Robinson, H. B. O. (North Shore Coll., Vancouver) 1947-48
Rogers, J. J. (Sedbergh) 1979-81
Ross, C. J. (Wanganui CS and Wellington U., NZ) (Capt. in 1980) 1978-80
Royle, V. P. F. A. (Rossall) 1875-76
Rucker, C. E. S. (Charterhouse) 1914
Rucker, P. W. (Charterhouse) 1919
Rudd, C. R. D. (Eton) 1949
Rumbold, J. S. (St Andrew's Coll., NZ) 1946

Sabine, P. N. B. (Marlborough) 1963
Sale, R. (Repton) 1910
Sale, R. (Repton) 1939, 1946
Sanderson, J. F. W. (Westminster) 1980
Saunders, C. J. (Lancing) 1964
Savage, R. Le Q. (Marlborough) 1976-78
Sayer, D. M. (Maidstone GS) 1958-60
Scott, K. B. (Winchester) 1937
Scott, M. D. (Winchester) 1957
Scott, R. S. G. (Winchester) 1931
Seamer, J. W. (Marlborough) 1934-36
Sinclair, E. H. (Winchester) 1924
Singleton, A. P. (Shrewsbury) (Capt. in 1937) 1934-37
Siviter, K. (Liverpool) 1976
Skeet, C. H. L. (St Paul's) 1920
Skene, R. W. (Sedbergh) 1928
Smith, A. C. (King Edward's, Birmingham) (Capt. in 1959-60) 1958-60
Smith, G. O. (Charterhouse) 1895-96
Smith, M. J. K. (Stamford) (Capt. in 1956) 1954-56
Stainton, R. G. (Malvern) 1933
Stallibrass, M. J. D. (Lancing) 1974
Stanning, J. (Winchester) 1939
Stephenson, J. S. (Shrewsbury) 1925-26
Stevens, G. T. S. (UCS) (Capt. in 1922) 1920-23
Stewart-Brown, P. H. (Harrow) 1925-26
Sutcliffe, S. P. (King George V GS, Southport) 1980-81
Sutton, M. A. (Ampleforth) 1946

Tavaré, C. J. (Sevenoaks) 1975-77
Taylor, C. H. (Westminster) 1923-26
Taylor, T. J. (Stockport GS) 1981-82
Thackeray, P. R. (St Edward's, Oxford and Exeter U.) 1974
Thomas, R. J. A. (Radley) 1965
Tindall, R. G. (Winchester) 1933-34
Toft, D. P. (Tonbridge) 1966-67
Toogood, G. J. (N. Bromsgrove HS) 1982
Topham, R. D. N. (Shrewsbury and Australian National U., Canberra) 1976
Townsend, D. C. H. (Winchester) 1933-34
Travers, B. H. (Sydney U.) 1946, 1948
Tuff, F. N. (Malvern) 1910
Twining, R. H. (Eton) (Capt. in 1912) 1910-13

van der Bijl, P. G. (Diocesan Coll., SA) 1932
Van Ryneveld, C. B. (Diocesan Coll., SA) (Capt. in 1949) 1948-50
Varey, J. G. (Birkenhead) 1982

Wagstaffe, M. C. (Rossall and Exeter U.) 1972

Waldock, F. A. (Uppingham) 1919-20
Walford, M. M. (Rugby) 1936, 1938
Walker, D. F. (Uppingham) (Capt. in 1935) 1933-35
Waller, G. de W. (Hurstpierpoint) 1974
Walsh, D. R. (Marlborough) 1967-69
Walshe, A. P. (Milton HS, Rhodesia) 1953, 1955-56
Walton, A. C. (Radley) (Capt. in 1957) 1955-57
Ward, H. P. (Shrewsbury) 1919, 1921
Ward, J. M. (Newcastle-u-Lyme HS) 1971-73
Warner, P. F. (Rugby) 1895-96
Watson, A. G. M. (St Lawrence) 1965-66, 1968
Webb, H. E. (Winchester) 1948
Webbe, A. J. (Harrow) (Capt. in 1877-78) 1875-78
Wellings, E. M. (Cheltenham) 1929, 1931
Westley, S. A. (Lancaster RGS) 1968-69
Wheatley, G. A. (Uppingham) 1946
Whitcombe, P. A. (Winchester) 1947-49
Whitcombe, P. J. (Worcester RGS) 1951-52
Whitehouse, P. M. (Marlborough) 1938
Wiley, W. G. E. (Diocesan Coll., SA) 1952
Williams, C. C. P. (Westminster) (Capt. in 1955) 1953-55
Wilson, P. R. B. (Milton HS, Rhodesia and Cape Town U.) 1968, 1970
Wilson, R. W. (Warwick) 1957
Wingfield Digby, A. R. (Sherborne) 1971, 1975-77
Winn, C. E. (KCS, Wimbledon) 1948-51
Woodcock, R. G. (Worcester RGS) 1957-58
Wookey, S. M. (Malvern and Cambridge U.) 1978
Wordsworth, Chas. (Harrow) (Capt. both years, first Oxford Capt.) 1827, 1829
Worsley, D. R. (Bolton) (Capt. in 1964) 1961-64
Wrigley, M. H. (Harrow) 1949

Young, D. E. (KCS, Wimbledon) 1938

CAMBRIDGE

Acfield, D. L. (Brentwood) 1967-68
Aers, D. R. (Tonbridge) 1967
Aird, R. (Eton) 1923
Alexander, F. C. M. (Wolmer's Coll., Jamaica) 1952-53
Allbrook, M. E. (Tonbridge) 1975-78
Allen, A. W. (Eton) 1933-34
Allen, B. O. (Clifton) 1933
Allen, G. O. (Eton) 1922-23
Allom, M. J. C. (Wellington) 1927-28
Ashton, C. T. (Winchester) (Capt. in 1923) 1921-23
Ashton, G. (Winchester) (Capt. in 1921) 1919-21
Ashton, H. (Winchester) (Capt. in 1922) 1920-22
Atkins, G. (Challenors GS) 1960
Austin, H. M. (Melbourne) 1924
Aworth, C. J. (Tiffin) (Capt. in 1975) 1973-75

Bagnell, H. F. (Harrow) 1923
Bailey, T. E. (Dulwich) 1947-48
Baker, R. K. (Brentwood) 1973-74
Bannister, C. S. (Caterham) 1976
Barber, R. W. (Ruthin) 1956-57
Barford, M. T. (Eastbourne) 1970-71
Barrington, W. E. J. (Lancing) 1982
Bartlett, H. T. (Dulwich) (Capt. in 1936) 1934-36
Beaumont, D. J. (West Bridgford GS and Bramshill Coll.) 1978
Benke, A. F. (Cheltenham) 1962
Bennett, B. W. P. (Welbeck and RMA Sandhurst) 1979
Bennett, C. T. (Harrow) (Capt. in 1925) 1923, 1925
Bernard, J. R. (Clifton) 1958-60
Bhatia, A. N. (Doon School, India) 1969
Blake, J. P. (Aldenham) 1939
Bligh, Hon. Ivo F. W. (Lord Darnley) (Eton) (Capt. in 1881) 1878-81
Block, S. A. (Marlborough) 1929
Blofeld, H. C. (Eton) 1959
Blundell, E. D. (Waitaki, NZ) 1928-29
Bodkin, P. E. (Bradfield) (Capt. in 1946) 1946
Boyd-Moss, R. J. (Bedford) 1980-82
Brearley, J. M. (City of London) (Capt. in 1963-64) 1961-64
Brocklebank, J. M. (Eton) 1936
Brodhurst, A. H. (Malvern) 1939
Brodie, J. B. (Union HS, SA) 1960
Brodrick, P. D. (Royal GS, Newcastle) 1961
Bromley, R. C. (Christ's Coll. and Canterbury U., NZ) 1970
Brooker, M. E. W. (Lancaster RGS and Burnley GS) 1976
Brooke-Taylor, G. P. (Cheltenham) 1919-20
Brown, F. R. (The Leys) 1930-31
Browne, F. B. R. (Aldro School and Eastbourne) 1922
Bryan, J. L. (Rugby) 1921
Burnett, A. C. (Lancing) 1949
Burnup, C. J. (Malvern) 1896-98
Bushby, M. H. (Dulwich) (Capt. in 1954) 1952-54
Butterworth, H. R. W. (Rydal Mount) 1929
Calthorpe, Hon. F. S. G. (Repton) 1912-14, 1919

Cameron, J. H. (Taunton) 1935-37
Cangley, B. G. M. (Felsted) 1947
Carling, P. G. (Kingston GS) 1968, 1970
Carris, B. D. (Harrow) 1938-39
Carris, H. E. (Mill Hill) 1930
Cawston, E. (Lancing) 1932
Chambers, R. E. J. (Forest) 1966
Chapman, A. P. F. (Oakham and Uppingham) 1920-22
Christopherson, J. C. (Uppingham) 1931
Close, P. A. (Haileybury) 1965
Cobbold, P. W. (Eton) 1896
Cobbold, R. H. (Eton) 1927
Cobden, F. C. (Harrow) 1870-72
Cockett, J. A. (Aldenham) 1951
Coghlan, T. B. L. (Rugby) 1960
Colbeck, L. G. (Marlborough) 1905-06
Collins, D. C. (Wellington Coll, NZ) 1910-11
Comber, J. T. H. (Marlborough) 1931-33
Conradi, E. R. (Oundle) 1946
Cook, G. W. (Dulwich) 1957-58
Cooper, N. H. C. (St Brendan's, Bristol and East Anglia U.) 1979
Cosh, N. J. (Dulwich) 1966-68
Cottrell, G. A. (Kingston GS) (Capt. in 1968) 1966-68
Cottrell, P. R. (Chislehurst and Sidcup GS) 1979
Coverdale, S. P. (St Peter's, York) 1974-77
Craig, E. J. (Charterhouse) 1961-63
Crawford, N. C. (Shrewsbury) 1979-80
Crawley, E. (Harrow) 1887-89
Crawley, L. G. (Harrow) 1923-25
Croft, P. D. (Gresham's) 1955
Crookes, D. V. (Michaelhouse, SA) 1953
Cumberlege, B. S. (Durham) 1913

Daniell, J. (Clifton) 1899-1901
Daniels, D. M. (Rutlish) 1964-65
Datta, P. B. (Asutosh Coll., Calcutta) 1947
Davies, G. B. (Rossall) 1913-14
Davies, J. G. W. (Tonbridge) 1933-34
Dawson, E. W. (Eton) (Capt. in 1927) 1924-27
Day, S. H. (Malvern) (Capt. in 1901) 1899-1902
Dewes, A. R. (Dulwich) 1978
Dewes, J. G. (Aldenham) 1948-50
Dexter, E. R. (Radley) (Capt. in 1958) 1956-58
Dickinson, D. C. (Clifton) 1953
Dickinson, P. J. (KCS, Wimbledon) 1939
Doggart, A. G. (Bishop's Stortford) 1921-22
Doggart, G. H. G. (Winchester) (Capt. in 1950) 1948-50
Doggart, S. J. G. (Winchester) 1980-82
Douglas-Pennant, S. (Eton) 1959
Downes, K. D. (Rydal) 1939
Duleepsinhji, K. S. (Cheltenham) 1925-26, 1928

Edmonds, P. H. (Gilbert Rennie HS, Lusaka, Skinner's and Cranbrook) (Capt. in 1973) 1971-73
Edwards, T. D. W. (Sherborne) 1981
Elgood, B. C. (Bradfield) 1948
Ellison, C. C. (Tonbridge) 1982
Enthoven, H. J. (Harrow) (Capt. in 1926) 1923-26
Estcourt, N. S. D. (Plumtree, Southern Rhodesia) 1954
Evans, R. G. (King Edward's, Bury St Edmunds) 1921

Fabian, A. H. (Highgate) 1929-31
Fairbairn, G. A. (Church of England GS, Geelong) 1913-14, 1919
Falcon, M. (Harrow) (Capt. in 1910) 1908-11
Farnes, K. (Royal Liberty School, Romford) 1931-33
Fiddian-Green, C. A. (The Leys) 1921-22
Field, M. N. (Bablake) 1974
Fitzgerald, J. F. (St Brendan's, Bristol) 1968
Ford, A. F. J. (Repton) 1878-81
Ford, F. G. J. (Repton) (Capt. in 1889) 1887-90
Ford, W. J. (Repton) 1873
Fosh, M. K. (Harrow) 1977-78
Francis, T. E. S. (Tonbridge) 1925
Franklin, W. B. (Repton) 1912
Fraser, T. W. (Jeppe, SA) 1937
Fry, K. R. B. (Cheltenham) 1904

Gardiner, S. J. (St Andrew's, Bloemfontein) 1978
Gibb, P. A. (St Edward's, Oxford) 1935-38
Gibson, C. H. (Eton) 1920-21
Gillespie, D. W. (Uppingham) 1939
Gilligan, A. E. R. (Dulwich) 1919-20
Goldie, C. F. E. (St Paul's) 1981-82
Goodfellow, A. (Marlborough) 1961-62
Goonesena, G. (Royal Coll., Colombo) (Capt. in 1957) 1954-57
Grace, W. G., jun. (Clifton) 1895-96
Grant, G. C. (Trinidad) 1929-30
Grant, R. S. (Trinidad) 1933
Green, D. J. (Burton GS) (Capt. in 1959) 1957-59
Greig, I. A. (Queen's Coll., SA) (Capt. in 1979) 1977-79
Grierson, H. (Bedford GS) 1911
Griffith, M. G. (Marlborough) 1963-65
Griffith, S. C. (Dulwich) 1935
Griffiths, W. H. (Charterhouse) 1946-48
Grimshaw, J. W. T. (King William's Coll., Isle of Man) 1934-35

Hadingham, A. W. G. (St Paul's) 1932
Hadley, R. J. (Sanfields CS) 1971-73
Hall, J. E. (Ardingly) 1969
Hall, P. J. (Geelong) 1949

Harbinson, W. K. (Marlborough) 1929
Harvey, J. R. W. (Marlborough) 1965
Hawke, Hon. M. B. (Eton) (Capt. in 1885) 1882-83, 1885
Hayes, P. J. (Brighton) 1974-75, 1977
Hays, D. L. (Highgate) 1966, 1968
Hayward, W. I. D. (St Peter's Coll., Adelaide) 1950-51, 1953
Haywood, D. C. (Nottingham HS) 1968
Hazelrigg, A. G. (Eton) (Capt. in 1932) 1930-32
Henderson, S. P. (Downside and Durham U.) 1982
Hewan, G. E. (Marlborough) 1938
Hignell, A. J. (Denstone) (Capt. in 1977-78) 1975-78
Hill-Wood, W. W. (Eton) 1922
Hobson, B. S. (Taunton) 1946
Hodgson, K. I. (Oundle) 1981-82
Hodson, R. P. (QEGS, Wakefield) 1972-73
Holliday, D. C. (Oundle) 1979-81
Hopley, G. W. V. (Harrow) 1912
Hotchkin, N. S. (Eton) 1935
Howat, M. G. (Abingdon) 1977, 1980
Howland, C. B. (Dulwich) (Capt. in 1960) 1958-60
Hughes, G. (Cardiff HS) 1965
Human, J. H. (Repton) (Capt. in 1934) 1932-34
Human, R. H. C. (Repton) 1930-31
Hunt, R. G. (Aldenham) 1937
Hurd, A. (Chigwell) 1958-60
Hutton, R. A. (Repton) 1962-64
Huxter, R. J. A. (Magdalen Coll. Sch.) 1981

Insole, D. J. (Monoux, Walthamstow) (Capt. in 1949) 1947-49
Irvine, L. G. (Taunton) 1926-27

Jackson, E. J. W. (Winchester) 1974-76
Jackson, F. S. (Harrow) (Capt. in 1892-93) 1890-93
Jagger, S. T. (Malvern) 1925-26
Jahangir Khan (Lahore), 1933-36
James, R. M. (St John's, Leatherhead) 1956-58
Jameson, T. E. N. (Taunton and Durham U.) 1970
Jarrett, D. W. (Wellington and Oxford U.) 1976
Jefferson, R. I. (Winchester) 1961
Jenner, Herbert (Eton) (Capt. in 1827, First Cambridge Capt.) 1827
Jephson, D. L. A. (Manor House, Clapham) 1890-92
Jessop, G. L. (Cheltenham GS) (Capt. in 1899) 1896-99
Johnson, P. D. (Nottingham HS) 1970-72
Johnstone, C. P. (Rugby) 1919-20
Jones, A. O. (Bedford Modern) 1893
Jorden, A. M. (Monmouth) (Capt. in 1969-70) 1968-70

Judd, A. K. (St Paul's) 1927
Kaye, M. A. C. P. (Harrow) 1938
Kelland, P. A. (Repton) 1950
Kemp-Welch, G. D. (Charterhouse) (Capt. in 1931) 1929-31
Kendall, M. P. (Gillingham GS) 1972
Kenny, C. J. M. (Ampleforth) 1952
Kerslake, R. C. (Kingswood) 1963-64
Khanna, B. C. (Lahore) 1937
Killick, E. T. (St Paul's) 1928-30
King, F. (Dulwich) 1934
Kirby, D. (St Peter's, York) (Capt. in 1961) 1959-61
Kirkman, M. C. (Dulwich) 1963
Knight, R. D. V. (Dulwich) 1967-70
Knightley-Smith, W. (Highgate) 1953

Lacey, F. E. (Sherborne) 1882
Lacy-Scott, D. G. (Marlborough) 1946
Lagden, R. B. (Marlborough) 1912-14
Langley, J. D. A. (Stowe) 1938
Lawrence, A. S. (Harrow) 1933
Lewis, A. R. (Neath GS) (Capt. in 1962) 1960-62
Lewis, L. K. (Taunton) 1953
Littlewood, D. J. (Enfield GS) 1978
Lockhart, J. H. B. (Sedbergh) 1909-10
Longfield, T. C. (Aldenham) 1927-28
Longrigg, E. F. (Rugby) 1927-28
Lowe, R. G. H. (Westminster) 1925-27
Lowry, T. C. (Christ's College, NZ) (Capt. in 1924) 1923-24
Lumsden, V. R. (Munro College, Jamaica) 1953-55
Lyon, M. D. (Rugby) 1921-22
Lyttelton, 4th Lord (Eton) 1838
Lyttelton, Hon. Alfred (Eton) (Capt. in 1879) 1876-79
Lyttelton, Hon. C. F. (Eton) 1908-09
Lyttelton, Hon. C. G. (Lord Cobham) (Eton) 1861-64
Lyttelton, Hon. Edward (Eton) (Capt. in 1878) 1875-78
Lyttelton, Hon. G. W. S. (Eton) 1866-67

McAdam, K. P. W. J. (Prince of Wales, Nairobi and Millfield) 1965-66
MacBryan, J. C. W. (Exeter) 1920
McCarthy, C. N. (Maritzburg Coll., SA) 1952
McDowall, J. I. (Rugby) 1969
MacGregor, G. (Uppingham) (Capt. in 1891) 1888-91
Machin, R. S. (Lancing) 1927
Mackinnon, F. A. (Harrow) 1870
McLachlan, A. A. (St Peter's, Adelaide) 1964-65
McLachlan, I. M. (St Peter's, Adelaide) 1957-58
Majid J. Khan (Aitchison Coll., Lahore and Punjab U.) (Capt. in 1971-72) 1970-72

Malalasekera, V. P. (Royal Coll., Colombo) 1966-67
Mann, E. W. (Harrow) (Capt. in 1905) 1903-05
Mann, F. G. (Eton) 1938-39
Mann, F. T. (Malvern) 1909-11
Mann, J. E. F. (Geelong) 1924
Mansfield, J. W. (Winchester) 1883-84
Marlar, R. G. (Harrow) (Capt. in 1953) 1951-53
Marriott, C. S. (St Columba's) 1920-21
Mathews, K. P. A. (Felsted) 1951
May, P. B. H. (Charterhouse) 1950-52
Melluish, M. E. L. (Rossall) (Capt. in 1956) 1954-56
Meyer, R. J. O. (Haileybury) 1924-26
Miller, M. E. (Prince Henry GS, Hohne, WG) 1963
Mills, J. M. (Oundle) (Capt. in 1948) 1946-48
Mills, J. P. C. (Oundle) (Capt. in 1982) 1979-82
Mischler, N. M. (St Paul's) 1946-47
Mitchell, F. (St Peter's, York) (Capt. in 1896) 1894-97
Morgan, J. T. (Charterhouse) (Capt. in 1930) 1928-30
Morgan, M. N. (Marlborough) 1954
Morris, R. J. (Blundell's) 1949
Morrison, J. S. F. (Charterhouse) (Capt. in 1919) 1912, 1914, 1919
Moses, G. H. (Ystalyfera GS) 1974
Moylan, A. C. D. (Clifton) 1977
Mubarak, A. M. (Royal Coll., Colombo and Sri Lanka U.) 1978-80
Murray, D. L. (Queen's RC, Trinidad) (Capt. in 1966) 1965-66
Murrills, T. J. (The Leys) (Capt. in 1976) 1973-74, 1976

Naumann, J. H. (Malvern) 1913, 1919
Nelson, R. P. (St George's, Harpenden) 1936
Nevin, M. R. S. (Winchester) 1969
Norris, D. W. W. (Harrow) 1967-68

O'Brien, R. P. (Wellington) 1955-56
Odendaal, A. (Queen's Coll. and Stellenbosch U., SA) 1980
Owen-Thomas, D. R. (KCS, Wimbledon) 1969-72

Palfreman, A. B. (Nottingham HS) 1966
Palmer, R. W. M. (Bedford) 1982
Parker, G. W. (Crypt, Gloucester) (Capt. in 1935) 1934-35
Parker, P. W. G. (Collyer's GS) 1976-78
Parry, D. M. (Merchant Taylors') 1931
Parsons, A. B. D. (Brighton) 1954-55
Partridge, N. E. (Malvern) 1920
Paull, R. K. (Millfield) 1967
Pawle, J. H. (Harrow) 1936-37
Payne, A. U. (St Edmund's, Canterbury) 1925
Payne, M. W. (Wellington) (Capt. in 1907) 1904-07
Payton, W. E. G. (Nottingham HS) 1937
Pearman, H. (King Alfred's and St Andrew's U.) 1969
Pearson, A. J. G. (Downside) 1961-63
Peck, I. G. (Bedford) (Capt. in 1980-81) 1980-81
Pelham, A. G. (Eton) 1934
Pepper, J. (The Leys) 1946-48
Pieris, P. I. (St Thomas's, Colombo) 1957-58
Pollock, A. J. (Shrewsbury) 1982
Ponniah, C. E. M. (St Thomas's, Colombo) 1967-69
Ponsonby, Hon. F. G. B. (Lord Bessborough) (Harrow) 1836
Popplewell, N. F. M. (Radley) 1977-79
Popplewell, O. B. (Charterhouse) 1949-51
Powell, A. G. (Charterhouse) 1934
Pretlove, J. F. (Alleyn's) 1954-56
Prideaux, R. M. (Tonbridge) 1958-60
Pringle, D. R. (Felsted) (Capt. in 1982, when he did not play v Oxford owing to Test selection) 1979-81
Pritchard, G. C. (King's, Canterbury) 1964
Pryer, B. J. K. (City of London) 1948
Pyemont, C. P. (Marlborough) 1967

Ranjitsinhji, K. S. (Rajkumar Coll., India) 1893
Ratcliffe, A. (Rydal) 1930-32
Reddy, N. S. K. (Doon School, India) 1959-61
Rees-Davies, W. R. (Eton) 1938
Riddell, V. H. H. (Clifton) 1926
Rimell, A. G. J. (Charterhouse) 1949-50
Robins, R. W. V. (Highgate) 1926-28
Roebuck, P. M. (Millfield) 1975-77
Roopnaraine, R. (Queen's RC, BG) 1965-66
Rose, M. H. (Pocklington) 1963-64
Ross, N. P. G. (Marlborough) 1969
Rotherham, G. A. (Rugby) 1919
Rought-Rought, D. C. (Private) 1937
Rought-Rought, R. C. (Private) 1930, 1932
Roundell, J. (Winchester) 1973
Russell, D. P. (West Park GS, St Helens) 1974-75
Russell, S. G. (Tiffin) (Capt. in 1967) 1965-67
Russom, N. (Huish's GS) 1980-81

Seabrook, F. J. (Haileybury) (Capt. in 1928) 1926-28
Seager, C. P. (Peterhouse, Rhodesia) 1971
Selvey, M. W. W. (Battersea GS and Manchester U.) 1971
Shelmerdine, G. O. (Cheltenham) 1922
Sheppard, D. S. (Sherborne) (Capt. in 1952) 1950-52
Sherwell, N. B. (Tonbridge) 1923-25

Shirley, W. R. de la C. (Eton) 1924
Shirreff, A. C. (Dulwich) 1939
Short, R. L. (Denstone) 1969
Shuttleworth, G. M. (Blackburn GS) 1946-48
Silk, D. R. W. (Christ's Hospital) (Capt. in 1955) 1953-55
Singh, S. (Khalsa Coll. and Punjab U.) 1955-56
Sinker, N. D. (Winchester) 1966
Slack, J. K. E. (UCS) 1954
Smith, C. S. (William Hulme's GS) 1954-57
Smith, D. J. (Stockport GS) 1955-56
Smyth, R. I. (Sedbergh) 1973-75
Snowden, W. (Merchant Taylors', Crosby) (Capt. in 1974) 1972-75
Spencer, J. (Brighton and Hove GS) 1970-72
Steele, H. K. (King's Coll., NZ) 1971-72
Stevenson, M. H. (Rydal) 1949-52
Studd, C. T. (Eton) (Capt. in 1883) 1880-83
Studd, G. B. (Eton) (Capt. in 1882) 1879-82
Studd, J. E. K. (Eton) (Capt. in 1884) 1881-84
Studd, P. M. (Harrow) (Capt. in 1939) 1937-39
Studd, R. A. (Eton) 1895
Subba Row, R. (Whitgift) 1951-53
Surridge, D. (Richard Hale and Southampton U.) 1979
Swift, B. T. (St Peter's, Adelaide) 1957

Taylor, C. R. V. (Birkenhead) 1971-73
Thompson, J. R. (Tonbridge) 1938-39
Thomson, R. H. (Bexhill) 1961-62
Thwaites, I. G. (Eastbourne) 1964
Tindall, M. (Harrow) (Capt. in 1937) 1935-37
Tomlinson, W. J. V. (Felsted) 1923
Tordoff, G. G. (Normanton GS) 1952
Trapnell, B. M. W. (UCS) 1946
Tufnell, N. C. (Eton) 1909-10
Turnbull, M. J. (Downside) (Capt. in 1929) 1926, 1928-29

Urquhart, J. R. (King Edward VI School, Chelmsford) 1948

Valentine, B. H. (Repton) 1929
Varey, D. W. (Birkenhead) 1982

Wait, O. J. (Dulwich) 1949, 1951
Warr, J. J. (Ealing County GS) (Capt. in 1951) 1949-52
Watts, H. E. (Downside) 1947
Webster, J. (Bradford GS) 1939
Webster, W. H. (Highgate) 1932
Weedon, M. J. H. (Harrow) 1962
Wells, T. U. (King's Coll., NZ) 1950
Wheatley, O. S. (King Edward's, Birmingham) 1957-58
Wheelhouse, A. (Nottingham HS) 1959
White, A. F. T. (Uppingham) 1936
White, A. H. (Geelong) 1924
White, R. C. (Hilton Coll., SA) (Capt. in 1965) 1962-65
Wilcox, D. R. (Dulwich) (Capt. in 1933) 1931-33
Wild, J. V. (Taunton) 1938
Wilenkin, B. C. G. (Harrow) 1956
Wilkin, C. L. A. (St Kitts GS) 1970
Willard, M. J. L. (Judd) 1959-61
Willatt, G. L. (Repton) (Capt. in 1947) 1946-47
Wilson, G. (Harrow) 1919
Windows, A. R. (Clifton) 1962-64
Winlaw, R. de W. K. (Winchester) 1932-34
Wood, G. E. C. (Cheltenham) (Capt. in 1920) 1914, 1919-20
Wookey, S. M. (Malvern) 1975-76
Wooller, W. (Rydal) 1935-36
Wright, C. C. G. (Tonbridge), 1907-08
Wright, P. A. (Wellingborough) 1922-24
Wright, S. (Mill Hill) 1973
Wykes, N. G. (Oundle) 1928

Yardley, N. W. D. (St Peter's, York) (Capt. in 1938) 1935-38
Young, R. A. (Repton) (Capt. in 1908) 1905-08

CRICKET ASSOCIATIONS AND SOCIETIES

AUSTRALIAN CRICKET SOCIETY

ADELAIDE BRANCH: *Secretary* Christopher Harte, GPO Box 696, Adelaide 5001, South Australia.

BRISBANE BRANCH: *Secretary* Robert Spence, GPO Box 1498, Brisbane 4001, Queensland.

CANBERRA BRANCH: *Secretary* Julian Oakky, 38 Holden Crescent, Wanniassa, ACT 2903.

MELBOURNE BRANCH: *Secretary* Gary Hartman, 13 Turner Road, Langwarrin 3910, Victoria.

PERTH BRANCH: *Secretary* Bruce Castellas, 5 Colibri Court, Burrendah Gardens, Willetton, 6155, Western Australia.

SYDNEY BRANCH: *Secretary* Ronald Cardwell, 24 New Street, Balgowlah Heights 2093, New South Wales.

BLACKLEY CRICKET SOCIETY: *Secretary* D. Butterfield, 7 Bayswater Terrace, West Yorkshire, HX3 0NB.

BOSTON CRICKET LOVERS' SOCIETY: *Secretary* L. A. Brooks, 7 Tawney Street, Boston, Lincolnshire.

CAMBRIDGE UNIVERSITY CRICKET SOCIETY: *Secretary* A. Short. St John's College, Cambridge CB2 1TP.

CHESTERFIELD CRICKET LOVERS' SOCIETY: *Secretary* B. Holling, 24 Woodland Way, Old Tupton, Chesterfield, Derbyshire.

COUNCIL OF CRICKET SOCIETIES, THE: *Secretary* P. T. Roberts, 21 Hadrian Close, Lodge Park, Witham, Essex, CM8 1XA.

CRICKET SOCIETY, THE: *Secretary* E. C. R. Rice, 11 Clive Court, Babington Road, London SW16 6AL.

CRICKET STATISTICIANS, ASSOCIATION OF: *Secretary* P. Wynne-Thomas, The Bungalow, Haughton Mill, Retford, Nottinghamshire.

DULWICH COLLEGE CRICKET SOCIETY: *Secretary* D. Jerome, 4 Silverton Lodge, 118 Church Road, London, SE19 2UE.

EAST RIDING CRICKET SOCIETY: *Secretary* H. K. Cooke, 104 Well Lane, Willerby, Kingston upon Hull, East Yorkshire.

ESSEX CRICKET SOCIETY: *Secretary* P. T. Roberts, 21 Hadrian Close, Lodge Park, Witham, Essex, CM8 1XA.

FYLDE COAST CRICKET SOCIETY: *Secretary* S. Kennedy, 36 Torquay Avenue, Marton, Blackpool, Lancashire.

HAMPSHIRE CRICKET SOCIETY: *Secretary* F. Bailey, 7 Lightfoot Grove, Basingstoke, Hampshire.

HEAVY WOOLLEN CRICKET SOCIETY: *Secretary* G. S. Cooper, 27 Milford Grove, Gomersal, Cleckheaton, West Yorkshire.

LANCASHIRE AND CHESHIRE CRICKET SOCIETY: *Secretary* H. W. Pardoe, Crantock, 117a Barlow Moor Road, Didsbury, Manchester, M20 8TS.

LIMITED-OVERS INFORMATION GROUP: *Secretary* T. Allcock, 57 Low Road, Rivelin, Sheffield, S6 5FY.

LINCOLNSHIRE CRICKET LOVERS' SOCIETY: *Secretary* C. Kennedy, ACP, 26 Eastwood Avenue, Grimsby, South Humberside, DN34 5BE.

NORTHERN CRICKET SOCIETY: *Secretary* R. Marsh, 113 Cross Gate Lane, Leeds, Yorkshire, LS15 7PJ.

NOTTINGHAM CRICKET SOCIETY: *Secretary* G. Blagdurn, 2 Inham Circus, Chilwell, Beeston, Nottinghamshire, NG9 4FN.

OXFORD UNIVERSITY CRICKET SOCIETY: *Secretary* Harriet Monkhouse, Corpus Christi College, Oxford.

ROTHERHAM CRICKET SOCIETY: *Secretary* J. A. R. Atkin, 15 Gallow Tree Road, Rotherham, South Yorkshire, S65 3EE.

SCOTLAND, CRICKET SOCIETY OF: *Secretary* A. J. Robertson, 19 Barlae Avenue, Eaglesham, Glasgow, G76 0DA.

SOMERSET WYVERNS: *Secretary* M. Richards, "Wyvern", 3 Ash Road, Tring, Hertfordshire.

SOPHIANS, THE: *Secretary* A. K. Hignell, 79 Coed Gardens Road, Llanishen, Cardiff.

STOURBRIDGE AND DISTRICT CRICKET SOCIETY: *Secretary* R. Barber, 6 Carlton Avenue, Stourbridge, DY9 9ED.

SUSSEX CRICKET SOCIETY: *Secretary* A. A. Dumbrell, 6 Southdown Avenue, Brighton, East Sussex, BN1 6EG.

SYDNEY BARNES CRICKET SOCIETY: *Secretary* J. D. Scholfield, 331 Turnhurst Road, Packmoor, Stoke-on-Trent, S77 4LA.

UPPINGHAM SCHOOL CRICKET SOCIETY: *Secretary* Dr E. J. R. Boston, The Common Room, Uppingham School, Rutland.

WALES, CRICKET SOCIETY OF: *Secretary* C. N. Fookes, 5 Melrose Close, St Mellons, Cardiff, CF3 9SW.

WEST LANCASHIRE CRICKET SOCIETY: *Secretary* D. H. Stringfellow, 36 Cardigan Road, Southport, Merseyside, PR8 4SF.

WOMBWELL CRICKET LOVERS' SOCIETY: *Secretary* J. Sokell, 42 Woodstock Road, Barnsley, South Yorkshire, S75 1DX.

ZIMBABWE, CRICKET SOCIETY OF: *Secretary* L. G. Morgenrood, 10 Elsworth Avenue, Balgravie, Harare, Zimbabwe.

OTHER MATCHES, 1982

†At Eglinton, Co. Derry, June 19, 20, 21. Drawn. Ireland 147 for three dec. (E. A. McDermott 40, R. T. Wills 40, M. A. Masood 39 not out) and 216 for five dec. (M. A. Masood 57 not out, J. F. Short 37; J. W. Stewart three for 77); MCC 155 for eight dec. (G. W. Sandrock 52, D. R. Owen-Thomas 36; J. D. Monteith five for 56) and 190 for nine (D. R. Owen-Thomas 70, G. W. Sandrock 44; S. C. Corlett five for 76, J. D. Monteith three for 58).

THE TILCON TROPHY

Northamptonshire, losing finalists in 1981, dramatically beat Yorkshire on the first day of the Harrogate Festival when, with a single needed off the last ball to level the scores, Allan Lamb hit Hartley to the boundary, having earlier led a recovery from 88 for five, his 93 containing one 6 and nine 4s. The holders, Worcestershire, were comprehensively beaten by Gloucestershire who, despite the loss of their last seven wickets for 29, had been assured of a challenging total by Broad and Romaines. The final, reduced by rain to ten overs a side, was won by Northamptonshire.

June 30. Northamptonshire won by one wicket. Yorkshire 181 (55 overs) (D. L. Bairstow 34, S. N. Hartley 32, G. Boycott 31, J. D. Love 30; B. J. Griffiths four for 25, T. M. Lamb three for 31); Northamptonshire 184 for nine (55 overs) (A. J. Lamb 93, G. Cook 44; G. B. Stevenson five for 31). *Man of the Match:* A. J. Lamb.

July 1. Gloucestershire won by 101 runs. Gloucestershire 226 (54.5 overs) (B. C. Broad 72, P. W. Romaines 71; J. D. Inchmore four for 50, A. E. Warner three for 27); Worcestershire 125 (38.2 overs) (D. J. Humphries 39; J. N. Shepherd three for 15, F. D. Stephenson three for 38). *Man of the Match:* B. C. Broad.

July 2. Northamptonshire won by 13 runs. Northamptonshire 101 for three (10 overs) (A. J. Lamb 45 not out); Gloucestershire 88 for five (10 overs).

†At Rathmines, Dublin, July 27, 28, 29. Ireland won by 49 runs. Ireland 301 (M. A. Masood 109, J. A. Prior 70, R. Torrens 39; M. Heames three for 66, G. Ellis three for 67) and 213 for four dec. (J. F. Short 103, E. A. McDermott 80); Wales 214 (W. Harris 64, G. Ellis 44; J. D. Monteith four for 52) and 251 (G. Edwards 71, N. Robert 62; J. D. Monteith four for 28, P. M. O'Reilly three for 84).

SCOTLAND v IRELAND

At Myreside, Edinburgh, August 7, 8, 9. Scotland won by eight wickets. On a wicket which at the start produced unpredictable bounce but became benign as play progressed, Ireland struggled for runs, owing much to a fourth-wicket partnership of 83 between Wills and Monteith, and to a late flurry by the tailenders. Two century partnerships and four individual half-centuries enabled Scotland to take a first-innings lead of 112. Rain interrupted play on the second day, and on the third Ireland, with all their recognised batsmen back in the pavilion, appeared to be heading for an innings defeat until Corlett and Jackson added 84 for the eighth wicket in three hours. Scotland were never troubled by their target of 56 in approximately an hour and a half, and have now won 18 matches against Ireland's 17, with 26 drawn.

Ireland

J. F. Short run out	10	– c and b Clark	30
E. A. McDermott c Brown b Clark	18	– b Clark	0
R. T. Wills c Ker b Rhind	43	– c Warner b Clark	0
I. J. Anderson b Rhind	9	– b Snodgrass	3
*J. D. Monteith c Brown b Snodgrass	45	– c Warner b Morton	15
J. A. Prior c Snodgrass b Morton	13	– c Loudon b Clark	11
S. C. Corlett c Brown b Clark	4	– not out	39
†P. B. Jackson lbw b Clark	7	– lbw b Loudon	46
R. Torrens c Ker b Rhind	17	– b Loudon	0
M. Halliday c Brown b Clark	30	– b Snodgrass	6
P. M. O'Reilly not out	1	– lbw b Loudon	0
B 1, n-b 5	6	B 5, l-b 5, n-b 7	17
1/26 2/30 3/44 4/127 5/141 6/145 7/146 8/159 9/173	203	1/9 2/31 3/36 4/53 5/53 6/59 7/81 8/165 9/165	167

Bowling: *First Innings*—Rhind 23–5–62–3; Snodgrass 18–6–50–1; Clark 15.1–3–24–4; Morton 16–5–44–1; Loudon 5–4–7–0; Donald 2–0–10–0. *Second Innings*—Rhind 17–10–23–0; Snodgrass 18–9–30–2; Clark 27–9–55–4; Morton 16–5–38–1; Loudon 5.1–4–4–3.

Scotland

W. A. Donald c Halliday b O'Reilly	6	– not out	34
C. J. Warner c Short b Corlett	55	– b Torrens	0
*R. G. Swan c Jackson b Corlett	66	– c Monteith b Torrens	2
R. S. Weir c Jackson b Corlett	65	– not out	14
A. B. M. Ker b Halliday	58		
†A. Brown c and b Corlett	1		
W. D. G. Loudon c McDermott b Corlett	21		
D. L. Snodgrass c Short b Corlett	6		
W. A. Morton c Short b Halliday	3		
J. Clark c Prior b Corlett	3		
P. A. Rhind not out	2		
B 3, l-b 13, w 4, n-b 9	29	B 1, l-b 5	6
1/15 2/136 3/145 4/264 5/271 6/299 7/301 8/309 9/313	315	1/4 2/6 (2 wkts)	56

Bowling: *First Innings*—Corlett 42–12–82–7; O'Reilly 6–1–14–1; Torrens 30–7–81–0; Monteith 24–4–58–0; Halliday 13.4–4–32–2; Prior 6–0–19–0. *Second Innings*—Corlett 6–1–19–0; Torrens 7–2–21–2; Monteith 5.2–2–6–0; Halliday 3–2–4–0.

THE ASDA TROPHY

The initial match of the Asda Trophy, contested for the first time at the Scarborough Festival, was marred by rain, Yorkshire losing to Lancashire on the toss of a coin after O'Shaughnessy had compiled his best limited-overs score of 80. The second day saw Miller and Barnett take Derbyshire to victory over Nottinghamshire with a stand of 143 in 23 overs after half their side had gone for 93 in 26 overs. Earlier Nottinghamshire had looked to be winners when Hadlee (four 6s, three 4s) and Birch (22) added 63 in five overs.

September 5. Lancashire won on the toss of a coin. Lancashire 212 for eight (45 overs) S. J. O'Shaughnessy 80, J. Abrahams 38 not out; C. M. Old three for 24); Yorkshire 17 for two (7 overs).

September 6. Derbyshire won by five wickets. Nottinghamshire 234 for six (50 overs) (B. Hassan 58, R. T. Robinson 58, R. J. Hadlee 47); Derbyshire 236 for five (49 overs) (G. Miller 87 not out, K. J. Barnett 54 not out, J. G. Wright 40).

September 7. Derbyshire won by nine wickets. Lancashire 163 for seven (50 overs) (C. H. Lloyd 57, J. Simmons 32); Derbyshire 164 for one (34.3 overs) (J. G. Wright 59, B. Wood 50 not out, P. N. Kirsten 49 not out).

NATWEST BANK TROPHY, 1982

Surrey, in their fourth final at Lord's in successive years, at last enjoyed the taste of success when they defeated Warwickshire by nine wickets in a disappointing final before a capacity crowd. They received, in addition to the NatWest Bank Trophy, a cheque for £12,000, while Warwickshire received £5,500. The losing semi-finalists, Middlesex and Yorkshire, each received £3,250, and Essex, Gloucestershire, Hampshire and Somerset, the losing quarter-finalists, each received £1,600.

David Thomas, of Surrey, received £300 as Man of the Match in the final. The Man of the Match in each semi-final received £200; in each quarter-final £150; and in each first and second round match £100.

FIRST ROUND

BEDFORDSHIRE v SOMERSET

At Bedford, July 3. Somerset won by four wickets. Garner and Moseley predictably proved too fast and straight for Bedfordshire's top batsmen, but the middle order took advantage of the later bowling, and the ninth-wicket pair, Dethridge and Williams, made a match of it. Somerset slipped to 77 for five just after tea, when Lines took his third wicket, and it needed application from Rose and Marks to right the situation with a stand of 58.

Man of the Match: F. R. Dethridge.

Bedfordshire

M. G. Stedman c Taylor b Garner	7
*D. M. Daniels c Roebuck b Garner	7
M. E. Gear c Rose b Moseley	0
S. J. Lines c Botham b Moseley	1
A. S. Pearson b Richards	39
R. G. Abeynaike lbw b Richards	26
M. Morgan b Dredge	13
K. V. Jones c Rose b Richards	3
F. R. Dethridge run out	31
C. Williams not out	20
B 2, l-b 2, w 1, n-b 1	6
1/15 2/17 3/17 4/37 5/76 6/93 7/101 8/101 9/153 (9 wkts, 60 overs)	153

†P. G. M. August did not bat.

Bowling: Garner 12–4–24–2; Botham 11–2–29–0; Moseley 10–1–38–2; Dredge 12–3–18–1; Marks 6–0–23–0; Richards 9–4–15–3.

Somerset

P. M. Roebuck c August b Lines	21
P. W. Denning lbw b Jones	20
I. V. A. Richards c Abeynaike b Jones	6
*B. C. Rose not out	28
I. T. Botham c August b Lines	6
N. F. M. Popplewell b Lines	15
V. J. Marks c Lines b Dethridge	31
†D. J. S. Taylor not out	15
L-b 3, w 6, n-b 3	12
1/39 2/49 3/50 4/56 5/77 6/135 (6 wkts, 48.2 overs)	154

J. Garner, C. H. Dredge and H. R. Moseley did not bat.

Bowling: Williams 12–1–47–0; Dethridge 7–1–21–1; Jones 11.2–7–22–2; Lines 10–2–28–3; Morgan 3–0–16–0; Abeynaike 5–3–8–0.

Umpires: J. Birkenshaw and D. O. Oslear.

LEICESTERSHIRE v NORFOLK

At Leicester, July 3. Leicestershire won by eight wickets. Handley, who had been given a trial by Leicestershire twelve years earlier, gave Norfolk a good start after they had elected to bat. However, with his dismissal their innings stagnated; Steele proved difficult to hit, and Parvez Mir's 55 occupied 41 overs. Gower, with ten 4s in his unbeaten 65, speeded up Leicestershire's innings as he saw his side comfortably home.

Man of the Match: D. I. Gower.

Norfolk

F. L. Q. Handley c Garnham b Taylor. 22
S. G. Plumb c and b Wenlock............ 12
R. D. Huggins c Wenlock b Taylor..... 24
Parvez Mir b Taylor.......................... 55
J. Barratt lbw b Parsons.................... 1
N. D. Cook not out 31
*P. J. Sharpe lbw b Taylor................ 0
D. G. Pilch b Parsons....................... 6
†D. E. Mattocks not out.................... 2
B 3, l-b 7, n-b 1....................... 11

1/31 2/49 3/81 4/101 5/149 6/149 7/162 (7 wkts, 60 overs) 164

E. Wright and T. H. Barnes did not bat.

Bowling: Taylor 12–3–34–4; Parsons 12–1–40–2; Steele 12–3–16–0; Wenlock 12–2–27–1; Higgs 12–2–36–0.

Leicestershire

J. C. Balderstone c Mattocks b Barnes. 39
N. E. Briers lbw b Pilch.................... 20
D. I. Gower not out.......................... 65
B. F. Davison not out....................... 33
L-b 7, n-b 2........................... 9

1/54 2/110 (2 wkts, 48.2 overs) 166

*R. W. Tolchard, †M. A. Garnham, J. F. Steele, D. A. Wenlock, G. J. Parsons, K. Higgs and L. B. Taylor did not bat.

Bowling: Wright 9–2–19–0; Parvez Mir 9.2–1–37–0; Plumb 12–2–33–0; Barnes 12–4–34–1; Pilch 6–1–34–1.

Umpires: D. G. L. Evans and D. J. Constant.

MIDDLESEX v CHESHIRE

At Enfield, July 3. Middlesex won by eight wickets. As early as the sixth over, Edmonds and Emburey were operating together to exploit the considerable spin in a pitch which had taken plenty of rain in preceding days. Cheshire, put in, found Edmonds virtually unplayable as he returned his best one-day figures. The visitors' spinners, Rodger and Bailey, could not achieve similar spin as the pitch dried quickly, and with Slack supervising the formalities, Middlesex won before four o'clock.

Man of the Match: P. H. Edmonds.

Cheshire

P. A. Tipton b Edmonds.................. 2
R. M. O. Cooke c Brearley b Emburey. 13
D. Bailey b Edmonds....................... 0
S. C. Wundke c Radley b Edmonds.... 0
*N. T. O'Brien c Gatting b Edmonds.. 10
J. Hitchmough b Daniel.................... 5
K. R. Harris lbw b Hughes............... 17
M. Watkinson b Edmonds................ 6
R. C. Rodger c Radley b Hughes....... 16
I. J. Gemmell not out....................... 20
†J. K. Pickup lbw b Selvey............... 5
B 2, l-b 7, n-b 1..................... 10

1/9 2/17 3/17 4/19 5/34 6/36 7/45 8/73 9/88 (51 overs) 104

Bowling: Selvey 6–2–11–1; Hughes 10–3–24–2; Edmonds 12–7–12–5; Emburey 12–2–26–1; Daniel 9–3–15–1; Gatting 2–1–6–0.

Middlesex

*J. M. Brearley c Tipton b Bailey	12
W. N. Slack not out	54
C. T. Radley st Pickup b O'Brien	16
M. W. Gatting not out	16
L-b 2, w 2, n-b 4	8
1/35 2/72 (2 wkts, 31.3 overs)	106

R. O. Butcher, J. E. Emburey, P. H. Edmonds, †P. R. Downton, M. W. W. Selvey, W. W. Daniel and S. P. Hughes did not bat.

Bowling: Wundke 3–0–6–0; Gemmell 3–1–4–0; Rodger 7–1–13–0; Bailey 9–1–36–1; O'Brien 6–3–16–1; Watkinson 3.3–0–23–0.

Umpires: R. Palmer and N. T. Plews.

NORTHAMPTONSHIRE v IRELAND

At Northampton, July 3. Northamptonshire won by seven wickets. In fading light after an earlier stoppage for rain, Willey (one 6 and seven 4s) decided the issue by hammering Torrens for 18 off five balls. Until Willey's unbroken stand of 85 with Williams, Ireland had fought bravely with bat and ball, achieving a creditable total after electing to bat.

Man of the Match: P. Willey.

Ireland

J. F. Short lbw b T. M. Lamb	37
E. A. McDermott c Cook b Steele	9
R. T. Wills b Steele	13
I. J. Anderson lbw b Griffiths	14
M. A. Masood c Sharp b Mallender	29
T. Harpur c Larkins b Williams	0
†C. C. J. Harte lbw b Williams	7
S. C. Corlett c Sharp b Mallender	9
*J. D. Monteith b T. M. Lamb	8
R. Torrens b T. M. Lamb	9
M. Halliday not out	0
B 3, l-b 16, n-b 1	20
1/54 2/61 3/76 4/102 5/112 6/126 7/128 8/139 9/151 (56.3 overs)	155

Bowling: Griffiths 8–2–22–1; Mallender 11–4–22–2; T. M. Lamb 8.3–2–25–3; Willey 12–1–24–0; Steele 12–2–25–2; Williams 5–0–17–2.

Northamptonshire

*G. Cook lbw b Corlett	2
W. Larkins c Harte b Corlett	30
P. Willey not out	72
A. J. Lamb b Halliday	11
R. G. Williams not out	31
L-b 9, n-b 1	10
1/6 2/55 3/71 (3 wkts, 39.5 overs)	156

D. J. Capel, D. S. Steele, †G. Sharp, N. A. Mallender, T. M. Lamb and B. J. Griffiths did not bat.

Bowling: Corlett 12–2–34–2; Torrens 4.5–0–47–0; Monteith 10–3–23–0; Halliday 11–4–27–1; Anderson 2–0–15–0.

Umpires: B. Leadbeater and K. E. Palmer.

SURREY v DURHAM

At The Oval, July 3. Surrey won by 111 runs. Durham conjured up a moment of magic as their Australian fast-medium bowler Davis dismissed Pauline, Clinton and Knight for 12 runs in his first six overs, justifying Riddell's decision to put Surrey in. However, from 16 for three the total soared, with Lynch hitting three 6s and six 4s in two and a quarter hours and Roope helping in a stand of 166 in 107 minutes. Durham were 114 runs behind with eight overs and four wickets left when a violent thunderstorm flooded the wicket, and although Riddell was prepared to concede the match, Knight felt it should be played out. Both agreed to the use of slow bowling and to few or no runs being scored to protect the Test pitch to be used five days later, and at 8.25 p.m. the players resumed for eight overs while 3 runs were scored – 2 from the bat and a wide.

Man of the Match: M. A. Lynch.

Surrey

D. B. Pauline c Birtwisle b Davis	10	D. J. Thomas not out	0
G. S. Clinton c Smith b Davis	2	†C. J. Richards not out	20
*R. D. V. Knight c Mercer b Davis	2		
D. M. Smith b Smith	27	B 1, l-b 3, w 3	7
M. A. Lynch c Richards b Davis	129		—
G. R. J. Roope lbw b Johnston	77	1/8 2/15 3/16 (7 wkts, 60 overs)	279
S. T. Clarke c Birtwisle b Davis	5	4/84 5/250 6/256 7/258	

K. S. Mackintosh and G. Monkhouse did not bat.

Bowling: Davis 12–2–51–5; Johnston 12–3–40–1; Lander 12–2–78–0; Greensword 12–3–42–0; Smith 12–0–61–1.

Durham

G. Hurst b Thomas	1	J. G. D. Smith c Richards b Mackintosh	3
I. M. Richards c Monkhouse b Mackintosh	9	†R. A. D. Mercer not out	1
S. Greensword c Smith b Mackintosh	73	B 1, l-b 13, w 10, n-b 2	26
*N. A. Riddell b Thomas	22		—
P. C. Birtwisle lbw b Thomas	0	1/7 2/44 3/98 4/98 (6 wkts, 60 overs)	168
A. S. Patel not out	33	5/144 6/157	

B. R. Lander, S. P. Davis and J. Johnston did not bat.

Bowling: Clarke 8–2–15–0; Thomas 10–2–16–3; Mackintosh 10–3–27–3; Monkhouse 11–1–38–0; Knight 12–1–43–0; Lynch 5–4–1–0; Clinton 4–2–2–0.

Umpires: R. S. Herman and K. Ibadulla.

SUSSEX v NOTTINGHAMSHIRE

At Hove, July 3. Nottinghamshire won by nine wickets. Sussex, electing to bat, were tumbled out for 113 after a match-winning spell by Rice – his first bowl of the season – in which he took six wickets for 18 runs. Todd and Robinson then opened with confidence and enterprise, taking Nottinghamshire towards their target before tea.

Man of the Match: C. E. B. Rice.

Sussex

G. D. Mendis c Birch b Hendrick	0	C. P. Phillipson c Hendrick b Rice	16
A. M. Green b Rice	41	C. E. Waller not out	1
C. M. Wells c French b Cooper	1	G. G. Arnold b Rice	0
P. W. G. Parker c Hendrick b Rice	11		
†I. J. Gould b Rice	4	B 5, l-b 5, w 2, n-b 3	15
G. S. le Roux run out	10		—
I. A. Greig c French b Hendrick	3	1/0 2/1 3/34 4/49 (51.1 overs)	113
*J. R. T. Barclay c and b Rice	11	5/62 6/80 7/81 8/111 9/112	

Bowling: Hendrick 8–2–14–2; Cooper 9–4–10–1; Saxelby 10–0–37–0; Rice 11.1–3–18–6; Hemmings 12–7–19–0.

Nottinghamshire

P. A. Todd b Greig	34
R. T. Robinson not out	44
D. W. Randall not out	16
L-b 4, w 7, n-b 9	20
1/89 (1 wkt, 29.4 overs)	114

B. Hassan, *C. E. B. Rice, J. D. Birch, †B. N. French, E. E. Hemmings, K. Saxelby, K. E. Cooper and M. Hendrick did not bat.

Bowling: le Roux 9–2–32–0; Arnold 8–4–10–0; Greig 10–2–37–1; Wells 2.4–0–15–0.

Umpires: M. J. Kitchen and C. T. Spencer.

WARWICKSHIRE v CAMBRIDGESHIRE

At Birmingham, July 3. Warwickshire won by 120 runs. After winning the toss, Cambridgeshire put up a stout fight but were destroyed by Amiss, whose 135, containing three 6s and sixteen 4s, was the highest score to date by a Warwickshire player in limited-overs cricket. McEvoy distinguished himself in reply but Cambridgeshire never threatened the home side's total.

Man of the Match: D. L. Amiss.

Warwickshire

D. L. Amiss c Miller b Rice	135
T. A. Lloyd b Wing	64
A. I. Kallicharran c Saggers b Wing	8
†G. W. Humpage c Gadsby b Brown	52
K. D. Smith b Wing	7
Asif Din c Gadsby b Brown	13
P. R. Oliver not out	5
G. C. Small not out	8
L-b 3, w 5	8
1/141 2/157 3/262 4/266 5/286 6/288 (6 wkts, 60 overs)	300

*R. G. D. Willis, J. Cumbes and S. P. Sutcliffe did not bat.

Bowling: Brown 12–1–44–2; Parker 12–0–55–0; Parry 12–0–54–0; Rice 12–1–89–1; Wing 12–2–50–3.

Cambridgeshire

G. V. Miller c and b Kallicharran	21
M. S. A. McEvoy c Humpage b Small	52
N. T. Gadsby b Kallicharran	0
D. R. Parry c Kallicharran b Sutcliffe	43
D. H. J. Baker b Cumbes	23
*A. M. Ponder st Humpage b Sutcliffe	6
G. S. Rice lbw b Cumbes	4
†M. L. Saggers b Small	1
I. J. Parker run out	2
M. Brown b Sutcliffe	0
D. C. Wing not out	11
B 3, l-b 5, n-b 9	17
1/54 2/56 3/119 4/143 5/154 6/160 7/164 8/167 9/168 (50.1 overs)	180

Bowling: Willis 7–1–28–0; Small 9.1–5–12–2; Kallicharran 12–2–44–2; Cumbes 12–3–39–2; Sutcliffe 10–1–40–3.

Umpires: C. Cook and P. J. Eele.

SECOND ROUND

ESSEX v KENT

At Chelmsford, July 14. Essex won by 130 runs. Fletcher, superb as he guided Essex through to the quarter-finals, batted for 146 minutes, hitting two 6s – one into the Pearce stand and another over extra cover against Underwood – before he was caught attempting a third. Following an encouraging start from Potter and Taylor, Kent's hopes were ruined by Turner, whose swing bowling reaped him a rich harvest. Phillip made sure there was no recovery.

Man of the Match: K. W. R. Fletcher.

Essex

G. A. Gooch b Underwood	30
B. R. Hardie c Knott b Dilley	41
*K. W. R. Fletcher c Benson b Underwood	97
K. S. McEwan lbw b Penn	19
N. Phillip c Asif b Dilley	29
K. R. Pont b Underwood	14
S. Turner b Jarvis	0
D. R. Pringle not out	7
†D. E. East not out	2
B 4, l-b 21, w 4, n-b 1	30
1/69 2/92 3/128 4/194 5/230 6/233 7/265 (7 wkts, 60 overs)	269

R. E. East and J. K. Lever did not bat.

Bowling: Jarvis 12–1–61–1; Dilley 12–1–45–2; Penn 12–1–34–1; Underwood 12–3–40–3; Johnson 12–0–59–0.

Kent

L. Potter c and b R. E. East	45
N. R. Taylor b Turner	20
C. J. Tavaré b Turner	12
M. R. Benson c R. E. East b Turner	24
*Asif Iqbal c Fletcher b Turner	5
†A. P. E. Knott b R. E. East	2
G. W. Johnson lbw b Phillip	3
C. Penn b Phillip	5
G. R. Dilley b Phillip	9
D. L. Underwood not out	1
K. B. S. Jarvis b Phillip	0
L-b 7, w 3, n-b 3	13
1/54 2/81 3/91 4/110 5/117 6/121 7/121 8/138 9/139 (41 overs)	139

Bowling: Lever 6–1–18–0; Phillip 7–0–26–4; Pringle 8–0–37–0; Turner 12–1–23–4; R. E. East 8–1–22–2.

Umpires: R. Julian and C. T. Spencer.

GLAMORGAN v WARWICKSHIRE

At Cardiff, July 14, 15. Warwickshire won by six wickets. Rain delayed play until after lunch on the first day when Glamorgan, put in, struggled against an accurate attack in poor light. Warwickshire, 107 for two overnight, easily qualified for the quarter-finals on the second day.

Man of the Match: T. A. Lloyd.

Glamorgan

A. Jones c Amiss b Sutcliffe............. 8
J. A. Hopkins c Sutcliffe b Kallicharran.. 13
D. A. Francis c Lloyd b Small............ 34
R. C. Ontong c Sutcliffe b Willis........ 54
C. J. C. Rowe st Humpage b Kallicharran.. 2
A. L. Jones run out......................... 0
M. A. Nash c Small b Sutcliffe........... 0
†E. W. Jones c Asif Din b Lethbridge. 11
*B. J. Lloyd c and b Small................ 12
S. R. Barwick b Small...................... 6
W. W. Davis not out........................ 2
B 11, l-b 7, w 1, n-b 8............ 27

1/20 2/48 3/107 4/116 5/117 6/120 7/141 8/145 9/160 (60 overs) 169

Bowling: Willis 12–4–21–1; Small 12–2–22–3; Sutcliffe 12–2–27–2; Lethbridge 12–1–37–1; Kallicharran 12–1–35–2.

Warwickshire

D. L. Amiss c E. W. Jones b Nash..... 12
T. A. Lloyd c Lloyd b Nash.............. 52
A. I. Kallicharran b Rowe................ 28
†G. W. Humpage lbw b Lloyd........... 39
K. D. Smith not out......................... 28
Asif Din not out.............................. 2
B 3, l-b 3, w 2, n-b 1............... 9

1/20 2/60 3/130 4/154 (4 wkts, 57 overs) 170

P. R. Oliver, C. Lethbridge, G. C. Small, *R. G. D. Willis and S. P. Sutcliffe did not bat.

Bowling: Davis 12–3–21–0; Nash 10–5–14–2; Ontong 11–1–43–0; Lloyd 12–1–40–1; Rowe 12–1–43–1.

Umpires: H. D. Bird and P. J. Eele.

HAMPSHIRE v DERBYSHIRE

At Southampton, July 14. Hampshire won by six wickets. Kirsten, missed when 25, played a splendid innings to score the first century by a Derbyshire batsman in the 60-overs competition, after his side had been put in. In 142 minutes he hit one 6 and eleven 4s, ending with 20 out of 21 off the last over from Emery. Hampshire moved easily into their stride thanks to the splendid batting of Greenidge (three 6s), who was patiently assisted by Rice. Wood applied a brief check by taking three wickets in fourteen balls, but Derbyshire's hopes were short-lived.

Man of the Match: P. N. Kirsten.

Derbyshire

*B. Wood c Emery b Tremlett........... 21
J. G. Wright c Marshall b Jesty.......... 56
P. N. Kirsten not out........................110
J. H. Hampshire lbw b Tremlett......... 18
G. Miller c Parks b Jesty................... 0
K. J. Barnett c Parks b Emery........... 15
W. P. Fowler not out........................ 9
B 1, l-b 6, w 1, n-b 2.............. 10

1/59 2/105 3/153 4/154 5/191 (5 wkts, 60 overs) 239

†R. W. Taylor, C. J. Tunnicliffe, P. G. Newman and S. Oldham did not bat.

Bowling: Marshall 12–1–48–0; Emery 12–0–69–1; Jesty 12–2–28–2; Tremlett 12–4–34–2; Cowley 12–0–50–0.

Hampshire

C. G. Greenidge lbw b Wood	83	*N. E. J. Pocock not out	40
J. M. Rice c Kirsten b Tunnicliffe	59	B 1, l-b 6, w 3, n-b 6	16
M. C. J. Nicholas c Barnett b Wood	0		—
T. E. Jesty c Miller b Wood	0	1/137 2/137 3/137 (4 wkts, 56.4 overs)	242
R. E. Hayward not out	44	4/172	

N. G. Cowley, M. D. Marshall, †R. J. Parks, T. M. Tremlett and K. St J. D. Emery did not bat.

Bowling: Oldham 10–2–47–0; Tunnicliffe 10.4–1–62–1; Newman 9–0–36–0; Miller 12–4–37–0; Wood 12–3–23–3; Kirsten 3–0–21–0.

Umpires: W. E. Alley and K. E. Palmer.

MIDDLESEX v LANCASHIRE

At Lord's, July 14, 15, 16. Middlesex won by 2 runs on the third afternoon, the first day having been lost to rain and the second abandoned following a torrential downpour after the Middlesex innings. Of the Middlesex batsmen, only Brearley, through 46 overs, coped comfortably with the demands of a slow wicket and tight bowling personified by Simmons, whose off-spin accounted for Slack and Butcher the moment they tried to attack. On the third morning Cowans, in only his second match of the season, sent back Fowler and Maynard in his first fifteen balls, and with Selvey giving nothing away it required all the experience of the middle order to keep Lancashire in the hunt. From 62 for three after 30 overs, they wanted 109 off twenty and then 71 from ten. Twice Cowans came back to take a wicket, there were three run-outs in the final seven overs, and in a gripping finish Croft was left with the task of hitting 3 off the last ball.

Man of the Match: N. G. Cowans.

Middlesex

*J. M. Brearley b Reidy	66	M. W. W. Selvey not out	10
W. N. Slack lbw b Simmons	13	N. G. Cowans c sub b Folley	0
M. W. Gatting lbw b Allott	5	S. P. Hughes not out	1
R. O. Butcher run out	17		
C. T. Radley c Maynard b Allott	23	B 12, l-b 8, w 3	23
G. D. Barlow b Reidy	11		—
J. E. Emburey c Hughes b Allott	9	1/48 2/53 3/98 (9 wkts, 60 overs)	204
†P. R. Downton c C. H. Lloyd b Folley	26	4/138 5/156 6/158 7/181 8/201 9/202	

Bowling: Croft 12–1–37–0; Folley 10–1–38–2; Allott 12–5–26–3; Simmons 12–5–20–1; Reidy 12–1–48–2; Abrahams 2–0–12–0.

Lancashire

D. Lloyd lbw b Cowans	48	P. J. W. Allott run out	3
G. Fowler b Cowans	0	I. Folley not out	3
†C. Maynard c Downton b Cowans	1	C. E. H. Croft not out	2
*C. H. Lloyd c Downton b Selvey	11		
D. P. Hughes c Butcher b Emburey	42	B 2, l-b 6, w 9, n-b 2	19
J. Abrahams b Cowans	35		—
J. Simmons run out	16	1/7 2/12 3/31 4/104 (9 wkts, 60 overs)	202
B. W. Reidy run out	22	5/118 6/157 7/182 8/187 9/200	

Bowling: Selvey 12–4–17–1; Cowans 12–3–26–4; Emburey 12–1–47–1; Hughes 12–1–50–0; Slack 8–1–27–0; Gatting 4–0–16–0.

Umpires: C. Cook and A. Jepson.

NOTTINGHAMSHIRE v GLOUCESTERSHIRE

At Nottingham, July 14, 15. Gloucestershire won by nine wickets. Nottinghamshire, without Hadlee and Hendrick as well as three other first-team players, gave a dismal batting display after winning the toss. Rain stopped play after three overs of the Gloucestershire innings but on the second day Broad and Stovold made light work of their task, hitting 126 in 46 overs.

Man of the Match: A. W. Stovold.

Nottinghamshire

B. Hassan run out	27
R. T. Robinson c Hignell b Surridge	16
D. W. Randall c Brassington b Surridge	0
*C. E. B. Rice c Graveney b Doughty	4
J. D. Birch c Brassington b Shepherd	12
M. A. Fell b Shepherd	6
†B. N. French c Hignell b Shepherd	18
E. E. Hemmings b Bainbridge	7
I. L. Pont not out	7
N. G. B. Illingworth b Stephenson	0
K. E. Cooper c and b Stephenson	11
B 3, l-b 12, w 14, n-b 5	34
1/47 2/53 3/60 4/83 5/85 6/91 7/117 8/117 9/120 (55 overs)	142

Bowling: Stephenson 10–3–17–2; Surridge 12–3–17–2; Doughty 9–1–32–1; Bainbridge 12–0–26–1; Shepherd 12–3–16–3.

Gloucestershire

B. C. Broad c French b Cooper	59
A. W. Stovold not out	76
P. W. Romaines not out	2
L-b 3, w 3, n-b 2	8
1/26 (1 wkt, 51.4 overs)	145

P. Bainbridge, A. J. Hignell, *D. A. Graveney, J. N. Shepherd, F. D. Stephenson, D. Surridge, †A. J. Brassington and R. J. Doughty did not bat.

Bowling: Cooper 12–6–21–1; Illingworth 7.4–0–38–0; Pont 9–2–25–0; Hemmings 12–5–17–0; Fell 11–0–36–0.

Umpires: J. Birkenshaw and J. van Geloven.

SOMERSET v LEICESTERSHIRE

At Taunton, July 14, 15. Somerset won by 63 runs. Thunderstorms delayed the start until three o'clock, and water which had leaked on to the pitch made batting awkward throughout. Somerset, put in, owed much to a third-wicket stand between Denning and Rose, followed by big hitting from Botham (four 6s) and Marks, who took 22 off the final over. Garner and Botham subdued Leicestershire's start on the second day, and as Dredge broke through, only a delightful 60 in 28 overs from Gower troubled Somerset. Balderstone struggled gamely for 24 overs, and a light-hearted swing by Roberts delayed the ending.

Man of the Match: V. J. Marks.

Somerset

P. W. Denning b Taylor	73
P. M. Roebuck run out	0
I. V. A. Richards b Taylor	8
*B. C. Rose c Tolchard b Roberts	48
I. T. Botham c Balderstone b Roberts	45
V. J. Marks not out	51
J. W. Lloyds not out	28
B 2, l-b 6, w 9, n-b 1	18
1/1 2/12 3/138 4/142 5/210 (5 wkts, 60 overs)	271

†D. J. S. Taylor, J. Garner, C. H. Dredge and H. R. Moseley did not bat.

Bowling: Roberts 12–0–71–2; Taylor 12–2–55–2; Higgs 12–0–34–0; Steele 12–1–41–0; Parsons 12–1–52–0.

Leicestershire

J. C. Balderstone lbw b Dredge	16	G. J. Parsons c Richards b Garner	6
J. F. Steele c Taylor b Garner	1	L. B. Taylor not out	5
D. I. Gower c Lloyds b Marks	60	K. Higgs not out	6
B. F. Davison c Richards b Dredge	4		
N. E. Briers c Lloyds b Marks	13	L-b 7, w 5, n-b 1	13
*R. W. Tolchard b Garner	26		—
†M. A. Garnham c Botham b Garner	12	1/2 2/58 3/72 4/96 (9 wkts, 60 overs)	208
A. M. E. Roberts st Taylor b Richards	46	5/103 6/143 7/144 8/174 9/202	

Bowling: Garner 12–7–23–4; Botham 8–2–21–0; Dredge 12–1–34–2; Moseley 12–2–36–0; Marks 12–1–38–2; Richards 4–0–43–1.

Umpires: D. R. Shepherd and K. Ibadulla.

SURREY v NORTHAMPTONSHIRE

At The Oval, July 14, 15, 16. Surrey won by six wickets. There was no play on the first day and only three and a quarter hours on the second, when Northamptonshire were put in under a grey sky and scored 173 for two in 50 of their 60 overs. Despite the swing bowlers' getting a good deal of help, Cook and Larkins began with 93 in 107 minutes, after which Willey and Lamb consolidated. Surrey, batting in more favourable conditions, owed much to Smith, whose 103 not out came in 204 minutes with nine 4s.

Man of the Match: D. M. Smith.

Northamptonshire

*G. Cook c Monkhouse b Knight	50	R. J. Boyd-Moss not out	15
W. Larkins c Clarke b Monkhouse	49		
P. Willey c Butcher b Clarke	55	B 5, l-b 8, w 6, n-b 1	20
A. J. Lamb c Monkhouse b Jackman	42		—
Kapil Dev b Thomas	1	1/93 2/122 3/199 (5 wkts, 60 overs)	239
R. G. Williams not out	7	4/208 5/214	

†G. Sharp, N. A. Mallender, T. M. Lamb and B. J. Griffiths did not bat.

Bowling: Clarke 12–2–34–1; Jackman 12–4–42–1; Thomas 12–0–51–1; Monkhouse 12–0–51–1; Knight 12–0–41–1.

Surrey

A. R. Butcher b T. M. Lamb	41	G. R. J. Roope not out	9
G. P. Howarth c Sharp b Griffiths	10		
D. M. Smith not out	103	B 6, l-b 14, w 1, n-b 5	26
M. A. Lynch c Williams b Willey	17		—
*R. D. V. Knight c T. M. Lamb b Kapil Dev	36	1/15 2/108 3/141 (4 wkts, 58.5 overs) 4/226	242

†C. J. Richards, D. J. Thomas, S. T. Clarke, R. D. Jackman and G. Monkhouse did not bat.

Bowling: Kapil Dev 11.5–2–41–1; Griffiths 11–1–48–1; Mallender 7–1–25–0; T. M. Lamb 11–0–47–1; Willey 12–3–29–1; Williams 6–0–26–0.

Umpires: D. G. L. Evans and B. J. Meyer.

YORKSHIRE v WORCESTERSHIRE

At Leeds, July 14, 15. Yorkshire won by three wickets. Turner, with five early boundaries, set Worcestershire off at a gallop against disappointing seam bowling. Old did not even complete his allocation of overs. Yorkshire, at 40 for four, appeared well beaten when rain took the match into a second day, but Hartley and Bairstow led a recovery. Inchmore, after a spell of four for 14, was saved for the end, but Stevenson hit him for two huge 6s, and with Neale dropping Old, on 34, off Weston, Worcestershire were dramatically beaten.

Man of the Match: D. L. Bairstow.

Worcestershire

G. M. Turner b Boycott	105
M. S. Scott b Illingworth	33
*P. A. Neale run out	42
M. J. Weston b Stevenson	23
E. J. O. Hemsley c Illingworth b Boycott	0
D. N. Patel not out	25
†D. J. Humphries retired hurt	0
J. D. Inchmore not out	32
B 4, l-b 6, w 13, n-b 3	26
1/91 2/189 3/201 4/201 5/234 (5 wkts, 60 overs)	286

A. E. Warner, N. Gifford and S. P. Perryman did not bat.

Bowling: Old 6–0–30–0; Stevenson 10–1–30–1; Jarvis 12–0–80–0; Illingworth 12–1–42–1; Carrick 12–0–43–0; Boycott 8–1–35–2.

Yorkshire

G. Boycott lbw b Inchmore	2
R. G. Lumb c Humphries b Inchmore	16
C. W. J. Athey b Inchmore	5
J. D. Love b Inchmore	2
S. N. Hartley b Gifford	58
†D. L. Bairstow c Scott b Warner	92
P. Carrick c Hemsley b Gifford	5
C. M. Old not out	55
G. B. Stevenson not out	28
B 8, l-b 13, w 1, n-b 5	27
1/13 2/28 3/30 4/38 5/133 6/142 7/244 (7 wkts, 59.3 overs)	290

*R. Illingworth and P. W. Jarvis did not bat.

Bowling: Warner 11.3–2–45–1; Inchmore 12–2–47–4; Perryman 12–0–32–0; Weston 12–1–52–0; Gifford 10–0–68–2; Patel 2–0–19–0.

Umpires: R. S. Herman and D. O. Oslear.

QUARTER-FINALS

GLOUCESTERSHIRE v MIDDLESEX

At Bristol, August 4. Middlesex won by 3 runs. Gloucestershire made a brave chase of it, with Broad making a determined 98 in three and a half hours. Dudleston stayed with him through a crucial 28 overs to set up an exciting finish, when victory depended on Graveney's sending the last ball to the boundary. The turning-point had come when Downton, who had earlier scored an unbeaten 40 in the last eight overs of Middlesex's innings, brilliantly stumped Broad as he seemed set to win the match.

Man of the Match: B. C. Broad.

Middlesex

*J. M. Brearley c Dudleston b Childs	18	†P. R. Downton not out	40
W. N. Slack b Stephenson	10	N. G. Cowans b Shepherd	2
K. P. Tomlins c Dudleston b Surridge	9	W. W. Daniel not out	0
M. W. Gatting c Stovold b Childs	33	L-b 7, w 4, n-b 2	13
C. T. Radley c Dudleston b Shepherd	45		
R. O. Butcher b Graveney	27	1/14 2/35 3/63 (9 wkts, 60 overs)	215
J. E. Emburey run out	11	4/100 5/137 6/162 7/167	
P. H. Edmonds c Stovold b Stephenson	7	8/191 9/196	

Bowling: Stephenson 12–1–45–2; Surridge 12–5–25–1; Shepherd 12–1–47–2; Childs 12–4–43–2; Graveney 12–1–42–1.

Gloucestershire

A. W. Stovold c Downton b Cowans	0	F. D. Stephenson c and b Daniel	7
B. C. Broad st Downton b Slack	98	†R. C. Russell run out	10
P. W. Romaines lbw b Daniel	0	J. H. Childs not out	4
B. Dudleston c Edmonds b Emburey	31	L-b 11, w 5, n-b 1	17
A. J. Wright run out	14		
J. N. Shepherd c and b Cowans	9	1/0 2/5 3/95 4/138 (8 wkts, 60 overs)	212
*D. A. Graveney not out	22	5/161 6/167 7/179 8/198	

D. Surridge did not bat.

Bowling: Cowans 12–3–33–2; Daniel 9–2–39–2; Edmonds 12–1–34–0; Emburey 12–2–25–1; Gatting 3–0–13–0; Slack 12–1–51–1.

Umpires: H. D. Bird and A. G. T. Whitehead.

HAMPSHIRE v SURREY

At Southampton, August 4. Surrey won by eight wickets. Hampshire's fate was virtually sealed by losing the toss, which was of great significance in view of the ten o'clock start. The pitch stayed damp for a long while under overcast skies, enabling Jackman to move the ball off the seam; he removed Greenidge and Nicholas in his first three overs, going on to take six for 22. Only Turner gave the Hampshire innings respectability and the modest target offered no serious challenge to Surrey.

Man of the Match: R. D. Jackman.

Hampshire

C. G. Greenidge lbw b Jackman	2	T. M. Tremlett c Richards b Knight	6
J. M. Rice c Richards b Monkhouse	6	†R. J. Parks c Roope b Jackman	1
M. C. J. Nicholas c Richards b Jackman	2	K. St J. D. Emery not out	4
T. E. Jesty c Clarke b Monkhouse	12		
D. R. Turner c Lynch b Jackman	51	B 5, l-b 5, w 2, n-b 1	13
*N. E. J. Pocock c Clarke b Thomas	15		
N. G. Cowley c Roope b Jackman	7	1/5 2/9 3/17 4/38 (45.2 overs)	119
M. D. Marshall b Jackman	0	5/82 6/98 7/98 8/106 9/107	

Bowling: Clarke 9–2–11–0; Jackman 10.2–2–22–6; Monkhouse 12–2–20–2; Knight 7–1–26–1; Thomas 7–0–27–1.

Surrey

A. R. Butcher b Emery	1
G. P. Howarth lbw b Cowley	28
D. M. Smith not out	62
*R. D. V. Knight not out	23
B 1, l-b 2, w 1, n-b 2	6
1/1 2/73 (2 wkts, 33.2 overs)	120

M. A. Lynch, G. R. J. Roope, †C. J. Richards, D. J. Thomas, S. T. Clarke, R. D. Jackman and G. Monkhouse did not bat.

Bowling: Marshall 7–0–29–0; Emery 6–0–26–1; Jesty 5–0–17–0; Cowley 10–0–29–1; Tremlett 5.2–1–13–0.

Umpires: W. E. Alley and B. J. Meyer.

SOMERSET v WARWICKSHIRE

At Taunton, August 4, 5. Warwickshire won by five wickets. Somerset, put in on a fresh pitch in heavy overcast conditions, went uncertainly to 91 for four in 33 overs before Marks and, after a quiet start, Botham (four 6s, seven 4s) cut loose to add 148 in 24 overs. Rain intervened when Warwickshire were 74 for two, but after a delayed start on the second day, Kallicharran and Amiss carried their partnership to a decisive 153 in 31 overs. Kallicharran, batting magnificently and hitting one 6 and 24 4s, carried his side over the final hurdle when Dredge took two wickets with successive balls.

Man of the Match: A. I. Kallicharran.

Somerset

P. W. Denning c Amiss b Willis	4
P. M. Roebuck lbw b Ferreira	15
I. V. A. Richards c Smith b Lethbridge	31
*B. C. Rose c Oliver b Small	29
I. T. Botham b Small	85
V. J. Marks c and b Ferreira	55
N. F. M. Popplewell c and b Small	4
J. Garner b Ferreira	3
†D. J. S. Taylor not out	3
C. H. Dredge c and b Ferreira	0
B 12, l-b 14, n-b 4	30
1/11 2/37 3/79 4/91 5/239 6/243 7/253 8/259 9/259 (9 wkts, 60 overs)	259

H. R. Moseley did not bat.

Bowling: Willis 12–1–34–1; Small 12–3–56–3; Ferreira 12–1–53–4; Lethbridge 12–1–44–1; Kallicharran 12–1–42–0.

Warwickshire

T. A. Lloyd run out	21
K. D. Smith c Richards b Botham	8
A. I. Kallicharran not out	141
D. L. Amiss c Richards b Garner	59
†G. W. Humpage lbw b Dredge	17
P. R. Oliver c Taylor b Dredge	0
Asif Din not out	6
B 1, l-b 7, n-b 1	9
1/30 2/30 3/183 4/220 5/220 (5 wkts, 53.3 overs)	261

C. Lethbridge, G. C. Small, A. M. Ferreira and *R. G. D. Willis did not bat.

Bowling: Garner 12–2–45–1; Botham 12–1–59–1; Marks 12–1–41–0; Moseley 10–0–59–0; Dredge 7.3–1–48–2.

Umpires: D. J. Constant and W. L. Budd.

YORKSHIRE v ESSEX

At Leeds, August 4. Yorkshire won by nine wickets. After Essex, sent in under overcast skies, collapsed in dramatic fashion to steady seam bowling, Fletcher complained about the ten o'clock start, arguing that the toss settled the match. The batting was undistinguished until Turner and Ray East added 81 in 31 overs to set a new tenth-wicket record in 60-overs cricket. Moxon outshone even Boycott in Yorkshire's reply, which was concluded on a soaked ground in pouring rain.

Man of the Match: M. D. Moxon.

Essex

G. A. Gooch c Bairstow b Stevenson	10
B. R. Hardie c Bairstow b Old	0
*K. W. R. Fletcher lbw b Stevenson	4
K. S. McEwan c Athey b Boycott	8
K. R. Pont lbw b Stevenson	0
D. R. Pringle b Sidebottom	8
N. Phillip lbw b Sidebottom	1
A. W. Lilley lbw b Boycott	2
S. Turner not out	50
†D. E. East c Moxon b Sidebottom	5
R. E. East lbw b Old	33
L-b 8, w 1, n-b 2	11
1/9 2/15 3/18 4/18 5/28 6/30 7/36 8/43 9/51 (56.5 overs)	132

Bowling: Old 10.5–2–22–2; Stevenson 10–3–25–3; Boycott 9–2–12–2; Sidebottom 12–2–21–3; Hartley 7–0–16–0; Carrick 8–0–25–0.

Yorkshire

G. Boycott c Gooch b Pont	14
M. D. Moxon not out	78
C. W. J. Athey not out	33
L-b 2, w 5, n-b 1	8
1/41 (1 wkt, 39 overs)	133

J. D. Love, S. N. Hartley, †D. L. Bairstow, P. Carrick, C. M. Old, G. B. Stevenson, A. Sidebottom and *R. Illingworth did not bat.

Bowling: Phillip 9–3–21–0; Pringle 6.4–2–9–0; Gooch 6–1–15–0; Turner 11–3–39–0; Pont 4.2–0–27–1; R. E. East 1–1–0–0; Lilley 1–0–14–0.

Umpires: A. Jepson and R. Julian.

SEMI-FINALS

SURREY v MIDDLESEX

At The Oval, August 18, 19. Surrey won by 125 runs. Clarke, with four for 8 in his first six overs, initiated a Middlesex collapse from which there was no escape. The medium-pacers finished off the job and there was no need for Clarke to bowl a second spell, although he took two catches in hastening the end. Earlier Butcher and Smith laid the foundation for a reasonable Surrey total with a second-wicket stand of 88 after Howarth had been caught behind off the tenth ball of a first day limited to just under an hour by the weather.

Man of the Match: S. T. Clarke.

Surrey

A. R. Butcher run out	53	G. Monkhouse c Downton b Daniel	0
G. P. Howarth c Downton b Daniel	0	R. D. Jackman b Daniel	6
D. M. Smith b Edmonds	43	K. S. Mackintosh not out	0
*R. D. V. Knight c and b Emburey	8		
M. A. Lynch not out	29	B 4, l-b 11, w 10	25
†C. J. Richards c Downton b Gatting	10		
D. J. Thomas b Cowans	27	1/2 2/90 3/106 4/121 (9 wkts, 60 overs)	205
S. T. Clarke c and b Daniel	4	5/135 6/181 7/189 8/189 9/200	

Bowling: Cowans 10–0–43–1; Daniel 8–1–24–4; Emburey 12–3–25–1; Slack 6–0–22–0; Edmonds 12–1–34–1; Gatting 12–1–32–1.

Middlesex

W. N. Slack c Richards b Clarke	5	P. H. Edmonds not out	13
*J. M. Brearley c Richards b Clarke	3	N. G. Cowans c Lynch b Jackman	3
K. P. Tomlins lbw b Clarke	0	W. W. Daniel c Clarke b Monkhouse	0
M. W. Gatting c Butcher b Clarke	6		
C. T. Radley b Monkhouse	14	L-b 2, w 2, n-b 2	6
R. O. Butcher c Richards b Jackman	21		
J. E. Emburey c Clarke b Jackman	8	1/5 2/5 3/10 4/17 5/41 (41.5 overs)	80
†P. R. Downton c Richards b Monkhouse	1	6/54 7/59 8/69 9/78	

Bowling: Clarke 7–2–10–4; Jackman 12–4–20–3; Thomas 5–2–6–0; Mackintosh 6–3–11–0; Monkhouse 11.5–0–27–3.

Umpires: D. R. Shepherd and A. G. T. Whitehead.

WARWICKSHIRE v YORKSHIRE

At Birmingham, August 18. Warwickshire won by seven wickets. Yorkshire, put in, made a troubled start and Boycott had to fight to hold the innings together. Bairstow and Carrick then ensured a useful total, Bairstow remaining to see another 65 runs come off the last fourteen overs. When Warwickshire replied, Smith and Lloyd took their side steadily towards the final, Smith hitting his highest score in one-day cricket and his first century for two seasons.

Man of the Match: K. D. Smith.

Yorkshire

G. Boycott lbw b Ferreira	51	A. Sidebottom b Ferreira	8
R. G. Lumb c Lloyd b Small	1	C. M. Old run out	17
C. W. J. Athey lbw b Willis	4	*R. Illingworth not out	2
J. D. Love c Lloyd b Ferreira	2		
S. N. Hartley run out	5	B 6, l-b 16, w 3, n-b 5	30
G. B. Stevenson b Lethbridge	14		
†D. L. Bairstow not out	49	1/6 2/11 3/29 4/52 (9 wkts, 60 overs)	216
P. Carrick lbw b Kallicharran	33	5/81 6/99 7/151 8/166 9/198	

Bowling: Willis 12–5–23–1; Small 12–1–39–1; Ferreira 12–2–34–3; Lethbridge 12–2–44–1; Kallicharran 12–0–46–1.

Warwickshire

T. A. Lloyd c Hartley b Carrick	66	†G. W. Humpage not out	5
K. D. Smith c Boycott b Sidebottom	113	L-b 6, w 1, n-b 4	11
A. I. Kallicharran c Boycott b Carrick	0		
D. L. Amiss not out	24	1/139 2/139 3/208 (3 wkts, 55.3 overs)	219

P. R. Oliver, Asif Din, A. M. Ferreira, C. Lethbridge, G. C. Small and *R. G. D. Willis did not bat.

Bowling: Old 11–0–49–0; Stevenson 9.3–2–31–0; Sidebottom 12–1–47–1; Illingworth 12–2–34–0; Carrick 9–0–35–2; Boycott 2–1–12–0.

Umpires: R. Palmer and P. B. Wight.

FINAL

SURREY v WARWICKSHIRE

At Lord's, September 4. Surrey won by nine wickets. Although the toss, won by Surrey, was expected to be decisive, owing to the advantage of being able to bowl as early as ten o'clock on a dewy September morning, it was not so much this that brought about a Warwickshire batting collapse as the more basic reason of their being outclassed. After 29 overs Warwickshire were 74 for eight, without the ball having moved about anything like as much as it might have done. At 32 for one Smith and Kallicharran had looked to be laying a Warwickshire foundation, but Thomas, left arm over the wicket and distinctly fast, came on and removed Smith, Amiss and Humpage for 1 run, and two superb slip catches by Howarth saw to it that by noon the result, barring a remarkable turnabout, was disappointingly inevitable. Thanks to a ninth-wicket partnership of 62 in 24 overs by Asif Din and Small, Surrey were left to make 159 to win, and it was gone five o'clock, though only just, by the time they got them. Howarth, Smith and especially Butcher all batted well for Surrey, who were appearing for the fourth successive year in a Lord's one-day final but winning one for the first time since the Benson and Hedges Cup in 1974. Though Warwickshire and Surrey had not sold, in advance, all their separate allocations of 4,500 tickets, the ground, as usual, was full, the crowd being 23,517 and the takings £203,229.

Man of the Match: D. J. Thomas.

Warwickshire

K. D. Smith hit wicket b Thomas	12
T. A. Lloyd lbw b Jackman	2
A. I. Kallicharran c Howarth b Knight	19
D. L. Amiss b Thomas	0
†G. W. Humpage c Richards b Thomas	0
P. R. Oliver run out	2
Asif Din lbw b Jackman	45
A. M. Ferreira lbw b Clarke	8
C. Lethbridge c Howarth b Knight	4
G. C. Small c Richards b Clarke	33
*R. G. D. Willis not out	8
B 8, l-b 11, n-b 6	25
1/3 2/32 3/42 4/48 5/51 6/52 7/67 8/74 9/136 (57.2 overs)	158

Bowling: Clarke 11.2–5–17–2; Jackman 12–2–27–2; Thomas 11–1–26–3; Monkhouse 8–0–36–0; Knight 12–3–14–2; Mackintosh 3–0–13–0.

Surrey

A. R. Butcher not out	86
G. P. Howarth c Oliver b Lethbridge	31
D. M. Smith not out	28
L-b 4, n-b 10	14
1/80 (1 wkt, 33.4 overs)	159

*R. D. V. Knight, M. A. Lynch, †C. J. Richards, D. J. Thomas, G. Monkhouse, S. T. Clarke, R. D. Jackman and K. S. Mackintosh did not bat.

Bowling: Willis 7–0–23–0; Small 8–0–60–0; Ferreira 6–0–16–0; Lethbridge 6–1–23–1; Kallicharran 6.4–1–23–0.

Umpires: H. D. Bird and B. J. Meyer.

NATWEST BANK TROPHY RECORDS

(Including Gillette Cup, 1963-80)

Batting

Highest individual scores: 177, C. G. Greenidge, Hampshire v Glamorgan, Southampton, 1975; 146, G. Boycott, Yorkshire v Surrey, Lord's, 1965; 145, P. W. Denning, Somerset v Glamorgan, Cardiff, 1978; 143 not out, B. L. Reed, Hampshire v Buckinghamshire, Chesham, 1970; 141 not out, G. D. Mendis, Sussex v Warwickshire, Hove, 1980; 141 not out, A. I. Kallicharran, Warwickshire v Somerset, Taunton, 1982; 140, R. E. Marshall, Hampshire v Bedfordshire, Goldington, 1968; 139 not out, I. V. A. Richards, Somerset v Warwickshire, Taunton, 1978; 135, D. L. Amiss, Warwickshire v Cambridgeshire, Birmingham, 1982; 132, G. Robinson, Lincolnshire v Northumberland, Jesmond, 1971. (93 hundreds were scored in the Gillette Cup; 11 hundreds have been scored in the NatWest Bank Trophy.)

Fastest hundred: R. E. Marshall in 77 minutes at Goldington, 1968.

Highest innings total: 371 for four wickets off 60 overs, Hampshire v Glamorgan, Southampton, 1975; 330 for four off 60 overs, Somerset v Glamorgan, Cardiff, 1978; 327 for seven off 60 overs, Gloucestershire v Berkshire, Reading, 1966; 326 for six off 60 overs, Leicestershire v Worcestershire, Leicester, 1979; 321 for four off 60 overs, Hampshire v Bedfordshire, Goldington, 1968; 317 for four off 60 overs, Yorkshire v Surrey (in the final), Lord's, 1965.

The highest innings total in the NatWest Bank Trophy is 306 for eight off 60 overs by Essex v Hertfordshire, Hitchin, 1981.

Highest innings total by a minor county: 229 for five off 60 overs, Devon v Cornwall, Exeter, 1980.

Highest totals by a side batting second: 297 for four off 57.1 overs, Somerset v Warwickshire, Taunton, 1978; 290 for seven off 59.3 overs, Yorkshire v Worcestershire, Leeds, 1982; 287 for six off 59 overs, Warwickshire v Glamorgan, Birmingham, 1976; 287 off 60 overs, Essex v Somerset, Taunton, 1978; 282 for nine off 60 overs, Leicestershire v Gloucestershire, Leicester, 1975. Somerset's 297 for four v Warwickshire, Taunton, 1978 was the highest by a side batting second and winning the match.

Highest innings by a side batting first and losing: 292 for five off 60 overs, Warwickshire v Somerset, Taunton, 1978.

Lowest innings in the final at Lord's: 118 off 60 overs, Lancashire v Kent, 1974.

Lowest completed innings totals: 41 off 20 overs, Cambridgeshire v Buckinghamshire, Cambridge, 1972; 41 off 19.4 overs, Middlesex v Essex, Westcliff, 1972; 41 off 36.1 overs, Shropshire v Essex, Wellington, 1974.

The lowest innings total in the NatWest Bank Trophy is 75 off 45.5 overs, Ireland v Gloucestershire, Clontarf, Dublin, 1981.

Lowest total by a side batting first and winning: 98 off 56.2 overs, Worcestershire v Durham, Chester-le-Street, 1968.

Shortest innings: 10.1 overs (60 for one), Worcestershire v Lancashire, Worcester, 1963.

Matches re-arranged on a reduced number of overs are excluded from the above.

Record partnerships for each wicket

227 for 1st	R. E. Marshall and B. L. Reed, Hampshire v Bedfordshire at Goldington	1968
223 for 2nd	M. J. Smith and C. T. Radley, Middlesex v Hampshire at Lord's...	1977
160 for 3rd	B. Wood and F. C. Hayes, Lancashire v Warwickshire at Birmingham	1976

234* for 4th	D. Lloyd and C. H. Lloyd, Lancashire v Gloucestershire at Manchester	1978
166 for 5th	M. A. Lynch and G. R. J. Roope, Surrey v Durham at The Oval..	1982
105 for 6th	G. S. Sobers and R. A. White, Nottinghamshire v Worcestershire at Worcester..........	1974
107 for 7th	D. R. Shepherd and D. A. Graveney, Gloucestershire v Surrey at Bristol..........	1973
69 for 8th	S. J. Rouse and D. J. Brown, Warwickshire v Middlesex at Lord's	1977
87 for 9th	M. A. Nash and A. E. Cordle, Glamorgan v Lincolnshire at Swansea	1974
81 for 10th	S. Turner and R. E. East, Essex v Yorkshire at Leeds..........	1982

The record partnership for any wicket in the NatWest Bank Trophy is:

184 for 1st	G. A. Gooch and B. R. Hardie, Essex v Hertfordshire at Hitchin..	1981

Bowling

Hat-tricks: J. D. F. Larter, Northamptonshire v Sussex, Northampton, 1963; D. A. D. Sydenham, Surrey v Cheshire, Hoylake, 1964; R. N. S. Hobbs, Essex v Middlesex, Lord's, 1968; N. M. McVicker, Warwickshire v Lincolnshire, Birmingham, 1971.

Four wickets in five balls: D. A. D. Sydenham, Surrey v Cheshire, Hoylake, 1964.

Three wickets in four balls: J. D. Bannister, Warwickshire v Somerset, Birmingham, 1966.

Best analyses: seven for 15, A. L. Dixon, Kent v Surrey, The Oval, 1967; seven for 30, P. J. Sainsbury, Hampshire v Norfolk, Southampton, 1965; seven for 33, R. D. Jackman, Surrey v Yorkshire, Harrogate, 1970; six for 14, R. D. Healey, Devon v Hertfordshire, Stevenage, 1969; six for 14, J. A. Flavell, Worcestershire v Lancashire, Worcester, 1963; six for 15, F. S. Trueman, Yorkshire v Somerset, Taunton, 1965; six for 15, W. W. Daniel, Middlesex v Sussex, Hove, 1980; six for 18, T. J. P. Eyre, Derbyshire v Sussex, Chesterfield, 1969; six for 18, C. E. B. Rice, Nottinghamshire v Sussex, Hove, 1982.

Results

Largest victories in runs: Leicestershire by 214 runs v Staffordshire, Longton, 1975; Sussex by 200 runs v Durham, Hove, 1964; Essex by 191 runs v Hertfordshire, Hitchin, 1981; Surrey by 184 runs v Derbyshire, The Oval, 1967; and in the final by 175 runs, Yorkshire v Surrey, Lord's, 1965.

Quickest finishes: both at 2.20 p.m. Worcestershire beat Lancashire by nine wickets at Worcester, 1963; Essex beat Middlesex by eight wickets at Westcliff, 1972.

Scores level: Nottinghamshire 215, Somerset 215 for nine at Taunton, 1964; Surrey 196, Sussex 196 for eight at The Oval, 1970; Somerset 287 for six, Essex 287 at Taunton, 1978; Surrey 195 for seven, Essex 195 at Chelmsford, 1980; Essex 149, Derbyshire 149 for eight at Derby, 1981; Northamptonshire 235 for nine, Derbyshire 235 for six at Lord's, 1981. Under the rules the side which lost fewer wickets won.

Minor Counties: Durham became the first minor county to defeat a first-class county when they beat Yorkshire at Harrogate by five wickets in 1973. Lincolnshire became the second when they beat Glamorgan at Swansea by six wickets in 1974 and Hertfordshire the first minor county to reach the third round when they beat Essex at Hitchin by 33 runs in 1976. Cumberland is the only minor county that has not appeared in either competition.

PAST WINNERS

Gillette Cup

1963 SUSSEX beat Worcestershire by 14 runs.
1964 SUSSEX beat Warwickshire by eight wickets.
1965 YORKSHIRE beat Surrey by 175 runs.
1966 WARWICKSHIRE beat Worcestershire by five wickets.
1967 KENT beat Somerset by 32 runs.
1968 WARWICKSHIRE beat Sussex by four wickets.
1969 YORKSHIRE beat Derbyshire by 69 runs.
1970 LANCASHIRE beat Sussex by six wickets.
1971 LANCASHIRE beat Kent by 24 runs.
1972 LANCASHIRE beat Warwickshire by four wickets.
1973 GLOUCESTERSHIRE beat Sussex by 40 runs.
1974 KENT beat Lancashire by four wickets.
1975 LANCASHIRE beat Middlesex by seven wickets.
1976 NORTHAMPTONSHIRE beat Lancashire by four wickets.
1977 MIDDLESEX beat Glamorgan by five wickets.
1978 SUSSEX beat Somerset by five wickets.
1979 SOMERSET beat Northamptonshire by 45 runs.
1980 MIDDLESEX beat Surrey by seven wickets.

NatWest Bank Trophy

1981 DERBYSHIRE beat Northamptonshire by losing fewer wickets with the scores level.
1982 SURREY beat Warwickshire by nine wickets.

NATWEST BANK TROPHY RULES

(As applied in 1982)

The Playing Conditions for first-class matches in the United Kingdom will apply except where specified below. The matches are not, however, first-class.

Duration of Matches

The matches will consist of one innings per side and each innings will be limited to 60 overs. The matches are intended to be completed in one day, but three days (four days if Sunday play is scheduled) will be allocated in case of weather interference.

Matches scheduled to start on Saturday, but not completed on that day, may be continued or, if necessary, started on the Sunday during the hours of 2.00 p.m. to 7.00 p.m. Umpires may order extra time until 7.30 p.m. on the Sunday if, in their opinion, a finish can be obtained that day.

In the event of the Cup Final starting not less than 30 minutes nor more than 90 minutes late, owing to the weather or the state of the ground, each innings shall be limited to 50 overs. If, however, the start of play is delayed for more than 90 minutes, the 60 overs limit shall apply.

Hours of Play

Normal hours will be 10.30 a.m. to 7.30 p.m. in the first and second rounds and 10.00 a.m. to 7.00 p.m. in the later rounds. The umpires may order extra time if, in their opinion, a finish can be obtained on any day or in order to give the team batting second an opportunity to complete twenty overs. The captains of the two teams in the final will be warned that heavy shadows may move across the pitch towards the end of the day and that no appeal against the light will be considered in such circumstances.

Intervals

Lunch..................	12.30 p.m. to 1.10 p.m. if start of play is 10.00 a.m.; 12.45 p.m. to 1.25 p.m. if start of play is 10.30 a.m. These may be varied if, owing to the weather or state of the ground, an alteration has been agreed upon by the captains or ordered by the umpires.
Between innings.....	10 minutes.
Tea......................	20 minutes.

Note: The timing of any interval may be delayed for a maximum of fifteen minutes on the second or third day of a match, if the umpires consider that a finish can be obtained within that time.

Limitation of Overs by Any One Bowler

In a 60 overs match no bowler may bowl more than twelve overs in an innings. In a match where the start is delayed and the innings of both teams is restricted from the start to less than 60 overs, no bowler may bowl more than one fifth of the total overs allowed, except that where the total overs is not divisible by five, an additional over shall be allowed to the minimum number of bowlers necessary to make up the balance – e.g. in a 33 overs match, three bowlers may bowl a maximum of seven overs and no other bowler more than six overs. In the event of a bowler breaking down and being unable to complete an over, the remaining balls will be bowled by another bowler. Such part of an over will count as a full over only in so far as each bowler's limit is concerned.

The number of overs bowled by each individual bowler shall be indicated on the scoreboard, from the commencement of an innings.

Restriction on Placement of Fieldsmen

At the instant of delivery, a minimum of four fieldsmen (plus the bowler and wicket-keeper) must be within an area bounded by two semi-circles centred on each middle stump (each with a radius of 30 yards) and joined by a parallel line on each side of the pitch. In the event of an infringement, the square-leg umpire shall call "No-ball".

Law 14 – Declarations

Law 14 will not apply in this competition. The captain of the batting side may not declare his innings closed at any time during the course of a match.

Law 24.1 – No-ball – Mode of Delivery

Law 24.1 will apply in this competition, except that no bowler may deliver the ball underarm.

Law 25.1 – Wide Ball – Judging a Wide

Umpires are instructed to apply a very strict and consistent interpretation in regard to this Law in order to prevent negative bowling wide of the wicket or over the batsman's head.

The following criteria should be adopted as a guide to umpires:

1. If the ball passes either side of the wicket sufficiently wide to make it virtually impossible for the striker to play a "normal cricket stroke" both from where he is standing and from where he should normally be standing at the crease, the umpire should call and signal "Wide".

2. If the ball passes over head height of the striker standing upright at the crease, the umpire should call and signal "Wide".

Note: The above provisions do not apply if the striker makes contact with the ball, or if it passes below head height between the striker and the wicket.

The Result

1. A Tie

In the event of a tie, the following will apply:

(a) The side losing the lesser number of wickets shall be the winner.

(b) If both sides are all out, the side with the higher overall scoring-rate shall be the winner.

(c) If the result cannot be decided by (a) or (b), the winner shall be the side with the higher score (i) after 30 overs, or if still equal (ii) after 20 overs, or if still equal (iii) after 10 overs.

2. Unfinished Match

If a match remains unfinished after three days (four days if Sunday play is scheduled) the winner will be the side which has scored the faster in runs per over throughout the innings, provided that at least twenty overs have been bowled at the side batting second. If the scoring-rate is the same, the side losing the lesser number of wickets in the first twenty overs of each innings will be the winner.

If, however, at any time on the third day (fourth day if Sunday play is scheduled), the umpires are satisfied that there is insufficient time remaining to achieve a definite result or, where applicable, for the team batting second to complete its 60 overs, they shall order a new match to be started, allowing an equal number of overs per side (minimum 10 overs each side) bearing in mind the time remaining for play until the scheduled close of play.

In the event of no result being obtained within this rule and the captains are unable to reach agreement on an alternative method of achieving a result to the match, it shall be decided by the toss of a coin.

CAREER FIGURES OF PLAYERS RETIRING OR NOT RETAINED

BATTING

	M	*I*	*NO*	*R*	*HI*	*Avge*	*100s*
Asif Iqbal	441	703	76	23,375	196	37.28	45
A. G. E. Ealham	305	466	68	10,996	153	27.62	7
P. G. Lee	202	164	68	779	26	8.11	—
G. G. Arnold	365	379	90	3,952	73	13.69	—
J. Cumbes	161	133	67	499	43	7.56	—
R. A. White	413	642	105	12,452	116*	23.18	5

BOWLING AND FIELDING

	R	*W*	*Avge*	*BB*	*5 W/i*	*10 W/m*	*Ct*	*St*
Asif Iqbal	8,776	291	30.15	6–45	5	—	304	—
A. G. E. Ealham	189	3	63.00	1–1	—	—	175	—
P. G. Lee	15,339	599	25.60	8–34	28	7	29	—
G. G. Arnold	24,761	1,130	21.91	8–41	46	3	122	—
J. Cumbes	11,447	379	30.20	6–24	13	—	38	—
R. A. White	21,138	693	30.50	7–41	28	4	189	—

Note: The career figures of J. M. Brearley may be found following the article by John Arlott earlier in this Almanack.

BENSON AND HEDGES CUP, 1982

Somerset retained the Benson and Hedges Cup when they beat Nottinghamshire by nine wickets in 33.1 overs at Lord's in the eleventh final of the competition. In addition to the trophy, which they hold for another year, Somerset received £10,000 in prize-money, plus £1,155 from their three wins in the group matches. Nottinghamshire received £4,500 as runners-up.

The losing semi-finalists, Lancashire and Sussex, received £2,200 each, while Derbyshire, Kent, Leicestershire and Middlesex, the losing quarter-finalists, received £1,100 each. The winners of the group matches each won £385.

V. J. Marks, nominated by T. W. Graveney as the Gold Award winner for his economical off-spin bowling in the final, received £300. The Gold Award winners in the semi-finals each received £200; in the quarter-finals £150 each; and in the group matches £60 each.

Total prize-money for the competition was £42,400, an increase of £4,700 over 1981. Benson and Hedges increased their total sponsorship to the TCCB for 1982 to £207,000.

FINAL GROUP TABLES

Group A	*Played*	*Won*	*Lost*	*No Result*	*Points*
DERBYSHIRE	4	3	1	0	6
LEICESTERSHIRE	4	3	1	0	6
Worcestershire	4	2	2	0	4
Minor Counties	4	1	3	0	2
Yorkshire	4	1	3	0	2
Group B					
NOTTINGHAMSHIRE	4	4	0	0	8
LANCASHIRE	4	3	1	0	6
Warwickshire	4	2	2	0	4
Northamptonshire	4	1	3	0	2
Scotland	4	0	4	0	0
Group C					
KENT	4	3	1	0	6
SUSSEX	4	3	1	0	6
Essex	4	2	2	0	4
Surrey	4	2	2	0	4
Hampshire	4	0	4	0	0
Group D					
MIDDLESEX	4	4	0	0	8
SOMERSET	4	3	1	0	6
Gloucestershire	4	2	2	0	4
Glamorgan	4	1	3	0	2
Oxford & Cambridge Univs	4	0	4	0	0

The top two counties in each section qualified for the quarter-finals.

Where two or more teams finished with the same number of points, the position in the group was determined by their bowlers' striking-rate.

BOWLERS' STRIKING-RATES

Group A	*Balls*	*Wickets*	*Striking-Rate*
DERBYSHIRE	1,311	34	38.55
LEICESTERSHIRE	1,320	30	44.00
Worcestershire	1,281	28	45.75
Minor Counties	1,036	26	39.84
Yorkshire	1,224	23	53.21
Group B			
NOTTINGHAMSHIRE	1,284	37	34.70
LANCASHIRE	1,186	38	31.21
Warwickshire	1,309	33	39.66
Northamptonshire	1,099	23	47.78
Scotland	1,184	12	98.66
Group C			
KENT	1,289	36	35.80
SUSSEX	1,215	32	37.96
Essex	1,215	31	39.19
Surrey	1,309	31	42.22
Hampshire	1,311	35	37.45
Group D			
MIDDLESEX	1,165	31	37.58
SOMERSET	1,185	31	38.22
Gloucestershire	1,312	30	43.73
Glamorgan	1,134	31	36.58
Oxford & Cambridge Univs	1,067	12	88.91

GROUP A

LEICESTERSHIRE v DERBYSHIRE

At Leicester, May 8. Leicestershire won by five wickets. Despite an economical spell by Parsons, Derbyshire, put in on an easy-paced pitch, compiled a useful total. Balderstone played a valuable anchor role for Leicestershire, but 94 were still needed off fourteen overs when Garnham swung the game with a superb 55 off only 31 deliveries.

Gold Award: M. A. Garnham.

Derbyshire

J. G. Wright c and b Steele	60
A. Hill run out	21
P. N. Kirsten not out	77
J. H. Hampshire c Garnham b Parsons	2
*B. Wood c Agnew b Steele	20
G. Miller c Gower b Taylor	8
K. J. Barnett c Garnham b Taylor	8
†R. W. Taylor not out	20
L-b 6, w 3, n-b 7	16
1/88 2/91 3/106 4/135 5/173 6/183 (6 wkts, 55 overs)	232

P. G. Newman, S. Oldham and P. J. Hacker did not bat.

Bowling: Taylor 11–3–43–2; Agnew 11–0–59–0; Clift 11–1–48–0; Parsons 11–1–28–1; Steele 11–3–38–2.

Leicestershire

J. C. Balderstone not out	89	J. F. Steele not out	5
N. E. Briers lbw b Oldham	11		
D. I. Gower b Wood	7	B 19, l-b 1, n-b 4	24
B. F. Davison st Taylor b Miller	25		—
*R. W. Tolchard run out	17	1/28 2/62 3/109 (5 wkts, 54 overs)	233
†M. A. Garnham b Hacker	55	4/139 5/216	

P. B. Clift, G. J. Parsons, L. B. Taylor and J. P. Agnew did not bat.

Bowling: Newman 10–2–43–0; Oldham 11–1–34–1; Hacker 11–2–49–1; Wood 11–0–37–1; Miller 11–2–46–1.

Umpires: P. B. Wight and M. J. Kitchen.

YORKSHIRE v WORCESTERSHIRE

At Leeds, May 8. Worcestershire won by two wickets. Yorkshire's total never looked enough on an easy-paced pitch, where their early progress was checked by Patel's accurate slow bowling. Worcestershire were in trouble at 64 for five in the 23rd over, Ramage working up exceptional pace, but the inexperienced Weston, together with Humphries, led a recovery.

Gold Award: G. B. Stevenson.

Yorkshire

G. Boycott c Humphries b Perryman	19	P. Carrick not out	8
K. Sharp c Younis b Hemsley	71	A. Sidebottom b Perryman	1
G. B. Stevenson c Patel b Inchmore	6	A. Ramage not out	4
C. W. J. Athey st Humphries b Hemsley	57	B 6, l-b 8, n-b 1	15
J. D. Love b Inchmore	7		—
†D. L. Bairstow c Humphries b Pridgeon	9	1/50 2/59 3/152 (9 wkts, 55 overs)	209
*C. M. Old lbw b Perryman	10	4/161 5/169 6/172	
S. N. Hartley b Hemsley	2	7/192 8/194 9/199	

Bowling: Pridgeon 8–0–17–1; Inchmore 11–1–45–2; Perryman 9–2–25–3; Hemsley 6–0–30–3; Gifford 10–0–51–0; Patel 11–1–26–0.

Worcestershire

G. M. Turner c Bairstow b Ramage	5	J. D. Inchmore b Hartley	29
J. A. Ormrod b Stevenson	14	*N. Gifford not out	19
D. N. Patel lbw b Stevenson	18	A. P. Pridgeon not out	9
Younis Ahmed c Bairstow b Sidebottom	13	L-b 3, w 4, n-b 2	9
E. J. O. Hemsley c Bairstow b Stevenson	13		—
M. J. Weston lbw b Stevenson	40	1/13 2/35 3/46 4/54 (8 wkts, 54 overs)	210
†D. J. Humphries b Stevenson	41	5/68 6/135 7/173 8/187	

S. P. Perryman did not bat.

Bowling: Old 11–0–45–0; Ramage 11–3–21–1; Sidebottom 11–1–45–1; Stevenson 11–1–50–5; Hartley 9–0–30–1; Boycott 1–0–10–0.

Umpires: D. O. Oslear and C. T. Spencer.

DERBYSHIRE v MINOR COUNTIES

At Derby, May 15. Derbyshire won by eight wickets. Minor Counties, put in, were restricted to 201, owing mainly to an economical spell by Miller who, with an unbeaten 88, then took his side to victory with more than sixteen overs to spare.

Gold Award: G. Miller.

Minor Counties

M. D. Nurton c Taylor b Finney	36
J. G. Tolchard c Hampshire b Hacker	24
S. G. Plumb c and b Miller	15
P. D. Johnson c Miller b Finney	28
G. I. Burgess b Miller	0
*D. Bailey c Taylor b Hacker	6
N. A. Riddell c Hampshire b Oldham	34
N. T. O'Brien c Miller b Oldham	27
†F. E. Collyer c Wright b Oldham	4
I. J. Gemmell b Tunnicliffe	1
R. J. Hailey not out	1
B 1, l-b 12, w 7, n-b 5	25
1/62 2/66 3/98 4/108 5/118 6/123 7/191 8/195 9/200 (54.3 overs)	201

Bowling: Oldham 10.3–2–34–3; Tunnicliffe 11–1–38–1; Finney 11–1–44–2; Hacker 11–2–43–2; Miller 11–4–17–2.

Derbyshire

J. G. Wright c and b Burgess	45
G. Miller not out	88
P. N. Kirsten c Tolchard b Plumb	58
C. J. Tunnicliffe not out	0
B 1, l-b 4, w 6	11
1/75 2/193 (2 wkts, 38.5 overs)	202

*B. Wood, J. H. Hampshire, K. J. Barnett, R. J. Finney, †R. W. Taylor, S. Oldham and P. J. Hacker did not bat.

Bowling: Gemmell 8–0–44–0; O'Brien 6–1–25–0; Hailey 11–3–45–0; Burgess 7–0–39–1; Bailey 4–0–21–0; Plumb 2–0–9–1; Riddell 0.5–0–8–0.

Umpires: K. Ibadulla and B. J. Meyer.

WORCESTERSHIRE v LEICESTERSHIRE

At Worcester, May 15. Leicestershire won by 6 runs after a two-hour break for rain had delayed the conclusion until 9.05 p.m. A second-wicket partnership of 158 between Patel and Ormrod put Worcestershire within sight of victory, but in the gathering gloom, the final target of 58 off eight overs was just too much. Earlier, Balderstone had anchored the Leicestershire innings with a century containing only seven boundaries.

Gold Award: J. C. Balderstone.

Leicestershire

J. C. Balderstone c Hemsley b Pridgeon	100
N. E. Briers lbw b Patel	47
D. I. Gower c Hemsley b Gifford	37
B. F. Davison not out	69
†M. A. Garnham not out	4
B 6, l-b 8, w 6, n-b 1	21
1/107 2/165 3/261 (3 wkts, 55 overs)	278

J. F. Steele, *R. W. Tolchard, A. M. E. Roberts, G. J. Parsons, L. B. Taylor and K. Higgs did not bat.

Bowling: Pridgeon 9–1–44–1; Inchmore 7–1–35–0; Perryman 11–0–47–0; Weston 3–0–15–0; Gifford 11–0–54–1; Patel 11–0–42–1; Hemsley 3–0–20–0.

Worcestershire

G. M. Turner lbw b Taylor................ 2
J. A. Ormrod b Taylor..................... 87
D. N. Patel c Parsons b Higgs............ 90
Younis Ahmed c Tolchard b Higgs...... 19
E. J. O. Hemsley c Davison b Taylor.. 28
†D. J. Humphries c Gower b Taylor... 5
M. J. Weston b Taylor..................... 2
J. D. Inchmore not out..................... 4
*N. Gifford b Taylor........................ 0
A. P. Pridgeon not out..................... 13
B 1, l-b 18, w 2, n-b 1............ 22

1/3 2/161 3/193 (8 wkts, 55 overs) 272
4/238 5/249 6/255 7/256 8/256

S. P. Perryman did not bat.

Bowling: Roberts 11–3–46–0; Taylor 11–0–35–6; Higgs 11–0–56–2; Parsons 11–1–54–0; Steele 11–0–59–0.

Umpires: C. Cook and J. van Geloven.

LEICESTERSHIRE v YORKSHIRE

At Leicester, May 22. Leicestershire won by six wickets. With the exception of Boycott, Yorkshire were pinned down by Agnew and Parsons, so that Leicestershire were set a seemingly easy target. Yet, despite Balderstone's third half-century in three group matches, Davison's quick 32 was needed to stimulate the innings.

Gold Award: G. Boycott.

Yorkshire

G. Boycott c Balderstone b Steele...... 82
K. Sharp c Steele b Agnew............... 20
C. W. J. Athey c and b Clift............ 24
†D. L. Bairstow c Balderstone b Parsons 13
S. N. Hartley c Agnew b Taylor......... 12
J. D. Love b Parsons....................... 1
G. B. Stevenson b Parsons................ 0
*C. M. Old c Parsons b Clift............. 15
R. G. Lumb run out........................ 8
A. Sidebottom not out...................... 22
A. Ramage not out.......................... 1
L-b 7, n-b 2........................... 9

1/57 2/124 3/140 (9 wkts, 55 overs) 207
4/148 5/157 6/157
7/169 8/174 9/195

Bowling: Taylor 11–2–40–1; Parsons 11–2–28–3; Agnew 11–4–26–1; Clift 11–0–46–2; Steele 11–0–58–1.

Leicestershire

J. C. Balderstone b Sidebottom.......... 50
N. E. Briers c Bairstow b Ramage...... 6
D. I. Gower c Sharp b Ramage.......... 38
B. F. Davison lbw b Old.................. 32
†M. A. Garnham not out.................. 32
*R. W. Tolchard not out.................. 31
B 1, l-b 11, w 3, n-b 6............ 21

1/14 2/98 3/144 (4 wkts, 53 overs) 210
4/148

J. P. Agnew, P. B. Clift, J. F. Steele, G. J. Parsons and L. B. Taylor did not bat.

Bowling: Ramage 10–1–38–2; Old 11–2–30–1; Sidebottom 11–1–38–1; Stevenson 10–0–42–0; Hartley 11–0–41–0.

Umpires: C. T. Spencer and B. J. Meyer.

MINOR COUNTIES v WORCESTERSHIRE

At Wellington, May 22. Worcestershire won by 97 runs. Turner played with easy freedom, taking Worcestershire towards 146 for one in the 37th over. However, Patel and Ormrod were caught behind and Nicholls collected five wickets at a cost of 10 runs in three overs. In reply, Tolchard and Plumb scored fairly briskly until Perryman bowled Tolchard before tea and afterwards picked up the rest of the main batting.

Gold Award: D. G. Nicholls.

Worcestershire

G. M. Turner c Johnson b Nicholls..... 79
J. A. Ormrod c Collyer b O'Brien...... 45
D. N. Patel c Collyer b Gemmell....... 13
Younis Ahmed run out..................... 17
*P. A. Neale c Gemmell b Nicholls.... 7
E. J. O. Hemsley lbw b Nicholls......... 7
†D. J. Humphries c Bailey b Nicholls.. 4
A. E. Warner b Nicholls.................. 3
J. D. Inchmore run out..................... 11
A. P. Pridgeon c Collyer b Nicholls..... 5
S. P. Perryman not out..................... 5

B 1, l-b 18, w 9, n-b 2............. 30

1/125 2/146 3/172 4/177 (55 overs) 226
5/192 6/192 7/202 8/205 9/214

Bowling: Gemmell 11–1–53–1; Smith 11–1–41–0; Burgess 11–1–28–0; Nicholls 11–0–43–6; O'Brien 11–1–31–1.

Minor Counties

S. G. Plumb c Hemsley b Perryman.... 47
J. G. Tolchard b Perryman............... 26
P. D. Johnson c Humphries b Perryman.. 2
G. I. Burgess c Ormrod b Perryman.... 1
N. A. Riddell c Turner b Inchmore..... 9
*D. Bailey c Neale b Patel................ 7
N. T. O'Brien c Neale b Patel........... 0
†F. E. Collyer c and b Pridgeon......... 10
J. A. Smith not out.......................... 6
D. G. Nicholls b Inchmore................ 2
I. J. Gemmell c Turner b Warner....... 0

B 2, l-b 6, w 5, n-b 6............... 19

1/74 2/81 3/85 4/86 (48.3 overs) 129
5/95 6/95 7/117 8/119 9/128

Bowling: Pridgeon 8–2–18–1; Warner 7.3–4–15–1; Inchmore 11–4–28–2; Perryman 11–4–28–4; Patel 11–3–21–2.

Umpires: B. Leadbeater and N. T. Plews.

WORCESTERSHIRE v DERBYSHIRE

At Worcester, May 25. Derbyshire won by 6 runs, after being given a flying start by Wood, who put on a hundred for the second wicket in 22 overs with Kirsten and reached 106 (one 6, twelve 4s) in 157 minutes. Turner and Ormrod replied with an opening stand of 113, but thereafter only Younis could keep the momentum going and, needing 18 off the last over, Worcestershire could manage only 11.

Gold Award: B. Wood.

Derbyshire

J. G. Wright c Turner b Patel........... 19
*B. Wood st Humphries b Patel......... 106
P. N. Kirsten c Warner b Gifford....... 53
J. H. Hampshire lbw b Warner.......... 44
G. Miller b Warner.......................... 19
K. J. Barnett run out........................ 6
C. J. Tunnicliffe not out................... 10
†R. W. Taylor not out...................... 6

B 1, l-b 6, w 4, n-b 10............. 21

1/56 2/165 3/209 (6 wkts, 55 overs) 284
4/245 5/267 6/269

P. G. Newman, S. Oldham and P. J. Hacker did not bat.

Bowling: Pridgeon 11–1–51–0; Warner 11–1–47–2; Perryman 10–0–65–0; Patel 11–0–60–2; Gifford 11–0–35–1; Hemsley 1–0–5–0.

Worcestershire

G. M. Turner c Tunnicliffe b Newman	78	A. P. Pridgeon b Newman	6
J. A. Ormrod b Wood	45	N. Gifford c Wood b Oldham	5
Younis Ahmed c Newman b Tunnicliffe	39	S. P. Perryman not out	10
D. N. Patel b Newman	25	L-b 7, w 2, n-b 1	10
E. J. O. Hemsley lbw b Newman	2		—
*P. A. Neale c Barnett b Tunnicliffe	26	1/113 2/167 3/178 (9 wkts, 55 overs)	278
†D. J. Humphries c Taylor b Oldham	8	4/185 5/223 6/226	
A. E. Warner not out	24	7/232 8/239 9/258	

Bowling: Hacker 3–0–19–0; Oldham 10–0–51–2; Newman 11–0–48–4; Miller 11–0–40–0; Wood 11–2–49–1; Kirsten 5–0–29–0; Tunnicliffe 4–0–32–2.

Umpires: R. Palmer and P. J. Eele.

YORKSHIRE v MINOR COUNTIES

At Bradford, May 25, 26. Yorkshire won by six wickets. A determined fourth-wicket stand of 69 from eighteen overs between Riddell and Bailey gave the Minor Counties innings some respectability on a wicket that encouraged the seamers. Nicholls was the only bowler to threaten Yorkshire who, following the early loss of Boycott, were taken towards victory by Athey and Lumb.

Gold Award: C. W. J. Athey.

Minor Counties

J. G. Tolchard c Athey b Sidebottom	23	D. G. Nicholls c Athey b Stevenson	15
S. G. Plumb c Bairstow b Old	1	S. P. Davis not out	1
P. D. Johnson lbw b Sidebottom	13	I. J. Gemmell not out	4
*D. Bailey lbw b Stuchbury	34	L-b 11, w 6	17
N. A. Riddell c Bairstow b Ramage	63		—
W. M. Osman c Sharp b Stuchbury	21	1/6 2/44 3/45 (8 wkts, 55 overs)	192
†A. Griffiths c Bairstow b Stevenson	0	4/114 5/148 6/148 7/186 8/188	

R. W. Flower did not bat.

Bowling: Old 11–1–27–1; Ramage 11–3–34–1; Sidebottom 11–3–27–2; Stuchbury 11–0–46–2; Stevenson 11–1–41–2.

Yorkshire

G. Boycott c Tolchard b Gemmell	2	†D. L. Bairstow not out	18
K. Sharp c Flower b Nicholls	23	B 6, w 3, n-b 2	11
R. G. Lumb c Plumb b Nicholls	76		—
C. W. J. Athey not out	61	1/3 2/56 3/165 (4 wkts, 52.3 overs)	193
S. N. Hartley c Plumb b Nicholls	2	4/168	

S. Stuchbury, *C. M. Old, G. B. Stevenson, A. Sidebottom and A. Ramage did not bat.

Bowling: Gemmell 11–1–35–1; Davies 11–2–24–0; Nicholls 11–2–31–3; Flower 11–1–42–0; Plumb 7–0–38–0; Bailey 1.3–0–12–0.

Umpires: N. T. Plews and J. van Geloven.

DERBYSHIRE v YORKSHIRE

At Chesterfield, May 27. Derbyshire won by seven wickets. Yorkshire, needing to win and bowl out their opponents inside 30 overs if they were to qualify for the quarter-finals, were put in and outplayed by Derbyshire, who thus finished top of the group. Hampshire, playing for the first time against his former county, finished the match with a 6 off Stuchbury.

Gold Award: J. H. Hampshire.

Yorkshire

G. Boycott run out	7	*C. M. Old c Barnett b Wood	3
R. G. Lumb run out	36	A. Sidebottom c Taylor b Newman	10
C. W. J. Athey c Taylor b Miller	11	A. Ramage run out	8
J. D. Love c Kirsten b Newman	60	S. Stuchbury not out	6
K. Sharp st Taylor b Wood	5	L-b 6, w 6	12
†D. L. Bairstow c Hampshire b Tunnicliffe	10	1/21 2/41 3/72 (55 overs)	178
G. B. Stevenson c Tunnicliffe b Wood	10	4/89 5/108 6/121 7/135 8/156 9/165	

Bowling: Oldham 11–2–30–0; Newman 11–2–36–2; Tunnicliffe 11–1–42–1; Miller 11–2–33–1; Wood 11–3–25–3.

Derbyshire

A. Hill c Old b Ramage	0
J. G. Wright c Ramage b Sidebottom	19
P. N. Kirsten c Ramage b Stuchbury	48
J. H. Hampshire not out	66
G. Miller not out	47
W 1	1
1/0 2/41 3/74 (3 wkts, 42 overs)	181

*B. Wood, K. J. Barnett, †R. W. Taylor, C. J. Tunnicliffe, P. G. Newman and S. Oldham did not bat.

Bowling: Ramage 5–1–35–1; Old 9–0–35–0; Stevenson 7–1–37–0; Sidebottom 11–3–30–1; Stuchbury 10–0–43–1.

Umpires: J. Birkenshaw and A. Jepson.

MINOR COUNTIES v LEICESTERSHIRE

At Wellington, May 27. Minor Counties won by 131 runs after bowling Leicestershire out for the lowest score in the eleven years of the competition. By then, the pitch, which deteriorated badly after a two-and-a-half-hour rain-break, had been reported by the umpires to the TCCB. Having already qualified for the quarter-finals, Leicestershire's batsmen were in no mood for a testing struggle, and Davis and Smith ran swiftly through the order.

Gold Award: S. P. Davis.

Minor Counties

J. G. Tolchard c Balderstone b Parsons	1	J. A. Smith run out	17
S. G. Plumb lbw b Agnew	24	†A. Griffiths not out	13
P. D. Johnson c Parsons b Steele	12	B 9, l-b 10, w 10, n-b 8	37
*D. Bailey c Balderstone b Agnew	8		
N. A. Riddell c Gower b Parsons	31	1/29 2/41 3/63 (7 wkts, 55 overs)	187
W. M. Osman b Parsons	44	4/63 5/141 6/154 7/187	

S. P. Davis, B. Brain and R. W. Flower did not bat.

Bowling: Roberts 11–5–18–0; Taylor 11–4–16–0; Parsons 11–1–42–3; Agnew 11–2–35–2; Steele 5–2–14–1; Briers 6–1–25–0.

Leicestershire

J. C. Balderstone lbw b Brain	5
N. E. Briers c Griffiths b Davis	6
D. I. Gower lbw b Davis	0
†M. A. Garnham c Griffiths b Davis	0
B. F. Davison c Riddell b Davis	4
*R. W. Tolchard c Griffiths b Brain	9
J. F. Steele not out	1
A. M. E. Roberts c Riddell b Smith	0
G. J. Parsons lbw b Smith	7
J. P. Agnew b Smith	1
L. B. Taylor lbw b Smith	5
L-b 2, w 15, n-b 1	18
1/13 2/13 3/13 4/14 5/23 6/31 7/32 8/40 9/42 (26.2 overs)	56

Bowling: Davis 9–6–11–4; Brain 8–3–18–2; Smith 6.2–2–8–4; Flower 3–2–1–0.

Umpires: P. J. Eele and D. G. L. Evans.

GROUP B

LANCASHIRE v SCOTLAND

At Manchester, May 8. Lancashire won by ten wickets after Croft had proved too much for Scotland, whose last seven wickets fell for 49 runs. David Lloyd and Kennedy then took Lancashire to victory with an unbroken opening partnership.

Gold Award: C. E. H. Croft.

Scotland

C. J. Warner c Scott b Allott	0
R. R. Jones c Scott b Allott	2
*R. G. Swan c Scott b Croft	1
†A. Brown b Abrahams	47
O. Henry c Allott b D. Lloyd	59
H. G. F. Johnston lbw b Croft	10
W. D. G. Loudon not out	17
D. L. Snodgrass b Croft	9
J. E. Ker b Croft	0
G. F. Goddard b Croft	1
J. Clark c D. Lloyd b Croft	0
L-b 8	8
1/0 2/3 3/7 4/105 5/121 6/132 7/150 8/150 9/154 (54 overs)	154

Bowling: Abrahams 2–0–14–1; D. Lloyd 11–1–21–1; Reidy 6–0–28–0; Simmons 11–1–28–0; Allott 10–1–27–2; Croft 10–4–10–6; McFarlane 4–0–18–0.

Lancashire

A. Kennedy not out	72
D. Lloyd not out	76
L-b 5, w 2, n-b 1	8
(no wkt, 49.2 overs)	156

J. Abrahams, *C. H. Lloyd, D. P. Hughes, B. W. Reidy, J. Simmons, P. J. W. Allott, C. E. H. Croft, †C. J. Scott and L. L. McFarlane did not bat.

Bowling: Snodgrass 5.2–1–21–0; Loudon 7–1–26–0; Goddard 10–1–28–0; Clark 6–3–4–0; Henry 11–1–35–0; Ker 6–1–20–0; Johnston 4–0–14–0.

Umpires: D. J. Constant and J. van Geloven.

NORTHAMPTONSHIRE v NOTTINGHAMSHIRE

At Northampton, May 8. Nottinghamshire won by 39 runs. Their enterprising batting featured a lively third-wicket stand of 77 between Randall and Rice, followed by Birch's aggressive 69, which included one 6 and six 4s. Northamptonshire's batsmen had little answer to Hendrick's devastating bowling, apart from a magnificent effort by Allan Lamb, who hit 95 in 123 minutes with one 6 and eleven 4s.

Gold Award: A. J. Lamb.

Nottinghamshire

P. A. Todd c Steele b Sarfraz	5	E. E. Hemmings not out	9
R. T. Robinson c Yardley b Carter	12	K. E. Cooper not out	1
D. W. Randall b Steele	45		
*C. E. B. Rice c Lamb b Steele	44	B 5, l-b 12, w 1, n-b 1	19
J. D. Birch c Yardley b Sarfraz	69		
R. J. Hadlee b Carter	20	1/8 2/32 3/109 (7 wkts, 55 overs)	234
†B. N. French run out	10	4/134 5/175 6/202 7/230	

M. Hendrick and M. K. Bore did not bat.

Bowling: Sarfraz 11–1–42–2; Griffiths 11–2–39–0; Mallender 11–1–49–0; Carter 11–1–49–2; Steele 11–1–36–2.

Northamptonshire

*G. Cook lbw b Bore	7	Sarfraz Nawaz c Hadlee b Hendrick	3
W. Larkins c Rice b Hendrick	13	N. A. Mallender not out	6
R. G. Williams b Hendrick	4	B. J. Griffiths b Hendrick	6
A. J. Lamb b Hadlee	95		
T. J. Yardley c Hendrick b Cooper	11	L-b 6	6
D. S. Steele st French b Bore	19		
R. M. Carter c Hadlee b Hendrick	18	1/15 2/20 3/25 4/47 (53.3 overs)	195
†G. Sharp b Hendrick	7	5/90 6/172 7/174 8/183 9/188	

Bowling: Hadlee 10–2–36–1; Bore 11–5–11–2; Hendrick 10.3–1–33–6; Hemmings 11–0–55–0; Cooper 11–3–54–1.

Umpires: R. S. Herman and R. Julian.

NOTTINGHAMSHIRE v WARWICKSHIRE

At Nottingham, May 15. Nottinghamshire won by 39 runs. Following a collapse to 30 for four in eighteen overs, they owed their victory to a dominating fifth-wicket stand of 125 in 22 overs between Hadlee and Hassan, who would not have played but for a late injury to Birch. Hadlee then quickly removed Warwickshire's openers and, despite Humpage's vibrant 62 and an eighth-wicket stand of 78 between Asif Din and Willis, victory eluded the visitors.

Gold Award: B. Hassan.

Nottinghamshire

R. T. Robinson b Ferreira	11	E. E. Hemmings run out	10
P. A. Todd b Willis	1	K. E. Cooper not out	8
D. W. Randall c Humpage b Small	7		
*C. E. B. Rice c Humpage b Ferreira	2	B 6, l-b 7, w 8, n-b 1	22
B. Hassan not out	99		
R. J. Hadlee c and b Cumbes	70	1/5 2/12 3/21 4/30 (7 wkts, 55 overs)	244
†B. N. French c Ferreira b Cumbes	14	5/155 6/199 7/227	

M. Hendrick and M. K. Bore did not bat.

Bowling: Willis 11–4–26–1; Small 11–2–48–1; Ferreira 11–1–44–2; Hogg 11–0–49–0; Cumbes 11–0–55–2.

Warwickshire

D. L. Amiss c French b Hadlee	0
T. A. Lloyd c French b Hadlee	4
A. I. Kallicharran c Randall b Hendrick	12
P. R. Oliver c Randall b Hemmings	4
†G. W. Humpage c Robinson b Cooper	62
Asif Din c Hemmings b Hendrick	61
A. M. Ferreira c and b Hemmings	0
G. C. Small c Cooper b Hemmings	11
*R. G. D. Willis b Hendrick	37
J. Cumbes not out	1
W. Hogg run out	0
B 1, l-b 8, w 3, n-b 1	13
1/4 2/5 3/47 4/73 5/100 6/100 7/124 8/202 9/204 (50.3 overs)	205

Bowling: Hadlee 8.3–3–22–2; Bore 11–3–44–0; Hendrick 9–3–19–3; Cooper 11–0–68–1; Hemmings 11–2–39–3.

Umpires: H. D. Bird and A. G. T. Whitehead.

SCOTLAND v NORTHAMPTONSHIRE

At Glasgow, May 15. Northamptonshire won by 177 runs. Scotland were embarrassingly outclassed as Northamptonshire ran up their highest score in the competition before the Scots replied with their lowest, only Weir being able to progress. Larkins was past his hundred before lunch, and his alliance with Lamb of 153 for the third wicket featured dazzling strokeplay, each player making his highest score in the competition.

Gold Award: W. Larkins.

Northamptonshire

*G. Cook c Kunderan b Henry	11
W. Larkins lbw b Snodgrass	126
P. Willey c Warner b Goddard	1
A. J. Lamb run out	81
R. G. Williams not out	9
T. J. Yardley b Loudon	2
D. S. Steele not out	5
L-b 20, w 4	24
1/62 2/76 3/229 4/239 5/246 (5 wkts, 55 overs)	259

†G. Sharp, Sarfraz Nawaz, R. M. Carter and B. J. Griffiths did not bat.

Bowling: Clark 8–0–40–0; Snodgrass 10–0–43–1; Loudon 7–0–32–1; Henry 9–1–41–1; Goddard 11–3–37–1; Johnston 10–0–42–0.

Scotland

B. K. Kunderan lbw b Sarfraz	3
†A. Brown c Sharp b Sarfraz	0
C. J. Warner lbw b Carter	17
*R. G. Swan c Sharp b Sarfraz	3
O. Henry b Willey	1
R. S. Weir c Sharp b Sarfraz	31
H. G. F. Johnston b Willey	0
W. D. G. Loudon c Willey b Steele	0
D. L. Snodgrass c Yardley b Steele	6
G. F. Goddard c Cook b Steele	14
J. Clark not out	0
L-b 3, w 2, n-b 2	7
1/0 2/9 3/13 4/28 5/28 6/30 7/33 8/45 9/82 (39.2 overs)	82

Bowling: Sarfraz 9–1–21–4; Griffiths 4–0–5–0; Carter 5–2–8–1; Willey 11–5–14–2; Steele 10.2–1–27–3.

Umpires: J. Birkenshaw and A. Jepson.

NORTHAMPTONSHIRE v LANCASHIRE

At Northampton, May 22. Lancashire won by eight wickets. Put in on a wicket that suited seam bowlers, Northamptonshire had no answer to Lancashire's lethal attack, led by Reidy, who took four for 14 in one spell of 7.2 overs. The only resistance came from Lamb (nine 4s) who was ninth out after a valiant effort lasting 136 minutes. The game finished before tea, Lancashire having moved steadily to their comfortable target.

Gold Award: B. W. Reidy.

Northamptonshire

*G. Cook lbw b Folley	1
W. Larkins c C. H. Lloyd b Croft	7
P. Willey c Hughes b Allott	0
A. J. Lamb b Croft	63
R. G. Williams c Kennedy b Reidy	14
T. J. Yardley lbw b Reidy	5
D. S. Steele c Wallwork b Reidy	0
†G. Sharp c C. H. Lloyd b Reidy	0
Sarfraz Nawaz c Wallwork b Allott	5
N. A. Mallender not out	0
B. J. Griffiths b Croft	0
L-b 4, w 1, n-b 2	7
1/1 2/2 3/25 4/45 5/55 6/63 7/65 8/89 9/102 (37.5 overs)	102

Bowling: Allott 8–2–18–2; Folley 9–3–26–1; Croft 7.5–2–21–3; Reidy 11–3–27–4; D. Lloyd 2–0–3–0.

Lancashire

A. Kennedy not out	43
G. Fowler b Willey	18
D. Lloyd b Mallender	4
*C. H. Lloyd not out	29
L-b 6, w 4, n-b 1	11
1/36 2/51 (2 wkts, 36.1 overs)	105

I. Cockbain, D. P. Hughes, B. W. Reidy, I. Folley, P. J. W. Allott, C. E. H. Croft and †M. A. Wallwork did not bat.

Bowling: Sarfraz 7–1–16–0; Griffiths 9–2–23–0; Willey 11–2–21–1; Mallender 6–2–17–1; Williams 3–0–13–0; Yardley 0.1–0–4–0.

Umpires: W. E. Alley and K. Ibadulla.

WARWICKSHIRE v SCOTLAND

At Birmingham, May 22. Warwickshire won by nine wickets. Scotland's total was easily brushed aside as Amiss, whose half-century came in 64 minutes, reached 105 in 117 minutes with three 6s and twelve 4s.

Gold Award: D. L. Amiss.

Scotland

W. A. Donald b Ferreira	35
A. B. M. Ker c Humpage b Small	2
*R. G. Swan c and b Cumbes	14
R. S. Weir c Humpage b Ferreira	26
O. Henry c Lloyd b Lethbridge	37
†A. Brown c Humpage b Ferreira	6
W. D. G. Loudon b Ferreira	16
H. G. F. Johnston b Willis	6
D. L. Snodgrass b Willis	10
A. R. Taylor b Small	0
J. Clark not out	0
L-b 10, w 2, n-b 2	14
1/9 2/57 3/61 4/111 5/127 6/140 7/148 8/165 9/166 (53.1 overs)	166

Bowling: Willis 10–4–12–2; Small 10.1–3–34–2; Ferreira 11–1–42–4; Cumbes 11–2–27–1; Lethbridge 11–2–37–1.

Warwickshire

D. L. Amiss not out	105
T. A. Lloyd st Brown b Henry	29
A. I. Kallicharran not out	29
L-b 1, n-b 3	4
1/90 (1 wkt, 38 overs)	167

†G. W. Humpage, K. D. Smith, Asif Din, A. M. Ferreira, C. Lethbridge, G. C. Small, *R. G. D. Willis and J. Cumbes did not bat.

Bowling: Snodgrass 5–0–31–0; Loudon 8–2–23–0; Clark 7–1–21–0; Henry 11–1–47–1; Taylor 2–0–20–0; Johnston 5–0–21–0.

Umpires: R. Julian and M. J. Kitchen.

LANCASHIRE v WARWICKSHIRE

At Manchester, May 25. Lancashire won by 38 runs. Lancashire ensured a place in the quarter-finals with their third successive win, thanks mainly to Kennedy, who shared in a third-wicket stand of 102 with Clive Lloyd, and later dismissed Smith when it looked as if he might lead Warwickshire to victory.

Gold Award: A. Kennedy.

Lancashire

A. Kennedy c Cumbes b Small	79
G. Fowler lbw b Ferreira	7
D. Lloyd b Lethbridge	9
*C. H. Lloyd c Kallicharran b Humpage	60
I. Cockbain lbw b Lethbridge	0
B. W. Reidy c Asif Din b Ferreira	19
D. P. Hughes b Small	14
P. J. W. Allott b Ferreira	0
I. Folley not out	3
C. E. H. Croft not out	26
B 1, l-b 14, w 5, n-b 2	22
1/25 2/47 3/149 4/149 5/190 6/196 7/205 8/205 (8 wkts, 55 overs)	239

†M. A. Wallwork did not bat.

Bowling: Small 11–3–48–2; Hogg 5–1–12–0; Ferreira 11–1–44–3; Cumbes 11–1–29–0; Lethbridge 11–0–55–2; Humpage 6–1–29–1.

Warwickshire

*D. L. Amiss c Wallwork b Croft	18
T. A. Lloyd c D. Lloyd b Folley	0
A. I. Kallicharran b Folley	0
†G. W. Humpage lbw b Allott	6
K. D. Smith c D. Lloyd b Kennedy	83
Asif Din b D. Lloyd	20
A. M. Ferreira c Hughes b Folley	45
C. Lethbridge not out	13
G. C. Small b Folley	8
J. Cumbes b Croft	0
W. Hogg b Croft	0
L-b 5, w 3	8
1/3 2/3 3/20 4/32 5/78 6/171 7/184 8/198 9/201 (50.5 overs)	201

Bowling: Allott 9–3–22–1; Folley 9–1–34–4; Reidy 11–0–44–0; Croft 9.5–1–26–3; D. Lloyd 8–0–52–1; Kennedy 4–0–15–1.

Umpires: J. Birkenshaw and A. Jepson.

SCOTLAND v NOTTINGHAMSHIRE

At Glasgow, May 25. Nottinghamshire won by 93 runs. Clark's two early wickets gave hope to Scotland before Rice, batting with masterful disdain, constructed his highest Benson and Hedges Cup score. The formal Scottish innings was sustained by the solid Swan, but victory was never likely.

Gold Award: C. E. B. Rice.

Nottinghamshire

P. A. Todd c and b Snodgrass............ 59
R. T. Robinson b Clark.................... 0
D. W. Randall lbw b Clark............... 0
*C. E. B. Rice not out..................... 130
R. J. Hadlee c Swan b Snodgrass........ 32
M. A. Fell c Brown b Loudon........... 4
†B. N. French lbw b Snodgrass.......... 0
E. E. Hemmings not out................... 0
B 3, l-b 8, w 3, n-b 3.............. 17

1/3 2/6 3/167 4/211 5/223 6/232 (6 wkts, 55 overs) 242

K. Saxelby, M. Hendrick and M. K. Bore did not bat.

Bowling: Clark 6–0–32–2; Snodgrass 11–1–44–3; Loudon 11–1–53–1; Goddard 8–1–36–0; Henry 11–2–26–0; Johnston 8–0–34–0.

Scotland

W. A. Donald c Hendrick b Hadlee.... 3
A. B. M. Ker b Saxelby.................... 12
*R. G. Swan b Saxelby..................... 69
R. S. Weir run out.......................... 18
O. Henry st French b Hemmings........ 8
W. D. G. Loudon b Saxelby.............. 11
†A. Brown st French b Fell............... 2
H. G. F. Johnston not out................. 13
D. L. Snodgrass st French b Fell........ 0
B 4, l-b 7, w 1, n-b 1............... 13

1/8 2/30 3/60 4/82 5/107 6/109 7/143 8/149 (8 wkts, 55 overs) 149

J. Clark and G. F. Goddard did not bat.

Bowling: Hadlee 4–2–4–1; Hendrick 5–1–8–0; Bore 11–2–34–0; Saxelby 11–2–24–3; Hemmings 11–3–24–1; Fell 11–0–38–2; Randall 2–0–4–0.

Umpires: R. Julian and B. Leadbeater.

WARWICKSHIRE v NORTHAMPTONSHIRE

At Birmingham, May 27, 28. Warwickshire won by six wickets. Bad weather took the match into a second day, when Warwickshire, needing 90 from fifteen overs, were taken to victory by Oliver and Asif Din. On the first day Larkins scored a magnificent 132, his hundred coming in 33 overs.

Gold Award: W. Larkins.

Northamptonshire

*G. Cook c Oliver b Small................ 1
W. Larkins c and b Cumbes.............. 132
P. Willey c Humpage b Small............ 0
A. J. Lamb lbw b Smith.................. 25
D. J. Capel c Humpage b Lethbridge.. 25
D. S. Steele c Lethbridge b Cumbes.... 28
R. M. Carter c Humpage b Lethbridge. 0
D. J. Wild b Lethbridge.................... 2
†G. Sharp not out............................ 11
Sarfraz Nawaz not out...................... 20
B 1, l-b 12, n-b 1.................... 14

1/6 2/28 3/73 4/141 5/212 6/213 7/217 8/225 (8 wkts, 55 overs) 258

B. J. Griffiths did not bat.

Bowling: Small 11–2–27–2; Cumbes 11–0–48–2; Lethbridge 11–1–49–3; P. A. Smith 11–1–65–1; Sutcliffe 11–1–55–0.

Warwickshire

K. D. Smith b Sarfraz	12
T. A. Lloyd b Willey	40
*A. I. Kallicharran c Wild b Steele	86
†G. W. Humpage run out	40
P. R. Oliver not out	42
Asif Din not out	19
L-b 10, w 5, n-b 5	20
1/20 2/138 3/163 4/229 (4 wkts, 52.4 overs)	259

P. A. Smith, C. Lethbridge, G. C. Small, S. P. Sutcliffe and J. Cumbes did not bat.

Bowling: Sarfraz 10.4–2–36–1; Griffiths 11–0–82–0; Willey 11–2–43–1; Wild 8–1–41–0; Steele 11–0–31–1; Carter 1–0–6–0.

Umpires: R. S. Herman and B. Leadbeater.

NOTTINGHAMSHIRE v LANCASHIRE

At Nottingham, May 27. Nottinghamshire won by 22 runs in a match to decide the group winners, both counties having already qualified for the quarter-finals. A typically aggressive innings by Hadlee, who struck one 6 and five 4s in sixteen overs, took the home side towards a respectable total, after they had been put in. A third-wicket partnership of 108 in 30 overs between Fowler and Clive Lloyd gave Lancashire a chance, but once they had gone, the visitors' hopes faded with the light.

Gold Award: R. J. Hadlee.

Nottinghamshire

P. A. Todd c Wallwork b Allott	3
R. T. Robinson c D. Lloyd b Folley	26
D. W. Randall c Reidy b Croft	21
*C. E. B. Rice c Wallwork b Reidy	31
M. A. Fell b D. Lloyd	26
R. J. Hadlee c Cockbain b Reidy	56
†B. N. French b Croft	2
E. E. Hemmings c Cockbain b Croft	19
K. Saxelby not out	13
K. E. Cooper not out	0
B 5, l-b 8, w 3, n-b 3	19
1/4 2/54 3/54 4/115 5/139 6/150 7/186 8/211 (8 wkts, 55 overs)	216

M. Hendrick did not bat.

Bowling: Allott 11–0–39–1; Folley 11–2–33–1; Croft 11–2–35–3; Reidy 11–0–45–2; D. Lloyd 11–1–45–1.

Lancashire

G. Fowler b Cooper	59
A. Kennedy c Hendrick b Hadlee	3
D. Lloyd c French b Hendrick	0
*C. H. Lloyd st French b Hemmings	49
I. Cockbain c Hadlee b Saxelby	14
B. W. Reidy lbw b Hadlee	16
D. P. Hughes c Fell b Hadlee	4
P. J. W. Allott c French b Saxelby	10
I. Folley not out	11
C. E. H. Croft run out	10
†M. A. Wallwork not out	0
L-b 14, w 4	18
1/10 2/13 3/121 4/123 5/152 6/158 7/166 8/182 9/194 (9 wkts, 55 overs)	194

Bowling: Hadlee 11–2–39–3; Cooper 11–2–35–1; Hendrick 11–2–38–1; Saxelby 11–2–36–2; Hemmings 11–1–28–1.

Umpires: K. Ibadulla and B. J. Meyer.

GROUP C

KENT v HAMPSHIRE

At Canterbury, May 8. Kent won by 19 runs. Following a second-wicket stand of 75 off eighteen overs between Taylor and Tavaré, Kent slumped to 127 for six before Knott and Johnson revived the innings with a seventh-wicket stand of 67 off fourteen overs. Hampshire got off to a fine start, with Greenidge reaching 50 in 57 minutes (one 6, seven 4s), but although Rice batted for 178 minutes, with two 6s and five 4s, victory eluded them as the last four wickets fell for just 3 runs.

Gold Award: N. R. Taylor.

Kent

R. A. Woolmer run out	8
N. R. Taylor c Parks b Tremlett	61
C. J. Tavaré b Rice	29
M. R. Benson c Jesty b Rice	7
*Asif Iqbal c Rice b Tremlett	9
C. S. Cowdrey run out	8
†A. P. E. Knott not out	42
G. W. Johnson b Marshall	43
G. R. Dilley lbw b Emery	0
D. L. Underwood c Rice b Emery	0
K. B. S. Jarvis not out	0
B 2, l-b 6, w 2	10
1/16 2/91 3/107 4/107 5/125 6/127 7/194 8/195 9/195 (9 wkts, 55 overs)	217

Bowling: Marshall 11–1–40–1; Emery 11–1–30–2; Jesty 6–0–25–0; Tremlett 11–1–35–2; Cowley 5–0–27–0; Rice 11–2–50–2.

Hampshire

C. G. Greenidge c Johnson b Woolmer	56
J. M. Rice c Knott b Dilley	66
D. R. Turner run out	6
*T. E. Jesty run out	18
N. G. Cowley b Jarvis	11
V. P. Terry b Jarvis	3
R. E. Hayward not out	5
M. D. Marshall c Knott b Dilley	21
T. M. Tremlett c Knott b Dilley	0
†R. J. Parks c Benson b Jarvis	2
K. St J. D. Emery c and b Dilley	0
L-b 9, n-b 1	10
1/74 2/89 3/124 4/152 5/169 6/169 7/195 8/195 9/198 (53.3 overs)	198

Bowling: Jarvis 10–0–41–3; Dilley 10.3–1–44–4; Woolmer 11–1–28–1; Cowdrey 11–0–50–0; Underwood 11–4–25–0.

Umpires: W. L. Budd and W. E. Alley.

SURREY v ESSEX

At The Oval, May 8. Surrey won by 85 runs. Clinton, Howarth and Lynch provided the backbone to Surrey's total, while Knight batted, bowled and led the side with distinction. He took the important wicket of Gooch – captain in the absence of the injured Fletcher – whereupon the visitors' effort petered out.

Gold Award: M. A. Lynch.

Surrey

A. R. Butcher c D. E. East b Gooch	39
G. S. Clinton c Hardie b Pont	79
*R. D. V. Knight c Lilley b Lever	33
G. P. Howarth not out	51
M. A. Lynch c Lever b Phillip	45
S. T. Clarke b Lever	4
G. R. J. Roope c Gooch b Lever	0
†C. J. Richards not out	2
L-b 14, w 8, n-b 1	23
1/64 2/132 3/186 4/254 5/262 6/262 (6 wkts, 55 overs)	276

R. D. Jackman, P. I. Pocock and P. H. L. Wilson did not bat.

Bowling: Lever 11–1–54–3; Phillip 11–2–54–1; Turner 10–2–41–0; Gooch 5–0–23–1; Pont 7–0–28–1; R. E. East 11–0–53–0.

Essex

*G. A. Gooch lbw b Knight	66	S. Turner c Richards b Clarke	13
B. R. Hardie b Knight	16	†D. E. East b Wilson	9
R. J. Leiper b Pocock	7	R. E. East not out	0
K. S. McEwan run out	20	B 1, l-b 5, w 5, n-b 1	12
A. W. Lilley c sub b Pocock	11		—
N. Phillip not out	33	1/50 2/89 3/97 4/120 (8 wkts, 55 overs)	191
K. R. Pont c Pocock b Jackman	4	5/146 6/151 7/168 8/185	

J. K. Lever did not bat.

Bowling: Clarke 11–4–38–1; Jackman 10–0–40–1; Wilson 11–0–36–1; Knight 11–0–28–2; Pocock 11–2–31–2; Clinton 1–0–6–0.

Umpires: H. D. Bird and N. T. Plews.

ESSEX v KENT

At Chelmsford, May 15. Kent won by five wickets. Underwood led the destruction of Essex's middle order as McEwan ran out of partners, following an encouraging start. Kent were then launched towards their comfortable victory by Woolmer and Taylor.

Gold Award: D. L. Underwood.

Essex

G. A. Gooch c Asif b Jarvis	19	R. E. East c Cowdrey b Underwood	7
B. R. Hardie run out	23	†D. E. East c Knott b Jarvis	0
*K. W. R. Fletcher b Cowdrey	38	J. K. Lever c Cowdrey b Underwood	3
K. S. McEwan not out	55	L-b 9, w 2	11
A. W. Lilley b Underwood	2		—
N. Phillip run out	7	1/26 2/58 3/111 (51.3 overs)	178
K. R. Pont c Woolmer b Dilley	6	4/118 5/139 6/145	
S. Turner c Benson b Underwood	7	7/160 8/170 9/171	

Bowling: Jarvis 9–0–27–2; Dilley 10–2–20–1; Cowdrey 11–0–44–1; Woolmer 11–1–52–0; Underwood 10.3–3–24–4.

Kent

R. A. Woolmer c D. E. East b R. E. East	55	†A. P. E. Knott not out	20
N. R. Taylor c and b Gooch	14		
C. J. Tavaré c Gooch b Phillip	16	B 1, l-b 12, w 9, n-b 4	26
M. R. Benson not out	41		—
*Asif Iqbal b Turner	1	1/57 2/96 3/105 (5 wkts, 52.5 overs)	180
C. S. Cowdrey run out	7	4/112 5/134	

G. R. Dilley, D. L. Underwood, L. Potter and K. B. S. Jarvis did not bat.

Bowling: Lever 10.5–3–25–0; Phillip 11–1–32–1; Turner 11–3–29–1; Gooch 10–0–44–1; R. E. East 10–2–24–1.

Umpires: P. J. Eele and D. O. Oslear.

HAMPSHIRE v SUSSEX

At Bournemouth, May 15. Sussex won by 119 runs. Marshall and Emery struck early after Sussex had elected to bat, but Mendis and Parker (ten 4s) led a recovery with a third-wicket stand of 115 in 27 overs. After the early loss of Greenidge, there were only brief moments of hope for Hampshire, who were quickly bowled out.

Gold Award: P. W. G. Parker.

Sussex

G. D. Mendis c Parks b Cowley	45
*J. R. T. Barclay c Jesty b Marshall	0
C. M. Wells c Jesty b Emery	6
P. W. G. Parker c Terry b Cowley	77
Imran Khan c and b Cowley	0
I. A. Greig c Greenidge b Emery	23
†I. J. Gould run out	29
C. P. Phillipson not out	17
G. S. le Roux c Greenidge b Emery	13
A. C. S. Pigott b Marshall	0
C. E. Waller not out	3
B 14, l-b 16, w 4, n-b 1	35
1/3 2/13 3/128 4/134 5/160 6/211 7/213 8/239 9/245 (9 wkts, 55 overs)	248

Bowling: Marshall 11–3–35–2; Emery 11–3–34–3; Malone 5–0–30–0; Jesty 8–1–32–0; Cowley 11–2–39–3; Tremlett 9–0–43–0.

Hampshire

C. G. Greenidge c Gould b le Roux	13
T. M. Tremlett b Barclay	25
M. C. J. Nicholas c Gould b Greig	22
*T. E. Jesty c Gould b Pigott	18
D. R. Turner b Pigott	9
N. G. Cowley c Parker b Barclay	13
V. P. Terry c Gould b Pigott	9
M. D. Marshall not out	9
†R. J. Parks run out	2
K. St J. D. Emery b Barclay	0
S. J. Malone c Pigott b Waller	0
B 4, l-b 2, w 1, n-b 2	9
1/21 2/54 3/78 4/91 5/101 6/111 7/118 8/128 9/128 (43.4 overs)	129

Bowling: Imran 5–2–8–0; le Roux 4–1–10–1; Greig 6–0–20–1; Waller 8.4–2–25–1; Pigott 11–2–33–3; Barclay 9–2–24–3.

Umpires: M. J. Kitchen and D. R. Shepherd.

ESSEX v HAMPSHIRE

At Chelmsford, May 22. Essex won by one wicket, having looked to be heading for the lowest score in the competition when they collapsed sensationally to 14 for six in eight overs against Emery and Marshall. But Turner played a marvellous innings in bad light and pouring rain to take his side to victory with nine balls remaining.

Gold Award: S. Turner.

Hampshire

C. G. Greenidge c Hardie b Lever	4
J. M. Rice c Gooch b Lever	11
M. C. J. Nicholas run out	44
*T. E. Jesty b Lever	10
V. P. Terry lbw b Gooch	15
R. E. Hayward c and b Gooch	2
N. G. Cowley c D. E. East b Phillip	7
M. D. Marshall b R. E. East	14
†R. J. Parks c Turner b Phillips	7
T. M. Tremlett c Hardie b Lever	3
K. St J. D. Emery not out	1
L-b 6, w 5, n-b 1	12
1/16 2/20 3/34 4/84 5/94 6/94 7/113 8/117 9/127 (52.2 overs)	130

Bowling: Lever 9.2–4–19–4; Phillip 10–2–28–2; Turner 11–5–12–0; Gooch 11–1–25–2; R. E. East 11–1–34–1.

Essex

G. A. Gooch c Nicholas b Marshall	2	†D. E. East b Rice	30
B. R. Hardie c Parks b Emery	2	R. E. East b Emery	2
*K. W. R. Fletcher c Parks b Marshall	5	J. K. Lever not out	4
K. S. McEwan b Emery	0	B 2, l-b 2, w 5, n-b 6	15
A. W. Lilley c Parks b Emery	0		
K. R. Pont b Tremlett	15	1/4 2/6 3/7 (9 wkts, 53.3 overs)	131
N. Phillip c Parks b Emery	1	4/7 5/13 6/14 7/52	
S. Turner not out	55	8/123 9/126	

Bowling: Marshall 11–2–29–2; Emery 10–3–24–5; Tremlett 11–4–19–1; Jesty 11–4–13–0; Rice 8.3–1–26–1; Cowley 2–0–5–0.

Umpires: J. Birkenshaw and J. van Geloven.

SURREY v SUSSEX

At The Oval, May 22, 24. Sussex won by three wickets. Surrey, put in, were helped to a worthwhile total by Butcher and Knight, whereas Sussex looked in some difficulty at the start of the second day. However, they made light of their task as Phillipson featured in a stand of 92 with Gould, after which he found le Roux an active ally. The last of Pocock's eleven overs cost 18, with two 6s and a 4 to le Roux.

Gold Award: I. J. Gould.

Surrey

A. R. Butcher c Gould b le Roux	80	R. D. Jackman c Gould b Pigott	0
G. S. Clinton b Greig	23	P. I. Pocock not out	3
M. A. Lynch c Gould b Greig	0	P. H. L. Wilson b Imran	0
G. R. J. Roope c Phillipson b Greig	11	B 2, l-b 10, w 6	18
*R. D. V. Knight c Barclay b Pigott	57		
D. M. Smith b Imran	26	1/82 2/82 3/141 (55 overs)	231
S. T. Clarke run out	10	4/159 5/207 6/219	
†C. J. Richards b Imran	3	7/222 8/223 9/227	

Bowling: le Roux 11–3–35–1; Imran 11–2–38–3; Pigott 11–2–50–2; Greig 11–2–48–3; Barclay 11–1–42–0.

Sussex

G. D. Mendis c Butcher b Jackman	6	C. P. Phillipson not out	66
*J. R. T. Barclay c Lynch b Knight	9	G. S. le Roux not out	37
C. M. Wells c Clarke b Wilson	30	B 1, l-b 10, w 5, n-b 1	17
P. W. G. Parker c Richards b Jackman	0		
Imran Khan lbw b Pocock	11	1/14 2/19 3/21 (7 wkts, 53.2 overs)	235
I. A. Greig lbw b Knight	3	4/55 5/67 6/67	
†I. J. Gould c Knight b Pocock	56	7/159	

A. C. S. Pigott and C. E. Waller did not bat.

Bowling: Clarke 11–2–30–0; Jackman 11–3–20–2; Knight 11–0–29–2; Pocock 11–0–70–2; Wilson 8.2–0–62–1; Roope 1–0–7–0.

Umpires: R. S. Herman and D. O. Oslear.

KENT v SURREY

At Canterbury, May 25. Kent beat Surrey by one wicket. Surrey were reduced to 113 for five – four of the wickets falling to 18-year-old paceman Penn in his first game in the competition – before Jackman played a valuable innings, adding 55 in fourteen overs for the ninth wicket with Monkhouse. Kent also made a disappointing start, but were rescued by Benson and Cowdrey. Another collapse left them needing 8 off the last over, and Jarvis steered the winning 4 off the penultimate delivery.

Gold Award: C. S. Cowdrey.

Surrey

A. R. Butcher c Johnson b Penn	33
G. S. Clinton c Dilley b Penn	17
*R. D. V. Knight c Potter b Penn	31
D. M. Smith c Knott b Woolmer	0
M. A. Lynch lbw b Penn	13
G. R. J. Roope c Cowdrey b Dilley	20
†C. J. Richards c Knott b Jarvis	8
S. T. Clarke b Jarvis	11
R. D. Jackman c Knott b Cowdrey	46
G. Monkhouse not out	12
P. I. Pocock b Woolmer	3
L-b 9, w 11, n-b 3	23
1/55 2/60 3/60 4/102 5/113 6/128 7/144 8/154 9/209 (54.5 overs)	217

Bowling: Jarvis 11–1–33–2; Dilley 11–0–40–1; Woolmer 10.5–2–42–2; Penn 11–0–34–4; Cowdrey 9–0–34–1; Johnson 2–0–11–0.

Kent

R. A. Woolmer lbw b Jackman	11
L. Potter c Knight b Monkhouse	30
C. J. Tavaré b Monkhouse	6
M. R. Benson run out	65
*Asif Iqbal lbw b Monkhouse	3
C. S. Cowdrey lbw b Clarke	66
†A. P. E. Knott b Jackman	17
G. W. Johnson b Clarke	1
G. R. Dilley b Jackman	3
C. Penn not out	2
K. B. S. Jarvis not out	4
B 2, l-b 3, w 5, n-b 2	12
1/14 2/31 3/60 4/68 5/161 6/194 7/194 8/206 9/216 (9 wkts, 54.5 overs)	220

Bowling: Clarke 10.5–2–35–2; Jackman 11–1–50–3; Knight 11–1–56–0; Monkhouse 11–3–20–3; Pocock 11–0–47–0.

Umpires: H. D. Bird and D. G. L. Evans.

SUSSEX v ESSEX

At Hove, May 25. Essex won by 114 runs. After being put in, Gooch and Fletcher thrilled spectators with magnificent attacking cricket in a record unbroken third-wicket partnership of 268. Fletcher hit seven boundaries, while Gooch included five 6s and 22 4s in his 198 not out, the highest individual score in a one-day match in England. Sussex lost half their wickets for 62 before the tail wagged vigorously and defiantly. Gooch rounded off one of the great days of his career by taking three for 24 as Sussex suffered their first defeat of the season.

Gold Award: G. A. Gooch.

Essex

G. A. Gooch not out	198
B. R. Hardie run out	17
K. S. McEwan c Barclay b Pigott	0
*K. W. R. Fletcher not out	101
B 1, l-b 4, w 5, n-b 1	11
1/59 2/59 (2 wkts, 55 overs)	327

A. W. Lilley, K. R. Pont, N. Phillip, S. Turner, †N. Smith, J. K. Lever and N. A. Foster did not bat.

Bowling: Imran 11–1–62–0; le Roux 11–0–70–0; Greig 11–1–56–0; Pigott 11–3–66–1; Barclay 11–1–62–0.

Sussex

G. D. Mendis c Smith b Lever	1	*J. R. T. Barclay c and b Gooch	31
†I. J. Gould c Hardie b Turner	18	A. P. Wells c Foster b Gooch	23
C. M. Wells hit wkt b Phillip	2	A. C. S. Pigott not out	6
P. W. G. Parker c Lilley b Foster	13	B 7, l-b 14, w 6, n-b 3	30
Imran Khan c Lever b Turner	4		
I. A. Greig lbw b Turner	18	1/2 2/15 3/44 (42.2 overs)	213
C. P. Phillipson lbw b Gooch	25	4/61 5/62 6/75	
G. S. le Roux c Smith b Phillip	42	7/145 8/148 9/201	

Bowling: Lever 8–0–39–1; Phillip 10–0–41–2; Foster 11–0–43–1; Turner 9–0–36–3; Gooch 4.2–0–24–3.

Umpires: R. S. Herman and P. B. Wight.

HAMPSHIRE v SURREY

At Southampton, May 27. Surrey won by 13 runs. Economical bowling by Jesty and Tremlett reduced Surrey to 103 for six before Clarke and Roope added 63 in nine overs. Three 6s came from Roope, and Clarke cracked four, three of which cleared the pavilion roof. Following the early loss of Greenidge, Rice and Nicholas gave Hampshire some hope, but when they and Jesty had gone, the innings subsided and Hampshire had again failed to record a single victory in the competition.

Gold Award: G. R. J. Roope.

Surrey

A. R. Butcher c Greenidge b Jesty	17	S. T. Clarke run out	39
G. S. Clinton lbw b Jesty	15	R. D. Jackman not out	12
*R. D. V. Knight lbw b Tremlett	21	G. Monkhouse not out	2
D. M. Smith c and b Cowley	13	L-b 13, w 3, n-b 2	18
M. A. Lynch c Parks b Tremlett	14		
G. R. J. Roope b Marshall	53	1/32 2/59 3/61 4/89 (8 wkts, 55 overs)	207
†C. J. Richards b Rice	3	5/98 6/103 7/166 8/204	

P. I. Pocock did not bat.

Bowling: Marshall 11–0–34–1; Emery 10–2–53–0; Jesty 11–1–29–2; Tremlett 11–4–22–2; Cowley 7–1–21–1; Rice 5–0–30–1.

Hampshire

C. G. Greenidge c Knight b Clarke	1	M. D. Marshall c Smith b Jackman	10
J. M. Rice run out	56	†R. J. Parks not out	3
M. C. J. Nicholas b Pocock	35	B 10, l-b 11, n-b 2	23
*T. E. Jesty c Clinton b Jackman	41		
N. G. Cowley c Smith b Roope	1	1/6 2/82 3/121 (7 wkts, 55 overs)	194
V. P. Terry c Knight b Monkhouse	12	4/133 5/160 6/168	
R. E. Hayward not out	12	7/185	

T. M. Tremlett and K. St J. D. Emery did not bat.

Bowling: Clarke 11–3–25–1; Jackman 11–2–30–2; Knight 11–1–34–0; Monkhouse 6–0–32–1; Pocock 11–1–27–1; Roope 5–0–23–1.

Umpires: W. L. Budd and C. Cook.

SUSSEX v KENT

At Hove, May 27, 28. Sussex won by 53 runs and qualified for the quarter-finals, Kent already having done so. After a start delayed by rain, entertaining knocks from Wells, Gould and Imran built up a massive Sussex total. A sparkling innings by Taylor, who hit four 6s and thirteen 4s and who raced from 50 to his century in 25 minutes, made the target look less formidable, but Kent lost their last five wickets for only 20 runs as le Roux, bowling at a fiery pace from the sea end, took four wickets in twelve balls for 9 runs.

Gold Award: N. R. Taylor.

Sussex

G. D. Mendis c and b Dilley	10
†I. J. Gould c Asif b Johnson	72
C. M. Wells b Cowdrey	80
P. W. G. Parker b Johnson	4
Imran Khan not out	65
I. A. Greig c Cowdrey b Dilley	39
C. P. Phillipson c Knott b Jarvis	5
G. S. le Roux not out	11
L-b 12, w 7	19
1/33 2/153 3/169 4/189 5/251 6/259 (6 wkts, 55 overs)	305

*J. R. T. Barclay, A. C. S. Pigott and A. P. Wells did not bat.

Bowling: Jarvis 11–0–58–1; Dilley 11–0–71–2; Penn 11–1–48–0; Cowdrey 9–0–40–1; Asif 3–0–10–0; Johnson 10–0–59–2.

Kent

L. Potter b Barclay	49
N. R. Taylor b Barclay	121
C. J. Tavaré c Gould b Imran	3
D. G. Aslett b Pigott	19
*Asif Iqbal c C. M. Wells b Greig	4
C. S. Cowdrey c Mendis b le Roux	34
†A. P. E. Knott c Pigott b le Roux	2
G. W. Johnson b le Roux	3
G. R. Dilley b Imran	4
C. Penn not out	0
K. B. S. Jarvis b le Roux	0
B 1, l-b 8, n-b 4	13
1/162 2/175 3/183 4/195 5/221 6/232 7/242 8/250 9/252 (48.5 overs)	252

Bowling: le Roux 9.5–2–59–4; Pigott 11–0–59–1; Barclay 11–1–54–2; Greig 9–1–44–1; Imran 8–0–23–2.

Umpires: R. Palmer and M. J. Kitchen.

GROUP D

GLOUCESTERSHIRE v GLAMORGAN

At Bristol, May 8. Gloucestershire won by 4 runs, snatching victory in a dramatic final hour. Stovold's brisk innings gave Gloucestershire a good start after they had been put in, but although Bainbridge and Hignell consolidated after the cheap dismissal of Zaheer, the Glamorgan seamers swept away the last six wickets for only 18 runs. Glamorgan were coasting towards their target until Alan Jones was run out at 139. Miandad went a run later, an accurate spell from Childs induced panic in their ranks, and Graveney finally bowled Eifion Jones with the second ball of the last over to seal an unlikely win.

Gold Award: J. H. Childs.

Gloucestershire

A. W. Stovold c Nash b Holmes........ 59
B. C. Broad c E. W. Jones b Barwick. 12
Sadiq Mohammad c Rowe b Holmes... 16
Zaheer Abbas b Lloyd..................... 7
P. Bainbridge b Barwick.................. 31
A. J. Hignell c E. W. Jones b Barwick. 33
J. N. Shepherd b Nash..................... 9
*D. A. Graveney c E. W. Jones b Ontong. 2
†A. J. Brassington c A. Jones b Nash.. 1
J. H. Childs not out......................... 4
D. Surridge run out.......................... 0
B 4, l-b 8, w 1.......................... 13

1/33 2/85 3/103 (54.2 overs) 187
4/105 5/169 6/172
7/179 8/182 9/187

Bowling: Nash 6.2–1–25–2; Ontong 11–1–36–1; Barwick 11–1–30–3; Lloyd 11–2–29–1; Holmes 11–0–38–2; Rowe 4–0–16–0.

Glamorgan

A. Jones run out.............................. 67
J. A. Hopkins c Surridge b Bainbridge. 27
*Javed Miandad c Brassington b Surridge. 34
R. C. Ontong b Childs..................... 12
C. J. C. Rowe lbw b Childs............... 4
G. C. Holmes c and b Shepherd......... 7
M. J. Llewellyn b Childs.................. 2
†E. W. Jones b Graveney.................. 5
M. A. Nash run out.......................... 6
B. J. Lloyd b Shepherd..................... 1
S. R. Barwick not out....................... 0
B 1, l-b 15, w 2......................... 18

1/59 2/139 3/140 (54.2 overs) 183
4/156 5/164 6/168
7/168 8/177 9/181

Bowling: Surridge 11–2–16–1; Shepherd 11–2–33–2; Bainbridge 11–0–40–1; Childs 11–3–36–3; Graveney 10.2–0–40–1.

Umpires: K. E. Palmer and P. J. Eele.

SOMERSET v OXFORD & CAMBRIDGE UNIVS

At Taunton, May 8. Somerset won by eight wickets. Only Pringle, with a splendid innings, could make any real progress after his side had been put in on a dry, fast pitch; and when Somerset batted he was the only bowler to hamper the home side. Rose hit nine 4s in an hour, Denning proceeded briskly, and Richards capitalised on an escape when 8 by winning the match with 20.1 overs to spare. Taylor included three catches of the highest class in his total of eight – a world record for one-day cricket.

Gold Award: D. J. S. Taylor.

Oxford & Cambridge Univs

R. G. P. Ellis c Taylor b Botham....... 4
G. J. Toogood c Taylor b Marks........ 14
R. J. Boyd-Moss c Taylor b Moseley... 1
*D. R. Pringle b Roebuck................ 68
S. P. Henderson c Taylor b Marks...... 0
K. A. Hayes c Taylor b Dredge......... 7
S. J. G. Doggart lbw b Richards........ 16
J. G. Varey c Taylor b Moseley.......... 20
A. J. Pollock c Taylor b Roebuck....... 8
†C. F. E. Goldie c Taylor b Moseley... 0
I. J. Curtis not out........................... 0
B 2, l-b 6, w 1......................... 9

1/4 2/10 3/41 (50.2 overs) 147
4/41 5/64 6/113
7/127 8/147 9/147

Bowling: Botham 4–0–13–1; Moseley 9–2–13–3; Dredge 11–1–43–1; Marks 11–2–20–2; Popplewell 4–0–27–0; Richards 5–0–9–1; Roebuck 6.2–1–13–2.

Somerset

*B. C. Rose b Doggart	58
P. W. Denning c Varey b Henderson	39
I. V. A. Richards not out	36
P. M. Roebuck not out	13
B 1, l-b 1, w 1, n-b 1	4
1/84 2/103 (2 wkts, 34.5 overs)	150

J. W. Lloyds, I. T. Botham, V. J. Marks, N. F. M. Popplewell, †D. J. S. Taylor, C. H. Dredge and H. R. Moseley did not bat.

Bowling: Pollock 6.5–1–44–0; Pringle 5–1–8–0; Varey 7–0–37–0; Doggart 6–0–19–1; Curtis 6–1–9–0; Henderson 4–0–29–1.

Umpires: C. Cook and D. R. Shepherd.

MIDDLESEX v SOMERSET

At Lord's, May 15. Middlesex won by six wickets. The crowd of around 7,000, many of them hoping for entertainment from Richards and Botham, were disappointed. Somerset began promisingly, but the Middlesex attack was too straight on a pitch not quite trustworthy and Richards's was the second of three wickets to fall in twelve deliveries by Williams. The spinners eliminated any hopes of a recovery, leaving Middlesex with a small target, which they reached with some uncertainty just after tea.

Gold Award: N. F. Williams.

Somerset

*B. C. Rose c Downton b Selvey	18
P. W. Denning lbw b Selvey	20
I. V. A. Richards lbw b Williams	6
P. M. Roebuck c Gatting b Williams	0
N. F. M. Popplewell c Downton b Williams	3
I. T. Botham c Edmonds b Gatting	10
J. W. Lloyds b Edmonds	19
V. J. Marks not out	14
†D. J. S. Taylor b Edmonds	1
C. H. Dredge b Emburey	2
H. R. Moseley lbw b Emburey	0
L-b 3, w 1, n-b 1	5
1/41 2/42 3/43 4/50 5/51 6/71 7/83 8/85 9/98 (39.3 overs)	98

Bowling: Daniel 7–1–15–0; Selvey 11–3–22–2; Williams 9–1–31–3; Gatting 6–0–15–1; Slack 1–0–6–0; Edmonds 3–1–4–2; Emburey 2.3–2–0–2.

Middlesex

*J. M. Brearley lbw b Botham	2
W. N. Slack run out	26
G. D. Barlow c Dredge b Botham	14
M. W. Gatting not out	29
C. T. Radley retired hurt	2
J. E. Emburey c Denning b Richards	17
†P. R. Downton not out	0
B 3, l-b 3, n-b 3	9
1/9 2/29 3/57 4/93 (4 wkts, 37.4 overs)	99

P. H. Edmonds, N. F. Williams, M. W. W. Selvey and W. W. Daniel did not bat.

Bowling: Botham 8–2–22–2; Moseley 8–3–8–0; Dredge 4–1–13–0; Marks 11–1–31–0; Richards 4.4–2–10–1; Lloyds 2–0–6–0.

Umpires: D. G. L. Evans and R. S. Herman.

OXFORD & CAMBRIDGE UNIVS v GLOUCESTERSHIRE

At Oxford, May 15. Gloucestershire won by 84 runs. Gloucestershire, put in, burst away with 26 in four overs and reached 100 in the nineteenth. Stovold's crisp cutting and productive on-side play took him to 97 at lunch, his century coming soon after off 115 balls. After a depressing start Pringle ensured that his side went down with honour by hitting two 6s a long way over mid-wicket and six 4s.

Gold Award: A. W. Stovold.

Gloucestershire

A. W. Stovold c Goldie b Pringle	123
B. C. Broad c Goldie b Varey	53
Zaheer Abbas c Hodgson b Varey	21
J. N. Shepherd run out	16
Sadiq Mohammad not out	23
P. Bainbridge not out	28
B 3, l-b 18, w 11, n-b 4	36
1/154 2/186 3/244 4/250 (4 wkts, 55 overs)	300

A. J. Hignell, *D. A. Graveney, †A. J. Brassington, R. J. Doughty and D. Surridge did not bat.

Bowling: Hodgson 11–0–53–0; Pringle 11–1–52–1; Doggart 11–0–67–0; Curtis 9–0–41–0; Boyd-Moss 1–0–4–0; Varey 11–2–44–2; Henderson 1–0–3–0.

Oxford & Cambridge Univs

R. G. P. Ellis c Stovold b Shepherd	5
G. J. Toogood b Bainbridge	8
R. J. Boyd-Moss c Stovold b Shepherd	4
*D. R. Pringle c sub b Graveney	64
S. P. Henderson b Doughty	15
S. J. G. Doggart b Graveney	18
K. I. Hodgson c Graveney b Shepherd	41
K. A. Hayes c and b Bainbridge	10
J. G. Varey not out	33
†C. F. E. Goldie not out	3
L-b 11, w 2, n-b 2	15
1/6 2/15 3/28 4/87 5/112 6/134 7/146 8/210 (8 wkts, 55 overs)	216

I. J. Curtis did not bat.

Bowling: Shepherd 11–1–37–3; Surridge 11–2–33–0; Bainbridge 10–2–27–2; Doughty 11–0–62–1; Graveney 11–2–42–2; Sadiq 1–1–0–0.

Umpires: K. E. Palmer and R. Palmer.

GLAMORGAN v OXFORD & CAMBRIDGE UNIVS

At Cardiff, May 22. Glamorgan won by 146 runs. Glamorgan reached a useful total, thanks mainly to Hopkins, and the Universities never looked happy. They were quickly reduced to 5 for three, and with Pringle top-scorer with 22 they faded away to 86.

Gold Award: J. A. Hopkins.

Glamorgan

A. Jones b Doggart	27
J. A. Hopkins c Henderson b Curtis	70
R. C. Ontong c and b Pollock	27
*Javed Miandad c Henderson b Varey	49
C. J. C. Rowe c Henderson b Varey	13
M. A. Nash not out	17
G. C. Holmes not out	0
B 10, l-b 11, w 5, n-b 3	29
1/57 2/135 3/143 4/190 5/228 (5 wkts, 55 overs)	232

†T. Davies, B. J. Lloyd, A. E. Cordle and S. R. Barwick did not bat.

Bowling: Pollock 11–0–39–1; Pringle 11–1–41–0; Doggart 11–0–31–1; Varey 11–0–62–2; Curtis 11–2–30–1.

Oxford & Cambridge Univs

R. G. P. Ellis b Cordle	0
G. J. Toogood c Hopkins b Cordle	1
R. J. Boyd-Moss lbw b Nash	1
*D. R. Pringle st Davies b Lloyd	22
S. P. Henderson c Davies b Ontong	18
K. A. Hayes b Lloyd	6
S. J. G. Doggart c Holmes b Barwick	4
J. G. Varey c Hopkins b Lloyd	6
A. J. Pollock st Davies b Lloyd	18
†C. F. E. Goldie c Davies b Barwick	3
I. J. Curtis not out	1
B 2, l-b 2, w 2	6
1/2 2/4 3/5 4/43 5/51 6/54 7/62 8/62 9/70 (28.4 overs)	86

Bowling: Nash 5–3–20–1; Cordle 5–1–18–2; Lloyd 9.4–3–26–4; Ontong 5–2–11–1; Barwick 4–1–5–2.

Umpires: W. L. Budd and K. E. Palmer.

GLOUCESTERSHIRE v MIDDLESEX

At Bristol, May 22, 24. Middlesex won by four wickets. Gloucestershire, put in after a delayed start, batted consistently with Andrew Stovold, Sadiq and Hignell making contrasting half-centuries. Middlesex were troubled by Childs and Graveney, but Brearley coolly saw the score to 162 before he was fifth out, leaving Emburey and Edmonds to end Gloucestershire's hopes.

Gold Award: J. M. Brearley.

Gloucestershire

A. W. Stovold b Edmonds	65
B. C. Broad c Downton b Selvey	16
Sadiq Mohammad b Edmonds	62
A. J. Hignell not out	56
M. W. Stovold not out	18
B 4, l-b 5	9
1/36 2/133 3/154 (3 wkts, 55 overs)	226

P. Bainbridge, J. N. Shepherd, *D. A. Graveney, †A. J. Brassington, J. H. Childs and D. Surridge did not bat.

Bowling: Daniel 11–1–63–0; Selvey 11–3–24–1; Williams 11–2–64–0; Edmonds 11–2–29–2; Emburey 11–0–37–0.

Middlesex

W. N. Slack b Surridge	5
*J. M. Brearley run out	70
G. D. Barlow st Brassington b Graveney	33
M. W. Gatting c Bainbridge b Childs	7
C. T. Radley run out	18
J. E. Emburey not out	44
P. H. Edmonds c Brassington b Graveney	36
†P. R. Downton not out	2
B 1, l-b 11, w 2	14
1/9 2/83 3/96 4/132 5/162 6/220 (6 wkts, 54.2 overs)	229

W. W. Daniel, M. W. W. Selvey and N. F. Williams did not bat.

Bowling: Shepherd 11–3–46–0; Surridge 11–1–31–1; Bainbridge 7.2–0–38–0; Childs 11–1–30–1; Graveney 9–0–38–2; Broad 5–0–32–0.

Umpires: D. J. Constant and A. G. T. Whitehead.

GLAMORGAN v SOMERSET

At Swansea, May 25. Somerset won by 12 runs. Roebuck, with a half-century spread over 31 overs, provided the backbone of Somerset's innings after they had been put in. Chasing a modest total, Glamorgan were devastated by Botham, who captured the first three wickets for 2 runs in seven overs.

Gold Award: I. T. Botham.

Somerset

P. M. Roebuck c and b Barwick......... 50
P. W. Denning c Barwick b Nash....... 8
I. V. A. Richards c Holmes b Barwick. 29
*B. C. Rose run out......................... 15
I. T. Botham c Lloyd b Barwick......... 16
N. F. M. Popplewell c Hopkins b Lloyd. 2
V. J. Marks c Davies b Ontong.......... 6
J. W. Lloyds c Ontong b Cordle......... 28
†D. J. S. Taylor not out.................. 4
C. H. Dredge not out....................... 10
B 1, l-b 3, w 2....................... 6

1/20 2/85 3/94 4/116 (8 wkts, 55 overs) 174
5/118 6/126 7/136 8/158

H. R. Moseley did not bat.

Bowling: Nash 11–1–31–1; Cordle 11–0–49–1; Ontong 11–0–35–1; Barwick 11–3–28–3; Lloyd 11–3–25–1.

Glamorgan

A. Jones c Marks b Botham.............. 3
J. A. Hopkins lbw b Botham............. 2
R. C. Ontong c Taylor b Botham....... 0
*Javed Miandad c Popplewell b Dredge. 41
C. J. C. Rowe b Moseley.................. 54
G. C. Holmes c Botham b Marks....... 1
M. A. Nash c Taylor b Dredge........... 0
A. E. Cordle c Popplewell b Richards. 10
B. J. Lloyd not out.......................... 28
†T. Davies run out.......................... 10
S. R. Barwick b Moseley.................. 3
B 1, l-b 9.............................. 10

1/4 2/4 3/11 4/85 5/93 (54.3 overs) 162
6/94 7/112 8/122 9/155

Bowling: Botham 11–5–24–3; Moseley 10.3–1–27–2; Richards 11–3–35–1; Dredge 11–1–27–2; Marks 9–1–32–1; Popplewell 2–1–7–0.

Umpires: D. J. Constant and A. G. T. Whitehead.

OXFORD & CAMBRIDGE UNIVS v MIDDLESEX

At Cambridge, May 25. Middlesex won by nine wickets. On a pitch of lively bounce, Edmonds, Selvey and Williams thrived. The Universities added to their troubles when Pringle was needlessly run out for 0, and although Boyd-Moss did his best to compensate for his calling error with some crisp strokes and Varey batted aggressively, their total was never enough. Brearley and Slack took their time against a presentable attack and the only wicket fell to Pringle, experimenting with off-breaks, as Brearley sought the winning boundary.

Gold Award: P. H. Edmonds.

Oxford & Cambridge Univs

R. G. P. Ellis b Selvey..................... 0
G. J. Toogood c Gatting b Edmonds... 10
R. J. Boyd-Moss c Brearley b Edmonds. 30
*D. R. Pringle run out..................... 0
S. P. Henderson b Edmonds............. 1
K. A. Hayes c Gatting b Williams...... 7
S. J. G. Doggart b Williams.............. 3
J. G. Varey c Brearley b Selvey......... 27
A. J. Pollock c Emburey b Williams.... 11
†C. F. E. Goldie lbw b Selvey........... 0
C. C. Ellison not out........................ 0
B 1, l-b 9, w 3, n-b 3.............. 16

1/2 2/40 3/40 4/41 (44.4 overs) 105
5/54 6/56 7/61 8/105 9/105

Bowling: Daniel 8–1–17–0; Selvey 5–0–20–3; Edmonds 11–6–9–3; Emburey 11–3–20–0; Williams 8.4–3–16–3; Gatting 1–0–7–0.

Middlesex

*J. M. Brearley lbw b Pringle	39
W. N. Slack not out	60
G. D. Barlow not out	4
B 1, l-b 1, w 2	4
1/103 (1 wkt, 33 overs)	107

M. W. Gatting, C. T. Radley, J. E. Emburey, P. H. Edmonds, †P. R. Downton, N. F. Williams, M. W. W. Selvey and W. W. Daniel did not bat.

Bowling: Pollock 6–0–18–0; Pringle 6–1–7–1; Boyd-Moss 6–0–25–0; Doggart 5–1–19–0; Ellison 5–0–20–0; Varey 5–0–14–0.

Umpires: C. T. Spencer and K. Ibadulla.

MIDDLESEX v GLAMORGAN

At Lord's, May 27, 28. Middlesex won by seven wickets. Glamorgan's openers toiled well beyond the halfway point and thereafter only Miandad successfully combated increasingly restrictive bowling. Nash then bowled his overs straight off with great economy, and with Slack taking 38 overs to score 41, the burden fell on Gatting until Butcher, producing a succession of spectacular strokes, helped him score the final 84 runs in just twelve overs.

Gold Award: M. W. Gatting.

Glamorgan

A. Jones b Williams	52
J. A. Hopkins c Selvey b Emburey	32
*Javed Miandad c Slack b Daniel	59
A. L. Jones c Barlow b Williams	8
R. C. Ontong run out	1
C. J. C. Rowe c Barlow b Selvey	7
M. A. Nash b Daniel	6
A. E. Cordle not out	5
B. J. Lloyd b Daniel	0
B 4, l-b 10, w 9, n-b 2	25
1/75 2/120 3/128 4/137 5/163 6/180 7/194 8/195 (8 wkts, 55 overs)	195

†T. Davies and S. R. Barwick did not bat.

Bowling: Daniel 11–4–13–3; Selvey 11–2–42–1; Williams 11–0–49–2; Edmonds 11–2–26–0; Emburey 11–1–40–1.

Middlesex

*J. M. Brearley c Davies b Cordle	10
W. N. Slack b Lloyd	41
M. W. Gatting not out	88
G. D. Barlow run out	1
R. O. Butcher not out	50
L-b 8, w 1	9
1/21 2/108 3/112 (3 wkts, 51 overs)	199

J. E. Emburey, P. H. Edmonds, †P. R. Downton, N. F. Williams, M. W. W. Selvey and W. W. Daniel did not bat.

Bowling: Cordle 9–2–25–1; Nash 11–2–22–0; Barwick 11–1–47–0; Lloyd 11–0–40–1; Ontong 9–0–56–0.

Umpires: C. T. Spencer and P. B. Wight.

SOMERSET v GLOUCESTERSHIRE

At Taunton, May 27. Somerset won by 13 runs. Somerset, put in on a perfect pitch, made their highest Benson and Hedges Cup score, with Denning featuring in two partnerships of 124 and hitting eleven 4s in 48 overs. Productive bowling by Davis halted Gloucestershire's progress until Bainbridge (two 6s, eight 4s) and Shepherd (one 6, six 4s) added 105 in

thirteen thrilling overs. When Bainbridge was brilliantly caught, 72 were needed in five overs, but despite Graveney's fine onslaught of two 6s and six 4s, it was beyond Gloucestershire's reach. The aggregate of 601 runs was a new record for the competition.
Gold Award: P. W. Denning.

Somerset

P. M. Roebuck c and b Childs	44
P. W. Denning c A. W. Stovold b Bainbridge	129
I. V. A. Richards c Graveney b Surridge	72
I. T. Botham b Surridge	15
*B. C. Rose c Graveney b Surridge	2
N. F. M. Popplewell not out	23
J. W. Lloyds run out	4
L-b 13, w 5	18
1/124 2/248 3/270 4/278 5/287 6/307 (6 wkts, 55 overs)	307

†D. J. S. Taylor, C. H. Dredge, H. R. Moseley and M. R. Davis did not bat.

Bowling: Shepherd 11–0–70–0; Surridge 11–0–49–3; Bainbridge 11–1–56–1; Childs 11–0–45–1; Graveney 6–0–40–0; Broad 5–0–29–0.

Gloucestershire

A. W. Stovold c Denning b Moseley	3
B. C. Broad b Davis	27
Sadiq Mohammad c Popplewell b Botham	9
A. J. Hignell lbw b Richards	34
M. W. Stovold b Davis	13
P. Bainbridge c Botham b Popplewell	80
J. N. Shepherd c Botham b Dredge	47
*D. A. Graveney not out	49
†A. J. Brassington not out	5
B 1, l-b 21, w 5	27
1/3 2/21 3/62 4/95 5/95 6/200 7/236 (7 wkts, 55 overs)	294

J. H. Childs and D. Surridge did not bat.

Bowling: Botham 11–1–62–1; Moseley 11–2–60–1; Davis 11–1–25–2; Dredge 11–1–66–1; Richards 8–1–41–1; Popplewell 3–0–13–1.

Umpires: W. E. Alley and D. J. Constant.

QUARTER-FINALS

DERBYSHIRE v SUSSEX

At Derby, June 16. Sussex won by four wickets. Derbyshire were unable to master spinners Waller and Barclay on a slow pitch, and, when Sussex replied, Parker steered his side to victory, running expertly between the wickets and receiving good support from Mendis and le Roux. Unnecessary confusion between the scorers and umpires had led to the scoreboard incorrectly showing Derbyshire's total as 189, and there was some bewilderment when, Sussex having scored 190, umpire Bird ordered that another ball be bowled.
Gold Award: P. W. G. Parker.

Derbyshire

*B. Wood c Parker b Waller	22
J. G. Wright c Wells b Barclay	33
P. N. Kirsten lbw b le Roux	60
J. H. Hampshire c Barclay b Waller	3
G. Miller b Imran	33
K. J. Barnett c Barclay b Greig	6
W. P. Fowler b Greig	4
†R. W. Taylor run out	8
C. J. Tunnicliffe c Wells b le Roux	12
P. G. Newman not out	1
S. Oldham run out	1
L-b 6, w 1	7
1/50 2/63 3/77 4/138 5/147 6/162 7/170 8/184 9/189 (55 overs)	190

Bowling: Imran 11–4–31–1; le Roux 11–2–57–2; Greig 11–1–34–2; Waller 11–2–38–2; Barclay 11–1–23–1.

Sussex

G. D. Mendis lbw b Miller	46	I. A. Greig not out	20
Imran Khan c Miller b Oldham	0	C. P. Phillipson not out	2
C. M. Wells c Wood b Newman	3	L-b 6, w 1, n-b 1	8
P. W. G. Parker lbw b Oldham	72		—
†I. J. Gould c Tunnicliffe b Kirsten	14	1/0 2/6 3/79 (6 wkts, 53.5 overs)	194
G. S. le Roux c and b Wood	29	4/106 5/154 6/186	

*J. R. T. Barclay, A. C. S. Pigott and C. E. Waller did not bat.

Bowling: Oldham 10–2–30–2; Newman 10.5–2–40–1; Wood 11–2–34–1; Tunnicliffe 9–1–36–0; Miller 11–2–36–1; Kirsten 2–0–10–1.

Umpires: H. D. Bird and A. Jepson.

KENT v SOMERSET

At Canterbury, June 16. Somerset won by three wickets. Kent, put in, owed much to Taylor (thirteen 4s), who dominated the Kent innings and was joined by Cowdrey – the only other Kent player to reach double figures – in a fifth-wicket stand of 119 in 27 overs. Thereafter Garner, with three for 11 in twenty balls, and Botham, with three for 6 in eleven balls, wrapped up the Kent innings as the last six wickets crashed for 34 runs. Somerset cruised towards their target, Rose and Botham adding 60 runs off nine overs, and a late thrust by Kent was in vain.

Gold Award: N. R. Taylor.

Kent

R. A. Woolmer c Denning b Botham	8	G. R. Dilley c Roebuck b Botham	3
N. R. Taylor b Botham	121	D. L. Underwood not out	3
C. J. Tavaré c Taylor b Dredge	3	K. B. S. Jarvis b Garner	0
L. Potter c Moseley b Marks	5	L-b 7, w 3, n-b 2	12
*Asif Iqbal c Garner b Marks	2		—
C. S. Cowdrey lbw b Garner	40	1/24 2/31 3/50 (54.2 overs)	207
†A. P. E. Knott c Denning b Botham	7	4/54 5/173 6/190	
G. W. Johnson b Garner	3	7/198 8/200 9/205	

Bowling: Garner 10.2–4–22–3; Botham 11–1–52–4; Dredge 11–0–41–1; Marks 11–1–31–2; Moseley 8–1–37–0; Richards 3–0–12–0.

Somerset

P. M. Roebuck c and b Woolmer	50	†D. J. S. Taylor not out	8
P. W. Denning c Knott b Jarvis	3	J. Garner not out	1
I. V. A. Richards lbw b Jarvis	12		
*B. C. Rose c Cowdrey b Dilley	52	B 4, l-b 9, w 4, n-b 2	19
I. T. Botham c Woolmer b Jarvis	42		—
J. W. Lloyds c Tavaré b Cowdrey	7	1/12 2/24 3/107 (7 wkts, 54.4 overs)	208
V. J. Marks c Cowdrey b Dilley	14	4/167 5/184 6/185 7/200	

H. R. Moseley and C. H. Dredge did not bat.

Bowling: Jarvis 11–0–44–3; Dilley 10.4–2–43–2; Woolmer 11–3–29–1; Underwood 11–2–21–0; Cowdrey 8–0–27–1; Johnson 3–0–25–0.

Umpires: P. B. Wight and D. R. Shepherd.

MIDDLESEX v LANCASHIRE

At Lord's, June 16. Lancashire won by 52 runs as Middlesex experienced their first defeat of the season in nineteen matches. Clive Lloyd reacted to Gatting's capture of two wickets in consecutive overs by playing a decisive innings, loyally supported in a stand of 74 in fourteen overs by Simmons, who later took two wickets in his first over. Following an early collapse, Middlesex needed Radley and Edmonds to gather runs swiftly, but Simmons bowled economically and once Hayes had run Edmonds out, the match ended swiftly.

Gold Award: C. H. Lloyd.

Lancashire

G. Fowler c Downton b Daniel	4	P. J. W. Allott b Edmonds	2
A. Kennedy b Gatting	20	C. E. H. Croft not out	9
F. C. Hayes st Downton b Gatting	6	I. Folley not out	3
*C. H. Lloyd b Selvey	66	B 5, l-b 7, w 1, n-b 3	16
D. P. Hughes b Edmonds	13		—
J. Simmons c Brearley b Emburey	33	1/8 2/32 3/35 4/72 (9 wkts, 55 overs)	191
B. W. Reidy run out	6	5/146 6/156 7/170	
†C. Maynard b Daniel	13	8/176 9/180	

Bowling: Daniel 11–2–32–2; Selvey 11–3–21–1; Gatting 10–1–33–2; Emburey 11–2–43–1; Edmonds 11–2–36–2; Slack 1–0–10–0.

Middlesex

*J. M. Brearley c Maynard b Croft	0	†P. R. Downton not out	2
W. N. Slack c Maynard b Folley	7	M. W. W. Selvey run out	1
C. T. Radley b Folley	66	W. W. Daniel b Folley	0
M. W. Gatting lbw b Reidy	10		
R. O. Butcher b Simmons	18	B 1, l-b 3, w 1	5
G. D. Barlow c and b Simmons	0		—
P. H. Edmonds run out	18	1/1 2/16 3/32 4/59 5/59 (48 overs)	139
J. E. Emburey b Folley	12	6/100 7/135 8/138 9/139	

Bowling: Croft 8–1–22–1; Folley 10–2–18–4; Allott 8–1–31–0; Reidy 11–0–46–1; Simmons 11–2–17–2.

Umpires: R. Palmer and A. G. T. Whitehead.

NOTTINGHAMSHIRE v LEICESTERSHIRE

At Nottingham, June 16, 17. Nottinghamshire won by 2 runs. After five previous quarter-final failures Nottinghamshire reached the semi-finals for the first time, although in a low-scoring match the result was in the balance until the final delivery when Leicestershire, needing 4 runs, managed only 2. Nottinghamshire, without Hadlee and batting on a slower Trent Bridge wicket, made a useful start, but fell away against some tight bowling highlighted by Parsons's economical return. Facing a modest target Leicestershire were in no hurry, but Hendrick, Cooper and Bore put them on the defensive. Although Gower and Davison improved matters, they were again slipping when bad light stopped play early. On the following morning, Parsons and Steele threatened to steer Leicestershire home, but Steele fell to a brilliant catch by wicket-keeper French, Higgs was run out by Randall, and Parsons and Taylor just failed to score the 10 runs needed off the final over.

Gold Award: G. J. Parsons.

Nottinghamshire

R. T. Robinson c Garnham b Higgs.... 12
B. Hassan b Steele.......................... 48
D. W. Randall c Garnham b Higgs..... 23
*C. E. B. Rice c Tolchard b Parsons... 24
J. D. Birch run out.......................... 14
†B. N. French run out...................... 0
E. E. Hemmings c Garnham b Roberts. 9
K. Saxelby c and b Taylor................. 3
K. E. Cooper c Garnham b Taylor...... 14
M. K. Bore c Gower b Taylor........... 3
M. Hendrick not out......................... 0
L-b 3, w 3.............................. 6

1/34 2/84 3/84 4/109 5/112 6/132 7/137 8/138 9/156 (53.4 overs) 156

Bowling: Roberts 10–2–31–1; Parsons 11–3–14–1; Higgs 11–2–32–2; Taylor 10.4–0–45–3; Steele 11–2–28–1.

Leicestershire

J. C. Balderstone c French b Bore...... 14
N. E. Briers c Birch b Cooper............ 0
D. I. Gower c Bore b Hemmings........ 34
B. F. Davison c Saxelby b Bore.......... 32
*R. W. Tolchard b Hendrick............. 13
†M. A. Garnham c Cooper b Bore..... 1
A. M. E. Roberts c Saxelby b Hendrick. 8
J. F. Steele c French b Saxelby........... 16
G. J. Parsons not out........................ 18
K. Higgs run out............................... 0
L. B. Taylor not out.......................... 2
B 3, l-b 9, w 2, n-b 2............... 16

1/3 2/29 3/74 4/97 5/102 6/106 7/116 8/143 9/144 (9 wkts, 55 overs) 154

Bowling: Hendrick 11–3–18–2; Cooper 11–3–25–1; Bore 11–1–21–3; Saxelby 11–1–42–1; Hemmings 11–1–32–1.

Umpires: W. E. Alley and B. J. Meyer.

SEMI-FINALS

NOTTINGHAMSHIRE v LANCASHIRE

At Nottingham, June 30. Nottinghamshire won by four wickets. They reached their first-ever one-day final at Lord's in a thrilling victory that owed everything to the brilliance of Hadlee. Chasing 183, Nottinghamshire lost four wickets for 23 runs, and at one time the asking-rate was 8 an over. Yet, despite the handicap of a hamstring injury that had restricted his bowling, Hadlee played himself in sensibly before launching into a fierce display of strokeplay. His 55 came in 78 minutes and, with the considerable assistance of Hemmings, he saw Nottinghamshire safely home. Earlier, the Lancashire innings was held together by a splendid effort from Maynard, and when Croft removed Robinson and Hassan cheaply, Lancashire had looked set to visit Lord's.

Gold Award: R. J. Hadlee.

Lancashire

G. Fowler c French b Saxelby............ 18
A. Kennedy c Hadlee b Hemmings..... 31
†C. Maynard c French b Saxelby........ 60
*C. H. Lloyd c French b Hadlee......... 5
D. P. Hughes c French b Hadlee........ 0
D. Lloyd b Hendrick........................ 23
J. Simmons b Hemmings................... 6
B. W. Reidy b Cooper...................... 9
C. E. H. Croft run out...................... 13
P. J. W. Allott b Saxelby.................. 2
I. Folley not out.............................. 3
B 1, l-b 8, w 3....................... 12

1/33 2/88 3/110 4/114 5/127 6/140 7/158 8/171 9/175 (54.4 overs) 182

Bowling: Hadlee 11–2–24–2; Cooper 11–4–30–1; Hendrick 10.4–1–37–1; Saxelby 11–1–51–3; Hemmings 11–2–28–2.

Nottinghamshire

B. Hassan c Simmons b Croft............ 6
R. T. Robinson b Croft.................... 1
D. W. Randall st Maynard b Simmons 43
*C. E. B. Rice b Reidy.................... 34
J. D. Birch lbw b Reidy.................... 8
R. J. Hadlee not out........................ 55
†B. N. French b Croft...................... 6
E. E. Hemmings not out.................... 15
B 4, l-b 7, w 3, n-b 2.............. 16

1/3 2/23 3/93 4/97 5/105 6/116 (6 wkts, 53.1 overs) 184

K. Saxelby, K. E. Cooper and M. Hendrick did not bat.

Bowling: Croft 10.1–2–33–3; Allott 10–2–35–0; Reidy 11–0–53–2; Folley 11–1–20–0; Simmons 11–4–27–1.

Umpires: W. L. Budd and K. E. Palmer.

SOMERSET v SUSSEX

At Taunton, June 30. Somerset won by eight wickets. Without Imran Khan, Parker and Pigott, Sussex, put in on a bland pitch with a slow outfield, were overwhelmed before tea. Garner, taking two wickets and a sharp gully catch within ten deliveries, began their discomfiture in company with Botham, and the visitors never recovered, although a stout performance by le Roux held things together for 27 overs. However, Marks dismissed him and Phillipson in one over and Garner completed the demolition. An opening partnership between Denning, who hit seven 4s despite an injured knee, and Roebuck virtually settled matters, though two excellent catches and useful containing spells from the spinners gave Sussex some consolation.

Gold Award: J. Garner.

Sussex

G. D. Mendis lbw b Garner............... 6
*J. R. T. Barclay c Garner b Botham.. 3
A. M. Green b Garner..................... 0
C. M. Wells c Richards b Marks......... 11
†I. J. Gould b Botham...................... 8
G. S. le Roux st Taylor b Marks........ 46
I. A. Greig c Taylor b Garner............ 13
C. P. Phillipson c Popplewell b Marks. 0
A. P. Wells not out.......................... 5
C. E. Waller b Dredge..................... 7
A. N. Jones b Garner....................... 2
B 1, l-b 3, w 3, n-b 2.............. 9

1/8 2/8 3/10 4/20 5/62 6/94 7/94 8/96 9/107 (41.1 overs) 110

Bowling: Garner 9.1–1–24–4; Botham 6–1–20–2; Dredge 4–0–12–1; Moseley 11–5–20–0; Marks 11–3–25–3.

Somerset

P. M. Roebuck c Barclay b A. P. Wells. 33
P. W. Denning not out..................... 68
I. V. A. Richards c and b Green........ 9
*B. C. Rose not out......................... 1
L-b 1.................................... 1

1/91 2/106 (2 wkts, 36.1 overs) 112

I. T. Botham, N. F. M. Popplewell, V. J. Marks, J. Garner, †D. J. S. Taylor, C. H. Dredge and H. R. Moseley did not bat.

Bowling: le Roux 5–0–22–0; Greig 4–1–14–0; Barclay 11–3–25–0; Waller 11–1–29–0; Green 3–1–4–1; A. P. Wells 2.1–1–17–1.

Umpires: R. Julian and D. O. Oslear.

FINAL

NOTTINGHAMSHIRE v SOMERSET

At Lord's, July 24. Somerset won by nine wickets, thus easily retaining the trophy. For Nottinghamshire it was a disappointing first one-day final at Lord's. Asked to bat first by Rose (as Surrey had been the previous year), Nottinghamshire were struggling at 89 for four at lunch, after 35 overs, and eventually failed to bat out their 55 overs. Garner made the initial breakthrough, yorking Todd in his second over, but Robinson and Randall were slowly but soundly building the innings when Robinson pulled a short-pitched ball to mid-wicket. In the next over, the eighteenth, Randall stepped back to cut Marks's second ball and was bowled. So, too, was Rice, yorking himself as Marks invited him to repeat an earlier 6. This was intelligent bowling by Marks, employing flight to restrict the tentative Nottinghamshire batsmen, and it meant they had to strike out in the afternoon. The result was a continuation of dismissals against full-length deliveries. The main interest in Somerset's innings was not whether they would win, but whether Roebuck, Richards or both would reach fifty. A brace of 4s in the 27th over took Roebuck closer and brought up Somerset's 100; next over Richards unleashed three marvellous 4s off Hadlee. A lofted drive off Hemmings took Roebuck past 50, and a moment later Richards flicked Cooper off his legs to bring the Somerset supporters racing on to the field and the players and umpires racing from it without the acknowledgment that Richards's carefree cameo deserved. It was still not half past five.

Gold Award: V. J. Marks.

Nottinghamshire

P. A. Todd b Garner	2	E. E. Hemmings b Botham	1
R. T. Robinson c Richards b Dredge	13	K. E. Cooper b Garner	3
D. W. Randall b Marks	19	M. Hendrick not out	0
B. Hassan c Taylor b Dredge	26	L-b 5, w 7, n-b 1	13
*C. E. B. Rice b Marks	27		
J. D. Birch b Moseley	7	1/3 2/40 3/40 (50.1 overs)	130
R. J. Hadlee b Garner	11	4/86 5/102 6/106	
†B. N. French c Taylor b Botham	8	7/122 8/123 9/130	

Bowling: Garner 8.1–1–13–3; Botham 9–3–19–2; Dredge 11–2–35–2; Moseley 11–2–26–1; Marks 11–4–24–2.

Somerset

P. M. Roebuck not out	53
P. W. Denning c French b Hendrick	22
I. V. A. Richards not out	51
B 5, w 1	6
1/27 (1 wkt, 33.1 overs)	132

*B. C. Rose, I. T. Botham, V. J. Marks, N. F. M. Popplewell, †D. J. S. Taylor, J. Garner, C. H. Dredge and H. R. Moseley did not bat.

Bowling: Hadlee 9–0–37–0; Hendrick 8–0–26–1; Cooper 5.1–0–41–0; Rice 6–2–11–0; Hemmings 5–0–11–0.

Umpires: D. J. Constant and D. G. L. Evans.

BENSON AND HEDGES CUP RECORDS

Highest individual scores: 198 not out, G. A. Gooch, Essex v Sussex, Hove, 1982; 173 not out, C. G. Greenidge, Hampshire v Minor Counties (South), Amersham, 1973; 158 not out, B. F. Davison, Leicestershire v Warwickshire, Coventry, 1972. (94 hundreds have been scored in the competition.)

Highest totals in 55 overs: 350 for three, Essex v Oxford & Cambridge Univs, Chelmsford, 1979; 327 for four, Leicestershire v Warwickshire, Coventry, 1972; 327 for two, Essex v Sussex, Hove, 1982; 321 for one, Hampshire v Minor Counties (South), Amersham, 1973.

Highest match aggregate: 593 for fourteen wickets, Gloucestershire (282) v Hampshire (311-4), Bristol, 1974.

Lowest totals: 56 in 26.2 overs, Leicestershire v Minor Counties at Wellington, 1982; 60 in 26 overs, Sussex v Middlesex, Hove, 1978; 62 in 26.5 overs, Gloucestershire v Hampshire, Bristol, 1975; 63 in 37.4 overs, Minor Counties (East) v Sussex, Eastbourne, 1978.

Best bowling: Seven for 12, W. W. Daniel, Middlesex v Minor Counties (East), Ipswich, 1978; seven for 22, J. R. Thomson, Middlesex v Hampshire, Lord's, 1981; seven for 32, R. G. D. Willis, Warwickshire v Yorkshire, Birmingham, 1981.

Hat-tricks: G. D. McKenzie, Leicestershire v Worcestershire, Worcester, 1972; K. Higgs, Leicestershire v Surrey in the final, Lord's, 1974; A. A. Jones, Middlesex v Essex, Lord's, 1977; M. J. Procter, Gloucestershire v Hampshire, Southampton, 1977; W. Larkins, Northamptonshire v Oxford & Cambridge Univs, Northampton, 1980; E. A. Moseley, Glamorgan v Kent, Cardiff, 1981.

Record partnerships for each wicket

241 for 1st	S. M. Gavaskar and B. C. Rose, Somerset v Kent at Canterbury...	1980
285* for 2nd	C. G. Greenidge and D. R. Turner, Hampshire v Minor Counties (South) at Amersham..	1973
268* for 3rd	G. A. Gooch and K. W. R. Fletcher, Essex v Sussex at Hove.......	1982
184* for 4th	D. Lloyd and B. W. Reidy, Lancashire v Derbyshire at Chesterfield	1980
134 for 5th	M. Maslin and D. N. F. Slade, Minor Counties (East) v Nottinghamshire at Nottingham..	1976
114 for 6th	Majid J. Khan and G. P. Ellis, Glamorgan v Gloucestershire at Bristol..	1975
149* for 7th	J. D. Love and C. M. Old, Yorkshire v Scotland at Bradford........	1981
109 for 8th	R. E. East and N. Smith, Essex v Northamptonshire at Chelmsford	1977
81 for 9th	J. N. Shepherd and D. L. Underwood, Kent v Middlesex at Lord's	1975
80* for 10th	D. L. Bairstow and M. Johnson, Yorkshire v Derbyshire at Derby	1981

WINNERS 1972–82

1972 LEICESTERSHIRE beat Yorkshire by five wickets.
1973 KENT beat Worcestershire by 39 runs.
1974 SURREY beat Leicestershire by 27 runs.
1975 LEICESTERSHIRE beat Middlesex by five wickets.
1976 KENT beat Worcestershire by 43 runs.
1977 GLOUCESTERSHIRE beat Kent by 64 runs.
1978 KENT beat Derbyshire by six wickets.
1979 ESSEX beat Surrey by 35 runs.
1980 NORTHAMPTONSHIRE beat Essex by 6 runs.
1981 SOMERSET beat Surrey by seven wickets.
1982 SOMERSET beat Nottinghamshire by nine wickets.

WINS BY OXFORD AND CAMBRIDGE UNIVERSITIES

1973 OXFORD beat Northamptonshire at Northampton by two wickets.
1975 OXFORD & CAMBRIDGE beat Worcestershire at Cambridge by 66 runs.
1975 OXFORD & CAMBRIDGE beat Northamptonshire at Oxford by three wickets.
1976 OXFORD & CAMBRIDGE beat Yorkshire at Barnsley by seven wickets.

WINS BY MINOR COUNTIES

1980 MINOR COUNTIES beat Gloucestershire at Chippenham by 3 runs.
1981 MINOR COUNTIES beat Hampshire at Southampton by 3 runs.
1982 MINOR COUNTIES beat Leicestershire at Wellington by 131 runs.

BENSON AND HEDGES CUP RULES

(As applied in 1982)

The Playing Conditions for first-class matches in the United Kingdom will apply, with the following exceptions. Matches are not considered first-class.

Duration of Matches

The matches will consist of one innings per side, each innings being limited to 55 overs. All matches will be completed in one day, if possible, but two days will be allocated for group league matches and three days for knockout matches in case of weather interference. Matches scheduled to start on Saturday, but not completed on that day, may be continued on the Sunday, only with the approval of the TCCB.

Hours of Play

Normal hours will be 11 a.m. to 7.30 p.m. (start at 2.00 p.m. on Sundays). The umpires may order extra time if they consider a finish can be obtained on any day, or in order to give the team batting second an opportunity to complete twenty overs.

Intervals

Lunch..................................	1.15 p.m.–1.55 p.m.
Between innings....................	10 minutes.
Tea......................................	20 minutes.

(a) In an uninterrupted match, or a match where, in spite of interruptions, the umpires consider that the match can be completed on that day, the tea interval will be taken at 4.30 p.m. or after 25 overs of the team batting second, whichever is the later. (If a wicket falls in the 25th over of the team batting second, tea will be taken immediately.)

(b) In a match where the start is delayed or play is suspended to such an extent that it is impracticable to adopt (a) above, owing to the unlikelihood of completing the match on that day, the tea interval will be taken at 4.30 p.m.

Note: The timing of any interval may be delayed for a maximum of fifteen minutes on the second or third day of a match, if the umpires consider that a finish can be obtained within that time.

Limitation of Overs by any one Bowler

In a 55 overs match no bowler may bowl more than eleven overs in an innings. In a match in which the start is delayed and the innings of both teams is restricted from the start to fewer than 55 overs, no bowler may bowl more than one fifth of the total overs allowed, except that where the total overs is not divisible by five, an additional over shall be allowed to the minimum number of bowlers necessary to make up the balance – e.g. in a 33 overs match, three bowlers may bowl a maximum of seven overs and no other bowler more than six overs.

In the event of a bowler breaking down and being unable to complete an over, the remaining balls will be bowled by another bowler. Such part of an over will count as a full over only in so far as each bowler's limit is concerned.

The number of overs bowled by each individual bowler shall be indicated on the score-board, from the commencement of an innings.

Restriction on Placement of Fieldsmen

At the instant of delivery, a minimum of four fieldsmen (plus the bowler and wicket-keeper) must be within an area bounded by two semi-circles centred on each middle stump (each with a radius of 30 yards) and joined by a parallel line on each side of the pitch. In the event of an infringement, the square-leg umpire shall call "No-ball".

Declarations

Law 14 will not apply in this competition. The captain of the batting side may not declare his innings closed at any time during the course of a match.

Mode of Delivery

Law 24.1 applies, except that no bowler may deliver the ball underarm.

Wide Ball – Judging a Wide

Umpires are instructed to apply a very strict and consistent interpretation in regard to Law 25.1 in order to prevent negative bowling wide of the wicket or over the batsman's head.

The following criteria should be adopted as a guide to umpires:

(a) If the ball passes either side of the wicket sufficiently wide to make it virtually impossible for the striker to play a "normal cricket stroke" both from where he is standing and from where he should normally be standing at the crease, the umpire should call and signal "Wide".
(b) If the ball passes over head height of the striker standing upright at the crease, the umpire should call and signal "Wide".

Note: The above provisions do not apply if the striker makes contact with the ball, or if it passes below head height between the striker and the wicket.

The Result

(a) *Unfinished Match*

If a match remains unfinished after the last scheduled day for play, the winner will be the side which has scored the faster in runs per over throughout the innings, provided that at least twenty overs have been bowled at the side batting second. If the scoring-rate is the same, the side losing the lesser number of wickets in the first twenty overs of each innings will be the winner.

If, however, at any time on the last day, the umpires are satisfied that there is insufficient time remaining to achieve a definite result or, where applicable, for the team batting second to complete its 55 overs, they shall order a new match to be started, allowing an equal number of overs per side (minimum ten overs each side), bearing in mind the time remaining for play until 7.30 p.m. In this event, team selection for the new match will be restricted to the eleven players and twelfth man originally chosen unless authorised otherwise in advance by the Secretary of the TCCB.

If it is impossible to achieve a result in a group league match, it shall be declared "No result".

In the event of no result being obtained within this rule in a knockout match, and the captains are unable to reach agreement on an alternative method of achieving a result to the match, it shall be decided by the toss of a coin.

(b) *A Tie*

In the event of a tie, the following shall apply:

(a) The side taking the greater number of wickets shall be the winner.
(b) If both sides are all out, the side with the higher overall scoring-rate shall be the winner.
(c) If the result cannot be decided by (a) or (b), the winner shall be the side with the higher score (i) after thirty overs, or if still equal (ii) after twenty overs, or if still equal (iii) after ten overs.

Points Scoring Systems for Group League Matches

(a) The team winning the match to score two points.

(b) In a "No result" match, each team to score one point.

(c) In the event of two or more teams in any group having an equal number of points, their positions in the table shall be based on the faster rate of taking wickets in all group league matches (to be calculated by total balls bowled, divided by wickets taken).

ERRATA IN WISDEN, 1982

Page 301	A. R. Butcher's 116 for Surrey v Kent was at Folkestone.
Page 305	N. A. Mallender's six for 37 for Northamptonshire v Yorkshire was at Wellingborough.
Page 736	In the John Player League match, Gloucestershire v Yorkshire, M. Johnson was in the Yorkshire team; not C. Johnson.
Page 935	In Pakistan's second innings, Sadiq Mohammad was lbw b Croft; not Clarke. In the Pakistan innings, the bowling figures should be as follows: First innings: Clarke 22–3–69–0 (not 68–0); Croft 28–4–91–3 (not 89–3); Marshall 22.4–4–88–3 (not 91–3). Second innings: Clarke 12–2–26–2 (not 3); Croft 20–7–37–1 (not 38–0); Richards 11–4–19–2 (not 20–2).
Page 941	The opening paragraph of the match report on the fourth Test states that the start of play was delayed by the late arrival of an umpire. This is incorrect. Such a delay occurred at the start of play on the fourth day of the third Test at Karachi.
Page 964	In New Zealand's first innings, there were 17 leg-byes (not 18) and 17 no-balls (not 16); in the second innings, there were 10 leg-byes (not 9) and 2 no-balls (not 3).
Page 966	In India's innings, Hadlee bowled 33 overs (not 23) and Troup bowled 6 maidens (not 5). In New Zealand's innings, there were 6 byes (not 4) and 8 leg-byes (not 10). Doshi bowled 49 over (not 69).
Page 967	In India's second innings, Snedden conceded 40 runs (not 41) and Cairns bowled 35.5 overs (not 34.4) and conceded 47 runs (not 46).
Page 968	In New Zealand's first innings, there were 14 byes (not 15) and 7 no-balls (not 6). Shastri bowled 56 overs (not 55)
Page 1209	Jack Redman should read Jim Redman. He was christened James.
Page 1260	*Totteridge Cricket Club 1881-1981* was "put together" by Ken Hughes, the club's Hon. Secretary; not Ken Green as stated.

John Player
League
Every Sunday
8th May–11th September
THE
JOHN
PLAYER
LEAGUE
DANGER: Government Health WARNING:
CIGARETTES CAN SERIOUSLY DAMAGE YOUR HEALTH

JOHN PLAYER LEAGUE, 1982

Sussex won the John Player League for the first time, and in doing so established records for the highest number of wins (14) and most points (58). The record for wins had been held by Lancashire (1970), Hampshire (1975) and Leicestershire (1977), while Leicestershire's 54 points in 1974 were the previous highest. In addition Sussex suffered only one defeat; to Worcestershire in June.

They had been unbeaten at the end of May, along with Kent and Middlesex, but a month later Middlesex had moved six points clear. On July 25, when Derbyshire and defending champions Essex moved alongside Kent into third place, Middlesex lost for the second successive week and Sussex, with a game in hand, took up the running. (They had also led in 1981 before falling away badly in August.) They began August six points ahead of their London rivals, and at the end of the month they made sure of the title when their defeat of Middlesex took them twelve points clear with only two games to be played.

Middlesex held second place without undue trouble, but the struggle for third and fourth places continued until the final Sunday, when Leicestershire beat Kent to leapfrog over them and Nottinghamshire. Nottinghamshire's defeat by Sussex left them out of the money after they had made steady progress following a poor start. For the first time in the competition, prize-money was awarded for fourth place. Another innovation was the use of fielding circles, as in the other limited-overs competitions, to discourage defensive tactics. One result of this was that 541 6s were hit, bettering the previous record of 438 set in 1970.

A feature of the season was the prolific form of Leicestershire's David Gower, whose 669 runs (average 95.57) included three hundreds and three fifties in nine innings. But for his absence on Test duty, he might have

FINAL TABLE

		P	*W*	*L*	*T*	*NR*	*Pts*	*6s*	*4w*
1	Sussex (5)	16	14	1	0	1	58	50	4
2	Middlesex (15)	16	11	4	0	1	46	22	6
3	Leicestershire (14)	16	9	6	0	1	38	17	6
4	Kent (7)	16	9	7	0	0	36	17	3
5	Essex (1)	16	9	7	0	0	36	43	2
5	Hampshire (6)	16	8	6	2	0	36	29	3
5	Nottinghamshire (10)	16	8	6	1	1	36	34	2
8	Northamptonshire (17)	16	8	7	0	1	34	54	2
9	Somerset (2)	16	8	8	0	0	32	54	5
10	Glamorgan (10)	16	6	7	0	3	30	14	2
10	Lancashire (10)	16	6	7	1	2	30	28	4
12	Derbyshire (4)	16	6	9	0	1	26	26	3
12	Surrey (7)	16	6	9	1	0	26	44	3
14	Gloucestershire (16)	16	5	9	0	2	24	9	1
15	Worcestershire (10)	16	5	10	0	1	22	36	2
16	Yorkshire (7)	16	3	10	1	2	18	38	1
17	Warwickshire (3)	16	3	11	0	2	16	26	1

1981 positions in brackets.

Kent finished in fourth place over Essex, Hampshire and Nottinghamshire by virtue of their greater number of away wins. This criteria applied only for the first four placings.

approached the record aggregate of 814 runs, by Clive Rice in 1977. The Nottinghamshire captain again scored the most runs in the League, 692 from sixteen games, while Ken McEwan of Essex was the only other to top 600 runs. Peter Denning of Somerset and Northamptonshire's Wayne Larkins both passed the 500 mark, Larkins's 158 against Worcestershire being the season's highest score.

No Sussex batsman featured in the top twenty in the League averages, which underlined their overall batting strength, but their South African fast bowler, Garth le Roux, was the season's most economical wicket-taker (29 wickets at 13.65 each). He was followed by Norbert Phillip of Essex (32 at 14.00) and Somerset's Joel Garner (16 at 14.43). Tony Pigott added to Sussex's firepower by claiming 28 wickets. Phillip returned the best figures of the season with six for 13 against Lancashire.

CHAMPIONS: 1969-82

1969	Lancashire	1976	Kent
1970	Lancashire	1977	Leicestershire
1971	Worcestershire	1978	Hampshire
1972	Kent	1979	Somerset
1973	Kent	1980	Warwickshire
1974	Leicestershire	1981	Essex
1975	Hampshire	1982	Sussex

DISTRIBUTION OF PRIZE-MONEY

The total prize-money was £56,000.

£12,000 and John Player Trophy: SUSSEX.
£5,500 to runners-up: MIDDLESEX.
£2,500 to third placing: LEICESTERSHIRE.
£1,300 to fourth placing: KENT.
£250 each match to the winners – shared if tied or no result: 124 wins, 3 ties, 9 no results.

Batting award: £350 to W. Larkins (Northamptonshire) who hit seventeen 6s in the season.

Other leading 6-hitters:

16 – I. T. Botham (Somerset), A. J. Lamb (Northamptonshire).
15 – K. S. McEwan (Essex), C. E. B. Rice (Nottinghamshire).
14 – G. S. le Roux (Sussex).
12 – C. H. Lloyd (Lancashire).
11 – P. W. G. Parker (Sussex), I. V. A. Richards (Somerset), J. G. Wright (Derbyshire).
10 – T. E. Jesty (Hampshire), M. A. Lynch (Surrey).
9 – C. G. Greenidge (Hampshire).
8 – G. A. Gooch (Essex).

Fastest televised match fifty

38 balls – M. W. Gatting, Middlesex v Somerset, Weston-super-Mare, August 8.

Bowling award: £350 to G. J. Parsons (Leicestershire) who took four wickets or more in an innings on three occasions.

Other bowlers to take four wickets or more in an innings were:

2 – P. B. Clift (Leicestershire), J. E. Emburey (Middlesex), K. B. S. Jarvis (Kent), I. R. Payne (Surrey), N. Phillip (Essex), A. C. S. Pigott (Sussex), M. W. W. Selvey (Middlesex), B. Wood (Derbyshire).

1 – P. Bainbridge (Gloucestershire), I. T. Botham (Somerset), D. J. Capel (Northamptonshire), N. G. Cowans (Middlesex), C. E. H. Croft (Lancashire), W. W. Daniel (Middlesex), W. W. Davis (Glamorgan), C. H. Dredge (Somerset), K. St J. D. Emery (Hampshire), J. Garner (Somerset), I. A. Greig (Sussex), E. E. Hemmings (Nottinghamshire), N. J. B. Illingworth (Nottinghamshire), T. E. Jesty (Hampshire), T. M. Lamb (Northamptonshire), G. S. le Roux (Sussex), C. Lethbridge (Warwickshire), L. L. McFarlane (Lancashire), K. S. Mackintosh (Surrey), M. D. Marshall (Hampshire), H. R. Moseley (Somerset), S. Oldham (Derbyshire), R. C. Ontong (Glamorgan), D. N. Patel (Worcestershire), S. P. Perryman (Worcestershire), B. W. Reidy (Lancashire), I. V. A. Richards (Somerset), J. Simmons (Lancashire), J. F. Steele (Leicestershire), S. Stuchbury (Yorkshire), D. L. Underwood (Kent).

DERBYSHIRE

At Leicester, May 9. DERBYSHIRE lost to LEICESTERSHIRE by 67 runs.

DERBYSHIRE v ESSEX

At Derby, May 16. Derbyshire won by four wickets. Wood's remarkable bowling, on a pitch which assisted the bowlers, had Essex in trouble after they had been put in, and it required a stand of 65 between East and Lever for a respectable total. With Kirsten taking command, Derbyshire were seldom in danger.

Essex

G. A. Gooch b Tunnicliffe	10
B. R. Hardie c Oldham b Wood	32
K. S. McEwan c Miller b Wood	28
*K. W. R. Fletcher b Oldham	7
N. Phillip c Miller b Oldham	2
A. W. Lilley st Taylor b Wood	9
K. R. Pont c Taylor b Oldham	0
S. Turner b Wood	1
†D. E. East run out	43
J. K. Lever not out	15
L-b 8, n-b 5	13
1/18 2/70 3/79 4/84 5/94 6/94 7/95 8/95 9/160 (9 wkts, 40 overs)	160

N. A. Foster did not bat.

Bowling: Oldham 8–1–23–3; Tunnicliffe 8–0–46–1; Newman 8–0–35–0; Hacker 4–0–22–0; Wood 8–2–8–4; Miller 4–0–13–0.

Derbyshire

J. G. Wright c D. E. East b Phillip	7
J. H. Hampshire b Phillip	2
P. N. Kirsten c Fletcher b Phillip	72
G. Miller c D. E. East b Foster	32
K. J. Barnett run out	26
*B. Wood c Gooch b Lever	1
C. J. Tunnicliffe not out	3
†R. W. Taylor not out	1
L-b 4, w 10, n-b 3	17
1/11 2/12 3/76 4/156 5/157 6/157 (6 wkts, 38.5 overs)	161

P. G. Newman, S. Oldham and P. J. Hacker did not bat.

Bowling: Lever 7.5–0–39–1; Phillip 7–0–21–3; Turner 8–0–38–0; Foster 8–1–24–1; Gooch 8–2–22–0.

Umpires: K. Ibadulla and B. J. Meyer.

At Taunton, May 23. DERBYSHIRE beat SOMERSET by seven wickets.

DERBYSHIRE v WARWICKSHIRE

At Chesterfield, May 30. Derbyshire won by seven wickets. Wood again won the toss and, following his customary tactics, put Warwickshire in. The pitch was good but only Asif Din showed the necessary application. With Wright, Hampshire and Kirsten in good form, it seemed that Derbyshire would cruise home. But they lost their rhythm and only two balls remained when Barnett hit the winning runs.

Warwickshire

D. L. Amiss c Wood b Newman	10	C. Lethbridge not out	20
T. A. Lloyd b Wood	10	G. C. Small not out	7
A. I. Kallicharran c Miller b Tunnicliffe	21		
*G. W. Humpage c Taylor b Miller	27	B 1, l-b 9, w 3	13
K. D. Smith c and b Miller	20		—
Asif Din c and b Newman	43	1/22 2/39 3/73 (7 wkts, 40 overs)	183
P. A. Smith c Miller b Wood	12	4/98 5/100 6/119 7/174	

*R. G. D. Willis and J. Cumbes did not bat.

Bowling: Newman 8–1–40–2; Oldham 8–2–23–0; Wood 8–0–46–2; Miller 8–1–23–2; Tunnicliffe 8–0–38–1.

Derbyshire

J. G. Wright b Kallicharran	43	K. J. Barnett not out	17
J. H. Hampshire c Amiss b P. A. Smith	79	B 1, l-b 4, w 3	8
P. N. Kirsten c Willis b P. A. Smith	28		—
G. Miller not out	12	1/98 2/154 3/159 (3 wkts, 39.4 overs)	187

*B. Wood, †R. W. Taylor, C. J. Tunnicliffe, P. G. Newman, S. Oldham and R. J. Finney did not bat.

Bowling: Willis 8–1–39–0; Small 8–1–30–0; Cumbes 3–0–17–0; Lethbridge 8–0–36–0; Kallicharran 7–0–36–1; P. A. Smith 5.4–0–21–2.

Umpires: D. G. L. Evans and A. G. T. Whitehead.

At Worcester, June 6. DERBYSHIRE beat WORCESTERSHIRE by eight wickets.

At Portsmouth, June 13. DERBYSHIRE lost to HAMPSHIRE by one wicket.

At Canterbury, June 20. DERBYSHIRE lost to KENT by 7 runs.

DERBYSHIRE v YORKSHIRE

At Derby, June 27. Yorkshire won by 19 runs. Illingworth registered his first victory after taking over the Yorkshire captaincy at the age of 50; at the other end of the scale, Jarvis, two days short of his seventeenth birthday, performed the hat-trick. Yorkshire, put in, did not make the most of an excellent opening partnership, but Derbyshire's batting was even more disappointing.

Yorkshire

C. W. J. Athey c Fowler b Oldham	76	S. N. Hartley not out	3
G. Boycott c Wood b Fowler	54		
J. D. Love c Kirsten b Wood	3	B 4, l-b 16, w 5	25
†D. L. Bairstow not out	17		—
C. M. Old b Oldham	6	1/123 2/131 3/144 (5 wkts, 40 overs)	202
G. B. Stevenson c Oldham b Tunnicliffe	18	4/150 5/188	

P. W. Jarvis, P. Carrick, *R. Illingworth and S. J. Dennis did not bat.

Bowling: Newman 8–1–34–0; Tunnicliffe 8–1–23–1; Wood 8–0–33–1; Kirsten 4–0–27–0; Oldham 8–0–38–2; Fowler 4–0–22–1.

Derbyshire

J. G. Wright c Hartley b Illingworth	31	†B. J. M. Maher b Jarvis	0
A. Hill run out	19	P. G. Newman not out	19
P. N. Kirsten c Athey b Stevenson	44	S. Oldham not out	10
C. J. Tunnicliffe run out	5	L-b 2	2
J. H. Hampshire b Illingworth	12		
*B. Wood c Athey b Stevenson	31	1/44 2/63 3/71 (9 wkts, 40 overs)	183
K. J. Barnett b Jarvis	10	4/94 5/134 6/154	
W. P. Fowler b Jarvis	0	7/154 8/154 9/154	

Bowling: Old 6–0–16–0; Dennis 4–0–31–0; Jarvis 8–0–39–3; Carrick 8–0–29–0; Illingworth 8–0–36–2; Stevenson 6–0–30–2.

Umpires: P. J. Eele and N. T. Plews.

DERBYSHIRE v LANCASHIRE

At Derby, July 4. Derbyshire won on faster scoring-rate. Barnett, opening with Wright, hit his maiden century in an exciting exhibition against Lancashire's erratic attack. Rain during the interval caused Lancashire's target to be amended to 186 from 33 overs, but they had no answer to Oldham in his best Sunday League performance.

Derbyshire

J. G. Wright c sub b Simmons	61	W. P. Fowler b McFarlane	0
K. J. Barnett run out	111	B 4, l-b 5, n-b 2	11
*P. N. Kirsten b McFarlane	30		
J. H. Hampshire not out	11	1/132 2/197 3/220 (5 wkts, 40 overs)	225
G. Miller run out	1	4/225 5/225	

I. S. Anderson, †R. W. Taylor, P. G. Newman, P. J. Hacker and S. Oldham did not bat.

Bowling: Allott 8–0–25–0; McFarlane 8–0–33–2; Croft 8–0–60–0; Folley 7–0–53–0; Simmons 8–0–35–1; Kennedy 1–0–8–0.

Lancashire

*C. H. Lloyd lbw b Hacker	5	I. Folley not out	5
G. Fowler b Oldham	31	L. L. McFarlane c Fowler b Hacker	2
†C. Maynard c Wright b Oldham	28	A. Kennedy absent hurt	
D. Lloyd run out	7	B 1, l-b 13, w 3, n-b 1	18
D. P. Hughes b Oldham	0		
J. Simmons b Oldham	0	1/15 2/58 3/77 (27.5 overs)	122
P. J. W. Allott st Taylor b Miller	14	4/77 5/78 6/79	
C. E. H. Croft b Oldham	12	7/111 8/114 9/122	

Bowling: Newman 6–0–19–0; Hacker 5.5–1–17–2; Miller 8–1–31–1; Oldham 8–1–37–5.

Umpires: D. Archer and B. J. Meyer.

At Lord's, July 18. DERBYSHIRE beat MIDDLESEX by seven wickets.

DERBYSHIRE v SURREY

At Derby, August 1. Surrey won by 56 runs. Roope batted through Surrey's innings and the scoring-rate was lifted by shrewd hitting from Knight and Needham. Derbyshire could not recover after losing three wickets in successive overs, and Payne took five wickets for the first time in this competition.

Surrey

A. R. Butcher c Maher b Finney	26
G. R. J. Roope not out	74
D. M. Smith c Moir b Finney	10
M. A. Lynch st Maher b Wood	10
*R. D. V. Knight c Anderson b Wood	31
D. J. Thomas lbw b Wood	0
†C. J. Richards b Newman	5
A. Needham c Kirsten b Oldham	25
B 2, l-b 15, w 7	24
1/43 2/67 3/90 4/151 5/152 6/169 7/205 (7 wkts, 40 overs)	205

K. S. Mackintosh, G. Monkhouse and I. R. Payne did not bat.

Bowling: Newman 8–0–36–1; Oldham 8–1–41–1; Finney 4–0–22–2; Kirsten 4–0–13–0; Moir 8–3–34–0; Wood 8–0–35–3.

Derbyshire

K. J. Barnett c Payne b Mackintosh	12
J. G. Wright c Richards b Monkhouse	19
P. N. Kirsten b Payne	43
J. H. Hampshire c Richards b Monkhouse	4
*B. Wood lbw b Payne	29
I. S. Anderson b Payne	20
R. J. Finney c Monkhouse b Knight	7
P. G. Newman c Roope b Payne	2
†B. J. M. Maher c Butcher b Payne	0
D. G. Moir c Butcher b Mackintosh	0
S. Oldham not out	4
B 1, l-b 5, w 2, n-b 1	9
1/33 2/37 3/42 4/108 5/119 6/140 7/142 8/142 9/143 (37.2 overs)	149

Bowling: Monkhouse 8–0–29–2; Thomas 4–0–16–0; Mackintosh 5–0–15–2; Needham 6–0–27–0; Knight 8–0–32–1; Payne 6.2–0–21–5.

Umpires: J. Birkenshaw and J. van Geloven.

At Milton Keynes, August 15. DERBYSHIRE lost to NORTHAMPTONSHIRE by five wickets.

DERBYSHIRE v SUSSEX

At Chesterfield, August 22. Sussex won by three wickets. Rain restricted the match to 28 overs each and, after good batting by Wood, Sussex had to score at 5.4 an over. Colin Wells drove effectively before falling to a fine return catch and Sussex won with three balls to spare. This left them needing one more victory to take the title.

Derbyshire

K. J. Barnett c Gould b le Roux	5
J. G. Wright c Gould b C. M. Wells	16
P. N. Kirsten c Phillipson b Greig	3
G. Miller c Greig b Barclay	27
*B. Wood c Waller b le Roux	41
I. S. Anderson c and b Pigott	28
C. J. Tunnicliffe c Gould b le Roux	10
R. J. Finney run out	10
†R. W. Taylor not out	0
L-b 10, w 1	11
1/15 2/24 3/29 4/70 5/131 6/131 7/150 8/151 (8 wkts, 28 overs)	151

P. G. Newman and S. Oldham did not bat.

Bowling: Pigott 5–0–27–1; le Roux 6–0–33–3; Greig 6–0–32–1; C. M. Wells 6–1–20–1; Barclay 5–0–28–1.

Sussex

G. D. Mendis c Miller b Tunnicliffe	26	*J. R. T. Barclay not out	7
†I. J. Gould c Taylor b Oldham	16	A. P. Wells not out	4
C. M. Wells c and b Newman	57	B 4, l-b 9, w 1, n-b 1	15
P. W. G. Parker c Finney b Oldham	9		
G. S. le Roux c Barnett b Oldham	0	1/27 2/72 3/113 (7 wkts, 27.3 overs)	155
C. P. Phillipson c Finney b Wood	11	4/113 5/118	
I. A. Greig b Wood	10	6/132 7/145	

C. E. Waller and A. C. S. Pigott did not bat.

Bowling: Newman 6–0–25–1; Oldham 6–0–23–3; Tunnicliffe 6–0–31–1; Wood 5–0–27–2; Miller 4.3–0–34–0.

Umpires: W. L. Budd and R. Palmer.

At Nottingham, August 29. DERBYSHIRE lost to NOTTINGHAMSHIRE by six wickets.

DERBYSHIRE v GLOUCESTERSHIRE

At Derby, September 5. No result.

DERBYSHIRE v GLAMORGAN

At Derby, September 12. Glamorgan won by four wickets. Derbyshire, put in, struggled against Nash and Davis before Wood joined Barnett to improve the scoring-rate. Alan Jones and Rowe, with his highest Sunday score since leaving Kent, pointed Glamorgan towards their first Sunday League victory in Derbyshire, despite the loss of three wickets in successive overs.

Derbyshire

K. J. Barnett run out	66	†R. W. Taylor c E. W. Jones b Ontong	0
J. G. Wright c E. W. Jones b Davis	1	D. G. Moir c E. W. Jones b Davis	4
P. N. Kirsten lbw b Davis	0	S. Oldham st E. W. Jones b Ontong	0
I. S. Anderson run out	5	L-b 5, w 5, n-b 10	20
G. Miller c Nash b Ontong	10		
C. J. Tunnicliffe c Davis b Barwick	7	1/5 2/7 3/29 (38.2 overs)	180
*B. Wood not out	50	4/50 5/69 6/139	
P. G. Newman b Davis	17	7/167 8/174 9/180	

Bowling: Nash 8–3–12–0; Davis 7–2–24–4; Barwick 8–0–39–1; Ontong 7.2–0–54–3; Lloyd 8–0–31–0.

Glamorgan

A. Jones c Kirsten b Miller	55	†E. W. Jones not out	22
A. L. Jones c Wright b Newman	8	*B. J. Lloyd not out	2
C. J. C. Rowe c Wood b Newman	61	B 1, l-b 6, w 1	8
R. C. Ontong b Kirsten	14		
D. A. Francis run out	6	1/29 2/105 3/130 (6 wkts, 38.2 overs)	182
J. A. Hopkins c Wright b Wood	6	4/146 5/149 6/161	

S. R. Barwick, M. A. Nash and W. W. Davis did not bat.

Bowling: Newman 7.2–0–33–2; Tunnicliffe 3–0–18–0; Moir 8–0–29–0; Oldham 4–0–30–0; Miller 8–1–20–1; Wood 6–0–38–1; Kirsten 2–1–6–1.

Umpires: B. Leadbeater and J. van Geloven.

ESSEX

At Hove, May 9. ESSEX lost to SUSSEX by five wickets.

At Derby, May 16. ESSEX lost to DERBYSHIRE by four wickets.

ESSEX v HAMPSHIRE

At Chelmsford, May 23. Hampshire won on faster scoring-rate. Stoppages were frequent, but Greenidge brightened the gloom with a powerfully struck 64 containing a 6 and five 4s. Given a target of 101 in 23 overs, Essex lost Gooch in Marshall's opening over, and Fletcher was just getting into his stride when further rain stopped play.

Hampshire

C. G. Greenidge c Hardie b Turner	64	R. E. Hayward not out	6
J. M. Rice b Lever	3	†R. J. Parks not out	4
M. C. J. Nicholas b Turner	10	B 1, l-b 4, w 3, n-b 1	9
N. G. Cowley c Smith b Phillip	19		
*T. E. Jesty b Foster	17	1/8 2/48 (7 wkts, 33 overs)	144
V. P. Terry c Fletcher b Lever	10	3/94 4/108	
M. D. Marshall c Hardie b Foster	2	5/122 6/124 7/137	

T. M. Tremlett and K. St J. D. Emery did not bat.

Bowling: Lever 8–2–26–2; Phillip 8–1–34–1; Turner 8–1–25–2; Foster 8–0–43–2; Gooch 1–0–7–0.

Essex

G. A. Gooch b Marshall	0	K. R. Pont not out	1
B. R. Hardie lbw b Marshall	14		
K. S. McEwan c Parks b Emery	7	L-b 3, w 4	7
*K. W. R. Fletcher not out	17		
N. Phillip c Parks b Jesty	3	1/2 2/20 3/32 (5 wkts, 15 overs)	52
A. W. Lilley b Jesty	3	4/37 5/43	

S. Turner, †N. Smith, N. A. Foster and J. K. Lever did not bat.

Bowling: Marshall 7–2–15–2; Emery 4–0–17–1; Jesty 3–0–11–2; Tremlett 1–0–2–0.

Umpires: J. Birkenshaw and J. van Geloven.

At Lord's, May 30. ESSEX lost to MIDDLESEX by 51 runs.

ESSEX v SOMERSET

At Chelmsford, June 6. Essex won by 1 run. This ten-overs-per-side affair took place only after supporters and the fire brigade had bailed out the ground. Their enterprise was rewarded with a thrilling tussle in doubt to the very last ball. Essex, at 88, lost five wickets in as many deliveries with Richards dismissing Phillip, McEwan and Fletcher for his hat-trick. Somerset began as if they would win with ease, even though Richards went in the same over as he struck Phillip for two 6s. However, Gooch and Pringle applied the brake, and Turner's direct hit from deep cover ran out Botham at a crucial stage.

Essex

G. A. Gooch c Richards b Popplewell	21	D. R. Pringle not out	2
B. R. Hardie c Dredge b Popplewell	11	†D. E. East lbw b Botham	0
S. Turner run out	18	J. K. Lever run out	1
A. W. Lilley b Richards	7	L-b 6, w 2	8
N. Phillip c Russom b Richards	10		
K. S. McEwan c Russom b Richards	14	1/31 2/37 3/62 (10 overs)	92
K. R. Pont b Botham	0	4/62 5/88 6/88	
*K. W. R. Fletcher b Richards	0	7/88 8/88 9/88	

Bowling: Botham 2–0–11–2; Dredge 2–0–19–0; Davis 2–0–19–0; Popplewell 2–0–26–2; Richards 2–0–9–4.

Somerset

I. V. A. Richards b Phillip	18	P. W. Denning run out	4
I. T. Botham run out	36	†D. J. S. Taylor not out	0
N. F. M. Popplewell c Fletcher b Turner	11	B 1, l-b 6, w 1, n-b 1	9
*B. C. Rose b Gooch	3		
V. J. Marks b Pringle	6	1/25 2/55 3/61 (6 wkts, 10 overs)	91
J. W. Lloyds not out	4	4/79 5/84 6/90	

N. Russom, C. H. Dredge and M. R. Davis did not bat.

Bowling: Lever 2–0–10–0; Phillip 2–0–26–1; Pringle 2–0–15–1; Gooch 2–0–12–1; Turner 2–0–19–1.

Umpires: D. J. Constant and C. Cook.

At Manchester, June 13. ESSEX beat LANCASHIRE by 82 runs.

ESSEX v WORCESTERSHIRE

At Ilford, June 20. Essex won by 109 runs. McEwan's sixth John Player League century took just 90 minutes, despite the slow pitch, and contained two 6s and six 4s. His partnership with Lilley, who hit four 6s off Gifford, brought 69 runs in only four overs. Worcestershire's hopes were destroyed by Pringle, who claimed a wicket in each of his opening three overs.

Essex

G. A. Gooch run out	23	S. Turner c Inchmore b Pridgeon	5
B. R. Hardie b Hemsley	45		
K. S. McEwan not out	105	L-b 5, w 2	7
N. Phillip c D'Oliveira b Inchmore	20		
*K. W. R. Fletcher c Weston b Gifford	6	1/41 2/123 3/158 (6 wkts, 40 overs)	247
A. W. Lilley c Inchmore b Gifford	36	4/170 5/239 6/247	

K. R. Pont, R. E. East, †D. E. East and D. R. Pringle did not bat.

Bowling: Pridgeon 8–0–62–1; Inchmore 8–0–33–1; Gifford 8–1–52–2; Weston 5–0–33–0; Patel 7–0–40–0; Hemsley 4–0–20–1.

Worcestershire

G. M. Turner lbw b Pringle	4	J. D. Inchmore c Gooch b Pont	30
J. A. Ormrod c D. E. East b Pringle	12	N. Gifford b Pont	6
D. N. Patel c D. E. East b Pringle	3	A. P. Pridgeon not out	0
E. J. O. Hemsley b R. E. East	16	L-b 3, w 1, n-b 1	5
*P. A. Neale c D. E. East b Phillip	1		
M. J. Weston lbw b Pont	51	1/5 2/13 3/22 (32 overs)	138
D. B. D'Oliveira c Phillip b R. E. East	6	4/23 5/49 6/63	
†D. J. Humphries c Phillip b R. E. East	4	7/73 8/125 9/134	

Bowling: Phillip 4–0–14–1; Pringle 4–0–11–3; Turner 4–1–12–0; R. E. East 8–0–17–3; Gooch 8–1–53–0; Pont 4–0–26–3.

Umpires: D. G. L. Evans and C. T. Spencer.

ESSEX v LEICESTERSHIRE

At Harlow, June 27. Essex won by 19 runs in a match reduced to 30 overs each. Essex, put in on a very wet pitch, were in dire straits at five for 28 after thirteen overs, but Phillip and Turner saved the day with 77 off fifteen overs. Phillip then displayed his ability with the ball, taking four for 11 in his six overs as Essex pocketed their fourth consecutive victory.

Essex

G. A. Gooch run out........................ 10
B. R. Hardie c Agnew b Parsons........ 2
K. S. McEwan c Agnew b Steele......... 10
*K. W. R. Fletcher c Garnham b Higgs 3
N. Phillip c Balderstone b Parsons...... 44
A. W. Lilley c Garnham b Higgs........ 0
S. Turner c Wenlock b Parsons.......... 35
K. R. Pont b Parsons........................ 4
†D. E. East not out.......................... 0
R. E. East not out............................ 0
B 1, l-b 4, w 1........................ 6

1/10 2/18 3/25 4/28 (8 wkts, 30 overs) 114
5/28 6/105 7/111 8/113

J. K. Lever did not bat.

Bowling: Taylor 6–1–26–0; Parsons 6–0–19–4; Higgs 6–1–12–2; Steele 6–1–8–1; Agnew 3–0–18–0; Balderstone 3–0–25–0.

Leicestershire

B. F. Davison b Gooch..................... 6
N. E. Briers lbw b R. E. East............ 3
*R. W. Tolchard run out.................. 0
†M. A. Garnham c Gooch b Phillip.... 39
J. C. Balderstone c D. E. East b Turner 18
J. F. Steele b Phillip......................... 4
G. J. Parsons c McEwan b Phillip....... 3
D. A. Wenlock c Lilley b Phillip........ 2
J. P. Agnew not out.......................... 3
L. B. Taylor not out......................... 0
B 4, l-b 6, w 7........................ 17

1/18 2/18 3/24 (8 wkts, 30 overs) 95
4/55 5/82 6/87 7/89 8/95

K. Higgs did not bat.

Bowling: Lever 6–1–9–0; Phillip 6–1–11–4; R. E. East 6–1–14–1; Gooch 6–0–17–1; Turner 6–0–27–1.

Umpires: W. E. Alley and P. B. Wight.

At Scarborough, July 11. ESSEX beat YORKSHIRE by five wickets.

ESSEX v SURREY

At Southend, July 18. Essex won by 31 runs. Phillip was the star of Essex's sixth successive Sunday win, hitting seven boundaries as he spearheaded a revival and later sending back Butcher and Knight in his opening three overs. Monkhouse underlined the virtues of line and length to have Essex struggling early on.

Essex

G. A. Gooch c Butcher b Monkhouse. 0
B. R. Hardie b Mackintosh............... 6
K. S. McEwan b Monkhouse............ 26
*K. W. R. Fletcher c Lynch
b Mackintosh. 7
N. Phillip c Needham b Mackintosh.... 56
K. R. Pont c Richards b Wilson......... 21
A. W. Lilley b Thomas..................... 22
S. Turner c Roope b Mackintosh........ 22
†D. E. East not out.......................... 16
R. E. East c Lynch b Wilson............. 0
J. K. Lever not out........................... 1
L-b 13, w 3, n-b 1................... 17

1/0 2/27 3/38 4/44 (9 wkts, 38 overs) 194
5/91 6/145 7/155 8/178 9/184

Bowling: Monkhouse 8–2–15–2; Wilson 7–0–41–2; Mackintosh 7–1–37–4; Thomas 8–0–39–1; Knight 4–0–25–0; Payne 4–0–20–0.

Surrey

A. R. Butcher b Phillip	0
A. Needham c Pont b Gooch	55
*R. D. V. Knight b Phillip	5
M. A. Lynch b Gooch	2
G. R. J. Roope c Hardie b R. E. East	18
*C. J. Richards b Turner	24
D. J. Thomas c R. E. East b Phillip	33
I. R. Payne b Lever	4
K. S. Mackintosh run out	1
G. Monkhouse not out	5
P. H. L. Wilson c Fletcher b Lever	0
L-b 8, w 4, n-b 4	16
1/2 2/14 3/22 4/69 5/108 6/115 7/133 8/155 9/163 (36.3 overs)	163

Bowling: Lever 7.3–1–22–2; Phillip 7–3–32–3; Gooch 7–0–43–2; Turner 7–2–30–1; R. E. East 8–1–20–1.

Umpires: D. O. Oslear and Khizar Hayat.

At Cardiff, August 1. ESSEX beat GLAMORGAN by 16 runs.

At Canterbury, August 8. ESSEX beat KENT by ten wickets.

At Cheltenham, August 15. ESSEX lost to GLOUCESTERSHIRE by 5 runs.

ESSEX v WARWICKSHIRE

At Colchester, August 22. Warwickshire won by four wickets with just three balls to spare, and in doing so they became the first side in the competition to top 300 when batting second. Smith and Lloyd gave them a tremendous start in just under twenty overs, and Humpage and Asif Din later added 94 in only nine overs. Earlier, McEwan had set an Essex record with his 156 not out (five 6s, seventeen 4s) in 106 minutes. His last 24 came in the final over from Ferreira, whose eight overs for 85 were the most expensive ever in a John Player League match.

Essex

G. A. Gooch lbw b Willis	10
B. R. Hardie c Humpage b Willis	75
K. S. McEwan not out	156
N. Phillip b Small	13
S. Turner b Lethbridge	16
*K. W. R. Fletcher not out	12
B 7, l-b 6, w 2, n-b 2	17
1/30 2/177 3/208 4/263 (4 wkts, 40 overs)	299

D. R. Pringle, K. R. Pont, †D. E. East, R. E. East and J. K. Lever did not bat.

Bowling: Willis 8–1–35–2; Small 8–0–43–1; Lethbridge 6–0–51–1; Ferreira 8–0–85–0; Kallicharran 8–0–52–0; Lloyd 2–0–16–0.

Warwickshire

K. D. Smith c and b Turner	73
T. A. Lloyd c Turner b Pringle	66
A. I. Kallicharran b Gooch	11
†G. W. Humpage c Pringle b Phillip	74
P. R. Oliver c Lever b Pringle	19
Asif Din b Lever	32
A. M. Ferreira not out	3
P. A. Smith not out	9
B 2, l-b 10, w 2	14
1/135 2/153 3/159 4/193 5/287 6/287 (6 wkts, 39.3 overs)	301

C. Lethbridge, G. C. Small and *R. G. D. Willis did not bat.

Bowling: Lever 8–0–66–1; Phillip 5.3–0–36–1; R. E. East 8–0–54–0; Turner 7–0–48–1; Pringle 7–0–50–2; Gooch 4–0–33–1.

Umpires: K. E. Palmer and P. J. Eele.

ESSEX v NOTTINGHAMSHIRE

At Chelmsford, September 5. Nottinghamshire won by seven wickets with nearly five overs to spare. Hassan and Robinson, with his best in the competition to date, launched them with an opening stand of 74 until the eighteenth over, and Rice made sure their good work was not wasted. An inspired spell by Hadlee had Essex struggling, and they never looked like achieving a winning total.

Essex

G. A. Gooch c French b Hadlee	18	K. R. Pont b Bore	1
B. R. Hardie lbw b Hadlee	19	S. Turner not out	18
K. S. McEwan not out	66	L-b 8	8
*K. W. R. Fletcher c Randall b Hadlee	12	1/32 2/41 3/69 (5 wkts, 39 overs)	159
N. Phillip b Bore	17	4/106 5/116	

D. R. Pringle, †D. E. East, R. E. East and J. K. Lever did not bat.

Bowling: Cooper 8–0–33–0; Bore 8–0–32–2; Hadlee 8–1–16–3; Saxelby 7–0–41–0; Hemmings 8–2–29–0.

Nottinghamshire

B. Hassan b Pringle	40	J. D. Birch not out	12
R. T. Robinson c Turner b Phillip	56	L-b 7, w 1, n-b 1	9
R. J. Hadlee run out	3		
*C. E. B. Rice not out	40	1/74 2/78 3/124 (3 wkts, 35.3 overs)	160

D. W. Randall, †B. N. French, E. E. Hemmings, K. Saxelby, K. E. Cooper and M. K. Bore did not bat.

Bowling: Lever 6–0–20–0; Phillip 8–0–23–1; R. E. East 8–0–35–0; Pringle 8–0–43–1; Turner 5.3–0–30–0.

Umpires: D. G. L. Evans and C. T. Spencer.

ESSEX v NORTHAMPTONSHIRE

At Chelmsford, September 12. Essex won by five wickets. A 6 by Pont off the first ball of the final over secured victory for Essex. Earlier, Gooch, Hardie and Fletcher had batted enterprisingly, but none could overshadow Allan Lamb, whose 93-minute 104 not out off 73 balls featured five 6s and eight 4s.

Northamptonshire

W. Larkins b R. E. East	8	D. J. Wild run out	0
P. Willey c Pont b Lever	0	T. M. Lamb run out	0
*G. Cook b R. E. East	21	N. A. Mallender not out	0
A. J. Lamb not out	104	B 2, l-b 9, w 7, n-b 1	19
R. G. Williams b Gooch	19		
R. J. Boyd-Moss c R. E. East b Gooch	4	1/0 2/25 3/60 (9 wkts, 40 overs)	189
D. J. Capel b Phillip	2	4/110 5/114 6/117	
†G. Sharp b Phillip	12	7/180 8/181 9/187	

Bowling: Lever 8–2–40–1; Phillip 7–1–16–2; R. E. East 8–0–25–2; Turner 4–0–20–0; Pringle 6–0–29–0; Gooch 7–0–40–2.

Essex

G. A. Gooch c Sharp b Wild............. 51
B. R. Hardie b Capel....................... 41
K. S. McEwan b Willey.................... 8
*K. W. R. Fletcher c Larkins
b T. M. Lamb. 46
N. Phillip b T. M. Lamb.................. 9
K. R. Pont not out.......................... 9
S. Turner not out............................ 16
B 1, l-b 10............................. 11

1/82 2/95 3/130 4/165 5/166 (5 wkts, 39.1 overs) 191

D. R. Pringle, †D. E. East, R. E. East and J. K. Lever did not bat.

Bowling: Mallender 7–0–35–0; T. M. Lamb 7.1–0–33–2; Williams 8–0–36–0; Willey 8–0–35–1; Wild 7–0–32–1; Capel 2–0–9–1.

Umpires: B. J. Meyer and N. T. Plews.

GLAMORGAN

At Manchester, May 9. GLAMORGAN lost to LANCASHIRE by seven wickets.

At Canterbury, May 16. GLAMORGAN lost to KENT by seven wickets.

GLAMORGAN v LEICESTERSHIRE

At Cardiff, May 23. No result. Put in to bat, Leicestershire opened with Gower, who had scored half their runs when a thunderstorm put an end to the match.

Leicestershire

D. I. Gower not out......................... 44
N. E. Briers c Davies b Cordle.......... 14
†M. A. Garnham c Miandad b Nash... 0
B. F. Davison c Davies b Barwick...... 22
*R. W. Tolchard not out.................. 0
L-b 5, w 3.............................. 8

1/28 2/31 3/88 (3 wkts, 25 overs) 88

J. C. Balderstone, P. B. Clift, J. F. Steele, D. A. Wenlock, G. J. Parsons and L. B. Taylor did not bat.

Bowling: Cordle 6–1–12–1; Nash 8–0–18–1; Ontong 6–0–25–0; Barwick 5–0–25–1.

Glamorgan

A. L. Jones, J. A. Hopkins, R. C. Ontong, *Javed Miandad, C. J. C. Rowe, A. E. Cordle, G. C. Holmes, †T. Davies, M. A. Nash, B. J. Lloyd, and S. R. Barwick.

Umpires: W. L. Budd and K. E. Palmer.

GLAMORGAN v SOMERSET

At Swansea, May 30. Somerset won by seven wickets. Glamorgan, put in, failed to build on a good start, 110 runs coming from 25 overs for the loss of two wickets. Denning guided Somerset to their first Sunday win of the season, which was hastened by Botham's lively 39 off 21 balls.

Glamorgan

J. A. Hopkins run out....................... 56
A. L. Jones run out.......................... 19
R. C. Ontong c Popplewell b Davis.... 24
*Javed Miandad c Botham b Dredge... 2
C. J. C. Rowe b Dredge.................... 19
G. C. Holmes lbw b Dredge............... 26
M. A. Nash c Botham b Dredge......... 17
S. A. B. Daniels not out.................... 1
L-b 17, w 4, n-b 1.................. 22

1/46 2/110 3/114 4/129 5/147 6/183 7/186 (7 wkts, 40 overs) 186

†T. Davies, B. J. Lloyd and S. R. Barwick did not bat.

Bowling: Botham 8–1–30–0; Moseley 8–0–29–0; Marks 8–0–30–0; Davis 8–0–43–1; Dredge 8–0–32–4.

Somerset

P. W. Denning not out	84	I. T. Botham not out	39
J. W. Lloyds c Ontong b Lloyd	29	B 2, l-b 3, w 1	6
I. V. A. Richards lbw Ontong	25		—
*B. C. Rose c Lloyd b Nash	4	1/60 2/112 3/133 (3 wkts, 34.5 overs)	187

M. R. Davis, N. F. M. Popplewell, V. J. Marks, †D. J. S. Taylor, C. H. Dredge and H. R. Moseley did not bat.

Bowling: Nash 8–1–42–1; Daniels 3–0–20–0; Barwick 6–0–33–0; Lloyd 8–0–28–1; Ontong 6.5–0–37–1; Rowe 3–0–21–0.

Umpires: A. Jepson and N. T. Plews.

At Bradford, June 6. YORKSHIRE v GLAMORGAN. No result.

At Hastings, June 20. GLAMORGAN lost to SUSSEX by 119 runs.

GLAMORGAN v GLOUCESTERSHIRE

At Ebbw Vale, June 27. No result.

GLAMORGAN v HAMPSHIRE

At Cardiff, July 11. Hampshire won by eight wickets. Glamorgan, still seeking their first League win of the season, were again beaten at home. They struggled through their own innings, and in the field they found Greenidge in majestic form, hitting three 6s and nine 4s.

Glamorgan

A. Jones st Parks b Tremlett	37	*B. J. Lloyd run out	17
J. A. Hopkins c Parks b Marshall	4	†E. W. Jones not out	1
A. L. Jones c Parks b Tremlett	48	B 5, l-b 12, w 3	20
M. J. Llewellyn c Marshall b Cowley	5		—
C. J. C. Rowe c Pocock b Tremlett	4	1/8 2/104 (8 wkts, 40 overs)	164
R. C. Ontong c Jesty b Emery	23	3/109 4/109 5/118	
M. A. Nash b Emery	5	6/130 7/162 8/163	

S. R. Barwick and W. W. Davis did not bat.

Bowling: Marshall 8–2–24–1; Emery 8–1–28–2; Jesty 8–0–38–0; Cowley 8–0–25–1; Tremlett 8–0–29–3.

Hampshire

C. G. Greenidge not out	92	L-b 2, w 4, n-b 3	9
J. M. Rice c and b Barwick	21		—
T. E. Jesty c Rowe b Barwick	12	1/69 2/83 (2 wkts, 38.5 overs)	165
M. C. J. Nicholas not out	31		

N. G. Cowley, *N. E. J. Pocock, R. E. Hayward, M. D. Marshall, †R. J. Parks, T. M. Tremlett and K. St J. D. Emery did not bat.

Bowling: Nash 8–1–25–0; Davis 7.5–1–30–0; Ontong 8–1–21–0; Lloyd 7–1–40–0; Barwick 8–0–40–2.

Umpires: D. J. Constant and P. J. Eele.

At Worcester, July 18. GLAMORGAN beat WORCESTERSHIRE by 1 run.

GLAMORGAN v MIDDLESEX

At Swansea, July 25. Glamorgan won by 39 runs. This was Glamorgan's best one-day performance at home during a disappointing season. Put in, they batted better than normally, but their total did not appear beyond the reach of Middlesex. However, the visitors found Glamorgan outstanding in the field, holding several near-impossible catches, and the winning margin was a handsome reward.

Glamorgan

A. Jones c Butcher b Merry	52	*B. J. Lloyd b Edmonds	12
A. L. Jones c Merry b Edmonds	30	J. G. Thomas not out	4
M. J. Llewellyn run out	18	B 9, l-b 18, w 3, n-b 1	31
D. A. Francis run out	3		
R. C. Ontong b Emburey	1	1/86 2/115 3/124 (6 wkts, 38 overs)	172
C. J. C. Rowe not out	21	4/124 5/128 6/150	

S. A. B. Daniels, †E. W. Jones and W. W. Davis did not bat.

Bowling: Selvey 7–1–25–0; Cowans 8–1–34–0; Merry 7–1–25–1; Edmonds 8–0–29–2; Emburey 8–0–28–1.

Middlesex

*J. M. Brearley c Daniels b Davis	9	M. W. W. Selvey not out	8
C. T. Radley c Francis b Daniels	31	N. G. Cowans b Lloyd	3
M. W. Gatting c and b Davis	0	W. G. Merry b Davis	13
†R. O. Butcher c Ontong b Thomas	16	B 4, l-b 4, w 2, n-b 1	11
K. P. Tomlins run out	13		
J. E. Emburey c Francis b Daniels	15	1/18 2/19 3/58 (35.4 overs)	133
W. N. Slack c Llewellyn b Lloyd	9	4/66 5/85 6/102	
P. H. Edmonds b Daniels	5	7/109 8/109 9/112	

Bowling: Davis 6.4–0–17–3; Thomas 8–0–26–1; Ontong 5–0–29–0; Daniels 8–0–32–3; Lloyd 8–2–18–2.

Umpires: D. J. Constant and K. Ibadulla.

GLAMORGAN v ESSEX

At Cardiff, August 1. Essex won by 16 runs. Batting first, Essex had scored only 91 from 31 overs, but their last nine overs saw them to 200, McEwan and Phillip saving the innings with a stand of 123 in 22 overs. Glamorgan's opening pair got them off to a good start but the later batsmen could not maintain the tempo.

Essex

G. A. Gooch c Rowe b Ontong	7	S. Turner not out	10
C. Gladwin c A. L. Jones b Thomas	0	†D. E. East not out	7
K. S. McEwan run out	68	B 1, l-b 4, w 2, n-b 6	13
*K. W. R. Fletcher b Ontong	7		
N. Phillip c Rowe b Ontong	84	1/4 2/17 3/34 (6 wkts, 40 overs)	200
K. R. Pont c and b Davis	4	4/157 5/161 6/191	

P. J. Prichard, R. E. East and J. K. Lever did not bat.

Bowling: Davis 8–3–36–1; Thomas 8–2–24–1; Ontong 8–0–24–3; Lloyd 8–2–35–0; Daniels 8–0–68–0.

Glamorgan

A. Jones c D. E. East b Phillip 55	*B. J. Lloyd c and b R. E. East 0
A. L. Jones c and b Turner 33	J. G. Thomas not out 15
D. A. Francis lbw b Gooch 5	B 2, l-b 16, w 2, n-b 3 23
R. C. Ontong c R. E. East b Lever..... 37	—
J. A. Hopkins st D. E. East b R. E. East. 2	1/57 2/77 3/137 (7 wkts, 40 overs) 184
C. J. C. Rowe b Phillip 14	4/153 5/153 6/158 7/184

S. A. B. Daniels, †E. W. Jones and W. W. Davis did not bat.

Bowling: Lever 8–1–34–1; Phillip 8–0–33–2; R. E. East 8–0–38–2; Turner 8–0–26–1; Gooch 8–0–30–1.

Umpires: D. R. Shepherd and A. G. T. Whitehead.

At Birmingham, August 8. GLAMORGAN beat WARWICKSHIRE by nine wickets.

GLAMORGAN v NOTTINGHAMSHIRE

At Swansea, August 22. Nottinghamshire won by nine wickets after winning the toss in a match reduced to ten overs a side. Rice and Birch hit freely in the rush for victory, which came with two balls to spare.

Glamorgan

A. Jones c Birch b Pont 29	R. C. Ontong not out 6
A. L. Jones b Hemmings 25	L-b 6 6
J. G. Thomas c Cooper b Hassan 1	—
J. A. Hopkins run out 5	
C. J. C. Rowe not out 17	1/59 2/59 3/63 4/71 (4 wkts, 10 overs) 89

M. A. Nash, *B. J. Lloyd, †E. W. Jones, S. R. Barwick and W. W. Davis did not bat.

Bowling: Saxelby 2–0–14–0; Pont 2–0–16–1; Hemmings 2–0–16–1; Cooper 2–0–16–0; Hassan 2–0–21–1.

Nottinghamshire

*C. E. B. Rice not out 46
R. J. Hadlee lbw b Ontong 4
J. D. Birch not out 29
B 4, l-b 6, n-b 1 11

—

1/11 (1 wkt, 9.4 overs) 90

R. T. Robinson, D. W. Randall, B. Hassan, E. E. Hemmings, †B. N. French, K. Saxelby, I. L. Pont and K. E. Cooper did not bat.

Bowling: Ontong 1.4–0–15–1; Nash 2–0–18–0; Barwick 2–0–14–0; Thomas 1–0–13–0; Davis 2–0–12–0; Lloyd 1–0–7–0.

Umpires: C. T. Spencer and D. O. Oslear.

At The Oval, August 29. GLAMORGAN beat SURREY by eight wickets.

GLAMORGAN v NORTHAMPTONSHIRE

At Abergavenny, September 5. Glamorgan won on faster scoring-rate. A splendid century by Ontong took Glamorgan to their fifth Sunday win in seven matches, after they had been put in. Rain interrupted Northamptonshire's innings at 95 for four, and their target was adjusted to 178 off 31 overs – in effect, 83 off eight remaining overs.

Glamorgan

A. Jones c Boyd-Moss b T. M. Lamb	2	*B. J. Lloyd not out	13
A. L. Jones c Sharp b Willey	14	†E. W. Jones not out	6
D. A. Francis run out	36	L-b 14, w 5, n-b 1	20
R. C. Ontong c Cook b Mallender	100		
J. A. Hopkins c Sharp b Mallender	17	1/8 2/29 (7 wkts, 40 overs)	229
J. G. Thomas b Capel	5	3/97 4/144 5/160	
C. J. C. Rowe b Capel	16	6/182 7/220	

M. A. Nash and W. W. Davis did not bat.

Bowling: Mallender 8–0–56–2; T. M. Lamb 8–3–20–1; Willey 6–0–35–1; Wild 8–0–35–0; Capel 8–0–39–2; Larkins 2–0–24–0.

Northamptonshire

W. Larkins lbw b Davis	4	D. J. Capel run out	9
P. Willey c Rowe b Nash	4	D. J. Wild not out	0
A. J. Lamb c Francis b Nash	25	B 4, l-b 2, w 1, n-b 4	11
G. Cook c A. L. Jones b Ontong	29		
R. G. Williams c E. W. Jones b Ontong	42	1/8 2/8 (7 wkts, 31 overs)	153
R. J. Boyd-Moss run out	15	3/48 4/91 5/112	
†G. Sharp not out	14	6/137 7/153	

T. M. Lamb and N. A. Mallender did not bat.

Bowling: Nash 8–1–21–2; Davis 8–0–41–1; Thomas 3–0–24–0; Ontong 8–0–39–2; Lloyd 4–0–17–0.

Umpires: D. R. Shepherd and A. G. T. Whitehead.

At Derby, September 12. GLAMORGAN beat DERBYSHIRE by four wickets.

GLOUCESTERSHIRE

GLOUCESTERSHIRE v MIDDLESEX

At Bristol, May 9. Middlesex won by 20 runs. Their win looked improbable at 51 for six, but Radley and Edmonds rescued them with a partnership of 90. Radley's unbeaten century, achieved in the final over, took him past 5,000 runs in the competition. Although Broad and Zaheer flourished briefly, Gloucestershire could not break the grip imposed by tight bowling and alert fielding.

Middlesex

*J. M. Brearley run out	10	P. H. Edmonds c Stovold b Shepherd	33
W. N. Slack c Brassington b Shepherd	0	*P. R. Downton not out	7
M. W. Gatting b Surridge	0		
R. O. Butcher lbw b Shepherd	7		
C. T. Radley not out	107	B 1, l-b 6, w 2	9
G. D. Barlow b Bainbridge	7		
J. E. Emburey st Brassington b Graveney	4	1/6 2/6 3/14 (7 wkts, 40 overs)	184
		4/18 5/34 6/51 7/141	

W. G. Merry and W. W. Daniel did not bat.

Bowling: Surridge 8–0–30–1; Shepherd 8–0–49–3; Bainbridge 8–0–27–1; Graveney 8–1–33–1; Childs 8–0–36–0.

Gloucestershire

A. W. Stovold run out	1	†A. J. Brassington not out	11
B. C. Broad b Slack	43	J. H. Childs run out	2
Zaheer Abbas c Barlow b Edmonds	23	D. Surridge run out	1
Sadiq Mohammad c Daniel b Slack	7	L-b 10, n-b 8	18
J. N. Shepherd run out	3		—
P. Bainbridge st Downton b Edmonds	19	1/8 2/52 3/78 (39.2 overs)	164
A. J. Hignell c and b Edmonds	17	4/82 5/91 6/123	
*D. A. Graveney b Merry	19	7/129 8/154 9/156	

Bowling: Daniel 8–2–18–0; Merry 5.2–1–29–1; Edmonds 8–0–33–3; Emburey 8–0–25–0; Gatting 2–0–9–0; Slack 8–0–32–2.

Umpires: P. J. Eele and K. E. Palmer.

At Manchester, May 16. GLOUCESTERSHIRE lost to LANCASHIRE by 106 runs.

GLOUCESTERSHIRE v WORCESTERSHIRE

At Bristol, May 23. Gloucestershire won on faster scoring-rate after their target had twice been adjusted because of rain. They were eventually asked to make 128 in 24 overs. Broad followed up his unexpected bowling success by making a punishing half-century. When 10, Turner became the first player to reach 6,000 runs in the Sunday League, and his century opening partnership with Ormrod was the basis of Worcestershire's score.

Worcestershire

G. M. Turner c Shepherd b Broad	73	*P. A. Neale run out	21
J. A. Ormrod c Graveney b Broad	46	†D. J. Humphries not out	12
Younis Ahmed c Graveney b Bainbridge	25	L-b 5, w 1, n-b 1	7
E. J. O. Hemsley c M. W. Stovold b Broad	15	1/102 2/148 3/154 (6 wkts, 38 overs)	202
D. N. Patel c Bainbridge b Childs	3	4/168 5/170 6/202	

J. D. Inchmore, A. E. Warner, A. P. Pridgeon and S. P. Perryman did not bat.

Bowling: Shepherd 7–0–29–0; Surridge 8–0–40–0; Bainbridge 8–0–31–1; Childs 6–0–34–1; Graveney 2–0–15–0; Broad 7–0–46–3.

Gloucestershire

A. W. Stovold st Humphries b Patel	16	P. Bainbridge not out	13
B. C. Broad c Hemsley b Perryman	54	J. N. Shepherd not out	8
Sadiq Mohammad c Hemsley b Pridgeon	22	L-b 12, n-b 1	13
A. J. Hignell run out	2	1/48 2/84 3/99 (5 wkts, 23.1 overs)	128
M. W. Stovold c Ormrod b Pridgeon	0	4/100 5/105	

*D. A. Graveney, †A. J. Brassington, J. H. Childs and D. Surridge did not bat.

Bowling: Pridgeon 8–1–31–2; Warner 4–0–19–0; Perryman 4–0–21–1; Patel 4–0–27–1; Inchmore 3.1–0–17–0.

Umpires: D. J. Constant and A. G. T. Whitehead.

GLOUCESTERSHIRE v SUSSEX

At Gloucester, May 30. Sussex won by three wickets. With ten overs left Sussex still needed 75, but a rapid 43 by le Roux saw them home with nine balls to spare. Imran, though unable to bowl, had chipped in with a valuable 37. Stovold and Broad gave Gloucestershire a flying start, and Sussex were always struggling to get on terms until le Roux's onslaught.

Gloucestershire

A. W. Stovold b le Roux	85
B. C. Broad c Gould b Greig	59
Zaheer Abbas lbw b Greig	0
A. J. Hignell b Greig	41
P. Bainbridge not out	4
J. N. Shepherd not out	2
B 5, l-b 12, w 1	18
1/113 2/113 3/199 4/207 (4 wkts, 40 overs)	209

E. J. Cunningham, *D. A. Graveney, †A. J. Brassington, J. H. Childs and D. Surridge did not bat.

Bowling: le Roux 8–0–33–1; Pigott 8–0–40–0; Barclay 8–0–33–0; Waller 8–0–32–0; Greig 8–1–53–3.

Sussex

G. D. Mendis c Brassington b Bainbridge	18
†I. J. Gould b Shepherd	16
C. M. Wells lbw b Childs	31
P. W. G. Parker c Broad b Graveney	20
Imran Khan c Broad b Surridge	37
I. A. Greig c Graveney b Surridge	25
G. S. le Roux not out	43
C. P. Phillipson c Childs b Surridge	3
*J. R. T. Barclay not out	0
B 1, l-b 15, w 1	17
1/28 2/65 3/75 4/111 5/151 6/174 7/194 (7 wkts, 38.3 overs)	210

C. E. Waller and A. C. S. Pigott did not bat.

Bowling: Surridge 7.3–0–35–3; Shepherd 7–0–39–1; Childs 8–1–30–1; Bainbridge 8–0–49–1; Graveney 8–0–40–1.

Umpires: R. Julian and J. Birkenshaw.

At The Oval, June 13. GLOUCESTERSHIRE lost to SURREY by 28 runs.

At Ebbw Vale, June 27. GLAMORGAN v GLOUCESTERSHIRE. No result.

At Leeds, July 4. GLOUCESTERSHIRE lost to YORKSHIRE on faster scoring-rate.

At Birmingham, July 11. GLOUCESTERSHIRE beat WARWICKSHIRE by five wickets.

GLOUCESTERSHIRE v NORTHAMPTONSHIRE

At Bristol, July 18. Northamptonshire won by 5 runs. Williams was the key figure for Northamptonshire, picking up their flagging innings with twelve 4s in his 82, made on a green pitch over 32 overs, and then taking two for 16 with his off-spinners as Gloucestershire fell behind the required rate. Graveney and Stephenson brought them within range with a partnership of 65 in ten overs, but it was too late.

Northamptonshire

*G. Cook b Stephenson 2
W. Larkins b Bainbridge 6
P. Willey b Surridge 4
R. G. Williams lbw b Shepherd 82
R. J. Boyd-Moss b Childs 28
D. J. Capel not out 34
†G. Sharp b Stephenson 2
R. M. Carter run out 2
T. M. Lamb not out 0
B 1, l-b 14, w 5 20

1/10 2/16 3/22 4/102 5/168 6/171 7/173 (7 wkts, 40 overs) 180

B. J. Griffiths and N. A. Mallender did not bat.

Bowling: Stephenson 8–1–25–2; Surridge 8–2–14–1; Bainbridge 8–0–40–1; Shepherd 8–1–46–1; Childs 8–0–35–1.

Gloucestershire

A. W. Stovold b Mallender 12
B. C. Broad c Sharp b Williams 28
P. W. Romaines lbw b Williams 19
A. J. Hignell c Cook b Willey 0
P. Bainbridge run out 4
J. N. Shepherd lbw b T. M. Lamb 5
*D. A. Graveney c Cook b Griffiths ... 41
F. D. Stephenson c Boyd-Moss b T. M. Lamb. 26
†A. J. Brassington not out 14
D. Surridge b T. M. Lamb 3
J. H. Childs not out 7
B 4, l-b 7, w 4, n-b 1 16

1/23 2/58 3/59 4/69 5/72 6/84 7/149 8/150 9/163 (9 wkts, 40 overs) 175

Bowling: Griffiths 8–0–49–1; Mallender 8–0–32–1; Willey 8–0–26–1; Williams 8–0–16–2; T. M. Lamb 8–0–36–3.

Umpires: W. L. Budd and C. Cook.

GLOUCESTERSHIRE v HAMPSHIRE

At Bristol, July 25. Gloucestershire won by eight wickets. Once Greenidge was out, Gloucestershire had little trouble beating opponents who struggled to come to terms with a typically slow Bristol pitch. Gloucestershire's batsmen played with fewer inhibitions, beginning at 4 an over and winning with four overs to spare after some lusty strokes by Romaines.

Hampshire

C. G. Greenidge c Wright b Shepherd. 41
J. M. Rice b Stephenson 7
M. C. J. Nicholas b Stephenson 6
T. E. Jesty b Shepherd 26
D. R. Turner lbw b Childs 3
N. G. Cowley b Graveney 6
*N. E. J. Pocock not out 24
T. M. Tremlett c Russell b Childs 4
M. D. Marshall b Stephenson 13
†R. J. Parks lbw b Shepherd 4
K. St J. D. Emery not out 3
L-b 8 8

1/14 2/24 3/69 4/83 5/87 6/98 7/103 8/127 9/136 (9 wkts, 39 overs) 145

Bowling: Surridge 7–1–35–0; Stephenson 8–0–36–3; Shepherd 7–0–27–3; Childs 8–0–23–2; Graveney 8–3–11–1; Bainbridge 1–0–5–0.

Gloucestershire

A. W. Stovold b Jesty 49
B. C. Broad st Parks b Cowley 35
P. W. Romaines not out 41
A. J. Wright not out 9
B 1, l-b 8, w 3 12

1/88 2/106 (2 wkts, 35 overs) 146

P. Bainbridge, J. N. Shepherd, F. D. Stephenson, *D. A. Graveney, †R. C. Russell, J. H. Childs and D. Surridge did not bat.

Bowling: Marshall 6–1–33–0; Emery 2–0–6–0; Tremlett 8–3–12–0; Jesty 8–0–33–1; Cowley 8–0–39–1; Rice 3–0–11–0.

Umpires: K. E. Palmer and A. G. T. Whitehead.

At Leicester, August 1. GLOUCESTERSHIRE lost to LEICESTERSHIRE by 32 runs.

GLOUCESTERSHIRE v NOTTINGHAMSHIRE

At Cheltenham, August 8. Nottinghamshire won by 47 runs. They owed much to Hadlee, whose first century in the competition contained three 6s and ten 4s. He followed a valuable partnership of 96 with Hassan by taking two important wickets, despite a hamstring strain. Wright and Shepherd batted bravely, but 106 from the last ten overs was too demanding.

Nottinghamshire

D. W. Randall run out 31
B. Hassan c Shepherd b Trembath...... 54
R. J. Hadlee not out.......................100
*C. E. B. Rice st Brassington b Childs. 8
J. D. Birch c and b Stephenson.......... 1
R. T. Robinson lbw b Stephenson....... 1
†B. N. French run out...................... 14
L-b 1, w 2, n-b 2 5

1/56 2/152 3/164 4/171 5/174 6/214 (6 wkts, 40 overs) 214

E. E. Hemmings, K. Saxelby, K. E. Cooper and N. J. B. Illingworth did not bat.

Bowling: Stephenson 8–0–35–2; Surridge 8–0–33–0; Shepherd 8–0–59–0; Childs 8–0–31–1; Trembath 8–0–51–1.

Gloucestershire

A. W. Stovold c Randall b Hadlee...... 27
P. W. Romaines st French b Rice....... 23
B. Dudleston b Hemmings................ 16
A. J. Hignell c Illingworth b Hemmings. 15
F. D. Stephenson lbw b Hadlee.......... 0
*J. N. Shepherd c Rice b Illingworth... 32
A. J. Wright c French b Hemmings..... 33
C. R. Trembath c Birch b Illingworth.. 7
†A. J. Brassington b Saxelby 2
J. H. Childs b Illingworth................. 2
D. Surridge not out......................... 1
B 2, l-b 6, n-b 1..................... 9

1/53 2/54 3/85 4/85 5/85 6/144 7/162 8/162 9/165 (38.1 overs) 167

Bowling: Saxelby 5–0–17–1; Cooper 8–0–41–0; Illingworth 7.1–0–28–3; Rice 2–0–6–1; Hadlee 8–1–33–2; Hemmings 8–0–33–3.

Umpires: A. Jepson and B. Leadbeater.

GLOUCESTERSHIRE v ESSEX

At Cheltenham, August 15. Gloucestershire won by 5 runs. Gloucestershire's score did not look large enough to deny Essex a ninth successive Sunday win, but the return of Shepherd for his second spell and the cheap dismissals of Lilley and Turner ended East Anglian aspirations.

Gloucestershire

A. W. Stovold b Lever.................... 14
B. C. Broad c Hardie b Gooch.......... 28
P. W. Romaines b Turner................. 24
A. J. Wright b Lever....................... 52
A. J. Hignell run out....................... 0
*J. N. Shepherd c Gooch b Phillip...... 34
F. D. Stephenson run out.................. 1
†A. J. Brassington not out................ 0
R. J. Doughty c Gooch b Lever......... 13
C. R. Trembath not out.................... 2
L-b 8, w 1............................ 9

1/34 2/59 3/75 4/91 5/147 6/161 7/161 8/177 (8 wkts, 39 overs) 177

J. H. Childs did not bat.

Bowling: Lever 8–0–43–3; Phillip 8–0–48–1; Turner 8–3–13–1; Gooch 8–0–30–1; R. E. East 7–0–34–0.

Essex

G. A. Gooch b Shepherd	24	S. Turner run out	9
B. R. Hardie c Brassington b Shepherd	20	†D. E. East not out	2
K. S. McEwan b Doughty	32	R. E. East not out	1
N. Phillip b Trembath	16	B 8, w 1, n-b 2	11
*K. W. R. Fletcher c Hignell b Doughty	20		
K. R. Pont c Shepherd b Stephenson	29	1/42 2/58 3/91 4/109 (8 wkts, 39 overs)	172
A. W. Lilley b Shepherd	8	5/133 6/152 7/168 8/171	

J. K. Lever did not bat.

Bowling: Stephenson 8–0–42–1; Doughty 8–0–40–2; Shepherd 8–0–24–3; Childs 8–0–25–0; Trembath 7–1–30–1.

Umpires: W. L. Budd and K. Ibadulla.

At Folkestone, August 22. GLOUCESTERSHIRE lost to KENT by 106 runs.

GLOUCESTERSHIRE v SOMERSET

At Bristol, August 29. Gloucestershire won on faster scoring-rate. Richards (ten 4s) was in dominant form as Somerset compiled a useful total. However, when rain and bad light, having already interrupted play, finally ended the match, Gloucestershire were fractionally ahead on scoring-rate.

Somerset

J. W. Lloyds lbw b Shepherd	0	J. Garner c Bainbridge b Doughty	3
P. M. Roebuck c Russell b Trembath	37	C. H. Dredge not out	1
I. V. A. Richards b Doughty	88		
*B. C. Rose c Russell b Doughty	0	L-b 9, w 3	12
N. F. M. Popplewell c Wright b Trembath	20	1/0 2/80 3/87 (6 wkts, 32 overs)	179
P. A. Slocombe not out	18	4/125 5/160 6/175	

G. V. Palmer, †T. Gard and H. R. Moseley did not bat.

Bowling: Shepherd 8–0–50–1; Surridge 8–0–41–0; Doughty 7–0–34–3; Trembath 5–0–31–2; Bainbridge 4–0–11–0.

Gloucestershire

A. W. Stovold c Gard b Garner	47
B. C. Broad run out	15
P. Bainbridge not out	5
A. J. Wright not out	0
L-b 1, w 3	4
1/55 2/71 (2 wkts, 12.4 overs)	71

A. J. Hignell, J. N. Shepherd, *D. A. Graveney, C. R. Trembath, †R. C. Russell, R. J. Doughty and D. Surridge did not bat.

Bowling: Garner 6.4–1–31–1; Moseley 3–0–16–0; Dredge 3–0–20–0.

Umpires: H. D. Bird and D. O. Oslear.

At Derby, September 5. DERBYSHIRE v GLOUCESTERSHIRE. No result.

HAMPSHIRE

At Nottingham, May 9. HAMPSHIRE beat NOTTINGHAMSHIRE by 15 runs.

HAMPSHIRE v MIDDLESEX

At Bournemouth, May 16. Middlesex won by four wickets. Radley's 80-minute innings, containing only three 4s, steered Middlesex to victory with ten balls to spare in a largely colourless match. With Greenidge not in touch with his timing, the Hampshire innings never really took off.

Hampshire

C. G. Greenidge lbw b Selvey	32	M. D. Marshall c Brearley b Daniel	21
V. P. Terry c Barlow b Selvey	18	†R. J. Parks not out	2
N. G. Cowley run out	32		
*T. E. Jesty c Downton b Daniel	7	L-b 9, w 5	14
D. R. Turner st Downton b Emburey	9		
M. C. J. Nicholas not out	32	1/49 2/64 3/78 (7 wkts, 40 overs)	185
R. E. Hayward c Radley b Daniel	18	4/101 5/108 6/133 7/180	

T. M. Tremlett and K. St J. D. Emery did not bat.

Bowling: Selvey 8–0–26–2; Williams 8–0–45–0; Emburey 8–2–23–1; Gatting 7–0–27–0; Daniel 8–0–40–3; Slack 1–0–10–0.

Middlesex

*J. M. Brearley c Parks b Marshall	13	J. E. Emburey b Emery	2
W. N. Slack c Jesty b Cowley	16	†P. R. Downton not out	10
M. W. Gatting c Parks b Tremlett	28		
C. T. Radley not out	60	B 4, l-b 13, w 2	19
R. O. Butcher c Greenidge b Tremlett	24	1/32 2/67 3/85 (6 wkts, 38.2 overs)	186
G. D. Barlow b Jesty	14	4/129 5/153 6/156	

N. F. Williams, M. W. W. Selvey and W. W. Daniel did not bat.

Bowling: Emery 7.2–0–24–1; Marshall 7–1–32–1; Jesty 8–1–31–1; Cowley 8–0–36–1; Tremlett 8–0–44–2.

Umpires: M. J. Kitchen and D. R. Shepherd.

At Chelmsford, May 23. HAMPSHIRE beat ESSEX on faster scoring-rate.

At Leicester, June 6. HAMPSHIRE lost to LEICESTERSHIRE by 9 runs.

HAMPSHIRE v DERBYSHIRE

At Portsmouth, June 13. Hampshire won by one wicket. Hampshire seemed to be cruising to victory at 103 for two in the 24th over, but the pendulum swung with the dismissal of Jesty, Rice, Pocock and Marshall for 19 runs in five overs. However, Cowley and Parks added 34 in seven overs, and then Tremlett batted with cool authority, finally despatching the penultimate ball for 4. The backbone of the Derbyshire innings was provided by Wright and John Hampshire, who put on 101 in 25 overs before falling in successive overs.

Derbyshire

A. Hill run out	6	*B. Wood not out	18
J. G. Wright c and b Tremlett	67		
P. N. Kirsten c Parks b Emery	1	B 3, l-b 6, w 1, n-b 3	13
J. H. Hampshire c Parks b Malone	41		—
G. Miller c Tremlett b Emery	29	1/12 2/18 3/119 (5 wkts, 40 overs)	193
K. J. Barnett not out	18	4/120 5/165	

†B. J. M. Maher, C. J. Tunnicliffe, P. G. Newman and S. Oldham did not bat.

Bowling: Marshall 8–1–27–0; Emery 8–1–53–2; Malone 8–1–48–1; Jesty 8–2–19–0; Tremlett 8–1–33–1.

Hampshire

C. G. Greenidge c Maher b Wood	29	T. M. Tremlett not out	18
J. M. Rice c Kirsten b Tunnicliffe	37	K. St J. D. Emery b Tunnicliffe	1
M. C. J. Nicholas b Newman	14	S. J. Malone not out	1
T. E. Jesty c Wright b Tunnicliffe	19	L-b 12, w 4	16
N. G. Cowley c Maher b Oldham	25		—
*N. E. J. Pocock b Wood	1	1/48 2/72 3/103 (9 wkts, 39.5 overs)	194
M. D. Marshall run out	0	4/119 5/122 6/122	
†R. J. Parks c Wood b Oldham	33	7/156 8/176 9/189	

Bowling: Newman 8–0–26–1; Oldham 8–0–36–2; Tunnicliffe 7.5–0–58–3; Miller 8–0–31–0; Wood 8–1–27–2.

Umpires: W. L. Budd and A. G. T. Whitehead.

HAMPSHIRE v KENT

At Basingstoke, June 27. Hampshire won on faster scoring-rate. Marshall, who took five wickets and ran out Asif, played a major role in this rain-affected match. Kent, having had their target re-adjusted, came to the sixteenth and last over needing 3 to win with two wickets standing. Facing Emery, Underwood failed to score off four balls and was then caught off a skier to cover. Taylor could manage only 2 off the last ball and Hampshire were home by 0.02 of a run. Jesty wisely insured this, his benefit match, against the weather, and the terms of his policy meant he collected £5,000 on his premium of £600.

Hampshire

J. M. Rice c and b Dilley	38	*N. E. J. Pocock not out	1
D. R. Turner b Penn	12		
M. C. J. Nicholas c Taylor b Woolmer	18	L-b 4, w 1	5
			—
T. E. Jesty not out	30	1/49 2/55 3/80 (4 wkts, 22 overs)	116
N. G. Cowley c Cowdrey b Woolmer	12	4/107	

V. P. Terry, M. D. Marshall, †R. J. Parks, T. M. Tremlett and K. St J. D. Emery did not bat.

Bowling: Dilley 8–0–35–1; Jarvis 6–1–24–0; Penn 5–0–35–1; Woolmer 3–0–17–2.

Kent

L. Potter b Marshall	18	C. Penn lbw b Marshall	0
R. A. Woolmer c Tremlett b Marshall	24	D. L. Underwood c Nicholas b Emery	1
M. R. Benson run out	2	K. B. S. Jarvis not out	0
*Asif Iqbal run out	6	B 1, l-b 3, w 1, n-b 3	8
C. S. Cowdrey lbw b Marshall	4		
†A. P. E. Knott c Turner b Emery	0	1/37 2/42 3/52	(9 wkts, 16 overs) 84
N. R. Taylor not out	14	4/56 5/57 6/60	
G. R. Dilley c Parks b Marshall	7	7/74 8/81 9/82	

Bowling: Marshall 8–0–31–5; Emery 8–0–45–2.

Umpires: K. Ibadulla and R. Palmer.

At Cardiff, July 11. HAMPSHIRE beat GLAMORGAN by eight wickets.

HAMPSHIRE v LANCASHIRE

At Southampton, July 18. Tied. A pulsating final over saw Hampshire scramble 3 runs and Lancashire take two wickets. Marshall was run out off the second ball; Parks caught at short mid-wicket off the fourth; Emery took a single off the fifth; and from the last ball Tremlett, helped by a misfield by Clive Lloyd at deep backward point, collected 2. That Hampshire went so close was largely thanks to Nicholas and Rice, who put on 68 in thirteen overs. For Lancashire, David Lloyd and Hughes enjoyed a third-wicket partnership of 81 in twelve overs. Jesty took two wickets to become the first player ever to achieve 200 wickets and 3,000 runs in the John Player League.

Lancashire

D. Lloyd b Emery	79	J. Simmons c and b Tremlett	23
G. Fowler c Pocock b Jesty	26	L-b 7, w 3, n-b 1	11
*C. H. Lloyd c Rice b Jesty	21		
D. P. Hughes c Rice b Marshall	39	1/57 2/91	(5 wkts, 39 overs) 215
J. Abrahams not out	16	3/172 4/181 5/215	

†C. Maynard, B. W. Reidy, S. J. O'Shaughnessy, I. Folley and L. L. McFarlane did not bat.

Bowling: Emery 8–0–37–1; Marshall 7–1–43–1; Jesty 8–1–30–2; Cowley 8–0–36–0; Tremlett 8–0–58–1.

Hampshire

C. G. Greenidge c D. Lloyd b McFarlane	17	†R. J. Parks c D. Lloyd b McFarlane	5
J. M. Rice c Hughes b Simmons	42	T. M. Tremlett not out	2
M. C. J. Nicholas b McFarlane	76	K. St J. D. Emery not out	1
T. E. Jesty c McFarlane b D. Lloyd	23	B 3, l-b 11, w 2	16
N. G. Cowley b Simmons	23		
*N. E. J. Pocock b McFarlane	0	1/28 2/96 3/135	(9 wkts, 39 overs) 215
R. E. Hayward run out	2	4/189 5/189 6/197	
M. D. Marshall run out	8	7/212 8/212 9/212	

Bowling: McFarlane 8–0–18–4; Folley 8–0–42–0; Reidy 6–0–31–0; Simmons 8–0–45–2; O'Shaughnessy 2–0–16–0; D. Lloyd 4–0–24–1; Abrahams 3–0–23–0.

Umpires: K. Ibadulla and R. Palmer.

At Bristol, July 25. HAMPSHIRE lost to GLOUCESTERSHIRE by eight wickets.

HAMPSHIRE v SOMERSET

At Portsmouth, August 1. Hampshire won by six wickets, aided principally by the power of Greenidge and the bowling of Jesty. After putting Somerset in, Jesty came on to bowl when Somerset's opening stand was gaining momentum and took four wickets in five overs. Greenidge, hitting two 6s and five 4s, raced to his 84 off 86 balls as Hampshire brushed aside Marks's breakthrough.

Somerset

P. M. Roebuck c Tremlett b Jesty	27	†D. J. S. Taylor not out	5
P. W. Denning c Marshall b Jesty	40	J. Garner not out	15
I. V. A. Richards c Marshall b Jesty	13	L-b 14, w 7, n-b 1	22
*B. C. Rose c Greenidge b Jesty	16		—
V. J. Marks c Greenidge b Tremlett	12	1/79 2/83 3/112 (6 wkts, 39 overs)	177
J. W. Lloyds b Emery	27	4/113 5/154 6/158	

M. R. Davis, C. H. Dredge and H. R. Moseley did not bat.

Bowling: Marshall 8–2–27–0; Emery 7–1–19–1; Tremlett 8–0–32–1; Cowley 8–1–32–0; Jesty 8–0–45–4.

Hampshire

C. G. Greenidge b Garner	84	N. G. Cowley not out	7
J. M. Rice c Dredge b Marks	1	B 2, l-b 12, w 1, n-b 2	17
M. C. J. Nicholas c Richards b Marks	6		—
*T. E. Jesty b Lloyds	33	1/26 2/51 (4 wkts, 37.2 overs)	180
D. R. Turner not out	32	3/114 4/138	

R. E. Hayward, M. D. Marshall, T. M. Tremlett, †R. J. Parks and K. St J. D. Emery did not bat.

Bowling: Garner 8–1–26–1; Davis 4–0–19–0; Marks 8–1–27–2; Moseley 3–0–24–0; Dredge 8–0–27–0; Lloyds 6.2–0–40–1.

Umpires: N. T. Plews and C. T. Spencer.

At Eastbourne, August 8. HAMPSHIRE lost to SUSSEX by 13 runs.

HAMPSHIRE v WORCESTERSHIRE

At Southampton, August 15. Worcestershire won by 11 runs. Patel's maiden John Player League century (125 off 132 balls), his part in the record partnership for any wicket in the competition – 224 with Ormrod – and his League best return of four for 39 helped Worcestershire end a run of six successive defeats. Worcestershire's opening partnership faced all but the last nine balls. Hampshire did well to come so close, but a requirement of 16 off the last over was too much.

Worcestershire

J. A. Ormrod not out	92
D. N. Patel b Malone	125
Younis Ahmed not out	3
L-b 14, w 2	16
	—
1/224 (1 wkt, 40 overs)	236

*P. A. Neale, E. J. O. Hemsley, †D. J. Humphries, D. A. Banks, N. Gifford, A. P. Pridgeon, S. P. Perryman and A. J. Webster did not bat.

Bowling: Marshall 8–1–29–0; Malone 8–1–43–1; Cowley 7–0–37–0; Rice 4–0–25–0; Jesty 8–0–37–0; Tremlett 5–0–49–0.

Hampshire

C. G. Greenidge c Younis b Gifford	34	T. M. Tremlett c Hemsley b Patel	0
J. M. Rice lbw b Perryman	25	†R. J. Parks run out	31
D. R. Turner b Patel	12	S. J. Malone not out	2
T. E. Jesty b Patel	38	B 1, l-b 21, w 3	25
M. C. J. Nicholas b Patel	7		
*N. E. J. Pocock c Banks b Hemsley	19	1/62 2/76 3/106	(39.4 overs) 225
N. G. Cowley run out	3	4/130 5/151 6/157	
M. D. Marshall b Pridgeon	29	7/164 8/172 9/223	

Bowling: Pridgeon 7.4–1–25–1; Webster 4–0–34–0; Perryman 5–0–25–1; Gifford 8–1–27–1; Patel 8–0–39–4; Hemsley 7–0–50–1.

Umpires: P. J. Eele and A. Jepson.

At Northampton, August 22. HAMPSHIRE lost to NORTHAMPTONSHIRE by 82 runs.

HAMPSHIRE v YORKSHIRE

At Southampton, August 29. Hampshire won by 14 runs. Jesty drew on his rich vein of runs by scoring his third century in four days. His unbeaten 110 (three 6s, twelve 4s) was his best Sunday League score, and he was given excellent support by Nicholas in a fourth-wicket partnership of 144 in twenty overs. Yorkshire made a commendable effort to meet a formidable target and were going particularly well while Sharp, whose 62 included three 6s, and Bairstow were adding 66 in ten overs for the fifth wicket. When they went in successive overs, Carrick hit his best John Player League score to keep Yorkshire in with an outside chance, but at the start of the final over he fell to Tremlett, who with the last ball bowled Illingworth.

Hampshire

C. G. Greenidge c Athey b Stevenson	10	*N. E. J. Pocock not out	7
J. M. Rice b Old	41	B 4, l-b 10, w 3	17
D. R. Turner c Sharp b Illingworth	13		
T. E. Jesty not out	110	1/39 2/73	(4 wkts, 40 overs) 248
M. C. J. Nicholas c Boycott b Stevenson	50	3/75 4/219	

M. D. Marshall, T. M. Tremlett, †R. J. Parks, S. J. Malone and N. G. Cowley did not bat.

Bowling: Ramage 8–0–46–0; Stevenson 7–0–31–2; Old 8–0–40–1; Illingworth 4–0–13–1; Carrick 5–0–36–0; Hartley 8–0–65–0.

Yorkshire

G. Boycott b Marshall	8	C. M. Old b Tremlett	8
C. W. J. Athey c Nicholas b Malone	9	A. Ramage not out	7
J. D. Love c Tremlett b Cowley	19	*R. Illingworth b Tremlett	1
K. Sharp c Greenidge b Marshall	62	B 8, l-b 13, w 5	26
G. B. Stevenson c Pocock b Jesty	17		
†D. L. Bairstow c Pocock b Jesty	27	1/18 2/33 3/63	(40 overs) 234
S. N. Hartley c Rice b Malone	11	4/86 5/152 6/160	
P. Carrick lbw b Tremlett	39	7/194 8/215 9/232	

Bowling: Malone 8–1–56–2; Marshall 8–1–21–2; Tremlett 8–0–32–3; Cowley 8–0–46–1; Jesty 8–0–53–2.

Umpires: W. E. Alley and J. Birkenshaw.

At The Oval, September 5. HAMPSHIRE tied with SURREY.

HAMPSHIRE v WARWICKSHIRE

At Bournemouth, September 12. Hampshire won by four wickets. Tidy Hampshire bowling, particularly by Tremlett and Jesty, prevented Warwickshire from making the progress they would have liked, and after four wickets had fallen for 64, it was left to Asif Din to play the major role. Hampshire, too, began with no great confidence, but there were useful contributions from Greenidge and Jesty before Pocock, the captain, steered them to their eighth Sunday victory.

Warwickshire

T. A. Lloyd b Tremlett	20	A. M. Ferreira c and b Marshall	17
K. D. Smith b Malone	14	C. Lethbridge not out	11
A. I. Kallicharran c Greenidge b Jesty	14	L-b 7, w 3	10
D. L. Amiss c Parks b Tremlett	23		—
G. W. Humpage c Cowley b Jesty	1	1/25 2/49 3/57 (6 wkts, 40 overs)	166
Asif Din not out	56	4/64 5/104 6/143	

†G. A. Tedstone, G. C. Small and *R. G. D. Willis did not bat.

Bowling: Malone 8–0–36–1; Marshall 8–0–37–1; Tremlett 8–0–20–2; Jesty 8–1–23–2; Rice 8–0–40–0.

Hampshire

C. G. Greenidge c Lethbridge b Ferreira	22	M. D. Marshall b Willis	19
J. M. Rice c and b Lethbridge	7	V. P. Terry not out	6
D. R. Turner b Lethbridge	17	B 4, l-b 7, w 2, n-b 1	14
T. E. Jesty c Smith b Kallicharran	31		—
N. G. Cowley c Willis b Ferreira	11	1/25 2/40 3/66 (6 wkts, 39 overs)	170
*N. E. J. Pocock not out	43	4/87 5/104 6/150	

†R. J. Parks, T. M. Tremlett and S. J. Malone did not bat.

Bowling: Willis 8–2–21–1; Small 8–3–18–0; Ferreira 7–0–28–2; Lethbridge 8–0–32–2; Humpage 3–0–26–0; Kallicharran 5–0–31–1.

Umpires: D. J. Constant and D. C. Oslear.

KENT

At The Oval, May 9. KENT beat SURREY by 107 runs.

KENT v GLAMORGAN

At Canterbury, May 16. Kent won by seven wickets. Glamorgan, put in, recovered through a partnership of 154 in 26 overs from Ontong (one 6 and seven 4s in 100 minutes) and Miandad (six 4s in 91 minutes). Kent also started badly, but when Asif joined Tavaré the Glamorgan attack was thrashed for 124 in sixteen overs. Asif reached 50 in 53 minutes, while Tavaré hit a 6 and seven 4s in reaching his century at a run a minute.

Glamorgan

A. Jones c Knott b Woolmer............. 14
J. A. Hopkins c Woolmer b Dilley...... 7
R. C. Ontong c Cowdrey b Jarvis....... 84
*Javed Miandad c Potter b Dilley....... 70
C. J. C. Rowe not out...................... 8
D. A. Francis c Benson b Jarvis......... 3
G. C. Holmes c Tavaré b Dilley......... 1
†E. W. Jones not out......................... 0
B 1, l-b 11, w 4, n-b 2............. 18

1/16 2/35 3/189 4/194 5/200 6/204 (6 wkts, 40 overs) 205

M. A. Nash, B. J. Lloyd and S. R. Barwick did not bat.

Bowling: Jarvis 8–0–38–2; Dilley 8–1–34–3; Woolmer 8–0–25–1; Penn 8–0–34–0; Cowdrey 4–0–26–0; Potter 4–0–30–0.

Kent

R. A. Woolmer c E. W. Jones b Nash 22
N. R. Taylor lbw b Nash.................. 1
C. J. Tavaré not out.........................103
M. R. Benson c Lloyd b Barwick....... 11
*Asif Iqbal not out........................... 56
L-b 9, w 4.............................. 13

1/1 2/59 3/82 (3 wkts, 35 overs) 206

C. S. Cowdrey, †A. P. E. Knott, L. Potter, G. R. Dilley, C. Penn and K. B. S. Jarvis did not bat.

Bowling: Nash 8–2–25–2; Ontong 6–0–22–0; Lloyd 8–0–57–0; Barwick 5–0–27–1; Holmes 2–0–23–0; Miandad 3–0–18–0; Rowe 3–0–21–0.

Umpires: P. J. Eele and D. O. Oslear.

At Worcester, May 30. KENT beat WORCESTERSHIRE by 30 runs.

At Birmingham, June 6. KENT beat WARWICKSHIRE by seven wickets.

At Northampton, June 13. KENT lost to NORTHAMPTONSHIRE by 61 runs.

KENT v DERBYSHIRE

At Canterbury, June 20. Kent won by 7 runs. Put in, Kent batted consistently, accelerating in a fifth-wicket stand of 56 off eight overs between Woolmer and Cowdrey. Derbyshire, tied down by Woolmer and Underwood, needed 48 off the last five overs, but then Fowler and Taylor lashed out, taking 17 off one over from Dilley. Needing 8 to win off the final over Derbyshire lost their last wicket to the first ball.

Kent

L. Potter c Oldham b Wood.............. 27
N. R. Taylor c Wood b Miller............ 44
C. J. Tavaré c Taylor b Tunnicliffe..... 25
R. A. Woolmer c Miller b Oldham..... 33
*Asif Iqbal c Taylor b Tunnicliffe....... 3
C. S. Cowdrey c Wood b Newman...... 33
†A. P. E. Knott c Wright b Oldham.... 0
G. R. Dilley not out......................... 14
C. Penn not out............................... 0
B 3, l-b 10, w 1....................... 14

1/46 2/93 3/107 4/113 5/169 6/169 7/187 (7 wkts, 38 overs) 193

D. L. Underwood and K. B. S. Jarvis did not bat.

Bowling: Oldham 8–0–34–2; Newman 8–0–29–1; Wood 6–0–42–1; Tunnicliffe 8–0–33–2; Miller 8–1–41–1.

Derbyshire

J. G. Wright c and b Penn	13	C. J. Tunnicliffe b Dilley	4
J. H. Hampshire b Underwood	25	P. G. Newman not out	0
P. N. Kirsten c Cowdrey b Woolmer	37	S. Oldham c Dilley b Jarvis	1
G. Miller c Potter b Woolmer	23		
K. J. Barnett b Penn	19	L-b 4, w 4, n-b 1	9
*B. Wood c Knott b Jarvis	11		
W. P. Fowler b Jarvis	29	1/14 2/79 3/85 (37.1 overs)	186
†R. W. Taylor run out	15	4/115 5/134 6/138 7/180 8/183 9/185	

Bowling: Dilley 5–0–39–1; Jarvis 7.1–0–45–3; Penn 8–1–35–2; Underwood 8–0–26–1; Woolmer 8–0–31–2; Cowdrey 1–0–1–0.

Umpires: W. L. Budd and R. S. Herman.

At Basingstoke, June 27. KENT lost to HAMPSHIRE on faster scoring-rate.

KENT v SUSSEX

At Maidstone, July 4. Kent lost by 73 runs. Sussex, put in, were given a magnificent start as Mendis and Gould hit 110 off nineteen overs. Only Underwood could check the flow of runs. Parker, square-cutting a 6 into the press box, helped Mendis add 57 off seven overs, and Mendis hit eight 4s and two 6s in his 120-minute stay. With Sussex taking some splendid catches and fielding brilliantly, Kent were never allowed to recover from a bad start.

Sussex

G. D. Mendis c Cowdrey b Dilley	121	C. P. Phillipson not out	12
†I. J. Gould c Tavaré b Cowdrey	52		
C. M. Wells c Tavaré b Underwood	14	L-b 8, w 2	10
P. W. G. Parker c Knott b Dilley	29		
G. S. le Roux c and b Dilley	1	1/110 2/157 3/214 (5 wkts, 40 overs)	254
I. A. Greig not out	15	4/216 5/229	

A. C. S. Pigott, *J. R. T. Barclay, G. G. Arnold and C. E. Waller did not bat.

Bowling: Dilley 8–0–53–3; Jarvis 8–1–74–0; Ellison 4–0–24–0; Penn 4–0–24–0; Cowdrey 8–0–43–1; Underwood 8–1–26–1.

Kent

M. R. Benson c Gould b le Roux	0	C. Penn c Greig b Waller	40
N. R. Taylor c Waller b Pigott	13	D. L. Underwood c Mendis b Pigott	3
C. J. Tavaré c Barclay b Arnold	27	K. B. S. Jarvis not out	2
*Asif Iqbal b Barclay	46		
C. S. Cowdrey run out	13	L-b 3, w 3, n-b 1	7
†A. P. E. Knott b Pigott	4		
R. M. Ellison c Barclay b le Roux	24	1/6 2/36 3/48 (38.2 overs)	181
G. R. Dilley c Waller b Barclay	2	4/71 5/77 6/110 7/116 8/143 9/148	

Bowling: Arnold 8–0–27–1; le Roux 8–0–26–2; Pigott 8–0–42–3; Greig 8–1–32–0; Barclay 6–0–45–2; Waller 0.2–0–2–1.

Umpires: A. Jepson and D. R. Shepherd.

KENT v SOMERSET

At Maidstone, July 11. Kent won by 1 run. Put in, Kent had lost half their side for 81 in 24 overs before Johnson (50 in 51 minutes with five 4s) and Knott rescued them with 90 off fifteen overs. Somerset cruised to 64 off fifteen overs, faltered and then recovered well through Popplewell and Marks. However, five wickets went for 24 in five overs and Moseley, needing to hit the last ball for 6, could manage only a 4.

Kent

N. R. Taylor b Davis	4	G. W. Johnson not out	54
L. Potter lbw b Marks	24	R. M. Ellison not out	1
M. R. Benson c Taylor b Moseley	19	B 1, l-b 10, w 4, n-b 3	18
*Asif Iqbal c Richards b Moseley	15		
C. S. Cowdrey c Taylor b Moseley	12	1/7 2/49 3/57 (6 wkts, 40 overs)	181
†A. P. E. Knott c Garner b Dredge	34	4/81 5/81 6/171	

C. Penn, D. L. Underwood and K. B. S. Jarvis did not bat.

Bowling: Garner 8–3–29–0; Davis 7–1–32–1; Marks 8–0–24–1; Moseley 8–2–25–3; Dredge 8–2–43–1; Richards 1–0–10–0.

Somerset

P. M. Roebuck run out	36	C. H. Dredge c sub b Jarvis	1
P. W. Denning c Penn b Underwood	30	H. R. Moseley not out	4
I. V. A. Richards c sub b Cowdrey	11	M. R. Davis not out	0
*B. C. Rose c Potter b Underwood	3	B 4, l-b 12, w 4, n-b 2	22
N. F. M. Popplewell c Knott b Penn	20		
V. J. Marks c Potter b Jarvis	43	1/64 2/71 3/78 (9 wkts, 40 overs)	180
J. Garner c Benson b Penn	10	4/94 5/156 6/168	
†D. J. S. Taylor c Potter b Jarvis	0	7/173 8/176 9/176	

Bowling: Jarvis 8–2–32–3; Penn 8–0–24–2; Ellison 1.5–0–4–0; Asif 2.1–0–18–0; Underwood 8–1–23–2; Cowdrey 8–0–33–1; Johnson 4–0–24–0.

Umpires: W. E. Alley and D. G. L. Evans.

KENT v YORKSHIRE

(A. G. E. Ealham's Benefit Match)

At Canterbury, July 25. Yorkshire won by five wickets. Put in to bat, Kent made a sound start, had lost half their side for 108 in 27 overs, and were saved by Knott, who was one of three wickets claimed by Jarvis for 3 runs in twelve balls. Yorkshire began badly, but Athey hit 51 out of 73 in 75 minutes and then Boycott, with 71 needed off the last ten overs, steered them home, his stand with Hartley realising 46 off seven overs.

Kent

L. Potter c and b Carrick	32	C. Penn b Stuchbury	1
N. R. Taylor run out	13	D. L. Underwood b Jarvis	0
C. J. Tavaré b Carrick	22	K. B. S. Jarvis not out	1
M. R. Benson c Bairstow b Illingworth	21	B 1, l-b 7, w 5, n-b 2	15
*Asif Iqbal run out	2		
C. S. Cowdrey c Bairstow b Sidebottom	8	1/36 2/76 3/83 (38 overs)	162
†A. P. E. Knott b Jarvis	31	4/89 5/108 6/120	
G. R. Dilley c Illingworth b Jarvis	16	7/153 8/161 9/161	

Bowling: Stuchbury 7–1–37–1; Jarvis 7–0–24–3; Sidebottom 8–0–22–1; Carrick 8–0–19–2; Illingworth 8–1–45–1.

Yorkshire

C. W. J. Athey b Penn.................... 59
M. D. Moxon c and b Cowdrey.......... 8
J. D. Love c Asif b Underwood......... 3
†D. L. Bairstow b Penn.................... 19
G. Boycott not out............................ 34
S. N. Hartley c Dilley b Penn........... 22
P. Carrick not out............................ 4
L-b 12, w 3............................ 15

1/17 2/32 3/86 4/101 5/147 (5 wkts, 37 overs) 164

A. Sidebottom, P. W. Jarvis, *R. Illingworth and S. Stuchbury did not bat.

Bowling: Jarvis 8–0–41–0; Dilley 7–0–24–0; Cowdrey 8–0–28–1; Underwood 6–0–21–1; Penn 8–0–35–3.

Umpires: P. B. Wight and Khizar Hayat.

At Lord's, August 1. KENT beat MIDDLESEX by 1 run.

KENT v ESSEX

At Canterbury, August 8. Kent lost by ten wickets. Kent struggled from the start against the pace and seam of Lever and Phillip, and although Johnson tried to hold the innings together, the target was never going to trouble Essex. Hardie, with seven 4s, raced to 50 in 51 minutes, outscoring his partner, but it was Gooch who ended the match abruptly by moving from 48 to 83 off just nine balls. One of his three 6s smashed a car windscreen.

Kent

M. R. Benson st D. E. East b R. E. East. 33
N. R. Taylor lbw b Lever.................. 1
C. J. Tavaré c D. E. East b Phillip..... 1
D. G. Aslett c Hardie b Gooch.......... 34
G. W. Johnson b Phillip.................... 36
*C. S. Cowdrey b Turner.................. 0
†A. P. E. Knott c R. E. East b Turner. 6
E. A. Baptiste b Lever...................... 8
R. A. Woolmer not out..................... 7
D. L. Underwood lbw b Phillip.......... 0
K. B. S. Jarvis not out...................... 8
L-b 16, w 2............................ 18

1/9 2/18 3/66 4/98 5/99 6/107 7/121 8/141 9/141 (9 wkts, 39 overs) 152

Bowling: Lever 8–0–26–2; Phillip 7–0–27–3; Pringle 4–0–11–0; Turner 8–0–24–2; Gooch 8–1–24–1; R. E. East 4–0–22–1.

Essex

G. A. Gooch not out........................ 83
B. R. Hardie not out........................ 67
L-b 3, w 1............................ 4

(no wkt, 28 overs) 154

*K. W. R. Fletcher, K. S. McEwan, D. R. Pringle, N. Phillip, K. R. Pont, S. Turner, †D. E. East, R. E. East and J. K. Lever did not bat.

Bowling: Jarvis 6–1–43–0; Baptiste 6–0–28–0; Woolmer 8–0–36–0; Cowdrey 3–0–17–0; Underwood 5–0–26–0.

Umpires: D. J. Constant and P. J. Eele

At Nottingham, August 15. KENT lost to NOTTINGHAMSHIRE by nine wickets.

KENT v GLOUCESTERSHIRE

At Folkestone, August 22. Kent won by 106 runs. Kent, put in, were given a fine start by Woolmer and Taylor, who reached his 50 in 63 minutes, and then Tavaré, hitting a 6 and fourteen 4s in 79 minutes, added 100 off eleven overs with Benson. Gloucestershire were never in with a chance after losing half their side for 88 in 23 overs, with Baptiste taking three for 12 in 22 balls.

Kent

R. A. Woolmer c Wright b Trembath	32
N. R. Taylor c Graveney b Trembath	74
C. J. Tavaré c M. W. Stovold b Doughty	90
M. R. Benson c A. W. Stovold b Broad	44
E. A. Baptiste c M. W. Stovold b Broad	0
G. W. Johnson not out	21
*C. S. Cowdrey not out	2
L-b 6, w 1, n-b 1	8
1/65 2/145 3/245 4/247 5/250 (5 wkts, 40 overs)	271

†A. P. E. Knott, G. R. Dilley, D. L. Underwood and K. B. S. Jarvis did not bat.

Bowling: Shepherd 8–1–48–0; Doughty 8–0–56–1; Trembath 8–0–55–2; Childs 6–0–40–0; Graveney 2–0–16–0; Broad 8–0–48–2.

Gloucestershire

A. W. Stovold b Baptiste	20
B. C. Broad c Benson b Jarvis	23
P. W. Romaines c Knott b Baptiste	13
M. W. Stovold b Baptiste	10
A. J. Wright c Knott b Woolmer	14
J. N. Shepherd c Dilley b Underwood	22
*D. A. Graveney not out	32
C. R. Trembath b Underwood	6
R. J. Doughty c Baptiste b Cowdrey	0
†A. J. Brassington b Underwood	3
J. H. Childs b Underwood	1
L-b 16, w 2, n-b 3	21
1/37 2/59 3/63 4/88 5/88 6/126 7/140 8/141 9/163 (38.5 overs)	165

Bowling: Dilley 5–0–15–0; Jarvis 5–0–19–1; Woolmer 8–1–27–1; Baptiste 8–0–32–3; Underwood 6.5–2–15–4; Cowdrey 6–0–36–1.

Umpires: R. Julian and N. T. Plews.

At Manchester, August 29. KENT beat LANCASHIRE by five wickets.

KENT v LEICESTERSHIRE

At Canterbury, September 12. Leicestershire won by 22 runs to leapfrog into third place in the table ahead of Kent. They were given a sound start by Briers and Gower, who ended a wonderful summer of Sunday scores with an unbeaten 88 in 120 minutes (seven 4s). He and Davison put on 68 off ten overs. After Kent's dismal start, Aslett and Cowdrey added 51 off nine overs, but with ten overs remaining the requirement was 99. Despite 45 off five overs from Knott and Ellison, it was too demanding.

Leicestershire

N. E. Briers b Jarvis	28
D. I. Gower not out	88
I. P. Butcher c Dilley b Underwood	22
B. F. Davison c Cowdrey b Dilley	38
A. M. E. Roberts not out	6
B 1, l-b 15, w 1, n-b 4	21
1/56 2/123 3/191 (3 wkts, 38 overs)	203

*R. W. Tolchard, †M. A. Garnham, J. F. Steele, P. B. Clift, G. J. Parsons and L. B. Taylor did not bat.

Bowling: Dilley 7–1–22–1; Ellison 7–0–40–0; Baptiste 8–0–60–0; Jarvis 8–1–27–1; Underwood 8–0–33–1.

Kent

M. R. Benson st Garnham b Steele	19	G. R. Dilley b Parsons	28
N. R. Taylor b Parsons	8	D. L. Underwood c Butcher b Parsons	4
*C. J. Tavaré c Roberts b Steele	0	K. B. S. Jarvis not out	5
D. G. Aslett c Davison b Clift	43		
C. S. Cowdrey lbw b Roberts	18	L-b 6	6
E. A. Baptiste run out	2		
†A. P. E. Knott b Roberts	27	1/22 2/25 3/30 4/81 (37.2 overs)	181
R. M. Ellison c Gower b Taylor	21	5/92 6/92 7/137 8/155 9/175	

Bowling: Taylor 8–1–34–1; Parsons 6.2–0–20–3; Steele 7–1–34–2; Clift 8–0–42–1; Roberts 8–0–45–2.

Umpires: R. S. Herman and K. E. Palmer.

LANCASHIRE

LANCASHIRE v GLAMORGAN

At Manchester, May 9. Lancashire won by seven wickets. Rowe and Ontong provided the only resistance to Lancashire's capable attack. Clive Lloyd, opening the innings for the first time, hit a 6 and ten 4s in a stand of 97 with Abrahams.

Glamorgan

A. L. Jones c Croft b Reidy	9	†E. W. Jones c and b Allott	6
J. A. Hopkins c C. H. Lloyd b McFarlane	0	M. A. Nash not out	2
R. C. Ontong run out	35	B. J. Lloyd b Simmons	3
*Javed Miandad b McFarlane	0	S. R. Barwick b Croft	3
C. J. C. Rowe b Simmons	54	B 4, l-b 12, w 4	20
D. A. Francis c Simmons b McFarlane	6	1/1 2/33 3/34 (38.4 overs)	148
G. C. Holmes c Hughes b Simmons	10	4/79 5/109 6/129 7/139 8/139 9/144	

Bowling: Reidy 8–3–23–1; McFarlane 8–1–24–3; Simmons 8–1–35–3; Allott 7–1–17–1; Croft 7.4–0–29–1.

Lancashire

A. Kennedy c E. W. Jones b Ontong	0	D. P Hughes not out	16
*C. H. Lloyd run out	64	L-b 2, w 2	4
J. Abrahams c Hopkins b Miandad	43		
D. Lloyd not out	25	1/3 2/100 3/131 (3 wkts, 35.1 overs)	152

B. W. Reidy, J. Simmons, L. L. McFarlane, †M. A. Wallwork, P. J. W. Allott and C. E. H. Croft did not bat.

Bowling: Nash 8–1–24–0; Ontong 8–2–17–1; Lloyd 5.1–0–33–0; Barwick 4–0–24–0; Rowe 3–0–19–0; Holmes 4–0–21–0; Miandad 3–0–10–1.

Umpires: D. J. Constant and J. van Geloven.

LANCASHIRE v GLOUCESTERSHIRE

At Manchester, May 16. Lancashire won by 106 runs. A century opening partnership between Kennedy and Clive Lloyd was followed by a sparkling innings from Cockbain, who hit an unbeaten 53 in nine overs. Gloucestershire, who have won only three of 23 limited-overs games against Lancashire, lost wickets steadily from the start.

Lancashire

A. Kennedy b Graveney	54	B. W. Reidy not out	12
*C. H. Lloyd c Bainbridge b Broad	72	L-b 5, w 2, n-b 1	8
J. Abrahams c Doughty b Graveney	5		
D. Lloyd b Shepherd	12	1/102 2/128 3/140 (4 wkts, 39 overs)	216
I. Cockbain not out	53	4/165	

J. Simmons, P. J. W. Allott, C. E. H. Croft, †M. A. Wallwork and L. L. McFarlane did not bat.

Bowling: Surridge 8–0–51–0; Shepherd 7–0–36–1; Doughty 5–0–23–0; Bainbridge 8–0–47–0; Broad 4–0–19–1; Graveney 7–0–32–2.

Gloucestershire

A. W. Stovold b McFarlane	9	*D. A. Graveney c C. H. Lloyd b Simmons	8
B. C. Broad c Allott b Reidy	15	R. J. Doughty not out	18
Sadiq Mohammad c Wallwork b Croft	11	†A. J. Brassington not out	11
P. Bainbridge c Wallwork b Croft	9	B 1, l-b 7	8
A. J. Hignell c D. Lloyd b Allott	4		
E. J. Cunningham c Cockbain b Simmons	12	1/28 2/28 3/39 (8 wkts, 39 overs)	110
J. N. Shepherd c Abrahams b Simmons	5	4/52 5/54 6/69 7/69 8/87	

D. Surridge did not bat.

Bowling: McFarlane 8–1–20–1; Reidy 8–2–24–1; Allott 7–0–26–1; Croft 7–0–19–2; Simmons 8–2–13–3; Abrahams 1–1–0–0.

Umpires: R. Julian and B. Leadbeater.

At Bedford School, May 23. NORTHAMPTONSHIRE v LANCASHIRE. No result.

LANCASHIRE v SUSSEX

At Manchester, June 6. Sussex won by seven wickets. Sussex asked Lancashire to bat in beautiful weather, but after 40 minutes, with Lancashire 50 for two from 13.2 overs, rain held up play and reduced the game to one of eighteen overs each. Lancashire added 43, but Sussex, despite losing two early wickets and having only four balls to spare, continued their unbeaten run.

Lancashire

A. Kennedy c Gould b Imran	30	B. W. Reidy not out	3
*C. H. Lloyd c Gould b Imran	10	B 1, l-b 4, w 2	7
G. Fowler b Imran	30		
D. Lloyd run out	4	1/40 2/41 3/51 (4 wkts, 18 overs)	93
D. P. Hughes not out	9	4/88	

J. Simmons, I. Folley, P. J. W. Allott, C. E. H. Croft and †M. A. Wallwork did not bat.

Bowling: Imran 7–0–29–3; le Roux 5–0–29–0; Greig 6–1–28–0.

Sussex

G. D. Mendis c Folley b Simmons	46	G. S. le Roux not out	1
†I. J. Gould c Kennedy b Folley	2	B 4, l-b 4, w 2	10
Imran Khan run out	2		—
P. W. G. Parker not out	36	1/9 2/14 3/85 (3 wkts, 17.2 overs)	97

*J. R. T. Barclay, C. M. Wells, I. A. Greig, C. P. Phillipson, A. C. S. Pigott and C. E. Waller did not bat.

Bowling: Allott 7–0–36–0; Folley 3–0–14–1; Croft 5–0–18–0; Simmons 2.2–0–19–1.

Umpires: J. Birkenshaw and R. S. Herman.

LANCASHIRE v ESSEX

At Manchester, June 13. Essex won by 82 runs. Essex's total was the highest ever recorded against Lancashire in the John Player competition. Gooch had his best-ever Sunday League innings, sharing in century stands with Hardie and McEwan. Lancashire struggled from the start, and only Hayes showed real resistance before being struck in the face by a ball from Phillip and hitting his own wicket.

Essex

G. A. Gooch c and b Croft	122	A. W. Lilley not out	1
B. R. Hardie c Maynard b Croft	53	B 3, l-b 11, w 2, n-b 1	17
K. S. McEwan run out	76		—
N. Phillip not out	0	1/107 2/268 3/268 (3 wkts, 40 overs)	269

*K. W. R. Fletcher, K. R. Pont, S. Turner, R. E. East, †D. E. East and D. L. Acfield did not bat.

Bowling: McFarlane 7–0–44–0; Folley 7–1–47–0; Reidy 8–1–39–0; Croft 8–0–43–2; Simmons 7–0–52–0; Hughes 3–0–27–0.

Lancashire

A. Kennedy b Phillip	6	I. Folley not out	8
*C. H. Lloyd c D. E. East b Phillip	3	C. E. H. Croft c Gooch b Phillip	13
G. Fowler c D. E. East b Phillip	5	L. L. McFarlane b Phillip	3
F. C. Hayes hit wkt b Phillip	87	L-b 3, w 2, n-b 1	6
D. P. Hughes c Lilley b R. E. East	17		—
J. Simmons b Gooch	21	1/7 2/13 3/18 4/49 (36.2 overs)	187
B. W. Reidy st D. E. East b Pont	11	5/93 6/132 7/152	
†C. Maynard c R. E. East b Pont	7	8/164 9/180	

Bowling: Phillip 6.2–0–13–6; Turner 6–0–27–0; Gooch 8–0–38–1; R. E. East 8–0–48–1; Acfield 5–0–35–0; Pont 3–0–20–2.

Umpires: A. Jepson and N. T. Plews.

At Lord's, June 20. LANCASHIRE lost to MIDDLESEX by 20 runs.

At Worcester, June 27. LANCASHIRE beat WORCESTERSHIRE by 22 runs.

At Derby, July 4. LANCASHIRE lost to DERBYSHIRE on faster scoring-rate.

LANCASHIRE v SURREY

At Manchester, July 11. Lancashire won by seven wickets. Two quick wickets by Reidy forced Surrey to struggle, and only a fifth-wicket stand between Roope and Richards enabled them to reach 172. An opening partnership of 72, followed by an aggressive half-century from Clive Lloyd, gave Lancashire a comfortable win.

Surrey

G. S. Clinton lbw b O'Shaughnessy	18	S. T. Clarke b Reidy	2
D. B. Pauline b Reidy	4	G. Monkhouse c Abrahams b McFarlane	6
*R. D. V. Knight c Maynard b Reidy	1		
M. A. Lynch lbw b O'Shaughnessy	21	P. H. L. Wilson not out	3
G. R. J. Roope b McFarlane	35	L-b 14, w 3, n-b 1	18
†C. J. Richards b Hughes	52		
D. J. Thomas c and b Abrahams	3	1/7 2/11 3/43 4/52 (39.5 overs)	172
A. Needham c C. H. Lloyd b Reidy	9	5/121 6/126 7/154 8/158 9/165	

Bowling: McFarlane 6.5–0–15–2; Reidy 8–0–28–4; Simmons 8–0–34–0; O'Shaughnessy 6–1–27–2; Abrahams 7–1–25–1; Hughes 4–0–25–1.

Lancashire

G. Fowler b Needham	31	D. P. Hughes not out	17
D. Lloyd c Lynch b Needham	40	B 4, l-b 13, w 6	23
*C. H. Lloyd not out	61		
†C. Maynard c and b Needham	2	1/72 2/97 3/107 (3 wkts, 35.3 overs)	174

J. Abrahams, B. W. Reidy, J. Simmons, K. A. Hayes, L. L. McFarlane and S. J. O'Shaughnessy did not bat.

Bowling: Wilson 7–0–37–0; Monkhouse 8–2–20–0; Thomas 6–0–17–0; Needham 8–0–41–3; Clarke 6–1–33–0; Lynch 0.3–0–3–0.

At Southampton, July 18. LANCASHIRE tied with HAMPSHIRE.

LANCASHIRE v WARWICKSHIRE

At Manchester, July 25. Lancashire won by 18 runs. A second-wicket partnership of 121 between the Lloyds enabled Lancashire to reach their best total of the season. Warwickshire's Lloyd was also in good form but Lancashire, despite a weakened attack, stayed in control.

Lancashire

G. Fowler c Humpage b Willis	6	B. W. Reidy c Lloyd b Willis	1
D. Lloyd c Asif Din b Small	93		
*C. H. Lloyd c Kallicharran b Small	70	B 2, l-b 6, w 5	13
D. P. Hughes c Lethbridge b Sutcliffe	25		
J. Abrahams c Humpage b Willis	9	1/19 2/140 3/205 (6 wkts, 40 overs)	225
J. Simmons not out	8	4/212 5/223 6/225	

†C. Maynard, I. Folley, S. J. O'Shaughnessy and L. L. McFarlane did not bat.

Bowling: Willis 8–0–30–3; Small 8–1–40–2; Lethbridge 8–0–32–0; Kallicharran 8–0–45–0; Sutcliffe 8–0–65–1.

Warwickshire

D. L. Amiss b McFarlane	11	Asif Din not out	55
T. A. Lloyd b Reidy	55	S. H. Wootton not out	28
A. I. Kallicharran c O'Shaughnessy b Folley.	12	L-b 17, w 2	19
†G. W. Humpage b Reidy	17	1/17 2/49 3/95 4/107 5/117	(5 wkts, 40 overs) 207
R. I. H. B. Dyer c Fowler b Abrahams.	10		

C. Lethbridge, G. C. Small, *R. G. D. Willis and S. P. Sutcliffe did not bat.

Bowling: Folley 8–1–29–1; McFarlane 8–0–46–1; Simmons 8–1–27–0; Reidy 8–0–46–2; Abrahams 8–0–40–1.

Umpires: N. T. Plews and J. van Geloven.

At Nottingham, August 1. LANCASHIRE beat NOTTINGHAMSHIRE by 6 runs.

LANCASHIRE v YORKSHIRE

At Manchester, August 8. No result. On a day of stops and starts Lancashire openers David Lloyd and Fowler did well to stay undefeated through 24 overs. Yorkshire were about to start the task of making 52 from ten overs when a final downpour ended the game.

Lancashire

D. Lloyd not out	53
G. Fowler not out	59
B 5, l-b 5, n-b 2	12
(no wkt, 24 overs)	124

*C. H. Lloyd, D. P. Hughes, J. Abrahams, J. Simmons, S. J. O'Shaughnessy, B. W. Reidy, †C. Maynard, P. J. W. Allott and C. E. H. Croft did not bat.

Bowling: Old 8–1–20–0; Stuchbury 5–0–30–0; Sidebottom 7–0–40–0; Stevenson 4–1–22–0.

Yorkshire

G. Boycott, S. Stuchbury, C. W. J. Athey, J. D. Love, S. N. Hartley, †D. L. Bairstow, P. Carrick, C. M. Old, G. B. Stevenson, *R. Illingworth and A. Sidebottom .

Umpires: B. J. Meyer and D. R. Shepherd.

At Leicester, August 15. LANCASHIRE lost to LEICESTERSHIRE by 24 runs.

LANCASHIRE v KENT

At Manchester, August 29. Kent won by five wickets. Lancashire, struggling for runs against an accurate attack, needed a fifth-wicket partnership between Abrahams and Simmons to give them encouragement. However, a run-rate of just over 4 an over proved easy for Kent, who thus maintained their position with the leaders.

Lancashire

D. Lloyd b Woolmer	14	P. J. W. Allott not out	7
I. Cockbain b Woolmer	12		
*C. H. Lloyd b Jarvis	19	B 1, l-b 6, w 2, n-b 1	10
S. J. O'Shaughnessy c and b Jarvis	1		
J. Abrahams not out	47	1/27 2/34 3/45 (5 wkts, 36 overs)	148
J. Simmons c Aslett b Dilley	38	4/58 5/138	

N. H. Fairbrother, †C. Maynard, I. Folley and M. Watkinson did not bat.

Bowling: Dilley 8–1–33–1; Ellison 8–0–39–0; Woolmer 6–1–22–2; Jarvis 8–0–30–2; Underwood 6–1–14–0.

Kent

N. R. Taylor c Maynard b Watkinson	33	*G. W. Johnson not out	11
R. A. Woolmer b Watkinson	12	†A. P. E. Knott not out	17
M. R. Benson c Fairbrother b Simmons	34	L-b 9, w 2	11
D. G. Aslett c Maynard b Allott	24	1/30 2/86 3/94 (5 wkts, 33.5 overs)	151
S. G. Hinks lbw b Simmons	9	4/119 5/129	

R. M. Ellison, G. R. Dilley, D. L. Underwood and K. B. S. Jarvis did not bat.

Bowling: Allott 6.5–2–27–1; Folley 4–0–17–0; Watkinson 8–1–26–2; O'Shaughnessy 8–0–39–0; Simmons 7–0–31–2.

Umpires: R. S. Herman and B. Leadbeater.

At Taunton, September 12. LANCASHIRE lost to SOMERSET by seven wickets.

LEICESTERSHIRE

LEICESTERSHIRE v DERBYSHIRE

At Leicester, May 9. Leicestershire won by 67 runs. Gower's run-a-minute hundred was the highlight of Leicestershire's formidable total from only 38 overs, though Davison slammed a 6 and six 4s as the last ten overs yielded 92. Derbyshire never recovered after Kirsten's run-out.

Leicestershire

D. I. Gower st Taylor b Oldham	100	T. J. Boon not out	6
N. E. Briers lbw b Newman	49	B 5, l-b 10, w 1, n-b 3	19
B. F. Davison b Hacker	53		
†M. A. Garnham c Newman b Hacker	10	1/140 2/206 3/226 (4 wkts, 38 overs)	239
*R. W. Tolchard not out	2	4/231	

D. A. Wenlock, J. F. Steele, G. J. Parsons, L. B. Taylor and K. Higgs did not bat.

Bowling: Hacker 7–0–38–2; Oldham 8–0–49–1; Wood 7–0–46–0; Miller 8–0–35–0; Newman 8–0–52–1.

Derbyshire

J. G. Wright c Garnham b Parsons	17	P. G. Newman c Garnham b Parsons	9
J. H. Hampshire c Gower b Steele	28	S. Oldham b Higgs	6
P. N. Kirsten run out	22	P. J. Hacker not out	6
G. Miller c Garnham b Steele	19	B 4, l-b 5, w 4, n-b 2	15
K. J. Barnett c Boon b Steele	18		
*B. Wood c Garnham b Higgs	22	1/29 2/65 3/79 (35.3 overs)	172
R. J. Finney c Gower b Steele	5	4/104 5/117 6/128	
†R. W. Taylor c Boon b Taylor	5	7/144 8/154 9/162	

Bowling: Taylor 7–0–27–1; Parsons 6.3–0–33–2; Higgs 8–0–35–2; Wenlock 7–0–38–0; Steele 7–1–24–4.

Umpires: M. J. Kitchen and P. B. Wight.

LEICESTERSHIRE v YORKSHIRE

At Leicester, May 16. Leicestershire won by 1 run. Yorkshire's left-arm seamer Stuchbury finished with a remarkable five for 16 from two four-over spells, while for Leicestershire, in their 100th John Player game at Grace Road, only Gower and Davison looked comfortable. Yorkshire, who had put Leicestershire in, fell behind the asking-rate, and then wickets tumbled as they tried to force the pace. Still, only 5 were needed off the last five balls, but Clift bowled Bairstow with the first of these and, with 2 needed to tie the match off the last, Sidebottom could only scramble a leg-bye.

Leicestershire

D. I. Gower c Sidebottom b Stuchbury	45
N. E. Briers c and b Hartley	10
†M. A. Garnham c Bairstow b Stuchbury	2
B. F. Davison c Sharp b Old	33
*R. W. Tolchard b Stuchbury	5
T. J. Boon c Hartley b Stuchbury	29
P. B. Clift c Moxon b Stevenson	4
J. F. Steele c Bairstow b Stuchbury	5
D. A. Wenlock run out	4
G. J. Parsons not out	6
L. B. Taylor not out	1
B 2, l-b 15, w 3, n-b 5	25
1/31 2/68 3/79 4/89 5/129 6/142 7/154 8/161 9/162 (9 wkts, 40 overs)	169

Bowling: Old 8–1–24–1; Stevenson 8–0–29–1; Sidebottom 8–0–38–0; Hartley 8–0–37–1; Stuchbury 8–1–16–5.

Yorkshire

K. Sharp b Clift	19
C. W. J. Athey st Garnham b Steele	54
J. D. Love lbw b Wenlock	9
*C. M. Old c Steele b Taylor	21
S. N. Hartley b Wenlock	6
†D. L. Bairstow b Clift	27
G. B. Stevenson b Clift	3
P. Carrick b Clift	9
M. D. Moxon not out	6
A. Sidebottom not out	1
B 3, l-b 6, w 2, n-b 2	13
1/35 2/64 3/96 4/106 5/131 6/136 7/150 8/165 (8 wkts, 40 overs)	168

S. Stuchbury did not bat.

Bowling: Taylor 8–1–32–1; Parsons 8–1–22–0; Clift 8–1–35–4; Wenlock 8–0–37–2; Steele 8–0–29–1.

Umpires: C. Cook and J. van Geloven.

At Cardiff, May 23. GLAMORGAN v LEICESTERSHIRE. No result.

At The Oval, May 30. LEICESTERSHIRE lost to SURREY by 1 run.

LEICESTERSHIRE v HAMPSHIRE

At Leicester, June 6. Leicestershire won by 9 runs. Gower, dropped twice, took his Sunday aggregate for the season to 400 with 96 (eight 4s) before becoming the first of Emery's three victims from four balls in the final over. Parsons set back Hampshire's prospects with three early wickets, and thereafter the visitors were always behind the run-rate.

Leicestershire

D. I. Gower b Emery	96	P. B. Clift b Emery	0
N. E. Briers b Malone	58	B 1, l-b 15, w 7, n-b 1	24
B. F. Davison c Greenidge b Emery	30		—
*R. W. Tolchard not out	3	1/130 2/199 3/211 (5 wkts, 40 overs)	211
†M. A. Garnham b Emery	0	4/211 5/211	

D. A. Wenlock, J. F. Steele, J. P. Agnew, G. J. Parsons and K. Higgs did not bat.

Bowling: Marshall 8–3–24–0; Emery 8–2–21–4; Malone 8–1–37–1; Tremlett 8–0–40–0; Jesty 5–0–43–0; Cowley 3–0–22–0.

Hampshire

C. G. Greenidge c Briers b Parsons	3	†R. J. Parks not out	36
J. M. Rice b Parsons	13	T. M. Tremlett c Agnew b Wenlock	16
N. G. Cowley c Garnham b Parsons	11	K. St J. D. Emery not out	0
*T. E. Jesty c Gower b Higgs	49	L-b 8, w 2, n-b 2	12
M. C. J. Nicholas b Steele	12		—
V. P. Terry lbw b Clift	4	1/5 2/25 3/33 (8 wkts, 40 overs)	202
M. D. Marshall b Higgs	46	4/54 5/77 6/113 7/162 8/194	

S. J. Malone did not bat.

Bowling: Agnew 8-0-36-0; Parsons 8–0–32–3; Steele 8–0–33–1; Clift 8–0–34–1; Higgs 7–0–43–2; Wenlock 1–0–12–1.

Umpires: R. Julian and M. J. Kitchen.

LEICESTERSHIRE v MIDDLESEX

At Leicester, June 13. Middlesex won by four wickets. Middlesex had Radley to thank as they retained their unbeaten record in the League. His 58 not out from 28 overs contained only one boundary, but his steady acquisition brought them through when they still needed 48 from seven overs. Leicestershire missed the impetus given them in recent weeks by Gower (on Test duty), for Briers's 61 was a 36-overs affair containing 29 singles.

Leicestershire

N. E. Briers c Selvey b Emburey	61	D. A. Wenlock run out	0
J. C. Balderstone c Butcher b Gatting	17	G. J. Parsons not out	5
†M. A. Garnham b Merry	0	L. B. Taylor not out	0
B. F. Davison b Gatting	31	L-b 14	14
*R. W. Tolchard c Brearley b Daniel	4		—
A. M. E. Roberts b Selvey	15	1/51 2/55 3/98 (8 wkts, 40 overs)	172
J. F. Steele c Butcher b Selvey	25	4/103 5/133 6/139 7/145 8/170	

K. Higgs did not bat.

Bowling: Daniel 8–2–21–1; Selvey 8–0–27–2; Merry 8–0–44–1; Gatting 8–1–21–2; Emburey 8–0–45–1.

Middlesex

J. M. Brearley c Garnham b Parsons	17	J. E Emburey c Higgs b Steele	9
W. N. Slack b Higgs	9	†P. R. Downton not out	14
G. D. Barlow b Taylor	29	L-b 10, w 1	11
C. T. Radley not out	58		—
R. O. Butcher lbw b Steele	5	1/23 2/38 3/90 (6 wkts, 39.1 overs)	173
M. W. Gatting c Steele b Roberts	21	4/97 5/125 6/146	

W. G. Merry, M. W. W. Selvey and W. W. Daniel did not bat.

Bowling: Roberts 8–0–43–1; Taylor 8–1–24–1; Higgs 7.1–0–26–1; Parsons 8–0–36–1; Steele 8–0–33–2.

Umpires: W. E. Alley and C. T. Spencer.

At Harlow, June 27. LEICESTERSHIRE lost to ESSEX by 19 runs.

LEICESTERSHIRE v WARWICKSHIRE

At Leicester, July 4. Leicestershire won by six wickets. Gower's third Sunday century in six innings, containing eleven 4s and a 6, improved a League average that stood at 100 before the game. For the visitors, Humpage, whose boundary tally matched Gower's, and Kallicharran put on 95 in only fourteen overs, the major sufferers being Higgs and Parsons.

Warwickshire

D. L. Amiss c Taylor b Steele	25	S. H. Wootton not out	7
T. A. Lloyd c Taylor b Steele	29	B 1, l-b 14, w 2, n-b 1	18
A. I. Kallicharran c Garnham b Taylor	45		—
†G. W. Humpage not out	87	1/47 2/72 3/167 (4 wkts, 37 overs)	213
Asif Din lbw b Taylor	2	4/179	

R. I. H. B. Dyer, S. P. Sutcliffe, G. C. Small, *R. G. D. Willis and J. Cumbes did not bat.

Bowling: Taylor 8–0–16–2; Parsons 8–0–60–0; Steele 8–0–37–2; Wenlock 6–0–27–0; Higgs 7–0–55–0.

Leicestershire

D. I. Gower c Wootton b Sutcliffe	107	T. J. Boon not out	0
N. E. Briers b Small	38	B 9, l-b 6, w 4, n-b 2	21
B. F. Davison b Sutcliffe	37		—
†M. A. Garnham c sub b Willis	1	1/100 2/186 (4 wkts, 34.3 overs)	214
*R. W. Tolchard not out	10	3/195 4/208	

J. F. Steele, D. A. Wenlock, G. J. Parsons, K. Higgs and L. B. Taylor did not bat.

Bowling: Willis 8–1–22–1; Small 8–0–42–1; Kallicharran 8–0–56–0; Sutcliffe 8–0–52–2; Dyer 2.3–0–21–0

Umpires: D. J. Constant and D. G. L. Evans.

At Nottingham, July 11. LEICESTERSHIRE lost to NOTTINGHAMSHIRE by five wickets.

At Hove, July 18. LEICESTERSHIRE lost to SUSSEX by 14 runs.

LEICESTERSHIRE v GLOUCESTERSHIRE

At Leicester, August 1. Leicestershire won by 32 runs to extend their long run of success over Gloucestershire, who have not beaten them in the League since 1969. On a slow pitch, Briers's 82, containing seven boundaries, occupied all but two of the 39 overs bowled. Gloucestershire's reply was immediately undermined by Parsons, whose initial five-over spell removed both openers and cost only 7 runs.

Leicestershire

N. E. Briers run out	82	T. J. Boon not out	2
I. P. Butcher lbw b Shepherd	19	B 10, w 3, n-b 4	17
*R. W. Tolchard c Stovold b Bainbridge	20		
B. F. Davison b Stephenson	32	1/42 2/96 3/154 (4 wkts, 39 overs)	196
†M. A. Garnham not out	24	4/173	

J. F. Steele, G. J. Parsons, N. G. B. Cook, J. P. Agnew and D. A. Wenlock did not bat.

Bowling: Surridge 6–0–36–0; Stephenson 8–0–34–1; Broad 5–0–26–0; Shepherd 7–0–26–1; Graveney 6–0–25–0; Bainbridge 7–0–32–1.

Gloucestershire

A. W. Stovold c Steele b Parsons	0	*D. A. Graveney c Steele b Agnew	10
B. C. Broad c Briers b Parsons	8	F. D. Stephenson b Parsons	18
P. W. Romaines c Tolchard b Wenlock	55	†R. C. Russell not out	7
A. J. Wright st Garnham b Steele	0	D. Surridge not out	1
P. Bainbridge c Steele b Wenlock	21	L-b 6, w 5, n-b 1	12
A. J. Hignell b Wenlock	3	1/0 2/24 3/25 (9 wkts, 39 overs)	164
J. N. Shepherd b Parsons	29	4/69 5/75 6/107 7/137 8/139 9/163	

Bowling: Parsons 8–1–33–4; Agnew 7–0–22–1; Steele 8–3–24–1; Wenlock 8–0–32–3; Cook 8–0–41–0.

Umpires: M. J. Kitchen and D. O. Oslear.

At Stourbridge, August 8. LEICESTERSHIRE beat WORCESTERSHIRE by eight wickets.

LEICESTERSHIRE v LANCASHIRE

At Leicester, August 15. Leicestershire won by 24 runs. Garnham, having taken twenty overs over 40, almost doubled his tally in the last six overs, whereupon Clift, out of action for two months with an Achilles' tendon injury, took three for 7 in his first four overs. From 63 for five, Simmons and Reidy revived Lancashire, and even with the last man in, Reidy still threatened Leicestershire with his lusty hitting until, sending up a skier off Steele, he was well caught by Tolchard.

Leicestershire

N. E. Briers c Maynard b McFarlane	0	J. F. Steele c D. Lloyd b Allott	10
I. P Butcher run out	0	G. J. Parsons run out	2
*R. W. Tolchard c Fowler b O'Shaughnessy	17	D. A. Wenlock b Allott	2
B. F. Davison lbw b Reidy	47	B 11, w 1	12
†M. A. Garnham not out	79	1/0 2/3 3/42 4/107 (8 wkts, 40 overs)	173
T. J. Boon b Reidy	4	5/115 6/162 7/169 8/173	

P. B. Clift and L. B. Taylor did not bat.

Bowling: McFarlane 8–0–50–1; O'Shaughnessy 8–1–21–1; Allott 8–1–32–2; Reidy 8–0–32–2; Simmons 8–0–26–0.

Lancashire

D. Lloyd c Tolchard b Clift	10	†C. Maynard c Garnham b Taylor	2
G. Fowler c and b Clift	33	P. J. W. Allott b Taylor	3
*C. H. Lloyd c Garnham b Clift	1	L. L. McFarlane not out	2
D. P. Hughes c and b Steele	0		
J. Abrahams b Clift	8	B 1, l-b 4, w 3, n-b 2	10
J. Simmons c Tolchard b Wenlock	21		—
B. W. Reidy c Tolchard b Steele	50	1/37 2/43 3/44 (36.3 overs)	149
S. J. O'Shaughnessy c Tolchard b Wenlock	9	4/46 5/63 6/95 7/105 8/115 9/128	

Bowling: Taylor 8–0–19–2; Parsons 8–0–36–0; Steele 6.3–0–26–2; Clift 8–1–17–4; Wenlock 6–0–41–2.

Umpires: D. R. Shepherd and P. B. Wight.

At Taunton, August 22. LEICESTERSHIRE lost to SOMERSET by six wickets.

LEICESTERSHIRE v NORTHAMPTONSHIRE

At Leicester, August 29. Leicestershire won by four wickets. Northamptonshire, after choosing to bat, looked anything but the side with the highest John Player League run-rate, though Nick Cook, in a rare Sunday appearance, bowled extremely well and with great economy. Griffiths's early injury while fielding limited Northamptonshire's bowling options, but Leicestershire had to bat in poor light. Butcher (eight 4s) and Tolchard appeared to have settled the match with 91 in sixteen overs, but there were only nine balls to spare when Tolchard made the winning hit.

Northamptonshire

W. Larkins b Roberts	5	†G. Sharp not out	19
P. Willey c Cook b Wenlock	39	T. M. Lamb not out	12
R. J. Boyd-Moss b Roberts	0	B 9, l-b 3, w 1, n-b 1	14
*G. Cook run out	24		—
R. G. Williams b Clift	20	1/11 2/11 (7 wkts, 40 overs)	166
Kapil Dev c Roberts b Wenlock	25	3/66 4/84 5/121	
D. J. Capel c Boon b Wenlock	8	6/126 7/141	

N. A. Mallender and B. J. Griffiths did not bat.

Bowling: Parsons 8–0–40–0; Roberts 8–0–35–2; Cook 8–2–15–0; Clift 8–1–29–1; Wenlock 8–0–33–3.

Leicestershire

N. E. Briers c sub b Willey	11	A. M. E. Roberts b Kapil Dev	2
I. P. Butcher lbw b Mallender	71	P. B. Clift not out	9
†M. A. Garnham b Williams	2	B 6, l-b 4, n-b 1	11
B. F. Davison b Willey	7		—
*R. W. Tolchard not out	57	1/26 2/34 3/49 (6 wkts, 38.4 overs)	170
T. J. Boon b Kapil Dev	0	4/140 5/143 6/143	

N. G. B. Cook, G. J. Parsons and D. A. Wenlock did not bat.

Bowling: Kapil Dev 8–1–38–2; Lamb 8–1–25–0; Willey 8–1–31–2; Williams 8–0–39–1; Mallender 6.4–1–26–1.

Umpires: R. Palmer and K. Ibadulla.

At Canterbury, September 12. LEICESTERSHIRE beat KENT by 22 runs.

MIDDLESEX

At Bristol, May 9. MIDDLESEX beat GLOUCESTERSHIRE by 20 runs.

At Bournemouth, May 16. MIDDLESEX beat HAMPSHIRE by four wickets.

MIDDLESEX v NOTTINGHAMSHIRE

At Lord's, May 23. No result. Todd's Lord's miseries continued when he followed his "King Pair" in the opening game with another cheap dismissal. After rain halted events for a long time, Middlesex were required to score 62 off ten overs. They lost Radley and Gatting in the first over, Butcher in the second, and the contest was neatly balanced when further rain ended it.

Nottinghamshire

P. A. Todd lbw b Daniel	1		L-b 5, w 3	8
R. T. Robinson not out	45			—
*C. E. B. Rice not out	58	1/2	(1 wkt, 18.1 overs)	112

D. W. Randall, M. A. Fell, R. J. Hadlee, †B. N. French, E. E. Hemmings, K. Saxelby, M. Hendrick and M. K. Bore did not bat.

Bowling: Daniel 7.1–0–39–1; Selvey 5–0–20–0; Edmonds 3–0–21–0; Gatting 2–0–16–0; Emburey 1–0–8–0.

Middlesex

G. D. Barlow not out	18	P. H. Edmonds not out		0
C. T. Radley c Fell b Hadlee	0			
M. W. Gatting run out	0	L-b 4		4
R. O. Butcher c Randall b Hendrick	1			—
*J. M. Brearley run out	8	1/1 2/1 3/12	(5 wkts, 5 overs)	32
J. E. Emburey b Hadlee	1	4/27 5/32		

W. N. Slack, †P. R. Downton, M. W. W. Selvey and W. W. Daniel did not bat.

Bowling: Hadlee 3–0–14–2; Hendrick 2–0–14–1.

Umpires: D. O. Oslear and R. Palmer

MIDDLESEX v ESSEX

At Lord's, May 30. Middlesex won by 51 runs. A large crowd, estimated at 12,000, saw Middlesex achieve their tenth win in eleven matches in a triumphant May. Slack, dropped first ball, and Brearley saw them past 100 in the fifteenth over after Fletcher put them in, and Butcher hooked Phillip for two 6s in an over to raise 200. Brearley took a deft catch to dismiss Gooch and Edmonds collected two spectacular catches — first off Phillip and then to end a stand of 75 in eleven overs between McEwan and Lilley.

Middlesex

*J. M. Brearley c D. E. East b Foster	98	P. H. Edmonds not out	11
W. N. Slack b Gooch	52		
M. W. Gatting b Gooch	24	B 3, l-b 8, w 2	13
R. O. Butcher c Gooch b Phillip	29		—
C. T. Radley c Phillip b Foster	7	1/136 2/170 (5 wkts, 37 overs)	245
J. E. Emburey not out	11	3/211 4/217 5/226	

†P. R. Downton, N. J. Kemp, M. W. W. Selvey and W. W. Daniel did not bat.

Bowling: Lever 7–0–59–0; Phillip 6–0–52–1; Foster 8–0–45–2; Turner 8–0–45–0; Gooch 8–0–31–2.

Essex

G. A. Gooch c Brearley b Selvey	17	S. Turner c Downton b Kemp	13
B. R. Hardie c Downton b Selvey	7	†D. E. East run out	0
K. S. McEwan c Downton b Kemp	69	N. A. Foster c Downton b Kemp	10
*K. W. R. Fletcher c Edmonds b Selvey	1	J. K. Lever b Gatting	10
		L-b 11, w 9	20
N. Phillip c Edmonds b Selvey	7		—
A. W. Lilley c and b Edmonds	22	1/26 2/29 3/36 (37 overs)	194
K. R. Pont not out	18	4/55 5/130 6/143 7/163 8/164 9/183	

Bowling: Daniel 6–0–23–0; Selvey 8–0–27–4; Edmonds 8–0–28–1; Emburey 5–0–32–0; Kemp 8–0–47–3; Gatting 2–0–17–1.

Umpires: W. E. Alley and P. J. Eele.

At Leicester, June 13. MIDDLESEX beat LEICESTERSHIRE by four wickets.

MIDDLESEX v LANCASHIRE

At Lord's, June 20. Middlesex won by 20 runs. Slack, unusually sedate for a Sunday game, contributed only 1 run for every 2 by his partners, and Middlesex were grateful for a late effort from Emburey and Downton. Brearley's experiment of pairing Emburey with Selvey in response to Clive Lloyd's appearance as opener was not a success, and Lancashire were promisingly placed on 95 for one at halfway. Then Lloyd was run out by Daniel's throw from long-off, after which Daniel completed the job with a five-wicket burst.

Middlesex

W. N. Slack b Croft	63	J. E. Emburey not out	18
*J. M. Brearley c C. H. Lloyd b Croft	24	†P. R. Downton not out	7
M. W. Gatting b Simmons	42		
R. O. Butcher c Fowler b Folley	16	B 4, l-b 12, w 2	18
C. T. Radley c Abrahams b Folley	3		—
G. D. Barlow b Simmons	1	1/44 2/114 3/137 (7 wkts, 39 overs)	198
P. H. Edmonds c and b Croft	6	4/152 5/153 6/164 7/179	

M. W. W. Selvey and W. W. Daniel did not bat.

Bowling: Allott 7–0–33–0; Folley 8–0–37–2; Croft 8–1–34–3; Reidy 8–0–43–0; Simmons 8–0–33–2.

Lancashire

A. Kennedy c Barlow b Daniel	26	C. E. H. Croft c Gatting b Selvey	1
*C. H. Lloyd run out	52	P. J. W. Allott not out	12
G. Fowler c and b Emburey	30	I. Folley c Edmonds b Daniel	2
D. P. Hughes b Daniel	18	L-b 5, w 2	7
B. W. Reidy b Edmonds	6		
J. Simmons b Daniel	7	1/55 2/95 3/130 (37.3 overs)	178
J. Abrahams c Emburey b Daniel	0	4/130 5/139 6/139	
†C. Maynard c Barlow b Selvey	17	7/150 8/163 9/163	

Bowling: Selvey 6–0–28–2; Emburey 8–1–50–1; Daniel 7.3–0–27–5; Gatting 8–0–29–0; Edmonds 8–0–37–1.

Umpires: D. Archer and K. E. Palmer.

MIDDLESEX v SURREY

At Lord's, June 27. Middlesex won by three wickets. Lynch thumped 42 from 39 balls in his usual scintillating fashion, and Smith's half-century took 82 balls as he tried to maintain the momentum. Although Brearley and Radley gave Middlesex a crisp start, batting was never easy, and, with 13 needed from the last two overs, it required all Downton's coolness to bring victory.

Surrey

*R. D. V. Knight b Merry	19	R. D. Jackman b Selvey	4
G. P. Howarth c Brearley b Selvey	2	G. Monkhouse not out	1
D. M. Smith c Downton b Daniel	50	P. H. L. Wilson b Selvey	0
M. A. Lynch c Tomlins b Daniel	42	B 2, l-b 5	7
G. R. J. Roope c Brearley b Gatting	8		
S. T. Clarke b Emburey	1	1/9 2/27 3/91 (38 overs)	161
†C. J. Richards b Gatting	4	4/102 5/108 6/123	
D. J. Thomas c Merry b Selvey	23	7/143 8/159 9/160	

Bowling: Selvey 7–0–32–4; Merry 8–1–37–1; Gatting 8–0–30–2; Emburey 8–1–32–1; Daniel 7–0–23–2.

Middlesex

C. T. Radley st Richards b Jackman	29	K. P Tomlins run out	0
*J. M. Brearley st Richards b Monkhouse	32	†P. R. Downton not out	14
M. W. Gatting b Jackman	36	M. W. W. Selvey not out	1
R. O. Butcher c Roope b Clarke	9	B 9, l-b 7, w 3	19
W. N. Slack b Thomas	16	1/49 2/91 3/108 (7 wkts, 37.3 overs)	162
J. E. Emburey b Clarke	6	4/134 5/144 6/146 7/148	

W. W. Daniel and W. G. Merry did not bat.

Bowling: Monkhouse 8–0–27–1; Thomas 7.3–0–25–1; Wilson 6–0–28–0; Jackman 8–0–39–2; Clarke 8–1–24–2.

Umpires: J. Birkenshaw and W. L. Budd.

MIDDLESEX v NORTHAMPTONSHIRE

At Lord's, July 11. Middlesex won by 16 runs. Middlesex sustained a run-rate of more than 5 an over, which went above 6 in the Brearley–Gatting stand of 79 in twelve overs. Larkins and Willey matched their strokeplay, but then Slack caught Larkins off Hughes, who expressed his thanks by holding Williams off Slack in the next over. Willey stayed until four overs were left, but the challenge had dwindled to the extent that Steele's two 6s in the last over were irrelevant.

Middlesex

C. T. Radley c Steele b Mallender	26	J. E. Emburey not out	17
*J. M. Brearley c and b Carter	74	L-b 4, w 6, n-b 1	11
M. W. Gatting c Griffiths b Carter	36		—
R. O. Butcher not out	44	1/63 2/142 (4 wkts, 40 overs)	214
G. D. Barlow c and b Mallender	6	3/153 4/165	

W. N. Slack, †P. R. Downton, M. W. W. Selvey, S. P. Hughes and W. G. Merry did not bat.

Bowling: Griffiths 8–0–45–0; T. M. Lamb 8–0–33–0; Mallender 8–0–37–2; Capel 8–0–44–0; Willey 2–0–15–0; Carter 6–1–29–2.

Northamptonshire

W. Larkins c Slack b Hughes	60	*†G. Sharp c Butcher b Selvey	2
P. Willey c and b Slack	76	N. A. Mallender c Brearley b Emburey	4
R. G. Williams c Hughes b Slack	1	T. M. Lamb not out	2
D. J. Capel run out	9	L-b 7, w 2	9
R. J. Boyd-Moss c Barlow b Hughes	7		—
R. M. Carter b Emburey	3	1/116 2/118 3/133 (8 wkts, 40 overs)	198
D. S. Steele not out	25	4/153 5/162 6/171 7/174 8/180	

B. J. Griffiths did not bat.

Bowling: Selvey 8–0–38–1; Merry 5–0–23–0; Emburey 7–1–28–2; Gatting 4–0–22–0; Slack 8–0–34–2; Hughes 8–0–44–2.

Umpires: D. R. Shepherd and J. van Geloven.

MIDDLESEX v DERBYSHIRE

At Lord's, July 18. Derbyshire won by seven wickets. Wood, omitted from the Prudential series against Pakistan, typically took the chance to display at Lord's his expertise as a one-day bowler. Moir, on his début in limited-overs cricket, arrested early Middlesex progress with two wickets in three balls, and Maher achieved two stumpings among his five victims. Barnett's sound innings provided an ideal complement to the easier approach of Kirsten and Hampshire.

Middlesex

*J. M. Brearley c Maher b Tunnicliffe	16	M. W. W. Selvey lbw b Wood	1
W. N. Slack st Maher b Moir	31	W. W. Daniel not out	7
C. T. Radley st Maher b Wood	34	W. G. Merry lbw b Wood	1
R. O. Butcher b Moir	0	L-b 4, w 1	5
K. P. Tomlins c Moir b Wood	14		—
G. D. Barlow c Maher b Oldham	7	1/25 2/67 3/67 (33.5 overs)	135
J. E. Emburey c Maher b Wood	12	4/90 5/105 6/109	
†P. R. Downton b Oldham	7	7/124 8/126 9/128	

Bowling: Newman 3–0–17–0; Tunnicliffe 6–1–21–1; Moir 8–1–29–2; Kirsten 4–0–19–0; Wood 6.5–0–20–5; Oldham 6–0–24–2.

Derbyshire

J. G. Wright hit wkt b Daniel	4	*B. Wood not out	6
K. J. Barnett run out	40	L-b 3, n-b 1	4
P. N. Kirsten lbw b Emburey	36		—
J. H. Hampshire not out	47	1/6 2/56 3/127 (3 wkts, 35.4 overs)	137

R. J. Finney, †B. J. M. Maher, C. J. Tunnicliffe, P. G. Newman, S. Oldham and D. G. Moir did not bat.

Bowling: Selvey 8–1–21–0; Daniel 8–2–28–1; Merry 4–0–16–0; Slack 5–0–32–0; Emburey 8–1–15–1; Tomlins 1–0–11–0; Brearley 1–0–6–0; Butcher 0.4–0–4–0.

Umpires: M. J. Kitchen and P. B. Wight.

At Swansea, July 25. MIDDLESEX lost to GLAMORGAN by 39 runs.

MIDDLESEX v KENT

At Lord's, August 1. Kent won by 1 run. On a slow pitch Johnson took 28 overs to score his runs and the first boundary came only in the 35th over – from Dilley. All the main Middlesex batsmen were swept aside for 13, and although Cook, Emburey and Downton toiled hard to repair the innings, 11 were needed from Dilley's last over. Downton took 2 off each of the first four balls, but was run out attempting a ninth, as was Cook, going for the run which would have tied the scores.

Kent

N. R. Taylor c Radley b Selvey	11	G. R. Dilley st Downton b Edmonds	24
L. Potter lbw b Cowans	6	C. Penn c Butcher b Cowans	8
G. W. Johnson b Daniel	29	D. L. Underwood not out	0
*Asif Iqbal c Downton b Cowans	6	L-b 10, w 3, n-b 3	16
C. S. Cowdrey b Daniel	1		—
†A. P. E. Knott c Downton b Emburey	8	1/20 2/22 3/30 (38.1 overs)	119
D. G. Aslett b Daniel	6	4/36 5/46 6/61	
R. M. Ellison b Edmonds	4	7/70 8/97 9/119	

Bowling: Selvey 8–2–12–1; Cowans 7.1–0–29–3; Daniel 8–0–23–3; Emburey 8–0–16–1; Edmonds 7–0–23–2.

Middlesex

*J. M. Brearley lbw b Dilley	2	†P. R. Downton run out	17
C. T. Radley c Potter b Ellison	2	N. G. Cowans not out	0
G. D. Barlow c Knott b Ellison	0	L-b 6, w 2, n-b 3	11
C. R. Cook run out	45		—
R. O. Butcher c Knott b Dilley	1	1/4 2/7 3/7 (8 wkts, 39 overs)	118
J. E. Emburey c and b Potter	29	4/13 5/62 6/87	
P. H. Edmonds b Underwood	11	7/117 8/118	

M. W. W. Selvey and W. W. Daniel did not bat.

Bowling: Dilley 8–2–26–2; Ellison 8–3–14–2; Penn 8–2–26–0; Potter 7–0–27–1; Underwood 8–3–14–1.

Umpires: B. J. Meyer and R. Palmer.

At Weston-super-Mare, August 8. MIDDLESEX beat SOMERSET by 14 runs.

At Birmingham, August 15. MIDDLESEX beat WARWICKSHIRE by 102 runs.

MIDDLESEX v YORKSHIRE

At Lord's, August 22. Middlesex won by 21 runs. Brearley played a typical innings while the other batsmen bustled on. Cowans then took two early wickets, Athey was run out, and when Boycott's solid innings ended, the match seemed settled. However, Hartley and Ramage provided marvellous entertainment in their John Player League record ninth-wicket stand of 88. They began with 15 from an over by Gatting, and Hartley hit two 6s and seven 4s in an innings that received a standing ovation.

Middlesex

W. N. Slack b Old	23	J. E. Emburey c Boycott b Stevenson	13
*J. M. Brearley c and b Carrick	73	†P. R. Downton not out	8
C. T. Radley b Hartley	6	L-b 7, w 2	9
M. W. Gatting st Bairstow b Carrick	23		—
R. O. Butcher c Illingworth b Carrick	11	1/60 2/67 3/112 (6 wkts, 40 overs)	198
C. R. Cook not out	32	4/139 5/152 6/182	

P. H. Edmonds, N. G. Cowans and W. W. Daniel did not bat.

Bowling: Ramage 4–0–20–0; Stevenson 5–0–26–1; Old 8–1–19–1; Hartley 8–0–46–1; Carrick 7–0–38–3; Illingworth 8–0–40–0.

Yorkshire

C. W. J. Athey run out	0	P. Carrick b Gatting	4
K. Sharp lbw b Cowans	4	A. Ramage not out	32
J. D. Love b Edmonds	22	*R. Illingworth not out	2
†D. L. Bairstow c Downton b Cowans	0	B 1, l-b 5, w 2	8
G. Boycott c Downton b Slack	31		—
C. M. Old c Emburey b Edmonds	6	1/1 2/12 3/12 (9 wkts, 40 overs)	177
G. B. Stevenson c Gatting b Edmonds	1	4/49 5/63 6/67	
S. N. Hartley c Brearley b Daniel	67	7/67 8/84 9/172	

Bowling: Cowans 8–0–47–2; Daniel 8–1–27–1; Edmonds 8–1–21–3; Slack 6–0–21–1; Emburey 7–0–34–0; Gatting 3–0–19–1.

Umpires: C. Cook and Khizar Hayat.

At Hove, August 29. MIDDLESEX lost to SUSSEX by 23 runs.

At Worcester, September 12. MIDDLESEX beat WORCESTERSHIRE by 17 runs.

NORTHAMPTONSHIRE

NORTHAMPTONSHIRE v SOMERSET

At Northampton, May 9. Northamptonshire won by 12 runs. Their openers, Cook and Larkins, began steadily with 66 in seventeen overs, but it needed a fifth-wicket stand of 52 by veterans Yardley and Steele to ensure a useful total. Somerset, initially behind the home rate, threatened to take charge until Botham was caught at long-on. Sarfraz, back for his final spell, settled the issue with three quick wickets.

Northamptonshire

*G. Cook c and b Moseley	31	†G. Sharp run out	1
W. Larkins c Denning b Dredge	28	R. M. Carter not out	7
A. J. Lamb c Rose b Popplewell	25	B 1, l-b 13, w 1, n-b 1	16
R. G. Williams c Moseley b Popplewell	23		
T. J. Yardley not out	43	1/66 2/74 3/107 (6 wkts, 40 overs)	196
D. S. Steele b Dredge	22	4/128 5/180 6/181	

Sarfraz Nawaz, D. J. Wild and B. J. Griffiths did not bat.

Bowling: Botham 8–0–38–0; Davis 8–0–33–0; Moseley 8–1–24–1; Dredge 8–0–48–2; Roebuck 4–0–19–0; Popplewell 4–0–18–2.

Somerset

*B. C. Rose c Sarfraz b Griffiths	6	C. H. Dredge not out	7
P. W. Denning st Sharp b Steele	45	H. R. Moseley b Sarfraz	0
N. F. M. Popplewell run out	29	M. R. Davis not out	1
I. T. Botham c Sarfraz b Carter	22	L-b 5, w 1, n-b 3	9
J. W. Lloyds lbw b Griffiths	31		
V. J. Marks c Lamb b Carter	15	1/13 2/72 3/84 (9 wkts, 40 overs)	184
P. M. Roebuck c Yardley b Sarfraz	10	4/109 5/146 6/160	
†D. J. S. Taylor c Cook b Sarfraz	9	7/170 8/179 9/180	

Bowling: Sarfraz 8–1–26–3; Griffiths 8–0–29–2; Carter 8–0–33–2; Steele 8–0–43–1; Wild 8–0–44–0.

Umpires: R. S. Herman and R. Julian.

NORTHAMPTONSHIRE v LANCASHIRE

At Bedford School, May 23. No result. Before thunder and hail-storms put an end to the game, Larkins had brilliantly run out Kennedy in the third over and Fowler had just been caught near the boundary.

Lancashire

A. Kennedy run out	1	L-b 1, w 1, n-b 1	3
*C. H. Lloyd not out	25		
G. Fowler c Wild b Willey	27	1/2 2/56 (2 wkts, 13.2 overs)	56

I. Cockbain, D. Lloyd, D. P. Hughes, B. W. Reidy, P. J. W. Allott, C. E. H. Croft, †M. A. Wallwork and I. Folley did not bat.

Bowling: Sarfraz 4–0–11–0; Griffiths 4–1–11–0; Carter 3–0–17–0; Willey 2.2–0–14–1.

Northamptonshire

*G. Cook, W. Larkins, R. G. Williams, A. J. Lamb, P. Willey, D. J. Wild, T. J. Yardley, †G. Sharp, Sarfraz Nawaz, R. M. Carter and B. J. Griffiths.

Umpires: W. E. Alley and K. Ibadulla.

At Nottingham, June 30. NORTHAMPTONSHIRE lost to NOTTINGHAMSHIRE by 23 runs.

NORTHAMPTONSHIRE v KENT

At Northampton, June 13. Northamptonshire won by 61 runs in wicket-keeper George Sharp's benefit match. Capel, a local nineteen-year-old, hit 79 in 94 minutes (one 6 and seven 4s), his initial first-team half-century, and figured in a century stand with Williams. Kent, previously unbeaten, struck early trouble against Sarfraz and Griffiths, and then fell to the spin of Willey and Williams. Only Cowdrey offered lengthy resistance.

Northamptonshire

W. Larkins c Knott b Jarvis	27	R. M. Carter not out	4
P. Willey lbw b Dilley	5	Sarfraz Nawaz not out	11
R. G. Williams run out	66	L-b 7, w 3	10
D. J. Capel b Jarvis	79		
T. J. Yardley c and b Jarvis	1	1/9 2/46 3/161 (6 wkts, 40 overs)	203
D. J. Wild b Jarvis	0	4/166 5/190 6/190	

*†G. Sharp, T. M. Lamb and B. J. Griffiths did not bat.

Bowling: Jarvis 8–0–39–4; Dilley 8–0–51–1; Woolmer 7–0–31–0; Cowdrey 8–0–37–0; Underwood 8–2–28–0; Potter 1–0–7–0.

Kent

R. A. Woolmer c Larkins b Griffiths	5	G. R. Dilley c and b Sarfraz	33
L. Potter c Sharp b Sarfraz	0	D. L. Underwood lbw b Willey	6
D. G. Aslett c Larkins b Williams	7	K. B. S. Jarvis not out	1
*Asif Iqbal b Williams	18		
C. S. Cowdrey b Willey	40	B 4, l-b 5, w 3, n-b 1	13
†A. P. E. Knott b Williams	8		
S. G. Hinks c Carter b Willey	4	1/0 2/11 3/23 4/48 5/66 (34.2 overs)	142
G. W. Johnson run out	7	6/77 7/94 8/102 9/118	

Bowling: Sarfraz 5.2–2–9–2; Griffiths 5–2–7–1; T. M. Lamb 8–0–44–0; Williams 8–1–38–3; Willey 8–1–31–3.

Umpires: J. Birkenshaw and D. O. Oslear.

At Middlesbrough, June 20. NORTHAMPTONSHIRE beat YORKSHIRE by 55 runs.

At Birmingham, June 27. NORTHAMPTONSHIRE lost to WARWICKSHIRE on faster scoring-rate.

NORTHAMPTONSHIRE v SURREY

At Tring, July 4. Northamptonshire won by 32 runs. Both sides began well and then collapsed. Northamptonshire's attempts to accelerate saw five wickets fall in the last six overs, but Surrey's decline was even more decisive. Seven batsmen fell in 34 balls for 20, the last four at the same total.

Northamptonshire

*G. Cook lbw b Knight	38	N. A. Mallender b Wilson	0
W. Larkins c and b Monkhouse	23	T. M. Lamb not out	1
P. Willey lbw b Clarke	17	B. J. Griffiths not out	11
A. J. Lamb c Lynch b Knight	9	B 4, l-b 7, w 4	15
R. G. Williams b Thomas	32		
D. J. Capel c Roope b Clarke	11	1/45 2/83 3/83 (9 wkts, 40 overs)	164
D. S. Steele c Pauline b Wilson	5	4/103 5/135 6/145	
†G. Sharp b Thomas	2	7/150 8/150 9/151	

Bowling: Thomas 8–2–39–2; Monkhouse 8–3–12–1; Wilson 8–0–40–2; Knight 8–0–26–2; Clarke 8–0–32–2.

Surrey

D. B. Pauline c Cook b Mallender	30	A. Needham lbw b Steele	0
*R. D. V. Knight b Mallender	22	G. Monkhouse not out	0
D. M. Smith st Sharp b Williams	30	P. H. L. Wilson b T. M. Lamb	0
M. A. Lynch b Mallender	2	B 7, l-b 8, w 6, n-b 1	22
D. J. Thomas b Griffiths	6		
S. T. Clarke c Mallender b Williams	10	1/43 2/84 3/96 (36.4 overs)	132
G. R. J. Roope c Sharp b T. M. Lamb	7	4/112 5/122 6/123	
†C. J. Richards st Sharp b Steele	3	7/132 8/132 9/132	

Bowling: Griffiths 6–0–9–1; T. M. Lamb 6.4–1–16–2; Mallender 8–0–27–3; Willey 8–1–24–0; Steele 5–0–18–2; Williams 3–0–16–2.

Umpires: B. Leadbeater and K. E. Palmer.

At Lord's, July 11. NORTHAMPTONSHIRE lost to MIDDLESEX by 16 runs.

At Bristol, July 18. NORTHAMPTONSHIRE beat GLOUCESTERSHIRE by 5 runs.

NORTHAMPTONSHIRE v SUSSEX

At Northampton, July 25. Sussex won by four wickets, thanks to le Roux, who went in at 29 for three and struck six mighty 6s in his 86 off 80 balls. Later Phillipson hit out to see Sussex home with a 6 off the last ball of the 39th over.

Northamptonshire

*G Cook c Greig b le Roux	13	D. J. Capel not out	1
W. Larkins c Gould b Pigott	59		
P. Willey c Mendis b le Roux	53	B 1, l-b 16, w 2, n-b 1	20
A. J. Lamb c Pigott b Barclay	45		
R. G. Williams not out	22	1/36 2/98 3/164 4/207 (4 wkts, 40 overs)	213

D. S. Steele, †G. Sharp, N. A. Mallender, T. M. Lamb and D. J. Wild did not bat.

Bowling: Arnold 6–0–22–0; le Roux 8–0–39–2; Waller 8–0–17–0; Greig 5–0–33–0; Barclay 7–0–47–1; Pigott 6–0–35–1.

Sussex

G. D. Mendis c Mallender b Willey.... 11
†I. J. Gould c Sharp b Mallender........ 17
C. M. Wells c Capel b Wild.............. 45
P. W. G. Parker lbw b Mallender....... 0
G. S le Roux c Wild b T. M. Lamb..... 85
I. A. Greig lbw b Wild...................... 0
C. P. Phillipson not out..................... 44
*J. R. T. Barclay not out.................. 7
L-b 4, w 2.............................. 6

1/29 2/29 3/29 4/132 5/132 6/179 (6 wkts, 39 overs) 215

G. G. Arnold, A. C. S. Pigott and C. E. Waller did not bat.

Bowling: T. M. Lamb 8–0–48–1; Mallender 7–1–31–2; Willey 6–1–27–1; Wild 7–1–43–2; Williams 5–0–23–0; Capel 4–0–23–0; Steele 2–0–14–0.

Umpires: D. G. L. Evans and B. J. Meyer.

NORTHAMPTONSHIRE v WORCESTERSHIRE

At Luton, August 1. Northamptonshire won by 52 runs. They set Worcestershire a formidable target, thanks to a magnificent 158 by Larkins (six 6s, twelve 4s), who shared with Williams a record third-wicket stand of 215 off 25 overs. Worcestershire lost three wickets in the first three overs, and although Neale hit a fighting century in two hours, with one 6 and eight 4s, Mallender, Willey and Lamb proved too much for the other batsmen.

Northamptonshire

W. Larkins c Humphries b Pridgeon... 158
P. Willey c Hemsley b Alleyne........... 9
R. J. Boyd-Moss c Humphries b Perryman. 8
R. G. Williams not out..................... 79
*G. Cook not out............................. 5
B 2, l-b 5, w 6........................ 13

1/16 2/37 3/252 (3 wkts, 40 overs) 272

D. S. Steele, D. J. Capel, †G. Sharp, N. A. Mallender, T. M. Lamb and D. J. Wild did not bat.

Bowling: Alleyne 8–1–28–1; Pridgeon 8–0–43–1; Perryman 8–0–63–1; Patel 8–0–48–0; Hemsley 4–0–31–0; Weston 4–0–46–0.

Worcestershire

M. J. Weston c Boyd-Moss b Mallender. 0
M. S. Scott c Sharp b T. M. Lamb...... 2
*P. A. Neale b Mallender................. 102
E. J. O. Hemsley lbw b Mallender...... 0
D. N. Patel c Larkins b Willey........... 16
D. B. D'Oliveira st Sharp b Willey..... 23
T. S. Curtis c Sharp b Willey............ 1
†D. J. Humphries c Williams b Wild... 35
H. L. Alleyne b T. M. Lamb............. 17
A. P. Pridgeon run out..................... 8
S. P. Perryman not out..................... 2
B 1, l-b 12, n-b 1.................... 14

1/2 2/4 3/5 4/41 5/89 6/91 7/170 8/207 9/211 (39.5 overs) 220

Bowling: Mallender 8–0–31–3; T. M. Lamb 7.5–1–38–2; Willey 8–1–32–3; Wild 8–0–47–1; Steele 4–0–29–0; Williams 4–0–29–0.

Umpires: D. J. Constant and Khizar Hayat.

NORTHAMPTONSHIRE v DERBYSHIRE

At Milton Keynes, August 15. Northamptonshire won by five wickets. Facing a stiff target, Willey shared profitable stands with Larkins and Cook before being joined by Kapil Dev, whose 75 came off 48 balls, with four 6s and eight 4s. Boyd-Moss finished the game with a 6 over the sightscreen. Earlier Wright (four 6s, three 4s) and Barnett had given Derbyshire a sound start, and after faltering briefly, the visitors' innings ended with the last ten overs yielding 92 runs, Tunnicliffe's unbeaten half-century coming off only 27 balls.

Derbyshire

K. J Barnett c and b Kapil Dev	47	I. S. Anderson not out	14
J. G. Wright c Cook b Willey	75		
P. N. Kirsten b Mallender	1	B 5, l-b 5, w 3	13
*B. Wood c Cook b Willey	8		
C. J. Tunnicliffe not out	51	1/124 2/125 3/140 (5 wkts, 40 overs)	233
G. Miller run out	24	4/144 5/189	

†B. J. M. Maher, D. G. Moir, P. G. Newman and S. Oldham did not bat.

Bowling: Griffiths 8–0–43–0; Kapil Dev 8–0–52–1; Lamb 7–0–42–0; Wild 5–0–22–0; Willey 7–0–24–2; Mallender 5–0–37–1.

Northamptonshire

P. Willey c Moir b Wood	58	†G. Sharp not out	2
W. Larkins c Kirsten b Miller	39		
*G. Cook c Barnett b Tunnicliffe	32	B 1, l-b 1, n-b 1	3
Kapil Dev c Barnett b Oldham	75		
R. G. Williams b Wood	7	1/62 2/120 3/184 (5 wkts, 39 overs)	238
R. J. Boyd-Moss not out	22	4/198 5/223	

D. J. Wild, T. M. Lamb, N. A. Mallender and B. J. Griffiths did not bat.

Bowling: Newman 8–1–33–0; Oldham 6–1–38–1; Miller 5–0–33–1; Moir 7–0–54–0; Tunnicliffe 5–0–37–1; Wood 8–0–40–2.

Umpires: R. Julian and A. G. T. Whitehead.

NORTHAMPTONSHIRE v HAMPSHIRE

At Northampton, August 22. Northamptonshire won by 82 runs. Hampshire collapsed against the medium-fast pace of Tim Lamb, who took three wickets in five balls. Cowley and Marshall rallied them with a fighting stand of 60, but Lamb returned to dismiss them both, and there was no further challenge. Earlier Northamptonshire's innings began with an excellent 51 in 73 minutes from Larkins (six 4s) and ended with aggressive hitting from Sharp.

Northamptonshire

W. Larkins c Parks b Tremlett	51	†G. Sharp run out	32
P. Willey c Parks b Marshall	17	T. M. Lamb not out	15
*G. Cook c Southern b Tremlett	33	L-b 5, w 1, n-b 1	7
A. J. Lamb c Parks b Marshall	40		
Kapil Dev c Parks b Tremlett	5	1/20 2/107 3/108 (8 wkts, 40 overs)	205
R. G. Williams c Tremlett b Jesty	5	4/122 5/140 6/140	
R. J. Boyd-Moss b Jesty	0	7/173 8/204	

N. A. Mallender and B. J. Griffiths did not bat.

Bowling: Emery 8–0–40–0; Marshall 8–1–18–2; Southern 2–0–11–0; Tremlett 8–1–34–3; Jesty 6–1–48–2; Cowley 8–0–47–0.

Hampshire

C. G. Greenidge c Larkins b Mallender	8	T. M. Tremlett not out	2
J. M. Rice c Sharp b Griffiths	2	J. W. Southern lbw b Willey	1
D. R. Turner b T. M. Lamb	17	K. St J. D. Emery b Kapil Dev	0
*N. E. J. Pocock lbw b T. M. Lamb	0	B 7, l-b 3, w 4	14
T. E. Jesty lbw b T. M. Lamb	0		
N. G. Cowley c Mallender b T. M. Lamb	34	1/7 2/34 3/34 (34.3 overs)	123
M. D. Marshall b T. M. Lamb	32	4/34 5/35 6/95	
†R. J. Parks c Boyd-Moss b Griffiths	13	7/114 8/121 9/122	

Bowling: Kapil Dev 5–0–10–1; Griffiths 5.3–0–12–2; T. M. Lamb 8–0–25–5; Mallender 8–0–44–1; Willey 8–1–18–1.

Umpires: J. Birkenshaw and P. B. Wight.

At Leicester, August 29. NORTHAMPTONSHIRE lost to LEICESTERSHIRE by four wickets.

At Abergavenny, September 5. NORTHAMPTONSHIRE lost to GLAMORGAN on faster scoring-rate.

At Chelmsford, September 12. NORTHAMPTONSHIRE lost to ESSEX by five wickets.

NOTTINGHAMSHIRE

NOTTINGHAMSHIRE v HAMPSHIRE

At Nottingham, May 9. Hampshire won by 15 runs. Jesty's all-round performance gave Hampshire a more comfortable victory than the final score suggested. His 79 in 66 minutes rescued them from a slow start, and an unbroken stand of 59 between Marshall and Hayward in nine overs took them past 200. When Hassan threatened to switch the initiative, Jesty again played a decisive hand.

Hampshire

C. G. Greenidge c French b Hendrick	14	R. E. Hayward not out	30
J. M. Rice c Rice b Hadlee	6	M. D. Marshall not out	30
N. G. Cowley c Bore b Hemmings	8	L-b 15, w 1	16
*T. E. Jesty c Randall b Illingworth	79		
D. R. Turner lbw b Bore	18	1/18 2/25 3/85 (6 wkts, 40 overs)	201
V. P. Terry c Hendrick b Illingworth	0	4/118 5/121 6/142	

†R. J. Parks, T. M. Tremlett and K. St J. D. Emery did not bat.

Bowling: Hadlee 8–3–21–1; Bore 8–0–22–1; Hendrick 8–1–36–1; Hemmings 8–0–48–1; Illingworth 8–1–58–2.

Nottinghamshire

B. Hassan c Parks b Jesty	48	E. E. Hemmings not out	23
D. W. Randall c Greenidge b Marshall	6	N. J. B. Illingworth not out	8
*C. E. B. Rice c Parks b Tremlett	23		
J. D. Birch c Tremlett b Jesty	17	L-b 9, w 7	16
R. J. Hadlee c Parks b Rice	20		
R. T. Robinson b Marshall	24	1/12 2/58 3/95 (7 wkts, 40 overs)	186
†B. N. French c Cowley b Jesty	1	4/102 5/124 6/135 7/168	

M. Hendrick and M. K. Bore did not bat.

Bowling: Marshall 8–1–16–2; Emery 7–0–36–0; Tremlett 8–0–33–1; Cowley 5–0–26–0; Jesty 8–0–40–3; Rice 4–0–19–1.

Umpires: B. Leadbeater and A. Jepson.

NOTTINGHAMSHIRE v WORCESTERSHIRE

At Nottingham, May 16. Worcestershire won by six wickets. The fragility of Nottinghamshire's batting was exposed by Worcestershire's attack, spearheaded by Pridgeon. French's top score of 18 told the sorry story. With Turner and Ormrod sharing an opening stand of 88, Worcestershire were able to canter to victory.

Nottinghamshire

R. T. Robinson run out	16	K. Saxelby b Pridgeon	6
D. W. Randall c Turner b Pridgeon	0	M. Hendrick c Humphries b Warner	12
*C. E. B. Rice c Turner b Pridgeon	7	M. K. Bore not out	9
B. Hassan c Humphries b Inchmore	12	L-b 8, w 3	11
M. A. Fell c Humphries b Patel	2		
R. J. Hadlee c Patel b Perryman	17	1/0 2/14 3/35 (36.5 overs)	118
†B. N. French c and b Perryman	18	4/41 5/45 6/66	
E. E. Hemmings c Patel b Warner	8	7/83 8/89 9/104	

Bowling: Pridgeon 6.5–1–20–3; Warner 8–0–36–2; Patel 8–0–18–1; Inchmore 7–0–18–1; Perryman 7–1–15–2.

Worcestershire

G. M. Turner b Hadlee	50	*P. A. Neale not out	4
J. A. Ormrod c Rice b Rose	44	L-b 4, w 2	6
D. N. Patel b Hadlee	0		
Younis Ahmed b Hemmings	0	1/88 2/88 (4 wkts, 36.1 overs)	122
E. J. O. Hemsley not out	18	3/89 4/105	

†D. J. Humphries, J. D. Inchmore, A. E. Warner, A. P. Pridgeon and S. P. Perryman did not bat.

Bowling: Hadlee 8–1–27–2; Hendrick 8–0–27–0; Saxelby 6–0–20–0; Bore 6·1–2–24–1; Hemmings 8–0–18–1.

Umpires: H. D. Bird and A. G. T. Whitehead.

At Lord's, May 23. MIDDLESEX v NOTTINGHAMSHIRE. No result.

NOTTINGHAMSHIRE v NORTHAMPTONSHIRE

At Nottingham, May 30. Nottinghamshire won by 23 runs. Rice inspired Nottinghamshire's first John Player League win of the season with a memorable 117 (three 6s, twelve 4s) which spanned 30 overs and was just 3 runs short of the highest by a Nottinghamshire player in the competition. Cook and Lamb made a gallant attempt to keep Northamptonshire in contention, but the return of Hadlee and Hendrick was decisive.

Nottinghamshire

R. T. Robinson st Sharp b Steele	28	†B. N. French not out	1
M. A. Fell c Sharp b Sarfraz	4		
*C. E. B. Rice c Capel b Sarfraz	117	B 1, l-b 12, w 4, n-b 3	20
J. D. Birch c Sarfraz b Capel	24		
D. W. Randall c Sarfraz b Griffiths	20	1/16 2/73 3/143 (5 wkts, 40 overs)	230
R. J. Hadlee not out	16	4/213 5/226	

E. E. Hemmings, K. Saxelby, M. Hendrick and M. K. Bore did not bat.

Bowling: Sarfraz 8–2–32–2; Mallender 8–1–55–0; Griffiths 8–0–21–1; Willey 8–0–45–0; Steele 5–0–29–1; Capel 3–0–28–1.

Northamptonshire

*G. Cook c Fell b Bore	71
W. Larkins b Hadlee	16
P. Willey c Rice b Saxelby	29
A. J. Lamb c Hemmings b Hendrick	45
R. M. Carter b Bore	6
D. J. Capel b Bore	6
†G. Sharp b Hendrick	15
Sarfraz Nawaz c French b Hadlee	4
D. S. Steele not out	3
N. A. Mallender not out	2
B 2, l-b 7, w 1	10
1/21 2/98 3/134 4/155 5/165 7/196 8/204 (8 wkts, 40 overs)	207

B. J. Griffiths did not bat.

Bowling: Hadlee 8–2–22–2; Bore 7–0–38–3; Hemmings 8–0–26–0; Hendrick 8–0–32–2; Saxelby 5–0–44–1; Fell 4–0–35–0.

Umpires: H. D. Bird and D. R. Shepherd.

At Hull, June 13. NOTTINGHAMSHIRE tied with YORKSHIRE.

NOTTINGHAMSHIRE v WARWICKSHIRE

At Nottingham, June 20. Nottinghamshire won by 22 runs. On a drying pitch, Nottinghamshire's modest total was more than a match for Warwickshire, despite some bold hitting by Willis and Cumbes. Nottinghamshire, put in, owed much to the power and improvisation of Rice and Birch; and later Hemmings and Bore capitalised on the conditions.

Nottinghamshire

B. Hassan run out	19
R. T. Robinson c Humpage b Small	2
*C. E. B. Rice b Cumbes	43
J. D. Birch c Amiss b Willis	47
D. W. Randall c and b Lethbridge	14
†B. N. French c Asif Din b Lethbridge	3
E. E. Hemmings b Small	17
N. J. B. Illingworth not out	5
K. Saxelby c Humpage b Willis	0
K. E. Cooper run out	4
L-b 4, w 2, n-b 1	7
1/5 2/44 3/82 4/108 5/112 6/149 7/153 8/153 9/161 (9 wkts, 40 overs)	161

M. K. Bore did not bat.

Bowling: Willis 8–2–10–2; Small 8–1–28–2; Lethbridge 8–0–42–2; Cumbes 7–0–40–1; Kallicharran 8–1–22–0; Asif Din 1–0–12–0.

Warwickshire

D. L. Amiss b Bore	23
T. A. Lloyd c Randall b Hemmings	9
A. I. Kallicharran c and b Bore	2
†G. W. Humpage b Illingworth	12
Asif Din c Randall b Illingworth	2
K. D. Smith c Cooper b Hemmings	18
S. H. Wootton c Cooper b Hemmings	8
C. Lethbridge b Saxelby	14
G. C. Small c Hemmings b Cooper	1
*R. G. D. Willis not out	25
J. Cumbes not out	14
L-b 6, w 4, n-b 1	11
1/26 2/33 3/38 4/51 5/53 6/68 7/89 8/95 9/112 (9 wkts, 40 overs)	139

Bowling: Cooper 8–2–31–1; Saxelby 8–0–33–1; Bore 8–1–17–2; Hemmings 8–3–17–3; Illingworth 8–0–30–2.

Umpires: P. J. Eele and B. J. Meyer.

At Bath, June 27. NOTTINGHAMSHIRE lost to SOMERSET by 113 runs.

NOTTINGHAMSHIRE v LEICESTERSHIRE

At Nottingham, July 11. Nottinghamshire won by five wickets. For Nottinghamshire, without six regular players and with Rice unable to bowl, this was an excellent win. Leicestershire, who chose to bat first, were left a bowler short when Higgs top-edged a ball into his face. Although the game was in the balance with Nottinghamshire 64 for five, Birch and French comfortably steered them to victory.

Leicestershire

J. C. Balderstone b Bore.................. 8
N. E. Briers c Pont b Illingworth........ 21
*R. W. Tolchard lbw b Bore............. 7
B. F. Davison b Illingworth............... 9
†M. A. Garnham c Bore b Fell.......... 11
T. J. Boon run out........................... 26
A. M. E. Roberts b Illingworth.......... 1
J. F. Steele b Illingworth.................. 5
G. J. Parsons not out....................... 7
L. B. Taylor c Robinson b Cooper...... 2
K. Higgs c Robinson b Cooper.......... 7
B 2, l-b 4, w 3, n-b 1............... 10

1/13 2/31 3/43 4/51 5/83 6/84 7/92 8/93 9/104 (40 overs) 114

Bowling: Cooper 8–0–29–2; Bore 8–2–11–2; Illingworth 8–2–15–4; Pont 8–0–27–0; Fell 8–0–22–1.

Nottinghamshire

B. Hassan run out........................... 2
R. T. Robinson c Tolchard b Taylor.... 19
M. A. Fell c Briers b Roberts............ 0
*C. E. B. Rice c Garnham b Taylor.... 21
J. D. Birch not out.......................... 40
P. Johnson b Steele.......................... 4
†B. N. French not out...................... 16
B 1, l-b 5, w 9, n-b 1............... 16

1/14 2/14 3/56 4/57 5/64 (5 wkts, 36.3 overs) 118

I. L. Pont, N. J. B. Illingworth, K. E. Cooper and M. K. Bore did not bat.

Bowling: Roberts 8–2–13–1; Taylor 8–2–22–2; Parsons 8–0–29–0; Steele 8–4–7–1; Briers 4–0–25–0; Balderstone 0.3–0–6–0.

Umpires: C. Cook and R. Palmer.

At The Oval, July 25. NOTTINGHAMSHIRE lost to SURREY by 7 runs.

NOTTINGHAMSHIRE v LANCASHIRE

At Nottingham, August 1. Lancashire won by 6 runs. Lancashire, put in to bat under grey skies, profited through David Lloyd, who faced the first ball and was out to the last. Clive Lloyd's 33 gave Lancashire the acceleration that Nottinghamshire failed to match, despite Hassan's unbeaten 96 (two 6s, nine 4s), but the ultimate match-winner was Simmons, who bowled seven overs for 25 runs when Nottinghamshire needed in excess of 8 an over.

Lancashire

D. Lloyd c Birch b Rice.................... 80
A. Kennedy c and b Rice.................. 26
*C. H. Lloyd b Cooper...................... 33
I. Cockbain c Johnson b Illingworth.... 4
D. P. Hughes c French b Saxelby....... 0
J. Abrahams c Cooper b Rice............ 26
J. Simmons not out.......................... 13
B 2, l-b 5, w 2, n-b 1.............. 10

1/57 2/107 3/119 4/119 5/172 6/192 (6 wkts, 40 overs) 192

†C. J. Scott, I. Folley, P. G. Lee and S. J. O'Shaughnessy did not bat.

Bowling: Hadlee 8–1–25–0; Cooper 8–0–34–1; Saxelby 8–1–22–1; Rice 8–0–43–3; Illingworth 8–0–58–1.

Nottinghamshire

B. Hassan not out........................... 96
P. Johnson c Abrahams b O'Shaughnessy. 16
*C. E. B. Rice b O'Shaughnessy........ 1
J. D. Birch b O'Shaughnessy............ 13
R. J. Hadlee b Abrahams................. 13
P. A. Todd run out.......................... 30
M. A. Fell c Scott b Folley................ 2
K. E. Cooper not out....................... 0
L-b 13, w 2.......................... 15

1/59 2/64 3/101 4/121 5/174 6/186 (6 wkts, 40 overs) 186

K. Saxelby, †B. N. French and N. J. B. Illingworth did not bat.

Bowling: Lee 8–1–32–0; Folley 6–0–29–1; Lloyd 8–0–26–0; O'Shaughnessy 8–0–36–3; Simmons 7–1–25–0; Abrahams 3–1–23–1.

Umpires: D. Archer and H. D. Bird.

At Cheltenham, August 8. NOTTINGHAMSHIRE beat GLOUCESTERSHIRE by 47 runs.

NOTTINGHAMSHIRE v KENT

At Nottingham, August 15. Nottinghamshire won by nine wickets, romping to victory in a match reduced to 36 overs each after a 25-minute stoppage for rain. Kent had flourished before the stoppage with Potter and Benson scoring at 5 an over, but the innings lost its way after the resumption. Robinson and Hassan, dropped at 7, put on 45 in nine overs, and then Hassan and Rice saw Nottinghamshire home with an unbroken century stand.

Kent

L. Potter c Pont b Rice..................... 28
M. R. Benson c Johnson b Fell.......... 77
D. G. Aslett run out........................ 2
G. W. Johnson c Hadlee b Fell.......... 11
*C. S. Cowdrey b Saxelby................. 5
†A. P. E. Knott c Todd b Saxelby...... 15
E. A. Baptiste b Saxelby.................. 2
G. R. Dilley c Saxelby b Pont........... 1
D. L. Underwood run out................. 1
K. B. S. Jarvis run out..................... 0
R. M. Ellison not out....................... 10
L-b 7, w 4, n-b 1.................... 12

1/74 2/81 3/101 4/116 5/126 6/138 7/142 8/158 9/163 (35 overs) 164

Bowling: Saxelby 8–0–38–3; Cooper 6–0–16–0; Rice 5–0–28–1; Pont 8–0–31–1; Fell 8–0–39–2.

Nottinghamshire

R. T. Robinson c Underwood b Dilley. 18
B. Hassan not out........................... 71
*C. E. B. Rice not out..................... 59
L-b 11, w 1, n-b 8................... 20

1/45 (1 wkt, 33 overs) 168

R. J. Hadlee, P. A. Todd, P. Johnson, M. A. Fell, †B. N. French, K. Saxelby, I. L. Pont and K. E. Cooper did not bat.

Bowling: Dilley 7–0–34–1; Jarvis 6–0–29–0; Baptiste 6–0–28–0; Ellison 5–0–27–0; Underwood 8–2–29–0; Johnson 1–0–1–0.

Umpires: C. Cook and R. S. Herman.

At Swansea, August 22. NOTTINGHAMSHIRE beat GLAMORGAN by nine wickets.

NOTTINGHAMSHIRE v DERBYSHIRE

At Nottingham, August 29. Nottinghamshire won by six wickets. Derbyshire, put in to bat, were reduced to 60 for six until Wood, with a typically gritty 47, and Tunnicliffe brought them some respectability. Hassan and Robinson shared an opening stand of 58 in Nottinghamshire's reply, but with rain threatening they were dangerously under the asking-rate for some time. The clouds cleared, however, and Birch and Rice put Nottinghamshire on the path to their fourth successive League victory.

Derbyshire

K. J. Barnett c Fell b Cooper	2
J. G. Wright c and b Hendrick	16
P. N. Kirsten c Fell b Cooper	19
J. H. Hampshire lbw b Hendrick	5
G. Miller run out	1
*B. Wood c Birch b Saxelby	47
I. S. Anderson c French b Hadlee	2
C. J. Tunnicliffe lbw b Hemmings	25
†B. J. M. Maher lbw b Hadlee	0
D. G. Moir b Cooper	11
S. Oldham not out	2
L-b 6, w 4, n-b 5	15
1/4 2/39 3/41 4/43 5/57 6/60 7/105 8/106 9/138 (37.1 overs)	145

Bowling: Saxelby 7–0–33–1; Cooper 6.1–0–22–3; Hendrick 8–2–23–2; Hadlee 8–0–26–2; Hemmings 8–0–26–1.

Nottinghamshire

B. Hassan b Wood	35
R. T. Robinson st Maher b Moir	21
*C. E. B. Rice c Anderson b Oldham	34
J. D. Birch not out	40
R. J. Hadlee c Wright b Wood	5
M. A. Fell not out	3
L-b 7, w 1, n-b 3	11
1/58 2/62 3/130 4/140 (4 wkts, 39.1 overs)	149

†B. N. French, E. E. Hemmings, K. Saxelby, K. E. Cooper and M. Hendrick did not bat.

Bowling: Oldham 8–0–26–1; Tunnicliffe 7.1–0–31–0; Wood 8–0–38–2; Moir 8–0–23–1; Miller 8–0–20–0.

Umpires: D. G. L. Evans and M. J. Kitchen.

At Chelmsford, September 5. NOTTINGHAMSHIRE beat ESSEX by seven wickets.

At Hove, September 12. NOTTINGHAMSHIRE lost to SUSSEX by six wickets.

SOMERSET

At Northampton, May 9. SOMERSET lost to NORTHAMPTONSHIRE by 12 runs.

At Hove, May 16. SOMERSET lost to SUSSEX by 19 runs.

SOMERSET v DERBYSHIRE

At Taunton, May 23. Derbyshire won by seven wickets. Somerset, put in, recovered remarkably through Botham, who hit six 6s and twelve fours in 27 overs, passing 100 in 77 balls, including 30 in one over from Finney. Marks hit two 6s and five 4s in a lively six overs. After a brisk opening at 4 an over, Miller, with two 6s and nine 4s in sixteen overs, and Hampshire, who batted throughout with nine 4s, put on 118 in sixteen overs, virtually deciding the issue.

Somerset

P. W. Denning c Newman b Wood	39	V. J. Marks not out	49
P. M. Roebuck c Taylor b Oldham	0	J. W. Lloyds not out	7
I. V. A. Richards c Taylor b Tunnicliffe	9	B 1, l-b 4, w 2	7
*B. C. Rose c Wood b Tunnicliffe	5		—
I. T. Botham c Hampshire b Oldham	105	1/6 2/25 3/37 (6 wkts, 40 overs)	235
N. F. M. Popplewell b Miller	14	4/75 5/170 6/207	

†D. J. S. Taylor, C. H. Dredge and H. R. Moseley did not bat.

Bowling: Tunnicliffe 8–0–42–2; Oldham 8–1–35–2; Wood 8–2–10–1; Newman 8–0–45–0; Finney 2–0–37–0; Barnett 2–0–24–0; Miller 4–0–35–1.

Derbyshire

J. G. Wright c Botham b Marks	22	*B. Wood not out	27
J. H. Hampshire not out	91	L-b 9, w 2	11
P. N. Kirsten b Moseley	4		—
G. Miller c Marks b Dredge	81	1/53 2/62 3/180 (3 wkts, 38.3 overs)	236

K. J. Barnett, †R. W. Taylor, C. J. Tunnicliffe, P. G. Newman, S. Oldham and R. J. Finney did not bat.

Bowling: Botham 7.3–0–43–0; Moseley 8–0–28–1; Marks 8–0–46–1; Richards 7–0–47–0; Dredge 8–0–61–1.

Umpires: D. R. Shepherd and P. B. Wight.

At Swansea, May 30. SOMERSET beat GLAMORGAN by seven wickets.

At Chelmsford, June 6. SOMERSET lost to ESSEX by 1 run.

At Birmingham, June 13. SOMERSET beat WARWICKSHIRE by 84 runs.

SOMERSET v SURREY

At Bath, June 10. Somerset won by four wickets. After a second-wicket stand of 65 in fourteen overs, Surrey, put in, faltered until Roope and Richards revived the innings. Somerset faced defeat at 94 for six after 25 overs, but Rose was steady and Garner won the match in astonishing style, striking Needham for four 6s in one over. In all he hit six 6s and two 4s, facing only 48 balls for his 59 not out.

Surrey

A. R. Butcher c Taylor b Botham	1	A. Needham c Marks b Botham	0
G. P. Howarth c Popplewell b Moseley	38	G. Monkhouse not out	20
*R. D. V. Knight b Marks	32	P. H. L. Wilson b Botham	0
M. A. Lynch lbw b Moseley	3	B 4, l-b 6, w 4	14
G. R. J. Roope c Richards b Botham	26		—
D. J. Thomas b Moseley	7	1/3 2/68 3/79 (39.5 overs)	175
†C. J. Richards c Taylor b Garner	34	4/92 5/108 6/133	
S. T. Clarke b Garner	0	7/145 8/146 9/160	

Bowling: Garner 8–2–12–2; Botham 7.5–0–47–4; Richards 6–0–31–0; Moseley 8–0–24–3; Marks 8–0–34–1; Dredge 2–0–13–0.

Somerset

P. W. Denning c Richards b Monkhouse	5	†D. J. S. Taylor c Richards b Knight	11
P. M. Roebuck st Richards b Monkhouse	30	J. Garner not out	59
I. V. A. Richards b Monkhouse	0	B 1, l-b 7, n-b 2	10
*B. C. Rose not out	49		—
I. T. Botham lbw b Clarke	15	1/15 2/15 3/48 (6 wkts, 38.2 overs)	179
V. J. Marks b Clarke	0	4/68 5/68 6/94	

N. F. M. Popplewell, H. R. Moseley and C. H. Dredge did not bat.

Bowling: Thomas 6–0–19–0; Monkhouse 8–1–39–3; Clarke 8–1–21–2; Needham 5–0–39–0; Knight 8–0–32–1; Wilson 3.2–0–19–0.

Umpires: K. Ibadulla and B. Leadbeater.

SOMERSET v NOTTINGHAMSHIRE

At Bath, June 27. Somerset won by 113 runs. Put in, Somerset were given a fine start by Denning, missed when 1, and Roebuck. After 6.3 overs, rain intervened and reduced the match to 28 overs each. Hemmings benefited from the chase for runs and from a fine catch by Fell. Accurate bowling by Garner and Moseley, aided by two good catches from Popplewell and Rose, beset Nottinghamshire with difficulties. Garner, who had run out Robinson in his first over, clean bowled the last four batsmen in two overs.

Somerset

P. W. Denning st French b Hemmings	71	V. J. Marks not out	14
P. M. Roebuck c Bore b Hendrick	41	J. W. Lloyds not out	13
I. V. A. Richards b Hemmings	15	B 8, w 1, n-b 1	10
J. Garner c Bore b Hemmings	12		—
*B. C. Rose c Fell b Hemmings	9	1/92 2/129 3/143 (6 wkts, 28 overs)	185
N. F. M. Popplewell b Hemmings	0	4/155 5/155 6/162	

†D. J. S. Taylor, H. R. Moseley and C. H. Dredge did not bat.

Bowling: Cooper 8–1–43–0; Bore 3–0–16–0; Hendrick 5–1–30–1; Saxelby 6–0–42–0; Hemmings 6–0–44–5.

Nottinghamshire

B. Hassan c Popplewell b Moseley	4	K. E. Cooper b Garner	0
R. T. Robinson run out	0	M. K. Bore b Garner	0
*C. E. B. Rice c Rose b Moseley	32	M. Hendrick b Garner	0
J. D. Birch c Dredge b Moseley	16	L-b 10, w 1	11
M. A. Fell c Popplewell b Moseley	8		—
†B. N. French b Moseley	0	1/0 2/20 3/58 (19 overs)	72
E. E. Hemmings b Garner	1	4/63 5/64 6/71	
K. Saxelby not out	0	7/72 8/72 9/72	

Bowling: Garner 6–3–6–4; Moseley 8–0–40–5; Dredge 5–2–15–0.

Umpires: D. J. Constant and R. Julian.

At Maidstone, June 11. SOMERSET lost to KENT by 1 run.

SOMERSET v YORKSHIRE

At Taunton, June 18. Somerset won by six wickets. Put in, Yorkshire recovered remarkably from 24 for three with Bairstow, improvising brilliantly, batting for 22 overs and leading a partnership of 105 in twenty overs with Hartley. Stevenson and Carrick continued the attack as the last eighteen overs brought 152 runs. After an ideal start, a combination of poor light and Stevenson's taking two wickets in two balls saw Somerset in difficulties. Richards was well caught, at long-leg, first ball in his benefit match. However, Marks (one 6, six 4s) and Popplewell (two 6s, three 4s) won the match with a superb century partnership in thirteen overs.

Yorkshire

C. W. J. Athey c Taylor b Garner	1
G. Boycott c Slocombe b Dredge	10
J. D. Love b Moseley	9
†D. L. Bairstow c Marks b Richards	64
S. N. Hartley c Popplewell b Dredge	56
G. B. Stevenson b Dredge	28
C. M. Old run out	13
P. Carrick not out	21
P. W. Jarvis not out	0
L-b 5, w 2, n-b 1	8
1/5 2/19 3/24 4/129 5/170 6/187 7/192 (7 wkts, 40 overs)	210

*R. Illingworth and S. Stuchbury did not bat.

Bowling: Garner 8–2–18–1; Dredge 8–0–47–3; Marks 8–1–19–0; Moseley 8–0–60–1; Richards 8–0–58–1.

Somerset

P. W. Denning c Bairstow b Stevenson	46
P. M. Roebuck c Bairstow b Jarvis	49
*I. V. A. Richards c Athey b Stevenson	0
J. W. Lloyds c Bairstow b Illingworth	5
V. J. Marks not out	56
N. F. M. Popplewell not out	49
L-b 4, w 4	8
1/92 2/96 3/105 4/107 (4 wkts, 38.2 overs)	213

P. A. Slocombe, †D. J. S. Taylor, J. Garner, C. H. Dredge and H. R. Moseley did not bat.

Bowling: Old 6.2–0–43–0; Stuchbury 8–0–47–0; Stevenson 7–0–42–2; Illingworth 8–0–31–1; Carrick 1–0–11–0; Jarvis 8–0–31–1.

Umpires: J. Birkenshaw and R. Julian.

SOMERSET v WORCESTERSHIRE

At Taunton, July 25. Somerset won by 2 runs. Marks, hitting ten 4s, and the steady Roebuck, in 38 overs, each achieved his highest John Player score to build a large total after Somerset, put in on a fast pitch, had faltered at first. Weston's maiden county century (five 6s, seven 4s) gave Worcestershire a good start, overcame a mid-innings collapse and prompted a final all-out attack. When he was brilliantly removed by Botham, 43 were needed from four overs, just too much of a side sorely beset by injury.

Somerset

P. W. Denning c Humphries b Alleyne	14	J. W. Lloyds c Patel b Alleyne	3
P. M. Roebuck c Scott b Warner	83	†D. J. S. Taylor not out	4
I. V. A. Richards c Weston b Perryman	17	J. Garner not out	2
*B. C. Rose c Scott b Patel	23	L-b 8, w 9	17
I. T. Botham c Weston b Patel	5	1/16 2/56 3/95 (7 wkts, 38 overs)	240
V. J. Marks run out	72	4/104 5/219 6/229 7/234	

C. H. Dredge and H. R. Moseley did not bat.

Bowling: Alleyne 8–0–46–2; Warner 7–0–49–1; Pridgeon 8–0–44–0; Perryman 8–0–43–1; Patel 7–0–41–2.

Worcestershire

M. S. Scott run out	8	†D. J. Humphries b Garner	19
M. J. Weston c and b Botham	109	H. L. Alleyne not out	17
E. J. O. Hemsley c Richards b Marks	23	A. E. Warner not out	4
*P. A. Neale c Lloyds b Dredge	3	B 4, l-b 12, w 6	22
D. N. Patel lbw b Marks	0	1/28 2/97 3/100 (7 wkts, 38 overs)	238
D. B. D'Oliveira c Garner b Botham	33	4/102 5/182 6/198 7/220	

A. P. Pridgeon and S. P. Perryman did not bat.

Bowling: Garner 8–0–25–1; Botham 8–0–59–2; Marks 8–0–25–2; Moseley 6–0–49–0; Dredge 8–0–58–1.

Umpires: A. Jepson and C. Cook.

At Portsmouth, August 1. SOMERSET lost to HAMPSHIRE by six wickets.

SOMERSET v MIDDLESEX

At Weston-super-Mare, August 8. Middlesex won by 14 runs. Put in, they were indebted to a second-wicket partnership of 120 through eighteen overs from Gatting, who hit two 6s and seven 4s in 51 balls, and Slack, whose innings lasted 39 overs. Botham, with a 6 and seven 4s in thirteen overs, and Richards gave Somerset hope with a third-wicket partnership of 67 in thirteen overs, but then Emburey struck. In gloomy light, Popplewell, Dredge and finally Davis strove to recover from 133 for eight after 31 overs, but Somerset still wanted 36 from the final two overs.

Middlesex

*J. M. Brearley c Popplewell b Marks	13	P. H. Edmonds b Botham	1
W. N. Slack run out	77	N. G. Cowans not out	3
M. W. Gatting c Roebuck b Davis	72	W. W. Daniel not out	1
R. O. Butcher c Taylor b Davis	1	B 3, l-b 10, w 1, n-b 2	16
C. T. Radley b Dredge	2		
†P. R. Downton lbw b Garner	16	1/30 2/150 3/152 (9 wkts, 40 overs)	211
K. P. Tomlins c Taylor b Botham	9	4/155 5/186 6/205	
J. E. Emburey run out	0	7/206 8/207 9/208	

Bowling: Garner 8–0–24–1; Botham 8–1–32–2; Marks 8–0–54–1; Davis 8–0–50–2; Dredge 8–0–35–1.

Somerset

P. W. Denning c Downton b Cowans	10
P. M. Roebuck c and b Daniel	2
I. V. A. Richards b Emburey	27
I. T. Botham c Edmonds b Emburey	44
*B. C. Rose c Tomlins b Emburey	7
V. J. Marks c Daniel b Emburey	27
N. F. M. Popplewell c Emburey b Cowans	29
J. Garner c and b Slack	0
†D. J. S. Taylor run out	3
C. H. Dredge not out	25
M. R. Davis run out	11
L-b 7, w 4, n-b 1	12
1/17 2/19 3/86 4/94 5/111 6/127 7/128 8/133 9/176 (39.2 overs)	197

Bowling: Cowans 7.2–1–24–2; Daniel 8–2–26–1; Edmonds 8–0–31–0; Slack 6–0–33–1; Emburey 8–0–50–4; Gatting 2–0–21–0.

Umpires: W. L. Budd and J. van Geloven.

SOMERSET v LEICESTERSHIRE

At Taunton, August 22. Somerset won by six wickets with two balls to spare. Put in, Leicestershire recovered well from a poor start. Gower, batting for 27 overs, received useful help from Davison (three 6s) and Butcher before rain reduced the match to 37 overs each. Steele and Parsons (two 6s) added an important 51 in eight overs. Rose and Roebuck produced an ideal start of 89 in twenty overs, but when Taylor took two wickets in his final over and Botham's breezy four overs ended, the requirement was 45 from seven overs. However, Marks remained unruffled, and Popplewell enterprisingly achieved the target to the excitement of an unexpectedly large crowd.

Leicestershire

N. E. Briers b Garner	0
D. I. Gower st Gard b Marks	58
*R. W. Tolchard c Garner b Marks	5
B. F. Davison b Moseley	28
†M. A. Garnham b Marks	1
I. P. Butcher c Gard b Richards	27
J. F. Steele not out	27
G. J. Parsons c Gard b Garner	23
D. A. Wenlock run out	1
L-b 7, w 3	10
1/1 2/23 3/65 4/71 5/120 6/127 7/178 8/180 (8 wkts, 37 overs)	180

P. B. Clift and L. B. Taylor did not bat.

Bowling: Garner 8–0–22–2; Botham 8–0–46–0; Marks 8–0–36–3; Palmer 8–0–44–0; Moseley 4–1–21–1; Richards 1–0–1–1.

Somerset

P. M. Roebuck c Steele b Taylor	36
*B. C. Rose c Parsons b Wenlock	54
I. V. A. Richards c Garnham b Taylor	13
I. T. Botham c and b Clift	18
V. J. Marks not out	36
N. F. M. Popplewell not out	16
L-b 10	10
1/89 2/111 3/111 4/136 (4 wkts, 36.4 overs)	183

P. A. Slocombe, †T. Gard, J. Garner, G. V. Palmer and H. R. Moseley did not bat.

Bowling: Taylor 8–0–30–2; Parsons 8–0–42–0; Clift 7.4–0–41–1; Wenlock 5–0–23–1; Steele 8–0–37–0.

Umpires: R. S. Herman and A. G. T. Whitehead.

At Bristol, August 29. SOMERSET lost to GLOUCESTERSHIRE on faster scoring-rate.

SOMERSET v LANCASHIRE

At Taunton, September 12. Somerset won by seven wickets with 16.3 overs to spare. Put in on a dry, responsive pitch, Lancashire never came to terms with a tight attack well supported in the field, Richards and Lloyds taking unusually fine catches. Only Cockbain, in four overs, and O'Shaughnessy, with a spirited effort which included a 6 and three 4s, made significant progress. Allott and the unlucky Folley made Somerset's start shaky, but Richards (three 6s, eight 4s) and Botham put on 50 in twelve overs against the change bowlers, and then smashed 65 from their final four overs together. Botham ended the match with two of his five 6s, having already hit five 4s.

Lancashire

D. Lloyd c Moseley b Marks............. 14
G. Fowler c Garner b Marks............. 14
*C. H. Lloyd c Richards b Marks....... 11
D. P. Hughes c Taylor b Moseley....... 7
I. Cockbain c Lloyds b Moseley.......... 18
J. Abrahams c Taylor b Moseley........ 10
S. J. O'Shaughnessy not out.............. 45
H. Pilling c Taylor b Botham............. 3
P. J. W. Allott b Botham.................. 10
†C. Maynard c Moseley b Botham...... 1
I. Folley not out.............................. 0
L-b 7, w 2, n-b 1.................... 10

1/23 2/32 3/43 4/67 5/73 6/82 7/97 8/119 9/141 (9 wkts, 40 overs) 143

Bowling: Garner 8–0–21–0; Botham 8–0–44–3; Marks 8–0–25–3; Moseley 8–3–7–3; Dredge 8–0–36–0.

Somerset

J. W. Lloyds lbw b Allott................. 1
P. M. Roebuck c Maynard b Allott..... 4
I. V. A. Richards c Folley b D. Lloyd. 69
*I. T. Botham not out...................... 67
V. J. Marks not out.......................... 0
L-b 1, w 2.............................. 3

1/3 2/16 3/131 (3 wkts, 23.3 overs) 144

P. A. Slocombe, N. F. M. Popplewell, †D. J. S. Taylor, J. Garner, C. H. Dredge and H. R. Moseley did not bat.

Bowling: Folley 5–0–17–0; Allott 5–2–18–2; O'Shaughnessy 4–0–14–0; C. H. Lloyd 3–0–11–0; D. Lloyd 3–0–39–1; Abrahams 2–0–29–0; Fowler 1–0–1–0; Pilling 0.3–0–12–0.

Umpires: J. Birkenshaw and C. T. Spencer.

SURREY

SURREY v KENT

At The Oval, May 9. Kent won by 107 runs. Benson, dropped by Richards off Clarke when 10, went on to a personal Sunday League-best 97 (nine 4s) in an hour and threequarters. Asif, 33 in 27 minutes, and Cowdrey, 48 in 30, were others to soften up Surrey, for whom only Roope, with three 6s in his 51 not out, showed any form with the bat.

Kent

L. Potter c Monkhouse b Knight........ 23
N. R. Taylor b Monkhouse................ 7
C. J. Tavaré b Thomas..................... 5
M. R. Benson c and b Thomas........... 97
*Asif Iqbal c Smith b Pocock............ 33
C. S. Cowdrey b Thomas.................. 48
†A. P. E. Knott run out................... 3
G. W. Johnson not out...................... 1
B 2, l-b 13, w 2, n-b 1............. 18

1/15 2/20 3/79 4/143 5/231 6/234 7/235 (7 wkts, 38 overs) 235

G. R. Dilley, D. L. Underwood and K. B. S. Jarvis did not bat.

Bowling: Thomas 8–1–36–3; Monkhouse 8–0–27–1; Clarke 7–1–32–0; Knight 5–0–33–1; Pocock 7–0–58–1; Wilson 3–0–31–0.

Surrey

A. R. Butcher c Taylor b Cowdrey	24	D. J. Thomas b Potter	1
*R. D. V. Knight c Underwood b Jarvis	3	S. T. Clarke st Knott b Underwood	8
M. A. Lynch c Knott b Dilley	8	G. Monkhouse not out	15
D. M. Smith c Knott b Cowdrey	3	L-b 5, w 6, n-b 3	14
G. R. J. Roope not out	51	1/8 2/29 3/39 (7 wkts, 38 overs)	128
†C. J. Richards c and b Potter	1	4/57 5/63 6/65 7/90	

P. H. L. Wilson and P. I. Pocock did not bat.

Bowling: Jarvis 7–0–16–1; Dilley 7–0–32–1; Cowdrey 8–1–19–2; Potter 8–2–27–2; Underwood 8–1–20-1.

Umpires: H. D. Bird and N. T. Plews.

At Birmingham, May 16. SURREY beat WARWICKSHIRE by 88 runs.

SURREY v LEICESTERSHIRE

At The Oval, May 30. Surrey won by 1 run. Gower scored his second League century of the season but was out going for a second run which would have brought a tie. So his brilliant 115 (one 6, nine 4s) off 103 balls was in vain. Loose bowling by Wenlock, Higgs and Parsons, which allowed Lynch and Smith to hit 48 off four overs, had enabled Surrey to compile a reasonable total after being put in to bat.

Surrey

A. R. Butcher c Tolchard b Clift	29	D. J. Thomas not out	2
G. S. Clinton c Garnham b Wenlock	32	G. R. J. Roope b Parsons	5
*R. D. V. Knight c Davison b Croft	8	B 1, l-b 8, w 3	12
M. A. Lynch c Higgs b Clift	49		
D. M. Smith c Parsons b Taylor	57	1/50 2/70 3/86 (7 wkts, 40 overs)	214
S. T. Clarke b Taylor	20	4/161 5/207 6/207 7/214	

†C. J. Richards, A. Needham and G. Monkhouse did not bat.

Bowling: Taylor 7–0–31–2; Parsons 8–0–43–1; Higgs 8–0–41–0; Clift 8–0–43–3; Steele 5–0–14–0; Wenlock 4–0–30–1.

Leicestershire

D. I. Gower run out	115	D. A. Wenlock c Richards b Clarke	5
N. E. Briers c Butcher b Knight	32	D. J. Parsons not out	7
*R. W. Tolchard b Needham	19	B 2, l-b 8, w 2	12
B. F. Davison run out	3		
†M. A. Garnham c Thomas b Knight	5	1/74 2/117 3/128 (8 wkts, 40 overs)	213
P. B. Clift c Needham b Clarke	3	4/139 5/144 6/188	
J. F. Steele b Knight	12	7/196 8/213	

K. Higgs and L. B. Taylor did not bat.

Bowling: Monkhouse 8–0–40–0; Thomas 8–0–42–0; Clarke 8–1–36–2; Needham 8–0–37–1; Knight 8–0–46–3.

Umpires: R. S. Herman and K. E. Palmer.

SURREY v GLOUCESTERSHIRE

At The Oval, June 13. Surrey won by 28 runs. When a superb one-handed catch by Hignell on the boundary ended a second-wicket stand of 84 between Butcher and Knight, Lynch launched an attack in which he hit three 6s and four 4s. Gloucestershire were replying well until Clarke, entering the attack for the twelfth over, took two for 8 in five overs and their momentum went.

Surrey

A. R. Butcher c Hignell b Graveney... 55	G. R. J. Roope c Stovold b Doughty... 1
G. P. Howarth c Shepherd b Broad.... 14	S. T. Clarke not out.......................... 8
*R. D. V. Knight c Bainbridge b Graveney. 49	B 2, l-b 10, w 5, n-b 2............ 19
M. A. Lynch not out........................ 55	1/34 2/118 (5 wkts, 38 overs) 210
D. J. Thomas c Brassington b Doughty. 9	3/140 4/166 5/188

A. Needham, †C. J. Richards, G. Monkhouse and P. H. L. Wilson did not bat.

Bowling: Shepherd 8–1–25–0; Doughty 7–0–38–2; Broad 4–0–27–1; Bainbridge 4–0–19–0; Graveney 8–0–31–2; Surridge 7–0–51–0.

Gloucestershire

A. W. Stovold b Clarke.................... 25	J. N. Shepherd not out..................... 14
B. C. Broad c Butcher b Clarke......... 25	
Zaheer Abbas not out...................... 63	B 1, l-b 13, w 2, n-b 1............ 17
A. J. Hignell c and b Knight............. 8	
P. Bainbridge c Roope b Needham..... 8	1/52 2/55 (5 wkts, 38 overs) 182
E. J. Cunningham c Richards b Thomas. 22	3/90 4/104 5/159

*D. A. Graveney, †A. J. Brassington, R. J. Doughty and D. Surridge did not bat.

Bowling: Thomas 8–0–48–1; Monkhouse 5–0–23–0; Knight 8–0–32–1; Clarke 8–1–16–2; Wilson 6–0–28–0; Needham 3–0–18–1.

Umpires: D. J. Constant and P. J. Eele.

At Bath, June 20. SURREY lost to SOMERSET by four wickets.

At Lord's, June 27. SURREY lost to MIDDLESEX by three wickets.

At Tring, July 4. SURREY lost to NORTHAMPTONSHIRE by 32 runs.

At Manchester, July 11. SURREY lost to LANCASHIRE by seven wickets.

At Southend, July 18. SURREY lost to ESSEX by 31 runs.

SURREY v NOTTINGHAMSHIRE

At The Oval, July 25. Surrey won by 7 runs and so ended a miserable weekend for Nottinghamshire, who the previous day had lost the final of the Benson and Hedges Cup. Rice and Birch did their best to bring about a change in fortune by adding 103 for the third wicket, but that ended when a former Nottinghamshire player, Mackintosh, took his third wicket. Lynch had provided the highlight of the Surrey innings with a 43-minute 50 which included two 6s and four 4s.

Surrey

A. R. Butcher c Cooper b Illingworth . 44
D. B. Pauline c French b Rice........... 17
*R. D. V. Knight c Hemmings b Cooper. 34
M. A. Lynch c Hendrick b Rice......... 50
G. R. J. Roope not out.................... 22
†C. J. Richards not out..................... 15
L-b 5, w 5, n-b 1.................... 11

1/30 2/83 3/121 4/164 (4 wkts, 39 overs) 193

I. R. Payne, A. Needham, K. S. Mackintosh, P. H. L. Wilson and G. Monkhouse did not bat.

Bowling: Hendrick 8–1–21–0; Rice 8–0–62–2; Hemmings 8–2–30–0; Illingworth 8–0–29–1; Cooper 7–1–40–1.

Nottinghamshire

B. Hassan c Richards b Mackintosh 10
R. T. Robinson b Mackintosh............ 15
*C. E. B. Rice b Payne.................... 62
J. D. Birch c Payne b Mackintosh....... 44
D. W. Randall b Wilson................... 18
M. A. Fell st Richards b Payne.......... 9
†B. N. French c Mackintosh b Wilson . 7
E. E. Hemmings not out................... 9
L-b 12................................. 12

1/24 2/29 3/132 4/158 5/162 6/176 7/186 (7 wkts, 39 overs) 186

N. J. B. Illingworth, K. E. Cooper and M. Hendrick did not bat.

Bowling: Monkhouse 8–1–23–0; Wilson 8–0–38–2; Mackintosh 6–1–27–3; Knight 6–0–34–0; Needham 3–0–14–0; Payne 8–0–38–2.

Umpires: R. S. Herman and M. J. Kitchen.

At Derby, August 1. SURREY beat DERBYSHIRE by 56 runs.

SURREY v SUSSEX

At Guildford, August 15. Sussex won by four wickets to maintain a six-point advantage at the top of the table. But it was a close thing. They had only four balls to spare in a match reduced to 33 overs a side through rain. Despite a run-a-minute innings from Knight, Surrey could muster only 133, Pigott's spell after the rain producing three for 0 in four balls. Sussex, at 87 for six with eight overs left and the clouds threatening, looked to have lost their grip, but Parker and Barclay saw them home.

Surrey

A. R. Butcher b C. M. Wells............ 18
G. R. J. Roope c and b Pigott........... 26
D. M. Smith c Green b C. M. Wells... 0
*R. D. V. Knight c Green b Pigott..... 57
M. A. Lynch c Barclay b Pigott......... 15
†C. J. Richards c Barclay b le Roux.... 1
D. J. Thomas c C. M. Wells b Pigott... 0
S. T. Clarke b Pigott........................ 0
I. R. Payne lbw b le Roux................ 1
G. Monkhouse not out..................... 1
K. S. Mackintosh not out.................. 5
B 1, l-b 6, w 1, n-b 1.............. 9

1/28 2/30 3/76 4/118 5/121 6/123 7/123 8/124 9/127 (9 wkts, 33 overs) 133

Bowling: C. M. Wells 8–1–20–2; le Roux 6–0–28–2; Barclay 8–0–23–0; Waller 4–0–25–0; Pigott 7–0–28–5.

Sussex

G. D. Mendis b Clarke..................... 10
†I. J. Gould c Richards b Clarke........ 4
C. M. Wells c Smith b Monkhouse...... 19
P. W. G. Parker not out.................. 49
G. S. le Roux lbw b Monkhouse........ 10
C. P. Phillipson run out.................... 11
A. P. Wells c Thomas b Payne........... 2
*J. R. T. Barclay not out.................. 18
L-b 8, w 3............................ 11

1/16 2/19 3/50 4/66 5/85 6/87 (6 wkts, 32.2 overs) 134

A. M. Green, C. E. Waller and A. C. S. Pigott did not bat.

Bowling: Clarke 8–1–21–2; Thomas 5–0–15–0; Monkhouse 8–1–28–2; Mackintosh 8–0–37–0; Payne 3.2–0–22–1.

Umpires: B. J. Meyer and R. Palmer.

At Worcester, August 22. SURREY lost to WORCESTERSHIRE on faster scoring-rate.

SURREY v GLAMORGAN

At The Oval, August 29. Glamorgan won by eight wickets, doing so with considerable ease. The two Jones put them on the right path with 96 in eighteen overs, and Rowe, who hit two 6s in one over from Payne, built on this strong foundation. Earlier Nash equalled a Glamorgan record in the League by conceding only 8 runs in his eight overs, but others were more expensive as Pauline and Lynch put on 110 in 65 minutes in a spirited third-wicket stand.

Surrey

G. P. Howarth c Rowe b Davis	3
D. B. Pauline not out	74
D. M. Smith c E. W. Jones b Barwick	4
M. A. Lynch b Ontong	56
D. J. Thomas b Ontong	1
†C. J. Richards b Ontong	1
*R. D. V. Knight c Lloyd b Ontong	7
A. Needham not out	7
B 1, l-b 11, w 6, n-b 3	21
1/12 2/19 3/129 4/131 5/135 6/149 (6 wkts, 37 overs)	174

I. R. Payne, G. Monkhouse, and K. S. Mackintosh did not bat.

Bowling: Nash 8–4–8–0; Davis 8–0–30–1; Barwick 6–0–32–1; Lloyd 7–0–46–0; Ontong 8–0–37–4.

Glamorgan

A. Jones c Smith b Thomas	34
A. L. Jones c Smith b Needham	60
C. J. C. Rowe not out	52
D. A. Francis not out	6
B 8, l-b 9, w 6	23
1/96 2/137 (2 wkts, 30.3 overs)	175

R. C. Ontong, J. A. Hopkins, S. R. Barwick, †E. W. Jones, *B. J. Lloyd, M. A. Nash and W. W. Davis did not bat.

Bowling: Thomas 7–0–28–1; Monkhouse 7–1–21–0; Mackintosh 6–0–32–0; Payne 4–0–32–0; Needham 6.3–0–39–1.

Umpires: C. T. Spencer and Khizar Hayat.

SURREY v HAMPSHIRE

At The Oval, September 5. Tied. Having beaten Warwickshire in the NatWest final the previous day, Surrey completed an interesting weekend with a tie. When the last over – from Monkhouse – began, with 2 runs needed, everything favoured Hampshire. But Rice, who had batted throughout for 64, was caught three balls later and Tremlett, in going for a single for victory off the last ball, skied a catch to mid-wicket. Not only were the scores level; each side had lost nine wickets in 39 overs. Also of note was the dismissal of Smith, out "handled the ball" when, with a reflex action, he stopped the ball from looping on to his wicket off his bat.

Surrey

A. R. Butcher c Parks b Jesty	24	I. R. Payne c Parks b Marshall	0
G. P. Howarth c Parks b Marshall	20	K. S. Mackintosh b Marshall	2
D. M. Smith handled the ball	8	P. I. Pocock not out	6
M. A. Lynch lbw b Jesty	4	L-b 7, w 7	14
*R. D. V. Knight b Cowley	3		
†C. J. Richards c Greenidge b Jesty	11	1/39 2/59 3/61 (9 wkts, 39 overs)	139
D. J. Thomas not out	38	4/64 5/80 6/80	
G. Monkhouse c Marshall b Tremlett	9	7/98 8/107 9/113	

Bowling: Emery 8–1–47–0; Marshall 8–3–17–3; Tremlett 8–1–23–1; Jesty 8–4–12–3; Cowley 7–1–26–1.

Hampshire

C. G. Greenidge c Payne b Knight	14	M. D. Marshall b Knight	2
J. M. Rice c Payne b Monkhouse	64	T. M. Tremlett c Lynch b Monkhouse	2
D. R. Turner c Richards b Payne	21	†R. J. Parks not out	0
T. E. Jesty lbw b Payne	0	B 6, l-b 12, w 5	23
M. C. J. Nicholas run out	2		
*N. E. J. Pocock c Knight b Monkhouse	11	1/37 2/89 3/89 4/97 (9 wkts, 39 overs)	139
N. G. Cowley run out	0	5/125 6/126 7/137 8/139 9/139	

K. St J. D. Emery did not bat.

Bowling: Thomas 6–2–20–0; Monkhouse 6–0–22–3; Knight 8–0–26–2; Payne 8–1–17–2; Mackintosh 3–0–14–0; Pocock 8–0–17–0.

Umpires: W. E. Alley and M. J. Kitchen.

SURREY v YORKSHIRE

At The Oval, September 12. Surrey won by 7 runs. Roope marked his last appearance for Surrey with a typically brilliant catch on the boundary as Sidebottom tried for a third successive 4. He had already hit 4s off the first two balls of the last over, which began with Yorkshire needing 20 to win. Earlier Butcher had continued his run of powerful form with an entertaining 70, to which Athey, in a different way, replied with 71 for Yorkshire.

Surrey

A. R. Butcher c Bairstow b Jarvis	70	D. J. Thomas not out	31
G. P. Howarth b Stevenson	12	B 1, l-b 10, w 1	12
D. M. Smith b Illingworth	28		
M. A. Lynch not out	52	1/34 2/106 3/139 (3 wkts, 40 overs)	205

*R. D. V. Knight, †C. J. Richards, I. R. Payne, G. Monkhouse, G. R. J. Roope and P. I. Pocock did not bat.

Bowling: Dennis 8–0–25–0; Jarvis 8–0–45–1; Stevenson 8–1–52–1; Illingworth 8–1–29–1; Sidebottom 8–0–42–0.

Yorkshire

G. Boycott c Richards b Thomas	0	A. Sidebottom c Roope b Monkhouse	32
M. D. Moxon c Richards b Payne	22	S. J. Dennis not out	9
C. W. J. Athey c Butcher b Payne	71	P. W. Jarvis not out	1
G. B. Stevenson b Payne	1	B 2, l-b 12, w 1, n-b 3	18
S. N. Hartley b Knight	22		
J. D. Love b Payne	0	1/0 2/54 3/66 4/123 (8 wkts, 40 overs)	198
†D. L. Bairstow c Smith b Knight	22	5/124 6/133 7/177 8/194	

*R. Illingworth did not bat.

Bowling: Thomas 8–0–32–1; Monkhouse 8–0–40–1; Knight 8–0–46–2; Pocock 8–1–31–0; Payne 8–0–31–4.

Umpires: K. Ibadulla and A. G. T. Whitehead.

SUSSEX

SUSSEX v ESSEX

At Hove, May 9. Sussex won by five wickets. Essex, sent in on a slightly green wicket, quickly lost wickets, and not even resistance from the middle order could ensure anything but a modest total. Nevertheless, Sussex made rather heavy weather of their task until Greig and Phillipson pushed the scoring along.

Essex

G. A. Gooch c Greig b Imran........... 1
B. R. Hardie c Greig b le Roux......... 4
K. S. McEwan c Gould b Imran......... 4
*K. W. R. Fletcher c Gould b Pigott... 7
N. Phillip c A. P. Wells b Imran........ 7
A. W. Lilley c A. P. Wells b C. M. Wells. 26
K. R. Pont c Phillipson b C. M. Wells. 16
S. Turner c Phillipson b C. M. Wells... 22
†D. E. East c Gould b le Roux.......... 2
J. K. Lever not out.......................... 8
N. A. Foster c Pigott b Phillipson....... 8
L-b 6, w 4.............................. 10

1/4 2/12 3/12 4/22 5/53 6/54 7/92 8/94 9/98 (38.5 overs) 115

Bowling: Imran 8–1–14–3; le Roux 8–1–21–2; Greig 8–0–25–0; Pigott 8–1–21–1; C. M. Wells 5–0–18–3; Phillipson 1.5–0–6–1.

Sussex

G. D. Mendis c Lilley b Lever........... 8
†I. J. Gould lbw b Turner................. 36
C. M. Wells run out......................... 9
P. W. G. Parker c D. E. East b Lever. 8
Imran Khan c D. E. East b Foster...... 13
I. A. Greig not out.......................... 22
C. P. Phillipson not out..................... 14
L-b 5, n-b 1............................ 6

1/22 2/46 3/61 4/75 5/83 (5 wkts, 34.3 overs) 116

*J. R. T. Barclay, G. S. le Roux, A. C. S. Pigott and A. P. Wells did not bat.

Bowling: Lever 8–2–19–2; Phillip 8–1–33–0; Turner 8–1–22–1; Foster 8–1–20–1; Gooch 2.3–0–16–0.

Umpires: W. E. Alley and W. L. Budd.

SUSSEX v SOMERSET

At Hove, May 16. Sussex won by 19 runs. If Sussex, sent in, had experienced difficulties after Mendis and Gould had sent them racing away with 46 off seven overs, Somerset experienced even worse setbacks. Richards and Botham were out for only 1 run between them, receiving just five balls, and five wickets were down for 57 before Popplewell and Taylor raised Somerset's hopes. Moseley lashed a 6 in the final over, but Sussex's meagre fare had proved sufficient.

Sussex

G. D. Mendis lbw b Marks............... 35
†I. J. Gould c Taylor b Moseley......... 18
C. M. Wells b Dredge....................... 2
P. W. G. Parker lbw b Marks............ 2
Imran Khan c Taylor b Dredge.......... 7
I. A. Greig run out.......................... 0
C. P. Phillipson lbw b Moseley........... 17
G. S. le Roux lbw b Moseley............. 39
*J. R. T. Barclay not out.................. 13
A. P. Wells c and b Botham.............. 1
A. C. S. Pigott b Botham................. 8
L-b 5, w 5, n-b 1................... 11

1/46 2/60 3/60 4/68 5/68 6/70 7/126 8/134 9/137 (38.3 overs) 153

Bowling: Botham 7.3–0–40–2; Moseley 8–0–29–3; Marks 8–3–19–2; Dredge 8–2–14–2; Richards 5–0–15–0; Popplewell 2–0–25–0.

Somerset

P. W. Denning c Phillipson b Imran	2	†D. J. S. Taylor b Imran	27
J. W. Lloyds lbw b le Roux	11	C. H. Dredge not out	13
I. V. A. Richards lbw b le Roux	1	H. R. Moseley not out	6
N. F. M. Popplewell lbw b Barclay	30	B 5, l-b 1, w 1	7
P. A. Slocombe b Barclay	14		
I. T. Botham c and b Barclay	0	1/7 2/8 3/23 (9 wkts, 40 overs)	134
*B. C. Rose c Barclay b Pigott	15	4/57 5/57 6/70	
V. J. Marks lbw b Greig	8	7/87 8/87 9/127	

Bowling: Imran 8–0–30–2; le Roux 8–2–16–2; Barclay 8–0–24–3; Greig 8–3–16–1; Pigott 8–1–41–1.

Umpires: D. G. L. Evans and R. S. Herman.

At Gloucester, May 30. SUSSEX beat GLOUCESTERSHIRE by three wickets.

At Manchester, June 6. SUSSEX beat LANCASHIRE by seven wickets.

SUSSEX v WORCESTERSHIRE

At Horsham, June 13. Worcestershire won by three wickets. Nearly 4,000 spectators on this lovely ground saw Worcestershire end a run of three successive defeats by inflicting the first reverse of the campaign on Sussex. The home total was highlighted by the batting of Parker, who went to school at Horsham and was coached on this ground, and looked to be a winning one after the early dismissals of Turner and Younis. However, 50 runs were plundered off the last four overs, Pigott conceding 31 in his final two.

Sussex

G. D. Mendis c Humphries b Pridgeon	0	C. P. Phillipson not out	36
†I. J. Gould c Humphries b Inchmore	12	*J. R. T. Barclay b Pridgeon	0
C. M. Wells c Humphries b Weston	46	A. C. S. Pigott not out	8
P. W. G. Parker c Hemsley b Gifford	73	B 1, l-b 8, w 2	11
Imran Khan c Neale b Weston	11	1/3 2/35 3/85 (8 wkts, 40 overs)	206
I. A. Greig st Humphries b Younis	2	4/107 5/116 6/129	
G. S. le Roux run out	7	7/180 8/184	

C. E. Waller did not bat.

Bowling: Pridgeon 8–0–39–2; Inchmore 4–0–22–1; Weston 8–0–36–2; Gifford 7–1–32–1; Patel 1–0–13–0; Younis 7–0–27–1; Hemsley 5–0–26–0.

Worcestershire

G. M. Turner b le Roux	5	†D. J. Humphries c and b Pigott	9
J. A. Ormrod b Barclay	28	J. D. Inchmore not out	19
Younis Ahmed run out	12		
D. N. Patel b Waller	36	L-b 7, w 3, n-b 1	11
E. J. O. Hemsley c Parker b Imran	32		
*P. A. Neale not out	46	1/9 2/43 3/66 (7 wkts, 39 overs)	208
M. J. Weston c le Roux b Imran	10	4/109 5/137 6/156 7/175	

N. Gifford and A. P. Pridgeon did not bat.

Bowling: Imran 8–1–17–2; le Roux 7–0–37–1; Pigott 7–0–62–1; Greig 8–0–36–0; Barclay 4–0–24–1; Waller 5–0–21–1.

Umpires: C. Cook and K. Ibadulla.

SUSSEX v GLAMORGAN

At Hastings, June 20. Sussex won by 119 runs. A standing ovation greeted le Roux following his thrilling innings of 88, scored off 56 balls in only 42 minutes with three towering 6s and ten 4s. He and Wells (one 6, six 4s) raced to a fourth-wicket stand of 118 off fifteen overs, demoralising the Glamorgan fieldsmen, who dropped four catches near the boundary line in quick succession.

Sussex

G. D. Mendis run out	2	I. A. Greig not out	18
‡I. J. Gould c and b Lloyd	48	L-b 6, w 6, n-b 1	13
C. M. Wells not out	81		
P. W. G. Parker c Ontong b Lloyd	1	1/3 2/89 3/93 (4 wkts, 40 overs)	251
G. S. le Roux b Ontong	88	4/211	

C. P. Phillipson, *J. R. T. Barclay, A. P. Wells, A. C. S. Pigott and C. E. Waller did not bat.

Bowling: Nash 8–0–50–0; Daniels 8–1–35–0; Ontong 8–0–59–1; Barwick 7–0–37–0; Lloyd 8–0–37–2; Rowe 1–0–20–0.

Glamorgan

J. A. Hopkins c Gould b le Roux	6	S. A. B. Daniels b Pigott	0
A. L. Jones b Pigott	4	†T. Davies b Parker	10
C. J. C. Rowe run out	11	S. R. Barwick not out	12
R. C. Ontong c and b Barclay	21	L-b 7, w 8	15
M. J. Llewellyn c Gould b Pigott	24		
M. A. Nash b Barclay	3	1/11 2/14 3/41 (39.1 overs)	132
G. C. Holmes c le Roux b Greig	3	4/56 5/63 6/81	
*B. J. Lloyd b Greig	23	7/95 8/95 9/113	

Bowling: le Roux 3–0–8–1; Pigott 8–1–14–3; Waller 8–0–31–0; Barclay 8–1–23–2; Greig 8–0–29–2; Phillipson 3–0–10–0; Parker 1.1–0–2–1.

Umpires: D. J. Constant and P. B. Wight.

At Maidstone, July 4. SUSSEX beat KENT by 73 runs.

SUSSEX v LEICESTERSHIRE

At Hove, July 18. Sussex won by 14 runs. Despite a third-wicket stand of 82 by Parker and Wells, Leicestershire's target was only 184. And when Briers and Balderstone comfortably scored 80 off eighteen overs, the task looked well within reach. As in the Sussex innings, though, a slump followed, and with five overs left Leicestershire still needed 45 with four wickets standing. With Greig in lively form, they failed to check Sussex's challenge for their first title.

Sussex

G. D. Mendis c and b Steele	27	*J. R. T. Barclay not out	10
*I. J. Gould b Parsons	4	A. C. S. Pigott c Tolchard b Parsons	2
C. M. Wells lbw b Wenlock	45	C. E. Waller b Parsons	0
P. W. G. Parker c Wenlock b Higgs	54	L-b 12, w 4	16
G. S. le Roux c Higgs b Taylor	6		—
I. A. Greig b Higgs	2	1/22 2/43 3/125 (9 wkts, 38 overs)	183
C. P. Phillipson b Parsons	17	4/150 5/152 6/152 7/179 8/183 9/183	

G. G. Arnold did not bat.

Bowling: Taylor 7–1–38–1; Parsons 7–0–27–4; Wenlock 8–1–33–1; Steele 8–0–26–1; Higgs 8–0–43–2.

Leicestershire

N. E. Briers c Gould b Pigott	34	G. J. Parsons c and b Greig	0
J. C. Balderstone c Gould b Greig	52	L. B. Taylor not out	9
B. F. Davison c Waller b Barclay	2	K. Higgs not out	1
*R. W. Tolchard st Gould b Barclay	12	B 1, l-b 7, w 1, n-b 2	11
†M. A. Garnham c Barclay b Greig	8		—
T. J. Boon hit wkt b le Roux	19	1/80 2/83 3/100 (9 wkts, 38 overs)	169
J. F. Steele c Pigott b Greig	14	4/113 5/122 6/150	
D. A. Wenlock lbw b Greig	7	7/152 8/153 9/164	

Bowling: Arnold 4–0–15–0; le Roux 6–0–27–1; Pigott 8–0–29–1; Waller 4–0–20–0; Barclay 8–1–25–2; Greig 8–0–42–5.

Umpires: D. Archer and C. T. Spencer.

At Northampton, July 25. SUSSEX beat NORTHAMPTONSHIRE by four wickets.

At Scarborough, August 1. SUSSEX beat YORKSHIRE by 55 runs.

SUSSEX v HAMPSHIRE

At Eastbourne, August 8. Sussex won by 13 runs. Sussex pottered uneasily to just 75 for three off twenty overs against steady bowling, but a burst of scoring off the last six produced a decisive 63 runs. Hampshire, too, made a slow start, Greenidge needing 24 overs for his 32, and, despite a bold and entertaining 36 from Nicholas, they still wanted 19 runs off the last over, with two wickets standing.

Sussex

G. D. Mendis c and b Jesty	23	*J. R. T. Barclay b Emery	19
†I. J. Gould c Parks b Jesty	29	A. P. Wells not out	26
C. M. Wells c Greenidge b Cowley	5	L-b 7, n-b 6	13
P. W. G. Parker c Pocock b Tremlett	21		—
G. S. le Roux run out	33	1/55 2/58 (7 wkts, 40 overs)	192
C. P. Phillipson not out	23	3/62 4/117 5/124	
I. A. Greig b Tremlett	0	6/124 7/162	

A. C. S. Pigott and C. E. Waller did not bat.

Bowling: Marshall 8–0–37–0; Emery 8–0–46–1; Cowley 8–1–28–1; Jesty 8–0–44–2; Tremlett 8–2–24–2.

Hampshire

C. G. Creenidge c A. P. Wells b C. M. Wells	32	M. D. Marshall c Phillipson b le Roux	2
J. M. Rice run out	27	T. M. Tremlett not out	12
M. C. J. Nicholas b le Roux	36	†R. J. Parks c Gould b Pigott	13
T. E. Jesty c Mendis b Greig	25	K. St J. D. Emery b Pigott	0
D. R. Turner c and b Greig	2	B 1, l-b 8, w 1, n-b 2	12
*N. E. J. Pocock c and b Pigott	13	1/48 2/75 3/128 4/128 (39.5 overs)	179
N. G. Cowley b Pigott	5	5/132 6/144 7/144 8/154 9/178	

Bowling: Pigott 7.5–0–33–4; le Roux 8–0–41–2; Waller 8–0–22–0; Greig 8–0–24–2; Barclay 6–0–36–0; C. M. Wells 2–0–11–1.

Umpires: D. G. L. Evans and K. Ibadulla.

At Guildford, August 15. SUSSEX beat SURREY by four wickets.

At Chesterfield, August 22. SUSSEX beat DERBYSHIRE by three wickets.

SUSSEX v MIDDLESEX

At Hove, August 29. Sussex won by 23 runs to capture the John Player Trophy for the first time. Before a crowd of 6,500, a Sunday League record for Hove, Mendis and Gould, with swift running between the wickets, gave Sussex a magnificent start, Mendis hitting nine 4s in his entertaining 100. Cowans bowled well for his four wickets, and Emburey was at his most economical. Despite the splendid fast bowling of le Roux, Pigott and Greig, Middlesex matched the Sussex scoring-rate until the closing overs.

Sussex

G. D. Mendis run out	100	I. A. Greig c Slack b Cowans	2
†I. J. Gould c Radley b Slack	58	*J. R. T. Barclay not out	0
C. M. Wells b Slack	2	B 2, l-b 13, w 1, n-b 2	18
P. W. G. Parker b Cowans	17		
G. S. le Roux c Cook b Cowans	23	1/134 2/150 3/194 (7 wkts, 40 overs)	228
C. P. Phillipson c Downton b Cowans	8	4/205 5/224 6/226 7/228	

A. P. Wells, A. C. S. Pigott and C. E. Waller did not bat.

Bowling: Daniel 8–0–56–0; Cowans 8–0–44–4; Slack 8–0–43–2; Emburey 8–1–20–0; Hughes 8–0–47–0.

Middlesex

W. N. Slack lbw b Barclay	31	W. W. Daniel b Pigott	6
*J. M. Brearley lbw b le Roux	8	N. G. Cowans not out	14
R. O. Butcher b Greig	59	S. P. Hughes run out	2
†P. R. Downton b Pigott	40	B 2, l-b 11, w 2, n-b 1	16
R. G. P. Ellis b Greig	6		
C. T. Radley c and b le Roux	18	1/22 2/80 3/142 (39.1 overs)	205
C. R. Cook c Gould b le Roux	3	4/158 5/160 6/179	
J. E. Emburey run out	2	7/182 8/185 9/197	

Bowling: Wells 6–0–23–0; le Roux 7.1–0–27–3; Greig 7–0–44–2; Barclay 8–0–36–1; Waller 3–0–16–0; Pigott 8–0–43–2.

Umpires: N. T. Plews and A. G. T. Whitehead.

At Birmingham, September 5. WARWICKSHIRE v SUSSEX. No result.

SUSSEX v NOTTINGHAMSHIRE

At Hove, September 12. Sussex won by six wickets, so taking their points in the competition to a record 58. Following entertaining batting from Robinson and Rice, whose stand of 82 occupied only eighteen overs, Nottinghamshire lost six wickets for just 27 runs and their final total was disappointing. In reply, Colin Wells hit a boundary-studded 65, Parker gave him enthusiastic support in a lively century stand, and le Roux, who had destroyed Nottinghamshire with four wickets for 18, hit the winning run off the last ball of the match.

Nottinghamshire

B. Hassan b C. M. Wells	14	K. Saxelby not out	10
R. T. Robinson c Waller b Pigott	47	K. E. Cooper run out	1
*C. E. B. Rice c and b Waller	59	M. K. Bore not out	2
R. J. Hadlee c Green b Pigott	22	B 1, l-b 8, w 2, n-b 1	12
J. D. Birch c Barclay b le Roux	5		
D. W. Randall c Mendis b le Roux	2	1/26 2/108 3/148 (9 wkts, 39 overs)	185
†B. N. French c Greig b le Roux	4	4/155 5/158 6/165	
E. E. Hemmings b le Roux	7	7/166 8/176 9/178	

Bowling: C. M. Wells 8–0–28–1; le Roux 7–0–18–4; Greig 8–0–34–0; Barclay 5–0–32–0; Pigott 8–0–44–2; Waller 3–0–17–1.

Sussex

†G. D. Mendis c Randall b Cooper	7	A. P. Wells not out	4
A. M. Green c and b Cooper	19	L-b 11, w 2, n-b 2	15
C. M. Wells c Hemmings b Saxelby	65		
P. W. G. Parker b Saxelby	52	1/14 2/36 (4 wkts, 39 overs)	186
G. S. le Roux not out	24	3/141 4/179	

C. P. Phillipson, I. A. Greig, *J. R. T. Barclay, A. C. S. Pigott and C. E. Waller did not bat.

Bowling: Cooper 8–0–25–2; Bore 8–1–49–0; Saxelby 7–0–32–2; Hemmings 8–0–32–0; Hadlee 8–0–33–0.

Umpires: P. J. Eele and M. J. Kitchen.

WARWICKSHIRE

WARWICKSHIRE v SURREY

At Birmingham, May 16. Surrey won by 88 runs. A bold 63 by Clinton, followed by 7-an-over scoring, put Surrey in a strong position, especially when they disposed of Amiss and Humpage cheaply. Pocock took three for 20 and held two catches as Warwickshire subsided to a convincing defeat.

Surrey

A. R. Butcher run out	2	A. Needham not out	13
G. S. Clinton c Smith b Ferreira	63	G. Monkhouse not out	18
*R. D. V. Knight b Ferreira	39		
M. A. Lynch c Small b Ferreira	31	L-b 13, w 4, n-b 1	18
G. R. J. Roope c Lethbridge b Small	22		
S. T. Clarke b Willis	15	1/3 2/74 3/142 (7 wkts, 40 overs)	229
†C. J. Richards b Willis	8	4/150 5/177 6/194 7/194	

P. H. L. Wilson and P. I. Pocock did not bat.

Bowling: Willis 8–0–34–2; Small 8–0–36–1; Hogg 8–0–39–0; Smith 4–0–27–0; Ferreira 5–0–43–3; Lethbridge 7–1–32–0.

Warwickshire

D. L. Amiss c Roope b Monkhouse	1	G. C. Small c Pocock b Wilson	4
T. A. Lloyd st Richards by Pocock	26	*R. G. D. Willis c Pocock b Wilson	0
A. I. Kallicharran c Richards b Clarke	24	W. Hogg b Clarke	2
†G. W. Humpage b Pocock	0	B 8, l-b 9, w 2, n-b 1	20
Asif Din c Richards b Needham	14		
A. M. Ferreira c Clinton b Needham	38	1/10 2/65 3/65 (36.3 overs)	141
P. A. Smith st Richards b Pocock	1	4/69 5/92 6/107	
C. Lethbridge not out	11	7/130 8/133 9/138	

Bowling: Wilson 6–2–14–2; Monkhouse 8–0–24–1; Needham 8–0–36–2; Pocock 8–1–20–3; Clarke 6.3–0–27–2.

Umpires: K. E. Palmer and R. Palmer.

At Bradford, May 23. WARWICKSHIRE beat YORKSHIRE by six wickets.

At Chesterfield, May 30. WARWICKSHIRE lost to DERBYSHIRE by seven wickets.

WARWICKSHIRE v KENT

At Birmingham, June 6. Kent won by seven wickets. After a steady start, with Dilley proving costly, Warwickshire were tied up by Underwood. The limitations of the home bowling were then exposed as Kent cantered home with overs to spare.

Warwickshire

D. L. Amiss c Knott b Woolmer	21	P. A. Smith c Knott b Dilley	7
T. A. Lloyd c and b Penn	26	G. C. Small not out	14
A. I. Kallicharran c and b Underwood	15	*R. G. D. Willis run out	1
†G. W. Humpage c Penn b Woolmer	2	L-b 6, w 7, n-b 3	16
P. R. Oliver c and b Underwood	11		
Asif Din c Tavaré b Jarvis	19	1/49 2/54 3/59 (9 wkts, 40 overs)	164
A. M. Ferreira run out	32	4/74 5/87 6/127 7/147 8/157 9/164	

J. Cumbes did not bat.

Bowling: Jarvis 8–0–25–1; Dilley 8–1–55–1; Woolmer 8–0–29–2; Penn 8–0–31–1; Underwood 8–4–8–2.

Kent

R. A. Woolmer c Asif Din b Small	1	*Asif Iqbal not out	41
L. Potter c Humpage b Smith	45	B 2, l-b 5, w 2, n-b 1	10
C. J. Tavaré c Amiss b Smith	36		
D. G. Aslett not out	33	1/10 2/77 3/88 (3 wkts, 34.3 overs)	166

C. Penn, C. S. Cowdrey, †A. P. E. Knott, G. R. Dilley, D. L. Underwood and K. B. S. Jarvis did not bat.

Bowling: Willis 7.3–1–30–0; Small 6–2–29–1; Ferreira 4–0–12–0; Cumbes 2–0–23–0; Kallicharran 8–1–34–0; Smith 6–1–21–2; Asif Din 1–0–7–0.

Umpires: H. D. Bird and P. B. Wight.

WARWICKSHIRE v SOMERSET

At Birmingham, June 13. Somerset won by 84 runs. Denning's unbeaten century and a quick-fire 79 by Richards, after Somerset had been put in, set the scene for another Warwickshire defeat. Their stad put on 148 in nineteen overs after tidy bowling had contained Somerset to 76 at the halfway stage. Warwickshire's total owed much to Lethbridge for his face-saving 57 not out.

Somerset

P. W. Denning not out	112	J. W. Lloyds not out	3
P. M. Roebuck c Humpage b Lethbridge	24	B 3, l-b 10, w 4, n-b 1	18
I. V. A. Richards b Small	79	1/58 2/206 3/258	(3 wkts, 40 overs) 261
*B. C. Rose b Lethbridge	25		

N. F. M. Popplewell, V. J. Marks, J. Garner, †D. J. S. Taylor, C. H. Dredge and M. R. Davis did not bat.

Bowling: Small 8–0–49–1; P. A. Smith 8–0–66–0; Cumbes 8–0–33–0; Lethbridge 8–0–43–2; Humpage 4–1–29–0; Kallicharran 4–0–23–0.

Warwickshire

*D. L. Amiss c Richards b Garner	3	†G. A. Tedstone b Garner	2
T. A. Lloyd c Lloyds b Davis	2	G. C. Small b Roebuck	0
A. I. Kallicharran c Roebuck b Marks	6	J. Cumbes c Rose b Roebuck	3
G. W. Humpage c Roebuck b Marks	16	L-b 8	8
Asif Din c Rose b Marks	31		
K. D. Smith c Lloyds b Popplewell	13	1/6 2/6 3/22 4/35 5/72 6/75 7/146 8/166 9/167	(40 overs) 177
P. A. Smith b Garner	36		
C. Lethbridge not out	57		

Bowling: Garner 8–2–17–3; Davis 8–0–32–1; Marks 8–0–19–3; Popplewell 6–0–32–1; Lloyds 3–0–9–0; Dredge 4–0–49–0; Roebuck 2–0–4–2; Richards 1–0–7–0.

Umpires: B. Leadbeater and D. R. Shepherd.

At Nottingham, June 20. WARWICKSHIRE lost to NOTTINGHAMSHIRE by 22 runs.

WARWICKSHIRE v NORTHAMPTONSHIRE

At Birmingham, June 27. Warwickshire won on faster scoring-rate. Lloyd's 79, which included three 6s, boosted Warwickshire to their highest Sunday total of the season and their second victory. Two stoppages by rain reduced Northamptonshire's target to 193 in 34 overs, and they were well placed at 124 for one after 23 overs. But Lethbridge and Small effected a breakthrough and Northamptonshire, requiring 19 off the last two overs, failed by 7 runs.

Warwickshire

*D. L. Amiss c Sharp b Capel	38	P. R. Oliver run out	18
T. A. Lloyd c Mallender b Capel	79	L-b 12, w 2	14
A. I. Kallicharran c Larkins b Capel	23		
†G. W. Humpage not out	45	1/92 2/132 3/153 4/165 5/227	(5 wkts, 40 overs) 227
Asif Din c Larkins b T. M. Lamb	10		

S. H. Wootton, C. Lethbridge, G. C. Small, J. Cumbes and K. R. Maguire did not bat.

Bowling: Griffiths 8-1-32-0; Mallender 8–0–53–0; Willey 8–0–43–0; T. M. Lamb 8–0–38–1; Capel 8–0–47–3.

Northamptonshire

P. Willey c Lloyd b Lethbridge	89	D. J. Wild c Humpage b Lethbridge	0
W. Larkins lbw b Lethbridge	16	N. A. Mallender b Small	5
R. G. Williams c Amiss b Maguire	30	T. M. Lamb b Lethbridge	7
D. J. Capel c Small b Cumbes	10	B. J. Griffiths not out	1
R. J. Boyd-Moss b Small	1	L-b 11, w 6, n-b 2	19
R. M. Carter c Humpage b Lethbridge	4	1/50 2/124 3/144 (33.5 overs)	185
*†G. Sharp b Small	3	4/155 5/160 6/170 7/170 8/174 9/183	

Bowling: Small 7.5–1–20–3; Maguire 8–0–43–1; Lethbridge 8–0–47–5; Cumbes 8–0–41–1; Kallicharran 2–0–15–0.

Umpires: D. Archer and A. G. T. Whitehead.

At Leicester, July 4. WARWICKSHIRE lost to LEICESTERSHIRE by six wickets.

WARWICKSHIRE v GLOUCESTERSHIRE

At Birmingham, July 11. Gloucestershire won by five wickets. A stand of 78 between Lloyd and Humpage was the backbone of the Warwickshire innings, in which Stephenson bowled well for the visitors. Romaines and Broad replied with 81 for the first wicket and Gloucestershire, needing 13 off the last two overs, got them with one ball to spare.

Warwickshire

*D. L. Amiss lbw b Shepherd	18	S. H. Wootton b Stephenson	0
T. A. Lloyd b Stephenson	83	C. Lethbridge not out	9
A. I. Kallicharran c Brassington b Shepherd	4	G. C. Small not out	3
G. W. Humpage c Broad b Bainbridge	41	B 5, l-b 7, w 1	13
Asif Din b Stephenson	10	1/56 2/62 3/140 (6 wkts, 39 overs)	181
		4/162 5/162 6/165	

†G. A. Tedstone, P. J. Hartley and S. P. Sutcliffe did not bat.

Bowling: Stephenson 8–3–18–3; Surridge 8–2–46–0; Bainbridge 8–0–39–1; Shepherd 7–0–27–2; Childs 5–0–16–0; Doughty 3–0–22–0.

Gloucestershire

P. W. Romaines c and b Kallicharran	52	J. N. Shepherd not out	18
B. C. Broad c and b Lethbridge	35	F. D. Stephenson not out	2
A. J. Hignell c and b Asif Din	23	B 4, l-b 6, w 4	14
P. Bainbridge b Small	35		
A. J. Wright c Asif Din b Kallicharran	6	1/81 2/106 3/135 (5 wkts, 38.5 overs)	185
		4/144 5/168	

R. J. Doughty, †A. J. Brassington, *J. H. Childs and D. Surridge did not bat.

Bowling: Small 7.5–1–39–1; Hartley 4–1–19–0; Sutcliffe 8–0–29–0; Lethbridge 7–0–35–1; Kallicharran 8–1–31–2; Asif Din 4–1–18–1.

Umpires: B. Leadbeater and P. B. Wight.

At Manchester, July 25. WARWICKSHIRE lost to LANCASHIRE by 18 runs.

WARWICKSHIRE v GLAMORGAN

At Birmingham, August 8. Glamorgan won by nine wickets. Put in, Warwickshire lost five wickets for 51 before Oliver hit a bold 44 to boost them to their vulnerable total of 137. Glamorgan made light of their task, A. L. Jones making his highest score in the competition, and they needed only 1 run to win when their first wicket fell.

Warwickshire

T. A. Lloyd c E. W. Jones b Nash..... 7
K. D. Smith lbw b Nash.................. 7
A. I. Kallicharran c Nash b Davis....... 2
D. L. Amiss lbw b Thomas............... 17
†G. W. Humpage b Nash.................. 11
Asif Din c E. W. Jones b Thomas...... 16
P. R. Oliver b Davis........................ 44
P. A. Smith b Davis........................ 8
C. Lethbridge not out...................... 4
G. C. Small not out......................... 4
B 1, l-b 5, w 8, n-b 3.............. 17

1/8 2/11 3/22 4/45 5/51 6/83 7/122 8/127 (8 wkts, 40 overs) 137

*R. G. D. Willis did not bat.

Bowling: Nash 8–2–26–3; Davis 8–2–17–3; Thomas 8–0–28–2; Lloyd 8–0–19–0; Ontong 8–0–30–0.

Glamorgan

A. Jones not out............................. 43
A. L. Jones c Asif Din b Small.......... 82
D. A. Francis not out........................ 0
B 1, l-b 2, w 5, n-b 5.............. 13

1/137 (1 wkt, 27 overs) 138

R. C. Ontong, C. J. C. Rowe, J. G. Thomas, J. A. Hopkins, †E. W. Jones, *B. J. Lloyd, M. A. Nash and W. W. Davis did not bat.

Bowling: Willis 7–2–14–0; Small 7–0–39–1; Lethbridge 6–1–24–0; P. A. Smith 3–0–26–0; Kallicharran 4–0–22–0.

Umpires: R. S. Herman and Khizar Hayat.

WARWICKSHIRE v MIDDLESEX

At Birmingham, August 15. Middlesex won by 102 runs. Fielding an injury-weakened side Warwickshire were beaten for the tenth time on a Sunday after Middlesex had built steadily on a second-wicket stand of 108 between Slack and Tomlins. Warwickshire's chances were considerably diminished when Kallicharran was struck behind the left ear, hooking at Daniel, and had to retire.

Middlesex

C. T. Radley c Tedstone b Small........ 0
W. N. Slack b Kallicharran................ 56
K. P. Tomlins run out....................... 58
R. O. Butcher c Maguire b P. A. Smith. 51
P. H. Edmonds b P. A. Smith........... 11
C. R. Cook c Cumbes b P. A. Smith... 0
†P. R. Downton c Small b Cumbes..... 13
*J. E. Emburey not out.................... 26
M. W. W. Selvey b Small................. 13
W. W. Daniel run out...................... 0
W. G. Merry not out....................... 0
L-b 11, n-b 4......................... 15

1/8 2/109 3/148 4/180 5/180 6/202 7/205 8/233 9/234 (9 wkts, 38 overs) 243

Bowling: Small 7–0–40–2; Maguire 8–0–42–0; Ferreira 7–0–46–0; Cumbes 4–0–32–1; Kallicharran 8–0–47–1; P. A. Smith 4–0–21–3.

Warwickshire

T. A. Lloyd b Edmonds	36	G. C. Small not out	3
K. D. Smith c Emburey b Selvey	5	J. Cumbes b Edmonds	2
A. I. Kallicharran retired hurt	2	K. R. Maguire b Emburey	0
*D. L. Amiss st Downton b Emburey	30	B 4, l-b 6, n-b 1	11
Asif Din c Radley b Edmonds	27		
A. M. Ferreira c Cook b Emburey	1	1/10 2/76 3/90 (30.4 overs)	141
P. A. Smith b Emburey	1	4/91 5/92 6/132	
†G. A. Tedstone b Merry	23	7/137 8/140 9/141	

Bowling: Selvey 6–0–28–1; Daniel 4–0–14–0; Merry 5–0–33–1; Emburey 7.4–2–25–4; Edmonds 8–1–30–3.

Umpires: W. E. Alley and B. Leadbeater.

At Colchester, August 22. WARWICKSHIRE beat ESSEX by four wickets.

At Worcester, August 29. WORCESTERSHIRE v WARWICKSHIRE. No result.

WARWICKSHIRE v SUSSEX

At Birmingham, September 5. No result.

At Bournemouth, September 12. WARWICKSHIRE lost to HAMPSHIRE by four wickets.

WORCESTERSHIRE

At Huddersfield, May 9. WORCESTERSHIRE beat YORKSHIRE by two wickets.

At Nottingham, May 16. WORCESTERSHIRE beat NOTTINGHAMSHIRE by six wickets.

At Bristol, May 23. WORCESTERSHIRE lost to GLOUCESTERSHIRE on faster scoring-rate.

WORCESTERSHIRE v KENT

At Worcester, May 30. Kent won by 30 runs. Worcestershire's three tailenders all had personal League-best scores but could not atone for an inept performance from the front-line batsmen. Cowdrey complemented his unbeaten half-century with a brilliant catch at deep mid-wicket to dismiss Hemsley and signal the end of Worcestershire's hopes. It seemed hard to believe that Worcestershire had scored 501 for one the previous day.

Kent

R. A. Woolmer c and b Inchmore	8	†A. P. E. Knott c Hemsley b Inchmore	36
N. R. Taylor b Gifford	33	G. R. Dilley not out	23
C. J. Tavaré b Inchmore	3	L-b 3, w 2	5
L. Potter c Patel b Hemsley	21		
*Asif Iqbal c Humphries b Perryman	29	1/17 2/23 3/50 (6 wkts, 40 overs)	219
C. S. Cowdrey not out	61	4/81 5/114 6/161	

C. Penn, D. L. Underwood and K. B. S Jarvis did not bat.

Bowling: Pridgeon 7–0–53–0; Inchmore 8–0–51–3; Perryman 6–0–30–1; Gifford 8–0–21–1; Hemsley 6–0–26–1; Patel 5–0–33–0.

Worcestershire

G. M. Turner b Jarvis	18
J. A. Ormrod c Tavaré b Jarvis	6
Younis Ahmed c Knott b Dilley	8
D. N. Patel c Dilley b Underwood	13
E. J. O. Hemsley c Cowdrey b Penn	40
*P. A. Neale c Knott b Penn	30
†D. J. Humphries c Underwood b Cowdrey	0
J. D. Inchmore b Penn	4
N. Gifford c Tavaré b Jarvis	31
A. P. Pridgeon c Knott b Jarvis	17
S. P. Perryman not out	19
L-b 2, w 1	3
1/11 2/33 3/35 4/57 5/114 6/116 7/116 8/122 9/165 (38.1 overs)	189

Bowling: Jarvis 7.1–0–41–4; Dilley 6–0–32–1; Underwood 8–1–15–1; Woolmer 8–0–30–0; Penn 5–0–45–3; Cowdrey 4–0–23–1.

Umpires: W. L. Budd and C. Cook.

WORCESTERSHIRE v DERBYSHIRE

At Worcester, June 6. Derbyshire won by eight wickets. A superb 103 by Wright, his highest score in the competition, set up a runaway Derbyshire victory. He and Kirsten raced to a century stand in fourteen overs, and went on to a record partnership of 154 for Derbyshire's second wicket in one-day cricket. Worcestershire, without the injured Turner, had recovered well to reach 200, but their bowling was taken apart.

Worcestershire

†D. J. Humphries run out	15
J. A. Ormrod c Taylor b Oldham	5
Younis Ahmed b Miller	49
D. N. Patel lbw b Miller	5
E. J. O. Hemsley b Oldham	41
*P. A. Neale c Wright b Newman	48
M. J. Weston c Hill b Newman	8
H. L. Alleyne not out	18
N. Gifford not out	1
L-b 6, w 3, n-b 2	11
1/17 2/28 3/38 4/105 5/171 6/171 7/186 (7 wkts, 38 overs)	201

A. P. Pridgeon and S. P. Perryman did not bat.

Bowling: Newman 7–0–39–2; Oldham 7–0–27–2; Miller 8–0–34–2; Wood 8–0–40–0; Tunnicliffe 6–0–43–0; Kirsten 2–0–7–0.

Derbyshire

J. G. Wright c Neale b Pridgeon	103
J. H. Hampshire b Gifford	18
P. N. Kirsten not out	64
G. Miller not out	0
B 1, l-b 6, w 4, n-b 7	18
1/45 2/199 (2 wkts, 31.2 overs)	203

*B. Wood, K. J. Barnett, †R. W. Taylor, P. G. Newman, C. J. Tunnicliffe, S. Oldham and A. Hill did not bat.

Bowling: Alleyne 6–1–19–0; Pridgeon 7–0–44–1; Gifford 5–0–23–1; Perryman 8–0–50–0; Patel 3–0–31–0; Hemsley 2–0–14–0; Neale 0.2–0–4–0.

Umpires: D. Archer and R. Palmer.

At Horsham, June 13. WORCESTERSHIRE beat SUSSEX by three wickets.

At Ilford, June 20. WORCESTERSHIRE lost to ESSEX by 109 runs.

WORCESTERSHIRE v LANCASHIRE

At Worcester, June 27. Lancashire won by 22 runs. From the seemingly invincible position of 95 for one, Worcestershire lost nine wickets for 42 in thirteen overs as they slithered to an embarrassing defeat. Simmons returned a Sunday-best five for 17, and Croft took the last three wickets in four balls. Lancashire were indebted to Lloyd and Fowler for a second-wicket stand of 104 before rain reduced the match to 34 overs a side.

Lancashire

A. Kennedy b Inchmore	6
G. Fowler c Inchmore b Patel	59
†C. Maynard run out	0
*D. Lloyd lbw b Weston	46
D. P. Hughes not out	14
J. Simmons not out	13
B 1, l-b 11, w 8, n-b 2	22
1/24 2/25 3/129 4/131 (4 wkts, 34 overs)	160

J. Abrahams, B. W. Reidy, C. E. H. Croft, L. L. McFarlane and I. Folley did not bat.

Bowling: Warner 6–1–20–0; Inchmore 4–1–9–1; Webster 8–1–21–0; Weston 8–1–46–1; Patel 8–0–42–1.

Worcestershire

G. M. Turner c Fowler b McFarlane	17
M. S. Scott c Fowler b Simmons	39
Younis Ahmed c Croft b Simmons	29
D. N. Patel b Simmons	6
*P. A. Neale c Reidy b Croft	24
J. D Inchmore st Maynard b Simmons	0
M. J. Weston b Simmons	2
†D. J. Humphries c D. Lloyd b Croft	4
A. E. Warner b Croft	1
A. J. Webster not out	1
D. B. D'Oliveira b Croft	0
L-b 10, w 5	15
1/33 2/95 3/98 4/122 5/128 6/128 7/135 8/137 9/137 (33 overs)	138

Bowling: Folley 5–0–20–0; McFarlane 4–0–15–1; Reidy 8–0–42–0; Croft 8–0–29–4; Simmons 8–2–17–5.

Umpires: D. G. L. Evans and K. E. Palmer.

WORCESTERSHIRE v GLAMORGAN

At Worcester, July 18. Glamorgan won by 1 run. This was Worcestershire's sixth successive defeat in one-day cricket at New Road, Glamorgan's first win in 23 games against county opposition, and their first-ever Sunday success at Worcester. Sound early batting reduced Worcestershire's target to 48 off nine overs, but 14 were still needed from the last two. In the final over Ontong yorked Patel, Humphries was run out, and Glamorgan scraped home.

Glamorgan

A. Jones c Humphries b Webster	31
A. L. Jones b Inchmore	13
D. A. Francis run out	30
R. C. Ontong c Inchmore b Warner	35
C. J. C. Rowe run out	3
M. J. Llewellyn b Perryman	31
*B. J. Lloyd not out	6
M. A. Nash b Perryman	2
†E. W. Jones b Perryman	1
S. A. B. Daniels not out	4
B 2, l-b 20, w 7, n-b 2	31
1/24 2/82 3/99 4/107 5/171 6/174 7/176 8/180 (8 wkts, 40 overs)	187

W. W. Davis did not bat.

Bowling: Inchmore 8–1–25–1; Warner 8–0–41–1; Perryman 8–1–26–3; Webster 8–0–35–1; Patel 8–0–29–0.

Worcestershire

G. M. Turner b Nash	8	J. D. Inchmore not out	1
M. S. Scott lbw b Davis	12	A. E. Warner not out	1
*P. A. Neale c Francis b Lloyd	41		
E. J. O. Hemsley c Francis b Ontong	77	L-b 6, w 6	12
D. N. Patel b Ontong	20		
D. B. D'Oliveira lbw b Davis	0	1/13 2/30 3/142 (7 wkts, 40 overs)	186
†D. J. Humphries run out	14	4/160 5/160 6/178 7/184	

A. J. Webster and S. P. Perryman did not bat.

Bowling: Nash 8–3–17–1; Davis 8–1–43–2; Daniels 8–1–45–0; Lloyd 8–0–38–1; Ontong 8–0–31–2.

Umpires: W. E. Alley and A. Jepson.

At Taunton, July 25. WORCESTERSHIRE lost to SOMERSET by 2 runs.

At Luton, August 1. WORCESTERSHIRE lost to NORTHAMPTONSHIRE by 52 runs.

WORCESTERSHIRE v LEICESTERSHIRE

At Stourbridge, August 8. Leicestershire won by eight wickets. Put in to bat, Worcestershire never recovered from the loss of Weston to the first ball. Throughout, the swing of Taylor and Parsons posed greater problems than the rain-affected wicket. Worcestershire's total soon looked inadequate as Gower and Briers put on 40 in ten overs, and when Tolchard joined Briers, 71 were added in 58 minutes as Leicestershire coasted home.

Worcestershire

M. J. Weston c Garnham b Taylor	0	H. L. Alleyne b Roberts	0
M. S. Scott c Gower b Taylor	12	A. P. Pridgeon c Taylor b Wenlock	2
*P. A. Neale c Garnham b Parsons	1	A. J. Webster not out	3
E. J. O. Hemsley c Garnham b Parsons	11		
D. N. Patel b Parsons	43	B 2, l-b 4, w 3	9
D. B. D'Oliveira b Roberts	11		
†D. J. Humphries b Wenlock	1	1/0 2/3 3/19 4/25 (37.3 overs)	119
J. D. Inchmore c Garnham b Roberts	26	5/40 6/54 7/85 8/85 9/100	

Bowling: Taylor 8–2–11–2; Parsons 6.3–0–23–3; Steele 8–0–37–0; Roberts 8–2–10–3; Wenlock 7–1–29–2.

Leicestershire

D. I. Gower c and b Pridgeon	16
N. E. Briers c Humphries b Webster	58
*R. W. Tolchard not out	32
B. F. Davison not out	2
B 1, l-b 3, w 5, n-b 3	12
1/40 2/111 (2 wkts, 31.4) overs	120

†M. A. Garnham, T. J. Boon, J. F. Steele, A. M. E. Roberts, G. J. Parsons, L. B. Taylor and D. A. Wenlock did not bat.

Bowling: Alleyne 5–0–28–0; Pridgeon 6–0–15–1; Inchmore 5–0–18–0; Webster 8–1–26–1; Patel 7.4–0–21–0.

Umpires: W. E. Alley and H. D. Bird.

At Southampton, August 15. WORCESTERSHIRE beat HAMPSHIRE by 11 runs.

WORCESTERSHIRE v SURREY

At Worcester, August 22. Worcestershire won on faster scoring-rate after four interruptions because of rain. It was their first home win of the season in limited-overs cricket. Butcher hit nine 4s in his 72 out of 125, before being sixth out. Worcestershire had to score at 4.3 runs an over, and were 65 for two off thirteen overs when the rain returned.

Surrey

A. R. Butcher c Webster b Perryman	72	A. Needham c Pridgeon b Alleyne	7
G. R. J. Roope c Ormrod b Webster	13	G. Monkhouse c Hemsley b Pridgeon	4
D. M. Smith lbw b Webster	10	I. R. Payne not out	0
M. A. Lynch run out	3	K. S. Mackintosh b Pridgeon	4
*R. D. V. Knight c Humphries b Patel	9	B 1, l-b 8, w 5, n-b 5	19
†C. J. Richards b Perryman	4	1/41 2/70 3/78 4/109 (34.4 overs)	156
D. J. Thomas lbw b Alleyne	11	5/114 6/125 7/139 8/151 9/152	

Bowling: Alleyne 7–0–28–2; Pridgeon 5.4–0–25–2; Webster 8–0–26–2; Perryman 8–1–27–2; Patel 6–0–31–1.

Worcestershire

J. A. Ormrod c and b Monkhouse	0
D. N. Patel c Smith b Mackintosh	26
Younis Ahmed not out	33
*P. A. Neale not out	2
L-b 2, w 2	4
1/0 2/61 (2 wkts, 13 overs)	65

M. J. Weston, E. J. O. Hemsley, †D. J. Humphries, H. L. Alleyne, A. P. Pridgeon, A. J. Webster and S. P. Perryman did not bat.

Bowling: Monkhouse 4–1–18–1; Thomas 3–0–21–0; Mackintosh 3–1–7–1; Knight 3–0–15–0.

Umpires: B. J. Meyer and M. J. Kitchen.

WORCESTERSHIRE v WARWICKSHIRE

At Worcester, August 29. No result. Smith and Lloyd made a valiant effort to score the 61 needed off ten overs to win the game for Warwickshire on faster scoring-rate, but in the end the rain was the only winner.

Worcestershire

J. A. Ormrod c Lloyd b Ferreira	9	A. E. Warner not out	2
D. N. Patel c Tedstone b Lethbridge	41	R. K. Illingworth run out	0
Younis Ahmed b Humpage	32	A. J. Webster b Ferreira	0
*P. A. Neale c Lethbridge b Small	57	B 4, l-b 13, w 5, n-b 3	25
E. J. O. Hemsley c Lloyd b Small	45		
M. J. Weston c and b Ferreira	7	1/40 2/87 3/107 (9 wkts, 40 overs)	242
†D. J. Humphries b Small	24	4/202 5/204 6/239 7/241 8/241 9/242	

S. P. Perryman did not bat.

Bowling: Small 8–1–26–3; Ferreira 8–1–39–3; Lethbridge 6–0–42–1; P. A. Smith 4–0–34–0; Kallicharran 8–0–40–0; Humpage 6–0–36–1.

Warwickshire

K. D. Smith not out........................ 23
T. A. Lloyd not out.......................... 19
L-b 1, w 2, n-b 1.................... 4

(no wkt, 8.1 overs) 46

*A. I. Kallicharran, G. W. Humpage, P. R. Oliver, Asif Din, A. M. Ferreira, C. Lethbridge, †G. A. Tedstone, G. C. Small and P. A. Smith did not bat.

Bowling: Warner 4.1–0–22–0; Webster 4–0–20–0.

Umpires: D. R. Shepherd and J. van Geloven.

WORCESTERSHIRE v MIDDLESEX

At Worcester, September 12. Middlesex won by 17 runs. Turner returned after his appendix operation to make his final appearance for Worcestershire but could not save them from defeat. In typical fashion he bludgeoned 26 of the first 30 runs and helped Patel put on 68 off eight overs for the first wicket. Weston hit Cowans for 18 off four balls during his quick-fire 45, but after his dismissal Worcestershire were always behind the clock.

Middlesex

W. N. Slack b Perryman................... 5
*J. M. Brearley b Perryman.............. 20
C. T. Radley lbw b Perryman............ 5
R. O. Butcher c Humphries b Webster. 42
M. W. Gatting c Perryman b Hemsley. 40
R. G. P. Ellis b Perryman................ 21
*P. R. Downton not out.................. 58
J. E. Emburey not out...................... 29
L-b 5, w 4............................. 9

1/16 2/25 3/42 4/90 5/130 6/171 (6 wkts, 40 overs) 229

P. H. Edmonds, N. G. Cowans and N. F. Williams did not bat.

Bowling: Warner 8–1–44–0; Perryman 8–0–31–4; Illingworth 8–0–45–0; Webster 8–0–51–1; Hemsley 4–0–26–1; Weston 4–0–23–0.

Worcestershire

G. M. Turner st Downton b Edmonds. 29
D. N. Patel c and b Edmonds............ 42
Younis Ahmed c Gatting b Slack........ 16
*P. A. Neale c Downton b Emburey... 29
E. J. O. Hemsley b Slack.................. 2
M. J. Weston b Williams.................. 45
†D. J. Humphries c Edmonds b Emburey. 6
A. E. Warner run out...................... 0
R. K. Illingworth b Cowans.............. 21
S. P. Perryman st Downton b Emburey. 1
A. J. Webster not out...................... 9
L-b 6, w 3, n-b 3.................... 12

1/68 2/89 3/95 4/105 5/145 6/157 7/157 8/179 9/182 (38.5 overs) 212

Bowling: Cowans 6.5–0–48–1; Williams 6–0–30–1; Edmonds 8–2–31–2; Emburey 8–0–42–3; Slack 8–0–32–2; Gatting 2–0–17–0.

Umpires: D. G. L. Evans and R. Palmer.

YORKSHIRE

YORKSHIRE v WORCESTERSHIRE

At Huddersfield, May 9. Worcestershire won by two wickets. Old and Bairstow, with 72 from ten overs, rescued Yorkshire from a slow start on a pitch that allowed some turn.

Worcestershire, in reply, collapsed, but Neale played himself in and some erratic seam bowling enabled Worcestershire to collect 76 runs from the last ten overs.

Yorkshire

K. Sharp lbw b Inchmore	4	G. B. Stevenson c Younis b Pridgeon	0
C. W. J. Athey c Humphries b Pridgeon	1	P. Carrick c and b Gifford	20
J. D. Love c Patel b Hemsley	32	M. D. Moxon not out	1
S. N. Hartley c Hemsley b Patel	20	B 1, w 1, n-b 1	3
†D. L. Bairstow b Pridgeon	55	1/5 2/9 3/34 (7 wkts, 39 overs)	185
*C. M. Old not out	49	4/81 5/153 6/154 7/182	

S. J. Dennis and P. W. Jarvis did not bat.

Bowling: Pridgeon 7–2–26–3; Inchmore 5–1–23–1; Perryman 7–0–41–0; Hemsley 4–0–21–1; Patel 8–0–31–1; Gifford 8–1–40–1.

Worcestershire

G. M. Turner c Bairstow b Old	47	J. D. Inchmore b Stevenson	21
J. A. Ormrod b Jarvis	8	N. Gifford c Hartley b Dennis	5
Younis Ahmed lbw b Jarvis	4	A. P. Pridgeon not out	2
†D. J. Humphries b Dennis	30	B 4, l-b 3, w 3, n-b 1	11
D. N. Patel b Old	13		
E. J. O. Hemsley c Sharp b Old	2	1/29 2/35 3/82 (8 wkts, 38.3 overs)	188
*P. A. Neale not out	45	4/106 5/108 6/111 7/150 8/167	

S. P. Perryman did not bat.

Bowling: Old 8–1–23–3; Stevenson 7.3–2–42–1; Jarvis 8–1–34–2; Dennis 8–0–58–2; Carrick 7–0–20–0.

Umpires: D. O. Oslear and C. T. Spencer.

At Leicester, May 16. YORKSHIRE lost to LEICESTERSHIRE by 1 run.

YORKSHIRE v WARWICKSHIRE

At Bradford, May 23. Warwickshire won by six wickets. Yorkshire appeared to be in control as Athey and Sharp made 60 from the first eleven overs on a slow pitch. But with the rest of the batsmen trying to maintain this rate, four wickets fell for 27 in six overs. Amiss and Humpage, who was caught off a no-ball when 6, thrived on some inaccurate bowling as Warwickshire advanced to their target.

Yorkshire

K. Sharp c Oliver b Cumbes	40	A. Sidebottom c Kallicharran b Small	10
C. W. J. Athey c Humpage b Ferreira	19	A. Ramage b Ferreira	15
J. D. Love c Hogg b Cumbes	1	S. Stuchbury not out	2
†D. L. Bairstow c Humpage b Hogg	35		
S. N. Hartley c Small b Cumbes	10	B 1, l-b 17, w 4	22
*C. M. Old b Lethbridge	13		
G. B. Stevenson c Amiss b Hogg	6	1/60 2/61 3/85 (9 wkts, 37 overs)	193
P. Carrick not out	20	4/118 5/134 6/138 7/144 8/161 9/191	

Bowling: Small 7–0–41–1; Hogg 7–1–27–2; Ferreira 8–0–33–2; Cumbes 8–2–36–3; Lethbridge 7–0–34–1.

Warwickshire

*D. L. Amiss b Hartley.................... 60
T. A. Lloyd c Bairstow b Stuchbury.... 14
A. I. Kallicharran c Hartley b Stuchbury. 8
†G. W. Humpage not out................. 74
P. R. Oliver run out........................ 14
Asif Din not out.............................. 13
B 1, l-b 3, w 4, n-b 3.............. 11

1/50 2/66 3/109 4/159 (4 wkts, 33.4 overs) 194

A. M. Ferreira, C. Lethbridge, G. C. Small, J. Cumbes, and W. Hogg did not bat.

Bowling: Ramage 5–0–32–0; Old 8–1–44–0; Stevenson 4.4–0–31–0; Stuchbury 7–0–29–2; Hartley 4–1–20–1; Carrick 5–0–27–0.

Umpires: B. J. Meyer and C. T. Spencer.

YORKSHIRE v GLAMORGAN

At Bradford, June 6. No result.

YORKSHIRE v NOTTINGHAMSHIRE

At Hull, June 13. Tied. Yorkshire, put in on a slow wicket, scored freely. Love, in spectacular form, hit four 6s and six 4s, adding 59 from eleven overs with Sharp and making 42 out of 47 with Bairstow. Nottinghamshire, hurried on their way by Rice (three 6s, five 4s), needed 2 from Stuchbury's last ball but managed only 1 as the bowler dived to field Saxelby's mis-hit drive.

Yorkshire

K. Sharp run out.............................. 40
C. W. J. Athey c Robinson b Saxelby.. 24
J. D. Love b Saxelby........................ 70
†D. L. Bairstow c French b Bore........ 18
*C. M. Old c French b Hendrick........ 45
G. B. Stevenson b Hendrick.............. 1
S. N. Hartley not out....................... 15
G. Boycott not out........................... 2
L-b 16, w 1............................ 17

1/40 2/99 3/146 4/173 5/185 6/230 (6 wkts, 40 overs) 232

P. Carrick, A. Sidebottom and S. Stuchbury did not bat.

Bowling: Hadlee 8–2–33–0; Bore 8–0–52–1; Hendrick 8–1–38–2; Saxelby 8–0–48–2; Hemmings 8–2–44–0.

Nottinghamshire

R. T. Robinson lbw b Sidebottom...... 25
B. Hassan c Bairstow b Old.............. 1
*C. E. B. Rice b Sidebottom............ 82
J. D. Birch c Sharp b Stevenson......... 45
R. J. Hadlee c Sharp b Stuchbury....... 6
M. A. Fell run out........................... 28
†B. N. French run out...................... 7
E. E. Hemmings lbw b Stevenson....... 4
K. Saxelby not out........................... 9
M. Hendrick not out........................ 3
B 3, l-b 15, w 4..................... 22

1/14 2/41 3/171 4/172 5/199 6/214 7/215 8/219 (8 wkts, 40 overs) 232

M. K. Bore did not bat.

Bowling: Old 8–1–29–1; Stuchbury 7–0–44–1; Hartley 4–0–28–0; Sidebottom 8–1–39–2; Stevenson 8–0–46–2; Carrick 5–0–24–0.

Umpires: R. Julian and K. E. Palmer.

YORKSHIRE v NORTHAMPTONSHIRE

At Middlesbrough, June 20. Northamptonshire won by 55 runs. Yorkshire, after winning the toss, conceded the highest total made against them in the competition. An opening stand of 128 from 21 overs was the prelude to Allan Lamb hitting five 6s and six 4s in his unbeaten 67 from only 36 balls. There were 31 from Stevenson's last over – 27 to the bat and four wides – and only a late flourish by Carrick and Sidebottom, plus four missed chances, brought Yorkshire to within a respectable distance.

Northamptonshire

*G. Cook c Bairstow b Old	73	D. J. Capel not out	12
W. Larkins c Hartley b Stevenson	79	B 2, l-b 8, w 4	14
P. Willey b Carrick	25		
A. J. Lamb not out	67	1/128 2/183 3/185 (4 wkts, 40 overs)	282
R. G. Williams run out	12	4/222	

B. J. Griffiths, R. M. Carter, †G. Sharp, N. A. Mallender and T. M. Lamb did not bat.

Bowling: Old 8–0–40–1; Stuchbury 4–0–24–0; Sidebottom 7–0–45–0; Dennis 4–0–24–0; Hartley 2–0–28–0; Carrick 6–0–34–1; Stevenson 8–0–63–1; Boycott 1–0–10–0.

Yorkshire

G. Boycott run out	7	A. Sidebottom not out	52
C. W. J. Athey c Sharp b Capel	45	S. J. Dennis b Carter	7
J. D. Love c Larkins b Griffiths	5	S. Stuchbury run out	0
†D. L. Bairstow c Williams b Capel	24		
*C. M. Old st Sharp b Willey	34	B 1, l-b 11, w 2, n-b 1	15
G. B. Stevenson b Capel	0		
S. N. Hartley c A. J. Lamb b Capel	4	1/19 2/32 3/84 4/89 5/89 (39.4 overs)	227
P. Carrick b T. M. Lamb	34	6/111 7/132 8/186 9/213	

Bowling: Mallender 8–0–41–0; Griffiths 5–1–8–1; T. M. Lamb 7–0–38–1; Capel 6–1–30–4; Willey 8–0–42–1; Carter 5.4–0–53–1.

Umpires: H. D. Bird and J. van Geloven.

At Derby, June 27. YORKSHIRE beat DERBYSHIRE by 19 runs.

YORKSHIRE v GLOUCESTERSHIRE

At Leeds, July 4. Yorkshire won on faster scoring-rate. Yorkshire, sent in on a slow pitch, thrashed some poor bowling and again benefited from four missed chances. Boycott and Athey made 74 from nineteen overs to set the pace. Rain reduced the visitors' target to 140 in 24 overs, but a burst from Stuchbury reduced them to 33 for five and ended the contest.

Yorkshire

G. Boycott b Bainbridge	48	G. B. Stevenson b Stephenson	30
C. W. J. Athey c Graveney b Broad	50	P. Carrick run out	0
J. D. Love c and b Bainbridge	29	P. W. Jarvis not out	0
†D. L. Bairstow c Brassington b Bainbridge	11	L-b 6, w 2, n-b 1	9
S. N. Hartley c Brassington b Stephenson	16	1/74 2/120 3/135 (8 wkts, 40 overs)	233
C. M. Old c and b Bainbridge	40	4/144 5/192 6/218 7/233 8/233	

*R. Illingworth and S. Stuchbury did not bat.

Bowling: Surridge 8–0–26–0; Stephenson 8–0–47–2; Childs 8–0–48–0; Broad 8–0–37–1; Bainbridge 8–0–66–4.

Gloucestershire

A. W. Stovold b Old........................ 4
B. C. Broad run out........................ 0
P. W. Romaines c Boycott b Stuchbury. 7
A. J. Hignell lbw b Jarvis................. 12
P. Bainbridge b Stuchbury................. 8
E. J. Cunningham b Stuchbury.......... 0
F. D. Stephenson b Stevenson........... 27
*D. A. Graveney c Bairstow b Stevenson. 14
†A. J. Brassington c Illingworth b Jarvis. 12
J. H. Childs not out......................... 2
D. Surridge not out.......................... 2
L-b 5, w 2............................. 7

1/12 2/13 3/15 4/33 5/33 6/44 7/76 8/85 9/93 (9 wkts, 24 overs) 95

Bowling: Old 5–0–16–1; Stuchbury 6.1–1–21–3; Jarvis 7–1–25–2; Stevenson 4.5–0–25–2; Boycott 1–0–1–0.

Umpires: H. D. Bird and R. Julian.

YORKSHIRE v ESSEX

At Scarborough, July 11. Essex won by five wickets. The loss of five wickets for 17 in mid-innings condemned Yorkshire to defeat on an easy-paced pitch. Only Love, Bairstow, who was injured in the process, and Sidebottom challenged steady Essex bowling. Although Essex had their problems, Fletcher and Phillip hit 51 from fifteen overs to settle the issue.

Yorkshire

C. W. J. Athey c D. E. East b Phillip. 12
G. Boycott run out.......................... 1
J. D Love b Gooch.......................... 28
†D. L. Bairstow c Fletcher b Lever..... 31
C. M. Old c Lilley b R. E. East......... 1
G. B. Stevenson c Turner b Gooch..... 1
*S. N. Hartley c R. E. East b Turner.. 8
P. Carrick run out.......................... 2
A. Sidebottom not out...................... 23
P. W. Jarvis c D. E. East b Phillip...... 4
S. Stuchbury not out........................ 9
B 1, l-b 6, w 4, n-b 2.............. 13

1/1 2/17 3/61 4/65 5/67 6/82 7/88 8/103 9/112 (9 wkts, 40 overs) 133

Bowling: Lever 8–0–20–1; Phillip 8–1–29–2; Turner 8–0–28–1; R. E. East 8–3–21–1; Gooch 8–1–22–2.

Essex

G. A. Gooch b Carrick..................... 14
B. R. Hardie b Stuchbury................. 8
K. S. McEwan b Jarvis..................... 7
*K. W. R. Fletcher c Athey b Stuchbury. 36
N. Phillip b Stuchbury...................... 24
A. W. Lilley not out........................ 21
S. Turner not out............................ 14
B 1, l-b 9.............................. 10

1/12 2/28 3/40 4/91 5/98 (5 wkts, 36.2 overs) 134

K. R. Pont, R. E. East, †D. E. East and J. K. Lever did not bat.

Bowling: Old 6.2–1–28–0; Stuchbury 8–0–23–3; Stevenson 6–0–18–0; Jarvis 6–0–28–1; Carrick 8–0–15–1; Boycott 2–0–12–0.

Umpires: R. S. Herman and D. O. Oslear.

At Taunton, July 18. YORKSHIRE lost to SOMERSET by six wickets.

At Canterbury, July 25. YORKSHIRE beat KENT by five wickets.

YORKSHIRE v SUSSEX

At Scarborough, August 1. Sussex won by 55 runs. Sent in, Sussex started confidently, stumbled in the middle, and finished at the gallop. Parker played with great dash, adding 68 in eight overs with Phillipson. Bairstow and Stevenson hit 63 from nine overs in Yorkshire's reply, but otherwise the innings lacked authority against steady bowling.

Sussex

G. D. Mendis c Love b Jarvis	25	A. M. Green not out	8
†I. J. Gould b Jarvis	13	C. E. Waller not out	0
C. M. Wells hit wkt b Sidebottom	30		
P. W. G. Parker c Love b Stevenson	77	B 6, l-b 11, w 5, n-b 1	23
G. S. le Roux b Boycott	15		
C. P. Phillipson c Old b Stevenson	31	1/30 2/71 3/76 (7 wkts, 40 overs)	222
*J. R. T. Barclay lbw b Sidebottom	0	4/113 5/181 6/183 7/219	

G. G. Arnold and A. C. S. Pigott did not bat.

Bowling: Old 8–1–22–0; Stevenson 7–0–55–2; Jarvis 8–0–37–2; Carrick 3–1–21–0; Sidebottom 8–1–36–2; Boycott 5–0–19–1; Hartley 1–0–9–0.

Yorkshire

G. Boycott c Barclay b Arnold	11	A. Sidebottom c Waller b le Roux	7
C. W. J. Athey b Arnold	0	P. W. Jarvis c Gould b le Roux	0
J. D. Love b le Roux	4	*R. Illingworth not out	1
†D. L. Bairstow b Barclay	54	L-b 10	10
G. B. Stevenson b Pigott	43		
S. N. Hartley c le Roux b Barclay	5	1/3 2/12 3/26 (33.5 overs)	167
P. Carrick b Pigott	19	4/89 5/116 6/124	
C. M. Old c Gould b Pigott	13	7/150 8/165 9/165	

Bowling: Arnold 8–0–27–2; le Roux 6–0–13–3; Waller 7–0–52–0; Pigott 6.5–0–41–3; Barclay 6–0–24–2.

Umpires: A. Jepson and R. Julian.

At Manchester, August 8. LANCASHIRE v YORKSHIRE. No result.

At Lord's, August 22. YORKSHIRE lost to MIDDLESEX by 21 runs.

At Southampton, August 29. YORKSHIRE lost to HAMPSHIRE by 14 runs.

At The Oval, September 12. YORKSHIRE lost to SURREY by 7 runs.

JOHN PLAYER LEAGUE RECORDS

Batting

Highest score: 163* – C. G. Greenidge, Hampshire v Warwickshire (Birmingham), 1979. (191 hundreds have been scored in the League.)

Most runs in a season: 814 – C. E. B. Rice (Nottinghamshire), 1977.

Most sixes in an innings: 10 – C. G. Greenidge, Hampshire v Warwickshire (Birmingham), 1979.

Most sixes by a team in an innings: 14 – Leicestershire v Somerset (Frome), 1970.

Most sixes in a season: 26 – I. V. A. Richards (Somerset), 1977.

Highest total: 307 for four – Worcestershire v Derbyshire (Worcester), 1975.

Highest total – batting second: 301 for six – Warwickshire v Essex (Colchester), 1982.

Highest match aggregate: 600 – Essex (299 for four) v Warwickshire (301 for six) (Colchester), 1982.

Lowest total: 23 – Middlesex v Yorkshire (Leeds), 1974.

Shortest completed innings: 16 overs – Northamptonshire 59 v Middlesex (Tring), 1974.

Shortest match: 2 hr 13 min (40.3 overs) – Essex v Northamptonshire (Ilford), 1971.

Biggest victories: 190 runs, Kent beat Northamptonshire (Brackley), 1973.
There have been seventeen instances of victory by ten wickets – by Derbyshire, Essex, Glamorgan, Hampshire, Kent, Leicestershire (twice), Middlesex (twice), Somerset, Surrey (twice), Warwickshire (twice), Worcestershire and Yorkshire (twice).

Ties: Nottinghamshire v Kent (Nottingham), 1969, in match reduced to 20 overs.
Gloucestershire v Hampshire (Bristol), 1972.
Gloucestershire v Northamptonshire (Bristol), 1972.
Surrey v Worcestershire (Byfleet), 1973.
Middlesex v Lancashire (Lord's), 1974.
Sussex v Leicestershire (Hove), 1974.
Lancashire v Worcestershire (Manchester), 1975.
Somerset v Glamorgan (Taunton), 1975.
Warwickshire v Kent (Birmingham), 1980.
Kent v Lancashire (Maidstone), 1981.
Yorkshire v Nottinghamshire (Hull), 1982.
Hampshire v Lancashire (Southampton), 1982.
Surrey v Hampshire (The Oval), 1982.

Record Partnerships for each Wicket

224 for 1st	J. A. Ormrod and D. N. Patel, Worcestershire v Hampshire at Southampton	1982
179 for 2nd	B. W. Luckhurst and M. H. Denness, Kent v Somerset at Canterbury	1973
215 for 3rd	W. Larkins and R. G. Williams, Northamptonshire v Worcestershire at Luton	1982
175* for 4th	M. J. K. Smith and D. L. Amiss, Warwickshire v Yorkshire at Birmingham	1970
179 for 5th	I. T. Botham and I. V. A. Richards, Somerset v Hampshire at Taunton	1981
121 for 6th	C. P. Wilkins and A. J. Borrington, Derbyshire v Warwickshire at Chesterfield	1972
101 for 7th	S. J. Windaybank and D. A. Graveney, Gloucestershire v Nottinghamshire at Nottingham	1981
95* for 8th	D. Breakwell and K. F. Jennings, Somerset v Nottinghamshire at Nottingham	1976
86 for 9th	D. P. Hughes and P. Lever, Lancashire v Essex at Leyton	1973
57 for 10th	D. A. Graveney and J. B. Mortimore, Gloucestershire v Lancashire at Tewkesbury	1973

Bowling

Best analyses: eight for 26, K. D. Boyce, Essex v Lancashire at Manchester, 1971; seven for 15, R. A. Hutton, Yorkshire v Worcestershire at Leeds, 1969; seven for 39, A. Hodgson, Northamptonshire v Somerset at Northampton, 1976; six for 6, R. W. Hooker, Middlesex v Surrey at Lord's, 1969; six for 7, M. Hendrick, Derbyshire v Nottinghamshire at Nottingham, 1972.

Four wickets in four balls: A. Ward, Derbyshire v Sussex at Derby, 1970.

Hat-tricks: A. Ward, Derbyshire v Sussex at Derby, 1970; R. Palmer, Somerset v Gloucestershire at Bristol, 1970; K. D. Boyce, Essex v Somerset at Westcliff, 1971; G. D. McKenzie, Leicestershire v Essex at Leicester, 1972; R. G. D. Willis, Warwickshire v Yorkshire at Birmingham, 1973; W. Blenkiron, Warwickshire v Derbyshire at Buxton, 1974; A. Buss, Sussex v Worcestershire at Hastings, 1974; J. M. Rice, Hampshire v Northamptonshire at Southampton, 1975; M. A. Nash, Glamorgan v Worcestershire at Worcester, 1975; A. Hodgson, Northamptonshire v Somerset at Northampton, 1976; A. E. Cordle, Glamorgan v Hampshire at Portsmouth, 1979; C. J. Tunnicliffe, Derbyshire v Worcestershire at Derby, 1979; M. D. Marshall, Hampshire v Surrey at Southampton, 1981; I. V. A. Richards, Somerset v Essex at Chelmsford, 1982; P. W. Jarvis, Yorkshire v Derbyshire at Derby, 1982.

Most economical analysis: 8–8–0–0; B. A. Langford, Somerset v Essex at Yeovil, 1969.

Most expensive analysis: 8–0–85–0; A. M. Ferreira, Warwickshire v Essex at Colchester, 1982.

Most wickets in a season: 34 – R. J. Clapp (Somerset) 1974.

RULES OF THE JOHN PLAYER LEAGUE

(As applied in 1982)

Hours of Play

All matches shall commence at 2.00 p.m., with a tea interval of twenty minutes at 4.10 p.m., or between innings, whichever is the earlier. The duration and time of the tea interval can be varied in the case of an interrupted match. Close of play shall normally be at 6.40 p.m., but play may continue after that time if, in the opinion of the umpires, the overs remaining to be bowled can be completed by 7.00 p.m.

Length of Innings

(i) In an uninterrupted match:
  (a) Each team shall bat for 40 overs unless all out earlier.
  (b) In the possible event of the team fielding first failing to bowl 40 overs by 4.10 p.m., the over in progress shall be completed and the innings of the team batting second shall be limited to the same number of overs as the innings of the team batting first. See Note 1.
  (c) If the team batting first is all out and its last wicket falls within two minutes of the scheduled time for the tea interval, the innings of the side batting second shall be limited to the same number of overs as the innings of the team batting first (the over in which the last wicket falls to count as a complete over).

(ii) In matches where the start is delayed or play is suspended:

(a) The object shall always be to rearrange the number of overs so that both teams have the opportunity of batting for the same number of overs (minimum ten overs each team). The calculation of the number of overs to be bowled shall be based on an average rate of eighteen overs per hour (one over per 3⅓ minutes or part thereof) in the time remaining before close of play at 6.40 p.m. See Note 2.

(b) If the start is delayed by not more than one hour and the innings of both teams is thereby reduced to not less than 30 overs per team, the time of close of the first innings (and start of the tea interval) shall be fixed, allowing three and a half minutes for each over to be bowled. If the team fielding first fails to bowl the revised number of overs by the agreed time for the close of the innings, the principles set out in Rule (i) (b & c) will apply. If the number of overs of the side batting first is reduced in any other circumstances, no fixed time will be specified for the close of their innings.

(c) If, owing to a suspension of play during the innings of the team batting second, it is not possible for that team to have the opportunity of batting for the same number of overs as the team batting first, they will bat for a number of overs to be calculated as in (ii) (a).

(d) In the event of a suspension occurring in the middle of an over, the full number of overs to be bowled in the time remaining will be calculated as in (ii) (a), any balls remaining to be bowled in the over during which play was suspended being added.

(e) The team batting second shall not bat for a greater number of overs than the first team, unless the latter has been all out in fewer than the agreed number of overs.

Note 1: All teams are normally required to bowl at an average rate of twenty overs per hour. It is appreciated, however, that in certain exceptional circumstances it may not be possible to attain this average, and a short additional period for each innings is allowed in the Hours of Play. If, at 6.40 p.m. more than three overs remain to be bowled, play may continue as allowed in Hours of Play, but the matter will be referred to the Discipline Committee. If the umpires report that a team fielding first has failed to bowl its full quota of overs on account of unnecessary "time-wasting", the matter will also be referred to the Discipline Committee.

Note 2: Umpires will notify the home authority of the time of resumption of play, following any delay or suspension, immediately they have reached a decision. The home authority will provide a representative who will be responsible for assisting umpires in calculating the revised number of overs to be played in the match and for notifying the decision of the umpires immediately to all concerned.

The Result

(1) A result can be achieved only if both teams have batted for at least ten overs, unless one team has been all out in less than ten overs or unless the team batting second scores enough runs to win in fewer than ten overs. All other matches in which one or both teams have not had an opportunity of batting for a minimum of ten overs shall be declared "No Result" matches.

(ii) In matches in which both teams have had an opportunity of batting for the agreed number of overs (i.e. 40 overs each, in an uninterrupted match, or a lesser number of overs in an interrupted match) the team scoring the higher number of runs shall be the winner. If the scores are equal, the result shall be a "Tie" and no account shall be taken of the number of wickets which have fallen.

(iii) If, due to suspension of play, the number of overs in the innings of the side batting second has to be revised to a lesser number than that allotted to the side batting first, their target score, which they must exceed to win the match, shall be calculated by multiplying the reduced number of overs by the average runs per over scored by the side batting first. If the target score involves a fraction of a run, the final scores cannot be equal and the result cannot be a Tie.

(iv) If a match is abandoned before the side batting second have received their allotted number of overs and they have neither been all out, nor have passed their opponents' score, the result shall be decided on the average run-rate throughout both innings.

(v) In the event of the team batting first being all out in less than their full quota of overs, the calculation of their average run-rate shall be based on the full quota of overs to which they would have been entitled and not on the number of overs in which they were dismissed.

Number of Overs per Bowler

If a match starts as a 40 overs match, no bowler may bowl more than eight overs in an innings and this allowance shall not be reduced even though the total overs may subsequently be restricted owing to weather interference. If, however, the start of a match is delayed and the overs of both teams are restricted to fewer than 40 overs, no bowler may bowl more than one fifth of the total overs allowed, except that where the total overs is not divisible by five, an additional over shall be allowed to the minimum number of bowlers necessary to make up the balance – e.g. in a 33 overs match, three bowlers may bowl a maximum of seven overs and no other bowler more than six overs. In a match where the innings of either or both teams is reduced after the start of the match, the maximum number of overs allowed per bowler shall remain as at the start of the match.

In the event of a bowler breaking down and being unable to complete an over, the remaining balls will be bowled by another bowler. Such part of an over will count as a full over only in so far as each bowler's limit is concerned.

The number of overs bowled by each individual bowler shall be indicated on the scoreboard, from the commencement of an innings.

Limitation of the Bowler's Run-up

The bowler's run-up, including his preliminary approach, shall be limited to fifteen yards, to be measured from the wicket. A white line will mark the maximum distance allowed.

Restriction on Placement of Fieldsmen

At the instant of delivery a minimum of four fieldsmen (plus the bowler and wicket-keeper) must be within an area bounded by two semi-circles centred on each middle stump (each with a radius of 30 yards) and joined by a parallel line on each side of the pitch. In the event of an infringement the square-leg umpire shall call "No-ball".

Law 14 – Declarations

Law 14 will not apply in this competition. The captain of the batting side may not declare his innings closed at any time during the course of a match.

Law 24.1 – No-Ball – Mode of Delivery

Law 24.1 will apply in this competition, except that no bowler may deliver the ball underarm.

Law 25.1 – Wide Ball – Judging a Wide

Umpires are instructed to apply a very strict and consistent interpretation in regard to this Law in order to prevent negative bowling wide of the wicket or over the batsman's head.

The following criteria should be adopted as a guide to umpires:

(i) If the ball passes either side of the wicket sufficiently wide to make it virtually impossible for the striker to play a "normal cricket stroke" both from where he is standing and from where he should normally be standing at the crease, the umpire should call and signal "Wide".

(ii) If the ball passes over head height of the striker standing upright at the crease, the umpire should call and signal "Wide".

Note: The above provisions do not apply if the striker makes contact with the ball, or if it passes below head height between the striker and the wicket.

Other Playing Conditions

Except as specified in these Playing Conditions, the Playing Conditions for first-class matches in the United Kingdom will apply. Matches in the John Player League are not, however, first-class.

Scoring of Points

(i) The team winning the match to score four points.

(ii) In the event of a "Tie", each team to score two points.

(iii) In a "No Result" match, each team to score two points.

(iv) In the event of two or more teams finishing with an equal number of points for any of the first three places, their final positions will be decided by:

(a) The most wins or, if still equal
(b) The most away wins or, if still equal
(c) The higher run-rate throughout the season.

LORDS AND COMMONS CRICKET, 1982

The first two matches of the season were missed because of emergency debates on the Falklands crisis, but thereafter the rest of the fixture list was played, with four wins, two draws, four losses and only one match rained off.

The tour to the Netherlands resulted in one handsome victory against the Dutch Parliament and a favourable draw, when large hailstones in a freak storm scattered the cricketers in record speed. For a late June fixture, it was an extraordinary sight to see the pitch completely white after five minutes. Most pleasing were the first win ever against the Harrow Wanderers and a very favourable draw against the Guards.

Eighteen members of Parliament appeared in one or more matches and there was a welcome increase of Clerks and other staff of the House. Special mention must be made of Lord Orr-Ewing, who has turned out for the club for more than 30 years and who played a full season. He celebrated his 70th birthday in February, 1982.

St Paul's School and Westminster School – matches cancelled owing to Falklands emergency debates.

Lords and Commons 130; Mandarin CC 116. Lords and Commons won by 14 runs.

Lords and Commons 178; Conservative Agents 174. Lords and Commons won by 4 runs.

BBC 166 for nine dec.; Lords and Commons 108. BBC won by 58 runs.

Dutch Parliament 131; Lords and Commons 132 for four. Lords and Commons won by six wickets.

Lords and Commons 137; Dutch Parliament 125 for seven. Drawn (rain).

Lords and Commons 224; Guards CC 133 for nine. Drawn.

MCC 249 for five dec.; Lords and Commons 239. MCC won by 10 runs.

Eton Ramblers – match abandoned because of rain.

Lords and Commons 213 for nine dec.; Old Westminsters 214 for nine. Old Westminsters won by one wicket.

Lords and Commons 121; Law Society CC 124 for five. Law Society CC won by five wickets.

Harrow Wanderers 109; Lords and Commons 110 for eight. Lords and Commons won by two wickets.

MINOR COUNTIES CHAMPIONSHIP, 1982

The loss of L. L. McFarlane to Lancashire and the frequent absence of S. E. Blott left the **Bedfordshire** attack considerably weakened, although veteran K. V. Jones worked hard and effectively. The batsmen, often chasing large totals, failed to score runs quickly enough, although A. S. Pearson and captain D. M. Daniels played some sound innings.

Berkshire, who moved up to fourth place, owed their strength to the batting, led by new captain J. F. Harvey, with M. L. Simmons, who scored his first century for the side, and J. A. Claughton, previously with Warwickshire, who was specially registered. Notable partnerships between openers M. Lickley and A. Dindar included 173 against Devon at Torquay, when Dindar reached 100. S. Burrow made runs, took wickets and fielded brilliantly, although the rest of the fielding tended to be patchy, apart from G. E. J. Child, who upheld his fine standard of wicket-keeping. The burden of the bowling fell upon J. H. Jones, who took the most wickets, and P. Bradburn, who tended to be expensive. The best return came from M. Hinchcliffe with eight for 66 against Wiltshire.

Buckinghamshire, who with only one win dropped to nineteenth position, were unable to muster a regular team, although many young players benefited from the opportunities they received. There were distinguished batting performances from P. G. C. Harvey and Cambridge Blue K. I. Hodgson, both of whom hit maiden centuries, Harvey's coming in the match against Suffolk at Ipswich, when P. Dolphin also reached three figures. Other consistent batsmen were D. E. Smith, M. E. Milton and J. B. Turner. Although C. A. Connor showed improved form and A. W. Lyon took six Bedfordshire wickets for 54, the lack of penetrative bowling was a handicap.

The loss of D. Collard weakened **Cambridgeshire's** attack, in which M. Brown was the most successful bowler, his 31 wickets including seven for 42 against Lincolnshire and six for 79 against Bedfordshire. M. S. A. McEvoy, recruited from Essex to strengthen the batting, did so admirably with 961 runs, including two hundreds in the match against Bedfordshire. He was well supported by G. V. Miller, who hit 104 not out against Norfolk.

Two wins in their last three games enabled **Cheshire** to finish in fifteenth place, nine lower than in 1981. The early loss of openers Mudassar Nazar, to the Pakistani touring team, and J. A. Sutton, injured, was a blow to the side, although considerable success was achieved by their replacements, P. A. Tipton and Cambridge Blue D. W. Varey. Sutton, in the second game against Cumberland, reached his 10,000th run and 150th catch for the side in 24 seasons. The bowling tended to be expensive, but I. J. Gemmell gained a place in the Minor Counties touring team to East Africa.

Cornwall, whose potentially strong side had hopes of reaching a high position in 1982, were handicapped by the absence of key players and settled next to the bottom of the table. However, encouragement came from the excellent batting of M. S. T. Dunstan and E. G. Willcock, who took over the captaincy when J. M. H. Graham-Brown was not available. D. A. Toseland bowled effectively, and opportunities were given to a number of younger players.

The season was a disappointing one for **Cumberland**, who crashed from ninth place to last, the position they had occupied in 1980. They remain the only Minor County never to have qualified for the Gillette Cup or NatWest Bank Trophy.

Devon improved on their dismal performance of 1981, when they finished bottom, to qualify for the NatWest Bank Trophy in 1983 by virtue of a storming finish, in which they defeated eventual champions Oxfordshire, with a run-out off the last ball, and had the better of a drawn match against Somerset II. Sound batting came from G. Wallen and captain B. L. Matthews, who hit 120 not out against Berkshire. D. I. Yeabsley, in his 24th season, was disappointing with the ball, but the attack was strengthened by the return from Argentina of M. J. Goulding. Spinner A. W. Allin's nineteen wickets included seven for 49 in the crucial match against Oxfordshire at Sidmouth.

Dorset, who shot up from twentieth to third position, owed their success to the advent of C. Stone, whose 43 wickets included a return of six for 104 against Berkshire, and who, with

C. W. Allen, took 72 of the 99 wickets to fall. The batting was sound, with centuries from Stone and R. V. Lewis, who scored the most runs. Valuable support came from S. J. Halliday and the young R. J. Scott, while M. C. Wagstaffe was an astute captain.

Without the services of many key players, defending champions **Durham** dropped to ninth position in their centenary year and ended their record of 65 Championship matches without defeat when they succumbed to Staffordshire at Stockton-on-Tees in mid-August. The batting was disappointing, only three batsmen averaging more than 30. S. R. Atkinson made his highest score of 155 not out against Cheshire and all-rounder A. S. Patel hit 108 not out against Cumberland, as well as taking eighteen wickets. S. Greensword also gave an excellent all-round performance with 501 runs and twenty wickets, while pace bowlers J. Johnston and Australian S. P. Davis collected 25 wickets apiece. R. A. D. Mercer kept wicket with his customary skill.

For **Hertfordshire**, who moved up twelve places to fifth, D. G. Ottley scored 605 runs at an average of 75.62, including 108 against Suffolk. Other three-figure innings came from N. P. G. Wright, C. S. Bannister and W. M. Osman, whose 103 against Bedfordshire at Henlow was accompanied by a return of seven for 58 from R. L. Johns. R. J. Hailey, who with Johns and T. S. Smith took the most wickets, captured seven Norfolk wickets for 63 at Watford.

In their last season in the Championship, **Lancashire II** suffered more than most from the weather, three of their matches producing no result. None the less, they moved up six places, with hundreds coming from I. Cockbain (129), F. C. Hayes (105) and K. A. Hayes (116). P. G. Lee's match analysis of seven for 87, with J. Simmons's six for 117, earned the side their only victory – against Cheshire.

The weak batting of **Lincolnshire**, for whom the only century was G. Robinson's 119 against Norfolk, placed a heavy responsibility on the bowlers. This was borne chiefly by G. A. Cope, whose 34 wickets included six for 65 against Staffordshire, and R. O. Estwick, whose 28 featured returns of eight for 59 against Norfolk and six for 46 against Northumberland.

Another county to experience difficulty over the availability of players was **Norfolk**, runners-up in 1981, who slipped to fourteenth position. However, fine performances came from S. C. Plumb, who scored over 200 runs more than anyone else, and leading wicket-taker T. A. Barnes, formerly with Lincolnshire, who achieved the feat of taking more than 200 wickets for each of two Minor Counties.

Northumberland, whose matches were badly affected by rain, dropped to eighteenth place. Outstanding of the bowlers was J. N. Graham, with 45 wickets, while T. R. Etwaroo, a West Indian from Guyana, again headed the batting averages.

Champions for the third time in 1982, **Oxfordshire** previously won the Championship in 1929 and 1974. They owed much to the fine leadership of captain P. J. Garner, who scored the most runs, including an unbeaten 102 against Berkshire at Oxford. R. A. Evans took six for 61 in the same match and six for 37 against Cornwall, while a return of eight for 39, against Berkshire at Boyne Hill, came from K. Arnold. These two bowlers, with leading wicket-taker S. R. Porter, D. G. Gallop and R. N. Busby, enabled the side comfortably to bowl out their opponents. M. D. Nurton and P. A. Fowler were sound opening batsmen and P. J. Densham reached 105 not out against Cornwall.

Despite winning only one game, **Shropshire** were never in danger of defeat in their seven drawn games, but dropped four places to eleventh. Sri Lankan D. S. de Silva was outstanding, his 489 runs including a century and his 38 wickets featuring a return of six for 45 against Bedfordshire. J. S. Johnson made 103 not out in the same match.

Despite falling to eighth position, **Somerset II** were encouraged by the performance of some of their younger players. I. Cox and J. Wyatt both batted well, M. D. Harman bowled his off-breaks effectively, and sixteen-year-old G. V. Palmer had an excellent all-round season with the second-highest batting aggregate and the most wickets, including seven for 47 against Dorset.

In a moderate season, **Staffordshire's** batting suffered from the absence for six matches of captain P. N. Gill with a fractured cheek-bone. Mushtaq Mohammad, engaged with a view to strengthening the bowling, failed to come up to expectations with the ball but had a successful season with the bat, scoring almost twice as many runs as the next batsman. R. W. Flower was the leading wicket-taker, his haul of 33 featuring match figures of ten for 95 against Cheshire. D. Cartledge was a useful all-rounder when available and A. Griffiths maintained his excellent form behind the stumps.

An effective all-round performance took **Suffolk** to sixth position in a season which saw the introduction of younger players. C. Rutterford, in his first season as captain, took the most wickets, while new pace bowler R. Green was also successful. However, the injured R. J. Robinson was often missed. The most consistent batsmen were R. F. Howlett and S. M. Clements, though new opener P. D. Barker scored the most runs, his maiden century for the county being the side's only three-figure innings.

Runners-up **Wiltshire**, with no professional, enjoyed a successful season in their centenary year. Consistent batting featured notable contributions from P. Thorn, B. H. White and J. Newman, whose maiden century came at a crucial time against Oxfordshire. Outstanding was G. I. Burgess, who topped the batting averages with the most runs, including a century, and took seven for 36 against his old county at Taunton. Leading wicket-taker was D. Crisp who, in his first season, collected eleven for 80 against Cornwall at Penzance, against whom A. M. Barker took seven for 53 at Swindon. Able assistance came from R. J. Gulliver, but the absence of a class spinner was evident.

MINOR COUNTIES CHAMPIONSHIP, 1983

In 1983 the Minor Counties Championship, sponsored for the first time by the United Friendly Insurance Company plc, will be known as the United Friendly Insurance County Championship. It will be contested in two divisions as follows:
East – Bedfordshire, Cambridgeshire, Cumberland, Durham, Hertfordshire, Lincolnshire, Norfolk, Northumberland, Staffordshire, Suffolk.
West – Berkshire, Buckinghamshire, Cheshire, Cornwall, Devon, Dorset, Oxfordshire, Shropshire, Somerset II, Wiltshire.

Each county will play every other county in its own division once, all matches being two-innings games played over two days. The leaders in each division will meet in a final play-off at Worcestershire County Ground. This match will be a one-day single-innings limited-overs match.

MINOR COUNTIES IN EAST AFRICA, 1982

A Minor Counties side, under the captaincy of M. D. Nurton and managed by C. G. Howard, toured East Africa in October-November 1982, playing matches in Kenya, Malawi, Zambia and Tanzania. The party consisted of: M. D. Nurton (*captain*, Oxfordshire), C. G. Howard (*manager*), J. A. R. Oliver (*assistant-manager*), R. W. Flower (Staffordshire), I. J. Gemmell (Cheshire), A. Griffiths (Staffordshire), F. L. Q. Handley (Norfolk), R. F. Howlett (Suffolk), R. D. Huggins (Norfolk), P. D. Johnson (Lincolnshire), A. W. Lyon (Buckinghamshire), M. S. A. McEvoy (Cambridgeshire), D. G. Nicholls (Staffordshire), A. S. Pearson (Bedfordshire), S. R. Porter (Oxfordshire) and J. A. Smith (Shropshire).

MINOR COUNTIES CHAMPIONSHIP, 1982

	Played	Won	Lost	Drawn Won 1st Inns[1]	Drawn Lost 1st Inns[1]	Drawn Tied 1st Inns[1]	No Result	Points	Average Points
Oxfordshire NW	10	4	2†	3	1	0	0	56	5.60
Wiltshire NW	10	4	4*T	2	0	0	0	51	5.10
Dorset NW	10	4	1	1	3	0	1	48	4.80
Berkshire NW	10	3	4†T	3	0	0	0	47	4.70
Hertfordshire NW	10	3	0	4	1	1	1	47	4.70
Suffolk NW	10	3	2†	2	2	1	0	46	4.60
Cambridgeshire NW	10	3	2*	3	2	0	0	44	4.40
Somerset II	8	2	0	2	3	0	1	31	3.87
Durham NW	10	1	1*	8	0	0	0	37	3.70
Lincolnshire NW	8	2	2	1	3	0	0	26	3.25
Shropshire NW	10	1	0	5	2	0	2	31	3.10
Lancashire II	8	1	0	2	2	0	3	24	3.00
Devon NW	10	2	3	1	2	0	2	29	2.90
Norfolk NW	10	1	2*	4	2	0	1	29	2.90
Cheshire NW	12	2	1	2	6	0	1	34	2.83
Staffordshire	10	1	0	2	5	0	2	25	2.50
Bedfordshire	10	1	3*	2	4	0	0	23	2.30
Northumberland	12	0	2*	3	3	1	3	23	1.91
Buckinghamshire	12	1	5*	0	6	0	0	19	1.58
Cornwall	10	0	3	2	3	0	2	13	1.30
Cumberland	8	0	2	1	3	1	1	10	1.25

[1] *After 55 overs completed.*
* *Signifies 1st-innings lead in* ONE *match lost.*
† *Signifies 1st-innings lead in* TWO *matches lost.*
T *Signifies tie on first innings in* ONE *match lost.*
NW *Signifies qualified for NatWest Bank Trophy in 1983.*

The two top counties having already played each other in the competition, no Challenge Match was played.

*In the averages that follow, * against a score signifies not out, * against a name signifies the captain, and † signifies wicket-keeper.*

BEDFORDSHIRE

Secretary – G. L. B. AUGUST, 24 Furzefield, Putnoe, Bedford

Matches 10: Won – Buckinghamshire. Lost – Shropshire, Suffolk (twice). Won on first innings – Buckinghamshire, Cambridgeshire. Lost on first innings – Cambridgeshire, Hertfordshire (twice), Shropshire.

Batting Averages

	I	NO	R	HI	Avge
*D. M. Daniels	19	3	563	63	35.18
A. S. Pearson	9	0	251	64	27.88
K. V. Gentle	14	0	371	82	26.50
R. G. Abeynaike	19	2	450	79*	26.47
M. Morgan	19	1	449	83	24.94
M. E. Gear	7	1	139	41	23.16
T. Thomas	16	2	314	65*	22.42
S. J. Lines	14	0	274	52	19.57
F. R. Dethridge	11	5	93	24*	15.50
K. V. Jones	17	6	169	26*	15.36
†P. G. M. August	11	7	54	21	13.50

Also batted: S. E. Blott, A. Fordham, J. Kettleborough, R. Loft, C. Musson, I. G. Peck, M. G. Stedman, P. M. Taylor, A. Wagner, C. Williams.

Bowling Averages

	O	M	R	W	Avge
C. Williams	58.5	16	169	11	15.36
K. V. Jones	291	99	781	28	27.89
S. E. Blott	63	14	181	6	30.16
R. Loft	78	13	261	8	32.62
A. Wagner	117.5	22	395	12	32.91
F. R. Dethridge	175	30	706	19	37.15
R. G. Abeynaike	117	29	355	9	39.44
M. Morgan	92.4	21	326	8	40.75

Also bowled: S. J. Lines 57–13–220–5; A. S. Pearson 28–2–96–3; T. Thomas 1–0–5–0.

BERKSHIRE

Secretary – C. F. V. MARTIN, Paradise Cottage, Paradise Road, Henley-on-Thames, Oxon RG9 1UB

Matches 10: Won – Buckinghamshire, Devon, Wiltshire. Lost – Dorset, Oxfordshire (twice), Wiltshire. Won on first innings – Buckinghamshire, Devon, Dorset.

Batting Averages

	I	NO	R	HI	Avge
*J. F. Harvey	20	7	636	96	48.92
M. L. Simmons	16	6	487	113*	48.70
J. A. Claughton	12	2	451	79	45.10
M. Lickley	20	1	501	72	26.36
A. Dindar	18	0	457	100	25.38
D. Gorman	8	0	177	67	22.12
S. Burrow	18	3	328	65*	21.86
J. Woollhead	13	1	218	40	18.16
†G. E. J. Child	9	2	89	25*	12.71

Also batted: P. Bradburn, M. Hewett, M. Hinchcliffe, T. James, J. H. Jones, G. P. Knight, M. D. Mence, P. New, R. Owen, M. Richardson, A. Rollins.

Bowling Averages

	O	M	R	W	Avge
M. Richardson.........	45	10	121	9	13.44
P. New..................	97	36	217	15	14.46
M. Hinchcliffe..........	75.1	12	284	13	20.84
M. Hewett..............	51	17	133	6	22.16
T. James.................	56	15	149	6	24.83
S. Burrow...............	140.3	28	436	17	25.64
J. H. Jones..............	228.2	46	812	23	35.30
P. Bradburn............	185	51	452	10	45.20

Also bowled: J. Alldis 15–5–33–0; A. Dindar 15–2–58–2; M. Lickley 11–2–47–1; M. D. Mence 22.1–3–62–4; A. Rollins 21–3–92–3; M. L. Simmons 55–8–204–5; J. Woollhead 62–14–189–4.

BUCKINGHAMSHIRE

Secretary – P. M. M. SLATTER, FIB,
The White Cottage, Framewood Road, Stoke Poges SL2 4QR

Matches 12: Won – Suffolk. Lost – Bedfordshire, Berkshire, Hertfordshire (twice), Oxfordshire. Lost on first innings – Bedfordshire, Berkshire, Norfolk (twice), Oxfordshire, Suffolk.

Batting Averages

	I	NO	R	HI	Avge
P. Dolphin..............	24	4	666	100	33.30
M. E. Milton...........	14	2	360	128*	30.00
P. G. C. Harvey.......	8	1	202	102	28.85
*D. E. Smith...........	20	2	509	109*	28.27
J. B. Turner............	18	1	467	70	27.47
†R. G. Humphrey.....	8	0	206	84	25.75
K. I. Hodgson..........	8	0	197	109	24.62
S. A. Mehar............	8	1	164	47	23.42
N. G. Hames...........	13	1	214	65	17.83
†T. P. Russell..........	9	2	110	39	15.71
S. J. Renshaw..........	11	2	138	38	15.33
A. J. Herrington.......	6	2	61	21	15.25
C. A. Connor...........	7	2	60	28	12.00
A. W. Lyon.............	11	4	75	22*	10.71
J. K. S. Edwards......	6	0	64	23	10.66
R. J. Dell...............	8	1	53	28*	7.57
J. M. Coles.............	8	5	11	9*	3.66

Also batted: M. J. J. Cox, N. W. Farrow, A. J. Field, †V. A. P. Flynn, D. C. Hopkins, P. J. Newport, J. N. Potter, S. P. Ridge.

Bowling Averages

	O	M	R	W	Avge
M. E. Milton...........	132.1	45	331	14	23.64
A. W. Lyon.............	266.5	71	756	29	26.06
C. A. Connor...........	246.5	52	806	28	28.78
S. A. Mehar............	170	33	546	18	30.33
S. P. Ridge.............	62.4	15	218	7	31.14
K. I. Hodgson..........	144	34	391	12	32.58

Also bowled: J. M. Coles 145–21–546–9; A. J. Field 31–2–149–1; P. G. C. Harvey 19.5–4–70–3; D. C. Hopkins 49–14–142–5; P. J. Newport 14–1–49–0; S. J. Renshaw 54–6–249–3; D. E. Smith 8–0–49–3.

CAMBRIDGESHIRE

Secretary – P. W. GOODEN,
The Redlands, Oakington Road, Cottenham, Cambridgeshire

Matches 10: Won – Lincolnshire, Norfolk, Suffolk. Lost – Hertfordshire, Suffolk. Won on first innings – Bedfordshire, Lincolnshire, Norfolk. Lost on first innings – Bedfordshire, Hertfordshire.

Batting Averages

	I	*NO*	*R*	*HI*	*Avge*
M. S. A. McEvoy......	19	2	961	140*	56.52
D. R. Parry.............	12	4	338	66	42.25
G. V. Miller............	19	1	607	104*	33.72
*A. M. Ponder.........	13	2	326	57	29.63
N. T. Gadsby...........	10	1	251	49	27.88
D. H. J. Baker.........	15	4	287	77*	26.09
P. J. Malkin............	8	5	66	18*	22.00
†M. L. Saggers.........	7	3	86	32	21.50
P. Redfarn..............	8	2	121	37*	20.16
G. S. Rice...............	6	2	79	34	19.75
I. J. Parker.............	8	2	107	66	17.83
D. R. Vincent..........	5	0	59	24	11.80

Also batted: M. Brown, D. C. Collard, H. Mumford, D. J. Smallwood.

Bowling Averages

	O	*M*	*R*	*W*	*Avge*
P. J. Malkin............	85	16	252	14	18.00
M. S. A. McEvoy......	87	19	256	13	19.69
M. Brown................	225	44	717	31	23.12
G. S. Rice...............	156	37	390	16	24.37
I. J. Parker.............	151	42	355	13	27.30
D. R. Parry.............	249	53	691	19	36.36
D. Wing..................	171.4	34	454	9	50.44

Also bowled: D. H. J. Baker 4.1–0–17–1; D. C. Collard 26–6–58–2; N. T. Gadsby 1–0–8–0; M. Gray 26–5–98–2; H. Mumford 24–6–73–5; A. M. Ponder 10.5–5–36–1.

CHESHIRE

Secretary – J. B. PICKUP,
2 Castle Street, Northwich, Cheshire CW8 1AB

Matches 12: Won – Cumberland, Northumberland. Lost – Lancashire II. Won on first innings – Cumberland, Staffordshire. Lost on first innings – Durham (twice), Northumberland, Shropshire (twice), Staffordshire. No result – Lancashire.

Batting Averages

	I	*NO*	*R*	*HI*	*Avge*
Mudassar Nazar	8	1	422	110*	60.28
S. C. Wundke	12	4	344	107*	43.00
D. W. Varey	13	1	461	99*	38.41
*J. A. Sutton	4	0	124	86	31.00
P. A. Tipton	17	0	503	76	29.58
D. Bailey	7	0	164	58	23.42
N. T. O'Brien	21	3	415	76	23.05
J. Hitchmough	14	0	266	69	19.00
M. Watkinson	14	2	208	36	17.33
R. M. O. Cooke	21	1	338	67*	16.90
K. R. Harris	6	0	76	34	12.66
I. Cowap	8	1	76	20*	10.85
I. J. Gemmell	8	2	62	19	10.33

Also batted: J. D. Carpenter, S. T. Crawley, S. C. M. Douglas, K. J. McCullagh, S. L. Milner, †J. K. Pickup, R. C. Rodger, G. M. Taylor, T. J. Taylor, J. G. Varey, P. G. Wakefield.

Bowling Averages

	O	*M*	*R*	*W*	*Avge*
J. A. Sutton	62	27	118	9	13.11
R. M. O. Cooke	140.5	44	426	24	17.75
S. C. Wundke	54	17	130	7	18.57
N. T. O'Brien	173.3	49	461	19	24.26
I. J. Gemmell	175.2	42	563	23	24.47
R. C. Rodger	202	57	633	16	39.56
M. Watkinson	172.3	39	569	12	47.41

Also bowled: D. Bailey 25–6–63–1; J. D. Carpenter 15–2–45–0; S. C. M. Douglas 24–3–135–3; K. R. Harris 1–0–2–0; J. Hitchmough 48–6–172–3; S. L. Milner 5–1–23–0; Mudassar Nazar 27–6–93–0; T. J. Taylor 32–4–106–2; P. A. Tipton 7–3–33–1; J. G. Varey 4–2–7–0; P. G. Wakefield 15–2–57–2.

CORNWALL

Secretary – T. D. MENEER, Falbridge, Penvale Cross, Penryn

Matches 10: Lost – Devon, Wiltshire (twice). Won on first innings – Dorset, Somerset II. Lost on first innings – Oxfordshire (twice), Somerset II. No result – Devon, Dorset.

Batting Averages

	I	*NO*	*R*	*HI*	*Avge*
M. S. T. Dunstan	18	1	653	111	38.41
*E. G. Willcock	16	1	471	130*	31.40
T. J. Angove	17	0	386	57	22.70
C. J. Trudgeon	16	1	302	116*	20.13
C. H. Rowe	6	0	112	34	18.66
D. A. Toseland	13	4	148	30	16.44
J. F. Rowe	7	2	81	50	16.20
*J. M. H. Graham-Brown	8	0	121	29	15.12
†T. L. Gall	14	2	168	48*	14.00
F. T. Willetts	11	0	141	28	12.81

Also batted: P. A. Coombe, D. J. Halfyard, D. Jenkin, P. I. Johns, A. Machin, V. K. Meneer, M. C. Rowe, M. O. Trenwith, A. H. Watts, G. G. Watts.

Bowling Averages

	O	*M*	*R*	*W*	*Avge*
P. I. Johns	112.5	35	282	14	20.14
A. H. Watts	174.3	33	585	28	20.89
D. A. Toseland	296.5	87	717	31	23.12
J. M. H. Graham-Brown	87	21	237	9	26.33

Also bowled: P. A. Coombe 52–12–152–3; D. J. Halfyard 55–13–145–3; D. Jenkin 57–11–236–5; A. Machin 21–2–80–0; V. K. Meneer 24–9–83–1; M. O. Trenwith 25–6–78–0; G. G. Watts 14–1–55–2; F. T. Willetts 2–0–15–1.

CUMBERLAND

Secretary – N. WISE, 18 Banklands, Workington, Cumbria

Matches 8: Lost – Cheshire, Durham. Won on first innings – Lancashire II. Lost on first innings – Cheshire, Durham, Lancashire II. Tied on first innings – Northumberland. No result – Northumberland.

Batting Averages

	I	*NO*	*R*	*HI*	*Avge*
L. Baichan	13	1	472	95*	39.33
R. Entwistle	11	1	279	93	27.90
R. M. Ratcliffe	9	2	174	54	24.85
J. R. Moyes	10	1	219	51	24.33
D. Halliwell	8	3	100	26	20.00
M. D. Woods	9	1	109	39	13.62

Also batted: D. L. Ash, M. Battersby, N. Boustead, I. Cooper, D. J. Lupton, G. McMeekin, D. J. Parsons, K. Sample, S. Sharp, C. Stockdale, D. Walters, A. G. Wilson, P. Wood.

Bowling Averages

	O	*M*	*R*	*W*	*Avge*
M. D. Woods	50.2	9	154	6	25.66
R. M. Ratcliffe	186.1	36	589	20	29.45
D. J. Parsons	131	25	463	15	30.86
D. Halliwell	109.1	17	403	10	40.30

Also bowled: D. L. Ash 37.4–5–149–2; D. J. Lupton 58–13–163–4; K. Sample 28–7–89–2; P. Wood 3–0–26–1.

DEVON

Secretary – Rev. K. J. WARREN,
49 Highfield, Lapford, Crediton, Devon EX17 6PY

Matches 10: Won – Cornwall, Oxfordshire. Lost – Berkshire, Dorset, Oxfordshire. Won on first innings – Somerset II. Lost on first innings – Berkshire, Dorset. No result – Cornwall, Somerset II.

Batting Averages

	I	*NO*	*R*	*HI*	*Avge*
N. R. Gaywood........	6	2	178	56	44.50
G. Wallen...............	15	3	510	92*	42.50
J. G. Tolchard..........	11	0	407	94	37.00
*B. L. Matthews.......	13	1	419	120*	34.91
R. F. Harriott...........	8	3	149	64*	29.80
R. C. Tolchard.........	10	0	273	78	27.30
N. A. Folland..........	7	1	145	64	24.16
M. Olive.................	9	0	209	65	23.22
A. W. Allin.............	7	1	83	41*	13.83
M. J. Goulding.........	6	2	49	24*	12.25

Also batted: P. A. Brown, P. G. Considine, C. A. Edwards, J. H. Edwards, †R. M. Oliver, †M. E. Stevens, A. Thomas, D. I. Yeabsley. N. J. Mountford kept wicket in one match but did not bat.

Bowling Averages

	O	*M*	*R*	*W*	*Avge*
M. J. Goulding.........	222.1	30	823	28	29.39
A. W. Allin.............	167	34	611	19	32.15
D. I. Yeabsley..........	239.4	54	726	21	34.57
P. A. Brown............	66.4	6	312	7	44.57

Also bowled: P. G. Considine 59–11–202–5; N. A. Folland 2–0–14–0; N. R. Gaywood 5–0–8–0; R. F. Harriott 33–4–110–3; B. L. Matthews 2–0–4–0; A. Thomas 40–5–165–2; R. C. Tolchard 8–1–34–1; G. Wallen 7.2–1–34–0.

DORSET

Secretary – D. J. W. BRIDGE,
Long Acre, Tinney's Lane, Sherborne, Dorset DT9 3DY

Matches 10: Won – Berkshire, Devon, Wiltshire (twice). Lost – Somerset. Won on first innings – Devon. Lost on first innings – Berkshire, Cornwall, Somerset II. No result – Cornwall.

Batting Averages

	I	*NO*	*R*	*HI*	*Avge*
R. V. Lewis.............	17	2	726	114*	48.40
S. J. Halliday...........	11	2	349	67	38.77
C. Stone..................	19	7	410	142*	34.16
C. A. Graham..........	14	3	309	78	28.09
R. J. Scott...............	19	3	406	73	25.37
†V. B. Lewis...........	18	0	433	64	24.05
*M. C. Wagstaffe......	8	3	116	60*	23.20
D. R. Baty...............	9	0	185	53	20.55

Also batted: C. W. Allen, J. F. Blackburn, R. V. J. Coombes, J. M. Guymer, D. R. Hayward, P. M. Howard, †D. A. Ridley, M. Rushworth, I. Stuart, J. Wilson, A. R. Wingfield Digby.

Bowling Averages

	O	*M*	*R*	*W*	*Avge*
C. Stone	273.2	55	807	43	18.76
C. W. Allen	247.3	48	832	29	28.68
A. R. Wingfield Digby	58	13	203	6	33.83
R. V. J. Coombes	119.1	32	375	9	41.66

Also bowled: D. R. Baty 3–0–15–0; J. F. Blackburn 1–0–14–0; A. Evans 4–0–22–0; C. A. Graham 3–0–9–0; S. J. Halliday 2–0–18–0; D. R. Hayward 56–13–168–4; P. M. Howard 22–9–51–1; R. V. Lewis 3–0–15–0; V. B. Lewis 10–0–66–2; M. Rushworth 55–13–163–2; R. J. Scott 29–2–115–2; I. Stuart 4–0–21–0; M. C. Wagstaffe 20–3–113–2.

DURHAM

Secretary – J. ILEY,
Roselea, Springwell Avenue, Durham City DH1 4LY

Matches 10: Won – Cumberland. Lost – Staffordshire. Won on first innings – Cheshire (twice), Cumberland, Northumberland (twice), Shropshire (twice), Staffordshire.

Batting Averages

	I	*NO*	*R*	*HI*	*Avge*
S. R. Atkinson	12	2	505	155*	50.50
S. Greensword	17	2	574	73	38.26
A. S. Patel	16	3	426	108*	32.76
J. G. D. Smith	6	1	130	42*	26.00
*N. A. Riddell	16	2	333	65	23.78
D. C. Jackson	12	0	285	85	23.75
G. Hurst	14	1	219	54	16.84
P. J. Kippax	6	1	70	29	14.00

Also batted: P. C. Birtwisle, P. J. Crane, S. P. Davis, †A. R. Fothergill, G. Johnson, J. Johnston, †R. A. D. Mercer, W. B. Parker, D. D. Parsana, I. M. Richards, I. Robson, Wasim Raja. †S. A. Rooke played in one match but did not bat.

Bowling Averages

	O	*M*	*R*	*W*	*Avge*
D. D. Parsana	144.3	62	242	16	15.12
A. S. Patel	104	21	328	18	18.22
J. Johnston	217.3	63	499	26	19.19
S. P. Davis	195.5	44	578	30	19.26
G. Johnson	115	31	320	13	24.61
S. Greensword	229.4	93	495	20	24.75
P. J. Kippax	78	21	253	7	36.14

Also bowled: I. E. Conn 18–3–78–2; P. J. Crane 26–5–62–1; D. C. Jackson 3–1–6–0; B. R. Lander 12–2–78–0; N. A. Riddell 3–0–13–0; I. Robson 1–0–9–0; J. G. D. Smith 34–2–168–4; Wasim Raja 35.5–11–76–4; J. S. Wilkinson 23–4–68–0.

Note: Averages include NatWest Bank Trophy match v Surrey.

HERTFORDSHIRE

Secretary – C. A. HARRISON, 147A High Street, Waltham Cross, Hertfordshire

Matches 10: Won – Buckinghamshire (twice), Cambridgeshire. Won on first innings – Bedfordshire (twice), Cambridgeshire, Suffolk. Lost on first innings – Norfolk. Tied on first innings – Suffolk. No result – Norfolk.

Batting Averages

	I	*NO*	*R*	*HI*	*Avge*
D. G. Ottley	11	3	605	108	75.62
W. M. Osman	13	1	663	103	55.25
C. S. Bannister	8	3	247	102*	49.40
*†F. E. Collyer	12	3	252	52	28.00
N. P. G. Wright	12	1	276	126	25.09
B. G. Evans	4	0	94	48	23.50
A. R. Garofall	10	1	203	49	22.55
T. S. Smith	11	3	135	62*	16.87
R. H. Pomphrey	5	1	65	20	16.25
A. C. Bagguley	5	0	56	28	11.20

Also batted: R. G. Ashby, I. R. Beven, D. Bithray, A. R. Brown, J. D. Carr, B. G. Collins, D. P. Doyle, S. P. J. Dymoke, A. R. L. Emerton, N. J. Gandon, R. J. Hailey, R. L. Johns, K. R. King, E. P. Neal, D. J. Smith, J. D. W. Wright.

Bowling Averages

	O	*M*	*R*	*W*	*Avge*
J. D. W. Wright	50.1	15	140	11	12.72
R. L. Johns	124.1	34	372	20	18.60
T. S. Smith	184.3	53	466	21	22.19
R. J. Hailey	187	57	508	19	26.73
K. R. King	98	16	371	13	28.53
A. R. Garofall	126	36	299	10	29.90

Also bowled: R. G. Ashby 7–2–33–1; I. R. Beven 43–13–107–1; B. G. Collins 61–16–140–4; D. P. Doyle 5–0–17–0; E. P. Neal 2–0–13–0; D. G. Ottley 5–0–25–0.

LANCASHIRE SECOND ELEVEN

Secretary – C. D. HASSELL, Old Trafford, Manchester M16 0PX

Matches 8: Won – Cheshire. Won on first innings – Cumberland, Northumberland. Lost on first innings – Cumberland, Shropshire. No result – Cheshire, Northumberland, Shropshire.

Batting Averages

	I	*NO*	*R*	*HI*	*Avge*
N. V. Radford	9	4	275	74	55.00
A. Kennedy	6	0	226	86	37.66
P. A. Davis	7	0	189	80	27.00
R. G. Watson	8	1	153	42	21.85
B. Thorpe	8	0	141	48	17.62

Also batted: I. Cockbain, A. Darlington, N. H. Fairbrother, J. Hartley, F. C. Hayes, K. A. Hayes, P. G. Lee, S. J. O'Shaughnessy, †D. Pearson, *H. Pilling, B. W. Reidy, †C. J. Scott, G. J. Speak, J. Stanworth, †M. A. Wallwork. L. Joyce and L. L. McFarlane each played in one match but did not bat.

Bowling Averages

	O	M	R	W	Avge
A. Kennedy	42	9	71	9	7.89
A. Murphy	36	14	83	6	13.83
P. G. Lee	80.5	26	172	12	14.33
J. Simmons	61	26	117	6	19.50
R. G. Watson	45.5	4	182	7	26.00
N. V. Radford	88	18	278	8	34.75

Also bowled: I. Folley 31–9–84–3; J. Hartley 39–10–102–4; K. A. Hayes 3–1–12–0; S. Jones 14–1–53–3; S. J. O'Shaughnessy 28.3–5–90–0; B. W. Reidy 38.2–5–130–2; G. J. Speak 46.4–8–142–4; B. Thorpe 15–4–59–0.

LINCOLNSHIRE

Secretary – C. H. WARMAN,
22 Charles Avenue, Grimsby, South Humberside

Matches 8: Won – Norfolk, Northumberland. Lost – Cambridgeshire, Norfolk. Won on first innings – Staffordshire. Lost on first innings – Cambridgeshire, Northumberland, Staffordshire.

Batting Averages

	I	NO	R	HI	Avge
†R. G. Draper	9	5	200	55*	50.00
G. Robinson	16	0	489	119	30.56
†J. G. Franks	16	2	302	60	21.57
H. Pougher	12	1	230	56*	20.90
R. G. White	10	2	144	67*	18.00
*P. D. Johnson	16	2	249	86*	17.78
G. A. Cope	9	5	70	15	17.50
S. T. Lawrence	15	3	209	65	17.41
D. Marshall	10	1	127	25	14.11
H. S. Stroud	4	0	53	27	13.25

Also batted: S. Braithwaite, R. L. Burton, R. O. Estwick, J. C. Munton, T. F. Nicholls, A. Priestley, J. C. Taylor, P. L. Tillison.

Bowling Averages

	O	M	R	W	Avge
R. O. Estwick	172.1	40	490	28	17.50
G. A. Cope	285.1	95	639	34	18.79
R. L. Burton	157.2	40	423	13	32.53
D. Marshall	184.5	47	530	16	33.12

Also bowled: S. Braithwaite 13–3–52–0; S. T. Lawrence 31–4–134–5; S. J. Mollin 4–0–29–0; T. F. Nicholls 12–3–43–0; P. L. Tillison 13–2–43–0.

NORFOLK

Secretary – D. J. M. ARMSTRONG, Thorpe Cottage, Mill Common, Ridlington, North Walsham NR28 9TY

Matches 10: Won – Lincolnshire. Lost – Cambridgeshire, Lincolnshire. Won on first innings – Buckinghamshire (twice), Hertfordshire, Suffolk. Lost on first innings – Cambridgeshire, Suffolk. No result – Hertfordshire.

Batting Averages

	I	*NO*	*R*	*HI*	*Avge*
S. G. Plumb	14	2	640	112*	53.33
T. L. Powell	7	2	212	115	42.40
Parvez Mir	15	5	366	89*	36.60
*P. J. Sharpe	10	4	212	117*	35.33
R. D. Huggins	12	3	312	79*	34.66
F. L. Q. Handley	14	1	436	122	33.53
N. D. Cook	8	3	148	66*	29.60
†D. E. Mattocks	8	4	111	40*	27.75
P. J. Ringwood	7	1	130	35	21.66
D. G. Pilch	7	1	116	53	19.33

Also batted: A. C. Agar, T. H. Barnes, J. Barrett, I. N. Battelley, R. L. Bradford, R. F. Innes, B. A. Meigh, P. A. Motum, P. W. Thomas, E. Wright. †J. H. Riley played in two matches but did not bat.

Bowling Averages

	O	*M*	*R*	*W*	*Avge*
T. H. Barnes	294.5	109	630	42	15.00
B. A. Meigh	67	18	215	12	17.91
D. G. Pilch	59.2	11	202	9	22.44
R. F. Innes	134.5	36	386	16	24.12
Parvez Mir	318.1	45	605	25	24.20
S. G. Plumb	182	38	543	19	28.57

Also bowled: A. C. Agar 26–1–119–3; I. N. Battelley 7–2–22–0; N. D. Cook 1–0–13–0; F. L. Q. Handley 1–0–6–0; P. A. Motum 14–3–42–4; P. J. Sharpe 2–2–0–0; P. W. Thomas 13–4–37–1; E. Wright 18–2–75–5.

NORTHUMBERLAND

Secretary – R. E. WOOD, Osborne Avenue, Jesmond, Newcastle upon Tyne NE2 1JS

Matches 12: Lost – Cheshire, Lincolnshire. Won on first innings – Cheshire, Lincolnshire, Staffordshire. Lost on first innings – Durham (twice), Lancashire. Tied on first innings – Cumberland. No result – Cumberland, Lancashire II, Staffordshire.

Batting Averages

	I	*NO*	*R*	*HI*	*Avge*
T. R. Etwaroo..........	8	2	349	130*	58.16
G. D. Halliday.........	16	4	427	156*	35.58
G. R. Morris............	8	2	183	53*	30.50
*A. S. Thompson......	18	2	458	100*	28.62
K. Pearson..............	15	0	425	85	28.33
J. S. Charleton.........	17	0	456	76	26.82
M. E. Younger.........	5	1	84	61*	21.00
R. D. Dodds............	9	0	183	49	20.33
S. G. Lishman..........	13	2	207	42*	18.81
A. Hardy.................	11	5	104	40*	17.33
M. N. Elliott............	4	0	55	33	13.75

Also batted: M. B. Anderson, †K. Corby, †N. C. D. Craig, P. C. Graham, J. N. Graham, D. W. Lilly, A. Maitra, †W. G. Robson, J. Shotton.

Bowling Averages

	O	*M*	*R*	*W*	*Avge*
J. N. Graham...........	372.1	110	980	45	21.77
R. D. Dodds............	114.3	8	422	16	26.37
A. Hardy.................	157.5	47	490	16	30.62
P. C. Graham..........	270.2	72	781	23	33.95
S. G. Lishman..........	89.5	13	363	7	51.85

Also bowled: G. D. Halliday 25.2–10–79–3; K. Pearson 1–1–0–0; M. E. Younger 3–0–18–0.

OXFORDSHIRE

Secretary – J. E. O. SMITH,
2 The Green, Horton-cum-Studley, Oxfordshire

Matches 10: Won – Berkshire (twice), Buckinghamshire, Devon. Lost – Devon, Wiltshire. Won on first innings – Buckinghamshire, Cornwall (twice). Lost on first innings – Wiltshire.

Batting Averages

	I	*NO*	*R*	*HI*	*Avge*
*P. J. Garner...........	18	3	720	102*	48.00
M. D. Nurton..........	14	2	431	69*	35.91
P. A. Fowler............	15	1	493	88	35.21
J. Manger................	7	1	191	63	31.83
B. J. Collis...............	11	4	192	47*	27.42
S. R. Porter.............	14	5	198	43	22.00
†A. Crossley............	13	3	183	40	18.30
C. Clements.............	8	1	110	27	15.71
K. Arnold................	7	0	83	32	11.85
R. N. Busby.............	5	0	55	22	11.00

Also batted: S. Brennecke, P. J. Densham, R. A. Evans, D. G. Gallop, M. Thomas, M. D. Thomas.

Bowling Averages

	O	M	R	W	Avge
D. G. Gallop	126	35	367	21	17.47
R. N. Busby	188	53	460	25	18.40
R. A. Evans	271	81	627	32	19.59
S. R. Porter	274	73	719	34	21.14
P. Goldring	67	8	225	10	22.50
K. Arnold	204	59	559	22	25.40

Also bowled: P. Bradbury 10–2–35–0; B. J. Collis 34–12–93–3; P. J. Densham 13.2–5–27–3; P. J. Garner 9.2–1–28–2; G. R. Hobbins 43–13–120–4.

SHROPSHIRE

Secretary – H. BOTFIELD, 1 The Crescent, Much Wenlock

Matches 10: Won – Bedfordshire. Won on first innings – Bedfordshire, Cheshire (twice), Lancashire II, Staffordshire. Lost on first innings – Durham (twice). No result – Lancashire II, Staffordshire.

Batting Averages

	I	NO	R	HI	Avge
C. N. Boyns	5	1	229	71	57.25
D. S. de Silva	14	3	489	109	44.45
*J. S. Johnson	16	2	501	103*	35.78
S. P. Henderson	10	2	256	67*	32.00
B. J. Perry	9	5	119	36	29.75
D. Williamson	4	0	98	43	24.50
J. B. R. Jones	17	1	386	82	24.12
J. Foster	15	2	232	51	17.84
S. C. Gale	13	3	161	33*	16.10
J. P. Dawson	7	2	72	18	14.40
P. L. Ranells	7	3	50	21*	12.50

Also batted: †D. J. Ashley, A. S. Barnard, B. M. Brain, M. Davies, J. A. Hulme, J. A. Smith, C. B. M. Williams. S. J. Mason played in one match but did not bat.

Bowling Averages

	O	M	R	W	Avge
D. S. de Silva	238	62	626	38	16.47
A. S. Barnard	60	21	120	7	17.14
C. N. Boyns	77.4	19	221	11	20.09
J. A. Smith	231	58	589	29	20.31
J. P. Dawson	161.4	54	407	18	22.61
B. J. Perry	215.3	59	586	21	27.90
P. L. Ranells	65	7	226	7	32.28

Also bowled: B. M. Brain 36–9–99–1; S. P. Henderson 3–1–12–0; J. B. R. Jones 2–0–5–0.

SOMERSET SECOND ELEVEN

Secretary – A. S. BROWN, County Cricket Ground, Taunton

Matches 8: Won – Dorset, Wiltshire. Won on first innings – Cornwall, Dorset. Lost on first innings – Cornwall, Devon, Wiltshire. No result – Devon.

Batting Averages

	I	*NO*	*R*	*HI*	*Avge*
I. Cox....................	6	3	195	73*	65.00
R. L. Ollis..............	14	1	565	103*	43.46
N. A. Felton...........	6	1	192	109*	38.40
G. V. Palmer...........	9	1	253	75	31.62
J. Wyatt.................	8	0	247	78	30.87
A. J. H. Dunning.....	6	0	175	85	29.16
N. F. M. Popplewell..	4	0	103	49	25.75
N. Russom..............	8	4	92	20	23.00
I. R. Bussey............	8	2	124	76	20.66
†G. E. Joyce...........	4	0	50	34	12.50

Also batted: T. J. Ackland, D. Breakwell, M. Bryant, P. W. Denning, †T. Gard, M. D. Harman, J. King, R. J. McCool, P. J. Robinson, P. A. Slocombe, A. W. J. Spiller, R. C. Talbot, †S. Turner.

Bowling Averages

	O	*M*	*R*	*W*	*Avge*
G. V. Palmer..........	148.5	37	418	27	15.48
P. J. Robinson.........	62.1	25	124	8	15.50
T. J. Ackland..........	61	13	201	12	16.75
M. Bryant...............	75.1	14	211	9	23.44
M. D. Harman.........	87.2	11	292	12	24.33
R. J. McCool..........	128.3	32	412	14	29.42
N. Russom..............	62.1	14	183	6	30.50

Also bowled: D. Breakwell 24–5–72–0; I. R. Bussey 10–2–40–0; I. Cox 5–2–9–0; N. A. Felton 2–0–4–1; R. L. Ollis 7–0–60–1; N. F. M. Popplewell 8–3–26–1; R. C. Talbot 2–1–4–0.

STAFFORDSHIRE

Secretary – L. W. HANCOCK,
4 Kingsland Avenue, Oakhill, Stoke-on-Trent ST4 5LA

Matches 10: Won – Durham. Won on first innings – Cheshire, Lincolnshire. Lost on first innings – Cheshire, Durham, Lincolnshire, Northumberland, Shropshire. No result – Northumberland, Shropshire.

Batting Averages

	I	*NO*	*R*	*HI*	*Avge*
Mushtaq Mohammad.	18	1	703	98*	41.35
D. Cartledge...........	9	0	326	94	36.22
P. A. Marshall.........	11	1	366	65	36.60
N. J. Archer............	16	4	347	44	28.91
G. S. Warner..........	14	0	366	62	26.14
*P. N. Gill.............	5	0	127	48	25.40
D. G. Nicholls.........	8	4	84	31*	21.00
S. J. Dawson...........	6	2	79	43*	19.75
†A. Griffiths...........	16	4	209	41	17.41
N. D. Croft.............	7	0	107	36	15.28
N. Hodgkinson.........	6	0	76	25	12.66
D. Blank................	8	4	42	13	10.50

Also batted: R. B. Allison, S. Bailey, M. E. W. Brooker, S. J. Dean, R. W. Flower, G. R. S. Hall, D. A. Hancock, P. W. Junkin, N. Penton.

Bowling Averages

	O	M	R	W	Avge
D. Blank	140	39	350	19	18.42
R. W. Flower	285.2	112	624	33	18.90
M. E. W. Brooker	149	42	411	18	22.83
D. G. Nicholls	132	33	363	15	24.20
Mushtaq Mohammad	241.4	54	687	21	32.71

Also bowled: N. J. Archer 2–1–8–0; P. R. Bagley 12–0–62–0; D. Cartledge 19–6–37–2; J. H. Durber 23–10–71–1; P. N. Gill 2–1–1–1; R. I. James 28–7–69–3; P. W. Junkin 59–11–161–3; P. A. Marshall 2–0–23–0.

SUFFOLK

Secretary – R. S. BARKER,
Harthill, 301 Henley Road, Ipswich IP1 6TB

Matches 10: Won – Bedfordshire (twice), Cambridgeshire. Lost – Buckinghamshire, Cambridgeshire. Won on first innings – Buckinghamshire, Norfolk. Lost on first innings – Hertfordshire, Norfolk. Tied on first innings – Hertfordshire.

Batting Averages

	I	NO	R	HI	Avge
R. F. Howlett	18	4	567	61*	40.50
S. M. Clements	20	4	586	95	36.62
P. D. Barker	20	3	603	108*	35.47
R. J. Bond	14	2	360	62	30.00
†S. A. Westley	11	4	189	73	27.00
J. W. Edrich	8	1	182	70	26.00
*C. Rutterford	8	5	73	19*	24.33
P. J. Hayes	19	2	367	56	21.58
P. J. Caley	15	1	271	51	19.35
R. N. S. Hobbs	6	1	68	28	13.60
R. Green	11	6	55	19*	11.00

Also batted: M. L. Clinch, †N. Crane, D. H. Knights, P. C. Rice, R. J. Robinson, A. G. Warrington.

Bowling Averages

	O	M	R	W	Avge
R. J. Robinson	44	9	74	9	8.22
P. J. Hayes	136.3	26	431	22	19.59
R. Green	241.3	39	624	24	26.00
C. Rutterford	290.2	53	717	27	26.55
R. N. S. Hobbs	121.2	26	424	13	32.61
P. D. Barker	107	24	403	12	33.58

Also bowled: P. J. Caley 79–14–347–9; S. M. Clements 44–4–181–5; J. W. Edrich 0.3–0–6–0; C. G. Graham 19–3–55–2; R. F. Howlett 15–0–95–3; S. A. Westley 1–0–11–0.

WILTSHIRE

Secretary – J. C. GREENWOOD,
35 Rowden Hill, Chippenham, Wiltshire

Matches 10: Won – Berkshire, Cornwall (twice), Oxfordshire. Lost – Berkshire, Dorset (twice), Somerset II. Won on first innings – Oxfordshire, Somerset II.

Batting Averages

	I	*NO*	*R*	*HI*	*Avge*
G. I. Burgess	19	0	676	115	35.57
P. Thorn	18	3	495	109*	33.00
J. Newman	16	3	396	100*	30.46
B. H. White	15	2	375	86	28.84
P. Donald	16	2	298	68*	21.28
D. Mercer	17	3	203	37	14.50
†G. E. Meale	14	4	132	47	13.20
D. Crisp	17	5	157	40	13.08
A. M. Barker	6	0	66	28	11.00

Also batted: *R. G. Gulliver.

Bowling Averages

	O	*M*	*R*	*W*	*Avge*
A. M. Barker	95	35	219	15	14.60
R. J. Gulliver	185	67	457	26	17.57
G. I. Burgess	139	52	314	16	19.62
D. Crisp	262	61	815	36	22.63
R. Wilson	55	14	166	7	23.71
P. Thorn	129	31	409	13	31.46
A. J. Spencer	110.4	27	343	8	42.87

Also bowled: A. Crouch 42.4–12–116–5.

LEADING MINOR COUNTIES AVERAGES – 1982

BATTING

(Qualification: 8 innings; average 40.00)

	I	*NO*	*R*	*HI*	*Avge*
D. G. Ottley (*Hertfordshire*)	11	3	605	108	75.62
Mudassar Nazar (*Cheshire*)	8	1	422	110*	60.28
M. S. A. McEvoy (*Cambridgeshire*)	19	2	961	140*	56.52
W. M. Osman (*Hertfordshire*)	13	1	663	103	55.25
N. V. Radford (*Lancashire II*)	9	4	275	74	55.00
S. G. Plumb (*Norfolk*)	14	2	640	112*	53.33
S. R. Atkinson (*Durham*)	12	2	505	155*	50.50
J. F. Harvey (*Berkshire*)	20	7	636	96	48.92
M. L. Simmons (*Berkshire*)	16	6	487	113*	48.70
R. V. Lewis (*Dorset*)	17	2	726	114*	48.40
P. J. Garner (*Oxfordshire*)	18	3	720	102*	48.00
J. A. Claughton (*Berkshire*)	12	2	451	79	45.10
D. S. de Silva (*Shropshire*)	14	3	489	109	44.45
R. L. Ollis (*Somerset II*)	14	1	565	103*	43.46

	I	*NO*	*R*	*HI*	*Avge*
S. C. Wundke (*Cheshire*)	12	4	344	107*	43.00
G. Wallen (*Devon*)	15	3	510	92*	42.50
D. R. Parry (*Cambridgeshire*)	12	4	338	66	42.25
Mushtaq Mohammad (*Staffordshire*)	18	1	703	98*	41.35
R. F. Howlett (*Suffolk*)	18	4	567	61*	40.50

BOWLING

(Qualification: 20 wickets; average 20.00)

	O	*M*	*R*	*W*	*Avge*
T. H. Barnes (*Norfolk*)	294.5	109	630	42	15.00
G. V. Palmer (*Somerset II*)	148.5	37	418	27	15.48
D. S. de Silva (*Shropshire*)	238	62	626	38	16.47
D. G. Gallop (*Oxfordshire*)	126	35	367	21	17.47
R. O. Estwick (*Lincolnshire*)	172.1	40	490	28	17.50
R. J. Gulliver (*Wiltshire*)	185	67	457	26	17.57
R. M. O. Cooke (*Cheshire*)	140.5	44	426	24	17.75
J. Johnston (*Durham*)	205.3	60	459	25	18.36
R. N. Busby (*Oxfordshire*)	188	53	460	25	18.40
R. L. Johns (*Hertfordshire*)	124.1	34	372	20	18.60
C. Stone (*Dorset*)	273.2	55	807	43	18.76
G. A. Cope (*Lincolnshire*)	285.1	95	639	34	18.79
R. W. Flower (*Staffordshire*)	285.2	112	624	33	18.90
R. A. Evans (*Oxfordshire*)	271	81	627	32	19.59
P. J. Hayes (*Suffolk*)	136.3	26	431	22	19.59

PRUDENTIAL WORLD CUP

As in the previous two tournaments for the Prudential Cup, in 1975 and 1979, the 1983 tournament, which commences on June 9, will be contested in two groups: Group A – England, New Zealand, Pakistan and Sri Lanka; Group B – Australia, India, West Indies and Zimbabwe. Each country in each group will meet the others twice, after which the leading two teams in each group will go forward into the semi-finals, to be played on June 22. The final, at Lord's, will be on June 25.

The winners of the Prudential Cup will receive £20,000, double the prize-money received by West Indies in 1979. The losing finalists will receive £8,000, and the losing semi-finalists £4,000. In addition, the winning team in each of the 24 group matches will receive £1,000. The Man of the Match in the final will receive £600, in the semi-finals £400, and in the group matches £200.

PREVIOUS FINALS

1975 West Indies beat Australia by 17 runs.
1979 West Indies beat England by 92 runs.

SECOND ELEVEN CHAMPIONSHIP, 1982

Derbyshire's unbeaten record of the previous two seasons was ended by Northamptonshire at Finedon, and a further defeat saw them tumble five places to the middle of the table. John Morris was their most prolific batsman, with hundreds against Lancashire and Nottinghamshire, and Iain Anderson proved his all-round worth with 100 not out against Nottinghamshire and a return of seven for 67 against Warwickshire.

After Neil Foster suffered a back injury early in the season, **Essex** were hampered by the lack of fast bowling support for Gary Sainsbury, whose 46 wickets included eleven Surrey wickets for 105. Also successful were Terry Foley, Andrew Golding and off-spinner Michael Field-Buss, who took seven for 73 against Nottinghamshire. Left-handers Chris Gladwin and Robert Leiper were the leading scorers, each making three centuries, as did Australian Steve Smith, on an Esso Scholarship, who headed both batting and bowling averages.

Opportunities were given to many young players by **Glamorgan,** who, without a win, subsided to the bottom of the table. Geoff Holmes and John Derrick were the leading wicket-takers, while Gary Thomas, formerly of Warwickshire, scored the most runs. Alan Lewis Jones hit 221 not out against Kent at Neath.

The promotion of Tony Wright and Paul Romaines to the First Eleven weakened **Gloucestershire**'s potentially strong side, who were disappointed to finish no higher than eighth. Barry Dudleston excelled against Glamorgan at Bristol, scoring 223 not out and taking four for 28. Of the younger players, Edward Cunningham, the Marlborough captain of two years earlier, showed ability to take on any attack, and Robert "Jack" Russell shared his considerable wicket-keeping talents between Gloucestershire's First and Second Elevens and Young England.

After two outright wins, **Hampshire**'s efforts to retain the Championship title fell away when several matches were drawn. Their strength lay in the batting, with fifteen three-figure innings being played and six batsmen averaging over 50. The most prolific was Chris Smith, followed by his hard-hitting brother, Robin, and Paul Terry, who scored 140 and 113 in the match against Sussex at Hove. The attack sometimes lacked penetration, although Steve Malone's 46 wickets included nine for 61 in the match against Gloucestershire at Bournemouth, John Southern took seven for 84 and six for 56 against Essex and Sussex respectively and Simon Massey returned seven for 64 against Northamptonshire.

The batting strength of **Kent,** under the captaincy of Alan Ealham, took them to third place. Simon Hinks had an outstanding season with three hundreds in his record 1,165 runs, while double-centuries were scored by Richard Ellison (218 not out against Essex) and Eldine Baptiste (201 not out against Surrey). Of the younger players, Derek Aslett, Ellison, Steven Marsh, Laurie Potter and Chris Penn acquitted themselves well in the First Eleven, the promising Penn being awarded a Whitbread Scholarship. Slow left-armer Lindsay Wood was the most successful bowler, his 34 wickets including six for 86 against Middlesex.

Under the challenging leadership of Harry Pilling, **Lancashire** shot from sixteenth to second place. Formidable opponents, they accumulated fourteen centuries, five from Andrew Kennedy and four from Ian Cockbain, who passed 1,000 runs. Neal Radford, with 55 wickets, including seven for 38 against Glamorgan, and Peter Lee, whose 42 wickets featured seven for 64 against Nottinghamshire, spearheaded the attack, ably supported by Steve O'Shaughnessy and Oxford Blue Timothy Taylor (slow left-arm).

For **Leicestershire,** who remained in tenth position, Mike Haysman was the most prolific batsman, closely followed by J. J. Whitaker and Ian Butcher. Several notable individual performances came in the match against Nottinghamshire at Leicester, where Tim Boon compiled 170, Mike Garnham hit 102 and David Wenlock, the side's leading wicket-taker, enjoyed match figures of nine for 64.

Substantial innings for **Middlesex** came from Keith Tomlins, with 169 against Hampshire, and Colin Cook, who made 162 against Warwickshire at Nuneaton, where the side made their highest total, 391 for five, having been bowled out for 97 by Surrey in their previous game. New Zealander Richard Hoskin collected 176 runs in his two matches and Norman Cowans took twenty wickets in his four appearances. The best return came from Kevan James with six for 56 against Sussex.

After three years at the bottom of the table, **Northamptonshire** lifted themselves to thirteenth position. The side was enhanced by the inclusion of R. Heritage, who bore the brunt of the bowling, and Martin Bamber, who scored 1,080 runs. David Capel and Duncan Wild showed the benefit of their First Eleven experience, but the young bowlers were again disappointing. Neil Mallender, who appeared only briefly, took seven for 28 against Derbyshire at Finedon.

Although **Nottinghamshire**'s results were disappointing, satisfaction came from seeing a large number of players in action, a long casualty list resulting in 43 players being called upon. Paul Johnson's 1,432 runs included a record-breaking 236 against Leicestershire at Steetly, Paul Todd made 216 against Sussex, David Saxelby approached 1,000 runs, and Mark Fell, who made ten Championship appearances for the First Eleven, scored 121 and 100 against Lancashire at Manchester. The bowling was less effective, but there were a number of useful individual performances, among them S. Mahboob's seven for 46 against Leicestershire.

Lack of experience on the part of **Somerset**'s young team left them in fifteenth place. Phil Slocombe's sound batting early in the season won him back his place in the First Eleven and Neil Russom, who started well with 154 against Nottinghamshire, was unlucky to fracture his jaw. Mark Davis's left-arm seam bowling showed an encouraging improvement, but Michael Bryant, from Cornwall, was a disappointment and Australian Russel McCool's leg-breaks proved expensive.

The loss of Graham Monkhouse and Kevin Mackintosh to the First Eleven was a blow to **Surrey,** who dropped to seventh place after winning four of their first matches. Duncan Pauline (200) and David Smith (175 including nine 6s) put on 336 for the third wicket against Sussex at Norbury where, in the match against Yorkshire, Dave Thomas and Graham Roope both reached three figures and J. Handley took seven for 32. Geoff Howarth, who appeared in only two matches, hit 106 against Essex and Alec Stewart made his first century for the side with 154 against Kent.

Another frustrating season saw **Sussex** slip to sixteenth place, owing in part to injuries to senior players and to a loss of confidence by others. On the credit side were hard-hit innings from Alan Wells, with hundreds against Middlesex and Surrey, against whom Paul Phillipson, who headed the batting averages, also reached three figures. Alan Willows bowled consistently for his 36 wickets and Chris Waller took six for 84 against Hampshire. Adrian Jones was plagued throughout the summer by a back injury.

Warwickshire were disappointed by the performances of batsmen Robin Dyer and Simon Wootton, although Geoff Tedstone showed improvement. Malcolm Dolman, on an Esso Scholarship from Australia, bowled left-arm chinamen to good effect to take 42 wickets in just six matches, including a return of eleven for 130 against Leicestershire at Birmingham, when he also scored 82. Simon Sutcliffe took seven for 61 in the first innings against Somerset at Keynsham, where David (D. M.) Smith took seven for 28 in the second innings, and hundreds came against the same side at Birmingham from Phil Oliver, Gordon Lord and Neal Abberley.

Worcestershire, led variously by Mark Scott, Tim Curtis and Vanburn Holder, were convincing champions, although they needed to win their last match, against Warwickshire, to secure the title. In a successful batting line-up, Damian D'Oliveira was the most prolific, with hundreds against Gloucestershire and Nottinghamshire. The skill and experience with the ball of Hartley Alleyne and Steve Perryman proved too much for many opposing batsmen, and encouraging contributions were made by pace bowlers Alan Warner, Andrew Webster, Philip Newport and David Slater, each in his first season. Sixteen-year-old schoolboy, Ricardo Ellcock, bowled with exceptional pace and fully justified his selection for the First Eleven, as did left-arm spin bowler Richard Illingworth, who received a Whitbread Scholarship. Peter Moores was a successful and enthusiastic wicket-keeper.

No one player was outstanding for **Yorkshire,** although the highly rated Martyn Moxon passed 1,000 runs. The second-highest aggregate came from the promising left-hander, Neil Lloyd, who died tragically in September from a mystery virus. He was the only player to score two hundreds for the side in 1982 – 128 against Lancashire at Liverpool and 100 not out against the same county at Bradford.

SECOND ELEVEN CHAMPIONSHIP FINAL TABLE

	Played	*Won*	*Lost*	*Drawn*	*Bonus Points* *Batting*	*Bonus Points* *Bowling*	*Total Points*	*Average*
Worcestershire.....	15	6	1	8	36	52	184	12.2
Lancashire...........	14	5	1	8	34	46	160	11.4
Kent....................	16	6	3	7	39	35	170	10.6
Middlesex............	13	4	2	7	28	33	125	9.6
Hampshire...........	13	3	1	9	38	39	125	9.6
Warwickshire.......	18	5	5	8	34	53	167	9.2
Surrey................	14	4	2	8	25	39	128	9.1
Gloucestershire....	11	2	3	6	31	38	101	9.1
Derbyshire..........	13	3	2	8	31	37	116	8.9
Leicestershire.......	10	1	2	7	33	33	82	8.2
Nottinghamshire...	18	3	6	9	49	48	145	8.0
Essex..................	12	2	4	6	27	30	89	7.4
Northamptonshire.	13	2	2	9	30	30	92	7.0
Yorkshire............	16	2	3	11	37	42	111	6.9
Somerset.............	12	2	4	6	18	30	80	6.6
Sussex................	13	1	6	6	27	34	77	5.9
Glamorgan..........	13	0	4	9	23	40	63	4.8

Notes: The averages to determine the positions in the Championship are worked to one, uncorrected decimal place.

The following matches were abandoned without a ball being bowled: Middlesex v Leicestershire, Nottinghamshire v Warwickshire, Worcestershire v Glamorgan, all on June 23, 24, 25.

*In the averages that follow, * against a score signifies not out, * against a name signifies the captain and † signifies wicket-keeper.*

DERBYSHIRE SECOND ELEVEN

Matches 13: Won – Northamptonshire, Warwickshire, Yorkshire. Lost – Lancashire, Northamptonshire. Drawn – Lancashire, Leicestershire (twice), Nottinghamshire (twice), Worcestershire (twice), Yorkshire.

Batting Averages

	I	*NO*	*R*	*Avge*
A. Hill....................................	13	3	619	61.90
I. S. Anderson............................	11	1	534	53.40
J. Morris..................................	21	1	802	40.10
A. J. Borrington..........................	16	3	391	30.07
K. G. Brooks..............................	21	2	521	27.42
R. J. Finney...............................	10	2	217	27.12
†B. J. M. Maher..........................	13	3	234	23.40
W. P. Fowler..............................	17	1	258	16.12
S. J. Farrell...............................	9	3	69	11.50
A. Watts...................................	13	4	98	10.88

Also batted: P. J. Hacker, D. G. Moir, P. G. Newman, *P. E. Russell, C. J. Tunnicliffe.

Bowling Averages

	O	*M*	*R*	*W*	*Avge*
P. G. Newman..........	75.3	27	154	13	11.84
A. Hill....................	98.2	13	170	9	18.88
A. Watts.................	256.5	79	683	35	19.51
W. P. Fowler............	352.1	104	827	42	19.69
R. J. Finney.............	100	33	220	11	20.00
D. G. Moir..............	83	31	173	8	21.62
I. S. Anderson..........	183.5	59	476	18	26.44
S. J. Farrell.............	234	68	661	21	31.47

Also bowled: K. G. Brooks 82–27–201–2; P. J. Hacker 126.2–22–361–5; C. J. Tunnicliffe 63.2–23–170–5.

ESSEX SECOND ELEVEN

Matches 12: Won – Kent, Nottinghamshire. Lost – Kent, Middlesex, Surrey (twice). Drawn – Hampshire, Middlesex, Northamptonshire (twice), Sussex (twice).

Batting Averages

	I	*NO*	*R*	*HI*	*Avge*
S. B. Smith.............	9	1	620	110	77.50
C. Gladwin.............	20	2	978	122	54.33
R. J. Leiper............	18	3	689	128	45.93
A. W. Lilley...........	9	1	361	69	45.12
P. J. Prichard..........	15	1	410	73	29.28
K. R. Pont..............	7	1	167	100	27.83
*†N. Smith..............	14	0	354	90	25.28
M. R. Gouldstone.....	10	1	168	45*	18.66
M. Field-Buss..........	8	3	92	29	18.40
G. E. Sainsbury........	9	2	101	29*	14.42
S. Ferguson............	4	0	57	22	14.25

Also batted: D. L. Acfield, N. Burns, N. Cooper, M. H. Denness, T. Foley, N. A. Foster, I. Gray, A. K. Golding, M. Hussain, F. Joseph, R. Miller, K. Moye, D. A. Wilson. T. Taiani played in one match but did not bat.

Bowling Averages

	O	*M*	*R*	*W*	*Avge*
S. B. Smith.............	36	11	108	6	18.00
G. E. Sainsbury........	355.2	121	849	46	18.45
A. K. Golding..........	72.5	19	221	9	24.55
T. Foley..................	201.3	57	520	18	28.88
K. R. Pont..............	82.4	23	199	6	33.16
K. Moye..................	156.3	35	502	14	35.85
M. Field-Buss..........	179	41	560	15	37.33

Also bowled: D. L. Acfield 38–10–80–3; N. Cooper 33–6–108–1; S. Ferguson 57–12–197–0; N. A. Foster 24–5–66–2; C. Gladwin 20–2–128–1; R. Haynes 20–3–89–2; M. Hussain 123–43–309–5; A. W. Lilley 7.1–2–37–0; R. Miller 95–10–387–7; B. Pinkerton 9–3–36–0; N. Smith 9–3–36–0; D. A. Wilson 24–3–108–0.

GLAMORGAN SECOND ELEVEN

Matches 13: Lost – Gloucestershire, Somerset, Warwickshire, Worcestershire. Drawn – Gloucestershire, Hampshire, Kent, Lancashire, Somerset, Surrey, Warwickshire, Yorkshire (twice). Abandoned – Worcestershire.

Batting Averages

	I	*NO*	*R*	*HI*	*Avge*
D. A. Francis..........	4	0	320	127	80.00
A. L. Jones............	6	1	296	221*	59.20
G. P. Thomas..........	15	2	595	128*	45.76
M. J. Llewellyn........	17	3	464	153*	33.14
*G. Ellis.................	10	3	232	62*	33.14
M. Cohen................	12	3	296	62	32.88
G. C. Holmes..........	14	0	374	54	26.71
M. N. Davies...........	20	1	445	98*	23.42
†T. Davies...............	15	1	322	118	23.00
J. Derrick................	17	2	343	112	22.86
A. Cottey................	4	0	72	33	18.00
I. Smith..................	4	0	58	40	14.50
S. A. B. Daniels.......	11	1	117	26	11.70

Also batted: S. R. Barwick, R. Benjamin, P. Britten, A. Cottey, C. Dickenson, G. Edwards, C. Elward, E. W. Jones, J. Kelly, C. McKay, S. Maddock, P. Murphy, J. Roberts, C. J. C. Rowe, I. Smith, J. G. Thomas, S. Watkins, C. White, M. Williams.

Bowling Averages

	O	*M*	*R*	*W*	*Avge*
C. J. C. Rowe..........	40.4	20	70	6	11.66
P. J. Lawlor............	56.4	13	192	10	19.20
J. G. Thomas...........	53	17	125	6	20.83
G. C. Holmes..........	175.3	58	440	20	22.00
J. Jacques...............	52	7	159	7	22.71
S. R. Barwick..........	84.3	21	198	8	24.75
J. Derrick................	181.3	41	627	20	31.35
G. Ellis...................	104.2	31	251	7	35.85
S. A. B. Daniels.......	188.4	51	501	12	41.75

Also bowled: R. Benjamin 62.3–8–225–5; P. Britten 37–11–123–2; A. F. Corbin 110–13–442–8; W. W. Davis 29.2–16–48–3; D. Dickenson 8–2–21–0; G. Edwards 5–1–20–0; T. Foley 24–5–79–4; J. John 33–11–107–1; A. L. Jones 1–0–7–0; J. Kelly 15–3–33–1; M. J. Llewellyn 25.5–8–66–2; S. Maddock 37–8–157–1; E. A. Moseley 11–2–24–2; P. Murphy 8–0–44–1; M. A. Nash 27–12–53–4; P. North 16–0–85–2; I. Smith 16–3–49–1; S. Watkins 68.2–13–219–4; C. White 13–2–44–0; N. Zaidi 6–0–59–1.

GLOUCESTERSHIRE SECOND ELEVEN

Matches 11: Won – Glamorgan, Warwickshire. Lost – Hampshire, Worcestershire (twice). Drawn – Glamorgan, Hampshire, Kent, Somerset (twice), Warwickshire.

Batting Averages

	I	NO	R	HI	Avge
*B. Dudleston..........	10	5	557	223*	111.40
A. J. Hignell...........	8	2	354	109	59.00
M. W. Stovold.........	13	2	529	114	48.09
P. W. Romaines........	6	0	237	95	39.50
E. J. Cunningham.....	18	3	571	132	38.06
A. J. Wright.............	10	0	323	85	32.30
S. J. Windaybank......	18	1	407	79	23.94
P. G. Roebuck.........	9	1	180	49	22.50
J. M. Tavaré...........	7	0	152	64	21.71
D. P. Simpkins.........	11	4	150	43*	21.42
†R. C. Russell..........	10	3	129	30	18.42
C. R. Trembath........	6	1	85	33	17.00
R. J. Doughty..........	11	1	145	37	14.50

Also batted: R. Berry, A. J. Brassington, J. S. Brooks, I. G. Broome, D. Crisp, H. Ellison, D. V. Lawrence, M. Lickley, K. G. Rice, Sadiq Mohammad, W. M. Smith, A. H. Wilkins.

Bowling Averages

	O	M	R	W	Avge
B. Dudleston...........	108.5	40	207	15	13.80
D. V. Lawrence........	94	29	278	14	19.85
E. J. Cunningham.....	80.3	25	203	9	22.55
I. G. Broome..........	144	33	517	21	24.61
R. J. Doughty..........	235.3	51	655	25	26.20
D. P. Simpkins.........	214.1	63	563	21	26.80
A. H. Wilkins...........	104.4	35	290	9	32.22
C. R. Trembath........	104	21	304	8	38.00

Also bowled: J. H. Childs 15–5–35–4; D. Crisp 19–5–81–0; K. G. Rice 1–0–16–0; P. G. Roebuck 27–9–57–0; Sadiq Mohammad 21–2–57–2; G. E. Sainsbury 32–12–66–3; M. W. Stovold 16.3–6–53–0; S. J. Windaybank 97–23–322–6; A. J. Wright 7–1–43–0.

HAMPSHIRE SECOND ELEVEN

Matches 13: Won – Gloucestershire, Somerset, Sussex. Lost – Somerset. Drawn – Essex, Glamorgan, Gloucestershire, Kent (twice), Middlesex, Surrey (twice), Sussex.

Batting Averages

	I	NO	R	HI	Avge
R. A. Smith.............	16	6	854	157	85.40
R. E. Hayward.........	14	5	592	100*	65.78
C. L. Smith.............	17	2	980	156	65.33
D. R. Turner...........	16	3	765	156	58.85
V. P. Terry.............	18	1	959	140	56.41
T. M. Tremlett.........	6	2	206	109	51.50
J. J. E. Hardy..........	16	2	379	76	27.07
K. Stevenson............	11	6	125	48	25.00
M. J. Bailey.............	11	1	230	81	23.00
S. N. C. Massey........	8	3	68	36	13.60
J. W. Southern.........	7	1	80	32	13.33

Also batted: S. Andrew, R. Clayton, R. Coombs, †R. Hall, M. Hussein, R. Keeble, S. J. Malone, T. Middleton, M. C. J. Nicholas, N. E. J. Pocock, †M. J. Poland, R. Scott, M. D. Smith.

Bowling Averages

	O	M	R	W	Avge
T. M. Tremlett	101	37	188	9	20.89
S. J. Malone	338.1	79	973	46	21.15
J. W. Southern	253.5	88	609	27	22.56
S. N. C. Massey	195.1	55	622	25	24.88
M. J. Bailey	338.4	90	997	33	30.21
K. Stevenson	297.4	71	833	25	33.32

Also bowled: S. Andrew 25–4–93–0; R. Clayton 12–3–30–0; R. Coombs 22–4–93–0; D. Hartley 19–4–68–0; R. E. Hayward 26.5–10–57–2; M. Hussein 62–21–153–3; R. Keeble 17–2–61–0; C. L. Smith 20–3–90–2; R. A. Smith 10–0–63–0; D. R. Turner 3–0–19–0.

KENT SECOND ELEVEN

Matches 16: Won – Essex, Lancashire, Middlesex, Surrey, Sussex (twice). Lost – Essex, Middlesex, Yorkshire. Drawn – Glamorgan, Gloucestershire, Hampshire (twice), Lancashire, Surrey, Yorkshire.

Batting Averages

	I	NO	R	HI	Avge
R. M. Ellison	11	4	460	218*	65.71
L. Potter	6	0	354	146	59.00
S. Goldsmith	10	3	373	84*	53.28
S. G. Hinks	26	4	1,165	161*	52.95
D. G. Aslett	8	1	316	94	45.14
*A. G. E. Ealham	18	4	602	102	43.00
E. A. Baptiste	16	3	469	201*	36.07
†S. Marsh	16	3	437	59	33.61
†S. N. V. Waterton	16	1	399	154	26.60
R. Sharma	25	2	542	54	23.56
R. Pepper	7	1	108	66*	18.00

Also batted: K. Masters, L. J. Wood.

Bowling Averages

	O	M	R	W	Avge
C. Penn	108.5	38	276	21	13.14
G. D. Spelman	115.4	23	416	16	26.00
C. Dale	132	46	342	13	26.30
R. M. Ellison	157.3	43	384	13	29.53
L. J. Wood	387.2	121	1,086	34	31.94
E. A. Baptiste	257	53	794	24	33.08
K. Masters	367.1	71	1,256	32	39.25

Also bowled: H. Butler-Gallie 54–13–198–4; S. G. Hinks 53–14–200–3; R. Sharma 172.4–49–529–10.

LANCASHIRE SECOND ELEVEN

Matches 14: Won – Derbyshire, Northamptonshire, Nottinghamshire, Warwickshire, Yorkshire. Lost – Kent. Drawn – Derbyshire, Glamorgan, Kent, Nottinghamshire, Surrey, Worcestershire (twice), Yorkshire.

Batting Averages

	I	NO	R	HI	Avge
I. Cockbain	18	5	1,093	182	84.07
A. Kennedy	16	5	911	174*	82.81
K. A. Hayes	6	1	314	180	62.80
*H. Pilling	14	7	325	64	46.42
S. J. O'Shaughnessy	14	4	405	101*	40.50
N. V. Radford	17	3	460	108*	32.85
†C. J. Scott	9	3	163	66*	27.16
R. G. Watson	20	4	356	103*	22.25
B. Thorpe	8	1	140	41	20.00
S. T. Crawley	13	1	209	60	17.41
B. W. Reidy	5	0	81	42	16.20
P. A. Davis	14	2	178	74	14.83
†M. A. Wallwork	6	0	68	24	11.33

Also batted: J. Abrahams, A. Darlington, S. Douglas, N. H. Fairbrother, G. Fowler, F. C. Hayes, D. P. Hughes, S. Jones, W. Joyce, P. G. Lee, †J. Macaulay, L. L. McFarlane, †C. Maynard, A. Murphy, J. Simmons, G. J. Speak, T. J. Taylor, D. W. Varey, J. G. Varey, †T. Wallwork, M. Whelan, J. Whitehead, A. Wild.

Bowling Averages

	O	M	R	W	Avge
J. Simmons	58	30	94	10	9.40
D. P. Hughes	32.5	13	85	7	12.14
B. W. Reidy	109	37	262	16	16.37
N. V. Radford	352	107	913	55	16.60
A. Kennedy	54.4	23	116	6	19.33
P. G. Lee	356.5	109	907	42	21.59
T. J. Taylor	391.1	158	749	28	26.75
S. J. O'Shaughnessy	212.5	58	593	21	28.23
R. G. Watson	157	31	449	12	37.41

Also bowled: J. Abrahams 10–1–45–3; S. T. Crawley 3–0–17–0; A. Darlington 4–1–6–0; S. Douglas 95.3–34–195–5; N. H. Fairbrother 3–0–13–0; S. Jones 30–3–128–1; L. L. McFarlane 10–1–46–1; A. Murphy 30–5–103–2; G. J. Speak 37–12–103–2; B. Thorpe 3–0–12–0; A. Wild 19–4–72–0.

LEICESTERSHIRE SECOND ELEVEN

Matches 10: Won – Nottinghamshire. Lost – Northamptonshire, Warwickshire. Drawn – Derbyshire (twice), Northamptonshire, Nottinghamshire, Warwickshire, Worcestershire (twice). Abandoned – Middlesex.

Batting Averages

	I	NO	R	HI	Avge
M. D. Haysman	13	1	629	100	52.41
J. J. Whitaker	17	4	620	103*	47.69
†I. P. Butcher	13	0	589	129	45.30
T. J. Boon	9	0	404	170	44.88
D. Da Silva	7	3	178	62	44.50
R. A. Cobb	6	0	222	91	37.00
P. B. Clift	7	0	177	62	25.28
G. Forster	9	3	140	35	23.33
N. R. Newman	11	3	153	35*	19.12
D. A. Wenlock	14	3	177	51*	16.09
J. Addison	7	0	112	35	16.00

Also batted: J. P. Agnew, D. C. Allett, R. Berry, N. G. B. Cook, †G. Franks, †M. A. Garnham, K. Higgs, R. Jones, W. Munden, T. J. Munton, G. J. Parsons, M. Schepens, †M. G. Tebbutt, M. Whitmore.

Bowling Averages

	O	*M*	*R*	*W*	*Avge*
P. B. Clift	135	36	301	20	15.05
T. J. Boon	38	9	119	6	19.83
D. A. Wenlock	271.4	104	611	29	21.06
J. Addison	82.3	26	224	9	24.88
J. P. Agnew	122.3	30	379	14	27.07
M. D. Haysman	133.2	32	453	9	50.33

Also bowled: D. C. Allett 35–8–107–2; I. P. Butcher 33–4–155–5; N. G. B. Cook 51–19–102–2; K. Higgs 42–16–76–2; P. Higgs 6–0–34–2; R. Jones 19–7–26–0; W. Munden 38–11–90–1; T. J. Munton 36–8–122–3; N. R. Newman 59–16–153–4: R. Spiers 7–2–18–1; A. Sygrove 15–2–65–1.

MIDDLESEX SECOND ELEVEN

Matches 13: Won – Essex, Kent, Sussex (twice). Lost – Kent, Surrey. Drawn – Essex, Hampshire, Northamptonshire (twice), Surrey, Warwickshire (twice). Abandoned – Leicestershire.

Batting Averages

	I	*NO*	*R*	*HI*	*Avge*
K. P. Tomlins	8	1	378	169	54.00
R. G. P. Ellis	10	1	376	96	41.77
K. D. James	18	8	382	58	38.20
A. G. Smith	22	1	752	88	35.80
N. J. Kemp	18	5	455	76	35.00
C. R. Cook	15	1	482	162	34.42
†K. R. Brown	8	3	150	61	30.00
*G. D. Barlow	14	0	370	104	26.42
G. M. Ritchie	10	1	199	63	22.11
N. G. Cowans	4	0	80	53	20.00
R. J. Maru	11	3	135	34	16.87
†C. P. Metson	6	1	51	32*	10.20

Also batted: M. Blackett, R. N. Berry, B. Bishop, R. O. Butcher, A. Fawden, S. P. Gatting, R. Haynes, R. N. Hoskin, S. P. Hughes, N. Jackett, J. Leppard, W. G. Merry, G. D. Moss, A. Neal, R. Patel, G. D. Rose, M. W. W. Selvey, W. M. Tebbit, N. F. Williams, S. M. N. Zaidi.

Bowling Averages

	O	*M*	*R*	*W*	*Avge*
N. G. Cowans	99.4	25	348	20	17.40
W. G. Merry	226.5	66	496	27	18.37
K. D. James	206.5	46	598	29	20.62
N. J. Kemp	160	47	497	15	33.13
N. F. Williams	106.1	20	314	9	34.88
R. J. Maru	237	63	717	18	39.83

Also bowled: G. D. Barlow 2–0–13–0; C. R. Cook 3–2–4–0; R. G. P. Ellis 3–0–13–0; A. Fawden 7.4–0–43–0; R. Haynes 9–1–47–0; S. P. Hughes 23–5–60–1; N. Jackett 9–4–23–2; G. D. Moss 4–2–9–1; A. Neal 27–9–39–3; R. Patel 23.3–8–55–4; G. M. Ritchie 4–0–14–1; G. D. Rose 2–1–1–0; M. W. W. Selvey 62.4–19–144–5; A. G. Smith 2–0–8–0; W. M. Tebbit 25–8–52–1; K. P. Tomlins 28–9–67–1; S. M. N. Zaidi 3–0–13–0.

NORTHAMPTONSHIRE SECOND ELEVEN

Matches 13: Won – Derbyshire, Leicestershire. Lost – Derbyshire, Lancashire. Drawn – Essex (twice), Leicestershire, Middlesex (twice), Nottinghamshire (twice), Yorkshire (twice).

Batting Averages

	I	*NO*	*R*	*HI*	*Avge*
M. J. Bamber	23	4	1,080	161	56.84
D. J. Wild	15	3	611	176	50.91
D. J. Capel	9	0	456	123	50.66
S. J. Lines	18	2	668	117	41.75
R. M. Carter	11	0	393	153	35.72
*T. J. Yardley	9	2	183	36	26.14
C. Pickles	10	2	194	102*	24.25
R. J. Bailey	15	2	282	60	21.69
R. Heritage	13	4	119	35	13.22
†A. Harlow	9	2	77	26	11.00

Also batted: R. Ashton, G. Austin, R. Bunting, D. C. N. Eland, N. Gilbert, A. Hagger, M. Hall, L. Hodgson, S. Holroyd, S. T. Jefferies, N. A. Mallender, J. P. C. Mills, D. Priestley, B. L. Reynolds, D. Ripley, M. Roseberry, D. Smith, D. S. Steele, A. Storr, A. Walker, M. Wheeler, R. G. Williams. R. Millard and P. Mores each played in one match but did not bat.

Bowling Averages

	O	*M*	*R*	*W*	*Avge*
N. A. Mallender	62.2	17	154	11	14.00
R. M. Carter	104.3	27	351	16	21.93
R. Heritage	257	70	699	26	26.88
D. C. N. Eland	84.1	15	248	8	31.00
D. J. Capel	115	25	436	11	39.63
M. Wheeler	110	19	401	8	50.12
D. J. Wild	173	39	471	9	52.33
R. J. Bailey	143.3	36	377	6	62.83
R. Bunting	134	17	510	6	85.00

Also bowled: R. Ashton 20–4–82–0; G. Austin 9–0–28–0; M. J. Bamber 50–13–150–1; S. Dean 14–0–87–1; M. Hall 33–10–107–5; L. Hodgson 15–3–84–1; S. Holroyd 13–3–63–0; S. T. Jefferies 15–1–54–0; T. M. Lamb 59–10–147–2; S. J. Lines 59–13–183–5; C. Pickles 0.2–0–1–0; D. Priestley 33–4–122–2; D. S. Steele 14–6–37–3; A. Walker 41–5–166–3; R. G. Williams 18–4–52–1.

NOTTINGHAMSHIRE SECOND ELEVEN

Matches 18: Won – Somerset, Sussex, Worcestershire. Lost – Essex, Lancashire, Leicestershire, Warwickshire, Worcestershire, Yorkshire. Drawn – Derbyshire (twice), Lancashire, Leicestershire, Northamptonshire (twice), Somerset, Sussex, Yorkshire. Abandoned – Warwickshire.

Batting Averages

	I	*NO*	*R*	*HI*	*Avge*
P. A. Todd	12	0	640	216	53.33
M. A. Fell	18	3	728	122*	48.53
R. A. White	15	10	237	44	47.40
P. Johnson	31	0	1,432	236	46.19
J. D. Birch	6	0	260	110	43.33
D. I. Saxelby	23	1	916	122	41.63
K. Evans	5	0	178	78	35.60
N. J. B. Illingworth	12	7	145	33*	29.00
K. Saxelby	9	1	231	61*	28.87
C. D. Fraser-Darling	14	4	285	52*	28.50
I. L. Pont	28	7	551	85*	26.23
†C. W. Scott	28	5	578	58	25.13
N. I. Weightman	18	2	378	114*	23.62
M. Newell	6	1	87	57	17.40
S. Mahboob	17	1	247	76	15.43
R. I. Frost	6	0	76	43	12.66

Also batted: R. Baker, D. J. Billington, M. K. Bore, K. E. Cooper, D. E. Coote, D. Donaldson, †B. N. French, N. French, N. Gilbert, N. Harah, M. J. Harris, P. N. Harvey, M. Hendrick, R. Ingham, R. McCreery, T. W. McEwan, Z. Nasir, R. A. Pick, I. Renshaw, P. C. Richardson, R. T. Robinson, N. A. Stent, P. M. Such, D. Sutton, S. J. Turrill. T. Wallace and M. Wintle each played in one match but did not bat.

Bowling Averages

	O	*M*	*R*	*W*	*Avge*
M. K. Bore	90.3	39	144	12	12.00
K. E. Cooper	72.5	26	130	9	14.44
R. Baker	141.3	30	460	22	20.90
R. A. Pick	112.1	23	384	16	24.00
K. Saxelby	169	48	436	15	29.06
C. D. Fraser-Darling	85	25	231	7	33.00
S. Mahboob	308.4	66	991	29	34.17
N. I. Weightman	247.4	45	890	22	40.45
N. J. B. Illingworth	196.3	51	615	15	41.00
I. L. Pont	287.3	69	884	21	42.09
P. M. Such	187.1	35	604	10	60.40

Also bowled: K. Evans 9–1–22–0; M. A. Fell 118.5–38–308–7; N. French 7–2–20–0; R. I. Frost 4–0–25–0; N. Gilbert 6–1–26–0; N. Harah 24–2–102–1; P. N. Harvey 56–12–200–4; M. Hendrick 24–7–45–0; P. Johnson 7–0–54–0; R. McCreery 47–7–144–5; Z. Nasir 32–4–120–3; P. C. Richardson 19–3–77–1; D. Sutton 21–2–109–0; P. A. Todd 15.1–3–37–2; S. J. Turrill 24–4–70–2; T. Wallace 32–4–120–1; R. A. White 123.5–40–233–5.

SOMERSET SECOND ELEVEN

Matches 12: Won – Glamorgan, Hampshire. Lost – Hampshire, Nottinghamshire, Warwickshire (twice). Drawn – Glamorgan, Gloucestershire (twice), Nottinghamshire, Worcestershire (twice).

Batting Averages

	I	*NO*	*R*	*HI*	*Avge*
P. A. Slocombe	12	2	508	153	50.80
R. Richardson	6	2	177	66	44.25
N. F. M. Popplewell	6	1	169	48	33.80
P. J. Robinson	9	6	100	46	33.33
N. Russom	16	1	429	154	28.60
N. A. Felton	9	0	251	108	27.88
A. J. H. Dunning	18	0	473	62	26.28
M. R. Davis	12	1	277	76	25.18
R. L. Ollis	23	1	420	64*	19.09
G. V. Palmer	5	0	89	44	17.80
†T. Gard	15	2	183	27	14.09
A. W. J. Spiller	10	2	92	24	11.50
M. Bryant	9	0	98	16	10.90

Also batted: T. J. Ackland, N. Berry, P. Browne, M. Clements, T. Dodd, †P. Gill, M. D. Harman, K. F. Jennings, D. Langford, J. W. Lloyds, R. J. McCool, M. Murfin, †N. Priestley, M. Richardson, R. J. Scott, C. Smart, R. C. Talbot, M. Turner, C. Westcott, C. Wilkinson, J. Wyatt.

Bowling Averages

	O	*M*	*R*	*W*	*Avge*
M. D. Harman	53	16	138	6	23.00
M. R. Davis	164.5	33	576	20	28.80
N. Russom	284.4	58	863	24	35.96
J. W. Lloyds	78	16	263	7	37.57
R. J. McCool	195.5	51	602	16	37.62
M. Bryant	165	27	514	11	46.73

Also bowled: T. J. Ackland 44–6–165–1; M. Clements 0.3–0–6–0; D. Compton 1–0–2–0; T. Dodd 28–3–86–0; N. A. Felton 3–0–23–0; K. F. Jennings 33.2–9–111–4; M. Murfin 3–0–35–0; R. L. Ollis 1–0–4–0; G. V. Palmer 76–4–325–7; N. F. M. Popplewell 34–9–114–3; M. Richardson 36–12–94–2; R. Richardson 6–0–22–0; P. J. Robinson 59–5–162–3; R. J. Scott 1.3–0–8–0; P. A. Slocombe 13.4–2–38–1; A. W. J. Spiller 78–22–251–3; R. C. Talbot 6–0–15–0; M. Turner 8–1–39–0; C. Westcott 61–17–193–2.

SURREY SECOND ELEVEN

Matches 14: Won – Essex (twice), Middlesex, Yorkshire. Lost – Kent, Sussex. Drawn – Glamorgan, Hampshire (twice), Kent, Lancashire, Middlesex, Sussex, Yorkshire.

Batting Averages

	I	*NO*	*R*	*HI*	*Avge*
G. R. J. Roope	8	1	316	113	45.14
D. J. Thomas	5	0	220	100	44.00
G. S. Clinton	6	2	159	96	39.75
I. R. Payne	20	2	650	76	36.11
D. B. Pauline	23	1	728	200	33.09
†A. J. Stewart	23	1	639	154	29.04
K. S. Mackintosh	9	1	214	68	26.75
N. J. Falkner	18	4	306	64	21.85
G. Monkhouse	9	4	96	33*	19.20
R. G. L. Cheatle	14	5	159	29	17.66
P. B. Taylor	11	2	132	49*	14.66
*A. Needham	16	0	230	39	14.37
G. Morgan	10	1	99	35	11.00

Also batted: A. M. Babington, A. M. Bredin, C. K. Bullen, M. A. Feltham, J. A. W. Fry, J. Handley, G. P. Howarth, G. J. Irwin, M. A. Lynch, C. D. Mathews, R. A. Milne, P. I. Pocock, J. Robinson, D. M. Smith, D. I. Starkey, D. M. Ward, P. H. L. Wilson.

Bowling Averages

	O	*M*	*R*	*W*	*Avge*
J. Handley	76.2	27	163	12	13.58
G. Monkhouse	171.4	47	426	30	14.20
D. J. Thomas	130	36	327	15	21.80
A. Needham	160	57	418	19	22.00
R. G. L. Cheatle	247.4	64	683	25	27.32
K. S. Mackintosh	163	48	404	14	28.85
D. B. Pauline	135	26	383	11	34.81
P. H. L. Wilson	193	55	533	13	41.00

Also bowled: A. M. Babington 18–4–59–0; C. K. Bullen 71–22–190–5; M. A. Feltham 32–4–144–1; G. J. Irwin 0.3–0–4–0; M. A. Lynch 5–1–16–0; C. D. Mathews 16.4–5–52–3; I. R. Payne 134–42–358–5; P. I. Pocock 74.3–31–177–4; G. R. J. Roope 27–8–89–2; D. I. Starkey 6–0–32–0; A. J. Stewart 1–0–10–1.

SUSSEX SECOND ELEVEN

Matches 13: Won – Surrey. Lost – Hampshire, Kent (twice), Middlesex (twice), Nottinghamshire. Drawn – Essex (twice), Hampshire, Nottinghamshire, Surrey, Warwickshire.

Batting Averages

	I	*NO*	*R*	*HI*	*Avge*
C. P. Phillipson	6	1	421	142	84.20
N. J. Lenham	9	2	368	123*	52.57
A. P. Wells	15	2	522	110*	40.15
D. Standing	6	0	217	71	36.16
A. M. Green	13	1	389	88	32.41
†D. J. Smith	16	2	359	66*	25.64
J. J. Groome	18	3	350	86	23.33
K. Macleay	6	0	139	44	23.16
T. D. Booth Jones	11	0	230	73	20.90
R. S. Cowan	14	1	269	56	20.69
J. R. P. Heath	18	1	345	74	20.29

Also batted: R. Berry, D. Cannon, J. Coles, M. R. Donald, C. Fletcher, C. Hartridge, D. Hartley, J. Kureishi, C. Matthews, L. Moody, S. Packard, N. Pattison, M. Sutton, C. E. Waller.

Bowling Averages

	O	*M*	*R*	*W*	*Avge*
C. E. Waller	49	18	127	9	14.11
K. Macleay	52	15	109	6	18.16
R. S. Cowan	113	25	330	15	22.00
C. Hartridge	120	22	437	16	27.31
C. P. Phillipson	64	19	182	6	30.33
A. Willows	404	126	1,132	36	31.44
J. R. P. Heath	116	21	408	12	34.00
A. N. Jones	161	32	555	16	34.68
A. P. Wells	154	22	602	10	60.20

Also bowled: D. Cannon 59–10–196–5; J. Coles 43–4–180–3; C. Fletcher 32–6–105–5; N. Gilbert 37–2–196–1; A. M. Green 20–2–106–2; D. Hartley 15–1–75–0; S. Packard 26–2–134–3; N. Pattison 86–16–331–6; N. Trestrail 3–1–11–0.

WARWICKSHIRE SECOND ELEVEN

Matches 18: Won – Glamorgan, Leicestershire, Nottinghamshire, Somerset (twice). Lost – Derbyshire, Gloucestershire, Lancashire, Worcestershire (twice). Drawn – Glamorgan, Gloucestershire, Leicestershire, Middlesex (twice), Sussex, Yorkshire (twice). Abandoned – Nottinghamshire.

Batting Averages

	I	*NO*	*R*	*HI*	*Avge*
P. R. Oliver	11	0	598	121	54.36
*R. N. Abberley	19	6	590	110*	45.38
†G. A. Tedstone	17	3	588	88	42.00
K. D. Smith	10	1	285	71	31.66
G. J. Lord	17	1	477	112	29.81
M. C. Dolman	8	2	174	82	29.00
R. I. H. B. Dyer	24	2	610	120	27.72
S. H. Wootton	28	3	662	101*	26.48
D. M. Smith	18	10	200	49	25.00
P. A. Smith	6	0	121	64	20.16
P. J. Hartley	11	2	164	33	18.22
H. A. Page	10	1	154	93	17.11
K. B. K. Ibadulla	26	0	405	64	15.57
D. Marsh	18	2	220	63	13.75

Also batted: Asif Din, M. Bryant, G. Charlesworth, D. Cousins, G. L. Davies, G. Franks, D. S. Hoffman, W. Hogg, A. Hough, C. Lethbridge, P. J. Lewington, K. R. Maguire, W. J. P. Matthews, †C. Maynard, S. Mollin, G. J. Plimmer, M. W. Plummer, E. F. Pugh, J. Robinson, M. Roseberry, C. Rudd, I. K. Smith, I. Stokes, S. P. Sutcliffe, D. A. Thorne, P. H. L. Wilson.

Bowling Averages

	O	*M*	*R*	*W*	*Avge*
W. Hogg	41	15	68	8	8.50
S. H. Wootton	42.1	14	104	10	10.40
C. Lethbridge	74	20	145	12	12.08
M. C. Dolman	193.4	44	586	42	13.95
S. P. Sutcliffe	104	43	207	13	15.92
K. B. K. Ibadulla	69.2	21	203	9	22.55
D. M. Smith	363.1	115	932	34	27.41
P. J. Lewington	187	62	385	14	27.50
K. R. Maguire	333.2	69	945	30	31.50
H. A. Page	146.4	47	366	11	33.27
P. J. Hartley	232.1	72	692	19	36.42

Also bowled: R. N. Abberley 5–4–1–0; Asif Din 39.3–10–125–5; M. Bryant 11–2–38–1; G. Charlesworth 6–0–25–0; D. Cousins 6–2–15–0; R. I. H. B. Dyer 15.1–4–76–4; D. S. Hoffmann 41–14–107–4; G. J. Lord 39–9–114–3; D. Marsh 167–37–493–9; S. Mollin 33–3–99–2; M. W. Plummer 3–1–6–1; E. F. Pugh 34–8–107–0; K. D. Smith 1–1–0–0; P. A. Smith 29–3–111–3; D. A. Thorne 47–11–132–4; P. H. L. Wilson 21–5–72–1.

WORCESTERSHIRE SECOND ELEVEN

Matches 15: Won – Glamorgan, Gloucestershire (twice), Nottinghamshire, Warwickshire (twice). Lost – Nottinghamshire. Drawn – Derbyshire (twice), Lancashire (twice), Leicestershire (twice), Somerset (twice). Abandoned – Glamorgan.

Batting Averages

	I	*NO*	*R*	*HI*	*Avge*
†D. B. D'Oliveira.....	21	4	871	145	51.23
M. J. Weston...........	9	1	372	89	46.50
*M. S. Scott............	18	2	555	97	34.68
A. E. Warner...........	7	1	205	66	34.16
S. G. Watkins..........	24	3	649	72	30.90
D. A. Banks............	23	1	679	100	30.86
R. K. Illingworth......	10	2	234	98	29.25
D. J. Walker............	8	0	223	85	27.87
S. P. Perryman.........	6	2	99	59	24.75
P. J. Newport...........	12	1	254	75	23.09
†P. Moores..............	10	1	199	55*	22.11
V. A. Holder...........	8	2	121	44*	20.16
†M. C. D. Vaughan...	11	3	144	50	18.00
H. V. Patel.............	4	0	46	18	11.50

Also batted: H. L. Alleyne, T. S. Curtis, R. M. Ellcock, N. Gifford, J. B. R. Jones, M. S. A. McEvoy, W. Morton, A. P. Pridgeon, G. E. Sainsbury, D. Shorter, D. A. Slater, A. J. Webster, J. Wright, Younis Ahmed.

Bowling Averages

	O	*M*	*R*	*W*	*Avge*
H. L. Alleyne..........	213.3	75	482	29	16.62
S. P. Perryman.........	235.5	70	492	26	18.92
D. A. Slater.............	156.4	35	447	20	22.35
R. M. Ellcock..........	141	26	409	18	22.72
A. E. Warner...........	157.2	28	519	21	24.71
A. J. Webster..........	303	86	685	26	26.34
P. J. Newport...........	250.1	64	640	23	27.82
R. K. Illingworth......	298	109	652	23	28.34

Also bowled: D. A. Banks 5–0–25–0; D. B. D'Oliveira 111–30–296–7; D. C. N. Eland 12–2–63–1; N. Gifford 26–6–100–3; V. A. Holder 63–21–126–1; W. Morton 13–6–22–1; A. P. Pridgeon 56–12–131–5; G. E. Sainsbury 34–8–94–5; M. S. Scott 6–1–20–0; D. Shorter 36–5–120–2; D. J. Walker 17–2–58–1; S. G. Watkins 16–2–51–1; M. J. Weston 50–14–132–4; J. Wright 26–8–61–3.

YORKSHIRE SECOND ELEVEN

Matches 16: Won – Kent, Nottinghamshire. Lost – Derbyshire, Lancashire, Surrey. Drawn – Derbyshire, Glamorgan (twice), Kent, Lancashire, Northamptonshire (twice), Nottinghamshire, Surrey, Warwickshire (twice).

Batting Averages

	I	*NO*	*R*	*HI*	*Avge*
J. D. Love	6	2	364	148*	91.00
M. D. Moxon	25	6	1,060	131*	55.78
K. Sharp	6	2	183	92	45.75
A. Ramage	7	2	201	114*	40.20
†S. P. Coverdale	12	3	322	110*	35.77
*C. Johnson	22	8	493	78*	35.21
N. Lloyd	21	2	623	128*	32.78
A. Tate	9	1	254	54	31.75
P. G. Ingham	14	3	345	86	31.36
S. J. Dennis	7	2	136	67	27.20
A. A. Metcalfe	17	2	370	65	24.66
†S. J. Rhodes	12	4	197	49	24.62
I. Swallow	9	0	173	41	19.22
J. P. Whiteley	14	3	147	44	13.36
P. A. Jackson	5	0	66	47	13.20

Also batted: A. P. Arundell, C. W. J. Athey, S. Booth, P. Carrick, A. Dalby, S. Fletcher, S. N. Hartley, P. W. Jarvis, R. G. Lumb, G. B. Stevenson, N. S. Taylor, A. P. Threadleton.

Bowling Averages

	O	*M*	*R*	*W*	*Avge*
S. Booth	41	14	107	6	17.83
P. Carrick	112	46	186	9	20.66
P. A. Jackson	143	49	363	14	25.92
N. S. Taylor	297	50	1,048	38	27.57
P. A. Booth	34	6	113	4	28.25
P. W. Jarvis	175	54	440	15	29.33
A. Ramage	145	40	421	13	32.38
J. P. Whiteley	522	176	1,230	33	37.27
S. J. Dennis	281	77	741	19	39.00

Also bowled: A. P. Arundell 63–16–245–2; S. Fletcher 36–11–122–1; S. N. Hartley 9–2–25–0; P. G. Ingham 1–0–13–0; J. D. Love 5–0–23–1; A. A. Metcalfe 10–0–40–1; M. D. Moxon 18–1–93–0; G. B. Stevenson 31–11–85–1; I. Swallow 88–32–216–5; A. Tate 90–18–333–7; A. P. Threadleton 39–6–118–1.

THE COMMERCIAL UNION/NAYC UNDER-19 CHAMPIONSHIP

1980 Kent beat Sussex by 13 runs.
1981 Lancashire beat Surrey by 3 runs.
1982 Middlesex 204 for seven (J. Leppard 82 not out, M. Blackett 43) beat Kent (176 for nine) (C. Pickers 36 not out, G. Brown five for 63) by 28 runs.

WARWICK UNDER-25 COMPETITION, 1982

By ARTHUR WIGGETT

Zone A: Lancashire, enjoying their most successful season for some years, easily qualified for the semi-final. Emphatic victories over Yorkshire, Derbyshire (twice) and Nottinghamshire ensured them an almost unassailable position halfway through the competition. A four-wicket away defeat by Yorkshire was their only reverse. Yorkshire, who had dominated the northern group for four successive seasons, were less consistent than usual but showed occasional glimpses of their true form and finished with three wins to their credit. Nottinghamshire marginally improved on their dismal 1981 record by winning two matches, their one-wicket success over Yorkshire on the pleasant College ground at Worksop giving much satisfaction. Derbyshire had an unsatisfactory season, their opening match being abandoned through rain when they had a reasonable chance of victory over Yorkshire. Some degree of success was achieved with a victory in their final fixture over Nottinghamshire.

Zone B: Middlesex got off to the best possible start by beating their chief rivals, Leicestershire, in their opening zonal fixture at Grace Road. Greg Ritchie, the young Australian batsman, contributed a sound 54. Successive defeats by Essex and Leicestershire, the former by the narrowest of margins, were only temporary setbacks and a successful programme was completed with five straight wins. Leicestershire, to their credit, chased Middlesex throughout, both counties finishing with identical records and Middlesex qualifying by virtue of a superior away record. Leicestershire owed much of their success to the consistent batting of T. J. Boon, R. A. Cobb, M. A. Garnham and M. D. Haysman. Essex and Northamptonshire both disappointed, although the former were involved in four close finishes, of which only one resulted in an Essex victory. Northamptonshire's indifferent home form spoilt any chances of this promising young side challenging for a semi-final place, although D. J. Wild again underlined his batting potential. Warwickshire, newcomers to this zone, never found any kind of form. Their only successes were gained at the expense of Northamptonshire and Essex, the latter by two wickets in a thrilling finish with Asif Din scoring an unbeaten 121.

Zone C: Chastened by a surprise seven-wicket defeat at Bournemouth in their opening match, Kent, a side full of all-round ability, proceeded to win their remaining fixtures by wide margins. Able to call on many players with county experience, they were always favourites to win this section. L. Potter, an all-rounder of great ability, D. G. Aslett and N. R. Taylor were consistent performers. Hampshire once again were disappointing. Their win over Kent was followed by two successive defeats which effectively ended their challenge. The young South African, Robin Smith, who is qualifying for the county, again batted well. Surrey, the 1981 finalists, suffered the frustration of having three of their matches abandoned without a ball being bowled and would have lost a fourth but for a last-minute change of venue. Sussex promised much by winning their two opening games, but they lost all their remaining matches. A. P. Wells was an effective all-rounder.

Zone D: In this the most competitive section, the successful young Worcestershire team just had the edge over Gloucestershire, qualifying by the smallest possible margin. Both sides set high standards throughout and it was left until the final zonal match to decide which would reach the semi-finals. In the end Worcestershire beat Somerset in the crucial game, but Gloucestershire could reflect on their season with the satisfaction of knowing that they were the most improved side in the competition. Their exciting one-run victory over the holders, Glamorgan, gave them the confidence and incentive for three additional successes, but an abandoned home fixture against Somerset cost them a possible four points. For Worcestershire, D. B. D'Oliveira, M. S. Scott and M. J. Weston were always prominent. Gloucestershire, too, fielded several young players of much promise. After Glamorgan's successes of the two previous seasons, 1982 was a year of anti-climax for them. Off to an indifferent start, it was well into July before they registered their first success, over Somerset, whom they were to beat again in their final fixture. Returning to the competition after a five-year absence, Somerset fielded a young and inexperienced side. Although unable to register a win, they acquitted themselves well in the two Glamorgan matches, losing only marginally on both occasions.

Semi-final: *Kent v Worcestershire; at Canterbury, August 15.* Kent won by 5 runs. On a fine but breezy day and a good wicket, Kent, who were put in, did not find scoring easy against accurate bowling backed by excellent fielding. However, Kent's middle order did not lack determination, S. G. Hinks setting a fine example with an innings of 82. Worcestershire replied with some spirited batting which raised the hopes of their supporters, but despite a good 74 by Scott, going in first, they were narrowly beaten.

Kent 185 for eight (39 overs); Worcestershire 180 for six (39 overs).

Semi-final: *Lancashire v Middlesex; at Old Trafford, August 15.* Lancashire won by 97 runs. Middlesex had to waive advantage of a home draw, Lord's being unavailable on the day. Lancashire opened on a good easy-paced pitch in cloudy conditions, P. A. Davis making a confident 62 against a comparatively inexperienced Middlesex attack. A brief interruption caused by rain reduced the match to one of 35 overs with Middlesex being set a target of 169 runs. They were never able to cope with the keen Lancashire bowling, their reply lasting only eighteen overs to end a disappointing match.

Lancashire 173 for five (36 overs); Middlesex 76 (18 overs).

FINAL

KENT v LANCASHIRE

At Birmingham, August 22. Kent won by 53 runs. In a match reduced by rain to 28 overs, Kent were invited to bat on an easy-paced wicket in damp and overcast conditions. Recovering from the loss of an early wicket, the captain, Aslett, and Hinks, a powerful left-hander, added 86 for the second wicket. With the famous Edgbaston cover being used to protect the playing area from successive and heavy showers, no more than 80 minutes were lost. Lancashire's batsmen, apart from the promising Hartley, never looked equal to the task of scoring in excess of 6 an over.

Kent

*D. G. Aslett b Watkinson	69
†S. N. V. Waterton b Speak	7
S. G. Hinks c Hartley b Watkinson	42
R. M. Ellison not out	34
C. Penn b Watkinson	1
S. Goldsmith b Watkinson	0
G. R. Cowdrey not out	2
L-b 12, w 4	16
1/13 2/99 3/167 4/169 5/169 (5 wkts, 28 overs)	171

S. Marsh, G. D. Spelman, L. J. Wood and K. Masters did not bat.

Bowling: Speak 8–1–17–1; Murphy 6–0–36–0; Watkinson 8–0–48–4; O'Shaughnessy 6–0–54–0.

Lancashire

*I. Cockbain c Waterton b Ellison	1
P. A. Davis run out	10
S. J. O'Shaughnessy run out	20
S. T. Crawley run out	1
N. H. Fairbrother c Aslett b Spelman	0
M. Watkinson c Marsh b Spelman	6
J. Hartley b Masters	40
†C. J. Scott c Aslett b Penn	19
G. J. Speak b Penn	2
T. J. Taylor run out	3
A. Murphy not out	0
L-b 16	16
1/1 2/23 3/28 4/30 5/40 6/48 7/108 8/111 9/117 (26.1 overs)	118

Bowling: Spelman 8–0–30–2; Ellison 8–0–31–1; Penn 7–0–19–2; Masters 3.1–0–22–1.

Umpires: D. J. Constant and D. G. L. Evans.

THE UAU CHAMPIONSHIP, 1982

The UAU competition was once more played with characteristic determination. Apart from Oxford and Cambridge and certain of the London Colleges, all English and Welsh universities enter the competition, and with a number of university players now reaching both county and national ranks, standards of play are occasionally high.

The Championship, as in 1981, began in April with matches initially confined to a set of regionally restricted mini-leagues. In mid-May the top two teams from each league entered an open draw played on a knockout basis. Weather and other conditions permitting, games were limited to a maximum of 60 overs per team, with no restriction on the number of overs bowled by any player.

By early June, eight teams remained: Exeter, Sussex, Manchester, Lancaster, Leeds, Southampton, Durham and Loughborough. In the first of the quarter-finals Exeter had an easy passage against Sussex. Batting first they made 240 for four off 60 overs, Paul Taylor making 59 and their captain, Mark Richardson, 88. In reply Sussex were dismissed for 162, Matthew Wheeler taking four for 42 with his fast-medium deliveries. In the second quarter-final Lancaster were outplayed by Manchester. Batting first they could manage only 56 in less than 30 overs, Manchester's captain, Simon Bellm, returning seven for 25. Manchester required only fifteen overs to pass this total for the loss of a single wicket, Matthew Cheetham hitting 37 not out. The third quarter-final was equally one-sided. Visiting Leeds, Southampton struggled to 132 all out in 58.3 overs, Winston Hunter contributing to their downfall with six for 53. Leeds' openers, Ian Whitehouse (54 not out) and Robert Iliffe (74 not out), were untroubled by this target.

Of recent years Durham have displayed a penchant for cliffhangers, some of which they do not survive. Having coasted into the quarter-finals, they met Loughborough at the Racecourse. Loughborough, put in on a moist wicket, were never comfortable and against the pace of Simon Hughes and Jake Pugh subsided to 88 for eight. But then tailender Tim Dodd struck a rapid 56 to see his team to a healthier 164 all out. Dodd, four for 45, also contributed to an early collapse that left Durham 8 for three. Opener Tim Curtis (53) steadied the position, but Loughborough's captain, Simon Sutcliffe, kept on the pressure and, in a palpitating finish, Durham were 1 run short with one wicket remaining. It was Durham's first competitive defeat at the Racecourse for eleven years.

By contrast both semi-finals were sedate affairs. Loughborough comfortably overcame Leeds at Liverpool University by 94 runs. In a match reduced to 55 overs Loughborough reached 205 for five, Tony Robery making 43 and Robert Meyer 41 not out. In reply Leeds could muster only 111 in 43 overs, Mark Bayman finishing with four for 18. The second semi-final was played at Bath University. With the weather particularly bad in late June, it was restricted to 40 overs, in which time Exeter accumulated 132 for eight, their opener Michael Wilcock scoring an invaluable 60. For Manchester, Bellm bowled throughout and finished with five for 60. Under the conditions Exeter's modest total was beyond Manchester's reach and they succumbed for 91 in 36 overs, Wheeler returning six for 27 in seventeen overs.

FINAL

EXETER v LOUGHBOROUGH

At Bath, June 29. Exeter won by 81 runs. The weather reduced the game to 50 overs each. Exeter batted first and Tim Dodd removed opener Michael Wilcock and Richard Ellison in his first over. This shaky start produced a splendid response from captain Richardson, who battled to an admirable 66 and held Exeter's innings together. It was, in fact, a match-winning innings, for Loughborough, faced with the skilful and accurate opening attack of Ellison and Wheeler, could not make the necessary headway towards their target. Two run-outs only added to their problems and, after 40 overs, Loughborough were dismissed for 70.

Man of the Match: M. A. Richardson.

Exeter

M. C. Wilcock b Dodd	0	K. R. Thompson st Beard b Sutcliffe	2
M. A. Richardson c Rowlands b Dodd	66	D. S. Dean not out	4
R. M. Ellison b Dodd	2		
J. D. Hall lbw b Sutcliffe	21	Extras	12
K. D. Young c Felton b Sutcliffe	31		—
N. J. Marment b Sutcliffe	13	(7 wkts, 50 overs)	151

M. D. Smith, D. C. S. Everall and M. B. H. Wheeler did not bat.

Bowling: Dodd 12–3–35–3; Stubbs 16–5–40–0; Bayman 5–0–21–0; Sutcliffe 17–2–43–4.

Loughborough

N. A. Felton lbw b Wheeler	11	S. P. Sutcliffe c Richardson b Young	4
R. A. Savage c Thompson b Wheeler	5	M. Bayman st Everall b Ellison	5
T. Robery c Hall b Wheeler	5	C. J. Stubbs run out	2
H. O'Keefe b Ellison	17	K. Beard not out	0
R. Meyer run out	11	Extras	3
D. A. Rowlands b Young	1		—
T. P. Dodd c and b Ellison	6	(40 overs)	70

Bowling: Ellison 20–8–35–3; Wheeler 15–7–16–3; Young 5–0–16–2.

Umpires: C. Mitchell and K. Hopley.

PREVIOUS WINNERS

1927 Manchester
1928 Manchester
1929 Nottingham
1930 Sheffield
1931 Liverpool
1932 Manchester
1933 Manchester
1934 Leeds
1935 Sheffield
1936 Sheffield
1937 Nottingham
1938 Durham
1939 Durham
1940-45 *No competition*
1946 *Not completed*
1947 Sheffield
1948 Leeds
1949 Leeds
1950 Manchester
1951 Manchester
1952 Loughboro Colleges
1953 Durham
1954 Manchester
1955 Birmingham
1956 *Null and void*
1957 Loughboro Colleges
1958 *Null and void*
1959 Liverpool
1960 Loughboro Colleges
1961 Loughboro Colleges
1962 Manchester
1963 Loughboro Colleges
1964 Loughboro Colleges
1965 Hull
1966 Southampton & Newcastle
1967 Manchester
1968 Southampton
1969 Southampton
1970 Southampton
1971 Loughboro Colleges
1972 Durham
1973 Loughboro Colleges & Leicester
1974 Durham
1975 Loughboro Colleges
1976 Loughborough
1977 Durham
1978 Manchester
1979 Manchester
1980 Exeter
1981 Durham
1982 Exeter

THE LANCASHIRE LEAGUES, 1982

By CHRIS ASPIN

Although runs came easily and often prolifically in the two major leagues – there were 47 individual centuries – the honours again went to sides strong in bowling. Rawtenstall retained the Lancashire League championship, just a point ahead of Lowerhouse, who enjoyed their best season since the League was formed in 1892. Todmorden took the Martini Trophy in an exciting final at Haslingden, scoring a bye off the last ball as darkness closed in and the street lights shone brightly round the ground. The run levelled the scores at 168, but Todmorden had lost only seven wickets against Haslingden's eight.

The season will long be remembered for the many brilliant feats of the Colne professional, Collis King, who scored 1,362 runs to beat Bill Alley's 33-year-old club record by 84. A third of King's runs came from 6s. In one over against East Lancashire, he hit 42 runs and completed his 50 in nine minutes. He also made the season's highest score – 179 against Todmorden.

King's nearest rival was Robert Bentley, of Natal, the Haslingden professional, who scored 982 runs. He and the Haslingden captain, Brian Knowles – again the leading amateur with 935 runs (average 42.50) – took part in five opening stands of more than 100; their unbroken partnership of 200 at Church in the Martini Trophy game was the highest in the League for 27 years.

Yet in spite of this excellent batting, both Colne and Haslingden finished in the lower half of the table. It was the hostile bowling of the Barbadian fast bowler, Franklyn Stephenson, which clinched the championship for Rawtenstall. He took 99 wickets, a total equalled only by his fellow West Indian, Rod Estwick of Todmorden. The Lowerhouse professional, Evan Gray from New Zealand, showed that a spin bowler need not be expensive in limited-overs cricket; he headed the League bowling averages with 69 wickets at 10.97. Another professional who caught the eye was Kamal Singh from Guyana, a last-minute replacement at Rishton for Michael Holding. Though he missed three matches, he scored 792 runs and took 70 wickets.

In the amateur ranks, nineteen amateurs topped 500 runs, but only two bowlers, Pat Calderbank of Nelson and Barry Hill of Rishton, took more than 50 wickets; each had 56. The best individual performance was nine for 42 (eight bowled) by the Haslingden medium-pacer, Rod Taylor, at Colne.

Oldham, for whom Larry Gomes did the double, won the Central Lancashire League championship, nine points in front of Middleton. After six years the Wood Cup returned to Littleborough, Andy Roberts taking eight for 25 in the final against Royton. In its second season with sixteen clubs, the CLL saw centuries scored almost every week. The final tally was 28, of which thirteen were made by amateurs.

Seven professionals scored more than 1,000 runs, and for the first time in the League's history two amateurs did so as well. They were Chris Dearden of Littleborough (1,029, average 34.30) and nineteen-year-old Mark Chadwick of Milnrow (1,011, average 38.88). The feat was last achieved in 1955 by Jimmy Hyde of Middleton. Another outstanding batsman was Stuart Meredith of Oldham: in 22 innings he made 913 runs (average 45.65) and set up a club record. He scored four centuries, including 176 against Hyde, only three short of the season's highest individual score, the 179 against Walsden by Werneth's West Indian professional, Les Reifer. This was a limited-overs record and included 140 in boundaries.

Andy Roberts, who topped the bowling averages with 105 wickets at 10.51, was one of six professionals to take more than 100 wickets. Two spinners, Bob Cooke of Heywood and Somachandra de Silva of Middleton, followed Roberts in the averages. The leading amateur bowler was Mel Whittle, of Crompton, whose 69 wickets cost 16.11 runs each. Fourteen other amateurs took 50 or more wickets, while Cooke's nine for 41 against Milnrow was the season's best return.

MATTHEW BROWN LANCASHIRE LEAGUE

	P	*W*	*L*	*NR*	*Pts*	*Professional*	*Runs*	*Avge*	*Wkts*	*Avge*
Rawtenstall	26	17	6	3	81	F. D. Stephenson	519	23.59	99	12.96
Lowerhouse	26	17	6	3	80	E. J. Gray	538	23.39	69	10.97
Ramsbottom	26	16	6	3*	74	A. L. F. de Mel	670	35.26	63	16.92
Rishton	26	16	10	0	71	Kamal Singh	792	41.68	70	17.01
Todmorden	26	15	10	1	67	R. Estwick	372	20.67	99	15.12
Nelson	26	13	11	1*	65	N. V. Radford	409	20.45	94	13.18
East Lancs	26	13	11	2	60	I. W. Callen	353	27.15	57	17.74
Burnley	26	11	12	3	54	G. K. Robertson	566	26.95	75	16.53
Haslingden	26	11	13	2	49	R. M. Bentley	982	46.76	38	25.55
Colne	26	10	13	3	47	C. L. King	1,362	61.91	78	17.08
Enfield	26	9	15	2	41	R. A. Austin	588	28.00	58	19.97
Church	26	7	17	2	35	B. McArdle	868	45.68	48	22.15
Bacup	26	6	19	1	29	E. J. Hodkinson	427	20.33	82	15.96
Accrington	26	5	17	4	27	D. Smith	382	18.19	45	21.27

**Includes tied game.*

Note: One bonus point awarded for bowling out the opposition.

MARTINI CENTRAL LANCASHIRE LEAGUE

	P	*W*	*L*	*NR*	*Pts*	*Professional*	*Runs*	*Avge*	*Wkts*	*Avge*
Oldham	30	22	5	3	95	H. A. Gomes	1,459	81.05	103	15.26
Middleton	30	21	6	3	86	D. S. de Silva	951	47.55	114	13.07
Crompton	30	17	11	2	81	M. Amarnath	1,000	47.61	68	17.11
Rochdale	30	19	9	2	79	R. Sutcliffe	506	28.11	49	20.10
Royton	30	18	8	4	76	N. Phillips	860	33.07	115	13.42
Heywood	30	16	11	3	73	R. H. Cooke	1,223	55.59	89	11.13
Werneth	30	16	12	2	70	L. N. Reifer	1,449	60.37	33	30.12
Littleborough	30	16	10	4	68	A. M. E. Roberts	948	35.11	105	10.51
Milnrow	30	13	15	2	55	C. C. Alleyne	103	7.35	114	13.57
Walsden	30	11	16	3	52	R. Skeete	1,244	46.07	51	22.15
Stockport	30	8	17	3	49	K. Bowden	655	23.39	111	14.05
Castleton Moor	30	8	19	3	41	D. Schofield	1,211	52.65	87	13.91
Ashton	30	7	17	6*	36	R. Otto	705	23.50	30	26.13
Hyde	30	7	19	4	33	J. C. Allen	1,261	54.82	38	31.07
Radcliffe	30	7	20	3*	33	S. Adams	762	27.21	44	25.31
Norden	30	6	19	5	31	P. G. Wood	868	31.00	57	26.64

**Includes tied game.*

Note: Five points awarded for an outright win; three for a limited win.

WEST INDIES YOUNG CRICKETERS IN ENGLAND, 1982

The fourth West Indies Young Cricketers side to tour England since 1970 retained the Agatha Christie Trophy, beating Young England quite convincingly in two of the three four-day "Tests" with honours even in the rain-ruined match at Scarborough. The side was ably captained by Harper. Young England, as some compensation, won both one-day "internationals", and from their ranks David Capel (Northamptonshire), Richard Illingworth (Worcestershire) and Chris Penn (Kent) were later awarded Whitbread Scholarships to play in the 1982-83 Australian season.

A heartening aspect of the matches was the emphasis placed on spin bowling to win matches, with Haynes (leg-spin) the most successful and Pragg, purveyor of left-arm Chinamen and googlies, the most colourful. During the tour Ferris, a genuinely fast, senior Test prospect, was signed by Leicestershire to join his fellow-Antiguan and mentor, Andy Roberts. The tour was sponsored by Agatha Christie Ltd, in conjunction with the National Cricket Association and Lord's Taverners. The weather, especially during the middle part of the tour, was unkind, and one or two of the county clubs on whose grounds the matches were played could have made better preparations.

The tour party was: Rodill Clarke (*manager*, Trinidad & Tobago), Seymour Nurse (*coach and assistant manager*, Barbados), Roger Harper (*captain*, Guyana), Andrew Jackman (*vice-captain*, Guyana), Mark Bowers, George Ferris, Anthony Merrick (all Antigua), David Cumberbatch, Raymond Denny (both Barbados), Haille Edgings (St Kitts), Robert Haynes, Patrick Harris, Courtney Walsh (all Jamaica), Deonarine Persaud (Guyana), Philip Simmons, David Williams, Shervan Pragg (all Trinidad & Tobago).

RESULTS

Matches 15: Won 5, Lost 2, Drawn 7, Abandoned 1.

Note: None of the matches played was first-class.

v Sussex Young Cricketers: at Hove, July 26. West Indians won by four wickets. Sussex YC 137; WIYC 139 for six.

v English Schools CA (South): at South Hampstead, July 27. West Indians won by nine wickets. ESCA (South) 160 (R. Pepper 67 not out; C. A. Walsh four for 16, R. A. Harper three for 18); WIYC 164 for one (P. Simmons 94 not out, M. Bowers 31, A. Jackman 37 not out).

v Combined Services: at RAF Uxbridge, July 28. West Indians won by six wickets. Combined Services 188 (R. Moylan-Jones 56, A. Izzard 46; R. C. Haynes three for 43); WIYC 189 for four (M. Bowers 85, P. Harris 63).

v MCC Young Cricketers: at Ealing, July 30. Drawn (rain stopped play). MCC YC 177 (M. Hussain 35, M. Valetta 33; R. C. Haynes six for 57); WIYC 83 for three (R. Denny 51).

v English Schools Cricket Association: at Fenner's, July 31, August 1, 2. Drawn. ESCA 220 (H. Morris 66, G. V. Palmer 55 not out; S. A. Pragg five for 68) and 257 (H. Morris 100; S. A. Pragg five for 40); WIYC 229 (D. Williams 49, R. Denny 42, R. A. Harper 37; R. A. Pick three for 51, A. K. Golding three for 29) and 179 for six (P. Simmons 55, R. A. Harper 32).

v Headmasters' Conference Schools: at Bedford School, August 4, 5. Drawn (no play on the second day because of rain). WIYC 210 for four dec. (P. Simmons 127); HMC Schools 133 for five dec. (W. J. P. Matthews 36).

ENGLAND YOUNG CRICKETERS v WEST INDIES YOUNG CRICKETERS

First "Test"

At Northampton, August 7, 8, 9. West Indies Young Cricketers won by 62 runs. With the wicket provided at the county ground, having been used previously, taking spin in unpredictable degrees from early on the first day, Harper's decision to bat first was to prove decisive. Illingworth's ten wickets included a hat-trick and the match ended before lunch on the third of the four days allocated, the faster bowlers having taken only seven wickets between them. K. A. Hayes (Lancashire) was injured fielding close to the wicket and did not play again in the series.

West Indies Young Cricketers

M. Bowers c Jarvis b Folley	43	– lbw b Illingworth	9
P. Simmons b Folley	25	– c Folley b Illingworth	11
A. Jackman b Penn	6	– c Penn b Illingworth	0
H. Edgings c Potter b Capel	12	– c Capel b Illingworth	13
*R. A. Harper c Russell b Bullen	14	– c Capel b Bullen	34
S. A. Pragg c Jarvis b Illingworth	5	– run out	21
†D. Williams b Illingworth	18	– lbw b Illingworth	9
D. A. Cumberbatch c sub b Bullen	6	– st Russell b Bullen	14
R. C. Haynes b Illingworth	12	– not out	10
C. A. Walsh not out	1	– b Bullen	3
G. Ferris lbw b Illingworth	0	– st Russell b Illingworth	6
B 9, l-b 6, w 5, n-b 4	24	B 6, l-b 6, n-b 1	13
1/52 2/81 3/82 4/110 5/121 6/123 7/147 8/159 9/166	166	1/16 2/16 3/27 4/36 5/95 6/99 7/115 8/133 9/136	143

Bowling: *First Innings*—Jarvis 7–1–20–0; Penn 12–4–30–1; Folley 15–5–31–2; Capel 5–2–7–1; Illingworth 19.3–9–35–4; Bullen 10–3–19–2. *Second Innings*—Jarvis 3–1–8–0; Folley 8–3–17–0; Illingworth 18.1–5–47–6; Bullen 19–4–57–3; Penn 1–0–1–0.

England Young Cricketers

*L. Potter (Kent) c and b Pragg	24	– lbw b Ferris	6
P. J. Prichard (Essex) b Ferris	4	– b Haynes	1
D. J. Capel (Northants) c Simmons b Cumberbatch	32	– c Simmons b Pragg	9
D. J. Wild (Northants) b Cumberbatch	0	– c Harper b Haynes	11
R. K. Illingworth (Worcs.) lbw b Cumberbatch	0	– c Williams b Haynes	35
†R. C. Russell (Glos.) c Jackman b Pragg	2	– c Williams b Haynes	25
K. A. Hayes (Lancs.) c and b Pragg	7	– b Ferris	4
C. Penn (Kent) b Haynes	5	– c sub b Haynes	4
C. K. Bullen (Surrey) c Edgings b Haynes	11	– not out	14
I. Folley (Lancs.) st Williams b Pragg	16	– st Williams b Pragg	0
P. W. Jarvis (Yorks.) not out	7	– c Williams b Haynes	0
B 6, w 1, n-b 2	9	B 9, l-b 3, w 7, n-b 2	21
1/5 2/55 3/55 4/55 5/60 6/67 7/76 8/86 9/106	117	1/8 2/21 3/41 4/41 5/42 6/47 7/89 8/108 9/118	130

Bowling: *First Innings*—Walsh 6–1–17–0; Ferris 6–1–20–1; Cumberbatch 10–3–23–3; Pragg 11.2–4–34–4; Haynes 5–2–14–2. *Second Innings*—Walsh 5–2–12–0; Ferris 11–4–27–2; Haynes 21.5–12–36–6; Harper 5–1–7–0; Pragg 14–6–27–2; Cumberbatch 4–4–0–0.

Umpires: R. Julian and N. T. Plews.

v Welsh Schools Cricket Association: at Gowerton, August 12, 13. Drawn (no play on the second day). Welsh Schools CA 205 for six dec. (A. Storey 107; D. A. Cumberbatch three for 38); WIYC 100 for seven (P. Simmons 31; S. Watkins three for 21).

v Wales Under-19: at Swansea, August 15. Abandoned.

v Midland Club Cricket Conference: at Stratford-upon-Avon, August 17. Drawn WIYC 173 (A. Jackman 68; P. Wright five for 67); Midland CCC 147 for seven (H. Green 55; A. Merrick four for 33).

v England Young Cricketers – 1st One-day "International": at Nuneaton, August 18. England YC won by four wickets in a match reduced to 46 overs from 55 because of early morning rain. West Indies Young Cricketers 163 (A. Jackman 43, H. Edgings 42); England Young Cricketers 166 for six (37.5 overs) (L. Potter 49, P. J. Prichard 40 not out).

ENGLAND YOUNG CRICKETERS v WEST INDIES YOUNG CRICKETERS

Second "Test"

At Scarborough, August 20, 21, 22, 23. Drawn. England, having won the toss, batted for the first three rain-affected days before declaring. Highlights of the second day were a fine 117 from Capel and a third-wicket stand of 116 with Wild, his Northamptonshire colleague. West Indies lost early wickets to Folley and Jarvis, but Harper calmly steered his team clear of the follow-on.

England Young Cricketers

*L. Potter (Kent) c Edgings b Walsh	13	– c Harper b Ferris	20
P. Johnson (Notts.) lbw b Ferris	13	– c Williams b Walsh	7
D. J. Capel (Northants) c Denny b Walsh	117	– c Williams b Haynes	43
D. J. Wild (Northants) c Williams b Haynes	52	– c Williams b Ferris	0
P. J. Prichard (Essex) c Bowers b Haynes	15	– c Simmons b Haynes	33
H. Morris (Glam.) c Jackman b Walsh	27	– not out	11
R. K. Illingworth (Worcs.) c Simmons b Walsh	4	– not out	6
†R. C. Russell (Glos.) not out	27		
C. K. Bullen (Surrey) not out	3		
B 4, l-b 8, w 14, n-b 6	32	B 6, l-b 5, w 1, n-b 1	13
1/23 2/39 3/155 4/181 5/245 6/251 7/278 (7 wkts dec.)	303	1/18 2/56 3/36 4/108 5/119 (5 wkts dec.)	133

I. Folley (Lancs.) and P. W. Jarvis (Yorks.) did not bat.

Bowling: *First Innings*—Ferris 21.4–3–57–1; Walsh 19–5–62–4; Harper 12–3–43–0; Cumberbatch 26–8–46–0; Haynes 22–12–63–2. *Second Innings*—Ferris 12–4–24–2; Walsh 5–0–40–1; Cumberbatch 10–2–29–0; Haynes 9–2–27–2.

West Indies Young Cricketers

M. Bowers b Folley	1
P. Simmons c Russell b Jarvis	67
R. O. Denny c Potter b Folley	21
A. Jackman c and b Folley	24
H. Edgings lbw b Jarvis	4
†D. Williams c Russell b Jarvis	45
*R. A. Harper c Capel b Folley	48
D. A. Cumberbatch lbw b Jarvis	0
R. C. Haynes run out	1
C. A. Walsh not out	10
G. Ferris lbw b Folley	0
L-b 8	8
1/5 2/51 3/102 4/120 5/121 6/202 7/202 8/208 9/229	229

Bowling: Jarvis 18–6–64–4; Folley 25.2–4–69–5; Capel 7–1–28–0; Illingworth 16–3–49–0; Bullen 4–0–11–0.

Umpires: J. van Geloven and B. Leadbeater.

v National Association of Young Cricketers: at Mitchell and Butler's, Birmingham, August 25, 26, 27. Drawn (abandoned because of rain). NAYC 166 for seven (C. K. Bullen 72 not out, P. Caley 35; C. A. Walsh five for 59): WIYC 273 for five (P. Harris 60, P. Simmons 65, D. Persaud 54, A. Jackman 51).

v England Young Cricketers – 2nd One-day "International". At The Saffrons, Eastbourne, August 31. England Young Cricketers won by 105 runs. England Young Cricketers 205 for eight (55 overs) (D. J. Capel 54, R. K. Illingworth 54 not out); West Indies Young Cricketers 100 (36.5 overs) (M. Bowers 32; R. K. Illingworth five for 17, I. Folley three for 21).

ENGLAND YOUNG CRICKETERS v WEST INDIES YOUNG CRICKETERS

Third "Test"

At Hove, September 1, 2, 3, 4. West Indies Young Cricketers won by four wickets after England had won the toss and elected to bat first. Haynes, a leg-spinner turned batsman, played a large part in his side's victory, scoring 131 runs for once out. But the game was marred by on-field incidents in which the umpires intervened.

England Young Cricketers

*L. Potter (Kent) c and b Haynes	43	– c Simmons b Ferris	41
N. Lloyd (Yorks.) c Harper b Ferris	24	– lbw b Walsh	0
D. J. Capel (Northants) c Harper b Cumberbatch	30	– c Williams b Ferris	4
D. J. Wild (Northants) c Williams b Pragg	16	– c Persaud b Ferris	10
H. Morris (Glam.) st Williams b Pragg	9	– lbw b Ferris	28
P. J. Prichard (Essex) b Pragg	0	– c Bowers b Pragg	17
R. K. Illingworth (Worcs.) c and b Pragg	4	– c Persaud b Haynes	23
†R. C. Russell (Glos.) b Harper	11	– c Williams b Ferris	0
C. Penn (Kent) c Williams b Ferris	46	– c Pragg b Haynes	5
I. Folley (Lancs.) c Williams b Walsh	17	– not out	2
P. W. Jarvis (Yorks.) not out	0	– c Williams b Haynes	0
B 9, l-b 3, w 5, n-b 9	26	B 8, l-b 3, w 4, n-b 7	22
1/42 2/118 3/118 4/144 5/144 6/145 7/148 8/175 9/226	226	1/2 2/11 3/34 4/96 5/98 6/99 7/127 8/148 9/150	152

Bowling: *First Innings*—Ferris 14–2–41–2; Walsh 9.4–3–21–1; Persaud 10–5–23–0; Cumberbatch 28–13–29–1; Haynes 23–6–47–1; Pragg 14–7–21–4; Harper 3–1–18–1. *Second Innings*—Ferris 13–2–45–5; Walsh 7–3–17–1; Pragg 17–7–36–1; Haynes 15–5–28–3; Cumberbatch 6–4–4–0.

West Indies Young Cricketers

M. Bowers lbw b Folley	16	– lbw b Jarvis	9
P. Simmons c Morris b Folley	20	– c Potter b Jarvis	8
A. Jackman c Russell b Penn	20	– c and b Illingworth	40
†D. Williams lbw b Folley	11	– run out	6
*R. A. Harper c Russell b Penn	0	– not out	32
D. Persaud c Morris b Illingworth	9	– c Jarvis b Illingworth	6
S. A. Pragg c Russell b Penn	4	– c Morris b Illingworth	8
D. A. Cumberbatch c Capel b Folley	4		
R. C. Haynes c Prichard b Illingworth	80	– not out	51
C. A. Walsh c Russell b Penn	25		
G. Ferris not out	11		
L-b 6, w 2, n-b 3	11	B 1, l-b 5, w 3	9
1/27 2/50 3/63 4/71 5/78 6/84 7/90 8/120 9/168	211	1/14 2/30 3/51 4/75 5/88 6/110	(6 wkts) 169

Bowling: *First Innings*—Jarvis 14–4–65–0; Folley 25–8–50–4; Penn 23–6–55–4; Illingworth 19.2–10–30–2. *Second Innings*—Jarvis 19.4–7–56–2; Folley 5–2–10–0; Illingworth 30–12–64–3; Penn 16–3–30–0.

Umpires: P. B. Wight and R. Palmer.

BUT NOT A DUCK IN SIGHT

During the John Player League match between Warwickshire and Kent at Edgbaston on June 6, a fox – a stray Leicestershire supporter perhaps – ran around the ground behind the arm of the bowler, Derek Underwood, before disappearing into the crowd.

A week later, at The Oval where Surrey were playing Gloucestershire, a pigeon crept up behind the Surrey batsman Monte Lynch into the closest of short-leg positions, causing him to move away from the crease just as the bowler was about to deliver the ball.

As has happened with animals of the human variety, word of these invasions of the field of play spread quickly around the kingdom. At Trent Bridge in August, a rabbit ran on to the pitch, where it was apprehended by the Derbyshire captain Barry Wood.

SCHOOLS CRICKET IN 1982

The English Schools Cricket Association Under-19 team was undefeated in 1982. After their convincing eight-wicket victory over HMC Schools at Eastbourne, the same team met Welsh Schools at Pontardulais in the first game of the triangular Michael Gerard Schools "Test" Series. England had the better of a drawn game, featuring in their first innings a second-wicket stand of 98 between H. Morris, an accomplished left-hander, and N. Folland and a third-wicket stand of 72 between Morris and N. H. Fairbrother. Wales were troubled by the pace of R. A. Pick, and after Morris and Fairbrother had contributed an unbroken partnership of 136, Fairbrother reaching 84 in even time, Wales made no attempt to make 240 in 75 minutes plus twenty overs. Pick took his match return to seven for 84.

When English Schools met West Indies Young Cricketers at Fenner's, the Schools achieved an honourable draw after West Indies YC, chasing 247 in three hours, had managed only 181 for six. Batting first, English Schools reached 200, and then reduced their opponents to 128 for seven before a recovery took them to 229. English Schools' second innings was held together by Morris's 100, which took five hours, while for the West Indians S. Pragg took five wickets for the second time in the match with his left-arm Chinamen and googlies. G. R. Cowdrey, injured, was unable to play, but represented HMC Schools two days later in the rain-affected drawn match against the touring side at Bedford School, when he and N. J. Lenham bowled well after M. P. Hickson broke down. A. Fordham, W. J. P. Matthews and Lenham batted resolutely against the excellent spin of R. Haynes and the slow left-arm bowling of D. Cumberbatch before Cowdrey made a telling contribution.

Scotland CU Colts, having defeated Wales, needed only to draw with English Schools to win the Michael Gerard Series, when they met at West Bromwich Dartmouth. England, put in, declared at 200 for one, after Morris (103 not out) and M. R. Gouldstone (83 not out) had added 180 for the second wicket. Scotland were dismissed for 119 and again for 171 after England had declared a second time at 185 for three. Pick returned match figures of seven for 53, and England's victory by 95 runs gave them the series.

The batting of the England side was generally superior to the bowling with Morris outstanding, well supported by Fairbrother, a promising stroke-player. Gouldstone fulfilled his potential as an opening bat, and N. Folland, G. D. Rose and G. V. Palmer all made useful contributions. Of the bowlers, Pick was the quickest, Rose achieved most movement through the air, A. K. Golding had the best individual performance with five for 38 at Lord's, and the most interesting was the leg-spin of R. C. Talbot, who bowled the most overs. Helped by good fielding and catching and the excellent wicket-keeping of P. Gill, the bowlers were never totally mastered by opponents. Again, under the unobtrusive captaincy of Morris, team spirit was always high.

HMC SOUTHERN SCHOOLS v THE REST

At College Field, Eastbourne, July 17, 18. Tied.

The Rest

A. Fordham (*Bedford Modern*) retired	70	– c Lenham b Pinkerton	34
J. P. Stephenson (*Felsted*) c Cowdrey b Lenham	32	– (7) c Ellcock b Robins	40
W. J. P. Matthews (*Bablake*) retired	75	– (8) not out	14
P. C. Maclarnon (*Loughborough*) c Hickson b Russell-Vick	35	– c Coulman b Hickson	12
B. G. Evans (*Berkhamsted*) not out	8	– (3) b Robins	41
S. R. Gorman (*St Peter's, York*) not out	1	– (2) c Ansell b Ellcock	9
†J. M. Robinson (*Solihull*) (did not bat)		– (5) lbw b Pinkerton	14
S. A. J. Kippax (*Woodhouse Grove*) (did not bat)		– (6) b Ellcock	3
J. R. Prentis (*Eastbourne*) (did not bat)		– (9) c Lenham b Robins	3
G. D. Moss (*Radley*) (did not bat)		– (10) not out	3
Extras	13	Extras	7
(4 wkts dec.)	234	(8 wkts dec.)	180

R. M. Ellcock (*Malvern*), P. R. C. Robinson (*Tiffin*) and I. S. Bishop (*Rendcomb*) did not bat.

Bowling: *First Innings*—Hickson 11–3–27–0; Moss 13–2–36–0; Cowdrey 6–2–18–0; Pinkerton 13–7–26–0; Lenham 10–3–54–1; Russell-Vick 8–0–30–1; Robins 8–1–30–0. *Second Innings*—Ellcock 13–2–40–2; Hickson 11–1–38–1; Lenham 6–0–27–0; Pinkerton 11–3–15–2; Robins 14–6–24–3; Cowdrey 7–0–29–0.

HMC Southern Schools

N. J. Lenham (*Brighton*) c Maclarnon b P. R. C. Robinson	31	– c J. M. Robinson b Moss	15
M. D. Smith (*Canford*) c Stephenson b Ellcock	5	– (4) c Gorman b Kippax	1
J. R. Ansell (*Epsom*) run out	27	– (2) lbw b Kippax	42
*G. R. Cowdrey (*Tonbridge*) b Kippax	5	– (5) b Moss	117
M. T. Russell-Vick (*Sutton Valence*) not out	50	– (3) run out	3
C. W. V. Robins (*Clifton*) c Fordham b Ellcock	18	– (7) c Prentis b Kippax	32
†M. W. C. Olley (*Felsted*) b Ellcock	4	– (8) lbw b Kippax	1
M. P. Hickson (*Tonbridge*) not out	26	– (9) lbw b Kippax	5
†E. M. Coulman (*Winchester*) (did not bat)		– (6) b Moss	0
B. H. Pinkerton (*Felsted*) (did not bat)		– not out	0
R. M. Ellcock (*Malvern*) (did not bat)		– (10) b Moss	5
Extras	14	Extras	13
	(6 wkts dec.) 180		234

G. D. Moss (*Radley*) did not bat.

Bowling: *First Innings*—Ellcock 12–3–32–3; Bishop 10–1–35–0; Kippax 10–2–35–1; P. R. C. Robinson 11–0–34–1; Gorman 12–5–30–0. *Second Innings*—Moss 19–1–82–4; Prentis 5–1–9–0; Kippax 18–3–107–5; Gorman 9–7–23–0.

After the first day's play Ellcock and Moss changed sides, and Prentis replaced Bishop, who was injured.

ESCA v HMC SCHOOLS

At The Saffrons, Eastbourne, July 19, 20. ESCA won by eight wickets. Electing to bat, HMC Schools made a steady start until Talbot took three wickets in two overs and, despite some resistance from Robins, Pick and Waring demolished the tail, five wickets falling for 3 runs. ESCA compiled a lead of 135 in their 60 overs, thanks to Morris, Gouldstone and Fairbrother, whose 85 not out came in 97 minutes. A contrasting innings was seen from Matthews when HMC Schools batted again. He took three and a half hours over his first 50 and reached his hundred in four and a half hours. Other useful scores came from Lenham, Ansell and Fordham as the Schools offered greater resistance than in their first innings. However, it was not enough, and the target of 123 in almost two hours was comfortably achieved by ESCA with 23 balls to spare.

HMC Schools

J. P. Stephenson (*Felsted*) c Rose b Talbot	25	– retired hurt	5
A. Fordham (*Bedford Modern*) c Golding b Talbot	24	– c Gill b Pick	24
W. J. P. Matthews (*Bablake*) b Rose	4	– c Pick b Talbot	103
*G. R. Cowdrey (*Tonbridge*) c and b Talbot	0	– b Rose	33
N. J. Lenham (*Brighton*) c Golding b Talbot	12	– b Golding	8
C. W. V. Robins (*Clifton*) b Pick	39	– c Morris b Waring	0
J. R. Ansell (*Epsom*) lbw b Waring	0	– b Pick	27
M. P. Hickson (*Tonbridge*) lbw b Pick	0	– c Morris b Rose	7
†J. M. Robinson (*Solihull*) b Pick	0	– b Rose	0
R. M. Ellcock (*Malvern*) b Waring	0	– c Talbot b Rose	18
G. D. Moss (*Radley*) not out	0	– not out	6
B 1, l-b 5, w 1, n-b 1	8	B 5, l-b 4, w 7, n-b 10	26
	112		257

Bowling: *First Innings*—Waring 9–4–21–2; Pick 7.3–4–23–3; Talbot 12–4–30–4; Rose 9–1–29–1; Golding 2–1–1–0. *Second Innings*—Waring 14–2–34–1; Pick 15–4–40–2; Talbot 21–8–53–1; Rose 17.3–3–59–4; Golding 13–3–37–1; Palmer 8–5–8–0.

ESCA

N. Folland (*Exmouth Comprehensive and Devon*) c Matthews b Hickson.	29	– c and b Ellcock	16
M. R. Gouldstone (*Braintree College and Essex*) c Robinson b Ellcock.	38	– not out	48
*H. Morris (*Blundell's and Devon*) lbw b Hickson.	55	– c Fordham b Ellcock	26
N. H. Fairbrother (*Lymm Oughtrington HS and Cheshire*) not out.	85	– not out	21
G. V. Palmer (*Queen's, Taunton and Somerset*) b Cowdrey.	6		
G. D. Rose (*Northumberland Park and Middlesex*) lbw b Cowdrey.	3		
R. C. Talbot (*Richard Huish College, Taunton and Somerset*) not out.	15		
B 2, l-b 11, n-b 3	16	B 5, l-b 6, n-b 2	13
(5 wkts)	247	(2 wkts)	124

A. K. Golding (*Colchester RGS and Essex*), †P. Gill (*Grange, Oldham and Lancashire*), R. A. Pick (*High Pavement and Nottinghamshire*) and I. Waring (*Tupton Hall, Chesterfield and Derbyshire*) did not bat.

Bowling: *First Innings*—Ellcock 20–3–72–1; Moss 11–2–48–0; Hickson 11–2–52–2; Cowdrey 7–2–25–2; Robins 11–1–34–0. *Second Innings*—Ellcock 13–4–30–2; Moss 3–1–11–0; Hickson 3–0–13–0; Cowdrey 3–1–8–0; Robins 6.1–0–33–0; Lenham 3–0–16–0.

Umpires: J. R. Cave and J. A. Larby.

Details of the match between MCC Schools and the National Association of Young Cricketers may be found in Other Matches at Lord's, 1982.

Reports from the Schools

Abingdon, with wins over St Bartholomews, Newbury, Berkhamsted, RGS Colchester, Bloxham and Douai, were encouraged by the performance of fifteen-year-old M. T. Boobbyer, who marked his début by scoring 106 v MCC. **Alleyn's**, whose bowlers often failed to consolidate on a sound start from the batsmen, reported a disappointing season, as did **Allhallows**, whose captain, P. M. B. Zealey, headed the batting averages. All-rounders P. M. Tuck and T. J. B. Dutton-Cox did well with bat and ball, and the side's strength lay in the bowling, J. P. Knapman's leg-spinners providing welcome variety and the young E. R. M. Gard making an impressive début as an opening bowler. An inexperienced **Ampleforth** side, which defeated Stonyhurst, Pocklington and Bootham, scored more than 3,000 runs in a season for only the second time in the school's history, although the bowling lacked bite. **Arnold School**, with wins v King's Macclesfield, Kirkham GS, Baines and Ipswich, owed much to P. A. Webb, whose two hundreds were the first for the side in ten years and who took 38 wickets with his medium-pace bowling.

Bablake, unbeaten by a school for the fourth consecutive season, retained the Warwickshire and Birmingham Under-19 Cup, also for the fourth time in succession. Seven of the XI were in the side that won the Barclays Bank ESCA Under-17 National Cup from an entry of 300 schools, while W. J. P. Matthews represented HMC Schools and, with all-rounder G. Charlesworth and D. A. Thorne, played for Warwickshire Second XI. Matthews took his aggregate for the First XI to a school record of 2,469. An experienced **Bancroft's** side enjoyed a successful season, with S. W. Gant turning in match-winning performances with bat and ball. All-rounder I. P. Debnam played a faultless unbeaten 104 v Incogniti and M. G. de Jode's unbeaten 141 v Forest School broke his own school record. W. J. Head, a colt playing in the first XI, batted with considerable maturity and skill. With a strong batting side, **Barnard Castle School** were encouraged by wins over Pocklington and Strathallan, although with M. Coates unable to bowl fast, the attack lacked penetration. Enjoyable tours took the side to the Isle of Man, Scotland and the Midlands.

Despite the absence of any outstanding performances, **Bedford School** enjoyed a successful season. The fielding was excellent, with many difficult catches held. Their nine victories included those v The Leys, Haileybury, Stowe, Uppingham, Repton and **Bedford Modern School**, who none the less achieved a record nine wins, including those v Kimbolton, Wesley College, Manchester GS, Bedfordshire Colts, Loughborough GS, Wolverhampton GS and RGS Worcester. The batting was dominated by A. Fordham, who played for HMC Schools v ESCA and v Young West Indies, as well as for Bedfordshire. His aggregate of 1,042 was a school record and included three centuries in eight days – 146 v Oundle, 114 v Old Bedford Modernians and 110 v Wolverhampton GS – as well as 95 not out v Clare College, Cambridge. The attack was more hostile than of late, led by captain A. K. G. Jones (right-arm medium) and J. O. R. Jones (right-arm fast), while the emergence of off-spinner P. A. Garratt gave encouragement for the future.

Berkhamsted ended an otherwise disappointing season with wins v Framlingham, Kimbolton and St Lawrence at the Ramsgate Festival. Captain B. G. Evans, who scored two centuries, was given sound support by J. R. Neal (left-hand opening bat and right-arm fast-medium bowler) and played for The Rest v Southern Schools. **Birkenhead**, who had exciting drawn games v Liverpool College, King's Macclesfield and William Hulme's GS, recorded eight wins under the captaincy of right-hand bat and off-spinner S. M. Holroyd, who played for Northamptonshire Second XI. He received valuable support from off-spinner S. McGowan, while M. P. Gamet topped the batting averages and shared in four century opening stands with P. C. Barber. Outstanding fielding, notably that of G. E. B. Swayne, and the leadership of G. K. Smith were the key to wins by a young **Bishop's Stortford College** side over The Perse, Kimbolton, Framlingham and Hymer's College. Lacking the bowling to secure many victories, **Bloxham's** powerful batting side featured centuries from captain T. J. Abraham v Bromsgrove and Hipperholme.

The season at **Blundell's**, unbeaten for the second successive year and whose victories included those v Clifton, Oundle and Ampleforth, was notable for the contribution of captain and left-hand bat H. Morris, who played for Glamorgan in the County Championship, MCC Schools and NAYC. His 1,032 runs were 569 more than the next highest aggregate and included three hundreds as well as nine other innings over 50. He also took 25 wickets (right-arm medium), including a return of six for 53 v Sherborne. Also bowling well were A. Morris (medium), off-spinner M. C. Coe and H. B. Day (medium), who took five for 18 v Taunton. The leading batsman for **Bradfield College** was opener M. J. Gent, a respected captain whose aggregate of 1,401 over three years is the highest since G. R. J. Roope's 1,846 in 1962-64. The batting was otherwise disappointing, but bowling intelligently on all types of wicket, A. J. Johnston (right-arm medium away-swing) took 44 wickets and was well supported in the field. A positive approach characterised a young **Bradford GS** side, who were rewarded with seven wins. The batting was sound – notably that of S. T. Firth and C. J. Hewitt – and the weakness was in their failure to bowl out the opposition, opening bowlers T. Welsh and A. M. Broadbent lacking consistent support.

High points of a disappointing season for **Brentwood** were an opening partnership of 116 between P. Preston and left-hander M. Wedge as well as the fast-medium bowling of S. C. Smith, who came into the side in June to top the averages. He returned six for 27 in the victory over Incogniti. A young **Brighton College** side, moulded into a formidable team by captain S. C. B. Withers, achieved a record twelve wins. J. A. Gorton (fast-medium) took 49 wickets and N. J. Lenham was outstanding with 34 wickets and 1,076 runs, breaking the school record which had stood since 1935. He played for HMC Schools and Sussex Second XI. The brightest feature for **Bristol GS** was the batting of D. J. Woolley, whose aggregate of 672 runs was more than three times the next highest and included two hundreds. **Bromsgrove School**, whose only win was over Wrekin, depended much on left-hander D. M. Meredith with the bat and S. W. Williams with the ball. The XL Club, Dauntsey's, Milton Abbey, Kingswood and Canford were defeated by the **Bryanston** side, who were never bowled out. G. Binns, in his first season, was selected for Southern Schools Under-16 XI.

A young **Canford** side, with victories v King's Taunton, Downside and King's Bruton, relied heavily on their captain, M. D. Smith, who scored twice as many runs as anyone else, including two hundreds, and who played for Southern Schools v The Rest. A return of seven for 50 v Bradfield by P. G. Edwards (slow left-arm) emphasised his considerable promise. For **Charterhouse**, a disappointing start to the season was overcome by wins v Portsmouth, Winchester and Westminster. The middle order could not match the consistency of openers C. A. Anderson and D. M. Bennett, although P. R. Durnford gave evidence that he is an exciting prospect. R. J. Rogers took 41 wickets with his left-arm spin and, with P. D. Newman (left-arm fast-medium) who took 46, provided a varied and penetrating attack. The **Cheltenham College** attack, sensibly handled by captain P. C. D. Sykes, regularly bowled out opponents, and with E. A. H. P. Rowland, R. P. W. Thompson and H. D. E. Evans excellent run-chasers, some notable victories were achieved, including those v Repton and Clifton.

In a season of rebuilding, **Christ College, Brecon**, were encouraged to win nine matches, thanks largely to captain and all-rounder S. W. Harvey, who captained the Welsh Schools and whose unbeaten 102 out of 149 v Bromsgrove deserves mention. Positive cricket was played by a young **Christ's Hospital** side, who were let down by erratic batting. However, the bowling was steady, with K. M. Cook taking eight for 55 v Lancing and M. R. Joyner returning seven for 69 v Sussex Martlets. A tour to Bermuda, where four matches were won, ended the season for **Clifton College**, whose C. W. V. Robins played for HMC Schools. Brittle batting hampered an inexperienced **Colfe's School** side, for whom captain A. Rodgers opened the bowling effectively, enjoying a haul of 49 wickets. **Colston's School** attributed their success v Bristol GS, Bristol Cathedral School and Dauntsey's to the prolific batting of W. M. Smith, captain N. H. Parnell and L. M. Roll, whose 757 runs were a school record.

In a mediocre season for **Dauntsey's**, only their captain, J. D. Livingstone, shone, batting well and bowling his off-breaks to good effect. **Dean Close**, too, had a disappointing season, though two sixteen-year-olds showed promise: P. M. Vincent with the bat and R. N. K. O. A. Lindsay (fast-medium) with the ball. Some exciting drawn matches enlivened the season of **Denstone College**, whose attack lacked sufficient depth to back up the penetrative spells of A. J. Little. A highlight was the win v a South African touring team from Woodridge College. A tidy and varied attack, backed by sound fielding, encouraged **Dover College** in a transitional year, but the batting too often revealed its lack of experience. **Downside**, without a win, entertained Wesley College, Australia. **Durham**, unbeaten by a school, achieved a record ten wins, among them v Fettes, Pocklington, Ashville, St Bees, Norwich and Merchiston. Their strength was in depth, although the averages were dominated by captain N. P. Tubbs (slow left-arm) and fifteen-year-old M. A. Roseberry, whose aggregate of 839 runs was more than double the next highest and who took the most wickets with his right-arm medium bowling.

The batting of **Eastbourne College** was stylishly led by J. R. Prentis and left-hander M. H. Edwardes-Evans, whose opening stand of 122 contributed to the defeat of Lancing in the final of the Sussex Schools Knockout Cup. Another highlight was M. O. Simpson's unbeaten century v Sussex Martlets. A limited attack was spearheaded by Prentis (fast-medium), well supported by J. C. Wallace (medium) and colt S. R. Davis (slow left-arm). For **Edinburgh Academy**, whose wins included those v Barnard Castle, Loretto and QEGS Wakefield, left-arm spinner B. J. M. Clube collected 52 wickets in his first season, including seven for 42 v Oxford University Authentics. I. D. Zuill hit a maiden century v Mill Hill and G. R. Mawdsley, who had a fine all-round season, formed a successful opening partnership with his brother, R. A. Mawdsley. A well-balanced **Ellesmere College** side were ably led by wicket-keeper A. I. Crow, who recorded eleven catches and nine stumpings. In the victory v William Hulme's GS, T. J. R. Petty scored an unbeaten 80 out of 160 before G. L. Home took seven for 12.

A memorable season for **Eltham College** brought seventeen wins, with captain M. R. Surguy and M. J. Holcombe becoming the most prolific batsmen in the school's history, aggregating 1,159 and 1,039 runs respectively. Holcombe's 155 not out v St Dunstan's was a school record, as were wicket-keeper R. J.Hunt's 64 dismissals (50ct, 14st) in three years. An inexperienced **Emanuel** side, whose twelve wins included those v Reigate GS and RGS Guildford, were runners-up in both the London Schools and Surrey Schools knockout competitions. The absence of all-rounder R. Carter, with a broken leg, for much of the season hampered a young **Enfield GS** side, whose sound fielding and bowling were not matched by some fragile batting. None the less, wins were recorded v Chigwell, Colchester

RGS, Latymer, St Albans and Watford GS.

Three new records set for **Epsom College** were an aggregate of 1,013 runs by captain R. M. C. Williams, a first-wicket partnership of 202 from J. R. Ansell and M. B. Finnigan, and a fourth-wicket stand of 157 between Finnigan and R. V. Williams. Ansell was selected for the Southern Schools and R. M. C. Williams captained Surrey Schools. M. J. Morris showed tremendous stamina in the attack, while D. G. Henwood, moving the ball both ways, created problems for opposing batsmen. **Eton**, unbeaten, recorded eight wins, among them those v Bradfield, Marlborough and Winchester. The strength of the side lay in bowling out the opposition, M. V. Fleming, a hard-hitting opening bat and prolific swing bowler, dominating in both respects and captain C. A. Watt bowling his off-spin maturely for 33 wickets. Although the bowlers of **Exeter School** sometimes struggled to dismiss their opponents, their batsmen, led by captain P. Hodgson, often successfully chased large targets in their most successful season for some years.

Felsted, unbeaten by a school, owed much to openers J. P. Stephenson and A. B. Mitchell, who compiled five century opening stands, 176 being the highest. Selected for Southern Schools was B. H. Pinkerton (left-arm orthodox spin), who led the attack, ably supported by Stephenson and A. J. Haynes. The fielding was sound, inspired by the outstanding wicket-keeping of M. W. C. Olley, who, with Stephenson, played for HMC Schools. A win over MCC was a highlight for **Fettes College**, who also defeated The Leys. **Forest School**, with wins v Brentwood, City of London, RGS Colchester, Chigwell, St Edmunds Canterbury and Wellingborough, could recall with satisfaction the performance of fourteen-year-old M. D. I. Sheppard, whose 501 runs included an unbeaten century.

The strength of the **Glenalmond** side lay in its team spirit under the outstanding captaincy of left-hand bat J. Everett, who scored fine hundreds v Fettes and Strathallan. S. J. Lewis (off-spin) and M. H. Alexander (slow left-arm) took many wickets as wins were recorded v Merchiston Castle, Loretto, Downside, RGS Lancaster, MCC, the XL Club and Christ's College, Cambridge. Everett played for Scotland Under-19, while J. Sutton captained and A. M. Stevenson played for Scotland Under-16. Memorable in an enjoyable season for **Giggleswick School** were all-rounder J. B. Newsome's leadership and R. M. White's 131 not out v Hipperholme. **Gordonstoun's** young side were encouraged by the performance of leading wicket-taker K. M. Mordue (slow left-arm) and captain R. P. J. Heyes's unbeaten century v The Abbey School, Fort Augustus.

An enjoyable winter tour to Sri Lanka, with three matches won and three lost, preceded a season in which **Haberdashers' Aske's, Elstree**, were defeated by a school – Bancroft's – for the first time in five years, although nine wins followed. The batting was strong, with valuable contributions from N. J Wood, D. J. Price, N. J. Churchman and left-hander A. J. Moulding, while the bowling, led by Moulding (right-arm in-swing) improved considerably. An enjoyable aspect of the **Haileybury** attack was the leg-spin of T. P. Jackson-Feilden, ably backed by wicket-keeper S. L. Feast, who made fourteen stumpings. J. E. Harding was a mature captain and led the batting. **Hampton School**, astutely captained by E. M. Turnill, played positive cricket to remain unbeaten by a school. Turnill and T. R. Eastaugh played match-winning innings, and there was much pleasure to be taken from the controlled slow left-arm spin of fifteen-year-old J. Shepherd.

Unbeaten for a second successive season, **Harrow** boasted a strong batting side, but the attack often lacked penetration, as did that of **Highgate School**, for whom A. C. Fawden took six for 32 v Old Cholmeleians. **Hereford Cathedral School**, in a season curtailed by the poor weather, had several matches which were in an interesting position when time ran out. **Hipperholme GS** began the season with convincing wins v Bradford GS and Woodhouse Grove, but later the attack failed to capitalise on the consistent batting of D. F. Rayner, R. S. Butterworth and left-hander K. D. Booth, who was also a sound wicket-keeper. **Hurstpierpoint** followed a winter tour of India with wins v Whitgift and Worth, but other opportunities were missed owing to inconsistent batting and wayward bowling. Exceptions were J. B. Buckeridge and M. D. Foulds, who scored the side's only century, and G. J. Alexander, who returned seven for 34 v Whitgift. A young and inexperienced **Ipswich School** side made considerable progress during the season, T. Rollett developing into a sound opening bat to score the school's only three-figure innings. S. Priscott (left-arm medium) showed promise, his 25 wickets including seven for 45 v Gresham's, while

J. Nicholls emerged as an accurate off-spin bowler who also batted tenaciously.

Apart from S. A. Sharpe, who was outstanding with both bat and ball, **Kimbolton's** batting was disappointing. The fielding, however, was competent and the bowling adequate, with P. A. J. Brittain (slow left-arm) taking six for 25 v MCC. A. W. Gilbert, captain of **King Edward VI School, Southampton**, scored his maiden century for the school and captained Hampshire Schools, while wicket-keeper R. P. Headington played for West of England Schools and Hampshire Schools. **King Edward VI College, Stourbridge**, owed their success to a strong attack, headed by D. J. Bullock and off-spinner D. J. Shorter, who took six for 46 for Midland Schools v The North and was selected for England Schools v The Army. Notable batsmen were D. M. Anderson and opener R. N. Tolley.

For **King Edward VII School, Lytham**, G. Cartmell scored 107 v Solihull School, against whom A. Thornton made 104, reaching three figures with two consecutive 6s. Of the bowlers, A. Gregson and J. Evans (both fast) and N. D. W. McDonnell (off-spin) excelled. With wins v Wrekin, Solihull and Denstone, **King Edward's School, Birmingham**, depended heavily on all-rounders M. K. Hughes and C. Ibbetson. N. A. Willetts, who scored the school's only hundred, played for ESCA Under-15 v Scotland. **King William's College, Isle of Man**, reported a disappointing season in which lack of a penetrative attack frustrated a strong batting side, for whom opener S. C. Watson scored two centuries. In a successful season, **King's College, Taunton**, defeated Wellington (Somerset), the XL Club, Queen's Taunton, MCC, Taunton School, Allhallows, Monmouth and Downside. Their strength lay in the bowling, with R. J. Harden (left-arm medium) taking 48 wickets, including a hat-trick v Queen's Taunton, a feat also performed by H. D. Wordsworth (right-arm medium) v Christ's Hospital. The forceful batting was led by Harden, who passed 90 on three occasions; he received valuable support from left-hander N. D. Everest, who also kept wicket.

King's College School, Wimbledon, owed their success to all-round depth, although notable performances came from J. H. Frost with the bat and N. P. Montgomery and fifteen-year-old P. S. Noble with the ball. Careless fielding hampered **King's School, Bruton**, for whom I. C. D. Stuart and R. C. Gainher scored the most runs, while Stuart and P. F. McIntyre were the leading wicket-takers. **The King's School, Canterbury**, defeated only by Sutton Valence, fielded a strong batting side, featuring P. G. Bromley, D. J. R. Hildick-Smith and P. J. Cranston-Smith, and a varied attack, with leg-spinner R. W. G. Oliver taking the most wickets. Wicket-keeper P. J. Whyte's performances encouraged good displays in the field. The **King's School, Ely**, also defeated only once, were indebted to the all-round excellence of T. S. May (right-hand bat and right-arm off-spin), whose 103 v Ely Diocese was their highest innings. J. P. Hulme, captain and opening bowler (right-arm in-swing) followed a fine season by playing for Cambridgeshire Under-19. In the junior section, eleven-year-old R. Bickell hit 30 runs in one over off Mr T. King in the match v the Fathers. In a season of rebuilding, P. A. Manning was outstanding for **The King's School, Macclesfield.**

King's School, Worcester, were disappointed to win only one match, their problem being mainly an inability to bowl out the opposition. The performance of J. S. Fleming appeared to suffer from his responsibilities as captain, and of the batsmen only D. P. E. Rogers played consistently. A young **Kingston GS** side were encouraged to win five matches, including one by four wickets v Tiffin as part of a sponsored contest in aid of the Lord's Taverners' Charities. Three centuries resulted from enterprising batting, two by D. E. Jenkins and one by S. H. Clayson. The outstanding bowler was R. C. Marshall (left-arm medium), backed up by captain S. J. Nicholls (medium).

Lancing College's record twelve wins included defeats of Charterhouse, Brighton College, Free Foresters and MCC. Off-spinner C. S. Mays took a record 58 wickets, while A. N. McPherson also had a rewarding season. Fifteen-year-old left-hander J. D. Robinson's 700 runs were the highest aggregate since 1957 and considerable depth to the batting came from J. G. Wills, I. C. Martin, J. J. S. Withyman and wicket-keeper C. P. Heaslip, the only member of the side not expected to return in 1983. An unbeaten tour to the Channel Islands was enjoyed in the summer. Positive cricket brought **Leeds GS** ten wins, among them those v Hipperholme GS, QEGS Wakefield, Ashville College, Bootham and Archbishop Holgate

GS, York. Their innings were given a sound start from J. K. Bowman and A. F. Tyler, who reached three figures twice. A. M. Watson took six for 5 v Silcoates School and four wickets in five balls v Archbishop Holgate GS.

The batting of **The Leys** was the strongest for some years, notable performances coming from G. C. Mackintosh (90 v The Perse) and J. D. R. Benson, who made 110 not out v the XL Club and whose 90 v Highgate came in 80 minutes, with eight 6s. He also captained HMC Schools Under-15. A successful **Liverpool College** side, who held their catches well, owed much to the formidable opening partnership of D. M. Fletcher and P. D. Williams, as well as the opening attack of T. F. Groom and Williams. A young **Lord Wandsworth College** side received encouragement from the performances of T. R. Jermyn (left-hand bat and right-arm off-spinner). Another young side, **Lord Williams's School, Thame,** were less successful, depending too heavily on S. J. Lewis. For **Loretto**, captain D. J. M. Orr excelled, making 105 not out v George Heriot's and taking five for 22 v Glenalmond.

Two all-rounders, S. Mendes and M. Barrow, headed the averages for **Magdalen College School,** who were planning a tour of the West Indies. Barbados-born R. M. Ellcock was outstanding for **Malvern College,** taking five wickets in an innings on six occasions, including returns of six for 31 v Dean Close, six for 41 v Radley and six for 57 v Clifton College. He played county cricket for Worcestershire and represented HMC Schools. Leading bowlers for **Manchester GS** were M. A. P. Jefferson and captain S. C. Williams, while the side's only three-figure innings came from R. E. Johnston v Arnold School. A potentially strong **Marlborough** side, who could none the less muster only one win, were let down by fragile middle-order batting and an attack which was rarely more than steady. The batting of a young **Merchant Taylors', Crosby,** side was disappointing, with only fifteen-year-old M. J. Cooke passing fifty. The bowling, often inaccurate, was led by D. J. Walmsley (slow right-arm) and L. N. J. Heathcliff-Core (left-arm fast-medium), while M. J. Clinton took six for 30 v Liverpool College. Some excellent catches were taken, particularly by D. H. Cooke at first slip.

Merchant Taylors', Northwood, unbeaten for the second successive season, owed their success to all-round strength. A strong batting side was invariably given a sound start by openers S. P. Ducat and left-hander D. J. Jenkins, who shared two century stands. Five accurate and attacking bowlers, who gave the opposition no respite, were backed by superb fielding inspired by Jenkins behind the stumps. **Merchiston Castle School** reported a disappointing season, with the side too often bowled out cheaply. Opening batsman J. E. Hamilton distinguished himself v Edinburgh Academy, when he was on the field throughout, scoring 74 not out and 47 not out. The seam bowling was rarely incisive enough and D. A. G. Watson (slow left-arm orthodox) and N. S. Hockborn (off-breaks) were often introduced too late to be effective. For **Mill Hill** opening bat P. A. Robin averaged 70.85 and was unfortunate to miss 1,000 runs for the school season.

A successful **Millfield** side owed much to all-rounder P. A. C. Bail, who represented ESCA West. Although the middle-order batting tended to be fragile, J. E. M. Nicholson made three centuries, and of the bowlers the accurate N. Brown deserved more success. A young **Milton Abbey** side often failed to sustain a sound start from promising opening batsmen J. M. Hopkins and N. J. Coppen, but they did reach the fifth round of the Barclays Bank Under-17 Cup. Leading bowlers were fifteen-year-old R. W. Gamble (fast-medium) and captain C. W. Moyle, whose right-arm leg-spin was both a match-winner and served to keep other matches interestingly open. The talented players of **Monkton Combe School** often failed to play to their full potential, although I. G. Osborne emerged as a fine all-rounder and S. A. M. Prentice played some fine attacking innings. Inability to bowl out the opposition often restricted **Monmouth School,** for whom captain K. G. Lewis made 119 not out v Christ College Brecon. All-rounder M. F. Kear captained the Welsh Under-15 side.

Norwich School's season, which featured a win by 3 runs v Gresham's, was rounded off with a tour to Durham, where the maturity of S. P. Bowling and P. D. Nicholls was supported by the promise of fourteen-year-old N. J. Foster with both bat and ball. The **Nottinghamshire High School** side, who equalled the school record of sixteen wins, played attractive, attacking cricket, ably led by R. Poole, whose 895 runs included two hundreds.

For **Oundle,** who defeated Mill Hill and St Edward's Oxford, a weak middle order failed to support openers A. S. A. Townsend and left-hander D. C. Boyce. Apart from leg-spinner J. S. Carr, the attack lacked penetration. For **The Perse School**, whose only win came v RGS Newcastle, J. M. C. Stenner was in fine form with the bat. Aggressive cricket brought **Pocklington School** eleven wins: J. D. St J. Lang and R. T. Nuttall were reliable opening batsmen and R. M. Aram (slow left-arm) established a school record with 69 wickets. Another fine season for **Queen's College, Taunton,** featured the all-round performance of G. V. Palmer, son of Test umpire Ken Palmer, who headed both batting and bowling averages and made his début for Somerset. Also outstanding with bat and ball was P. Graham.

Highlights for **Radley** were wins v Sherborne, St Edward's, Abingdon and Free Foresters, against whom R. G. Butler scored 111. Captain G. D. Moss, son of Alan Moss (Middlesex and England) played for HMC Schools and for Middlesex Under-25. With L. S. N. George he formed the side's best opening attack for over a decade, but the later bowlers failed to prise out opposing tailenders. E. J. B. Popplewell (brother of Somerset's N.F.M.) was a talented wicket-keeper-batsman. A season of rebuilding for **Ratcliffe College** ended with a successful tour to Blackpool. Above-average fielding supported notable performances from D. M. Prior, who scored 101 v Hutton GS, and P. W. Tarimo, with seven for 26 v Cotton College. **Reading School** relied heavily on captain E. P. O'Leary, who headed both batting and bowling averages and took five for 16 v Abingdon, the only school to be beaten by the side.

A young **Reed's School** side performed better than expected, thanks mainly to the accurate slow bowling of captain M. R. Dunn (off-spin) and C. R. Notton (leg-spin). The batting was steady, with opening bat G. A. Hatton excelling. A successful tour to the Channel Islands ended the season for **Reigate GS,** whose attack was often handicapped by injuries. Two all-rounders were outstanding – C. M. Allen and left-arm wrist-spinner P. W. Gritton. A weak attack brought **Repton** a frustrating season in which no school was beaten. The most successful batsman was C. Benn, while captain T. R. Barlow took 22 catches behind the stumps. Highlights for **Rossall** were victories v Sedbergh, Stonyhurst and Arnold School. R. I. Kanhai led the team by example, heading both batting and bowling averages, and was given valuable support by K. C. Stiles (right-arm fast-medium).

Royal GS, Newcastle, with a young side, had an encouraging season. Apart from S. J. Sill (off-spin) and J. N. J. Anderson (leg-spin), the bowling was expensive and the batting, although strong in depth, lacked consistency. **Royal GS, Worcester,** benefited from the aggressive strokeplay of openers S. D. Cairney (112 v King's School, Worcester) and P. Bent (115 not out v Christ College, Brecon). Although I. G. Jinks (right-arm fast-medium) was hostile in the right conditions, the attack rarely dominated. **Rugby,** with no wins over schools, were beaten only by St Edward's Oxford. **Rydal** had a disappointing record, although keenness and determination often made up for technical deficiencies. The absence through injury of T. P. Forster at the beginning of the season was critical.

St Albans School, with only four drawn games, owed much to the attacking captaincy of all-rounder A. P. Latham. Off-spinner W. J. Dean collected a post-war record of 50 wickets, including returns of seven for 45 v Bedford Modern and six for 41 v Verulam. A high standard of wicket-keeping came from M. D. Lynes and J. C. Simpson, and in the middle order H. S. F. Thompson often steadied the innings under pressure. A strong batting line-up at **St Dunstan's** was built around No. 3, C. Denny, but C. Tooley failed to fulfil his potential as an opening bat. Fifteen-year-old G. Pointer showed promise as a fast left-arm bowler and S. Cross took 25 wickets with his slow off-cutters. For **St Edmund's, Canterbury,** who in a season of rebuilding defeated Sir Roger Manwood's School, Duke of York's RHS and Cranbrook, S. A. A. Roche's six for 39 v Dover College was an outstanding performance. Had some of their senior colours, especially the batsmen, produced their true form, **St Edward's, Oxford,** might have enjoyed a more rewarding term. Except for R. Franklin (left-arm chinaman and googly), the bowling was weak. **St George's, Weybridge,** found a useful off-break bowler in S. E. Jones, and fifteen-year-old T. J. O'Gorman, with the side's only three-figure innings, promised much for the future.

St John's, Leatherhead, achieved wins v KCS Wimbledon and Christ's Hospital, with captain M. T. Sibley scoring the most runs and taking the most wickets with his off-breaks. Unbeaten by a school, **St Peter's, York,** were indebted to spinners R. J. Kirby (left-arm) and S. R. Gorman (off-spin), who topped both batting and bowling averages and played for HMC Schools. In a successful season, **Sedbergh's** young side played positive cricket, being particularly successful at chasing targets and achieving notable wins v Ampleforth and MCC. Captain C. James played fine attacking innings, and M. T. Alban, W. D. C. Carling, J. C. Foster and S. R. Paton gave him good support. The varied attack featured M. G. Burgess (fast), J. C. R. Binks (left-arm fast-medium) and Alban (leg-break).

The strength of **Sevenoaks School's** side lay in the attack, with R. P. Roberts (right-arm fast-medium) taking the most wickets. The batting was dominated by the consistent J. G. Perks, with D. B. Thresher and left-hander N. P. Thomas in support. A highlight for **Sherborne,** defeated only by Radley, was an unbroken first-wicket partnership of 205 v Downside between M. M. C. F. Jones and captain T. J. Dudgeon. P. L. Garlick proved to be a tireless fast bowler and T. J. Billington's accurate, slow left-arm spin reaped its reward. **Shrewsbury** suffered a frustrating season. They had an inadequate attack, despite the contribution of R. J. P. Burton, who took 56 wickets with his out-swing, including five wickets in an innings on five occasions. **Simon Langton GS,** who suffered their first defeat in three years, depended heavily on S. C. Goldsmith, who scored three hundreds in his 938 runs, took 27 wickets and played for Kent Second XI. For **Sir Roger Manwood's School,** M. I. A. Howell (right-arm fast-medium) collected seven for 39 v Dover College. The batting was carried principally by the captain, K. B. G. Boland, and a promising fifteen-year-old, G. W. Laslett.

With a strong bowling side, **Solihull** recorded five wins, including those v MCC and Barnard Castle, against whom C. M. Jowsey took six for 38 with his off-spinners. M. Whitehead (right-arm fast-medium) took six Bromsgrove wickets for 32 and M. C. Duck (right-arm fast-medium) produced a sensational victory over King's Worcester with three wickets in the final over and match figures of five for 8. The batting, however, was brittle, although J. M. Robinson scored an unbeaten 97 in the victory over King William's College and played for the Rest v Southern Schools. An experienced **Stamford School** side, with wins v Kimbolton, the XL Club, Spalding GS and Bishop's Stortford College, was centred around captain D. W. Browne, who hit 117 v Clitheroe GS. I. D. Stafford had an excellent season behind the stumps (16ct, 3st) and most wickets fell to fast bowlers I. R. Plant and J. N. Ralphs: the rest of the attack tended to be expensive. A tour of Australia was planned for the winter.

Stockport GS were unbeaten, noteworthy wins coming v Manchester GS and King William's College, against whom the hostile opening bowler, R. A. Samarji, claimed six for 32. Leading batsmen were T. P. R. Reeman, P. H. Wickenden and captain R. P. Nicholson. **Strathallan,** with twelve wins and only one defeat – at the hands of Barnard Castle School – were given outstanding example by their captain and all-rounder M. J. de G. Allingham, who scored 721 runs at 103.00 and took 45 wickets at 10.55. A superb season for **Sutton Valence** left the side undefeated with twelve wins, including those v St Lawrence, King's Rochester, Dover College, King's Canterbury, Trinity Croydon, William Hulme's GS and Culford. To the fore were all-rounders A. R. Shaw and M. T. Russell-Vick, a fine captain who made 114 v Dover College, against whom Shaw took six for 13. Russell-Vick played for HMC Schools.

From a young **Taunton School** side, who defeated Clifton, Canford, Monmouth, Rutlish and a Stowe XI, J. C. Pike and R. J. Bartlett were selected for England Schools Under-15. **Tiffin** suffered a disappointing season. Owing to a lack of form among the fast bowlers, the burden of the attack fell upon the left-arm orthodox spinners, W. B. Shermer and N. M. Williams. Run-making was prolific at times, with P. R. C. Robinson excelling. **Tonbridge,** again unbeaten by a school, defeated Charterhouse, Bedford, Haileybury, Clifton, Eastbourne, Wellington, Lancing and Sevenoaks. Four batsmen scored five centuries between them, with G. R. Cowdrey and M. P. Hickson outstanding; both played for HMC Schools. The bowling was equally strong, 114 wickets being shared between four seamers, well supported by wicket-keeper M. Cooper, who collected 27 victims. **Trent College** owed their excellent season to three fast bowlers: W. Fox (on Leicestershire's books), who took seven for 31 v Pocklington, the promising M. Davison (son of I. M. Davison and on Nottinghamshire's books) and accurate swing bowler N. J. S. Booth. They were ably assisted by some brilliant catching from S. J. Kinselle (on Derby County's books as a goalkeeper), as well as some aggressive outcricket. Seven consecutive wins, four on a Dutch tour, gave **Trinity** a total of fourteen wins, with only three defeats; the result of a strong team effort. P. J. Stapley equalled the school record of four hundreds in a season. **Truro School,** with only one defeat, were ably led by T. Manhire, who made a valuable all-round contribution.

With a well-balanced side and depth to their batting, **Uppingham,** unbeaten, defeated Haileybury, Repton, Shrewsbury, Ampleforth and Oundle. New records were set for **Victoria College, Jersey,** who defeated Elizabeth College to win the Sullivan Trophy. Captain W. Jenner established a post-war record with 1,227 runs, while pace bowler J. M. W. Giles's 71 wickets were the best return in a term.

Warwick School, after a slow start, defeated King's Worcester, MCC, the XL Club, Dean Close and Solihull. Runs were scored quickly, with two centuries coming from J. C. Ball and one from N. C. B. Robinson. There was a shortage of slow bowlers, the emphasis of the attack being the formidable opening partnership of A. C. Nunn and B. J. Barnfather, well supported by A. Knight. Inconsistent batting restricted **Wellingborough School** to two wins against schools – v Bedford Modern and Lord Williams's Thame. **Wellington College, Crowthorne,** found runs hard to come by, but good catching and a penetrative attack brought six victories. Early promise was not fulfilled by **Westminster**, although the promotion of attacking right-hand batsman R. J. Levy brought a fine late victory v Free Foresters. Weak batting restricted **Whitgift,** although good wins were achieved v Trinity and St George's Weybridge. The leading bowler was captain R. D. Ronald (slow left-arm), who collected 41 wickets.

William Hulme's GS played positive cricket, with bowlers' performances often winning matches; I. D. Thorpe was the most consistent, A. D. Brown claimed six for 12 in the win v King's Macclesfield, and N. J. Fairfax (leg-spin) and R. G. McLaren (medium) were responsible for the wins v Rydal and Loughborough GS respectively. R. P. Thornton and H. Fryman scored the most runs, but large scores generally eluded the side. **Winchester** reported a disappointing season, the batting fragile and the bowling often ineffective. However, W. E. J. Holland scored three centuries – 150 not out v Eastbourne, 108 not out v Harrow and 107 v Clifton – and captain and wicket-keeper E. M. Coulman was selected for Southern Schools. After a poor start to the season, **Woodbridge School** achieved some exciting wins, including those in the final over v RHS Holbrook and Norwich, against whom R. W. Bensly made 100 not out. He scored the most runs as well as taking the most wickets, but the side generally had difficulty in bowling out the opposition, although R. A. Jack emerged as a promising off-spinner and S. Leask's seam bowling proved effective later in the season.

Woodhouse Grove beat Bootham, Ashville and Giggleswick, I. W. Stott emerging as the most successful batsman for ten years and receiving sound support from the Percy brothers. S. A. J. Kippax bowled his leg-spin to good effect and was selected for the Rest v Southern Schools, while B. S. Percy (seam and off-spin) and left-arm opening bowler S. Cockerill enjoyed good returns. E. M. Greenwood was a competent wicket-keeper. Highlights for **Worksop College** were S. N. Waddington's 132 not out v Denstone and 100 not out by his younger brother, W. M. Waddington, at Repton. **Wrekin** reported many exciting finishes and good wins v Worksop, Stonyhurst and MCC. Captain J. R. Mackenzie took more than 50 wickets and scored over 500 runs for the second season in succession, while O. N. E. Harvey also made a valuable contribution. A young **Wycliffe College** side did better than expected, with J. R. Bodington playing a gloriously aggressive innings v Colston's, going from 50 to 70 in one over. R. B. Hair had a promising first season with the ball, and after a poor start captain S. J. Shorthose recovered form to top the bowling averages.

THE SCHOOLS

(Qualification: Batting 100 runs; Bowling 10 wickets)

**On name indicates captain.* **On figures indicates not out.*

Note: The line for batting reads Innings–Not Outs–Runs–Highest Innings–Average; that for bowling reads Overs–Maidens–Runs–Wickets–Average.

ABINGDON SCHOOL

Played 16: Won 8, Lost 4, Drawn 4. Abandoned 1

Master i/c: N. H. Payne

Batting—M. T. Boobbyer 4–0–233–106–58.25; B. E. Woolley 13–6–191–60*–27.28; R. I. McCreery 11–1–264–62–26.40; *C. C. Newmark 15–0–292–59–19.46; N. G. Rice 15–2–237–59–18.23; R. M. R. Suggate 13–0–186–54–14.30; S. J. Rushton 16–1–209–61–13.93; D. R. Newman 13–0–140–50–10.76.

Bowling—D. H. Phillips 114.2–31–264–29–9.10; R. I. McCreery 134–35–324–27–12.00; T. D. Winter 151.2–51–342–28–12.21; M. A. Marsden 96.5–33–195–12–16.25.

ALDENHAM SCHOOL

Played 15: Won 4, Lost 4, Drawn 7. Abandoned 1

Master i/c: P. K. Smith Cricket professional: F. J. Titmus

Batting—P. A. Stenning 15–3–387–68–32.25; C. Y. Appenteng 8–1–180–59*–25.71; C. R. Bateson 14–0–353–68–25.21; S. W. H. Vickers 11–1–196–81–19.60; S. P. Radin 13–5–156–61*–19.50; J. M. Edwards 10–1–158–64–17.55; *A. P. O. Cotton 14–2–205–40–17.08; J. M. Aukett 10–1–107–32–11.88.

Bowling—S. W. H. Vickers 158–36–423–22–19.22; P. A. Stenning 185–35–636–31–20.51; J. M. Edwards 118–24–344–11–31.27.

ALLEYN'S SCHOOL

Played 16: Won 4, Lost 6, Drawn 6

Master i/c: J. F. C. Nash

Batting—J. Graham 8–4–118–49*–29.50; J. Weaver 16–0–437–82–27.31; S. Harmer 16–0–426–54–26.62; R. Preston 14–3–216–41–19.63; S. Geere 14–2–235–45–19.58; P. Messent 13–1–222–49–18.50; D. Malam 12–1–168–48*–15.27; B. Preston 12–0–101–30–8.41.

Bowling—G. Hamilton 190–62–449–24–18.70; J. Graham 168–35–528–27–19.55; W. Grigg 68.5–17–225–11–20.45; S. Geere 116.2–25–345–15–23.00; *W. Postlethwaite 144.5–42–419–18–23.27.

ALLHALLOWS SCHOOL

Played 19: Won 4, Lost 10, Drawn 5

Master i/c: P. L. Petherbridge

Batting—*P. M. B. Zealey 18–1–462–71*–27.17; T. J. B. Dutton-Cox 17–3–313–54–22.35; G. Spark 16–3–253–42–19.46; P. M. Tuck 17–1–262–41–16.37; J. P. Knapman 16–3–178–40–13.69; D. N. H. Smith 16–0–157–47–9.81.

Bowling—P. M. Tuck 194.2–63–436–35–12.45; T. J. B. Dutton-Cox 203–50–560–32–17.50; E. R. M. Gard 126–28–406–23–17.65; J. P. Knapman 55–2–275–15–18.33.

AMPLEFORTH COLLEGE

Played 17: Won 3, Lost 4, Drawn 10

Masters i/c: J. G. Willcox and Rev. J. F. Stephens

Batting—*J. M. Carter 17–1–558–99–34.87; C. L. Macdonald 16–2–389–65*–27.78; W. Beardmore-Gray 18–2–376–88–23.50; M. L. Roberts 15–5–225–50–22.50; N. Read 13–0–261–54–20.07; R. Rigby 16–0–303–46–18.93; C. Crossley 17–3–248–46*–17.71.

Bowling—J. M. Carter 124–27–326–22–14.81; M. L. Roberts 167–31–474–29–16.34; E. Soden-Bird 163–50–441–25–17.64; J. Perry 99–16–277–14–19.78; J. Porter 117–33–294–14–21.00.

ARDINGLY COLLEGE

Played 15: Won 7, Drawn 7, Lost 1

Master i/c: N. D. Duncan

Batting—A. T. Baiden 15–4–614–123–55.81; W. A. Musk 13–7–240–41*–40.00; P. S. Germain 14–2–457–89–38.08; S. Jacobsen 14–1–495–110–38.07; H. Teague 10–4–164–70*–27.33; A. J. Harris 15–0–292–63–19.46.

Bowling—I. Stringer 211.3–69–521–44–11.84; R. D. Newcomb 96.4–23–269–15–17.93; G. R. Emmerson 162–33–500–21–23.80; G. L. Calvert Lee 104.2–20–317–13–24.38.

ARNOLD SCHOOL

Played 18: Won 5, Lost 4, Drawn 9. Abandoned 2

Master i/c: S. T. Godfrey

Batting—P. A. Webb 17–3–571–103–40.78; A. J. Cardwell 16–3–359–61*–27.61; *S. A. W. Clark 17–2–402–79–26.80; J. F. Nicholson 11–5–114–31*–19.00; R. Southern 15–1–263–78–18.78; S. Beckwith 12–1–206–94–18.72.

Bowling—P. A. Webb 223–64–563–38–14.81; R. Southern 137–26–449–19–23.63; C. A. Hoskisson 136–31–403–13–31.00; S. E. Davies 100–17–318–10–31.80.

ASHVILLE COLLEGE

Played 17: Won 3, Lost 8, Drawn 6. Abandoned 2

Master i/c: J. M. Bromley

Batting—J. C. Lister 14–2–466–104–38.83; *S. H. Walsh 17–3–286–50–20.42; I. M. Feetam 12–3–132–39–14.66; C. D. Brawn 17–1–217–27–13.56; I. D. Hopper 15–4–140–41*–12.72; T. L. Holgate 12–0–134–44–11.16; D. A. Kindon 14–0–134–47–9.57.

Bowling—E. J. London 155–43–394–27–14.59; A. D. Reaks 74–14–252–17–14.82; S. H. Walsh 64–16–225–15–15.00; A. Perkins 133–42–366–22–16.63; I. D. Hopper 183–45–471–22–21.40.

BABLAKE SCHOOL

Played 18: Won 11, Lost 0, Drawn 7. Abandoned 5

Master i/c: R. A. Fewtrell

Batting—*W. J. P. Matthews 17–5–570–94*–47.50; D. A. Thorne 15–3–551–108*–45.91; M. D. White 10–5–187–63*–37.40; M. Twigger 16–1–388–66–25.86; G. Charlesworth 14–3–257–72–23.36; P. Percival 10–4–124–49–20.66.

Bowling—G. Charlesworth 142.5–38–381–41–9.29; W. J. P. Matthews 113.1–24–277–24–11.54; P. Percival 99–32–201–16–12.56; D. A. Thorne 173–56–387–29–13.34; L. J. Paul 135–36–322–24–13.41.

BANCROFT'S SCHOOL

Played 15: Won 7, Lost 4, Drawn 4. Abandoned 1

Master i/c: J. G. Bromfield

Batting—S. W. Gant 14–5–292–65*–32.44; *M. G. de Jode 15–1–430–141*–30.71; I. P. Debnam 16–4–363–104*–30.25; G. M. Fleet 16–1–345–97–23.00; J. P. Thomas 5–0–111–50–22.20; W. J. Head 13–3–217–54*–21.70; S. P. Laiker 14–1–282–46–21.69.

Bowling—S. W. Gant 196–58–410–36–11.38; M. G. de Jode 100–35–219–19–11.52; I. P. Debnam 187–57–479–38–12.60; R. S. Patel 90–29–235–12–19.58.

BARNARD CASTLE SCHOOL

Played 20: Won 9, Lost 4, Drawn 7. Abandoned 1

Master i/c: R. T. Mardon

Batting—G. Underwood 18–3–520–104–34.66; R. Butcher 14–0–421–87–30.05; M. Coates 9–5–107–30–26.75; D. Swinbank 18–1–443–86–26.05; J. Ashman 5–0–111–68–22.20; T. Blackburn 17–1–327–60–20.43; S. Nicholson 15–5–190–54*–19.00; A. Harvey 13–3–153–41*–15.30.

Bowling—M. Coates 225–82–504–34–14.82; R. Blamire 95–21–264–15–17.60; S. Crowther 207–63–529–28–18.89; P. Coulthard 107–15–245–12–20.41; D. Swinbank 131–14–430–10–43.00.

BEDFORD SCHOOL

Played 17: Won 9, Lost 2, Drawn 6. Abandoned 2

Master i/c: P. D. Briggs

Batting—C. J. Bell 16–4–364–70–30.33; M. C. Nutt 18–2–456–68*–28.50; D. C. R. Waterfield 19–1–457–77*–25.38; R. J. Howe 13–3–244–49*–24.40; E. Castenskiold 16–1–320–59–21.33; *S. M. Smith 19–3–326–47–20.37.

Bowling—C. J. Bell 219–57–552–44–12.54; I. T. Osborne 131–41–273–19–14.36; D. Stroud 74–20–232–14–16.57; C. Stevens 160–44–371–20–18.55; M. Singh 166–56–433–20–21.65; E. Castenskiold 126–31–287–12–23.91.

BEDFORD MODERN SCHOOL

Played 22: Won 9, Lost 4, Drawn 9. Abandoned 4

Master i/c: A. D. Curtis

Batting—A. Fordham 22–3–1,042–146–54.84; T. M. Lord 22–3–591–92–31.10; *A. K. G. Jones 22–4–502–72–27.88; S. D. Philbrook 21–7–374–53*–26.71; A. P. Oakley 17–6–215–32*–19.54.

Bowling—A. K. G. Jones 147–44–358–27–13.25; J. O. R. Jones 233.4–75–553–38–14.55; A. P. Oakley 132–42–326–19–17.15; A. D. Tyler 202.3–66–526–29–18.13; P. A. Garratt 160.3–45–401–22–18.22; D. F. Fishwick 101–11–419–15–27.93.

BERKHAMSTED SCHOOL

Played 14: Won 4, Lost 3, Drawn 7. Abandoned 2

Master i/c: F. J. Davis

Batting—*B. G. Evans 13–4–610–120–67.77; J. R. Neal 13–1–342–80*–28.50; P. Brown 11–2–220–59*–24.44; R. Hudson 10–3–120–24–17.14; P. Beard 11–2–137–45–15.22; S. Pearce 11–1–101–32–10.10.

Bowling—R. Hudson 65–9–186–15–12.40; B. G. Evans 76–14–233–16–14.56; J. R. Neal 166.4–35–418–26–16.07; N. Cowley 140–29–465–22–21.13; T. Warren 163–43–449–18–24.94.

BIRKENHEAD SCHOOL

Played 16: Won 8, Lost 1, Drawn 7. Abandoned 1

Master i/c: M. H. Bowyer

Batting—M. P. Gamet 15–1–646–89–46.14; P. J. Sylvester 13–7–197–39–32.83; E. R. Hamilton 13–5–235–70–29.37; P. C. Barber 14–0–329–73–23.50; *S. M. Holroyd 14–2–223–59–18.58; C. D. Fletcher 11–1–185–35–18.50.

Bowling—S. McGowan 77–19–215–24–8.95; S. M. Holroyd 150.3–42–358–30–11.93; M. McGowan 116.1–18–356–23–15.47; N. V. Jeffreys 75–17–202–10–20.20; M. P. Gamet 121–27–379–16–23.68.

BISHOP'S STORTFORD COLLEGE

Played 14: Won 4, Lost 2, Drawn 8. Abandoned 1

Master i/c: D. A. Hopper — Cricket professional: E. G. Witherden

Batting—S. E. Kok 9–3–200–43–33.33; *G. K. Smith 14–3–338–72–30.72; G. E. B. Swayne 11–2–239–51–26.55; R. S. Banks 10–1–185–85*–20.55; G. L. Chapman 7–1–120–45–20.00.

Bowling—A. C. Simpson 102.2–30–259–19–13.63; R. S. Banks 163–47–325–19–17.10; G. L. Chapman 124.3–35–283–14–20.21.

BLOXHAM SCHOOL

Played 12: Won 2, Lost 4, Drawn 6

Master i/c: M. J. Tideswell

Batting—*T. J. Abraham 12–4–538–103*–67.25; T. M. Cooper 12–2–363–80–36.30; G. B. Civil 7–1–136–64*–22.66; N. J. Reynolds 11–0–152–50–13.81; J. F. Benfield 12–0–161–59–13.41.

Bowling—S. M. Gomes 53–15–114–11–10.36; I. R. Davies 52–14–119–11–10.81; M. E. B. Brown 111–22–388–22–17.63; T. M. Cooper 107.2–21–327–14–23.35.

BLUNDELL'S SCHOOL

Played 15: Won 5, Lost 0, Drawn 10. Abandoned 1

Master i/c: E. D. Fursdon — Cricket professional: E. Steele

Batting—*H. Morris 15–7–1,032–129*–129.00; R. J. Taverner 12–5–311–73*–44.42; P. S. Selley 12–1–463–100*–42.09; R. B. Hughes 16–2–279–67–19.92; M. C. Coe 14–2–111–30–9.25.

Bowling—H. Morris 152.5–40–439–25–17.56; M. C. Coe 129.2–32–386–20–19.30; H. B. Day 152.2–26–452–23–19.65; A. Morris 170.3–45–417–20–20.85; R. J. Taverner 113.4–19–458–15–30.53.

BRADFIELD COLLEGE

Played 15: Won 3, Lost 3, Drawn 9. Abandoned 1

Master i/c: R. A. Brookes Cricket professional: J. F. Harvey

Batting—*M. J. Gent 15–0–529–114–35.26; R. S. C. Blumire 15–1–302–56–21.57; M. P. Silcock 14–1–263–55*–20.23; M. E. Wills 15–2–258–54–19.84; A. J. Johnston 14–2–230–46–19.16; M. J. Taylor 14–2–219–84*–18.25.

Bowling—A. J. Johnston 262.3–69–599–44–13.61; J. R. E. Ricketts 181.4–44–440–27–16.29; M. J. Gent 121–42–276–14–19.71.

BRADFORD GRAMMAR SCHOOL

Played 22: Won 7, Lost 8, Drawn 7. Abandoned 3

Master i/c: A. G. Smith

Batting—S. T. Firth 22–3–474–73–24.94; R. A. Scott 14–2–244–66–20.33; J. B. Gray 19–0–378–72–19.89; C. J. Hewitt 22–2–394–64*–19.70; A. M. Broadbent 14–3–201–58–18.27; G. M. Bentley 18–5–232–59*–17.84; C. E. Nichols 20–2–271–51–15.05; R. D. Nerurkar 8–0–111–33–13.87; *R. J. Basham 18–3–154–35–10.26.

Bowling—T. Welsh 243.2–60–686–45–15.24; A. M. Broadbent 196–47–601–34–17.67; R. A. Scott 54.2–7–235–12–19.58; C. J. Hewitt 166–32–579–20–28.95; T. R. Adams 92–10–453–15–30.20.

BRENTWOOD SCHOOL

Played 18: Won 3, Lost 11, Drawn 4. Abandoned 1

Master i/c: A. Guyver Cricket professional: K. Preston

Batting—S. Moore 18–8–262–35*–26.20; P. Preston 19–1–363–69*–20.16; P. Lindley 13–0–252–66–19.38; M. Wedge 9–0–172–56–19.11; P. Smaje 18–2–305–55*–19.06; R. Loughland 16–0–272–61–17.00; *W. Gear 17–0–287–39–16.88; P. Grief 9–0–106–32–11.77; T. Pryke 11–1–113–42–11.30; D. Pauffley 15–2–117–29–9.00.

Bowling—S. C. Smith 111.4–23–354–23–15.39; D. Pauffley 194.2–49–515–27–19.07; J. Dykes 131–30–405–13–31.15; P. Smaje 93–25–322–10–32.20; S. Moore 108.3–14–423–12–35.25.

BRIGHTON COLLEGE

Played 16: Won 12, Lost 1, Drawn 3. Abandoned 1

Master i/c: J. Spencer

Batting—N. J. Lenham 16–2–1,076–112–76.85; *S. C. B. Withers 15–2–403–85*–31.00; J. Appleton 9–5–101–25*–25.25; M. G. Simmonds 13–4–191–35–21.22; D. G. Shaw 14–1–266–81*–20.46; K. M. Harrison 15–2–247–65*–19.00; M. A. Bewick 11–5–114–37*–19.00.

Bowling—J. A. Gorton 248.1–68–569–49–11.61; N. J. Lenham 231–62–607–34–17.85; M. A. Bewick 110.3–30–269–15–17.93; D. J. O'Hara 126–32–394–19–20.73.

BRISTOL GRAMMAR SCHOOL

Played 15: Won 4, Lost 6, Drawn 5

Master i/c: A. J. Booth

Batting—D. J. Woolley 15–2–672–117*–51.69; T. M. Evans 9–1–140–28–17.50; D. J. Tanner 12–2–141–47–14.10; C. Nicholson 11–1–135–30*–13.50; A. M. C. Feltham 14–0–188–50–13.42; M. D. Gray 13–0–163–45–12.53.

Bowling—D. J. Tanner 99.4–20–304–19–16.00; R. P. Yelland 128.2–32–358–19–18.84; J. G. Beale 138–39–467–23–20.30.

BROMSGROVE SCHOOL

Played 14: Won 1, Lost 3, Drawn 10. Abandoned 1

Master i/c: P. R. Sawtell

Batting—D. M. Meredith 13–2–340–84*–30.90; C. E. Rostrup 13–6–176–32*–25.14; A. J. Morgan 13–0–279–79–21.46; M. R. Dudley 13–2–202–51–18.36; M. R. Thomas 11–1–141–29–14.10; C. E. Sellers 12–0–136–42–11.33.

Bowling—*S. W. Williams 186.2–41–617–39–15.82; C. E. Rostrup 78.4–18–259–14–18.50; J. D. Hart 129.1–28–459–23–19.95.

BRYANSTON SCHOOL

Played 13: Won 5, Lost 2, Drawn 6. Abandoned 1

Master i/c: M. C. Wagstaffe

Batting—*M. Guymer 13–2–435–70–39.54; G. Binns 13–0–434–81–33.38; R. Stanbrook 13–5–249–50–31.12; P. Partridge 13–1–259–91*–21.58.

Bowling—P. Partridge 103–20–317–30–10.56; P. Sprague 119.5–29–388–22–17.63; J. Quinn 136–28–350–18–19.44; G. Locke 96.3–23–308–14–22.00; N. Davis 63.2–11–239–10–23.90.

CANFORD SCHOOL

Played 14: Won 6, Lost 5, Drawn 3

Master i/c: H. A. Jarvis — Cricket professional: D. Shackleton

Batting—*M. D. Smith 14–0–749–123–53.50; J. A. Norris 14–2–344–81*–28.66; D. Barker 14–1–261–51–20.07; J. R. Doble 10–1–105–35–11.66; D. J. S. Page 14–0–135–26–9.64.

Bowling—A. J. Paddock 145.3–35–402–24–16.75; P. G. Edwards 152.3–33–493–28–17.60; D. G. le Sueur 109.2–13–350–18–19.44; D. Barker 106.3–20–380–15–25.33.

CHARTERHOUSE

Played 21: Won 4, Lost 4, Drawn 13. Abandoned 1

Master i/c: M. F. D. Lloyd — Cricket professional: R. V. Lewis

Batting—C. A. Anderson 23–2–819–104–39.00; D. M. Bennett 19–1–615–91–34.16; P. R. Durnford 21–3–479–74–26.61; *S. H. O'Brien 22–3–423–54–22.26; J. W. Gard 15–5–173–38–17.30; A. J. Challen 10–0–154–61–15.40; J. C. Davis 20–4–240–39–15.00; T. J. Stilwell 13–1–162–40–13.50; P. D. Newman 17–2–197–38–13.13.

Bowling—P. D. Newman 275.3–70–693–46–15.06; N. T. Kingston 130–42–383–19–20.15; R. J. Rogers 284.3–83–846–41–20.63; J. C. Davis 83–20–270–10–27.00; J. D. Reid 202–46–565–19–29.73.

CHELTENHAM COLLEGE

Played 14: Won 7, Lost 1, Drawn 6. Abandoned 4

Master i/c: R. D. Knight Cricket professional: G. A. Edrich

Batting—E. A. H. P. Rowland 14–3–607–121*–55.18; C. J. Edwards 9–2–234–58*–33.42; R. P. W. Thompson 14–1–425–107*–32.69; S. P. E. Churchfield 8–4–116–42*–29.00; H. D. E. Evans 14–2–326–78*–27.16; A. J. Brettell 6–2–108–42–27.00; P. N. Richardson 10–1–157–60–17.44.

Bowling—B. D. J. Kent 145.3–52–342–26–13.15; *P. C. D. Sykes 167.3–33–543–25–21.72; R. P. W. Thompson 145.3–38–648–27–24.00; P. G. Gent 63–16–245–10–24.50; P. D. Richardson 95.1–36–324–13–24.92.

CHIGWELL SCHOOL

Played 11: Won 4, Lost 3, Drawn 4. Abandoned 2

Master i/c: D. N. Morrison

Batting—J. M. W. Yates 11–1–459–86–45.90; *D. A. Leiper 11–0–348–75–31.63; J. R. Maskey 9–2–132–39–18.85; J. P. Amos 9–2–122–29–17.42; I. M. Zilesnick 9–3–102–21–17.00; D. E. Rogers 11–1–137–27–13.70; R. C. Noble 9–0–103–33–11.44.

Bowling—M. Beaver 59–15–161–14–11.50; J. M. W. Yates 214.4–56–483–38–12.71; D. A. Leiper 126.4–37–333–17–19.58.

CHRIST COLLEGE, BRECON

Played 18: Won 9, Lost 4, Drawn 5

Master i/c: C. W. Kleiser

Batting—*S. W. Harvey 16–3–520–102*–40.00; G. E. R. Jones 14–4–256–67*–25.60; K. Noble 12–4–123–23*–15.37; P. S. Burgess 17–2–227–64*–15.13; A. B. Evans 16–2–202–62–14.42; A. P. Johnson 14–0–190–45–13.57.

Bowling—J. W. Lewis 56.5–12–103–17–6.05; S. W. Harvey 145–56–312–23–13.56; J. W. Thomas 127.5–37–324–22–14.72; P. D. Thomas 163.2–40–446–27–16.51; K. Noble 43.4–9–171–10–17.10; N. P. Gibson 128–25–432–21–20.57.

CHRIST'S HOSPITAL

Played 14: Won 3, Lost 9, Drawn 2

Master i/c: G. M. Baldwin

Batting—B. A. F. James 15–0–373–48–24.86; *T. A. P. Godfrey 16–0–300–57–18.75; P. J. Goodwin 15–2–235–55–18.07; S. C. Wilson 16–0–236–28–14.75; J. D. Brown 16–8–104–28–13.00; P. N. Castledine 15–1–166–36–11.85; J. O. J. Bennett 12–1–113–40–10.27; T. I. Chrishop 14–1–126–39–9.69.

Bowling—J. O. J. Bennett 68–15–203–16–12.68; K. M. Cook 62.1–13–224–13–17.23; M. R. Joyner 95.1–24–311–17–18.29; T. I. Chrishop 221.2–48–635–30–21.16; P. J. Goodwin 141.3–22–473–19–24.89.

CITY OF LONDON SCHOOL

Played 14: Won 1, Lost 8, Drawn 5. Abandoned 1

Master i/c: L. M. Smith Cricket professional: L. M. Smith

Batting—W. M. Tebbit 9–0–151–57–16.77; I. Rodin 12–2–150–52*–15.00; *D. L. Berger 10–0–129–60–12.90; J. H. Whiteson 13–3–124–34–12.40; J. S. Statham 14–0–161–46–11.50.

Bowling—J. H. Whiteson 124–30–349–17–20.52; W. M. Tebbit 107.1–25–363–13–27.92; G. A. Townson 127.1–23–465–14–33.21.

CLIFTON COLLEGE

Played 16: Won 3, Lost 7, Drawn 6. Abandoned 3

Master i/c: D. C. Henderson Cricket professional: F. J. Andrew

Batting—*C. W. V. Robins 16–0–618–158–38.62; C. T. J. Manners 10–4–137–42*–22.83; D. R. Brown 15–1–290–62–20.71; J. A. Connick 17–2–285–39–19.00; J. S. Matthews 16–0–290–63–18.12; S. C. Hazlitt 12–3–158–35*–17.55; J. A. S. Crawford 15–1–237–51–16.92; J. C. de L. Wright 17–1–253–61–15.81; C. J. Downing 10–1–139–41*–15.44.

Bowling—C. W. V. Robins 252–77–648–42–15.42; J. C. de L. Wright 213–51–556–30–18.53; S. C. Hazlitt 86–8–345–16–21.56; D. R. Brown 109–21–387–13–29.76.

COLFE'S SCHOOL

Played 19: Won 5, Lost 4, Drawn 10

Batting—G. Tomkins 17–2–410–89–27.33; A. Byers 17–0–432–105–25.41; A. Saleemi 13–3–229–51*–22.90; *A. Rodgers 17–5–242–64*–20.16; K. Weir 17–0–228–60–13.41; T. Bloomfield 13–2–135–33–12.27; N. Bryan 14–1–113–29–8.69.

Bowling—D. Beszant 127–36–302–29–10.41; A. Rodgers 263–87–635–49–12.95; M. Davies 27–0–147–10–14.70; A. Byers 93–15–303–17–17.82.

COLSTON'S SCHOOL

Played 17: Won 7, Lost 3, Drawn 7. Abandoned 2

Master i/c: M. P. B. Tayler Cricket professional: R. A. Sinfield

Batting—L. M. Roll–17–6–757–101*–68.81; W. M. Smith 17–2–750–105*–50.00; *N. H. Parnell 14–2–566–114–47.16; S. R. Thomas 11–7–132–35*–33.00; D. C. Kettlewell 13–2–244–66*–22.18.

Bowling—I. Coles 47.3–3–194–11–17.63; R. Lawrence 93.4–10–415–22–18.86; N. H. Parnell 132.1–16–567–27–21.00; S. Luxton 115.3–16–451–18–25.05; L. M. Roll 183.5–33–684–26–26.30.

CRANBROOK SCHOOL

Played 14: Won 0, Lost 9, Drawn 5. Abandoned 1

Masters i/c: T. Gunn and J. Furminger

Batting—S. Shaw 5–0–134–64–26.80; A. Ward 14–2–206–63*;–17.16; *A. Mullins 14–0–214–59–15.28; H. Youngman 14–0–191–59–13.64; J. Gurney 14–0–178–72–12.71; D. Patten 13–0–152–36–11.69; J. Brown 14–1–126–37–9.69.

Bowling—A. Ward 179–38–544–33–16.48; C. Coleman 206.5–47–643–35–18.37; C. Brotherton 103–26–319–14–22.78.

CULFORD SCHOOL

Played 14: Won 7, Lost 2, Drawn 5. Abandoned 2

Batting—*R. Guy 16–4–467–100*–38.91; P. Rackham 15–5–312–104–31.20; K. Spencer 15–2–350–66–26.92; P. Hazell 12–0–178–51–14.83; A. Dahl 16–1–218–49–14.53; D. Carey 10–2–108–46*–13.50.

Bowling—K. Spencer 92.3–22–252–19–13.26; P. Hazell 108–22–332–19–17.47; C. Williams 158.4–43–435–24–18.12.

DAUNTSEY'S SCHOOL

Played 13: Won 3, Lost 3, Drawn 7. Abandoned 2

Master i/c: M. K. F. Johnson Cricket professional: P. Hough

Batting—I. Hassall 6–3–117–60*–39.00; R. L. Baker 13–2–294–86*–26.72; *J. D. Livingstone 13–1–272–55–22.66; P. R. Holford 10–2–138–58–17.25.

Bowling—D. C. Masters 94.5–17–315–17–18.52; P. R. Holford 159–20–588–24–24.50.

DEAN CLOSE SCHOOL

Played 15: Won 2, Lost 5, Drawn 8. Abandoned 1

Master i/c: C. M. Kenyon Cricket professional: V. A. Holder

Batting—P. M. Vincent 13–2–380–105*–34.54; *M. P. A. Crawshaw 15–2–419–129–32.23; D. J. H. Leng 11–0–195–41–17.72; N. Butt 7–0–101–29–14.42; H. M. Davies-Thomas 13–0–144–63–11.07; C. R. Torrens 11–0–107–26–9.72.

Bowling—R. N. K. O. A. Lindsay 117–26–265–15–17.66; P. M. Vincent 122.3–24–398–19–20.94; O. J. Barkes 95–11–376–16–23.50; J. F. Eveleigh 102–24–344–10–34.40.

DENSTONE COLLEGE

Played 18: Won 5, Lost 2, Drawn 11. Abandoned 4

Master i/c: D. J. Dexter Cricket professional: H. J. Rhodes

Batting—M. N. Aris 15–2–583–110–44.84; S. A. Roy 13–3–383–98*–38.30; A. J. Little 14–3–230–66–20.90; C. M. Ireland 14–2–207–60*–17.25; M. R. Bollard 11–0–124–42–11.27.

Bowling—A. J. Little 253.2–72–598–43–13.90; *J. P. D. Cadman 170.4–45–469–25–18.76; M. N. Aris 212–61–497–25–19.88.

DOVER COLLEGE

Played 17: Won 3, Lost 8, Drawn 6. Abandoned 3

Master i/c: R. S. Quinton-Jones Cricket professional: A. H. Drake

Batting—*J. Corbett 14–3–251–36*–22.81; B. Slater 16–3–292–75*–22.46; J. Tatt 15–2–263–67–20.23.

Bowling—D. Carrion 183–58–392–31–12.64; A. Iliasu 209–60–543–28–19.39; N. Coupland 92–19–284–12–23.66; J. Tatt 94–10–410–12–34.16.

DOWNSIDE SCHOOL

Played 11: Won 0, Lost 7, Drawn 4. Abandoned 1

Master i/c: D. Baty

Batting—*P. A. N. Dougall 11–1–233–66*–23.30; A. G. M. Wates 6–1–112–30–22.40; N. R. J. Mackenzie 11–0–226–72–20.54; C. D. Chignell 9–1–127–43*–15.87; A. P. Smerdon 11–2–125–34–13.88; S. C. Vyvyan 11–0–146–35–13.27.

Bowling—M. J. Smith 120.1–22–477–11–43.36.

DURHAM SCHOOL

Played 18: Won 10, Lost 1, Drawn 7

Master i/c: W. J. R. Allen Cricket professional: M. Hirsch

Batting—M. A. Roseberry 16–3–839–137*–64.53; *N. P. Tubbs 14–4–391–63–39.10; C. R. Mayes 17–2–402–81–26.80; J. Foley 13–3–223–61*–22.30; B. M. Hume 16–5–227–44–20.63; G. D. Dawson 12–1–205–61–18.63; J. M. Alderson 12–4–116–33–14.50.

Bowling—M. A. Roseberry 183.1–68–432–38–11.36; N. P. Tubbs 213–81–474–30–15.80; A. G. Hay 132–34–347–16–21.68; J. M. Alderson 194.2–73–409–18–22.72; B. M. Hume 195.4–52–538–23–23.39.

EASTBOURNE COLLEGE

Played 19: Won 8, Lost 4, Drawn 7

Master i/c: C. F. A. T. Halliday Cricket professional: A. E. James

Batting—J. R. Prentis 18–0–580–87–32.22; T. G. Bevan-Thomas 18–2–489–86–30.56; M. O. Simpson 18–2–455–101*–28.43; M. H. Edwardes-Evans 18–0–408–82–22.66; S. M. Wheeler 16–2–269–51–19.21; *S. K. Kiley-Worthington 16–4–183–51*–15.25; J. C. Wallace 17–7–139–20–13.90; D. J. W. Lush 13–2–117–25–10.63.

Bowling—J. R. Prentis 282.3–75–781–43–18.16; J. C. Wallace 163.3–50–411–22–18.68; S. R. Davis 251.2–56–851–35–24.31.

THE EDINBURGH ACADEMY

Played 16: Won 5, Lost 5, Drawn 6

Master i/c: A. R. Dyer

Batting—G. R. Mawdsley 18–2–571–83*–35.68; *I. D. Zuill 18–3–446–104–29.73; J. F. Richardson 16–3–343–71–26.38; R. A. Mawdsley 18–1–367–53–21.58; J. D. Kudianavala 12–4–131–28–16.37; A. L. Paton 15–3–186–34–15.50; A. F. Gunn 12–0–151–42–12.58; J. McFlynn 13–1–121–34–10.08.

Bowling—B. J. M. Clube 319.3–73–909–52–17.48; R. J. A. Coleman 167–45–409–20–20.45; G. R. Mawdsley 228.1–52–620–27–22.96; J. D. Kudianavala 153–44–384–15–25.60.

ELLESMERE COLLEGE

Played 17: Won 5, Lost 1, Drawn 11. Abandoned 1

Master i/c: R. K. Sethi

Batting—R. T. Millinchip 15–5–307–103*–30.70; T. J. R. Petty 17–2–453–80*–30.20; D. M. P. Maisey 15–9–180–51–30.00; G. L. Home 17–3–404–75*–28.85; *A. I. Crow 16–2–286–60*–20.42; J. P. P. Maisey 17–1–260–70*–16.25.

Bowling—G. L. Home 100–27–292–20–14.60; D. M. P. Maisey 127–37–330–22–15.00; T. J. R. Petty 128.3–29–364–17–21.41; D. V. Millward-Hopkins 148.5–26–433–20–21.65; M. N. G. Stubbs 120–11–521–20–26.05.

ELIZABETH COLLEGE, GUERNSEY

Played 14: Won 1, Lost 5, Drawn 8

Master i/c: A. Croft

Batting—*D. J. Mechem 14–2–415–52–34.58; C. D. Waldron 13–1–366–61–30.50; G. Mellor 14–0–262–52–18.71; B. A. Mauger 14–1–220–60–16.92; A. Tapp 12–0–175–84–14.58.

Bowling—N. M. Mechem 67.3–19–174–15–11.60; S. Blake 66.1–11–161–10–16.10; B. A. Mauger 108.4–26–352–17–20.70; J. Mattinson 118.5–28–421–18–23.38; D. J. Mechem 157.5–37–457–18–25.38; A. Tapp 135–12–527–12–43.91.

ELTHAM COLLEGE

Played 25: Won 17, Lost 2, Drawn 6. Abandoned 2

Master i/c: P. C. McCartney and B. M. Withecombe

Batting—*M. R. Surguy 23–9–1,159–119*–82.78; M. J. Holcombe 22–4–1,039–155*–57.72; B. A. Holcombe 17–6–287–59*–26.09; I. Whalley 16–6–211–50*–21.10; M. G. Pratt 13–6–132–47*–18.85; J. R. S. Brown 7–0–116–43–16.57; T. Haden-Scott 11–3–111–37–13.87; A. Baidya 17–6–133–27–12.09; N. S. Williams 11–0–116–33–10.54; W. H. Wright 13–1–126–39–10.50.

Bowling—N. S. Williams 73.5–15–194–17–11.41; M. G. Pratt 141.3–28–433–33–13.12; M. R. Surguy 216.4–79–403–30–13.43; B. A. Holcombe 169–48–370–25–14.80; M. J. Holcombe 232.5–60–608–41–14.82; T. Haden-Scott 124.3–37–272–15–18.13.

EMANUEL SCHOOL

Played 28: Won 12, Lost 9, Drawn 7. Abandoned 2

Master i/c: M. J. Stewart

Batting—*D. I. K. Blyth 27–3–711–119*–29.62; I. M. Carrick 25–3–536–72–24.36; A. J. Flind 7–0–153–86–21.85; S. Sharma 25–0–513–72–20.52; F. Ahmed 24–1–382–92–16.60; A. J. Hope 15–6–133–36*–14.77; G. G. DiLullo 18–3–198–25*–13.20; G. P. Piddington 16–4–149–38–12.41; S. J. Park 21–3–153–29–8.50; R. D. Hinkson 21–3–136–19–7.55; P. T. Williams 21–5–108–14–6.75.

Bowling—A. J. Hope 101–20–316–27–11.70; P. T. Williams 103.3–19–438–34–12.88; G. P. Piddington 149.1–31–456–32–14.25; T. J. Harmer 53–9–185–12–15.41; W. C. Passanisi 80–19–288–16–18.00; D. I. K. Blyth 160.2–34–486–24–20.25; I. M. Carrick 240–53–691–33–20.93; F. Ahmed 113–33–262–12–21.83.

ENFIELD GRAMMAR SCHOOL

Played 19: Won 8, Lost 4, Drawn 7. Abandoned 2

Master i/c: J. J. Conroy

Batting—G. Allen 15–2–454–86–34.92; *B. Conway 16–4–408–76*–34.00; R. Carter 5–1–131–62–32.75; N. Jackett 12–2–173–38–17.30; A. Gibbens 14–1–207–59–15.92; G. Jardine 12–0–177–64–14.75.

Bowling—R. Carter 64–22–167–18–9.27; T. Phocou 40.5–8–124–13–9.53; R. Low 141.3–43–290–26–11.15; S. Humphries 199.5–64–462–30–15.40; N. Jackett 155–26–489–17–28.76.

EPSOM COLLEGE

Played 18: Won 10, Lost 2, Drawn 6

Master i/c: J. T. J. Houlson

Batting—*R. M. C. Williams 19–5–1,013–131–72.35; J. R. Ansell 14–0–626–124–44.71; R. V. Williams 17–2–415–121*–27.66; P. R. Hedge 14–2–328–51*–27.33; M. B. Finnigan 16–5–296–72–26.90; C. D. R. Hartigan 11–2–124–34–13.77; M. J. Morris 15–4–135–22–12.27.

Bowling—M. J. Morris 240–56–645–38–16.97; D. G. Henwood 147–32–506–24–21.08; D. A. Harris 85–15–324–11–29.45; J. N. Barnado 117–17–473–15–31.53; R. M. C. Williams 99–16–418–13–32.15; C. D. R. Hartigan 129–28–482–14–34.42.

ETON COLLEGE

Played 15: Won 8, Lost 0, Drawn 7. Abandoned 1

Master i/c: P. R. Thackeray Cricket professional: V. H. D. Cannings

Batting—M. V. Fleming 17–3–648–90–46.28; *C. A. Watt 8–4–149–42–37.25; J. P. Berry 15–5–339–54–33.90; M. H. Brooks 16–3–325–71*–25.00; W. A. B. Russell 9–4–110–23–22.00.

Bowling—M. V. Fleming 282.5–130–490–36–13.61; C. E. Pettifer 134.4–36–318–20–15.90; J. W. M. Barlow 85–24–229–14–16.35; C. A. Watt 202.1–46–597–33–18.09; Hon. E. Brassey 179–47–443–20–22.15.

EXETER SCHOOL

Played 10: Won 5, Lost 2, Drawn 3. Abandoned 3

Master i/c: T. J. Dewes

Batting—*P. Hodgson 10–2–397–79*–49.62; D. Cox 10–1–221–50–24.55; T. Nash 9–0–219–56–24.33; R. Hudson 9–2–136–38*–19.42.

Bowling—P. Clarke 84.1–19–284–18–15.77; I. Hayter 91–29–245–14–17.50; R. Hudson 61.2–13–215–12–17.91.

FELSTED SCHOOL

Played 15: Won 10, Lost 1, Drawn 4

Master i/c: T. P. Woods Cricket professional: G. O. Barker

Batting—J. P. Stephenson 15–4–873–131–79.36; A. B. Mitchell 15–2–570–82–43.84; M. W. C. Olley 12–3–316–67–35.11; E. C. Dodson 12–4–260–44–32.50; P. M. Rigby 9–2–156–71–22.28.

Bowling—J. P. Stephenson 127.1–42–322–24–13.41; *B. H. Pinkerton 269.4–84–624–46–13.56; A. J. Haynes 167.2–46–527–31–17.00; G. A. Lambert 173–34–550–16–34.37.

FETTES COLLEGE

Played 12: Won 4, Lost 3, Drawn 5

Master i/c: J. G. Begg

Batting—*G. F. Barnet 13–1–405–72–33.75; C. W. D. Scott 13–0–356–71–27.38; D. F. M. Stewart 12–2–233–64*–23.30; A. J. M. Gilfillan 13–1–249–66–20.75; C. J. Barker 10–1–148–37–16.44; N. I. S. Jones 12–0–133–35–11.08; N. M. Ferguson 12–2–110–27*–11.00.

Bowling—R. N. Cheape 98–19–318–21–15.14; C. J. Barker 124.1–30–396–22–18.00; I. C. S. Ramsay 117.5–28–348–17–20.47.

FOREST SCHOOL

Played 16: Won 9, Lost 3, Drawn 4. Abandoned 2

Master i/c: M. Surridge Cricket professional: W. B. Morris

Batting—M. D. I. Sheppard 14–2–501–101*–41.75; R. J. Harnack 13–2–384–69*–34.90; *I. Crossley 14–3–373–75*–33.90; B. S. Watts 10–7–101–49*–33.66; A. Hussain 15–3–385–65–32.08; C. M. Elliott 14–1–391–77–30.07; A. C. Cundy 12–2–208–47–20.80.

Bowling—N. Hussain 180–47–448–32–14.00; S. Shivalkar 113–28–335–20–16.75; C. M. Elliott 65–11–251–14–17.92; M. Phillips 84–18–233–12–19.41; I. Crossley 157–33–490–25–19.60.

FRAMLINGHAM COLLEGE

Played 18: Won 6, Lost 6, Drawn 6. Abandoned 2

Master i/c: S. A. Westley Cricket professional: C. Rutterford

Batting—N. C. J. Holmes 17–0–416–78–24.47; M. R. Brearey 12–4–168–43–21.00; J. R. Gubbins 13–4–186–29–20.66; T. J. Mayhew 18–0–370–47–20.55; A. C. Pulham 16–3–267–77*–20.53; *C. G. S. Pattinson 16–4–227–54–18.91; J. L. Arthur 12–0–204–56–17.00; A. J. Phillips 10–1–146–53*–16.22; D. A. Rimmer 14–0–192–35–13.71.

Bowling—P. M. Hunter 256.5–63–551–34–16.20; C. G. S. Pattinson 239–52–644–39–16.51; N. C. J. Holmes 165.5–41–501–23–21.78; J. R. Gubbins 126.5–27–395–18–21.94.

GIGGLESWICK SCHOOL

Played 13: Won 4, Lost 3, Drawn 6. Abandoned 3

Master i/c: J. Mayall Cricket professional: I. W. Callen

Batting—R. M. White 12–1–371–131*–33.72; *J. B. Newsome 13–2–369–59–33.54; N. C. Westhead 13–1–151–42–12.58; M. J. Nuttall 13–0–125–23–9.61.

Bowling—J. B. Newsome 142.2–37–353–27–13.07; N. C. Westhead 58.2–3–230–16–14.37; B. L. Baldwin 94.4–19–253–14–18.07; C. A. Chapman 156–24–463–24–19.29.

GLENALMOND

Played 15: Won 8, Lost 3, Drawn 4. Abandoned 1

Master i/c: Alwyn James Cricket professional: W. J. Dennis

Batting—*J. Everett 14–2–633–112–52.75; J. Sutton 15–1–417–75–29.78; C. B. G. Watson 13–1–313–65–26.08; S. J. Lewis 15–0–329–57–21.93; M. H. Alexander 11–4–133–27–19.00; E. M. T. Crichton 13–0–123–52–9.46.

Bowling—S. J. Lewis 100.2–13–345–23–15.00; J. M. MacLean 164.3–40–461–29–15.89; J. F. Alexander 159–36–397–21–18.90; M. H. Alexander 115.2–16–408–16–25.50; C. B. G. Watson 73–15–263–10–26.30.

GORDONSTOUN SCHOOL

Played 13: Won 7, Lost 4, Drawn 2

Master i/c: P. S. Larkman

Batting—*R. P. J. Heyes 11–1–345–106*–34.50; R. L. W. Alexander 10–2–143–52*–17.87; M. B. Johnston 10–0–139–30–13.90; M. S. Halbert 11–1–109–27–10.90.

Bowling—R. P. J. Heyes 52.5–13–142–17–8.35; C. R. Mason 66–18–161–19–8.47; K. M. Mordue 55.3–5–247–26–9.50.

THE HABERDASHERS' ASKE'S SCHOOL, ELSTREE

Played 16: Won 9, Lost 1, Drawn 6. Abandoned 4

Master i/c: D. I. Yeabsley

Batting—D. J. Price 12–3–404–77*–44.88; N. J. Churchman 13–4–357–79*–39.66; *N. J. Wood 16–1–523–89–34.86; A. J. Moulding 15–5–342–56–34.20; E. Addy 11–4–198–37–28.28; D. G. Price 12–2–268–57*–26.80.

Bowling—A. J. Moulding 133.1–38–374–33–11.33; D. G. Price 82–22–236–14–16.85; R. A. Pitt 150.3–34–448–26–17.23; A. Dawtrey 150.4–47–368–21–17.52; N. J. Churchman 105–19–302–11–27.45.

HAILEYBURY COLLEGE

Played 16: Won 5, Lost 4, Drawn 7. Abandoned 3

Master i/c: M. S. Seymour Cricket professional: P. M. Ellis

Batting—*J. E. Harding 17–1–506–76–31.62: M. J. Churchill 15–1–387–70*; 27.64; I. C. West 13–2–277–78–25.18; S. L. Feast 13–3–205–45–20.50; R. J. O. Graham 17–3–254–53*–18.14; D. M. Sawney 11–0–189–53–17.18.

Bowling—T. P. Jackson-Feilden 218–37–615–48–12.81; J. W. S. Meacock 131–27–274–14–19.57; J. E. Harding 214–51–554–26–21.30; J. R. Jackman 153–29–438–14–31.28.

HAMPTON SCHOOL

Played 21: Won 9, Lost 3, Drawn 9

Master i/c: G. R. Cocksworth

Batting—T. R. Eastaugh 12–3–334–99*–37.11; *E. M. Turnill 18–2–537–103*–33.56; S. A. Bishop 14–3–345–70*–31.36; C. Hind 15–2–325–61*–25.00; P. Burnham 12–1–243–63–22.09; S. Edwards 14–2–197–42–16.41; G. J. Collins 11–1–134–29–13.40; M. Turner 16–0–136–26–8.50.

Bowling—J. Shepherd 127.1–31–342–24–14.25; T. R. Eastaugh 159.2–29–513–29–17.68; C. Hind 78–28–242–12–20.16; P. Johnstone 123.5–20–382–18–21.22; G. M. W. Stacey 111–19–310–13–23.84; G. J. Collins 144.4–40–397–12–33.08.

HARROW SCHOOL

Played 14: Won 2, Lost 0, Drawn 12. Abandoned 2

Master i/c: G. M. Attenborough — Cricket professional: P. Davis

Batting—J. M. H. Ford 13–3–433–89–43.30; W. A. Menpes-Smith 9–3–229–58–38.16; J. W. S. Raper 14–2–443–101*–36.91; N. F. M. Hay 10–2–192–55–24.00; J. D. R. Field 11–4–155–31–22.14; *J. F. Turner 13–1–234–35–19.50.

Bowling—P. R. G. Murray 227–50–600–38–15.78; J. W. S. Raper 129–28–311–19–16.36; D. St J. B. Beard 219–74–467–27–17.29; N. F. M. Hay 85–23–240–11–21.81.

HEREFORD CATHEDRAL SCHOOL

Played 8: Won 2, Lost 3, Drawn 3. Abandoned 2

Master i/c: M. V. Howlett

Batting—J. Ferguson 6–0–129–34–21.50; S. Makin 7–1–102–33–17.00.

Bowling—D. Phillips 56.3–12–181–17–10.64; N. Startin 32–8–107–10–10.70.

HIGHGATE SCHOOL

Played 15: Won 2, Lost 6, Drawn 7

Master i/c: R. W. Halstead

Batting—N. Rathbone 9–6–119–30–39.66; *K. E. Kenny 13–0–432–61–33.23; T. K. Crick 13–0–255–63–19.61; A. Walton 12–0–203–41–16.91; A. Ferrari 13–1–193–87*–16.08; N. J. Banks 10–1–127–42*–14.11; A. C. Fawden 13–1–163–40–13.58.

Bowling—A. C. Fawden 192–38–500–28–17.85; K. E. Kenny 163–24–503–22–22.86.

HIPPERHOLME GRAMMAR SCHOOL

Played 18: Won 7, Lost 4, Drawn 7. Abandoned 1

Master i/c: J. M. Edwards

Batting—D. F. Rayner 18–4–491–71*–35.07; K. D. Booth 18–3–310–66–20.66; C. A. Thompson 14–2–248–46–20.66; *R. S. Butterworth 17–1–327–75*–20.43; E. J. Armitage 15–5–162–30–16.20; *J. B. Lunn 16–0–154–40–9.62.

Bowling—R. S. Butterworth 63.3–19–174–15–11.60; J. R. N. Broster 186.1–55–469–28–16.75; R. E. Shaw 106.2–21–376–22–17.09; M. J. Hopwood 129–25–388–20–19.40; P. Deegan 182–48–496–23–21.56.

HURSTPIERPOINT COLLEGE

Played 15: Won 3, Lost 5, Drawn 7. Abandoned 1

Master i/c: M. E. Allbrook Cricket professional: D. J. Semmence

Batting—M. D. Foulds 14–5–418–115*–46.44; J. B. Buckeridge 15–5–380–73–38.00; J. P. Graham 7–1–149–64–24.83; *T. J. Thorne 11–2–192–45–21.33; A. J. L. Sawers 15–1–262–58–18.71; A. P. Subba Row 10–1–152–53–16.88; J. P. Terry 8–1–100–31–14.28.

Bowling—G. J. Alexander 152.5–19–571–32–17.84; J. R. C. Lamb 59.3–9–246–13–18.92; S. R. Taubman 105.2–19–353–15–23.53; D. A. Procter 77–10–322–10–32.20.

IPSWICH SCHOOL

Played 13: Won 2, Lost 7, Drawn 4

Master i/c: P. M. Rees

Batting—J. Nicholls 12–4–257–74*–32.12; T. Rollett 12–1–351–108*–31.90; E. Downie 12–0–317–78–26.41; B. Caley 11–3–170–48–21.25; *M. Prior 9–3–107–30–17.83.

Bowling—M. Prior 49.1–9–197–10–19.70; M. Mitson 80.1–17–216–10–21.60; J. Nicholls 161.4–33–523–23–22.73; S. Priscott 204.2–42–581–25–23.24.

KIMBOLTON SCHOOL

Played 15: Won 3, Lost 6, Drawn 6. Abandoned 1

Master i/c: I. J. Burton Cricket professional: J. W. Hart

Batting—S. A. Sharpe 15–3–441–77*–36.75; R. A. Johnson 15–2–249–53*–19.15; B. B. G. D. Aylott 15–1–243–58–17.35; S. L. Simpson 15–1–210–46–15.00; *A. C. Whitman 15–0–208–45–13.86; A. J. Cox 14–0–147–33–10.50.

Bowling—P. A. J. Brittain 62.4–16–161–12–13.41; S. A. Sharpe 186–72–466–29–16.06; S. R. P. Doyle 92.5–24–242–15–16.13; R. A. Johnson 116.4–26–366–16–22.87; C. J. Street 119.3–25–340–11–30.90.

KING EDWARD VI SCHOOL, SOUTHAMPTON

Played 22: Won 8, Lost 3, Drawn 11

Master i/c: M. H. May

Batting—*A. W. Gilbert 17–2–735–100–49.00; M. E. O'Connor 13–2–422–86*–38.36; M. P. Board 14–3–287–65*–26.09; S. P. Arnold 20–1–436–58–22.94; R. M. A. Metcalfe 16–3–227–66–17.46; R. P. Headington 15–3–207–50–17.25; P. A. Watkins 14–3–135–31–12.27; R. T. Minns 15–3–120–31–10.00.

Bowling—J. E. Merrill 138–30–379–31–12.22; S. P. Arnold 86.3–20–273–14–19.50; R. J. Cross 106.3–23–397–20–19.85; S. D. Lambert 130.3–16–581–24–24.20; R. T. Minns 81–12–320–10–32.00.

KING EDWARD VI COLLEGE, STOURBRIDGE

Played 16: Won 6, Lost 1, Drawn 9. Abandoned 4

Master i/c: M. L. Ryan

Batting—D. M. Anderson 13–5–295–63*–36.87; D. J. Bullock 13–7–186–39*–31.00; R. N. Tolley 14–3–307–58*–27.90; D. J. Shorter 13–1–262–45–21.83; J. Hill 13–1–220–68–18.33; P. J. T. Miles 14–0–196–47–14.00.

Bowling—D. J. Shorter 202–62–428–44–9.75; D. J. Bullock 167.2–54–362–34–10.64; M. J. Price 69–16–209–13–16.07; *P. N. Shillingford 139.1–32–358–18–19.88.

KING EDWARD VII SCHOOL, LYTHAM

Played 21: Won 5, Lost 3, Drawn 13. Abandoned 3

Master i/c: J. A. Liggett

Batting—G. Cartmell 21–3–587–107–32.61; A. Thornton 21–2–509–104–26.78; N. D. W. McDonnell 21–3–415–79*–23.05; M. Lees 18–2–283–53*–17.68; G. Banning 16–4–125–26–10.41; T. Williamson 15–1–136–25–9.71.

Bowling—A. Gregson 172.1–49–443–34–13.02; N. D. W. McDonnell 129–22–402–25–16.08; J. Cooper 76.1–21–203–12–16.91; J. Evans 226.5–52–586–34–17.23; G. Cartmell 71.3–16–257–14–18.35.

KING EDWARD'S SCHOOL, BATH

Played 9: Won 2, Lost 1, Drawn 6. Abandoned 1

Master i/c: D. J. Kemp

Batting—N. Cahn 7–3–199–64*–49.75; *N. Walker 9–1–226–53–28.25; P. Beresford 7–0–170–88–24.28; R. Vowles 9–0–170–40–18.88; C. Woods 9–0–134–35–14.88.

Bowling—N. Cahn 51–14–208–18–11.55; J. Brown 75–18–122–10–12.20; M. Lowe 72–12–194–11–17.63; M. Thomas 83–22–241–12–20.08.

KING EDWARD'S SCHOOL, BIRMINGHAM

Played 15: Won 5, Lost 3, Drawn 7. Abandoned 3

Master i/c: D. H. Benson Cricket professional: A. Smith

Batting—M. K. Hughes 16–5–529–71–48.09; C. Ibbetson 16–4–312–51–26.00; N. A. Willetts 14–2–301–116–25.08; J. R. Bishop 16–0–272–57–17.00; N. V. Subhedar 13–5–112–38*–14.00; *S. J. Laugharne 15–0–161–44–10.73.

Bowling—P. W. Nienow 51–16–136–10–13.60; C. Ibbetson 139.1–46–331–21–15.76; M. K. Hughes 143.3–35–380–22–17.27; J. G. Masters 100.5–36–254–13–19.53; D. C. Tyler 123.1–17–449–21–21.38; A. N. Marshall 118.5–28–327–11–29.72.

KING HENRY VIII SCHOOL, COVENTRY

Played 17: Won 3, Lost 5, Drawn 9. Abandoned 4

Master i/c: G. P. C. Courtois

Batting—P. M. Smith 16–2–339–69*–24.21; K. L. Culligan 15–0–322–43–21.46; D. R. Sewell 16–1–255–43–17.00; E. A. Ansari 13–4–144–28–16.00; J. G. Bieszczad 16–1–203–41–13.53; *I. L. Robertson 15–1–175–51–12.50; A. C. Wallbridge 12–1–134–33–12.18.

Bowling—P. C. Williams 39.5–5–145–11–13.18; I. L. Robertson 195.2–69–499–32–15.59; C. J. J. Harrison 196.2–67–486–25–19.44; E. A. Ansari 76.2–14–243–11–22.09.

KING WILLIAM'S COLLEGE, I. of M.

Played 20: Won 3, Lost 4, Drawn 13

Master i/c: A. Q. Bashforth Cricket professional: D. Mark

Batting—S. C. Watson 22–3–857–103*–45.10; N. A. R. Watson 20–3–534–101*–31.41; A. J. A. Turnbull 20–4–372–47–23.25; R. K. Corkill 21–2–398–66–20.94; D. N. J. Turnbull 14–6–150–53*–18.75; N. R. J. Cowley 13–1–159–30*–13.25.

Bowling—R. J. S. Talavera 104–26–274–18–15.22; D. A. J. Butterfield 134.5–43–316–20–15.80; N. A. R. Watson 194.5–41–574–34–16.88; A. J. A. Turnbull 293.1–66–804–31–25.93; *G. L. Russell 157.4–29–550–18–30.55.

KING'S COLLEGE, TAUNTON

Played 15: Won 9, Lost 1, Drawn 5

Master i/c: P. A. Dossett Cricket professional: R. E. Marshall

Batting—*R. J. Harden 16–1–633–92–42.20; N. D. Everest 16–2–412–57–29.42; J. M. A. Cassell 10–4–172–42*–28.66; S. J. Kaye 16–1–311–51–20.73; G. R. N. Drayton 14–3–197–47*–17.90; J. W. M. Bell 14–0–161–58–11.50; G. T. W. Cashell 11–2–103–29–11.44.

Bowling—R. J. Harden 226.1–80–446–48–9.29; A. J. Willson 117.2–35–364–22–16.54; G. R. N. Drayton 68–14–221–12–18.41; J. R. G. Bird 199.5–46–489–26–18.80; J. A. Turner 124–29–376–15–25.06.

KING'S COLLEGE SCHOOL, WIMBLEDON

Played 20: Won 10, Lost 3, Drawn 7. Abandoned 2

Master i/c: A. G. P. Lang Cricket professional: R. A. Dare

Batting—J. H. Frost 18–2–444–91–27.75; R. Alikhan 17–2–363–67–24.20; P. J. Morse 18–2–386–103–24.12; *S. W. J. Silvester 19–1–405–55–22.50; N. P. Montgomery 12–5–132–32–18.85; J. D. Lamb 14–0–253–54–18.07; J. A. Casale 12–4–142–28*–17.75; M. J. Jayarajah 8–1–100–42–14.28; P. S. Noble 13–4–122–33*–13.55.

Bowling—J. D. Lamb 42.1–9–133–10–13.30; N. P. Montgomery 226.4–67–528–38–13.89; P. S. Noble 206.3–56–485–32–15.15; R. Alikhan 100–16–209–13–16.07; S. A. C. Hammer 154–36–429–25–17.16; P. J. Morse 78–24–193–11–17.54; M. Woolnough 129.5–43–304–17–17.88.

KING'S SCHOOL, BRUTON

Played 11: Won 4, Lost 3, Drawn 4. Abandoned 3

Master i/c: A. S. Linney

Batting—I. C. D. Stuart 11–3–433–88–54.12; S. H. Maxwell 9–3–201–84*–33.50; C. E. Budgett 8–3–148–50*–29.60; R. C. Gainher 11–1–288–106*–28.80; S. T. Harvey 11–0–186–49–16.90; C. G. Weir 9–0–124–40–13.77.

Bowling—I. C. D. Stuart 141.1–23–425–25–17.00; J. D. M. Bruce 68–15–224–13–17.23; C. G. Weir 90.3–23–206–11–18.72; *P. F. McIntyre 162–37–464–24–19.33; R. C. Gainher 68.5–9–263–10–26.30.

THE KING'S SCHOOL, CANTERBURY

Played 15: Won 8, Lost 1, Drawn 6

Master i/c: A. W. Dyer Cricket professional: D. V. P. Wright

Batting—D. J. R. Hildick-Smith 13–2–500–92–45.45; P. G. Bromley 15–3–532–97–44.33; *P. J. Cranston Smith 15–2–446–75–34.30; D. J. Pritchard 9–3–145–46*–24.16; S. J. S. Lark 12–4–148–44*–18.50; R. W. G. Oliver 15–2–237–38–18.23; J. H. A. Albin 14–1–235–62*–18.07.

Bowling—C. J. Wheeler 70–20–191–17–11.23; D. N. S. Kenney 112.5–45–238–19–12.52; D. J. Pritchard 143.2–30–339–26–13.03; R. W. G. Oliver 119–22–535–33–16.21; S. M. Parrott 135.2–32–407–23–17.69.

THE KING'S SCHOOL, ELY

Played 12: Won 5, Lost 1, Drawn 6

Master i/c: R. M. Parsons

Batting—T. S. May 12–4–335–103–41.87; A. R. J. Manktelow 11–1–201–37–20.10; A. G. Woodcock 12–0–211–37–17.58; J. A. T. Lankfer 9–2–112–37*–16.00; M. Chamberlain 10–1–138–33–15.33.

Bowling—*J. P. Hulme 137–45–273–24–11.37; M. Chamberlain 45–5–174–15–11.60; T. S. May 131–21–428–33–12.96.

THE KING'S SCHOOL, MACCLESFIELD

Played 22: Won 5, Lost 9, Drawn 8. Abandoned 4

Master i/c: I. A. Wilson

Batting—P. A. Manning 22–3–615–101*–32.36; C. J. R. Eccles 18–6–282–41–23.50; S. R. Hope 20–0–379–55–18.95; S. A. Hoole 20–4–297–59–18.56; T. I. Moore 21–1–319–56–15.95; R. A. D. Laughton 17–3–214–53*–15.28; A. J. Cornford 15–0–134–35–8.93; D. J. H. Fitches 19–0–144–40–7.57.

Bowling—T. I. Moore 109.3–24–328–21–15.61; R. A. D. Laughton 187–48–547–30–18.23; R. N. Wilson 107.1–25–325–17–19.11; C. J. R. Eccles 87.2–18–272–12–22.66; *McAlpine J. J. 246.4–61–720–28–25.71; S. A. Hoole 133.2–31–452–13–34.76.

KING'S SCHOOL, ROCHESTER

Played 16: Won 4, Lost 2, Drawn 10. Abandoned 3

Master i/c: John S. Irvine

Batting—R. D. Barrett 16–3–592–105*–45.53; R. P. Mernagh 12–5–174–92*–24.85; T. W. Collard 13–3–247–59*–24.70; *A. G. Watson 13–5–195–42–23.87; A. S. Brown 11–0–217–60–19.72.

Bowling—M. Fairbank 101–19–261–20–13.05; R. P. Mernagh 153–32–473–34–13.91; N. Q. Miller 190.1–37–527–35–15.05; M. E. Rowe 87–16–293–12–24.41.

KING'S SCHOOL, WORCESTER

Played 16: Won 1, Lost 3, Drawn 12. Abandoned 1

Master i/c: D. P. Iddon

Batting—D. P. E. Rogers 15–3–493–80*–41.08; D. G. Vivian 13–2–264–52*–24.00; R. D. Jones 16–1–340–73–22.66; S. D. Preston 11–1–198–109*–19.80; P. A. G. Day 7–2–116–38*–16.57; D. A. G. Bishop 12–1–156–40–14.18; *J. S. Fleming 12–2–133–33*–13.30.

Bowling—A. Suckling 24–3–71–10–7.10; K. D. Andrews 162.4–38–520–30–17.33; J. S. Fleming 181.4–45–477–20–23.85; N. Fisher 117.5–30–361–15–24.06; J. Hodgson 95.2–22–296–12–24.66.

KINGSTON GRAMMAR SCHOOL

Played 19: Won 5, Lost 6, Drawn 8. Abandoned 1

Master i/c: R. J. Sturgeon

Batting—S. H. Clayson 18–1–602–113*–35.41; D. E. Jenkins 19–3–516–103*–32.25; G. B. Foreman 18–5–374–69–28.76; A. S. K. Ghauri 19–1–361–66–20.05; *S. J. Nicholls 14–7–109–18*–15.57; R. J. Gornall 17–0–224–45–13.17; J. P. Molloy 13–0–171–27–13.15; R. A. Ukiah 18–1–155–22–9.11.

Bowling—R. C. Marshall 236–60–665–44–15.11; S. J. Nicholls 239.1–60–686–34–20.17; M. R. Bradford 204.3–44–629–27–23.29.

KINGSWOOD SCHOOL

Played 14: Won 1, Lost 5, Drawn 8

Master i/c: R. J. Lewis

Batting—R. W. Ward 14–0–311–40–22.21; C. J. Huxtable 13–0–267–62–20.53; *P. A. Hurt 14–2–195–44–16.25; J. W. Rogers 14–1–167–50*–12.84; A. C. Hymer 13–0–161–48–12.38; J. F. Ducker 14–0–172–57–12.28; A. W. McLennan 10–0–106–32–10.60.

Bowling—R. H. Vowles 70.5–20–186–18–10.33; R. W. Ward 105.5–20–328–23–14.26; T. S. Hammond 136.2–30–357–25–14.28; A. C. Hymer 184.2–47–400–27–14.81.

LANCING COLLEGE

Played 19: Won 12, Lost 4, Drawn 3

Master i/c: E. A. Evans-Jones — Cricket professional: D. V. Smith

Batting—J. D. Robinson 19–2–700–90*–41.17; J. G. Wills 18–0–431–95–23.94; *I. C. Martin 19–1–356–69–19.77; J. J. S. Withyman 16–0–298–61–18.62; C. P. Heaslip 19–0–294–46–15.47; C. S. Mays 16–5–163–42*–14.81; P. G. Sealey 18–2–229–50–14.31; J. N. P. Davies 15–5–131–30*–13.10.

Bowling—C. S. Mays 244–66–573–58–9.87; A. N. McPherson 214.5–57–508–41–12.39; P. G. Sealey 126.1–26–340–20–17.00; J. Baker 103–18–301–13–23.15; J. N. P. Davies 89.3–16–273–11–24.81.

LEEDS GRAMMAR SCHOOL

Played 19: Won 10, Lost 4, Drawn 5. Abandoned 3

Master i/c: I. R. Briars

Batting—A. F. Tyler 17–3–668–117*–47.71; J. K. Bowman 19–2–673–85–39.58; *D. H. Innes 16–3–377–88–29.00; D. C. Barker 13–5–183–59–22.87; S. A. Gray 15–4–217–58–19.72; J. D. E. Weston 14–1–196–44–15.07; J. E. Cook 15–1–165–54–11.78.

Bowling—D. A. Smith 127.3–27–423–30–14.10; A. M. Watson 143.3–46–381–25–15.24; S. A. Gray 46–4–233–13–17.92; N. J. Pridmore 144–25–510–26–19.61; D. C. Barker 130.4–30–462–23–20.08; R. S. J. Tovey 132.5–22–413–16–25.81.

LEIGHTON PARK SCHOOL

Played 14: Won 3, Lost 5, Drawn 6

Master i/c: G. C. Shaw

Batting—*N. A. S. Unsworth 12–2–311–92–31.10; P. D. R. Berridge 14–1–383–75*–29.46; D. Doraisamy 10–1–146–52–16.22; R. J. Dworzak 13–2–170–45–15.45; C. A. J. Allan 11–0–103–32–9.36.

Bowling—S. I. Mahendra 78–14–263–18–14.61; D. Doraisamy 116.4–26–358–23–15.56; R. C. Newell Price 77.3–6–269–12–22.41; R. J. Dworzak 122.5–22–406–18–22.55.

THE LEYS SCHOOL

Played 19: Won 5, Lost 7, Drawn 7. Abandoned 1

Master i/c: P. R. Chamberlain

Batting—*G. C. Mackintosh 19–2–631–106*–37.11; J. D. R. Benson 18–3–464–110*–30.93; J. G. Mitchell 14–2–344–63–28.66; J. H. E. Griffith 18–1–437–86*–25.70; T. H. P. Kerkham 17–4–313–70–24.07; G. R. Webb 17–2–220–57*–14.66; M. P. Fernandez 12–0–105–28–8.75.

Bowling—T. G. Gray 73–19–323–18–17.94; M. Gardner 160–26–550–30–18.33; J. D. R. Benson 150–33–395–20–19.75; M. P. Fernandez 118–27–380–16–23.75; G. C. Mackintosh 144–18–504–20–25.20.

LIVERPOOL COLLEGE

Played 18: Won 8, Lost 3, Drawn 7

Master i/c: J. R. H. Robertson Cricket professional: W. Clutterbuck

Batting—D. M. Fletcher 16–0–623–115–38.93; *N. K. Pyne 16–3–393–89*–30.23; T. F. Groom 16–5–297–65*–27.00; P. D. Williams 19–3–423–66*–26.43; I. M. Lawless 7–1–122–53–20.33; M. Llewellyn 11–4–114–32–16.28; R. Llewellyn 13–1–115–32–9.58.

Bowling—P. D. Williams 187.5–43–484–45–10.75; T. F. Groom 191–43–607–39–15.56; A. P. Hanson 122.5–35–314–19–16.52; R. B. Green 82.2–8–354–20–17.70; M. Llewellyn 81.3–19–242–11–22.00.

LLANDOVERY COLLEGE

Played 11: Won 2, Lost 5, Drawn 4. Abandoned 2

Master i/c: Tom Marks

Batting—N. Whiskerd 10–1–250–66*–27.77; *D. A. Williams 10–0–133–35–13.30; S. Meredith 11–0–141–34–12.81.

Bowling—G. E. Owen 196–62–359–41–8.75; T. B. Williams 137–39–354–24–14.75; J. Moseley 72–14–195–13–15.00.

LORD WANDSWORTH COLLEGE

Played 12: Won 4, Lost 2, Drawn 6

Master i/c: S. R. Davidson

Batting—T. R. Jermyn 12–4–492–116*–61.50; *S. D. Bentley 12–3–369–104*–41.00; N. C. Wright 6–1–150–53–30.00; A. M. Blows 11–4–131–34*–18.71; C. G. Marston 8–0–145–45–18.12.

Bowling—S. E. Meadows-Smith 76.1–19–206–14–14.71; M. J. Pritchard 101–20–298–20–14.90; T. R. Jermyn 124.1–29–442–29–15.24; S. G. Saunders 62–10–205–12–17.08.

LORD WILLIAMS'S SCHOOL, THAME

Played 13: Won 4, Lost 6, Drawn 3

Masters i/c: G. M. D. Howat and A. M. Brannan

Batting—S. J. Lewis 11–3–237–58–29.62; A. J. Deans 11–0–218–72–19.81; *S. V. Cox 12–1–186–62–16.90; C. M. Payne 11–2–129–44*–14.33.

Bowling—J. P. H. Pawsey 68–15–160–12–13.33; S. Porter 62–7–172–10–17.20; S. J. Lewis 116–14–388–21–18.47.

LORETTO SCHOOL

Played 11: Won 1, Lost 6, Drawn 4. Abandoned 1

Master i/c: R. G. Selley Cricket professional: A. D. Gaekwad

Batting—*D. J. M. Orr 9–1–336–105*–42.00; J. I. Mahler 8–3–134–58*–26.80; A. G. D. Aitchison 8–2–136–33–22.66; P. D. Stevenson 10–0–211–39–21.10; R. G. S. Prenter 9–0–138–34–15.33.

Bowling—J. I. Mahler 103–22–282–14–20.14; D. J. M. Orr 111–22–377–16–23.56; A. G. D. Aitchison 123–18–407–12–33.91.

MAGDALEN COLLEGE SCHOOL

Played 17: Won 5, Lost 3, Drawn 9

Master i/c: E. P. L. Sandbach

Batting—M. Barrow 18–2–790–103–49.37; *S. Mendes 18–3–601–114*–40.06; M. Mackinlay 6–2–132–35*–33.00; J. Atkins 7–2–151–68*–30.20; S. Kilgour 13–2–261–59–23.72; R. Buchanan 14–2–196–37–16.33; P. Witts 13–1–184–39–15.33.

Bowling—M. Barrow 174–51–607–42–14.45; S. Mendes 171–50–699–46–15.19; S. Hazell 152–49–450–20–22.50.

MALVERN COLLEGE

Played 18: Won 4, Lost 1, Drawn 13. Abandoned 1

Master i/c: A. J. Murtagh Cricket professional: G. D. Morton

Batting—N. R. C. Maclaurin 4–0–158–58–39.50; R. C. W. Mason 16–0–579–93–36.18; R. A. F. Bache 13–3–292–91*–29.20; A. H. Lewis 15–5–250–78*–25.00; *S. R. Shenkman 14–3–255–53*–23.18; S. J. Creffield 14–2–224–51–18.66; M. C. J. Smith 15–1–252–60–18.00; R. M. Ellcock 13–2–196–62–17.81.

Bowling—R. M. Ellcock 283–83–754–57–13.22; R. C. W. Mason 205–60–581–27–21.51; P. S. R. Wootton 108–20–396–16–24.75; M. T. Lock 127–30–377–10–37.70.

MANCHESTER GRAMMAR SCHOOL

Played 21: Won 5, Lost 5, Drawn 11. Abandoned 1

Master i/c: D. Moss

Batting—M. A. Atherton 16–1–535–96–35.66; C. D. James 15–3–379–53*–31.58; E. M. C. Alexander 9–3–179–58–29.83; R. E. Johnston 20–1–493–144–25.94; C. M. Rogers 15–1–356–61–25.42; *S. C. Williams 13–7–123–36–20.50; M. J. C. Barnes 20–4–299–70–18.68; P. J. Oldham 12–3–125–53–13.88.

Bowling—S. C. Williams 162–35–459–31–14.80; S. A. Corbett 79.5–17–259–17–15.23; M. A. P. Jefferson 278.2–64–848–37–22.91; D. A. Newton 108–28–333–10–33.30; M. A. Atherton 182–52–528–15–35.20.

MARLBOROUGH COLLEGE

Played 13: Won 1, Lost 2, Drawn 10

Master i/c: P. J. Lough

Batting—R. J. P. Young 16–2–427–95*–30.50; *C. S. L. Olver 16–1–388–77–25.86; J. T. Burrell 17–0–439–64–25.82; A. J. Makin 14–5–209–66–23.22; R. T. Thicknesse 14–2–264–51–22.00; M. J. K. Hickman 10–1–142–35–15.77.

Bowling—R. Stafford 67–11–200–12–16.66; A. F. D. Coplestone 201–56–507–25–20.28; A. J. Makin 184–44–514–23–22.34; R. T. Thicknesse 118–21–405–15–27.00.

MERCHANT TAYLORS' SCHOOL, CROSBY

Played 20: Won 0, Lost 14, Drawn 6. Abandoned 1

Master i/c: Rev. D. A. Smith

Batting—M. J. Cooke 12–1–214–54–19.45; D. H. Cooke 20–1–281–40–14.78; L. N. J. Heathcliff-Core 20–1–247–41–13.00; R. A. Saundry 17–3–180–47–12.85; D. R. Drury 17–0–195–40–11.47; M. J. Clinton 15–1–160–42–11.42; I. M. Kerr 20–1–192–36–10.10; *G. Clarke 19–0–138–17–7.26.

Bowling—D. J. Walmsley 200.2–44–654–36–18.16; M. J. Clinton 108.4–23–319–16–19.93; D. H. Cooke 128.1–39–349–15–23.26; L. N. J. Heathcliff-Core 203.3–39–636–24–26.50; A. T. Williams 163.5–42–457–17–26.88.

MERCHANT TAYLORS' SCHOOL, NORTHWOOD

Played 14: Won 11, Lost 0, Drawn 3. Abandoned 4

Master i/c: R. B. Hawkey

Batting—S. P. Ducat 15–5–662–79–66.20; A. A. G. Mee 12–4–309–63–38.62; D. J. Jenkins 15–2–454–68*–34.92; J. H. Armstrong 9–1–192–70*–24.00.

Bowling—P. Jack 113.1–37–275–23–11.95; A. Cornish 84.2–27–212–15–14.13; J. H. Armstrong 99.4–29–265–18–14.72; A. Roberts 175–49–443–29–15.27; J. W. Walter 109.3–34–324–21–15.42.

MERCHISTON CASTLE SCHOOL

Played 13: Won 3, Lost 5, Drawn 5. Abandoned 2

Master i/c: M. C. L. Gill   Cricket professional: R. Ratcliffe

Batting—*P. K. Young 15–1–398–81–28.42; D. A. G. Watson 15–2–301–83–23.15; D. C. Kennedy 10–3–160–55–22.85; A. P. Cunningham 14–0–317–61–22.64; J. E. Hamilton 15–1–294–74–21.00; G. Maxwell 11–3–153–38–19.12; N. S. Hockborn 10–3–127–57–18.14; I. D. Rose 10–1–100–29–11.11.

Bowling—I. D. Rose 34.4–5–127–11–11.54; C. E. Dishington 125–20–383–24–15.95; D. A. G. Watson 144.3–28–501–21–23.85; N. S. Hockborn 109–17–410–15–27.33; G. Maxwell 127–29–347–10–34.70.

MILL HILL SCHOOL

Played 19: Won 3, Lost 5, Drawn 11

Master i/c: C. Dean

Batting—P. A. Robin 17–3–992–164*–70.85; *S. C. M. Harley 19–3–537–85–33.56; G. R. W. Hawley 14–5–208–63*–23.11; I. A. Adebayo 12–1–209–57–19.00; R. S. W. Roberts 13–3–154–36–15.40; R. V. Ram 12–1–155–37–14.09.

Bowling—L. N. E. Smith 30.5–7–103–10–10.30; N. Gerasimidis 43–8–122–10–12.20; G. R. W. Hawley 106.2–35–238–12–19.83; C. E. F. Kent 56–6–203–10–20.30; P. A. Robin 253.1–62–664–26–25.53; R. S. W. Roberts 200.1–50–549–18–30.50.

MILLFIELD SCHOOL

Played 21: Won 7, Lost 3, Drawn 11. Abandoned 1

Master i/c: F. N. Fenner   Cricket professional: G. Wilson

Batting—N. E. R. Hutchinson 7–1–228–50*–38.00; J. E. M. Nicolson 18–1–596–109*–35.05; P. A. C. Bail 19–2–560–71*–32.94; R. M. Cooper 19–2–399–93–23.47; D. Pyemont 14–7–164–28*–23.42; J. R. Ravenscroft 13–1–264–63–22.00; R. A. Hawes 11–1–102–34–10.20.

Bowling—N. Brown 206.2–61–377–28–13.46; J. R. Ravenscroft 132.4–23–523–29–18.03; P. A. C. Bail 243.1–62–788–30–26.26; S. E. Hull 178–48–462–17–27.17; A. M. Hassall 183.2–24–616–19–32.42.

MILTON ABBEY SCHOOL

Played 20: Won 7, Lost 8, Drawn 5. Abandoned 2

Master i/c: S. T. Smail

Batting—C. G. Bevan 11–1–250–64*–25.00; J. M. Hopkins 18–0–411–72–22.83; N. J. Coppen 20–0–337–53–16.85; J. W. Lovell 12–2–165–50*–16.50; *C. W. Moyle 18–0–268–45–14.88.

Bowling—G. C. Birkbeck 80–13–264–22–12.00; C. W. Moyle 198–34–694–49–14.16; R. W. Gamble 200–59–486–30–16.20; D. A. Meredith 82–15–279–16–17.43; R. D. Barrington 102–18–306–18–17.00.

MONKTON COMBE SCHOOL

Played 16: Won 3, Lost 3, Drawn 10. Abandoned 1

Master i/c: P. C. Sibley Cricket professional: P. D. Marsden

Batting—S. A. M. Prentice 15–2–349–73*–26.84; I. G. Osborne 15–1–312–64–22.28; A. R. C. Batterham 11–5–124–46*–20.66; A. P. S. McDougal 12–4–138–50*–17.25; A. P. Fussell 13–1–190–65–15.83; A. G. Lea 11–1–149–26*–14.90; R. H. Miller 10–2–113–36–14.12; J. J. A. Beales 13–1–164–43*–13.66; *J. B. East 15–1–119–25–8.50.

Bowling—J. J. A. Beales 85.4–32–209–21–9.95; J. B. East 49.2–6–180–14–12.85; A. R. C. Batterham 201.1–42–494–38–13.00; S. A. M. Prentice 80–27–194–13–14.92; A. M. Owen 76–7–225–12–18.75; I. G. Osborne 153–43–427–19–22.47.

MONMOUTH SCHOOL

Played 16: Won 2, Lost 6, Drawn 8

Masters i/c: P. D. R. Anthony and P. Dennis-Jones Cricket professional: G. I. Burgess

Batting—*K. G. Lewis 13–1–362–119*–30.16; R. S. Kear 13–1–327–80*–27.25; A. G. Nicholas 12–2–248–84–24.80; A. C. Olney 12–0–227–60–18.91; M. F. Kear 13–2–194–35–17.63; D. W. Joseph 13–3–172–30–17.20.

Bowling—M. F. Kear 178.1–41–542–25–21.68; A. G. Douglass 138–39–335–14–23.92; D. W. Joseph 117–32–386–16–24.12; G. A. Davies 180.2–43–580–21–27.61.

NORWICH SCHOOL

Played 16: Won 3, Lost 7, Drawn 6

Master i/c: P. J. Henderson

Batting—D. R. Glasbey 4–1–231–75–77.00; *S. P. Bowling 14–1–447–69–34.38; N. J. Kedar 11–5–145–33*–24.16; N. J. Foster 8–1–167–56–23.85; P. D. Nicholls 16–0–368–64–23.00; A. J. Clarke 14–0–178–60–12.71; S. Windsor 15–0–184–36–12.26; S. Cook 15–5–116–13*–11.60; J. A. Cooper 14–2–120–20–10.00.

Bowling—N. J. Kedar 119.5–26–445–28–15.89; P. D. Nicholls 169–37–544–29–18.75; N. J. Foster 95.3–15–382–18–21.22; G. P. Sargent 132–25–457–18–25.38.

NOTTINGHAM HIGH SCHOOL

Played 26: Won 16, Lost 2, Drawn 8. Abandoned 3

Master i/c: J. E. Sadler Cricket professional: K. J. Poole

Batting—R. P. Rhodes 12–8–241–46*–60.25; *R. Poole 27–5–895–113–40.68; R. C. Elgie 24–6–491–83*–27.27; J. G. Morris 24–2–456–70–20.72; R. J. Briggs 17–2–272–65*–18.13; G. D. Harding 16–3–216–46*–16.61; R. M. Mousley 22–3–303–42–15.94; R. J. Sadler 20–3–233–65–13.70.

Bowling—G. D. Harding 281–85–511–47–10.87; R. P. Rhodes 296–91–746–52–14.34; R. J. Briggs 270–81–601–36–16.69; T. J. Deas 92–22–276–16–17.25; R. M. Mousley 132–34–364–16–22.75; N. A. M. Garden 192–58–504–21–24.00; T. D. Jackman 172–43–503–20–25.15.

OAKHAM SCHOOL

Played 20: Won 3, Lost 2, Drawn 15

Master i/c: J. Wills Cricket professional: I. H. S. Balfour

Batting—A. C. Douglass 16–3–651–95–50.07; *E. G. Sly 20–6–425–56*–30.35; M. Steans 19–2–504–114*–29.64; C. A. Selby 15–9–121–33*–20.16; S. P. Stephenson 14–4–176–27–17.60; T. P. Jones 16–0–263–52–16.43; S. Wood 15–0–214–54–14.26; S. R. Ratcliffe 14–0–177–31–12.64.

Bowling—D. A. Lewis 124.2–26–372–23–16.17; E. G. Sly 242.2–88–544–33–16.48; J. M. Wratten 87–18–241–12–20.08; S. P. Stephenson 150–31–430–18–23.88; J. S. England 106–25–321–10–32.10.

OUNDLE SCHOOL

Played 17: Won 4, Lost 6, Drawn 7. Abandoned 1

Master i/c: M. J. Goatly Cricket professional: A. J. Watkins

Batting—D. C. Boyce 15–1–577–141*–41.21; A. S. A. Townsend 16–2–537–107–38.35; E. J. Pickard 15–2–338–68*–26.00; W. M. O. Massey 15–1–248–71–17.71; J. A. MacMillan 13–3–174–62*–17.40; R. C. Merrikin 15–1–202–58–14.42.

Bowling—J. S. Carr 222.2–46–873–35–24.94; J. A. MacMillan 166.4–41–513–19–27.00; J. R. Waters 107.2–22–370–12–30.83; M. J. D. Walliker 205–50–612–14–43.71.

THE PERSE SCHOOL

Played 15: Won 2, Lost 2, Drawn 11

Master i/c: A. W. Billinghurst

Batting—A. R. Young 9–3–249–66*–41.50; J. M. C. Stenner 13–2–366–67–33.27; J. D. Steele 13–1–297–62–24.75; *A. R. Wass 14–0–313–94–22.35; P. W. Sterland 12–2–217–50–21.70.

Bowling—A. R. Young 116–38–262–25–10.48; G. D. A. Clayson 131–35–403–20–20.15; C. A. Riley 114.3–39–277–11–25.18; A. R. Wass 97–24–322–11–29.27; R. Hanka 161.1–42–427–13–32.84.

PLYMOUTH COLLEGE

Played 17: Won 5, Lost 5, Drawn 7. Abandoned 5

Master i/c: T. J. Stevens

Batting—*M. Tall 16–2–421–100*–30.07; J. Chislett 16–1–428–70–28.53; S. Luffman 15–0–409–64–27.26; N. Trobridge 15–6–218–38–24.22; R. Seymour 15–2–256–60–19.69; C. Stevens 16–3–199–37*–15.30.

Bowling—M. Sprague 103.4–24–378–26–14.53; G. Hooper 65–19–202–12–16.83; C. Rose 148.4–24–580–30–19.33; A. Luffman 124.3–21–402–20–20.10.

POCKLINGTON SCHOOL

Played 25: Won 11, Lost 8, Drawn 6

Master i/c: D. Nuttall

Batting—J. D. St J. Lang 24–2–692–100*–31.45; R. T. Nuttall 23–0–566–75–24.60; S. J. Hall 20–1–403–99–21.21; R. M. Picknett 23–2–395–53*–18.80; *M. N. Townend 24–3–375–77*–17.85; C. J. Lewis 20–4–251–39–15.68; D. Ellinor 19–5–179–25–12.78.

Bowling—R. M. Aram 349.3–96–955–69–13.84; P. J. Buckley 242–80–564–40–14.10; S. D. R. Beynon 113.4–20–367–21–17.47; S. J. Hall 257–66–685–34–20.14.

QUEEN ELIZABETH GRAMMAR SCHOOL, WAKEFIELD

Played 15: Won 8, Lost 6, Drawn 1

Master i/c: C. W. M. Furniss Cricket professional: H. Hariharan

Batting—*J. S. Young 15–5–459–100*–45.90; R. Adams 7–3–114–50*–28.50; A. K. Das 14–2–203–37*–16.91; A. M. Taylor 15–1–233–74–16.64; S. Jubb 12–2–125–25–12.50.

Bowling—J. Tunnicliffe 82–22–186–21–8.85; A. M. Smith 32–6–103–11–9.36; R. Hattersley 243–65–576–33–17.45; P. Hesseltine 173–31–570–26–21.92.

QUEEN'S COLLEGE, TAUNTON

Played 12: Won 5, Lost 1, Drawn 6. Abandoned 1

Master i/c: J. W. Davies

Batting—G. V. Palmer 9–2–362–116–51.71; P. Graham 11–1–382–130–38.20; A. Free 11–1–195–72–19.50; M. Swift 11–0–201–44–18.27; *A. Bloxham 12–1–184–50–16.72; R. Irish 11–2–106–31–11.77.

Bowling—G. V. Palmer 161–49–325–33–9.84; P. Graham 135–38–327–25–13.08; M. Swift 149–35–407–28–14.53.

RADLEY COLLEGE

Played 17: Won 4, Lost 1, Drawn 12. Abandoned 1

Master i/c: C. H. Hirst Cricket professional: A. G. Robinson

Batting—E. J. B. Popplewell 16–3–446–68–34.30; R. G. Butler 15–1–467–111–33.35; J. A. G. Fawcett 16–1–368–60*–24.53; J. R. L. Ballantyne 13–5–183–57*–22.87; R. C. H. Reed 16–1–340–53*–22.66; J. S. Male 12–2–214–65*–21.40; C. C. H. Phillips 16–4–250–66*–20.83; J. H. Nash 8–1–113–37–16.14.

Bowling—*G. D. Moss 242.3–67–608–40–15.20; S. N. A. Leefe 60–10–204–13–15.69; J. S. Male 58–12–213–12–17.75; L. S. N. George 195.3–45–486–27–18.00; J. A. G. Fawcett 159.3–39–434–23–18.86; J. H. Nash 98–18–330–11–30.00.

RATCLIFFE COLLEGE

Played 17: Won 3, Lost 4, Drawn 10. Abandoned 2

Master i/c: C. W. Swan

Batting—*J. A. Foulds 12–2–250–85*–25.00; D. H. Mestecky 14–4–249–63*–24.90; D. M. Prior 17–2–367–101–24.46; G. J. O'Connor 16–4–212–37–17.66.

Bowling—D. H. Mestecky 99–25–308–21–14.66; P. W. Tarimo 209–55–499–34–14.67; D. M. Prior 109–16–331–15–22.06.

READING SCHOOL

Played 14: Won 1, Lost 6, Drawn 7. Abandoned 1

Master i/c: R. G. Owen Cricket professional: A. Dindar

Batting—*E. P. O'Leary 10–2–308–87*–38.50; K. W. Seymour 14–1–306–70–23.53; D. G. Purslow 14–1–283–58–21.76; E. L. Weekes 14–5–182–47–20.22; A. C. Dray 13–0–240–71–18.46; D. B. K. Williams 14–0–234–35–16.71; M. W. Allen 8–1–104–56–14.85; R. I. West 13–1–107–28*–8.91.

Bowling—*E. P. O'Leary 80–22–234–14–16.71; E. L. Weekes 141–30–468–17–27.52; G. M. Cox 166–42–521–18–28.94; R. I. West 85–17–333–10–33.30.

REED'S SCHOOL

Played 14: Won 5, Lost 4, Drawn 5. Abandoned 1

Master i/c: G. R. Martin

Batting—G. A. Hatton 12–1–460–77–41.81; A. P. Shiells 14–1–282–53–21.69; *M. R. Dunn 13–3–205–39–20.50; A. M. J. Glass 13–2–224–58–20.36; L. N. Onyesoh 12–2–202–51–20.20; J. M. A. Price 11–2–150–26*–16.66.

Bowling—M. R. Dunn 200.1–58–475–39–12.17; C. R. Notton 136.4–22–451–35–12.88; R. P. A. Maddock 119–25–372–15–24.80.

REIGATE GRAMMAR SCHOOL

Played 23: Won 7, Lost 2, Drawn 14. Abandoned 3

Master i/c: D. C. R. Jones

Batting—P. W. Gritton 14–5–316–59–35.11; *P. N. J. Downman 21–2–622–65–32.73; D. G. C. Downman 18–4–404–65*–28.85: D. McG. Gilbertson 7–2–119–57–23.80; C. M. Allen 20–4–377–72–23.56; D. R. Cawthrow 21–2–418–61–22.00; J. M. G. Baird 21–0–455–57–21.66; S. A. Bedell 21–1–298–67–14.90.

Bowling—A. C Bradley 111–19–383–23–16.65; M. Peckham 76–17–184–10–18.40; C. M. Allen 249–48–730–38–19.21; P. W. Gritton 253.3–48–841–41–20.51; I. M. Brimicombe 105.1–16–420–13–32.30.

REPTON SCHOOL

Played 18: Won 3, Lost 5, Drawn 10. Abandoned 1

Master i/c: J. F. M. Walker Cricket professional: M. Kettle

Batting—C. Benn 17–3–649–120–46.35; C. V. Berriman 18–3–462–108*–30.80; S. W. Lovell 18–1–460–119–27.05; J. C. Gibbow 8–2–138–38–23.00; S. C. Robinson 16–0–312–56–19.50; A. S. J. Pass 10–2–133–33–16.62; M. S. H. Smith 13–4–137–43–15.22; *T. R. Barlow 11–2–127–33–14.11.

Bowling—G. P. J. Emmerson 156–19–635–24–26.45; M. S. H. Smith 264.1–45–947–32–29.59; N. F. Slater 241.1–33–951–29–32.79.

ROSSALL SCHOOL

Played 14: Won 7, Lost 4, Drawn 3

Master i/c: R. J. Clapp

Batting—*R. I. Kanhai 14–5–360–81*–40.00; S. L. Corlett 9–4–186–50*–37.20; F. D. Merry 11–1–221–37–22.10; A. B. Efiong 15–1–243–72–17.35; N. V. Salvi 14–2–170–26–14.16; L. M. Clube 14–1–146–48–11.23.

Bowling—R. I. Kanhai 173–48–428–35–12.22; C. J. D. Lees 61–20–165–10–16.50; K. C. Stiles 197–50–513–29–17.68; H. B. Mellor 123–42–230–13–17.69.

ROYAL GRAMMAR SCHOOL, NEWCASTLE

Played 22: Won 6, Lost 5, Drawn 11

Master i/c: D. W. Smith Cricket professional: J. N. Graham

Batting—S. D. Pyle 21–4–436–61–25.64; A. S. Latimer 10–1–186–41–20.66; M. A. Reed 21–0–422–83–20.09; R. H. J. Milbank 16–4–237–41*–19.75; A. V. F. Nargol 13–2–202–50–18.36; J. A. Bruce 21–1–353–40–17.65; I. D. Lumley 19–1–284–84*–15.77; L. D. Anderson 20–0–234–32–11.70; S. J. Sill 19–4–169–37*–11.26.

Bowling—S. D. Pyle 22–6–83–10–8.30; S. J. Sill 102–14–377–23–16.39; A. V. F. Nargol 136–27–409–24–17.04; *J. N. J. Anderson 64–13–238–13–18.30; J. A. Bruce 155.2–41–436–19–22.94; A. P. Manley 95.2–18–291–12–24.25.

ROYAL GRAMMAR SCHOOL, WORCESTER

Played 20: Won 11, Lost 4, Drawn 5. Abandoned 2

Master i/c: B. M. Rees

Batting—P. Bent 19–2–643–115*–37.82; S. D. Cairney 19–0–644–112–33.89; M. C. W. Jones 17–1–354–59–22.12; D. C. Richmond 17–6–243–55–22.09; J. S. Phillips 19–2–308–55*–18.11; G. A. Powell 14–1–228–46–17.53; *S. P. Madzarevic 12–2–115–28–11.50.

Bowling—D. C. Richmond 86.1–19–236–15–15.73; I. G. Jinks 206–55–563–28–20.10; A. C. Madzarevic 162.3–51–396–18–22.00; P. Bent 263.4–70–695–29–23.96; A. R. Hill 138–33–360–15–24.00; J. S. Phillips 102.5–18–293–12–24.41.

RUGBY SCHOOL

Played 16: Won 1, Lost 2, Drawn 13

Master i/c: G. A. Tiffin Cricket professional: W. J. Stewart

Batting—P. J. Leaver 16–3–396–103*–30.46; *F. G. A. Mitchell 16–4–356–59–29.66; A. J. Stewart 9–3–166–58–27.66; D. P. W. Umbers 17–1–363–53–22.68; I. A. Hunter 17–1–314–50–19.62; J. G. A. Squire 13–2–209–37–19.00; D. J. Cleverley 10–3–106–60*–15.14.

Bowling—N. C. W. Fenton 228.3–55–514–32–16.06; *F. G. A. Mitchell 185–51–440–27–16.29; J. D. D. Allan 77–15–203–11–18.45; D. J. Cleverley 91.3–25–241–11–21.90.

RYDAL SCHOOL

Played 15: Won 1, Lost 7, Drawn 7

Master i/c: M. J. Darlington Cricket professional: R. W. C. Pitman

Batting—N. S. Lawrence 9–2–172–44–24.57; N. B. Morgan 11–0–237–85–21.54; *D. P. Johnson 12–0–232–74–19.33; J. T. Owen 13–0–227–63–17.46; N. J. Dale 12–0–177–58–14.75; J. M. Tunstall 13–0–121–35–9.30.

Bowling—D. P. Johnson 44–6–164–11–14.90; T. P. Forster 94–34–231–15–15.40; J. M. Sherrington 100–24–357–18–19.83; N. B. Morgan 108–24–341–15–22.73; A. P. Sherrington 115–17–416–15–27.73.

ST ALBANS SCHOOL

Played 15: Won 6, Lost 5, Drawn 4. Abandoned 4

Master i/c: N. J. Pritchard

Batting—H. S. F. Thompson 13–7–152–29–25.33; W. J. Dean 13–0–320–51–24.61; *A. P. Latham 15–1–314–55–22.42; M. D. Lynes 11–1–210–66–21.00; S. R. Dobson 13–0–137–40–10.53; A. I. Bird 13–1–112–17*–9.33; N. J. Roper 13–0–107–32–8.23.

Bowling—W. J. Dean 269–74–629–50–12.58; A. P. Latham 201–52–504–25–20.16.

ST DUNSTAN'S COLLEGE

Played 13: Won 4, Lost 2, Drawn 7. Abandoned 3

Master i/c: C. Matten

Batting—C. Denny 13–2–449–84–40.81; P. Slade 11–3–224–37*–28.00; C. Tooley 15–2–305–65*–23.46; S. Cross 11–3–166–41*–20.75; P. White 11–0–196–58–17.81; I. Jack 12–3–144–35*–16.00; A. Rouse 12–1–140–34–12.72; *M. Jeffcoat 12–0–124–29–10.33.

Bowling—S. Cross 107–27–343–25–13.72; G. Pointer 174–48–414–20–20.70; W. Beavington 65–15–216–10–21.60; H. Phillips 229–48–705–28–25.17.

ST EDMUND'S SCHOOL, CANTERBURY

Played 15: Won 3, Lost 5, Drawn 7. Abandoned 3

Master i/c: R. Woodberry Cricket professional: D. V. P. Wright

Batting—R. A. L. Fields 13–1–350–74*–29.16; J. M. Carr 13–0–330–70–25.38; S. D. Beckett 15–4–251–57*–22.81; P. Samakatunga 15–1–295–50–21.07; A. P. Walton 11–1–185–49–18.50.

Bowling—A. P. Walton 87–14–309–20–15.45; *J. C. Mankey 183–46–528–30–17.60; S. A. A. Roche 137–31–455–17–26.76.

ST EDWARD'S SCHOOL, OXFORD

Played 11: Won 3, Lost 2, Drawn 6. Abandoned 2

Master i/c: P. G. Badger Cricket professional: B. A. Edrich

Batting—T. de Putron 7–0–263–62–37.57; D. Soper 12–0–360–64–30.00; D. Arkell 12–1–224–58–20.36; S. Smith 12–1–217–57–19.72; A. Lamb 12–0–213–77–17.75; A. Cane 10–2–121–29–15.12; P. Bishop 10–2–115–29–14.37; P. Blanchard 12–2–126–49–12.60.

Bowling—T. Rayne 134.5–38–348–23–15.13; R. Franklin 185.2–35–570–31–18.38; D. Soper 75–18–233–11–21.18; R. Mitchell 102.4–28–273–10–27.30.

ST GEORGE'S COLLEGE, WEYBRIDGE

Played 17: Won 5, Lost 6, Drawn 6. Abandoned 2

Master i/c: B. O'Gorman

Batting—T. J. O'Gorman 15–6–420–100*–46.66; D. A. Hamer 8–1–216–55*–30.85; M. J. Johnson 10–3–204–69–29.14; J. M. Jones 16–0–359–68–22.43; M. J. Collins 17–2–312–50*–20.80; M. J. Inman 12–1–218–60–19.81; A. P. Jansen 15–3–222–56*–18.50; S. E. Jones 17–0–283–43–16.64; R. P. McBride 13–2–112–32–10.18.

Bowling—A. P. Jansen 57.4–13–165–11–15.00; P. Davis 195–68–459–27–17.00; S. E. Jones 177–34–651–38–17.13; M. J. Johnson 117.3–39–328–18–18.22; D. A. Hamer 100.5–26–355–17–20.88.

ST JOHN'S SCHOOL, LEATHERHEAD

Played 12: Won 2, Lost 3, Drawn 7. Abandoned 2

Master i/c: M. E. C. Comer Cricket professional: E. Shepperd

Batting—*M. T. Sibley 12–3–271–66*–30.11; P. A. Sidwell 10–3–203–61–29.00; P. J. Warren 11–2–199–39–22.11; J. M. Downing 11–0–223–41–20.27; G. C. Blows 12–0–174–42–14.50; D. W. M. Canning 9–0–128–32–14.22.

Bowling—D. B. Millard 94–32–253–16–15.81; C. D. Lane 110–16–326–14–23.28; J. M. Downing 130–43–359–15–23.93; M. T. Sibley 200–59–575–23–25.00.

ST LAWRENCE COLLEGE

Played 15: Won 0, Lost 6, Drawn 9

Master i/c: N. O. S. Jones

Batting—P. R. Hobcraft 16–3–348–72*–26.76; *M. J. Marchant 16–1–309–69–20.60; J. M. G. Barber 10–3–120–44*–17.14; R. H. Mayger 14–1–212–61–16.30; N. A. Crush 15–4–160–48*–14.54; J. L. Binfield 15–1–142–39–10.14; S. W. Cook 15–0–151–27–10.06.

Bowling—D. R. Joyce 164–41–470–20–23.50; M. J. Marchant 170.1–29–575–21–27.38; P. R. Hobcraft 121.1–26–359–13–27.61; J. M. G. Barber 120.3–21–423–12–35.25.

ST PAUL'S SCHOOL

Played 14: Won 2, Lost 2, Drawn 10. Abandoned 2

Master i/c: G. Hughes Cricket professional: E. W. Whitfield

Batting—N. H. D. Macklin 11–4–245–62–35.00; R. W. D. Hampton 13–0–404–87–31.07; J. T. K. Evans 13–1–356–69–29.66; *W. B. Boulton 13–1–274–45–22.83; M. G. A. Woodward 10–2–135–32–16.87.

Bowling—P. M. Wright 200–51–571–26–21.96; A. J. Kemp 134.4–30–361–14–25.78; I. W. Ross Russell 148–32–445–14–31.78; J. P. Clayman 112–22–391–11–35.54.

ST PETER'S SCHOOL, YORK

Played 19: Won 8, Lost 2, Drawn 9. Abandoned 1

Master i/c: D. Kirby Cricket professional: K. Mohan

Batting—S. R. Gorman 20–2–737–120–40.94; *E. F. J. Wright 18–3–373–77*–24.86; M. D. Willink 16–2–341–65*–24.35; A. G. Jackson 20–3–313–55–18.41; S. P. Burdass 17–3–240–47*–17.14.

Bowling—S. R. Gorman 234.3–76–664–58–11.44; G. Y. Taylor 145.3–56–332–24–13.83; R. F. Dibb 110.1–26–319–14–22.78; D. W. Thomas 201.1–72–477–20–23.85; R. J. Kirby 242.4–84–588–23–25.56.

SEDBERGH SCHOOL

Played 14: Won 7, Lost 4, Drawn 3. Abandoned 1

Master i/c: J. O. Morris

Batting—*C. James 12–1–379–64–34.45; M. T. Alban 14–2–331–80*–27.58; W. D. C. Carling 11–3–200–64–25.00; J. C. Foster 13–0–293–51–22.53; S. R. Paton 11–0–229–67–20.81.

Bowling—J. C. R. Binks 149–49–223–22–10.13; M. G. Burgess 172.4–53–359–28–12.82; N. R. Leeming 85–30–255–11–23.18; M. T. Alban 136–21–493–21–23.47; J. P. Cheetham 151–54–416–17–24.47.

SEVENOAKS SCHOOL

Played 11: Won 5, Lost 1, Drawn 5. Abandoned 2

Master i/c: I. J. B. Walker

Batting—*J. G. Perks 11–3–325–64–40.62; N. P. Thomas 11–2–271–65*–30.11; D. B. Thresher 11–0–267–61–24.27; R. C. Withers 9–0–175–37–19.44.

Bowling—R. P. Roberts 133–37–363–37–9.81; A. J. Bell 71.5–26–164–16–10.25; D. B. Thresher 92.4–31–199–18–11.05; J. H. Page 66.5–17–174–11–15.81.

SHERBORNE SCHOOL

Played 14: Won 6, Lost 1, Drawn 7. Abandoned 1

Master i/c: D. F. Gibbs Cricket professional: C. Stone

Batting—R. W. Lloyd 11–5–321–87*–53.50; M. M. C. F. Jones 14–2–530–94*–44.16; *T. J. Dudgeon 14–3–374–101*–34.00; R. A. Rydon 12–1–251–43–22.81; D. W. Thorne 13–1–237–40–19.75; M. C. Bennett 11–3–125–38*–15.62; G. A. Tice 8–0–111–74–13.87.

Bowling—T. J. Billington 167.5–55–468–31–15.09; P. L. Garlick 186.3–52–462–30–15.40; I. P. M. Sharpe 162–44–456–21–21.71.

SHREWSBURY SCHOOL

Played 20: Won 4, Lost 3, Drawn 13. Abandoned 3

Master i/c: C. M. B. Williams Cricket professional: P. H. Bromley

Batting—J. C. C. Pettegree 11–2–342–92–38.00; M. P. Dickson 9–4–190–61*–38.00; R. S. M. Shepherd 14–4–328–69*–32.80; I. M. Garrard 13–3–304–72*–30.40; R. J. P. Burton 18–3–421–60*–28.06; I. J. F. Hutchinson 18–0–435–81–24.16; A. J. Everall 16–1–361–76–24.06; A. D. Hobson 8–2–127–36–21.16; *P. Wozencroft 14–1–274–53–21.07.

Bowling—R. J. P. Burton 292.2–92–709–56–12.66; I. J. F. Hutchinson 98.5–21–279–15–18.60; T. G. Sillar 210.1–45–600–31–19.35; S. M. K. Goodman 109–14–402–15–26.80; R. P. Holt 87.4–14–325–12–27.08.

SIMON LANGTON GRAMMAR SCHOOL

Played 24: Won 8, Lost 1, Drawn 15

Master i/c: R. F. Harriott

Batting—*S. C. Goldsmith 22–3–938–121–49.36; S. Newlyn 16–5–327–58*–29.72; M. Judge 15–4–191–46–17.36; S. Munday 18–1–284–78–16.70; R. James 21–1–323–37–16.15; G. Wiskar 15–1–224–61–16.00; N. Owen 14–5–125–26*–13.88.

Bowling—J. Blair 62.3–19–129–20–6.45; M. Dobson 40.1–6–109–11–9.90; J. Richards 121.4–32–314–27–11.62; S. Goldsmith 165.3–46–388–27–14.37; A. Castle 201.4–58–579–36–16.08; N. Owen 55–8–203–12–16.91; S. Newlyn 103.5–30–268–12–22.33.

SIR ROGER MANWOOD'S SCHOOL

Played 11: Won 3, Lost 3, Drawn 5. Abandoned 1

Master i/c: P. W. Kullman

Batting—G. W. Laslett 7–4–163–62*–54.33; *K. B. G. Boland 11–4–224–65–32.00.

Bowling—K. B. G. Boland 35–6–92–10–9.20; S. D. Baldock 91–24–220–23–9.56; D. J. Stevens 60.3–12–161–16–10.06; M. I. A. Howell 67.5–9–227–20–11.35.

SOLIHULL SCHOOL

Played 17: Won 5, Lost 4, Drawn 8. Abandoned 1

Master i/c: M. R. Brough

Batting—J. M. Robinson 15–1–499–97*–35.64; R. Hamilton 15–1–391–50*–27.92; D. Lloyd 10–1–211–68*–23.44; C. Too Chung 8–2–137–49–22.83; *A. J. McNeish 9–0–188–56–20.88; I. Berry 15–2–255–60–19.61; R. Cohen 12–1–195–57–17.72; S. A. J. Frost 10–1–141–45–15.66; A. Morton 13–2–139–38–12.63.

Bowling—M. C. Duck 142–42–324–21–15.42; C. M. Jowsey 149.2–22–578–26–22.23; M. Whitehead 142–29–422–18–23.44; A. Morton 169.4–37–499–19–26.26.

STAMFORD SCHOOL

Played 16: Won 5, Lost 3, Drawn 8

Master i/c: H. K. Bell

Batting—I. D. Stafford 7–4–148–64–49.33; *D. W. Browne 15–1–643–117–45.92; R. P. Alston 14–1–273–13–21.00; M. A. Welch 15–1–292–81*–20.85; J. S. Gibson 11–2–172–38–19.11; M. A. Bryant 12–3–142–42–15.77; C. P. Richardson 12–2–140–29–14.00.

Bowling—I. R. Plant 192.3–63–435–35–12.42; J. N. Ralphs 125.5–33–343–18–19.05; R. P. Alston 78.3–20–234–11–21.27; N. J. Tyers 86–12–285–11–25.90.

STOCKPORT GRAMMAR SCHOOL

Played 15: Won 6, Lost 0, Drawn 9. Abandoned 2

Master i/c: L. P. Kynaston

Batting—P. H. Wickenden 10–4–290–83*–48.33; T. P. R. Reeman 15–3–496–67–41.33; *R. P. Nicholson 14–1–386–66–29.69; C. R. Thompson 13–1–200–66–16.66; T. Ambler 10–1–142–50–15.77; T. Firth 11–0–170–45–15.45; T. J. Chalmers 11–2–110–44–12.22.

Bowling—S. J. Merricks 34.1–15–67–10–6.70; R. A. Samarji 169–61–343–37–9.27; J. G. P. Roughton 140.1–44–404–22–18.36; T. Firth 150.2–47–336–16–21.00.

STOWE SCHOOL

Played 19: Won 4, Lost 5, Drawn 10

Master i/c: L. E. Weston — Cricket professional: C. Oakes

Batting—W. J. Lord 19–1–508–77–28.22; *P. K. E. Steward 17–1–434–90–27.12; J. H. M. Claydon 14–5–226–43*–25.11; J. N. A. Davies 16–5–259–61*–23.54; D. M. W. Thomas 16–1–318–52*–21.20; A. M. Morrison 17–1–322–51*–20.12; D. A. Steward 17–1–269–45–16.81; M. M. Ivison 8–0–103–35–12.87.

Bowling—C. W. F. Farquhar 76.1–20–139–11–12.63; D. A. Steward 182.3–43–557–30–18.56; A. M. Morrison 310.1–98–928–43–21.58.

STRATHALLAN SCHOOL

Played 17: Won 12, Lost 1, Drawn 4. Abandoned 1

Master i/c: R. J. W. Proctor

Batting—*M. J. de G. Allingham 15–8–721–117–103.00; R. W. N. Kilpatrick 17–1–619–139–38.68; J. A. R. Coleman 9–4–176–72–35.20; G. S. B. Corbett 16–1–473–66*–31.53; N. H. McKee 11–3–223–65*–27.87; G. E. McClung 11–4–173–40–24.71.

Bowling—M. J. de G. Allingham 217.1–68–475–45–10.55; J. A. R. Coleman 207–57–520–40–13.00; R. W. N. Kilpatrick 120.1–32–370–17–21.76; G. W. A. Truter 74.3–18–262–10–26.20.

SUTTON VALENCE SCHOOL

Played 19: Won 12, Lost 0, Drawn 7

Master i/c: G. G. Able

Batting—*M. T. Russell-Vick 18–8–739–114*–73.90; A. R. Shaw 17–5–560–113*–46.66; T. R. Sunnucks 11–6–208–39*–41.60; I. S. Ekuza 5–0–131–49–26.20; S. J. Norris 12–3–215–56–23.88; R. J. H. Thomas 17–3–315–50–22.50; D. I. W. Usendorff 15–2–283–77–21.76; D. G. Curtis 8–1–124–47–17.71.

Bowling—M. T. Russell-Vick 125.3–43–251–36–6.97; A. R. Shaw 200.4–66–381–38–10.02; R. J. Mee 142–47–307–23–13.34; R. D. Coate 149.4–45–384–23–16.69; T. R. Sunnucks 93–29–188–10–18.80.

TAUNTON SCHOOL

Played 14: Won 5, Lost 2, Drawn 7

Master i/c: R. P. Smith Cricket professional: J. A. Jameson

Batting—J. C. Pike 11–3–345–71*–43.12; R. C. E. Grant 10–4–171–48*–28.50; R. P. Copestick 10–1–250–111–27.77; N. J. Pringle 12–0–286–68–23.83; R. J. Bartlett 13–1–268–56*–22.33; A. N. Challacombe 13–1–260–89*–21.66; M. E. Masters 13–2–210–73–19.09; *A. J. Blake 12–0–126–36–10.50.

Bowling—J. C. Pike 210–73–466–33–14.12; D. A. Law 105–29–298–16–18.62; R. C. E. Grant 270–77–683–36–18.97; P. Gibb 95–29–273–13–21.00.

TIFFIN SCHOOL

Played 19: Won 3, Lost 6, Drawn 10

Master i/c: M. J. Williams

Batting—*P. R. C. Robinson 18–2–806–101*–50.37; P. A. Shepherd 17–1–370–64–23.12; N. A. Legg 17–3–289–50–20.64; A. S. Thurman 18–2–319–48–19.93; M. J. Campbell 16–1–287–36–19.13; M. I. Rathjen 12–2–166–26–16.60; D. R. Hickman 10–2–106–34–13.25.

Bowling—W. B. Shermer 220–67–587–34–17.26; N. M. Williams 172.5–46–528–30–17.60; P. R. C. Robinson 261.1–75–637–28–22.75.

TONBRIDGE SCHOOL

Played 15: Won 10, Lost 0, Drawn 5. Abandoned 1

Master i/c: D. R. Walsh

Batting—M. P. Hickson 14–6–478–101*–59.75; *G. R. Cowdrey 14–0–691–143–49.35; J. N. C. Budden 14–3–398–105*–36.18; A. M. Spurling 12–5–204–100*–29.14; A. M. M. Wilmot 13–2–259–49–23.54.

Bowling—G. R. Cowdrey 157–55–332–29–11.44; A. D. H. Grimes 159–49–379–32–11.84; R. C. G. Spurgeon 169–66–343–27–12.70; M. P. Hickson 156–42–409–26–15.73; R. Owen-Browne 63–18–178–10–17.80; M. A. Newnham 84–19–290–10–29.00.

TRENT COLLEGE

Played 13: Won 7, Lost 2, Drawn 4. Abandoned 2

Master i/c: M. F. Sayer Cricket professional: H. Cartwright

Batting—B. S. Hazzledine 6–2–180–50*–45.00; T. Bullement 7–3–117–55–29.25; S. J. Kinselle 8–2–152–50*–25.33; R. T. Lawless 12–4–189–57*–23.62; *P. O. Burge 11–2–164–73–18.22; S. B. Carlisle 11–1–170–37–17.00; P. C. Newman 13–1–106–27–8.83.

Bowling—W. Fox 90.2–30–212–27–7.85; B. S. Hazzledine 45.1–2–154–19–8.10; N. J. S. Booth 78–25–187–15–12.46; T. Bullement 63–16–178–10–17.80.

TRINITY SCHOOL

Played 26: Won 14, Lost 3, Drawn 9. Abandoned 2

Master i/c: B. Widger

Batting—P. J. Stapley 25–4–788–105–37.52; N. W. F. Redwood 25–4–522–67–24.85; D. H. Cooper 23–4–463–81*–24.36; T. P. Firth 12–6–144–58–24.00; *J. R. Collison 24–1–473–77*–20.56; P. J. Smith 24–0–461–92–19.20; M. P. Cuin 19–5–255–68–18.21; R. J. Elliott 17–5–214–40*–17.83; D. W. Price 11–2–105–40–11.66.

Bowling—P. J. Stapley 47.5–12–105–10–10.50; C. J. Holder 122.5–38–225–19–11.84; P. D. Bone 321.5–97–736–50–14.72; R. J. Elliott 301–73–697–47–14.82; B. S. Lees 95–16–324–18–18.00; T. P. Firth 274.3–86–585–30–19.50; N. W. F. Redwood 155.4–27–469–24–19.54.

TRURO SCHOOL

Played 12: Won 5, Lost 1, Drawn 6. Abandoned 4

Master i/c: A. J. D. Aldwinckle

Batting—M. Blomfield 9–5–135–41–33.75; *T. Manhire 9–2–215–54*;–30.71; A. Jones 10–2–196–54–24.50; D. Morton 11–2–151–34–16.77; J. Stick 11–0–111–58–10.09.

Bowling—T. Manhire 107–40–209–24–8.70; I. Berridge 70–20–155–16–9.68; D. Aldwickle 114–46–201–19–10.57; J. Hall 72–21–163–13–12.53.

UPPINGHAM SCHOOL

Played 12: Won 5, Lost 0, Drawn 7. Abandoned 1

Master i/c: G. A. Wheatley Cricket professional: M. R. Hallam

Batting—C. W. Clarke 11–3–421–103*–52.62; D. J. Kennedy 13–2–359–59–32.63; R. M. Sunderland 8–1–216–78–30.85; *J. P. Green 11–3–218–50*–27.25; J. S. Williams 12–1–296–78*–26.90.

Bowling—J. G. K. Stratton 154–47–322–24–13.41; C. R. S. Phillips 75–17–237–14–16.92; M. A. F. Riddington 196–62–571–30–19.03; C. R. J. Timm 130–32–357–17–21.00; J. S. Williams 123–36–361–14–25.78.

VICTORIA COLLEGE, JERSEY

Played 28: Won 15, Lost 0, Drawn 13

Master i/c: D. A. R. Ferguson

Batting—C. M. Graham 11–8–169–45*–56.33; *W. Jenner 28–6–1,227–123*–55.77; P. L. Lalor 21–6–487–82*–32.46; D. A. Oliver 26–6–569–74–28.45; G. B. Gothard 23–7–334–50*–20.87; A. J. Sugden 21–0–327–66–15.57; S. G. Clarke 13–3–140–50*–14.00; B. Vincent 15–0–154–72–10.26; J. M. W. Giles 17–3–118–26*–8.42.

Bowling—J. M. W. Giles 262–81–708–71–9.97; C. M. Graham 70–18–214–18–11.88; G. A. Holmes 162–45–419–31–13.51; I. St C. Morgan 99–20–416–28–14.85; D. A. Oliver 113–20–481–31–15.51; S. G. Clarke 169–42–436–27–16.14.

WARWICK SCHOOL

Played 13: Won 7, Lost 2, Drawn 4. Abandoned 1

Master i/c: I. B. Moffatt Cricket professional: N. Horner

Batting—J. C. Ball 11–1–504–142*–50.40; N. C. B. Robinson 11–3–318–103*–39.75; B. J. Barnfather 7–3–142–52–35.50; R. M. Sadiq 10–3–184–87*–26.28; A. C. Nunn 13–2–273–80–24.81; *R. A. Horner 12–0–230–54–19.16; S. D. Dyde 12–1–133–29–12.09.

Bowling—A. Knight 64–19–158–20–7.90; A. C. Nunn 162.3–40–459–30–15.30; D. J. Coldron 57–16–177–10–17.70; B. J. Barnfather 149–35–441–22–20.45.

WELLINGBOROUGH SCHOOL

Played 19: Won 3, Lost 7, Drawn 9. Abandoned 5

Master i/c: C. J. Ford

Batting—T. P. Cosford 19–1–439–69*–24.38; R. H. Woodhall 15–2–291–40–22.38; R. S. Minto 18–3–276–48*–18.40; *R. H. Lucas 18–1–244–33–14.35; R. T. H. Gane 10–1–121–37–13.44; A. M. Hants 17–0–183–51–10.76; I. Tinson 18–1–173–31–10.17; D. S. Smith 12–1–107–31–9.72.

Bowling—A. M. Hants 204–49–598–35–17.08; R. H. Lucas 172–50–482–26–18.53; R. Harston 146–39–405–19–21.31; R. H. Woodhall 145–30–443–19–23.31; J. S. Baker 128–41–422–13–32.46.

WELLINGTON COLLEGE, CROWTHORNE

Played 16: Won 6, Lost 4, Drawn 6. Abandoned 2

Master i/c: D. J. Mordaunt Cricket professional: P. J. Lewington

Batting—P. S. Wollocombe 15–3–390–65*–32.50; R. C. Fedrick 17–2–375–91–25.00; *R. A. C. Mallinson 13–1–281–80–23.41; G. R. L. Spackman 17–1–365–101*–22.81; B. A. M. Wessely 11–2–169–76*–18.77; G. I. G. Sharp 16–3–199–51–15.30; P. K. O'Toole 13–3–102–19*–10.20.

Bowling—P. K. O'Toole 71–19–185–16–11.56; G. R. L. Spackman 60.2–16–173–12–14.41; R. C. Fedrick 196.2–61–493–34–14.50; J. T. Ansell 150.3–39–446–26–17.15; B. A. M. Wessely 61.5–14–193–10–19.30; R. E. K. Marshall 184.5–62–431–19–22.68.

WESTMINSTER SCHOOL

Played 10: Won 1, Lost 3, Drawn 6. Abandoned 3

Master i/c: J. A. Cogan Cricket professional: R. Gilson

Batting—R. J. Levy 5–2–157–57*–52.33; *R. S. Rutnagur 10–1–289–48–32.11; S. D. Warshaw 10–1–230–68–25.55; C. J. Duffell 8–3–117–50*–23.40; D. D. W. Martin 10–1–209–52–23.22; G. G. Weston 9–2–134–38–19.14; N. Coleman 9–0–167–52–18.55; S. Craft 8–0–100–51–12.50.

Bowling—R. S. Rutnagur 102–29–287–14–20.50; T. E. Lunn 100.2–19–356–17–20.94; G. G. Weston 72.2–15–233–10–23.30; C. J. Duffell 105–19–352–15–23.46.

WHITGIFT SCHOOL

Played 19: Won 6, Lost 8, Drawn 5. Abandoned 1

Master i/c: P. C. Fladgate

Batting—A. D. Vokes 19–2–569–87–33.47; P. W. J. Ellingham 20–0–474–63–23.70; R. J. Ward 12–3–209–44–23.22; M. A. Lenton 19–0–338–58–17.78; R. I. Taylor 20–1–252–36–13.26; D. N. Drinkwater 16–3–154–29*–11.84; A. D. H. Marshall 20–0–212–28–10.60; R. B. Weller 16–0–144–19–9.00.

Bowling—D. N. Drinkwater 118–17–400–27–14.81; *R. D. Ronald 243.5–78–619–41–15.09; S. Talbot 172.5–41–472–29–16.27; A. D. Vokes 133.4–28–408–20–20.40; R. J. Ward 91.3–15–340–10–34.00.

WILLIAM HULME'S GRAMMAR SCHOOL

Played 23: Won 8, Lost 7, Drawn 8

Master i/c: I. J. Shaw

Batting—R. P. Thornton 21–1–493–70*–24.65; H. Fryman 22–0–500–81–22.72; R. G. McLaren 17–3–229–35–16.35; N. W. Roberts 18–3–204–42–13.60; *D. K. Smythe 20–1–245–48–12.89; J. Braddock 14–1–149–38–11.46; J. D. Sealy 20–3–173–37–10.17; J. Wade 17–4–120–28*–9.23.

Bowling—I. D. Thorpe 214–48–623–45–13.84; N. J. Fairfax 174–24–563–30–18.76; A. D. Brown 223–47–625–28–22.32; R. G. McLaren 176–41–565–23–24.56.

WINCHESTER COLLEGE

Played 19: Won 2, Lost 7, Drawn 10. Abandoned 2

Master i/c: J. F. X. Miller Cricket professional: V. Broderick

Batting—W. E. J. Holland 20–3–753–150*–44.29; I. L. M. Henry 17–1–344–48*–21.50; C. N. N. Smith 20–3–354–54*–20.82; S. Nicklin 13–0–242–53–18.61; *E. M. Coulman 19–2–285–58*–16.76; A. J. de Q. Adams 17–3–211–43–15.07; C. E. R. M. Hall 13–3–138–45–13.80; R. B. M. Heyworth 19–2–158–25*–9.29.

Bowling—I. L. M. Henry 64–8–211–10–21.10; T. P. Smail 167–34–591–28–21.10; J. D. Dean 109–30–373–17–21.94; A. J. de Q. Adams 94–22–275–11–25.00; J. D. C. Douglas-Hamilton 186–36–592–23–25.73; C. E. R. M. Hall 144–33–506–16–31.62.

WOODBRIDGE SCHOOL

Played 15: Won 6, Lost 3, Drawn 6. Abandoned 1

Master i/c: J. Bidwell Cricket professional: J. Pugh

Batting—*R. W. Bensly 14–4–424–100*–42.40; E. A. H. Griffiths 14–1–299–79–23.00; S. Parker 14–0–315–78–22.50; R. H. Kemsley 12–2–215–57–21.50; J. A. Speedman 11–5–129–37*–21.50; S. N. Mayhew 9–1–107–38–13.37.

Bowling—S. Leask 30–4–101–10–10.10; R. A. Jack 95–16–260–12–21.66; R. W. Bensly 82.5–10–336–15–22.40.

WOODHOUSE GROVE SCHOOL

Played 12: Won 5, Lost 2, Drawn 5. Abandoned 2

Master i/c: J. F. Clay Cricket professional: P. J. Kippax

Batting—I. W. Stott 11–1–488–89–48.80; B. S. Percy 11–5–215–59*–35.83; A. G. Percy 12–2–287–72–28.70; *S. A. J. Kippax 11–0–194–42–17.63.

Bowling—B. S. Percy 104.4–30–215–24–8.95; S. Cockerill 120–47–222–23–9.65; S. A. J. Kippax 131.4–34–326–31–10.51; A. D. Ratcliffe 106.1–30–266–12–22.16.

WORKSOP COLLEGE

Played 13: Won 2, Lost 2, Drawn 9

Master i/c: N. S. Broadbent

Batting—W. M. Waddington 13–3–533–100*–53.30; *S. N. Waddington 12–2–412–132*–41.20; J. T. Mair 10–3–220–66*–31.42; J. W. Wolstenholme 11–2–156–30–17.33; D. Manger 10–3–100–37–14.28; J. E. Broadbent 13–0–160–40–12.30; J. S. Cooper 10–1–105–65–11.66.

Bowling—E. R. Hughes 89–20–222–22–10.09; D. Manger 89.5–18–320–17–18.82; S. N. Waddington 165–49–422–18–23.44; J. H. Wilks 157.5–32–517–16–32.31.

WREKIN COLLEGE

Played 22: Won 7, Lost 5, Drawn 10

Master i/c: E. C. Gower Cricket professional: J. Smith

Batting—*J. R. Mackenzie 21–4–527–72–31.00; C. S. Joyner 20–1–481–87–25.31; O. N. E. Harvey 16–5–274–57–24.90; A. W. Hartley 17–1–336–51–21.00; R. G. R. Boddington 18–3–274–46–18.26; D. A. Wells 19–0–276–45–14.52.

Bowling—P. R. Mitchell 118–24–325–24–13.54; O. N. E. Harvey 389–120–764–52–14.69; J. R. Mackenzie 359–89–882–50–17.64.

WYCLIFFE COLLEGE

Played 11: Won 2, Lost 3, Drawn 6. Abandoned 3

Master i/c: H. W. Scott

Batting—J. R. Bodington 11–1–298–75–29.80; P. J. Rowley 11–0–299–78–27.18; J. F. Gowen 11–4–155–35*–22.14; *S. J. Shorthose 11–1–156–46–15.60; R. B. Hair 11–0–112–20–10.18.

Bowling—S. J. Shorthose 96–20–245–21–11.66; R. B. Hair 56–16–173–11–15.72; C. A. Vaux 60–11–217–13–16.69; J. R. Bodington 76–16–235–13–18.07; C. C. E. Byers 114–30–329–15–21.93.

WYGGESTON AND QUEEN ELIZABETH I COLLEGE

Played 11: Won 3, Lost 4, Drawn 4

Master i/c: G. G. Wells

Batting—*R. J. Mee 11–6–298–130*–59.60; D. K. Santaney 5–1–150–50–37.50; N. Patel 8–0–250–79–31.25; N. Vyas 7–0–163–44–23.28; R. G. Long 10–0–106–53–10.60.

Bowling—D. A. Silver 75–22–219–20–10.95; A. Jones 59.1–17–139–12–11.58; S. G. Allcock 102.1–26–289–18–16.05.

OVERSEAS CRICKET, 1981-82

Note: Throughout this section, matches not first-class are denoted by the use of a dagger.

ENGLAND IN INDIA AND SRI LANKA, 1981-82

By JOHN THICKNESSE

The first sentiment to be expressed about England's tour of India is relief that Mrs Gandhi, India's Prime Minister, allowed it to take place. Because of the presence among Fletcher's sixteen players of Boycott and Cook, who had both been in South Africa in the recent past, the tour was in doubt until days before the party left London's Heathrow airport. The Cricket Boards of both countries feared that cancellation might lead to a black-white split in cricket, and in the fortnight following an announcement by the Indian government that Boycott and Cook were "unacceptable", there was ceaseless activity in London, Delhi and Bombay to ward off that disaster. Boycott's absence in Hong Kong on holiday added to the difficulties, but after a week of suspense he joined Cook in declaring his repugnance to apartheid, and Mrs Gandhi was placated.

In the event Boycott failed to see the tour out, flying home a fortnight after overtaking Sir Garfield Sobers's Test record aggregate on grounds of "physical and mental tiredness". In view of his part in secretly setting up the tour of South Africa which, to the surprise and concern of the Test and County Cricket Board, began within days of the England party returning from Sri Lanka, it should be said in mitigation that neither Boycott nor Cook (who was among those who turned down the invitation) was asked for an undertaking not to revisit the Republic.

Early in the tour Boycott made a tactless comment to an Indian journalist about South Africa, for which he was taken to task by Raman Subba Row, the manager, but in sixteen weeks there was no further trouble on that score. Although a plodding series in India produced five draws and only one positive result, and England's itinerary gave them far too little time off duty, it was by and large a happy tour, culminating in a delightful fortnight in Sri Lanka, where Emburey and Underwood bowled England to their only Test win.

For the huge crowds who came to watch in India, the disappointment of the series was that, after losing the first Test on a poor pitch in Bombay, England lacked the penetration to harry a confident Indian side who, with batting down to No. 10, were content to hold on to their lead. Of the last five Tests, the only one that looked like reaching a result was that in Calcutta, where England's declaration left them six hours to bowl India out on a pitch on which the ball was keeping low and turning. But with 70 minutes lost to smog on the final morning, and Gavaskar once again immovable, that game also petered out. Nevertheless, even though the best session of the series was the first morning of the fifth Test at Madras, Calcutta remained the best match of the six because of its fair balance between bat and ball. No attendance figures were given, but it was estimated to have been watched by 394,000, surpassing the official record of 350,532 for Australia against England at Melbourne in 1936-37.

Botham's ineffectiveness with the ball – he had nine for 133 at Bombay, but only eight more wickets, at 65 each, in the last five Tests – was a telling blow to England's chance of levelling the series; as was Fletcher's misplaced confidence that India could be overcome by pace. Yet the major factor was the deadness of the pitches. Even Madras had become a perfect batting surface by tea on the first day, while at Bangalore (second Test), New Delhi (third) and Kanpur (sixth), the conditions were loaded so heavily in favour of the bat that first innings was still in progress on the final day.

The over-rate by both sides was abominable – about thirteen an hour throughout the series. However, the pitches were so true and short of bounce that even if the rate had reached sixteen, which because of hourly drinks breaks may be the maximum in India, the results would probably still have been the same. Although the series re-emphasised the need for an agreed daily over-rate, it is also to be hoped that the Indian Board recognise the need to put some ginger in their pitches before their crowds start losing interest. There was little sign of that on this tour; but with the increasing popularity of one-day cricket, bolstered by India's unexpected 2-1 victory in the one-day series, it could happen.

At Bombay, where Fletcher lost his one toss of the series, England had cause for grievance over the umpiring, and made it in the form of an official protest the day after the match. It was a rare, if not unprecedented, action by an England touring team and was widely criticised. However, I felt it justified. K. B. Ramaswamy, the umpire objected to, did not stand again in Tests, although he made an unannounced appearance in the final one-day international, and the umpiring in the last five games was adequate. None the less, as is usual for a touring team, England believed they came off second-best.

Granted that the pitches would have frustrated most attacks, Botham's inconsistent bowling was at the root of England's inability to mount a proper challenge. He compensated with the bat, pipping Gooch in the averages through a mature mixture of disciplined stockpiling and fierce hitting, but his failure as a bowler threw too great a load on Willis. At 32, the vice-captain made good use of the new ball, matching hostility with accuracy, but both ends had to be in business to make a dent in India's solid early batting. After Willis, Allott (though, owing to missed catches, his figures did not show it) was the pick of the quicker bowlers. His line was nearly always excellent, and during the tour he looked to gain a yard of pace.

In a series dominated by the bat, Gavaskar confirmed his stature as the soundest opener in world cricket by his handling of Willis. India were a well-knit side under his direction, needing only a bowler of greater pace than Madan Lal, as support for Kapil Dev, to become as hard to beat abroad as in their own conditions. Viswanath, after a shaky start, refound his wristy touch with hundreds at New Delhi and Madras, Yashpal Sharma made a solid comeback, while Roy and Malhotra emerged as batsmen of clear talent. Doshi bowled with flight and guile, Kirmani's wicket-keeping equalled Taylor's, and in the nineteen-year-old Shastri, 6ft 2in tall, India have an accurate slow left-armer who also bats with obdurate maturity.

England's main gains were the consistency of Gower, Botham's acknowledgement that he has the game to play a measured innings, and Allott's ability to hit the seam at a lively pace. But Fletcher's lack of flexibility as captain and the suspension of Gooch, Emburey and Underwood, for playing in South Africa, were a reminder to the new chairman of selectors, Peter May, that there are always fresh problems to be solved.

ENGLAND TOUR RESULTS

In India

Test matches – Played 6: Lost 1, Drawn 5.
First-class matches – Played 13: Won 2, Lost 1, Drawn 10.
Wins; – India Under-22 XI, Board of Control President's XI.
Loss – India.
Draws – India (5), West Zone, South Zone, North Zone, East Zone, Central Zone.
Non first-class matches – Played 4: Won 2, Lost 2. Wins – CCI President's XI, India. Losses – India (2).

Note: The England team played a limited-overs Benefit match in India following the Sri Lankan section of the tour. This match was not included in the official itinerary of the tour and has not been included in the above results.

In Sri Lanka

Test matches – Played 1: Won 1.
First-class matches – Played 2: Won 1, Drawn 1.
Win – Sri Lanka.
Draw – Sri Lanka Board President's XI.
Non first-class matches – Played 2: Won 1, Lost 1. *Win* – Sri Lanka. *Loss* – Sri Lanka.

TEST MATCH AVERAGES

INDIA v ENGLAND

INDIA – BATTING

	M	*I*	*NO*	*R*	*HI*	*Avge*
Yashpal Sharma........	2	3	1	220	140	110.00
S. M. Gavaskar.........	6	9	1	500	172	62.50
G. R. Viswanath.......	6	8	0	466	222	58.25
Kapil Dev................	6	8	2	318	116	53.00
D. B. Vengsarkar......	6	8	1	292	71*	41.71
P. Roy.....................	2	3	1	71	60*	35.50
R. J. Shastri............	6	6	1	140	93	28.00
Madan Lal...............	6	5	2	69	44	23.00
K. Srikkanth............	4	6	0	119	65	19.83
S. M. H. Kirmani.....	6	6	1	99	67	19.80
S. M. Patil..............	4	6	1	95	31	19.00
Kirti Azad..............	3	4	0	71	24	17.75
A. Malhotra............	2	2	0	31	31	15.50
D. R. Doshi............	6	5	2	14	7*	4.66

Played in one Test: N. S. Yadav 5.

**Signifies not out.*

BOWLING

	O	M	R	W	Avge
D. R. Doshi............	267.5	103	468	22	21.27
Madan Lal...............	159	34	432	14	30.85
Kapil Dev................	243.5	40	835	22	37.95
R. J. Shastri............	233	73	462	12	38.50

Also bowled: Kirti Azad 48-10-153-1; S. M. Gavaskar 4-0-14-0; S. M. Patil 17-2-60-1; K. Srikkanth 6-1-10-0; N. S. Yadav 20-7-53-0.

ENGLAND – BATTING

	M	I	NO	R	HI	Avge
I. T. Botham............	6	8	0	440	142	55.00
G. A. Gooch...........	6	10	1	487	127	54.11
D. I. Gower.............	6	9	1	375	85	46.87
G. Boycott...............	4	8	1	312	105	44.57
C. J. Tavaré.............	6	9	0	349	149	38.77
K. W. R. Fletcher.....	6	9	2	252	69	36.00
G. R. Dilley.............	4	5	0	70	52	14.00
M. W. Gatting.........	5	6	1	68	32	13.60
R. G. D. Willis........	5	4	2	26	13	13.00
D. L. Underwood.....	6	7	4	38	13*	12.66
R. W. Taylor............	6	7	1	57	33	9.50

Played in three Tests: J. E. Emburey 0, 1, 1, 2; in two Tests: J. K. Lever 1,2; in one Test: P. J. W. Allott 6.

**Signifies not out.*

BOWLING

	O	M	R	W	Avge
J. K. Lever.............	73	16	204	7	29.14
R. G. D. Willis........	129.1	29	381	12	31.75
J. E. Emburey..........	99	31	222	6	37.00
I. T. Botham............	240.3	52	660	17	38.82
D. L. Underwood.....	228	99	438	10	43.80
G. R. Dilley.............	105.	17	350	7	50.00

Also bowled: P. J. W. Allott 31-4-135-0; K. W. R. Fletcher 6-2-20-1; M. W. Gatting 1-0-4-0; G. A. Gooch 33.1-6-77-2; D. I. Gower 2-0-2-1; C. J. Tavaré 2-0-11-0; R. W. Taylor 2-0-6-0.

ENGLAND AVERAGES

FIRST-CLASS MATCHES IN INDIA AND SRI LANKA

BATTING

	M	*I*	*NO*	*R*	*HI*	*Avge*
G. Boycott	8	14	5	701	105	77.88
I. T. Botham	11	15	1	760	142	54.28
G. A. Gooch	13	21	3	967	127	53.72
D. I. Gower	13	18	3	755	94	50.33
C. J. Richards	6	6	4	97	46	48.50
K. W. R. Fletcher	13	18	6	581	108	48.41
G. Cook	7	10	1	372	104*	41.33
C. J. Tavaré	13	19	0	761	149	40.05
M. W. Gatting	12	14	1	509	127	39.15
G. R. Dilley	10	11	2	204	52	22.66
R. W. Taylor	11	10	2	132	40	16.50
D. L. Underwood	11	10	5	74	22*	14.80
R. G. D. Willis	10	6	3	26	13	8.66
J. E. Emburey	12	12	2	79	33	7.90
J. K. Lever	8	6	1	36	16	7.20
P. J. W. Allott	7	5	1	22	9*	5.50

BOWLING

	O	*M*	*R*	*W*	*Avge*
D. L. Underwood	385.3	150	784	34	23.05
J. E. Emburey	380.1	96	1,063	42	25.30
R. G. D. Willis	242.1	62	687	24	28.62
J. K. Lever	214	45	664	20	33.20
I. T. Botham	317.2	64	928	25	37.12
P. J. W. Allott	181.4	40	601	15	40.06
G. R. Dilley	210.2	29	767	15	51.13

Also bowled: G. Cook 6.5-1-21-2; K. W. R. Fletcher 29-2-121-2; M. W. Gatting 11-1-40-1; G. A. Gooch 58.1-14-150-2; D. I. Gower 5-2-6-1; C. J. Richards 2-0-5-0; C. J. Tavaré 4-0-18-0; R. W. Taylor 2-0-6-0.

FIELDING

R. W. Taylor 28 (27ct, 1st); C. J. Richards 12 (11ct, 1st); G. A. Gooch 10, C. J. Tavaré 10, K. W. R. Fletcher 9, I. T. Botham 7, D. I. Gower 7, G. Cook 5, J. E. Emburey 5, M. W. Gatting 5, P. J. W. Allott 3, G. Boycott 3, G. R. Dilley 3, D. L. Underwood 3, R. G. D. Willis 3, J. K. Lever 2.

HUNDREDS FOR ENGLAND

The following twelve three-figure innings were played for the England team on their tour of India and Sri Lanka.

I. T. Botham (2)
142 v India at Kanpur (Sixth Test)
122 v Central Zone at Indore

G. Boycott (2)
105 v India at New Delhi (Third Test)
101* v Indian Under-22 XI at Pune

G. Cook (2)
104* v Central Zone at Indore
104 v Sri Lanka Board President's XI at Kandy

M. W. Gatting (2)
127 v East Zone at Jamshedpur
111 v Central Zone at Indore

G. A. Gooch (2)
127 v India at Madras (Fifth Test)
119* v South Zone at Hyderabad

K. W. R. Fletcher (1)
108 v South Zone at Hyderabad

C. J. Tavaré (1)
149 v India at New Delhi (Third Test)

**Signifies not out.*

HUNDREDS AGAINST ENGLAND

The following seven three-figure innings were played against the England team on their tour of India and Sri Lanka.

G. R. Viswanath (2)
222 for India at Madras (Fifth Test)
107 for India at New Delhi (Third Test)

S. M. Gavaskar (1)
172 for India at Bangalore (Second Test)

Gursharan Singh (1)
101* for India Under-22 XI at Pune

Kapil Dev (1)
116 for India at Kanpur (Sixth Test)

R. S. Madugalle (1)
142* for Sri Lanka Board President's XI at Kandy

Yashpal Sharma (1)
140 for India at Madras (Fifth Test)

**Signifies not out.*

†CCI PRESIDENT'S XI v AN ENGLAND XI

At Bombay, November 11. An England XI won by 47 runs. An England XI 154 for nine (48 overs) (G. Cook 56; S. V. Nayak three for 17, R. J. Shastri three for 21); CCI President's XI 107 (42.2 overs) (G. A. Gooch three for 20).

INDIA UNDER-22 XI v AN ENGLAND XI

At Pune, November 13, 14, 15. An England XI won by six wickets. A typical innings by Botham, whose 98 off 67 balls included five 6s and ten 4s, enabled the touring side to cruise home with four overs to spare after being set a target of 301 in three and a half hours. India's Under-22 team had made most of the running in conditions which gave bowlers little chance after the first morning, Srikkanth carving 87 off 53 balls in 95 minutes and Gursharan Singh, a pint-sized eighteen-year-old student from Delhi, showing excellent concentration in making an undefeated hundred on his first-class début. Boycott occupied four and a half hours over his 101 not out, but Fletcher's declaration kept the match open and at lunch on the third day Srikkanth reciprocated. Gower and Gatting were frustrated by defensive fields and a slow over-rate, but Botham, missed at slip when 1, was uncontainable, and his stand of 144 in seventeen overs with Gower decided the match.

Indian Under-22 XI

*K. Srikkanth c Richards b Allott	87	– b Emburey	74
S. K. Khandekar b Dilley	41	– c sub b Dilley	37
L. Rajput c Richards b Willis	38	– not out	30
Gursharan Singh not out	101	– not out	31
R. N. Dani c Richards b Emburey	12		
†S. Viswanath c Dilley b Botham	11		
G. Sharma b Emburey	7		
R. S. Ghai c Willis b Gatting	26		
V. Sinha not out	5		
L-b 2, n-b 9	11	L-b 1, n-b 7	8
1/88 2/147 3/182 4/221 5/252 6/275 7/322	(7 wkts dec.) 339	1/97 2/136	(2 wkts dec.) 180

S. Gudge and Maninder Singh did not bat.

Bowling: *First Innings*—Willis 11–1–65–1; Botham 11–2–55–1; Allott 18–1–67–1; Dilley 12–1–58–1; Emburey 23–7–67–2; Gatting 6–1–16–1. *Second Innings*—Willis 4–0–18–0; Botham 3–0–26–0; Allott 8–2–25–0; Dilley 7–0–43–1; Emburey 17–3–51–1; Fletcher 2–0–9–0.

England XI

G. Boycott not out	101		
C. J. Tavaré c Ghai b Maninder	56		
*K. W. R. Fletcher not out	56		
D. I. Gower (did not bat)		– (1) run out	94
M. W. Gatting (did not bat)		– (2) lbw b Srikkanth	42
I. T. Botham (did not bat)		– (3) c Gudge b Sinha	98
G. R. Dilley (did not bat)		– (4) not out	36
†C. J. Richards (did not bat)		– (6) not out	18
J. E. Emburey (did not bat)		– (5) c Sinha b Maninder	10
N-b 6	6	B 1, n-b 4	5
1/113	(1 wkt dec.) 219	1/77 2/221 3/257 4/278	(4 wkts) 303

P. J. W. Allott and R. G. D. Willis did not bat.

Bowling: *First Innings*—Ghai 17.4–4–39–0; Sinha 5–0–12–0; Srikkanth 4–1–13–0; Maninder 24–5–57–1; Sharma 15–1–42–0; Gudge 14–0–50–0. *Second Innings*—Ghai 7–0–33–0; Sinha 12–0–83–1; Srikkanth 4–0–21–1; Maninder 13–0–90–1; Sharma 2–0–20–0; Gudge 9–0–51–0.

Umpires: Hanumantha Rao and Swaroop Kishen.

BOARD OF CONTROL PRESIDENT'S XI v AN ENGLAND XI

At Nagpur, November 17, 18, 19. An England XI won by five wickets. The spinners dominated this low-scoring game on a pitch which gave them turn throughout and, until it lost pace on the second evening, an awkward, variable bounce. Underwood achieved match figures of eleven for 136, and 22-year-old Kirti Azad, bowling his off-spin at a brisk pace, returned a career-best seven for 63 in England's first innings. With seven of the first eight wickets, he looked like running through the side before Emburey, Underwood and Lever added 71 to give England an important lead. Until Fletcher steered England home, with an "old pro's" 35 not out, only Tavaré and Cook of the Englishmen and Srikkanth, Vengsarkar and Yashpal Sharma, for the home side, had shown any conviction in coping with the uneven bounce.

President's XI

K. Srikkanth c Tavaré b Underwood	66	– b Underwood	1
Sanjeeva Rao c Taylor b Dilley	17	– b Lever	0
*D. B. Vengsarkar c Botham b Emburey	37	– c Botham b Emburey	25
Arun Lal b Underwood	6	– c Taylor b Lever	0
Yashpal Sharma c Fletcher b Underwood	6	– (6) not out	61
Kirti Azad c Lever b Emburey	5	– (7) c Gooch b Underwood	24
R. M. H. Binny c Gooch b Emburey	21	– (8) b Emburey	10
D. Chopra c Taylor b Underwood	8	– (5) b Emburey	35
G. Sharma c Taylor b Underwood	22	– c Botham b Underwood	1
†Z. Parkar not out	1	– c Gatting b Underwood	0
Randhir Singh b Underwood	3	– lbw b Underwood	10
B 3, l-b 1, n-b 6	10	L-b 4, n-b 5	9
1/35 2/123 3/128 4/134 5/143 6/147 7/163 8/187 9/198	202	1/1 2/5 3/10 4/45 5/75 6/112 7/135 8/136 9/136	176

Bowling: *First Innings*—Dilley 6–0–31–1; Botham 6–0–27–0; Lever 8–0–27–0; Underwood 21.1–7–64–6; Emburey 14–1–43–3. *Second Innings*—Lever 6–2–19–2; Underwood 29.4–7–72–5; Emburey 24–5–76–3.

England XI

G. A. Gooch c Sharma b Randhir	17	– b Kirti Azad	16
G. Cook c Arun Lal b Kirti Azad	39	– b Kirti Azad	30
C. J. Tavaré c Vengsarkar b Kirti Azad	51	– st Parkar b Sharma	7
†R. W. Taylor c Sharma b Kirti Azad	4		
*K. W. R. Fletcher c Vengsarkar b Kirti Azad	2	– (4) not out	35
M. W. Gatting c and b Kirti Azad	2	– (5) c Vengsarkar b Sharma	8
I. T. Botham c Chopra b Kirti Azad	32	– (6) b Chopra	25
G. R. Dilley b Kirti Azad	3	– (7) not out	5
J. E. Emburey c and b Chopra	33		
D. L. Underwood not out	22		
J. K. Lever b Sharma	16		
B 14, l-b 4, n-b 4	22	B 5, l-b 4, n-b 1	10
1/19 2/94 3/98 4/106 5/120 6/121 7/159 8/172 9/213	243	1/44 2/49 3/61 4/79 5/115	(5 wkts) 136

Bowling: *First Innings*—Binny 6–0–22–0; Randhir 4–1–20–1; Chopra 22–7–60–1; Sharma 23.1–10–56–1; Kirti Azad 27–7–63–7. *Second Innings*—Binny 2–0–17–0; Chopra 3–0–8–1; Sharma 14–3–30–2; Kirti Azad 19–1–71–2; Yashpal 0.1–0–0–0.

Umpires: K. B. Ramaswamy and J. Gothaskar.

WEST ZONE v AN ENGLAND XI

At Baroda, November 21, 22, 23. Drawn. England lost only six wickets in the match, two of them being Gooch's when he was given out lbw to balls he seemed to hit. But on a slow pitch that lasted better than expected, the touring side were only briefly in contention for their fourth successive win, when West Zone, making no attempt to score 271 in three and a half hours, were 91 for four with eighty minutes left. Then Nayak, a wristy left-hander, took the battle to the bowlers and with Satham added 106. Boycott looked like making his second consecutive hundred until he was caught ankle-high at short mid-on, and Tavaré ended four and a half hours of relentless concentration with a hoick to deep mid-wicket. In the conditions, the main credit belonged to England's bowlers for, although West Zone were without Gavaskar, Vengsarkar and Patil, it needed a concerted effort in great heat to bowl them out in their first innings in 280 minutes. Dilley, despite bowling fourteen no-balls, bowled better than his figures suggested.

England XI

G. A. Gooch lbw b Satham	17	– lbw b Parsana	32
G. Boycott c Mankad b Joshi	66	– not out	73
C. J. Tavaré c Parkar b Joshi	96		
D. I. Gower c Parkar b Parsana	39	– not out	33
*K. W. R. Fletcher not out	39		
I. T. Botham not out	6	– (3) b Parsana	24
B 4, l-b 6, w 1, n-b 4	15	L-b 3, n-b 6	9
1/39 2/116 3/183 4/262 (4 wkts dec.)	278	1/49 2/106 (2 wkts dec.)	171

G. R. Dilley, J. E. Emburey, †R. W. Taylor, D. L. Underwood and R. G. D. Willis did not bat.

Bowling: *First Innings*—Ghavri 11–1–40–0; Satham 9–3–26–1; Parsana 32–7–77–1; Nayak 8–2–17–0; Bhalekar 2–0–4–0; Joshi 30–8–62–2; Mankad 8–1–37–0. *Second Innings*—Ghavri 11–0–45–0; Satham 1–0–3–0; Parsana 16–4–40–2; Nayak 3–0–15–0; Joshi 13–2–43–0; Gaekwad 3–0–16–0.

West Zone

A. D. Gaekwad lbw b Dilley	14	– c Gower b Underwood	20
G. A. Parkar c Gooch b Botham	9	– b Botham	1
R. B. Bhalekar c Boycott b Willis	6	– c Tavaré b Emburey	30
*A. V. Mankad c Botham b Emburey	49	– (5) c Taylor b Emburey	17
S. V. Nayak b Emburey	22	– (4) not out	77
N. Y. Satham not out	26	– not out	42
K. D. Ghavri c Taylor b Botham	2		
†K. More run out	1		
D. D. Parsana c Taylor b Willis	24		
U. C. Joshi b Underwood	1		
D. P. Nanavati absent ill			
B 2, l-b 5, n-b 18	25	N-b 10	10
1/16 2/25 3/46 4/116 5/130 6/133 7/138 8/178 9/179	179	1/14 2/47 3/59 4/91 (4 wkts)	197

Bowling: *First Innings*—Willis 12–4–28–2; Botham 16–4–30–2; Dilley 11–0–47–1; Underwood 4.5–0–16–1; Emburey 17–6–33–2. *Second Innings*—Willis 5–0–16–0; Botham 7–2–26–1; Dilley 8–0–38–0; Underwood 13–5–25–1; Emburey 17–1–59–2; Gooch 7–2–23–0.

Umpires: P. R. Punjabi and J. D. Ghosh.

†INDIA v ENGLAND

First One-day International

At Ahmedabad, November 25. England won by five wickets. A fifth-wicket stand of 65 off 20.4 overs between Fletcher and Gatting was at the heart of a win which looked unlikely when four wickets fell for 61. India, without Kapil Dev who had a back strain, did well to run England close after being put in on a pitch moist with dew on a hazy morning. Vengsarkar and Kirti Azad repaired the loss of early wickets with a stand of 52, but Underwood gave nothing away. The loss of three wickets to Binny made England's task of scoring 157 in 46 overs harder than it should have been over a fast outfield, and with Shastri and Doshi bowling tightly, the score after 30 overs was only 89 for four. However, Fletcher and Gatting were rewarded for their patience, and Botham finished the match off with thirteen balls to spare by sweeping and pulling Binny for successive 6s.

Man of the Match: M. W. Gatting.

India

*S. M Gavaskar c Gooch b Willis	0	R. J. Shastri run out	19
K. Srikkanth b Botham	0	R. M. H. Binny not out	2
D. B. Vengsarkar c and b Underwood	46		
G. R. Viswanath c Cook b Gooch	8	B 4, l-b 13, w 7, n-b 3	27
Kirti Azad b Botham	30		
Madan Lal c Lever b Underwood	6	1/2 2/8 3/39 4/91 (7 wkts, 46 overs)	156
†S. M. H. Kirmani not out	18	5/113 6/119 7/154	

D. R. Doshi and Randhir Singh did not bat.

Bowling: Willis 9-3-17-1; Botham 10-4-20-2; Lever 10-0-46-0; Gooch 7-0-28-1; Underwood 10-3-18-2.

England

G. A. Gooch c Kirmani b Binny	23	I. T. Botham not out	25
G. Boycott lbw b Madan Lal	5		
G. Cook c Viswanath b Binny	13	L-b 7, w 2, n-b 4	13
D. I. Gower c and b Binny	8		
*K. W. R. Fletcher b Doshi	26	1/5 2/43 (5 wkts, 43.5 overs)	160
M. W. Gatting not out	47	3/46 4/61 5/126	

†C. J. Richards, J. K. Lever, D. L. Underwood and R. G. D. Willis did not bat.

Bowling: Madan Lal 10-2-30-1; Randhir 6-0-18-0; Binny 7.5-3-35-3; Shastri 10-1-24-0; Doshi 10-1-40-1.

Umpires: M. V. Gothaskar and Hanumantha Rao.

INDIA v ENGLAND

First Test Match

At Bombay, November 27, 28, 29, December 1. India won by 138 runs. Fine bowling by Kapil Dev and Madan Lal on the fourth morning gave India a deceptively big win in what had been a close match. When it finished 50 minutes after lunch that day, it became the fourth successive Test at the Wankhede Stadium to end in four days. The bounce, uneven from the start, became more variable as the game progressed, several batsmen falling lbw to balls that hit them ankle-high.

There was a time on the second day when Gavaskar must have wondered whether he would have done better not to have won the toss. Having seen India bowled out for 179 in four and a half hours, Boycott and Tavaré, intent only on occupation, built a solid answer with a stand of 92 in 59 overs. At 95 for two, England seemed well placed for a lead that might have made certain of the match, but a series of controversial decisions changed the picture. Gower was adjudged run out by Srikkanth, retrieving in the short-leg area, whereupon Doshi, abetted by umpire Ramaswamy, removed Fletcher, Botham and Emburey as they tried to sweep. Nine wickets fell in two and threequarter hours, and on the third morning India's prospects were further helped in the fifth over when Gavaskar, on the back foot, survived an lbw appeal from a ball by Willis which came back and kept low. Shastri, promoted four places, impressively consolidated India's advantage by batting for two and a half hours, permitting himself only strokes which could be made straight-batted. It was a fine innings from a nineteen-year-old in only his fourth Test.

England were still strongly in the game when India fell back to 157 for eight. But Kapil Dev, hitting through the line with a certainty unmatched by either set of batsmen, added 46 in even time with Madan Lal, and on the fourth morning Madan Lal and Doshi, by careful and determined batting, put on another 24.

Psychologically, those extra 70 runs were vital. Though time was no object, England approached the task of scoring 241 in a defeatist frame of mind, lacking confidence in both the pitch and the umpires, although in the event it was a fine opening spell by Kapil Dev which undid them. In contrast to the first innings, he swung the new ball away from the right-handers, and in his first and second overs he removed Gooch and Tavaré to catches at the wicket and at second slip. Gower played freely for a time, but Madan Lal had Boycott and Fletcher lbw with break-backs that kept low, and at 42 for five the innings was in tatters.

Only a last-wicket stand of 27 between Underwood and Willis spared England the indignity of their lowest score in a Test against India – 101 at The Oval in 1971. Their previous lowest in India was 159 in Madras in 1972–73. Botham, who bowled unchanged through India's first innings, deserved better figures than he achieved. When he reached 16 in England's second innings, he completed the "double double" of 2,000 runs and 200 wickets in Tests, in seven fewer matches than Benaud (49) and 38 fewer than Sobers (80).

India

*S. M. Gavaskar c Taylor b Botham	55	– c Taylor b Botham	14
K. Srikkanth c Fletcher b Willis	0	– run out	13
D. B. Vengsarkar c Tavaré b Dilley	17	– c Tavaré b Botham	5
G. R. Viswanath c Boycott b Botham	8	– c Taylor b Botham	37
S. M. Patil lbw b Botham	17	– lbw b Botham	13
Kirti Azad c sub (Gatting) b Underwood	14	– (7) lbw b Emburey	17
Kapil Dev c Taylor b Botham	38	– (8) lbw b Willis	46
†S. M. H. Kirmani lbw b Dilley	12	– (9) c Taylor b Emburey	0
Madan Lal c Taylor b Dilley	0	– (10) not out	17
R. J. Shastri not out	3	– (6) lbw b Dilley	33
D. R. Doshi c Taylor b Dilley	0	– b Botham	7
L-b 5, n-b 10	15	B 8, l-b 8, n-b 9	25
1/1 2/40 3/70 4/104 5/112 6/164 7/164 8/168 9/179	179	1/19 2/24 3/43 4/72 5/90 6/138 7/154 8/157 9/203	227

Bowling: *First Innings*—Willis 12–5–33–1; Botham 28–6–72–4; Dilley 13–1–47–4; Underwood 4–2–12–1. *Second Innings*—Willis 13–4–31–1; Botham 22.3–3–61–5; Dilley 18–5–61–1; Underwood 11–4–14–0; Emburey 13–2–35–2.

England

G. A. Gooch b Madan Lal	2	– c Kirmani b Kapil Dev	1
G. Boycott c Srikkanth b Kirti Azad	60	– lbw b Madan Lal	3
C. J. Tavaré c Shastri b Doshi	56	– c Gavaskar b Kapil Dev	0
D. I. Gower run out	5	– lbw b Kapil Dev	20
*K. W. R. Fletcher lbw b Doshi	15	– lbw b Madan Lal	3
I. T. Botham c Gavaskar b Doshi	7	– c Kirti Azad b Kapil Dev	29
J. E. Emburey lbw b Doshi	0	– c Gavaskar b Madan Lal	1
G. R. Dilley b Shastri	0	– b Madan Lal	9
†R. W. Taylor not out	9	– b Madan Lal	1
D. L. Underwood c Kirmani b Kapil Dev	8	– not out	13
R. G. D. Willis c Gavaskar b Doshi	1	– c Kirmani b Kapil Dev	13
B 1, l-b 2	3	B 4, l-b 3, n-b 2	9
1/3 2/95 3/105 4/131 5/143 6/146 7/147 8/147 9/163	166	1/2 2/4 3/28 4/29 5/42 6/50 7/73 8/74 9/75	102

Bowling: *First Innings*—Kapil Dev 22–10–29–1; Madan Lal 12–2–24–1; Doshi 29.1–12–39–5; Shastri 19–6–27–1; Patil 3–0–9–0; Kirti Azad 15–4–35–1. *Second Innings*—Kapil Dev 13.2–0–70–5; Madan Lal 12–6–23–5; Doshi 1–1–0–0.

Umpires: K. B. Ramaswamy and Swaroop Kishen.

SOUTH ZONE v AN ENGLAND XI

At Hyderabad, December 4, 5, 6. Drawn. Despite three declarations, a positive result was always unlikely and the game petered out when England made no attempt to meet a target of 303 in 230 minutes. Willis, digging the ball in, made an opening on the first day with a spell of 6–4–5–3, but the stylish Narasimha Rao, strongly supported by the tail, effected a recovery. On the second day Gooch took advantage of the best batting conditions since Pune to score his first hundred of the tour, but Boycott took 218 minutes over 55 and to keep the game open, Fletcher declared 61 behind. Runs were readily conceded in South Zone's second innings, but when off-spinner Yadav dismissed Gower and Cook (first ball), England settled for practice. Fletcher and Gatting added 154 in almost three hours, Fletcher's hundred coming in 216 minutes.

South Zone

K. Srikkanth c Gooch b Willis	21	– c Allott b Willis	31
V. Sivaramakrishnan lbw b Allott	38	– c Gatting b Emburey	30
V. Mohan Raj c Gatting b Willis	20	– b Emburey	59
A. V. Jayaprakash c Cook b Willis	31	– (6) st Richards b Cook	12
*B. P. Patel c Emburey b Willis	0	– lbw b Emburey	68
M. V. Narasimha Rao not out	51	– (4) lbw b Fletcher	12
R. M. H. Binny c Richards b Lever	1	– not out	9
†B. Reddy c Richards b Lever	6	– (9) not out	14
N. S. Yadav b Emburey	24		
D. Meher Baba b Emburey	31	– (8) c Allott b Cook	0
K. Bharatkumar not out	7		
L-b 8, n-b 9	17	L-b 3, w 2, n-b 1	6
1/49 2/77 3/115 4/119 5/124 6/134 7/140 8/188 9/236	(9 wkts dec.) 247	1/40 2/76 3/109 4/172 5/209 6/221 7/221	(7 wkts dec.) 241

Bowling: *First Innings*—Willis 17–6–35–4; Lever 19–2–83–2; Gooch 5–0–26–0; Allott 16–3–48–1; Emburey 15–3–38–2. *Second Innings*—5–0–31–1; Lever 5–0–24–0; Allott 3–1–9–0; Emburey 24–8–71–3; Fletcher 20–0–82–1; Cook 3.5–0–18–2.

England XI

G. A. Gooch not out	119		
G. Boycott not out	55		
*K. W. R. Fletcher (did not bat)	–	(2) lbw b Yadav	108
D. I. Gower (did not bat)	–	(1) c Reddy b Yadav	8
G. Cook (did not bat)	–	(3) lbw b Yadav	0
M. W. Gatting (did not bat)	–	(4) c Reddy b Narasimha Rao	71
J. E. Emburey (did not bat)	–	(5) not out	11
†C. J. Richards (did not bat)	–	(6) not out	11
B 5, l-b 3, n-b 4	12	B 4, l-b 8, n-b 2	14
(no wkt dec.)	186	1/29 2/29 3/183 4/209 (4 wkts)	223

P. J. W. Allott, J. K. Lever and R. G. D. Willis did not bat.

Bowling: *First Innings*—Binny 7–1–30–0; Bharatkumar 7–2–23–0; Meher Baba 11–1–38–0; Srikkanth 2–0–10–0; Yadav 19–2–48–0; Narasimha Rao 11–3–25–0. *Second Innings*—Binny 5–1–24–0; Bharatkumar 8–2–19–0; Meher Baba 6–0–20–0; Yadav 32–6–97–3; Narasimha Rao 17–0–49–1.

Umpires: D. N. Dotiwala and Mohammad Ghouse.

INDIA v ENGLAND

Second Test Match

At Bangalore, December 9, 10, 12, 13, 14. Drawn. In normal circumstances, it is a dull match that sees only 23 wickets fall in a full five days, but the second Test, though an almost certain draw from lunch-time on the third day, will long be remembered for the batting of Gavaskar. In the longest innings ever played for India – 11 hours, 48 minutes – he gave a flawless exhibition of the defensive arts, batting chancelessly from the first ball of the third day until mid-morning on the fifth. His concentration was unwavering and his perfect balance and coordination in defence, plus the unerring selection and beautiful execution of his attacking strokes, made it a connoisseur's delight. Of his 21 4s, mostly through the covers off the front foot or between square leg and fine leg off his hip, all but one came from the middle of the bat.

Justification for Gavaskar's slowness lay in an England score of 400 which occupied two days and all but insured them against losing. To that end they played an extra batsman, Gatting, at the expense of a bowler, Emburey, from the side that lost the first Test, setting their sights no higher than a draw even before Willis, suffering from chest and stomach troubles, cried off on the morning of the match. He was replaced by Lever.

Gooch and Boycott gave the innings a buoyant start by scoring 84 in the first two hours after Fletcher had won the toss; but in the afternoon and evening Tavaré, dropping a dead bat even on half-volleys, consumed three hours making 22. Gower, after a shaky start against the left-arm spinners, played well to reach 50 in 101 minutes. Then he, too, gave best to Doshi and Shastri, spending 140 minutes adding 32 before Shastri had him lbw on the second morning with what, to the left-hander, was a perfect off-break which turned and hurried.

Half an hour later Fletcher, given out caught at the wicket when he swept at Shastri, so far forgot the standards expected of an England captain that he used his bat to cuff the stumps awry as he turned for the pavilion, sure he had not hit the ball. It was an unworthy reaction from someone who had been at pains to tell his team to accept the umpiring for what it was and he later wrote a letter of apology to the Indian Board. However, on balance England benefited from various questionable decisions in the match. A controlled 55 by Botham, and a positive ninth-wicket stand of 69 between Dilley and Taylor, took England to 400 just before the close.

Despite the slowness of the pitch, England might have put India under pressure by taking wickets early in their innings. But Srikkanth won the initiative with 65 off only 87 balls, and by the close the Indians were safe at 189 for one. Lever, rediscovering his in-swinger with the second new ball, took four wickets in eight overs next morning, but Gavaskar remained immovable. Only four and threequarter hours were left for England's second innings, when Boycott passed Cowdrey's world record of 188 Test innings, and a match watched by more than 200,000 petered to a draw.

England

G. A. Gooch c Gavaskar b Shastri	58	– lbw b Kapil Dev	40
G. Boycott c Gavaskar b Kapil Dev	36	– b Doshi	50
C. J. Tavaré lbw b Madan Lal	22	– c Patil b Shastri	31
D. I. Gower lbw b Shastri	82	– not out	34
J. K. Lever lbw b Kapil Dev	1		
*K. W. R. Fletcher c Kirmani b Shastri	25	– (5) not out	12
I. T. Botham c Madan Lal b Doshi	55		
M. W. Gatting lbw b Kapil Dev	29		
G. R. Dilley c Gavaskar b Shastri	52		
†R. W. Taylor c Kapil Dev b Doshi	33		
D. L. Underwood not out	2		
L-b 2, n-b 3	5	L-b 6, n-b 1	7
1/88 2/96 3/180 4/181 5/223 6/230 7/278 8/324 9/393	400	1/59 2/105 3/152 (3 wkts dec.)	174

Bowling: *First Innings*—Kapil Dev 40–3–136–3; Madan Lal 24–7–46–1; Doshi 39–15–83–2; Kirti Azad 12–1–47–0; Shastri 43–14–83–4. *Second Innings*—Kapil Dev 12–2–49–1; Madan Lal 4–2–14–0; Doshi 21–8–37–1; Kirti Azad 12–3–36–0; Shastri 20–7–31–1.

India

*S. M. Gavaskar c and b Underwood	172
K. Srikkanth c Gooch b Botham	65
D. B. Vengsarkar c Taylor b Lever	43
G. R. Viswanath lbw b Lever	3
R. J. Shastri lbw b Lever	1
S. M. Patil lbw b Lever	17
Kirti Azad c Fletcher b Underwood	24
Kapil Dev c Taylor b Lever	59
†S. M. H. Kirmani lbw b Botham	9
Madan Lal not out	7
D. R. Doshi c Boycott b Underwood	0
B 2, l-b 15, n-b 8, w 3	28
1/102 2/195 3/208 4/214 5/242 6/284 7/376 8/412 9/428	428

Bowling: Botham 47–9–137–2; Dilley 24–4–75–0; Lever 36–9–100–5; Underwood 43–21–88–3.

Umpires: M. V. Gothaskar and P. R. Punjabi.

NORTH ZONE v AN ENGLAND XI

At Jammu, December 16, 17, 18. Drawn. A draw was always the likely result on a slow pitch which seamed in the morning mist and spun throughout; but an England collapse from 76 for no wicket to 154 all out on the second morning gave the match an unexpected twist and interest. Despite the absence of Kapil Dev, Madan Lal and Kirti Azad, North Zone looked likely winners when they started the last day 101 ahead at 88 for two. However, Willis, captaining the side while Fletcher rested, conceded only 9 runs in a spell of fourteen overs against unambitious batting, and the chance passed. England, set 214 in 130 minutes, were 70 without loss at the beginning of the last twenty overs, but the control of sixteen-year-old Maninder Singh, a promising slow left-arm bowler, persuaded Gooch and Boycott to opt for practice. Ashok Malhotra, a 5ft 4in right-hander, quick-footed and wristy, was another to impress in the first match a touring side had played in the twin state of Jammu and Kashmir.

North Zone

C. P. S. Chauhan lbw b Allott	8	– b Emburey	43
R. Lamba lbw b Lever	1	– c Gatting b Emburey	34
†S. C. Khanna lbw b Lever	2		
M. Amarnath b Allott	16	– (7) not out	30
*Yashpal Sharma c Richards b Allott	3	– c Gatting b Emburey	1
A. Malhotra b Lever	80	– not out	67
Gursharan Singh c Richards b Allott	0	– (4) b Emburey	5
D. Chopra lbw b Allott	17	– (3) c Tavaré b Willis	14
R. C. Shukla lbw b Lever	28		
S. Talwar b Emburey	5		
Maninder Singh not out	0		
B 3, l-b 2, w 1, n-b 1	7	L-b 5, n-b 1	6
1/6 2/8 3/30 4/33 5/40 6/40 7/80 8/150 9/167	167	1/71 2/88 3/101 4/101 5/114 (5 wkts dec.)	200

Bowling: *First Innings*—Lever 19–7–57–4; Willis 11–4–21–0; Allott 16–4–54–5; Gooch 12–6–21–0; Emburey 3.1–0–7–1. *Second Innings*—Lever 12–1–59–0; Willis 20–8–22–1; Allott 17.5–8–41–0; Emburey 25–6–72–4.

England XI

G. A. Gooch lbw b Yashpal	42	– not out	58
G. Boycott lbw b Amarnath	35	– not out	59
M. W. Gatting c Khanna b Amarnath	26		
C. J. Tavaré c Shukla b Yashpal	7		
D. I. Gower run out	0		
G. Cook lbw b Maninder	8		
J. E. Emburey c Shukla b Amarnath	2		
J. K. Lever b Maninder	15		
†C. J. Richards c Amarnath b Chopra	5		
P. J. W. Allott c Chauhan b Chopra	4		
*R. G. D. Willis not out	0		
B 8, l-b 2, n-b 1	10	B 4, l-b 6	10
1/76 2/95 3/110 4/120 5/121 6/123 7/131 8/146 9/150	154	(no wkt)	127

Bowling: *First Innings*—Amarnath 28–6–75–3; Lamba 2–0–20–0; Maninder 15–6–27–2; Talwar 2–1–4–0; Shukla 1–0–2–0; Yashpal 14–6–12–2; Chopra 1.3–1–4–2. *Second Innings*—Amarnath 3–0–13–0; Maninder 18–8–28–0; Talwar 5–0–24–0; Shukla 10–2–19–0; Yashpal 2–1–5–0; Chopra 3–1–12–0; Chauhan 1–0–6–0; Malhotra 1–0–10–0.

Umpires: B. Ganguli and M. G. Subramaniam.

†INDIA v ENGLAND

Second One-day International

At Jullundur, December 20. India won by six wickets. Vengsarkar's lovely driving, mostly through the covers, took India to their first victory over England in five limited-overs contests since 1974. Yet the touring side fought hard to preserve their record, and defending a low score they required India to make 8 off the final seven deliveries. However, Yashpal clubbed Botham straight for 6, leaving Vengsarkar the deserved honour of finishing the match with the last of many 4s past extra-cover. Earlier, a stand of 110 in seventeen overs between Gower and Gatting, who drove Shastri for four 6s in one over, produced England's only batting of quality. A full house of 25,000 watched the game, but Jullundur in mid-winter was an unfortunate venue for a 50-overs contest: morning mist reduced the match to 36 overs a side, and the end came in an eerie half-light at 5.17, only minutes before sunset.

Man of the Match: D. B. Vengsarkar.

England

G. A. Gooch b Madan Lal	12	G. Cook b Kapil Dev	1
G. Boycott run out	6	†C. J. Richards lbw b Kapil Dev	0
I. T. Botham lbw b Madan Lal	5		
*K. W. R. Fletcher c Kirti Azad b Patil	5	B 2, l-b 4, w 1, n-b 1	8
D. I. Gower run out	53	1/18, 2/22, 3/25, 4/48, 5/158, 6/161, 7/161 (7 wkts, 36 overs)	161
M. W. Gatting not out	71		

D. L. Underwood, J. K. Lever and R. G. D. Willis did not bat.

Bowling: Kapil Dev 8–1–26–2; Madan Lal 7–0–33–2; Nayak 7–2–25–0; Patil 7–0–16–1; Shastri 7–0–53–0.

India

K. Srikkanth lbw b Botham	17	Yashpal Sharma not out	28
D. B. Vengsarkar not out	88	B 3, l-b 3, n-b 2	8
Kirti Azad c Gower b Gooch	14		
S. M. Patil b Gooch	3	1/41, 2/69, 3/78, 4/89 (4 wkts, 35.3 overs)	164
Kapil Dev c Willis b Underwood	6		

*S. M. Gavaskar, S. V. Nayak, Madan Lal, †S. M. H. Kirmani and R. J. Shastri did not bat.

Bowling: Willis 7.3–2–41–0; Lever 7–0–31–0; Gooch 7–0–25–2; Botham 7–0–33–1; Underwood 7–1–26–1.

Umpires: Swaroop Kishen and J. D. Ghosh.

INDIA v ENGLAND

Third Test Match

At New Delhi, December 23, 24, 26, 27, 28. Drawn. This time only nineteen wickets fell and it *was* dull. At the root of it lay the type of pitch that makes 450-500 the "par" first-innings score – and an over-rate that underlined how necessary it is to introduce a daily minimum. England managed just 13.06, which was nothing to be proud of, but that India, with only one bowler above medium pace, should be allowed to average 12.79 without interference from the umpires made a travesty of cricket; especially as Gavaskar was to admit afterwards that this was a preconceived policy, calculated to limit India's batting time once Gooch and Boycott had given England a solid foundation with a stand of 132 after Fletcher had again won the toss.

The day before the match the Indian board upheld England's objection to Mohammad Ghouse and substituted Swaroop Kishen, who had stood at Bombay. It excited some unfavourable comment in the local press, but the match itself was played in good spirit, produced batting records rather than controversy and, apart from the disregard of the torpid over-rates, was well umpired.

Of the records set, the most notable was by Boycott, who, on his way to equalling Hammond's and Cowdrey's tally of 22 Test hundreds for England, became, when 82, the most prolific of all Test batsmen, passing Sobers's 8,032 runs for West Indies. (Boycott needed 190 innings to Sobers's 160). For India, Shastri shared in two record partnerships against England – 128 for the eighth wicket with Kirmani and 104 for the ninth with Madan Lal – as India compiled their highest total against England in India.

For Tavaré, in his seventh Test match, there was an enterprising maiden hundred: under orders not to hang about he needed only 303 balls for his 149. Boycott's 105 came off 278 balls. However, the best batting was provided by the artistic Viswanath (107 off 200 balls) in his 74th successive Test for India, and by the mighty Botham who, with a declaration in the offing, clubbed 66 off 48 balls with five 6s, three of them 30 yards beyond the line.

The match was shaped not only by the pitch and the over-rate but also by the reluctance of the ball to swing, which was unusual for Delhi and in sharp contrast to England's last two Tests there. Changes of ball were commonplace as, with the acquiescence of the umpires, both sides probed for one that swung. But of the dozen tried, no more than three fulfilled the bowlers' hopes and then only briefly. One of these was being used during the sole period in five days when either side was vulnerable: through a combination of careless strokes and determined England bowling, India sank to 254 for seven. But with India needing only another 23 to save the follow-on, Lever bowled four bad overs to give Kirmani and Shastri a footing. On so placid a pitch, though, England would have been hard pressed to win even if India had been obliged to bat again.

England

G. A. Gooch c Kapil Dev b Doshi	71	– not out	20
G. Boycott c Madan Lal b Doshi	105	– not out	34
C. J. Tavaré b Madan Lal	149		
D. I. Gower lbw b Madan Lal	0		
*K. W. R. Fletcher b Patil	51		
I. T. Botham c Kirti Azad b Madan Lal	66		
M. W. Gatting b Madan Lal	5		
†R. W. Taylor lbw b Madan Lal	0		
J. K. Lever b Kapil Dev	2		
D. L. Underwood not out	2		
L-b 15, n-b 10	25	B 9, n-b 5	14
1/132 2/248 3/248 (9 wkts dec.)	476	(no wkt dec.)	68
4/368 5/459 6/465 7/465 8/474 9/476			

R. G. D. Willis did not bat.

Bowling: *First Innings*—Kapil Dev 40.4–5–126–1; Madan Lal 32–4–85–5; Doshi 40–15–68–2; Shastri 27–3–109–0; Kirti Azad 9–2–35–0; Patil 8–1–28–1. *Second Innings*—Kapil Dev 4–1–18–0; Madan Lal 3–1–4–0; Patil 3–1–10–0; Srikkanth 6–1–10–0; Gavaskar 3–0–12–0.

India

*S. M. Gavaskar c Taylor b Lever	46
K. Srikkanth b Willis	6
D. B. Vengsarkar c Fletcher b Underwood	8
G. R. Viswanath b Botham	107
S. M. Patil b Willis	31
Kirti Azad st Taylor b Underwood	16
Kapil Dev c Gooch b Botham	16
R. J. Shastri lbw b Gooch	93
†S. M. H. Kirmani lbw b Lever	67
Madan Lal b Gooch	44
D. R. Doshi not out	0
B 20, l-b 8, w 4, n-b 21	53
1/11 2/41 3/89 4/174 5/213 6/237 7/254 8/382 9/486	487

Bowling: Willis 26–3–99–2; Lever 37–7–104–2; Underwood 48–18–97–2; Botham 41–6–122–2; Gooch 8.1–1–12–2.

Umpires: Swaroop Kishen and Hanumantha Rao.

INDIA v ENGLAND

Fourth Test Match

At Calcutta, January 1, 2, 3, 5, 6. Drawn. England had their best chance to date of levelling the series when a brisk, inventive 60 not out by Fletcher enabled him to leave his bowlers six hours to bowl India out a second time – or India to score 306 to win on a slow pitch with the ball keeping low. But on the last morning the smog from the nearby River Hooghlie, drifting like bonfire smoke into Eden Gardens, spared India 70 minutes of batting and took the pressure out of what could have been a tense last day. England might still have won had Gavaskar gone early; but after an anxious start, in which he survived two close lbws, he batted imperturbably through the day.

It was a fine match, watched on all five days by a notably well-behaved capacity crowd of 78,800. India made their first change of the series, preferring Yadav to Kirti Azad, who had taken only one wicket with his brisk off-spin. England, convinced it would not be another stalemate but in doubt as to which bowlers would be best suited to a suspect pitch, brought in Emburey for Lever, partly in deference to Underwood's known liking to be supported by another spinner.

Kapil Dev, after being firmly hooked for 4 by Boycott – who began with unfamiliar levity – produced his best bowling of the series as, settling into a relentless line around off stump, he had Boycott, Tavaré and, on the second morning, Gatting caught at the wicket off balls that left the bat. He finished with six for 91. England, having elected to bat, were content to let Doshi and Shastri dictate, but the 93 Fletcher and Botham added for the fifth wicket was the only stand of note. When the last five wickets fell for 32, the innings ended lamely at lunchtime on the second day.

Though Underwood hit Gavaskar's off stump through a defensive stroke, India looked well placed to take control when they were 105 for two at the close. Next morning, however, Underwood had Kapil Dev caught at slip, patting a late cut, just as he was threatening mayhem, and the innings fell apart. The crucial wicket was that of Vengsarkar, who, after a slow 50 in 267 minutes, was driving and hitting off his legs with graceful fluency and power when, on the stroke of lunch, he was adjudged caught at the wicket off the second new ball off a snick he thought had failed to carry.

England used the heavy roller in the hope of opening the cracks and breaking up the pitch. Boycott, pushing forward, was lbw to Madan Lal, but with a lead of 89 they spent the rest day hopeful that the ball's increasingly low bounce would make 250 out of range in India's second innings. India averaged 13.5 overs an hour, Doshi and Shastri justifying Gavaskar's faith in their ability to keep control to defensive fields. Gower was tied down, but Fletcher cleverly restored the impetus Gooch had given the innings. The declaration came 40 minutes from the close, but the smog, Gavaskar and the pitch's failure to deteriorate ended all hopes of an England victory.

England

G. A. Gooch c Viswanath b Doshi	47	– b Doshi	63
G. Boycott c Kirmani b Kapil Dev	18	– lbw b Madan Lal	6
C. J. Tavaré c Kirmani b Kapil Dev	7	– run out	25
D. I. Gower c Kirmani b Shastri	11	– run out	74
*K. W. R. Fletcher lbw b Madan Lal	69	– (6) not out	60
I. T. Botham c Gavaskar b Kapil Dev	58	– (5) c Yadav b Doshi	31
D. L. Underwood c Patil b Kapil Dev	13		
M. W. Gatting c Kirmani b Kapil Dev	0	– (7) not out	2
J. E. Emburey lbw b Kapil Dev	1		
†R. W. Taylor c Vengsarkar b Doshi	6		
R. G. D. Willis not out	11		
L-b 3, n-b 4	7	L-b 4	4
1/25 2/39 3/68 4/95 5/188 6/216 7/218 8/224 9/230	248	1/24 2/88 3/107 4/154 5/259 (5 wkts dec.)	265

Bowling: *First Innings*—Kapil Dev 31–6–91–6; Madan Lal 20–4–58–1; Doshi 19.2–8–28–2; Yadav 17–7–42–0; Shastri 21–10–22–1. *Second Innings*—Kapil Dev 21–3–81–0; Madan Lal 19–3–58–1; Doshi 27–5–63–2; Yadav 3–0–11–0; Shastri 17–4–35–0; Patil 3–0–13–0.

India

*S. M. Gavaskar b Underwood	42	– not out	83
K. Srikkanth b Underwood	10	– c Botham b Emburey	25
D. B. Vengsarkar c Taylor b Botham	70	– c Tavaré b Fletcher	32
G. R. Viswanath c and b Emburey	15	– c Gooch b Emburey	0
S. M. Patil c Fletcher b Emburey	0	– not out	17
Kapil Dev c Tavaré b Underwood	22		
R. J. Shastri run out	8		
†S. M. H. Kirmani b Botham	10		
Madan Lal c Gooch b Willis	1		
N. S. Yadav c Taylor b Willis	5		
D. R. Doshi not out	7		
B 2, l-b 4, w 1, n-b 11	18	L-b 2, n-b 11	13
1/33 2/83 3/117 4/117 5/143 6/180 7/184 8/187 9/196	208	1/48 2/117 3/120	(3 wkts) 170

Bowling: *First Innings*—Willis 14–3–28–2; Botham 27–8–63–2; Underwood 29–13–45–3; Emburey 24–11–44–2; Gooch 6–1–10–0. *Second Innings*—Willis 6–0–21–0; Botham 11–3–26–0; Underwood 31–18–38–0; Emburey 30–11–62–2; Gooch 2–0–4–0; Fletcher 3–1–6–1.

Umpires: Swaroop Kishen and M. V. Gothaskar.

EAST ZONE v AN ENGLAND XI

At Jamshedpur, January 8, 9, 10. Drawn. Gooch, captaining an England side for the first time while Fletcher, Willis and Botham rested, put East Zone in; but though the pitch was quick and bouncy, its help for seam bowling failed to match its greenness. Pranab Roy, son of the old Test player, Pankaj, and himself just picked for the Madras Test that followed, left in the second over, padding up to Lever; but Nandy, making up in concentration what he lacked in elegance, held an end for five hours and ten minutes, despite another good display by Allott, who was unlucky not to do better than five for 77. Cook, rusty after so little cricket, made a determined effort to play himself into the departed Boycott's Test place, Gooch hit powerfully, and Gatting made his first tour hundred (in 328 minutes) as England opted for batting practice.

East Zone

P. Roy lbw b Lever	3	– not out	35
P. Nandy c and b Allott	97	– not out	30
Arun Lal b Dilley	17		
H. Gidwani c Gooch b Allott	26		
R. Venkat c Richards b Dilley	7		
K. Das c Richards b Dilley	2		
†S. Banerjee c Tavaré b Allott	23		
S. Sahu c Tavaré b Allott	10		
*Paramjit Singh c Emburey b Allott	38		
Randhir Singh run out	6		
S. Sinha not out	0		
B 4, l-b 4, n-b 5	13	L-b 1, n-b 8	9
1/3 2/53 3/98 4/140 5/146 6/176 7/189 8/211 9/228	242	1/113 2/125 3/215 4/252 5/279 6/253 7/355 8/356	(no wkt) 74

Bowling: *First Innings*—Dilley 29–3–93–3; Lever 20–3–46–1; Allott 26.5–6–77–5; Emburey 8–3–13–0. *Second Innings*—Dilley 5–2–6–0; Lever 3–2–10–0; Allott 6–3–7–0; Gatting 4–0–20–0; Cook 3–1–3–0; Tavaré 2–0–7–0; Gower 3–2–4–0; Richards 2–0–5–0; Gooch 1–0–3–0.

England XI

*G. A. Gooch c Banerjee b Paramjit	79
G. Cook c Venkat b Sahu	37
M. W. Gatting c Das b Paramjit	127
D. I. Gower c Roy b Sinha	57
C. J. Tavaré c Banerjee b Nandy	15
J. E. Emburey lbw b Paramjit	7
G. R. Dilley c Banerjee b Paramjit	23
†C. J. Richards not out	1
P. J. W. Allott b Paramjit	0
J. K. Lever not out	0
L-b 3, n-b 7	10
1/113 2/125 3/215 4/252 5/279 6/353 7/355 8/356	(8 wkts dec.) 356

R. W. Taylor did not bat.

Bowling: Randhir 5–0–17–0; Sinha 38–9–121–1; Sahu 14–0–68–1; Paramjit 35–9–108–5; Das 2–0–9–0; Nandy 5–1–22–1; Gidwani 1–0–1–0.

Umpires: K. C. Mahra and P. D. Reporter.

INDIA v ENGLAND

Fifth Test

At Madras, January 13, 14, 15, 17, 18. Drawn. A pitch similar to those at Bangalore and New Delhi tilted the match unrealistically in favour of the bat, the inevitable upshot being a high-scoring, slow-paced draw in which only seventeen wickets fell. Viswanath, whose 222 was the highest by an Indian against England (beating Gavaskar's 221 at The Oval in 1979), and Gooch, who reached his hundred off 140 balls, played the best innings of the match.

For India's third wicket, 415 runs were added by three batsmen: Viswanath, the common denominator, Vengsarkar, who was obliged to retire hurt at 150 when he ducked into a low-flying bouncer from Willis, and Yashpal Sharma, who in 492 minutes of stolid accumulation helped Viswanath add the remaining 316. The entire stand, scored at 3.44 an over, spanned ten and a quarter hours, during which time the population of India was said to have risen by 75,000. The 316 put on by Viswanath and Yashpal was a third-wicket record for India in all Tests, and the highest for any wicket in Tests between England and India.

Viswanath batted for 632 minutes, a wristy, rounded innings marred only by a missed slip catch at 141 (one of three dropped off the hapless Allott) and an uppish leg-glance off Dilley at 103, which on his best day Taylor might have caught. Towards the end of India's innings, when they were pressing for a declaration, Yashpal opened up, hooking and picking up Allott for 6s off successive balls; but he was overshadowed first by Viswanath and then by Gooch, who with a series of cleanly hit drives off Kapil Dev, front foot and back, passed 50 in an hour on his way to 127 in three and threequarter hours. By contrast Tavaré, taking Boycott's place as Gooch's partner, took Fletcher's invitation to bat as long as possible so literally that his 35 lasted five and a half hours.

Despite the batting of Viswanath and Gooch, the best session of the match was the first, in which India, put in, scored a numerically trivial but none the less vital 49 for the loss of only Roy off 24 overs. Its highlight was a superb duel between Gavaskar and Willis, who on a pitch that was then extremely lively, turned the clock back years with a spell of scalding pace and straightness. Roy, under less pressure from a wayward Botham (threequarters fit following a day in bed and an almost sleepless night), held on for a crucial 82 minutes, and by lunch, with Gavaskar and Vengsarkar still there, England's chance had gone. Had

Gavaskar not played so skilfully, and had the catches stuck, India might have been 45 for five at lunch. Yet, with the pitch developing into a featherbed so soon, it would have needed a major effort by England's bowlers to dismiss them a second time.

India

*S. M. Gavaskar c Taylor b Willis	25	– c Botham b Willis	11
P. Roy c Taylor b Dilley	6	– not out	60
D. B. Vengsarkar retired hurt	71		
G. R. Viswanath b Willis	222		
Yashpal Sharma c Tavaré b Botham	140	– (4) c Botham b Underwood	25
Kapil Dev not out	6	– (5) not out	15
A. Malhotra (did not bat)		– (3) run out	31
L-b 1, w 1, n-b 9	11	B 12, l-b 1, n-b 5	18
1/19 2/51 3/466 4/481 (4 wkts dec.)	481	1/19 2/69 3/122 (3 wkts dec.)	160

R. J. Shastri, †S. M. H. Kirmani, Madan Lal and D. R. Doshi did not bat.

Bowling: *First Innings*—Willis 28.1–7–79–2; Botham 31–10–83–1; Dilley 31–4–87–1; Allott 31–4–135–0; Underwood 22–7–59–0; Gooch 9–2–27–0. *Second Innings*—Willis 7–2–15–1; Botham 8–1–29–0; Dilley 5–1–13–0; Underwood 15–8–30–1; Gooch 8–2–24–0; Fletcher 1–0–9–0; Taylor 2–0–6–0; Tavaré 2–0–11–0; Gower 1–0–1–0; Gatting 1–0–4–0.

England

G. A. Gooch c and b Shastri	127
C. J. Tavaré c Gavaskar b Doshi	35
*K. W. R. Fletcher b Doshi	3
D. I. Gower lbw b Shastri	64
I. T. Botham c Kirmani b Shastri	52
M. W. Gatting c Viswanath b Doshi	0
G. R. Dilley c and b Kapil Dev	8
†R. W. Taylor b Doshi	8
D. L. Underwood c Kirmani b Kapil Dev	0
P. J. W. Allott c Roy b Kapil Dev	6
R. G. D. Willis not out	1
B 1, l-b 11, n-b 12	24
1/155 2/164 3/195 4/279 5/283 6/307 7/307 8/311 9/320	328

Bowling: Kapil Dev 25.5–7–88–3; Madan Lal 9–1–41–0; Shastri 63–23–104–3; Doshi 57–31–69–4; Gavaskar 1–0–2–0.

Umpires: B. Ganguli and Hanumantha Rao.

CENTRAL ZONE v AN ENGLAND XI

At Indore, January 22, 23, 24. Drawn. The touring side's priority was for Botham to recapture the rhythm and penetration of his bowling in their last three-day match before the final Test. Instead, in an innings of premeditated violence, he bludgeoned 122 in 55 minutes, including a drinks break, his hundred, thought to be the fastest ever made in India, coming in 50 minutes off 48 balls. In all, Botham received 55 balls, of which seven went for 6 – mainly pulled drives and sweeps – sixteen for 4, three for 2, and ten for singles. It was of no help to England's prospects at Kanpur, however, that he bowled only a handful of fast overs in the match. Gatting came into his own after Botham was caught at deep mid-wicket and hit the three longest 6s of the match. Central Zone saved the follow-on with one effective wicket standing, and in the last two sessions Cook, out in dubious circumstances in the first innings, made up for previous disappointments with a chanceless 104 not out – the first time he had passed 40 on the tour.

England

G. Cook c Sanjeeva Rao b Mathur	39	– not out 101
C. J. Tavaré c Bhanot b Mathur	14	– c sub b Hans 81
*K. W. R. Fletcher c Vedraj b G. Sharma	32	
M. W. Gatting b Aslam Ali	111	
I. T. Botham c Chaturvedi b P. Sharma	122	
R. W. Taylor st Vedraj b G. Sharma	40	
G. R. Dilley c Deshpande b Mathur	52	
J. E. Emburey not out	9	
†C. J. Richards (did not bat)		– (3) not out 16
B 8, l-b 2, n-b 7	17	B 2, l-b 5, n-b 2 9
1/33 2/87 3/87 4/224 5/351 6/388 7/436	(7 wkts dec.) 436	1/164 (1 wkt dec.) 210

D. L. Underwood and J. K. Lever did not bat.

Bowling: *First Innings*—Aslam Ali 17–2–68–1; Deshpande 3–1–9–0; Mathur 27.3–4–82–3; Hans 14–4–91–0; G. Sharma 26–4–107–2; P. Sharma 6–0–62–1. *Second Innings*—Aslam Ali 9–0–30–0; Mathur 11–2–34–0; Hans 14–2–59–1; G. Sharma 17–1–70–0; Bhanot 1–0–8–0.

Central Zone

Sanjeeva Rao retired hurt	17
S. Khandkar c Taylor b Botham	29
S. Chaturvedi c Richards b Underwood	33
A. Bhanot c and b Underwood	40
A. P. Deshpande run out	20
*P. Sharma b Emburey	20
A. Mathur c Cook b Emburey	12
†P. Vedraj hit wkt b Lever	59
G. Sharma c and b Emburey	18
Aslam Ali c Taylor b Dilley	48
R. S. Hans not out	6
B 1, l-b 4, n-b 4	9
1/40 2/97 3/132 4/160 5/173 6/203 7/247 8/287 9/311	311

Bowling: Botham 9–2–39–1; Dilley 13.2–4–57–1; Lever 24–6–73–1; Underwood 12–2–29–2; Emburey 21–5–94–3; Fletcher 1–0–10–0.

Umpires: V. Vikramraju and S. D. Ghosh.

†INDIA v ENGLAND

Third One-day International

At Cuttack, January 27. India won by five wickets. The one-day decider followed the pattern of its predecessors, with the side lucky with the toss electing to field and winning by several wickets. Only a tremendous thrash by Fletcher and Botham gave India any challenge, for on a dampish, seaming pitch England were only 118 for four after 35 overs. The last eleven brought another 112 as Fletcher (four 6s) and Botham (two 6s) threw the bat against the medium-pacers, Kapil Dev returning only at the end. Although the pitch had eased when India batted, England might still have snatched a win had Botham not dropped Gavaskar at 6 off an awkward, swirling caught and bowled which he chased into the covers. India's captain went on to take brilliant advantage of the Indian playing condition that required seven men in the fielding circle for fifteen overs.

Man of the Match: S. M. Gavaskar.

England

G. A. Gooch c Arun Lal b Madan Lal	3
G. Cook c Nayak b Patil	30
C. J. Tavaré c Madan Lal b Shastri	11
D. I. Gower c and b Patil	42
I. T. Botham b Nayak	52
*K. W. R. Fletcher b Madan Lal	69
M. W. Gatting not out	8
†R. W. Taylor not out	2
L-b 9, n-b 3, w 1	13
1/13 2/33 3/86 4/101 5/181 6/228 (6 wkts., 46 overs)	230

J. K. Lever, D. L. Underwood and R. G. D. Willis did not bat.

Bowling: Kapil Dev 8–3–23–0; Madan Lal 8–0–56–2; Nayak 10–1–51–1; Shastri 10–1–34–1; Patil 10–0–53–2.

India

*S. M. Gavaskar st Taylor b Underwood	71
Arun Lal c Gooch b Botham	9
D. B. Vengsarkar c Willis b Gooch	13
S. M. Patil b Underwood	64
Yashpal Sharma not out	34
Kapil Dev c Gooch b Underwood	0
A. Malhotra not out	28
L-b 7, n-b 3, w 2	12
1/16 2/59 3/135 4/184 5/184 (5 wkts, 42 overs)	231

†S. M. H. Kirmani, S. V. Nayak, Madan Lal and R. J. Shastri did not bat.

Bowling: Willis 6–1–29–0; Botham 8–0–48–1; Lever 10–0–55–0; Gooch 8–0–39–1; Underwood 10–0–48–3.

Umpires: K. B. Ramaswamy and P. R. Punjabi.

INDIA v ENGLAND

Sixth Test Match

At Kanpur, January 30, 31, February 1, 3, 4. Drawn. The loss of 9 hours, 40 minutes did no more than turn probability into certainty that the final Test would be drawn. It was played at a time of year when rain is not uncommon on the Ganges, and apart from the first morning and the last afternoon, when the sun broke through, the weather was miserable. True to Kanpur tradition the pitch, clay-based and nearly grassless, lacked pace and bounce, offering no more to bowlers at the end than it had at the beginning.

England brought back Emburey for the sick Allott and when Fletcher won his fifth toss in a row, Gooch gave them a flying start by reaching 50 off 55 balls in 90 minutes; however, seventeen minutes later he attempted to force Doshi off the back foot and was bowled off an inside edge when the ball kept low. On a cloudy afternoon, an old ball swung and seamed for the first time since Bombay, but Gower played very well, and despite the loss of twenty minutes through bad light England, 213 for three at the close, had compiled the highest first-day total of the series.

Three of the next four sessions were lost to drizzle, which removed virtually any chance of a result, and on the third afternoon Botham completed his ninth Test hundred, playing an exemplary innings in which discipline and opportunism were balanced flawlessly. A late assault on Doshi, whom he on-drove for two gigantic 6s, took him to 142 off 214 balls in just over five and a half hours. He followed up by bowling Roy in the final over of the day with a fine ball that straightened off the pitch.

When India continued their innings after an hour's delay on the fourth morning, the pitch was greener than at any stage before or after. Yet the ball neither swung nor seamed, and Gavaskar, playing second string to Vengsarkar and then Viswanath, made sure India had no trouble saving the follow-on.

After the loss of two hours to pea-soup fog, Willis began the last afternoon by taking three for 7 with the second new ball. But Kapil Dev, struck painfully on the elbow as soon as he came in, responded with a superb piece of controlled hitting (one 6, fourteen 4s), reaching his 100 off 83 balls – by 57 balls the fastest of the series. Batting like a racquets player, he hit wristily through the line off almost any length. His seventh-wicket partnership of 169 with Yashpal was an Indian record against England.

England

G. A Gooch b Doshi	58
C. J. Tavaré b Doshi	24
*K. W. R. Fletcher b Kapil Dev	14
D. I. Gower lbw b Kapil Dev	85
I. T. Botham st Kirmani b Doshi	142
M. W. Gatting c Madan Lal b Doshi	32
G. R. Dilley lbw b Shastri	1
†R. W. Taylor b Shastri	0
J. E. Emburey run out	2
D. L. Underwood not out	0
B 2, l-b 5, w 6, n-b 7	20
1/82 2/89 3/121 4/248 5/349/6/354 7/354 8/360 9/378	(9 wkts dec.) 378

R. G. D. Willis did not bat.

Bowling: Kapil Dev 34–3–147–2; Madan Lal 24–4–79–0; Doshi 34.2–8–81–4; Shastri 23–6–51–2.

India

*S. M. Gavaskar run out	52
P. Roy b Botham	5
D. B. Vengsarkar c Fletcher b Dilley	46
G. R. Viswanath c Gower b Willis	74
Yashpal Sharma not out	55
A. Malhotra lbw b Willis	0
R. J. Shastri c Taylor b Willis	2
Kapil Dev c Dilley b Gower	116
†S. M. H. Kirmani not out	1
B 1, l-b 7, w 2, n-b 16	26
1/12 2/79 3/166 4/197 5/197 6/207 7/376	(7 wkts dec.) 377

Madan Lal and D. R. Doshi did not bat.

Bowling: Willis 23–5–75–3; Botham 25–6–67–1; Dilley 14–2–67–1 Underwood 25–8–55–0; Emburey 32–7–81–0; Fletcher 2–1–5–0; Gower 1–0–1–1.

Umpires: D. N. Dotiwala and M. V. Gothaskar.

SRI LANKA BOARD PRESIDENT'S XI v AN ENGLAND XI

At Kandy, February 9, 10, 11. Drawn. Although England's first game in Sri Lanka was in no more danger of reaching a positive result than the last five Tests in India, there were compensations for the home side in the promising form of Madugalle and Ratnayeke. Madugalle, a slender 22-year-old, showed an engaging disrespect for reputations, confidently using the air to punish the spin of Emburey and Underwood, while the wide-shouldered Ratnayeke, a year younger than Madugalle, was full value for his five for 120. Without straining for pace he bowled a full fast-medium and maintained a good line. For England, Cook continued his staunch battle for Test recognition with a chanceless 104 in three and threequarter hours, his second first-class hundred in succession. A newly laid pitch played fairly true, if slow, but the natural beauty of what was to be Sri Lanka's second Test ground was marred by a bare and bumpy outfield.

Sri Lanka Board President's XI

S. R. de S. Wettimuny c Gower b Allott	12	– c and b Lever	0
S. Warnakulasuriya b Lever	6	– (3) lbw b Allott	15
†R. S. A. Jayasekera b Lever	0	– (2) b Underwood	52
R. S. Madugalle not out	142	– c and b Emburey	9
*L. R. D. Mendis c Underwood b Allott	28	– lbw b Emburey	0
A. Ranatunga c Richards b Emburey	15	– not out	33
J. B. N. Perera not out	56	– c Dilley b Emburey	6
R. G. C. E. Wijesuriya (did not bat)		not out	0
B 9, l-b 3, n-b 2	14	B 9, l-b 1	10
	—		—
1/17 2/17 3/33 4/82 5/109 (5 wkts dec.)	273	1/6 2/45 3/82 4/82 5/88 6/113 (6 wkts)	125

S. Jeganathan, J. R. Ratnayeke and V. John did not bat.

Bowling: *First Innings*—Lever 18–4–45–2; Allott 21–4–70–2; Underwood 16–6–37–0; Dilley 7–1–26–0; Emburey 18–3–81–1. *Second Innings*—Lever 7–2–17–1; Allott 5–0–24–1; Underwood 5–3–8–1; Dilley 7–1–18–0; Emburey 11–2–48–3.

England XI

G. A. Gooch b Ratnayeke	47
G. Cook b Wijesuriya	104
*K. W. R. Fletcher c sub b Ratnayeke	12
D. I. Gower c Jayasekera b Ratnayeke	18
M. W. Gatting b Ratnayeke	54
†C. J. Richards lbw b Jeganathan	46
G. R. Dilley b Wijesuriya	15
J. E. Emburey c Mendis b Ratnayeke	3
D. L. Underwood run out	14
P. J. W. Allott not out	9
J. K. Lever run out	2
B 12, l-b 7, n-b 17	36
	—
1/77 2/105 3/123 4/243 5/269 6/301 7/317 8/343 9/350	360

Bowling: John 19–1–87–0; Ratnayeke 29–4–120–5; Jeganathan 11.4–4–45–1; Wijesuriya 23–6–72–2.

Umpires: E. Seneviratne and S. Ponnadurai.

†SRI LANKA v ENGLAND

First One-day International

At Sinhalese Sports Club, Colombo, February 13. England won by 5 runs. Sri Lanka's loss of three wickets for 8 runs in the middle of their innings prevented them from achieving their target, although a stand of 68 at 6 an over between Madugalle and Ranasinghe kept them in the game, and some strong hitting by the tail sustained interest until the final over. Earlier the home side had been let down by their fielding when, after putting England in, they missed Gooch three times – the first left-handed by wicket-keeper Jayasekera off de Mel's first ball. Gooch went on to share in a third-wicket stand with Botham that at one time produced 43 in five overs, but England's later batting disintegrated and, on a sun-baked, close-cropped outfield, their final score was disappointing.

Man of the Match: I. T. Botham.

England

G. A. Gooch b G. R. A. de Silva	64
G. Cook c G. R. A. de Silva b Kaluperuma	28
D. I. Gower run out	15
I. T. Botham b de Mel	60
*K. W. R. Fletcher b D. S. de Silva	12
M. W. Gatting c Mendis b de Mel	3
†C. J. Richards b G. R. A. de Silva	3
J. E. Emburey lbw b de Mel	0
P. J. W. Allott run out	0
D. L. Underwood b de Mel	4
R. G. D. Willis not out	2
B 6, l-b 2, w 2, n-b 10	20
	—
1/55 2/83 3/152 4/191 5/197 6/202 7/205 8/205 9/205 (44.4 overs)	211

Bowling: de Mel 8.4–1–34–4; Ranasinghe 8–2–20–0; Kaluperuma 7–0–35–1; D. S. de Silva 9–0–31–1; G. R. A. de Silva 9–0–56–2; Wettimuny 3–0–15–0.

Sri Lanka

*B. Warnapura c Gower b Allott	10	A. L. F. de Mel not out	13
S. Wettimuny c Richards b Allott	46	L. W. Kaluperuma not out	14
†R. S. A. Jayasekera c Gooch b Willis	17		
R. L. Dias c and b Underwood	4	B 5, l-b 10, w 2, n-b 2	19
L. R. D. Mendis c Gower b Underwood	2		—
R. S. Madugalle b Willis	22	1/34 2/75 3/84 (8 wkts, 45 overs)	206
A. N. Ranasinghe c Cook b Botham	51	4/92 5/92 6/160	
D. S. de Silva b Botham	8	7/175 8/187	

G. R. A. de Silva did not bat.

Bowling: Willis 9–1–32–2; Botham 9–0–45–2; Emburey 5–0–18–0; Allott 9–0–40–2; Gooch 6–1–18–0; Underwood 7–0–34–2.

Umpires: E. C. B. Anthony and H. C. Felsinger.

†SRI LANKA v ENGLAND

Second One-day International

At Sinhalese Sports Club, Colombo, February 14. Sri Lanka won by 3 runs. Another capacity crowd of 22,000 saw their side avenge the previous day's defeat when England, needing 14 off the last two overs, lost four of their remaining five wickets to run-outs and the last to a skied catch. Having elected to field, England could have won the match in the first hour if even half the balls that beat the bat had found the edge. However, Sidath Wettimuny, younger brother of Sunil who played in Kandy, battled through and went on to pace the innings with skill and opportunism. With five wickets down and needing 46 at nearly 9 an over, England looked beaten until Fletcher and Gatting together plundered 34 off an over apiece from the de Silvas. Then victory was suddenly there for the taking.

Man of the Match: S. Wettimuny.

Sri Lanka

*B. Warnapura c Taylor b Botham	4	R. S. Madugalle c Taylor b Lever	12
S. Wettimuny not out	86	A. L. F. de Mel run out	14
L. R. D. Mendis c and b Botham	0	D. S. de Silva not out	9
R. L. Dias hit wkt b Lever	26	B 2, l-b 18, w 1, n-b 1	22
A. Ranatunga run out	42		—
A. N. Ranasinghe c Gooch b Underwood	0	1/5 2/5 3/43 (7 wkts, 45 overs)	215
		4/130 5/130 6/158 7/186	

†H. M. Goonatillake and G. R. A. de Silva did not bat.

Bowling: Willis 9–1–26–0; Botham 9–4–29–2; Lever 9–0–51–2; Gooch 9–0–50–0; Underwood 9–0–37–1.

England

G. A. Gooch st Goonatillake b G. R. A. de Silva	74	†R. W. Taylor run out	3
G. Cook st Goonatillake b G. R. A. de Silva	32	J. K. Lever not out	2
D. I. Gower lbw b de Mel	6	D. L. Underwood run out	0
I. T. Botham c and b Warnapura	13	R. G. D. Willis c Madugalle b de Mel	0
*K. W. R. Fletcher run out	38	L-b 19, w 1, n-b 1	21
C. J. Tavaré b D. S. de Silva	5	1/109 2/122 3/122 (44.5 overs)	212
M. W. Gatting run out	18	4/147 5/170 6/203 7/206 8/211 9/211	

Bowling: de Mel 8.5–0–14–2; Ranasinghe 9–0–37–0; Warnapura 9–0–42–1; D. S. de Silva 9–0–54–1; G. R. A. de Silva 9–1–44–2.

Umpires: P. W. Vidanegama and K. T. Francis.

SRI LANKA v ENGLAND

Inaugural Test Match

At Saravanamuttu Oval, Colombo, February 17, 18, 20, 21. England won by seven wickets. Although they were beaten five minutes from the end of the fourth day, following a headlong collapse in which seven wickets fell for 8 runs, Sri Lanka did enough in their first Test to show they deserved elevation to full membership of the International Cricket Conference. Apart from the frustration when, in threequarters of an hour, Emburey destroyed their hopes with a spell of five for 5, the only disappointment of a long-awaited moment in the island's history was the smallness of the crowds. On only two of the four days was the 25,000-capacity ground even threequarters full, this being variously attributed to high admission prices, television coverage and, disturbingly, the public's preference for one-day cricket. The consequence was a saddening lack of atmosphere, except briefly on the fourth morning when Sri Lanka, 160 ahead with seven wickets standing on a turning pitch, seemed to have the makings of a winning score. Ultimately, both the batting and the spin bowling failed to rise to the occasion, but their overall performance left little doubt that in batsmen Dias, Madugalle and Ranatunga, an eighteen-year-old left-hander still at school, and opening bowler de Mel, Sri Lanka have a handful of promising young players.

England made two changes from the side which drew at Kanpur, Cook deservedly winning his first cap, although Gatting was unlucky to be displaced, while Allott came in for Dilley. Sri Lanka played ten of the team that won the second one-day international, with off-spinner Kaluperuma replacing Ranasinghe. By overlooking Ratnayeke the Sri Lankan selectors gave their captain an unbalanced attack in which only de Mel was more than medium pace.

The lack of a second fast bowler may have been a factor in Warnapura's decision to bat on a pitch still damp from heavy watering the previous morning. Whatever his reasons, it might have been fatal to Sri Lanka's chances had England bowled better and held two catches off the ill-starred Allott, the second of them a vital one overhead to Emburey in the gully when Madugalle was 2. Although the ball bounced unevenly, three of the four wickets lost before lunch fell to poor strokes, only Warnapura being blameless; but in easing conditions Madugalle and Ranatunga batted through the afternoon. The recovery was going smoothly when, in the over after tea, Ranatunga shouldered arms to Underwood and was bowled. Underwood's five for 28 was his first such return in his twelve post-Packer Tests.

Brisk and with good variation, de Mel reduced England to 40 for three with three wickets in seven balls, and had Fletcher missed at short-leg four balls later. The match may have been decided at that moment, for with Sri Lanka's slow left-armer, Ajith de Silva, unable to make use of the rough outside leg stump – like Underwood he bowled over the wicket – Fletcher and Gower added 80. Gower went on to a mature 89 in four hours, twenty minutes, but the lead that was in prospect at 200 for five vanished when D. S. de Silva deceived him with a top-spinner.

Dias, steadily backed by Warnapura, handled Underwood with rare brilliance in the second innings, his cover-driving proving flawless. Both partners fell after tea on the third day, but Sri Lanka were certainly no worse than level-pegging when, half an hour into the fourth day, Emburey went round the wicket. In eight overs of sharply turning, flighted off-spin, he polished off the innings.

After the early loss of Cook, to a questionable lbw, England might still have had a battle if Sri Lanka's spinners had matched the bounce, control and turn of England's on a pitch now badly scarred at both ends. But they couldn't, and Tavaré, in stands of 81 and 83 with Gooch and Gower respectively, steered England home with an innings smoother and no less secure than any he had played in Tests.

Sri Lanka

*B. Warnapura c Gower b Willis	2	– c Gooch b Emburey	38
S. Wettimuny c Taylor b Botham	6	– b Willis	9
R. L. Dias c Cook b Willis	0	– c Taylor b Underwood	77
L. R. D. Mendis lbw b Botham	17	– c Willis b Emburey	27
R. S. Madugalle c Gower b Underwood	65	– c Cook b Emburey	3
A. Ranatunga b Underwood	54	– c Fletcher b Emburey	2
D. S. de Silva c Gower b Underwood	3	– c Fletcher b Underwood	1
A. L. F. de Mel c Fletcher b Underwood	19	– c Gower b Emburey	2
L. W. Kaluperuma c Cook b Underwood	1	– c Taylor b Emburey	0
†H. M. Goonatillake not out	22	– not out	2
G. R. A. de Silva c Emburey b Botham	12	– c Willis b Underwood	0
B 2, l-b 4, w 2, n-b 9	17	L-b 6, n-b 8	14
1/9 2/11 3/29 4/34 5/133 6/149 7/181 8/183 9/190	218	1/30 2/113 3/140 4/167 5/169 6/170 7/172 8/173 9/174	175

Bowling: *First Innings*—Willis 19–7–46–2; Botham 12.5–1–28–3; Allott 13–4–44–0; Emburey 19–3–55–0; Underwood 18–6–28–5. *Second Innings*—Willis 9–3–24–1; Botham 12–1–37–0; Emburey 25–9–33–6; Underwood 37.5–15–67–3.

England

G. A. Gooch lbw b de Mel	22	– b G. R. A. de Silva	31
G. Cook c Kaluperuma b de Mel	11	– lbw b de Mel	0
C. J. Tavaré b de Mel	0	– st Goonatillake b G. R. A. de Silva	85
D. I. Gower c Goonatillake b D. S. de Silva	89	– not out	42
*K. W. R. Fletcher c Warnapura b G. R. A. de Silva	45	– not out	0
I. T. Botham b de Mel	13		
†R. W. Taylor not out	31		
J. E. Emburey lbw b G. R. A. de Silva	0		
P. J. W. Allott c Kaluperuma b D. S. de Silva	3		
D. L. Underwood c Mendis b D. S. de Silva	0		
R. G. D. Willis run out	0		
L-b 3, n-b 6	9	B 7, l-b 5, n-b 1	13
1/34 2/34 3/40 4/120 5/151 6/200 7/207 8/216 9/216	223	1/3 2/84 3/167	

Bowling: *First Innings*—de Mel 17–2–70–4; Warnapura 3–1–9–0; D. S. de Silva 27.5–11–54–3; Kaluperuma 9–1–29–0; G. R. A. de Silva 30–12–52–2. *Second Innings*—de Mel 13.1–4–33–1; Warnapura 1–0–1–0; D. S. de Silva 15–5–38–0; Kaluperuma 12–3–40–0; G. R. A de Silva 17–6–46–2.

Umpires: H. C. Felsinger and K. T. Francis.

THE PAKISTANIS IN AUSTRALIA, 1981-82

By BRIAN OSBORNE

Pakistan's visit to Australia was restricted to eight first-class matches, including three Tests, plus a programme of Benson and Hedges World Series Cup one-day games, coinciding with a West Indian tour. The team performed moderately well, twelve of them having taken part in Pakistan's short tour to Australia three years earlier.

In the World Series Cup, Pakistan only narrowly missed reaching the final with West Indies. Zaheer hit a fine 108 against Australia at Sydney, to bring victory to his side, and scored the most runs in the series. Miandad, Mudassar and Imran also batted well. Mudassar collected twelve wickets and headed the one-day bowling averages, while Imran, Sarfraz and Sikander all did quite creditably with the ball. An unfortunate aspect of the visit was the decline in public interest in the Test matches between Australia and Pakistan, this being most marked in the third Test at Melbourne, which Pakistan won, when the attendance on each of the five-days play was below 10,000. The three Tests attracted only 88,369 spectators.

Javed Miandad led the side and batted well throughout, although his confrontation with Lillee during the Perth Test was a wretched affair and he did not appear to have the full support of his whole team at all times. He was also involved in strong but unsuccessful requests by the Pakistani management to have the umpires replaced for the second Test.

The confrontation between Miandad and Lillee was one of the most undignified incidents in Test history. Miandad, batting to Lillee, had turned a ball to the on side and was in the course of completing a comfortable single when he was obstructed by Lillee. In the ensuing fracas Lillee kicked Miandad, who responded by shaping to strike him with his bat. The Australian team imposed a $200 fine (£120 approx.) on Lillee and sought an apology from Miandad for his part in the affair. However, the umpires, who had assisted in quelling the incident, objected to the penalty as being too lenient and the matter was dealt with at a Melbourne hearing before Mr R. Merriman, the coordinator of the Australian Cricket Board's cricket sub-committee. His ruling was that Lillee's penalty, set by the players, was not sufficient and he imposed a suspension from Australia's two ensuing one-day internationals – against Pakistan and West Indies. No apology was forthcoming from Miandad, whose participation in the incident was also referred to in the umpires' report.

Zaheer Abbas maintained his customary form with some crisp and effective batting, while Majid Khan batted soundly and his replacement as opening batsman, Mansoor Akhtar, showed promise. The youthful Rizwan-uz-Zaman had distinct ability as an opening batsman, hitting hundreds against South Australia and Tasmania. Mudassar Nazar batted soundly, playing the role of sheet-anchor, and Wasim Raja showed glimpses of form on occasions.

Imran Khan became Pakistan's highest Test wicket-taker in the Melbourne Test with 144 dismissals. His fast bowling throughout the tour was excellent, and in the view of many he was the outstanding cricketer of the Australian season. He was ably supported by the angular fast bowler, Sikander Bakht, and the veteran, Sarfraz Nawaz, both of whom performed in stout-hearted fashion. Iqbal Qasim, the side's only top-class slow bowler, headed the bowling averages with 23 wickets. He bowled particularly well in the third Test in Melbourne while taking seven wickets. He was supported by the all-rounder, Ijaz Faqih, who bowled right-arm off-spinners, as well as batting quite usefully.

PAKISTANI TOUR RESULTS

Test matches – Played 3: Won 1, Lost 2.

First-class matches – Played 8: Won 2, Lost 2, Drawn 4.

Wins – Australia, Tasmania.

Losses – Australia (2).

Draws – Western Australia, Queensland, Victoria, South Australia.

Non first-class matches – Played 13: Won 6, Lost 6, Drawn 1. *Wins* – Australia (3), West Indies, South Australian Country XI, Victorian Country XI. *Losses* – West Indies (4), Australia (2). *Draw* – Australian Capital Territory.

TEST MATCH AVERAGES

AUSTRALIA – BATTING

	T	*I*	*NO*	*R*	*HI*	*Avge*
G. M. Wood	3	6	1	255	100	51.00
G. S. Chappell	3	5	0	251	201	50.20
B. M. Laird	3	6	1	246	85	49.20
K. J. Hughes	3	5	0	193	106	38.60
R. W. Marsh	3	5	0	142	47	28.40
D. M. Wellham	2	3	0	75	36	25.00
J. R. Thomson	3	5	3	49	22*	24.50
A. R. Border	3	5	0	84	37	16.80
B. Yardley	3	5	0	53	22	10.60
T. M. Alderman	3	4	3	10	5*	10.00
D. K. Lillee	3	5	1	39	16	9.75

Played in one Test: G. N. Yallop 20, 38.

* *Signifies not out.*

BOWLING

	O	*M*	*R*	*W*	*Avge*
D. K. Lillee	104.3	22	332	15	22.13
B. Yardley	130.5	26	399	18	22.16
T. M. Alderman	93.2	23	252	8	31.50
J. R. Thomson	69	12	219	5	43.80

Also bowled: A. R. Border 5–1–17–0; G. S. Chappell 12–3–23–2; K. J. Hughes 3–1–2–0; B. M. Laird 1–0–9–0.

PAKISTAN – BATTING

	T	*I*	*NO*	*R*	*HI*	*Avge*
Zaheer Abbas	2	3	0	170	90	56.66
Javed Miandad	3	5	0	205	79	41.00
Wasim Raja	3	5	0	181	50	36.20
Mudassar Nazar	3	5	0	169	95	33.80
Imran Khan	3	5	1	108	70*	27.00
Majid J. Khan	3	5	0	121	74	24.20
Mohsin Khan	2	3	0	71	43	23.66
Iqbal Qasim	2	3	1	25	16*	12.50
Sarfraz Nawaz	3	5	0	52	26	10.40
Wasim Bari	3	5	1	40	20	10.00
Sikander Bakht	3	4	3	6	3*	6.00

Played in one Test: Ijaz Faqih 34, 21; Mansoor Akhtar 6, 36; Rizwan-uz-Zaman 0, 8.

**Signifies not out.*

BOWLING

	O	*M*	*R*	*W*	*Avge*
Imran Khan	150.2	39	312	16	19.50
Iqbal Qasim	108	33	235	10	23.50
Sarfraz Nawaz	118	32	306	9	34.00
Sikander Bakht	71	9	217	5	43.40
Wasim Raja	88	13	233	4	58.25

Also bowled: Ijaz Faqih 22–1–76–1; Javed Miandad 6–0–29–0; Majid J. Khan 15–2–36–0; Mudassar Nazar 4–1–11–0.

PAKISTANI AVERAGES – FIRST-CLASS MATCHES

BATTING

	M	*I*	*NO*	*R*	*HI*	*Avge*
Javed Miandad	7	11	2	682	158*	75.77
Zaheer Abbas	7	9	1	461	117	57.62
Mansoor Akhtar	4	7	0	345	86	49.28
Imran Khan	6	7	2	244	93*	48.80
Rizwan-uz-Zaman	6	10	0	431	126	43.10
Ijaz Faqih	4	6	2	164	61*	41.00
Salim Malik	3	5	1	159	62	39.75
Mudassar Nazar	6	9	1	295	95	36.87
Majid J. Khan	6	9	0	264	110	29.33
Mohsin Khan	3	5	1	99	43	24.75
Wasim Raja	7	10	0	239	50	23.90
Tahir Naqqash	4	3	1	39	25*	19.50
Ashraf Ali	2	4	2	35	17	17.50
Wasim Bari	6	8	1	68	26	9.71
Sarfraz Nawaz	6	7	0	63	26	9.00
Iqbal Qasim	5	4	1	25	16*	8.33
Sikander Bakht	6	7	4	21	11	7.00

**Signifies not out.*

BOWLING

	O	*M*	*R*	*W*	*Avge*
Iqbal Qasim.............	214.4	56	532	23	23.13
Imran Khan.............	281.2	67	686	28	24.50
Ijaz Faqih................	124.4	20	324	9	36.00
Tahir Naqqash..........	81	15	272	6	45.33
Sikander Bakht.........	146.3	26	454	10	45.40
Sarfraz Nawaz..........	208	52	590	12	49.16
Wasim Raja.............	163	30	480	7	68.57

Also bowled: Javed Miandad 38–4–137–1; Majid J. Khan 56–13–137–2; Mansoor Akhtar 2–1–3–0; Mudassar Nazar 22–6–78–0; Rizwan-uz-Zaman 6–1–15–0; Salim Malik 7–0–33–0; Wasim Bari 2–1–1–0.

FIELDING

Wasim Bari 15 (12ct, 3st), Javed Miandad 6, Ashraf Ali 5, Majid J. Khan 5, Mudassar Nazar 5, Zaheer Abbas 5, Ijaz Faqih 4, Iqbal Qasim 4, Mohsin Khan 2, Wasim Raja 2, Imran Khan 1, Mansoor Akhtar 1, Rizwan-uz-Zaman 1, Salim Malik 1, Sarfraz Nawaz 1, Tahir Naqqash 1.

HUNDREDS FOR PAKISTANIS

The following seven three-figure innings were played for the Pakistanis on their tour of Australia, one of which was not first-class.

Javed Miandad (2)
158* v Tasmania at Launceston
138 v Queensland at Brisbane

Rizwan-uz-Zaman (2)
126 v South Australia at Adelaide
118 v Tasmania at Launceston

Zaheer Abbas (2)
117 v South Australia at Adelaide
†108 v Australia at Sydney (B & H World Series Cup)

Majid J. Khan (1)
110 v Western Australia at Perth

**Signifies not out. †Not first-class.*

HUNDREDS AGAINST PAKISTANIS

The following nine three-figure innings were played against the Pakistanis on their tour of Australia, one of which was not first-class.

G. S. Chappell (2)
201 for Australia at Brisbane (Second Test)
162 for Queensland at Brisbane

G. M. Wood (2)
151 for Western Australia at Perth
100 for Australia at Melbourne (Third Test)

W. M. Darling (1)
132 for South Australia at Adelaide

C. G. Greenidge (1)
†103 for West Indies at Melbourne (B & H World Series Cup)

K. J. Hughes (1)
106 for Australia at Perth (First Test)

W. B. Phillips (1)
106 for South Australia at Adelaide

G. Shipperd (1)
131 for Western Australia at Perth

†*Not first-class.*

WESTERN AUSTRALIA v PAKISTANIS

At Perth, October 23, 24, 25, 26. Drawn. Rain, reducing play to 115 minutes on the last day, washed out the match, played on an easy-paced wicket. After Mudassar Nazar and Rizwan-uz-Zaman had opened with a sound century partnership, Majid Khan reached his 70th first-class century in 169 minutes with some delightful strokeplay. For Western Australia, Laird and Wood opened well with 109, Wood exhibiting some fine driving and hooking during his 382 minutes' stay for 151. Shippard's 131 occupied 364 minutes.

Pakistanis

Mudassar Nazar c Marsh b Malone	57	– not out	48
Rizwan-uz-Zaman b Baker	44	– c Marsh b Malone	11
Zaheer Abbas c and b Malone	24	– b Malone	15
*Javed Miandad c Hughes b Yardley	6	– not out	11
Majid J. Khan b Malone	110		
Wasim Raja lbw b Malone	0		
Imran Khan lbw b Yardley	43		
Ijaz Faqih not out	61		
†Wasim Bari c Baker b Yardley	26		
Tahir Naqqash c Laird b Yardley	4		
B 1, l-b 2, w 1, n-b 1	5	B 3, l-b 2, w 1, n-b 1	7
1/104 2/110 3/123 4/159 5/156 6/236 7/313 8/374 9/380	(9 wkts dec.) 380	1/34 2/56	(2 wkts) 92

Iqbal Qasim did not bat.

Bowling: *First Innings*—Malone 36–10–111–4; Baker 27–5–101–1; Yardley 35–10–100–4; Porter 17–3–56–0; O'Neill 2–1–7–0. *Second Innings*—Malone 10–3–35–2; Baker 9–0–41–0; Yardley 3–0–9–0.

Western Australia

G. M. Wood c Mudassar b Tahir	151
B. M. Laird c and b Qasim	47
*G. Shipperd c Ijaz b Qasim	131
K. J. Hughes st Bari b Ijaz	55
M. D. O'Neill b Qasim	1
C. S. Serjeant b Qasim	24
†R. W. Marsh c and b Majid	34
G. D. Porter not out	23
B. Yardley st Bari b Ijaz	32
M. F. Malone c Zaheer b Qasim	15
D. J. Baker b Ijaz	3
B 4, l-b 11, w 2, n-b 12	29
1/109 2/289 3/387 4/400 5/413 6/471 7/473 8/515 9/536	545

Bowling: Imran 36–6–92–0; Tahir 26–1–97–1; Ijaz 31.4–1–93–3; Qasim 44–5–136–5; Mudassar 9–3–22–0; Raja 7–2–12–0; Miandad 8–3–21–0; Rizwan 3–0–7–0; Majid 21–9–36–1.

Umpires: A. Claydon and P. McConnell.

QUEENSLAND v PAKISTANIS

At Brisbane, October 30, 31, November 1, 2. Drawn. Some splendid batting marked this match until it was spoilt by the loss of the third and fourth days to rain. On the opening day, a flowing century by the Pakistani captain, Javed Miandad, was ably supplemented by a top-class 84 from Zaheer Abbas. Miandad hit one 6 and twenty 4s. The remaining batsmen failed to contribute much, Lillie taking four wickets with leg-spin. After Wessels was run out early, Kent and Queensland's captain, Greg Chappell, overcame injuries to put on 192, Chappell hitting two 6s and twenty 4s in his 66th first-class century.

Pakistanis

Mudassar Nazar c Chappell b Thomson	20
Rizwan-uz-Zaman c Border b Dymock	0
Zaheer Abbas c Border b Thomson	84
*Javed Miandad c Dymock b Thomson	138
Majid J. Khan c Chappell b Lillie	26
Wasim Raja c Thomson b Lillie	9
†Wasim Bari c Broad b Lillie	0
Sarfraz Nawaz c Phillips b Lillie	4
Tahir Naqqash not out	25
Iqbal Qasim b Dymock	0
Sikander Bakht b Hohns	11
B 3, l-b 1, n-b 7	11
1/0 2/45 3/141 4/203 5/233 6/233 7/240 8/304 9/308	328

Bowling: Thomson 22–5–76–3; Dymock 28–7–74–2; Chappell 3–1–8–0; Broad 10–3–35–0; Border 1–0–3–0; Hohns 11–0–44–1; Lillie 20–3–77–4.

Queensland

K. C. Wessels run out	9
M. F. Kent c Bari b Sarfraz	91
*G. S. Chappell c and b Majid	162
W. R. Broad c Miandad b Qasim	11
G. M. Ritchie not out	44
T. V. Hohns c Miandad b Sikander	32
A. R. Border not out	0
B 4, l-b 8, n-b 14	26
1/21 2/213 3/256 4/312 5/375	(5 wkts) 375

†R. B. Phillips, G. Dymock, D. J. Lillie and J. R. Thomson did not bat.

Bowling: Sarfraz 20–5–74–1; Sikander 15–5–43–1; Qasim 19–3–76–1; Raja 15–2–55–0; Majid 20–2–65–1; Miandad 2–0–21–0; Rizwan 2–0–8–0; Mudassar 2–0–7–0.

Umpires: M. W. Johnson and J. T. C. Taylor.

VICTORIA v PAKISTANIS

At Melbourne, November 6, 7, 8 , 9. Drawn. Wiener and Watts opened impressively for Victoria with a partnership of 57 before the Pakistanis' best bowler, Imran Khan, had Watts caught at second slip. Yallop helped Wiener add a further 102 before both were caught by wicket-keeper Ashraf Ali. On the second morning, Robinson was unbeaten with 71 when Scholes declared. Pakistan's teenage opening batsman, Rizwan-uz-Zaman, pressed for Test selection with a sound half-century, Salim Malik contributed a stylish 62, and there was a hard-hit 93 by Imran Khan. In Victoria's second innings, Yallop scored an attractive 68 in a 123-run partnership with Watts, before a declaration was made on the final day with Victoria leading by 236 runs. After Mansoor and Rizwan-uz-Zaman had started brightly with 56 runs in 73 minutes, Walker began a collapse; and after a rain-extended tea interval it was left to Ijaz Faqih and Ashraf Ali to hold on until bad light stopped play.

Victoria

J. M. Wiener c Ashraf b Raja	83	– lbw b Sarfraz	2
G. M. Watts c Zaheer b Imran	29	– c Majid b Ijaz	59
G. N. Yallop c Ashraf b Raja	36	– c and b Ijaz	68
P. J. Davies c Ashraf b Imran	12	– c sub b Ijaz	0
*J. W. Scholes b Raja	25	– lbw b Imran	6
†R. D. Robinson not out	71	– c Ijaz b Sarfraz	29
S. F. Graf b Imran	3	– not out	32
R. J. Bright b Imran	28	– c Rizwan b Sikander	15
M. H. N. Walker c Raja b Imran	9		
L-b 5, w 1, n-b 9	15	B 11, l-b 12, n-b 8	31
1/57 2/159 3/162 4/178 5/222 6/230 7/295 8/311 (8 wkts dec.)	311	1/22 2/145 3/145 4/154 5/168 6/201 7/242 (7 wkts dec.)	242

R. J. McCurdy and J. D. Higgs did not bat.

Bowling: *First Innings*—Imran 28–5–89–5; Sarfraz 21–4–64–0; Raja 21–8–49–3; Sikander 16–4–53–0; Ijaz 8–2–22–0; Salim 4–0–19–0. *Second Innings*—Imran 19–5–50–1; Sarfraz 18–2–49–2; Raja 14–3–45–0; Sikander 15.3–4–35–1; Ijaz 24–10–32–3.

Pakistanis

Rizwan-uz-Zaman run out	50	– c Watts b Graf	27
Mansoor Akhtar c Bright b Walker	33	– b Walker	30
Salim Malik c Robinson b Walker	62	– b Walker	0
Majid J. Khan run out	5	– c Robinson b Walker	2
Wasim Raja c and b Higgs	38	– lbw b Walker	10
Imran Khan not out	93		
Ijaz Faqih run out	1	– (6) not out	18
†Ashraf Ali lbw b Graf	17	– (7) not out	10
Sarfraz Nawaz c Davies b Graf	7		
Sikander Bakht st Robinson b Higgs	0		
Zaheer Abbas absent hurt			
B 1, l-b 7, n-b 3	11	L-b 2	2
1/66 2/103 3/111 4/152 5/224 6/225 7/288 8/306 9/317	317	1/56 2/56 3/60 4/64 5/78 (5 wkts)	99

Bowling: *First Innings*—McCurdy 17–1–86–0; Graf 25–6–52–2; Higgs 23.3–8–69–2; Bright 23–6–54–0; Walker 14.5–5–37–2; Scholes 3.1–0–8–0. *Second Innings*—McCurdy 4–0–22–0; Graf 12–3–29–1; Bright 2–1–1–0; Walker 18–5–45–4.

Umpires: R. C. Bailhache and R. V. Whitehead.

AUSTRALIA v PAKISTAN

First Test Match

At Perth, November 13, 14, 15, 16, 17. Australia won by 286 runs. Australia won the first Test effortlessly after being sent in to bat by Miandad. But the match was marred by a lamentable confrontation between fast bowler Lillee and the Pakistan captain.

In reasonable batting conditions Australia scored only 154 for seven on the first day, off a miserly 74 overs. The Australian innings finished quickly on the second morning preparatory to a sensational batting collapse by Pakistan before the pace of Lillee and Alderman, who reduced them to 26 for eight wickets. Sarfraz, batting at No.8, made 26, but the innings petered out at 62 – Pakistan's lowest total in a Test match. Lillee took five for 18, Alderman four for 36 including the first-ball dismissal of Rizwan-uz-Zaman, making his début. At the close of the second day Australia led by 288 with eight second-innings wickets standing, Chappell having gone cheaply.

Laird batted 298 minutes for 85 and Hughes 271 minutes for 106. Yallop batted with assurance for 38 and Border for 37 before being brilliantly caught low down at square leg by Mudassar Nazar. Marsh made an aggressive 47. Set to score 543 to win, Pakistan lost two early batsmen before Mansoor and Miandad took the score to 96, when Mansoor was dismissed by Thomson. There then followed the Lillee–Miandad fracas, after which Yardley's clever off-spin removed six batsmen in a row, including Miandad, top-scorer with 79, Wasim Raja and Imran Khan, to bring Australia a sweeping victory.

The total attendance was 29,284, of whom 9,049 were present on the second day.

Australia

B. M. Laird c Bari b Imran	27	– (2) c Bari b Imran	85
G. M. Wood lbw b Sikander	33	– (1) b Qasim	49
*G. S. Chappell lbw b Imran	22	– b Imran	6
K. J. Hughes b Sarfraz	14	– c Majid b Imran	106
G. N. Yallop c and b Qasim	20	– c Imran b Sikander	38
A. R. Border c Bari b Sarfraz	3	– c Mudassar b Sikander	37
†R. W. Marsh c Qasim b Sikander	16	– c Mansoor b Raja	47
B. Yardley c Bari b Imran	9	– st Bari b Qasim	22
D. K. Lillee c Bari b Raja	16	– not out	4
J. R. Thomson b Imran	2	– not out	5
T. M. Alderman not out	0		
L-b 5, w 1, n-b 12	18	B 1, l-b 9, w 1, n-b 14	25
1/45 2/81 3/89 4/113 5/119 6/136 7/154 8/165 9/180	180	1/92 2/105 3/192 4/262 5/327 6/360 7/412 8/416 (8 wkts dec.)	424

Bowling: *First Innings*—Imran 31.4–8–66–4; Sarfraz 27–10–43–2; Sikander 21–4–47–2; Qasim 3–1–6–1; Raja 1–1–0–1. *Second Innings*—Imran 39–12–90–3; Sarfraz 27–5–88–0; Sikander 23–3–79–2; Qasim 26–4–81–2; Raja 20–3–58–1; Miandad 1–0–2–0; Mudassar 2–1–1–0.

Pakistan

Mudassar Nazar c Marsh b Lillee	0	– lbw b Alderman	5
Rizwan-uz-Zaman lbw b Alderman	0	– c Marsh b Alderman	8
Mansoor Akhtar c Marsh b Alderman	6	– c Hughes b Thomson	36
*Javed Miandad c Hughes b Alderman	6	– b Yardley	79
Majid J. Khan c Marsh b Lillee	3	– c Marsh b Yardley	0
Wasim Raja c Thomson b Lillee	4	– c Hughes b Yardley	48
Imran Khan c Yardley b Lillee	4	– c Alderman b Yardley	31
Sarfraz Nawaz c Marsh b Alderman	26	– c and b Yardley	9
†Wasim Bari c Marsh b Lillee	1	– c Border b Yardley	20
Iqbal Qasim c Alderman b Thomson	5	– c Alderman b Lillee	4
Sikander Bakht not out	3	– not out	0
N-b 4	4	L-b 1, n-b 15	16
1/1 2/1 3/14 4/17 5/21 6/25 7/25 8/26 9/57	62	1/8 2/27 3/96 4/99 5/174 6/198 7/229 8/236 9/254	256

Bowling: *First Innings*—Lillee 9–3–18–5; Alderman 10.2–2–36–4; Thomson 2–1–4–1. *Second Innings*—Lillee 20–3–78–1; Alderman 16–4–43–2; Thomson 12–4–35–1; Yardley 25.5–5–84–6.

Umpires: A. R. Crafter and M. W. Johnson.

†At Melbourne, November 21. PAKISTAN lost to WEST INDIES by 18 runs (See Benson and Hedges World Series Cup section).

†At Melbourne, November 22. PAKISTAN beat AUSTRALIA by four wickets (See Benson and Hedges World Series Cup section).

†AUSTRALIAN CAPITAL TERRITORY v PAKISTANIS

At Canberra, November 23, 24. Drawn. Pakistanis 200 for six dec. (Salim Malik 51 not out, Zaheer Abbas 41; N. Bulger three for 40) and 153 for three (Zaheer Abbas 91 not out); Australian Capital Territory 200 for seven dec. (P. Bowler 42, N. Bulger 42, G. Irvine 32; Wasim Raja three for 49).

AUSTRALIA v PAKISTAN

Second Test Match

At Brisbane, November 27, 28, 29, 30, December 1. Australia won by ten wickets. Pakistan made three changes, Rizwan-uz-Zaman, Mansoor Akhtar and Iqbal Qasim being replaced by Mohsin Khan, Zaheer Abbas and Ijaz Faqih. However, despite protests from the touring party, the first-Test umpires, A. R. Crafter and M. W. Johnson, were retained.

On winning the toss, Chappell sent Pakistan in. After a slow but steady opening, they had declined to 111 for four before Zaheer Abbas and Wasim Raja added 125 for the fifth wicket, Raja batting breezily before skying an attempted hook. Zaheer drove, hooked and pulled splendidly to become top-scorer with 80, and Lillee claimed his 300th Test wicket in his 56th appearance for Australia.

On the second day, Laird and Wood opened well with a partnership of 109, the prelude to a brilliant 201 from Chappell, who was aided by useful contributions from Border, Hughes, Wellham and Marsh as the score reached 512 by declaration time. Mudassar Nazar and Mohsin Khan started Pakistan's second innings with a stand of 72; but once Mudassar had been well caught by Laird off a fine Lillee delivery, the fast bowler, helped by off-spinner Yardley, finished off Pakistan's innings in under four hours. With the resolution to be expected of a Test side, Pakistan would have saved the match which, poorly attended, attracted only 25,342 spectators.

Pakistan

Mudassar Nazar c Marsh b Lillee	36	– c Laird b Lillee	33
Mohsin Khan c Border b Chappell	11	– c Marsh b Lillee	43
Majid J. Khan c Chappell b Lillee	29	– c Chappell b Yardley	15
*Javed Miandad b Lillee	20	– lbw b Lillee	38
Zaheer Abbas b Lillee	80	– lbw b Yardley	0
Wasim Raja c Laird b Lillee	43	– b Lillee	36
Imran Khan c Marsh b Alderman	0	– c Wellham b Yardley	3
Ijaz Faqih b Yardley	34	– c Chappell b Thomson	21
Sarfraz Nawaz c Border b Alderman	4	– c Alderman b Yardley	13
†Wasim Bari c Marsh b Thomson	7	– not out	4
Sikander Bakht not out	1	– b Thomson	2
B 12, l-b 1, w 1, n-b 12	26	B 2, l-b 3, w 1, n-b 9	15
1/40 2/60 3/105 4/111 5/236 6/237 7/245 8/263 9/285	291	1/72 2/90 3/115 4/115 5/177 6/178 7/189 8/216 9/219	223

Bowling: *First Innings*—Lillee 20–3–81–5; Alderman 25–6–74–2; Thomson 15–2–52–1; Chappell 3–1–6–1; Yardley 15–1–51–1; Border 1–0–1–0. *Second Innings*—Lillee 19–4–51–4; Alderman 15–3–37–0; Thomson 15–3–43–2; Yardley 24–4–77–4.

Australia

B. M. Laird c Zaheer b Ijaz	44	– (2) not out	3
G. M. Wood c Mudassar b Raja	72	– (1) not out	0
*G. S. Chappell c Zaheer b Sikander	201		
A. R. Border b Imran	36		
K. J. Hughes b Imran	28		
D. M. Wellham b Imran	36		
†R. W. Marsh c Zaheer b Imran	27		
B. Yardley b Sarfraz	2		
D. K. Lillee b Sarfraz	14		
J. R. Thomson not out	22		
T. M. Alderman not out	5		
B 1, l-b 5, w 2, n-b 17	25		
1/109 2/149 3/219 4/298 5/429 6/448 7/469 8/470 9/492 (9 wkts dec.)	512	(no wkt)	3

Bowling: *First Innings*—Imran 40–6–92–4; Sarfraz 35–4–121–2; Sikander 24–2–81–1; Ijaz 22–1–76–1; Raja 17–0–68–1; Mudassar 2–0–10–0; Miandad 3–0–18–0; Majid 9–1–21–0. *Second Innings*—Imran 1.2–1–2–0; Sikander 1–0–1–0.

Umpires: A. R. Crafter and M. W. Johnson.

†SOUTH AUSTRALIAN COUNTRY XI v PAKISTANIS

At Port Lincoln, December 3. Pakistanis won by eight wickets and batted on. South Australian Country XI 161 for eight (50 overs) (P. Schmeri 50, R. Johnson 39); Pakistanis 214 for four (Ijaz Faqih 83, Iqbal Qasim 51).

†At Adelaide, December 5. PAKISTAN beat WEST INDIES by 8 runs (See Benson and Hedges World Series Cup section).

†At Adelaide, December 6. PAKISTAN lost to AUSTRALIA by 38 runs (See Benson and Hedges World Series Cup section).

AUSTRALIA v PAKISTAN

Third Test Match

At Melbourne, December 11, 12, 13, 14, 15. Pakistan won by an innings and 82 runs. Australia preferred a fast-bowling attack on the controversial MCG pitch, though they came to regret it. There was nothing to encourage them as Pakistan scored 245 for three on the opening day, and finally closed their first innings at 500 for eight on the second evening. Mohsin Khan lifted a simple catch just before lunch on the opening morning, but Mudassar and Majid added 141 for the second wicket, Mudassar batting 273 minutes before failing to control a sweep shot. Miandad and Zaheer put on 128 in 143 minutes before Zaheer – earlier dropped by Wood – was caught and bowled for 90. Wasim Raja and Imran also enjoyed themselves before Miandad declared. The faster bowlers, Lillee, Thomson and Alderman, bowled 88.3 overs between them without taking a wicket, whereas Yardley, with off-breaks, took seven for 187 in 66 overs, bowling with great perseverance.

Having scored 15 runs without loss at the end of the second day, Australia batted slowly to add a further 182 while losing four wickets on the third. Wood and Laird put on 75, Wood going on to his century next morning, scored in 368 minutes off 298 balls with just three 4s – the third-slowest century on record by an Australian batsman. Australia's innings faded when they had appeared likely to save the follow-on, their last four wickets falling for 7 runs; and when they batted a second time, only Laird, with a fighting 52, offered any opposition.

In Australia's first innings, Imran Khan became Pakistan's highest wicket-taker with 142 dismissals, finishing the match with 144. Iqbal Qasim, slow orthodox left-arm, took seven wickets in a convincing Pakistan victory. Greg Chappell, Australia's captain, complained to the Australian Cricket Board about the condition of the Melbourne pitch, being supported in this by the Pakistan captain, Javed Miandad.

On no single day did the crowd number 10,000. The total match attendance was 33,743, a serious decline on previous years.

Pakistan

Mudassar Nazar c Lillee b Yardley	95
Mohsin Khan c Thomson b Yardley	17
Majid J. Khan c Wood b Yardley	74
*Javed Miandad lbw b Yardley	62
Zaheer Abbas c and b Yardley	90
Wasim Raja c Laird b Yardley	50
Imran Khan not out	70
Sarfraz Nawaz c Yardley b Chappell	0
†Wasim Bari b Yardley	8
Iqbal Qasim not out	16
B 1, l-b 5, n-b 12	18
1/40 2/181 3/201 4/329 5/363 6/443 7/444 8/457 (8 wkts dec.)	500

Sikander Bakht did not bat.

Bowling: Lillee 36.3–9–104–0; Alderman 27–8–62–0; Thomson 25–2–85–0; Yardley 66–16–187–7; Border 4–1–16–0; Chappell 9–2–17–1; Hughes 3–1–2–0; Laird 1–0–9–0.

Australia

B. M. Laird lbw b Qasim	35	– (2) c Sarfraz b Qasim	52
G. M. Wood c Mohsin b Sarfraz	100	– (1) c Bari b Sarfraz	1
*G. S. Chappell c Bari b Raja	22	– c Miandad b Sarfraz	0
A. R. Border run out	7	– run out	1
K. J. Hughes c and b Qasim	34	– c Majid b Qasim	11
D. M. Wellham c Mudassar b Sarfraz	26	– b Sarfraz	13
†R. W. Marsh c Mudassar b Imran	31	– c Mohsin b Qasim	21
B. Yardley b Qasim	20	– b Imran	0
D. K. Lillee lbw b Imran	1	– c Bari b Qasim	4
J. R. Thomson not out	3	– b Imran	17
T. M. Alderman lbw b Imran	1	– not out	4
B 4, l-b 6, n-b 3	13	B 1	1
1/75 2/118 3/127 4/173 5/232 6/235 7/286 8/288 9/288	293	1/1 2/9 3/13 4/29 5/77 6/78 7/79 8/92 9/121	125

Bowling: *First Innings*—Imran 24.1–7–41–3; Sarfraz 14–3–43–2; Raja 37–7–73–1; Qasim 55–17–104–3; Sikander 2–0–9–0; Majid 2–0–10–0. *Second Innings*—Imran 14.1–5–21–2; Sarfraz 15–10–11–3; Raja 13–2–34–0; Qasim 24–11–44–4; Majid 4–1–5–0; Miandad 2–0–9–0.

Umpires R. C. Bailhache and R. A. French.

†At Sydney, December 17. PAKISTAN beat AUSTRALIA by six wickets (See Benson and Hedges World Series Cup section).

†At Perth, December 19. PAKISTAN lost to WEST INDIES by seven wickets (See Benson and Hedges World Series Cup section).

SOUTH AUSTRALIA v PAKISTANIS

At Adelaide, December 26, 27, 28, 29. Drawn. No fewer than 649 runs were scored on the first two days for the loss of six wickets. Rizwan-uz-Zaman, ably supported by Mansoor Akhtar in an opening stand of 139, scored his first hundred in Australia, though Mansoor was the more aggressive of the two. Javed Miandad batted on into the second day. South Australia opened with a double-century partnership by Darling and Phillips, the latter being one of the four Australian Cricket Board's Esso Scholarship winners chosen to visit England in 1981. Darling's 132 was his first first-class century in two seasons.

Pakistanis

Mansoor Akhtar c Hookes b Vincent	81	– (2) c Parkinson b Sleep	86
Rizwan-uz-Zaman b Parkinson	126	– (7) c Hookes b Winter	47
Salim Malik run out	16	– c and b Parkinson	30
*Javed Miandad c Phillips b Winter	90	– (6) c Hookes b Winter	74
Zaheer Abbas not out	36	– (8) b Crowe	117
Mudassar Nazar (did not bat)		– (1) lbw b Parkinson	1
Wasim Raja (did not bat)		– (5) run out	1
Ijaz Faqih (did not bat)		– (4) run out	29
Tahir Naqqash (did not bat)		– (10) c and b Winter	10
†Wasim Bari (did not bat)		– (9) lbw b Winter	2
Sikander Bakht (did not bat)		– not out	4
L-b 1, w 4, n-b 4	9	B 6, l-b 5, w 2, n-b 1	14
1/139 2/176 3/283 4/358	(4 wkts dec.) 358	1/4 2/66 3/142 4/147 5/160 6/256 7/291 8/293 9/339	415

Bowling: *First Innings*—Parkinson 21–2–79–1; Winter 16–4–41–1; Vincent 19–3–75–1; Hookes 9–0–18–0; Lewis 25–3–69–0; Dugan 20–5–41–0; Sleep 10–6–26–0. *Second Innings*—Parkinson 26–5–88–2; Winter 24–3–89–4; Vincent 9–0–37–0; Hookes 4–0–27–0; Lewis 17–5–39–0; Sleep 12–3–41–1; Inverarity 31–11–70–0; Crowe 0.4–0–10–1.

South Australia

W. M. Darling c Bari b Tahir	132	– not out	58
†W. B. Phillips c Bari b Sikander	106	– c Raja b Ijaz	54
J. J. Crowe run out	28	– not out	9
*D. W. Hookes c Bari b Sikander	91		
P. R. Sleep b Ijaz	7		
R. J. Inverarity c Miandad b Sikander	4		
B. A. Vincent not out	7		
G. J. Winter not out	2		
B 4, l-b 6, n-b 17	27	N-b 4	4
1/228 2/261 3/308 4/362 5/393 6/394	(6 wkts dec.) 404	1/100	(1 wkt) 125

K. J. Lewis, S. D. H. Parkinson and R. W. Dugan did not bat.

Bowling: *First Innings*—Sikander 24–3–93–3; Tahir 24–5–84–1; Ijaz 27–4–74–1; Raja 12–2–59–0; Miandad 14–0–46–0; Mudassar 2–0–21–0. *Second Innings*—Sikander 5–1–13–0; Tahir 6–3–19–0; Ijaz 12–2–27–1; Raja 6–0–27–0; Mudassar 5–2–17–0; Salim 3–0–14–0; Bari 2–1–1–0; Rizwan 1–1–0–0; Mansoor 2–1–3–0.

Umpires: P. M. Cronin and M. G. O'Connell.

TASMANIA v PAKISTANIS

At Launceston, January 1, 2, 3, 4. Pakistanis won by ten wickets. The Pakistanis gained their first win of the tour against an Australian state when they defeated Tasmania. Tasmania batted first, but after a useful second-wicket partnership of 105 between Jeffery and the island's up-and-coming star, Boon, they collapsed to lose eight wickets for 49 runs to the pace bowling of Imran and the spin of Qasim. Rizwan-uz-Zaman and Mansoor Akhtar gave the Pakistani innings impetus by adding 146 in 177 minutes. Miandad was also in command, racing to 158 before declaring. Boon again batted well in Tasmania's second innings, as did Davison, who, after being felled by a rising ball from Imran in the first innings, scored 72 before being lbw to a boot-high delivery.

Tasmania

I. R. Beven b Imran	0	– lbw b Tahir	21
R. F. Jeffery c Miandad b Qasim	64	– lbw b Imran	37
D. C. Boon run out	34	– c Qasim b Miandad	49
*B. F. Davison retired hurt	15	– lbw b Imran	72
†R. D. Woolley b Imran	0	– c Miandad b Qasim	37
N. J. Allanby b Imran	0	– (7) b Qasim	8
P. J. Mancell lbw b Qasim	12	– (8) c Salim b Imran	2
F. D. Stephenson b Qasim	12	– (9) c sub b Tahir	9
S. L. Saunders c Ashraf b Qasim	4	– (10) not out	2
P. A. Blizzard not out	1	– (11) lbw b Tahir	4
P. M. Clough b Qasim	0	– (6) c Ashraf b Tahir	34
B 4, l-b 3, w 1, n-b 8	16	B 19, l-b 9, w 2, n-b 11	41
1/4 2/109 3/113 4/114 5/114 6/148 7/157 8/158 9/158	158	1/46 2/88 3/170 4/217 5/256 6/273 7/289 8/303 9/311	316

Bowling: *First Innings*—Imran 18–4–59–3; Sarfraz 12–3–40–0; Tahir 2–0–12–0; Qasim 21.4–8–31–5. *Second Innings*—Imran 30–8–84–3; Sarfraz 19–6–57–0; Tahir 23–6–60–4; Qasim 22–7–54–2; Miandad 8–1–20–1.

Pakistanis

Rizwan-uz-Zaman lbw b Blizzard	118		
Mohsin Khan b Stephenson	28	– (1) not out	0
Mansoor Akhtar lbw b Blizzard	73		
*Javed Miandad not out	158		
Zaheer Abbas b Clough	15		
†Ashraf Ali c Woolley b Allanby	4	– (2) not out	4
Salim Malik not out	51		
B 4, l-b 7, w 6, n-b 8	25		
1/53 2/199 3/286 4/338 5/378 (5 wkts dec.)	472	(no wkt)	4

Imran Khan, Sarfraz Nawaz, Tahir Naqqash and Iqbal Qasim did not bat.

Bowling: *First Innings*—Stephenson 25–4–85–1; Blizzard 27–6–94–2; Mancell 13–4–38–0; Clough 23–4–96–1; Saunders 17–4–46–0; Allanby 19–2–53–1; Beven 10–2–35–0. *Second Innings*—Woolley 2–2–0–0; Mancell 1.1–1–4–0.

F. D. Stephenson kept wicket in Pakistan's second innings.

Umpires: S. Gane and M. Hull.

†VICTORIAN COUNTRY XI v PAKISTANIS

At Stawell, January 6. Pakistanis won by five wickets. Victorian Country XI 178 for eight (R. Scott 52, W. Walsh 50 not out, P. Neville 31; Tahir Naqqash six for 32); Pakistanis 179 for five (Zaheer Abbas 81 not out, Ijaz Faqih 35 not out; R. Davis four for 50).

†At Melbourne, January 9. PAKISTAN beat AUSTRALIA by 25 runs (See Benson and Hedges World Series Cup section).

†At Sydney, January 12. PAKISTAN lost to WEST INDIES by seven wickets (See Benson and Hedges World Series Cup section).

†At Sydney, January 14. PAKISTAN lost to AUSTRALIA by 76 runs (See Benson and Hedges World Series Cup section).

†At Brisbane, January 16. PAKISTAN lost to WEST INDIES on faster scoring-rate (See Benson and Hedges World Series Cup section).

AUSTRALIA v ENGLAND, 1982-83

By winning the second and third matches of the five-Test series, against England's victory in the fourth, Australia, under the captaincy of G. S. Chappell, regained the Ashes, which England had held since 1977. Public interest in the Test matches was encouragingly high, with an overall attendance of more than half a million people reflecting the best figures in Australia since the mid-1970s.

First Test: at Perth, November 12, 13, 14, 16, 17. Drawn. England 411 (C. J. Tavaré 89, D. W. Randall 78, D. I. Gower 72, A. J. Lamb 46, G. Miller 30; B. Yardley five for 107, D. K. Lillee three for 96) and 358 (D. W. Randall 115, A. J. Lamb 56, D. R. Pringle 47 not out, N. G. Cowans 36, R. W. Taylor 31; G. F. Lawson five for 108, B. Yardley three for 101); Australia 424 for nine dec. (G. S. Chappell 117, K. J. Hughes 62, D. W. Hookes 56, J. Dyson 52, G. F. Lawson 50; G. Miller four for 70, R. G. D. Willis three for 95) and 73 for two (A. R. Border 32 not out).

Second Test: at Brisbane, November 26, 27, 28, 30, December 1. Australia won by seven wickets. England 219 (A. J. Lamb 72, I. T. Botham 40, D. W. Randall 37; G. F. Lawson six for 47) and 309 (G. Fowler 83, G. Miller 60, D. I. Gower 34; J. R. Thomson five for 73, G. F. Lawson five for 87); Australia 341 (K. C. Wessels 162, G. S. Chappell 53, B. Yardley 53; R. G. D. Willis five for 66, I. T. Botham three for 105) and 190 for three (D. W. Hookes 66 not out, K. C. Wessels 46, K. J. Hughes 39 not out).

Third Test: at Adelaide, December 10, 11, 12, 14, 15. Australia won by eight wickets. Australia 438 (G. S. Chappell 115, K. J. Hughes 88, K. C. Wessels 44, J. Dyson 44, B. Yardley 38, D. W. Hookes 37; I. T. Botham four for 114) and 83 for two (J. Dyson 27 not out); England 216 (A. J. Lamb 82, D. I. Gower 60, I. T. Botham 35; G. F. Lawson four for 56, J. R. Thomson three for 51) and 304 (D. I. Gower 114, I. T. Botham 58, G. Fowler 37; G. F. Lawson five for 66).

Fourth Test: at Melbourne, December 26, 27, 28, 29, 30. England won by 3 runs. England 284 (C. J. Tavaré 89, A. J. Lamb 83; R. M. Hogg four for 69, B. Yardley four for 89) and 294 (G. Fowler 65, I. T. Botham 46, D. R. Pringle 42, R. W. Taylor 37; G. F. Lawson four for 66, R. M. Hogg three for 64, J. R. Thomson three for 74); Australia 287 (K. J. Hughes 66, D. R. Hookes 53, R. W. Marsh 53, K. C. Wessels 47; R. G. D. Willis three for 38, G. Miller three for 44) and 288 (D. W. Hookes 68, A. R. Border 62 not out, K. J. Hughes 48, J. Dyson 31; N. G. Cowans six for 77).

Fifth Test: at Sydney, January 2, 3, 4, 6, 7. Drawn. Australia 314 (A. R. Border 89, J. Dyson 79, G. S. Chappell 35; I. T. Botham four for 75, E. E. Hemmings three for 68) and 382 (K. J. Hughes 137, A. R. Border 83, K. C. Wessels 53, R. W. Marsh 41; E. E. Hemmings three for 116, G. Miller three for 133); England 237 (D. I. Gower 70, D. W. Randall 70, G. Miller 34; J. R. Thomson five for 50, G. F. Lawson three for 70) and 314 (E. E. Hemmings 95, D. W. Randall 44, I. T. Botham 32; B. Yardley four for 139).

Full details of the England tour of Australia will appear in the 1984 edition of Wisden.

THE WEST INDIANS IN AUSTRALIA, 1981-82

By HENRY BLOFELD

There was evidence during their tour of Australia that the powers of Clive Lloyd's West Indian side had begun to decline. Although they won the triangular Benson and Hedges limited-overs competition with something to spare, they were less convincing in the series of three Test matches against Australia, which they drew one-all.

The success of Lloyd's side over the last few years has centred round their great fast bowling strength. They have continually been able to field sides containing four fast bowlers, Roberts, Holding, Croft and Garner, with Marshall and sometimes Clarke in reserve. Yet in Australia, on several occasions, they were no longer so effective, failing to finish off an innings when the first three or four wickets had fallen cheaply.

Advancing years may be one of the reasons for this. Another, almost certainly, is that the side has been spoiled by its own remarkable success. In Australia the players no longer had, perhaps, the same biting urge to succeed. There was evidence of this in the batting as well as the bowling. Richards, for such an exceptional player, did not have an outstanding tour. Often he would come in and start trying to hit the ball to all parts of the ground without bothering to play himself in. Greenidge, handicapped for much of the time by a knee injury, was another who did not go on to make big scores, and Haynes was a disappointment.

In the end, the batting was saved by Lloyd himself, who played with cool authority and was always a wonderful example to his side on the field of play, and Gomes, who, assured at last of a regular Test place, thrived on the confidence that this gave him, scoring centuries in the second and third Tests.

The other batting success was the newcomer from Jamaica and reserve wicket-keeper, Jeff Dujon. In six innings in the Test series the lowest score he was out for was 41, although the fact that he reached the forties four times and fifty once indicated that he still has to learn about the need to concentrate. Nevertheless he scored his runs in the most impressive way. Perhaps his best innings came in a one-day international against Australia on a nasty pitch in Melbourne. Even Richards was defeated by it, but Dujon played as if he was batting in the Jamaican nets, taking West Indies to victory in a match they might well have lost.

Roberts went to Australia mainly to play in the limited-overs matches. However, injuries forced him to play in the first Test, and when he did not play in the second it was noticeable how much he was missed. Holding bowled magnificently throughout and took five or more wickets in an innings four times in six innings. West Indies' failure to bowl a side out when they had begun the job well may have been more than anything the result of Croft and Garner not being quite the bowlers they were, Croft's decline being due partly to injury.

With a well-established Test side, the reserves had little chance of much worthwhile cricket. Bacchus batted well at the end of the tour, revealing himself to be a handsome stroke-maker, but he hardly looked the part when called upon to open in place of the injured Greenidge. Logie's wonderful fielding made him an almost permanent twelfth man, but Joseph, the wrist-spinner from Trinidad, made few appearances. It was a happy tour, well managed by Stephen Camacho, from Guyana, who formed an excellent partnership with Lloyd.

WEST INDIAN TOUR RESULTS

Test matches – Played 3: Won 1, Lost 1, Drawn 1.

First-class matches – Played 7: Won 4, Lost 1, Drawn 2.

Wins – Australia, South Australia, New South Wales, Queensland.

Loss – Australia.

Draws – Tasmania, Australia.

Non first-class matches – Played 17: Won 12, Lost 4, Drawn 1. *Wins* – Australia (6), Pakistan (4), New South Wales Country XI, Queensland Country XI. *Losses* – Australia (3), Pakistan. *Draw* – Victorian Country XI.

TEST MATCH AVERAGES

AUSTRALIA – BATTING

	T	*I*	*NO*	*R*	*HI*	*Avge*
A. R. Border	3	6	1	336	126	67.20
J. Dyson	2	4	1	166	127*	55.33
K. J. Hughes	3	6	1	226	100*	45.20
B. M. Laird	3	6	0	200	78	33.33
G. M. Wood	3	6	1	130	63	26.00
R. W. Marsh	3	5	0	117	39	23.40
B. Yardley	3	5	0	93	45	18.60
G. S. Chappell	3	6	0	86	61	14.33
J. R. Thomson	2	3	1	26	18*	13.00
T. M. Alderman	2	3	0	11	10	3.66
D. K. Lillee	3	5	0	8	4	1.60

Played in one Test: G. F. Lawson 2, 0*; L. S. Pascoe 10, 0*; D. M. Wellham 17, 2.

* *Signifies not out.*

BOWLING

	O	*M*	*R*	*W*	*Avge*
D. K. Lillee	121.3	26	317	16	19.81
B. Yardley	142.5	28	446	20	22.30
J. R. Thomson	83.1	9	317	9	35.22
T. M. Alderman	69	17	196	5	39.20

Also bowled: A. R. Border 6–1–19–0; G. S. Chappell 2–2–0–0; G. F. Lawson 26–5–64–1; L. S. Pascoe 52–6–178–4.

WEST INDIES – BATTING

	T	*I*	*NO*	*R*	*HI*	*Avge*
H. A. Gomes	3	6	1	393	126	78.60
C. H. Lloyd	3	6	1	275	77*	55.00
P. J. Dujon	3	6	1	227	51	45.40
C. G. Greenidge	2	4	0	134	66	33.50
I. V. A. Richards	3	6	0	160	50	26.66
A. M. E. Roberts	2	3	0	70	42	23.33
D. L. Haynes	3	6	0	125	51	20.83
D. A. Murray	2	4	1	56	32*	18.66
S. F. A. Bacchus	2	4	0	28	27	7.00
M. A. Holding	3	5	0	26	9	5.20
J. Garner	3	5	0	20	12	4.00
C. E. H. Croft	3	5	3	4	4*	2.00

Played in one Test: S. T. Clarke 14, 5.

**Signifies not out.*

BOWLING

	O	*M*	*R*	*W*	*Avge*
M. A. Holding	140.3	37	344	24	14.33
J. Garner	122	37	275	12	22.91
A. M. E. Roberts	76	24	178	6	29.66
C. E. H. Croft	138.1	25	361	7	51.57

Also bowled: S. T. Clarke 32–13–76–1; H. A. Gomes 45–12–87–3; I. V. A. Richards 49–13–109–0.

WEST INDIAN AVERAGES – FIRST-CLASS MATCHES

BATTING

	M	*I*	*NO*	*R*	*HI*	*Avge*
H. A. Gomes	7	10	2	712	200*	89.00
C. H. Lloyd	5	8	1	394	77*	56.28
P. J. Dujon	5	8	2	332	104*	55.33
I. V. A. Richards	7	11	1	436	121	43.60
S. F. A Bacchus	6	10	2	319	85	39.87
D. L . Haynes	6	11	0	383	139	34.81
D. A. Murray	4	6	2	139	72	34.75
M. D. Marshall	2	2	0	66	66	33.00
A. M. E. Roberts	4	5	1	103	42	25.75
C. G. Greenidge	5	8	0	179	66	22.37
A. L. Logie	3	4	0	81	43	20.25
C. E. H. Croft	6	8	4	48	34	12.00
M. A. Holding	6	7	0	56	24	8.00
J . Garner	5	7	0	50	18	7.14
S. T. Clarke	4	3	0	19	14	6.33
H. Joseph	2	2	0	11	7	5.50

**Signifies not out.*

BOWLING

	O	M	R	W	Avge
M. D. Marshall	46	14	105	11	9.54
J. Garner	165.3	51	372	23	16.17
M. A. Holding	214.3	49	535	32	16.71
A. M. E. Roberts	147	44	318	13	24.46
S. T. Clarke	89	18	261	9	29.00
H. A. Gomes	72	13	169	5	33.80
C. E. H. Croft	251.5	43	673	18	37.38
H. Joseph	91	25	217	5	43.40
I. V. A. Richards	120.5	28	304	6	50.66

FIELDING

D. A. Murray 29 (all ct, 1 sub), P. J. Dujon 16 (all ct, 1 sub), S. F. A. Bacchus 4, J. Garner 4, I. V. A. Richards 4, C. E. H. Croft 3, C. G. Greenidge 3, D. L. Haynes 3, M. A. Holding 3, C. H. Lloyd 3, H. A. Gomes 1, H. Joseph 1, A. M. E. Roberts 1.

HUNDREDS FOR WEST INDIANS

The following eight three-figure innings were played for the West Indians during the tour, two of which were not first-class.

H. A. Gomes (3)
200* v Queensland at Brisbane
126 v Australia at Sydney (Second Test)
124* v Australia at Adelaide (Third Test)

S. F. A. Bacchus (1)
†103* v Queensland Country XI at Caloundra

P. J. Dujon (1)
104* v New South Wales at Sydney

C. G. Greenidge (1)
†103 v Pakistan at Melbourne (B & H World Series Cup)

D. L. Haynes (1)
139 v New South Wales at Sydney

I. V. A. Richards (1)
121 v Queensland at Brisbane

**Signifies not out.* *† Not first-class.*

HUNDREDS AGAINST WEST INDIANS

The following five three-figure innings were played against the West Indians during the tour, one of which was not first-class.

J. Dyson (2)
127* for Australia at Sydney (Second Test)
123 for New South Wales at Sydney

A. R. Border (1)
126 for Australia at Adelaide (Third Test)

K. J. Hughes (1)
100* for Australia at Melbourne (First Test)

B. M. Laird (1)
†117 for Australia at Sydney (B & H World Series Cup)

**Signifies not out.* *† Not first-class.*

SOUTH AUSTRALIA v WEST INDIANS

At Adelaide, November 13, 14, 15, 16. West Indians won by 226 runs. Although the West Indians were quick to confirm the strength of their fast bowling, their batting was not so convincing. At 106 for five on the first day they were in trouble before Gomes and Murray added 165 for the sixth wicket with some attractive strokeplay. Winter, at just above medium pace, was rewarded for his accuracy with first-innings figures of seven for 65 against batsmen short of practice. Garner, Croft, Clarke and Marshall gave the West Indians a first-innings lead of 215, but Richards, captaining the side in the absence of Lloyd who had remained in England because his wife was ill, settled for more batting practice rather than enforcing the follow-on. South Australia, set to score 452 to win, were given a fine start by Darling and Harris, but thereafter only Hookes, South Australia's new captain, batted with any freedom.

West Indians

C. G. Greenidge run out	28	– c Harris b Parkinson	4
D. L. Haynes c Phillips b Sayers	44	– c Wright b Parkinson	53
*I. V. A. Richards c Phillips b Winter	1		
S. F. A. Bacchus c Crowe b Parkinson	12	– not out	58
H. A. Gomes lbw b Winter	95		
A. L. Logie c Dugan b Winter	5	– (5) lbw b Dugan	4
†D. A. Murray c Wright b Winter	72		
C. E. H. Croft not out	4	– (3) c Phillips b Sleep	34
M. D. Marshall c Wright b Winter	0	– (6) run out	66
S. T. Clarke lbw b Winter	0		
J. Garner c Darling b Winter	18		
B 2, l-b 3, n-b 10	15	B 2, l-b 8, w 5, n-b 2	17
1/58 2/70 3/82 4/99 5/105 6/271 7/273 8/273 9/273	294	1/26 2/99 3/114 4/123 5/236 (5 wkts dec.)	236

Bowling: *First Innings*—Parkinson 28–5–87–1; Winter 36–15–65–7; Sayers 14–4–50–1; Sleep 14–6–37–0; Dugan 19–3–40–0. *Second Innings*—Parkinson 18–5–52–2; Winter 19–7–42–0; Sayers 16–7–34–0; Sleep 12–3–35–1; Dugan 16.3–4–56–1.

South Australia

W. M. Darling c Greenidge b Marshall	7	– c Murray b Garner	88
K. P. Harris c Murray b Garner	19	– c Murray b Croft	49
J. J . Crowe c Garner b Clarke	1	– b Croft	9
W. B. Phillips b Marshall	19	– lbw b Garner	10
*D. W. Hookes c Croft b Clarke	8	– c Murray b Marshall	42
P. R. Sleep c Croft b Clarke	4	– lbw b Garner	0
†K. J. Wright lbw b Marshall	0	– lbw b Garner	1
G. J. Winter c Richards b Croft	5	– b Garner	4
S. D. H. Parkinson c Greenidge b Garner	1	– c sub b Marshall	0
R. W. Dugan c Richards b Garner	3	– not out	0
D. K. Sayers not out	1	– b Marshall	0
B 4, l-b 2, n-b 5	11	B 5, l-b 5, n-b 12	22
1/7 2/14 3/35 4/46 5/51 6/52 7/64 8/65 9/78	79	1/141 2/154 3/156 4/193 5/193 6/201 7/222 8/222 9/222	225

Bowling: *First Innings*—Clarke 11–2–28–3; Marshall 10–2–23–3; Croft 6–3–11–1; Garner 6–3–6–3. *Second Innings*—Clarke 10–0–43–0; Marshall 12–3–29–3; Croft 21–1–86–2; Garner 18–6–45–5.

Umpires: P. M. Cronin and B. E. Martin.

†VICTORIAN COUNTRY XI v WEST INDIANS

At Mildura, November 18. Drawn. West Indians 250 for five dec. (A. L. Logie 57 not out, C. H. Lloyd 55, C. G. Greenidge 51, H. A. Gomes 46); Victorian Country XI 92 for eight (H. Joseph four for 13).

†At Melbourne, November 21. WEST INDIES beat PAKISTAN by 18 runs (See Benson and Hedges World Series Cup section).

†At Sydney, November 24. WEST INDIES lost to AUSTRALIA by seven wickets (See Benson and Hedges World Series Cup section).

NEW SOUTH WALES v WEST INDIANS

At Sydney, November 27, 28, 29, 30. West Indians won by nine wickets. Left to score 116 to win in 22 overs on the last afternoon, the West Indians hit them off 17.1 overs in 57 minutes against a somewhat strange selection of bowlers. McCosker, captaining New South Wales, wanted to use an old ball for this final innings, and when the West Indians did not agree to this, he opened the bowling with two gentle medium-pacers, Beard and Chappell. McCosker said after the match that he thought he would try something different but that it had not worked. Centuries by Haynes, his first in three visits to Australia, and another by Dujon assured the West Indians of a big lead. Dyson, after failing by 2 to reach his hundred in New South Wales's first innings, compiled a painstaking 123 in five hours in the second. In an exciting last session, Bacchus and Richards took the West Indians to victory.

New South Wales

*R. B. McCosker c Richards b Croft	64	– (2) lbw b Joseph	23
J. Dyson c Haynes b Roberts	98	– (1) c sub b Richards	123
T. M. Chappell c Dujon b Clarke	6	– lbw b Roberts	44
I. C. Davis b Holding	15	– b Roberts	52
P. M. Toohey c Dujon b Roberts	11	– c Haynes b Croft	44
G. R. Beard c Bacchus b Joseph	4	– run out	2
†S. J. Rixon c Croft b Gomes	25	– lbw b Roberts	2
M. Ray not out	21	– not out	11
L. S. Pascoe b Holding	23	– c Dujon b Roberts	0
M. R. Whitney b Croft	0	– (11) b Croft	0
A. J. Skilbeck (did not bat)		– (10) lbw b Croft	0
B 2, l-b 7, w 1, n-b 1	11	B 5, l-b 7, w 3, n-b 3	18
1/102 2/109 3/163 4/185 5/206 6/206 7/236 8/277 9/278	(9 wkts dec.) 278	1/49 2/170 3/211 4/293 5/302 6/302 7/310 8/318 9/319	319

Bowling: *First Innings*—Clarke 11–1–40–1; Holding 16–2–44–2; Roberts 14–4–30-2; Croft 17–3–43–2; Joseph 31–8–89–1; Richards 1–0–4–0; Gomes 5–0–17–1. *Second Innings*—Roberts 33–11–48–4; Croft 41.4–10–78–3; Joseph 33–8–73–1; Richards 33–8–71–1; Gomes 11–1–31–0.

West Indians

D. L. Haynes b Pascoe .... 139 – c Dyson b Chappell 10
S. F. A. Bacchus c Davis b Chappell .... 83 – not out 53
H. A. Gomes c McCosker b Beard 13
A. L. Logie c Skilbeck b Pascoe 43
†P. J. Dujon not out 104
A. M. E. Roberts c Davis b Pascoe 33
*I. V. A. Richards c Toohey b Ray .... 44 – (3) not out 53
H. Joseph c Toohey b Ray 7
B 2, l-b 6, n-b 8 .... 16 L-b 1 1

1/168 2/191 3/285 4/308 5/367 6/460 7/482 (7 wkts dec.) 482 1/11 (1 wkt) 117

S. T. Clarke, M. A. Holding and C. E. H. Croft did not bat.

Bowling: *First Innings*—Pascoe 26–4–112–3; Whitney 16–2–79–0; Skilbeck 14–4–41–0; Ray 33.5–8–112–2; Beard 31–8–71–1; Chappell 14–3–34–1; McCosker 3–1–17–0. *Second Innings*—Beard 4–0–26–0; Chappell 5-0-40-1; Ray 4–0–20–0; McCosker 3.1–0–29–0; Toohey 1–0–1–0.

Umpires M. Jay and A. G. Watson.

†NEW SOUTH WALES COUNTRY XI v WEST INDIANS

At Orange, December 2. West Indians won by 54 runs. West Indians 235 for six (45 overs) (M. D. Marshall 65 not out, A. L. Logie 63 not out, D. L. Haynes 46; J. Culverson three for 54); New South Wales Country XI 181 for eight (45 overs) (R. Oakley 78).

†At Adelaide, December 5. WEST INDIES lost to PAKISTAN by 8 runs (See Benson and Hedges World Series Cup section).

TASMANIA v WEST INDIANS

At Hobart, December 7, 8, 9. Drawn. After the first day had been almost entirely lost to rain, Tasmania struggled to 204, only Mancell with a determined 50 making a significant contribution. The West Indian batsmen were then given a shock by one of their fellow-countrymen, Franklyn Stephenson from Barbados, a young fast bowler who in the previous two seasons had taken 100 wickets in the Lancashire Leagues. He took the three West Indian wickets to fall on the second evening and finished with five for 46 as Tasmania gained a first-innings lead of 1 run. Another feature of the West Indians' innings was the fielding of Tasmania's twelfth man, Robinson, who held four catches.

Tasmania

I. R. Beven lbw b Croft .... 40 – not out 37
R. F. Jeffery not out 10
N. J. Allanby c Murray b Holding .... 9 – (2) c Joseph b Croft 10
D. C. Boon b Joseph .... 21 – not out 40
*B. F. Davison lbw b Garner 9
†R. D. Woolley c Holding b Croft .... 24 – (3) b Holding 4
P. Mancell c Murray b Garner 50
F. D. Stephenson c Murray b Joseph 13
S. L. Saunders b Holding 2
D. Mullett b Garner 13
P. M. Clough lbw b Joseph 0
B 4, l-b 3, w 1, n-b 5 .... 13 B 4, l-b 3, n-b 2 9

1/50 2/73 3/82 4/97 5/136 6/166 7/171 8/193 9/196 204 1/34 2/41 (2 wkts) 100

Bowling: *First Innings*—Holding 20–3–48–2; Croft 17–0–52–2; Garner 16.3–5–41–3; Joseph 21–7–45–3; Gomes 1–0–5–0. *Second Innings*—Holding 9–2–34–1; Croft 11–1–42–1; Garner 3–0–5–0; Joseph 6–2–10–0.

West Indians

C. G. Greenidge c Beven b Clough	12	J. Garner c Davison b Clough	12
S. F. A. Bacchus c and b Stephenson	0	M. A. Holding c Mullett b Stephenson	6
I. V. A. Richards c sub b Stephenson	57	H. Joseph lbw b Stephenson	4
C. E. H. Croft c Saunders b Stephenson	6	L-b 2, n-b 2	4
H. A. Gomes c sub b Clough	11		—
*C. H. Lloyd c sub b Saunders	51	1/3 2/21 3/32	203
A. L. Logie c sub b Saunders	29	4/61 5/118 6/170	
†D. A. Murray not out	11	7/171 8/186 9/197	

Bowling: Stephenson 17.5–3–46–5; Clough 19–4–48–3; Mullett 7–2–21–0; Mancell 13–1–54–0; Saunders 9–1–30–2.

Umpires: J. Stevens and S. Randell.

QUEENSLAND v WEST INDIANS

At Brisbane, December 11, 12, 13, 14. West Indians won by an innings and 92 runs. Dropped twice while spending half an hour reaching double figures, Richards found his best form in a brilliant innings of 121 made in 152 minutes with eighteen 4s and one 6. He and Gomes added 127 for the third wicket after De Jong had dismissed Haynes with his second ball in first-class cricket. Gomes went on to his first-ever double-century. Queensland's batting had no answer in their first innings to Marshall, who took five for 31; only Ritchie passed 50 in a determined innings. When they followed on 374 behind, Wessels, Ritchie and Phillips made fifties, while Richards took five for 88 with his off-breaks.

West Indians

C. G. Greenidge c Kerr b Dymock	1	†P. J. Dujon lbw b Hohns	1
D. L. Haynes c Phillips b De Jong	12	A. M. E. Roberts not out	0
I. V. A. Richards c Ritchie b Hohns	121		
H. A. Gomes not out	200	B 4, l-b 4, n-b 19	27
S. F. A. Bacchus c Kerr b Maguire	85		—
M. A. Holding c Ritchie b Lillie	24	1/1 2/40 3/167 4/350 (7 wkts dec.)	539
*C. H. Lloyd c Phillips b De Jong	68	5/385 6/521 7/526	

M. D. Marshall and S. T. Clarke did not bat.

Bowling: Maguire 27–6–97–1; Dymock 30–10–73–1; De Jong 16–2–71–2; Lillie 32–3–166–1; Hohns 37.4–9–105-2; Wessels 1–1–0–0.

Queensland

K. C. Wessels c Bacchus b Roberts	13	– b Richards	57
R. B. Kerr lbw b Holding	20	– c Dujon b Clarke	16
M. A. Gaskell c Dujon b Clarke	0	– b Richards	6
G. M. Ritchie b Holding	55	– b Holding	71
A. D. Parker c Dujon b Marshall	8	– c Lloyd b Richards	0
T. V. Hohns c Lloyd b Marshall	18	– b Richards	18
H. K. De Jong lbw b Marshall	1	– c Roberts b Richards	20
†R. B. Phillips not out	16	– lbw b Clarke	51
*G. Dymock c Dujon b Marshall	10	– b Gomes	8
J. N. Maguire run out	0	– lbw b Clarke	0
D. J. Lillie b Marshall	0	– not out	15
B 10, l-b 4, n-b 10	24	B 12, l-b 4, n-b 4	20
	—		—
1/20 2/23 3/96 4/97	165	1/62 2/80 3/85 4/85	282
5/125 6/136 7/143 8/164 9/165		5/148 6/207 7/250 8/250 9/261	

Bowling: *First Innings*—Clarke 7–1–23–1; Roberts 12–4–26–1; Marshall 18–8–31–5; Holding 12–3–29–2; Richards 15–3–32–0. *Second Innings*—Clarke 18–1–51–3; Roberts 12–1–36–0; Marshall 6–1–22–0; Holding 17–2–36–1; Richards 22.5–4–88–5; Gomes 10–0–29–1.

Umpires: M. W. Johnson and C. D. Timmins.

†QUEENSLAND COUNTRY XI v WEST INDIANS

At Caloundra, December 16. West Indians won by 68 runs. West Indians 214 for seven (45 overs) (S. F. A. Bacchus 103 not out); Queensland Country XI 146 for eight (45 overs).

†At Perth, December 19. WEST INDIES beat PAKISTAN by seven wickets (See Benson and Hedges World Series Cup section).

†At Perth, December 20. WEST INDIES beat AUSTRALIA by eight wickets (See Benson and Hedges World Series Cup section).

AUSTRALIA v WEST INDIES

First Test Match

At Melbourne, December 26, 27, 28, 29, 30. Australia won by 58 runs. Australia made one change from the side which had lost to Pakistan ten days earlier on the same ground, bringing in Lawson for Thomson. The indications were that the toss would prove decisive, but the pitch, two away from that used against Pakistan, had been amply watered with the result that there was enough moisture on the first two days to help the faster bowlers.

In the fifth over of the match, after Australia had chosen to bat, Holding dismissed Laird and Chappell with successive balls, this being the Australian captain's fourth successive 0 for Australia since the last Test against Pakistan. Soon Australia were 26 for four, and it needed a superb innings by Hughes to effect some sort of recovery. Holding, in particular, was extremely fast. Yet Hughes was determined not just to concentrate on passive defence. When the ninth wicket fell at 155 Hughes had reached 71, but Alderman kept his head down and his bat straight while his partner played some marvellous strokes, reaching his hundred with a thrilling square cut for 4 off Garner. Hughes batted for 262 minutes and hit eleven 4s.

West Indies were left with 35 minutes' batting on the first evening, which produced most dramatic cricket as Alderman and Lillee took four wickets for 10 runs. Alderman had Bacchus, opening in place of Greenidge whose knee injury had not mended, caught at fourth slip; Lillee, who began the match needing five wickets to beat Lance Gibbs's record of 309 Test wickets, then had Haynes splendidly caught by Border above his head at second slip. Croft, the night-watchman, was leg before, shuffling across his stumps in the same over. And with the last ball of the day Lillee bowled Richards off the inside edge as he tried to drive.

Lillee thus began the second day needing two more wickets for his record. Dujon, having batted excitingly well, was the first, being caught at deep backward square leg off a hook that would have been a big 6 on many grounds. Lillee got his record when Gomes was caught by Chappell at first slip.

West Indies were eventually all out for 201, which gave them a first-innings lead of 3. But by then the pitch had dried after the rain storms which had punctuated the second day, and for the next four hours Australia seemed to be building a sizeable score as Wood, Laird and Border all played useful innings. Chappell failed again, this time being caught behind glancing at Garner. Four wickets fell in the last hour of the third day as the pitch began to behave awkwardly, and Holding quickly finished off the innings the next morning. His eleven for 107 in the match was a fine reward for some wonderful bowling and the best ever by a West Indian against Australia. David Murray, behind the stumps, took his tally of catches for the match to nine, a figure exceeded in Test cricket only by Bob Taylor's ten at Bombay in 1979-80.

West Indies final target was 220, but after Alderman had had Bacchus leg before and bowled Richards in the second over of the innings they never looked likely to win. The only time Australia had any anxiety was when Dujon played a second fine innings, this time concentrating for the most part on defence, though never wasting the chance to play a stroke that did not involve a risk.

During the match the Melbourne Cricket Club announced that the committee had decided to relay the square over the next three years, beginning as soon as the current Australian season was over. This was also the last match before the old MCG scoreboard was taken down, to be replaced by an electronic one.

Attendance: 136,464.

Australia

B. M. Laird c Murray b Holding	4	(2) lbw b Croft	64
G. M. Wood c Murray b Roberts	3	(1) c Murray b Garner	46
*G. S. Chappell c Murray b Holding	0	c Murray b Garner	6
A. R. Border c Murray b Holding	4	b Holding	66
K. J. Hughes not out	100	b Holding	8
D. M. Wellham c sub (Logie) b Croft	17	lbw b Holding	2
†R. W. Marsh c Richards b Garner	21	c Murray b Holding	2
B. Yardley b Garner	21	b Garner	13
D. K. Lillee c Gomes b Holding	1	c Murray b Holding	0
G. F. Lawson b Holding	2	not out	0
T. M. Alderman c Murray b Croft	10	b Holding	1
B 1, l-b 5, n-b 8	15	B 5, l-b 4, w 1, n-b 4	14
1/4 2/4 3/8 4/26 5/59 6/115 7/149 8/153 9/155	198	1/82 2/106 3/139 4/184 5/190 6/199 7/215 8/218 9/220	222

Bowling: *First Innings*—Holding 17–3–45–5; Roberts 15–6–40–1; Garner 20–6–59–2; Croft 16.1–3–39–2. *Second Innings*—Holding 21.3–5–62–6; Roberts 18–4–31–0; Garner 18–5–37–3; Croft 20–2–61–1; Richards 5–0–17–0.

West Indies

D. L. Haynes c Border b Lillee	1	c Lillee b Yardley	28
S. F. A. Bacchus c Wood b Alderman	1	lbw b Alderman	0
C. E. H. Croft lbw b Lillee	0	(11) not out	0
I. V. A. Richards b Lillee	2	(3) b Alderman	0
*C. H. Lloyd c Alderman b Yardley	29	(4) c Border b Lawson	19
H. A. Gomes c Chappell b Lillee	55	(5) b Yardley	24
P. J. Dujon c Hughes b Lillee	41	(6) c Marsh b Yardley	43
†D. A. Murray not out	32	(7) c Marsh b Yardley	10
A. M. E. Roberts c Marsh b Lillee	18	(8) lbw b Lillee	10
M. A. Holding c and b Alderman	2	(9) lbw b Lillee	7
J. Garner c Laird b Lillee	7	(10) lbw b Lillee	0
B 1, l-b 3, n-b 9	13	B 1, l-b 10, n-b 9	20
1/3 2/5 3/6 4/10 5/62 6/134 7/147 8/174 9/183	201	1/4 2/4 3/38 4/80 5/88 6/116 7/150 8/154 9/154	161

Bowling: *First Innings*—Lillee 26.3–3–83–7; Alderman 18–3–54–2; Lawson 9–2–28–0; Chappell 2–2–0–0; Yardley 7–2–23–1. *Second Innings*—Lillee 27.1–8–44–3; Alderman 9–3–23–2; Lawson 17–3–36–1; Yardley 21–7–38–4.

Umpires: A. R. Crafter and R. C. Bailhache.

AUSTRALIA v WEST INDIES

Second Test Match

At Sydney, January 2, 3, 4, 5, 6. Drawn. For four days this match was as exciting as the first Test in Melbourne. When, on the last day, Australia were 169 for four in their second innings with no chance of winning, the West Indian fast bowlers would have been expected a few years earlier to have finished them off.

Both sides made two changes for the match, Australia bringing in Dyson for Wellham and Thomson for Lawson while West Indies played Greenidge, whose knee had not completely mended, for Bacchus and Clarke for Roberts.

Lloyd batted on winning the toss and it was soon clear that playing Greenidge, who made a fine 66, was a worthwhile gamble. But the West Indian batsmen mostly got themselves out when well set, and instead of the huge score that once or twice looked likely they had to be content with 384. For that they were indebted to a long innings by Gomes, whose 126 took 444 minutes.

When Australia batted they were given a good start by Wood, but then fell away badly against some more hostile bowling from Holding. At one point they were in danger of having to follow on, but were saved from this by an innings of handsome strokes from Yardley, now close to being a genuine all-rounder, and a typically determined effort from Border. After gaining a lead of 117, West Indies promised more in their second innings than they in fact achieved. Haynes, Gomes, Lloyd and Dujon moved into the 40s or 50s before being undone through carelessness. The innings was finished off by a remarkable spell of off-spin bowling by Yardley: in 77 balls he took seven for 37, one from an amazing, leaping, overhead catch by Dyson to remove Clarke after a dash of some 25 yards. For one who did not turn to bowling off-breaks until he was 27, Yardley, now 34, has developed quickly.

Left to score 373 to win, Australia's second innings revolved round a mammoth defensive effort by Dyson, whose second Test hundred made sure of a draw. However, there were anxious moments on the last day when Laird and Chappell were out in the same over from Croft. Chappell, pushing forward to his first ball, was brilliantly caught by Murray diving across first slip to extend his run of failures. Hughes and Border were also out cheaply during the afternoon, but any chance the West Indian fast bowlers might have had of pressing their advantage home was ended when bad light prevented more than half an hour's play after tea. In his undefeated 127, occupying 377 minutes, Dyson hit eleven 4s.

Attendance: 115,161.

West Indies

C. G. Greenidge c Laird b Lillee	66	– c Yardley b Lillee	8
D. L. Haynes lbw b Thomson	15	– lbw b Lillee	51
I. V. A. Richards c Marsh b Lillee	44	– c Border b Alderman	22
H. A. Gomes c Chappell b Yardley	126	– c Border b Yardley	43
*C. H. Lloyd c Marsh b Thomson	40	– c Hughes b Yardley	57
P. J. Dujon c and b Thomson	44	– c and b Yardley	48
†D. A. Murray b Yardley	13	– c Laird b Yardley	1
M. A. Holding lbw b Lillee	9	– c Dyson b Yardley	5
S. T. Clarke b Yardley	14	– c Dyson b Yardley	5
J. Garner c Marsh b Lillee	1	– (11) b Yardley	0
C. E. H. Croft not out	0	– (10) not out	4
L-b 3, n-b 9	12	L-b 1, w 5, n-b 5	11
1/37 2/128 3/133 4/229 5/325 6/346 7/363 8/379 9/380	384	1/29 2/52 3/112 4/179 5/208 6/225 7/231 8/246 9/255	255

Bowling: *First Innings*—Lillee 39–6–119–4; Alderman 30–9–73–0; Thomson 20–1–93–3; Yardley 26.2–3–87–3; Border 1–1–0–0. *Second Innings*—Lillee 20–6–50–2; Alderman 12–2–46–1; Thomson 15–3–50–0; Yardley 31.4–6–98–7.

Australia

B. M. Laird c Dujon b Garner	14	– c Murray b Croft	38
G. M. Wood c Murray b Holding	63	– (6) not out	7
J. Dyson lbw b Holding	28	– (2) not out	127
*G. S. Chappell c Dujon b Holding	12	– (3) c Murray b Croft	0
T. M. Alderman b Clarke	0		
K. J. Hughes b Garner	16	– (4) lbw b Gomes	13
A. R. Border not out	53	– (5) b Gomes	9
†R. W. Marsh c Holding b Gomes	17		
B. Yardley b Holding	45		
D. K. Lillee c Garner b Holding	4		
J. R. Thomson run out	8		
B 1, l-b 2, w 2, n-b 2	7	B 2, l-b 1, n-b 3	6
1/38 2/108 3/111 4/112 5/128 6/141 7/172 8/242 9/246	267	1/104 2/104 3/149 4/169	(4 wkts) 200

Bowling: *First Innings*—Holding 29–9–64–5; Clarke 16–4–51–1; Garner 20–4–52–2; Croft 20–7–53–0; Richards 13–7–21–0; Gomes 9–1–19–1. *Second Innings*—Holding 19–6–31–0; Clarke 16–9–25–0; Garner 12–3–27–0; Croft 27–5–58–2; Richards 13–3–33–0; Gomes 15–7–20–2.

Umpires: R. A. French and M. W. Johnson.

†At Melbourne, January 10. WEST INDIES beat AUSTRALIA by five wickets (See Benson and Hedges World Series Cup section).

†At Sydney, January 12. WEST INDIES beat PAKISTAN by seven wickets (See Benson and Hedges World Series Cup section).

†At Brisbane, January 16. WEST INDIES beat PAKISTAN on faster scoring-rate (See Benson and Hedges World Series Cup section).

†At Brisbane, January 17. WEST INDIES beat AUSTRALIA by five wickets (See Benson and Hedges World Series Cup section).

†At Sydney, January 19. WEST INDIES lost to AUSTRALIA on faster scoring-rate (See Benson and Hedges World Series Cup section).

†At Melbourne, January 23. WEST INDIES beat AUSTRALIA by 86 runs (See Benson and Hedges World Series Cup section).

†At Melbourne, January 24. WEST INDIES beat AUSTRALIA by 128 runs (See Benson and Hedges World Series Cup section).

†At Sydney, January 26. WEST INDIES lost to AUSTRALIA by 46 runs (See Benson and Hedges World Series Cup section).

†At Sydney, January 27. WEST INDIES beat AUSTRALIA by 18 runs (See Benson and Hedges World Series Cup section).

AUSTRALIA v WEST INDIES

Third Test Match

At Adelaide, January 30, 31, February 1, 2, 3. West Indies won by five wickets. This was a superb game of cricket, played a few days after Mr Lynton Taylor, Managing Director of the Packer company which markets Australian cricket, had said that he doubted whether Test cricket could be saved. Australia brought in Pascoe for Alderman; Murray was unfit to keep wicket for West Indies, Dujon, though also injured, taking the gloves. Bacchus and Roberts, both missing from the West Indian team for the second Test, also played.

After being put in on a slightly green pitch, Australia lost their first four wickets for 17. Chappell, however, chose this moment to play his best innings for several weeks, and Australia were 204 for six at the end of the first day. Marsh, making his 80th Test appearance for Australia and so passing Harvey as his country's most-capped player, also played well before being hit on the side of his helmet by Croft and having to retire temporarily. He was the first of several injuries suffered by Australia in the game. Roberts and Holding quickly finished off the Australian innings on the second morning.

Careless strokes caused the loss of West Indies' first four wickets for 92 before Lloyd and the ever-improving Gomes steadied the innings. On the third day Gomes received invaluable help from Dujon, who once again made batting seem easy in reaching 51, and Roberts, with whom he added 82 for the eighth wicket as West Indies progressed to a lead of 151.

Australia made another bad start, losing Wood and Dyson for 35 before Laird and Border stayed together for almost four hours in a determined stand of 166 to give Australia a chance of saving the match. Hughes and Marsh carried on the good work, and at the close of the fourth day Australia, at 341 for four, were 190 ahead. They needed only a draw to win the series and the match looked almost safe. Next morning, though, their last six wickets fell for 24 runs, Garner taking four for 5 in nine overs and Holding claiming the other two. West Indies were thus left to score 236 to win in four and a half hours.

Following the early loss of Haynes, another excellent stand between Richards and Greenidge looked like taking them to an unhurried victory. Both were then out within 7 runs of each other and serious doubts appeared in the West Indians' batting. Fortunately for them a series of important catches were dropped, the most vital of them when Lloyd, on 18, was put down behind the wicket by Marsh, diving to his left, off Thomson. In the closing stages Bacchus was also dropped, and Lloyd twice more. The winning runs came with seventeen balls to spare, leaving Lloyd 77 not out after what was expected to be his last Test innings in Australia. The three West Indian fast bowlers, Holding, Garner and Croft, chaired him off the field.

Attendance: 107,769.

Australia

B. M. Laird c Dujon b Roberts	2	– (2) c Dujon b Croft	78
G. M. Wood c Garner b Roberts	5	– (1) c and b Holding	6
J. Dyson c Dujon b Holding	1	– c Lloyd b Garner	10
K. J. Hughes c Greenidge b Holding	5	– (5) c Bacchus b Garner	84
*G. S. Chappell c Garner b Holding	61	– (7) lbw b Holding	7
A. R. Border c Dujon b Roberts	78	– (4) c Dujon b Roberts	126
†R. W. Marsh c Dujon b Holding	39	– (6) c Haynes b Holding	38
B. Yardley b Croft	8	– b Garner	6
D. K. Lillee b Roberts	2	– c Dujon b Garner	1
J. R. Thomson not out	18	– c Bacchus b Garner	0
L. S. Pascoe b Holding	10	– not out	0
B 1, l-b 2, w 1, n-b 5	9	B 7, l-b 10, n-b 13	30
1/3 2/8 3/8 4/17 5/122 6/193 7/206 8/209 9/210	238	1/10 2/35 3/201 4/267 5/362 6/373 7/383 8/383 9/383	386

Bowling: *First Innings*—Holding 25–5–72–5; Roberts 19–7–43–4; Croft 23–4–60–1; Garner 17–4–44–0; Gomes 7–3–10–0. *Second Innings*—Holding 29–9–70–3; Roberts 24–7–64–1; Croft 32–4–90–1; Garner 35–15–56–5; Gomes 14–1–38–0; Richards 18–3–38–0.

West Indies

C. G. Greenidge c Border b Thomson	8	– c Marsh b Thomson 52
D. L. Haynes c Marsh b Thomson	26	– c Marsh b Thomson 4
I. V. A. Richards c Laird b Yardley	42	– b Pascoe 50
H. A. Gomes not out	124	– b Pascoe 21
S. F. A. Bacchus c Laird b Pascoe	0	– (6) c Lillee b Pascoe 27
*C. H. Lloyd c Marsh b Thomson	53	– (5) not out 77
C. E. H. Croft b Thomson	0	
†P. J. Dujon c Thomson b Yardley	51	– (7) not out 0
A. M. E. Roberts c sub (Hookes) b Yardley	42	
M. A. Holding b Yardley	3	
J. Garner c Wood b Yardley	12	
B 4, l-b 7, w 3, n-b 14	28	L-b 2, w 1, n-b 5 8
1/12 2/72 3/85 4/92 5/194 6/194 7/283 8/365 9/369	389	1/7 2/107 3/114 4/176 5/235 (5 wkts) 239

Bowling: *First Innings*—Lillee 4.5–3–4–0; Thomson 29–1–112–4; Yardley 40.5–10–132–5; Pascoe 30–3–94–1; Border 5–0–19–0. *Second Innings*—Lillee 4–0–17–0; Thomson 19.1–5–62–2; Yardley 16–0–68–0; Pascoe 22–3–84–3.

Umpires: R. C. Bailhache and M. W. Johnson.

THE AUSTRALIANS IN NEW ZEALAND, 1981-82

By R. T. BRITTENDEN

There has been no more successful tour of New Zealand in terms of public relations, gate receipts and even results than the 1981–82 tour by Australia. The visitors set out to remedy the damage done the previous summer in Australia – the season of two hotly disputed catches and of the underarm incident in the third of the Benson and Hedges final series matches, in Melbourne. They succeeded admirably, and for this much credit is due to the captain, Greg Chappell, and his industrious, amiable manager, Alan Crompton. It was a measure of Chappell's determination to make amends that he won the award of nearly £1,700 for the Sportsman of the Series.

The Australians overcame grounds for complaint. In the opening match of the one-day series, at Auckland, New Zealand's top scorer, Edgar, was almost certainly bowled when only 7, but was given not out. After his splendid century in that match, Chappell was accidentally knocked over as he left the pitch by one of the horde of spectators who invaded the ground. At the Christchurch Test he had his cap snatched from his head by a youthful spectator. Yet there was no murmur of complaint about these and other incidents, and the New Zealand players matched the Australians in their behaviour. It made for a most pleasant summer.

Paid attendances totalled more than 200,000 and the crowd of 42,000 at the first one-day international at Auckland surpassed by some 12,000 the previous New Zealand record. New Zealand's success in that match led to a ground record of 15,000 for the second game of the one-day series in Dunedin. If New Zealand's defeat there and in the deciding one-day match at Wellington, followed by some bad weather and a washed-out first Test, also at Wellington, rather took the cream off the financial cake, the New Zealand Cricket Council still showed a healthy profit of some £58,000 on the venture.

By drawing the Test series one-all, New Zealand maintained their recent good record at home. They have won two and shared two of their last five domestic series. The rained-out first Test suggested that the teams were evenly matched. Australia batted badly at Auckland, and lost; New Zealand bowled and batted wretchedly at Christchurch, and Australia won. In addition, the drawn series was very satisfactory for the New Zealand public, which seldom hopes for more than evidence that its Test team can foot it with the other cricket countries.

There were some fine individual performances in the Test series. Edgar made 161 at Auckland, the highest score by a New Zealander against Australia and the best in a Test at Eden Park. There were also memorable centuries at Christchurch by Chappell and Wright. By and large, however, the batting was sketchy. Chappell was head and shoulders above all his colleagues except, perhaps, Wood. Edgar capped a very successful season, while the New Zealand captain, Howarth, played some useful innings. However, there were too many Test failures by players chosen for their batting.

Although the Australians seldom had Lillee fully fit, there was some very fast bowling by Thomson. The most successful Australian bowler, however, was the energetic and aggressive off-spinner, Yardley, who maintained his

Australian form by taking thirteen wickets in the three Tests. New Zealand had the best bowler of the series in Richard Hadlee, winner of the Man of the Series award, a car valued at £5,900. This gave New Zealand players about £14,000 and the Australians £12,600 of the most substantial prize-money ever offered in New Zealand.

AUSTRALIAN TOUR RESULTS

Test matches – Played 3: Won 1, Lost 1, Drawn 1.

First-class matches – Played 5: Won 1, Lost 1, Drawn 3.

Win – New Zealand.

Loss – New Zealand.

Draws – New Zealand, North Island, NZCC President's XI.

Non first-class matches – Played 6: Won 3, Lost 3. *Wins* – New Zealand (2), Nelson-Marlborough. *Losses* – New Zealand, Northern Districts, Central Districts.

TEST MATCH AVERAGES

NEW ZEALAND – BATTING

	T	*I*	*NO*	*R*	*HI*	*Avge*
B. A. Edgar............	3	5	0	278	161	55.60
G. P. Howarth.........	3	5	1	183	58*	45.75
J. G. Wright............	3	5	0	200	141	40.00
M. C. Snedden.........	3	3	1	70	32	35.00
R. J. Hadlee...........	3	5	1	92	40	23.00
B. L. Cairns............	3	5	1	86	34	21.50
J. V. Coney............	3	5	1	79	73	19.75
J. F. M. Morrison.. ..	3	5	0	46	15	9.20
M. D. Crowe...........	3	4	0	20	9	5.00
I. D. S. Smith..........	3	4	0	16	11	4.00

Played in two Tests: G. B. Troup 4, 0*, 8*. Played in one Test: E. J. Chatfield did not bat.

* *Signifies not out.*

BOWLING

	O	*M*	*R*	*W*	*Avge*
R. J. Hadlee...........	91.5	25	226	14	16.14
J. F. M. Morrison.....	39.5	16	62	2	31.00
G. B. Troup............	44.3	8	166	5	33.20
M. C. Snedden.........	50	10	176	4	44.00
B. L. Cairns............	100	25	245	5	49.00

Also bowled: E. J. Chatfield 8–5–7–0; J. V. Coney 13–3–23–1; M. D. Crowe 4.3–1–14–0; G. P. Howarth 5–2–12–0; J. G. Wright 1–0–2–0.

AUSTRALIA – BATTING

	T	*I*	*NO*	*R*	*HI*	*Avge*
G. S. Chappell	3	4	1	235	176	78.33
G. M. Wood	3	5	0	229	100	45.80
B. M. Laird	3	5	1	147	39	36.75
J. Dyson	3	5	2	93	33	31.00
R. W. Marsh	3	3	0	59	33	19.66
A. R. Border	3	3	0	44	38	14.66
J. R. Thomson	3	3	0	42	25	14.00
B. Yardley	3	3	0	33	25	11.00
K. J. Hughes	3	3	0	29	17	9.66
D. K. Lillee	3	3	0	21	9	7.00
T. M. Alderman	3	3	3	1	1*	—

**Signifies not out.*

BOWLING

	O	*M*	*R*	*W*	*Avge*
A. R. Border	15.3	7	34	4	8.50
B. Yardley	113.4	41	311	13	23.92
D. K. Lillee	79	23	183	7	26.14
J. R. Thomson	89	31	192	6	32.00
T. M. Alderman	117.5	33	311	8	38.87

Also bowled: G. S. Chappell 31–9–51–1.

AUSTRALIAN AVERAGES – FIRST-CLASS MATCHES

BATTING

	M	*I*	*NO*	*R*	*HI*	*Avge*
G. S. Chappell	5	6	2	317	176	79.25
G. M. Wood	5	7	0	388	100	55.42
B. M. Laird	4	6	1	155	39	31.00
J. Dyson	4	6	2	124	33	31.00
K. J. Hughes	5	5	0	115	66	23.00
R. W. Marsh	5	4	1	59	33	19.66
A. R. Border	5	5	0	91	38	18.20
J. R. Thomson	5	4	0	51	25	12.75
B. Yardley	5	4	0	42	25	10.50
D. K. Lillee	4	3	0	21	9	7.00
T. M. Alderman	5	4	4	6	5*	—

Played in two matches: R. J. Bright 27. Played in one match: L. S. Pascoe 1.

**Signifies not out.*

BOWLING

	O	M	R	W	Avge
A. R. Border	20.3	7	52	4	13.00
D. K. Lillee	79	23	183	7	26.14
B. Yardley	150.2	50	462	17	27.17
J. R. Thomson	109	39	238	8	29.75
T. M. Alderman	136.5	37	362	12	30.16

Also bowled: R. J. Bright 42–10–156–2; G. S. Chappell 35–10–58–1; J. Dyson 3–0–18–1; K. J. Hughes 2–1–3–1; L. S. Pascoe 29–3–110–3.

FIELDING

R. W. Marsh 7 (all ct), G. S. Chappell 4, G. M. Wood 4, K. J. Hughes 3, D. K. Lillee 3 (1 sub.), B. Yardley 3, T. M. Alderman 2, A. R. Border 2, R. J. Bright 1, J. Dyson 1, B. M. Laird 1.

HUNDREDS FOR AUSTRALIANS

The following three three-figure innings were played for the Australians on their tour of New Zealand, one of which was not first-class.

G. S. Chappell (2)
176 v New Zealand at Christchurch (Third Test)
†108 v New Zealand at Auckland (First One-day International)

G. M. Wood (1)
100 v New Zealand at Auckland (Second Test)

†*Not first-class.*

HUNDREDS AGAINST AUSTRALIANS

The following three three-figure innings were played against the Australians in first-class matches.

V. R. Brown (1)
121* for NZCC President's XI at Christchurch

B. A. Edgar (1)
161 for New Zealand at Auckland (Second Test)

J. G. Wright (1)
141 for New Zealand at Christchurch (Third Test)

* *Signifies not out.*

NEW ZEALAND v AUSTRALIA

First One-Day International

At Auckland, February 13. New Zealand won by 46 runs. Australia were well beaten, despite a century by Chappell. Although New Zealand had some luck, with Edgar being given not out when 7, and the Australian innings ending in poor light, it was an assertive performance by the home side. With one-third of their 50 overs bowled, they had scored only 37, but Chappell and a strangely ineffective Lillee yielded 113 runs from their twenty overs as New Zealand's fortunes revived. Australia soon left New Zealand's scoring-rate behind. Chappell, after a diffident start, batted magnificently, but Border's dismissal in the 40th over began a collapse, Australia losing their last six wickets in as many overs. Chappell was given a mixed reception when he led his team out, and when he came out to begin his own innings, an ebonite wood, as in bowls, was sent from the fence across the turf. The noisy crowd delayed the progress of the game and spectators persisted in invading the ground at the fall of every Australian wicket, which detracted from the enjoyment of one of New Zealand's most exciting cricket days.

Man of the Match: G. S. Chappell.

Attendance: 42,000. *Takings:* £75,860.

New Zealand

J. G. Wright run out.......................... 18
B. A. Edgar b Pascoe........................ 79
J. F. Reid c Alderman b Chappell...... 20
*G. P. Howarth c Marsh b Lillee........ 34
J. V. Coney run out.......................... 45
R. J. Hadlee b Alderman.................. 11
B. L. Cairns not out.......................... 18
L-b 13, w 1, n-b 1................ 15

1/28 2/89 3/148 4/164 5/210 6/240 (6 wkts, 50 overs) 240

M. D. Crowe, †I. D. S. Smith, M. C. Snedden and G. B. Troup did not bat.

Bowling: Thomson 10–2–36–0; Alderman 10–3–41–1; Pascoe 10–0–35–1; Chappell 10–0–57–1; Lillee 10–0–56–1.

Australia

G. M. Wood run out.......................... 1
B. M. Laird c Crowe b Cairns............ 11
J. Dyson c Crowe b Troup................ 32
*G. S. Chappell c Howarth b Troup.... 108
K. J. Hughes c Crowe b Coney.......... 16
A. R. Border b Crowe...................... 6
†R. W. Marsh b Troup...................... 1
J. R. Thomson c Snedden b Troup...... 0
D. K. Lillee c Wright b Crowe........... 1
L. S. Pascoe not out.......................... 2
T. M. Alderman b Snedden............... 1
B 4, l-b 9, n-b 2.................. 15

1/1 2/21 3/109 4/144 5/182 6/187 7/189 8/190 9/192 (44.5 overs) 194

Bowling: Cairns 10–1–31–1; Hadlee 8–3–15–0; Snedden 7.5–1–35–1; Coney 7–0–45–1; Troup 10–1–44–4; Crowe 2–0–9–2.

Umpires: B. A. Bricknell and J. B. R. Hastie.

NORTHERN DISTRICTS v AUSTRALIANS

At Hamilton, February 14. Northern Districts won by 24 runs. Lack of batting application completed a disappointing weekend for the Australians.

Northern Districts 260 (46 overs) (G. P Howarth 72, J. G. Wright 38, B. L. Cairns 35; B. Yardley five for 58); Australians 236 (47.2 overs) (J. Dyson 79, B. M. Laird 63, A. R. Border 34; C. W. Dickeson three for 43).

NEW ZEALAND v AUSTRALIA

Second One-Day International

At Dunedin, February 17. Australia won by six wickets. Injuries caused Reid and Troup to withdraw from the New Zealand team just before the start, bringing in Chatfield and Blair, a left-hand batsman from Otago. Although Thomson was no-balled ten times, the Australian bowling was much sharper than it had been at Auckland and made the most of a pitch with an erratic bounce on which New Zealand prospered only during a fifth-wicket stand of 85 between Coney and Blair. With the pitch playing fewer tricks, Australia had a relatively simple task, though at 45 for four the game was still very much alive, Hadlee having dismissed Chappell and Hughes in successive overs. However, Laird, batting solidly, and Border, driving handsomely, shared an unbroken partnership of 115.

Man of the Match: A. R. Border.
Attendance: 15,000. *Takings:* £25,810.

New Zealand

B. A. Edgar lbw b Alderman	3
J. G. Wright b Lillee	5
M. D. Crowe c Hughes b Alderman	3
*G. P. Howarth c Chappell b Thomson	12
J. V. Coney b Alderman	54
B. R. Blair c Laird b Lillee	29
R. J. Hadlee b Lillee	7
†I. D. S. Smith not out	14
B. L. Cairns c Dyson b Pascoe	3
M. C. Snedden run out	3
E. J. Chatfield not out	2
L-b 11, w 1, n-b 12	24
1/14 2/16 3/27 4/39 5/124 6/132 7/136 8/143 9/150 (9 wkts, 49 overs)	159

Bowling: Thomson 10–1–30–1; Alderman 10–3–22–3; Lillee 10–3–24–3; Chappell 10–1–30–0; Pascoe 9–0–29–1.

Australia

G. M. Wood b Chatfield	4
B. M. Laird not out	71
J. Dyson c Smith b Cairns	18
*G. S. Chappell c Howarth b Hadlee	0
K. J. Hughes b Hadlee	5
A. R. Border not out	53
L-b 8, n-b 1	9
1/12 2/37 3/39 4/45 (4 wkts, 45 overs)	160

†R. W. Marsh, D. K. Lillee, J. R. Thomson, L. S. Pascoe and T. M. Alderman did not bat.

Bowling: Chatfield 10–1–30–1; Hadlee 9–3–24–2; Snedden 9–1–41–0; Coney 9–1–32–0; Cairns 8–1–24–1.

Umpires: F. R. Goodall and D. A. Kinsella.

NEW ZEALAND v AUSTRALIA

Third One-Day International

At Wellington, February 20. Australia won by eight wickets. Having won the toss in both the earlier one-day internationals, Chappell, reckoning it was his turn to call wrong, delegated Hughes to toss for him. The ruse worked, enabling Chappell to send New Zealand in on a pitch tailor-made for his seamers. Alderman, keeping the ball well up to the bat, took five for 17, the best figures of any bowler in fourteen one-day matches between the two countries. Lillee, bowling flat out, gave excellent support and New Zealand were all out for 74 in 29 overs, 34 of these runs coming in a half-hour stand for the eighth wicket between Hadlee and Cairns. Australia had no difficulty in achieving their target and so won the Rothmans Cup.

Man of the Match: T. M. Alderman.
Attendance: 17,000. *Takings:* £34,800.

New Zealand

J. G. Wright c Alderman b Thomson	0	B. L. Cairns c Alderman b Pascoe	14
B. A. Edgar b Alderman	11	M. C. Snedden b Lillee	1
M. D. Crowe c Laird b Alderman	7	G. B. Troup not out	2
*G. P. Howarth b Alderman	7		
J. V. Coney c Hughes b Lillee	3	L-b 6, w 1, n-b 2	9
B. R. Blair lbw b Alderman	2		
†I. D. S. Smith c Border b Alderman	0	1/0 2/20 3/23 4/30 (29 overs)	74
R. J. Hadlee c Hughes b Lillee	18	5/32 6/35 7/37 8/71 9/71	

Bowling: Thomson 5–1–11–1; Alderman 10–2–17–5; Lillee 10–3–14–3; Pascoe 4–1–23–1.

Australia

B. M. Laird lbw b Hadlee	10	L-b 5, w 2, n-b 5	12
†R. W. Marsh b Cairns	3		
J. Dyson not out	26	1/4 2/28 (2 wkts, 20.3 overs)	75
*G. S. Chappell not out	24		

K. J. Hughes, A. R. Border, B. Yardley, D. K. Lillee, J. R. Thomson, L. S. Pascoe and T. M. Alderman did not bat.

Bowling: Hadlee 8.3–2–25–1; Cairns 4–1–12–1; Troup 6–1–23–0; Snedden 2–1–3–0.

Umpires: S. J. Woodward and F. R. Goodall.

NORTH ISLAND v AUSTRALIANS

At Napier, February 22, 23, 24. Drawn. Only 50 overs were bowled before rain washed out the match, there being no play on the second and third days. Wood found form for the first time on the tour, but it was an unsatisfactory trial for the touring team.

Australians

B. M. Laird lbw b Chatfield	8	†R. W. Marsh not out	0
G. M. Wood c Crowe b Coney	66		
*K. J. Hughes b Snedden	20	B 2, l-b 3, w 1, n-b 9	15
A. R. Border c Morrison b Coney	21		
G. S. Chappell not out	4	1/38 2/82 3/130 4/134 (4 wkts)	134

R. J. Bright, B. Yardley, J. R. Thomson, D. K. Lillee and T. M. Alderman did not bat.

Bowling: Carrington 7–1–27–0; Snedden 14–4–33–1; Chatfield 15–5–27–1; Gray 7–1–19–0; Coney 7–1–13–2.

North Island

J. G. Wright, T. J. Franklin, *J. F. M. Morrison, J. R. Wiltshire, J. V. Coney, E. J. Gray, M. D. Crowe, †E. B. McSweeney, M. C. Snedden, M. C. Carrington and E. J. Chatfield.

Umpires: D. A. Kinsella and G. Reardon.

NEW ZEALAND v AUSTRALIA

First Test Match

At Wellington, February 26, 27, 28, March 1, 2. Drawn. Rain restricted play to less than eleven hours with no play on the first day, only four hours on the second, 51 minutes on the third, none on the fourth, and a full six hours on the last day. The covers, quite inadequate for a Test ground, had been blown off by a typically vigorous Wellington wind the night before the match was due to begin, and the pitch was saturated.

When, eventually, the Australians won their sixth successive toss of the tour and sent New Zealand in, the pitch played more easily than expected, and there was some inaccurate bowling and sloppy fielding from the Australians. The New Zealand left-hand opening combination of Edgar and Wright seemed to put Lillee and Thomson out of their stride, both of them bowling very wide of the off stump. By the close of this second day New Zealand were 107 for one from 60 overs; on the third, 20 runs were added for the loss of Morrison; and on the fifth, Edgar went to a self-denying half-century in 310 minutes – one of the slowest fifties in Test history. Howarth, missed twice, played some pleasant shots.

For Australia, Thomson produced occasional bursts of great pace but Lillee retired with a back injury after one over on the third day.

By the time New Zealand declared and Australia began their first innings, it was nearly three o'clock on the final day. The Australian batsmen were seldom in trouble.

Attendance: 22,000. *Takings:* £18,340.

New Zealand

B. A. Edgar lbw b Alderman	55
J. G. Wright c Chappell b Yardley	38
J. F. M. Morrison b Thomson	15
*G. P. Howarth not out	58
J. V. Coney lbw b Yardley	1
M. D. Crowe run out	9
R. J. Hadlee b Thomson	21
†I. D. S. Smith c Chappell b Yardley	11
B. L. Cairns not out	19
B 5, l-b 19, w 4, n-b 11	39
(7 wkts dec.)	266

1/86 2/120 3/149 4/162 5/186 6/212 7/246

M. C. Snedden and E. J. Chatfield did not bat.

Bowling: Thomson 26–13–35–2; Alderman 44–20–93–1; Lillee 15–5–32–0; Chappell 8–2–18–0; Yardley 23–10–49–3.

Australia

G. M. Wood b Cairns	41
B. M. Laird not out	27
J. Dyson not out	12
L-b 2, n-b 3	5
1/65 (1 wkt)	85

*G. S. Chappell, K. J. Hughes, A. R. Border, †R. W. Marsh, D. K. Lillee, B. Yardley, T. M. Alderman and J. R. Thomson did not bat.

Bowling: Hadlee 7–2–15–0; Snedden 8–1–24–0; Cairns 11–4–20–1; Chatfield 8–5–7–0; Crowe 4–1–14–0.

Umpires: F. R. Goodall and S. J. Woodward.

NELSON-MARLBOROUGH v AUSTRALIANS

At Nelson, March 4. Australians won by 63 runs. Australians 195 (49.3 overs) (J. Dyson 97; D. C. Aberhart four for 37); Nelson-Marlborough 132 (37.2 overs) (G.S. Chappell three for 26).

NZCC PRESIDENT'S XI v AUSTRALIANS

At Christchurch, March 6, 7, 8. Drawn. The Australians, having lost the toss for the first time, had some much-needed batting practice on a good pitch with the President's Eleven offering unexpected resistance. It was an unusually constructed home team, containing only two seam bowlers and five spinners. One of the faster men, former Test player Brendon Bracewell, was in his eleventh over when he was banned from further bowling because of damaging the pitch in his follow-through. Chappell was in masterly form, Wood sound but slow. The match was a triumph for Brown, New Zealand's first "Young Cricketer of the Year" who had spent a season on the Lord's groundstaff; he scored 173 in the match for only once out.

NZCC President's XI

P. N. Webb lbw b Alderman	7	– c Hughes b Yardley	25
T. J. Franklin c Marsh b Thomson	27	– lbw b Alderman	3
J. F. M. Morrison c Marsh b Pascoe	24	– c Border b Yardley	48
B. R. Blair b Thomson	9	– b Bright	11
E. J. Gray lbw b Alderman	21	– c Wood b Pascoe	45
V. R. Brown c Bright b Pascoe	52	– not out	121
*†W. K. Lees lbw b Alderman	0	– c Hughes b Yardley	25
J. G. Bracewell c sub b Yardley	62	– c Hughes b Dyson	29
G. K. Robertson c Yardley b Bright	28	– lbw b Hughes	4
B. P. Bracewell run out	0	– not out	13
S. L. Boock not out	6		
B 5, l-b 6, n-b 3	14	B 5, l-b 8, w 1	14
1/19 2/55 3/77 4/78 5/131 6/131 7/166 8/227 9/227	250	1/11 2/66 3/79 4/95 5/213 6/252 7/318 8/323	(8 wkts) 338

Bowling: *First Innings*—Thomson 15–5–44–2; Alderman 12–2–35–3; Pascoe 13–1–53–2; Chappell 4–1–7–0; Yardley 6.4–2–31–1; Bright 20–5–66–1. *Second Innings*—Thomson 5–3–2–0; Alderman 7–2–16–1; Pascoe 16–2–57–1; Yardley 30–7–120–3; Bright 22–5–90–1; Border 5–0–18–0; Dyson 3–0–18–1; Hughes 2–1–3–1.

Australians

G. M. Wood c Boock b J. G. Bracewell	93
†J. Dyson c Lees b B. P. Bracewell	31
*K. J. Hughes c Lees b Blair	66
A. R. Border c Blair b Robertson	26
†G. S. Chappell c Lees b Gray	78
R. J. Bright c Blair b Robertson	27
B. Yardley b Robertson	9
J. R. Thomson b Gray	9
T. M. Alderman not out	5
L. S. Pascoe c Boock b J. G. Bracewell	1
R. W. Marsh absent injured	
L-b 4, n-b 8	12
1/77 2/167 3/215 4/255 5/333 6/337 7/342 8/352 9/357	357

Bowling: B. P. Bracewell 11–3–40–1; Robertson 26–6–84–3; Boock 22–6–69–0; J. G. Bracewell 19.3–3–64–2; Blair 12–4–31–1; Gray 22–6–45–2; Brown 4–0–12–0.

Umpires: F. R. Goodall and I. C. Higginson.

CENTRAL DISTRICTS v AUSTRALIANS

At New Plymouth, March 9. Central Districts won by one wicket. A delayed flight from Christchurch had the Australians eating breakfast on the way to Pukekura Park, and they took the 45-over match so light-heartedly that Marsh opened the batting, with Wood at No. 11, and Marsh was bowling when the winning run was made off the second-last ball of the match.

Australia 171 (43 overs) (A. R. Border 76, J. Dyson 40; D. C. Aberhart three for 35; W. G. Hodgson three for 42); Central Districts 172 for nine (44.5 overs) (R. W. Anderson 36, W. G. Hodgson 33, I. D. Smith 31; T. M. Alderman four for 21).

NEW ZEALAND v AUSTRALIA

Second Test Match

At Auckland, March 12, 13, 14, 15, 16. New Zealand won by five wickets. Howarth won the toss and sent Australia in, but it was no more the pitch than a couple of poor shots and two suicidal attempts at quick runs that led to Australia being dismissed for 210. Laird batted briskly, Dyson watchfully, Chappell extravagantly. Australia regained some ground by taking two wickets for 35 late on the first day, but on the second Edgar batted with certainty, his innings lasting more than eight and a half hours in all; because of intervals and stoppages for bad light, he had to start and restart nine times. His concentration was admirable, and he played many attractive strokes, passing 1,000 runs in Tests. An aggressive Howarth helped him add 87 for the third wicket, and Coney joined him in a partnership of 154 in 217 minutes for the fourth. Edgar was seventh out after Hadlee had hit two 6s off Yardley, the second one thought to be the longest drive seen at Eden Park.

An opening stand of 106 between Wood and Laird – the first century opening partnership by Australia against New Zealand – put Australia back in the game when they batted again 177 behind. With nothing in the pitch for the faster bowlers, they had reached 167 before losing their second wicket. Wood scored his century in 260 minutes, and at the end of the fourth day Australia were 64 ahead on 241 for four.

On the final morning, Chappell was out first ball, checking a drive at Hadlee and being taken at cover-point. This success so inspired the New Zealanders, particularly Hadlee, that the eighth wicket fell at 260 and the home side were left needing only 104 to win. At 17 for two a close finish was in prospect, but Cairns, promoted to No. 5, hit out successfully, adding 53 in 32 minutes with Edgar. Cairns hit two 6s and Hadlee finished the match with another one. It was New Zealand's thirteenth Test victory, their second over Australia.

Attendance: 49,000. *Takings:* £55,000.

Australia

B. M. Laird c Smith b Troup	38	– (2) lbw b Hadlee	39
G. M. Wood c Smith b Cairns	9	– (1) c Snedden b Cairns	100
J. Dyson b Snedden	33	– b Cairns	33
K. J. Hughes c Smith b Troup	0	– b Cairns	17
*G. S. Chappell run out	32	– c Edgar b Hadlee	24
A. R. Border run out	0	– c Howarth b Morrison	38
†R. W. Marsh b Troup	33	– c Crowe b Hadlee	3
B. Yardley b Hadlee	25	– c Coney b Hadlee	0
J. R. Thomson lbw b Hadlee	13	– lbw b Hadlee	4
D. K. Lillee c Crowe b Troup	9	– c Smith b Morrison	5
T. M. Alderman not out	0	– not out	0
L-b 2, n-b 16	18	B 4, l-b 5, n-b 8	17
1/19 2/75 3/76 4/120 5/120 6/131 7/173 8/187 9/203	210	1/106 2/167 3/196 4/202 5/241 6/254 7/254 8/260 9/277	280

Bowling: *First Innings*—Hadlee 20–7–38–2; Troup 18.3–3–82–4; Cairns 17–7–38–1; Snedden 12–5–26–1; Howarth 1–0–8–0. *Second Innings*—Hadlee 28–9–63–5; Troup 15–4–31–0; Cairns 42–10–85–3; Snedden 8–2–22–0; Howarth 4–2–4–0; Coney 4–1–6–0; Morrison 34.5–15–52–2.

New Zealand

B. A. Edgar c and b Yardley	161	– c Lillee b Yardley 29
J. G. Wright c Yardley b Lillee	4	– c Laird b Alderman 4
J. F. M. Morrison b Lillee	11	– c Marsh b Lillee 8
*G. P. Howarth run out	56	– c Chappell b Yardley 19
J. V. Coney b Yardley	73	– (6) not out 5
M. D. Crowe c Wood b Lillee	2	
R. J. Hadlee c Chappell b Yardley	25	– not out 6
†I. D. S. Smith lbw b Yardley	5	
B. L. Cairns c Lillee b Alderman	14	– (5) b Border 34
M. C. Snedden not out	18	
G. B. Troup c Border b Alderman	4	
B 4, l-b 7, w 1, n-b 2	14	L-b 4 4
1/15 2/35 3/122 4/276 5/291 6/326 7/345 8/352 9/366	387	1/4 2/17 3/44 4/97 5/103 (5 wkts) 109

Bowling: *First Innings*—Thomson 23–8–52–0; Alderman 24.3–5–59–2; Lillee 39–7–106–3; Yardley 56–22–142–4; Border 3–2–11–0; Chappell 5–2–3–0. *Second Innings*—Alderman 7–0–30–1; Lillee 13–5–32–1; Yardley 7.4–2–40–2; Border 2–1–3–1.

Umpires: S. J. Woodward and B. A. Bricknell.

NEW ZEALAND v AUSTRALIA

Third Test Match

At Christchurch, March 19, 20, 21, 22. Australia won by eight wickets. Howarth again sent Australia in, and although Wood scored swiftly, New Zealand made good progress on a grassy pitch. Wood, with a diverting display, scored 64, reaching his half-century from only 58 balls. After an uncertain start on the first afternoon, Chappell was magnificent on the second morning when, in 106 minutes, he added 100 to his overnight 76. His 176 came from 218 balls in 260 minutes with two 6s and 23 4s.

If, with the exception of Hadlee's splendid bowling, New Zealand's performance in the field was disappointing, so was their batting. The Australians were all hostility, Thomson in particular bowling very fast, but New Zealand reached 50 with only one wicket down. Then six were lost in an hour, despite another knee injury to Lillee, whose last victim, caught by Marsh, gave the Australian wicket-keeper his 300th Test dismissal, 88 of them catches off Lillee.

At the close of the second day New Zealand were 98 for eight, needing another 56 runs to avoid the follow-on. Hadlee and Snedden scored all but 5 of them with some assertive batting, but both were out at 149 to give Australia a first-innings lead of 204. In Lillee's absence Chappell thought deeply before enforcing the follow-on. He opened the bowling himself, in order to rest Thomson, and when a stand of 93 between Wright and Howarth took New Zealand to 129 for two, a full recovery was in sight. Howarth was then given out caught at silly mid-on, a decision which caused considerable discussion, from which point New Zealand lost ground rapidly. Wright, driving beautifully, was 91 not out at the end of the day, with New Zealand 181 for seven. On the fourth morning he hit ten 4s in adding another 50, totalling seventeen 4s in his second Test century, but Australia, needing only 69 to win, had squared the series by mid-afternoon.

Attendance: 36,000. *Takings:* £41,000.

Australia

B. M. Laird c Smith b Troup	12	(2) c Edgar b Snedden	31
G. M. Wood c Crowe b Hadlee	64	(1) c Coney b Hadlee	15
J. Dyson c Hadlee b Snedden	1	not out	14
*G. S. Chappell c Smith b Coney	176	not out	3
K. J. Hughes b Hadlee	12		
A. R. Border b Snedden	6		
†R. W. Marsh c Cairns b Hadlee	23		
B. Yardley c Cairns b Hadlee	8		
J. R. Thomson b Hadlee	25		
D. K. Lillee c and b Hadlee	7		
T. M. Alderman not out	1		
B 2, l-b 8, n-b 8	18	B 2, l-b 2, n-b 2	6
1/50 2/57 3/82 4/128 5/145 6/237 7/256 8/340 9/352	353	1/24 2/60	(2 wkts) 69

Bowling: *First Innings*—Hadlee 28.5–5–100–6; Troup 11–1–53–1; Snedden 18–2–89–2; Cairns 21–3–74–0; Coney 8–2–15–1; Morrison 3–0–4–0. *Second Innings*—Hadlee 8–2–10–1; Snedden 4–0–15–1; Cairns 9–1–28–0; Coney 1–0–2–0; Morrison 2–1–6–0; Wright 1–0–2–0; Crowe 0.3–0–0–0.

New Zealand

B. A. Edgar c Dyson b Alderman	22	c Marsh b Alderman	11
J. G. Wright c Marsh b Lillee	13	b Alderman	141
J. F. M. Morrison lbw b Thomson	8	lbw b Chappell	4
*G. P. Howarth c Alderman b Thomson	9	c Wood b Border	41
J. V. Coney b Lillee	0	b Border	0
M. D. Crowe c Marsh b Lillee	0	b Yardley	9
R. J. Hadlee c Marsh b Thomson	40	c Alderman b Yardley	0
†I. D. S. Smith b Thomson	0	c Wood b Yardley	0
B. L. Cairns run out	3	lbw b Yardley	16
M. C. Snedden b Alderman	32	b Border	20
G. B. Troup not out	0	not out	8
B 8, l-b 2, w 1, n-b 11	22	B 4, l-b 7, w 2, n-b 9	22
1/33 2/57 3/57 4/57 5/67 6/82 7/82 8/87 9/149	149	1/21 2/36 3/129 4/133 5/162 6/166 7/166 8/215 9/249	272

Bowling: *First Innings*—Thomson 21–5–51–4; Alderman 19.2–3–63–2; Lillee 12–6–13–3. *Second Innings*—Alderman 23–5–66–2; Chappell 18–5–30–1; Thomson 19–5–54–0; Yardley 27–7–80–4; Border 10.3–4–20–3.

Umpires: D. A. Kinsella and F. R. Goodall.

THE SRI LANKANS IN PAKISTAN, 1981-82

By GEOFFREY SAULEZ

Two days after the England team left Colombo for home, the Sri Lankans left for Pakistan, their first tour as a Test-playing country. This comprised a concentrated itinerary, with an opening three-day match – in the event, abandoned through rain – three Test matches and three one-day internationals in five weeks. With so many international games, it was inevitable that some of the team had little cricket; and indeed Perera did not play in any match, appearing only as substitute fieldsman, which assignment he accomplished brilliantly.

From Sri Lanka's point of view the results were perhaps disappointing, with one draw in the Tests and one win in the one-day matches to set against two defeats in each. More resolute batting on the last day could have saved the first Test, and the second Test might have been won had they switched to attack sooner, rather than using de Mel to bowl to a defensive field, with one slip, long after all possibility of defeat had vanished. When D. S. de Silva was brought on for the last over before tea, with only the last twenty overs to come afterwards, he took three wickets in that one over, but by then it was too late.

The main batting successes of the team were Dias and Wettimuny. To Wettimuny, succeeding his elder brother as Sri Lanka's opening batsman, fell the distinction of scoring Sri Lanka's first Test century. He showed the application necessary for Test cricket in batting throughout the first day's play. Dias was the foremost stroke-player in the team, and he was very consistent with it, scoring a fifty in every match but the last, when he was out for 49. In addition he was a fine fielder in the covers. Madugalle also showed much promise as a correct player in the middle order. The more experienced players, Warnapura and Mendis, were somewhat disappointing. Warnapura, troubled by a finger injury, played only one innings of note, in the first one-day match, and Mendis too often got out to a rash stroke.

The bowling was built around the spin of the two unrelated de Silvas, D. S. (leg-spin) and G. R. A. (slow left-arm) and the brisk medium pace of de Mel. It was encouraging to see leg-spin used so freely at Test level, but D. S. de Silva, well as he bowled, was handicapped by having to be the team's stock bowler as well as the main attacker. His namesake rather lacked penetration in the Tests, but was useful in keeping an end going economically. de Mel kept going through long spells, moving the ball both ways and never giving up. For these three there was little support, although Ratnayeke, rather above medium pace, improved as the tour progressed. The ground fielding was mostly good, with Dias, Ranasinghe and Perera outstanding, but there were too many dropped catches, including one which may well have cost Sri Lanka the last one-day international.

The Pakistan team was involved in a dispute before the tour started, all ten of the side which had beaten Australia in Melbourne a few weeks earlier, under Javed Miandad's captaincy, refusing to play unless there was a change in captaincy for the tour of England, due later in the year. Three of them subsequently withdrew their objection and were selected; the others did not play until the last Test, enabling new players to be introduced, one of whom,

Salim Malik, only eighteen, scored a century on his Test début. Pakistan's bowling for the first two Tests was based on Iqbal Qasim's spin, but the last Test was dominated by Imran Khan, whose fourteen wickets in the match established a Pakistan record.

The Sri Lankan team was managed by A. P. B. Tennekoon, with E. R. Fernando as his assistant. They had been captain and vice-captain respectively on Sri Lanka's last tour of Pakistan eight years earlier.

SRI LANKAN TOUR RESULTS

Test matches–Played 3: Lost 2, Drawn 1.
First-class matches–Played 3: Lost 2, Drawn 1, Abandoned 1.
Losses–Pakistan (2).
Draw–Pakistan.
Abandoned–BCCP President's XI.
Non first-class matches–Played 3: Won 1, Lost 2. *Win*–Pakistan.
Losses–Pakistan (2).

TEST MATCH AVERAGES

PAKISTAN–BATTING

	T	*I*	*NO*	*R*	*HI*	*Avge*
Ashraf Ali	2	3	2	132	58	132.00
Rashid Khan	2	3	2	105	59	105.00
Mohsin Khan	2	3	0	215	129	71.66
Haroon Rashid	2	3	0	178	153	59.33
Salim Malik	2	4	1	139	100*	46.33
Javed Miandad	3	5	0	176	92	35.20
Rizwan-uz-Zaman	2	4	0	104	42	26.00
Tahir Naqqash	3	4	1	72	57	24.00
Tauseef Ahmed	3	2	1	23	18	23.00
Iqbal Qasim	3	3	0	62	56	20.66
Wasim Raja	3	5	1	66	31	16.50

Played in one Test: Imran Khan 39; Majid J. Khan 63; Mansoor Akhtar 6, 23; Mudassar Nazar 37; Salim Yousuf 4; Zaheer Abbas 134.

BOWLING

	O	*M*	*R*	*W*	*Avge*
Imran Khan	52.2	11	116	14	7.28
Rizwan-uz-Zaman	17	5	39	3	13.00
Iqbal Qasim	151.1	46	329	15	21.93
Tauseef Ahmed	96.4	22	264	11	24.00
Wasim Raja	45	14	117	3	39.00
Rashid Khan	48	13	134	3	44.66
Tahir Naqqash	96	19	354	7	50.57

Also bowled: Javed Miandad 1–0–1–0; Majid J. Khan 1–1–0–0; Mudassar Nazar 8–1–23–0.

FIELDING

Salim Yousuf 7 (5ct, 2st), Ashraf Ali 6 (4ct, 2st), Javed Miandad 4, Salim Malik 4, Tauseef Ahmed 3, Mohsin Khan 2, Haroon Rashid 1, Imran Khan 1, Majid J. Khan 1, Mansoor Akhtar 1, Mudassar Nazar 1, Rashid Khan 1, Rizwan-uz-Zaman 1, Wasim Raja 1.

SRI LANKA–BATTING

	T	*I*	*NO*	*R*	*HI*	*Avge*
S. Wettimuny...........	3	6	0	316	157	52.66
R. L. Dias...............	3	6	0	295	109	49.16
R. S. Madugalle........	3	6	1	155	91*	31.00
H. M. Goonatillake...	3	6	0	146	56	24.33
D. S. de Silva...........	3	6	1	114	36*	22.80
L. R. D. Mendis.......	3	6	0	116	54	19.33
G. R. A. de Silva.....	2	3	2	15	10*	15.00
A. L. F. de Mel........	3	6	1	74	34	14.80
A. Ranatunga..........	2	4	0	48	33	12.00
B. Warnapura..........	2	4	0	46	26	11.50
J. R. Ratnayeke.......	2	4	1	25	24	8.33

Played in one Test: R. S. A. Jayasekera 0, 2; L. W. Kaluperuma 0, 11*; A. N. Ranasinghe 6, 5; R. G. C. E. Wijesuriya 0, 3.

BOWLING

	O	*M*	*R*	*W*	*Avge*
D. S. de Silva..........	153	20	492	17	28.94
A. L. F. de Mel........	119.2	14	488	11	44.36
J. R. Ratnayeke........	49.4	11	190	4	47.50
G. R. A. de Silva.....	95.2	21	209	3	69.66

Also bowled: L. W. Kaluperuma 6–0–24–0; A. N. Ranasinghe 12–1–40–1; B. Warnapura 2–0–9–0; S. Wettimuny 2–0–21–0; R. G. C. E. Wijesuriya 24–2–105–0.

FIELDING

H. M. Goonatillake 8 (6ct, 2st), R. S. Madugalle 5, A. L. F. de Mel 3, L. R. D. Mendis 3, Substitutes 3, S. Wettimuny 2, R. L. Dias 1, A. Ranatunga 1.

HUNDREDS FOR SRI LANKANS

The following two three-figure innings were played for the Sri Lankans.

R. L. Dias (1)
109 v Pakistan at Lahore (Third Test)

S. Wettimuny (1)
157 v Pakistan at Faisalabad (Second Test)

HUNDREDS AGAINST SRI LANKANS

The following five three-figure innings were played against the Sri Lankans, four in first-class matches and one in a non first-class match.

Zaheer Abbas (2)
134 for Pakistan at Lahore (First Test)
†123 for Pakistan at Lahore (Second One-day International)

Haroon Rashid (1)
153 for Pakistan at Karachi (First Test)

Mohsin Khan (1)
129 for Pakistan at Lahore (Third Test)

Salim Malik (1)
100* for Pakistan at Karachi (First Test)

**Signifies not out.* †*Not first-class.*

BCCP PRESIDENT'S XI v SRI LANKANS

At Rawalpindi, February 28, March 1, 2. Abandoned.

PAKISTAN v SRI LANKA

First Test Match

At Karachi, March 5, 6, 7, 9, 10. Pakistan won by 204 runs. Sri Lanka made one change from the team which had played against England, preferring pace bowler Ratnayeke to off-spinner Kaluperuma; Pakistan, with several leading players unavailable, introduced four new caps, Salim Malik, Salim Yousuf, Rashid Khan and Tahir Naqqash.

Pakistan won the toss, but lost Mansoor Akhtar in the first over, edging de Mel, who got some lift in his first spell, to the wicket-keeper. In spite of a steady innings from Rizwan-uz-Zaman and an attacking 31 off 37 balls by Wasim Raja, Pakistan were in trouble at 126 for six before Haroon Rashid led a recovery in which the last four wickets added 270. Attacking the bowling, Haroon put on 104 with Tahir Naqqash in 97 minutes off 23.3 overs, the first 50 coming off seven overs, and a further 127 in even time with Rashid Khan. Haroon batted for 319 minutes, hitting sixteen 4s and three 6s.

Sri Lanka made a spirited reply. After losing Warnapura, lbw offering no stroke, Wettimuny and Dias added 96 in 73 minutes, Dias reaching 50 in 64 minutes before he too was lbw without offering a stroke. On the third morning, Ratnayeke, the night-watchman, batted for two hours and Madugalle for two and a half hours, but the tempo of the previous day was not maintained, only Mendis developing an innings.

Batting again, Pakistan soon lost Rizwan-uz-Zaman, and Mansoor Akhtar at 53 the next day, but the batsmen then took command. Iqbal Qasim, the night-watchman, reached his first Test fifty before giving a simple catch to square leg, and Salim Malik and Javed Miandad put Pakistan in an impregnable position. On the last day Miandad declared when Salim Malik reached his century, the third Pakistani, after Khalid Ibadulla and Miandad, to do so in his first Test. He had batted for nearly five hours and hit ten 4s in a chanceless innings.

Sri Lanka, set to make 354 in 236 minutes and twenty overs, lost Warnapura in the first over, and wickets fell at regular intervals, the batsmen making little attempt to close the game up until the position was hopeless. Although six of the first seven reached double figures, only one, the eighteen-year-old Ranatunga, passed 20, and his 33 off 41 balls contained five 4s and one 6. The match, which was watched by a total of fewer than 15,000 people, finished with two hours to spare.

Pakistan

Mansoor Akhtar c Goonatillake b de Mel	6 – c Mendis b D. S. de Silva	23
Rizwan-uz-Zaman c Goonatillake b Ratnayeke	42 – c Goonatillake b de Mel	10
Salim Malik b D. S. de Silva	12 – (4) not out	100
*Javed Miandad c Goonatillake b de Mel	4 – (5) st Goonatillake b D. S. de Silva.	92
Wasim Raja c Dias b de Mel	31 – (6) not out	12
Haroon Rashid run out	153	
†Salim Yousuf st Goonatillake b D. S. de Silva	4	
Tahir Naqqash c Mendis b D. S. de Silva	57	
Iqbal Qasim lbw b D. S. de Silva	1 – (3) c sub b D.S. de Silva	56
Rashid Khan c Madugalle b G. R. A. de Silva.	59	
Tauseef Ahmed not out	5	
L-b 9, w 4, n-b 9	22 B 5, l-b 1, w 1, n-b 1	8
1/6 2/46 3/53 4/72 5/113 6/126 7/230 8/232 9/359	396 1/16 2/53 3/107 4/269 (4 wkts dec.)	301

Bowling: *First Innings*—de Mel 28–2–124–3; Ratnayeke 16–6–49–1; D. S. de Silva 38–8–102–4; G. R. A. de Silva 17.2–2–69–1; Warnapura 2–0–9–0; Wettimuny 2–0–21–0. *Second Innings*—de Mel 23.2–3–100–1; Ratnayeke 5.4–2–20–0; D. S. de Silva 26–3–99–3; G. R. A. de Silva 35–5–74–0.

Sri Lanka

*B. Warnapura lbw b Tahir	13 – b Tahir	0
S. Wettimuny c Mansoor b Rashid Khan	71 – c Salim Yousuf b Rashid Khan.	14
R. L. Dias lbw b Qasim	53 – lbw b Tahir	19
R. S. Madugalle c Salim Yousuf b Rashid Khan	29 – c Tauseef b Qasim	18
J. R. Ratnayeke c Rizwan b Qasim	24 – (10) c Salim Malik b Raja	0
L. R. D. Mendis c Rashid Khan b Tahir	54 – (5) c Salim Yousuf b Qasim	15
A. Ranatunga st Salim Yousuf b Tauseef	13 – (6) c Salim Yousuf b Tauseef	33
D. S. de Silva b Tauseef	26 – (7) st Salim Yousuf b Qasim	12
†H. M. Goonatillake c Salim Yousuf b Tahir	14 – c Haroon b Raja	13
A. L. F. de Mel run out	9 – (8) c Miandad b Qasim	2
G. R. A. de Silva not out	10 – not out	0
B 1, l-b 12, w 3, n-b 12	28 B 9, l-b 11, w 1, n-b 2	23
1/24 2/120 3/152 4/199 5/221 6/242 7/285 8/308 9/322	344 1/1 2/27 3/41 4/68 5/91 6/121 7/125 8/139 9/149	149

Bowling: *First Innings*—Tahir 32–11–83–3; Rashid Khan 26–7–53–2; Qasim 28–7–88–2; Tauseef 21.4–6–64–2; Raja 5–1–28–0. *Second Innings*—Tahir 9–1–34–2; Rashid Khan 8–3–25–1; Qasim 15.1–8–27–4; Tauseef 12–1–39–1; Raja 3–2–1–2.

Umpires: Amanullah Khan and Mahboob Shah.

†PAKISTAN v SRI LANKA

First One-day International

At Karachi, March 12. Pakistan won by eight wickets. Play was marred by crowd disturbances and invasions of the playing area, resulting in a reduction of the match from 40 to 33 overs. Pakistan won the toss and, deciding to field, took the wicket of Wettimuny in the second over. After a slow start Warnapura and Dias added 139 in 27 overs. Soon afterwards crowd disturbances, and tear gas fired by the police, caused the match to be suspended with Sri Lanka 147 for two after 29 overs. The umpires rescheduled the match for 35 overs, only to come off after 33 overs. Sri Lanka having lost momentum through the interruptions to their innings, Pakistan were quickly up with the required scoring-rate. After Mansoor Akhtar was out in Wijesuriya's first over, Javed Miandad, promoting himself to No. 3, soon lofted Wijesuriya for 6 and Mohsin Khan also scored freely.

Man of the Match: Mohsin Khan.

Sri Lanka

*B. Warnapura b Qasim	77	A. Ranatunga not out	15
S. Wettimuny b Jalal-ud-Din	2	B 10, l-b 1, w 1, n-b 3	15
R. L. Dias c and b Tahir	57		—
L. R. D. Mendis not out	5	1/5 2/144 3/151 (3 wkts, 33 overs)	171

R. S. Madugalle, †R. S. A. Jayasekera, D. S. de Silva, A. L. F. de Mel, J. R. Ratnayeke and R. G. C. E. Wijesuriya did not bat.

Bowling: Tahir 6–0–19–1; Jalal-ud-Din 5–1–14–1; Rashid Khan 8–0–40–0; Qasim 5–0–32–1; Raja 5–0–29–0; Miandad 4–0–22–0.

Pakistan

Mansoor Akhtar b Wijesuriya	20	B 3, l-b 5, w 2, n-b 3	13
Mohsin Khan c Mendis b Ratnayeke	85		—
*Javed Miandad not out	56	1/52 2/157 (2 wkts, 20.2 overs)	174
Wasim Raja not out	0		

Salim Malik, Haroon Rashid, †Salim Yousuf, Tahir Naqqash, Jalal–ud–Din, Iqbal Qasim and Rashid Khan did not bat.

Bowling: de Mel 6–2–28–0; Ratnayeke 6.2–0–40–1; Wijesuriya 8–0–48–1; de Silva 6–0–30–0; Ranatunga 3–0–15–0.

Umpires: Shakil Khan and Tariq Atta.

PAKISTAN v SRI LANKA

Second Test Match

At Faisalabad, March 14, 15, 16, 18, 19. Drawn. Each side made two changes, Pakistan including Mohsin Khan, now available, for Mansoor Akhtar and Ashraf Ali for the injured Salim Yousuf. Sri Lanka played Ranasinghe and Kaluperuma for Warnapura (injured) and Ratnayeke, Mendis taking over the captaincy. Sri Lanka won the toss and, batting first on a grassless pitch, made a good start, with makeshift opener Goonatillake staying until nearly lunch-time before being caught at gully. This was Pakistan's only success on the first day as Wettimuny and Dias took the score to 270 for one. Wettimuny reached Sri Lanka's first Test century with a sweep to the boundary off Tauseef Ahmed, but was dropped when 109 in the gully and 111 at long-leg, both off Iqbal Qasim. He scored most of his runs behind the wicket on the leg side, whereas Dias excelled with his off-driving. Both were out early on the second day, having added 217 in four hours, Wettimuny hitting 21 4s and Dias fifteen 4s.

Sri Lanka lost three more wickets before lunch, Iqbal Qasim taking his 100th Test wicket when he had Ranasinghe caught at silly-point. Apart from D. S. de Silva, Madugalle could find little support and was left with 91 not out, including fifteen 4s, the last three wickets having fallen for 8 runs to Rizwan-uz-Zaman's gentle spin.

Pakistan soon lost Mohsin Khan, skying a hook to second slip, on the second evening; and, apart from a dour innings of three and a half hours from Rizwan-uz-Zaman, none of the main batsmen stayed for long. However, Ashraf Ali, in his first Test, was severe on the spinners and had reached his fifty before bad light ended play 30 minutes early. When he was out next morning, 35 were still needed to avoid the follow-on, but Tauseef Ahmed and Rashid Khan proved equal to the task.

Sri Lanka's second innings was held together by a determined innings from Goonatillake, who stood firm for nearly three and a half hours while wickets fell at regular intervals. He was finally eighth out at 114, and the declaration came after 30 minutes on the last morning, setting Pakistan to make 339 in approximately four and a half hours. The match was proceeding quietly to a draw until D. S. de Silva took three wickets in an over which spanned the tea interval, and dismissed Javed Miandad, who completed 3,000 Test runs, in the fourth of the last twenty overs. However, Ashraf Ali and Tahir Naqqash made sure that there would not be a dramatic victory for Sri Lanka.

The overall attendance, approximately 40,000, was a considerable improvement over the first Test.

Sri Lanka

S. Wettimuny b Raja	157	– c Ashraf b Tahir	13
†H. M. Goonatillake c Salim b Qasim	27	– b Qasim	56
R. L. Dias c Salim b Qasim	98	– c Mohsin b Tahir	7
R. S. Madugalle not out	91	– lbw b Qasim	12
*L. R. D. Mendis b Qasim	16	– run out	0
A. Ranatunga b Qasim	0	– c Ashraf b Tauseef	2
A. N. Ranasinghe c Miandad b Qasim	6	– c Miandad b Tauseef	5
A. L. F. de Mel c Salim b Qasim	4	– (9) not out	25
D. S. de Silva lbw b Rizwan	25	– (8) st Ashraf b Tauseef	8
L. W. Kaluperuma b Rizwan	0	– not out	11
G. R. A. de Silva lbw b Rizwan	5		
L-b 11, w 2, n-b 12	25	L-b 9, w 1, n-b 5	15
1/77 2/294 3/304 4/341 5/341 6/355 7/385 8/446 9/448	454	1/19 2/44 3/82 4/82 5/86 6/104 7/114 8/114 (8 wkts dec.)	154

Bowling: *First Innings*—Tahir 26–4–108–0; Rashid Khan 13–3–52–0; Qasim 65–18–141–6; Tauseef 12–3–35–0; Raja 26–6–66–1; Miandad 1–0–1–0; Rizwan 12–3–26–3. *Second Innings*—Tahir 13–3–53–2; Rashid Khan 1–0–4–0; Qasim 30–9–51–2; Rizwan 5–2–13–0; Tauseef 14–4–18–3.

Pakistan

Rizwan-uz-Zaman b G. R. A. de Silva	36	– b de Mel	16
Mohsin Khan c Wettimuny b de Mel	12	– c de Mel b D. S. de Silva	74
Salim Malik b de Mel	23	– lbw b de Mel	4
*Javed Miandad c Ranatunga b D. S. de Silva	18	– c Madugalle b D. S. de Silva	36
Wasim Raja c Madugalle b D. S. de Silva	22	– c Wettimuny b D. S. de Silva	0
Haroon Rashid c de Mel b D. S. de Silva	25	– b D. S. de Silva	0
†Ashraf Ali b Ranasinghe	58	– not out	29
Tahir Naqqash c de Mel b G. R. A. de Silva	1	– c sub b D. S. de Silva	13
Iqbal Qasim run out	5		
Rashid Khan not out	43	– (9) not out	3
Tauseef Ahmed c Madugalle b D. S. de Silva	18		
L-b 1, n-b 8	9	B 3, l-b 7, n-b 1	11
1/19 2/54 3/83 4/116 5/124 6/154 7/156 8/185 9/222	270	1/24 2/40 3/132 4/132 5/132 6/137 7/174 (7 wkts)	186

Bowling: *First Innings*—de Mel 23–4–73–2; Ranasinghe 7–1–23–1; D. S. de Silva 32–3–103–4; G. R. A. de Silva 24–10–38–2; Kaluperuma 6–0–24–0. *Second Innings*—de Mel 17–2–71–2; Ranasinghe 5–0–17–0; D. S. de Silva 18–2–59–5; G. R. A. de Silva 19–4–28–0.

Umpires: Javed Akhtar and Khizer Hayat.

PAKISTAN v SRI LANKA

Third Test Match

At Lahore, March 22, 23, 25, 26, 27. Pakistan won by an innings and 102 runs. Pakistan, now able to play their full team after Javed Miandad had announced that he was unavailable as captain for the tour of England, proved too strong for Sri Lanka. Majid Khan, Zaheer Abbas, Mudassar Nazar and Imran Khan were included, those making way being Salim Malik, Haroon Rashid, Rizwan-uz-Zaman and Rashid Khan. Sri Lanka recalled Warnapura and Ratnayeke, and included Jayasekera and Wijesuriya for their Test débuts, omitting G. R. A. de Silva (injured), Ranatunga, Ranasinghe and Kaluperuma.

After a start delayed by an hour following overnight rain, Pakistan put Sri Lanka in to bat and struck twice in Imran Khan's third over, with Warnapura caught at short-leg and

Jayasekera bowled by a break-back. Imran continued to dominate, and only a magnificent innings by Dias saved his side from collapse. He reached a chanceless century shortly before the close of the first day and when caught at cover-point early next morning had batted for 260 minutes. His 109 included fourteen 4s and one 6. Imran maintained his speed over long spells; his eight for 58 represented his career-best figures and the best in a Test in Pakistan.

Pakistan's experienced batting found little difficulty from Sri Lanka's bowlers, who were not helped by missed chances. Mohsin Khan, in a fluent, maiden Test century, drove strongly and hit sixteen 4s before being bowled off his pads. His partnership with Majid, who earlier had been caught at cover only 15 runs short of Hanif Mohammad's Pakistan record of 3,915 Test runs, added 151.

Sri Lanka were reasonably well placed at tea with Pakistan 306 for five, but Zaheer and Imran put on a quick 100, Ashraf Ali joined in, and the declaration came soon after Zaheer, having batted for four and a half hours with two 6s and twelve 4s, was bowled attempting a big hit.

Sri Lanka, needing 260 to save the innings defeat, showed more resolution in their early batting, and at tea on the fourth day had reached 71 for the loss of Warnapura. They lost their chance of saving the match when, in just over half an hour before the close, they lost four more wickets. Imran's match figures of fourteen for 116 were a record for Pakistan. In the penultimate over of the match, Ashraf Ali conceded his first byes in two Tests, having kept wicket without a bye while 998 runs were scored. The total attendance was approximately 35,000.

Sri Lanka

*B. Warnapura c Mohsin b Imran	7	– c Miandad b Tauseef	26
S. Wettimuny c Qasim b Imran	20	– c Majid b Imran	41
R. S. A. Jayasekera b Imran	0	– (6) b Imran	2
R. L. Dias c Tauseef b Imran	109	– (3) c Raja b Tauseef	9
R. S. Madugalle c Ashraf b Imran	0	– (4) b Tauseef	5
L. R. D. Mendis c and b Tauseef	26	– (5) c Mudassar b Tauseef	5
D. S. de Silva b Imran	7	– not out	36
A. L. F. de Mel st Ashraf b Qasim	34	– lbw b Imran	0
†H. M. Goonatillake b Imran	15	– c and b Imran	21
J. R. Ratnayeke not out	1	– b Imran	0
R. G. C. E. Wijesuriya lbw b Imran	0	– b Imran	3
L-b 11, w 6, n-b 4	21	B 4, l-b 2, w 1, n-b 3	10
1/17 2/17 3/79 4/83 5/141 6/171 7/209 8/231 9/239	240	1/56 2/78 3/84 4/90 5/93 6/95 7/96 8/142 9/142	158

Bowling: *First Innings*—Imran 29.3–8–58–8; Tahir 10–0–54–0; Qasim 12–4–21–1; Mudassar 8–1–23–0; Tauseef 12–1–50–1; Raja 5–1–13–0. *Second Innings*—Imran 22.5–3–58–6; Tahir 6–0–22–0; Tauseef 25–7–58–4; Qasim 1–0–1–0; Raja 6–4–9–0; Majid 1–1–0–0.

Pakistan

Mudassar Nazar c Madugalle b de Silva	37
Mohsin Khan b Ratnayeke	129
Majid J. Khan c sub b Ratnayeke	63
*Javed Miandad c Goonatillake b de Mel	26
Zaheer Abbas b Ratnayeke	134
Wasim Raja c Goonatillake b de Mel	1
Imran Khan c Mendis b de Mel	39
†Ashraf Ali not out	45
Tahir Naqqash not out	1
B 5, l-b 5, w 5, n-b 10	25
1/79 2/230 3/247 4/297 5/306 6/406 7/494 (7 wkts dec.)	500

Iqbal Qasim and Tauseef Ahmed did not bat.

Bowling: de Mel 28–3–120–3; Ratnayeke 28–3–121–3; de Silva 39–4–129–1; Wijesuriya 24–2–105–0.

Umpires: Khizer Hayat and Shakoor Rana.

†PAKISTAN v SRI LANKA

Second One-day International

At Lahore, March 29. Sri Lanka won on faster scoring-rate. Sri Lanka, electing to field first, removed Mohsin Khan in the sixth over, but Zaheer Abbas, twice dropped early on, again batted freely. After Mudassar Nazar and Javed Miandad, brilliantly run out by Goonatillake, had left in quick succession, Haroon Rashid helped Zaheer to add 122 in eighteen overs. Zaheer's innings, lasting 32 overs, included three 6s and fifteen 4s. Despite an economical opening spell by Imran and Sikander, Sri Lanka were soon scoring well, with 21 runs coming from Tahir's third over. Dias again excelled with powerful driving, hitting twelve 4s in his 81, scored off 60 balls, and he and Mendis put on 73 inside ten overs. Madugalle kept up the scoring-rate, the last two overs before bad light stopped play – bowled by Sikander and Imran – producing 21 runs. At that point Sri Lanka needed 13 runs off seven overs, and they won the match with an overall scoring-rate of 6.87 runs per over against Pakistan's 5.97.

Man of the Match: R. L. Dias.

Pakistan

Mudassar Nazar b de Silva	27
Mohsin Khan run out	6
Zaheer Abbas c Madugalle b Ratnayeke	123
*Javed Miandad run out	1
Haroon Rashid not out	63
Imran Khan not out	9
L-b 2, w 8	10
1/14 2/86 3/92 4/215 (4 wkts, 40 overs)	239

Mansoor Akhtar, †Ashraf Ali, Tahir Naqqash, Rashid Khan and Sikander Bakht did not bat.

Bowling: de Mel 8–1–31–0; Ratnayeke 8–1–42–1; Ranasinghe 6–0–33–0; Warnapura 2–0–21–0; de Silva 8–0–49–1; Ranatunga 8–0–53–1.

Sri Lanka

*B. Warnapura c Miandad b Sikander	5
S. Wettimuny c Ashraf b Mudassar	32
R. L. Dias c Imran b Mudassar	81
L. R. D. Mendis b Tahir	52
R. S. Madugalle not out	36
A. Ranatunga not out	5
L-b 7, w 7, n-b 2	16
1/10 2/87 3/160 4/185 (4 wkts, 33 overs)	227

A. N. Ranasinghe, D. S. de Silva, A. L. F. de Mel, †H. M. Goonatillake and J. R. Ratnayeke did not bat.

Bowling: Imran 5–1–20–0; Sikander 5–1–15–1; Tahir 8–0–65–1; Mudassar 8–0–56–2; Rashid Khan 7–0–55–0.

Umpires: Mian Mohammad Aslam and Rab Nawaz.

†PAKISTAN v SRI LANKA

Third One-day International

At Karachi, March 31. Pakistan won by five wickets. Both captains were unfit, Zaheer and Mendis deputising, and Pakistan, winning the toss, put Sri Lanka in. Goonatillake left early, but once the opening bowlers were withdrawn, after six overs, the batsmen had little difficulty in keeping the score moving. However, Sri Lanka lost their last four wickets in thirteen balls for 7 runs. Mudassar and Mohsin soon put Pakistan on top, and Mansoor Akhtar helped maintain the scoring-rate despite some economical bowling by Ranasinghe. When Imran joined Wasim Raja, 49 runs were needed off the last ten overs, but Sri Lanka lost their last chance when Wasim Raja, then 11, was dropped at long-on off de Mel.

Man of the Match: Mudassar Nazar.

Sri Lanka

S. Wettimuny c Mansoor b Mudassar	27	D. S. de Silva run out	2
†H. M. Goonatillake c Imran b Sikander	5	J. R. Ratnayeke not out	0
R. L. Dias b Mudassar	49	G. R. A. de Silva b Sikander	1
*L. R. D. Mendis b Tauseef	44	L-b 4, w 5	9
R. S. Madugalle st Salim b Raja	46		—
A. Ranatunga b Imran	6	1/7 2/54 3/113 (38.3 overs)	218
A. N. Ranasinghe c and b Imran	24	4/147 5/170	
A. L. F. de Mel run out	5	6/198 7/211 8/213 9/214	

Bowling: Imran 7–1–10–2; Sikander 5.3–0–34–2; Rashid Khan 4–0–37–0; Mudassar 8–0–42–2; Tauseef 8–0–41–1; Raja 6–0–45–1.

Pakistan

Mudassar Nazar c sub b Ranatunga	79	Wasim Raja not out	41
Mohsin Khan c Madugalle b Ranasinghe	36	Imran Khan not out	15
*Zaheer Abbas b G. R. A. de Silva	1	L-b 10, w 2, n-b 3	15
Mansoor Akhtar st Goonatillake b G. R. A. de Silva	31		—
Haroon Rashid c and b G. R. A. de Silva	4	1/90 2/91 (5 wkts, 38.1 overs)	222
		3/154 4/162 5/170	

†Salim Yousuf, Rashid Khan, Sikander Bakht and Tauseef Ahmed did not bat.

Bowling: de Mel 7–0–35–0; Ratnayeke 4.1–0–34–0; Ranasinghe 8–1–27–1; D. S. de Silva 4–0–34–0; Ranatunga 7–0–36–1; G. R. A. de Silva 8–0–41–3.

Umpires: Ghafoor Butt and Shakil Khan.

CORINTHIAN-CASUALS CENTENARY

With 1982-83 being the centenary season of the Corinthian-Casuals Football Club, Bob Willis's captaincy of, plus his catching for, and Doug Insole's managership of the England team in Australia had a double significance. Willis is in line with a great tradition of Corinthian-Casuals cricketing goalkeepers, from the C. B. Fry days of W. R. Moon and G. B. Railes to the strong Surrey strain of D. R. Jardine, P. G. H. Fender, H. H. Garland-Wells, Graham Roope and Willis himself. Insole played with another Corinthian-Casuals Test match cricketer, F. C. M. (Gerry) Alexander, the West Indies wicket-keeper, in the FA Amateur Cup final before 80,000 at Wembley in 1956. They are all part of the great tradition embodied by R. E. Foster, whose 287 in 1903-04 is the highest Test innings *in Australia* by an Englishman. Foster is the only amateur ever to have captained England's professionals at both soccer and cricket.

BENSON AND HEDGES WORLD SERIES CUP, 1981-82

†PAKISTAN v WEST INDIES

At Melbourne, November 21. West Indies won by 18 runs. After their heavy defeat in the first Test against Australia, Pakistan did well to come within measurable distance of beating West Indies. When West Indies were put in to bat, it looked as if openers Greenidge and Haynes would run away with the match as they put on 182 for the first wicket in 39 overs. However, Haynes's dismissal precipitated a collapse. For Pakistan, Rizwan and Mudassar had fifty on the board from fifteen overs, and the hundred came in a slightly faster time than West Indies'; but then Richards bowled ten overs of off-breaks with surprising economy and Pakistan were never quite up with the clock.

Man of the Match: C. G. Greenidge. *Attendance:* 6,415.

West Indies

C. G. Greenidge c Rizwan b Sarfraz	103
D. L. Haynes b Mudassar	84
I. V. A. Richards b Imran	17
S. F. A. Bacchus c Rizwan b Sarfraz	8
*C. H. Lloyd b Sarfraz	10
A. M. E. Roberts c Mansoor b Imran	0
J. Garner c Ashraf b Imran	0
M. D. Marshall not out	9
H. A. Gomes c and b Sarfraz	0
†D. A. Murray not out	1
L-b 13	13
1/182 2/203 3/222 4/223 5/223 6/224 7/244 8/244 (8 wkts, 50 overs)	245

C. E. H. Croft did not bat.

Bowling: Sarfraz 9–2–37–4; Imran 10–2–23–3; Sikander 9–0–46–0; Qasim 10–0–49–0; Majid 5–0–34–0; Mudassar 7–0–43–1.

Pakistan

Mudassar Nazar b Marshall	51
Rizwan-uz-Zaman c Roberts b Garner	14
*Javed Miandad c Murray b Roberts	74
Mansoor Akhtar b Marshall	2
Majid J. Khan c Bacchus b Roberts	56
Imran Khan c Murray b Roberts	0
Wasim Raja not out	10
†Ashraf Ali not out	1
B 2, l-b 7, w 4, n-b 6	19
1/53 2/120 3/124 4/212 5/212 6/221 (6 wkts, 50 overs)	227

Sarfraz Nawaz, Sikander Bakht and Iqbal Qasim did not bat.

Bowling: Roberts 10–1–42–3; Marshall 10–1–27–2; Garner 10–0–30–1; Croft 10–1–57–0; Richards 10–0–52–0.

Umpires: R. C. Bailhache and R. A. French.

†AUSTRALIA v PAKISTAN

At Melbourne, November 22. Pakistan won by four wickets. Australia, put in, battled hard to reach 209 against an economical attack in which Sikander reaped the highest reward. For Pakistan, Mudassar Nazar and Javed Miandad added 105 for the third wicket, the latter batting particularly well, and Imran Khan and Ashraf Ali knocked off the runs required for victory.

Man of the Match: Javed Miandad. *Attendance:* 20,671.

Australia

G. M. Wood run out........................ 23
W. M. Darling c Sarfraz b Sikander.... 41
*G. S. Chappell c Wasim b Sikander... 3
A. R. Border b Sikander.................... 6
K. J. Hughes c Mudassar b Sikander... 67
†R. W. Marsh b Sarfraz.................... 15
B. Yardley b Imran.......................... 28
S. F. Graf run out........................... 8
G. F. Lawson not out........................ 4
J. R. Thomson run out..................... 3
B 2, l-b 3, w 3, n-b 3.............. 11

1/48 2/51 3/71 4/80 (9 wkts, 50 overs) 209
5/102 6/188 7/197 8/204 9/209

T. M. Alderman did not bat.

Bowling: Imran 10–1–42–1; Sarfraz 10–0–44–1; Tahir 10–0–46–0; Sikander 10–1–34–4; Ijaz 10–1–32–0.

Pakistan

Mudassar Nazar c Marsh b Chappell... 44
Mansoor Akhtar c Yardley b Alderman. 12
*Zaheer Abbas c Marsh b Alderman... 2
Javed Miandad c Lawson b Chappell... 72
Wasim Raja c Darling b Chappell...... 8
Imran Khan not out......................... 28
Ijaz Faqih b Thomson....................... 17
†Ashraf Ali not out.......................... 15
L-b 7, w 3, n-b 2.................... 12

1/19 2/21 3/126 (6 wkts, 49.2 overs) 210
4/139 5/151 6/184

Tahir Naqqash, Sikander Bakht and Sarfraz Nawaz did not bat.

Bowling: Thomson 9.2–0–47–1; Alderman 10–0–20–2; Graf 10–0–34–0; Lawson 8–1–43–0; Yardley 3–0–21–0; Chappell 9–1–33–3.

Umpires: B. E. Martin and R. V. Whitehead.

†AUSTRALIA v WEST INDIES

At Sydney, November 24. Australia won by seven wickets. A fine innings by Laird, who had often been left out of Australian sides for one-day matches because he was thought to be too slow a scorer, took Australia to a remarkable victory. West Indies, given a good start, faltered in mid-innings, but a fourth-wicket stand of 72 between Richards and a superb Lloyd looked to have given them enough runs. Australia lost Darling and Chappell quickly, only for Laird and Border to give the innings a foundation. When Border was thrown out by Haynes, Hughes continued his splendid form of the previous ten days, he and Laird adding 147 and taking Australia to victory with two overs to spare. Having bowled only 49 overs in three and a half hours the Australians were fined $600 of their prize-money.

Man of the Match: B. M. Laird. *Attendance:* 27,008.

West Indies

C. G. Greenidge b Thomson............. 39
D. L. Haynes c and b Thomson......... 30
I. V. A. Richards run out................. 47
S. F. A. Bacchus c Hughes b Thomson. 4
*C. H. Lloyd c Thomson b Lawson..... 63
†D. A. Murray c Graf b Lawson........ 5
M. D. Marshall not out.................... 16
A. M. E. Roberts run out................. 15
J. Garner lbw b Alderman................ 1
M. A. Holding not out..................... 2
L-b 7, w 5, n-b 2.................... 14

1/64 2/89 3/98 (8 wkts, 49 overs) 236
4/170 5/197 6/197 7/229 8/232

C. E. H. Croft did not bat.

Bowling: Lawson 10–2–28–2; Alderman 10–2–35–1; Thomson 10–0–55–3; Graf 9–0–56–0; Chappell 10–0–48–0.

Australia

B. M. Laird not out	117
W. M. Darling c Murray b Holding	5
*G. S. Chappell lbw b Roberts	1
A. R. Border run out	29
K. J. Hughes not out	62
B 1, l-b 13, w 4, n-b 5	23
1/7 2/8 3/90 (3 wkts, 47 overs)	237

G. M. Wood, †R. W. Marsh, S. F. Graf, G. F. Lawson, J. R. Thomson and T. M. Alderman did not bat.

Bowling: Holding 10–0–34–1; Roberts 9–0–44–1; Marshall 10–0–45–0; Garner 9–0–43–0; Croft 9–0–48–0.

Umpires: A. R. Crafter and M. W. Johnson.

†PAKISTAN v WEST INDIES

At Adelaide, December 5. Pakistan won by 8 runs, a remarkable victory, coming as it did immediately after they had been overwhelmed by Australia in the second Test. Pakistan were put in to bat and after sixteen overs had been reduced to 35 for five. A patient innings by Zaheer, helped first by Ijaz Faqih and then by Sarfraz, produced a total which saved face but hardly seemed adequate. However, West Indies' batsmen paid the penalty for over-confidence as their first three wickets went for 38. Lloyd and Bacchus tilted the balance West Indies' way, but a brilliant falling catch by Tahir at deep square leg accounted for Lloyd, and Dujon soon followed. The rest of the batting was then disposed of most improbably by the leg-spin of Wasim Raja.

Man of the Match: Wasim Raja. *Attendance:* 6,133.

Pakistan

Mudassar Nazar c Greenidge b Holding	11
Mohsin Khan run out	11
*Zaheer Abbas c Murray b Roberts	46
Javed Miandad lbw b Marshall	1
Wasim Raja b Garner	1
Imran Khan c Murray b Marshall	1
Ijaz Faqih c Lloyd b Holding	20
†Ashraf Ali c Bacchus b Richards	3
Sarfraz Nawaz not out	34
Tahir Naqqash run out	1
Sikander Bakht run out	3
B 1, l-b 4, w 2, n-b 1	8
1/16 2/27 3/31 4/34 5/35 6/63 7/68 8/125 9/127 (49 overs)	140

Bowling: Roberts 10–3–19–1; Holding 10–1–28–2; Garner 10–3–32–1; Marshall 9–0–18–2; Richards 10–1–35–1.

West Indies

C. G. Greenidge b Sarfraz	4
D. L. Haynes c Ashraf b Tahir	7
I. V. A. Richards c Ashraf b Sarfraz	9
S. F. A. Bacchus b Raja	37
*C. H. Lloyd c Tahir b Ijaz	28
P. J. Dujon b Raja	0
M. D. Marshall b Raja	20
†D. A. Murray lbw b Raja	0
A. M. E. Roberts b Imran	4
M. A. Holding c Raja b Imran	8
J. Garner not out	1
L-b 7, w 2, n-b 5	14
1/7 2/19 3/38 4/85 5/88 6/107 7/108 8/120 9/120 (38.5 overs)	132

Bowling: Imran 9.5–0–13–2; Sarfraz 6–0–24–2; Sikander 4–0–11–0; Tahir 6–0–25–1; Ijaz 6–0–20–1; Raja 7–0–25–4.

Umpires: A. R. Crafter and B. E. Martin.

†AUSTRALIA v PAKISTAN

At Adelaide, December 6. Australia won by 38 runs to share the lead in the series with Pakistan. Had it not been for fielding lapses midway through the Pakistan innings, the margin of victory might have been greater. Put in, Australia's batsmen produced a series of consistent innings, with Chappell showing a welcome return to form. After a sound start by Mudassar and Mohsin, the Pakistan innings fell behind the required run-rate, which rose to more than seven an over from the final ten overs.

Man of the Match: G. S. Chappell. *Attendance:* 20,566.

Australia

B. M. Laird lbw b Sikander	20	D. K. Lillee c Sarfraz b Imran	7
W. M. Darling run out	35	J. R. Thomson b Imran	6
*G. S. Chappell c Raja b Ijaz	38	T. M. Alderman c Ashraf b Imran	1
A. R. Border c Raja b Mudassar	25	L-b 2, w 3, n-b 2	7
K. J. Hughes c Mudassar b Sarfraz	14		—
G. M. Wood not out	43	1/43 2/84 3/103 (48.3 overs)	208
†R. W. Marsh c Ashraf b Mudassar	10	4/136 5/136 6/169 7/176	
G. F. Lawson b Sarfraz	2	8/187 9/199	

Bowling: Imran 9.3–3–19–3; Sarfraz 10–0–44–2; Sikander 9–0–29–1; Ijaz 7–0–43–1; Tahir 6–0–41–0; Mudassar 7–0–25–2.

Pakistan

Mudassar Nazar run out	14	Sarfraz Nawaz c Darling b Chappell	5
Mohsin Khan c Marsh b Chappell	27	Tahir Naqqash not out	21
*Zaheer Abbas c Alderman b Lawson	38	†Ashraf Ali not out	11
Javed Miandad c Alderman b Chappell	4	L-b 8, w 1, n-b 3	12
Wasim Raja c Darling b Lawson	2		—
Imran Khan c Darling b Alderman	18	1/41 2/57 3/79 4/84 (8 wkts, 50 overs)	170
Ijaz Faqih c Marsh b Thomson	18	5/91 6/121 7/134 8/138	

Sikander Bakht did not bat.

Bowling: Alderman 10–1–26–1; Lawson 10–1–33–2; Chappell 10–1–31–3; Lillee 10–0–23–0; Thomson 10–0–45–1.

Umpires: R. C. Bailhache and R. A. French.

†AUSTRALIA v PAKISTAN

At Sydney, December 17. Pakistan won by six wickets, just two days after their comprehensive victory in the third Test at Melbourne. Sent in on an easy-paced wicket, Australia were struck down in the middle order by all-rounder Mudassar, and owed much to Darling, whose innings ended in a run-out mix-up with Wellham. Marsh contributed some hefty blows in the later stages. The early loss of Mohsin was compensated for by the flamboyant strokeplay of Mudassar and a typically aggressive century by Zaheer which always kept Pakistan in advance of the run-rate.

Man of the Match: Mudassar Nazar. *Attendance:* 11,413.

Australia

W. M. Darling run out	74	†R. W. Marsh not out	54
B. M. Laird b Sikander	12		
G. M. Wood b Mudassar	25	B 2, l-b 7, w 1, n-b 3	13
A. R. Border c Ashraf b Mudassar	2		—
D. M. Wellham run out	42	1/40 2/106 3/110 (6 wkts, 50 overs)	222
*G. S. Chappell c Miandad b Mudassar	0	4/132 5/132 6/222	

D. K. Lillee, G. F. Lawson, J. R. Thomson and T. M. Alderman did not bat.

Bowling: Imran 10–0–47–0; Sikander 8–0–48–1; Sarfraz 9–0–38–0; Tahir 3–0–21–0; Majid 10–0–35–0; Mudassar 10–4–20–3.

Pakistan

Mudassar Nazar c Alderman b Thomson.	50
Mohsin Khan b Lawson	2
Zaheer Abbas b Chappell	108
*Javed Miandad lbw b Chappell	22
Majid J. Khan not out	20
Wasim Raja not out	9
B 2, l-b 5, w 4, n-b 1	12
1/15 2/120	
3/174 4/205 (4 wkts, 43.2 overs)	223

Imran Khan, Sarfraz Nawaz, †Ashraf Ali, Tahir Naqqash and Sikander Bakht did not bat.

Bowling: Lawson 9–0–43–1; Alderman 10–1–41–0; Lillee 8–1–38–0; Thomson 7–0–27–1; Border 3–0–24–0; Chappell 6.2–0–38–2.

Umpires: R. A. French and M. W. Johnson.

†PAKISTAN v WEST INDIES

At Perth, December 19. West Indies won by seven wickets. The day before the match Clive Lloyd had spoken strongly to his side about the poor start they had made to their tour. The results were immediate, this being as convincing a West Indian victory as it sounds. After getting away to a good start, Pakistan, who chose to bat, collapsed. Three of their batsmen paid the penalty of trying to slog Richards, and Garner and Marshall were too much for the lower order. West Indies had an anxious moment when Bacchus and Richards went early in their innings, but Haynes played responsibly and had excellent support from Lloyd and Gomes.

Man of the Match: D. L. Haynes. *Attendance:* 6,005.

Pakistan

Mudassar Nazar c Richards b Marshall	30
Mohsin Khan c Lloyd b Garner	6
Zaheer Abbas c Dujon b Richards	35
*Javed Miandad c Bacchus b Richards.	21
Wasim Raja c Haynes b Richards	17
Imran Khan not out	29
Ijaz Faqih c Haynes b Garner	2
Sarfraz Nawaz c Roberts b Garner	0
†Wasim Bari run out	4
Sikander Bakht c Dujon b Marshall	0
Majid J. Khan absent injured	
B 4, l-b 3, w 2, n-b 7	16
1/29 2/61 (44.4 overs)	160
3/106 4/107 5/148	
6/151 7/152 8/156 9/160	

Bowling: Holding 8–1–15–0; Roberts 8–1–21–0; Garner 9–1–23–3; Marshall 9.4–0–33–2; Richards 10–0–52–3.

West Indies

D. L. Haynes not out	82
S. F. A. Bacchus c Bari b Imran	4
I. V. A. Richards c Bari b Sarfraz	8
*C. H. Lloyd c and b Raja	32
H. A. Gomes not out	26
B 1, l-b 3, w 2, n-b 3	9
1/12 2/28 3/101 (3 wkts, 42.2 overs)	161

†P. J. Dujon, A. L. Logie, M. D. Marshall, A. M. E. Roberts, M. A. Holding and J. Garner did not bat.

Bowling: Imran 8.2–0–38–1; Sarfraz 10–1–29–1; Sikander 6–0–27–0; Mudassar 1–0–1–0; Ijaz 6–0–30–0; Raja 10–1–26–1; Miandad 1–0–1–0.

Umpires: B. E. Martin and R. V. Whitehead.

†AUSTRALIA v WEST INDIES

At Perth, December 20. West Indies won by eight wickets with no less than twenty overs to spare to complete a highly successful weekend. Lloyd put the Australians in to bat on a fast pitch, and after Holding had dismissed Darling and Chappell with successive balls in his third over, they collapsed to 80 for six. A fighting stand of 70 between the two West Australians, Wood and Lillee, enabled Australia to reach 188 for nine. West Indies lost Bacchus and Haynes for 37, whereupon Richards and Lloyd began to bat at their most brilliant best.

Man of the Match: C. H. Lloyd. *Attendance:* 30,000 (estimated).

Australia

W. M. Darling b Holding	7	G. F. Lawson b Garner	0
B. M. Laird lbw b Marshall	7	J. R. Thomson run out	5
*G. S. Chappell c Haynes b Holding	0	T. M. Alderman not out	9
A. R. Border c Bacchus b Marshall	27	L-b 12, w 5, n-b 2	19
K. J. Hughes c Holding b Marshall	18		
G. M. Wood run out	54	1/10 2/10 (9 wkts, 50 overs)	188
†R. W. Marsh c Logie b Richards	0	3/30 4/62 5/78 6/80	
D. K. Lillee not out	42	7/150 8/150 9/166	

Bowling: Holding 10–0–37–2; Roberts 10–1–26–0; Garner 10–1–32–1; Marshall 10–0–31–3; Richards 10–0–43–1.

West Indies

D. L. Haynes c Chappell b Lillee	9
S. F. A. Bacchus c Thomson b Alderman	21
I. V. A. Richards not out	72
*C. H. Lloyd not out	80
W 4, n-b 4	8
1/13 2/37 (2 wkts, 30 overs)	190

H. A. Gomes, †P. J. Dujon, A. L. Logie, M. D. Marshall, A. M. E. Roberts, M. A. Holding and J. Garner did not bat.

Bowling: Lillee 6–1–36–1; Alderman 8–1–41–1; Thomson 5–0–24–0; Lawson 6–0–46–0; Chappell 5–0–35–0.

Umpires: R. C. Bailhache and A. R. Crafter.

†AUSTRALIA v PAKISTAN

At Melbourne, January 9. Pakistan won by 25 runs. Australia, having asked Pakistan to bat, must have been well satisfied to restrict them to 218, a total which owed much to a scintillating 84 in 110 minutes by Zaheer, who was dropped at mid-off off Thomson when he was 29. Laird, the culprit, added to his woes by his early run-out, the forerunner of a minor epidemic which felled later Australian batsmen. Border, hitting an unbeaten 75 off 83 balls in 106 minutes, showed what could be done, but he ran out of partners.

Man of the Match: Zaheer Abbas. *Attendance:* 18,039.

Pakistan

Mudassar Nazar lbw b Thomson	40	Ijaz Faqih run out	1
Mansoor Akhtar c Marsh b Alderman	5	Sarfraz Nawaz not out	14
Zaheer Abbas c Laird b Thomson	84	L-b 10, w 1, n-b 4	15
*Javed Miandad c Darling b Lillee	37		
Imran Khan run out	3	1/10 2/79 3/169 4/172 (6 wkts, 50 overs)	218
Wasim Raja not out	19	5/193 6/194	

†Wasim Bari, Tahir Naqqash and Sikander Bakht did not bat.

Bowling: Lawson 10–0–36–0; Alderman 10–0–37–1; Lillee 10–1–37–1; Chappell 10–0–38–0; Thomson 10–0–55–2.

Australia

G. M. Wood c Raja b Mudassar	38	G. F. Lawson run out	1
B. M. Laird run out	4	J. R. Thomson b Imran	2
J. Dyson lbw b Sikander	11	T. M. Alderman b Sikander	0
*G. S. Chappell b Ijaz	35	B 4, l-b 8	12
A. R. Border not out	75		—
W. M. Darling run out	5	1/5 2/41	(49 overs) 193
†R. W. Marsh c Miandad b Ijaz	2	3/74 4/135 5/147	
D. K. Lillee run out	8	6/153 7/175 8/182 9/190	

Bowling: Imran 9–2–21–1; Sarfraz 8–0–34–0; Tahir 8–0–35–0; Sikander 8–0–33–2; Mudassar 6–0–24–1; Ijaz 10–0–34–2.

Umpires: A. R. Crafter and R. V. Whitehead.

†AUSTRALIA v WEST INDIES

At Melbourne, January 10. West Indies won by five wickets, a brilliant innings by Dujon bringing them a victory which was less comfortable than the final margin suggests. Batting was never easy on another poor Melbourne pitch and Australia reached 146 after winning the toss only because Chappell played a determined innings for two hours, twenty minutes. West Indies, too, made a bad start, and with Richards able to make little of the slow, uneven pitch and the outstanding bowling of Malone, a last-minute replacement for the injured Alderman, it was left to Dujon to overcome the difficulties. He found attacking strokes for almost every ball (he faced 80) and a solid partner in Lloyd, whose calming influence was as always invaluable to West Indies. The match was watched by 78,142 spectators, a world record for a one-day match.

Man of the Match: P. J. Dujon. *Attendance:* 78,142.

Australia

B. M. Laird hit wkt b Holding	4	D. K. Lillee c Holding b Roberts	1
G. M. Wood c Greenidge b Holding	3	G. F. Lawson not out	0
R. B. McCosker run out	20	M. F. Malone b Holding	1
*G. S. Chappell c Logie b Roberts	59	L-b 4, w 1, n-b 4	9
A. R. Border b Marshall	6		—
W. M. Darling c Holding b Gomes	20	1/7 2/16 3/33	(42.5 overs) 146
†R. W. Marsh c Logie b Gomes	0	4/41 5/99 6/101 7/140	
B. Yardley c Logie b Holding	23	8/144 9/145	

Bowling: Holding 7.5–1–32–4; Roberts 7–0–23–2; Garner 6–0–13–0; Marshall 5–0–12–1; Richards 10–1–31–0; Gomes 7–1–26–2.

West Indies

C. G. Greenidge c Border b Malone	9	†P. J. Dujon not out	51
D. L. Haynes lbw b Lawson	1	M. D. Marshall not out	5
I. V. A. Richards c Lawson b Yardley	32	L-b 3, w 1, n-b 1	5
H. A. Gomes c Laird b Malone	7	1/8 2/18 3/48	—
*C. H. Lloyd lbw b Lawson	37	4/52 5/137	(5 wkts, 47.1 overs) 147

A. L. Logie, A. M. E. Roberts, M. A. Holding and J. Garner did not bat.

Bowling: Lillee 10–0–34–0; Lawson 9.1–0–31–2; Malone 10–5–9–2; Chappell 9–1–33–0; Yardley 6–0–25–1; Border 3–0–10–0.

Umpires: R. C. Bailhache and B. E. Martin.

†WEST INDIES v PAKISTAN

At Sydney, January 12. West Indies won by seven wickets. Pakistan were handicapped by the absence of Mudassar, who was unwell, and of Sarfraz, who apparently felt he would be unable to see properly under the floodlights when wearing glasses. This was Pakistan's first game under the lights. Imran Khan's best innings of the tour enabled Pakistan to reach a modest 191 for seven, but with Greenidge, Richards and Lloyd batting freely, West Indies won with almost eight overs to spare.

Man of the Match: C. G. Greenidge. *Attendance:* 10,995.

Pakistan

Mohsin Khan b Marshall	12	Ijaz Faqih b Garner	5
Mansoor Akhtar run out	13	Tahir Naqqash not out	23
Zaheer Abbas run out	1		
*Javed Miandad c Dujon b Garner	26	B 1, l-b 5, w 7, n-b 3	16
Wasim Raja c Logie b Roberts	33		—
Salim Malik b Garner	0	1/26 2/32 3/32 (7 wkts, 50 overs)	191
Imran Khan not out	62	4/75 5/75 6/122 7/144	

†Wasim Bari and Sikander Bakht did not bat.

Bowling: Holding 10–1–37–0; Roberts 10–0–47–1; Marshall 10–1–33–1; Garner 10–1–17–3; Richards 10–0–41–0.

West Indies

C. G. Greenidge lbw b Imran	84	H. A. Gomes not out	15
D. L. Haynes b Imran	2	B 1, l-b 4, w 5, n-b 5	15
I. V. A. Richards b Tahir	41		—
*C. H. Lloyd not out	35	1/37 2/107 3/155 (3 wkts, 42.1 overs)	192

†P. J. Dujon, A. L. Logie, M. D. Marshall, A. M. E. Roberts, M. A. Holding and J. Garner did not bat.

Bowling: Imran 10–0–42–2; Sikander 7–1–40–0; Raja 9.1–0–37–0; Tahir 10–0–31–1; Ijaz 6–0–27–0.

Umpires: M. W. Johnson and B. E. Martin.

†AUSTRALIA v PAKISTAN

At Sydney, January 14. Australia won by 76 runs. Sent in to bat, Australia opened with 80 from Wood and Laird, and some crisp strokeplay from Chappell and Hughes established the innings with a fourth-wicket stand of 87 in 59 minutes. Australia's 230 for five was their highest score in the 50-overs matches, and poor early batting by the Pakistanis never threatened it. Only Mansoor Akhtar, 40, and Imran Khan, 39, showed the necessary application. Chappell probably decided the match when he had Miandad lbw and in his next over induced a catch from Mansoor to mid-on.

Man of the Match: K. J. Hughes. *Attendance:* 27,978.

Australia

G. M. Wood b Mudassar	42	A. R. Border not out	11
B. M. Laird c Bari b Mudassar	45		
R. B. McCosker lbw b Mudassar	13	B 3, l-b 8, w 3, n-b 3	17
*G. S. Chappell c Raja b Sikander	36		—
K. J. Hughes not out	63	1/80 2/108 3/111 (5 wkts, 50 overs)	230
†R. W. Marsh c Zaheer b Imran	3	4/198 5/206	

D. K. Lillee, G. F. Lawson, J. R. Thomson and M. F. Malone did not bat.

Bowling: Imran 10–0–37–1; Sarfraz 9–0–45–0; Tahir 5–2–20–0; Sikander 9–0–43–1; Mudassar 10–0–36–3; Ijaz 7–0–32–0.

Pakistan

Mudassar Nazar b Lillee	5	Tahir Naqqash c Lillee b Lawson	13
Mansoor Akhtar c Lawson b Chappell	40	†Wasim Bari retired hurt	9
Zaheer Abbas c Border b Lawson	12	Sikander Bakht not out	0
*Javed Miandad lbw b Chappell	8		
Wasim Raja b Malone	16	L-b 6, w 1	7
Imran Khan b Thomson	39		
Ijaz Faqih c Marsh b Malone	0	1/8 2/30 3/66 4/71 (40.3 overs)	154
Sarfraz Nawaz c Hughes b Lillee	5	5/89 6/89 7/99 8/129 9/150	

Bowling: Lillee 7.3–1–23–2; Thomson 7–1–19–1; Lawson 8–0–45–2; Malone 10–2–36–2; Chappell 8–0–24–2.

Umpires: R. A. French and R. V Whitehead.

†WEST INDIES v PAKISTAN

At Brisbane, January 16. West Indies won on faster scoring-rate. A storm reduced an exciting match to a 30-over affair after Pakistan had been put in to bat and kept to 177 for nine in 50 overs. West Indies' target after the rain was 107 in 30 overs and they almost failed to achieve it, still needing 2 runs to win when the last man. Garner, came to the wicket. A fine opening spell from Sarfraz removed Greenidge, Haynes and Richards, and after nineteen overs West Indies were 61 for five. Bacchus then began to go for his strokes, after being missed at long-on off Sarfraz when 3. Had Pakistan won, they would have been in the finals of the competition at Australia's expense.

Man of the Match: S. F. A. Bacchus. *Attendance:* 11,102.

Pakistan

Mudassar Nazar run out	40	Sarfraz Nawaz c Clarke b Garner	10
Mansoor Akhtar c Greenidge b Holding	4	Iqbal Qasim c Greenidge b Garner	2
Zaheer Abbas c Lloyd b Richards	17	Sikander Bakht not out	1
*Javed Miandad c Lloyd b Roberts	25	B 2, l-b 12, w 6, n-b 2	22
Imran Khan c Dujon b Garner	31		
Wasim Raja retired hurt	12	1/16 2/57 3/101 (50 overs)	177
Majid J. Khan c Dujon b Holding	10	4/111 5/115 6/161 7/165	
†Ashraf Ali run out	3	8/175 9/177	

Bowling: Holding 10–3–23–2; Clarke 10–2–28–0; Roberts 10–1–33–1; Garner 10–1–19–3; Richards 10–0–52–1.

West Indies

C. G. Greenidge b Sarfraz	7	S. T. Clarke c Ashraf b Imran	1
D. L. Haynes c sub b Sarfraz	13	M. A. Holding c Ashraf b Mudassar	8
I. V. A. Richards c Imran b Sarfraz	0	J. Garner not out	1
H. A. Gomes b Sikander	13	B 4, l-b 4, w 5	13
*C. H. Lloyd c Mudassar b Sikander	1		
S. F. A. Bacchus not out	36	1/12 2/12 3/36 (9 wkts, 28.5 overs)	107
A. M. E. Roberts c Sarfraz b Mudassar	1	4/38 5/61 6/69	
†P. J. Dujon c and b Sikander	13	7/83 8/91 9/105	

Bowling: Imran 10–1–23–1; Sarfraz 10–1–31–3; Sikander 6.5–1–29–3; Mudassar 2–0–11–2.

Umpires: R. A. French and R. V. Whitehead.

†AUSTRALIA v WEST INDIES

At Brisbane, January 17. West Indies won by five wickets with eight balls to spare in a wonderful finish. Australia were put in to bat by Richards, captaining West Indies instead of Lloyd, who was not feeling well although he played. Midway through Australia's innings a storm caused the match to be reduced to 40 overs, and Australia were indebted to Chappell's best innings since his 201 in Brisbane in the second Test against Pakistan in November for their useful total. West Indies soon lost both openers, and Richards played a rather desperate innings before the third wicket fell at 94. However, sensible batting by Gomes, with help from Bacchus and Lloyd, took West Indies to victory in front of a capacity crowd of 22,610 – the biggest at the 'Gabba since its new stands were finished.

Man of the Match: H. A. Gomes. *Attendance:* 22,610.

Australia

B. M. Laird b Garner	26	D. K. Lillee c Holding b Garner	11
G. M. Wood c Lloyd b Richards	15	G. F. Lawson not out	4
R. B. McCosker c Bacchus b Clarke	18	M. F. Malone not out	0
*G. S. Chappell c Greenidge b Garner	61	B 2, l-b 9, w 9, n-b 1	21
K. J. Hughes st Dujon b Richards	2		—
A. R. Border c Garner b Holding	20	1/51 2/58 3/97 (9 wkts, 40 overs)	185
†R. W. Marsh c Greenidge b Garner	7	4/113 5/159	
J. R. Thomson b Holding	0	6/161 7/165 8/181 9/181	

Bowling: Holding 8–1–38–2; Clarke 9–1–22–1; Garner 9–0–45–4; Roberts 5–1–11–0; Richards 7–0–36–2; Gomes 2–0–12–0.

West Indies

C. G. Greenidge c Wood b Chappell	16	†P. J. Dujon not out	6
D. L. Haynes c Marsh b Lillee	11		
*I. V. A Richards c Lillee b Thomson	34	L-b 7, w 4, n-b 2	13
H. A. Gomes not out	56		—
S. F. A Bacchus run out	20	1/27 2/32 3/94 (5 wkts, 38.4 overs)	186
C. H. Lloyd c Border b Thomson	30	4/116 5/174	

A. M. E. Roberts, S. T. Clarke, J. Garner and M. A. Holding did not bat.

Bowling: Lillee 9–2–32–1; Thomson 10–2–40–2; Malone 10–1–34–0; Chappell 4–0–22–1; Lawson 5.4–0–45–0.

Umpires: A. R. Crafter and M. W. Johnson.

†AUSTRALIA v WEST INDIES

At Sydney, January 19. Australia won on faster scoring-rate when rain ended the game, just before ten o'clock at night, in the 44th over of Australia's innings when they needed another 22 to win from 41 balls. With Australia having to win the match to reach the finals of the competition, this provided a frantic climax for a record crowd for a night match at Sydney. West Indies, without Lloyd who had flu, were put in and saved from a low score by Richards and later Marshall. Australia, chasing 190, lost an early wicket before Dyson and Darling put on 51. Roberts, bowling splendidly, then removed Darling and Chappell for his sixth duck in twelve innings. Australia, with five wickets standing, needed 47 from the last ten overs. The 42nd and 43rd overs, bowled by Holding and Garner respectively, produced 22 runs, and after one ball of the 44th it began to rain heavily. Realising they were ahead of the required rate, for the first time in their innings, the Australian batsmen raced for the pavilion and so joined West Indies in the finals, an achievement which was expected to make a difference of anything up to £500,000 to the Australian Cricket Board. A series of final matches between West Indies and Pakistan would have been much less of a money-spinner from the one now in prospect between Australia and West Indies.

Man of the Match: A. M. E. Roberts. *Attendance:* 52,053.

West Indies

C. G. Greenidge b Lillee	1
D. L. Haynes b Malone	5
*I. V. A. Richards b Thomson	64
H. A. Gomes c Marsh b Pascoe	3
S. F. A. Bacchus c Hughes b Malone	20
†P. J. Dujon b Thomson	30
M. D. Marshall not out	32
A. M. E. Roberts c Wood b Pascoe	9
M. A. Holding c Marsh b Pascoe	0
S. T. Clarke b Lillee	16
J. Garner run out	2
L-b 5, w 1, n-b 1	7
1/2 2/23 3/40 4/79 5/103 6/137 7/155 8/156 9/182	(50 overs) 189

Bowling: Lillee 10–0–47–2; Thomson 10–1–36–2; Pascoe 10–0–44–3; Malone 10–1–27–2; Chappell 10–0–28–0.

Australia

G. M. Wood c Roberts b Holding	1
W. M. Darling c Clarke b Roberts	34
J. Dyson b Garner	37
*G. S. Chappell lbw b Roberts	0
K. J. Hughes b Roberts	25
A. R. Border not out	30
†R. W. Marsh c Greenidge b Marshall	12
D. K. Lillee b Holding	6
L. S. Pascoe not out	0
L-b 16, w 5, n-b 2	23
1/6 2/57 3/61 4/97 5/125 6/144 7/157	(7 wkts, 43.1 overs) 168

J. R. Thomson and M. F. Malone did not bat.

Bowling: Holding 6.1–0–34–2; Clarke 10–1–20–0; Marshall 10–0–43–1; Roberts 10–3–15–3; Garner 7–0–33–1.

Umpires: R. C. Bailhache and M. W. Johnson.

QUALIFYING TABLE

	P	*W*	*L*	*Pts*
West Indies	10	7	3	14
Australia	10	4	6	8
Pakistan	10	4	6	8

Australia qualified for the finals by virtue of a faster scoring-rate.

FINAL MATCHES

†AUSTRALIA v WEST INDIES

First Final Match

At Melbourne, January 23. West Indies won by 86 runs. Chappell put West Indies in on yet another bad Melbourne pitch with an uneven bounce and complete lack of pace. West Indies won principally because of two outstanding innings, by Richards and Greenidge who both gave a wonderful exhibition of how to bat in such conditions. Their footwork and improvisation were a joy to watch. The Australians, having made a bad start to their innings, were easily bowled out. The smallness of the crowd was a big disappointment.

Attendance: 24,981.

West Indies

C. G. Greenidge b Lillee	59
D. L. Haynes c Marsh b Pascoe	13
I. V. A. Richards c Wood b Chappell	78
*C. H. Lloyd c Pascoe b Thomson	20
S. F. A. Bacchus c Marsh b Thomson	2
†P. J. Dujon c Hughes b Pascoe	6
H. A. Gomes run out	6
A. M. E. Roberts run out	5
M. A. Holding not out	7
S. T. Clarke not out	0
L-b 5, w 12, n-b 3	20
1/26 2/138 3/179 4/184 5/197 6/198 7/204 8/210 (8 wkts, 49 overs)	216

J. Garner did not bat.

Bowling: Lillee 10–3–35–1; Thomson 10–1–44–2; Malone 10–2–25–0; Pascoe 9–1–33–2; Chappell 10–0–59–1.

Australia

W. M. Darling c Bacchus b Garner	14
G. M. Wood run out	19
J. Dyson b Clarke	0
*G. S. Chappell lbw b Garner	4
K. J. Hughes b Richards	4
A. R. Border c and b Gomes	16
†R. W. Marsh c Bacchus b Clarke	32
D. K. Lillee b Clarke	11
J. R. Thomson b Holding	5
L. S. Pascoe not out	3
M. F. Malone st Dujon b Gomes	10
B 4, l-b 5, w 2, n-b 1	12
1/20 2/30 3/43 4/43 5/56 6/64 7/107 8/110 9/117 (37.4 overs)	130

Bowling: Holding 8–1–19–1; Roberts 5–1–16–0; Clarke 9–1–22–3; Garner 6–3–7–2; Richards 5–1–29–1; Gomes 4.4–0–25–2.

Umpires: M. W. Johnson and R. V. Whitehead.

†AUSTRALIA v WEST INDIES

Second Final Match

At Melbourne, January 24. West Indies won by 128 runs. For the second day running Australia were overwhelmed on another bad pitch and before another disappointing crowd (25,661). As on the previous day the heat was intense, which may have kept spectators away. After winning the toss West Indies were given a fine start by Greenidge, Haynes and then Richards. Greenidge and Haynes put on 65 for the first wicket, Haynes and Richards 85 for the second, and Richards and Bacchus 50 for the third, all four giving a fine exhibition of batting in difficult conditions. With a total of 235 always likely to be far beyond Australia's reach, their batsmen went in as if they were already resigned to defeat. The West Indian fast bowlers took the first six Australian wickets before Gomes finished the match off by taking four wickets with his gentle off-breaks.

Attendance: 25,661.

West Indies

C. G. Greenidge c Marsh b Malone	47
D. L. Haynes c Dyson b Pascoe	52
I. V. A. Richards c Dyson b Chappell	60
S. F. A. Bacchus c Malone b Thomson	31
*C. H. Lloyd not out	22
†P. J. Dujon b Lillee	5
A. M. E. Roberts b Pascoe	0
S. T. Clarke b Pascoe	5
M. A. Holding b Pascoe	0
J. Garner run out	0
B 2, l-b 9, w 2	13
1/65 2/150 3/200 4/204 5/220 6/225 7/235 8/235 9/235 (9 wkts, 50 overs)	235

H. A. Gomes did not bat.

Bowling: Lillee 10–0–53–1; Pascoe 10–1–39–4; Thomson 10–1–31–1; Malone 10–0–37–1; Chappell 10–0–62–1.

Australia

G. M. Wood c Haynes b Clarke	7	J. R. Thomson b Gomes	15
B. M. Laird c Haynes b Roberts	13	L. S. Pascoe lbw b Gomes	0
A. R. Border c Dujon b Roberts	13	M. F. Malone not out	15
*G. S. Chappell b Garner	1		
K. J. Hughes lbw b Garner	0	B 2, l-b 3, w 4, n-b 1	10
J. Dyson b Clarke	18		
†R. W. Marsh b Gomes	15	1/14 2/42 3/43 4/43 (32.2 overs)	107
D. K. Lillee c Dujon b Gomes	0	5/43 6/65 7/65 8/81 9/81	

Bowling: Holding 10–3–25–0; Clarke 6.2–1–15-2; Garner 5–2–10–2; Roberts 5–1–16–2; Gomes 6–1–31–4.

Umpires: R. C. Bailhache and R. A. French.

†AUSTRALIA v WEST INDIES

Third Final Match

At Sydney, January 26. Australia won by 46 runs. This was a splendid fight-back by Australia after they had been put in to bat and lost Chappell for yet another duck. Even so, a total of 214 was by no means out of West Indies' reach. But Lillee, with the roar of the Hill behind him, gave Australia a magnificent start, having both Greenidge and Richards leg before in his first spell. He received excellent support from Thomson, Pascoe and Malone, and although Lloyd did his best to prop up the innings, West Indies were never at any stage on terms with their target. Australia's victory brought them back into the finals after their two disastrous games in Melbourne.

Attendance: 29,484.

Australia

B. M. Laird c Richards b Clarke	14	D. K. Lillee b Clarke	1
G. M. Wood c and b Gomes	45	J. R. Thomson c Dujon b Roberts	7
*G. S. Chappell b Garner	0	L. S. Pascoe not out	15
K. J. Hughes b Holding	28	L-b 13, n-b 1	14
A. R. Border not out	69		
D. W. Hookes c Dujon b Holding	1	1/19 2/20 3/94 (8 wkts, 50 overs)	214
†R. W. Marsh b Clarke	20	4/100 5/103 6/145 7/147 8/167	

M. F. Malone did not bat.

Bowling: Holding 10–2–32–2; Clarke 10–2–30–3; Garner 10–0–42–1; Roberts 10–1–50–1; Gomes 10–0–46–1.

West Indies

C. G. Greenidge lbw b Lillee	5	M. A. Holding c Thomson b Chappell	6
D. L. Haynes c Chappell b Pascoe	26	S. T. Clarke run out	16
I. V. A. Richards lbw b Lillee	4	J. Garner c sub b Pascoe	3
H. A. Gomes c Marsh b Thomson	0		
*C. H. Lloyd not out	63	B 1, l-b 3, w 9, n-b 2	15
S. F. A. Bacchus run out	19		
†P. J. Dujon c sub b Malone	10	1/20 2/34 3/41 4/41 (42.5 overs)	168
A. M. E. Roberts lbw b Chappell	1	5/68 6/88 7/95 8/113 9/164	

Bowling: Lillee 10–4–18–2; Thomson 6–0–38–1; Pascoe 6.5–1–21–2; Malone 10–1–33–1; Chappell 10–1–43–2.

Umpires: A. R. Crafter and B. E. Martin.

†AUSTRALIA v WEST INDIES
Fourth Final Match

At Sydney, January 27. West Indies won by 18 runs, a victory achieved more easily than the margin suggests and one that gave West Indies the Benson and Hedges Cup for the second time in the three years of its existence. They were assured of a good total by another fine partnership between Greenidge and Richards, who put on 138 for the second wicket, and later in the innings Lloyd, playing very well, took them to an almost impregnable total. Wood again batted well for Australia, but whenever they looked anything like getting on top a wicket fell.

Man of the Finals: I. V. A. Richards. *Attendance:* 19,984.

West Indies

C. G. Greenidge b Malone	64	A. M. E. Roberts b Thomson	5
D. L. Haynes lbw b Lillee	8	S. T. Clarke not out	2
I. V. A. Richards run out	70	L-b 14	14
S. F. A. Bacchus b Thomson	17		
*C. H. Lloyd not out	41	1/13 2/151 3/155 (6 wkts, 50 overs)	234
†P. J. Dujon b Pascoe	13	4/198 5/224 6/229	

M. A. Holding, J. Garner and H. A. Gomes did not bat.

Bowling: Lillee 10–4–30–1; Thomson 10–0–60–2; Pascoe 10–1–46–1; Malone 10–1–50–1; Chappell 10–2–34–0.

Australia

G. M. Wood c Lloyd b Holding	69	J. R. Thomson not out	19
B. M. Laird lbw b Garner	13	D. K. Lillee b Roberts	4
*G. S. Chappell c Richards b Clarke	10	M. F. Malone not out	5
K. J. Hughes c Lloyd b Richards	27	B 4, l-b 10, w 2, n-b 1	17
A. R. Border b Richards	23		
D. W. Hookes c Greenidge b Garner	17	1/37 2/57 3/102 (9 wkts, 50 overs)	216
†R. W. Marsh c Gomes b Roberts	5	4/135 5/163 6/173	
L. S. Pascoe b Roberts	7	7/176 8/194 9/198	

Bowling: Holding 10–1–36–1; Clarke 10–3–40–1; Garner 10–1–27–2; Roberts 10–0–48–3; Richards 10–0–48–2.

Umpires: A. R. Crafter and B. E. Martin.

CRICKET IN AUSTRALIA, 1981-82

By PETER MACKINNON

With a remarkable late-season run of success, South Australia won the Sheffield Shield for the first time since 1975-76. It was a victory excitingly achieved against the odds and in the final game of the season, and brought with it prize-money of $56,000 (approx. £32,000).

Prior to the start of the summer, the Australian Cricket Board decided to make a number of changes to the Shield format. These changes included the replacement of a bonus points system, which had been introduced in 1971-72, with a more simple method which awarded four points for a first-innings lead and an additional twelve points for an outright win. Other innovations involved a requirement that at least 100 balls be bowled each hour, the taking of a new ball after 85 overs, and the scrapping of the five-man limitation on fieldsmen on the leg side.

The arrangement of the 1981-82 fixtures played a major part in the winning of the Shield. The programme was drawn up so that, once the series of Test matches and one-day internationals had begun, those selected for Australia had little further chance of playing for their states. This obviously severely penalised those states with several Test representatives.

Without the participation of the leading players of the day and more enthusiastic promotion, the survival of the Shield competition will be in doubt. Administrators tend to give top priority to whatever wins television ratings. Thus, while the marketing men concentrate on one-day or day/night cricket, the down-grading of the Sheffield Shield continues, a trend which is unhealthy for Australian cricket. For the 1982-83 season, an attempt to increase public interest was made by changing the method by which the champion state is decided. Although a table system still applied, the Shield champions were henceforth to be decided by a four-day challenge match between the states finishing in first and second place in the table.

A close finish to the competition should have ensured a reasonable level of public interest to the season's end. Only in South Australia, however, was this evident, followers elsewhere showing no greater appetite for Shield cricket in 1981-82 than they had in the previous summer. This was despite some half-hearted television coverage (there had been none in 1980-81) and some experimentation with playing venues. In Tasmania, Shield games were played in Devonport as well as Hobart and Launceston; in New South Wales, one game was transferred to Newcastle, while in Victoria the inadequacies of the MCG pitch caused two games to be switched to nearby St Kilda and two others to Geelong.

Early in the season, the Western Australians were hot favourites to win the Shield, and certainly, when able to field a full side, they looked well-nigh invincible. At the season's halfway point they still seemed probable winners, and after five games they appeared to have an unassailable lead. In the event, their challenge faded so badly that they took only four points from their last four games.

As Western Australia fell from contention, it appeared possible that New South Wales might achieve their first Shield win since 1965-66. The latter had players possessing considerable experience, much of it gained at Test level, and yet were relatively unaffected by the demands of the Australian selectors. However, they were capable of unexpectedly erratic performance, as a consequence of which they never realised their full potential. Bad weather, particularly in the early part of the season, also denied them several point-scoring opportunities.

South Australia started the season more slowly than anyone else, six points from their first four games giving little hint of what was to come. However, with maximum points from four of their last five matches, they finished in aggressive and determined style. Fortunate to have the experienced Inverarity as his guide and mentor, Hookes led his team by example, and some of his batting was reminiscent of his brilliant form of 1976-77. South Australia's triumph was all the more remarkable considering that they finished last in the competition in 1980-81 and when the new season began were without Mallett, Attenborough and Prior, each of whom had retired, and Hogg, who was injured. During the season Prior came out of retirement to play in two matches but he did so without spectacular results. Hogg remained unavailable for the entire summer. Much of South Australia's success was attributable to their spinners, Sleep and Inverarity. That Sleep, after an indifferent beginning, should have taken important wickets was to be expected, but the performance of Inverarity was a revelation. He has probably seldom had so much bowling to do. A third spinner, Dolman, made a promising start but was less effective towards the end of the season.

After a dismal performance in the opening game, South Australia's batsmen played with greater consistency and usually scored more freely than those of other states. Except for Sleep, each of the recognised batsmen scored at least one century. Both Darling and Phillips had excellent seasons; they were the most successful pair of opening batsmen in the competition. Darling's cricket showed more maturity than hitherto; as an example of this, he avoided running himself out in any Shield innings. Phillips's batting showed the benefit of a season in England on an Esso scholarship. Crowe, besides exhibiting a partiality for the bowlers of New South Wales, made other important runs, and Hookes, Inverarity, Sleep and Wright formed a middle order which was usually able to capitalise upon the opportunities created by the earlier batsmen. Harris, a newcomer, made the most of limited opportunities.

For runners-up New South Wales, McCosker had a marvellous summer with the bat, four centuries (three of them not out) and a ninety making this one of his best seasons. Toohey and Davis each displayed some of the form that has, in the past, won them Test selection, while Dyson, Chappell and Beard often made useful runs, though seldom in the quantity expected of them. Wellham, however, had a wretched season and, unable to find early form, lost his place in the side. His replacement, Smith, looked a player of considerable promise. New South Wales depended heavily on Lawson and Holland for bowling success. Lawson had a frustrating summer, spending much of the time as twelfth man for Australia, though when given the opportunity at state level he bowled with pace and enthusiasm. This was especially valuable early in the season when Pascoe was unfit and out of form. Of the other new-ball bowlers, Whitney and Skilbeck did best. Beard as usual bowled economically, while Holland proved to be the most successful leg-spinner in the country.

Western Australia found it impossible, not surprisingly, to replace players of the calibre of Hughes, Lillee, Marsh, Wood, Laird, Alderman and Yardley when on Test duty. Of those who did play regularly, Serjeant, who took over the captaincy of the side, found runs less plentiful than in 1980-81 and Shipperd also had a lean time in comparison with the previous summer. Langer and Geoff Marsh were the most successful of the batsmen and Clements made an encouraging début in the final match. In the latter part of the summer, the most useful bowling performances came from the spinner Hogan, a protégé of Tony Lock.

Tasmania again had an abbreviated programme, and not a particularly well-planned one. After achieving a splendid victory against Victoria in late October, they had to wait until mid-January for their next Shield game. Additionally, this gave Tasmanians little chance of pressing their claims for Test selection. It was disappointing that, after such a good start, Tasmania could win only four more points from their four remaining games. Woolley, returned from injury, was easily the state's most successful batsman. Several times a poor score was boosted by unexpected contributions from the late-order batsmen. Saunders was thrice responsible for such a recovery, and on another occasion Tasmania's fortunes were improved by a whirlwind contribution from Stephenson, a tall West Indian fast bowler who came to Tasmania on the recommendation of Clive Lloyd and was the find of the season. An altercation with authority led to Clough being suspended for the last two matches.

Queensland were another state whose Shield performances were adversely affected by Test calls. Without Chappell, Border and Thomson, their fortunes slumped alarmingly, four points from a first-innings lead against Tasmania being all they had to show from their last six games. Their batting was carried largely by Wessels and Ritchie, who scored five and three centuries respectively and should soon be on the fringe of Test selection. Wessels became only the seventh player to score 1,000 runs in a Shield season. In the absence of the injured Kent, Kerr came into the side and made three hundreds (two of them in the last game of the season), which was a commendable start in Shield cricket. Of the remaining batsmen, Hohns occasionally made runs, as did wicket-keeper Phillips, who scored his maiden first-class hundred against Victoria. In the twilight of his career, Dymock also reached three figures for the first time – on his home ground against South Australia. The shortcomings of their attack were the principal reason for Queensland's failure to win matches. The highlight of their summer was the winning of the McDonald's Cup when, although Broad's batting won him the Man of the Match award, an inspired spell from Dymock undermined the New South Wales innings.

The Victorians had a summer they would probably prefer to forget, failing to win a game and managing points only on the four occasions when a first-innings lead was obtained. As no Victorians were lost to the Test side, the overall performance was even more disappointing. During the season, the Victorian selectors turned from experience to youth; Robinson, Walker and Moss were replaced by Sacristani, Hughes and Green, a policy which failed to produce dividends. Wiener, after a slow start, scored more heavily than anyone else and did well in the one-day cricket, but Yallop showed only glimpses of his best form and Watts, Scholes and Moss failed to make the most of many opportunities. Green looked to be the best of the younger brigade. The bowling was boosted by the return of Callen, who had a fine season.

There were fewer "unseemly" incidents than in the previous season. As before, most charges of misconduct were heard by the miscreant's fellow players, a system which was not considered wholly satisfactory. The confrontation between Pascoe and Hughes in Perth occurred off as well as on the field and culminated in Pascoe being suspended for one match. As there were doubts about Pascoe's fitness at this time, it is possible that he would have missed the match anyway. For his display of petulance at the conclusion of the South Australia-New South Wales game in Sydney, Hookes went unpunished by his colleagues but was fined $130 (£75) by a less sympathetic Australian Cricket Board. Clough of Tasmania received a four-week suspension for abusing an official during a one-day match in a domestic competition. The South Australian, Prior, received a similar penalty for the same offence in Adelaide.

FIRST-CLASS AVERAGES, 1981-82

BATTING

(Qualification: 300 runs)

	M	*I*	*NO*	*R*	*HI*	*100s*	*Avge*
W. M. Darling (*SA*)........	9	17	3	1,011	134	3	72.21
R. B. McCosker (*NSW*)...	9	15	3	796	146*	4	66.33
K. C. Wessels (*Qld*)........	11	18	0	1,094	220	5	60.77
G. M. Ritchie (*Qld*)........	10	16	2	833	136*	3	59.50
J. Dyson (*NSW*).............	8	14	1	709	127*	3	54.53
G. R. Marsh (*WA*)..........	5	10	0	545	176	2	54.50
J. M. Wiener (*Vic*)..........	9	17	1	847	221*	3	52.93
K. J. Hughes (*WA*).........	9	15	1	706	113	3	50.42
J. J. Crowe (*SA*)............	10	18	4	704	157	3	50.28
W. B. Phillips (*SA*).........	10	19	1	857	260	2	47.61
R. B. Kerr (*Qld*)............	8	14	1	613	158	3	47.15
B. M. Laird (*WA*)...........	9	16	2	659	110*	1	47.07
P. M. Toohey (*NSW*).......	8	13	2	511	137	1	46.45
J. K. Moss (*Vic*)............	5	9	1	358	200*	1	44.75
D. W. Hookes (*SA*).........	11	17	1	703	106	1	43.93
D. C. Boon (*Tas*)............	7	13	2	473	88	0	43.00
G. Shipperd (*WA*)..........	10	17	2	613	131	1	40.86
A. R. Border (*Qld*).........	9	15	2	530	126	1	40.76
G. M. Wood (*WA*)..........	9	16	2	569	151	2	40.64
B. C. Green (*Vic*)..........	5	10	2	318	82	0	39.75
K. J. Wright (*SA*)..........	9	14	4	392	104*	1	39.20
R. S. Langer (*WA*)..........	8	14	1	506	140	1	38.92
R. J. Inverarity (*SA*).......	9	12	3	348	100*	1	38.66
T. M. Chappell (*NSW*).....	10	17	3	533	89	0	38.07
G. N. Yallop (*Vic*)..........	9	18	1	647	111*	1	38.05
I. C. Davis (*NSW*)..........	9	14	0	523	133	2	37.35
R. D. Woolley (*Tas*)........	7	13	0	482	116	1	37.07
B. F. Davison (*Tas*).........	7	12	1	397	86	0	36.09
G. S. Chappell (*Qld*).......	9	15	0	532	201	2	35.46
S. J. Rixon (*NSW*)..........	10	12	3	310	124	1	34.44
G. R. Beard (*NSW*)........	10	13	2	378	75	0	34.36

	M	*I*	*NO*	*R*	*HI*	*100s*	*Avge*
R. B. Phillips (*Qld*).........	11	16	3	414	111*	1	31.84
W. J. Scholes (*Vic*)..........	10	18	1	505	94	0	29.70
T. V. Hohns (*Qld*)..........	11	18	3	442	89	0	29.46
P. R. Sleep (*SA*).............	11	16	1	438	78	0	29.20
C. S. Serjeant (*WA*)........	10	16	3	376	106	1	28.92
S. L. Saunders (*Tas*)........	7	12	1	308	106	1	28.00
R. F. Jeffery (*Tas*)..........	7	12	1	305	67	0	27.72
G. M. Watts (*Vic*)...........	10	19	1	495	71	0	27.50
R. W. Marsh (*WA*).........	9	14	0	342	47	0	24.42

**Signifies not out.*

BOWLING

(Qualification: 15 wickets)

	O	*M*	*R*	*W*	*Avge*
T. M Alderman..............	241.2	60	627	37	16.94
F. D. Stephenson (*Tas*)....	229.5	56	630	36	17.50
R. J. Inverarity (*SA*).......	343.2	117	639	30	21.30
P. M. Clough (*Tas*).........	148.3	42	390	18	21.66
D. K. Lillee (*WA*)..........	300	65	819	37	22.13
G. F. Lawson (*NSW*).......	200.4	48	533	24	22.20
B. Yardley (*WA*)............	360.4	73	1,105	49	22.55
R. G. Holland (*NSW*)......	332.4	128	661	27	24.48
I. W. Callen (*Vic*)...........	265.1	45	789	31	25.45
G. J. Winter (*SA*)...........	318.4	97	773	29	26.65
S. D. H. Parkinson (*SA*)..	310.5	81	851	28	30.39
M. G. Hughes (*Vic*)........	192.4	37	567	18	31.50
L. S. Pascoe (*NSW*)........	234.4	45	761	23	33.08
P. R. Sleep (*SA*).............	343.3	96	878	26	33.76
G. R. Beard (*NSW*)........	355	116	747	22	33.95
A. L. Mann (*WA*)...........	220.4	60	533	15	35.53
T. G. Hogan (*WA*).........	303.3	83	735	20	36.75
R. J. Bright (*Vic*)............	350.1	109	742	20	37.10
J. R. Thomson (*Qld*).......	246.1	47	788	21	37.52
J. D. Higgs (*Vic*).............	391.3	82	1,141	29	39.34
S. F. Graf (*Vic*)..............	244.3	49	671	17	39.47
M. F. Malone (*WA*)........	264	45	763	19	40.15
G. Dymock (*Qld*)...........	382.2	107	919	22	41.77
J. N. Maguire (*Qld*).........	276	61	773	18	42.94
T. V. Hohns (*Qld*)..........	368.1	62	1,178	23	51.21

WICKET-KEEPING

R. W. Marsh (*WA*) 37 (37ct); K. J. Wright (*SA*) 34 (32ct, 2st); S. J. Rixon (*NSW*) 24 (21ct, 3st); R. B. Phillips (*Qld*) 16 (16ct); T. J. Zoehrer (*WA*) 16 (13ct, 3st); R. D. Woolley (*Tas*) 14 (12ct, 2st); R. D. Robinson (*Vic*) 10 (7ct, 3st); P. G. Sacristani (*Vic*) 10 (9ct, 1st).

SHEFFIELD SHIELD, 1981-82

	P	*W*	*D*	*L*	*Lead on 1st inns*	*Drawn on 1st inns*	*Pts*
South Australia	9	4	4	1	6	1	74
New South Wales	9	4	4	1	5	2	72
Western Australia	9	3	5	1	4	1	54
Tasmania	5	1	1	3	2	0	36
Queensland	9	1	6	2	1	2	20
Victoria	9	0	4	5	4	0	16

Points: win = 12; lead on 1st innings = 4; draw on 1st innings = 2.
Tasmania's points have been multiplied by 1.8.

QUEENSLAND v VICTORIA

At Brisbane, October 16, 17, 18, 19. Queensland won by 63 runs. Queensland 12 pts, Victoria 4 pts. After dismissing Queensland for 247, a total that owed most to the tail, Victoria at one stage were 187 for two and seemingly set for a big score. Yallop was in fine touch, but with their middle batting failing, the visitors' first-innings lead was only 68. The second half of the game was dominated first by Wessels and then by the Queensland spinners, Hohns and Lillie, who enjoyed more success than their Victorian counterparts, the internationals, Bright and Higgs. Wessels, missed at 43, batted superbly, scoring his runs in less than five hours.

Queensland

K. C. Wessels b McCurdy	11	– c sub b Higgs	168
M. F. Kent c Watts b McCurdy	25	– retired hurt	25
*G. S. Chappell b Walker	10	– c and b Graf	21
A. R. Border c Moss b McCurdy	0	– c Yallop b Bright	52
G. M. Ritchie run out	49	– lbw b Walker	14
W. R. Broad c and b Walker	18	– c Robinson b Higgs	13
T. V. Hohns c Robinson b Walker	36	– not out	58
†R. B. Phillips st Robinson b Bright	19	– c Robinson b Graf	27
G. Dymock b Higgs	22		
J. R. Thomson c Scholes b Higgs	45	– not out	9
D. J. Lillie not out	4		
B 5, l-b 3	8	B 1, l-b 3, w 5, n-b 3	12
1/16 2/45 3/47 4/47 5/72 6/147 7/166 8/177 9/212	247	1/91 2/214 3/251 4/272 5/317 6/377 (6 wkts dec.)	399

Bowling: *First Innings*—McCurdy 16–2–60–3; Walker 24–2–89–3; Graf 9–3–22–0; Bright 20–8–42–1; Higgs 4.4–0–26–2. *Second Innings*—McCurdy 8–1–45–0; Walker 20.2–2–106–1; Graf 15–1–66–2; Bright 31–5–96–1; Higgs 24–6–74–2.

Victoria

P. A. Hibbert c Hohns b Dymock	26	– c Border b Hohns	89
G. M. Watts b Hohns	60	– b Dymock	2
G. N. Yallop lbw b Dymock	82	– c sub b Dymock	31
J. K. Moss c Phillips b Thomson	12	– c Phillips b Lillie	16
*W. J. Scholes run out	13	– c Border b Hohns	1
S. F. Graf lbw b Hohns	4	– c Dymock b Hohns	25
†R. D. Robinson b Dymock	30	– c Chappell b Hohns	0
R. J. Bright lbw b Thomson	39	– lbw b Thomson	23
M. H. N. Walker b Thomson	0	– lbw b Lillie	31
R. J. McCurdy b Hohns	30	– c Dymock b Lillie	32
J. D. Higgs not out	0	– not out	0
L-b 2, w 3, n-b 14	19	B 6, l-b 3, w 1, n-b 8	18
1/72 2/144 3/187 4/203 5/209 6/219 7/251 8/257 9/313	315	1/7 2/49 3/99 4/100 5/101 6/162 7/182 8/221 9/256	268

Bowling: *First Innings*—Thomson 29–6–76–3; Dymock 31–6–82–3; Chappell 14–4–43–0; Lillie 8–4–21–0; Hohns 24.3–4–74–3. *Second Innings*—Thomson 19–5–47–1; Dymock 8–1–33–2; Chappell 8–0–17–0; Lillie 15.2–3–68–3; Hohns 29–7–85–4.

Umpires: M. W. Johnson and R. B. Philippe.

WESTERN AUSTRALIA v SOUTH AUSTRALIA

At Perth, October 16, 17, 18, 19. Western Australia won by 152 runs. Western Australia 16 pts. With nine Test players in their side, Western Australia were not expected to have much difficulty in overcoming opposition whose attack had virtually no first-class experience; yet their victory was not achieved without some anxious moments. Sent in to bat, Western Australia reached only 186, of which Lillee scored an unexpected half-century. Much of the second day was lost through bad weather and, on the third morning, Alderman and Lillee quickly disposed of the South Australians, whose last eight wickets added only 38 runs, Alderman returning career-best figures of seven for 49. Hughes then batted in his most commanding style and, with a patient contribution from Laird, the home side were able to set a target of 333, in response to which South Australia's second innings was notable only for a determined but unavailing effort from McLean. The bowling of Winter, on his début, provided an encouraging feature for South Australia.

Western Australia

G. M. Wood b McLellan	4	– c Wright b Winter	12
B. M. Laird run out	26	– not out	110
G. Shipperd run out	24	– c Wright b Winter	3
*K. J. Hughes c Wright b Sayers	39	– c Sincock b Winter	80
M. D. O'Neill c Wright b Winter	7	– c Inverarity b Winter	1
C. S. Serjeant b Sayers	9	– not out	9
†R. W. Marsh c Phillips b Winter	3	– c Darling b McLellan	7
B. Yardley c Wright b Winter	3	– b Sincock	26
D. K. Lillee not out	54		
M. F. Malone c Sleep b Winter	8		
T. M. Alderman c McLean b Winter	8		
N-b 1	1	L-b 3, w 1, n-b 1	5
1/4 2/51 3/63 4/78 5/99 6/104 7/116 8/116 9/156	186	1/43 2/57 3/170 4/187 5/228 6/243 (6 wkts dec.)	253

Bowling: *First Innings*—McLellan 10–3–30–1; Sincock 12–1–40–0; Winter 36.4–10–67–5; Sayers 21–8–43–2; Sleep 4–2–5–0. *Second Innings*—McLellan 11–3–47–1; Sincock 20–4–70–1; Winter 25–5–76–4; Sayers 4–0–19–0; Sleep 6–0–36–0.

South Australia

W. M. Darling c Marsh b Lillee	23	– c Marsh b Alderman	32
W. B. Phillips c Wood b Alderman	13	– c Marsh b Alderman	4
I. R. McLean c Serjeant b Alderman	13	– c Malone b Yardley	70
*D. W. Hookes b Alderman	7	– c Serjeant b Yardley	10
R. J. Inverarity lbw b Alderman	18	– c Lillee b Yardley	9
P. R. Sleep c Marsh b Alderman	0	– c Marsh b Lillee	1
G. J. Winter c Marsh b Lillee	1	– b Yardley	2
A. T. Sincock c Marsh b Lillee	0	– run out	6
†K. J. Wright c Serjeant b Alderman	7	– c Serjeant b Alderman	21
R. M. McLellan c Marsh b Alderman	5	– not out	14
D. K. Sayers not out	5	– c Hughes b Malone	1
L-b 12, n-b 3	15	B 4, l-b 6	10
1/34 2/46 3/69 4/77 5/80 6/89 7/94 8/94 9/98	107	1/4 2/60 3/91 4/105 5/106 6/144 7/152 8/156 9/161	180

Bowling: *First Innings*—Lillee 25–6–43–3; Alderman 24.2–5–49–7. *Second Innings*—Lillee 16–4–38–1; Alderman 19–6–43–3; Malone 11.2–1–35–1; Yardley 20–4–54–4.

Umpires: P. McConnell and D. G. Weser.

NEW SOUTH WALES v QUEENSLAND

At Newcastle, October 22, 23, 24, 25. Drawn. New South Wales 2 pts, Queensland 2 pts. With the Sydney Cricket Ground unavailable, this game was played in Newcastle, and although the crowd of 7,292 was probably larger than would have attended in Sydney, the game was ruined by rain, which caused the loss of the first two days. When play did begin, the New South Wales batsmen showed little sense of urgency; Dyson, Chappell, Davis and Beard each made half-centuries, but McCosker delayed his declaration until the fourth day. Queensland made a brisk start, Wessels and Border being in excellent form. However, at 195 for two the situation was suddenly changed by Beard, who took five quick wickets with his off-spinners, and the game ended on an exciting note with the last pair, Dymock and Brabon, holding out to deny New South Wales a first-innings win.

New South Wales

*R. B. McCosker lbw b Brabon	18	G. R. Beard run out	62
J. Dyson c Phillips b Brabon	65	†S. J. Rixon not out	4
T. M. Chappell lbw b Chappell	58	L-b 9, w 1, n-b 13	23
D. M. Wellham c Phillips b Dymock	24		
P. M. Toohey run out	16	1/32 2/134 3/158 4/181 5/208 6/310 (6 wkts dec.)	322
I. C. Davis run out	52		

L. S. Pascoe, M. R. Whitney and D. W. Hourn did not bat.

Bowling: Thomson 24–9–53–0; Dymock 33–14–75–1; Brabon 22–4–58–2; Chappell 11–4–42–1; Hohns 10–0–38–0; Border 6–1–20–0; Broad 3–0–13–0.

Queensland

M. F. Kent c McCosker b Whitney	26	G. Dymock not out	22
K. C. Wessels c Rixon b Beard	103	J. R. Thomson lbw b Pascoe	0
*G. S. Chappell c Toohey b Whitney	2	G. W. Brabon not out	1
A. R. Border st Rixon b Beard	58		
G. M. Ritchie lbw b Pascoe	22	B 1, l-b 7, w 4, n-b 14	26
W. R. Broad b Beard	0		
T. V. Hohns b Beard	4	1/71 2/84 3/195 4/213 5/220 6/225 7/237 8/257 9/257 (9 wkts)	269
†R. B. Phillips b Beard	5		

Bowling: Pascoe 13–5–28–2; Whitney 17–3–65–2; Beard 24–5–67–5; Hourn 25.2–7–70–0; Chappell 5.4–1–13–0.

Umpires: M. Jay and A. G. Watson.

WESTERN AUSTRALIA v NEW SOUTH WALES

At Perth, October 30, 31, November 1. Western Australia won by an innings and 35 runs. Western Australia 16 pts. Another splendid exhibition of bowling by Alderman was instrumental in Western Australia's victory with a day to spare. New South Wales never recovered from a collapse to 22 for four in their first innings, Alderman having taken four for 2 and only Beard batting with any distinction. In reply, Western Australia were rescued from an indifferent start by Hughes and Langer, who added 188 for the fifth wicket, Hughes playing with great circumspection, taking four hours to score 113. Of the New South Welsh bowlers, Lawson was easily the most impressive. The second New South Wales innings was even more disappointing than the first and, once again, it was Alderman who did the damage, his match figures of fourteen for 87 being the best ever recorded by a Western Australian bowler in Shield cricket.

New South Wales

*R. B. McCosker c Marsh b Alderman	0	– c Serjeant b Alderman	4
J. Dyson c Laird b Alderman	10	– c Laird b Lillee	19
T. M. Chappell c Marsh b Alderman	31	– b Alderman	12
I. C. Davis c Yardley b Alderman	0	– c Serjeant b Alderman	36
D. M. Wellham c Marsh b Alderman	2	– c Laird b Yardley	0
G. R. Beard c Serjeant b Alderman	75	– c Laird b Yardley	30
†S. J. Rixon c Marsh b Lillee	18	– c Shipperd b Alderman	7
G. F. Lawson b Malone	4	– c Marsh b Alderman	0
L. S. Pascoe b Yardley	39	– not out	5
D. W. Hourn c Shipperd b Alderman	24	– c Serjeant b Alderman	0
M. R. Whitney not out	3	– c Marsh b Alderman	0
L-b 3, w 1, n-b 5	9	L-b 2, n-b 2	4
1/9 2/15 3/15 4/22 5/73 6/108 7/113 8/178 9/208	215	1/5 2/19 3/49 4/54 5/86 6/110 7/112 8/117 9/117	117

Bowling: *First Innings*—Alderman 18.4–4–59–7; Lillee 21–4–49–1; Yardley 15–3–52–1; Malone 13–2–46–1. *Second Innings*—Alderman 17–5–28–7; Lillee 13–3–40–1; Yardley 14–2–45–2.

Western Australia

B. M. Laird b Whitney	30
G. M. Wood c Rixon b Lawson	17
G. Shipperd c Dyson b Lawson	3
*K. J. Hughes lbw b Hourn	113
C. S. Serjeant c Rixon b Lawson	8
R. S. Langer c Rixon b Lawson	77
†R. W. Marsh b Whitney	39
B. Yardley c McCosker b Lawson	19
D. K. Lillee not out	24
M. F. Malone b Lawson	2
T. M. Alderman run out	1
B 4, l-b 9, w 8, n-b 13	34
1/37 2/54 3/75 4/92 5/270 6/313 7/325 8/347 9/353	367

Bowling: Pascoe 17–5–46–0; Whitney 28–4–89–2; Lawson 22–6–70–6; Hourn 15.5–2–63–1; Beard 22–2–65–0.

Umpires: P. McConnell and D. G. Weser.

SOUTH AUSTRALIA v NEW SOUTH WALES

At Adelaide, November 7, 8, 9, 10. Drawn. South Australia 2 pts, New South Wales 2 pts. Conditions for batting could hardly have been more favourable, and South Australia were confronted by a New South Welsh attack in which, without Pascoe (suspended), Lawson posed the greatest threat. Taking advantage of this, Crowe and Hookes each made a welcome return to form with fine centuries. South Australia's innings having continued until late on the second day, New South Wales made no effort to score quickly. Not that this mattered much in the end, for rain washed out most of the final day after Dyson and McCosker had taken almost six hours over an opening stand of 191.

South Australia

W. M. Darling lbw b Lawson	71	G. J. Winter c Davis b Hourn	4
I. R. McLean run out	43	S. D. H. Parkinson c Chappell b Lawson	26
J. J. Crowe c Rixon b Hourn	157	R. W. Dugan not out	1
R. J. Inverarity c Rixon b Lawson	54	L-b 11, n-b 16	27
*D. W. Hookes c Wellham b Chappell	106		
P. R. Sleep c Rixon b Beard	29	1/123 2/129 3/333 (9 wkts dec.)	551
†K. J. Wright b Beard	33	4/364 5/441 6/517 7/519 8/523 9/551	

D. K. Sayers did not bat.

Bowling: Lawson 34.5–9–87–3; Whitney 31–6–85–0; Done 26–2–117–0; Hourn 37–5–153–2; Beard 32–8–75–2; Chappell 4–2–7–1.

New South Wales

*R. B. McCosker c Wright b Parkinson	90
J. Dyson c Wright b Parkinson	108
T. M. Chappell not out	4
D. M. Wellham not out	7
B 1, l-b 4, w 1, n-b 5	11
1/191 2/210 (2 wkts)	220

I. C. Davis, G. R. Beard, †S. J. Rixon, R. P. Done, D. W. Hourn, G. F. Lawson and M. R. Whitney did not bat.

Bowling: Parkinson 34.2–10–69–2; Winter 8–2–15–0; Sayers 17–8–26–0; Dugan 23–14–21–0; Sleep 20–2–54–0; Inverarity 19–7–24–0.

Umpires: A. R. Crafter and B. E. Martin.

VICTORIA v TASMANIA

At Melbourne, October 30, 31, November 1. Tasmania won by 96 runs. Tasmania 16 pts. History was made when, for the first time since being admitted to the Sheffield Shield in 1977, Tasmania achieved an outright win on the mainland, doing so with a day to spare. It was a victory thoroughly deserved, notwithstanding the extraordinary deterioration of another Melbourne pitch on which batsmen struggled throughout to survive, the run-rate seldom rising above 2 per over. In Tasmania's first innings, Boon gave further evidence of his potential, his 79 being the only score of over fifty in the match. Victoria's batsmen failed to master the West Indian, Stephenson, in either innings; he was impressive in the first and often unplayable in the second.

Tasmania

D. B. Robinson lbw b Graf	7	– lbw b Graf	12
R. F. Jeffery c and b McCurdy	4	– c Yallop b Higgs	32
R. L. Knight run out	7	– lbw b Graf	0
D. C. Boon c Scholes b Bright	79	– c Scholes b Bright	1
*B. F. Davison c Robinson b Higgs	27	– run out	15
†R. D. Woolley c Yallop b Higgs	6	– c Scholes b Bright	37
P. J. Mancell c Scholes b Higgs	2	– c Yallop b Higgs	6
S. L. Saunders lbw b Walker	21	– b McCurdy	15
F. D. Stephenson b Graf	26	– c Moss b Bright	5
M. B. Scholes not out	24	– not out	1
P. M. Clough b Graf	1	– c and b Higgs	15
B2, l-b 6, n-b 3	11	B 9, l-b 7	16
1/5 2/16 3/20 4/80 5/94 6/118 7/154 8/184 9/190	215	1/29 2/33 3/38 4/59 5/76 6/91 7/109 8/149 9/149	155

Bowling: *First Innings*—McCurdy 9–3–26–1; Walker 15–3–31–1; Graf 18.3–7–37–3; Higgs 29–6–71–3; Bright 23–7–39–1. *Second Innings*—McCurdy 9–2–28–1; Walker 5–1–17–0; Graf 15–5–31–2; Higgs 23–7–40–3; Bright 29.2–18–23–3; Yallop 1–1–0–0.

Victoria

J. M. Wiener c Robinson b Stephenson	2	– b Mancell	4
G. M. Watts lbw b Saunders	46	– c and b Clough	4
G. N. Yallop st Woolley b Saunders	46	– b Stephenson	3
J. K. Moss c Jeffery b Saunders	23	– b Stephenson	5
*W. J. Scholes lbw b Stephenson	22	– lbw b Stephenson	13
†R. D. Robinson c Knight b Saunders	2	– c Stephenson b Mancell	8
S. F. Graf c Woolley b Stephenson	7	– c Boon b Saunders	24
R. J. Bright b Stephenson	0	– lbw b Stephenson	5
M. H. N. Walker c Scholes b Clough	11	– b Stephenson	0
R. J. McCurdy c Woolley b Clough	3	– lbw b Stephenson	0
J. D. Higgs not out	0	– not out	5
B 11, l-b 8, n-b 10	29	B 8, l-b 2, n-b 2	12
1/13 2/92 3/131 4/148 5/158 6/173 7/173 8/183 9/188	191	1/8 2/11 3/17 4/27 5/36 6/46 7/68 8/70 9/70	83

Bowling: *First Innings*—Stephenson 18–9–27–4; Clough 13.1–8–19–2; Mancell 16–6–13–0; Saunders 22–1–82–4; Scholes 3–0–21–0. *Second Innings*—Stephenson 15–7–19–6; Clough 10–2–20–1; Mancell 18–8–22–2; Saunders 3–0–10–1.

Umpires: R. A. French and R. V. Whitehead.

QUEENSLAND v WESTERN AUSTRALIA

At Brisbane, November 20, 21, 22, 23. Drawn. Queensland 2 pts, Western Australia 2 pts. The demands of Test cricket caused each side to make extensive changes, Western Australia being without Hughes, Wood, Laird, Marsh, Lillee, Alderman and Yardley and Queensland losing Chappell, Border and Thomson as well as the injured Kent. Owing to adverse weather, which completely washed out the first day, there seemed little prospect of anything other than a first-innings result. In the end, not even this was achieved as, in an exciting conclusion, the last two Queensland batsmen denied Western Australia the points. Western Australia's innings owed much to Langer, who batted for more than five hours for his century; for Queensland Wessels continued his impressive early-season form. Of the bowlers the leg-spinners, Hohns and Mann, were the most effective.

Western Australia

G. D. Porter b Brabon	12	†T. J. Zoehrer c Broad b Hohns	13
M. D. O'Neill c Parker b Maguire	15	M. F. Malone not out	27
G. Shipperd c Wessels b Brabon	47	W. W. Daniel c Kerr b Hohns	21
*C. S. Serjeant c Wessels b Maguire	10		
R. S. Langer b Broad	140	B 4, 1-b 5, n-b 5	14
K. H. MacLeay b Hohns	16		—
A. L. Mann lbw b Hohns	31	1/23 2/31 3/60 4/134 5/173	351
D. J. Baker c Parker b Dymock	5	6/276 7/284 8/302 9/302	

Bowling: Maguire 35–11–90–2; Dymock 39–19–66–1; Brabon 19–6–56–2; Broad 18–8–28–1; Hohns 27.3–3–97–4.

Queensland

K. C. Wessels c Mann b Malone	72	*G. Dymock st Zoehrer b Mann	33
R. B. Kerr c Porter b Malone	4	J. N. Maguire not out	0
M. A. Gaskell b Mann	19	G. W. Brabon not out	0
G. M. Ritchie c Serjeant b Baker	44		
A. D. Parker b Malone	6	B7, 1-b 3, n-b 16	26
W. R. Broad c Baker b Mann	33		—
T. V. Hohns c Zoehrer b Daniel	25	1/12 2/73 3/120 4/130 (9 wkts)	308
†R. B. Phillips c Daniel b Mann	46	5/171 6/197 7/232 8/282 9/307	

Bowling: Daniel 30–9–66–1; Malone 29–5–72–3; Baker 23–5–51–1; Mann 30–5–78–4; Porter 6–1–15–0; Langer 1–1–0–0.

Umpires: C. E. Harvey and J. T. C. Taylor.

VICTORIA v WESTERN AUSTRALIA

At Melbourne, November 27, 28, 29, 30. Drawn. Victoria 4 pts. After the venue for this game had been switched from the much-criticised Melbourne Cricket Ground to St Kilda, records were established during a Victorian innings which proved to be a statisticians' delight. Wiener and Moss, both of whom had hitherto been out of form, each scored a double-century and shared in an unbroken third-wicket partnership of 390. This surpassed the previous Australian record for the third wicket (389 by Ponsford and McCabe against MCC at Lord's in 1934) and was a record for any wicket for Victoria in Shield cricket. When Western Australia batted it was discovered that water had seeped under the covers and damaged the pitch, an incident which caused them to redouble their match-saving efforts. Porter played two dogged and determined innings for Western Australia; Higgs achieved match figures of seven for 79 off 43 overs and Callen made a welcome return to first-class cricket.

Victoria

J. M. Wiener not out	221
G. M. Watts lbw b Malone	4
P. A. Hibbert run out	38
J. K. Moss not out	200
L-b 7, w 1, n-b 16	24
	—
1/8 2/97 (2 wkts dec.)	487

*W. J. Scholes, †I. L. Maddocks, S. F. Graf, R. J. Bright, M. H. N. Walker, I. W. Callen and J. D. Higgs did not bat.

Bowling: Daniel 33–4–114–0; Malone 41.4–6–102–1; Porter 20–3–66–0; Mann 11–1–39–0; Hogan 25–2–77–0; MacLeay 17–2–58–0; Langer 2–0–7–0.

Western Australia

G. D. Porter c Maddocks b Callen	64	– lbw b Walker	51
M. D. O'Neill c Watts b Walker	26	– c Scholes b Higgs	39
G. Shipperd c Graf b Callen	33	– c Graf b Callen	4
A. L. Mann b Bright	2	– not out	40
*C. S. Serjeant b Callen	1	– c Moss b Higgs	3
R. S. Langer b Graf	10	– c Watts b Callen	48
K. H. MacLeay c Scholes b Higgs	34	– c Scholes b Higgs	1
†T. J. Zoehrer c Scholes b Higgs	23	– not out	4
M. F. Malone not out	2		
T. G. Hogan c Scholes b Higgs	0		
W. W. Daniel st Maddocks b Higgs	2		
B 1, l-b 2, w 1, n-b 7	11	B 6, l-b 9, n-b 4	19
1/50 2/126 3/131 4/131 5/132 6/147 7/201 8/204 9/206	208	1/76 2/92 3/97 4/116 5/126 6/196	(6 wkts) 209

Bowling: *First Innings*—Graf 15–3–41–1; Walker 19–7–36–1; Callen 23–8–54–3; Higgs 14–7–24–4; Bright 26–11–42–1. *Second Innings*—Graf 11–2–19–0; Walker 21–7–42–1; Callen 18–4–46–2; Higgs 29–5–55–3; Bright 21–9–22–0; Scholes 1–0–3–0; Wiener 1–0–3–0.

Umpires: R. A. French and R. C. Bailhache.

NEW SOUTH WALES v SOUTH AUSTRALIA

At Sydney, December 10, 11, 12, 13. Drawn. New South Wales 4 pts. A splendid game ended in controversy when, in conditions which seemed by no means unplayable, the umpires and the New South Wales fieldsmen ran off the field, leaving behind two frustrated South Australian batsmen with their side only 11 short of victory and probably needing no more than one over in which to get the runs. Although soon afterwards the rain did get heavier, the South Australians could justifiably have considered themselves "robbed". In the first New South Wales innings, Toohey batted with some of his old authority, but on a pitch always responsive to spin it was Inverarity, taking five for 40, who achieved the outstanding performance. South Australia's reply was held together by Phillips and Sleep, but the slow bowlers continued to call the tune, Holland recording six for 64 off 32 overs. When New South Wales batted a second time, McCosker maintained the form that had recently brought him many runs in all classes of cricket, and his declaration left South Australia a day in which to score 256 – a task which most considered beyond the capabilities of a young and relatively inexperienced side. However, Crowe made an exciting 137 not out in only 216 minutes and took South Australia to within reach of victory.

New South Wales

*R. B. McCosker c Prior b Winter	49	– not out	146
J. Dyson b Prior	5	– lbw b Parkinson	26
T. M. Chappell c Wright b Parkinson	34	– c Lewis b Inverarity	18
I. C. Davis c Winter b Prior	0	– c and b Inverarity	1
P. M. Toohey c Hookes b Inverarity	84	– b Lewis	39
G. R. Beard c Crowe b Inverarity	48	– c Sleep b Inverarity	2
†S. J. Rixon c Wright b Inverarity	17	– not out	14
M. Ray c Crowe b Inverarity	17		
L. S. Pascoe b Lewis	4		
R. G. Holland b Inverarity	2		
M. R. Whitney not out	1		
L-b 4, w 1, n-b 5	10	B 2, w 1, n-b 3	6
1/12 2/79 3/81 4/124 5/201 6/247 7/247 8/251 9/270	271	1/122 2/129 3/188 4/189 5/197	(5 wkts dec.) 252

Bowling: *First Innings*—Prior 18–2–53–2; Parkinson 17–4–43–1; Winter 13–2–41–1; Lewis 21–6–54–1; Inverarity 12.3–2–40–5; Sleep 3–1–14–0; Hookes 5–0–16–0. *Second Innings*—Prior 8–0–47–0; Parkinson 13–4–38–1; Winter 6–1–23–0; Lewis 21–4–60–1; Inverarity 26–8–51–3; Sleep 11–4–27–0.

South Australia

W. B. Phillips lbw b Holland	79	– c and b Beard	41
†K. J. Wright b Beard	38		
J. J. Crowe c Rixon b Holland	1	– not out	137
R. J. Inverarity c Ray b Holland	2		
*D. W. Hookes b Holland	11	– not out	7
P. R. Sleep c Rixon b Whitney	65		
W. M. Darling c McCosker b Ray	16	– lbw b Pascoe	52
W. Prior c Rixon b Ray	0		
G. J. Winter c Dyson b Holland	19		
S. D. H. Parkinson c Pascoe b Holland	12		
K. J. Lewis not out	2		
B 1, l-b 5, n-b 17	23	B 1, l-b 2, n-b 5	8
1/86 2/107 3/109 4/131 5/148 6/193 7/193 8/238 9/262	268	1/125 2/231	(2 wkts) 245

Bowling: *First Innings*—Pascoe 14–2–51–0; Whitney 15–4–49–1; Holland 32–13–64–6; Ray 13–7–17–2; Beard 37–13–64–1. *Second Innings*—Pascoe 8.4–0–53–1; Whitney 3–0–10–0; Holland 15–2–67–0; Ray 20–6–46–0; Beard 19–5–59–1; Chappell 1–0–2–0.

Umpires: M. Jay and I. Jones.

NEW SOUTH WALES v VICTORIA

At Sydney, December 19, 20, 21, 22. New South Wales won by eight wickets. New South Wales 16 pts. Victoria were comprehensively defeated in a game in which New South Wales lost a total of only six wickets. The dominant player was McCosker, who continued to press his Test claims with two undefeated centuries, while Toohey and Dyson also scored runs stylishly. Of the New South Wales bowlers, Holland did particularly well; Beard, bowling as economically as he usually does, took important wickets in Victoria's second innings, and Skilbeck made an encouraging début with match figures of five for 73. For Victoria, the bowling was undistinguished and the batting disappointing, the latter especially as each of their recognised batsmen got a start in either the first or second innings without being able to convert a moderate score to an adequate one.

Victoria

J. M. Wiener c Rixon b Holland	72	– c Beard b Skilbeck	2
G. M. Watts b Pascoe	2	– b Beard	71
G. N. Yallop c Rixon b Skilbeck	24	– b Beard	10
J. K. Moss c Beard b Holland	30	– b Beard	67
*W. J. Scholes b Holland	15	– c McCosker b Holland	48
†R. D. Robinson c Toohey b Holland	22	– c Rixon b Holland	8
S. F. Graf c Dyson b Pascoe	13	– c Rixon b Skilbeck	0
R. J. Bright not out	35	– b Beard	6
M. H. N. Walker c Dyson b Skilbeck	28	– c Dyson b Holland	8
R. J. McCurdy lbw b Skilbeck	0	– not out	4
J. D. Higgs b Pascoe	0	– run out	0
L-b 4, n-b 9	13	L-b 4, n-b 4	8
1/9 2/74 3/133 4/138 5/169 6/176 7/203 8/249 9/251	254	1/2 2/86 3/98 4/199 5/210 6/211 7/218 8/228 9/228	232

Bowling: *First Innings*—Pascoe 27.4–3–93–3; Skilbeck 17–9–34–3; Holland 34–9–73–4; Ray 3–0–13–0; Chappell 2–0–11–0; Beard 17–9–17–0. *Second Innings*—Pascoe 16–3–47–0; Skilbeck 13–3–39–2; Holland 28–10–66–3; Beard 34.5–17–54–4; Ray 4–1–18–0.

New South Wales

*R. B. McCosker not out	123	– not out	118
J. Dyson c Watts b McCurdy	6	– st Robinson b Bright	83
T. M. Chappell c Watts b Walker	1	– b Higgs	10
S. B. Smith c Robinson b Bright	35		
P. M. Toohey run out	76	– not out	19
G. R. Beard not out	12		
L-b 1, n-b 1	2	B 1, l-b 2	3
1/9 2/10 3/87 4/222 (4 wkts dec.)	255	1/174 2/204 (2 wkts)	233

†S. J. Rixon, A. J. Skilbeck, L. S. Pascoe, M. Ray and R. G. Holland did not bat.

Bowling: *First Innings*—McCurdy 12–1–27–1; Walker 13–4–39–1; Graf 7–0–23–0; Bright 35–8–76–1; Higgs 30–5–88–0. *Second Innings*—McCurdy 3–1–4–0; Walker 17–6–40–0; Graf 9–3–26–0; Bright 29.3–7–69–1; Higgs 29–6–91–1.

Umpires: M. Jay and A. Marshall.

QUEENSLAND v SOUTH AUSTRALIA

At Brisbane, December 17, 18, 19, 20. Drawn. South Australia 4 pts. In a game in which declarations were a major factor, Dymock eventually left Queensland with just insufficient time to bowl out a South Australian side prepared to risk everything for quick runs. It was another exciting finish with the last pair having to survive the final over, still 37 runs short of victory. For most of the game the batsmen were well on top, with Queensland's Ritchie looking a Test prospect. It was Dymock, however, who provided the surprise of the first Queensland innings; with De Jong, he added 145 for the eighth wicket and in so doing scored his maiden first-class century, as did Kerr, whose undefeated 103 allowed Dymock to set the visitors a reasonable target. In South Australia's first innings, Inverarity reached his 21st hundred in first-class cricket. Their second innings was dominated by Harris who, in an encouraging Shield début, had almost carried his side to victory when Henschell took four quick wickets, after which South Australia struggled to avoid defeat.

Queensland

K. C. Wessels c Wright b Winter	23	– c Harris b Sleep	29
R. B. Kerr c Wright b Winter	6	– not out	103
R. N. Traves run out	25	– c Prior b Sleep	25
G. M. Ritchie c Harris b Inverarity	126	– c Hookes b Inverarity	47
T. V. Hohns c Inverarity b Prior	33	– c Hookes b Inverarity	10
A. B. Henschell c Hookes b Prior	19	– c Inverarity b Sleep	0
†R. B. Phillips c Wright b Prior	6	– lbw b Inverarity	14
H. K. De Jong c Crowe b Parkinson	41	– st Wright b Sleep	5
*G. Dymock not out	101	– not out	0
D. J. Lillie (did not bat)		– b Sleep	0
L-b 6, w 1, n-b 2	9	B 11, l-b 2, w 2, n-b 1	16
1/26 2/29 3/137 4/208 5/228 6/239 7/244 8/389 (8 wkts dec.)	389	1/61 2/132 3/152 4/159 5/178 6/201 7/244 8/245 (8 wkts dec.)	249

J. N. Maguire did not bat.

Bowling: *First Innings*—Prior 26–4–84–3; Parkinson 20–5–46–1; Winter 23–7–57–2; Lewis 26–8–63–0; Inverarity 21–7–50–1; Sleep 25–7–80–0. *Second Innings*—Parkinson 2–1–1–0; Winter 3–1–11–0; Lewis 20–7–58–0; Inverarity 20.1–8–46–3; Sleep 39–11–117–5.

South Australia

W. B. Phillips c Ritchie b Maguire	15	– c Lillie b De Jong	0
K. P. Harris c Dymock b Lillie	52	– c sub b Henschell	97
J. J. Crowe c Phillips b Maguire	24	– run out	16
*D. W. Hookes c Dymock b Hohns	51	– c De Jong b Lillie	32
P. R. Sleep b Hohns	78	– c and b Henschell	22
R. J. Inverarity not out	100	– not out	4
†K. J. Wright not out	64	– c Dymock b Hohns	3
W. Prior (did not bat)		– b Henschell	4
S. D. H. Parkinson (did not bat)		– c and b Henschell	7
G. J. Winter (did not bat)		– c Wessels b Lillie	0
K. J. Lewis (did not bat)		– not out	0
B 6, l-b 6, n-b 8	20	B 7, l-b 4, w 1, n-b 1	13
1/27 2/84 3/140 4/149 5/270 (5 wkts dec.)	404	1/0 2/49 3/100 4/157 5/161 6/174 7/187 8/197 9/198 (9 wkts)	198

Bowling: *First Innings*—Maguire 26–7–52–2; Dymock 21–7–38–0; Hohns 42–8–122–2; Lillie 31–5–122–1; De Jong 9–3–21–0; Henschell 11–4–28–0; Wessels 1–0–1–0. *Second Innings*—Maguire 3–2–3–0; Dymock 2–0–11–0; Hohns 21–6–58–1; Lillie 12–1–69–2; De Jong 2–1–2–1; Henschell 7–0–34–4; Wessels 2–0–8–0.

Umpires: R. B. Philippe and J. T. C. Taylor.

SOUTH AUSTRALIA v QUEENSLAND

At Adelaide, January 8, 9, 10. South Australia won by an innings and 93 runs. South Australia 16 pts. With a day to spare, South Australia scored a convincing victory, set up by Phillips and clinched by their spin bowlers, Dolman, Inverarity and Sleep. Despite a stomach upset, Phillips batted for almost seven and a half hours in a marathon innings which contained two 6s and 25 4s. He received useful support, notably from Hookes, who was especially severe on Lillie, at one stage hitting the leg-spinner for 6 off four consecutive balls. Although batting from the start of their innings to avoid the follow-on, Queensland failed to do so despite a patient innings from Ritchie, and in their second innings only Kerr offered serious resistance.

South Australia

K. P. Harris c and b Hohns	45	R. J. Inverarity not out	38
W. B. Phillips c Lillie b Dymock	260		
J. J. Crowe c Rackemann b Maguire	22	B 1, l-b 10, w 4, n-b 22	37
*D. W. Hookes b Maguire	88		
P. R. Sleep not out	62	1/168 2/208 3/386 4/475 (4 wkts dec.)	552

B. A. Vincent, †J. R. Davey, S. D. H. Parkinson, M. C. Dolman and G. J. Winter did not bat.

Bowling: Rackemann 27–6–114–0; Maguire 21–0–82–2; Dymock 36–3–95–1; Hohns 31–2–125–1; Lillie 7–1–54–0; Henschell 6–1–31–0; Wessels 1–0–4–0; Kerr 1–0–3–0; Traves 1–0–5–0; Ritchie 1–0–2–0.

Queensland

K. C. Wessels c Crowe b Winter	22	– c Inverarity b Vincent	4
R. B. Kerr c Davey b Winter	14	– st Davey b Sleep	66
R. N. Traves c Davey b Dolman	24	– lbw b Inverarity	7
G. M. Ritchie c Phillips b Dolman	103	– c Davey b Winter	1
A. B. Henschell c Hookes b Inverarity	50	– b Dolman	15
T. V. Hohns run out	26	– b Inverarity	4
†R. B. Phillips lbw b Inverarity	6	– c Harris b Dolman	27
*G. Dymock b Dolman	37	– c Harris b Sleep	6
J. N. Maguire b Parkinson	0	– c Davey b Sleep	19
D. J. Lillie not out	2	– st Davey b Sleep	1
C. G. Rackemann b Dolman	0	– not out	6
B 5, l-b 3, w 4, n-b 1	13	B 3, l-b 2, n-b 1	6
1/37 2/48 3/88 4/177 5/236 6/242 7/257 8/287 9/297	297	1/6 2/40 3/51 4/79 5/88 6/112 7/124 8/132 9/152	162

Bowling: *First Innings*—Parkinson 14–4–42–1; Winter 27–7–68–2; Dolman 26–2–114–4; Sleep 20–9–39–0; Inverarity 14–6–21–2. *Second Innings*—Parkinson 5–1–13–0; Winter 12–5–32–1; Dolman 11.1–1–47–2; Sleep 8–3–19–4; Inverarity 20–5–40–2; Vincent 3–1–5–1.

Umpires: P. M. Cronin and M. G. O'Connell.

WESTERN AUSTRALIA v TASMANIA

At Perth, January 9, 10, 11, 12. Western Australia won by five wickets. Western Australia 16 pts. Tasmania's chances of a high finish in the Sheffield Shield were heavily dependent on success in this game which, because of Test calls, was against virtually a Western Australian second eleven. However, although at one stage it seemed possible that they might escape with a draw, they never looked like winning. After batting first for a laborious 234, Tasmania did reasonably well to restrict Western Australia to a lead of only 94. Tasmania's second innings was even more disappointing than their first; of their recognised batsmen only Jeffery made runs, the rest finding the spinners, Mann and Hogan, too good for them. At 159 for nine and only 65 ahead, Tasmania looked beaten, but a tenth-wicket partnership between Saunders and Clough added 120 in three hours with Saunders scoring his maiden first-class hundred. This unexpected defiance left Western Australia a target of 186 runs at about a run a minute, which they achieved fairly comfortably.

Tasmania

D. B. Robinson c Serjeant b Mann	48	– c Shipperd b Boyd	4
I. R. Beven c Porter b Clark	12	– c Serjeant b Boyd	4
R. F. Jeffery c Serjeant b Mann	31	– lbw b Clark	67
D. C. Boon b Mann	37	– c Serjeant b Hogan	24
*B. F. Davison c Zoehrer b MacLeay	68	– b Hogan	25
†R. D. Woolley c Zoehrer b Boyd	12	– c Zoehrer b Hogan	1
P. J. Mancell c Zoehrer b MacLeay	6	– c Serjeant b Mann	4
S. L. Saunders c Zoehrer b Boyd	0	– b Hogan	106
F. D. Stephenson c Serjeant b Boyd	1	– c Boyd b Mann	2
P. A. Blizzard c Hogan b MacLeay	4	– b Mann	0
P. M. Clough not out	0	– not out	31
B 6, l-b 5, w 1, n-b 3	15	L-b 4, n-b 7	11
1/23 2/82 3/117 4/160 5/190 6/205 7/223 8/225 9/232	234	1/7 2/17 3/80 4/124 5/126 6/129 7/145 8/147 9/159	279

Bowling: *First Innings*—Boyd 17–3–40–3; Clark 11–1–27–1; Porter 12–2–23–0; MacLeay 22.2–6–34–3; Mann 27–6–72–3; Hogan 12–5–23–0. *Second Innings*—Boyd 16–2–68–2; Clark 30–5–63–1; Porter 3–1–5–0; MacLeay 13–5–14–0; Mann 34–17–54–3; Hogan 37.1–18–64–4; Langer 2–2–0–0.

Western Australia

G. D. Porter c Stephenson b Blizzard	14	– c Robinson b Clough	6
G. Shipperd lbw b Clough	3	– lbw b Beven	67
G. R. Marsh c Saunders b Clough	24	– c Beven b Stephenson	7
R. S. Langer c Woolley b Jeffery	75	– c Woolley b Stephenson	46
*C. S. Serjeant c Woolley b Stephenson	19	– not out	29
K. H. MacLeay not out	83		
A. L. Mann c Davison b Beven	47	– not out	14
†T. J. Zoehrer c Clough b Mancell	3		
W. M. Clark b Stephenson	3		
D. L. Boyd c Stephenson b Mancell	37	– c Stephenson b Clough	4
T. G. Hogan c Boon b Clough	4		
B 12, l-b 2, w 1, n-b 1	16	B 6, l-b 6, n-b 1	13
1/6 2/40 3/46 4/86 5/151 6/242 7/253 8/265 9/317	328	1/12 2/33 3/127 4/151 5/156	(5 wkts) 186

Bowling: *First Innings*—Stephenson 26–8–67–2; Clough 26.2–7–64–3; Blizzard 9–2–34–1; Beven 12–3–26–1; Mancell 24–7–59–2; Saunders 12–3–49–0; Jeffery 3–1–13–1. *Second Innings*—Stephenson 17.4–1–72–2; Clough 13–3–44–2; Blizzard 3–0–10–0; Beven 15–4–47–1.

Umpires: P. McConnell and D. G. Weser.

VICTORIA v SOUTH AUSTRALIA

At Geelong, January 15, 16, 17, 18. Drawn. South Australia 4 pts. Neither side made any strenuous efforts to win the match, which was transferred from Melbourne to Geelong. After South Australia had batted slowly on the first day, Victoria replied in even more pedestrian fashion, the spin bowlers, Inverarity and Sleep, commanding particular respect. With a lead of 84, South Australia might then have been expected to score quickly, but although Darling made a sound century, it took him over five and a half hours. Eventually, Hookes left Victoria a target of 364 at about a run a minute, a task obviously beyond a side which lacked the necessary form and experience. Easily the best of their batsmen was Green, whose recall to the side followed the mid-season retirement from first-class cricket of Walker and Robinson.

South Australia

W. M. Darling b Hughes	46	– c Hughes b Callen	134
W. B. Phillips b Callen	14	– b Callen	8
J. J. Crowe c Maddocks b Callen	1	– st Maddocks b Higgs	62
*D. W. Hookes c Moss b Hughes	21	– c Maddocks b Callen	34
P. R. Sleep c Green b Bright	42	– st Maddocks b Bright	4
R. J. Inverarity c Yallop b Bright	0	– b Bright	11
†K. J. Wright c Wiener b Bright	59	– not out	16
B. A. Vincent b Callen	47	– not out	7
G. J. Winter c Bright b Callen	5		
S. D. H. Parkinson c Maddocks b Hughes	1		
M. C. Dolman not out	0		
B 3, l-b 5	8	L-b 3	3
1/29 2/33 3/75 4/92 5/101 6/143 7/207 8/243 9/244	244	1/23 2/166 3/229 4/236 5/246 6/262	(6 wkts dec.) 279

Bowling: *First Innings*—Callen 26.1–2–76–4; Hughes 21–5–53–3; Bright 30–9–65–3; Higgs 21–6–40–0; Green 2–0–2–0. *Second Innings*—Callen 25–3–81–3; Hughes 19–3–52–0; Bright 27–9–62–2; Higgs 14–0–62–1; Green 2–0–7–0; Yallop 4–1–12–0.

Victoria

J. M. Wiener c Wright b Parkinson	3	– c Hookes b Parkinson	25
G. M. Watts c Phillips b Parkinson	6	– b Sleep	64
*W. J. Scholes run out	32	– lbw b Inverarity	37
G. N. Yallop b Parkinson	19	– c Winter b Dolman	9
J. K. Moss c Parkinson b Hookes	5	– c Inverarity b Dolman	0
B. C. Green b Inverarity	39	– not out	63
R. J. Bright b Inverarity	34	– b Parkinson	26
†I. L. Maddocks c Winter b Sleep	6	– not out	16
I. W. Callen c Hookes b Inverarity	0		
M. G. Hughes not out	1		
J. D. Higgs lbw b Sleep	0		
B 2, l-b 12, w 1	15	B 2, l-b 4, w 1, n-b 5	12
1/8 2/11 3/44 4/54 5/77 6/147 7/150 8/154 9/158	160	1/36 2/104 3/122 4/128 5/153 6/212	(6 wkts) 252

Bowling: *First Innings*—Parkinson 12–4–20–3; Winter 12–2–28–0; Hookes 13–5–22–1; Vincent 5–1–8–0; Dolman 14–3–38–0; Inverarity 16–9–15–3; Sleep 9–3–14–2. *Second Innings*—Parkinson 21–4–66–2; Winter 14–5–26–0; Hookes 7–5–5–0; Dolman 24–8–53–2; Inverarity 33–12–45–1; Sleep 16–4–44–1; Phillips 1–0–1–0.

Umpires: B. Guy and R. Isherwood.

TASMANIA v NEW SOUTH WALES

At Hobart, January 15, 16, 17, 18. New South Wales won by 63 runs. New South Wales 12 pts, Tasmania 4 pts. In a match of fluctuating fortunes, each side appeared more than once to have the game won. At 219 for no wicket, in almost even time, New South Wales seemed set for a huge total. Davis was back to his best form, but with the remaining batsmen unable to cope with the pace of Stephenson and Clough, the last nine wickets fell for the addition of just 62 runs. Tasmania were rescued from a bad start by Davison, Woolley and Saunders, whose batting continued to belie his low position in the order. Their first-innings lead of 64 was far more than seemed likely at 134 for six. When New South Wales batted again, although most batsmen got a start, only the reliable Beard passed 50 and Tasmania, needing to score 199 to win, had hopes of victory. However, they were shattered by Pascoe, whose career-best eight for 41 saw his restoration to the Test side.

New South Wales

I. C. Davis c Mancell b Clough	133	– c and b Stephenson	6
T. M. Chappell c Jeffery b Stephenson	81	– lbw b Stephenson	12
D. M. Wellham c Woolley b Clough	1	– st Woolley b Mancell	25
S. B. Smith c Woolley b Clough	7	– c Robinson b Mancell	46
P. M. Toohey c Beven b Clough	11	– c Stephenson b Mancell	20
D. A. H. Johnston run out	13	– b Clough	14
G. R. Beard lbw b Mancell	0	– lbw b Allanby	67
*†S. J. Rixon c Davison b Stephenson	5	– lbw b Clough	39
L. S. Pascoe b Stephenson	1	– not out	10
R. G. Holland lbw b Stephenson	1	– c Robinson b Stephenson	5
A. J. Skilbeck not out	6	– run out	2
B 7, l-b 11, n-b 4	22	B 10, l-b 2, n-b 4	16
1/219 2/227 3/227 4/247 5/254 6/254 7/267 8/270 9/271	281	1/15 2/28 3/74 4/114 5/115 6/133 7/234 8/242 9/253	262

Bowling: *First Innings*—Stephenson 17.2–6–51–4; Clough 23–9–57–4; Allanby 12–0–50–0; Saunders 14–5–42–0; Beven 4–1–15–0; Mancell 13–3–31–1; Jeffery 5–1–13–0. *Second Innings*—Stephenson 25–2–78–3; Clough 21–5–42–2; Allanby 11–5–18–1; Saunders 6–0–18–0; Beven 3–1–8–0; Mancell 23–4–66–3; Jeffery 3–1–9–0; Robinson 2–0–7–0.

Tasmania

D. B. Robinson b Skilbeck	1	– lbw b Pascoe	0
I. R. Beven lbw b Chappell	15	– lbw b Pascoe	5
P. M. Clough b Pascoe	11	– lbw b Pascoe	2
R. F. Jeffery b Pascoe	31	– lbw b Skilbeck	9
D. C. Boon run out	12	– not out	63
*B. F. Davison c Chappell b Beard	48	– c Rixon b Pascoe	9
†R. D. Woolley c Johnston b Skilbeck	83	– b Holland	26
N. J. Allanby b Holland	26	– c Wellham b Pascoe	0
S. L. Saunders c Johnston b Skilbeck	84	– b Pascoe	0
P. J. Mancell c Toohey b Skilbeck	16	– b Pascoe	14
F. D. Stephenson not out	1	– c Holland b Pascoe	0
B 1, l-b 10, n-b 6	17	B 1, l-b 4, w 1, n-b 1	7
1/1 2/26 3/42 4/63 5/108 6/134 7/199 8/248 9/344	345	1/0 2/13 3/15 4/36 5/79 6/80 7/80 8/127 9/127	135

Bowling: *First Innings*—Pascoe 38–7–111–2; Skilbeck 27–3–94–4; Beard 16–8–25–1; Holland 33–14–63–1; Chappell 10–1–35–1; Toohey 1–1–0–0. *Second Innings*—Pascoe 22.1–10–41–8; Skilbeck 17–3–54–1; Beard 15–4–19–0; Holland 12–6–14–1.

Umpires: S. Randell and J. Stevens.

QUEENSLAND v NEW SOUTH WALES

At Brisbane, January 29, 30, 31, February 1. New South Wales won by eight wickets. New South Wales 16 pts. After a reasonable start on a rain-affected first day, the later Queensland batsmen fell to Lawson, 147 for three becoming 183 all out. New South Wales quickly showed that this would be an inadequate total; first Davis, after surviving a chance to second slip when 4, made a fine century and then Toohey thrashed some dispirited bowling to even greater effect. Queensland began their second innings well, but too much depended on Wessels, whose 106 was made out of only 148, and with his departure the middle order collapsed to Lawson, leaving Hohns to try to save the day. He almost succeeded, but the loss of three quick wickets to Beard finally left New South Wales with sufficient time to score the 70 they needed to give them their first victory in Brisbane since 1970.

Queensland

K. C. Wessels c McCosker b Skilbeck	8	– c Davis b Chappell	106
R. B. Kerr st Rixon b Holland	37	– c McCosker b Lawson	26
R. N. Traves c Rixon b Gordon	28	– lbw b Lawson	4
G. M. Ritchie c Davis b Gordon	52	– c Holland b Lawson	8
T. V. Hohns c Holland b Lawson	23	– b Beard	89
A. B. Henschell c Rixon b Beard	0	– c McCosker b Gordon	38
H. K. De Jong c Toohey b Lawson	14	– b Holland	19
†R. B. Phillips c Davis b Lawson	0	– c Davis b Skilbeck	22
*G. Dymock c Rixon b Lawson	10	– c Lawson b Beard	0
J. N. Maguire c Gordon b Holland	4	– b Beard	4
C. G. Rackemann not out	0	– not out	0
B 1, l-b 3, w 2, n-b 1	7	B 5, l-b 7, n-b 6	18
1/19 2/79 3/79 4/147 5/152 6/156 7/163 8/174 9/183	183	1/138 2/142 3/148 4/154 5/178 6/270 7/306 8/317 9/333	334

Bowling: *First Innings*—Lawson 23.1–8–37–4; Skilbeck 12–2–33–1; Gordon 16–3–49–2; Beard 10–4–22–1; Holland 18–6–35–2. *Second Innings*—Lawson 28–5–83–3; Skilbeck 15–3–46–1; Gordon 15–5–34–1; Beard 25.1–7–56–3; Holland 44–15–93–1; Chappell 2–1–4–1.

New South Wales

*R. B. McCosker c Rackemann b Maguire	20	– run out	6
I. C. Davis c Phillips b Maguire	113	– c Wessels b Dymock	11
T. M. Chappell c Phillips b Maguire	26	– not out	22
S. B. Smith c Phillips b De Jong	50		
P. M. Toohey c De Jong b Hohns	137	– not out	26
G. R. Beard lbw b Maguire	40		
†S. J. Rixon not out	18		
G. F. Lawson not out	14		
B 1, l-b 3, w 1, n-b 25	30	L-b 7	7
1/67 2/171 3/176 4/313 5/403 6/412 (6 wkts dec.)	448	1/11 2/41 (2 wkts)	72

E. Gordon, A. J. Skilbeck and R. G. Holland did not bat.

Bowling: *First Innings*—Maguire 29–6–86–4; Dymock 26–7–59–0; De Jong 13–1–62–1; Rackemann 13–3–55–0; Hohns 30–1–110–1; Henschell 13–1–45–0; Wessels 1–0–1–0. *Second Innings*—Maguire 8–0–25–0; Dymock 8–2–26–1; De Jong 0.3–0–14–0.

Umpires: J. T. C. Taylor and C. D. Timmins.

WESTERN AUSTRALIA v VICTORIA

At Perth, January 29, 30, 31, February 1. Drawn. Victoria 4 pts. Western Australia were again without their Test players and, with Victoria depleted by injury and retirement, neither team bore much resemblance to that with which they had started the season. Western Australia's first innings began inauspiciously, but recovered through Serjeant and, later, Hogan and Boyd, whose 102 in even time was a record ninth-wicket partnership for their state. In contrast, the Victorian innings was a dour affair; Green made 82 in almost four hours and they owed their narrow first-innings lead to a last-wicket partnership of 31 between Callen and Higgs. After Western Australia had gone for runs in their second innings, Victoria were left with 210 minutes in which to score 255 runs but, apart from the openers, they made no effort for victory.

Western Australia

G. D. Porter c Sacristani b Callen	13	– c Green b Callen	11
G. Shipperd c Yallop b Hughes	43	– c Green b Bright	69
G. R. Marsh c and b Callen	1	– lbw b Callen	67
R. S. Langer c Watts b Bright	3	– c Yallop b Higgs	21
*C. S. Serjeant run out	80	– c Bright b Higgs	23
K. H. MacLeay c Sacristani b Hughes	3	– b Bright	27
A. L. Mann c Green b Callen	17	– c Jones b Higgs	24
†T. J. Zoehrer c Watts b Bright	13	– b Higgs	2
T. G. Hogan c Bright b Callen	70	– c Green b Higgs	3
D. L. Boyd c Callen b Bright	42	– st Sacristani b Bright	6
W. M. Clark not out	0	– not out	1
B 5, l-b 9, w 1, n-b 7	22	B 1, l-b 3, n-b 5	9
1/30 2/32 3/48 4/86 5/94 6/138 7/149 8/201 9/303	307	1/18 2/156 3/156 4/199 5/206 6/208 7/245 8/258 9/261	263

Bowling: *First Innings*—Callen 30–5–88–4; Hughes 25–5–60–2; Bright 28.2–8–59–3; Higgs 23–4–68–0; Jones 3–1–10–0. *Second Innings*—Callen 18–3–52–2; Hughes 11–2–41–0; Bright 25–3–92–3; Higgs 18.2–4–68–5; Green 2–1–1–0.

Victoria

J. M. Wiener c Serjeant b MacLeay	42	c Hogan b Clark	33
G. M. Watts c Mann b Clark	6	c Porter b Hogan	20
*W. J. Scholes b Boyd	0	c Serjeant b Hogan	25
G. N. Yallop c and b Hogan	55	c and b Hogan	7
D. M. Jones c Zoehrer b MacLeay	39	c Shipperd b Clark	6
B. C. Green b Hogan	82	not out	15
R. J. Bright run out	30	lbw b Mann	6
†P. G. Sacristani c Zoehrer b Hogan	3	not out	3
M. G. Hughes st Zoehrer b Mann	4		
I. W. Callen c MacLeay b Mann	34		
J. D. Higgs not out	10		
B 2, l-b 1, n-b 8	11	B 1, l-b 1, n-b 3	5
1/12 2/13 3/106 4/106 5/241 6/262 7/264 8/269 9/285	316	1/48 2/54 3/63 4/75 5/103 6/112	(6 wkts) 120

Bowling: *First Innings*—Boyd 18–6–37–1; Clark 19–6–50–1; MacLeay 16–3–40–2; Porter 13–6–23–0; Hogan 45–12–92–3; Mann 29.4–12–63–2; Langer 1–1–0–0. *Second Innings*—Boyd 7–1–30–0; Clark 11–1–26–2; MacLeay 4–0–5–0; Hogan 27–14–33–3; Mann 11–5–15–1; Langer 3–2–2–0; Serjeant 1–0–4–0.

Umpires: P. McConnell and A. Claydon.

NEW SOUTH WALES v WESTERN AUSTRALIA

At Sydney, February 11, 12, 13, 14. Drawn. New South Wales 4 pts. Intent on denying New South Wales outright victory, Western Australia batted for more than ten hours in a first innings which was dominated by a record fourth-wicket partnership of 260 between Geoff Marsh and Serjeant. Marsh, who had taken a long time to fulfil his obvious promise, batted for nine hours in an innings which included one 6 and 21 4s, while Serjeant took five and a half hours over 106. Once the partnership was broken, the last seven wickets added only another 55 runs. What by then had become virtually a one-innings match was eventually settled in New South Wales' favour after McCosker had scored his fourth Shield century of the season.

Western Australia

R. R. McFarlane c Rixon b Lawson	22	c Toohey b Holland	10
G. R. Marsh c and b Holland	176	b Holland	20
G. Shipperd b Holland	21	not out	16
R. S. Langer b Holland	31	not out	2
*C. S. Serjeant c Smith b Beard	106		
A. L. Mann lbw b Holland	4		
K. H. MacLeay run out	11		
T. G. Hogan b Beard	2		
†T. J. Zoehrer c Smith b Beard	19		
M. F. Malone not out	17		
W. M. Clark lbw b Lawson	0		
B 10, l-b 9, w 1, n-b 10	30	L-b 1, n-b 7	8
1/24 2/49 3/124 4/384 5/384 6/393 7/400 8/401 9/435	439	1/27 2/46	(2 wkts) 56

Bowling: *First Innings*—Lawson 23.4–6–67–2; Skilbeck 22–8–56–0; Holland 68–26–124–4; Gordon 14–1–47–0; Beard 54–19–109–3; Chappell 5–3–6–0. *Second Innings*—Skilbeck 8–4–13–0; Holland 12–8–6–2; Gordon 10–3–28–0; Smith 1–0–1–0.

New South Wales

*R. B. McCosker c McFarlane b Hogan	130
I. C. Davis c Serjeant b MacLeay	72
T. M. Chappell b Hogan	89
S. B. Smith c Shipperd b Mann	60
P. M. Toohey c McFarlane b Langer	1
G. R. Beard c and b Hogan	17
†S. J. Rixon c McFarlane b Hogan	37
G. F. Lawson c Serjeant b Mann	25
E. Gordon not out	30
A. J. Skilbeck b Clark	34
R. G. Holland not out	12
B 3, l-b 4, n-b 9	16
1/145 2/274 3/343 4/348 5/377 6/400 7/435 8/447 9/504 (9 wkts dec.)	523

Bowling: Clark 24–3–64–1; Malone 39–8–76–0; Hogan 60–15–154–4; Mann 52–10–139–2; MacLeay 17–2–46–1; Langer 8–0–28–1.

Umpires: M. Jay and A. Marshall.

VICTORIA v QUEENSLAND

At Geelong, February 12, 13, 14, 15. Drawn. Victoria 4 pts. On the first day, Victoria's opening bowlers gave their side an advantage which would have been greater still had Phillips not made an unbeaten century in four hours. In reply, Wiener and Scholes added 209 in only three hours for Victoria's second wicket, and later, while Yallop struggled to find his touch, Green helped to maintain the momentum with some powerful driving. A first-innings lead of 254 gave Victoria a good chance of recording their first outright win for the season, but their hopes were thwarted by Wessels who, although dropped twice, batted splendidly for five and a half hours. He and Hohns were instrumental in Victoria being left insufficient time in which to make the 87 they needed to win.

Queensland

K. C. Wessels c Yallop b Hughes	2	b Callen	173
R. B. Kerr c Sacristani b Graf	24	lbw b Graf	9
R. N. Traves c Sacristani b Callen	4	lbw b Graf	27
G. M. Ritchie c Callen b Hughes	40	c Wiener b Higgs	21
T. V. Hohns c Sacristani b Hughes	0	not out	48
A. B. Henschell c Sacristani b Callen	33	c Callen b Higgs	16
†R. B. Phillips not out	111	b Callen	12
I. D. C. Kelly b Green	31	c Wiener b Hughes	15
*G. Dymock lbw b Hughes	1	b Hughes	0
J. N. Maguire lbw b Green	1	lbw b Hughes	5
G. W. Brabon b Callen	6	lbw b Callen	0
B 4, l-b 17, w 4, n-b 4	29	B 4, l-b 5, n-b 5	14
1/3 2/9 3/72 4/80 5/83 6/145 7/228 8/229 9/236	282	1/26 2/168 3/211 4/249 5/253 6/288 7/318 8/318 9/333	340

Bowling: *First Innings*—Callen 21.5–5–43–3; Hughes 24–7–69–4; Graf 22–4–54–1; Higgs 20–3–71–0; Green 9–3–16–2. *Second Innings*—Callen 28–4–74–3; Hughes 20–2–73–2; Graf 25–5–68–3; Higgs 41–8–107–2; Green 2–1–4–0.

Victoria

G. M. Watts c Phillips b Brabon	42	– not out	11
J. M. Wiener c Phillips b Dymock	165	– b Dymock	8
*W. J. Scholes c Wessels b Brabon	94	– not out	11
G. N. Yallop not out	111	– b Maguire	20
B. C. Green c Phillips b Maguire	64	– b Maguire	0
P. J. Davies c Phillips b Maguire	9		
S. F. Graf c Traves b Brabon	12		
†P. G. Sacristani c Maguire b Brabon	12		
I. W. Callen not out	2		
L-b 13, n-b 12	25	B 1, l-b 6	7
1/68 2/277 3/341 4/459 5/481 6/510 7/532 (7 wkts dec.)	536	1/26 2/34 3/34 (3 wkts)	57

M. G. Hughes and J. D. Higgs did not bat.

Bowling: *First Innings*—Maguire 34–5–102–2; Dymock 32–9–57–1; Brabon 23–2–106–4; Kelly 26–3–77–0; Hohns 32–2–130–0; Henschell 10–0–39–0. *Second Innings*—Maguire 4–0–21–2; Dymock 4–0–29–1.

Umpires: B. Guy and A. Nicosia.

TASMANIA v SOUTH AUSTRALIA

At Launceston, February 12, 13, 14, 15. South Australia won by five wickets. South Australia 16 pts. Tasmania's first innings was notable for Davison's return to something like his punishing form of the previous season – 72 of his 86 runs came in boundaries and the last 30 in 26 minutes after lunch – as well as for a promising début by Reid. Darling and Phillips gave South Australia an excellent start before Crowe, Sleep and Winter each contributed half-centuries towards a first-innings lead of 164. Batting a second time, Tasmania made a disastrous start and, with Vincent taking three quick wickets, an innings defeat seemed probable. This was averted by the efforts of the consistent Woolley and by Saunders, who finished the game in a blaze of glory, following another impressive innings with a return of four for 29 as South Australia made hard work of reaching their target.

Tasmania

R. F. Jeffery c Sleep b Parkinson	9	– c Wright b Vincent	11
I. R. Beven c Phillips b Vincent	0	– c Darling b Winter	5
D. C. Boon b Sleep	25	– c Wright b Vincent	0
*B. F. Davison b Parkinson	88	– c Harris b Vincent	9
†R. D. Woolley c Winter b Dolman	53	– b Parkinson	83
S. Reid not out	65	– c Wright b Vincent	21
P. J. Mancell c Wright b Sleep	2	– lbw b Parkinson	38
S. L. Saunders lbw b Sleep	0	– c Vincent b Sleep	70
F. D. Stephenson c Parkinson b Vincent	33	– b Parkinson	0
G. J. Wilson b Dolman	7	– c Wright b Parkinson	5
M. F. Leedham c Crowe b Sleep	3	– not out	4
B 7, l-b 3, w 2, n-b 3	15	B 6, l-b 8, w 5	19
1/3 2/18 3/127 4/157 5/201 6/205 7/205 8/263 9/289	298	1/16 2/16 3/25 4/37 5/118 6/143 7/254 8/255 9/260	265

Bowling: *First Innings*—Parkinson 15–1–59–2; Vincent 17–1–64–2; Winter 13–3–44–0; Dolman 22–6–56–2; Sleep 17.4–4–60–4. *Second Innings*—Parkinson 17.3–7–50–4; Vincent 22–5–64–4; Winter 7–5–9–1; Dolman 12–2–60–0; Sleep 33–14–60–1; Crowe 1–0–3–0.

South Australia

W. M. Darling c Davison b Stephenson	88	– not out	52
W. B. Phillips b Beven	67	– b Mancell	16
J. J. Crowe c Davison b Stephenson	79	– b Saunders	3
*D. W. Hookes c Woolley b Wilson	26	– b Saunders	9
P. R. Sleep c Woolley b Stephenson	66	– b Saunders	0
K. P. Harris c Woolley b Stephenson	0	– c Boon b Saunders	13
†K. J. Wright lbw b Stephenson	22	– not out	6
B. A. Vincent c Woolley b Saunders	23		
G. J. Winter not out	50		
S. D. H. Parkinson c Reid b Beven	4		
M. C. Dolman run out	6		
B 5, l-b 19, n-b 7	31	B 2, n-b 1	3
1/163 2/167 3/208 4/299 5/299 6/359 7/380 8/399 9/445	462	1/32 2/61 3/67 4/81 5/81	(5 wkts) 102

Bowling: *First Innings*—Stephenson 32–9–97–5; Wilson 21–3–68–1; Mancell 21–5–59–0; Saunders 15–2–68–1; Leedham 12–1–50–0; Beven 22–5–61–2; Reid 5–0–20–0; Jeffery 1–0–8–0. *Second Innings*—Stephenson 5–0–30–0; Wilson 2–0–17–0; Mancell 11.2–4–23–1; Saunders 9–0–29–4.

Umpires: M. Hull and S. Randell.

SOUTH AUSTRALIA v WESTERN AUSTRALIA

At Adelaide, February 19, 20, 21, 22. South Australia won by nine wickets. South Australia 16 pts. South Australia dominated the match from start to finish. A large first-innings total was the foundation for victory and their bowlers pressed home the advantage, the spinners being effective in Western Australia's first innings and medium-pacer Sincock, a late replacement for the injured Vincent, doing well in the second. For South Australia, Darling played his best Shield innings of the season, Inverarity enacted his customary sheet-anchor role, Hookes batted with the aggression of old, and Wright, with assistance from Winter, lifted the total past 500. By now a draw was the best Western Australia could hope for, but after being 91 for five in their first innings, they never looked quite like achieving it. Having followed on 262 behind, they struggled stubbornly but unavailingly in their second innings. With an undefeated century, seven catches and a stumping, Wright had an outstanding game for South Australia.

South Australia

W. M. Darling lbw b Hogan	121	– not out	8
W. B. Phillips b Malone	20	– c Zoehrer b Boyd	7
J. J. Crowe c Serjeant b Malone	0	– not out	4
R. J. Inverarity lbw b Boyd	75		
*D. W. Hookes c Shipperd b Malone	97		
P. R. Sleep c Shipperd b Boyd	5		
†K. J. Wright not out	104		
G. J. Winter c Serjeant b Malone	64		
A. T. Sincock not out	6		
B 6, l-b 5, w 2, n-b 2	15		
1/62 2/92 3/175 4/307 5/326 6/326 7/489 (7 wkts dec.)	507	1/15	(1 wkt) 19

M. C. Dolman and S. D. H. Parkinson did not bat.

Bowling: *First Innings*—Boyd 23–1–125–2; Malone 42–5–134–4; MacLeay 13–4–37–0; Hogan 46–10–121–1; Mann 26–4–73–0; Langer 1–0–2–0. *Second Innings*—Boyd 2–0–9–1; Malone 1–0–10–0.

Western Australia

R. R. McFarlane lbw b Inverarity	6	– b Inverarity	13
G. R. Marsh c Wright b Inverarity	20	– lbw b Sincock	59
G. Shipperd b Dolman	1	– c Wright b Sincock	30
R. S. Langer c Wright b Sleep	27	– b Dolman	3
*C. S. Serjeant lbw b Sleep	23	– c Wright b Sincock	18
K. H. MacLeay c Inverarity b Parkinson	24	– lbw b Sleep	24
†T. J. Zoehrer c Wright b Parkinson	34	– b Inverarity	46
A. L. Mann b Hookes	40	– c Wright b Winter	17
T. G. Hogan not out	19	– c Wright b Sincock	49
D. L. Boyd st Wright b Sleep	17	– not out	0
M. F. Malone c Crowe b Inverarity	6	– lbw b Sincock	0
B 8, l-b 12, w 5, n-b 3	28	B 3, l-b 9, w 1, n-b 8	21
1/29 2/36 3/36 4/80 5/91 6/149 7/168 8/200 9/236	245	1/36 2/108 3/118 4/138 5/139 6/173 7/198 8/277 9/280	280

Bowling: *First Innings*—Parkinson 13–6–24–2; Winter 9–5–13–0; Sincock 7–1–21–0; Hookes 4–0–13–1; Inverarity 35.4–15–67–3; Sleep 22–2–33–3; Dolman 20–7–46–1. *Second Innings*—Parkinson 5–4–4–0; Winter 15–8–26–1; Sincock 25.4–8–56–5; Hookes 7–1–15–0; Inverarity 33–9–63–2; Sleep 28–4–59–1; Dolman 18–8–36–1.

Umpires: A. R. Crafter and P. M. Cronin.

TASMANIA v QUEENSLAND

At Devonport, February 19, 20, 21, 22. Drawn. Queensland 4pts. The loss of most of the second day through bad weather turned the match into a battle for first-innings points. Tasmania's only innings was a mixture of collapse and recovery, Boon and Woolley improving a bad start with a partnership of 137 for the fifth wicket. Then, following a second collapse, the big West Indian, Stephenson, blazed his way to within 10 runs of a maiden century. For Queensland, Wessels and Ritchie made sure of the first-innings lead with a record third-wicket partnership of 304, which beat the previous best for Queensland – 296 by Burge and MacKay against South Australia in Adelaide in 1961. Wessels's marathon innings lasted eight and a half hours and included eighteen boundaries.

Tasmania

R. F. Jeffery b Dymock	0
D. A. Smith c Henschell b Dymock	12
P. J. Mancell b De Jong	27
D. C. Boon lbw b Dymock	88
*B. F. Davison b Maguire	14
†R. D. Woolley run out	116
S. Reid c Wessels b Brabon	9
S. L. Saunders b Maguire	4
E. Benjamin c Ritchie b Hohns	6
F. D. Stephenson c and b Hohns	90
G. J. Wilson not out	19
B 1, l-b 8, n-b 11	20
1/2 2/25 3/47 4/71 5/208 6/279 7/279 8/283 9/323	405

Bowling: Dymock 43–13–88–3; Maguire 42–9–105–2; De Jong 9–1–31–1; Brabon 24–5–68–1; Kelly 6–2–16–0; Hohns 28.3–4–77–2; Henschell 1–1–0–0.

Queensland

K. C. Wessels b Stephenson	220
R. B. Kerr b Stephenson	29
H. K. De Jong c Boon b Stephenson	0
G. M. Ritchie not out	136
A. B. Henschell lbw b Stephenson	1
T. V. Hohns not out	2
B 2, l-b 6, w 2, n-b 13	23
1/91 2/91 3/395 4/397	(4 wkts) 411

†R. B. Phillips, I. D. C. Kelly, *G. Dymock, G. W. Brabon and J. N. Maguire did not bat.

Bowling: Stephenson 31–7–58–4; Wilson 21–6–51–0; Mancell 27–7–63–0; Saunders 29–5–93–0; Benjamin 23–0–81–0; Jeffery 6–0–18–0; Smith 1–0–6–0; Boon 3–0–18–0.

Umpires: R. Marshall and S. Randell.

VICTORIA v NEW SOUTH WALES

At St Kilda, Melbourne, February 19, 20, 21, 22. New South Wales won by eight wickets. New South Wales 16 pts. With New South Wales needing to take maximum points to have a chance of winning the Shield, the achievements of their recognised batsmen, and also Victoria's, were mostly undistinguished. Victoria started badly and had Graf to thank for their recovery from 75 for seven. In reply, New South Wales were held together by Rixon, who had gone in as night-watchman on the first evening and stayed for more than six and a half hours to compile a patient 124. In the second Victorian innings, Yallop seemed back to his most fluent form, until a ball from Whitney broke a bone in his right wrist. Thereafter there was brief resistance from Green, Davies and Graf, but the innings was brought to an abrupt conclusion by Chappell, who followed his bowling success with a brisk partnership with Smith which carried his side to an easy win.

Victoria

J. M. Wiener c Toohey b Chappell	26	– c Rixon b Whitney	1
G. M. Watts c McCosker b Whitney	10	– c Toohey b Whitney	20
*W. J. Scholes c Chappell b Lawson	6	– c Holland b Skilbeck	22
G. N. Yallop c McCosker b Lawson	14	– c Chappell b Lawson	54
B. C. Green b Lawson	0	– st Rixon b Holland	37
P. J. Davies run out	0	– c McCosker b Chappell	33
S. F. Graf c and b Whitney	55	– c Beard b Holland	39
†P. G. Sacristani c Rixon b Skilbeck	2	– lbw b Chappell	0
I. W. Callen b Lawson	26	– lbw b Chappell	0
M. G. Hughes c Chappell b Holland	17	– c Davis b Chappell	1
J. D. Higgs not out	0	– not out	1
W 2, n-b 3	5	B 6, l-b 6, w 6, n-b 9	27
1/25 2/39 3/49 4/49 5/49 6/60 7/75 8/132 9/161	161	1/5 2/40 3/68 4/114 5/175 6/211 7/211 8/215 9/235	235

Bowling: *First Innings*—Lawson 21–5–63–4; Skilbeck 12–3–36–1; Whitney 20.1–6–33–2; Chappell 3–1–10–1; Holland 15–10–13–1; Beard 2–1–1–0. *Second Innings*—Lawson 22–4–62–1; Skilbeck 6–2–19–1; Whitney 18–3–55–2; Chappell 8–5–12–4; Holland 21.4–9–43–2; Beard 12–6–17–0.

New South Wales

*R. B. McCosker c Sacristani b Callen	5	– lbw b Callen	0
I. C. Davis lbw b Hughes	16	– c Higgs b Hughes	16
†S. J. Rixon lbw b Hughes	124		
T. M. Chappell c Yallop b Callen	38	– not out	47
S. B. Smith lbw Hughes	17	– not out	30
P. M. Toohey b Hughes	27		
G. R. Beard run out	19		
G. F. Lawson c Scholes b Graf	2		
A. J. Skilbeck not out	33		
B 1, l-b 10, w 2, n-b 11	24		
1/17 2/39 3/95 4/139 5/184 6/230 7/239 8/305 (8 wkts dec.)	305	1/11 2/19 (2 wkts)	93

R. G. Holland and M. R. Whitney did not bat.

Bowling: *First Innings*—Callen 31–4–120–2; Hughes 30.4–6–71–4; Higgs 7–1–24–0; Green 2–2–0–0; Graf 27–5–66–1. *Second Innings*—Callen 4–0–25–1; Hughes 3–0–19–1; Higgs 6–0–22–0; Green 6–0–27–0.

Umpires: R. A. French and R. V. Whitehead.

WESTERN AUSTRALIA v QUEENSLAND

At Perth, February 26, 27, 28, March 1. Drawn. Western Australia 4 pts. Had the states had their Test players available for a majority of Shield games, this could have been the climax of the season. Instead, it did little more than provide an opportunity to blood promising younger players. In Western Australia's first innings Marsh and Clements provided a good start, but the later batsmen failed rather tediously to make the most of their chances. When Queensland batted Wessels reached 1,000 runs for the Shield season, his 62 containing some exhilarating strokeplay. In contrast, Kerr played a painstaking knock: when last out for 158, he had batted for almost seven hours. The tempo increased when Western Australia batted a second time, Marsh and Clements reaching 171 in two hours and Shipperd, who had been extremely slow in the first innings, showing that he, too, was capable of aggressive cricket by making 70 in only 97 minutes. To score 324 to win in 274 minutes Queensland needed a dashing contribution from Wessels, but for once he failed. So the game ended in an unexciting draw, though not before Kerr had recorded his second hundred of the match.

Western Australia

G. R. Marsh run out	51	– c Phillips b Dymock	120
S. Clements c Traves b Hohns	73	– c Traves b Brabon	86
G. Shipperd lbw b Dymock	48	– not out	70
R. S. Langer c Broad b Hohns	20	– b Dymock	3
*C. S. Serjeant b Dymock	3	– not out	11
K. H. MacLeay c Kerr b Dymock	19		
G. A. Millar c Kelly b Dymock	20		
†T. J. Zoehrer b Brabon	31		
T. G. Hogan c Kerr b Maguire	12		
D. L. Boyd not out	43		
M. F. Malone run out	11		
B 3, l-b 13, n-b 6	22	B 1, l-b 2, w 1, n-b 7	11
1/127 2/127 3/159 4/163 5/224 6/229 7/260 8/294 9/308	353	1/171 2/263 3/283 (3 wkts dec.)	301

Bowling: *First Innings*—Maguire 33–11–55–1; Dymock 33–9–86–3; Brabon 14.3–0–57–2; Broad 4–2–14–0; Hohns 40–16–81–2; Kelly 19–8–38–0. *Second Innings*—Maguire 14–4–55–0; Dymock 8.2–0–27–2; Brabon 16–1–72–1; Broad 4–0–32–0; Hohns 4–1–36–0; Kelly 8–0–56–0; Wessels 2–0–8–0; Henschell 1–0–4–0.

Queensland

K. C. Wessels c Malone b MacLeay	62	– c Shipperd b Malone	12
R. B. Kerr b Hogan	158	– run out	101
W. R. Broad b MacLeay	22	– c Zoehrer b Boyd	19
R. N. Traves st Zoehrer b Hogan	6	– c Serjeant b MacLeay	29
T. V. Hohns c Clements b Hogan	4	– c Serjeant b MacLeay	10
A. B. Henschell b Hogan	15	– c Langer b Hogan	76
†R. B. Phillips c Zoehrer b Boyd	40	– not out	12
I. D. C. Kelly c Zoehrer b Boyd	1	– run out	3
*G. Dymock c Hogan b Malone	10	– not out	0
J. N. Maguire c Zoehrer b Malone	2		
G. W. Brabon not out	1		
L-b 7, w 1, n-b 2	10	B 2, l-b 10, w 1, n-b 1	14
1/101 2/147 3/169 4/186 5/205 6/288 7/300 8/323 9/327	331	1/15 2/36 3/100 4/114 5/259 6/260 7/267 (7 wkts)	276

Bowling: *First Innings*—Boyd 21–4–56–2; Millar 12–2–40–0; Malone 21–2–72–2; Hogan 28.2–4–103–4; MacLeay 23–7–50–2. *Second Innings*—Boyd 9–1–41–1; Millar 7–1–37–0; Malone 20–3–70–1; Hogan 23–3–68–1; MacLeay 19–5–46–2.

Umpires: P. McConnell and D. G. Weser.

SOUTH AUSTRALIA v VICTORIA

At Adelaide, February 26, 27, 28, March 1. South Australia won by nine wickets. South Australia 16 pts. To win the Sheffield Shield, South Australia needed maximum points, which they eventually achieved in convincing and exciting fashion. Early on, it seemed that Victoria might provide unexpectedly stern opposition. Wiener played a sound innings and, after only four hours, with the score at 230 for one, a large total seemed likely. Nine wickets then fell for only 67 runs. When South Australia batted, they wasted no time in chasing runs, Crowe and Hookes being particularly severe on the Victorian bowlers, of whom only Callen looked dangerous. South Australia declared 126 ahead with a day and a half left for play, and by the end of the third day, with Victoria 145 for two, they seemed to have barely a half-chance of victory. However, on the final morning, the recognised Victorian batsmen were quickly dismissed. Only wicket-keeper Sacristani and Callen offered serious resistance and South Australia eventually had 44 overs in which to score 161 runs. Some fine batting by Darling, Phillips and Crowe saw them home with nine overs to spare.

Victoria

J. M. Wiener run out	116	– lbw b Inverarity	42
G. M. Watts c Crowe b Inverarity	35	– c Sleep b Parkinson	4
*W. J. Scholes b Parkinson	64	– c Hookes b Sleep	71
P. J. Davies b Sincock	32	– c Hookes b Sleep	57
D. M. Jones b Parkinson	0	– lbw b Inverarity	8
B. C. Green c Crowe b Inverarity	12	– run out	6
S. F. Graf lbw b Sincock	8	– c Parkinson b Inverarity	8
†P. G. Sacristani c Wright b Sincock	0	– c Hookes b Vincent	36
I. W. Callen not out	6	– c Crowe b Vincent	34
M. G. Hughes c Wright b Sincock	0	– not out	1
J. D. Higgs c Wright b Hookes	0	– c Wright b Sleep	6
B 5, l-b 8, w 2, n-b 9	24	B 4, l-b 3, w 1, n-b 5	13
1/95 2/230 3/237 4/237 5/261 6/288 7/289 8/290 9/290	297	1/13 2/74 3/168 4/193 5/193 6/207 7/209 8/273 9/280	286

Bowling: *First Innings*—Parkinson 17–7–44–2; Vincent 8–2–26–0; Hookes 9.3–5–15–1; Inverarity 25–5–38–2; Sincock 22–3–85–4; Sleep 12–0–35–0; Dolman 14–5–30–0. *Second Innings*—Parkinson 12–2–26–1; Vincent 16–5–41–2; Inverarity 37–13–69–3; Sincock 17–4–82–0; Sleep 21.5–8–43–3; Dolman 6–2–12–0.

South Australia

W. M. Darling c Jones b Callen	36	– c Scholes b Higgs	47
W. B. Phillips b Callen	40	– not out	84
J. J. Crowe lbw b Callen	126	– not out	25
R. J. Inverarity b Hughes	33		
*D. W. Hookes b Graf	63		
P. R. Sleep run out	53		
†K. J. Wright b Hughes	18		
B. A. Vincent c Sacristani b Callen	23		
A. T. Sincock not out	11		
S. D. H. Parkinson not out	9		
B 4, l-b 4, n-b 3	11	L-b 3, n-b 2	5
1/75 2/78 3/141 4/269 5/326 6/354 7/403 8/403 (8 wkts dec.)	423	1/101 (1 wkt)	161

M. C. Dolman did not bat.

Bowling: *First Innings*—Callen 32–7–98–4; Hughes 31–6–97–2; Graf 25–2–108–1; Higgs 26–6–82–0; Green 6–1–27–0. *Second Innings*—Callen 8–0–32–0; Hughes 8–1–32–0; Graf 9–0–59–0; Higgs 9–0–29–1; Scholes 1–0–4–0.

Umpires: B. E. Martin and M. G. O'Connell.

SHEFFIELD SHIELD WINNERS

1892-93	Victoria	1928-29	New South Wales
1893-94	South Australia	1929-30	Victoria
1894-95	Victoria	1930-31	Victoria
1895-96	New South Wales	1931-32	New South Wales
1896-97	New South Wales	1932-33	New South Wales
1897-98	Victoria	1933-34	Victoria
1898-99	Victoria	1934-35	Victoria
1899-1900	New South Wales	1935-36	South Australia
1900-01	Victoria	1936-37	Victoria
1901-02	New South Wales	1937-38	New South Wales
1902-03	New South Wales	1938-39	South Australia
1903-04	New South Wales	1939-40	New South Wales
1904-05	New South Wales	1940-46	No competition
1905-06	New South Wales	1946-47	Victoria
1906-07	New South Wales	1947-48	Western Australia
1907-08	Victoria	1948-49	New South Wales
1908-09	New South Wales	1949-50	New South Wales
1909-10	South Australia	1950-51	Victoria
1910-11	New South Wales	1951-52	New South Wales
1911-12	New South Wales	1952-53	South Australia
1912-13	South Australia	1953-54	New South Wales
1913-14	New South Wales	1954-55	New South Wales
1914-15	Victoria	1955-56	New South Wales
1915-19	No competition	1956-57	New South Wales
1919-20	New South Wales	1957-58	New South Wales
1920-21	New South Wales	1958-59	New South Wales
1921-22	Victoria	1959-50	New South Wales
1922-23	New South Wales	1960-61	New South Wales
1923-24	Victoria	1961-62	New South Wales
1924-25	Victoria	1962-63	Victoria
1925-26	New South Wales	1963-64	South Australia
1926-27	South Australia	1964-65	New South Wales
1927-28	Victoria	1965-66	New South Wales

1966-67	Victoria	1974-75	Western Australia
1967-68	Western Australia	1975-76	South Australia
1968-69	South Australia	1976-77	Western Australia
1969-70	Victoria	1977-78	Western Australia
1970-71	South Australia	1978-79	Victoria
1971-72	Western Australia	1979-80	Victoria
1972-73	Western Australia	1980-81	Western Australia
1973-74	Victoria	1981-82	South Australia

New South Wales have won the Shield 36 times, Victoria 24, South Australia 12, Western Australia 8, Queensland 0, Tasmania 0.

†McDONALD'S CUP, 1981-82

At Brisbane, November 7. Queensland won by seven wickets. Tasmania 225 for seven (R. F. Jeffery 58, D. C. Boon 53, N. J. Allanby 31 not out); Queensland 229 for three (G. S. Chappell 92, A. R. Border 55 not out).

At Brisbane, November 8. Queensland won by six wickets. Western Australia 148 for eight (R. W. Marsh 48); Queensland 149 for four (R. B. Kerr 50, A. R. Border 31).

At Sydney, November 19. New South Wales won by 47 runs. New South Wales 260 for two (R. B. McCosker 111 not out, J. Dyson 78, I. C. Davis 32); Victoria 213 (J. M. Wiener 108 not out, G. R. Beard three for 49).

At Sydney, December 3. New South Wales won by 111 runs. New South Wales 310 for four (R. B. McCosker 164, J. Dyson 100, P. M. Toohey 30 not out); South Australia 199 (P. R. Sleep 90; T. M. Chappell three for 37).

At Adelaide, January 1. Victoria won by six wickets. South Australia 249 for five (P. R. Sleep 81, D. W. Hookes 56, R. J. Inverarity 54 not out, W. B. Phillips 33); Victoria 253 for four (J. M. Wiener 89, W. J. Scholes 62 not out, G. M. Watts 52).

At Perth, January 7. Western Australia won by 13 runs. Western Australia 215 for three (R. S. Langer 99 not out, G. Shipperd 86); Tasmania 202 for nine (B. F. Davison 41, D. C. Boon 31; D. L. Boyd four for 35).

Semi-Finals

At Brisbane, February 7. Queensland won by 21 runs. Queensland 238 for eight (W. R. Broad 59, A. R. Border 59, R. B. Kerr 37, G. M. Ritchie 31; I. W. Callen four for 7); Victoria 217 for seven (J. M. Wiener 79, W. J. Scholes 60; J. R. Thomson three for 34).

At Perth, February 6. New South Wales won by 59 runs. New South Wales 245 for five (J. Dyson 101, R. B. McCosker 67, I. C. Davis 51; T. M. Alderman three for 39); Western Australia 186 (B. M. Laird 56; T. M. Chappell four for 35, G. R. Beard three for 43).

Consolation Final

At Melbourne, March 6. Western Australia won by 2 wickets. Victoria 171 for eight (G. M. Watts 41; M. F. Malone three for 19); Western Australia 172 for eight (S. Clements 35, G. A. Millar 30; S. F. Graf three for 28).

FINAL

†NEW SOUTH WALES v QUEENSLAND

At Sydney, March 7. Queensland won by 27 runs.

Man of the Match: W. R. Broad.

Queensland

K. C. Wessels c Beard b Lawson	2	H. K. De Jong not out	12
R. B. Kerr c Beard b Whitney	1	*G. Dymock b Chappell	11
W. R. Broad run out	85		
M. A. Gaskell c McCosker b Chappell	26	B 6, l-b 12, w 7, n-b 3	28
T. V. Hohns b Beard	11		—
A. B. Henschell c Chappell b Lawson	45	1/2 2/8 3/89 (8 wkts, 47 overs)	224
†R. B. Phillips lbw b Skilbeck	3	4/111 5/181 6/184 7/203 8/224	

G. W. Brabon and J. N. Maguire did not bat.

Bowling: Lawson 10–2–33–2; Whitney 10–0–36–1; Skilbeck 10–1–46–1; Beard 8–0–36–1; Chappell 9–0–45–2.

New South Wales

*R. B. McCosker b Dymock	4	G. F. Lawson b Dymock	5
I. C. Davis lbw b Dymock	1	A. J. Skilbeck not out	6
T. M. Chappell b Dymock	7	M. R. Whitney run out	4
P. M. Toohey b Maguire	66		
S. B. Smith c De Jong b Maguire	0	L-b 12, w 3, n-b 4	19
D. M. Wellham c and b Brabon	21		—
†S. J. Rixon c Kerr b Dymock	41	1/3 2/10 3/13 4/14 5/78 (44 overs)	197
G. R. Beard c Wessels b De Jong	23	6/128 7/178 8/181 9/186	

Bowling: Maguire 10–1–29–2; Dymock 8.4–1–27–5; Brabon 9–0–38–1; De Jong 9–1–43–1; Broad 8–0–41–0.

Umpires: M. Jay and A. G. Watson.

KNOCKOUT COMPETITION WINNERS

Australasian Knockout

1969-70 New Zealand
1970–71 Western Australia
1971-72 Victoria
1972-73 New Zealand

McDonald's Cup

1979-80 Victoria
1980–81 Queensland
1981–82 Queensland

Gillette Cup

1973-74 Western Australia
1974-75 New Zealand
1975-76 Queensland
1976-77 Western Australia
1977-78 Western Australia
1978-79 Tasmania

CRICKET IN SOUTH AFRICA, 1981-82

By PETER SICHEL

The South African season, which concluded at the later than usual time of early April, turned out to be a triumph for Western Province, who performed the "double" for the first time by winning the Currie Cup, fairly convincingly, and the Datsun Shield, the premier one-day competition. Special praise must go to Stuart Leary, formerly of Kent, the Union's coach, and Peter Kirsten, who captained the side with wisdom and maturity. Apart from his qualities of leadership, Kirsten's contribution with the bat was enormous, and his work in the field often miraculous. Between them, Leary and Kirsten blended a young but experienced side into a winning combination.

The potential of players such as Adrian Kuiper and Stephen Jefferies was realised: both won Springbok "colours" against the touring SAB English side. Jefferies and the experienced Garth le Roux, who had a fine season, formed a lethal new-ball combination. Kuiper's performance in completing five half-centuries was meritorious, several of them being scored in adversity. He demonstrated a fine technique, courage and determination.

Every player in the team provided a match-winning performance at some stage of the season. There was Ken McEwan's 117 against Natal at Newlands, Allan Lamb's scintillating 106 not out against Eastern Province at Port Elizabeth when batting points were eagerly sought, Stephen Bruce's exciting 89, including five sixes and eight fours, against Transvaal at Newlands, and le Roux's splendid fast bowling which earned for him five wickets in an innings on no fewer than five occasions.

Transvaal, ably assisted by the West Indian, Alvin Kallicharran, fought every inch of the way and were always in contention to win the Currie Cup. Injuries to key players at vital stages of the season retarded their progress, but they were at all times a difficult side to beat. Together with Kallicharran, batting honours belonged to Clive Rice, with two hundreds, Graeme Pollock and Kevin McKenzie. Pollock, not quite as devastating as of old, nevertheless inspired confidence by his very presence at the wicket. Rice, who led the side very well, batted with both authority and assurance, in spite of a nagging neck injury which caused him to give up bowling, temporarily, before the season ended. Rupert Hanley, Alan Kourie and Neal Radford all bowled well, admirably supported behind the stumps by Ray Jennings.

Natal, reinforced by Barry Richards, were favoured by many to retain the trophy, but with Mike Procter and Richards himself out with injuries, and Chris Wilkins failing to maintain his form of the previous season, their returns were somewhat disappointing. Richards showed glimpses of his finest form, particularly in the match against Northern Transvaal at Pietermaritzburg, where he made scores of 62 and 87 not out, but an injury at New Year forced him out of the game for five weeks, a setback both for himself and Natal. Procter soldiered on, though without being able to bowl anything like his fastest. His quiet, undemonstrative leadership was an inspiration. Daryl Bestall enjoyed a splendid season, Neville Daniels performed most creditably, producing several fine all-round performances, but Rob Bentley, from whom much was expected, fell away after a promising start. Vintcent van der Bijl was once again magnificent. Ably supported by Les Taylor, on winter leave from Leicestershire, he again captured more than 50 Currie Cup wickets, including five in an innings seven times and ten in a match on three occasions. His departure for Transvaal for the 1982–83 season was likely to be a tremendous loss to Natal.

Northern Transvaal did better than in 1980–81, but once again, despite an abundance of talent, they were able to win only one match outright. Individually, Vernon du Preez played several innings of great merit. Brian Whitfield and Craig Stirk also demonstrated their undeniable skill, each playing innings of class, but Norman Featherstone, Anton Ferreira and Rodney Ontong, apart from flashes, failed to live up to their potential. Among the bowlers, Chris Old of Yorkshire, Frank Joubert, Ferreira and Ontong were steady, but it was left to young Trevor Wheelwright, who gained selection for the last match of the season, to provide the desired penetration, capturing five for 47 in the first innings against Natal at Berea Park, Pretoria.

Eastern Province were extremely, not to say mysteriously, disappointing. Robbie Armitage, who enjoyed a vintage season, had developed into a fine player. His courage and dedication brought him hundreds against Northern Transvaal and Natal, and his performances were often in adverse circumstances. Simon Bezuidenhout, too, showed skill and a fine technique in putting together a brilliant hundred against Western Province. Kenny Watson, so often the spearhead of the Eastern Province attack, suffered a reversal of form which was a reflection of the Eastern Province season.

Now that the South African Cricket Union have given their blessing to the inclusion of two overseas players in each provincial team, the balance of power could be more evenly distributed, making for a better and more evenly contested Currie Cup tournament.

FIRST-CLASS AVERAGES, 1981-82

BATTING

(Qualification: 400 runs, average 30)

	I	*NO*	*R*	*HI*	*100s*	*Avge*
M. J. D. Doherty (*Griqualand W.*)	10	2	556	113*	1	69.50
R. G. Pollock (*Transvaal*)	14	5	586	124	1	65.11
P. N. Kirsten (*W. Province*)	19	3	948	151	4	59.25
A. I. Kallicharran (*Transvaal*)	10	1	484	129	2	53.77
E. J. Barlow (*Boland*)	12	1	584	202*	2	53.09
C. E. B. Rice (*Transvaal*)	16	4	561	108	2	46.75
P. D. Swart (*Boland*)	11	1	433	92	0	43.30
A. J. Lamb (*W. Province*)	14	3	472	106*	1	42.90
C. L. Smith (*Natal*)	13	1	513	112	1	42.75
B. A. Richards (*Natal*)	16	4	475	87*	0	39.58
D. Bestall (*Natal*)	15	1	528	80*	0	37.71
L. Seeff (*W. Province*)	18	3	547	79	0	36.46

	I	*NO*	*R*	*HI*	*100s*	*Avge*
S. J. Cook (*Transvaal*)	19	3	576	114	1	36.00
R. L. S. Armitage (*E. Province*)	14	1	465	171*	2	35.76
K. S. McEwan (*W. Province*)	14	1	430	117	1	33.07
A. P. Kuiper (*W. Province*)	15	1	457	90	0	32.64
V. F. du Preez (*N. Transvaal*)	16	1	471	115	1	31.40

**Signifies not out.*

BOWLING

(Qualification: 20 wkts, average 20)

	R	*W*	*Avge*	*5 W/i*	*BB*
I. F. Weideman (*Transvaal B*)	261	21	12.42	0	4-39
J. D. du Toit (*W. Province B*)	496	39	12.71	3	6-26
G. S. le Roux (*W. Province*)	677	49	13.81	5	6-44
P. Anker (*Boland*)	731	50	14.62	5	6-83
V. A. P. van der Bijl (*Natal*)	1,119	75	14.92	10	8-47
S. A. Jones (*Boland*)	389	25	15.56	0	3-15
P. J. Marneweck (*N. Transvaal*)	340	21	16.19	1	6-12
H. W. Raath (*N. Transvaal*)	435	26	16.73	2	6-95
C. J. Coetzee (*Boland*)	527	31	17.00	0	4-49
R. W. Hanley (*Transvaal*)	605	33	18.33	2	6-33
C. E. B. Rice (*Transvaal*)	504	27	18.66	1	5-45
O. Henry (*W. Province/WP B*)	695	37	18.78	2	7-22
N. V. Radford (*Transvaal*)	543	25	21.72	0	4-20
L. B. Taylor (*Natal*)	610	28	21.78	1	5-61
G. E. McMillan (*Transvaal/Tvl B*)	483	22	21.95	0	4-43
S. T. Jefferies (*W. Province*)	1,166	52	22.42	1	5-46
W. M. van der Merwe (*OFS*)	483	20	24.15	0	4-37
E. J. Hodkinson (*Natal/Natal B*)	604	25	24.16	1	6-68
R. R. Lawrenson (*W. Province B*)	654	27	24.22	1	5-50
C. J. P. G. van Zyl (*OFS*)	537	22	24.40	1	5-42
J. A. Carse (*E. Province*)	544	22	24.72	1	6-50
A. J. Kourie (*Transvaal*)	712	25	28.48	2	6-88
I. Ebrahim (*Natal B*)	636	22	28.90	2	5-57
A. M. Ferreira (*N. Transvaal*)	667	23	29.00	1	5-63
W. K. Watson (*E. Province*)	655	22	29.77	0	4-52
D. L. Hobson (*W. Province*)	776	26	29.84	1	5-82
H. Liebenberg (*Griqualand W.*)	627	21	29.85	1	5-55

SAB CURRIE CUP, 1981-82

					Bonus Points		*Total*
	Played	*Won*	*Lost*	*Drawn*	*Batting*	*Bowling*	*Points*
Western Province (3)	8	5	1	2	31	35	116
Transvaal (2)	8	4	1	3	37	30	107
Natal (1)	8	4	2	2	12	33	85
Northern Transvaal (5)	8	1	4	3	9	33	52
Eastern Province (4)	8	0	6	2	8	29	37

1980-81 positions in parentheses.

NORTHERN TRANSVAAL v TRANSVAAL

At Berea Park, Pretoria, October 30, 31, November 2. Drawn. Transvaal 8 pts, Northern Transvaal 5 pts.

Northern Transvaal

B. J. Whitfield c Jennings b Rice	31	– b Hanley	3
A. Barrow lbw b Radford	13	– c Jennings b Hanley	37
V. F. du Preez c Jennings b Hanley	115	– (8) lbw b Rice	33
C. S. Stirk c Cook b Hanley	124	– c Rice b Radford	11
*N. G. Featherstone c Pollock b Rice	9	– b Radford	4
R. C. Ontong c Hanley b McMillan	18	– c Rice b Radford	4
A. M. Ferreira b Radford	0	– c Cook b Rice	12
C. M. Old c McMillan b Radford	1	– (9) c Barnard b Hanley	30
†B. McBride b Radford	2	– (3) lbw b Hanley	5
W. F. Morris not out	6	– c Jennings b Barnard	27
F. E. Joubert b McMillan	12	– not out	3
Extras	25	Extras	12
1/30 2/62 3/286 4/295 5/317 6/318 7/320 8/337 9/337	356	1/18 2/32 3/59 4/63 5/70 6/83 7/85 8/143 9/166	181

Bowling: *First Innings*—Rice 28–10–60–2; Hanley 41–15–79–2; McMillan 26.4–11–44–2; Radford 28–4–93–4; Barnard 22–7–55–0. *Second Innings*—Rice 19–4–64–2; Hanley 20–8–34–4; McMillan 2–1–8–0; Radford 13–2–53–3; Barnard 6.4–4–10–1.

Transvaal

S. J. Cook lbw b Joubert	9	– b Joubert	19
A. I. Kallicharran c McBride b Ferreira	34	– c McBride b Joubert	0
H. R. Fotheringham c McBride b Ferreira	12	– c Featherstone b Old	12
R. G. Pollock c Old b Ontong	65	– not out	14
K. A. McKenzie lbw b Old	67	– b Old	1
*C. E. B. Rice c Old b Ferreira	66	– not out	16
L. J. Barnard b Ferreira	36		
†R. V. Jennings b Old	1		
N. V. Radford not out	16		
G. E. McMillan c Whitfield b Ferreira	13		
R. W. Hanley not out	12		
Extras	16	Extras	4
1/31 2/50 3/69 4/194 5/212 6/303 7/303 8/304 9/326	(9 wkts dec.) 347	1/10 2/33 3/33 4/36	(4 wkts) 66

Bowling: *First Innings*—Old 23–3–108–2; Joubert 14–3–51–1; Ferreira 25–8–63–5; Ontong 21–4–65–1; Morris 8–0–44–0. *Second Innings*—Old 6–1–26–2; Joubert 6–0–28–2; Ferreira 3–0–8–0.

Umpires: A. A. Mathews and G. Hawkins.

WESTERN PROVINCE v EASTERN PROVINCE

At Newlands, Cape Town, November 6, 7, 9. Western Province won by ten wickets. Western Province 17 pts, Eastern Province 2 pts.

Eastern Province

D. Broad b le Roux	10	– c Ryall b Jefferies	12
K. W. Gradwell c Ryall b Jefferies	4	– lbw b le Roux	23
R. L. S. Armitage c Lamb b Jefferies	20	– (4) c Ryall b Jefferies	37
R. J. D. Whyte c Ryall b le Roux	8	– (5) c Henry b Hobson	1
I. Foulkes c McEwan b le Roux	20	– (6) b le Roux	4
D. H. Howell c Ryall b le Roux	6	– (7) c Ryall b Jefferies	18
*D. J. Brickett c Seeff b Henry	55	– (8) c Henry b Hobson	12
G. Long b le Roux	0	– (3) c Ryall b Jefferies	0
†J. W. Stephenson c McEwan b Henry	1	– c Jefferies b Hobson	21
W. K. Watson run out	36	– st Ryall b Hobson	10
J. A. Carse not out	6	– not out	0
Extras	6	Extras	20
1/15 2/15 3/23 4/52 5/70 6/91 7/91 8/94 9/160	172	1/15 2/22 3/63 4/72 5/87 6/96 7/119 8/123 9/158	158

Bowling: *First Innings*—le Roux 19–4–30–5; Jefferies 20.3–5–56–2; Pienaar 11–4–11–0; Hobson 9–3–29–0; Henry 18–5–40–2. *Second Innings*—le Roux 18–9–22–2; Jefferies 28–9–51–4; Hobson 27.1–11–65–4.

Western Province

L. Seeff lbw b Watson	47	– not out	20
M. J. Nel c Foulkes b Brickett	5	– not out	19
*P. N. Kirsten b Watson	114		
†R. J. Ryall b Brickett	7		
A. J. Lamb c Brickett b Foulkes	32		
K. S. McEwan c Gradwell b Watson	21		
R. F. Pienaar b Carse	4		
O. Henry c Broad b Armitage	6		
G. S. le Roux c Foulkes b Carse	12		
S. T. Jefferies not out	3		
D. L. Hobson b Watson	2		
Extras	31	Extras	11
1/21 2/115 3/132 4/205 5/253 6/256 7/265 8/266 9/279	284		(no wkt) 50

Bowling: *First Innings*—Watson 26–5–52–4; Carse 20–3–52–2; Brickett 11–2–21–2; Long 28–4–58–0; Foulkes 16–3–45–1; Armitage 7–1–25–1. *Second Innings*—Watson 6–1–14–0; Carse 7.4–3–23–0; Armitage 3–2–2–0.

Umpires: H. R. Martin and O. R. Schoof.

EASTERN PROVINCE v NORTHERN TRANSVAAL

At St George's Park, Port Elizabeth, November 13, 14, 15. Northern Transvaal won by 30 runs. Northern Transvaal 15 pts, Eastern Province 7 pts.

Northern Transvaal

B. J. Whitfield c Richardson b Watson	0	– b Watson	3
A. Barrow c Ogilvie b Carse	6	– c Brickett b Carse	7
V. F. du Preez lbw b Carse	0	– c Richardson b Carse	70
C. S. Stirk c Fensham b Carse	1	– lbw b van Vuuren	5
*N. G. Featherstone c Richardson b Ogilvie	14	– lbw b Ogilvie	7
R. C. Ontong run out	75	– c Richardson b van Vuuren	4
P. D. de Vaal lbw b Watson	15	– c Richardson b Watson	19
A. M. Ferreira c Richardson b Carse	4	– c Carse b van Vuuren	40
C. M. Old c Fensham b Carse	20	– c Richardson b Carse	7
†B. McBride not out	0	– c Ogilvie b Watson	1
F. E. Joubert lbw b Carse	6	– not out	9
Extras	36	Extras	11
1/12 2/14 3/15 4/30 5/40 6/79 7/122 8/168 9/171	177	1/8 2/12 3/36 4/45 5/56 6/109 7/135 8/143 9/144	183

Bowling: *First Innings*—Watson 16–10–11–2; Carse 17.5–5–50–6; van Vuuren 11–3–30–0; Ogilvie 14–2–50–1. *Second Innings*—Watson 22–11–27–3; Carse 18–4–67–3; van Vuuren 11.4–1–29–3; Ogilvie 13–3–42–1; Armitage 4–2–7–0.

Eastern Province

K. W. Gradwell lbw b Old	2	– run out	2
T. G. Shaw lbw b Ontong	7	– c Stirk b Old	2
R. L. S. Armitage c Stirk b Old	1	– lbw b Joubert	4
R. J. D. Whyte c Featherstone b Ontong	8	– lbw b Old	2
†D. J. Richardson c Whitfield b Ferreira	47	– lbw b Ontong	18
R. G. Fensham c McBride b Joubert	37	– b Old	0
*D. J. Brickett c de Vaal b Ferreira	5	– c Stirk b Old	6
W. K. Watson c Stirk b Old	27	– c and b Ontong	24
J. D. Ogilvie lbw b Ontong	21	– c Featherstone b Ferreira	17
M. K. van Vuuren c Whitfield b Old	25	– b Ferreira	10
J. A. Carse not out	0	– not out	16
Extras	36	Extras	13
1/2 2/4 3/20 4/25 5/123 6/133 7/133 8/174 9/204	216	1/3 2/8 3/12 4/14 5/18 6/41 7/43 8/84 9/91	114

Bowling: *First Innings*—Old 19.5–9–54–4; Joubert 21–8–37–1; Ferreira 26–9–43–2; Ontong 19–4–46–3. *Second Innings*—Old 17–5–29–4; Joubert 10–6–15–1; Ferreira 10–5–21–2; Ontong 8.5–1–26–2; de Vaal 6–3–10–0.

Umpires: J. W. Peacock and C. M. P. Coetzee.

NORTHERN TRANSVAAL v WESTERN PROVINCE

At Berea Park, Pretoria, November 27, 28, 30. Western Province won by an innings and 31 runs. Western Province 19 pts, Northern Transvaal 4 pts.

Northern Transvaal

B. J. Whitfield c McEwan b During	24	– c Ryall b Hobson	70
A. Barrow c Ryall b le Roux	1	– c Hobson b le Roux	45
V. F. du Preez c McEwan b Jefferies	48	– (4) c Kirsten b Hobson	1
C. S. Stirk c Kirsten b Hobson	0	– (5) c Ryall b Jefferies	24
P. D. de Vaal c Ryall b Jefferies	13	– (6) c Lamb b Hobson	6
*N. G. Featherstone lbw b Jefferies	19	– (7) b Hobson	11
R. C. Ontong c Seeff b Jefferies	8	– (8) not out	36
A. M. Ferreira c and b le Roux	8	– (9) c Ryall b During	1
C. M. Old c Ryall b Jefferies	0	– (10) c Ryall b During	2
†B. McBride not out	4	– (3) lbw b Hobson	0
F. E. Joubert c During b le Roux	0	– c and b le Roux	3
Extras	4	Extras	9
1/3 2/54 3/59 4/86 5/89 6/115 7/125 8/125 9/129	129	1/105 2/105 3/107 4/138 5/148 6/155 7/162 8/175 9/179	208

Bowling: *First Innings*—le Roux 14.4–5–22–3; Jefferies 20–6–46–5; During 18–7–33–1; Hobson 14–3–24–1. *Second Innings*—le Roux 18.4–6–31–2; Jefferies 21–6–51–1; During 13–4–20–2; Hobson 30–11–82–5; Pienaar 6–0–11–0; Kuiper 2–1–4–0.

Western Province

L. Seeff b Ontong	37
R. F. Pienaar c McBride b Old	3
*P. N. Kirsten c Featherstone b Ferreira	86
A. J. Lamb b Joubert	38
K. S. McEwan c sub b de Vaal	53
A. P. Kuiper c McBride b Ontong	27
G. S. le Roux c Ontong b Ferreira	6
J. During c McBride b Ferreira	29
S. T. Jefferies run out	63
†R. J. Ryall not out	4
D. L. Hobson not out	11
Extras	11
1/9 2/90 3/147 4/183 5/226 6/239 7/269 8/345 9/355	(9 wkts dec.) 368

Bowling: Old 23–4–80–1; Joubert 15–1–59–1; Ontong 23–2–83–2; Ferreira 29–5–81–3; de Vaal 15–2–54–1.

Umpires: E. A. Carter and A. J. Norton.

TRANSVAAL v WESTERN PROVINCE

At The Wanderers, Johannesburg, December 5, 6, 7. Drawn. Transvaal 8 pts, Western Province 4 pts.

Western Province

L. Seeff lbw b Fairclough	20	– not out	57
R. F. Pienaar c Radford b Rice	20	– lbw b Kourie	8
*P. N. Kirsten c Jennings b Hanley	14	– c McKenzie b Rice	38
A. J. Lamb c Rice b Fairclough	62	– not out	9
K. S. McEwan run out	4		
A. P. Kuiper b Rice	63		
J. During c McKenzie b Kourie	4		
G. S. le Roux lbw b Fairclough	34		
S. T. Jefferies c Kourie b Fairclough	14		
†R. J. Ryall not out	13		
D. L. Hobson c Jennings b Fairclough	4		
Extras	17	Extras	6
1/46 2/54 3/84 4/97 5/155 6/179 7/229 8/243 9/251	269	1/12 2/100	(2 wkts) 118

Bowling: *First Innings*—Rice 21–9–43–2; Hanley 28–8–70–1; Radford 25–10–45–0; Fairclough 29–12–44–5; Kourie 16–4–50–1. *Second Innings*—Rice 10–4–16–1; Hanley 7.4–1–17–0; Radford 5–1–14–0; Fairclough 8–0–19–0; Kourie 22–6–46–1.

Transvaal

S. J. Cook b During	48	A. J. Kourie not out	10
M. Yachad c Kuiper b Jefferies	8	†R. V. Jennings not out	23
A. I. Kallicharran b During	129	Extras	26
R. G. Pollock b Hobson	70		—
*C. E. B. Rice c McEwan b During	70	1/27 2/86 3/241 4/331 (6 wkts dec.)	397
K. A. McKenzie c Ryall b During	13	5/361 6/366	

N. V. Radford, R. W. Hanley and J. Fairclough did not bat.

Bowling: le Roux 8–3–18–0; Jefferies 35–7–128–1; During 35–6–114–4; Hobson 15–2–55–1; Pienaar 14–1–56–0.

Umpires: J. W. Peacock and D. A. Sansom.

NATAL v NORTHERN TRANSVAAL

At Pietermaritzburg, December 5, 6, 7. Drawn. Natal 6 pts, Northern Transvaal 4 pts.

Natal

B. A. Richards c Ferreira b Joubert	62	not out	87
C. P. Wilkins c Joubert b Old	10	c and b Old	5
R. M. Bentley b Ferreira	88	b Joubert	21
D. Bestall c McBride b de Vaal	31	run out	8
*M. J. Procter c McBride b Ferreira	1	c Whitfield b Ontong	10
N. P. Daniels c Joubert b Ferreira	3	b Ferreira	14
†A. J. S. Smith b Joubert	47		
P. B. Clift c du Preez b de Vaal	14		
V. A. P. van der Bijl not out	53	(8) st McBride b de Vaal	12
K. R. Cooper not out	38	(7) b de Vaal	16
Extras	11	Extras	11
	—		—
1/27 2/117 3/182 4/189 (8 wkts dec.)	358	1/19 2/64 3/98 (7 wkts dec.)	184
5/197 6/208 7/245 8/295		4/113 5/143 6/168 7/184	

L. B. Taylor did not bat.

Bowling: *First Innings*—Old 18–2–79–1; Joubert 16–1–69–2; Ferreira 32–9–92–3; Ontong 10–2–36–0; de Vaal 25–8–71–2. *Second Innings*—Old 7–0–21–1; Joubert 12–2–36–1; Ferreira 7–0–40–1; Ontong 11–1–51–1; de Vaal 2.3–0–25–2.

Northern Transvaal

B. J. Whitfield lbw b Taylor	100	not out	58
A. Barrow c Smith b van der Bijl	6	lbw b Clift	19
P. D. de Vaal c Smith b Clift	64		
C. S. Stirk b Clift	0		
V. F. du Preez c and b Procter	12	(3) not out	33
R. C. Ontong c Richards b Clift	38		
*N. G. Featherstone run out	10		
A. M. Ferreira b Procter	30		
C. M. Old c Wilkins b Clift	4		
†B. McBride not out	0		
F. E. Joubert c Smith b Procter	0		
Extras	13	Extras	10
	—		—
1/11 2/147 3/147 4/182 5/203	277	1/33 (1 wkt)	120
6/217 7/261 8/271 9/277			

Bowling: *First Innings*—van der Bijl 31–9–56–1; Taylor 22–9–50–1; Procter 16.5–7–30–3; Cooper 13–1–47–0; Clift 22–10–45–4; Daniels 11–3–32–0; Bentley 4–2–4–0. *Second Innings*—van der Bijl 11–2–22–0; Taylor 11–4–23–0; Procter 14–5–30–0; Cooper 4–0–12–0; Clift 11–2–21–1; Wilkins 1–0–2–0.

Umpires: B. C. Smith and A. J. Norton.

TRANSVAAL v EASTERN PROVINCE

At The Wanderers, Johannesburg, December 26, 27, 28. Transvaal won by an innings and 101 runs. Transvaal 22 pts, Eastern Province 3 pts.

Eastern Province

S. J. Bezuidenhout c Jennings b Fairclough	38	– c Jennings b Hanley	3
J. A. Hopkins c Pollock b Fairclough	7	– lbw b Radford	3
R. L. S. Armitage c Jennings b Fairclough	26	– c Jennings b Radford	0
R. G. Fensham run out	15	– c Jennings b Hanley	0
R. J. D. Whyte lbw b Radford	7	– lbw b Rice	3
†D. J. Richardson c Jennings b Fairclough	20	– c Hanley b Radford	38
I. Foulkes b Kourie	6	– c Jennings b Rice	5
*D. J. Brickett c McKenzie b Fairclough	4	– not out	11
W. K. Watson b Hanley	23	– c Jennings b Radford	0
J. A. Carse c Fairclough b Kourie	2	– c Jennings b Hanley	9
C. Wulfsohn not out	17	– b Rice	1
Extras	13	Extras	7
1/46 2/53 3/84 4/93 5/106 6/121 7/130 8/141 9/146	178	1/6 2/6 3/6 4/6 5/25 6/39 7/61 8/61 9/75	80

Bowling: *First Innings*—Rice 13–7–16–0; Hanley 12.2–5–20–1; Radford 9–1–30–1; Fairclough 27–10–52–5; Kourie 23–7–47–2. *Second Innings*—Rice 10.3–2–18–3; Hanley 15–6–23–3; Radford 13–5–20–4; Fairclough 8–4–4–0; Kourie 7–3–8–0.

Transvaal

S. J. Cook lbw b Watson	15
H. R. Fotheringham lbw b Carse	8
A. I. Kallicharran b Wulfsohn	42
R. G. Pollock c Armitage b Brickett	124
*C. E. B. Rice c Foulkes b Watson	108
K. A. McKenzie not out	5
A. J. Kourie not out	13
Extras	44
1/27 2/29 3/132 4/329 5/343 (5 wkts dec.)	359

†R. V. Jennings, N. V. Radford, J. Fairclough and R. W. Hanley did not bat.

Bowling: Watson 28–7–79–2; Carse 20–3–78–1; Wulfsohn 19–1–81–1; Brickett 15–1–39–1; Armitage 7–0–38–0.

Umpires: B. C. Smith and S. G. Moore.

NATAL v WESTERN PROVINCE

At Kingsmead, Durban, December 26, 27, 28. Natal won by five wickets. Natal 15 pts, Western Province 5 pts.

Western Province

L. Seeff c Smith b Taylor	0	– lbw b van der Bijl	4
R. F. Pienaar b van der Bijl	1	– c Procter b van der Bijl	0
*P. N. Kirsten lbw b van der Bijl	3	– c Wilkins b van der Bijl	19
A. J. Lamb c Wilkins b Cooper	8	– lbw b van der Bijl	28
K. S. McEwan c Smith b van der Bijl	1	– b Procter	34
A. P. Kuiper c Clift b van der Bijl	89	– b Procter	9
J. During c Daniels b van der Bijl	6	– c Smith b Taylor	9
G. S. le Roux b van der Bijl	1	– c Smith b Taylor	8
†R. J. Ryall c Cooper b van der Bijl	0	– c Procter b Taylor	6
S. T. Jefferies not out	17	– not out	0
D. L. Hobson lbw b Clift	4	– b Taylor	0
Extras	27	Extras	27
1/3 2/3 3/12 4/16 5/24 6/83 7/92 8/120 9/145	157	1/4 2/9 3/53 4/66 5/82 6/123 7/123 8/137 9/139	144

Bowling: *First Innings*—van der Bijl 23.5–10–31–7; Taylor 14–3–43–1; Cooper 10–3–25–1; Clift 8–2–31–1. *Second Innings*—van der Bijl 23–9–33–4; Taylor 19.5–6–47–4; Cooper 5–2–9–0; Clift 7–2–13–0; Procter 17–11–15–2.

Natal

B. A. Richards c Ryall b Jefferies	6	– c Kuiper b Jefferies	3
C. P. Wilkins run out	10	– c Kuiper b Jefferies	1
R. M. Bentley c Kuiper b Pienaar	39	– b Kuiper	48
D. Bestall c McEwan b le Roux	25	– c Seeff b Jefferies	57
*M. J. Procter c Kirsten b During	11	– b Jefferies	24
N. P. Daniels b Pienaar	8	– not out	8
†A. J. S. Smith c Ryall b Pienaar	1	– not out	0
P. B. Clift c le Roux b Pienaar	29		
V. A. P. van der Bijl b Pienaar	4		
K. R. Cooper not out	3		
L. Taylor b Jefferies	2		
Extras	5	Extras	19
1/17 2/17 3/64 4/83 5/99 6/103 7/120 8/136 9/141	143	1/7 2/10 3/109 4/146 5/152	(5 wkts) 160

Bowling: *First Innings*—le Roux 10–0–37–1; Jefferies 15.4–4–49–2; During 18–5–28–1; Pienaar 12–4–24–5. *Second Innings*—le Roux 5–0–14–0; Jefferies 15–5–50–4; During 6.5–1–28–0; Pienaar 9–3–28–0; Kuiper 5–2–8–1; Hobson 3–0–13–0.

Umpires: D. H. Bezuidenhout and P. R. Hurwitz.

EASTERN PROVINCE v NATAL

At St George's Park, Port Elizabeth, January 1, 2, 3. Drawn. Eastern Province 7 pts, Natal 5 pts.

Eastern Province

S. J. Bezuidenhout lbw b van der Bijl	25
J. A. Hopkins c Bentley b van der Bijl	19
R. L. S. Armitage c Clift b Taylor	118
R. G. Fensham c Clift b Procter	4
R. J. D. Whyte lbw b Clift	48
†D. J. Richardson c Smith b van der Bijl	5
I. Foulkes b Taylor	40
*D. J. Brickett lbw b Cooper	20
W. K. Watson c Daniels b Cooper	2
J. A. Carse b Cooper	4
C. Wulfsohn not out	3
Extras	7
1/41 2/46 3/51 4/121 5/140 6/237 7/276 8/278 9/287	295

Bowling: van der Bijl 34–6–74–3; Taylor 21.5–7–59–2; Cooper 23–7–56–3; Procter 12–3–40–1; Clift 27–11–52–1; Bentley 4–2–7–0.

Natal

†A. J. S. Smith c Whyte b Watson	2	– c and b Foulkes	39
C. P. Wilkins b Foulkes	29	– c Richardson b Watson	37
R. M. Bentley b Carse	13	– c Hopkins b Armitage	39
D. Bestall b Foulkes	32	– b Foulkes	19
†M. J. Procter c Fensham b Wulfsohn	6	– c Watson b Wulfsohn	76
N. P. Daniels c Richardson b Wulfsohn	7	– not out	20
B. A. Richards not out	39		
P. B. Clift b Wulfsohn	9	– (7) not out	11
V. A. P. van der Bijl c Richardson b Wulfsohn	4		
K. R. Cooper b Wulfsohn	0		
L. B. Taylor b Wulfsohn	0		
Extras	4	Extras	13
1/8 2/36 3/50 4/67 5/79 6/104 7/133 8/143 9/143	145	1/72 2/102 3/153 4/215 5/235 (5 wkts)	254

Bowling: *First Innings*—Watson 16–5–34–1; Carse 13–3–44–1; Foulkes 16–6–32–2; Wulfsohn 12–4–18–6; Brickett 6–3–12–0; Armitage 1–0–1–0. *Second Innings*—Watson 17–1–54–1; Carse 9–2–27–0; Foulkes 38–15–71–2; Wulfsohn 21–5–40–1; Brickett 9–0–23–0; Armitage 15–5–26–1.

Umpires: P. R. Hurwitz and A. J. Norton.

WESTERN PROVINCE v TRANSVAAL

At Newlands, Cape Town, January 1, 2, 4. Drawn. Western Province 9 pts, Transvaal 6 pts.

Western Province

L. Seeff b Kourie	44	– c Jennings b Radford	31
R. F. Pienaar lbw b Rice	7	– c Radford b Kourie	8
*P. N. Kirsten c and b Kourie	22	– c McKenzie b Kourie	14
A. J. Lamb c and b Kourie	4	– c Barnard b Radford	1
K. S. McEwan c Fairclough b Kourie	3	– c Cook b Kourie	42
A. P. Kuiper b Fairclough	72	– st Jennings b Kourie	28
†S. D. Bruce lbw b Fairclough	89	– not out	15
G. S. le Roux b Kourie	43	– c Johnson b Kourie	10
O. Henry c Barnard b Kourie	53	– not out	30
J. During not out	0		
Extras	16	Extras	7
1/19 2/71 3/83 4/84 5/90 6/247 7/258 8/350 9/353 (9 wkts dec.)	353	1/18 2/53 3/54 4/55 5/126 6/135 7/150 (7 wkts dec.)	186

S. T. Jefferies did not bat.

Bowling: *First Innings*—Rice 22–6–43–1; Radford 13–2–58–0; Fairclough 26–4–87–2; Kourie 25.3–9–88–6; Johnson 17–3–61–0. *Second Innings*—Rice 14–4–20–0; Radford 10–2–21–2; Fairclough 12–3–27–0; Kourie 33.5–11–102–5; Johnson 2–0–9–0.

Transvaal

S. J. Cook c and b Jefferies	72	– b Henry	28
H. R. Fotheringham c Lamb b le Roux	12	– lbw b le Roux	5
†R. V. Jennings c Bruce b le Roux	3		
K. A. McKenzie c McEwan b Pienaar	78	– (3) c Kuiper b Henry	23
R. G. Pollock c During b le Roux	2	– (4) not out	41
*C. E. B. Rice lbw b Jefferies	35	– (5) not out	17
L. J. Barnard b le Roux	5		
A. J. Kourie b Henry	3		
G. W. Johnson lbw b Jefferies	9		
N. V. Radford c Jefferies b le Roux	12		
J. Fairclough not out	9		
Extras	11	Extras	4
1/16 2/22 3/173 4/177 5/177 6/189 7/202 8/224 9/231	251	1/20 2/57 3/62	(3 wkts) 118

Bowling: *First Innings*—le Roux 27.3–6–63–5; Jefferies 32–6–73–3; Henry 27–9–53–1; During 4–0–21–0; Kirsten 2–0–12–0; Pienaar 9–1–18–1. *Second Innings*—le Roux 8–0–27–1; Jefferies 11–4–29–0; Henry 15–5–28–2; Kirsten 3–0–17–0; Pienaar 3–0–3–0; Seeff 2–0–10–0.

Umpires: A. T. Maasch and D. D. Schoof.

NATAL v TRANSVAAL

At Kingsmead, Durban, January 16, 17, 18. Natal won by two wickets. Natal 15 pts, Transvaal 7 pts.

Transvaal

S. J. Cook c Daniels b Taylor	30	– c Wilkins b van der Bijl	2
A. J. Kourie c Procter b Cooper	11	– c Cooper b van der Bijl	29
A. I. Kallicharran c A. J. S. Smith b Cooper	24	– c Procter b van der Bijl	29
*C. E. B. Rice c A. J. S. Smith b Clift	34	– c Bentley b van der Bijl	20
K. A. McKenzie c van der Bijl b Cooper	7	– c Procter b van der Bijl	4
H. R. Fotheringham c Daniels b van der Bijl	4	– lbw b Cooper	9
N. T. Day lbw b van der Bijl	26	– b van der Bijl	10
†R. V. Jennings c A. J. S. Smith b Clift	0	– c A. J. S. Smith b van der Bijl	23
G. E. McMillan c A. J. S. Smith b Taylor	33	– c Wilkins b Daniels	13
N. V. Radford c A. J. S. Smith b Taylor	21	– b Daniels	0
R. W. Hanley not out	2	– not out	0
Extras	17	Extras	12
1/31 2/62 3/91 4/99 5/111 6/128 7/128 8/160 9/197	209	1/6 2/32 3/57 4/61 5/70 6/97 7/115 8/151 9/151	151

Bowling: *First Innings*—van der Bijl 23–6–42–2; Procter 9–4–14–0; Taylor 14.5–3–55–3; Clift 15–6–28–2; Cooper 19–5–53–3. *Second Innings*—van der Bijl 32.3–11–64–7; Taylor 13–2–29–0; Clift 7–0–25–0; Cooper 11–3–20–1; Daniels 1–0–1–2.

Natal

†A. J. S. Smith lbw b Radford	11	– run out	18
C. P. Wilkins c Jennings b Radford	2	– c Fotheringham b Rice	32
R. M. Bentley b McMillan	18	– not out	4
D. Bestall b Hanley	41	– b Radford	34
*M. J. Procter c Radford b Hanley	55	– c Hanley b Rice	0
R. A. Smith c Jennings b Hanley	6	– lbw b Kourie	10
N. P. Daniels b Hanley	5	– run out	31
P. B. Clift b Kourie	0	– c Jennings b Rice	28
V. A. P. van der Bijl not out	18	– not out	17
K. R. Cooper c Jennings b Hanley	3	– b Radford	1
L. B. Taylor b Hanley	12		
Extras	3	Extras	12
1/6 2/15 3/39 4/122 5/134 6/135 7/138 8/144 9/156	174	1/29 2/65 3/65 4/88 5/115 6/149 7/178 8/179	(8 wkts) 187

Bowling: *First Innings*—Rice 15–5–51–0; Radford 14–4–40–2; Hanley 19–4–33–6; McMillan 9–0–33–1; Kourie 5–1–14–1. *Second Innings*—Rice 10–1–37–3; Radford 8–1–24–2; Hanley 13–2–63–0; Kourie 15–1–51–1.

In Natal's second innings Bentley retired hurt before he had scored and resumed at the fall of the eighth wicket.

Umpires: O. R. Schoof and D. H. Bezuidenhout.

TRANSVAAL v NORTHERN TRANSVAAL

At The Wanderers, Johannesburg, January 23, 24, 25. Transvaal won by ten wickets. Transvaal 18 pts, Northern Transvaal 5 pts.

Northern Transvaal

B. J. Whitfield c Jennings b McMillan	5	– b Radford	6
J. P. Ackermann lbw b Radford	14	– lbw b Radford	2
V. F. du Preez b McMillan	5	– lbw b Rice	0
C. S. Stirk c Fotheringham b Rice	25	– c McKenzie b Hanley	5
A. M. Ferreira run out	11	– c Day b Rice	20
*N. G. Featherstone lbw b Rice	2	– lbw b Rice	26
R. C. Ontong c Rice b Hanley	3	– c Cook b Hanley	33
C. P. L. de Lange b Hanley	1	– lbw b Rice	0
C. M. Old b Hanley	4	– c McKenzie b Hanley	6
†B. McBride not out	2	– c Jennings b Rice	15
F. E. Joubert b Rice	1	– not out	22
Extras	13	Extras	18
1/22 2/33 3/35 4/64 5/67 6/72 7/77 8/79 9/85	86	1/13 2/14 3/18 4/26 5/64 6/98 7/108 8/108 9/119	153

Bowling: *First Innings*—Rice 15.2–4–19–3; Radford 10–2–30–1; Hanley 13–6–10–3; McMillan 8–4–14–2. *Second Innings*—Rice 21.3–5–45–5; Radford 13–3–23–2; Hanley 21–4–51–3; McMillan 7–3–16–0.

Transvaal

S. J. Cook lbw b Ferreira	34	– not out	9
M. S. Venter c McBride b Ontong	9	– not out	4
N. T. Day c McBride b Ontong	4		
*C. E. B. Rice c McBride b Joubert	9		
K. A. McKenzie b Ontong	56		
H. R. Fotheringham c Featherstone b Ontong	16		
A. J. Kourie lbw b Ontong	10		
†R. V. Jennings c Stirk b Old	5		
G. E. McMillan not out	43		
N. V. Radford c McBride b Old	0		
R. W. Hanley lbw b du Preez	6		
Extras	34	Extras	1
1/44 2/65 3/67 4/106 5/143 6/164 7/168 8/173 9/173	226	(no wkt)	14

Bowling: Old 24–8–35–2; Joubert 10–1–29–1; Ferreira 20–4–51–1; Ontong 27–10–69–5; Ackermann 2–1–4–0; du Preez 1.4–0–4–1. *Second Innings*—du Preez 2–0–9–0; Featherstone 2.4–0–4–0.

Umpires: D. A. Sansom and C. J. Mitchley.

WESTERN PROVINCE v NORTHERN TRANSVAAL

At Newlands, Cape Town, January 29, 30, February 1. Western Province won by an innings and 96 runs. Western Province 21 pts, Northern Transvaal 7 pts.

Northern Transvaal

B. J. Whitfield c Kirsten b le Roux	53	– lbw b le Roux	5
J. P. Ackermann lbw b le Roux	5	– lbw b Jefferies	2
V. F. du Preez lbw b le Roux	24	– c Bruce b le Roux	4
C. S. Stirk b le Roux	4	– c Seeff b le Roux	2
A. M. Ferreira c Seeff b Hobson	2	– (8) c Kirsten b Hobson	0
*N. G. Featherstone lbw b Jefferies	99	– (7) b Jefferies	18
R. C. Ontong c Bruce b Hobson	0	– (9) c Lamb b Hobson	4
C. P. L. de Lange c Kirsten b Henry	19	– (5) b Kirsten	6
W. F. Morris c McEwan b le Roux	16	– (10) b Jefferies	0
C. M. Old b le Roux	4	– (11) not out	14
†B. McBride not out	10	– (6) c Seeff b Jefferies	12
Extras	15	Extras	8
1/7 2/74 3/88 4/91 5/95 6/95 7/148 8/232 9/236	251	1/4 2/9 3/12 4/21 5/21 6/52 7/53 8/53 9/53	75

Bowling: *First Innings*—le Roux 21.4–7–44–6; Jefferies 18–5–41–1; Hobson 30–10–84–2; Pienaar 6–4–6–0; Henry 11–1–45–1; du Toit 5–2–9–0; Kirsten 1–0–7–0. *Second Innings*—le Roux 14–7–23–3; Jefferies 14–6–25–4; Hobson 15.2–6–19–2; Kirsten 3–3–0–1.

Western Province

L. Seeff c McBride b Old	50
R. F. Pienaar b Old	5
*P. N. Kirsten lbw b Morris	130
A. J. Lamb st McBride b Morris	12
K. S. McEwan c Old b Ferreira	61
†S. D. Bruce c Old b Ontong	7
O. Henry lbw b Old	31
J. D. du Toit lbw b Ferreira	8
G. S. le Roux c Featherstone b Ackermann	42
S. T. Jefferies not out	35
Extras	41
1/13 2/121 3/144 4/277 5/289 6/296 7/315 8/366 9/422 (9 wkts dec.)	422

D. L. Hobson did not bat.

Bowling: Old 30–9–75–3; Ferreira 31–8–114–2; Morris 24–2–76–2; Ontong 20–5–96–1; Featherstone 1–0–11–0; Ackermann 1–0–9–0.

Umpires: B. C. Smith and N. M. Paterson.

NATAL v EASTERN PROVINCE

At Kingsmead, Durban, January 30, 31, February 1. Natal won by ten wickets. Natal 20 pts, Eastern Province 5 pts.

Natal

†A. J. S. Smith c Brickett b Ogilvie	25	– not out	8
C. P. Wilkins c Whyte b Watson	2	– not out	0
R. M. Bentley c Hopkins b Carse	16		
D. Bestall b Carse	1		
*M. J. Procter c Hopkins b Brickett	22		
R. A. Smith c Ogilvie b Armitage	91		
N. P. Daniels c Whyte b Watson	40		
D. K. Pearse b Carse	11		
V. A. P. van der Bijl c Furstenburg b Carse	42		
K. R. Cooper lbw b Armitage	6		
L. B. Taylor not out	0		
Extras	23		
1/8 2/46 3/46 4/49 5/76 6/161 7/199 8/268 9/277	279		8

Bowling: *First Innings*—Watson 21–5–62–2; Brickett 18–2–40–1; Carse 17–3–59–4; Ogilvie 13–2–63–1; Armitage 11.2–3–32–2. *Second Innings*—Carse 0.4–0–8–0.

Eastern Province

J. W. Furstenburg c A. J. S. Smith b van der Bijl	2	– c Cooper b van der Bijl	0
J. A. Hopkins c Wilkins b Taylor	25	– lbw b van der Bijl	5
R. L. S. Armitage c Bentley b van der Bijl	0	– c A. J. S. Smith b Procter	2
S. J. Bezuidenhout c A. J. S. Smith b van der Bijl	0	– c sub b van der Bijl	22
J. A. Carse b van der Bijl	0	– (11) b Daniels	19
R. G. Fensham lbw b Taylor	10	– (5) c A. J. S. Smith b Procter	6
R. J. D. Whyte c Cooper b van der Bijl	1	– (7) c A. J. S. Smith b van der Bijl	17
†D. J. Richardson lbw b Taylor	21	– (6) c Bentley b Cooper	32
*D. J. Brickett c A. J. S. Smith b Procter	17	– (8) c Cooper b Taylor	5
J. D. Ogilvie b Procter	23	– (9) not out	21
W. K. Watson not out	0	– (10) lbw b van der Bijl	13
Extras	21	Extras	22
1/8 2/8 3/15 4/15 5/32 6/33 7/77 8/78 9/115	120	1/0 2/3 3/8 4/22 5/58 6/92 7/105 8/105 9/126	164

Bowling: *First Innings*—van der Bijl 23–7–48–5; Taylor 20–9–26–3; Cooper 6–1–16–0; Procter 4.4–1–9–2. *Second Innings*—van der Bijl 21–8–56–5; Taylor 13–3–38–1; Cooper 11–3–28–1; Procter 8–5–10–2; Pearse 7–6–1–0; Daniels 2.2–1–9–1.

Umpires: D. D. Schoof and K. E. Liebenberg.

EASTERN PROVINCE v TRANSVAAL

At St George's Park, Port Elizabeth, February 6, 7, 8. Transvaal won by nine wickets. Transvaal 21 pts, Eastern Province 5 pts.

Eastern Province

S. J. Bezuidenhout c McMillan b Hanley	31	– c McKenzie b Rice	43
J. A. Hopkins c Jennings b Hanley	5	– b Radford	33
R. L. S. Armitage c Kallicharran b Hanley	3	– c Venter b Radford	24
†D. J. Richardson st Jennings b McMillan	5	– lbw b Radford	39
R. G. Fensham lbw b McMillan	6	– b McMillan	6
R. J. D. Whyte c Rice b McMillan	58	– c Jennings b Rice	23
I. Foulkes c Pollock b Hanley	0	– c Kallicharran b Hanley	38
*D. J. Brickett b McMillan	13	– (9) c Jennings b Rice	15
J. D. Ogilvie not out	42	– (8) c Pollock b Radford	6
W. K. Watson c Hanley b Rice	0	– c Radford b Rice	8
J. A. Carse c Pollock b Hanley	0	– not out	3
Extras	19	Extras	11
1/5 2/9 3/32 4/42 5/68 6/70 7/107 8/158 9/181	182	1/70 2/100 3/105 4/115 5/154 6/208 7/214 8/227 9/240	249

Bowling: *First Innings*—Hanley 15.3–7–31–5; Radford 12–0–39–0; Rice 12–1–23–1; McMillan 20–9–43–4; Kourie 10–3–27–0. *Second Innings*—Hanley 19–5–51–1; Radford 17–4–53–4; Rice 19.4–4–49–4; McMillan 20–5–55–1; Kourie 20–9–30–0.

Transvaal

S. J. Cook c Richardson b Carse	9	– not out	28
M. S. Venter lbw b Carse	18	– c sub b Watson	3
A. I. Kallicharran st Richardson b Armitage	61	– not out	45
R. G. Pollock c Ogilvie b Carse	72		
*C. E. B. Rice c Carse b Watson	22		
K. A. McKenzie not out	101		
G. E. McMillan lbw b Brickett	2		
†R. V. Jennings run out	14		
A. J. Kourie b Watson	25		
N. V. Radford not out	3		
Extras	27	Extras	2
1/33 2/48 3/147 4/187 5/216 6/237 7/282 8/339 (8 wkts dec.)	354	1/9 (1 wkt)	78

R. W. Hanley did not bat.

Bowling: *First Innings*—Watson 28–6–73–2; Carse 21–3–74–3; Brickett 18–2–41–1; Ogilvie 14–2–63–0; Armitage 13–0–58–1; Foulkes 3–0–18–0. *Second Innings*—Watson 7–0–33–1; Brickett 6–0–14–0; Ogilvie 2.3–0–15–0; Foulkes 2–1–14–0.

Umpires: A. A. Mathews and B. C. Smith.

WESTERN PROVINCE v NATAL

At Newlands, Cape Town, February 12, 13, 15. Western Province won by seven wickets. Western Province 18 pts, Natal 3 pts.

Natal

B. A. Richards b le Roux	38	– c During b Hobson	34
C. P. Wilkins c During b le Roux	22	– c Kuiper b Hobson	15
R. M. Bentley c During b Jefferies	6	– c Bruce b Hobson	24
D. Bestall c Seeff b Henry	43	– lbw b Jefferies	37
R. A. Smith c Lamb b Henry	2	– lbw b Jefferies	0
*M. J. Procter c During b Hobson	20	– c Hobson b Jefferies	63
†A. J. S. Smith c Seeff b Henry	0	– c Bruce b le Roux	0
N. P. Daniels c Bruce b Jefferies	1	– b le Roux	32
P. B. Clift c McEwan b Henry	17	– b Jefferies	4
V. A. P. van der Bijl c Bruce b Jefferies	6	– c During b le Roux	0
L. B. Taylor not out	2	– not out	6
Extras	12	Extras	28
1/52 2/74 3/84 4/118 5/131 6/131 7/132 8/139 9/155	169	1/46 2/53 3/123 4/153 5/196 6/196 7/197 8/215 9/216	243

Bowling: *First Innings*—le Roux 17–5–50–2; Jefferies 23–11–40–3; During 10–3–14–0; Hobson 7–1–31–1; Henry 10.5–4–22–4. *Second Innings*—le Roux 19–4–64–3; Jefferies 21.3–7–65–4; Hobson 31–17–53–3; Henry 14–8–26–0; Kirsten 9–6–7–0.

Western Province

L. Seeff lbw b Taylor	10	– lbw b Daniels	6
J. During c Bestall b Procter	5	– lbw b Clift	10
*P. N. Kirsten c A. J. S. Smith b Taylor	5	– not out	28
A. J. Lamb b Daniels	89	– not out	4
K. S. McEwan b Daniels	117		
†S. D. Bruce c sub b Daniels	5		
A. P. Kuiper c Bestall b Clift	50	– c Daniels b A. J. S. Smith	0
G. S. le Roux c and b Clift	3		
O. Henry not out	22		
S. T. Jefferies c A. J. S. Smith b Procter	12		
D. L. Hobson c R. A. Smith b Procter	5		
Extras	40	Extras	3
1/12 2/18 3/36 4/188 5/202 6/317 7/319 8/324 9/343	363	1/12 2/24 3/41 (3 wkts)	51

Bowling: *First Innings*—van der Bijl 30–9–61–0; Procter 20–3–61–3; Taylor 14–3–34–2; Clift 23–3–78–2; Daniels 27–3–78–3; Bentley 6–3–11–0. *Second Innings*—van der Bijl 6–2–15–0; Clift 4–2–10–1; Daniels 5–1–13–1; A. J. S. Smith 1–0–4–1; R. A. Smith 0.5–0–6–0.

Umpires: E. Hunt and P. R. Hurwitz.

NORTHERN TRANSVAAL v EASTERN PROVINCE

At Berea Park, Pretoria, February 12, 13, 15. Drawn. Northern Transvaal 5 pts, Eastern Province 6 pts.

Northern Transvaal

B. J. Whitfield c Richardson b Brickett	8	– lbw b Carse	0
K. Jennings c Foulkes b Carse	18	– c Bezuidenhout b Armitage	25
V. F. du Preez b Ogilvie	8	– b Foulkes	84
P. J. A. Visagie run out	47	– c Brickett b Armitage	12
*N. G. Featherstone lbw b Ogilvie	5	– c Richardson b Foulkes	0
C. S. Stirk c Armitage b Foulkes	45	– b Foulkes	59
A. M. Ferreira st Richardson b Foulkes	60	– b Armitage	12
R. C. Ontong c Whyte b Armitage	5	– lbw b Brickett	12
C. M. Old c Fensham b Armitage	1	– b Foulkes	2
†N. Rynners not out	13	– not out	16
F. E. Joubert c Ogilvie b Foulkes	0	– c and b Armitage	13
Extras	10	Extras	11
1/25 2/37 3/45 4/51 5/106 6/162 7/186 8/188 9/220	220	1/1 2/89 3/113 4/139 5/139 6/156 7/205 8/215 9/221	246

Bowling: *First Innings*—Watson 12–2–25–0; Carse 19–5–48–1; Brickett 12–3–17–1; Ogilvie 13–3–35–2; Foulkes 19.4–4–60–3; Armitage 11–3–25–2. *Second Innings*—Watson 12–5–31–0; Carse 13–3–14–1; Brickett 6–2–13–1; Ogilvie 8–4–20–0; Foulkes 38–11–92–4; Armitage 37.1–11–65–4.

Eastern Province

S. J. Bezuidenhout lbw b Ontong	34	b Joubert	2
J. A. Hopkins lbw b Old	20	c Featherstone b Joubert	2
R. L. S. Armitage not out	171		
†D. J. Richardson c Featherstone b Ontong	0		
R. G. Fensham c Ontong b Ferreira	28	– b Joubert	0
R. J. D. Whyte c Stirk b Ferreira	12	– not out	7
I. Foulkes c Rynners b Joubert	53		
*D. J. Brickett not out	11		
Extras	21	Extras	3
1/38 2/70 3/70 4/145 5/183 6/339 (6 wkts dec.)	350	1/3 2/14 3/14 (3 wkts)	14

J. D. Ogilvie, W. K. Watson and J. A. Carse did not bat.

Bowling: *First Innings*—Old 18–5–35–1; Joubert 25–3–82–1; Ontong 19–7–62–2; Ferreira 32–7–89–2; du Preez 13–2–46–0; Featherstone 4–1–12–0; Stirk 1–0–3–0. *Second Innings*—Old 2–0–8–0; Joubert 1.3–0–3–3.

Umpires: E. A. Carter and A. T. Maasch.

NORTHERN TRANSVAAL v NATAL

At Berea Park, Pretoria, March 8, 9, 10. Natal won by six wickets. Natal 14 pts, Northern Transvaal 7 pts.

Northern Transvaal

B. J. Whitfield lbw b van der Bijl	30	– lbw b van der Bijl	8
K. Jennings c Cooper b van der Bijl	26	– b van der Bijl	1
*V. F. du Preez lbw b van der Bijl	18	– c Richards b van der Bijl	16
P. J. A. Visagie b Clift	5	– c Clift b van der Bijl	0
C. S. Stirk lbw b van der Bijl	27	– lbw b van der Bijl	31
A. M. Ferreira c Smith b Clift	29	– b van der Bijl	0
R. C. Ontong c Wilkins b Daniels	45	– b Clift	20
†G. Tullis c Wilkins b Hodkinson	21	– b van der Bijl	22
H. W. Raath not out	6	– c Wilkins b Daniels	1
A. Wilkins c Clift b van der Bijl	2	– b van der Bijl	2
T. Wheelwright c Daniels b van der Bijl	2	– not out	1
Extras	10	Extras	8
1/40 2/45 3/88 4/92 5/125 6/169 7/204 8/216 9/219	221	1/5 2/26 3/26 4/27 5/27 6/73 7/94 8/99 9/105	110

Bowling: *First Innings*—van der Bijl 29–8–64–6; Hodkinson 13–3–29–1; Cooper 12–1–44–0; Clift 18–6–35–2; Procter 12–4–36–0; Daniels 4–1–3–1. *Second Innings*—van der Bijl 21–6–47–8; Hodkinson 6–1–14–0; Clift 11–2–22–1; Daniels 13–6–19–1.

Natal

B. A. Richards c Stirk b Wheelwright	5	– (5) b du Preez	32
C. P. Wilkins b Wilkins	6	– c Tullis b Raath	33
R. M. Bentley c Tullis b Wheelwright	4	– c Raath b Wheelwright	5
P. B. Clift c Wheelwright b Ontong	35	– (1) c Tullis b Wheelwright	9
D. Bestall c Stirk b Ontong	35	– (4) not out	80
*M. J. Procter b Ontong	9	– not out	17
N. P. Daniels not out	20		
†A. J. S. Smith c Tullis b Ferreira	10		
V. A. P. van der Bijl c Tullis b Ferreira	3		
K. R. Cooper b Wheelwright	17		
E. J. Hodkinson c Tullis b Wheelwright	0		
Extras	4	Extras	10
1/11 2/13 3/25 4/86 5/98 6/100 7/117 8/127 9/148	148	1/10 2/15 3/96 4/164	(4 wkts) 186

Bowling: *First Innings*—Wilkins 13–5–27–1; Wheelwright 16.4–2–47–5; Ferreira 17–5–31–2; Ontong 11–1–39–2. *Second Innings*—Wilkins 15–4–46–0; Wheelwright 13–4–34–2; Ferreira 26–12–34–0; Ontong 6–3–17–0; Raath 12.1–3–31–1; du Preez 6–1–14–1.

Umpires: G. Hawkins and O. R. Schoof.

TRANSVAAL v NATAL

At The Wanderers, Johannesburg, March 31, April 1, 2. Transvaal won by three wickets. Transvaal 17 pts, Natal 7 pts.

Natal

C. P. Wilkins st Jennings b Kourie	46	– c Cook b Fairclough	44
C. L. Smith b Hanley	112	– c Jennings b Hanley	6
R. M. Bentley c McKenzie b Kourie	0	– run out	12
D. Bestall b McKenzie	68	– c Pollock b Kallicharran	17
N. P. Daniels b McMillan	66	– b Page	51
*B. A. Richards lbw b Hanley	2	– not out	31
†A. J. S. Smith c Rice b Hanley	4		
D. K. Pearse c Pollock b McMillan	3		
K. R. Cooper c Kallicharran b McMillan	36		
V. A. P. van der Bijl not out	13		
E. J. Hodkinson run out	1		
Extras	20	Extras	14
1/67 2/75 3/217 4/260 5/266 6/274 7/281 8/353 9/369	371	1/17 2/58 3/67 4/117 5/175 (5 wkts dec.)	175

Bowling: *First Innings*—Hanley 23.5–5–95–3; Fairclough 22–4–53–0; Kourie 24.4–9–44–2; Page 15–1–50–0; Kallicharran 6–1–16–0; McMillan 20–3–74–3; McKenzie 4–0–19–1. *Second Innings*—Hanley 13–2–28–1; Fairclough 8–2–21–1; Page 7.1–1–18–1; Kallicharran 13–0–35–1; McMillan 10–2–25–0; McKenzie 8–2–34–0.

Transvaal

S. J. Cook c Richards b Daniels	50	– c A. J. S. Smith b van der Bijl	28
†R. V. Jennings lbw b van der Bijl	3	– b van der Bijl	1
A. I. Kallicharran lbw b Cooper	103	– lbw b van der Bijl	17
*C. E. B. Rice b van der Bijl	1	– (5) not out	102
K. A. McKenzie st A. J. S. Smith b Daniels	5	– (6) lbw b Daniels	30
R. G. Pollock not out	72	– (4) c Richards b van der Bijl	26
H. Page b van der Bijl	3	– b Daniels	26
G. E. McMillan b van der Bijl	0	– c and b van der Bijl	6
A. J. Kourie not out	27	– not out	12
Extras	13	Extras	22
1/3 2/137 3/142 4/161 5/187 6/191 7/191 (7 wkts dec.)	277	1/25 2/30 3/69 4/84 5/160 6/209 7/230 (7 wkts)	270

R. W. Hanley and J. Fairclough did not bat.

Bowling: *First Innings*—van der Bijl 28–8–62–4; Hodkinson 6–0–20–0; Daniels 28–4–75–2; C. L. Smith 1–0–14–0; Wilkins 1–0–8–0; Cooper 14–0–57–1; Pearse 2–0–14–0; Bentley 4–0–14–0. *Second Innings*—van der Bijl 23.1–2–129–5; Hodkinson 1–0–21–0; Daniels 11–3–42–2; Cooper 9–1–39–0; Bentley 2–0–17–0.

Umpires: C. J. Mitchley and D. D. Schoof.

EASTERN PROVINCE v WESTERN PROVINCE

At St George's Park, Port Elizabeth, March 31, April 1, 2. Western Province won by ten wickets. Western Province 23 pts, Eastern Province 2 pts.

Eastern Province

S. J. Bezuidenhout b le Roux	10	lbw b le Roux	110
J. W. Furstenburg c Bruce b Jefferies	9	c Henry b Kuiper	15
R. L. S. Armitage c Bruce b Kuiper	25	c Pienaar b Jefferies	34
†D. J. Richardson c Kuiper b Jefferies	16	c Bruce b Henry	34
R. J. D. Whyte c Bruce b Jefferies	0	(6) c Lamb b le Roux	46
I. Foulkes c Kuiper b Jefferies	5	(5) c Bruce b le Roux	3
R. G. Fensham not out	38	c Henry b Jefferies	39
*D. J. Brickett c Pienaar b le Roux	4	lbw b le Roux	1
J. D. Ogilvie c Pienaar b le Roux	6	lbw b Jefferies	0
W. K. Watson lbw b le Roux	0	c Kirsten b le Roux	13
M. K. van Vuuren c Kirsten b le Roux	0	not out	0
Extras	7	Extras	12
1/20 2/22 3/65 4/69 5/69 6/70 7/96 8/112 9/112	120	1/33 2/153 3/179 4/183 5/223 6/284 7/286 8/287 9/307	307

Bowling: *First Innings*—le Roux 18.3–8–28–5; Jefferies 19–8–48–4; Hobson 4–2–14–0; Pienaar 6–2–11–0; Kuiper 3–1–12–1. *Second Innings*—le Roux 20.3–1–51–5; Jefferies 23–2–88–3; Hobson 28–3–68–0; Pienaar 8–0–43–0; Kuiper 3–1–10–1; Henry 11–2–35–1.

Western Province

L. Seeff b Watson	79	not out	21
R. F. Pienaar c Whyte b Watson	7	not out	25
*P. L. Kirsten c Armitage b Brickett	151		
A. J. Lamb not out	106		
K. S. McEwan not out	28		
Extras	13		
1/14 2/203 3/279 (3 wkts dec.)	384	(no wkt)	46

A. P. Kuiper, †S. D. Bruce, G. S. le Roux, O. Henry, S. T. Jefferies and D. L. Hobson did not bat.

Bowling: *First Innings*—Watson 25–4–81–2; van Vuuren 18–1–81–0; Foulkes 11–0–66–0; Brickett 22–2–65–1; Ogilvie 9–1–56–0; Armitage 6–0–22–0. *Second Innings*—van Vuuren 5–1–16–0; Ogilvie 5–1–19–0; Fensham 1–0–7–0; Furstenburg 0.1–0–4–0.

Umpires: A. A. Mathews and D. A. Sansom.

CURRIE CUP WINNERS

1889-90	Transvaal	1923-24	Transvaal
1890-91	Griqualand West	1925-26	Transvaal
1892-93	Western Province	1926-27	Transvaal
1893-94	Western Province	1929-30	Transvaal
1894-95	Transvaal	1931-32	Western Province
1896-97	Western Province	1933-34	Natal
1897-98	Western Province	1934-35	Transvaal
1902-03	Transvaal	1936-37	Natal
1903-04	Transvaal	1937-38	Natal/Transvaal (Tied)
1904-05	Transvaal	1946-47	Natal
1906-07	Transvaal	1947-48	Natal
1908-09	Western Province	1950-51	Transvaal
1910-11	Natal	1951-52	Natal
1912-13	Natal	1952-53	Western Province
1920-21	Western Province	1954-55	Natal
1921-22	Transvaal/Natal/W. Prov. (Tied)	1955-56	Western Province

1958-59	Transvaal	1971-72	Transvaal
1959-60	Natal	1972-73	Transvaal
1960-61	Natal	1973-74	Natal
1962-63	Natal	1974-75	Western Province
1963-64	Natal	1975-76	Natal
1965-66	Natal/Transvaal (Tied)	1976-77	Natal
1966-67	Natal	1977-78	Western Province
1967-68	Natal	1978-79	Transvaal
1968-69	Transvaal	1979-80	Transvaal
1969-70	Transvaal/Western Province (Tied)	1980-81	Natal
1970-71	Transvaal	1981-82	Western Province

SAB BOWL, 1981-82

North	Played	Won	Lost	Drawn	Bonus Points Batting	Bonus Points Bowling	Total Points
Boland	6	4	2	0	11	30	81
Northern Transvaal B	6	3	1	2	10	30	70
Transvaal B	6	2	2	2	14	29	63
Eastern Province B	6	2	2	2	17	25	62
Border	6	1	5	0	3	22	35

South	Played	Won	Lost	Drawn	Bonus Points Batting	Bonus Points Bowling	Total Points
Western Province B	6	3	1	2	12	30	72
Orange Free State	6	2	1	3	13	26	59
Natal B	6	0	1	5	17	24	41
Griqualand West	6	0	2	4	15	25	40

Boland beat Western Province B by 149 runs in the final.

SAB BOWL, 1981-82

Northern Section

At The Wanderers, Johannesburg, October 30, 31, November 2. Transvaal B won by six wickets. Northern Transvaal B 173 and 207 (J. P. Ackermann 52; I. F. Weideman four for 39); Transvaal B 260 (M. Yachad 154; H. W. Raath five for 53) and 121 for four (M. Yachad 59). *Transvaal B 19 pts, Northern Transvaal B 5 pts.*

At Kemsley Park, Port Elizabeth, November 7, 8, 9. Eastern Province B won by an innings and 93 runs. Border 113 (I. L. Howell four for 22) and 133; Eastern Province B 339 (I. L. Howell 112, M. K. van Vuuren 75, R. G. Fensham 68; M. J. Hartley four for 57). *Eastern Province B 22 pts, Border 5 pts.*

At Oude Libertas, Stellenbosch, November 12, 13, 15. Boland won by an innings and 61 runs. Boland 346 for three dec. (A. du Toit 117, E. J. Barlow 107; H. N. Basson 64); Border 116 and 169 (R. Kent 52, G. L. Hayes 52; P. Anker six for 83, E. J. Barlow four for 25). *Boland 21 pts, Border 1 pt.*

At Oude Libertas, Stellenbosch, December 4, 5, 7. Northern Transvaal B won by 81 runs. Northern Transvaal B 241 (J. P. Ackermann 61, P. J. Marneweck 54; P. Anker four for 42) and 172 (P. J. A. Visagie 95; P. Anker four for 55); Boland 164 (P. D. Swart 54; H. W. Raath four for 25, W. F. Morris four for 67) and 168 (H. W. Raath four for 41). *Northern Transvaal B 18 pts, Boland 5 pts.*

At Jan Smuts Ground, East London, December 26, 28, 29. Northern Transvaal B won by an innings and 75 runs. Border 110 (P. J. Marneweck six for 12) and 158 (P. J. Marneweck four for 37); Northern Transvaal B 343 for nine dec. (C. P. L. de Lange 112, W. F. Morris 99; G. M. Gower five for 66). *Northern Transvaal B 17 pts, Border 3 pts.*

At Uitenhage, December 26, 27, 28. Drawn. Transvaal B 149 and 297 (L. J. Barnard 69, N. T. Day 63); Eastern Province B 232 (H. Losper seven for 86) and 177 for nine (J. W. Furstenburg 57). *Eastern Province B 8 pts, Transvaal B 5 pts.*

At Jan Smuts Ground, East London, December 31, January 1, 2. Border won by four wickets. Transvaal B 230 (N. T. Day 78, G. E. McMillan 64) and 203 (N. E. Wright 65); Border 335 (E. T. Laughlin 101, R. B. C. Ranger 75) and 102 for six. *Border 17 pts, Transvaal B 6 pts.*

At The Wanderers, Johannesburg, January 15, 16, 18. Boland won by six wickets. Transvaal B 106 and 135; Boland 169 (E. J. Barlow 65; I. F. Weideman four for 55) and 73 for four. *Boland 15 pts, Transvaal B 5 pts.*

At Berea Park, Pretoria, January 22, 23, 25. Drawn. Transvaal B 268 (A. Videgauz 57; H. W. Raath six for 95) and 249 for three dec. (N. E. Wright 85, L. J. Barnard 65); Northern Transvaal B 219 (I. F. Weideman four for 52) and 121 for three. *Transvaal B 9 pts, Northern Transvaal B 7 pts.*

At Berea Park, Pretoria, January 1, 2, 4. Drawn. Northern Transvaal B 284 (D. N. Edwards 62, C. P. L. de Lange 61; L. Reid-Ross six for 78) and 221 for six dec. (D. N. Edwards 50); Eastern Province B 195 and 251 for six. (G. S. Cowley 98 not out). *Northern Transvaal B 6 pts, Eastern Province B 4 pts.*

At Uitenhage, January 30, February 1, 2. Boland won by nine wickets. Eastern Province B 263 (J. W. Stephenson 83; P. Anker five for 55) and 136 (P. Anker five for 50); Boland 378 for six dec. (E. J. Barlow 202 not out) and 22 for one. *Boland 17 pts, Eastern Province B 7 pts.*

At Jan Smuts Ground, East London, February 4, 5, 6. Boland won by 46 runs. Boland 191 (S. A. Jones 59) and 240 for seven dec. (P. D. Swart 92; M. J. Hartley four for 56); Border 136 (C. J. Coetzee four for 49) and 249 (D. S. Scott 62, E. T. Laughlin 56). *Boland 16 pts, Border 5 pts.*

At The Wanderers, Johannesburg, February 5, 6, 7. Transvaal B won by an innings and 55 runs. Transvaal B 305 for seven dec. (H. R. Fotheringham 115); Eastern Province B 146 (H. A. Page four for 47) and 104 (H. A. Page four for 49). *Transvaal B 19 pts, Eastern Province B 4 pts.*

At Oude Libertas, Stellenbosch, February 26, 27, March 1. Eastern Province B won by 50 runs. Eastern Province B 212 and 202 (G. Long 98, D. H. Howell 54; P. Anker five for 70); Boland 201 (J. de Villiers 61, P. D. Swart 57; M. K. van Vuuren five for 38) and 163. *Eastern Province B 17 pts, Boland 7 pts.*

At Berea Park, Pretoria, February 26, 27, March 1. Northern Transvaal B won by 108 runs. Northern Transvaal B 215 (C. P. L. de Lange 72) and 190 (A. H. Jordaan 57; B. M. Osborne seven for 25); Border 144 and 153. *Northern Transvaal B 17 pts, Border 4 pts.*

Southern Section

At Ramblers Ground, Bloemfontein, October 16, 17, 19. Orange Free State won by seven wickets. Griqualand West 247 (T. Smit 52 not out; J. van Heerden four for 45) and 243 (M. J. D. Doherty 53, A. D. Methven 67); Orange Free State 309 (J. J. Strydom 85, G. W. Humpage 64) and 182 for three (G. W. Humpage 61 not out, R. J. East 53 not out). *Orange Free State 19 pts, Griqualand West 7 pts.*

At Kingsmead, Durban, November 7, 8, 9. Drawn. Griqualand West 242 (A. P. Beukes 55) and 91 for two; Natal B 313 (P. H. Williams 67, D. K. Pearse 55 not out; A. P. Beukes five for 101). *Natal B 10 pts, Griqualand West 7 pts.*

At Ramblers Ground, Bloemfontein, November 6, 7, 9. Orange Free State won by two wickets. Western Province B 129 (C. J. P. G. van Zyl six for 50) and 278 (H. M. Ackerman 86 not out, T. A. Clarke 82; A. Sidebottom five for 50); Orange Free State 218 (R. J. East 54; J. D. du Toit five for 46) and 190 for eight. *Orange Free State 17 pts, Western Province B 5 pts.*

At Burt Oval, Constantia, November 27, 28, 30. Western Province B won by five wickets. Griqualand West 108 (J. D. du Toit six for 26) and 203 (M. J. D. Doherty 82; J. D. du Toit four for 41); Western Province B 210 (T. A. Clarke 54; T. Smit five for 68) and 104 for five. *Western Province B 17 pts, Griqualand West 5 pts.*

At Country Club, Kimberley, November 12, 13, 14. Drawn. Western Province B 282 for eight dec. (P. M. Thompson 90, E. Muntingh 69) and 166 for five (P. M. Thompson 52); Griqualand West 288 (A. D. Methven 68, M. J. D. Doherty 55; T. A. Clarke five for 30). *Griqualand West 7 pts, Western Province B 7 pts.*

At Burt Oval, Constantia, December 4, 5, 7. Western Province B won by 243 runs. Western Province B 252 (A. Sidebottom four for 36, W. M. van der Merwe four for 38) and 215 for eight dec. (W. M. van der Merwe four for 37); Orange Free State 92 (O. Henry five for 34) and 132 (J. D. du Toit four for 24, O. Henry four for 48). *Western Province B 19 pts, Orange Free State 5 pts.*

At Newlands, Cape Town, December 26, 28, 29. Western Province B won by ten wickets. Western Province B 349 for five dec. (J. Seeff 113 not out, S. D. Bruce 100 not out, P. M. Thompson 55) and 14 for no wkt; Natal B 99 (R. R. Lawrenson five for 50) and 260 (M. D. Tramontino 69, M. Hedley 53; J. L. Louw four for 52). *Western Province B 17 pts, Natal B 2 pts.*

At Kingsmead, Durban, January 1, 2, 3. Drawn. Natal B 295 for seven dec. (P. J. Allan 75 not out, D. K. Pearse 70, R. A. Smith 58) and 160 for seven dec.; Orange Free State 250 (J. van Heerden 57, I. Ebrahim five for 75) and 81 for one. *Natal B 6 pts, Orange Free State 5 pts.*

At Ramblers Ground, Bloemfontein, January 23, 25, 26. Drawn. Natal B 238 (T. R. Madsen 55; A. Sidebottom four for 43) and 346 for seven dec. (M. D. Logan 107 not out); Orange Free State 249 (A. Sidebottom 66, E. J. Hodkinson four for 76) and 204 for five (S. N. Hartley 72 not out, R. J. East 53). *Orange Free State 8 pts, Natal B 8 pts.*

At Country Club, Kimberley, January 28, 29, 30. Drawn. Griqualand West 296 (F. W. Swarbrook 71, A. D. Methven 57; M. Clare four for 61) and 236 for seven dec. (F. W. Swarbrook 70, M. J. D. Doherty 62; I. Ebrahim five for 57); Natal B 251 for eight dec. (T. R. Madsen 92; H. Liebenberg five for 55) and 245 for eight (C. L. Smith 78). *Griqualand West 8 pts, Natal B 7 pts.*

At Jan Smuts Oval, Pietermaritzburg, February 13, 14, 15. Drawn. Western Province B 212 (T. A. Clarke 63; E. J. Hodkinson four for 31) and 281 for nine dec. (R. R. Lawrenson 87; E. J. Hodkinson six for 68); Natal B 238 (C. L. Smith 65, K. D. Verdoorn 61) and 176 for eight (H. M. Ackerman four for 61). *Natal B 8 pts, Western Province B 7 pts.*

At Country Club, Kimberley, February 25, 26, 27. Drawn. Orange Free State 202 (R. A. le Roux 67; A. P. Beukes four for 49) and 215 for four (R. A. le Roux 100 not out); Griqualand West 246 for eight dec. (M. J. D. Doherty 113 not out, H. Liebenberg 63). *Griqualand West 6 pts, Orange Free State 5 pts.*

Final

At Oude Libertas, Stellenbosch, March 24, 25, 26, 27. Boland won by 149 runs. Boland 237 (T. A. Clarke four for 35) and 291 (P. D. Swart 89; J. L. Louw seven for 57); Western Province B 115 and 264 (E. Muntingh 67, M. D. Mellor 60; P. Anker five for 73).

OTHER FIRST-CLASS MATCH

At Newlands, Cape Town, December 14, 15, 17. Western Province won by 84 runs. Western Province 130 and 309 (A. J. Lamb 69, L. Seeff 56; J. D. du Toit five for 59); South African Universities 249 (R. J. East 63; R. F. Pienaar four for 64) and 106 (O. Henry seven for 22).

DATSUN SHIELD, 1981-82

First Round

At Newlands, Cape Town, October 24. Orange Free State won by 20 runs. Orange Free State 253 for six (G. W. Humpage 99); Western Province B 233 (P. Rayner 143; W. M. van der Merwe four for 49).

At Berea Park, Pretoria, October 24. Northern Transvaal won by 171 runs. Northern Transvaal 232 for four (N. G. Featherstone 70); Border 61 (F. E. Joubert three for 11).

Second Round

At Ramblers Ground, Bloemfontein, October 31. Natal won by six wickets. Orange Free State 153 (L. W. Griessel 59 not out; L. B. Taylor four for 15); Natal 157 for four (B. A. Richards 66).

At Country Club, Kimberley, October 31. Transvaal won by 69 runs. Transvaal 237 for five (R. G. Pollock 66); Griqualand West 168 for six.

At Newlands, Cape Town, October 31. Western Province won by eight wickets. Northern Transvaal 98 (S. T. Jefferies three for 17); Western Province 101 for two.

At St George's Park, Port Elizabeth, October 31. Boland won by 66 runs. Boland 184 for eight (J. A. Carse three for 21); Eastern Province 118 (H. Bergins four for 18).

Semi-Finals – First Leg

At Newlands, Cape Town, December 19. Western Province won by 74 runs. Western Province 258 for four (A. J. Lamb 90, R. F. Pienaar 67, P. N. Kirsten 57 not out); Boland 184 for nine (P. D. Swart 51; A. P. Kuiper three for 16, R. F. Pienaar three for 32).

At The Wanderers, Johannesburg, December 19. Transvaal won by six wickets. Natal 230 for eight (C. P. Wilkins 66; N. V. Radford four for 25); Transvaal 234 for four (A. I. Kallicharran 70 not out, S. J. Cook 60).

Semi-Finals – Second Leg

At Oude Libertas, Stellenbosch, January 9. Western Province won by 118 runs. Western Province 236 for nine (S. A. Jones four for 52); Boland 118 (S. T. Jefferies four for 34).

At Kingsmead, Durban, January 9. Natal won by 8 runs. Natal 191 (C. P. Wilkins 84; C. E. B. Rice three for 29); Transvaal 183 for nine.

Replay

At Kingsmead, Durban, January 13. Natal won by three wickets. Transvaal 165 for nine (C. E. B. Rice 76; K. R. Cooper four for 24); Natal 166 for seven (N. V. Radford three for 37).

FINAL
WESTERN PROVINCE v NATAL

At The Wanderers, Johannesburg, February 20. Western Province won by 2 runs.

Western Province

L. Seeff c Smith b Procter	1	G. S. le Roux b Taylor	8
R. F. Pienaar lbw b Taylor	12	O. Henry not out	17
*P. N. Kirsten c Bestall b Clift	35	S. T. Jefferies not out	1
A. J. Lamb run out	16	Extras	30
K. S. McEwan run out	3		—
A. P. Kuiper c Richards b Taylor	38	1/1 2/35 3/63 4/69 (8 wkts, 55 overs)	178
†S. D. Bruce b Taylor	17	5/109 6/136 7/143 8/177	

J. During did not bat.

Bowling: van der Bijl 11–1–39–0; Procter 11–5–15–1; Taylor 11–3–26–4; Cooper 11–0–51–0; Clift 11–1–17–1.

Natal

†A. J. S. Smith b Jefferies	0	P. B. Clift run out	3
C. P. Wilkins run out	0	V. A. P. van der Bijl not out	1
R. M. Bentley c Bruce b Pienaar	28	K. R. Cooper not out	3
D Bestall c Kirsten b le Roux	47	Extras	18
B. A. Richards c Jefferies b le Roux	29		—
*M. J. Procter c Seeff b Jefferies	24	1/0 2/1 3/74 4/117 (8 wkts, 55 overs)	176
N. P. Daniels b Jefferies	23	5/118 6/167 7/172 8/172	

L. B. Taylor did not bat.

Bowling: Jefferies 11–3–17–3; le Roux 11–5–21–2; Kuiper 6–1–14–0; Kirsten 4–0–16–0; Pienaar 10–0–40–1; During 11–0–45–0; Henry 2–0–5–0.

Umpires: P. R. Hurwitz and O. R. Schoof.

SAB ENGLISH TEAM IN SOUTH AFRICA, 1981-82

On February 27, 1982, a party of English cricketers slipped out of London, having taken every precaution to keep their departure a secret, to play a series of matches in South Africa. Before their first fixture, less than a week later, strenuous efforts were made to dissuade them from their venture. From the Test and County Cricket Board went a cable urging them, if it was not too late, to think again. Implicit in this was a warning that they were hazarding their cricketing futures, a threat which was duly implemented when, on March 9, a three-year ban from Test cricket was imposed on them.

Not only was the tour fiercely controversial; the cricket itself was disappointing, and as an exercise in public relations the whole operation left much to be desired. The best of the seven games was the first of three one-day matches, played before a capacity crowd at Port Elizabeth. The first of the three four-day games, at The Wanderers Stadium in Johannesburg, fell well short of being the expected sell-out.

Although extensive television coverage was thought to be responsible for this, when, on the Sunday (the third day of the match) the cricket was not screened, a crowd of around 20,000 was still 10,000 fewer than hoped for. It was the same story elsewhere, with the moderate form of the English players detracting from the success of the operation. They went through the tour without a victory. Of the four-day matches, the first resulted in an easy victory for the home side; the last two, though more closely contested, were rain-affected.

The only English batsman to do himself justice was Gooch, who, soon after the team's arrival, was elected captain by his fellow-players. His powerful strokeplay won him many admirers. The rest were only spasmodically impressive. The furore their visit created may have been one of the reasons for this. Of the fifteen players who took part, five (Boycott, Emburey, Gooch, Lever and Underwood) had just been with the England team in India; five (Humpage, Old, Sidebottom, Taylor and Woolmer) were already in South Africa, where they had been coaching and playing; and five (Amiss, Hendrick, Knott, Larkins and Willey) had spent most of their winter in England.

Woolmer, Humpage, Taylor and Sidebottom were recruited after the tour had started, having first contacted their counties to advise them of what they had in mind. In each case the players concerned were told that although their county futures would, in all likelihood, be unharmed, they would be risking their chances of representative selection. An abortive attempt was also made by the English players to persuade the sponsors of the tour, the South African Breweries, to allow Alvin Kallicharran, who was under contract to the Transvaal Cricket Union, to join them. Besides strengthening the batting of the team, there were those who felt that Kallicharran's presence might have acted as a political poultice.

The matches served as a reminder that South Africa, given the chance, could still hold their own in the international arena. They were not as strong, however, as when they last played Test cricket, in 1969-70. Procter, a shadow of his old self, eventually withdrew with injury, and Richards and Graeme Pollock were much less commanding. Barlow failed to find a place in the South African XI, all of whom were awarded Springbok colours.

Of the new school, Kirsten, well known in English county cricket, made 114 in the four-day game in Cape Town, while Cook, an opening batsman, Jefferies, a medium-paced bowler, Kourie, an orthodox left-arm spinner, and Jennings, the wicket-keeper, all created a favourable impression. The best bowler on either side was van der Bijl. Rice, one of the world's leading all-rounders, was unfit to bowl.

With the Currie Cup regulations being revised to allow provincial sides to include two overseas players, a majority of the English players were expected to return to South Africa for the English winter of 1982-83, this time as individuals rather than as a team and so with the customary approval of the TCCB. For their unapproved tour, the players were paid on a sliding scale, sums, it was thought, of between £10,000 and £40,000 each. – J.W.

SAB ENGLISH XI AVERAGES – FIRST-CLASS MATCHES

BATTING

	M	*I*	*NO*	*R*	*HI*	*Avge*
D. L. Amiss	4	7	2	308	73*	61.60
G. A. Gooch	4	7	0	396	109	56.57
W. Larkins	4	7	0	231	95	33.00

	M	I	NO	R	HI	Avge
G. Boycott	4	7	0	204	95	29.14
R. A. Woolmer	4	7	1	168	100	28.00
J. K. Lever	4	5	3	41	10*	20.50
P. Willey	3	4	0	79	39	19.75
A. P. E. Knott	4	6	0	63	27	10.50
C. M. Old	4	6	1	48	20	9.60
L. B. Taylor	3	3	1	10	10*	5.00
D. L. Underwood	2	3	0	14	8	4.66
M. Hendrick	2	2	1	1	1	1.00

Played in one match: J. E. Emburey 13; G. W. Humpage 1, 10. A. Sidebottom did not play in a first-class match.

* *Signifies not out.*

BOWLING

	O	M	R	W	Avge
L. B. Taylor	91.3	22	206	11	18.72
J. E. Emburey	47.5	10	153	6	25.50
G. A. Gooch	33	6	114	4	28.50
J. K. Lever	107	25	335	11	30.45
M. Hendrick	61.4	16	144	4	36.00
C. M. Old	102	34	258	5	51.60

Also bowled: G. W. Humpage 2–0–6–0; A. P. E. Knott 1–0–5–0; W. Larkins 11.1–0–47–1; D. L. Underwood 45–10–128–2; P. Willey 4–1–8–0.

FIELDING

A. P. E. Knott 17; G. A. Gooch 6, D. L. Amiss 1, G. Boycott 1, J. E. Emburey 1, M. Hendrick 1, G. W. Humpage 1, C. M. Old 1, P. Willey 1, R. A. Woolmer 1.

SPRINGBOK CAPS

The following players were awarded Springbok caps for representing South Africa in the three four-day matches against the SAB English XI: S. J. Cook (3), D. L. Hobson (1), S. T. Jefferies (2), R. V. Jennings (3), P. N. Kirsten (3), A. J. Kourie (3), A. P. Kuiper (2), G. S. le Roux (2), R. G. Pollock (3), M. J. Procter (1), C. E. B. Rice (3), B. A. Richards (3), V. A. P. van der Bijl (3), W. K. Watson (1).

†SOUTH AFRICAN UNDER-25 XI v SAB ENGLISH XI

At Pretoria, March 3, 4. Drawn. SAB English XI 152 for seven dec. (A. P. Kuiper five for 22) and 32 for two; South African Under-25 XI 170 for eight dec. (B. Whitfield 37).

†SOUTH AFRICA v SAB ENGLISH XI

At Port Elizabeth, March 6. South Africa won by seven wickets. SAB English XI 240 for five (50 overs) (G. A. Gooch 114, D. L. Amiss 71 not out); South Africa 244 for three (47.2 overs) (S. J. Cook 82, B. A. Richards 62, R. G. Pollock 57 not out).

WESTERN PROVINCE v SAB ENGLISH XI

At Cape Town, March 8, 9, 10. Drawn.

Western Province

L. Seeff c Knott b Emburey	12	c Humpage b Emburey	48
R. F. Pienaar run out	0	(9) not out	2
*P. N. Kirsten c Knott b Emburey	10	(6) not out	67
K. S. McEwan b Emburey	0	(3) c Knott b Old	2
A. P. Kuiper b Gooch	90	c Emburey b Hendrick	1
†S. D. Bruce c Boycott b Gooch	42	c and b Gooch	10
T. A. Clarke c Knott b Old	41	(8) b Gooch	11
O. Henry not out	33	(2) c Knott b Old	6
S. T. Jefferies b Emburey	17	(4) c Woolmer b Emburey	45
J. During not out	10		
L-b 8	8	B 1, l-b 6, w 1, n-b 4	12
1/7 2/22 3/22 4/24 5/100 6/195 7/203 8/242 (8 wkts)	263	1/21 2/26 3/103 4/108 5/110 6/184 7/196 (7 wkts dec.)	204

Bowling: *First Innings*—Old 18–7–61–1; Lever 0.2–0–0–0; Hendrick 16.4–2–52–0; Gooch 17–4–54–2; Emburey 26–7–88–4. *Second Innings*—Old 11–5–26–2; Hendrick 12–2–27–1; Gooch 14–2–45–2; Emburey 21.5–3–65–2; Larkins 6.1–0–23–0; Humpage 2–0–6–0.

SAB English XI

*G. Boycott c Clarke b Jefferies	20	run out	95
W. Larkins b Jefferies	24	c Kuiper b Hobson	22
D. L. Amiss b Hobson	52	(5) b Henry	30
R. A. Woolmer lbw b Hobson	3	(3) c Seeff b Pienaar	27
†A. P. E. Knott lbw b Jefferies	27	(4) c Kirsten b Jefferies	0
G. A. Gooch c McEwan b Clarke	58	c Jefferies b Pienaar	0
J. E. Emburey c Kirsten b Clarke	13		
G. W. Humpage b Hobson	1	(7) c During b Henry	10
C. M. Old not out	5	(8) c Kuiper b Hobson	20
M. Hendrick b Hobson	1	not out	0
J. K. Lever absent hurt	–	(9) not out	10
B 6, l-b 4, n-b 5	15	L-b 4, w 1, n-b 6	11
1/45 2/52 3/72 4/133 5/133 6/134 7/202 8/215 9/219	219	1/62 2/135 3/138 4/165 5/165 6/190 7/211 8/220 (8 wkts)	225

Bowling: *First Innings*—Jefferies 19–3–47–3; Kuiper 3–0–15–0; Pienaar 11–4–24–0; During 5–2–7–0; Hobson 21.1–8–57–4; Henry 8–3–34–0; Clarke 4–1–20–2. *Second Innings*—Jefferies 13–1–37–1; Kuiper 9–2–20–0; Pienaar 16–2–41–2; Hobson 21–6–48–2; Henry 11–1–61–2; Clarke 2–0–2–0; Kirsten 1–0–5–0.

Umpires: O. R. Schoof and A. T. Maasch.

SOUTH AFRICA v SAB ENGLISH XI

At Johannesburg, March 12, 13, 14, 15. South Africa won by eight wickets, having won the toss and elected to bat first.

South Africa

B. A. Richards c Amiss b Underwood	66	– (2) lbw b Lever	4
S. J. Cook c Gooch b Taylor	114	– (1) c and b Old	2
P. N. Kirsten c Gooch b Taylor	88	– not out	20
R. G. Pollock not out	64	– not out	9
C. E. B. Rice c Knott b Taylor	1		
*M. J. Procter c Knott b Lever	1		
A. J. Kourie lbw b Old	14		
†R. V. Jennings c Knott b Lever	24		
G. S. le Roux not out	6		
L-b 17, w 4, n-b 1	22	L-b 2	2
1/117 2/278 3/286 4/290 5/295 6/331 7/388 (7 wkts dec.)	400	1/8 2/14 (2 wkts)	37

S. T. Jefferies and V. A. P. van der Bijl did not bat.

Bowling: *First Innings*—Taylor 31–7–73–3; Old 28–10–76–1; Lever 32–3–122–2; Underwood 23–1–92–1; Gooch 2–0–15–0. *Second Innings*—Old 6–1–8–1; Lever 5.4–1–27–1.

SAB English XI

*G. A. Gooch b le Roux	30	– c Jennings b van der Bijl	109
G. Boycott c Cook b van der Bijl	5	– lbw b van der Bijl	36
W. Larkins lbw b van der Bijl	2	– c Kourie b van der Bijl	20
D. L. Amiss not out	66	– c Procter b Jefferies	24
R. A. Woolmer c Jennings b Kourie	14	– lbw b le Roux	21
P. Willey lbw b Jefferies	1	– lbw b le Roux	24
D. L. Underwood c Cook b van der Bijl	8	– (10) lbw b van der Bijl	6
†A. P. E. Knott c Richards b van der Bijl	5	– (7) lbw b van der Bijl	9
C. M. Old c Kourie b van der Bijl	1	– (8) b le Roux	11
J. K. Lever b Kourie	9	– (9) not out	10
L. B. Taylor b Jefferies	0	– c Pollock b le Roux	0
B 1, l-b 5, w 2, n-b 1	9	B 4, l-b 3, w 2, n-b 4	13
1/38 2/38 3/42 4/73 5/80 6/90 7/124 8/130 9/142	150	1/119 2/174 3/179 4/207 5/229 6/252 7/258 8/267 9/278	283

Bowling: *First Innings*—van der Bijl 22–8–25–5; Jefferies 20–5–59–2; Kourie 11–2–19–2; le Roux 10–2–38–1. *Second Innings*—van der Bijl 31–9–79–5; Jefferies 27–4–88–1; Kourie 16–7–53–0; le Roux 22.2–5–44–4; Procter 6–3–6–0.

Umpires: P. R. Hurwitz and B. C. Smith.

†SOUTH AFRICA v SAB ENGLISH XI

At Durban, March 17. South Africa won by 79 runs. South Africa 231 for six (50 overs) (R. G. Pollock 41, S. J. Cook 35, B. A. Richards 34, M. J. Procter 30); SAB English XI 152 (43.2 overs) (W. Larkins 47, P. Willey 31; V. A. P. van der Bijl three for 19).

SOUTH AFRICA v SAB ENGLISH XI

At Cape Town, March 19, 20, 21, 22. Drawn. The SAB English XI won the toss and batted first. Only two and threequarter hours' play was possible on the first day because of rain.

SAB English XI

*G. A. Gooch hit wicket b Kourie	83	– c Kourie b Hobson	68
G. Boycott c Kuiper b Kourie	16	– c Jennings b Jefferies	1
W. Larkins c Richards b Kourie	29	– lbw b Kirsten	95
D. L. Amiss c Jennings b Jefferies	13	– not out	73
R. A. Woolmer c and b Kourie	2	– not out	1
P. Willey c Kourie b van der Bijl	39		
†A. P. E. Knott b van der Bijl	16		
C. M. Old c Jennings b Jefferies	1		
J. K. Lever b Jefferies	8		
D. L. Underwood c Richards b van der Bijl	0		
L. B. Taylor not out	10		
L-b 2, w 2, n-b 2	6	B 4, l-b 7	11
1/27 2/104 3/140 4/144 5/148 6/189 7/199 8/205 9/207	223	1/8 2/112 3/231 (3 wkts dec.)	249

Bowling: *First Innings*—van der Bijl 33–12–61–3; Jefferies 24.4–9–56–3; Hobson 13–3–48–0; Kourie 32–15–52–4. *Second Innings*—van der Bijl 21–6–53–0; Jefferies 14–5–39–1; Hobson 30–7–86–1; Kourie 16–4–38–0; Kirsten 4–2–7–1; Kuiper 8–2–15–0.

South Africa

S. J. Cook c Knott b Lever	18		
*B. A. Richards lbw b Taylor	8		
P. N. Kirsten lbw b Lever	114		
R. G. Pollock c Knott b Lever	0		
C. E. B. Rice lbw b Taylor	12		
A. P. Kuiper c Willey b Underwood	1	– (2) not out	9
A. J. Kourie c Knott b Lever	18		
†R. V. Jennings c sub b Lever	32	– (1) not out	28
S. T. Jefferies c Knott b Lever	3		
V. A. P. van der Bijl not out	4		
D. L. Hobson b Taylor	2		
L-b 6, w 1, n-b 16	23	L-b 1	1
1/11 2/43 3/43 4/85 5/87 6/144 7/212 8/218 9/232	235	(no wkt)	38

Bowling: *First Innings*—Taylor 27–8–49–3; Lever 37–11–86–6; Old 18–6–33–0; Underwood 22–9–36–1; Willey 4–1–8–0. *Second Innings*—Lever 3–0–22–0; Old 4–0–15–0.

Umpires: O. R. Schoof and B. C. Smith.

†SOUTH AFRICA v SAB ENGLISH XI

At Johannesburg, March 24. South Africa won on faster scoring-rate. South Africa 243 for five (50 overs) (S. J. Cook 62, C. E. B. Rice 58 not out, A. P. Kuiper 54, P. N. Kirsten 32; A. Sidebottom three for 35); SAB English XI 111 for seven (23 overs) (G. A. Gooch 38; V. A. P. van der Bijl three for 30).

SOUTH AFRICA v SAB ENGLISH XI

At Durban, March 26, 27, 28, 29. Drawn. Gooch won the toss and put South Africa in on a green Kingsmead pitch. Rain prevented any play on the third day.

South Africa

S. J. Cook c Gooch b Lever	11	– not out	50
*B. A. Richards c Knott b Hendrick	41	– retired hurt	17
P. N. Kirsten c Gooch b Hendrick	11	– c Knott b Lever	14
R. G. Pollock b Taylor	15	– c Hendrick b Larkins	12
C. E. B. Rice c Gooch b Hendrick	9	– not out	39
A. P. Kuiper b Taylor	0		
A. J. Kourie not out	50		
†R. V. Jennings c Knott b Taylor	22		
G. S. le Roux c Knott b Taylor	0		
V. A. P. van der Bijl c Knott b Taylor	0		
W. K. Watson not out	4		
L-b 11, w 7	18	L-b 4, n-b 7	11
1/48 2/61 3/77 4/92 5/92 6/111 7/168 8/170 9/170 (9 wkts dec.)	181	1/61 2/91 (2 wkts)	143

Bowling: *First Innings*—Taylor 25.3–5–61–5; Lever 13–1–53–1; Old 11–3–21–0; Hendrick 21–9–28–3. *Second Innings*—Taylor 8–2–23–0; Lever 16–9–25–1; Old 6–2–18–0; Hendrick 12–3–37–0; Larkins 5–0–24–1; Knott 1–0–5–0.

SAB English XI

*G. A. Gooch c Kourie b le Roux	48
G. Boycott c Jennings b van der Bijl	31
W. Larkins lbw b van der Bijl	39
D. L. Amiss c Cook b van der Bijl	50
R. A. Woolmer c Kourie b Watson	100
P. Willey b Watson	15
†A. P. E. Knott c Kirsten b van der Bijl	6
C. M. Old c Rice b van der Bijl	10
J. K. Lever not out	4
L-b 7, w 1	8
1/67 2/95 3/137 4/217 5/259 6/270 7/301 8/311 (8 wkts dec.)	311

L. B. Taylor and M. Hendrick did not bat.

Bowling: van der Bijl 40–14–97–5; Watson 25.1–4–79–2; le Roux 24–5–71–1; Kourie 17–3–43–0; Kuiper 3–1–8–0; Kirsten 2–1–5–0.

Umpires: D. D. Schoof and O. R. Schoof.

CRICKET IN THE WEST INDIES, 1981-82

By TONY COZIER

Barbados have so dominated the Shell Shield tournament since its inception in 1966 that their tenth triumph in 1982 was hardly a surprise. It was one of their less convincing performances, however, and unquestionably the team of the season was the Windward Islands.

After playing together since 1970 as the Combined Islands, the Leeward and Windward Islands were split into separate teams, a decision by the West Indies Cricket Board of Control which was expected to leave the Windwards the weakest team in the Shield. The Combined team, the 1981 champions, had flourished mainly under the influence of players from the Leewards, principally the Test caps, Vivian Richards, Andy Roberts and Derick Parry. In contrast, the Windwards would have not a single contemporary Test player, and yet, having narrowly lost their first match to the Leewards, they proceeded to humble the mighty Barbadians in Bridgetown, an historic victory which so lifted the team's morale that Trinidad & Tobago and Jamaica were also subsequently beaten.

Equatorial weather which left Guyana sodden almost throughout the season, and caused all three Shield matches scheduled there to be abandoned, proved a frustrating intervention for both Barbados and the Windwards – not to mention the home team themselves who managed to complete only their two away matches.

Barbados clinched the championship through their victories over Trinidad & Tobago, the Leewards and Jamaica, but they had to fight tooth and nail batting second to win the first two. Playing for the first time with their four leading fast bowlers available, Barbados finally demonstrated their power with an innings decision over Jamaica. After winning both home matches, Jamaica fell away disappointingly, while neither the Leeward Islands nor Trinidad & Tobago seriously challenged for the championship.

Despite the increase in the number of teams and the corresponding growth of the tournament from ten to fifteen matches, and although there was no international home series as a counter-attraction, the Shield proved generally disappointing. It was hoped that all of those who had been involved in the preceding tour of Australia would provide a stimulus to competition, but injury prevented both Michael Holding and Malcolm Marshall from playing at all while Clive Lloyd was available for only one match and Joel Garner, Gordon Greenidge and Sylvester Clarke were missing at various times. What is more, there was no really outstanding individual performance, and any conclusive evidence about West Indian players of the future was left until another time.

The leaders of the averages were, by and large, already well established. Everton Mattis and Herbert Chang of Jamaica, Vivian Richards, the Leeward Islands captain, and Richard Gabriel, the Trinidad & Tobago opener, were the only ones to accumulate more than 400 runs. All were Shield veterans. Of the bowlers, the Trinidadian policeman, Ranjie Nanan, set a new record of 32 wickets in a Shield season in his ninth year of first-class cricket, while others of long-standing, such as fast bowlers Andy Roberts (24 wickets for the Leewards), Norbert Phillip (21 wickets for the Windwards) and Garner (16 wickets in two matches for Barbados) were key men in their teams.

Fortunately, there were a few relatively new names in the scorebooks to attract attention. Winston Davis, a slim, tall 24-year-old fast bowler from St Vincent, contributed greatly to the Windwards' successes with 22 wickets earned from genuine speed and hostility. In the teenagers Courtenay Walsh and Robert Haynes, Jamaica possessed two bowlers of immense promise. Both are over six feet tall. Walsh bowled with pace and commonsense to head his team's averages while Haynes's leg-spin claimed twenty wickets in the two matches on the favourable Sabina Park pitch. He used his height to great advantage and varied his pace cleverly. When he develops more confidence to attempt his googly regularly, he could fill the wrist-spin bowling position in the West Indies team which has become virtually extinct.

The most exciting newcomer to the tournament was Franklyn Stephenson, a dynamic Barbadian with the energy and attitude of a modern Keith Boyce. Having enjoyed an outstanding season for Tasmania in the Sheffield Shield, he returned to play his first first-class match in the West Indies against the Leewards. Finding himself in the unaccustomed position of night-watchman on the first evening, he destroyed the opposing attack with four 6s and twenty 4s in 165, scored in three and a half hours. He bowled at lively pace, with a deceptive slower ball used to good effect, and was seldom out of the action. Those who remember Boyce's contribution to West Indies' cricket in the 1970s will follow the development of his possible successor closely.

In the limited-overs Geddes Grant/Harrison Line tournament, the Leeward Islands beat Barbados convincingly in the final. Their fast-medium bowler, Eldine Baptiste, did the hat-trick and former Test off-spinner Parry took four wickets for 5 runs from ten overs on a blameless pitch. Barbados fell for an embarrassingly low 94 and the Leewards won by five wickets.

Administratively, the presidency of the West Indies Cricket Board of Control changed hands as Jeffrey B. Stollmeyer, who had held the post since 1975, retired and was replaced by Allan F. Rae, the president of the Jamaican Cricket Association. The two formed one of the most reliable opening pairs West Indies have ever had, during their playing days, and have subsequently been caring and dedicated workers in the cause of West Indies cricket. Rae, who has his own legal office in Kingston, has a strong cricketing background: his father was Ernest A. Rae, who played for Jamaica in the 1920s, toured England with the West Indians of 1928, and was a leading figure in Jamaican cricket for many years.

For the first time, the Board has appointed a permanent secretary, Stephen G. Camacho, who, like Rae, is a former West Indies opening batsman – if of somewhat more recent vintage – and has a strong family background in the game. His grandfather, G. C. Learmond, toured England with the West Indian teams of 1900 and 1906, and his father, George Camacho, is a former British Guiana captain and Cricket Board president.

FIRST-CLASS AVERAGES, 1981-82

BATTING

(Qualification: 150 runs, average 30)

	M	*I*	*NO*	*R*	*HI*	*Avge*
S. F. A. Bacchus (*Guyana*)	3	5	1	326	126	81.50
F. D. Stephenson (*Barbados*)	3	3	0	187	165	62.33
I. V. A. Richards (*Leeward I*)	4	7	0	433	167	61.85
D. A. Murray (*Barbados*)	3	5	2	179	55*	59.66
C. G. Greenidge (*Barbados*)	3	4	0	216	101	54.00
C. L. King (*Barbados*)	5	7	1	319	88*	53.16
A. E. Greenidge (*Barbados*)	5	7	1	315	172	52.50
E. H. Mattis (*Jamaica*)	5	10	1	441	98	49.00
K. G. d'Heurieux (*T & T*)	3	5	1	193	70*	48.25
H. S. Chang (*Jamaica*)	5	9	0	426	155	47.33
C. W. Fletcher (*Jamaica*)	3	6	1	232	122	46.40
R. S. Gabriel (*T & T*)	5	9	0	408	85	45.33
A. L. Logie (*T & T*)	4	7	0	317	171	45.28
Timur Mohamed (*Guyana*)	3	5	0	221	102	44.20
W. N. Slack (*Windward I*)	4	8	1	290	68*	41.42
H. A. Gomes (*T & T*)	5	9	0	367	92	40.77
G. Powell (*Jamaica*)	2	4	0	157	95	39.25
P. J. Dujon (*Jamaica*)	5	9	2	270	81	38.57
L. D. John (*Windward I*)	3	6	0	223	69	37.16
A. A. Lyte (*Guyana*)	4	7	0	259	103	37.00
A. L. Kelly (*Leeward I*)	4	8	0	288	71	36.00
N. Phillip (*Windward I*)	4	7	1	186	62	31.00
S. W. Julien (*Windward I*)	4	8	1	213	58	30.42

BOWLING

(Qualification: 10 wickets)

	O	*M*	*R*	*W*	*Avge*
J. Garner (*Barbados*)	91.5	24	251	16	15.68
N. Phillip (*Windward I*)	121	24	342	21	16.28
A. M. E. Roberts (*Leeward I*)	142.4	37	398	24	16.58
C. E. H. Croft (*Guyana*)	111.2	27	255	13	19.61
B. D. Julien (*T & T*)	128	18	422	21	20.09
R. Nanan (*T & T*)	310.3	105	677	32	21.15
T. Kentish (*Windward I*)	121.2	23	305	14	21.78
W. W. Davis (*Windward I*)	173	34	501	22	22.77
N. C. Guishard (*Leeward I*)	178.3	45	448	18	24.88
C. A. Walsh (*Jamaica*)	114.1	21	378	15	25.20
A. L. Padmore (*Barbados*)	168	45	360	14	25.71
E. A. Moseley (*Barbados*)	161.2	28	476	18	26.44
R. C. Haynes (*Jamaica*)	184.5	34	624	23	27.13
S. J. Hinds (*Windward I*)	151	28	450	15	30.00
R. R. Wynter (*Jamaica*)	121.1	18	460	14	32.85
D. R. Parry (*Leeward I*)	192	46	525	13	40.38

Note: Matches taken into account are the Shell Shield and Jones Cup matches.

SHELL SHIELD, 1981-82

	Won	Lost	Drawn	1st Inns lead	1st Inns arrears	Aban'd	Pts
Barbados	3	1	0	1*	0	1	57
Windward Islands	3	1	0	0	0	1	52
Jamaica	2	2	1	0	1	0	36
Guyana	0	1	1	2*	0	3	25
Leeward Islands	1	2	1	0	1	1	24
Trinidad & Tobago	0	2	3	2	1	0	20

* *First innings lead in one match lost outright.*

Win = 16pts; first innings win in match lost outright = 5pts; first innings lead in drawn match = 8pts; first innings arrears in drawn match = 4pts; abandoned match = 4pts each.

WINDWARD ISLANDS v LEEWARD ISLANDS

At Windsor Park, Roseau, March 4, 5, 6, 7. Leeward Islands won by 57 runs. Leeward Islands 16 pts.

Leeward Islands

E. E. Lewis c Slack b Davis	15	– b Davis	4
A. L. Kelly c Hinds b Phillip	71	– c Slack b Kentish	49
R. M. Otto c Julien b Hinds	62	– c Slack b Phillip	5
*I. V. A. Richards st Cadette b Hinds	92	– (6) c Phillip b Kentish	1
J. C. Allen c Hinds b Davis	8	– (4) lbw b Phillip	34
†S. I. Williams c Sebastien b Kentish	18	– (5) c Cadette b Phillip	2
D. R. Parry lbw b Davis	11	– c Slack b Phillip	5
E. A. Baptiste c Shillingford b Kentish	46	– b Phillip	0
N. C. Guishard c Texeira b Slack	14	– (10) b Phillip	0
A. M. E. Roberts c Shillingford b Slack	22	– (9) not out	2
J. B. Harris not out	0	– b Phillip	0
B 14, l-b 3, n-b 8	25	B 8, l-b 3, n-b 2	13
1/29 2/157 3/157 4/175 5/216 6/251 7/326 8/347 9/380	384	1/12 2/25 3/100 4/102 5/106 6/107 7/109 8/115 9/115	115

Bowling: *First Innings*—Phillip 21–4–80–1; Davis 30–5–88–3; Kentish 32–8–85–2; Hinds 31–4–91–2; Slack 6.1–2–15–2. *Second Innings*—Phillip 13–0–33–7; Davis 8–2–30–1; Hinds 7–1–22–0; Kentish 12–3–12–2; Slack 1–0–5–0.

Windward Islands

L. C. Sebastien c Richards b Roberts	0	– lbw b Roberts	34
L. A. Lewis c Roberts b Guishard	115	– lbw b Roberts	2
S. W. Julien lbw b Roberts	5	– c and b Roberts	19
*I. T. Shillingford c Baptiste b Harris	48	– lbw b Guishard	11
W. N. Slack c Parry b Guishard	13	– b Richards	23
A. Texeira c Lewis b Guishard	16	– b Guishard	2
N. Phillip c Kelly b Guishard	2	– c Kelly b Guishard	10
†I. Cadette c Richards b Parry	3	– lbw b Roberts	17
T. Kentish not out	31	– b Roberts	7
S. J. Hinds c Otto b Guishard	47	– not out	6
W. W. Davis b Guishard	8	– c Kelly b Parry	1
B 2, l-b 7, n-b 5	14	B 6, l-b 2	8
1/0 2/12 3/132 4/181 5/201 6/209 7/214 8/214 9/282	302	1/4 2/52 3/61 4/84 5/88 6/102 7/112 8/130 9/133	140

Bowling: *First Innings*—Roberts 22–6–59–2; Harris 14–1–73–1; Parry 27–9–78–1; Baptiste 8–1–30–0; Richards 6–2–15–0; Guishard 25–9–33–6. *Second Innings*—Roberts 18–7–52–5; Harris 5–2–9–0; Parry 13–2–29–1; Baptiste 3–0–4–0; Richards 5–2–11–1; Guishard 18–7–27–3.

Umpires: T. Baptiste and J. Simon.

BARBADOS v TRINIDAD & TOBAGO

At Kensington Oval, Bridgetown, March 5, 6, 7, 8. Barbados won by five wickets. Barbados 16 pts.

Trinidad & Tobago

R. S. Gabriel c Clarke b Moseley	34	– c Trotman b Clarke	71
K. S. Miller c Reifer b Clarke	1	– c Murray b Daniel	44
*H. A. Gomes b Clarke	26	– lbw b Clarke	19
A. L. Logie c Reifer b Padmore	42	– c Clarke b Moseley	24
P. Moosai c Reifer b Padmore	23	– b Moseley	28
T. Cuffy c Moseley b Padmore	0	– c C. G. Greenidge b Moseley	88
B. D. Julien c Murray b Moseley	19	– c C. G. Greenidge b Daniel	7
R. Sampath c Reifer b Daniel	24	– c Murray b King	20
R. Nanan c Murray b Daniel	4	– not out	6
†J. R. Lyon not out	0	– c Murray b King	1
H. Joseph b Moseley	4	– c A. E. Greenidge b King	5
B 4, l-b 1, w 1, n-b 10	16	B 1, l-b 4, n-b 11	16
1/9 2/66 3/68 4/135 5/137 6/140 7/181 8/185 9/185	193	1/82 2/131 3/157 4/177 5/224 6/243 7/309 8/319 9/321	329

Bowling: *First Innings*—Clarke 19–5–45–2; Daniel 14–3–40–2; Moseley 15.2–1–67–3; Padmore 11–5–25–3. *Second Innings*—Clarke 31–7–99–2; Daniel 23–4–81–2; Moseley 21–7–58–3; Padmore 29–9–56–0; King 6.4–1–19–3.

Barbados

C. G. Greenidge c Moosai b Nanan	101	– c Cuffy b Nanan	25
D. L. Haynes c Gabriel b Julien	34	– lbw b Nanan	16
A. E. Greenidge b Joseph	31	– not out	48
E. N. Trotman c Moosai b Joseph	3	– b Nanan	5
C. L. King c Lyon b Julien	42	– c Julien b Nanan	56
L. N. Reifer c Gabriel b Joseph	0	– c Gabriel b Gomes	41
†D. A. Murray lbw b Julien	38		
S. T. Clarke c Cuffy b Joseph	7	– (7) not out	0
*A. L. Padmore lbw b Nanan	25		
E. A. Moseley not out	16		
W. W. Daniel b Nanan	5		
B 5, l-b 6, w 1, n-b 12	24	B 1, l-b 4, n-b 1	6
1/88 2/129 3/145 4/211 5/221 6/239 7/246 8/300 9/316	326	1/37 2/42 3/48 4/126 5/195 (5 wkts)	197

Bowling: *First Innings*—Julien 26–3–100–3; Gomes 20–8–46–0; Nanan 38.2–18–59–3; Joseph 33–7–97–4. *Second Innings*—Julien 8–0–38–0; Gomes 9–0–44–1; Nanan 18.3–6–64–4; Joseph 9–1–45–0.

Umpires: S. E. Parris and D. M. Archer.

JAMAICA v GUYANA

At Sabina Park, Kingston, March 5, 6, 7, 8. Jamaica won by 52 runs. Jamaica 16 pts. Guyana 5 pts.

Jamaica

R. A. Austin c Bacchus b Croft	2	– run out	118
G. Powell c Harper b Kallicharran	48	– c Harper b Croft	2
E. H. Mattis c Harper b Butts	98	– c Lloyd b Kallicharran	41
*L. G. Rowe c Timur b Croft	3	– (5) c Lloyd b Harper	13
†P. J. Dujon c Harper b Kallicharran	20	– (7) not out	66
H. S. Chang c Bacchus b Kallicharran	19	– c Lloyd b Harper	155
M. C. Neita c Pydanna b Harper	6	– (8) not out	12
M. A. Tucker not out	2	– (4) lbw b Harper	3
C. U. Thompson lbw b Harper	4		
R. C. Haynes lbw b Croft	1		
R. R. Wynter b Croft	0		
L-b 1, w 1, n-b 6	8	B 6, l-b 8, n-b 11	25
1/6 2/79 3/87 4/126 5/169 6/204 7/208 8/210 9/211	211	1/17 2/89 3/92 4/108 5/267 6/414 (6 wkts dec.)	435

Bowling: *First Innings*—Croft 12.2–0–26–4; Joseph 11–1–50–0; Harper 10–5–15–2; Kallicharran 20–3–71–3; Butts 12–3–31–1; Etwaroo 2–0–10–0. *Second Innings*—Croft 24–6–81–1; Joseph 11–2–58–0; Harper 40–10–95–3; Kallicharran 29–3–116–1; Butts 16–2–60–0.

Guyana

A. A. Lyte st Dujon b Haynes	44	– c Chang b Haynes	69
T. R. Etwaroo c Rowe b Thompson	11	– c Chang b Haynes	8
Timur Mohamed c Chang b Haynes	17	– (5) c Powell b Haynes	22
*S. F. A. Bacchus c Dujon b Wynter	50	– (6) c Powell b Tucker	79
C. H. Lloyd c Rowe b Haynes	0	– (4) run out	38
†M. R. Pydanna c Rowe b Haynes	37	– (7) c Powell b Haynes	17
I. D. Kallicharran c Chang b Haynes	21	– (8) c Dujon b Haynes	13
R. A. Harper lbw b Thompson	7	– (9) b Wynter	9
C. Butts c Rowe b Mattis	35	– (3) c Wynter b Haynes	14
C. E. H. Croft not out	27	– run out	1
R. F. Joseph c and b Austin	2	– not out	0
B 20, l-b 8, n-b 6	34	B 20, l-b 11, n-b 8	39
1/39 2/67 3/101 4/107 5/151 6/192 7/199 8/221 9/267	285	1/34 2/84 3/147 4/148 5/176 6/227 7/247 8/300 9/304	309

Bowling: *First Innings*—Wynter 20–3–69–1; Thompson 15–2–25–2; Austin 6.1–1–39–1; Haynes 29–5–87–5; Tucker 13–3–30–0; Mattis 2–1–1–1. *Second Innings*—Wynter 12–0–43–1; Thompson 10–3–28–0; Austin 11–3–31–0; Haynes 34–7–119–6; Tucker 13.2–1–49–1.

Umpires: D. Sang Hue and R. Bell.

BARBADOS v WINDWARD ISLANDS

At Kensington Oval, Bridgetown, March 12, 13, 14, 15. Windward Islands won by four wickets. Windward Islands 16 pts. Barbados 5 pts.

Barbados

C. G. Greenidge lbw b Kentish	64	(6) lbw b Phillip	26
D. L. Haynes c Shillingford b Hinds	34	(1) c Hinds b Phillip	11
A. E. Greenidge b Kentish	39	(2) c Shillingford b Kentish	12
E. N. Trotman c sub b Kentish	7	(5) b Hinds	11
C. L. King c Davis b Kentish	87	(4) c Lewis b Hinds	24
L. N. Reifer c and b Kentish	22	(3) c Phillip b Hinds	19
†D. A. Murray c Julien b Davis	2	c Cadette b Phillip	55
G. L. Linton c Cadette b Davis	0	absent injured	
E. A. Moseley c John b Kentish	5	(8) lbw b Phillip	9
*A. L. Padmore c Cadette b Davis	3	(9) b Kentish	3
W. W. Daniel not out	0	(10) not out	0
L-b 1, w 1, n-b 4	6	L-b 2, n-b 12	14
1/68 2/122 3/134 4/163 5/216 6/219 7/219 8/236 9/247	269	1/20 2/38 3/60 4/83 5/84 6/168 7/173 8/184 9/184	184

Bowling: *First Innings*—Phillip 11–3–44–0; Davis 19–3–86–3; Hinds 18–6–64–1; Kentish 16.1–2–69–6. *Second Innings*—Phillip 14–5–21–4; Davis 19–6–43–0; Hinds 24–6–62–3; Kentish 18.3–2–44–2.

Windward Islands

L. C. Sebastien c and b Daniel	6	c Moseley b Padmore	60
L. A. Lewis lbw b Padmore	38	run out	1
L. D. John b Padmore	34	c Murray b Moseley	2
S. W. Julien c sub b Padmore	52	c Trotman b Padmore	20
W. N. Slack lbw b Moseley	12	not out	68
*I. T. Shillingford c Murray b Daniel	10	(8) not out	5
N. Phillip c Murray b Moseley	2	c A. E. Greenidge b Moseley	62
†I. Cadette c Murray b Moseley	21	(6) lbw b Daniel	8
T. Kentish c Trotman b King	0		
S. J. Hinds not out	21		
W. W. Davis b Moseley	0		
B 1, l-b 1, w 6, n-b 9	17	B 2, l-b 7, w 3, n-b 3	15
1/6 2/81 3/82 4/117 5/134 6/141 7/176 8/179 9/196	213	1/6 2/12 3/53 4/101 5/110 6/223	(6 wkts) 241

Bowling: *First Innings*—Daniel 15–0–73–2; Moseley 23.5–4–66–4; Padmore 21–6–37–3; Linton 6–4–7–0; King 6–2–13–1. *Second Innings*—Daniel 21–4–76–1; Moseley 36–6–66–2; Padmore 42–12–71–2; King 10–5–13–0.

Umpires: S. E. Parris and N. Harrison.

TRINIDAD & TOBAGO v GUYANA

At Guaracara Park, Pointe-á-Pierre, March 12, 13, 14, 15. Drawn. Trinidad & Tobago 4 pts, Guyana 8 pts.

Guyana

A. A. Lyte c Lyon b Julien	0	– lbw b Julien	1
T. R. Etwaroo c Julien b Nanan	38	– c Jumadeen b Julien	10
Timur Mohamed c Furlonge b Joseph	102	– c Julien b Nanan	45
*S. F. A. Bacchus c Jumadeen b Joseph	59	– run out	126
M. A. Harper c Julien b Nanan	5	– c Cuffy b Nanan	2
†M. R. Pydanna lbw b Nanan	1	– lbw b Jumadeen	2
I. D. Kallicharran c Julien b Nanan	19	– lbw b Nanan	6
R. A. Harper lbw b Jumadeen	37	– c Nanan b Jumadeen	34
C. Butts not out	5	– c Joseph b Jumadeen	20
C. E. H. Croft b Jumadeen	1	– c Julien b Jumadeen	15
R. F. Joseph not out	2	– not out	0
B 4, l-b 3, n-b 3	10	B 6, l-b 2	8
1/3 2/91 3/194 4/208 5/214 6/214 7/270 8/270 9/273 (9 wkts dec.)	279	1/11 2/11 3/93 4/99 5/110 6/139 7/223 8/235 9/264	269

Bowling: *First Innings*—Julien 9–1–34–1; Gomes 9–3–25–0; Nanan 34–14–78–4; Jumadeen 19–5–50–2; Joseph 16–0–82–2. *Second Innings*—Julien 8–1–30–2; Gomes 7–1–22–0; Nanan 48–17–75–3; Joseph 19–2–76–0; Jumadeen 21.3–4–58–4.

Trinidad & Tobago

R. S. Gabriel c Butts b Joseph	44	– c R. A. Harper b Croft	39
D. C. Furlonge c sub b Kallicharran	23	– c Pydanna b R. A. Harper	71
A. Rajah c Etwaroo b Kallicharran	25	– (6) run out	21
*H. A. Gomes c Etwaroo b Kallicharran	16	– (3) b Croft	93
T. Cuffy c Butts b Kallicharran	0	– (4) c Kallicharran b R. A. Harper	42
P. Moosai b Butts	7	– (7) b Croft	0
B. D. Julien c Pydanna b R. A. Harper	37	– (5) run out	2
R. Nanan b R. A. Harper	24	– not out	11
†J. R. Lyon run out	1		
S. Jumadeen c Pydanna b Kallicharran	10	– (9) not out	0
H. Joseph not out	0		
L-b 2, n-b 7	9	B 13, l-b 9, n-b 12	34
1/57 2/93 3/109 4/109 5/119 6/137 7/174 8/177 9/196	196	1/85 2/168 3/257 4/272 5/276 6/276 7/307 (7 wkts)	313

Bowling: *First Innings*—Croft 14–2–33–0; Joseph 9–2–40–1; Kallicharran 28–6–63–5; Butts 14–5–40–1; R. A. Harper 6.2–2–11–2. *Second Innings*—Croft 31–5–83–3; Joseph 8–1–34–0; R. A. Harper 28–5–63–2; Kallicharran 16–2–69–0; Butts 21–10–30–0; Bacchus 1–1–0–0.

Umpires: C. Cumberbatch and Sadiq Mohammad.

JAMAICA v LEEWARD ISLANDS

At Sabina Park, Kingston, March 12, 13, 14, 15. Jamaica won by 263 runs. Jamaica 16 pts.

Jamaica

R. A. Austin c Williams b Roberts	0	– c Richards b Roberts	55
G. Powell c Baptiste b Guishard	95	– c Lewis b Baptiste	12
E. H. Mattis c Lewis b Baptiste	21	– lbw b Baptiste	77
*L. G. Rowe b Guishard	29	– c Richards b Guishard	1
H. S. Chang c Richards b Roberts	15	– c Richards b Parry	57
†P. J. Dujon c Guishard b Roberts	81	– not out	35
M. C. Neita c Kelly b Roberts	84	– not out	48
D. O. Malcolm c Kelly b Roberts	3		
R. C. Haynes b Baptiste	11		
C. A. Walsh b Roberts	15		
R. R. Wynter not out	2		
B 8, l-b 4, n-b 4	16	B 10, l-b 7, n-b 3	20
1/0 2/63 3/142 4/165 5/167 6/315 7/335 8/342 9/364	372	1/23 2/108 3/117 4/191 5/230 (5 wkts dec.)	305

Bowling: *First Innings*—Roberts 21–7–54–6; Baptiste 20–3–105–2; Richards 10–1–29–0; Parry 16–1–72–0; Guishard 35–8–96–2. *Second Innings*—Roberts 13–1–26–1; Baptiste 16–2–57–2; Richards 4–0–9–0; Parry 31–4–82–1; Guishard 38–5–105–1; Eddy 2–0–6–0.

Leeward Islands

E. E. Lewis lbw b Austin	2	– b Wynter	11
A. L. Kelly c Dujon b Haynes	64	– c and b Walsh	20
R. M. Otto b Austin	3	– c Austin b Haynes	32
V. A. Eddy c Mattis b Haynes	6	– c sub b Haynes	15
*I. V. A. Richards b Austin	73	– (6) c sub b Malcolm	50
J. C. Allen c Wynter b Haynes	25	– (5) lbw b Wynter	2
D. R. Parry lbw b Wynter	20	– (8) c and b Haynes	15
†S. I. Williams c Rowe b Haynes	10	– (7) c and b Malcolm	12
E. A. Baptiste not out	28	– b Haynes	0
A. M. E. Roberts b Wynter	3	– c Malcolm b Haynes	2
N. C. Guishard c Rowe b Malcolm	2	– not out	0
B 1, l-b 2, n-b 1	4	B 6, l-b 2, n-b 7	15
1/57 2/65 3/69 4/86 5/170 6/174 7/192 8/229 9/235	240	1/24 2/34 3/36 4/90 5/129 6/139 7/161 8/161 9/174	174

Bowling: *First Innings*—Wynter 7–1–45–2; Walsh 10–2–52–0; Austin 20–7–54–3; Haynes 23–6–68–4; Malcolm 6.1–0–17–1. *Second Innings*—Wynter 15–4–46–2; Walsh 8–2–16–1; Haynes 20–5–72–5; Malcolm 13–7–25–2.

I. V. A. Richards took 3 catches as wicket-keeper during Jamaica's second innings.

In Leeward Islands' second innings, Otto retired hurt at 34 for one and returned at the fall of the fourth wicket.

Umpires: D. Sang Hue and J. Gayle.

TRINIDAD & TOBAGO v JAMAICA

At Queen's Park Oval, Port-of-Spain, March 19, 20, 21, 22. Drawn. Trinidad & Tobago 8 pts, Jamaica 4 pts.

Jamaica

R. A. Austin c Gabriel b Julien	5	– c Lyon b Julien	2
C. W. Fletcher c Lyon b Julien	122	– not out	24
E. H. Mattis lbw b Jumadeen	51	– not out	50
*L. G. Rowe b Julien	73		
H. S. Chang b Julien	6		
†P. J. Dujon c Jumadeen b Julien	25		
M. C. Neita c d'Heurieux b Julien	4		
D. O. Malcolm c Gabriel b Julien	5		
R. C. Haynes c sub b Julien	16		
C. A. Walsh lbw b Julien	21		
R. R. Wynter not out	3		
B 8, l-b 5, n-b 2	15	N-b 1	1
1/13 2/104 3/226 4/238 5/276 6/286 7/300 8/301 9/325	346	1/2 (1 wkt)	77

Bowling: *First Innings*—Julien 32.2–4–97–9; Sampath 18–3–67–0; Gomes 15–1–47–0; Nanan 31–6–76–0; Jumadeen 24–6–44–1. *Second Innings*—Julien 8–3–12–1; Sampath 4–0–29–0; Nanan 7–2–13–0; Jumadeen 4–2–4–0; Rajah 1–0–1–0; Lyon 5–0–13–0; Gabriel 2–0–4–0.

Trinidad & Tobago

R. S. Gabriel lbw b Walsh	13
K. R. Bainey c Fletcher b Walsh	12
A. Rajah b Malcolm	52
A. L. Logie b Austin	171
*H. A. Gomes b Walsh	59
K. G. d'Heurieux b Walsh	61
B. D. Julien c Rowe b Austin	0
R. Sampath c Neita (w-k) b Wynter	40
R. Nanan lbw b Wynter	40
S. Jumadeen not out	2
B 6, l-b 12, w 1, n-b 11	30
1/16 2/32 3/154 4/279 5/380 6/393 7/396 8/477 (9 wkts dec.)	480

†J. R. Lyon did not bat.

Bowling: Walsh 35–8–119–4; Wynter 31.1–6–98–2; Haynes 18–3–69–0; Malcolm 15–0–77–1; Fletcher 2–0–8–0; Austin 28–2–79–2.

Umpires: C. Cumberbatch and D. Fereira.

LEEWARD ISLANDS v BARBADOS

At Warner Park, Basseterre, March 20, 21, 22, 23. Barbados won by four wickets. Barbados 16 pts.

Leeward Islands

A. L. Kelly c Payne b Garner	47	– b Stephenson	8
R. B. Richardson c Payne b Garner	0	– lbw b Garner	76
R. M. Otto lbw b Stephenson	18	– (4) c Murray b Moseley	38
J. C. Allen b Garner	48	– (6) c L. N. Reifer b Stephenson	28
*I. V. A. Richards c Padmore b Garner	4	– c Murray b Moseley	46
†S. I. Williams c Murray b Moseley	0	– (7) run out	13
D. R. Parry not out	27	– (8) b Garner	25
E. A. Baptiste b Padmore	25	– (9) c L. N. Reifer b Padmore	3
A. M. E. Roberts c King b Padmore	4	– (10) c G. N. Reifer b Padmore	0
N. C. Guishard c sub b Garner	1	– (3) lbw b Padmore	13
J. B. Harris run out	1	– not out	13
B 2, l-b 3, n-b 14	19	B 4, l-b 9, n-b 8	21
1/2 2/49 3/87 4/91 5/98 6/151 7/183 8/191 9/192	194	1/23 2/71 3/113 4/196 5/201 6/233 7/245 8/252 9/252	284

Bowling: *First Innings*—Garner 23.2–8–56–5; Moseley 15–4–44–1; Stephenson 13–4–39–1; Padmore 14–5–22–2; King 3–1–14–0. *Second Innings*—Garner 22.2–5–65–2; Stephenson 24–5–58–2; Moseley 14–1–57–2; Padmore 29–6–83–3.

Barbados

D. L. Haynes c Richards b Parry	32	– b Parry	26
G. N. Reifer c Williams b Harris	0	– lbw b Harris	0
A. E. Greenidge c Baptiste b Roberts	5	– (4) c Allen b Parry	8
F. D. Stephenson run out	165	– (3) lbw b Roberts	12
T. R. O. Payne c Richards b Parry	2	– c Allen b Parry	3
C. L. King lbw b Roberts	6	– not out	88
L. N. Reifer c Richards b Roberts	0	– c Richardson b Roberts	1
†D. A. Murray not out	55	– not out	29
E. A. Moseley c Richards b Guishard	29		
*A. L. Padmore c Richards b Guishard	5		
J. Garner b Roberts	0		
B 1, l-b 2, n-b 6	9	L-b 2, n-b 4	6
1/0 2/8 3/107 4/129 5/154 6/154 7/238 8/300 9/308	308	1/0 2/27 3/46 4/50 5/70 6/73	(6 wkts) 173

Bowling: *First Innings*—Roberts 20.2–4–53–4; Harris 12–1–36–1; Baptiste 9–0–43–0; Parry 36–7–92–2; Guishard 20–6–63–2; Richards 7–2–12–0. *Second Innings*—Roberts 16–1–53–2; Harris 4–0–14–1; Parry 27–7–49–3; Guishard 12–2–49–0; Richards 1–0–2–0.

Umpires: R. Whyte and A. Weekes.

GUYANA v WINDWARD ISLANDS

At Albion, March 20, 21, 22, 23. Abandoned. Guyana 4 pts, Windward Islands 4 pts.

BARBADOS v JAMAICA

At Kensington Oval, Bridgetown, March 27, 28, 29. Barbados won by an innings and 95 runs. Barbados 16 pts.

Barbados

D. L. Haynes c Dujon b Walsh	11
C. A. Best c Wynter b Malcolm	75
A. E. Greenidge lbw b Walsh	172
E. N. Trotman b Wynter	55
C. L. King b Wynter	16
†R. L. Skeete c Mattis b Walsh	32
F. D. Stephenson c Malcolm b Wynter	10
E. A. Moseley c Dujon b Walsh	21
S. T. Clarke c Rowe b Walsh	31
*A. L. Padmore not out	8
J. Garner b Walsh	0
B 3, l-b 5, w 5, n-b 21	34
1/18 2/187 3/303 4/323 5/368 6/380 7/421 8/434 9/464	465

Bowling: Walsh 31.1–7–95–6; Wynter 20–1–98–3; Austin 10–0–50–0; Haynes 29–2–107–0; Malcolm 25–3–80–1; Mattis 1–0–1–0.

Jamaica

R. A. Austin c Skeete b Clarke	20	– c Moseley b Stephenson	19
C. W. Fletcher lbw b Garner	43	– c Skeete b Stephenson	5
E. H. Mattis c Best b Stephenson	18	– (5) c Skeete b Moseley	24
*L. G. Rowe c Trotman b Garner	21	– b Clarke	0
H. S. Chang c Moseley b Garner	97	– (3) c Skeete b Moseley	26
†P. J. Dujon b Garner	0	– c Skeete b Garner	0
M. C. Neita b Garner	4	– b Garner	16
D. O. Malcolm lbw b Stephenson	5	– run out	19
R. C. Haynes c Skeete b Moseley	16	– c Stephenson b Garner	5
C. A. Walsh c King b Garner	0	– c Best b Stephenson	0
R. R. Wynter not out	0	– not out	5
B 6, l-b 5, w 1, n-b 6	18	B 2, l-b 3, n-b 4	9
1/34 2/81 3/86 4/143 5/143 6/153 7/165 8/234 9/242	242	1/16 2/35 3/36 4/69 5/70 6/108 7/112 8/119 9/119	128

Bowling: *First Innings*—Clarke 18–4–50–1; Moseley 20–3–48–1; Garner 26.5–5–73–6; Stephenson 14–4–24–2; Padmore 8–1–29–0. *Second Innings*—Clarke 8–0–33–1; Stephenson 8–1–27–3; Moseley 6–0–35–2; Garner 6.2–1–24–3.

Umpires: D. M. Archer and L. Barker.

GUYANA v LEEWARD ISLANDS

At Georgetown, March 27, 28, 29, 30. Abandoned. Guyana 4 pts, Leeward Islands 4 pts.

WINDWARD ISLANDS v TRINIDAD & TOBAGO

At Queen's Park, St George's, March 27, 28, 29, 30. Windward Islands won by 85 runs. Windward Islands 16 pts.

Windward Islands

L. C. Sebastien lbw b Nanan	50	– c Jumadeen b Nanan	33
L. D. John st Lyon b Nanan	69	– c Rajah b Nanan	32
L. A. Lewis lbw b Nanan	0	– lbw b Nanan	0
W. N. Slack b Jumadeen	47	– c Julien b Gomes	40
S. W. Julien c Gabriel b Nanan	58	– c Gomes b Nanan	5
*I. T. Shillingford lbw b Julien	34	– b Jumadeen	2
N. Phillip not out	43	– lbw b Nanan	23
T. Kentish c Cuffy b Julien	0	– (9) b Julien	24
†I. Cadette c Lyon b Gomes	7	– (8) lbw b Gomes	11
S. J. Hinds c d'Heurieux b Julien	4	– not out	1
W. W. Davis lbw b Julien	4	– c Lyon b Gomes	0
B 6, l-b 7, n-b 3	16	B 13, l-b 4, n-b 4	21
1/100 2/100 3/141 4/222 5/242 6/298 7/301 8/310 9/315	332	1/55 2/59 3/75 4/93 5/100 6/147 7/148 8/189 9/191	192

Bowling: *First Innings*—Julien 18.4–2–59–4; Gomes 16–3–47–1; Nanan 39–11–98–4; Jumadeen 33–8–112–1. *Second Innings*—Julien 18–4–52–1; Gomes 11.2–4–30–3; Nanan 35–10–51–5; Jumadeen 19–8–38–1.

Trinidad & Tobago

R. S. Gabriel lbw b Davis	13	– c sub b Davis	34
D. C. Furlonge c Slack b Phillip	4	– c Cadette b Davis	8
*H. A. Gomes c Slack b Hinds	72	– lbw b Davis	31
A. L. Logie b Phillip	7	– st Cadette b Hinds	17
A. Rajah run out	44	– retired hurt	0
K. G. d'Heurieux not out	70	– b Hinds	12
T. Cuffy lbw b Davis	22	– lbw b Davis	19
B. D. Julien b Davis	1	– retired hurt	1
R. Nanan run out	19	– not out	13
†J. R. Lyon lbw b Hinds	11	– lbw b Davis	0
S. Jumadeen b Hinds	2	– st Cadette b Hinds	8
B 3, l-b 3, n-b 10	16	B 3, l-b 6, w 1, n-b 5	15
1/15 2/19 3/36 4/139 5/150 6/176 7/178 8/219 9/279	281	1/34 2/57 3/98 4/98 5/129 6/139 7/140 8/158	158

Bowling: *First Innings*—Phillip 24–3–68–2; Davis 31–4–97–3; Hinds 21.4–2–60–3; Kentish 18–3–40–0. *Second Innings*—Davis 26–5–42–5; Phillip 1–0–4–0; Sebastien 3–0–14–0; Hinds 24.2–4–72–3; Kentish 6–1–11–0.

In Trinidad & Tobago's second innings, Rajah retired hurt at 98 for three and Julien at 133.

Umpires: S. Forsythe and G. Johnson.

GUYANA v BARBADOS

At Bourda Oval, Georgetown, April 2, 3, 4, 5. Abandoned. Guyana 4 pts, Barbados 4 pts.

Guyana

A. A. Lyte run out	103
T. R. Etwaroo c Garner b Stephenson	20
Timur Mohamed b Padmore	35
*S. F. A. Bacchus not out	12
W. Whyte not out	1
L-b 4, n-b 1	5
1/47 2/148 3/175 (3 wkts)	176

K. Singh, †M. R. Pydanna, I. D. Kallicharran, C. Butts, R. A. Harper and C. E. H. Croft did not bat.

Bowling: Clarke 8–1–40–0; Moseley 9–2–35–0; Stephenson 5–1–26–1; Garner 13–5–33–0; Padmore 14–1–37–1.

Barbados

C. G. Greenidge, D. L. Haynes, C. A. Best, A. E. Greenidge, C. L. King, †R. L. Skeete, S. T. Clarke, E. A. Moseley, *A. L. Padmore, F. D. Stephenson and J. Garner.

Umpires: C. F. Vyfhuis and D. Narine.

LEEWARD ISLANDS v TRINIDAD & TOBAGO

At Antigua Recreation Ground, April 2, 3, 4, 5. Drawn. Leeward Islands 4 pts, Trinidad & Tobago 8 pts.

Trinidad & Tobago

R. S. Gabriel lbw b Roberts	75	– c Williams b Roberts	85
D. C. Furlonge b White	9	– b Guishard	49
*H. A. Gomes st Williams b Guishard	51	– c Parry b Baptiste	1
A. L. Logie c Kelly b Parry	29	– c Williams b Baptiste	27
K. G. d'Heurieux c and b Parry	23	– c sub b Parry	27
T. Cuffy c Richards b White	42	– c White b Parry	0
R. Sampath b Baptiste	34	– c Williams b Baptiste	31
R. Nanan c White b Guishard	2	– lbw b Parry	3
†J. R. Lyon lbw b Baptiste	18	– c Parry b Guishard	4
P. Ramnath c Williams b Roberts	6	– b Roberts	13
K. Williams not out	0	– not out	0
B 4, l-b 6, n-b 5	15	B 3, l-b 5, n-b 5	13
1/44 2/111 3/149 4/185 5/210 6/248 7/256 8/293 9/302	304	1/118 2/119 3/153 4/199 5/200 6/202 7/208 8/217 9/245	253

Bowling: *First Innings*—Roberts 17.2–5–45–2; Baptiste 17–3–48–2; White 13–0–64–2; Richards 5–1–19–0; Parry 21–5–86–2; Guishard 12–4–27–2. *Second Innings*—Roberts 16–3–56–2; Baptiste 17–3–62–3; Parry 26–11–37–3; White 6–0–31–0; Guishard 19–4–48–2; Richards 4–0–6–0.

Leeward Islands

A. L. Kelly c Furlonge b Nanan	25	– b Williams	4
R. B. Richardson c Furlonge b Nanan	24	– lbw b Ramnath	11
R. M. Otto c Furlonge b Nanan	13	– lbw b Nanan	24
*I. V. A. Richards c Lyon b Williams	167		
S. Liburd c Sampath b Nanan	7	– not out	48
†S. I. Williams st Lyon b Ramnath	2		
D. R. Parry st Lyon b Nanan	17	– (6) not out	6
E. A. Baptiste c sub b Nanan	24		
A. C. M. White run out	11		
A. M. E. Roberts b Nanan	2		
N. C. Guishard not out	4	– (4) st Lyon b Nanan	43
B 3, l-b 3	6	B 1, l-b 9	10
1/46 2/57 3/90 4/116 5/121 6/198 7/264 8/292 9/296	302	1/4 2/29 3/75 4/128 (4 wkts)	146

Bowling: *First Innings*—Williams 17–2–65–1; Gomes 1–1–0–0; Sampath 6–1–25–0; Nanan 34.4–11–109–7; Ramnath 25–2–97–1. *Second Innings*—Williams 5–0–21–1; Sampath 2–0–6–0; Nanan 25–10–54–2; Ramnath 21–5–51–1; Gomes 4–1–4–0.

Umpires: P. Whyte and A. Weekes.

WINDWARD ISLANDS v JAMAICA

At Arnos Vale, St Vincent, April 2, 3, 4. Windward Islands won by seven wickets. Windward Islands 16 pts.

Jamaica

R. A. Austin c Kentish b Davis	2	– b Phillip	2
C. W. Fletcher lbw b Phillip	7	– c Kentish b Davis	31
E. H. Mattis b Phillip	30	– lbw b Kentish	31
*L. G. Rowe c Cadette b Phillip	16	– (5) hit wkt b Davis	22
H. S. Chang c Sebastien b Phillip	1	– (4) b Davis	50
†P. J. Dujon c Cadette b Davis	17	– (7) run out	26
M. C. Neita lbw b Phillip	0	– (8) c Texeira b Hinds	8
D. O. Malcolm c Texeira b Davis	12	– (9) b Kentish	21
R. C. Haynes c Cadette b Phillip	28	– (6) lbw b Hinds	19
C. A. Walsh b Davis	2	– lbw b Hinds	0
R. R. Wynter not out	5	– not out	0
B 6, l-b 4, n-b 12	22	L-b 2, n-b 1	3
1/4 2/17 3/53 4/55 5/70 6/70 7/100 8/110 9/128	142	1/14 2/50 3/96 4/129 5/140 6/175 7/188 8/207 9/207	213

Bowling: *First Innings*—Phillip 19–6–41–6; Davis 18–3–45–4; Hinds 8–1–34–0. *Second Innings*—Phillip 18–3–51–1; Davis 22–6–70–3; Hinds 17–4–45–3; Kentish 18.4–3–44–2.

Windward Islands

L. C. Sebastien c Dujon b Wynter	4	– b Walsh	0
L. D. John c Fletcher b Wynter	57	– lbw b Walsh	29
W. N. Slack c Dujon b Walsh	45	– c Dujon b Haynes	42
S. W. Julien c Dujon b Malcolm	4	– not out	51
A. Texeira b Malcolm	0	– not out	13
*I. T. Shillingford c Malcolm b Walsh	2		
N. Phillip c and b Wynter	44		
†I. Cadette c Wynter b Haynes	3		
T. Kentish run out	8		
S. J. Hinds c Rowe b Haynes	18		
W. W. Davis not out	10		
B 7, l-b 4, w 4, n-b 7	22	N-b 4	4
1/4 2/68 3/88 4/88 5/95 6/136 7/144 8/180 9/205	217	1/2 2/46 3/95	(3 wkts) 139

Bowling *First Innings*—Wynter 13.2–0–41–3; Walsh 21–1–70–2; Haynes 24–5–57–2; Austin 6–2–12–0; Malcolm 7–0–15–2. *Second Innings*—Walsh 9–1–26–2; Wynter 3–0–20–0; Haynes 7.5–1–45–1; Malcolm 7–2–29–0; Austin 4–0–15–0.

Umpires: M. Hippolyte and T. Baptiste.

SHELL SHIELD WINNERS

1965-66	Barbados
1966-67	Barbados
1968-69	Jamaica
1969-70	Trinidad
1970-71	Trinidad
1971-72	Barbados
1972-73	Guyana
1973-74	Barbados
1974-75	Guyana
1975-76	Trinidad / Barbados
1976-77	Barbados
1977-78	Barbados
1978-79	Barbados
1979-80	Barbados
1980-81	Combined Islands
1981-82	Barbados

JONES CUP, 1981-82

BERBICE v DEMERARA

At Georgetown, October 23, 24, 25, 26. Drawn.

Demerara

A. A. Lyte b Lambert	34	– c Kallicharran b Lambert	8
†S. Bamfield lbw b Lambert	12	– lbw b Joseph	0
*M. A. Harper b Lambert	0	– not out	100
W. Whyte b Joseph	15	– lbw b Joseph	17
A. Jackman c Pydanna b Singh	21	– lbw b Ganouri	40
L. Harper b Kallicharran	139	– lbw b Kallicharran	1
R. A. Harper c Baichan b Kallicharran	15	– not out	18
C. Butts c Joseph b Kallicharran	28		
G. Gomes c Baichan b Reginald Etwaroo	48		
C. E. H. Croft c Lambert b Kallicharran	15		
O. Gordon not out	0		
B 10, l-b 2, n-b 6	18	B 14, l-b 6, w 1, n-b 7	28
1/20 2/20 3/52 4/73 5/98 6/145 7/215 8/327 9/345	345	1/1 2/9 3/34 4/109 5/112	(5 wkts) 212

Bowling: *First Innings*—Joseph 16–2–71–1; Lambert 15–3–53–3; Singh 18–6–45–1; Reginald Etwaroo 17–4–49–1; Ganouri 26–8–52–0; Kallicharran 29.1–6–57–4. *Second Innings*—Joseph 10–2–28–2; Lambert 6–0–45–1; Singh 9.4–2–29–0; Reginald Etwaroo 2–0–10–0; Ganouri 14–4–26–1; Kallicharran 10–2–46–1.

Berbice

L. Baichan b Croft	55
T. R. Etwaroo c M. A. Harper b Gordon	52
A. Ramcharitar b Croft	29
D. I. Kallicharran lbw b Croft	11
K. Singh c and b R. A. Harper	24
*Romain Etwaroo c Lyte b Croft	20
†M. R. Pydanna c Whyte b Butts	57
Reginald Etwaroo c Bamfield b Gordon	14
S. Ganouri not out	52
L. Lambert c Whyte b Gordon	9
R. F. Joseph c Bamfield b Gordon	0
B 5, l-b 6, n-b 8	19
1/105 2/145 3/149 4/166 5/188 6/217 7/257 8/326 9/342	342

Bowling: Croft 26–5–71–4; Gordon 25.5–8–58–4; M. A. Harper 2–0–7–0; Butts 35–14–66–1; Gomes 17–2–45–0; R. A. Harper 30–5–69–1; Whyte 3–0–7–0.

CRICKET IN NEW ZEALAND, 1981-82

By C. R. BUTTERY

The Shell Trophy was won in a most convincing manner by Wellington, who gained six outright victories in seven games. This was their first major success since 1973-74, although they had been runners-up in 1978-79 and 1979-80. The reason for their success can be summed up in two words, consistency and application. Unlike the other teams they suffered no wholesale batting collapses. Five Wellington batsmen featured in the first ten in the national averages, and when wickets began to fall quickly someone was always on hand to prevent a rout.

Much of the credit must go to John Morrison. Apart from scoring 498 runs at an average of 49.80 in the Shell series, he led his side well and ensured that bright, attractive cricket was played. Ewen Chatfield and Evan Gray also deserve special mention. Chatfield maintained his usual high standard in collecting 47 wickets at a low cost, while Gray averaged 45.00 with the bat and picked up 22 wickets with his left-arm spinners.

Many people expected the competition to be won by Northern Districts, who looked particularly strong on paper. However, despite the achievements of John Parker and John Wright, the side could manage only second place. Parker had a golden summer, easily his best since he entered first-class cricket. He failed to reach double figures only once, and in thirteen innings scored 618 runs at an average of 103.00. Wright also scored well, but these two did not get the support they needed from the lower-order batsmen and the bowling generally lacked penetration.

As expected, Richard Hadlee dominated the New Zealand bowling scene. Bowling from his short run, he showed that he had lost none of his hostility and he headed the averages with 45 wickets at a cost of only 14.31 runs apiece. Even so this was not enough to lift a weak Canterbury side into contention for major honours. Admittedly Canterbury experienced more than their share of injuries, but their fourth placing must have disappointed those of their supporters who could recall the great Canterbury teams of the past.

Perhaps the less said about Otago and Central Districts the better. Each side often looked outclassed, although Otago ended up with a seven–wicket victory over Canterbury after being 79 runs behind on the first innings. The failure of both teams was due to the inability of their batsmen to provide the basis of a respectable total. No-one from either team averaged over 30 in a season in which little seemed to go right for them. Both sides also relied heavily on spin, but Stephen Boock, John Bracewell and David O'Sullivan were unable to repeat their successes of the previous year.

The previous season's winners, Auckland, started well with a comfortable eight-wicket win against Central Districts then faded as the season got under way and could manage only third place. The veteran leg-spinner, John McIntyre, had another satisfactory season but the brightest spot was undoubtedly the progress shown by Martin Crowe. He scored 525 runs at an average of 43.75 and fully justified the faith shown in him by those who saw his début as a seventeen-year-old two seasons earlier.

Over recent years more and more cricketers are spending the off-season in

England in order to improve their game. This is a trend which it is hoped will continue, as the experience gained by playing in English conditions, whether it be for club or county, will prove invaluable. At least twelve cricketers playing in the Shell series in 1981–82 had just returned from a summer's cricket in England.

FIRST-CLASS AVERAGES, 1981-82

BATTING

(Qualification: 5 complete innings; average 35.00)

	I	*NO*	*R*	*HI*	*Avge*
J. M. Parker (*Northern Districts*)	13	7	618	117	103.00
B. A. Edgar (*Wellington*)	19	1	934	161	51.88
J. G. Wright (*Northern Districts*)	18	0	872	141	48.44
J. F. Reid (*Auckland*)	14	1	585	95	45.00
E. B. McSweeney (*Wellington*)	10	3	295	96*	42.14
V. R. Brown (*Canterbury*)	8	2	250	121*	41.66
E. J. Gray (*Wellington*)	15	0	623	126	41.53
M. C. Snedden (*Auckland*)	15	6	342	49*	38.00
R. W. Ormiston (*Wellington*)	14	3	411	93	37.36
J. F. M. Morrison (*Wellington*)	20	3	616	100*	36.23

BOWLING

(Qualification: 20 wickets)

	O	*M*	*R*	*W*	*Avge*
R. J. Hadlee (*Canterbury*)	424.4	128	870	59	14.74
E. J. Chatfield (*Wellington*)	386.2	135	868	51	17.01
D. C. Aberhart (*Central Districts*)	206	79	455	23	19.78
B. L. Cairns (*Northern Districts*)	371.2	111	816	41	19.90
S. L. Boock (*Otago*)	236	84	592	27	21.92
M. C. Carrington (*Northern Districts*)	202.4	39	611	26	23.50
J. G. Bracewell (*Otago*)	239.4	74	661	28	23.60
G. B. Troup (*Auckland*)	272.1	61	827	34	24.32
L. W. Stott (*Auckland*)	265.3	76	657	27	24.33
C. W. Dickeson (*Northern Districts*)	240	84	498	20	24.90
J. A. Williams (*Wellington*)	188.2	43	555	22	25.22
M. C. Snedden (*Auckland*)	341.5	73	1,051	40	26.27
E. J. Gray (*Wellington*)	265.1	86	661	24	27.54

SHELL TROPHY

Win = 12 points†	*Played*	*Won*	*Lost*	*Drawn*	*Bonus Batting*	*Bonus Bowling*	*Total*
Wellington	7	6	0	1	19	26	116*
Northern Districts	7	4	1	2	17	27	92
Auckland	7	3	2	2	15	28	78*
Canterbury	7	1	5	1	15	24	51
Otago	7	1	2	4	8	22	47*
Central Districts	7	0	5	2	9	19	33*

* *Wellington, Auckland, Otago and Central Districts were each penalised one point.*

† *Otago and Central Districts each received 6 match points for their rain-affected game on January 23, 24, 25.*

AUCKLAND v CENTRAL DISTRICTS

At Eden Park, Auckland, December 27, 28, 29. Auckland won by eight wickets. Auckland 17 pts, Central Districts 3 pts.

Central Districts

R. W. Anderson lbw b McIntyre	73	–	c and b McIntyre	20
A. H. Jones c Scott b Snedden	0	–	c Hellaby b Troup	0
M. H. Toynbee c Crowe b Snedden	0	–	c Crowe b McIntyre	20
G. N. Edwards c Crowe b Troup	33	–	c Troup b McIntyre	57
J. R. Wiltshire c Webb b Stott	12	–	c Reid b Troup	12
W. G. Hodgson b Troup	21	–	b Snedden	27
†I. D. Smith lbw b Stott	5	–	b Snedden	22
G. K. Robertson b Stott	8	–	c Snedden b McIntyre	8
D. C. Aberhart c Webb b Stott	1	–	b Snedden	0
*D. R. O'Sullivan b McIntyre	20	–	b Snedden	1
M. F. Gill not out	4	–	not out	0
L-b 7, n-b 7	14		B 2, l-b 10, n-b 2	14
1/0 2/8 3/41 4/80 5/140 6/158 7/166 8/166 9/167	191		1/18 2/34 3/65 4/120 5/121 6/163 7/178 8/178 9/181	181

Bowling: *First Innings*—Troup 16–2–51–2; Snedden 14–6–40–2; Stott 19–6–57–4; Hellaby 2–0–5–0; McIntyre 12.2–5–24–2. *Second Innings*—Troup 13–2–45–2; Snedden 16.1–5–28–4; Stott 8–2–17–0; McIntyre 31–12–63–4; Reid 2–0–14–0.

Auckland

A. E. W. Parsons b Aberhart	40	–	not out	34
T. J. Franklin c and b O'Sullivan	36	–	lbw b Gill	21
*J. F. Reid c and b Robertson	43	–	b Toynbee	26
M. D. Crowe c Anderson b O'Sullivan	36	–	not out	1
P. N. Webb lbw b O'Sullivan	11			
A. T. R. Hellaby b O'Sullivan	46			
M. C. Snedden c Wiltshire b Aberhart	33			
J. M. McIntyre b Robertson	7			
L. W. Stott c Wiltshire b Robertson	13			
†N. A. Scott not out	6			
G. B. Troup lbw b Robertson	0			
B 4, l-b 6, n-b 5, w 2	17		L-b 2, n-b 1	3
1/69 2/83 3/141 4/166 5/173 6/244 7/260 8/264 9/288	288		1/47 2/83	(2 wkts) 85

Bowling: *First Innings*—Robertson 29.4–8–57–4; Gill 17–3–66–0; O'Sullivan 42–15–88–4; Aberhart 25–12–32–2; Toynbee 13–4–28–0. *Second Innings*—Robertson 7–2–12–0; Gill 4–0–26–1; O'Sullivan 14.4–0–38–0; Toynbee 3–1–6–1.

Umpires: B. V. Dennison and J. D. Matheson.

OTAGO v NORTHERN DISTRICTS

At Molyneaux Park, Alexandra, December 27, 28, 29. Drawn. Northern Districts 7 pts, Otago 6 pts.

Northern Districts

†M. J. E. Wright run out	7	– b Boock	30
J. G. Wright c and b J. G. Bracewell	124	– lbw b Boock	20
*G. P. Howarth c W. Blair b Boock	58	– lbw b Boock	16
B. G. Cooper lbw b Boock	21	– c Dawson b J. G. Bracewell	12
J. M. Parker c Hills b J. G. Bracewell	47	– not out	44
A. D. G. Roberts lbw b J. G. Bracewell	3	– c Lees b B. P. Bracewell	12
D. J. White lbw b Boock	4	– c and b Boock	20
B. L. Cairns b J.G. Bracewell	2	– b Boock	58
C. W. Dickeson c B. Blair b J. G. Bracewell	6	– lbw b J. G. Bracewell	1
S. R. Gillespie b J. G. Bracewell	2	– b J. G. Bracewell	6
S. J. Scott not out	0	– st Lees b Boock	4
B 2, l-b 7, n-b 3	12	L-b 3, n-b 1	4
1/21 2/159 3/215 4/215 5/227 6/236 7/245 8/265 9/283	286	1/45 2/54 3/67 4/95 5/95 6/103 7/135 8/209 9/218	227

Bowling: *First Innings*—B. P. Bracewell 11–4–25–0; Hills 8–2–30–0; Abernathy 9–4–17–0; J. G. Bracewell 34–7–91–6; Boock 34–5–111–3. *Second Innings*—B. P. Bracewell 11–2–30–1; Hills 3–1–13–0; Abernathy 4–2–8–0; J. G. Bracewell 31–10–77–3; Boock 39–18–95–6.

Otago

I. A. Rutherford b Roberts	20	– c Scott b Dickeson	29
J. G. Bracewell c Cooper b Roberts	15	– c and b Howarth	33
R. N. Hoskin run out	27	– c Gillespie b Dickeson	33
B. R. Blair c Howarth b White	82	– c and b Dickeson	52
W. L. Blair c Cooper b White	22	– lbw b Dickeson	9
G. J. Dawson lbw b White	4	– not out	27
*†W. K. Lees b White	8	– c Howarth b Dickeson	0
B. A. Abernathy c Howarth b White	6	– not out	31
B. P. Bracewell b White	8		
P. W. Hills not out	4		
S. L. Boock not out	8		
B 7, l-b 6, n-b 11	24	B 3, l-b 4, w 1, n-b 4	12
1/45 2/46 3/134 4/170 5/180 6/196 7/197 8/210 9/215	(9 wkts dec.) 228	1/66 2/68 3/130 4/165 5/170 6/170	(6 wkts) 226

Bowling: *First Innings*—Gillespie 14–5–25–0; Cairns 18–6–29–0; Scott 12–4–42–0; Roberts 9–5–12–2; Dickeson 24–8–42–0; White 22–10–45–6; Howarth 6–3–9–0. *Second Innings*—Gillespie 11–3–21–0; Cairns 14–1–42–0; Roberts 4–2–14–0; Dickeson 38–16–59–5; White 19–2–55–0; Howarth 13–4–22–1; Cooper 1–0–1–0.

Umpires: W. Garrick and N. F. Tapper.

WELLINGTON v CANTERBURY

At Basin Reserve, Wellington, December 27, 28, 29. Wellington won by six wickets. Wellington 20 pts, Canterbury 4 pts.

Canterbury

D. A. Dempsey b Chatfield	3	c Coney b Gray	63
P. J. Rattray c Cederwall b Williams	36	c Gray b Williams	1
V. R. Brown c Morrison b Chatfield	0	c Maguiness b Chatfield	6
P. E. McEwan lbw b Chatfield	20	c McSweeney b Chatfield	49
R. T. Latham c Maguiness b Cederwall	5	c Maguiness b Gray	23
*C. L. Bull c and b Chatfield	42	c Ormiston b Gray	0
D. W. Stead c McSweeney b Williams	12	b Maguiness	37
R. J. Hadlee not out	61	c and b Chatfield	35
S. Bateman b Maguiness	25	b Chatfield	2
†J. M. Mackle b Coney	6	b Gray	13
S. R. McNally run out	1	not out	0
B 2, l-b 7, n-b 13	22	B 9, l-b 3, w 1, n-b 6	19
1/5 2/5 3/50 4/61 5/85 6/121 7/169 8/202 9/232	233	1/8 2/32 3/109 4/143 5/155 6/155 7/202 8/210 9/248	248

Bowling: *First Innings*—Chatfield 28–9–67–4; Williams 18–4–57–2; Cederwall 6–2–17–1; Maguiness 5–0–15–1; Gray 9–2–23–0; Coney 16–1–32–1. *Second Innings*—Chatfield 35–13–76–4; Williams 8–1–31–1; Maguiness 6.4–4–11–1; Gray 37–11–92–4; Coney 14–7–19–0.

Wellington

B. A. Edgar c Mackle b McNally	30	c McEwan b Stead	9
R. H. Vance b McNally	3	c Brown b Hadlee	17
J. V. Coney c Mackle b McNally	72	c Dempsey b Stead	5
B. W. Cederwall b Hadlee	1		
*J. F. M. Morrison c McEwan b Hadlee	2	not out	45
E. J. Gray c Stead b Bateman	18	c Dempsey b Hadlee	11
R. W. Ormiston lbw b Hadlee	80	not out	33
†E. B. McSweeney not out	96		
S. J. Maguiness c McEwan b Hadlee	1		
J. A. Williams b Hadlee	0		
E. J. Chatfield c Bateman b McNally	3		
B 13, l-b 24, w 2, n-b 11	50	B 4, l-b 1, n-b 4	9
1/8 2/65 3/66 4/85 5/137 6/165 7/319 8/331 9/331	356	1/32 2/32 3/41 4/61 (4 wkts)	129

Bowling: *First Innings*—Hadlee 35–10–81–5; McNally 30.1–10–57–4; McEwan 12–0–44–0; Bateman 18–7–54–1; Stead 7–1–42–0; Brown 13–6–28–0. *Second Innings*—Hadlee 16–6–24–2; McNally 9–4–32–0; Stead 13–2–47–2; Brown 4–1–4–0; Dempsey 1–0–9–0; Latham 0.2–0–4–0.

Umpires: A. H. Hart and S. J. Woodward.

OTAGO v AUCKLAND

At Carisbrook, Dunedin, January 1, 2, 3. Drawn. Auckland 7 pts, Otago 2 pts.

Auckland

A. E. W. Parsons lbw b B. R. Blair	41
T. J. Franklin lbw b Abernathy	30
*J. F. Reid b Abernathy	95
M. D. Crowe c Boock b Abernathy	72
M. C. Snedden c Dawson b J. G. Bracewell	5
A. T. R. Hellaby not out	5
J. M. McIntyre c Dawson b Abernathy	3
A. J. Hunt not out	10
B 2, l-b 5, w 1, n-b 18	26
1/64 2/127 3/261 4/261 5/269 6/277 (6 wkts dec.)	287

G. B. Troup, †N. A. Scott and I. T. Donnelly did not bat.

Bowling: B. P. Bracewell 8–3–13–0; Abernathy 31–9–85–4; Walker 23–5–78–0; B. R. Blair 11–3–17–1; Boock 14–6–32–0; J. G. Bracewell 13–2–36–1.

Otago

I. A. Rutherford c Donnelly b Troup	0	c Reid b McIntyre	27
J. G. Bracewell c Scott b Snedden	10	c Crowe b Hellaby	26
G. J. Dawson c Franklin b Troup	1	c Crowe b McIntyre	49
R. N. Hoskin b Troup	0	c Crowe b Troup	0
B. R. Blair c Reid b Hellaby	42	b Troup	4
S. L. Boock c Hellaby b Snedden	0		
W. L. Blair c Scott b Troup	17	c Hellaby b Snedden	5
*†W. K. Lees b Hellaby	3	c Scott b Troup	63
B. A. Abernathy c Parsons b Hellaby	1	not out	16
D. J. Walker not out	0	not out	0
B. P. Bracewell c Reid b Hellaby	4		
B 1, l-b 1, w 2, n-b 3	7	B 6, l-b 6, w 6, n-b 6	24
1/4 2/12 3/12 4/17 5/17 6/75 7/77 8/80 9/81	85	1/42 2/53 3/59 4/70 5/70 6/166 7/214 (7 wkts)	214

Bowling: *First Innings*—Troup 14–5–29–4; Snedden 9–1–32–2; Hellaby 6–1–17–4. *Second Innings*—Troup 26.1–6–53–3; Snedden 30–10–58–1; Hellaby 29–15–30–1; McIntyre 24–17–30–2; Donnelly 8–2–19–0.

Umpires: G. Morris and F. R. Goodall.

WELLINGTON v CENTRAL DISTRICTS

At Basin Reserve, Wellington, January 1, 2, 3. Wellington won by an innings and 15 runs. Wellington 18 pts, Central Districts 3 pts.

Central Districts

R. W. Anderson c McSweeney b Maguiness	47	c McSweeney b Maguiness	9
A. H. Jones c Coney b Williams	2	c Gray b Chatfield	38
M. H. Toynbee c Coney b Chatfield	0	lbw b Maguiness	3
G. N. Edwards c McSweeney b Maguiness	15	c Gray b Chatfield	10
J. R. Wiltshire b Williams	45	run out	29
W. G. Hodgson lbw b Chatfield	49	b Chatfield	6
†I. D. Smith c Vance b Chatfield	24	b Chatfield	36
G. K. Robertson c Maguiness b Coney	2	b Williams	0
D. C. Aberhart not out	8	c Ormiston b Gray	11
*D. R. O'Sullivan c McSweeney b Chatfield	0	c Williams b Chatfield	12
M. F. Gill c McSweeney b Williams	7	not out	0
B 3, l-b 3, n-b 10	16	B 1, l-b 7, w 1, n-b 5	14
1/9 2/9 3/58 4/89 5/113 6/187 7/198 8/199 9/200	215	1/18 2/23 3/66 4/81 5/88 6/100 7/134 8/136 9/161	168

Bowling: *First Innings*—Williams 16.4–2–48–3; Chatfield 29–9–69–4; Cederwall 3–0–33–0; Maguiness 11–2–37–2; Coney 12–7–12–1. *Second Innings*—Williams 17–3–47–1; Chatfield 19.4–7–29–5; Maguiness 21–5–40–2; Coney 4–3–1–0; Gray 9–4–29–1; Morrison 2–0–8–0.

Wellington

R. H. Vance c Smith b Aberhart	24
B. A. Edgar lbw b Robertson	64
J. V. Coney b Aberhart	13
B. W. Cederwall c Smith b Aberhart	0
*J. F. M. Morrison lbw b Aberhart	7
E. J. Gray run out	126
R. W. Ormiston c sub b Toynbee	93
†E. B. McSweeney c Aberhart b O'Sullivan	7
S. J. Maguiness c Anderson b Toynbee	6
J. A. Williams st Edwards b Toynbee	13
E. J. Chatfield not out	19
B 2, l-b 17, w 6, n-b 1	26
1/71 2/89 3/89 4/114 5/120 6/346 7/352 8/364 9/365	398

Bowling: Robertson 28–9–86–1; Gill 24–5–72–0; O'Sullivan 25–7–73–1; Aberhart 38–10–94–4; Hodgson 3–0–13–0; Toynbee 9.1–2–34–3.

G. N. Edwards kept wicket in the absence of I. D. Smith.

Umpires: S. J. Woodward and A. H. Hart.

CANTERBURY v NORTHERN DISTRICTS

At Lancaster Park, Christchurch, January 1, 2, 3. Northern Districts won by 61 runs. Northern Districts 16 pts, Canterbury 4 pts.

Northern Districts

†M. J. E. Wright b Hadlee	13	b Hadlee	9
J. G. Wright b Hadlee	4	lbw b Hadlee	23
*G. P. Howarth c Mackle b Hadlee	2	b Brown	53
B. G. Cooper b McNally	20	st Mackle b Brown	14
J. M. Parker not out	41	b Stead	17
A. D. G. Roberts c Ritchie b McEwan	14	c Ritchie b McNally	42
D. J. White c Mackle b McEwan	4	lbw b McNally	8
B. L. Cairns c Bull b McEwan	10	b McNally	16
C. W. Dickeson b Hadlee	4	c Hadlee b Stead	5
S. R. Gillespie b Hadlee	2	c Dempsey b Stead	0
M. C. Carrington c Mackle b Bateman	7	not out	0
B 2, l-b 6, n-b 3	11	B 5, l-b 8, n-b 2	15
1/7 2/10 3/36 4/45 5/68 6/72 7/87 8/109 9/119	132	1/29 2/48 3/86 4/123 5/141 6/176 7/194 8/201 9/201	202

Bowling: *First Innings*—Hadlee 26–8–49–5; Bateman 21.3–13–23–1; McEwan 7–2–25–3; McNally 13–4–24–1. *Second Innings*—Hadlee 22–6–46–2; Bateman 9–3–22–0; McEwan 5–1–14–0; McNally 18–8–35–3; Brown 16–3–31–2; Stead 20.3–6–39–3.

Canterbury

P. J. Rattray c Parker b Gillespie	0	c Cooper b Carrington	5
D. A. Dempsey c White b Carrington	13	lbw b Gillespie	16
V. R. Brown b Carrington	42	c Cairns b Gillespie	1
P. E. McEwan b Cairns	3	c M. J. E. Wright b Cairns	7
D. W. Stead c Parker b Cairns	21	c Roberts b Cairns	16
*C. L. Bull c Carrington b Roberts	5	c Dickeson b Roberts	7
R. J. Hadlee c Parker b Carrington	4	c Parker b Howarth	68
B. D. Ritchie c Parker b Cairns	17	c Roberts b Cairns	2
G. C. Bateman lbw b Cairns	1	lbw b Cairns	0
†J. M. Mackle not out	1	not out	21
S. R. McNally b Cairns	1	c J. G. Wright b Gillespie	6
N-b 1	1	B 6, l-b 3, w 1, n-b 5	15
1/0 2/18 3/40 4/75 5/80 6/98 7/106 8/106 9/107	109	1/18 2/19 3/32 4/45 5/58 6/60 7/72 8/94 9/103	164

Bowling: *First Innings*—Gillespie 8–3–18–1; Carrington 13–1–49–3; Roberts 9–5–7–1; Howarth 1–0–2–0; Cairns 18.4–5–32–5. *Second Innings*—Gillespie 18–6–41–3; Carrington 15–2–42–1; Roberts 7–1–21–1; Howarth 5.1–3–5–1; Cairns 26–9–39–4; Dickeson 1–0–1–0.

Umpires: I. C. Higginson and R. Hoskin.

NORTHERN DISTRICTS v WELLINGTON

At Harry Barker Reserve, Gisborne, January 6, 7, 8. Drawn. Northern Districts 9 pts, Wellington 5 pts.

Northern Districts

†M. J. E. Wright b Holland	62	c Cederwall b Gray	27
J. G. Wright c Maguiness b Coney	90	c Coney b Chatfield	31
A. D. G. Roberts c and b Maguiness	59	not out	65
B. G. Cooper b Coney	0	c Morrison b Gray	26
J. M. Parker not out	80	c Edgar b Chatfield	38
B. L. Cairns c Cederwall b Coney	25	lbw b Chatfield	17
*G. P. Howarth not out	20		
B 1, l-b 9, n-b 8	18	L-b 4, n-b 5	9
1/139 2/175 3/183 4/273 5/318 (5 wkts dec.)	354	1/62 2/71 3/118 4/193 5/213 (5 wkts dec.)	213

C. W. Dickeson, D. J. White, S. J. Scott and M. C. Carrington did not bat.

Bowling: *First Innings*—Williams 13–3–46–0; Chatfield 26–4–79–0; Maguiness 15–2–65–1; Coney 20–3–54–3; Gray 12–2–52–0; Holland 12–2–40–1. *Second Innings*—Williams 6–1–19–0; Chatfield 11–2–71–3; Maguiness 1–0–4–0; Coney 2–0–12–0; Gray 27–8–82–2; Holland 2–0–16–0.

Wellington

P. J. Holland c M. J. E. Wright b Cairns	1		
R. H. Vance c J. G. Wright b White	50	c White b Dickeson	23
†E. B. McSweeney b Cairns	0		
B. A. Edgar not out	141	c Parker b Howarth	41
J. V. Coney c Dickeson b White	0	not out	76
*J. F. M. Morrison c M. J. E. Wright b Dickeson	24	not out	47
E. J. Gray c Parker b Dickeson	0		
R. W. Ormiston b Dickeson	5		
S. J. Maguiness c M. J. E. Wright b Cairns	2		
J. A. Williams lbw b Dickeson	3		
E. J. Chatfield not out	23		
B 4, l-b 8, n-b 1	13	B 5, l-b 2, n-b 1	8
1/1 2/1 3/123 4/123 5/180 6/180 7/204 8/207 9/218 (9 wkts dec.)	262	1/66 2/70 (2 wkts)	195

Bowling: *First Innings*—Carrington 10–1–35–0; Cairns 22–6–55–3; Scott 13–3–38–0; Dickeson 33–12–56–4; White 11–3–34–2; Howarth 12–2–31–0. *Second Innings*—Carrington 5–1–27–0; Scott 4–0–30–0; Dickeson 23–8–60–1; White 5–1–32–0; Howarth 15–5–26–1; J. G. Wright 5–1–12–0.

Umpires: G. I. J. Cowan and T. McCall.

CENTRAL DISTRICTS v OTAGO

At McLean Park, Napier, January 6, 7, 8. Drawn. Otago 6 pts, Central Districts 5 pts.

Otago

J. G. Bracewell lbw b Aberhart	12	c Edwards b Aberhart	15
I. A. Rutherford c Smith b Aberhart	92	c Edwards b Hodges	11
R. N. Hoskin lbw b Gill	15	lbw b Gill	7
B. R. Blair b Gill	10	c Smith b Aberhart	22
W. L. Blair c sub b Aberhart	13	b Aberhart	10
G. J. Dawson c sub b Aberhart	15	c Hodgson b Gill	5
*†W. K. Lees c O'Sullivan b Aberhart	14	not out	66
B. A. Abernathy b Gill	19	not out	57
B. P. Bracewell lbw b O'Sullivan	1		
P. W. Hills c Aberhart b O'Sullivan	20		
S. L. Boock not out	2		
B 7, l-b 4	11	L-b 11, w 1	12
1/38 2/71 3/85 4/131 5/152 6/181 7/182 8/212 9/224	224	1/19 2/26 3/56 4/59 5/67 6/82 (6 wkts dec.)	205

Bowling: *First Innings*—Robertson 10–5–9–0; Gill 27–9–60–3; Aberhart 29–13–61–5; O'Sullivan 33.5–12–83–2. *Second Innings*—Gill 26–10–49–2; Aberhart 29–12–44–3; O'Sullivan 46–15–66–0; Hodgson 8–0–34–1.

Central Districts

R. W. Anderson c Rutherford b Hills	19	b Abernathy	11
A. H. Jones c Lees b Hills	3	b Hills	6
J. R. Wiltshire b Boock	23	run out	0
D. C. Aberhart lbw b B. P. Bracewell	11	not out	4
G. N. Edwards c Hoskin b B. P. Bracewell	0	b Boock	10
C. Webb b Boock	14	c Hills b J. G. Bracewell	21
W. G. Hodgson c Dawson b Boock	48	b J. G. Bracewell	10
†I. D. Smith lbw b J. G. Bracewell	13	b J. G. Bracewell	63
S. J. Gill not out	17	lbw b J. G. Bracewell	60
*D. R. O'Sullivan b B. P. Bracewell	0	not out	1
G. K. Robertson b B. P. Bracewell	4		
L-b 3, n-b 2	5	L-b 2, n-b 3	5
1/14 2/31 3/50 4/50 5/72 6/85 7/126 8/152 9/153	157	1/18 2/18 3/19 4/33 5/61 6/61 7/184 8/186 (8 wkts)	191

Bowling: *First Innings*—B. P. Bracewell 15–4–41–4; Hills 10–4–27–2; J. G. Bracewell 11–5–36–1; Boock 14–3–36–3; Abernathy 2–0–12–0. *Second Innings*—B. P. Bracewell 4–1–5–0; Hills 14–4–52–1; J. G. Bracewell 32–16–51–4; Boock 30–13–62–1; Abernathy 8–3–16–1.

Umpires: D. A. Kinsella and B. Blommaart.

CANTERBURY v AUCKLAND

At Lancaster Park, Christchurch, January 6, 7, 8. Drawn. Canterbury 6 pts, Auckland 6 pts.

Canterbury

D. A. Dempsey c Hellaby b Troup	0	– b McIntyre	41
P. J. Rattray b McIntyre	44	– c Troup b McIntyre	36
P. E. McEwan c Crowe b Snedden	19	– run out	7
*C. L. Bull c Scott b Stott	15	– c McIntyre b Stott	2
V. R. Brown c Crowe b Troup	16	– not out	12
R. T. Latham b Snedden	24	– c Scott b Stott	4
D. W. Stead lbw b Stott	32	– not out	42
R. J. Hadlee c Scott b Stott	32	– b Snedden	24
†B. D. Ritchie run out	40		
S. R. McNally b McIntyre	39		
G. C. Bateman not out	0		
B 6, l-b 12, n-b 6	24	B 6, l-b 6	12
1/7 2/33 3/78 4/103 5/139 6/189 7/196 8/219 9/284	285	1/76 2/83 3/89 4/101 5/102 6/148 (6 wkts dec.)	180

Bowling: *First Innings*—Troup 17–4–68–2; Snedden 21–3–77–2; Stott 20–9–44–3; Hellaby 6–2–17–0; McIntyre 31.4–14–55–2. *Second Innings*—Troup 4–0–13–0; Snedden 12–2–47–1; Stott 29–10–63–2; McIntyre 22–7–45–2.

Auckland

A. E. W. Parsons b McNally	31	– b Hadlee	5
T. J. Franklin b Bateman	11	– c sub b Hadlee	0
M. D. Crowe b Bateman	24	– lbw b McNally	9
A. J. Hunt b Stead	58	– b Bateman	32
A. T. R. Hellaby c Ritchie b McNally	15	– c sub b Hadlee	3
*J. F. Reid c Latham b Stead	17	– lbw b Hadlee	12
M. C. Snedden not out	41	– b Hadlee	1
J. M. McIntyre b Stead	7	– not out	1
L. W. Stott not out	27	– lbw b Hadlee	0
†N. A. Scott (did not bat)		– not out	0
B 7, l-b 6, n-b 1	14	B 4, l-b 8, n-b 2	14
1/31 2/49 3/100 4/131 5/165 6/170 7/183 (7 wkts dec.)	245	1/1 2/11 3/23 4/46 5/48 6/48 7/67 8/77 (8 wkts)	77

G. B. Troup did not bat.

Bowling: *First Innings*—Hadlee 31–9–72–0; Bateman 28–9–57–2; McNally 16–3–44–2; Stead 24–11–58–3; McEwan 1–1–0–0. *Second Innings*—Hadlee 22–6–26–6; Bateman 11–6–8–1; McNally 8–1–19–1; Stead 10.1–7–10–0.

Umpires: B. L. Aldridge and R. L. McHarg.

CENTRAL DISTRICTS v CANTERBURY

At Fitzherbert Park, Palmerston North, January 11, 12, 13. Canterbury won by seven wickets. Canterbury 18 pts, Central Districts 6 pts.

Central Districts

R. A. Pierce c Leggat b Hadlee	0	lbw b Hadlee	4
R. W. Anderson c Rattray b Bateman	17	b Hadlee	80
J. R. Wiltshire b McEwan	16	c Latham b McEwan	14
G. N. Edwards b McNally	37	c Leggat b McEwan	10
C. Webb c Stead b Dempsey	44	b Leggat	25
G. J. Langridge b Bateman	76	b Hadlee	0
S. J. Gill c McEwan b Bateman	2	st Mackle b Leggat	15
†I. D. Smith lbw b Bateman	4	lbw b Hadlee	28
D. C. Aberhart lbw b Hadlee	5	c McEwan b Hadlee	1
*D. R. O'Sullivan c Dempsey b Bateman	22	b Hadlee	0
M. F. Gill not out	4	not out	1
B 6, l-b 7, n-b 1	14	B 3, l-b 5, n-b 1	9
1/0 2/24 3/61 4/79 5/193 6/203 7/209 8/214 9/217	241	1/23 2/51 3/61 4/72 5/120 6/152 7/175 8/183 9/186	187

Bowling: *First Innings*—Hadlee 26–7–63–2; Bateman 18.1–2–60–5; McEwan 7–1–15–1; McNally 14–4–49–1; Stead 9–0–39–0; Dempsey 1–0–1–1. *Second Innings*—Hadlee 19.1–6–40–6; Bateman 7–3–10–0; McEwan 7–2–22–2; McNally 20–4–48–0; Stead 5–1–11–0; Leggat 13–1–47–2.

Canterbury

P. J. Rattray c S. J. Gill b M. F. Gill	7	c Webb b O'Sullivan	82
D. A. Dempsey c Smith b S. J. Gill	2	lbw b M. F. Gill	2
P. E. McEwan c Anderson b M. F. Gill	3	not out	103
*C. L. Bull c Smith b Aberhart	31		
D. W. Stead c S. J. Gill b M. F. Gill	56		
†J. M. Mackle c Smith b M. F. Gill	11	lbw b O'Sullivan	1
R. T. Latham c Webb b Aberhart	2	not out	6
R. J. Hadlee not out	83		
R. I. Leggat c Smith b M. F. Gill	0		
S. R. McNally c Anderson b O'Sullivan	1		
G. C. Bateman c Edwards b M. F. Gill	16		
L-b 7, w 1, n-b 5	13	B 5, l-b 4, w 1, n-b 1	11
1/6 2/12 3/17 4/78 5/111 6/120 7/132 8/137 9/166	225	1/3 2/8 3/182	(3 wkts) 205

Bowling: *First Innings*—M. F. Gill 25.3–11–56–6; S. J. Gill 11–1–55–1; Aberhart 24–6–70–2; O'Sullivan 15–6–31–1. *Second Innings*—M. F. Gill 15–2–64–1; Aberhart 15–8–49–0; O'Sullivan 19.4–2–71–2; Pierce 6–2–10–0.

Umpires: G. Reardon and R. Trott.

AUCKLAND v NORTHERN DISTRICTS

At Eden Park, Auckland, January 12, 13, 14. Northern Districts won by five wickets. Northern Districts 20 pts, Auckland 6 pts.

Auckland

A. E. Barrons c White b Gillespie	1	– not out	53
T. J. Franklin b Carrington	0	– lbw b Dickeson	22
*J. F. Reid c M. J. E. Wright b Carrington	58	– b Dickeson	82
M. D. Crowe c Parker b Gillespie	99	– c J. G. Wright b White	60
P. N. Webb c M. J. E. Wright b Carrington	9	– st M. J. E. Wright b White	116
A. J. Hunt c Roberts b Carrington	0	– c Dickeson b Parker	0
W. P. Fowler c Dickeson b Gillespie	29	– b Dickeson	6
M. C. Snedden c Cooper b Dickeson	16	– not out	14
L. W. Stott c Howarth b Gillespie	0		
†N. A. Scott c Parker b White	17		
G. B. Troup not out	11		
L-b 5, n-b 4	9	B 2, l-b 4, n-b 8	14
1/1 2/1 3/143 4/159 5/180 6/199 7/206 8/210 9/228	249	1/67 2/214 3/237 4/238 5/325 6/336 (6 wkts dec.)	367

Bowling: *First Innings*—Carrington 22–4–57–4; Gillespie 25–9–64–4; Cairns 21–4–64–0; Roberts 2–0–9–0; Dickeson 20–5–40–1; White 1.5–0–6–1. *Second Innings*—Carrington 13–5–27–0; Gillespie 6–1–15–0; Cairns 17–6–39–0; Roberts 8–6–16–0; Dickeson 37–8–106–3; White 21–2–96–2; Howarth 7–1–23–0; Parker 8–0–31–1.

Northern Districts

†M. J. E. Wright b Troup	36	– c Scott b Troup	9
J. G. Wright run out	113	– lbw b Snedden	105
B. G. Cooper b Snedden	25	– c Webb b Stott	56
*G. P. Howarth c Crowe b Stott	41	– b Fowler	41
J. M. Parker not out	45	– not out	14
A. D. G. Roberts c and b Stott	7	– not out	15
D. J. White lbw b Snedden	6		
B. L. Cairns b Stott	38	– b Fowler	29
C. W. Dickeson b Stott	0		
S. R. Gillespie c and b Snedden	1		
M. C. Carrington b Stott	4		
L-b 14, n-b 5	19	B 3, l-b 10	13
1/48 2/120 3/277 4/259 5/270 6/317 7/319 8/330 9/330	335	1/14 2/109 3/208 4/250 5/252 (5 wkts)	282

Bowling: *First Innings*—Troup 23–8–58–1; Snedden 28–3–95–3; Stott 38.5–13–115–5; Crowe 3–0–19–0; Fowler 7–0–29–0. *Second Innings*—Troup 9–0–60–1; Snedden 13–0–76–1; Stott 12–0–66–1; Fowler 13–0–65–2; Reid 0.2–0–2–0.

Umpires: K. M. Wallis and J. D. Matheson.

WELLINGTON v OTAGO

At Basin Reserve, Wellington, January 12, 13, 14. Wellington won by four wickets. Wellington 19 pts, Otago 7 pts.

Otago

I. A. Rutherford c Ormiston b Cederwall	13	– c Ormiston b Chatfield	51
J. G. Bracewell c and b Chatfield	0	– lbw b Chatfield	23
B. R. Blair b Chatfield	12	– c Ormiston b Gray	4
W. L. Blair c Cederwall b Gray	132	– lbw b Gray	1
R. N. Hoskin c Morrison b Chatfield	17	– c Vance b Williams	25
G. J. Dawson b Gray	48	– c Cederwall b Williams	52
*†W. K. Lees c and b Gray	7	– b Cederwall	41
B. A. Abernathy c Ormiston b Cederwall	2	– c and b Chatfield	9
B. P. Bracewell c Gray b Cederwall	12	– lbw b Cederwall	19
P. W. Hills not out	6	– not out	3
S. L. Boock b Cederwall	12		
B 4, l-b 6, n-b 3	13	B 4, l-b 10, n-b 4	18
1/9 2/22 3/39 4/91 5/223 6/231 7/246 8/261 9/274	274	1/79 2/80 3/84 4/92 5/141 6/174 7/202 8/231 9/246 (9 wkts dec.)	246

Bowling: *First Innings*—Williams 15–5–36–0; Chatfield 24–6–58–3; Cederwall 26.4–5–65–4; Coney 8–4–27–0; Wheeler 3–0–17–0; Gray 23–7–58–3. *Second Innings*—Williams 21–8–49–2; Chatfield 28–12–68–3; Cederwall 7.5–1–26–2; Coney 2–0–16–0; Wheeler 7–2–13–0; Gray 38–18–56–2.

Wellington

R. H. Vance lbw b B. P. Bracewell	12	– c Lees b Abernathy	18
B. A. Edgar c Abernathy b Hills	14	– st Lees b J. G. Bracewell	58
J. V. Coney c B. P. Bracewell b Abernathy	48	– c Lees b Abernathy	28
*J. F. M. Morrison c Lees b Hills	11	– c W. L. Blair b Boock	43
E. J. Gray c Hoskin b B. P. Bracewell	35	– c W. L. Blair b Boock	13
R. W. Ormiston c Rutherford b B. P. Bracewell	6	– not out	21
†E. B. McSweeney c B. R. Blair b Boock	29	– not out	60
B. W. Cederwall c Dawson b Boock	38	– c B. R. Blair b Boock	0
G. Wheeler not out	32		
J. A. Williams b Boock	18		
E. J. Chatfield c Rutherford b Boock	4		
B 2, l-b 1, n-b 3	6	B 8, l-b 15, n-b 5	28
1/21 2/37 3/91 4/92 5/112 6/137 7/171 8/200 9/246	253	1/55 2/99 3/146 4/182 5/220 6/220 (6 wkts)	269

Bowling: *First Innings*—B. P. Bracewell 25–5–45–3; Hills 14–3–43–2; B. R. Blair 10–2–27–0; Abernathy 4–0–17–1; J. G. Bracewell 22–4–87–0; Boock 13.5–4–28–4. *Second Innings*—B. P. Bracewell 3–0–10–0; Hills 3–1–5–0; Abernathy 20–1–96–2; J. G. Bracewell 5–0–43–1; Boock 19.4–2–87–3.

Umpires: S. C. Cowman and S. J. Woodward.

NORTHERN DISTRICTS v CENTRAL DISTRICTS

At Tauranga Domain, January 17, 18, 19. Northern Districts won by 99 runs. Northern Districts 18 pts, Central Districts 6 pts.

Northern Districts

†M. J. E. Wright c Webb b Stirling	1	– c Edwards b Jamieson	46
J. G. Wright c Smith b Jamieson	26	– c Langridge b Jamieson	22
*G. P. Howarth c Langridge b Stirling	11	– c Edwards b O'Sullivan	0
B. G. Cooper c Anderson b Stirling	8	– c Wiltshire b Gill	9
J. M. Parker c Smith b Jamieson	117	– not out	102
A. D. G. Roberts c Jamieson b Gill	28	– c Edwards b Stirling	56
D. J. White c Pierce b Stirling	0	– c Edwards b Gill	16
B. L. Cairns c Langridge b O'Sullivan	0	– not out	14
C. W. Dickeson c Anderson b Stirling	1		
S. R. Gillespie not out	18		
M. C. Carrington c Jamieson b Stirling	23		
L-b 4, n-b 4	8	B 4, l-b 6, n-b 3	13
1/8 2/39 3/40 4/54 5/156 6/174 7/177 8/186 9/207	241	1/65 2/70 3/70 4/182 5/202 6/248 (6 wkts dec.)	278

Bowling: *First Innings*—Stirling 20.1–3–75–6; Gill 14–4–37–1; Jamieson 23–6–44–2; O'Sullivan 26–7–65–1; Pierce 5–2–12–0. *Second Innings*—Stirling 14–2–41–1; Gill 19–2–69–2; Jamieson 31–12–61–2; O'Sullivan 23.2–5–66–1; Pierce 10–3–28–0.

Central Districts

R. W. Anderson c Parker b Carrington	1	– c M. J. E. Wright b Gillespie	25
R. A. Pierce c Howarth b Carrington	29	– c Howarth b Cairns	13
C. Webb c Dickeson b Cairns	7	– b Cairns	45
G. N. Edwards c J. G. Wright b Cairns	0	– c Parker b Carrington	14
J. R. Wiltshire c M. J. E. Wright b Carrington	29	– c White b Dickeson	23
M. D. Jamieson c M. J. E. Wright b Gillespie	59	– c Gillespie b Dickeson	7
G. J. Langridge c J. G. Wright b Roberts	21	– b Dickeson	18
†I. D. Smith b Cairns	74	– c M. J. E. Wright b Gillespie	1
D. Stirling c and b Cairns	0	– not out	0
M. F. Gill not out	0	– c Carrington b White	16
D. R. O'Sullivan lbw b Cairns	0	– c M. J. E. Wright b Cairns	20
B 1, l-b 4, n-b 3	8	B 4, l-b 5, n-b 1	10
1/4 2/27 3/27 4/53 5/74 6/107 7/226 8/226 9/226	228	1/62 2/63 3/91 4/129 5/133 6/138 7/158 8/176 9/176	192

Bowling: *First Innings*—Carrington 12–1–45–3; Gillespie 19–6–53–1; Cairns 28–10–48–5; Roberts 6–4–7–1; Dickeson 7–1–27–0; White 10–3–30–0; Howarth 3–1–10–0. *Second Innings*—Carrington 12–6–32–1; Gillespie 18–5–33–2; Cairns 17–3–35–3; Roberts 7–1–26–0; Dickeson 25–14–35–3; White 5.3–0–21–1.

Umpires: J. B. R. Hastie and N. W. Stoupe.

OTAGO v CANTERBURY

At Carisbrook, Dunedin, January 17, 18, 19. Otago won by seven wickets. Otago 16 pts, Canterbury 6 pts.

Canterbury

P. J. Rattray c B. P. Bracewell b B. R. Blair	20	c Dawson b Osborne	20
D. A. Dempsey c Lees b Hills	16	b B. R. Blair	34
P. E. McEwan c Osborne b Hills	11	c Dawson b J. G. Bracewell	52
*C. L. Bull b Hills	0	c W. L. Blair b J. G. Bracewell	4
D. W. Stead c B. R. Blair b B. P. Bracewell	35	c Osborne b J. G. Bracewell	5
R. T. Latham c Hills b J. G. Bracewell	95	c Hills b Boock	0
R. J. Hadlee c sub b Hills	22	c Boock b J. G. Bracewell	0
R. I. Leggat lbw b Boock	23	c Boock b J. G. Bracewell	1
†A. W. Hart not out	13	c W. L. Blair b J. G. Bracewell	0
S. R. McNally c Dawson b Boock	0	c Dawson b J. G. Bracewell	2
A. I. Farrant c Hoskin b B. P. Bracewell	2	not out	1
B 6	6	L-b 2	2
1/22 2/33 3/39 4/62 5/92 6/136 7/217 8/232 9/232	243	1/44 2/78 3/94 4/117 5/117 6/117 7/117 8/117 9/120	121

Bowling: *First Innings*—B. P. Bracewell 12.3–3–33–2; Hills 16–2–71–4; Osborne 16–6–35–0; B. R. Blair 20–8–52–1; Boock 9–3–22–2; J. G. Bracewell 10–4–24–1. *Second Innings*—B. P. Bracewell 6–1–20–0; Hills 8–1–27–0; B. R. Blair 12–2–47–1; Osborne 7–2–10–1; Boock 8–6–6–1; J. G. Bracewell 10.1–6–9–7.

Otago

I. A. Rutherford c Leggat b McNally	1	lbw b McNally	0
J. G. Bracewell c McEwan b Stead	51	c Stead b McNally	8
W. L. Blair st Hart b Stead	6	lbw b Hadlee	29
B. R. Blair b Hadlee	20	not out	98
R. N. Hoskin lbw b Hadlee	0	not out	62
G. J. Dawson c Stead b Hadlee	15		
*†W. K. Lees not out	25		
G. C. Osborne b Hadlee	8		
B. P. Bracewell b Farrant	23		
P. W. Hills c Stead b McEwan	0		
S. L. Boock lbw b McEwan	0		
B 3, l-b 10, n-b 2	15	B 4, l-b 1, n-b 2	7
1/33 2/54 3/81 4/83 5/88 6/99 7/121 8/159 9/164	164	1/5 2/12 3/75	(3 wkts) 204

Bowling: *First Innings*—Hadlee 19–5–32–4; McNally 14–5–46–1; Stead 16–9–28–2; Farrant 14–6–27–1; Leggat 1–0–10–0; McEwan 3.5–1–6–2. *Second Innings*—Hadlee 22–12–34–1; McNally 15.5–4–46–2; Stead 16–4–50–0; Farrant 10–2–19–0; Leggat 4–1–16–0; McEwan 9–2–26–0; Latham 1–0–6–0.

Umpires: G. Morris and I. C. Higginson.

AUCKLAND v WELLINGTON

At Eden Park, Auckland, January 17, 18, 19. Wellington won by 146 runs. Wellington 19 pts, Auckland 5 pts.

Wellington

B. A. Edgar c Webb b Snedden	20	c and b Stott	31
R. H. Vance c Kelly b Snedden	2		
J. V. Coney c Crowe b Snedden	1	lbw b Troup	0
*J. F. M. Morrison c Donnelly b Stott	18	run out	83
E. J. Gray c Parsons b Donnelly	114	lbw b Stott	43
R. W. Ormiston lbw b Snedden	1	b Troup	4
P. J. Holland lbw b Donnelly	4	run out	4
†E. B. McSweeney lbw b Stott	68	not out	16
S. J. Maguiness c Snedden b Donnelly	24	b Stott	0
J. A. Williams not out	5		
E. J. Chatfield c Snedden b Donnelly	3		
B 4, l-b 6, w 1, n-b 6	17	B 5, l-b 12, w 1, n-b 5	23
1/8 2/10 3/29 4/58 5/60 6/73 7/215 8/268 9/268	277	1/19 2/19 3/66 4/169 5/185 6/202 7/204 (7 wkts dec.)	204

Bowling: *First Innings*—Troup 13–3–37–0; Snedden 20–5–58–4; Stott 29–6–57–2; Hellaby 10–3–26–0; Donnelly 22.2–2–70–4; Reid 3–1–5–0; Crowe 2–0–7–0. *Second Innings*—Troup 9–2–24–2; Snedden 19–4–62–0; Stott 24.5–6–56–3; Hellaby 7–1–22–0; Donnelly 7–2–17–0.

Auckland

A. E. W. Parsons lbw b Chatfield	5	lbw b Chatfield	53
P. N. Webb lbw b Williams	16	b Chatfield	1
T. J. Franklin c McSweeney b Maguiness	20	c Ormiston b Chatfield	4
*J. F. Reid c and b Chatfield	37	b Gray	27
M. D. Crowe b Maguiness	4	c McSweeney b Gray	3
A. T. R. Hellaby c McSweeney b Maguiness	1	c Holland b Gray	16
†P. J. Kelly c Morrison b Holland	14	c sub b Holland	11
M. C. Snedden c Morrison b Gray	12	c Ormiston b Williams	39
L. W. Stott lbw b Chatfield	32	run out	13
G. B. Troup c McSweeney b Chatfield	4	b Gray	1
I. T. Donnelly not out	0	not out	1
B 2, l-b 2, n-b 8	12	B 1, l-b 3, w 1, n-b 4	9
1/33 2/71 3/79 4/85 5/92 6/96 7/110 8/134 9/152	157	1/19 2/88 3/88 4/92 5/93 6/120 7/122 8/167 9/171	178

Bowling: *First Innings*—Williams 10–4–42–1; Chatfield 25.3–12–30–4; Gray 13–6–28–1; Maguiness 13–3–24–3; Holland 5–1–21–1. *Second Innings*—Williams 10–0–35–1; Chatfield 23–7–45–3; Gray 27–8–58–4; Maguiness 5–1–17–0; Holland 5–2–8–1; Coney 1–0–6–0.

Umpires: B. A. Bricknell and B. V. Dennison.

WELLINGTON v NORTHERN DISTRICTS

At Hutt Recreation Ground, Lower Hutt, January 23, 24, 25. Wellington won by 154 runs. Wellington 19 pts, Northern Districts 5 pts.

Wellington

R. H. Vance lbw b Pollock	15	c Parker b Cairns	52
B. A. Edgar c M. J. E. Wright b Cairns	26	lbw b Carrington	12
J. V. Coney b Cairns	1	lbw b Carrington	0
*J. F. M. Morrison c M. J. E. Wright b Gillespie	41	b Cairns	56
E. J. Gray run out	71	c sub b Carrington	43
R. W. Ormiston b Dickeson	48	c Parker b Pollock	18
†E. B. McSweeney lbw b Pollock	4	c Parker b Cairns	6
B. W. Cederwall not out	17	b Carrington	19
S. J. Maguiness c Roberts b Dickeson	0	not out	12
J. A. Williams not out	18	c Dickeson b Carrington	8
E. J. Chatfield (did not bat)		c sub b Dickeson	3
B 1, l-b 8, n-b 1	10	B 8, l-b 24, n-b 1	33
1/26 2/33 3/47 4/130 5/182 6/193 7/221 8/221	(8 wkts dec.) 251	1/25 2/25 3/130 4/139 5/184 6/200 7/234 8/234 9/249	262

Bowling: *First Innings*—Carrington 18–4–46–0; Gillespie 18–7–31–1; Pollock 15–3–48–2; Cairns 23.3–8–61–2; Dickeson 17–5–40–2; Roberts 8–2–15–0. *Second Innings*—Carrington 26–5–69–5; Gillespie 13–2–34–0; Pollock 14–4–45–1; Cairns 25–8–43–3; Dickeson 15–7–32–1; Roberts 4–2–6–0.

Northern Districts

†M. J. E. Wright c Morrison b Chatfield	41	c Ormiston b Williams	13
J. G. Wright c Coney b Maguiness	26	b Maguiness	88
*G. P. Howarth b Chatfield	3	b Chatfield	6
B. G. Cooper c Coney b Chatfield	5	lbw b Chatfield	5
J. M. Parker not out	57	c Ormiston b Maguiness	12
A. D. G. Roberts c McSweeney b Chatfield	10	lbw b Williams	0
B. L. Cairns c Vance b Williams	3	c Vance b Gray	13
C. W. Dickeson b Williams	1	c Vance b Williams	0
S. R. Gillespie c McSweeney b Williams	9	lbw b Gray	8
M. C. Carrington b Williams	0	c McSweeney b Williams	5
N. Pollock b Chatfield	24	not out	0
B 5, l-b 5, n-b 11	21	L-b 4, n-b 5	9
1/72 2/76 3/82 4/82 5/96 6/104 7/130 8/151 9/153	200	1/34 2/51 3/93 4/126 5/139 6/140 7/144 8/145 9/159	159

Bowling: *First Innings*—Williams 20–6–39–4; Maguiness 18–7–52–1; Chatfield 27–11–42–5; Cederwall 15–2–38–0; Gray 1–0–8–0. *Second Innings*—Williams 12–6–26–4; Maguiness 10–1–29–2; Chatfield 16–5–54–2; Cederwall 1–0–8–0; Gray 11.1–4–33–2.

Umpires: S. C. Cowman and R. L. McHarg.

AUCKLAND v CANTERBURY

At Eden Park, Auckland, January 23, 24, 25. Auckland won by three wickets. Auckland 17 pts, Canterbury 6 pts.

Canterbury

P. J. Rattray c Kelly b Troup	4	c sub b Stott	35
D. W. Stead b Troup	12	run out	50
P. E. McEwan c Crowe b McIntyre	55	not out	42
R. T. Latham b Snedden	40	c Troup b McIntyre	2
*C. L. Bull lbw b Snedden	29	not out	0
D. J. Boyle c Crowe b Troup	58		
R. J. Hadlee c Snedden b Stott	0	c Troup b Stott	31
D. G. Farrant st Kelly b Stott	33		
†A. W. Hart run out	24		
S. R. McNally c Parsons b Troup	0		
G. C. Bateman not out	4		
L-b 10, n-b 12	22	L-b 2, n-b 1	3
1/12 2/29 3/105 4/125 5/153 6/154 7/202 8/262 9/262	281	1/69 2/87 3/110 4/149 (4 wkts dec.)	163

Bowling: *First Innings*—Troup 24.3–5–63–4; Snedden 30–9–93–2; Stott 26–3–49–2; McIntyre 18–7–40–1; Hunt 3–0–14–0. *Second Innings*—Troup 6–1–19–0; Snedden 11–3–17–0; Stott 24.5–7–71–2, McIntyre 17–6–53–1.

Auckland

A. E. W. Parsons b Bateman	1	c Hadlee b Bateman	2
T. J. Franklin c Hart b McNally	7	lbw b Hadlee	47
*J. F. Reid c Hart b Hadlee	11	c McNally b Farrant	72
M. D. Crowe c Hart b Bateman	25	b Bateman	34
P. N. Webb lbw b Bateman	21	c Farrant b Bateman	12
A. J. Hunt b Hadlee	53	b Bateman	9
M. C. Snedden not out	46	not out	49
†P. J. Kelly c Stead b Hadlee	10	c Hadlee b McNally	6
L. W. Stott lbw b Hadlee	0		
J. M. McIntyre not out	0	not out	11
B 2, l-b 8	10	B 10, l-b 8, w 1, n-b 1	20
1/1 2/20 3/22 4/66 5/71 6/178 7/184 8/184 (8 wkts dec.)	184	1/2 2/105 3/152 4/169 5/176 6/197 7/212 (7 wkts)	262

G. B. Troup did not bat.

Bowling: *First Innings*—Hadlee 22–9–27–4; Bateman 20–9–29–3; McEwan 4–3–1–0; Stead 27–6–76–0; Farrant 5–0–14–0; McNally 17–7–27–1. *Second Innings*—Hadlee 26.3–10–62–1; Bateman 15–3–49–4; McEwan 4–0–20–0; Stead 9–2–26–0; Farrant 6–1–31–1; McNally 20–3–54–1.

Umpires: J. B. R. Hastie and J. D. Matheson.

OTAGO v CENTRAL DISTRICTS

At Queens Park, Invercargill, January 23, 24, 25. Drawn. Otago 6 pts, Central Districts 6 pts. Only 3 hours, 59 minutes of play were possible, rain washing out all the first day and much of the third, as well as interrupting the second.

Otago

J. G. Bracewell lbw b Aberhart......... 15	B. A. Abernathy not out.................. 6
S. J. McCullum c Smith b Jamieson.... 12	B. P. Bracewell not out.................... 16
W. L. Blair b Aberhart.................... 10	
B. R. Blair b Aberhart..................... 4	L-b 3.................................... 3
R. N. Hoskin c Edwards b O'Sullivan.. 53	
*†W. K. Lees b Aberhart.................. 0	1/26 2/32 3/40 4/47 (7 wkts) 161
G. J. Dawson c Edwards b Aberhart... 42	5/57 6/127 7/145

P. W. Hills and S. L. Boock did not bat.

Bowling: Stirling 8–0–31–0; Jamieson 17–4–33–1; Aberhart 26–11–46–5; O'Sullivan 17–7–48–1.

Central Districts

R. A. Pierce, C. Webb, R. W. Anderson, G. N. Edwards, J. R. Wiltshire, M. D. Jamieson, †I. D. Smith, D. C. Aberhart, *D. R. O'Sullivan, D. Stirling, M. F. Gill.

Umpires: N. F. Tapper and J. Fitzgerald.

CANTERBURY v WELLINGTON

At Lancaster Park, Christchurch, January 29, 30, 31. Wellington won by six wickets. Wellington 16 pts, Canterbury 7 pts.

Canterbury

P. J. Rattray c Edgar b Williams.....................	4	– c McSweeney b Maguiness........	14
D. W. Stead lbw b Chatfield..........................	88	– c and b Chatfield.....................	11
P. E. McEwan c Coney b Chatfield................	19	– lbw b Williams.........................	0
R. T. Latham c McSweeney b Chatfield..........	0	– not out..................................	72
*C. L. Bull c Morrison b Coney......................	46	– lbw b Maguiness.......................	2
B. D. Ritchie b Coney..................................	2	– b Chatfield..............................	0
R. J. Hadlee c Ormiston b Gray.....................	41	– c Cederwall b Maguiness..........	7
D. G. Farrant lbw b Chatfield........................	0	– c Ormiston b Chatfield.............	0
†A. W. Hart c Morrison b Gray......................	6	– b Maguiness............................	13
S. R. McNally b Williams..............................	40	– c Maguiness b Gray..................	15
G. C. Bateman not out.................................	3	– c Chatfield b Coney..................	10
L-b 4, n-b 8..	12	B 2, l-b 7, n-b 5.............	14
1/5 2/47 3/47 4/169 5/169 6/175 7/193 8/217 9/218	261	1/19 2/23 3/34 4/40 5/41 6/60 7/86 8/137 9/137	158

Bowling: *First Innings*—Williams 9.4–1–41–2; Chatfield 23–3–74–4; Maguiness 24–4–62–0; Cederwall 4–1–11–0; Gray 9–2–37–2; Coney 7–2–24–2. *Second Innings*—Williams 12–2–39–1; Chatfield 19–10–31–3; Maguiness 13–2–42–4; Gray 13–5–26–1; Coney 5–2–6–1.

Wellington

B. A. Edgar c McEwan b Bateman	2	– c sub b Farrant	65
R. H. Vance c Rattray b Hadlee	4	– lbw b Hadlee	27
J. V. Coney c Hart b Farrant	11	– lbw b Stead	14
*J. F. M. Morrison run out	21	– not out	100
E. J. Gray lbw b Hadlee	21		
R. W. Ormiston b Hadlee	18	– not out	59
†E. B. McSweeney c Hart b Hadlee	9		
B. W. Cederwall lbw b Hadlee	0		
J. A. Williams lbw b Stead	7	– c Hart b Hadlee	2
S. J. Maguiness st Hart b Stead	15		
E. J. Chatfield not out	7		
B 1, l-b 7	8	B 13, l-b 16, n-b 1	30
1/3 2/9 3/38 4/43 5/74 6/93 7/93 8/96 9/100	123	1/69 2/75 3/104 4/163 (4 wkts)	297

Bowling: *First Innings*—Hadlee 20–5–35–5; Bateman 10–2–20–1; McNally 7–1–18–0; Farrant 6–2–7–1; Stead 12–3–35–2. *Second Innings*—Hadlee 26–4–53–2; Bateman 20–7–42–0; McNally 18–1–59–0; Farrant 17–6–32–1; Stead 36–17–72–1; Latham 2–0–5–0; Rattray 1–0–4–0.

Umpires: B. L. Aldridge and I. C. Higginson.

NORTHERN DISTRICTS v OTAGO

At Seddon Park, Hamilton, January 30, 31, February 1. Northern Districts won by ten wickets. Northern Districts 17 pts, Otago 4 pts.

Otago

G. J. Dawson c J. G. Wright b Carrington	2	– lbw b Howarth	38
J. G. Bracewell c M. J. E. Wright b Gillespie	36	– c Howarth b Carrington	0
W. L. Blair c M. J. E. Wright b Gillespie	5	– c Parker b Gillespie	17
B. R. Blair c M. J. E. Wright b Cairns	0	– c Dickeson b Howarth	0
R. N. Hoskin c Parker b Gillespie	5	– c Kuggeleijn b Cairns	3
*†W. K. Lees b Cairns	0	– b Cairns	0
J. K. Lindsay c Parker b Carrington	42	– lbw b Cairns	5
B. A. Abernathy c M. J. E. Wright b Roberts	10	– not out	8
B. P. Bracewell c sub b Carrington	3	– b Cairns	0
P. W. Hills b Carrington	7	– lbw b Cairns	0
S. L. Boock not out	1	– c Kuggeleijn b Cairns	6
N-b 3	3	B 1, l-b 2, w 1, n-b 1	5
1/20 2/40 3/46 4/46 5/46 6/56 7/95 8/103 9/111	114	1/9 2/51 3/51 4/54 5/54 6/66 7/66 8/76 9/82	82

Bowling: *First Innings*—Carrington 13.4–2–43–4; Gillespie 11–3–36–3; Cairns 15–8–24–2; Roberts 3–2–8–1. *Second Innings*—Carrington 7–1–22–1; Gillespie 11–3–31–1; Cairns 14.1–8–19–6; Howarth 5–3–5–2.

Northern Districts

†M. J. E. Wright c Hills b J. G. Bracewell	31		
J. G. Wright b Hills	0		
*G. P. Howarth lbw b Hills	9		
B. G. Cooper c B. R. Blair b Boock	19	– not out	6
J. M. Parker c B. R. Blair b Boock	4		
A. D. G. Roberts b Boock	59	– not out	1
C. M. Kuggeleijn lbw b B. P. Bracewell	17		
B. L. Cairns c Hoskin b B. P. Bracewell	31		
C. W. Dickeson b Boock	1		
S. R. Gillespie c Lees b B. P. Bracewell	4		
M. C. Carrington not out	0		
B 4, l-b 5, n-b 9	18		
1/0 2/24 3/71 4/71 5/79 6/131 8/190 9/194	193	(no wkt)	7

Bowling: *First Innings*—B. P. Bracewell 15–2–55–3; Hills 6–1–21–2; Boock 32.3–18–44–4; J. G. Bracewell 24–9–55–1. *Second Innings*—Lees 1–1–0–0; Dawson 0.3–0–7–0.

Umpires: G. I. J. Cowan and B. A. Bricknell.

CENTRAL DISTRICTS v AUCKLAND

At Pukekura Park, New Plymouth, January 30, 31, February 1. Auckland won by seven wickets. Auckland 20 pts, Central Districts 4 pts. M. D. Crowe, whose 150 was his maiden first-class hundred, hit 102 before lunch on the second day.

Central Districts

R. A. Pierce lbw b Snedden	52	– run out	17
C. Webb lbw b Hellaby	12	– not out	20
R. W. Anderson c Kelly b Hellaby	0	– lbw b Hellaby	38
G. N. Edwards c Hunt b Troup	10	– b Snedden	0
J. R. Wiltshire c Hellaby b Stott	73	– st Kelly b Stott	33
G. J. Langridge b Snedden	5	– c Kelly b Troup	12
†I. D. Smith c Kelly b Snedden	0	– lbw b Stott	32
D. C. Aberhart b McIntyre	18	– c Franklin b Snedden	27
*D. R. O'Sullivan c Stott b McIntyre	3	– b Snedden	4
M. D. Jamieson not out	1	– b McIntyre	3
M. F. Gill b McIntyre	0	– c Franklin b McIntyre	0
B 11, n-b 9	20	B 3, l-b 5, n-b 6	14
1/28 2/28 3/44 4/125 5/132 6/132 7/180 8/192 9/194	194	1/60 2/64 3/65 4/91 5/139 6/142 7/178 8/181 9/194	200

Bowling: *First Innings*—Troup 14–4–26–1; Snedden 16-4–39–3; Hellaby 15–6–33–2; Stott 21–8–38–1; McIntyre 23.4–11–38–3. *Second Innings*—Troup 16–5–51–1; Snedden 16–2–58–3; Hellaby 8–2–22–1; Stott 13–6–24–2; McIntyre 16–9–31–2.

Auckland

P. N. Webb lbw b Gill	32	– c Langridge b Gill	16
T. J. Franklin lbw b Gill	57	– b Jamieson	6
*J. F. Reid c and b O'Sullivan	29	– not out	9
M. D. Crowe c and b Aberhart	150	– c Stirling b Gill	8
A. J. Hunt st Smith b O'Sullivan	6	– not out	14
A. T. R. Hellaby c Pierce b O'Sullivan	29		
M. C. Snedden c Smith b Aberhart	6		
†P. J. Kelly c sub b O'Sullivan	4		
L. W. Stott not out	7		
J. M. McIntyre not out	14		
L-b 4, n-b 4	8		
1/73 2/103 3/139 4/186 5/303 6/310 7/317 8/319 (8 wkts dec.)	342	1/22 2/22 3/36 (3 wkts)	53

N. A. Scott did not bat.

Bowling: *First Innings*—Gill 24–5–79–2; Jamieson 19–5–52–0; Aberhart 20–7–59–2; O'Sullivan 40–9–118–4; Pierce 7–2–26–0. *Second Innings*—Gill 6–2–26–2; Jamieson 5–0–15–1; Edwards 2–1–4–0; Wiltshire 1–0–4–0; Anderson 2–1–1–0; Smith 0.1–0–3–0.

Umpires: D. A. Kinsella and R. Trott.

NEW ZEALAND v THE REST

At Basin Reserve, Wellington, February 8, 9, 10. New Zealand won by an innings and 160 runs.

New Zealand

B. A. Edgar c Ormiston b J. G. Bracewell	143
P. N. Webb c Gray b Carrington	70
J. F. Reid b Carrington	67
*G. P. Howarth c Lees b B. P. Bracewell	20
J. V. Coney b Carrington	36
M. D. Crowe b Blair	37
†I. D. Smith b Carrington	5
B. L. Cairns b B. P. Bracewell	14
M. C. Snedden not out	10
G. B. Troup lbw b B. P. Bracewell	0
E. J. Chatfield b Blair	1
B 1, l-b 12, n-b 6	19
1/143 2/281 3/312 4/321 5/381 6/396 7/399 8/415 9/415	422

Bowling: B. P. Bracewell 31–11–76–3; Carrington 29–5–90–4; Stirling 15–4–66–0; Blair 23.2–9–68–2; J. G. Bracewell 28–8–88–1; Gray 7–2–15–0.

The Rest

R. W. Ormiston c Smith b Troup	8	– lbw b Cairns	17
T. J. Franklin hit wkt b Snedden	2	– c Smith b Chatfield	9
G. N. Edwards c Edgar b Troup	5	– b Troup	0
E. J. Gray b Snedden	1	– c Howarth b Troup	61
B. R. Blair c Smith b Troup	11	– run out	17
*J. R. Wiltshire b Snedden	1	– lbw b Troup	15
†W. K. Lees c Smith b Snedden	3	– not out	19
J. G. Bracewell not out	19	– c Howarth b Snedden	1
B. P. Bracewell b Cairns	10	– c Reid b Chatfield	15
D. Stirling lbw b Cairns	4	– c Smith b Snedden	5
M. C. Carrington b Chatfield	6	– b Snedden	0
B 4, n-b 6	10	B 1, l-b 12, n-b 10	23
1/12 2/19 3/20 4/22 5/23 6/37 7/44 8/55 9/61	80	1/24 2/25 3/30 4/68 5/77 6/119 7/149 8/173 9/182	182

Bowling: *First Innings*—Snedden 8–1–15–4; Troup 9–2–23–3; Chatfield 9.1–4–18–1; Cairns 6–3–14–2. *Second Innings*—Snedden 14.4–1–47–3; Troup 14–4–41–3; Chatfield 20–11–23–2; Cairns 6–1–27–1; Crowe 15–7–19–0; Coney 5–3–2–0.

Umpires: S. J. Woodward and S. C. Cowman.

CRICKET IN INDIA, 1981-82

By P. N. SUNDARESAN

Normally, peak interest in cricket in India is reached during a Test series, but the countless fans who flocked to see the Tests against England in the 1981-82 season felt disappointed. Fortunately for them, the knockout matches of the Ranji Trophy championship, taken up after the Englishmen had departed, proved lively and keen, with the final between Delhi and Karnataka providing a fitting climax.

Delhi were declared winners on their first-innings lead, but what a match of high drama it turned out to be! Under the rules of the championship the final is a five-day affair, but in the event of the first innings of the two teams not being completed on the fifth day, the match may be prolonged until a result on first innings is obtained. It was on the afternoon of the sixth day when Delhi succeeded in their exciting bid to overtake Karnataka's first-innings score of 705. This was the first occasion on which such an extension of play had had to be made.

Unfortunately, it was not just the exciting nature of the cricket that drew attention to the later stages of the Ranji Trophy. Some matches were marred by the disorderly behaviour of unruly elements. Umpire Reporter's decision to uphold a close-in catch against T. E. Srinivasan, who was batting in his best style in Tamilnadu's first innings against Delhi, led to a vociferous demonstration at the end of the day's play. A section of the crowd threatened to disrupt play if the umpire failed to change his decision. Next day, the simmering discontent of the spectators exploded into a minor riot when a similar decision was given against Vasudevan, to which the batsman, as in the other earlier case, showed his displeasure. The spectators marched on to the ground, and one of the umpires was assaulted. Play had to be called off shortly before lunch and was resumed only after the Tamilnadu captain, Venkataraghavan, and others had pacified the crowd.

A decision by umpire Rajan Mehra against Viswanath, the local favourite, sparked off trouble at Bangalore in Karnataka's semi-final against Bombay. Viswanath, reputed to be a "walker", stayed a while before leaving after being given out caught. Later he explained that it was a gesture of disappointment at getting out when he was in good form, but the incident provoked the spectators to rush on to the ground, mob the two umpires, and set fire to one of the sightscreens. This riot forced the abandonment of play fifteen minutes before the end of the second day, and only after strong appeals from officials of the Karnataka Cricket Association was it resumed on the following morning. Another unacceptable incident in the same match concerned Gavaskar, Viswanath's brother-in-law. Entering at No. 7 in Bombay's second innings, he batted alternately left- and right-handed. Although this did not offend the Laws of Cricket, it was in poor taste, and Gavaskar was later censured for his conduct by the Working Committee of the Indian Board. The Umpires Advisory Panel, in a report to the Board, said that Gavaskar's gesture was not in keeping with a cricketer of distinction and should be termed as a bad example for the young cricketers of India.

At the end of the season the umpires sub-committee of the Indian Cricket

Board met to discuss the incidents, and held the players responsible. It felt that the mob was infuriated by their gesticulations against the umpires. The committee was also of the view that mob violence sometimes resulted from adverse comments by commentators on the decisions of umpires, and wrote to the Ministry of Information and Broadcasting to frame guidelines for the commentators so that they should confine themselves to the factual description of matches.

Gavaskar had the highest aggregate of 632 runs in the Ranji Trophy, but perhaps the credit for outstanding batsmanship should go to Mohinder Amarnath. After his two efforts in the quarter-final against Tamilnadu on a turning pitch, and his great innings of 185 runs in 487 minutes in the final, there was keen disappointment when he was not included in the Indian team to England.

While the season confirmed the form of established players, it also threw up a number of future Test prospects. Of these, Gursharan Singh and Maninder Singh of Delhi and L. Sivaramakrishnan of Tamilnadu stood out. Gursharan Singh, a stocky, turbaned Sikh, hit the headlines with a century against the touring England team at the start of the season and ended it with another in the Ranji Trophy final against Karnataka. His bold approach and his range of strokes created a fine impression. Maninder Singh, a tall young bowler on the lines of Bedi, showed much promise and perseverance. In his first season in the championship he collected 40 wickets, including a return of fourteen for 122 against Punjab in the North Zone league. Sivaramakrishnan, in the only match he played for Tamilnadu, revealed great promise as an orthodox leg-spinner. These three youngsters are all ripe to be blooded in Test cricket.

Both Ashok Ghosh of Bihar and Zulfiqar Parkar of Bombay established new wicket-keeping records of ten dismissals in a match. Ghosh's feat was against Assam and Parkar's against Maharashtra. In each case, nine of the dismissals were catches.

The Irani Cup match, the Duleep Trophy championship, the Wills Trophy limited-overs tournament and the Deodhar Trophy limited-overs zonal tournament were all played at the start of the season. Bombay, the Ranji Trophy champions of 1980-81, won the Irani Cup match, with left-arm spinner Shastri establishing a new record for the series by taking nine wickets in an innings. West Zone won the Duleep Trophy while Bombay annexed the Wills Trophy. The Deodhar Trophy went to South Zone. The C. K. Nayudu Trophy for under-22 sides was won by North Zone, and the All-India Inter-University tournament by Delhi University.

FIRST-CLASS AVERAGES, 1981-82

BATTING

(Qualification: 500 runs)

	I	*NO*	*R*	*HI*	*100s*	*Avge*
S. M. Gavaskar (*Bombay*)............	21	4	1,471	340	5	86.52
G. A. Parkar (*Bombay*)...............	11	1	624	156	2	62.40
Yashpal Sharma (*Punjab*)............	15	4	672	140	3	61.09

	I	*NO*	*R*	*HI*	*100s*	*Avge*
B. P. Patel (*Karnataka*)................	12	1	532	126	2	48.36
R. Lamba (*Delhi*)........................	12	1	527	205*	1	47.90
D. B. Vengsarkar (*Bombay*).........	20	1	885	142	2	46.57
S. M. Patil (*Bombay*)..................	17	1	704	125	2	44.00
P. Roy (*Bengal*)..........................	17	3	566	136	1	40.42
Arun Lal (*Bengal*).......................	14	0	550	109	2	39.28
G. R. Viswanath (*Karnataka*)........	20	1	738	222	2	38.84
R. M. H. Binny (*Karnataka*).........	15	1	522	115	1	37.28
K. Srikkanth (*Tamilnadu*).............	21	0	695	101	1	33.09

**Signifies not out.*

BOWLING

(Qualification: 25 wickets)

	O	*M*	*R*	*W*	*Avge*
D. Chopra (*Punjab*).....................	193	78	363	30	12.10
R. Goel (*Haryana*)......................	209.3	61	427	34	12.55
Hyder Ali (*Railways*)...................	212.5	74	412	26	15.84
Maninder Singh (*Delhi*)...............	365.3	102	785	44	17.84
S. Venkataraghavan (*Tamilnadu*)...	316.2	100	635	31	20.48
R. S. Hans (*Uttar Pradesh*)..........	240	65	642	31	20.70
Raghuram Bhat (*Karnataka*).........	402	104	870	41	21.21
B. S. Sandhu (*Bombay*)...............	221	57	539	25	21.56
D. D. Parsana (*Saurashtra*)..........	321.5	102	618	28	22.07
D. R. Doshi (*Bengal*)..................	650	190	1,403	63	22.26
Madan Lal (*Delhi*)......................	347.1	79	897	39	23.00
A. Mathur (*Uttar Pradesh*)...........	205.1	39	608	26	23.38
B. Vijayakrishna (*Karnataka*)........	330.3	94	714	27	26.44
R. J. Shastri (*Bombay*)................	639.3	179	1,307	48	27.22
Kapil Dev (*Haryana*)..................	352.1	70	1,089	33	33.00

Note: Matches taken into account are Ranji Trophy, Duleep Trophy, Irani Trophy, and those against the England team which toured India during the season.

RANJI TROPHY, 1981-82

Central Zone

At Pilibhit, November 22, 23, 24. Uttar Pradesh won by eight wickets. Vidarbha 107 (R. S. Hans eight for 25) and 176 (A. Bhagwat 61; G. Sharma four for 40, A. Mathur three for 34); Uttar Pradesh 145 for eight dec. (A. P. Deshpande six for 45) and 139 for two (S. Chaturvedi 57, V. Chopra 52 not out). *Uttar Pradesh 8 pts.*

At Nagpur, December 1, 2, 3. Railways won by an innings and 58 runs. Railways 441 for five dec. (M. I. Ansari 136, A. Burrows 103, R. Vats 55, M. Tarif 43); Vidarbha 238 (S. Phadkar 77, P. Pankule 41, P. Sahasrabudhe 41; S. Madhavan five for 70, Aslam Ali four for 32) and 145 (Riaz three for 15, S. Madhavan three for 35). *Railways 9 pts, including 1 bonus point.*

At Agra, December 5, 6, 7. Uttar Pradesh won by seven wickets. Rajasthan 125 (V. Dutt four for 66, G. Sharma three for 30) and 157 (K. Mathur 41; A. Mathur four for 31, R. S. Hans three for 39); Uttar Pradesh 173 (G. Sharma 50 not out, A. Bambi 40; S. Mobar five for 40, K. R. Gattani three for 36) and 110 for three. *Uttar Pradesh 8 pts.*

At Bilaspur, December 6, 7, 8. Drawn. Madhya Pradesh 228 (S. Saxena 54, M. Hasan 40; S. Riaz four for 37) and 260 for nine dec. (S. M. Jagdale 90; Hyder Ali three for 71); Railways 251 (A. Burrows 56; A. Patel four for 103) and 152 for two (M. Tarif 72 not out, A. Burrows 61). *Railways 5 pts, Madhya Pradesh 3 pts.*

At Jabalpur, December 11, 12, 13. Drawn. Madhya Pradesh 345 (R. Dave 65, S. M. Jagdale 61, S. Naqvi 43; S. Sharma three for 56) and 340 (S. Saxena 97, S. Gulrez Ali 70, M. Hasan 68; V. Dutta three for 39, S. Sharma three for 69); Uttar Pradesh 332 (G. Sharma 58, V. Chopra 40; N. Shirke three for 70, S. Gulrez Ali three for 77, A. Patel three for 86) and 17 for no wkt. *Madhya Pradesh 5 pts, Uttar Pradesh 3 pts.*

At Delhi, December 12, 13, 14. Railways won by an innings and 14 runs. Rajasthan 86 (Padam Shastri 43; Hyder Ali five for 12) and 81 (Aslam Ali four for 24, P. Banerjee three for 21); Railways 181 (P. Sharma three for 39). *Railways 8 pts.*

At Nagpur, December 16, 17, 18. Drawn. Vidarbha 265 (A. P. Deshpande 68, S. Takale 57; Gopal Rao four for 27) and 44 for one; Madhya Pradesh 270 (Sanjeeva Rao 119, S. Naqvi 68; H. Wasu six for 69, A. P. Deshpande three for 81). *Madhya Pradesh 5 pts, Vidarbha 3 pts.*

At Beawar, December 25, 26, 27. Rajasthan won by nine wickets. Madhya Pradesh 212 (M. Hasan 69, Sanjeeva Rao 56; K. R. Gattani three for 22) and 61 (P. Sharma five for 19); Rajasthan 184 (S. Mudkavi 51; N. Shirke three for 36, S. Gulrez Ali three for 54) and 90 for one (S. Mudkavi 47 not out). *Rajasthan 8 pts.*

At Khatrinagar, December 29, 30, 31. Rajasthan won by eight wickets. Vidarbha 66 (K. R. Gattani four for 25, P. Sharma three for 9) and 54 (K. R. Gattani six for 20, S. Joshi three for 27); Rajasthan 78 (H. Wasu four for 9) and 44 for two. *Rajasthan 8 pts.*

At Delhi, December 17, 18, 19. Drawn. Railways 231 (P. Vedraj 65; R. S. Hans four for 98, G. Sharma three for 49) and 255 (M. I. Ansari 112, R. Vats 62; V. Dutt four for 76, A. Mathur three for 43, R. S. Hans three for 70); Uttar Pradesh 204 (S. Chaturvedi 102, G. Sharma 46; Hyder Ali six for 61, Aslam Ali three for 43) and 185 for four (S. Anand 52 not out). *Railways 5 pts, Uttar Pradesh 3 pts.*

Railways 27 points, Uttar Pradesh 22, Rajasthan 16, Madhya Pradesh 13, Vidarbha 3. Railways and Uttar Pradesh qualified for the knockout stage.

East Zone

At Bhagalpur, December 5, 6, 7. Bihar won by an innings and 2 runs. Assam 166 (G. Das 54; S. Sinha four for 38, V. Venkatram three for 45) and 181 (K. Das 52; S. Sinha four for 54); Bihar 349 for eight dec. (V. Joseph 110, S. Roy 46 not out; S. Uzir three for 54). *Bihar 8 pts.*

At Baripada, December 5, 6, 7. Drawn. Bengal 503 (Arun Lal 82, S. Banerjee 76, Raja Venkat 40; S. Sahu four for 50, H. Praharaj three for 47) and 194 for four dec. (Farasatulla 70); Orissa 253 (R. Panda 57; M. Ghosh four for 53, A. Bhattacharjee three for 49) and 78 for three. *Bengal 5 pts, Orissa 3 pts.*

At Jamshedpur, December 11, 12, 13. Drawn. Bengal 375 for six dec. (P. Roy 136, Arun Lal 72, Pronab Nandy 51 not out, S. Banerjee 46; S. Sinha three for 93); Bihar 229 for four (H. Gidwani 89, R. Saxena 76 not out). No decision could be made on first innings. *Bengal 2 pts, Bihar 2 pts.*

At Sambalpur, December 11, 12, 13. Orissa won by eight wickets. Assam 80 (Sabir Hussain three for 26) and 227 (P. Hazarika 57, N. Konwar 53 not out, B. Bharali 41; A. Jayaprakash five for 61, Paramjit Singh three for 50); Orissa 270 (A. Bharadwaj 72, R. Praharaj 64; M. Kakoti five for 69, N. Singh three for 69) and 38 for two. *Orissa 8 pts.*

At Berhampur, December 18, 19, 20. Bihar won by an innings and 123 runs. Bihar 251 (S. Roy 57, S. Nair 54; A. Jayaprakash four for 72, Paramjit Singh three for 90); Orissa 64 (V. Venkatram five for 15, M. R. Bhalla five for 20) and 64 (Randhir Singh three for 28, M. R. Bhalla three for 5). *Bihar 8 pts.*

At Krishnanagar, December 18, 19, 20. Bengal won by an innings and 18 runs. Bengal 290 (Pronab Nandy 81, Farasatulla 72, R. Venkat 40; N. Konwar three for 70, K. Das three for 82); Assam 112 (D. R. Doshi five for 45, B. Burman three for 12) and 160 (S. Uzir 56, B. Bharali 43; D. R. Doshi five for 75, S. Shome three for 29). *Bengal 8 pts.*

Bihar 18 points, Bengal 15, Orissa 11, Assam 0. Bihar and Bengal qualified for the knockout stage.

North Zone

At Delhi, November 7, 8, 9. Drawn. Delhi 428 for six dec. (Madan Lal 116 not out, R. C. Shukla 103 not out, R. Lamba 79, R. Amarnath 41 not out; J. S. Bakshi three for 108); Services 270 (B. Ghosh 131, Chander Vijay 63; Kirti Azad three for 41) and 184 for three (Gaurishankar 62, Ratan Das 50). *Delhi 5 pts, Services 3 pts.*

At Chandigarh, November 7, 8, 9. Drawn, with a tie on first innings. Haryana 170 (R. Chadda 53; D. Chopra six for 59) and 106 for four; Punjab 170 (D. Chopra 62 not out; R. Goel five for 56). *Haryana 4 pts, Punjab 4 pts.*

At Amritsar, November 12, 13, 14. Punjab won by an innings and 54 runs. Services 115 (P. Sur 42 not out; Umesh Kumar six for 32) and 91 (D. Chopra six for 43, Umesh Kumar four for 22); Punjab 260 (Yashpal Sharma 100 not out, R. Handa 51; J. S. Bakshi seven for 87). *Punjab 8 pts.*

At Delhi, November 12, 13, 14. Drawn. Delhi 111 (Kapil Dev five for 34. R. Goel four for 65) and 99 for three (R. Lamba 45, S. Amarnath 43 not out); Haryana 66 (M. Amarnath six for 25, Madan Lal three for 24). *Delhi 5 pts, Haryana 3 pts.*

At Patiala, November 22, 23, 24. Drawn. Punjab 156 (Yashpal Sharma 74; Maninder Singh eight for 48) and 195 (Satish Kumar 51; Maninder Singh four for 74); Delhi 265 for seven dec. (S. C. Khanna 119, Gursharan Singh 47; Yashpal Sharma three for 108) and 54 for six. *Delhi 5 pts, Punjab 3 pts.*

At Faridabad, November 22, 23, 24. Haryana won by ten wickets. Services 171 (A. Jha 51; R. Goel five for 66, Sharanjit Singh five for 82) and 261 (Chandrasekhar 104 not out, Gaurishankar 50, Chander Vijay 40; R. Goel seven for 122); Haryana 430 for six dec. (A. Malhotra 200 not out, R. Chadda 104, Sarabjit Singh 46; Chandrasekhar three for 67) and four for no wkt. *Haryana 8 pts.*

At Patiala, November 26, 27, 28. Punjab won by an innings and 79 runs. Jammu and Kashmir 83 (A. Ajaj 42; D. Chopra six for 27) and 48 (D. Chopra five for 26, Satish Kumar four for 17); Punjab 210 for two dec. (Yashpal Sharma 100 not out, Navjot Singh 85). *Punjab 9 pts, including 1 bonus point.*

At Delhi, November 30, December 1, 2. Services won by nine wickets. Jammu and Kashmir 142 (A. Ajaj 43; J. S. Bakshi five for 42, V. Chavan three for 12) and 106 (Murlidharan five for 17, J. S. Bakshi four for 16); Services 217 (Chander Vijay 108; Mehboob Iqbal seven for 80) and 33 for one. *Services 8 pts.*

At Delhi, December 4, 5, 6. Delhi won by an innings and 177 runs. Jammu and Kashmir 91 (Maninder Singh five for 26) and 81 (Maninder Singh four for 20, Kirti Azad three for 31); Delhi 349 for three dec. (R. Lamba 205 not out, C. P. S. Chauhan 75). *Delhi 9 pts, including 1 bonus point.*

At Rohtak, December 8, 9, 10. Haryana won by an innings and 20 runs. Jammu and Kashmir 129 (A. Ajaj 43; R. Goel seven for 40, S. Talwar three for 39) and 69 (R. Jolly five for 31, R. Goel four for 33); Haryana 218 for nine dec. (Aman Kumar 67, R. Chadda 48; M. Iqbal three for 53, Ashinder Kaul three for 65). *Haryana 9 pts, including 1 bonus point.*

Delhi 24 points, Punjab 24, Haryana 24, Services 11, Jammu and Kashmir 0. Delhi and Punjab qualified for the knockout stage by virtue of the quotient rule.

South Zone

At Davanagere, October 10, 11, 12. Karnataka won by ten wickets. Kerala 177 (P. Balachandran 54; Raghuram Bhat four for 63) and 171 (Raghuram Bhat five for 38); Karnataka 338 for eight dec. (G. R. Viswanath 72, C. Saldana 59 not out, B. Vijayakrishna 45) and 13 for no wkt. *Karnataka 9 pts, including 1 bonus point.*

At Kothagudem, November 13, 14, 15. Hyderabad won by 134 runs. Hyderabad 341 (K. A. Qayyum 106, M. V. Narasimha Rao 65, Shahid Akbar 50; J. K. Ghiya four for 45, K. Chandrasekhar Rao four for 94) and 190 for seven dec. (M. V. Narasimha Rao 74; K. Chandrasekhar Rao three for 31); Andhra 195 (K. B. Ramamurthy 75; M. V. Narasimha Rao three for 44) and 202 (M. N. Ravikumar 52, G. J. J. Raju 49; M. V. Narasimha Rao four for 61, N. S. Yadav three for 62). *Hyderabad 8 pts.*

At Bangalore, November 13, 14, 15. Drawn. Tamilnadu 416 (A. G. Harjinder Singh 59, K. Bharatkumar 55 not out, P. S. Moses 55, M. O. Parthasarathy 43; Raghuram Bhat four for 125, R. M. H. Binny three for 83, B. Vijayakrishna three for 88) and 60 for one; Karnataka 357 (A. V. Jayaprakash 93, J. Abhiram 70, R. Sudhakar Rao 49, Raghuram Bhat 47 not out; K. Bharatkumar three for 58, S. Venkataraghavan three for 88). *Tamilnadu 5 pts, Karnataka 3 pts.*

At Nizamabad, November 21, 22, 23. Drawn. Karnataka 483 (A. V. Jayaprakash 119, R. M. H. Binny 81, R. Sudhakar Rao 70, B. Vijayakrishna 53; N. S. Yadav four for 128) and 36 for one; Hyderabad 412 (Hariprasad 72, Arshad Ayub 69, Faiz Baig 66, Shahid Akbar 42, N. S. Yadav 42; J. Anhiram three for 60, R. M. H. Binny three for 117). *Karnataka 5 pts, Hyderabad 3 pts.*

At Vijayawada, December 18, 19, 20. Tamilnadu won by 132 runs. Tamilnadu 243 (A. Jabbar 69, A. Bharat Reddy 56, T. E. Srinivasan 52; D. Meher Baba three for 98) and 221 for eight dec. (V. Sivaramakrishnan 112; D. Meher Baba four for 63, K. Chandrasekhar Rao three for 63); Andhra 134 (S. Valson eight for 40) and 198 (J. K. Ghiya 55; T. A. Sekhar four for 62). *Tamilnadu 8 pts.*

At Tellicherry, January 3, 4, 5. Hyderabad won by eight wickets. Kerala 199 (P. Balachandran 83, K. Jayaram 40; Kanwaljit Singh three for 34) and 156 (Arshad Ayub three for 27, A. B. Wahab three for 31); Hyderabad 253 (Azhar-ud-Din 59, Faiz Baig 40 not out; V. Hariharan six for 99, T. R. Narayanan three for 65) and 106 for two (K. A. Qayyum 60 not out). *Hyderabad 9 pts, including 1 bonus point.*

At Coimbatore, January 8, 9, 10. Drawn. Hyderabad 160 (M. V. Narasimha Rao 49; S. Vasudevan five for 47, S. Venkataraghavan three for 23) and 290 for six (V. Mohanraj 81, K. A. Qayyum 50, Shahid Akbar 48); Tamilnadu 368 for nine dec. (P. S. Moses 90, A. Bharat Reddy 55, T. E. Srinivasan 46; M. V. Narasimha Rao four for 104). *Tamilnadu 5 pts, Hyderabad 3 pts.*

At Tellicherry, January 9, 10, 11. Kerala won by 71 runs. Kerala 251 (R. Thomas 88; J. K. Ghiya four for 25) and 186 (P. Balachandran 57, K. Jayaram 42; J. K. Ghiya six for 61); Andhra 155 (K. B. Ramamurthy 42; T. R. Narayanan five for 48, V. Hariharan three for 60) and 211 (D. Meher Baba 70; S. Ramesh four for 54, V. Hariharan four for 56). *Kerala 8 pts.*

At Vizianagram, January 23, 24, 25. Karnataka won by six wickets. Andhra 220 (V. Chamundeswarnath 60; Raghuram Bhat three for 58) and 249 (V. Chamundeswarnath 68, D. Meher Baba 51; M. R. Srinivasaprasad three for 16, B. Vijayakrishna three for 49); Karnataka 292 (M. R. Srinivasaprasad 57, B. P. Patel 46; D. Meher Baba four for 87, G. V. S. Raju three for 76) and 180 for four (R. M. H. Binny 74, G. R. Viswanath 47 not out). *Karnataka 8 pts.*

At Madras, January 24, 25, 26. Tamilnadu won by 239 runs. Tamilnadu 249 (A. Bharat Reddy 88, A. Jabbar 48; T. R. Narayanan three for 75) and 217 for five dec. (A Jabbar 59, A. G. Harjinder Singh 41 not out; P. S. Moses 41); Kerala 114 (K. Bharatkumar four for 37, S. Venkataraghavan three for 23) and 113 (S. Valson three for 41). *Tamilnadu 9 pts, including 1 bonus point.*

Tamilnadu 27 points, Karnataka 25, Hyderabad 23, Kerala 8, Andhra 0. Tamilnadu and Karnataka qualified for the knockout stage.

West Zone

At Bombay, October 23, 24, 25. Bombay won by an innings and 61 runs. Maharashtra 188 (S. V. Nayak three for 29, R. Thakkar three for 30) and 110 (R. Thakkar six for 33); Bombay 359 for six dec. (A. V. Mankad 100 not out, S. M. Patil 67, S. Hattangadi 50). *Bombay 9 pts including 1 bonus point.*

At Bhavnagar, October 23, 24, 25. Saurashtra won by 107 runs. Saurashtra 205 (Yajurvindra Singh 103, D. P. Nanavati 43; N. Y. Satham three for 45) and 192 (B. Jadeja 51 not out; N. Y. Satham four for 49, D. V. Pardeshi three for 45); Baroda 193 (R. V. Hazare 50) and 97 (D. D. Parsana four for 26, D. Jadeja four for 29). *Saurashtra 8 pts.*

At Bombay, November 13, 14, 15. Drawn. Bombay 389 for four dec. (D. B. Vengsarkar 142, S. M. Patil 98, S. Hattangadi 56) and 67 for one; Saurashtra 313 (D. P. Nanavati 78, K. Chauhan 46, S. Keshwala 46, R. Jadeja 40; S. V. Nayak three for 58, R. Thakkar three for 65). *Bombay 5 pts, Saurashtra 3 pts.*

At Bulsar, November 13, 14, 15. Drawn. Gujarat 250 (S. Talati 54; S. Oak three for 37, N. Khaniwale three for 55) and 301 for four dec. (S. Talati 109, J. Bakrania 91, J. Desai 42; S. Oak three for 90); Maharashtra 216 (S. Nimbalkar 68, M. D. Gunjal 41; A. Joshi three for 46) and 127 for three (S. F. Saldana 50, R. B. Bhalekar 47 not out). *Gujarat 5 pts, Maharashtra 3 pts.*

At Nadiad, November 4, 5, 6. Bombay won by an innings and 24 runs. Bombay 316 for three dec. (G. A. Parkar 148 not out, D. B. Vengsarkar 83); Gujarat 142 (J. Desai 53; S. V. Nayak three for 32, B. S. Sandhu three for 35) and 150 (A. Shroff 45; K. D. Ghavri three for 27, B. S. Sandhu three for 70). *Bombay 8 pts.*

At Sholapur, December 4, 5, 6. Drawn. Maharashtra 185 (D. V. Pardeshi five for 39, A. Petiwale three for 47) and 291 for six dec. (M. D. Gunjal 113 not out, R. G. Borde 70 not out; D. V. Pardeshi three for 56); Baroda 173 (R. V. Deshmukh 42, C. R. Mohite 40; R. G. Borde five for 30, S. Gudge five for 71) and 130 for five (R. V. Hazare 59). *Maharashtra 5 pts, Baroda 3 pts.*

At Baroda, December 16, 17, 18. Drawn. Bombay 385 for four dec. (A. V. Mankad 129 not out, S. M. Gavaskar 127, G. A. Parkar 40) and 76 for two (S. Hattangadi 42); Baroda 324 (A. D. Gaekwad 83, N. Y. Satham 75, K. More 41; R. Thakkar six for 77). *Bombay 5 pts, Baroda 3 pts.*

At Jamnagar, December 16, 17, 18. Saurashtra won by ten wickets. Gujarat 144 (R. Jadeja five for 44) and 178 (P. Desai 74; D. D. Parsana five for 30, U. C. Joshi four for 56); Saurashtra 310 (N. Parsana 80, D. P. Nanavati 70, S. Keshwala 66; B. Mistry four for 54, J. Pandya three for 80) and 16 for no wkt. *Saurashtra 8 pts.*

At Pune, January 8, 9, 10. Drawn. Saurashtra 359 (A. Patel 68 not out, S. Keshwala 68, D. P. Nanavati 67, B. Jadeja 47, D. D. Parsana 41; S. Oak five for 75) and 82 for three; Maharashtra 575 for five dec. (R. B. Bhalekar 207 not out, R. G. Borde 134 not out, M. Dixit 87, S. Nimbalkar 62, M. D. Gunjal 43). *Maharashtra 5 pts, Saurashtra 3 pts.*

At Baroda, January 8, 9, 10. Baroda won by an innings and 110 runs. Gujarat 139 (A. D. Gaekwad four for 33, H. Kahar four for 40) and 50 (D. V. Pardeshi eight for 17); Baroda 299 for four dec. (S. Parikh 104, R. V. Hazare 86, A. D. Gaekwad 62). *Baroda 8 pts.*

Bombay 27 points, Saurashtra 22, Baroda 14, Maharashtra 13, Gujarat 5. Bombay and Saurashtra qualified for the knockout stage.

KNOCKOUT STAGES

TAMILNADU v UTTAR PRADESH

At Madras, February 11, 12, 13, 14. Tamilnadu won by 241 runs. Having won the toss and batted first, Tamilnadu were rescued by their lanky left-hander, Vasudevan, who hit an unbeaten hundred and then turned in a fine all-round performance by finishing with match figures of eight for 99 on a pitch responsive to spin. Venkat, the Tamilnadu captain, took five wickets in each innings.

Tamilnadu

V. Sivaramakrishnan c Sharma b Mathur	2	– run out	35
K. Srikkanth c Khan b Dutt	25	– c Khandkar b Hans	101
T. E. Srinivasan lbw b Mathur	1	– c Chaturvedi b Hans	10
P. S. Moses c Bhanot b Dutt	35	– c Anand b Hans	0
A. Jabbar c Chopra b Mathur	5	– c Dutt b Sharma	73
P. Vijaykumar c Sharma b Dutt	0	– b Hans	84
†B. Reddy c Bhanot b Sharma	16	– c sub b Sharma	8
S. Vasudevan not out	115	– c and b Sharma	22
*S. Venkataraghavan c Bhanot b Sharma	30	– lbw b Hans	22
T. A. Sekhar st Chopra b Sharma	30	– c Dutt b Sharma	10
S. Valson c Sharma b Mathur	6	– not out	5
B 13, l-b 2, w 4, n-b 3	22	B 4, l-b 2, n-b 2	8
1/3 2/5 3/63 4/68 5/69 6/76 7/150 8/222 9/240	287	1/76 2/102 3/108 4/178 5/277 6/309 7/319 8/355 9/371	378

Bowling: *First Innings*—Dutt 22–2–94–3; Mathur 20–2–67–4; Sharma 20–3–57–3; Hans 22–6–47–0. *Second Innings*—Dutt 9–0–46–0; Mathur 13–0–62–0; Sharma 36–1–151–4; Hans 34.5–3–102–5; Anand 1–0–9–0.

Uttar Pradesh

S. Khandkar b Vasudevan	50	– c Sivaramakrishnan b Venkataraghavan	77
S. Chaturvedi c Bharat Reddy b Sekhar	11	– c Sivaramakrishnan b Vasudevan	15
A. Bhanot c Sivaramakrishnan b Venkataraghavan	34	– b Vasudevan	23
†V. Chopra c Vasudevan b Venkataraghavan	0	– c Vijaykumar b Venkataraghavan	7
*A. Mathur c Jabbar b Venkataraghavan	23	– lbw b Vasudevan	10
A. Bambi c Jabbar b Vasudevan	24	– c Venkataraghavan b Vasudevan	76
G. Sharma c Vijaykumar b Venkataraghavan	7	– c Sivaramakrishnan b Vasudevan	5
S. Anand c Jabbar b Vasudevan	7	– c Jabbar b Venkataraghavan	5
P. A. Khan not out	13	– c Jabbar b Venkataraghavan	0
R. S. Hans c Sivaramakrishnan b Vasudevan	6	– c Vijaykumar b Venkataraghavan	1
V. Dutt c Jabbar b Venkataraghavan	10	– not out	0
B 4, l-b 1, n-b 5	10	B 9, l-b 1	10
1/19 2/100 3/100 4/100 5/152 6/152 7/162 8/168 9/180	195	1/44 2/85 3/120 4/163 5/163 6/178 7/192 8/221 9/225	229

Bowling: *First Innings*—Sekhar 8–1–27–1; Valson 9–1–38–0; Venkataraghavan 29–4–76–5; Vasudevan 23–6–44–4. *Second Innings*—Valson 6–1–33–0; Sekhar 7–1–31–1; Vasudevan 32.2–12–55–4; Venkataraghavan 32–5–98–5; Jabbar 1–0–2–0.

Umpires: M. G. Mukherjee and S. K. Ghosh.

BENGAL v RAILWAYS

At Delhi, February 15, 16, 17, 18. Bengal won by six wickets. Toss won by Railways, who foundered in their first innings against the medium-fast bowling of Barun Burman and the spin of Dilip Doshi. They rallied in the second innings through a century from opener Alfred Burrows but Bengal, after an early collapse, moved into the quarter-finals with half-centuries from Pronab Nandy and Raja Venkat.

Railways

A. Burrows c Arun Lal b Burman	3	– c Arun Lal b Doshi	106
M. I. Ansari b Burman	4	– c Banerjee b Doshi	40
R. M. Manohar c Roy b Burman	5	– c Banerjee b Porel	10
R. Vats lbw b Doshi	33	– c Burman b Doshi	13
†P. Vedraj st Banerjee b Doshi	18	– lbw b Burman	12
M. Tarif c Banerjee b Burman	16	– lbw b Porel	24
Aslam Ali st Banerjee b Doshi	23	– c Pronab Nandy b Burman	18
*Hyder Ali run out	24	– b Doshi	19
Mohammad Riaz c Dalvi b Burman	5	– b Doshi	16
Jaswinder Singh c and b Doshi	13	– b Burman	0
P. Banerjee not out	1	– not out	46
B 1, n-b 9	10	B 6, l-b 5, w 1, n-b 9	21
	155		325
Penalty for 4 overs short	16		
1/7 2/11 3/18 4/70 5/73 6/97 7/121 8/127 9/148	171	1/15 2/100 3/159 4/192 5/216 6/223 7/257 8/261 9/262	

Bowling: *First Innings*—Burman 13–2–54–5; Porel 7–2–19–0; Doshi 14–3–42–4; Shome 8–1–30–0. *Second Innings*—Burman 16–3–44–3; Porel 12–2–41–2; Doshi 48.2–8–138–5; Shome 30–7–59–0; Palash Nandy 2–1–10–0; Pronab Nandy 3–1–12–0.

Bengal

P. Roy c Aslam Ali b Hyder Ali	43	– b Jaswinder	15
Arun Lal c Vedraj b Hyder Ali	37	– c sub b Banerjee	43
Palash Nandy b Hyder Ali	29	– c Jaswinder b Hyder Ali	4
M. K. Dalvi c Vedraj b Hyder Ali	32	– c Hyder Ali b Banerjee	34
Raja Venkat c Vedraj b Hyder Ali	8	– not out	67
Pronab Nandy lbw b Banerjee	20	– not out	52
†S. Banerjee b Banerjee	30		
B. Burman b Banerjee	8		
*D. R. Doshi b Banerjee	0		
S. Shome c Burrows b Banerjee	8		
S. Porel not out	5		
B 5, l-b 11, n-b 8	24	B 18, l-b 11, n-b 9	38
1/62 2/111 3/130 4/160 5/161 6/205 7/222 8/222 9/225	244	1/25 2/30 3/100 4/107	(4 wkts) 253

Bowling: *First Innings*—Aslam Ali 13–2–46–0; Banerjee 9.3–2–28–5; Vats 7–2–15–0; Hyder Ali 37–12–59–5; Jaswinder 24–6–44–0; Riaz 5–0–28–0. *Second Innings*—Aslam Ali 9–2–25–0; Banerjee 10–4–12–2; Hyder Ali 26–9–49–1; Jaswinder 31–12–57–1; Riaz 13–2–45–0; Tarif 4–0–9–0; Vats 5–2–11–0; Burrows 1–0–7–0.

Umpires: A. L. Narasimha and M. Y. Gupte.

QUARTER-FINALS

BIHAR v SAURASHTRA

At Jamshedpur, February 25, 26, 27, 28. Drawn. Bihar declared winners by virtue of their first-innings lead. Toss won by Saurashtra.

Saurashtra

K. Chauhan c Gidwani b Randhir	38	– not out	114
†D. P. Nanavati c Sinha b Randhir	23	– run out	35
A. Patel lbw b Gidwani	51	– not out	4
S. Keshwala c Venkatram b Bhalla	45		
B. Jadeja c Ghosh b Sinha	34		
R. Jadeja c Ghosh b Randhir	49		
N. Jadeja c Ghosh b Randhir	30		
D. D. Parsana c Joseph b Randhir	47		
N. Parsana not out	27		
D. Jadeja run out	26		
*U. C. Joshi b Randhir	0		
B 3, l-b 4, n-b 6	13	N-b 2	2
1/62 2/67 3/158 4/164 5/248 6/252 7/319 8/334 9/381	383	1/110	(1 wkt) 155

Bowling: *First Innings*—Randhir 45–6–141–6; Sinha 30–2–99–1; Bhalla 33–10–47–1; Venkatram 31–10–55–0; Gidwani 10.2–1–28–1. *Second Innings*—Randhir 6–2–32–0; Sinha 6–0–43–0; Venkatram 6–0–42–0; Bhalla 6–0–21–0; Gidwani 4–0–13–0; Saxena 2–1–2–0; Das 1–1–0–0.

Bihar

V. Joseph run out	99
*S. Das b D. D. Parsana	8
H. Gidwani c N. Parsana b Patel	160
R. Saxena b Joshi	131
S. Roy c Chauhan b Patel	1
S. Nair not out	100
V. Venkatram not out	52
B 10, l-b 3, n-b 17	30
1/20 2/250 3/329 4/335 5/493	(5 wkts dec.) 581

†A. Ghosh, Randhir Singh, M. R. Bhalla and S. Sinha did not bat.

Bowling: R. Jadeja 29–4–100–0; N. Parsana 10–3–19–0; D. D. Parsana 46–9–88–1; Joshi 73–20–136–1; D. Jadeja 11–2–43–0; B. Jadeja 12.1–1–48–0; Patel 28–3–96–3; Chauhan 5–2–21–0.

Umpires: R. B. Gupta and R. Mrutyunjayan.

KARNATAKA v PUNJAB

At Bangalore, February 25, 26, 27, 28. Karnataka won by an innings and 167 runs. Toss won by Punjab. Steady batting, backed up by penetrative spin bowling, saw Karnataka move smoothly into the semi-final round.

Punjab

R. Handa c Kirmani b Bhat	14 – st Kirmani b Bhat	2
R. Rathore b Abhiram	0 – b Binny	6
S. C. Khanna b Bhat	6 – lbw b Binny	0
*Yashpal Sharma lbw b Vijayakrishna	46 – b Bhat	0
D. Chopra c Srinivasaprasad b Bhat	32 – c Kirmani b Bhat	5
K. P. Amarjeet not out	21 – c Srinivasaprasad b Vijayakrishna	28
Y. Dutta c Saldana b Vijayakrishna	0 – c Binny b Vijayakrishna	0
Satish Kumar c Binny b Bhat	0 – c Abhiram b Srinivasaprasad	5
R. S. Ghai c Sudhakar Rao b Vijayakrishna	2 – c Patel b Bhat	66
Umesh Kumar c Binny b Vijayakrishna	0 – not out	1
†A. Sharma lbw b Bhat	0 – c Viswanath b Vijayakrishna	7
L-b 6, n-b 3	9 L-b 1, n-b 4	5
1/5 2/17 3/40 4/82 5/119 6/119 7/120 8/128 9/130	130 1/0 2/19 3/40 4/40 5/43 6/43 7/111 8/124 9/124	125

Bowling: *First Innings*—Binny 7–3–12–0; Abhiram 8–6–6–1; Vijayakrishna 26–13–46–4; Bhat 24.2–8–45–5; Srinivasaprasad 1–0–12–0. *Second Innings*—Binny 4–1–21–2; Vijayakrishna 14–3–46–3; Abhiram 2–0–9–0; Bhat 13.4–4–35–4; Srinivasaprasad 4–0–9–1.

Karnataka

R. M. H. Binny c Ghai b Umesh	92
M. R. Srinivasaprasad c Handa b Umesh	56
A. V. Jayaprakash lbw b Yashpal	25
*G. R. Viswanath run out	28
B. P. Patel c Amarjeet b Umesh	1
C. Saldana c Umesh b Ghai	37
R. Sudhakar Rao b Yashpal	51
†S. M. H. Kirmani run out	12
B. Vijayakrishna c Amarjeet b Ghai	3
J. Abhiram not out	63
A. Raghuram Bhat b Yashpal	21
B 23, l-b 5, w 1, n-b 4	33
1/154 2/163 3/207 4/217 5/231 6/308 7/327 8/328 9/331	422

Bowling: Ghai 17–1–60–2; Satish 9–1–28–0; Chopra 12–1–46–0; Umesh 60–12–157–3; Yashpal 48–11–98–3.

Umpires: P. G. Pandit and K. S. Sundaram.

TAMILNADU v DELHI

At Madras, February 25, 26, 27, 28. Delhi won by 20 runs. This was the most exciting match of the round, played on a pitch which deteriorated rapidly as the game progressed. Delhi, having elected to bat, looked in a useful position when they established a first-innings lead of 116, but brilliant leg-spin bowling by Sivaramakrishnan, making his debut in the competition, brought about their collapse in the second innings. Only Mohinder Amarnath, using his feet to the spinners, showed any sign of mastering the turning ball. Requiring 234 to win, Tamilnadu batted determinedly, chipping away at the target, only to finish 20 runs short as the left-arm spinner, Maninder Singh, reaped six wickets.

Delhi

C. P. S. Chauhan b Venkataraghavan	83	– b Vasudevan 8
R. Lamba lbw b Bharatkumar	8	– c V. Sivaramakrishnan b Vasudevan. 24
*M. Amarnath c V. Sivaramakrishnan b Venkataraghavan.	99	– c Bharatkumar b L. Sivaramakrishnan. 40
S. Amarnath c Vasudevan b Venkataraghavan	32	– c V. Sivaramakrishnan b Vasudevan. 0
Kirti Azad b Venkataraghavan	77	– st Bharat Reddy b L. Sivaramakrishnan. 27
Madan Lal c Jabbar b Venkataraghavan	0	– c Jabbar b L. Sivaramakrishnan. 5
Gursharan Singh c Jabbar b Venkataraghavan	0	– c Venkataraghavan b L. Sivaramakrishnan. 0
R. C. Shukla c V. Sivaramakrishnan b Venkataraghavan.	9	– c Bharatkumar b L. Sivaramakrishnan. 2
†S. C. Khanna lbw b L. Sivaramakrishnan	77	– c Srikkanth b L. Sivaramakrishnan. 5
Deepak Sharma lbw b L. Sivaramakrishnan	13	– not out 3
Maninder Singh not out	0	– c Bharatkumar b L. Sivaramakrishnan. 2
L-b 7, w 2, n-b 7	16	L-b 1 1
1/19 2/195 3/200 4/265 5/267 6/268 7/293 8/371 9/407	414	1/32 2/37 3/37 4/90 5/96 6/102 7/112 8/112 9/115 117

Bowling: *First Innings*—Bharatkumar 19–2–52–1; Moses 6–1–16–0; Srikkanth 10–1–22–0; Venkataraghavan 61–13–145–7; Vasudevan 23-6-71-0; L. Sivaramakrishnan 25.1–4–77–2; Jabbar 9–3–15–0. *Second Innings*—Bharatkumar 3–2–2–0; Srikkanth 3–1–13–0; Venkataraghavan 16–7–45–0; S. Vasudevan 9–4–28–3; L. Sivaramakrishnan 11.3–3–28–7.

Tamilnadu

T. E. Srinivasan c Khanna b Shukla	87	– lbw b Shukla 20
K. Srikkanth c S. Amarnath b Madan Lal	4	– b Maninder 23
V. Sivaramakrishnan b Deepak Sharma	72	– lbw b Maninder 20
P. S. Moses st Khanna b Shukla	18	– lbw b Shukla 7
A. Jabbar lbw b Maninder	53	– c Shukla b Maninder 38
P. Vijaykumar c and b Maninder	5	– not out 52
S. Vasudevan c Khanna b Kirti Azad	15	– c Chauhan b Maninder 4
†B. Reddy b Kirti Azad	0	– c Chauhan b Maninder 5
*S. Venkataraghavan c Chauhan b Maninder	14	– c Gursharan b Madan Lal 15
K. Bharatkumar c Deepak Sharma b Kirti Azad.	1	– c Shukla b Maninder 11
L. Sivaramakrishnan not out	4	– run out 8
B 13, l-b 12	25	B 2, l-b 4 6
	298	209
		Penalty for 1 over short 4
1/5 2/175 3/191 4/204 5/213 6/246 7/252 8/281 9/282		1/33 2/41 3/63 4/81 5/112 6/130 7/134 8/144 9/192 213

Bowling: *First Innings*—Madan Lal 7–2–28–1; M. Amarnath 7–1–31–0; Maninder 27.1–10–82–3; Shukla 18–4–44–2; Kirti Azad 23–4–55–3; Deepak Sharma 8–1–33–1. *Second Innings*—Madan Lal 7–1–40–1; Maninder 30.5–8–80–6; Shukla 17–2–62–2; Kirti Azad 10–2–21–0.

Umpires: P. D. Reporter and S. R. Bose.

BOMBAY v BENGAL

At Bombay, February 25, 26, 27, 28. Bombay won by an innings and 181 runs. Bombay's captain Gavaskar was in commanding form, his 340 being his highest first-class score. In all, he batted for 543 minutes and hit two 6s and 46 4s. Ghulam Parkar, with whom he shared a massive opening partnership of 421 runs, suffered only in comparison with his captain, hitting thirteen 4s in a stay of 410 minutes. Bengal, who had won the toss and batted first, were unable to match such prodigious batting feats against the medium pace of the Sikh, Balwinder Singh Sandhu, and the left-arm spin of Shastri.

Bengal

P. Roy run out	11	– b Sandhu	8
Arun Lal c Z. Parkar b Sandhu	8	– c Z. Parkar b Sandhu	21
Palash Nandy c and b Nayak	50	– c Z. Parkar b Shastri	62
M. K. Dalvi lbw b Ghavri	41	– lbw b Shastri	6
R. Venkat b Sandhu	49	– b Shastri	39
Pronab Nandy lbw b Shastri	23	– c Z. Parkar b Shastri	1
†S. Banerjee c Z. Parkar b Nayak	10	– run out	17
S. Shome c Mankad b Sandhu	0	– c Z. Parkar b Sandhu	0
B. Burman lbw b Sandhu	10	– lbw b Shastri	33
*D. R. Doshi lbw b Ghavri	20	– not out	15
P. Neogi not out	12	– c Thakkar b Shastri	0
B 4, l-b 3, n-b 11	18	B 4, l-b 5, n-b 8	17
1/16 2/43 3/105 4/141 5/180 6/208 7/208 8/208 9/224	252	1/28 2/50 3/50 4/134 5/136 6/148 7/155 8/200 9/211	219

Bowling: *First Innings*—Ghavri 15–7–32–2; Sandhu 19–5–57–4; Nayak 18–5–45–2; Shastri 23–7–49–1; Thakkar 19–5–51–0; Mankad 1–1–0–0. *Second Innings*—Ghavri 10–3–24–0; Sandhu 16–5–48–3; Nayak 6–2–24–0; Shastri 19.3–6–61–6; Thakkar 16–2–45–0.

Bombay

*S. M. Gavaskar st Banerjee b Doshi	340
G. A. Parkar lbw b Burman	156
D. B. Vengsarkar st Banerjee b Doshi	43
S. M. Patil c Banerjee b Shome	6
S. V. Nayak c Banerjee b Doshi	26
K. D. Ghavri c Pronab Nandy b Doshi	40
R. J. Shastri not out	18
†Z. Parkar not out	2
B 2, l-b 7, n-b 12	21
1/421 2/543 3/550 4/574 5/599 6/642 (6 wkts dec.)	652

A. V. Mankad, B. S. Sandhu and R. Thakkar did not bat.

Bowling: Burman 24–3–127–1; Neogi 24–0–131–0; Doshi 57–8–196–4; Shome 49–9–155–1; Pronab Nandy 5–1–13–0; Palash Nandy 2–0–9–0.

Umpires: B. Nagaraj Rao and R. V. Ramani.

SEMI-FINALS

KARNATAKA v BOMBAY

At Bangalore, March 11, 12, 13, 14. Drawn. Karnataka were declared winners by virtue of their first-innings lead. On the eve of the match, Karnataka made an unsuccessful appeal to B. S. Chandrasekhar to come out of retirement, but such misgivings about the quality of their attack were shown to be without foundation as the left-arm spinner, Raghuram Bhat, worked his way through the Bombay innings after the Ranji Trophy holders had won the toss and chosen to bat. His eight wickets in the first innings included a hat-trick.

Bombay

*S. M. Gavaskar c Viswanath b Bhat	41	– not out	18
G. A. Parkar lbw b Bhat	84	– c Kirmani b Bhat	68
D. B. Vengsarkar b Bhat	7	– c Viswanath b Bhat	41
S. M. Patil lbw b Bhat	117	– lbw b Vijayakrishna	11
A. V. Mankad c Viswanath b Bhat	0	– c Viswanath b Bhat	8
S. V. Nayak b Bhat	0	– c and b Bhat	9
R. J. Shastri c and b Bhat	12	– b Viswanath	24
†Z. Parkar c Binny b Vijayakrishna	8	– c Srinivasaprasad b Vijayakrishna.	2
B. S. Sandhu c Kirmani b Vijayakrishna	0	– c Abhiram b Viswanath	0
R. V. Kulkarni lbw b Bhat	1	– lbw b Bhat	7
R. Thakkar not out	0	– not out	8
L-b 1	1	B 1, l-b 2, n-b 1	4
1/62 2/82 3/183 4/183 5/183 6/235 7/270 8/270 9/271	271	1/72 2/107 3/126 4/134 5/139 6/160 7/169 8/169 9/176 (9 wkts)	200

Bowling: *First Innings*—Binny 12–1–28–0; Abhiram 6–2–18–0; Vijayakrishna 48–11–92–2; Bhat 49.1–10–123–8; Sudhakar Rao 2–0–9–0. *Second Innings*—Binny 3–0–28–0; Abhiram 2–0–6–0; Vijayakrishna 31–10–56–2; Bhat 37.5–9–77–5; Srinivasaprasad 6–4–8–0; Viswanath 4–2–21–2.

Karnataka

R. M. H. Binny run out	25
M. R. Srinivasaprasad run out	42
A. V. Jayaprakash c Vengsarkar b Mankad.	22
*G. R. Viswanath c Vengsarkar b Mankad.	37
B. P. Patel c Vengsarkar b Nayak	78
C. Saldana c Mankad b Shastri	12
R. Sudhakar Rao not out	155
†S. M. H. Kirmani c Shastri b Nayak	32
J. Abhiram c Z. Parkar b Nayak	0
B. Vijayakrishna b Sandhu	10
A. Raghuram Bhat run out	30
B 5, l-b 10, w 1, n-b 11	27
1/69 2/79 3/133 4/136 5/195 6/272 7/345 8/345 9/379	470

Bowling: Kulkarni 4–0–18–0; Sandhu 29–3–61–1; Shastri 53–5–156–1; Thakkar 50–17–90–0; Nayak 25–5–64–3; Mankad 23–1–39–2; Gavaskar 3–0–9–0; Vengsarkar 1–0–1–0; Patil 1.4–1–5–0.

Umpires: J. D. Ghosh and Rajan Mehra.

BIHAR v DELHI

At Jamshedpur, March 11, 12, 13, 14. Drawn. Delhi declared winners by virtue of their first-innings lead. Toss won by Bihar.

Delhi

C. P. S. Chauhan run out	4
R. Lamba c Nair b Randhir	1
*M. Amarnath c Ghosh b Sinha	7
R. Peter c Ghosh b Sinha	0
Gursharan Singh b Randhir	15
S. Amarnath c Nair b Venkatram	131
Kirti Azad c Joseph b Randhir	132
Madan Lal not out	100
†S. C. Khanna c Bhalla b Venkatram	12
R. C. Shukla not out	74
L-b 5, n-b 2	7
1/1 2/12 3/12 4/20 5/31 6/281 7/318 8/340 (8 wkts dec.)	483

Maninder Singh did not bat.

Bowling: Randhir 44–11–143–3; Sinha 28.2–5–122–2; Bhalla 42–10–92–0; Venkatram 37–4–117–2; Gidwani 1–0–2–0.

Bihar

V. Joseph b M. Amarnath	14	– c Madan Lal b Maninder	25
*S. Das c Khanna b M. Amarnath	4	– b Madan Lal	0
H. Gidwani b M. Amarnath	5	– c Khanna b M. Amarnath	4
S. Roy st Khanna b Maninder	65	– b M. Amarnath	0
R. Saxena c Khanna b M. Amarnath	2	– b Shukla	37
S. Nair lbw b Peter	14	– c sub b Shukla	41
V. Venkatram c Shukla b Madan Lal	36	– c M. Amarnath b Maninder	7
†A. Ghosh c M. Amarnath b Madan Lal	2	– c sub b Maninder	1
Randhir Singh not out	12	– lbw b Maninder	7
M. R. Bhalla lbw b Madan Lal	2	– not out	4
S. Sinha c Gursharan b M. Amarnath	5	– not out	0
B 8, l-b 3, n-b 4	15	B 4, n-b 3	7
	176	(9 wkts)	133
Penalty for 1 over short	4		
1/13 2/19 3/37 4/59 5/86 6/152 7/156 8/157 9/165	180	1/0 2/10 3/10 4/70 5/86 6/111 7/113 8/123 9/129	

Bowling: *First Innings*—Madan Lal 22–5–38–3; M. Amarnath 28.5–7–74–5; Peter 12–2–37–1; Maninder 7–6–1–1; Shukla 10–7–11–0. *Second Innings*—Madan Lal 6–5–5–1; M. Amarnath 11–5–15–2; Peter 9–6–16–0; Maninder 32–13–48–4; Kirti Azad 9–3–18–0; Shukla 18–11–24–2.

Umpires: Mohammad Ghouse and V. Vikramraju.

FINAL

DELHI v KARNATAKA

At Delhi, March 24, 25, 26, 27, 28, 29. Drawn. Delhi declared winners by virtue of their first-innings lead. The Ferozsha Kotal ground pitch was even more lifeless than it had been for the Test against England and favoured the batsmen throughout. Maninder Singh and Shukla bowled 87.5 and 63 overs respectively for Delhi, while Vijayakrishna and Raghuram Bhat, the left-arm spinners, delivered 71 and 94 overs respectively for Karnataka, Raghuram Bhat beating the record of C. S. Nayudu, who bowled 88 overs in an innings for Holkar in the final against Bombay in 1944-45. At the end of the second day, with Karnataka 332 for five after electing to bat, there was no indication of the course the match would take; but next day, with Kirmani and Khanvilkar hitting centuries, they pushed on to 679 for nine. The innings ended on the fourth morning at 705, Karnataka's highest in the championship. Delhi were given a flying start by Lamba, and with a fluent century from the young Gursharan Singh, accompanied by the Amarnath brothers, they reached 302 for three by the close. A day later they were 543 for six, with Mohinder Amarnath unbeaten on 181. He came out next morning with a stiff knee, and with Khanna as runner, but he added only 4 before Binny bowled him with an in-swinger and seemingly ended Delhi's prospects. However, Madan Lal and Shukla added 41 before Rajesh Peter, chosen more for his medium-paced bowling, joined Shukla and set about the bowling with forthright strokes, taking Delhi to victory in the afternoon. Delhi's 706 for eight was also their best in the championship.

Karnataka

R. M. H. Binny lbw b Shukla............ 115
M. R. Srinivasaprasad lbw b Shukla.... 35
A. V. Jayaprakash b Shukla.............. 6
*G. R. Viswanath lbw b Maninder...... 0
B. P. Patel c Peter b Madan Lal......... 124
R. Sudhakar Rao c Kirti Azad b Madan Lal. 71
†S. M. H. Kirmani c Shukla b Maninder.116
R. Khanvilkar c and b Chauhan......... 113
J. Abhiram not out........................ 75
B. Vijayakrishna b Chauhan............. 0
A. Raghuram Bhat b Maninder.......... 15
B 15, l-b 16, n-b 1, w 3............ 35

1/109 2/123 3/124 4/215 5/232 6/412 7/568 8/659 9/659 — 705

Bowling: Madan Lal 40–8–112–2; M. Amarnath 23–3–62–0; Maninder 87.5–18–204–3; Peter 15–4–38–0; Shukla 63–10–158–3; Kirti Azad 18–2–62–0; Chauhan 7–0–24–2; Gursharan 2–0–10–0.

Delhi

C. P. S. Chauhan c Viswanath b Vijayakrishna. 36
R. Lamba b Khanvilkar.................... 61
Gursharan Singh c Sudhakar Rao b Binny.101
S. Amarnath lbw b Binny.................. 22
*M. Amarnath b Binny..................... 185
Kirti Azad b Khanvilkar.................... 50
†S. C. Khanna c Khanvilkar b Vijayakrishna. 31
Madan Lal b Bhat............................ 48
R. C. Shukla not out........................ 69
R. Peter not out.............................. 66
B 10, l-b 17, n-b 10................ 37

1/95 2/137 3/302 4/308 5/406 6/466 7/548 8/589 — (8 wkts) 706

Maninder Singh did not bat.

Bowling: Binny 28–1–134–3; Abhiram 8–0–28–0; Khanvilkar 33.4–3–138–2; Vijayakrishna 71–18–141–2; Bhat 94–24–179–1; Viswanath 6–1–18–0; Srinivasaprasad 9–1–24–0; Sudhakar Rao 3–1–7–0.

Umpires: D. N. Dotiwala and P. G. Pandit.

DULEEP TROPHY, 1981-82

SOUTH ZONE v NORTH ZONE

At Trivandrum, October 23, 24, 25, 26. South Zone won by spin of the coin, rain having ended play after lunch on the second day. Toss won by South Zone.

South Zone

V. Sivaramakrishnan c Kapil Dev b Madan Lal. 1
K. Srikkanth c M. Amarnath b Kapil Dev. 1
T. E. Srinivasan c Khanna b Madan Lal 0
*G. R. Viswanath lbw b Madan Lal.... 3
B. P. Patel lbw b Madan Lal.............126
M. V. Narasimha Rao lbw b Madan Lal 32
R. M. H. Binny c Khanna b Madan Lal 23
†S. M. H. Kirmani c Chopra b Shukla. 26
N. S. Yadav st Khanna b Shukla........ 6
S. Venkataraghavan b Madan Lal....... 2
S. Valson not out........................... 0
B 4, n-b 1............................ 5

1/1 2/1 3/7 4/9 5/66 6/118 7/167 8/187 9/222 — 225

Bowling: Kapil Dev 17–2–53–1; Madan Lal 21.2–6–49–7; Ghai 5–1–21–0; S. Amarnath 8–2–14–0; Kirti Azad 6–0–31–0; Chopra 12–4–23–0; Shukla 8–0–29–2.

North Zone

C. P. S. Chauhan c Narasimha Rao b Binny	11
†S. C. Khanna c Yadav b Binny	24
M. Amarnath lbw b Narasimha Rao	16
Yashpal Sharma b Venkataraghavan	20
Kirti Azad c Venkataraghavan b Narasimha Rao	0
A. Malhotra not out	21
*Kapil Dev not out	19
B 4, l-b 2, n-b 1	7
1/32 2/39 3/74 4/74 5/74 (5 wkts)	118

R. C. Shukla, D. Chopra, R. S. Ghai and S. Amarnath did not bat.

Bowling: Valson 6–2–16–0; Binny 11–1–29–2; Shivlal Yadav 5–5–0–0; Venkataraghavan 17–6–25–1; Narasimha Rao 15–1–41–2.

Umpires: B. Ganguli and S. K. Ghosh.

SEMI-FINALS

EAST ZONE v SOUTH ZONE

At Cuttack, October 29, 30, 31, November 1. East Zone won by 55 runs. Toss won by East Zone.

East Zone

P. Roy c Yadav b Binny	2	not out	96
K. Dubey c Yadav b Valson	20	c Srikkanth b Narasimha Rao	56
Arun Lal c and b Binny	104	c Viswanath b Meher Baba	31
R. Venkat c Srikkanth b Yadav	34	b Binny	4
U. Banerjee b Narasimha Rao	3	run out	5
A. Bharadwaj c Kirmani b Binny	15	st Mohanraj b Meher Baba	2
A. Jayaprakash c Meher Baba b Narasimha Rao	14	b Binny	1
†S. Banerjee c Viswanath b Binny	12		
B. Burman run out	1		
*D. R. Doshi b Valson	5	run out	6
Randhir Singh not out	13		
B 2, l-b 7, n-b 5	14	B 18, l-b 9, n-b 5	32
	237	(7 wkts dec.)	233
		Penalty for 2 overs short	8
1/7 2/38 3/125 4/136 5/188 6/191 7/204 8/205 9/213		1/122 2/192 3/195 4/200 5/213 6/233 7/233	241

Bowling: *First Innings*—Valson 22–7–43–2; Binny 21–4–55–4; Srikkanth 4–1–9–0; Yadav 17–5–37–1; Meher Baba 9–1–23–0; Narasimha Rao 20–3–53–2; Viswanath 1–0–3–0. *Second Innings*—Valson 13–1–58–0; Binny 12.4–2–42–2; Narasimha Rao 20–2–45–1; Meher Baba 16–4–35–2; Yadav 8–2–21–0.

South Zone

K. Srikkanth c U. Banerjee b Randhir	81	– c and b Jayaprakash	51
V. Mohan Raj c Randhir b Doshi	67	– c Arun Lal b Doshi	2
T. E. Srinivasan lbw b Doshi	13	– b Doshi	24
*G. R. Viswanath c U. Banerjee b Doshi	1	– b Jayaprakash	15
B. P. Patel retired ill	31	– absent ill	
M. V. Narasimha Rao c Dubey b Randhir	3	– c Arun Lal b Doshi	0
R. M. Binny c Arun Lal b Doshi	34	– c Arun Lal b Jayaprakash	1
†S. M. H. Kirmani c Bharadwaj b Doshi	9	– c and b Jayaprakash	19
D. Meher Baba c Bharadwaj b Jayaprakash	0	– c Arun Lal b Jayaprakash	11
N. S. Yadav c Randhir b Doshi	24	– not out	9
S. Valson not out	2	– c Arun Lal b Jayaprakash	4
B 7, l-b 5, n-b 4	16	B 1, l-b 2, n-b 3	6
1/123 2/146 3/148 4/204 5/226 6/249 7/249 8/262 9/281	281	1/73 2/81 3/83 4/88 5/91 6/116 7/123 8/130 9/142	142

Bowling: *First Innings*—Burman 4–1–16–0; Randhir 34–9–109–2; Roy 1–0–16–0; Doshi 44.5–9–78–6; Jayaprakash 16–4–46–1. *Second Innings*—Randhir 7–1–27–0; Burman 9–3–16–0; Doshi 31–13–55–3; Jayaprakash 23.5–7–38–6.

Umpires: M. Y. Gupte and K. S. Sundaram.

CENTRAL ZONE v WEST ZONE

At Nagpur, October 30, 31, November 1, 2. West Zone won by an innings and 54 runs. Toss won by Central Zone.

Central Zone

Sanjeeva Rao c Yajurvindra b Parsana	1	– c Shastri b Ghavri	6
S. Khandekar c Yajurvindra b Parsana	13	– c Shroff b Parsana	46
S. Chaturvedi c Shastri b Ghavri	24	– lbw b Ghavri	1
*P. Sharma b Parsana	5	– c Shastri b Ghavri	17
†V. Chopra c Shastri b Parsana	43	– c and b Shastri	10
S. Mudkavi c Vengsarkar b Parsana	7	– c Shroff b Ghavri	4
A. Mathur c Yajurvindra b Parsana	13	– c Gaekwad b Shastri	19
P. Vedraj c G. A. Parkar b Shastri	6	– c Shroff b Shastri	18
G. Sharma not out	19	– c and b Shastri	10
Aslam Ali run out	1	– c Gaekwad b Parsana	14
R. S. Hans b Parsana	1	– not out	3
B 5, l-b 1, n-b 5	11	L-b 3, n-b 7	10
1/5 2/24 3/39 4/66 5/89 6/114 7/119 8/129 9/131	144	1/6 2/19 3/30 4/68 5/89 6/91 7/129 8/129 9/154	158

Bowling: *First Innings*—Ghavri 10–2–38–1; Parsana 26.1–9–46–7; Patil 5–2–5–0; Shastri 20–6–44–1. *Second Innings*—Ghavri 14–3–54–4; Parsana 14.5–3–62–2; Shastri 13–2–32–4.

West Zone

A. D. Gaekwad c Chaturvedi b P. Sharma	17
G. A. Parkar c Vedraj b G. Sharma	36
*S. M. Gavaskar not out	164
S. M. Patil c Mathur b P. Sharma	54
D. B. Vengsarkar run out	26
A. V. Mankad lbw b Hans	11
Yajurvindra Singh lbw b Hans	19
R. J. Shastri c Chaturvedi b Mathur	16
K. D. Ghavri not out	10
B 2, n-b 1	3
1/40 2/66 3/168 4/238 5/256 6/287 7/320 (7 wkts dec.)	356

D. D. Parsana and †A. Shroff did not bat.

Bowling: Aslam Ali 19–5–52–0; Mathur 13–2–35–1; Hans 49–15–71–2; P. Sharma 19–1–51–2; G. Sharma 41–3–139–1; Mudkavi 1–0–5–0.

Umpires: M. G. Subramaniam and V. Vikramraju.

FINAL

WEST ZONE v EAST ZONE

At Bombay, November 5, 6, 7, 8. Drawn. West Zone were declared winners by virtue of their first-innings lead. Toss won by East Zone.

East Zone

P. Roy c Z. Parkar b Sandhu	90	– b Sandhu	16
K. Dubey c Vengsarkar b Sandhu	1	– c Z. Parkar b Shastri	19
Arun Lal c Sandhu b Shastri	109	– b Ghavri	16
R. Venkat lbw b Shastri	5	– c Patil b Parsana	27
A. Bharadwaj c Z. Parkar b Sandhu	2	– c and b Parsana	6
U. Banerjee c Gaekwad b Sandhu	29	– not out	21
A. Jayaprakash b Ghavri	2	– not out	18
†S. Banerjee st Z. Parkar b Parsana	21		
*D. R. Doshi c and b Shastri	22		
Randhir Singh not out	10		
S. Porel c Ghavri b Shastri	6		
B 3, l-b 6, n-b 14, w 7	30	B 3, l-b 2, n-b 10	15
1/4 2/199 3/217 4/228 5/230 6/244 7/278 8/304 9/314	327	1/33 2/44 3/70 4/92 5/99	(5 wkts) 138

Bowling: *First Innings*—Ghavri 18–6–47–1; Sandhu 27–9–50–4; Shastri 45–7–103–4; Parsana 42–12–86–1; Patil 2–0–6–0; A. V. Mankad 3–0–5–0. *Second Innings*—Ghavri 13–3–22–1; Sandhu 13–3–24–1; Shastri 22–9–37–1; Parsana 21–7–24–2; Gaekwad 6–4–3–0; Gavaskar 5–0–10–0; Patil 6–5–2–0; Vengsarkar 2–0–1–0.

West Zone

A. D. Gaekwad c Arun Lal b Doshi	42
G. A. Parkar c Arun Lal b Doshi	43
*S. M. Gavaskar c Arun Lal b Randhir	23
S. M. Patil c Venkat b Doshi	2
A. V. Mankad c Dubey b Randhir	13
†Z. Parkar c Dubey b Randhir	2
D. B. Vengsarkar b Doshi	108
R. J. Shastri lbw b Porel	134
K. D. Ghavri run out	35
B. S. Sandhu c S. Banerjee b Randhir	8
D. D. Parsana not out	6
B 7, l-b 5, n-b 3	15
1/77 2/114 3/114 4/118 5/125 6/136 7/315 8/395 9/408	431

Bowling: Randhir 51–15–147–4; Porel 19–5–50–1; Doshi 73–19–131–4; Jayaprakash 31–3–84–0; U. Banerjee 1–0–4–0.

Umpires: Swaroop Kishen and R. B. Gupta.

IRANI TROPHY, 1981-82

RANJI TROPHY CHAMPIONS (BOMBAY) v REST OF INDIA

At Indore, October 16, 17, 18, 19. Drawn. Bombay were declared winners by virtue of their first-innings lead. Toss won by Bombay.

Bombay

*S. M. Gavaskar c Yadav b Madan Lal	50	– not out	102
G. A. Parkar c Sanjeeva Rao b Madan Lal	22	– b Kapil Dev	17
D. B. Vengsarkar lbw b Kapil Dev	47	– c Chauhan b Kapil Dev	1
S. M. Patil c Doshi b Madan Lal	125	– c Sanjeeva Rao b Chauhan	68
R. V. Mankad c Kirmani b Doshi	22		
A. V. Mankad c Kirmani b Doshi	50	– lbw b Doshi	14
R. J. Shastri b Yadav	80	– not out	4
K. D. Ghavri c Chauhan b Yadav	24		
B. S. Sandhu c Kirmani b Doshi	6		
†Z. Parkar c Kapil Dev b Doshi	2		
K. D. Mokashi not out	9		
B 2, l-b 6	8	L-b 8, n-b 2	10
1/71 2/76 3/176 4/230 5/300 6/334 7/393 8/404 9/414	445	1/30 2/32 3/66 4/196 (4 wkts dec.)	216

Bowling: *First Innings*—Kapil Dev 29–6–100–1; Burman 6–1–30–0; Madan Lal 26–0–83–3; Doshi 49–13–101–4; Yadav 40.2–2–123–2. *Second Innings*—Kapil Dev 13–3–30–2; Madan Lal 5–0–21–0; Yadav 18–2–52–0; Doshi 26–6–74–1; Chauhan 5–0–18–1; Viswanath 5–0–11–0.

Rest of India

C. P. S. Chauhan c R. V. Mankad b Shastri	19	– c sub b Shastri	20
Sanjeeva Rao b Shastri	14	– c Patil b Shastri	25
S. Amarnath c R. V. Mankad b Shastri	18	– lbw b Mokashi	66
*G. R. Viswánath lbw b Shastri	2		
A. Malhotra c Vengsarkar b Shastri	24	– c Ghavri b Mokashi	34
Madan Lal not out	97	– not out	21
Kapil Dev b Shastri	41	– c Sandhu b A. V. Mankad	25
†S. M. H. Kirmani c Vengsarkar b Shastri	8		
N. S. Yadav st Z. Parkar b Shastri	6		
B. Burman c sub b Ghavri	9	– not out	7
D. R. Doshi c Ghavri b Shastri	15		
L-b 3, nb 5	8	B 9, n-b 3	12
1/25 2/48 3/55 4/56 5/103 6/167 7/183 8/193 9/220	261	1/46 2/61 3/145 4/158 5/194 (5 wkts)	210

Bowling: *First Innings*—Ghavri 23–6–51–1; Sandhu 8–3–13–0; Shastri 45–8–101–9; Mokashi 27–4–82–0; A. V. Mankad 1–0–6–0. *Second Innings*—Ghavri 12–0–33–0; Sandhu 4–3–6–0; Shastri 15–3–46–2; Mokashi 15–1–53–2; A. V. Mankad 10–0–40–1; Patil 7–3–17–0; Vengsarkar 1–0–3–0.

Umpires: S. R. Bose and Rajan Mehra.

CRICKET IN PAKISTAN, 1981-82

By GHULAM MUSTAFA KHAN

Bank sides dominated domestic cricket in Pakistan in 1981-82, three of the six participating banks laying claim to major honours. The Quaid-e-Azam Trophy was won by National Bank, the PACO Cup by Habib Bank and the Patron's Trophy by Allied Bank.

National Bank, whose team consisted mainly of former Test players and was without Iqbal Qasim and Wasim Raja, took the Quaid-e-Azam Trophy for the third time, winning seven of their nine games and losing only one. Their captain, Shafiq Ahmad, scored 754 runs in the competition, Ali Zia was their leading all-rounder with 635 runs, 24 wickets and 13 catches, while Ehtesham-ud-Din bowled well, narrowly missing the 50-wickets mark. United Bank, their closest rivals, did not lose a game, but with a high number of drawn or abandoned games were pushed to second place. Lahore and Karachi settled at the bottom of the table, Karachi being the only team to lose all nine of their matches. Rawalpindi, participating for the first time in two years, did well to reach seventh place and PIA achieved good results, despite the absence of Majid Khan, Zaheer Abbas, Wasim Raja, Imran Khan and Rizwan-uz-Zaman, who were in Australia.

Railways fielded two ineligible players – Khalid Masood, who played in the match against Muslim Commercial Bank (MCB), and Gulfraz Khan, who played in seven matches and who topped the side's batting averages. Complaints to the BCCP were made only by MCB and Habib Bank, each of whom were awarded an additional ten bonus points, while 21 were deducted from Railways.

Shoaib Mohammad topped the batting averages for the competition, with 711 runs at 88.87, although Agha Zahid scored the most runs (853). Mohammad Nazir achieved a bowling average of 14.67, taking two fewer wickets than Abdul Qadir (58), who did the hat-trick as did Jalal-ud-Din. PIA's Anil Dalpat was the leading wicket-keeper, while Gulfraz Khan of Railways set a new Pakistani fielding record when he took six catches in an innings against MCB.

Habib Bank won the second PACO pentangular tournament, finishing ten points ahead of their nearest rivals – United Bank. Habib Bank players Azhar Khan and Abdul Qadir topped the competition's batting and bowling averages respectively. In the match between Rawalpindi and United Bank, Mudassar Nazar and Mansoor Akhtar shared in a first-wicket stand of 389 for United Bank, who totalled 485 for two. At Lahore, MCB, following on 163 behind National Bank and struggling at 132 for six, were saved by Asif Ali and Nadeem Yousaf who added 238 for the seventh wicket: Nadeem went on to compile a Pakistan-record 196 for the last wicket with Maqsood Kundi, both batsmen scoring a maiden century.

The place of Railways, disqualified for their earlier infringement of national rules, was taken by MCB, while PIA, who with nine players abroad were unable to raise a team, were replaced by Rawalpindi.

The Patron's Trophy, no longer deemed to be first-class, was won by Allied Bank, who easily beat Karachi Whites in the final. In Group A, Sukkur failed by one point to qualify for the knockout stages when they drew with Karachi Whites in their last match. Bahawalpur, LDCA and Allied Bank, however, all had easy passages. The lowest score of the tournament came from Karachi Greens, dismissed for 28 by Bahawalpur, who later lost their semi-final match against Karachi Whites by 1 run. Karachi Whites and Allied Bank qualified to play in the Quaid-e-Azam tournament in 1982-83.

The season's leading batsman in the national averages was Shoaib Mohammad with an average of 88.87, and five batsmen passed 1,000 runs, Agha Zahid being the most prolific with 1,281. Abdul Qadir and Tauseef Ahmed took the most wickets with 87 apiece, but the averages were headed by Mohammad Nazir. Salim Yousuf of IDBP was the leading wicket-keeper with 26 catches and 3 stumpings, and Sultan Rana of Habib Bank took the most catches by a non-wicket-keeper (26).

FIRST-CLASS AVERAGES, 1981-82

BATTING

(Qualification: 600 runs, average 35)

	M	*I*	*NO*	*R*	*HI*	*Avge*
Shoaib Mohammad (*PIA*)............	7	12	4	711	177*	88.87
Nasir Valika (*United Bank*)..........	13	22	8	931	109	66.50
Mudassar Nazar (*United Bank*)......	7	11	1	624	241	62.40
Mohsin Khan (*Habib Bank*)..........	12	20	1	1,160	129	61.05
Agha Zahid (*Habib Bank*)...........	13	24	3	1,218	136	58.00
Arshad Pervez (*Habib Bank*)........	13	24	4	1,102	164	55.10
Shafiq Ahmad (*National Bank*)......	13	26	3	1,058	161	46.00
Qasim Omar (*MCB*)....................	11	22	0	966	145	43.90
Imtinan Zamir (*Rawalpindi*)..........	8	14	0	613	120	43.78
Ali Zia (*National Bank*)..............	13	24	3	904	157	43.04
Haroon Rashid (*United Bank*).......	15	25	2	967	153	42.04
Anwarul Haq (*MCB*)..................	13	26	1	1,037	147	41.48
Salim Yousuf (*IDBP*)..................	10	19	0	706	115	37.15
Masood Anwar (*Rawalpindi*).........	13	26	2	876	144	36.50
Mahmood Rashid (*United Bank*)....	13	21	4	610	73	35.88
Saleem Pervez (*National Bank*)......	10	20	2	645	142*	35.83

* *Signifies not out.*

BOWLING

(Qualification: 30 wickets)

	O	*M*	*R*	*W*	*Avge*
Mohammad Nazir (*Railways*)........	504	171	822	56	14.67
Abdul Raqeeb (*Habib Bank*).........	449.3	113	1,123	62	18.11
Ehtesham-ud-Din (*National Bank*)..	436.5	88	1,400	77	18.18
Tauseef Ahmed (*United Bank*)......	715.1	195	1,586	87	18.22
Iqbal Qasim (*National Bank*).........	315.3	86	752	41	18.34
Abdul Qadir (*Habib Bank*)...........	596.4	132	1,609	87	18.49
Afzaal Butt (*Railways*)................	301	60	936	47	19.91
Khurshid Akhtar (*United Bank*).....	373.5	104	884	41	21.56
Shahid Mahboob (*IDBP*).............	248.4	32	918	41	22.39

	O	*M*	*R*	*W*	*Avge*
Zahid Ahmad (*PIA*)	319.2	67	823	34	24.20
Iqbal Sikandar (*PIA*)	304.3	62	807	33	24.45
Mohi-ud-Din (*Karachi*)	259.3	31	960	36	26.66
Liaqat Ali (*Habib Bank*)	331.4	56	1.040	38	27.36
Ilyas Khan (*MCB*)	412.3	102	988	34	29.05
Jalal-ud-Din (*IDBP*)	234.4	26	905	30	30.16
Ali Zia (*National Bank*)	435	75	1,314	40	32.85
Rizwan Khatib (*Rawalpindi*)	424.4	84	1,280	35	36.57
Mohammad Riaz (*Rawalpindi*)	416.1	79	1,224	33	37.09
Raja Afaq (*Rawalpindi*)	413.3	60	1,294	29	44.62

QUAID-E-AZAM TROPHY WINNERS

1953-54	Bahawalpur	1969-70	PIA
1954-55	Karachi	1970-71	Karachi Blues
1956-57	Punjab	1972-73	Railways
1957-58	Bahawalpur	1973-74	Railways
1958-59	Karachi	1974-75	Punjab A
1959-60	Karachi	1975-76	National Bank
1961-62	Karachi B	1976-77	United Bank
1962-63	Karachi A	1977-78	Habib Bank
1963-64	Karachi Blues	1978-79	National Bank
1964-65	Karachi Blues	1979-80	PIA
1966-67	Karachi	1980-81	United Bank
1968-69	Lahore	1981-82	National Bank

QUAID-E-AZAM TROPHY, 1981-82

The competition was contested on a league basis, between Pakistan's top ten sides, with the Trophy decided on points.

	Played	*Won*	*Drawn*	*Lost*	*Bonus Points Batting*	*Bonus Points Bowling*	*Total Points*
National Bank	9	7	1	1	27	31	128
United Bank	9	6	3	0	34	31	125
Habib Bank	9	5	2	2	35	37	122*
PIA	9	5	2	2	25	27	102
MCB	9	2	2	5	29	30	79*
Railways	9	5	2	2	11	18	79†
Rawalpindi	9	2	1	6	25	28	73
IDBP	9	2	2	5	20	28	68
Lahore	9	3	1	5	18	18	66
Karachi	9	0	0	9	11	27	38

* *5 batting points and 5 bowling points added for games against Railways, who fielded ineligible players.*

† *11 batting and 10 bowling points deducted for fielding ineligible players.*

Note: First innings closed at 85 overs.

At Bahawalpur, September 19, 20, 21, 22. United Bank won by 130 runs. United Bank 264 for six (Nasir Valika 102 not out, Haroon Rashid 99) and 266 for seven dec. (Haroon Rashid 128; Farrukh Zaman three for 60); MCB 179 (Salah-ud-Din 56, Asif Ali 44; Tauseef Ahmed five for 58, Khurshid Akhtar five for 71); and 221 (Zaigham Burki 79; Khurshid Akhtar four for 93). *United Bank 18 pts, MCB 3 pts.*

At LCCA Ground, Lahore, September 19, 20, 21, 22. Railways won by 248 runs. Railways 264 for eight (Ejaz Ahmad 101 not out; Ali Ahmad three for 47) and 378 for six dec. (Abdul Sami 94, Saadat Ali 88, Asad Rauf 63); Lahore 253 for six (Mansoor Rana 89, Shahzad Bashir 65) and 141 (Mian Fayyaz 68; Mohammad Nazir three for 19). *Railways 16 pts, Lahore 6 pts.*

At Rawalpindi, September 19, 20, 21, 22. PIA won by 29 runs. PIA 177 (Anil Dalpat 34 not out; Mohammad Riaz five for 61, Sabih Azhar three for 12) and 166 (Rashid Israr 43; Raja Afaq four for 36); Rawalpindi 147 (Mohammad Riaz 42; Naeem Ahmad five for 56) and 167 (Raja Sarfraz 54; Aftab Baloch five for 30). *PIA 15 pts, Rawalpindi 4 pts.*

At Bahawalpur, September 26, 27, 28, 29. Drawn. MCB 294 for nine dec. (Anwarul Haq 147, Zaigham Burki 45; Shahid Mahboob four for 72) and 296 for five dec. (Babar Basharat 81, Anwarul Haq 59, Salah-ud-Din 40 not out); IDBP 251 for nine dec. (Anwar Miandad 63; Ilyas Khan six for 73) and 267 for eight (Ashfaq Malik 64 not out, Shahid Mahboob 59, Salim Yousuf 46). *MCB 7 pts, IDBP 7 pts.*

At LCCA Ground, Lahore, September 26, 27, 28, 29. National Bank won by 310 runs. National Bank 206 (Saleem Pervez 46; Nasir Abbas six for 96) and 393 (Maqsood Ahmad 161, Mohammad Jamil 80; Mohsin Kamal four for 54); Lahore 143 (Iqbal Butt six for 28) and 146 (Nasir Abbas 42 not out; Ali Zia five for 71, Iqbal Butt four for 42). *National Bank 16 pts, Lahore 4 pts.*

At Sialkot, September 26, 27, 28, 29. PIA won by 16 runs. PIA 189 (Feroze Mehdi 58; Abdul Qadir five for 47) and 265 (Iqbal Sikandar 90, Feroze Mehdi 51, Aftab Baloch 48; Liaqat Ali four for 54); Habib Bank 273 for eight (Mohsin Khan 89, Masood Iqbal 46) and 165 (Azhar Khan 57; Zahid Ahmad five for 37). *PIA 13 pts, Habib Bank 8 pts.*

At Rawalpindi, September 26, 27, 28, 29. Railways won by eight wickets. Rawalpindi 292 for nine dec. (Mohammad Riaz 107, Rizwan Khatib 37 not out; Afzaal Butt three for 56) and 158 (Azmat Jalil 52; Mohammad Nazir three for 15); Railways 279 for eight dec. (Ejaz Ahmad 104 not out, Asad Rauf 57, Saadat Ali 43; Asif Afridi four for 33) and 172 for two (Abdul Sami 78 not out, Akbar Siddiq 70 not out). *Railways 17 pts, Rawalpindi 6 pts.*

At National Stadium, Karachi, October 4, 5, 6, 7. MCB won by 177 runs. MCB 301 for five dec. (Qasim Omar 145, Anwarul Haq 64; Mohi-ud-Din three for 59) and 312 for six dec. (Anwarul Haq 132, Salah-ud-Din 69, Asif Ali 53; Obaid Kadir three for 69); Karachi 274 for nine dec. (Mohi-ud-Din 105; Ilyas Khan four for 107) and 162 (Ghulam Abbas 47 not out; Zaigham Burki five for 69). *MCB 17 pts, Karachi 5 pts.*

At Bahawalpur, October 3, 4, 5, 6. Habib Bank won by 216 runs. Habib Bank 278 for eight (Arshad Pervez 137 not out; Tanveer Ali four for 94) and 321 for six dec. (Agha Zahid 130, Mohsin Khan 127; Shahid Mahboob four for 46); IDBP 177 (Mohindar Kumar 42 not out; Abdul Qadir three for 54) and 206 (Salim Yousuf 42; Abdul Qadir five for 54, Abdul Raqeeb four for 58). *Habib Bank 18 pts, IDBP 3 pts.*

At Sialkot, October 3, 4, 5, 6. Drawn. Railways 232 for nine dec. (Shahid Pervez 84 not out; Rashid Khan three for 59) and 230 for six (Ejaz Ahmad 93, Gulfraz Khan 74 not out; Zahid Ahmad three for 69); PIA 250 for three (Shoaib Mohammad 102 not out, Feroze Mehdi 61, Naeem Ahmad 46 not out). *Railways 4 pts, PIA 7 pts.*

At Rawalpindi, October 3, 4, 5, 6. National Bank won by nine wickets. Rawalpindi 194 (Imtinan Zamir 120, Ehtesham-ud-Din three for 43) and 219 (Raja Afaq 95, Fazeelur Rehman 49 not out; Ali Zia four for 50); National Bank 355 for seven (Ali Zia 81, Mohammad Jamil 59 not out, Mahmood Arshad 50, Saleem Pervez 45, Anwar Khan 43) and 62 for one. *National Bank 18 pts, Rawalpindi 3 pts.*

At Hyderabad, October 12, 13, 14, 15. Habib Bank won by ten wickets. MCB 153 (Babar Basharat 35; Abdul Raqeeb four for 30) and 289 (Salah-ud-Din 103 not out, Qasim Omar 40, Sajid Abbasi 40; Abdul Qadir six for 92); Habib Bank 259 for five (Agha Zahid 94, Sultan Rana 46 not out; Nadeem Wahab three for 84) and 189 for no wkt (Agha Zahid 100 not out, Arshad Pervez 78 not out). *Habib Bank 18 pts, MCB 1 pt.*

At Multan, October 12, 13, 14, 15. United Bank won by four wickets. United Bank 343 (Nasir Valika 109; Tanveer Ali five for 52) and 73 for six (Shahid Mahboob three for 23); IDBP 145 (Khurshid Akhtar four for 41) and 270 (Salim Yousuf 115, Munirul Haq 44; Amin Lakhani three for 43). *United Bank 18 pts, IDBP 4 pts.*

At Faisalabad, October 13, 14, 15, 16. National Bank won by 27 runs. National Bank 288 for two (Afzaal Ahmad 155 not out, Shafiq Ahmad 110) and 250 (Ali Zia 48; Iqbal Sikandar six for 100); PIA 268 for six (Asif Mohammad 81, Iqbal Sikandar 59, Shoaib Mohammad 55, Aftab Baloch 43) and 243 (Naeem Ahmad 112; Ehtesham-ud-Din four for 63, Ali Zia four for 79). *National Bank 16 pts, PIA 4 pts.*

At LCCA Ground, Lahore, October 12, 13, 14, 15. Lahore won by 69 runs. Lahore 235 for seven (Rameez Raja 105, Shahzad Bashir 42; Mohammad Riaz four for 71) and 297 (Saleem Taj 80, Shahzad Bashir 63, Mansoor Rana 49, Khalid Khan 45; Rizwan Khatib four for 67); Rawalpindi 262 for five dec. (Masood Anwar 118 not out, Imtinan Zamir 56; Mohammad Riaz 54) and 201 (Imtinan Zamir 69, Mohammad Riaz 56; Nasir Abbas five for 94). *Lahore 14 pts, Rawalpindi 6 pts.*

At National Stadium, Karachi, October 18, 19, 20. IDBP won by seven wickets. Karachi 119 (Shahid Mahboob six for 33, Jalal-ud-Din four for 49 including the hat-trick) and 163 (Jalal-ud-Din five for 62); IDBP 212 (Shahid Mahboob 48, Mohammad Afzal 43; Atiqur Rehman six for 74) and 73 for three (Shahid Mahboob 45 not out). *IDBP 16 pts, Karachi 4 pts.*

At Faisalabad, October 18, 19, 20, 21. United Bank won by 144 runs. United Bank 218 (Nasir Shah 56, Nasir Valika 53; Mohammad Nazir six for 78) and 157 (Mohammad Nazir six for 57); Railways 115 (Tauseef Ahmad five for 36, Khurshid Akhtar four for 22) and 116 (Farooq Shera six for 41). *United Bank 16 pts, Railways 4 pts.*

At Gaddafi Stadium, Lahore, October 18, 19, 20, 21. National Bank won by three wickets. Habib Bank 266 for nine dec. (Agha Zahid 90, Mohsin Khan 50; Ehtesham-ud-Din four for 44) and 208 (Mohsin Khan 125); National Bank 234 for eight dec. (Ali Zia 70, Taslim Arif 61, Mahmood Arshad 45; Abdul Raqeeb four for 103) and 242 for seven (Taslim Arif 73, Ali Zia 59 not out, Saleem Pervez 44). *National Bank 16 pts, Habib Bank 6 pts.*

At LCCA Ground, Lahore, October 18, 19, 20. PIA won by nine wickets. PIA 354 for four (Shoaib Mohammad 177 not out, Rashid Israr 64, Zahid Ahmad 52 not out) and 39 for one; Lahore 139 (Iqbal Sikandar nine for 81) and 250 (Saleem Taj 82 not out, Nasir Abbas 52; Iqbal Sikandar five for 118, Naeem Ahmad four for 38). *PIA 18 pts, Lahore 1 point.*

At National Stadium, Karachi, October 24, 25, 26, 27. PIA won by ten wickets. Karachi 206 (Ejaz Mir 46, Khalid Alvi 43) and 273 (Ejaz Mir 84, Khalid Alvi 59; Rashid Khan four for 63); PIA 397 for five (Asif Mohammad 132, Shoaib Mohammad 117, Feroze Mehdi 56) and 83 for no wkt (Feroze Mehdi 51 not out). *PIA 18 pts, Karachi 3 pts.*

At Hyderabad, October 24, 25, 26, 27. Drawn. National Bank 336 for four (Shafiq Ahmad 113 not out, Afzaal Ahmad 68, Saleem Pervez 68, Taslim Arif 47) and 338 for six dec. (Ali Zia 100 not out, Taslim Arif 92, Saleem Pervez 68, Shafiq Ahmad 40); IDBP 264 for eight (Salim Yousuf 86, Saghir Abbas 57; Shafiq Ahmad four for 58) and 348 for six (Saghir Abbas 108 not out, Salim Yousuf 104, Ashfaq Malik 61 not out, Mohammad Afzal 40). *National Bank 6 pts, IDBP 5 pts.*

At LCCA Ground, Lahore, October 24, 25, 26, 27. Lahore won by eight wickets. MCB 250 for eight dec. (Anwarul Haq 104; Nadeem Ghauri four for 77) and 196 (Salah-ud-Din 64, Qasim Omar 61, Nadeem Ghauri five for 40); Lahore 186 (Mohammad Akram 44; Zaigham Burki five for 72) and 263 for two (Tanveer Ahmad 110, Saleem Taj 92). *Lahore 13 pts, MCB 8 pts.*

At Rawalpindi, October 24, 25, 26, 27. United Bank won by five wickets. Rawalpindi 254 for eight (Imtinan Zamir 83) and 177 (Azmat Jalil 53; Tauseef Ahmed six for 67, Khurshid Akhtar four for 76); United Bank 266 (Mahmood Rashid 73; Rizwan Khatib six for 99) and 166 for five (Haroon Rashid 73). *United Bank 16 pts, Rawalpindi 8 pts.*

At Hyderabad, October 31, November 1, 2, 3. PIA won by 153 runs. PIA 233 (Asif Mohammad 59, Anil Dalpat 48) and 319 for six dec. (Shoaib Mohammad 126 not out, Iqbal Sikandar 46, Zahid Ahmad 42 not out); IDBP 211 (Iqbal Chippa 59, Anwar Miandad 59) and 188 (Salim Yousuf 79). *PIA 17 pts, IDBP 6 pts.*

At Bahawalpur, October 31, November 1, 2, 3. National Bank won by six wickets. Railways 254 (Asad Rauf 130; Ali Zia four for 74) and 293 for nine dec. (Ejaz Ahmad 74, Gulfraz Khan 64 not out); National Bank 263 for nine dec. (Ijaz Ahmad 102, Shafiq Ahmad 80; Mohammad Nazir five for 104) and 290 for four (Saleem Pervez 142 not out, Ali Zia 46). *National Bank 18 pts, Railways 7 pts.*

At Gaddafi Stadium, Lahore, October 31, November 1, 2, 3. Drawn. United Bank 289 for four (Arif-ud-Din 77, Khalid Irtiza 73, Haroon Rashid 67 not out) and 277 for four dec. (Arif-ud-Din 99); Lahore 228 (Saleem Taj 65, Rameez Raja 47) and 0 for no wkt. *United Bank 8 pts, Lahore 4 pts.*

At Rawalpindi, October 31, November 1, 2. Habib Bank won by ten wickets. Rawalpindi 167 (Masood Anwar 49; Abdul Raqeeb seven for 40) and 228 (Mohammad Riaz 106, Raja Sarfraz 48; Abdul Qadir four for 62); Habib Bank 270 (Mohsin Khan 116) and 127 for no wkt (Arshad Pervez 75 not out, Agha Zahid 47 not out). *Habib Bank 18 pts, Rawalpindi 4 pts.*

At National Stadium, Karachi, November 9, 10, 11. Railways won by 95 runs. Railways 220 (Naveed Anjam 40) and 200 (Asad Rauf 69; Tariq Nazar six for 52); Karachi 116 (Shahid Pervez four for 44) and 209 (Khalid Alvi 46, Kamal Najamuddin 41; Mohammad Nazir seven for 35). *Railways 16 pts, Karachi 4 pts.*

At Faisalabad, November 9, 10, 11. Habib Bank won by an innings and 59 runs. Lahore 130 (Tanveer Ahmad 53; Abdul Raqeeb five for 34, Adbul Qadir four for 34) and 146 (Ali Ahmad 53; Abdul Qadir seven for 44 including the hat-trick); Habib Bank 335 for six (Arshad Pervez 144, Azhar Khan 87; Ali Ahmad five for 112). *Habib Bank 18 pts, Lahore 2 pts.*

At Rawalpindi, November 9, 10, 11, 12. Drawn. MCB 259 for eight dec. (Azmat Rana 100, Anwarul Haq 68, Qasim Omar 45; Abdul Wahab five for 70) and 279 for five dec. (Azmat Rana 100 not out, Babar Basharat 56 not out, Salah-ud-Din 48; Rizwan Khatib four for 100); Rawalpindi 264 for eight dec. (Imtinan Zamir 102, Raja Afaq 53 not out; Ilyas Khan four for 89) and 90 for three (Azmat Jalil 55). *MCB 6 pts, Rawalpindi 6 pts.*

At National Stadium, Karachi, November 16, 17, 18. Lahore won by an innings and 98 runs. Karachi 122 (Khalid Alvi 41; Ghaffar Kazmi five for 48, Ali Ahmad four for 32) and 185 (Feroze Najamuddin 60, Kamal Najamuddin 44); Lahore 405 for four (Tanveer Ahmad 182, Mansoor Rana 69, Saleem Taj 64, Nasir Chughtai 52). *Lahore 18 pts, Karachi 1 pt.*

At Gaddafi Stadium, Lahore, November 14, 15, 16, 17. Drawn. United Bank 314 for seven (Kamal Merchant 73 not out, Siddiq Patni 71, Mahmood Rashid 60) and 193 (Mahmood Rashid 56 not out, Arif-ud-Din 43; Abdul Qadir five for 37); Habib Bank 253 for five dec. (Agha Zahid 100, Mohsin Khan 91; Saud Khan four for 52) and 210 for seven (Agha Zahid 82 not out, Arshad Pervez 56). *United Bank 5 pts, Habib Bank 6 pts.*

At Sialkot, November 15, 16, 17, 18. Railways won by eight wickets. MCB 102 (Afzaal Butt four for 41, Naveed Anjam four for 49) and 254 (Qasim Omar 57, Azmat Rana 45; Afzaal Butt five for 60, Mohammad Nazir four for 74); Railways 255 for nine dec. (Gulfraz Khan 69 not out; Mohammad Sabir 57) and 104 for two. *Railways 18 pts, MCB 3 pts.*

At Rawalpindi, November 14, 15, 16, 17. Rawalpindi won by ten wickets. IDBP 237 (Ashfaq Malik 49; Abdul Wahab four for 42) and 138 (Abdul Wahab five for 41); Rawalpindi 328 for nine dec. (Imtinan Zamir 101, Azmat Jalil 66, Shahid Munir 45 not out) and 51 for no wkt. *Rawalpindi 18 pts, IDBP 6 pts.*

At Hyderabad, November 21, 22, 23, 24. United Bank won by six wickets. National Bank 102 (Ali Zia 43; Tauseef Ahmed seven for 28) and 275 (Saleem Pervez 58, Ijaz Ahmad 50, Anwar Khan 46; Tauseef Ahmed five for 122); United Bank 252 (Mahmood Rashid 50, Haroon Rashid 49; Ehtesham-ud-Din five for 72) and 128 for four (Iqbal Butt three for 43). *United Bank 18 pts, National Bank 4 pts.*

At Bahawalpur, November 21, 22, 23, 24. MCB won by 200 runs. MCB 274 (Qasim Omar 104, Azmat Rana 62, Salah-ud-Din 56; Naeem Ahmad five for 49) and 238 (Babar Basharat 56, Azmat Rana 44; Zahid Ahmad four for 84); PIA 201 for nine (Hasan Jamil 42) and 111 (Ilyas Khan five for 46). *MCB 17 pts, PIA 6 pts.*

At Sialkot, November 21, 22, 23, 24. Drawn. Habib Bank 202 for nine dec. (Sultan Rana 42, Masood Iqbal 42; Mohammad Nazir four for 57) and 260 for nine dec. (Raees Ahmad 48 not out, Sultan Rana 48; Mohammad Nazir four for 62, Afzaal Butt four for 94); Railways 183 (Gulfraz Khan 41 not out; Abdul Qadir six for 62) and 263 for eight (Abdul Sami 70, Asad Rauf 66, Gulfraz Khan 46). *Habib Bank 6 pts, Railways 4 pts.*

At LCCA Ground, Lahore, November 22, 23, 24, 25. IDBP won by 6 runs. IDBP 279 for five dec. (Salim Yousuf 105, Ashfaq Malik 68, Qaisar Hussain 56) and 156 (Qaisar Hussain 54 not out; Ghaffar Kazmi five for 61); Lahore 225 for nine dec. (Saleem Taj 73) and 204 (Nasir Chughtai 77; Mohindar Kumar five for 56, Shahid Mahboob four for 63). *IDBP 17 pts, Lahore 4 pts.*

At Hyderabad, November 28, 29, 30, December 1. Drawn. United Bank 279 for seven (Siddiq Patni 61, Farooq Shera 54 not out, Waheed Mirza 45; Zahid Ahmad four for 97) and 257 (Nasir Valika 64, Arif-ud-Din 47; Naeem Ahmad five for 97); PIA 222 (Aftab Baloch 53; Khurshid Akhtar five for 68, Tauseef Ahmed five for 97) and 244 for eight (Anil Dalpat 47, Zahid Ahmad 44 not out; Shahid Aziz four for 67). *United Bank 8 pts, PIA 4 pts.*

At LCCA Ground, Lahore, November 28, 29, 30, December 1. Rawalpindi won by 190 runs. Rawalpindi 283 (Mohammad Riaz 123; Tariq Nazar four for 74) and 259 (Shahid Munir 62, Raja Afaq 45; Feroze Najamuddin four for 59); Karachi 198 (Feroze Najamuddin 81; Abdul Wahab seven for 71) and 154 (Feroze Najamuddin 55; Raja Afaq five for 52). *Rawalpindi 18 pts, Karachi 5 pts.*

At University Ground, Lahore, November 28, 29, 30, December 1. Railways won by eight wickets. IDBP 137 (Ashfaq Malik 78; Afzaal Butt seven for 60) and 109 (Mohammad Nazir five for 31, Afzaal Butt four for 38); Railways 89 (Jalal-ud-Din seven for 43) and 162 for two (Naveed Anjam 80 not out, Asad Rauf 51). *Railways 14 pts, IDBP 4 pts.*

At National Stadium, Karachi, November 28, 29, 30, December 1. National Bank won by 94 runs. National Bank 258 (Ali Zia 66, Ijaz Ahmad 65 not out, Taslim Arif 44) and 276 (Shafiq Ahmad 161; Ilyas Khan four for 85); MCB 239 (Qasim Omar 72; Ehtesham-ud-Din seven for 90) and 201 (Qasim Omar 72; Ehtesham-ud-Din four for 84). *National Bank 18 pts, MCB 7 pts.*

At Karachi Gymkhana, Karachi, December 5, 6, 7. National Bank won by 113 runs National Bank 201 (Ijaz Ahmad 66 not out; Mohi-ud-Din five for 74) and 164 (Shafiq Ahmad 46; Mansoor Ahmad five for 35); Karachi 207 (Ghulam Abbas 42; Anwar Khan three for 43) and 45 (Ehtesham-ud-Din six for 24). *National Bank 16 pts, Karachi 6 pts.*

At Karachi Gymkhana, Karachi, December 13, 14, 15. Habib Bank won by nine wickets. Karachi 85 (Aslam Qureshi four for 20, Liaqat Ali four for 37) and 180 for nine dec. (Bharat Kumar 62); Habib Bank 137 (Atiqur Rehman four for 40, Mohi-ud-Din four for 48) and 131 for one (Agha Zahid 48, Arshad Pervez 45 not out). *Habib Bank 14 pts, Karachi 4 pts.*

At National Stadium, Karachi, December 26, 27, 28. United Bank won by an innings and 148 runs. Karachi 204 (Ejaz Mir 54; Saud Khan six for 87) and 75 (Farooq Shera five for 24); United Bank 427 (Farooq Shera 136, Haroon Rashid 53, Arif-ud-Din 48; Mansoor Ahmad five for 105). *United Bank 18 pts, Karachi 6 pts.*

PACO CUP, 1981-82

The pentangular tournament, sponsored by Pakistan Automobile Corporation, was played on a league basis, with the trophy decided on points. The five leading sides in the Quaid-e-Azam Trophy tournament qualify to compete for the PACO Cup, but in 1981-82 the place of Railways was taken by MCB and that of PIA by Rawalpindi:

					Bonus Points		*Total*
	Played	*Won*	*Drawn*	*Lost*	*Batting*	*Bowling*	*Points*
Habib Bank	4	3	0	1	12	12	54
United Bank	4	2	1	1	13	11	44
National Bank	4	1	2	1	12	10	32
Rawalpindi	4	1	1	2	13	5	28
MCB	4	0	2	2	5	7	12

Note: First innings closed at 85 overs.

PACO Awards

Batting — Nasir Valika (United Bank); *Bowling* — Abdul Qadir (Habib Bank); *Fielding* — Zaheer Ahmed (Habib Bank).

NATIONAL BANK v UNITED BANK

At Gaddafi Stadium, Lahore, January 17, 18, 19, 20. Drawn. National Bank 6 pts, United Bank 5 pts.

United Bank

†Arif-ud-Din lbw b Jehanzeb	17	– c Jamil b Ehtesham	22
Nasir Shah c Ali Zia b Jehanzeb	3	– c Jamil b Ehtesham	5
Waheed Mirza c Ali Zia b Ehtesham	5	– c Shafiq b Ehtesham	5
*Haroon Rashid c Ali Zia b Ehtesham	15	– c Ali Zia b Anwar	50
Nasir Valika c Jamil b Iqbal	61	– b Jehanzeb	84
Mahmood Rashid c Mahmood b Ali Zia	66	– c and b Ali Zia	42
Kamal Merchant b Ehtesham	62	– c Mahmood b Anwar	18
Farooq Shera c Jamil b Ehtesham	0	– not out	60
Saud Khan not out	27	– b Ijaz	2
Tauseef Ahmed (did not bat)		– st Jamil b Ali Zia	6
B 8, l-b 6, w 1, n-b 2	17	L-b 16, n-b 10	26
1/6 2/15 3/41 4/43 5/171 6/205 7/210 8/273	(8 wkts dec.) 273	1/16 2/27 3/66 4/104 5/168 6/202 7/295 8/299 9/320	(9 wkts dec.) 320

Khurshid Akhtar did not bat.

Bowling: *First Innings*—Ehtesham 27.4–4–93–4; Jehanzeb 11–3–18–2; Anwar 9–0–32–0; Iqbal 18–2–57–1; Shafiq 11–1–29–0; Ali Zia 8–1–27–1. *Second Innings*—Ehtesham 25–5–79–3; Jehanzeb 15–4–42–1; Anwar 18–3–80–2; Iqbal 18–4–43–0; Shafiq 3–0–6–0; Ali Zia 10–3–24–2; Ijaz 7–1–20–1.

National Bank

Afzaal Ahmad lbw b Farooq	17	– b Saud	0
Taslim Arif c Farooq b Tauseef	78	– c Haroon b Khurshid	72
*Shafiq Ahmad c Saud b Tauseef	76	– c Waheed b Farooq	14
Ali Zia c Tauseef b Kamal	33	– lbw b Saud	22
Mahmood Arshad not out	28	– c Waheed b Khurshid	25
Ijaz Ahmad c Tauseef b Khurshid	9	– not out	22
†Mohammad Jamil not out	0	– not out	5
L-b 3, w 4, n-b 2	9	B 11, n-b 8	19
1/36 2/172 3/183 4/222 5/247	(5 wkts dec.) 250	1/4 2/43 3/88 4/128 5/161	(5 wkts) 179

Anwar Khan, Iqbal Butt, Jehanzeb Khan and Ehtesham-ud-Din did not bat.

Bowling: *First Innings*—Saud 4–1–21–0; Farooq 7–0–35–1; Kamal 22–6–55–1; Khurshid 15–3–65–1; Tauseef 26.4–7–65–2. *Second Innings*—Saud 14–1–68–2; Farooq 10–1–47–1; Tauseef 9–4–24–0; Khurshid 14–6–15–2; Kamal 3–1–3–0; Nasir Valika 4–1–3–0; Nasir Shah 1–1–0–0.

Waheed Mirza kept wicket in National Bank's second innings when Arif-ud-Din was injured.

RAWALPINDI v MCB

At Bagh-e-Jinnah Ground, Lahore, January 17, 18, 19, 20. Drawn. Rawalpindi 7 pts, MCB 5 pts.

MCB

Qasim Omar c Azmat b Khatib	13	– b Riaz	110
*Anwarul Haq not out	111	– c Khalid b Khatib	0
Babar Basharat lbw b Khatib	6	– b Riaz	29
Salah-ud-Din b Khatib	0	– b Afaq	9
Asif Ali b Afaq	36	– c Azmat b Sabih	64
†Sajid Abbasi lbw b Afaq	5	– lbw b Riaz	22
Pervez Akhtar run out	1	– c Azmat b Asif	53
Nadeem Yousuf c Khalid b Khatib	3	– (9) c Shahid b Asif	13
Maqsood Kundi run out	47	– (8) c Azmat b Riaz	4
Nadeem Wahab lbw b Khatib	1	– not out	53
Farrukh Zaman not out	0	– not out	1
B 3, l-b 5, w 2, n-b 1	11	B 17, l-b 6, w 1, n-b 7	31
1/21 2/33 3/38 4/108 5/122 6/132 7/143 8/228 9/234	(9 wkts dec.) 234	1/5 2/57 3/78 4/221 5/242 6/261 7/277 8/296 9/354	(9 wkts dec.) 389

Bowling: *First Innings*—Khatib 27–3–78–5; Asif 4–1–7–0; Sabih 5–1–6–0; Riaz 21–4–53–0; Afaq 25.1–3–79–2. *Second Innings*—Khatib 44–16–89–1; Sabih 13–2–43–1; Asif 20–6–66–2; Riaz 30–10–83–4; Afaq 17–2–70–1; Khalid 1–0–1–0; Sarfraz 1–0–6–0.

Rawalpindi

Azmat Jalil lbw b Babar	39	– (2) not out	83
Masood Anwar b Babar	66	– (1) lbw b Nadeem Wahab	3
Iqtidar Khwaja c Sajid b Babar	6	– not out	64
Mohammad Riaz c Maqsood b Farrukh	45		
Raja Afaq c Qasim b Babar	61		
Qazi Khalid b Farrukh	5		
Raja Sarfraz run out	57		
†Shahid Munir c Salah-ud-Din b Nadeem Wahab	7		
*Rizwan Khatib not out	12		
B 1, l-b 4, w 2, n-b 3	10	B 4, l-b 2, w 1, n-b 1	8
1/93 2/112 3/127 4/174 5/186 6/283 7/287 8/308	(8 wkts dec.) 308	1/7	(1 wkt) 158

Sabih Azhar and Asif Afridi did not bat.

Bowling: *First Innings*—Nadeem Wahab 16.3–3–62–1; Nadeem Yousuf 10–3–39 0; Farrukh 28–5–90–2; Babar 29–3–93–4; Anwar 4–0–14–0. *Second Innings*—Nadeem Yousuf 4–0–30–0; Nadeem Wahab 4–0–36–1; Farrukh 4–0–29–0; Babar 5–0–16–0; Anwar 4–0–26–0; Salah-ud-Din 1–0–8–0; Qasim 1–0–5–0.

NATIONAL BANK v RAWALPINDI

At Gaddafi Stadium, Lahore, January 21, 22, 23, 24. National Bank won by nine wickets. National Bank 17 pts, Rawalpindi 5 pts.

Rawalpindi

Masood Anwar b Ijaz	113	– b Ehtesham	79
Azmat Jalil b Ehtesham	0	– c Jamil b Jehanzeb	10
Iqtidar Khwaja c Jehanzeb b Ehtesham	18	– lbw b Ali Zia	59
Mohammad Riaz b Ehtesham	4	– c Iqbal b Jehanzeb	8
Qazi Khalid c Ali Zia b Anwar	81	– c Taslim b Ehtesham	5
Raja Afaq lbw b Iqbal	13	– c Jamil b Ehtesham	1
Raja Sarfraz c Ali Zia b Ijaz	12	– b Ehtesham	17
†Shahid Munir c and b Ijaz	9	– b Ehtesham	7
Masood Afzal b Ehtesham	6	– b Ehtesham	4
*Rizwan Khatib not out	15	– not out	23
Asif Afridi (did not bat)		– c Ehtesham b Ali Zia	0
L-b 1, n-b 2	3	B 4, l-b 5, w 1, n-b 6	16
1/17 2/41 3/49 4/217 5/217 6/236 7/246 8/254 9/274	(9 wkts dec.) 274	1/32 2/151 3/160 4/169 5/171 6/178 7/197 8/201 9/220	229

Bowling: *First Innings*—Ehtesham 9–0–52–4; Jehanzeb 5–0–26–0; Iqbal 13–2–42–1; Ali Zia 10–1–42–0; Shafiq 11–2–49–0; Anwar 16–5–31–1; Ijaz 11–3–29–3. *Second Innings*—Ehtesham 22–3–109–6; Jehanzeb 14–2–32–2; Iqbal 4–1–11–0; Ali Zia 17.1–8–23–2; Shafiq 3–0–14–0; Anwar 5–0–23–0; Ijaz 2–1–1–0.

National Bank

Afzaal Ahmad lbw b Riaz	49	– (2) lbw b Khatib	10
Taslim Arif c and b Riaz	51	– (1) not out	64
*Shafiq Ahmad run out	26	– not out	51
Ali Zia b Riaz	0		
Mahmood Arshad not out	136		
Ijaz Ahmad not out	97		
B 2, l-b 4, w 6, n-b 3	15	B 2, lb 2, w 1	5
1/92 2/123 3/135 4/137	(4 wkts) 374	1/15	(1 wkt) 130

†Mohammad Jamil, Anwar Khan, Iqbal Butt, Jehanzeb Khan and Ehtesham-ud-Din did not bat.

Bowling: *First Innings*—Khatib 22–5–81–0; Asif 18–4–79–0; Riaz 32–4–103–3; Afaq 19–3–83–0; Masood Afzal 4–0–13–0. *Second Innings*—Khatib 7–0–34–1; Asif 3–0–13–0; Sarfraz 4–0–21–0; Afaq 4–0–24–0; Riaz 4–0–16–0; Masood Anwar 1–0–4–0; Khalid 1–0–13–0.

HABIB BANK v MCB

At LCCA Ground, Lahore, January 21, 22, 23, 24. Habib Bank won by 60 runs. Habib Bank 18 pts, MCB 2 pts.

Habib Bank

Agha Zahid lbw b Nadeem Wahab	16	– c and b Nadeem Yousuf	7
Arshad Pervez c Salah-ud-Din b Farrukh	112	– c Maqsood b Qasim	46
Tehsin Javed lbw b Babar	53	– c Maqsood b Farrukh	34
Azhar Khan not out	83	– c Maqsood b Farrukh	8
Sultan Rana not out	3	– (6) run out	0
Raees Ahmed (did not bat)		– (5) c Salah-ud-Din b Nadeem Wahab	55
†Zaheer Ahmed (did not bat)		– c Maqsood b Nadeem Wahab	36
Abdul Qadir (did not bat)		– not out	7
Jamshed Hussain (did not bat)		– c Babar b Nadeem Yousuf	2
B 5, l-b 6	11	B 6, l-b 5, w 2, n-b 3	16
1/28 2/125 3/271 (3 wkts)	278	1/9 2/96 3/103 4/116 5/120 6/188 7/206 8/211 (8 wkts dec.)	211

*Abdul Raqeeb and Liaqat Ali did not bat.

Bowling: *First Innings*—Nadeem Wahab 11–3–31–1; Nadeem Yousuf 10–1–26–0; Babar 26–5–70–1; Farrukh 31-1-111-1; Anwar 6–0–27–0; Qasim 1–0–2–0. *Second Innings*—Nadeem Wahab 12–1–30–2; Nadeem Yousuf 9–0–57–2; Babar 13–0–49–0; Qasim 4–0–11–1; Farrukh 14–8–9–2; Anwar 6–1–23–0; Salah-ud-Din 6–0–16–0.

MCB

Qasim Omar c Zaheer b Raqeeb	13	– st Zaheer b Raqeeb	25
*Anwarul Haq c Azhar b Raqeeb	53	– b Raqeeb	36
Nadeem Wahab lbw b Azhar	30	– (10) c Tehsin b Liaqat	4
Babar Basharat c Tehsin b Azhar	46	– (3) c Sultan b Raqeeb	0
Salah-ud-Din b Qadir	8	– (4) c Sultan b Raqeeb	6
Asif Ali c Jamshed b Qadir	1	– (5) lbw b Qadir	70
†Maqsood Kundi run out	23	– (6) c Zaheer b Liaqat	28
Sajid Abbasi c Sultan b Qadir	4	– (9) lbw b Liaqat	2
Pervez Akhtar lbw b Qadir	0	– (8) c Zaheer b Liaqat	2
Nadeem Yousuf c Zahid b Qadir	0	– (7) b Liaqat	30
Farrukh Zaman not out	9	– not out	4
B 3, l-b 2, n-b 7	12	B 9, l-b 2, n-b 12	23
1/48 2/73 3/113 4/140 5/142 6/179 7/184 8/184 9/184	199	1/51 2/51 3/63 4/88 5/119 6/191 7/193 8/201 9/211	230

Bowling: *First Innings*—Liaqat 2–0–27–0; Jamshed 4–0–8–0; Qadir 31–9–72–5; Raqeeb 23.3–6–58–2; Azhar 11–2–22–2. *Second Innings*—Liaqat 19–3–48–5; Jamshed 4–1–14–0; Qadir 27–5–82–1; Raqeeb 16–4–52–4; Raees 5–1–11–0; Zahid 1–1–0–0.

RAWALPINDI v UNITED BANK

At Gaddafi Stadium, Lahore, January 26, 27, 28. United Bank won by an innings and 155 runs. United Bank 18 pts, Rawalpindi 1 pt.

Rawalpindi

Masood Anwar c Farooq b Sikander	4	– b Mudassar	31
Iqtidar Khwaja c Mudassar b Sikander	0	– b Sikander	0
Qazi Khalid c Haroon b Farooq	10	– lbw b Mudassar	33
Mohammad Riaz b Mudassar	2	– c Tauseef b Mudassar	3
Raja Afaq b Farooq	1	– lbw b Sikander	1
†Shahid Munir c Farooq b Khurshid	32	– (7) c Farooq b Khurshid	26
Raja Sarfraz c Mahmood b Tauseef	13	– (6) c Ashraf b Sikander	0
*Rizwan Khatib c Ashraf b Tauseef	17	– b Sikander	14
Sabih Azhar lbw b Mudassar	47	– c Mahmood b Tauseef	14
Nasim Iqbal not out	43	– c Ashraf b Tauseef	7
Abdul Wahab run out	7	– not out	1
B 3, l-b 6, n-b 8	17	B 1, l-b 3, n-b 3	7
1/4 2/11 3/15 4/17 5/30 6/65 7/69 8/104 9/176	193	1/1 2/62 3/66 4/69 5/69 6/69 7/87 8/122 9/136	137

Bowling: *First Innings*—Sikander 18–5–72–2; Farooq 8–4–19–2; Mudassar 9.1–3–19–2; Tauseef 17–6–31–2; Khurshid 13–6–19–1; Nasir 4–3–1–0; Kamal 3–0–15–0. *Second Innings*—Sikander 15–2–63–4; Farooq 4–1–12–0; Tauseef 14.2–2–30–2; Mudassar 8–3–13–3; Khurshid 7–2–12–1.

United Bank

Mudassar Nazar c Shahid b Sabih	241
Mansoor Akhtar c and b Riaz	176
*Haroon Rashid not out	50
†Ashraf Ali not out	8
B 6, l-b 3, w 1	10
1/389 2/440 (2 wkts dec.)	485

Nasir Valika, Mahmood Rashid, Kamal Merchant, Farooq Shera, Sikander Bakht, Tauseef Ahmed and Khurshid Akhtar did not bat.

Bowling: Khatib 17–1–67–0; Sabih 7–1–40–1; Wahab 19–0–97–0; Sarfraz 1–0–5–0; Nasim 7–0–48–0; Afaq 13–0–71–0; Riaz 29–0–147–1.

Umpires: Ikram Rabbani and Javed Akhtar.

HABIB BANK v NATIONAL BANK

At Bagh-e-Jinnah Ground, Lahore, January 26, 27, 28. Habib Bank won by an innings and 94 runs. Habib Bank 17 pts, National Bank 1 pt.

National Bank

Taslim Arif c Zaheer b Liaqat	19	– (2) c Liaqat b Qadir	38
Afzaal Ahmad c and b Raqeeb	15	– (1) c Sultan b Liaqat	8
*Shafiq Ahmad run out	25	– c Arshad b Qadir	10
Ali Zia b Raqeeb	14	– st Zaheer b Qadir	34
Mahmood Arshad c Raqeeb b Liaqat	24	– c Jamshed b Qadir	0
Ijaz Ahmad b Qadir	5	– b Qadir	22
†Mohammad Jamil c Raqeeb b Liaqat	1	– c Qadir b Raqeeb	51
Anwar Khan c Zahid b Qadir	1	– c Zaheer b Raqeeb	60
Iqbal Butt not out	0	– c Arshad b Qadir	12
Jehanzeb Khan lbw b Qadir	0	– (11) not out	9
Ehtesham-ud-Din (did not bat)		– (10) c Zahid b Qadir	5
B 9, l-b 2, n-b 7	18	B 4, l-b 1, w 1, n-b 9	15
1/35 2/44 3/61 4/114 5/114 6/119 7/122 8/122 9/122 (9 wkts dec.)	122	1/48 2/52 3/80 4/97 5/102 6/131 7/226 8/246 9/250	264

Bowling: *First Innings*—Liaqat 18–7–51–3; Raqeeb 10–1–42–2; Jamshed 3–1–7–0; Qadir 4.3–2–4–3. *Second Innings*—Liaqat 14–3–55–1; Jamshed 5–3–17–0; Qadir 28.1–5–114–7; Raqeeb 14–1–57–2; Javed 2–0–6–0.

Habib Bank

Agha Zahid c Shafiq b Ehtesham	84	Sultan Rana not out	28
Arshad Pervez st Jamil b Taslim	164	†Zaheer Ahmed not out	13
Tehsin Javed st Jamil b Ali Zia	92	B 2, l-b 11, w 1, n-b 4	18
*Javed Miandad c sub b Ehtesham	52		
Azhar Khan retired hurt	29	1/153 2/324 3/377 4/424 (4 wkts)	480

Abdul Qadir, Jamshed Hussain, Abdul Raqeeb and Liaqat Ali did not bat.

Bowling: Ehtesham 27.3–3–105–2; Jehanzeb 13–4–44–0; Ali Zia 15–0–55–1; Anwar 28–4–102–0; Iqbal 35–6–91–0; Shafiq 7–0–23–0; Ijaz 2–0–21–0; Taslim 7–1–21–1.

Umpires: Mian Aslam and Iqbal Athar.

HABIB BANK v UNITED BANK

At LCCA Ground, Lahore, January 30, 31, February 1, 2. Habib Bank won by 94 runs. Habib Bank 13 pts, United Bank 3 pts.

Habib Bank

Agha Zahid b Khurshid	18	– c Farooq b Shahid	36
Arshad Pervez st Ashraf b Khurshid	16	– c Haroon b Tauseef	14
Mohsin Khan run out	7	– run out	71
*Javed Miandad st Ashraf b Tauseef	4	– c Mahmood b Tauseef	107
Tehsin Javed c Mudassar b Khurshid	1	– (6) b Shahid	1
Sultan Rana c Mahmood b Shahid	36	– (5) lbw b Tauseef	36
†Zaheer Ahmed c Farooq b Tauseef	4	– b Sikander	19
Abdul Qadir b Tauseef	0	– c Mahmood b Tauseef	0
Abdul Raqeeb not out	0	– not out	20
Jamshed Hussain (did not bat)		– c Farooq b Shahid	0
Liaqat Ali (did not bat)		– c Mahmood b Tauseef	0
B 4, l-b 2	6	B 4, l-b 8, n-b 12	24
1/28 2/44 3/49 4/50 5/56 6/61 7/66 8/92 (8 wkts dec.)	92	1/89 2/158 3/241 4/262 5/274 6/291 7/291 8/322 9/326	328

Bowling: *First Innings*—Sikander 5–1–14–0; Farooq 3–1–10–0; Khurshid 16–3–37–3; Tauseef 14–4–25–3; Shahid 0.2–0–0–1. *Second Innings*—Sikander 21–3–67–1; Khurshid 16–3–58–0; Tauseef 44–9–100–5; Shahid 22–7–79–3.

United Bank

Mudassar Nazar c Sultan b Raqeeb	9	– c Zaheer b Liaqat	11
*Haroon Rashid b Liaqat	0	– (3) c Zaheer b Raqeeb	32
Mahmood Rashid c Miandad b Liaqat	8	– (5) c sub b Qadir	1
Nasir Valika not out	66	– c Miandad b Raqeeb	24
†Ashraf Ali c Sultan b Liaqat	7	– (6) c Zahid b Raqeeb	40
Mansoor Akhtar st Zaheer b Raqeeb	12	– (2) c and b Raqeeb	15
Shahid Aziz c sub b Raqeeb	9	– (10) b Qadir	0
Farooq Shera b Raqeeb	11	– (7) run out	0
Sikander Bakht lbw b Raqeeb	23	– (8) c Liaqat b Qadir	5
Tauseef Ahmed st Zaheer b Raqeeb	16	– (9) b Qadir	1
Khurshid Akhtar (did not bat)		– not out	1
B 4, w 2, n-b 10	16	B 5, l-b 4, w 2, n-b 8	19
1/8 2/11 3/31 4/64 5/78 6/78 7/94 8/143 9/177 (9 wkts dec.)	177	1/29 2/43 3/82 4/85 5/122 6/131 7/140 8/147 9/148	149

Bowling: *First Innings*—Liaqat 21–3–57–3; Raqeeb 31.4–6–71–6; Qadir 10–2–33–0; Miandad 1–1–0–0. *Second Innings*—Liaqat 8–0–36–1; Raqeeb 24–6–61–4; Qadir 17–6–33–4.

Umpires: Rab Nawaz and Khalid Khan.

NATIONAL BANK v MCB

At Gaddafi Stadium, Lahore, January 30, 31, February 1, 2. Drawn. National Bank 8 pts, MCB 2 pts.

National Bank

Taslim Arif c Sajid b Nadeem	5	– (3) c Sajid b Tahir	4
Saleem Pervez c Ijaz b Tahir	5	– (1) c Ijaz b Nadeem	15
*Shafiq Ahmad b Tahir	101	– (6) c Salah-ud-Din b Tahir	1
Ali Zia c Babar b Tahir	157	– (2) c Farrukh b Tahir	9
Mahmood Arshad c sub b Farrukh	25	– c Sajid b Tahir	39
Maqsood Ahmad c and b Farrukh	5	– (4) b Tahir	0
†Mohammad Jamil st Sajid b Farrukh	0	– not out	19
Anwar Khan not out	3	– c Asif Ali b Ijaz	11
Iqbal Butt b Tahir	1	– not out	0
Ehtesham-ud-Din not out	4		
B 1, l-b 1, n-b 2	4	B 13, l-b 1, w 5, n-b 6	25
1/7 2/11 3/248 4/290 5/295 6/297 7/304 8/305	(8 wkts) 310	1/29 2/33 3/33 4/33 5/57 6/88 7/113	(7 wkts) 123

Nasir Malik did not bat.

Bowling: *First Innings*—Tahir 25–5–81–4; Nadeem 10–2–41–1; Ijaz 12–1–53–0; Farrukh 27–3–93–3; Babar 11–0–38–0. *Second Innings*—Tahir 15–5–40–5; Nadeem 6–2–28–1; Ijaz 15–12–11–1; Farrukh 7–2–19–0.

MCB

Qasim Omar c Saleem b Ehtesham	5	– c sub b Anwar	49
Anwarul Haq c Shafiq b Ehtesham	19	– c Iqbal b Anwar	17
Babar Basharat c Jamil b Ehtesham	19	– c Nasir b Iqbal	25
*Ijaz Faqih b Nasir	13	– (5) b Anwar	0
Salah-ud-Din lbw b Ehtesham	0	– (4) c Jamil b Anwar	3
Asif Ali c Shafiq b Ehtesham	2	– b Ehtesham	145
Maqsood Kundi c Jamil b Nasir	0	– (11) not out	109
Tahir Naqqash run out	42	– (7) c Anwar b Iqbal	5
Nadeem Yousuf not out	32	– (8) not out	202
†Sajid Abbasi c Jamil b Ehtesham	6	– lbw b Ehtesham	2
Farrukh Zaman b Anwar	0	– (9) c Jamil b Ehtesham	3
L-b 1, w 1, n-b 7	9	B 3, l-b 7, w 3, n-b 7	20
1/25 2/29 3/61 4/61 5/63 6/64 7/76 8/130 9/144	147	1/57 2/74 3/80 4/80 5/118 6/132 7/370 8/382 9/384	(9 wkts dec.) 580

Bowling: *First Innings*—Ehtesham 18–4–64–6; Nasir 12–5–29–2; Anwar 7.5–0–36–1; Iqbal 2–0–9–0. *Second Innings*—Ehtesham 36–8–135–3; Nasir 9–2–32–0; Anwar 38–11–98–4; Iqbal 27–5–89–2; Ali Zia 24–3–128–0; Shafiq 14–2–43–0; Taslim 2–0–11–0; Maqsood 3–0–18–0; Mahmood 1–0–6–0.

Umpires: Agha Saadat and Athar Zaidi.

MCB v UNITED BANK

At LCCA Ground, Lahore, February 4, 5, 6, 7. United Bank won by ten wickets. United Bank 18 pts, MCB 3 pts.

MCB

Qasim Omar b Sikander	19	– c Mudassar b Sikander	0
Anwarul Haq b Tauseef	19	– b Haroon	59
Babar Basharat c Mudassar b Sikander	33	– (4) c Haroon b Tauseef	73
Asif Ali b Tauseef	16	– (7) not out	28
Salah-ud-Din c Farooq b Sikander	36	– c Mahmood b Tauseef	11
*Ijaz Faqih b Tauseef	7	– c sub b Haroon	11
Nadeem Yousuf c Waheed b Tauseef	7	– (8) lbw b Sikander	13
Tahir Naqqash b Tauseef	11	– (9) c Shahid b Haroon	4
Maqsood Kundi c Waheed b Sikander	2	– (10) c Mahmood b Tauseef	2
†Sajid Abbasi c Waheed b Sikander	7	– (3) c Waheed b Farooq	5
Farrukh Zaman not out	4	– c sub b Tauseef	0
B 9, l-b 8, n-b 1	18	B 5, n-b 2	7
1/34 2/42 3/82 4/99 5/108 6/132 7/151 8/158 9/171	179	1/0 2/8 3/140 4/140 5/156 6/171 7/198 8/206 9/209	213

Bowling: *First Innings*—Sikander 28.3–11–51–5; Farooq 3–1–13–0; Tauseef 31–6–77–5; Amin 7–2–20–0. *Second Innings*—Sikander 10–4–21–2; Farooq 7–1–20–1; Shahid 19–5–44–0; Tauseef 26.5–5–64–4; Amin 11–3–23–0; Haroon 11–4–34–3.

United Bank

Mudassar Nazar b Farrukh	59		
†Waheed Mirza b Tahir	19	– (1) not out	27
*Haroon Rashid c Qasim b Ijaz	11		
Nasir Valika not out	100		
Mahmood Rashid b Farrukh	8		
Kamal Merchant b Tahir	31	– (2) not out	9
Farooq Shera run out	102		
Sikander Bakht not out	5		
B 9, l-b 9, n-b 5	23	W 1	1
1/42 2/66 3/119 4/137 5/182 6/342	(6 wkts dec.) 358		(no wkt) 37

Tauseef Ahmed, Amin Lakhani and Shahid Aziz did not bat.

Bowling: *First Innings*—Tahir 22–2–87–2; Nadeem 5–1–15–0; Ijaz 29–6–91–1; Farrukh 35–5–102–2; Babar 9–1–40–0. *Second Innings*—Tahir 2–0–6–0; Nadeem 2–0–10–0; Qasim 1–0–8–0; Sajid 1–0–8–0; Asif 0.1–0–4–0.

RAWALPINDI v HABIB BANK

At Gaddafi Stadium, Lahore, February 4, 5, 6, 7. Rawalpindi won by two wickets. Rawalpindi 15 pts, Habib Bank 6 pts.

Habib Bank

Agha Zahid run out	136	– c Iqtidar b Riaz	68
Arshad Pervez b Khatib	12	– c Iqtidar b Sabih	60
Raees Ahmad c Iqtidar b Afaq	34	– lbw b Sabih	22
*Mohsin Khan not out	98	– lbw b Sabih	7
Masood Iqbal not out	1	– (8) c Riaz b Sabih	3
Sultan Rana (did not bat)		– (5) c Khalid b Sabih	12
Tehsin Javed (did not bat)		– (6) b Riaz	25
†Zaheer Ahmed (did not bat)		– (7) c sub b Sabih	14
Abdul Qadir (did not bat)		– not out	6
Aslam Qureshi (did not bat)		– c Afaq b Sabih	0
Liaqat Ali (did not bat)		– run out	2
B 1, l-b 9, w 1, n-b 1	12	B 6, l-b 2, w 4, n-b 2	14
1/32 2/109 3/284	(3 wkts) 293	1/101 2/146 3/158 4/169 5/177 6/195 7/224 8/224 9/224	233

Bowling: *First Innings*—Khatib 31-4-98-1; Sabih 5-0-16-0; Nasim 2-0-14-0; Riaz 34-6-104-0; Afaq 13-2-49-1. *Second Innings*—Khatib 19-4-63-0; Sabih 21-3-61-7; Riaz 27-5-61-2; Afaq 8-0-34-0.

Rawalpindi

Masood Anwar c Zaheer b Qadir	144	– c Mohsin b Qadir	10
Azmat Jalil run out	45	– lbw b Liaqat	3
†Iqtidar Khwaja c Tehsin b Zahid	9	– b Liaqat	0
Mohammad Riaz c Masood b Qadir	40	– c Tehsin b Liaqat	30
Qazi Khalid not out	91	– (6) not out	49
Raja Afaq c Sultan b Aslam	0	– (7) lbw b Qadir	4
Shahid Munir st Zaheer b Qadir	12	– (9) c Raees b Qadir	4
*Rizwan Khatib c Masood b Qadir	4	– (5) b Qadir	5
Sabih Azhar not out	1	– (10) not out	1
Raja Sarfraz c Sultan b Qadir	0	– (8) lbw b Raees	28
B 3, l-b 15, w 4, n-b 8	30	B 10, l-b 2, w 3, n-b 4	19
1/99 2/142 3/215 4/306 5/307 6/309 7/363 8/371	(8 wkts) 376	1/10 2/10 3/15 4/53 5/67 6/84 7/139 8/144	(8 wkts) 153

Nasim Iqbal did not bat.

Bowling: *First Innings*—Liaqat 16-2-78-0; Aslam 8-0-45-1; Arshad 3-0-12-0; Sultan 6-2-16-0; Zahid 14-3-43-1; Qadir 23-4-90-5; Mohsin 4-2-12-0; Raees 11-0-50-0. *Second Innings*—Liaqat 20-2-63-3; Aslam 2-0-8-0; Qadir 22-7-53-4; Raees 4.3-0-10-1.

PATRON'S TROPHY, 1981-82

The tournament was contested on a league basis, with teams placed in four groups, and the four group winners then playing a knockout round. No longer considered to have first-class status, the tournament is used as a qualifying tournament for the Quaid-e-Azam Trophy competition.

Group A: Hyderabad, Karachi Whites, Quetta, Rawalpindi II, Sukkur.
Group B: Bahawalpur, Karachi Greens, Lahore Blues, Multan, Sargodha.
Group C: Hazara, HBFC, Lahore I, LDCA, Peshawar, Universities.
Group D: Allied Bank, PWD, Services, State Bank, WAPDA.

Semi-Finals

At National Stadium, Karachi, January 27, 28, 29, 30. Drawn, Karachi Whites won on first innings lead. Karachi Whites 250 (Shaukat Mirza 59, Junaid Alvi 57; Shahid Hussain five for 98) and 378 (Omar Rashid 100, Raja Akbar 84 not out, Javed Zaidi 60; Shahid Hussain six for 124); Bahawalpur 249 (Azhar Abbas 51, Naseer Ahmad 51; Fahim Sani five for 68) and 254 for six (Wasim Khurshid 71, Naseer Ahmad 64; Mahboobul Haq four for 73).

At Moghalpura Institute, Lahore, January 27, 28, 29, 30. Allied Bank won by 318 runs. Allied Bank 249 (Zafar Mehdi 50, Salman Qizalbash 39; Raja Sadiqullah four for 45) and 356 for nine dec. (Farooq Rashid 109, Shoaib Habib 64); LDCA 165 (Ziaur Rehman 56; Zafar Mehdi four for 59) and 122 (Rais-ud-Din six for 53).

Final

At Bahawalpur, February 2, 3, 4, 5, 6. Allied Bank won by nine wickets. Karachi Whites 185 for nine dec. (Tahir Rashid 90 not out; Shoaib Habib six for 79) and 141 (Shaukat Mirza 33; Ali Akbar four for 36, Zafar Mehdi four for 50); Allied Bank 295 for nine (Talat Masood 86, Shoaib Habib 60, Farooq Rashid 49; Fahim Sani seven for 99) and 34 for one.

INTERNATIONAL XI IN PAKISTAN

An International XI, managed by V. Lewis and captained by Rohan Kanhai, visited Pakistan in September-October, 1981. The party consisted of R. B. Kanhai (captain), B. S. Bedi, R. O. Butcher, T. R. Etwaroo, I. J. Gould, F. C. Hayes, E. E. Hemmings, M. A. Holding, C. L. King, M. A. Lynch, G. D. Mendis, M. W. W. Selvey, W. N. Slack, G. C. Small and J. A. Williams.

PAKISTAN XI v INTERNATIONAL XI

At Karachi, September 21, 22, 23, 24. International XI won by 207 runs. International XI elected to bat on a docile wicket.

International XI

G. D. Mendis not out	124	– c and b Qasim	44
W. N. Slack c Ijaz b Rashid	17	– lbw b Sikander	15
R. O. Butcher c Majid b Qasim	35	– b Qasim	15
M. A. Lynch c Mudassar b Ijaz	44	– lbw b Rashid	6
C. L. King c Majid b Qasim	34	– c Qasim b Ijaz	11
*R. B. Kanhai b Qasim	7	– (7) c Raja b Qasim	5
†I. J. Gould b Raja	0	– (6) c Mudassar b Ijaz	17
E. E. Hemmings lbw b Qasim	0	– (10) c Raja b Qasim	12
J. A. Williams c Bari b Raja	0	– c Raja b Qasim	12
M. W. W. Selvey c Bari b Sikander	40	– (8) not out	26
M. A. Holding not out	39	– c Raja b Ijaz	2
B 1, l-b 9, n-b 17	27	B 2, l-b 6, n-b 8	16
1/52 2/99 3/164 4/208 5/216 6/217 7/218 8/219 9/300	(9 wkts dec.) 367	1/31 2/64 3/85 4/96 5/104 6/121 7/123 8/151 9/178	181

Bowling: *First Innings*—Sikander 15–0–88–1; Rashid 21–4–67–1; Mudassar 12–3–33–0; Qasim 24–6–81–4; Ijaz 5–2–32–1; Raja 19–6–39–2. *Second Innings*—Sikander 8–1–33–1; Rashid 10–1–30–1; Mudassar 2–0–14–0; Qasim 23–7–47–5; Ijaz 13.5–2–28–3; Raja 5–1–10–0; Rizwan 1–0–3–0.

Pakistan XI

Mudassar Nazar c Butcher b Hemmings	31	– lbw b Williams	23
Rizwan-uz-Zaman c Gould b Holding	28	– b Holding	6
Mohsin Khan run out	47	– c Williams b Holding	0
Wasim Raja c Gould b King	26	– c Slack b Holding	4
*Majid J. Khan retired hurt	66	– c Kanhai b Hemmings	11
Salim Malik c and b Selvey	1	– c Mendis b Holding	36
Ijaz Faqih b Selvey	2	– b Holding	1
†Wasim Bari c Slack b Hemmings	4	– c Lynch b Hemmings	11
Rashid Khan c Gould b King	0	– c Slack b Hemmings	0
Iqbal Qasim c Gould b Holding	2	– c Butcher b Holding	12
Sikander Bakht not out	2	– not out	4
L-b 4, w 2, n-b 2	8	B 4, l-b 8, w 1, n-b 3	16
1/64 2/68 3/120 4/163 5/175 6/179 7/200 8/207 9/217	217	1/17 2/17 3/27 4/49 5/50 6/62 7/81 8/81 9/100	124

Bowling: *First Innings*—Holding 10.1–4–26–2; Williams 8–1–28–0; Selvey 17–3–36–2; Hemmings 26–5–66–2; King 16–2–53–2. *Second Innings*—Holding 15–3–49–6; Williams 5–2–9–1; Selvey 2–0–9–0; Hemmings 21–10–30–3; King 4–2–9–0; Lynch 2–1–2–0.

R. O. Butcher kept wicket in Pakistan XI's second innings.

Umpires: Amanullah Khan and Javed Akhtar.

PAKISTAN XI v INTERNATIONAL XI

At Hyderabad, September 27, 28, 29, 30. Pakistan XI won by nine wickets. International XI won the toss.

International XI

G. D. Mendis c Tahir b Ijaz	15	– st Bari b Ijaz	38
W. N. Slack c Mudassar b Sikander	0	– c Bari b Tahir	0
R. O. Butcher b Tahir	5	– b Ijaz	3
F. C. Hayes b Qasim	38	– b Ijaz	1
M. A. Lynch c Raja b Ijaz	27	– c Majid b Qasim	1
*R. B. Kanhai c Qasim b Raja	14	– c Bari b Ijaz	9
†I. J. Gould lbw b Sikander	26	– b Qasim	31
M. A. Holding lbw b Sikander	67	– c Majid b Qasim	23
G. C. Small not out	21	– c Tahir b Ijaz	13
E. E. Hemmings c Bari b Qasim	5	– c Qasim b Sikander	5
B. S. Bedi b Tahir	0	– not out	3
L-b 3, n-b 7	10	L-b 2, n-b 11	13
1/2 2/7 3/31 4/68 5/106 6/106 7/163 8/202 9/217	228	1/3 2/11 3/19 4/24 5/33 6/89 7/93 8/125 9/133	140

Bowling: *First Innings*—Sikander 13–3–40–3; Tahir 6.3–2–20–2; Qasim 28–11–68–2; Ijaz 19–5–60–2; Raja 8–3–30–1. *Second Innings*—Sikander 3.2–1–4–1; Tahir 9–1–19–1; Qasim 21–3–47–3; Ijaz 23–7–46–5; Raja 4–0–11–0.

Pakistan XI

Mansoor Akhtar b Hemmings	25	– st Butcher b Lynch	2
Rizwan-uz-Zaman b Bedi	11	– not out	8
Mudassar Nazar c and b Bedi	50	– not out	11
Wasim Raja b Lynch	24		
*Majid J. Khan st Gould b Bedi	44		
Salim Malik c Slack b Small	38		
Ijaz Faqih b Hemmings	38		
†Wasim Bari c Kanhai b Bedi	14		
Tahir Naqqash c Butcher b Bedi	14		
Iqbal Qasim c Butcher b Bedi	40		
Sikander Bakht not out	21		
B 1, l-b 5, n-b 10	16	L–b 2, n–b 11	13
1/42 2/46 3/79 4/162 5/163 6/214 7/251 8/271 9/272	335	1/17	(1 wkt) 34

Bowling: *First Innings*—Holding 21–4–69–0; Small 14–4–31–1; Bedi 45.2–14–117–6; Hemmings 29–5–70–2; Lynch 14–5–32–1. *Second Innings*—Small 4–0–6–0; Lynch 3–0–15–1.

Umpires: Amanullah Khan and Javed Akhtar.

†PAKISTAN XI v INTERNATIONAL XI

At Karachi, October 2. International XI won by seven wickets. Pakistan XI 63 (27.3 overs) (G. C. Small three for 18); International XI 64 for three (12.3 overs).

†PAKISTAN XI v INTERNATIONAL XI

At Lahore, October 4. Pakistan XI won by virtue of losing fewer wickets. Pakistan XI 168 for six (40 overs) (Rizwan-uz-Zaman 60); International XI 168 (39.5 overs) (C. L. King 55 not out; Iqbal Qasim four for 13).

†PAKISTAN XI v INTERNATIONAL XI

At Quetta, October 6. Pakistan XI won by seven wickets. International XI 135 for nine (40 overs) (C. L. King 49; Tahir Naqqash three for 9); Pakistan XI 137 for three (31.4 overs) (Javed Miandad 58 not out).

PAKISTAN XI v INTERNATIONAL XI

At Lahore, October 8, 10, 11, 12, 13. Pakistan won by 296 runs, thanks mainly to Iqbal Qasim, who took nine wickets in International XI's second innings and caught the tenth batsman. The International XI again won the toss.

Pakistan

Mudassar Nazar lbw b Williams	1	– c Etwaroo b Bedi	151
Rizwan-uz-Zaman c Mendis b Small	32	– st Gould b Hemmings	65
Mansoor Akhtar b Bedi	23	– not out	75
*Javed Miandad st Gould b Bedi	177	– c and b Bedi	1
Majid J. Khan b Bedi	5	– c Etwaroo b Bedi	32
Wasim Raja c Hayes b Small	144	– not out	24
Ijaz Faqih c Gould b Bedi	1		
†Wasim Bari b Small	4		
Sarfraz Nawaz lbw b Williams	3		
Tahir Naqqash c Hayes b Williams	1		
Iqbal Qasim not out	1		
L-b 2, n-b 14	16	B 2, l-b 3, w 1, n-b 2	8
1/6 2/60 3/64 4/89 5/351 6/354 7/372 8/380 9/402	408	1/160 2/271 3/275 4/321	(4 wkts dec.) 356

Bowling: *First Innings*—Williams 22–2–76–3; Small 19–2–83–3; Butcher 3–1–12–0; Bedi 25.3–2–134–4; Hemmings 16–1–66–0; Kanhai 1–0–4–0; Lynch 3–0–17–0. *Second Innings*—Williams 18–2–50–0; Small 10–2–41–0; Bedi 28–3–114–3; Hemmings 21–1–84–1; Kanhai 2–0–13–0; Lynch 7–0–46–0.

International XI

G. D. Mendis c Mudassar b Sarfraz	5	– b Qasim	38
T. R. Etwaroo c Mansoor b Sarfraz	136	– c Bari b Qasim	12
M. A. Lynch c Bari b Tahir	0	– lbw b Qasim	0
F. C. Hayes b Ijaz	18	– c Bari b Qasim	16
R. O. Butcher st Bari b Qasim	7	– (6) c Miandad b Qasim	27
*R. B. Kanhai c Miandad b Qasim	54	– (7) c Miandad b Qasim	46
†I. J. Gould run out	4	– (8) c Qasim b Ijaz	15
J. A. Williams c Miandad b Ijaz	3	– (9) c Rizwan b Qasim	0
E. E. Hemmings c Ijaz b Qasim	9	– (10) not out	20
G. C. Small not out	16	– (5) c Tahir b Qasim	4
B. S. Bedi c Mudassar b Sarfraz	8	– c Miandad b Qasim	9
B 1, l-b 3, w 1, n-b 9	14	B 2, l-b 3, n-b 2	7
1/18 2/19 3/60 4/73 5/188 6/192 7/198 8/223 9/260	274	1/31 2/31 3/66 4/73 5/90 6/117 7/148 8/149 9/176	194

Bowling: *First Innings*—Sarfraz 17.4–7–44–3; Tahir 12–3–50–1; Qasim 38–7–100–3; Ijaz 21–4–56–2; Raja 6–1–10–0. *Second Innings*—Sarfraz 4–1–12–0; Tahir 4–0–15–0; Qasim 30.2–5–80–9; Ijaz 22–3–60–1; Raja 6–0–15–0; Mudassar 2–0–5–0.

Umpires: Shakoor Rana and Mahboob Shah.

CRICKET IN SRI LANKA, 1981-1982

By GERRY VAIDYASEKERA

With the promotion of Sri Lanka to Test status, the Board of Control for Cricket in Sri Lanka devised plans for the laying of turf pitches in several provincial capitals, a Sri Lanka Cricket Foundation, a Cricket Secretariat, an Inter-Provincial Cricket Tournament of four-day and five-day matches, and tours of India, Australia, New Zealand and Zimbabwe.

Matches in the final round of the premier cricket tournament, the P. Saravanamuttu Trophy, were extended to three days for the first time in its 33-year history. The Trophy was won for the second successive year by the Bloomfield Cricket and Athletic Club, led by Test captain Bandula Warnapura. The runners-up were Sinhalese Sports Club, led by the Test vice-captain, Duleep Mendis. However, most of the clubs suffered in the final round when their leading players were touring Pakistan. To compensate for this, the Maharashtra state captain from India, Raju Bhalekar, played for Bloomfield, and Tim Boon and Gordon Parsons of Leicestershire for Colombo Cricket Club. In eight innings Boon totalled 434 runs at an average of 72.33 with two hundreds.

Colts Cricket Club, under the leadership of Beverley Paul, ran out easy winners of the Rahaman Hathy Trophy, maintaining an unbeaten record in all their eight matches. Moors Sports Club, who lost only to Colts, were runners-up.

The Donovan Andree Trophy was won by Bloomfield, their second major trophy, with Colombo Cricket Club as runners-up. Gehan Karunaratne of the Colombo club topped the batting for the tournament with an average of 221.50, hitting two hundreds and totalling 443 runs with seven not outs in nine innings. The Macan Markar Challenge Trophy for the highest individual score was won by Warnapura with an innings of 220 against the Police. Tissa Wijeratne, of Kandy Cricket Club, hitting a hundred in 98 minutes against Moratuwa, won the V.V.T. Fernando Challenge Trophy for the fastest century.

As many as 78 hundreds were hit in the season, shared by 52 batsmen. Four of them were double-hundreds. Mithra Wettimuny of the Sinhalese Sports Club scored four hundreds, while Hemal Mendis of the Saracens and Rohan Jayasekera of the Tamils knocked three each. Mithra Wettimuny, Hemal Mendis, Athula Samarasekera, and Lanka Perera aggregated over 1,000 runs for the season. Mumtaz Yusuf of the Colts headed the bowling with 39 wickets at 12.97 apiece and Bloomfield's Vinodhan John had the largest haul with 48 wickets at an average of 15.41. Nineteen bowlers captured more than 50 wickets each in the season, with Jayantha Amerasinghe of the Nomads the highest with 80 wickets (average 19.72).

A new record first-wicket partnership of 352 was set up by Athula Samarasekera (192) and Wayne Jansz (157) for the Tamils against the Police.

CRICKET IN ZIMBABWE, 1981-82

By ARTHUR HOLDEN

Zimbabwe operated in its new status as an Associate Member of the International Cricket Conference, having been elected as such at the Annual General Meeting of the ICC at Lord's on July 23, 1981. The Board of Control having resolved to continue a policy of staging two tours to the country each season, to ensure a good standard at national level and maintain enthusiasm, arrangements were made for visits by Young West Indies and the Pakistan International Airways.

The Young West Indian side, managed by the former Test player, C. W. Smith, contained six players already chosen to tour Australia shortly afterwards – Faoud Bacchus, the captain, Desmond Haynes, the vice-captain, Jeff Dujon, Harold Joseph, Augustine Logie and Malcolm Marshall. Of the three one-day "internationals" the visitors won two and Zimbabwe one. In the three-day matches, the West Indians were the winners of the first and the other two were drawn with honours even.

PIA, though without several of their leading players, who were engaged in the Test series between Pakistan and Sri Lanka, provided interesting opposition. The first of the three-day matches was drawn, thanks to a fine first-innings century by Mushtaq Mohammad, captaining PIA, and another in the second innings by Asif Mohammad. Of the four one-day matches, when the Zimbabwe selectors were experimenting with an eye on the forthcoming tour of England for the ICC Trophy, each team won one; two, somewhat unusually, were drawn, no provision having been made in the rules for the rain and bad light which affected them.

With the bat, Andy Pycroft, Robin Brown and David Houghton turned in some good performances, while Vince Hogg, Duncan Fletcher and John Traicos (off-spin) bowled well. Against every touring team in the last two seasons Pycroft has been outstandingly successful. The form shown by the Zimbabweans provided grounds for optimism for the tour to England and these were duly justified when the ICC Trophy was won, bringing with it qualification for the 1983 World Cup.

YOUNG WEST INDIES IN ZIMBABWE

The Young West Indies side which toured Zimbabwe in October 1981 consisted of: C. W. Smith (manager), S. F. A. Bacchus (captain), H. L. Alleyne, I. Cadette, W. W. Daniel, P. J. Dujon, D. L. Haynes, H. Joseph, A. L. Logie, M. D. Marshall, E. H. Mattis, E. A. Moseley, M. C. Neita, Timur Mohamed and M. A. Tucker.

†At Salisbury, October 7. Young West Indies won by seven wickets. Zimbabwe Country Districts 132 for six (40 overs) (G. Paterson 31); Young West Indies 134 for three (36.5 overs) (E. H. Mattis 55 not out, S. F. A. Bacchus 31).

ZIMBABWE v YOUNG WEST INDIES

At Salisbury, October 9, 10, 12. Young West Indies won by seven wickets.

Zimbabwe

J. G. Heron c Dujon b Marshall	24	– c Haynes b Daniel	11
G. Paterson c Dujon b Alleyne	0	– b Tucker	12
†R. D. Brown c Mattis b Daniel	13	– c Bacchus b Tucker	18
A. J. Pycroft not out	61	– c Alleyne b Tucker	17
*D. A. G. Fletcher b Joseph	17	– b Joseph	7
G. C. Wallace c Mattis b Alleyne	5	– c Mohamed b Tucker	2
†D. L. Houghton b Alleyne	1	– c Haynes b Daniel	87
K. M. Curran lbw b Daniel	6	– c Dujon b Joseph	4
A. J. Traicos c Dujon b Marshall	10	– c Dujon b Daniel	3
V. R. Hogg c Dujon b Daniel	0	– b Tucker	21
R. H. Kaschula c Bacchus b Tucker	13	– not out	2
B 3, l-b 4, n-b 6	13	B 7, l-b 10	17
1/2 2/38 3/40 4/68 5/91 6/95 7/107 8/120 9/121	163	1/20 2/39 3/48 4/67 5/73 6/81 7/90 8/110 9/197	201

Bowling: *First Innings*—Daniel 16–5–46–3; Alleyne 15–3–27–3; Marshall 13–2–46–2; Joseph 9–1–30–1; Tucker 1.1–0–1–1. *Second Innings*—Daniel 16.2–3–43–3; Alleyne 13–7–18–0; Marshall 6–1–16–0; Joseph 18–3–57–2; Tucker 32–15–50–5.

Young West Indies

D. L. Haynes c Houghton b Curran	3	– c Kaschula b Hogg	5
*S. F. A. Bacchus c Pycroft b Fletcher	13		
Timur Mohamed c Pycroft b Curran	11	– c Traicos b Hogg	16
E. H. Mattis c Fletcher b Kaschula	106		
A. L. Logie c Houghton b Hogg	5	– (4) not out	21
†P. J. Dujon c Heron b Traicos	60	– (2) c sub b Hogg	12
M. D. Marshall st Houghton b Traicos	34		
M. A. Tucker lbw b Traicos	30	– (5) not out	6
H. L. Alleyne c Brown b Traicos	0		
W. W. Daniel b Traicos	27		
H. Joseph not out	2		
B 2, l-b 4, n-b 5	11	L-b 1, n-b 2	3
1/3 2/19 3/33 4/38 5/151 6/240 7/242 8/248 9/281	302	1/10 2/25 3/36	(3 wkts) 63

Bowling: *First Innings*—Hogg 22–3–70–1; Curran 11–1–32–2; Fletcher 12–6–28–1; Kaschula 25–3–88–1; Traicos 26.3–5–73–5. *Second Innings*—Hogg 5–0–23–3; Curran 2–0–11–0; Kaschula 4–0–25–0; Traicos 1.1–1–1–0.

Umpires: K. Kanjee and P. Latham.

†At Salisbury, October 11. Young West Indies won by three wickets. Zimbabwe 183 for six (50 overs) (A. J. Pycroft 63, G. Paterson 39); Young West Indies 189 for seven (46.5 overs) (S. F. A. Bacchus 51, E. H. Mattis 32, I. Cadette 31 not out, A. L. Logie 31).

†At Gwelo, October 14. Young West Indies won by 97 runs. Young West Indies 270 for four (50 overs) (D. L. Haynes 89, E. H. Mattis 78, Timur Mohamed 59 not out); Zimbabwe XI 173 for seven (50 overs) (G. C. Wallace 48, S. Kuhn 35 not out, J. G. Heron 35; D. L. Haynes three for 30).

ZIMBABWE v YOUNG WEST INDIES

At Bulawayo, October 16, 17, 19. Drawn.

Young West Indies

D. L. Haynes lbw b Kaschula	17	– c sub b Kaschula	69
*S. F. A. Bacchus c Houghton b Hogg	29	– b Hogg	4
E. H. Mattis c Brown b Fletcher	0	– lbw b Hogg	4
Timur Mohamed c Traicos b Hogg	28	– st Brown b Kaschula	23
A. L. Logie lbw b Kaschula	29	– c Brown b Hogg	20
†P. J. Dujon c Traicos b Hogg	9	– st Brown b Kaschula	29
M. D. Marshall c Kaschula b Fletcher	19	– c Houghton b Pycroft	109
M. A. Tucker lbw b Traicos	21	– b Traicos	25
H. L. Alleyne c Fletcher b Kaschula	24	– c Brown b Kaschula	19
W. W. Daniel b Hogg	13	– not out	4
H. Joseph not out	16		
L-b 7, w 2, n-b 1	10	B 4, l-b 6 n-b 2	12
1/34 2/35 3/69 4/79 5/90 6/134 7/138 8/183 9/183	215	1/23 2/31 3/92 4/127 5/127 6/196 7/245 8/306 9/318 (9 wkts dec.)	318

Bowling: *First Innings*—Hogg 17–8–33–4; Curran 3–0–26–0; Fletcher 12–0–41–2; Kaschula 16–1–78–3; Traicos 7–0–27–1. *Second Innings*—Hogg 15–3–50–3; Curran 11–0–51–0; Fletcher 5–2–20–0; Kaschula 39–9–116–4; Traicos 31–6–69–1; Pycroft 3–0–0–1.

Zimbabwe

*D. A. G. Fletcher lbw b Alleyne	35
G. Paterson b Daniel	7
†R. D. Brown lbw b Alleyne	102
A. J. Pycroft c Bacchus b Joseph	30
J. G. Heron lbw b Alleyne	0
G. C. Wallace lbw b Tucker	14
D. L. Houghton lbw b Marshall	46
K. M. Curran not out	13
A. J. Traicos b Joseph	3
V. R. Hogg lbw b Joseph	0
R. H. Kaschula c Haynes b Joseph	4
B 5, l-b 11, w 5, n-b 4	25
1/22 2/49 3/110 4/112 5/147 6/249 7/256 8/267 9/271	279

Bowling: Marshall 22–7–46–1; Daniel 18–6–43–1; Joseph 28–8–69–4; Alleyne 20–7–35–3; Tucker 17–5–52–1; Mohamed 2–0–9–0.

Umpires: P. Latham and I. Robinson.

†At Bulawayo, October 18. Zimbabwe won by 53 runs. Zimbabwe 227 for five (50 overs) (D. A. G. Fletcher 54, J. G. Heron 44, G. C. Wallace 40 not out, T. W. Dunk 33); Young West Indies 174 (38.3 overs) (S. F. A. Bacchus 48, D. L. Haynes 45; D. Streak four for 45, V. R. Hogg three for 43).

†At Umtali, October 21. Young West Indies won by 118 runs. Young West Indies 283 (50 overs) (D. L. Haynes 122, Timur Mohamed 44; M. Jarvis three for 40); Zimbabwe XI 165 (45.4 overs) (G. Scott 44, J. Meyer 31, A. J. Pycroft 30; Timur Mohamed four for 13 including the hat-trick, M. D. Marshall three for 11).

ZIMBABWE v YOUNG WEST INDIES

At Salisbury, October 23, 24, 26. Drawn.

Zimbabwe

T. W. Dunk lbw b Marshall	7	– c Mattis b Davis	0
*D. A. G. Fletcher b Davis	1	– c Dujon b Daniel	26
†R. D. Brown c Dujon b Davis	8	– c Dujon b Daniel	11
A. J. Pycroft run out	94	– c Mohamed b Daniel	59
D. L. Houghton c Mohamed b Joseph	23	– c Mattis b Daniel	45
G. Paterson run out	4	– not out	43
G. C. Wallace b Davis	4	– not out	35
K. M. Curran c Logie b Marshall	24		
A. J. Traicos not out	5		
V. R. Hogg c Tucker b Marshall	0		
R. H. Kaschula b Marshall	0		
B 4, l-b 2, w 1, n-b 17	24	B 13, l-b 11, w 1, n-b 11	36
1/4 2/17 3/29 4/96 5/107 6/114 7/184 8/194 9/194	194	1/1 2/45 3/51 4/158 5/167 (5 wkts dec.)	255

Bowling: *First Innings*—Marshall 16.4–2–39–4; Davis 11.2–2–27–3; Daniel 11–2–28–0; Tucker 5.4–0–31–0; Joseph 15–4–33–1; Mattis 2–0–5–0; Mohamed 1–0–7–0. *Second Innings*—Marshall 23–8–45–0; Davis 11–3–24–1; Daniel 16–3–38–4; Tucker 15–0–54–0; Joseph 15–1–58–0; Haynes 1–1–0–0.

Young West Indies

D. L. Haynes c Brown b Fletcher	35	– not out	40
†P. J. Dujon c Hogg b Curran	0	– run out	14
E. H. Mattis c and b Hogg	8		
A. L. Logie c Brown b Fletcher	12		
W. W. Daniel b Kaschula	24		
Timur Mohamed b Kaschula	59	– (3) c Pycroft b Kaschula	54
M. D. Marshall c and b Hogg	13		
M. A. Tucker b Curran	1		
W. W. Davis b Hogg	5		
*S. F. A. Bacchus not out	23		
H. Joseph c Curran b Traicos	15		
B 3, l-b 5, w 1, n-b 10	19	B 8	8
1/2 2/29 3/49 4/87 5/119 6/136 7/137 8/148 9/191	214	1/44 2/116 (2 wkts)	116

Bowling: *First Innings*—Hogg 24–4–68–3; Curran 8–2–21–2; Fletcher 11.3–2–26–2; Traicos 12.5–4–27–1; Kaschula 14.3–3–53–2. *Second Innings*—Hogg 4–0–11–0; Curran 2–1–2–0; Traicos 9–1–34–0; Kaschula 10.5–3–61–1.

Umpires: A. Wilmot and K. Kanjee.

†At Salisbury, October 25. Young West Indies won by 126 runs. Young West Indies 231 for seven (50 overs) (A. L. Logie 73, M. C. Neita 46); Zimbabwe 105 (33.1 overs).

PIA IN ZIMBABWE

The PIA side, captained by Mushtaq Mohammad, which toured Zimbabwe in March-April, 1982, consisted of: Aftab Baloch, Aquil Memon, Asif Mohammad, Feroze Mehdi, Ghulam Abbas, Hasan Jamil, Liaqat Ali, Mushtaq Mohammad, Naeem Ahmad, Shahid Mohammad, Rashid Israr, Yahya Toor, Zafar Ahmed, Zahid Ahmad.

†At Salisbury South, March 17. Zimbabwe Country Districts won by 32 runs. Zimbabwe Country Districts 250 for eight (50 overs) (G. Paterson 60, I. P. Butchart 55, B. Oldrieve 48); PIA 218 (47.2 overs) (Asif Mohammad 54, Aftab Baloch 37; M. Seager five for 56).

ZIMBABWE v PIA

At Salisbury, March 19, 20, 22. Drawn.

Zimbabwe

†D. L. Houghton c Israr b Mushtaq	62	– b Naeem	36
J. G. Heron c Israr b Liaqat	1	– c Naeem b Toor	41
R. D. Brown b Toor	29	– b Toor	10
A. J. Pycroft c Mushtaq b Liaqat	71	– not out	42
*D. A. G. Fletcher c Asif b Liaqat	56	– not out	39
G. C. Wallace b Liaqat	0	– (5) b Mushtaq Mohammad	14
K. M. Curran lbw b Jamil	25		
L. L. de Grandhomme run out	13		
A. J. Traicos not out	13		
V. R. Hogg b Jamil	0		
E. J. Hough run out	4		
B 12, l-b 9, n-b 4	25	L-b 6, n-b 5	11
1/8 2/62 3/122 4/228 5/230 6/249 7/278 8/285 9/292	299	1/75 2/88 3/95 4/126 (4 wkts dec.)	193

Bowling: *First Innings*—Liaqat 17–5–35–4; Jamil 18–4–51–2; Toor 15–0–54–1; Mushtaq 15–3–57–1; Zahid 7–1–24–0; Naeem 11–2–33–0; Aftab 7–2–20–0. *Second Innings*—Liaqat 15–3–44–0; Jamil 7–2–21–0; Naeem 10–2–33–1; Toor 12–3–34–2; Mushtaq 7–0–36–1; Aftab 2–0–14–0.

PIA

Asif Mohammad c de Grandhomme b Fletcher	26	– not out	100
Feroze Mehdi lbw b Hogg	16	– b Fletcher	18
Rashid Israr c Traicos b Curran	8	– c Houghton b Hough	0
Aftab Baloch c de Grandhomme b Traicos	2	– c Heron b Hough	1
Mushtaq Mohammad c Heron b Fletcher	101	– b Hough	9
Naeem Ahmad b Hogg	1	– not out	28
Hasan Jamil c Brown b Hough	27		
Zahid Ahmad b de Grandhomme	10		
Yahya Toor c Brown b Hogg	1		
†Aquil Memon not out	33		
Liaqat Ali not out	4		
B 2, l-b 6, w 1, n-b 9	18	L-b 1, w 2, n-b 4	7
1/33 2/59 3/59 4/74 5/78 6/130 7/163 8/166 9/236 (9 wkts dec.)	247	1/46 2/49 3/51 4/80 (4 wkts)	163

Bowling: *First Innings*—Hogg 25–6–50–3; Hough 14–3–26–1; Traicos 24–7–53–1; Fletcher 16–2–56–2; Curran 6–1–24–1; de Grandhomme 7–2–20–1. *Second Innings*—Hogg 5–0–22–0; Hough 17–3–51–3; Fletcher 2–0–5–1; Traicos 15–6–33–0; de Grandhomme 4–0–21–0; Wallace 5–0–21–0; Curran 2–1–3–0.

Umpires: P. Latham and K. Kanjee.

†At Salisbury, March 21. PIA won by three wickets. Zimbabwe 203 for eight (50 overs) (T. W. Dunk 81); PIA 204 for seven (47.4 overs) (Mushtaq Mohammad 95 not out).

†At Umtali, March 24. Tied. A Zimbabwe XI 200 (48 overs) (G. Langlois 42, K. M. Curran 31; Liaqat Ali three for 38); PIA 200 (49 overs) (Naeem Ahmad 74, Ghulam Abbas 58; G. C. Wallace four for 14).

†At Bulawayo, March 27. Zimbabwe won by three wickets. PIA 205 (48 overs) (Hasan Jamil 65, Ghulam Abbas 49; D. A. G. Fletcher three for 30, K. M. Curran three for 34); Zimbabwe 208 for seven (46.5 overs) (C. A. T. Hodgson 52, R. D. Brown 42, A. J. Pycroft 31; Naeem Ahmad three for 51).

†At Bulawayo, March 28. Drawn. Zimbabwe 275 for eight (50 overs) (A. J. Pycroft 66, R. D. Brown 63, I. P. Butchart 41; Naeem Ahmad three for 34); PIA 239 for eight (46.1 overs) (Ghulam Abbas 77, Naeem Ahmad 38 not out, Asif Mohammad 38; V. R. Hogg three for 33).

†At Triangle, March 31. PIA won by 38 runs. PIA 178 (49.5 overs) (Shahid Mohammad 59; P. W. E. Rawson three for 31); A Zimbabwe XI 140 (44.2 overs) (J. G. Heron 38; Liaqat Ali three for 14).

ZIMBABWE v PIA

At Salisbury, April 2, 3, 5. Zimbabwe won by an innings and 45 runs.

PIA

Asif Mohammad c Fletcher b Hough	6	– c Hodgson b Hogg	9
Feroze Mehdi run out	6	– b Hogg	8
Shahid Mohammad c Houghton b Hough	18	– lbw b Hough	0
Mushtaq Mohammad c Butchart b Traicos	46	– c Butchart b Fletcher	18
Ghulam Abbas c Pycroft b Hogg	0	– (6) c Brown b Hough	40
Naeem Ahmad c and b Hogg	2	– (8) c and b Traicos	14
Aftab Baloch c Heron b Fletcher	19	– c Brown b Hough	5
Zafar Ahmed c Pycroft b Curran	11	– (9) c Heron b Curran	31
Zahid Ahmad c Curran b Fletcher	22	– (10) lbw b Hough	4
†Aquil Memon not out	7	– (4) c Brown b Butchart	55
Liaqat Ali b Fletcher	5	– not out	0
L-b 6, w 2, n-b 9	17	B 6, n-b 5	11
1/17 2/19 3/42 4/43 5/45 6/88 7/122 8/122 9/150	159	1/12 2/13 3/41 4/74 5/128 6/140 7/145 8/178 9/183	195

Bowling: *First Innings*—Hogg 23–5–48–2; Hough 17–3–35–2; Fletcher 14.4–4–28–3; Curran 4–1–19–1; Butchart 3–0–8–0; Traicos 6–3–4–1. *Second Innings*—Hogg 21–5–51–2; Hough 24–10–48–4; Traicos 23–14–38–1; Fletcher 11–5–25–1; Curran 5.4–1–19–1; Butchart 6–4–3–1.

Zimbabwe

†D. L. Houghton lbw b Mushtaq........ 83	I. P. Butchart c Zahid b Mushtaq....... 14
J. G. Heron c Naeem b Liaqat........... 43	K. M. Curran not out....................... 6
R. D. Brown st Memon b Naeem....... 0	B 5, l-b 13, w 2....................... 20
A. J. Pycroft c Shahid b Mushtaq....... 133	—
*D. A. G. Fletcher b Naeem............. 13	1/113 2/114 3/154 (7 wkts dec.) 399
C. A. T. Hodgson lbw b Mushtaq....... 87	4/177 5/337 6/377 7/399

A. J. Traicos, V. R. Hogg and E. J. Hough did not bat.

Bowling: Liaqat 30–4–111–1; Asif 4–1–14–0; Naeem 25–4–85–2; Mushtaq 20.3–2–103–4; Zafar 3–0–13–0; Zahid 3–0–30–0; Aftab 6–1–23–0.

Umpires: P. Latham and K. Kanjee.

†At Salisbury, April 4. Drawn. Zimbabwe 272 for six (50 overs) (D. A. G. Fletcher 95, C. A. T. Hodgson 59, A. J. Pycroft 42; Hasan Jamil three for 50); PIA 200 for six (37 overs) (Mushtaq Mohammad 59, Asif Mohammad 43; D. A. G. Fletcher three for 33).

MCC TOURS

An MCC team, captained by M. G. Griffith and managed by Lt-Col. J. R. Stephenson, toured East and Central Africa in October, 1981. Three countries of the East African Cricket Conference (Tanzania, Zambia and Malawi) were visited before the team travelled to Kenya for the last leg of their tour. Of the twelve matches played, MCC won nine and lost three, two of their defeats being at the hands of the Kenya Cricket Association. The team's most successful batsman was J. H. Hampshire, the vice-captain, who scored 574 runs at an average of 71.75.

The team was: M. G. Griffith *(captain)*, Lt-Col J. R. Stephenson *(manager)*, Asif Din, S. P. Coverdale, S. J. Dennis, S. Dyson, J. H. Hampshire, J. M. M. Hooper, R. J. Lanchbury, W. G. Merry, J. D. Monteith, M. C. J. Nicholas, R. LeQ. Savage and P. H. L. Wilson.

★ ★ ★ ★

An MCC team also paid a short visit to the Far East in October, 1981, playing four matches in Hong Kong, two in Singapore and one in Thailand. Three of the games were won, including a two-day game against the Singapore Cricket Association President's XI, and the others drawn. The team was: A. C. D. Ingleby-Mackenzie *(captain)*, J. A. Bailey *(manager)*, N. E. Briers, E. A. Clark, N. G. B. Cook, M. H. Denness, P. J. Kippax, M. D. Mence, N. E. J. Pocock, H. J. Rhodes, M. O. C. Sturt, F. J. Titmus and D. C. Wing.

★ ★ ★ ★

In September and October 1982, an MCC team toured the United States, playing ten matches in New Jersey, Washington, Philadelphia, Chicago, Los Angeles and San Francisco. Nine matches were won, including the two-day match against the United States Cricket Association XI, and one was drawn. The team was: A. R. Lewis (*captain*), F. W. Millett (*player/manager*), N. G. B. Cook, S. J. Dennis, C. F. E. Goldie, S. P. Henderson, R. P. Hodson, J. A. Jameson, W. G. Merry, Mushtaq Mohammad, N. E. J. Pocock, N. P. D. Ross and F. J. Titmus.

IRISH CRICKET IN 1982

By DEREK SCOTT

Ireland's record of 1981, played seven, won one, drawn three, lost three, was exactly repeated in 1982. The victory came against the same opponents, Wales. The blot on the escutcheon was the defeat by Scotland, the first such anywhere since 1977 and the first on Scottish soil since 1966. The venue was a new one, Myreside in Edinburgh (Ireland's previous seven matches in Edinburgh having been at the Grange club), but the change did not affect Ireland's luck, because a win has yet to be recorded in Edinburgh.

The Indians visited Ormeau, Belfast, in late May, the first Test-playing tourists to Northern Ireland since 1969, and played two one-day limited-overs matches. The first was washed out by a fifteen-minute downpour after India had made 179 for two (P. Roy 84 not out), and this same rain caused a late start to the second match, which was reduced from 55 to 50 overs each. Ireland reached 92 for three (E. A. McDermott 50) but subsided to 134 for nine, Doshi causing this collapse with four for 11 in nine overs. India won by five wickets in the 42nd over (R. J. Shastri 37).

For these matches Ireland retained their 1981 team, except for B. A. O'Brien who had retired. M. Halliday again captained the team in the continued absence of Monteith, who was not selected because he was still contracted to Middlesex for the NatWest Bank Trophy.

MCC came to Eglinton in the North-West somewhat short of bowling, not helped by the injury to Don Wilson. Rain cut the first day and also the first innings of both teams, so the match did not begin in earnest until the middle of the second day. Ireland made 216 for five, of which M. A. Masood, on his début, made 57 not out. Masood, a Pakistani who has lived in Dublin for five years, made 96 runs altogether in this match without being out. MCC needed 209 to win in 131 minutes, plus twenty overs (or one hour), and with ten of these bowled 62 runs were still needed. Then Corlett took five wickets in his last six overs, seven wickets went down in eleven overs and the last MCC man had to face the final ball of the match at 190 for nine. He survived.

Monteith, now available, had returned as captain in this match, while Shaun Bradley of the local club won a cap as wicket-keeper when P. B. Jackson was injured. Bradley had been a reserve on seventeen occasions, extending back to 1970. J. F. Short reached 2,000 runs for Ireland, the fourth to do so after Bergin, Anderson and O'Riordan, and also the quickest to do so.

The NatWest Bank Trophy match at Northampton followed the course of the previous two years, a reasonable performance but, as is said in school reports, "could have done better". Having won the toss Ireland were 54 without loss from nineteen overs, but they then subsided to 155 all out in 56.3 overs and have yet to go the distance. Northamptonshire, with five Test batsmen, got the runs for the loss of three wickets after being 71 for three. Corlett took two for 34 in ten overs and was unlucky not to have even better figures. Once again the generosity of Aer Lingus was greatly appreciated.

In the match against Wales at Rathmines, Dublin, in late July, the selectors restored the exciting John Prior to the team and introduced Peter O'Reilly, an eighteen-year-old fast bowler. Anderson and Corlett were not available. When

Ireland were put in, Masood made 109 in 173 minutes but was upstaged by Prior, who made 70 in 68 minutes. A score of 301 was sufficient to provide an 87-run lead, and in Ireland's second innings Short and McDermott put on 155 for the first wicket, 6 short of a 103-year-old record. Short hit his third century for Ireland (in 197 minutes) and his second in successive matches against Wales. Wales, needing 301 to win, got 251 and took the match aggregate to only 21 runs short of 1,000. Monteith took eight wickets in the match for 80 runs. It was his 23rd match as captain and his eighth win, equalling the wins as captain of A. J. O'Riordan.

Much as Ireland disliked being beaten by Scotland in August, Scotland won well and deserved to do so. McDermott, dropped after his 80 against Wales, came back when Masood cried off, and Jackson returned as wicket-keeper after his injury. Anderson, too, was again available. Unfortunately O'Reilly became ill on the first day and took very little part in the match, which saw Monteith's first defeat in 24 matches as captain, other than to the West Indians, Northamptonshire and Middlesex. (Match report and scorecard of Scotland v Ireland may be found on page 689.)

A batting extravaganza with a tinge of frustration was the outcome of the last match of the season, against Warwickshire at Rathmines. The first day produced 614 runs with nineteen 6s, Warwickshire leading off with 345 for four declared. K. D. Smith hit ten 6s in making 161 not out in 172 minutes, while Kallicharran needed only 68 minutes for his 96. Then came the most remarkable innings ever played by an Irish batsman for his country. John Prior, 22, of Dublin University and Old Belvedere, hammered 119 runs in 66 minutes off 66 balls, hitting four 6s and 21 4s in a series of marvellous strokes off back and front foot. His 50 came in 26 minutes, 100 in 51 minutes, and he went from 25 to 113 by means of boundaries only.

Ireland declared overnight at 269 for six and at one stage had the visitors 110 for eight, but Kallicharran prevented further ignominy with 51 not out in 43 minutes. The declaration set Ireland 239 in three hours, an exciting prospect if Prior could strike again; but he did not get in. Rain prevented play for an hour and the match petered out.

Mark Cohen and Stephen Warke returned to the Irish side for this match, for the first time in 1982. Warke, indeed, was at his work in Belfast when the match began, J. F. Short having called off only fifteen minutes earlier.

Five batsmen scored between 200 and 260 runs and Masood had the highest aggregate and the best average, 259 at 64.75. Monteith took seventeen wickets and now has 287, twenty short of J. C. Boucher's record. Corlett had the best average, 18.20 from fifteen wickets.

The inaugural Under-23 international against Cheshire at Sale was ruined by rain. The match against the Welsh Schools was played in Dublin and, for the first time, over three days. Ireland won relatively easily (their second successive win) by 97 runs, runs coming from Lewis and Rea, wickets from Lewis, Shannon and O'Reilly.

The Interprovincial tournament (Guinness Cup) was won by North Leinster, who won four and lost one of the five matches. It was their fourth win in all, the last being in 1975. Masood, in four innings, made two centuries and his 281 runs broke the competition record for runs in a season. McDermott also contributed runs and the wickets fell to O'Reilly, Halliday and Kirwan. Munster won two matches, a feat they had never achieved before, and finished second.

The Schweppes Cup, another innovation of the 1982 season, featured almost all the senior clubs in Ireland (32). Matches were of 50-overs-a-side duration and the Cup was contested on a knockout basis. In the first round it was stipulated that a team could not meet an opponent from its own area. The competition was a splendid success, except for the final, which was rain affected and became a 21-overs match which was won by North of Ireland club from Leinster club. This victory gave North of Ireland a cup double, as they had already won the Benson and Hedges-sponsored Northern Cricket Union Cup. Waringstown retained the League title.

In Munster, Limerick and Harlequins, respectively, won the Bank of Ireland-sponsored Cup and League, each for the first time. Donemana retained the North-West League while St Johnston, a team from Donegal, overwhelmed Strabane in the Cup final. Ian Rankin scored 167 in this final for St Johnston. The most consistent team in the Leinster area were Malahide. In the Tyler League they finished second to Leinster club (who retained their title); they lost the Cup final to Phoenix; and they shared the Wiggins Teape League with Old Belvedere.

M. A. Masood scored 1,010 runs for Phoenix, a new amateur record and within 128 runs of the professional record held by N. P. Daniels (Natal and Carlisle), set in 1981.

The Esso Cup, an Under-19 interprovincial competition, was shared by North-West and North Leinster. At Under-15 level, Leinster province won the interprovincial series for the fourth successive year.

In all, it was a poor summer for weather, but the game continued to grow and develop.

SCOTTISH CRICKET IN 1982

By WATSON BLAIR

Scotland's third season in the Benson and Hedges Cup again proved fruitless. With Brian Close still at the helm, it was anticipated that the Scots would improve on the promise shown in 1981, but apart from some fine individual performances, the reverse was the case.

Continuing the practice of the previous two years, Worcestershire provided Scotland's squad with two one-day practice matches, and in these some of the new players looked good. When the campaign proper started at Old Trafford, a fourth-wicket partnership of 98 between Omar Henry, the Western Province player in his third year as a professional with Poloc, and Sandy Brown raised Scottish hopes. Henry's 59 was the highest score in the competition for Scotland, and remained so until the final game, against Nottinghamshire at Titwood, when the Scottish captain, Richard Swan, brightened a sorry day for the Scots with a fine 69. Not one of the four matches was won, and throughout the competition Scotland's lack of bowlers with pace and penetration put them at a distinct disadvantage. The batting, too, was inconsistent.

Yet the team's critics were confounded by a fine performance against Worcestershire at Broughty Ferry. Batting first, the county declared, after only 72.3 overs, at 369 for eight. Turner, despite suffering from a bad cold, had raced to 50 in 40 minutes and 34 minutes later topped his century, well before lunch. Scotland's reply was positive. Aberdeenshire's Willie Donald, following an early-season injury, led the way with a sterling 92, featuring prominently with Swan in a third-wicket stand of 133 in 37 overs. And another century stand, 103 for the fifth wicket by Scott Weir and Andrew Ker, enabled the Scots to declare at 316 for five. The spin duo of veteran George Goddard and new cap Willie Morton halted the county's efforts to apply an early declaration, and when this did come, at 189 for eight, there was insufficient time to produce a result. Scotland's 128 for three, however, was heartening.

The rail strike created difficulties for the Scottish party travelling from Broughty Ferry to Arundel Castle and Lord's, but by plane and hired coach both fixtures were fulfilled. Donald was again Scotland's top scorer with 51 in a total of 235 for seven declared, while Lavinia, Duchess of Norfolk's XI were well in arrears at 172 for eight when play ended. At Lord's, two unbeaten centuries from R. A. B. Ezekowitz and S. G. Plumb allowed MCC a commanding declaration at 233 without loss, and despite two further declarations, a draw was inevitable. Scott Weir was Scotland's star, following his first-innings 61 with 102 not out in the second.

Rain ruined the Titwood two-day encounter with the Pakistani tourists. Wasim Raja scored an unbeaten 174 out of 351 for four declared, while Donald, with 53 not out, dominated Scotland's reply of 111 for five.

The disappointments of the season were almost erased with a fine eight-wicket win over Ireland at Myreside. Half-centuries by Chris Warner, Swan, Weir and Ker put Scotland in the driving seat with 315, a first-innings lead of 112, and Ireland's poor response of 167 left Scotland with 90 minutes to score 56. Donald, 34 not out, steered his side to success in the 22nd over, Scotland's first home win over Ireland since 1966.

A restricted "B" programme produced draws against Durham University and the SCU Hon. President's XI. Scotland's under 19s beat the Welsh Schools at Titwood but lost to the English Schools at Birmingham.

The Senior District Championship for the British Reserve Insurance Cup was won by the North.

The 1983 season sees the inauguration of a League Cup embracing the twenty leading clubs throughout Scotland. After the four groups have completed their programme, the top two clubs from each will participate in knockout rounds, with the winner receiving The Scottish Cup. The competition will be sponsored by Knight, Frank & Rutledge, who provided the finance for the 1982 cup, which was played in a knockout format only. In an interesting final at Raeburn Place, Drumpellier beat Stenhousemuir by 28 runs. Former Indian Test wicket-keeper, Budhi Kunderan, and Tom Porteous laid the foundations with a second-wicket partnership of 82, and a swashbuckling 60 off just nine overs from Dick McDougall and Billy McPate enabled the Coatbridge club to reach 213 for seven in the allotted overs. Stenhousemuir were always behind the rate, but until Morrison Zuill, playing a stubborn innings, was brilliantly run out by McDougall when 44, they were not completely out of the hunt.

Ayr set the pace in the D. M. Hall & Son Western Union, but by July Greenock were in the lead and finished clear winners. Ayr, Ferguslie and Clydesdale followed in that order. The new champions were indebted to Australian Peter Clifford whose tally of runs, 892, was only 53 short of the record aggregate set by Omar Henry in 1981. Altogether eleven centuries were scored in the Union. The awards to the top amateur batsman and bowler went to Don O'Connor (Clydesdale) and Billy McPate (Drumpellier) respectively.

The West League Cup was also won by Greenock, who beat Clydesdale comfortably in the final. The Glasgow club gained some consolation by defeating Poloc in the Rowan Charity Cup final. The Western Union 2nd XI championship was won by Clydesdale and Ferguslie were successful in the 3rd XI competition.

For the sixth successive year Heriot's FP carried off the Ryden & Partners East League, closely followed by Carlton. Stenhousemuir and Watsonians were respectively third and fourth. Edinburgh Academicals and Royal High were both relegated while Leith Franklin and Kirkcaldy move up. The Masterton Trophy was won by Carlton at the expense of Stenhousemuir.

There was an exciting conclusion to the Beneagles Scottish Counties. Aberdeenshire and West Lothian jostled each other for leadership right up to the final match, when the two clubs met and Aberdeenshire won by 58 runs at home to deprive their rivals of the title. Forfarshire, county champions in 1981, finished in third place but won the Beneagles Quaich with a narrow victory over Stirling County in the final. Ross Chapman, Stirling County's Australian professional, scored 773 runs in the championship, while the most successful bowler was Scottish international Peter Rhind, of Forfarshire, with 38 wickets.

The habit of deciding the champions of the North of Scotland CA on the last day of the season was continued. In the end Northern Counties finished on top and in addition won the Reserve League. Runners-up in the senior championship were Huntly. Elgin won the Knockout Cup with an easy win over Keith. The Batting Averages Cup changed hands but remained with Huntly, the successful player being Norman Rough. The runner-up, Dave Whincup of RAF Lossiemouth, had the satisfaction of winning the Macrae Aggregate Cup with a total of 587 runs, the only player to score over 500 runs in the season. Scott Campbell (Elgin) retained the Bowling Averages Cup while Phil Nealer (Fochabers) with 73 wickets obtained the Alex Smith Cup.

Prestwick and Helensburgh qualified for the new Scottish Cup by finishing first and second in the Abbey Life Glasgow and District League. Prestwick completed the double by winning the Knockout Competition.

The Grasshopper Strathmore Union title went to Aberdeen GSFP with Dundee HSFP in second place. The other competitions in that Union – the Flotex Three Counties Cup and the Six-a-side Tournament – were won by Mannofield XI and Arbroath United respectively.

Finally, Selkirk had a successful treble in the Blacklock Farries Border League, winning the Championship, the Border Knockout Cup and the Border Six-a-side Tournament. Kelso finished runners-up in the League while Peebles County finished at the top of the Reserve League.

There was a noteworthy event early in the season when, for the first time ever, a Test-playing country opened its United Kingdom programme with a match in Scotland. On Sunday, June 20, the Pakistani touring team played a Noor Mahal President's XI at Hamilton Crescent. A delightful innings of 64 by Mohsin Khan highlighted the visitors' 198 for six, to which the home side replied with 163 for six. The tourists were extremely popular both on and off the field, their visit provided Glasgow with a preview of the undoubted talent in the side, and Bader Islam, a Glasgow restauranteur, deserves much credit for bringing his fellow-countrymen to Scotland for that one-day match.

WOMEN'S CRICKET, 1982

by NETTA RHEINBERG

The 1982 World Cup

Australia proved just too good for England in the World Cup final in New Zealand in February, beating them by three wickets in the penultimate over. An exciting match, played in brilliant weather at Lancaster Park, Christchurch, before a crowd of some 3,000, the final provided attractive cricket from both teams and was given live TV coverage. Five teams – Australia, New Zealand, India, England, and an International XI – competed in the five-week, limited-overs-match series covering both North and South Islands, each side playing the others three times. England won seven matches, lost three and tied two.

In retrospect, the general opinion is that Australia deserved to win, that India showed remarkable progress and enthusiasm and have become worthy competitors, and that England are mistaken if they consider themselves able to fend off all challengers. The outcome has been continued efforts to foster cricket at junior level and this is already showing promising signs for the future.

WORLD CUP TABLE

	Played	*Won*	*Tied*	*Lost*	*Pts*
Australia	12	11	1	0	46
England	12	7	2	3	32
New Zealand	12	6	1	5	26
India	12	4	0	8	16
International XI	12	0	0	12	0

AUSTRALIA v ENGLAND

World Cup Final

At Christchurch, February 7. Australia won by three wickets.

England

*S. Goatman b Fullston	29	G. Hullah not out	1
J. Brittin c and b Cornish	17	B 5, l-b 7, w 1	13
C. Watmough c Kennare b Fullston	9		—
J. Southgate c Hill b Tredrea	53	1/42 2/54 (5 wkts, 60 overs)	151
R. Heyhoe-Flint c Fullston b Tredrea	29	3/63 4/150 5/151	

C. Hodges, E. Bakewell, J. Tedstone, A. Starling and †S. Hodges did not bat.

Bowling: Tredrea 12–2–36–2; Martin 12–2–31–0; Cornish 12–6–17–1; Thompson 12–2–34–0; Fullston 12–3–20–2.

Australia

P. Vercoe c Goatman b Starling	7	R. Thompson run out	3
S. Hill c Goatman b Starling	12	L. Fullston not out	0
J. Kennare run out	4	B 2, l-b 3, w 1, n-b 2	8
K. Read c Southgate b Tedstone	32		
*S. Tredrea c S. Hodges b C. Hodges	25	1/18 (7 wkts, 59 overs)	152
J. Jacobs run out	37	2/22 3/28 4/82	
M. Cornish not out	24	5/97 6/134 7/145	

†T. Russell and D. Martin did not bat.

Bowling: Tedstone 12–4–24–1; Starling 11–3–21–2; Hullah 11–0–35–0; Bakewell 12–3–26–0; C. Hodges 12–1–33–1; Watmough 1–0–5–0.

Umpires: H. D. Bird and F. R. Goodall.

England Captaincy

After returning from the World Cup, Sue Goatman (Kent), the England captain, announced her retirement. She led the team for three years, having previously captained Young England, and was a capable leader and first-class player with six centuries in major games to her credit. One of these was notched up in 130 minutes against the Australians in 1976. Her successor is Jan Southgate (Sussex), a prolific scorer and experienced player who made an impressive and memorable 201 not out for the South in a trial match at Oakham School in May, double-centuries being a rarity in women's cricket. With England following their visit to the West Indies for a Test series in February 1983 with a tour to Australia in 1984, to celebrate the Golden Jubilee of the Australian Women's Cricket Council, her captaincy will be watched with interest.

Sponsorship

Sponsorship, or rather the lack of it, continues to be a major problem. There are very few members willing, or indeed in a position, to interest sponsors in providing the right sort of money for home or overseas visits, and such are circumstances now that the Women's Cricket Association cannot prepare or organise tours of the desired standard without recourse to sponsorship.

New Zealand recently royally entertained teams in the World Cup. They were helped by sponsorship from a soft drinks firm and a grant from the New Zealand government towards a total cost in the region of £70,000. Women cricketers are amateurs who do not earn their living from the game and have to resort to sponsorship and to raising funds to fulfil the role of hostess (or visitors) to other countries. This situation brings many conflicting views to the fore and this year, owing to this problem, there have been serious misunderstandings among officers, leading to resignations from the WCA committee.

Except for a visit for the World Cup in 1973, New Zealand's last tour to England for a Test series was in 1966, and the WCA is most conscious of the fact that an invitation to them is long overdue. Already a tentative invitation issued to them for 1982 could not, for financial reasons, be ratified. At the time of writing, an effort is being made to raise £20,000 by January 1983 to swell the

General Tour and Hospitality Fund, with a view to renewing the invitation for 1984. Clubs and counties have all taken part, each having been given a specific target, added to which a number of matches against men have been organised. The latter prove good fund raisers; provided, of course, the weather is good.

Other member countries of the International Women's Cricket Council have similar problems, with the exception perhaps of India. For instance, Australia will host the next World Cup tournament in 1986 and this, together with the Golden Jubilee of the Australian Women's Cricket Council in 1984, places a heavy burden on their organisation. In this connection it is worth mentioning that there has been a change of officials in the IWCC, and all are now Australians.

Season 1982

At home, the season was an active one. The County Championship was won by West Midlands, who beat East Anglia by five wickets. The National Club Championship was won for the fourth consecutive year by Gunnersbury, who beat North Riding by 73 runs.

The Dutch National XI visited England at the end of July, playing East Anglia, Kent and Young England in a rain-interrupted tour, the last two games being at the St Lawrence Ground, Canterbury.

With more than twenty women's cricket clubs in Ireland, of which fourteen are in the Dublin area, an inter-provincial competition has been established. An interesting and detailed history of women's cricket in Ireland has been compiled by Isolda Howard, who has been a mainstay of women's cricket in that country for many years and is an avid follower of the game.

Denmark's women's team may well soon come to the notice of the cricketing public. Pioneered and coached by Peter Hargreaves, they are planning matches on their home ground against both Dutch and young England players in 1983.

BIRTHS AND DEATHS OF CRICKETERS

The qualifications are as follows:

1. All players who have appeared in a Test match.

2. Players who have appeared in 50 or more first-class matches during their career and did not die prior to 1973. Owing to the difficulty in obtaining records from India and Pakistan, these countries are not included under this qualification.

3. Players who appeared in fifteen or more first-class matches in the 1982 English season.

4. English county captains, county caps and captains of Oxford and Cambridge Universities who did not die prior to 1973.

5. Oxford and Cambridge Blues of the last ten years. Earlier Blues may be found in previous *Wisdens*.

6. All players chosen as *Wisden* Cricketers of the Year, including the Public Schoolboys chosen for the 1918 and 1919 Almanacks. Cricketers of the Year are identified by the italic notation *CY* and year of appearance.

7. Players or personalities not otherwise qualified who are of sufficient fame or interest to merit inclusion.

Although the country is given for most overseas players, it is not done so for England players. There is a full list of Test Cricketers from page 113.

Aamer Hameed (Oxford U.) b Oct. 18, 1954
Abberley, R. N. (Warw.) b April 22, 1944
A'Beckett, E. L. (Australia) b Aug. 11, 1907
Abdul Kadir (Pakistan) b May 5, 1944
Abdul Qadir Khan (Pakistan) b Sept. 15, 1955
Abel, R. (Surrey; *CY 1890*) b Nov. 30, 1857, d Dec. 10, 1936
Abell, Sir G. E. B. (Oxford U., Worcs. and N. India) b June 22, 1904
Aberdare, 3rd Lord (*see* Bruce, Hon. C. N.)
Abid Ali, S. (India) b Sept. 9, 1941
Abrahams, J. (Lancs.) b July 21, 1952
Absolom, C. A. (Camb. U. and Kent) b June 7, 1846, d July 30, 1889
Acfield D. L. (Camb. U. and Essex) b July 24, 1947
Achong, E. (W. Indies) b Feb. 16, 1904
Ackerman, H. M. (Border, NE Transvaal, Northants, Natal and W. Province) b April 28, 1947
A'Court, D. G. (Glos.) b July 27, 1937
Adam, Sir Ronald, 2nd Bt (Pres. MCC 1946-47) b Oct. 30, 1885, d Dec. 26, 1982
Adams, P. W. (Cheltenham and Sussex; *CY 1919*) b 1900, d Feb. 28, 1962
Adcock, N. A. T. (S. Africa; *CY 1961*) b March 8, 1931
Adhikari, Col. H. R. (India) b July 31, 1919
Afaq Hussain (Pakistan) b Dec. 31, 1939
Aftab Baloch (Pakistan) b April 1, 1953
Aftab Gul (Pakistan) b March 31, 1946
Agha Saadat Ali (Pakistan) b June 21, 1929
Agha Zahid (Pakistan) b Jan. 7, 1953
Agnew, J. P. (Leics.) b April 4, 1960
Ainsworth, Lt-Cdr M. L. Y. (Worcs.) b May 13, 1922, d Aug. 28, 1978
Aird, R. (Camb. U. and Hants; Sec. MCC 1953-62, Pres. MCC 1968-69) b May 4, 1902
Aitchison, Rev. J. K. (Scotland) b May 26, 1920
Alabaster, G. D. (Canterbury, N. Districts and Otago) b Dec. 10, 1933
Alabaster, J. C. (N. Zealand) b July 11, 1930
Alcock, C. W. (Sec. Surrey CCC 1872-1907, Editor *Cricket* 1882-1907) b Dec. 2, 1842, d Feb. 26, 1907
Alderman, A. E. (Derby.) b Oct. 30, 1907
Alderman, T. M. (Australia; *CY 1982*) b June 12, 1956
Aldridge, K. J. (Worcs. and Tasmania) b March 13, 1935
Alexander of Tunis, 1st Lord (Pres. MCC 1955-56) b Dec. 10, 1891, d June 16, 1969
Alexander, F. C. M. (Camb. U. and W. Indies) b Nov. 2, 1928
Alexander, G. (Australia) b April 22, 1851, d Nov. 6, 1930

Alexander, H. H. (Australia) b June 9, 1905
Alim-ud-Din (Pakistan) b Dec. 15, 1930
Allan, D. W. (W. Indies) b Nov. 5, 1937
Allan, F. E. (Australia) b Dec. 2, 1849, d Feb. 9, 1917
Allan, J. M. (Oxford U., Kent, Warw. and Scotland) b April 2, 1932
Allan, P. J. (Australia) b Dec. 31, 1935
Allbrook, M. E. (Camb. U., Kent and Notts.) b Nov. 15, 1954
Allcott, C. F. W. (N. Zealand) b Oct. 7, 1896, d Nov. 21, 1973
Allen, A. W. (Camb. U. and Northants) b Dec. 22, 1912
Allen, B. O. (Camb. U. and Glos.) b Oct. 13, 1911, d May 1, 1981
Allen, D. A. (Glos.) b Oct. 29, 1935
Allen, G. O. (Camb. U. and Middx; Pres. MCC 1963-64) b Sydney July 31, 1902
Allen, J. C. (Leeward I.) b Aug. 18, 1951
Allen, M. H. J. (Northants and Derby.) b Jan. 7, 1933
Allen, R. C. (Australia) b July 2, 1858, d May 2, 1952
Alletson, E. B. (Notts.) b March 6, 1884, d July 5, 1963
Alley, W. E. (NSW and Somerset; *CY 1962*) b Feb. 3, 1919
Alleyne, H. L. (Barbados and Worcs.) b Feb. 28, 1957
Allom, M. J. C. (Camb. U. and Surrey; Pres. MCC 1969-70) b March 23, 1906
Allott, P. J. W. (Lancs.) b Sept. 14, 1956
Altham, H. S. (Oxford U., Surrey and Hants; Pres. MCC 1959-60) b Nov. 30, 1888, d March 11, 1965
Amarnath, Lala (India) b Sept. 11, 1911
Amarnath, M. (India) b Sept. 24, 1950
Amarnath, S. (India) b Dec. 30, 1948
Amar Singh, L. (India) b Dec. 4, 1910, d May 20, 1940
Ames, L. E. G. (Kent; *CY 1929*) b Dec. 3, 1905
Amir Elahi (India and Pakistan) b Sept. 1, 1908, d Dec. 28, 1980
Amiss, D. L. (Warw.; *CY 1975*) b April 7, 1943
Anderson, I. S. (Derby.) b April 24, 1960
Anderson, J. H. (S. Africa) b April 26, 1874, d March 11, 1926
Anderson, R. W. (N. Zealand) b Oct. 2, 1948
Anderson, W. McD. (N. Zealand) b Oct. 8, 1919, d Dec. 21, 1979
Andrew, K. V. (Northants) b Dec. 15, 1929
Andrews, B. (N. Zealand) b April 4, 1945
Andrews, T. J. E. (Australia) b Aug. 26, 1890, d Jan. 28, 1970
Andrews, W. H. R. (Somerset) b April 14, 1908
Angell, F. L. (Somerset) b June 29, 1922
Anwar Hussain (Pakistan) b July 16, 1920
Anwar Khan (Pakistan) b Dec. 24, 1955
Appleyard, R. (Yorks.; *CY 1952*) b June 27, 1924
Apte, A. L. (India) b Sept. 29, 1934
Apte, M. L. (India) b Oct. 5, 1932
Archer, A. G. (Worcs.) b Dec. 6, 1871, d July 15, 1935
Archer, K. A. (Australia) b Jan. 18, 1928
Archer, R. G. (Australia) b Oct. 25, 1933
Arif Butt (Pakistan) b May 17, 1944
Arlott, John, (Writer and Broadcaster) b Feb. 25, 1914
Armitage, R. L. S. (E. Province and N. Transvaal) b July 9, 1955
Armitage, T. (Yorks.) b April 25, 1848, d Sept. 21, 1922
Armstrong, N. F. (Leics.) b Dec. 22, 1892
Armstrong, T. R. (Derby.) b Oct. 13, 1909
Armstrong, W. W. (Australia; *CY 1903*) b May 22, 1879, d July 13, 1947
Arnold, E. G. (Worcs.) b Nov. 7, 1876, d Oct. 25, 1942
Arnold, G. G. (Surrey and Sussex; *CY 1972*) b Sept. 3, 1944
Arnold, J. (Hants) b Nov. 30, 1907
Arnold, A. P. (Canterbury and Northants) b Oct. 16, 1926
Arnott, T. (Glam.) b Feb. 16, 1902, d Feb. 2, 1975
Asgarali, N. (W. Indies) b Dec. 12, 1922
Ashdown, W. H. (Kent) b Dec. 27, 1898, d Sept. 15, 1979
Ashley, W. H. (S. Africa) b Feb. 10, 1862, d July 14, 1930
Ashraf Ali (Pakistan) b April 22, 1958
Ashton, Sqdn-Ldr C. T. (Camb. U. and Essex) b Feb. 19, 1901, d Oct. 31, 1942
Ashton, G. (Camb. U. and Worcs.) b Sept. 27, 1896, d Feb. 6, 1981
Ashton, Sir H. (Camb. U. and Essex; *CY 1922*; Pres. MCC 1960-61) b Feb. 13, 1898, d June 17, 1979
Asif Din. M. (Warw.) b Sept. 21, 1960
Asif Iqbal (Kent and Pakistan; *CY 1968*) b June 6, 1943
Asif Masood, S. (Pakistan) b Jan. 23, 1946
Aslett, D. G. (Kent) b Feb. 12, 1958
Aspinall, R. (Yorks.) b Nov. 27, 1918
Astill, W. E. (Leics.; *CY 1933*) b March 1, 1888, d Feb. 10, 1948
Athey, C. W. J. (Yorks.) b Sept. 27, 1957
Atkinson, C. R. M. (Somerset) b July 23, 1931
Atkinson, D. St E. (W. Indies) b Aug. 9, 1926
Atkinson, E. St E. (W. Indies) b Nov. 6, 1927
Atkinson, G. (Somerset and Lancs.) b March 29, 1938
Atkinson, T. (Notts.) b Sept. 27, 1930

Attenborough, G. R. (S. Australia) b Jan. 17, 1951
Attewell, W. (Notts.; *CY 1892*) b June 12, 1861, d June 11, 1927
Austin, Sir H. B. G. (Barbados) b July 15, 1877, d July 27, 1943
Austin, R. A. (W. Indies) b Sept. 5, 1954
Avery, A. V. (Essex) b Dec. 19, 1914
Aworth, C. J. (Camb. U. and Surrey) b Feb. 19, 1953
Aylward, J. (Hants and All-England) b 1741, d Dec. 27, 1827
Azhar Khan (Pakistan) b Sept. 7, 1955
Azmat Rana (Pakistan) b Nov. 3, 1951

Bacchus, S. F. A. (W. Indies) b Jan. 31, 1954
Bacher, Dr A. (S. Africa) b May 24, 1942
Badcock, C. L. (Australia) b April 10, 1914
Badcock, F. T. (N. Zealand) b Aug. 9, 1898
Baggallay, R. R. C. (Derby.) b May 4, 1884, d Dec. 12, 1975
Bagnall, H. F. (Camb. U. and Northants) b Feb. 18, 1904, d Sept. 2, 1974
Baichan, L. (W. Indies) b May 12, 1946
Baig, A. A. (Oxford U., Somerset and India) b March 19, 1939
Bailey, D. (Durham, Lancs. and Cheshire) b Sept. 9, 1944
Bailey, Sir Derrick (D. T. L.) (Glos.) b August 5, 1918
Bailey, J. (Hants) b April 6, 1908
Bailey, J. A. (Essex and Oxford U.; Sec. MCC 1974-) b June 22, 1930
Bailey, T. E. (Essex and Camb. U.; *CY 1950*) b Dec. 3, 1923
Bainbridge, P. (Glos.) b April 16, 1958
Bairstow, D. L. (Yorks. and Griqualand W.) b Sept. 1, 1951
Baker, C. S. (Warw.) b Jan. 5, 1883, d Dec. 16 1976
Baker, R. K. (Camb. U. and Essex) b April 28, 1952
Baker, R. P. (Surrey) b April 9, 1954
Bakewell, A. H. (Northants; *CY 1934*) b Nov. 2, 1908
Balaskas, X. C. (S. Africa) b Oct. 15, 1910
Balderstone, J. C. (Yorks. and Leics.) b Nov. 16, 1940
Baldry, D. O. (Middx and Hants) b Dec. 26, 1931
Baldwin, H. G. (Surrey; Umpire) b March 16, 1893, d March 7, 1969
Banerjee, S. A. (India) b Nov. 1, 1919
Banerjee, S. N. (India) b Oct. 3, 1913, d Oct. 14, 1980
Bannerman, A. C. (Australia) b March 21, 1854, d Sept. 19, 1924
Bannerman, Charles (Australia) b Woolwich, Kent July 23, 1851, d Aug. 20, 1930
Bannister, C. S. (Camb. U.) b May 22, 1956
Bannister, J. D. (Warw.) b Aug. 23, 1930
Barber, A. T. (Oxford U. and Yorks.) b June 17, 1905
Barber, R. T. (N. Zealand) b June 23, 1925
Barber, R. W. (Lancs., Camb. U. and Warw.; *CY 1967*) b Sept. 26, 1935
Barber, W. (Yorks.) b April 18, 1901, d Sept. 10, 1968
Barclay, J. R. T. (Sussex and Orange Free State) b Jan. 22, 1954
Bardsley, W. (Australia; *CY 1910*) b Dec. 7, 1882, d Jan. 20, 1954
Baring, A. E. G. (Hants) b Jan. 21, 1910
Barker, G. (Essex) b July 6, 1931
Barling, T. H. (Surrey) b Sept. 1, 1906
Barlow, A. (Lancs.) b Aug. 31, 1915
Barlow, E. A. (Oxford U. and Lancs.) b Feb. 24, 1912, d June 27, 1980
Barlow, E. J. (Derby. and S. Africa) b Aug. 12, 1940
Barlow, G. D. (Middx) b March 26, 1950
Barlow, R. G. (Lancs.) b May 28, 1851, d July 31, 1919
Barnard, H. M. (Hants) b July 18, 1933
Barnes, A. R. (Sec. Australian Cricket Board 1960-81) b Sept. 12, 1916
Barnes, S. F. (Warw. and Lancs.; *CY 1910*) b April 19, 1873, d Dec. 26, 1967
Barnes, S. G. (Australia) b June 5, 1916, d Dec. 16, 1973
Barnes, W. (Notts.; *CY 1890*) b May 27, 1852, d March 24, 1899
Barnett, B. A. (Australia) b May 23, 1908, d June 29, 1979
Barnett, C. J. (Glos.; *CY 1937*) b July 3, 1910
Barnett, K. J. (Derby.) b July 17, 1960
Barnwell, C. J. P. (Somerset) b June 23, 1914
Baroda, Maharaja of (Manager, India in England, 1959) b April 2, 1930
Barratt, Fred (Notts.) b April 12, 1894, d Jan. 29, 1947
Barratt, R. J. (Leics.) b May 3, 1942
Barrett, A. G. (W. Indies) b Jan. 4, 1944
Barrett, J. E. (Australia) b Oct. 15, 1866, d Feb. 9, 1916
Barrick, D. W. (Northants) b April 28, 1926
Barrington, K. F. (Surrey; *CY 1960*) b Nov. 24, 1930, d March 14, 1981
Barrington, W. E. J. (Camb. U.) b Jan. 4, 1960
Barron, W. (Lancs. and Northants) b Oct. 26, 1917
Barrow, A. (Natal) b Jan. 23, 1955
Barrow, I. (W. Indies) b Jan. 6, 1911, d April 2, 1979
Bartholomew, P. C. S. (Trinidad) b Oct. 9, 1939

Bartlett, E. L. (W. Indies) b March 18, 1906, d Dec. 21, 1976
Bartlett, G. A. (N. Zealand) b Feb. 3, 1941
Bartlett, H. T. (Camb. U., Surrey and Sussex; *CY 1939*) b Oct. 7, 1914
Bartley, T. J. (Umpire) b March 19, 1908, d April 2, 1964
Barton, M. R. (Oxford U. and Surrey) b Oct. 14, 1914
Barton, P. T. (N. Zealand) b Oct. 9, 1935
Barton, V. A. (Kent and Hants) b Oct. 6, 1867, d March 23, 1906
Barwick, S. R. (Glam.) b Sept. 6, 1960
Bates, D. L. (Sussex) b May 10, 1933
Bates, W. (Yorks.) b Nov. 19, 1855, d Jan. 8, 1900
Bath, B. F. (Transvaal) b Jan. 16, 1947
Baumgartner, H. V. (S. Africa) b Nov. 17, 1883, d April 8, 1938
Baxter, A. D. (Devon, Lancs., Middx and Scotland) b Jan. 20, 1910
Bean, G. (Notts. and Sussex) b March 7, 1864, d March 16, 1923
Bear, M. J. (Essex and Canterbury) b Feb. 23, 1934
Beard, D. D. (N. Zealand) b Jan. 14, 1920, d July 15, 1982
Beard, G. R. (Australia) b Aug. 19, 1950
Beauclerk, Lord Frederick (Middx, Surrey and MCC) b May 8, 1773, d April 22, 1850
Beaufort, 10th Duke of (Pres. MCC 1952-53) b April 4, 1900
Beaumont, D. J. (Camb. U.) b Sept. 1, 1944
Beaumont, R. (S. Africa) b Feb. 4, 1884, d May 25, 1958
Beck, J. E. F. (N. Zealand) b Aug. 1, 1934
Bedford, P. I. (Middx) b Feb. 11, 1930, d Sept. 18, 1966
Bedi, B. S. (Northants and India) b Sept. 25, 1946
Bedser, A. V. (Surrey; *CY 1947*) b July 4, 1918
Bedser, E. A. (Surrey) b July 4, 1918
Beet, G. (Derby.; Umpire) b April 24, 1886, d Dec. 13, 1946
Begbie, D. W. (S. Africa) b Dec. 12, 1914
Beldham, W. (Hambledon and Surrey) b Feb. 5, 1766, d Feb. 20, 1862
Bell, A. J. (S. Africa) b April 15, 1906
Bell, J. T. (Yorks. and Glam.) b June 16, 1896, d Aug. 8, 1974
Bell, R. V. (Middx and Sussex) b Jan. 7, 1931
Bell, W. (N. Zealand) b Sept. 5, 1931
Bellamy, B. W. (Northants) b April 22, 1891
Benaud, J. (Australia) b May 11, 1944
Benaud, R. (Australia; *CY 1962*) b Oct. 6, 1930
Bennett, B. W. P. (Camb. U.) b Feb. 6, 1955
Bennett, C. T. (Camb. U., Surrey and Middx) b Aug. 10, 1902, d Feb. 3, 1978
Bennett, D. (Middx) b Dec. 18, 1933
Bennett, G. M. (Somerset) b Dec. 17, 1909, d July 26, 1982
Bennett, N. H. (Surrey) b Sept. 23, 1912
Bennett, R. (Lancs.) b June 16, 1940
Benson, M. R. (Kent) b July 6, 1958
Bensted, E. C. (Queensland) b Feb. 11, 1901, d Jan. 21, 1980
Bernard, Dr. J. R. (Camb. U. and Glos.) b Dec. 7, 1938
Berry, L. G. [G. L.] (Leics.) b April 28, 1906
Berry, R. (Lancs., Worcs. and Derby.) b Jan. 29, 1926
Beslee, G. P. (Kent) b March 27, 1904
Bessant, J. G. (Glos.) b Nov. 11, 1895, d Jan. 18, 1982
Bestall, D. (N. Transvaal, Natal and E. Province) b May 28, 1952
Betancourt, N. (W. Indies) b June 4, 1887, d Oct. 12, 1947
Bezuidenhout, S. J. (E. Province) b July 11, 1946
Bhandari, P. (India) b Nov. 27, 1935
Bick, D. A. (Middx) b Feb. 22, 1936
Bickmore, A. F. (Oxford U. and Kent) b May 19, 1899, d March 18, 1979
Biddulph, K. D. (Somerset) b May 29, 1932
Biggs, A. L. (E. Province) b April 26, 1946
Bilby, G. P. (N. Zealand) b May 7, 1941
Binks, J. G. (Yorks.; *CY 1969*) b Oct. 15, 1935
Binny, R. M. H. (India) b July 19, 1955
Binns, A. P. (W. Indies) b July 24, 1929
Birch, J. D. (Notts.) b June 18, 1955
Bird, H. D. (Yorks. and Leics.; umpire) b April 19, 1933
Bird, M. C. (Lancs. and Surrey) b March 25, 1888, d Dec. 9, 1933
Bird, R. E. (Worcs.) b April 4, 1915
Birkenshaw, J. (Yorks., Leics. and Worcs.) b Nov. 13, 1940
Birkett, L. S. (W. Indies) b April 14, 1904
Birrell, H. B. (E. Province, Rhodesia and Oxford U.) b Dec. 1, 1927
Bisset, Sir Murray (S. Africa) b April 14, 1876, d Oct. 24, 1931
Bissett, G. F. (S. Africa) b Nov. 5, 1905, d Nov. 14, 1965
Bissex, M. (Glos.) b Sept. 28, 1944
Blackham, J. McC. (Australia; *CY 1891*) b May 11, 1853, d Dec. 27, 1932
Blackie, D. D. (Australia) b April 5, 1882, d April 18, 1955
Blackledge, J. F. (Lancs.) b April 15, 1928
Blair, R. W. (N. Zealand) b June 23, 1932

Blair, W. L. (Otago) b May 11, 1948
Blake, D. E. (Hants) b April 27, 1925
Blake, Rev. P. D. S. (Oxford U. and Sussex) b May 23, 1927
Blanckenberg, J. M. (S. Africa) b Dec. 31, 1893, 'presumed dead'
Bland, K. C. (S. Africa; *CY 1966*) b April 5, 1938
Blenkiron, W. (Warw.) b July 21, 1942
Bligh, Hon. Ivo F. W. (*see* 8th Earl of Darnley)
Block, S. A. (Camb. U. and Surrey) b July 15, 1908, d Oct. 7, 1979
Blofeld, H. C. (Camb. U.; Writer and Broadcaster) b Sept. 23, 1939
Blundell, Sir E. D. (Camb. U. and N. Zealand) b May 29, 1907
Blunt, R. C. (N. Zealand; *CY 1928*) b Durham, England Nov. 3, 1900, d London June 22, 1966
Blythe, C. (Kent; *CY 1904*) b May 30, 1879, d Nov. 8, 1917
Board, J. H. (Glos.) b Feb. 23, 1867, d at sea April 16, 1924
Bock, E. G. (S. Africa) b Sept. 17, 1908, d Sept. 5, 1961
Boddington, R. A. (Lancs.) b June 30, 1892, d Aug. 5, 1977
Bodkin, P. E. (Camb. U.) b Sept. 15, 1924
Bolton, B. A. (N. Zealand) b May 31, 1935
Bolus, J. B. (Yorks., Notts. and Derby.) b Jan. 31, 1934
Bond, G. E. (S. Africa) b April 5, 1909, d Aug. 27, 1965
Bond, J. D. (Lancs. and Notts.; *CY 1971*) b May 6, 1932
Bonnor, G. J. (Australia) b Feb. 25, 1855, d June 27, 1912
Boock, S. L. (N. Zealand) b Sept. 20, 1951
Booth, A. (Yorks.) b Nov. 3, 1902, d Aug. 17, 1974
Booth, B. C. (Australia) b Oct. 19, 1933
Booth, B. J. (Lancs. and Leics.) b Dec. 3, 1935
Booth, F. S. (Lancs.) b Feb. 12, 1907, d Jan. 21, 1980
Booth, M. W. (Yorks.; *CY 1914*) b Dec. 10, 1886, d July 1, 1916
Booth, P. (Leics.) b Nov. 2, 1952
Booth, R. (Yorks. and Worcs.) b Oct. 1, 1926
Borde, C. G. (India) b July 21, 1934
Border, A. R. (Glos. and Australia; *CY 1982*) b July 27, 1955
Bore, M. K. (Yorks. and Notts.) b June 2, 1947
Borrington, A. J. (Derby.) b Dec. 8, 1948
Bosanquet, B. J. T. (Oxford U. and Middx; *CY 1905*) b Oct. 13, 1877, d Oct. 12, 1936
Boshier, B. S. (Leics.) b March 6, 1932
Botham, I. T. (Somerset; *CY 1978*) b Nov. 24, 1955
Botten, J. T. (S. Africa) b June 21, 1938
Botton, N. D. (Oxford U.) b June 21, 1954
Boucher, J. C. (Ireland) b Dec. 22, 1910
Bourne, W. A. (Barbados and Warw.) b Nov. 15, 1952
Bowden, M. P. (Surrey and Transvaal) b Nov. 1, 1865, d Feb. 19, 1892
Bowditch, M. H. (W. Province) b Aug. 30, 1945
Bowes, W. E. (Yorks.; *CY 1932*) b July 25, 1908
Bowley, E. H. (Sussex and Auckland; *CY 1930*) b June 6, 1890, d July 9, 1974
Bowley, F. L. (Worcs.) b Nov. 9, 1873, d May 31, 1943
Bowman, R. (Oxford U. and Lancs.) b Jan. 26, 1934
Box, T. (Sussex) b Feb. 7, 1808, d July 12, 1876
Boyce, K. D. (Essex and W. Indies; *CY 1974*) b Oct. 11, 1943
Boycott, G. (Yorks. and N. Transvaal; *CY 1965*) b Oct. 21, 1940
Boyd-Moss, R. J. (Camb. U. and Northants) b Dec. 16, 1959
Boyes, G. S. (Hants) b March 31, 1899, d Feb. 11, 1973
Boyle, H. F. (Australia) b Dec. 10, 1847, d Nov. 21, 1907
Bracewell, B. P. (N. Zealand) b Sept. 14, 1959
Bracewell, J. G. (N. Zealand) b April 15, 1958
Bradburn, W. P. (N. Zealand) b Nov. 24, 1938
Bradley, W. M. (Kent) b Jan. 2, 1875, d June 19, 1944
Bradman, Sir D. G. (Australia; *CY 1931*) b Aug. 27, 1908
Bradshaw, J. C. (Leics.) b Jan. 25, 1902
Brain, B. M. (Worcs. and Glos.) b Sept. 13, 1940
Brann, W. H. (S. Africa) b April 4, 1899, d Sept. 22, 1953
Brassington, A. J. (Glos.) b Aug. 9, 1954
Bratchford, J. D. (Queensland) b Feb. 2, 1929
Braund, L. C. (Surrey and Somerset; *CY 1902*) b Oct. 18, 1875, d Dec. 22, 1955
Bray, C. (Essex) b April 6, 1898
Brayshaw, I. J. (W. Australia) b Jan. 14, 1942
Brazier, A. F. (Surrey and Kent) b Dec. 7, 1924
Breakwell, D. (Northants and Somerset) b July 2, 1948
Brearley, J. M. (Camb. U. and Middx; *CY 1977*) b April 28, 1942
Brearley, W. (Lancs.; *CY 1909*) b March 11, 1876, d Jan. 30, 1937
Brennan, D. V. (Yorks.) b Feb. 10, 1920

Brettell, D. N. (Oxford U.) b March 10, 1956
Brickett, D. J. (E. Province) b Dec. 9, 1950
Bridge, W. B. (Warw.) b May 29, 1938
Bridger, Rev. J. R. (Hants) b April 8, 1920
Brierley, T. L. (Glam. and Lancs.) b June 15, 1910
Briers, N. E. (Leics.) b Jan. 15, 1955
Briggs, John (Lancs.; *CY 1889*) b Oct. 3, 1862, d Jan. 11, 1902
Bright, R. J. (Australia) b July 13, 1954
Briscoe, A. W. (S. Africa) b Feb. 6, 1911, d April 22, 1941
Broad, B. C. (Glos.) b Sept. 29, 1957
Broadbent, R. G. (Worcs.) b June 21, 1924
Brocklebank, Sir J. M. Bt (Camb. U. and Lancs.) b Sept. 3, 1915, d Sept. 13, 1974
Brocklehurst, B. G. (Somerset) b Feb. 18, 1922
Brockwell, W. (Kimberley and Surrey; *CY 1895*) b Jan. 21, 1865, d July 1, 1935
Broderick, V. (Northants) b Aug. 17, 1920
Brodhurst, A. H. (Camb. U. and Glos.) b July 21, 1916
Bromfield, H. D. (S. Africa) b June 26, 1932
Bromley, E. H. (Australia) b Sept. 2, 1912, d Feb. 1, 1967
Bromley-Davenport, H. R. (Camb. U., Cheshire and Middx) b Aug. 18, 1870, d May 23, 1954
Brooker, M. E. W. (Camb. U.) b March 24, 1954
Brookes, D. (Northants; *CY 1957*) b Oct. 29, 1915
Brookes, W. H. (Editor of *Wisden* 1936-39) b Dec. 5, 1894, d May 28, 1955
Brooks, E. W. J. (Surrey) b July 6, 1898, d Feb. 10, 1960
Brooks, R. A. (Oxford U. and Somerset) b June 14, 1943
Brown, A. (Kent) b Oct. 17, 1935
Brown, A. S. (Glos.) b June 24, 1936
Brown, D. J. (Warw.) b Jan. 30, 1942
Brown, D. W. J. (Glos.) b Feb. 26, 1942
Brown, E. (Warw.) b Nov. 27, 1911
Brown, F. R. (Camb. U., Surrey and Northants; *CY 1933*; Pres. MCC 1971-72) b Lima, Peru Dec. 16, 1910
Brown, George (Sussex and England) b April 27, 1783, d June 25, 1857
Brown, G. (Hants) b Oct. 6, 1887, d Dec. 3, 1964
Brown, J. (Scotland) b Sept. 24, 1931
Brown, J. T. (Yorks.; *CY 1895*) b Aug. 20, 1869, d Nov. 4, 1904
Brown, L. S. (S. Africa) b Nov. 24, 1910
Brown, S. M. (Middx) b Dec. 8, 1917
Brown, W. A. (Australia; *CY 1939*) b July 31, 1912
Brown, W. C. (Northants) b Nov. 13, 1900
Browne, C. R. (W. Indies) b Oct. 8, 1890, d Jan. 12, 1964
Bruce, Hon. C. N. (3rd Lord Aberdare) (Oxford U. and Middx) b Aug. 2, 1885, d Oct. 4, 1957
Bruce, S. D. (W. Province and Orange Free State) b Jan. 11, 1954
Bruce, W. (Australia) b May 22, 1864, d Aug. 3, 1925
Bruyns, A. (W. Province and Natal) b Sept. 19, 1946
Bryan, Brig. G. J. (Kent) b Dec. 29, 1902
Bryan, J. L. (Camb. U. and Kent; (*CY 1922*) b May 26, 1896
Bryan, R. T. (Kent) b July 30, 1898, d July 27, 1970
Buckenham, C. P. (Essex) b Jan. 16, 1876, d Feb. 23, 1937
Buckingham, J. (Warw.) b Jan. 21, 1903
Buckston, R. H. R. (Derby.) b Oct. 10, 1908, d May 16, 1967
Budd, E. H. (Middx and All-England) b Feb. 23, 1785, d March 29, 1875
Budd, W. L. (Hants) b Oct. 25, 1913
Buggins, B. L. (W. Australia) b Jan. 29, 1935
Bull, C. L. (Canterbury) b Aug. 19, 1946
Bull, D. F. E. (Queensland) b Aug. 13, 1935
Bull, F. G. (Essex; *CY 1898*) b April 2, 1875, d Sept. 16, 1910
Buller, J. S. (Yorks. and Worcs.) b Aug. 23, 1909, d Aug. 7, 1970
Burden, M. D. (Hants) b Oct. 4, 1930
Burge, P. J. (Australia; *CY 1965*) b May 17, 1932
Burger, C. G. de V. (S. Africa) b July 12, 1935
Burgess, G. I. (Somerset) b May 5, 1943
Burgess, M. G. (N. Zealand) b July 17, 1944
Burke, C. (N. Zealand) b March 22, 1914
Burke, J. W. (Australia; *CY 1957*) b June 12, 1930, d Feb. 2, 1979
Burke, S. F. (S. Africa) b March 11, 1934
Burki, Javed (Oxford U. and Pakistan) b May 8, 1938
Burn, K. E. (Australia) b Sept. 17, 1862, d July 20, 1956
Burnet, J. R. (Yorks.) b Oct. 11, 1918
Burnup, C. J. (Camb. U. and Kent; *CY 1903*) b Nov. 21, 1875, d April 5, 1960
Burrough, H. D. (Somerset) b Feb. 6, 1909
Burrow, B. W. (Griqualand W.) b Feb. 8, 1940
Burton, D. C. F. (Yorks.) b Sept. 13, 1887, d Sept. 24, 1971
Burton, F. J. (Australia) b 1866, d Aug. 25, 1929
Burtt, J. W. (C. Districts) b June 11, 1944
Burtt, T. B. (N. Zealand) b Jan. 22, 1915
Bury, T. E. O. (Oxford U.) b May 14, 1958
Buse, H. T. F. (Somerset) b Aug. 5, 1910

Bushby, M. H. (Camb. U.) b July 29, 1931
Buss, A. (Sussex) b Sept. 1, 1939
Buss, M. A. (Sussex and Orange Free State) b Jan. 24, 1944
Buswell, J. E. (Northants) b July 3, 1909
Butcher, A. R. (Surrey) b Jan. 7, 1954
Butcher, B. F. (W. Indies; *CY 1970*) b Sept. 3, 1933
Butcher, R. O. (Middx and Barbados) b Oct. 14, 1953
Butler, H. J. (Notts.) b March 12, 1913
Butler, L. C. (Wellington) b Sept. 2, 1934
Butler, L. S. (W. Indies) b Feb. 9, 1929
Butt, H. R. (Sussex) b Dec. 27, 1865, d Dec. 21, 1928
Butterfield, L. A. (N. Zealand) b Aug. 29, 1913
Buxton, I. R. (Derby.) b April 17, 1938
Buys, I. D. (S. Africa) b Feb. 3, 1895
Bynoe, M. R. (W. Indies) b Feb. 21, 1941

Caccia, Lord (Pres. MCC 1973-74) b Dec. 21, 1905
Caesar, Julius (Surrey and All-England) b March 25, 1830, d March 6, 1878
Caffyn, W. (Surrey and NSW) b Feb. 2, 1828, d Aug. 28, 1919
Caine, C. Stewart (Editor of *Wisden* 1926-33) b Oct. 28, 1861, d April 15, 1933
Cairns, B. L. (N. Zealand) b Oct. 10, 1949
Calder, H. L. (Cranleigh; *CY 1918*) b 1900
Callaway, S. T. (Australia) b Feb. 6, 1868, d Nov. 25, 1923
Callen, I. W. (Australia) b May 2, 1955
Calthorpe, Hon. F. S. Gough- (Camb. U., Sussex and Warw.) b May 27, 1892, d Nov. 19, 1935
Camacho, G. S. (W. Indies) b Oct. 15, 1945
Cameron, F. J. (W. Indies) b June 22, 1923
Cameron, F. J. (N. Zealand) b June 1, 1932
Cameron, H. B. (S. Africa; *CY 1936*) b July 5, 1905, d Nov. 2, 1935
Cameron, J. H. (Camb. U., Somerset and W. Indies) b April 8, 1914
Campbell, K. O. (Otago) b March 20, 1943
Campbell, T. (S. Africa) b Feb. 9, 1882, d Oct. 5, 1924
Cannings, V. H. D. (Warw. and Hants) b April 3, 1919
Caple, R. G. (Middx and Hants) b Dec. 8, 1939
Cardus, Sir Neville (Cricket Writer) b April 2, 1889, d Feb. 27, 1975
Carew, G. McD. (W. Indies) b 1910, d Dec. 9, 1974
Carew, M. C. (W. Indies) b Sept. 15, 1937
Carkeek, W. (Australia) b Oct. 17, 1878, d Feb. 20, 1937
Carlson, P. H. (Australia) b Aug. 8, 1951
Carlstein, P. R. (S. Africa) b Oct. 28, 1938
Carmody, D. K. (NSW and W. Australia) b Feb. 16, 1919, d Oct. 21, 1977
Carpenter, D. (Glos.) b Sept. 12, 1935
Carpenter, R. (Cambs. and Utd England XI) b Nov. 18, 1830, d July 13, 1901
Carr, A. W. (Notts.; *CY 1923*) b May 21, 1893, d Feb. 7, 1963
Carr, D. B. (Oxford U. and Derby.; *CY 1960*; Sec. TCCB 1974-) b Dec. 28, 1926
Carr, D. W. (Kent; *CY 1910*) b March 17, 1872, d March 23, 1950
Carrick, P. (Yorks. and E. Province) b July 16, 1952
Carrigan, A. H. (Queensland) b Aug. 26, 1917
Carrington, E. (Derby.) b March 25, 1914
Carter, C. P. (S. Africa) b April 23, 1881, d Nov. 8, 1952
Carter, H. (Australia) b Halifax, Yorks. March 15, 1878, d June 8, 1948
Carter, R. G. (Warw.) b April 14, 1933
Carter, R. G. M. (Worcs.) b July 11, 1937
Carter, R. M. (Northants) b May 25, 1960
Carter, W. (Derby.) b May 14, 1896, d Nov. 1, 1975
Cartwright, H. (Derby.) b May 12, 1951
Cartwright, T. W. (Warw., Somerset and Glam.) b July 22, 1935
Carty, R. A. (Hants) b July 28, 1922
Cass, G. R. (Essex and Worcs.) b April 23, 1940
Castell, A. T. (Hants) b Aug. 6, 1943
Castle, F. (Somerset) b April 9, 1909
Catt, A. W. (Kent and W. Province) b Oct. 2, 1933
Catterall, R. H. (S. Africa; *CY 1925*) b July 10, 1900, d Jan. 2, 1961
Causby, J. P. (S. Australia) b Oct. 27, 1942
Cave, H. B. (N. Zealand) b Oct. 10, 1922
Chadwick, D. (W. Australia) b March 29, 1941
Chalk, F. G. H. (Oxford U. and Kent) b Sept. 7, 1910, d Feb. 20, 1943
Challenor, G. (W. Indies) b June 28, 1888, d July 30, 1947
Chandrasekhar, B. S. (India; *CY 1972*) b May 18, 1945
Chang, H. S. (W. Indies) b July 22, 1952
Chapman, A. P. F. (Uppingham, Camb. U. and Kent; *CY 1919*) b Sept. 3, 1900, d Sept. 16, 1961
Chapman, H. W. (S. Africa) b June 30, 1890, d Dec. 1, 1941
Chapman, T. A. (Leics. and Rhodesia) b May 14, 1919, d Feb. 19, 1979
Chappell, G. S. (Somerset and Australia; *CY 1973*) b Aug. 7, 1948
Chappell, I. M. (Lancs. and Australia; *CY 1976*) b Sept. 26, 1943
Chappell, T. M. (Australia) b Oct. 12, 1952

Chapple, M. E. (N. Zealand) b July 25, 1930
Charlton, P. C. (Australia) b April 9, 1867, d Sept. 30, 1954
Charlwood, H. R. J. (Sussex) b Dec. 19, 1846, d June 6, 1888
Chatfield, E. J. (N. Zealand) b July 3, 1950
Chatterton, W. (Derby.) b Dec. 27, 1861, d March 19, 1913
Chauhan, C. P. S. (India) b July 21, 1947
Cheatle, R. G. L. (Sussex and Surrey) b July 31, 1953
Cheetham, J. E. (S. Africa) b May 26, 1920, d Aug. 21, 1980
Chester, F. (Worcs.; Umpire) b Jan. 20, 1895, d April 8, 1957
Chesterton, G. H. (Oxford U. and Worcs.) b July 15, 1922
Chevalier, G. A. (S. Africa) b March 9, 1937
Childs, J. H. (Glos.) b Aug. 15, 1951
Childs-Clarke, A. W. (Middx and Northants) b May 13, 1905, d Feb. 19, 1980
Chipperfield, A. G. (Australia) b Nov. 17, 1905
Chisholm, R. H. E. (Scotland) b May 22, 1927
Chowdhury, N. R. (India) b May 23, 1923, d Dec. 14, 1979
Christiani, C. M. (W. Indies) b Oct. 28, 1913, d April 4, 1938
Christiani, R. J. (W. Indies) b July 19, 1920
Christopherson, S. (Kent; Pres. MCC 1939-45) b Nov. 11, 1861, d April 6, 1949
Christy, J. A. J. (Queensland and S. Africa) b Dec. 12, 1904, d Feb. 1, 1971
Chubb, G. W. A. (S. Africa) b April 12, 1911, d Aug. 28, 1982
Clark, D. G. (Kent; Pres. MCC 1977-78) b Jan. 27, 1919
Clark, E. A. (Middx) b April 15, 1937
Clark, E. W. (Northants) b Aug. 9, 1902, d April 28, 1982
Clark, L. S. (Essex) b March 6, 1914
Clark, T. H. (Surrey) b Oct. 4, 1924, d June 15, 1981
Clark, W. M. (Australia) b Sept. 19, 1953
Clarke, Dr C. B. (Northants, Essex and W. Indies) b April 7, 1918
Clarke, R. W. (Northants) b April 22, 1924, d Aug. 3, 1981
Clarke, S. T. (Barbados, Surrey and W. Indies) b Dec. 11, 1954
Clarke, William (Notts.; founded All-England XI and Trent Bridge ground) b Dec. 24, 1798, d Aug. 25, 1856
Clarkson, J. A. (Yorks. and Somerset) b Sept. 5, 1939
Claughton, J. A. (Oxford U. and Warw.) b Sept. 17, 1956
Clay, J. C. (Glam.) b March 18, 1898, d Aug. 12, 1973
Clay, J. D. (Notts.) b Oct. 15, 1924
Clayton, G. (Lancs. and Somerset) b Feb. 3, 1938
Clements, S. M. (Oxford U.) b April 19, 1956
Cleverley, D. C. (N. Zealand) b Dec. 23, 1909
Clift, Patrick B. (Rhodesia, Leics. and Natal) b July 14, 1953
Clift, Philip B. (Glam.) b Sept. 3, 1919
Clinton, G. S. (Kent, Surrey and Zimbabwe-Rhodesia) b May 5, 1953
Close, D. B. (Yorks. and Somerset; *CY 1964*) b Feb. 24, 1931
Cobb, R. A. (Leics.) b May 18, 1961
Cobden, F. C. (Camb. U.) b Oct. 14, 1849, d Dec. 7, 1932
Cobham, 10th Visct (Hon. C. J. Lyttelton) (Worcs.; Pres. MCC 1954) b Aug. 8, 1909, d March 20, 1977
Cochrane, J. A. K. (S. Africa) b July 15, 1909
Cockbain, I. (Lancs.) b April 19, 1958
Coen, S. K. (S. Africa) b Oct. 14, 1902, d Jan. 28, 1967
Colah, S. M. H. (India) b Sept. 22, 1902, d Sept. 11, 1950
Colchin, Robert ("Long Robin") (Kent and All-England) b Nov. 1713, d April 1750
Coldwell, L. J. (Worcs.) b Jan. 10, 1933
Coleman, C. A. R. (Leics.) b July 7, 1906, d June 14, 1978
Colley, D. J. (Australia) b March 15, 1947
Collin, T. (Warw.) b April 17, 1911
Collinge, R. O. (N. Zealand) b April 2, 1946
Collins, H. L. (Australia) b Jan. 21, 1889, d May 28, 1959
Collins, R. (Lancs.) b March 10, 1934
Colquhoun, I. A. (N. Zealand) b June 8, 1924
Comber, J. T. H. (Camb. U.) b Feb. 26, 1911, d May 3, 1976
Commaille, J. M. M. (S. Africa) b Feb. 21, 1883, d July 27, 1956
Compton, D. C. S. (Middx; *CY 1939*) b May 23, 1918
Compton, L. H. (Middx) b Sept. 12, 1912
Coney, J. V. (N. Zealand) b June 21, 1952
Congdon, B. E. (N. Zealand; *CY 1974*) b Feb. 11, 1938
Coningham, A. (Australia) b July 4, 1863, d June 1939
Connolly, A. N. (Middx and Australia) b June 29, 1939
Constable, B. (Surrey) b Feb. 19, 1921
Constant, D. J. (Kent and Leics.; Umpire) b Nov. 9, 1941
Constantine, Lord L. N. (W. Indies; *CY 1940*) b Sept. 21, 1902, d July 1, 1971

Constantine, L. S. (Trinidad) b May 25, 1874, d Jan. 5, 1942
Contractor, N. J. (India) b March 7, 1934
Conyngham, D. P. (S. Africa) b May 10, 1897
Cook, C. (Glos.) b Aug. 23, 1921
Cook, F. J. (S. Africa) b 1870, ass. dead
Cook, G. (Northants and E. Province) b Oct. 9, 1951
Cook, G. G. (Queensland) b June 29, 1910
Cook, N. G. B. (Leics.) b June 17, 1956
Cook, S. J. (Transvaal) b July 31, 1953
Cook, T. E. (Sussex) b Feb. 5, 1901, d Jan. 15, 1950
Coope, M. (Somerset) b Nov. 28, 1917, d July 5, 1974
Cooper, A. H. C. (S. Africa) b Sept. 2, 1893, d July 18, 1963
Cooper, B. B. (Middx, Kent and Australia) b March 15, 1844, d Aug. 7, 1914
Cooper, F. S. Ashley- (Cricket Historian) b March 17, 1877, d Jan. 31, 1932
Cooper, G. C. (Sussex) b Sept. 2, 1936
Cooper, H. P. (Yorks. and N. Transvaal) b April 17, 1949
Cooper, K. E. (Notts.) b Dec. 27, 1957
Cooper, K. R. (Natal) b April 1, 1954
Cooper, N. H. C. (Glos. and Camb. U.) b Oct. 14, 1953
Cooper, W. H. (Australia) b Sept. 11, 1849, d April 5, 1939
Cope, G. A. (Yorks.) b Feb. 23, 1947
Copson, W. H. (Derby.; *CY 1937*) b April 27, 1908, d Sept. 14, 1971
Cordle, A. E. (Glam.) b Sept. 21, 1940
Corling, G. E. (Australia) b July 13, 1941
Cornford, J. H. (Sussex) b Dec. 9, 1911
Cornford, W. L. (Sussex) b Dec. 25, 1900, d Feb. 6, 1963
Cornwallis, Capt. Hon. W. S. (2nd Lord Cornwallis) (Kent) b March 14, 1892, d Jan. 4, 1982
Corrall, P. (Leics.) b July 16, 1906
Corran, A. J. (Oxford U. and Notts.) b Nov. 25, 1936
Cosh, N. J. (Camb. U. and Surrey) b Aug. 6, 1946
Cosier, G. J. (Australia) b April 25, 1953
Cottam, J. T. (Australia) b Sept. 5, 1867, d Jan. 30, 1897
Cottam, R. M. H. (Hants and Northants) b Oct. 16, 1944
Cotter, A. (Australia) b Dec. 3, 1883, d Oct. 31, 1917
Cotton, J. (Notts. and Leics.) b Nov. 7, 1940
Cottrell, G. A. (Camb. U.) b March 23, 1945
Cottrell, P. R. (Camb. U.) b May 22, 1957
Coulson, S. S. (Leics.) b Oct. 17, 1898, d Oct. 3, 1981
Coulthard, G. (Australia) b Aug. 1, 1856, d Oct. 22, 1883
Coventry, Hon. C. J. (Worcs.) b Feb. 26, 1867, d June 2, 1929
Coverdale, S. P. (Camb. U. and Yorks.) b Nov. 20, 1954
Cowan, M. J. (Yorks.) b June 10, 1933
Cowan, R. S. (Oxford U. and Sussex) b March 30, 1960
Cowans, N. G. (Middx) b April 17, 1961
Cowdrey, C. S. (Kent) b Oct. 20, 1957
Cowdrey, M. C. (Oxford U. and Kent; *CY 1956*) b. Dec. 24, 1932
Cowie, J. (N. Zealand) b March 30, 1912
Cowley, N. G. (Hants) b March 1, 1953
Cowper, R. M. (Australia) b Oct. 5, 1940
Cox, A. L. (Northants) b July 22, 1908
Cox, G., jun. (Sussex) b Aug. 23, 1911
Cox, G. R. (Sussex) b Nov. 29, 1873, d March 24, 1949
Cox, J. L. (S. Africa) b June 28, 1886, d July 4, 1971
Coxon, A. (Yorks.) b Jan. 18, 1916
Crabtree, H. P. (Essex) b April 30, 1906, d May 28, 1982
Craig, E. J. (Camb. U. and Lancs.) b March 26, 1942
Craig, I. D. (Australia) b June 12, 1935
Cranfield, L. M. (Glos.) b Aug. 29, 1909
Cranmer, P. (Warw.) b Sept. 10, 1914
Cranston, J. (Glos.) b Jan. 9, 1859, d Dec. 10, 1904
Cranston, K. (Lancs.) b Oct. 20, 1917
Crapp, J. F. (Glos.) b Oct. 14, 1912, d Feb. 15, 1981
Crawford, J. N. (Surrey, S. Australia, Wellington and Otago; *CY 1907*) b Dec. 1, 1886, d May 2, 1963
Crawford, N. C. (Camb. U.) b Nov. 26, 1958
Crawford, W. P. A. (Australia) b Aug. 3, 1933
Crawley, A. M. (Oxford U. and Kent; Pres. MCC 1972-73) b April 10, 1908
Crawley, L. G. (Camb. U., Worcs. and Essex) b July 26, 1903, d July 9, 1981
Cray, S. J. (Essex) b May 29, 1921
Creese, W. L. C. (Hants) b Dec. 28, 1907, d March 9, 1974
Cresswell, G. F. (N. Zealand) b March 22, 1915, d Jan. 10, 1966
Cripps, G. (S. Africa) b Oct. 19, 1865, d July 27, 1943
Crisp, R. J. (Worcs. and S. Africa) b May 28, 1911
Croft, C. E. H. (Lancs. and W. Indies) b March 15, 1953
Cromb, I. B. (N. Zealand) b June 25, 1905
Crookes, N. S. (Natal) b Nov. 15, 1935
Cross, G. F. (Leics.) b Nov. 15, 1943
Crowe, M. D. (N. Zealand) b Sept. 22, 1962

Crump, B. S. (Northants) b April 25, 1938
Crush, E. (Kent) b April 25, 1917
Cumbes, J. (Lancs., Surrey, Worcs. and Warw.) b May 4, 1944
Cunis, R. S. (N. Zealand) b Jan. 5, 1941
Cunningham, K. G. (S. Australia) b July 26, 1939
Curnow, S. H. (S. Africa) b Dec. 16, 1907
Curtis, I. J. (Oxford U.) b May 13, 1959
Cushing, V. G. B. (Oxford U.) b Jan. 17, 1950
Cuthbertson, G. B. (Middx, Sussex and Northants) b March 28, 1901
Cutmore, J. A. (Essex) b Dec. 28, 1898
Cuttell, W. R. (Lancs.; *CY 1898*) b Sept. 13, 1864, d Dec. 9, 1929

Da Costa, O. C. (W. Indies) b Sept. 11, 1907, d Oct. 1, 1936
Dacre, C. C. R. (Auckland and Glos.) b May 15, 1899, d Nov. 2, 1975
Daer, A. G. (Essex) b Nov. 22, 1906
Daft, Richard (Notts. and All-England) b Nov. 2, 1835, d July 18, 1900
Dakin, G. F. (E. Province) b Aug. 13, 1935
Dalmeny, Lord (6th Earl of Rosebery) (Middx and Surrey) b Jan. 8, 1882, d May 30, 1974
Dalton, E. L. (S. Africa) b Dec. 2, 1906, d June 3, 1981
Dani, H. T. (India) b May 24, 1933
Daniel, W. W. (Barbados, Middx, W. Australia and W. Indies) b Jan. 16, 1956
Dansie, H. N. (S. Australia) b July 2, 1928
D'Arcy, J. W. (N. Zealand) b April 23, 1936
Dare, R. (Hants) b Nov. 26, 1921
Darling, J. (Australia; *CY 1900*) b Nov. 21, 1870, d Jan. 2, 1946
Darling, L. S. (Australia) b Aug. 14, 1909
Darling, W. M. (Australia) b May 1, 1957
Darnley, 8th Earl of (Hon. Ivo Bligh) (Camb. U. and Kent; Pres. MCC 1900) b March 13, 1859, d April 10, 1927
Davey, J. (Glos.) b Sept. 4, 1944
Davidson, A. K. (Australia; *CY 1962*) b June 14, 1929
Davies, Dai (Glam.) b Aug. 26, 1896, d July 16, 1976
Davies, Emrys (Glam.) b June 27, 1904, d Nov. 10, 1975
Davies, E. Q. (S. Africa) b Aug. 26, 1909, d Nov. 11, 1976
Davies, G. R. (NSW) b July 22, 1946
Davies, H. D. (Glam.) b July 23, 1932
Davies, H. G. (Glam.) b April 23, 1913
Davies, J. G. W. (Camb. U. and Kent) b Sept. 10, 1911
Davis, B. A. (Glam. and W. Indies) b May 2, 1940
Davis, C. A. (W. Indies) b Jan. 1, 1944
Davis, E. E. (Northants) b March 8, 1922
Davis, I. C. (Australia) b June 25, 1953
Davis, P. C. (Northants) b May 24, 1915
Davis, R. C. (Glam.) b Jan. 1, 1946
Davison, B. F. (Rhodesia, Leics. and Tasmania) b Dec. 21, 1946
Davison, I. (Notts.) b Oct. 4, 1937
Dawkes, G. O. (Leics. and Derby.) b July 19, 1920
Dawson, E. W. (Camb. U. and Leics.) b Feb. 13, 1904, d June 4, 1979
Dawson, O. C. (S. Africa) b Sept. 1, 1919
Day, A. P. (Kent; *CY 1910*) b April 10, 1885, d Jan. 22, 1969
Day, H. L. V. (Hants) b Aug. 12, 1898, d June 15, 1972
Dean, H. (Lancs.) b Aug. 13, 1884, d March 12, 1957
Deane, H. G. (S. Africa) b July 21, 1895, d Oct. 21, 1939
De Caires, F. I. (W. Indies) b May 12, 1909, d Feb. 2, 1959
De Courcy, J. H. (Australia) b April 18, 1927
Deed, J. A. (Kent) b Sept. 12, 1901, d Oct. 19, 1980
Delisle, G. P. S. (Middx and Oxford U.) b Dec. 25, 1934
Dell, A. R. (Australia) b Lymington, Hants Aug. 10, 1947
de Mel, A. L. F. (Sri Lanka) b May 9, 1959
Dempster, C. S. (Leics., Warw. and N. Zealand; *CY 1932*) b Nov. 15, 1903, d Feb. 14, 1974
Dempster, E. W. (N. Zealand) b Jan. 25, 1925
Denness, M. H. (Scotland, Kent and Essex; *CY 1975*) b Dec. 1, 1940
Dennett, E. G. (Glos.) b April 27, 1880, d Sept. 14, 1937
Denning, P. W. (Somerset) b Dec. 16, 1949
Dennis, F. (Yorks.) b June 11, 1907
Denton, D. (Yorks.; *CY 1906*) b July 4, 1874, d Feb. 17, 1950
Denton, J. S. (Northants) b Nov. 2, 1890, d April 9, 1971
Denton, W. H. (Northants) b Nov. 2, 1890, d April 23, 1979
Depeiaza, C. C. (W. Indies) b Oct. 10, 1927
Desai, R. B. (India) b June 29, 1939
De Saram, F. C. (Oxford U. and Ceylon) b Sept. 1912
de Schmidt, R. (W. Province; oldest surviving Currie Cup player) b Nov. 24, 1883
de Silva, D. S. (Sri Lanka) b June 11, 1944
de Silva, G. R. A. (Sri Lanka) b Dec. 12, 1952
De Vaal, P. D. (Transvaal) b Dec. 3, 1945
Devereux, L. N. (Middx, Worcs. and Glam.) b Oct. 20, 1931

Dewdney, C. T. (W. Indies) b Oct. 23, 1933
Dewes, A. R. (Camb. U.) b June 2, 1957
Dewes, J. G. (Camb. U. and Middx) b Oct. 11, 1926
Dews, G. (Worcs.) b June 5, 1921
Dexter, E. R. (Camb. U. and Sussex; *CY 1961*) b May 15, 1935
Dias, R. L. (Sri Lanka) b Oct. 18, 1952
Dick, A. E. (N. Zealand) b Oct. 10, 1936
Dickeson, C. W. (N. Districts) b March 26, 1955
Dickinson, G. R. (N. Zealand) b March 11, 1903, d March 17, 1978
Dilley, G. R. (Kent) b May 18, 1959
Diment, R. A. (Glos. and Leics.) b Feb. 9, 1927
Dipper, A. E. (Glos.) b Nov. 9, 1885, d Nov. 7, 1945
Divecha, R. V. (Oxford U., Northants and India) b Oct. 18, 1927
Diver, A. J. D. (Cambs., Middx, Notts. and All-England) b June 6, 1824, d March 25, 1876
Dixon, A. L. (Kent) b Nov. 27, 1933
Dixon, C. D. (S. Africa) b Feb. 12, 1891, d Sept. 9, 1969
Dodds, T. C. (Essex) b May 29, 1919
Doggart, A. G. (Camb. U., Durham and Middx) b June 2, 1897, d June 7, 1963
Doggart, G. H. G. (Camb. U. and Sussex; Pres. MCC 1981-82) b July 18, 1925
Doggart, S. J. G. (Camb. U.) b Feb. 8, 1961
Doherty, M. J. D. (Griqualand W.) b March 14, 1947
D'Oliveira, B. L. (Worcs.; *CY 1967*) b Oct. 4, 1931
Dollery, H. E. (Warw. and Wellington; *CY 1952*) b Oct. 14, 1914
Dollery, K. R. (Queensland, Auckland, Tasmania and Warw.) b Dec. 9, 1924
Dolphin, A. (Yorks.) b Dec. 24, 1885, d Oct. 24, 1942
Donnan, H. (Australia) b Nov. 12, 1864, d Aug. 13, 1956
Donnelly, M. P. (Middx, Warw., Oxford U. and N. Zealand; *CY 1948*) b Oct. 17, 1917
Dooland, B. (Notts. and Australia; *CY 1955*) b Nov. 1, 1923, d Sept. 8, 1980
Dorrinton, W. (Kent and All-England) b April 29, 1809, d Nov. 8, 1848
Dorset, 3rd Duke of (Kent) b March 24, 1745, d July 19, 1799
Doshi, D. R. (Notts., Warw. and India) b Dec. 22, 1947
Douglas, J. W. H. T. (Essex; *CY 1915*) b Sept. 3, 1882, d Dec. 19, 1930
Dovey, R. R. (Kent) b July 18, 1920, d Dec. 27, 1974
Dowding, A. L. (Oxford U.) b April 4, 1929
Dowe, U. G. (W. Indies) b March 29, 1949
Dower, R. R. (S. Africa) b June 4, 1876, d Sept. 15, 1964
Dowling, D. F. (Border, NE Transvaal and Natal) b July 25, 1914
Dowling, G. T. (N. Zealand) b March 4, 1937
Downton, P. R. (Kent and Middx) b April 4, 1957
Draper, E. J. (E. Province and Griqualand W.) b Sept. 27, 1934
Draper, R. G. (S. Africa) b Dec. 24, 1926
Dredge, C. H. (Somerset) b Aug. 4, 1954
Druce, N. F. (Camb. U. and Surrey; *CY 1898*) b Jan. 1, 1875, d Oct. 27, 1954
Drybrough, C. D. (Oxford U. and Middx) b Aug. 31, 1938
D'Souza, Antao (Pakistan) b Jan. 1, 1938
Ducat, A. (Surrey; *CY 1920*) b Feb. 16, 1886, d July 23, 1942
Duckworth, C. A. R. (S. Africa) b March 22, 1933
Duckworth, G. (Lancs.; *CY 1929*) b May 9, 1901, d Jan. 5, 1966
Dudleston, B. (Leics., Glos. and Rhodesia) b July 16, 1945
Duff, R. A. (Australia) b Aug. 17, 1878, d Dec. 13, 1911
Dujon, P. J. (W. Indies) b May 28, 1956
Duleepsinhji, K. S. (Camb. U. and Sussex; *CY 1930*) b June 13, 1905, d Dec. 5, 1959
Dumbrill, R. (S. Africa) b London Nov. 19, 1938
Duminy, J. P. (Oxford U. and S. Africa) b Dec. 16, 1897, d Jan. 31, 1980
Duncan, J. R. F. (Australia) b March 25, 1944
Dunell, O. R. (S. Africa) b July 15, 1856, d Oct. 21, 1929
Dunning B. (N. Districts) b March 20, 1940
Dunning, J. A. (Oxford U. and N. Zealand) b Feb. 6, 1903, d June 24, 1971
Du Preez, J. H. (S. Africa) b Nov. 14, 1942
Durani, S. A. (India) b Dec. 11, 1934
Durose, A. J. (Northants) b Oct. 10, 1944
Durston, F. J. (Middx) b July 11, 1893, d April 8, 1965
Du Toit, J. F. (S. Africa) b April 5, 1868, d July 10, 1909
Dye, J. C. J. (Kent, Northants and E. Province) b July 24, 1942
Dyer, D. D. (Natal and Transvaal) b Dec. 3, 1946
Dyer, D. V. (S. Africa) b April 2, 1914
Dymock, G. (Australia) b July 21, 1946
Dyson, A. H. (Glam.) b July 10, 1905, d June 7, 1978
Dyson, J. (Lancs.) b July 8, 1934
Dyson, John (Australia) b June 11, 1954

Eady, C. J. (Australia) b Oct. 29, 1870, d Dec. 20, 1945
Eagar, E. D. R. (Oxford U., Glos. and Hants) b Dec. 8, 1917, d Sept. 13, 1977
Eagar, M. A. (Oxford U. and Glos.) b March 20, 1934
Eaglestone, J. T. (Middx and Glam.) b July 24, 1923
Ealham, A. G. E. (Kent) b Aug. 30, 1944
East, D. E. (Essex) b July 27, 1959
East, R. E. (Essex) b June 20, 1947
Eastman, G. F. (Essex) b April 7, 1903
Eastman, L. C. (Essex and Otago) b June 3, 1897, d April 17, 1941
Eastwood, K. H. (Australia) b Nov. 23, 1935
Ebeling, H. I. (Australia) b Jan. 1, 1905, d Jan. 12, 1980
Eckersley, P. T. (Lancs.) b July 2, 1904, d Aug. 13, 1940
Edgar, B. A. (N. Zealand) b Nov. 23, 1956
Edinburgh, HRH Duke of (Pres. MCC 1948-49, 1974-75) b June 10, 1921
Edmeades, B. E. A. (Essex) b Sept. 17, 1941
Edmonds, P. H. (Camb. U., Middx and E. Province) b March 8, 1951
Edmonds, R. B. (Warw.) b March 2, 1941
Edrich, B. R. (Kent and Glam.) b Aug. 18, 1922
Edrich, E. H. (Lancs.) b March 27, 1914
Edrich, G. A. (Lancs.) b July 13, 1918
Edrich, J. H. (Surrey; *CY 1966*) b June 21, 1937
Edrich, W. J. (Middx; *CY 1940*) b March 26, 1916
Edwards, F. (Surrey) b May 23, 1885, d July 10, 1970
Edwards, G. N. (N. Zealand) b May 27, 1955
Edwards, J. D. (Australia) b June 12, 1862, d July 31, 1911
Edwards, M. J. (Camb. U. and Surrey) b March 1, 1940
Edwards, R. (Australia) b Dec. 1, 1942
Edwards, R. M. (W. Indies) b June 3, 1940
Edwards, T. D. W. (Camb. U.) b Dec. 6, 1958
Edwards, W. J. (Australia) b Dec. 23, 1949
Eele, P. J. (Somerset) b Jan. 27, 1935
Eggar, J. D. (Oxford U., Hants and Derby.) b Dec. 1, 1916
Ehtesham-ud-Din (Pakistan) b Sept. 4, 1950
Elgie, M. K. (S. Africa) b March 6, 1933
Elliott, C. S. (Derby.) b April 24, 1912
Elliott, H. (Derby.) b Nov. 2, 1891, d Feb. 2, 1976
Elliott, Harold (Lancs.; Umpire) b June 15, 1904
Ellis, G. P. (Glam.) b May 24, 1950
Ellis, J. L. (Victoria) b May 9, 1890, d July 26, 1974
Ellis, R. G. P. (Oxford U. and Middx) b Oct. 20, 1960
Ellison, C. C. (Camb. U.) b Feb. 11, 1962
Elms, R. B. (Kent and Hants) b April 5, 1949
Emburey, J. E. (Middx) b Aug. 20, 1952
Emery, K. St J. D. (Hants) b Feb. 28, 1960
Emery, R. W. G. (N. Zealand) b March 28, 1915
Emery, S. H. (Australia) b Oct. 16, 1886, d Jan. 7, 1967
Emmett, G. M. (Glos.) b Dec. 2, 1912, d Dec. 18, 1976
Emmett, T. (Yorks.) b Sept. 3, 1841, d June 29, 1904
Endean, W. R. (S. Africa) b May 31, 1924
Engineer, F. M. (Lancs. and India) b Feb. 25, 1938
Enthoven, H. J. (Camb. U. and Middx) b June 4, 1903, d June 29, 1975
Evans, A. J. (Oxford U., Hants and Kent) b May 1, 1889, d Sept. 18, 1960
Evans, D. G. L. (Glam.; Umpire) b July 27, 1933
Evans, E. (Australia) b March 6, 1849, d July 2, 1921
Evans, G. (Oxford U., Glam. and Leics.) b Aug. 13, 1915
Evans, J. B. (Glam.) b Nov. 9, 1936
Evans, T. G. (Kent; *CY 1951*) b Aug. 18, 1920
Evans, V. J. (Essex) b March 4, 1912, d March 28, 1975
Every, T. (Glam.) b Dec. 19, 1909
Eyre, T. J. P. (Derby.) b Oct. 17, 1939
Ezekowitz, R. A. B. (Oxford U.) b Jan. 19, 1954

Faber, M. J. J. (Oxford U. and Sussex) b Aug. 15, 1950
Fagg, A. E. (Kent) b June 18, 1915, d Sept. 13, 1977
Fairbairn, A. (Middx) b Jan. 25, 1923
Fairbairn, G. A. (Camb. U. and Middx) b June 26, 1892, d Nov. 5, 1973
Fairfax, A. G. (Australia) b June 16, 1906, d May 17, 1955
Fairservice, C. (Kent and Middx) b Aug. 21, 1909
Fairservice, W. J. (Kent) b May 16, 1881, d June 26, 1971
Falcon, M. (Camb. U.) b July 21, 1888, d Feb. 27, 1976
Fallows, J. A. (Lancs.) b July 25, 1907, d Jan. 20, 1974
Fane, F. L. (Oxford U. and Essex) b April 27, 1875, d Nov. 27, 1960
Fantham, W. E. (Warw.) b May 14, 1918
Farnes, K. (Camb. U. and Essex; *CY 1939*) b July 8, 1911, d Oct. 20, 1941

Farooq Hamid (Pakistan) b March 3, 1945
Farrer, W. S. (S. Africa) b Dec. 8, 1936
Farrimond, W. (Lancs.) b May 23, 1903, d Nov. 14, 1979
Farrukh Zaman (Pakistan) b April 2, 1956
Faulkner, G. A. (S. Africa) b Dec. 17, 1881, d Sept. 10, 1930
Favell, L. E. (Australia) b Oct. 6, 1929
Fazal Mahmood (Pakistan; *CY 1955*) b Feb. 18, 1927
Fearnley, C. D. (Worcs.) b April 12, 1940
Featherstone, N. G. (Transvaal, N. Transvaal, Middx and Glam.) b Aug. 20, 1949
'Felix', N. (Wanostrocht) (Kent, Surrey and All-England) b Oct. 4, 1804, d Sept. 3, 1876
Fellows-Smith, J. P. (Oxford U., Northants and S. Africa) b Feb. 3, 1932
Fender, P. G. H. (Sussex and Surrey; *CY 1915*) b Aug. 22, 1892
Fenley, S. (Surrey and Hants) b Jan. 4, 1896, d Sept. 2, 1972
Fenner, D. (Border) b March 27, 1929
Ferguson, W. (W. Indies) b Dec. 14, 1917, d Feb. 23, 1961
Fernandes, M. P. (W. Indies) b Aug. 12, 1897, d May 8, 1981
Ferrandi, J. H. (W. Province) b April 3, 1930
Ferreira, A. M. (N. Transvaal and Warw.) b April 13, 1955
Ferris, J. J. (Glos., Australia and England; *CY 1889*) b May 21, 1867, d Nov. 21, 1900
Fichardt, C. G. (S. Africa) b March 20, 1870, d May 30, 1923
Fiddian-Green, C. A. F. (Camb. U., Warw. and Worcs.) b Dec. 22, 1898, d Sept. 5, 1976
Fiddling, K. (Yorks. and Northants) b Oct. 13, 1917
Field, M. N. (Camb. U. and Warw.) b March 23, 1950
Fielder, A. (Kent; *CY 1907*) b July 19, 1877, d Aug. 30, 1949
Findlay, T. M. (W. Indies) b Oct. 19, 1943
Findlay, W. (Oxford U. and Lancs.; Sec. Surrey CCC, Sec. MCC 1926-36) b June 22, 1880, d June 19, 1953
Fingleton, J. H. (Australia) b April 28, 1908, d Nov. 22, 1981
Finlason, C. E. (S. Africa) b Feb. 19, 1860, d July 31, 1917
Firth, J. (Yorks. and Leics.) b June 27, 1918, d Sept. 6, 1981
Firth, Rev. Canon J. D'E. E. (Winchester, Oxford U. and Notts.; *CY 1918*) b Jan. 21, 1900, d Sept. 21, 1957
Fisher, B. (Queensland) b Jan. 20, 1934, d April 1980
Fisher, F. E. (N. Zealand) b July 28, 1924
Fisher, P. B. (Oxford U., Middx and Worcs.) b Dec. 19, 1954
Fishlock, L. B. (Surrey; *CY 1947*) b Jan. 2, 1907
Fitzroy-Newdegate, Cdr. Hon. J. M. (Northants) b March 20, 1897, d May 7, 1976
Flanagan, J. P. D. (Transvaal) b Sept. 20, 1947
Flavell, J. A. (Worcs.; *CY 1965*) b May 15, 1929
Fleetwood-Smith, L. O'B. (Australia) b March 30, 1910, d March 16, 1971
Fletcher, D. A. G. (Rhodesia, Zimbabwe) b Sept. 27, 1948
Fletcher, D. G. W. (Surrey) b July 6, 1924
Fletcher, K. W. R. (Essex; *CY 1974*) b May 20, 1944
Floquet, C. E. (S. Africa) b Nov. 3, 1884, d Nov. 22, 1963
Flowers, W. (Notts.) b Dec. 7, 1856, d Nov. 1, 1926
Foat, J. C. (Glos.) b Nov. 21, 1952
Foley, H. (N. Zealand) b Jan. 28, 1906, d Oct. 16, 1948
Folley, I. (Lancs.) b Jan. 9, 1963
Foord, C. W. (Yorks.) b June 11, 1924
Forbes, C. (Notts.) b Aug. 9, 1936
Ford, D. A. (NSW) b Dec. 12, 1930
Ford, F. G. J. (Camb. U. and Middx) b Dec. 14, 1866, d Feb. 7, 1940
Ford. N. M. (Oxford U., Derby. and Middx) b Nov. 18, 1906
Ford, R. G. (Glos.) b March 3, 1907, d Oct. 1981
Foreman, D. J. (W. Province and Sussex) b Feb. 1, 1933
Fosh, M. K. (Camb. U. and Essex) b Sept. 26, 1957
Foster, D. G. (Warw.) b March 19, 1907, d Oct. 13, 1980
Foster, F. R. (Warw.; *CY 1912*) b Jan. 31, 1889, d May 3, 1958
Foster, G. N. (Oxford U., Worcs. and Kent) b Oct. 16, 1884, d Aug. 11, 1971
Foster, H. K. (Oxford U. and Worcs.; *CY 1911*) b Oct. 30, 1873, d June 23, 1950
Foster, M. K. (Worcs.) b Jan. 1, 1889, d Dec. 3, 1940
Foster, M. L. C. (W. Indies) b May 9, 1943
Foster, P. G. (Kent) b Oct. 9, 1916
Foster, R. E. (Oxford U. and Worcs.; *CY 1901*) b April 16, 1878, d May 13, 1914
Fothergill, A. J. (Somerset) b Aug. 26, 1854, d Aug. 1, 1932
Fotheringham, H. R. (Natal and Transvaal) b April 4, 1953
Foulkes, I. (Border and Orange Free State) b Feb. 22, 1955
Fowler, A. J. B. (Middx) b April 1, 1891, d May 7, 1977

Fowler, G. (Lancs.) b April 20, 1957
Francis, B. C. (Essex and Australia) b Feb. 18, 1948
Francis, D. A. (Glam.) b Nov. 29, 1953
Francis, G. N. (W. Indies) b Dec. 7, 1897, d Jan. 12, 1942
Francis, H. H. (S. Africa) b May 26, 1868, d Jan. 7, 1936
Francke, F. M. (Sri Lanka and Queensland) b March 29, 1941
Francois, C. M. (S. Africa) b June 20, 1897, d May 26, 1944
Frank, C. N. (S. Africa) b Jan. 27, 1891, d Dec. 26, 1961
Frank, W. H. B. (S. Africa) b Nov. 23, 1872, d Feb. 16, 1945
Franklin, H. W. F. (Oxford U., Surrey and Essex) b June 30, 1901
Frederick, M. C. (Derby. and W. Indies) b May 6, 1927
Fredericks, R. C. (Glam. and W. Indies; *CY 1974*) b Nov. 11, 1942
Freeman, A. P. (Kent; *CY 1923*) b May 17, 1888, d Jan. 28, 1965
Freeman, D. L. (N. Zealand) b Sept. 8, 1914
Freeman, E. W. (Australia) b July 13, 1944
Freer, F. W. (Australia) b Dec. 4, 1915
French, B. N. (Notts.) b Aug. 13, 1959
Frost, G. (Notts.) b Jan. 15, 1947
Fry, C. A. (Oxford U., Hants and Northants) b Jan. 14, 1940
Fry, C. B. (Oxford U., Sussex and Hants; *CY 1895*) b April 25, 1872, d Sept. 7, 1956
Fuller, E. R. H. (S. Africa) b Aug. 2, 1931
Fuller, R. L. (W. Indies) b Jan. 30, 1913
Fullerton, G. M. (S. Africa) b Dec. 8, 1922
Funston, G. K. (NE Transvaal and Griqualand W.) b Nov. 21, 1948
Funston, K. J. (S. Africa) b Dec. 3, 1925
Furlonge, H. A. (W. Indies) b June 19, 1934
Fursdon, E. D. (Oxford U.) b Dec. 20, 1952

Gabriel, R. S. (Trinidad) b June 5, 1952
Gadkari, C. V. (India) b Feb. 3, 1928
Gaekwad, A. D. (India) b Sept. 23, 1952
Gaekwad, D. K. (India) b Oct. 27, 1928
Gaekwad, H. G. (India) b Aug. 29, 1923
Gale, R. A. (Middx) b Dec. 10, 1933
Gallichan, N. (N. Zealand) b June 3, 1906, d March 25, 1969
Gamsy, D. (S. Africa) b Feb. 17, 1940
Gandotra, A. (India) b Nov. 24, 1948
Gannon, J. B. (Australia) b Feb. 2, 1947
Ganteaume, A. G. (W. Indies) b Jan. 22, 1921
Gardiner, H. A. B. (Rhodesia) b Jan. 3, 1944
Gardiner, S. J. C. (Camb. U.) b March 19, 1947
Gardner, F. C. (Warw.) b June 4, 1922, d Jan. 13, 1979
Gardner, L. R. (Leics.) b Feb. 23, 1934
Garland-Wells, H. M. (Oxford U. and Surrey) b Nov. 14, 1907
Garlick, R. G. (Lancs. and Northants) b April 11, 1917
Garner, J. (Somerset and W. Indies; *CY 1980*) b Dec. 16, 1952
Garnham, M. A. (Glos. and Leics.) b Aug. 20, 1960
Garrett, T. W. (Australia) b July 26, 1858, d Aug. 6, 1943
Gaskin, B. M. (Manager, W. Indies in England, 1963) b March 21, 1908, d May 2, 1979
Gatting, M. W. (Middx) b June 6, 1957
Gaunt, R. A. (Australia) b Feb. 26, 1934
Gavaskar, S. M. (Somerset and India; *CY 1980*) b July 10, 1949
Gay, L. H. (Camb. U., Hants and Somerset) b March 24, 1871, d Nov. 1, 1949
Geary, A. C. T. (Surrey) b Sept. 11, 1900
Geary, G. (Leics.; *CY 1927*) b July 9, 1893, d March 6, 1981
Gedye, S. G. (N. Zealand) b May 2, 1929
Gehrs. D. R. A. (Australia) b Nov. 29, 1880, d June 25, 1953
Ghavri, K. D. (India) b Feb. 28, 1951
Ghazali, Mohammad E. Z. (Pakistan) b June 15, 1924
Ghorpade, J. M. (India) b Oct. 2, 1930, d March 29, 1978
Ghulam Abbas (Pakistan) b May 1, 1947
Ghulam Ahmed (India) b July 4, 1922
Gibb, P. A. (Camb. U., Scotland, Yorks. and Essex) b July 11, 1913, d Dec. 7, 1977
Gibbons, H. H. I. (Worcs.) b Oct. 10, 1904, d Feb. 16, 1973
Gibbs, G. L. (W. Indies) b Dec. 27, 1925, d Feb. 21, 1979
Gibbs, L. R. (Warw., S. Australia and W. Indies; *CY 1972*) b Sept. 29, 1934
Gibbs, P. J. K. (Oxford U. and Derby.) b Aug. 17, 1944
Gibson, C. H. (Eton, Camb. U. and Sussex; *CY 1918*) b Aug. 23, 1900, d Dec. 31, 1976
Gibson, D. (Surrey) b May 1, 1936
Gibson, J. G. (N. Districts and Auckland) b Nov. 12, 1948
Giffen, G. (Australia; *CY 1894*) b March 27, 1859, d Nov. 29, 1927
Giffen, W. F. (Australia) b Sept. 10, 1863, d June 29, 1949
Gifford, N. (Worcs.; *CY 1975*) b March 30, 1940

Gilchrist, R. (Jamaica, Hyderabad and W. Indies) b June 28, 1934
Giles, R. J. (Notts.) b Oct. 17, 1919
Gill, A. (Notts.) b Aug. 4, 1940
Gilhouley, K. (Yorks. and Notts.) b Aug. 8, 1934
Gilliat, R. M. C. (Oxford U. and Hants) b May 20, 1944
Gilligan, A. E. R. (Camb. U., Surrey and Sussex; *CY 1924*; Pres. MCC 1967-68) b Dec. 23, 1894, d Sept. 5, 1976
Gilligan, A. H. H. (Sussex) b June 29, 1896, d May 5, 1978
Gilligan, F. W. (Oxford U. and Essex) b Sept. 20, 1893, d May 4, 1960
Gilmour, G. J. (Australia) b June 26, 1951
Gimblett, H. (Somerset; *CY 1953*) b Oct. 19, 1914, d March 30, 1978
Gladstone, G. (W. Indies) (*see* Marais, G. G.)
Gladwin, C. (Derby.) b April 3, 1916
Gleeson, J. W. (E. Province and Australia) b March 14, 1938
Gleeson, R. A. (S. Africa) b Dec. 6, 1873, d Sept. 27, 1919
Glover, G. K. (S. Africa) b May 13, 1870, d Nov. 15, 1938
Glover, T. R. (Oxford U.) b Nov. 26, 1951
Goddard, G. F. (Scotland) b May 19, 1938
Goddard, J. D. C. (W. Indies) b April 21, 1919
Goddard, T. L. (S. Africa) b Aug. 1, 1931
Goddard, T. W. (Glos.; *CY 1938*) b Oct. 1, 1900, d May 22, 1966
Goldie, C. F. E. (Camb. U.) b Nov. 20, 1960
Goldstein, F. S. (Oxford U., Northants, Transvaal and W. Province) b Oct. 14, 1944
Gomes, H. A. (Middx and W. Indies) b July 13, 1953
Gomes, S. A. (Trinidad) b Oct. 18, 1950
Gomez, G. E. (W. Indies) b Oct. 10, 1919
Gooch, G. A. (Essex; *CY 1980*) b July 23, 1953
Goodway, C. C. (Warw.) b July 10, 1909
Goodwin, K. (Lancs.) b June 25, 1938
Goodwin, T. J. (Leics.) b Jan. 22, 1929
Goonatillake, H. M. (Sri Lanka) b Aug. 16, 1952
Goonesena, G. (Ceylon, Notts., Camb. U. and NSW) b Feb. 16, 1931
Gopalan, M. J. (India) b June 6, 1909
Gopinath, C. D. (India) b March 1, 1930
Gordon, N. (S. Africa) b Aug. 6, 1911
Gore, A. C. (Eton and Army; *CY 1919*) b May 14, 1900
Gothard, E. J. (Derby.) b Oct. 1, 1904, d Jan. 17, 1979
Gould, I. J. (Middx, Auckland and Sussex) b Aug. 19, 1957
Gover, A. R. (Surrey; *CY 1937*) b Feb. 29, 1908
Gower, D. I. (Leics.; *CY 1979*) b April 1, 1957
Gowrie, 1st Lord (Pres. MCC 1948-49) b July 6, 1872, d May 2, 1955
Grace, Dr Alfred b May 17, 1840, d May 24, 1916
Grace, Dr Alfred H. (Glos.) b March 10, 1866, d Sept. 16, 1929
Grace, C. B. (Clifton) b March 1882, d June 6, 1938
Grace, Dr E. M. (Glos.) b Nov. 28, 1841, d May 20, 1911
Grace, Dr Edgar M. (MCC) (son of E. M. Grace) b Oct. 6, 1886, d Nov. 24, 1974
Grace, G. F. (Glos.) b Dec. 13, 1850, d Sept. 22, 1880
Grace, Dr Henry (Glos.) b Jan. 31, 1833, d Nov. 15, 1895
Grace, Dr H. M. (father of W. G., E. M. and G. F.) b Feb. 21, 1808, d Dec. 23, 1871
Grace, Mrs H. M. (mother of W. G., E. M. and G. F.) b July 18, 1812, d July 25, 1884
Grace, Dr W. G. (Glos.; *CY 1896*) b July 18, 1848, d Oct. 23, 1915
Grace, W. G., jun. (Camb. U. and Glos.) b July 6, 1874, d March 2, 1905
Graf, S. F. (Victoria and Hants) b May 19, 1957
Graham, H. (Australia) b Nov. 29, 1870, d Feb. 7, 1911
Graham, J. N. (Kent) b May 8, 1943
Graham, R. (S. Africa) b Sept. 16, 1877, d April 21, 1946
Grant, G. C. (Camb. U., Rhodesia and W. Indies) b May 9, 1907, d Oct. 26, 1978
Grant, R. S. (Camb. U. and W. Indies) b Dec. 15, 1909, d Oct. 18, 1977
Graveney, D. A. (Glos.) b Jan. 21, 1953
Graveney, J. K. R. (Glos.) b Dec. 16, 1924
Graveney, T. W. (Glos., Worcs. and Queensland; *CY 1953*) b June 16, 1927
Graves, P. J. (Sussex and Orange Free State) b May 19, 1946
Gray, E. J. (Wellington) b Nov. 18, 1954
Gray, J. R. (Hants) b May 19, 1926
Gray, L. H. (Middx) b Dec. 16, 1915
Greasley, D. G. (Northants) b Jan. 20, 1926
Green, D. J. (Derby. and Camb. U.) b Dec. 18, 1935
Green, D. M. (Oxford U., Lancs. and Glos.; *CY 1969*) b Nov. 10, 1939
Green, Brig. M. A. (Glos. and Essex; Manager MCC in S. Africa 1948-49, MCC in Australia 1950-51) b Oct. 3, 1891, d Dec. 28, 1971
Greenhough, T. (Lancs.) b Nov. 9, 1931

Greenidge, A. E. (W. Indies) b Aug. 20, 1956
Greenidge, C. G. (Hants and W. Indies; *CY 1977*) b May 1, 1951
Greenidge, G. A. (Sussex and W. Indies) b May 26, 1948
Greensmith, W. T. (Essex) b Aug. 16, 1930
Greenwood, A. (Yorks.) b Aug. 20, 1847, d Feb. 12, 1889
Greenwood, F. E. (Yorks.) b Sept. 28, 1905, d July 30, 1963
Greenwood, H. W. (Sussex and Northants) b Sept. 4, 1909
Greenwood, P. (Lancs.) b Sept. 11, 1924
Greetham, C. M. H. (Somerset) b Aug. 28, 1936
Gregory, David W. (Australia; first Australian captain) b April 15, 1845, d Aug. 4, 1919
Gregory, E. J. (Australia) b May 29, 1839, d April 22, 1899
Gregory, J. M. (Australia; *CY 1922*) b Aug. 14, 1895, d Aug. 7, 1973
Gregory, R. G. (Australia) b Feb. 26, 1916, d June 10, 1942
Gregory, R. J. (Surrey) b Aug. 26, 1902, d Oct. 6, 1973
Gregory, S. E. (Australia; *CY 1897*) b April 14, 1870, d July 31, 1929
Greig, A. W. (Border, E. Province and Sussex; *CY 1975*) b Oct. 6, 1946
Greig, I. A. (Camb. U., Border and Sussex) b Dec. 8, 1955
Grell, M. G. (W. Indies) b Dec. 18, 1899, d Jan. 11, 1976
Greswell, W. T. (Somerset and Ceylon) b Oct. 15, 1889, d Feb. 12, 1971
Grieve, B. A. F. (England) b May 28, 1864, d Nov. 19, 1917
Grieves, K. J. (NSW and Lancs.) b Aug. 27, 1925
Grieveson, R. E. (S. Africa) b Aug. 24, 1909
Griffin, G. M. (S. Africa) b June 12, 1939
Griffith, C. C. (W. Indies; *CY 1964*) b Dec. 14, 1938
Griffith, G. ("Ben") (Surrey and Utd England XI) b Dec. 20, 1833, d May 3, 1879
Griffith, H. C. (W. Indies) b Dec. 1, 1893, d March 18, 1980
Griffith, K. (Worcs.) b Jan. 17, 1950
Griffith, M. G. (Camb. U. and Sussex) b Nov. 25, 1943
Griffith, S. C. (Camb. U., Surrey and Sussex; Sec. MCC 1962-74; Pres. MCC 1979-80) b June 16, 1914
Griffiths, B. J. (Northants) b June 13, 1949
Griffiths, Sir W. H. (Camb. U. and Glam.) b Sept. 26, 1923
Grimmett, C. V. (Wellington and Australia; *CY 1931*) b Dec. 25, 1891, d May 2, 1980
Grimshaw, N. (Northants) b May 5, 1911
Gripper, R. A. (Rhodesia) b July 7, 1938
Groube, T. U. (Australia) b Sept. 2, 1857, d Aug. 5, 1927
Grout, A. T. W. (Australia) b March 30, 1927, d Nov. 9, 1968
Grove, C. W. (Warw. and Worcs.) b Dec. 16, 1912, d Feb. 15, 1982
Grover, J. N. (Oxford U.) b Oct. 15, 1915
Groves, B. S. (Border and Natal) b March 1, 1947
Groves, M. G. M. (Oxford U., Somerset and W. Province) b Jan. 14, 1943
Grundy, J. (Notts. and Utd England XI) b March 5, 1824, d Nov. 24, 1873
Guard, G. M. (India) b Dec. 12, 1925, d March 13, 1978
Guest, C. E. J. (Australia) b Oct. 7, 1937
Guha, S. (India) b Jan. 31, 1946
Guillen, S. C. (W. Indies and N. Zealand) b Sept. 24, 1924
Guise, J. L. (Oxford U. and Middx) b Nov. 25, 1903
Gul Mahomed (Pakistan and India) b Oct. 15, 1921
Gunn, G. (Notts.; *CY 1914*) b June 13, 1879, d June 28, 1958
Gunn, G. V. (Notts.) b June 21, 1905, d Oct. 14, 1957
Gunn, J. (Notts.; *CY 1904*) b July 19, 1876, d Aug. 21, 1963
Gunn, T. (Sussex) b Sept. 27, 1935
Gunn, William (Notts.; *CY 1890*) b Dec. 4, 1858, d Jan. 29, 1921
Gupte, B. P. (India) b Aug. 30, 1934
Gupte, S. P. (India) b Dec. 11, 1929
Gurr, D. R. (Oxford U. and Somerset) b March 27, 1956
Guy, J. W. (Northants and N. Zealand) b Aug. 29, 1934

Hacker, P. J. (Notts., Derby. and Orange Free State) b July 16, 1952
Hadlee, B. G. (Canterbury) b Dec. 14, 1941
Hadlee, D. R. (N. Zealand) b Jan. 6, 1948
Hadlee, R. J. (Notts. and N. Zealand; *CY 1982*) b July 3, 1951
Hadlee, W. A. (N. Zealand) b June 4, 1915
Hadley, R. J. (Camb. U. and Glam.) b Oct. 22, 1951
Hafeez, A. (*see* Kardar)
Haig, N. E. (Middx) b Dec. 12, 1887, d Oct. 27, 1966
Haigh, S. (Yorks.; *CY 1901*) b March 19, 1871, d Feb. 27, 1921
Halfyard, D. J. (Kent and Notts.) b April 3, 1931
Hall, A. E. (S. Africa) b Jan. 23, 1896, d Jan. 1, 1964
Hall, G. G. (S. Africa) b May 24, 1938

Hall, I. W. (Derby.) b Dec. 27, 1939
Hall, Louis (Yorks.; *CY 1890*) b Nov. 1, 1852, d Nov. 19, 1915
Hall, T. A. (Derby. and Somerset) b Aug. 19, 1930
Hall, W. W. (Queensland and W. Indies) b Sept. 12, 1937
Hallam, A. W. (Lancs. and Notts.; *CY 1908*) b Nov. 12, 1869, d July 24, 1940
Hallam, M. R. (Leics.) b Sept. 10, 1931
Halliday, S. J. (Oxford U.) b July 13, 1960
Halliwell, E. A. (Middx and S. Africa; *CY 1905*) b Sept. 7, 1864, d Oct. 2, 1919
Hallows, C. (Lancs.; *CY 1928*) b April 4, 1895, d Nov. 10 1972
Hallows, J. (Lancs.; *CY 1905*) b Nov. 14, 1873, d May 20, 1910
Halse, C. G. (S. Africa) b Feb. 28, 1935
Hamblin, C. B. (Oxford U.) b April 14, 1952
Hamence, R. A. (Australia) b Nov. 25, 1915
Hamer, A. (Yorks. and Derby.) b Dec. 8, 1916
Hamilton, A. C. (Oxford U.) b Sept. 23, 1953
Hammond, H. E. (Sussex) b Nov. 7, 1907
Hammond, J. R. (Australia) b April 19, 1950
Hammond, W. R. (Glos.; *CY 1928*) b June 19, 1903, d July 2, 1965
Hampshire, J. H. (Yorks., Derby. and Tasmania) b Feb. 10, 1941
Hands, P. A. M. (S. Africa) b March 18, 1890, d April 27, 1951
Hands, R. H. M. (S. Africa) b July 26, 1888, d April 20, 1918
Hands, W. C. (Warw.) b Dec. 20, 1886, d Aug. 31, 1974
Hanif Mohammad (Pakistan; *CY 1968*) b Dec. 21, 1934
Hanley, M. A. (S. Africa) b Nov. 10, 1918
Hanley, R. W. (E. Province, Orange Free State and Transvaal) b Jan. 29, 1952
Hanumant Singh (India) b March 29, 1939
Hardie, B. R. (Scotland and Essex) b Jan. 14, 1950
Hardikar, M. S. (India) b Feb. 8, 1936
Hardinge, H. T. W. (Kent; *CY 1915*) b Feb. 25, 1886, d May 8, 1965
Hardstaff, J. (Notts.) b Nov. 9, 1882, d April 2, 1947
Hardstaff, J., jun. (Notts. and Auckland; *CY 1938*) b July 3, 1911
Harfield, L. (Hants) b Aug. 16, 1905
Harford, N. S. (N. Zealand) b Aug. 30, 1930, d March 30, 1981
Harford, R. I. (N. Zealand) b May 30, 1936
Harman, R. (Surrey) b Dec. 28, 1941
Haroon Rashid (Pakistan) b March 25, 1953
Harper, H. (Worcs.; believed to be oldest surviving County Championship cricketer) b Feb. 1, 1889
Harris, 4th Lord (Oxford U. and Kent; Pres. MCC 1895) b Trinidad Feb. 3, 1851, d March 24, 1932
Harris, David (Hants and All-England) b 1755, d May 19, 1803
Harris, C. B. (Notts.) b Dec. 6, 1907, d Aug. 8, 1954
Harris, M. J. (Middx, Notts., E. Province and Wellington) b May 25, 1944
Harris, P. G. Z. (N. Zealand) b July 18, 1927
Harris, R. M. (N. Zealand) b July 27, 1933
Harris, T. A. (S. Africa) b Aug. 27, 1916
Harrison, L. (Hants) b June 8, 1922
Harry, J. (Australia) b Aug. 1, 1857, d Oct. 27, 1919
Hart, G. E. (Middx) b Jan. 13, 1902
Hartigan, G. P. D. (S. Africa) b Dec. 30, 1884, d Jan. 7, 1955
Hartigan, R. J. (Australia) b Dec. 12, 1879, d June 7, 1958
Hartkopf, A. E. V. (Australia) b Dec. 28, 1889, d May 20, 1968
Hartley, A. (Lancs.; *CY 1911*) b April 11, 1879, d Oct. 1918
Hartley, J. C. (Oxford U. and Sussex) b Nov. 15, 1874, d March 8, 1963
Hartley, S. N. (Yorks. and Orange Free State) b March 18, 1956
Harty, I. D. (Border) b May 7, 1941
Harvey, J. F. (Derby.) b Sept. 27, 1939
Harvey, M. R. (Australia) b April 29, 1918
Harvey, P. F. (Notts.) b Jan. 15, 1923
Harvey, R. L. (S. Africa) b Sept. 14, 1911
Harvey, R. N. (Australia; *CY 1954*) b Oct. 8, 1928
Harvey-Walker, A. J. (Derby.) b July 21, 1944
Haseeb Ahsan (Pakistan) b July 15, 1939
Hassan, B. (Notts.) b March 24, 1944
Hassett, A. L. (Australia; *CY 1949*) b Aug. 28, 1913
Hastings, B. F. (N. Zealand) b March 23, 1940
Hathorn, C. M. H. (S. Africa) b April 7, 1878, d May 17, 1920
Hawke, 7th Lord (Camb. U. and Yorks.; *CY 1909*; Pres. MCC 1914-18) b Aug. 16, 1860, d Oct. 10, 1938
Hawke, N. J. N. (Australia) b June 27, 1939
Hawker, Sir Cyril (Essex; Pres. MCC 1970-71) b July 21, 1900
Hawkins, D. G. (Glos.) b May 18, 1935
Hawtin, A. P. R. (Northants) b Feb. 1, 1883, d Jan. 15, 1975
Hayes, E. G. (Surrey and Leics.; *CY 1907*) b Nov. 6, 1876, d Dec. 2, 1953
Hayes, F. C. (Lancs.) b Dec. 6, 1946

Hayes, J. A. (N. Zealand) b Jan. 11, 1927
Hayes, K. A. (Oxford U. and Lancs.) b Sept. 26, 1962
Hayes, P. J. (Camb. U.) b May 20, 1954
Haygarth, A. (Sussex; Historian) b Aug. 4, 1825, d May 1, 1903
Haynes, D. L. (W. Indies) b Feb. 15, 1956
Haynes, R. W. (Glos.) b Aug. 27, 1913, d Oct. 16, 1976
Hayward, T. (Cambs. and All-England) b March 21, 1835, d July 21, 1876
Hayward, T. W. (Surrey; *CY 1895*) b March 29, 1871, d July 19, 1939
Haywood, P. R. (Leics.) b March 30, 1947
Hazare, V. S. (India) b March 11, 1915
Hazell, H. L. (Somerset) b Sept. 30, 1909
Hazlerigg, Lord, formerly Hon. A. G. (Camb. U. and Leics.) b Feb. 24, 1910
Hazlitt, G. R. (Australia) b Sept. 4, 1888, d Oct. 30, 1915
Headley, G. A. (W. Indies; *CY 1934*) b Panama May 30, 1909
Headley, R. G. A. (Worcs. and W. Indies) b June 29, 1939
Heal, M. G. (Oxford U.) b Sept. 7, 1948
Heane, G. F. H. (Notts.) b Jan. 2, 1904, d Oct. 24, 1969
Hearn, P. (Kent) b Nov. 18, 1925
Hearne, Alec (Kent; *CY 1894*) b July 22, 1863, d May 16, 1952
Hearne, Frank (Kent, England and S. Africa) b Nov. 23, 1858, d July 14, 1949
Hearne, G. A. L. (S. Africa) b March 27, 1888, d Nov. 13, 1978
Hearne, George G. (Kent) b July 7, 1856, d Feb. 13, 1932
Hearne, J. T. (Middx; *CY 1892*) b May 3, 1867, d April 17, 1944
Hearne, J. W. (Middx; *CY 1912*) b Feb. 11, 1891, d Sept. 13, 1965
Hearne, Thos. (Middx) b Sept. 4, 1826, d May 13, 1900
Hearne, Thos., jun. (Lord's Ground Superintendent) b Dec. 29, 1849, d Jan. 29, 1910
Heath, G. E. M. (Hants) b Feb. 20, 1913
Heath, M. (Hants) b March 9, 1934
Hedges, B. (Glam.) b Nov. 10, 1927
Hedges, L. P. (Tonbridge, Oxford U., Kent and Glos.; *CY 1919*) b July 13, 1900, d Jan. 12, 1933
Heine, P. S. (S. Africa) b June 28, 1928
Hemmings, E. E. (Warw. and Notts.) b Feb. 20, 1949
Hemsley, E. J. O. (Worcs.) b Sept. 1, 1943
Henderson, M. (N. Zealand) b Aug. 2, 1895, d June 17, 1970
Henderson, R. (Surrey; *CY 1890*) b March 30, 1865, d Jan. 29, 1931
Henderson, S. P. (Camb. U. and Worcs.) b Sept. 24, 1958
Hendren, E. H. (Middx; *CY 1920*) b Feb. 5, 1889, d Oct. 4, 1962
Hendrick, M. (Derby. and Notts.; *CY 1978*) b Oct. 22, 1948
Hendriks, J. L. (W. Indies) b Dec. 21, 1933
Hendry, H. S. T. L. (Australia) b May 24, 1895
Henwood, P. P. (Orange Free State and Natal) b May 22, 1946
Herman, O. W. (Hants) b Sept. 18, 1907
Herman, R. S. (Middx, Border, Griqualand W. and Hants) b Nov. 30, 1946
Heron, J. G. (Zimbabwe) b Nov. 8, 1948
Heseltine C. (Hants) b Nov. 26, 1869, d June 13, 1944
Hever, N. G. (Middx and Glam.) b Dec. 17, 1924
Hewetson, E. P. (Oxford U. and Warw.) b May 27, 1902, d Dec. 26, 1977
Hewett, H. T. (Oxford U. and Somerset; *CY 1893*) b May 25, 1864, d March 4, 1921
Hibbert, P. A. (Australia) b July 23, 1952
Higgins, H. L. (Worcs.) b Feb. 24, 1894, d Sept. 15, 1979
Higgs, J. D. (Australia) b July 11, 1950
Higgs, K. (Lancs. and Leics.; *CY 1968*) b Jan. 14, 1937
Hignell, A. J. (Camb. U. and Glos.) b Sept. 4, 1955
Hilditch, A. M. J. (Australia) b May 20, 1956
Hill, Alan (Derby. and Orange Free State) b June 29, 1950
Hill, Allen (Yorks.) b Nov. 14, 1843, d Aug. 29, 1910
Hill, A. J. L. (Camb. U. and Hants) b July 26, 1871, d Sept. 6, 1950
Hill, Clement (Australia; *CY 1900*) b March 18, 1877, d Sept. 5, 1945
Hill, E. (Somerset) b July 9, 1923
Hill, G. (Hants) b April 15, 1913
Hill, J. C. (Australia) b June 25, 1923, d Aug, 11. 1974
Hill, L. W. (Glam.) b April 14, 1942
Hill, M. (Notts., Derby. and Somerset) b Sept. 14, 1935
Hill, N. W. (Notts.) b Aug. 22, 1935
Hill, W. A. (Warw.) b April 27, 1910
Hills, J. J. (Glam.; Umpire) b Oct. 14, 1897, d Oct. 1969
Hills, R. W. (Kent) b Jan. 8, 1951
Hill-Wood, C. K. B. H. (Oxford U. and Derby.) b June 5, 1907
Hill-Wood, Sir W. W. H. (Camb. U. and Derby.) b Sept. 8, 1901, d Oct. 10, 1980
Hilton, C. (Lancs. and Essex) b Sept. 26, 1937
Hilton, J. (Lancs. and Somerset) b Dec. 29, 1930
Hilton, M. J. (Lancs.; *CY 1957*) b Aug. 2, 1928

Hime, C. F. W. (S. Africa) b Oct. 24, 1869, d Dec. 6, 1940
Hindlekar, D. D. (India) b Jan. 1, 1909, d March 30, 1949
Hirst, G. H. (Yorks.; *CY 1901*) b Sept. 7, 1871, d May 10, 1954
Hitch, J. W. (Surrey; *CY 1914*) b May 7, 1886, d July 7, 1965
Hitchcock, R. E. (Canterbury and Warw.) b Nov. 28, 1929
Hoad, E. L. G. (W. Indies) b Jan. 29, 1896
Hoare, D. E. (Australia) b Oct. 19, 1934
Hobbs, Sir J. B. (Surrey; *CY 1909, special portrait 1926*) b Dec. 16, 1882, d Dec. 21, 1963
Hobbs, R. N. S. (Essex and Glam.) b May 8, 1942
Hobson, D. L. (E. Province and W. Province) b Sept. 3, 1951
Hodges, J. H. (Australia) b July 31, 1856, d Jan. 17, 1933
Hodgkinson, G. F. (Derby.) b Feb. 19, 1914
Hodgson, A. (Northants) b Oct. 27, 1951
Hodgson, K. I. (Camb. U.) b Feb. 24, 1960
Hodson, R. P. (Camb. U.) b April 26, 1951
Hofmeyr, M. B. (Oxford U. and NE Transvaal) b Dec. 9, 1925
Hogg, R. M. (Australia) b March 5, 1951
Hogg, W. (Lancs. and Warw.) b July 12, 1955
Hohns, T. V. (Queensland) b Jan. 23, 1954
Holder, V. A. (Worcs. and W. Indies) b Oct. 8, 1945
Holding, M. A. (Lancs. and W. Indies: *CY 1977*) b Feb. 16, 1954
Holdsworth, R. L. (Oxford U., Warw. and Sussex) b Feb. 25, 1899, d June 20, 1976
Hole, G. B. (Australia) b Jan. 6, 1931
Holford, D. A. J. (W. Indies) b April 16, 1940
Holliday, D. C. (Camb. U.) b Dec. 20, 1958
Hollies, W. E. (Warw.; *CY 1955*) b June 5, 1912, d April 16, 1981
Hollingdale, R. A. (Sussex) b March 6, 1906
Holmes, A. J. (Sussex) b June 30, 1899, d May 21, 1950
Holmes, E. R. T. (Oxford U. and Surrey; *CY 1936*) b Aug. 21, 1905, d Aug. 16, 1960
Holmes, G. C. (Glam.) b Sept. 16, 1958
Holmes, Percy (Yorks.; *CY 1920*) b Nov. 25, 1886, d Sept. 3, 1971
Holt, A. (Hants) b April 8, 1911
Holt, J. K., jun. (W. Indies) b Aug. 12, 1923
Home of the Hirsel, Lord (Middx; Pres. MCC 1966-67) b July 2, 1903
Hone, Sir B. W. (S. Australia and Oxford U.) b July 1, 1907, d May 28, 1978
Hone, L. (MCC) b Jan. 30, 1853, d Dec. 31, 1896
Hooker, J. E. H. (NSW) b March 6, 1898, d Feb. 12, 1982
Hooker, R. W. (Middx) b Feb. 22, 1935
Hookes, D. W. (Australia) b May 3, 1955
Hopkins, A. J. Y. (Australia) b May 4, 1874, d April 25, 1931
Hopkins, J. A. (Glam.) b June 16, 1953
Hopkins, V. (Glos.) b Jan. 21, 1911
Hopwood, J. L. (Lancs.) b Oct. 30, 1903
Horan, T. P. (Australia) b March 8, 1854, d April 16, 1916
Hordern, H. V. (Australia) b Feb. 10, 1884, d June 17, 1938
Hornby, A. N. (Lancs.) b Feb. 10, 1847, d Dec. 17, 1925
Horner, N. F. (Yorks. and Warw.) b May 10, 1926
Hornibrook, P. M. (Australia) b July 27, 1899, d Aug. 25, 1976
Horsfall, R. (Essex and Glam.) b June 26, 1920, d Aug. 25, 1981
Horsley, J. (Notts. and Derby.) b Jan. 4, 1890, d Feb. 13, 1976
Horton, H. (Worcs. and Hants) b April 18, 1923
Horton, J. (Worcs.) b Aug. 12, 1916
Horton, M. J. (Worcs. and N. Districts) b April 21, 1934
Hossell, J. J. (Warw.) b May 25, 1914
Hough, K. W. (N. Zealand) b Oct. 24, 1928
Howard, A. B. (W. Indies) b Aug. 27, 1946
Howard, A. H. (Glam.) b Dec. 11, 1910
Howard, B. J. (Lancs.) b May 21, 1926
Howard, K. (Lancs.) b June 29, 1941
Howard, N. D. (Lancs.) b May 18, 1925, d May 31, 1979
Howard, Major R. (Lancs.; MCC Team Manager) b April 17, 1890, d Sept. 10, 1967
Howarth, G. P. (Surrey and N. Zealand) b March 29, 1951
Howarth, H. J. (N. Zealand) b Dec. 25, 1943
Howat, M. G. (Camb. U.) b March 2, 1958
Howell, H. (Warw.) b Nov. 29, 1890, d July 9, 1932
Howell, M. (Oxford U. and Surrey) b Sept. 9, 1893, d Feb. 23, 1976
Howell, W. P. (Australia) b Dec. 29, 1869, d July 14, 1940
Howland, C. B. (Camb. U., Sussex and Kent) b Feb. 6, 1936
Howorth, R. (Worcs.) b April 26, 1909, d April 2, 1980
Hughes, D. P. (Lancs. and Tasmania) b May 13, 1947
Hughes, K. J. (Australia; *CY 1981*) b Jan. 26, 1954

Huish, F. H. (Kent) b Nov. 15, 1869, d March 16, 1957
Hulme, J. H. A. (Middx) b Aug. 26, 1904
Human, J. H. (Camb. U. and Middx) b Jan. 13, 1912
Humpage, G. W. (Warw. and Orange Free State) b April 24, 1954
Humphries, D. J. (Leics. and Worcs.) b Aug. 6, 1953
Humphries, J. (Derby.) b May 17, 1876, d May 8, 1946
Hunt, A. V. (Scotland and Bermuda) b Oct. 1, 1910
Hunt, W. A. (Australia) b Aug. 26, 1908
Hunte, C. C. (W. Indies; *CY 1964*) b May 9, 1932
Hunte, E. A. C. (W. Indies) b Oct. 3, 1905, d Aug. 1967
Hunter, David (Yorks.) b Feb. 23, 1860, d Jan. 11, 1927
Hunter, Joseph (Yorks.) b Aug. 3, 1855, d Jan. 4, 1891
Hurd, A. (Camb. U. and Essex) b Sept. 7, 1937
Hurst, A. G. (Australia) b July 15, 1950
Hurst, R. J. (Middx) b Dec. 29, 1933
Hurwood, A. (Australia) b June 17, 1902, d Sept. 26, 1982
Hussain, M. Dilawar (India) b March 19, 1907, d Aug. 26, 1967
Hutchings, K. L. (Kent; *CY 1907*) b Dec. 7, 1882, d Sept. 3, 1916
Hutchinson, J. M. (Derby.) b Nov. 29, 1896
Hutchinson, P. (S. Africa) b Jan. 26, 1862, d Sept. 30, 1925
Hutton, Sir Leonard (Yorks.; *CY 1938*) b June 23, 1916
Hutton, R. A. (Camb. U., Yorks. and Transvaal) b Sept. 6, 1942
Huxford, P. N. (Oxford U.) b Feb. 17, 1960
Huxter, R. J. A. (Camb. U.) b Oct. 29, 1959
Hylton, L. G. (W. Indies) b March 29, 1905, d May 17, 1955
Ibadulla, K. (Warw., Tasmania, Otago and Pakistan) b Dec. 20, 1935
Ibrahim, K. C. (India) b Jan. 26, 1919
Iddon, J. (Lancs.) b Jan. 8, 1902, d April 17, 1946
Ijaz Butt (Pakistan) b March 10, 1938
Ijaz Faqih (Pakistan) b March 24, 1956
Ikin, J. T. (Lancs.) b March 7, 1918
Illingworth, R. (Yorks. and Leics.; *CY 1960*) b June 8, 1932
Imran Khan Niazi (Oxford U., Worcs., Sussex and Pakistan; *CY 1983*) b Nov. 25, 1952
Imtiaz Ahmed (Pakistan) b Jan. 5, 1928
Imtiaz Ali (W. Indies) b July 28, 1954
Inchmore, J. D. (Worcs. and N. Transvaal) b Feb. 22, 1949
Indrajitsinhji, K. S. (India) b June 15, 1937
Ingle, R. A. (Somerset) b Nov. 5, 1903
Ingleby-Mackenzie, A. C. D. (Hants) b Sept. 15, 1933
Ingram, E. (Middx and Ireland) b Aug. 14, 1910, d March 13, 1973
Inman, C. C. (Ceylon and Leics.) b Jan. 29, 1936
Innes, G. A. S. (W. Province and Transvaal) b Nov. 16, 1931, d July 19, 1982
Inshan Ali (W. Indies) b Sept. 25, 1949
Insole, D. J. (Camb. U. and Essex; *CY 1956*) b April 18, 1926
Intikhab Alam Khan (Surrey and Pakistan) b Dec. 28, 1941
Inverarity, R. J. (Australia) b Jan. 31, 1944
Iqbal Qasim (Pakistan) b Aug. 6, 1953
Irani, J. K. (India) b Aug. 18, 1923
Iredale, F. A. (Australia) b June 19, 1867, d April 15, 1926
Iremonger, J. (Notts.; *CY 1903*) b March 5, 1876, d March 25, 1956
Ironmonger, H. (Australia) b April 7, 1882, d May 31, 1971
Ironside, D. E. J. (S. Africa) b May 2, 1925
Irvine, B. L. (Natal, Essex and Transvaal) b March 9, 1944
Israr Ali (Pakistan) b May 1, 1927
Iverson, J. B. (Australia) b July 27, 1915, d Oct. 24, 1973

Jackman, R. D. (Surrey, W. Province and Rhodesia; *CY 1981*) b Aug. 13, 1945
Jackson, A. (Australia) b Scotland Sept. 5, 1909, d Feb. 16, 1933
Jackson, A. B. (Derby.) b Aug. 21, 1933
Jackson, Sir A. H. M. (Derby.) b Nov. 9, 1899
Jackson, E. J. W. (Camb. U.) b March 26, 1955
Jackson, Rt Hon. Sir F. S. (Camb. U. and Yorks.; *CY 1894*; Pres. MCC 1921) b Nov. 21, 1870, d March 9, 1947
Jackson, G. R. (Derby.) b June 23, 1896, d Feb. 21, 1966
Jackson, H. L. (Derby.; *CY 1959*) b April 5, 1921
Jackson, John (Notts. and All-England) b May 21, 1833, d Nov. 4, 1901
Jackson, P. F. (Worcs.) b May 11, 1911
Jacques, T. A. (Yorks.) b Feb. 19, 1905
Jahangir Khan, Dr (Camb. U. and India) b Feb. 1, 1910
Jai, L. P. (India) b April 1, 1902, d Jan. 29, 1968
Jaisimha, M. L. (India) b March 3, 1939
Jakeman, F. (Yorks. and Northants) b Jan. 10, 1920
James, A. E. (Sussex) b Aug. 7, 1924
James, K. C. (Northants and N. Zealand) b March 12, 1904, d Aug. 21, 1976

James, R. M. (Camb. U. and Wellington) b Oct. 2, 1934
Jameson, J. A. (Warw.) b June 30, 1941
Jamshedji, R. J. D. (India) b Nov. 18, 1892, d April 5, 1976
Jardine, D. R. (Oxford U. and Surrey; *CY 1928*) b Oct. 23, 1900, d June 18, 1958
Jardine, M. R. (Oxford U. and Middx) b June 8, 1869, d Jan. 16, 1947
Jarman, B. N. (Australia) b Feb. 17, 1936
Jarrett, D. W. (Oxford U. and Cambridge U.) b April 19, 1952
Jarvis, A. H. (Australia) b Oct. 18, 1860, d Nov. 15, 1933
Jarvis, K. B. S. (Kent) b April 23, 1953
Jarvis, T. W. (N. Zealand) b July 29, 1944
Javed Akhtar (Pakistan) b Nov. 21, 1940
Javed Miandad Khan (Sussex, Glam. and Pakistan; *CY 1982*) b June 12, 1957
Jayantilal, K. (India) b Jan. 13, 1948
Jayasekera, R. S. A. (Sri Lanka) b Dec. 7, 1957
Jayasinghe, S. (Ceylon and Leics.) b Jan. 19, 1931
Jefferson, R. I. (Camb. U. and Surrey) b Aug. 15, 1941
Jenkins, R. O. (Worcs.; *CY 1950*) b Nov. 24, 1918
Jenkins, V. G. J. (Oxford U. and Glam.) b Nov. 2, 1911
Jenner, T. J. (Australia) b Sept. 8, 1944
Jennings, C. B. (Australia) b June 5, 1884, d June 20, 1950
Jennings, K. F. (Somerset) b Oct. 5, 1953
Jennings, R. V. (Transvaal) b Aug. 9, 1954
Jepson, A. (Notts.) b July 12, 1915
Jessop, G. L. (Camb. U. and Glos.; *CY 1898*) b May 19, 1874, d May 11, 1955
Jesty, T. E. (Hants, Border and Griqualand W; *CY 1983*) b June 2, 1948
Jewell, Major M. F. S. (Sussex and Worcs.) b Sept. 15, 1885, d May 28, 1978
Jilani, M. Baga Khan (India) b July 20, 1911, d July 2, 1941
Johnson, C. (Yorks.) b Sept. 5, 1947
Johnson, C. L. (S. Africa) b 1871, d May 31, 1908
Johnson, G. W. (Kent and Transvaal) b Nov. 8, 1946
Johnson, H. H. H. (W. Indies) b July 17, 1910
Johnson, H. L. (Derby.) b Nov. 8, 1927
Johnson, I. W. (Australia) b Dec. 8, 1918
Johnson, L. A. (Surrey and Northants) b Aug. 12, 1936
Johnson, L. J. (Australia) b March 18, 1919, d April 20, 1977
Johnson, P. D. (Camb. U. and Notts.) b Nov. 12, 1949
Johnson, T. F. (W. Indies) b Jan. 10, 1917
Johnston, W. A. (Australia; *CY 1949*) b Feb. 26, 1922
Johnstone, C. P. (Camb. U., Kent and Madras) b Aug. 19, 1895, d June 23, 1974
Jones, A. (Glam., W. Australia, N. Transvaal and Natal; *CY 1978*) b Nov. 4, 1938
Jones, A. A. (Sussex, Somerset, Middx, Glam., N. Transvaal and Orange Free State) b Dec. 9, 1947
Jones, A. K. C. (Oxford U. and Warw.) b April 20, 1951
Jones, A. L. (Glam.) b June 1, 1957
Jones, A. O. (Notts. and Camb. U.; *CY 1900*) b Aug. 16, 1872, d Dec. 21, 1914
Jones, B. J. R. (Worcs.) b Nov. 2, 1955
Jones, C. M. (W. Indies) details not known
Jones, Ernest (Australia) b Sept. 30, 1869, d Nov. 23, 1943
Jones, E. C. (Glam.) b Dec. 14, 1912
Jones, E. W. (Glam.) b June 25, 1942
Jones, I. J. (Glam.) b Dec. 10, 1941
Jones, K. V. (Middx) b March 28, 1942
Jones, P. E. (W. Indies) b June 6, 1917
Jones, P. C. H. (Oxford U.) b Aug. 19, 1948
Jones, P. H. (Kent) b June 19, 1935
Jones, S. P. (Auckland and Australia) b Aug. 1, 1861, d July 14, 1951
Jones, W. E. (Glam.) b Oct. 31, 1916
Jordan, A. B. (C. Districts) b Sept. 5, 1949
Jordan, J. M. (Lancs.) b Feb. 7, 1932
Jorden, A. M. (Camb. U. and Essex) b Jan. 28, 1947
Jordon, R. C. (Victoria) b Feb. 17, 1937
Joshi, P. G. (India) b Oct. 27, 1926
Joshi, U. C. (Gujerat and Sussex) b Dec. 23, 1944
Joslin, L. R. (Australia) b Dec. 13, 1947
Jowett, D. C. P. R. (Oxford U.) b June 24, 1931
Judd, A. K. (Camb. U. and Hants) b Jan. 1, 1904
Judge, P. F. (Middx, Glam. and Bengal) b May 23, 1916
Julian, R. (Leics.) b Aug. 23, 1936
Julien, B. D. (Kent and W. Indies) b March 13, 1950
Jumadeen, R. R. (W. Indies) b April 12, 1948
Jupp, H. (Surrey) b Nov. 19, 1841, d April 8, 1889
Jupp, V. W. C. (Sussex and Northants; *CY 1928*) b March 27, 1891, d July 9, 1960

Kallicharran, A. I. (Warw., Queensland and W. Indies; *CY 1983*) b March 21, 1949
Kaluperuma, L. W. (Sri Lanka) b June 25, 1949
Kanhai, R. B. (Warw., W. Australia, Tasmania and W. Indies; *CY 1964*) b Dec. 26, 1935

Kanitkar, H. S. (India) b Dec. 8, 1942
Kapil Dev (Northants and India; *CY 1983*) b Jan. 6, 1959
Kaplan, C. J. (Orange Free State) b Jan. 26, 1909
Kardar, A. H. (formerly Abdul Hafeez) (Oxford U., Warw., India and Pakistan) b Jan. 17, 1925
Katz, G. A. (Natal) b Feb. 9, 1947
Kayum, D. A. (Oxford U.) b Oct. 13, 1955
Keeton, W. W. (Notts.; *CY 1940*) b April 30, 1905, d Oct. 9, 1980
Keighley, W. G. (Oxford U. and Yorks.) b Jan. 10, 1925
Keith, G. L. (Somerset, W. Province and Hants) b Nov. 19, 1937, d Dec. 26, 1975
Keith, H. J. (S. Africa) b Oct. 25, 1927
Kelleher, H. R. A. (Surrey and Northants) b March 3, 1929
Kelleway, C. (Australia) b April 25, 1889, d Nov. 16, 1944
Kelly, J. (Notts.) b Sept. 15, 1930
Kelly, J. J. (Australia; *CY 1903*) b May 10, 1867, d Aug. 14, 1938
Kelly, J. M. (Lancs. and Derby.) b March 19, 1922, d Nov. 13, 1979
Kelly, T. J. D. (Australia) b Ireland May 3, 1844, d July 20, 1893
Kempis, G. A. (S. Africa) b Aug. 4, 1865, d May 19, 1890
Kendall, T. (Australia) b Bedford, England Aug. 24, 1851, d Aug. 17, 1924
Kennedy, A. (Lancs.) b Nov. 4, 1949
Kennedy, A. S. (Hants; *CY 1933*) b Jan. 24, 1891, d Nov. 15, 1959
Kenny, R. B. (India) b Sept. 29, 1930
Kent, M. F. (Australia) b Nov. 23, 1953
Kentish, E. S. M. (Oxford U. and W. Indies) b Nov. 21, 1916
Kenyon, D. (Worcs.; *CY 1963*) b May 15, 1924
Kerr, J. (Scotland) b April 8, 1885, d Dec. 27, 1972
Kerr, J. L. (N. Zealand) b Dec. 28, 1910
Kerslake, R. C. (Camb. U. and Somerset) b Dec. 26, 1942
Kettle, M. K. (Northants) b March 18, 1944
Khalid Hassan (Pakistan) b July 14, 1937
Khalid Ibadulla, (*see* Ibadulla, K.)
Khalid Wazir Ali (Pakistan) b April 27, 1936
Khan Mohammad (Somerset and Pakistan) b Jan. 1, 1928
Kidd, E. L. (Camb. U. and Middx) b Oct. 18, 1889
Killick, Rev. E. T. (Camb. U. and Middx) b May 9, 1907, d May 18, 1953
Kilner, Norman (Yorks. and Warw.) b July 21, 1895, d April 28, 1979
Kilner, Roy (Yorks.; *CY 1924*) b Oct. 17, 1890, d April 5, 1928
Kimpton, R. C. M. (Oxford U. and Worcs.) b Sept. 21, 1916
King, C. L. (Glam. and W. Indies) b June 11, 1951
King, F. McD. (W. Indies) b Dec. 14, 1926
King, I. M. (Warw. and Essex) b Nov. 10, 1931
King, J. B. (Philadelphia) b Oct. 19, 1873, d Oct. 17, 1965
King, J. H. (Leics.) b April 16, 1871, d Nov. 20, 1946
King, L. A. (Jamaica, Bengal and W. Indies) b Feb. 27, 1939
Kingsley, Sir Patrick (PGT) (Oxford U.) b May 26, 1908
Kinneir, S. P. (Warw.; *CY 1912*) b May 13, 1871, d Oct. 16, 1928
Kippax, A. F. (Australia) b May 25, 1897, d Sept. 5, 1972
Kirby, D. (Camb. U. and Leics.) b Jan. 18, 1939
Kirmani, S. M. H. (India) b Dec. 29, 1949
Kirsten, P. N. (W. Province, Sussex and Derby.) b May 14, 1955
Kirti Azad (India) b Jan. 2, 1959
Kirton, K. N. (Border and E. Province) b Feb. 24, 1928
Kischenchand, G. (India) b April 14, 1925
Kitchen, M. J. (Somerset) b Aug. 1, 1940
Kline, L. F. (Australia) b Sept. 29, 1934
Knight, A. E. (Leics.; *CY 1904*) b Oct. 8, 1872, d April 25, 1946
Knight, B. R. (Essex and Leics.) b Feb. 18, 1938
Knight, D. J. (Oxford U. and Surrey; *CY 1915*) b May 12, 1894, d Jan. 5, 1960
Knight, J. M. (Oxford U.) b March 16, 1958
Knight, R. D. V. (Camb. U., Surrey, Glos. and Sussex) b Sept. 6, 1946
Knight, W. H. (Editor of *Wisden* 1870-79) b Nov. 29, 1812, d Aug. 16, 1879
Knott, A. P. E. (Kent and Tasmania; *CY 1970*) b April 9, 1946
Knott, C. H. (Oxford U. and Kent) b March 20, 1901
Knott, C. J. (Hants) b Nov. 26, 1914
Knott, F. H. (Oxford U., Kent and Sussex) b Oct. 30, 1891, d Feb. 10, 1972
Knowles, J. (Notts.) b March 25, 1910
Knox, G. K. (Lancs.) b April 22, 1937
Knox, N. A. (Surrey; *CY 1907*) b Oct. 10, 1884, d March 3, 1935
Kortright, C. J. (Essex) b Jan. 9, 1871, d Dec. 12, 1952
Kotze, J. J. (S. Africa) b Aug. 7, 1879, d July 7, 1931
Kourie, A. J. (Transvaal) b July 30, 1951
Kripal Singh, A. G. (India) b Aug. 6, 1933
Krishnamurthy, P. (India) b July 12, 1947
Kulkarni, U. N. (India) b March 7, 1942

Kumar, V. V. (India) b June 22, 1935
Kunderan, B. K. (India) b Oct. 2, 1939
Kuys, F. (S. Africa) b March 21, 1870, d Sept. 12, 1953

Lacey, Sir F. E. (Camb. U. and Hants; Sec. MCC 1898-1926) b Oct. 19, 1859, d May 26, 1946
Laird, B. M. (Australia) b Nov. 21, 1951
Laker, J. C. (Surrey, Auckland and Essex; *CY 1952*) b Feb. 9, 1922
Lall Singh (India) b Dec. 12, 1909
Lamb, A. J. (W. Province and Northants; *CY 1981*) b June 20, 1954
Lamb, T. M. (Oxford U., Middx and Northants) b March 24, 1953
Lambert, G. E. E. (Glos. and Somerset) b May 11, 1919
Lambert, R. H. (Ireland) b July 18, 1874, d March 24, 1956
Lambert, Wm (Surrey) b 1779, d April 19, 1851
Lampard, A. W. (Victoria and AIF; oldest living Sheffield Shield player) b July 3, 1885
Lance, H. R. (S. Africa) b June 6, 1940
Langdon, C. W. (W. Australia) b July 4, 1922
Langdale, G. R. (Derby. and Somerset) b March 11, 1916
Langford, B. A. (Somerset) b Dec. 17, 1935
Langley, G. R. A. (Australia; *CY 1957*) b Sept. 19, 1919
Langridge, James (Sussex; *CY 1932*) b July 10, 1906, d Sept. 10, 1966
Langridge, J. G. (Sussex; *CY 1950*) b Feb. 10, 1910
Langridge, R. J. (Sussex) b April 13, 1939
Langton, A. B. C. (S. Africa) b March 2, 1912, d Nov. 27, 1942
Larkins, W. (Northants) b Nov. 22, 1953
Larter, J. D. F. (Northants) b April 24, 1940
Larwood, H. (Notts.; *CY 1927*) b Nov. 14, 1904
Lashley, P. D. (W. Indies) b Feb. 11, 1937
Latchman, A. H. (Middx and Notts.) b July 26, 1943
Laughlin, T. J. (Australia) b Jan. 30, 1951
Laver, F. (Australia) b Dec. 7, 1869, d Sept. 24, 1919
Lawrence, G. B. (S. Africa) b March 31, 1932
Lawrence, J. (Somerset) b March 29, 1914
Lawry, W. M. (Australia; *CY 1962*) b Feb. 11, 1937
Lawson, G. F. (Lancs. and Australia) b Dec. 7, 1957
Leadbeater, B. (Yorks.) b Aug. 14, 1943
Leadbeater, E. (Yorks. and Warw.) b Aug. 15, 1927
Leary, S. E. (Kent) b April 30, 1933
Lee, C. (Yorks. and Derby.) b March 17, 1924
Lee, F. S. (Middx and Somerset) b July 24, 1905, d March 30, 1982
Lee, G. M. (Notts. and Derby.) b June 7, 1887, d Feb. 29, 1976
Lee, H. W. (Middx) b Oct. 26, 1890, d April 21, 1981
Lee, I. S. (Victoria) b March 24, 1914
Lee, J. W. (Middx and Somerset) b Feb. 1, 1904, d June 20, 1944
Lee, P. G. (Northants and Lancs.; *CY 1976*) b Aug. 27, 1945
Lee, P. K. (Australia) b Sept. 15, 1904, d Aug. 9, 1980
Lee, R. J. (Oxford U.) b March 6, 1950
Lees, W. K. (N. Zealand) b March 19, 1952
Lees, W. S. (Surrey; *CY 1906*) b Dec. 25, 1875, d Sept. 10, 1924
Leese, Sir Oliver W. H., 3rd Bt (Pres. MCC 1965-66) b Oct. 27, 1894, d Jan. 20, 1978
Legall, R. A. (W. Indies) b Dec. 1, 1925
Legard, E. (Warw.) b Aug. 23, 1935
Leggat, I. B. (N. Zealand) b June 7, 1930
Leggat, J. G. (N. Zealand) b May 27, 1926, d March 8, 1973
Lenham, L. J. (Sussex) b May 24, 1936
le Roux, F. L. (S. Africa) b Feb. 5, 1882, d Sept. 22, 1963
le Roux, G. S. (W. Province and Sussex) b Sept. 4, 1955
le Roux, R. A. (Orange Free State) b May 27, 1950
Leslie, C. F. H. (Oxford U. and Middx) b Dec. 8, 1861, d Feb. 12, 1921
Lester, E. I. (Yorks.) b Feb. 18, 1923
Lester, G. (Leics.) b Dec. 27, 1915
Lester, Dr J. A. (Philadelphia) b Cumberland, England Aug. 1, 1871, d Sept. 3, 1969
L'Estrange, M. G. (Oxford U.) b Oct. 12, 1952
Lethbridge, C. (Warw.) b June 23, 1961
Lever, J. K. (Essex; *CY 1979*) b Feb. 24, 1949
Lever, P. (Lancs. and Tasmania) b Sept. 17, 1940
Leveson Gower, Sir H. D. G. (Oxford U. and Surrey) b May 8, 1873, d Feb. 1, 1954
Levett, W. H. V. (Kent) b Jan. 25, 1908
Lewington, P. J. (Warw.) b Jan. 30, 1950
Lewis, A. R. (Camb. U. and Glam.) b July 6, 1938
Lewis, C. (Kent) b July 27, 1908
Lewis, D. J. (Oxford U. and Rhodesia) b July 27, 1927
Lewis, D. M. (W. Indies) b Feb. 21, 1946
Lewis, E. B. (Warw.) b Jan. 5, 1918

Lewis, E. J. (Glam. and Sussex) b Jan. 31, 1942
Lewis, P. T. (S. Africa) b Oct. 2, 1884, d Jan. 30, 1976
Lewis, R. V. (Hants) b Aug. 6, 1947
Leyland, M. (Yorks.; *CY 1929*) b July 20, 1900, d Jan. 1, 1967
Liaqat Ali Khan (Pakistan) b May 21, 1955
Liddicutt, A. E. (Victoria) b Oct. 17, 1891
Lightfoot, A. (Northants) b Jan. 8, 1936
Lill, J. C. (S. Australia) b Dec. 7, 1933
Lillee, D. K. (Australia; *CY 1973*) b July 18, 1949
Lilley, A. A. (Warw.; *CY 1897*) b Nov. 28, 1866, d Nov. 17, 1929
Lilley, B. (Notts.) b Feb. 11, 1895, d Aug. 4, 1950
Lillywhite, Fred (Sussex; Editor of *Lillywhite's Guide to Cricketers*) b July 23, 1829, d Sept. 15, 1866
Lillywhite, F. W. ("William") (Sussex) b June 13, 1792, d Aug. 21, 1854
Lillywhite, James, jun. (Sussex) b Feb. 23, 1842, d Oct. 25, 1929
Lindsay, D. T. (S. Africa) b Sept. 4, 1939
Lindsay, J. D. (S. Africa) b Sept. 8, 1909
Lindsay, N. V. (S. Africa) b July 30, 1886, d Feb. 2, 1976
Lindwall, R. R. (Australia; *CY 1949*) b Oct. 3, 1921
Ling, W. V. S. (S. Africa) b Oct. 3, 1891, d Sept. 26, 1960
Lissette, A. F. (N. Zealand) b Nov. 6, 1919, d Jan. 24, 1973
Lister, J. (Yorks. and Worcs.) b May 14, 1930
Lister, W. H. L. (Lancs.) b Oct. 7, 1911
Littlewood, D. J. (Cambridge U.) b Oct. 28, 1955
Livingston, L. (NSW and Northants) b May 3, 1920
Livingstone, D. A. (Hants) b Sept. 21, 1933
Livsey, W. H. (Hants) b Sept. 23, 1893, d Sept. 12, 1978
Llewellyn, C. B. (Hants and S. Africa; *CY 1911*) b Sept. 26, 1876, d June 7, 1964
Llewellyn, M. J. (Glam.) b Nov. 27, 1953
Lloyd, B. J. (Glam.) b Sept. 6, 1953
Lloyd, C. H. (W. Indies and Lancs.; *CY 1971*) b Aug. 31, 1944
Lloyd, D. (Lancs.) b March 18, 1947
Lloyd, M. F. D. (Oxford U.) b June 6, 1954
Lloyd, T. A. (Warw. and Orange Free State) b Nov. 5, 1956
Lloyds, J. W. (Somerset) b Nov. 17, 1954
Loader, P. J. (Surrey and W. Australia; *CY 1958*) b Oct. 25, 1929
Lobb, B. (Warw. and Somerset) b Jan. 11, 1931
Lock, G. A. R. (Surrey, Leics. and W. Australia; *CY 1954*) b July 5, 1929
Lock, H. C. (Surrey) b May 8, 1903, d May 18, 1978
Lockwood, Ephraim (Yorks.) b April 4, 1845, d Dec. 19, 1921
Lockwood, W. H. (Notts. and Surrey; *CY 1899*) b March 25, 1868, d April 26, 1932
Lockyer, T. (Surrey and All-England) b Nov. 1, 1826, d Dec. 22, 1869
Logan, J. D. (S. Africa) b June 24, 1880, d Jan. 3, 1960
Lohmann, G. A. (Surrey, W. Province and Transvaal; *CY 1889*) b June 2, 1865, d Dec. 1, 1901
Lomax, J. G. (Lancs. and Somerset) b May 5, 1925
Long, A. (Surrey and Sussex) b Dec. 18, 1940
Longfield, T. C. (Camb. U. and Kent) b May 12, 1906, d Dec. 21, 1981
Longrigg, E. F. (Camb. U. and Somerset) b April 16, 1906, d July 23, 1974
Lord, Thomas (Middx; founder of Lord's) b Nov. 23, 1755, d Jan. 13, 1832
Love, H. S. B. (Australia) b Aug. 10, 1895, d July 22, 1969
Love, J. D. (Yorks.) b April 22, 1955
Lowndes, W. G. L. F. (Oxford U. and Hants) b Jan 24, 1898, d May 23, 1982
Lowry, T. C. (Camb. U., Somerset and N. Zealand) b Feb. 17, 1898, d July 20, 1976
Lowson, F. A. (Yorks.) b July 1, 1925
Loxton, S. J. E. (Australia) b March 29, 1921
Lucas, A. P. (Camb. U., Surrey, Middx and Essex) b Feb. 20, 1857, d Oct. 12, 1923
Luckes, W. T. (Somerset) b Jan. 1, 1901, d Oct. 27, 1982
Luckhurst, B. W. (Kent; *CY 1971*) b Feb. 5, 1939
Luddington, R. S. (Oxford U.) b April 8, 1960
Lumb, R. G. (Yorks.) b Feb. 27, 1950
Lundie, E. B. (S. Africa) b March 15, 1888, d Sept. 12, 1917
Lynch, M. A. (Surrey) b May 21, 1958
Lyon, B. H. (Oxford U. and Glos.; *CY 1931*) b Jan. 19, 1902, d June 22, 1970
Lyon, J. (Lancs.) b May 17, 1951
Lyon, M. D. (Cambridge U. and Somerset) b April 22, 1898, d Feb. 17, 1964
Lyons, J. J. (Australia) b May 21, 1863, d July 21, 1927
Lyons, K. J. (Glam.) b Dec. 18, 1946
Lyttelton, Rt Hon. Alfred (Camb. U. and Middx; Pres. MCC 1898) b Feb. 7, 1857, d July 5, 1913
Lyttelton, Rev. Hon. C. F. (Camb. U. and Worcs.) b Jan. 26, 1887, d Oct. 3, 1931
Lyttelton, Hon. C. J. (*see* 10th Visct Cobham)

Lyttelton, Hon. R. H. (Eton) b Jan. 18, 1854, d Nov. 7, 1939

McAlister, P. A. (Australia) b July 11, 1869, d May 10, 1938
Macartney, C. G. (Australia; *CY 1922*) b June 27, 1886, d Sept. 9, 1958
Macaulay, G. G. (Yorks.; *CY 1924*) b Dec. 7, 1897, d Dec. 14, 1940
Macaulay, M. J. (S. Africa) b April 19, 1939
MacBryan, J. C. W. (Camb. U. and Somerset; *CY 1925*) b July 22, 1892
McCabe, S. J. (Australia; *CY 1935*) b July 16, 1910, d Aug. 25, 1968
McCanlis, M. A. (Oxford U., Surrey and Glos.) b June 17, 1906
McCarthy, C. N. (Camb. U. and S. Africa) b March 24, 1929
McConnon, J. (Glam.) b June 21, 1922
McCool, C. L. (Somerset and Australia) b Dec. 9, 1915
McCorkell, N. T. (Hants) b March 23, 1912
McCormick, E. L. (Australia) b May 16, 1906
McCosker, R. B. (Australia; *CY 1976*) b Dec. 11, 1946
McDonald, C. C. (Australia) b Nov. 17, 1928
McDonald, E. A. (Lancs. and Australia; *CY 1922*) b Jan. 6, 1891, d July 22, 1937
McDonnell, P. S. (Australia) b London Nov. 13, 1858, d Sept. 24, 1896
McEvoy, M. S. A. (Essex) b Jan. 25, 1956
McEwan, K. S. (E. Province, W. Province, Essex and W. Australia; *CY 1978*) b July 16, 1952
McEwan, P. E. (N. Zealand) b Dec. 19, 1953
McGahey, C. P. (Essex; *CY 1902*) b Feb. 12, 1871, d Jan. 10, 1935
MacGibbon, A. R. (N. Zealand) b Aug. 28, 1924
McGirr, H. M. (N. Zealand) b Nov. 5, 1891, d April 14, 1964
McGlew, D. J. (S. Africa; *CY 1956*) b March 11, 1929
MacGregor, G. (Camb. U. and Middx; *CY 1891*) b Aug. 31, 1869, d Aug. 20, 1919
McGregor, S. N. (N. Zealand) b Dec. 18, 1931
McHugh, F. P. (Yorks. and Glos.) b Nov. 15, 1925
McIlwraith, J. (Australia) b Sept. 7, 1857, d July 5, 1938
Macindoe, D. H. (Oxford U.) b Sept. 1, 1917
McIntyre, A. J. W. (Surrey; *CY 1958*) b May 14, 1918
McIntyre, J. M. (Auckland and Canterbury) b July 4, 1944
MacKay, K. D. (Australia) b Oct. 24, 1925, d June 13, 1982
McKay-Coghill, D. (Transvaal) b Nov. 4, 1941
McKenzie, G. D. (Leics. and Australia; *CY 1965*) b June 24, 1941
McKenzie, K. A. (NE Transvaal and Transvaal) b July 16, 1948
McKibbin, T. R. (Australia) b Dec. 10, 1870, d Dec. 15, 1939
McKinnon, A. H. (S. Africa) b Aug. 20, 1932
MacKinnon, F. A. (Camb. U. and Kent) b April 9, 1848, d Feb. 27, 1947
McLachlan, I. M. (Camb. U. and S. Australia) b Oct. 2, 1936
MacLaren, A. C. (Lancs.; *CY 1895*) b Dec. 1, 1871, d Nov. 17, 1944
McLaren, J. W. (Australia) b Dec. 24, 1887, d Nov. 17, 1921
McLaughlin, J. J. (Queensland) b Feb. 18, 1930
Maclean, J. A. (Australia) b April 27, 1946
McLean, R. A. (S. Africa; *CY 1961*) b July 9, 1930
McLeod, C. E. (Australia) b Oct. 24, 1869, d Nov. 26, 1918
McLeod, E. G. (N. Zealand) b Oct. 14, 1900
McLeod, R. W. (Australia) b Jan. 19, 1868, d June 15, 1907
McMahon, J. W. (Surrey and Somerset) b Dec. 28, 1919
McMahon, T. G. (N. Zealand) b Nov. 8, 1929
McMaster, J. E. P. (England) b March 16, 1861, d June 7, 1929
McMillan, Q. (S. Africa) b June 23, 1904, d July 3, 1948
McMorris, E. D. A. (W. Indies) b April 4, 1935
McNally, J. P. (Griqualand W.) b Nov. 27, 1907
McRae, D. A. N. (N. Zealand) b Dec. 25, 1912
McShane, P. G. (Australia) b 1857, d Dec. 11, 1903
McVicker, N. M. (Warw. and Leics.) b Nov. 4, 1940
McWatt, C. A. (W. Indies) b Feb. 1, 1922
Madan Lal (India) b March 20, 1951
Maddocks, L. V. (Australia) b May 24, 1926
Madray, I. S. (W. Indies) b July 2, 1934
Madson, M. B. (Natal) b Sept. 29, 1949
Madugalle, R. S. (Sri Lanka) b April 22, 1959
Mahmood Hussain (Pakistan) b April 2, 1932
Mailey, A. A. (Australia) b Jan. 3, 1886, d Dec. 31, 1967

Majid J. Khan (Camb. U., Glam., Queensland and Pakistan; *CY 1970*) b Sept. 28, 1946
Maka, E. S. (India) b March 5, 1922
Makepeace, H. (Lancs.) b Aug. 22, 1881, d Dec. 19, 1952
Malhotra, A. (India) b June 26, 1957
Mallender, N. A. (Northants) b Aug. 13, 1961
Mallett, A. A. (Australia) b July 13, 1945
Mallett, A. W. H. (Oxford U. and Kent) b Aug. 29, 1924
Mallett, N. V. H. (Oxford U.) b Oct. 30, 1956
Malone, M. F. (Australia and Lancs.) b Oct. 9, 1950
Manjrekar, V. L. (India) b Sept. 26, 1931
Mankad, A. V. (India) b Oct. 12, 1946
Mankad, V. (M. H.) (India; *CY 1947*) b April 12, 1917, d Aug. 21, 1978
Mann, A. L. (Australia) b Nov. 8, 1945
Mann, F. G. (Camb. U. and Middx) b Sept. 6, 1917
Mann, F. T. (Camb. U. and Middx) b March 3, 1888, d Oct. 6, 1964
Mann, J. P. (Middx) b June 13, 1919
Mann, N. B. F. (S. Africa) b Dec. 28, 1920, d July 31, 1952
Manning, J. S. (S. Australia and Northants) b June 11, 1924
Manning, T. E. S. (Northants) b Sept. 2, 1884, d Nov. 22, 1975
Mansell, P. N. F. (S. Africa) b Shropshire March 16, 1920
Mansoor Akhtar (Pakistan) b Dec. 25, 1956
Mantri, M. K. (India) b Sept. 1, 1921
Maqsood Ahmed (Pakistan) b March 26, 1925
Marais, G. G. ("G. Gladstone") (W. Indies) b Jan. 14, 1901, d May 19, 1978
Marie, G. V. (Oxford U.) b Feb. 17, 1945
Markham, L. A. (S. Africa) b Sept. 12, 1924
Marks, V. J. (Oxford U. and Somerset) b June 25, 1955
Marlar, R. G. (Camb. U. and Sussex) b Jan. 2, 1931
Marlow, W. H. (Leics.) b Feb. 13, 1900, d Dec. 16, 1975
Marner, P. T. (Lancs. and Leics.) b March 31, 1936
Marr, A. P. (Australia) b March 28, 1862, d March 15, 1940
Marriott, C. S. (Camb. U., Lancs. and Kent) b Sept. 14, 1895, d Oct. 13, 1966
Marsden, R. (Oxford U.) b April 2, 1959
Marsden, Tom (England) b 1805, d Feb. 27, 1843
Marsh, F. E. (Derby.) b July 7, 1920
Marsh, R. W. (Australia; *CY 1982*) b Nov. 4, 1947
Marshal, Alan (Queensland and Surrey; *CY 1909*) b June 12, 1883, d July 23, 1915
Marshall, J. M. A. (Warw.) b Oct. 26, 1916
Marshall, M. D. (Hants and W. Indies; *CY 1983*) b April 18, 1958
Marshall, N. E. (W. Indies) b Feb. 27, 1924
Marshall, R. E. (Hants and W. Indies; *CY 1959*) b April 25, 1930
Martin, E. J. (Notts.) b Aug. 17, 1925
Martin, F. (Kent; *CY 1892*) b Oct. 12, 1861, d Dec. 13, 1921
Martin, F. R. (W. Indies) b Oct. 12, 1893, d Nov. 23, 1967
Martin, J. D. (Oxford U. and Somerset) b Dec. 23, 1941
Martin, J. W. (Australia) b July 28, 1931
Martin, J. W. (Kent) b Feb. 16, 1917
Martin, S. H. (Worcs., Natal and Rhodesia) b Jan. 11, 1909
Martindale, E. A. (W. Indies) b Nov. 25, 1909, d March 17, 1972
Marx, W. F. E. (S. Africa) b July 4, 1895, d June 2, 1974
Mason, J. R. (Kent; *CY 1898*) b March 26, 1874, d Oct. 15, 1958
Massie, H. H. (Australia) b April 11, 1854, d Oct. 12, 1938
Massie, R. A. L. (Australia; *CY 1973*) b April 14, 1947
Matheson, A. M. (N. Zealand) b Feb. 27, 1906
Mathias, Wallis (Pakistan) b Feb. 4, 1935
Matthews, A. D. G. (Northants and Glam.) b May 3, 1904, d July 29, 1977
Matthews, C. S. (Notts.) b Oct. 17, 1929
Matthews, T. J. (Australia) b April 3, 1884, d Oct. 14, 1943
Mattis, E. H. (W. Indies) b April 11, 1957
Maudsley, R. H. (Oxford U. and Warw.) b April 8, 1918, d Sept. 29, 1981
May, B. (Oxford U.) b Nov. 1, 1944
May, P. B. H. (Camb. U. and Surrey; *CY 1952*; Pres. MCC 1980-81) b Dec. 31, 1929
Mayer, J. H. (Warw.) b March 2, 1902, d Sept. 6, 1981
Mayes, R. (Kent) b Oct. 7, 1921
Maynard, C. (Warw. and Lancs.) b April 8, 1958
Mayne, E. R. (Australia) b July 2, 1884, d Oct. 26, 1961
Mayne, L. C. (Australia) b Jan. 26, 1942
Mead, C. P. (Hants; *CY 1912*) b March 9, 1887, d March 26, 1958
Mead, W. (Essex; *CY 1904*) b March 25, 1868, d March 18, 1954
Meads, E. A. (Notts.) b Aug. 17, 1916
Meale, T. (N. Zealand) b Nov. 11, 1928
Meckiff, I. (Australia) b Jan. 6, 1935
Meher-Homji, K. R. (India) b Aug. 9, 1911, d Feb. 10, 1982

Mehra, V. L. (India) b March 12, 1938
Meintjes, D. J. (S. Africa) b June 9, 1890, d July 17, 1979
Melle, M. G. (S. Africa) b June 3, 1930
Melluish, M. E. L. (Camb. U. and Middx) b June 13, 1932
Melville, A. (Oxford U., Sussex and S. Africa; *CY 1948*) b May 19, 1910
Mence, M. D. (Warw. and Glos.) b April 30, 1944
Mendis, G. D. (Sussex) b April 20, 1955
Mendis, L. R. D. (Sri Lanka) b Aug. 25, 1952
Mendonca, I. L. (W. Indies) b July 13, 1934
Mercer, J. (Sussex, Glam. and Northants; *CY 1927*) b April 22, 1895
Merchant, V. M. (India; *CY 1937*) b Oct. 12, 1911
Merritt, W. E. (Northants and N. Zealand) b Aug. 18, 1908, d June 9, 1977
Merry, C. A. (W. Indies) b Jan. 20, 1911, d April 19, 1964
Meuleman, K. D. (Australia) b Sept. 5, 1923
Meuli, E. M. (N. Zealand) b Feb. 20, 1926
Meyer, B. J. (Glos.) b Aug. 21, 1932
Meyer, R. J. O. (Camb. U., Somerset and W. India) b March 15, 1905
Mian Mohammad Saaed (Pakistan's first captain) b Aug. 31, 1910, d Aug. 23, 1979
Middleton, J. (S. Africa) b Sept. 30, 1865, d Dec. 23, 1913
Midwinter, W. E. (Victoria, Glos., Australia and England) b Forest of Dean, England June 19, 1851, d Dec. 3, 1890
Milburn, B. D. (N. Zealand) b Nov. 24, 1943
Milburn, C. (Northants and W. Australia; *CY 1967*) b Oct. 23, 1941
Milkha Singh, A. G. (India) b Dec. 31, 1941
Miller, A. M. (England) b Oct. 19, 1869, d June 26, 1959
Miller, G. (Derby.) b Sept. 8, 1952
Miller, K. R. (Notts. and Australia; *CY 1954*) b Nov. 28, 1919
Miller, L. S. M. (N. Zealand) b March 31, 1923
Miller, R. (Warw.) b Jan. 6, 1941
Miller, R. C. (W. Indies) b Dec. 24, 1924
Milligan, F. W. (Yorks.) b March 19, 1870, d March 31, 1900
Millman, G. (Notts.) b Oct. 2, 1934
Mills, C. H. (Surrey and S. Africa) b Nov. 26, 1867, d July 26, 1948
Mills, G. H. (Otago) b Aug. 1, 1916
Mills, J. E. (N. Zealand) b Sept. 3, 1905, d Dec. 11, 1972
Mills, J. M. (Camb. U. and Warw.) b July 27, 1921
Mills, J. P. C. (Camb. U. and Northants) b Dec. 6, 1958
Milner, J. (Essex) b Aug. 22, 1937
Milton, C. A. (Glos.; *CY 1959*) b March 10, 1928
Milton, W. H. (S. Africa) b Dec. 3, 1854, d March 6, 1930
Minnett, R. B. (Australia) b June 13, 1888, d Oct. 21, 1955
"Minshull", John (scorer of first recorded century) b *circa* 1741, d Oct. 1793
Miran Bux, M. (Pakistan) b April 20, 1907
Misson, F. M. (Australia) b Nov. 19, 1938
Mitchell, A. (Yorks.) b Sept. 13, 1902, d Dec. 25, 1976
Mitchell, B. (S. Africa; *CY 1936*) b Jan. 8, 1909
Mitchell, C. G. (Somerset) b Jan. 27, 1929
Mitchell, F. (Camb. U., Yorks., England and S. Africa; *CY 1902*) b Aug. 13, 1872, d Oct. 11, 1935
Mitchell, T. B. (Derby.) b Sept. 4, 1902
Mitchell-Innes, N. S. (Oxford U. and Somerset) b Sept. 7, 1914
Mobey, G. S. (Surrey) b March 5, 1904
Modi, R. S. (India) b Nov. 11, 1924
Mohammad Aslam (Pakistan) b Jan. 5, 1920
Mohammad Farooq (Pakistan) b April 8, 1938
Mohammad Ilyas (Pakistan) b March 19, 1946
Mohammad Munaf (Pakistan) b Nov. 2, 1935
Mohammad Nazir (Pakistan) b March 8, 1946
Mohsin Khan (Pakistan) b March 15, 1955
Moir, A. McK. (N. Zealand) b July 17, 1919
Moir, D. G. (Derby. and Scotland) b April 13, 1957
Mold, A. W. (Lancs.; *CY 1892*) b May 27, 1863, d April 29, 1921
Moloney, D. A. R. (N. Zealand) b Aug. 11, 1910, d July 15, 1942
Monckton of Brenchley, 1st Lord (Pres. MCC 1956-57) b Jan. 17, 1891, d Jan. 9, 1965
Monks, C. I. (Glos.) b March 4, 1912, d Jan. 23, 1974
Moodie, G. H. (W. Indies) b Nov. 25, 1915
Moon, L. J. (Camb. U. and Middx) b Feb. 9, 1878, d Nov. 23, 1916
Mooney, F. L. H. (N. Zealand) b May 26, 1921
Moore, D. N. (Oxford U. and Glos.) b Sept. 26, 1910
Moore, H. I. (Notts.) b Feb. 28, 1941
Moore, R. H. (Hants) b Nov. 14, 1913
Morgan, D. C. (Derby.) b Feb. 26, 1929

Morgan, J. T. (Camb. U. and Glam.) b May 7, 1907, d Dec. 18, 1976
Morgan, M. (Notts.) b May 21, 1936
Morgan, R. W. (N. Zealand) b Feb. 12, 1941
Morkel, D. P. B. (S. Africa) b Jan. 25, 1906, d Oct. 6, 1980
Morley, F. (Notts.) b Dec. 16, 1850, d Sept. 28, 1884
Morley, J. D. (Sussex) b Oct. 20, 1950
Moroney, J. R. (Australia) b Oct. 10, 1919
Morrill, N. D. (Oxford U.) b Dec. 9, 1957
Morris, A. R. (Australia; *CY 1949*) b Jan. 19, 1922
Morris, H. M. (Camb. U. and Essex) b April 16, 1898
Morris, R. E. T. (W. Province) b Jan. 28, 1947
Morris, S. (Australia) b June 22, 1855, d Sept. 20, 1931
Morrisby, R. O. G. (Tasmania) b Jan. 12, 1915
Morrison, B. D. (N. Zealand) b Dec. 17, 1933
Morrison, J. F. M. (N. Zealand) b Aug. 27, 1947
Mortimore, J. B. (Glos.) b May 14, 1933
Mortlock, W. (Surrey and Utd England XI) b July 18, 1832, d Jan. 23, 1884
Moseley, E. A. (Glam. and Barbados) b Jan. 5, 1958
Moseley, H. R. (Somerset) b May 28, 1948
Moses, G. H. (Camb. U.) b Sept. 24, 1952
Moses, H. (Australia) b Feb. 13, 1858, d Dec. 7, 1938
Moss, A. E. (Middx) b Nov. 14, 1930
Moss, J. K. (Australia) b June 29, 1947
Motz, R. C. (N. Zealand; *CY 1966*) b Jan. 12, 1940
Moulding, R. P. (Oxford U. and Middx) b Jan. 3, 1958
Moule, W. H. (Australia) b Jan. 31, 1858, d Aug. 24, 1939
Moylan, A. C. D. (Camb. U.) b June 26, 1955
Mubarak, A. M. (Camb. U.) b July 4, 1951
Mudassar Nazar (Pakistan) b June 26, 1956
Muddiah, V. M. (India) b June 8, 1929
Mufasir-ul-Haq (Pakistan) b Aug. 16, 1944
Muncer, B. L. (Middx and Glam.) b Oct. 23, 1913, d Jan. 18, 1982
Munden, V. S. (Leics.) b Jan. 2, 1928
Munir Malik (Pakistan) b July 10, 1934
Murdoch, W. L. (Sussex, Australia and England) b Oct. 18, 1854, d Feb. 18, 1911
Murray, A. R. A. (S. Africa) b April 30, 1922
Murray, B. A. G. (N. Zealand) b Sept. 18, 1940
Murray, D. A. (W. Indies) b May 29, 1950
Murray, D. L. (Camb. U., Notts., Warw. and W. Indies) b May 20, 1943
Murray, J. T. (Middx; *CY 1967*) b April 1, 1935
Murray-Willis, P. E. (Worcs. and Northants) b July 14, 1910
Murray-Wood, W. (Oxford U. and Kent) b June 30, 1917, d Dec. 21, 1968
Murrell, H. R. (Kent and Middx) b Nov. 19, 1879, d Aug. 15, 1952
Murrills, T. J. (Camb. U.) b Dec. 22, 1953
Musgrove, H. (Australia) b Nov. 27, 1860, d Nov. 2, 1931
Mushtaq Ali, S. (India) b Dec. 17, 1914
Mushtaq Mohammad (Northants and Pakistan; *CY 1963*) b Nov. 22, 1943
Muzzell, R. K. (W. Province, Transvaal and E. Province) b Dec. 23, 1945
Mynn, Alfred (Kent and All-England) b Jan. 19, 1807, d Oct. 31, 1861

Nadkarni, R. G. (India) b April 4, 1932
Nagel, L. E. (Australia) b March 6, 1905, d Nov. 23, 1971
Naik, S. S. (India) b Feb. 21, 1945
Nanan, R. (W. Indies) b May 29, 1953
Naoomal Jaoomal, M. (India) b April 17, 1904, d July 18, 1980
Narasimha Rao, M. V. (India) b Aug. 11, 1954
Nash, J. E. (S. Australia) b April 16, 1950
Nash, L. J. (Australia) b May 2, 1910
Nash, M. A. (Glam.) b May 9, 1945
Nasim-ul-Ghani (Pakistan) b May 14, 1941
Naushad Ali (Pakistan) b Oct. 1, 1943
Navle, J. G. (India) b Dec. 7, 1902, d Sept. 7, 1979
Nayak, S. V. (India) b Oct. 20, 1954
Nayudu, Col. C. K. (India; *CY 1933*) b Oct. 31, 1895, d Nov. 14, 1967
Nayudu, C. S. (India) b April 18, 1914
Nazar Mohammad (Pakistan) b Aug. 5, 1921
Nazir Ali, S. (Sussex and India) b June 8, 1906, d Feb. 1975
Neale, P. A. (Worcs.) b June 5, 1954
Neblett, J. M. (W. Indies) b Nov. 13, 1901, assumed dead
Neilson, D. R. (Transvaal) b Dec. 17, 1948
Nel, J. D. (S. Africa) b July 10, 1928
Nelson, G. W. (Border) b Nov. 14, 1941
Nelson, R. P. (Camb. U. and Northants) b Aug. 7, 1912, d Oct. 29, 1940
Nevell, W. T. (Middx, Surrey and Northants) b June 13, 1916
Newberry, C. (S. Africa) b 1889, d Aug. 1, 1916
Newdick, G. A. (Wellington) b Jan. 11, 1949
Newham, W. (Sussex) b Dec. 12, 1860, d June 26, 1944

Newland, Richard (Sussex) b *circa* 1718, d May 29, 1791
Newman, G. C. (Oxford U. and Middx) b April 26, 1904, d Oct. 13, 1982
Newman, J. (N. Zealand) b July 3, 1902
Newman, J. A. (Hants and Canterbury) b Nov. 12, 1884, d Dec. 21, 1973
Newman, P. A. (Derby.) b Jan. 10, 1959
Newsom, E. S. (S. Africa) b Dec. 2, 1910
Newstead, J. T. (Yorks.; *CY 1909*) b Sept. 8, 1877, d March 25, 1952
Niaz Ahmed (Pakistan) b Nov. 11, 1945
Nicholas, M. C. J. (Hants) b Sept. 29, 1957
Nicholls, D. (Kent) b Dec. 8, 1943
Nicholls, R. B. (Glos.) b Dec. 4, 1933
Nichols, M. S. (Essex; *CY 1934*) b Oct. 6, 1900, d Jan. 26, 1961
Nicholson, A. G. (Yorks.) b June 25, 1938
Nicholson, F. (S. Africa) b Sept. 17, 1909, d July 30, 1982
Nicolson, J. F. W. (S. Africa) b July 19, 1899, d Dec. 13, 1935
Nissar, Mahomed (India) b Aug. 1, 1910, d March 11, 1963
Nitschke, H. C. (Australia) b April 14, 1905, d Sept. 29, 1982
Niven, R. A. (Oxford U.) b April 28, 1948
Noble, M. A. (Australia; *CY 1900*) b Jan. 28, 1873, d June 21, 1940
Noblet, G. (Australia) b Sept. 14, 1916
Noreiga, J. M. (W. Indies) b April 15, 1936
Norfolk, 16th Duke of (Pres. MCC 1957-58) b May 30, 1908, d Jan. 31, 1975
Norman, M. E. J. C. (Northants and Leics.) b Jan. 19, 1933
Norton, N. O. (S. Africa) b May 11, 1881, d June 27, 1968
Nothling, O. E. (Australia) b Aug. 1, 1900, d Sept. 26, 1965
Nourse, A. D. ("Dudley") (S. Africa; *CY 1948*) b Nov. 12, 1910, d Aug. 14, 1981
Nourse, A. W. ("Dave") (S. Africa) b Croydon, Surrey Jan. 26, 1878, d July 8, 1948
Nugent, 1st Lord (Pres. MCC 1962-63) b Aug. 11, 1895, d April 27, 1973
Nunes, R. K. (W. Indies) b June 7, 1894, d July 22, 1958
Nupen, E. P. (S. Africa) b Jan. 1, 1902, d Jan. 29, 1977
Nurse, S. M. (W. Indies; *CY 1967*) b Nov. 10, 1933
Nutter, A. E. (Lancs. and Northants) b June 28, 1913
Nyalchand, S. (India) b Sept. 14, 1919
Nye, J. K. (Sussex) b May 23, 1914
Nyren, John (Hants) b Dec. 15, 1764, d June 28, 1837
Nyren, Richard (Hants and Sussex) b 1734, d April 25, 1797

Oakes, C. (Sussex) b Aug. 10, 1912
Oakes, J. (Sussex) b March 3, 1916
Oakman, A. S. M. (Sussex) b April 20, 1930
Oates, T. W. (Notts.) b Aug. 9, 1875, d June 18, 1949
Oates, W. F. (Yorks. and Derby.) b June 11, 1929
O'Brien, F. P. (Canterbury and Northants) b Feb. 11, 1911
O'Brien, L. P. J. (Australia) b July 2, 1907
O'Brien, Sir T. C. (Oxford U. and Middx) b Nov. 5, 1861, d Dec. 9, 1948
Ochse, A. E. (S. Africa) b March 11, 1870, d April 11, 1918
Ochse, A. L. (S. Africa) b Oct. 11, 1899, d May 6, 1949
O'Connor, J. (Essex) b Nov. 6, 1897, d Feb. 22, 1977
O'Connor, J. D. A. (Australia) b Sept. 9, 1875, d Aug. 23, 1941
Odendaal, A. (Camb. U. and Boland) b May 4, 1954
Ogilvie, A. D. (Australia) b June 3, 1951
O'Keefe, K. J. (Somerset and Australia) b Nov. 25, 1949
Old, C. M. (Yorks.; *CY 1979*) b Dec. 22, 1948
Oldfield, N. (Lancs. and Northants) b May 5, 1911
Oldfield, W. A. (Australia; *CY 1927*) b Sept. 9, 1894, d Aug. 10, 1976
Oldham, S. (Yorks. and Derby.) b July 26, 1948
Oldroyd, E. (Yorks.) b Oct. 1, 1888, d Dec. 27, 1964
O'Linn, S. (Kent and S. Africa) b May 5, 1927
Oliver, P. R. (Warw.) b May 9, 1956
O'Neill, N. C. (Australia; *CY 1962*) b Feb. 19, 1937
Ontong, R. C. (Border, Transvaal, N. Transvaal and Glam.) b Sept. 9, 1955
Ord, J. S. (Warw.) b July 12, 1912
Orders, J. O. D. (Oxford U.) b Aug. 12, 1957
O'Reilly, W. J. (Australia; *CY 1935*) b Dec. 20, 1905
O'Riordan, A. J. (Ireland) b July 20, 1940
Ormrod, J. A. (Worcs.) b Dec. 22, 1942
Oslear, D. O. (Umpire) b March 3, 1929
O'Sullivan, D. R. (Hants and N. Zealand) b Nov. 16, 1944
Outschoorn, L. (Worcs.) b Sept. 26, 1918
Overton, G. W. F. (N. Zealand) b June 8, 1919
Owen-Smith, H. G. O. (Oxford U., Middx and S. Africa; *CY 1930*) b Feb. 18, 1909
Owen-Thomas, D. R. (Camb. U. and Surrey) b Sept. 20, 1948
Oxenham, R. K. (Australia) b July 28, 1891, d Aug. 16, 1939

Packe, M. St J. (Leics.) b Aug. 21, 1916, d Dec. 20, 1978
Padgett, D. E. V. (Yorks.) b July 20, 1934
Padmore, A. L. (W. Indies) b Dec. 17, 1946
Page, D. A. C. (Glos.) b April 11, 1911, d Sept. 2, 1936
Page, J. C. T. (Kent) b May 20, 1930
Page, M. H. (Derby.) b June 17, 1941
Page, M. L. (N. Zealand) b May 8, 1902
Pai, A. M. (India) b April 28, 1945
Paine, G. A. E. (Middx and Warw.; *CY 1935*) b June 11, 1908, d March 30, 1978
Pairaudeau, B. H. (N. Districts and W. Indies) b April 14, 1931
Palairet, L. C. H. (Oxford U. and Somerset; *CY 1893*) b May 27, 1870, d March 27, 1933
Palairet, R. C. N. (Oxford U. and Somerset; Joint-Manager MCC in Australia 1932-33) b June 25, 1871, d Feb. 11, 1955
Palia, P. E. (India) b Sept. 5, 1910, d Sept. 9, 1981
Palm, A. W. (S. Africa) b June 8, 1901, d Aug. 17, 1966
Palmer, C. H. (Worcs. and Leics.; Pres. MCC 1978-79) b May 15, 1919
Palmer, G. E. (Australia) b Feb. 22, 1860, d Aug. 22, 1910
Palmer, K. E. (Somerset) b April 22, 1937
Palmer, R. (Somerset) b July 12, 1942
Palmer, R. W. M. (Camb. U.) b June 4, 1960
Pardon, Charles Frederick (Editor of *Wisden* 1887-90) b March 28, 1850, d April 18, 1890
Pardon, Edgar S. (12 years associated with *Wisden*) b Sept. 28, 1859, d July 16, 1898
Pardon, Sydney H. (Editor of *Wisden* 1891-1925) b Sept. 23, 1855, d Nov. 20, 1925
Parfitt, P. H. (Middx; *CY 1963*) b Dec. 8, 1936
Paris, C. G. A. (Hants; Pres. MCC 1975-76) b Aug. 20, 1911
Parish, R. J. (Aust. Administrator) b May 7, 1916
Park, R. L. (Australia) b July 30, 1892, d Jan. 23, 1947
Parkar, G. A. (India) b Oct. 24, 1955
Parkar, R. D. (India) b Oct. 31, 1946
Parker, C. W. L. (Glos.; *CY 1923*) b Oct. 14, 1882, d July 11, 1959
Parker, E. F. (Rhodesia and Griqualand W.) b April 26, 1939
Parker, G. M. (S. Africa) b May 27, 1899, d May 1, 1969
Parker, G. W. (Camb. U. and Glos.) b Feb. 11, 1912
Parker, J. F. (Surrey) b April 23, 1913
Parker, J. M. (Worcs. and N. Zealand) b Feb. 21, 1951
Parker, J. P. (Hants) b Nov. 29, 1902
Parker, N. M. (N. Zealand) b Aug. 28, 1948
Parker, P. W. G. (Camb. U., Sussex and Natal) b Jan. 15, 1956
Parkhouse, W. G. A. (Glam.) b Oct. 12, 1925
Parkin, C. H. (Yorks. and Lancs.; *CY 1924*) b Feb. 18, 1886, d June 15, 1943
Parkin, D. C. (S. Africa) b Feb. 18, 1870, d March 20, 1936
Parks, H. W. (Sussex) b July 18, 1906
Parks, J. H. (Sussex and Canterbury; *CY 1938*) b May 12, 1903, d Nov. 21, 1980
Parks, J. M. (Sussex and Somerset; *CY 1968*) b Oct. 21, 1931
Parks, R. J. (Hants) b June 15, 1959
Parr, F. D. (Lancs.) b June 1, 1928
Parr, George (Notts. and All-England) b May 22, 1826, d June 23, 1891
Parry, D. R. (W. Indies) b Dec. 22, 1954
Parsana, D. D. (India) b Dec. 2, 1947
Parsons, A. B. D. (Camb. U. and Surrey) b Sept. 20, 1933
Parsons, A. E. W. (Auckland and Sussex) b Glasgow Jan. 9, 1949
Parsons, G. J. (Leics.) b Oct. 17, 1959
Parsons, Canon J. H. (Warw.) b May 30, 1890, d Feb. 2, 1981
Partridge, J. T. (S. Africa) b Dec. 9, 1932
Partridge, N. E. (Malvern, Camb. U. and Warw.; *CY 1919*) b Aug. 10, 1900, d March 10, 1982
Partridge, R. J. (Northants) b Feb. 11, 1912
Pascoe, L. S. (Australia) b Feb. 13, 1950
Passailaigue, C. C. (W. Indies) b Aug. 1902, d Jan. 7, 1972
Patankar, C. T. (India) b Nov. 24, 1930
Pataudi, Iftikhar Ali, Nawab of (Oxford U., Worcs., England and India; *CY 1932*) b March 16, 1910, d Jan. 5, 1952
Pataudi, Mansur Ali, Nawab of (Oxford U., Sussex and India; *CY 1968*) b Jan. 5, 1941
Patel, B. P. (India) b Nov. 24, 1952
Patel, D. N. (Worcs.) b Oct. 25, 1958
Patel, J. M. (India) b Nov. 26, 1924
Paterson, R. F. T. (Essex) b Sept. 8, 1916, d May 29, 1980
Pathmanathan, G. (Oxford U. and Sri Lanka) b Jan. 23, 1954
Patiala, Yuvraj of (India) b Jan. 17, 1913
Patil, S. M. (India) b Aug. 18, 1956
Patil, S. R. (India) b Oct. 10, 1933
Paulsen, R. G. (Queensland and W. Australia) b Oct. 18, 1947
Paver, R. G. L. (Oxford U.) b April 4, 1950
Pawson, A. G. (Oxford U. and Worcs.; oldest living Blue) b May 30, 1888

Pawson, H. A. (Oxford U. and Kent) b Aug. 22, 1921
Payn, L. W. (Natal) b May 6, 1915
Paynter, E. (Lancs.; *CY 1938*) b Nov. 5, 1901, d Feb. 5, 1979
Payton, D. H. (C. Districts) b Feb. 19, 1945
Payton, W. R. D. (Notts.) b Feb. 13, 1882, d May 2, 1943
Pearce, G. (Sussex) b Oct. 27, 1908
Pearce, J. P. (Oxford U.) b April 18, 1957
Pearce, T. A. (Kent) b Dec. 18, 1910, d Aug. 11, 1982
Pearce, T. N. (Essex) b Nov. 3, 1905
Pearse, C. O. C. (S. Africa) b Oct. 10, 1884, d May 7, 1953
Pearson, D. B. (Worcs.) b March 29, 1937
Peate, E. (Yorks.) b March 2, 1856, d March 11, 1900
Peck I. G. (Camb. U. and Northants) b Oct. 18, 1957
Peebles, I. A. R. (Oxford U., Middx and Scotland; *CY 1931*) b Jan. 20, 1908, d Feb. 28, 1980
Peel, R. (Yorks.; *CY 1889*) b Feb. 12, 1857, d Aug. 12, 1941
Pegler, S. J. (S. Africa) b July 28, 1888, d Sept. 10, 1972
Pellew, C. E. (Australia) b Sept. 21, 1893, d May 9, 1981
Penn, F. (Kent) b March 7, 1851, d Dec. 26, 1916
Pepper, C. G. (NSW and Aust. Services; Umpire) b Sept. 15, 1918
Perkins, C. G. (Northants) b June 4, 1911
Perks, R. T. D. (Worcs.) b Oct. 4, 1911, d Nov. 22, 1977
Perrin, P. A. (Essex; *CY 1905*) b May 26, 1876, d Nov. 20, 1945
Perryman, S. P. (Warw. and Worcs.) b Oct. 22, 1955
Pervez Sajjad (Pakistan) b Aug. 30, 1942
Petherick, P. J. (N. Zealand) b Sept. 25, 1942
Petrie, E. C. (N. Zealand) b May 22, 1927
Pfuhl, G. P. (W. Province) b Aug. 27, 1947
Phadkar, D. G. (India) b Dec. 12, 1925
Phebey, A. H. (Kent) b Oct. 1, 1924
Phelan, P. J. (Essex) b Feb. 9, 1938
Philipson, H. (Oxford U. and Middx) b June 8, 1866, d Dec. 4, 1935
Phillip, N. (Essex and W. Indies) b June 22, 1949
Phillipps, J. H. (N. Zealand Manager 1949, 1958; Manager MCC in N. Zealand 1960-61) b Jan. 1, 1898, d June 8, 1977
Phillipson, C. P. (Sussex) b Feb. 10, 1952
Phillipson, W. E. (Lancs.) b Dec. 3, 1910
Philpott, P. I. (Australia) b Nov. 21, 1934
Piachaud, J. D. (Oxford U., Hants and Ceylon) b March 1, 1937
Pickles, L. (Somerset) b Sept. 17, 1932
Pierre, L. R. (W. Indies) b June 5, 1921
Pigott, A. C. S. (Sussex) b June 4, 1958
Pilch, Fuller (Norfolk and Kent) b March 17, 1804, d May 1, 1870
Pilling, H. (Lancs.) b Feb. 23, 1943
Pilling, R. (Lancs.; *CY 1891*) b July 5, 1855, d March 28, 1891
Pinch, C. J. (NSW and S. Australia) b June 23, 1921
Pithey, A. J. (S. Africa) b July 17, 1933
Pithey, D. B. (Oxford U., Northants and S. Africa) b Oct. 10, 1936
Pitman, R. W. C. (Hants) b Feb. 21, 1933
Place, W. (Lancs.) b Dec. 7, 1914
Platt, R. K. (Yorks. and Northants) b Dec. 21, 1932
Playle, W. R. (W. Australia and N. Zealand) b Dec. 1, 1938
Pleass, J. E. (Glam.) b May 21, 1923
Plimsoll, J. B. (S. Africa) b Oct. 27, 1917
Pocock, N. E. J. (Hants) b Dec. 15, 1951
Pocock, P. I. (Surrey and N. Transvaal) b Sept. 24, 1946
Pollard, R. (Lancs.) b June 19, 1912
Pollard, V. (N. Zealand) b Burnley Sept. 7, 1945
Pollock, A. J. (Camb. U.) b April 19, 1962
Pollock, P. M. (S. Africa; *CY 1966*) b June 30, 1941
Pollock, R. G. (S. Africa; *CY 1966*) b Feb. 27. 1944
Ponsford, W. H. (Australia; *CY 1935*) b Oct. 19, 1900
Pont, K. R. (Essex) b Jan. 16, 1953
Poole, C. J. (Notts.) b March 13, 1921
Pooley, E. (Surrey and first England tour) b Feb. 13, 1838, d July 18, 1907
Poore, M. B. (N. Zealand) b June 1, 1930
Poore, Brig-Gen. R. M. (Hants and S. Africa; *CY 1900*) b March 20, 1866, d July 14, 1938
Pope, A. V. (Derby.) b Aug. 15, 1909
Pope, G. H. (Derby.) b Jan. 27, 1911
Pope, R. J. (Australia) b Feb. 18, 1864, d July 27, 1952
Popplewell, N. F. M. (Camb. U. and Somerset) b Aug. 8, 1957
Portal of Hungerford, 1st Lord (Pres. MCC 1958-59) b May 21, 1893, d April 22, 1971
Porter, A. (Glam.) b March 25, 1914
Porter, G. D. (W. Australia) b March 18, 1955
Porter, S. R. (Oxford U.) b Aug. 9, 1950
Pothecary, E. A. (Hants) b March 1, 1906
Pothecary, J. E. (S. Africa) b Dec. 6, 1933
Potter, G. (Sussex) b Oct. 26, 1931
Potter, J. (Victoria) b April 13, 1938
Pougher, A. D. (Leics.) b April 19, 1865, d May 20, 1926

Pountain, F. R. (Sussex) b April 23, 1941
Powell, A. G. (Camb. U. and Essex) b Aug. 17, 1912, d June 7, 1982
Powell, A. W. (S. Africa) b July 18, 1873, d Sept. 11, 1948
Prasanna, E. A. S. (India) b May 22, 1940
Pratt, R. C. E. (Surrey) b May 5, 1928, d June 7, 1977
Pratt, R. L. (Leics.) b Nov. 15, 1938
Preece, C. R. (Worcs.) b Dec. 15, 1888, d Feb. 5, 1976
Prentice, F. T. (Leics.) b April 22, 1912, d July 10, 1978
Pressdee, J. S. (Glam. and N. E. Transvaal) b June 19, 1933
Preston, Hubert (Editor of *Wisden* 1944-51) b Dec. 16, 1868, d Aug. 6, 1960
Preston, K. C. (Essex) b Aug. 22, 1925
Preston, Norman (Editor of *Wisden* 1951-80) b March 18, 1903, d March 6, 1980
Pretlove, J. F. (Camb. U. and Kent) b Nov. 23, 1932
Price, E. J. (Lancs. and Essex) b Oct. 27, 1918
Price, J. S. E. (Middx) b July 22, 1937
Price, V. R. (Oxford U. and Surrey) b May 22, 1895, d May 29, 1973
Price, W. F. F. (Middx) b April 25, 1902, d Jan. 12, 1969
Prideaux, R. M. (Camb. U., Kent, Northants, Sussex and Orange Free State) b July 31, 1939
Pridgeon, A. P. (Worcs.) b Feb. 22, 1954
Prince, C. F. H. (S. Africa) b Sept. 11, 1874, d March 5, 1948
Pringle, D. R. (Camb. U. and Essex) b Sept. 18, 1958
Pritchard, T. L. (Wellington, Warw. and Kent) b March 10, 1917
Procter, M. J. (Glos. and S. Africa; *CY 1970*) b Sept. 15, 1946
Prodger, J. M. (Kent) b Sept. 1, 1935
Promnitz, H. L. E. (S. Africa) b Feb. 23, 1904
Prouton, R. O. (Hants) b March 1, 1926
Puckett, C. W. (W. Australia) b Feb. 21, 1911
Pugh, C. T. M. (Glos.) b March 13, 1937
Pullan, D. A. (Notts.) b May 1, 1944
Pullar, G. (Lancs. and Glos.; *CY 1960*) b Aug. 1, 1935
Pullinger, G. R. (Essex) b March 14, 1920
Puna, N. (N. Zealand) b Oct. 28, 1929
Punjabi, P. H. (India) b Sept. 20, 1921
Pydanna, M. (Guyana) b Jan. 27, 1950

Quaife, B. W. (Warw. and Worcs.) b Nov. 24, 1899
Quaife, William ("W. G.") (Warw. and Griqualand W.; *CY 1902*) b March 17, 1872, d Oct. 13, 1951
Quick, I. W. (Victoria) b. Nov. 5, 1933
Quinn, N. A. (S. Africa) b Feb. 21, 1908, d Aug. 5, 1934

Rabone, G. O. (N. Zealand) b Nov. 6, 1921
Radley, C. T. (Middx; *CY 1979*) b May 13, 1944
Rae, A. F. (W. Indies) b Sept. 30, 1922
Rai Singh, K. (India) b Feb. 24, 1922
Rait Kerr, Col. R. S. (Sec. MCC 1936-52) b April 13, 1891, d April 2, 1961
Rajindernath, V. (India) b Jan. 7, 1928
Rajinder Pal (India) b Nov. 18, 1937
Ralph, L. H. R. (Essex) b May 22, 1920
Ramadhin, S. (Lancs. and W. Indies; *CY 1951*) b May 1, 1929
Ramaswami, C. (India) b June 18, 1896
Ramchand, G. S. (India) b July 26, 1927
Ramji, L. (India) b 1900, d Dec. 20, 1948
Ramsamooj, D. (Trinidad and Northants) b July 5, 1932
Ranasinghe, A. N. (Sri Lanka) b Oct. 13, 1956
Ranatunga, A. (Sri Lanka) b Dec. 1, 1963
Randall, D. W. (Notts.; *CY 1980*) b Feb. 24, 1951
Randhir Singh (Bihar and Indian tourist) b Aug. 16, 1957
Rangachari, C. R. (India) b April 14, 1916
Rangnekar, K. M. (India) b June 27, 1917
Ranjane, V. B. (India) b July 22, 1937
Ranjitsinhji, Kumar Shri, afterwards H. H. the Jam Saheb of Nawanagar (Camb. U. and Sussex; *CY 1897*) b Sept. 10, 1872, d April 2, 1933
Ransford, V. S. (Australia; *CY 1910*) b March 20, 1885, d March 19, 1958
Ransom, V. J. (Hants and Surrey) b March 17, 1918
Rashid Khan (Pakistan) b Dec. 15, 1959
Ratcliffe, R. M. (Lancs.) b Nov. 29, 1951
Ratnayeke, J. R. (Sri Lanka) b May 2, 1960
Rayment, A. W. H. (Hants) b May 29, 1928
Raymer, V. N. (Queensland) b May 4, 1918
Read, H. D. (Surrey and Essex) b Jan. 28, 1910
Read, J. M. (Surrey; *CY 1890*) b Feb. 9, 1859, d Feb. 17, 1929
Read, W. W. (Surrey; *CY 1893*) b Nov. 23, 1855, d Jan. 6, 1907
Reddick, T. B. (Middx, Notts. and W. Province) b Feb. 17, 1912, d June 1, 1982
Reddy, B. (India) b Nov. 12, 1954
Redman, J. (Somerset) b March 1, 1926, d Sept. 19, 1981
Redmond, R. E. (N. Zealand) b Dec. 29, 1944
Redpath, I. R. (Australia) b May 11, 1941

Reed, B. L. (Hants) b Sept. 9, 1937
Reedman, J. C. (Australia) b Oct. 9, 1865, d March 25, 1924
Rees, A. (Glam.) b Feb. 17, 1938
Reeves, W. (Umpire) b Jan. 22, 1875, d March 22, 1944
Rege, M. R. (India) b March 18, 1924
Rehman, S. F. (Pakistan) b June 11, 1935
Reid, J. F. (N. Zealand) b March 3, 1956
Reid, J. R. (N. Zealand; *CY 1959*) b June 3, 1928
Reid, K. P. (E. Province and Northants) b July 24, 1951
Reid, N. (S. Africa) b Dec. 26, 1890, d June 10, 1947
Reidy, B. W. (Lancs.) b Sept. 18, 1953
Relf, A. E. (Sussex and Auckland; *CY 1914*) b June 26, 1874, d March 26, 1937
Renneburg, D. A. (Australia) b Sept. 23, 1942
Revill, A. C. (Derby. and Leics.) b March 27, 1923
Reynolds, B. L. (Northants) b June 10, 1932
Reynolds, G. R. (Queensland) b Aug. 24 1936
Rhodes, A. E. G. (Derby.) b Oct. 10, 1916
Rhodes, H. J. (Derby.) b July 22, 1936
Rhodes, S. D. (Notts.) b March 24, 1910
Rhodes, Wilfred (Yorks.; *CY 1899*) b Oct. 29, 1877, d July 8, 1973
Rice, C. E. B. (Transvaal and Notts.; *CY 1981*) b July 23, 1949
Rice, J. M. (Hants) b Oct. 23, 1949
Richards, A. R. (S. Africa) b 1868, d Jan. 9, 1904
Richards, B. A. (Glos., Hants, S. Australia and S. Africa; *CY 1969*) b July 21, 1945
Richards, C. J. (Surrey) b Aug. 10, 1958
Richards G. (Glam.) b Nov. 29, 1951
Richards, I. V. A. (Somerset, Queensland and W. Indies; *CY 1977*) b March 7, 1952
Richards, W. H. M. (S. Africa) b Aug. 1862, d Jan 4, 1903
Richardson, A. J. (Australia) b July 24, 1888, d Dec. 23, 1973
Richardson, A. W. (Derby.) b March 4, 1907
Richardson, D. W. (Worcs.) b Nov. 3, 1934
Richardson, G. W. (Derby.) b April 26, 1938
Richardson, P. E. (Worcs. and Kent; *CY 1957*) b July 4, 1931
Richardson, T. (Surrey and Somerset: *CY 1897*) b Aug. 11, 1870, d July 2, 1912
Richardson, V. Y. (Australia) b Sept. 7, 1894, d Oct. 29, 1969
Riches, N. V. H. (Glam.) b June 9, 1883, d Nov. 6 1975
Richmond, T. L. (Notts.) b June 23, 1890, d Dec. 29, 1957
Rickards, K. R. (Essex and W. Indies) b Aug. 23, 1923
Riddington, A. (Leics.) b Dec. 22, 1911
Ridge, S. P. (Oxford U.) b Nov. 23, 1961
Ridgway, F. (Kent) b Aug. 10, 1923
Ridings, P. L. (S. Australia) b Oct. 2, 1917
Rigg, K. E. (Australia) b May 21, 1906
Ridley, G. N. S. (Oxford U. and Kent) b Nov. 27, 1944
Riley, H. (Leics.) b Oct. 3, 1902
Ring, D. T. (Australia) b Oct. 14, 1918
Rist, F. H. (Essex) b March 30, 1914
Ritchie, G. G. (Transvaal) b Sept. 16, 1933
Rixon, S. J. (Australia) b Feb. 25, 1954
Rizwan-uz-Zaman (Pakistan) b Sept. 4, 1962
Roach, C. A. (W. Indies) b March 13, 1904
Roberts, A. D. G. (N. Zealand) b May 6, 1947
Roberts, A. M. E. (Hants, Leics., NSW and W. Indies; *CY 1975*) b Jan. 29, 1951
Roberts, A. T. (W. Indies) b Sept. 18, 1937
Roberts, A. W. (N. Zealand) b Aug. 20, 1909, d May 13, 1978
Roberts, Pascal (Trinidad) b Dec. 15, 1937
Roberts, W. B. (Lancs. and Victory Tests) b Sept. 27, 1914, d Aug. 24, 1951
Robertson, J. B. (S. Africa) b June 5, 1906
Robertson, J. D. (Middx; *CY 1948*) b Feb. 22, 1917
Robertson, S. D. (Rhodesia) b May 1, 1947
Robertson, W. R. (Australia) b Oct. 6, 1861, d June 24, 1938
Robertson-Glasgow, R. C. (Oxford U. and Somerset) b July 15, 1901, d March 4, 1965
Robins, R. V. C. (Middx) b March 13, 1935
Robins, R. W. V. (Camb. U. and Middx; *CY 1930*) b June 3, 1906, d Dec. 12, 1968
Robinson, A. L. (Yorks.) b Aug. 17, 1946
Robinson, Emmott (Yorks.) b Nov. 16, 1883, d Nov. 17, 1969
Robinson, Ellis P. (Yorks. and Somerset) b Aug. 10, 1911
Robinson, H. B. O. (Oxford U. and Canada) b March 3, 1919
Robinson, M. (Glam. and Warw.) b July 16, 1921
Robinson, P. J. (Worcs. and Somerset) b Feb. 9, 1943
Robinson, Ray (Writer) b July 8, 1908, d July 6, 1982
Robinson, R. D. (Australia) b June 8, 1946
Robinson, R. H. (Australia) b March 26, 1914, d Aug. 10, 1965
Robinson, R. T. (Notts.) b Nov. 21, 1958
Robson, E. (Somerset) b May 1, 1870, d May 23, 1924
Rochford, P. (Glos.) b Aug. 27, 1928
Rodriguez, W. V. (W. Indies) b June 25, 1934

Roe, B. (Somerset) b Jan. 27, 1939
Roebuck, P. M. (Camb. U. and Somerset) b March 6, 1956
Rogers, J. J. (Oxford U.) b Aug. 20, 1958
Rogers, N. H. (Hants) b March 9, 1918
Rogers, R. E. (Queensland) b Aug. 24, 1916
Roope, G. R. J. (Surrey and Griqualand W.) b July 12, 1946
Root, C. F. (Derby. and Worcs.) b April 16, 1890, d Jan. 20, 1954
Rorke, G. F. (Australia) b June 27, 1938
Rose, B. C. (Somerset; *CY 1980*) b June 4, 1950
Rosebery, 6th Earl of (*see* Dalmeny, Lord)
Rose-Innes, A. (S. Africa) b Feb. 16, 1868, d Nov. 22, 1946
Rosendorff, N. (OFS) b Jan. 22, 1945
Ross, C. J. (Wellington and Oxford U.) b June 24, 1954
Rotherham, G. A. (Rugby, Camb. U., Warw. and Wellington; *CY 1918*) b May 28, 1899
Roundell, J. (Camb. U.) b Oct. 23, 1951
Rouse, S. J. (Warw.) b Jan. 20, 1949
Routledge, R. (Middx) b July 7, 1920
Routledge, T. W. (S. Africa) b April 18, 1867, d May 9, 1927
Rowan, A. M. B. (S. Africa) b Feb. 7, 1921
Rowan, E. A. B. (S. Africa; *CY 1952*) b July 20, 1909
Rowe, C. G. (N. Zealand) b June 30, 1915
Rowe, C. J. C. (Kent) b May 5, 1953
Rowe, E. J. (Notts.) b July 21, 1920
Rowe, G. A. (S. Africa) b June 15, 1874, d Jan. 8, 1950
Rowe, L. G. (Derby. and W. Indies) b Jan. 8, 1949
Roy, A. (India) b June 5, 1945
Roy, Pankaj (India) b May 31, 1928
Roy, Pranab (India) b Feb. 10, 1957
Royle, Rev. V. P. F. A. (Oxford U. and Lancs.) b Jan. 29, 1854, d May 20, 1929
Rumsey, F. E. (Worcs., Somerset and Derby.) b Dec. 4, 1935
Russell, A. C. [C. A. G.] (Essex; *CY 1923*) b Oct. 7, 1887, d March 23, 1961
Russell, D. P. (Camb. U.) b June 4, 1951
Russell, P. E. (Derby.) b May 9, 1944
Russell, S. E. J. (Middx and Glos.) b Oct. 4, 1937
Russell, S. G. (Camb. U. and Surrey) b March 11, 1945
Russell, W. E. (Middx) b July 3, 1936
Russom, N. (Camb. U. and Somerset) b Dec. 3, 1958
Rutherford, I. A. (Worcs. and Otago) b June 30, 1957
Rutherford, J. W. (Australia) b Sept. 25, 1929
Ryan, M. (Yorks.) b June 23, 1933
Ryan, M. L. (Canterbury) b June 7, 1943
Ryder, J. (Australia) b Aug. 8, 1889, d April 3, 1977

Sadiq Mohammad (Tasmania, Glos., Essex and Pakistan) b May 3, 1945
Sadler, W. C. H. (Surrey) b Sept. 24, 1896
Saeed Ahmed (Pakistan) b Oct. 1, 1937
Saggers, R. A. (Australia) b May 15, 1917
Sainsbury, P. J. (Hants; *CY 1974*) b June 13, 1934
St Hill, E. L. (W. Indies) b March 9, 1904, d May 21, 1957
St Hill, W. H. (W. Indies) b July 6, 1893, d 1957
Salah-ud-Din (Pakistan) b Feb. 14, 1947
Sale, R. (Oxford U. and Derby.) b June 21, 1889, d Sept. 7, 1970
Sale, R. jun. (Oxford U., Warw. and Derby.) b Oct. 4 1919
Saleem Altaf (Pakistan) b March 23, 1944
Salim Malik (Pakistan) b April 16, 1963
Salim Yousuf (Pakistan) b Dec. 7, 1959
Salter, M. G. (Oxford U. and Glos.) b May 10, 1887, d June 15, 1973
Sampson, H. (Yorkshire and All-England) b March 13, 1813, d March 29, 1885
Samuelson, S. V. (S. Africa) b Nov. 21, 1883, d Nov. 18, 1958
Sanderson, J. F. W. (Oxford U.) b Sept. 10, 1954
Sandham, A. (Surrey; *CY 1923*) b July 6, 1890, d April 20, 1982
Sandman, D. McK. (Canterbury) b Nov. 3, 1889, d Jan. 29, 1973
Sardesai, D. N. (India) b Aug. 8, 1940
Sarfraz Nawaz (Northants and Pakistan) b Dec. 1, 1948
Sarwate, C. T. (India) b June 22, 1920
Saunders, J. V. (Australia) b Feb. 3, 1876, d Dec. 21, 1927
Savage, J. S. (Leics. and Lancs.) b March 3, 1929
Savage, R. Le Q. (Oxford U. and Warw.) b Dec. 10, 1955
Savill, L. A. (Essex) b June 30, 1935
Saville, G. J. (Essex) b Feb. 5, 1944
Saxena, R. C. (India) b Sept. 20, 1944
Sayer, D. M. (Oxford U. and Kent) b Sept. 19, 1936
Scarlett, R. O. (W. Indies) b Aug. 15, 1934
Schmidt, E. (E. Province and Orange Free State) b Sept. 21, 1950
Schofield, R. M. (C. Districts) b Nov. 6, 1939
Scholes, W. J. (Victoria) b Feb. 5, 1950
Schonegevel, D. J. (Orange Free State and Griqualand W.) b Oct. 9, 1934
Schultz, S. S. (Camb. U. and Lancs.) b Aug. 29, 1857, d Dec. 17, 1937

Schwarz, R. O. (Middx and S. Africa; *CY 1908*) b Lee, Kent May 4, 1875, d Nov. 18, 1918
Scott, A. P. H. (W. Indies) b July 29, 1934
Scott, Christopher J. (Lancs.) b Sept. 16, 1959
Scott, Colin J. (Glos.) b May 1, 1919
Scott, H. J. H. (Australia) b Dec. 26. 1858, d Sept. 23, 1910
Scott, M. E. (Northants) b May 8, 1936
Scott, O. C. (W. Indies) b Aug. 25, 1893, d June 16, 1961
Scott, R. H. (N. Zealand) b March 6, 1917
Scott, R. S. G. (Oxford U. and Sussex) b April 26, 1909, d Aug. 26, 1957
Scott, S. W. (Middx; *CY 1893*) b March 24, 1854, d Dec. 8, 1933
Scott, V. J. (N. Zealand) b July 31, 1916, d Aug. 2, 1980
Scotton, W. H. (Notts.) b Jan. 15, 1856, d July 9, 1893
Seabrook, F. J. (Camb. U. and Glos.) b Jan. 9, 1899, d Aug. 7, 1979
Sealey, B. J. (W. Indies) b Aug. 12, 1899, d Sept. 12, 1963
Sealy, J. E. D. (W. Indies) b Sept. 11, 1912, d Jan. 3, 1982
Seamer, J. W. (Somerset and Oxford U.) b June 23, 1913
Sebastian, L. C. (Windwards) b Oct. 31, 1955
Seccull, A. W. (S. Africa) b Sept. 14, 1868, d July 20, 1945
Selby, J. (Notts.) b July 1, 1849, d March 11, 1894
Sellers, A. B. (Yorks.; *CY 1940*) b March 5, 1907, d Feb. 20, 1981
Sellers, R. H. D. (Australia) b Aug. 20, 1940
Selvey, M. W. W. (Camb. U., Surrey, Middx and Orange Free State) b April 25, 1948
Sen, P. (India) b May 31, 1926, d Jan. 27, 1970
Sen Gupta, A. K. (India) b Aug. 3, 1939
Serjeant, C. S. (Australia) b Nov. 1, 1951
Seymour, James (Kent) b Oct. 25, 1879, d Sept. 30, 1930
Seymour, M. A. (S. Africa) b June 5, 1936
Shackleton, D. (Hants; *CY 1959*) b Aug. 12, 1924
Shafiq Ahmad (Pakistan) b March 28, 1949
Shafqat Rana (Pakistan) b Aug. 10, 1943
Shahid Israr (Pakistan) b March 1, 1950
Shahid Mahmoud (Pakistan) b March 13, 1939
Shalders, W. A. (S. Africa) b Feb. 12, 1880, d March 18, 1917
Sharma, P. (India) b Jan. 5, 1948
Sharp, A. T. (Leics.) b March 23, 1889, d Feb. 15, 1973
Sharp, G. (Northants) b March 12, 1950
Sharp, H. P. H. (Middx) b Oct 6, 1917
Sharp, J. (Lancs.) b Feb. 15, 1878, d Jan. 27, 1938
Sharp, K. (Yorks. and Griqualand W.) b April 6, 1959
Sharpe, D. (Pakistan) b Aug. 3, 1937
Sharpe, J. W. (Surrey and Notts.; *CY 1892*) b Dec. 9, 1866, d June 19, 1936
Sharpe, P. J. (Yorks. and Derby.; *CY 1963*) b Dec. 27, 1936
Shastri, R. J. (India) b May 27, 1962
Shaw, Alfred (Notts. and Sussex) b Aug. 29, 1842, d Jan. 16, 1907
Shaw, J. H. (Victoria) b Oct. 18, 1932
Sheahan, A. P. (Australia) b Sept. 30, 1946
Sheffield, J. R. (Essex and Wellington) b Nov. 19, 1906
Shepherd, B. K. (Australia) b April 23, 1938
Shepherd, D. J. (Glam.; *CY 1970*) b Aug. 12, 1927
Shepherd, D. R. Glos.) b Dec. 27, 1940
Shepherd, J. N. (Kent, Glos., Rhodesia and W. Indies; *CY 1979*) b Nov. 9, 1943
Shepherd, T. F. Surrey) b Dec. 5, 1889, d Feb. 13, 1957
Sheppard, Rt Rev. D. S. (Bishop of Liverpool) (Camb. U. and Sussex; *CY 1953*) b March 6, 1929
Shepstone, G. H. (S. Africa) b April 8, 1876, d July 3, 1940
Sherwell, P. W. (S. Africa) b Aug. 17, 1880, d April 17, 1948
Sherwin, M. (Notts.; *CY 1891*) b Feb. 26, 1851, d July 1910
Shillingford, G. C. (W. Indies) b Sept. 25, 1944
Shillingford, I. T. (W. Indies) b April 18, 1944
Shinde, S. G. (India) b Aug. 18, 1923, d June 22, 1955
Shipman, A. W. (Leics.) b March 7, 1901, d Dec. 12, 1979
Shirreff, A. C. (Camb. U., Hants, Kent and Somerset) b Feb. 12, 1919
Shivnarine, S. (W. Indies) b May 13, 1952
Shodhan, R. H. (India) b Oct. 18, 1928
Short, A. M. (Natal) b Sept. 27, 1947
Shortland, N. A. (Warw.) b July 6, 1916, d March 14, 1973
Shrewsbury, Arthur (Notts.; *CY 1890*) b April 11, 1856, d May 19, 1903
Shrimpton, M. J. F. (N. Zealand) b June 23, 1940
Shuja-ud-Din, Col. (Pakistan) b April 10, 1930
Shuter, J. (Kent and Surrey) b Feb. 9, 1855, d July 5, 1920
Shuttleworth, K. (Lancs. and Leics.) b Nov. 13, 1944

Sibbles, F. M. (Lancs.) b March 15, 1904, d July 20, 1973
Sidebottom, A. (Yorks. and Orange Free State) b April 1, 1954
Siedle, I. J. (S. Africa) b Jan. 11, 1903, d Aug. 24, 1982
Sievers, M. W. (Australia) b April 13, 1912, d May 10, 1968
Sikander Bakht (Pakistan) b Aug. 25, 1957
Silk, D. R. W. (Camb. U. and Somerset) b Oct. 8, 1931
Sime, W. A. (Notts.) b Feb. 8, 1909
Simmons, J. (Lancs. and Tasmania) b March 28, 1941
Simpson, R. B. (Australia; *CY 1965*) b Feb. 3, 1936
Simpson, R. T. (Notts. and Sind; *CY 1950*) b Feb. 27, 1920
Simpson-Hayward, G. H. (Worcs.) b June 7, 1875, d Oct. 2, 1936
Sims, Sir Arthur (Canterbury) b July 22, 1877, d April 27, 1969
Sims, J. M. (Middx) b May 13, 1903, d April 27, 1973
Sinclair, B. W. (N. Zealand) b Oct. 23, 1936
Sinclair, I. McK. (N. Zealand) b June 1, 1933
Sinclair, J. H. (S. Africa) b Oct. 16, 1876, d Feb. 23, 1913
Sincock, D. J. (Australia) b Feb. 1, 1942
Sinfield, R. A. (Glos.) b Dec. 24, 1900
Singh, Charan K. (West Indies) b 1938
Singh, Swaranjit (Camb. U., Warw., E. Punjab and Bengal) b July 18, 1931
Singleton, A. P. (Oxford U., Worcs. and Rhodesia) b Aug. 5, 1914
Siviter, K. (Oxford U.) b Dec. 10, 1953
Skeet, C. H. L. (Oxford U. and Middx) b Aug. 17, 1895, d April 20, 1978
Skelding, Alec (Leics.) b Sept. 5, 1886, d April 17, 1960
Skinner, A. F. (Derby. and Northants) b April 22, 1913, d Feb. 28, 1982
Skinner, D. A. (Derby.) b March 22, 1920
Skinner, L. E. (Surrey and Guyana) b Sept. 7, 1950
Slack, W. N. (Middx and Windward Islands) b Dec. 12, 1954
Slade, D. N. F. (Worcs.) b Aug. 24, 1940
Slade, W. D. (Glam.) b Sept. 27, 1941
Slater, K. N. (Australia) b March 12, 1935
Sleep, P. R. (Australia) b May 4, 1957
Slight, J. (Australia) b Oct. 20, 1855, d Dec. 9, 1930
Slocombe, P. A. (Somerset) b Sept. 6, 1954
Smailes, T. F. (Yorks.) b March 27, 1910, d Dec. 1, 1970
Smales, K. (Yorks. and Notts.) b Sept. 15, 1927
Small, G. C. (Warw.) b Oct. 18, 1961
Small, John, sen. (Hants and All-England) b April 19, 1737, d Dec. 31, 1826
Small, J. A. (W. Indies) b Nov. 3, 1892, d April 26, 1958
Smart, C. C. (Warw. and Glam.) b July 23, 1898, d May 21, 1975
Smart, J. A. (Warw.) b April 12, 1891, d Oct. 3, 1979
Smedley, M. J. (Notts.) b Oct. 28, 1941
Smith, A. C. (Oxford U. and Warw.) b Oct. 25, 1936
Smith, A. J. S. (Natal) b Feb. 8, 1951
Smith, Sir C. Aubrey (Camb. U., Sussex and Transvaal) b July 21, 1863, d Dec. 20, 1948
Smith, C. I. J. (Middx; *CY 1935*) b Aug. 25, 1906, d Feb. 8, 1979
Smith, C. J. E. (S. Africa) b Dec. 25, 1872, d March 27, 1947
Smith, C. L. (Natal, Glam. and Hants) b Oct. 15, 1958
Smith, C. S. (Camb. U. and Lancs.) b Oct. 1, 1932
Smith, C. W. (W. Indies) b July 29, 1933
Smith, Denis (Derby.; *CY 1936*) b Jan. 24, 1907, d Sept. 12, 1979
Smith, D. B. M. (Australia) b Sept. 14, 1884, d July 29, 1963
Smith, D. H. K. (Derby. and Orange Free State) b June 29, 1940
Smith, D. M. (Surrey) b Jan. 9, 1956
Smith, D. R. (Glos.) b Oct. 5, 1934
Smith, D. V. (Sussex) b June 14, 1923
Smith, Edwin (Derby.) b Jan. 2, 1934
Smith, E. J. (Warw.) b Feb. 6, 1886, d Aug. 31, 1979
Smith, F. B. (N. Zealand) b March 13, 1922
Smith, F. W. (S. Africa) No details of birth or death known
Smith, G. (Kent) b Nov. 30, 1925
Smith, G. J. (Essex) b April 2, 1935
Smith, Harry (Glos.) b May 21, 1890, d Nov. 12, 1937
Smith, H. D. (N. Zealand) b Jan. 8, 1913
Smith, I. D. S. (N. Zealand) b Feb. 28, 1957
Smith, K. D. (Warw.) b July 9, 1956
Smith, L. D. (Otago) b Dec. 23, 1914
Smith, M. J. (Middx) b Jan. 4, 1942
Smith, M. J. K. (Oxford U., Leics. and Warw.; *CY 1960*) b June 30, 1933
Smith, N. (Yorks. and Essex) b April 1, 1949
Smith, O. G. (W. Indies; *CY 1958*) b May 5, 1933, d Sept. 9, 1959
Smith, Ray (Essex) b Aug. 10, 1914
Smith, Roy (Somerset) b April 14, 1930
Smith, R. C. (Leics.) b Aug. 3, 1935
Smith, Sydney (Manager Australians in England 1921 and 1926) b March 1, 1880, d April 11, 1972

Smith, S. G. (Trinidad, Northants and Auckland; *CY 1915*) b Jan. 15, 1881, d Oct. 25, 1963
Smith, T. P. B. (Essex; *CY 1947*) b Oct. 30, 1908, d Aug. 4, 1967
Smith, V. I. (S. Africa) b Feb. 23, 1925
Smith, W. A. (Surrey) b Sept. 15, 1937
Smith, W. C. (Surrey; *CY 1911*) b Oct. 4, 1877, d July 16, 1946
Smithson, G. A. (Yorks. and Leics.) b Nov. 1, 1926, d Sept. 6, 1970
Smythe, R. I. (Camb. U.) b Nov. 19, 1951
Snedden, C. A. (N. Zealand) b Jan. 7, 1918
Snedden, M. C. (N. Zealand) b Nov. 23, 1958
Snellgrove, K. L. (Lancs.) b Nov. 12, 1941
Snooke, S. D. (S. Africa) b Nov. 11, 1878, d April 4, 1959
Snooke, S. J. (S. Africa) b Feb. 1, 1881, d Aug. 14, 1966
Snow, J. A. (Sussex; *CY 1973*) b Oct. 13, 1941
Snowden, A. W. (Northants) b Aug. 15, 1913, d May 7, 1981
Snowden, W. (Camb. U.) b Sept. 27, 1952
Sobers, Sir G. St A. (Notts., S. Australia and W. Indies; *CY 1964*) b July 18, 1936
Sohoni, S. W. (India) b March 5, 1918
Solanky, J. W. (E. Africa and Glam.) b June 30, 1942
Solkar, E. D. (Sussex and India) b March 18, 1948
Solomon, J. S. (W. Indies) b Aug. 26, 1930
Solomon, W. R. T. (S. Africa) b April 23, 1872, d July 12, 1964
Sood, M. M. (India) b July 6, 1939
Southern, J. W. (Hants) b Sept. 2, 1952
Southerton, James (Surrey, Hants and Sussex) b Nov. 16, 1827, d June 16, 1880
Southerton, S. J. (Editor of *Wisden* 1934-35) b July 7, 1874, d March 12, 1935
Sparling, J. T. (N. Zealand) b July 24, 1938
Spencer, C. T. (Leics.) b Aug. 18, 1931
Spencer, J. (Camb. U. and Sussex) b Oct. 6, 1949
Spencer, T. W. (Kent) b March 22, 1914
Sperry, J. (Leics.) b March 19, 1910
Spofforth, F. R. (Australia) b Sept. 9, 1853, d June 4, 1926
Spooner, R. H. (Lancs.; *CY 1905*) b Oct. 21, 1880, d Oct. 2, 1961
Spooner, R. T. (Warw.) b Dec. 30, 1919
Springall, J. D. (Notts.) b Sept. 19, 1932
Squires, H. S. (Surrey) b Feb. 22, 1909, d Jan. 24, 1950
Srikkanth, K. (India) b Dec. 21, 1959
Srinivasan, T. E. (India) b Oct. 26, 1950
Stackpole, K. R. (Australia; *CY 1973*) b July 10, 1940
Stallibrass, M. J. D. (Oxford U.) b June 28, 1951
Standen, J. A. (Worcs.) b May 30, 1935
Stanyforth, Lt-Col. R. T. (Yorks.) b May 30, 1892, d Feb. 20, 1964
Staples, S. J. (Notts.; *CY 1929*) b Sept. 18, 1892, d June 4, 1950
Starkie, S. (Northants) b April 4, 1926
Statham, J. B. (Lancs.; *CY 1955*) b June 16, 1930
Stayers, S. C. (Guyana, Bombay and W. Indies) b June 9, 1937
Stead, B. (Yorks., Essex, Notts. and N. Transvaal) b June 21, 1939, d April 15, 1980
Stead, D. W. (Canterbury) b May 26, 1947
Steel, A. G. (Camb. U. and Lancs.; Pres. MCC 1902) b Sept. 24, 1858, d June 15, 1914
Steele, D. S. (Northants and Derby.; *CY 1976*) b Sept. 29, 1941
Steele, J. F. (Leics. and Natal) b July 23, 1946
Stephens, E. J. (Glos.) b March 23, 1910
Stephens, F. G. (Warw.) b April 26, 1889, d Aug. 9, 1970
Stephenson, G. R. (Derby. and Hants) b Nov. 19, 1942
Stephenson, H. H. (Surrey and All-England) b May 3, 1832, d Dec. 17, 1896
Stephenson, H. W. (Somerset) b July 18, 1920
Stephenson, Lt-Col. J. W. A. (Essex and Worcs.) b Aug. 1, 1907, d May 20, 1982
Stevens, Edward ("Lumpy") (Hants) b *circa* 1735, d Sept. 7, 1819
Stevens, G. B. (Australia) b Feb. 29, 1932
Stevens, G. T. S. (UCS, Oxford U. and Middx; *CY 1918*) b Jan. 7, 1901, d Sept. 19, 1970
Stevenson, G. B. (Yorks.) b Dec. 16, 1955
Stevenson, K. (Derby. and Hants) b Oct. 6, 1950
Stevenson, M. H. (Camb. U. and Derby.) b June 13, 1927
Stewart, M. J. (Surrey; *CY 1958*) b Sept. 16, 1932
Stewart, R. B. (S. Africa) b Sept. 3, 1856, d Sept. 12, 1913
Stewart, R. W. (Glos. and Middx) b Feb. 28, 1945
Stewart, W. J. (Warw. and Northants) b Aug. 31, 1934
Stocks, F. W. (Notts.) b Nov. 6, 1917
Stoddart, A. E. (Middx; *CY 1893*) b March 11, 1863, d April 3, 1915
Stollmeyer, J. B. (W. Indies) b April 11, 1921
Stollmeyer, V. H. (W. Indies) b Jan. 24, 1916
Storer, W. (Derby.; *CY 1899*) b Jan. 25, 1867, d March 5, 1912
Storey, S. J. (Surrey and Sussex) b Jan. 6, 1941

Stott, L. W. (Auckland) b Dec. 8, 1946
Stott, W. B. (Yorks.) b July 18, 1934
Stovold, A. W. (Glos. and Orange Free State) b March 19, 1953
Street, G. B. (Sussex) b Dec. 6, 1889, d April 24, 1924
Stricker, L. A. (S. Africa) b May 26, 1884, d Feb. 5, 1960
Stringer, P. M. (Yorks. and Leics.) b Feb. 23, 1943
Strudwick, H. (Surrey; *CY 1912*) b Jan. 28, 1880, d Feb. 13, 1970
Strydom, W. T. (Orange Free State) b March 21, 1942
Studd, C. T. (Camb. U. and Middx) b Dec. 2, 1860, d July 16, 1931
Studd, G. B. (Camb. U. and Middx) b Oct. 20, 1859, d Feb. 13, 1945
Studd, Sir Peter M. (Camb. U.) b Sept. 15, 1916
Sturt, M. O. C. (Middx) b Sept. 12, 1940
Subba Row, R. (Camb. U., Surrey and Northants; *CY 1961*) b Jan. 29, 1932
Subramanya, V. (India) b July 16, 1936
Sueter, T. (Hants and Surrey) b *circa* 1749, d Feb. 17, 1827
Sugg, F. H. (Yorks., Derby. and Lancs.; *CY 1890*) b Jan. 11, 1862, d May 29, 1933
Sullivan, J. (Lancs.) b Feb. 5, 1945
Sully, H. (Somerset and Northants) b Nov. 1, 1939
Sunderram, G. R. (India) b March 29, 1930
Sunnucks, P. R. (Kent) b June 22, 1916
Surendranath, R. (India) b Jan. 4, 1937
Surridge, D. (Camb. U. and Glos.) b Jan. 6, 1956
Surridge, W. S. (Surrey; *CY 1953*) b Sept. 3, 1917
Surti, R. F. (Queensland and India) b May 25, 1936
Susskind, M. J. (Middx and S. Africa) b June 8, 1891, d July 9, 1957
Sutcliffe, B. (N. Zealand; *CY 1950*) b Nov. 17, 1923
Sutcliffe, H. (Yorks.; *CY 1920*) b Nov. 24, 1894, d Jan. 22, 1978
Sutcliffe, S. P. (Oxford U. and Warw.) b May 22, 1960
Sutcliffe, W. H. H. (Yorks.) b Oct. 10, 1926
Suttle, K. G. (Sussex) b Aug. 25, 1928
Sutton, R. E. (Auckland) b May 30, 1940
Swamy, V. N. (India) b May 23, 1924
Swanton, E. W. (Middx; Writer) b Feb. 11, 1907
Swarbrook, F. W. (Derby., Griqualand W. and Orange Free State) b Dec. 17, 1950
Swart, P. D. (Rhodesia, W. Province and Glam.) b April 27, 1946
Swetman, R. (Surrey, Notts. and Glos.) b Oct. 25, 1933
Sydenham, D. A. D. (Surrey) b April 6, 1934
Symington, S. J. (Leics.) b Sept. 16, 1926

Taber, H. B. (Australia) b April 29, 1940
Taberer, H. M. (S. Africa) b Oct. 7, 1870, d June 5, 1932
Tahir Naqqash (Pakistan) b June 28, 1959
Tait, A. (Northants and Glos.) b Dec. 27, 1953
Talat Ali (Pakistan) b May 29, 1950
Talbot, R. O. (Canterbury and Otago) b Nov. 26, 1903
Tallon, D. (Australia; *CY 1949*) b Feb. 17, 1916
Tamhane, N. S. (India) b Aug. 4, 1931
Tancred, A. B. (S. Africa) b Aug. 20, 1865, d Nov. 23, 1911
Tancred, L. J. (S. Africa) b Oct. 7, 1876, d July 28, 1934
Tancred, V. M. (S. Africa) b 1875, d June 3, 1904
Tapscott, G. L. (S. Africa) b Nov. 7, 1889, d Dec. 13, 1940
Tapscott, L. E. (S. Africa) b March 18, 1894, d July 7, 1934
Tarapore, K. K. (India) b Dec. 17, 1910
Tarbox, C. V. (Worcs.) b July 2, 1891, d June 15, 1978
Tarrant, F. A. (Victoria and Middx; *CY 1908*) b Dec. 11, 1880, d Jan. 29, 1951
Tarrant, George F. (Cambs. and All-England) b Dec. 7, 1838, d July 2, 1870
Taslim Arif (Pakistan) b May 1, 1954
Tate, F. W. (Sussex) b July 24, 1867, d Feb. 24, 1943
Tate, M. W. (Sussex; *CY 1924*) b May 30, 1895, d May 18, 1956
Tattersall, R. (Lancs.) b Aug. 17, 1922
Tauseef Ahmed (Pakistan) b May 10, 1960
Tavaré, C. J. (Oxford U. and Kent) b Oct. 27, 1954
Tayfield, A. (Natal, Transvaal and NE Transvaal) b June 21, 1931
Tayfield, H. J. (S. Africa; *CY 1956*) b Jan. 30, 1929
Taylor, A. I. (S. Africa) b July 25, 1925
Taylor, B. (Essex; *CY 1972*) b June 19, 1932
Taylor, B. R. (N. Zealand) b July 12, 1943
Taylor, C. R. V. (Camb. U., Warw. and Middx.) b Oct. 3, 1951
Taylor, Daniel (S. Africa) b Jan. 9, 1887, d Jan. 24, 1957
Taylor, D. D. (Warw. and N. Zealand) b March 2, 1923, d Dec. 5, 1980
Taylor, D. J. S. (Surrey, Somerset and Griqualand W.) b Nov. 12, 1942
Taylor, G. R. (Hants) b Nov. 25, 1909
Taylor, H. W. (S. Africa; *CY 1925*) b May 5, 1889, d Feb. 8, 1973

Taylor, J. M. (Australia) b Oct. 10, 1895, d May 12, 1971
Taylor, J. O. (W. Indies) b Jan. 3, 1932
Taylor, K. (Yorks. and Auckland) b Aug. 21, 1935
Taylor, K. A. (Warw.) b Sept. 29, 1916
Taylor, L. B. (Leics. and Natal) b Oct. 25, 1953
Taylor, M. L. (Lancs.) b July 16, 1904, d March 14, 1978
Taylor, M. N. S. (Notts. and Hants) b Nov. 12, 1942
Taylor, N. R. (Kent) b July 21, 1959
Taylor, R. M. (Essex) b Nov. 30, 1909
Taylor, R. W. (Derby.; *CY 1977*) b July 17, 1941
Taylor, T. J. (Oxford U. and Lancs.) b March 28, 1961
Taylor, T. L. (Camb. U. and Yorks.; *CY 1901*) b May 25, 1878, d March 16, 1960
Taylor, W. (Notts.) b Jan. 24, 1947
Tennekoon, A. P. B. (Sri Lanka) b Oct. 29, 1946
Tennyson, 3rd Lord (Hon. L. H.) (Hants; *CY 1914*) b Nov. 7, 1889, d June 6, 1951
Thackaray, P. R. (Oxford U.) b Sept. 26, 1950
Theunissen, N. H. (S. Africa) b May 4, 1867, d Nov. 9, 1929
Thomas, D. J. (Surrey and N. Transvaal) b June 30, 1959
Thomas, G. (Australia) b March 21, 1938
Thompson, A. W. (Middx) b April 17, 1916
Thompson, G. J. (Northants; *CY 1906*) b Oct. 27, 1877, d March 3, 1943
Thompson, J. R. (Camb. U. and Warw.) b May 10, 1918
Thompson, Nathaniel (Australia) b Birmingham, England April 21, 1838, d Sept. 2, 1896
Thompson, R. G. (Warw.) b Sept. 26, 1932
Thoms, G. R. (Australia) b March 22, 1927
Thomson, A. L. (Australia) b Dec. 2, 1945
Thomson, J. R. (Middx and Australia) b Aug. 16, 1950
Thomson, K. (N. Zealand) b Feb. 26, 1941
Thomson, N. I. (Sussex) b Jan. 23, 1929
Thornton, C. I. (Camb. U., Kent and Middx) b March 20, 1850, d Dec. 10, 1929
Thornton, P. G. (Yorks., Middx and S. Africa) b Dec. 24, 1867, d Jan. 31, 1939
Thurlow, H. M. (Australia) b Jan. 10, 1902, d Dec. 3, 1975
Tilly, H. W. (Middx) b May 25, 1932
Timms, B. S. V. (Hants and Warw.) b Dec. 17, 1940
Timms, J. E. (Northants) b Nov. 3, 1906, d May 18, 1980
Timms, W. W. (Northants) b Sept. 28, 1902
Tindall, M. (Camb. U. and Middx) b March 31, 1914
Tindall, R. A. E. (Surrey) b Sept. 23, 1935
Tindill, E. W. T. (N. Zealand) b Dec. 18, 1910
Titmus, F. J. (Middx, Surrey and Orange Free State; *CY 1963*) b Nov. 24, 1932
Todd, L. J. (Kent) b June 19, 1907, d Aug. 20, 1967
Todd, P. A. (Notts.) b March 12, 1953
Tolchard, J. G. (Leics.) b March 17, 1944
Tolchard, R. W. (Leics.) b June 15, 1946
Tomlinson, D. S. (S. Africa) b Sept. 4, 1910
Tompkin, M. (Leics.) b Feb. 17, 1919, d Sept. 27, 1956
Toogood, G. J. (Oxford U.) b Nov. 19, 1961
Toohey, P. M. (Australia) b April 20, 1954
Topham, R. D. N. (Oxford U.) b July 17, 1952
Tordoff, G. G. (Camb. U. and Somerset) b Dec. 6, 1929
Toshack, E. R. H. (Australia) b Dec. 15, 1914
Towell, E. F. (Northants) b July 5, 1901, d June 2, 1972
Townsend, A. (Warw.) b Aug. 26, 1921
Townsend, A. F. (Derby.) b March 29, 1912
Townsend, C. L. (Glos.; *CY 1899*) b Nov. 7, 1876, d Oct. 17, 1958
Townsend, D. C. H. (Oxford U.) b April 20, 1912
Townsend, L. F. (Derby.; *CY 1934*) b June 8, 1903
Traicos, A. J. (S. Africa) b May 17, 1947
Trapnell, B. M. W. (Camb. U. and Middx) b May 18, 1924
Travers, J. P. F. (Australia) b Jan. 10, 1871, d Sept. 15, 1942
Tremlett, M. F. (Somerset and C. Districts) b July 5, 1923
Tremlett, T. M. (Hants) b July 26, 1956
Tribe, G. E. (Northants and Australia; *CY 1955*) b Oct. 4, 1920
Trim, J. (W. Indies) b Jan. 24, 1915, d Nov. 12, 1960
Trimble, S. C. (Queensland) b Aug. 16, 1934
Trimborn, P. H. J. (S. Africa) b May 18, 1940
Trott, A. E. (Middx, Australia and England; *CY 1899*) b Feb. 6, 1873, d July 30, 1914
Trott, G. H. S. (Australia; *CY 1894*) b Aug. 5, 1866, d Nov. 10, 1917
Troup, G. B. (N. Zealand) b Oct. 3, 1952
Trueman, F. S. (Yorks.; *CY 1953*) b Feb. 6, 1931
Trumble, H. (Australia; *CY 1897*) b May 12, 1867, d Aug. 14, 1938
Trumble, J. W. (Australia) b Sept. 16, 1863, d Aug. 17, 1944

Trumper, V. T. (Australia; *CY 1903*) b Nov. 2, 1877, d June 28, 1915
Truscott, P. B. (N. Zealand) b Aug. 14, 1941
Tuckett, L. (S. Africa) b Feb. 6, 1919
Tuckett, L. R. (S. Africa) b April 19, 1885, d April 8, 1963
Tufnell, N. C. (Camb. U. and Surrey) b June 13, 1887, d Aug. 3, 1951
Tuke, Sir Anthony (Pres. MCC 1982-83) b Aug. 22, 1920
Tunnicliffe, C. J. (Derby.) b Aug. 11, 1951
Tunnicliffe, H. T. (Notts.) b March 4, 1950
Tunnicliffe, J. (Yorks.; *CY 1901*) b Aug. 26, 1866, d July 11, 1948
Turnbull, M. J. (Camb. U. and Glam.; *CY 1931*) b March 16, 1906, d Aug. 5, 1944
Turner, A. (Australia) b July 23, 1950
Turner, C. (Yorks.) b Jan. 11, 1902, d Nov. 19, 1968
Turner, C. T. B. (Australia; *CY 1889*) b Nov. 16, 1862, d Jan. 1, 1944
Turner, D. R. (Hants and W. Province) b Feb. 5, 1949
Turner, F. M. (Leics.) b Aug. 8, 1934
Turner, G. M. (Worcs. and N. Zealand; *CY 1971*) b May 26, 1947
Turner, S. (Essex and Natal) b July 18, 1943
Twentyman-Jones, P. S. (S. Africa) b Sept. 13, 1876, d March 8, 1954
Twining, R. H. (Oxford U. and Middx; Pres. MCC 1964-65) b Nov. 3, 1889, d Jan. 3, 1979
Tyldesley, E. (Lancs.; *CY 1920*) b Feb. 5, 1889, d May 5, 1962
Tyldesley, J. T. (Lancs.; *CY 1902*) b Nov. 22, 1873, d Nov. 27, 1930
Tyldesley, R. K. (Lancs.; *CY 1925*) b March 11, 1897, d Sept. 17, 1943
Tylecote, E. F. S. (Oxford U. and Kent) b June 23, 1849, d March 15, 1938
Tyler, E. J. (Somerset) b Oct. 13, 1864, d Jan. 21, 1917
Tyson, F. H. (Northants; *CY 1956*) b June 6, 1930

Ufton, D. G. (Kent) b May 31, 1928
Ulyett, G. (Yorks.) b Oct. 21, 1851, d June 18, 1898
Umrigar, P. R. (India) b March 28, 1926
Underwood, D. L. (Kent; *CY 1969*) b June 8, 1945
Unwin, F. St G. (Essex) b April 23, 1911

Valentine, A. L. (W. Indies; *CY 1951*) b April 29, 1930
Valentine, B. H. (Camb. U. and Kent) b Jan. 17, 1908
Valentine, V. A. (W. Indies) b April 4, 1908, believed dead
van der Bijl, P. G. V. (S. Africa) b Oct. 21, 1907, d Feb. 16, 1973
van der Bijl, V. A. P. (Natal and Middx; *CY 1981*) b March 19, 1948
Van der Gucht, P. I. (Glos.) b Nov. 2, 1911
Van der Merwe, E. A. (S. Africa) b Nov. 9, 1904, d Feb. 28, 1971
Van der Merwe, P. L. (S. Africa) b March 14, 1937
van Geloven, J. (Yorks. and Leics.) b Jan 4, 1934
Van Ryneveld, C. B. (Oxford U. and S. Africa) b March 19, 1928
Varachia, R. (First Pres. S. African Cricket Union) b Oct. 12, 1915, d Dec. 11, 1981
Varey, D. W. (Camb. U.) b Oct. 15, 1961
Varey, J. G. (Oxford U.) b Oct. 15, 1961
Varnals, G. D. (S. Africa) b July 24, 1935
Vaulkhard, P. (Notts. and Derby.) b Sept. 15, 1911
Vengsarkar, D. B. (India) b April 6, 1956
Veivers, T. R. (Australia) b April 6, 1937
Venkataraghavan, S. (Derby. and India) b April 21, 1946
Verity, Capt. H. (Yorks.; *CY 1932*) b May 18, 1905, d July 31, 1943
Vernon, G. F. (Middx) b June 20, 1856, d Aug. 10, 1902
Vernon, M. T. (W. Australia) b Feb. 9, 1937
Vials, G. A. T. (Northants) b March 18, 1887, d April 26, 1974
Vigar, F. H. (Essex) b July 7, 1917
Viljoen, K. G. (S. Africa) b May 14, 1910, d Jan. 21, 1974
Vincent, C. L. (S. Africa) b Feb. 16, 1902, d Aug. 24, 1968
Vine, J. (Sussex; *CY 1906*) b May 15, 1875, d April 25, 1946
Vintcent, C. H. (S. Africa) b Sept. 2, 1866, d Sept. 28, 1943
Virgin, R. T. (Somerset and Northants; *CY 1971*) b Aug. 26, 1939
Viswanath, G. R. (India) b Feb. 12, 1949
Vivian, G. E. (N. Zealand) b Feb. 28, 1946
Vivian, H. G. (N. Zealand) b Nov. 4, 1912
Voce, W. (Notts.; *CY 1933*) b Aug. 8, 1909
Vogler, A. E. E. (Middx and S. Africa; *CY 1908*) b Nov. 28, 1876, d Aug. 9, 1946
Vizianagram, Maharaj Sir Vijaya of (India) b Dec. 28, 1905, d Dec. 2, 1965

Waddington, A. (Yorks.) b Feb. 4, 1893, d Oct. 27, 1959
Waddington, J. E. (Griqualand W.) b Dec. 30, 1918
Wade, H. F. (S. Africa) b Sept. 14, 1905, d Nov. 22, 1980
Wade, T. H. (Essex) b Nov. 24, 1910
Wade, W. W. (S. Africa) b June 18, 1914
Wadekar, A. L. (India) b April 1, 1941

Wadsworth, K. J. (N. Zealand) b Nov. 30, 1946, d Aug. 19, 1976
Wainwright, E. (Yorks.; *CY 1894*) b April 8, 1865, d Oct. 26, 1919
Waite, J. H. B. (S. Africa) b Jan. 19, 1930
Waite, M. G. (Australia) b Jan. 7, 1911
Walcott, C. L. (W. Indies; *CY 1958*) b Jan. 17, 1926
Walcott, L. A. (W. Indies) b Jan. 18, 1894
Walden, F. I. (Northants; Umpire) b March 1, 1888, d May 3, 1949
Walford, M. M. (Oxford U. and Somerset) b Nov. 27, 1915
Walker, A. K. (NSW and Notts.) b Oct. 4, 1925
Walker, C. (Yorks. and Hants) b June 27, 1920
Walker, C. W. (S. Australia) b Feb. 19, 1909, d Dec. 21, 1942
Walker, I. D. (Middx) b Jan. 8, 1844, d July 6, 1898
Walker, M. H. N. (Australia) b Sept. 12, 1948
Walker, P. M. (Glam., Transvaal and W. Province) b Feb. 17, 1936
Walker, W. (Notts.) b Nov. 24, 1892
Wall, T. W. (Australia) b May 13, 1904, d March 26, 1981
Wallace, W. M. (N. Zealand) b Dec. 19, 1916
Waller, C. E. (Surrey and Sussex) b Oct. 3, 1948
Waller, G. de W. (Oxford U.) b Feb. 10, 1950
Walsh, J. E. (NSW and Leics.) b Dec. 4, 1912, d May 20, 1980
Walter, K. A. (S. Africa) b Nov. 5, 1939
Walters, C. F. (Glam. and Worcs.; *CY 1934*) b Aug. 28, 1905
Walters, F. H. (Australia) b Feb. 9, 1860, d June 1922
Walters, J. (Derby.) b Aug. 7, 1949
Walters, K. D. (Australia) b Dec. 21, 1945
Walton, A. C. (Oxford U. and Middx) b Sept. 26, 1933
Waqar Hassan (Pakistan) b Sept. 12, 1932
Ward, Alan (Derby., Leics. and Border) b Aug. 10, 1947
Ward, Albert (Yorks. and Lancs.; *CY 1890*) b Nov. 21, 1865, d Jan. 6, 1939
Ward, B. (Essex) b Feb. 28, 1944
Ward, D. (Glam.) b Aug. 30, 1934
Ward, F. A. (Australia) b Feb. 23, 1909, d March 25, 1974
Ward, J. M. (Oxford U. and Derby.) b Sept. 14, 1948
Ward, J. T. (N. Zealand) b March 11, 1937
Ward, T. A. (S. Africa) b Aug. 2, 1887, d Feb. 16, 1936
Ward, William (MCC and Hants) b July 24, 1787, d June 30, 1849
Wardle, J. H. (Yorks.; *CY 1954*) b Jan. 8, 1923
Warnapura, B. (Sri Lanka) b March 1, 1953
Warne, F. B. (Worcs., Victoria and Transvaal) b Oct. 3, 1906
Warner, Sir Pelham (Oxford U. and Middx; *CY 1904, special portrait 1921*) b Oct. 2, 1873, d Jan. 30, 1963
Warr, J. J. (Camb. U. and Middx) b July 16, 1927
Warren, A. (Derby.) b April 2, 1875, d Sept. 3, 1951
Washbrook, C. (Lancs.; *CY 1947*) b Dec. 6, 1914
Wasim Bari (Pakistan) b March 23, 1948
Wasim Raja (Pakistan) b July 3, 1952
Wass, T. G. (Notts.; *CY 1908*) b Dec. 26, 1873, d Oct. 27, 1953
Wassell, A. (Hants) b April 15, 1940
Watkins, A. J. (Glam.) b April 21, 1922
Watkins, J. C. (S. Africa) b April 10, 1923
Watkins, J. R. (Australia) b April 16, 1943
Watson, C. (Jamaica, Delhi and W. Indies) b July 1, 1938
Watson, F. B. (Lancs.) b Sept. 17, 1898, d Feb. 1, 1976
Watson, G. D. (Australia) b March 8, 1945
Watson, G. G. (NSW and Worcs.) b Jan. 29, 1955
Watson, G. S. (Kent and Leics.) b April 10, 1907, d April 1, 1974
Watson, W. (Yorks. and Leics.; *CY 1954*) b March 7, 1920
Watson, W. (Australia) b Jan. 31, 1931
Watson, W. K. (Border, N. Transvaal, E. Province and Notts.) b May 21, 1955
Watt, A. E. (Kent) b June 19, 1907, d Feb. 3, 1974
Watt, L. (N. Zealand) b Sept. 17, 1924
Watts, E. A. (Surrey) b Aug. 1, 1911, d May 2, 1982
Watts, H. E. (Camb. U. and Somerset) b March 4, 1922
Watts, P. D. (Northants and Notts.) b March 31, 1938
Watts, P. J. (Northants) b June 16, 1940
Wazir Ali, S. (India) b Sept. 15, 1903, d June 17, 1950
Wazir Mohammad (Pakistan) b Dec. 22, 1929
Webb, M. G. (N. Zealand) b June 22, 1947
Webb, P. N. (N. Zealand) b July 14, 1957
Webb, R. T. (Sussex) b July 11, 1922
Webb, S. G. (Manager Australians in England 1961) b Jan. 31, 1900, d Aug. 5, 1976
Webbe, A. J. (Oxford U. and Middx) b Jan. 16, 1855, d Feb. 19, 1941
Webster, J. (Camb. U. and Northants) b Oct. 28, 1917
Webster, Dr R. V. (Warw. and Otago) b June 10, 1939

Webster, W. H. (Camb. U. and Middx; Pres. MCC 1976-77) b Feb. 22, 1910
Weekes, E. D. (W. Indies; *CY 1951*) b Feb. 26, 1925
Weekes, K. H. (W. Indies) b Jan. 24, 1912
Weeks, R. T. (Warw.) b April 30, 1930
Weir, G. L. (N. Zealand) b June 2, 1908
Wellard, A. W. (Somerset; *CY 1936*) b April 8, 1902, d Dec. 31, 1980
Wellham, D. M. (Australia) b March 13, 1959
Wellings, E. M. (Oxford U. and Surrey) b April 6, 1909
Wells, B. D. (Glos. and Notts.) b July 27, 1930
Wells, C. M. (Sussex and Border) b March 3, 1960
Wenman, E. G. (Kent and England) b Aug. 18, 1803, d Dec. 31, 1879
Wensley, A. F. (Sussex) b May 23, 1898, d June 17, 1970
Wesley, C. (S. Africa) b Sept. 5, 1937
Wessels, K. C. (Orange Free State, W. Province, N. Transvaal, Sussex and Queensland) b Sept. 14, 1957
West, G. H. (Editor of *Wisden* 1880-86) b 1851, d Oct. 6, 1896
Westcott, R. J. (S. Africa) b Sept. 19, 1927
Weston, M. J. (Worcs.) b April 8, 1959
Wettimuny, S. (Sri Lanka) b Aug. 12, 1956
Wharton, A. (Lancs. and Leics.) b Apil 30, 1923
Whatmore, D. F. (Australia) b March 16, 1954
Wheat, A. B. (Notts.) b May 13, 1898, d May 20, 1973
Wheatley, K. J. (Hants) b Jan. 20, 1946
Wheatley, O. S. (Camb. U., Warw. and Glam.; *CY 1969*) b May 28, 1935
Whitaker, Haddon (Editor of *Wisden* 1940-43) b Aug. 30, 1908, d Jan. 5, 1982
Whitcombe, P. A. (Oxford U. and Middx) b April 23, 1923
White, A. F. T. (Camb. U., Warw. and Worcs.) b Sept. 5, 1915
White, D. W. (Hants and Glam.) b Dec. 14, 1935
White, E. C. S. (NSW) b July 14, 1913
White, G. C. (S. Africa) b Feb. 5, 1882, d Oct. 17, 1918
White, J. C. (Somerset; *CY 1929*) b Feb. 19, 1891, d May 2, 1961
White, Hon. L. R. (5th Lord Annally) (Middx and Victory Test) b March 15, 1927
White, R. A. (Middx and Notts.) b Oct. 6, 1936
White, R. C. (Camb. U., Glos. and Transvaal) b Jan. 29, 1941
White, W. A. (W. Indies) b Nov. 20, 1938
Whitehead, J. P. (Yorks. and Worcs.) b Sept. 3, 1925
Whitehouse, J. (Warw.) b April 8, 1949
Whitelaw, P. E. (N. Zealand) b Feb. 10, 1910
Whitfield, E. W. (Surrey and Northants) b May 31, 1911
Whiting, N. H. (Worcs.) b Oct. 2, 1920
Whitington, R. S. (S. Australia and Victory Tests; Writer) b June 30, 1912
Whitney, M. R. (Glos. and Australia) b Feb. 24, 1959
Whittaker, G. J. (Surrey) b May 29, 1916
Whittingham, N. B. (Notts.) b Oct. 22, 1940
Whitty, W. J. (Australia) b Aug. 15, 1886, d Jan. 30, 1974
Whysall, W. W. (Notts.; *CY 1925*) b Oct. 31, 1887, d Nov. 11, 1930
Wiener, J. M. (Australia) b May 1, 1955
Wight, C. V. (W. Indies) b July 28, 1902, d 1969
Wight, G. L. (W. Indies) b May 28, 1929
Wight, P. B. (B. Guiana, Somerset and Canterbury) b June 25, 1930
Wijesuriya, R. G. C. E. (Sri Lanka) b Feb. 18, 1960
Wilcox, D. R. (Camb. U. and Essex) b June 4, 1910, d Feb. 6, 1953
Wiles, C. A. (W. Indies) b Aug. 11, 1892
Wilkins, A. H. (Glam., Glos. and N. Transvaal) b Aug. 22, 1953
Wilkins, C. P. (Derby., E. Province and Natal) b July 31, 1944
Wilkinson, C. T. A. (Surrey) b Oct. 4, 1884, d Dec. 16, 1970
Wilkinson, L. L. (Lancs.) b Nov. 5, 1916
Wilkinson, P. A. (Notts.) b Aug. 23, 1951
Wilkinson, Col. W. A. C. (Oxford U.) b Dec. 6, 1892
Willatt, G. L. (Camb. U., Notts. and Derby.) b May 7, 1918
Willett, E. T. (W. Indies) b May 1, 1953
Willett, M. D. (Surrey) b April 21, 1933
Willey, P. (Northants) b Dec. 6, 1949
Williams, A. B. (W. Indies) b Nov. 21, 1949
Williams, C. B. (Barbados) b March 8, 1926
Williams, C. C. P. (Oxford U. and Essex) b Feb. 9, 1933
Williams, D. L. (Glam.) b Nov. 20, 1946
Williams, E. A. V. (W. Indies) b April 10, 1914
Williams, R. G. (Northants) b Aug. 10, 1957
Williams, R. J. (S. Africa) b April 12, 1912
Williamson, J. G. (Northants) b April 4, 1936
Willis, R. G. D. (Surrey, Warw. and N. Transvaal; *CY 1978*) b May 30, 1949
Willoughby, J. T. (S. Africa) b Nov. 7, 1874, d *circa* 1955

Willsher, E. (Kent and All-England) b Nov. 22, 1828, d Oct. 7, 1885
Wilmot, A. L. (E. Province) b June 1, 1943
Wilmot, K. (Warw.) b April 3, 1911
Wilson, A. (Lancs.) b April 24, 1921
Wilson, A. E. (Middx and Glos.) b May 5, 1912
Wilson, Rev. C. E. M. (Camb. U. and Yorks.) b May 15, 1875, d Feb. 8, 1944
Wilson, D. (Yorks. and MCC) b Aug. 7, 1937
Wilson, E. F. (Surrey) b June 24, 1907, d March 3, 1981
Wilson, E. R. (Camb. U. and Yorks.) b March 25, 1879, d July 21, 1957
Wilson, J. V. (Yorks.; *CY 1961*) b Jan. 17, 1921
Wilson, J. W. (Australia) b Aug. 20, 1922
Wilson, R. C. (Kent) b Feb. 18, 1928
Wimble, C. S. (S. Africa) b Jan. 9, 1864, d Jan. 28, 1930
Windows, A. R. (Glos. and Camb. U.) b Sept. 25, 1942
Winfield, H. M. (Notts.) b June 13, 1933
Wingfield Digby, A. R. (Oxford U.) b July 25, 1950
Winlaw, Sqn Ldr R. de W. K. (Camb. U. and Surrey) b March 28, 1912, d Oct. 31, 1942
Winn, C. E. (Oxford U. and Sussex) b Nov. 13, 1926
Winrow, H. F. (Notts.) b Jan. 17, 1916, d Aug. 19, 1973
Winslow, P. L. (Sussex and S. Africa) b May 21, 1929
Wisden John (Sussex; founder John Wisden and Co. and *Wisden's Cricketers' Almanack*) b Sept. 5, 1826, d April 5, 1884
Wishart, K. L. (W. Indies) b Nov. 28, 1908, d Oct. 18, 1972
Wolton, A. V. G. (Warw.) b June 12, 1919
Wood, A. (Yorks.; *CY 1939*) b Aug. 25, 1898, d April 1, 1973
Wood, B. (Yorks., Lancs., Derby. and E. Province) b Dec. 26, 1942
Wood, C. J. B. (Leics.) b Nov. 21, 1875, d June 5, 1960
Wood, D. J. (Sussex) b May 19, 1914
Wood, G. E. C. (Camb. U. and Kent) b Aug. 22, 1893, d March 18, 1971
Wood, G. M. (Australia) b Nov. 6, 1956
Wood, H. (Kent and Surrey; *CY 1891*) b Dec. 14, 1854, d April 30, 1919
Wood, R. (Lancs. and Victoria) b March 7, 1860, d Jan. 6, 1915
Woodcock, A. J. (Australia) b Feb. 27, 1948
Woodfull, W. M. (Australia); *CY 1927*) b Aug. 22, 1897, d Aug. 11, 1965
Woodhead, F. G. (Notts.) b Oct. 30, 1912
Woodhouse, G. E. S. (Somerset) b Feb. 15, 1924
Woods, S. M. J. (Camb. U., Somerset, Australia and England; *CY 1889*) b April 14, 1867, d April 30, 1931
Wookey, S. M. (Camb. U. and Oxford U.) b Sept. 2, 1954
Wooler, C. R. D. (Leics. and Rhodesia) b June 30, 1930
Wooller, W. (Camb. U. and Glam.) b Nov. 20, 1912
Woolley, C. N. (Glos. and Northants) b May 5, 1886, d Nov. 3, 1962
Woolley, F. E. (Kent; *CY 1911*) b May 27, 1887, d Oct. 18, 1978
Woolmer, R. A. (Kent, Natal and W. Province; *CY 1976*) b May 14, 1948
Worrall, J. (Australia) b May 12, 1863, d Nov. 17, 1937
Worrell, Sir F. M. M. (W. Indies; *CY 1951*) b Aug. 1, 1924, d March 13, 1967
Worsley, D. R. (Oxford U. and Lancs.) b July 18, 1941
Worsley, Sir W. A. 4th Bt. (Yorks.; Pres. MCC 1961-62) b April 5, 1890, d Dec. 4, 1973
Worthington, T. S. (Derby.; *CY 1937*) b Aug. 21, 1905, d Aug. 31, 1973
Wright, A. (Warw.) b Aug. 25, 1941
Wright, C. W. (Camb. U. and Notts.) b May 27, 1863, d Jan. 10, 1936
Wright, D. V. P. (Kent; *CY 1940*) b Aug. 21, 1914
Wright, J. G. (Derby. and N. Zealand) b July 5, 1954
Wright, K. J. (Australia) b Dec. 27, 1953
Wright, L. G. (Derby.; *CY 1906*) b June 15, 1862, d Jan. 11, 1953
Wright, M. J. E. (N. Districts) b Jan. 17, 1950
Wright, S. (Camb. U.) b Feb. 4, 1952
Wyatt, R. E. S. (Warw. and Worcs.; *CY 1930*) b May 2, 1901
Wynne, O. E. (S. Africa) b June 1, 1919, d July 13, 1975
Wynyard, E. G. (Hants) b April 1, 1861, d Oct. 30, 1936

Yadav, N. S. (India) b Jan. 26, 1957
Yajurvindra Singh, (India) b Aug. 1, 1952
Yallop, G. N. (Australia) b Oct. 7, 1952
Yardley, B. (Australia) b Sept. 7, 1947
Yardley, N. W. D. (Camb. U. and Yorks.; *CY 1948*) b March 19, 1915
Yardley, T. J. (Worcs. and Northants) b Oct. 27, 1946
Yarnold, H. (Worcs.) b July 6, 1917, d Aug. 13, 1974
Yashpal Sharma (India) b Aug. 11, 1954
Yawar Saeed (Somerset and Punjab) b Jan. 22, 1935
Yograj Singh (India) b March 25, 1958

Young, D. M. (Worcs. and Glos.) b April 15, 1924
Young, H. I. (Essex) b Feb. 5, 1876, d Dec. 12, 1964
Young, J. A. (Middx) b Oct. 14, 1912
Young, R. A. (Camb. U. and Sussex) b Sept. 16, 1885, d July 1, 1968
Younis Ahmed, M. (Surrey, Worcs., S. Australia and Pakistan) b Oct. 21, 1947
Yuile, B. W. (N. Zealand) b Oct. 29, 1941

Zaheer Abbas (Glos. and Pakistan; *CY 1972*) b July 24, 1947
Zulch, J. W. (S. Africa) b Jan. 2, 1886, d May 19, 1924
Zulfiqar Ahmed (Pakistan) b Nov. 22, 1926

UMPIRES FOR 1983

TEST MATCH UMPIRES

With only four Test matches scheduled for the series against New Zealand in 1983, the list of Test match umpires was reduced to four, K. Palmer and A. G. T. Whitehead being omitted from those who stood in the Test series against India and Pakistan in 1982. The full list consists of: H. D. Bird, D. J. Constant, D. G. L. Evans and B. J. Meyer.

PRUDENTIAL CUP UMPIRES

Both Whitehead and Palmer were included in the list of umpires for the Prudential Cup matches in 1983, the latter being joined by his brother Roy. After serving only one summer on the list of first-class umpires, J. Birkenshaw and M. J. Kitchen were also included in the list. The full Prudential Cup panel is: H. D. Bird, J. Birkenshaw, D. J. Constant, D. G. L. Evans, M. J. Kitchen, B. Leadbeater, B. J. Meyer, D. O. Oslear, K. E. Palmer, R. Palmer, D. R. Shepherd and A. G. T. Whitehead.

FIRST-CLASS UMPIRES

Three new umpires joined the first-class list for 1983: J. H. Harris, who played for Somerset and also in Minor Counties cricket for Devon and Suffolk; J. W. Holder, formerly of Hampshire; and R. A. White, who played for Middlesex and Nottinghamshire. The full list is: W. E. Alley, H. D. Bird, J. Birkenshaw, D. J. Constant, C. Cook, P. J. Eele, D. G. L. Evans, J. H. Harris, J. W. Holder, K. Ibadulla, A. Jepson, R. Julian, M. J. Kitchen, B. Leadbeater, B. J. Meyer, D. O. Oslear, K. E. Palmer, R. Palmer, N. T. Plews, D. R. Shepherd, C. T. Spencer, J. van Geloven, R. A. White, A. G. T. Whitehead and P. B. Wight.

MINOR COUNTIES UMPIRES

N. P. Atkins, K. A. Beaumont, F. Bingley, C. J. Chapman, D. C. Conners, Dr D. Fawkner-Corbett, D. J. Dennis, R. H. Duckett, D. J. A. Edwards, W. H. Gillingham, D. J. Halfyard, D. B. Harrison, C. L. Head, B. Knight, J. E. Lawton, S. Levison, M. E. Manning, G. I. McLean, S. J. Noble, D. Norton, K. S. Shenton, C. Smith, P. S. G. Stevens, D. S. Thompsett, T. V. Wilkins, R. T. Wilson, T. G. Wilson.

OBITUARIES

ADAM, GENERAL SIR RONALD FORBES, BT, GCB, DSO, who died on December 26, 1982, aged 97, was President of MCC in 1946. He was the oldest living member of I Zingari, to which he was elected in 1935.

ARKELL, HENRY JOHN DENHAM, died at Oxford on March 12, 1982, aged 83. He played a couple of matches for Northamptonshire in 1921. He also played hockey for the county.

AUSTIN, HAROLD McPHERSON, who died on July 31, 1980, aged 77, was a valuable member of the Cambridge side in 1924, his only year in residence. Coming from Australia, he made his place virtually secure in the first match of the season, against Sussex, scoring 30 not out and 60 against Tate and Gilligan, the England opening pair, and he finished with the useful record of 444 runs for an average of 29.60 and 34 wickets at 23.17. Against Oxford he made 51 and took three wickets. A tall and immensely powerful man, he was essentially an attacking batsman and, with his bat impeccably straight, a fine driver on both sides of the wicket. He was a splendid field and for a man of his size a very fast runner. He bowled slow leg-breaks and top-spinners which, if not always accurate, took many valuable wickets. Returning to Australia he was a member of the Victoria side which toured New Zealand in 1924–25, but he never appeared in the Sheffield Shield.

BADER, GROUP CAPTAIN SIR DOUGLAS, CBE, DSO, DFC, the famous airman, who died on September 5, 1982, aged 72, was captain of St Edward's School, Oxford, in 1928. A good attacking bat and a useful fast-medium bowler, he later played for the RAF and in 1931 made 65, the top score, for them against the Army, a fixture which in those days had first-class status. He gained greater distinction at rugger, and at the time of the accident the following winter which cost him his legs he was in the running for an England cap.

BEARD, DONALD DEREK, who died on July 15, 1982, aged 62, while on a visit to England, was a member of the first New Zealand side ever to win a Test match – against West Indies at Auckland in March, 1956. He made a useful all-round contribution, scoring 31 and 6 not out at No. 9 and taking one for 20 in West Indies' first innings and three for 22 in fifteen overs in the second. New Zealand had waited 26 years and 45 Tests for this success. An accurate, medium-paced right-hand bowler, capable of late swing, and a lively hitter of the ball, in his four Test appearances he scored 101 runs at an average of 20.20 and captured nine wickets at 33.55 apiece. In all first-class cricket (for both Central and Northern Districts) he took 278 wickets (average 21.58) and scored 2,166 runs (average 22.10).

BENNETT, MAJOR GEOFFREY MICHAEL, died in Toronto on July 26, 1982, aged 72. After having a fine all-round record in the Eleven at King's School, Bruton, he had a few trials for Somerset in 1928, the year he left school, and 1929, but it was not until 1932 that he gained a regular place in the side. From then until 1939 he played frequently, at one time acting as vice-captain to R. A. Ingle. His best season was 1934 when he scored 735 runs with an average of 19.86, including 71 and 73 (his highest score for the county) against Gloucestershire at Bath. Another fine innings was against Kent at Maidstone in 1939, when, after seven wickets were down for 47, a brave 72 enabled his side to reach 185. He hit the ball well, especially in front of the wicket, and was a fine field. Little use was made in county cricket of his bowling, though in 1934 he took four for 39 against Nottinghamshire at Taunton. In all he made 2,330 runs for Somerset with an average of 15.33. After the war he emigrated to Canada.

BESSANT, JOHN, who died on January 18, 1982, aged 86, played for Gloucestershire as a fast-medium bowler from 1921 to 1928. In 1921 he took 34 wickets at 25.73, but thereafter could never produce an average of under 30 and, after three seasons as a regular member of the side, had increasing difficulty in keeping his place. One of his competitors was Tom Goddard, who seeing no real future as a fast bowler, altered his style and became a great slow off-spinner. As a bat Bessant, a useful hitter, enjoyed one triumph: against Somerset at Bristol in 1923 he made 50, putting on 131 for the last wicket (still a Gloucestershire record) in just over an hour with W. R. Goldsworthy. Altogether for the county he scored 1,200 runs with an average of 10.26 and took 130 wickets at 35.50. For many years he was groundsman to Bristol University.

BLAGRAVE, HERBERT HENRY GRATWICKE, died on March 21, 1982, aged 82. A member of the Cheltenham Eleven in 1917, he appeared in one match for Gloucestershire in 1922. He was a prominent figure in the horse-racing world.

BRETT, PATRICK JOHN, who died at Hook Heath, Woking, on December 9, 1982, aged 72, was in the Winchester Eleven in 1927 and 1928 and got his Blue at Oxford in 1929. For Winchester v Eton in 1928 he scored 55 and took twelve for 115. As a batsman, at this time he was chiefly an on-side player. He bowled medium-pace right-arm, could swing the ball late both ways and came quickly off the pitch. At Oxford he was given a trial halfway through the term, largely as an opening bowler, but in that capacity was a complete failure. However, in his first match he made 30 and 75 not out against Leicestershire, in the second innings putting on 137 for the first wicket with I. Akers-Douglas. In the next match, against Middlesex, he followed this with 79, adding 143 for the fourth wicket with N. M. Ford. So strong, however, was the Oxford batting that even after this his place was in doubt: he clinched it with innings of 57 and 106 against H. D. G. Leveson Gower's XI at Eastbourne, which was for once a strong bowling side. By now he had become a fine driver on both sides of the wicket and particularly good past extra cover. Unfortunately a bad car accident stopped him from playing cricket in 1930 and his first-class career came to an end after one season.

BROUGHTON, ERNEST ALFRED, who died on February 19, 1982, aged 76, played a number of times for Leicestershire from 1928 to 1933. A useful hard-hitting batsman, against Worcestershire in 1932 he made 61 at Worcester and 52 at Hinckley. He did much valuable work for the county in captaining Second Eleven and Club and Ground sides, was on the Committee for many years and a Vice-President, and from 1974 to 1981 was Hon. Treasurer.

BULL, AMY, CBE, who died in Surrey on August 6, 1982, aged 80, learnt her cricket at Roedean, being one of three cricketing sisters, and continued to play as one of the first members of the newly founded WCA. In 1929, she played in the first-ever public match for London & District v Rest of England, making 73 not out and taking three for 31. As a captain, she infected her team with determination and enthusiasm, accompanied by a keen sense of humour. Amy Bull served the WCA twice as Chairman and was twice President of the Association of Headmistresses. Her services to nursing (during the war) and to education brought her the award of the CBE in 1963.

BURNETT, HAROLD JOHN BEVERLEY, who died in Diego Martin, Trinidad, on December 18, 1981, at the age of 66, was, from 1974 till 1981, the efficient and affable Secretary of the West Indian Cricket Board of Control. During this time he had a difficult course to steer over the Packer Affair, which he did with his customary consideration. In 1963 he was assistant-manager of Frank Worrell's West Indian team to England, in his estimation the strongest of all West Indian sides. An outstanding games-player as a schoolboy at Queen's Royal College, Trinidad, he became for several years, as an off-spinner and middle-order batsman, a regular member of the Trinidad team. He also played football for the island.

CHUBB, GEOFFREY WALTER ASHTON, who died in East London on August 28, 1982, at the age of 71, played five times for South Africa against England in England in 1951 and served two terms as President of the South African Cricket Association. At 40 years 56 days he was the oldest South African to make a Test début. It happened at Trent Bridge, and when England went in late on the second day, facing a total of 483, he had Ikin caught at slip with his third ball and finished with four for 146 off 46 overs. He and McCarthy reduced England from 375 for three to 419 all out and gave South Africa the chance to record their first win in England for sixteen years. Chubb's best Test figures came at Old Trafford when he took six for 51 in England's first innings. With 21 wickets in the series at 27.47 apiece, he headed the bowling averages for South Africa. He was also their leading wicket-taker in all first-class matches on the tour, capturing 72 at 26.84 apiece and bowling over 150 overs more than anyone else.

Born in Rhodesia, Chubb began his first-class career as an opening batsman for Border in 1931–32, but on moving to Johannesburg concentrated on his bowling. He worked hard at perfecting his medium-paced seamers and developing a high degree of accuracy. Fair-haired, studious and bespectacled, he was a disarmingly effective bowler and immensely popular. After his retirement in 1951, at the end of his tour of England, he devoted his energies to cricket administration, becoming a national selector and, from 1955 to 1957 and again from 1959 to 1960, President of the SACA. In all first-class cricket he took 160 wickets at an average of 23.91, scored 835 runs (average 18.15) and held twelve catches.

CLARK, EDWARD WINCHESTER, inevitably known as "Nobby", who died on April 28, 1982, near King's Lynn, aged 79, possessed every qualification of a great bowler except temperament. With a lovely loose left arm, which almost brushed his ear as it came over, he had a classic action, his right shoulder pointing straight at the batsman. He was at his best really fast and, though he was well capable of bowling, like Voce, to a leg-side field, was probably most effective round the wicket when the ball, swinging in and breaking away, would produce catches in the slips if the batsman was good enough to touch it. But he was a perfectionist and anything outside his control which interfered with that perfection – a dropped catch, an insecure foothold, a tactless word from his captain or one of his companions – was quite sufficient to put him off. It was his misfortune that his county, Northamptonshire, was throughout his career one of the weakest sides that has ever played in the Championship: not only did he have to do more than his fair share of bowling, but perhaps no fast bowler since Buckenham of Essex had so many chances dropped off him. A further annoyance to him was the rate at which his *vis-à-vis*, that splendid bowler Albert Thomas, got through his overs, an undue proportion of which were maidens, thus robbing Clark of what he considered as a rightful rest. His cricket began and ended with his bowling: neither batting nor fielding did he regard as any business of his.

Though he was born near Peterborough, it was success in league cricket in Yorkshire, where he was an engineering apprentice, that brought him to the notice of the Northamptonshire authorities and he made a promising start in 1922, heading the averages with twenty wickets at 17.10. There followed two or three seasons of varying fortune, but in 1925 he came right to the front with 84 wickets at 17.79 and began to be talked of as a Test match prospect. He played in the Test trials in 1927, but in 1928, handicapped by injury, he had a poor season and he had to wait till 1929 for his first Test, against South Africa at The Oval, where he was criticised for overdoing leg-theory. A row with Northamptonshire, whom he left temporarily for league cricket, spoiled his chances of playing against the Australians in 1930. However, he returned to the county in 1932, and in 1933 he played at The Oval and Old Trafford against West Indies, bowling well without spectacular success. That winter he had a successful tour in India under D. R. Jardine and in 1934 was picked at Old Trafford and again at The Oval against Australia. At Old Trafford he bowled well without any luck, but in the second innings at The Oval he took five for 98, his victims being Ponsford, Brown, McCabe, Kippax and Chipperfield, while he twice failed by only the narrowest margin to bowl Bradman. This was his last Test, but he continued to bowl with success until 1936. In 1937, handicapped by injury, he had a poor season and dropped out of the county side, but he returned in 1946 to bowl with at least some trace of his former greatness. A few matches in 1947 concluded his career. In all first-class cricket he took 1,203 wickets at 21 runs each.

CLOVER-BROWN, CHARLES, who died on October 6, 1982, aged 75, captained Harrow in 1927, his third year in the Eleven. Later, working in Colombo until the war, he represented All Ceylon and against D. R. Jardine's side to Australia in 1932, though he himself made only 15, helped W. T. Brindley to put on 79 for the first wicket, a record for Ceylon in these matches. Against G. O. Allen's side in 1936 he made 31. While on leave in England he appeared with some success for Buckinghamshire. He was a solid and consistent opening batsman and in club cricket a useful leg-spinner.

CONIBERE, WILLIAM JACK, who died early in September, 1982, aged 59, had a trial for Somerset as an amateur in 1950. A fast-medium left-armer, who batted right-hand, he took six wickets against Warwickshire but met with little success in his three remaining matches.

CORNWALLIS, THE RIGHT HON. WYKEHAM STANLEY, 2ND BARON, died at his home, Ashurst Park, Kent, on January 4, 1982, aged 89. A genuinely fast bowler with an easy, if slightly low and slinging action, he played for Kent from 1919 to 1926, captaining them in his last three seasons. At a time when there was a desperate shortage of fast bowling, not only in Kent but in the country as a whole, he might have been a great asset had he remained sound. But he was 27 when his first-class career started and since leaving Eton, where he was not in the Eleven, had been a regular soldier with only limited opportunities of playing (and none in the last five years): his muscles had not had the work and training to enable them to stand the strain of county cricket. He was constantly breaking down, and during his three years as captain could bowl only 560 overs in all. What he could do when sound he had shown at Tonbridge in 1920 when he took five for 40 against the strong Lancashire batting side, his victims including Makepeace and Ernest Tyldesley, both clean bowled, and he bowled well next year at the start of the Australian innings at Canterbury. He was a good field and, not normally regarded as a batsman, enjoyed one triumph, against Essex at Canterbury in 1926. When he came in, Kent, facing a total of 267, were 189 for seven and Collins had retired ill. Cornwallis helped Hardinge to put on 130 and then added another 77 with Collins, who had returned: he himself made 91, largely by carefree off-side hitting, the total reached 413 and Kent won by an innings.

Later, besides holding a number of directorships, he was tireless in public life in Kent, of which he was for years Lord-Lieutenant, but interest in the game never flagged. In 1948 he was President both of Kent and MCC, and only a week or two before the commencement of his last illness he was watching IZ, of which he was a Freeman, playing Lavinia, Duchess of Norfolk's XI at Arundel, as full of life and of cricket reminiscences as ever. A man deservedly popular wherever he went and a great public servant, he will be widely missed.

COULSON, SYDNEY SAMUEL, died at Gainsborough on October 3, 1981, aged 82. After a good trial for Leicestershire in 1923, he was a regular member of the side in 1924 and 1925, showing some promise as a steady bat who could, if wanted, open the innings. Unfortunately this promise was never fulfilled, and after a few matches in 1926 and 1927 he dropped out of the side. His highest score was 80, against Derbyshire at Leicester in 1925, when he hit eleven 4s and put on 99 for the sixth wicket with Geary. In all matches for the county he scored 1,094 runs with an average of 12.43. Later he was for some years professional and groundsman at Gainsborough.

CRABTREE, HARRY POLLARD, MBE, died at Great Baddow, Essex, on May 28, 1982, aged 76. A Yorkshireman by birth, he came south as a schoolmaster to Westcliff-on-Sea, where he was a prolific scorer in club cricket. He had made a stray appearance for Essex in 1931, but most of his cricket for the county was played in the summer holidays of 1946 and 1947. In 1946 he made 793 runs with an average of 49.56, including three centuries. In 1947, though he scored 117 against the South Africans, he was less successful and he did not appear for the county after that year. A sound opening bat, he had an impeccable technique and was especially strong on the leg side. For many years he served on the Essex Committee. He will be particularly remembered for the work he did to encourage cricket coaching in state schools and as the instigator of the MCC's highly successful group coaching scheme. His friendliness and enthusiasm reassured and inspired many a young cricketer.

CRUTCHLEY, EDWARD, who died in a nursing home at Guildford on October 18, 1982, aged 60, was a stylish batsman who made 115 for Harrow against Eton at Lord's in 1939. This was in the first innings when he and G. F. Anson came together at 102 for four, with the match hanging in the balance, and added 117 in an hour. Crutchley was at the wicket in the second innings when the winning run was scored to give Harrow a historic victory, their first in the match since 1908 when his father, G. E. V. Crutchley, was in the Harrow Eleven. In 1940 Crutchley was again in the Harrow side, but for such a good player he had a disappointing season. He played in war-time matches for Oxford before service in the Army, but apart from two appearances for Middlesex against the Universities in 1947 he played little cricket after the war.

DE KLERK, THEO, who died in Durban on July 2, 1982, aged 75, was a useful all-rounder who scored 791 runs at an average of 17.57 and took 89 wickets for Western Province in 33 matches between 1925 and 1936. He made his first-class début in 1925–26, for Western Province against Orange Free State, making what was to remain his highest first-class score, 79, in Western Province's first innings. His best season was 1931–32 when his 33 wickets cost 16.42 apiece. In later years he became one of South Africa's leading racehorse trainers, saddling over 1,000 winners. A versatile sportsman, he also played first league rugger and first league soccer. He had a vivid personality and was a sought-after speaker.

DE SILVA, J. A. ("BERTIE"), who has died in Sri Lanka at the age of 84, was one of his country's best all-rounders between the wars. Coming up to Oxford in 1924, he played twice for the University, once that year and once in 1925, without getting a Blue. A left-handed batsman, he was 14 not out when Oxford beat Kent by six wickets in The Parks in 1924. The Kent side included Chapman, Freeman, Woolley, Ashdown and Hardinge.

DUNDAS, SIR ROBERT WHYTE MELVILLE, BT, died on October 10, 1981, within three weeks of his 100th birthday. He was captain of an unbeaten Glenalmond Eleven in 1899. At the age of 90 he caught, at cover-point, while playing for Comrie, an opponent 70 years his junior.

FELTON, ROBERT, died after a long illness on October 5, 1982, aged 72. He made many runs for St Paul's, where he was four years in the Eleven, and, after proving himself a valuable member of the Middlesex Second Eleven, played a number of times for the county between 1935 and 1948, scoring in all 496 runs with an average of 27.56. He played one outstanding innings of 171 against Cambridge at Fenner's in 1937, reaching his hundred in 110 minutes and putting on 138 with Hulme for the fifth wicket in just over an hour. Altogether he batted for 160 minutes. He had a beautiful pair of wrists and was a particularly good cutter. For years he was a heavy scorer in club cricket around London.

FEWIN, HENRY, who died on August 25, 1980, aged 84, played one game for Queensland (against Victoria) in 1929–30 as a right-hand batsman. He fell in each innings to Ironmonger, for 7 and 11.

FITZMAURICE, DESMOND MICHAEL JOHN, who died on January 19, 1981, aged 63, played twice for Victoria in 1947–48 as a medium-paced bowler. He toured India in 1949–50 with a strong Commonwealth team, opening the bowling in two of the five unofficial Tests, and played for a while as a professional in the Central Lancashire League. He also took a coaching appointment in Kimberley, South Africa. In all he played in seventeen first-class matches, scoring 272 runs at an average of 17 and taking 28 wickets at 28.50 apiece. He was the younger brother of D. J. A. Fitzmaurice, who also played for Victoria.

FORD, REGGIE GILBERT, who died in Bristol in October, 1981, aged 74, played in 57 matches for Gloucestershire between 1929 and 1936. At the outset of his career he was expected to develop into a sound bat and, as a medium-pace right-armer, was often given the new ball. But as his final record for the county was 496 runs, with an average of 10.55 and a highest score of 37 not out, and as his ten wickets cost him 49.30 runs each, he can hardly be said to have fulfilled his promise.

FORDHAM, MICHAEL, who died suddenly from a heart attack at Miami, Florida, on February 7, 1982, aged 53, had just delivered the copy and corrected the proofs for his statistical contributions to *Wisden, Playfair Cricket Annual* and *The Cricketer Quarterly.* A local government officer, his early involvement in statistics was in association with the late Roy Webber, on whose death in 1962 he took over as chief statistician for the Playfair publications. He provided the statistical background for a great variety of publications – biographies, brochures and magazines – and his biographical notes and career records of current county players in the *Playfair Cricket Annual* were a regular feature of each season, providing invaluable up-to-date information for all those interested in cricket. He led and organised the team of statisticians for *The Cricketer Quarterly* from its inception in 1973, and had looked after the records section for *Wisden* since 1979. Fordham was a founder member of the Association of Cricket Statisticians and was frequently consulted in connection with its publications and the vexed question of the definition of first-class matches. In addition to his statistical work he acted as scorer for sound radio and BBC TV. He was a member of MCC and all seventeen first-class counties, but never had any pretensions as a player. – B.M.

FRANCOIS, HUGH AUGUST, who died in Johannesburg on July 17, 1982, aged 77, played sixteen times for Border from 1923 to 1928, scoring 484 runs at an average of 18.61 and taking 26 wickets at 41.26 apiece. Born at Tsolo in Transkei, he was one of three brothers to play first-class cricket, the others being C. M. and S. H.. (C. M. played in all five Tests against England in 1922–23.) A middle-order batsman and off-spin bowler, H. A.

turned in several useful performances for Border: his top score was 61 against Orange Free State, his best bowling analysis seven for 79, also against the Free State, two seasons later. In his last first-class match, against R. T. Stanyforth's MCC side, he made a top score of 40 and in an MCC innings of 362 for five declared claimed the wickets of Holmes, E. Tyldesley and Dawson for 114 runs.

FRANKLIN, RONALD CHRISTIAN, who made one appearance for Essex in 1924, died at Prestwood, Buckinghamshire, on September 28, 1982, aged 78. A medium-pace right-arm bowler, he was younger brother of H. W. F. Franklin, of Oxford University and Essex.

FRANKS, BRIAN MORTON FORSTER, died on May 6, 1982, aged 71. A member of the Eton Eleven in 1929, he was a steady fast-medium bowler who had some life off the wicket.

GILLESPIE, DEREK WILLIAM, who died on August 21, 1981, aged 64, was captain of Uppingham in 1936 and gained the last place in the Cambridge side of 1939. Though he was a useful, solid batsman, who made 60 in three hours against the Free Foresters, he owed his Blue largely to his bowling. Starting the season as a fast-medium opener, he changed in June to slower off-breaks and, Cambridge being desperately short of spin, was picked for Lord's. However, he met with little success in the match. His best performance was to dismiss four of the first five Warwickshire batsmen at Birmingham, where he finished with four for 48.

GRACE, COLONEL HUGH RAYMOND, OBE, who died at Crundale, near Canterbury, on February 2, 1982, was in the Marlborough Eleven of 1929. A staunch supporter of Kent, he was their Librarian for some years and President of the county in 1979.

GREENWOOD, LEONARD WARWICK, who died at Astley, near Stourport-on-Severn, on July 20, 1982, aged 83, was a good opening bat in the Winchester Eleven in 1916 and 1917. In 1917 he played a fine innings of 141 against Harrow. In 1919 he played for Oxford against the Gentlemen of England (the first first-class match to be played after the Great War), but failed to get a Blue. However, he represented Somerset against the University in 1920 and between 1923 and 1926 appeared three times for Worcestershire without much success. For many years he was a master at Abberley Hall, near Worcester.

GRIFFITHS, JOHN VESEY CLAUDE, died at Wedmore, Somerset, on February 18, 1982, aged 50. A left-hand bat and a slow left-arm bowler, he had a number of trials for Gloucestershire between 1952 and 1957 but met with little success and failed to secure a regular place in the side.

GROVE, CHARLES WILLIAM, who died at Solihull on February 15, 1982, aged 69, did much good work for Warwickshire between 1938 and 1953. He showed promise before the war, but then came an eight-year gap and he did not resume his place in the side till 1947 when, with 98 wickets, even if they were somewhat expensive, he showed himself a very useful member of the attack. Again in 1949 and 1950 he topped 90 wickets and in 1950 had much to do with Warwickshire being the only county to beat the West Indians, taking eight for 38 in the first innings. However, it was in his last three years for the county that his best work was accomplished. In 1951, his benefit year, with 110 wickets at 18.52, he played a big part in Warwickshire winning the Championship, and he followed it with 118 at 17.53 in 1952 and in 1953 with 83 at 18.50. A big man, he was an extremely accurate fast-medium opening bowler, who could move the ball both ways, and a useful tail-end hitter, whose big performance was an innings of 104 not out in 80 minutes against Leicestershire at Leicester in 1948. Leaving Warwickshire, the county of his birth, at the end of 1953, he played in 1954 for Worcestershire with only moderate success and then went into the Birmingham League. In his first-class career he took 744 wickets at an average of 22.67. From 1974 to 1981 he was the Warwickshire scorer.

HAVEWALLA DADY RUSTOMJI, who died in Bombay on July 21, 1982, aged 70, was a big-hitting left-handed batsman. His innings of 515, including 32 6s and 55 4s, for the BB and CI Railway against St Xavier's College in the Times of India Shield in December

1933, was for a long time a record in any class of Indian cricket. He was always keen to derive the utmost enjoyment from his tenure of the crease and was very popular with the crowds. C. G. Macartney's tribute to him when he scored a rapid 71 against Ryder's Australian team in 1935–36 was fulsome. "I can truly say", wrote the great Australian, "that I have seldom seen finer hitting than that by Havewalla". Another notable effort was his 106 in 93 minutes for the Maharaja of Patiala's team against Lord Tennyson's at Patiala in 1937–38. This effort earned him a place in the Indian team for the fourth and fifth unofficial Tests at Madras and Bombay. In the Madras match, which India won by an innings, he made 44, the second highest score for the side. Havewalla played for Bombay in the Ranji Trophy from 1934–35 to 1941–42, his best score being 103 against Western India in 1935–36. He had started his career as a left-arm medium bowler, and took 27 wickets in the Ranji Trophy.

HELE, GEORGE, who has died in Australia at the age of 91, umpired sixteen Test matches between 1928 and 1933, ten of them between England and Australia. He stood in all five Tests in the 1932–33 Bodyline series, subsequently expressing his disapproval of the leg-theory tactics employed by some of the English fast bowlers. Himself one of the best umpires produced by Australia, his father, Andy, was also a first-class umpire, as was his son, Ray.

HENDERSON, ERNEST JAMES, DSO, MC, who died on March 29, 1982, aged 91, was a legendary figure in club cricket in Surrey. Having joined Sutton in 1905, he captained them from 1927–37, 1947–50 and again, at the age of 65, in 1957, their centenary year. Despite a limp, the result of being wounded in the Great War, he was a fine fielder and a powerful hitter. He was President, up to his death, of the both the Sutton Cricket Club and the Sutton Rugby Football Club.

HILL-WOOD, DENIS JOHN CHARLES, MC, died on May 4, 1982, aged 75. Never in the Eleven at Eton, he got a Blue at Oxford in 1928, owing his place to the need for finding a solid rather than a stroke-playing opening partner for A. M. Crawley, and, though the side's batting that year was so strong that the Nawab of Pataudi failed to get in, he fully justified his choice. In his first match he helped Crawley to put on 197 against the Free Foresters, of which his share was 44, and at The Oval they put on 153. His contribution at Lord's was a useful 23 in each innings. Altogether he made 286 runs with an average of 26, his highest score being 62 against Essex at Colchester. In both 1928 and 1929 he appeared for Derbyshire without success. In 1928 he was also a member of the Oxford soccer side and since 1959 had been Chairman of the Arsenal. He was one of four brothers (three of them Blues) who had played for Derbyshire: their father had captained the county.

HOOKER, JOHN EDWARD HALFORD ("HAL"), died in Sydney on February 12, 1982, aged 83. A right-arm medium-paced bowler, capable of swinging the ball both ways, he was regarded by many as one of the best bowlers never to play for Australia. He made his first-class début for New South Wales against Victoria in Melbourne in 1924–25 and in his seventeen first-class matches, including one Test Trial, took 63 wickets at 29 apiece. He is best remembered for having partnered Alan Kippax in what still stands as the world record tenth-wicket partnership of 307 against Victoria at Melbourne in 1928. He joined Kippax late on Christmas Eve, when New South Wales were 113 for nine in reply to Victoria's first-innings total of 376. On Christmas Day a sparse crowd gathered to see Victoria capture the remaining wicket and enforce the follow-on. But by lunch Hooker was still there, on 18, and by tea he had advanced to 22. When eventually, on Boxing Day morning, he was dismissed for 62 (caught Ryder bowled A'Beckett) he had batted for 304 minutes, New South Wales had scored 420 and Kippax was 260 not out. The match was drawn. A month later, the return match was played at Sydney, and again Hooker made a remarkable contribution. Batting first New South Wales declared at 713 for six; Victoria were then dismissed for 265, Hooker finishing off the innings with a hat-trick (Ebeling, Gamble and Ironmonger). When Victoria followed on Hooker took a wicket (Austin) with his first ball, thus becoming the only person ever to have claimed four wickets with consecutive balls in Sheffield Shield cricket. Three of his victims were bowled, the other caught and bowled. Hooker had one other claim to cricketing fame. After a long and unsuccessful stint, bowling at Ponsford, he complained light-heartedly to the umpire that Ponsford's bat exceeded the legal width. The bat, when measured later, was found to be fractionally in excess of the regulation size of four and a quarter inches. On his retirement from first-class cricket Hooker worked for almost twenty years as a sporting commentator for the Australian Broadcasting Commission.

HORSFIELD, GORDON CAMERON, who died in Sydney in September 1982, aged 69, was a left-handed batsman who played five times for New South Wales between 1934–35 and 1941–42, though with modest success.

HUSKINSON, GEOFFREY NEVILLE BAYLEY, died at Hinton Waldrist on June 17, 1982, aged 82. In the Oundle Eleven from 1915 to 1917, he did not get a Blue at Oxford but played for Nottinghamshire in their first two matches in 1922 and in the second made 33 against Glamorgan. He also appeared a number of times for Nottinghamshire Second Eleven, occasionally acting as captain. He was a useful bat and a good field at slip or cover and was related by marriage to the great Richard Daft. A member of the county Committee from 1943 to 1958, he was President in 1959 and 1960 and a Vice-President from 1961. At his home, Langar Hall, he used to grow cricket bat willows. He had also been a first-class rugger player, and, when advancing years forced him to give up cricket, he made himself into a good enough croquet player to represent Nottinghamshire at that game too.

HUSSAIN, SYED MAHMUD, who died at Hyderabad on July 2, 1982, at the age of 80, was a sound and attractive stroke-player who proved himself against three visiting teams. He scored 90 against the first official MCC team to visit India in 1926–27 at Madras, 73 for Moin-ud-Doela's XI against Ryder's Australian team at Secunderabad in 1935–36, and in 1937–38, for the same team, 55 against Lord Tennyson's team, also at Secunderabad. About his performance against Ryder's team, C. G. Macartney wrote: "The best innings of the day was played by Hussain, who had the misfortune to be run out when his valiant display deserved the coveted century." Hussain played in one unofficial Test against Ryder's team at Calcutta, but failed on a rain-affected pitch. He was a member of the Indian team to England in 1936, when his best effort was an innings of 55 against Worcestershire. He was captain of Hyderabad in the Ranji Trophy from the start in 1934–35 to 1941–42 and had the distinction of leading the side to its only championship victory in 1942–43. He belonged to the landed classes.

HUTTON, NORMAN HARVEY, who died in Adelaide on June 7, 1980, aged 67, was a member of a well-known cricketing family. As a fast-medium bowler he played twice for South Australia in 1934–35. His father, Percy, had played for the state in 1905–06, as did his two brothers, Maurice and Mervyn, in 1928–29 and 1930–31 respectively.

INGLIS, RUSSELL, who died of a heart attack at Chester-le-Street on April 28, 1982, aged 45, was a sound right-hand batsman who played 140 games for Durham between 1956 and 1973, when a severe illness caused his premature retirement. His total of 6,626 runs for Durham remains a record for the county. Inglis appeared in three first-class matches – for the Minor Counties against the South Africans in 1965, the Pakistanis in 1967 and the West Indians in 1969, his best score being a sound 43 out of 134 against the South Africans at Jesmond. His club cricket was played for Durham City and Chester-le-Street.

INNES, GERALD ALFRED SKERTEN, who died in Cape Town after a long illness on July 19, 1982, aged 50, was a widely respected and much-liked figure in South African cricket. Born in Cape Town, he was educated at Diocesan College, Rondebosch, and the University of Cape Town. An outstanding schoolboy cricketer, he captained the "Bishop's" Eleven in his last two years at school, as well as the Western Province Nuffield Shield side, which he had the rare distinction of representing for four consecutive seasons. He also captained the South African Schools representative side. In January, 1951, he was given a trial for that year's South African tour to England, batting competently for 49 but failing to make the team. After a fine season for Western Province in 1951–52, in which he completed his first first-class hundred, 139 against Eastern Province, he toured Australia with J. E. Cheetham's side in 1952–53. His best score was 109 against Victoria at Melbourne. Although he never played in a Test match, he was chosen by the *South African Cricket Annual* as one of its cricketers of the year in 1958–59, having made hundreds for Western Province against both Natal and Transvaal. In 1959 he assumed the captaincy of Western Province. Having transferred to Johannesburg in 1963, he played for Transvaal in 1963–64, making 140 not out against Natal at Durban. After retiring from first-class cricket in 1965, he became a Transvaal selector, and upon returning to Cape Town he served Western Province in the same capacity. His warmth, friendliness and good humour made him popular wherever he went and with cricketers of all ages.

JACKSON, KENNETH LESLIE TATTERSALL, who died on March 21, 1982, aged 69, was captain of the Rugby Eleven in 1932 and got a Blue at Oxford in 1934. A right-arm fast-medium bowler, with a good high action, and a useful bat in the lower half of the order, he was preferred at the last moment to J. H. Dyson, a slow-left-armer who had been in the side as it was originally chosen, but, overbowled on unresponsive wickets, had lost his effectiveness. Jackson failed to keep his place in 1935. He was well known as a Scottish rugger international. On coming down from Oxford he became a schoolmaster.

JENKINSON, CECIL VICTOR, died late in 1980 at the age of 89. Keeping wicket for Essex on a few occasions in 1922 and 1923, he created a favourable impression and might have been invaluable had he been able to play more frequently, as the side at that time lacked a reliable wicket-keeper until Frank Gilligan was available in August.

JORDAN, CORTEZ, who died in Barbados on September 8, 1982, aged 61, umpired in 22 Test matches between 1953 and 1974. He was the only man to no-ball Charlie Griffith for throwing in a first-class match. It happened on the day when, playing for Barbados against the Indian touring team at Bridgetown in 1962, Griffith had inflicted serious injury on Nari Contractor, the Indian captain, whom he hit over the right ear with a bouncer. Jordan's appointment to the Georgetown Test of 1964–65 between West Indies and Australia broke new ground. Until then no umpire had stood in a Test match in West Indies outside his home territory. In protest at this new departure, the local umpire, Cecil Kippins, who had been appointed to stand with Jordan, was ordered by the British Guiana Umpires' Association to withdraw from the match. This led to Gerry Gomez, a former Test player and then a West Indian selector, having to officiate. Although the holder of an umpiring certificate, Gomez had not previously stood in a first-class match. Quiet and efficient, Jordan always umpired in a white panama hat and dark glasses.

LANCASHIRE, WALTER, died on July 7, 1981, aged 78. A Yorkshireman by birth, he played in eighteen matches for Hampshire, as an amateur, between 1935 and 1937, scoring 471 runs with an average of 16.82. His most notable performance was against Essex at Southampton in 1936, when he followed a first innings of 32 with 66 out of 83 in the second innings, made in 50 minutes and containing a 6 and ten 4s. Later in the season he made a valuable 54 against Middlesex at Lord's.

LEE, FRANK STANLEY, who died suddenly on March 30, 1982, was the youngest of three brothers who attained distinction in first-class cricket. The eldest, Harry, went in first for Middlesex for years. Jack and Frank, seeing no opening in Middlesex, migrated to Somerset, where they opened the innings together for several seasons and on one occasion put up a hundred together thrice in four days. Jack was killed in action in Normandy. Frank had a couple of trials for Middlesex in August 1925, but although in his first innings he scored a valuable 42 in two hours against Worcestershire, was not persevered with. He started to play for Somerset in 1929 and within a few weeks had shown his value with innings of 62 and 107 against Hampshire. He finished the season with 852 runs and an average of 19.81. After a disappointing year in 1930, he got his thousand runs for the first time in 1931: indeed, the three Lees provided the first instance of three professional brothers achieving the feat in the same season. It was in that year, too, that Luckes, the regular wicket-keeper, being out of action, Frank Lee, always a good fielder, took over his position and emerged from the ordeal without discredit. His great season was 1938, when he became the first Somerset player to score 2,000 runs in a summer and also the first to make three hundreds in successive innings: his final figures were 2,019 runs with an average of 44.86. His highest innings for the county was 169 against Nottinghamshire at Trent Bridge in 1946. Somerset went in 209 runs in arrears, but Lee, batting for six hours, averted any danger of defeat. One of his best performances was against the Australians in 1934, when he went in first and carried his bat for 59 out of a total of 116 against O'Reilly on a damp wicket. In 1947 he had a record benefit for the county, but his own form was poor and he retired at the end of the season.

He and his brother were, apart from Braund and A. Young, almost the first professionals to play for the county mainly as batsmen, but they were certainly not in the adventurous Somerset tradition. Frank was a solid rather than an entertaining left-hander, but, as his record shows, there could be no doubt about his value. In his first-class career he scored 15,310 runs with an average of 27.93, including 23 centuries. Not normally regarded as a bowler, he took five for 53 against Warwickshire at Taunton in 1933 and in the next match was given the new ball. He bowled right-arm medium-pace. From 1948 to 1963 he was a first-class umpire and quickly became recognised as one of the best and most respected on the list, standing in 29 Tests. He will be especially remembered for his fearless no-balling of Griffin, the South African, in the Lord's Test in 1960, the first time a member of a touring team had been no-balled in England.

LITCHFIELD, ERIC, was in the process of completing his first *Protea Cricket Annual of South Africa* (formerly the *South African Cricket Annual*) as editor when he died in Cape Town in July, 1982, at the age of 61. A good footballer and useful wicket-keeper, Litchfield moved from England to South Africa after the Second War. He wrote cricket for the *Rand Daily Mail* from 1949 to 1970 and at the time of his death was also the cricket correspondent of the *Cape Times*. He wrote *Cricket Grand Slam*, an account of South Africa's last triumphant Test series against Australia in 1969–70, and collaborated with D. J. McGlew in *Six for Glory*.

LLOYD, NEIL, who died at Wakefield, of an unidentified virus, on September 17, 1982, aged 17, was a left-handed batsman of great promise. He had played for three years for Yorkshire Second Eleven and barely a fortnight before his death had gone in first for Young England against Young West Indies in the third of last season's "Test" matches. He was awarded his Yorkshire Second Eleven cap posthumously.

LOWNDES, WILLIAM GEOFFREY LOWNDES FRITH, died at Newbury on May 23, 1982, aged 84. A member of the Eton Eleven in 1915 and 1916, he got a place in the strong Oxford batting side of 1921, of which he was the last survivor. He was a late choice. Playing for the Free Foresters against the University in the last match but one of the term, he scored 29 and 21 and took three wickets, with the result that he was picked for the next match against the Army. An innings of 88 secured him a further trial and he clinched his place by making 52 at Hove and 216 against H. D. G. Leveson Gower's XI at Eastbourne, where he and H. P. Ward put on 218 in just over 90 minutes. Though he failed at Lord's, he finished second in the University averages. He first appeared for Hampshire in 1924, but played little more first-class cricket until he was persuaded to succeed the Hon. L. H. Tennyson as captain of the county in 1934. Though the side, then in a state of transition, did not meet with great success, he was a popular captain and had no reason to be dissatisfied with his own efforts. He made three centuries, the most notable being 140 against the 1934 Australians. On this occasion he reached his hundred in 75 minutes and with Mead added 247 in under three hours for the fourth wicket. In 1935 he made 118 before lunch against Kent in two hours on the first day of the season, but scored very few runs thereafter and resigned at the end of the year. In fact, he found a full season's cricket rather more than he wanted, and in neither of his years as captain did he play in more than two-thirds of the matches. He was a natural cricketer: an attacking batsman and a particularly fine driver, at his best on fast wickets; a useful fast-medium away-swinger, who sometimes took the new ball and might perhaps have used himself more; and a good mid-off. In his attitude to the game he was typical of the amateur of his own and earlier periods – to him it was fun and he tried to make it fun for others.

LUCKES, WALTER THOMAS, who died at Bridgwater on October 27, 1982, aged 81, kept wicket for Somerset from 1924 to 1949. When he first appeared, the bulk of the 'keeping was done by M. D. Lyon and M. L. Hill, and it was not till 1927 that Luckes (pronounced Luckies) gained a regular place. Hardly had he done so than his career was nearly terminated by ill-health. In 1929 and 1930 he could play little, in 1931 not at all, and it was not until part way through 1932 that he was fit to resume his place. Condemned then by the doctors to bat at No. 11, he came second in the batting averages, mainly owing to fifteen not out innings. However, one of these was 58 against Yorkshire. As far back as 1927, an innings of 45 against McDonald at his best had shown what he could do, and later, in his benefit year, 1937, being allowed for some reason to go in at No. 5 against Kent at

Bath, he made 121 not out, driving in great form. For the most part, however, he had to resign himself to causing unwelcome delay to the opposition just when they thought the innings was as good as over. As a wicket-keeper he ranked high, higher indeed than the general public ever realised. Quiet in method and, except in appealing, wholly undemonstrative, he made the job look so easy that only the experts or those out in the middle could see how often he brought off as a matter of course what was in fact a brilliant catch or stumping. To others he might seem only one who seldom made an obvious mistake. Fortunately, after 1932 he suffered no interruptions on account of his health and it was only in 1949, when he was 48, that he made way for Stephenson. His first-class cricket was confined to Somerset, for whom he caught 586 batsmen and stumped 241, besides making 5,640 runs with an average of 16.02.

MACKAY, KENNETH DONALD, MBE, who died on June 13, 1982, aged 56, was one of the best and most popular cricketers ever produced by Queensland. As a left-handed middle-order batsman, he possessed a highly distinctive style, this endearing him to crowds which otherwise might have found his rate of scoring unendurably slow. At the crease he stood impassively, cap at a rakish angle, knees slightly bent, chewing compulsively. He employed negligible backlift and was an uncanny judge of line, often leaving balls that seemed to make the bails quiver. When a stroke was required, his most prolific were a deflection wide of cover-point's right hand and a type of "shovel" shot past mid-wicket. He was more often a match-saver than a match-winner. Very occasionally he would play an innings of remarkable and unexpected aggression and unorthodoxy, one such being at Lord's against Middlesex in 1961 when he made a whirlwind 168. As a right-arm medium-paced bowler, he became in the early sixties a useful member of the Australian attack, possessing the ability to contain batsmen for long periods and often taking good wickets. He had a stealthy, almost apologetic approach to the wicket, but the innocuous appearance of his deliveries masked subtle variations of pace and swing.

"Slasher" MacKay first played grade cricket in Brisbane at the age of fifteen. By 1946 he had won a place in the Queensland side, the start of a first-class career that lasted for eighteen years and included 100 appearances for his state and 37 for Australia. He became captain of Queensland in 1954–55 and in 1956 toured England with Ian Johnson's side. He made his Test début at Lord's, in the only Test won by Australia that summer, batting for more than seven hours in the match, yet scoring only 38 and 31. In his second innings, which lasted for 264 minutes, he fulfilled what was to become a familiar sheet-anchor role while Benaud played a brilliant innings of 97. MacKay's performance in the next two Tests threatened his international career: at Headingly he made 2 and 2, at Old Trafford Laker dismissed him for a "pair". He was dropped for the last Test at The Oval and was not an original selection for Ian Craig's team to tour South Africa in 1957–58. However, he was added to Craig's side at the last moment and, with Test scores of 3, 65 not out, 63, 32, 52 not out, 83 not out and 77 not out, he justified his selection.

MacKay's best Test performances were achieved on a tour of Pakistan and India in 1959–60. On a matting wicket at Dacca he helped Australia to gain their first Test win in Pakistan, recording in the second innings the remarkable bowling figures of 45–27–42–6. Against India at Madras he made his highest Test score, 89 – ended, somewhat surprisingly, when he was stumped. His best-remembered Test innings must have been against West Indies at Adelaide in 1961, the series of the tied Test. With 100 minutes of the game remaining Australia, trailing by many runs, lost their ninth wicket. As Lindsay Kline joined MacKay a West Indian victory seemed assured. However, dour defence by both batsmen frustrated all the efforts of Worrell's side and the game ended with Australia's last pair still together, MacKay undefeated with 62, made in almost four hours. He played his last Test against England at Adelaide in January, 1963, and not long afterwards announced his retirement from first-class cricket, his final appearance being for Queensland against Victoria in 1964. "In affection and gratitude", the people of Brisbane contributed some £20,000 to a "bob in for Slasher" campaign, conducted by the city's morning paper. For fifteen years after his retirement MacKay was a state selector, and in 1977 he was appointed state coach for Queensland. In 1962 he was made an MBE for his services to cricket.

MACKLEY, ALAN, who has died in Perth, aged 69, was the first Western Australian to stand in a Test match, officiating in the fourth Test between England and Australia at Adelaide in 1962–63. He became, subsequently, a member of the Western Australian Cricket Association Appeals Board and also of the Umpires Appointments Board.

MEHER-HOMJI, KHURSHED RUSTOMJI, who died in Bombay on February 10, 1982, aged 70, toured England as a wicket-keeper with the Maharaj Kumar of Vizianagram's Indian team in 1936, playing in the second Test match at Old Trafford. That was his only appearance for India. At home he played for the Parsis in the Bombay Tournament and for West India and Bombay in the Ranji Trophy. His uncle, Rustomji Meher-Homji, toured England with the 1911 All-India side.

MILES, ERIC VICTOR, who has died at the age of 83, represented Border in twelve matches between 1920 and 1930. A left-handed batsman and right-arm bowler he scored 419 runs in first-class cricket, took four wickets, and held four catches. His highest score, 69, was made against Eastern Province in 1925–26. Against S. B. Joel's English touring team in 1924–25 he made top score in each innings, 44 and 33. His brother, Lawrence, had a longer career in provincial cricket. Once, after spending the night in Cathcart, before a league match, they turned up at the ground to find themselves the only members of the Whittlesea team present, the others having been delayed by a river in flood. Unabashed, they went in to bat, and when their team-mates arrived had made a century apiece and were still going strong.

MUNCER, BERNARD LEONARD, died suddenly on January 18, 1982, aged 68. When he left Middlesex in 1946 at the age of 33 after thirteen seasons, his career seemed a failure. Nor had a spell on the Burma-Siam Railway, as a prisoner-of-war, improved his prospects. He had played fairly regularly in 1934 and 1935 with moderate success, but since then he had failed to keep his place: his highest score was 85 against Northamptonshire in 1937 and his 23 wickets had cost over 28 runs each. Yet when he retired in 1954 after eight seasons with Glamorgan, he had five times taken over 100 wickets, once being the first in England to reach that target, he had made four centuries, he had had much to do with his county winning the Championship in 1948, and in 1952 he had done the double. Moreover, at one period some regarded him as the best slow spinner in England and in 1948 he had played for the Players at Lord's. The main reason for this dramatic development was that he had switched from leg-breaks and googlies to off-breaks. With these, besides the cardinal gifts of length, flight and spin, he had the rarer virtue of making the batsman play six balls an over. To add to his value he was a good slip. His highest score was 135 against Somerset at Swansea in 1952. Later the emergence of McConnon, also an off-spinner, restricted his opportunities and, having been awarded a benefit in 1954, he left the county at the end of the season and returned to Lord's, where he eventually became Head Coach. A cheerful, friendly man, he was deservedly popular.

NASH, PHILIP GEOFFREY ELWIN, CBE, died at Old Basing on December 8, 1982, aged 76. A good bat and a slow-medium opening bowler, he was captain of the St Paul's Eleven in 1925 and later did useful work for Berkshire.

NEWMAN, GEORGE CHRISTOPHER, who died on October 13, 1982, aged 78, had the unusual experience of getting into the Eton Eleven so late in his last year at school, 1923, that he played two innings only, against Winchester and against Harrow. He owed his selection to the advice of R. A. Young, then master-in-charge of cricket, who had spotted, beneath a style which did not wholly conform to the strict Eton canons of orthodoxy, possibilities of a fine attacking batsman. His judgement proved, as so often, right: Newman, after making 22 at Winchester, did at Lord's exactly what was wanted – going in No. 9, he hit some erratic Harrow bowling all over the ground to score 82 not out. This early success was typical of his later career, even though it did not secure him any kind of trial in The Parks during his first two years at Oxford. He had to wait till his third year when, given a chance on the tour, he made his place secure with an innings of 66 at The Oval, where he helped C. H. Taylor to add 141. He failed at Lord's, but in 1927, after starting with 92 against the full bowling strength of Lancashire, that year's champions (an innings described as "one of the best played in The Parks since the war"), he came second in the Oxford averages with 481 runs at an average of 40.08. Again he failed at Lord's and so it came as a surprise to many when, given a trial by Middlesex in 1929, he played a brilliant innings in his third match, 112 out of 168 in just over two hours against Gloucestershire at Lord's. He should have been stumped off Parker first ball, but immediately retaliated by hitting Goddard for two 6s off consecutive balls with pulled drives towards the Tavern. The match was, in fact, otherwise notable as the occasion on which Goddard, taking thirteen for 120, first demonstrated that an indifferent fast bowler had in one season's absence from county cricket changed himself into a great slow off-spinner. Newman made two more fine centuries in 1930, against Warwickshire and Essex, and continued to play for the county until 1936, though never regularly; indeed after 1931 for a match or two a year only. In 1937 he captained an MCC side in Canada. A tall man, who made full use of his reach, he was a fine striker of the ball in front of the wicket, but also a good cutter and a glorious off-side fieldsman with a beautiful return. He was a natural athlete who had represented Oxford in the high jump and the low hurdles and been President of the OUAC. He had also played in the first two squash matches against Cambridge. In later life he did valuable work on the MCC Committee and had been one of the club's Trustees since 1970. He was also, from 1963 to 1976, President of Middlesex.

NICHOLSON, FRANK ("NIPPER"), who died in Port Elizabeth on July 30, 1982, aged 72, kept wicket four times for South Africa against Australia in 1935–36. From 1927 until 1947 he represented Griqualand West, captaining them for several seasons. A neat wicket-keeper and more than adequate batsman, he accounted for 64 victims and scored 2,353 runs at an average of 24.76 in a first-class career of 52 matches. His highest score of 185 was made against Orange Free State. His best season was 1933–34 when, in four Currie Cup matches, he scored 353 runs for an average of 44.12, caught seven batsmen and stumped 15. On the death of H. B. Cameron he took over briefly as South Africa's wicket-keeper, in a losing series against Australia. With K. G. Viljoen he established what still stands as the third-wicket record for Griqualand West – 212 against Western Province in 1929–30 – and his total of 54 wicket-keeping victims for Griqualand West in Currie Cup matches is unsurpassed.

NITSCHKE, HOLMEDALE CARL ("JACK" or "SLINGER"), who died in Australia on September 29, 1982, aged 77, was an attacking left-hand batsman who played twice for Australia against South Africa in 1931–32, scoring 6 in the first Test and 47 in the second. For several years he made enough runs for South Australia to have been chosen considerably more often for a weaker Australian side, but his best years coincided with those of Bradman, Ponsford, Woodfull, Jackson, McCabe and Kippax. In 1932–33, in two matches for South Australia against D. R. Jardine's MCC side he scored 67, 28, 38 and 87 with a dash and confidence which caused the Englishmen to believe he would have done better in the Test matches than some of those who played. For four successive seasons he scored centuries for South Australia against New South Wales, carrying his bat in the last of them, at Sydney in 1933–34, for 130 out of a total of 246. In 1934–35 he was one of four batsmen – the first four in the order – to score centuries for South Australia against Queensland in Adelaide, the others being V. Y. Richardson, Lonergan and Badcock. In all first-class cricket he scored 3,320 runs (average 42.03), including nine centuries. He became, after his retirement, an outstandingly successful race-horse breeder.

PARRINGTON, WILLIAM FERGUSON, who died at Northallerton on May 7, 1980, aged 90, played a few matches for Derbyshire as a bat in 1926, his highest score being 47 against Warwickshire at Derby. He had been in the Rossall Eleven in 1907 and 1908 and in 1914 had appeared for Durham, the county of his birth.

PARTRIDGE, NORMAN ERNEST, who died at Aberystwyth on March 10, 1982, aged 81, was an outstanding schoolboy cricketer. For Malvern in 1918 he scored 514 runs with an average of 102.80 and in 1919 took 71 wickets at 12.98. In 1919 he and G. T. S. Stevens of University College School were both asked to play for the Gentlemen, Stevens at Lord's and Partridge at The Oval. They are believed to have been the first schoolboys so honoured since R. A. H. Mitchell in 1861. Stevens played, but, the match being in term-time, Malvern refused leave to Partridge, just as Eton had to Mitchell. Going up to Cambridge, Partridge duly got his Blue in a very strong side, but, though his final record of a batting average of 25 and 38 wickets at 21.60 was respectable, he hardly achieved as much as had been hoped of him. This was his only summer in residence, but between 1921 and 1937 he played for Warwickshire, for a few seasons frequently but later seldom for more than a match or two. Yet he generally did something either as a batsman or a bowler that showed what a loss it was that he could not play regularly. In all he scored 2,352 runs for the county with an average of 18.52 and took 347 wickets at 22.27. His highest score and his only century was 102 against Somerset at Edgbaston in 1925, made in 100 minutes: he and R. E. S. Wyatt put on 138 in an hour and a half for the seventh wicket. Bowling fast-medium in-swingers, he had, like many of his type, a rather ugly action which, though he was never no-balled, was regarded by some as slightly suspect. It is said that a batsman whom he had comprehensively bowled said indignantly to "Tiger" Smith behind the wicket, "He threw that". "Yes", said "Tiger". "And bloody well too."

PEARCE, THOMAS ALEXANDER, died in hospital at Tunbridge Wells on August 11, 1982, aged 71. He was three years in the Charterhouse Eleven and, after playing a number of matches for Kent in 1930 and 1931, won a regular place in the side in 1932, when he scored 581 runs with an average of 24.13, his highest score being 83 against Northamptonshire at Tunbridge Wells: he and Ames put on 194 for the seventh wicket "by brilliant cricket". At the end of the season he went out to join his father's business in Hong Kong, but reappeared in the county side when home on leave in 1937 and 1946. Captured in the siege of Hong Kong, he spent the rest of the war as a prisoner, and it was therefore no mean performance when in his third match in 1946 he made 106 in two and threequarter hours against Northamptonshire at Northampton. This was his only hundred in first-class cricket. A natural games-player, who had been in the rackets pair at school and a scratch golfer, he relied largely on the typical rackets player's off-side strokes and county bowlers soon found ways of keeping him relatively quiet, though he was a prolific scorer in club cricket. To Kent his main value was his glorious fielding in any position, a more important consideration than it would be in these days when the average age is so much lower. He was for many years a leading figure in cricket in Hong Kong and after his retirement to England he served on the Kent Committee and was President in 1978. Altogether for Kent he scored 1,177 runs with an average of 17.05

PEARSE, ALAN A., who died on June 14, 1981, aged 67, played occasionally for Somerset from 1936 to 1938 as an amateur. In nine matches his batting average was 5.79 and his highest score 20 against Kent in his first innings for the county.

PEDEN, MRS MARGARET, who died in 1981, was a founder member of the Australian Cricket Council. In 1937 she captained the first Australian team to tour England, and she maintained her interest and support for the game, especially in her home state of New South Wales, until her death.

PILKINGTON, THOMAS ALEC, who has died at the age of 74, was a member of P. F. Warner's MCC side to South America in 1926–27. A notable all-round sportsman, he played for Eton in 1925, though not against Harrow.

POLLARD, MARJORIE, OBE, who died on March 21, 1982, aged 81, was a foremost figure in the fight for the establishment and recognition of women's team games. She was a founder member of the Women's Cricket Association, the first official reporter of women's cricket in the national press and the first woman radio commentator on the game. For twenty years she produced and edited the magazine *Women's Cricket*. She was herself a fine all-round player and a shrewd captain. Her OBE, awarded in 1965, was for services to sport.

POWELL, ADAM GORDON, who died at his home in Sandwich on June 7, 1982, aged 69, was regarded by some good judges as one of the outstanding English wicket-keepers of his time. A pupil of Strudwick, to whom he always acknowledged a great debt, he stood up to all but the fastest bowlers and was so neat and quiet, making the whole job look so simple, that it was easy to underestimate him. He was also a useful attacking bat: with beautiful wrists, a lovely cover drive and an effective golf-shot over mid-on, he was particularly good against fast bowling. When Essex beat Yorkshire at Southend by an innings in 1934, he contributed 62 not out and had an unfinished partnership of 113 in 90 minutes with Peter Smith for the ninth wicket. In the next year he scored 47 against Larwood and Voce: on this occasion his partner, an England batsman, was inclined to leave to him the playing of Larwood.

After three years in the Charterhouse side he went up to Cambridge, but got his Blue only in his third year, 1934: many thought he should have had it earlier. Between 1932 and 1937 he played frequently for Essex and in 1935 went as one of the two wicket-keepers with E. R. T. Holmes's MCC side to Australia and New Zealand: unfortunately he missed much of the tour with a sprained ankle. His county career ended when in 1937 the doctors forbade him to play serious first-class cricket. In 1939 he appeared for Suffolk and captained them in 1946 when they won the Minor Counties Championship for the first time. He continued for many years to play club cricket and also to represent MCC and Free Foresters in first-class matches. He was a member of the MCC sides to Canada in 1937 and 1951 and also toured Egypt with Hubert Martineau's XI.

PULLE, JOHN, who has died at the age of 70, represented Ceylon against the Australians, who were on their way to England, in both 1934 and 1938. A forthright opening batsman and a good captain, he spent much of his life in England.

REDDICK, TOM BOCKENHAM, died in Cape Town on June 1, 1982, aged 70. Born in Shanghai, he had a varied and unusual career as player and coach, spread over half a century. After showing unusual promise as an all-rounder while on the staff of G. A. Faulkner's cricket school in London, he appeared twice for Middlesex in 1931, while still in his teens; but although his Championship appearances extended over nearly two decades he had only two full seasons of county cricket. Both were for Nottinghamshire, whom he joined in 1946 as player-coach after war service with the RAF. One of the mainstays of a weak side he scored more runs (994) in 1946 than anyone except Keeton and Harris, playing one specially good fighting innings of 131 against Lancashire. In the following year he made 1,206 runs: captaining the side for the first time, against Kent, he scored 139, sharing in a fifth-wicket partnership of 244 with Winrow. After that he spent almost all his cricketing life in South Africa, appearing for Western Province in the Currie Cup and making a great reputation in the coaching field. After returning to England for two summers as chief coach to Lancashire, he settled permanently in the Cape, where his flair as a teacher of the game unearthed and developed the talents of countless young players who later made their mark, Basil D'Oliveira among them. A main reason for Reddick not having played more first-class cricket in England was his engagement by Sir Julien Cahn, for whom he played from 1930 to 1939, scoring over 1,500 runs in three successive seasons in a competitive environment. A man of charm, modesty and wit, Reddick for many years wrote a weekly column for the *Cape Times*. In 1979 he had published an autobiography, *Never Cross a Bat*.

ROBINSON, RAY, who died at the Royal North Shore Hospital, Sydney, on July 6, 1982, two days before his 77th birthday, was one of cricket's most prolific and felicitous writers. He had to steel himself to be critical of those about whom he wrote. Born in Victoria, he started his career in journalism with the *Melbourne Herald*, in 1925, before becoming chief cricket writer for the *Melbourne Star* in 1930. The first of his many overseas tours was to England with Woodfull's team in 1934. Moving to Sydney, he joined the *Sydney Daily Telegraph* during the Second War, after which he worked for the *Sydney Sun*, the *Sydney Morning Herald* and the *Sun-Herald*. He had a namesake, for whom he was sometimes mistaken, who played once for Australia.

"Robbie", as Ray Robinson was called by all who knew him, loved cricket. His industry was remarkable, his conscientiousness unquestioned. He was read with pleasure throughout the cricket world, his sentences being as full of facts as they were of happy phrases. He left technical analysis to others, realising that that was not his forte and being respected for doing so. His strength lay not in saying how, for example, Bill Edrich may have had a technical weakness on the off side, or why, but in writing about his background, his appearance, his war record, the weight of his bat and the most carefully catalogued statistics of his innings. No cricket writer was ever more reticent about entering a dressing-room than Robinson; none less likely to be shown the door. The players knew they could trust him implicitly. He was a copious maker of seemingly illegible notes, as often as not in the margins of a newspaper. In recent years, owing to fading eyesight, he watched a day's play glued to his binoculars, sometimes fighting to keep awake. He had a soft voice, with a Scottish lilt, and he never took a taxi when there might be a bus on the way. The remarkable success of his first book, *Between Wickets* (1945), he put down, with characteristic modesty, to the post-war enthusiasm for cricket. He also wrote *From the Boundary* (1950), *Green Sprigs* (1954), *The Wit of Sir Robert Menzies* (1966), *The Wildest Tests* (1972) and *On Top Down Under* (1976). The last of these, a detailed study of all Australia's Test captains, won him the Cricket Society's Silver Jubilee Literary Award. – J. W.

SANDHAM, ANDREW, who died in hospital on April 20, 1982, aged 91, might, had things turned out differently, have been for years a regular and successful Test match batsman. It was his misfortune that, slow to develop, owing partly to the great pressure for places as batsmen in the Surrey side, partly to the Great War, he was over 30 when he first came into serious consideration, and by then his rival as Hobbs's partner was Sutcliffe. By the time Hobbs retired from international cricket Sandham was too old to be his replacement. And so he will be remembered as a wonderful servant of Surrey and as Hobbs's partner for the county for fifteen years.

His career began as long ago as 1911 when in his first match he made 53 against Cambridge and in his second 60 against Lancashire, creating a great impression. None the less in 1912 he had only one match for the county. In 1913 he scored 196 against Sussex, adding 298 with Harrison for the sixth wicket, and one might have supposed that this would have made his place secure, but a month later he was dropped for D. J. Knight, who had just left Malvern, and in 1914 he appeared in only five matches. Even in 1919 he was dropped for some matches, but an innings of 175 not out against Middlesex at the beginning of August at last ensured him a regular place, which he retained until 1937 when, having made a century against Sussex at Hove in the last match of the season, he left it to the Surrey Committee to announce his retirement. By then he had made in all first-class matches 41,284 runs with an average of 44.83, including 107 centuries. Twenty times he had exceeded a thousand runs, two of these occasions being on tours abroad, and his 219 for Surrey in 1934 is still the highest score made for a county against the Australians.

His first Test match was against Australia at The Oval in 1921, when he made a useful 21 at No. 5. In 1922–23 he went to South Africa, where he played in all five Tests as an opener, but did little, although taking the tour as a whole he was the most consistent bat on the side, and in 1924 he played twice against South Africa, scoring 46 in his only innings. That winter he was a member of Arthur Gilligan's side in Australia. Hobbs and Sutcliffe were now in their prime as an opening pair and Sandham in his two Tests, going in lower down, met with no success. Finally in 1929–30 he went to West Indies and played innings of 152 at Bridgetown and 325 at Kingston. These matches were classified as Tests only at a later date: at the time they were called Representative matches and in fact only one of the English team played in the Tests in England in the following summer. So, unluckily, he never had the chance of opening for England with Hobbs. To Surrey, Hobbs and Sandham meant what Hobbs and Sutcliffe did to England. They put up 100 for the first wicket 63 times, their highest partnership being 428 against Oxford University in 1926. Sandham was the ideal partner, content to stay there and let Hobbs take the applause and as much of the bowling as he wanted. When, against Somerset at Taunton in 1925, Hobbs, having equalled W. G.'s number of centuries in the first innings, had a chance of beating it in the second, Sandham saw to it that he got the bowling, thus sacrificing a possible hundred for himself. He was the least selfish of players.

He had formed his style in his early days by watching Tom Hayward, much of whose skill on the leg side he had inherited, and he perfected it by association with Hobbs. Like many small men he was quick on his feet and a fine and fearless hooker: this, with his mastery of the cut, in which he always made full use of such height as he had, made him a particularly good player of fast bowling. Of his other strokes perhaps the best was a square drive. He was also a magnificent outfield with a fast and low return, whose value was even greater in the days when the whole area of The Oval was used more often than it is now.

His services to Surrey did not end with his playing career. From 1946 to 1958 he was their coach and then for another twelve years their scorer. An Honorary Member at The Oval since 1961 and a Vice-President since 1979, he continued to watch the play there till the end of his life. He was also an Honorary Member of MCC. A quiet man with a great sense of humour, who set himself and expected of others a high standard of behaviour, he was much respected.

SEALY, JAMES EDWARD DEREK, who died in Trinidad on January 3, 1982, aged 69, was something of an infant prodigy. When he first played for West Indies, against England at Bridgetown in 1929–30, he was 17 years 122 days, at the time the youngest-ever Test cricketer. He still is the youngest to have played for West Indies. He was to become more than a very good, quick-footed batsman, occasionally bowling effectively at medium pace and twice (against England in 1939) keeping wicket in Test matches. He epitomised the natural cricketing ability of so many West Indians, his cap at a rakish angle, the bat seeming to be an extension of himself, often smiling, always friendly. As a boy, in his first Test match, he was placed in the order between Headley and Constantine and scored 58 against an England attack which included Voce, Rhodes and Stevens. In Australia in 1930–31 he had a disappointing tour and was not chosen to go to England in 1933. In 1934–35, by when he was 22, he averaged 45 in the four Test matches against R. E. S. Wyatt's England team, only Headley, with whom he added 202 for West Indies' third wicket at Kingston in the fourth Test match, doing better. In England in 1939 he made his highest first-class score, 181 in three and a half hours against Middlesex at Lord's, although more was expected of him as a batsman than he achieved. "Sealy", wrote *Wisden*, "not unlike Headley in appearance at the wicket, and somewhat similar in forcing tactics, showed less ability to score when playing back, but he gave some attractive displays". In 1941–42, for Barbados against Trinidad in Bridgetown, he had a large share in a remarkable record, taking eight wickets for 8 runs as Trinidad were bowled out for 16 on a sticky wicket. After the war, having moved to Trinidad, he made no particular impact on West Indian cricket. He continued, however, to bring happiness wherever he went. In eleven Tests he scored 478 runs (average 28.11), with a highest score of 92 against England at Port-of-Spain in 1934–35, and took three wickets for 94 runs. His overall first-class record was 3,831 runs at an average of 30.40 and 63 wickets at 28.60 apiece.

SEVERN, DR CLIFFORD BRILL, who died in California in February, 1981, aged 90, was a pioneer of cricket in Southern California. One of the founders, in 1931, of the Hollywood Cricket Club, he was an Honorary Member of MCC. For more than half a century he worked hard to keep cricket in America alive.

SIEDLE, IVAN JULIAN ("JACK"), who died in Durban on August 24, 1982, aged 79, was South Africa's oldest surviving Test cricketer at the time of his death. He had the unique distinction of scoring the first century on a turf pitch in South Africa in both a Currie Cup match and a Test match. The first, 114 for Natal against Border at Durban, was in December, 1926. The second was at Newlands in Cape Town in 1930–31 when he and Bruce Mitchell shared a record first-wicket partnership of 260 against England, Siedle making 141, his one Test century. A right-handed opening batsman, solid and watchful, he made his first-class début for Natal on the day after he turned nineteen, scoring 6 and 8 against the 1922–23 MCC team. In 1924–25 he appeared in three unofficial Tests against S. B. Joel's English team, scoring 52 in the final match. In 1926–27 he and J. F. W. Nicolson shared in a first-wicket stand of 424 for Natal against Orange Free State at Bloemfontein, a record to this day. Nicolson scored 252 not out, Siedle 174. Siedle's 265 not out, also for Natal against Orange Free State, in 1929–30 was the highest score made in the Currie Cup until J. E. Cheetham's 271 not out for Western Province against Orange Free State in 1950–51, a figure passed within five days by E. A. B. Rowan (277 not out for Transvaal against Griqualand West). Siedle's first Test match was against England at Durban in 1927–28, but he was dropped after scoring 11 and 10 as H. W. Taylor's opening partner. Selected for the 1929 tour of England, he finished second in the batting averages, totalling 1,579 runs at an average of 35.88 with centuries against Leicestershire and Yorkshire. He missed two of the five Tests through injury. In his first full home series, against England in 1930–31, he scored 384 runs (average 42.66). Unavailable for the 1931–32 tour of Australia, he made his second trip to England in 1935, starting in fine form and becoming the first member of the side to reach 1,000 runs, these including three successive hundreds – against Surrey, Oxford University and MCC. In the third of them he carried his bat for 132 not out in a total of 297. He was less successful in the Tests, one of which he missed through injury. Against the all-conquering Australian team in South Africa in 1935–36 he was second to A. D. Nourse in both Test average and Test aggregate. That was the finish of his Test career, and at the end of the 1936–37 season, after successive scores of 105, 111 and 207, he retired. His seventeen first-class centuries included three of over 200. In all first-class matches he scored 7,730 runs with an average of 40.05. In eighteen Tests he made 977 runs at an average of 28.73. He was a fine all-round fielder and had a wide range of strokes. His son John (J. R.) hit a century on his début in first-class cricket, for Western Province against Eastern Province in 1955–56.

SINCOCK, HAROLD, who died in Adelaide on February 3, 1982, aged 74, played twice for South Australia as a leg-spinner and forceful batsman in 1929–30, the first of his appearances being against A. H. H. Gilligan's visiting MCC team. In his nine overs in the match he took four wickets for 72 runs. His son, David, played three times for Australia as a left-arm wrist spinner. Another son, Peter, also made five appearances for South Australia.

SKINNER, ALAN FRANK, who died in the West Suffolk Hospital on February 28, 1982, aged 68, did much useful work for Derbyshire between 1931 and 1938. Captain of the Leys School side in 1931, he had trials for the county that year and the next without achieving much, but in 1933, his second year at Cambridge, who had not yet given him a match, he scored 788 runs with an average of 28. Next year he did have a trial for Cambridge but failed to get his Blue: however, in all first-class matches he made 1,019 runs with an average of 27.54, including the only century of his career, 102 for Derbyshire against Gloucestershire at Gloucester. From 1935 to 1938 his opportunities were more limited, but in 1935 his 550 runs and an average of 36.66 suggested what he might have done had he been able to devote his whole time to the game. Though he watched the ball carefully, he was a good stroke-player and could be the most attractive bat on the side, equally prepared to open or to go in lower down. He was also a fine slip. On a number of occasions he captained the county. After the war his first-class cricket was confined to one match for Northamptonshire in 1949. Later he was for many years Clerk of the West Suffolk County Council. His younger brother, David, captained Derbyshire in 1949.

SMITH, EDGAR FRANK, who died in hospital at Slough on December 16, 1982 was a past President of the Club Cricket Conference.

STEPHENSON, LT-COL. JOHN WILLIAM ARTHUR, DSO, died at his home at Pulborough on May 20, 1982, aged 73. If there were more cricketers like him, there would always have been fewer empty grounds. There could never, when he was in action, be a dull moment; nor, as far as he was concerned, would there be a slow over-rate. Whatever he was doing he was the very personification of energy and enthusiasm. Bowling brisk fast-medium seamers with a high action and a full follow-through, he seemed almost to hurl himself down the pitch after the ball. He could move it both ways, making it come off the ground at a remarkable pace. He was a serviceable attacking batsman in the lower half of the order and, as R. C. Robertson-Glasgow put it, "ran three when the book said two" and "was dangerous for a partner with short legs or a weak heart". A brilliant and untiring field, he never took a rest whether bowling or not, and he was popularly supposed to go to bed with his fingers wrapped round a cricket ball.

Originally playing for Buckinghamshire, he started to appear for Essex in 1934 and his first big performance was against the South Africans at Southend in the following year when, deputising for H. D. Read, who was resting for The Oval Test, he took seven for 66 and three for 44. But the feat for which he will always be remembered was to take nine for 46 in the first innings for the Gentlemen at Lord's in 1936, one of the most notable bowling performances by an amateur in the history of the match. After this he must have been a serious candidate for G. O. Allen's team to Australia in the following winter and there were those who thought that he should have been preferred to Copson, who, with Allen himself, Farnes and Voce in the side, was really superfluous. Stephenson continued to play when his military duties allowed until 1939, and in that year he was one of three amateurs who shared the Essex captaincy between them. The war virtually ended his serious cricket, though he did play one match for Worcestershire in 1947. He would never have lingered on once he found his energy and activity gradually abating. In later years he played much golf in a style peculiarly his own, giving equal enjoyment to himself and his friends, putting one-handed back-hand from any part of the green and holing, if not a proportion that would have satisfied a champion, at least as many as more orthodox players in his own class. It was no surprise to learn from tributes after his death what a splendid and inspiring leader he had shown himself in the war and how much his men had liked him. In all first-class cricket he scored 2,582 runs with an average of 21.34 and took 311 wickets at 23.99.

TOLHURST, EDWARD KEITH, who has died in Melbourne, aged 86, played first-class cricket for Victoria as a batsman in 1930–31, his best score being 63 against G. C. Grant's touring West Indians. In 1930 he toured Canada and the USA in a team captained by Arthur Mailey and which included Bradman. He was closely connected with the Melbourne Cricket Club, finally as an Honorary Life Member.

TOMKINS, ERIC FELTHAM, who died on July 20, 1980, had a few trials for Northamptonshire as a batsman in 1920 and 1921, his highest score being 50 not out against Leicestershire at Leicester in 1920. He was better known as a hard-working halfback in the strong Northampton Town football team before and after the Great War. By profession he was a schoolmaster at Rushden.

TRUMPER, VICTOR (JUN.), the only son of his legendary father, died in Sydney on August 31, 1981, at the age of 67. A fast out-swing bowler, with few pretensions to batting, he played for New South Wales in 1940–41, though not in the Sheffield Shield, which was suspended for the duration of the Second World War.

VARACHIA, RASHID, who died in Johannesburg on December 11, 1981, aged 66, had been President of the South African Cricket Union since its formation as the non-racial controlling body of South African cricket in September, 1977. A highly successful businessman, born in Bombay, he was previously President of the South African Cricket Board of Control (SACBOC), administering Indians and Coloureds. Latterly he had worked under the handicap of a heart condition but had travelled the world, frail of body but intensely sincere of purpose, putting South Africa's claims for a return to international cricket. He withstood many rebuffs and was even amused when, because of his connection with South African cricket, the Australian government refused him a visa to visit Sydney where his son lived. At first he was frustrated not so much by his lack of success in approaches to the ICC but by the ignorance of South Africa shown by representatives of some member-countries and by their unwillingness to learn more about it or even discuss it. His last rebuff, in July 1981, was a heavy blow for one of fragile health to bear.

VAULKHARD, DENIS HENRY, a member of the well-known midland cricketing family, who died at Nottingham on May 19, 1982, aged 73, played for Sir Julien Cahn's XI from 1924 to 1929 and also appeared for Nottinghamshire Second Eleven. He was a useful bat and medium-pace bowler. From 1949 to 1960 he was a member of the Nottinghamshire Committee.

WATTS, EDWARD ALFRED, was found dead in his home at Cheam on May 2, 1982. He was 70. Coming out for Surrey as an amateur in 1933, he immediately showed how valuable he was going to be if he could play regularly, scoring 318 runs with an average of 39.75 and taking 28 wickets at 24.85. In 1934 he joined the staff and with 928 runs and 91 wickets made it clear that he had not been over-estimated: moreover, against the powerful Yorkshire attack at Bradford he made 123 in under two hours, with four 6s and fourteen 4s. His only other century for the county, 116 not out against Hampshire at Bournemouth in 1936, also took less than two hours. He continued as an essential member of the side up to the war, heading the bowling averages in 1938 with 114 wickets in county matches at 17.69 and in 1939 taking ten for 67 in the second innings against Warwickshire at Edgbaston. After the war he was less effective, but continued to give useful assistance when required. He retired at the end of 1949, having received a benefit. Later he ran a sports shop. A strongly built man, he bowled fast-medium, could swing the ball both ways and got plenty of life off the wicket: to these gifts he added a shrewd bowling brain. He was a good striker of the ball, particularly through the covers, and a reliable slip. He was a brother-in-law of Alf Gover. All told he scored 6,158 runs at an average of 21.41 and took 729 wickets at 26.06 apiece.

WEST, LESLIE HAROLD, who died suddenly on November 12, 1982, aged 77, at a cricket dinner, had a trial for Essex as a professional in 1928. A stylish batsman, he made many runs later in club cricket, first for Ilford and then for Wanstead, and after his retirement he did wonderful work in coaching and inspiring young players.

WESTLEY, ROGER BANCROFT, who was master-in-charge of cricket at Haileybury, died on May 12, 1982, aged 35. In 1969, when his brother, Stuart, got a Blue, he played in five matches for Oxford without success. The two provide one of the comparatively few instances of twins appearing together in first-class cricket. They were educated at Lancaster Grammar School.

WHEATLEY, JACK BRIAN, who died at Sellescombe, Sussex, on April 29, 1982, aged 78, appeared for Middlesex against Oxford University in 1925 and then in 1928 played in seven matches for the county, making 62 against Worcestershire at Lord's in the first of them but doing little later. A batsman who played straight and was a good driver, he was also a useful slow left-arm change bowler. He had been in the Eleven at St Paul's School but did not get a Blue at Oxford.

WHITAKER, EDGAR HADDON, OBE, who died at his home at Roehampton on January 5, 1982, was editor of *Wisden Cricketers' Almanack* from 1940 to 1943. He was Chairman of J. Whitaker and Sons, publishers of *Whitaker's Almanack* and from 1938 to 1978 of *Wisden*.

WILSON, ERNEST FREDERICK, who died on March 3, 1981, aged 73, was one of several professional batsmen who might have made a name with other counties but were unable to secure a place in the tremendously strong pre-war Surrey batting sides. Having played an innings of 240 in three and a half hours for the Second Eleven against Devon at The Oval in 1928, he was given a trial for the county at Northampton and scored 99. Surrey declared at 530 for nine. The Northamptonshire bowling, never at that period strong (it was the first of three consecutive innings in which they fielded out to totals of over 500), was in the absence of Jupp, Thomas and Clark, so perhaps Wilson's success was not taken very seriously. At any rate, it was his only game for the side that season. In 1929 he had a good trial and scored 660 runs with an average of 25.42, his outstanding performance being 110 against Kent at Blackheath, the only century of his career, in the course of which he put on 154 in 95 minutes for the fifth wicket with P. G. H. Fender. Afforded another fair trial in 1930 he was disappointing and for the next few years appeared only spasmodically, playing occasionally a good innings but never really fulfilling his promise. Some had seen in him the successor to Sandham. He watched the ball well, had a good defence and scored mainly in front of the wicket. Perhaps his fielding did not help: he had a safe pair of hands, but was a slow mover. His last appearance was in 1936. In all matches for Surrey he made 2,516 runs with an average of 23.30.

WILSON, PETER, who died at Palma, Majorca, on October 5, 1981, aged 68, was for many years Sports Columnist of the *Daily Mirror*, in which capacity he wrote occasionally, and usually affectionately, of cricket. His father, F. B. Wilson, who captained Harrow and Cambridge at cricket, wrote about numerous games for *The Times*. His son is Julian Wilson, the horse-racing commentator.

WOODMAN, REGINALD GEORGE, died on May 20, 1980, aged 84. He played two matches for Gloucestershire in 1925 as a batsman, but without success.

THE LAWS OF CRICKET

(1980 CODE)

INDEX TO THE LAWS

LAW 1. THE PLAYERS

1. Number of Players and Captain

A match is played between two sides each of eleven players, one of whom shall be captain. In the event of the captain not being available at any time, a deputy shall act for him.

2. Nomination of Players

Before the toss for innings, the captain shall nominate his players, who may not thereafter be changed without the consent of the opposing captain.

Note

(a) More or Less than Eleven Players a Side
A match may be played by agreement between sides of more or less than eleven players, but not more than eleven players may field.

LAW 2. SUBSTITUTES AND RUNNERS: BATSMAN OR FIELDSMAN LEAVING THE FIELD: BATSMAN RETIRING: BATSMAN COMMENCING INNINGS

1. Substitutes

Substitutes shall be allowed by right to field for any player who, during the match, is incapacitated by illness or injury. The consent of the opposing captain must be obtained for the use of a substitute if any player is prevented from fielding for any other reason.

2. Objection to Substitutes

The opposing captain shall have no right of objection to any player acting as substitute in the field, nor as to where he shall field, although he may object to the substitute acting as wicket-keeper.

3. Substitute not to Bat or Bowl

A substitute shall not be allowed to bat or bowl.

4. A Player for whom a Substitute has Acted

A player may bat, bowl or field even though a substitute has acted for him.

5. Runner

A runner shall be allowed for a batsman who, during the match, is incapacitated by illness or injury. The person acting as runner shall be a member of the batting side and shall, if possible, have already batted in that innings.

6. Runner's Equipment

The person acting as runner for an injured batsman shall wear batting gloves and pads if the injured batsman is so equipped.

7. Transgression of the Laws by an Injured Batsman or Runner

An injured batsman may be out should his runner break any one of Laws 33 (Handled the Ball), 37 (Obstructing the Field) or 38 (Run Out). As striker he remains himself subject to the Laws. Furthermore, should he be out of his ground for any purpose and the wicket at the wicket-keeper's end be put down he shall be out under Law 38 (Run Out) or Law 39 (Stumped), irrespective of the position of the other batsman or the runner, and no runs shall be scored.

When not the striker, the injured batsman is out of the game and shall stand where he does not interfere with the play. Should he bring himself into the game in any way, then he shall suffer the penalties that any transgression of the Laws demands.

8. Fieldsman Leaving the Field

No fieldsman shall leave the field or return during a session of play without the consent of the umpire at the bowler's end. The umpire's consent is also necessary if a substitute is required for a fieldsman, when his side returns to the field after an interval. If a member of the fielding side leaves the field or fails to return after an interval and is absent from the field for longer than fifteen minutes, he shall not be permitted to bowl after his return until he has been on the field for at least that length of playing time for which he was absent. This restriction shall not apply at the start of a new day's play.

9. Batsman Leaving the Field or Retiring

A batsman may leave the field or retire at any time owing to illness, injury or other unavoidable cause, having previously notified the umpire at the bowler's end. He may resume his innings at the fall of a wicket, which for the purposes of this Law shall include the retirement of another batsman.

If he leaves the field or retires for any other reason he may resume his innings only with the consent of the opposing captain.

When a batsman has left the field or retired and is unable to return owing to illness, injury or other unavoidable cause, his innings is to be recorded as "retired, not out". Otherwise it is to be recorded as "retired, out".

10. Commencement of a Batsman's Innings

A batsman shall be considered to have commenced his innings once he has stepped on to the field of play.

Note

(a) Substitutes and Runners
For the purpose of these Laws, allowable illnesses or injuries are those which occur at any time after the nomination by the captains of their teams.

LAW 3. THE UMPIRES

1. Appointment

Before the toss for innings, two umpires shall be appointed, one for each end, to control the game with absolute impartiality as required by the Laws.

2. Change of Umpires

No umpire shall be changed during a match without the consent of both captains.

3. Special Conditions

Before the toss for innings, the umpires shall agree with both captains on any special conditions affecting the conduct of the match.

4. The Wickets

The umpires shall satisfy themselves before the start of the match that the wickets are properly pitched.

5. Clock or Watch

The umpires shall agree between themselves and inform both captains before the start of the match on the watch or clock to be followed during the match.

6. Conduct and Implements

Before and during a match the umpires shall ensure that the conduct of the game and the implements used are strictly in accordance with the Laws.

7. Fair and Unfair Play

The umpires shall be the sole judges of fair and unfair play.

8. Fitness of Ground, Weather and Light

(a) The umpires shall be the sole judges of the fitness of the ground, weather and light for play.

(i) However, before deciding to suspend play, or not to start play, or not to resume play after an interval or stoppage, the umpires shall establish whether both captains (the batsmen at the wicket may deputise for their captain) wish to commence or to continue in the prevailing conditions; if so, their wishes shall be met.

(ii) In addition, if during play the umpires decide that the light is unfit, only the batting side shall have the option of continuing play. After agreeing to continue to play in unfit light conditions, the captain of the batting side (or a batsman at the wicket) may appeal against the light to the umpires, who shall uphold the appeal only if, in their opinion, the light has deteriorated since the agreement to continue was made.

(b) After any suspension of play, the umpires, unaccompanied by any of the players or officials, shall, on their own initiative, carry out an inspection immediately the conditions improve and shall continue to inspect at intervals. Immediately the umpires decide that play is possible they shall call upon the players to resume the game.

9. Exceptional Circumstances

In exceptional circumstances, other than those of weather, ground or light, the umpires may decide to suspend or abandon play. Before making such a decision the umpires shall establish, if the circumstances allow, whether both captains (the batsmen at the wicket may deputise for their captain) wish to continue in the prevailing conditions; if so, their wishes shall be met.

10. Position of Umpires

The umpires shall stand where they can best see any act upon which their decision may be required.

Subject to this over-riding consideration, the umpire at the bowler's end shall stand where he does not interfere with either the bowler's run-up or the striker's view.

The umpire at the striker's end may elect to stand on the off instead of the leg side of the pitch, provided he informs the captain of the fielding side and the striker of his intention to do so.

11. Umpires Changing Ends

The umpires shall change ends after each side has had one innings.

12. Disputes

All disputes shall be determined by the umpires, and if they disagree the actual state of things shall continue.

13. Signals

The following code of signals shall be used by umpires who will wait until a signal has been answered by a scorer before allowing the game to proceed.

Boundary	– by waving the arm from side to side.
Boundary 6	– by raising both arms above the head.
Bye	– by raising an open hand above the head.
Dead Ball	– by crossing and re-crossing the wrists below the waist.
Leg-bye	– by touching a raised knee with the hand.
No-ball	– by extending one arm horizontally.
Out	– by raising the index finger above the head. If not out, the umpire shall call "not out".
Short run	– by bending the arm upwards and by touching the nearer shoulder with the tips of the fingers.
Wide	– by extending both arms horizontally.

14. Correctness of Scores

The umpires shall be responsible for satisfying themselves on the correctness of the scores throughout and at the conclusion of the match. See Law 21.6 (Correctness of Result).

Notes

(a) Attendance of Umpires
The umpires should be present on the ground and report to the ground executive or the equivalent at least thirty minutes before the start of a day's play.

(b) Consultation between Umpires and Scorers
Consultation between umpires and scorers over doubtful points is essential.

(c) Fitness of Ground
The umpires shall consider the ground as unfit for play when it is so wet or slippery as to deprive the bowlers of a reasonable foothold, the fieldsmen, other than the deep-fielders, of the power of free movement, or the batsmen of the ability to play their strokes or to run between the wickets. Play should not be suspended merely because the grass and the ball are wet and slippery.

(d) Fitness of Weather and Light
The umpires should suspend play only when they consider that the conditions are so bad that it is unreasonable or dangerous to continue.

LAW 4. THE SCORERS

1. Recording Runs

All runs scored shall be recorded by scorers appointed for the purpose. Where there are two scorers they shall frequently check to ensure that the score sheets agree.

2. Acknowledging Signals

The scorers shall accept and immediately acknowledge all instructions and signals given to them by the umpires.

LAW 5. THE BALL

1. Weight and Size

The ball, when new, shall weigh not less than $5\frac{1}{2}$ ounces/155.9g, nor more than $5\frac{3}{4}$ ounces/163g; and shall measure not less than $8\frac{13}{16}$ inches/22.4cm, nor more than 9 inches/22.9cm in circumference.

2. Approval of Balls

All balls used in matches shall be approved by the umpires and captains before the start of the match.

3. New Ball

Subject to agreement to the contrary, having been made before the toss, either captain may demand a new ball at the start of each innings.

4. New Ball in Match of Three or More Days' Duration

In a match of three or more days' duration, the captain of the fielding side may demand a new ball after the prescribed number of overs has been bowled with the old one. The governing body for cricket in the country concerned shall decide the number of overs applicable in that country, which shall be not less than 75 six-ball overs (55 eight-ball overs).

5. Ball Lost or Becoming Unfit for Play

In the event of a ball during play being lost or, in the opinion of the umpires, becoming unfit for play, the umpires shall allow it to be replaced by one that in their opinion has had a similar amount of wear. If a ball is to be replaced, the umpires shall inform the batsman.

Note

(a) **Specifications**
The specifications, as described in 1 above, shall apply to top-grade balls only. The following degrees of tolerance will be acceptable for other grades of ball.

(i) *Men's Grades 2–4*
Weight: $5\frac{5}{16}$ ounces/150g to $5\frac{13}{16}$ ounces/165g.
Size: $8\frac{11}{16}$ inches/22.0cm to $9\frac{1}{16}$ inches/23.0cm.

(ii) *Women's*
Weight: $4\frac{15}{16}$ ounces/140g to $5\frac{5}{16}$ ounces/150g.
Size: $8\frac{1}{4}$ inches/21.0cm to $8\frac{7}{8}$ inches/22.5cm.

(iii) *Junior*
Weight: $4\frac{5}{16}$ ounces/133g to $5\frac{1}{16}$ ounces/143g.
Size: $8\frac{1}{16}$ inches/20.5cm to $8\frac{11}{16}$ inches/22.0cm.

LAW 6. THE BAT

1. Width and Length

The bat overall shall not be more than 38 inches/96.5cm in length; the blade of the bat shall be made of wood and shall not exceed $4\frac{1}{4}$ inches/10.8cm at the widest part.

Note

(a) The blade of the bat may be covered with material for protection, strengthening or repair. Such material shall not exceed $\frac{1}{16}$ inch/1.56mm in thickness.

LAW 7. THE PITCH

1. Area of Pitch

The pitch is the area between the bowling creases – see Law 9 (The Bowling and Popping Creases). It shall measure 5ft/1.52m in width on either side of a line joining the centre of the middle stumps of the wickets – see Law 8 (The Wickets).

2. Selection and Preparation

Before the toss for innings, the executive of the ground shall be responsible for the selection and preparation of the pitch; thereafter the umpires shall control its use and maintenance.

3. Changing Pitch

The pitch shall not be changed during a match unless it becomes unfit for play, and then only with the consent of both captains.

4. Non-Turf Pitches

In the event of a non-turf pitch being used, the following shall apply:

(a) Length: That of the playing surface to a minimum of 58ft/17.68m.

(b) Width: That of the playing surface to a minimum of 6ft/1.83m.

See Law 10 (Rolling, Sweeping, Mowing, Watering the Pitch and Re-marking of Creases) Note (a).

LAW 8. THE WICKETS

1. Width and Pitching

Two sets of wickets, each 9 inches/22.86cm wide, and consisting of three wooden stumps with two wooden bails upon the top, shall be pitched opposite and parallel to each other at a distance of 22 yards/20.12m between the centres of the two middle stumps.

2. Size of Stumps

The stumps shall be of equal and sufficient size to prevent the ball from passing between them. Their tops shall be 28 inches/71.1cm above the ground, and shall be dome-shaped except for the bail grooves.

3. Size of Bails

The bails shall be each $4\frac{3}{8}$ inches/11.1cm in length and when in position on the top of the stumps shall not project more than $\frac{1}{2}$ inch/1.3cm above them.

Notes

(a) Dispensing with Bails
In a high wind the umpires may decide to dispense with the use of bails.

(b) Junior Cricket
For junior cricket, as defined by the local governing body, the following measurements for the wickets shall apply:

Width – 8 inches/20.32cm.
Pitched – 21 yards/19.20m.
Height – 27 inches/68.58cm.
Bails – each $3\frac{7}{8}$ inches/9.84cm in length and should not project more than $\frac{1}{2}$ inch/1.3cm above the stumps.

LAW 9. THE BOWLING, POPPING AND RETURN CREASES

1. The Bowling Crease

The bowling crease shall be marked in line with the stumps at each end and shall be 8 feet 8 inches/2.64m in length, with the stumps in the centre.

2. The Popping Crease

The popping crease, which is the back edge of the crease marking, shall be in front of and parallel with the bowling crease. It shall have the back edge of the crease marking 4 feet/ 1.22m from the centre of the stumps and shall extend to a minimum of 6 feet/1.83m on either side of the line of the wicket.

The popping crease shall be considered to be unlimited in length.

3. The Return Crease

The return crease marking, of which the inside edge is the crease, shall be at each end of the bowling crease and at right angles to it. The return crease shall be marked to a minimum of 4 feet/1.22m behind the wicket and shall be considered to be unlimited in length. A forward extension shall be marked to the popping crease.

LAW 10. ROLLING, SWEEPING, MOWING, WATERING THE PITCH AND RE-MARKING OF CREASES

1. Rolling

During the match the pitch may be rolled at the request of the captain of the batting side, for a period of not more than seven minutes before the start of each innings, other than the first innings of the match, and before the start of each day's play. In addition, if, after the toss and before the first innings of the match, the start is delayed, the captain of the batting side shall have the right to have the pitch rolled for not more than seven minutes.

The pitch shall not otherwise be rolled during the match.

The seven minutes' rolling permitted before the start of a day's play shall take place not earlier than half an hour before the start of play and the captain of the batting side may delay such rolling until ten minutes before the start of play should he so desire.

If a captain declares an innings closed less than fifteen minutes before the resumption of play, and the other captain is thereby prevented from exercising his option of seven minutes' rolling or if he is so prevented for any other reason, the time for rolling shall be taken out of the normal playing time.

2. Sweeping

Such sweeping of the pitch as is necessary during the match shall be done so that the seven minutes allowed for rolling the pitch, provided for in 1 above, is not affected.

3. Mowing

(a) Responsibilities of Ground Authority and of Umpires
All mowings which are carried out before the toss for innings shall be the responsibility of the ground authority; thereafter they shall be carried out under the supervision of the umpires. See Law 7.2 (Selection and Preparation).

(b) Initial Mowing
The pitch shall be mown before play begins on the day the match is scheduled to start, or in the case of a delayed start on the day the match is expected to start. See 3(a) above (Responsibilities of Ground Authority and of Umpires).

(c) Subsequent Mowings in a Match of Two or More Days' Duration
In a match of two or more days' duration, the pitch shall be mown daily before play begins. Should this mowing not take place because of weather conditions, rest days or other reasons, the pitch shall be mown on the first day on which the match is resumed.

(d) Mowing of the Outfield in a Match of Two or More Days' Duration
In order to ensure that conditions are as similar as possible for both sides, the outfield shall normally be mown before the commencement of play on each day of the match, if ground and weather conditions allow. See Note (b) to this Law.

4. Watering

The pitch shall not be watered during a match.

5. Re-marking Creases

Whenever possible the creases shall be re-marked.

6. Maintenance of Foot-holes

In wet weather, the umpires shall ensure that the holes made by the bowlers and batsmen are cleaned out and dried whenever necessary to facilitate play. In matches of two or more days' duration, the umpires shall allow, if necessary, the re-turfing of foot-holes made by the bowler in his delivery stride, or the use of quick-setting fillings for the same purpose, before the start of each day's play.

7. Securing of Footholds and Maintenance of Pitch

During play, the umpires shall allow either batsman to beat the pitch with his bat and players to secure their footholds by the use of sawdust, provided that no damage to the pitch is so caused, and Law 42 (Unfair Play) is not contravened.

Notes

(a) Non-turf Pitches
The above Law 10 applies to turf pitches.

The game is played on non-turf pitches in many countries at various levels. Whilst the conduct of the game on these surfaces should always be in accordance with the Laws of Cricket, it is recognised that it may sometimes be necessary for governing bodies to lay down special playing conditions to suit the type of non-turf pitch used in their country.

In matches played against touring teams, any special playing conditions should be agreed in advance by both parties.

(b) Mowing of the Outfield in a Match of Two or More Days' Duration
If, for reasons other than ground and weather conditions, daily and complete mowing is not possible, the ground authority shall notify the captains and umpires, before the toss for innings, of the procedure to be adopted for such mowing during the match.

(c) Choice of Roller
If there is more than one roller available, the captain of the batting side shall have a choice.

LAW 11. COVERING THE PITCH

1. Before the Start of a Match

Before the start of a match, complete covering of the pitch shall be allowed.

2. During a Match

The pitch shall not be completely covered during a match unless prior arrangement or regulations so provide.

3. Covering Bowlers' Run-up

Whenever possible, the bowlers' run-up shall be covered, but the covers so used shall not extend further than 4 feet/1.22m in front of the popping crease.

Note

(a) Removal of Covers
The covers should be removed as promptly as possible whenever the weather permits.

LAW 12. INNINGS

1. Number of Innings

A match shall be of one or two innings of each side according to agreement reached before the start of play.

2. Alternate Innings

In a two-innings match each side shall take their innings alternately except in the case provided for in Law 13 (The Follow-on).

3. The Toss

The captains shall toss for the choice of innings on the field of play not later than fifteen minutes before the time scheduled for the match to start, or before the time agreed upon for play to start.

4. Choice of Innings

The winner of the toss shall notify his decision to bat or to field to the opposing captain not later than ten minutes before the time scheduled for the match to start, or before the time agreed upon for play to start. The decision shall not thereafter be altered.

5. Continuation after One Innings of Each Side

Despite the terms of 1 above, in a one-innings match, when a result has been reached on the first innings, the captains may agree to the continuation of play if, in their opinion, there is a prospect of carrying the game to a further issue in the time left. See Law 21 (Result).

Notes

(a) Limited Innings – One-innings Match
In a one-innings match, each innings may, by agreement, be limited by a number of overs or by a period of time.

(b) Limited Innings – Two-innings Match
In a two-innings match, the first innings of each side may, by agreement, be limited to a number of overs or by a period of time.

LAW 13. THE FOLLOW-ON

1. Lead on First Innings

In a two-innings match the side which bats first and leads by 200 runs in a match of five days or more, by 150 runs in a three-day or four-day match, by 100 runs in a two-day match, or by 75 runs in a one-day match, shall have the option of requiring the other side to follow their innings.

2. Day's Play Lost

If no play takes place on the first day of a match of two or more days' duration, 1 above shall apply in accordance with the number of days' play remaining from the actual start of the match.

LAW 14. DECLARATIONS

1. Time of Declaration

The captain of the batting side may declare an innings closed at any time during a match, irrespective of its duration.

2. Forfeiture of Second Innings

A captain may forfeit his second innings, provided his decision to do so is notified to the opposing captain and umpires in sufficient time to allow seven minutes' rolling of the pitch. See Law 10 (Rolling, Sweeping, Mowing, Watering the Pitch and Re-marking of Creases). The normal ten-minute interval between innings shall be applied.

LAW 15. START OF PLAY

1. Call of Play

At the start of each innings and of each day's play, and on the resumption of play after any interval or interruption, the umpire at the bowler's end shall call "play".

2. Practice on the Field

At no time on any day of the match shall there be any bowling or batting practice on the pitch.

No practice may take place on the field if, in the opinion of the umpires, it could result in a waste of time.

3. Trial Run-up

No bowler shall have a trial run-up after "play" has been called in any session of play, except at the fall of a wicket when an umpire may allow such a trial run-up if he is satisfied that it will not cause any waste of time.

LAW 16. INTERVALS

1. Length

The umpire shall allow such intervals as have been agreed upon for meals, and ten minutes between each innings.

2. Luncheon Interval – Innings Ending or Stoppage within Ten Minutes of Interval

If an innings ends or there is a stoppage caused by weather or bad light within ten minutes of the agreed time for the luncheon interval, the interval shall be taken immediately.

The time remaining in the session of play shall be added to the agreed length of the interval but no extra allowance shall be made for the ten-minute interval between innings.

3. Tea Interval – Innings Ending or Stoppage within Thirty Minutes of Interval

If an innings ends or there is a stoppage caused by weather or bad light within thirty minutes of the agreed time for the tea interval, the interval shall be taken immediately.

The interval shall be of the agreed length and, if applicable, shall include the ten-minute interval between innings.

4. Tea Interval – Continuation of Play

If, at the agreed time for the tea interval, nine wickets are down, play shall continue for a period not exceeding thirty minutes or until the innings is concluded.

5. Tea Interval – Agreement to Forgo

At any time during the match, the captains may agree to forgo a tea interval.

6. Intervals for Drinks

If both captains agree before the start of a match that intervals for drinks may be taken, the option to take such intervals shall be available to either side. These intervals shall be restricted to one per session, shall be kept as short as possible, shall not be taken in the last hour of the match, and in any case shall not exceed five minutes.

The agreed times for these intervals shall be strictly adhered to, except that if a wicket falls within five minutes of the agreed time then drinks shall be taken out immediately.

If an innings ends or there is a stoppage caused by weather or bad light within thirty minutes of the agreed time for a drinks interval, there will be no interval for drinks in that session.

At any time during the match the captains may agree to forgo any such drinks interval.

Notes

(a) Tea Interval – One-day Match
In a one-day match, a specific time for the tea interval need not necessarily be arranged, and it may be agreed to take this interval between the innings of a one-innings match.

(b) Changing the Agreed Time of Intervals
In the event of the ground, weather or light conditions causing a suspension of play, the umpires, after consultation with the captains, may decide in the interests of time-saving to bring forward the time of the luncheon or tea interval.

LAW 17. CESSATION OF PLAY

1. Call of Time

The umpire at the bowler's end shall call "time" on the cessation of play before any interval or interruption of play, at the end of each day's play, and at the conclusion of the match. See Law 27 (Appeals).

2. Removal of Bails

After the call of "time", the umpires shall remove the bails from both wickets.

3. Starting a Last Over

The last over before an interval or the close of play shall be started provided the umpire, after walking at his normal pace, has arrived at his position behind the stumps at the bowler's end before time has been reached.

4. Completion of the Last Over of a Session

The last over before an interval or the close of play shall be completed unless a batsman is out or retires during that over within two minutes of the interval or the close of play or unless the players have occasion to leave the field.

5. Completion of the Last Over of a Match

An over in progress at the close of play on the final day of a match shall be completed at the request of either captain, even if a wicket falls after time has been reached.

If, during the last over, the players have occasion to leave the field, the umpires shall call "time" and there shall be no resumption of play and the match shall be at an end.

6. Last Hour of Match – Number of Overs

The umpires shall indicate when one hour of playing time of the match remains according to the agreed hours of play. The next over after that moment shall be the first of a minimum of 20 six-ball overs (15 eight-ball overs), provided a result is not reached earlier or there is no interval or interruption of play.

7. Last Hour of Match – Intervals between Innings and Interruptions of Play

If, at the commencement of the last hour of the match, an interval or interruption of play is in progress or if, during the last hour, there is an interval between innings or an interruption of play, the minimum number of overs to be bowled on the resumption of play shall be reduced in proportion to the duration, within the last hour of the match, of any such interval or interruption.

The minimum number of overs to be bowled after the resumption of play shall be calculated as follows:

(a) In the case of an interval or interruption of play being in progress at the commencement of the last hour of the match, or in the case of a first interval or interruption, a deduction shall be made from the minimum of 20 six-ball overs (or 15 eight-ball overs).

(b) If there is a later interval or interruption, a further deduction shall be made from the minimum number of overs which should have been bowled following the last resumption of play.

(c) These deductions shall be based on the following factors:

- (i) The number of overs already bowled in the last hour of the match or, in the case of a later interval or interruption, in the last session of play.
- (ii) The number of overs lost as a result of the interval or interruption allowing one six-ball over for every full three minutes (or one eight-ball over for every full four minutes) of interval or interruption.
- (iii) Any over left uncompleted at the end of an innings to be excluded from these calculations.
- (iv) Any over left uncompleted at the start of an interruption of play to be completed when play is resumed and to count as one over bowled.
- (v) An interval to start with the end of an innings and to end ten minutes later; an interruption to start on the call of "time" and to end on the call of "play".

(d) In the event of an innings being completed and a new innings commencing during the last hour of the match, the number of overs to be bowled in the new innings shall be calculated on the basis of one six-ball over for every three minutes or part thereof remaining for play (or one eight-ball over for every four minutes or part thereof remaining for play); or alternatively on the basis that sufficient overs be bowled to enable the full minimum quota of overs to be completed under circumstances governed by (a), (b) and (c) above. In all such cases the alternative which allows the greater number of overs shall be employed.

8. Bowler Unable to Complete an Over during Last Hour of the Match

If, for any reason, a bowler is unable to complete an over during the period of play referred to in 6 above, Law 22.7 (Bowler Incapacitated or Suspended during an Over) shall apply.

LAW 18. SCORING

1. A Run

The score shall be reckoned by runs. A run is scored:

(a) So often as the batsmen, after a hit or at any time while the ball is in play, shall have crossed and made good their ground from end to end.

(b) When a boundary is scored. See Law 19 (Boundaries).

(c) When penalty runs are awarded. See 6 below.

2. Short Runs

(a) If either batsman runs a short run, the umpire shall call and signal "one short" as soon as the ball becomes dead and that run shall not be scored. A run is short if a batsman fails to make good his ground on turning for a further run.

(b) Although a short run shortens the succeeding one, the latter, if completed, shall count.

(c) If either or both batsmen deliberately run short the umpire shall, as soon as he sees that the fielding side have no chance of dismissing either batsman, call and signal "dead ball" and disallow any runs attempted or previously scored. The batsmen shall return to their original ends.

(d) If both batsmen run short in one and the same run, only one run shall be deducted.

(e) Only if 3 or more runs are attempted can more than one be short and then, subject to (c) and (d) above, all runs so called shall be disallowed. If there has been more than one short run the umpires shall instruct the scorers as to the number of runs disallowed.

3. Striker Caught

If the striker is caught, no run shall be scored.

4. Batsman Run Out

If a batsman is run out, only that run which was being attempted shall not be scored. If, however, an injured striker himself is run out, no runs shall be scored. See Law 2.7 (Transgression of the Laws by an Injured Batsman or Runner).

5. Batsman Obstructing the Field

If a batsman is out Obstructing the Field, any runs completed before the obstruction occurs shall be scored unless such obstruction prevents a catch being made, in which case no runs shall be scored.

6. Runs Scored for Penalties

Runs shall be scored for penalties under Laws 20 (Lost Ball), 24 (No-ball), 25 (Wide-ball), 41.1 (Fielding the Ball) and for boundary allowances under Law 19 (Boundaries).

7. Batsman Returning to Wicket he has Left

If, while the ball is in play, the batsmen have crossed in running, neither shall return to the wicket he has left, even though a short run has been called or no run has been scored as in the case of a catch. Batsmen, however, shall return to the wickets they originally left in the cases of a boundary and of any disallowance of runs and of an injured batsman being, himself, run out. See Law 2.7 (Transgression by an Injured Batsman or Runner).

Note

(a) Short Run

A striker taking stance in front of his popping crease may run from that point without penalty.

LAW 19. BOUNDARIES

1. The Boundary of the Playing Area

Before the toss for innings, the umpires shall agree with both captains on the boundary of the playing area. The boundary shall, if possible, be marked by a white line, a rope laid on the ground, or a fence. If flags or posts only are used to mark a boundary, the imaginary line joining such points shall be regarded as the boundary. An obstacle, or person, within the playing area shall not be regarded as a boundary unless so decided by the umpires before the toss for innings. Sightscreens within, or partially within, the playing area shall be regarded as the boundary and when the ball strikes or passes within or under or directly over any part of the screen, a boundary shall be scored.

2. Runs Scored for Boundaries

Before the toss for innings, the umpires shall agree with both captains the runs to be allowed for boundaries, and in deciding the allowance for them, the umpires and captains shall be guided by the prevailing custom of the ground. The allowance for a boundary shall normally be 4 runs, and 6 runs for all hits pitching over and clear of the boundary line or fence, even though the ball has been previously touched by a fieldsman. 6 runs shall also be scored if a fieldsman, after catching a ball, carries it over the boundary. See Law 32 (Caught) Note (a). 6 runs shall not be scored when a ball struck by the striker hits a sightscreen full pitch if the screen is within, or partially within, the playing area, but if the ball is struck directly over a sightscreen so situated, 6 runs shall be scored.

3. A Boundary

A boundary shall be scored and signalled by the umpire at the bowler's end whenever, in his opinion:

(a) A ball in play touches or crosses the boundary, however marked.

(b) A fieldsman with ball in hand touches or grounds any part of his person on or over a boundary line.

(c) A fieldsman with ball in hand grounds any part of his person over a boundary fence or board. This allows the fieldsman to touch or lean on or over a boundary fence or board in preventing a boundary.

4. Runs Exceeding Boundary Allowance

The runs completed at the instant the ball reaches the boundary shall count if they exceed the boundary allowance.

5. Overthrows or Wilful Act of a Fieldsman

If the boundary results from an overthrow or from the wilful act of a fieldsman, any runs already completed and the allowance shall be added to the score. The run in progress shall count provided that the batsmen have crossed at the instant of the throw or act.

Note

(a) Position of Sightscreens
Sightscreens should, if possible, be positioned wholly outside the playing area, as near as possible to the boundary line.

LAW 20. LOST BALL

1. Runs Scored

If a ball in play cannot be found or recovered, any fieldsman may call "lost ball" when 6 runs shall be added to the score; but if more than 6 have been run before "lost ball" is called, as many runs as have been completed shall be scored. The run in progress shall count provided that the batsmen have crossed at the instant of the call of "lost ball".

2. How Scored

The runs shall be added to the score of the striker if the ball has been struck, but otherwise to the score of byes, leg-byes, no-balls or wides as the case may be.

LAW 21. THE RESULT

1. A Win – Two-innings Matches

The side which has scored a total of runs in excess of that scored by the opposing side in its two completed innings shall be the winners.

2. A Win – One-innings Matches

(a) One-innings matches, unless played out as in 1 above, shall be decided on the first innings, but see Law 12.5 (Continuation after One Innings of Each Side).

(b) If the captains agree to continue play after the completion of one innings of each side in accordance with Law 12.5 (Continuation after One Innings of Each Side) and a result is not achieved on the second innings, the first innings result shall stand.

3. Umpires Awarding a Match

(a) A match shall be lost by a side which, during the match, (i) refuses to play, or (ii) concedes defeat, and the umpires shall award the match to the other side.

(b) Should both batsmen at the wickets or the fielding side leave the field at any time without the agreement of the umpires, this shall constitute a refusal to play and, on appeal, the umpires shall award the match to the other side in accordance with (a) above.

4. A Tie

The result of a match shall be a tie when the scores are equal at the conclusion of play, but only if the side batting last has completed its innings.

If the scores of the completed first innings of a one-day match are equal, it shall be a tie but only if the match has not been played out to a further conclusion.

5. A Draw

A match not determined in any of the ways as in 1, 2, 3 and 4 above shall count as a draw.

6. Correctness of Result

Any decision as to the correctness of the scores shall be the responsibility of the umpires. See Law 3.14 (Correctness of Scores).

If, after the umpires and players have left the field in the belief that the match has been concluded, the umpires decide that a mistake in scoring has occurred, which affects the result, and provided time has not been reached, they shall order play to resume and to continue until the agreed finishing time unless a result is reached earlier.

If the umpires decide that a mistake has occurred and time has been reached, the umpires shall immediately inform both captains of the necessary corrections to the scores and, if applicable, to the result.

7. Acceptance of Result

In accepting the scores as notified by the scorers and agreed by the umpires, the captains of both sides thereby accept the result.

Notes

(a) Statement of Results

The result of a finished match is stated as a win by runs, except in the case of a win by the side batting last when it is by the number of wickets still then to fall.

(b) Winning Hit or Extras

As soon as the side has won, see 1 and 2 above, the umpire shall call "time", the match is finished, and nothing that happens thereafter other than as a result of a mistake in scoring (see 6 above) shall be regarded as part of the match.

However, if a boundary constitutes the winning hit – or extras – and the boundary allowance exceeds the number of runs required to win the match, such runs scored shall be credited to the side's total and, in the case of a hit, to the striker's score.

LAW 22. THE OVER

1. Number of Balls

The ball shall be bowled from each wicket alternately in overs of either six or eight balls according to agreement before the match.

2. Call of "Over"

When the agreed number of balls has been bowled, and as the ball becomes dead or when it becomes clear to the umpire at the bowler's end that both the fielding side and the batsmen at the wicket have ceased to regard the ball as in play, the umpire shall call "over" before leaving the wicket.

3. No-ball or Wide-ball

Neither a no-ball nor a wide-ball shall be reckoned as one of the over.

4. Umpire Miscounting

If an umpire miscounts the number of balls, the over as counted by the umpire shall stand.

5. Bowler Changing Ends

A bowler shall be allowed to change ends as often as desired, provided only that he does not bowl two overs consecutively in an innings.

6. The Bowler Finishing an Over

A bowler shall finish an over in progress unless he be incapacitated or be suspended under Law 42.8 (The Bowling of Fast Short-pitched Balls), 9 (The Bowling of Fast High Full Pitches), 10 (Time Wasting) and 11 (Players Damaging the Pitch). If an over is left incomplete for any reason at the start of an interval or interruption of play, it shall be finished on the resumption of play.

7. Bowler Incapacitated or Suspended during an Over

If, for any reason, a bowler is incapacitated while running up to bowl the first ball of an over, or is incapacitated or suspended during an over, the umpire shall call and signal "dead ball" and another bowler shall be allowed to bowl or complete the over from the same end, provided only that he shall not bowl two overs, or part thereof, consecutively in one innings.

8. Position of Non-striker

The batsman at the bowler's end shall normally stand on the opposite side of the wicket to that from which the ball is being delivered, unless a request to do otherwise is granted by the umpire.

LAW 23. DEAD BALL

1. The Ball Becomes Dead

When:

(a) It is finally settled in the hands of the wicket-keeper or the bowler.

(b) It reaches or pitches over the boundary.

(c) A batsman is out.

(d) Whether played or not, it lodges in the clothing or equipment of a batsman or the clothing of an umpire.

(e) A ball lodges in a protective helmet worn by a member of the fielding side.

(f) A penalty is awarded under Law 20 (Lost Ball) or Law 41.1 (Fielding the Ball).

(g) The umpire calls "over" or "time".

2. Either Umpire Shall Call and Signal "Dead Ball"

When:

(a) He intervenes in a case of unfair play.

(b) A serious injury to a player or umpire occurs.

(c) He is satisfied that, for an adequate reason, the striker is not ready to receive the ball and makes no attempt to play it.

(d) The bowler drops the ball accidentally before delivery, or the ball does not leave his hand for any reason.

(e) One or both bails fall from the striker's wicket before he receives delivery.

(f) He leaves his normal position for consultation.

(g) He is required to do so under Law 26.3 (Disallowance of Leg-byes).

3. The Ball Ceases to be Dead

When:

(a) The bowler starts his run-up or bowling action.

4. The Ball is Not Dead

When:

(a) It strikes an umpire (unless it lodges in his dress).

(b) The wicket is broken or struck down (unless a batsman is out thereby).

(c) A unsuccessful appeal is made.

(d) The wicket is broken accidentally either by the bowler during his delivery or by a batsman in running.

(e) The umpire has called "no-ball" or "wide".

Notes

(a) Ball Finally Settled
Whether the ball is finally settled or not – see 1(a) above – must be a question for the umpires alone to decide.

(b) Action on Call of "Dead Ball"

(i) If "dead ball" is called prior to the striker receiving a delivery, the bowler shall be allowed an additional ball.

(ii) If "dead ball" is called after the striker receives a delivery, the bowler shall not be allowed an additional ball, unless a "no-ball" or "wide" has been called.

LAW 24. NO-BALL

1. Mode of Delivery

The umpire shall indicate to the striker whether the bowler intends to bowl over or round the wicket, overarm or underarm, right- or left-handed. Failure on the part of the bowler to indicate in advance a change in his mode of delivery is unfair and the umpire shall call and signal "no-ball".

2. Fair Delivery – The Arm

For a delivery to be fair the ball must be bowled, not thrown – see Note (a) below. If either umpire is not entirely satisfied with the absolute fairness of a delivery in this respect he shall call and signal "no-ball" instantly upon delivery.

3. Fair Delivery – The Feet

The umpire at the bowler's wicket shall call and signal "no-ball" if he is not satisfied that in the delivery stride:

(a) The bowler's back foot has landed within and not touching the return crease or its forward extension; or

(b) Some part of the front foot whether grounded or raised was behind the popping crease.

4. Bowler Throwing at Striker's Wicket before Delivery

If the bowler, before delivering the ball, throws it at the striker's wicket in an attempt to run him out, the umpire shall call and signal "no-ball". See Law 42.12 (Batsman Unfairly Stealing a Run) and Law 38 (Run Out).

5. Bowler Attempting to Run Out Non-striker before Delivery

If the bowler, before delivering the ball, attempts to run out the non-striker, any runs which result shall be allowed and shall be scored as no-balls. Such an attempt shall not count as a ball in the over. The umpire shall not call "no-ball". See Law 42.12 (Batsman Unfairly Stealing a Run).

6. Infringement of Laws by a Wicket-keeper or a Fieldsman

The umpire shall call and signal "no-ball" in the event of the wicket-keeper infringing Law 40.1 (Position of Wicket-keeper) or a fieldsman infringing Law 41.2 (Limitation of On-side Fieldsmen) or Law 41.3 (Position of Fieldsmen).

7. Revoking a Call

An umpire shall revoke the call "no-ball" if the ball does not leave the bowler's hand for any reason. See Law 23.2 (Either Umpire Shall Call and Signal "Dead Ball").

8. Penalty

A penalty of 1 run for a no-ball shall be scored if no runs are made otherwise.

9. Runs from a No-ball

The striker may hit a no-ball and whatever runs result shall be added to his score. Runs made otherwise from a no-ball shall be scored no-balls.

10. Out from a No-ball

The striker shall be out from a no-ball if he breaks Law 34 (Hit the Ball Twice) and either batsman may be run out or shall be given out if either breaks Law 33 (Handled the Ball) or Law 37 (Obstructing the Field).

11. Batsman Given Out off a No-ball

Should a batsman be given out off a no-ball the penalty for bowling it shall stand unless runs are otherwise scored.

Notes

(a) Definition of a Throw
A ball shall be deemed to have been thrown if, in the opinion of either umpire, the process of straightening the bowling arm, whether it be partial or complete, takes place during that part of the delivery swing which directly precedes the ball leaving the hand. This definition shall not debar a bowler from the use of the wrist in the delivery swing.

(b) No-ball Not Counting in Over
A no-ball shall not be reckoned as one of the over. See Law 22.3 (No-ball or Wide-ball).

LAW 25. WIDE-BALL

1. Judging a Wide

If the bowler bowls the ball so high over or so wide of the wicket that, in the opinion of the umpire, it passes out of the reach of the striker, standing in a normal guard position, the umpire shall call and signal "wide-ball" as soon as it has passed the line of the striker's wicket.

The umpire shall not adjudge a ball as being wide if:

(a) The striker, by moving from his guard position, causes the ball to pass out of his reach.

(b) The striker moves and thus brings the ball within his reach.

2. Penalty

A penalty of 1 run for a wide shall be scored if no runs are made otherwise.

3. Ball Coming to Rest in Front of the Striker

If a ball which the umpire considers to have been delivered comes to rest in front of the line of the striker's wicket, "wide" shall not be called. The striker has a right, without interference from the fielding side, to make one attempt to hit the ball. If the fielding side interfere, the umpire shall replace the ball where it came to rest and shall order the fieldsmen to resume the places they occupied in the field before the ball was delivered.

The umpire shall call and signal "dead ball" as soon as it is clear that the striker does not intend to hit the ball, or after the striker has made an unsuccessful attempt to hit the ball.

4. Revoking a Call

The umpire shall revoke the call if the striker hits a ball which has been called "wide".

5. Ball Not Dead

The ball does not become dead on the call of "wide-ball" – see Law 23.4 (The Ball is Not Dead).

6. Runs Resulting from a Wide

All runs which are run or result from a wide-ball which is not a no-ball shall be scored wide-balls, or if no runs are made 1 shall be scored.

7. Out from a Wide

The striker shall be out from a wide-ball if he breaks Law 35 (Hit Wicket), or Law 39 (Stumped). Either batsman may be run out and shall be out if he breaks Law 33 (Handled the Ball), or Law 37 (Obstructing the Field).

8. Batsman Given Out off a Wide

Should a batsman be given out off a wide, the penalty for bowling it shall stand unless runs are otherwise made.

Note

(a) Wide-ball Not Counting in Over
A wide-ball shall not be reckoned as one of the over – see Law 22.3 (No-ball or Wide-ball).

LAW 26. BYE AND LEG-BYE

1. Byes

If the ball, not having been called "wide" or "no-ball", passes the striker without touching his bat or person, and any runs are obtained, the umpire shall signal "bye" and the run or runs shall be credited as such to the batting side.

2. Leg-byes

If the ball, not having been called "wide" or "no-ball", is unintentionally deflected by the striker's dress or person, except a hand holding the bat, and any runs are obtained the umpire shall signal "leg-bye" and the run or runs so scored shall be credited as such to the batting side.

Such leg-byes shall be scored only if, in the opinion of the umpire, the striker has:

(a) Attempted to play the ball with his bat; or

(b) Tried to avoid being hit by the ball.

3. Disallowance of Leg-byes

In the case of a deflection by the striker's person, other than in 2(a) and (b) above, the umpire shall call and signal "dead ball" as soon as 1 run has been completed or when it is clear that a run is not being attempted, or the ball has reached the boundary.

On the call and signal of "dead ball" the batsmen shall return to their original ends and no runs shall be allowed.

LAW 27. APPEALS

1. Time of Appeals

The umpires shall not give a batsman out unless appealed to by the other side which shall be done prior to the bowler beginning his run-up or bowling action to deliver the next ball. Under Law 23.1 (f) (The Ball Becomes Dead), the ball is dead on "over" being called; this does not, however, invalidate an appeal made prior to the first ball of the following over provided "time" has not been called – see Law 17.1 (Call of Time).

2. An Appeal "How's That?"

An appeal "How's That?" shall cover all ways of being out.

3. Answering Appeals

The umpire at the bowler's wicket shall answer appeals before the other umpire in all cases except those arising out of Law 35 (Hit Wicket) or Law 39 (Stumped) or Law 38 (Run Out) when this occurs at the striker's wicket.

When either umpire has given a batsman not out, the other umpire shall, within his jurisdiction, answer the appeal on a further appeal, provided it is made in time in accordance with 1 above (Time of Appeals).

4. Consultation by Umpires

An umpire may consult with the other umpire on a point of fact which the latter may have been in a better position to see and shall then give his decision. If, after consultation, there is still doubt remaining the decision shall be in favour of the batsman.

5. Batsman Leaving his Wicket under a Misapprehension

The umpires shall intervene if satisfied that a batsman, not having been given out, has left his wicket under a misapprehension that he has been dismissed.

6. Umpire's Decision

The umpire's decision is final. He may alter his decision, provided that such alteration is made promptly.

7. Withdrawal of an Appeal

In exceptional circumstances the captain of the fielding side may seek permission of the umpire to withdraw an appeal provided the outgoing batsman has not left the playing area. If this is allowed, the umpire shall cancel his decision.

LAW 28. THE WICKET IS DOWN

1. Wicket Down

The wicket is down if:

(a) Either the ball or the striker's bat or person completely removes either bail from the top of the stumps. A disturbance of a bail, whether temporary or not, shall not constitute a complete removal, but the wicket is down if a bail in falling lodges between two of the stumps.

(b) Any player completely removes with his hand or arm a bail from the top of the stumps, provided that the ball is held in that hand or in the hand of the arm so used.

(c) When both bails are off, a stump is struck out of the ground by the ball, or a player strikes or pulls a stump out of the ground, provided that the ball is held in the hand(s) or in the hand of the arm so used.

2. One Bail Off

If one bail is off, it shall be sufficient for the purpose of putting the wicket down to remove the remaining bail, or to strike or pull any of the three stumps out of the ground in any of the ways stated in 1 above.

3. All the Stumps Out of the Ground

If all the stumps are out of the ground, the fielding side shall be allowed to put back one or more stumps in order to have an opportunity of putting the wicket down.

4. Dispensing with Bails

If owing to the strength of the wind, it has been agreed to dispense with the bails in accordance with Law 8, Note (a) (Dispensing with Bails), the decision as to when the wicket is down is one for the umpires to decide on the facts before them. In such circumstances and if the umpires so decide, the wicket shall be held to be down even though a stump has not been struck out of the ground.

Note

(a) Remaking the Wicket
If the wicket is broken while the ball is in play, it is not the umpire's duty to remake the wicket until the ball has become dead – see Law 23 (Dead Ball). A member of the fielding side, however, may remake the wicket in such circumstances.

LAW 29. BATSMAN OUT OF HIS GROUND

1. When out of his Ground

A batsman shall be considered to be out of his ground unless some part of his bat in his hand or of his person is grounded behind the line of the popping crease.

LAW 30. BOWLED

1. Out Bowled

The striker shall be out *Bowled* if:

(a) His wicket is bowled down, even if the ball first touches his bat or person.

(b) He breaks his wicket by hitting or kicking the ball on to it before the completion of a stroke, or as a result of attempting to guard his wicket. See Law 34.1 (Out Hit the Ball Twice).

Note

(a) Out Bowled – Not lbw
The striker is out bowled if the ball is deflected on to his wicket even though a decision against him would be justified under Law 36 (lbw).

LAW 31. TIMED OUT

1. Out Timed Out

An incoming batsman shall be out *Timed Out* if he wilfully takes more than two minutes to come in – the two minutes being timed from the moment a wicket falls until the new batsman steps on to the field of play.

If this is not complied with and if the umpire is satisfied that the delay was wilful and if an appeal is made, the new batsman shall be given out by the umpire at the bowler's end.

2. Time to be Added

The time taken by the umpires to investigate the cause of the delay shall be added at the normal close of play.

Notes

(a) Entry in Scorebook
The correct entry in the scorebook when a batsman is given out under this Law is "timed out", and the bowler does not get credit for the wicket.

(b) Batsmen Crossing on the Field of Play
It is an essential duty of the captains to ensure that the in-going batsman passes the out-going one before the latter leaves the field of play.

LAW 32. CAUGHT

1. Out Caught

The striker shall be out *Caught* if the ball touches his bat or if it touches below the wrist his hand or glove, holding the bat, and is subsequently held by a fieldsman before it touches the ground.

2. A Fair Catch

A catch shall be considered to have been fairly made if:

(a) The fieldsman is within the field of play throughout the act of making the catch.

(i) The act of making the catch shall start from the time when the fieldsman first handles the ball and shall end when he both retains complete control over the further disposal of the ball and remains within the field of play.

(ii) In order to be within the field of play, the fieldsman may not touch or ground any part of his person on or over a boundary line. When the boundary is marked by a fence or board the fieldsman may not ground any part of his person over the boundary fence or board, but may touch or lean over the boundary fence or board in completing the catch.

(b) The ball is hugged to the body of the catcher or accidentally lodges in his dress or, in the case of the wicket-keeper, in his pads. However, a striker may not be caught if a ball lodges in a protective helmet worn by a fieldsman, in which case the umpire shall call and signal "dead ball". See Law 23 (Dead Ball).

(c) The ball does not touch the ground even though a hand holding it does so in effecting the catch.

(d) A fieldsman catches the ball, after it has been lawfully played a second time by the striker, but only if the ball has not touched the ground since being first struck.

(e) A fieldsman catches the ball after it has touched an umpire, another fieldsman or the other batsman. However, a striker may not be caught if a ball has touched a protective helmet worn by a fieldsman.

(f) The ball is caught off an obstruction within the boundary provided it has not previously been agreed to regard the obstruction as a boundary.

3. Scoring of Runs

If a striker is caught, no run shall be scored.

Notes

(a) Scoring from an Attempted Catch
When a fieldsman carrying the ball touches or grounds any part of his person on or over a boundary marked by a line, 6 runs shall be scored.

(b) Ball Still in Play
If a fieldsman releases the ball before he crosses the boundary, the ball will be considered to be still in play and it may be caught by another fieldsman. However, if the original fieldsman returns to the field of play and handles the ball, a catch may not be made.

LAW 33. HANDLED THE BALL

1. Out Handled the Ball

Either batsman on appeal shall be out *Handled the Ball* if he wilfully touches the ball while in play with the hand not holding the bat unless he does so with the consent of the opposite side.

Note

(a) Entry in Scorebook
The correct entry in the scorebook when a batsman is given out under this Law is "handled the ball', and the bowler does not get credit for the wicket.

LAW 34. HIT THE BALL TWICE

1. Out Hit the Ball Twice

The striker, on appeal, shall be out *Hit the Ball Twice* if, after the ball is struck or is stopped by any part of his person, he wilfully strikes it again with his bat or person except for the sole purpose of guarding his wicket: this he may do with his bat or any part of his person other than his hands, but see Law 37.2 (Obstructing a Ball From Being Caught).

For the purpose of this Law, a hand holding the bat shall be regarded as part of the bat.

2. Returning the Ball to a Fieldsman

The striker, on appeal, shall be out under this Law if, without the consent of the opposite side, he uses his bat or person to return the ball to any of the fielding side.

3. Runs from Ball Lawfully Struck Twice

No runs except those which result from an overthrow or penalty – see Law 41 (The Fieldsman) – shall be scored from a ball lawfully struck twice.

Notes

(a) Entry in Scorebook
The correct entry in the scorebook when the striker is given out under this Law is "hit the ball twice", and the bowler does not get credit for the wicket.

(b) Runs Credited to the Batsman
Any runs awarded under 3 above as a result of an overthrow or penalty shall be credited to the striker, provided the ball in the first instance has touched the bat, or, if otherwise, as extras.

LAW 35. HIT WICKET

1. Out Hit Wicket

The striker shall be out *Hit Wicket* if, while the ball is in play:

(a) His wicket is broken with any part of his person, dress, or equipment as a result of any action taken by him in preparing to receive or in receiving a delivery, or in setting off for his first run, immediately after playing, or playing at, the ball.

(b) He hits down his wicket whilst lawfully making a second stroke for the purpose of guarding his wicket within the provisions of Law 34.1 (Out Hit the Ball Twice).

Notes

(a) Not Out Hit Wicket
A batsman is not out under this Law should his wicket be broken in any of the ways referred to in 1(a) above if:

(i) It occurs while he is in the act of running, other than in setting off for his first run immediately after playing at the ball, or while he is avoiding being run out or stumped.

(ii) The bowler after starting his run-up or bowling action does not deliver the ball; in which case the umpire shall immediately call and signal "dead ball".

(iii) It occurs whilst he is avoiding a throw-in at any time.

LAW 36. LEG BEFORE WICKET

1. Out lbw

The striker shall be out *lbw* in the circumstances set out below:

(a) Striker Attempting to Play the Ball
The striker shall be out lbw if he first intercepts with any part of his person, dress or equipment a fair ball which would have hit the wicket and which has not previously touched his bat or a hand holding the bat, provided that:

(i) The ball pitched in a straight line between wicket and wicket or on the off side of the striker's wicket, or in the case of a ball intercepted full pitch would have pitched in a straight line between wicket and wicket; and

(ii) The point of impact is in a straight line between wicket and wicket, even if above the level of the bails.

(b) Striker Making No Attempt to Play the Ball
The striker shall be out lbw even if the ball is intercepted outside the line of the off stump if, in the opinion of the umpire, he has made no genuine attempt to play the ball with his bat, but has intercepted the ball with some part of his person and if the circumstances set out in (a) above apply.

LAW 37. OBSTRUCTING THE FIELD

1. Wilful Obstruction

Either batsman, on appeal, shall be out *Obstructing the Field* if he wilfully obstructs the opposite side by word or action.

2. Obstructing a Ball From Being Caught

The striker, on appeal, shall be out should wilful obstruction by either batsman prevent a catch being made.

This shall apply even though the striker causes the obstruction in lawfully guarding his wicket under the provisions of Law 34. See Law 34.1 (Out Hit the Ball Twice).

Notes

(a) Accidental Obstruction
The umpires must decide whether the obstruction was wilful or not. The accidental interception of a throw-in by a batsman while running does not break this Law.

(b) Entry in Scorebook
The correct entry in the scorebook when a batsman is given out under this Law is "obstructing the field", and the bowler does not get credit for the wicket.

LAW 38. RUN OUT

1. Out Run Out

Either batsman shall be out *Run Out* if in running or at any time while the ball is in play – except in the circumstances described in Law 39 (Stumped) – he is out of his ground and his wicket is put down by the opposite side. If, however, a batsman in running makes good his ground he shall not be out run out if he subsequently leaves his ground, in order to avoid injury, and the wicket is put down.

2. "No-ball" Called

If a no-ball has been called, the striker shall not be given run out unless he attempts to run.

3. Which Batsman Is Out

If the batsmen have crossed in running, he who runs for the wicket which is put down shall be out; if they have not crossed, he who has left the wicket which is put down shall be out. If a batsman remains in his ground or returns to his ground and the other batsman joins him there, the latter shall be out if his wicket is put down.

4. Scoring of Runs

If a batsman is run out, only that run which is being attempted shall not be scored. If, however, an injured striker himself is run out, no runs shall be scored. See Law 2.7 (Transgression of the Laws by an Injured Batsman or Runner).

Notes

(a) Ball Played on to Opposite Wicket
If the ball is played on to the opposite wicket, neither batsman is liable to be run out unless the ball has been touched by a fieldsman before the wicket is broken.

(b) Entry in Scorebook
The correct entry in the scorebook when a batsman is given out under this Law is "run out", and the bowler does not get credit for the wicket.

LAW 39. STUMPED

1. Out Stumped

The striker shall be out *Stumped* if, in receiving the ball, not being a no-ball, he is out of his ground otherwise than in attempting a run and the wicket is put down by the wicket-keeper without the intervention of another fieldsman.

2. Action by the Wicket-keeper

The wicket-keeper may take the ball in front of the wicket in an attempt to stump the striker only if the ball has touched the bat or person of the striker.

Note

(a) Ball Rebounding from Wicket-keeper's Person
The striker may be out stumped if, in the circumstances stated in 1 above, the wicket is broken by a ball rebounding from the wicket-keeper's person or equipment or is kicked or thrown by the wicket-keeper on to the wicket.

LAW 40. THE WICKET-KEEPER

1. Position of Wicket-keeper

The wicket-keeper shall remain wholly behind the wicket until a ball delivered by the bowler touches the bat or person of the striker, or passes the wicket, or until the striker attempts a run.

In the event of the wicket-keeper contravening this Law, the umpire at the striker's end shall call and signal "no ball" at the instant of delivery or as soon as possible thereafter.

2. Restriction on Actions of the Wicket-keeper

If the wicket-keeper interferes with the striker's right to play the ball and to guard his wicket, the striker shall not be out except under Laws 33 (Handled the Ball), 34 (Hit the Ball Twice), 37 (Obstructing the Field), 38 (Run Out).

3. Interference with the Wicket-keeper by the Striker

If in the legitimate defence of his wicket, the striker interferes with the wicket-keeper, he shall not be out, except as provided for in Law 37.2 (Obstructing a Ball From Being Caught).

LAW 41. THE FIELDSMAN

1. Fielding the Ball

The fieldsman may stop the ball with any part of his person, but if he wilfully stops it otherwise, 5 runs shall be added to the run or runs already scored; if no run has been scored 5 penalty runs shall be awarded. The run in progress shall count provided that the batsmen have crossed at the instant of the act. If the ball has been struck, the penalty shall be added to the score of the striker, but otherwise to the scores of byes, leg-byes, no-balls or wides as the case may be.

2. Limitation of On-side Fieldsmen

The number of on-side fieldsmen behind the popping crease at the instant of the bowler's delivery shall not exceed two. In the event of infringement by the fielding side the umpire at the striker's end shall call and signal "no-ball" at the instant of delivery or as soon as possible thereafter.

3. Position of Fieldsmen

Whilst the ball is in play and until the ball has made contact with the bat or the striker's person or has passed his bat, no fieldsman, other than the bowler, may stand on or have any part of his person extended over the pitch (measuring 22 yards/20.12m × 10 feet/3.05m). In the event of a fieldsman contravening this Law, the umpire at the bowler's end shall call and signal "no-ball" at the instant of delivery or as soon as possible thereafter. See Law 40.1 (Position of Wicket-keeper).

Note

(a) Batsmen Changing Ends
The 5 runs referred to in 1 above are a penalty and the batsmen do not change ends solely by reason of this penalty.

LAW 42. UNFAIR PLAY

1. Responsibility of Captains

The captains are responsible at all times for ensuring that play is conducted within the spirit of the game as well as within the Laws.

2. Responsibility of Umpires

The umpires are the sole judges of fair and unfair play.

3. Intervention by the Umpire

The umpires shall intervene without appeal by calling and signalling "dead ball" in the case of unfair play, but should not otherwise interfere with the progress of the game except as required to do so by the Laws.

4. Lifting the Seam

A player shall not lift the seam of the ball for any reason. Should this be done, the umpires shall change the ball for one of similar condition to that in use prior to the contravention. See Note (a).

5. Changing the Condition of the Ball

Any member of the fielding side may polish the ball provided that such polishing wastes no time and that no artificial substance is used. No-one shall rub the ball on the ground or use any artificial substance or take any other action to alter the condition of the ball.

In the event of a contravention of this Law, the umpires, after consultation, shall change the ball for one of similar condition to that in use prior to the contravention.

This Law does not prevent a member of the fielding side from drying a wet ball, or removing mud from the ball. See Note (b).

6. Incommoding the Striker

An umpire is justified in intervening under this Law and shall call and signal "dead ball" if, in his opinion, any player of the fielding side incommodes the striker by any noise or action while he is receiving the ball.

7. Obstruction of a Batsman in Running

It shall be considered unfair if any fieldsman wilfully obstructs a batsman in running. In these circumstances the umpire shall call and signal "dead ball" and allow any completed runs and the run in progress, or alternatively any boundary scored.

8. The Bowling of Fast Short-pitched Balls

The bowling of fast short-pitched balls is unfair if, in the opinion of the umpire at the bowler's end, it constitutes an attempt to intimidate the striker. See Note (d).

Umpires shall consider intimidation to be the deliberate bowling of fast short-pitched balls which by their length, height and direction are intended or likely to inflict physical injury on the striker. The relative skill of the striker shall also be taken into consideration.

In the event of such unfair bowling, the umpire at the bowler's end shall adopt the following procedure:

(a) In the first instance the umpire shall call and signal "no-ball", caution the bowler and inform the other umpire, the captain of the fielding side and the batsmen of what has occurred.

(b) If this caution is ineffective, he shall repeat the above procedure and indicate to the bowler that this is a final warning.

(c) Both the above caution and final warning shall continue to apply even though the bowler may later change ends.

(d) Should the above warnings prove ineffective the umpire at the bowler's end shall:

- (i) At the first repetition call and signal "no-ball" and when the ball is dead direct the captain to take the bowler off forthwith and to complete the over with another bowler, provided that the bowler does not bowl two overs or part thereof consecutively. See Law 22.7 (Bowler Incapacitated or Suspended during an Over).
- (ii) Not allow the bowler, thus taken off, to bowl again in the same innings.
- (iii) Report the occurrence to the captain of the batting side as soon as the players leave the field for an interval.
- (iv) Report the occurrence to the executive of the fielding side and to any governing body responsible for the match, who shall take any further action which is considered to be appropriate against the bowler concerned.

9. The Bowling of Fast High Full Pitches

The bowling of fast high full pitches is unfair. See Note (e).

In the event of such unfair bowling the umpire at the bowler's end shall adopt the procedures of caution, final warnings, action against the bowler and reporting as set out in 8 above.

10. Time Wasting

Any form of time wasting is unfair.

(a) In the event of the captain of the fielding side wasting time or allowing any member of his side to waste time, the umpire at the bowler's end shall adopt the following procedure:

(i) In the first instance he shall caution the captain of the fielding side and inform the other umpire of what has occurred.

(ii) If this caution is ineffective he shall repeat the above procedure and indicate to the captain that this is a final warning.

(iii) The umpire shall report the occurrence to the captain of the batting side as soon as the players leave the field for an interval.

(iv) Should the above procedure prove ineffective the umpire shall report the occurrence to the executive of the fielding side and to any governing body responsible for that match, who shall take appropriate action against the captain and the players concerned.

(b) In the event of a bowler taking unnecessarily long to bowl an over the umpire at the bowler's end shall adopt the procedures, other than the calling of "no-ball", of caution, final warning, action against the bowler and reporting.

(c) In the event of a batsman wasting time (See Note (f)) other than in the manner described in Law 31 (Timed Out), the umpire at the bowler's end shall adopt the following procedure:

(i) In the first instance he shall caution the batsman and inform the other umpire at once, and the captain of the batting side, as soon as the players leave the field for an interval, of what has occurred.

(ii) If this proves ineffective, he shall repeat the caution, indicate to the batsman that this is a final warning and inform the other umpire.

(iii) The umpire shall report the occurrence to both captains as soon as the players leave the field for an interval.

(iv) Should the above procedure prove ineffective, the umpire shall report the occurrence to the executive of the batting side and to any governing body responsible for that match, who shall take appropriate action against the player concerned.

11. Players Damaging the Pitch

The umpires shall intervene and prevent players from causing damage to the pitch which may assist the bowlers of either side. See Note (c).

(a) In the event of any member of the fielding side damaging the pitch, the umpire shall follow the procedure of caution, final warning, and reporting as set out in 10(a) above.

(b) In the event of a bowler contravening this Law by running down the pitch after delivering the ball, the umpire at the bowler's end shall first caution the bowler. If this caution is ineffective the umpire shall adopt the procedures, other than the calling of "no-ball", of final warning, action against the bowler and reporting.

(c) In the event of a batsman damaging the pitch the umpire at the bowler's end shall follow the procedures of caution, final warning and reporting as set out in 10(c) above.

12. Batsman Unfairly Stealing a Run

Any attempt by the batsman to steal a run during the bowler's run-up is unfair. Unless the bowler attempts to run out either batsman – see Law 24.4 (Bowler Throwing at Striker's Wicket before Delivery) and Law 24.5 (Bowler Attempting to Run Out Non-striker before Delivery) – the umpire shall call and signal "dead ball" as soon as the batsmen cross in any such attempt to run. The batsmen shall then return to their original wickets.

13. Player's Conduct

In the event of a player failing to comply with the instructions of an umpire, criticising his decisions by word or action, or showing dissent, or generally behaving in a manner which might bring the game into disrepute, the umpire concerned shall, in the first place, report the matter to the other umpire and to the player's captain requesting the latter to take action. If this proves ineffective, the umpire shall report the incident as soon as possible to the executive of the player's team and to any governing body responsible for the match, who shall take any further action which is considered appropriate against the player or players concerned.

Notes

(a) The Condition of the Ball
Umpires shall make frequent and irregular inspections of the condition of the ball.

(b) Drying of a Wet Ball
A wet ball may be dried on a towel or with sawdust.

(c) Danger Area
The danger area on the pitch, which must be protected from damage by a bowler, shall be regarded by the umpires as the area contained by an imaginary line 4 feet/1.22m from the popping crease, and parallel to it, and within two imaginary and parallel lines drawn down the pitch from points on that line 1 foot/30.48cm on either side of the middle stump.

(d) Fast Short-pitched Balls
As a guide, a fast short-pitched ball is one which pitches short and passes, or would have passed, above the shoulder height of the striker standing in a normal batting stance at the crease.

(e) The Bowling of Fast Full Pitches
The bowling of one fast, high full pitch shall be considered to be unfair if, in the opinion of the umpire, it is deliberate, bowled at the striker, and if it passes or would have passed above the shoulder height of the striker when standing in a normal batting stance at the crease.

(f) Time Wasting by Batsmen
Other than in exceptional circumstances, the batsman should always be ready to take strike when the bowler is ready to start his run-up.

INTERNATIONAL CRICKET CONFERENCE

On June 15, 1909, representatives of cricket in England, Australia and South Africa met at Lord's and founded the Imperial Cricket Conference. Membership was confined to the governing bodies of cricket in countries within the British Commonwealth where Test cricket was played. India, New Zealand and West Indies were elected as members on May 31, 1926, Pakistan on July 21, 1953, and Sri Lanka on July 21, 1981. South Africa ceased to be a member of the ICC on leaving the British Commonwealth in May, 1961.

On July 15, 1965, the Conference was renamed the International Cricket Conference and new rules were adopted to permit the election of countries from outside the British Commonwealth.

CONSTITUTION

Chairman: The President of MCC for the time being or his nominee.
Secretary: The Secretary of MCC.
Foundation members: United Kingdom and Australia.
Full members: India, New Zealand, West Indies, Pakistan and Sri Lanka.
Associate members*: Argentina (1974), Bangladesh (1977), Bermuda (1966), Canada (1968), Denmark (1966), East Africa (1966), Fiji (1965), Gibraltar (1969), Hong Kong (1969), Israel (1974), Kenya (1981), Malaysia (1967), Netherlands (1966), Papua New Guinea (1973), Singapore (1974), USA (1965), West Africa (1976) and Zimbabwe (1981).

* *Year of election shown in parentheses.*

MEMBERSHIP

The following governing bodies for cricket shall be eligible for election.

Foundation Members: The governing bodies for cricket in the United Kingdom and Australia are known as Foundation Members, and while being Full Members of the Conference such governing bodies have certain additional rights as set out in the rules of the Conference.

Full Members: The governing body for cricket recognised by the Conference of a country, or countries associated for cricket purposes, of which the representative teams are accepted as qualified to play official Test matches.

Associate Members: The governing body for cricket recognised by the Conference of a country, or countries associated for cricket purposes, not qualifying as Full Members but where cricket is firmly established and organised.

Chairman: P. A. Snow (Fiji). *Deputy Chairman:* J. Buzaglo (Gibraltar). *Hon. Treasurer:* G. Davis (Israel).

TEST MATCHES

1. Duration of Test Matches

Within a maximum of 30 hours' playing time, the duration of Test matches shall be a matter for negotiation and agreement between the two countries in any particular series of Test matches.

When agreeing the Playing Conditions prior to the commencement of a Test series, the participating countries may:

(a) Extend the playing hours of the last Test beyond the limit of 30 hours, in a series in which, at the conclusion of the penultimate match, one side does not hold a lead of more than one match.

(b) Allow an extension of play by one hour on any of the first four days of a Test match, in the event of play being suspended for one hour or more on that day, owing to weather interference.

(c) Play on the rest day, conditions and circumstances permitting, should a full day's play be lost on either the second or third scheduled days of play.

(d) Make up time lost in excess of five minutes in each day's play owing to circumstances outside the game, other than acts of God.

Note. The umpires shall determine when such time shall be made up. This could, if conditions and circumstances permit, include the following day.

2. Qualification Rules

A cricketer is qualified to play in a Test match either by birth or residence.

(a) Qualification by birth. A cricketer, unless debarred by the Conference, is always eligible to play for the country of his birth.

(b) Qualification by residence. A cricketer, unless debarred by the Conference, shall be eligible to play for any country in which he is residing and has been residing during the four immediately preceding years, provided that he has not played for the country of his birth during that period.

Note. Notwithstanding anything hereinbefore contained, any player who has once played in a Test match for any country shall not afterwards be eligible to play in a Test match against that country, without the consent of its governing body.

FIRST-CLASS MATCHES

1. Definitions

(a) A match of three or more days' duration between two sides of eleven players officially adjudged first-class shall be regarded as a first-class fixture.

(b) In the following Rules the term "governing body" is restricted to Foundation Members, Full Members and Associate Members of the conference.

2. Rules

(a) Foundation and Full Members of the ICC shall decide the status of matches of three or more days' duration played in their countries.

(b) In matches of three or more days' duration played in countries which are not Foundation Members or Full Members of the ICC:

(i) If the visiting team comes from a country which is a Foundation or Full Member of the ICC, that country shall decide the status of matches.

(ii) If the visiting team does not come from a country which is a Foundation or Full Member of the ICC, or is a Commonwealth team composed of players from different countries, the ICC shall decide the status of matches.

Notes

(a) Governing bodies agree that the interest of first-class cricket will be served by ensuring that first-class status is *not* accorded to any match in which one or other of the teams taking part cannot on a strict interpretation of the definition be adjudged first-class.

(b) In case of any disputes arising from these Rules, the Secretary of the ICC shall refer the matter for decision to the Conference, failing unanimous agreement by postal communication being reached.

3. First-class Status

The following matches shall be regarded as first-class, subject to the provisions of Definitions (a) being completely complied with:

(a) In the British Isles and Eire

The following matches of three or more days' duration shall automatically be considered first-class:

(i) County Championship matches.

(ii) Official representative tourist matches from Full Member countries unless specifically excluded.

(iii) MCC v any first-class county.

(iv) Oxford v Cambridge and either University against first-class counties.

(v) Scotland v Ireland.

(b) In Australia

(i) Sheffield Shield matches.

(ii) Matches played by teams representing states of the Commonwealth of Australia between each other or against opponents adjudged first-class.

(c) In India

(i) Ranji Trophy matches.

(ii) Duleep Trophy matches.

(iii) Irani Trophy matches.

(iv) Matches played by teams representing state or regional associations affiliated to the Board of Control between each other or against opponents adjudged first-class.

(v) All three-day matches played against representative visiting sides.

(d) In New Zealand

(i) Shell Trophy matches.

(ii) Matches played by teams representing provinces or the North or South Islands between each other or against opponents adjudged first-class.

(e) In Pakistan

(i) Matches played by teams representing divisional associations affiliated to the Board of Control, between each other or against teams adjudged first-class.

(ii) Matches between the divisional associations and the Universities past and present XI.

(iii) Quaid-e-Azam Trophy matches.

(iv) BCCP Trophy Tournament matches.

(v) Pentangular Trophy Tournament matches.

(f) In Sri Lanka

(i) Matches of three days or more against touring sides adjudged first-class.

At the time of going to press details of domestic competitions with first-class status were not available.

(g) In West Indies

(i) Matches played by teams representing Barbados, Guyana, Jamaica, Trinidad, the Windward Islands and the Leeward Islands, either for the Shell Shield or against other opponents adjudged first-class.

(ii) The final of the inter-county tournament for the Jones Cup in Guyana between Berbice, Demerara and Essequibo.

(h) In all Foundation and Full Member countries represented on the Conference

(i) Test matches and matches against teams adjudged first-class played by official touring teams.

(ii) Official Test Trial matches.

(iii) Special matches between teams adjudged first-class by the governing body or bodies concerned.

MEETINGS IN 1982

TCCB SPRING MEETING

Delegates at the Spring Meeting of the TCCB, held at Lord's on March 9, spent much of their time formulating a policy for penalising the cricketers who were in South Africa on their unofficial tour. A meeting to settle this issue was scheduled for ten days later, but the Board were told that the financial implications could be crippling if either summer tour was jeopardised. Mr S. K. Wankhede, chairman of the Board of Control for Cricket in India, let it be known that their visit to England depended on a firm line being taken against Graham Gooch and his "rebel" team. (After a special meeting of the Board on March 19, it was announced that the fifteen players participating in the unofficial tour of South Africa were to be banned from selection for England for three years. "We are trying to maintain multi-racial barriers", said the chairman, Mr F. G. Mann. "The players have broken no law, none of our rules. We are not trying to penalise them, merely taking the minimum steps needed to protect cricket.")

Having failed to obtain the consent of Australia for a minimum of 100 overs on each Test day in 1981, the Board were pleased to reach agreement with both India and Pakistan for a daily minimum, weather permitting, of 96 overs.

A plan to cut the number of overs bowled to a side who had first failed to bowl their own 40 overs in the John Player League was abandoned. The idea had been mooted at the previous Winter Meeting, but the Board considered that it would place an extra burden on already over-taxed umpires.

Norman Gifford was confirmed as a Test selector, and P. B. H. May, the chairman of the panel, began his duties by seeking the counties' cooperation in producing Test players, stressing the important role of coaches and county managers. A. V. Bedser and A. C. Smith completed the selection committee.

INTERNATIONAL CRICKET CONFERENCE

Although delegates of the South African Cricket Union were in London at the time, they were not given a hearing by the International Cricket Conference during their meeting at Lord's on July 21 and 22. While referring to "various shades of opinion" within the Conference, regarding the strength of South Africa's case for re-election, Mr J. A. Bailey, secretary of the ICC, said that it was generally felt there was nothing constructive to be achieved by calling the South Africans to the meeting.

The draw for the Prudential World Cup, to be played in England from June 9–25, 1983, was made, with England and West Indies, as the finalists in 1979, being seeded to appear in separate groups, as, with their consent, were Zimbabwe, who had qualified as winners of the ICC Trophy, and Sri Lanka. To reduce the chances of a "freak result", caused by bad weather, it was decided that in the group matches each side should play one another twice. Group A would consist of England, New Zealand, Pakistan and Sri Lanka, and Group B of Australia, India, West Indies and Zimbabwe.

A move to make statutory in Test cricket the bowling of a minimum of 96 overs in a day, weather permitting, was rejected, objections to it being based on the shortness of the twilight in West Indies and on the Indian sub-continent. Sub-committees were to be set up, with a view to their reporting back to the next ICC meeting, to consider the merits of an international panel of umpires and the idea of an international code of conduct.

Neutral observers at Test matches were to be discontinued. They had, in any event, been only occasionally in evidence. Although discussed, the suggestion that a bowler's run-up should, by degrees, be reduced to a maximum of 25 yards failed to find favour. The excessive use of short-pitched bowling was deplored, and each member undertook, as before, to urge its representatives to aim at an average of 16.5 overs an hour. It was agreed that it should be written into the Laws of Cricket that if a ball strikes a helmet lying loose on the field it shall cost the fielding side 5 runs. When not being worn, helmets must be placed either behind the wicket-keeper or below ground.

The Conference declared its unanimous approval of the three-year ban from Test cricket imposed on those English players who had toured South Africa. They also reiterated that on no account should there be political interference by one country in the selection of the team of another.

TCCB WINTER MEETING

One theme emerging from the TCCB's Winter Meeting on December 14 was the need to obtain full value for spectators from touring teams' matches. Counties who failed to play their strongest available side in such matches were warned that their fixtures against future visitors could be jeopardised. It was assumed that, by this threat, the Board could attract a sponsor to replace Holts Products, who had ceased underwriting county matches against touring sides after 1981.

Following the success of the 96-overs-a-day experiment in the 1982 Test series, the Board planned to offer New Zealand a scheme for a minimum of 100 overs each day in the 1983 Tests. The experiment of Sunday play in Tests, with no rest day, would be continued in two of the four Tests against New Zealand.

An urgent review of the structure of the first-class game was established, even before the adjusted programme of 24 Championship fixtures in 1983 was given a trial. Normally, the outline for 1984 would have been floated for discussion, at least, by December 1982; but as they looked forward to two extra matches, some counties were already having second thoughts. Peter Lush said: "Counties are finding that the recession is starting to bite fairly sharply, and staging extra matches can be expensive. Some captains, too, have expressed reservations about increasing their commitments."

The registrations of various categories of cricketers came under review. At Yorkshire's request, a prohibition was imposed on any county approaching a young player born in another first-class county until the boy in question reached the age of sixteen. With regard to the rule on overseas players, Glamorgan asked for it to be reconsidered. They felt that the intended final reduction to one overseas player per county would take effect so slowly that some counties would find themselves at a disadvantage in the near future.

It was agreed that Test umpires' schedules would be planned so that the umpires had a break before and after Test matches.

The hours of play in the last three rounds of the NatWest Bank Trophy were adjusted so that the start would be at 10.30 a.m. instead of 10.00 a.m., which had been tried in 1982. The latest tea interval in the John Player League was put back from 4.10 p.m. to 4.15 p.m.

CRICKET BOOKS, 1982

A total of 72 titles was sent for review in 1982: and they quite certainly represent the highest general standard ever observed in one of these reviews.

At long intervals, cricket books appear which make most of the rest look ordinary. One such, even in as rich a year as this, is *The Roses Matches 1919–1939* (Souvenir Press; £9.95) by Neville Cardus; a posthumous collection of his reports on Yorkshire-Lancashire between the two wars; written for what he always regarded as *The Manchester Guardian*. They have a period – indeed, an elegant – quality about them, and certainly Sir Neville always wrote his accounts in the same, unabbreviated, flowing hand. He had, though, deadlines to meet; deadlines as strict as those of today. His work demands no allowances on that score. Here are his daily stories, sometimes as much as 2,000 words long, yet with an air of unhurried contemplation; rich in turn of phrase, humanity, humour; yet, also, sharp cricketing observation and – sometimes acerbic – criticism. Long hidden in the files of his newspaper, these reports have about them, at once, freshness and nostalgia. The great characters of the two counties – Ted Macdonald, Herbert Sutcliffe, Harry Makepeace, Wilfred Rhodes, Dick Tyldesley, Emmott Robinson, Eddie Paynter, George Macaulay, Cecil Parkin, Maurice Leyland, Dick Pollard, Len Hutton, Cyril Washbrook, Bill Bowes, "Buddy" Oldfield, Hedley Verity – not only bat and bowl but are their own three-dimensional figures again. Perhaps Sir Neville Cardus created a mythology of cricket. If it is a mythology it is an absorbing, nostalgic, masterly, utterly readable and moving mythology; such as no-one else has ever matched.

Benny Green's *Wisden Anthology 1940–1963* (Queen Anne Press; £25) is the third of his – physically – weighty collections from the running story of cricket history. Mr Green is a master anthologist; enthusiastic, yet balanced in judgement; infallibly thorough – he must have read every page of all those solid tomes to come up with the best – yet never ponderous. Even those few who possess a full set of *Wisden* are hardly likely, in the course of casual reading, to come up with such relishable pieces in such quantity. It is tragic, yet in the cricketing nature of things, that a considerable number of the most important items are obituary; but surveys, match reports (most patiently unearthed), tour accounts and wider essays, the histories of the centenary volume, and a perceptive introduction, extend the range of, surely, the finest bedside books ever created for cricketers. They will look forward with enthusiasm to the fourth volume.

Cricket art receives relatively slight attention from the game's writers; perhaps because neither its quality nor its quantity is great. It has two main groups; the mid-nineteenth century lithographs of C. J. Basébé, John Corbett Anderson and "Felix"; and the *Vanity Fair* cartoons which were an important facet of the social pattern of the latter quarter of that century. *The Cricketers of Vanity Fair* (Webb & Bower; £9.95) by Russell March is the first work devoted to the subject, and it deals, in thoroughly informed fashion, with all its aspects. For many it will seem most satisfactory that it reproduces in their original size and colouring 40 of the caricatures. They include several, some even as important as The Hon. Ivo Bligh – who is shown as Lord Darnley – not represented as cricketers: all with their accompanying text. There is, too, most valuable to collectors, a list of those of cricketing significance – not solely as players but, for instance, presidents of MCC – who would be included in a complete collection of *Vanity Fair* cricketers. Mr March provides, as well, notes on the artists, and background information on the magazine and its editorship. The 69 persons with cricketing connections among more than 2,000 caricatured in *Vanity Fair* may not seem a particularly important theme. These prints, though, are collected; they do, in fact, command relatively high prices; and no catalogue of them was available. It is a subject on which an increasing number of people want information; and here, at the first attempt, is the authoritative work on it.

Mike Brearley was different from other cricket captains. It can now be observed that he is different, also, from other cricket writers. Hitherto he had written in happy collaboration with Dudley Doust. *Phoenix from the Ashes* (Hodder & Stoughton; £7.95), though, is not only his own work; it is himself. It would seem difficult – if not impossible – for anyone to write modestly about a Test series in which, as soon as he took over the captaincy, the whole course of the rubber was reversed and it was won. To do that was a major triumph. He is rare, not merely among cricketers, but among human beings, in being capable of standing back and observing himself.

This book will be listed as an account of a Test series. It is, though, much more absorbing as a quite unusual self-examination by a cricketer. It is never more revealing than on his reactions to his treatment by the crowds in Australia in 1978-79, which was so offensive that even an Australian confessed himself disgusted. Brearley was never a bigger man than in his behaviour then.

The reader looking for an account of the Tests will find all he could reasonably demand. Proceeding from the general of the overall situation to the particular of separate matches, Brearley examines the series dispassionately and illuminates it with perceptive comments on personalities and tactics. Book and man are probably best epitomised in a single caption, to a photo of the author in action: "Batting at Lord's, May 1980. The beard grown to roughen my exterior for contacts with the rebarbative Australians, is still there, as is a career-long tendency to lean back when driving. The left shoulder has fallen away and the right shoulder came through too soon." It may be noted that rebarbative means, give or take a barb or two, unattractive. This is a thoughtful, and a thought-provoking, book; one not simply to read, but, rarely among cricket books, to re-read.

Not surprisingly, publishers have marked the centenary year of The Ashes – actually, of the first use of the term in, of course, *The Sporting Times* – with several titles. Historically that is untidy for it excludes, by definition, the eight Tests of 1876-77, 1878-79, 1880 and 1881-82, which are the essential foundation of England-Australia.

A Hundred Years of The Ashes (Rothmans; £12.95) by Doug Ibbotson and Ralph Dellor, with a foreword by Richie Benaud, is edited by David Frith, who was no doubt responsible for the generous and impressive range of illustrations. Doug Ibbotson covers the first period, though he leads with the epic series of 1981 before reverting to 1882–1938; Ralph Dellor deals with 1946–1979. The historical survey is sound and attractively presented – from "Captain Bligh's Bounty" to "The 'Okker' Age" – and there is an appendix of summarised results.

The Ashes: A Centenary (Collins; £7.95) by Ray Illingworth and Kenneth

Gregory is a collaboration between writer and Test cricketer. The period to 1900 is treated lightly and amusingly; that to the end of the inter-war period, ruminatively, anecdotally and somewhat obliquely – all of which makes for variety from the often repeated processional story. After 1945 the touch is still light but the story is strengthened by the personal observation of Ray Illingworth; especially and illuminatingly on the series in which he captained England. The authors have done well to avoid the hackneyed on so familiar a theme.

England versus Australia (Lutterworth, £15) is the third, revised, edition of David Frith's history of the entire series of those Tests. By comparison with his first edition (1977) it covers four subsequent series (including that of 1981) and the two Centenary matches in another 24 pages; and, of course, there are many more illustrations. Although there is a textual summary of each series, this is primarily, and uniquely, a pictorial record. If it is to be kept up to date and reprinted, it would be improved by an index.

England on Tour (Hamlyn; £8.95) by Peter Wynne-Thomas is, perhaps surprisingly, a novel theme. Most faithfully handled, it is an exhaustive record of tours by English teams overseas – or, at least, outside Europe. It includes those to Egypt, Bangladesh, Kenya, Uganda, Bermuda, and Burma, as well as the more obvious countries; and those by the teams of Julian Cahn, H. M. Martineau, Incogniti and the Arabs; from the Pickering/George Parr side to North America in 1859 to that organised by the South African Breweries to South Africa under Graham Gooch in 1981-82. The facts are as carefully marshalled and clearly laid out as would be expected of the secretary of the Association of Cricket Statisticians. A most valuable record, not available elsewhere, it is quite admirably produced and illustrated.

Calypso Summer (Wedneil Publications, 7 Louise Court, Seaford, Victoria, 3198, Australia; £7 airmail, £5 seamail), by Ken Piesse and Jim Main, is another fresh record for the cricket history bookshelves. A chronological record of Australia-West Indies Test cricket, it contains substantial biographical notes on the leading players on both sides; reviews, scores and averages of all series between the two countries from the first in 1930-31 to the "World Series" of 1977–79. A 201-page octavo paperback, it is pleasingly produced and well illustrated.

Cricketing Bygones (Shire Books; 95p) by Stephen Green, Curator of the MCC collection, is a scholarly survey of cricket literature, art, documents and cricketana. Its 32 well-produced pages contain well-compressed information of value to both students and collectors.

Yet another book marked by outstanding production and pictorial quality is *Test Decade 1972–1982* (World's Work; £12.95), a gathering of Patrick Eagar's work over that period, with his own captions; and a sympathetic and lucid accompanying text by Graeme Wright. The range of these photographs – not only from Lord's to Lahore, Bridgetown and Karachi; but from the furious exhibitionism of Lillee to the tranquil decorum of a stand full of Pakistani ladies – is a measure of his appreciation, and the quality of his selection, as well as his skill in the mechanical performance of photography. Patrick Eagar is the best cricket photographer and this book proves it beyond question.

Two impressively extensive, painstaking and apparently meticulous volumes of statistical history have emerged from Queensland. The first is *Queensland Cricket and Cricketers 1862–1981* (from Roger Page, 55 Tarcoola Drive,

WISDEN

CRICKET MONTHLY

Edited by David Frith

- **A focus on today's action**
- **A mirror on the past**
- **A probe into the future**

The finest of cricket coverage— in words, figures and pictures— the perfect complement to *Wisden Cricketers' Almanack*

MONTHLY THROUGHOUT THE YEAR

Yallambie, Victoria 3085, Australia; $A12.50), by Warwick Torrens and based on his original research for the Association of Cricket Statisticians' publication, *Queensland Cricketers 1892–1979*. The first match in this substantially larger (209-page) book is that between Brisbane and the migrant ship *Flying Cloud* at Green Hills, Brisbane, in January 1863. All first-class matches, including Sheffield Shield as well as the main non-first-class matches, are accorded a summarised score; and there are detailed records. Most impressive, though, is the list of every cricketer and umpire it has been possible to trace, identify and describe technically – and indicate their relationships (very frequent) with other Queensland players – who took part in all matches of importance played by or within the state.

The second is *A Cricket Centenary: England in Queensland* (from Roger Page, 55 Tarcoola Drive, Yallambie, Victoria 3085, Australia; $A8.50), also by Warwick Torrens. On February 2, 1883, the Hon. Ivo Bligh's team began their match against eighteen of Queensland on Eagle Farm Racecourse, Brisbane. Mr Torrens has recorded it and every subsequent match played by English sides in the state, including Wide Bay v England and Gympie v England which, like some others, did not rank as first-class: and, of course, Test matches. He gives full scores, analyses, and a list of the major records.

Queensland versus Western Australia (available in Australia from the author, 112 Forrest Street, South Perth, WA, 6151; $A4.00: in the UK from E. K. Brown, Bevois Mount, Church Street, Liskeard, Cornwall; £2.50), by John King, is a painstaking 24-page quarto of most full and careful statistics of that series of matches.

Ralph Barker proved his considerable skill in the reconstruction of cricket events with *Ten Great Innings* and *Ten Great Bowlers. Innings of a Lifetime* (Collins; £7.95), cast in the same mould, emphasises that ability. Taking ten great batting performances between 1955 and 1980, it sets them and their makers in human and historic perspective. It is most effectively and readably done.

Derek Lodge has made himself a reputation in that small but highly internecine world of cricket statisticians as one who is not interested in figures for figures' sake; but rather for what they show. He has demonstrated that particular capacity in publications of the Association of Cricket Statisticians and, to a wider public, in *Wisden Cricket Monthly;* and now in *Figures on the Green* (Allen & Unwin; £8.95). In the course of some 25 essays, whose character is indicated by such sample headings as "The Burden of Captaincy", "Night Watchmen", "Some records that will never be equalled (and some that are getting easier)" and "Never selected", he uses figures absorbingly to correct some fallacies and to present some theories.

Derbyshire County Cricket Club (Breedon Books, 45 Overdale Road, Derby; £1.50) by Anton Rippon and John Grainger is a 44-page, paperback quarto which celebrates the county's NatWest Trophy win of 1981 with a well-produced history of the club. It is at once balanced in perspective and admirably condensed; the illustrations, too, are well chosen and revealing.

Derbyshire Cricketers 1871–1981 (Association of Cricket Statisticians; £1.50) is yet another in the growing and valuable series issued by the Association. In 38 pages it provides a list of well-researched records of all the county's players in a specified period, together with the figures of their batting and bowling, both in first-class matches for the county and in all first-class cricket. In that

last comparison, needless to say, the figures of Venkataraghavan show a striking variation. Spofforth played for Derbyshire only in second-class matches during the period 1888 to 1893, when they were not regarded as among the first-class counties.

Warwickshire Cricket Record Book (Association of Cricket Statisticians; £3 post free) by Robert Brooke is not in the same series as the previous title. It is an exhaustive statistical record of 96 pages, including as appendices a list of the county's players in first-class cricket and their county career averages.

Cumberland County Cricket Club: A History (from the author, "Rimington", Netherend Road, Penrith, Cumbria; £2.50 post free) by John Hurst is a workmanlike, 120-page study, beginning in the 1820s and continuing down to the present. The current secretary, Norman Wise, once said that "Running a Minor Counties cricket team in this far flung, North-Western outpost of civilization is a prospect to daunt the stoutest hearted. Our gates are negligible, our population thin and widely scattered amidst Cumbria's hills and dales. However, all connected with the club are fanatic and, although daunted and 'bloody headed' we are unbowed." The county now includes the former Westmorland; they then used to play in combination. Former players include Charles Toppin, Harry Halliday, Geoffrey Edrich, Peter Broughton, John Waring, Barry Whittingham, David Ashe, Robert Entwistle, Leonard Baichan, Allan Wharton, Tom Atkinson, Peter Judge, and latterly Graham Monkhouse, now of Surrey.

A healthy crop of club histories begins, alphabetically, with *Cogenhoe Cricket Club; a Centenary History* (from the secretary, 100 Holcot Lane, Syrwell, Northamptonshire; 50p plus p & p) by Tim Street. It is a 44-page octavo; a workmanlike account, with that major figure of Northamptonshire cricket, G. J. Thompson, figuring large in its early days.

"Silver Billy" Beldham, the finest batsman of the Hambledon period, once told the Rev. James Pycroft "In those days the Hambledon Club could beat all England; but our three parishes around Farnham at last beat Hambledon". Two hundred years of cricket are the basis of *Farnham Cricket Club 1782–1982* (Farnham Castle Newspapers; £2 post free) by Graham Collyer, sub-titled "A bi-centenary history also featuring the life of 'Silver Billy' Beldham and cricket in the villages". Mr Collyer, a native of Farnham and assistant editor of a Surrey newspaper, has a good story to tell, and tells it skilfully in a 96-page octavo, in which famous cricketers appear for and against, and visit, Farnham.

The cover of *The History of I Zingari* (Stanley Paul; £12.95), by R. L. Arrowsmith and B. J. W. Hill, bears a reproduction of that famous portrait of the three impossibly patrician-looking founders of the club; Sir Spencer Ponsonby-Fane, J. L. Baldwin (in a bath chair) and Lord Bessborough. I Zingari is Italian for "the gypsies": its history is a 144-page octavo, amusingly illustrated, brightly written and punctuated with the appearance of great players in their colours – black, red and gold – which represent "out of darkness, through fire, into light". It is explained that, in IZ, victory is celebrated with due modesty; but "defeat is taken with quiet resignation, and consolation sought in the festivities provided". The preface is by Lord Home of the Hirsel, "Governor of the 4th wicket Down", and publication was subsidised by Hambro's Bank.

"A Happy Memory of Cricket" (Lloyd's Register Cricket & Tennis Club, 71 Fenchurch Street, London EC3M 4BS; 48p) by Dennis Kidd is sub-titled "100

years of cricket at Lloyd's Register". A 44-page octavo, written with warmth and knowledge, it consists of impressions and recollections rather than a strict chronological account. Probably the most famous of the author's "Five Players of the Century" is W. M. Bradley, who appeared five times for England and claimed to know every church and pub in the south of England.

175 Years of Lymington Cricket Club (Eon Graphics, Highcliffe, Dorset) by Norman Gannaway is a solid, 219-page octavo. Sound, companionable, it traces the story with immense fidelity and illustrates it with some excellent period pictures.

One Hundred Years of Local Cricket (Skipton Church Institute, no price given) by Terry Hennigan is the centenary booklet of Skipton Church Institute Cricket Club. A 56-page octavo, it contains, in addition to Mr Hennigan's story, club photographs and many letters of congratulation on its anniversary.

History of the Tunbridge Wells Cricket Club (from C. F. Openshaw, 85 Warwick Park, Tunbridge Wells, Kent; £2 post free), edited by Carl Openshaw, celebrates the bi-centenary of the historically famous club which played first on the Common below Mount Ephraim, and subsequently on the Nevill. The great Kent cricketers of the nineteenth century took part in the club's matches and Kent, too, have long played county fixtures there. The history is an attractively produced 128-page octavo, relevantly illustrated, and with a handsome coloured cover picture of the Nevill Ground.

Innings Established (1956-57–1981-82) (The Secretary, Northern Districts Cricket Association, PO Box 1347, Hamilton, New Zealand; $NZ5) is the silver jubilee souvenir history of Northern Districts. Among its players have been Richard Collinge, Hedley and Geoff Howarth, Bert Sutcliffe, Bruce Pairaudeau, Andrew Roberts, John Parker, Eric Gillott, Eric Petrie, John Wright, Glenn Turner, David O'Sullivan, and Martin Horton. They won the Plunket Shield in 1962-63; the Shell Cup in 1976-77 and 1979-80; the Shell Trophy in 1979-80. The history is a brightly written and enthusiatic 48-page quarto, with many illustrations.

This Curious Game of Cricket (Allen & Unwin; £5.95) by George Mell is a collection of odd facts and events – some extremely odd – which have occurred in cricket matches. The foreword is by Brian Johnston; illustrations by Bill Tidy. It will, undoubtedly, provoke many "I say, listen to this"es; great interest; and some disagreement.

Tom Graveney's Top Ten Cricket Book (Harrap; £6.95) edited by Norman Giller is a substantial volume, listing Tom Graveney's rankings of the master players of all types, periods, counties and countries. In some categories, he divides his cricketers into old time, pre-war (meaning the 1939–45 war), and post-war. Like most cricket followers he confesses "I have never been able to resist selecting a team" and adds that he has chosen these groups "using *feelings* rather than *facts* as my guide". There are, though, many biographical facts and figures; and spaces for the reader's choice.

Botham's Choice (Collins; £5.95) by Ian Botham and Kenneth Gregory is a collection of snippets, ideas, anecdotes, theories and interviews, ending with a sketch of Botham by his fellow-author. It is diverting, sometimes sage, always readable, and charmingly illustrated by Haro.

The Spinner's Turn (Dent; £7.95) by Patrick Murphy is a thoughtful and thought-provoking survey of spin bowling in the past, through its recent period

of change, to the present day. The author has been tireless in gathering evidence from the most knowledgeable observers and practitioners still alive, from as many periods as possible. He has, too, the knack of extracting the most relevant comments; of assessing importance and significance; and of drawing sound conclusions. As his deepest concern is for the health of the game itself, he regrets the decline in the amount – and, he would argue, the quality – of spin bowling. He balances opinions with shrewdly selected statistics. The result is a wise and readable survey of a crucial, and historically important, department of the game.

County Champions (Heinemann; £7.95) is a collection of essays on each of the seventeen first-class counties, by their supporters; who are, of course, inevitably but healthily, hopelessly biassed. Charles Palmer writes on Leicestershire; Colin Cowdrey on Kent; Trevor Bailey on Essex; Alan Gibson on Gloucestershire; so much might have been expected. Leslie Thomas on Glamorgan; Barry Norman on Middlesex; Ted Moult on Derbyshire; and Bill Tidy – with pencil – on Lancashire, might not have been anticipated. The result is a highly readable present for the cricket enthusiast.

The Wit of Cricket (André Deutsch; £4.50) is by Ian Brayshaw, for many years all-rounder, and, latterly, captain of Western Australia; and who was in six of their Sheffield Shield-winning teams. He has remained close to the game and is now a radio commentator for the ABC. No-one could produce a 111-page book of entirely fresh cricket stories, but an impressive proportion of these will be new to most readers.

Every year Nico Craven comes out of Cumbria to pay a visit to his native Gloucestershire and especially to its cricket fields. Each year, too, as an act of homage, he writes a book about his pilgrimage. *Playing a Supporting Role* (from the author, The Coach House, Ponsonby, Cumbria; £5.95) is the sixteenth of them. In addition to his usual match reports, it contains pen portraits of six eminent Gloucestershire cricketers, from Charles Barnett to Zaheer Abbas, and of his seven foreword writers.

The Game of the Season (Oxford University Press; £2.50), by Hugh de Selincourt, is a re-issue of that author's follow-up to his classic *The Cricket Match*. Lighter in touch than its predecessor, it consists of two long and four shorter short stories. They are mellow; and if they seem dated, they are also charmingly nostalgic.

Slices of Cricket (Allen & Unwin; £7.95) by Peter Roebuck introduces a fresh cricket-book writer. That is not, of itself, important. When, however, the writer is a first-class cricketer with a sense of humour and a capacity for both clarity and irony, the matter assumes some significance. In a first book, the author is, superficially at least, fittingly modest about it; he prefaces his dedication with 'As this could be the only book I write . . .'. If he can endure the prodigious physical and mental chore which is writing a book of any kind, it will not be the only one. These are pleasing and well-observed studies; none better than the profiles of Viv Richards and Ian Botham. The first book is one matter; the second is a different; but anyone with an appetite for cricket writing will await Peter Roebuck's sequel with considerable interest.

Summer of the All-Rounder (Collins; £5.95) is another collection of Patrick Eagar's cricket photographs with text by Alan Ross. Similar in format to his *A Summer To Remember,* it deals in the main with the England-India and England-Pakistan Test series of 1982 which were, of course, dominated by the three all-rounders, Kapil Dev, Imran Khan and Ian Botham, in a quite rare emergence of highly capable and entertaining pace bowler-batsmen. The 128 quarto pages consist mainly of photographs with captions, rather than a running story, by Alan Ross. The section of "extras" at the back is interesting, entertaining, well worthwhile and affords an illuminating micro-survey of the season. All the photographs are in black and white: such is the quality of his work that Patrick Eagar does not need colour; but he deserves it.

Glorious Battle (Hemal Publication, 10 Radhanput Society, Bhairavnath Road, Ahmedabad 380028; Rs 16.00) by Sudhir Talati, an All-India Radio commentator, is an account of the India *versus* Pakistan Test series of 1979-80. It is a faithful story of the matches; written diligently and individually. Here is another writer at the outset of a career; but in a very different situation; faced with different demands. He has, though, probably the most devoted cricket audience in the world. He is not to be judged by English standards, but by those of his own people.

The English view of a series in the sub-continent is *Cricket Wallah* (Hodder & Stoughton; £8.95), an account of England in India 1981-82 by Scyld Berry, cricket correspondent of *The Observer*. He is valuably content, from time to time, to take his eye off the ball and write about India and Indians. He does so, too, with a dry humour which may not please everyone; humour never pleases everyone. No-one else, though, has so fairly caught the atmosphere of cricket in India; and his book is not only worth while reading for that reason: play is sympathetically linked to its background.

The Dictionary of National Biography 1961–1970 (Oxford University Press; £40) is the seventh supplement to that major, 21-volume, work of reference. This issue deals with British subjects who died between January 1, 1961 and December 31, 1970. Thus, it includes Sir Winston Churchill, Lord Attlee, Pandit Nehru, T. S. Eliot, and Augustus John. There are, also, six substantial and authoritative biographies of cricketers: Sir Jack Hobbs, Sir Frank Worrell, Sir Pelham Warner, S. F. Barnes, Walter Hammond, and H. S. Altham; as well as Lord Birkett.

Literary fashions change; whether at the behest of the public, or of publishers, has never been clearly established; perhaps both are involved. It is, though, most noticeable that, while only a few years ago the autobiographical/biographical titles in this notice consisted largely of – sometimes premature – "ghosted" autobiographies, only two such items are present this year. On the contrary, of the eleven titles, six are studies of already dead persons whom the author generally has researched as distinct from writing from first-hand knowledge; two are "straight" biographies; and one a statistical evaluation.

The first of the "historical" biographies is *Bobby Abel; Professional Batsman* (Secker & Warburg; £9.95) by David Kynaston, whose label is that of historian rather than cricket writer. As the statistical appendix shows, Abel was a highly successful batsman for Surrey and England between 1881 and 1905. No-one now alive is entitled to pass a first-hand critical opinion on his batting; but Mr Kynaston has researched his subject most thoroughly, and built a credible, revealing, and sometimes moving, picture. Nothing, though, is more revealing than the sociological chapter "A Pro's Lot". Anyone interested in the human side of Victorian cricket should read it. Albert Craig, "The Cricket Poet" who hawked his work broadsheets round The Oval, was a great admirer of Abel: and three of his pieces form another appendix.

An act of affectionate homage is *Ken Barrington: a Tribute* (Harrap; £7.95) by Brian Scovell. It consists of a tidy biographical account entitled "The Colonel"; followed by 75 pages of recollections – some humorous, some admiring, most moving, all affectionate – by his contemporaries and friends. There is, too, a substantial record of his considerable achievements – not forgetting his bowling – but especially as a monumentally conscientious and reliable batsman.

The number of books by, "by", and about Geoffrey Boycott must now, surely, exceed those credited to any other English cricketer. *Boycott: a Cricketing Legend* (Pelham; £7.95) by John Callaghan, cricket correspondent of *The Yorkshire Evening Post*, is probably the best of them. Mr Callaghan, covering Yorkshire and English Test cricket since 1972, has had an unusual opportunity to observe his subject; and they have collaborated on several books. As he observes, "for almost twenty years he has enjoyed the undisputed ranking as England's senior batsman". "It is time to redress the balance", Mr Callaghan writes, and he adds: "I am aware of no single instance when Boycott has failed to tell the truth." Out of experience, observation and consultation, he illuminates his enigmatic subject with understanding and sympathy. It is a readable, absorbing and revealing study; worth a place on any bookshelf of contemporary cricket.

The Geoffrey Boycott File (Hamlyn; £2.25) by Steven Sheen is simply that. It records every innings he has ever played in first-class and major over-limit cricket; his score; how out; the totals; and the match result; followed by 105 analyses, tabulations and arrangements of his batting; including the heading "Boycott's Pair". It runs to 191 pages; but Boycott is not done yet. Is it all to be done over again when – if – he calls it a day?

Samuel Britcher: the Hidden Scorer (from J. R. Batten, 9 Windmill Lane, Lewes Road, East Grinstead, West Sussex; £11.50 post free) by David Rayvern Allen was issued in a limited, signed and numbered edition of 100 copies. A 16-page octavo, it is the result of painstaking research into the work and publications of the scorer, and score-publisher, whose publications – the hushed tones, rare fifteen volumes 1790 to 1804 of *Britchers Scores* – are more often discussed than seen. Mr Allen identifies Britcher as an innovator: "a highly educated individual, who ignored the old method for the pencil". "The old method" was, of course, cutting notches in a stick. A collector's piece; and one for the archivists.

'Tich' Freeman and the Decline of the Leg Break Bowler (Allen & Unwin; £7.95), by David Lemmon, is a study of the most successful of all leg-spinners, set against the background of an English cricket world which now, apparently, has little time for his kind. By far the greater proportion of wrist-spin bowled in English cricket in 1982 was from Pakistanis – either with their national team, or, in the cases of Sadiq Mohammad and Javed Miandad, for English counties – and the Ugandan Asian, Asif Din of Warwickshire. "Tich", the little philosopher who took punishment with the bland and justified confidence that he would extort his price, once took 304 wickets in a season; sent down 2,039 overs in another. Only Wilfred Rhodes exceeded his career aggregate of 3,776 wickets. Mr Lemmon tells a thoroughly researched and persuasive story which will become one of the standard biographies of the game.

David Foot has sub-titled *Harold Gimblett* (Heinemann; £7.95) "Tormented Genius of Cricket" and his biography justifies it. This is no cosy recital of runs

or wickets, of comfortable success; but of the mental agony of one man who, despite his outstanding cricket gifts, never gained the satisfaction they seemed to offer. Mr Foot is an experienced journalist; and, just as this is not a comfortable book, neither is it a sentimental one. In a way it is an autobiography, for the man recorded much of his agony and indecision on tapes. There is no other book like it in cricket literature; no-one else has ever gone – or honestly attempted to go – down into the pit with a cricketer. Because it is so honest, because it has a tragic and not a happy ending, this may never be a "popular" book; but it is fine, compassionate and wise. Mr Foot deserves the admiration and thanks of all who care for human truth in a game which does not always face facts.

In compiling *My Cricket Diary '81* (Stanley Paul; £6.95) Graham Gooch had the assistance of that conscientious and observant cricket journalist, Alan Lee. It is a fair inside view of a first-class cricketer's year, home and abroad. In the background of the reader's mind, though, there must always be the thought that, while the diary was being written, Gooch himself was making the arrangements to go on the "pirate" tour of South Africa in the following close season. That makes the chapter on "Ashes and Apartheid" seem unreal; and undermines the reader's trust.

The Gloves of Irony (Pelham Books; £5.95) by Rodney Marsh is a "pop" journalistic, personal account of some of the headline events – both on and off the field – in which the Australian wicket-keeper has been concerned. The title stems from the nickname given to Marsh in his early days – "Old Iron Gloves" – and which he has lived down in the most capable possible way. Written with the acknowledged assistance of Austin Robertson, it has a spectacularly brash dust-wrapper; cartoons, press photographs, reproductions of newspaper front pages. The opening chapter, entitled "A Man Called Peter" is devoted to an incident in which a person called Peter Jenkins, after the Australian defeat at Edgbaston in 1981, apparently barracked the team from part way up a barbed-wire fence: and Marsh "gave him a burst that even in these permissive days could only make the pages of this book as an asterisk". That occupies six pages. A photograph of Marsh with a bandaged knee is captioned "Sometimes it hurts – but the pay cheque eases the pain!" He is not so tough as he pretends; sometimes he seems a veritable teddy-bear of a man.

Keith Miller – The Golden Nugget (Rigby Publishers, Adelaide, South Australia; $A9.95) by R. S. Whitington is a happy, factual, lively, reminiscent, essentially familiar book. Opening batsman for South Australia from 1932 to 1940, Dick Whitington played with Keith Miller in the Australian Services side in the "Victory" Tests in England in 1945 and on the tour through India and round the Australian states. They collaborated in six cricket books, of which Miller said "I mean to read one of them one day"; and this biography germinated for many years. It is a substantial – 312 page – book; but there was enough material – the entire background of Australian cricket of the period – stored up in the author's mind to have made one three times as long. This is to be relished as its subject was; most spectacularly joyous, and one of the most likeable of post-war Test cricketers.

David Rayvern Allen, cricket scholar, BBC variety producer, student of popular song, films and theatre, found his natural subject in C. Aubrey Smith. His *Sir Aubrey* (Elm Tree Books; £12.50) is sub-titled "A biography of C. Aubrey Smith, England cricketer, West End actor, Hollywood film star", and in each of those fields, and as a man, he does his subject informed justice. Aubrey Smith's first-class cricket career, which began at Cambridge University in 1881, took him to Sussex, Australia, South Africa; he acted in London; and he became – in both cricketing and acting terms – "The Grand Old Man of Hollywood". That completes surely the best hand of cricket biographies in any post-war year.

In *Travelling Reserve* (Collins; £5.95) Ian Wooldridge discources discursively about his 24-year experience as a sports writer. He has covered many different sports, and for seven years he was a cricket correspondent. His observation is sharp; his mind is clear; he has high standards, few prejudices; he is one of the most conscientious workers in any press box. If this book seems light in tone, that is because he is such a careful writer – and has a splendid sense of humour. *Travelling Reserve* is really about people – as all the best books are: here sport is the link between them and the many splendid anecdotes. This must surely emerge as the most amusing sports book of the year.

Cricketers in the Making (Queen Anne Press; £7.95) by Trevor Bailey is an instructional book for boys, based on one of the same title which Mr Bailey wrote in collaboration with the late D. R. Wilcox in 1950. For this edition, however, the text has been revised and brought up to date; and there are fresh illustrations (as can be deduced from the hair length of the juvenile models). All the boys were under fourteen when they were photographed (by Patrick Eagar); and they demonstrated exactly what the author wanted. It is interesting, too, that of the six, one became a regular member of Essex Second Eleven; another was chosen for the England under fifteen cricket team; and a third has already appeared for Arsenal at football. The book, which has a separate chapter on soft-ball cricket, is orthodox, precise, full of wisdom, and will be helpful both to boys and their teachers.

Benson & Hedges Cricket Year (Pelham Books; £9.95), edited by David Lemmon with Tony Lewis as assistant, is not outwardly dated, but is described on the cover as "First Edition". Clearly, however, it inherits directly from *Pelham Cricket Year* (which it "incorporates"): same editor, same publisher and, similarly, it sets out, with high-speed timing, to produce the full details of the English season within little more than two months of its end. It runs from September 1981 to September 1982; and, in 480 quarto pages, covers eight Test series; the domestic seasons of England, Australia, West Indies and South Africa (including the SAB tour by English players). An immense effort of compilation and production, its illustration – a fair proportion of it in colour – is generous.

The Daily Telegraph Cricket Year Book '82 (Daily Telegraph; £3.95), by Michael Melford, E. W. Swanton, Bill Frindall and Michael Carey, contests the same ground. It, too, tackles the editorial problems of the increasingly complex pattern of world cricket at speed. It is an octavo paperback of 224 pages; containing some thoughtful features; dealing with the domestic seasons of all the ICC countries and all the Test series; reviewing the counties and "Looking Forward".

Playfair Cricket Annual 1982 (Queen Anne Press; £1.10) continues in its 35th edition under the editorship of Gordon Ross. In its convenient, pocket-sized format it is a most valuable reference with its county biographies and averages; and especially its first-class and Test career averages. It was, sadly, the last edition to which the late Michael Fordham contributed.

The West Indies Cricket Annual 1982 (Caribbean Communications, 32 Walton

Lane, Weybridge, Surrey; £2.50), in its thirteenth edition and still edited by Tony Cozier, is sponsored by Benson & Hedges. It continues in its generous, large quarto format, concentrating wisely and usefully on coverage of West Indian cricket at all levels. The Who's Who section is careful, valuable, and not available anywhere else. The Five Cricketers of the Year are Winston Davis, Joel Garner, Larry Gomes, Ranjie Nanan and Norbert Phillip. The editor never takes his eye off the ball. Production and illustration are pleasing.

The 1981 Shell Cricket Almanack of New Zealand (available in the UK from E. K. Brown, Bevois Mount, Church Street, Liskeard, Cornwall; £4.60) goes into its 34th year under the continuing editorship of the indefatigable Arthur Carman. Within 206 pages, his coverage of domestic play at all worthwhile levels once more is complete and immaculate. There are biographical notes on Shell Shield players and match reports at several levels. The Batsman of the Year is J. F. Reid; the bowler, J. M. McIntyre. This almanack is established beyond all question as the authoritative record of the game in New Zealand.

Indian Cricket 1981 (published by Kasturi & Sons of Madras; available in the UK from E. K. Brown, Bevois Mount, Church Street, Liskeard, Cornwall; £2.75), edited by S. Thyagarajan, is remarkably good money's-worth. Quite massive coverage – 327 pages – is devoted to domestic play, making this the essential reference book to Indian cricket. The four Cricketers of the Year are Kirti Azad, Ravi Shastri, Ghulam Parkar and V. Sivaramakrishnan; and there is a special feature on Ajit Wadekar.

The 1981 Protea Cricket Annual of South Africa (available in the UK from E. K. Brown, Bevois Mount, Church Street, Liskeard, Cornwall; £4.15), published with the co-operation of the South African Cricket Union, is edited by Michael Owen-Smith, with Peter Sichel as his associate; and is "Volume 28". It covers, within its 374 well-printed pages, all levels of play within South Africa. Its editorial is understandably concerned with the cricket/politics relationship; and it is clear-minded but not optimistic. There are three weighty obituaries – of Dudley Nourse, Herbie Wade and Eric Dalton – and special tributes to Eddie Barlow and D. R. Neilson. The Cricketers of the Year are S. J. Cook, K. R. Cooper, N. T. Day and L. Seeff: no doubt good players but names in isolation.

Derbyshire County Cricket Year Book 1982 (Derbyshire County Cricket Supporters' Club, County Cricket Ground, Nottingham Road, Derby; £1.50 post free), under the familiar editorship of F. G. Peach and A. F. Dawn, is a special souvenir edition to mark the county's winning the NatWest Trophy of 1981. It is the editors' invariably thorough job; as sound a county yearbook as any. There is a "farewell" by Michael Carey; a piece on Walter Goodyear by Gerald Mortimer; and complete and up-to-date statistics.

Hampshire Handbook 1982 (Hampshire CCC, County Ground, Southampton; £1.40), determinedly put together by Peter Marshall, has a seasonal review by John Hughes, father-son features on the Tremletts, the Parks and the Eagars; and a nostalgic reminiscence of Philip Mead by Ronnie Aird. The records are provided by the diligent and precise Victor Isaacs.

Rothmans Club Cricket Handbook 1982 (Rothmans Publications; £5.50), edited by Martin Burgess and Patrick Allen, had a vast void to fill. In their first attempt, working under county headings with information about competitions and performances and providing a basic list of addresses, they have already rendered a service to the ordinary cricket club. There are, too, notes on some

of the play of 1981. They have far to go; but they will be helped by their subjects.

India v/s England Bumper Cricket Souvenir (from the Editor, Parwati Niwas, Hanuman Road, Vile Parle (East), Bombay 400 057, India; Rs 4), edited by Mrunal Desai, is a 60-page quarto. A typical Indian cricket souvenir, it has statistical records, biographical notes on all the members of the touring England side, and a series of feature articles by Suresh Saraiya, Madhav Mantri, Ramakant Desai, Bal Pandit and E. W. Swanton.

The general health of the game may be inferred from the continuing progress of its periodicals. The senior, of course, is *The Cricketer International* (Beech Hanger, Ashurst, Tunbridge Wells, Kent, TN3 9ST; £11.85 for twelve monthly numbers, or £1.10 per issue). Now 61 years old, and edited by Christopher Martin-Jenkins, it has become, in journalistic parlance, "harder" than it was; and its condensed scores, if unglamorous, are nevertheless useful. Regular contributors are E. W. Swanton, Robert Brooke, Alan Lee, Reg Hayter. Its correspondence columns are invariably interesting; and the features have readable variety.

Its competitor is *Wisden Cricket Monthly* (Subscription Dept, Watling Street, Bletchley, Milton Keynes, MK2 2BW; £10 for twelve issues, or 75p per issue), under the editorship of David Frith. His editorial board of contributors includes Ted Dexter, David Gower, Jim Laker, Bob Willis and the photographer, Patrick Eagar. There are sound county notes. The editor himself contributes a considerable proportion of the news items and the nostalgic "Picture Gallery" from his own extensive collection of photographs; he has a significant bibliographical bias as far as book reviews are concerned. His correspondence columns, too, are entertaining.

Cricketer (NEWSPRESS Pty Ltd, PO Box 628E, Melbourne, 3001, Victoria, Australia) – "Australia's national cricket magazine" – has undergone a few changes in the period to its "tenth birthday issue" of 1982. The latest edition indicates "five monthly issues from December 1982 to April 1983 – plus '100 Summers' and 'Cricket's Finest Years'. Seven publications in all cost $A12.20; overseas surface mail $A17.00 for seven publications; England airmail $A32.50 for seven publications". This continues as a lively, sometimes controversial, and substantial (78-page) magazine. The editor is Ken Piesse. Among his regular correspondents are Paul Sheahan, Frank Tyson, Don Neely, Ashley Mallett, Ian Brayshaw and Phil Wilkins. The Club Review is highly competent. The measure of *Cricketer*'s success is the appearance of a competitor.

The first issue of *Australian Cricket* (Murray Publishers, 152-156 Clarence Street, Sydney, 2000, Australia; $A1.50 per issue) appeared in September 1982. Its period of publication is "out every fortnight during summer". It is edited by Brad Boxall, with Phil Tresidder as consultant. The special writers are John Benaud, Tony Greig, Allan Border and David Hookes. Its format is that of a tabloid newspaper and the issue so far seen was of 30 lively pages within a colour wrapper.

The Cricket Player (PO Box 28-280, Remuera, Auckland, New Zealand; $NZ9.75 for eight issues) continues under the editorship of Robin Craze; with Dick Brittenden still a contributor as well as Richard Hadlee. The editorial content of the technically well-produced magazine is sound and increasingly lively. An interesting recent feature was entitled "Allan Stimpson in Ireland", about a Northern Districts player who spent the summer of 1981 as a professional with the Pembroke Cricket Club in Eire. His 91 wickets at 9.71 broke the Leinster Cricket Union bowling record. Generally, though, the material is home-produced and the more valuable for that fact.

A newcomer to this field is *Zimbabwe Cricketer* (Glen Byrom Public Relations, Box BE 14, Belvedere, Harare; annual subscription Z$4 for four quarterly issues), edited by Mike Rogan, the official journal of the Zimbabwe Cricket Union. Volume 1, number 1, dated November 1982, a 36-page quarto, is much, and understandably, concerned with Zimbabwe's performance in winning the ICC Trophy in England in 1982, when they beat Bermuda by five wickets in the final.

Cathedral End (from the Secretary, Adelaide Branch of the Australian Cricket Society, 28 Glenalvon Drive, Flagstaff Hill, SA, 5159, Australia: gratis to members, $A2.00 to non-members) is the quarterly journal of the branch. Running to about 72 cyclostyled foolscap pages, it is an extremely ambitious magazine; reporting fully the talks and answers to questions of their visiting speakers. Its range, though, is wide; the issue for Spring 1982, for instance, contained an account of visits to grounds of the seventeen English first-class counties. Primarily, of course, its interests lie in Australia, and especially in South Australia, and it is for that local information that the journal will be of most interest to students of cricket.

FIXTURES, 1983

** Indicates Sunday play.   † Not first-class.*

Wednesday, April 20

Cambridge	Univ. v Glam.

Saturday, April 23

Cambridge	Univ. v Leics.
Oxford	Univ. v Lancs.

Wednesday, April 27

Lord's	MCC v Middx
Cambridge	Univ. v Essex
Oxford	Univ. v Somerset

Saturday, April 30

Derby*	Derby. v Glos.
Manchester	Lancs. v Glam.
Leicester*	Leics. v Hants
Lord's	Middx v Essex
Nottingham*	Notts. v Somerset
The Oval*	Surrey v Kent
Birmingham	Warw. v Northants
Worcester*	Worcs. v Yorks.
Oxford	Univ. v Sussex

Sunday, May 1

Manchester	†Lancs. v Glam. (1 day)

Wednesday, May 4

Cardiff	Glam. v Essex
Bristol	Glos. v Surrey
Leicester	Leics. v Derby.
Lord's	Middx v Lancs.
Northampton	Northants v Hants
Taunton	Somerset v Worcs.
Hove	Sussex v Notts.
Leeds	Yorks. v Warw.
Cambridge	Univ. v Kent

Saturday, May 7

†**Benson and Hedges Cup** (1 day)

Chesterfield	Derby. v Yorks.
Southampton	Hants v Essex
Manchester	Lancs. v Warw.
Northampton	Northants v Glos.
Cambridge	Oxford & Cam. U. v Kent
Taunton	Somerset v Sussex
The Oval	Surrey v Middx
Worcester	Worcs. v Leics.

Wednesday, May 11

Chesterfield	Derby. v Lancs.
Chelmsford	Essex v Kent
Gloucester	Glos. v Sussex
Southampton	Hants v Warw.
Lord's	Middx v Yorks.
Northampton	Northants v Notts.
The Oval	Surrey v Leics.
Worcester	Worcs. v Somerset
Cambridge	†Univ. v MCC
Oxford	Univ. v Glam.

Saturday, May 14

†**Benson and Hedges Cup** (1 day)

Chelmsford	Essex v Somerset
Gloucester	Glos. v Leics.
Canterbury	Kent v Middx
Oxford	Oxford & Cam. U. v Glam.
Aberdeen	Scotland v Worcs.
Hove	Sussex v Minor C.
Birmingham	Warw. v Derby.
Bradford	Yorks. v Notts.

Tuesday, May 17

†**Benson and Hedges Cup** (1 day)

Canterbury	Kent v Surrey
Leicester	Leics. v Northants
Lord's	Middx v Glam.
Slough	Minor C. v Essex
Nottingham	Notts. v Derby.
Glasgow (Titwood)	Scotland v Glos.
Taunton	Somerset v Hants
Leeds	Yorks. v Lancs.

Thursday, May 19

†**Benson and Hedges Cup** (1 day)

Derby	Derby. v Lancs.
Chelmsford	Essex v Sussex
Cardiff	Glam. v Surrey
Bournemouth	Hants v Minor C.
Leicester	Leics. v Scotland
Lord's	Middx v Oxford & Cam. U.
Nottingham	Notts. v Warw.
Worcester	Worcs. v Northants

Saturday, May 21

†**Benson and Hedges Cup** (1 day)

Swansea	Glamorgan v Kent
Bristol	Glos. v Worcs.
Manchester	Lancs. v Notts.
Slough	Minor C. v Somerset
Northampton	Northants v Scotland
The Oval	Surrey v Oxford & Cam. U.
Hove	Sussex v Hants
Birmingham	Warw. v Yorks.

Wednesday, May 25

Southampton	Hants v Worcs.
Leicester	Leics. v Essex
Lord's	Middx v Glam.
Taunton	Somerset v Sussex
The Oval	Surrey v Lancs.
Birmingham	Warw. v Glos.
Bradford	Yorks. v Northants
Oxford	†Univ. v MCC

Saturday, May 28

Chelmsford	Essex v Surrey
Swansea	Glam. v Glos.
Canterbury	Kent v Hants
Manchester	Lancs. v Yorks.
Lord's	Middx v Sussex
Northampton	Northants v Leics.
Nottingham	Notts. v Derby.
Worcester	Worcs. v Warw.

Sunday, May 29

Oxford	†Univ. v Free Foresters

Wednesday, June 1

†**Benson and Hedges Cup – Quarter-Finals** (1 day)

Saturday, June 4

Derby	Derby. v Hants
Dartford	Kent v Middx
Nottingham	Notts. v Leics.
Taunton	Somerset v Essex
Hove	Sussex v Worcs.
Birmingham	Warw. v Lancs.
Middlesbrough	Yorks. v Glam.
Oxford	†Univ. v Combined Services

Wednesday, June 8

Chelmsford	Essex v Notts.
Bristol	Glos. v Somerset
Bournemouth	Hants v Lancs.
Leicester	Leics. v Yorks.
Uxbridge	Middx v Derby.
Hove	Sussex v Kent
Worcester	Worcs. v Surrey
Cambridge	Univ. v Warw.
Oxford	Univ. v Northants

Thursday, June 9

†**Prudential World Cup** (1 day)

Nottingham	Australia v Zimbabwe
The Oval	England v New Zealand
Swansea	Pakistan v Sri Lanka
Manchester	West Indies v India

Saturday, June 11

†**Prudential World Cup** (1 day)

Taunton	England v Sri Lanka
Leicester	India v Zimbabwe
Birmingham	Pakistan v New Zealand
Leeds	West Indies v Australia

Derby	Derby. v Leics.
Cardiff	Glam. v Warw.
Tunbridge Wells	Kent v Essex
Manchester	Lancs. v Notts.
Northampton	Northants v Glos.
The Oval	Surrey v Middx
Hove	Sussex v Somerset
Oxford	Univ. v Hants

Monday, June 13

†**Prudential World Cup** (1 day)

Lord's	England v Pakistan
Nottingham	India v Australia
Bristol	New Zealand v Sri Lanka
Worcester	West Indies v Zimbabwe

Wednesday, June 15

†**Prudential World Cup** (1 day)

Birmingham	England v New Zealand
The Oval	West Indies v India

Derby	Derby. v Essex
Swansea	Glam. v Somerset
Tunbridge Wells	Kent v Sussex
Manchester	Lancs. v Warw.
Leicester	Leics. v Glos.
Uxbridge	Middx v Hants
Nottingham	Notts. v Surrey
Cambridge	Univ. v Northants
Oxford	Univ. v Worcs.

Thursday, June 16

†**Prudential World Cup** (1 day)

Southampton	Australia v Zimbabwe
Leeds	Pakistan v Sri Lanka

Saturday, June 18

†**Prudential World Cup** (1 day)

Manchester	England v Pakistan
Tunbridge Wells	India v Zimbabwe
Derby	New Zealand v Sri Lanka
Lord's	West Indies v Australia

Bristol	Glos. v Kent
Southampton	Hants v Yorks.
Northampton	Northants v Warw.
Bath	Somerset v Derby.
Horsham	Sussex v Lancs.
Worcester	Worcs. v Middx
Cambridge	Univ. v Notts.
The Oval*	Surrey v Oxford U.

Monday, June 20

†**Prudential World Cup** (1 day)

Chelmsford	Australia v India
Leeds	England v Sri Lanka
Nottingham	New Zealand v Pakistan
Birmingham	West Indies v Zimbabwe

Wednesday, June 22

†**Prudential World Cup – Semi-Finals** (1 day)

Manchester and The Oval

Ilford	Essex v Northants
Abergavenny	Glam. v Worcs.
Basingstoke	Hants v Sussex
Leicester	Leics. v Surrey
Nottingham	Notts. v Kent
Bath	Somerset v Glos.
Sheffield	Yorks. v Derby.
Cambridge	Univ. v Middx
Birmingham	Warw. v Oxford U.

Saturday, June 25

Lord's	†PRUDENTIAL WORLD CUP FINAL (1 day)
Chesterfield	Derby. v Middx
Ilford	Essex v Sussex
Bristol	Glos. v Hants
Hinckley	Leics. v Glam.
Nottingham	Notts. v Lancs.
The Oval	Surrey v Northants
Birmingham	Warw. v Yorks.
Worcester	Worcs. v Cambridge U.

Wednesday, June 29

Lord's	Oxford v Cambridge

†**NatWest Bank Trophy – First Round** (1 day)

Reading	Berks. v Yorks.
Wisbech	Cambs. v Middx
Bournemouth (Dean Park)	Dorset v Essex
Chester-le-Street	Durham v Lancs.
Bristol	Glos. v Scotland
Hitchin	Herts. v Hants
Dublin (Castle Ave)	Ireland v Sussex
Canterbury	Kent v Cheshire
Leicester	Leics. v Devon
Sleaford	Lincs. v Surrey
Norwich	Norfolk v Glam.
Wellington	Salop. v Somerset
Bury St Edmunds	Suffolk v Derby.
Birmingham	Warw. v Oxon.
Swindon	Wilts. v Northants
Worcester	Worcs. v Notts.

Thursday, June 30

Portsmouth	†Combined Services v New Zealanders (2 days)

Saturday, July 2

Taunton*	Somerset v New Zealanders
Derby	Derby. v Worcs.
Canterbury	Kent v Glam.
Liverpool	Lancs. v Hants
Nottingham	Notts. v Essex
The Oval	Surrey v Glos.
Hove	Sussex v Northants
Birmingham	Warw. v Middx
Harrogate	Yorks. v Leics.

Wednesday, July 6

Bristol	Glos. v New Zealanders (or New Zealanders v another county if Glos. in B & H Cup semi-final)

†**Benson and Hedges Cup – Semi-Finals** (1 day)

Harrogate	†Tilcon Trophy (3 days)

Saturday, July 9

Lord's*	Middx v New Zealanders
Cardiff	Glam. v Sussex
Bristol	Glos. v Derby.
Southampton	Hants v Surrey
Maidstone	Kent v Lancs.
Leicester	Leics. v Somerset
Northampton	Northants v Yorks.
Nuneaton	Warw. v Essex
Worcester	Worcs. v Notts.

Wednesday, July 13

Southend	Essex v Hants
Swansea	Glam. v Lancs.
Bristol	Glos. v Middx
Maidstone	Kent v Somerset
Nottingham	Notts. v Northants
Birmingham	Warw. v Derby.
Hereford	Worcs. v Leics.
Leeds	Yorks. v Sussex

Thursday, July 14

The Oval*	ENGLAND v NEW ZEALAND (1st Cornhill Test, 5 days)

Saturday, July 16

Derby*	Derby. v Northants
Southend	Essex v Glam.
Bournemouth	Hants v Notts.
Manchester	Lancs. v Worcs.
Lord's	Middx v Leics.
Taunton	Somerset v Surrey
Sheffield	Yorks. v Kent

Wednesday, July 20

Nottingham or Worcester	Notts. v New Zealanders (or Worcs. v New Zealanders if Notts. in NatWest Bank Trophy second round)

†NatWest Bank Trophy – Second Round (1 day)

Reading or Leeds	Berks. or Yorks. v Wilts. or Northants
Bournemouth (Sports Club) or Chelmsford	Dorset or Essex v Kent or Cheshire
Chester-le-Street or Manchester	Durham or Lancs. v Salop. or Somerset
Ireland or Hove	Ireland or Sussex v Worcs. or Notts.
Leicester or Torquay	Leics. or Devon v Glos. or Scotland
Lincoln or The Oval	Lincs. or Surrey v Warw. or Oxon.
Norwich or Swansea	Norfolk or Glam. v Herts. or Hants
Bury St Edmunds or Derby	Suffolk or Derby. v Cambs. or Middx

Saturday, July 23

Lord's	†BENSON & HEDGES CUP FINAL (1 day)
Birmingham	Warw. v New Zealanders (or another county v New Zealanders if Warw. in B & H Cup Final)

Wednesday, July 27

Portsmouth	Hants v Derby.
Southport	Lancs. v Glos.
Northampton	Northants v Somerset
The Oval	Surrey v Notts.
Hove	Sussex v Essex
Birmingham	Warw. v Kent
Worcester	Worcs. v Glam.

Thursday, July 28

Leeds	ENGLAND v NEW ZEALAND (2nd Cornhill Test, 5 days)

Saturday, July 30

Chesterfield	Derby. v Kent
Swansea	Glam. v Surrey
Portsmouth	Hants v Glos.
Manchester	Lancs. v Somerset
Leicester	Leics. v Sussex
Lord's	Middx v Warw.
Northampton	Northants v Worcs.
Worksop	Notts. v Yorks.

Wednesday, August 3

Northampton	Northants v New Zealanders (or another county v New Zealanders if Northants in NatWest Bank Trophy quarter-finals)

†NatWest Bank Trophy – Quarter-Finals (1 day)

Friday, August 5

Lord's	†England Young Cricketers v Australian Young Cricketers (1 day)

Saturday, August 6

Bournemouth*	Hants v New Zealanders
Chelmsford	Essex v Middx
Cheltenham	Glos. v Glam.
Canterbury	Kent v Worcs.
Leicester	Leics. v Notts.
Weston-super-Mare	Somerset v Northants
The Oval	Surrey v Warw.
Eastbourne	Sussex v Derby.
Leeds	Yorks. v Lancs.
Nottingham	†England Young Cricketers v Australian Young Cricketers (4 days)

Sunday, August 7

†Warwick Under-25 Competition Semi-Finals (1 day) (or Sunday, August 14)

Wednesday, August 10

Chelmsford	Essex v Leics.
Ebbw Vale	Glam. v Notts.
Cheltenham	Glos. v Warw.
Canterbury	Kent v Surrey
Northampton	Northants v Middx
Weston-super-Mare	Somerset v Yorks.
Eastbourne	Sussex v Hants
Worcester	Worcs. v Lancs.

Thursday, August 11

Lord's	ENGLAND v NEW ZEALAND (3rd Cornhill Test, 5 days)

Saturday, August 13

Derby — Derby. v Somerset
Cardiff — Glam. v Kent
Cheltenham — Glos. v Yorks.
Manchester — Lancs. v Middx
Wellingborough — Northants v Essex
Nottingham — Notts. v Hants
Guildford — Surrey v Worcs.
Birmingham — Warw. v Leics.

Sunday, August 14

†Warwick Under-25 Competition Semi-Finals (1 day) (if not played on August 7)

Wednesday, August 17

Chelmsford — Essex v New Zealanders (or another county if Essex in NatWest Bank Trophy semi-finals)

†NatWest Bank Trophy – Semi-Finals (1 day)

Scarborough — †England Young Cricketers v Australian Young Cricketers (4 days)
Glasgow (Titwood) — †Scotland v MCC

Saturday, August 20

Leicester* — Leics. v New Zealanders
Colchester — Essex v Glos.
Swansea — Glam. v Derby.
Folkestone — Kent v Warw.
Lord's — Middx v Somerset
Northampton — Northants v Lancs.
Hove — Sussex v Surrey
Worcester — Worcs. v Hants
Bradford — Yorks. v Notts.

Sunday, August 21

Birmingham — †Warwick Under-25 Competition Final (1 day)

Monday, August 22

Derby — †England Young Cricketers v Australian Young Cricketers (1 day)

Wednesday, August 24

Colchester — Essex v Worcs.
Bournemouth — Hants v Somerset
Folkestone — Kent v Leics.
Blackpool — Lancs. v Derby.
Lord's — Middx v Surrey
Northampton — Northants v Glam.
Birmingham — Warw. v Sussex
Scarborough — Yorks. v Glos.

Thursday, August 25

Nottingham* — ENGLAND v NEW ZEALAND (4th Cornhill Test, 5 days)

Saturday, August 27

Chesterfield — Derby. v Yorks.
Bristol — Glos. v Notts.
Bournemouth — Hants v Kent
Leicester — Leics. v Northants
Taunton — Somerset v Glam.
The Oval — Surrey v Essex
Hove — Sussex v Middx
Birmingham — Warw. v Worcs.

Wednesday, August 31

Scarborough — D. B. Close's XI v New Zealanders
Cardiff — Glam. v Northants
Bristol — Glos. v Worcs.
Manchester — Lancs. v Essex
Leicester — Leics. v Kent
Nottingham — Notts. v Warw.
Taunton — Somerset v Hants
The Oval — Surrey v Sussex
Leeds — Yorks. v Middx
Canterbury — †England Young Cricketers v Australian Young Cricketers (4 days)

Saturday, September 3

Lord's — †NATWEST BANK TROPHY FINAL (1 day)

Sunday, September 4

Scarborough — †Yorks. v Lancs. (1 day, ASDA Cricket Challenge)

Monday, September 5

Scarborough — †Essex v Hants (1 day, ASDA Cricket Challenge)

Tuesday, September 6

Scarborough — †ASDA Cricket Challenge Final (1 day)

Wednesday, September 7

Derby — Derby. v Notts.
Lord's — Middx v Northants

Taunton Somerset v Kent
Hove Sussex v Leics.
Birmingham Warw. v Glam.
Worcester Worcs. v Glos.
Scarborough Yorks. v Surrey

Saturday, September 10

Chelmsford Essex v Yorks.
Southampton Hants v Glam.
Canterbury Kent v Northants
Manchester Lancs. v Leics.
Nottingham Notts. v Middx
Taunton Somerset v Warw.
The Oval Surrey v Derby.
Worcester Worcs. v Sussex

NEW ZEALAND TOUR, 1983

JUNE

30 Portsmouth †v Combined Services (2 days)

JULY

2 Taunton* v Somerset
6 Bristol v Glos. (or v another county if Glos. in B & H semi-finals)
9 Lord's* v Middx
14 The Oval* v ENGLAND (1st Cornhill Test, 5 days)
20 Nottingham (or Worcester v Notts. (or Worcs. if Notts. in NatWest Bank Trophy second round)
23 Birmingham v Warw. (or v another county if Warw. in B & H Cup Final)
28 Leeds v ENGLAND (2nd Cornhill Test, 5 days)

AUGUST

3 Northampton v Northants (or v another county if Northants in NatWest Bank Trophy quarter-finals)
6 Bournemouth* v Hants
11 Lord's v ENGLAND (3rd Cornhill Test, 5 days)
17 Chelmsford v Essex (or v another county if Essex in NatWest Bank Trophy semi-finals)
20 Leicester* v Leics.
25 Nottingham* v ENGLAND (4th Cornhill Test, 5 days)
31 Scarborough v D. B. Close's XI

†JOHN PLAYER SUNDAY LEAGUE, 1983

MAY

8 – Hants v Essex (Southampton); Kent v Surrey (Canterbury); Lancs. v Derby. (Manchester); Leics. v Worcs. (Leicester); Middx v Glam. (Lord's); Northants v Notts. (Northampton); Somerset v Sussex (Taunton); Warw. v Yorks. (Birmingham).

15 – Derby. v Northants (Derby); Essex v Lancs. (Chelmsford); Glam. v Warw. (Swansea); Glos. v Leics. (Gloucester); Middx v Hants (Lord's); Notts. v Somerset (Nottingham); Sussex v Kent (Hove); Yorks. v Surrey (Leeds).

22 – Essex v Derby. (Chelmsford); Hants v Northants (Bournemouth); Leics. v Kent (Leicester); Surrey v Somerset (The Oval); Warw. v Lancs. (Birmingham); Worcs. v Glos. (Worcester); Yorks. v Middx (Hull).

29 – Glam. v Lancs. (Swansea); Kent v Hants (Canterbury); Middx v Sussex (Lord's); Northants v Leics. (Northampton); Notts. v Surrey (Nottingham); Yorks. v Somerset (Bradford).

JUNE

5 – Glos. v Surrey (Bristol); Lancs. v Northants (Manchester); Middx v Worcs. (Lord's); Notts. v Glam. (Nottingham); Somerset v Essex (Taunton); Warw. v Derby. (Courtaulds, Coventry); Yorks. v Hants (Middlesbrough).

12 – Derby. v Leics. (Derby); Essex v Kent (Chelmsford); Glam. v Yorks. (Cardiff); Lancs. v Notts. (Manchester); Northants v Glos. (Northampton); Surrey v Middx (The Oval); Sussex v Warw. (Hove).

19 – Glos. v Kent (Bristol); Hants v Leics. (Basingstoke); Northants v Warw. (Luton); Somerset v Glam. (Bath); Sussex v Lancs. (Horsham); Worcs. v Essex (Worcester).

26 – Derby. v Middx (Chesterfield); Essex v Sussex (Ilford); Kent v Notts. (Canterbury); Leics. v Glam. (Leicester); Somerset v Glos. (Bath); Surrey v Northants (Imber Court, East Molesey); Warw. v Hants (Birmingham); Worcs. v Yorks. (Worcester).

JULY

3 – Derby. v Worcs. (Derby); Lancs. v Hants (Manchester); Middx v Glos. (Lord's); Notts. v Essex (Nottingham); Sussex v Northants (Hastings); Yorks. v Leics. (Scarborough).

10 – Glam. v Sussex (Cardiff); Glos. v Derby. (Bristol); Hants v Surrey (Portsmouth); Kent v Lancs. (Maidstone); Leics. v Somerset (Leicester); Northants v Yorks. (Tring); Warw. v Essex (Birmingham); Worcs. v Notts. (Hereford).

17 – Essex v Glam. (Southend); Glos. v Warw. (Bristol or Moreton-in-Marsh); Hants v Notts. (Portsmouth); Lancs. v Worcs. (Manchester); Middx v Leics. (Lord's); Yorks. v Kent (Scarborough).

24 – Derby. v Notts. (Derby); Kent v Middx (Canterbury); Leics. v Essex (Leicester); Northants v Glam. (Northampton); Somerset v Hants (Taunton); Surrey v Lancs. (The Oval); Sussex v Yorks. (Hove); Warw. v Worcs. (Birmingham).

31 – Derby. v Kent (Chesterfield); Glam. v Surrey (Swansea); Hants v Glos. (Bournemouth); Lancs. v Somerset (Manchester); Leics. v Sussex (Leicester); Middx v Warw. (Lord's); Notts. v Yorks. (Nottingham); Worcs. v Northants (Worcester).

AUGUST

7 – Essex v Middx (Chelmsford); Glos. v Glam. (Cheltenham); Kent v Worcs. (Canterbury); Leics. v Notts. (Leicester); Somerset v Northants (Weston-super-Mare); Surrey v Warw. (The Oval); Sussex v Derby. (Eastbourne); Yorks. v Lancs. (Leeds).

14 – Derby. v Somerset (Heanor); Glam. v Kent (Cardiff); Glos. v Yorks. (Cheltenham); Lancs. v Middx (Manchester); Northants v Essex (Wellingborough); Notts. v Sussex (Nottingham); Surrey v Worcs. (Guildford); Warw. v Leics. (Birmingham).

21 – Essex v Glos. (Colchester); Glam. v Derby. (Swansea); Kent v Warw. (Folkestone); Middx v Somerset (Lord's); Sussex v Surrey (Hove); Worcs. v Hants (Worcester).

28 – Glam. v Worcs. (Cardiff); Glos. v Lancs. (Bristol); Hants v Sussex (Southampton); Northants v Middx (Milton Keynes); Somerset v Kent (Taunton); Surrey v Essex (The Oval); Warw. v Notts. (Birmingham); Yorks. v Derby. (Bradford).

SEPTEMBER

4 – Derby. v Hants (Derby); Leics. v Surrey (Leicester); Notts. v Middx (Cleethorpes); Sussex v Glos. (Hove); Worcs. v Somerset (Worcester).

11 – Essex v Yorks. (Chelmsford); Hants v Glam. (Bournemouth); Kent v Northants (Canterbury); Lancs. v Leics. (Manchester); Notts. v Glos. (Nottingham); Somerset v Warw. (Taunton); Surrey v Derby. (The Oval); Worcs. v Sussex (Worcester).

MINOR COUNTIES CHAMPIONSHIP, 1983

Sponsored by United Friendly Insurance

All matches are of two days' duration

MAY

29 – Berks. v Salop. (Reading University); Lincs. v Herts. (Sleaford).

31 – Durham v Herts. (Hartlepool).

JUNE

5 – Northumb. v Cambs. (Bebwell Hill); Salop. v Cheshire (Wellington).

7 – Cumb. v Cambs. (Carlisle).

12 – Lincs. v Cumb. (Bourne).

14 – Herts. v Cumb. (Hitchin); Salop. v Somerset II (St Georges, Telford).

15 – Cambs. v Norfolk (Wisbech).

16 – Cheshire v Somerset II (Boughton Hall, Chester).

19 – Durham v Norfolk (Chester-le-Street); Northumb. v Lincs. (Jesmond).

21 – Northumb. v Norfolk (Jesmond).

22 – Herts. v Cambs. (Watford).

26 – Staffs. v Herts. (Walsall).

JULY

2 – Herts. v Beds. (Clarence Park, St Albans).

3 – Bucks. v Salop. (Slough); Oxon. v Cheshire (Morris Motors, Oxford).

5 – Wilts. v Cheshire (Swindon).

6 – Staffs. v Cambs. (Knypersley).

10 – Cumb. v Staffs. (Millom); Lincs. v Norfolk (Stamford); Somerset II v Bucks. (Taunton).

12 – Northumb. v Cumb. (Jesmond).

17 – Beds. v Lincs. (Bedford School); Cornwall v Devon (Helston); Dorset v Bucks. (Bournemouth Sports Club); Oxon. v Berks. (Christ Church, Oxford).

20 – Suffolk v Cambs. (GRE, Ipswich).

21 – Devon v Dorset (Sidmouth).

24 – Cheshire v Dorset (Bowdon); Cornwall v Berks. (Truro); Lincs. v Durham (Lincoln); Oxon. v Bucks. (St Edward's, Oxford); Suffolk v Cumb. (GRE, Ipswich).

25 – Staffs. v Northumb. (Brewood); Wilts. v Somerset II (Chippenham).

26 – Cambs. v Beds. (Royston); Devon v Berks. (Exmouth); Norfolk v Cumb. (Lakenham); Salop. v Dorset (Newport); Suffolk v Herts. (Felixstowe).

28 – Norfolk v Beds. (Lakenham).

31 – Berks. v Wilts. (Courage, Reading); Durham v Northumb. (Durham City); Oxon. v Salop. (Shipton-under-Wychwood).

AUGUST

1 – Cornwall v Bucks. (Falmouth); Norfolk v Staffs. (Lakenham).

2 – Wilts. v Salop. (Trowbridge).

3 – Cambs. v Lincs. (March); Devon v Bucks. (Torquay); Norfolk v Herts. (Lakenham); Suffolk v Staffs. (Bury St Edmunds).

4 – Berks. v Dorset (Finchampstead).

5 – Norfolk v Suffolk (Lakenham).

8 – Beds. v Durham (Wardown Park, Luton); Herts. v Northumb. (Balls Park, Hertford); Somerset II v Devon (Taunton).

9 – Cheshire v Cornwall (Toft).

10 – Beds. v Staffs. (Dunstable); Cambs. v Durham (Peterborough); Dorset v Somerset II (Dean Park, Bournemouth); Suffolk v Northumb. (Mildenhall); Wilts. v Oxon. (Devizes).

11 – Salop. v Cornwall (Bridgenorth).

14 – Bucks. v Cheshire (Stowe School); Lincs. v Suffolk (Grimsby); Northumb. v Beds. (Jesmond).

15 – Cornwall v Oxon. (St Austell); Staffs. v Durham (Stone); Wilts. v Dorset (Bemerton, Salisbury).

16 – Berks. v Cheshire (Reading CC); Cumb. v Beds. (Kendal).

17 – Devon v Oxon. (Newton Abbot).

18 – Somerset II v Berkshire (Westlands, Weston-super-Mare).

21 – Bucks. v Wilts. (High Wycombe); Cumb. v Durham (Netherfield); Dorset v Oxon. (Canford School); Staffs. v Lincs. (Longton).

23 – Cheshire v Devon (Nantwich); Dorset v Cornwall (Weymouth); Somerset II v Oxon. (Keynsham).

24 – Durham v Suffolk (Stockton-on-Tees).

25 – Salop. v Devon (London Road, Shrewsbury); Somerset II v Cornwall (Wells).

28 – Beds. v Suffolk (Southill Park); Bucks. v Berks. (Amersham); Cornwall v Wilts. (Wadebridge).

30 – Devon v Wilts. (Bovey Tracey).

The top county in the Eastern Division will meet the top county in the Western Division in a one-day match to decide the Championship, at Worcestershire County Cricket Ground, probably on September 18. The composition of the two divisions may be found on page 851.

†MINOR COUNTIES KNOCKOUT COMPETITION, 1983

English Industrial Estates Trophy

Qualifying Round

May 22 Bucks. v Cornwall (Monks Risborough); Northumb. v Cumb. (Jesmond); Staffs. v Beds. (Stone).

First Round

June 5 Lincs. v Beds. or Staffs.
June 12 Cumb. or Northumb. v Durham; Devon v Bucks. or Cornwall (Torquay); Herts. v Cheshire. (Bishop's Stortford); Norfolk v Berks. (Pinebanks, Norwich); Oxon. v Dorset; Suffolk v Cambs. (Ransomes, Ipswich); Wilts. v Salop.

Quarter-Finals to be played on August 7.

Semi-Finals to be played on September 9, 10.

Final to be played at Jesmond, Newcastle upon Tyne, on September 11.

†SECOND ELEVEN CHAMPIONSHIP, 1983

All matches are of three days' duration.

APRIL

27 – Somerset v Warw. (Taunton).

MAY

4 – Lancs. v Northants (Manchester), Leics. v Middx (Hinckley), Warw. v Yorks. (Birmingham).

11 – Derby. v Northants (Bass Ground, Burton upon Trent), Middx v Essex (Enfield CC), Lancs. v Glam. (Manchester), Notts. v Warw. (Nottingham), Somerset v Hants (Taunton), Sussex v Kent (Eastbourne), Yorks. v Surrey (Harrogate).

18 – Glos. v Somerset (Bristol), Hants v Sussex (Southampton), Northants v Middx (Wellingborough), Notts. v Essex (Collingham), Warw. v Leics. (Birmingham), Worcs. v Lancs. (Dudley), Yorks. v Derby. (Elland).

25 – Derby. v Lancs. (Buxton), Essex v Hants (Chelmsford), Glam. v Yorks. (Ebbw Vale), Glos. v Warw. (Bristol), Kent v Surrey (Orpington), Sussex v Middx (Hove).

JUNE

1 – Hants v Somerset (Bournemouth), Notts. v Lancs. (Steetly, Shireoaks), Warw. v Middx (Knowle & Dorridge), Worcs. v Glos. (Worcester), Yorks. v Glam. (Bradford).

8 – Glam. v Glos. (Usk), Middx v Hants (Southgate), Northants v Essex (Milton Keynes), Notts. v Derby. (Coleston), Somerset v Worcs. (Street), Sussex v Surrey (Eastbourne), Yorks. v Lancs. (Elland).

15 – Northants v Lancs. (Horton), Notts. v Leics. (Worksop), Surrey v Middx (Banstead), Sussex v Essex (Hastings), Yorks. v Warw. (Marske-by-Sea).

22 – Derby. v Notts. (Heanor), Glam. v Somerset (Neath), Glos. v Worcs. (Bristol), Kent v Lancs. (Folkestone), Leics. v Northants (Market Harborough), Surrey v Yorks. (Guildford), Sussex v Hants. (Hove).

28 – Glam. v Warw. (Cardiff), Leics. v Notts. (Lutterworth).

29 – Essex v Kent (Eton Manor, Leyton), Lancs. v Derby. (Manchester), Northants v Yorks. (Northampton), Surrey v Hants (Guildford), Worcs. v Somerset (Kidderminster).

JULY

4 – Glos. v Somerset (Bristol), Northants v Middx (Northampton), Notts. v Yorks. (Caythorpe CC), Surrey v Hants (Farnham CC), Sussex v Kent (Hastings).

6 – Essex v Northants (Chelmsford), Glam. v Lancs. (BP Llandarcy), Hants v Kent (Bournemouth), Leics. v Derby. (Coalville), Middx v Surrey (South Hampstead), Warw. v Sussex (Moseley CC).

13 – Kent v Yorks. (Canterbury), Leics. v Lancs. (Leicester), Middx v Sussex (Hornsey), Somerset v Glos. (Bristol Imperial), Warw. v Notts. (Olton & Warshire CC), Worcs. v Glam. (Worcester).

20 – Hants v Surrey (Southampton), Kent v Essex (Dartford), Northants v Leics. (Northampton), Somerset v Glam. (Taunton), Warw. v Lancs. (Leamington CC).

27 – Derby. v Leics. (Derby), Essex v Surrey (South Church Park, Southend), Glos. v Glam. (Bristol), Kent v Sussex (Gore Court, Sittingbourne), Middx v Northants (Harefield), Notts. v Yorks. (Nottingham), Somerset v Lancs. (Taunton), Warw. v Worcs. (Moseley CC).

AUGUST

3 – Lancs. v Yorks. (Heywood), Middx v Kent (Uxbridge), Notts. v Sussex (Nottingham High School), Surrey v Essex (Barclays Bank, Norbury), Worcs. v Warw. (Worcester).

10 – Glam. v Worcs. (Swansea), Lancs. v Leics. (Manchester), Northants v Notts. (Horton), Surrey v Kent (The Oval), Warw. v Glos. (Griff & Coton, Nuneaton).

17 – Glam. v Hants (Cardiff), Kent v Middx (Dover), Lancs. v Warw. (Fleetwood), Worcs. v Leics. (Old Hill), Northants v Derby. (Bretton Gate, Peterborough), Surrey v Sussex (Guildford), Yorks. v Notts. (Harrogate).

24 – Glos. v Hants (Bristol), Middx v Warw. (Lensbury Club), Notts. v Northants (Steetly, Shireoaks), Surrey v Lancs. (The Oval).

31 – Derby. v Yorks. (Chesterfield), Essex v Middx (Eton Manor, Leyton), Kent v Glam. (Bowaters, Sittingbourne), Lancs. v Notts. (Preston), Warw. v Somerset (Courtaulds, Coventry).

SEPTEMBER

7 – Essex v Sussex (Chelmsford), Lancs. v Surrey (Manchester), Warw. v Glam. (Stratford-upon-Avon).

†WARWICK UNDER-25 COMPETITION

All matches of one day's duration.

MAY

9 – Essex v Northants (Chigwell), Glos. v Glam. (Bristol).

10 – Somerset v Glos. (Weston-super-Mare), Worcs. v Warw. (Worcester).

16 – Worcs. v Somerset (Worcester).

17 – Warw. v Glam. (Birmingham).

23 – Hants v Kent (Bournemouth), Leics. v Essex (Leicester).

24 – Glos. v Worcs. (Bristol), Northants v Leics. (Northampton), Somerset v Warw. (Taunton).

JUNE

6 – Essex v Leics. (Chelmsford), Worcs. v Glos. (Worcester).

13 – Kent v Hants (Tonbridge School), Middx v Northants (St Albans).

14 – Glam. v Worcs. (Croesyceiliog).

20 – Leics. v Middx (Leicester), Notts. v Derby. (Caythorpe CC).

21 – Glam. v Somerset (Swansea).

27 – Glam. v Glos. (Cardiff), Hants v Sussex (Southampton), Northants v Essex (Northampton), Surrey v Kent (Banstead), Warw. v Somerset (Moseley CC).

JULY

1 – Glam. v Warw. (Pontardulais), Middx v Leics. (Enfield).

4 – Lancs. v Derby. (Manchester).

8 – Somerset v Worcs. (Street).

11 – Kent v Surrey (Cornhill Sports Ground, Beckenham), Lancs. v Notts. (Manchester), Middx v Essex (Uxbridge), Sussex v Hants (Arundel), Yorks. v Derby. (Doncaster).

12 – Yorks. v Lancs. (Hull)

18 – Kent v Sussex (Folkestone), Warw. v Glos. (Birmingham), Yorks. v Notts. (York).

19 – Derby. v Lancs. (Darley Dale), Glos. v Warw. (Bristol), Hants v Surrey (Southampton), Somerset v Glam. (Wells).

25 – Derby. v Notts. (Derby), Essex v Middx (Chelmsford), Lancs. v Yorks. (Manchester), Leics. v Northants (Leicester), Surrey v Sussex (The Oval), Worcs. v Glam. (Worcester).

26 – Derby. v Yorks. (Derby), Notts. v Lancs. (JP Ground, Nottingham), Warw. v Worcs. (Knowle & Dorridge).

AUGUST

1 – Sussex v Surrey (Hove).

7 – Semi-final.

14 – Semi-final.

21 – FINAL (Birmingham).

Limp edition ISBN 0356 09382 4 *Cased edition* ISBN 0356 09381 6

Filmset by Waterlow Limited, Dunstable

Printed and bound in Great Britain by Hazell, Watson and Viney Ltd, Aylesbury, Bucks.

Slazenger in action
Allan Lamb
Peter Willey
Alan Knott
Geoffrey Boycott
Desmond Haynes
Slazenger
the sports people